CW00494842

# Writer's
# Market UK
# 2008

# Writer's Market UK

# 2008

## THE ONLY GUIDE TO WRITING AND PUBLISHING YOU'LL EVER NEED

EDITOR: MICHAEL CADY

David and Charles

David and Charles would like to thank all of the people who have worked on and contributed to *Writer's Market*. Particular thanks go to our editorial team: Jennifer Fox-Proverbs, Bethany Dymond, Louise Clark, Emily Rae, Demelza Hookway, Neil Baber and Jane Trollope. Thanks also to Pip Leahy for her compilation work, and to Ellie Irwin for her patience and resourcefulness with the proofreading. Many thanks to the article writers, all of whom wrote brilliant pieces at short notice. Grateful thanks to Nigel Hanson of Foot Anstey for his work on the contractual notes. Many thanks to Hal Robinson, David Wilcockson, Neville Mooney, David Lewis and Michael Hatt. And extra  special thanks to Anthony Pearson for his pivotal work throughout the project.

A DAVID & CHARLES BOOK
Copyright © David & Charles Limited 2007

David & Charles is an F+W Publications Inc. company
4700 East Galbraith Road
Cincinnati, OH 45236

First published in the UK in 2007

All rights reserved. No part of this publication may be reproduced, stored in a retrieval system, or transmitted, in any form or by any means, electronic or mechanical, by photocopying, recording or otherwise, without prior permission in writing from the publisher.

Any views expressed in this book do not necessarily represent those of the publisher. The publisher takes no responsibility for any errors or omissions.

A catalogue record for this book is available from the British Library.

ISBN-13: 978-0-7153-2661-9
ISBN-10: 0-7153-2661-9

Printed in Great Britain by CPD (Wales) Ltd, Ebbw Vale
for David & Charles Ltd.
Brunel House, Newton Abbot, Devon

Head of Publishing: Ali Myer
Editor: Mic Cady
Project Editor: Emily Pitcher
Lead Compiler: Sarah Wedlake
Compiler: James Brooks
Technical Editor: Anthony Pearson
Art Editor: Marieclare Mayne
Proofreader: Ellie Irwin
Indexer: Lisa Footitt
Production Director: Roger Lane

Visit our website at www.davidandcharles.co.uk

David & Charles books are available from all good bookshops; alternatively you can contact our Orderline on 0870 9908222 or write to us at FREEPOST EX2 110, D&C Direct, Newton Abbot, TQ12 4ZZ (no stamp required UK only);
US customers call 800-289-0963 and
Canadian customers call 800-840-5220.

www.writersmarket.co.uk

David and Charles

# www.writersmarket.co.uk

# www.writersmarket.co.uk
## is an exciting new online resource for writers

Whether you're a published author, an author wanting to be published or simply enjoy reading and writing, this is the site for you

**Features include:**

- More articles and expert advice from some of the top agents, authors, editors, and producers in the business

- Constantly updated directory listings, providing you with all the information available to help you get your writing seen by the right people

- Poet's Corner, featuring regular reviews and articles by Andy Brown, with opportunities to post your own poetry for him to review and give advice on

- Agent's Corner, with regular articles and insider info from an industry professional, helping you to keep abreast of what's selling and who's buying it

- Got a great idea for a book? Want a job in publishing? Want to know more about how the industry works? Then use the live Advice Centre, where you can ask any of the D & C team your question and receive advice, hints and tips on what to do next and how to go about it

- Daily news feed, keeping you up-to-date with all the happenings in the industry

- Ever-growing online community of members, with forums to post your work for review and get advice, hints and tips from fellow writers and industry professionals

- Easy-to-use, searchable database, enabling you to look for specific genres of listing, or search for specific entries

- Personalise your Writer's Market site, and store your favourite listings, articles and threads for quick and easy reference

- Submission tracker to help you keep on top of your correspondence and submissions

**TO RECEIVE YOUR FREE 30-DAY TRIAL, VISIT WWW.WRITERSMARKET.CO.UK AND FOLLOW THE LINK FROM THE HOME PAGE. YOU WILL NEED TO SUBMIT A VALID EMAIL ADDRESS, AND ENTER THE CODE WMBC7 WHEN PROMPTED**

## www.writersmarket.co.uk
## Make the most of your writing talent

# CONTENTS

# ON WRITING

## PETER ACKROYD

Writing is a strange business, if you can call it a business at all. It is an occupation, in the sense that it occupies one's time. It occupies the time of others. It is a trade, in the sense that the writer is paid to produce an article that others will consume. There are even writers' guilds, on the model of the medieval trade guilds. It is a craft, in the sense that the writer must learn certain essential skills. It is a profession, in the sense that the writer has a definite status in the world. The writer is considered somehow apart.

But writing is also an obsession, in the sense that you – now I will address you, the aspiring or existing writer – you can never do enough of it. You can never think of anything else you would rather do. You will never abandon it – probably not even in remote old age. Even if you were paralysed, you would somehow still manage to write. If you were deprived of the opportunity or ability to write, you would probably go mad.

Writing is a vocation. You are drawn to your work as if by a shining light that directs you forward. You believe that this is the one thing on earth that you were meant to be doing. It is your birthright. It is your destiny that it would be folly to shun. Most writers seem destined to their craft from earliest childhood; like infant prodigies in music or mathematics, there seems to be a definite type of child who will one day become a writer. He or she is often an only child; he or she is by nature solitary; he or she soon discovers a passion for reading that is never shaken off. How many writers recall the earliest books of childhood, read as if for life?

Writing is a dream, in the sense that you are always planning to embark upon the next book that will be the summit, the climax of your ambition and achievement. Nothing will surpass that next book. Writing is a career. Some authors find fame and wealth and even notoriety. Certain authors also acquire public honours and public respect. These honours, in themselves, of course mean nothing. If a writer is not happy with his work, then no public recognition will allay the sorrow.

But writing can also lead to poverty and failure, to the endless round of rejected manuscripts and unfinished books. There are many fine novels devoted to the plight of the unsuccessful and unrecognised author, among them Knut Hamsun's *Hunger* and George Gissing's *New Grub Street*. When I was young, they were the stuff of my nightmares. One of the great impulses of the young writer is fear – fear of failure, fear of rejection, fear of poverty. On the other side must be mustered energy, ambition, determination and the ability to work. Good health is an advantage, although not a prerequisite. But there must also be self-confidence. You must find your star and let it guide you. Never be down-hearted. Never be cowed by bad reviews.

Writing is also a delusion and a despair, when each book fails to achieve the impossible hopes and expectations that you placed upon it. Every book is finally abandoned; every book is a kind of failure. But then every book leads to the next one, and the next, in a continual sequence of imaginative life.

Writing is an imprisonment, since you are in a sense doomed to write. You cannot imagine doing anything else. Any time not spent writing is time wasted. You begrudge holidays, dinner parties, trips to the cinema, anything that keeps you away from the act of composition. But it is also omnivorous – any experience can be used and deployed. Any part of your life can become material for the act of writing. Nothing is taboo. Nothing is too trivial – or, even, too grand.

Writing can be a burden, but a burden often placed upon others. You should pity the spouse, or lover, or partner, of a writer. They are always the third party in a marriage or a relationship. The writing always comes first. It is a question of time – the writer needs time to compose, to contemplate, to revise. It is a question of attention – writers have that absent or preoccupied look, which can be so galling to a partner who requires a response. It is also a question of love – whom do you love

**8**

most, your partner or your work? Which would be the most difficult to abandon? For some it would be a difficult choice to make. The partner is there to make life easier, to provide food and a bed, to listen to the writer's complaints. But the partner knows also when to withdraw on silent feet, and to leave the writer alone in reverie or excitement. It is a hard role, which is why the biographies are filled in particular with the horrendous lives of the wives of famous authors. They came to love, but they were forced to serve. It is also on a technical level a question of space – the writer needs a room, a study, a desk, a table, where he or she can commune.

I have known some writers, however, who can work in any circumstance – who can work in a kitchen crowded with children, in a hotel room, in an aeroplane, in a public bar. These are what I call the 'lifers' for whom writing has become a duty as much as a pleasure. It is indeed a lifetime sentence, to be served twenty four hours a day. Even dreams are taken hostage by the writer's imagination. I am writing this article now, early in the morning, having experienced a particularly vivid dream about – about what? As far as I remember it was about writers and writing, people whom I did not know but were writing or were planning to write books. One of them said to me, 'You must give more attention to your people'. By which she meant, I assume, that I do not engage enough in the analysis of character. Another berated me for the use of horror. And then I found myself as a young man in a lecture theatre, questioning an academic about T. S. Eliot. The academic said, 'so this is the young man who has written a biography of Eliot'. And in my dream all these books – as well as those written by the other participants in my dream – came together. I awoke, and immediately began writing this article.

So you cannot escape the writer's curse, or destiny. Of course I am not complaining. I cannot imagine a task I could or would enjoy more. I cannot imagine living in any other fashion. I could no more give up writing – or retire from the fray – than I can imagine cutting off my right hand. It is also a delight as well as a burden. There is something infinitely satisfying about the act of expression – I do not necessarily call it self-expression, because the mundane 'self' may have very little to do with it. To have expressed a theme – a subject – an intuition – is a wonderful thing. To have expressed it successfully to a public is even more wonderful. And then you may become part of a process – part of a living tradition that stretches back for many centuries. You are part of a dialogue with your fellows, living or dead. You carry on the discourse of the imagination. The writer may seem alone, but he or she is not alone at all. The presence of his predecessors is somewhere around.

The house of literature, therefore, has many rooms. There are no laws concerning how you should write, what you should write, when you should write, or even why you should write. You must follow your own star. I am sometimes asked, for example, whether I prefer writing fiction to biography, or biography to cultural history or (in more recent days) cultural history to drama. But for me these are not separate or separable activities. They are all part of the same process. They are part of the same project. No one would ever ask a composer of music to remain in the field of the concerto rather than the sonata, or the opera rather than the quartet. Music is music – it defines itself and is not defined by any particular form. The same is the case with writing. It should not be compartmentalised and degraded into one specific activity. It is encompassing. That is why each book is never finished. When one text is completed, then another one opens out. The line continues. Each book is, rather, a separate chapter in the book that will only be completed at the moment of my death. Until that moment comes, I will continue writing. And so must you.

# INTRODUCTION

Writing and reading are among the greatest gifts and pleasures of civilised life. Indeed, you could make a very good case for saying that without writing there wouldn't *be* any such thing as a civilised life. It won't take you long to write a list of recent and present world regimes where suppression of the freedom to write, publish and read are sure signs of fear, repression and the removal of basic rights and freedoms.

So, when Peter Ackroyd, in his astonishing and passionate Foreword to *Writer's Market*, links all writers past and present in a vital intellectual network, he's not just talking about the business of writing, he's talking about what it is that makes us civilised and what it is that ensures we stay civilised.

Peter's Foreword sets the tone for all of the articles in *Writer's Market*. Their authors make it clear time and again that it is passion, commitment and tenacity that keep them going. This is regardless of the task at hand; be it technical writing or poetry, research or science fiction, editing or novels, all of our contributors are devoted to what they do. Like Peter, most of us could not imagine doing anything else. I've worked in publishing in one way or another for 30 years and I don't regret any of it. That's not to say I have not chewed my fair share of carpets or wanted to run screaming from the office some days...

## WRITERS AND PUBLISHERS

*Writer's Market* is for writers, so in the articles at the beginning of the book I have set out to describe the world of publishing for the benefit of writers and from my own perspective as an editor. It's not an objective view: I've written based on my own experience. For example, you will quickly see that for some areas of writing I believe that the nature of the relationship between author and editor is almost as important as the writing itself.

I've been very fortunate throughout my career in publishing, in that I've usually worked with authors who write superbly and who are also extremely nice people. I've also worked with authors whose writing is not going to set the literary world ablaze but who write to length, deliver on time and whose company I enjoy.

There have been a few times when I've ended up working with the famous 'difficult author'. If I've been able to avoid working with them again I have, regardless of the quality of their writing.

If I were writing from the perspective of an editor with a stable of world-ranking novelists or poets I might see things differently. Maybe their foibles are as nothing compared to their work. Maybe.

## DOING THE JOB

Commissioning editors have to have a grasp of commercial realities, but I'm no salesperson. Selling books is a tough job and it gets tougher all the time, especially in a business where very often you don't know whether any given book will succeed or fail. Salespeople and the financial team have to look at what they do and the books themselves from a commercial perspective – that's their job.

In the end, I see my job – and your job as the writer – as providing the salesperson with the best possible book we can, regardless of the subject matter. 'Best possible' has to have flexible meanings in my world: it might be a lead title where we've pulled out all the stops; it might also be a small, cheap book that fits a particular market or niche.

I've worked on books that I've been really proud of and which have had excellent reviews, but they haven't gone on to be great sellers. And I've worked on books that were modest in their scope, but whose sales made the publishers very happy.

All this is a reminder that publishing is not just a business; it's much more important and complex than that.

## WRITING MATTERS

We can't afford to be complacent about writing and reading. There are constant threats to both, some trivial and hardly noticed, some at the heart of our society. We all know about the corrosive effects of those parts of the media which seem to relish the dumbing down of language and communication. We have all read about, and maybe learned at first hand, how some of our citizens struggle with basic literacy. It's not just in deprived areas, as the Royal Literary Fund's excellent and thought-provoking report into writing in Higher Education, *Writing Matters* made clear: students in universities often struggle to write coherently. Writing and reading are essential communication skills, but shockingly many of us don't have those skills, or don't have them at advanced enough levels.

I think writers of all sorts have a role to play here.

A great story, well told, pulls readers out of their own world and into its own, specially created world. Once captured, they're likely to want to read more, and another person joins the global community of readers and writers. The story can be very simple – read Richard Powell's article on books for pre-schoolers to learn how he crafts picture stories of 50 words and less. The story may be factual, complex and even controversial – read Alison Benjamin's article on her work at *The Guardian*. These writers work in very different disciplines but it is narrative and storytelling, and a dedication and love of what they do, that links them.

Stories can be novels, poems, newspaper and magazine articles, scripts for TV, film and radio, and much else, as all the articles in this book illustrate.

Good stories, good writing and good books are cornerstones and foundations of society. Let's keep it that way.

*Mic Cady*

---

Please join us at www.writersmarket.co.uk. As well as all the information and inspiration that can be found in this book, you'll find much more: daily news about the world of writing and publishing, regular updates and additions to the directory listings, and a growing community of writers.

# INSIDE A PUBLISHING HOUSE
## WHO DOES WHAT, AND HOW

Mic Cady explains how the key decisions that might affect your book are made, who makes them, and more importantly, why they are made

Book publishing is an art, not a science, despite what the accountants would like. No one predicted the success of the first *Harry Potter* book, or Dan Brown's string of books, or even *50 Ways to Kill a Slug*. They just happened.

Sarah Ford, an Editor at Hamlyn and author of *50 Ways to Kill a Slug*, had the idea for the book turned down by her own publisher, and had to do a personal marketing campaign to get the idea reconsidered and eventually accepted. The book went on to be a bestseller.

So how do book ideas get accepted, and who makes the decisions? How do ideas become manuscripts, and how do manuscripts become books on the shelves of your local WH Smiths or Waterstones? Who does the work, and how is it done?

There is no industry standard in publishing. Every publisher has its own structure, culture, way of doing things, and even language. These idiosyncrasies are rooted in the origins of each Publishing House, and can often be traced back to the founder. For example, Dorling Kindersley was pretty much the creation of Peter Kindersley, a genius with a singular vision for what illustrated information books should do and what they should look like. He was driven by what he called 'lexigraphics', the unique look and feel of DK books. The company structure he created had much more to do with what he considered to be the best way to make books than it had to do with business efficiency. While PK (as most of his staff called him when they were feeling polite) was at the helm, and while his vision remained solid it worked, despite the eccentricities of the company structure. When his vision wobbled, the whole company trembled and nearly collapsed. Years after he had gone, DK still struggled to rid itself of PK's persistent and troubling ghost.

### THE VISION THING

Peter Kindersley had a vision of what DK should be, and drove the company to international success. There are similar stories inside almost every Publishing House. The visionaries come and go, and when they go – or are kicked out – the company had better watch out because things are going to get tricky.

This reinforces the fact that publishing is a subjective industry, not an objective one. A visionary leader can drive a company to success. Publishing Houses run by weak or timid leaders run out of good books fast, and those run by committees tend to stall, because no one makes decisions.

AA Publishing is a case in point. In the 1980s, a succession of dithering directors aided by corporate meandering left it in serious danger of sinking entirely. In the early 90s along came a new MD in the imposing shape of John Howard. Armed with one clear vision – to turn AA Publishing into one of the world's leading travel book publishers – he did just that, often by dragging a reluctant and tetchy staff along in his wake. When John retired at the end of the century the company almost immediately lost direction once more, leaving a trail of job losses and missed opportunities in its wandering path. Today, once more, it may have a Publisher who is prepared to think, take risks, listen, and be adventurous. Similar stories can be told about many publishing companies.

## WHAT'S IN A NAME: PUBLISHING HOUSE STRUCTURES

Publishing Houses come in every imaginable shape and size, from multinational mega corporations to the proverbial one man and a dog. Usually – but not always – they have at the helm a person called (this might not come as a surprise) The Publisher. The Publisher is the monarch of all he or she surveys, and often has an ego to match. It takes a strong willed Publisher not to succumb to egomania, arrogance and selective vision. Remarkably, some of them remain almost like normal human beings. A good Publisher sets the overall vision for the company and makes all the big decisions.

Next in the pecking order come a slew of directors and senior managers, with the Finance, working closely with the Publisher and the various marketing and sales managers. They have to walk a fine line between a pure 'the world needs this book' kind of mindset and the 'but how much money will we make' attitude of those craven types in the finance and sales offices. It's a walk that for many has got trickier and trickier as more and more books are published, and as discounts, supermarkets, the internet and other nasty things have shrunk the opportunities and the profit margins.

The ivory towers that Commissioning Editors used to inhabit are now likely to be low-rise, low-rent bunkers, with Commissioning Editors cowering together and whimpering about the unfairness of it all, and how come the Sales Director makes all the decisions anyway?

> "THERE IS NO INDUSTRY STANDARD IN PUBLISHING. EVERY PUBLISHER HAS ITS OWN STRUCTURE, CULTURE, WAY OF DOING THINGS, AND EVEN LANGUAGE."

Marketing, and UK Sales and Overseas Sales directors often near the top of the pile. A fairly recent new kid on the block in most Houses will be the IT Manager. IT is a key function, though there are still many senior managers in other departments who do not take IT seriously enough, even with the internet hammering on the front door.

Commissioning Editors are key personnel in some Publishing Houses; non-existent in others. In some Houses they are demi-gods, very close to the Publisher, and often the ones who decide whether a book proposal gets past the intray or email inbox. It's usually to them that hopeful authors write. The myth about 'publishing lunches' where Commissioning Editors left the office at eleven and came rolling back full of good humour and wine at four were once reality, but sadly these days they are glued to their keyboards just like everyone else. So don't expect to hear back from them tomorrow or even next month. Proposals can fester in the famous slush pile for a year.

### PUBLISH AND BE DAMNED, OR AT LEAST GET SHOUTED AT

Commissioning Editors are very often the holders of the vision for their particular subject area,

In many Houses, notably non-fiction Houses, Managing Editors and Senior Editors take many of the roles of Commissioning Editors. Typically, their skills will focus on project and people management. They are much less likely to be precious about their vision, which can mean they are ultra pragmatic in their views of whose work gets published, and may be quite content to employ hacks on a flat fee basis; don't expect cosy lunches or long phone calls with these people – for them time really is money. The last thing they want is 'difficult' authors; if you get a reputation for being difficult your chances of repeat work (unless you are one of the few outstanding ones) are very small.

### AN ASIDE ON THE CRUEL TRUTH

It's time to underline again that Publishing is not the gentle, gentlemanly business it once was. It is a very tough world out there – spend a few minutes in your local big book chain and look at the sheer number of books available on everything. Fiction dominates, of course, but how many of the books are three-for-two offers or some such special deal? Each of those deals chews a bit more off the bottom line for the publisher. And how many will actually reap a profit? Not much poetry? It's not there because it wouldn't sell if that was, so it is not worth the shelf space. Take a look at that fat, illustrated non-fiction book. If it looks good, is well made, on decent paper, with high quality images and add-ons such as maps, tinted panels and so on, it will have cost a lot of money to make. Photographs, illustrations and excellent design all carry a premium. Making books like that is a serious investment upfront with no certainty that it will make a good return. Fashions change. A competing book may appeal more. For some reason the book may just die (good books die just as often as bad ones do). As many as 70 per cent of all books fail; in other words they make nothing for the Publisher. Keep that in mind next time you think your Publisher/Editor is being timid.

## EMAIL RULES OK?

Publishing offices these days tend to be as silent as monasteries, with the loudest noise being the rattle of keyboards. It's because of email. Most work is done using it. Whether it's talking to authors or agents or other external people, or whether it is the strings and strands of interminable internal communications, it's email that rules.

Why? First and foremost because it's quick – emails typically take a fraction of the time of a phone call. It's a written record of what was said, and when. You can include multiple recipients. You can work with anyone, anywhere, anytime. That's why most Editors will want email to be the standard means of communication. It's not that they are being unfriendly or stand-offish, which a surprising number of authors still don't understand.

There's another reason: for Editors it's words, and words are their natural milieu; they'll feel more confident and be more accurate in an email, probably. But there may be spelling mistakes since many Editors are self-confessed rotten spellers – they leave that stuff to the poor copy editor!

Of course, there are times when face-to-face meetings are essential and the only right thing to do. Book planning meetings are a prime example, where the entire team will gather to decide exactly what goes where and who does what. Commissioning Editors will also want to create a close relationship with their authors, and Agents often insist that the early contact is by phone first, followed by a meeting.

## WELCOME TO THE FACTORY

If Senior Managers and Editors are at the top of the publishing pile, what of the rest?

Below the Senior Editors are Desk Editors, Assistant Editors and Editorial Assistants (in pretty much that order, although their titles may vary from House to House). These are the people doing much of the hands-on work. They'll handle liaison with the author and the rest of the internal and external team; they'll prepare the advance information sheets and other promotional and selling materials; manage the schedules and generally keep the House moving. The day-to-day call/email you get from your Publisher is likely to be from someone such as this. (Aside: in an industry traditionally dominated by women, most workers are still likely to be female.)

Across the corridor or room may be the art/design department, usually with a structure very like the editorial one. Designers these days are valued as much for their technical skills as they are for their design eyes. Designers are unlikely to get far without very high skills in InDesign or Quark (the industry standard DTP applications), Photoshop, and maybe an application such as Illustrator.

No one is going to be sitting around being 'creative' and staring into space; or if they are their days are likely to be numbered. Publishing Houses are like factories, albeit very quiet factories; that is until the resident precious Designer throws a predictable tantrum because their latest cover ideas were laughed out of the marketing meeting.

Much work will go straight out to the army of freelancers that keeps the publishing world going. Copy editing, proofreading, indexing, and often the actual project management will typically go to freelancers – see Sue Gordon's article on p66 for more on this.

## BOOK LOOK

There are age-old arguments about the selling strength of book covers, but there is little doubt that in a bookshop heaving with temptingly-priced books, a clever, bright, startling or original cover gets that book noticed and picked up. A Designer capable of coming up with strong covers is going to be sought after.

There is no doubt that the insides of popular non-fiction stand or fall by the interior design. 'Book look' is crucial, even when the reader is blissfully unaware that they are being ever so gently tempted. DK is the most famous case in this regard, with countless stories of the book look dictating the editorial content. Inside the DK 'factory' the look of

> **A LUKEWARM RESPONSE TO A PUBLISHING PROPOSAL FROM A SENIOR SALES PERSON CAN MEAN INSTANT DEATH TO THE IDEA**

each and every page is assessed and re-assessed again and again.

Pictures and other illustrative elements are just one aspect of good design: typography and page layout can make every difference between a book that looks the part and one that looks like it was just tailored for the bargain basement.

Paper, binding and cover material are also crucial parts of the book as an object. It's as much about message as anything. What does the publisher want this book to be seen as: classy and modern? A timeless classic? A quirky one-off? Cheap and cheerful?

Decisions made in the production department count for a lot here. Print buyers/production controllers (as in the rest of the industry, names may not be the same from company to company) decide who will do the 'repro' – the essential work of turning computer files into pages – and deciding on paper, board, and printer. Designers, and sometimes Editors, do and should have influence on paper and board. And increasingly, there is a trend to create pages as PDFs internally, test

internally, and export direct to the printer – known as ctp (Computer to Plate). This saves money, but on 'quality' books is likely to get caring Designers and Editors taking even more nerve pills than usual, as they will be worrying whether they'll get the print quality they want.

But print quality generally has never been higher; Far Eastern printers can achieve marvels at costs no European printer can come close to. This does not mean European printers aren't used – for black and white, for special jobs, for jobs at off-peak times they can be best for quality and a close match on cost.

As everywhere, competition on cost and the ever-increasing power and capability of IT means that senior managers are looking for as many cost saving IT solutions as can reasonably (sometimes unreasonably) be achieved.

## SALES, PUBLICITY, MARKETING & PR

Books rarely sell themselves; most need all the help they can get. And many books would sink without trace (even more than many do already) if they were only sold in traditional 'trade' outlets.

In publishing-speak 'The Trade' is High Street bookshops. Non traditional outlets are 'special', hence Special Sales Departments, which can include targeting anything from the National Trust (classy shops with a classy clientele) to CTNs (Confectionary, Tobacco, News outlets), and from garden centres to craft shops. Then there are sales to book clubs (at eye-wateringly big discounts), and if things are going well, overseas sales and co-publishing deals. And don't forget the supermarkets – even though we'd all like to.

All this selling stuff usually comes under one umbrella. So, the UK Sales Director is likely to have marketers, publicists and the various sales forces – including the reps who visit The Trade – in his department. International Sales might have its own senior manager, as might Special Sales.

## PUBLISHING DECISIONS

Some of these people are going to be hugely important in the 'shall we publish' conversation. A lukewarm response to a publishing proposal from a senior sales person can mean instant death to the idea. And it's still not science; they might hate it this week but love a near-identical idea next week. It can drive Editors to drink, distraction, rage, and possibly all three.

**15**

Of course, it can be the Editor's fault; 'selling' the idea in a slipshod, boring or flat way can be an effective way of killing the idea at birth. Because that is what Commissioning and Senior/Managing Editors do – a key part of their job is to convince sceptical sales people and other senior managers that they should sign up for this book.

But sales people are prone to unfortunate lemming-like tendencies. *Schott's Original Miscellany* was a clever, witty, one-off that sold in millions, to everyone's surprise. To no surprise it was promptly followed by other publishers rushing to the same place – they hoped. Soon the bookshops were sagging under the weight of not very clever, struggling to be witty clones that probably sold poorly. *Eats, Shoots & Leaves* was another big surprise – who would have thought it? But inevitably it was followed by very similar 'quirky' titles. It's not always as suicidal as it sounds – crumbs from the tables of the big sellers can be very nice (= profitable) crumbs to have. Or not. It's all just part of the gamble.

## WHAT GETS A BOOK IDEA APPROVED?

The arrival of the post each morning is a mixed blessing for Editors. Does that big brown parcel contain something exciting, or is it a completely inappropriate idea that we would never publish? Worse still, is it just plain awful? Both things happen, unfortunately.

> ## *SCHOTT'S ORIGINAL MISCELLANY WAS A CLEVER, WITTY, ONE-OFF THAT SOLD IN MILLIONS TO EVERYONE'S SURPRISE.*

Sending the wrong kind of book idea to a publisher is a waste of time and money for everyone. It does not take long to find out what a publisher does and doesn't do – websites often tell you a lot, for example. *Writer's Market* and its

## BOOK SALES: A CATEGORY CASE STUDY

Every year, more books are published than the previous year. There seems to be an endless demand for new books on every conceivable subject.

But there are casualties; only a tiny percentage of books become best sellers. Some wash their faces and keep the publisher in business; a horrifyingly big percentage (some say as much as 70 per cent or even more) make no money.

There are sobering stories: for years gardening was a reliable staple for many publishing houses. Helped by popular TV and radio gardening programmes it was one of the healthiest categories, with respectable sales for mainstream authors and potentially enormous sales for the biggest names – the names on TV, usually. But two years or so ago it reached saturation point and sales began to drop. Even the big names could not help sales. The slide in sales became a collapse. Why? The consensus is that so many gardening books were published that readers became bored – they'd got one, two, three on their shelves. Why would they need more? Unless, of course, they had specialist interests; sales of gardening monographs (clematis, say, or orchids) have always been modest, but have kept fairly constant while general gardening books have collapsed. The result has been a massive retrenchment in gardening books, with some publishers pulling out entirely, and bookshops reducing the shelf space allocated to gardening. But what goes around comes around: look at the number of books now on growing vegetables and allotments and so on; it's the bandwagon being jumped on all over again.

website provide you with very detailed information, whenever and wherever we have been able to find it. If in any doubt, a phone call or email should make the position clear. Do those things first before sending in that parcel.

Sometimes, of course, 'wild cards' do happen. A completely off-the-wall idea might fire the imagination of an Editor and give them the courage to go out on a limb and take a risk. But it almost goes without saying that such an idea is going to be truly outstanding.

And the way that idea is presented is crucial. Shoddily presented work is always going to be viewed negatively, no matter how good the idea.

With few exceptions, a poor idea is a poor idea, and it will be immediately obvious that no one is going to publish it. This is where the sender of the idea needs to try to be objective. Journals and reminiscences are the areas perhaps most prone to poor judgement. The only way to get an objective view is to ask outside of a close circle of family and friends, or possibly to send the manuscript to a reputable assessment company. It is difficult, but it should be done. If the author is using the publisher to get that kind of assessment then he should be prepared for a blunt letter – eventually. And accept that he may never hear, the Publisher/Editor having been so appalled they can't bring themselves to do or say anything.

## OK, WE'LL DO IT!

Once the decision to publish has been made, usually with the joint agreement of the Editor, Publisher and sales people, the book becomes part of the factory production line. (The decision can take a long, long time; six months is not unusual; a year is possible – really.)

Decision made, the book needs a schedule, publicity and sales blurbs, a refinement of what it is going to look like and feel like (the 'spec', specification). It needs the author to be contracted; probably mollified over the low advance but cheered by the prospects of years of royalties (but, realistically, take the idea of royalties rolling in with a pinch of salt).

Every book is a new challenge, with its own problems and puzzles, rewards and pleasures. Mostly, the hands-on Editors and Designers will give it their best shot. The fiction Editor will read it as carefully as they can, and compile queries in a

---

## TOP BESTSELLING BOOKS OF ALL TIME

**The Bible**
Possibly as many as six billion copies printed, but no one knows for sure.

**Quotations from Chairman Mao Zedong (Little Red Book)**
Once compulsory reading in China.

**Xinhua Zidian**
China's top-selling dictionary.

**The Quran**
The central religious text of Islam.

**The Book of Common Prayer**
Closely followed by Bunyan's Pilgrim's Progress.

*Source: Wikipedia*

---

careful way so as not to irritate the proud author. The non-fiction Editor will be looking for facts to check as well as spelling and grammar to correct. The Designer will be thinking about book look, not words. The production team will be sourcing the best, but hopefully cheapest, print and paper deals.

The publicity and marketing people will be thinking about angles to get it publicity, where best to sell it, who might review it, whether it merits in-store PoS (Point of Sale) materials or advertising in the national or special press. Is the author going to be any good at self-publicity and selling? This will make a difference – book sales can be transformed by proactive, determined authors, even against the odds. A shy, retiring, overly modest author can sink a book. Is there a special story to sell? And today's Holy Grail of Publishing: will it get on *Richard and Judy*? Probably not, to be honest.

And in nine months, or a year, or two years depending on the book complexity, publisher plans and so on, a day comes when the advance copies arrive. 'It looks great!' we all say, and the author is delighted.

But soon it's on its own, out there competing with the tens of thousands of other books vying for the attention of readers and reviewers. We wish it well. We hope it will make it, but we won't hold our breath…

## PUBLISHERS AND READERS

What is the relationship between what publishers publish and what readers want, or think they want? Or even more crucially, what do readers actually buy? This brings us back to the black arts of publishing: no book is guaranteed success (not entirely true; some publishers try very hard to pre-sell books, perhaps to book clubs or as foreign co-editions; and then there are the Harry Potters…). Publishers and senior creative people do their best to have a pulse on their area or genre; they watch what's going up and what's coming down. They pour over sales figures – both their own and their competitors'. They know the bookshops are key account HQ, where he sells his company's books to one central buyer. That buyer is hugely powerful: one opinion can bring a book, or book idea, down.

It is another facet of the business that drives Editors to distraction: buyers are often in place for only short times; they may know very little about the book or its genre, yet they have the power of life or death. They may have moved on in a month, and what do you know, the new buyer likes that idea after all…as we said at the start, publishing is not a science. Even the statistics we all use don't actually tell the whole story. The industry standard source for book sales is Nielsen BookData. It gathers data

> **" EDITORS SEE WORDS WHERE DESIGNERS SEE GREY BLOCKS THAT HELP TO MAKE THEIR DESIGNS LOOK NICE "**

doing the same; a rep walking into a head office or bookshop with a title that is similar in concept to one whose sales have been poor is going to struggle. The book the rep has might be hugely better than the poor seller; it makes no odds, he's asking the bookseller to gamble, when he'd rather have a sure-fire hit.

And it's a tougher and tougher call. Some sales people have what are called 'key accounts'. WH Smith is a key account; Waterstones is one; as is Borders; so are some of the non-trade companies, those providing books to, say, garden centres. In these cases, the sales person has to make one trip: to the direct from the tills, but not yet all the tills; there are still some areas it does not gather data from. But try telling that to a new and inexperienced buyer and you'll get a wary look back.

Yet, despite all that, publishers keep publishing, and readers do keep reading.

The internet – predicted by some to destroy publishing as we know it – is actually good for books. You can go to Amazon (the world's biggest bookseller) and buy pretty much whatever you like from the comfort of your home, and for less than you'd pay in the bricks and mortar shops. (Discounts again; the publisher picks up the tab here, of course.) Or if that's not to your taste, you can try the specialist

## DESIGN V EDITORIAL – THE OLDEST PUNCH-UP IN PUBLISHING

Editors see words where Designers see grey blocks that help to make their designs look nice. Editors want more room for more words where Designers want that picture to be bigger and that white space to be even more effective. It's all part of what is politely called 'creative tension' with scalpels at dawn sometimes the outcome. And where is the author in this ongoing family brawl? Lucky if they get a look in, especially if their words have been bought for a flat fee. In that case the Editors and Designers can fight as much as they like, without any reference to the hack who churned it out in the first place. So, if authors want a say in a book's look, they should make sure their contract includes a clause that incorporates an approval stage.

## BOOK NUMBERS
### Numbers published per year in the UK:

| | | | |
|---|---|---|---|
| 1990 | 65,000 | 2000 | 116,000 |
| 1995 | 95,000 | 2005 | 206,000 |

*Source: Nielsen BookData*

online sellers, or maybe go direct to the publisher's own website (whose sales might in reality go through Amazon). Secondhand bookselling has been transformed by the internet and has become hugely successful, with the fascinating consequence that some of the most successful online secondhand booksellers are opening actual bricks and mortar shops where you indulge in that most pleasurable of pursuits: browsing. And we all know that electronic sales have transformed academic and educational publishing.

## LONG TAIL STORY

And then there is the 'long tail'. This is *Wired*'s Editor Chris Anderson's by now rightly famous idea, cum article, cum blog, cum bestselling book called *The Long Tail*. The book is wise and witty and packed with good things, but at its heart is the notion that because of the internet anyone can potentially buy anything, and that thus, a tiny, niche book might over time become a bestseller that no bricks and mortar shop would have dreamed of stocking.

Of course, the niche market that would be interested in that book needs to know that the book exists, and that is where such things as blogs can be so powerful. Example: you've written a book on the history of bone buttons, and you've got a publisher to publish it, somehow. It's not selling, but you know that out there somewhere are thousands of people who would really like to have a book about buttons made of bone. Of course they might 'Google' the subject, and if your book is on your publisher's website they might trip across it (aside: ask your publishers if their website has metatags; now go and check metatags online). But if there were a mini-website or blog dedicated to bone buttons, with lots of lovely content about such things, and the opportunity to talk with other bone button nuts, that would be a natural place for such nuts to gather, and a natural place for you to promote your book. So why don't you create that little site or blog?

## CHANGE ON THE STREETS

Bricks and mortar bookshops are doing OK, too, for now at least. We all know that WH Smith has gone through rocky times; after all, we've all been in them and thought 'whatever on earth do they think they are doing', but WHSmith could thrive, perhaps, if it did not try to emulate the 'offer' from the supermarkets. Waterstones, having sucked up Ottakars, is the leading chain bookseller, with shops of all shapes and sizes, some more like boutiques or cafes than traditional bookshops. And that works – drink a coffee, eat a bun, buy flowers or a t-shirt in between looking; very civilised. Good for people; good for books! So far, we don't have the extraordinary, vast book 'hangars' such as those owned by Barnes & Noble and Borders in the US. But we do have the supermarkets taking a bigger and bigger share of the market. Top titles and big discounts are the fare here, and probably always will be; like it or loathe it, it's here to stay. They and the internet are bound to be the biggest players, but clever High Street shops could succeed still with lots of lateral thinking and an emphasis on quality at every level.

And the Independents? Going, going, gone? Or some going, good/lucky ones staying? A loyal customer base can make a huge difference. As can a friendly, 'browsy' ambience. And maybe specializing. Certainly, the knowledge and enthusiasm of the staff are going to be hugely important. But they are at risk, no doubt about that.

Print on demand? Ebooks? Yes, both have their place. And clever Independents will make sure their place is in their store. But 'proper' books – paper and board – are going to be here for a good long while. They are convenient, practical, good to give and receive, they feel nice, they look good; they even smell nice! How many other 'products' give so much?

## PUBLISHING SHORTHAND

- **USP = Unique Selling Point**
- **POS = Point Of Sale**
- **ROI = Return On Investment**
- **OP = Out of Print**
- **AI = Advance Information**
- **BLAD = basic layout and design**

# GETTING ON WITH THE PUBLISHER
## THERE'S MORE TO BEING AN AUTHOR THAN JUST WRITING

Building a good and positive relationship with your publisher is a key to long-term success

The first contact you as writer will have with a potential publisher is most likely to be by letter, by phone or by email. In rare cases you may meet each other socially or even by chance. Once you are signed up, you should nurture the relationship.

### HOW SHOULD THE FIRST CONTACT BE MADE?

Contact by phone: only use this to find out if they are interested in your idea, and to find out who to send it to if they are. Keep it brief, polite and to the point. Don't boast and don't ramble.

Contact by email: introduce yourself and explain how you got the person's email address. Outline your idea, tell them a bit about yourself, and ask if they'd like to see more. Wait for them to reply. If they haven't replied in two weeks send a polite reminder. If they suggest that you send them an attachment containing ideas, etc then all well and good. But some Publishing House systems block or can't cope with large attachments, and some

## BUILDING THE RELATIONSHIP

- Once you have got through the initial proposal stage and your book idea has been accepted and signed off, the good author will go on to build a positive relationship with her Editor and the publishing team.
- The good author does not fire volleys of emails or phone calls again and again. The good author understands that the editorial team is up against it on a daily basis and will get back to her as soon as they can.
- The good author will listen to the team's queries and suggestions and take them seriously. She'll know that these are professional people who are asking things for a reason and because they are trying to make the book better.
- The good author is patient over things like late payments, especially as she will have

- realized that the editorial team have very little to do with the accounts dept on a day-to day basis.
- The good author makes a real effort to help the publicist and agrees to signings, interviews and the like in a cheerful, positive way, and also has lots of good publicity suggestions herself.
- The good author writes genuinely amusing emails and makes sweet phone calls and generally lightens the day. Sounds cheesy? But it works.
- The good author is rewarded in all this because the team will want to work with her again. Relationships like this can last for many years, and can even survive and thrive should the Editor move to another Publishing House, taking her authors with her.

## SOME PROPOSAL LETTER DON'TS:

Don't talk money in the first letter; it is entirely inappropriate and will put the Editor off.

Don't bother writing if your idea is vague or just a kind of pipedream.

Don't boast; you'll get a very negative response.

Don't rant; a surprising numbers of would-be authors do just that and it rings all the alarm bells saying 'difficult author'.

Editors would rather you sent it all in as paper anyway. Once you are signed up, email will likely be the main form of communication.

Contact by letter: this remains the way that many Editors would like to receive your proposal.

You'll need: 1) a covering letter introducing yourself and your book; 2) a concept/contents document explaining in detail what the book is and does; 3) sample chapters. If yours is an illustrated idea and you have illustrations/photos you should include some examples.

The more evidence you can produce that you have done a substantial amount of work already will count in your favour. As will evidence that you've looked to see what your competition is. As will your ideas for selling and marketing the book, so long as they are realistic.

A good title for your idea can be really beneficial. If your title is clever, witty, and/or catchy and so long as it is actually appropriate you are helping the Editor a lot. And helping the Editor is exactly what you want to be doing. The Editor has to be enthused by your idea; she has to want to publish it, and she has to want to 'sell' the idea to the publisher and to the appropriate salespeople. The more you do to help her in each of those things the more chance your idea stands.

See page 103 for examples of query letters.

## THE 'DIFFICULT' AUTHOR

No Editor wants to work with difficult authors. It's not pleasant and we all avoid it if we possibly can. So what counts as difficult?

- **Grumpy/Rude.** It's just not on to be grumpy or rude with anyone in the Publishing House. If you are rude to the receptionist you can be sure the Editor will get to hear about it sooner or later. If you are grumpy or rude to the Editor herself she will probably do her best not to work with you in the future, or at all if you are at the proposal stage.
- **Arrogant.** Many Editors will have had to work with arrogant authors at some point and they will do anything they can to avoid it happening again. Arrogance of this kind often manifests itself in treating junior staff inside the Publishing House with contempt or as if they are idiots. If you reduce a Junior Editor to tears (and this does happen) her boss will get to know very soon and your popularity will plummet.
  - **Mad.** You might think you are charmingly eccentric but we have not got the time or stamina to deal with that kind of thing. Ranting puts you straight in the mad category.
- **Dithering/Inefficient.** Everyone in publishing these days works long, hard hours. We just don't need people who break deadline promises, forget to post their work, and so on. Sorry.

And yet we have all heard stories about the successful authors who are famously repulsive to work with. They get away with it only because they make a lot of money for the publisher. It's not because they are loveable rogues or geniuses. Their behaviour is still completely unacceptable, and maybe if they knew how disliked they are they would change. But there is a type of author who positively relishes their unpopular reputation and behaves even worse in a quite calculated way. If the world was fair they would be marooned on a desert island with a group of people as revolting as themselves.

# THE PUBLISHING PROCESS

## HOW BOOKS ARE PUT TOGETHER

From manuscript to the final proofs

No Publisher works in quite the same way as another Publisher. Each has its own ways of working, and each will have its own language and jargon to describe different parts of the process. What follows is as close to a generic (and very simplified) 'workflow' as possible, regardless of genre or company.

### SCHEDULE

Once the book has been signed off, a series of meetings will take place to fix its place in the overall publishing schedule. Publishers have two main seasons: spring and autumn. Both are a bit of a moveable feast, but the autumn one is almost certainly directed towards Christmas. Nearly all 'gift' books are published for Christmas. There are exceptions: a wedding book will probably do better in spring, for example. Some books are published to coincide with anniversaries or film tie-ins, and in those cases the sales people will want the book delivered well enough in advance of the critical date to have the books in the shops at the right time, when the subject is on the 'radar' of potential readers.

Getting the overall publishing schedule right is tricky. You can't publish all your books in the autumn, because the company would be frantic at one time and idle at another. This affects the entire team, from Editors and Designers through to sales reps. There are specialist Publishers who work to specific times and specific events. The reps work to regular 'cycles' which affect everything they do and which can have a huge impact on sales. If the book or books miss their dates it can throw the finances of the company completely askew. Just one key book disappearing from a scheduled publishing date can knock thousands, even ten of thousands, off the bottom line.

So, Publishers take schedules and scheduling very seriously.

Most Publishers work about a year in advance. In other words, they are working on a list that will be published over the following year. Some books are signed off early, but you'll find that in those cases they are put on the backburner until the Editors need to kick them back into life when their production schedules begin.

A big, illustrated book may take two years or more to put together, and will require a complex schedule for the whole of that time. In many houses, much of the work will actually be done by contributors and freelancers, so the impact inhouse may look minimal, at least early in the schedule.

Some books – say by big name authors – will be given royal treatment and will be slotted into the schedule with as much deference to the author and the work as possible. A few Publishers still work on the 'we'll publish it when you've finished it' principle, but most mainstream Publishers and their mainstream authors have to work to structured schedules. In the end, it all comes down to money: no books published = no money coming in.

### MANUSCRIPT, DELIVERY AND EDITING

If the book is a traditional one, ie it is a manuscript written by one named author who delivers it on the agreed date, its progress through the House will depend on what kind of book it is.

Fiction and poetry should, in theory, have traditional editorial and proofreading processes applied to them. A 'light touch' will be the general rule here. But the team will be looking for the obvious things like typos and (accidental) bad grammar, and, depending on the book, may have a query sheet.

This is where a good Editor can really come into her own. That 'light touch' may have been the result of many reads of the whole manuscript, sleepless nights worrying about tiny detail, and, eventually, a careful letter to the author.

If the author is a 'tricky' one, whom the Publisher values but fears, then there will be intense conversations within the Publishing House about how any query will be worded, and who will get

## DESIGN

All books are designed. (Of, course they might be badly designed.) Even a standard text book needs decisions on typography and page layout.

Novels need to 'feel nice' to read, and the Designer will do a subtle, behind-the-scenes job in deciding on typeface, percentage of 'white space' (those areas without type) and so forth.

Large illustrated books can take a very long time to design.

Usually, the picture research job of getting in a selection of pictures from which the Designers can choose their shortlists will have taken place while the author was writing, the author (or project Editor/manager) having been asked to provide a picture list before writing.

> ## IF THE BOOK OR BOOKS MISS THEIR DATES IT CAN THROW THE FINANCES OF THE COMPANY COMPLETELY ASKEW

in touch. Generally, this is going to be a job for the Commissioning Editor.

For general illustrated books, there will also probably be a day on which the manuscript arrives. The commissioning process will have involved planning meetings, where the books was specified in detail – length, word count, main text, boxes, side bars, panels, etc. But usually that changes quite a lot once the design stages begin.

Some illustrated books are written around the designs. In other words, a lot of the work is done without a word being in place. The pictures are chosen, the layouts (page designs) are done, and then the author or authors set to work. This is skilled, painstaking work, requiring the writers to write exactly to length – to fit their text to the areas specified by the Designer. This will extend to caption length. Writing meaningful short captions is one of the great skills in this kind of publishing. As is writing long, 'story' captions that are not waffle.

For this kind of work the Publisher will generally use trusted old hands, people who have had years of experience. Writers who have specific subject expertise (natural history, travel, etc) and who can write to length at speed are never going to be short of work.

Once words and pictures are inhouse, the Designers can begin the task of designing the pages. This will usually be to an agreed 'book look', in other words, the Publisher knows what kind of appearance the book will have. Sometimes, this look evolves as the book develops, but usually the team and/or Commissioning/Senior Editor knows what kind of look they are aiming for.

## FIRST PAGES

Whether poetry, a novel, or an illustrated reference book, there comes a stage known as 'first pages'. With simple books this is often pretty much what the book will look like when complete, but with complex books it can look a real mess – too much material (overmatter); too little (undermatter); stubby little lines of type ('widows' and 'orphans' depending where they are) and much else besides.

This tidying up work is usually done by Editors rather than by writers, but that depends on the way the Publisher works and on the skills to hand.

If it is felt that the designs need to be amended, perhaps to fit more words in, then lots of interaction between Editors and Designers will happen. Sometimes this becomes acrimonious because Editors stand up for words while Designers stand up

## BOOK CREATION JARGON

***Spread (aka double page spread)***
Two facing pages.

***Part title***
Usually a spread, marking a major division within the book; often just has a full bleed image (full bleed = the images going over all four edges) and the name of the section (part) to come.

***Chapter opener***
Rather like a part title, but most often using only the full right hand page.

***Body text***
The main text on the page.

***Box (aka box-out)***
A standalone piece of text (possibly including a picture) that is boxed off from the main text, sometimes with a tint or grey background.

***Panel***
Big box!

***Side bars***
Rather like elongated boxes, but running down the outer edges of a page.

for illustrations and the wonderful but mysterious 'white space'.

This highly skilled work is what provides the job satisfaction for many Editors and Designers. It's why they work long, hard hours on very modest salaries. They get a professional thrill from fitting that essential little phrase in *there* and drawing out that subtle little point *there*.

## SECOND PAGES

Once all the work above has been done, a second set of page proofs is run out. By this stage, everyone in the team will expect most of the editorial and design problems to have been solved, but there is still usually further tidying up to do, and the author is still likely to be involved at this stage. Most people will hope that it does not mean a third set of pages, but this is sometimes unavoidable. Eventually final pages are produced.

## REPRO

This is short for reproduction; also known as origination. This is a key date for virtually all Publishers, even when there is no actual repro to be done. Usually it means the day on which all the final pages (as electronic files), any trannies and artwork and so forth are handed over to the production department.

The production department checks that everything is there that should be there, is in the correct format, and is properly labelled, packages it all up, and sends it of for repro. (In bigger houses the production team will make sure the digital files are correctly named. This sounds tedious and is, but it is also crucial – wrong file names can cause major disasters.)

Repro itself is traditionally the process by which trannies (transparencies) and any other physical materials are scanned by a specialist repro house to become printable digital files. It's also the stage at which computer dtp files in Quark or InDesign are finalized for printing, and the colour that you see on screen is processed so that it can be printed on paper correctly. This used to be output as film, which was then used to photographically expose a plate for printing.

This part of the book production process is the one that is changing most in publishing, and there are many different ways now of getting from final pages to printer's proofs.

For example, most Publishers now make digital PDF files at repro and output either direct to plate for printed wet proofs or direct to digital contract proofs for the final printer to match for colour. The logical end to this streamlining of what we'll probably still call 'repro' for a while is for the House Designers machines to speak directly to the computer connected to the printer; the ultimate 'computer to plate' (ctp). Already it is possible to print PDF files straight through to a digital printer for on demand printing. Some Publishers have full PDF workflows and/or content management systems designed to automate and speed up this entire process.

## PROOFS

Depending on the technologies used as simplified and outlined above, proofs come back from the printer. For books with only one colour – text black – these proofs can be a simple checking phase to

# PROOFREADING

Any writing work you do must be proofread before it is submitted to a potential publisher. This is a cardinal rule of any writing of whatever sort.

You should read your own writing in the cold light of the day after you wrote it (some authors lock their finished work away for a week at least before bringing it out for one last read). Ideally you won't do your own proofreading; you'll get someone else to do it for you. And they are not just looking for those inevitable spelling mistakes, they are looking for wonky grammar and things that just don't make sense; a good proofreader asks questions.

Never try to proofread on screen. This is one of the ancient chestnuts of publishing, but ask any old hand at the job and they'll say the same: the only way to proofread properly is on paper. The old-fashioned way was to do a 'ruler read': you held a ruler against the lines of type and moved the ruler down as you read. It's time consuming but can be very accurate.

It's a live issue inside publishing house again at the moment because there are software tools that are specially developed to enable 'soft' reading (soft = reading onscreen; hard = reading on paper). It's tempting for publishers because in theory it saves both time and the cost of printing for the proofreader.

Proofreading is a specialist skill and requires a particular mindset: methodical, painstaking, questioning and with meticulous attention to detail.

(PS: don't trust the spell checker and grammar checker in your word processing application. It probably won't pick up that you typed our when you meant out, or that you typed god when you meant good, for example.)

make sure everything is in place. For more complex books it means a detailed check by the entire team, including to check that any colour is accurately rendered. If trannies have been used the production department will check each one against its scanned image in the proofs and will mark up any required changes to get the colour correct.

These proofs are very often sent out to the author and to the freelance team. Any necessary changes to the text are made by re-supplying amended dtp files.

## THE WHOLE BOOK WILL COME BACK COMPLETE FOR ONE LAST 'ULCER' CHECK

Once the proofs have gone back to the printer, only those pages that have been changed will be re-proofed and seen again by the Publishers.

### PLOTTERS/OZALIDS
The whole book will come back complete for one last 'ulcer' check. These are machine 'imposed' pages, with the book in its print sections (usually the standard 32 pages). These are not full quality colour pages, although any pictures will be in place so that the team can check that everything is present and correct.

Changes made at this stage are very expensive, so Editors quake in their shoes if they see a last minute 'grolly' or error.

### ADVANCE COPIES
When printing and binding are complete, a few advance copies will be specially shipped to the publishers. These are for the predilection of the senior managers, for key account sales, and to send out to the author and any other important contributors.

Beyond that it's distribution and publication.

# THE AGENT'S VIEW
## THE ROLE OF THE LITERARY AGENT IN PUBLISHING

Mandy Little of leading agency Watson, Little gives the lowdown on working with and using agents

### MANDY LITTLE

Mandy is managing director of Watson, Little Ltd, a medium-sized agency established originally in 1970 that handles a wide range of adult and juvenile fiction and non-fiction. She has been an agent for 26 years.

If the expression you most want to be able to say (after 'follow that car...') is `speak to my agent...` you will already know how ideal it is that your authorial affairs are handled by a literary agent. But what do these people actually do, and how do they do it? Why do you need one? How do you get one? Are they all the same? Which one would be right? These are some of the questions you might be asking yourself, so let's delve into the world of the agent to find out how it all works.

## WHAT DO AGENTS DO?

Agents are not employment agents (sorry!), but you could expect a reputable agent to manage your career as an author, building it as your developing talent and the market allow. This is a tall order, so if an agent takes you on it means he or she has considerable faith in your writing since agencies take on only those clients whose work they are confident they can sell (they'd go bust if they did anything else as their commission is paid only on sold work). If you get taken on by a good agent be very pleased indeed; some say it's harder to get a good agent than it is to find a publisher.

Your agent should explain commission rates to you and the roles of other staff in the agency. Also the boundaries between themselves and any associates, what expenses they are entitled to charge etc. Everything should be formally recorded in a letter of engagement signed by you both (all agents/agencies belonging to the Association of Authors' Agents will automatically do this).

## THE MAIN PARTS OF AN AGENT'S JOB ARE:

- To make sure your work is editorially fit to show to a publisher or newspaper and that it has the right selling points, structure and grammar.

- To sell your idea, synopsis and sample chapters or typescript (newspaper column perhaps) either individually or by auction. Your agent is looking for the best advance, and deal in general, and also for an Editor who will really champion you and your work.

- To negotiate the 'big print', the advance and royalties, and take you through what is good, bad

> **TIP**
>
> *Go through with your agent at the outset just how you are going to work together, identifying what is permissible and desirable on both sides in order to avoid misunderstandings or frustration. Never work with an agent you haven't met.*

**TIP**

*Agents are a necessary evil: generally you gain more than you lose.*

## WHY DO YOU NEED AN AGENT?

You might be thinking you could probably do some of the placing of your work yourself and, if you have the time and have been published before, you might be right. But the main reasons you need an agent are:

- Publishers take more seriously submissions from agents, who have already picked out what they consider to be saleable in the current marketplace. Agents know Commissioning Editors; they know who is buying what and what it might be worth. Your agent's reputation should help yours

- If you don't have an agent you will have to let your publisher sell most or all subsidiary rights for you (just how good are your contacts in

or indifferent about the offer before going back to the publisher to get the best possible deal. (An agent will not accept or decline an offer at any stage without your permission, so you're still in control of your own work.) Then there's the 'small print', actually not so small if, say, someone comes out of the woodwork accusing you of plagiarism just because he or she feels like making some money out of you. The wording on the contract should protect you from the world's literary headcases and most 'small print' is there because

## AGENTS KNOW COMMISSIONING EDITORS; THEY KNOW WHO IS BUYING WHAT AND WHAT IT MIGHT BE WORTH. YOUR AGENT'S REPUTATION SHOULD HELP YOURS

something once went wrong for someone. A reputable agency will use its own contract form wherever possible .

- To sell other rights attached to the work, the idea being to exploit as much as possible from one piece of writing. These may be serial or overseas rights not leased to the publisher, television or film, perhaps computer games or merchandizing.

- To handle the financial side of the sale of your work, which includes checking every royalty statement and chasing invoices.

- To revert the rights when the book is at the end of its life so that you can use the material again in some form, assuming the copyright remains yours – your agent will have seen to it that this is the case in 99 per cent of work sold.

These are the broad areas of work for a principal literary agent but there will be variations depending on your intended markets and what the particular agency covers, and how it operates.

Japan?) and they'll charge a lot more to do it than your agent will. For example, if you've let your publisher have film/television or overseas rights they may well charge you 50 per cent of what they make for selling them. But your agent would typically lease UK & Commonwealth rights only in a non-illustrated book to a British publisher, retaining other major rights for their own staff to sell or place via an associate.

- You are free to have a fragrant, purely editorial, relationship with your Editor, leaving your agent to go after that vital extra £1,000 your bank manager seems so keen you repay.

- The agent deals with all the business side of being an author, leaving you free to focus just on your writing.

- Your agent will support you over any differences with your publisher, provided you've done nothing illegal or immoral. Say your book has been edited into some kind of nonsense you barely recognize? I imagine most authors wouldn't fancy tackling that kind of problem unaided, particularly if the contract has to be cancelled.

## HOW DO YOU GET AN AGENT?

Talk to other writers; there is nothing like the personal experience of another author in the same field who works with an agent already. Whether or not you know other authors try the Association of Authors' Agents (*www.agentsassoc.co.uk*) which will help point you in the right direction, or the Society of Authors (*www.societyofauthors.net*).

- Know your own markets. You can have more than one but be sure you're focused.

- Target only those agencies which handle the kind of writing you do.

- Ring your chosen agencies to enquire about procedure specific to that company.

**TIP**

*You might try to go for relatively recently established agencies – see the Agents directory listings in this book – or those where there is a young agent building a stable of clients.*

## HOW TO GET THE BEST FROM YOUR AGENT

- Keep phone calls and emails brief and to the point. Only make them if they really are necessary.

- Inform your agent of anything you do which might help raise your profile. Never do anything behind your agent's back.

- Send a hard copy of anything which needs reading (or editing) and don't expect a verdict within hours; you are not your agent's only client.

# THERE IS NOTHING LIKE THE PERSONAL EXPERIENCE OF ANOTHER AUTHOR IN THE SAME FIELD WHO WORKS WITH AN AGENT ALREADY

- Try to speak to the agent you have in mind, asking permission to send in material.

- Write a well-worded, succinct letter briefly outlining your work and include a synopsis, together with three polished chapters (no typos or grammatical mistakes) and a brief CV. The agent will ask for more if he or she is interested.

- Don't make your initial approach by email, or send material in as an attachment unless asked to. These will often be overlooked and nobody will thank you for clogging up their inbox with your manuscript. Send an SAE if you want your work returned.

- Remain courteous if there's a problem. Problems happen and you'd be nuts to alienate the person most able or willing to help.

- Don't keep asking how the agent is getting on. From time to time is fine and you will be told immediately there is interest from a publisher; no news is no news.

- Don't ring up to go through your next book prior to sending it in just because you can't finish a sentence or need a coffee break and fancy a chat.

**TIP**

*Agents hate having their time wasted, and love a bit of appreciation now and again.*

# PUBLICITY AND HOW TO GET IT
## AN INSIDER'S VIEW

Publicist Rosalie Macfarlane explains how it's done

## ROSALIE MACFARLANE

Rosalie's career in publishing began at Harper & Row in London in 1976, where she was Publicity Assistant. In 1980, she joined Macmillan as a Publicity Executive where she promoted the Macmillan hardbacks before heading up publicity for the Papermac imprint. In 1984 she became Publicity Manager at Souvenir Press and then left at the end of 1986 to join Macdonald. The company was owned by Robert Maxwell, and when he died it was bought by Little, Brown and remained part of the Time Warner publishing group until 2006 when they were sold to Hachette Livres. She is currently Group Publicity Director, heading up a team of nine publicists, including a Publicity Manager in Ireland, publicizing titles for the following imprints: Little, Brown, Abacus, Virago and Sphere.

Writing is a solitary process; publishing a book is a team effort. Nowadays, we actively encourage authors to become involved in helping to promote their own work, as books are in fierce competition with every section of the entertainment industry, who all use the media to spread the word.

## YOUR CAMPAIGN

The tough fact is that marketing budgets are very tight, as marketing is expensive and campaigns have to be big to make a real impact. However, do not be daunted, as publicity, on the other hand, is 'free' and will only involve your time and effort. Every publishing company has a Publicity department and you will be assigned a publicist who will seek your co-operation in helping to promote your new book.

At Little, Brown we want our authors to feel they are part of the team aiming to make their book a success, and publicity can be a vital key to making a book sell. I contact authors well ahead of publication, as knowing how we can work together is essential to planning a publicity campaign.

## PUBLICITY IDEA

I will usually have read the whole typescript at this stage, and at our meeting (or during a telephone or email conversation) will discuss what makes this book different, as the media are always on the look out for something new, topical or revealing.

### AMONG THE QUESTIONS I'LL ASK ARE THE FOLLOWING:

- Are you willing to do publicity for your book, including interviews and writing features for the press or magazines?

- Does the book have any unique or news-related angles?

- Is there anything exceptional in your background that would make a good article?

- Did you interview someone for the book with a fascinating story to tell?

- Did you discover anything interesting or new in your research?

- Is there a significant anniversary to tie in with publication?

- Is the location of the story somewhere you have lived or know well?

- Do you have any interesting personal anecdotes related to the book?

## BIOGRAPHICAL INFORMATION

I always ask a new author to provide biographical material, as we are not only selling your book via the media, but you as well. Any information you can give about yourself from when you first took up writing to your research for this particular book all helps you to shape ideas for getting media attention.

## RADIO

I think radio is the most powerful broadcasting medium for promoting books and authors. BBC Radio 4 offers a number of opportunities from programmes with guest authors (eg Woman's Hour or Front Row), to slots for dramatizations or straight readings. But I don't neglect the popular BBC Radio 2 or Radio 5 live programmes for interviews, and I also approach BBC local radio stations for face-to-face interviews or arrange for recordings down-the-line from another BBC station, such as Broadcasting House in London.

## TELEVISION

Television shows come and go, but topical books are excellent for the national news programmes, and authors with a moving human interest story or unique experience appear on daytime shows.

## FESTIVALS, BOOKSHOP AND LIBRARY EVENTS OFFER WRITERS A GREAT OPPORTUNITY TO TALK TO AN AUDIENCE AS WELL AS SELLING COPIES OF YOUR BOOK.

## CONTACT

If you have good contacts with the media or know someone useful in the public eye, then don't hold back from giving your publicist a full list of names, as this will help get your book noticed.

This is the stage you can raise all sorts of suggestions for getting publicity, but they must be related to the book, as publicity for its own sake may provide fodder for the media but not lead to sales.

## NEWSPAPERS AND MAGAZINES

I regret that not all books are reviewed in the national press as each broadsheet paper receives about 400 books a week from different publishers, and Literary Editors have to be very selective. But there are other opportunities for getting into print outside the book pages. I have a large database of editors and journalists from different sections of the paper, so will target the relevant person with the ideas and angles I will have discussed with my authors, which may lead to an interview or a commission to write a feature.

## PUBLIC SPEAKING EVENTS

Festivals, bookshop and library events offer writers a great opportunity to talk to an audience as well as selling copies of the book. I am keen on this means for promoting authors as it is a brilliant way of keeping in touch with your readers, and, at festivals in particular, of meeting other authors. The usual format is to give a talk for about forty minutes, and then take questions from the audience.

## BOOKING INTERVIEWS

After sending out information or proofs to my media contacts, I will need to chase them, as they rarely come to me begging to interview authors. They all work to different deadlines, which means that they are making decisions at different times. The monthly magazines work to the longest deadlines, and while broadcasting producers like to get material early, they may not decide until closer to publication, and daily newspapers will work about a week ahead. I start drawing up a schedule as soon as the first interview is agreed, but would urge authors not to be too dismayed if your schedule

## PUBLICITY CASE STUDIES

### Five examples from Rosalie Macfarlane's files

#### *Rebecca's Tale*, Sally Beauman

Sally Beauman had met Kits Browning, son of Daphne du Maurier, who suggested that she wrote a 'prequel' to *Rebecca*. She was the ideal choice, as her knowledge of du Maurier's works, and her insights into the much-loved classic *Rebecca*, not only resulted in a brilliant novel that was much more than a mere 'prequel' but gave all her talks and interviews a refreshing depth.

#### *The Historian*, Elizabeth Kostova

This fascinating debut novel, based on the history of the real Dracula took Elizabeth Kostova ten years to write. It was a challenge trying to persuade journalists and producers to read the novel, but she gave me invaluable background material – such as how her father's stories about Dracula told to her as a young girl lit the first flame of inspiration, to her research into the historical Dracula – which enabled me to attract their interest, and led to some excellent publicity interviews.

#### *The No 1 Ladies' Detective Agency*, Alexander McCall Smith

Alexander McCall Smith had written over fifty books before he enjoyed overnight success with this series featuring the wise and indomitable Mma Ramotswe. We gave the paperbacks a striking new look and gradually the excellent reviews led to a word-of-mouth expansion of his readership. Best of all, he is as thoughtful and humorous as his novels, and continues to be generous and engaging in all his interviews and public talks.

#### *The Pilot's Wife*, Anita Shreve

All of Anita Shreve's publishers lost money on her novels, in spite of the good reviews from the national newspapers. At Little, Brown she had a firm following, and we were reluctant to cease publishing them. We are the only publishers who remained loyal to her, and since the publication of *The Pilot's Wife*, we have been rewarded with consistently high sales.

#### *The Night Watch*, Sarah Waters

It is exhilarating to see a novelist gradually grow more successful with each novel, and especially thrilling to see it happening to Sarah Waters, who made a dramatic move from the Victorian period that had made her first three novels so popular to an entirely new setting for *The Night Watch*. The accolades from reviewers and the public alike showed that her writing is much admired whether she uses Victorian pastiche or sets her story in the 1940s.

looks bare for weeks, as many interviews are not confirmed until a week or two before publication.

## MEDIA TRAINING

There are some subjects that will be of much interest to the media and it is vital to get the right message across to them, for example autobiographies or books on sensitive topics. I have recommended media training to authors who have found it invaluable because you can practise what you are trying to convey and ensure that your message or story is clear and compelling.

## AFTER PUBLICATION

You won't lose touch with your publicist immediately after publication, as we always send reviews or features that appear in the press. We are open to further ideas, especially if you notice something in the news related to your book or expertise which would make a good feature for a national newspaper, or a broadcasting programme. On the whole media interest dries up after publication, though don't forget that there might be more opportunities when the paperback is published.

## TIPS FOR AUTHORS

- Talk to your publicist about your expectations, most books are not suited to all media outlets. *Feng Shui for Cats*, for instance, would not be reviewed in the broadsheets, but the tabloid press might love it.

> ## IF YOU ARE A GUEST ON THE PROGRAMME, REMEMBER THAT YOUR ROLE IS TO ENTERTAIN THE AUDIENCE WITH A CLEAR MESSAGE, BACKED UP BY EXAMPLES, BRIEF ANECDOTES OR RELEVANT FACTS AND FIGURES

- Most problems arising with publicity are to do with poor communication, so talk to your publicist at the outset and make it clear that you want to be kept in the loop. If you are experiencing difficulties, talk to him or her directly and then the Editor, before complaining to your agent.

- Be very clear about topics or issues you would prefer not to be raised during interviews, so that there is no mention of them in letters or press releases from the publisher.

- If you are approached directly by a festival or other event organiser, contact your publicist before agreeing to appear. It is much easier for you if the event is controlled via the publishers as the publicist can say no on your behalf, vet the organizer, liaise over who is dealing with book sales, and lastly ensure that you don't have a burdensome schedule which would take up too much of your time.

- The author biography form may look intimidating, but do provide your publicist with as much information as possible about your background, your writing career, places where you have lived or know well, other achievements, previous publications etc.

- Prepare yourself well in advance before giving radio and television interviews. If you are a guest on the programme, remember that your role is to entertain the audience with a clear message, backed up by examples, brief anecdotes or relevant facts and figures.

- Do not keep saying 'in my book' in radio interviews as the interviewer will usually mention your title at the end of the conversation.

- Remember that you are talking to one viewer or one listener and speak to that person, and tell the story you want to tell in addition to answering the interviewer's questions.

- Beware of speaking 'off the record' unless you know and trust the journalist. If they require background information you may decide to comply, but it is a gamble, and if in doubt, play safe.

- At festivals or bookshop events, it's much better to give a talk (referring to your notes if necessary) rather than read from the book – though a brief reading to illustrate a point can be very effective.

- If you have never spoken in public before, practise hard and get some feedback about your performance. It will make all the difference to the effect you have on your audience.

- Consider setting up your own website, which can then be linked into your publishing company's own site.

- Be prepared to work hard around publication, and maintain a good relationship with your publicist who will provide professional guidance over the selection of interviews and events, and will act as the main link with your publishers while you are promoting your book.

Good Luck!

# A WRITER'S VIEW
## SECRETS OF A NOVELIST

Nia Williams comes clean and confesses to being a writer, and gives you her insights into a succesful writing regime

## NIA WILLIAMS

Nia's first novel, *The Glass Pier*, was published to critical acclaim in 2001. Her second, *Persons Living or Dead*, was published in 2005 and longlisted for the Welsh Book of the Year Award. Her short stories appear in numerous anthologies and magazines, and are broadcast on radio.

I'm a writer. No coy shrugs or self-deprecating snorts: after 20 years or so, I'm finally out of the literary closet.

What kept me in there all that time? Well, for starters, it took me so long to knuckle down and finish anything – let alone get it published –that even 'aspiring writer' seemed overblown. And when I did get into print, there was no question of dropping the day job. I'm certainly not in it for the money – it's much more important than that! So far, my earnings from fiction just about cover my printer's ink.

Still, the more I write the clearer it is to me that this is what makes me tick. So without blush or apology, here's my account of Becoming a Writer.

## LIGHTBULB MOMENT (1)

I was crossing a footbridge over the A3010. I was in my 30s, and for 15 years or so I'd wanted to be a writer. If only I had the time and the security. If only I could pay off the mortgage, finish that project at work, retire … Halfway across the footbridge, I realized I had a choice. I could carry on with an OK job and shelve the writing fantasy along with the Olympic gold and a dance with Fred Astaire. Or I could get cracking.

Once that was settled, I had to write something. This was precisely what I'd failed to do during all those pre-footbridge years. Diaries, yes, and jottings, and teen-angst verse, and a few rainforests' worth of abandoned novels and half-baked plots. Nothing remotely fit for publication. Everything I produced was lame, pompous or dull, and petered out after a couple of paragraphs. I didn't know how a proper writer should write.

## LIGHTBULB MOMENT (2)

It's the weekly life-drawing class. I'm at my easel trying to do justice to Ken, our 70-something life model, who's striking poses by his electric heater. The teacher assesses my efforts: 'Hmmm… Never mind. Keep what you've got and make it work'.

Ping!

## FINISHING AND SUBMITTING TIPS

• Write something every day, even if it's only 10 words. If it's rubbish, you can change it later.
• When the first draft is done, hide it for a month. Then go back and read it with a fresh eye.
• Proofread your work. Typos, spelling mistakes and clunky grammar will irritate your readers.

• Submit a neat manuscript, typed in double-spacing on one side of A4, with numbered pages and secure but loose binding (such as treasury tags). Include a polite and friendly covering note.
• If you don't like the rules, break them. After all, it's your book.

While I was waiting for the muse to descend, I'd forgotten the golden rule: practice makes it better.

Actually, I'm no great fan of golden rules (see tips box). But this one holds true. Writing is a craft like any other: you have to work at it. If the text is feeble, fix it. Those binned sheets of purple prose aren't signs of failure – they're a resource. Having grasped the uncomfortable fact that Becoming a Writer would involve hard graft, I was ready to start producing something with a beginning, a middle and – hallelujah! – an end.

## WHAT SHALL I WRITE ABOUT?

Six words to chill a writer's blood: 'Where do you get your ideas'? The most honest reply might be

grief. Writing is a very private business. Even if your work is pure invention, it's come from the deepest recesses of your warped imagination. You don't necessarily want that waved about. Unfortunately, there's no way round this one. Going public is scary, but it has to be done.

One way to ease yourself in is to join a creative writing group. You might recoil in horror from the prospect of reading your work to an audience – I did. But everyone I know who's been brave enough to try has found it stimulating and helpful. My own way of breaking the feedback barrier was to give my first drafts to a few trusted friends.

Taking criticism seriously while knowing your own mind is a difficult balance to maintain.

> # " TAKING CRITICISM SERIOUSLY WHILE KNOWING YOUR OWN MIND IS A DIFFICULT BALANCE TO MAINTAIN. "

'I'll tell you when I get some', but a more useful and practical one is 'everywhere'.

As soon as I started attending to the nuts and bolts of writing, the subject matter took care of itself. It didn't have to be new or clever or earth-shattering – it just had to catch my interest.

## NOTHING CATCHING YOUR INTEREST? TRY THIS EXERCISE.

- Find a café, buy yourself a coffee and take a seat by the window.
- Count the first 10 passers-by.
- When you get to number 10, take a mental snapshot of your subject and his or her surroundings.
- Get out your notebook and describe your snapshot in every detail. Clothes, gait, facial expression, hair. People in the background. Street, traffic, weather, sounds, smells.
- Give your passer-by a name. Let's say Florence.
- Ask yourself where Florence was going, where she'd been, who she was thinking about.
- You get the idea. By now you're probably halfway into a story of your own.

## FEEDBACK

I haven't got statistics to prove it, but I'd guess this is the fence where most budding writers come to

My method is to throw a minor tantrum, then let the suggestions percolate. If any of them are still niggling a week later, they're probably right. In any case, it's as well to elicit some opinions before hitting the publishers and agents, if only for the sake of your self-esteem.

Professionals approach your manuscript not as counsellors or teachers but as readers, so it's worth considering their comments – even if, ultimately,

### NIA'S FIVE FAVOURITE NOVELS

*Middlemarch,* **George Eliot**
Humane, intelligent and thoroughly involving.

*Our Mutual Friend,* **Charles Dickens**
Moody and cinematically vivid.

*Lord of the Flies,* **William Golding**
The book that first showed me the power of literature.

*An Artist of the Floating World,* **Kazuo Ishiguro**
Small, subtle, beautifully formed.

*The Peculiar Memories of Thomas Penman,* **Bruce Robinson**
Funny and disturbing.

you disagree. Remember, though, that feedback of any kind from publishers is relatively rare. You're more likely to get, at most, a standard letter – and even that could take months. If you're after impartial views of your work you might want to consider paying for the reading services offered by some agencies and websites.

## WHERE SHALL I SEND IT?

A little preliminary research saves a lot of time, money and disappointment. Most agents and publishers are very clear about what they will and won't consider. A quick look at their websites or listings will ensure that you don't send your futuristic psychodrama to a cookery-book imprint.

Some firms require a letter in the first instance, setting out brief details of your experience and the work you're offering. Others might want a synopsis – usually a page – of the plot, and a couple of sample chapters. A few will take full manuscripts. Most insist on hard copies, rather than electronic files.

If you're starting, as I did, with short stories, I'd recommend reading a selection of the huge range of small-press magazines catering for story-writers and poets, because:

## FIVE HANDY WEBSITES

**www.societyofauthors.net**
Website of the long-established society, with information on grants and an extensive directory.

**www.bbc.co.uk/dna/getwriting/ and www.bbc. co.uk/writersroom/**
Packed with guidance for new writers.

**www.booktribes.com**
An innovative online community where book lovers can share their passion for books.

**www.booksellers.org.uk**
Useful information about the book trade, and good links to other information.

**www.writersmarket.co.uk**
The online companion to this book.

• They're are always bulging with news about competitions, grants, festivals and other outlets – all good incentives to keep writing

• Reading other people's work is a great way of sparking off your own ideas

• Many small-press magazines focus on particular genres or geographical areas, which might limit their readership but also increases your chances of inclusion.

• Just being in print gives you confidence and opens that closet door a little wider.

## SMALL PRESSES

They're underfunded and overworked and not great for name-dropping at parties. But here are a few reasons to celebrate the small-fry companies who keep the literary world alive:

• By and large, they're staffed by people who care more about books than about market trends. So they're more likely to read your manuscript, even if it's not the next *Harry Potter*.

• Published work is easier to promote than unpublished work, whoever produces it. Despite minimal print-runs, my novels led to interviews, literary festivals and tours, commissions and reviews, which – judiciously edited – provide handy blurbs for future submissions.

• Distribution may be trickier for smaller companies, but the internet has changed everything. For all the legitimate worries of independent booksellers, online sales are an undeniable boon to small-scale writers, making their books available everywhere, at the click of a mouse.

## FINALLY

This is one small cog's account of the machine, and your experience may be entirely different. I think it's safe to say, though, that it will entail a certain degree of frustration, insecurity and grumpiness. If you already know all that, and are still writing, stop procrastinating – I know your little game. Get back to that desk. You're a writer!

# YOUR NOVEL: THE ESSENTIAL TICK LIST
## GETTING THE BASICS RIGHT

Jane Friedman discusses some of the tried and tested rules and ways of working for novelists, in any genre

## JANE FRIEDMAN

Jane is Editorial Director for Writer's Digest Books, America's leading publisher of 'how to' and inspirational books for writers of all sorts.

Writing for publication is a business. If the beginning novelist will accept this fact, he'll be one step closer to success. It is not necessary to learn a great mass of rules in order to become a writer, but it is necessary that each writer recognize the principles underlying the profession he seeks to enter. It is necessary that a story should be so put together that it catches the interest at the outset, holds the mind alert and expectant until the climax is reached, and ends with the reader satisfied. If you can break the rules and still produce a manuscript that will grip the attention from the first sentence to the last, you need not fear rejection.

Writers develop their skill at novel writing – or fiction craft and technique – over many years of practice. Novel writing does not become easier after the first attempt. Nearly every accomplished novelist will tell you that she's not sure how she did it the first time (or the second or third time). Each novelist begins all over again with each new novel attempt, not knowing the outcome or if they will finish successfully. But one does learn much more about the art of novel writing after the first attempt – after every attempt – and you'll find that many

published first novels aren't actually an author's first novel at all. Those first and second novels (or third or fourth) are still tucked in a desk drawer or under the bed – often where they rightfully belong.

The following 'tick list' for novel writing offers a brief glimpse of the most essential elements of novel writing, which often inspire lively debate among working writers and successful authors.

## OUTLINING

An outline is like a blueprint for writing your novel. It details the developing plot and action, sometimes scene-by-scene, and often includes sketches of all characters. Outlines tend to be unique to each writer – they can be a few pages or more than a hundred. Many genre writers like to prepare an outline so detailed that it practically serves as a first draft.

Should you create an outline before you start writing your novel? Some writers swear by their outlining methods, while others say it results in contrived plots and characters. Whether outlining

> ## ONCE YOU'VE FINISHED YOUR NOVEL, WHAT YOU HAVE IS A FIRST DRAFT

is a good idea for you depends upon the kind of writer you are or what kind of novel you're writing. Novels with fast-paced plots (or 'high-concept' plots) and numerous subplots would likely benefit from an initial outline. If you believe, however, that stories should be organic and spontaneous in their growth (if your characters tend to rebel against what you have in store for them), then outlining may not be productive for you. Do consider: if you're a non-outliner who has experienced countless novel revisions and drafts due to poor plotting, structure, or pace, try a little pre-planning. Outlining doesn't have to be drudgery or a strict blueprint – it can act as a baseline, a way to keep you focused and on track.

## BEGINNINGS

Start quickly – make the problem/conflict apparent from the first chapter. Don't get bogged down in background detail at the beginning. Weave it into the story as you go. Whatever you do, avoid the urge to start with a prologue, flashback, or other

whether internal or external, and the protagonist's conflict should boil down to a choice. How will the protagonist decide? At all costs you must avoid a *deus ex machina* outcome (one that is left to the gods); the outcome should be the result of characters' actions. It is through characters that you can most highly appeal to your readers and make the most lasting impression. If you want to produce novels that go to the heart of your reader, you must have vivid, convincing characterization.

## DIALOGUE

Dialogue reveals the skill of a writer immediately. Dialogue tags should say who's speaking, but little more. They should only be there to keep things clear, and they don't need to be repeated over and over again if it's clear who is speaking.

> A STORY CAN REQUIRE AN UNLIMITED NUMBER OF REVISIONS TO REACH ITS FULL POTENTRIAL

device that's primarily informational.

After the first chapter or so, no one should have to wonder who your protagonist is. Strangely, this can be a big problem for writers. Make clear whose story it is, who we should really care about. Your opening scene should establish an emotional connection with your readers. This initial connection should intensify as the story progresses, so it's crucial that you ground it early in a particular character (maybe two).

## PLOT AND CHARACTER

The relationship between plot and character can be one of the most vexing for the novelist, and you'll find disagreement among successful authors on whether character or plot should drive your novel. At the very least, though, no matter how interesting your characters, no matter how beautiful and unique your setting, no matter how fresh and pleasing the action you have gathered together, you have no material for any kind of story unless your characters have an obstacle to overcome (or are at war with one another).

Your story should be driven forward by conflict,

The biggest mistake in dialogue is to use it as a form of exposition in which characters deliver information (usually back story or technical explanation) to the reader. Don't have your characters talk about things they already know about and wouldn't explain to each other.

Finally, dialogue should be dramatic. Eliminate all commonplace dialogue; if dialogue copied real-life exchanges, it would be very boring. Don't do it. Only use dialogue that furthers the plot of the story or tells us something about the characters.

## POINT OF VIEW

Don't go from first-person point-of-view ('I') to third-person point-of-view ('he' or 'she') in the same story or novel. Choose one and stick with it. A more difficult problem is switching viewpoints between characters. Beginners should choose one viewpoint character and not switch to another. That means: you may get inside one person's head (such as your protagonist's), and relate that person's feelings throughout the course of the story – but you should never reveal what's going on inside other characters' heads. One of the most common problems for new writers is abruptly switching between characters' viewpoints in the same scene.

I have heard people ask a thousand times why it is that all guides on writing declare against shifting viewpoint when successful writers allow their viewpoint to shift about. The reason is that successful writers who break such rules succeed not because of their breaking the rules, but because their style, characterization, or mastery of the craft overcomes the inherent problems involved with the shifting of the viewpoint.

If you do switch between characters' viewpoints, try to make the switch during chapter breaks, or indicate it within a chapter by using *** or a visual indicator.

## RESEARCH

Good research is what makes your finished work come alive with realism and truth. Each interview, each trip to the library (or website) is what adds excitement and authenticity to your finished piece. There are only so many subjects you can write about from personal experience, and there are only so many subjects you can learn firsthand. Fortunately, to learn everything else you can rely on others' expertise through interviews, the internet, and books and magazines. In the end, the quality of what you write will be based on the quality of what you know and learn.

## REVISION

Once you've finished your novel, what you have is a first draft. A major key to getting your fiction published is learning to revise that first draft, as well as the second, third, and infinite number of drafts that follow. It can be easy in the afterglow of a finished story to want to rush it out into the world, to share your enthusiasm for your creation with readers. This is never a good idea. Few editors and agents have time to work with writers on promising stories – only polished ones.

A story can require an unlimited number of revisions to reach its full potential. Celebrated US author Joyce Carol Oates is known to revise work of her own that has already been published. Give the manuscript time to become as polished as you can make it. Joining a writer's critique group may be helpful, or look for a mentor or a colleague who

is a careful and responsive reader. Just be sure not to rely on the opinions of your family and close friends; they will not be able to give you an honest assessment of your work.

## FINAL THOUGHTS

When I find an author who is glad to be shown his defects but who also declares that no amount of adverse criticism can induce him to stop writing, that author possesses two key elements of a successful writing career. A writer should so love his work that he would go on writing even if he knew that his efforts would never bring him a word of praise or a cent of money. Editors have a deep respect for that kind of writer.

## WRITING DISCIPLINE

Most successful writers have a routine; a daily way of weaving their writing into their lives so that it is a job like any other. Here are four starting points from which to proceed:

• Have a plan and sets of goals. What are you going to write, and by when?

• Set aside specific times for writing. Many of us are at our best early in the morning, but some writers work best at dead of night. Either end of the day is usually good as those are when you are most likely to get peace and quiet. Get into a pattern of working and stick to it.

• Set yourself a specific minimum number of words to aim for; even if it's only 50 you'll still see your manuscript growing over time.

• Make good use of any unexpected 'spare' time. If that train or plane is going to be delayed don't just sit there – write. Of course this means your notebook needs to be with you at all times; it might well be your most important piece of equipment.

# SHORT STORIES
## WRITING IN THE SCIENCE FICTION, FANTASY AND HORROR GENRES

Linda Acaster gives pointers for success in three very popular genres

## LINDA ACASTER

Linda has published seventy short stories across a selection of genres, three historical novels and a host of articles on the techniques of writing fiction. Her fantasy tends to have its roots in early medieval history, her science fiction is extrapolated from tidbits of information that snag her interest, and her horror from any daily newspaper she has the misfortune to open.

While the markets for other types of short fiction have diminished, markets for the three genres known collectively as speculative fiction have grown rampant. There are reasons for this: readers care enough to sacrifice inordinate amounts of their time, not simply to print-reading, but to supporting their favoured sub-genres via associations, conventions, author readings, pro-zines and fanzines, and writing it themselves; writers, particularly household-name novelists, continue to embrace the short story form, so producing a huge catalogue of short fiction that readers can enjoy, and new writers can study.

## SPECULATIVE FICTION

You're not interested in speculative fiction? I'm sceptical of that. Depending on the criteria used as a guide, the three genres spawn between 20 and 30 subgenres. From alternate history to humorous fantasy, magic realism to psychological horror, utopian fiction to hard science fiction, there is a niche to light the imagination of any writer. As all fiction is, by definition, fantasy because it is not verbatim reality, how much of a nudge do you need to slip through the self-imposed barriers of your comfort zone and unfurl your creative wings?

## DOING IT THE SAME BUT DIFFERENTLY

Writing is communication, and communicating on the page differs little no matter the genre. A writer creates a mental, emotionally experienced reality, encodes it into a written language, passes it for distribution where it is taken by a reader, who decodes the written language so as to emotionally experience the reality as it was experienced in the writer's mind. Nothing to it, really. For illustration I'll describe the birth-pangs of three of my own short stories: *Doppelganger* (fantasy), *Harvester World TZ29-4* (science fiction) and *The Donor* (horror).

## STARTING WITH A PREMISE

Writers who concentrate on one particular category of speculative fiction will be on the lookout for a premise that compliments that category, something that has caught their imaginations and they want to explore. Because I write short fiction in a number of different genres I look for a premise that doesn't fit easily elsewhere: the effect of hypnosis on multiple personalities; extrapolating society's obsession with genetic engineering; in donating our organs on death, do we truly die?

## CHARACTER

Character is paramount. Readers are complex beings, so protagonists need to be, too. I'm a 'show', not a 'tell', writer, but I've used both techniques to convey fiction on the page. My characters have to be emotionally motivated so that readers

The choice of gender – or alien or animal – is made partly on the scenery coalescing about the premise and the emotional motivation of the character, and partly on my cold calculation as to the possibilities that character can offer a story, and that story the reader. This takes brainstorming

> ## "CHARACTER IS PARAMOUNT. BECAUSE READERS ARE COMPLEX BEINGS, PROTAGONISTS NEED TO BE, TOO"

experience, not watch; empathize, not sympathize. For *Doppelganger* I settled on an ineffectual character tired of being humiliated; for *Harvester World TZ29-4* a childless woman euphoric on being offered motherhood; for *The Donor* a near-death experience changing a character's outlook on life.

as each possibility is chased down using what if? and why? Taking the hypnosis and multiple personalities premise, females come ready-faceted by expectations of society: they should be caring nurturers while assertive and self-fulfilling, their wardrobe is expected to mimic that of a cross-

## TEN TIPS FOR A SUCCESSFUL SHORT STORY

- Read. Speculative fiction is a congested super-genre with a long and innovative backlist. Don't try to add to it without knowing what's already out there.

- Think first, write second. Lack of thinking leads to use of clichés.

- Keep it simple. A short story should elucidate a single train of events, not a man's, or a world's, history.

- Openings should provide anchors for readers to link into and so let slip their own reality to immerse themselves in your fictional reality: an indication of time, place, focus character and problem.

- Keep it focused. Choose the viewpoint character to gain maximum drama – usually the one with the biggest problem – and stick to it. Don't head-hop, and don't allow the author on the page.

- Write in specifics so that readers can build true mental images, not fuzzy outlines. Humans have five senses, not just sight, and you can let them help your word pictres.

- Don't summarize, dramatize. Readers can't experience a bullet-pointed list.

- Beware info-dumps. Are you showing off your research or your lack of planning? If the information is pertinent to the story and not simply dressing, thread it into the story a strip at a time.

- Choose words with care. Ensure the level of vocabulary is in keeping with the viewpoint character. A rash of adverbs or extravagant dialogue tags is a sure sign that there is a problem.

- Become your characters, and write. Pacing, dialogue, description and the rest will be much easier to juggle.

dresser, and so on. The effect society's expectations has on males isn't so obvious. There is also the added ingredient that I'm female so exploring a male's psyche holds a certain fascination. The questions continue: if a man wants to change his personality but is so ineffectual that he relies on a hypnotist to do the changing for him, what other insecurities does he harbour? What other personalities are on offer, and if he does change what happens to his ineffectual self? What if? and why? again and again and again.

## BUDDIES, ANTAGONISTS AND OUTSIDE INFLUENCES

It is at this brainstorming stage that the original character can split into protagonist and antagonist, or protagonist and buddy. The female desperate

### LINDA PICKS FIVE FAVOURITE AUTHORS

Five favourites across three genres with nearly 30 subgenres between them? I'll be arbitrary. Keeping to UK authors and ignoring the upper pantheon...

*Chaz Brenchley*
Whether it is straight fiction, crime, magic realism or historical fantasy, there is a distinct and individual tone to each novel with subtexts subtly conveyed.

*Ken MacLeod*
Usually wary of hard SF, I like his because I can empathize with his characters.

*Simon Clark*
If you like your horror with plenty of gore, this is your man.

*Gwyneth Jones*
You name it, she writes it, through all three genres, including as Ann Halam for teenagers.

*Robert Holdstock*
The blinkers came off with his 1984 novel, *Mythago Wood*, showing me that my love of history could be a mere portal. It remains my comfort zone icon, to be relaxed with at regular intervals.

to be a mother spawned a male suspicious of the circumstances, but I didn't know why until I read an article on progeria, a medical condition where an infant's growth is interrupted and its aging process accelerated. What if this misstep of nature was planned? By whom? Why? What if the female wasn't a 'woman' in the accepted sense but a product of genetic engineering – a clone or manufactured drone? What if all the characters were? The time and place ingredients, not yet considered, immediately moved into the future and off-planet.

While a buddy can act as the sounding board for underlying thoughts and fears the protagonist does not wish to face but the reader needs to take into consideration, an antagonist can be a direct opposite in motivation and temperament. If a character has its life-view altered due to a near-death experience, could another character similarly have its life-view entrenched? A news report on the serious injury of two joy-riders proved to be the catalyst for *The Donor*, and the gender and age of the lead characters were set, as were their relationship and shared sub-culture. But their roles needed to be reversed. While I'd been concentrating on the changed life-viewer as protagonist, adding in the new information made it obvious that the character with the entrenched life-view would offer far more scope for drama.

## STORYLINE

With premise, lead characters and setting cast, foundations are firm enough to consider the storyline evolving in the background. It is given a cursory examination to ensure that it is workable, but that's all. I don't produce an outline. When I first started writing fiction I began with ideas for a storyline, tinkered until a reasonable premise presented itself, and then went in search of characters to delineate it. The routine rarely produced fiction of satisfying depth. It was when I stopped directing and started acting that the change occurred.

As I would once have done, it is at this point that an exuberant writer rushes to the keyboard, yet the planning is only half complete.

## TONE, GENRE, MARKET

Is the story of the ineffectual man seeking a different personality going to be comic fantasy, erotic fantasy, paranormal, or psychological horror? Choice of tone will either become the overall decider, or the choice of genre or subgenre will lead to a decision on tone. However, this pairing cannot be agreed in isolation if a particular market is being targeted. The market's requirements must be able to accommodate the chosen genre and may influence the depth of tone used to convey the story. In turn the tone's resonance will depend on the choice of individual words and the length and syntax of the sentences. There's no point marking out an area for hopscotch if I'm supposed to be undertaking the hop, skip and jump.

Do I always adhere to this complicated shuffle? If I know the market – have immersed myself in its fiction by studying back issues – it becomes

> **WITH PREMISE, LEAD CHARACTERS AND SETTING CAST, FOUNDATIONS ARE FIRM ENOUGH TO CONSIDER THE STORYLINE EVOLVING IN THE BACKGROUND**

part of the automatic creative process that by usage seldom fails me. This does not mean that the story is on course for an acceptance, only that I can be confident that it is walking in the right neighbourhood. If I'm trying out a technique or type of story that I have little experience with, then giving it my best is the priority. If it works successfully I'll keep an eye open for likely markets and rewrite as necessary.

## SHOW AND TELL, VIEWPOINT AND TENSE

The individual elements are now primed so it is back to the characters for a final tweaking. Do I know them inside out, their fears and attitudes, their back-stories, where and how they live? On the page is not the place to work this out, it is the place

to be credible. And to be credible I don't set the characters in motion and write telling readers what I see happening to them, I become the viewpoint character and write showing what happens to me. More or less. There is a decent amount of sleight-of-hand and fancy footwork going on to accomplish this, but the trick is not to let the reader know it's happening.

A way of achieving this is to make choices on viewpoint and tense that compliment the storyline and the tone. The ineffectual man in *Doppelganger* was an ideal candidate for first person viewpoint narration as I wanted the least distance possible between him and the reader so as to enhance the claustrophobic tone. I set him in a dead-end job in a grey office environment where his opportunities for interaction with other people were minimal. In short, I isolated him so his natural instinct was to retreat inside himself, taking the reader with him. Past tense was used to convey the story until the final scene when the tense was shifted into present to underline his sense of being lost, physically, mentally and spiritually – a living death.

First person viewpoint and past tense was again chosen for the joy-rider in *The Donor*, this time to convey the man's anger and corruption of spirit after five years of obsessing on the outcome of a crash. Everything – the people, the places, the sounds, the smells – was filtered through his festering mindset by the use of a conversational delivery using short sentences littered with colloquialisms. Readers became 'one of the boys' from the start so that by the end they also shared the burden.

It is not often that I contemplate a storyline which takes place across years. It is difficult to achieve in the short story form as so much needs explaining, yet incidents seem inconsequential when taken in isolation. Info-dumping becomes a real hazard. The genetics story, *Harvester World TZ29-4*, was written using parallel time-frames: past events, conveyed in past tense using the usual dialogue/narrative mix, and present events conveyed in present tense using a controlled inner narrative, each leapfrogging the other with a single first person narrator acting as the link. Inconsequential incidents in the past became robed with significance by being reflected in the mirror of the present, allowing readers to build a third picture of their own from the information.

And there we are. Nothing to it, really. All it takes is a bit of practice.

# WRITING BIOGRAPHY
## HOW DO YOU GO ABOUT IT?

Writing biography is like having an affair, argues Margaretta Jolly

## DR MARGARETTA JOLLY

Margaretta is the editor of *The Encyclopedia of Life Writing, Dear Laughing Motorbyke: Letters from Women Welders of the Second World War* and *Critical Perspectives on Pat Barker*. She has also published on the art of letter writing, ghost biography and coming out stories. She lectures in contemporary literature at Exeter University.

To write biography is to write history, drama and fiction all at once. As Virginia Woolf put it, you must combine the granite of fact with the rainbow of personality, something she herself admitted was an impossible task. You may spend years interviewing eccentric relatives and busying about in archives, to discover you cannot make a good story out of the life of a quiet sensible writer. On the other hand, you may suspect that Queen Victoria was in fact a cross-dressing highwaywoman but you can't prove it.

### A LOW-LIFE GENRE FOR THE LOW LIFE

No doubt it is this duality that makes biography writing vulnerable to other writers' condescension. Novelists condemn it as the form for those who can't make things up. Historians believe it reduces theories of causality to pop psychology. And everybody judges it for being tabloid journalism with pretensions. Ian Hamilton's *In Search of J.D. Salinger* made a virtue of this by turning himself into two people, the humble critic wanting to honour a great writer, and the compulsive detective-fan who

doesn't know when to let well enough alone. J.D. wasn't charmed: he sued Hamilton for unauthorized quoting of his letters, and Hamilton was forced to rewrite the whole thing. (It's still fabulous.)

Those who are driven to write – and to read – biographies know the genre's limits. But they also know what makes its particular quest and romance so special.

### THE MYSTERY OF OTHER PEOPLE

Writing biography is to confront a person's otherness, often discovering oneself in the process. The mystery this involves is why so many biographers talk about falling in love with their subject. Leon Edel, who spent a lifetime writing the biography of Henry James, said the key was to uncover a subject's 'personal myth' – for him, James' homo-erotic desires were a distraction. But the back-weave need not be psychological. Many of the best biographies find the pattern in the individual's times. Hannah Arendt found in the life of concentration-camp designer Adolf Eichmann a means to analyse the 'banality of evil'. Virginia Woolf comically revealed the stuffy hypocrisy of Victorian Britain by writing the life of Elizabeth Barrett Browning's cocker spaniel Flush. Claire Tomalin won the 2004 Whitbread Prize for *Pepys, The Unequalled Self* because she said everything the diarist didn't about 17th-century London.

### CHOOSING YOUR SUBJECT

Pepys was a good choice for a subject. Almost everyone has heard of him, but there was no accessible biography. Similarly, Hilary Spurling's life of Matisse had a ready-made market. Choosing the right subject is crucial to successful biography. You have to be fascinated by their society, and you have to understand what they did. Don't write about Wole

**43**

Soyinka if you don't understand Nigerian politics. Do write about your unknown great-aunt, but be prepared for private publication and an audience of family and friends. Biographies of writers have the advantage that the subject will probably be quotable and might have left stashes of letters, diaries and drafts. On the other hand, a life of action may provide plot but inarticulacy. Football ace Wayne Rooney's 'autobiography' garnered an advance of millions but hasn't sold. Which brings me on to….

## AUTHORIZED, UNAUTHORIZED, GHOSTED OR TOASTED: WHOSE LIFE IS IT ANYWAY?

The ghost-written 'autobiography' of a celebrity marks the extreme end of the biographer's subservience to the biographee. They, not you, decide what the public shall know, and you will be paid a fee rather than a royalty. With an authorized biography, commissioned by the subject or their family, you are still somewhat the hired hand, although you may cultivate a relationship that allows you your voice and their archives. The best contract is the unauthorized biography, in which you may write what you like, within the laws of libel. You need to be able to defend your facts as 'provable truth', should you be so unlucky as to end in court. You cannot libel the dead, but you can upset their descendents. Copyright laws prove another challenge. If the subject has been dead for less than 75 years, all their letters, diaries and published works are owned by their estate, and you may need to pay to quote. The law of Fair Use does allow a free 250–1000 words, but each case will be different.

Overcoming these practical and stylistic hurdles without compromising either respect for your subject or your own art requires intense discipline. That's why biography is in the end a relationship that is much more than an affair.

## FIVE BIOGRAPHICAL SURPRISES

John Aubrey's *Brief Lives* shows you that even 17th-century biography thrived on anecdotes and the detail of a forgotten hat.

Sylvia Townsend Warner's *T.H. White* remains a classic for balancing story-telling with scrupulous respect, though White was a grumpy man who loved boys, and to whom little happened after his thirties.

Janet Malcolm's *The Silent Woman* tells you as much about biographical sleuthing as the Plath-Hughes marriage.

Julian Barnes' *Flaubert's Parrot* is the funniest, pithiest example of post-modern biography.

Peter Ackroyd's *London: The Biography* reminds us that people are not the only beings to live, love and die.

## TIPS FOR BIOGRAPHERS

- Be careful whom you fall for: you're going to have to live with them for a long time and, worse, you may discover somebody else has fallen for them too!

- Be realistic about the market. A biography will be judged and bought for who it is about, not who it is by.

- Read the *Oxford Dictionary of National Biography*, burrow in the British Library. Find addresses in phone books and www.192.com, via Friends United or trade unions.

- Experiment with point of view. What changes if you put yourself in the picture? Or tell the story of their house, pet or mother?

- Prioritise interviewing those who are over 80, test your tape recorder and record the date and place of interview. Write up interview notes the same day.

- Decide how far to hypothesize. Will you allow speculative dialogue?

# WRITING NON-FICTION
## WISDOM FROM A BESTSELLING NATURAL HISTORY AUTHOR

Dr Paul Sterry explains how his passion and hobby also earn him his living. Paul's insights apply to all areas of non-fiction publishing

## DR PAUL STERRY

Paul did a degree and PhD in Zoology at Imperial College, London before working as a research fellow at the University of Sussex for five years. He became a freelancer in the 1980s and now owns and manages the photolibrary Nature Photographers Ltd, while pursuing a writing career. In recent years, this has been mainly as the creator of photographic field guides for HarperCollins.

From an early age I can remember being almost as fascinated by natural history books as I was by the subjects they were describing. Like many of my peers, I started off collecting and using titles in the Observers series before progressing, when funds would permit, to their older cousins in Warne's Wayside and Woodland series. For me the books I possessed were objects of beauty in their own right as well as sources of reference. Never once did I imagine I would write anything in the same vein myself.

### THE FIRST BREAK
My first writing break came in the early 1980s when, out of the blue, I was approached to write a book called *Pond Watching*. At the time I still had a 'proper' job and my immediate reaction, having never written anything for public consumption before, was 'I can't do that'. Fortunately, however, long-forgotten advice about 'never turning down an opportunity' stirred in the back of my mind and before commonsense could prevail I said 'yes' to the offer. Thank goodness I did. In those days, manuscripts had to be hand-written and then typed, and so much of the process was unbelievably tedious. Nevertheless, the writing bug had bitten me.

### FINDING WORK
As in all spheres of freelance life, there is competition aplenty for writing jobs, as any budding author or jobbing writer will tell you. In this sense, writing natural history books is no different from writing on any other subject, except perhaps that the potential pool of unpublished authors is bigger than in most other spheres of interest. Discounting books that are generated by TV tie-ins or celebrities, work for the everyday author comes in two forms – either a publisher will come up with an idea and then look for a suitable writer, or an author dreams up a concept for a book and then approaches the publisher. So how do you actually convince a publisher that either you are the person for the job they have in mind or that the idea you have approached them with is worth pursuing?

When considering potential authors, most publishers are looking for somebody who can write accurately and speedily, and who recognises the need to stick to agreed deadlines. Before you can convince a publisher that you have these qualities

**45**

you need to build up a track record. Therein lies the problem for the aspiring, but unpublished author. In terms of your qualifications to write on any given subject, peer recognition can play an important part – so get out there and make yourself known. When it comes to the writing side of things, write anything and everything, be it magazine articles or minor contributions to larger books. At this stage in your career, don't necessarily worry too much about the financial side of things – think of it as an investment.

## STICK TO WHAT YOU KNOW ABOUT

I should perhaps qualify the statement 'write anything and everything' by stressing that it is important to recognize your area of expertise: play to your strengths, and don't expose your weaknesses. Also ask yourself why you want to write. If it is because you want to get a message across or embark on a personal crusade then, unless you are extremely lucky, or have a genuine gift for literary expression, you are unlikely to succeed. With a few exceptions in terms or subjects and authors, natural history writing is not an area

where the inexperienced author is likely to shine unless he or she writes about things in a factual and informative manner; a professional approach if you like.

## ADDED VALUE

It is also worth asking yourself if you can supply 'added value' in any way. In my case, I did this, and still do this, by supplying photographs to accompany the text. This was never a problem – rather, it was a pleasure – since wildlife photography had always been a passion of mine and it made perfect sense to publish pictures in my own books, rather than contribute them to books written by other people. Most publishers find the prospect of a complete 'package' extremely appealing, not to mention good value for money. Taking this to its logical extreme, most of the books I work on nowadays are done in conjunction with an editorial partner and together we supply the publisher with PDF files ready for printing. A decade ago, this approach would have been unthinkable so it is important to move with the times, and take advantage of technological advances.

# SURVIVAL TIPS FOR WRITERS

- Recognize the most creative time of day for you to write and set aside that period to the exclusion of all else.

- Recognize that writing is a job – indeed sometimes nothing more than a chore.

- If you are easily distracted, disconnect the phone while writing and move your desk so that it faces a blank wall.

- If in doubt about how to write something, rather than agonize, just clear your mind and imagine you are in an exam situation and have to finish in a given time limit.

- It is far easier to edit and improve something than it is to agonize over every last word as you go along.

- Always re-read what you have written, ideally a day or two later and in conjunction with text written before and after. This helps maintain a continuity of style.

- Write in the same way as you would speak to somebody – it is all too easy to acquire literary pretensions that are inappropriate in the context of most non-fiction writing.

- Stick to the matter in hand and remain professional, by which I mean don't let your personal opinions influence the way you write.

- Don't get too precious about your writing – your text is just one part of the complex process of book publishing.

- Never read reviews of your own books!

# ON POETRY
## WHAT IS POETRY FOR ANYWAY?

Andy Brown discusses some important reasons for writing poetry

### ANDY BROWN

Andy is Director of the Centre for Creative Writing & Arts at Exeter University. His eight books include *Fall of the Rebel Angels: Poems 1996 – 2006* and *Goose Music*, co-written with John Burnside (both Salt International Editions). He also writes short stories, reviews and poetry criticism.

### REMEMBRANCE, ROMANCE AND RUDENESS

In one of his lyric essays, the US poet and undertaker Thomas Lynch asserts that poetry has three main purposes: 'breaking bread with the dead', 'wooing our loved ones', and 'poxing our enemies'. I've written all three kinds – poems of Remembrance, Romance and Rudeness – and can recommend them all: the eulogy consoles; the love poem gets results ('Reader, I married her') and the third is, let's face it, more creative than a fashionable poetry punch-up. But let me expand on Lynch's Trinity…

### SINGING

Poets have always commemorated their dead, penning eulogies, epitaphs, dirges and prayers, threnodies, obsequies and, lastly, laments. When not doing so, they've praised the living with elegies, panegyrics, encomiums and odes. To my mind, there's not enough Praise Poetry around any more, so I urge you to sing someone or something's praises whenever you can. It's good for the soul.

If not singing, then voicing your poems is imperative. Poetry is all about breath, and the sounds breath carries. It is not about ideas. Poetry is a physical sound. And reading and writing are both physical acts. That makes poems very real things.

One doesn't, however, have to descend to the level of greetings-card doggerel to write a good poem celebrating life's landmarks. And lest all this seem too earnest for our oh-so-ironic age, then vent your spleen with a Curse or a Complaint. Get it off your poetic chest. Or take the current advice of the shrinks: laughter is good for you and can be the best medicine – even in a poem.

### GETTING BETTER?

Talking of medicine, there's been much debate about whether or not poetry should be cathartic, therapeutic, or confessional. Wherever you stand on this, poetry certainly seems to satisfy a deep need, both individually and socially. In an age when our language has been so debased by political

## 10 TIPS ON POETRY

1. Poetry is made of Things, not Ideas.
2. Poetry is a sound.
3. Poetry is the best words in the best order.
4. Poetry happens in the white spaces.
5. Poetry brings us out of ourselves and directs us to the World.
6. Celebrate, lament, love, curse. Laugh.
7. Write like you were unafraid.
8. Write what you mean, and mean what you write.
9. If you can't take a risk in a poem, where can you?
10. Poetry points in the wrong direction and heads off there regardless; for the sheer pleasure of it.

47

spin, advertising, journalese and text messaging (amongst other evils), poetry is a way of restoring language to health. Poems give language a thorough work out. All great poets have enriched the language and ours is a duty to make the language work in the best possible, new ways.

## FOR WHOM?

Cyril Connolly once said: 'Better to write for yourself and have no public, than to write for the public and have no self'. He was right, to a degree: one should never write poetry with an eye on being popular. Not least because the public couldn't care

> **A POEM IS FINISHED ONLY WHEN IT NO LONGER NEEDS YOU; WHEN IT WOULD COLLAPSE IF YOU CUT A SINGLE WORD MORE**

less if you write it or not. Poetry sales are minimal. Paradoxically, that frees us up, neither to write the greatest Everyman Poem of the New Millennium, nor to chase the popular success of the current gang of poetry darlings, but to write exactly as we wish. Poets are only going to be read by a few, so 'to thine own self be true'.

But Connolly was also wrong. Writing is about others. It's about Readers. Even if it's only one. Never underestimate them. 'Your reader is at least as intelligent as you are' advised the poet Basil Bunting. Poetry communicates something in heightened language to someone else. Poetry is therefore about them, not you. Copernicus showed that the Earth wasn't at the centre of the Universe. The same holds for poets: the poem is at the centre, not the poet. It's all about the words, and about what your readers make of them.

## WORDS WORDS WORDS WORDS WORDS

Remember, poems are just words; material that could be expressed in any number of ways. The poet's job is to find the best form and expression for that material. The duty is to the words, not 'truth to the experience', or 'sincerity of feeling', but making the words sound right with depth.

Hemingway was once asked why the last page of one of his books needed re-writing some 39 times. 'What was wrong?' asked the interviewer. 'Getting the words right,' the reply. Hemingway wasn't being glib. It's hard work. A poem is finished only when it no longer needs you; when it would collapse if you cut a single word more. It is finished when it sounds right. Poetry is above all a sound.

## 'I CAN'T NOT WRITE POEMS'

If you agree with that statement, you're a poet. But if we knew what the next poem was going to be like, we wouldn't need to write it. And if we knew it was going to be another one like the last, there wouldn't be any point either. 'Poetry is words in new configurations, fresh to the senses', wrote William Carlos Williams. He was right too. Poets must firstly surprise themselves, which means playing, seriously, with language. Experimenting. Having fun. Pushing it as far as you can. Challenging yourself.

## ANDY'S TOP FIVE RECENT UK POETRY BOOKS

**Selected Poems, John Burnside**
Sublime, lyric poems exploring our wonder at nature and our belonging in the world.

**How to Disappear, Amanda Dalton**
Moving, strange, disquieting poems, with a great dramatic sequence 'Room of Leaves' adapted for Radio 4.

**Collected Poems, Lee Harwood**
'Britain's best kept secret' according to John Ashbery. 40 years of fabulously inventive work here.

**Dart, Alice Oswald**
A journey along the Dart, weaving verse, prose poetry and the voices of the people, animals and spirits who inhabit the river.

**Full Stretch, Anthony Wilson**
Warm, witty, generous poems, skillfully crafted, great fun and respectful of their readers.

# SPECIALITY BOOKS FOR PRE-SCHOOLERS
## EXAMINING A GROWING NICHE MARKET

Books for the under-fives have seen a huge rise in popularity in recent years, but before you jump on the bandwagon (or ride-on)...

### RICHARD POWELL

Richard has been making books for pre-school children for twenty or so years, and is co-founder of the small independent publisher, Treehouse Children's Books. His own books for pre-schoolers have sold 37 million copies worldwide and have been published in 35 languages.

**Why You Shouldn't Write for Pre-schoolers.**
**Let's get the harsh reality bit over first of all.**
There's no money in it. There's no celebrity to be gained. Your friends will ask 'Do you ever write proper books?' once they learn your magnum opus is just ten pages long, contains under fifty words and has a target audience of nappy wetting illiterates. The less polite will simply rib you to death. Don't mention it at parties.

'So it's not glamorous, but with a readership like that it must be easy at least, and it's still a book, printed, in the high street, with my name on it.'

Well, yes and no. It's true that 50 words is a lot easier to write than 50,000, but then again it means those 50 have to be chosen pretty carefully, as each one rather stands out among so few companions.

And, of course, your readership does have a limited life experience, thus the subject matter has to be somewhat constrained too.

'I don't care, I have resigned myself to a literary life based around ridicule, farm animals and talking tractors. What can I do that might get published?'

There are three options. Board books, picture books or novelty books. For very young children there are three basic stages of book development:

1. For babies there are board books of clear pictures and few rhyming, rhythmic words, and cloth books and bath books which are a novelty development of these (for children from birth to one, although age grading is dangerous as children develop at such different rates and many books can serve more than one age range).

2. For toddlers, as they grow more curious and dexterous, there are more sophisticated board books and novelty books, before they graduate to...

3. First picture books.

Now, unless you are an exceptional illustrator and/or writer preferably with a cast-iron reputation and a good sales record, loved by reviewers and librarians, an ordinary board book or picture book just ain't going to cut it. Editors can knock out straight board books themselves, thus not having to pay an author, can choose tailor-made subject material and commission just the right illustrator for the intended market. For picture books, illustrations or text have to be exceptional and the author or illustrator lucky - the competition is staggeringly tough. And its no good saying but my son/daughter/grandson/daughters absolutely adore my stories and/or pictures, because let's be honest, they're going to love anything you write or draw. They would squeal with delight if you read them the shipping forecast. What you need is what we call in the trade 'something extra', which is where the novelty book comes in.

## WHAT IS A NOVELTY BOOK?

This is a book, often made of card or board, which has pages, yes, but also the addition of other elements, from simple lift-up flaps, shaped pages or holes cut in the pages to custom manufactured electronic sound and light modules built into the book design.

## WHAT'S THE FUN IN CREATING A NOVELTY BOOK?

In a novelty book the graphic design, the physical object, and sometimes the mechanics or paper engineering included within it are all equally important in creating a unified, satisfactory, entertaining whole. Making a pre-school novelty book is a bit like being an inventor. There's something of a challenge for the illustrator, the designer and the wordsmith, and anyone can be the instigator of a successful idea.

> **FOR PICTURE BOOKS, ILLUSTRATIONS OR TEXT HAVE TO BE EXCEPTIONAL AND THE AUTHOR OR ILLUSTRATOR LUCKY – THE COMPETITION IS STAGGERINGLY TOUGH**

## WHAT THE PUBLISHER LOOKS FOR:

1. An original novelty concept, design or novel use of an existing novelty 'form' or material.

2. The right kind of subject matter for the right age group.

3. The right word count/extent for the age group – a line or two max per page.

4. A rhythmic or rhyming text that is fun to say out loud for both the reader and the listener

5. Humour/charm – don't forget the poor adult who will have to read this thing again and again and again...

6. An original and novel twist on presenting early learning subjects.

7. Practicality – don't ask for animated 3D laser generated atomic-powered holograms.

8. Each spread working as an entertainment on its own.

9. Every spread linked by a common thread/storyline/theme.

10. Ideally, a prototype which demonstrates how the novelty element works.

11. Subjects that will work internationally. These books are often published simultaneously in several countries for economic reasons.

12. A book that will be safe – safety regulations for books of this nature are as stringent as those for toys. The publisher will know the details but a heavy application of common sense to your idea will get you most of the way.

## DO I NEED TO REGRESS TO BABYHOOD TO WRITE FOR BABIES?

No, because you need to be able to read and write.

Seriously, to get myself into the right frame of mind I imagine myself sat comfortably in a deep armchair with a toddler on my knee staring at a completely blank book. I pick a theme. Story time begins and I ask myself what can I do on that blank page that will grab the attention of the imaginary wriggling, enthusiastic baby or toddler (invariably one of my two sons, which revelation will crease them up with embarrassment as they are both young men now) sat on my lap. I think of a picture that might capture their imaginations, and then I think how to animate that picture and what words would enhance it and how to introduce an element of surprise, of peekaboo, of hide-and-seek, something that will make them giggle. If I hear the imaginary giggle, I know I'm on the right track. Well, it works for me. Then I have to figure out how to make what I imagined work in the real world. It's a good idea to have an idea of the style of illustration that would suit, but the publisher will be more than happy to choose their own illustrator if you are not a professional.

## RICHARD'S FIVE FAVOURITE BOOKS FOR PRE-SCHOOLERS

### Amazing Baby
Series of books for babies and toddlers that encapsulate the best in contemporary publishing for these age groups.

### Hungry Caterpillar, Eric Carle
A perfect mix of novelty, text and illustration, each element supporting each other to tell the story with humour and suspense.

### Dear Zoo, Rod Campbell
So simple but effective flap book with a classic twist at the end and ever so slightly off the wall.

### Where The Wild Things Are, Maurice Sendak and Each Peach Pear Plum, Janet and Allan Ahlberg
Typify the very best in classic first picture books.

## WHAT'S THE POINT OF MAKING BOOKS FOR CHILDREN TOO YOUNG TO READ?

They can often be the beginning of a lifelong love affair with the book. Not so long ago the novelty book was derided by the great and good of the children's book world who wrote them off as gimmicky, of no literary merit, and more like toys than books. Well, actually, that's the point. Children like toys, more than they like books – at first, anyway. Things that move, pictures hidden then suddenly revealed, noises, shiny surfaces and bits that sparkle or are soft or squidgy to touch

## CHILDREN LIKE TOYS, MORE THAN THEY LIKE BOOKS – AT FIRST, ANYWAY

attract the curious baby and toddler, they draw them in to this thing Mum or Dad calls a book, make them familiar with the way pages turn, with sequences, with the concept of a beginning, a middle and an end. There is no better 'quality time' that can be spent between adult and child than when sharing a book. And of course many early learning concepts can be physically illustrated by a moving part in a picture, by a texture, by a sound even, and the reinforcement provided by the surprise and fun of a paper tiger actually jumping out from behind a cardboard tree when a tab is pulled, like the expression on the young reader's face, is priceless. With the greatly increased interest in early years development the value of these kinds of books is now generally agreed upon and every major children's publisher publish some of them alongside the traditional first picture books and straightforward board books.

## THE WORTHY CAUSE

The toy-like qualities of novelty books attract very young children, but just as importantly they intrigue the adults that buy them, often appealing to those who are not normally book buyers, and therefore introduce books into households where perhaps books might not otherwise appear alongside the plethora of toys every young child is showered with. And that can't be a bad thing.

51

# WRITING FOR NEWSPAPERS
## FIVE ESSENTIAL QUESTIONS FOR NEWSPAPER JOURNALISTS

Alison Benjamin of the *The Guardian* gets to the heart of the journalist's motivation

## ALISON BENJAMIN

Alison is deputy editor of *The Guardian*'s weekly *Society* section. Her job entails both writing and commissioning features. She was a regular freelancer for the section before joining the staff in 2002. She has written extensively on social issues for *The Guardian*, ranging from homelessness, to child poverty and drugs policy. She also writes on corporate social responsibility for *Guardian Unlimited*'s environment website. Her journalism career began on a local newspaper in Kent, almost 20 years ago, after graduating in History from Sussex University.

I always wanted to write for a newspaper. As an inquisitive teenager I learnt about the world through the pages of *The Guardian*, which landed on the doormat each morning (except for Sundays when an *Observer* took its place). Burying my head in their broadsheet pages informed me about the burning social issues of the day; issues that seemed a million miles from the sleepy suburbs where I grew up. I wanted to meet the people that inhabited this world, to expose injustices, to indulge my passion in writing to raise awareness of what was going on in society and, more importantly, why. And here I am thirty years later fulfilling that dream.

## WHY, HOW, WHAT, WHEN, WHO?

Journalism boils down to asking and answering five questions Why? How? What? When? and Who? So what better way to structure a chapter about writing for newspapers than to use these questions.

## WHY WRITE FOR A NEWSPAPER?

Every journalist has a different motive. One colleague told me that she wanted to be able to tell the truth, to set the record straight; another said it was the thrill of getting a scoop; a third quipped 'It's better than working'. They all agreed that no one does it for the financial rewards. Aside from a few national newspaper editors and popular columnists, journalism does not offer big bucks. But its other benefits more than outweigh a hefty salary. Author and journalist, George Orwell, in his essay Why I Write, said: 'because there is some lie that I want to expose, some fact to which I want to draw attention, and my initial concern is to get a hearing'.

For myself, the attraction was the prospect of an exciting job, where I could use my initiative and writing skills, meet incredibly interesting and inspiring people, and hold powerful people and institutions to account. But in reality it is much more than that. It is constantly challenging, stimulating, creative, fast-paced and endlessly fascinating. There is no clock watching. No one day is the same. You are always learning. You can wake up one day knowing little about a subject and by the end of the day, after having spoken to a few experts and asked pertinent questions, written an informative article about it.

As a feature writer, my role on a newspaper is less about uncovering news, although that can happen while researching a story, and more about shedding light on an issue that is already in the public domain, or raising awareness about a little-known fact.

Yes, there is a thrill seeing your byline in print and a kudos attached to being a newspaper journalist, but for me the satisfaction comes with writing an informative and probing article that has the potential to influence and shape the debate. Knowledge is Power. That is why a free press is one of the cornerstones of democracy. How free the press actually is in this country given its ownership and dependency on advertising revenue is beyond the scope of this article, but if one of my pieces makes a government minister think differently, or equips readers with the information to challenge the status quo, then I am doing my job well. And with the spread of the internet your writing now has a global audience and the opportunity to make more of a difference on the world stage.

But let's not lose sight among these lofty aspirations that writing for newspapers is also great fun. You are surrounded by highly intelligent, witty, sceptical, irreverent, like-minded people. I have never felt so at home in my life as I did the day I walked into *The Guardian* offices to see dishevelled journalists beavering away behind mountains of papers and books.

## HOW DO YOU WRITE FOR NATIONAL NEWSPAPERS?

Ted Bottomley and Anthony Loftus in *A Journalist's Guide to the Use of English* say that the key to writing well for newspapers – whether you are writing news, features, or comment – is 'clarity and accuracy allied to a simplicity of style which conveys meaning quickly and with an impact which compels the reader's attention'. My favourite quote from their book – which is one of the few tools of the trade on my bookshelves – is 'Call a spade a spade. Do not call it a horticultural implement.'

It helps if you are an experienced journalist. You can gain experience in a number of ways. A well-worn path is to get yourself onto a post-graduate journalism course after completing university; from there cut your teeth on a local newspaper or trade magazine, or these days a web-based news site or magazine, then use the skills and knowledge you have acquired and contacts you have developed to offer some stories to the nationals. Build up a good relationship with a Commissioning Editor, or the news desk, and when a position becomes free they may recommend you for the job.

Like many professions, knowing the right people often helps. Many jobs on national newspapers are never advertised. An editor may have a few candidates in mind, external and internal, whose track record has impressed them so much that they will call them in for

## TOP TIPS FOR JOURNALISTS

- Always write up notes and interviews straight away. However good your shorthand is, it is much easier to write up notes when they are fresh in your mind, and you could lose the notebook.

- Shorthand is not essential for a feature writer. You can record interviews and develop your own form of speed writing.

- Fix a time and date ahead to interview someone for a feature. Don't leave it to chance that they will be there when you make a call.

- If you don't understand something, your readers won't. So always ask an interviewee to clarify a point if it is not clear to you. Remember you are writing for the lay reader. I will often say, 'I'm sure I'm being stupid but can you just explain that again', then I will paraphrase what they have told me back to them just to be clear we have both understood what has been said.

- Like most things, writing for newspapers takes practice, experience and confidence.

an interview. I got my break at *The Guardian* by building a good relationship with the editor of the section I freelanced for. I suggested many ideas, of which the majority were rejected. For those that were accepted, the editor could trust me to deliver an accurate, diligent and well-written story to the length commissioned, on deadline, and with little fuss.

day, and trade journals in my field each week, and most importantly, I talk to people. I speak to my contacts to see what reports, campaigns or anniversaries are coming up that could make a potential story or be a hook for a story. I keep abreast of government policy. Often stories are pegged to a government bill, a target that the government is introducing or has missed, or to

# "ALL NEWSPAPERS VARY IN STYLE, POLITICAL STANCE, AND THEREFORE READERSHIP"

All newspapers vary in style, political stance, and therefore readership. This will determine whether your story idea and the way that you write it is suitable for a particular newspaper. So after building your experience, confidence and contacts, get to know your newspapers. Many of the stories I write for *The Guardian* would never get published in other newspapers because they cover issues in which other papers don't think their readers are interested.

Where do you find your ideas? I listen to the radio, watch television, and read the papers each

something the government is trying to hide. I check my emails see if any of the story ideas proposed by PR executives, press officers and freelance journalists meet the mark i.e. are timely (we work about two weeks ahead), cover our field (social policy) and throw new light on a subject. Once I have exhausted all my sources, I discuss story ideas with my editor at our weekly meeting. I then explore some of the ideas myself, and commission freelance journalists to pursue some of the others. The ideas will become feature articles, or provide material for comment or analysis pieces.

## TOOLS OF THE TRADE

You do not have to be a computer expert to write for newspapers. A computer word processing package and email are all that a freelance journalist needs to write and send a story, although for speedy research the internet is a journalist's best friend. For example, *www.saidwhat.co.uk* has just informed me that Otto Von Bismark is credited with saying: 'Never believe anything in politics until it has been officially denied'. A maxim all journalists should remember.

Staff writers will use a newspaper's inhouse design software. Unless you are a sub-editor (who lays out pages, and writes headlines and stand firsts) you need only know the basics of the software.

## WHAT DO YOU WRITE?

Unless you are a general news reporter, sent off on stories by the news editor, what you write will depend to some extent on your knowledge and interests. I have always written about social affairs because it is a field in which I have always taken

## ALISON'S FIVE FAVOURITE BOOKS

***Homage to Catalonia*, George Orwell**
The master of English political prose at his finest.

***Scoop*, Evelyn Waugh**
Hilarious satirical novel about Fleet Street.

***Wild Swans*, Jung Chang**
Extraordinary biography that reveals the history of 20th-century China.

***The Bookseller of Kabul*, Asne Seierstad**
A journalist's fascinating portrait of an Afghan family.

***My Trade: A Short History of British Journalism*, Andrew Marr**
The most insightful and entertaining guide to modern journalism told through the author's own experiences.

## TIPS FOR PITCHING STORIES

- Make sure your idea for a pitch is relevant by reading very carefully the section of the paper at which it is aimed.

- Find out how far in advance the section is commissioned to ensure your idea will not be too late for inclusion.

- Find out when the section is put to bed (goes to press) and don't call the editor with an idea on press day.

- Pitch the idea by email and follow up with a phone call later that day.

- Don't propose a story that you can't deliver by the deadline required.

- Don't be deterred if your idea is turned down. Try to find out the reason and use this information to formulate future pitches

a keen interest. Over the years I have covered the subject for trade journals and developed contacts and expertise. I couldn't imagine working on the city desk or being a sports or a fashion writer. But interests do change and broaden.

I prefer writing features to news because of the scope it gives to explore a story in more depth and the opportunity to be more creative.

Although my views do come across in the way I tell the story, and I am sometimes called upon to air my opinions in comment pieces, I am first and foremost a feature writer. I see one of my roles as a journalist as giving a voice to the powerless. For many journalists, however, it is the thrill of breaking a story or wielding the sword of justice that inspires them.

What you write, therefore, is determined by your motives for being a journalist.

## WHEN DO YOU WRITE?
You pitch the idea to your editor. Or they come to you with a story. Either way, you discuss it and the editor gives you a brief that includes the number of words, the deadline and the angle for the story. On

a newspaper the deadline can be very tight. For a news story, you will have a few hours to interview people and file the piece. For a comment you may have an afternoon to turn it around in if it is for next day's paper; the same goes for a feature that is pegged to today's news. More often with features, however, there is a longer deadline as the article is hooked to a forthcoming report, anniversary or event. Yet journalists are trained to write for deadlines. Although you may have two weeks to write a story, most journalists will write it the day before the deadline. It can be helpful to give yourself a little more time, just in case you have to double check any facts or figures.

## WHO TO WRITE FOR?
Many journalists don't care which newspaper they write for. The challenges, the kudos, the excitement of bagging an exclusive are the same. For others the politics of a newspaper, or its culture, may influence them. Tabloid papers traditionally have a more macho culture than the broadsheets. The Guardian has more of the air of a library than a busy testosterone-fuelled newsroom. The terms and conditions of work will also vary from newspaper to newspaper and may have a bearing on which one to work for. I chose The Guardian, because it was one of the few newspapers that covers the issues I want to write about in a sensitive way.

## WHO SHOULD WRITE FOR NEWSPAPERS?
It is a competitive world, not for the faint hearted. You have to be prepared to work long and unpredictable hours. It is not a nine to five job. You need to be tenacious, resourceful, and a bit thick skinned, to take the knock backs, and have lots of initiative. It is not a job for someone who likes to be told what to do. It also helps if you are fearless and irreverent. The most important thing is to have the desire and determination to do it and to keep plugging away. A good test to assess whether you have journalistic potential is to go back to what my colleague said about it being better than working. Ask yourself this question. Would I want to be a journalist if no one was paying me? If the answer is yes then you should be writing for newspapers.

I can't think of anything else I would rather do for a living.

# BEGINNING IN JOURNALISM
## TENACITY IS CRUCIAL

Jo Grobel looks back at the route she took to becoming a journalist and the decisions she made along the way

## JO GROBEL

Following an English degree, Jo went to City University, London where she gained the post-graduate diploma in Periodical Journalism. Her first job as a journalist was as a reporter for *The Grocer* magazine, the only paid-for weekly magazine to service the food and drink retail sector. From there, she moved to *Convenience Store* magazine, where she spent a year and a half, before moving into the drinks trade, as a features writer for the pub-trade magazine, the *Morning Advertiser*.

My reason for starting out in journalism was simple: it was a combination of a love of writing, a curiosity of people and things, and a desire to uncover the real story.

From the age of eight or nine I wrote mini manuals on how to care for your cat, or holiday diaries of, for instance, walking in the Lake District with the family. These subject-matters clearly were not going to win me any prizes but the writing, recording and analysing of events definitely helped me later on.

## GETTING SOMETHING PUBLISHED

The first key to starting out in journalism is to get something published, and this means anything; anything that will help you build up a portfolio of cuttings to show to a future employer.

At school, I wrote a few articles for the school magazine. At university I wrote for my student newspaper, and also did unpaid freelance work for the arts magazine, *Proof*, which was then edited by journalist and broadcaster Bel Mooney. I chose not to do an undergraduate degree in journalism as firstly, sitting around reading books for three years was very appealing, and secondly, everyone advised me to specialize in journalism later.

## FINDING WORK EXPERIENCE

Work experience is essential to becoming a journalist. Apart from building a cuttings portfolio, it also helps you make contacts and work out what sort of publication you'd like to write for.

In my third year at university I did work experience at London's *Evening Standard* for a couple of weeks during the Christmas holidays. This wasn't organized through a 'friend of Daddy's' who edited the paper, it was just a phone-call to the paper three months beforehand, to find out if it was possible. I was perhaps lucky, but I had also called and written to several magazines which all said no.

Work experience can be notoriously difficult to organize: editors often ask you to send in cuttings first, when that's often why you are organizing the work experience. But keep trying – there are lots of editors out there who are more than happy to provide work experience for a week or two.

## WORKING TO A DEADLINE

After a two-week stint at the 'Londoner's Diary' section of the *Evening Standard* I was offered shift work for when I finished university. I decided, though, to do the post-grad diploma in magazine journalism at City University, as I thought it would give me better training. Journalism is unfortunately

## JO'S FIVE FAVOURITE BOOKS

**An Unexpected Light, Jason Elliott**
Beautiful descriptions of daily life in
Afghanistan in the late Seventies.

**Waterland, Graham Swift**
Richly vivid tale focusing on the
cyclical nature of life.

**The Promise of Happiness, Justin Cartwright**
Disturbing, but incredibly real, descriptions
of human relationships.

**The Universal Journalist, David Randall**
The best, down-to-earth, book on
journalism there is.

**Rebecca, Daphne Du Maurier**
One long sitting needed to read it.
Chilling but thoroughly involving.

how to work under pressure to a deadline.

I quickly learnt that writer's block is not something journalists are allowed to get – there isn't time. I also found out – through trial and error – what I wanted to specialize in.

## DECIDING WHAT SUBJECT TO SPECIALIZE IN

My original plan to go into women's lifestyle glossies was shattered after a miserable month working on a well-known title for 30-something women. I was sent out regularly, Devil-Wears-Prada-style, to run all sorts of errands in the snow, carrying various mystery parcels back and forth down Oxford Street. After writing my one feature there, I was told I had gone into too much depth, that I should 'keep things more on the surface'. All I could think was, 'Err, hello, so this isn't journalism then?'

For my next work experience, I took the other extreme: B2B (or trade magazines) here we come, spending a couple of weeks on the grocery trade bible, *The Grocer*. No more ridiculous errands or making tea for the editor before she arrived in the morning – the majority of my time was spent writing or interviewing people and then seeing my work published. It was through this work experience that I got my first job there.

So much of starting out in journalism comes from chance encounters, but to experience these you obviously need to put yourself out there in the first place. Call people up and say you want some work experience. Send a CV in. Call again. And again. The worse they can say is no.

a very popular career choice, so a qualification helps differentiate you from others.

While on-the-job training is invaluable, I still believe that I learnt more in my year at City than I could have done in the same time on a paper or magazine. Journalists are busy people and can't afford anywhere near the same amount of time as the tutors gave us at City. If a piece wasn't up to scratch, they would go through it line by line, explaining how it could be improved.

The course was tough, much harder work than the student life I knew, but it provided me with an excellent grounding in journalism. It also taught me

## TOP TIPS FOR GETTING WORK EXPERIENCE

- To get ideas for publications you would like to write for, go to your largest local newsagent and spend an hour or so browsing the shelves.
- Call the magazine to find out who organizes work experience.
- If you have cuttings, send these with a CV and brief covering letter to the relevant person, asking for work experience.
- Make sure the name is spelt correctly – you wouldn't believe how many people mis-spell the editor's name.
- Call the person three days later, to check they have received your letter.
- Be determined: if a week later you still haven't heard anything, call again.
- Maintain your contacts. Email suggestions for stories, or just drop them a line to say hello. They could be useful in the future.

# TRAVEL WRITING
## HOW TRAVEL WRITERS FIND WORK AND THINK WIDE TO EARN A LIVING

Tim Locke reveals that travel writing can be a pleasure, but it can also come at a price

## TIM LOCKE

Tim has worked for over 20 years as a freelance writer and editor, specializing in travel in Britain. He has also branched out into other subjects such as history books for children, sustainable tourism itineraries, walks calendars and guidebooks to Thailand and New England. A member of the British Guild of Travel Writers, he began by writing walking guides, and has worked for AA Publishing, Thomas Cook, Visit Britain, Cadogan Guides, The Good Pub Guide and Reader's Digest.

I was relaxing in a hot tub under the stars, with snowflakes landing gently on my face as I reflected on a day spent cross-country skiing in the backwoods of Vermont. Life seemed pretty perfect: I was doing what I wanted and getting paid for it – as a travel writer with a commission to update my guidebook to New England. So, I reflected, there really is such a thing as a free lunch…

Yet a couple of summers previously in the same area I spent a gruelling ten weeks researching the same guidebook. I visited over 180 museums and scores of hotels, working non-stop from breakfast to late at night, driving thousands of miles and getting lost repeatedly, amassing impressions and speaking notes into my Dictaphone all the while. Curiosity about places and wanting to tell the world about them is what drives travel writers to do this extraordinary and often hectic job. More people are travelling more than ever before and there are plenty of opportunities for travel writing, though it is a very competitive and sometimes exasperating business. Getting started as a freelance travel journalist is not easy: simply writing about where you went on holiday and hoping to find an outlet for it is not likely to be the way forward. A better plan is to research who publishes the sort of material you could write, find out if they take freelance writers, find some ideas that might appeal to a publisher and email round proposals to editors.

Travel writing comes in many guises, and its purpose can be to provide information such as a consumerist angle, to advertise or just to entertain or evoke places.

## UPS AND DOWNS

Yes, this job can be exciting, boring, relaxing, dangerous, frustrating or satisfying. One thing it isn't is predictable.

On the upside, you have the opportunity to see new places, meet new people and maybe find out something about yourself. There's an exhilarating can-do sense of freedom: you are your own boss, can work (maybe) when you like and beyond retirement age. There may be spin-offs such as broadcasting ventures, and you might win a travel writing award. And the sheer satisfaction of getting your name in print and broadcasting your ideas to the world can be elating. Then if all goes well and you've published something successfully, you can start building up contacts and maybe establishing your niche as an expert in one field, perhaps recycling and developing your knowledge for future projects.

It's a competitive business both for staff writers and freelancers. The money, it has to be said, is not great, and you need to be able to market yourself – striking the right balance between being a bit pushy and being diplomatic at the same time.

## WHAT TO WRITE FOR

Many professional freelance travel writers write for a range of outlets. My own work sometimes spills into areas peripheral to travel – such as features about history for coffee-table travel books about Britain.

### NEWSPAPERS AND MAGAZINES

Think wider than the conventional travel magazines: many other publications such as religious newspapers and antiques or lifestyle magazines have travel features. It can be a hard world to break into, though: many travel editors have piles of spare articles, and others (particularly national newspapers) may not give work to non-staff writers. If you don't know the editor, you need bright ideas to get you noticed: find out what's new or about to happen, and try to get ahead of the others.

### INTERNET

Writing for websites can be lucrative, and it's an ever-expanding field. However, much is written for free. Beware of obscure sites that ask for travel pieces on the understanding that you get paid each

time someone accesses your article: this may be more hassle than it's worth.

### ADVERTISING AND MARKETING

Writing for holiday brochures and tourist organizations can be financially rewarding. I have earned useful money using my general knowledge of Britain to write for hotel and tour operators' brochures, and for major tourism bodies.

### GUIDEBOOKS

There's plenty of scope in guidebook writing, but bear in mind that books are generally published as part of a series, and publication lists are drawn up years in advance, though commissioning is often done fairly late in the process. As well as

> ## YOU NEED BRIGHT IDEAS TO GET YOU NOTICED: FIND OUT WHAT'S NEW OR ABOUT TO HAPPEN AND GET AHEAD OF THE REST

writing a whole book or parts of it, you might find opportunities for updating, verifying and editing. Publishers have been nervous of competition from the internet, but good guidebook series will probably survive.

### TRAVELOGUES

It all started with the likes of Johnson and Boswell penning travelogues as they ventured to little-known places in the 18th Century. The form continues into the present with writers such as Bill Bryson, Nicholas Crane and Tony Hawks, all providing the ultimate armchair travel. The travelogue-style book is probably the hardest field to get into: you need to find a theme that hasn't been done before, to have the skill, time and funding to get it carried out and to get a publisher interested in taking it on.

### GETTING PAID

There's no hard and fast rule about how much or how (or even if) you get paid for travel writing, and whether it's negotiable. Per thousand words

## TYPES OF TRAVEL WRITING INCLUDE

- Destination reports (for independent or package holidays) on a city or area
  - Places to stay and to eat
    - Consumerist angles
- Walks, cycle rides and other activities
- Themed tours such as ancient cultures, natural history or vineyards
- Modes of transport such as cruises or rail journeys

> ## THINK WIDER THAN THE CONVENTIONAL TRAVEL MAGAZINES: MANY OTHER PUBLICATIONS SUCH AS RELIGIOUS NEWSPAPERS AND ANTIQUES OR LIFESTYLE MAGAZINES HAVE TRAVEL FEATURES

## TEN TOP TIPS

1. Tell editors where and when you are travelling: a lot of travel writing commissions are done at short notice, and you might pick up several commissions for one trip.

2. Polish up a specialism – a particular subject or a geographical area.

3. Don't forget the domestic travel market, which is huge for short breaks. In Britain even the traditional seaside resorts are looking up as summers are warmer and visitors can avoid airport hassles (making it particularly appealing to young families). If you're bilingual you might be able to write about Britain for an overseas market.

4. Never miss a deadline. Even a great piece of writing may not be appreciated by an editor if it's late. Allow yourself enough time for travel (there's no substitute for actually visiting places – even places you think you know), writing and checking.

5. Take notes wherever you travel (even on holiday) for future projects, and file them away meticulously. I write restaurant and pub reports on the backs of postcards – that way staff never notice I'm doing anything but writing postcards. Dictaphones can be useful for hands-free note taking, if you're hiking for instance.

6. Massage your contacts. Editors do move on to work on other publications, and take lists of their favourite writers with them.

7. Keep an eye on press releases and websites to see what's up and coming: a new hotel, a revamped museum, a major event or an emerging destination that wants publicity. Be aware of new tourism markets: travel by Chinese tourists, for instance, is set to boom.

8. Suggest offbeat, quirky subjects rather than straightforward destination reports, and always have your readers' needs in mind. Also remember that articles are often accompanied by adverts for that location – so pitch subjects according to what a paper or magazine could sell in terms of advertising.

9. If you want to suggest an idea for a new travel book, research the market thoroughly (see *www.amazon.com* and search for similar subjects) and think of likely publishers. Send the publisher a synopsis, explain who it's intended for, and write a sample chapter. Ask the publisher who to send a proposal to, and try to get an idea of how long they'll take to come to a decision.

10. If you're writing to length and are concerned that the editor might massacre your copy, show optional cuts (for example, by underlining text that could be cut), or produce a long version and a short version of the same text. This also makes it a lot easier for the editor, and everything you do to help the editor is good for your career.

it's often more lucrative to write articles than guidebooks, but with the latter at least you get a guaranteed large chunk of work. Usually, but not always, the publisher or editor suggests the fee.

There's similar flexibility about when you get paid for writing an article. Normally, it is payable once you send in your final copy – or (worse) when the article is published (which may be never). If you get paid only on publication and the newspaper or magazine decides not to publish your article, things could get sticky. Whether you want to enforce the contract and sue if necessary (perhaps souring relations forever with that editor), or just accept a smaller 'kill fee' is a matter of judgment.

With books, the norm is to get paid in instalments – on signature of contract, on submission of final copy and then either on dealing with editor's queries or on publication.

## COVERING THE COSTS

The perennial struggle for the travel writer is how to write about places without blowing the budget. Travel writing contracts normally don't cover

## TIPS FROM A TRAVEL GUIDE EDITOR

Travel guide editors are not looking for great art; they are looking for accurate, fresh material delivered on time without fuss. Here's a list of essential requirements:

- **Don't cheat** – if you get your info secondhand (such as only from brochures) we'll find out.

- **Deliver on time** – travel publishing is done to tight schedules and depends on meeting dates. Miss dates and your reputation drops like a stone.

- **Don't be a pain** – once commissioned just get on with the job.

- **Don't be greedy** – if you don't like the offered fee just say so and we'll find someone who will do it for the money.

## TIM'S FIVE TOP TRAVEL BOOKS

**The Great Railway Bazaar, Paul Theroux**
Brilliantly observant travelogue about riding trains through Asia – more about the people he meets rather than the places he visits.

**Rough Guides**
My favourite guidebook series, which gets just the right balance between down to earth advice and background information, helping you get the most out of a destination.

**Two Degrees West, Nicholas Crane**
An admirably ingenious concept: a walk through a dead straight cross-section of Britain, getting an angle on Britain that hovers between the mundane and the bizarre.

**Sorrento and the Amalfi Coast, Julian Tippett**
One of many walking guides I could mention: this one helped us take some magnificently scenic walks which we'd have never found in an area where footpath information is otherwise poor.

**A Walk in the Woods, Bill Bryson**
Humorous and self-deprecating account of a very tough trek, making the ultimately armchair read.

expenses. Help is at hand in the form of public relations companies and tourist organisations, who can provide all-expenses paid travel and press trips. This is on the understanding that you'll give favourable press coverage – which can compromise what you really want to write. It's generally easier to get such useful freebies for articles than for guidebooks, as readership figures are so much greater. Even then, you may only get two or three hundred pounds for an article that takes several days to research and write: accordingly it's worth picking up extra information as you travel for use in other writing projects.

Taking photos is a handy sideline. The publisher might pay for your travel images (though this is sadly not universal practice), or you could sell them to someone else later on.

# WRITING FOR RADIO
## GETTING YOUR WORK BROADCAST

Producer and writer Roger Elsgood explains how to succeed in a tough area

## ROGER ELSGOOD

Roger grew up listening to radio drama. Charles Chiltern's *Journey Into Space* (every episode) remains the most riveting radio experience he ever had. His independent company, Art and Adventure, has written, adapted, directed and produced many dramas for BBC Radio. Some have been stories needing to be told – Anne Michaels' *Fugitive Pieces* (broadcast on Holocaust Remembrance Day); some have been productions with stellar companies – John Berger's *To The Wedding*, a collaboration with Complicite (broadcast on World AIDS Day); others have been bursting with talent – *Shooting Stars And Other Heavenly Bodies* starring Clive Owen, Michael Sheen and Michael Gambon and directed by Mike Hodges. In 2007 he was in India recording an adaptation of Shakespeare's *The Two Gentlemen of Verona* (Valasna actually!) with The Industrial Theatre of Mumbai. Look for Art and Adventure at: *www.artandadventure.org*.

'It ain't easy; but then if it was, everyone would be doing it'. John Lennon's words echo down the time tunnel. But to make it just a bit easier to get your play produced on radio, this is what you need to know.

There are three routes

**Route One** is to network with the BBC's Writers Room, which seeks to encourage and develop writers for radio. They run workshops and create opportunities for first and second-time writers. It's probably the best way for new writers to get their head above the parapet and then avoid the slings and arrows and get their talent and work known. The Writer's Room provides real opportunities for new writers, particularly with the Radio 3 strand 'The Wire'.

**Route Two** is to submit your script to BBC inhouse departments that have output guarantees for drama. These departments have traditionally established quotas of drama production and produce around 90 per cent of all drama heard on BBC radio. The level of submission of scripts is considerable and many good plays fall without being offered-up to the annual commissioning rounds.

**Route Three** is to submit your work through independent production companies. Indies have, in theory, around 10 per cent access to BBC network production and therefore have to try harder. Indies have to come up with outstanding proposals and exceptional productions. If they didn't they wouldn't get work. No indie production company has output guarantees. Working with an indie supplier means that getting a play commissioned is difficult, especially for a new writer, but if your play does get greenlighted then the prospect of a high value production is assured.

## HARD FACTS

All plays heard on BBC radio networks are subject to commissioning rounds. These are rigorous, annual processes (biannual in the case of R4), in which producers, both inhouse and independent, submit proposals developed against finely-drawn criteria to specialist BBC commissioners for rigorous appraisal. The criteria used by commissioners when considering the merits of a proposal are not just related to the intrinsic creative or entertainment qualities of the work. Factors such as similarity of idea or closeness in time to other productions, concepts or treatments not matching current focus issues or writing failing to meet the very specific strand criteria will cause work to be rejected. Often the very volume of good plays submitted will cause gems to be laid on the 'rejected' pile. Some rejected proposals may be requested to be re-submitted in a subsequent round when circumstances could be different, but so often a 'rejected' can be the end of the road as there is nowhere else to take a radio play.

Writing a play for radio is a very particular process. You need to know the territory. Plays have to fit both the time slot and the network criteria for each programme strand.

## KNOWING THE TERRITORY

Radio 3 has two drama strands, The Sunday Play, which showcases major dramatic works, Shakespeare, the dramatic greats, international gems, transfers from current stage productions and serious contemporary drama by internationally renown writers. Radio 3 also broadcasts The Wire, which features work by new writers many whom have worked with The BBC Writer's Room.

The World Service tends to commission dramas with a strong international flavour often by writers living and working outside the UK.

Radio 4 has five drama strands each with its very specific criteria. The Woman's Hour strand is deemed to be the province of experienced radio dramatists due to the complexities of the storytelling required. The Friday Play is focused on strong contemporary stories often written by outstanding established talent. The Saturday Play is more generalist and populist and often provides dramatizations of much-loved novels and plays. The Classic Serial is exactly that, no opportunity for the new or aspiring writer there. The most likely opportunity for aspiring writers is The Afternoon Play; the slot most numerous in terms of potential commissions and a strand open to ideas from new sources.

This is what Radio 4 is currently seeking for the Afternoon Play slot: 'Contemporary and period drama; comedy; biography; issue-driven plays; drama-documentary; family plays; crime and thrillers; poetry; romance and fantasy'. R4 is also looking for strong contemporary, domestically-set

series with identifiable iconic characters. However, no detectives, no hospitals or historicals. Whether it be for a series or for the more familiar one-offs, the need is for stories about life as experienced by the Radio 4 audience or those which will give a window onto their lives. Above all the requirement is simply for a good story very well told.

If it all seems a bit formidable, it is. But don't be daunted. Good writing always gets noticed and there's always space at the table for new talent.

## BEAR THESE IN MIND

In writing for radio you are writing for the blind. Your audience cannot see what is going on. You have to help them. Keep characters to a minimum. Make them differentiated. Make it clear who is present (and who is absent), entrances and exits are not obvious on radio. Manipulate comings and goings avoiding the 'Look Jill, here comes Shula. Hello Shula, we were just saying to David a moment ago' routine. Give thought to important but non-visual plot points, pace the much-quoted 'The gun in my left hand sir, is still smoking' without doing just that. (I once had a pivotal moment in a radio play dependent on an envelope being silently slipped under a door!). The ability to marry the natural way people talk and behave with the need to keep the listener informed of evolving events is the mark of a good dramatist. Be circumspect with epic scenarios and crowds, they rarely sound convincing. Similarly physical sex. Narrative flashbacks and dream sequences can provide challenges for the radio audience

> ## IN WRITING FOR RADIO YOU ARE WRITING FOR THE BLIND. YOUR AUDIENCE CANNOT SEE WHAT IS GOING ON

as do lines spoken but not addressed to other characters.

Get the writing wrong and nothing can prevent a disaster. Get the writing right and everything falls into place. That's all you have to do. And keep on doing it.

# WRITING FOR THE SCREEN
## THE ART OF SHOWING, NOT TELLING

Sue Teddern inspires aspiring scriptwriters

### SUE TEDDERN

Sue came to scriptwriting after a brief blip as a window dresser and a career in magazine journalism. She has written numerous radio plays and serials. Her screen credits include *Birds of a Feather*, *Happy Together*, *My Parents are Aliens*, *Sister Frances*, *Bosom Pals* and *My Family*. She is also an experienced script editor. Sue is currently Screenwriter in Residence for the Creative Writing and Arts programme, Department of English, University of Exeter, where she also teaches the MA in Developing a Feature Screenplay.

William Goldman famously wrote in *Adventures in the Screen Trade* that: 'Nobody knows anything'. But if you've (mis)spent your life couch-potatoed in front of the telly or at the local Odeon, you will know instinctively when a movie works and when it doesn't. Want to be a scriptwriter? Just type: INT. BEDROOM – DAY and see where it takes you.

Years ago, I did something rather clever. I was completing the final scene of a sitcom and the dialogue was pouring out, almost faster than I could type it. The scene was between two women who had drifted apart and desperately wanted to be best friends again.

As I wrote one particularly poignant line, I heard myself say out loud: 'I love this!' I didn't mean that I loved the line - although I'm sure I was rather pleased with it. I meant that I loved this; the process, the business of creating people from scratch, with real thoughts and motivations and quirks and histories.

The clever bit was remembering precisely which words sparked my outburst. And so, a few months later, when I watched the episode being recorded and the appropriate actress uttered the line I had so loved writing, I recalled that joyful feeling. Whenever I watch a tape of this sitcom, it gets me every time. I love this.

## THE WRITE FEELING

Anyone who writes will know the feeling I've just described. It may come when you're crafting a sonnet or composing a jingle for Krunchy Munch cereal. You will have an affinity with words or you

### FIVE KEY SCRIPTS

These are all currently on my bookshelves and I love them. And yes, I'm surprised and disappointed too that none are by women…

*Fargo*, Ethan & Joel Coen

*The Apartment*, Billy Wilder and I.A. L Diamond

*Sideways*, Alexander Payne & Jim Taylor

*The Sopranos Scriptbook*, David Chase

*The Chain/The Knowledge/Ready when You are Mr McGill*, Jack Rosenthal

## TEN TIPS FOR SCRIPTWRITERS

- Never forget: you can't write an Alan Bennett (or whoever) script better than him and he can't write a 'You' script better than You.

- Hurrah, you've finished your first draft. But it's still only your first draft.

- If you get an avalanche of notes from a script editor, only dig in your heels about the really important stuff.

- If you wouldn't want to watch it, will you want to write it?

- Writing can be a solitary business; find a script buddy to show drafts to and take criticism from. You can help them too.

- It's probably over-written. What can you cut? Come back to it later with a fresh eye.

- Avoid stereotypes. Everyone has a surprise up his/her sleeve!

- Don't send off a script as soon as you've finished writing it. Sleep on it and read it through the next day. You will always find things to finesse.

- If one person rejects your script, they might be wrong. If 20 people reject your script, maybe they have a point?

- Love what you're doing. Or just go and do something else.

wouldn't be reading this book.

So why choose scriptwriting? Maybe it chooses you, because of those couch potato moments you've relished over the years. Certainly, if you are successful, writing scripts can be highly lucrative. A few years' regular work on a soap opera will afford you a very comfortable, if stressful, life. Scriptwriting is the genre to choose if you hope to make a reasonable living from your talents. However, that isn't a good enough reason to write for the screen.

I can write prose. I have written prose. But the idea of filling a whole novel fills me with dread. So many words. A script, on the other hand, is lean and spare. The directions (also called the blackstuff) don't contain thoughts or feelings.

### CALLING CARD

If you have an aptitude for scriptwriting and a dogged, pragmatic and mostly uncynical approach, write your calling card script and send it to an agent. If it shows promise, you will be taken on. It's unlikely that the first gig you get will be to write that big star-studded movie. But with an agent on your side, you'll get to hear about interesting writing jobs and meet producers and development people. With any luck, you'll be writing the scenes and telling the stories that will make couch potatoes out of the rest of us.

### IMAGES AND ACTIONS

A woman walks into a bedroom, still in her coat, and lies on the bed. This might be the entirety of scene 1 of your script. You are building up images and actions for the viewer to store, process and make sense of. Maybe she's unhappy or brokenhearted or terminally ill. Maybe she's just cold and tired.

Some writers instantly take to this form of storytelling, while others prefer to explore the inner landscapes of their characters – and that's what makes them novelists. They might also baulk at what seem like the restrictions of a script's classic three-act structure. It feels too didactic, too formulaic.

Summed up in a few words, a well-structured script should be about a character who wants to do something and ends up succeeding/failing/changed. This essential truth sums up films as diverse as *The Apartment*, *Sweet Sixteen*, *Witness*, *The Motorcycle Diaries* … or any number of other great movies you'd kill to have written.

# ON BEING A FREELANCER

## INVALUABLE ADVICE FOR ALL FREELANCERS OF WHATEVER KIND

Sue Gordon has been both a staff editor and a freelancer. With wisdom and insight, she provides lists of essential freelancer dos and don'ts

### SUE GORDON

Sue is an inveterate freelance editor, writer and project manager. She has also worked on the other side of the desk, in several publishing houses, and knows what stressed inhouse editors really appreciate in their freelancers. Since 1996 she has been a partner in OutHouse Publishing, a small team of freelancers who specialize in the project management and packaging of illustrated non-fiction books.

Feelancing is a lifestyle, with pros and cons that are never fully understood by those who have not experienced them. For me it is the only civilized way of working. For others, it spells isolation and uncertainty.

### WHAT IS A FREELANCER?

Freelancers are self-employed and work for a number of clients, usually from home.

The publishing industry would not exist without writers, of course, who are per se freelancers. Elsewhere in the book-production chain, and fundamental to the creation process, are freelance copy editors, designers, picture researchers, illustrators, verifiers, proofreaders, indexers and project managers.

Being freelance does not preclude you from working inhouse part-time or on a specific project, but it is essential that you and the publisher are aware that you will fall foul of Her Majesty's Revenue and Customs IR35 regulations if you are contracted to only one client and could be regarded as acting like one of their employees.

### THE PROS

● You are your own boss. It is you who determines your pattern and conditions of work.

● You work to your own timetable. Take time out when you wish and catch up by starting at 5am, shutting down at midnight, working at the weekends or on bank holidays.

● There is no risk of becoming embroiled in office politics or suffocated by corporate culture.

● You are not stuck with the same colleagues day in, day out. Working with several clients means working with a variety of people and types of organization.

● You have the opportunity to work on a much wider range of books than you do inhouse.

● You are there when your children are ill or their school has a staff training day.

## DO IT NOW

Download electronic files as soon as you receive them from your client, even if you are not free to start work immediately. If you don't, it could be that when you do load them you find you have a corrupt file and have to reveal to your client that you haven't yet started work. You, of course, know that you will complete the work on time, but your client may be alarmed.

- You have the perfect excuse to build your own reference library.

- You can hang out the washing while your printer is spitting out proofs.

## THE CONS

- There will be peaks and troughs in your cashflow and your workload.

- Your net income will not be as high as that of a full-time inhouse employee (see Finances).

- You are on your own, fully responsible for yourself and your work.

- You may feel isolated. You do not have colleagues beside you, with brains to pick, shoulders to cry on, jokes to share.

- No one updates your computer for you.

- No one offers you professional training.

- Your work may be varied, but if you want career development, think again.

- You have to pay for your own reference library.

- You have to pay for your own subscription to *The Bookseller* or *Publishers Weekly* if you want to keep up to date with the world of publishing.

- You may get little or no appreciative feedback from your clients.

- You have to pay your own office running costs.

- You have to do your own accounts.

- It may be hard to keep work and home life separate.

- Juggling children and work can be stressful.

- Taking the script or the CD to the post office may be the only time you set foot outside the house all week.

## THE FINANCES

There are those who make a living from freelance work in publishing. A far higher proportion does not earn enough to make a living. If this is a problem, another string to the bow may be a good idea. This might be in the shape of a partner employed in a better-paid industry (and, ideally, tolerant of pre-deadline tension and unconventional working hours).

A freelancer is self-employed and responsible for submitting annual tax returns and for paying income tax and National Insurance contributions.

## UNPAID WORK

It has been estimated that realistically a freelancer is earning money for as little as a third of the hours spent 'working'. You are not paid for time spent:
- keeping records and accounts
- getting your computer sorted
- going to and from the post office, bank, copy shop, stationers
- dealing with emails and phone calls
- taking a tea or lunch break

## YOU WORK TO YOUR OWN TIMETABLE. TAKE TIME OUT WHEN YOU WISH AND CATCH UP BY STARTING AT 5AM, FINISHING AT MIDNIGHT OR WORKING WEEKENDS

- taking a holiday
- chasing publishers for work, updates on schedules, and payment
- and, unless you are assertive, attending meetings

While you may be able to claim for postage and possibly for the cost of travel to an inhouse meeting, you will almost certainly not be reimbursed for:

- upgrading or replacing your computer, printer, software and any other office equipment
- use of telephone and internet
- stationery, including CDs
- photocopying
- petrol and motoring expenses
- heating and lighting
- contributions to a pension scheme
- National Insurance contributions
- subscription to professional journals
- membership of professional bodies
- training courses
- days off sick or on maternity leave

So if your client mutters that your hourly rate is higher than that of the inhouse staff, draw this to

## FIVE KEY BOOKS FOR FREELANCE EDITORS

In addition to a range of dictionaries, a good encyclopedia and the largest *Times Atlas of the World* you can afford:

*Copy-editing: The Cambridge Handbook for Editors, Authors and Publishers,* Judith Butcher
The editors' indispensable bible

*The New Oxford Dictionary for Writers and Editors:*
*The Essential A-Z Guide to the Written Word,*
R M Ritter, Angus Stevenson, and Lesley Brown

*The Oxford Guide to Style, Robert Ritter*

*Fowler's Modern English Usage, 3rd edn,*
ed. R.W. Burchfield

*Usage and Abusage: A Guide to Good English,*
Eric Partridge

## PAY THAT TAX!

Income tax is payable at the end of January and the end of July. Either put 25 per cent of each fee aside or assign the fee for one particular job to tax. If you don't plan ahead, you could find that in order to meet your tax bill you must look for extra work in December, a point in the publishing year when there is often little freelance work to be found.

their attention. As employees, they probably have no idea how much it adds up to.

The publisher is your client, so theoretically you state your terms. In practice, rates of pay are fixed inhouse, may not be negotiable, and inevitably are significantly lower than NUJ recommended minimum rates.

Inhouse project managers, with budgets to control, like to offer lump sums. The good thing for the freelancer is that you don't have to keep track of your hours and you don't have to worry about possible disputes over the invoice since the publisher knows what to expect. The bad thing is that you may not be paid for every hour you work: projects are often more time-consuming than you expect, and the fee can then represent a very poor hourly rate indeed.

## GETTING WORK

In the vast majority of cases, those who establish themselves as freelancers most successfully have worked inhouse and have become competent at their job. Competition for freelance work can be intense, so inhouse staff have plenty of choice. They will usually plump for someone they already know and trust, or a freelancer recommended by someone else in the industry. Former colleagues are therefore likely to be your principal clients for the first year or two, but it is wise to try to widen your client base.

- Do a mailshot and send it to all the publishers you might like to work for. Follow them up.

- First impressions are all-important. Write on professional-looking headed paper. Check for any spelling or grammatical mistakes.

- Try to get into the office to meet someone. Your face will be more memorable than an email.

- If you can get your feet under a desk inhouse for a while, even if the work is menial, you may find yourself first in line when a more challenging job comes up. Trusty freelancers are sometimes asked to do maternity cover.

## STAYING IN WORK

- Be a whore – work for anyone who pays.

- Never say 'no' (unless you are well-established and confident they will come back another time).

- Network, even when you don't feel like it.

- Remember that reliability and a professional attitude are as vital as excellent standards of work

Until you are well established, accept that you cannot afford, in any sense, to pick and choose. Say yes to that boring job, do it well and, who knows, the next offer may well be much more attractive.

Once you are in favour with a particular inhouse editor or art director, you should be OK until he or she leaves. Perhaps she is moving to another publisher: (a) if you hear about it in time, make sure she knows you are still interested in working with her and (b) introduce yourself to her successor as someone familiar with the books she worked on.

If you have an unscheduled gap – perhaps a job you had booked in for a particular slot has been delayed or even cancelled – let other clients know.

Never miss a deadline, even if this means working excessive and unsocial hours: if you can see you are not going to be able to meet the deadline, let your client know in good time. Maybe you can offer to feed the work through in batches.

Your client has a budget to keep. However, you don't do yourself or other freelancers any favours by working for love, so let your client know if your hours look like exceeding the estimate. If you have proved yourself valuable to them, they may be willing to negotiate on a little more money.

## DOS AND DON'TS

- Do use decent headed notepaper, compliment slips and invoices. You may be answering the phone in your pyjamas and working at the kitchen table or in a corner of the bedroom… It doesn't matter (provided you are doing a professional job) because the client can't see any of that. What they can see is your stationery.

- Do make sure your answerphone message is appropriately business-like.

- Do remember that your book is just one of several that the inhouse staff have in hand; if you have a query, don't expect them to remember the minutiae of your particular project.

- If you are working on paper and use a pencil, do use a 2B so your marks are clearly legible by the keyboarder.

- Copy editors: when you think you have finished the script, do read it through again before you send it in: you may think you have done a thorough job, but you will undoubtedly find something you missed.

- Proofreaders: don't send a proof back to the inhouse editor covered with queries. Suggest solutions for as many as you can. This is a fraught time for inhouse editors and the last thing they need is dozens of queries to sort.

- Do ask for feedback when you return work.

- Don't be afraid to ask for a copy of the book you have worked on. It is a marketing tool.

- Do respect your client's request for confidentiality. Be discreet.

## FIVE ESSENTIAL FREELANCER QUALITIES

- Self-motivation
- Self-discipline
- Willingness to take risks
- Willingness to work unsocial and excessive hours at times
- Acceptance that workflow will be like the proverbial bus – nothing for a while, then three jobs come at once

# RESEARCHING
## FINDING THE FACTS TO GET WRITING RIGHT

Research is pivotal in many areas of writing. Nick Channer tells you why, and how to go about it efficiently and accurately

### NICK CHANNER

Nick began his writing career in the late 1970s. Since then he has written more than 40 books, many of them walking and travel guides. He has written for the *Daily Telegraph*, *Country Life* and *The Scots Magazine*, among others, and has worked on local radio and BBC Radio 4. Walking, social history and literary landscapes are his main specialist subjects

The advice to budding novelists is generally 'write about what you know.' In the field of non-fiction, perhaps it should be 'know what you write about.'

Getting an idea for a magazine feature, a newspaper article or a book is one thing but doing the research is quite another. In other words, the initial flash of inspiration is the easy bit – the hard work comes later.

You might ask 'Why Research?' Quite simply, without it there is no end result. In other words, one is totally dependent on the other. Research may be time consuming and demanding but it can also be fun, entertaining and very informative. You never stop listening and learning. If you enjoy what you do and take a pride in your work, then the effort is certainly worthwhile. Besides, no self-respecting writer would ever dare contemplate submitting a manuscript or a feature without undertaking meticulous research.

There are several crucial tools of the trade to help make the task of research easier. I never go anywhere without a good, reliable pocket notebook and a trusty mini tape-recorder. Even in this fast, hi-tech age, there is nothing to beat making copious notes. The tape-recorder comes in handy for conversations, more formal interviews and as an aide-memoire. A laptop is invaluable too, but it is the internet, of course, that is the writer's greatest asset today.

The trick with research is not to waste time – be efficient and adopt a professional, business-like approach to the task. Try to use every moment to your advantage. Newspapers and magazines don't pay a fortune for an average 1,000-word feature and if you don't manage your time properly, you'll find yourself seriously out of pocket. A book might be more lucrative but don't forget there is almost certainly going to be a great deal more research involved.

But whether it's a book, a magazine or a newspaper, thorough and exhaustive research is the key. Plan what you need to do before actually getting down to the business of writing, work out how best to gain the vital information you need, talk to those with the answers and make sure your work has the stamp of accuracy and authority it needs to maintain your credibility as a writer.

## WRITING AND WALKING

I began my writing career a long time ago, and over the years I have never doubted the need to do my homework – and to do it right. There's nothing worse than sloppy research, inaccurate information, a job half done. It shows in the end result and may well reflect badly on your reputation.

## FIVE RESEARCH TOOLS

- Use a laptop computer – it's especially useful if you are researching away from home for any length of time.

- Build up a good personal reference library at home ie biographical directory, slang dictionary, Thesaurus, books on where famous people are buried, etc.

- Take a notebook wherever you go, and a simple but good quality mini tape-recorder. If recording telephone conversations, you can buy electronic recording equipment at reputable electrical stores.

- Create your own website to help increase work offers and improve your credibility.

- Take plenty of photographs to help you as an aide-memoire and perhaps submit some of them with your work.

My first published book was a modest walking guide. I had absolutely no journalistic background and no proven track record as a writer, though to a naïve 22-year-old the task sounded straightforward and relatively undemanding. How wrong I was. Walking guides require a great deal of research undertaken on foot, as well as many hours studying books, maps, and websites.

All the routes in a walking guide have to be physically checked and re-checked. Many are walked again when and if there are reprints. With

## A CENTURY OF CHANGE

Back at the start of the new millennium, I embarked on a walking assignment with a difference. I had read Hilaire Belloc's book *The Four Men*, dealing with his 90-mile journey on foot across Sussex in 1902, and my long-held ambition had been to retrace his rural odyssey in order to examine a century of change in the countryside. Exactly 100 years after Belloc's walk and with several magazine and newspaper commissions secured, I set off in the footsteps of the great man. But Belloc's hike alone would not yield what I needed. If my piece was to focus on the effects of social and economic upheaval in the villages and farming communities of Sussex, I would need to concentrate on very detailed research.

Along the way I chatted to villagers, publicans and farmers – in fact, anyone I could find to help me fill in the vital detail. I even knocked on doors for snippets of background information. My efforts paid off. I learnt all about pub, shop and school closures, changes in farming methods and much more besides. Everyone I met chatted away quite amiably, some seemingly grateful to talk to an outsider about increased traffic levels and gentrification in the Sussex countryside – among a whole range of other rural topics.

## RESEARCH ON THE STREETS

Around this time, a Wiltshire-based publisher commissioned me to write a social history of Farnham, my narrative strongly influenced by the company's archive of fascinating black and white photographs of the Surrey town dating back to the turn of the century. I signed the contract, but I knew that working on the book would be a daunting task. I had rarely been to Farnham and had no friends

## "THOROUGH AND EXHAUSTIVE RESEARCH IS THE KEY

the huge growth in leisure activities in recent years, information on visitor attractions and places of interest on or near the routes is often part of the remit, and this involves gathering details and data along the way and contacting local tourist information centres. All this in the name of research – but research that is sessential to the success of the book.

or contacts in the town. I suppose, in a sense, that made the challenge even more irresistible.

Where to begin? I assumed the role of history detective and tramped the streets of Farnham, comparing the subjects of the photographs with the reality on the ground. That was the easy bit. Far harder was unearthing the facts behind the pictures. On my travels around the town, I made

## TEN TIPS TO HELP WITH RESEARCH

- Read as much as you can on the subject – books, articles and features. If it's a news story, read all the relevant newspapers and visit appropriate websites.

- Record interviews when possible but pick the right moment. Telephone interviews are fine but it's easier by email or in person. Emailing a set of questions allows more time for reply.

- Always try to visit the setting you are writing about. It's important to experience the atmosphere and the sense of place.

- Establish contact with those who are in a position to help you - ie archivist, tourist information staff – and explain what you are doing. The more open you are the better the result.

- Use the internet as much as possible for research. It saves so much time and effort. The site for the National Archives of the UK includes an online catalogue and plenty of research information (*www. nationalarchives. gov.uk*) – and try wikipedia, the biggest multi-lingual free-content encyclopedia on the net.

- Join organisations to help you with contacts and setting up press trips to do your research ie *www. wpu. org.uk* or *www.owpg.org.uk*.

- Get as much additional information when on a press visit in case you can find another market for the piece.

- Plan an itinerary before the trip if you are travelling under your own steam.

- Make PR contacts to help create work opportunities.

- If it's a walking guide you are researching always make sure you work off an OS map, as these are the most accurate available, but never, ever, plagiarize them.

a point of making myself known to the librarians and to those who worked in the tourist information centre. I engaged in casual conversation with staff and customers in the town's shops and cafes and gradually word began to spread that there was a stranger in town, a writer who was eager for information, anxious to build a composite picture of Farnham both past and present.

As a result of my efforts, I met several of the town's 'trustees' or 'town fathers' – leading figures in the community who have influenced its growth and development over the years. Their help was invaluable. A retired architect invited me to lunch during which he extolled Farnham's virtues and mourned the effects of social upheaval on the town in the most eloquent terms. One elderly lady I met in a Farnham tearoom took me on trust and invited me to her home to tell me about life in the town during the Second World War.

Her fascinating personal account revealed far more about Farnham at that time than any book or archive newspaper story. By the time I returned home, I knew I had more than enough material to start writing. True, I spent many hours in the town library, pouring over half a dozen or more books about Farnham, but more than anything my research proved the importance of cultivating contacts and finding what you need through simple, informal conversation.

### DELVING ON THE SANDS

Several years ago I went to Lancashire to write a magazine article about Cedric Robinson, the Queen's Official Guide to Morecambe Bay. Since 1963 this quietly spoken Cumbrian has been guiding groups of 300 or more people across the treacherous sands at low tide. I knew what I wanted to ask him but I definitely wouldn't be doing it while he was busy concentrating on guiding us to safety. The following day, in the comfort of his nearby home, Cedric provided me with plenty of colourful background to Morecambe Bay.

But I needed more detail – stranded victims, grim statistics and scientific data on the terrifying speed of the tide. Also, at the request of the magazine editor, I had to come up with '10 Things You Never Knew About Morecambe Bay'. I had a word with the local tourist information office and they pointed me in the direction of Lancaster's maritime museum

plunged to his death; to Le Touquet in France – possibly the model for the town of Royale-les-Eaux in Ian Fleming's first Bond novel *Casino Royale*; and to Scotland to try and pinpoint the route taken by fugitive Richard Hannay through Dumfries & Galloway in John Buchan's famous adventure spy story *The Thirty-Nine Steps*. In all three cases, the

> # THE TRICK WITH RESEARCH IS NOT TO WASTE TIME – BE EFFICIENT AND ADOPT A PROFESSIONAL, BUSINESS-LIKE APPROACH TO THE TASK

where I spent an entire morning reading about lost lives, constantly shifting sandbanks and mail coaches stuck in the mud on this inhospitable stretch of coast.

## TRAVEL WRITING

Research depends on your field of writing and expertise. It is about people and history and culture. It is about places too, and in particular the sense of atmosphere and adventure they evoke. In recent years I have added travel writing to my range of professional activities. I felt the time was right to spread my wings and so I joined an organisation called Writers and Photographers Unlimited to give me the right contacts to set up press trips overseas. My first assignment took me to the Faroe Islands, midway between Iceland and Norway. Once I'd sold the idea of a feature to a magazine editor and been formally commissioned, I approached the tourism office by email to arrange a visit.

They made all the arrangements and set up an itinerary for my 3-day trip. If you think this sounds like the perfect way to get a free holiday, you couldn't be more wrong. It was three days of hard, non-stop work. My main objective was to see and experience as much as I could in the time I had, set up interviews with one or two colourful local characters and gather as much published material as my luggage limit would allow.

## LITERARY LANDSCAPES

Playing literary detective is one of my great loves when it comes to travel writing. I've been fortunate enough to travel to the Reichenbach Falls in Switzerland where Sherlock Holmes apparently

internet, local tourist offices and dedicated experts whose knowledge of the subject knows no bounds helped me in equal measure with my research. Naturally, I have taken my well-thumbed copies of the novels along too.

The preparation so crucial to creating the main body of any work falls into different categories – as does the nature of my job. Sometimes I'm a travel writer, sometimes I'm a campaigning journalist, sometimes I'm a social historian, but whatever hat I'm wearing, they all require me to complete painstaking but rewarding research.

## YOUR SPACE

Having a space set aside for your writing work is a good part of the discipline of writing.

Many of us don't have the benefit of a whole room to write in, but many of us could turn part of a room into a writing area. Maybe it's part of the living room, if that's not too much at the heart of a buzzing family life. Maybe it's part of a bedroom. In most modern households the one thing to get as far away from as possible is the TV.

So far as equipment goes, you don't need much more than a writing/computer surface, something to sit on, decent lighting, and an electric socket close by if you use a computer. Anything else is pure luxury!

RESEARCHING

# TECHNICAL WRITING
## IF YOU ARE PASSIONATE ABOUT ACCURACY AND DETAIL, TECHNICAL WRITING MAY BE THE JOB FOR YOU

Tom Marshall shines a spotlight on a lesser-known career for writers

## TOM MARSHALL

Tom is a freelance technical writer living in Thailand, with clients in Europe and Asia. His first two careers were in publishing and computing, which add up to his third and probably final career in technical writing. User manuals often get a bad name. Tom appreciates the opportunity to make a difference and enjoys the challenge of writing good manuals. He is very happy to be a technical writer; it means he can be his own boss and live any place he likes the look of.

When people ask me what I do, I say 'I'm a writer.' 'Oh, really? How interesting!' comes the enthusiastic reply. 'What do you write?' I pause, and wonder what it would be like to be a best-selling novelist, shortlisted for the Booker Prize. 'I write computer manuals,' I say.

'Oh, really…' The enthusiasm evaporates and eyes scan the room for an exit.

Technical writing probably won't put your name on a title page, and you probably won't find yourself in bookshops, surreptitiously rearranging your titles more prominently (I believe writers of other genres do this in their spare time). But if you recognize yourself in the description below, technical writing could be the career for you (first tip: the bullet point is a technical writer's best friend).

DO YOU:
● have a technical or scientific outlook

● grasp new concepts quickly and have a desire to tell others about them

● communicate easily with people of all ranks and abilities

● believe in detail

● have a compulsion for accuracy

● have impeccable grammar

● have solid writing skills, but can't think of a plot?

If so, technical writing can be a very satisfying and well paid job. It is always a challenge, requiring business acumen, diplomacy and a range of personal skills. It could take you anywhere in the world, or you could work from home.

## WHAT IS TECHNICAL WRITING?

A technical writer creates documentation to support a product. Documentation is produced for several reasons: ranging from legal requirements (for safe use of a product) to lower support costs. Employing technical writers costs money, but in the long run, it costs less than after-sales support, loss of business or law suits if a product is supplied without documentation.

Ultimately, technical writing aims to deliver documentation that allows the user to operate a product safely and efficiently.

Technical writers are in demand in many industries, for example:
- Manufacturing
- Computing
- Automotive
- Aerospace
- Military
- Financial
- Medical

The product you write about could be anything: an electric toothbrush, a software program, an industrial component or a jumbo jet. In my case it is an X-ray machine. Whatever your prior technical skill or interest, you will find plenty of opportunities to write.

## TOOLS OF THE TRADE
Documentation takes many forms: a printed manual, an electronic file, a web page or an online help system, for example. Below are some specific tools for particular formats.

### MANUALS
Adobe FrameMaker is regarded as the industry standard for creating technical manuals, but it represents a significant investment. Microsoft Word or WordPerfect are widely used alternatives.

### ELECTRONIC FILES
File distribution using PDF (Portable Document Format) is popular and a technical writer should become familiar with PDF creation. Adobe Acrobat is the standard tool for this, but alternatives are available at lower cost.

### ONLINE HELP
Online help is widely used when documenting software, and many employers ask specifically for this skill. Tools such as RoboHelp or AuthorIT are used to create an online help file. The help file is usually integrated with the software being documented. Try pressing 'F1' on your keyboard now

## THE SECRET LIFE OF DOCUMENTATION
Documentation goes through several stages on its journey to the user.

### UNDERSTAND THE REQUIREMENTS
Project requirements describe what kind of product you will write about, its intended use and the level of understanding of the users. From this you can decide on the correct format for your documentation, the correct level of language to pitch it at, and what kind of information to include.

### UNDERSTAND THE PRODUCT
Before they build something, product developers usually write down what their product will do, and how it will do it. These are the product

## TOM'S FIVE FAVOURITE (NON TECHNICAL!) BOOKS

**Lord Jim, Joseph Conrad**
Mortal danger on the high seas, and a moment of moral weakness sets a young man on an epic journey to erase the stain of cowardice. What would you have done, in his place?

**Zen and the Art of Motorcycle Maintenance, Robert M Pirsig**
Not a user manual, but a guide to life: a thought-provoking journey along America's back roads and across the threshold of psychosis into… madness or clarity?

**Woe To Live On, Daniel Woodrell**
An American tale: an evocative and authentic account of those just trying to get by amid the insanity of civil war.

**Man Plus, Frederik Pohl**
A surgically enhanced man is our only hope of colonizing Mars before Earth self-destructs: monstrous and alien, his greatest survival trait is his humanity, the only part the surgeons could not cut from his body.

**Time Out of Joint, Philip K Dick**
When you can't trust reality, what else is left? Dick is a genius, read everything he wrote.

## TIP

### *The golden rules of technical writing*

The ISTC members' forum discussed this topic recently, giving a good indication of what is expected:

- KNOW YOUR AUDIENCE
  - BE CONCISE
  - BE CONSISTENT
  - BE CURIOUS
  - BE CORRECT
  - KEEP IT SIMPLE
  - AVOID JARGON
- PROVIDE GOOD NAVIGATION
  - BE PROFESSIONAL
- AND FINALLY, NEVER PROOFREAD YOUR OWN WORK!

## START WRITING!

This is the fun part, and be sure to take pride in what you do.

### TESTING TIMES

Your documentation must be checked and verified by the project team. You create draft versions for developers to test against the product, and they respond with corrections. Technical writers and product developers do not always agree. Within the project team, the writer is usually outnumbered and considered bottom of the food chain (no offence). But you have a responsibility to the user to influence good usability. Starting arguments in project meetings won't change minds, but intelligent reasoning and persistence will. Stubborn diplomacy is a core skill of the technical writer.

### LEAD THE WAY

Documentation is rarely read cover to cover. You must construct a navigation system to direct the user to specific sections. This includes:
- a table of contents
- a logical hierarchy of headings
- bullet points!
- step by step procedures

specifications, and they are your key to understanding how a product works.

### READ ALL ABOUT IT

Specifications can be complex documents, and you may need to read them five times before they make sense. That is precisely why you have been hired: as

## "STARTING ARGUMENTS IN PROJECT MEETINGS WON'T CHANGE MINDS, BUT INTELLIGENT REASONING AND PERSISTENCE WILL"

a technical writer, you have the desire to find out how a product works, and you have the ability to communicate that to others.

### GETTING A HANDLE ON IT

You may get hands-on experience of the product, but don't rely on that. After all, you will be writing the documentation alongside development of the product itself. You may even be expected to deliver the final text before the product is completed. This is not ideal, but it is quite normal. If your product is a jumbo jet, you probably won't get your hands on it even after it is finished. To date, no one has let me loose on an X-ray machine. If the specification documents are well written, you can write good user documentation.

- cross references
- data tables
- illustrations
- appendices
- a comprehensive index.

A good technical writer has an eye for page layout; good design techniques can unlock the documentation for the user.

### RELEASE IT INTO THE WILD

When you have completed your edits, reviews and corrections, your documentation is almost complete. Read it through one last time, and then deliver it to the project manager in the agreed format.

## WRITING DISCIPLINE

Most successful writers have a routine, a daily way of weaving their writing into their lives so that it is a job like any other. Here are three starting points from which to proceed:

• Have a plan and sets of goals. What are you going to write, and by when?

• Set aside specific times for writing. Many of us are at our best early in the morning, but some writers work best at dead of night. Get into a pattern of working and stick to it.

• Set yourself a specific minimum number of words to aim for; even if it's only 50 you'll still see your manuscript growing over time.

## YOU WANT TO BE A TECHNICAL WRITER?

As a small child, you probably didn't want to grow up to be a technical writer. Older and wiser, and never destined to be an astronaut, you have acquired knowledge of a product in a different role, and the time has come when you want to write about it for the benefit of others.

### TRAINING OR EXPERIENCE?

There are opportunities to study technical writing, but degree courses are few and far between. There are many short commercial training courses available, but in reality, experience counts for more than qualifications.

### DO IT YOURSELF

To get experience, you might find small documentation projects are available in your current role. These projects give you a taste of what you are in for, and count as experience when applying for a position as a writer. There is nothing to stop you writing your own texts about things that interest you. How about product reviews, or procedures describing tasks you perform at work?

## FINDING WORK

There are several employment agencies dedicated to finding posts for technical writers, and the job promises flexible working opportunities.

### PERMANENT

There are many new junior and senior positions advertised every week. Salaries for permanent posts range between £20,000 and £40,000, depending on experience.

### CONTRACT

There is an active contract market for technical writers, with contracts from a few weeks (urgently required!) to several months and longer regularly available.

### FREELANCE

Technical writing could be your chance to go it alone. As with any freelance enterprise, you need business skills and good self-marketing, but the benefits of working for yourself are immense.

## FIND YOUR OWN SPACE

Technical writing is as much about communicating with your colleagues as it is about writing documentation, and you may find yourself working in a busy development team. Writing can also be a solitary occupation, and much time is spent staring out of a window waiting for inspiration to pay a visit. Working at home is a possibility, although this depends on your employer, and your ability to fulfil team-oriented responsibilities.

Further afield, technical writing is in demand around the world. There are many positions available throughout Europe. If you ever wanted to travel, technical writing can open the door for you.

## RESOURCES

**ISTC**
**Institute of Scientific and Technical Communicators**
**www.istc.org.uk**
Technical writers are represented by the ISTC, which brings professionals together as a community and provides useful resources, including information about training.

**SfEP**
**Society for Editors and Proofreaders**
**www.sfep.co.uk**
Grammar must be the bedrock of your writing. Visit the SfEP website for details of courses covering all aspects of English language usage.

# SELF PUBLISHING DOS AND DON'TS
## ADVICE FROM A SCEPTICAL EXPERT

Bestselling author and Antiques Roadshow expert Paul Atterbury shares his experience of self publishing

## PAUL ATTERBURY

Paul is a writer, lecturer, historian and occasional broadcaster with a lifelong enthusiasm for books. He has been a graphic designer, writer, publisher, editor, photographer, and has worked in the printing industry. Thus, he knows quite a bit about books and book production! As an art historian and antiques expert, he has written books on ceramics and design, and has worked on the BBC's *Antiques Roadshow* for seventeen years. A life-long railway enthusiast, he has produced a series of books on railways for David & Charles: *Branch Line Britain, Along Country Lines,* and *Tickets Please!* Others are in the pipeline.

I became a self publisher by mistake. A friend and I had a contract with a well known name to produce an architectural guide to the north of France. When we delivered the manuscript and the photographs, the publisher changed their mind. As we had done all the work, we decided to publish it ourselves.

Luckily, I knew about publishing and printing, having worked in both sides of the industry. Producing the book was great fun, selling it a bit of a nightmare as it needed good publicity and nationwide sales. In the end we did break even, thanks largely to the selling of a French language edition. After a few years we remaindered the outstanding stock, getting 50p per copy (they had cost us £2.75 per copy to produce). Overall it was an enjoyable experience and so I have done it several times since, notably with a series of little books showing the history of local Dorset villages through old postcards, produced via our Postcard Press imprint. These are ideal for self publishing as all the sales are local, so distribution is just a couple of hours in the car from time to time.

## WHY SELF PUBLISH?

Most books are best published through conventional channels. However, self publishing has always been an option and, prior to the nineteenth century, it was actually quite common. Today, this option is both tempting and accessible, thanks to modern computer technology. However, the downside of the desktop revolution is that everyone thinks they can write, design and produce books, which blurs the boundaries. Anyone considering the self publishing route should first ask themselves why. The reasons should be quite specific: first, that the proposed book is relatively obscure, personal or limited to a specific or local market to which the self publisher has good access and, second, vanity – the desire to publish for private reasons material that is likely to be otherwise unpublishable. A third reason, never enough on its own, is to have complete control of content, style and production. A pre-requisite of any self publishing venture is a full understanding of all the processes of book production, publishing, marketing and distribution. Anyone without this necessary knowledge or experience should not even think about it.

## TECHNICAL KNOWLEDGE

Self publishing is not difficult and can be enjoyable and even efficient, providing the rules are followed. A well-developed knowledge of computers is also essential.

Here are the rules. Write or prepare the text to as final a form as possible. Find a friendly and experienced editor to work on the text – self editing is never easy and is usually inefficient, for editing is a highly professional skill. Select and prepare illustrations, which may be drawings, photographs, colour transparencies or prints, or artwork of other kinds. Make sure the quality is high – a badly composed, out of focus photograph will always be exactly that. The next stage is the laying out of the material and the design of the book. Anyone without advanced computer skills should find a designer, for this is a complex process involving

> **MANY SELF PUBLISHING VENTURES COME TO GRIEF IN A GHASTLY MUDDLE OF PRIVATE AND BUSINESS FINANCES**

layouts, type size and specification, picture scanning and possibly Photoshop, and on-screen page assembly, which can include folios and running heads, pagination, footnotes, and prelim pages. The aim is to produce the complete book on a CD or DVD, ready for the printer.

There are a number of other tasks to be undertaken before this final stage. The self publisher has to choose an imprint or name, such as the Rosemary Press, and this should be registered to ensure no one else can use it. Once the name is established, the book can be registered for an ISBN, the international numbering system that issues every book with a unique reference number that is used by wholesalers and book shops when they order individual titles. It is also important to make sure that all necessary permissions have been obtained for the use and reproduction of pictures and text quotations from

published works. Copyright law is now complex and strict, and ignorance is no excuse.

## KNOW YOUR PRINTER

The next stage is the printing. It is sensible to ask for quotes from at least two printers, preferably local and with good reputations in the book production field. The key thing at this point is a fully detailed and accurate specification, identifying the size and number of pages, the quality and weight of paper, the style of binding (paper or hardback, thread sewn or glued sections), the number of illustrations, whether they're colour or black and white and their placing in the book, together with any other technical information that will affect the price. Now choose the printer on the basis of price and reputation, and discuss schedules, proofs, delivery details and payment terms. Everything at this stage must be in writing. The printer may ask for a credit check or insist on payment in advance. Such an advance should not exceed 50 per cent of the total price. Always remember that, after this stage, changes and extras are expensive.

Think about printing extra copies of the front jacket for publicity purposes or for overprinting as a leaflet.

## KEEP ACCOUNTS AND CHECK YOUR SUMS

Everything so far is straightforward but, before telling the printer to go ahead, the project must have been fully costed.

The total production budget should include the printing, all preparation costs – the author and any royalties, the services of designer and editor, photograph and reproduction fees and illustration costs – and sums to cover promotion and publicity. There are also overheads that can be included, such as the publisher's own time, the rent of premises, services and storage. There is no VAT on books at the moment.

Given this figure, it is possible to establish the selling price for the book, the unit cost, the possible breakeven point and any likely profit. The price structure is very simple. Booksellers and other retail outlets will usually require at least a 40 per cent discount, and sometimes more. To make this work, the selling price has to be about five times the cost price. The other element in this equation is the print run. In principle, the higher the number of books produced, the lower the unit cost. Thus, if it costs £5000 to produce 1000 books, the unit cost is £5, and the retail selling price should therefore be £25. To produce 2000 of the same book may cost £8000, with a unit cost of £4. The retail selling price can be lower, but there are more books to sell to reach a breakeven point. It is a matter of juggling figures and being realistic. Many self publishers are over optimistic and end up with a garage full of hard to sell books for years.

## YOU'VE GOT TO SELL THEM AS WELL, YOU KNOW

The most exciting moment for any publisher, or writer, is when the first finished copies arrive. However, this is also the end of the easy bit, for now all those books have to be sold, and all those costs repaid. The key thing to consider long before any actual books are produced is the method of distribution. How are the books going to be sold? There are, as ever, choices. Distribution can be sub-contracted to another publisher or distribution agent but this is usually expensive and not particularly efficient as any publisher will naturally sell their own books rather than someone else's. The other route is the do it yourself one, relatively easy if the book has a largely local interest, and virtually impossible if it is to be sold nationwide. Selling books nationwide means going on the road or employing sales people, establishing efficient packing, dispatch and invoicing systems and chasing payment from dilatory clients. It is possible to sell to major national chains such as W H Smith, but they will always demand huge discounts

and very generous payment terms which a small publisher cannot afford. Other options include a website and mail order, both of which require credit card payment facilities, and long days spent packing and posting assorted parcels.

Successful selling is dependent upon good publicity and so any small independent publisher has to devote plenty of time to promotion and marketing, and to be very persuasive on the telephone.

## WE DID IT!

When all is said and done, and the book goes well, the whole experience can be entertaining and rewarding. A crucial question then arises: reprint or not, and if so, how many copies. If the book is a failure, the choices are pretty stark: keep the stocks for ever, sell the whole edition to a remainder company, who may pay 50p per copy, or take a deep breath and pulp the lot. Alternatively, build an extension, for books make good wall insulation! The final thing to consider is the nature of the business. If the publishing venture is a one off, do not bother to start a limited company. If, on the other hand, publishing threatens to become a habit, then it might be a good idea. In any case, seek financial advice, and always have a separate bank account for the publishing venture. Most banks charge no costs for the first eighteen months for a small business account. Accurate record keeping is essential, of all costs, all sales and all income, both for tax purposes and for peace of mind. Many self publishing ventures come to grief in a ghastly muddle of private and business finances.

## TIPS FOR SELF PUBLISHING

- Make sure you know what you are doing and why. If in doubt, leave it to the professionals.

- Write the most comprehensive specification and stick to it. All changes and uncertainties cost money.

- Draw up a budget and stick to it. Cost control at every stage is vital.

- Organise the design/layout in ways that best suit the book, and make sure they are efficient

- Choose your printer with care. It is not just about cost – the cheapest is often not the best. Discuss the project thoroughly and make a proper and agreed schedule.

- Write everything down and have written agreements at all stages, rather than verbal.

# PUBLISHING SERVICES
## SOME DEFINITIONS

There is a bewildering number of companies out there offering all kinds of publishing services. What should you consider?

Paul's article on the previous pages is a realistic guide to doing it yourself. But if you intend to get help, perhaps by using one of the many companies that now call themselves self publishers, what should you look for?

Before you make any decisions, the first thing to do is consider carefully all the points that Paul makes: for example, do you know professional editors and designers? If you don't, how will you find people you can trust? Your first port of call should be the pages of *Writer's Market*. Here you will find companies of all sorts that provide a range of editorial and design services.

## WHAT IS A PACKAGER?

Some of the companies in theses listings are packagers, a word peculiar to publishing that means that they 'package' books, handling everything in the book creation and management process from manuscript to ready-to-print files.

Confusingly, some packagers are also publishers, in that they have their own imprints under which their books appear. Usually, packagers take the book through to print-ready digital files, leaving the production and print jobs to the publishers (who can usually source print more economically). But some packagers do the complete job, offering finished books.

The consideration for the writer here may be a simple one: cost. Packagers would normally charge industry rates. But, if they think your idea is a good one with commercial potential, some may take it on as part of their production cycle and bear the costs, in just the way that a publisher would.

If you think this is a possible way forward for you, you'll need to talk to individual companies to find out exactly the way they might work with you.

## VANITY PUBLISHING CAVEATS

Once, vanity publishing was relatively easy to understand: essentially it meant you as the writer wanted the book for whatever reason and knew that in order to have that book you would have to pay for it to be made and printed.

Fair enough. Except that you may have ended up with a bill for thousands, no rights in your own work, and possibly no sales either. Again, fair enough if you knew all of that upfront. Unfortunately, there were, and still are companies that do not make their terms and conditions clear at the outset. There are well-documented cases of writers paying thousands for poorly made books, or paying for books that never appeared because of small print in the contract disguising a host of reasons why the book would never appear.

These days vanity publishing may be disguised as 'subsidy', 'joint-venture', 'shared-responsibility' or even 'self' publishing. And this is where it can get very worrying indeed for writers who are considering working with such companies.

Don't work with companies like this unless you are completely satisfied with their terms and conditions and ways of working before you sign anything. If you have the slightest doubts you should not go ahead.

If you really want to make your book like this, consider working with one of the companies that offer fully costed short run print on demand services. Again, you need to be sure exactly what kind of agreement you are getting into.

Or read Paul's article again and do it yourself.

# WRITING FOR THE WEB
## TIPS FROM AN INTERNET VETERAN

Getting the words right on websites is a special skill. Anthony Pearson gives his expert advice.

### ANTHONY PEARSON

Anthony is a freelance producer, writer and editor with a specialism in online and interactive media. He has devised, written and produced content for the BBC, BT, FT.com, The Arts Council, Dorling Kindersley, Carphone Warehouse, Cahoot and many others.

> Stick to your point and keep it short. There's a bit more to writing for the web than that, but with those two points in mind you won't go far wrong. (If I hadn't been asked to write 1,500 words on the subject, I'd be tempted to stop here.)

People use the web to do things quickly and to get information quickly. People don't use the web to read from just for the pleasure of reading (which is why we still buy books) – the web is all about the message. So make sure you know what you want your readers to get out of your copy and then write your message using a few, simple words. And then go back and take half the words out. And then go back again and replace all the long words with short ones.

### GENERAL RULES

- Make your writing work. Be clear about what you want to achieve and re-read what you've written to make sure it delivers.

- Know your audience and use words and style they'll understand.

- Be positive (don't be negative).

- Be direct and confident. (It is, perhaps, best not to be indirect.)

- Use plain language. Buzzwords and jargon make your strategic innovations mission statements look unoriginal and insincere.

- Studiously avoid the loquacious, endeavour to shun baroque locutions and spurn labyrinthine grammatical structures else you may earn the disapprobation of your esteemed readership. (Don't show off. Keep it simple.)

- DUA (don't use acronyms) unless they really do save space and your audience will understand them. Even then, always explain what they mean the first time you use them. *Acronymfinder.com* is a good place to find out how ambiguous you are being – DUA also stands for Distal Uterine Artery and Dead or Unable to Attend.

- Contractions (you'll, we'll, they're) are good things – they save space and make your writing more direct.

- Avoid colons and semi-colons. Much as I love them in print, they usually mean your sentence is too complicated: Split your sentence into several, shorter ones; or write your points as a bulleted list.

- And don't worry about starting sentences with 'and' and 'but' – it makes your writing snappier.

Good grammar is important, but on the web accessible writing is more important.

Having said that, do brush up on your grammar. Quality counts on the web as much as it does in print. Knowing the difference between 'which' and 'that' and putting apostrophes and commas in the right places make all the difference. If your writing is clear and acurate (check your spelling), people will take notice of, and trust, your message.

important bits first so your readers don't have to scroll down to find them.

● Search engines look for keywords (words that describe what your site is about) at the top of pages. Writing meaningful headlines and first paragraphs helps your readers find your site.

● If you're repetitively repeating the same information under different headings, re-jig your site structure.

## PEOPLE DON'T USE THE WEB TO READ FROM JUST FOR THE PLEASURE OF READING (WHICH IS WHY WE STILL BUY BOOKS) – THE WEB IS ALL ABOUT THE MESSAGE

### SOME SPECIFICS

You'll need to adapt your writing to its destination. Here are a few varieties of web publishing, and some points to bear in mind.

### WEBSITES

Whether you are selling something, teaching something or inviting your friends to a birthday party, your site has a purpose. You've got a message – be clear about what it is.

Think advertising, think newspapers. Get the whole message across in the heading and the first paragraph and fill in the details later.

Have a look at the BBC News website (*news.bbc. co.uk*). For a start, its name says what it is. If your site's name isn't descriptive, tell people what it is in the first paragraph, or use a strapline (a short, descriptive line under the heading). Now have a look at any one of the news stories. The headline and first paragraph tells you the whole story. You only need to read the rest if you want the details.

● Be clear about your site's purpose, and tell people what that purpose is.

● Split your site into bite-sized chunks under meaningful headings. (That's your navigation sorted out.)

● It's hard to read long chunks of writing from a screen, so keep it short, break it up and put the

● Make links descriptive. Tell people why they should click on a link and what they'll find there.

● Test your site on as many people as you can. Take note of what they say – you may not agree, but the site is for your audience, not for you. Then change your site until it works for your audience.

### EMAILS

Just because it's quick and easy to send an email, it doesn't mean it's quick and easy to write them. Emails are permanent (once you've sent them they get saved all over the internet), and can be copied and forwarded – write in haste, repent at your leisure. If you are sending anything important, contentious or personal, slow down. Write your email, save it, then read it again in ten minutes. Do you really want to send that? Remember, the person you are sending it to can keep it and share it – imagine everyone you know and thousands of complete strangers reading it. It can happen.

● Keep it simple, focussed and accurate.

● Make the subject line meaningful – people get a lot of email and you need to tell them up-front why they should read yours.

● Don't send personal, especially financial, information by email. Email isn't secure and it isn't

83

private. Unless you run your own server, lots of people have access to every message you send.

- Make sure you are sending it to the right person – check the address before you hit the send button.

## FORUMS

As with emails, it's easy to send messages to a forum. And again, it's easy for something you'll regret writing to get published to the world. Have a look around any forum before you jump in with your penny's worth. Like walking into a pub, you'll soon get a feel for what sort of place a forum is, and how you should pitch your posts (messages). And if there are forum rules, read them.

- What you are writing will be published. Keep it simple, focussed and accurate.

- Keep to the forum's topic, and the specific point being discussed.

- Don't post contentious messages in haste.

- Don't get drawn into arguments ('flame wars'). Make your point clearly and concisely without getting personal.

- Don't post personal, especially financial, information.

- Be suspicious. Would you believe me if I told you I was an 18-year-old Adonis?

## ADS

If you are selling something, what you say about it matters. Hence the advertising industry. Writing adverts is an art, whether you are writing copy for banner ads or selling something on Ebay.

- Be snappy, direct and keep it simple – don't try to be too clever in your ads.

- Be honest about what you are selling.

- But be positive – there's no need to sell your item's faults.

- Know your audience, and sell them the benefits of the thing from their point of view. A lot of people sell technologies on the web, when they should be selling what the technology does.

- Check your spelling and grammar. If your writing is dodgy, people will think you are too.

## BLOGS

Blogging (from 'web logging', which means an online diary) sites - try *blogware.com* or *blogger. com* - make organizing and sharing your diary over the web easy. Unfortunately, this won't make you a Pepys. We are still reading Pepys' diary today because he had first-hand experience of momentous events, had a talent for writing about them and had the dedication to keep on writing. There are a lot of minority-interest blogs out there; there are a few blogs that approach the sort of mass-market, mildly entertaining Polyfilla that you'll find in a Sunday supplement; there are a handful that are by interesting people who can write. Random Acts of Reality (*http://randomreality.blogware.com/*) is a great example of a blog that works for a wide audience. Written by a paramedic who works for the London Ambulance Service, the entries are, well, read them and see.

Having said that, unless you are aiming for a huge audience, and especially if your blog covers a specific niche, you don't need to be a great writer. What matters is your content. Whether your blog contains photos you want to share with your friends or top tips on implementing the latest coding techniques, there will be an audience out there for you (just don't expect Hollywood to come knocking on your door offering millions for the film rights).

- Keep it simple, keep it focussed. (There is a theme emerging here… have you spotted it yet?)

- Write about something you know for an audience you understand.

- Stick with it – dedication is all when it comes to diaries.

- Think twice before sharing too much. Anything you write can be saved (don't rely on being able to delete it), copied and passed around.

And finally…you know what I'm going to say; stick to your point and keep it short.

# ELECTRONIC PUBLISHING
## WHAT MIGHT THAT BE, THEN?

Some pointers to the digital future and its impact on writers

Electronic publishing is a catch-all phrase that can include everything from interactive multimedia content on DVDs through to one-liners delivered on mobile phones.

At the heart of all electronic publishing is digital content. The digital revolution enabled publishers to think of new mixtures of content, delivered in different ways. 'Content' is a peculiar word that can include words, collections of words, whole books, pictures, video and sound, and any mixture of these things.

In the mid 1990s many publishers thought that their future lay in CD ROMs, not books. They were wrong. Spectacularly so.

Today many of the same publishers think their future lies online, but with the proviso that books still have a lot going for them, and that their online content might be delivered to a very wide range of products, not just desktop computers.

## DIGITAL BUSINESS MODELS

For many of these publishers the challenge now is not how to deliver non-book content to consumers, but how to make money from it. Some publishers have business models that work: educational publishers publish digitally on subscription models.

The subscription model might work for some other kinds of publishers, for example those who specialize in practical information. Examples here might be travel publishers, who could provide large amounts of bespoke information (say an itinerary for a weekend in Paris) to a computer, or very small amounts of information to a mobile phone (say a hotel recommendation, the hotel being close to wherever the phone is). Such information could reasonably be charged for.

## EBOOKS

Ebooks are not new; there have been perfectly workable handheld digital book readers for at least ten years. The reason they were not commercially successful is simply because most people would rather read a traditional, paper, book.

Maybe that's changing; many publishers now make at least some of their books available in digital format.

For authors the traditional financial models probably still work for you here; your work is simply going to be sold in a digital, rather than physical format. One wonders, however, whether the same 'challenges' will apply as to music, where once the digital files are out there, they are copied again and again – stolen as content owners see it.

## EARNINGS FOR THE WRITER IN THE DIGITAL WORLD?

If you write for a readership that accepts the need to pay you, perhaps as part of a subscription to a digital product for doctors, or scientists, or academics, then your earnings seem set to continue. Why wouldn't they?

If you write for a readership that wants a specific piece of information at a specific time, then they'll probably be prepared to pay.

If a new generation of readers would rather read your novel on a screen than on paper, then presumably you'll still be paid, but will have to accept that illegal copying is inevitable.

In nearly all publishing areas writers who have to make a living will be competing with increasing amounts of free information of all sorts.

But accurate, good, content is always likely to have value, and monetary value at that. You hope.

# STUDYING MEDIA AND PUBLISHING
## THE OPTIONS FOR STUDENTS AND POTENTIAL STUDENTS

Think out of the box: David Penfold examines the options for those wishing to further their writing and other creative skills via the academic route. And he gives crucial advice for those needing to write dissertations; advice that all who write in whatever sphere are likely to find invaluable

### DAVID PENFOLD

David has worked in publishing for many years, starting on scientific journals in the days when they were set with hot metal. He has provided consultancy, project management and editorial services to many of the UK's leading publishers. He now teaches on publishing courses at the London College of Communication (a college of the University of the Arts London) and supervizes research projects that are carried out in co-operation with publishers and related organizations.

There is an Indian fable in which blind philosophers feel the different parts of an elephant and draw different conclusions about what it is. One feels the leg and suggests the elephant is a tree, another feels the tusk and suggests it is a spear, and so on. Publishing and the media are rather like this. Someone who only has experience of magazine publishing, for example, will give a different view of the industry to that provided by another person, who has, say, spent their working life publishing fiction or academic monographs, not to mention the web designer, the film-maker, the photographer or the fashion designer.

So, if you want to have a career in publishing or the media, how do you go about finding out what it is about? Taking one of the many courses on media or publishing is one (and probably the best) way. Which course and at what level is something we will try and address in this article, along with a description of what courses include, particularly those in publishing.

There are literally hundreds of courses in media studies, particularly if those taken at school are included. These courses have various characteristics in common. First, they are intended to give an overview of what the media is, ie newspapers, magazines, broadcasting and now the World Wide Web. Then, in many cases they aim to provide an introduction to some of the skills required in jobs in the media. These range from writing computer games to creative writing and broadcast journalism. Similarly, publishing courses differ in their emphasis, some overlapping with journalism, some related more to the arts and others, such as the courses at the London College of Communication, very much vocationally based, including not only technical skills and production skills, but also business skills, including marketing and business planning.

### INDUSTRY SKILLS

The media industry involves three or four main skill areas, although there is some overlap. The main areas are:

- **Creative** This includes journalism and other kinds of writing, as well, for example, as design, photography and film direction.

- **Technical** This will include production (of all kinds) and skills such as web design, although of course in web design, as well as areas such as photography and film-making, there is an overlap with the creative area.

- **Editorial** It can be argued that this is part of the creative skills and in some ways it is. However,

In addition, there is the business side, but, if this is your interest, you would be better to consider a business or accountancy qualification.

So, if you want to study media or publishing, first you need to decide the level at which you are able to study, which will depend on either or both of your paper qualifications and your experience. It is worth noting that your experience may qualify you to take a particular course even though on paper you may not have the appropriate qualifications.

Once you have decided the level at which you want to study, you need to decide what you want

> ## THERE IS A TENDENCY TO READ WHAT YOU EXPECT TO READ WHEN YOU READ SOMETHING YOU HAVE WRITTEN YOURSELF

the term 'editing' means a number of different things, so while editing a film or a website may be creative, building publishing lists and commissioning books is more closely related to marketing.

- **Marketing** While marketing is a subject that can be studied on its own (and if it is marketing as a discipline that you are interested in, then you should consider this), there are aspects of marketing in all the media industries and each has its own special emphasis.

## WHAT ABOUT A DAY JOB?

Many writers have jobs that bring them steady money as well as pursuing their writing passion. T S Eliot famously worked for many years at Faber & Faber, for example. Some find the creative fulfilment that they require in these jobs and the writing eventually takes second place. These days, it is much easier to get work in the creative and media industries if you are formally qualified, as David Penfold's article on these pages makes clear.

to get out of a course. Only then can you study the prospectuses and web sites of the institutions you are interested in and review what they offer.

It is often rumoured that students choose their university or college on the basis of the social life, which may be as good a way as any if that's all you are looking for. However, if you want a qualification to form the basis of a career, then there needs to be more to it than this. Study the course outline provided by the institution. Today, you should be able to get hold of a course handbook, which will give you a lot of information about the content of the course and how it is assessed.

However, there can be more than this. It is worth finding out what facilities an institution can provide. Some universities, for example, have a broad range of faculties or schools and you may be able to do a joint honours degree in media and another subject if that is what you want. On the other hand, institutions like the London College of Communication (LCC) offer a much narrower range of courses, but therefore are able to offer a greater range of facilities. For example, the Media School at LCC has film and radio studios, photographic studios and a newspaper newsroom. In the newsroom journalism students produce a weekly newspaper for much of the academic year. The School of Printing and Publishing has printing and reprographic equipment, both traditional and digital, which means that publishing students are able to get hands-on experience of printing, which they are unlikely to get in any other way. Of course, other institutions will have their own Unique Selling Points (USPs).

## THE COURSE

So what will you get on the course? The answer to this is almost as broad as the type of course. Almost certainly you will get lectures or classes. The level of these will vary depending on the level of the qualification you are aiming for. If you take course leading to a foundation degree in the Arts (FdA) for example, you will be taught the curriculum in detail, while at Master's level, the information will be put in front of you, together with sources and places where you can find out more. Then it is up to you to manage your own learning. And a first degree will

be somewhere between the two. And, at any level, the responsibility is yours; the staff will help if you have difficulties, but if you don't make the effort, it is unlikely that anyone will come and chase you; at least not more than once or twice.

Students often query the relevance of parts of their course. However, remember that the aim is often to teach you why and what, rather than how. In other words, you need to know about a topic, but not necessarily how to implement it. A good example is XML (the technical markup language that is now regarded by many as an industry standard in many media areas). I have lost count of the number of past students on the MA in Publishing at LCC who have said to me that, at the time, they wondered why they needed to know about it, but, subsequently once they were in jobs,

## TOPICS COVERED IN COURSES IN MEDIA AND PUBLISHING

This list is probably not comprehensive, but gives some idea of the range of topics to choose from. It should also be noted that the same topics may be taught under different names and no course will include all of these topics

- Media
- Creative writing
- Writing for the media/ journalism
  Specialist areas of journalism, e.g. sports
  Broadcast journalism/writing for TV and radio
- Web authoring
- Website design, HTML and related languages and techniques
- Graphic design
- Video and film production
- Audio (and radio) production

- Print production and print management
- Multimedia production
- Interactive (computer) games
- Photography
- Animation
- Music programming
- Marketing, PR and publicity
- Publishing
- Creative writing
- Commissioning and list management for books
- Market research
- Print production techniques, including page composition, colour management and pre-press
- Digital production techniques
- Website design, HTML and related languages and techniques
- The Internet: basic principles; security; how it is used; e-commerce

- Book design
- Dealing with printers
- Rights
- Finance
- Distribution
- Project management
- Magazine management
- Magazine production
- Advertising in magazines and on the Web
- Marketing
- Academic journals (editing, peer review and production)
- Content management, structured documents and metadata
- XML, XSL and related languages
- Information Technology Management
- Publicity and PR
- Picture research
- Bookbinding
- Letterpress printing

*Note that there are also courses relating to printing, which we have not discussed here.*

they realized how relevant it as and they were very pleased that they listened.

You will probably also have practical classes and projects, although this will depend on the nature of the course and on the institution. Some of these may form part of the assessment, although you may also have exams to take as well. There is, however, a trend towards the use of assignments as a way of assessing students and, of course, at both master's level (and often at first degree level too) there is also

> ## REMEMBER THAT THE AIM IS OFTEN TO TEACH YOU WHY AND WHAT, RATHER THAN HOW

a dissertation based on research (see below).

The other trend is towards group work. Sometimes this is inevitable; you cannot produce a weekly paper on your own, while in other cases it provides a foretaste of the professional world in which students hope to be working. Sometimes students choose their own groups based on a commonality of interest or simply friendship, while at other times students will be allocated to groups with a particular brief. In the latter case, you may find you are in a group with someone you don't like or respect. This is something you will have to cope with, if only because it mirrors the professional world, although staff should be able to help you if there are real problems.

## THE BENEFITS OF STUDYING

Quite apart from the social life, the main benefits of studying are that you learn skills and you obtain a qualification. And to get a job, you need those things. It is, of course, possible to learn skills in other ways, but it is increasingly the case that you need a qualification to get a job. While there are those who blag their way into jobs in the industry (or even start their own companies) without any qualifications and still achieve great success, they are very much the minority and, if you look at the media industries, you will find that most successful people have a qualification of some kind.

The other big advantage of taking a recognized course in media or publishing is that you establish contacts within the industry. The Publishing MA at the London College of Communication, for example, has a placement scheme, through which students are able to obtain work experience. Thus, not only can they learn in a practical way, but they also have an opportunity to confirm that the job is what they thought it would be and that it interests them. In addition, students have the opportunity to hear and question visiting speakers from top-level management within the industry, some of whom are visiting professors. Speakers and visiting professors include Richard Charkin, CEO of Macmillan, Lynette Own, Rights Director of Pearson Education, Bryn Walls, Art Director of Dorling Kindersley, Andrew Franklin, publisher of *Eats, Shoots and Leaves*, and many other distinguished publishing professionals of many sorts.

## CAREER PROSPECTS

It is hard to say anything very useful about career prospects. Obviously, a few people do very well, a few fail disastrously, while the majority have modest (or not so modest) success. The University of the Arts London, the largest institution in the UK mainly devoted to art and design, lists successful alumnae on the inside of the programme for graduation ceremonies and the list is impressive. Doubtless, other institutions could produce equally impressive lists, but what is clear is that courses on media and publishing produce people who succeed in the media industry.

Of course, what your career prospects are will depend on the level of your qualification as well as on your skill set. And, even if having a higher degree does not enhance your prospect of actually getting a job, it can certainly help you to rise more quickly within an organization.

## THE INDUSTRY

The media industry is huge and it is difficult to identify the key players. Obviously the BBC and the national press (News International, Associated Newspapers and Trinity Mirror Group) are significant, but some of the largest web sites belong to companies whose main business is not publishing or media at all. They may produce these in house, but they may outsource them to a design agency, for example, and there are very many of these. There are no large film companies in the

UK and, of course, photography is essentially an individual art.

It is probably easier to identify the large companies in publishing, although there are many different types of publishing. Of magazine publishers, the largest are probably the National Magazine Company, Reed-Elsevier and Condé Nast, although there are a number of other quite large magazine publishers, such as Hachette Magazines, Haymarket and Future Publishing. In educational publishing, Pearson probably stands out, although Hodder (part of Hachette) is also large. When it comes to academic publishing (books and journals) Elsevier is the largest company, although Wiley's takeover of Blackwell Publishing puts them in second place. Other major academic publishers include Oxford and Cambridge University Presses (of course), Macmillan, Hodder (part of Hachette) and Taylor & Francis.

provide guidance on choosing your project (and will probably have the final say on the topic), but it does no harm to think about this right from the start of your course if you are a postgraduate or from the start of your final year if you are doing a first degree.

One advantage of focusing on your research topic fairly early on is that you may well be able to tailor other assignments so that they provide you with the opportunity to do some relevant work at that stage, rather than spending time other topics. On the other hand, if you are undecided about the topic of your major project, then looking at different areas as part of other assignments (or even work experience) may give you some ideas. Some people develop an idea quite early and slowly build it as the course goes on, often seeing almost everything in the light of this project. This can be good, although there is a danger of becoming

## " IT IS NO GOOD HAVING A FASCINATING RESEARCH QUESTION IF THERE IS NO POSSIBLE WAY THAT YOU CAN GET HOLD OF INFORMATION TO ANSWER IT "

In addition, there are hundreds of small companies, both in publishing and the media. Not only can they be very successful, growing into large companies, but they can also provide you with experience and a stepping stone in your career. One advantage of smaller companies is that you are likely to get a broader range of experience; in very small companies everyone does everything!

## YOUR DISSERTATION

Almost every masters' degree, and many undergraduate degrees as well, includes a major (research) project, which leads to a dissertation or research report. The main purpose of such a project is for students to learn what doing research is all about. However, there is no reason why the results of such research, limited as they may be, cannot provide useful input to the industry.

So, how do you choose your project and how do you carry it out. There are lots of books on actually doing the project and on choosing your project (see below). Your tutor or supervisor will certainly

blinkered. Other people have to cast around for a topic, so lectures, assignments and other activities, such as visiting speakers or visits or even simply something you see in the paper or on TV, can provide a stimulus that starts you thinking about a particular idea.

Above all, choose something that interests you. After all, you are going to be living and breathing this for weeks if not months and, if it doesn't really interest you, you are going to get bored and find it hard to produce quality work.

Other things you need to take into account, and your supervisor/tutor should be able to advise on these, are defining the scope of the project and assessing its feasibility; in the time you have available you are not going to be able to solve one of the world's major problems. Many students' initial ideas are much too broad in scope and also very hazy: 'I want to research the way magazine publishers operate' is perhaps broader than most but not really untypical. It is really important to define research questions (one or more) or to put forward hypotheses (again one or more). And in

# TEN TIPS FOR A GOOD DISSERTATION

- Give yourself time to plan the topic.

- Focus and state the research question(s); the smaller and better defined the problem is, the easier it is to solve.

- Choose a topic where you have a chance of getting some results.

- Make sure you understand the regulations.

- Make sure you understand the topic.

- Read the literature as widely as you can, but only include what is relevant. Then relate your findings back to what has been published previously.

- Be clear about the methodology and ensure that it is appropriate (read the reference books!).

- If English is not your first language (and probably even if it is), get someone else to read the dissertation.

- Proofread the dissertation; examiners find spelling, punctuation and typing errors irritating if they are present in large numbers.

- Take the advice of your supervisor/tutor

either case there must be a reasonable chance of being able to answer the questions or validate, or otherwise, the hypotheses. It is no good having a fascinating research question if there is no possible way that you can get hold of information to answer it.

## THE RESEARCH ITSELF

Research is all about structure. Research is essentially all about adding structure to information, which can be described as transforming information into knowledge. There are various different types of structure: the structure of the research itself, the structure of the information resources that you need to access and the structure of the final report or dissertation.

Why is structure important? First, as far as the research is concerned, it is by adding structure or interpreting structure that we understand issues and phenomena. However, there is more to it than that; structure helps you to organise your thought and your research and adding structure allows you to analyse your results. Finally, providing structure in your dissertation makes clear what you have done and helps the reader to understand it.

To create a structure one needs 'building blocks':
- What does the research seek to find out?
- What is the context?
- Which areas of knowledge is the research based on?
- What is already known?
- What are the sources of information?
- Also, what are the limits to the structure?
- What research resources are you able to access?

You need to determine the limits to the structure and you need to be clear about the time you have and resources (of all types) that you have available.

In order to create any structure, it is a good idea to have a plan – or several! First, you need a plan of the research territory. This will help you see how the areas you are researching fit together and how they fit into what other people have investigated; this is the purpose of the literature review, which we shall look at shortly. Creating a plan may help you focus so that you can see what can be done and what is outside the scope of your research (but may, nevertheless, be relevant to discuss).

The next plan you need is a timetable (a plan of how you are going to carry out the research). This is vital so that you can meet the deadline. You also need to document the research itself. Keep records of tutorials. It is quite possible, as we have mentioned above, that you will have had a lecture course on project management. Your research project gives you the opportunity to try out techniques such as activity flow charts and Gantt charts in practice.

**91**

Then you need a plan of how you are going to store your information. Again it is important to keep a record of the references that you read. Always note the source and try to categorize them (i.e. add a structure). This will also help you to identify the gaps and also save you a lot of time when you come to create the reference list or bibliography in your dissertation. (This is usually one of the last things to be done – or at least finalized – so anything that can reduce the pressure towards the end of the project is a good idea.) Incidentally, there are special programs, for example EndNote and ProCite, that can be used to organize and format references. If you have a lot of references, then you may find it useful to invest in one of these, particularly if you plan to continue in research (or even work in the area covered by your research topic). You will probably be able to get a student discount on such software!

Very important is a plan of how you are going to structure your report, which will be based on, but also determine, the structure of your research. A fairly common structure is the following:

- Introduction (aims, rationale, structure of report)
- Review of the context
- Review of the literature
- Design of research and the methodology
- Presentation and analysis of research findings
- Discussion
- Conclusions and recommendations
- References/bibliography
- Appendices

This structure is important because it should determine how you think. You will also, of course, have a title page, an abstract and a table of contents, but these will probably be the last items that you will add.

Let's look at each of these sections in turn.

## INTRODUCTION

Start by briefly stating the aim of this research and explain very briefly why the research topic is what it is and the scope. You may find it useful to state the research questions/hypotheses here (although not explain them).

It's also usual to explain the structure of the report or dissertation (how the sections/chapters are structured).

## REVIEW OF THE CONTEXT

This can be regarded as an introduction for someone who is not familiar with the area of the research (possibly whoever is marking it). It also serves to give people who are familiar with the research area a view on where you think the research is situated.

What actually goes into this section will depend very much on the subject area of your research. You may need to describe an industrial context; indeed

---

## RESEARCH RESOURCES

Some have already been mentioned, but other useful resources are:

*Managing Information for Research,*
**Elizabeth Orna with Graham Stevens**
Open University Press, 1997. This is good because it is aimed specifically at master's students and explains a lot of the detail of doing a research project

*Doing your Research Project:*
*A guide for first-time researchers in education and social science*
*(2nd edn),* **Judith Bell**
Open University Press, 1993. Does what 'it says on the tin'. Has useful advice about choosing a project.

*Research Project How to Write It*
*(4th edn),* **Ralph Bell**
Routledge Study Guides, 2004. Another good practical guide.

*Your Research Project: A Step-by-Step Guide for the First-Time Researcher (2nd edn),*
**Nicholas S.R. Walliman**
Sage, 2005. There is also *Your Undergraduate Dissertation: The Essential Guide for Success* (2004) by the same author. Another clear introduction.

*Methods in Behavioural Research (8th edn),*
**Paul C. Cozby**
McGraw-Hill, 2004. A rather more advanced, but established book in a particular area. Has an associated website:
http://methods.fullerton.edu/.

this section is quite often described as the industry review, but equally the context may be situational, social or academic.

You can have (and probably should have) references in your context review.

## LITERATURE REVIEW

In spite of the titles of this and the previous chapter, this is what really provides the context for your research. Sir Isaac Newton described himself as standing on the shoulders of giants. Although you shouldn't have delusions of grandeur, you need to be aware that almost all research builds on what has been done by others. You may, of course, find that your conclusions contradict or disagree with previous results, but that doesn't matter (although you need to be sure of your own results and be able to explain them – see below).

Another way of thinking of the literature

## "DON'T ASSUME THAT GOOGLE WILL PROVIDE YOU WITH ALL THE ANSWERS"

review is as a springboard that launches you into your research area. You need to know what has been published that is relevant to your research. If your literature review is not thorough, you may miss a publication that is relevant. Not only will this possibly invalidate or cast doubt on your conclusions, but it will make you look a bit silly! Try and include specific references rather than general ones.

So, how do you go about finding these references? It's much easier than it used to be, now that the World Wide Web means that there is information available at the desktop. Don't assume, however, that Google will provide you with all the answers, though Google Book Search and Google Scholar should make more information accessible. You should also be aware that you may not have access to some or even many of the articles that you need to read; not everything is free on the Web! Your institution will probably have a subscription to a scheme called Athens, which allows you to have

online access to journals to which the institution has subscribed. Ask in your library. In fact, don't ignore the library; not only will the staff be willing to help about online access to publications, but they will also remind you that printed resources are still a very valuable source of information!

If you do carry much of your literature search out over the web, remember that a large proportion of useful information resides in databases (often called the 'deep' or 'hidden' web). Google can't see these and you need to know how to access them. See *http://www.sc.edu/beaufort/library/pages/bones/bones.shtml* for a tutorial on ways to find information on the Web; Google is not the only answer. Other useful sites are:

- *www.digital-librarian.com*
- *Librarians' Index (www.lii.org)*
- The WWW Virtual Library *(http://vlib.org/)*
- *Intute (www.intute.ac.uk)*
- *www.completeplanet.com/*
- *www.weblens.org/invisible.html*

Quite a lot of information may be free, although you may have to register. Incidentally, you may find it useful to obtain either Google Desktop Search (see *http://www.google.com/options/*) or Copernic Desktop Search (see *http://www.copernic.com/en/products/desktop-search/*). Either of these will make it much easier to find information on your own computer.

If you carry out an effective literature review, it can lead you to the question(s) that you may wish to answer (or at least investigate) in your research. Remember also that this is a review and should, therefore, be critical/analytical and not just report what others have said. It should not just be a series of quotes and certainly not a 'cut and paste' from the Web!

Some of the references may be the same as those in the context review, but they are serving a different purpose. There they were setting the scene. Here they are providing information on which you can build and against which you will assess your results.

In theory, you should be able to write at least a first draft of most of your literature review before you begin the research in earnest. Indeed, you should try to do this because, as noted above, the literature review may well reveal research questions

# TEN TOP MISTAKES IN DISSERTATIONS

- Choosing a topic that is too broad.

- Not stating the research question(s)/hypothesis(es).

- Thinking that the Web is the only source of information and it can all be found using Google.

- Not considering research methods in enough detail.

- Thinking that you really only need to do secondary research (i.e. read what others have done). However, for some qualifications this may be acceptable.

- Not doing what the regulations require; your institution will provide precise regulations.

- Posing one research question and answering another.

- Not thinking clearly enough about how to present your results; what is the best way: pie charts, histograms, tables, graphs?

- Not leaving enough time if you are using a technique in which you require responses from people outside the institution.

- Not seeing your supervisor/tutor and/or ignoring his/her advice.

and even research methods that you had not previously considered.

## YOUR RESEARCH DESIGN AND THE METHODS USED

This is all about how you carried out the research (the methods and the sequence of events). I say 'carried out'; because this is how you write it up. Of course, these are the issues that you should consider when you are deciding which approach to use.

There are many different ways in which you can carry out research. These partly depend on the area in which you think your research falls; research projects that are covered by the term 'media' and even 'publishing' may be considered as social science, as economics, as business, even as behavioural science or, of course, as design. The difference between quantitative and qualitative research has been written about in many publications; two that you may like to read are: Burrell, B. and Morgan, G. (1979) *Sociological paradigms and organisational analysis*, published by Heinemann, and Hammersley, M. (1998); and 'The relationship between qualitative and quantitative research: paradigm loyalty versus methodological eclecticism' in Richardson, J.T.E., (Ed.). *Handbook of Qualitative Research Methods*

*for Psychological and the Social Sciences*, published by BPS Books. Alternatively, a quick summary can be found at *http://www.wilderdom.com/research/QualitativeVersusQuantitativeResearch.html*.

You need to explain why you used the approach(es) that you did, giving the advantages, disadvantages, implications and limitations of your approach(es) that you chose, as well ideally as the advantages, disadvantages, implications and limitations of other approaches that you could have used.

You also need to discuss the constraints on the research and any circumstances that affected the results.

This is an important area, often given too little attention and you can either do this here or it may be appropriate to include it as part of your conclusions.

## THE PRESENTATION AND ANALYSIS OF THE RESULTS AND THE DISCUSSION

This may be one section or two and is the heart of your research report. This is what you found out. Because you want this to be clear and readable, it may be better to include bulky results in appendices and present here the distilled essence of what you have found. Because research projects vary considerably, it is impossible to describe in any detail what this should look like. However, if you can present your findings using tables or as graphs or charts, then try to do so, particularly if the results are numeric in any way (and many results do have a numeric aspect, even if it is only the number of people who you spoke to or who completed questionnaires).

Of course, if your results are numeric, then there will be uncertainty (margin of error) associated with them. Statistical analysis is a good way to deal with this, but remember that, for statistical methods to apply, you must have a sufficient number of results. Many of the discussions of this are quite technical, but see *http://www.craighospital.org/SCI/METS/stats.asp* for a very readable discussion of statistics in a medical context, which it is easy to transfer to other contexts. However, if you are going to use statistics,

out and how it fits in with what was previously known. A bulleted list is quite a good way of doing this, but check with your supervisor that this is an acceptable approach.

You then need to make recommendations or predictions. Which these will be will depend on the topic and on your findings. It is also a good idea to include suggestions for future work if you can make any.

## BIBLIOGRAPHY/REFERENCES

A reference list is normally a listing of the references you have cited in the text, while a bibliography is list of related publications, not necessarily cited in the text. It is quite common to have a reference list at the end of each chapter or section, while a bibliography is given at the end of the dissertation. However, you can also give a single reference list

> # IF YOU CAN PRESENT YOUR FINDINGS USING TABLES OR AS GRAPHS OR CHARTS, THEN TRY TO DO SO, PARTICULARLY IF THE RESULTS ARE NUMERIC

you do need to understand what they are all about (and you may not have time to learn). *http://www.du.edu/psychology/methods/concepts/index.htm* has lots of links to websites about visualizing statistical concepts.

In the discussion section you discuss what you found out (of course). You compare the results with information that you presented earlier in the literature review and probably in the context review as well and explain why your results are in agreement with or differ from those previously published or possibly how they enhance them.

If you asked a question at the beginning, here you begin to give an answer. If you provided a hypothesis, here you indicate whether it has been shown to be true or false. It is essential that you present and discuss your results within the context that you set up earlier in the dissertation.

## CONCLUSIONS AND RECOMMENDATIONS

This section can be quite short. However, you should be able to summarize what you have found

covering all chapters. Check with your supervisor and the documentation issued by your institution to find out which approach is preferred. The other thing you need to check is the preferred reference style. There are two main approaches, one using the names of authors and the dates of the publications; this is called the Harvard style and the reference list is given in name and date order. The second approach is to number the citations (usually in the order in which they first appear in the text) and then the list is given in numerical order. This style is sometimes referred to as the Vancouver style. There are a number of variations on both styles, as well as variations in how the references themselves are punctuated and internally arranged. Your institution may or may not have rules as to how these things should be done and, if it does, you need to know what they are.

See also the comments above about programs for organizing your bibliographic references.

## APPENDICES

These include anything that is relevant, but does not form part of the flow of the main report.

## PRESENTATION

You need to think about the presentation of your report. There may be regulations about type size, layout and whether you print the dissertation single or double sided. If possible, relate the typographical design to the content, particularly since you are studying for a degree in media or publishing, in which the medium is at least part of the message!

Use a spellchecker, but use it intelligently. Remember that spellcheckers don't tell you if, for example, you have used 'their' when you should have used 'there' or 'effect' when you should have used 'affect'. The same applies to grammar checking and note that sometimes grammar checkers give incorrect or misleading advice.

It is a good idea to have someone else read your dissertation, however good a writer you are. Of checking that the dissertations you look at are the ones that received high marks!

The above is essentially concerned with dissertations that provide a written report of the research. It may, however, be the case that your research is practice based, so that an important part of it is an artefact of some kind. What this is will depend on the degree, but it may be photographs, graphic designs, a film or something else of this nature. Then, although you should still consider the issues discussed above, some aspects may be of less importance. Check the regulations and talk to your supervisor/tutor.

It is perhaps worth noting that many of the above considerations also apply to any research you carry out (for eventual publication or even for purely personal reasons), whether it is part of a formal course or not.

> ## USE A SPELLCHECKER, BUT USE IT INTELLIGENTLY. THE SAME APPLIES TO GRAMMAR CHECKING AND NOTE THAT SOME GRAMMAR CHECKERS GIVE INCORRECT OR MISLEADING ADVICE.

course, you may feel that you need someone to check your spelling, grammar and punctuation, but, even if you are confident about these aspects, there is a tendency to read what you expect to read when you read something you have written something yourself. A second pair of eyes can be very useful.

If English is not your first language, then the last paragraph is particularly important. You may want to use a professional editor, but remember that professional editors will want to charge professional fees. Also check with your supervisor or tutor about what is allowed in this respect. Some institutions have special departments that can help you with your language.

## BUT...

While your dissertation should almost certainly include all the elements discussed above, it does not necessarily have to be structured as described. There may be a more appropriate structure that fits your research. It may be worth looking at previous dissertations submitted for your degree to see what other students have done, although it's worth

## CONCLUSION

If you want a career in publishing or the media, you need to understand what the industries do and how they work in order that you can decide which area you wish to work in and, indeed, whether you want to work in the industry at all! There are places in the industry for people with many kinds of skills. Studying on a course not only helps you develop your skills, but it also provides you with information about the industry and, if you are lucky, leads to contacts with industry, work experience and even a job!

So check out what you can do with the qualifications and experience that you have. We wish you good luck with finding the niche and the career you want.

# EQUIPMENT
## THE WRITER'S TOOLBOX
And some simple tips that may save you time and money

Writers don't need many tools, usually. A pencil and a notebook can still be the key equipment, at least for ideas and outlines. Many writers would rather go out undressed than without their notebook and pencil; it's a good habit to have. Some very famous authors write their entire novels in pen in notebooks, feeling that the physical contact with the paper helps the creative process. So if they do it, why should you feel embarrassed to do the same? But, of course, no publisher these days is going to accept a handwritten manuscript; you'll need to get it word processed at some point.

### SOME SIMPLE IDEAS
Try having pencils or pens of different colours so you can annotate in different colours.

And you'll need a sharpener, and a proper, substantial pencil rubber. The one at the end of your pencil is hopeless.

A pad of 'stickies' can do many things: to do lists, chapter headings; and try using them as brainstorming tools – write your ideas/chapters/whatever on individual stickies and arrange them on a convenient surface. Very interactive!

### COMPUTERS
The industry standard machine in publishing is the 'Mac' (never called 'Apple Mac', by Pros by the way). Publishers use Macs for good reason: they were designed as publishing tools in the first place and they are easy to use.

The applications are pretty standard, regardless of whether it is a Mac or a Windows machine: Word dominates, of course. There are others: Apple's own Appleworks, is OK, for example. Very simple, basic text editors can be perfectly useable, with the wonderful advantage of no clutter or distractions of any sort.

The two industry tools for page layout and composition are QuarkXpress and Adobe's InDesign. Most writers and authors won't need either, and it is worth saying here that Publishers will usually not want their authors tiddling around with complex layouts and peculiar fonts – Keep it Simple, Stupid is a golden rule here as elsewhere. Any submission rigged out like the local scout group newsletter is destined for the darkest corner of the slush pile.

Laptops are brilliant, but two key tips: 1) they never last as long on the battery as you hope/think so always take the mains cable with you 2) don't leave your work on the laptop alone – back it up onto something else.

## BACK IT UP!

It happens to us all, and it will happen to you sooner or later. Either your machine will die or be stolen, or you'll accidentally delete a vital file, or some other disaster will befall.

These days, USB memory sticks and flash drives are cheap and can hold lots of data, so use one or more of those. Or have an external hard disk attached to your machine, and make sure you use it to back your work up on a regular basis (at least once a day).

If you do delete a vital file, stop working immediately. Do not do anything else. Computers don't wipe files just like that, they make the space the files takes up available to be overwritten. Anything you do after the mishap might overwrite your vital file. Then, either use one of the specialist recovery software programmes (look online), or get an expert to retrieve your data for you. Chances are you'll get it back. The downside is you'll probably get loads of rubbish back, too, and you will have to separate the wheat from the chaff, and that could take hours and hours.

# FINANCIAL TIPS
## KEEP ACCURATE ACCOUNTS

Some advice for writers from a publisher's perspective

If you do not have an employer, but you are working for yourself, and earning money (no matter how little) then you should register yourself as self employed. This means you are responsible for your own tax and other payments to government. You must also fill in your own tax return (or pay an accountant or financial advisor to do it for you). This is not so onerous these days as it once was.

But you must keep meticulous records. Mainly, this is for your own use, but it is just possible that the Inland Revenue will ask to see your records. Copies of every invoice that you submit, every payment you receive, should be filed. Use your computer to build a record of all such invoices and payments. Many writers use Excel to build themselves a document that they can use again and again. It need not be complex; it does need to be a complete record. It will help enormously with filling in your tax return. It can also help you to know who owes you money, when you invoiced, etc.

Keep these records separate from any other records. Do not muddle your payments up with any other financial matters you might have. Consider a separate bank account for your writing work.

### TAX KITTY

There will come a time when you have to pay tax against any earnings; be sure to have a strategy that arms you for that eventuality. Keep some money in the bank from each job, or put aside every fourth fee for tax, for example. (Sue Gordon's article on freelancing on page 66 has many valuable tips in this area.) This depends, of course, on how much you are earning. Many self-employed writers and publishing freelancers make sure their earnings are kept below tax thresholds.

If you are genuinely hopeless at this kind of thing then you need an accountant if your earnings are taxable.

A good accountant will also explain to you what you can reasonably (and legally) claim as expenses. Expenses are not (or should not be) a 'fiddle'. If you are working from home, using electricity to keep you warm and power your machine, for example, then some of that can be set against tax. The same applies to stationery, computer expenditure, necessary travel, etc. Sometimes, publishers will allow you to add 'reasonable expenses' to your invoice. This might be for postage, say, or for travel to a meeting. It is always worth asking. Keep any receipts in case proof is needed. Keeping receipts is good practise anyway.

## PUBLIC LENDING RIGHT

PLR is the system whereby authors and contributors are paid for their books being taken out of public libraries by readers.

If your name is on the title page of the book or if you are entitled to a royalty from the publisher, then you can qualify for PLR. You do not have to be the copyright holder in order to qualify.

It is not only sole authors who can qualify: writers who have contributed in part, illustrators and photographers, translators, adaptors, ghost writers and editors and compilers might also be eligible, possibly to a percentage share of the total monies available.

You have to apply for PLR. For more information and application forms, go to the PLR website: *www.plr.uk.com*.

## GETTING PAID

When you get work from a publisher, or magazine, or whatever, ask whether you will get a written agreement from them, or whether they will send you a Purchase Order, or if they expect you to invoice them. Those commissioning work from you should have such things near the top of their minds, but the reality is that often such things are forgotten, or put way down the priority order. Accounts departments also forget things or miss things, so if your payment is overdue, ask the person who commissioned the work from you.

Issues). This way they get to buy your words by the thousand, or even by the book full. Many old hands in the writing world will be more than happy with this arrangement. They get a guaranteed, agreed, fee. It's clean and clear to all. It's business.

Some types of publishing are pretty much built around the idea of flat fees. An example is travel publishing, where the publisher wants to have the maximum freedom to use and re-use the information you have gathered. Successful travel writers will accept such flat fees and the surrender of their rights, but they will expect a generous payment.

**FINANCIAL TIPS    FEATURE**

> ## IF YOU ARE AT THE BOTTOM OF THE WRITING LADDER YOU MIGHT BE WELL ADVISED TO DO YOUR FIRST JOBS FOR NOTHING, JUST TO GET SOMETHING ON YOUR CV

Reputable publishers don't cheat, and they don't hold payments back deliberately; the cock-up rather than conspiracy theory is nearly always the right one here.

But an insider tip from publishers to writers: getting stroppy or 'clever' with accounts departments within days of your payment being late is counter-productive. A vitriolic phone call will not usually help your cause. The best route is to ask the person who commissioned you to check on your behalf; only if they fail should you approach the accounts department yourself. Most publishers pay on regular cycles, and you will hear them talking about 'cheque runs'. But they can always issue cheques manually, so if your payment is overdue you should not have to wait until the next 'run'.

### HOW MUCH WILL WE PAY YOU?

Newspapers and some magazines may well pay you the going NUJ rates. Smaller magazines will pay what they can. Some will pay you nothing. As many of the articles in *Writer's Market* make clear, if you are the bottom of the writing ladder you might be well advised to do your first jobs for nothing just to get something on your CV.

Book publishers' rates vary a lot. More and more non-fiction publishers will offer you a flat, one-off, fee, wanting 'All Rights' (see Contracts and Legal

Fiction is pretty much built around the idea of royalties, and advances against royalties, of course. You or your agent will negotiate this with the publisher. First-time authors will naturally expect a modest advance. *The Bookseller* sometimes has stories of authors of first-time novels receiving enormous advances, but it's newsworthy simply because it's unusual. Some fiction houses are experimenting with the idea of royalty but no advance. This reduces the risk to the publisher and means that your book is more likely to be published by them. If it's a success then the royalties may start to come in, and you are much more likely to get a second book deal.

### A NOTE ON ROYALTIES

Do royalties happen? Established authors earn royalties. Bestselling authors earn a lot of royalties. Many authors whose books have sold in modest numbers never 'earn out' their advance: the royalty statement (usually sent twice a year – check your contract) will always be in the negative. Sometimes royalties are surprisingly/unexpectedly good. Many authors have stories of a book that they wrote years and years ago still selling in appreciable numbers and providing a comforting cheque on a regular basis. It does happen, but planning your pension round such an idea is risky.

# CONTRACTS AND LEGAL ISSUES
## A BRIEF OVERVIEW

What kinds of thing can the author expect; what should she look out for?

> Usually, the fee or contractual terms are not among the first things Commissioning Editors want to discuss.

It may be the case that during the early conversations about the book, the editor may not know how much they are in a position to offer. Nearly all publishers have a rough scale of advances and royalties that they offer, depending on the kind of book. They'll first apply that to see if it will work; if it doesn't they try to reduce other parts of the specification. If all else fails they'll offer the author a deal that the book can afford. Then it's often a case of polite haggling. Established authors are obviously in a much stronger position. Bestsellers can probably ask what they want.

Then there is the question of what kind of agreement you will have with your publisher. Will it be royalty based, or a flat fee? If it is a flat fee you may get a very simple written agreement; indeed if it is a very small, one-off job, such as an article, it may be a hand-written Purchase Order (PO). No matter how small the job, you should have extracted from your Editor a brief - how many words about what in what order and what tone, for example, might be the most simple of briefs.

More complex work will require a fuller, properly written-up brief from the Editor. Such a brief and its accompanying PO should tell you when you can invoice. Payment will usually be in three or four parts. Typically, this will be on signature, on delivery of any advance material, on delivery of the bulk of the work, and on publication.

## INVOICING

Your invoice can be a simple sheet of paper with your name and address, the name of the job, the sum being invoiced for, who you did the work for, and that all-important PO Order Number.

Increasingly, invoices are submitted by email. So long as the editor authorises it and it signs that will be fine for the accounts dept. If it's a one-off for a small fee, you will usually be paid by cheque.

## 'ALL RIGHTS'

If the agreement talks about 'All Rights resting with the Publisher' check what the publisher means by that. It probably means they want you to give them permission to use your words wherever, whenever and however they want, but check they don't mean your copyright is to be assigned to them. If you don't like what's proposed you must say immediately. Whether the editor continues with you or not will then largely depend on how much he wants you. If he can get someone else to agree to his terms he'll go elsewhere; it's a risk you'll take.

## ROYALTY CONTRACTS

If yours is a traditional advance against royalty deal, then the chances are you'll receive a standard publisher's contract. These days they are pretty much the same regardless of publisher. The royalty will probably be 10%. That will very possibly be against the net price of the book, not its cover price. In other words, the royalty is paid against what the publisher actually gets for the book. This can make a BIG difference if your book is sold to book clubs, for example. Their discounts are huge, so thinking 'wow, they've sold 10,000 copies of my book to the book club' might look more stark if the book club has taken it for a pittance, which is likely.

As you make your way through the contract, you'll find, probably, that you get less royalties for such things as co-publishing deals, paperbacking, serialisation or broadcasting, and a whole bunch of other types of related publication. The publisher makes less money on these deals, usually, so that is what is being reflected. It's all pretty standard stuff. But read it carefully before acceptance.

It is these kinds of percentages that wily agents will try to negotiate upwards on your behalf. That's if you have an agent. It can look impressive if the agent succeeds, but a cynical publisher might just be thinking that the chances of that particular book being snapped up by, let's say TV or for electronic use, are tiny at best. Still, good luck to the agent for being on the ball.

If you do have an agent you should expect her to go through the contract in minute deal for, and possibly with, you before the deal is struck.

The advance will vary, usually according to your value to the publisher, the kind of book it is, its potential market, and other key factors. Publishers do have rough rules of thumb about advances (as discussed above) and how much a 'typical' one for that area might be. But it does differ. What one author gets might not be the same as the publisher offers to another, and it might not be for straightforward reasons. Should you try to negotiate? With a reputable, mainstream publisher over a first book deal, probably not. They will have considered the offer with care. Many commissioning editors are quite prepared to discuss such things in an open way, but, of course, they will not tell you what they are paying their other authors. By the way, bigger publisher does not necessarily equal bigger advance; there are big names who pay very 'competitive' fees.

## YOUR COPYRIGHT

In a standard contract, the copyright in the work will typically remain yours. In other words, when the book is published the little 'c' symbol will be against your name. The default standard contract may say that you are responsible for the entire content of the book, including any pictures, illustrations, or maps, for example. In fact, the publisher may not escape liability as easily as this, but you obviously need to be aware of your own liability. In law, copyright may be infringed both by a publisher who publishes material without the permission of the copyright owner and also by any person, such as a writer, who authorises the publisher to do so. But what if you are not providing that sort of additional content? Some authors take a relaxed view of such things; they know the publisher is doing the design and providing all the visual materials and they trust that any clauses about content other than words will not be relied on by the publisher. Other authors will want any such clauses removed or amended.

You can hand amend a contract if the changes are small. Make the changes and initial them; ensure the editor or publisher counter-initial them to show their agreement. It's as simple as that, but it's important both sides are clear what they are agreeing to when the contract is formed.

Copyright carries responsibilities. Have you stolen someone else's words (plagiarised them)? Used any other content without permission – say a photograph? Broken the law in some way? If so you could be in serious trouble.

Plagiarism happens. Sometimes authors genuinely don't realise that what they have done constitutes breaching someone's copyright. For example, you cannot compile lots of other people's work into your own book without obtaining permission unless it constitutes 'fair dealing' for the purpose of criticism, review or news reporting. However, photographs cannot be subject to this 'fair dealing' exception, which is available under the Copyright, Designs and Patents Act 1988. This is a complex area, so take care. Ignorance is not acceptable. At the least, you might be subjected to the humiliation of the publisher discovering your wrongdoing and cancelling your contract, and demanding its money back. At the worst you could end up in court. In all the above instances, the publisher will be on the look out for wrongdoing. It is not in their interest to publish a book that may have to be withdrawn, or one that becomes the subject of a lawsuit. But the publisher can only do so much. So the 'rule' is that you must be honest and do everything in your power not to cheat or steal. Obvious, really.

The starting point is that the first owner of copyright is the author (or authors). So, independent writers will obviously be the initial owners of copyright in words they have written. But what about illustrations and the book's design? These may have been created by employees of the publisher (in which case the publisher will own copyright in them as employer) or by independent persons. If the publisher wants to spell out exactly who owns the copyright in what, then it may add another line or two in the agreement.

## LIBEL

Have you defamed a living person who is identifiable from the words or content you have submitted? If so, on publication both you and the publisher could be sued for damages for libel and could face an injunction. Usually the publisher will have any contentious passages 'legalled' to avoid the expense of having to pulp books following a claim, which often gives writers some reassurance, but you need to be aware of the risks yourself.

## DISCLAIMERS

If the book contain recipes or instructions, publishers will nearly always include a disclaimer along the lines of 'The Publisher can accept no responsibility for any accident or injury as a result of anyone using this book.' Would it stand up in court? It might. If the publisher is nervous that images may not have been traced back to their rightful owners, it may include some such caveat as 'The Publisher has made every reasonable effort to contact Rights owners, but…..' This may be an acceptable and reasonable thing to do. However, the bottom line is that both publisher and author could potentially be sued for breach of copyright.

## PROTECTING YOUR IDEAS

There is no copyright in ideas.
 Authors sometimes say that they have a great idea but they are not going to say what it is because the publisher might steal it. This is a dead-end argument. If you as the author are not going to share your idea, how can the publisher possibly know whether it is good, bad or indifferent?

Do publishers steal ideas? It has probably happened. But most reputable publishers would never consider doing such a thing. Very often, editors and publishers help authors to work up their ideas so that they become properly commercially viable. That is the ideal relationship between them, and that is what most publishers would seek to do.

In publishing, the view that there is no such thing as a new idea is widely held. It can be a sensible, practical view to have. An idea (or 'concept' as a worked-up publishing idea is often called) that has worked in the past may well work again – suitably updated and re-wrapped of course. And it can be more than that. In travel publishing, there are umpteen titles about – say – Paris. But each one is slightly different in approach, tone, design, etc. Sufficiently different for each to work on its own terms and to provide the choices the reader wants. Everyone is happy.

If you want to discuss a project that you want kept secret for a while, you could consider asking your confidant to sign a confidentiality agreement, but that might put them off – and is rare in publishing.

## STAYING IN PRINT, GOING OUT OF PRINT AND REVERTING

Your book may be a runaway success, or maybe even just a steady seller that sits on the 'back list' for years. Books like that are what both publisher and author want. If it's a novel it obviously does not need updating, if it's non-fiction it may need updating occasionally (or even often) but if it sells then the publisher will invest in the cost of the revision.

Some books that one would have thought need updating roll on for years for mysterious, unfathomable reasons. All part of the magic of publishing.

But, your book may not be doing quite well enough, or, possibly the publisher loses interest in it. In that case, the book will eventually go out of print, and in the fullness of time, depending on the agreement, the rights may revert to the author. This means the author can then take the book to another publisher. This happens quite often, and can be a success for both book and author.

All of these aspects of a book's life should be covered somewhere, somehow, in the contract for the book. The clauses may be couched in terms that are not easy to understand at first read, but the vast majority of the clauses in the contract will be rooted in common sense and pragmatism, underpinned with legal necessities. So read it with care, then read it again before deciding whether to accept the deal on those terms.

# GOOD AND BAD LETTERS
## YOUR LETTERS REVEAL A LOT ABOUT YOU

A good letter can bring success; a bad one will bring failure

Query and proposal letters are a key part of your communications with the publisher you want to work with. Whether you are writing to a tiny magazine or a leading book publisher, you want your letter to be taken seriously and to elicit a fast, positive response. A poorly written, clumsy letter will inevitably result in rejection, no matter how good or original your actual proposal. Even if your sample work is brilliant, the chances are it will not be read or appreciated if the covering letter is weak. The most important tip is to take the letter as seriously as the work itself.

Whenever possible, and no matter how experienced you are, always get someone else to read your letter objectively. Ask them to look for ambiguities, clumsiness, ramblings and anything that they think might need clarification or simplifying.

## STEPS ALONG THE WAY TO A GOOD (OR BAD) LETTER

Go to the website of the publisher you want to approach and find out what they do. There is no point sending an idea or query to a science fiction magazine if your idea is for an article on cookery.

Find out what format, or by which means, they wish writers to contact them. If they say by email only, don't write a letter; if they say by letter only, then only send a letter.

Try to find a contact name, and use it in your letter.

If you can't find the above from the publisher's website (and it has to be said that the websites of some companies are hopeless) then ring up and make your initial enquiry that way. Keep any phone conversation short, businesslike and to the point.

What follows is a broad indication of what you should say (and not say), and with suggestions about the order. It is not intended to be prescriptive.

You need to explain your idea in very clear terms right at the beginning so the reader wants to find out more. The last thing you want is for your opening to turn the reader off. This will happen if you are boastful, unrealistic, vague and/or mad.

## THE FIRST PARAGRAPH

Grab the attention of the reader; not by talking about yourself, but by putting across what is special about your idea. If appropriate, say how many words the article/book comes to. Tell the reader the title: a great, snappy title gets your idea noticed immediately.

Do not boast about yourself or the idea; do not mention money; do not say you've copyrighted the idea – all of these say 'amateur' very loudly.

## PARAGRAPH TWO

Go into more detail about the idea. Do it in a calm and structured way. Put across what the idea will achieve; précis the story. Explain any particularly noteworthy or unusual aspects of your idea in more detail than in paragraph one.

Do not say that this is going to be the greatest blockbuster in history; will become a box office sensation when it becomes a film, etc. Anything like that is off-putting for the publisher as they know it's flim-flam.

**103**

### PARAGRAPH THREE

Discuss any special marketing ideas or opportunities that you might have; but be realistic.

If you could sell or promote the story/book yourself via your website, for example, then say so. If the idea is particularly attractive to a specific audience that you know you could reach, say so.

The key thing here is to spend time thinking about how the idea could actually, realistically be marketed.

### PARAGRAPH FOUR

Make it clear that you know the work of the publisher you are approaching, you have studied what they publish and have read at least some of it.

Present your credentials: if you've been published elsewhere say what and by whom. Be specific.

### PARAGRAPH FIVE

Sign off, by saying thank you for considering the approach/proposal, and if appropriate, suggest that they contact you for more information, etc.

## BASIC RULES FOR LETTERS

- Include your name, address, phone number, email address and website, if you have one.
- Address a specific person if possible (check contact names online or by calling first).
- Limit your letter to one single-spaced page.
- Include self-addressed, stamped envelope for response with post submissions.
- Use a standard font and typeface, such as Times New Roman and 10- or 12-point type; don't use fancy fonts or 'clever' formatting.
- Use block paragraph format (no indentations).
- Thank the recipient for considering your query.

## EMAIL CONSIDERATIONS

- An email is not the same as a letter. This may sound obvious, but when you are writing to a potential publisher for the first time by email you should think about the information you need to provide, simply because we all tend to treat email as a more informal means of communication.
- So, in your first email you should include your full name, just as if it were a letter. In other words, don't sign off simply with your given name, leaving the publisher no idea what your family name is.
- Think about how you are going to address the recipient; you might get away with just the given name first time out, but caution might suggest you use both given and family name.
- In your first email, write as formally and thoughtfully as you would if it were a letter.
- One of the foibles of email writing is that many of us use many more exclamation marks and so forth than we would in a 'normal' letter. Don't do this in your first email approach – it won't be read as amusing or funny!

*There are more things that you should think through in your email:*

- Subject line: first, make sure there is one! Second: make it meaningful; no 'Hi Mic' or 'Here's a Great Idea'. If nothing else, the recipient is likely to think it might be spam and delete it. If it's a book proposal, why not say exactly that: 'Book Proposal for your consideration'.
- Your email name: 'funny' or 'amusing' email names are going to lead to failure, because you will not be taken seriously. Cryptic email names are similarly off-putting. Always go for the most straightforward.
- Finally, you might consider saying in your first email: 'Pardon me for adding to your inbox' or something like that.

# GLOSSARY

## Book Trade Terminology

**acquiring/acquisitions editor:** a person within a publishing house whose primary function is to identify and negotiate to acquire new titles for publication. Also known as a commissioning editor, or acquisitions editor.

**advance:** the non-returnable payment to authors by publishers against which the royalty earnings are offset.

**A format:** format of mass market paperbacks, most commonly with a trimmed page size of 178 x 111 mm (unsewn).

**agent:** see literary agent.

**AI:** (sometimes AIS) abbreviation for Advance Information (Sheet), a document produced by publishers for new titles to provide information for the purpose of subscription to book buyers and initiating promotional opportunities. Typical contents would include a blurb, author biography, review of the author's previous works, provisional specification, working cover, publication date and price.

**Amazon:** e-commerce company that was one of the first major companies to sell goods over the internet. Amazon.com began as an online bookstore, though it soon diversified its product lines, adding DVDs, CDs, computer software, video games, electronics, homewares, toys and more. Amazon has established separate websites in Canada, the United Kingdom, Germany, Austria, France, China and Japan. Its hourly-updated list of the top 100 book bestsellers is a well-used resource within the publishing industry, and is a good reflection of current market trends.

**appendix:** material which is not part of the main text appearing at the end of a book.

**archival:** papers specifically made for an extended lifespan which do not discolour or otherwise deteriorate; used in academic texts and other works of permanent value, and particularly favoured by library conservationists and US libraries, which often require their use.

**auction:** a process whereby a title is submitted, particularly by a literary agent, to a number of selected publishers in order to secure the best offer or highest price. Auctions sometimes run to several 'rounds' and may end with the exercise of topping rights.

**BA:** abbreviation for The Booksellers Association of Great Britain and Ireland, the trade association for booksellers.

**barcodes:** the machine readable image of lines of varying thickness which encodes a book's ISBN and which is printed on the back cover. When 'read' by electronic till equipment it plays a vital part in booksellers' EPOS systems for sales monitoring and stock control. Also used in distribution centres for various functions such as processing returns

**Berne Convention:** an international agreement made in 1886 for the respect of copyright between participating nations.

**B format:** a format for paperbacks particularly favoured for non-fiction and literary fiction, normally of a trimmed size 198 x 126 mm (unsewn).

**BIC:** see Book Industry Communication.

**binders pack:** the packing unit, either of kraft paper or increasingly shrink-wrap, used by binders when delivering books. Contains a variable number of copies depending on their size.

**BL:** see British Library.

**blad:** Basic Layout And Design – a term used to describe advance sales material, most commonly consisting of a jacket, sales blurb and a selection of pages of text and illustration, printed professionally.

**bleed:** term used for an illustration or image which extends beyond the trimmed page.

**blocking:** the use of metallic foils, much used on covers and jackets for visual impact or as a routine operation on the spine of a hardback book.

**blurb:** the brief description of a book which appears on the back of a paperback or on the inside front flap of a book jacket.

**Bologna Book Fair:** the pre-eminent book fair for children's publishers, particularly those buying and selling rights, held in Bologna in Italy each spring.

**Bookbank:** a bibliographic product on CD-ROM from Whitaker listing titles currently in print in the UK.

**book block:** the sewn or perfect bound pages of a hardback book before they are cased in.

**book club:** a mail order operation through which selected books are sold direct to the public at a price significantly below the RRP in return for a commitment to buy a particular number of books over a period.

**BookData:** company established in the UK to market bibliographical information supplied by participating publishers

**Book fairs:** exhibitions and conventions used by publishers as locations for meetings and business dealings. Many such fairs take place internationally, of widely differing purpose and focus, of which much the most important is Frankfurt.

**Book House Training Centre:** the book trade's training organisation, based in south London.

**Book Industry Communication:** a company set up by the Booksellers Association, the British Library, the Library Association and the Publishers Association to encourage the establishment of standards in the book trade. Among other activities, BIC has responsibility for bar codes and EDI standards.

**Book jacket:** the paper cover wrapped round a hardback book, and normally the publisher's main marketing tool.

**Book Marketing Ltd:** formed from the Book Marketing Council of the Publishers Association, this company provides statistical and market research information to the industry, notably in the form of the annual publication Books and the Consumer.

**Book proof:** a specially produced advance copy of the uncorrected text of a title, used by publishers' sales teams and as early review copies.

**Bookseller (The):** a weekly journal of the UK book trade, with up-to-date bestseller lists.

**BookTrack:** an operation set up by Whitaker to monitor sales out of bookshops and produce accurate bestseller lists.

**British Library:** the national book collection based in London and now being relocated from the British Museum building to its new site at St Pancras.

**bulk:** the thickness of a book.

**bulky news:** improved quality newsprint used for mass market paperbacks.

**byline:** the name of the author of a given piece, indicating credit for having written a book or article (most commonlyused in magazine publishing)

**cased:** hardback; derived from the case into which the book block is inserted (cased in) at the conclusion of hardback binding.

**CD-ROM:** compact disc with read-only memory; a non-interactive CD which is the platform for almost all offline electronic publishing.

**C format:** an imprecise term for any paperback format other than A and B, most often used to describe a paperback edition published simultaneously with, and in the same format as, the hardback original.

**CMYK:** Cyan, Magenta, Yellow and black – the four colours of ink used in four-colour printing.

**colophon:** originally the bibliographic information printed at the end of a book, the term is now used almost exclusively for the device or logo of the publisher commonly printed on the title-page and the spine of the cover or jacket.

**commissioning editor:** a person employed in a publishing house to seek out authors to write particular books for publication.

**contract:** the agreement drawn up between the publisher and the author to confirm payment terms, royalty, respective responsibilities etc. at the point of acquisition.

**copy editor:** the person employed in a publishing house who works on the detail of a book, ensuring accuracy and completeness and preparing it for typesetting.

**copyright:** the right of an author, artist, publisher etc. to retain ownership of works and to produce or contract others to produce copies. In 1996, the full term of copyright was extended throughout the European Union to 70 years (previously 50 years in the UK) from the end of the year in which the author died.

**consignment:** books sold on consignment are not invoiced to the customer but paid for as they are resold. Books consigned in this way are sometimes described as supplied 'see-safe'.

**counterpack:** presentation pack, comprising a small number of copies of a book, used for point of sale merchandising and intended to stand beside the bookshop till to encourage impulse purchase.

**Cover copy:** blurb that is written by the publishing house, generally on the back of paperbacks, or in the front flap of hard backs, to give the reader information on the book's content.

**Cromalin:** brand name of a form of dry colour proofing.

**Crown octavo:** book format, trimmed page size 189 x 123 mm sewn (120 mm unsewn), comparatively little used nowadays.

**Crown quarto:** book format, trimmed page size 246 x 189 mm, frequently an economical choice for illustrated books.

**Demy octavo:** very popular book format, trimmed page size 216 x 138 mm sewn (135 mm unsewn).

**discount:** the percentage reduction from the publisher's recommended retail price at which a book is sold to a bookseller.

**distribution centre:** location where orders from booksellers are received and processed and where books are stored and dispatched. Since the days when every publisher had its own warehouse and trade counter (from which local orders were supplied on demand), the trend has been towards large out of town distribution centres servicing the requirements of many publishers and imprints.

**DPI:** Dots Per Inch – a measure of printing resolution, in particular the number of individual dots of ink a printer or toner can produce within a linear one-inch (2.54 cm) space.

**DPS:** Double Page Spread.

**dues:** orders taken before a title is published or while it is for any reason unavailable which are fulfilled when stock is again available. Called in the US 'back orders'.

**dumpbin:** presentation stand, usually containing some 20-40 copies of a book, used for point of sale merchandising in bookshops.

**Dust jacket:** See Book jacket

**EAN:** European Article Numbering – the international convention of product numbering used throughout the world.

**edition:** the whole (usually first) printing of a title. See new edition, first edition.

**editorial:** the department within a publishing house responsible for the content of its titles, both by commissioning and acquiring but also subsequently ensuring accuracy and completeness of the finished publication.

**em:** a typographical measurement, so called because it represents the width of the widest character in the alphabet. In general use it is a synonym for pica em.

**en:** half an em; used as a measurement of the number of characters (text and spaces) in a given text.

**Endmatter:** the last pages at the end of the book, usually containing glossary, index, picture credits etc.

**endpaper:** the pages of heavy cartridge paper at the front and back of a hardback book which join the book block to the hardback binding; sometimes used for maps or carrying a decorative colour or design.

**EPOS:** Electronic Point of Sale

**erratum:** the correction of errors in a book, normally inserted as a slip of paper (an erratum slip) into the finished book.

**extent:** the number of pages in a book.

**Finish:** Special treatment which is usually applied to a book's cover. Can include gloss, matt etc. See lamination.

**firm sale:** books supplied on this basis may not be returned unsold by the bookseller.

**first edition:** first printing of a book; occasionally gains substantial secondhand value if the book or its author become especially collectable.

**floor:** an offer made for a book by a publishing company on the basis that after an auction of the rights in which it does not participate it may exercise topping rights to secure the acquisition.

**folio:** the page number which is printed at the top or bottom of each printed page.

**fore-edge:** the right-hand edge of a book when opened, opposite the spine.

**footnote:** explanatory note inserted at the foot of the page referring to a point within the text, usually indicated by symbols such as asterisks and daggers or by superior numerals.

**format:** the shape of a book defined by its height and depth.

**Frankfurt Book Fair:** the most important international book fair of the year, especially for the buying and selling of rights, held in Frankfurt at the beginning of October.

**frontispiece:** an illustration inserted to face the title-page.

**FTP:** File Transfer Protocol is used to connect two computers or a server and a client (computer) over the internet so that large files can be transferred. The client connects to the server by running FTP client software (such as Fetch or Cyberduck), and can then transfer the file to their computer. It is a common way for publishers to send large files to printers or repro houses, and sometimes for large files to be passed quickly between author and publisher.

**furnish:** the pulp and chemical components of a quality or grade of paper.

**half-title:** the first page of a book, on which the title is displayed, sometimes with a blurb or quotations from reviews.

**half-tone:** result of the process whereby continuous tone illustrations are broken down into dots for printing.

**headband:** a decorative strip of coloured material glued to the top of the spine of the book block of a hardback. Usually used in conjunction with a tailband.

**headline:** the line which commonly appears at the top of each printed page, typically showing the book title on the left-hand side and chapter title on the right; sometimes also incorporates the folio. Sometimes also known as a running head.

**High-res:** Picture resolution over 300dpi. Publishers will always want high-res images for printing as they have the best quality reproduction. The images can either be supplied to the publisher as digital files, or as transparencies for them to scan at an appropriate size.

**imposition:** the positioning of pages on a sheet or reel of paper when printed which produces the correct sequence of pages when folded.

**imprint:**
- the name of the publisher under which a title is issued. Increasingly in conglomerate publishing the term represents a publishing brand rather than a publishing company in its own right.
- also used to refer to the printer's name and address which by law must appear in all printed books.

**Independent Publishers Guild:** organisation which represents the interests of publishers in the UK which are independent of any owning group or consortium.

**InDesign:** A graphic design product similar to Quark Xpress, made by Adobe. It is now widely used in the book, magazine and newspaper industries for page design and layout.

**International Publishers Association:** an organisation representing the publishing industry worldwide.

**IPG:** see Independent Publishers Guild.

**ISBN:** universal abbreviation for International Standard Book Number, a ten digit unique identifier for each title published, which is used in a wide range of applications in all stages of the supply chain throughout the world. The number - made up of a language prefix (0 or 1 for the English language), followed by a publisher prefix, then a number relating to the individual title, and finally a check digit (used to validate the remainder of the code) - is customarily encoded in a bar code printed on the back of the book and normally appears also in the bibliographical details on the reverse of the title-page. The issuing agency for ISBNs in the United Kingdom is managed by Whitaker. In January 2007 ISBN-13 was introduced on all titles in the supply chain. Made up of 13 digits, rather than the traditional 10, this unique identifying number was introduced to expand the numbering capacity of the ISBN system, and to fully align the numbering system for books with the global standard system of identification, which is used to identify most other consumer goods worldwide. Most books carry the ISBN-10 and ISBN-13, although the ISBN-10 will be gradually phased out.

**ISSN:** abbreviation for International Standard Serials Number, the equivalent of the ISBN in the journal and magazine publishing business.

**jacket:** see bookjacket.

**JPEG/JPG:** A colour image compression format which allows the storage of high-quality images in relatively small files by balancing compression against loss of detail.

**Kill fee:** A fee paid by a magazine when it cancels a commissioned article. The fee is only a certain percentage of the agreed-on payment for the whole assignment (rarely more than 50 per cent). Not all publihsers pay kill fees, so any arrangements should be formally agreed in advance.

**LA:** abbreviation for The Library Association, the UK trade association for librarians.

**lamination:** the coating of film applied to bookjackets to give high gloss as well as added durability. A matt version is also available and is fashionable from time to time.

**landscape:** description of a format which is wider than it is deep.

**Large Crown octavo:** a hardback format with identical measurements to those of B format paperbacks, 198 x 129 mm sewn (126 mm unsewn).

**large print:** editions of existing titles redesigned for reading by those with impaired vision, produced specifically for the library market.

**lead time:** the time it takes from a publishing house accepting your work to its actual publication.

**leaf:** a page of the book comprising both recto and verso.

**legal deposit:** the legal requirement for publishers to deposit with the British Library and five regional libraries (University Library in Cambridge, the Bodleian Library in Oxford and the national libraries of Scotland, Wales and Ireland) a single copy of each publication.

**Library of Congress:** the USA's national book collection, based in Washington, DC.

**licence:** a subsidiary right usually granted for a fixed term or for a particular usage by the holder of the head contract in a work.

**limited edition:** a book published on the basis that a stated number of copies will be printed regardless of demand. Such titles are often individually numbered by hand and may achieve rarity value for collectors.

**literary agent:** a person or company looking after the interests of author clients and managing the exploitation of rights in an author's work. This includes submission of a book to publishers, perhaps in the form of an auction, negotiating a contract, collecting money due, and dealing with other rights not held by the publisher, such as (in many cases) broadcasting and film rights.

**London International Book Fair:** held annually in the Spring, this fair has grown rapidly as a meeting place for all those involved in the book trade in the UK and Europe.

**Low-res:** image file that is less than 300dpi in resolution size. Often used at this smaller size by designers for layout purposes, because they are smaller file sizes and use up less of the computer's memory than high-res images.

**Mac:** the common name for the Apple Mackintosh personal computer, much favoured by publishers' art and design departments for its flexibility and suitability for graphics programs.

**margin:** the white space surrounding a page of type.

**market:**
- the potential readership for a title.
- the territories of the world in which a title may be contractually sold.

**marketing:** the department in a publishing house with responsibility for promoting titles published; this may include the creation of point of sale display material, press and other advertising, and securing free coverage through PR and publicity.

**Matchprint:** brand name for a common form of digital colour proof.

**mechanical:** a paper made from mechanically treated woodpulp which has a limited life and tends to discolour with time; originally used only for paperbacks and other titles of ephemeral value but nowadays mechanical pulp is used in variable proportions in the furnish of many book papers. More explicitly called 'groundwood' in the US.

**merchandising:** the management of stock in supermarkets and other non-specialist sales outlets in order to ensure the display of the fastest selling titles.

**microfiche:** a sheet of microfilm pages to facilitate storage by libraries etc. now largely made redundant by computer technology.

**Minimum Terms Agreement:** a contractual agreement negotiated between the Society of Authors and a number of publishers laying down the minimum acceptable terms for individual book contracts. The most contentious ingredient is the requirement that the work should be contracted on a limited licence rather than for the full term of copyright.

**monochrome:** printing in one colour, usually black.

**MTA:** see Minimum Terms Agreement.

**NBA:** see Net Book Agreement.

**net, nett:** system of pricing whereby no retail price is recommended by the publisher; not subject to further discount.

**Net Book Agreement:** the agreement formerly administered by The Publishers Association whereby publishers in the UK were able to dictate the minimum price at which their titles were sold by bookshops; abandoned by publishers in 1995 and finally made illegal by the Restrictive Practices Court in 1997.

**new edition:** a reprint of an existing title incorporating substantial textual alterations, or republication of a title which has been out of print.

**Nielsen BookScan:** the industry-standard database providing weekly point-of-sale data with the highest possible degree of accuracy. The sales figures come from all the major booksellers. Nielsen BookScan functions as a central clearinghouse for book industry data, and enables its subscribers to access comprehensive and up-to-the-minute reports on a wide variety of perspectives within the industry. It is widely used by publishers as a central resource to track sales figures for similar titles when at the acquisitions process, and also to monitor sales of specific titles.

**NIP:** New In Paperback.

**non-net:** during the existence of the Net Book Agreement, not subject to a price established by the publisher, particularly used for educational textbooks.

**novelty:** a book or book-related toy either involving the use of paper engineering or diecut to an unusual shape; almost always aimed at the children's market.

**NYP:** common abbreviation for Not Yet Published; see answer codes.

**offprint:** a printed copy of an individual article in a learned journal, generally offered by publishers to authors.

**offset, offset fee:** so named after the process of offset lithography, which in the days when letterpress was still the predominant printing method was used for the reprinting of books when the metal type was no longer available. The term describes the practice of photographically reproducing the text of one edition of a book in order to create another (for instance, from the US edition to the UK edition, or from an original hardback to a reduced size paperback). Hence, offset fee, the charge made for the right to reproduce an existing text.

**OP:** universal abbreviation for Out Of Print; see answer codes.

**order processing:** the handling of customer orders within the distribution centre; involving the keying of customer and order details into the computer system in order to produce invoices for picking.

**ozalid:** a form of proof made from a film assembly used to check the position of text and illustrations as a final stage of approval before printing. Called in the US 'blues' after the colour of the image on the proof. Rarely used now thanks to digital printing.

**PA:** see Publishers Association.

**packager:** company which creates and originates, sometimes manufactures, books for publishers.

**page proof:** proof of the made-up pages in a book, often used not only to check accuracy of typesetting but also as an advance promotional tool.

**pallet:** the raised wooden platform on which books are delivered by binders and stored in distribution centres; handling requires the use of forklift trucks.

**paper engineering:** the devising of the mechanics of novelty books and pop-ups.

**part-title:** a page in a book which divides it into separate parts, usually printed with the name of the forthcoming section on the recto page but having a blank verso.

**partwork:** a publication which appears in weekly or fortnightly installments and which may be bound together to make a complete book.

**PDF:** Portable Document Format – a file format that maintains the original look of the document, regardless of the software it was created in, and allows it to be read on any machine that has Adobe Acrobat installed. Acrobat is available as a free download.

**perfect binding:** adhesive binding in which the individual pages of a book are glued together as opposed to section sewn; commonly called unsewn binding.

**perfector:** a sheet-fed printing machine which prints both sides of the paper in a single pass.

**permanent paper:** inaccurate but commonly used description of archival papers.

**permissions:** the granting of rights by one publisher to another to quote extracts from a previously published title; under normal circumstances a permission fee is charged.

**pica em:** typographical measurement, consisting of 12 points, approximately 5 mm.

**picture research:** the process of finding suitable illustrations for a book, normally involving contacts with photo libraries, art galleries, museums and so on.

**picking:** the process of collecting together in the distribution centre the titles to fulfil an order.

**plates:** illustrations printed separately from the text of a book and inserted in the appropriate place by the binder. These may appear as a single section, or be wrapped round text sections, or occasionally individually pasted in.

**PLC:** Paper Laminated Case. See PPC.

**point:** a size measurement for type. Most books are set in 10 or 11 point type. Twelve points equal one pica em.

**point of sale:** merchandizing display material provided by publishers to bookshops in order to promote particular titles.

**pop-up:** type of novelty book where a three dimensional image is created when the book is opened.

**portrait:** description of a format which is deeper than it is wide.

**POS:** see Point of Sale.

**PPC:** Paper Printed Case – printed paper cover adhered to book boards to create a casebound book, without the need for a protective jacket.

**prelims:** universal abbreviation for the preliminary pages of a book before the start of the main text, often numbered in roman numerals.

**print run:** the number of copies printed in a single impression.

**process colours:** the four colours used in printing to represent the full spectrum. See CMYK. Black is represented with a K because B is used for Blue in the RGB profile.

**production:** the department within a publishing house responsible for print and paper buying and cost and quality control; in some cases has responsibility for typographic design also.

**proof:** general description of any kind of check of accuracy and quality control of a book's content; might be used of typesetting (when normally takes the form of a photocopy), of the reproduction of illustrations, or as a final check before printing (see ozalid).

**proofreader:** person either employed in a publishing house or as a freelancer to read text proofs and ensure accuracy of typesetting.

**publicity:** the department within a publishing house which organises 'free' promotion of titles published, often through the sending out of review copies or soliciting coverage in the broadcast media; often nowadays in larger firms a part of the marketing department.

**Publishing News:** a weekly news magazine for the UK book trade.

**Pulping:** a system of destroying unsold books. If a book is not selling or has reached the end of its lifetime with excess stock, the publisher may let it go out of print, but destroy any copies they haven't been able to sell by the end of the financial year. The books are usually recycled into paper or cardboard products.

**Quark Xpress:** a graphic design software package, much used on the Apple Mac, which enables a designer to manipulate words and images to produce an integrated design concept.

**recommended retail price:** since the abolition of the Net Book Agreement, the price at which the publisher recommends that a book should be sold; to which the bookseller's discount is applied and on which the royalty payment to the author is customarily calculated.

**recto:** the right-hand page of an opening in a book.

**register:** the accurate printing of each of the four process colours on top of the others to produce a near-perfect representation of a colour original.

**remainder:** a publisher's overstock sold off cheaply for resale through bargain bookshops etc.

**reprint:** a second or subsequent printing of a title with minimal alteration to the text.

**repro:** a common abbreviation for the reproduction of illustrations; a company carrying out such work is called a 'repro house'.

**returns:** books returned unsold from bookshops to publishers for full credit.

**review copy:** advance copy of a book sent out without charge to the press or other media for the purposes of review.

**RGB:** Red, Green, Blue – the colors used by a computer monitor which is converted to CMYK for printing.

**ribbon marker:** a thin strip of coloured material bound into the head of the book block in order to mark the reader's place in the book; often used as a decorative feature.

**Royal octavo:** book format, 234 x 156 mm (153 mm unsewn), very common in all sectors of the market.

**royalty:** the payment made by publishers to authors and others on sales made; typically a percentage of the recommended retail price in the home market and of the monies received from export sales. These payments are frequently set off against an advance and accounted for at six monthly intervals.

**RRP:** Recommended Retail Price.

**running head:** see headline.

**sale or return:** the arrangement whereby books supplied by publishers to booksellers may be returned for credit if subsequently unsold.

**scanning:**
- the electronic process of breaking down a continuous tone image into dots for printing.
- the electronic process of reading a document into a digital memory, from which it can be retrieved and manipulated.

**scout:** a person employed in an overseas territory to identify possible acquisitions of new titles.

**screen:** the process of breaking down a photographic image into dots for printing; originally named from a patterned glass screen inserted between the illustration and the light source on a camera, and now used to describe the process and also the size of the dots created (hence the quality of the reproduction).

**section:** the unit of folded pages produced by the printing or folding machine, most often 16 or 32 pages, which is then sewn together to make a book block or gathered for perfect binding.

**serial rights:** a subsidiary right involving the sale of extracts from a title to a newspaper or magazine.

**sheetfed:** printing term for a machine printing individual sheets of paper.

**slipcase:** a cardboard box open at one end into which single copies of a book (or two or three related volumes) are inserted; nowadays used for decorative effect.

**spot varnish:** the varnishing of a particular part only of a cover or jacket image for visual impact.

**Society of Authors:** organisation representing the interests of writers of books in the UK.

**Society of Young Publishers:** society which provides a forum for young people employed in the publishing industry.

**spine:** the round edge of a book, where the title, author's and publisher's name or logo normally appear.

**Spread:** common name for a double page spread – ie two facing pages.

**Strip and re-bind:** process where a book which is already printed and bound has the cover stripped off and replaced with a new one. No changes are made to internal pages. This is generally done by publishers wanting to invigorate sales of existing stock, or to correct an error on a cover after printing.

**subscription:** the process whereby a title is sold to booksellers in advance of publication and orders taken which are held as dues until shortly before the publication date.

**subsidiary rights:** rights are acquired by publishers for resale, such as serial rights, translation rights, etc.

**SYP:** see Society of Young Publishers.

**tailband:** a decorative strip of coloured material glued to the bottom of the spine of the book block of a hardback. Always used in conjunction with a headband.

**terms:** the percentage discount from the recommended retail price given to the bookseller.

**TIFF/TIF:** Tagged Image File – a format for bitmapped colour images produced by a scanner. The most common image file format for the industry.

**title-page:** the page, normally the second leaf in a book, which displays the title, author and publisher's name.

**title verso:** the reverse of the title-page, on which the publisher's name and address, printing history, ISBN and other bibliographical details, and the printer's imprint are customarily printed.

**topping rights:** in an auction the opportunity given by a literary agent to a publisher to match (or in practice increase by an agreed percentage) the highest bid received from other participants.

**translation rights:** the right acquired to translate and publish a work into another language.

**typeface:** a style or design of type encompassing shape, weight and proportions that make it distinct from the many hundreds of other typefaces. There are around 20 that are commonly used in books.

**unsewn binding:** see perfect binding.

**UV varnish:** a varnish cured by ultraviolet light normally applied to covers and jackets as part of the printing process.

**verso:** the reverse of a page in a book, thus the left-hand page of an opening.

**web offset:** printing process which prints onto a reel, or web, of paper, and produces folded sections off the press.

**Whitaker:** J. Whitaker & Sons Ltd, the leading bibliographical publisher in the UK, publisher of the Bookseller and provider of a wide range of bibliographical services and book listings.

**wholesaler:** stockholding supplier of titles to booksellers whose business is based on buying from the publisher in quantity and supplying single copy or small orders.

**WIP:** see Women in Publishing.

**WIPO:** abbreviation for World Intellectual Property Organisation, a body concerned with international copyright.

**Women in Publishing:** organisation which works to promote the status of women employed in the publishing industry and provide a forum for them.

**woodfree:** paper made from chemically treated woodpulp and used for good quality book production because of its colour fastness and durability.

**wove:** a loose description nowadays for uncoated bulky book papers, as in antique wove, book wove etc.

**Writers Guild:** an organization representing the interests of writers in the UK.

**109**

In this section you'll find listings for UK and Irish book publishers (including poetry and music publishers), book packagers, UK and Irish magazines, and national and local newspapers. Also here is a selection of European and International publishers, and our choice of podcasting companies and blogs that cover the world of publishing. Where royalty details are given, they are expressed as fractions of a pound.

# BOOKS

## UK & IRISH BOOK PUBLISHERS

### 11:9
**Suite Ex 8, Pentagon Centre, 44 Washington Street, Glasgow, Scotland, G3 8AZ**
- 0141 221 1117
- 0141 221 5363
- info@nwp.co.uk
- www.nwp.co.uk

**Parent Company** Neil Wilson Publishing Ltd
**Insider Info** Catalogue and manuscript guidelines are available online.
**Fiction** Publishes Contemporary Scottish fiction and anthologies.
**Submission Guidelines** Does not accept submissions.
**Recent Title(s)** *Dead Letter House*, Drew Campbell (Novel)
**Tips** 11:9 is the contemporary fiction imprint of Neil Wilson Publishing and specialises in Scottish fiction and regional anthologies. 11:9 is not currently commissioning any further titles, but may do so in the future.

### A&C Black Publishers Ltd
**38 Soho Square, London, W1D 3HB**
- 020 7758 0200
- 020 7758 0222
- enquiries@acblack.com
- www.acblack.com

**Parent Company** Bloomsbury Publishing Plc
**Contact** Chairman/Chief Executive, Nigel Newton; Managing Director, Jill Coleman.
**Established** 1807
**Imprint(s)** Adlard Coles Nautical
Andrew Brodie Publications
Christopher Helm
Pica Press
T&D Poyser
Herbert Press
Methuen Drama
Fitness Trainers

**Insider Info** Publishes 170 titles per year. Receives approximately 3,000 queries and 650 manuscripts per year. Five per cent of books published are from first time authors and 70 per cent are from unagented authors. Offers an advance. Average lead time is nine months with simultaneous submissions accepted. Aims to respond within two months to proposals and manuscripts. Catalogue is free on request.
**Non-Fiction** Publishes Children's/Teenage, General Non-fiction, Gift books, How-to, Humour, Illustrated, Scholarly, Dictionary, Who's Who (Biography/Reference) and Reference titles on the following subjects:
 Language/Literature, Marine Subjects, Sports, Travel, Fitness Training, Arts & Crafts, Glass, Ceramics, Printmaking, Ornithology, Performing Arts and Stagecraft, Drama and Writing, Children's Educational.
**Fiction** Publishes Juvenile titles.
**Recent Title(s)** *159th Edition of Who's Who*; *Whitaker's Almanack*; *The Sunday Times Rich List 2006–2007*.
**Tips** A&C Black was acquired by Bloomsbury Publishing Plc in 2000. The editorial contact email addresses are displayed by subject on the website.

### AA Publishing
**Fanum House, Basingstoke, RG21 4EA**
- 01256 491524
- 01256 491974
- www.theaa.com

**Contact** Publishing Director, David Watchus
**Insider Info** AA Publishing is one of the world's leading publishers of travel guides and books on

Britain, as well as illustrated reference books, atlases and maps. Catalogue available online.

**Non-Fiction** Publishes Travel guides (including *Citypack, Essential, Explorer* and *Spiral* series and *Baedeker, National Geographic Travellers*); Maps and Atlases; Driving Test books; Lifestyle guides (including *Pub Guide, Hotel Guide, Bed & Breakfast Guide, Golf Course Guide*); Leisure guides; Walking; Illustrated Reference titles and Children's character books.

## Aard Press
**c/o Aardverx, 31 Mountearl Gardens, London, SW16 2NL**
**Contact** Managing Director, Dawn Redwood
**Established** 1971
**Non-Fiction** Publishes Booklets, General Non-fiction, Multimedia and Illustrated titles on the following subjects:
 Art/Architecture, Crafts, Creative Non-fiction, Literary Criticism.
**Fiction** Publishes Experimental and Picture Book titles.
**Poetry** Publishes Poetry titles.
**Recent Title(s)** *Actuary*, Dawn Redwood
**Tips** Aard Press only does small print runs and does not accept any form of unsolicited submission proposals, or even enquiries.

## Abacus
**Brettenham House, Lancaster Place, London, WC2E 7EN**
- 020 7911 8000
- 020 7911 8100
- info@littlebrown.co.uk
- www.littlebrown.co.uk
**Parent Company** Little, Brown Book Group
**Contact** Managing Director, Richard Beswick
**Established** 1973
**Insider Info** Submissions accompanied by SAE will be returned. Aims to respond to proposals within eight weeks. Catalogue available online.
**Non-Fiction** Publishes General Non-fiction on the following subjects:
 Memoirs, Nature/Environment, Science.
 * Began as a strictly non-fiction imprint with an ecological focus. Now publishes over a wider range of subjects.
**Submission Guidelines** Accepts query with SAE. Submit proposal package (including outline, three sample chapters and a covering letter).
**Fiction** Publishes Literary and Mainstream/Contemporary fiction.

* Publishes both original fiction and paperback editions of Little Brown's hardback fiction.
**Submission Guidelines** Accepts query with SAE. Submit proposal package (including outline, three sample chapters and a covering letter).
**Tips** Agented submissions strongly preferred. Publishes mainly in paperback.

## Abbey Press
**Courtney Hill, Newry, Co. Down, BT34 2ED, Northern Ireland**
- 028 3026 3142
- 028 3026 2514
- adrianrice@earthlink.net
- www.abbeypressbooks.com
**Contact** Co-Founder/Editor, Adrian Rice (Poetry/Essays); Co-Founder/Administrator, Mel McMahon (Poetry)
**Established** 1997
**Insider Info** Publishes three titles per year. Receives approximately 200 queries and 100 manuscripts per year. 20 per cent of books published are from first-time authors, and 75 per cent are from unagented authors. Does not publish author subsidy books. Authors paid by small fee, plus free books. Average lead time is seven months. Does not accept simultaneous submissions. Submissions accompanied by SAE will be returned. Aims to respond to queries, proposals and manuscript submissions within four months. Catalogue available online, or via email. Author guidelines available by sending SAE, online or via email.
**Non-Fiction** Publishes Autobiography, Biography and Scholarly titles on the following subjects:
 Art/Architecture, Community/Public Affairs, Contemporary Culture, Creative Non-fiction, Government/Politics, History, Humanities, Language/Literature, Literary Criticism, Memoirs, Multicultural, Music/Dance, Philosophy, Regional, Translation.
**Submission Guidelines** Accepts query with SAE. Submit proposal package (including outline, one sample chapter, your publishing history, author biography and SAE). Does not review artwork/photographs.
**Fiction** Publishes Historical, Literary, Mainstream/Contemporary, Multicultural, Plays, Regional and Short story collections.
**Poetry** Publishes poetry and poetry in translation.
 * Read poetry from existing authors to judge their taste.
**Submission Guidelines** Submit seven sample poems.

**Recent Title(s)** *The Rest is History*, Gerald Dawe (Paperback); *Whereabouts*, Mark Roper (Paperback)
**Tips** Target audience is literary/academic/poetry/history lovers.

## ABC-Clio
**PO Box 1437, Oxford, OX4 9AZ**
- 01865 481403
- 01865 481482
- salesuk@abc-clio.com
- www.abc-clio.com

**Contact** President and CEO (US), Ron Boehm
**Established** 1955
**Insider Info** Catalogue available online.
**Non-Fiction** Publishes Reference and Scholarly, (online subscription database), Education and General Reference works, focusing on History and Social sciences.
**Submission Guidelines** Contact Oxford office for information on submission methods.
**Recent Title(s)** *The Home Front Encyclopaedia*, James Ciment (Editor), Thaddeus Russell (Contributing Editor) (Reference – US, Britain and Canada in WWs I & II)
**Tips** The company is US based with an office in the UK. The website is US authored, but does contain information for UK authors and readers.

## Absolute Press
**Scarborough House, 29 James Street West, Bath, BA1 2BT**
- 01225 316013
- 01225 445836
- office@absolutepress.co.uk
- www.absolutepress.co.uk

**Contact** Publisher, Jon Croft; Commissioning Editor, Meg Avent
**Established** 1979
**Insider Info** Authors paid by royalty. Catalogue available online. No unsolicited manuscripts.
**Non-Fiction** Publishes Cookbooks, General Non-fiction, Gift books, How-to, Humour and Reference titles on the following subjects:
Cooking/Foods/Nutrition, Health/Medicine, House and Home, Travel.
**Recent Title(s)** *Meat & Two Veg*, Fiona Beckett (Cookery); *Aga Easy*, Lucy Young (Reference – Aga)
**Tips** Target audience is chefs, cooks, homeowners, etc. As well as not accepting unsolicited manuscripts, Absolute Press is also unable to offer any proofreading or copyediting commissions for freelancers.

## Abson Books London
**5 Sidney Square, London, E1 2EY**
- 020 7790 4737
- 020 7790 7346
- books@absonbooks.co.uk
- www.absonbooks.co.uk

**Contact** Publisher, M.J. Ellison
**Established** 1971
**Insider Info** Catalogue is available online.
**Non-Fiction** Publishes Language Glossaries, Literary Quiz, Puzzle Book and Curiosity titles.
**Recent Title(s)** *Rude Rhyming Slang*, Abson Books.
**Tips** The largest area of publishing is dialect and slang books.

## Academic Press
**The Boulevard, Langford Lane, Kidlington, Oxford, OX5 1GB**
- 01865 843000
- 01865 843010
- authorsupport@elsevier.com
- www.elsevier.com

**Parent Company** Elsevier Ltd (Science & Technology)
**Established** 1946
**Insider Info** Authors paid by royalty. Catalogue and author guidelines available online.
**Non-Fiction** Publishes Multimedia, Textbooks, Reference, Scholarly and Technical titles on the following subjects:
Education, Nature/Environment, Science, Social Sciences, Construction/Engineering.
**Submission Guidelines** Accepts query with SAE. Submit proposal package (including outline).
**Recent Title(s)** *International Review Of Cytology*, Kwang Jeon (Reference)
**Tips** Academic Press publishes books, periodicals, online services and CD-ROMs (from single volumes to multi-volume reference works in the fields of physical, applied and life sciences). Titles are aimed at scientists, researchers, engineers, and other professionals in industry and academia. Authors' proposals for books are welcomed. The first step is to discuss the proposal with the relevant Publishing Editor. Check the website for in-depth submission guidelines and a full list of editorial contacts.

## Academy of Light
**Unit 1c, Delta Centre, Mount Pleasant, Wembley, Middlesex, HA0 1UX**
- 020 8795 2695
- 020 8903 3748

**o** info@academyoflight.co.uk
**w** www.academyoflight.co.uk
**Contact** Managing Director, Dr Yubraj Sharma
**Established** 2000
**Non-Fiction** Publishes Children's/Juvenile, Illustrated, Reference and Scholarly titles on the following subjects:
Alternative Lifestyles, Art/Architecture, Health/Medicine, New Age, Spirituality.
**Recent Title(s)** *Spiritual Bioenergetics of Homeopathic Materia Medica Vol.1*, Dr Yubraj Sharma (Medical/Spirituality)
**Tips** Academy of Light is a specialist book publisher on homoeopathy and spirituality. It aims to integrate the many fields of alternative medicine into a holistic system of new age medicine.

## Acair Ltd

**Unit 7, St James Street, Stornoway, Isle of Lewis, HS1 2QN**
**o** 01851 703020
**o** 01851 703294
**o** info@acairbooks.com
**w** www.acairbooks.com
**Established** 1975
**Insider Info** Authors paid by royalty. Catalogue available online.
**Non-Fiction** Publishes Children's/Juvenile, General Non-fiction, Illustrated, Reference and Scholarly titles on the following subjects:
History, Military/War, Regional.
**Fiction** Publishes Juvenile, Young Adult and Gaelic (sometimes printed in Gaelic language) fiction titles.
**Poetry** Publish Poetry titles.
* See catalogue for more information on Acair poetry publishing.
**Recent Title(s)** *The Living Past*, Donald Macleod (Autobiography); *Aeolus*, Donald MacIntyre
**Tips** Acair is a bilingual publisher, printing books in both English and Gaelic languages, and targeted mainly at Gaelic primary school education. Looking to the future, Acair are keen to carry on producing quality Scottish books, and in order to do that are keen to promote talent from the Western Isles in particular, and Scotland in general.

## Accent Press

**The Old School, Upper High Street, Bedlinog, Mid Glamorgan, CF46 6SA**
**o** 01443 710930
**o** 01443 710940
**o** info@accentpress.co.uk
**w** www.accentpress.co.uk

**Contact** Managing Director, Hazel Cushion (Fiction/Non-Fiction)
**Established** 2003
**Imprint(s)** Xcite Books
**Insider Info** Publishes 36 titles per year. Receives approximately 500 queries and 750 manuscripts per year. Three per cent of books published are from first-time authors and ten per cent of books published are from unagented authors. Payment is via royalty (on retail price) with 0.1 (per £) maximum. Average lead time is six months, with simultaneous submissions not accepted. Submissions accompanied by SAE will be returned. Aims to respond to queries, proposals and manuscripts within six months, and all other enquiries within twelve months. A catalogue is free on request, and available online.
**Non-Fiction** Publishes Autobiography, Cookbooks, How-to and Self-help titles on the following subjects:
Child Guidance/Parenting, Cooking/Foods/Nutrition, Gay/Lesbian, Literary Criticism, Memoirs.
**Submission Guidelines** Accepts proposal package (including outline, three sample chapters, your publishing history, author biography, SAE and artworks/images (send digital files as jpegs).
**Fiction** Publishes Erotica (short stories), Historical, Literary, Mainstream/Contemporary, Romance, Crime and Thriller titles.
* Check the published titles catalogue to see what kind of fiction is of interest.
**Submission Guidelines** Accepts proposal package (including outline, with three sample chapters).
**Recent Title(s)** *Hole Kidnapped in Georgia*, Peter Shaw (Memoir); *Barefoot In The Dark*, Lynne Barrett Lee (Romance)
**Tips** Accent Press books have a mainstream and mass market readership. They do not publish any poetry, or short story collections, with the exception of erotica, and have a limited production schedule.

## Acorn Editions

**PO Box 60, Cambridge, CB1 2NT**
**o** 01223 350865
**o** 01225 366951
**o** publishing@lutterworth.com
**w** www.lutterworth.com
**Parent Company** The Lutterworth Press
**Insider Info** Publishes 50 titles per year. Catalogue available online.
**Non-Fiction** Publishes General Non-fiction on the following subjects:
History, Memoirs, Regional, Local and Minority Interest.

**Submission Guidelines** Submit proposal package (including outline and three sample chapters). No email submissions.

**Recent Title(s)** *From Anschluss to Albion: Memoirs of a Regufee Girl 1938–40*, Elizabeth Orsten (Memoir)

**Tips** Acorn Editions is a local and minority interest imprint of The Lutterworth Press, the UK's oldest independent publishing house. Unsolicited proposals are welcome, but read the guidelines on the website before submitting.

## Acumen Publishing Limited
**Stocksfield Hall, Stocksfield, NE43 7TN**

- 01661 844865
- 01661 844865
- enquiries@acumenpublishing.co.uk/ tristanpalmereditor@yahoo.co.uk/steven.gerrard@acumenpublishing.co.uk
- www.acumenpublishing.co.uk

**Contact** Publisher/Partner, Steven Gerrard; Senior Editor, Tristan Palmer

**Insider Info** Catalogue and author guidelines available online.

**Non-Fiction** Publishes scholarly titles and academic journals on the following subjects:
History, Philosophy, Aesthetics, Classics, Epistemology and Metaphysics, Logic and Mathematics, Mind and Language, Social Theory.

**Submission Guidelines** Submit proposal package (including outline, sample chapter(s) and author biography). Also submit a review of competing books and information about intended readership.

**Recent Title(s)** *Reading Nietzsche – An Analysis of Beyond Good and Evil*, Douglas Burnham (Academic non-fiction)

**Tips** Acumen Publishing's books are read by a worldwide higher education audience; students, lecturers and researchers. There is good submission information for authors on the website, including style and indexing downloads.

## Addison-Wesley
**Edinburgh Gate, Harlow, Essex, CM20 2JE**

- 01279 623623
- 01279 414130
- www.pearsoned.co.uk/imprints/addison-wesley

**Parent Company** Pearson Education

**Insider Info** Catalogue and manuscript guidelines are available online.

**Non-Fiction** Publishes Reference, Scholarly, Technical and Academic titles on the following subjects:

Astronomy, Computers, Economics, Electronics, Finance, Mathematics, Physics.

**Submission Guidelines** Accepts proposal package (including synopsis, sample chapters, market research, your publishing history and author biography).

**Recent Title(s)** *Scaling Software Agility*, Dean Leffingwell (Business/Management)

**Tips** Addison-Wesley is the world's leading technical publisher, authors are generally technology creators, proteges and acknowledged experts. The imprint's professional titles specialise in the area of computer programming, producing high quality and up to date information for programmers, developers, engineers, and system administrators. Addison-Wesley's academic titles specialise in the areas of astronomy and physics, computing, economics and finance, mathematics and statistics. See website for full list of submissions contacts.

## Adlard Coles Nautical
**38 Soho Square, London, W1D 3HB**

- 020 7758 0200
- 020 7758 0333
- adlardcoles@acblack.com
- www.acblack.com

**Parent Company** A & C Black

**Contact** Editorial Director, Janet Murphy

**Established** 1947

**Imprint(s)** Reeds Nautical Almanac (series)
Thomas Reed Publications (list)

**Insider Info** Catalogue available online.

**Non-Fiction** Publishes How-to, Humour, Almanacs, Illustrated, Reference and Technical titles on the following subjects:
Hobbies, Marine Subjects, Sports, Travel, Nautical/Sailing.

**Submission Guidelines** Accepts query with SAE.

**Recent Title(s)** *Reeds Nautical Almanac 2007*, Neville Featherstone and Peter Lambie eds.
(Technical Maritime)

**Tips** Adlard Coles Nautical publishes practical and technical books on all manner of nautical, maritime and sailing topics. The Thomas Reed list publishes practical sailing books aimed at both professional merchant sailors and the practical boating leisure market and the Nautical Almanac series is a long running series of practical and general nautical interest. Subjects are generally practical or technical in nature, so some working experience in the field would be useful for a prospective contributor, but they also publish some general interest and humorous books.

## African Books Collective

**Unit 13, King's Meadow, Ferry Hinksey Road, Oxford, OX2 0DP**

- ☎ 01865 726686
- ☏ 01865 793298
- ✉ abc@africanbookscollective.com
- 🌐 www.africanbookscollective.com

**Contact** Mary Jay
**Established** 1989
**Insider Info** Catalogue available online. Only accepts manuscripts from participating African publishers.
**Non-Fiction** Publishes Children's/Juvenile, General Non-fiction, How-to, Scholarly and Self-help titles on the following subjects:
 Art/Architecture, Child Guidance/Parenting, Counselling/Career, Education, Ethnic, Government/Politics, Health/Medicine, Humanities, Money/Finance, Regional, Science, Social Sciences, World Affairs.
**Fiction** Publishes Juvenile, Multicultural, Translation and Young Adult fiction.
**Recent Title(s)** *Democracy in the Time of Mbeki*, Richard Calland and Paul Graham (Social History); *Battles of Songs: Udje Tradition of the Urhobo*, G.G. Darah (World Culture)
**Tips** African Books Collective (ABC), founded, owned and governed by African publishers, seeks to strengthen indigenous African publishing through collective action, and to increase the visibility and accessibility of the wealth of African scholarship and culture. The collective is open to genuinely autonomous and independent African publishers, and ABC actively seeks suitable titles for distribution outside Africa.

## Age Concern Books

**1268 London Road, London, SW16 4ER**

- ☎ 020 8765 7200
- ☏ 020 8765 7211
- ✉ books@ace.org.uk
- 🌐 www.ace.org.uk

**Contact** Commissioning Editor, Becky Senior
**Established** 1973
**Insider Info** Catalogue available online.
**Non-Fiction** Publishes General Non-fiction, How-to, Reference and Self-help titles on the following subjects:
 Computers/Electronics, Counselling/Career, Health/Medicine, House and Home, Real Estate, Recreation, Geronotology.
**Submission Guidelines** Accepts query with SAE. Submit proposal package (including outline and SAE).
**Recent Title(s)** *Choices in Retirement*, Ro Lyon; *Your Rights: Working After 50*, Andrew Harrop and Susie Munro
**Tips** Age Concern Books addresses the needs of older people, their families and professional carers, as well as business and voluntary organisations. The aim of their titles is to provide accurate and up to date information to improve quality of life and standards of care. Although fiction submissions are not accepted, Age Concern will consider ideas for new practical handbooks that are aimed at the elderly generation in tone and content.

## Akros Publications

**33 Lady Nairn Avenue, Kirkcaldy, Fife, Scotland, KY1 2AW**

- ☎ 01592 651522
- ✉ akrospublications@blueyonder.co.uk
- 🌐 www.akrospublications.co.uk

**Contact** Publisher, Duncan Glen
**Established** 1965
**Insider Info** Publishes ten titles per year. Authors paid by royalty, twice yearly. Catalogue available online.
**Non-Fiction** Publishes Literary Criticism and Local History titles.
**Submission Guidelines** Accepts query with SAE. No unsolicited manuscripts.
**Poetry** Publishes Scottish Poetry titles.
**Submission Guidelines** Please contact for submission guidelines. No unsolicited manuscripts.
**Recent Title(s)** *Fife Photographs*, Duncan Glen; *Confessions of an Occasional Poet*, George Philip
**Tips** The main activity of Akros is to publish Scottish poets, and there are many well known names on the backlist. The local history books published are largely written by Duncan Glen himself.

## Alistair Sawday Publishing

**The Old Farmyard, Yanley Lane, Long Ashton, Bristol, BS41 9LR**

- ☎ 01275 395430
- ☏ 01275 393388
- ✉ specialplaces@sawdays.co.uk
- 🌐 www.sawdays.co.uk

**Contact** Publisher, Alistair Sawday
**Established** 1994
**Insider Info** Catalogue available online.
**Non-Fiction** Publishes Travel guides under the *Special Places to Stay* and *Fragile Earth* series.

**Recent Title(s)** *Green Places to Stay*, Alistair Sawday Publishing (Special Places to Stay).

**Tips** Alistair Sawday guides are aimed at discerning and interested travellers/holiday makers, who appreciate the vivid and honest style of the entries and are looking for a special, more unique places to stay.

## Allen Lane

**80 Strand, London, WC2R 0RL**

- 020 7010 3000
- 020 7010 6060
- customer.service@penguin.co.uk
- www.penguin.co.uk

**Parent Company** Penguin Press
**Established** 1967
**Insider Info** Catalogue is available online or by email.
**Non-Fiction** Publishes Autobiography, Biography, General Non-fiction and Illustrated titles.
**Submission Guidelines** Agented submissions only.
**Recent Title(s)** *Empire: How Britain Made the World*, Niall Ferguson (History)
**Tips** Allen Lane is expanding steadily and aims to publish accessible and excellent non-fiction books of lasting value.

## Allison and Busby Ltd

**13 Charlotte Mews, London, W1T 4EJ**

- 020 7580 1080
- 020 7580 1180
- susie@allisonandbusby.com
- www.allisonandbusby.ltd.uk

**Established** 1969
**Insider Info** Catalogue is available online.
**Non-Fiction** Publishes Autobiography, Biography, General Non-fiction, How-to, Encyclopedias and Reference titles on the following subjects: Computers/Electronics, Contemporary Culture, History, Language/Literature, Memoirs, Music/Dance, Psychology, Sex, Writing, Politics, Personalities, Crime, Film and Television.
**Submission Guidelines** Agented submissions only.
**Fiction** Publishes Literary, Mainstream/Contemporary and Crime fiction.
**Submission Guidelines** Agented submissions only.
**Recent Title(s)** *Kidnapping Ronnie, The 1981 kidnapping of Ronnie Biggs from Brazil*, Patrick King; *Little Children*, Tom Perrotta

## Allyn & Bacon

**Edinburgh Gate, Harlow, Essex, CM20 2JE**

- 01279 623623
- 01279 414130
- www.pearsoned.co.uk/Imprints/AllynBacon

**Parent Company** Pearson Education
**Insider Info** Catalogue and manuscript guidelines are available online.
**Non-Fiction** Publishes Reference, Scholarly and Textbook titles on the following subjects: Education, Humanities, Social Sciences.
**Submission Guidelines** Accepts proposal package (including synopsis, sample chapters, market research, your publishing history and author biography).
**Recent Title(s)** *Abnormal Psychology: International Edition (13th Edition)*, James Butcher, Susan Mineka and Jill Hooley (Education)
**Tips** Allyn & Bacon is a leading publisher for higher education in the areas of education, humanities and the social sciences. See website for full list of submission contacts.

## Alma Books Ltd

**London House, 243–253 Lower Mortlake Road, Richmond, Surrey, TW9 2LL**

- 020 8948 9550
- 020 8948 5599
- info@almabooks.com
- www.almabooks.com

**Contact** Publisher, Alessandro Gallenzi (Trade Fiction and Non-Fiction)
**Established** 2005
**Imprint(s)** Herla Publishing
**Insider Info** Publishes 25 titles per year. Receives 500 queries and 400 manuscripts per year. 30 per cent of books published are from first-time authors and 20 per cent are from unagented authors. Payment is via royalty (on retail price) with 0.1 (per £) minimum and 0.12 (per £) maximum. Advance offered is from £1,000–£5,000. Average lead time is 12 months, with simultaneous submissions accepted. Submissions accompanied by SAE will be returned. Aims to respond to queries within one day, proposals within one week and manuscripts within one month. Catalogue is free on request, and available online or via email. Manuscript guidelines are available online.
**Non-Fiction** Publishes Biography, General Non-fiction and Humour titles.
**Submission Guidelines** Accepts query with SAE, or proposal package (including outline, two sample

chapters, author biography and SAE) and artworks/ images (send photocopies).

**Fiction** Publishes Humour, Literary, Mainstream/ Contemporary, Short Story collections and Translation titles.

**Submission Guidelines** Accepts query with SAE or proposal package (including outline, two sample chapters).

**Poetry** Publishes some poetry including European translations.

**Submission Guidelines** Accepts query or proposal package (including five sample poems).

**Recent Title(s)** *Angus McBean: Facemaker*, Adrian Woodhouse (Biography); *Remainder*, Tom McCarthy (Literary Fiction)

## Amber Lane Press
**Cherol House, Church Street, Charlbury, OX7 3PR**
- 01608 810024
- 01608 810024
- info@amberlanepress.co.uk
- www.amberlanepress.co.uk

**Contact** Director/Managing Editor, Judith Scott
**Established** 1979
**Insider Info** Publishes four titles per year. Receives approximately ten queries per year, and six manuscripts. Approximately 20 per cent of books published are by first-time authors, and approximately ten per cent are by unagented authors. Authors paid by royalty. Average lead time is 18 months plus. Submissions accompanied by SAE will be returned. Catalogue available online. No unsolicited manuscripts.
**Non-Fiction** Publishes Biography, General Non-fiction, How-to, Reference and Scholarly titles on the following subjects:
 Art/Architecture, Drama/Theatre.
**Submission Guidelines** Submit proposal package (including outline and two sample chapters).
**Fiction** Publishes Plays.
**Recent Title(s)** *Bent*, Martin Sherman (Play); *Longitude*, Arnold Wesker (Play)
**Tips** Target audience is playwrights, theatre goers, dramatists, actors, acting enthusiasts, etc. Only plays that are scheduled for professional production will be considered for publication. In your submission, explain why the book would be different from anything else published on the subject.

## Andersen Press Ltd
**20 Vauxhall Bridge Road, London SW1V 2SA**
- 020 7840 8701

- 020 7233 6263
- andersenpress@randomhouse.co.uk
- www.andersenpress.co.uk

**Contact** Fiction Editor, Liz Maude (Children's Fiction); Editorial Director, Rona Selby (Children's Books)
**Established** 1976
**Insider Info** Publishes 64 titles per year. Receives approximately 200 queries and 500 manuscripts per year. 25 per cent of books published are from first-time authors and 30 per cent of books published are from unagented authors. Payment is via royalty (on retail price) with 0.075 (per £) minimum and 0.125 (per £) maximum. Advance offered is £2,000. Catalogue is free on request, and available online. Manuscript guidelines are free on request.
**Non-Fiction** Publishes Young Adult and Children's titles.
 * Publishes very little non-fiction.
**Submission Guidelines** Accepts proposal package (including outline, one sample chapter, author biography and SAE) and artworks/images (send digital files as jpegs or other formats).
**Fiction** Publishes Children's and Picture Book titles.
**Submission Guidelines** Accepts proposal package (including outline and one sample chapter)
**Recent Title(s)** *Sara's Face*, Melvin Burgess (Juvenile Fiction)
**Tips** Readership for Andersen Press books is children and young adults, between the ages of one and eighteen. They publish mainly picture books, for which the required text would be under 1000 words, a series of early readers fiction called Tigers which are about 3-5000 words long, and older fiction for which the text is about 15-50,000 words. Books are sold in conjunction with Random House Children's Books.

## Andre Deutsch
**20 Mortimer Street, London, W1T 3JW**
- 020 7612 0400
- 020 7612 0401
- enquiries@carltonbooks.co.uk
- www.carltonbooks.co.uk

**Parent Company** Carlton Publishing Group
**Established** 1950s
**Insider Info** Publishes four titles per year. Catalogue available online.
**Non-Fiction** Publishes Biography and General Non-fiction on the following subjects:
 History, Travel, Current affairs.
**Submission Guidelines** Submit proposal package (including outline, the first 20 pages or two sample chapters – whichever is shorter).

**Recent Title(s)** *Peter Kay: The Unauthorised Biography*, Johnny Dee; *The Treasures of Tutankhamun*, Jaromir Malek

**Tips** Although Andre Deutsch was created to publish high end non-fiction, it does not accept proposals for academic books.

Andre Deutsch, a European (Hungarian) émigré, started the distinguished publishing house in the 1950s. Deutsch died in 2000, but his name lives on through the high quality list from the Carlton Publishing Group.

## Andrew Brodie Publications

**38 Soho Square, London, W1D 3HB**
- 020 7758 0200
- 020 7758 0222
- childrens@acblack.com
- www.acblack.com

**Parent Company** A & C Black
**Insider Info** Catalogue available online.
**Non-Fiction** Publishes Children's/Juvenile, Illustrated books, Multimedia educational titles.
**Recent Title(s)** *Have a Go: English Tests*, Judy Richardson (Education)
**Tips** Andrew Brodie Publications publishes reference and education material for children of all ages. Also publishes photocopiable material for use in schools and libraries as teaching resources. Andrew Brodie books are practical and educational in nature, but must also be easily photocopiable for use as teaching materials.

## Andromeda Children's Books

**Winchester House, 259–269 Old Marylebone Road, London, NW1 5XJ**
- 020 7616 7200
- 020 7616 7201
- www.pinwheel.co.uk

**Parent Company** Pinwheel Limited
**Insider Info** Catalogue available online.
**Non-Fiction** Publishes Children's/Juvenile, Cloth, Novelty, Gift and Illustrated titles on the following subjects:
Children's and Baby's Early Learning.
**Fiction** Publishes Children's, Picture Books and Illustrated fiction titles.
**Recent Title(s)** *Secrets of the Master Magician* (Activity Pack); *The Beautiful Butterfly Book* (Illustrated Non-fiction)
**Tips** As part of Pinwheel, specialist children's publishers, the Andromeda imprint focuses on the three to twelve year old age group. Typical titles include wipe clean books for pre-schoolers and

novelty series such as *Beautiful Bugs*. Any picture book submissions should be directed to Gullane Children's Books (another imprint of Pinwheel) and not Andromeda.

## The Angels Share

**Suite Ex 8, Pentagon Centre, 44 Washington Street, Glasgow, Scotland, G3 8AZ**
- 0141 221 1117
- 0141 221 5363
- info@nwp.co.uk
- www.nwp.co.uk

**Parent Company** Neil Wilson Publishing Ltd
**Insider Info** Catalogue and manuscript guidelines are available online.
**Non-Fiction** Publishes General Non-fiction titles on the following subjects:
Cooking, Food and Drink, Scottish Cuisine, Whisky.
**Submission Guidelines** Submit proposal package (including outline, synopsis, one sample chapter, author biography, CV and SAE). Will accept artworks/images.
**Recent Title(s)** *The Whisky Barons*, Allen Andrews (Whisky)
**Tips** The Angels Share is the food and drink imprint of Neil Wilson Publishing and specialises in books on Scottish food and drink. The Angels Share is the leading publisher of books on whisky and takes its name from the high amount of spirit that evaporates from Scotland's warehouses every year, the so called 'Angels Share'.

## Anglo-Saxon Books

**25 Brocks Road, EcoTech Business Park, Swaffham, Norfolk, PE37 7XG**
- 0845 430 4200
- tony@asbooks.co.uk
- www.asbooks.co.uk

**Contact** Managing Editor, Tony Linsell
**Established** 1990
**Insider Info** Publishes five titles per year. Catalogue available online. No unsolicited manuscripts.
**Non-Fiction** Publishes General Non-fiction, Illustrated, Reference and Scholarly titles on the following subjects:
History, Language/Literature, Tolkien studies.
**Submission Guidelines** Query by phone only.
**Fiction** Publishes Tolkien related fiction and Old English Fiction titles.
**Poetry** Publishes poetry in translation and Old English poetry.
**Submission Guidelines** Query by phone only.

**Recent Title(s)** *Anglo-Saxon Attitudes*, J. A. Hilton (History/Culture); *Necessary Words*, Raymond Tong (History/Language)

**Tips** Anglo-Saxon Books was created to promote a greater awareness of, and interest in early English history, language and culture. It aims to publish good books at a reasonable price. Phone with query before any submissions.

## Anness Publishing

**Hermes House, 88–89 Blackfriars Road, London, SE1 8HA**

☏ 020 7401 2077
☏ 020 7633 9499
✉ info@anness.com
🌐 www.annesspublishing.com

**Contact** Chairman/Managing Director, Paul Anness; Publisher/Partner, Joanna Lorenz (Creative Issues)

**Established** 1988

**Imprint(s)** Lorenz Books
 Southwater
 Hermes House
 Peony Press

**Insider Info** Publish 300 titles per year. Catalogue available online.

**Non-Fiction** Publishes Children's/Juvenile, General Non-fiction, Gift, Illustrated and Reference titles on the following subjects:
 Child Guidance/Parenting, Contemporary Culture, Cooking/Foods/Nutrition, Crafts, Gardening, Health/Medicine, Hobbies, House and Home, Memoirs, New Age, Sports, Food and Drink, Lifestyle, Pets.
 * The Lorenz Books and Southwater imprints publish traditionally across the range of non-fiction topics, whereas Hermes House and Peony Press deal with non-trade sales, promotional sales and customised publishing for major customers.

**Recent Title(s)** *The Secrets of the Knights Templar*, Susie Hodge (Lorenz); *Easter: Recipes, Gifts and Decorations*, Tessa Evelegh (Southwater – Non-fiction); *Step Into: Ancient Egypt*, Philip Steele (Southwater – Children's Reference)

**Tips** Anness is the largest independent book publisher in the UK. The company has embarked on a major forestry project by managing and planting trees to replace the ones used to produce its books.

## Anova Books Company Ltd

**151 Freston Road, London, W10 6TH**

☏ 020 7314 1400
☏ 020 7314 1588
✉ pelmadani@anovabooks.com
🌐 www.anovabooks.com

**Contact** Senior Editor, Emily Preece-Morrison; Commissioning Editor, Michelle Lo (Craft); Commissioning Editor, Victoria Alers-Hankey (Reference, Health); Commissioning Editor, Barbara Phelan (Biography, Popular Culture); Senior Editor, Nicola Birtwisle; Editor, Kristy Richardson

**Established** 2005

**Imprint(s)** Batsford
 Robson
 Pavilion
 Conway Maritime Press
 Portico
 Collins & Brown
 National Trust Books
 Chrysalis Children's Books

**Insider Info** Publishes 150 titles per year. Receives approximately 40 queries and 200 manuscripts per year. 50 per cent of books published are from first-time authors and 50 per cent of books published are from unagented authors. Payment is via royalty (on retail price), with 0.075 (per £) maximum, or outright purchase. Advance offered will be up to £10,000. Average lead time is seven months, with simultaneous submissions not accepted. Submissions accompanied by SAE will be returned. Aims to respond to queries within one week, proposals within two weeks, and manuscripts within five weeks. Catalogue is free on request, and available online.

**Non-Fiction** Publishes Biography, Children's and Coffee table titles on the following subjects:
 Art/Architecture, Cooking/Foods/Nutrition, Crafts, Gardening, Health/Medicine, Memoirs, Military/War, Photography, Sports, Travel, Bridge/Chess, Fashion/Textiles, Popular Culture, History/Heritage, Lifestyle, Interiors Design, Maritime/Naval, Aviation, Mind, Body and Spirit.

**Submission Guidelines** Accepts proposal package (including outline and one sample chapter).

**Fiction** Publishes Erotica, Fantasy, Military/War, Spiritual and Sports titles.

**Submission Guidelines** Accepts proposal package (including outline and one sample chapter).

**Recent Title(s)** *The Sound of Music Companion*, Laurence Maslon with Rodgers & Hammerstein org

## Antique Collector's Club

**Sandy Lane, Old Martlesham, Woodbridge, IP12 4SD**

☏ 01394 389950
☏ 01394 389999
✉ sales@antique-acc.com
🌐 www.antique-acc.com

**Contact** Managing Director, Diana Steel

**Established** 1966

**Insider Info** Catalogue free on request, or available online.

**Non-Fiction** Publishes Children's/Juvenile, General Non-fiction, Gift and Illustrated titles on the following subjects:
Art/Architecture, Crafts, Gardening, Hobbies, Photography, Horology, Antiques/Collectables/ Museums.

**Recent Title(s)** *The English House*, John Steel and Michael Wright; *Great Exhibitions*, Jonathan Meyer

**Tips** Target audience antiques/art collectors. Will consider synopses or ideas for books. Also publishes a journal, *Antique Collecting*, which may be more likely to accept article submissions.

## Apex Publishing Ltd

**PO Box 7086, Clacton on Sea, Essex, CO15 5WN**

- ☎ 01255 428500
- 🖷 0870 046 6536
- ✉ enquiry@apexpublishing.co.uk
- 🌐 www.apexpublishing.co.uk

**Contact** Managing Editor, Susan Kidby; Production Manager, Chris Cowlin; Marketing Manager, Jackie Bright

**Established** 2002

**Insider Info** Publishes 20 titles per year. Receives approximately 500 queries and 500 manuscripts per year. 60 per cent of books published are from first-time authors and 90 per cent of books published are from unagented authors. 50 per cent of books published are author subsidy published based on potential sales. Payment is via royalty (on retail price). Average lead time is nine months, with simultaneous submissions accepted. Submissions accompanied by SAE will be returned. Aims to respond to queries within seven days, proposals within 14 days, manuscripts within 21 days, and any other enquiry within seven days. Catalogue and manuscript guidelines are free on request, and available online or by email.

**Non-Fiction** Publishes Autobiography, Biography, Cookbooks, General Non-fiction, Humour, Reference and Self-help titles on the following subjects:
Animals, Cooking/Foods/Nutrition, Education, History, Hobbies, Military/War, New Age, Philosophy, Psychology, Regional, Religion, Science, Sex, Social Sciences, Sociology, Sports, Travel, Young Adult.

**Submission Guidelines** Accepts query with SAE or completed manuscript (including publishing history, clips, author biography and SAE) and artworks/ images (send photocopies or digital files as jpegs).

**Fiction** Publishes Erotica, Fantasy, Horror, Humour, Regional, Science Fiction and Sports titles.

**Submission Guidelines** Accepts query with SAE or completed manuscript (including publishing history, clips, author biography and SAE).

## Apple Press

**Sheridan House, 112–116A Western Road, Hove, East Sussex, BN3 1DD**

- ☎ 01273 727268
- 🖷 01273 727269
- ✉ apple@rotovision.com
- 🌐 www.apple-press.com

**Contact** Editorial Manager, Liane Stark

**Established** 1976

**Insider Info** Catalogue free on request or available online.

**Non-Fiction** Publishes Children's/Juvenile, General Non-fiction and Illustrated titles on the following subjects:
Art/Architecture, Cooking/Foods/Nutrition, Crafts, Gardening, History, Hobbies, House and Home.

**Submission Guidelines** Query with SAE.

**Recent Title(s)** *500 Cupcakes & Muffins*, Fergal Connolly (Cookery); *Ice Cream Machine Book*, Rosemary Moon (Cookery)

**Tips** The hallmarks of Apple's books are clear, reliable and accessible content with fresh, modern design. Any submissions need to be aware of this ethos.

## Appletree Press Ltd

**The Old Potato Station, 14 Howard Street South, Belfast, BT7 1AP, Northern Ireland**

- ☎ 028 9024 3074
- 🖷 028 9024 6756
- ✉ reception@appletree.ie
- 🌐 www.appletree.ie

**Contact** Managing Director, John Murphy

**Established** 1974

**Insider Info** Payment is via royalty. Catalogue available online.

**Non-Fiction** Publishes Biography, General Non-fiction, Gift, How-to and Illustrated titles on the following subjects:
Art/Architecture, Cooking/Foods/Nutrition, Crafts, History, Music/Dance, Nature/Environment, Regional, Religion, Translation, Travel, Celtic.

**Submission Guidelines** Accepts query with SAE with proposal package (including outline).

**Recent Title(s)** *Great Irish Writers*, Martin Wallace (Literary); *Scottish Kitchen*, Paul Harris and Marion Maxwell (Cookery)

**Tips** Titles aimed at anyone Scottish, Irish or Celtic. Appletree Press does not accept unsolicited manuscripts, but will consider ideas or synopses for gift books or general interest Scottish or Irish non-fiction.

## Arcadia Books
**5–16 Nassau Street, London, W1W 7AB**
- 020 7436 9898
- 020 7436 9898
- info@arcadiabooks.co.uk
- www.arcadiabooks.co.uk

**Contact** Managing Director, Gary Pulsifer; Publishing Director, Daniela de Groote
**Established** 1996
**Imprint(s)** BlackAmber
 Bliss Books
 Eurocrime
**Insider Info** Catalogue available online.
**Non-Fiction** Publishes Autobiography, Biography, General Non-fiction titles on the following subjects:
 Memoirs, Travel.
**Submission Guidelines** Agented submissions only.
**Fiction** Publishes Ethnic, Gay/Lesbian, Literary, Mainstream/Contemporary, Multicultural, Short story collections, Suspense, Translation, European Crime Writing titles.
**Submission Guidelines** Agented submissions only.
**Recent Title(s)** *Back from Africa*, Corrine Hofmann (Autobiography, Bliss imprint); *The Locust Hunter*, Po Wah Lam (Fiction, BlackAmber imprint)
**Tips** Of the different imprints, Arcadia publishes fiction, translated world fiction, biography, memories, travel, and gay and gender studies. BlackAmber publishes multicultural literary fiction, non-fiction and translations. Bliss publishes popular best sellers, including biography and autobiography. Eurocrime publishes European crime writing. Arcadia Books do not consider poetry, plays, short stories, children's, teenage, science fiction, fantasy, horror, romance or self-help titles.

## Architectural Press
**The Boulevard, Langford Lane, Kidlington, Oxford, OX5 1GB**
- 01865 843000
- 01865 843010
- authorsupport@elsevier.com
- www.elsevier.com

**Parent Company** Elsevier Ltd (Science & Technology)
**Insider Info** Payment is via royalties. Catalogue and manuscript guidelines available online.
**Non-Fiction** Publishes Reference, Scholarly and Technical titles on the following subjects:
 Architecture, Building/Construction, Urban Design.
**Submission Guidelines** Accepts query with SAE with proposal package (including outline).
**Recent Title(s)** *Identity by Design*, Georgia Butina-Watson (Architecture)
**Tips** Architectural Press publishes technical, theoretical and practical books written by experts from around the globe. The list of titles covers the full range of topics within architecture, from new theory through to practical design guides, breaking new ground and aiding work and study. Architectural Press welcomes authors' proposals for books. The first step is to discuss the proposal with the relevant Publishing Editor. Check the website for in-depth submission guidelines and a full list of editorial contacts.

## Arcturus Foulsham
**The Publishing House, Bennetts Close, Cippenham, Slough, Berkshire, SL1 5AP**
- 01753 526769
- 01753 535003
- marketing@foulsham.com
- www.foulsham.com

**Parent Company** Foulsham Publishers
**Insider Info** Catalogue is free on request and available online.
**Non-Fiction** Pubilshes Children's/Juvenile, General Non-fiction, Illustrated, Reference and Self-help titles on he following subjects:
 Art/Architecture, Health/Medicine, History, Spirituality, Puzzles and Games, Practical Art and Manga, Real Crime.
**Submission Guidelines** Accepts proposal package (including outline, author biography, SAE, information on the market position of the book, including its competitors and its readership).
**Recent Title(s)** *The Complete Book of Ghosts: A Fascinating Exploration of the Spirit World from Animal Apparitions to Haunted Places* Paul Roland; *Smoking Sucks: Don't Let Your Child Become a Smoker*, Allen Carr
**Tips** Will not accept emailed submissions.

## The Arden Shakespeare
**High Holborn House, 50–51 Bedford Row, London, WC1R 4LR**
- 020 7067 2500
- 020 7067 2600
- margaret.bartley@thomson.com
- www.ardenshakespeare.com

**Parent Company** Thomson Learning (EMEA)

**Contact** Editors, Richard Proudfoot, Ann Thompson, David Scott Kastan
**Insider Info** Catalogue available online.
**Non-Fiction** Publishes Criticisms, Dictionaries of Quotations and Gift titles on Literary Criticism.
**Fiction** Publishes plays.
**Recent Title(s)** *Hamlet*, Ann Thompson and Neil Taylor

**Tips** Titles are aimed at teachers, scholars, students and general readers with an interest in Shakespeare's works. The Arden Shakespeare series was created by Methuen towards the end of the 19th Century. In 1995, The third series of The Arden Shakespeare was launched as an imprint. The publishers focus largely on the works of Shakespeare.

See Thomson Learning (EMEA) entry for further information.

## Argentum
**7 Greenland Street, London, NW1 0ND**
- 020 7284 7160
- 020 7845 4902
- www.aurumpress.co.uk

**Parent Company** Aurum Press
**Contact** Managing Director, Bill McCreadie; Consultant Editor, Eddie Ephraums (Argentum list, Photography).
**Insider Info** Catalogue is free on request and available online, or via an online request form. Manuscript guidelines are available by email.
**Non-Fiction** Publishes Coffee Table, General Non-fiction, How-to and Technical titles on Photography.
**Submission Guidelines** Accepts email with brief proposal in the first instance.

Submission details to: Eddie Ephraums at onephraums@uk2.net
**Recent Title(s)** *Working the Light*, Charlie Waite, Joe Cornish and David Ward (Illustrated Non-fiction)
**Tips** Argentum publishes high quality practical photography titless and is now recognised as a leading publisher for photography books.

## Arris Books
**12 Main Street, Adlestrop, Moreton in Marsh, Gloucestershire, GL56 0YN**
- 01608 659328
- 01608 659345
- info@arrisbooks.com/victoriama.huxley@btinternet.com
- www.arrisbooks.com

**Contact** Publishing Director, Victoria Huxley
**Established** 2003

**Insider Info** Submissions accompanied by SAE will be returned. Catalogue and manuscript guidelines available online.
**Non-Fiction** Publish General Non-fiction, Illustrated and Scholarly titles on the following subjects: Anthropology/Archaeology, Art/Architecture, Ethnic, Government/Politics, History, Language/Literature, Multicultural, Nature/Environment, Travel.
**Submission Guidelines** Accepts query with SAE with proposal package (including outline and one sample chapter). Do not email submissions.
**Fiction** Publishes Multicultural and Translated fiction titles.
**Submission Guidelines** Accepts query with SAE with proposal package (including outline and one sample chapter). Do not email submissions.
**Recent Title(s)** *Traveller's History of Poland*, John Radzilowski (Travel); *Traveller's Wine Guide to France*, Christopher Fielden and Jim Budd (Travel/Food and Drink/Culture)
**Tips** Titles aimed at travellers interested in world culture, not tourism. Despite having separate categories of history and politics, travel and world literature, Arris Books all follow the same thematic principles: 'One would need to travel, read the history of a country, as well as the literature to gain a genuine understanding of a people. Doing one of the three is never enough. It is very naive to think that one can truly understand a culture by reading an academic history book, or by going on a packaged holiday.' All submissions should reflect this principle.

## Arrow
**Random House, 20 Vauxhall Bridge Road, London, SW1V 2SA**
- 020 7840 8518
- 020 7233 6127
- arroweditorial@randomhouse.co.uk
- www.randomhouse.co.uk

**Parent Company** The Random House Group Ltd
**Contact** Publishing Director, Kate Elton
**Insider Info** Submissions accompanied by SAE will be returned. Catalogue available online, use advanced search to search by imprint.
**Non-Fiction** Publishes Autobiography, Biography and General Non-fiction titles.
**Submission Guidelines** Accepts proposal package (including outline, one sample chapter, SAE). Will accept artworks/images (send photocopies).
**Fiction** Publishes Mass-market paperback fiction titles.
**Submission Guidelines** Accepts proposal package (including outline, one sample chapter).

**Recent Title(s)** *Little Girl Lost*, Katie Flynn (Saga)

**Tips** No emailed submissions. Although unagented proposals are accepted, writers are recommended to approach agents with ideas first.

## Artech House
**46 Gillingham Street, London, SW1V 1AH**
- 020 7596 8750
- 020 7630 0166
- artech-uk@artechhouse.co.uk
- www.artechhouse.com

**Parent Company** Horizon House Publications Inc

**Contact** Commissioning Editor, Eric Willner

**Established** 1969

**Insider Info** Publish 65 titles per year. Payment is via royalty. Catalogue and manuscript guidelines available online.

**Non-Fiction** Publishes Reference, Scholarly, Technical and Textbook titles on the following subjects:
 Agriculture/Horticulture, Communications, Computers/Electronics, Science, Software, Nanotechnology, Bioinformatics/Biomedical Engineering.

**Submission Guidelines** Accepts query with SAE, or via email, with proposal package (including outline, one sample chapter, reference forms and details of equations/figures and your publishing history). You may also fill in the online submission form, or submit a completed manuscript.
 Submission details to: ewillner@artechhouse.co.uk

**Recent Title(s)** *ES3D: Electrostatic Field Solver for Multilayer Circuits*, Marija Nikolic, Antonije Djordevic and Milos Nikolic (Technical/Reference); *Information Warfare and Organizational Decision-Making*, Alexander Kott (Technical/Reference)

**Tips** Artech House is a leading publisher of high quality professional books with titles aimed at engineers and managers, as well as high technology professionals and students internationally. They accept practical and informed proposals, ideally from academic or industry professionals in the specified subject areas.

## Ashfield Press
**30 Linden Grove, Blackrock, Co. Dublin, Republic of Ireland**
- 00353 1 288 9808
- info@ashfieldpress.com
- www.ashfieldpress.com

**Contact** Director, Susan Waine

**Imprint(s)** Linden Press (Self-publishing)

**Insider Info** Catalogue available online.

**Non-Fiction** Publishes Autobiography, Biography, Cookbooks, General Non-fiction, Scholarly and Self-help titles on the following subjects:
 Art/Architecture, Cooking/Foods/Nutrition, History, Military/War, Regional, Travel, Irish folklore/ Irish history.

**Recent Title(s)** *Practical Parenting: An Irish Survival Guide*, Pat Rees (Guide/Parenting)

**Tips** Ashfield Press only publishes Irish non-fiction but, with sister company Linden Press, also offers various self-publishing services in Ireland, including proofreading and editing.

## Ashgate Publishing Group
**Gower House, Croft Road, Aldershot, Hampshire, GU11 3HR**
- 01252 331551
- info@ashgate.com, firstinitiallastname@ ashgate.com
- www.ashgate.com

**Contact** Publishers, Thomas Gray and John Smedley (History); Publisher, Erika Gaffney (Literary Studies to 17th Century, Women and Gender Studies); Publisher, Sarah Lloyd (Theology and Religious Studies); Publishing Director, Dymphna Evans (Social Sciences and Reference); Senior Commissioning Editor, Alison Kirk (Law and Legal Studies); Commissioning Editor, Guy Loft (Aviation)

**Established** 1967

**Imprint(s)** Gower
 Lund Humphries
 Ashgate

**Insider Info** Publishes 700 titles per year. Average lead time is between four and nine months. Catalogue and manuscript guidelines available online.

**Non-Fiction** Publishes Reference, Scholarly, Technical and Textbook titles on the following subjects:
 Art/Architecture, Business/Economics, Education, Ethnic, Government/Politics, History, Humanities, Language/Literature, Law, Music/Dance, Philosophy, Social Sciences, Sociology, and Aviation.
 \* The publishing programme is not centred around text books and journals but instead around ground breaking academic research publications, business practice guides and illustrated art books. Books published within the Ashgate programme are subject to peer review by recognised authorities in the field.

**Submission Guidelines** Accepts proposal package (including outline, table of contents, extent, illustration information, your publishing history, author biography, market research). Address proposals to the relevant commissioning editor (see contacts).

**Tips** Writers published within the Ashgate group are mostly experts in their fields and not necessarily career writers.

## Ashley Drake Publishing Ltd
**PO Box 733, Cardiff, CF14 7ZY**

- ☎ 07803 940867
- ☎ 0870 705 2582
- ✉ post@ashleydrake.com
- 🌐 www.ashleydrake.com

**Contact** Managing Director, Ashley Drake
**Established** 1994
**Imprint(s)** Welsh Academic Press
 Scandinavian Academic Press
 St. David's Press
 Welsh Educational Press
 Y Ddraig Fach (The Little Dragon)
**Insider Info** Publishes five titles per year. Receives approximately ten queries per year and ten manuscripts per year. Three per cent of books published are from first-time authors and 100 per cent of books published are from unagented authors. Payment is via net receipts. Average lead time is one year, with simultaneous submissions not accepted. Submissions accompanied by SAE will be returned. Aims to respond to queries within five days, proposals and manuscripts within one month. Catalogue is free on request, and available online or by email. Manuscript guidelines are available online.
**Non-Fiction** Publishes Autobiography, Biography, Scholarly and Textbook titles on the following subjects:
 Business/Economics, Education, Government/ Politics, History, Humanities, Language/Literature, Memoirs, Sports.
 * Welsh Academic Press and Scandinavian Academic Press focus on scholarly books; St. David's press is a trade imprint; Welsh Educational Press publishes educational books and Y Ddraig Fach has published children's books.
**Submission Guidelines** Accepts proposal package (including outline, one sample chapter, publishing history, author biography).
**Tips** Writers should ensure that their subject matter is relevant to what Ashley Drake publish by checking on their website. If your work is a departure from their usual editorial policy, do not submit your proposal.

## Ashmolean Museum Publications
**Ashmolean Museum, Beaumont Street, Oxford, OX1 2PH**

- ☎ 01865 278010
- ☎ 01865 278018
- ✉ publications@ashmus.ox.ac.uk
- 🌐 www.ashmolean.org

**Contact** Publications Manager, Declan McCarthy; Publications Deputy Manager, Emily Jolliffe; Photographic Services Orders Officer, Amanda Turner
**Insider Info** Catalogue available online.
**Non-Fiction** Publishes Children's/Juvenile, Gift books, Textbooks, Illustrated, Reference, Scholarly and Technical titles on the following subjects:
 Anthropology/Archaeology, Art/Architecture, Crafts, Education, History, Photography, Science.
**Recent Title(s)** *Pilgrimage: The Sacred Journey*, Ashmolean Museum (History)
**Tips** The Publications Department supports the Asmolean's mission to disseminate information and educate the public through its collection. Only books directly concerned with the museum's own collections are published. Most of the authors are staff at the Ashmolean Museum, although sometimes an academic from another institution is appointed to write a book, if they are experts on the particular subject. Authors are not generally encouraged to submit manuscripts.

## Atlantean Publishing
**38 Pierrot Steps, 71 Kursaal Way, Southend on Sea, Essex, SS1 2UY**

- ✉ atlanteanpublishing@hotmail.com
- 🌐 www.geocities.com/dj_tyrer/atlantean_pub

**Contact** David John Tyrer
**Insider Info** Authors are paid with a free copy of the publication. Does not accept simultaneous submissions. Submissions accompanied by SAE will be returned. Aims to respond to proposals within six weeks. Catalogue and author guidelines available online.
**Non-Fiction** Publishes General Non-fiction (Local interest) and How-to (Particularly on writing and publishing with small presses) titles.
 * It is Atlantean's intention to publish other non-fiction in the future, particularly on the topics of 'How To Be A Writer' and 'How To Start A Small Press Magazine'. All non-fiction is in the form of A5 booklets.
**Submission Guidelines** Submit proposal package by mail or email. Will review artworks/photographs as part of the proposal package. Include as A4 or A5

photocopies, or digital files as jpegs. Text should be single sided.

**Poetry** Publishes poetry booklets and single poet broadsheet style papers, *The Bards*.

**Submission Guidelines** Accepts queries with submit sample poems or complete manuscript. Submissions should either be by email or post, single sided pages only.

**Recent Title(s)** *Southend Living Legends*, Dee Gordon; *Dark Tower Volume 2*, Steve Sneyd

**Tips** Atlantean Publishing also publishes five magazines; *Monomyth*, *The Supplement*, *BARD*, *AWEN*, and *Garbaj*. Submissions should be made to the company overall, and are then published in whatever medium the editors feel most suitable. The company prefers first British serial rights, but will consider previously published work as long as it is declared. An SAE is recommended if you wish your work to be returned, but if you do not need it back you may include a return email address instead.

## Atlantic Books

**Ormond House, 26–27 Boswell Street, London, WC1N 2BP**

- 020 7269 1610
- 020 7430 0916
- enquiries@groveatlantic.co.uk
- www.groveatlantic.co.uk

**Parent Company** Grove/Atlantic Inc (see entry under European & International Publishers)

**Contact** Chairman, Morgan Entrekin; Managing Director/Publisher, Toby Mundy

**Established** 2000

**Insider Info** Publishing partner of *The Guardian* and *The Observer*.

**Non-Fiction** Publishes General Non-fiction titles on the following subjects:
History, Current affairs, Biography, Politics and Reference.

**Fiction** Publishes literary fiction.

**Tips** The Atlantic Books website is currently under construction, when completed check back for more information on the publisher.

## Atlas Press

**BCM Atlas Press, 27 Old Gloucester Street, London, WC1N 3XX**

- 020 7490 8742
- editor@atlaspress.co.uk
- www.atlaspress.co.uk

**Contact** Editor, Alastair Brotchie

**Established** 1983

**Insider Info** Catalogue available online.

**Non-Fiction** Publishes General Non-fiction and Scholarly titles on the following subjects:
Art/Architecture, History, Humanities, Language/Literature, Literary Criticism, Philosophy.

**Fiction** Publishes Experimental, Literary and Short Story Collection titles.

**Poetry** Publishes Poetry titles.

**Recent Title(s)** *Pataphysics*, Jean Baudrillard (Literary); *Circular Walks Around Rowley Hall*, Andrew Lanyon

**Tips** The writing published by Atlas Press is 'irrefutably modern, but never solemn; experimental, but not mere exercises in formalism; humorous but not (often) frivolous; it is extremist, demanding, delectable, sometimes appalling...' Proposals for publications must reflect this ethos.

## Atom

**Brettenham House, Lancaster Place, London, WC2E 7EN**

- 020 7911 8000
- 020 7911 8100
- atom.uk@twbg.co.uk
- www.atombooks.co.uk

**Parent Company** Little, Brown Book Group

**Contact** Publishing Director, Tim Holman

**Established** 2002

**Insider Info** Submissions accompanied by SAE will be returned. Aims to respond to proposals within 12 weeks. Catalogue available online.

**Fiction** Publishes Young Adult/Teenage fiction, including historical adventure, fantasy, science fiction and high school adventures.
\* Only able to read unsolicited submissions for novels in the science fiction genre. No other genres, short stories or poetry.

**Submission Guidelines** Send an outline and no more than 30 pages of double spaced text, and SAE.

**Recent Title(s)** *The Extraordinary and Unusual Adventures of Horatio Lyle*, Catherine Webb

**Tips** Writers are recommended to browse through some author websites for personal insights on writing for teenagers. No email submissions.

## Aureus Publishing Ltd

**Castle Court, Castle upon Alun, St. Brides Major, Vale of Glamorgan, CF32 0TN**

- 01656 880033
- 01656 880033
- info@aureus.co.uk
- www.aureus.co.uk

**Established** 1993

**Insider Info** Publishes two titles per year. Receives approximately 50 queries and 20 manuscripts per year. 80 per cent of books published are from first-time authors and 100 per cent of books published are from unagented authors. Payment is via royalty (on wholesale price) with 0.01 (Per £) minimum. Average lead time is one year, with simultaneous submissions accepted. Submissions accompanied by SAE will be returned. Aims to respond to queries and proposals within three days, and manuscripts within one week. Catalogue and manuscript guidelines are available online.

**Non-Fiction** Publishes Celebrity Autobiography and Celebrity Biography titles on the following subjects: Music/Dance, Sports, Entertainment.

**Submission Guidelines** Accepts query with SAE, or via preferably by email, with proposal package (including outline and SAE) and artworks/images (send digital files as jpegs). Synopsis should be no more than 250 words. If Aureus Publishing is interested then further material will be requested.

**Recent Title(s)** *Coghlan and Quo*, Steven Myatt (Rock Biography)

**Tips** Readership is generally males in their 30s. Prospective authors are expected to thoroughly know their subject. If the book has little sales value, and the author is willing to take the risk, then Aureus Publishing will consider taking a subsidy published book.

## Aurora Metro Publications

**2 Oriel Court, The Green, Twickenham, TW2 5AG**

- 020 8898 4488
- 020 8898 0735
- info@aurorametro.com
- www.aurorametro.com

**Contact** Publisher, Cheryl Robson (Drama, Fiction, Biography)

**Established** 1989

**Imprint(s)** Amp Books

**Insider Info** Publishes eight titles per year. Receives approximately 100 queries and 25 manuscripts per year. Ten per cent of books published are from first-time authors and 50 per cent of books published are from unagented authors. 20 per cent of books published are author-subsidy published, based on funding available from the Arts Council. Payment is via royalty (on retail price) or outright purchase. Average lead time is one year, with simultaneous submissions accepted. Submissions will not be returned. Aims to respond to queries within ten days, proposals within four months, and manuscripts within six months. Catalogue is free on request, or available by email.

**Non-Fiction** Publishes Biography, Children's, Cookbooks, General Non-fiction, Humour, Illustrated and Reference titles on the following subjects: Business/Economics, Contemporary Culture, Cooking/Foods/Nutrition, Creative Non-fiction, Education, Ethnic, Gay/Lesbian, History, Humanities, Language/Literature, Multicultural, Music/Dance, Translation, Women's Issues/Studies, Young Adult.

**Submission Guidelines** Accepts proposal package (including outline, synopsis, three sample chapters, author biography, reviews, your publishing history and clips) and artworks/images (send photocopies).

**Fiction** Publishes Adventure, Erotica, Ethnic, Experimental, Fantasy, Feminist, Gay/Lesbian, Gothic, Historical, Horror, Humour, Children's, Literary, Mainstream/Contemporary, Multicultural, Multimedia, Mystery, Plays, Regional, Romance, Science Fiction, Suspense, Translation and Young Adult titles.

**Submission Guidelines** Accepts proposal package (including outline, synopsis, three sample chapters, author biography and reviews).

**Recent Title(s)** *Theatre for Children*, Stuart Bennett (Theatre History); *Coming Back*, David Hill (Young Adult)

**Tips** Aurora Metro specialises in theatre and play scripts, and often seeks subsidies from the Arts Council for projects that fall within their funding criteria, e.g. translations.

## Aurum Press

**7 Greenland Street, London, NW1 0ND**

- 020 7284 7160
- 020 7485 4902
- editorial@aurumpress.co.uk
- www.aurumpress.co.uk

**Contact** Managing Director, Bill McCreadie; Editorial Director, Graham Coster; Consultant Editor, Eddie Ephraums (Photography - Argentum).

**Established** 1976

**Imprint(s)** Argentum
Jacqui Small

**Insider Info** Publishes 75 titles per year. Catalogue and manuscript guidelines are available online.

**Non-Fiction** Publishes Biography, General Non-fiction, Gift books, Illustrated and Reference titles on the following subjects: Art/Architecture, Health/Medicine, History, Military/War, Music/Dance, Sports, Travel, Current affairs, Film, Walking guides.

**Submission Guidelines** Accepts queries by email.

**Recent Title(s)** *Moveable Feasts (The Secret Journey Of The Things We Eat)*, Sarah Murray (Non-fiction, Topical).

**Tips** Aurum Press is a medium sized independent publishing company that has built a reputation for topical, original and critically-acclaimed non-fiction. Aurum Press also publishes titles alongside alliances such as Country Life and the National Trust for Scotland, as well as successfully collaborating with The Guardian and the Daily Telegraph.

## Austin & Macauley Publishers
**25 Canada Square, Canary Wharf, London, E14 5LB**
- 020 7038 8212
- 020 7038 8312
- editors@austinmacauley.com
- www.austinmacauley.com

**Contact** General Manager, Alan Forster; Managing Editors, Annette Longman and Brenda Barclay
**Established** 2005
**Insider Info** Publishes 25 titles per year. Authors paid by royalty, biannually. Aims to respond to queries and proposals within three weeks. Catalogue and author guidelines available online.
**Non-Fiction** Publishes Autobiography, Biography, General Non-fiction, Textbooks, Reference and Scholarly titles on the following subjects:
Business/Economics, Computers/Electronics, Contemporary Culture, Education, Government/Politics, History, Language/Literature, Memoirs, Military/War, Music/Dance, Religion, Sociology, Sports, World Affairs.
**Submission Guidelines** Accepts query with SAE. Submit proposal package (including outline, four sample chapters and SAE).
**Fiction** Publishes Horror, Humour, Literary, Military/War, Multimedia, Religious, Romance, Suspense, Crime and Women's fiction.
  * Does not consider or accept poetry, short stories or screenplays.
**Submission Guidelines** Accepts query with SAE. Submit proposal package (including outline, four sample chapters and SAE).
**Recent Title(s)** *Many Crosses*, Natalie Singer (Novel)
**Tips** Austin & Macauley is a publishing house dealing with the publication of books of current interest and impact. The Company is developing its publishing lists of the work of both younger and older authors. Austin Macauley is actively looking for established and new writers in a wide range of genres. It is particularly seeking authors for the expanding educational list. This encompasses a wide range of subjects, including computer studies and the internet.

## Australian Consolidated Press
**10 Scirroco Close, Moulton Park Office Village, Northampton, Northamptonshire, NN3 6AP**
- 01604 642200
- 01604 642300
- books@acpuk.com
- www.australian-womens-weekly.co.uk

**Insider Info** Catalogue is available online.
**Non-Fiction** Publishes General Non-fiction and How-to titles on the following subjects:
Cooking, Craft & Home, Foods, Gardening, Health & Nutrition, International Cuisine.
**Recent Title(s)** *Cheap Eats,* Australian Women's Weekly (Cooking); *Kid's Cooking,* Australian Women's Weekly (Cooking).
**Tips** Specialists in innovative cooking and food preparation books. New titles are often commissioned in-house. Also publishes some craft, health and gardening titles for an international market.
ACP Books UK distributes the *Australian Women's Weekly Cookbook* series throughout Europe and the Middle East.

## Authentic Media
**9 Holdom Avenue, Bletchley, Milton Keynes, MK1 1QR**
- 01908 364213
- 01908 648952
- info@authenticmedia.co.uk
- www.authenticmedia.co.uk

**Contact** Editor, Charlotte Huback
**Established** 1962
**Imprint(s)** Authentic Lifestyle
Paternoster Press
**Insider Info** Publishes 50 titles per year. Catalogue available online.
**Non-Fiction** Publishes Audio cassettes, Autobiography, Biography, Children's, General Non-fiction, Gift books, Illustrated books, Multimedia, e-books/i-books and Scholarly titles on the following subjects:
Alternative Lifestyles, Child Guidance/Parenting, Religion, Spirituality.
**Fiction** Publishes Juvenile, Multimedia, Religious, Spiritual and Young Adult titles.
**Recent Title(s)** *I'm Dying to Tell You*, Neil Hood (Religious); *Christmas by Candlelight*, David Thomson (Religious)
**Tips** Publishes Christian books to help all types of Christians, wherever they are on their spiritual journey. Welcomes unsolicited manuscripts or synopsis submissions for fiction or non-fiction, sent

by post or email to the Editor. Does not publish poetry.

## Autumn Publishing

**Appledram Barns, Birdham Road, Chichester, West Sussex, PO20 7EQ**

☎ 01243 531660
🖷 01243 774433
✉ autumn@autumnpublishing.co.uk
🌐 www.autumnpublishing.co.uk

**Contact** Editorial Director, Lyn Coutts
**Established** 1976
**Insider Info** Publishes 200 titles per year. Submissions will not be not returned. Catalogue available online.
**Non-Fiction** Publishes Children's, Illustrated books and Children's activity books.
**Fiction** Publishes Juvenile and Picture books.
**Recent Title(s)** *Bumper Star Learning Diploma*, Autumn; *Bath Time Books*, Autumn
**Tips** Titles aimed at giving children the chance to enjoy learning while they play. The creative teams work hard to ensure that the books are at the forefront of current trends and that the range is always fresh and vibrant. Focuses on younger childrens' and infants activity books, which are often in high demand.

## Award Publications

**The Old Riding School, The Welbeck Estate, Worksop, Nottinghamshire, S80 3LR**

☎ 01909 478170
🖷 01909 484632
✉ info@awardpublications.co.uk
🌐 www.awardpublications.co.uk

**Established** 1972
**Insider Info** Catalogue available online. Manuscript guidelines available online.
**Non-Fiction** Publishes Children's and Reference titles on the following subjects:
 Crafts, Creative Non-fiction, Education, Entertainment/Games.
**Submission Guidelines** Accepts query with SAE/proposal package (including outline, one to two sample chapters and SAE) and artwork/images via email or post.
**Fiction** Publishes Juvenile, Picture books, Religious, Short story collections and General children's titles.
**Submission Guidelines** Accepts query with SAE/proposal package (including outline, one to two sample chapters and SAE).

**Recent Title(s)** *My Own Picture Dictionary; More Adventures from Black Pony Inn,* Christine Pulleir-Thompson
**Tips** Titles aimed at children and infants, and parents. Always on the lookout, particularly for new illustrators and designers, so please send samples by post or email.

## Baillière Tindall

**32 Jamestown Road, Camden Town, London, NW1 7BY**

☎ 020 7424 4200
🖷 020 7482 2293
✉ m.ging@elsevier.com
🌐 www.intl.elsevierhealth.com/bt

**Parent Company** Elsevier Ltd (Health Sciences)
**Established** 1869
**Insider Info** Royalties paid. Catalogue available online. Manuscript guidelines available online.
**Non-Fiction** Publishes Multimedia, Scholarly, Technical, Textbook, Journal and Reference titles on the following subjects:
 Education, Health/Medicine, Care/Nursing, Midwifery.
**Submission Guidelines** Submission details to: c.makepeace@elsevier.com
**Recent Title(s)** *Foundations of Nursing Practice*, Chris Brooker and Anne Waugh (Nursing)
**Tips** The longest established publisher for all aspects of the nursing and midwifery professions. Baillière Tindall have always held the needs of nurses paramount, and have established a tradition of 'books for nurses, by nurses'. Baillière Tindall also publishes the renowned *Baillière's Best Practice & Research* series of journals. To submit a proposal to Baillière Tindall, fill in and return a Proposal Form, available on the website. Alternatively, authors may contact the Publishing Director or Editor prior to submission to discuss the proposal.

## Bantam Press

**61–63 Uxbridge Road, London, W5 5SA**

☎ 020 8579 2652
🖷 020 8579 5479
✉ info@transworld-publishers.co.uk
🌐 www.booksattransworld.co.uk

**Parent Company** Transworld Publishers
**Insider Info** Catalogue available online. Manuscript guidelines not available.
**Non-Fiction** Publishes General Non-fiction titles on the following subjects:
 Diet and Healthy eating.
**Submission Guidelines** Agented submissions only.

**Fiction** Publishes Historical, Mainstream/Contemporary, Military/War, Mystery, Romance and Suspense titles.
**Submission Guidelines** Agented submissions only.
**Recent Title(s)** *The F2 Diet*, Audrey Eyton; *The Chemistry Of Death*, Simon Beckett.
**Tips** Bantam Press publishes hardbacks only.

## The Barddas Society
**Pen-rhiw, 71 Ffordd Pentrepoeth, Treforys, Abertawe, Cymru, SA6 6AE**
✆ 01792 772636
✆ 01792 792829
**Non-fiction** Publishes Biography and General Non-fiction titles on the following subjects: Literature, Literary Criticism, Literary History.
* All titles are related to Welsh poetry.
**Poetry** * Publishes Welsh Poetry collections and anthologies.
**Recent Title(s)** *Paradwys*, Wiliam Owen Roberts
**Tips** The Barddas Society publishes an annual journal of poetry as well as books relating to Welsh poetry. It has produced over a hundred different titles, mainly focusing on poetry, literary criticism, literary history and biographies of well-known poets.

## Bardfield Press
**The Bardfield Centre, Great Bardfield, Essex, CM7 4SL**
✆ 01371 811309
✆ 01371 811393
✉ info@mileskelly.net
🌐 www.mileskelly.net
**Parent Company** Miles Kelly Publishing Ltd
**Non-Fiction** Publishes Children's titles.
**Submission Guidelines** Please do not send any unsolicited manuscripts.
**Fiction** Publishes Children's titles.
**Submission Guidelines** Please do not send any unsolicited manuscripts.
**Tips** An imprint of Miles Kelly Publishing focused specifically on children's books with a mass market appeal.

## Barefoot Books Ltd
**124 Walcot St, Bath, Somerset, BA1 5BG**
✆ 01225 322400
✆ 01225 322499
✉ info@barefootbooks.co.uk
🌐 www.barefootbooks.com
**Contact** Editor in Chief, Tessa Strickland (Picture Books, Young Fiction)

**Established** 1993
**Insider Info** Publishes 16 titles per year, 15 per cent of books published are from first-time authors and 75 per cent of books published are from unagented authors. Payment is via royalty (on wholesale price) with 0.025 (per £) minimum and 0.05 (per £) maximum. Advance offered is variable. Average lead time is over 18 months, with simultaneous submissions accepted. Submissions accompanied by SAE will be returned. Aims to respond to queries within eight weeks. Catalogue is free on request, and available online. Manuscript guidelines are available online.
**Non-Fiction** Publishes Cookbooks, Gift, Illustrated and Self-help titles on the following subjects: Multicultural, Nature/Environment, Spirituality, Travel.
**Submission Guidelines** Accepts query with SAE, or completed manuscript.

## Barny Books
**The Cottage, Hough on the Mill, Grantham, Lincolnshire, NG32 2BB**
✆ 01400 250246
✆ 01400 251737
✉ barnybooks@hotmail.com
🌐 www.barnybooks.biz
**Contact** Managing Director, Molly Burkett
**Established** 1980
**Insider Info** Catalogue available online. Too small to accept unsolicited manuscripts. Manuscript guidelines not available.
**Non-Fiction** Publishes Children's/Juvenile, Illustrated books and General Non-fiction titles on the following subjects: Cooking/Foods/Nutrition, Health /Medicine, History, Hobbies, Military/War.
**Submission Guidelines** Accepts query with SAE.
**Fiction** Publishes Historical, Juvenile, Military/War and Young Adult titles.
**Submission Guidelines** Accepts query with SAE.
**Recent Title(s)** *Enjoying Life*, Sue Ricks (Health/Spirituality); *Operation Firewall*, Glenda Abramson (Military)
**Tips** Aims to help and support writers from writing a book, through to publication. The writer is taken through the process of getting a book into print, advising how their book would look best and discussing the best places to sell their end product. This process can also include translation where the author's first language is not English, and help for those who are dyslexic, handicapped or the elderly. Although they cannot accept any unsolicited manuscripts due to their small size, Barny Books

does offer professional critiquing and editing services, as well as some self-publishing facilities.

## Barrington Stoke
**18 Walker Street, Edinburgh, EH3 7LP**
- 0131 225 4113
- 0131 225 4140
- barrington@barringtonstoke.co.uk
- www.barringtonstoke.co.uk

**Contact** Fiona Brown
**Established** 1998
**Insider Info** Catalogue available online or with SAE. Manuscript guidelines not available.
**Non-Fiction** Publishes Children's, How-to, Reference, Scholarly, Textbook and Self-help titles for teachers or parents of struggling readers on the following subjects:
Child Guidance/Parenting, Guidance, Education, Young Adult.
**Submission Guidelines** Please note that we are unable to accept unsolicited manuscripts.
Submission details to: fiona.brown@barringtonstoke.co.uk
**Fiction** Publishes Juvenile, Picture books, Short story collections, and Young Adult titles.
**Submission Guidelines** Please note that we are unable to accept unsolicited manuscripts.
**Recent Title(s)** *Primary Spelling Dictionary*, Christine Maxwell and Julia Rowlandson (Children's reference); *Cold Keep*, James Lovegrove (Children's fantasy)
**Tips** Titles aimed at children/young adults (struggling readers), children with dyslexia or a learning difficulty. Texts must be subtly adapted, so that these children do not feel patronised or short changed. Accessible language, a fast moving and unambiguous plot and clear presentation are essential.

## Batsford
**151 Freston Road, London, W10 6TH**
- 020 7314 1400
- 020 7314 1594
- krichardson@anovabooks.com
- www.chrysalisbooks.co.uk/imprint/batsford

**Parent Company** Anova Books Company Ltd
**Contact** Kristy Richardson (Submissions)
**Established** 1843
**Insider Info** Catalogue available online.
**Non-fiction** Publishes General and Illustrated titles on the following subjects:
Embroidery and Textiles, Chess, Heritage, Horticulture, Fashion and Design.

**Recent Title(s)** *Kasparov's Fighting Chess 1999-2005*, Tibor Károlyi and Nick Aplin (Chess/Non-fiction); *Delphiniums*, David and Shirley Bassett (Gardening)
**Tips** Titles are aimed at serious enthusiasts and professionals in many hobbyist areas.

## BBC Active
**Edinburgh Gate, Harlow, Essex, CM20 2JE**
- 01279 623623
- 01279 414130
- emma.shackleton@pearson.com
- www.bbcactive.com

**Parent Company** Pearson Education
**Contact** Editor, Emma Shackleton
**Insider Info** Catalogue and manuscript guidelines are available online.
**Non-Fiction** Publishes Multimedia, Scholarly and Textbooks titles on the following subjects:
Education, Home Learning, Language/Literature.
**Submission Guidelines** Accepts proposal package (including synopsis, sample chapters, market research, your publishing history and author biography).
**Recent Title(s)** *Get Into Spanish*, BBC Active (Language/Multimedia)
**Tips** BBC Active publishes learning resources for children and adults, at home, school and college. The imprint has developed a wide range of innovative and interactive ways of learning to suit all styles with DVDs, CD-ROMs and online products. Resource cover the school curriculum and adult learning across modern foreign languages, plus a variety of other skills.

## BBC Books
**Random House, 20 Vauxhall Bridge Road, London, SW1V 2SA**
- 020 7840 8400
- 020 7233 8791
- emarketing@randomhouse.co.uk
- www.randomhouse.co.uk

**Parent Company** The Random House Group Ltd
**Insider Info** Catalogue available online.
**Non-Fiction** Publishes Cookbooks, Gift books, Illustrated books, Television tie-ins and Reference titles covering a wide range of subjects, including Science fiction.
**Submission Guidelines** Submit proposal package (including outline, one sample chapter, SAE) and artworks/images (send photocopies).
**Fiction** Publishes Television tie-in titles.
**Recent Title(s)** *Low GI Vegetarian Cookbook*, Rose Elliot

**Tips** The vast majority of BBC Books are a direct non-fiction spin-offs from BBC televsion programmes, although not all. There are a few fiction books published, again television tie-ins, such as *Doctor Who* novels.

See The Random House Group Entry.

## BBC Children's Books
**80 Strand, London, WC2R ORL**
- 020 7010 3000
- 020 7010 6060
- customer.service@penguin.co.uk
- www.penguin.co.uk

**Parent Company** Penguin Group UK
**Contact** Managing Director, Sally Floyer
**Established** 2004
**Insider Info** Catalogue available online.
**Non-Fiction** Publishes Children's, General Non-fiction, Illustrated, Novelty and Television tie-in titles.
**Submission Guidelines** Agented submissions only.
**Fiction** Publishes Children's Television tie-in titles.
**Submission Guidelines** Agented submissions only.
**Recent Title(s)** *Lunar Jim: The Lunar Fluffies*, Lunar Jim Activity Book
**Tips** BBC Children's books publishes illustrated titles ranging from pre-school to older children. Most books and products are linked to BBC children's programmes. No unsolicited submissions.

## BC Decker
**32 Jamestown Road, Camden Town, London, NW1 7BY**
- 020 7424 4200
- 020 7482 2293
- m.ging@elsevier.com
- www.intl.elsevierhealth.com/bcdecker

**Parent Company** Elsevier Ltd (Health Sciences)
**Established** 1981
**Insider Info** Royalties paid. Catalogue and manuscript guidelines available online.
**Non-Fiction** Publishes Illustrated, Multimedia, Reference, Scholarly, Textbook and Technical titles on the following subjects:
 Education, Health/Medicine, Science, Dentistry, Oncology.
**Submission Guidelines** Use the online Proposal Form.
 Submission details to: t.horne@elsevier.com
**Recent Title(s)** *Herb-drug Interactions In Oncology*, Peter A. Cassileth (Medical/Oncology)
**Tips** BC Decker publishes a range of material in medicine, health science and dentistry. The company is the official publisher of the American Cancer Society and publishes a leading oncology list. Virtually all BC Decker books include, at no additional cost, a CD-ROM with full text and images. To submit a proposal to BC Decker, fill in and return a Proposal Form, available on the website. Alternatively authors may contact the Publishing Director or Editor prior to submission, to discuss the proposal.

## Beautiful Books
**117 Sugden Road, London, SW11 5ED**
- 020 7738 2428
- 020 3070 0764
- simon@beautiful-books.co.uk
- www.beautiful-books.co.uk

**Contact** Publisher, Simon Petherick
**Established** 2005
**Imprint(s)** Bloody Books
 Young Travellers Club
 Burning House
**Insider Info** Publishes 15 titles per year. Receives 500 queries and 300 manuscripts per year. 50 per cent of books published are from first-time authors and 90 per cent of books published are from unagented authors. Payment via royalty (on wholesale price) with 0.15 (per £) minimum and 0.20 (per £) maximum, or outright purchase. Advance offered is from £1–£1,000. Average lead time is eight months, with simultaneous submissions accepted. Submissions accompanied by SAE will be returned. Aims to respond to queries within seven days, proposals within 18 days and manuscripts within two months. Catalogue is free on request, and available online, or by email. Manuscript guidelines are available online.
**Non-Fiction** Publishes Children's, General Non-Fiction, Gift and Illustrated titles on the following subjects:
 Contemporary Culture, Gardening, Travel, Young Adult.
 * Children's travel guides are published under the Young Travellers Club imprint (see www.youngtravellersclub.co.uk).
**Submission Guidelines** Accepts query with SAE, or via email, and artworks/images (send photocopies or digital files as jpegs). All proposals will be considered on their merits.
 Submission details to: submissions@beautiful-books.co.uk
**Fiction** Publishes Confession, Erotica, Gay/Lesbian, Horror, Humour, Literary, Mainstream/Contemporary, Picture books, Translation and Young Adult titles.

* Horror fiction is published under the Bloody Books imprint whilst contemporary fiction will be published under the new Burning House imprint.

**Submission Guidelines** Accepts query with SAE or via email.

Submission details to: submissions@beautiful-books.co.uk

**Recent Title(s)** *Going Where My Pig Is Headed*, Sara Sharpe (Travel literature); *The Last Good Man*, Patience Swift (Literary fiction)

**Tips** When submitting to Beautiful Books be clear and patient, and give as much information about yourself as you can.

## Benjamin Cummings
**Edinburgh Gate, Harlow, Essex, CM20 2JE**
- 01279 623623
- 01279 414130
- www.pearsoned.co.uk/imprints/benjamincummings

**Parent Company** Pearson Education

**Insider Info** Catalogue and manuscript guidelines are available online.

**Non-Fiction** Publishes Reference, Scholarly and Textbook titles on the following subjects:
Anatomy, Biology, Health/Medicine, Physiology, Science.

**Submission Guidelines** Accepts proposal package (including synopsis, sample chapters, market research, your publishing history and author biography).

**Recent Title(s)** *Human Anatomy and Physiology Laboratory Manual (8th Edition)*, Elaine Marieb and Susan Mitchell (Anatomy/Physiology)

**Tips** Benjamin Cummings specialises in the areas of anatomy and physiology, biology, health, kinesiology, and microbiology. Work is published in both printed and electronic formats. See the website for a full list of submissions contacts.

## Berghahn Books
**3 Newtec Place, Magdalen Road, Oxford, OX4 1RE**
- 01865 250011
- 01865 250056
- publisher@berghahnbooks.com
- www.berghahn.com

**Contact** Publisher/Editor in Chief, Marion Berghahn; Managing Editor, Mark Stanton

**Established** 1994

**Insider Info** Publishes 90 titles per year. Catalogue and author guidelines available online. Prospective authors may download a copy of the 'New Book

Outline' to be filled out and faxed, or emailed as an attachment to our New York or Oxford offices.

**Non-Fiction** Publishes General Non-fiction, e-books and Scholarly titles on the following subjects:
Anthropology/Archaeology, Education, Government/Politics, History, Nature/Environment, Regional, Travel, World Affairs, Migration studies.

**Submission Guidelines** Accepts query with SAE/proposal package (including outline, sample chapter(s)). Use online 'New Book Outline' forms.

**Recent Title(s)** *Nationalism's Bloody Terrain*, George Baca (Anthropology); *State Practices and Zionist Images*, David A. Wesley (Anthropology)

**Tips** Thanks to our strong transatlantic position and our close links to Continental Europe, we see it as very important to further the dialogue between the European and the American scholar. Check the writers' guidelines on the website for style guides and publicity details.

## Berg Publishers
**1st Floor, Angel Court, 81 St. Clements Street, Oxford, OX4 1AW**
- 01865 245104
- 01865 791165
- enquiry@bergpublishers.com
- www.bergpublishers.com

**Contact** Editorial Director, Tristan Palmer (Culture and Media studies, Film); Senior Commissioning Editor, Kathleen May (Food, History and Politics); Assistant Editor, Hannah Shakespeare (Fashion & Dress, Anthropology); Publishing Assistant, Louise Butler (General Enquiries)

**Established** 1983

**Insider Info** Simultaneous submissions not accepted. Submissions accompanied by SAE will be returned. Catalogue and manuscript guidelines available online.

**Non-Fiction** Publishes General Non-fiction, Illustrated book, Reference and Scholarly titles on the following subjects:
Agriculture/Horticulture, Alternative Lifestyles, Anthropology/Archaeology, Art/Architecture , Cooking/Foods/Nutrition, Crafts, Entertainment/Games, Gay/Lesbian, Government/Politics, History, Hobbies, House and Home, Humanities, Language/Literature, Literary Criticism, Philosophy, Sociology, Sports, Women's Issues/Studies, World Affairs.

**Submission Guidelines** Accepts query with SAE/proposal package (including outline, sample chapter(s), SAE, your publishing history, and author biography) and artworks/images (send transparencies, digital files and other media as jpegs).

Submission details to: tpalmer@bergpublishers.com

**Recent Title(s)** *Barren States*, Carrie B. Douglass; *Shoes: A History of Sandals to Sneakers*, Giorgio Riello and Peter McNeill (eds.)

**Tips** Berg is an international independent publisher committed to innovative ideas in visual and material culture, including fashion and textiles, cultural/media studies, film, art and design, food, sport and anthropology. Send submission proposals in the post to the relevant editor enclosing an SAE. Be sure to be check the submission guidelines on the website thoroughly prior to posting a proposal.

## Berlitz Publishing

**APA Publications, 58 Borough High Street, London, SE1 1XF**

- 020 7403 0284
- 020 7403 0290
- www.berlitzpublishing.com

**Parent Company** Apa Publications (The Langenscheidt Publishing Group)

**Contact** Managing Director, Jeremy Westwood (Apa Publications)

**Established** 1970

**Insider Info** Catalogue is available online.

**Non-Fiction** Publishes Audio cassettes, Guidebooks, Multimedia and Reference titles on the following subjects:
 Travel guides and maps, Language Learning/Home Study, Phrasebooks, Travel packs, Specialist travel books.

**Submission Guidelines** Does not accept unsolicited material.

**Recent Title(s)** *French: Berlitz Concise Dictionary*, Berlitz Publishing (Language/Phrasebook); *Athens: Berlitz Pocket Guide,* Berlitz Publishing (Travel guide)

## Bernard Babani (Publishing) Ltd

**The Grampians, Shepherds Bush Road, London, W6 7NF**

- enquiries@babanibooks.com
- www.babanibooks.com

**Contact** Company Director, Michael Babani

**Established** 1942

**Insider Info** Catalogue is available online.

**Non-Fiction** Publishes How-to, Reference, Technical titles on the following subjects:
 Computing, Electronics, Radio, Robotics.

**Recent Title(s)** *Getting More from Your Microsoft XBOX 360*, A. Edney (Computing)

**Tips** Bernard Babani has only fairly recently added books on robotics to its list, it has been specialising in computer books since 1980. Prior to that the company only published radio and electronics titles. The publisher only commissions specialist expert authors for its titles.

## Between the Lines

**9 Woodstock Road, London, N4 3ET**

- 020 8374 5526
- 020 8374 5736
- btluk@aol.com
- www.interviews-with-poets.com

**Contact** Editor, Peter Dale; Editor, J.D. McClatchy; Editor, Philip Hoy; Editorial Assistant, Ryan Roberts

**Established** 1998

**Insider Info** Catalogue is available online.

**Non-Fiction** Publishes Literary interviews.
 * Interviews are around 10–20 lines and with well known poets and literary figures. They are often accompanied by career sketches, bibliographies, poems, quotations from critics and reviewers, and galleries of photographs.

**Poetry** Publishes Poetry titles.

**Tips** A list of past and present interviewers and interviewees is available on the website.

## BFI Publishing

**21 Stephen Street, London, W1T 1LN**

- 020 7957 4789
- 020 7636 2516
- www.bfi.org.uk

**Parent Company** British Film Institute

**Contact** Head of Publishing, Rebecca Barden

**Insider Info** Catalogue and manuscript guidelines are available online.

**Non-Fiction** Publishes Illustrated books, Reference and Scholarly titles on the following subjects:
 Film Classics, Modern Classics, Television Classics, Screen Classics, Film Criticism/History/Theory, Filmmakers, US Film and Television, British and Irish Film and Television, World Directors, Television Media and Cultural Studies, New Media, Teaching Resources, Understanding the Moving Image.

**Submission Guidelines** Accepts proposal package (including outline, one to two sample chapters, author biography and market research).

**Recent Title(s)** *100 European Horror Films*, Steven Jay Schneider (Film)

**Tips** BFI Publishing is the publishing arm of the British Film Institute, publishing a wide range of books and educational materials on cinema/television, and related matters. Titles are aimed at primary and secondary school pupils, undergraduates and teachers, although many titles are also aimed at a broader audience with an informed interest in cinema and television.

## Birlinn Ltd

**West Newington House, 10 Newington Road, Edinburgh, EH9 1QS**

- 0131 668 4371
- 0131 668 4466
- info@birlinn.co.uk
- www.birlinn.co.uk

**Contact** Managing Editor, Hugh Andrew
**Established**
1992

**Imprint(s)** Birlinn Military and Adventure
John Donald Publishers
Polygon

**Insider Info** Publishes 90 titles per year. Receives approximately 50 queries and 25 manuscripts per year. Average lead time is 12 months with simultaneous submissions accepted. Catalogue is available online. Manuscript guidelines are not available.

**Non-Fiction** Publishes Biography, General Non-fiction, Gift books, Humour, Illustrated books, Reference, Textbooks and Scholarly titles. Anthropology/Archaeology, Art/Architecture, Creative Non-fiction, Education, History, Military/War, Nature/Environment, Regional, Religion, Sociology, Sports, Travel, Scottish interest.

**Fiction** Publishes Adventure, Historical, Humour, Military/War, Scottish fiction and Gaelic fiction titles.
**Poetry** Publish Classic Scottish Poetry titles.
**Recent Title(s)** *Isolation Shepherd*, Iain R. Thomson (Agriculture/Scottish); *Macbeth And All That*, Allan Burnett (Drama/History)
**Tips** Birlinn publish a range of books of Scottish interest, including books on history, archaeology, customs and traditions, travel and folklore, modern and classic Scottish poetry and fiction. Ideas or synopses for either fiction or non-fiction are welcomed, providing they relate to Scottish interest. Please do not send any unsolicited manuscripts.

## Biscuit Publishing

**PO Box 123, Washington, Newcastle upon Tyne, NE37 2YW**

- info@biscuitpublishing.com
- www.biscuitpublishing.com

**Contact** Managing Director, Brian Lister
**Established** 2000
**Insider Info** Catalogue is available online.
**Non-Fiction** Publishes General Non-fiction titles on the following subjects:

History, Regional, Local Interest.
**Fiction** Publishes Adventure, Historical, Literary and Short story collection titles.
**Poetry** Publishes poetry titles.
**Recent Title(s)** *Chasing Angels*, Sally Zignmond; *On New Street*, Biscuit/Anthology (Short Story Collection)
**Tips** Biscuit Publishing is one of the UK's newest independent publishing houses, it is dedicated to finding and publishing new, talented authors. Mainly fiction, some non-fiction, and very occasionally poetry is published. All publications are by Biscuit prize winners, or by selected authors approached and commissioned by Biscuit. Therefore, it is best to enter a competition with Biscuit first. Some competitions say that they will 'consider' publishing a book by the winner; Biscuit promises it.

## Bitter Lemon Press

**37 Arundel Gardens, London, W11 2LW**

- 020 7727 7927
- 020 7460 2164
- books@bitterlemonpress.com
- www.bitterlemonpress.com

**Contact** Managing Editor, Laurence Colchester
**Established** 2003
**Insider Info** Publishes six titles per year. Catalogue and manuscript guidelines are available online.
**Fiction** Publishes Crime, Thriller and Noir/Roman Noir titles.
 * Must be foreign writers/fiction from abroad.
**Submission Guidelines** Accepts query with SAE/proposal package (including outline and two sample chapters). Submissions email: lcolchester@bitterlemonpress.com
**Recent Title(s)** *Havana Blue*, Leonardo Padura (Crime)
**Tips** Bitter Lemon Press aim to bring readers high quality thrillers and other contemporary fiction from abroad. The publisher is dedicated to the crime genre and publish dark, sexy and often humorous novels that expose the seamier side of society. Bitter Lemon Press is pleased to receive submissions in the literary crime and thriller area, though submissions should be through a literary agent. Please include a synopsis and a sample chapter in the first submission.

## Black & White Publishing

**99 Giles Street, Edinburgh, EH6 6BZ**

- 0131 625 4500
- 0131 625 4501
- mail@blackandwhitepublishing.com

@ www.blackandwhitepublishing.com
**Contact** Managing Director, Campbell Brown
**Established** 1990
**Imprint(s)** Chroma
  Itchy Coo
**Insider Info** Submissions accompanied with SAE will be returned. Aims to respond to queries and manuscript queries within three months. Catalogue and manuscript guidelines are available online.
**Non-Fiction** Publishes Biography, Cookbooks, General Non-fiction, Crosswords/Quizzes and Humour titles on the following subjects: Cooking/Foods/Nutrition, Crafts, Entertainment/Games, Sports, Travel, True crime, Scottish interest.
**Submission Guidelines** Accepts query with SAE/proposal package (including outline, sample chapter(s), 30 pages maximum, contact details and SAE).
**Fiction** Publishes Historical, Juvenile, Crime, Children's Scottish language and Scottish interest titles.
**Submission Guidelines** Accepts query with SAE/proposal package (including outline, sample chapter(s), 30 pages maximum, contact details and SAE).
**Recent Title(s)** *The Wee Book of Weegie Wit and Wisdom*, Ian Black (Humour); *The Cat's Whispers*, Cat Harvey
**Tips** Titles are aimed at anyone, especially Scottish language speakers and children. Unsolicited manuscripts are accepted, but please do not send complete manuscripts. For fiction and non-fiction submissions, please send a covering letter, a brief synopsis and sample chapters of no more than 30 pages and always include an SAE. At present poetry submissions are not accepted.

## Black Ace Books

**PO Box 7547, Perth, Scotland, PH2 1AU**
@ 01821 642822
@ 01821 642101
@ www.blackacebooks.com
**Contact** Managing Director, Hunter Steele.
**Insider Info** Catalogue and manuscript guidelines are available online.
**Non-Fiction** Publishes Biography, Anthologies and General Non-fiction titles on the following subjects: Art/Architecture, History, Philosophy, Psychology.
**Fiction** Publishes Mainstream/Contemporary and Scottish interest titles.
**Recent Title(s)** *Caryddwen's Cauldron*, Paul Hilton (Novel)
**Tips** Black Ace Books are not currently accepting submissions from new authors. Black Ace Books also

offers some honest self-publishing services, although they do not recommend this route for fiction titles.

## Black Amber

**15–16 Nassau Street, London, W1W 7AB**
@ 020 7436 9898
@ 020 7436 9898
@ info@arcadiabooks.co.uk
@ www.arcadiabooks.co.uk
**Parent Company** Arcadia Books
**Contact** Commissioning Editor, Rosemary Hudson
**Insider Info** Catalogue is available online.
**Non-Fiction** Publishes General Non-fiction titles on Language/Literature.
**Submission Guidelines** Accepts agented submissions only.
**Fiction** Publishes Literary and Translation titles.
**Submission Guidelines** Accepts agented submissions only.
**Recent Title(s)** *Brixton Rock*, Alex Wheatle; *The Undertaker's Daughter*, Yvonne Brewster
**Tips** Black Amber place strong emphasis on multicultural literary fiction and non-fiction.

## Blackhall Publishing

**33 Carysfort Avenue, Blackrock, Co. Dublin, Republic of Ireland**
@ 00 353 1 278 5090
@ 00 353 1 278 4446
@ info@blackhallpublishing.com
@ www.blackhallpublishing.com
**Contact** Commissioning Editor, Elizabeth Brennan
**Established** 1997
**Insider Info** Publishes 15 titles per year. Receives approximately 30 queries and 20 manuscripts per year. 90 per cent of published books are from first-time authors and 100 per cent of published books are from unagented authors. 20 per cent of published books are author subsidy published. Payment is via royalty on net revenue. Average lead time is four months, with simultaneous submissions accepted. Submissions accompanied by SAE will be returned. Aims to respond to queries within 14 days, proposals within 31 days and manuscripts within six weeks. Catalogue is available online. Manuscript guidelines are available with an SAE, or by email.
**Non-Fiction** Publishes General Non-fiction, Scholarly, Self-help, Textbook and Legal Statutes titles on the following subjects:
  Business/Economics, Communications, Computers/Electronics, Counselling/Career, Education, Government/Politics, Health/Medicine, Law, Money/

Finance, Philosophy, Psychology, Religion, Social Sciences, Software.

**Submission Guidelines** Accepts query with SAE and artworks/images (send digital files as jpegs).

**Recent Title(s)** *Know Your Rights*, Andrew McCann (Legal Reference)

**Tips** Blackhall's readership consists of third level students, academics, businesses, management and marketing personnel, parents and the general public.

## Black Spring Press

**Curtain House, 134–146 Curtain Road, London, EC2A 3AR**

➊ 020 7613 3066

➊ 020 7613 0028

➋ enquiries@blackspringpress.co.uk

➌ www.blackspringpress.co.uk

**Parent Company** Dexter Haven Associates

**Contact** Publisher, Robert Hastings (Fiction, Biography, Film)

**Established** 1985

**Insider Info** Publishes five titles per year. Receives approximately 100 queries and 80 manuscripts per year. 20 per cent of published books are from first-time authors and ten per cent of published books are from unagented authors. Payment is via royalty (on wholesale price). Average lead time is eight months, with simultaneous submissions accepted. Submission accompanied by SAE will be returned. Aims to respond to queries within two weeks, proposals and manuscripts within three months, and all other enquiries within five weeks. Catalogue is free on request, and available online.

**Non-Fiction** Publishes Autobiography, Biography and General Non-fiction titles.

**Fiction** Publishes Mainstream/Contemporary and Classic fiction titles.

**Poetry** Publishes Contemporary and Classic poetry titles.

**Tips** Specialises in contemporary, cutting edge literature as well as reviving classic works.

## Blackstaff Press

**4c Heron Wharf, Sydenham Business Park, Belfast, BT3 9LE, Northern Ireland**

➊ 028 9045 5006

➊ 028 9046 6237

➋ info@blackstaffpress.com

➌ www.blackstaffpress.com

**Contact** Managing Editor, Patsy Horton

**Established** 1971

**Imprint(s)** Beeline

**Insider Info** Publishes 20 titles per year. Submissions accompanied by SAE will be returned. Catalogue is available online.

**Non-Fiction** Publishes Biography, Cookbooks, General Non-fiction, How-to, Illustrated books, Reference and Scholarly titles on the following subjects: Agriculture/Horticulture, Animals, Anthropology/Archaeology, Art/Architecture, Cooking/Foods/Nutrition, Crafts, Education, Government/Politics, Health/Medicine, History, Humanities, Music/Dance, Nature/Environment, Nostalgia, Photography, Religion, Sex, Travel, Women's Issues/Studies, Irish interest, Northern Ireland.

**Submission Guidelines** Will accept artwork/photos (send transparencies or digital files as jpegs).

**Fiction** Publishes Comic Books, Erotica, Romance, Short story collections and Irish fiction titles.

**Poetry** Publishes poetry titles.

**Recent Title(s)** *The Butterflies and Moths of Northern Ireland*, Robert Thompson and Brian Nelson; *Call My Brother Back*, Michael McLaverty

**Tips** Since being launched in Belfast with a book of political cartoons, Blackstaff Press have published over 650 titles, covering a wide range of subjects (mainly but not exclusively of Irish Interest), from history and politics, to fiction, poetry and humour. The publisher is always on the lookout for good new writing, but please bear in mind that many hundreds of submissions are received annually, and it can take quite a long time to reach a decision.

## Black Swan

**61–63 Uxbridge Road, London, W5 5SA**

➊ 020 8579 2652

➊ 020 8579 5479

➋ info@transworld-publishers.co.uk

➌ www.booksattransworld.co.uk

**Parent Company** Transworld Publishers

**Insider Info** Catalogue is available online. Manuscript guidelines are not available.

**Fiction** Publishes Historical, Humour, Mainstream/Contemporary, Mystery, Romance, and Suspense titles.

**Submission Guidelines** Accepts agented submissions only.

**Recent Title(s)** *Sweet Gum*, Jo-Ann Goodwin; *The Boy in the Striped Pyjamas*, John Boyne

**Tips** Please do not send any unsolicited manuscripts.

## Blackwell Publishing Ltd

9600 Garsington Road, Oxford, OX4 2DQ

- 01865 776868
- 01865 714591
- info@oxon.blackwellpublishing.com
- www.blackwellpublishing.com

**Parent Company** John Wiley & Sons Inc (see entry under European & International Publishers)

**Contact** President, Robert Campbell; CEO, Rene Olivieri; Publisher, Mary Banks (BMJ Books)

**Established** 2001

**Imprint(s)** BMJ Books
Blackwell Futura

**Insider Info** Publishes 650 titles per year, and 805 Journals per year. Catalogue and manuscript guidelines are available online.

**Non-Fiction** Publishes Journals, Multimedia, Reference, Scholarly and Textbook titles on the following subjects:
Agriculture and Aquaculture, Animal Science, Applied Arts, Architecture, Art History and Theory, Business, Construction, Economics, Finance and Accounting, Humanities, Property, Engineering and Technology, Law and Criminology, Life and Physical Sciences, Mathematics and Statistics, Medicine, Music, Nursing Health and Dentistry, Performing Arts, Social and Behavioural Studies, Veterinary Medicine.

**Submission Guidelines** Accepts proposal package (including outline, sample chapters, your publishing history and author biography) by email to the relevant editorial contact, details of which may be found on the website.

**Recent Title(s)** *Cardiovascular Hemodynamics for the Clinician*, George Stouffer eds. (Medicine); *Literary Theory: A Practical Introduction (2nd Edition)*, Michael Ryan (Literature)

**Tips** Blackwell Publishing is the world's largest independent society publisher. The BMJ Books imprint publishes self-help and alternative medicine titles, and Blackwell Futura specialises in the dissemination of clinical 'state of the art' information throughout the medical community, via publications and electronic media.

There is an extensive list of departmental editorial contacts published on the website, which potential authors should consult in order to direct their email to the appropriate person. There is also detailed information on how to prepare proposals and how books and authors are dealt with at Blackwell.

## Bliss Books

5–16 Nassau Street, London, W1W 7AB

- 020 7436 9898
- 020 7436 9898
- info@arcadiabooks.co.uk
- www.arcadiabooks.co.uk

**Parent Company** Arcadia Books

**Contact** Managing Director, Gary Pulsifer

**Insider Info** Catalogue is available online.

**Non-Fiction** Publishes Biography and General Non-fiction titles on Memoirs.

**Submission Guidelines** Agented submissions only.

**Recent Title(s)** *The Real Diana*, Colin Campell; *The White Masai*, Corinne Hofmann

**Tips** Bliss Books publish mainly popular bestsellers. The publisher does not publish any poetry, plays, short stories, children's, teenage, science fiction, fantasy, horror, romance, spirituality or self-help titles.

## Bloody Books

117 Sugden Road, London, SW11 5ED

- 020 7738 2428
- 020 3070 0764
- simon@beautiful-books.co.uk
- www.beautiful-books.co.uk

**Parent Company** Beautiful Books

**Contact** Publisher, Simon Petherick; Curator, Adèle Hartley

**Established** 2006

**Insider Info** Publishes four titles per year. Catalogue is available online.

**Fiction** Publishes Horror fiction titles.

**Submission Guidelines** Check website for latest submission guidelines.

**Recent Title(s)** *Read by Dawn Volume 1*, Various; *Classic Tales of Horror Volume 2*, Various

**Tips** The Bloody Books imprint is curated by Adèle Hartley, the Director of *Dead By Dawn*, Scotland's International Horror Film Festival, held annually in Edinburgh (see www.deadbydawn.co.uk).

## Bloomsbury Publishing Plc

36 Soho Square, London, W1D 3QY

- 020 7494 2111
- 020 7434 0151
- csm@bloomsbury.com
- www.bloomsbury.com

**Contact** Chairman/Chief Executive, Nigel Newton; Publishing Director (Book Division), Liz Calder (Fiction); Editorial Director, Sarah Odedina (Children's Books); Editor in Chief, Alexandra Pringle.

**Established** 1986

**Imprint(s)** A&C Black Publishers Ltd
Peter Collin Publishing Ltd
Berlin Verlag GmbH (German Division)
Bloomsbury USA ( US Division)
Walker & Company (US Division)

**Insider Info** Payment is via royalties. Aims to respond to proposals within three months. Catalogue and manuscript guidelines are available online.

**Non-Fiction** Publishes Audio cassettes, Autobiography, Biography, Children's/Juvenile, Cookbooks, General Non-fiction, Gift book, Humour, Illustrated books, Multimedia and Reference titles on the following subjects: Art/Architecture, Gardening, Health/Medicine, History, House and Home, Memoirs, Music/Dance, Photography, Psychology, Science, Sports, Travel, Exploration, Film.

**Submission Guidelines** Accepts proposal package (including outline, two sample chapters, and SAE). Please send postal submissions only.

**Fiction** Publishes Juvenile, Literary, Mainstream/Contemporary, Short story collections, Translation, Young Adult and Classics titles.

**Submission Guidelines** Accepts proposal package (including outline, two sample chapters and SAE). Please send postal submissions only.

**Poetry** Publishes Poetry titles.

**Recent Title(s)** *An Inconvenient Truth*, Al Gore; *If Minds Had Toes*, Lucy Eyre

**Tips** Bloomsbury is a major publisher, perhaps best known for its publishing phenomenon, J.K. Rowling's *Harry Potter* books. Bloomsbury, and its various divisions, publishes a wide range of adult and children's books, both fiction and non-fiction. Currently Bloomsbury is not accepting unsolicited submissions for children's titles. The adult division accepts book proposals, but it is rare that an unsolicited book will be published. The Bloomsbury website has a writers' area which holds a wealth of advice and links for aspiring authors. Aside from its UK imprints, Bloomsbury also has a division in America and owns the American publisher Walker & Company and the German company Berlin Verlag GmbH.

## Bluechrome
**PO Box 109, Portishead, Bristol, BS20 7ZJ**
- 07092 273360
- 07092 273357
- pr@bluechrome.co.uk
- www.bluechrome.co.uk

**Established** 2002

**Insider Info** Publishes 20 titles per year. Receives approximately 2,000 queries per year. Submissions accompanied by an SAE will be returned. Aims to respond to queries within 12 months. Catalogue available online.

**Non-Fiction** Publishes General Non-fiction (often with a literary or writing connection) on the following subjects: Creative Non-fiction, Sports, Travel, Writing, Publishing and Poetry guides.

**Submission Guidelines** Agented submissions only.

**Fiction** Publishes Experimental and Literary titles.

**Submission Guidelines** Agented submissions only.

**Poetry** Publish Poetry titles.

 * Bluechrome are not currently accepting poetry submissions, despite a substantial proportion of their list being poetry. However, this may change in the near future – check their website for details. The company have recently put in place an editorial board to oversee the editing and production of poetry titles, and to commission established poets to appear alongside new writers.

**Recent Title(s)** *Light's List*, John Light; *Dr. Mooze*, Eric Ryman; *American Voodoo*, Michael Paul Hogan

**Tips** Keep checking the website for current positions on the acceptance of unagented submissions. In the case that the position changes, Bluechrome advise that email is the best way of querying or submitting proposals.

## The Bodley Head
**61–63 Uxbridge Road, London, W5 5SA**
- 020 8231 6800
- 020 8231 6767
- childrenseditorial@randomhouse.co.uk
- www.randomhouse.co.uk/childrens

**Parent Company** Random House Children's Books

**Insider Info** Submissions accompanied by SAE will be returned. Catalogue available online.

**Fiction** Publishes Picture books and Children's fiction titles.

**Submission Guidelines** Accepts proposal package (including outline, and one sample chapter). Will accept artworks/images (send photocopies).

**Recent Title(s)** *Sebastian Darke*, Philip Caveney; *Green Boy*, Susan Cooper

**Tips** Strongly prefer agented submissions. Publish almost entirely in hardback.

## The Book Castle
**12 Church Street, Dunstable, Bedfordshire, LU5 4RU**
- 01582 605670

● 01582 662431
● bc@book-castle.co.uk
● www.book-castle.co.uk
**Contact** Managing Editor, Paul Bowes; Sally Siddons
**Established** 1986
**Insider Info** Publishes ten titles per year. Payment is via royalties. Catalogue and manuscript guidelines available online.
**Non-Fiction** Publishes General Non-fiction titles on the following subjects:
History and Regional.
 * The Book Castle publish local interest and history books for the counties surrounding Bedfordshire.
**Submission Guidelines** Accepts query with SAE/ proposal package (including outline). Mark for the attention of Paul Bowes or Sally Siddons and include any other relevant information.
**Recent Title(s)** *From Country Boy to Weatherman*, George Jackson (Memoir)
**Tips** All publications must be of local interest, particularly focusing upon the counties of Bedfordshire, Buckinghamshire, Hertfordshire and Oxfordshire.

## Book Guild Publishing Ltd
**Pavilion View, 19 New Road, Brighton, East Sussex, BN1 1UF**
● 01273 720900
● 01273 723122
● info@bookguild.co.uk
● www.bookguild.co.uk
**Contact** Managing Director, Carol Biss; Managing Editor, Joanna Bentley
**Established** 1982
**Insider Info** Publishes 100 titles per year. 60 per cent of books publishes are from first-time authors. Payment is via royalties. Aims to respond to proposals and manuscripts within one month. Catalogue and manuscript guidelines are available online.
**Non-Fiction** Publishes Biography, Children's/ Juvenile and General Non-fiction titles on the following subjects: History, Memoirs, World Affairs.
 * Wish to publish vivid memoirs and biographies of highly interesting people, past and present, and timely books on current affairs.
**Submission Guidelines** Accepts query with SAE/ proposal package (including outline, two sample chapters, your publishing history, author biography and an SAE).
 Submissions email: joanna@bookguild.co.uk
**Fiction** Publishes General fiction titles.
 * Wish to publish engaging novels and stories for adult and children readers.

**Submission Guidelines** Accepts query with SAE/ proposal package (including outline, two sample chapters).
 Submissions email: joanna@bookguild.co.uk
**Recent Title(s)** *In Sickness and in Health*, Richard Bayliss (Memoir); *The Flyleaf Killer*, William Prater (Novel)
**Tips** The Book Guild is an independent publisher and most material is conventionally published, but 'Joint Venture' services, where the author contributes costs, as well as other production services. This option should be researched thoroughly.

## Booth-Clibborn Editions
**Studio 83, 235 Earls Court Road, London, SW5 9FE**
● 020 7565 0688
● 020 7244 1018
● info@booth-clibborn.com
● www.booth-clibborn.com
**Established** 1974
**Insider Info** Catalogue available online.
**Non-Fiction** Publishes General Non-fiction, Illustrated titles and Multimedia on the following subjects:
 Art/Architecture, Contemporary Culture, Photography.
**Recent Title(s)** *I Want to Spend the Rest of My Life Everywhere, with Everyone (One to One); Always, Forever (Now)*, Damien Hirst (Art/Photography)
**Tips** Booth-Clibborn Editions was founded in 1974 as a privately owned, wholly independent company publishing an outstanding list of books on the fine, media and decorative arts. Its policy is to commission first class creative work from the best of today's designers, whether they are renowned book specialists or innovative younger groups.

## Boulevard Books/Babel Guides
**71 Lytton Road, Oxford, OX4 3NY**
● 01865 712931
● 01865 712931
● raybabel@dircon.co.uk
● www.babelguides.com
**Contact** Managing Director, Ray Keenoy
**Established** 1990
**Insider Info** Catalogue is available online.
**Non-Fiction** Publishes General Non-fiction and Guidebook titles on the following subjects:
 Literary Guides, Literary Translation.
**Fiction** Publishes World Literature and Translated Fiction titles.

**Submission Guidelines** Accepts query with SAE.
**Recent Title(s)** *Yiddish After the Holocaust*, Joseph Sherman ed. (Yiddish Literature); *The Babel Guide to Brazilian Literature,* Babel Guides (Non-fiction).

## Bounty Books
**2–4 Heron Quays, London, E14 4JP**
- 020 7531 8400
- 020 7531 8607
- www.bountybooks.co.uk

**Parent Company** Octopus Publishing Group
**Contact** Publishing and International Sales Manager, Polly Manguel
**Non-Fiction** Publishes reprints of non-fiction titles.
**Tips** Bounty, the UK's first reprint company, is entirely based on reprints from across the Octopus Group's backlists.

## Boxtree
**20 New Wharf Road, London, N1 9RR**
- 020 7014 6000
- 020 7014 6001
- www.panmacmillan.com

**Parent Company** Pan Macmillan Publishers
**Established** 1990 (became an imprint of Pan Macmillan in 1996)
**Insider Info** Catalogue available online, as a downloadable pdf.
**Non-Fiction** Publishes Autobiography, Biography, General Non-fiction, Gift books, Humour and Illustrated titles on the following subjects: Entertainment, Film and Television tie-ins, Sport, Music.
**Submission Guidelines** Accepts agented submissions only.
**Recent Title(s)** *Purple Ronnie's Little Book for a Perfect Lover*, Giles Andreae (Gift book)
**Tips** Specialises in quirky entertainment related and branded non-fiction. Do not send in any unsolicited manuscripts.

## Boydell & Brewer Ltd
**PO Box 9, Woodbridge, Suffolk, IP12 3DF**
- 01394 610600
- 01394 610316
- editorial@boydell.co.uk
- www.boydell.co.uk

**Established** 1978
**Insider Info** Simultaneous submissions are not accepted. Catalogue is available free on request and online. Manuscript guidelines are available online.

**Non-Fiction** Publishes Autobiography, Biography, General Non-fiction, Illustrated books, Multimedia, Reference and Scholarly titles on the following subjects: Art/Architecture, Crafts, History, Hobbies, Humanities, Language/Literature, Literary Criticism, Military/War, Music/Dance, Philosophy, Photography, Religion.
**Submission Guidelines** Please use the downloadable submission form on the website.
**Recent Title(s)** *The Medieval Warrior Aristocracy*, Andrew Cowell (Military History)
**Tips** While embracing a philosophy of innovation and growth, Boydell & Brewer remains a defiantly independent publisher of scholarly works for the academic community and thought provoking, attractively produced books for the general reader. Medieval studies originally formed the core of the list, but it has rapidly expanded to embrace the humanities in all periods up to and including the 19th Century. The downloadable submission form provides the publisher with the information necessary to make an initial appraisal of your publication project. If it is decided that it is a possibility for the list, you will contacted with a request for further material for peer review. If the complete manuscript is not available, at least two sample chapters and a detailed breakdown of the rest of the book will be required.

## BPS Blackwell Publishing
**9600 Garsington Road, Oxford, OX4 2DQ**
- firstname.lastname@blackwellpublishing.com
- www.bpsblackwell.co.uk

**Contact** Commissioning Editor, Andrew McAleer; Development Editor, Elizabeth Johnston
**Insider Info** Publishes 12 titles per year. Receives approximately 30 queries and 15–20 manuscripts per year. 25 per cent of books published are from first time authors and 95 per cent are from unagented authors. Payment via royalty (on retail price) with 0.07 (per £) minimum and 0.12 (per £) maximum. Average lead time is one year with simultaneous submissions not accepted. Book catalogue and manuscript guidelines are available online.
**Non-fiction** Publishes Multimedia, Reference, Scholarly and Reference titles on the following subjects: Education, Psychology, Sociology.
**Submission Guidelines** Accepts proposal package (including outline, table of contents, market research and intended readership). Will accept initial query via email.

Submission details to: andrew.mcaleer@blackwellpublishing.com

**Recent Title(s)** *Personality and Individual Differences,* Tomas Chamorro-Premuzic (Undergraduate Textbook); *Educational Testing: A Competence-Based Approach*, James Boyle and Stephen Fisher

**Tips** A unique partnership between The British Psychological Society and Blackwell Publishers whose titles are aimed at managers, teachers, medical and healthcare professionals, students and practising psychologists. Do not publish self-help, popular psychology or fiction. Authors should be able to provide evidence of qualifications that enable them to write titles with authority. All submissions will go through an editorial board.

## Bradshaw Books

**Tigh Fili Art Centre, Thompson House, McCurtain Street, Cork, Republic of Ireland**

- 00353 21 450 9274
- 00353 21 455 1617
- info@tighfili.com
- www.tighfili.com/publishing.asp

**Contact** Artistic Director, Máire Bradshaw; Project Manager, Leslie Ryan

**Established** 1985

**Insider Info** Publishes eight titles per year. Submissions accompanied by SAE will be returned. Catalogue is available online.

**Poetry** Publishes Poetry titles.

 \* Concentrates on Irish poets. Also publishes the *Cork Literary Review* and the *Eurochild Anthologies*.

**Submission Guidelines** Accepts proposal package or entire manuscript by post or via email.

 Submission details to: admin@cwpc.ie

**Recent Title(s)** *Beowulf: An Adaptation*, Felix Nobis (Translation); *Toil the Dark Harvest*, Geraldine Mills (Poetry collection)

**Tips** Máire Bradshaw, founder and director of the company had become increasingly aware of the need for an outlet in publishing that was brave enough to take on new names in poetry. Bradshaw Books has continued this theme throughout its publishing history with the publication of many previously unknown writers who have gone on to greater success. Bradshaw encourages new and unknown Irish poets and welcomes unsolicited manuscripts or proposal submissions. Also publishes the *Cork Literary Review* which has various poetry/prose competitions, which can lead to publication by Bradshaw.

## Bradt Travel Guides

**23 High Street, Chalfont St. Peter, Bucks, SL9 9QE**

- 01753 893444
- 0753 892333
- info@bradtguides.com
- www.bradtguides.com

**Contact** Managing Director and Founder, Hilary Bradt; Publishing Director, Donald Greig; Commissioning Editor, Adrian Phillips

**Established** 1974

**Insider Info** Receives approximately 200 queries and 60 manuscripts per year. 30 per cent of books published are from first-time authors, 95 per cent of books published are from unagented authors. Payment is via royalty (on wholesale price). Advance is offered. Average lead time is eight months, with simultaneous submissions not accepted. Aims to respond to proposals and manuscripts within one month. Catalogue is available online. Manuscript guidelines are available by email.

**Non-Fiction** Publishes Guidebook and Reference titles on the following subjects:

 Activity and Adventure, Ancient Sites and Culture, City guides, Cruising, Destinations, General Travel, Health, Islands and Beaches, Offbeat and Eccentric Travel, Wildlife.

 \* Bradts travel guides cover a range of subjects from general interest travel and city guides, to eccentric or remote destinations for the dedicated traveller.

**Submission Guidelines** Accepts proposal package (including outline, market research, CV and travelling history).

**Recent Title(s)** *Eccentric Cambridge*, Benedict Le Vay (Eccentric Travel); *Zagreb,* Piers Letcher and Sarah Parkes (Ancient Sites and Culture)

**Tips** Bradts readership includes thinking, responsible travellers who are interested in destinations off the beaten track. Bradt aims to publish guides to unusual destinations, or unusual guides to rather more mainstream places. Bradt does not publish standard travel narratives.

## Brandon/Mount Eagle Publications

**Cooleen, Dingle, Co. Kerry, Republic of Ireland**

- 00353 66 915 1463
- 00353 66 915 1234
- www.brandonbooks.com

**Contact** Publisher, Steve MacDonogh

**Established** 1997

**Insider Info** Publishes 15 titles per year. Receives approximately 200 queries and 200 manuscripts per year. Submissions accompanies by SAE will be returned. Catalogue and manuscript guidelines are available online.

**Non-Fiction** Publishes Biography and General Non-fiction titles on the following subjects:
 Government/Politics, History, Memoirs, Regional, World Affairs.

**Submission Guidelines** Accepts query with SAE with proposal package (including outline, your publishing history, clips, author biography). Will accept artworks/images (send digital files as jpegs). No submissions by email or fax.

**Fiction** Publishes Regional and Irish fiction titles.

**Submission Guidelines** Accepts query with SAE with proposal package (including outline, sample chapter(s) or 40 sample pages, review quotes, author biography). No submissions by fax or email.

**Recent Title(s)** *The Story of Irish Dance*, Helen Brennan (History/Culture); *Miss Katie Regrets*, Jack Barry (Novel/Thriller)

**Tips** Titles are aimed at a wide readership, generally with an Irish focus. The company is looking principally for biography, memoirs, popular history, current affairs and modern politics proposals.

## Breedon Books Publishing Co
**3 The Parker Centre, Masfield Road, Derby, DE21 4SZ**
- 01332 384235
- 01332 292755
- susan.last@breedonpublishing.co.uk
- www.breedonbooks.co.uk

**Contact** Commissioning Editor, Susan Last
**Established** 1983
**Insider Info** Publishes 50 titles per year. Payment is via royalties (on retail price). Submissions accompanied by SAE will be returned. Catalogue is available online. Manuscript guidelines are available online via the website.

**Non-Fiction** Publishes Illustrated books and General Non-fiction titles on the following subjects:
 History, Photography and Sports.

**Submission Guidelines** Accepts query with SAE and proposal package (including outline, sample chapter(s) and SAE). Will accept images (send transparencies/digital files as jpegs).

**Recent Title(s)** *Yesterday's Whitefriars*, Paul Crampton (History)

**Tips** Before sending anything to Breedon Books, it is a good idea to have a look around their website to get an idea of the types of books published. Breedon concentrates on local history, motorsport and football titles, although there are always a few that fall outside these areas. Therefore, each submission will be looked at on its own merits.

## Breese Books Ltd
**10 Hanover Crescent, Brighton, BN2 9SB**
- 01273 687555
- martin@abracadabra.co.uk
- www.abracadabra.co.uk

**Contact** Chairman/Managing Director, Martin Ranciar-Breese
**Established** 1975
**Insider Info** Catalogue available online.
**Non-Fiction** Publishes General Non-fiction, How-to and Multimedia titles on the following subjects:
 Conjuring, Magic Tricks.

**Submission Guidelines** No unsolicited manuscripts accepted.

**Recent Title(s)** *Best of Spell-Binder*, Stephen Tucker (Magic tricks/How-to)

**Tips** Titles aimed at enthusiast magicians, or anyone interested in magic tricks and mentalism.

## Brewin Books Ltd
**Doric House, 56 Alcester Road, Studley, Warwickshire, B80 7NP**
- 01527 854228
- 01527 852746
- admin@brewinbooks.com
- www.brewinbooks.com

**Contact** Managing Director, Alan Brewin (Non-Fiction); Editor, Alistair Brewin (Regional History Magazines)
**Established** 1976
**Imprint(s)** History Into Print
 Brewin Junior
**Insider Info** Publishes 30 titles per year. Receives approximately 50 queries and 95 manuscripts per year. Payment is via royalty (on retail price). Average lead time is six months, with simultaneous submissions not accepted. Submissions accompanied by SAE will be returned. Catalogue is free on request, and available online or by email. Manuscript guidelines are free on request.

**Non-Fiction** Publishes Autobiography, Biography, Children's, General Non-fiction, Humour, Illustrated, Reference and Scholarly titles on the following subjects:
 Art/Architecture, Automotive, Communications, Cooking/Foods/Nutrition, Ethnic , Health/Medicine, History, Language/Literature, Memoirs, Military/War, Music/Dance, Nostalgia, Regional (Midlands), Social Sciences, Sports, Transportation, Travel.

**Submission Guidelines** Accepts proposal package (including outline, sample chapters, your publishing history, author biography and SAE) and artworks/images.

**Fiction** Publishes Regional (Midlands) titles.
**Submission Guidelines** Accepts proposal package (including outline, sample chapters, your publishing history, author biography and SAE).
**Recent Title(s)** *Sounds Unlikely - Music in Birmingham*, Margaret Handford (Music History); *More tea less Vicar!*, Jill Fraser (Humour/Midlands)
**Tips** Brewin Books publishes books with mass market appeal for a general readership.

## Brilliant Publications
**1 Church View, Sparrow Hall Farm, Edlesborough, Dunstable, Bedfordshire, LU6 2ES**
- 01525 222292
- 01525 222720
- priscilla@brilliantpublications.co.uk
- www.brilliantpublications.co.uk

**Contact** Publisher, Priscilla Hannaford
**Established** 1993
**Insider Info** Publishes 12 titles per year. Submissions accompanied by SAE will be returned. Catalogue and manuscript guidelines are free on request, and available online.
**Non-Fiction** Publishes Children's/Juvenile, General Non-fiction, Reference, Scholarly and Textbook titles on the following subjects:
 Education, Teaching/Textbooks (all school subjects).
 * Do not publish children's picture books.
**Submission Guidelines** Accepts query with SAE with proposal package (including outline, two sample chapters, author biography, market research, intended audience).
**Recent Title(s)** *How To Be Brilliant At Christmas Time*, Val Edgar
**Tips** Specialise in producing high quality, well designed materials that make teaching and learning enjoyable and rewarding, for both teachers and pupils. Brilliant Publications are always looking for new book ideas, including book series. Writers should try to sell both themselves and their book strongly in the proposal, and include plenty of information on what makes their book, or series, distinct.

## The British Academy
**10 Carlton House Terrace, London, SW1Y 5AH**
- 020 7969 5200
- 020 7969 5300
- pubs@britac.ac.uk
- www.britac.ac.uk

**Contact** Chairman of the Publications Committee, Dr. David McKitterick
**Established** 1902

**Insider Info** Publishes 20 titles per year. Payment is via royalties. Catalogue available online.
**Non-Fiction** Publishes Reference, Scholarly and Technical titles on the following subjects:
 Anthropology/Archaeology, Art/Architecture, Business/Economics, Ethnic, Government/Politics, History, Humanities, Language/Literature, Music/Dance, Philosophy, Psychology, Religion, Science, Social Sciences.
 * The Academy publishes a wide range of monographs, editions and catalogues, reflecting the breadth of its scholarly activities.
**Submission Guidelines** Accepts query with SAE.
**Recent Title(s)** *Britain's Pensions Crisis: History and Policy*, Hugh Pemberton (Pat Thane and Noel Whiteside eds.)
**Tips** The British Academy was established by Royal Charter under the full title of 'The British Academy for the Promotion of Historical, Philosophical and Philological Studies'. It is an independent and self-governing fellowship of scholars, elected for distinction and achievement in one or more branches of the academic disciplines, which make up the humanities and social sciences. The Academy's publishing programme is overseen by a Publications Committee and all new and recent titles are published worldwide by Oxford University Press. The Academy mostly publishes work within its existing series, details of which are available on the website.

## The British Computer Society
**First Floor, Block D, North Star House, North Star Avenue, Swindon, Wiltshire SN2 1FA**
- 01793 417417
- 01793 480270
- pubsenq@hq.bcs.org.uk
- www.bcs.org/books

**Contact** Commissioning Editor, Matthew Flynn (Business, IT)
**Established** 1957
**Insider Info** Publishes ten titles per year. Payment is via royalty (on wholesale price). Average lead time is five months, with simultaneous submissions accepted. Catalogue is free on request, and available online or via email: matthew.flynn@hq.bcs.org.uk Manuscript guidelines are free on request, and available online or via email.
**Non-Fiction** Publish Reference, Scholarly, Technical and Textbook titles on the following subjects:
 Business/Economics, Computers/Electronics.
**Submission Guidelines** Accepts proposal package (including outline, sample chapter(s), your

publishing history, author biography). Writers should download a book proposal form from the website.

Submission details to: matthew.flynn@hq.bcs.org.uk

**Tips** The leading body for those working in IT, they aim to promote the study and practice of computing, and advance the knowledge of, and education in IT, for the benefit of the public. BCS is also a registered charity. Publications should support the professional, academic, and practical needs of both BCS members and the wider IT community. Readership includes students or those undertaking professional exams, IT managers, and senior directors wanting a greater understanding of their IT systems.

## British Library
**96 Euston Road, London, NW1 2BD**
- 020 7412 7535
- 020 7412 7768
- blpublications@bl.uk
- www.bl.uk

**Contact** Head of Publishing, David Way; Publishing Manager, Catherine Britton; Managing Editor, Lara Speicher

**Established** 1973

**Insider Info** Publishes 50 titles per year. Receives approximately 500 queries per year. Average lead time is over 18 months. Catalogue is free on request, or by email.

**Non-Fiction** Publishes Biography, Illustrated, Reference and Scholarly titles on the following subjects:

Art/Architecture (Design), Typography, History (History of the Book), Humanities, Language/Literature, Literary Criticism, Religion (History of Sacred texts), Cartography (History of Maps and Exploration), Bibliography, Biography.

\* Titles are linked to the collections of the British Library.

**Submission Guidelines** Accepts proposal package (including outline, sample chapters, your publishing history, author biography, SAE).

**Recent Title(s)** *Medieval Dress and Fashion*, Margaret Scott (History)

## The British Museum Press
**38 Russell Square, London, WC1B 3QQ**
- 020 7323 1234
- 020 7436 7315
- www.britishmuseum.co.uk

**Parent Company** The British Museum

**Contact** Managing Director, Andrew Thatcher

**Established** 1973

**Insider Info** Catalogue is available online.

**Non-Fiction** Publishes Biography, Children's/Juvenile, Coffee Table, Gift, Illustrated, Reference, Scholarly, and Anthology titles on the following subjects:

Exhibition Catalogues, Collection Guidebooks, Religion, History, Archaeology, Ethnography, Fine and Decorative Arts, Numismatics.

**Poetry** Publish some Classical poetry titles.

**Recent Title(s)** *Hogarth*, Tim Clayton

## Brooklands Books
**PO Box 146, Cobham, Surrey, KT11 1LG**
- 01932 865051
- 01932 868803
- sales@brookland-books.com
- www.brooklandsbooks.com

**Contact** Managing Director, Ian Dowdesell

**Established** 1954

**Insider Info** Catalogue is available online.

**Non-Fiction** Publishes General Non-fiction, Reference and Technical titles on the following subjects: Automotive, History, Military/War, Aircraft.

**Recent Title(s)** *COMBAT LAND ROVERS Portfolio No. 1*, Bob Morrison (Reference manuals)

**Tips** As a company, Brooklands Books are dedicated to preserving motoring literature for enthusiasts. All these publications, it has to be stressed, are the real thing – not to be confused with the much advertised 'condensed' manuals which are fine for servicing and small repair jobs, but often fall woefully short when more detailed help is needed.

## Brown, Son & Ferguson
**4–10 Darnley Street, Glasgow, G41 2SD**
- 0141 429 1234
- 0141 420 1694
- enquiries@skipper.co.uk
- www.skipper.co.uk

**Contact** Managing Director, L. Ingram-Brown; Chairman/Joint Managing Director, T. Nigel Brown

**Established** 1850

**Insider Info** Catalogue available online.

**Non-Fiction** Publishes General Non-fiction, Reference, and Technical titles on the following subjects:

Marine Subjects, Travel and Nautical Reference.

**Fiction** Publishes Plays and Regional interest titles.

**Recent Title(s)** *Brown's Nautical Almanac 2007*, T. Nigel Brown (Nautical Reference); *A Song to Sing and a Tale to Tell*, Jean Brown (Novel)

**Tips** Brown, Son & Ferguson have been nautical publishers, printers and ships' stationers since 1832.

On the website you will find nautical textbooks, both technical and non-technical, books about the sea, historical books, information on old sailing ships and how to build model ships. Brown, Son & Ferguson publishes anything related to sailing or other nautical themes, and Scottish interest plays and non-fiction.

## Brown Skin Books
**PO Box 46504, London, N1 3YA**
- 020 8986 1115
- info@brownskinbooks.co.uk
- www.brownskinbooks.co.uk

**Contact** Managing Director, Vastiana Belfon
**Established** 2002
**Insider Info** Publishes seven titles per year. 75 per cent of books published are from first-time authors and 80 per cent are from unagented authors. Payment is via royalty (on retail price) or outright purchase with £750 minimum and £1,500 maximum. Average lead time is ten months with simultaneous submissions accepted. Submissions accompanied by SAE will be returned. Aims to respond to proposals and manuscripts within two months. Catalogue available online. Manuscript guidelines available online, by post or via email.
**Fiction** Publishes Erotica titles.
 * Do not publish any poetry.
**Submission Guidelines** Accepts query with SAE with proposal package (including outline and one sample chapter).
**Recent Title(s)** *A Darker Shade of Blue*, Angela Campion (Erotic novel)
**Tips** Titles are primarily aimed at women of colour aged 18–50, living in the US, Canada, Europe, Africa, and the Caribbean. There is a dedicated hints and tips section published on the website that writers should read before submitting. Also, make sure there is a strong story with believable characters, as this is just as important as the sex in Brown Skin Books publications.

## Brown Watson
**The Old Mill, 76 Fleckney Road, Kibworth Beauchamp, Leicestershire, LE8 OHG**
- 0116 279 6333
- books@brownwatson.co.uk
- www.brownwatson.co.uk

**Non-Fiction** Publishes Children's General Non-fiction and Picture Book titles.
**Fiction** Publishes Children's titles.
**Tips** Brown Watson is a small, family owned, children's book publisher and distributer.

## Brynterion Press
**Bryntirion, Bridgend, CF31 4DX**
- 01656 655886
- 01656 665919
- office@emw.org.uk
- www.emw.org.uk/books/bryntirionpress/default.htm

**Contact** Press Manager, Huw Kinsey
**Established** 1955
**Insider Info** Catalogue free on request and online.
**Non-Fiction** Publishes Children's/Juvenile, General Non-fiction, Illustrated book, Reference and Scholarly titles on the following subjects:
 Religion, Spirituality.
**Fiction** Religious.
**Recent Title(s)** *Christian Handbook*, Peter Jeffery (Religion/Reference); *They Beheld His Glory*, Peter Trumper (Bible stories)
**Tips** Titles aimed at the Evangelical/Welsh. Also publishes Christian books and magazines in the Welsh language, and Welsh language writers are in demand.

## Bureau of Freelance Photographers
**Focus House, 497 Green Lanes, London, N13 4BP**
- 020 8882 3315
- 020 8886 3933
- info@thebfp.com
- www.thebfp.com

**Insider Info** Catalogue is available online.
**Non-Fiction** Publishes How-to and Reference titles on the following subjects:
 Photography, Freelance photography market.
**Recent Title(s)** *The Freelance Photographer's Market Handbook 2007*, BFP Books (Directory)
**Tips** The Bureau of Freelance Photographers publishes titles aimed at professional freelance photographers and keen amateurs.

## Burning House
**117 Sugden Road, London, SW11 5ED**
- 020 7738 2428
- 020 3070 0764
- simon@beautiful-books.co.uk
- www.beautiful-books.co.uk

**Parent Company** Beautiful Books
**Contact** Publisher, Simon Petherick
**Established** 2007
**Fiction** Publishes contemporary fiction titles.
**Submission Guidelines** Accepts query with SAE or via email.

Submission details to: submissions@beautiful-books.co.uk

**Tips** Burning House is a brand new imprint, due to launch in March 2007, focusing entirely on contemporary fiction.

## Burns & Oates

**The Tower Building, 11 York Road, London, SE1 7NX**

- 020 7922 0880
- 020 7922 0881
- rbairdsmith@continuumbooks.com
- www.continuumbooks.com

**Parent Company** The Continuum International Publishing Group

**Contact** Publishing Director, Robin Baird-Smith (General Trade and Religion); Editor, Ben Hayes (General Trade and Religion)

**Established** 1847

**Insider Info** Catalogue and manuscript guidelines are available online.

**Non-Fiction** Publishes General Non-fiction of Roman Catholic interest, as well as official publications for the Catholic faith.

**Submission Guidelines** Accepts proposal package (including outline, your publishing history, published clips, author biography and market research). Send no more than four A4 sheets.

**Recent Title(s)** *The Catechism of the Catholic Church*, Burns & Oates (Religious); *The Compendium of Social Doctrine of the Catholic Church*, Burns & Oates (Religious)

**Tips** Burns & Oates is the premier Roman Catholic publishing imprint in Great Britain and publishes traditional and contemporary titles from Catholic writers. Designated 'Publishers to the Holy See' by Pope Leo XIII, Burns & Oates has also maintained a strong tradition of publishing official works for the Catholic Church in England and Wales.

## The Business Education Publishers Ltd

**The Teleport Doxford International, Sunderland, Tyne and Wear, SR3 3XD**

- 0191 525 2410
- 0191 520 1815
- info@bepl.com
- www.bepl.com

**Insider Info** Catalogue and manuscript guidelines are available online.

**Non-Fiction** Publishes titles on the following subjects:

Information Technology, Business, Education, Travel, Tourism and Leisure, Local Interest (Durham area).

**Submission Guidelines** Accepts proposal package (including outline, details of readership and competing titles and an electronic version).

**Recent Title(s)** *For you Tommy the War is Over*, Major Ian English and Harry Moses (Military)

**Tips** The Business Education Publishers are always interested in hearing from potential authors. As an independent publisher, they take a personal interest in each project and their staff work closely with authors to produce high quality work.

## Butterworth-Heinemann

**32 Jamestown Road, Camden Town, London, NW1 7BY**

- 020 7424 4200
- 020 7482 2293
- m.ging@elsevier.com
- www.intl.elsevierhealth.com/bh

**Parent Company** Elsevier Ltd (Health Sciences)

**Insider Info** Royalties paid. Catalogue and manuscript guidelines available online.

**Non-Fiction** Publishes Illustrated books, Multimedia, Reference, Scholarly, Textbook and Technical titles on the following subjects:

Education, Health/Medicine, Science, Veterinary Medicine, Optometry, Dentistry.

**Submission Guidelines** See the online Proposal Form.

Submission details to: t.horne@elsevier.com

**Recent Title(s)** *Butterworth Heinemann's Review Questions for the NBEO Examination: Part One*, Edward S. Bennett and Vasudevan Lakshminarayanan (Medical/Reference)

**Tips** A leading international publisher of medical and health professions books, software and visual aids. Specialist areas include anesthesiology and intensive care, dentistry, neurology, ophthalmology, optometry, nursing, physiotherapy and veterinary. To submit a proposal to Butterworth-Heinmann, fill in and return a 'Proposal Form', available on the website. Alternatively authors may contact the Publishing Director or Editor prior to submission, to discuss the proposal.

## Cadogan Guides

**2nd Floor, 233 High Holborn, London, C1V 7DN**

- 020 7611 4660
- 020 7611 4665
- info@cadoganguides.co.uk
- www.cadoganguides.com

**Parent Company** The Globe Pequot Press (Morris Communications Corporation)
**Insider Info** Catalogue is available online.
**Non-Fiction** Publishes Children's/Juvenile, Guidebook and Reference titles on the following subjects:
Children's Travel books, Destinations, General Travel Guides, Life Writing (Travel Biography), Living Abroad, Property Buying, Short Breaks, Travel Literature.
**Recent Title(s)** *Pick Your Brain About France*, Marian Pashley (Children's Travel); *There and Back Again: In the footsteps of J.R.R. Tolkien,* Matthew Lyons (Travel Literature)
**Tips** Cadogan Guides is part of The Globe Pequot Press book division of Morris Communications Corporation, an American multimedia business. Globe Pequot is one of the top three US publishers and distributors of books on travel and outdoor leisure. Cadogan publishes a wide range of travel writing for both children and adults, including the *In The Footsteps* series which traces the travels of well known historical literary figures.

## Calder Publications
**51 The Cut, London, SE1 8LF**
☎ 020 7633 0599
☎ 020 7928 5930
✉ info@calderpublications.com
🌐 www.calderpublications.com
**Contact** Managing Director, John Calder,
**Established** 1949
**Insider Info** Catalogue available online. Manuscript guidelines not available.
**Non-Fiction** Publishes Autobiography, Biography, Booklets, Illustrated and Scholarly titles on the following subjects:
Art/Architecture, Contemporary Culture, Creative Non-fiction, Government/Politics, History, Humanities, Language/Literature, Literary Criticism, Music/Dance, Philosophy, Sociology.
**Fiction** Publishes Experimental, Literary, Mainstream/Contemporary and Short story collection titles.
**Poetry** Publishes Poetry titles.
**Recent Title(s)** *Impressions of Africa*, Raymond Roussel (Adventure/Surrealism); *Watt*, Samuel Beckett (Philosophical Novel).
**Tips** Calder Publications continues to publish mostly experimental work with a cult or minority appeal.

## Cambridge Scholars Publishing
**15 Angerton Gardens, Newcastle upon Tyne, Tyne and wear, NE5 2JA**
☎ 0191 274 7224
✉ admin@c-s-p.org
🌐 www.c-s-p.org
**Established** 2001
**Insider Info** Publishes 120 titles per year. Receives approximately 1,200 manuscripts per year. 40 per cent of books published are from first-time authors and 100 per cent are from unagented authors. One per cent of books published are author subsidy published. Payment is via royalty (on wholesale price). Average lead time is four months, with simultaneous submissions accepted. Submissions accompanied by SAE will not be returned. Aims to respond to queries within seven days and proposals within one month. Catalogue is free on request, and available online. Manuscript guidelines are available online.
**Non-Fiction** Publishes Reference, Scholarly, Technical and Textbook titles on the following subjects:
Anthropology/Archaeology, Art/Architecture, Business/Economics, Communications, Contemporary Culture, Education, Ethnic, Government/Politics, History, Humanities, Language/Literature, Literary Criticism, Multicultural, Music/Dance, Nature/Environment, Philosophy, Photography, Psychology, Religion, Science, Social Sciences, Translation, Travel, Women's Issues/Studies.
**Submission Guidelines** Accepts proposal package (including outline, one to three sample chapters, author biography).
**Tips** Cambridge Scholars Publishing only publishes books aimed at professional academics and scholars.

## Cambridge University Press
**The Edinburgh Building, Shaftesbury Road, Cambridge, CB2 8RU**
☎ 01223 312393
☎ 01223 315052
✉ information@cambridge.org
🌐 www.cambridge.org/uk
**Contact** Chief Executive, Stephen R.R. Bourne; Managing Director - Europe, Middle East & Africa, Michael Holdsworth; Managing Director - Academic Publishing, Andrew Brown; Publishing Director, Richard Fisher (Humanities & Social Sciences); Publishing Director, Richard Barling (Science, Technology & Medicine)
**Established** 1534

**Insider Info** Publishes 1,200 titles peer year. Payment is via royalties. Catalogue available online. Manuscript guidelines available online, http://authornet.cambridge.org/information/proposaluk/hss/

**Non-Fiction** Publishes Reference, Scholarly and Technical titles on the following subjects: Anthropology/Archaeology, Business/Economics, Education, Government/Politics, Health/Medicine, History, Language/Literature, Law, Multicultural, Music/Dance, Nature/Environment, Philosophy, Psychology, Religion, Science, Transportation.

**Submission Guidelines** Accepts query with SAE/proposal package (including outline, two sample chapters, your publishing history, author biography, SAE).

**Recent Title(s)** *British or American English?*, John Algeo

**Tips** CUP publishes the finest academic and educational writing from around the world. As a department of the University of Cambridge, its purpose is to further the University's objective of advancing knowledge, education, learning, and research. They do not publish new fiction, poetry or other forms of creative writing, autobiography or memoir, overtly devotional or religious tracts (except for the Bible), political polemic, cookbooks, car handbooks or DIY manuals, or highly illustrated books for the general reader. Everything they do publish must have some educational and/or scholarly value.

## Camden Press
**43 Camden Passage, London, N1 8EA**
- 020 7226 4673

**Contact** Managing Director, Robert Borzello
**Established** 1985
**Non-Fiction** Publishes General Non-fiction titles on the following subjects: Community/Public Affairs, Social Sciences.
**Tips** Books may be launched in connection with major national conferences.

## Cameron & Hollis
**PO Box 1, Moffat, Dumfriesshire, DG10 9SU**
- 01683 220808
- 01683 220012
- editorial@cameronbooks.co.uk
- www.cameronbooks.co.uk

**Contact** Director, Ian A. Hamilton
**Established** 1976
**Insider Info** Catalogue available online.

**Non-Fiction** Publishes General Non-fiction, Illustrated and Scholarly titles on the following subjects: Art/Architecture, Crafts, Hobbies.

**Recent Title(s)** *Beyond Genre: Melodrama, Comedy and Romance in Hollywood Films*, Deborah Thomas (Academic); *Dictionary of Ornament*, Philippa Lewis and Gillian Darley (Art/Reference)

**Tips** Specialises in creating books in the fields of contemporary art, film criticism, the decorative arts, architecture, social history and the environment for publishers in Britain, continental Europe and North America. Operates abroad as well as in the UK, but only prints serious critical studies on the specified subject areas.

## Campbell Books
**20 New Wharf Road, London, N1 9RR**
- 020 7014 6000
- 020 7014 6001
- www.panmacmillan.com

**Insider Info** Catalogue available online.
**Fiction** Publishes Picture books and Children's interactive, moving and textured books.
**Submission Guidelines** Agented submissions only.
**Recent Title(s)** *Oh Dear!*, Rod Campbell (Book and Egg Cup Pack); *Noisy Jungle Babies: Little Zebra*, Rebecca Harry (Picture book with noise)
**Tips** Founded by Rod Campbell, the creator of the toddler classic, *Dear Zoo*. The imprint is a front-runner in the specialist pre-school market. No unsolicited submissions.

## Canongate Books Ltd
**14 High Street, Edinburgh, EH1 1TE**
- 0131 557 5111
- 0131 557 5211
- info@canongate.co.uk
- www.canongate.net

**Contact** Publisher, Jamie Byng; Managing Director, David Graham
**Established** 1973
**Imprint(s)** Canongate Classics
Canongate Crime
Canongate International
**Insider Info** Catalogue and manuscript guidelines available online.
**Non-Fiction** Publishes Biography, General Non-fiction and Scholarly titles on the following subjects: History, Language/Literature, Music/Dance, Regional, Religion, Travel.
* Lists full until 2008.
**Submission Guidelines** No submissions.

**Fiction** Publishes Literary, Regional, Religious, Short story collections, Crime and Scottish titles.

**Tips** We relish the opportunity to read new writing, but unfortunately are no longer accepting unsolicited submissions. With our lists currently full until 2008, we have reluctantly decided to stop accepting unsolicited material from authors.

## Canopus Publishing
**27 Queen Square, Bristol, BS1 4ND**

- 0117 922 6660
- 0117 922 6660
- robin@canopusbooks.com
- www.canopusbooks.com

**Contact** Director, Robin Rees; Commissioning Editor, Tom Spicer; Commissioning Editor, Jim Revill; Publishing Assistant, Julian Brigstocke

**Established** 1999

**Insider Info** Catalogue available online.

**Non-Fiction** Publishes General Non-fiction, Reference, Scholarly, Textbook and Technical titles on the following subjects:
 Science, Astronomy/Space.

**Recent Title(s)** *Dark Side of the Universe*, Iain Nicolson

**Tips** Canopus specialises in science and astronomy. Readers are anyone interested in space and astronomy. Canopus generally produces books and multimedia products for major publishing companies and institutions, but also publishes titles in the UK under its own imprint, selling rights in other territories.

## Capall Bann Publishing
**Auton Farm, Milverton, Somerset, TA4 1NE**

- 01823 401528
- 01823 401529
- enquiries@capallbann.co.uk
- www.capallbann.co.uk

**Contact** Publisher, Julia Day (Alternative Health, Angels, Spiritual Living, Folklore, Animals and Lore, Fairies); Publisher, Jon Day (Magic, Witchcraft, Earth Magic, Sacred Sites, Shamanism)

**Established** 1993

**Insider Info** Publishes 45 titles per year. Receives approximately 500 queries and 350 manuscripts per year. 50 per cent of books published are from first-time authors and 100 per cent of books published are from unagented authors. Five per cent of books published are author subsidy-published, depending on whether the title has special requirements, such as colour pictures. Payment is via royalty (on wholesale price) with 0.1 (per £). Average lead time is

six months, with simultaneous submissions accepted. Submissions accompanied by SAE will be returned. Catalogue is free on request, and available online or by email. Manuscript guidelines are available with an SAE or by email.

**Non-Fiction** Publishes Self-help and General Non-fiction titles on the following subjects:
 Alternative Health, Animals, Astrology/Psychic, Cooking/Foods/Nutrition, Folklore, Gardening, Health/Medicine, Mind, Body and Spirit, Nature/Environment, New Age, Philosophy, Religion (Pagan), Spirituality.

**Submission Guidelines** Accepts query with SAE or by email, or proposal package (including outline, two sample chapters and SAE) and artworks/images (send photocopies or digital files as jpegs).

**Tips** Capall Bann Publishing does not require an author to make submissions through a literary agent.

## Capstone Publishing
**8 Newtec Place, Magdalen Road, Oxford, OX4 1RE**

- 01865 798623
- 01865 240941
- info@wiley-capstone.co.uk
- www.capstoneideas.com

**Parent Company** John Wiley & Sons Inc

**Contact** Director, Mark Allin; Director, Richard Burton

**Established** 1997

**Insider Info** Catalogue is available online.

**Non-Fiction** Publishes General Non-fiction, Humour, Multimedia and Scholarly titles on Business/Economics.

**Submission Guidelines** Query with SAE or proposal package (including outline, sample chapter(s), author biography and SAE).

**Recent Title(s)** *Barefoot on Broken Glass*, John Timperley (Business)

**Tips** Capstone is a business publisher, making the ideas that are driving the new economy accessible and entertaining is its mission. The publisher, like the public, wants to find the right information quickly and easily and start putting it into practice.
 Articles for submission must work towards understanding the key ideas and decisions that are influencing the way business is developing in the 21st Century.

## Carcanet Press Ltd
**4th Floor, Alliance House, Cross Street, Manchester, M2 7AQ**

- 0161 834 8730

0161 832 0084
info@carcanet.co.uk
www.carcanet.co.uk
**Contact** Editorial and Managing Director, Michael Schmidt; Managing Editor, Judith Wilson
**Established** 1969
**Insider Info** Aims to respond to queries and proposals within six weeks. Catalogue and manuscript guidelines are available online.
**Non-Fiction** Publishes Biography and Scholarly titles.
**Fiction** Publishes Classic, Contemporary and Translation titles.
**Submission Guidelines** Accepts query with SAE/ proposal package (including outline, sample chapter(s)), or completed manuscript.
**Poetry** Publishes Poetry and Poetry Translation titles.
**Submission Guidelines** Accepts query/sample poems (6–10 pages).
**Recent Title(s)** *The Shepherd's Calendar*, John Clare
**Tips** Carcanet takes its bearing from Modernism. It bases its activities on the best practice of the last century, during which great lists were forged - some of which did not survive as independents into the changing 21st Century. Carcanet considers submissions and book proposals submitted in hard copy form only. No electronic submissions will be considered. Writers wishing to submit poetry should familiarise themselves with Carcanet's books.

## Cardiff Academic Press
**St. Fagans Road, Fairwater, Cardiff, CF5 3AE**
029 2056 0333
029 2056 0313
www.drakegroup.co.uk
**Parent Company** Drake Group
**Non-Fiction** Publishes Biography, Textbook and Scholarly titles on the following subjects: Cosmology, Education, Literature, Religious Studies, Women's Studies, Welsh History.
**Fiction** Publishes Literary titles.
**Recent Title(s)** *Can Darwinism Explain Morality?*, Daniel Oakey

## Carlton Books
**20 Mortimer Street, London, W1T 3JW**
020 7612 0400
020 7612 0401
enquiries@carltonbooks.co.uk
www.carltonbooks.co.uk
**Parent Company** Carlton Publishing Group

**Insider Info** Aims to respond to proposals within four weeks. Catalogue is available online.
**Non-Fiction** Publishes Humour, Illustrated books and Reference titles on the following subjects: Entertainment/Games, History, Sports, Lifestyle, Humour.
**Submission Guidelines** Accepts proposal package (including outline and the first 20 pages, or two chapters, whichever is shorter).
**Recent Title(s)** *The England Cricket Miscellany*, John White; *Bang! The Complete History of the Universe*, Brian May, Sir Patrick Moore and Chris Lintott
**Tips** Carlton Books do not publish any academic books. Please do not send a full manuscript other than via an agent.

## Carlton Publishing Group
**20 Mortimer Street, London, W1T 3JW**
020 7612 0400
020 7612 0401
enquiries@carltonbooks.co.uk
www.carltonbooks.co.uk
**Contact** Managing Director, Jonathan Goodman
**Established** 1992
**Imprint(s)** Carlton Books
Andre Deutsch
Prion
**Insider Info** Aims to respond to proposals within four weeks. Catalogue is available online.
**Non-Fiction** Publishes Autobiography, Biography, Children's/Juvenile, Coffee table books, Gift books, Humour, Illustrated books, Arts catalogues and Reference titles on the following subjects: Art/ Architecture, Cooking/Foods/Nutrition, Entertainment/Games, Health/Medicine, Military/ War, Music/Dance, Photography, Theatre and Drama, Mind, Body and Spirit, Criminology, Erotica.
 * Do not consider proposals for academic books.
**Submission Guidelines** Accepts query with SAE/ proposal package (including outline, author biography and two sample chapters, or 20 pages, whichever is shorter). Submission details to: pmurrayhill@carltonbooks.co.uk
**Fiction** Publishes Children's illustrated fiction.
 * Does not accept proposals.
**Recent Title(s)** *How to be a Princess*, Caitlin Matthews (Children's); *Vintage Fashion*, Harriet Quick (Illustrated Non-fiction); *John, Paul, George, Ringo and Me*, Tony Barrow (Biography)
**Tips** Please do not send full manuscript unless via an agent.

## Carroll & Brown Ltd

**20 Lonsdale Road, London, NW6 6RD**

☎ 020 7372 0900

☎ 020 7372 0460

✉ louise.dixon@carrollandbrown.co.uk

🌐 www.carrollandbrown.co.uk

**Contact** Editorial Director, Louise Dixon

**Established** 2000

**Insider Info** Catalogue is available online.

**Non-Fiction** Publishes Gift books, How-to, Illustrated books, Reference and Self-help titles on the following subjects: Pregnancy and Child care, Medical care, Alternative therapies, Fitness, Sex, Women's health issues, Pastimes, Crafts, Sports, Mind, Body and Spirit.

**Submission Guidelines** Accepts queries by email.

**Recent Title(s)** *The Dream Workbook*, Joe Friedman; *A Man's Guide to Babycare*, Colin Cooper (Childcare)

## Cassell Illustrated

**2–4 Heron Quays, London, E14 4JP**

☎ 020 7531 8400

☎ 020 7537 0858

✉ iain.macgregor@cassell-illustrated.com

🌐 www.cassell-illustrated.com

**Parent Company** Octopus Publishing Group

**Contact** Publishing Director, Iain MacGregor; Commissioning Editor, Laura Price

**Insider Info** Downloadable catalogue is available online.

**Non-Fiction** Publishes Coffee table books, Cookbooks, Gift books, How-to, Humour, Illustrated books, Reference and Self-help titles on the following subjects: Art/Architecture, Child Guidance/Parenting, Contemporary Culture, Cooking/Foods/Nutrition, Crafts, Gardening, Health/Medicine, History, House and Home, Psychology, Sex, Spirituality, Sports, Travel, Adventure, Television tie-ins.

**Submission Guidelines** Accepts email or phone submission ideas in the first instance. Submission details to: Iain.MacGregor@Cassell-Illustrated.co.uk

**Recent Title(s)** *The New Art of Erotic Massage*, Andrew Yorke

**Tips** Cassell Illustrated's commissioning team will consider exciting new talent. Please make contact with the relevant Commissioning Editor. No submission information is available on the website but relevant contact details are as listed, alternatively please look on the 'contact us' page of the website.

## Cassell Reference

**Orion House, 5 Upper St. Martins Lane, London, WC2H 9EA**

☎ 020 7240 3444

☎ 020 7240 4822

🌐 www.orionbooks.co.uk

**Parent Company** Weidenfeld & Nicholson (Orion Publishing Group)

**Insider Info** Catalogue is available online and as a downloadable pdf.

**Non-Fiction** Publishes Illustrated and Reference titles.

**Submission Guidelines** Accepts agented submissions only.

**Recent Title(s)** *Cassell's History of English Literature*

## Catholic Truth Society

**40–46 Harleyford Road, Vauxhall Road, London, SE11 5AY**

☎ 020 7640 0042

☎ 020 7640 0046

✉ editor@cts-online.org.uk

🌐 www.cts-online.org.uk/CTS.htm

**Contact** Chairman, Rev. Peter Smith; General Secretary, Fergal Martin

**Established** 1868

**Insider Info** Catalogue is available online.

**Non-Fiction** Publishes Biography, General Non-fiction, Gift books and Reference titles on the following subjects: Alternative Lifestyles, History, Religion.

**Fiction** Publishes Religious titles.

**Recent Title(s)** *The Rosary*, Juliette Levivier

**Tips** Publications appeal to many different age groups, to Catholic parishes and schools and to the wider Christian community, as well as to a wide range of other enquirers. The principal goal of CTS publications is to explain the Catholic faith. Hopefully the publications reveal something of the love of Jesus Christ and his Church for all mankind, and for the reader in particular.

## CBD Research

**Chancery House, 15 Wickham Road, Beckenham, Kent, BR3 5JS**

☎ 0871 222 3440

☎ 020 8650 0768

✉ cbd@cbdresearch.com

🌐 www.cbdresearch.com

**Established** 1961

**Imprint(s)** Chancery House Press

**Insider Info** Catalogue is available online.

**Non-Fiction** Publishes Multimedia, Directories and Reference titles.
**Recent Title(s)** *Directory of British Associations Edition 18*, CBD Research (Directory)
**Tips** CBD Research is an independent publisher of high quality reference books and CD-ROMS. Titles are aimed at Librarians, Media Researchers, Journalists, PR, Sales and Marketing professionals, and career changers.

## The Celtic Cross Press
**Ovins Well House, Lastingham, York, YO62 6TJ**
- 01751 417298
- 01751 417739
- info@celticcrosspress.com
- http://celticcrosspress.com

**Non-Fiction** Publish short works of prose.
**Fiction** Publish short works of prose.
**Poetry** Publish reprints of fine works.
**Recent Title(s)** *Angels*, Various; *A Thrill of Pleasure*, William Wordsworth
**Tips** The Celtic Cross Press mainly publish limited editions of fine books, poetry and prose, hand-printed by letterpress on fine paper and bound in full cloth covered boards. Every book is numbered and signed. All the original illustrations are printed from blocks cut in wood or lino, or from drawings made into metal line blocks. They are a member of the Fine Press Book Association.

## Century
**Random House, 20 Vauxhall Bridge Road, London, SW1V 2SA**
- 020 7840 8554
- 020 7233 6127
- centuryeditorial@randomhouse.co.uk
- www.randomhouse.co.uk

**Parent Company** The Random House Group Ltd
**Contact** Publishing Director, Mark Booth
**Insider Info** Submissions accompanied with SAE will be returned. Catalogue is available online.
**Non-Fiction** Publishes Autobiography, Biography, General Non-fiction and Self-help titles on the following subjects: History, Spirituality, Parenting.
**Submission Guidelines** Accepts query with SAE/ Submit proposal package (including outline, one sample chapter and SAE). Will accept artwork/ photos (send photocopies).
**Fiction** Publishes Mystery, Romance, Suspense, General fiction and 'Chick Lit' titles.
**Submission Guidelines** Submit proposal package (including outline, sample chapter(s) and an SAE).

**Recent Title(s)** *Step by Step Low Fat Cookbook*, Rosemary Conley; *Dawn of Empire*, Sam Barone (Historical fiction); *Cobra Gold*, Damien Lewis (Thriller)
**Tips** Please do not email submissions. View the Century section of the main Random House catalogue for examples of publishing lists.
Please see The Random House Group Ltd entry for submission information.

## Chambers Harrap Publishers Ltd
**7 Hopetoun Crescent, Edinburgh, EH7 4AY**
- 0131 556 5929
- 0131 556 5313
- admin@chambers.co.uk
- www.chambersharrap.co.uk

**Parent Company** Hachette Livre UK (see Hachette Livre entry under *European & International Publishers*)
**Contact** Managing Director and Publisher, Patrick White
**Established** 1819
**Insider Info** Catalogue is available online.
**Non-Fiction** Publishes Dictionary, Multimedia, Reference and Scholarly titles on the following subjects:
Biographical Reference, History, Factbooks, Language, Phrasebooks, Puzzles & Games, Quotations, Science, Thesaurus, Writing Guides.
**Recent Title(s)** *Chambers Book of Speeches*, Chambers Harrap (Quotation Anthology); *The Chambers Thesaurus*, Chambers Harrap (Thesaurus)

## Chancery House Press
**Chancery House, 15 Wickham Road, Beckenham, Kent, BR3 5JS**
- 0871 222 3440
- 020 8650 0768
- cbd@cbdresearch.com
- www.cbdresearch.com

**Parent Company** CBD Research
**Non-Fiction** Publishes Esoteric, Specialist Non-fiction and Reference titles.
**Recent Title(s)** *Adhesive Wafer Seals: A Transient Victorian Phenomenon*, Michael Champness and David Trapnell (Non-fiction)
**Tips** Chancery House titles are aimed at serious researchers and dedicated hobbyists. Publishes very specialist, niche books, often the products of detailed research or cataloguing exercises. Subjects have included records of hangings and wafer seals.

## Channel 4 Books

**61–63 Uxbridge Road, London, W5 5SA**

☎ 020 8579 2652

☎ 020 8579 5479

✉ info@transworld-publishers.co.uk

🌐 www.booksattransworld.co.uk

**Parent Company** Transworld Publishers

**Insider Info** Catalogue is available online.

**Non-Fiction** Publishes Illustrated books, Television tie-ins and General Non-fiction titles.

**Submission Guidelines** Accepts agented submissions only.

**Recent Title(s)** *10 Years Younger Cosmetic Surgery Bible*, Jan Stanek

**Tips** Publish mainly non-fiction books derived from popular Channel 4 lifestyle series.


## Chapman Publishing

**4 Broughton Place, Edinburgh, EH1 3RX**

☎ 0131 557 2207

✉ chapman-pub@blueyonder.co.uk

Submission details to: chapman-pub@blueyonder.co.uk

🌐 www.chapman-pub.co.uk

**Contact** General Editor, Joy Hendry (Poetry)

**Established** 1986

**Insider Info** Publishes three titles per year. Receives approximately 200 queries and 80 manuscripts per year. 30 per cent of books published are from first-time authors, 100 per cent are from unagented authors. Payment is via royalty (on retail price).

**Fiction** Publishes Regional (Scottish) and Short story titles.

**Poetry** Publishes Scottish Poetry titles.

**Recent Title(s)** *Winter Barley*, George Gunn (Poetry)

**Tips** Chapman publishes the *Chapman* literary magazines as well as publishing new short-fiction and poetry with an emphasis on Scottish writing and Gaelic. Chapman books usually come under one of various series, including the *Wild Women Series* and *New Writing Series*.


## Charlewood Press

**7 Weavers Place, Chandlers Ford, Eastleigh, Hampshire, SO53 1TU**

☎ 023 8026 1192

✉ gponting@clara.net

🌐 http://home.clara.net/gponting/index.html

**Contact** Managing Editor, Gerald Ponting; Managing Editor, Anthony Light

**Established** 1987

**Insider Info** Catalogue is available online.

**Non-Fiction** Publishes General Non-fiction titles on the following subjects: History, Regional, Local history, Local walks.

**Recent Title(s)** *The Chandler's Ford Story*, Barbara Hillier and Gerald Ponting (Local history)

**Tips** The publisher specialises in titles on guidebooks, local history, and archaeological sites.


## Chatto & Windus

**Random House, 20 Vauxhall Bridge Road, London, SW1V 2SA**

☎ 020 7840 8540

☎ 020 7233 6117

✉ chattoeditorial@randomhouse.co.uk

🌐 www.randomhouse.co.uk

**Parent Company** The Random House Group Ltd.

**Contact** Publishing Director, Alison Samuel

**Established** Founded in the 19th Century, part of The Random House Group since 1987

**Insider Info** Submissions accompanied by SAE will be returned. Catalogue is available online.

**Non-Fiction** Publishes General Non-fiction titles on the following subjects: Government/Politics, History, Memoirs, Philosophy, Biography.

**Submission Guidelines** Accepts proposal package (including outline, one sample chapter and SAE). Will accept artwork/photos (send photocopies).

**Fiction** Publishes Literary, Mainstream/Contemporary and Translation titles.

**Submission Guidelines** Accepts proposal package (including outline, one sample chapter and SAE).

**Poetry** Publishes Classic and Contemporary Poetry titles.

**Recent Title(s)** *Edith Wharton*, Hermione Lee; *Our Horses in Egypt*, Rosalind Belben

**Tips** Strongly prefer agented submissions and do not accept email submissions. Look at the Chatto & Windus section of the catalogue to get a feel for the list before submitting.


## The Cherry on the Top Press

**29 Vickers Road, Firth Park, Sheffield, S5 6UY**

☎ 0114 244 1202

✉ dgk@kennedyd.fsworld.co.uk

🌐 www.indigogroup.co.uk/llpp/cherry.html

**Contact** Publisher, David Kennedy

**Insider Info** Catalogue available free on request. No unsolicited manuscripts.

**Non-Fiction** Publishes Gift books.

**Fiction** Publishes Short story collections.

**Poetry** Publishes Poetry titles.

**Recent Title(s)** *Four True Prophecies of the New State*, David Kennedy; *A Walk Towards Spicer,* Stephen Vincent (Contemporary Poetry)

**Tips** The press publishes artist's books, small run pamphlets of innovative writing and a magazine of innovative poems in English called *The Paper*. The press is unable to consider unsolicited submissions.

## Chicken House Publishing
**2 Palmer Street, Frome, Somerset, BA11 1DS**
- 01373 454488
- 01373 454499
- chickenhouse@doublecluck.com
- www.doublecluck.com/index.php

**Contact** Publisher/Managing Director, Barry Cunningham; Deputy Managing Director, Rachel Hickman

**Established** 2000

**Insider Info** Aims to respond to proposals and manuscripts within three months. Catalogue and manuscript guidelines are available online.

**Fiction** Publishes Teenage, Picture books, and Children's titles.

**Submission Guidelines** Accepts query with SAE/Proposal package (including outline and three sample chapters). No email submissions.

**Recent Title(s)** *Candy*, Kevin Brooks (Novel)

**Tips** The Chicken House is a plucky, highly individual, children's book publishing company with an enthusiasm for finding new writers, artists and ideas. Chicken House books have found worldwide popularity with children, parents, teachers and librarians.

## Child's Play (International)
**Ashworth Road, Bridgemead, Swindon, Wiltshire, SN5 7YD**
- 01793 616286
- www.childs-play.com

**Contact** Chief Executive, Neil Burden

**Insider Info** Catalogue is free on request and available online or by email.

**Non-Fiction** Publishes Children's/Juvenile titles.

**Fiction** Publishes Picture books, Board books and Children's titles.

**Recent Title(s)** *Bear and Turtle and the Great Lake Race*, Andrew Fusek Peters (Children's)

**Tips** Child's Play is an independent publisher specialising in learning through play with a range of books, games, toys and other resources (aimed at Key Stage 1 & 2). Company products also support minority groups and languages.

## Chimera
**Sheraton House, Castle Park, Cambridge, CB3 0AX**
- 01223 370012
- 01223 370040
- editors@pegasuspublishers.com
- www.pegasuspublishers.com

**Parent Company** Pegasus Elliot MacKenzie Publishers Ltd

**Insider Info** Catalogue and manuscript details are available online.

**Fiction** Publishes Erotica titles.

**Submission Guidelines** Accepts proposal package (including outline and two sample chapters).

**Tips** Chimera publishes adult erotic fiction for over 18s and specialises in the work of 'previously unpublished first time authors from all over the world who have a good spanking tale to tell.' Chimera accepts submissions of erotic fiction from any author over the age of 18 as long as the content does not 'contravene the Law of the Land or International Law.'

## Christian Education
**1020 Bristol Road, Selly Oak, Birmingham, B29 6LB**
- 0121 472 4242
- 0121 472 7575
- editorial@christianeducation.org.uk
- www.christianeducation.org.uk

**Contact** Senior Editor, Anstice Hughes

**Insider Info** Catalogue is available online.

**Non-Fiction** Publishes Textbook, Worship resources and Scholarly titles on Religion.

**Fiction** Publishes Religious and Children's religious titles.

**Tips** Christian Education (CE) provides advice, resources and opportunities for teaching and learning in the school, the church and the family group, carrying forward the work of the National Christian Education Council (NCEC, formerly the National Sunday School Union) and the Christian Education Movement (CEM). The two organisations are now joining together to maximise their delivery of high quality training and resources for Christian educators and for teachers of Religious Education in schools. Works must be aimed at academic usage either for schools or church groups.

## Christian Focus Publications
**Geanies House, Fearn by Tain, Ross-shire, IV20 1TW**

☎ 01862 871011
🖷 01862 871699
✉ info@christianfocus.com
🌐 www.christianfocus.com
**Contact** Editorial Manager, Willie Mackenzie
**Established** 1979
**Imprint(s)** CF4Kids
Christian Heritage
Mentor
**Insider Info** Catalogue and manuscript guidelines are available online.
**Non-Fiction** Publishes Children's/Juvenile, General Non-fiction, Gift books, Scholarly books on religion and Religious titles.
**Submission Guidelines** Query with SAE/Proposal package (including outline, two sample chapters, author biography and SAE).
**Fiction** Publishes Children's titles.
**Recent Title(s)** *God in the Shadows*, Brain Morley (Religious)
**Tips** Titles are aimed at all ages and abilities. Christian Focus Publications (CFP) has been producing Christian books since the early 1970s, originally starting as a publisher of classic Scottish authors. The addition of children's colour Bible story books in the early 1980s prefaced an expansion of the company, with books by authors from five continents sold all around the world. CFP books have been translated into 40 different languages. Christian Focus Publications is a conservative, evangelical publishing house. It comes from a non-denominational reformed background and although it is not insisted that all authors call themselves reformed, anything that would be a polemic against the reformed faith would not be considered. CFP are committed to the historic foundations of the faith, the inerrancy of Scripture in its original manuscripts, the deity of Christ, His uniqueness as a means of salvation and the existence of hell.

## Christopher Davies Publishers
**PO Box 403, Swansea, SA1 4YF**
☎ 01792 648825
🖷 01792 648825
✉ editor@cdaviesbookswales.com
🌐 www.cdaviesbookswales.com/index.htm
**Contact** Director, Chris Talfan Davies; Editor; Morwenna Talfan Davies
**Insider Info** Catalogue is available online.
**Non-Fiction** Publishes General Non-fiction on the following subjects: History, Regional, Sports, Travel, Welsh interest.

**Recent Title(s)** *An A-Z of Wales and the Welsh*, Terry Breverton (Welsh interest/reference)
**Tips** Titles are aimed at anyone interested in books about Wales, her culture and her people. All books are of general Welsh interest or concerning Welsh history.

## Christopher Helm
**38 Soho Square, London, W1D 3HB**
☎ 020 7758 0200
🖷 020 7758 0222
✉ ornithology@acblack.com
🌐 www.acblack.com
**Parent Company** A&C Black Publishers Ltd
**Contact** Department Head, Nigel Redman; Publishing Director, Jonathan Glasspool (Reference, Theatre and Ornithology)
**Established** 1983
**Insider Info** Catalogue is available online.
**Non-Fiction** Publishes General Non-fiction, Illustrated books and Reference titles on the following subjects: Nature/Environment, Ornithology.
**Recent Title(s)** *Secret Lives of British Birds*, Dominic Couzens (Ornithology)
**Tips** Christopher Helm publishes taxonomic and geographic bird books, identification and field guides, and general interest nature books. Also publishes the 'Where to Watch' series and books for the RSPB. Along with the other A&C Black nature imprints, Christopher Helm is the largest bird book publisher in the English language. Christopher Helm publishes material from well known or celebrity naturalists, such as Bill Oddie, and books in conjunction with companies such as the RSPB. They do not generally consider unsolicited material.

## Chrysalis Children's Books
**151 Freston Road, London, W10 6TH**
☎ 020 7314 1400
🖷 020 7314 1401
🌐 www.anovabooks.com
**Parent Company** Anova Books Company Ltd
**Insider Info** Catalogue available online.
**Non-fiction** Publishes Children's Illustrated reference titles.
**Fiction** Publishes Children's Picture Book, Novelty and Classic titles.
**Recent Title(s)** *War Boy*, Michael Foreman (Wartime childhood memoir)
**Tips** Chrysalis Children's Books are published within the Anova Books Company and are separated into three divisions: Pre-school and Fiction; Education

and Non-Fiction. The age range covered is from infants to ten plus years.

## Churchill Livingstone
**32 Jamestown Road, Camden Town, London, NW1 7BY**
- 020 7424 4200
- 020 7482 2293
- m.ging@elsevier.com
- www.intl.elsevierhealth.com/cl

**Parent Company** Elsevier Ltd (Health Sciences)
**Established** 1972
**Insider Info** Payment is via royalties. Catalogue and manuscript guidelines are available online.
**Non-Fiction** Publishes Multimedia, Reference, Scholarly, Textbook, Journals and Technical titles on the following subjects: Education, Health/ Medicine, Science.
**Submission Guidelines** Accepts submissions via online proposal form.
Submissions email: c.makepeace@elsevier.com
**Recent Title(s)** *District Nursing: Providing Care in a Supportive Context*, Sally Lawton Jane Cantrell and Jane Harris (Healthcare/Reference)
**Tips** Churchill Livingstone is a global publisher of health and medical books, journals and CD-ROMs, including medical reference for health professionals and textbooks for lecturers and students. To submit a proposal to Churchill Livingstone fill in and return a proposal form, available on the website. Alternatively authors may contact the publishing director or editor prior to submission to discuss the proposal.

## Churchwarden Publications Ltd
**PO Box 420, Warminster, BA12 9XB**
- 01985 840189
- 01985 840243
**Contact** Managing Director, John Stidolph
**Established** 1974
**Insider Info** Publishes two titles per year.
**Tips** Publishes books and stationery aimed at Churchwardens and Administrators.

## Cicerone Press Ltd
**2 Police Square, Milnthorpe, Cumbria, LA7 7PY**
- 01539 562069
- 01539 563417
- info@cicerone.co.uk
- www.cicerone.co.uk
**Contact** Director, Jonathan Williams (all areas)
**Established** 1968

**Imprint(s)** Cicerone
**Insider Info** Publishes 30 titles per year. Receives approximately 400 queries and 50 manuscripts per year. 10 per cent of books are from first-time authors, 90 per cent are from unagented authors. Payment is via royalty (on wholesale price) 0.10 (per £) maximum (on retail price) 0.10 (per £). Average lead time is nine months. Submissions accompanied by SAE will be returned. Aims to respond to queries within seven days, proposals within 28 days, manuscripts within two days. Catalogue and manuscript guidelines are available free on request and online.
**Non-Fiction** Publishes walking guidebooks and titles on the following subjects: Guidance, Nature/ Environment, Recreation, Travel.
\* Almost exclusively guidebooks for walking, trekking, mountaineering and cycling.
**Submission Guidelines** Accepts proposal package (including outline, sample chapter(s), your publishing history, clips and author biography). Will accept artwork/photos (send digital files as jpegs). Submissions email: info@cicerone.co.uk
**Fiction** \* No fiction at this time.
**Recent Title(s)** *Tour of the Jungfrau Region*, Kev Reynolds (Guidebook)
**Tips** Titles are always aimed at adults.

## Cico Books
**1st Floor, 32 Great Sutton Street, London, EC1V 0NB**
- 020 7253 7960
- 020 7253 7967
**Contact** Managing Director, Mark Collins; Publisher, Lucinda Richards
**Established** 1999
**Non-Fiction** Publishes Illustrated book and General Non-fiction titles on the following subjects: Spirituality, Lifestyle/Interiors, Mind/Body/Spirit.
**Tips** Cico Books publish stylish, highly illustrated non-fiction for the worldwide co-edition market. They specialise in design, interiors, craft, health, mind, body and spirit, magic, history and gift books. Please do not send any unsolicited submissions.

## Cinnamon Press
**Meirion House, Glan yr afon, Tanygrisiau, Blaenau Ffestiniog, Gwynedd, LL41 3SU**
- firstname@cinnamonpress.com
- www.cinnamonpress.com
**Contact** Jan Fortune-Wood (Writers' queries); Mike Fortune-Wood (Trade/Publicity/Payment queries)

**Insider Info** Submissions accompanied by an SAE will be returned. Catalogue and manuscript guidelines are available online.

**Non-Fiction** Publishes General Non-fiction titles on no specific subject areas, but want to see manuscripts that are unique and thought provoking. No purely academic titles, or books with a strictly local appeal.

 * Past non-fiction titles have focused on alternative parenting and memoirs, but Cinnamon Press are open to a much wider range of books, providing they are well written.

**Submission Guidelines** Accepts full proposal my mail only (including details of intended market, synopsis, chapter outlines, first 5,000 words of the book, covering letter stating your writing aims, your publishing CV and SAE).

**Fiction** Publishes all genres except erotica, crime and horror.

 * Publish full length novels that are unique and affecting. No children's novels, although well written work for older teenagers will be considered.

**Submission Guidelines** Accepts proposal package (including outline, first three chapters double spaced, and your publishing CV).

**Poetry** Publish Poetry titles.

 * Poetry should be modern, have depth and an edge.

**Submission Guidelines** Submit ten sample poems.

**Tips** Books should have a wide audience appeal and the publishers state that they are particularly interested in authors who can demonstrate a willingness to actively promote their work to the widest possible audience, particularly through local and national media. All submissions should be made by post only. Although Cinnamon Press publish authors from around the world, they intend to strongly promote the voice of Welsh writers. Check the website for any specific calls for anthology contributions.

## CIPD Publishing
**151 The Broadway, London, SW19 1JQ**
- 020 8612 6562
- 020 8612 6201
- j.steventon@cipd.co.uk
- www.cipd.co.uk/bookstore

**Parent Company** CIPD Enterprises Ltd (Chartered Insititute of Personnel and Development)

**Contact** Commissioning Editor, Jenna Steventon (Student Textbooks); Commissioning Editor, Margaret Marriott (Professional Publications and Toolkits).

**Insider Info** Payment is via royalty (on wholesale price). Catalogue is available free on request and online. A hard copy catalogue/brochure can be ordered from the website.

**Non-Fiction** Publishes Textbooks, Subscription products, Toolkits, Electronic and General Non-fiction titles on the following subjects:
 Human Resources, Business Economics, Coaching, Learning and Development, General Management, Employment Law.

**Submission Guidelines** Accepts proposal package (including outline, two sample chapters, author biography, competition analysis and market research).

**Recent Title(s)** *Continuing Professional Development 2nd Edition*, David Megginson and Vivien Whitaker

**Tips** CIPD Publishing's readership consists of human resources practitioners, students and human resources training professionals. Author guidelines and instructions for initial proposal are available to download from the website.

## Cisco Press
**Edinburgh Gate, Harlow, Essex, CM20 2JE**
- 01279 623623
- 01279 414130
- www.pearsoned.co.uk/Imprints/CiscoPress

**Parent Company** Pearson Education

**Insider Info** Catalogue and manuscript guidelines are available online.

**Non-Fiction** Publishes Reference, Textbooks and Scholarly titles on the following subjects:
 Computers, Computer Networking, Electronics, Server Mechanics.

**Submission Guidelines** Accepts proposal package (including synopsis, sample chapters, market research, your publishing history and author biography).

**Recent Title(s)** *PacketCable Implementation*, Jeff Riddel (Networking)

**Tips** Cisco Press is a partnership between Cisco Systems and Pearson Education. Cisco Press is the Cisco Systems authorised book publisher of Cisco Networking Technology, Cisco Certification Self Study, and Cisco Networking Academy programme materials for students and professionals. Leading authorities from Cisco Systems, and other industry innovators write and contribute to the various titles and series, which make up the Cisco Press product family.

## CJ Fallon

**Ground Floor, Block B, Liffey Valley Office Campus, Dublin, Republic of Ireland**
☎ 00353 1 616 6400
☎ 00353 1 616 6499
✉ editorial@cjfallon.ie
🌐 www.cjfallon.ie
**Contact** Managing Director, H.J. McNicholas; Editorial Director, N. White
**Established** 1927
**Non-Fiction** Publishes Textbooks and Scholarly titles on Education.

## Clairview Books

**Hillside Lodge, The Square, Forest Row, East Sussex, RH18 5ES**
☎ 0870 486 3526
✉ office@clairviewbooks.com
🌐 www.clairviewbooks.com
**Parent Company** Temple Lodge Publishing
**Established** 2000
**Insider Info** Catalogue is free on request or available online.
**Non-Fiction** Publishes General Non-fiction titles on the following subjects:
Art, Current Affairs, Health and Healing, History, Politics, Spiritual Experience, World Affairs.
**Recent Title(s)** *The Oil Depletion Protocol*, Richard Heinberg (Politics/Current Affairs); *Birth and Breastfeeding,* Michel Odent (Childcare)
**Tips** Clairview Books publishes non-fiction titles that engage with contemporary issues and challenge conventional thinking.

## Co & Bear Productions

**565 Fulham Road, London, SW6 1ES**
☎ 020 7385 0888
☎ 020 7385 0101
✉ info@cobear.co.uk
**Contact** Publisher, Beatrice Vincenzini
**Established** 1996
**Imprint(s)** Scriptum Editions
Cartago
**Non-Fiction** Publishes Illustrated books on the following subjects: Alternative Lifestyles, Art/Architecture, Photography.

## Colin Smythe Limited

**PO Box 6, Gerrards Cross, Buckinghamshire, SL9 8XA**
☎ 01753 886000
☎ 01753 886469
✉ cs@colinsmythe.co.uk
🌐 www.colinsmythe.co.uk
**Contact** Managing Director, Colin Smythe
**Established** 1966
**Imprint(s)** Dolmen Press
Van Duren Publishers
**Insider Info** Publishes eight titles per year. Receives approximately 50–100 queries per year. Payment is via royalty (on retail price). Simultaneous submissions are not accepted. Submissions accompanied by SAE will be returned.
**Non-Fiction** Publishes General Non-fiction and illustrated titles on the following subjects: Biography, History, Literary Criticism, Theatre History, Parapsychology, Supernatural, Folklore, Heraldry, Mysticism.
**Fiction** Publishes Fantasy and Science fiction titles.

## Collins & Brown

**151 Freston Road, London, W10 6TH**
☎ 020 7314 1400
☎ 020 7314 1401
🌐 www.anovabooks.com
**Parent Company** Anova Books Company Ltd
**Contact** Tom Stainer
**Established** 1989
**Insider Info** Catalogue is available online.
**Non-Fiction** Publishes How-to, Illustrated books, Reference and Self-help titles on the following subjects: Art/Architecture, Cooking/Foods/Nutrition, Crafts, Gardening, Photography, Spirituality, Health, Lifestyle and Personal Development.
**Submission Guidelines** Submissions email: tstainer@anovabooks.com
**Recent Title(s)** *Heirloom Knits*, Judith McLeod-Odell
**Tips** The Collins & Brown imprint publishes high quality illustrated books that adopt a 'how-to' approach across a range of subjects. See Anova Books entry for more information about the company.

## Collins

**77–85 Fulham Palace Road, Hammersmith, London, W6 8JB**
☎ 020 8741 7070
☎ 020 8307 4440
✉ customerservice@harpercollins.co.uk
🌐 www.collins.co.uk
**Parent Company** HarperCollins Publishers Ltd
**Contact** Managing Director, Thomas Webster
**Established** 1819
**Imprint(s)** Collins Reference Books

Collins Dictionaries/COBUILD
Collins Education
Collins Maps & Atlases

**Insider Info** Catalogue available online.
**Non-Fiction** Publish Gift books, How-to, Multimedia, Reference, Self-help, Textbook, Guidebooks, Maps, Atlases and Dictionary titles on the following subjects: Animals, Art/Architecture, Astrology/Psychic, Child Guidance/Parenting, Contemporary Culture, Cooking/Foods/Nutrition, Education, Gardening, House and Home, Language/Literature, Military/War, Nature/Environment, Religion, Travel, DIY, Home Learning.
**Submission Guidelines** Accepts agented submissions only.
**Recent Title(s)** *Wine* (Collins Gem)

## Collins Dictionaries/COBUILD
**77–85 Fulham Palace Road, Hammersmith, London, W6 8JB**
- 020 8741 7070
- 020 8307 4440
- customerservice@harpercollins.co.uk
- www.collins.co.uk

**Parent Company** Collins (HarperCollins Publishers Ltd)
**Contact** Managing Director, Lorna Knight; Publishing Director, Michela Clari; Publishing Director, Helen Newstead (Online and Electonic Development)
**Insider Info** Catalogue is available online.
**Non-Fiction** Publishes Multimedia, Dictionaries and Reference titles on the following subjects: Language/Literature, Translation.
**Submission Guidelines** Accepts agented submissions only.
**Recent Title(s)** *Advanced Learner's English Dictionary (5th Edition)*, Collins COBUILD (Bilingual Dictionary)
**Tips** Publishes bilingual and English dictionaries, as well as the internationally successful Collins COBUILD series of dictionaries for foreign learners. Collins Dictionaries does not accept submissions.

## Collins Education
**77–85 Fulham Palace Road, Hammersmith, London, W6 8JB**
- 020 8741 7070
- 020 8307 4440
- editorial@collinseducation.com
- www.collinseducation.com

**Parent Company** Collins (HarperCollins Publishers Ltd)

**Contact** Managing Director, Jim Green; Publishing Director, Paul Cherry (Education); Publishing Director, Brenda Stones (Home Learning)
**Insider Info** Catalogue is available online.
**Non-Fiction** Publishes Children's/Juvenile, General Non-fiction and Multimedia titles on Education.
**Submission Guidelines** Accepts agented submissions only.
**Recent Title(s)** *Exam Practice: GCSE English (Series)*, John Reynolds (Education)
**Tips** Collins Education publishes books and electronic materials, including CD-ROMs and online resources for schools, colleges and universities, as well as students of any age, and home learners. Collins Education accepts queries and proposals from academic authors for educational books or materials. Contact by email with ideas in the first instance.

## Collins Maps & Atlases
**77–85 Fulham Palace Road, Hammersmith, London, W6 8JB**
- 020 8741 7070
- 020 8307 4440
- customerservice@harpercollins.co.uk
- www.collins.co.uk

**Parent Company** Collins (HarperCollins Publishers Ltd)
**Contact** Managing Director, Mike Cottingham; Publishing Director, Helen Gordon
**Insider Info** Catalogue is available online.
**Non-Fiction** Publishes Maps/Atlases/Street Guides and Reference titles on the following subjects: History, Military/War, Nature/Environment, Travel.
**Submission Guidelines** Accepts agented submissions only.
**Recent Title(s)** *Collins Atlas of World War II*, John Keegan (Military History/Atlas)
**Tips** Collins Maps & Atlases publish illustrated maps, atlases, road and leisure travel guides. HarperCollins only accepts submissions from literary agents or previously published authors, but may consider submissions that are accompanied by a positive assessment from a manuscript assessment agency.

## Collins Reference Books
**77–85 Fulham Palace Road, Hammersmith, London, W6 8JB**
- 020 8741 7070
- 020 8307 4440
- customerservice@harpercollins.co.uk
- www.collins.co.uk

**Parent Company** Collins (HarperCollins Publishers Ltd )

**Contact** Managing Director, Sarah Bailey; Publishing Director, Denise Bates

**Imprint(s)** Jane's
Times Books

**Insider Info** Catalogue is available online.

**Non-Fiction** Publishes General Non-fiction, Atlases, Illustrated and Reference titles on the following subjects: Animals, Art/Architecture, Cooking/Foods/Nutrition, Crafts, Gardening, History, Language/Literature, Military/War, Nature/Environment, Regional, Translation, Travel.

**Submission Guidelines** Accepts agented submissions only.

**Recent Title(s)** *Garden Natural History*, Collins New Naturalist Series (Natural History)

**Tips** The Jane's imprint publishes military reference and guidebooks while Times Books publishes educational books, as well as books on astronomy and the Times World Atlas series. Collins Reference has many series, including Collins New Naturalist, Collins Gem and the new Collins Need to Know? series. HarperCollins only accepts submissions from literary agents or previously published authors, but may consider submissions that are accompanied by a positive assessment from a manuscript assessment agency.

## The Collins Press

**West Link Park, Doughcloyne, Wilton, Cork, Republic of Ireland**

- 00353 21 434 7717
- 00353 21 434 7720
- enquiries@collinspress.ie
- www.collinspress.ie

**Contact** Con Collins

**Established** 1989

**Insider Info** Catalogue and manuscript guidelines available online.

**Non-Fiction** Publishes Biography, General Non-fiction, Illustrated and Reference titles on the following subjects:
Anthropology/Archaeology, Art/Architecture, Cooking/Foods/Nutrition, Health/Medicine, History, Hobbies, Memoirs, Music/Dance, Nature/Environment, Regional, Spirituality, Sports, Travel.

**Submission Guidelines** Accepts query with SAE/proposal package (including outline, three sample chapters, your publishing history and author biography). Submit completed manuscript.

**Recent Title(s)** *Little Lady, One Man, Big Ocean*, Paul Gleeson and Tori Holmes with Liam Gorman (Memoir)

**Tips** The Collins Press's interests as a publisher are not limited to specific subject areas. Their assessment of a book's worth is based upon the quality of the writing, how well it engages the interest of the reader and whether it has new, interesting or original material. They do not publish poetry, short stories, drama or literary criticism and are discontinuing adult fiction for the present. Unsolicited material in any of these categories will not be returned.

## Colourpoint Books

**Colourpoint House, Jubilee Business Park, 21 Jubilee Road, Newtownards, BT23 4YH, Northern Ireland**

- 028 9182 0505
- 028 9182 1900
- info@colourpoint.co.uk
- www.colourpoint.co.uk

**Contact** Partner, Sheila Johnston (Educational); Partner, Norman Johnston (Transportation/General); Partner, Malcolm Johnston; Partner, Wesley Johnston

**Established** 1993

**Insider Info** Publishes 25 titles per year. Aims to respond to proposals and manuscripts within two months. Catalogue and submission details are available online.

**Non-Fiction** Publishes General Non-fiction, Illustrated books, Textbooks and Scholarly titles on the following subjects: Education, Regional, Travel, Irish interest, Travel maps (UK), School textbooks.

**Submission Guidelines** Accepts query with SAE/proposal package (including outline, sample chapter(s), your publishing history and SAE). Will accepts emailed queries.
Submissions email: sheila@colourpoint.co.uk (write 'submissions query' as the subject line).

**Recent Title(s)** *Reading and Writing: GCSE English*, Freddy Clifford and Pat McGuckian

**Tips** Titles mainly aimed at students and teachers, or anyone involved with the education system. Before approaching the publisher with a proposal, be sure that it fits with the Colourpoint list, whose specialisms mainly lie in educational texbooks and transport subjects such as trains and buses.

## The Columba Press

**55a Spruce Avenue, Stillorgan Industrial Park, Blackrock, Dublin, Republic of Ireland**

- 00353 1 294 2556
- 00353 1 294 2564
- info@columba.ie

www.columba.ie
**Contact** Managing Director/Publisher, Sean O'Boyle
**Established** 1985
**Imprint(s)** Currach Press
**Insider Info** Publishes 30 titles per year. Payment is via royalties. Catalogue available online.
**Non-Fiction** Publishes General Non-fiction titles on the following subjects:
Counselling/Career, Religion, Spirituality, Prayer books/Hymnals.
**Submission Guidelines** Accepts query with SAE or via email.
Submission details to: sean@columba.ie
**Recent Title(s)** *Let the Reader Understand: The Sunday Readings of Year C*, Sean Goan
**Tips** Columba publishes across a broad range of areas, including pastoral resources, spirituality, theology, the arts and history. They often publish seasonal themed books, such as hymns for Christmas or Easter. Proposals should be tagged to specific seasons, and submitted far enough in advance to be effective.

## Comma Press
**3rd Floor, 24 Lever Street, Manchester, M1 1DW**
07792 564747
commapublications@yahoo.co.uk
www.commapress.co.uk
**Contact** Editor, Maria Crossan; Editor, Ra Page; Funding Manager, Jim Hinks; Consultant Editor, Sarah Eyre; Editorial Assistant, Tim Goodall
**Established** 2002
**Insider Info** Simultaneous submissions are not accepted. Submissions accompanied by an SAE will be returned. Manuscript guidelines are available.
**Fiction** Publishes Short story collections (No stories on coming of age, student life, drug taking, splitting up with a partner, or anecdotes).
* Comma Press seek new writers to contribute to short story anthologies and any specific calls for submissions will be on the website.
**Submission Guidelines** Accepts proposal package (including story between 800 and 5,000 words and full contact details via email, A4 one sided, double spaced hard copy via post). Submit completed manuscript. Submissions email: ra.page@commapress.co.uk
**Poetry** Publishes original, previously unpublished poetry from published writers.
* When submitting samples, try and be representative and include in the covering letter any magazine or anthology credits.
**Submission Guidelines** Submit six sample poems. Hard copies of the submission should be sent to:

Comma Poetry, 3 Vale Bower, Mytholmroyd, West Yorkshire, HX7 5EP.
Submissions email: ra.page@commapress.co.uk
**Recent Title(s)** *The Book of Leeds*, Maria Crossan and Tom Palmer (ed.)
**Tips** Comma Press is a not for profit publishing collective, with a particular focus on the short story. For potential contributors to anthologies, reading a sample of previously published short fiction is highly recommended. The website FAQ section contains detailed advice on what the editors do not like to see in new writing.

## Compendium Publishing
**43 Frith Street, London, W1D 4SA**
020 7287 4570
020 7494 0583
alan.greene@compendiumpublishing.com
**Contact** Managing Director, Alan Greene; Editorial Director, Simon Forty
**Established** 1996
**Non-Fiction** Publishes Children's/Juvenile, Illustrated books and General Non-fiction titles on the following subjects: Education, History, Hobbies, Transportation.
**Submission Guidelines** Accepts query with SAE.
**Tips** Compendium Publishing have a fast growing programme of high quality, illustrated non-fiction titles for the general trade, and educational and reference materials for schools and colleges. Generally publishes and packages for international publishing companies and does not accept unsolicited manuscripts. However, they will consider brief idea proposals.

## Connections Book Publishing
**St. Chad's House, 148 Kings Cross Road, London, WC1X 9DH**
020 7837 1968
020 7837 2025
info@connections-publishing.com
www.connections-publishing.com
**Contact** Nick Eddison
**Insider Info** Catalogue is available online.
**Non-Fiction** Publishes Gift books, Illustrated books, Box books and General Non-fiction titles on the following subjects: New Age, Spirituality.
**Recent Title(s)** *The Arturian Tarot*, Caitlín Matthews and John Matthews (Gift book/Tarot cards)
**Tips** Connections is a new imprint offering superbly produced titles to meet the growing demands of the new age market. The list comprises interactive book, plus kits, many of which have become market

leaders in their field, as well as beautifully illustrated and expertly written books in traditional areas. Specialises in gift book and curios such as 'books in a box'. Favours the unusual product, aimed at a new age market.

## Conran Octopus

**2–4 Heron Quays, London, E14 4JP**

☎ 020 7531 8400

☎ 020 7531 8627

✉ info@conran-octopus.co.uk

🌐 www.conran-octopus.co.uk

**Parent Company** Octopus Publishing Group

**Contact** Publishing Director, Lorraine Dickey; Art Director, Jonathan Christie

**Established** 1984

**Insider Info** Catalogue is available online.

**Non-Fiction** Publishes Illustrated titles on the following subjects:
 Crafts, Food and Drink, Gardens, Interiors and Design, Living.

**Recent Title(s)** *Wall Effects,* Katie Ebben (Interior Design); *Eat London: All About Food,* Terence Conran and Peter Prescott (Food/Culture)

**Tips** Conran Octopus is a leading illustrated book publisher. Conran aims to publish books which combine authoritative and informed writing with cutting edge design and sumptuous photography.

## Constable & Robinson Ltd

**3 The Lanchesters, 162 Fulham Palace Road, London, W6 9ER**

☎ 020 8741 3663

☎ 020 8748 7562

✉ enquiries@constablerobinson.com

🌐 www.constablerobinson.com

**Contact** Publisher and Managing Director, Nick Robinson; Commissioning Editor, Becky Hardie (Non-fiction); Editorial Director, Krystyna Green (True Crime, Crime Fiction); Editorial Director, Pete Duncan (Illustrated co-editions); Manager, Fritha Saunders (Overcoming CBT series); Commissioning Editor, Leo Hollis (Non-fiction)

**Insider Info** Publishes 160 titles per year. Receives approximately 3,000 queries and 1,000 manuscripts per year. Payment via royalty and advance is offered. Average lead time is one year with simultaneous submissions accepted. Aims to respond to proposals within one month and queries within three months. Catalogue is free on request.

**Non-Fiction** Publishes Autobiography, Biography, General Non-fiction and Illustrated titles on the following subjects:

Current Affairs, World Politics, Military History, Health, Psychology, Travel, Photography.
 * Publishes across a wide range of non-fiction areas. Well known for the Overcoming CBT series, a series of consumer friendly psychology and behavioural therapy books, designed to help people overcome mental illnesses.

**Submission Guidelines** Accepts query with SAE, or proposal package (including outline, one sample chapter). Will accept artworks/images (send photocopies).

**Fiction** Publishes Mainstream/Contemporary, Mystery, Suspense and Crime fiction titles.

**Submission Guidelines** Accepts query with SAE, or proposal package (including outline, one sample chapter).

**Tips** Constable & Robinson does not accept email submissions and does not accept children's fiction or any adult fiction other than crime.

## Contact Publishing

**Unit 346, 176 Finchley Road, London, NW3 6BT**

✉ info@contact-publishing.co.uk

🌐 www.contact-publishing.co.uk

**Contact** Anne Kontoyannis

**Established** 2003

**Insider Info** Aims to respond to proposals and manuscripts within one month. Catalogue and manuscript guidelines are available online.

**Non-Fiction** Publisher General Non-fiction and Self-help titles on the following subjects: Health/Medicine, Spirituality, Inspirational, Mind/Body/Spirit, Self-help.

**Submission Guidelines** Accepts query with SAE/proposal package (including outline, sample chapter(s) and SAE).

**Fiction** Publishes Short story collections and Spiritual titles.

**Submission Guidelines** Accepts query with SAE/proposal package (including outline, sample chapter(s) and SAE).

**Recent Title(s)** *A Suitcase of Adventures: The Inside Story,* Brendan Maguire (Travel/Humour); *The Tainted Shadow,* Maleeha Kamal (Novel)

**Tips** The mission of Contact Publishing is to highlight the diversity of new thought and perspective, whilst at the same time providing unknown and unpublished authors with an opportunity to reach the world with their stories and ideas. Every manuscript is read and every effort is made to respond to submissions within one month of receipt, though periodic backlog can result in delays to response times. Contact regret that the quantity of submissions received prevents the possibility of entering into correspondence concerning individual submissions.

## The Continuum International Publishing Group
**The Tower Building, 11 York Road, London, SE1 7NX**
- 020 7922 0880
- 020 7922 0881
- rbairdsmith@continuumbooks.com
- www.continuumbooks.com

**Contact** Publishing Director, Robin Baird-Smith (General Trade and Religion); Associate Publisher, Anna Sandeman (Literary Studies and Humanities); Commissioning Editor, Joanne Allcock (Academic Division, Education)
**Established** 1999
**Imprint(s)** Burns & Oates
Thoemmes Continuum
T & T Clark
**Insider Info** Publishes over 500 titles per year. Catalogue and manuscript guidelines are available online.
**Non-Fiction** Publishes General Non-fiction, Reference and Scholarly titles on the following subjects:
Education, Government/Politics, History, Language/Literature, Philosophy, Religion, Biblical studies, Theology, Popular Culture.
**Submission Guidelines** Accepts proposal package (including outline, your publishing history, author biography and market research). Send no more than four A4 sheets.
**Tips** Send submissions directly to the relevant editorial contact. See the company website for full contact details, downloads and submission guidelines. Also see individual imprint entries for more information.

## Conway Maritime Press
**151 Freston Road, London, W10 6TH**
- 020 7314 1400
- 020 7314 1401
- info@anovabooks.com
- www.anovabooks.com

**Parent Company** Anova Books Company Ltd
**Non-fiction** Publishes General Non-fiction and Illustrated titles on the following subjects:
History, Maritime, Military History, Transportation.
**Recent Title(s)** *Send a Gunboat*, Anthony Preston and John Major (Maritime/Military History)
**Tips** Focuses entirely on maritime and shipping culture, including military elements.

## Corgi
**61–63 Uxbridge Road, London, W5 5SA**
- 020 8579 2652
- 020 8579 5479
- info@transworld-publishers.co.uk
- www.booksattransworld.co.uk

**Parent Company** Transworld Publishers
**Insider Info** Catalogue is available online. Manuscript guidelines are not available.
**Non-Fiction** Publishes Biography and General Non-fiction titles on the following subjects: Sex, Relationships.
**Submission Guidelines** Accepts agented submissions only.
**Fiction** Publishes Historical, Humour, Mainstream/Contemporary, Mystery, Romance and Suspense titles.
**Submission Guidelines** Accepts agented submissions only.
**Recent Title(s)** *The Unknown Soldier*, Neil Hanson (Historical account); *The Crime Code*, Michael Cordy (Crime fiction); *Fred*, David Hall (Biography)
**Tips** Please do not send unsolicited submissions. See entry Transworld Publishers for more information. Individual imprint category information can be requested by email.

## Corgi Children's Books
**61–63 Uxbridge Road, London, W5 5SA**
- 020 8231 6439
- 020 8231 6767
- childrenseditorial@randomhouse.co.uk
- www.randomhouse.co.uk/childrens

**Parent Company** Random House Children's Books
**Insider Info** Catalogue is available online.
**Fiction** Publishes Children's and Teenage novels.
**Submission Guidelines** Accepts proposal package (including outline and one sample chapter).
**Recent Title(s)** *The Medici Seal*, Theresa Breslin; *The Intruders*, E.E. Richardson
**Tips** Agented submissions are strongly preferred.

## Cork University Press
**Youngline Industrial Estate, Pouladuff Road, Togher, Cork, Republic of Ireland**
- 00353 21 490 2980
- 00353 21 431 5329
- mike.collins@ucc.ie
- www.corkuniversitypress.com

**Contact** Publications Director, Mike Collins; Editor, Sophie Watson
**Established** 1925

**Insider Info** Catalogue and manuscript guidelines are available online.

**Non-Fiction** Publishes General Non-fiction, Illustrated, Reference and Scholarly titles on the following subjects:
Art/Architecture, Government/Politics, History, Language/Literature, Law, Music/Dance, Philosophy, Travel, Women's issues andstudies, Current Affairs, Film studies.

**Submission Guidelines** Downloadable proposal form and guidelines on website.

**Recent Title(s)** *Opening the Field: Irish Women Texts and Contexts,* Patricia Boyle Haberstroh and Christine St. Peter

## Corvo Books
**64 Duncan Terrace, London, N1 8AG**
- 020 7288 0651
- editor@corvobooks.com
- www.corvobooks.com

**Contact** Managing Editor, Julia Rochester; Publisher, Scott McDonald

**Established** 2002

**Insider Info** Publishes two titles per year. Receives approximately 500 queries and 100 manuscripts per year. 75 per cent of books published are from first-time authors and 75 per cent of books published are from unagented authors. Payment is via royalty (on retail price) with 0.08 (per £) minimum and 0.12 (per £) maximum. Advance offered is up to £1,500 maximum. Average lead time is one year, with simultaneous submissions accepted. Submissions accompanied by SAE will be returned. Aims to respond to queries with one month, and proposal and manuscripts within two months. Catalogue and manuscript guidelines available online.

**Non-Fiction** Publishes Autobiography, Biography and General Non-fiction titles on the following subjects:
Business/Economics, Government/Politics, Humanities, Memoirs, Military/War, Philosophy, Social Sciences, Travel, World Affairs.
* Publishes high quality, serious non-fiction.

**Submission Guidelines** Accepts query with SAE, or proposal package (including one to three sample chapters).

**Recent Title(s)** *A Very English Hangman*, Leonora Klein (Biography/History)

## The Cosmic Elk
**68 Elsham Crescent, Lincoln, LN6 3YS**
- 01522 820922
- post@cosmicelk.co.uk
- www.cosmicelk.co.uk

**Contact** Heather Hobden

**Established** 1988

**Non-Fiction** Publishes Multimedia, Reference, Scholarly and Technical titles on History and Science.

**Recent Title(s)** *The King of Siam's Eclipse,* Heather Hobden

**Tips** The Cosmic Elk is a small press that publishes books and booklets, and designs and maintains websites. The main topics are science, history and the history of science. All publications, print or web, are refered or are updates on previously published work.

## Council for British Archeology
**St. Mary's House, 66 Bootham, York, YO30 7BZ**
- 01904 671417
- 01904 671384
- info@britarch.ac.uk
- www.britarch.ac.uk

**Contact** Director, Mike Heyworth; Publications Officer, Jane Thorniley-Walker

**Established** 1944

**Insider Info** Catalogue and manuscript guidelines are available online.

**Non-Fiction** Publishes General Non-fiction and Scholarly titles on the following subjects: Anthropology/Archaeology, History.

**Submission Guidelines** Accepts query with SAE/proposal package (including outline, sample chapter(s), author biography and SAE). Will accept artwork/photos.

**Recent Title(s)** *Historic Mauchline: Archaeology and Development*, E. Patricia Dennison, Dennis Gallagher and Gordon Ewart (Historic/Archaeology)

**Tips** One of the main aims of the Council for British Archaeology (CBA) is to help facilitate communication between all those involved in archaeology in Britain. The CBA has a long established (but continuously developing) range of publication conventions and house style preferences. The CBA Notes for Authors, available on the website, provides details of our latest recommendations.

## Country Publications Ltd
**The Watermill, Broughton Hall, Skipton, BD23 3AG**
- 01756 701381
- 01756 701326
- editorial@dalesman.co.uk
- www.dalesman.co.uk

**Contact** CEO, Matthew Townsend; Managing Director, Robert Flanagan; Editor in Chief, Terry Fletcher

**Insider Info** Catalogue is available online.

**Non-Fiction** Publishes General Non-fiction and Magazine titles on the following subjects: Agriculture, Countryside, Regional interest, Walking guides.

**Recent Title(s)** *Yorkshire Dialect Classics*, Arnold Kellett (Anthology)

**Tips** Country Publications are regional publishers of regional interest titles and magazines, including *The Dalesman* and *Down Your Way*. Subjects encompass walking, literature and art, people and dialect, humour, history and craft.

## Countryside Books

**Highfield House, 2 Highfield Avenue, Newbury, Berkshire, RG14 5DS**

- 01635 43816
- 01635 551004
- info@countrysidebooks.co.uk
- www.countrysidebooks.co.uk

**Contact** Publisher, Nicholas Battle

**Established** 1976

**Insider Info** Catalogue and manuscript guidelines available online.

**Non-Fiction** Publishes General Non-fiction titles on the following subjects: Hobbies, Regional, Travel.

**Submission Guidelines** Accepts query with SAE/ proposal package (including outline, one sample chapter and SAE).

**Recent Title(s)** *A Rum Owd Dew!*, Charlie Haylock

**Tips** Countryside Books publish books of regional interest, usually based upon English counties. Book subjects range from country walks and pub walks, to memories of Second World War airfields. Two wider geographical series are aimed at people who want to discover more of England's living history, and at those researching their family tree. Book submissions are welcomed from all new authors who feel they have an idea that we might successfully publish. Firstly, check to make sure your book covers a subject that fits into the existing list. Note in particular that Countryside Books only publish non-fiction, and that most book titles relate to English counties.

## CRC Press

**24 Blades Court, Deodar Road, London, SW15 2NU**

- 020 7017 6000
- 020 7017 6747
- john.lavender@taylorandfrancis.com
- www.crcpress.com

**Parent Company** Taylor and Francis Group

**Contact** Senior Vice President Publishing, John Lavender; Editor, Rich O'Hanley (Business & Management, IT); Editor, Lindsey Hofmeister (Chemistry); Editor, Allison Shatkin (Engineering); Editor, Steve Wells (Electronic Publishing)

**Established** 1973

**Insider Info** Publishes 350 titles per year, and 32 journals per year. Catalogue and manuscript guidelines are available online.

**Non-Fiction** Publishes Journals, Multimedia, Reference, Scholarly, Technical and Textbook titles on the following subjects: Business and Management, Chemistry, Computer Science, Engineering, Environmental Science, Forensics & Criminal Justice, Food Science, Information Technology, Life Sciences, Mathematics, Nutrition, Pharmacology and Toxicology, Physics, Statistics, Electronic Publishing.

**Submission Guidelines** Accepts proposal package (including outline, one sample chapter and CV).

**Recent Title(s)** *Brain Aging: Models, Methods, and Mechanisms*, David R. Riddle (Neurosciences)

**Tips** CRC Press is a leading publisher of professional reference books and journals in the specialist areas of science, engineering and medicine. Detailed information on how to submit a proposal, or in some cases a camera ready manuscript, is available on the website. Full details and names of editors and their individual specialisms are also published on the website.

## Crecy Publishing

**1a Ringway Trading Estate, Shadowmoss Road, Manchester, M22 5LH**

- 0161 499 0024
- 0161 499 0298
- enquiries@crecy.co.uk
- www.crecy.co.uk

**Contact** Gillian Richardson

**Established** 1993

**Imprint(s)** Goodall
 Air Data Publications

**Insider Info** Publishes eight titles per year. Receives approximately 30 queries and 20 manuscripts per year. Eight per cent of books published are from first-time authors, 75 per cent of books published are from unagented authors. Payment is via royalty. Average lead time is one year, with simultaneous submissions accepted. Submissions accompanied by SAE will be returned. Aims to respond to queries within three days, proposals within two months and manuscripts within three months. Catalogue and manuscript guidelines are free on request.

**Non-Fiction** Publishes Autobiography, Biography, General Non-fiction, Illustrated and Reference titles on the following subjects:
 Aviation, History, Maritime (Naval), Military/War (WWII), Transportation.
 * Requires a number of photographs/illustration with every submission.

**Submission Guidelines** Accepts proposal package (including outline, two sample chapters) or completed manuscript, and artworks/images (send photocopies, digital files as jpegs).

**Recent Title(s)** *Fist from the Sky*, Peter C Smith (Military biography)

**Tips** Crecy Publishing publishes books for an adult readership only.

## Creme de la Crime
**PO Box 523, Chesterfield, S40 9AT**
☎ 01246 520835
✉ info@cremedelacrime.com
🌐 www.cremedelacrime.com
**Contact** Managing Director, Lynne Patrick (Debut Crime Fiction)
**Established** 2003
**Insider Info** Publishes six titles per year. Receives approximately 500 queries and 300 manuscripts per year. 60 per cent of books published are from first-time authors, 90 per cent of books published are from unagented authors. Payment is via royalty (on wholesale price). Average lead time is one year, with simultaneous submissions not accepted. Submissions accompanied by SAE will be returned. Aims to respond to queries within ten days and manuscripts within eight weeks. Catalogue is available online. Manuscript guidelines are available online, or by post for the cost of £2.50, with an A4 envelope and three first class stamps.
**Fiction** Publishes Crime, Mystery, Suspense and Thriller titles.
 * Creme de la Crime publishes crime fiction from both debut authors, and from a small stable of authors they have previously nurtured. All titles are 70–80,000 words in length.
**Submission Guidelines** Accepts proposal package (including outline, a one page synopsis and three sample chapters - approximately 10,000 words).
**Recent Title(s)** *Behind You!*, Linda Regan (Crime fiction)
**Tips** Creme de la Crime stipulates that all prospective authors must follow their submission guidelines carefully when preparing a proposal.

## Crescent Moon Publishing
**PO Box 393, Maidstone, Kent, ME14 5XU**
☎ 01622 729593
✉ cresmopub@yahoo.co.uk
🌐 www.crescentmoon.org.uk
**Contact** Director, Jeremy Robinson; Editor, C. Hughes; Editor, B.D. Barnacle
**Established** 1988
**Insider Info** Publishes 25 titles per year. Receives approximately 300 queries and 400 manuscripts per year. One per cent of books published are from first-time authors and one per cent are from unagented authors. Payment via royalty and an advance is offered. Average lead time is eighteen months with simultaneous submissions accepted. Aims to respond to proposals and manuscripts within four months. Catalogue and manuscript guidelines are available online.
**Non-Fiction** Publishes Biography, General Non-fiction, Illustrated books, and Scholarly titles on the following subjects: Art/Architecture, History, Hobbies, Humanities, Literary Criticism, Philosophy, Religion, Sociology, Translation, World Affairs, Politics.
**Submission Guidelines** Accepts query with SAE/ proposal package (including outline, one to two sample chapters, your publishing history, author biography and SAE). Will accept artworks/images (send photocopies).
**Fiction** Publishes Short Story Collections.
**Submission Guidelines** Accepts query with SAE/ proposal package (including outline and one to two sample chapters and SAE).
**Poetry** Publishes Poetry titles.
 * Prefer a very small selection of a writer's best work in the first instance and tend to favour free or non-rhyming material.
**Submission Guidelines** Accepts query (including six sample poems).
**Tips** Crescent Moon publishes a number of critical subject studies, including painters and artists, literature, and art. All submissions are carefully reviewed and should be replied to.

## Cressrelles Publishing Co. Ltd
**10 Station Road Industrial Estate, Coldwall, Malvern, WR13 6RN**
☎ 01684 540154
☎ 01684 540154
✉ simonsmith@cressrelles4drama.fsbusiness.co.uk
**Contact** Managing Director, Leslie Smith
**Established** 1973
**Imprint(s)** Actinic Press

J. Garnet Miller
Kenyon-Deane

**Insider Info** Publishes 10-20 titles per year. Catalogue free on request.

**Non-Fiction** Publishes General Non-fiction titles on the following subjects: Local Interest, Drama/Plays.

**Submission Guidelines** Accepts completed manuscript.

## Crocus Books

**6 Mount Street, Manchester, M2 5NS**
- 0161 832 3777
- 0161 832 2929
- crocus@commonword.org.uk
- www.commonword.org.uk

**Parent Company** Commonword and Cultureword

**Insider Info** Catalogue and manuscript guidelines are available online.

**Fiction** Publishes Mainstream/Contemporary and Short story collection titles from writers in the North West of the UK.

**Poetry** Publishes Contemporary Poetry titles.

**Recent Title(s)** *The Hat Check Boy*, Mike Duff (Novel)

**Tips** Crocus is the publishing imprint of Commonword and Cultureword, projects that coordinate a range of writing development and publishing projects. Cultureword was established in 1986 as a centre for Black creative writing in the North West of England, and Commonword is the virtual community of North West writers. Crocus Books often runs writing competitions offering cash prizes and publication.

## Crombie Jardine Publishing Ltd

**13 Nonsuch Walk, Cheam, SM2 7LG**
- 020 8393 5454
- catriona@crombiejardine.com
- www.crombiejardine.com

**Contact** Sales and Publishing Director, David Crombie; Publishing Director, Catriona Jardine

**Established** 2004

**Insider Info** Publishes six titles per year. Catalgoue is available online.

**Non-Fiction** Publishes General Non-fiction, Gift books and Humour titles on the follwing subjects: Adult Humour, Puzzles.

**Submission Guidelines** Accepts query with SAE/ proposal package (including outline, sample chapter(s) and SAE). Submit completed manuscript.

**Recent Title(s)** *Make Your Own Sex Toys*, Matt Pagett (Adult Humour)

**Tips** Titles are firmly aimed at the young adult humour market. Crombie and Jardine specialise in

impulse buy humour titles. Whatever title you are looking for has probably been covered by the publisher, or is about to be.

## Crossbridge Books

**Tree Shadow, Berrow Green, Martley, WR6 6PL**
- 01886 821128
- 01886 821128
- crossbridgebooks@btinternet.com
- www.crossbridgebooks.com

**Contact** Managing Director, Eileen Mohr

**Established** 1995

**Imprint(s)** Mohr Books

**Insider Info** Catalogue is available online.

**Non-Fiction** Publishes Children's/Juvenile, Illustrated books and General Non-fiction titles on Religion.

**Fiction** Publishes Religious titles.

**Recent Title(s)** *Total Healing*, Trevor Dearing (Christian faith); *Mother Twin*, Eileen Mohr (Novel)

**Tips** Titles are aimed at a predominantly Christian readership. Many of the publisher's books reveal the miraculous power of God, the Creator, through His Son Jesus Christ. Most of them show how lives can be turned around, from hopelessness to new zest for life, as people have put their trust in Jesus. It is anticipated that all future books will be Christian.

## Crown House Publishing Ltd

**Crown Buildings, Bancyfelin, Carmarthen, SA33 5ND**
- 01267 211345
- 01267 211882
- books@crownhouse.co.uk
- www.crownhouse.co.uk

**Contact** Managing Director, David Bowman

**Established** 1998

**Insider Info** Publishes 40 titles per year. Catalogue and manuscript guidelines are available online.

**Non-Fiction** Publishes Scholarly, Self-help, and Technical titles on the following subjects: Counselling/Career, Education, Health/Medicine, Spirituality, Hypnosis, Neuro-Linguistic Programming, Accelerated Learning.

**Submission Guidelines** Accepts query with SAE/ Proposal package (including outline, 3 sample chapters, online author questionnaire form, author biography and an SAE).

**Recent Title(s)** *Advanced Skills and Interventions in Therapeutic Counselling*, Gordon Emmerson

**Tips** Crown House Publishing is a rapidly growing publishing house specialising in the areas of neuro-linguistic programming (NLP), hypnosis, accelerated learning, stress management, health and well being and personal growth. There is an international list of authors, and an advanced network of global distributors ensuring the publisher's titles are directed towards, and available to, a worldwide audience. Crown House Publishing is a specialist publisher and ensures that if a book is published it will be worked upon and developed by people with a distinct knowledge of the subject area.

## The Crowood Press Ltd
**The Stable Block, Crowood Lane, Ramsbury, Wiltshire, SN8 2HR**
- 01672 520320
- 01672 520280
- enquiries@crowood.com
- www.crowoodpress.co.uk

**Contact** Chairman, John Dennis; Managing Director, Ken Hathway
**Established** 1982
**Imprint(s)** Farming Press
**Insider Info** Publishes 70 titles per year. Payment is via royalties. Catalogue available free on request and online. Manuscript guidelines available online.
**Non-Fiction** Publishes Biography, General Non-fiction, How-to, Illustrated and Reference titles on the following subjects:
 Agriculture/Horticulture, Art/Architecture, Automotive, Business/Economics, Crafts, Entertainment/Games, Gardening, Health/Medicine, History, Hobbies, House and Home, Military/War, Music/Dance, Nature/Environment, Sports, Transportation, Travel.
 * The Crowood Press initially published titles on Sport, Fishing, Equestrianism and Country Sports, but has since moved into Gardening, Farming, Dogs, Crafts, Motoring, Military History and Aviation.
**Submission Guidelines** Accepts query with SAE.
**Recent Title(s)** *Evolution of the Airliner*, Ray Whitford
**Tips** If you have an idea for a book that is within an appropriate subject area, the best approach is initially by letter, fax or email. Do not send complete manuscripts or photographs. More information will be requested if necessary.

## CRW Publishing
**69 Gloucester Crescent, London, NW1 7EG**
- 020 7485 5764
- marcus@niche2002.fsnet.co.uk
- www.crw-publishing.co.uk

**Contact** Editorial Director, Marcus Clapham.
**Established** 2003
**Fiction** Publishes reprints of classic fiction.

**Recent Title(s)** *Don Quixote*, Miguel de Cervantes (Classic world fiction); *Bleak House (Illustrated)*, Charles Dickens (Classic novel)
**Tips** CRW has a commitment to producing reasonably priced but beautifully produced, high quality hardback classics. Series produced by CRW Publishing include: *Book Blocks, Collector's Library, Essential Thinkers, Poetry Library, Myth and Legend, Who? What? Where? When?* Two million books were sold in the company's first year.

## Culva House Publications
**10 The Carrs, Sleights, Whitby, YO21 1RR**
- 01947 810819
- alan@culvahouse.co.uk
- www.culvahouse.co.uk

**Contact** Managing Editor, Alan Whitworth
**Established** 1986
**Non-Fiction** Publishes Biography and General Non-fiction titles on the following subjects: Art/Architecture, History, Local history.
**Submission Guidelines** Accepts query with SAE.

## Currach Press
**55a Spruce Avenue, Stillorgan Industrial Park, Blackrock, Dublin, Republic of Ireland**
- 00353 1 294 2560
- 00353 1 294 3564
- jo@currach.ie
- www.currach.ie

**Contact** Publisher, Jo O'Donoghue (General Non-fiction)
**Established** 2001
**Insider Info** Publishes 12 titles per year. Receives approximately 50 queries and 50 manuscripts per year. 20 per cent of books published are from first-time authors, 90 per cent of books published are from unagented authors. Payment is via royalty (on retail price). Average lead time is six months, with simultaneous submissions not accepted. Submissions accompanied by SAE will be returned. Aims to respond to queries within one week, proposals within two weeks, manuscripts within three weeks, and all other enquiries within two weeks. Catalogue available with an A5 SAE and an IRC (for outside of Ireland).
**Non-Fiction** Publishes Autobiography, Biography, Coffee table books, Cookbooks, General Non-fiction, Gift, Illustrated, Reference and Self-help titles on the following subjects: Alternative Lifestyles, Art/Architecture, Business/Economics, Contemporary Culture, Cooking/Foods/Nutrition, Gay/Lesbian, Government/Politics, History, House and Home,

Humanities, Memoirs, Money/Finance, Photography, Psychology, Regional, Travel.

**Submission Guidelines** Accepts proposal package (including outline, author biography, SAE), or completed manuscript.

**Recent Title(s)** *Style Source Ireland – Interiors*, Eoin Lyons (House and Home)

**Tips** Currach Press publishes books for a general interest adult readership.

## D&B Publishing

**PO Box 18, Hassocks, West Sussex, BN6 9WR**

- 01273 834680
- 01273 831629
- info@dandbpublishing.com
- www.dandbpublishing.com

**Contact** Publisher, Byron Jacobs (Poker, Puzzles, Games)

**Established** 2002

**Insider Info** Publishes eight titles per year. Receives approximately five queries per year. 20 per cent of books published are from first-time authors, 100 per cent of books published are from unagented authors. Payment is via royalty (on retail price). Average lead time is nine months, with simultaneous submissions accepted. Submissions accompanied by SAE will be returned. Aims to respond to queries within one day and proposals and manuscripts within one week. Catalogue is free on request and available online, or by email. Manuscript guidelines are available by email.

**Non-Fiction** Publishes Games/Puzzles, How-to and Multimedia titles on the following subjects: Card Games, Casino Games, Entertainment/Games, Gambling, Poker, Puzzles.

**Submission Guidelines** Accepts proposal package (including outline, two sample chapters and author biography).

**Recent Title(s)** *Secrets of Professional Pot-Limit Omaha*, Rolf Slotboom (Poker)

**Tips** D&B Publishing publishes books for poker players and puzzle enthusiasts in general. They determine whether an author should be subsidy published, by the quality of synopsis and sample chapters supplied.

## Dalesman Publishing Co. Ltd

**The Water Mill, Broughton Hall, Skipton, North Yorkshire, BD23 3AG**

- 01756 701381
- 01756 701326
- editorial@dalesman.co.uk
- www.dalesman.co.uk

**Contact** Managing Director, Robert Flanagan; Editor in Chief, Terry Fletcher

**Insider Info** Publishes ten titles per year. Catalogue is available online.

**Non-Fiction** Publishes Illustrated books and General Non-fiction titles on the following subjects: History, Hobbies, Regional, Travel, Local interest (Northern UK), Northern folklore.

**Submission Guidelines** Accepts query with SAE.

**Recent Title(s)** *Yorkshire Greats Special Edition*, Bernard Ingham (Regional interest)

**Tips** There's more to Dalesman Publishing than *Dalesman magazine*. As well as *Dalesman, Cumbria, Countryman* and *Down Your Way*, the publisher has always had a superb reputation for publishing a range of quality books and calendars. The Smith Settle publishing imprint was acquired in February 2003. As a result Dalesman Publishing holds the largest collection of Northern interest publications in the marketplace, providing an even wider range of books for all who have a special affection for the region. Ideas for submission will be considered providing they relate to the North in some way; walking guides or photo books are most popular.

## Darton Longman & Todd Ltd

**1 Spencer Court, 140–142 Wandsworth High Street, London, SW18 4JJ**

- 020 8875 0155
- 020 8875 0133
- editorial@darton-longman-todd.co.uk
- www.darton-longman-todd.co.uk

**Contact** Editorial Director, Brendan Walsh; Commissioning Editor, Virginia Hearn; Managing Editor, Helen Porter

**Established** 1959

**Insider Info** Catalogue and manuscript guidelines are available online.

**Non-Fiction** Publishes General Non-fiction titles on the following subjects: Religion, Spirituality, Prayer, Theology, Church Today, Personal Growth, Ministry, Counselling and Pastoral Care, Bereavement, Traditions of Christian Spirituality, Exploring Faith, Bibles.

**Submission Guidelines** Accepts queries and completed manuscripts by post only.

**Recent Title(s)** *Hostage In Iraq*, Norman Kember (Memoir); *Ordinary Work, Extraordinary Grace,* Scott Hahn (Religion)

**Tips** Darton Longman and Todd are the UK's leading independent publisher of high quality popular books on spirituality, religion and theology. The publisher's books come from many different backgrounds and traditions, but they all share a relish for opening up argument and debate. Darton Longman and Todd are always looking for writers with freshness, inquisitiveness, faithfulness and passion.

## David & Charles Publishers

**Brunel House, Newton Abbot, Devon, TQ12 4PU**
- 01626 323200
- 01626 364463
- ali.myer@davidandcharles.co.uk
- www.davidandcharles.co.uk

**Parent Company** F+W Publications
**Contact** Executive Editor, Cheryl Brown (Craft); Commissioning Editor, Jane Trollope (Equestrian); Commissioning Editor, Neil Baber (General, History, Reference); Commissioning Editor, Mic Cady (General, History, Reference); Commissioning Editor, Freya Dangerfield (Practical Art)
**Established** 1960
**Insider Info** Publishes 175 titles per year. Receives approximately 1,200–1,500 queries and 30–50 manuscripts per year. 30 per cent of books published are from first-time authors and 85 per cent of books published are from unagented authors. Payment is via royalty (on retail price), outright purchase from £400–£10,000. Advance offered is from £2,000–£10,000. Average lead time is two years, with simultaneous submissions accepted. Submissions accompanied by SAE will be returned. Aims to respond to queries, proposals and manuscripts within two months. Catalogue available via A4 SAE. Author guidelines not available.
**Non-Fiction** Publishes General Non-fiction, Gift, How-to, Illustrated and Reference titles on the following subjects:
Agriculture/Horticulture (very broad interest), Animals (Equestrian and Pet Care), Anthropology/Archaeology (Archaeology only), Art/Architecture, Astrology/Psychic (general titles only), Contemporary Culture, Cooking/Foods/Nutrition (very small list), Crafts (our core strength), Creative Non-fiction, Entertainment/Games, Gardening, History, Hobbies (broad interest), House and Home, Military/War, Nature/Environment, Nostalgia (broad interest), Photography (practical rather than coffee table), Sports, Transportation (mostly railways), Directories.
* As well as the areas mentioned above, will always look at new ideas and new areas. Will consider brief and concise ideas.
**Submission Guidelines** Accepts query with SAE or via email with proposal package (including outline, sample chapter(s), your publishing history, author biography) and artworks/images (send photocopies or digital files as jpegs).
Submission details to: ali.myer@davidandcharles.co.uk
**Tips** Titles aimed at people with a strong interest and/or hobby. Submissions should be brief, concise and to the point. A short biography of the author is extremely helpful and you should note any previously published material, be it books or magazine articles. Happily consider unagented authors. If your proposal is for a visual book e.g. art or photography, samples of your work should be included either as copies or on CD. Never send originals.

## David Fickling Books

**31 Beaumont Street, Oxford, OX1 2NP**
- 01865 339000
- 01865 339009
- DFickling@randomhouse.co.uk
- www.davidficklingbooks.co.uk

**Parent Company** Random House Children's Division
**Contact** Publisher, David Fickling; Senior Editor, Bella Pearson
**Insider Info** Catalogue available online.
**Fiction** Publish Children's/Juvenile titles.
**Submission Guidelines** Strongly prefer agented submissions.
**Recent Title(s)** *Lyra's Oxford*, Philip Pullman (Fantasy)
**Tips** David Fickling Books are a very small imprint within Random House, but they publish some very commercially successful authors. They are the first bicontinental children's publisher with books publishing simultaneously in the US and the UK.

## David Fulton Publishers

**2 Park Square, Milton Park, Abingdon, Oxford, OX14 4RN**
- 020 7017 6000
- 020 7017 6699
- tf.enquiries@informa.com
- www.routledge.com

**Parent Company** Routledge Education (Taylor & Francis Group)
**Insider Info** Manuscript guidelines available online.
**Non-fiction** Publishes How-to, Reference, Scholarly and Textbook titles on the following subjects:
Education, Teaching Resources.
**Submission Guidelines** Accepts proposal package (including outline, sample chapters, your publishing history and author biography).

**Tips** David Fulton Publishers publishes books for teacher training and continuing professional development, also a comprehensive range of resources for SENCOs, and teachers working with children with special educational needs.

## David Porteous Editions
**PO Box 5, Chudleigh, Newton Abbot, Devon, TQ13 0YZ**
- 01626 853310
- 01626 853663
- editorial@davidporteous.com
- www.davidporteous.com

**Non-Fiction** Publishes How-to, Illustrated titles on the following subjects:
 Arts and Crafts, Hobbies.
**Submission Guidelines** Accepts proposal package (including outline and short synopsis) by post or email.
**Recent Title(s)** *Dolls' Clothes*, Mette Jorgensen (Craft)
**Tips** David Porteous are constantly seeking new ideas and welcome ideas from experienced artists or craftspeople.

## Day Books
**Orchard Piece, Crawborough, Charlbury, Oxfordshire, OX7 3TX**
- 01608 811196
- 01608 811196
- lives@day-books.com
- www.day-books.com

**Contact** Managing Editor, James Sanderson
**Established** 1997
**Imprint(s)** Charlbury Press
 Leo Children's Books
**Insider Info** Receives approximately 200 queries and 100 manuscripts per year. Ten per cent of books published are from first-time authors and 80 per cent are from unagented authors. Payment via royalty (on wholesale price) with 0.1 (per £) maximum. Average lead time is one year with simultaneous submissions accepted. Aims to respond to proposals and manuscripts within one month.
**Non-Fiction** Publishes Biography, General Non-fiction, Diaries, and Local interest (Oxfordshire) titles.
**Submission Guidelines** Accepts query with SAE.
**Fiction** Publishes on the following subjects:
 Juvenile, Children's.
**Submission Guidelines** Accepts query with SAE.
**Recent Title(s)** *Lifting the Latch*, Sheila Stewart (Local interest); *Zoot*, Alan Fraser (Children's fiction)

**Tips** Day Books is an independent publishing company, established to publish a series of 'great diaries from around the world'. Since then they've branched out to include all kinds of personal writing; biography, autobiography, and collections of letters in well edited and well produced editions. The company can only respond to those who include return postage or provide an email address.

## Debrett's Limited
**18–20 Hill Rise, Richmond, Surrey, TW10 6UA**
- 020 8939 2250
- 020 8600 8322
- people@debretts.co.uk
- www.debretts.co.uk

**Contact** Managing Director, David C. Tennant; Editor in Chief, Charles Mosley
**Established** 1769
**Non-Fiction** Publishes General Non-fiction, Diary and Gift books on the following subjects:
 Etiquette/Culture
**Submission Guidelines** Query with SAE.
**Recent Title(s)** *Etiquette for Girls*
**Tips** Debrett's is one of the oldest publishing brands in the world. Established in 1769, Debrett's remains the arbiter of taste, manners and correct form to this day. Publishes mainly on high culture and society, etiquette, and similar topics.

## Dewi Lewis Publishing
**8 Broomfield Road, Heaton Moor, Stockport, SK4 4ND**
- 0161 442 9450
- 0161 442 9450
- mail@dewilewispublishing.com
- www.dewilewispublishing.com

**Contact** Director, Dewi Lewis
**Established** 1994
**Insider Info** Average lead time is 12 months. Catalogue and manuscript guidelines are available online.
**Non-Fiction** Publishes Illustrated book titles on Photography.
**Submission Guidelines** Accepts query with SAE/ proposal package (including outline, sample chapter(s), author biography) and artworks/images (send photocopies or digital files as jpegs).
**Fiction** Publishes Mainstream/Contemporary titles. However, no longer accepting fiction submissions.
**Recent Title(s)** *Between Dogs and Wolves*, Jodi Bieber (Photography); *Laughter in a Dark Wood*, Peter Gilbert (Novel)

**Tips** Founded in 1994 Dewi Lewis Publishing is internationally known for its photography list. The aim of the company is to bring to the attention of a wider public, accessible but challenging contemporary photography, by both established and lesser known practitioners. We're looking for projects of quality, which are fresh, powerful and unique. We are publishing books for an international audience and you should consider this when proposing a project. We are unlikely to be interested in something which is too specific to one country or geographical region.

## Digital Press
**The Boulevard, Langford Lane, Kidlington, Oxford, OX5 1GB**
- 01865 843000
- 01865 843010
- authorsupport@elsevier.com
- www.books.elsevier.com

**Parent Company** Elsevier Ltd (Science & Technology)
**Insider Info** Payment is via royalties. Catalogue and manuscript guidelines available online: www.elsevier.com/wps/find/authors.authors/bookauthorshome.
**Non-Fiction** Publishes How-to, Reference, Scholarly and Technical titles on the following subjects: Business/Economics, Computers/Electronics, Computer Troubleshooting/Tutorial Guides.
**Submission Guidelines** Accepts query with SAE, with proposal package (including outline).
**Recent Title(s)** *Developing Practical Wireless Applications*, Dean A. Gratton (Computing/Reference)
**Tips** Publishes books that bring practical and timely solutions to computing professionals working with critical projects and everyday challenges. Many authors are world renowned consultants and senior staff of companies such as Microsoft, HP Consulting and Integration Services and Nokia. Welcomes authors' proposals for books, the first step is to discuss the proposal with the relevant Publishing Editor. Check the website for a full list of editorial contacts.

## Dionysia Press
**127 Milton Road West, 7 Duddingston House, Edinburgh, EH15 1JG**
- 0131 661 1156
- 0131 661 1156
**Contact** Director, Denise Smith
**Established** 1989

**Fiction** Publishes Short stories, Translations and Novels.
**Poetry** Publishes Poetry Collections.
**Tips** Denise Smith is also the editor of *Understanding* magazine. Contact her directly for more information on her publications.

## Discovery Walking Guides
**10 Tennyson Close, Dallington, Northampton, NN5 7HJ**
- 01604 244869
- 01604 752576
- ask.discovery@ntlworld.com
- www.walking.demon.co.uk
**Contact** Chairman, Rosamund C. Brawn
**Established** 1994
**Insider Info** Catalogue available online.
**Non-Fiction** Publishes General Non-fiction and Technical titles on the following subjects: Hobbies, Travel, Walking guides, GPS guides.
**Submission Guidelines** Accepts query with SAE/proposal package (including outline, sample chapter(s))
**Recent Titles** *Walk! Dartmoor*, Alan Hobbs and Kate Hobbs
**Tips** Titles aimed at walking enthusiasts. Will accept proposals/ideas from experienced and technologically skilled walkers.

## Donhead Publishing
**Lower Coombe, Donhead St. Mary, Shaftesbury, SP7 9LU**
- 01747 828422
- 01747 828522
- jillpearce@donhead.com
- www.donhead.com
**Contact** Jill Pearce
**Established** 1990
**Insider Info** Publishes six titles per year. Catalogue available online and via email: sales@donhead.com
**Non-Fiction** Publishes General Non-fiction, Illustrated books and Scholarly titles on the following subjects: Art/Architecture, Building Conservation.
**Submission Guidelines** Query with SAE.
**Recent Title(s)** *Modern Practical Masonry*, Edmund George Warland
**Tips** Donhead is the leading independent publisher of building conservation, preservation and architecture books, specialising in publishing original material for professionals and academics. Welcomes unsolicited submissions from academic or technically experienced professionals.

## The Do-Not Press
**16 The Woodlands, London, SE13 6TY**
- 020 8698 7833
- 020 8698 7834
- info@thedonotpress.com
- www.thedonotpress.com

**Contact** Editor in Chief, Jim Driver
**Insider Info** Publishes 12 titles per year. Catalogue and manuscript guidelines available online. Unsolicited submissions are no longer accepted.
**Non-Fiction** Publishes General Non-fiction titles on the following subjects:
Art/Architecture, Music/Dance.
**Submission Guidelines** Accepts agented submissions only.
**Fiction** Publishes Erotica, Experimental, Mainstream/Contemporary, Mystery and Crime titles.
**Submission Guidelines** Accepts agented submissions only.
**Recent Title(s)** *Ike Turner: King of Rhythm*, John Collis (Music); *Judas Pig*, Horrace Silver (Novel)
**Tips** Proposals are not accepted for romantic fiction, science fiction, fantasy and horror genres, or titles written for children, businessmen, housewives and bankers. They specialise in crime fiction, but almost inevitably of the type that is modern, thought provoking and on the cutting edge of the genre. Please include a synopsis and SAE with any proposals. Manuscripts must be typed, not handwritten, and the publishers advise that prospective authors should not telephone to enquire on progress.

## Dorling Kindersley
**80 Strand, London, WC2R 0RL**
- 020 7010 3000
- 020 7010 6060
- adulteditorial@uk.dk.com, childreneditorial@uk.dk.com, travelguides@uk.dk.com
- www.dorlingkindersley-uk.co.uk

**Parent Company** Penguin Group (UK)
**Contact** CEO, Gary June; Global Managing Director, Andrew Welham
**Established** 1974
**Insider Info** Catalogue available as a pdf online.
**Non-Fiction** Publishes Children's, General Non-fiction, Gift, How-to, Illustrated, Multimedia, Self-help, Maps/Atlas, Guide, Dictionary, Encyclopedia and Reference titles on the following subjects:
Animals, Anthropology/Archaeology, Art/Architecture, Astrology/Psychic, Business/Economics, Child Guidance/Parenting, Computers/Electronics, Contemporary Culture, Cooking/Foods/Nutrition, Crafts, Entertainment/Games, Gardening, Health/Medicine, History, Hobbies, House and Home, Language/Literature, Marine Subjects, Military/War, Money/Finance, Nature/Environment, Philosophy, Photography, Recreation, Religion, Science, Sex, Sports, Travel, Young Adult, Relationships, Film and Television.
 * There are Dorling Kindersley (DK) illustrated guides on a huge variety of subjects with a readership age range from infants to mature adults.
**Submission Guidelines** No unsolicited submissions, agented submissions only.
**Recent Title(s)** *How to Raise an Amazing Child*, Tim Seldin (Parenting); *Rome: RealCity,* Real City Guides (Travel)
**Tips** Dorling Kindersley is the world leader in illustrated reference books. Dorling Kindersley books aim to inspire and teach people of all ages by using design, illustration and photography to make ideas come alive.

## Doubleday
**61–63 Uxbridge Road, London, W5 5SA**
- 020 8579 2652
- 020 8579 5479
- info@transworld-publishers.co.uk
- www.booksattransworld.co.uk

**Parent Company** Transworld Publishers
**Fiction** Publishes Ethnic, Historical, Humour, Literary, Mainstream/Contemporary and Multicultural titles.
**Submission Guidelines** No unsolicited manuscripts, agented submissions only.
**Recent Title(s)** *The Shoe Queen*, Anna Davis (Modern fiction)
**Tips** See Transworld Publishers for more detailed information.

## Doubleday Children's Books
**61–63 Uxbridge Road, London, W5 5SA**
- 020 8231 6800
- 020 8231 6767
- childrenseditorial@randomhouse.co.uk
- www.randomhouse.co.uk/childrens

**Parent Company** Random House Children's Books
**Insider Info** Manuscript guidelines available online.
**Fiction** Publishes Picture books and Children's fiction.
**Submission Guidelines** Accepts proposal package (including outline, one sample chapter, photocopied artwork if needed - do not send originals). Agented submissions are strongly preferred. No email submissions.

**Recent Title(s)** *Honeybee's Busy Day*, Richard Fowler (Illustrated children's); *Dexter Bexley and the Big Blue Beastie*, Joel Stewart (Illustrated children's)

## Dovecote Press Ltd
**Stanbridge, Wimborne Minster, Dorset, BH21 4JD**
- 01258 840549
- 01258 840958
- online@dovecotepress.com
- www.dovecotepress.com

**Contact** Editorial Director, David Burnett
**Established** 1974
**Insider Info** Catalogue available online. Manuscript guidelines available online.
**Non-Fiction** Publishes Autobiography, Biography, General Non-fiction and Illustrated titles on the following subjects:
 Art/Architecture, History, Hobbies, Nature/ Environment, English Counties.
**Submission Guidelines** In the first instance, please write to David Burnett with proposal package (including detailed synopsis or outline and SAE).
**Recent Title(s)** *The Rich Spoils of Time*, Frances Campbell-Preston
**Tips** The Dovecote Press was founded in 1974 in a Victorian barn on the edge of water meadows, near the Dorset market town of Wimborne Minster. Today, and over 200 books later, it is widely regarded as one of Britain's finest local interest publishers, and has been described as 'the very model of what a good local publishing house ought to be'. We pay proper royalties, and are always willing to make a small advance against royalties.

## Drake Educational Associates
**St. Fagans Road, Fairwater, Cardiff, CF5 3AE**
- 029 2056 0333
- 029 2055 4909
- drakegroup@btinternet.com
- www.btinternet.com/~drakegroup/drake02/ ed_products.htm

**Contact** Managing Director, R.G. Drake
**Established** 1974
**Non-Fiction** Publishes Multimedia, Textbook and Scholarly titles on Education.
**Tips** Drake Audio-Visual and Drake Educational Associates have been trading for 30 years.

## Dramatic Lines
**PO Box 201, Twickenham, TW2 5RQ**
- 020 8296 9502
- 020 8296 9503
- mail@dramaticlines.co.uk
- www.dramaticlines.co.uk

**Contact** Managing Editor, John Nicholas
**Non-Fiction** Publishes General Non-fiction, Reference and Scholarly titles on the following subjects:
 Education, Drama.
**Submission Guidelines** Query with SAE.
**Tips** Produces educational texts concerning varying aspects of drama and plays.

## Dref Wen
**28 Church Road, Whitchurch, Cardiff, CFI4 2EA**
- 029 2061 7860
- 029 2061 0507
- gwilym@drefwen.com

**Contact** Managing Director, G. Boore
**Established** 1970
**Non-Fiction** Publishes General Non-fiction, Scholarly, and Welsh language titles on the following subjects:
 Education, Translation, Welsh language educational.
**Fiction** Juvenile (Welsh language/bilingual).
**Tips** Titles aimed at Welsh language learners/ bilingual.

## Dublar Scripts
**204 Mercer Way, Romsey, Hampshire SO51 7QJ**
- 01794 501377
- 01794 502538
- scripts@dublar.freeserve.co.uk
- www.dublar.co.uk

**Contact** Managing Director, Bob Heather
**Established** 1994
**Imprint(s)** Sleepy Hollow Pantomimes
**Non-Fiction** Drama/Pantomimes.
**Recent Title(s)** *The Kings New Clothes*, Bob Heather (Pantomime)
**Tips** Has produced several pantomimes, performed all over Great Britain, Canada, Australia, and New Zealand, and a few in Malta, Poland, Spain and France. Traditional family pantomimes only.

## Duncan Baird Publishers
**Castle House, 75–76 Wells Street, London, W1T 3QH**
- 020 7323 2229
- 020 7580 5692
- enquiries@dbp.co.uk
- www.dbponline.co.uk

**Contact** Publisher, Duncan Baird; Editorial Director, Bob Saxton
**Established** 1992
**Imprint(s)** Watkins Publishing
**Insider Info** Catalogue available online.
**Non-Fiction** Publishes General Non-fiction, Illustrated books and Self-help titles on the following subjects:
 Health/Medicine, Religion, Spirituality, Mind/Body, World Culture/Civilisations.
**Tips** Duncan Baird Publishers is the leading independent publisher of illustrated books in the fields of mind, body and spirit, health and wellbeing, culture and civilizations, and religion and faith. We are committed to innovation, design, editorial excellence and imagination, creating unique books for today's readership.

## Duncan Petersen Publishing
**31 Ceylon Road, London, W14 OPY**
- 020 7371 2356
- 020 7371 2507
- dp@macunlimited.net
**Contact** Managing Director, Andrew Duncan; Editor, Fiona Duncan
**Established** 1986
**Non-Fiction** Publishes General Non-fiction titles on the following subjects:
 Art/Architecture, Business/Economics, Child Guidance/Parenting, Nature/Environment, Travel, Antiques, Walking.
**Submission Guidelines** Accepts query with SAE. Submit completed manuscript.
**Recent Title(s)** *Charming Small Hotel Guides*, Fiona Duncan ed. (Travel guides)
**Tips** *Charming Small Hotel Guides* were started in 1986 by Andrew Duncan and Mel Petersen and 20 years later remain one of the most important publishing activities of London co-edition publisher Duncan Petersen. Contact with a proposal for an unbiased and totally objective travel text, ideally including detailed photographs.

## Dunedin Academic Press Ltd
**Hudson House, 8 Albany Street, Edinburgh, PH10 6PY**
- 0131 473 2397
- mail@dunedinacademicpress.co.uk
- www.dunedinacademicpress.co.uk
**Contact** Director, Anthony Kinahan (Earth Sciences, Education, Singing, International Affairs, Social Sciences, Religious Studies)
**Established** 2000

**Insider Info** Publishes 20 titles per year. Receives approximately 100 queries and 40 manuscripts per year. 50 per cent of books published are from first-time authors, 100 per cent of books published are from unagented authors. Payment is via royalty (on wholesale price). Average lead time is one year, with simultaneous submissions not accepted. Submissions accompanied by SAE will be returned. Aims to respond to queries within five days, proposals within ten days and manuscripts within six months. Catalogue is free on request and available online. Manuscript guidelines are free on request.
**Non-Fiction** Publishes Scholarly titles (Tertiary level and upwards) on the following subjects:
 Anthropology/Archaeology, Education, Government/Politics, History, Music/Dance, Philosophy, Religion, Science (Earth Sciences), Social Sciences, Sociology, World Affairs.
**Submission Guidelines** Accepts artworks/images with submissions (send digital files as jpegs).
**Recent Title(s)** *Volcanoes and the Making of Scotland*, Brian Upton (Earth Science)
**Tips** Dunedin is an academic press, which only publishes scholarly texts aimed at undergraduate level scholars upwards. As it is based in Scotland, the Press will always reflect Scottish interests but its horizons are, in reality, far broader and its books tackle subjects from an international academic world.

## Earthscan Publications
**8–12 Camden High Street, London, NW1 0JH**
- 020 7387 8558
- 020 7387 8998
- earthinfo@earthscan.co.uk
- www.earthscan.co.uk
**Contact** Publishing Director, Jonathan Sinclair Wilson
**Insider Info** Catalogue free on request online or by email. Manuscript guidelines available online.
**Non-Fiction** Publishes Textbooks and Scholarly titles on the following subjects:
 Business/Economics, Nature/Environment, Sustainable development, Climate/Energy/Resource management.
**Submission Guidelines** Accepts query with SAE/proposal package (including outline, sample chapter(s), publishing history, and author biography and SAE) and artworks/images (send photocopies or digital files as jpegs).
 Submission details to: proposals@earthscan.co.uk
**Recent Title(s)** *The Atlas of Climate Change*, Kirstin Dow and Thomas E. Downing (Climate/Energy/Resource management)

**Tips** Through publishing a wide range of media - books, magazines, journals, directories, CD-ROMs and other electronic products - we seek to increase understanding of environmental issues and their implications at all levels. We seek to influence opinion and policy towards sustainable forms of development, and to promote the various businesses, industries and organisations that provide the infrastructure to make this happen. Our distribution is worldwide and our readership includes academics, professionals, business people, policy makers and general readers. We are always keen to work with new authors and to discuss projects for which you may have publishing plans. If you have a book proposal which you think may be suitable for Earthscan, then please ensure you send us as many relevant details as possible.

## Ebury Press
**Random House, 20 Vauxhall Bridge Road, London, SW1V 2SA**
- 020 7840 8400
- 020 7840 8406
- eburyeditorial@randomhouse.co.uk
- www.randomhouse.co.uk

**Parent Company** The Random House Group Ltd
**Contact** Publishing Director, Hannah MacDonald (Non-fiction); Publishing Director, Carey Smith (Illustrated)
**Insider Info** Submissions accompanied by SAE will returned. Catalogue available online.
**Non-Fiction** Publishes Autobiography, Biography, Cookbooks, General Non-fiction, Gift books, Humour, Illustrated books, Reference and Television tie-in titles.
**Submission Guidelines** Accepts query with SAE/proposal package (including outline, one sample chapter and SAE) and artworks/images (send photocopies).
**Recent Title(s)** *101 Incredible Experiments for the Shed Scientist*, Rob Beattie (Gift book)
**Tips** No emailed submissions. Agented submissions are preferred, although unagented submissions are accepted.
 Please see The Random House Group entry for submission information.

## Economist Books
**3a Exmouth House, Pine Street, Exmouth Market, London, EC1R OJH**
- 020 7841 6300
- 020 7833 3969
- stephen.brough@profilebooks.com

- www.profilebooks.co.uk
**Parent Company** Profile Books
**Contact** Editor, Stephen Brough
**Insider Info** Catalogue available online.
**Non-Fiction** Publishes General Non-fiction, Reference and Scholarly title on the following subjects:.
 Business/Economics.
 * All books are published on economy issues and are linked with *The Economist* newspaper brand.
**Submission Guidelines** Accepts proposal package (including outline, two sample chapters, SAE).
**Tips** Most material submitted to Profile Books as an overall company is through agents but unsolicited proposals following the guidelines set out above are accepted.

## Edgewell Publishing
**5a Front Street, Prudhoe, Northumberland, NE42 5HJ**
- 01661 835330
- 01661 835330
- keith@tynedale-languages.co.uk
- www.tynedale-languages.co.uk
**Contact** Editor, Keith Minton
**Established** 2005
**Insider Info** Submissions accompanied by SAE will be returned. Manuscript guidelines available by email and online.
**Non-Fiction** Publishes Reference, Scholarly, Textbook and Self-help titles on Education.
**Submission Guidelines** Accepts queries by phone or email.
**Fiction** Publishes Juvenile, Multicultural, Short story collections, Translation and Young Adult titles.
**Submission Guidelines** Accepts queries with SAE.
**Poetry** Pubish Poetry titles.
**Submission Guidelines** Accepts queries by phone or email.
**Recent Title(s)** *LIVELY TALES Magazine*, Edgewell Publishing (Short story magazine)
**Tips** Titles aimed at foreign language students/immigrants, young or new writers. Edgewell Publishing also offers a basic critiquing service which can then lead to being published in *LIVELY TALES Magazine* or as a stand alone book.

## Edinburgh University Press
**22 George Square, Edinburgh, Scotland, EH8 9LF**
- 0131 650 4218
- 0131 662 0053
- jackie.jones@eup.ed.ac.uk
- www.eup.ed.ac.uk

**Contact** Deputy Chief Executive and Head of Book Publishing, Jackie Jones (Literary Studies); Senior Commissioning Editor, Nicola Ramsey (Politics; Islamic Studies); Senior Commissioning Editor, Sarah Edwards (Linguistics, Film and Media Studies); Commissioning Editor, Carol MacDonald (Philosophy, Ancient History); Commissioning Editor, Esme Watson (Scottish History); Journals Publishing Manager, Diana Spencer (Journals)
**Established** 1946
**Insider Info** Publishes 105 titles per year. 15 per cent of books published are from first-time authors, 100 per cent of books published are from unagented authors. Five per cent of books published are author subsidy-published, based on expected gross profit. Payment is via net receipts. Advance offered is from £100 to £1,500. Average lead time is eight months, with simultaneous submissions accepted. Submissions accompanied by SAE will be returned. Aims to respond to queries within 14 days, proposals within two months and manuscripts within three months. Catalogue is free on request. Manuscript guidelines are free on request and available online, or by email.
**Non-Fiction** Publishes Journals, and Reference, Scholarly and Textbook titles on the following subjects:
 Anthropology/Archaeology (Journals and Scottish only), Contemporary Culture, Education (Scottish only), Government/Politics, History (Scottish History only), Humanities (Philosophy; Linguistics), Language/Literature (English, Scottish, Arabic language only); English, Scottish, American Literature, Law (Scottish only), Literary Criticism, Military/War (Scottish only), Philosophy, Regional (Scottish), Religion (Backlist only), Social Sciences (Politics only), Women's Issues/Studies (Backlist only), Islamic Studies, Film and Media, Ancient History, Scottish Studies.
**Submission Guidelines** Accepts proposal package (including outline, one to three sample chapters, your publishing history and author biography) and artworks/images (send photocopies, digital files as jpegs).
**Recent Title(s)** *The Edinburgh Companion to Ancient Greece and Rome*, ed. Bispham et al (Reference/scholarly)
**Tips** Proposals should be prepared according to the EUP guidelines and submitted via email attachment.

## The Educational Company of Ireland
**Ballymouth Road, Walkinstown, Dublin 12, Republic of Ireland**
☎ 00353 1 450 0611

☎ 00353 1 450 0993
✉ info@edco.ie
🌐 www.edco.ie
**Contact** Chief Executive, Frank Maguire; Publisher, Frank Fahy
**Established** 1910
**Insider Info** Catalogue and manuscript guidelines available online.
**Non-Fiction** Publishes Reference, Scholarly and Textbook titles on the following subjects:
 Education, Language/Literature, Translation.
**Recent Title(s)** *Aoibhneas Ardleibhéal*, Micheal O' Ruairc
**Tips** Publishes educational books and teaching resources on all subjects in both English and Irish. It is worth bearing in mind that educational publishers must keep an eye on the number of students taking a particular subject, in order to ensure that any publishing proposal is commercially viable.

## Educational Explorers
**PO Box 3391, Wokingham, RG41 5ZD**
☎ 0118 978 9680
☎ 0118 978 2335
✉ explorers@cuisenaire.co.uk
🌐 www.cuisenaire.co.uk
**Contact** Director, M.J. Hollyfield; Director. D.M. Gattegno
**Established** 1962
**Non-Fiction** Publishes Textbook and Scholarly titles.

## Educational Heretics Press
**113 Arundel Drive, Bramcote Hills, Nottingham, NG9 3FQ**
☎ 0115 925 7261
☎ 0115 925 7261
🌐 www.gn.apc.org/edheretics
**Contact** Director, Janet Meighan; Director, Roland Meighan
**Insider Info** Catalogue available online.
**Non-Fiction** Publishes Scholarly titles on Education.
**Tips** We are a small press that exists to question the dogmas and superstitions of mass, coercive schooling, with its roots in totalitarian thinking, with a view to developing the next modern, humane, flexible, personalised effective public learning system – one fit for a progressive democracy. Any submissions must, 'ask necessary questions about the fundamental processes of schooling.'

## Edward Elgar Publishing Ltd

**Glensanda House, Montpellier Parade, Cheltenham, Gloucestershire, GL5O 1UA**

- 01242 226934
- 01242 262111
- info@e-elgar.co.uk
- www.e-elgar.co.uk

**Contact** Managing Director, Edward Elgar
**Established** 1986
**Insider Info** Publishes 250 titles per year. Catalogue available on online. Submission guidelines available online.
**Non-fiction** Publishes general Non-fiction and Scholarly titles in the following subjects: Business/Economics, Government/Politics, Law, Money/Finance, Nature/Environment.
**Submission Guidelines** Accepts query with SAE and proposal package (including outline, sample chapter(s) or completed manuscript, author biography). See also the online proposal form. Submissions email: submissions@e-elgar.co.uk
**Recent Title(s)** *Complexity, Endogenous Money And Macroeconomic Theory,* Mark Setterfield (Economics)
**Tips** Founded in 1986, we are a leading international academic publisher in economics, management, law, environment, public and social policy. Specialising in research monographs, reference books and upper-level textbooks in a highly focused area, we are able to offer a unique service in terms of editorial, production and worldwide marketing. We are actively commissioning new titles and are always happy to consider and advise on ideas and proposals at any stage. If you would like to discuss your work, please feel free to contact us, we will reply promptly. We look forward to hearing from you and to working closely with you.

## Egg Box Publishing

**25 Brian Avenue, Norwich, NR1 2PH**

- 01603 470191
- mail@eggboxpublishing.com
- www.eggboxpublishing.com

**Contact** Managing Editor, Nathan Hamilton; Founder, Alexander Gordon Smith
**Established** 2001
**Insider Info** Receives approximately 5,000 manuscripts per year. Authors are paid around 30 per cent of the profits from their book.
**Non-Fiction** Publishes Non-fiction by unpublished writers only.
**Submission Guidelines** Postal submissions only.
**Fiction** Publishes Fiction by unpublished writers only.

**Submission Guidelines** Accepts postal submissions only.
**Poetry** Publish new poetry from unpublished writers only.
**Submission Guidelines** Accepts postal submissions only.
**Recent Title(s)** *Ahem,* Martin Figura (Poetry)
**Tips** Egg Box Publishing has recently become a limited company but is completely self funded, allowing brand new writers the chance to be published and possibly picked up by a more mainstream publisher. Authors must not have had any poetry collections or novels previously published anywhere. There are no guidelines for manuscripts as the ethos of the company is to encourage writing outside the usual constraints of mainstream publishing.

## Egmont Books

**239 Kensington High Street, London, W8 65A**

- 020 7761 3500
- 020 7761 3510
- info@egmont.co.uk
- www.egmont.co.uk

**Contact** Publishing Director, David Riley
**Established** 1878
**Insider Info** Publishes 500 titles per year. Catalogue available online. Manuscript guidelines available online.
**Non-Fiction** Publishes Gift books and Children's titles. No unsolicited manuscripts.
**Fiction** Picture books and Children's titles. No unsolicited manuscripts.
**Recent Title(s)** *A Series of Unfortunate Events: The End,* Lemony Snicket; *The Egyptians - Know It All Packs,* Know It All Packs
**Tips** Egmont Press is about turning writers into successful authors and children into passionate readers, producing books that enrich and entertain. Due to a huge backlog, we are unable to accept unsolicited manuscripts. You may wish to get a literary agent, to represent you to publishers.

## Eilish Press

**4 Collegiate Crescent, Broomhall Park, Sheffield, S10 2BA**

- 07973 353964
- eilishpress@hotmail.co.uk

**Contact** Dr. Suzi Kapadia (Women's Issues, Human Rights, Anti-Racism)
**Established** 2006

**Insider Info** Publishes five titles per year. Receives approximately 30 queries and five manuscripts per year. 100 per cent of books published are from unagented authors. Payment is via royalty (on wholesale price) or outright purchase. Catalogue available online or by email.

**Non-Fiction** Publishes Children's and Scholarly titles on the following subjects:

Ethnic, Health/Medicine, History, Women's Issues/Studies, Young Adult (all human rights orientated).

\* Eilish Press only accepts email proposals for children's non-fiction titles with human rights or anti-racism themes.

**Submission Guidelines** Accepts query by email. All unsolicited manuscripts are returned unopened. Accepts artworks/images (send digital files as jpegs).

**Fiction** Publishes Ethnic, Feminist, Historical, Multicultural and Young Adult titles.

\* Eilish Press only accepts email proposals for children's fiction titles with human rights or anti-racism themes.

**Recent Title(s)** *Conception Diary: Thinking About Pregnancy & Childbirth*, Dr Susan Hogan (Polemical Feminist, Humour)

**Tips** Eilish Press only publishes non-sexist, non-racist literature with humanitarian themes for children.

## Eland Publishing Ltd
**61 Exmouth Market, London, EC1R 4QL**
- 020 7833 0762
- 020 7833 4434
- info@travelbooks.co.uk
- www.travelbooks.co.uk

**Contact** Director, Rose Baring; Director, John Hatt; Director, Barnaby Rogerson

**Established** 1982

**Imprint(s)** Sickle Moon Books
Baring & Rogerson Books

**Insider Info** Catalogue available online.

**Non-Fiction** Publishes General Non-fiction in the following subjects:

Regional, Travel.

**Recent Title(s)** *Marrakesh: Through writers' eyes*, Barnaby Rogerson (Travel); *The Weather in Africa*, Martha Gellhorn (Travel/Novella)

**Tips** Eland specialises in keeping the classics of travel literature in print. Eland books open out our understanding of other cultures, interpret the unknown and reveal different environments, as well as celebrating the humour and occasional horrors of travel. Eland is a company with a mission; to keep the great works of travel literature in print. Eland only really publishes reprints.

## Elastic Press
**85 Gertrude Road, Norwich, Norfolk, NR3 4SG**
- 0845 398 3349
- elasticpress@elasticpress.com
- www.elasticpress.com

**Contact** Editor, Andrew Hook (Short fiction)

**Established** 2002

**Insider Info** Publishes five titles per year. Receives approximately 200 queries and 120 manuscripts per year. Ten per cent of books published are from first-time authors, 80 per cent of books published are from unagented authors. Payment is via royalty (on wholesale price). Average lead time is more than 18 months, with simultaneous submissions accepted. Submissions accompanied by SAE will be returned. Aims to respond to queries and proposals within two days, manuscripts within two months and all other enquiries within two days. Catalogue and manuscript guidelines are available with SAE or available online or by email.

**Fiction** Publishes Experimental (short stories only), Fantasy (short stories only), Gothic (short stories only), Horror (short stories only), Literary (short stories only), Mainstream/Contemporary (short stories only), Science Fiction (short stories only) and Short story collection titles.

\* Elastic Press operates a reading window system for submissions. See website for full details.

**Submission Guidelines** Accepts query with SAE or proposal package (including outline and synopsis), elasticpress@elasticpress.com

**Recent Title(s)** *Extended Play*, edited by Gary Couzens (Short fiction anthology)

**Tips** Elastic Press is a small publishing house dedicated to showcasing the talents of previously published independent press writers. Elastic Press publishes four times per year; on the 1st of February, May, August and November.

## Elliot Right Way Books
**Kingswood Buildings, Brighton Road, Tadworth, Surrey, KT20 6TD**
- 01737 832202
- 01737 830311
- info@right-way.co.uk
- www.right-way.co.uk

**Contact** Managing Director, A. Clive Elliot; Managing Director, Malcolm G. Elliot

**Established** 1946

**Imprint(s)** Right Way
Right Way Plus
Clarion

**Insider Info** Catalogue is available online. Manuscript guidelines are available online.

**Non-Fiction** Publishes General Non-fiction, How-to, Reference and Scholarly titles on the following subjects: Business/Economics, Child Guidance/ Parenting, Cooking/Foods/Nutrition, Counselling/ Career, Education, Hobbies, House and Home, Law, Etiquette.

**Submission Guidelines** Accepts query with SAE/ proposal package (including outline, sample chapter(s)).

**Recent Title(s)** *21st Century Babies' Names*, Jacqueline Harrod

**Tips** Titles are aimed at anyone and are widely known and respected for being informative, helpful and reasonably priced guides on an ever widening range of subjects. Always on the look out for interesting, informative and useful new titles. Get in touch with the publisher if you have specialist knowledge of your subject, and would like to share that it with readers all over the world. If you think your grammar and spelling are not as good as they should be, do not be discouraged, an excellent in-house editorial team may be able to help.

## Elliott & Thompson
**27 John Street, London, WC1N 2BX**
- 020 7831 5013
- 020 7831 5011
- gmo73@dial.pipex.com
- www.elliottthompson.com

**Contact** Publisher, David Elliott; Publisher, Brad Thompson
**Established** 2001
**Imprint(s)** Spitfire
 Gold Edition
 Young Spitfire

**Insider Info** Catalogue is available online. Manuscript guidelines are available online.

**Non-Fiction** Publishes Biography and Belles-Lettres titles.

**Submission Guidelines** Accepts query with SAE/ proposal package (including outline, sample chapter(s) and SAE).

**Fiction** Publishes Literary and Classic male writers titles.

**Submission Guidelines** Accepts query with SAE/ proposal package (including outline, sample chapter(s) and SAE).

**Recent Title(s)** *Russian Conspirators In Siberia*, Baron Andreas von Rosen (Historic account); *A Flag On the Abbey*, Rod Brammer (Novel)

**Tips** Elliott & Thompson publish within a finely chosen area of writing, once classified by the more traditional bookshops as 'belles-lettres'. The list includes works in the areas of fiction, memoir, biography, history, art, politics and travel. The publisher's catalogue may contain some surprises for the discerning reader. Please do not send unsolicited manuscripts, an outline with a sample chapter is sufficient. Please include SAE as no correspondence will be entered into unless full postal costs are included.

## Elm Publications/Training
**Seaton House, Kings Ripton, Huntingdon, Cambridgeshire, PE28 2NJ**
- 01487 773254
- 01487 773359
- elm@elm-training.co.uk
- www.elm-training.co.uk

**Parent Company** Elm Consulting Ltd
**Contact** Managing Director, Sheila Ritchie
**Established** 1977
**Insider Info** Publishes 30 titles per year. Catalogue is available online.

**Non-Fiction** Publishes Reference, Textbook and Technical titles on the following subjects: Business/ Economics, Counselling/Career, Education.

**Submission Guidelines** Accepts query with SAE/ proposal package (including outline and SAE).

**Recent Title(s)** *Drugs, Addiction and the Law*, Leonard Jason-Lloyd (Legal guidebook)

**Tips** Titles aimed at adults in education, training teams and businesses. The publisher actively seeks good, tested, training materials aimed at the public and private sectors and at adults in employment. Very pleased to hear from consultants and trainers who have tested materials and would like to extend their use through wider publication.

## Elsevier Ltd
**The Boulevard, Langford Lane, Kidlington, Oxford, OX5 1GB**
- 01865 843000
- 01865 843010
- authorsupport@elsevier.com
- www.elsevier.com

**Parent Company** Reed Elsevier Group Plc
**Contact** CEO, Erik Engstrom; CEO (Science & Technology), Herman van Campenhout; CEO (Health Sciences), Brian Nairn
**Established** 1880
**Imprint(s)** Elsevier Ltd (Health Sciences)
 Elsevier Ltd (Science & Technology)

**Insider Info** Publishes 1,900 books per year. Authors paid by royalty. Catalogue and author guidelines available online.

**Non-Fiction** Publishes Journals/Monographs, Illustrated books, Textbooks, Multimedia, Reference, Scholarly and Technical titles on the following subjects:
Anthropology/Archaeology, Art/Architecture, Business/Economics, Communications, Computers/Electronics, Education, Government/Politics, Health/Medicine, Humanities, Language/Literature, Law, Money/Finance, Nature/Environment, Psychology Science, Social Sciences, Sociology, Sports, Transportation, Technology, Physics/Astronomy, Leisure/Tourism.

**Submission Guidelines** Accepts query with SAE.

**Recent Title(s)** *Davidson's Principles and Practice of Medicine (20th edition)*, Nicholas Boon (Reference)

**Tips** Elsevier is the world's leading publisher of science and health information. The publishing operation is organised into two divisions: Science & Technology and Health Sciences. Elsevier publishes various products and services including electronic and print versions of journals, monographs, textbooks and reference works which cover the health, life, physical and social sciences. Elsevier welcomes authors' proposals for books. The first step is to discuss the proposal with the relevant Publishing Editor. Check the website for in-depth submission guidelines and a full list of editorial contacts. Note that most Elsevier publications are written by qualified academics.

## Elsevier Ltd (Health Sciences)
**32 Jamestown Road, Camden Town, London, NW1 7BY**
- 020 7424 4200
- 020 7482 2293
- m.ging@elsevier.com
- www.elsevier-health.com

**Parent Company** Elsevier Ltd

**Contact** CEO (Amsterdam), Brian Nairn; Managing Director, Mary Ging; Publishing Director, Caroline Makepeace (Health Professions); Publishing Manager, Timothy Horne (Medical Textbooks); Commissioning Editor, Michael Houston (Professional and Reference Medical Books)

**Imprint(s)** Baillière Tindall
Butterworth-Heinemann
BC Decker
Churchill Livingstone
Hanley & Belfus
Mosby
Saunders

**Insider Info** Payment is via royalties. Catalogue available online. Manuscript guidelines available online.

**Non-Fiction** Publishes Illustrated books, Multimedia, Reference, Scholarly, Textbook and Technical titles on the following subjects: Education, Health/Medicine, Psychology, Science, Social Sciences, Care, Veterinary Medicine, Midwifery, Complementary Therapies.

**Submission Guidelines** Use online proposal form.

**Recent Title(s)** *Gray's Dissection Guide for Human Anatomy (2nd edition)*, David Morton (Medical Reference)

**Tips** Elsevier Health Sciences is a leading publisher of health science books and journals, including online material and CD-ROMs. See individual entries for details of Health Sciences imprints. Elsevier Health Sciences accepts unsolicited proposals in their subject areas. To submit a proposal fill in a proposal form, available on the website, and return by email. Alternatively authors may contact the relevant editor prior to submission to discuss the proposal.

## Elsevier Ltd (Science & Technology)
**The Boulevard, Langford Lane, Kidlington, Oxford, OX5 1GB**
- 01865 843000
- 01865 843010
- authorsupport@elsevier.com
- www.elsevier.com

**Parent Company** Reed Elsevier Group Plc (Elsevier Ltd)

**Contact** CEO, Herman van Campenhout

**Imprint(s)** Academic Press
Architectural Press
Digital Press
Focal Press
Gulf Professional Publishing
Made Simple
Morgan Kauffman
Newnes
Pergamon Flexible Learning

**Insider Info** Payment is via royalties. Catalogue and manuscript guidelines available online.

**Non-Fiction** Publishes Illustrated, Multimedia, Reference, Scholarly, Technical and Textbook titles on the following subjects:
Art/Architecture, Business/Economics, Communications, Computers/Electronics, Education, Government/Politics, Humanities, Language/Literature, Law, Money/Finance, Psychology, Science, Sports, Transportation,

Technology, Construction/Engineering, Astronomy/ Physics, Leisure and Tourism.

**Submission Guidelines** Accepts query with SAE/ proposal package (including outline and SAE).

**Recent Title(s)** *Finance Director's Handbook*, Glynis Morris (Reference)

**Tips** Elsevier Science & Technology is a division of Elsevier Ltd and publishes printed material and digital resources over a wide range of scientific, financial and construction related subjects. They welcome authors' proposals for books. The first step is to discuss the proposal with the relevant Publishing Editor. Check the website for in-depth submission guidelines and a full list of editorial contacts.

## Emissary Publishing
**PO Box 33, London, NW1 7BY**
- 01869 323447
- 01869 324096

**Contact** Editorial Director, Val Miller
**Established** 1992
**Insider Info** Catalogue is available online at: http://website.lineone.net/~selfpublishuk/book_order_form.htm.
**Fiction** Publishes humour titles.
**Tips** Please do not send any unsolicited submissions.

## Emma Treehouse Ltd
**Old Brewhouse, Charlton Estate, Shepton Mallet, Somerset, BA4 5QE**
- 01749 330529
- 01749 330544
- info@emmatreehouse.com
- www.emmatreehouse.com

**Contact** Director, David Bailey; Creative and Editorial Director, Richard Powell
**Established** 1992
**Insider Info** Catalogue is available online.
**Non-Fiction** Publishes Gift books and Children's/Juvenile titles.
**Submission Guidelines** Accepts query with SAE.
**Fiction** Publishes Children's titles.
**Submission Guidelines** Accepts query with SAE.
**Recent Title(s)** *Crib Critters*, Ana Martin-Larranaga (Novelty/Children's)
**Tips** Emma Treehouse Ltd is a specialist creator of books for children from 0-5 years with a worldwide audience and international recognition for its innovative concepts. The company was founded in 1992 and has since produced over 36 million books, translated into 35 languages. Novelty, Cloth, Feel,

Flap and books with a sound concept are included in the company's list. Publishes in the UK as Treehouse Children's Books. Do not send unsolicited manuscript submissions, contact via email with ideas only.

## Enable Enterprises
**PO Box 1974, Coventry, CV3 1YF**
- 0800 358 8484
- 0870 133 2447
- writers@enableenterprises.com
- www.enableenterprises.com

**Contact** Chief Executive, Simon Stevens
**Non-Fiction** Publishes General Non-fiction titles on the following subjects: Health/Medicine, Disability.
**Submission Guidelines** Accepts query with SAE/completed manuscript.
**Tips** Enable Enterprises is a leading and now renowned award winning provider of disability and accessibility services including training, consultancy, research, advocacy, information, payroll and more. Unsolicited submissions related to health and disabilities are welcomed.

## Encyclopædia Britannica (UK) Ltd
**2nd Floor, Unity Wharf, Mill Street, London, SE1 2BH**
- 020 7500 7800
- 020 7500 7878
- http://info.britannica.co.uk

**Parent Company** Encyclopaedia Britannica Inc
**Year established** 1768
**Non-Fiction** Publishes Multimedia and Reference titles on the following subjects:
 Arts and Literature, The Earth, Geography, Health and Medicine, Philosophy, Religion, Sports and Recreation, Science, Mathematics, Life, Society, Technology, History.
**Tips** Primarily publishes the Encyclopædia Britannica, a major reference guide.

## English Heritage (Publishing)
**Kemble Drive, Swindon, SN2 2GZ**
- 01793 414497
- 01793 414769
- customers@english-heritage.org.uk
- www.english-heritage.org.uk

**Contact** Rob Richardson
**Insider Info** Catalogue is available online.
**Non-Fiction** Publishes General Non-fiction, Illustrated books, Scholarly books and Reference titles.

**Recent Title(s)** *Diary of a Victorian Gardener*, William Cresswell and Audley End (History)

**Tips** English Heritage exists to protect and promote England's spectacular historic environment and ensure that its past is researched and understood. All the titles relate directly to the work of the organisation, so unsolicited material is not accepted.

## Enitharmon Press

**26b Caversham Road, London, NW5 2DU**

☎ 020 7482 5967

✆ 020 7284 1787

✉ books@enitharmon.co.uk

🌐 www.enitharmon.co.uk

**Contact** Director, Stephen Stuart-Smith

**Established** 1967

**Imprint(s)** Enitharmon Editions

**Insider Info** Catalogue is available online.

**Non-Fiction** Publishes Illustrated and General Non-fiction titles on the following subjects: Art/Architecture, Literary Criticism, Photography.

**Fiction** Publishes Literary and Short story collections.

**Poetry** Publishes Poetry titles.

**Recent Title(s)** *The Apple That Astonished Paris*, Billy Collins (Poetry collection)

**Tips** Enitharmon commissions collaborations between distinguished artists and writers. These artists' books have earned an international reputation for their exceptional quality. Currently unsolicited submissions cannot be accepted.

## Epworth Press

**c/o Methodist Publishing House, 4 John Wesley Road, Werrington, Peterborough, Cambridgeshire, PE4 6ZP**

☎ 01733 325002

✆ 01733 384180

✉ sales@mph.org.uk

🌐 www.mph.org.uk

**Parent Company** MPH

**Contact** Commissioning Editor, Dr. Natalie Watson

**Established** 1800

**Insider Info** Publishes ten titles per year. Payment is via royalties (annually). Catalogue is available online at: http://secure2.cyberware.co.uk/%7Ecb537/acatalog/. Manuscript guidelines available online.

**Non-Fiction** Publishes Illustrated books and General Non-fiction titles on the following subjects: Religion, Methodist faith.

**Submission Guidelines** Accepts query with SAE submit proposal package (outline, two sample chapters, SAE).

**Recent Title(s)** *Living Hope: A Practical Theology of Hope for the Dying*, Russell Herbert

**Tips** With roots in John Wesley's 'Christian Library', Epworth publishes ten to twelve new titles a year on the Bible, worship, contemporary Christian issues and Methodism. Epworth is interested in hearing from new and aspiring authors. The publisher would be interested to hear from you if you are writing or have written something that might be of interest to a wider readership.

## The Erotic Print Society

**1st Floor, 17 Harwood Road, London, SW6 4QP**

☎ 020 773 65800

✆ 020 773 66330

✉ eps@leadline.co.uk

🌐 www.eroticprints.org

**Contact** Managing Director, Jamie Maclean; Society Secretary, Tilly Johnson

**Established** 1994

**Insider Info** Publishes 20 titles per year. Catalogue available online.

**Non-Fiction** Publishes Illustrated and Multimedia titles on Sex.

**Fiction** Publishes Erotica and Multimedia titles.

**Recent Title(s)** *Sister's Dirty Secret*, Meg Oliphant (Erotic Novel)

**Tips** Titles are aimed at men and women who appreciate the best in erotic books, art, photography and literature. The Erotic Print Society is now established as the leading source of collectable erotica worldwide and publish works such as pocket sized paperbacks and beautifully bound limited editions. They also publish several magazines, such as *SEx*, which can offer further publishing opportunities for shorter writing.

## EuroCrime

**5–16 Nassau Street, London, W1W 7AB**

☎ 020 7436 9898

✆ 020 7436 9898

✉ info@arcadiabooks.co.uk

🌐 www.arcadiabooks.co.uk

**Parent Company** Arcadia Books

**Insider Info** Catalogue available online.

**Fiction** Publishes Crime fiction titles.

**Submission Guidelines** Accepts agented submissions only.

**Recent Title(s)** *Dead Horsemeat*, Dominique Manotti

**Tips** Publishes European crime writing only (excluding the UK).

## Euromonitor International

**60–61 Britton Street, London, EC1M 5UX**

- 020 7251 8024
- 020 7608 3149
- info@euromonitor.com
- www.euromonitor.com

**Contact** Chairman, R.N. Senior; Managing Director, T.J. Fenwick

**Established** 1972

**Insider Info** Publishes 1,000 titles per year. Author's work is purchased outright. Catalogue is available free on request, online and via email.

**Non-Fiction** Publishes Multimedia, Reference and Technical titles on the following subjects: Business/Economics, Market reports/Analysis.

**Recent Title(s)** *European Marketing Data and Statistics*, Euromonitor (Market analysis)

**Tips** Euromonitor International's mission is to be the best provider of quality international market intelligence on industries, countries and consumers. Prospective authors must be highly experienced with a background in technical market analysis, or similar.

## Evans Brothers Ltd

**2a Portman Mansions, Chiltern Street, London, W1V 6NR**

- 020 7487 0920
- 020 7487 0921
- sales@evansbrothers.co.uk
- www.evansbooks.co.uk

**Contact** Managing Director, Stephen Pawley; Publisher, Su Swallow

**Established** 1908

**Imprint(s)** Cherrytree Books
Zero to Ten

**Insider Info** Publishes 120 titles per year. Payment is via royalties (annually). Catalogue is available online. Discounts are available for schools.

**Non-Fiction** Publishes Children's/Juvenile, Textbook and Scholarly titles on the following subjects: Education, Translation, Foreign language children's textbooks.

**Recent Title(s)** *Countdown!*, Kay Woodward (Children's)

**Tips** The publisher is committed to providing children, teachers and carers with books that help deliver key areas of the curriculum, whilst instilling a lifelong love of reading and learning in children and young people. Evans Brothers Ltd publish children's education books only.

## Everyman

**Random House, 20 Vauxhall Bridge Road, London, SW1V 2SA**

- 020 7840 8400
- 020 7840 8406
- sarah@everyman.uk.com
- www.randomhouse.co.uk

**Parent Company** The Random House Group Ltd

**Insider Info** Submissions accompanied by SAE will be returned. Catalogue is available online.

**Non-Fiction** Publishes Biography, Illustrated books and General Non-fiction titles on the following subjects: Memoirs, Nostalgia.

**Submission Guidelines** Submit proposal package (including outline, one sample chapter and SAE). Will accept artwork/photos (send photocopies).

**Fiction** Publish reprints of classic novels.

**Poetry** Publish reprinted collections from established poets.

**Recent Title(s)** *Big Money*, P. G Wodehouse (Novel); *Edwin Arlington Robinson Poems*, Edwin Arlington Robinson (Poetry collection)

**Tips** In terms of fiction, Everyman mainly publish reprints. Other imprints of Random House are more likely to be useful for new works of fiction. Please see the Random House Group entry for the list, and individual entries for detailed information.

## Everyman Classics

**5 Upper St. Martins Lane, London, WC2H 9EA**

- 020 7240 3444
- 020 7240 4822
- www.orionbooks.co.uk

**Parent Company** Orion Publishing Group Ltd

**Insider Info** Catalogue is available online.

**Non-Fiction** Publishes General Non-fiction titles on the following subjects: Creative Non-fiction, History, Literary Criticism, Philosophy, Regional. All are reprints of classic works of non-fiction.

**Fiction** Publishes Literary, Plays and Poetry titles. All arer eprints of classic fiction works.

**Poetry** Publishes reprints of poetry collections.

**Recent Title(s)** *A Treatise of Human Nature*, David Hume (Non-fiction); *Ruth*, Elizabeth Gaskell (Fiction); *Libertine Plays Of The Restoration*, Gillian Manning (ed.) (Drama anthology)

**Tips** Publishes reprints only, so no submissions please.

## Everyman's Library

**Northborough House, 10 Northborough Street, London, EC1V 0AT**

☎ 020 7566 6350
🖷 020 7490 3708
✉ books@everyman.uk.com
**Contact** Publisher, David Campbell
**Established** 1906
**Non-Fiction** Publishes General Non-fiction titles on Travel. No new titles, only publishes classic reprints.
**Fiction** Publishes Children's, Literary, Poetry and Translation titles. No new titles, only publishes classic reprints.
**Poetry** Publishes new poetry anthologies, but does not accept submissions.
**Tips** Titles aimed at anyone interested in classic literary/world writing. Submissions cannot be accepted since only reprints of 'classic' literature are published.

## Exley Publications Ltd
**16 Chalk Hill, Watford, WD19 4BG**
☎ 01923 248328
🖷 01923 800440
✉ editorial@exleypublications.co.uk
🌐 www.helenexleygiftbooks.com
**Contact** Editorial Director, Helen Exley
**Established** 1976
**Insider Info** Catalogue is available online.
**Non-Fiction** Publishes Gift books, Quotation anthologies and Humour titles.
**Submission Guidelines** No submissions accepted.
**Recent Title(s)** *The Thank You Book*, Helen Exley ed. (Gift book)
**Tips** At least 12 million people give, receive and read the gift books created by Exley Publications each year - about one in five hundred of all people in the world. The books are about family relationships, wisdom and personal values and are a great source of help to people in their journey through life. The company, whilst reaching out to the public on a worldwide basis, is still run as a family business from peaceful, creeper covered offices in Watford, UK. The publisher also has companies in the US, Belgium and Germany, where their joint owners are also family people who have the same goals and principles. As a family business unsolicited material will not be accepted.

## Faber & Faber Ltd
**3 Queen Square, London, WC1N 3AU**
☎ 020 7465 0045
🖷 020 7465 0034
✉ gapublicity@faber.co.uk
🌐 www.faber.co.uk

**Contact** Chief Executive, Stephen Page; Editorial Director, Lee Brackstone (Fiction); Editorial Director, Julian Loose (Non-fiction); Editor, Paul Keegan (Poetry); Editorial Director, Suzy Jenvy (Children's).
**Established** 1929
**Insider Info** Publishes 300 titles per year. Payment is via royalty, along with varying advances. Submissions accompanied by SAE will be returned. Aim to respond to manuscripts within 12 weeks. Catalogue is available online and via email: gacatalogue@faber.co.uk
**Non-Fiction** Publishes Biography, Children's/Juvenile, Coffee table books, Cookbooks, General Non-fiction, Anthologies and Humour titles on the following subjects: Art/Architecture, Contemporary Culture, Cooking/Foods/Nutrition, Creative Non-fiction, Entertainment/Games, Government/Politics, History, Humanities, Literary Criticism, Military/War, Multicultural, Music/Dance, Philosophy, Psychology, Recreation, Science, Sports, Travel, World Affairs, Young Adult, Film, Music.
 * Faber have rejuvenated their non-fiction lists in recent years and the film and drama books remain market leaders.
**Submission Guidelines** Accepts agented submissions only.
**Fiction** Publishes Adventure, Ethnic, Experimental, Historical, Literary, Mystery, Plays, Poetry, Short story collections, Sports, Suspense, Young Adult, Drama, Screenplays and Children's fiction titles.
**Submission Guidelines** Accepts agented submissions only.
**Poetry** Publishes Classic and Contemporary Poetry titles.
 * Poetry is the only area where Faber and Faber will accept unsolicited submissions.
**Submission Guidelines** Submit up to six sample poems.
**Recent Title(s)** *A Blow to the Heart*, Marcel Theroux (Novel); *The New Faber Book of Love Poems*, Introduced by James Fenton (Poetry).
**Tips** Faber & Faber will only accepted submissions for poetry titles, and then only by post with accompanying SAE for return. If you have not heard anything 12 weeks after sending submissions you may then send a further query.

## Fabian Society
**11 Dartmouth Street, London, SW1H 9BN**
☎ 020 7227 4900
🖷 020 7976 7153
✉ info@fabian-society.org.uk
🌐 www.fabian-society.org.uk

**Contact** General Secretary, Sunder Katwala; Editorial Director, Tom Hampson
**Established** 1884
**Insider Info** Catalogue is available online.
**Non-Fiction** Publishes Booklets, General Non-fiction, Reference, Policy reports and Scholarly titles on the following subjects: Business/Economics, Community/Public Affairs, Contemporary Culture, Education, Government/Politics, Money/Finance, Social Sciences, Sociology, World Affairs.
**Submission Guidelines** Submission details to: tom.hampson@fabian-society.org.uk
**Recent Title(s)** *The Real Deal: Drugs Policy that Works*, John Mann MP (Report)
**Tips** The Fabian Society has played a central role for more than a century in the development of political ideas and public policy on the left of centre. Analysing the key challenges facing the UK and the rest of the industrialised world, in a changing society and global economy, the Society's programme aims to explore the political ideas and the policy reforms which will define progressive politics in the new century. The Society is unique among think tanks, in being a democratically constituted membership organisation. It is affiliated to the Labour Party, but is editorially and organisationally independent. Through its publications, seminars and conferences, the Society provides an arena for open minded public debate. Proposals for publication must reflect this ethos.

## Facet Publishing
**7 Ridgemont Street, London, WC1E 7AE**
- 020 7255 0590
- 020 7255 0591
- info@facetpublishing.co.uk
- www.facetpublishing.co.uk
**Contact** Publishing Director, Helen Carley; Commissioning Editor, Sophie Baird
**Imprint(s)** Library Association Publishing
 Clive Bingley Books
**Insider Info** Publishes 25 titles per year. Payment is via royalties. Catalogue and manuscript guidelines are available online.
**Non-Fiction** Publishes Scholarly, Textbook, Directories/Bibliographies and Reference titles on the following subjects: Library and Information science, Information technology.
**Submission Guidelines** Accepts query with SAE/proposal package (including outline, two sample chapters, your publishing history, author biography and SAE). Submissions details to: sophie.baird@facetpublishing.co.uk

**Recent Title(s)** *Copyright for Records Managers and Archivists*, Tim Padfield (Reference)
**Tips** Facet Publishing is the leading international publisher of books for the library and information profession. The publisher provides dynamic, relevant and up to date books for information professionals wherever they may be, and acknowledge the need for high quality books that inform, instruct and inspire in the ever changing information world. The audiences of these books are industry professionals, so submissions need to reflect this.

## Fal Publications
**PO Box 74, Truro, Cornwall, TR1 1XS**
- 07887 560018
- info@falpublications.co.uk
- www.falpublications.co.uk
**Contact** Publisher, Victoria Field (Poetry, Cornish Interest)
**Established** 2004
**Insider Info** Publishes three titles per year. Receives approximately 12 queries per year. 50 per cent of books published are from first-time authors, 80 per cent of books published are from unagented authors. Payment is via royalty (on wholesale price). Simultaneous submissions not accepted. Submissions accompanied by SAE will be returned. Aims to respond to queries within seven days. Catalogue available online.
**Fiction** Publishes Cornwall related fiction titles.
**Poetry** Publishes Cornwall related poetry titles.
**Submission Guidelines** Accepts query by email.
**Recent Title(s)** *The Devil and the Floral Dance*, D.M. Thomas (Illustrated story about Cornwall; *Many Waters*, Victoria Field (Poems about Truro Cathedral).
**Tips** Fal Publications publishes general fiction and poetry for those interested in Cornwall.

## F.A. Thorpe (Publishing)
**The Green, Bradgate Road, Anstey, LE7 7FU**
- 0116 236 4325
- 0116 234 0205
**Contact** Group Chief Executive, Robert Thirlby
**Established** 1964
**Imprint(s)** Linford Mystery
 Linford Romance
 Linford Western
**Insider Info** Publishes 450 titles per year.
**Non-Fiction** Publishes General Non-fiction titles in the form of large print books for libraries.
 * No education, gardening, or any books unsuitable for large print.

**Submission Guidelines** Do not send any unsolicited submissions.
**Fiction** Publishes Mystery, Romance and Western titles.
 * Large print books for libraries. No books unsuitable for large print.
**Submission Guidelines** Do not send any unsolicited submissions.
**Tips** As part of the Ulverscroft Group, F.A. Thorpe supply large print books to libraries and other services. Unsolicited material cannot be accepted since only reprints supplied to libraries are published.

## Fernhurst Books
**The Atrium, Southern Gate, Chichester, West Sussex, PO19 8SQ**
- 01243 770372
- 01243 770481
- sdavison@wiley.co.uk
- www.fernhurstbooks.co.uk

**Parent Company** John Wiley & Sons Ltd
**Contact** Publisher, Simon Davison (Nautical Sports)
**Established** 1979
**Insider Info** Publishes 12 titles per year. Receives approximately 30 queries per year. 50 per cent of books published are from first-time authors and 90 per cent are from unagented authors. Payment via royalty with 0.1 (per £) maximum. An advance is offered. Average lead time is one year with simultaneous submissions not accepted. Catalogue is available online.
**Non-Fiction** Publishes General Non-fiction, How-to, Reference and Technical titles on the following subjects:
 Hobbies, Marine Subjects, Recreation, Sports, Transportation.
**Recent Title(s)** *The Brilliance of Sunbeams*, Peter Nicholson (Yachting); *Electrics Afloat*, Pat Manley (Reference)
**Tips** Titles are aimed at nautical sports/watersports/sailing enthusiasts and professional sailors. Fernhurst Books has recently been acquired by John Wiley & Sons, any submission enquiries must be directed through them.

## Fidra Books
**60 Craignook Road, Edinburgh, EH3 3PJ**
- 0131 343 3118
- info@fidrabooks.co.uk
- www.fidrabooks.co.uk

**Contact** Vanessa Robertson
**Insider Info** Catalogue is available online.

**Fiction** Publishes Children's and Young Adult titles.
 * Reprints of children's fiction only.
**Submission Guidelines** Accepts query with SAE.
**Recent Title(s)** *The Far Island*, Margot Pardoe
**Tips** Fidra Books is a new publishing company, specialising in reprinting some of the best children's fiction from the 20th Century. Please only approach Fidra if you are interested in reissuing a work of children's fiction. A background in book selling provides the publisher with an awareness of authors that are in demand, yet whose books are hard to find. There is a definite policy of only publishing books which the publisher likes.

## Fig Tree
**80 Strand, London, WC2R 0RL**
- 020 7010 3000
- 020 7010 6060
- customer.service@penguin.co.uk
- www.penguin.co.uk

**Parent Company** Penguin General
**Contact** Publishing Director, Juliet Annan
**Established** 2006
**Insider Info** Catalogue is available online.
**Fiction** Publishes Literary titles.
**Submission Guidelines** Agented submissions only.
**Recent Title(s)** *The Sea Lady,* Margaret Drabble (Literary novel); *No! I Don't Want to Join a Bookclub,* Virginia Ironside (Fictionalised diary)
**Tips** Fig Tree is a new Penguin imprint that specialises in literary books with commercial appeal. Fig Tree titles aim to be fresh, distinct, well written, clever, entertaining and sometimes funny.

## Findhorn Press
**305a The Park, Findhorn, Forres, Scotland, IV36 3TE**
- 01309 690582
- 01309 690036
- submissions@findhornpress.com
- www.findhornpress.com

**Contact** Director, Karin Biogolo; Director, Thierry Biogolo
**Established** 1971
**Insider Info** Publishes 20 titles per year. Receives approximately 1,000 queries per year. 50 per cent of books published are from first-time authors. Authors are paid royalties on the wholesale price of books with 0.1 (per £) minimum and 0.15 (per £) maximum. Average lead time is 12 months. Catalogue and manuscript guidelines are available online.
**Non-Fiction** Publishes General Non-fiction, Gift books and Self-help titles in the following subjects:

Alternative Lifestyles, Health/Medicine, New Age, Spirituality, Mind/Body/Spirit.

**Submission Guidelines** Accepts query with SAE/proposal package (including outline, two sample chapters, your publishing history, author biography and SAE). Will accept artwork/photos.

**Recent Title(s)** *Clearing,* Jim PathFinder Ewing

**Tips** Based on the Findhorn Community campus at Findhorn in Northeast Scotland, Findhorn Press is a small publishing house who offer books, sets of cards, cds and dvds that cover a wide range of 'mind, body and spirit' topics such as nature, spirituality, alternative health (for both people and for animals), self-help, etc. Before contacting the publisher, please take a good look at the type of books published to ensure your work is suitable. In particular, please note that they do not publish poetry or short stories.

## First and Best in Education
**Earlstrees Court, Earlstrees Road, Corby, Northamptonshire, NN17 4HH**
- 01536 399005
- 01536 399012
- info@firstandbest.co.uk
- www.firstandbest.co.uk

**Contact** Publisher, Tony Attwood; Editor, Anne Cockburn

**Established** 1992

**Imprint(s)** School Improvement Reports

**Insider Info** Payment via royalties. Catalogue and submission guidelines are available online.

**Non-Fiction** Publishes Reference, Textbook and Scholarly titles on Education.

\* Books must be photocopiable and aimed at education.

**Submission Guidelines** Accepts query with SAE/proposal package (including outline, two to four sample chapters and SAE).

**Recent Title(s)** *Ofsted Buster Departmental Handbook,* Francis Stapleton (Copiable book)

**Tips** Publishes photocopiable books and books on disk for teachers and parents. First and Best is interested in publishing the following types of educational books: Materials for teachers, drama, history, DT, PSHE and religious studies lesson materials, special needs and behaviour management materials, and information for school administrators. At this moment the publisher cannot consider any fiction or primary texts.

## Fitness Trainers
**38 Soho Square, London, W1D 3HB**
- 020 7758 0200

- 020 7758 0222
- rfoss@acblack.com
- www.acblack.com

**Parent Company** A & C Black Publishers Ltd

**Contact** Department Head and Commissioning Editor, Robert Foss; Commissioning Editor, Charlotte Croft; Editor, Lucy Beevor; Editor, Alex Hazle

**Established** 2003

**Insider Info** Catalogue is available online.

**Non-Fiction** Publishes General Non-fiction, Illustrated books and Reference titles in the following subjects: Health/Medicine, Sports, Fitness Training.

**Recent Title(s)** *The Complete Guide to Sports Training,* John Shepherd

**Tips** Fitness Trainers publishes practical fitness and sports guides, training schedules, and general interest books on sports for all age ranges and abilities. Fitness Trainers specialises in comprehensive guides written by well known experts in their relevant fields.

## Fitzgerald Publishing
**89 Ermine Road, Ladywell, London, SE13 7JJ**
- 020 8690 0597
- fitzgeraldbooks@yahoo.co.uk
- www.thebts.co.uk/fitzgerald_publishing.htm

**Contact** Managing Editor, Tim Fitzgerald; General Editor, Andrew Smith

**Established** 1974

**Insider Info** Publishes two titles per year. Catalogue is available online.

**Non-Fiction** Publishes Illustrated books and Scholarly titles on the following subjects: Nature/Environment, Spiders and Insects.

**Submission Guidelines** Accepts query with SAE. Will accept artwork/photos.

**Recent Title(s)** *Scorpions Of Medical Importance,* Prof. Keegan

**Tips** Aimed at those who study spiders and other insects, so titles are technical or academic in nature. Unsolicited submissions, or ideas for books are welcome, as are scripts for video documentaries (along with the video content).

## Fitzwarren Publishing
**51 Nicholson Drive, Leighton Buzzard, LU7 4HQ**
- 01525 384433
- pen2paper@btopenworld.com

**Contact** Julie Stretton

**Insider info** Publishes three titles per year. Payment is via royalties.

**Non-Fiction** Publishes Reference and Technical titles on Law.

* All books follow rigid 128 page format. Books are all legal handbooks.

**Submission Guidelines** Accepts query with SAE/proposal package (including outline, sample chapter(s), author biography and SAE).

**Recent Title(s)** *The Litigation Handbook*, Anthony Reeves (Legal handbook)

**Tips** Publishes mainly layman's handbooks on legal matters. Written approaches and synopses from prospective authors are welcome. Authors, although not necessarily legally qualified, are expected to know their subject as well as a lawyer would.

## Five Leaves Publications
**PO Box 8786, Nottingham, NG1 9AW**
- 0115 969 3597
- info@fiveleaves.co.uk
- www.fiveleaves.co.uk

**Contact** Ross Bradshaw
**Established** 1995
**Insider Info** Publishes eight titles per year. Payment is via royalties. Catalogue is available online.
**Non-Fiction** Publishes General Non-fiction titles on the following subjects: Government/Politics, History, Social Sciences, Jewish interest.
**Fiction** Publishes Historical, Literary, Religious, Short story collections, and Jewish fiction titles.
**Poetry** Publish Poetry titles.
**Tips** Five Leaves is a small publisher based in Nottingham. Interests include secular Jewish culture, writers from the East Midlands. Being small means non-commercial material can be published, hence the first British study of Yiddish film and how a book about the ideas of William Morris have come to fruition. Alongside these, books by well known commercial writers such as David Belbin, Michael Rosen and Marge Piercy are also published. The publisher's list also includes a Booker Prize winning novel; Holiday by Stanley Middleton. Five Leaves titles are almost always commissioned. Unsolicited material is generally not read. If you have a submission in keeping with the type of material published, then please make contact by email first.

## Flambard Press
**Stable Cottage, East Fourstones, Hexham, Northumberland, NE47 5DX**
- 01434 674360
- 01434 674178
- enquiries@flambardpress.co.uk
- www.flambardpress.co.uk

**Contact** Managing Editor, Peter Lewis
**Established** 1990
**Insider Info** Publishes five titles per year. Authors are paid royalties. Catalogue and manuscript guidelines are available online.
**Fiction** Publishes Literary and Short Story Collections titles.

* No genre fiction.

**Submission Guidelines** Accepts query with SAE/proposal package (including outline and two sample chapters).
**Poetry** Publish Poetry titles.
**Submission Guidelines** Accepts query with 15–20 sample poems.
**Recent Title(s)** So, What Kept You?, Various (Anthology); *Writing With Mercury,* Nancy Mattson (Poetry Collection)
**Tips** Margaret and Peter Lewis set up Flambard in 1990 as a small, independent press offering opportunities to new and neglected writers, especially in the North of England. From the outset Flambard has been keen to nourish developing talent. Poetry came first and is still the backbone of the list, but Flambard now publishes a small amount of fiction as well. Flambard publishes five or six books a year, so authors are very carefully selected. Only book length collections of poetry or short stories, and novels are considered. Children's books, science fiction, fantasy, romance, westerns or horror are not published by Flambard.

## Flame Tree Publishing
**Crabtree Hall, Crabtree Lane, London, SW6 6TY**
- 020 7386 4700
- 020 7386 4701
- info@flametreepublishing.com
- www.flametreepublishing.com

**Parent Company** The Foundry Creative Media Company Ltd
**Contact** Publisher/Creative Director, Nick Wells
**Established** 1992
**Insider Info** Catalogue is available online.
**Non-Fiction** Children's/Juvenile, Gift books and General Non-fiction titles on the following subjects: Art/Architecture, Cooking/Foods/Nutrition, Education, History, Hobbies, Music/Dance.
**Recent Title(s)** *Chocolate and Baking*, Gina Steer ed. (Cooking)
**Tips** Flame Tree Publishing aspire to create high quality books and stationery of great integrity and genuine value. The publisher aims to produce a body of work that will continue to provide benefit to our customers over many years. Illustrated reference books are favoured above others.

## Flicks Books

**29 Bradford Road, Trowbridge, Wiltshire, BAI4 9AN**

☎ 01225 767728

✉ flicks.books@dial.pipex.com

**Contact** Publisher, Matthew Stevens

**Established** 1986

**Non-Fiction** Publishes General Non-fiction titles on the following subjects: Entertainment/Games, Cinema/Television/Related media.

## Flipped Eye Publishing Limited

**PO Box 43771, London, W14 8ZY**

✉ books@flippedeye.net

🌐 www.flippedeye.net

**Contact** Editor, Sally Strong (Literary Fiction); Senior Editor, Nii Ayikwei Parkes (Poetry, Short Stories)

**Established** 2001

**Imprint(s)** Lubin and Kleyner

Waterways

Mouthmark Poetry (series)

**Insider Info** Publishes ten titles per year. Receives approximately 200 queries and 140 manuscripts per year. 90 per cent of books published are from first-time authors, 95 per cent of books published are from unagented authors. Payment is via royalty (on retail price). Advance offered is from £50 to £1,000. Average lead time is nine months, with simultaneous submissions not accepted. Submissions will not be returned. Aims to respond to queries and proposals within three months, manuscripts within six months and all other enquiries within 14 days. Catalogue is free on request and available online. Manuscript guidelines are available online.

**Fiction** Publishes Erotica, Fantasy, Literary, Mainstream/Contemporary, Multicultural, Short story collections and Translation titles.

**Submission Guidelines** Accepts query with SAE/ proposal package (including outline, three sample chapters and your publishing history).

Submission details to: newwork@flippedeye.net

**Poetry** * Publishes Poetry (Experience of reading to an audience required) and Poetry in translation (Short proposal must be sent first).

**Submission Guidelines** Accepts proposal package (including six sample poems).

Submission details to: newwork@flippedeye.net

**Recent Title(s)** *Tell Tales Volume 2*, Rajeev Balasubramanyam ed. (Poetry Anthology); *Communion*, Jacob Sam-La Rose (Pamphlet)

## Floris Books

**15 Harrison Gardens, Edinburgh, EH11 1SH**

☎ 0131 337 2372

☎ 0131 347 9919

✉ floris@florisbooks.co.uk

🌐 www.florisbooks.co.uk

**Contact** Managing Director, Christian Maclean; Editor, Gale Winskill; Editor Christopher Moore

**Established** 1977

**Imprint(s)** Flyways

Kelpies

**Insider Info** Payment via royalties. Catalogue and manuscript guidelines are available online.

**Non-Fiction** Publishes Children's/Juvenile, General Non-fiction, Illustrated books and Scholarly titles on the following subjects: Art/Architecture, Crafts, Education, Health/Medicine, History, Religion, Science, Social Sciences, Spirituality, Celtic studies.

**Submission Guidelines** Accepts query with SAE/ proposal package (including outline, three sample chapters and SAE). No email submissions.

**Fiction** Publishes Historical, Juvenile, Regional and Scottish titles.

**Submission Guidelines** Accepts query with SAE/ proposal package (including outline, three sample chapters and SAE). No email submissions.s

**Recent Title(s)** *Bees and Honey, from Flower to Jar*, Michael Weiler; *Story of the Wind Children*, Sibylle von Olfers (Picture Book)

**Tips** Floris Books publishes books for children and adults, including fiction and non-fiction books of predominantly Scottish interest. Subject matter is predominantly Scottish in content. Research has found that there is a huge demand for books encompassing modern settings, with contemporary situations and characters to which today's children can relate. That does not rule out historical fiction, but more modern titles are currently being prioritised.

## Flyleaf Press

**4 Spencer Villas, Glenageary, Dublin, Republic of Ireland**

☎ 00353 1 284 5906

✉ books@flyleaf.ie

🌐 www.circa.ie

**Contact** Managing Editor, Jim Ryan (Family History, Genealogy)

**Established** 1988

**Insider Info** Publishes three titles per year. Receives 20 queries and ten manuscripts per year. 75 per cent of books published are from first-time authors, 100 per cent of books published are from unagented authors. Payment is via royalty (on wholesale price) with 0.07 (per £) minimum and 0.1 (per £) maximum. Average lead time is eight months, with simultaneous submissions accepts. Submissions accompanied by SAE will be returned. Aims to respond to queries within five days, proposals within 30 days and manuscripts within six weeks. Catalogue available online and by email. Manuscript guidelines available by email.

**Non-Fiction** Publishes General Non-fiction and Reference titles on the following subjects: History (Irish Genealogical History), Hobbies, Family history and Genealogy (Irish family history and related local history).

 * Flyleaf is interested in any works that will assist readers with interests in Irish family history. Flyleaf is not usually interested in histories of a single family.

**Submission Guidelines** Accepts proposal package (including outline, clips, author biography and SAE).

**Recent Title(s)** *Tracing your Limerick Ancestors*, Margaret Franklin (Genealogy)

**Tips** Flyleaf's target readership is Irish family history and genealogy enthusiasts, and libraries and societies with genealogical interests.

## Focal Press

**The Boulevard, Langford Lane, Kidlington, Oxford, OX5 1GB**

- 01865 843000
- 01865 843010
- authorsupport@elsevier.com
- www.books.elsevier.com/uk//focalbooks

**Parent Company** Elsevier Ltd (Science & Technology)

**Established** 1946

**Insider Info** Payment via royalties. Catalogue available online.

**Non-Fiction** Publishes How-to, Illustrated, Textbook, Technical, and Reference titles on the following subjects: Art/Architecture, Communications, Computers/Electronics, Music/Dance, Photography, Digital Film/Media, Cinematography, Computer Animation, Theatre Technology.

**Submission Guidelines** Accepts query with SAE/ proposal package (including outline and SAE).

**Recent Title(s)** Prepare to Board! Creating Story and Characters for Animation Features and Shorts, Nancy Beiman (Animation)

**Tips** Titles aimed at professionals and students in many areas including; film and digital video production, photography, digital imaging, graphics, animation and new media, broadcast and media distribution technologies, music recording and production, mass communications and theatre technology. Focal Press welcomes authors' proposals for books. The first step is to discuss the proposal with the relevant Publishing Editor. Check the website for in-depth submission guidelines and a full list of editorial contacts.

## Fodor

**Random House, 20 Vauxhall Bridge Road, London, SW1V 2SA**

- 020 7840 8735
- 020 7840 8406
- www.randomhouse.co.uk

**Parent Company** The Random House Group Ltd

**Insider Info** Catalogue available online.

**Non-fiction** Publishes General Non-fiction and Guidebook titles on the following subjects: Travel, Travel destinations.

**Submission Guidelines** Accepts query with SAE with proposal package (including one sample chapter and outline). No email submissions.

**Recent Title(s)** *Fodor's Alaska 2007*

**Tips** Agented submissions are preferred, although unsolicited proposals are considered.

## Folens Ltd

**Apex Business Centre, Boscombe Road, Dunstable, Bedfordshire, LU5 4RL**

- 0870 609 1237
- 0870 609 1236
- folens@folens.com
- www.folens.com

**Contact** Publishing Director, Peter Burton

**Established** 1987

**Imprint(s)** Belair

**Insider Info** Publishes 150 titles per year. Catalogue and manuscript guidelines available online.

**Non-Fiction** Publishes General Non-fiction, Textbook and Scholarly titles on Education.

**Submission Guidelines** Accepts query with SAE/ proposal package (including outline, three sample chapters, market research, your author biography, and SAE)
 Submission details to: pburton@folens.com

**Recent Title(s)** Art Through Magic, Belair (Textbook)

**Tips** Folens are one of the leading publishers of primary and secondary educational texts, classroom resources and software for both students and teaching professionals. The publishers are pleased to receive suggestions for publications from teachers, or others involved in education. Please check the website for manuscript submission guidelines.

## Folens Publishers

**Hibernian Industrial Estate, Greenhills Road, Tallaght, Dublin 24, Republic of Ireland**

- 00353 1 413 7200
- 00353 1 413 7280
- info@folens.ie
- www.folens.ie

**Contact** Managing Director, John O'Connor
**Established** 1956
**Imprint(s)** Blackwater Press
Magic Emerald
**Insider Info** Catalogue available online.
**Non-Fiction** Publishes Children's, General Non-fiction and Scholarly titles on the following subjects: Education, Regional, Irish Interest.
**Fiction** Juvenile, Irish interest.
**Recent Title(s)** *Disappeared*, Seamus McKendry
**Tips** Publishes books in Irish and English for primary and secondary education, children's fiction and general Irish interest books.

## Footprint Handbooks

**6 Riverside Court, Lower Bristol Road, Bath, BA2 3DZ**

- 01225 469141
- 01225 469461
- webeditor@footprint.cix.co.uk
- www.footprints.com

**Contact** Managing Director, Patrick Dawson; Managing Editor, Sophie Blacksell
**Insider Info** Catalogue and manuscript guidelines available online.
**Non-Fiction** Publishes Travel booklets and Travel handbooks
**Submission Guidelines** Accepts query with SAE/proposal package (including outline, your publishing history, clips and author biography and SAE). Will review artwork/photos as part of the manuscript package.
**Recent Title(s)** *Snowboarding The World*, Matt Barr, Chris Moran and Ewan Wallace (Travel handbook)
**Tips** Footprint Handbooks like to ensure that they produce travel guides of the highest quality. The writing team comprises of over 30 authors and many contributors from around the globe. Authors all have first hand knowledge and prolonged experience of the regions they specialise in. Welcomes any feedback and CVs, marked for the attention of the Office Manager, including a sample of travel writing and highlighting any areas of particular interest.

## Forest Books

**The New Building, Ellwood Road, Milkwall, Coleford, Gloucestershire, GL16 7LE**

- 01594 833858
- 01594 833446
- Online form
- www.forestbooks.com

**Contact** Director, Doug McLean
**Established** 1989
**Insider Info** Catalogue available online and free on request.
**Non-Fiction** Publishes General Non-fiction, Scholarly and Self-help books on the following subjects: Education, Health/Medicine, Deafness/Disability and Sign language.
**Recent Title(s)** *Look at Me*, Lisa Mills
**Tips** Publishes books, videos, DVDs, CD-ROMs and software specialising in sign language and deaf issues. Forest Books upholds a worldwide reputation for a friendly, fast, helpful, expert and knowledgeable service.

## Fort Publishing Ltd

**Old Belmont House, 12 Robsland Avenue, Ayr, KA7 2RW**

- fortpublishing@aol.com
- www.fortpublishing.co.uk

**Contact** Director, James McCarroll
**Established** 1999
**Insider Info** Catalogue available online.
**Non-Fiction** Publishes Biography and General Non-fiction titles on the following subjects: History, Photography, Regional, Photography Sports, Local interest, Scottish interest and True Crime.
**Recent Title(s)** *Scotland's Most Wanted*, Douglas Skelton
**Tips** Fort Publishing are an independent book publishing company based in Ayr, in the Southwest of Scotland. Publishes non-fiction titles on sport, history, local interest, true crime and photography. Specialises in Scottish books, but has also published books on Yorkshire, East Anglia and Surrey.

## Foulsham Publishers (W Foulsham & Co Ltd)

**The Publishing House, Bennetts Close, Cippenham, Slough, Berkshire, SL1 5AP**

- 01753 526769
- 01753 535003
- marketing@foulsham.com

w www.foulsham.com
**Contact** Publisher/Managing Director, B.A.R. Belasco
**Established** 1819
**Imprint(s)** Quantum Foulsham
 Arcturus Foulsham
**Insider Info** Submissions accompanied by SAE will be returned. Catalogue available free on request and online. Manuscript guidelines available online (see 'Contact' for authors' information).
**Non-Fiction** Publishes Coffee table books, Cookbooks, General Non-fiction, How-to, Humour, Illustrated books, Reference, Self-help, and Textbooks on the following subjects:
 Art/Architecture, Astrology/Psychic, Child Guidance/Parenting, Contemporary Culture, Cooking/Foods/Nutrition, Counselling/Career, Guidance, Gardening, Gay/Lesbian, Health/Medicine, History, Hobbies, Money/Finance, Recreation, Spirituality, Travel, Young Adult, Antiques and Collectables, Babies and Children, Diet, Dreams, Drinks and Cocktails, Languages, Letter writing and e-matters, Mind Games and Puzzles, Mind, Body and Spirit, Self development, Weddings, Speeches and Toasts.
**Submission Guidelines** Accepts query with SAE/proposal package addressed to the Editorial Department (including outline, sample chapter(s), chapter breakdown showing proposed structure, consumer profile defining target market, information on other books in same area, explaining how your title is different, your author biography). No email submissions are accepted and material is not returned unless an SAE is enclosed.
**Recent Title(s)** *Secrets of the Vatican*, Cyrus Shahrad

## Fountain Press
**Old Sawmills Road, Faringdon, SN7 7DS**
o 01367 242411
o 01367 241124
o sales@newprouk.co.uk
w www.newprouk.co.uk
**Parent Company** Newpro UK Ltd
**Contact** Publisher, C.J. Coleman
**Established** 1923
**Insider Info** Publishes five titles per year. Catalogue available online.
**Non-Fiction** Publishes General Non-fiction, Illustrated books, Reference and Technical titles on the following subjects:
 Nature/Environment and Photography.
**Recent Title(s)** *Digital Photographer's Guide to Photoshop Elements*, Barry Beckham

**Tips** Titles aimed at photographers of any skill level or interest, seeking to learn technical skills and the history of their craft.

## Four Courts Press
**7 Malpas Street, Dublin 8, Republic of Ireland**
o 00353 1 453 4668
o 00353 1 453 4672
o info@four-courts-press.ie
w www.four-courts-press.ie
**Contact** Publishing Director, Michael Adams; Editor, Martin Fanning
**Established** 1970
**Insider Info** Publishes 70 titles per year. Receives approximately 200 queries and 100 manuscripts per year. 30 per cent of books published are from first-time authors and 90 per cent are from unagented authors. Payment is via royalty (on wholesale price) of 0.1 per £. Average lead time is six months with simultaneous submissions not accepted. Aims to respond to manuscripts within two months. Catalogue and manuscript guidelines available online.
**Non-Fiction** Publishes General Non-fiction and Scholarly titles on the following subjects:
 Anthropology/Archaeology, Art/Architecture, Education, Government/Politics, History, Language/Literature, Law, Music/Dance, Philosophy, Regional, Religion, Ancient History.
**Submission Guidelines** Accepts query with SAE or via email.
**Recent Title(s)** *Manuscripts and Ghosts: Essays on the Transmission of Medieval and Early Renaissance Literature*, John Scattergood
**Tips** Four Courts Press expanded rapidly from its theology base, first into Celtic and Medieval Studies and Ecclesiastical History, and then into Modern History, Art, Literature and Law. The publishers have strict guidelines as to the submission of manuscripts. They do not consider unsolicited manuscripts; therefore prospective authors should contact the publishers via email. For more information concerning the Four Courts Press house style, consult their guidelines.

## Fourth Estate
**77-85 Fulham Palace Road, Hammersmith, London, W6 8JB**
o 020 8307 4149
o 020 8307 4440
o michelle.kane@harpercollins.co.uk
w www.4thestate.co.uk

**Parent Company** HarperCollins Publishers Ltd, Press Books Division

**Contact** Publishing Director, Nick Pearson; Publicity Director, Michelle Kane

**Insider Info** Catalogue available online.

**Non-Fiction** Publishes Autobiography, Biography, General Non-fiction and Humour titles on the following subjects:
 Contemporary Culture, Government/Politics, Science, Social Sciences and World Affairs.

**Submission Guidelines** Accepts agented submissions only.

**Fiction** Publishes Literary and Mainstream/Contemporary titles.

**Submission Guidelines** Accepts agented submissions only.

**Recent Title(s)** The Great War for Civilisation: The Conquest of the Middle East, Robert Fisk (Current Affairs); *So He Takes The Dog*, Jonathan Buckley (Novel)

**Tips** Fourth Estate publishes cutting edge non-fiction and fiction, often with a controversial flavour. This includes Biography, Current Affairs, Popular Culture, Humour, Politics and Contemporary Fiction. Fourth Estate only accepts submissions from literary agents or previously published authors, but may consider submissions that are accompanied by a positive assessment from a manuscript assessment agency.

## Foxbury Press

**15 St. Michael's Road, Winchester, SO23 9JE**
❶ 01962 864037

**Contact** Managing Editor, Robert Cross.

**Established** 2000

**Non-Fiction** Publishes Reference and Scholarly titles on the following subjects:
 Education, History, Bibliography and Academic reference.

## Frances Lincoln

**4 Torriano Mews, Torriano Avenue, London, NW5 2RZ**
❶ 020 7284 4009
❶ 020 7485 0490
❶ reception@frances-lincoln.com
❶ www.franceslincoln.com

**Contact** Managing Director, John Nicoll

**Established** 1977

**Insider Info** Publishes 70 titles per year, Catalogue available online.

**Non-Fiction** Publishes Illustrated books and Children's titles on the following subjects:

Art/Architecture, Crafts, Gardening, Hobbies, Nature/Environment, Recreation and Walking.

**Submission Guidelines** Submit completed manuscript. Will review artwork photos as part of the manuscript package.
 Submission details to: michaelb@frances-lincoln.com

**Fiction** Publishes Children's books and Young Adult titles.

**Submission Guidelines** Submit completed manuscript.
 Submission details to: michaelb@frances-lincoln.com

**Recent Title(s)** *London High*, Herbert Wright (Political/Architecture); *Home Now*, Lesley Beake (Illustrated novel)

**Tips** The company was founded by Frances Lincoln in 1977 and the first books were published two years later. Frances Lincoln publish high quality illustrated books, with special emphasis on gardening, walking and the outdoors, art, architecture, design and landscape. In 1983 Frances Lincoln started to publish illustrated books for children and has since won many awards and prizes with both fiction and non-fiction children's books. Frances Lincoln do not have any submission guidelines as such for the adult department; any submissions should be addressed to the attention of Mr John Nicoll (Managing Director).

## Franklin Watts

 338 Euston Road
**London, NW1 3BH**
❶ 020 7873 6000
❶ 020 7873 6024
❶ www.wattspublishing.co.uk

**Parent Company** Hachette Children's Books (Hodder Headline)

**Established** 1972

**Insider Info** Catalogue available online.

**Non-Fiction** Publishes Children's/Juvenile and Illustrated titles, on the following subjects:
 All aspects of the National Curriculum.

**Submission Guidelines** Agented submissions only.

**Tips** Publishes children's information books, designed to engage, stimulate and entertain the more reluctant reader, and generally encourage a positive response to discovering the world around us.

## Free Association Books Ltd

**PO Box 37664, London, NW7 2XU**
❶ 020 8906 0396

◉ 020 8906 0006
◉ info@fabooks.com
◉ www.fabooks.com
**Contact** Managing Director/Publisher, T.E. Brown
**Established** 1984
**Insider Info** Payment is via royalties. Catalogue available free on request and online.
**Non-Fiction** Publishes Scholarly, Self-help, Textbook and Reference titles on the following subjects: Contemporary Culture, Education, Psychology, Social Sciences, Sociology.
**Submission Guidelines** Accepts query with SAE/ proposal package (including outline).
**Recent Title(s)** *Recovering From Childhood Wounds*, Jacques Lecompte
**Tips** Titles aimed at scholars and carers interested in theoretical analysis and practical application of various social sciences, including psychotherapy, sexuality and gender studies, women's studies, and psychoanalysis. Prospective writers should send a letter in the first instance, containing a brief outline of the project. Academic sources must be thoroughly referenced.

## Free Press
**Africa House, 64–78 Kingsway, London, WC2B 6AH**
◉ 020 7316 1900
◉ 020 7316 0332
◉ enquiries@simonandschuster.co.uk
◉ www.simonsays.co.uk
**Parent Company** Simon & Schuster UK Ltd
**Established** 2003
**Non-Fiction** Publishes Biography and General Non-fiction titles on the following subjects: Business/Economics, Government/Politics, History, World Affairs and Current Affairs.
**Submission Guidelines** Accepts agented submissions only.
**Recent Title(s)** *Who are We*, Samuel Huntington; *In the Blink of an Eye*, Andrew Parker
**Tips** Free Press is Simon & Schuster's 'serious' non-fiction imprint and publishes 'heavyweight' works on subjects including business, politics and world affairs..

## The Friday Project
**83 Victoria Street, London, SW1H 0HW**
◉ 020 3008 8472
◉ clareweber@thefridayproject.co.uk
◉ www.thefridayproject.co.uk
**Parent Company** Friday Project Media Plc

**Contact** Managing Director and Publishing Director, Clare Christian (Non-Fiction, Humour, Literary Fiction); Commercial Director, Scott Pack (Fiction, Humour, Non-Fiction); Publishing Editor, Heather Smith; Editor, Clare Weber
**Established** 2005
**Insider Info** Publish 50 titles per year. Receives approximately 400 queries per year and less than 30 unsolicited manuscripts per year. 60-70 per cent of books published are from first-time authors, less than five per cent are from unagented authors and less than five per cent are author subsidy published. Payment is via royalty (on wholesale price) with 0.12 (per £) minimum and 0.18 (per £) maximum. Average lead time is six months with simultaneous submissions accepted. Submissions accompanied by SAE will be returned. Aims to respond to queries within seven days, proposals within six weeks and manuscripts within two months. Catalogue is available online.
**Non-Fiction** Publishes Autobiography, Biography, Coffee Table, Cookbook, General Non-fiction, Gift and Humour titles on the following subjects: Contemporary Culture, Cooking/Foods/Nutrition, Government/Politics, Memoirs, Sex, Travel.
**Submission Guidelines** Accepts proposal package via email (including outline, sample chapters, your publishing history and author biography). Will not accept artworks/images.
Submission details to: authors@ thefridayproject.co.uk
**Fiction** Publishes Confession, Experimental, Gothic, Historical, Humour, Literary and Mainstream/ Contemporary titles.
**Submission Guidelines** Accepts proposal package via email (including outline, sample chapters, your publishing history and author biography).
Submission details to: authors@ thefridayproject.co.uk
**Recent Title(s)** *Gents,* Warwick Collins (Novel); *Life is a Cabaret*, James Innes-Smith (Non-fiction)
**Tips** The Friday Project develops much of its publishing programme from the most exciting and innovative web sites, properties and content already in existence, as well as from submissions.

## Frontier Publishing
**Windetts, Kirstead, NR15 1EG**
◉ 01508 558174
◉ frontier.pub@macunlimited.net
◉ www.frontierpublishing.co.uk
**Contact** Managing Editor, John Black
**Established** 1983

**Insider Info** Publishes four titles per year. Payment is via royalties. Catalogue available online.

**Non-Fiction** Publishes Illustrated books and General Non-fiction titles on the following subjects: Art/Architecture , History, Language/Literature and Travel.

**Submission Guidelines** Accepts query with SAE.

**Recent Title(s)** *The Obelisk - A Monumental Feature in Britain*, Richard Barnes

**Tips** Founded in Norfolk in 1986, Frontier aims to publish books about history, travel, poetry and sculpture for a world market. The company is based on medium and smaller print runs of attractive volumes, which are publicised in the UK press and sold in UK bookshops. Authors must be passionate about their chosen subject.

## FT Prentice Hall
**Edinburgh Gate, Harlow, Essex, CM20 2JE**
- 01279 623623
- 01279 414130
- tim_moore@prenhall.com
- www.pearsoned.co.uk/Imprints/FTPrenticeH

**Parent Company** Pearson Education

**Contact** Editor in Chief, Timothy C. Moore

**Insider Info** Catalogue and manuscript guidelines are available online.

**Non-Fiction** Publishes Reference, Scholarly and Textbook titles on the following subjects: Business, Accountancy.
 * FT Prentice Hall's list addresses all aspects of business, finance and investment and includes many of the business world's top authors.

**Submission Guidelines** Accepts proposal package (including synopsis, sample chapters, market research, your publishing history and author biography).

**Recent Title(s)** *Asset and Liability Management: The Banker's Guide to Value Creation and Risk Control 2nd Edition*, Jean Dermine

**Tips** FT Prentice Hall represents a powerful collaboration between the Financial Times and Pearson Education. Titles are aimed at both students and professionals. Authors are usually experts in their particular field.

## Gaia Books
**2–4 Heron Quays, London, E14 4JP**
- 020 7531 8400
- 020 7531 8650
- info-ho@hamlyn.co.uk
- www.gaiabooks.co.uk

**Parent Company** Hamlyn (Octopus Publishing Group)

**Contact** Publisher, Jane Birch; Executive Editor, Jo Godfrey Wood

**Established** Joined Octopus Publishing Group in 2004.

**Insider Info** Catalogue available online.

**Non-Fiction** Publishes Illustrated books on the following subjects: Gardening, Health/Medicine, Natural Health, Personal Growth, Earth and Ecology.

**Recent Title(s)** *Yoga for Stress Relief*, Swami Shivapremananda

**Tips** Gaia is the mind, body and spirit imprint of Hamlyn. The publisher's vision is to see the relationship of people and the planet more clearly understood. One of its bestselling titles is an atlas of planet management.

## Gairm Publications
**29 Waterloo Street, Glasgow, G2 6BZ**
- 0141 221 1971
- 0141 221 1971

**Non-Fiction** Publishes Biography, Children's/Juvenile, General Non-fiction, Illustrated books, Reference, Scholarly and Gaelic titles on the following subjects: Art/Architecture, Language/Literature, Music/Dance, Regional, Travel and Gaelic Language.
 * Texts are in Gaelic language only.

**Fiction** Publishes Adventure, Mainstream/Contemporary, Short story collections, Suspense and Crime titles.
 * Texts are in Gaelic language only.

**Poetry** Publishes Gaelic Language Poetry titles.

**Tips** Titles aimed at fluent Gaelic readers and students.

## Galactic Central Publications
**25a Copgrove Road, Leeds, West Yorkshire, LS8 2SP**
- 07968 851571
- gcp@philsp.com
- www.philsp.com

**Contact** Publisher, Phil Stephensen-Payne (Science-fiction Author Bibliographies)

**Established** 1985

**Insider Info** Publishes two titles per year. Receives approximately four queries and two manuscripts per year. 100 per cent of books published are from unagented authors. Average lead time is three months, with simultaneous submissions not accepted. Submissions accompanied by SAE will be

**197**

returned. Aims to respond to queries within one day, proposals and other enquiries within seven days, and manuscripts within one month. Catalogue available online.

**Non-Fiction** Publishes Bibliography titles on Science Fiction.

  * Submissions should be in keeping with the standard layout of GCP bibliographies.

**Submission Guidelines** Accepts queries by email.

**Recent Title(s)** *Barry N. Malzberg: Dweller in the Deeps: A Working Bibliography*, Phil Stephensen-Payne (Bibliography)

**Tips** Galactic Central Publications target readership is Science fiction fans and collectors. GCP does not offer payment to authors as the business generally runs at a loss.

## The Gallery Press

**Loughcrew, Oldcastle, Co. Meath, Republic of Ireland**

- 00353 49 854 1779
- 00353 49 854 1779
- contactus@gallerypress.com
- www.gallerypress.com

**Contact** Editor and Publisher, Peter Fallon

**Established** 1970

**Insider Info** Payment made by offer on advance, set against royalties on sales. Simultaneous submissions will be accepted. Submissions accompanied by SAE will be returned. Catalogue available online. Manuscript guidelines are available free on request and via email.

**Fiction** Publishes Plays (must have been professionally produced).

**Submission Guidelines** Submit completed manuscript.

**Poetry** Publishes Poetry titles.

  * The Gallery Press was established to publish the work of young Irish poets in particular, so submissions are currently accepted from Irish writers only.

**Submission Guidelines** Submit complete manuscript. No email or fax submissions will be accepted.

**Recent Title(s)** *Adaptions*, Derek Mahon (Poetry collection)

**Tips** Although The Gallery Press is primarily a poetry publisher, it now accepts plays as long as they have received a professional production. It publishes some fiction but only from its own long-standing authors. Writers are advised to build up a publishing resume in magazines and newspapers before approaching the publisher with a collection of poems. The editor requests that you make it clear if your work is being simultaneously submitted elsewhere, as they generally prefer a clear option on it.

## Galore Park

**19–21 Sayers Lane, Tenterden, Kent, TN30 6BW**

- 0870 234 2304
- 0870 234 2305
- info@galorepark.co.uk
- www.galorepark.co.uk

**Contact** Managing Director, Nicholas Oulton (Classics, English, History, Languages); Director, Louise Martine (Science, Maths)

**Established** 1999

**Insider Info** Publishes 15 titles per year. Catalogue available free on request, online and via email.

**Non-Fiction** Publishes Textbooks on the following subjects:

  Education (Prep School Textbooks).

  * Galore Park's textbooks are tailored to the prep school market and are endorsed by the ISEB. Non-prep school material is not published.

**Tips** Galore Park titles are aimed at prep school students.

## Garland Science

**2 Park Square, Milton Park, Abingdon, Oxfordshire, OX14 4RN**

- 020 7017 6000
- 020 7017 6699
- tf.enquiries@informa.com
- www.garlandscience.com

**Parent Company** Taylor and Francis Group

**Contact** Vice President (US), Denise Schanck.

**Insider Info** Catalogue and manuscript guidelines are available online and by email.

**Non-Fiction** Publishes Journals, Multimedia, Reference, Scholarly and Textbook titles on the following subjects:

  Cell Biology, Immunology, Molecular Biology, Protein Science, Science (Biology).

**Submission Guidelines** Accepts proposal package (including outline, synopsis, one-two sample chapters, market research and CV).

  Submission details to: denise.schanck@ taylorandfrancis.com (US)

**Recent Title(s)** *Biology of Disease*, Nessar Ahmed, Maureen Dawson, Chris Smith and Ed Wood (Biology)

**Tips** Garland Science has established itself as one of the leading textbook publishers in the fields of cell and molecular biology, immunology and protein science. Specific details of material to be included in your proposal are published on the website. It is useful to include a summary of a suitable competitor book.

## Garnet Publishing Ltd
**8 Southern Court, South Street, Reading, RG1 4QS**
- 0118 959 7847
- 0118 959 7356
- enquiries@garnetpublishing.co.uk
- www.garnetpublishing.co.uk

**Contact** Editorial Manager, Emma G. Hawker
**Established** 1992
**Imprint(s)** Ithaca Press
**Insider Info** Publishes 20 titles per year. Payment is via royalties.
**Non-Fiction** Publishes General Non-fiction, Illustrated books and Scholarly titles on the following subjects:
Art/Architecture, Cooking/Foods/Nutrition, History, Photography, Religion, Translation, Travel, World Affairs and Islamic culture.
**Submission Guidelines** Accepts query with SAE/proposal package (including outline, publishing history, author biography and SAE).
**Fiction** Publishes Religious and Translation titles.
**Submission Guidelines** Accepts query with SAE/proposal package (including outline).
**Tips** Mostly publishes general interest or academic non-fiction relating to various aspects of Middle Eastern culture. Ensure to enclose an up to date CV with any submissions, including any relevant publishing history.

## GB Publishing Services
**26 Percheron Drive, Spalding, PE11 3GH**
- 01775 768902
- garry.baker@btinternet.com

**Contact** Managing Editor, Garry Baker
**Established** 2004
**Insider Info** Payment via royalties.
**Non-Fiction** Publishes General Non-fiction titles.
**Fiction** Publishes Romance titles.
**Submission Guidelines** Accepts query with SAE/proposal package (including outline and three sample chapters).

## Geddes & Grosset
**David Dale House, New Lanark, ML11 9DJ**
- 01555 665000
- 01555 665694
- info@gandg.sol.co.uk

- www.geddesandgrosset.co.uk

**Contact** Publisher, Ron Grosset
**Established** 1989
**Non-Fiction** Publishes Children's/Juvenile and Reference titles.
**Submission Guidelines** Accepts query with SAE. Submit completed manuscript.
**Fiction** Publishes children's titles.
**Submission Guidelines** Accepts query with SAE. Submit completed manuscript.
**Tips** Unsolicited submissions will be accepted. Please note that Geddes & Grosset do not publish any adult fiction.

## The Geological Society Publishing House
**Unit 7, Brassmill Enterprise Centre, Brassmill Lane, Bath, BA1 3JN**
- 01225 445046
- 01225 442836
- angharad.hills@geolsoc.org.uk
- www.geolsoc.org.uk

**Contact** Commissioning Editor, Angharad Hills
**Established** 1998
**Insider Info** Publishes 30 titles per year. Author guidelines are available online. Catalogue is free on request, and available online or via email from: julie.webster@geolsoc.org.uk
**Non-Fiction** Publishes Reference, Scholarly and Technical titles on the following subjects:
Nature/Environment, Geology, Science (mainly Earth Sciences).
**Submission Guidelines** Accepts query with SAE with proposal package (including, outline, author biography, SAE). Will review artworks/images as part of proposal package.
**Recent Title(s)** *Whatever is Under the Earth: The Geological Society of London 1807 to 2007*, G.L. Herries Davies
**Tips** The society is a major international earth science publisher aiming to provide a high-quality service to earth scientists throughout the world. Books are mainly published as one of a series, but occasionally some 'one off' titles are published.

## George Ronald Publishers Ltd
**3 Rosecroft Lane, Oaklands, Welwyn, Hertfordshire, AL6 0UB**
- 01438 716062
- 0870 762 6242
- sales@grbooks.com
- www.grbooks.com

**Contact** Dr Wendi Momen

**Established** 1943

**Insider Info** Publishes eight titles per year. Receives approximately 30 queries and 40 manuscripts per year. 60 per cent of books published are from first-time authors, 90 per cent of books published are from unagented authors. Payment is via royalty (on wholesale price), with 0.1 per £. The advance offered is from £50 to £1,000. Simultaneous submissions are accepted. Submissions accompanied by SAE will be returned. Aims to respond to queries within two weeks and proposals and manuscripts within two months. Catalogue and manuscript guidelines are free on request, and available online, or by email.

**Non-Fiction** Publishes Autobiography, Biography, Children's/Juvenile, Coffee table, General Non-fiction, How-to, Illustrated, Reference, Scholarly and Self-help titles on the following subjects:
  Religion (Baha'i Faith).
  * George Ronald Publishers is only interested in manuscripts that have a connection with the Baha'i Faith.

**Submission Guidelines** Accepts completed manuscripts.

**Poetry** * Publishes some poetry titles that have a connection with the Baha'i Faith.

**Submission Guidelines** Accepts complete manuscripts.

**Recent Title(s)** *Against Incredible Odds*, Baharieh Maani (Biography/Autobiography); *Sonata of Spirit*, Michael Fitzgerald (Poetry)

**Tips** George Ronald books are aimed at Baha'is and those interested in the Baha'i Faith. See the 'submitting a manuscript' section on their website for further details.

## Gerald Duckworth & Co. Ltd

**1st Floor, East Wing, 90–93 Cowcross Street, London, EC1M 6BF**

- 020 7490 7300
- 020 7490 0080
- info@duckworth-publishers.co.uk
- www.ducknet.co.uk

**Contact** Eleanor Birne

**Established** 1898

**Imprint(s)** Ardis
  Duckworth Academic
  Overlook

**Insider Info** Aims to respond to proposals within 12 weeks and manuscripts within 12 weeks. Catalogue and manuscript guidelines available online.

**Non-Fiction** Publishes Biography, General Non-fiction and Scholarly titles on the following subjects:

Anthropology/Archaeology, Art/Architecture, History, Language/Literature, Literary Criticism, Philosophy.

**Submission Guidelines** Accepts query with SAE/proposal package (including outline and three sample chapters).

**Fiction** Publishes Literary titles.

**Submission Guidelines** Accepts query with SAE/proposal package (including outline and three sample chapters).

**Recent Title(s)** *The Devil's Guide To Hollywood*, Joe Eszterhas (Humour/Guidebook); *Shattering Glass*, Nancy-Gay Rotstein (Novel)

**Tips** Founded in 1898, Duckworth is an independent publisher with a general trade and academic list. Duckworth General publishes literary and commercial fiction and non-fiction, including history, biography and memoir. Prospective authors can submit a covering letter and three sample chapters, including return postage. The publishers request no phone calls, or email submissions.

## Gibson Square

**47 Lonsdale Square, London, N1 1EW**

- 020 7096 1100
- 020 7993 2214
- info@gibsonsquare.com
- www.gibsonsquare.com

**Contact** Publisher, Martin Rynja (Serious Non-fiction); Editorial Director, Dawn Schaefer (Women's Non-fiction)

**Established** 2001

**Insider Info** Publishes 25 titles per year. Payment via royalties. Average lead time is six months with simultaneous submissions not accepted. Submissions will not be returned. Catalogue available online. Manuscript guidelines are not available.

**Non-Fiction** Publishes Autobiography, Biography, Humour and General Non-fiction titles on the following subjects:
  Community/Public Affairs, Contemporary Culture, Creative Non-fiction, Gay/Lesbian, History, Memoirs, Military/War, Philosophy, Psychology, Sex, Travel, Women's Issues/Studies, World Affairs.

**Submission Guidelines** Accepts Proposal package (including outline, the first few sample chapters, your publishing history and author biography). It is suggested that authors include details about any book(s) used as a model for their own, if appropriate. Please note that due to the number of submissions received, only successful queries will receive a response. Will review photographs/artworks as part of the manuscript package (send photocopies).

**Recent Title(s)** *House of Bush House of Saud*, Craig Unger (Current Affairs)

## Giles de la Mare Publishers Ltd
**PO Box 25351, London, NW5 1ZT**
- 020 7485 2533
- 020 7485 3534
- gilesdelamare@dial.pipex.com
- www.gilesdelamare.co.uk

**Established** 1995

**Insider Info** Publishes two titles per year. Receives 250 queries per year. 100 per cent of books published are from unagented authors. Payment is via royalty (on retail price). Simultaneous submissions are accepted. Submissions accompanied by SAE will be returned. Catalogue and and manuscript guidelines are free on request, and available online.

**Non-Fiction** Publishes Autobiography, Biography, General Non-fiction and Illustrated titles on the following subjects:
Art/Architecture, History, Music/Dance, Travel.

**Submission Guidelines** Accepts queries by telephone initially. Artworks/images accepted with submission (send photocopies).

## Gill & Macmillan Ltd
**Hume Avenue, Park West, Dublin 12, Republic of Ireland**
- 00353 1 500 9500
- 00353 1 500 9596
- info@gillmacmillan.ie
- www.gillmacmillan.ie

**Contact** Commissioning Editor, Fergal Tobin
**Established** 1968
**Imprint(s)** Tivoli
**Insider Info** Catalogue available free on request, online and via email.

**Non-Fiction** Publishes Biography, General Non-fiction and Scholarly titles on the following subjects:
Cooking/Foods/Nutrition, Education, History, Language/Literature, Memoirs, Travel, World Affairs.

**Submission Guidelines** Accepts query with SAE/proposal package (including outline, two to three sample chapters and author biography).
Submission details to: ftobin@gillmacmillan.ie

**Fiction** Publishes Mainstream/Contemporary titles.

**Submission Guidelines** Accepts query with SAE/proposal package (including outline, two to three sample chapters and author biography).
Submission details to: ftobin@gillmacmillan.ie

**Recent Title(s)** *The Power of 'Negative' Thinking*, Tony Humphreys (Self-help); *The Mun: Growing Up in Ballymun*, Lynn Connolly (Memoir)

**Tipf** Gill & Macmillan is Ireland's leading publisher of further education, school textbooks and general books. First-time authors should check the website for tips on writing and submitting a book proposal for educational, fiction and non-fiction texts, as well as detailed advice on how to get published.

## Ginn and Co
**Halley Court, Jordan Hill, Oxford, OX2 8EJ**
- 01865 311366
- 01865 314641
- enquiries@harcourt.co.uk
- www.harcourt.co.uk

**Parent Company** Harcourt Education Ltd
**Non-Fiction** Publishes Children's/Juvenile, Reference, Textbook and Scholarly titles.

**Tips** Ginn has a strong tradition for publishing quality educational resources, mainly for children aged three to twelve, including the UK's most successful maths scheme, *Abacus*, and the new *Abacus Evolve*. Its literacy and science materials are also popular with teachers internationally.

## GlassHouse Press
**2 Park Square, Milton Park, Abingdon, Oxford, OX14 4RN**
- 07833 930626
- 020 7017 6699
- colin.perrin@informa.com
- www.cavendishpublishing.com/glasshouse

**Parent Company** Routledge-Cavendish (Taylor and Francis Group)
**Contact** Commissioning Editor, Colin Perrin
**Established** 2002
**Imprint(s)** Critical Approaches to Law (series)
Contemporary Issues in Public Policy (series)
Nomikoi: Critical Legal Thinkers (series)
Law, Science & Society (series)

**Insider Info** Publishes 30 titles per year. Catalogue and manuscript guidelines are available online.

**Non-Fiction** Publishes Scholarly and Technical titles on the following subjects:
Critical Legal Theory, Law/Legal, Socio-legal Studies.

**Submission Guidelines** Accepts proposal package (including outline, synopsis, one to two sample chapters, market research and CV).

**Recent Title(s)** *UK Election Law: A Critical Examination,* Bob Watt (Contemporary Issues in Public Policy).

**Tips** GlassHouse Press is a leading publisher of texts in the areas of socio-legal studies and critical legal theory. GlassHouse specialises in books that offer a fresh perspective on law and contemporary legal issues. Aside from individual titles GlassHouse also accepts proposals for titles for its four main series.

## Glosa Education Organisation

**PO Box 18, Richmond, Surrey, TW9 2GE**

- m001@glosa.org
- www.glosa.org

**Contact** Managing Editor, Wendy Ashby
**Established** 1981
**Insider Info** Catalogue available online.
**Non-Fiction** Publishes Booklets, Textbooks and Scholarly titles on the following subjects:
Language/Literature and Translation.
**Submission Guidelines** Accepts query with SAE/proposal package (including outline and SAE). Submit completed manuscript.
**Tips** Publishes textbooks, dictionaries, guidebooks and translations for teachers and speakers of the Glosa language, an international auxiliary language. Also publishes a newsletter and journal dedicated to developments in Glosa. All books are either written in Glosa, or are written in English about the Glosa language.

## Gloucester Publishers Plc

**Northburgh House, 10 Northburgh Street, London, EC1V 0AT**

- 020 7253 7887
- 020 7490 3708
- info@everymanchess.com
- www.everymanchess.com

**Contact** Managing Director, Mark Bicknall
**Established** 1998
**Insider Info** Publishes 30 titles per year. Payment is via royalties. Catalogue available online.
**Non-Fiction** Publishes Scholarly and Technical titles on Chess.
**Submission Guidelines** No unsolicited submissions are accepted.
**Recent Title(s)** *Garry Kasparov on Modern Chess: Revolution in the 70s*, Garry Kasparov
**Tips** Publish academic and leisure books relating to the game of chess for medium to high level players. The publishers do not use freelancers, or place any work outside their existing stable of collaborators.

## Godsfield Press

**2–4 Heron Quays, London, E14 4JP**

- 020 7531 8400
- 020 7531 8650
- info-ho@hamlyn.co.uk
- www.godsfieldpress.com

**Parent Company** Hamlyn (Octopus Publishing Group)
**Contact** Publisher, Jane Birch; Executive Editor, Sandra Rigby
**Established** Joined Octopus Publishing Group in 2004
**Insider Info** Catalogue available online.
**Non-Fiction** Publishes Gift books, Humour, Illustrated books, Reference, Self-help and Spiritual Development titles on the following subjects: Alternative Lifestyles, Astrology/Psychic, Health/Medicine, New Age, Religion, Sex, Spirituality, Magic and Witchcraft, Fortune Telling and Divination and the Bible.
**Recent Title(s)** *The Homeopathy Bible*, Ambika Wauters
**Tips** Godsfield Press publish books, packs and kits by highly regarded authors from the UK and the US. The publisher's aim is to promote and support spiritual growth.

## Gollancz

**Orion House, 5 Upper St. Martins Lane, London, WC2H 9EA**

- 020 7240 3444
- 020 7240 4822
- info@orionbooks.co.uk
- www.orionbooks.co.uk

**Parent Company** Orion Publishing Group Ltd
**Contact** Editorial Director, Simon Spanton; Editorial Director, Jo Fletcher
**Established** 1927 (incorporated into Orion in 1998)
**Imprint(s)** Gollancz Manga
**Insider Info** Catalogue available online (as a downloadable pdf or via the online catalogue request form).
**Fiction** Publishes Science Fiction and Manga.
* Gollancz specialises in fantasy and science fiction, and also publishes the *Masterworks* series of reprints of fantasy and science fiction classics. Also publishes illustrated books.
**Submission Guidelines** Accepts agented submissions only.
**Recent Title(s)** *Before They Are Hanged*, Joe Abercrombie (Noir Fantasy)

## Gomer Press/Gwasg Gomer

**Llandysul Enterprise Park, Llandysul, Ceredigion, SA44 4JL**

- 01559 362371
- 01559 363758
- gwasg@gomer.co.uk
- www.gomer.co.uk

**Contact** Publishing Director, Mairwen Prys Jones (English Books for Children, Pont Books); Editor, Ceri Wyn Jones (English Books for Adults); Editor, Bethan Mair (Welsh Books for Adults); Editor, Sioned Lleinau (Welsh Books for Primary School Children); Editor, Helen Evans (Welsh Books for Secondary School Children); Editor, Morys Rhys (Welsh Educational Resources for Children)

**Established** 1892

**Imprint(s)** Gomer
Pont Books

**Insider Info** Publishes 120 titles per year. Aims to respond to proposals and manuscripts within one month. Catalogue and manuscript guidelines available online.

**Non-Fiction** Publishes Biography, General Non-fiction, Textbooks and Scholarly titles on the following subjects:
Art/Architecture, Cooking/Foods/Nutrition, Education, History, Language/Literature and Travel.
* Many texts are in Welsh language.

**Submission Guidelines** Accepts query with SAE/proposal package (including outline, one sample chapter and your author biography).
Submission details to: ceri@gomer.co.uk

**Fiction** Publishes Juvenile, Young Adult and Welsh titles.

**Poetry** Publishes Welsh Poetry Collections.

**Submission Guidelines** Accepts query with SAE/proposal package (including outline, one sample chapter and your author biography).
Submission details to: firstname@gomer.co.uk (Adult's book proposals, see contacts for relevant editors), children@gomer.co.uk (Children's book proposals)

**Recent Title(s)** *Freeloading Cymru*, Tony Millin (Travel); *Nobody Asked Me!*, Jenny Sullivan (Children's novel)

**Tips** Gomer Press is Wales's largest independent publisher, publishing books from Wales, about Wales. They publish over 120 new titles every year, in Welsh and in English, for children and adults. Please do not send whole manuscripts to an editor, a sample chapter and a synopsis will be sufficient to start. It would also be useful to include a CV and an outline of the sales strengths of the proposal. As the publisher receives a large number of manuscripts for consideration every week, they advise authors to be patient. They aim to send an acknowledgement of receipt for manuscripts within one month.

## The Good Web Guide Ltd

**65 Bromfelde Road, London, SW4 6PP**

- 020 7720 8919
- 020 7738 5717
- marketing@thegoodwebguide.com
- www.thegoodwebguide.co.uk

**Contact** Managing Director, Sarah Mahaffy; Content and Editorial Director, Arabella Dymoke

**Established** 1999

**Insider Info** Publishes five titles per year. Payment is via royalties. Catalogue available online.

**Non-Fiction** Publishes Booklets, Multimedia and Reference titles on the Internet.

**Submission Guidelines** Accepts query with SAE/proposal package (including outline, clips and author biography).
Submission details to: a.dymoke@thegoodwebguide.com

**Tips** The Good Web Guide publishes guidebooks to the best sites on the internet. They aim to find out what is best about life online, across a wide range of lifestyle and consumer interests.

## Government Supplies Agency

**Publications Division, Office of Public Works, 51 St. Stephen's Green, Dublin 2, Republic of Ireland**

- 00353 1 647 6000
- 00353 1 647 6843
- info@opw.ie

**Non-fiction** Publishes Irish government publications.

## Gower Publishing Limited

**Gower House, Croft Road, Aldershot, Hampshire, GU11 3HR**

- 01252 331551
- 01252 344405
- info@gowerpub.com, firstinitiallastname@gowerpub.com
- www.gowerpub.com

**Parent Company** Ashgate Publishing Group

**Contact** Commissioning Editor, Jonathon Norman (Business and Management); Commissioning Editor, Brendan George (Higher Education Textbooks and Research Monographs)

**Insider Info** Publishes 70 titles per year. Catalogue available online.

**Non-Fiction** Publishes General Non-fiction, Textbooks, How-to, and Scholarly titles on the following subjects:
Business/Economics, Education, Law, Money/Finance, Management, Marketing and Human Resources.

\* Gower Publishing Limited is one of the world's leading publishers on management and business practice. They publish handbooks, popular paperbacks, training videos, activity manuals, and student skills materials, in conjunction with Ashgate Publishing.

**Submission Guidelines** Accepts proposal package (including outline, your publishing history, author biography, sample material in your proposed writing style and information about illustrations, the length of the book and the general appeal and purpose of the book).

**Recent Title(s)** *Age Discrimination in Employment*, Malcolm Sargeant (guide for Human Resources specialists and Employment lawyers).

**Tips** Writers will tend to be experts in their fields.

## Graffeg

**2 Radnor Court, 256 Cowbridge Road East, Cardiff, CF5 1GZ**
- 029 2037 7312
- info@graffeg.com
- www.graffeg.com

**Contact** Peter Gill

**Insider Info** Catalogue available online.

**Non-Fiction** General Non-fiction and Illustrated books on the following subjects:
Cooking/Foods/Nutrition, Crafts, Photography, Regional, Welsh photography.

**Recent Title(s)** *Landscape Wales: Tirlun Cymru*, Jeremy Moore (Photography)

**Tips** Graffeg publish illustrated books about Wales. Titles examine Welsh cities, towns and villages, focusing on local information, including landscapes, food, where to eat and stay, festivals and events, culture, heritage and the arts, and tourist information on what to see and do. Publications are photography based, and must therefore be accompanied by a range of suitable photographs illustrating 'just how wonderful Wales is'.

## Granta Books

**2–3 Hanover Yard, Noel Road, London, N1 8BE**
- 020 7704 9776
- 020 7704 0474
- info@granta.com
- www.granta.com

**Parent Company** Granta Publications

**Contact** Editorial Director, George Miller; Senior Editor, Sara Holloway; Assistant Editor, Bella Shand

**Established** 1979

**Insider Info** Publishes 40 titles a year. Payment is via royalties. Catalogue and manuscript guidelines available via the website.

**Non-Fiction** Publishes General Non-fiction and Scholarly titles on the following subjects:
Contemporary Culture, Government/Politics, History, Language/Literature, Literary Criticism, Memoirs, Social Sciences.

**Submission Guidelines** Accepts query with SAE. Submit proposal package (including outline and 50 sample pages).

**Fiction** Publishes Literary titles.
\* No genre fiction.

**Submission Guidelines** Accepts query with SAE/proposal package (including outline, 50 pages, or two sample chapters).

**Recent Title(s)** *Estates*, Lynsey Hanley (Social history); *The Year of the Jouncer*, Simon Gray (Novel)

**Tips** We publish a small list of approximately 40 new titles a year, and we are weighted more towards non-fiction publishing than fiction, with a ratio of about 70:30. Our non-fiction tends to fall into the categories of serious cultural, political and social history, narrative history, or memoir. We rarely publish straightforward biographies. Submissions should be made by post only. We don't accept faxes, or emails, and please don't send us your work on computer disc. Due to the large numbers of submissions we receive, it can take some time before we get back to you. We aim to respond within three months, and we do respond to every manuscript eventually.

## Grant Books

**The Coach House, New Road, Cutnall Green, Droitwich, Worcestershire, WR9 0PQ**
- 01299 851588
- 01299 851446
- golf@grantbooks.co.uk
- www.grantbooks.co.uk

**Contact** Managing Editor, H.R.J. Grant

**Established** 1978

**Insider Info** Publishes six titles per year. Payment is via royalties. Catalogue available online via the website.

**Non-Fiction** Publishes Biography and General Non-fiction on the following subjects:
Golf, Hobbies and Sports.

**Submission Guidelines** Accepts query with SAE. Submit proposal package (including outline and sample chapter(s)). Also accepts completed manuscripts.

**Recent Title(s)** *The Perfect Golfer*, H.N. Wethered

**Tips** Grant Books aim is to provide for the discerning reader the more unusual titles in the world of golf, new, old and out of print. Ideas and submissions welcome, but not for instructional material or fiction.

## Great Northern Publishing

**PO Box 202, Scarborough, North Yorkshire, YO11 3GE**

- ☎ 01723 581329
- ☎ 01723 581329
- ✉ books@greatnorthernpublishing.co.uk
- 🌐 www.greatnorthernpublishing.co.uk

**Contact** Production Manager, Mark Marsay; Senior Editor, Diane Crowther

**Established** 1999

**Insider Info** Payment is via royalties. Catalogue and manuscript guidelines available via the website.

**Non-Fiction** Publishes General Non-fiction titles on the following subjects:
History, Military/War.

**Submission Guidelines** Accepts query with SAE.

**Fiction** Publishes Erotica, Humour and Crime titles.

**Submission Guidelines** Accepts query with SAE.

**Recent Title(s)** *Bombardment! The Day The East Coast Bled,* Mark Marsay (Military History); *Geography,* Sophie Cunningham (Erotica)

**Tips** Great Northern Publishing is a fully independent, wholly family owned, award winning small publishing and production company, based in Scarborough, on the beautiful Yorkshire coast. We publish the much respected, bi-monthly magazines; *The Great War, The Second World War*, and the highly acclaimed international adult, erotic art and literature magazine *Jade*. If you are seriously considering using our services and submitting your work, then please take the time to study and implement the house style rules given in our guide.

## Green Books

**Foxhole, Dartington, Totnes, Devon, TQ9 6EB**

- ☎ 01803 863260
- ☎ 01803 863843
- ✉ edit@greenbooks.co.uk
- 🌐 www.greenbooks.co.uk

**Contact** Publisher, John Elford (General); Project Development, Amanda Cuthbert (Green Lifestyle and Gardening)

**Established** 1986

**Insider Info** Publishes 12 titles per year. Receives approximately 200–300 queries and 200–300 manuscripts per year. 15 per cent of books published are from first-time authors, 100 per cent of books published are from unagented authors. Five per cent of books published are author subsidy published, and are usually produced in association with other green organisations, rather than being unsolicited submissions. Payment is via royalty (on wholesale price). Advance offered is up to £2,000. Average lead time is six months, with simultaneous submissions accepted. Submissions accompanied by SAE will be returned. Aims to respond to queries within one week and proposals and manuscripts within two months. Catalogue is free on request, and available online. Manuscript guidelines are available online.

**Non-Fiction** Publishes Autobiography, (occasionally), Biography, (occasionally), How-to (e.g. eco-building), Illustrated (full colour), Reference (e.g. Organic Directory), Self-help and Technical titles on the following subjects:
Agriculture/Horticulture, Alternative Lifestyles, Art/Architecture , Business/Economics, Community/Public Affairs, Cooking/Foods/Nutrition (Organic/Green), Crafts, Education, Gardening, Government/Politics, Health/Medicine, House and Home, Language/Literature, Memoirs, Nature/Environment, Philosophy, Regional, Spirituality, World Affairs.
 * Prospective authors must follow the submission guidelines on the websites closely to ensure that all submissions are appropriate for Green Books.

**Submission Guidelines** Accepts email enquiries initially (including outline and one sample chapter), and artworks/images (send digital files as jpegs).

**Recent Title(s)** *Allotment Gardening: An organic guide for beginners*, Susan Berger (Gardening)

**Tips** Books are aimed at the general reader interested in environmental issues.

## Greenhill Books/Lionel Leventhal Ltd

**Park House, 1 Russell Gardens, London, NW11 9NN**

- ☎ 020 8458 6314
- ☎ 020 8905 5245
- ✉ info@greenhillbooks.com
- 🌐 www.greenhillbooks.com

**Contact** Director, Michael Leventhal

**Established** 1984

**Insider Info** Payment is via royalties. Catalogue and manuscript guidelines available via the website.

**Non-Fiction** Publishes General Non-fiction and Reference titles on the following subjects:
Military/War.
 * Publishes military history or related subjects only.

**Submission Guidelines** Accepts query with SAE. Submit proposal package (including outline, one sample chapter, your publishing history, clips, and author biography).

**Recent Title(s)** *A Mighty Fortress*, Chuck Alling (Military history)

**Tips** The idea behind Greenhill is that there are valuable, often important books in the military field that have stood the test of time, sometimes great reading in themselves, and in other cases presenting significant reference material, but they have been virtually impossible to obtain. What Greenhill sets out to do is to make such books available once more for the military enthusiast by reprinting the original text, where necessary adding new material to set the work in context, and also to republish when the market has renewed itself. If you are working on a book project on an area of military history, and feel that it might fit the Greenhill publishing list, please follow the step by step 'Guidelines For Submission' on the website. It is important that you take note of these points, to ensure that your typescript is given proper assessment.

## Grub Street Publishing

**4 Rainham Close, London, SW11 6SS**

- 020 7924 3966/7738 1008
- 020 7738 1009
- post@grubstreet.co.uk
- www.grubstreet.co.uk

**Contact** Managing Director, John B. Davies

**Established** 1982

**Insider Info** Publishes 20 titles per year. Payment is via royalties. Aims to respond to proposals and manuscripts within three months. Catalogue is free on request and available online. Manuscript guidelines available online.

**Non-Fiction** Publishes General Non-fiction and Reference titles on the following subjects: Cookery, Military Aviation History.

**Submission Guidelines** Accepts query with SAE. Submit proposal package (including outline, one sample chapter and author biography).

**Recent Title(s)** *Into Enemy Arms*, Michael Hingston (Military History)

**Tips** We enjoy a wealth of recognition and praise for our comprehensive range of food and wine and military aviation history titles. With acclaimed authors such as Colin Spencer, Jane Grigson, Marguerite Patten, Norman Franks and Christopher Shores, to name but a few, we have secured a loyal following of readers and enthusiasts. We believe as a small independent publisher that it is right for us to be open to outside suggestions. However, as we are

a small publishing company there are one or two points you should consider when sending a book proposal. Check the website for submission guidelines.

## GSSE

**11 Malford Grove, Gilwern, Abergavenny, Monmouthshire, NP7 0RN**

- 01873 830872
- gsse@zoo.co.uk
- www.gsse.org.uk

**Contact** Owner, Dr David P. Bosworth (Application of Educational Technology)

**Established** 1987

**Insider Info** Publishes one title per year. Receives approximately two queries and two manuscripts per year. One per cent of books published are from first-time writers, 100 per cent of books published are from unagented writers. Payment is via royalty (on retail price), with 0.05 (per £) minimum and 0.12 (per £) maximum. Average lead time is five months, with simultaneous submissions not accepted. Submissions accompanied by SAE will be returned. Aims to respond to queries and proposals within two weeks and manuscripts within two months. Catalogue is free on request, or available by email.

**Non-Fiction** Publishes Booklets and How-to (Educational Technology in Higher/Further Education teaching) titles on the following subjects: Education, Application of Educational Technology in Higher/Further Education.

**Submission Guidelines** Accepts query with SAE, and artworks/images (send digital files as jpegs).

**Recent Title(s)** *Citing Your References*, David P Bosworth (How-to)

**Tips** GSSE books are aimed at students and lecturers in higher/further education. Submissions should not be written in an 'academic' style and instead should be easily accessible to students and readers of any level.

## Guild of Master Craftsman Publications Ltd

**166 High Street, Lewes, East Sussex, BN7 1XU**

- 01273 477374
- 01273 478606
- pubs@thegmcgroup.com
- www.thegmcgroup.com

**Parent Company** GMC Services Ltd

**Contact** Managing Director, J.A.J. Phillips; Managing Director. J.A.B. Phillips

**Established** 1974

**Imprint(s)** Photographers' Institute Press (PIP)

**Insider Info** Publishes 40 titles per year. Payment is via royalties. Catalogue is free on request and available online.

**Non-Fiction** Publishes General Non-fiction, Illustrated, Reference and Technical titles on the following subjects:
Cooking/Foods/Nutrition, Crafts, Gardening, Hobbies, Photography.

**Submission Guidelines** Accepts query with SAE.

**Recent Title(s)** *Drawing Crime Noir: For Comics & Graphic Novels*, Christopher Hart

**Tips** The Guild of Master Craftsman Publications is a publisher and distributor of over 1,000 books and magazines that are valued by professional craftsmen and women, and enjoyed by keen amateurs. Titles cover photography, gardening, cookery, woodworking and related craft subjects such as toy making, dolls' house, upholstery, furniture restoration, needlework and cross stitch. Submissions and ideas welcome.

## Guinness World Records Ltd

**3rd Floor, 184–192 Drummond Street, London, NW1 3HP**

- 020 7891 4567
- 020 7891 4501
- info@guinnessrecords.com
- www.guinnessworldrecords.com

**Contact** Chief Operations Officer, Alistair Richards

**Established** 1954

**Insider Info** Publishes two titles per year.

**Recent Title(s)** *Guinness Book of World Records*, Guinness World Records Ltd (Reference)

**Tips** Company created to publish the *Guinness Book of World Records*, as well as the annual *British Hit Singles & Albums* book. Contact from prospective researchers is encouraged.

## Gulf Professional Publishing

**The Boulevard, Langford Lane, Kidlington, Oxford, OX5 1GB**

- 01865 843000
- 01865 843010
- authorsupport@elsevier.com
- www.books.elsevier.com/uk//gulf

**Parent Company** Elsevier Ltd (Science & Technology)

**Insider Info** Payment is via Royalties. Catalogue and manuscript guidelines available online.

**Non-Fiction** Publishes Reference, Scholarly and Technical titles on the following subjects:

Business/Economics, Computers/Electronics, Regional, Science, Engineering, Oil/Petroleum/ Natural Gas, Oil Technologies.

**Submission Guidelines** Accepts query with SAE. Submit proposal package (including outline).

**Recent Title(s)** *Activated Carbon*, Harry Marsh (Science)

**Tips** Gulf Professional Publications publishes books and reports covering the oil and petroleum industry, natural gas, offshore drilling, carbon research, plastics research, resource engineering, facility operations, cosmetics industry reports and Gulf region resources. Gulf Professional Publishing welcomes authors' proposals for books. The first step is to discuss the proposal with the relevant Publishing Editor. Check the website for in-depth submission guidelines and a full list of editorial contacts.

## Gullane Children's Books

**Winchester House, 259–269 Old Marylebone Road, London, NW1 5XJ**

- 020 7616 7200
- 020 7616 7201
- www.pinwheel.co.uk

**Parent Company** Pinwheel Limited

**Insider Info** Catalogue available online.

**Non-Fiction** Publishes Children's/Juvenile and Illustrated titles.

**Submission Guidelines** Accepts entire manuscript with SAE for children's picture books (up to 800 words).

**Fiction** Publishes Children's, Picture Book and Illustrated fiction titles.

**Submission Guidelines** Accepts entire manuscript with SAE for children's picture books (up to 800 words).

**Recent Title(s)** *Ten in the Bed,* Jane Cabrera (Picture Book)

**Tips** Within Pinwheel, a specialist children's publisher, the Gullane imprint publishes fairly traditional picture books for which submissions are sought. Titles submitted for consideration should be pitched at children aged seven or younger.

## Gwasg Carreg Gwalch

**12 Iard yr Orsaf, Llanrwst, LL26 0EH**

- 01492 642031
- 01492 641502
- llyfrau@carreg-gwalch.co.uk
- www.carreg-gwalch.co.uk

**Contact** Managing Editor, Myrddin ap Dafydd

**Established** 1980

**Insider Info** Publishes 60 titles per year. Payment is via royalties. Catalogue available online.
**Non-Fiction** Publishes General Non-fiction on the following subjects:
 History, Language/Literature, Nature/Environment, Regional, Translation, Welsh interest.
 * Publishes mainly in Welsh language.
**Submission Guidelines** Accepts query with SAE.
**Recent Title(s)** *Haunted Clwyd*, Richard Holland (Welsh interest)
**Tips** Gwasg Carreg Gwalch is a productive printing house, which publishes a variety of Welsh books and books of Welsh interest. Ideas and submissions welcome, if of Welsh interest.

## Gwasg Pantycelyn
**Lon Dewi, Caernarfon, Gwynedd, LL55 1ER**
- 01268 672081
- 01268 677823
- gwasgpantycelyn@ukonline.co.uk

**Non-Fiction** Publishes Welsh and English language books on the following subjects:
 Literature Studies, History, Theology.
**Fiction** Publishes Welsh and English language Fiction titles.
**Poetry** Publishes Welsh and English Poetry titles.
**Tips** Has published a collection of around 150 books for adults and children. The intended audience is all those who read for pleasure, those interested in a more analytical approach to literature and readers interested in the culture and social history of Wales.

## Hachette Children's Books
**338 Euston Road, London, NW1 3BH**
- 020 7873 6000
- 020 7873 6024
- www.hodderheadline.co.uk

**Parent Company** Hodder Headline Ltd
**Contact** Managing Director, Marlene Johnson
**Established** 2005
**Imprint(s)** Franklin Watts
 Orchard Books
 Wayland
**Insider Info** Catalogue available online (see www.wattspublishing.co.uk for Franklin Watts and Orchard Books imprints).
**Non-Fiction** Publishes Children's/Juvenile titles, Gift and Children's information titles on the following subjects:
 Animals, Crafts, History, Hobbies, Science, General Information including Special Needs, Reading Development, Citizenship and PSHE.
**Submission Guidelines** Agented submissions only.

**Fiction** Publishes Picture books, and Novelty titles.
**Submission Guidelines** Agented submissions only.

## Halban Publishers Ltd
**22 Golden Square, London, W1F 9JW**
- 020 7437 9300
- 020 7437 9512
- books@halbanpublishers.com
- www.halbanpublishers.com

**Contact** Director, Peter Halban; Director, Martine Halban
**Established** 1986
**Insider Info** Publishes eight titles per year. Payment is via royalties. Catalogue available online.
**Non-Fiction** Publishes Biography and General Non-fiction titles on the following subjects:
 History, Memoirs, Religion, Jewish Interest.
**Submission Guidelines** Accepts query with SAE.
**Fiction** Publishes Jewish interest titles.
**Submission Guidelines** Accepts query with SAE.
**Recent Title(s)** *Memoirs of a Fortunate Jew*, Dan Vittorio Segre (Memoir); *The Overseer*, Jonathan Rabb (Novel)
**Tips** Halban Publishers is an independent, London based publishing company, established in 1986. We publish fiction, memoirs, history, biography and books of Jewish interest. Welcomes proposals, but approach by letter first.

## Haldane Mason Ltd
**PO Box 34196, London, NW10 3YB**
- 020 8459 2131
- 020 8728 1216
- info@haldanemason.com
- www.haldanemason.com

**Contact** Director, Sydney Francis; Director, Ron Samuel
**Established** 1995
**Imprint(s)** Red Kite Books
**Non-Fiction** Publishes Children's/Juvenile and Gift titles.
**Submission Guidelines** Accepts query with SAE. Submit proposal package (including outline, sample chapter(s)).
**Tips** Publishes illustrated non-fiction books and gift books for children. We are currently commissioning in the area of illustrated non-fiction for children. Please post relevant proposals to Sydney Francis. All submissions must be accompanied by SAE if material is to be returned.

## Halsgrove

**Halsgrove House, Lower Moor Way, Tiverton Business Park, Tiverton, Devon, EX16 6SS**

☎ 01884 243242

🖷 01884 243325

✉ sales@halsgrove.com

🌐 www.halsgrove.co.uk

**Contact** Publisher, Simon Butler

**Established** 1990

**Insider Info** Publishes 150 titles per year. Payment is via royalties. Catalogue and manuscript guidelines are available online.

**Non-Fiction** Publishes Biography, General Non-fiction and Illustrated titles on the following subjects: Art/Architecture, Cooking/Foods/Nutrition, History, Regional/Local interest.

 * Mostly regional themed books.

**Submission Guidelines** Accepts query with SAE. Submit proposal package (including outline and sample chapter(s)).

 Submission details to: simonb@halsgrove.com

**Recent Title(s)** *My Life With Horses*, Alison Downes and Alan Childs, eds. (Biography); *Bod the Beast of Bodmin*, Endymion Beer (Local interest)

**Tips** Halsgrove is England's leading regional publisher. Each year we publish around 100 hardbacks celebrating the varied history, art, heritage and life of England's regions, cities, towns and villages. Individual authors are welcome to submit works. Halsgrove provide a complete publishing service to such clients, from editorial, design and production through marketing, promotion and distribution. In the first instance please contact the Publisher, Simon Butler.

## Hamish Hamilton

**80 Strand, London, WC2R 0RL**

☎ 020 7010 3000

🖷 020 7010 6060

✉ customer.service@penguin.co.uk

🌐 www.penguin.co.uk

**Parent Company** Penguin General

**Contact** Publishing Director, Simon Prosser

**Established** 1931

**Insider Info** Publishes 20 titles per year. Catalogue is available online.

**Non-Fiction** Publishes Literary Non-fiction titles.

**Submission Guidelines** Agented submissions only.

**Fiction** Publishes Literary Fiction titles.

**Submission Guidelines** Agented submissions only.

**Recent Title(s)** *At the Same Time*, Susan Sontag (Collection of letters and addresses); *What is the What*, Dave Eggars

**Tips** The Hamish Hamilton list is a small section of the Penguin group and focuses entirely on distinct, often unusual, literary fiction and non-fiction from an exciting and eclectic group of authors.

## Hamlyn

**2–4 Heron Quays, London, E14 4JP**

☎ 020 7531 8400

🖷 020 7531 8650

✉ info-ho@hamlyn.co.uk

🌐 www.hamlyn.co.uk

**Parent Company** Octopus Publishing Group

**Contact** Publisher, Jane Birch

**Established** 1950

**Imprint(s)** Gaia Books

 Godsfield Press

 Pyramid Paperbacks

**Insider Info** Catalogue available online.

**Non-Fiction** Publishes Coffee table, Cookery, Illustrated, Reference and Self-help titles on the following subjects:

 Child Guidance/Parenting, Cooking/Foods/Nutrition, Crafts, Gardening, Health/Medicine, House and Home, Sex, Sports, Weddings, General Reference – Children and Adults.

**Recent Title(s)** *Miracle Foods for Kids*, Juliette Kellow (Sunil Vijayakar)

**Tips** Two thirds of Hamlyn's business is in international, US and export markets, therefore books should potentially have an international appeal.

## Hammersmith Press Ltd

**496 Fulham Palace Road, London, SW6 6JD**

☎ 020 7736 9132

🖷 020 7348 7521

✉ gmb@hammersmithpress.co.uk

🌐 www.hammersmithpress.co.uk

**Contact** Publisher, Georgina Bentliff (Health, Nutrition, Medical Humanities)

**Established** 2004

**Insider Info** Publishes six titles per year. Receives approximately 40 queries and 30 manuscripts per year. 100 per cent of books published are from unagented authors. Payments is via royalty (on wholesale price). Average lead time is six months, with simultaneous submissions not accepted. Submissions accompanied by an SAE will be returned. Aims to respond to queries within five days, proposals within two weeks and manuscripts within one month. Manuscript guidelines available by email.

**Non-Fiction** Publishes Self-help titles on the following subjects:
 Health/Medicine.
 * Hammersmith books integrate conventional medicine with complementary/alternative medicine.
**Submission Guidelines** Accepts query by email with brief outline initially. Will not accept artwork/images.
**Recent Title(s)** *Your Thyroid and How to Keep it Healthy*, Dr Barry Durrant Peatfield (Self-help health)
**Tips** Hammersmith books are targeted at members of the general public with specific health problems and are generally written by specialists in the relevant area, rather than by general health writers.

## Hanley & Belfus
**32 Jamestown Road, Camden Town, London, NW1 7BY**
☎ 020 7424 4200
🖷 020 7482 2293
✉ m.ging@elsevier.com
🌐 www.intl.elsevierhealth.com/hanleyandbelfus
**Parent Company** Elsevier Ltd (Health Sciences)
**Insider Info** Payment via royalty. Catalogue and manuscript guidelines are available online.
**Non-Fiction** Publishes Scholarly, Technical, Textbook and Reference titles on the following subjects:
 Education, Health/Medicine, Science.
**Submission Guidelines** Submit using an Online Proposal Form.
 Submission details to: t.horne@elsevier.com
**Recent Title(s)** *Anaesthesia Secrets*, James Duke (Medical/Reference)
**Tips** Hanley & Belfus publishes textbooks and reference books, specialising in carefully edited publications for medical students, residents, practising physicians, biomedical scientists, and other healthcare professionals. Hanley & Belfus publishes a number of popular medical series, including the *Secrets* series. To submit a proposal to Hanley & Belfus, fill in and return a proposal form, available on the website. Alternatively authors may contact the Publishing Director or Editor prior to submission, to discuss the proposal.

## Harcourt Education
**Halley Court, Jordan Hill, Oxford, OX2 8EJ**
☎ 01865 311366
🖷 01865 314641
✉ uk.school@harcourteducation.co.uk
🌐 www.harcourteducation.co.uk

**Parent Company** Reed Elsevier Group Plc
**Contact** Chief Executive, Chris Jones
**Established** 2001
**Imprint(s)** Heinemann Educational
 Ginn & Co
 Rigby Heinemann
**Insider Info** Payment is via royalties. Catalogue available online.
**Non-Fiction** Publish Reference, Scholarly and Textbook titles on Education.
**Tips** Harcourt Education is an international publishing group with operations in the UK, Australia, New Zealand, Southern Africa and South East Asia. Titles are aimed at school pupils all over the world, and also for educators of all kinds. Only educational textbooks are published.

## Harlequin Mills & Boon Ltd
**Eton House, 18–24 Paradise Road, Richmond, TW9 1SR**
☎ 020 8288 2800
🖷 020 8288 2898
✉ andrea.grice@hmb.co.uk
🌐 www.millsandboon.co.uk
**Contact** Managing Director, Guy Hallowes; Editorial Director, Karin Stoecker; Senior Editor, Tessa Shapcott (Mills & Boon Modern Romance); Senior Editor, Kimberley Young (Mills & Boon Romance); Senior Editor, Sheila Hodgson (Mills & Boon Medical Romance); Senior Editor, Linda Fildew (Mills & Boon Historical Romance)
**Established** 1908
**Imprint(s)** Mills & Boon Modern Romance
 Mills & Boon Romance
 Mills & Boon Medical Romance
 Mills & Boon Historical Romance
**Insider Info** Publishes 600 titles per year. Receives approximately 2,000 manuscripts per year. Payment is via royalties. Simultaneous submissions not accepted. Submissions accompanied by SAE will be returned. Aims to respond to manuscripts within three months. Catalogue and manuscript guidelines available online. No non-fiction.
**Fiction** Publishes Erotica, Romance and Women's Fiction titles.
**Submission Guidelines** Accepts query with SAE. Submit proposal package (including outline).
**Recent Title(s)** *The Italian's Inexperienced Mistress*, Lynne Graham (Romance Novel)
**Tips** Harlequin Mills & Boon are a leading international publisher of romance fiction aimed at women. The Romance and Modern Romance imprints publish traditional romance novels, often set against a backdrop of luxury, wealth and

international locations. Medical Romance publishes romance novels set in or around the medical professions. Historical Romance publishes romance novels set in historical eras and includes chivalrous knights, roguish rakes and rugged cattlemen as the main focus of interest. Other imprints such as Silhouette and MIRA - which publish racier romance fiction and general women's fiction respectively - are available in the other international editorial offices. Harlequin Mills & Boon accept unsolicited submissions, and have substantial aspiring author information on their website, with detailed guidelines including word counts and proposal style guides, for each of their series.

## Harley Books

**Martins, Great Horkesley, Colchester, Essex, C06 4AH**

- 01206 271216
- 01206 271182
- harley@keme.co.uk
- www.harleybooks.com

**Contact** Managing Director, Basil Harley
**Established** 1983
**Insider Info** Payment is via royalties. Catalogue is available online.
**Non-Fiction** Publishes Reference and Scholarly titles on the following subjects:
 Science, Botany/Entomological.
**Submission Guidelines** Accepts query with SAE.
**Recent Title(s)** *The Dragonflies of Europe*, R.R. Askew
**Tips** Harley Books is an independent publisher of natural history books, specialising in Entomology and Botany, with an established reputation for excellence, and a worldwide market. The aim is to publish books of the highest editorial and production standards, many titles are regarded as definitive works in their fields and are likely to remain so for the foreseeable future. Query by post or email. Particular attention is paid to the quality of design, illustration, references and indexing.

## Harold Starke Publishers Ltd

**Pixey Green, Stadbroke, Eye, Suffolk, IP21 5NG**

- 01379 388334
- 01379 388335

**Contact** Naomi Galinski
**Non-Fiction** Publishes Textbooks, Coffee table and Scholarly titles on the following subjects:
 Education, Health/Medicine, Nature/Environment.
**Tips** Harold Starke's publishing house has made innovative forays into educational publishing and

gone on to specialise in high quality coffee table books.

## HarperCollins Publishers Ltd

**77–85 Fulham Palace Road, Hammersmith, London, W6 8JB**

- 020 8741 7070
- 020 8307 4440
- info@harpercollins.co.uk
- www.harpercollins.co.uk

**Parent Company** HarperCollins Worldwide (Division of News Corporation)
**Contact** Chief Executive and Publisher, Victoria Barnsley
**Established** 1819
**Imprint(s)** Collins (Division)
 General Books (Division)
 Press Books (Division)
**Insider Info** Publishes 1,500 titles per year. Catalogue and manuscript guidelines available online.
**Non-Fiction** Publishes Audio cassettes, Autobiography, Biography, Children's/Juvenile, Cookery, General Non-fiction, Gift, How-to, Humour, Illustrated, Multimedia, Reference, Scholarly, Self-help, Textbooks, Maps and Atlases; Guidebooks and Dictionaries on the following subjects:
 Alternative Lifestyles, Art/Architecture, Astrology/Psychic, Child Guidance/Parenting, Contemporary Culture, Cooking/Foods/Nutrition, Education, Entertainment/Games, Health/Medicine, History, Hobbies, Humanities, Language/Literature, Memoirs, Military/War, Music/Dance, Nature/Environment, Philosophy, Psychology, Recreation, Science, Sex, Social Sciences, Spirituality, Sports, Travel, World Affairs, Young Adult, Film and Television tie-ins, Mind, Body and Spirit, Lifestyle, Relationships.
**Submission Guidelines** Agented submissions only.
**Fiction** Publishes Adventure, Fantasy, Historical, Horror, Humour, Children's, Literary, Mainstream/Contemporary, Mystery, Romance, Science Fiction, Suspense, Young Adult and Thriller titles and Picture books.
**Submission Guidelines** Agented submissions only.
**Recent Title(s)** *Cancer Vixen*, Marisa Acocella Marchetto (Autobiography); *Next*, Michael Crichton (Novel)
**Tips** Harper Collins Publishers UK is one of the leading English language publishers in the world, and publishes the widest range of books of any of Britain's publishing groups. Anything is published, from contemporary fiction to thrillers, genre fiction including fantasy and science fiction, to children's stories and classics. It also publishes a wide range of

non-fiction including history, popular science, health and spirituality, celebrity biography and reference titles including dictionaries and atlases. Authors include many award winning and international bestsellers. In addition it publishes the complete works of J.R.R. Tolkein, C.S. Lewis and Agatha Christie. HarperCollins only accepts submissions from literary agents or previously published authors, but may consider submissions that are accompanied by a positive assessment from a manuscript assessment agency.

## HarperCollins Publishers Ltd – General Books Division

**77–85 Fulham Palace Road, Hammersmith, London, W6 8JB**

- 020 8741 7070
- 020 8307 4440
- customerservice@harpercollins.co.uk
- www.harpercollins.co.uk

**Parent Company** HarperCollins Publishers Ltd
**Contact** Managing Director, Amanda Ridout
**Imprint(s)** HarperFiction
  HarperCollins
  Voyager
  HarperThorsons
  HarperElement
  HarperEntertainment
  HarperSport
  Tolkien and Estates
  HarperCollins Children's Books
  HarperCollins Crime & Thrillers
  HarperCollins Audio
**Insider Info** Catalogues available online at: www.harpercollins.co.uk, www.voyager-books.co.uk, www.thorsens.com, www.harpercollinschildrensbooks.co.uk, www.collins-crime.co.uk, www.tolkien.co.uk
**Non-Fiction** Publishes Autobiography, Biography, Children's/Juvenile, General Non-fiction, How-to, Humour, Illustrated, Reference, Self-help, Television and Media Tie-in titles on the following subjects: Sports, Mind, Body and Spirit Lifestyle, Diet, Relationships, Work/Life Balance, Real life Issues, Film and Film Companions.
**Submission Guidelines** Accepts agented submissions only.
**Fiction** Publish Fantasy, Juvenile, Mainstream/ Contemporary, Picture book, Science Fiction, Young Adult, Crime and Thriller and Classic titles.
  * Books published under license include: *Mary-Kate and Ashley, Noddy, The Hulk, Spiderman, The Simpsons, The Magic Roundabout, Dr Seuss* and *Paddington Bear.*

**Submission Guidelines** Agented submissions only.
**Recent Title(s)** *Bobby Moore: By the Person Who Knew Him Best*, Tina Moore (Biography: HarperSport); *The Savage Garden*, Mark Mills (Thriller)
**Tips** The General Books division of HarperCollins Publishers Ltd publishes some of the most high profile writers around under the HarperFiction imprint from Josephine Cox, Tony Parsons to Sidney Sheldon and Tracey Chavalier. The Voyager imprint is the UK's leading science fiction and fantasy imprint. Non-fiction imprints include, HarperThorsons/ Harper Element with a list of well known brand name authors. HarperEntertainment produces humour and media related books, while HarperSport is the country's top sports imprint. The list of HarperCollins Children's Books includes much loved titles such as *The Tiger Who Came to Tea* and a wide range of children's fiction.

## HarperCollins Publishers Ltd - Press Books Division

**77–85 Fulham Palace Road, Hammersmith, London, W6 8JB**

- 020 8741 7070
- 020 8307 4440
- customerservice@harpercollins.co.uk
- www.harpercollins.co.uk

**Parent Company** HarperCollins Publishers Ltd
**Contact** Managing Director, John Bond
**Imprint(s)** Fourth Estate
  HarperPerennial
  HarperPress
**Insider Info** Catalogue available online.
**Non-Fiction** Publishes Autobiography, Biography, General Non-fiction and Humour on the following subjects: Contemporary Culture, Government/Politics, History, Memoirs, Science, Travel, World Affairs, Current Affairs.
**Submission Guidelines** Agented submissions only.
**Fiction** Publishes Humour, Literary, Mainstream/ Contemporary, Romance, Translation, Crime and Genre Fiction titles
**Submission Guidelines** Agented submissions only.
**Recent Title(s)** *Living with the Laird*, Belinda Rathbone (Harper Perennial – Memoir); *So He Takes the Dog*, Jonathan Buckley (Fourth Estate – Novel)
**Tips** Fourth Estate, acquired by HarperCollins in 2000, is one of the most innovative imprints in the industry. It has a reputation for selecting critically acclaimed titles; titles in the list are cutting edge non-fiction and fiction, often with a controversial flavour. HarperPerennial was launched in 2004 as the prestigious paperback literary imprint of

HarperCollins UK Press Books division. HarperPress, launched in 2005, publishes a wide range of award winning non-fiction and quality, commercial fiction. Press Books is a large division within HarperCollins and it is best to direct enquiries to the relevant imprint, rather than to the division as a whole.

## HarperCollins Children's Books

**77–85 Fulham Palace Road, Hammersmith, London, W6 8JB**

- 020 8741 7070
- 020 8307 4440
- enquiries@harpercollinschildrensbooks.co.uk
- www.harpercollinschildrensbooks.co.uk

**Parent Company** HarperCollins Publishers Ltd – General Books Division

**Contact** Managing Director, Sally Gritten; Publishing Director, Gillie Russel (Fiction); Publishing Director, Sue Buswell (Picture Books)

**Insider Info** Catalogue available online.

**Non-Fiction** Publishes Audiobooks and Children's/Juvenile titles.

**Submission Guidelines** Agented submissions only.

**Fiction** Publishes Picture books and Children's and Young Adult titles.

**Submission Guidelines** Agented submissions only.

**Recent Title(s)** *Lady Friday*, Garth Nix (Young Adult)

**Tips** HarperCollins Children's Books publishes fiction, picture books and audiobooks for children of all ages, including young adult. Various intellectual properties are also published under licence by the imprint including *Spiderman, Paddington Bear* and *The Simpsons*. HarperCollins only accepts submissions from literary agents or previously published authors, but may consider submissions that are accompanied by a positive assessment from a manuscript assessment agency.

## HarperCollins Crime & Thrillers

**77–85 Fulham Palace Road, Hammersmith, London, W6 8JB**

- 020 8741 7070
- 020 8307 4440
- customerservice@harpercollins.co.uk
- www.collins-crime.co.uk

**Parent Company** HarperCollins Publishers Ltd – General Books Division

**Contact** Publishing Director, Julia Wisdom

**Insider Info** Catalogue available online.

**Fiction** Publishes Mystery, Suspense, Crime and Thriller titles.

**Submission Guidelines** Agented submissions only.

**Recent Title(s)** *The Death of Dalziel*, Reginald Hill (Crime/Thriller)

**Tips** HarperCollins Crime & Thrillers publishes the best in modern crime fiction from popular writers such as Val McDermid, Reginald Hill and Robert Wilson. HarperCollins only accepts submissions from literary agents or previously published authors, but may consider submissions that are accompanied by a positive assessment from a manuscript assessment agency.

## HarperEntertainment

**77–85 Fulham Palace Road, Hammersmith, London, W6 8JB**

- 020 8741 7070
- 020 8307 4440
- customerservice@harpercollins.co.uk
- www.harpercollins.co.uk

**Parent Company** HarperCollins Publishers Ltd – General Books Division

**Contact** Managing Director and Publisher, Trevor Dolby; Publishing Director, Ben Dunn

**Imprint(s)** HarperCollins Audio
HarperCollins Entertainment
HarperSport

**Insider Info** Catalogue available online.

**Non-Fiction** Publishes Audio cassettes, Autobiography, Biography, Children's/Juvenile, General Non-fiction, Humour, Illustrated and Multimedia titles on the following subjects: Entertainment/Games, Memoirs, Sports, Film/Television tie-ins.

**Submission Guidelines** Agented submissions only.

**Fiction** Publishes Children's and Film/Television tie-in titles and Comic Books and Audio books.

**Submission Guidelines** Agented submissions only.

**Recent Title(s)** *Peter Jackson: A Film-maker's Journey*, Brian Sibley (Biography); *That Hideous Strength*, C.S. Lewis (Novel)

**Tips** HarperCollins Entertainment publishes humour and media related non-fiction books, from film companions to autobiographies, to various types of television and cinema tie-ins. HarperSport publishes sporting guides, biographies of athletes and sporting figures and general interest sports titles. HarperCollins Audio publishes recordings of HarperCollins fiction and non-fiction titles, for both children and adults. HarperCollins only accepts submissions from literary agents or previously published authors, but may consider submissions that are accompanied by a positive assessment from a manuscript assessment agency.

## HarperEstates

**77–85 Fulham Palace Road, Hammersmith, London, W6 8JB**

- ☎ 020 8741 7070
- ☎ 020 8307 4440
- ✉ customerservice@harpercollins.co.uk
- 🌐 www.harpercollins.co.uk

**Parent Company** HarperCollins Publishers Ltd – General Books Division

**Contact** Publishing Director, David Brawn

**Imprint(s)** Tolkien

**Insider Info** Catalogue available online.

**Fiction** Publishes Classic reprints.

**Tips** HarperEstates publishes the complete works of J.R.R. Tolkien, along with the complete works of both Agatha Christie and C.S. Lewis. HarperEstates exists solely to print the works of Tolkien, Lewis and Christie and therefore does not accept submissions.


## HarperFiction

**77–85 Fulham Palace Road, Hammersmith, London, W6 8JB**

- ☎ 020 8741 7070
- ☎ 020 8307 4440
- ✉ customerservice@harpercollins.co.uk
- 🌐 www.harpercollins.co.uk

**Parent Company** HarperCollins Publishers Ltd – General Books Division

**Contact** Publisher, Lynne Drew

**Imprint(s)** HarperCollins
HarperCollins Crime & Thrillers
HarperVoyager

**Insider Info** Catalogue available online.

**Fiction** Publishes Fantasy, Historical, Horror, Literary, Mainstream/Contemporary, Romance, Science Fiction, Suspense, Women's Writing, and Crime/Thriller titles.

**Submission Guidelines** Agented submissions only.

**Recent Title(s)** *The Ravenscar Dynsaty*, Barbara Taylor Bradford

**Tips** HarperFiction is the general fiction division under HarperCollins' General Books division. The HarperCollins imprint publishes general and contemporary fiction, historical fiction and women's writing. HarperCollins Crime & Thriller specialises in crime fiction from best selling authors.
HarperVoyager publishes a wide range of popular genre fiction, including fantasy, science fiction and horror. HarperCollins only accepts suubmissions from literary agents or previously published authors, but may consider submissions that are accompanied by a positive assessment from a manuscript assessment agency.

## HarperPerennial

**77–85 Fulham Palace Road, Hammersmith, London, W6 8JB**

- ☎ 020 8741 7070
- ☎ 020 8307 4440
- ✉ web.contact@harpercollins.co.uk
- 🌐 www.harperperennial.co.uk

**Parent Company** HarperCollins Publishers Ltd – Press Books Division

**Contact** Rachel Skerry

**Insider Info** Catalogue available online.

**Non-Fiction** Publishes Autobiography, Biography and General Non-fiction titles on the following subjects:
Contemporary Culture, Government/Politics, History, Memoirs, Science, Social Sciences, Travel.

**Submission Guidelines** Agented submissions only.

**Fiction** Publishes Literary, Mainstream/Contemporary and Genre fiction titles.

**Submission Guidelines** Agented submissions only.

**Recent Title(s)** *The Tribes Triumphant*, Charles Glass (World Affairs/Politics); *The Loneliness of the Long Distance Runner*, Alan Sillitoe (Novel)

**Tips** HarperPerennial is the literary paperback imprint for all Press Books titles. HarperPerennial offers the very best in new fiction and non-fiction from some of the most significant names of contemporary British and international writing. HarperPerennial only accepts submissions from literary agents or previously published authors, but may consider submissions that are accompanied by a positive assessment from a manuscript assessment agency.


## HarperPress

**77–85 Fulham Palace Road, Hammersmith, London, W6 8JB**

- ☎ 020 8741 7070
- ☎ 020 8307 4440
- ✉ customerservice@harpercollins.co.uk
- 🌐 www.harpercollins.co.uk

**Parent Company** HarperCollins Publishers Ltd – Press Books Division

**Contact** Publishing Director, Michael Fishwick

**Insider Info** Catalogue available online.

**Non-Fiction** Publishes Biography and General Non-fiction on the following subjects:
History, Memoirs, Travel.

**Submission Guidelines** Agented submissions only.

**Fiction** Publishes Mainstream/Contemporary titles.

**Submission Guidelines** Agented submissions only.

**Recent Title(s)** *Dusty Warriors: Modern Soldiers at War*, Richard Holmes (Military History)

**Tips** HarperPress publishes a wide range of popular non-fiction including biographies, history, military and current affairs. HarperPress also publishes commercial novels. HarperCollins only accepts submissions from literary agents or previously published authors, but may consider submissions that are accompanied by a positive assessment from a manuscript assessment agency.

## HarperSport
**77–85 Fulham Palace Road, Hammersmith, London, W6 8JB**
- 020 8741 7070
- 020 8307 4440
- customerservice@harpercollins.co.uk
- www.harpercollins.co.uk

**Parent Company** HarperCollins Publishers Ltd – General Books Division
**Contact** Publishing Director, Michael Doggart
**Insider Info** Catalogue available online.
**Non-Fiction** Publishes Autobiography, Biography, General Non-fiction and Illustrated titles on Sports.
**Submission Guidelines** Agented submissions only.
**Recent Title(s)** *FOUL!: The Secret World of FIFA: Bribes, Vote Rigging and Ticket Scandals*, Andrew Jennings (Sports)
**Tips** HarperSports publishes biographies, guidebooks, history and general interest sporting titles. HarperCollins only accepts submissions from literary agents or previously published authors, but may consider submissions that are accompanied by a positive assessment from a manuscript assessment agency.

## HarperThorsens/HarperElement
**77–85 Fulham Palace Road, Hammersmith, London, W6 8JB**
- 020 8741 7070
- 020 8307 4440
- customerservice@harpercollins.co.uk
- www.thorsons.com

**Parent Company** HarperCollins Publishers Ltd – General Books Division
**Contact** Publishing Director, Carole Tonkinson (Mind, Body and Spirit); Publishing Director, Wanda Whiteley (Health)
**Insider Info** Catalogue available online.
**Non-Fiction** Publishes Biography, General Non-fiction, Illustrated and Self-help titles on:
Alternative Lifestyles, Astrology/Psychic, Cooking/Foods/Nutrition, Guidance, Health/Medicine, Sex, Spirituality, Mind, Body and Spirit, Relationships.
**Submission Guidelines** Agented submissions only.

**Recent Title(s)** *Extreme Psychic*, Derek Acorah (Supernatural)
**Tips** HarperThorsons/HarperElement publishes a non-fiction list packed full of promotable brand name authors, and has a 'quality meets populism' attitude. Subjects include sex, relationships, diet and nutrition, health, mind, body and spirit, psychic and self-help. HarperCollins only accepts submissions from literary agents or previously published authors, but may consider submissions that are accompanied by a positive assessment from a manuscript assessment agency.

## HarperVoyager
**77–85 Fulham Palace Road, Hammersmith, London, W6 8JB**
- 020 8741 7070
- 020 8307 4440
- customerservice@harpercollins.co.uk
- www.voyager-books.co.uk

**Parent Company** HarperCollins Publishers Ltd – General Books Division
**Contact** Publishing Director, Jane Johnson
**Insider Info** Catalogue available online.
**Fiction** Publishes Fantasy, Gothic, Horror and Science Fiction titles.
**Submission Guidelines** Agented submissions only.
**Recent Title(s)** *Forest Mage*, Robin Hobb (Fantasy)
**Tips** HarperVoyager publishes the best in modern fantasy, horror and science-fiction, with authors including Terry Goodkind, David Eddings, Raymond E. Feist and Robin Hobb. HarperCollins only accepts submissions from literary agents or previously published authors, but may consider submissions that are accompanied by a positive assessment from a manuscript assessment agency.

## Harvard University Press
**Fitzroy House, 11 Chenies Street, London, WC1E 7EY**
- 020 7306 0603
- 020 7306 0604
- info@HUP-MITpress.co.uk
- www.hup.harvard.edu

**Contact** General Manager, Ann Sexsmith
**Established** 1913
**Insider Info** Catalogue and manuscript guidelines available online.
**Non-Fiction** Publishes Reference and Scholarly titles on the following subjects:
Art/Architecture, Business/Economics, Government/Politics, History, Language/Literature, Literary Criticism, Music/Dance, Philosophy,

**215**

Psychology, Science, Social Sciences, Sociology, Women's Issues/Studies.
**Submission Guidelines** Accepts query with SAE. Submit proposal package (including outline, sample chapter(s), publishing history, author biography and SAE).
**Recent Title(s)** *The Smaller Majority*, Piotr Naskrecki
**Tips** The European (UK) office of Harvard University Press publishes academic works in a range of subjects including politics, history, art and culture, science, and sociology. The website has very detailed submission guidelines. Please note that all manuscript submissions must be sent to the American office.

## Harvill Secker
**Random House, 20 Vauxhall Bridge Road, London, SW1V 2SA**
☏ 020 7840 8540
☏ 020 7233 6117
✉ harvillseckereditorial@randomhouse.co.uk
🌐 www.randomhouse.co.uk
**Parent Company** The Random House Group Ltd
**Contact** Publishing Director, Geoff Mulligan
**Insider Info** Submissions accompanied by SAE will be returned. Catalogue available online.
### Non-Fiction
Publishes General Non-fiction titles on the following subjects:
History, Literary Criticism and Memoirs.
**Submission Guidelines** Accepts query with proposal package (including outline, one sample chapter, author biography). Will accept artwork/images (send photocopies).
### Fiction
Publishes Literary and Mainstream/Contemporary titles.
**Submission Guidelines** Accepts query with SAE/proposal package (including outline, one sample chapter and SAE).
### Recent Title(s)
*King Henry*, Douglas Galbraith (Novel); *A Russian Diary*, Anna Politkovskaya (Memoir/Historical account)
**Tips** Please note emailed submissions are not accepted. Research the Harvill Secker section of the Random House catalogue for ideas about the types of fiction and non-fiction published.

## Haunted Library
**Flat 1, 36 Hamilton Street, Hoole, Chester, CH2 3JQ**
☏ 01244 313685

✉ pardos@globalnet.co.uk
🌐 www.users.globalnet.co.uk/~pardos/GS.html
**Contact** Managing Editor, Rosemary Pardoe; Assistant Editor, David Rowlands; Assistant Editor, Steve Duffy
**Established** 1979
**Tips** Publishes the *Ghosts and Scholars M.R. James Newsletter* several times a year. Features various articles, reviews and literary criticism. No longer publishes fiction.

## Haus Publishing
**26 Cadogan Court, Draycott Avenue, London, SW3 3BX**
☏ 020 7584 6738
☏ 020 7584 9501
✉ haus@hauspublishing.co.uk
🌐 www.hauspublishing.co.uk
**Contact** Managing Director, Barbara Schwepke
**Established** 2001
**Imprint(s)** Life & Times
Armchair Traveller
HBooks
**Insider Info** Publishes 20 titles per year. Payment is via royalties. Catalogue available online. Manuscript guidelines available online.
**Non-Fiction** Publishes Biography and Scholarly titles on the following subjects:
Biography, Literary Travel.
**Submission Guidelines** Accepts query with SAE and proposal package (including outline, one sample chapter, author biography).
**Recent Title(s)** *Pictures of the Surface of the Earth*, Wim Wenders (Photography/Travel)
**Tips** Specialising in biographies, Haus books tell the stories of those people who have shaped our lives, set within the context of their time and culture. From Beethoven to Dietrich, Caravaggio to Marie Curie, each authoritative, illustrated book is produced to the highest quality. Haus does accept unsolicited submissions direct from authors, but follow the submission guidelines from the website. We also publish a literary travel series, *The Armchair Traveller*, which is travel literature of a personal nature. These are not guidebooks.

## Haynes Publishing
**Sparkford, Yeovil, Somerset, BA22 7JJ**
☏ 01963 440635
☏ 01963 440825
✉ info@haynes.co.uk
🌐 www.haynes.co.uk

**Contact** Chairman, John H. Haynes OBE; Editorial Director, Matthew Minter; Editorial Director, Mark Hughes

**Established** 1960

**Imprint(s)** Haynes

Sutton Publishing Ltd

**Insider Info** Payment is via royalties. Catalogue available online.

**Non-Fiction** Publishes General Non-fiction, Reference and Technical titles on the following subjects:

Hobbies, Motoring/Engineering, Leisure.

**Submission Guidelines** Accepts query with SAE and proposal package (including outline, sample chapters, author biography).

**Recent Title(s)** *Lotus: A genius for innovation*, Russell Hayes

**Tips** Alongside our world famous car and motorcycle manuals, Haynes also publish a huge variety of books on many other motoring, transport, family and DIY related areas. These include; restoration, motor sport and maritime subjects, aviation, farm tractors, commercial vehicles, motorcycling, cycling, caravanning, camping, home decorating and DIY, health matters and American cars.

## Headland Publications

**38 York Avenue, West Kirkby, Wirral, CH48 3JF**

 0151 625 9128

 gladysmarycoles@talk21.com

**Contact** Director and Editor, Gladys Mary Coles

**Established** 1969

**Fiction** Publishes Short Story Collections and Mainstream/Contemporary titles.

**Submission Guidelines** Accepts query with SAE. No unsolicited manuscripts.

**Poetry** Publishes Poetry titles.

**Submission Guidelines** Accepts query with SAE. No unsolicited manuscripts.

## Headpress

**Suite 306, The Colourworks, 2a Abbott Street, London, E8 3DP**

 020 7275 6001

 020 7249 6395

 info@headpress.com

 www.headpress.com

**Established** 1991

**Insider Info** Publishes six titles per year. Receives approximately 50 queries and 50 manuscripts per year. 50 per cent of books published are from first-time authors, 100 per cent of books published are from unagented authors. Payment is via a flat fee. Catalogue available online.

**Non-Fiction** Publishes General Non-fiction titles on the following subjects:

Alternative Lifestyles, Contemporary Culture, Creative non-fiction, Music, Film, True Crime.

**Recent Title(s)** *Better to Reign in Hell: Serial Killers, Media Panics & the FBI*, Stephen Milligen (Crime, Popular Culture)

## Heart of Albion

**2 Cross Hill Close, Wymeswold, Loughborough, Leicestershire, LE12 6UJ**

 01509 880725

 01509 881715

 albion@indigogroup.co.uk

 www.hoap.co.uk

**Contact** Proprietor, R.N. Trubshaw (Folklore, Mythology, Cultural Studies)

**Established** 1989

**Imprint(s)** Explore Books

Alternative Albion

**Insider Info** Publishes 12 titles per year. Receives approximately 200 queries and 20 manuscripts per year. Ten per cent of books published are from first-time authors, 90 per cent of books published are from unagented authors. Five per cent of books published are author subsidy published, depending on subject matter and estimates of realistic sales. Payment is via royalty (on retail price), with 0.15 (per £) maximum. Average lead time is six months, with simultaneous submissions accepted. Submissions accompanied by SAE will be returned. Aims to respond to queries within five days and proposals, manuscripts and all other enquiries within ten days. Catalogue and manuscript guidelines are free on request, and available online.

**Non-Fiction** Publishes General Non-fiction, e-books and Multimedia titles on the following subjects:

Anthropology/Archaeology ('History of Ideas'), Art/ Architecture (Medieval Carvings and Effigies), Contemporary Culture, History (Folklore and Mythology), Humanities, Memoirs, Nature/ Environment (Cryptozoology), New Age, Philosophy (non-Western philosophies), Psychology, Religion (modern pagan and non-Western religions), Social Sciences (Emergence theories), Spirituality, and World Affairs.

* Heart of Albion's overall aim is to popularise current 'academic' thinking in folklore, mythology, cultural studies and related disciplines.

**Submission Guidelines** Accepts proposal package (including outline, one sample chapter and your publishing history) by email preferably.

**Recent Title(s)** *Cures and Curses*, Janet Bord (Holy Well research).

**Tips** Readership is 'thinking' adults, especially those drawn to alternative ideas.

## Heinemann Educational
**Halley Court, Jordan Hill, Oxford, OX2 8EJ**

- ☎ 01865 311366
- ☎ 01865 314641
- ✉ enquiries@harcourt.co.uk
- 🌐 www.heinemann.co.uk

**Parent Company** Harcourt Education

**Non-fiction** Publishes Children's/Juvenile, Reference, Scholarly and Textbook titles.

**Tips** Publishes educational titles aimed at primary and secondary school children, vocational and further education students, and library users and professionals. Publications need to fit with appropriate curriculum guidelines.

## Helicon Publishing
**RM Plc, 183 Milton Park, Abingdon, Oxfordshire, OX14 4SE**

- ☎ 0870 920 0200
- ☎ 01235 826999
- ✉ helicon@rm.com
- 🌐 www.helicon.co.uk

**Contact** General Manager, Caroline Dodds

**Established** 1992

**Insider Info** Catalogue available online on request.

**Non-Fiction** Publishes Reference titles.

**Tips** Helicon publishes and provides reference material – including the *Hutchinson Encyclopedia*, the UK's leading encyclopedia – in print, on CD-ROM, and online. Helicon specialises in electronic publishing, and maintains databases containing over 21 million words, ranging from serious subject reference to quizzes and memory joggers. As well as text, the databases contain thousands of maps, diagrams, illustrations, audio clips, and animations. With 21 million words and thousands of multimedia items, Helicon offers the very best content for any print or electronic publishing project.

## Helm Information Ltd
**Crowham Manor, Main Road, Westfield, Hastings, TN35 4SR**

- ☎ 01424 882422
- ☎ 01424 882817
- ✉ amandahelm@helm-information.co.uk
- 🌐 www.helm-information.co.uk

**Contact** Director, Amanda Helm; Director, Christopher Helm

**Established** 1990

**Insider Info** Payment is via royalties. Catalogue available online.

**Non-Fiction** Publishes Reference, Scholarly and Textbook titles.

**Submission Guidelines** Accepts query with SAE and proposal package (including outline).

**Recent Title(s)** *The Development of the Novel: Literary Sources & Developments*, Eleanor McNees (ed.)

**Tips** The main aim of the company is to publish books and collections of reference material in the humanities, presented in a helpful and structured format, primarily for academic libraries to give students access to material that would otherwise be difficult or impossible for them to find. Will consider proposals if they are in keeping with the regular Helm Series.

## Helter Skelter Publishing
**Southbank House, Black Prince Road, London, SE1 7SJ**

- ☎ 020 7463 2204
- ☎ 020 7463 2295
- ✉ sales@helterskelterpublishing.com
- 🌐 www.helterskelterbooks.com

**Contact** Sean Body

**Established** 1995

**Imprint(s)** Firefly Publishing

**Insider Info** Publishes 15 titles per year. Receives approximately 50 queries and 30 manuscripts per year. 50 per cent of books published are from first-time authors and 60 per cent are from unagented authors. Payment is via royalty (on retail price) of 0.08 (per £) minimum and 0.125 (per £) maximum. Average lead time is six months with simultaneous submissions accepted. Catalogue available online.

**Non-Fiction** Publishes General Non-fiction on Contemporary Culture, Music/Dance.

**Submission Guidelines** Accepts query with SAE. Submit proposal package (including outline, sample chapter(s)). Will accept artworks/images (send photocopies).

**Recent Title(s)** *Metal Box: Stories From John Lydon's Public Image Ltd*, Phil Strongman

**Tips** Even though the Helter Skelter music bookstore, like so many independent bookshops, is no more, Helter Skelter Publishing continues to go from strength to strength with a particular strength in music titles. Unsolicited submissions and ideas are welcome.

## Herbert Press

**38 Soho Square, London, W1D 3HB**

- ☎ 020 7758 0200
- 🖷 020 7758 0222
- ✉ llambert@acblack.com
- 🌐 www.acblack.com

**Parent Company** A & C Black Publishers Ltd
**Contact** Department Head and Commissioning Editor, Linda Lambert
**Insider Info** Catalogue available online.
**Non-Fiction** Publishes General Non-fiction, How-to, Illustrated books, Multimedia and Reference books on the following subjects:
Art/Architecture, History, Photography, Visual Arts, Design and Calligraphy.
**Recent Title(s)** *A Visual Language*, David Cohen (Practical/Art)
**Tips** Herbert Press publishes practical and general interest handbooks on all aspects of art and design, including visual arts, crafts, ceramics, calligraphy, printmaking and jewellery. It also publishes books on architecture and art history, as well as photography. Herbert Press has recently redesigned its *Draw Books* series which is a practical series offering tutorials and guidance for various art and craft techniques.

## Hesperus Press

**4 Rickett Street, London, SW6 1RU**

- ☎ 020 7610 3331
- 🖷 020 7610 3217
- ✉ info@hesperuspress.com
- 🌐 www.hesperuspress.com

**Contact** Managing Editor, Katherine Venn
**Established** 2001
**Insider Info** Publishes 40 titles per year. Payment via royalties. Catalogue available online.
**Fiction** Publishes Literary, Translation and Classics titles.
**Submission Guidelines** Accepts query with SAE.
**Recent Title(s)** *The Calligrapher's Night*, Yasmine Ghata (Novel/Translation)
**Tips** Hesperus Press is committed to bringing near what is far – far both in space and time. Works written by the greatest authors, and unjustly neglected or simply little known in the English speaking world, are made accessible through new translations and a completely fresh editorial approach. We don't generally accept proposals for new fiction, as mainly we publish classic literary fiction. If you're proposing a translation, send it to Katherine Venn via post or email, with as many details as possible.

## Highbury Nexus Special Interests

**Nexus House, Azalea Drive, Swanley, Kent, BR8 8HU**

- ☎ 01322 660070
- 🖷 01322 616319

**Contact** Publisher, Dawn Frosdick-Hopley
**Non-Fiction**
Publishes General Non-fiction titles on the following subjects:
Crafts, Hobbies, Military/War.
**Tips** Publishes books on model building/collecting, woodworking, arts, crafts and the military.

## High Stakes Publishing

**PO Box 394, Harpenden, AL5 1EQ**

- ☎ 01582 761264
- 🖷 01582 761264
- 🌐 www.highstakespublishing.co.uk

**Parent Company** Oldcastle books
**Established** 2002
**Insider Info** Catalogue available online on request.
**Non-Fiction** Publishes Biography, Reference and How-to books on Gambling.
**Recent Title(s)** *Thirteen Against the Bank*, Norman Leigh

## Hilmarton Manor Press

**Hilmarton Manor Press, Calne, Wiltshire, SN11 8SB**

- ☎ 01249 760208
- 🖷 01249 760379
- ✉ mailorder@hilmartonpress.co.uk
- 🌐 www.hilmartonpress.co.uk

**Contact** Managing Director, Charles Baile de Laperriere
**Established** 1964
**Insider Info** Payment via royalties. Catalogue available online.
**Non-Fiction** Publishes Reference titles on the following subjects:
Art/Architecture
**Tips** Publishes art reference books and directories only, including *Who's Who In Art*.

## Hobsons Publishing Plc

**Challenger House, 42 Adler Street, London, E1 1EE**

- ☎ 020 7958 5000
- 🖷 020 7958 5001
- 🌐 www.hobsons.com

**Contact** Chairman, Martin Morgan; Group Managing Director, Christopher Letcher

**Established** 1974

**Non-Fiction** Publishes Reference and Scholarly titles on Education.

 * Publishes educational and careers information databases under licence to the Careers and Research Advisory Centre (CRAC).

**Tips** Publishes educational and careers information databases under licence to the Careers and Research Advisory Centre (CRAC). Hobsons enables schools to market their programs and opportunities to a large number of students, and also works with them to recruit a high quality, diverse student body. Hobsons delivers both online and offline publications to help students learn more about the educational and career opportunities available to them.

## Hodder Headline Ltd
**338 Euston Road, London, NW1 3BH**

- 020 7873 6000
- 020 7873 6024
- www.hodderheadline.co.uk

**Parent Company** Hachette Livre UK (see Hachette Livre entry under European & International Publishers)

**Contact** Managing Director, Tim Hely Hutchinson.

**Established** 1993

**Imprint(s)** Divisions:
 Headline
 Hodder Education
 Hodder & Stoughton General
 Hodder & Stoughton Religious
 Hodder Headline Ireland
 Hodder Headline Scotland
 Hachette Children's
 John Murray

## Headline
**338 Euston Road, London, NW1 3BH**

- 020 7873 6000
- 020 7873 6024
- Use online form
- www.hodderheadline.co.uk

**Parent Company** Hodder Headline Ltd

**Contact** Managing Director, Martin Neild; Publishing Director, Jane Morpeth (Fiction); Publishing Director, Val Hudson (Non-Fiction)

**Established** 1986

**Insider Info** Does not accept simultaneous submissions. Submissions accompanied by SAE will be returned. Aims to respond to proposals within three weeks. Catalogue and manuscript guidelines are available online on request.

**Non-Fiction** Publishes Autobiography, Biography, General Non-fiction, Illustrated books and Multimedia titles on the following subjects:
 Contemporary Culture, Entertainment/Games, History, Science, Sports, Film/Media.

**Submission Guidelines** Accepts query with SAE and proposal package (including outline and first 100 pages).

**Fiction** Publishes Mainstream/Contemporary, Short story collections and literary titles.

**Submission Guidelines** Accepts query with SAE and proposal package (including outline and first 100 pages).

**Poetry** Publishes Poetry titles.

**Recent Title(s)** *Are Men Necessary?*, Maureen Dowd (Mainstream/Contemporary); *Singletini*, Amanda Trimble (Romance)

**Tips** Headline publishes best selling adult commercial and literary fiction, including romance. Its eclectic, popular non-fiction list includes autobiographies and television tie ins, humour and history titles. Headline will accept submissions of novels or non-fiction from first time writers, as long as they follow the guidelines on the website. However, they will only accept submissions of novellas, poetry and short story collections from established authors.

## Hodder Education
**338 Euston Road, London, NW1 3BH**

- 020 7873 6000
- 020 7873 6299
- educationenquiries@hodder.co.uk
- www.hoddereducation.co.uk

**Parent Company** Hodder Headline Ltd

**Contact** Managing Director, Philip Walters; Publishing Director, Lis Tribe (School Textbooks and Learning Materials); Publishing Director, John Mitchell (Scottish School Textbooks and Learning Materials); Publishing Director, Alexia Chan (College and University Textbooks and Learning Materials, Reference); Publishing Director, Katie Roden (Self-Improvement and Home Learning Materials); Publishing Director, Joanna Koster (Health Sciences Textbooks, Reference and Other Learning Materials)

**Established** 2001

**Imprint(s)** Hodder Arnold
 Hodder Murray
 Hodder Gibson
 Philip Allan Updates

**Insider Info** Catalogue available online, free on request.

**Non-Fiction** Publishes Audio cassettes, How-to, Multimedia, Reference, Scholarly, Self-help, Journals and Textbook titles on the following subjects: Computers/Electronics, Education, Health/Medicine, History, Humanities, Science, Home Learning, Self-Improvement.

**Submission Guidelines** Accepts proposal package (including outline, sample chapter(s), market research, publishing history, author biography and SAE).

**Recent Title(s)** *Hodder Graphics: A Kestrel for a Knave*, Phil Page (Graphic Text)

**Tips** Hodder Arnold publishes books and digital materials for the Further Education, Higher Education, Health Sciences and Consumer Education markets. It comprises Hodder Arnold Further & Higher Education, Hodder Arnold Consumer Education, and Hodder Arnold Health Sciences. It also publishes the popular *Teach Yourself* series. Hodder Murray publishes books, resources, digital materials and assessment for the schools market and is the second largest publisher for secondary education in the UK. Hodder Gibson publishes educational books and digital materials in Scotland. Philip Allan Updates runs conferences and courses, as well as publishing subject specific material for GCSE and A-Level studies across the UK. Hodder Education is always keen to hear from qualified writers with new educational books. Send a proposal along with market research and some personal information, including publishing history, to the relevant publishing contact (see website).

### Hodder & Stoughton General
**338 Euston Road, London, NW1 3BH**
- 020 7873 6000
- 020 7873 6024
- www.hodderheadline.co.uk

**Parent Company** Hodder Headline Ltd
**Contact** Managing Director, Jamie Hodder-Williams
**Established** 1868
**Insider Info** Catalogue available online.
**Submission Guidelines** Agented submissions only.
**Recent Title(s)** *Mr Jones' Rules for the Modern Man*, Dylan Jones; *Lisey's Story*, Stephen King
**Tips** Hodder & Stoughton publishes household names in fiction and non-fiction. The non-fiction list is particularly noted for biography and memoir, history, sport, entertainment and lifestyle.

### Hodder & Stoughton Religious
**338 Euston Road, London, NW1 3BH**
- 020 7873 6051

- 020 7873 6059
- relgious-sales@hodder.co.uk

**Parent Company** Hodder Headline Ltd
**Contact** Managing Director, Martin Mullin; Publishing Director, Judith Longman
**Established** 1868
**Imprint(s)** Hodder & Stoughton Hodder Christian Books
**Insider Info** Catalogue available free online on request.
**Non-Fiction** Publishes Audio cassettes, Autobiography, Biography, Children's/Juvenile, General Non-fiction, Multimedia and Reference titles on the following subjects: Guidance, Health/Medicine, Religion, Spirituality.

**Submission Guidelines** Accepts proposal package (including outline, sample chapter(s), author biography, SAE and marketing and/or publicity information, if available).

**Fiction** Publishes Spiritual, Children's/Juvenile religious titles.

**Recent Title(s)** *Prayer*, Philip Yancey (Religious); *Dinner With A Perfect Stranger*, David Gregory (Religious)

**Tips** Hodder Christian Books publishes various Christian books and bibles, as well as self-help and spirituality guides and religious teaching resources. The Hodder & Stoughton imprint focuses on more general interest titles. Hodder & Stoughton Religious accepts unsolicited manuscripts, ideally with in-depth market research of similar titles and a brief author biography and publishing history. Full details are available on the website.

### Hodder Headline Ireland
**8 Castlecourt, Castleknock, Dublin 15, Republic of Ireland**
- 00353 1 824 6288
- 00353 1 824 6289
- info@hhireland.ie
- www.hodderheadline.co.uk

**Parent Company** Hodder Headline Ltd

**Contact** Submissions Editor
**Established** 2003
**Insider Info** Catalogue available online on request. Manuscript guidelines available online via website.
**Non-Fiction** Publishes Autobiography, Biography, General Non-fiction, Humour, Self-help, Sports and Music titles on the following subjects: Health/Medicine, History, Regional, Sports, Music.

**Submission Guidelines** Accepts query with SAE/
proposal package (including outline, first 100
pages, SAE).
**Fiction** Publishes Literary and Mainstream/
Contemporary titles on the following subjects:
Crime, Irish Writing.
**Submission Guidelines** Accepts query with SAE/
proposal package (including outline, first 100
pages, SAE).
**Recent Title(s)** *In Search of John*, Marie Carthy;
*Forget*, Ruth Gilligan
**Tips** Hodder Headline Ireland publishes mainstream
and literary fiction, as well as sports, music, humour
and general interest non-fiction. Hodder Headline
Ireland is not currently accepting unsolicited fiction
from previously unpublished authors. Submission
details for published authors and general non-fiction
titles are available at, www.hodderheadline.co.uk

## Hodder Headline Scotland
**2a Christie Street, Paisley, PA1 1NB**
- bob.mcdevitt@hodder.co.uk
- www.hodderheadline.co.uk

**Parent Company** Hodder Headline Ltd
**Contact** Bob McDevitt
**Insider Info** Catalogue available online via website
on request.
**Non-Fiction** Publishes General Non-fiction,
Illustrated and Scottish Interest books on the
following subjects:
Contemporary Culture, History, Nature/
Environment, Regional, Travel, Scotland.
**Submission Guidelines** Accepts proposal package
by post or email (including outline, first 50 pages,
SAE if sending by post).
**Fiction** Publishes Literary, Mainstream/
Contemporary, Scottish Writing titles.
**Submissions Guidelines** Accepts proposal package
by post or email (including outline, first 50 pages,
SAE if sending by post).
**Tips** Hodder Headline Scotland publishes new
Scottish writing and non-fiction books of general
Scottish interest by Scottish writers. Hodder
Headline Scotland is looking to publish the best new
books by Scottish authors, or of Scottish interest.
Send or email synopsis and the first 50 pages of a
manuscript to Bob McDevitt.

## Hollis Publishing Ltd
**Harlequin House, 7 High Street, Teddington,
Middlesex, TW11 8EL**
- 020 8973 3400
- 020 8977 1133

- orders@hollis-pr.co.uk
- www.hollis-publishing.com

**Contact** Managing Director, Gary Zabel
**Established** 1967
**Insider Info** Catalogue available online via website
on request.
**Non-Fiction** Publishes Reference titles and
Directories.
**Recent Title(s)**
*Hollis UK PR Annual*, Hollis
**Tips** Hollis is the leading publisher of directories and
online information for public relations, media,
advertising, sponsorship and marketing fields.

## Honeyglen Publishing Ltd
**56 Durrels House, Warwick Gardens, London,
W14 8QB**
- 020 7602 2876
- 020 7602 2876

**Contact** Director, J. Poderegin; Director,
N.S. Poderegin
**Established** 1983
**Non-Fiction**
Publishes Biography and General Non-fiction titles
on the following subjects:
History, Philosophy.
**Submission Guidelines** Accepts query with SAE.
Submit completed manuscript.
**Fiction** Publishes Literary titles.
* No Science Fiction or Children's Fiction.
**Submission Guidelines** Accepts query with SAE.
Submit completed manuscript.
**Tips** A small house that handles biography, history
and philosophy of history, as well as some literary
fiction. Unsolicited submissions welcome, but due to
the small size of the publishers, output is usually
extremely limited.

## Honno Welsh Women's Press
**Canolfan Merched y Wawr, Vulcan Street,
Aberystwyth, SY23 1JH**
- 01970 623150
- 01970 623150
- post@honno.co.uk
- www.honno.co.uk

**Contact** Publishing Manager, Lindsay Ashford;
Editor, Caroline Oakley
**Established** 1986
**Insider Info** Publishes eight titles per year. Payment
is via royalties. Aims to respond to proposals and
manuscripts within three months. Catalogue
available online on request. Manuscript guidelines
available online via website.

**Fiction** Publishes Children's, Mainstream/ Contemporary, Regional, Short Story Collections, Translation, Young Adult and Welsh Fiction titles.
**Submission Guidelines** Accepts proposal package (including outline and 50 pages).
**Poetry** Publishes Poetry titles with a Welsh connection.
**Submission Guidelines** Accepts queries with complete manuscript.
**Recent Title(s)** *Safe World Gone*, Patricia Duncker and Janet Thomas eds. (Anthology)
**Tips** Honno is an independent cooperative press run by women and committed to publishing the best in Welsh women's writing. Most of Honno's titles are novels, autobiographies and short story anthologies in English, but it also publishes poetry, children's and teenage titles and books in Welsh. Honno only considers for publication the work of women who are Welsh, living in Wales, or have a significant Welsh connection. Please call if you are unsure if you meet this requirement, and they can advise you.

## Hopscotch Educational Publishing Ltd
**Unit 2, The Old Brushworks, 56 Pickwick Road, Corsham, Wiltshire, SN13 9BX**
- 01249 701701
- 01249 701987
- sales@hopscotchbooks.com
- www.hopscotchbooks.com

**Contact** Editorial Director, Margot O'Keeffe; Creative Director, Frances Mackay
**Established** 1997
**Insider Info** Catalogue available free on request and online. Manuscript guidelines are available online via the website.
**Non-Fiction** Publishes Reference, Scholarly and Textbook titles on the following subjects:
 Education and the National Curriculum.
**Submission Guidelines** Accepts query with SAE. Submit completed manuscript.
**Recent Title(s)** *The Puncs*, Hopscotch
**Tips** Hopscotch aims to produce high quality, value for money resources that enable teachers to teach with confidence. The aim of the books is to enable children to have fun and success in their learning. Accepts manuscripts and ideas from first-time authors. The in-house team of experts will guide writers through the publishing process. Please call the editorial department for further information or simply send in the manuscript. Never send original or valuable products through the post.

## House of Lochar
**Isle of Colonsay, Argyll, PA61 7YR**
- 01951 200232
- 01951 200232
- lochar@colonsay.org.uk
- www.houseoflochar.com

**Contact** Chairman, Kevin Byrne; Managing Director, Georgina Hobhouse
**Established** 1995
**Imprint(s)** Colonsay Books
 West Highland Series
**Insider Info** Payment via royalties. Catalogue available online. Manuscript guidelines available on the website.
**Non-Fiction** Publishes General Non-fiction titles on the following subjects:
 History, Hobbies, Regional, Transportation, Walking Guides, Scottish Interest.
**Submission Guidelines** Accepts query with SAE and proposal package (including outline and sample chapter(s)).
**Fiction** Publishes Mainstream/Contemporary, Regional and Scottish titles.
**Submission Guidelines** Accepts query with SAE and proposal package (including outline, sample chapter(s)).
**Recent Title(s)** *Jura: Language and Landscape*, Gary McKay (Photography); *The Blood is Strong*, Richenda Francis (Novel)
**Tips** House of Lochar is a specialist Scottish publisher with a particular remit to print quality books on a number of subjects, including Scottish history, traditions and other titles of general Scottish interest in both fiction and non-fiction. Approaching their twentieth birthday, they have gained a reputation for publishing books which are regarded as being of great value to the Scottish book publishing industry. The House of Lochar are always on the lookout for new material and potential book ideas are welcome. In the first instance please forward a copy of the synopsis and sample text to the marketing agents.

## House of Stratus
**Thirsk Industrial Park, Thirsk, North Yorkshire, Y07 3BX**
- 01845 527700
- 01845 527711
- info@houseofstratus.com
- www.houseofstratus.com

**Non-fiction** Publishes General Non-fiction titles.

**Submission Guidelines** Accepts query with SAE and proposal package (including outline, sample chapter(s), CV, author biography and SAE).
**Fiction** Publishes Literary and Mainstream/Contemporary titles.
**Submission Guidelines** Accepts query with SAE and proposal package (including outline, sample chapter(s), CV and SAE).

## How To Books Ltd
3 Newtec Place, Magdalen Road, Oxford, OX4 1RE
- 01865 793806
- 01865 248780
- info@howtobooks.co.uk
- www.howtobooks.co.uk

**Contact** Publisher, Giles Lewis; Editorial Director, Nikki Read
**Established** 1991
**Insider Info** Publishes 100 titles per year. Receives approximately 200 queries and 100 manuscripts per year. 80 per cent of books are from first-time authors and 90 per cent are from unagented authors. Accepts simultaneous submissions. Aims to respond to proposals within one month and manuscripts within two months. Catalogue is free on request and available online. Manuscript guidelines are free on request.
**Non-Fiction** Publishes How-to, Reference and Self-help titles.
**Submission Guidelines** Accepts query with SAE (include synopsis).
**Recent Title(s)** *The Mature Student's Study Guide*, Catherine Dawson
**Tips** How To Books have more than 250 titles in print, all of which aim to help readers achieve their dreams and their goals in their personal and working lives. They welcome proposals from authors with genuine experience of their subject.

## Hurst & Co (Publishers) Ltd
41 Great Russell Street, London, WC1B 3PL
- 020 7255 2201
- 020 7255 2204
- hurst@atlas.co.uk
- www.hurstpub.co.uk

**Contact** Managing Director, Michael J. Dwyer.
**Established** 1969
**Insider Info** Catalogue can be downloaded online.
**Non-Fiction** Publishes Biography, General Non-fiction, Reference and Scholarly titles on the following subjects:

Anthropology/Archaeology, Government/Politics, History, Memoirs, Religion, Current Affairs, International Relations and Diplomacy, Islamic Studies.
**Submission Guidelines** Accepts proposal package (including outline, sample chapters, market research and author biography). Do not send completed manuscripts.
**Recent Title(s)** *African Boundaries: A Legal and Diplomatic Encyclopaedia*, Ian Brownlie; *Architect of Global Jihad: The Life of Al-Qaeda Strategist Abu Mus'ab Al-Sur*, Brynjar Lia (Biography)
**Tips** Hurst's authors include scholars, journalists and other authors who illuminate contemporary concerns and provide historical, cultural and religious background. Hurst also publishes books of wider public interest and two series', one in conjunction with CERI (Centre d'Etudes et de Recherches Internationales) in Paris, and the other, *Crises in World Politics*, with the Centre of International Studies, University of Cambridge.

## Hutchinson
Random House, 20 Vauxhall Bridge Road, London, SW1V 2SA
- 020 7840 8564
- 020 7233 6117
- hutchinsoneditorial@randomhouse.co.uk
- www.randomhouse.co.uk

**Parent Company** The Random House Group Ltd
**Contact** Publishing Director, Sue Freestone
**Non-Fiction** Publishes Autobiography, Biography, Children's/Juvenile and History titles.
**Submission Guidelines** Accepts query with SAE with proposal package (including synopsis, one sample chapter). No email submissions.
**Fiction** Publishes General and Literary Fiction.
**Submission Guidelines** Accepts query with SAE with proposal package (including synopsis, one sample chapter). No email submissions.
**Recent Title(s)** *England's Mistress*, Kate Williams (History); *Pistache*, Sebastian Faulks (Humour)
**Tips** Agented submissions are generally preferred, but unsolicited submissions are accepted. All submissions should be addressed to the Hutchinson editorial department.

## Hutchinson Children's Books
61–63 Uxbridge Road, London, W5 5SA
- 020 7840 8648
- 020 7233 6058
- childrenseditorial@randomhouse.co.uk
- www.randomhouse.co.uk/childrens

**Parent Company** Random House Children's Books
**Insider Info** Catalogue is available online.
**Fiction** Publishes Children's fiction and
activity books.
**Submission Guidelines** Accepts proposal package
(including outline and one sample chapter).
**Recent Title(s)** *More and More Rabbits*, Nicholas
Allen (Picture Book); *Little Red Train Magnetic
Playbook,* Benedict Blathwayt (Activity Book).
**Tips** Hutchinson Children's Books specialises in
hardback children's books, including picture books
and activity books.

## Hymns Ancient & Modern Ltd
**St. Mary's Works, St. Mary's Plain, Norwich,
Norfolk, NR3 3BH**
- 01603 612914
- 01603 624483
- hymns@scm-canterburypress.co.uk
- www.hymnsam.co.uk/hymnsam.asp
**Contact** Publisher, Christine Smith
**Established** 1975
**Insider Info** Publishes over 100 titles per year.
Authors paid by royalty. Catalogue and author
guidelines available online.
**Non-Fiction** Publishes Booklets and Hymn Books.
**Submission Guidelines** Accepts query with SAE.
Submit proposal package (including outline, sample
chapter(s), author biography and SAE).
**Recent Title(s)** *One Hundred Years of the English
Hymnal: 1906–2006*, Alan Luff (ed.)
**Tips** SCM-Canterbury Press brings together four
distinct, but complementary religious publishing
lists: SCM Press; Canterbury Press; RMEP; and Hymns
Ancient & Modern. Among its lists you will find some
of the world's best known religious titles and
authors. Please don't send proposals for
dissertations, fiction, poetry, drama, children's books,
books of specialist local interest, or as a general rule,
multi authored collections of essays or
symposium papers.

## Ian Allan Publishing Ltd
**Riverdene Business Park, Molesey Road,
Hersham, Surrey, KT12 4RG**
- 01932 266600
- 01932 266601
- peter.waller@ianallanpublishing.co.uk
- www.ianallanpublishing.com
**Parent Company** Ian Allan Group Ltd
**Contact** Publisher, Peter Waller (Transport, Aviation,
Military, Sport and Leisure, Masonic)
**Established** 1942

**Imprint(s)** Ian Allan Publishing
 Lewis Masonic
 Midland Publishing
**Insider Info** Publishes 150 titles per year. Receives
approximately 300 queries and 50 manuscripts per
year. Five per cent of books published are from first-
time authors and 95 per cent are from unagented
authors. Average lead time is six months, with
simultaneous submissions accepted. Submissions
accompanied by SAE will be returned. Aims to
respond to queries, proposals, manuscripts and all
other enquiries within seven days. Catalogue is free
on request.
**Non-Fiction** Publishes General Non-fiction and
Illustrated titles on the following subjects:
 Aviation, Military/War, Sport and Leisure, Masonic,
Hobbies, Transportation.
**Submission Guidelines** Accepts query with SAE
and artworks/images (send photocopies).
**Tips** Ian Allan Publishing's target readership is
historians, enthusiasts, modellers and Freemasons.
Does not accept publish books with a significant
amount of personal reminiscence.

## Ian Henry Publications Ltd
**20 Park Drive, Romford, Essex, RM1 4LH**
- 01708 749119
- 01708 736213
- ianhenry@parishchest.com
- www.parishchest.com/en-gb/dept_1707.html
**Contact** Managing Director, Ian Wilkes
**Established** 1976
**Insider Info** Publishes ten titles per year. Authors
paid by royalty. Catalogue available online.
**Non-Fiction** Publishes General Non-fiction and
Humour titles on the following subjects:
 Health/Medicine, History, Regional, Transportation,
Essex, Conan Doyle.
**Submission Guidelines** Accepts query with SAE.
**Fiction** Sherlock Holmes pastiche.
**Submission Guidelines** Accepts query with SAE.
**Recent Title(s)** *A Ghost Hunter's guide to Essex*
**Tips** Ian Henry Publications was established in 1975
and has published in excess of 600 books since then.
Since 1984 it has specialised in books on the history
and topography of Essex and surrounding counties,
and is now recognised as the largest publisher of
books on a single county in the country. A further
specialism of Ian Henry Publications is books based
on Sir Arthur Conan Doyle's Sherlock Holmes, both
in pastiche form, novels, plays, television scripts, and
factual titles on both Doyle himself and his creation.

## iBall Press

**The Old Candlemakers, West Street, Lewes, East Sussex, BN7 2NZ**

☎ 01273 487440

☎ 01273 487441

✉ hook@ivy-group.co.uk

🌐 www.iballpress.co.uk

**Parent Company** The Ivy Group

**Contact** Publisher, Jason Hook

**Insider Info** Fees always paid for published work. Catalogue available online.

**Non-Fiction** Publishes Gift books, Humour, Illustrated books and Novelty titles.

 * A quirky imprint of the Ivy Group that publishes novelty books on a huge range of subjects.

**Submission Guidelines** Accepts proposal package (including a table of contents and sample text and author biography).

**Recent Title(s)** *Carma Sutra*, Alex Games and Esther Selsdon; *My Book of Hard Words*, Stella Hyde

**Tips** Look through the catalogue to get a feel for the unusual, humorous subjects that iBall press publish.

## I.B.Tauris & Co Ltd

**6 Salem Road, London, W2 4BU**

☎ 020 7243 1225

☎ 020 7243 1226

✉ mail@ibtauris.com

🌐 www.ibtauris.com

**Contact** Chairman and Publisher, Iradj Bagherzade; Managing Director, Jonathan McDonnell

**Established** 1984

**Imprint(s)** Tauris Parke Books/Paperbacks
British Academic Press/Tauris Academic Studies
Radcliffe Press

**Insider Info** Publishes 175 titles per year. Catalogue available free online, on request. Manuscript guidelines available online via website.

**Non-Fiction** Publishes Biography, General Non-fiction and Scholarly titles on the following subjects: Art/Architecture, Government/Politics, History, Religion, Travel, World Affairs, Film Studies, Middle Eastern Studies.

**Submission Guidelines** Accepts query with SAE and proposal package (including outline, sample chapter(s), author biography and SAE).

**Recent Title(s)** *Frontline Pakistan,* Zahid Hussain

**Tips** I.B.Tauris is an independent publishing house pioneering a distinctive approach to the publishing of both general non-fiction and new work in the humanities and social sciences. Produces about 175 new books a year and aim to publish books that appeal to academics, area specialists, students and researchers as well as to general readers. Please note that we do not publish fiction, poetry or children's books. Does not accept complete manuscripts, unless specifically requested. Unsolicited manuscripts will not be returned.

## Icon Books Ltd

**The Old Dairy, Brook Road, Thriplow, Cambridge, SG8 7RG**

☎ 01763 208008

☎ 01763 208080

✉ info@iconbooks.co.uk

🌐 www.iconbooks.co.uk

**Contact** Managing Director, Peter Pugh; Publishing Director, Simon Flynn; Editorial Director, Duncan Heath

**Established** 1992

**Non-Fiction** Publishes Children's/Teenage, General Non-fiction, Reference, Scholarly and Technical titles on the following subjects: Art/Architecture, Government/Politics, History, Philosophy, Psychology, Science.

**Submission Guidelines** Query with SAE. Please send submission proposals only, not full manuscripts.

**Fiction** Publishes children's fiction titles for ages seven and upwards.

**Submission Guidelines** Query with SAE.

**Recent Title(s)** *Googlies, Nutmegs & Bogeys: The Origins of Peculiar Sporting Lingo* (Bob Wilson)

**Tips** Icon Books is a small independent British publisher specialising in thought provoking books. Icon now publishes a wide variety of books in non-fiction. Having tended to publish in series, such as the lists of *Postmodern Encounters*, *Ideas in Psychoanalysis* and *Revolutions in Science*, Icon is now publishing more and more individual titles, such as our bestselling guide to the internet, *The Internet from A to Z* and the critically acclaimed *The Euro: Should Britain Join – Yes or No?*.

## ICSA Publishing

**16 Park Crescent, London, W1B 1AH**

☎ 020 7612 7020

☎ 020 7612 1032

✉ icsa.pub@icsa.co.uk

🌐 www.icsapublishing.co.uk

**Contact** Joint Managing Directors, Clare Grist Taylor and Susan Richards; Publishing Assistant, John Savage

**Established** 1981

**Insider Info** Catalogue and manuscript guidelines are available online.

**Non-Fiction** Publishes Reference and Technical titles on Business/Economics.

**Submission Guidelines** Submission details to: Accepts query with SAE and proposal package (including, outline, two sample chapters, your publishing history and author biography).
Submission details to: jsavage@icsa.co.uk

**Recent Title(s)** *The ICSA Companies Act 2006 Handbook*, Keith Walmsley (ed.)

**Tips** Specialise in information solutions for compliance in the corporate, not for profit and public sectors. ICSA publish a range of products in topic areas including corporate governance, company secretarial practice and law for business. ICSA Publishing is committed to providing high levels of support and advice to its authors. In most cases, potential authors will be preparing a proposal after initial discussions with ICSA Publishing. This is always preferable. Please contact Clare Grist Taylor for further guidance.

## Ignotus Press
**BCM-Writer, London, WC1N 3XX**
- 0845 230 2980
- 01638 662294
- ignotuspress@aol.com
- www.ignotuspress.com

**Contact** Commissioning Editor, Suzanne Ruthven
**Established** 1994
**Imprint(s)** Moonraker (Fiction)
Past Tomes
Alphard (LifeStyle)

**Insider Info** Publishes 20 titles per year. Receives approximately 200 queries and 100 manuscripts per year. 50 per cent of books published are from first-time authors and 100 per cent are from unagented authors. Royalty (on retail price), is a maximum of £1 per book. Average lead time is 12 months. Simultaneous submissions accepted. Submissions accompanied by SAE will be returned. Aims to respond to queries within seven days, proposals two weeks and manuscripts within one month. Book catalogue available online.

**Non-Fiction** Publishes Autobiographies, How-to, Mind, Body and Spirit subjects, Humour, Pagan related humour, Self-help, Metaphysical, and Reference titles with very specific guidelines, on the following subjects:
Agriculture/Horticulture, Alternative Lifestyles, Animals, Anthropology/Archaeology, Astrology/Psychic, Contemporary Culture, History, Nature/Environment, New Age, Nostalgia, Psychology, Regional, Religion, Spirituality.

* Any potential authors should obtain a copy of Ignotus Press guidelines before sending proposals/submissions.

**Submission Guidelines** Accepts query with SAE. Will review artwork/photographs as part of the manuscript package.

**Fiction** Publishes Fiction on the following subjects: Adventure, Gothic, Historical, Humour, Mystery, Occult, Regional, Spiritual.
* All Fiction proposals must be metaphysically based to appeal to the target audience.

**Submission Guidelines** Accepts query with SAE.

**Recent Title(s)** *Champagne & Slippers*, Garrett Kelly (Field sports autobiography); *The Wild Horseman*, Harri Slaymaker (Adventure set in WW2)

**Tips** Ignotus Press titles are aimed at those with an alternative lifestyle and an interest in genuine pagan/new age/metaphysical writing. Any prospective author should study the guidelines thoroughly before submission.

## Ilex Press
**The Old Candlemakers, West Street, Lewes, East Sussex, BN7 2NZ**
- 01273 487440
- 01273 487441
- campbell@ilex-press.com
- www.ilex-press.com

**Contact** Publisher, Alastair Campbell
**Insider Info** Always pays a fee for works published. Catalogue is free on request, or available via the website.

**Non-Fiction** Publishes Illustrated, Reference and Technical titles on the following subjects:
Art/Architecture, Photography, Web design, Computer design.
* Specialises in books on art, digital art, design and photography, aiming to eradicate technophobia and provide helpful resources for digital creativity.

**Submission Guidelines** Accepts queries with SAE. Include a brief outline, table of contents and sample text and author biography.
Submission details to: authors@ivy-group.co.uk

**Recent Title(s)** *Web Comics*, Steven Withrow and John Barber; *Layouts for Scrapbooking*, Helen Bradley

**Tips** Books shouldn't be too full of jargon, but should try to break down the technical and creative processes.

## Immanion Press
**8 Rowley Grove, Stafford, ST17 9BJ**
- 01785 613299
- editorial@immanionpress.wox.org

**Contact** Managing Editor, Storm Constantine
**Established** 2003
**Insider Info** Authors paid by royalty. Manuscript guidelines available online.
**Fiction** Publishes the following genres: Fantasy, Gothic, Horror, Science Fiction, Slipstream.
**Submission Guidelines** Accepts query with SAE. Submit proposal package (including outline and sample chapter(s)).
**Tips** Publishes mainly speculative fiction such as horror, fantasy and science fiction. Also publishes slipstream. Check the website for detailed submission guidelines before submitting by post or email.

## I.M.P. Fiction Ltd

**PO Box 69, Church Stretton, Shropshire, SY6 6WZ**

- 01694 720049
- 01694 720049
- info@impbooks.com
- www.impbooks.com

**Contact** Managing Director, Kaye Roach
**Established** 1998
**Insider Info** Authors paid by royalty. Catalogue and author guidelines available online.
**Fiction** Publishes Mainstream/Contemporary fiction.
 * Does not publish Science fiction, Horror, Crime or novels about Bands/Music.
**Submission Guidelines** Accepts query with SAE. Submit proposal package (including outline, three sample chapters and author biography). Does not accept email submissions.
**Recent Title(s)** *The Gravedigger's Story*, Ged Simmons
**Tips** I.M.P. Fiction has quickly established itself as one of the most innovative and cutting edge publishing houses in the country. Be aware that I.M.P. Fiction has a reputation for refreshing and original storytelling.

## Imprint Academic

**PO Box 200, Exeter, Devon, EX5 5YX**

- 01392 851550
- 01392 851178
- keith@imprint.co.uk
- www.imprint-academic.com

**Contact** Reverend Anthony Freeman (Philosophy, Psychology, Religion); Mr Keith Sutherland, (Politics, Cultural Studies)
**Established** 1980
**Imprint(s)** Imprint Academic

Imprint Arts
 Societas

**Insider Info** Publishes 30 titles per year. Receives approximately 200 queries and 200 manuscripts per year. Five per cent of books published are from first-time authors and 100 per cent of books are from unagented authors. Payment is via royalty (on wholesale price) with 0.35 (per £) minimum and 2.25 (per £) maximum. No advance offered. Average lead time is 12 months with simultaneous submissions accepted. Submissions accompanied by SAE will be returned. Aims to respond to queries within seven days, proposals within fourteen days and manuscripts within three months. Catalogue is free on request, and available online. Manuscript guidelines are available online, or via email.
**Non-Fiction** Publishes Booklets, General Non-fiction and Scholarly titles on the following subjects:
 Anthropology/Archaeology, Contemporary Culture, Education, Government/Politics, Philosophy, Psychology, Religion, Social Sciences, Sociology, Spirituality, World Affairs.
**Submission Guidelines** Accepts proposal package (including outline, one sample chapter, your publishing history, clips, author biography and SAE). Will not review artwork/images as part of the manuscript package.
**Tips** Titles aimed at an educated and academic audience.

## Independent Music Press

**PO Box 69, Church Stretton, Shropshire, SY6 6WZ**

- 01694 720049
- 01694 720049
- info@impbooks.com
- www.impbooks.com

**Contact** Managing Director, Martin Roach
**Established** 1992
**Insider Info** Independent Music Press was founded in 1992 by author/publisher Martin Roach, whose immersion in the punk and alternative music world brings an acute insight into breakthrough artists. Authors paid by royalty. Catalogue and author guidelines available online.
**Non-Fiction** Publishes Biography, General Non-fiction and Illustrated titles on the following subjects:
 Alternative Lifestyles, Contemporary Culture, Music/Dance.
**Submission Guidelines** Accepts query with SAE. Submit proposal package (including outline, three sample chapters and author biography).

**Recent Title(s)** *My Chemical Romance: Something Incredible This Way Comes*, Paul Stenning (Music Biography)

**Tips** Independent Music Press publishes high quality first biographies on bands such as Travis, Stereophonics, Beastie Boys, Dave Grohl, Prodigy, Shaun Ryder and Ian McCulloch. They publish music biographies and focus on youth culture, mainly rock/indie music and its surrounding sub-culture.

## Infinite Ideas

**36 St. Giles, Oxford, OX1 3LD**

- 01865 514888
- 01865 514777
- info@infideas.com
- www.infideas.com

**Contact** Co-Directors, David Grant and Richard Burton; Managing Editor, Rebecca Clare

**Established** 2004

**Insider Info** Publishes 40 titles per year. Always pays fees on published work. Catalogue and author guidelines are free on request, or available online.

**Non-Fiction** Publishes Self-help titles on the following subjects:
Alternative Lifestyles, Art/Architecture, Business/Economics, Counselling/Career, Entertainment/Games, Health/Medicine, Hobbies, Language/Literature, Music/Dance, Sex, Sports.

**Submission Guidelines** Accepts query with SAE. Submit proposal package (including outline and sample chapter(s)). Template available online.
Submission details to: richard@infideas.com

**Tips** Infinite Ideas ditches the drivel, banishes the boring and publishes books that make a real difference to the lives of real people. Its authors are leading writers and journalists who are specialists within their fields. The style of the books is deliberately informal and humorous, as well as informative, so reading them feels more like you're having a chat with an old friend or a mentor, rather than just reading an instruction manual. Infinite Ideas are always open to new ideas, even if they don't appear to fit into the series. Basically if you think you've got a real best seller on your hands get in touch (strictly non-fiction though!). Study the author brief, available on the website, beforehand.

## Informa Law

**Informa House, 30–32 Mortimer Street, London, W1T 3JH**

- 020 7017 4115
- victoria.ophield@informa.com
- www.informalaw.com

**Parent Company** T & F Informa Plc

**Contact** Publishing Director, Nicola Whyke; Editorial, Victoria Ophield and Eleanor Taylor

**Insider Info** Informa Law publishes a wide range of books, loose leafs, newsletters, conferences, seminars, distance learning courses, law reporting services and strategic management reports for legal professionals in areas as varied as Maritime and Commercial law, Construction law and Intellectual Property law. Catalogue available online.

**Non-Fiction** Publishes Booklets and Technical titles on Law.

**Recent Title(s)** *Bills of Lading*, Richard Aikens (Michael Bools and Richard Lord)

**Tips** Informa Law's publications are written and edited by independent experts, and read by senior legal professionals and executives in the legal fraternity worldwide. Parent company Informa Plc is the leading provider of specialist information to the global academic and scientific, professional communities.

## Inner Sanctum Publications

**75 Greenleaf Gardens, Polegate, BN26 6PQ**

- 01323 484058
- 1106@mhession.clara.co.uk
- www.innersanctumpublications.com

**Contact** Managing Editor, Mary Hession

**Established** 1999

**Insider Info** Catalogue available online.

**Fiction** Publishes Spiritual titles.

**Submission Guidelines** Accepts query with SAE.

**Recent Title(s)** *Adventures with Little Big Woman*, Lori Ann Kavanaugh (Spiritual)

**Tips** Welcomes submissions.

## In Pinn

**Suite Ex 8, Pentagon Centre, 44 Washington Street, Glasgow, Scotland, G3 8AZ**

- 0141 221 1117
- 0141 221 5363
- info@nwp.co.uk
- www.nwp.co.uk

**Parent Company** Neil Wilson Publishing Ltd

**Insider Info** Catalogue and manuscript guidelines are available online.

**Non-Fiction** Publishes General Non-fiction titles on the following subjects:
Outdoor Pursuits, Travel, Wilderness issues.

**Submission Guidelines** Submit proposal package (including outline, synopsis, one sample chapter, author biography, CV and SAE). Will accept artworks/images.

**Recent Title(s)** *Wilderness Dreams: The Call of Scotland's Last Wild Places*, Mike Cawthorne (Wilderness Issues)

**Tips** In Pinn is the outdoor pursuits imprint of Neil Wilson Publishing. It publishes non-fiction titles about outdoor pursuits and travel in the Scotland area.

## Insight Guides

**58 Borough High Street, London, SE1 1XF**

- ☎ 020 7403 0284
- ☎ 020 7403 0290
- ⊙ Online form.
- ⊛ www.insightguides.com

**Parent Company** Apa Publications (The Langenscheidt Publishing Group)

**Insider Info** Catalogue is free on request or available online.

**Non-Fiction** Publishes Travel guides, Maps and Atlases.

**Recent Title(s)** *Indian Wildlife Insight Guide*, Insight Guides (Travel/Nature).

**Tips** Insight Guides are the world's largest series of visual travel guidebooks and maps. With more than 600 travel guides and maps in print, Insight do not generally need aspiring travel writers. However, local updaters and researchers, to help maintain the topicality of titles, are always welcomed. As well as a detailed knowledge of a destination and its culture, an updater must know how to find information and fact check thoroughly and efficiently. Clear presentation of information is also important. Write to the Insight Guides office, for the attention of the Editorial Department. As well as sending your CV, include details of which destinations you know best, and include some short samples of your writing in *Insight Guides* style.

## Inspire

**c/o MPH, 4 John Wesley Road, Werington, Peterborough, PE4 6ZP**

- ☎ 01733 325002
- ☎ 01733 384180
- ⊙ comm.editor@mph.org.uk
- ⊛ www.mph.org.uk

**Parent Company** Methodist Publishing House

**Contact** Commissioning Editor, Natalie K. Watson

**Insider Info** Publishes 12 titles per year. Authors paid by royalty. Catalogue and author guidelines available online.

**Non-Fiction** Publishes General Non-fiction titles on the following subjects:
 Religion, Spirituality, Worship resources.

**Submission Guidelines** Accepts query with SAE. Submit proposal package (including, outline and two sample chapters).

**Recent Title(s)** *Prayer – A Christian Companion*, Susan Hibbins (ed.)

**Tips** Before submitting your manuscript, it is advisable to look at the catalogue to ensure suitability. Inspire does not publish fiction or children's books.

## Institute of Public Administration

**Vergemount Hall, Clonskeagh, Dublin 4, Republic of Ireland**

- ☎ 00353 1 240 3600
- ☎ 00353 1 269 8644
- ⊙ information@ipa.ie
- ⊛ www.ipa.ie

**Contact** Publisher, Declan McDonagh

**Established** 1957

**Insider Info** Catalogue available online.

**Non-Fiction** Publishes Reference, Scholarly and Technical titles on the following subjects:
 Business/Economics, Government/Politics, Law, Social Sciences, Administrative history, Public management.

**Recent Title(s)** *Innovation in the Irish Public Sector*, Orla O'Donnell

**Tips** The Institute of Public Administration is Ireland's only consultancy service focused exclusively on public sector development. It delivers its service through education and training, research and publishing, and direct consultancy. It tailors its services to the particular needs of the public service. Its blend of skill and experience means that it can develop and offer a service which meets public service needs precisely and effectively.

## Interpet Publishing

**Interpet House, Vincent Lane, Dorking, Surrey, SU6 6WZ**

- ⊙ customercare@interpet.co.uk
- ⊛ www.interpet.co.uk

**Established** 1998

**Non-Fiction** Publishes General Non-fiction, How-to and Reference titles on the following subjects:
 Nature/Environment, Pet care.

**Tips** Interpet Publishing has over 2,000 available titles in its catalogue. Interpet Publishing's philosophy is to provide both new and experienced pet keepers with the advice and information they need to care for their pets responsibly. Its experienced authors write with authority across the entire spectrum of pet keeping.

## Inter-Varsity Press

Norton Street, Nottingham, NG7 3HR

☎ 0115 978 1054

✉ sales@ivpbooks.com

🌐 www.ivpbooks.com

**Contact** Chief Executive, Brian Wilson;
Commissioning Editor, Sandra Byatt; Senior Project
Editor, Eleanor Trotter

**Established** 1930s

**Imprint(s)** IVP
  Apollos
  Crossway

**Insider Info** Publishes 50 titles per year. Authors
paid by royalty. Aims to respond to proposals and
manuscripts within three months. Catalogue and
author guidelines are available online.

**Non-Fiction** Publishes General Non-fiction and
Scholarly titles on Religion and Spirituality.

**Submission Guidelines** Accepts query with SAE.
Submit proposal package (including, outline, two
sample chapters and author biography).
  Submission details to: et@ivpbooks.com

**Recent Title(s)** *Integrity*, Jonathan Lamb

**Tips** Inter–Varsity Press (IVP) is the publishing arm of
UCCF (Universities and Colleges Christian
Fellowship). IVP publish books that are true to the
Bible and that communicate the gospel, develop
discipleship and strengthen the church for its
mission in the world. IVP welcomes suggestions for
new books and are happy to evaluate any proposals
that are submitted. It is better to draft an overall plan
and then talk to a commissioning editor at IVP,
rather than writing the whole book, and then
approaching an editor.

## Iolo

38 Chaucer Road, Bedford, MK40 2AJ

☎ 01234 301718

☎ 01234 301718

✉ newplays@dedwyddjones.screaming.net

**Contact** Managing Director, Dedwydd Jones

**Non-Fiction** Publishes Booklets and General Non-
fiction on Welsh theatre.

**Tips** Iolo publishes Welsh theatre related books, and
also campaigns for a Welsh National Theatre. Ideas
are welcome in writing, providing they are on the
theme of Welsh theatre.

## Irish Academic Press Ltd

44 Northumberland Road, Dublin 4, Republic of
Ireland

☎ 020 8952 9526

☎ 020 8952 9242

✉ info@iap.ie

🌐 www.irishacademicireland.com

**Contact** Editor, Lisa Hyde

**Established** 1974

**Imprint** Irish University Press

**Insider Info** Publishes 15 titles per year. Payment via
royalty. Catalogue available online. Manuscript
guidelines are free on request.

**Non-Fiction** Publishes Irish Interest Scholarly titles
on the following subjects:
  Art/Architecture, History, Language/Literature,
Military/War, Heritage, Women's Studies, Literature
and Culture.

**Submission Guidelines** Accepts query with SAE, or
via email. Submit proposal package (including
outline and sample chapter(s)).
  Submission details to: lisa.hyde@vmbooks.com

**Recent Title(s)** *The Presumption of Innocence and
Irish Criminal Law*, Claire Hamilton

**Tips** Irish Academic Press is a long established
Dublin based publisher, producing high quality
books of Irish interest. They welcome manuscript
proposals and ideas in all publishing subject areas.
These can be directed to the Editor, Lisa Hyde.

## Irish Management Institue (IMI)

Sandyford Road, Dublin 16, Republic of Ireland

☎ 00353 1 207 8400

☎ 00353 1 295 5150

✉ reception@imi.ie

🌐 www.imi.ie

**Contact** Dr Tom McCarthy

**Non-Fiction** Publishes General Non-fiction,
Reference and Technical titles on Business/
Economics.

**Tips** Research led and business focused, IMI is a
central element in the architecture of Ireland's
knowledge economy, through its management
development and executive education
programmes. Access to information, new thinking
and best practice is a critical resource for
organisations competing in a challenging business
environment.

## Iron Press

5 Marden Terrace, Cullercoats, North Shields,
Northumberland, NE30 4PD

☎ 0191 253 1901

☎ 0191 253 1901

✉ contact@ironpress.co.uk

🌐 www.ironpress.co.uk

**Contact** Peter Mortimer

**Established** 1973

**Insider Info** Submissions accompanied by SAE will be returned. Contact for catalogue.

**Fiction** Publishes Plays, and any fiction liked by the editors.

  \* Iron Press' lists are full two years ahead for fiction, poetry and plays.

**Submission Guidelines** Query with Peter Mortimer before submission.

**Poetry** Publishes Poetry titles.

**Submission Guidelines** Query with Peter Mortimer before submission.

**Recent Title(s)** *Storm Short Stories*, Peter Slater; *Utter Nonsense*, Peter Mortimer

**Tips** Iron Press' policy is to seek new writers from the North of England, the rest of the country and occasionally from overseas. It spurns literary competitions, prizes and mass market fiction.

## Isis Publishing Ltd

**7 Centremead, Osney Mead, Oxford, OX2 0ES**

- 01865 250333
- 01865 790358
- sales@isis-publishing.co.uk
- www.isis-publishing.co.uk

**Insider Info** Authors paid by royalty. Catalogue available online.

**Non-Fiction** Publishes Audio books.

**Fiction** Publishes Audio books.

**Recent Title(s)** *The Dead Hour*, Denise Mina (Audio book)

**Tips** Isis is the world's leading publisher of unabridged audio books. Also publishes large print reprints, both fiction and non-fiction. Cannot accept any submissions, as Isis does not undertake original titles.

## The Islamic Foundation

**Markfield Conference Centre, Ratby Lane, Markfield, Leicestershire, LE67 9SY**

- 01530 244944
- 01530 244946
- i.foundation@islamic-foundation.org.uk
- www.islamic-foundation.org.uk/

**Insider Info** Catalogue available online.

**Non-Fiction** Publishes Audio cassettes, Children's/ Juvenile, General Non-fiction, Multimedia, Reference, Scholarly, Posters, Cards and Maps on Islam

**Tips** The Islamic Foundation was established in 1973 as a centre for education, training, research and publication. The foundation promotes the highest standards of academic research and publications related to Islam. They publish subjects relating to Islam, including history, economics, contemporary politics, women and family.

## The Ivy Group

**The Old Candlemakers, West Street, Lewes, East Sussex, BN7 2NZ**

- 01273 487440
- 01273 487441
- surname@ivy-group.co.uk
- www.ivy-group.co.uk

**Contact** Group Managing Director, Stephen Paul; Group Creative Director, Peter Bridgewater

**Imprint(s)** iball Press

 Ivy Press

 Ixos Press

 Ilex Press

 Bridgewater Books

**Insider Info** Payment is via fees.

**Non-Fiction** Publishes General Non-fiction, Illustrated and Reference titles on the following subjects:

 Popular Culture, Art and Design, Digital Design, Photography, General Reference, Health and Parenting, Mind, Body and Spirit, Humour, Novelty.

**Submission Guidelines** Accepts proposal package (including outline, table of contents, sample text, author biography).

**Recent Title(s)** *How to Read Buildings*, Dr Elizabeth Kirk (Ivy Press); *In 10 Simple Lessons: Feng Shui*, Jane Butler-Biggs (Ixos); *Complete Guide to Light and Lighting in Digital Photography*, Michael Freeman (Ilex)

**Tips** The group will consider proposals from both published and unpublished writers. They also occasionally have opportunities for freelance writers to work on specific projects. Send a biography, a list of published titles, and explain areas of interest and expertise.

## Ivy Press

**The Old Candlemakers, West Street, Lewes, East Sussex, BN7 2NZ**

- 01273 487440
- 01273 487441
- hook@ivy-group.co.uk
- www.ivypress.co.uk

**Parent Company** Ivy Group

**Contact** Publisher, Jason Hook

**Insider Info** Always pays fees for published work. Catalogue and author guidelines are available online.

**Non-Fiction** Publishes General Non-fiction and Illustrated titles on the following subjects:

Child Guidance/Parenting, Contemporary Culture, Cooking/Foods/Nutrition, Health/Medicine, House and Home, Lifestyle.

* A lifestyle and general reference imprint of the Ivy Group. Will consider proposals from any writer, published or unpublished.

**Submission Guidelines** Accepts query with SAE. Submit proposal package (including, outline, one sample chapter, your publishing history and an author biography).

Submission details to: authors@ivy-group.co.uk

**Recent Title(s)** *The Tarot Directory*, Annie Lionnet

**Tips** Publishes illustrated books for an international market, therefore books should have an international appeal.

## Ivy Publications

**72 Hyperion House, Somers Road, London, SW2 1HZ**

☎ 020 8671 6872

☎ 020 8671 3391

**Contact** Proprietor, Ian Burton-Simmonds

**Established** 1989

**Insider Info** Authors paid by royalty.

**Non-Fiction** Publishes Children's/Juvenile and General Non-fiction on the following subjects:
Education, History, Literary Criticism, Philosophy, Science, Travel.

**Submission Guidelines** Accepts query with SAE. Submit proposal package (including outline, two sample chapters and SAE).

**Fiction** Publishes Historical, Juvenile, Literary, Mainstream/Contemporary fiction, Multimedia, Film scripts.

**Submission Guidelines** Accepts query with SAE. Submit proposal package (including outline, two sample chapters and SAE).

**Tips** Proposals preferable to full manuscripts. Send two sample chapters, one being from the main body of the text.

## Ixos Press

**The Old Candlemakers, West Street, Lewes, East Sussex, BN7 2NZ**

☎ 01273 403128

☎ 01273 487441

✉ alexander@ixospress.com

🌐 www.ixospress.com

**Contact** Publisher, Daniel Alexander

**Insider Info** Always pays fees for published work. Catalogue available online.

**Non-Fiction** Publishes General Non-fiction, How-to, Illustrated and Self-help titles on the following subjects:
Counselling/Career, Health/Medicine, New Age, Religion, Spirituality, Mind, Body and Spirit.

**Submission Guidelines** Submit proposal package (including outline, author biography, table of contents and some sample text).
Submission details to: authors@ivy-group.co.uk

**Recent Titles** *Meditations from Conversations with God*, Neale Donald Walsch (Prayer and Spirituality); *500 Ways to Change the World*, The Global Ideas Bank (Social change); *20,000 Dreams*, Mary Summer Rain (Dream Analysis)

**Tips** Works with both published and unpublished authors, and will read all proposals relating to the relevant subject areas.

## J.A. Allen & Co.

**Clerkenwell House, 45–47 Clerkenwell Green, London, EC1R 0HT**

☎ 020 7251 2661

☎ 020 7490 4958

✉ allen@halebooks.com

🌐 www.halebooks.com

**Contact** Publisher, Caroline Burt; Commissioning Editor, Cassandra Campbell

**Established** 1926

**Insider Info** Publishes 20 titles per year. Authors paid by royalty. Catalogue and author guidelines are available free on request, via email or online.

**Non-Fiction** Publishes General Non-fiction, Reference and Technical titles on Equine and Equestrian subjects.

**Submission Guidelines** Accepts query with SAE. Submit proposal package (including outline, and three sample chapters). No email submissions.

**Tips** Caters for beginners and experts in the equine world, publishing both academic and more basic texts.

## Jacqui Small

**7 Greenland Street, London, NW1 0ND**

☎ 020 7284 7160

☎ 020 7845 4902

✉ sales@jacquismallpub.com

🌐 www.aurumpress.co.uk

**Parent Company** Aurum Press

**Contact** Managing Director, Bill McCreadie.

**Insider Info** Catalogue and manuscript guidelines are free on request, or available online or by email.

**Non-Fiction** Publishes Coffee table and Illustrated titles on the following subjects:

Cooking/Foods/Nutrition, Crafts, Gardening, House and Home, Lifestyle.

**Submission Guidelines** Email a brief proposal to editorial@aurumpress.co.uk.

**Recent Title(s)** *Hot Homes*, Suzanne Trocme (Interiors)

**Tips** Jacqui Small publishes a range of upmarket illustrated lifestyle books. The books are written by the best authors in their field, photographed by the best photographers in the world and designed and edited by a team of informed and creative people.

## James Clarke & Co
**PO Box 60, Cambridge, CB1 2NT**
- 01223 350865
- 01223 366951
- publishing@jamesclarke.co.uk
- www.jamesclarke.co.uk

**Parent Company** The Lutterworth Press
**Established** 1859
**Insider Info** Publishes 12 titles per year. Submissions accompanied by SAE will be returned. Catalogue available online or via email.
**Non-Fiction** Publishes General Non-fiction, Reference and Scholarly titles on the following subjects:
History, Humanities, Religion.
**Submission Guidelines** Accepts query with SAE. Submit proposal package (including outline, sample chapter(s), author biography and SAE). No email submissions but email queries welcomed.
**Recent Title(s)** *Images of the Church in the New Testament*, Paul S. Menear
**Tips** Please make sure submissions are presented in an easily readable format, no handwritten submissions. Only considers scholarly books on the humanities, focusing particularly on theology, history, or works of reference. James Clarke & Co. generally expect to take on books that offer some original scholarship, or alternatively present a well argued and authoritative case for a re-interpretation.

## James Currey Publishers
**73 Botley Road, Oxford, OX2 0BS**
- 01865 244111
- 01865 246454
- editorial@jamescurrey.co.uk
- www.jamescurrey.co.uk

**Contact** Chairman, James Currey; Managing Director and Editorial Director, Douglas H. Johnson (Anthropology, Archaeology, Economics, Development, History, Politics); Editorial Manager, Lynn Taylor (Literary Criticism, Theatre and Film)

**Established** 1985
**Insider Info** Authors paid by royalty. Catalogue and author guidelines available online.
**Non-Fiction** Publishes Scholarly titles on the following subjects:
Anthropology/Archaeology, Business/Economics, Government/Politics, History, Literary Criticism, Sociology.
* All books concern Africa and the Third World.
**Submission Guidelines** Accepts query with SAE. Submit proposal package (including outline, author biography and SAE).
Submission details to: douglas.johnson@jamescurrey.co.uk
**Recent Title(s)** *Melodies of Mourning*, Fiona Magowan
**Tips** James Currey Publishers are leading academic publishers on Africa, specialising in archaeology, history, politics, development studies, economics, anthropology, gender studies, literary criticism, theatre and film studies. James Currey Publishers welcomes proposals for consideration before submission of a manuscript. Initial enquiries may be sent by post or email. Please do not send email attachments unless requested by the publishers.

## James Nisbet & Co. Ltd
**Pirton Court, Prior's Hill, Hitchin, Hertfordshire, SG5 3QA**
- 01462 713444
- 01462 713444
- alison@jamesnisbet.demon.co.uk

**Contact** Director, E.M. Mackenzie-Wood
**Established** 1810
**Insider Info** Publishes books on business management.

## Jane's Information Group
**Sentinel House, 163 Brighton Road, Coulsdon, Surrey, CR5 2YH**
- 020 8700 3700
- 020 8763 1006
- customerservices.uk@janes.com
- www.janes.com

**Contact** Managing Director, Alfred Rolington
**Established** 1898
**Insider Info** Authors paid by royalty. Catalogue available online.
**Non-Fiction** Publishes General Non-fiction, Reference and Technical titles on Military/War.
**Submission Guidelines** Accepts query with SAE. Submit proposal package (including outline and sample chapter(s)).

**Tips** Jane's Information Group is a world leading provider of intelligence and analysis on national and international defence, security and risk developments. Jane's is an independent organisation with an unrivalled reputation for accuracy, authority and impartiality.

## Jarrold Publishing
### Whitefriars, Norwich, NR3 1JR
- 01603 763300
- 01603 662748
- info@jarrold-publishing.co.uk
- www.jarrold-publishing.co.uk

**Contact** Managing Director, Margot Russell-King
**Established** 1770
**Imprint(s)** Pitkin
 Unichrome
**Insider Info** Publishes 30 titles per year. Catalogue available online.
**Non-Fiction** Biography, General Non-fiction, Guidebooks and Illustrated titles on the following subjects:
 History, Hobbies, Travel, Walking and Tourism.
**Submission Guidelines** Accepts query with SAE.
**Recent Title(s)** *Nelson*, Colin White and John McIlwain
**Tips** Jarrold Publishing has around 250 books currently in print, including walking and travel guides, history, biography and pictorial guides. Contact the editorial department before sending any submissions.

## Jessica Kingsley Publishers Ltd
### 116 Pentonville Road, London, N1 9JB
- 020 7833 2307
- 020 7837 2917
- post@jkp.com
- www.jkp.com

**Contact** Managing Director and Publisher, Jessica Kingsley; Senior Acquisitions Editor, Stephen Jones
**Established** 1987
**Insider Info** Publishes 100 titles per year. Receives approximately 500 queries and 30 manuscripts per year. 20 per cent of books published are from first-time authors and 99 per cent are from unagented authors. Authors paid by royalty (on wholesale price) with an advance offered. Average lead time is five months with simultaneous submissions not accepted. Aims to respond to proposals in one month and manuscripts within three months. Catalogue and author guidelines available online.

**Non-Fiction** Publishes General Non-fiction, Reference, Scholarly and Technical titles on the following subjects:
 Counselling/Career, Health/Medicine, Psychology, Disability, Mental illness.
**Submission Guidelines** Accepts query with SAE. Submit proposal package (including outline, author biography, your CV/resumé, and a completed copy of the 'New Book Proposals' form, available on the website).
**Recent Title(s)** *All Cats Have Asperger Syndrome*, Kathy Hoopmann
**Tips** Jessica Kingsley publish books for professional and general readers in a range of subjects. It is well known for its long established lists on the autism spectrum, social work, and on the arts therapies. More recently, they have published extensively in the fields of mental health, counselling, palliative care, and practical theology. Ideas for new books in the areas in which it publishes are welcome.

## John Blake Publishing Ltd
### 3 Bramber Court, 2 Bramber Road, London, W14 9PB
- 020 7381 0666
- 020 7381 6868
- words@blake.co.uk
- www.blake.co.uk

**Contact** Managing Director, John Blake; Editor in Chief, Michelle Signore
**Established** 1991
**Insider Info** Publishes 100 titles per year. Authors paid by royalty. Aims to respond to proposals and manuscripts within three months. Catalogue and author guidelines are free on request, or available online.
**Non-Fiction** Publishes Autobiography, Biography and General Non-fiction titles on the following subjects:
 Contemporary Culture, Cooking/Foods/Nutrition, Government/Politics, Health/Medicine, Spirituality, Celebrity Memoirs.
**Submission Guidelines** Accepts query with SAE. Submit proposal package (including outline, two sample chapters, your publishing history, author biography and SAE).
**Recent Title(s)** *Kylie – Story Of A Survivor*, Emily Herbert (Biography)
**Tips** John Blake Publishing specialises in high profile, mass market non-fiction. The bulk of its output centres on the biography and true crime lists, including the phenomenally successful true crime library and *Hard Men* series of books, as well as the ever popular stars, media and sports personality

**235**

titles. If you would like to submit your work for consideration, please check the website for guidelines and do not send a full manuscript. The commissioning criterion is, 'Could it be a bestseller?'

## John Donald Publishers Ltd
**West Newington House, 10 Newington Road, Edinburgh, EH9 1QS**
- 0131 668 4371
- 0131 668 4466
- info@birlinn.co.uk
- www.birlinn.co.uk

**Contact** Managing Director, Hugh Andrew
**Established** 1999
**Insider Info** Publishes 20 titles per year. Authors paid by royalty. Catalogue and author guidelines available online.
**Non-Fiction** Publishes General Non-fiction, Reference and Scholarly titles on the following areas: Anthropology/Archaeology, Art/Architecture, History, Regional, Social Sciences, Travel.
**Submission Guidelines** No unsolicited submissions.
**Recent Title(s)** *A Canticle of Love*, John Watts
**Tips** John Donald specialises in academic books on Scottish subjects, and the local history of East coast Scotland. It cannot accept any unsolicited submissions, and request that you do not send manuscripts or synopses for books at the moment. Check the website again at a later date.

## John Libbey Publishing
**PO Box 276, Eastleigh, SO50 5YS**
- 023 8065 0208
- 023 8065 0259
- john.libbey@libertysurf.fr
- www.johnlibbey.com

**Contact** Publisher, John Libbey
**Established** 1979
**Imprint(s)** John Libbey Eurotext Ltd (France)
**Insider Info** Catalogue is free on request, or available online.
**Non-Fiction** Publishes General Non-fiction, Reference and Scholarly titles on the following subjects: Art/Architecture, Cinema, Animation and Media, Medical.
**Submission Guidelines** Accepts query with SAE.
**Recent Title(s)** *Unsung Heroes of Animation*, Chris Robinson
**Tips** John Libbey Publishing publishes a range of books and journals for researchers, academics, students and professionals in the fields of cinema, animation and media. John Libbey also publishes the renowned series of *Media* books, formerly under the imprint of University of Luton Press.

## John Murray
**338 Euston Road, London, NW1 3BH**
- 020 7873 6000
- 020 7873 6024
- www.hodderheadline.co.uk

**Parent Company** Hodder Headline Ltd
**Established** 1768
**Insider Info** Catalogue available online.
**Non-Fiction** Publishes Biography and General Non-fiction titles on the following subjects: History, Memoirs, Travel, Current Affairs.
**Submission Guidelines** Agented submissions only.
**Fiction** Publishes Literary fiction.
**Submission Guidelines** Agented submissions only.
**Recent Title(s)** *Woman's Hour: From Joyce Grenfell to Sharon Osbourne*, Various; *The Brief History of the Dead*, Kevin Brockmeier (Fiction)

## Jonathan Cape
**Random House, 20 Vauxhall Bridge Road, London, SW1V 2SA**
- 020 7840 8563
- 020 7233 6117
- capeeditorial@randomhouse.co.uk
- www.randomhouse.co.uk

**Parent Company** The Random House Group Ltd
**Contact** Publishing Director, Dan Franklin
**Established** 1921
**Insider Info** Catalogue available online, use advanced search to search the online catalogue by imprint.
**Non-Fiction** Publishes titles on the following subjects: Government/Politics, History, Memoirs, Military/War, Photography, Travel, Current Affairs.
**Submission Guidelines** Accepts query with SAE/proposal package (including outline, one sample chapter and SAE), and artworks/images (send photocopies).
**Fiction** Publishes Literary, Picture books, Poetry, Children's fiction.
**Submission Guidelines** As for Non-fiction.
**Poetry** Publishes poetry titles.
 * Only publish around four-six titles per year.
**Submission Guidelines** Submit 40-60 sample poems.
**Recent Title(s)** *The Great Man Sir Robert Walpole*, Edward Pearce (Biography/Political); *Sunstroke and Other Stories*, Tessa Hadley (Modern fiction)

**Tips** Do not accept email submissions. Although unagented submissions are accepted, it is very unlikely that any will end up being published.

## Jonathan Cape Children's Books
**61–63 Uxbridge Road, London, W5 5SA**

- 020 7840 8648
- 020 7233 6058
- childrenseditorial@randomhouse.co.uk
- www.randomhouse.co.uk/childrens

**Parent Company** Random House Children's Books
**Insider Info** Catalogue is available online.
**Non-fiction** Publishes Children's and Young Adult titles on the following subjects:
Diary, General Interest, Interactive, Miscellaneous, Stationary.
**Fiction** Publishes Children's and Young Adult novels.
**Submission Guidelines** Accepts proposal package (including outline and one sample chapter).
**Recent Title(s)** *Roald Dahl Diary 2007*, Roald Dahl (Diary).
**Tips** Agented submissions are strongly preferred.

## Jordan Publishing Ltd
**21 St. Thomas Street, Bristol, BS1 6JS**

- 0117 923 0600
- 0117 925 0486
- achim.bosse@jordanpublishing.co.uk
- www.jordanpublishing.co.uk

**Contact** Managing Director, Caroline Vandridge-Ames
**Insider Info** Catalogue available online.
**Non-Fiction** Publishes Reference and Technical titles on the subject of Law.
**Recent Title(s)** *Companies Act 2006: The New Law*, Alistair Alcock (John Birds and Steve Gale)
**Tips** Jordan Publishing Ltd is the UK's leading privately owned law publisher. Under the Jordans and Family Law imprints, we have a reputation for providing a high standard of customer service in legal publishing, and we pride ourselves on being able to respond quickly to customer's needs.

## Josef Weinberger Plays Ltd
**12–14 Mortimer Street, London, W1T 3JJ**

- 020 7580 2827
- 020 7436 9016
- general.info@jwmail.co.uk
- www.josef-weinberger.com

**Contact** Editor, Christopher Moss
**Established** 1885

**Insider Info** Publishes 12 titles per year. Catalogue available online.
**Fiction** Publishes Plays.
**Tips** We publish the best of musical and dramatic theatre and music from the West End, Broadway and Concert Hall. We would only consider acquiring rights to a new play in the event that a large scale professional production is planned or underway. We then publish the script to coincide with the opening performance, and handle subsidiary rights on future productions.

## Kahn & Averill
**9 Harrington Road, London, SW7 3ES**

- 020 8743 3278
- 020 8743 3278
- kahn@averill23.freeserve.co.uk

**Contact** Managing Director, M. Khan
**Established** 1967
**Insider Info** Payment via royalties.
**Non-Fiction** Publishes General Non-fiction titles on the subject of Music/Dance.
**Submission Guidelines** Accepts query with SAE/proposal package (including outline and SAE).
**Tips** Originally published children's books, but now publishes only music books. Other categories in which they used to publish have now been dropped.

## Karnak House
**157 Dudden Hill Lane, London, NW10 1AU**

- 020 8830 8301
- 020 8830 8301
- karnakhouse@aol.com
- www.karnakhouse.co.uk

**Contact** Dr. Amon Saba Saakana
**Established** 1979
**Imprint(s)** The Intef Institute
**Insider Info** Publishes seven titles per year. Receives approximately 30 queries and 20 manuscripts per year. 15 per cent of books published are from first-time authors, 100 per cent of books published are from unagented authors. Payment is via royalty (on wholesale price), with 0.08 (per £) minimum. Advance offered is from £200 to £500. Average lead time is more than 18 months, with simultaneous submissions accepted. Submissions accompanied by SAE will be returned. Aims to respond to queries within seven days, proposals within 14 days and manuscripts within four months. Catalogue is available online. Manuscript guidelines are available by email.

**Non-Fiction** Publishes General Non-fiction (African/Caribbean context) titles on the following subjects: Anthropology/Archaeology, Art/Architecture, Communications, Contemporary Culture, Education, Egyptology, Health/Medicine, History, Language/Literature, Literary Criticism, Music/Dance, Philosophy, Religion, Science, Sociology, Women's Issues/Studies, Academic.

 * Specialists in African and Caribbean Studies. No other subject area should be submitted.

**Submission Guidelines** Accepts query with SAE/proposal package (including outline, contents page, two sample chapters and SAE).

**Fiction** Publishes African/Caribbean and Children's Fiction titles.

**Submission Guidelines** Accepts query with SAE/proposal package (including outline, contents page, two sample chapters and SAE).

**Poetry** Publishes African/Caribbean Poetry titles.

## The Kates Hill Press

**126 Watson's Green Road, Kates Hill, Dudley, West Midlands, DY2 7LG**

- 01384 255973
- 01384 255973
- kateshillpress@blueyonder.co.uk
- www.kateshillpress.pwp.blueyonder.co.uk

**Contact** Greg Stokes
**Established** 1992
**Insider Info** Payment is via royalties.
**Non-Fiction** Publishes Social Histories of the West Midlands.
**Submission Guidelines** Accepts proposal package (including outline and sample chapter(s)).
**Fiction** Publishes Regional and Short story collections on a West Midlands theme, or by a West Midlands writer.
**Submission Guidelines** Accepts proposal package (including sample chapter(s)).
**Poetry** Publishes Poetry titles with a West Midlands connection.
**Submission Guidelines** Submit sample poems.
**Recent Title(s)** *A Pack of Saftness*, Greg Stokes; *Cor Yow Shurrup a Minit Billy!,* Billy Spakemon
**Tips** The Kates Hill Press cannot begin work on any new books until Summer 2007, but are still accepting proposals. Any work submitted should also be available in electronic format. Responses to proposals may take a while as the press is a part time venture.

## Kenilworth Press

**Addington, Buckingham, Buckinghamshire, MK18 4R**

- 01296 715101
- 01296 715148
- editorial@kenilworthpress.co.uk
- www.kenilworthpress.co.uk

**Contact** Managing Director, Andrew Johnston
**Established** 1989
**Insider Info** Publishes ten titles per year. Ten per cent of books published are from first-time authors and 95 percent of books published are from unagented authors. Approximately five per cent of books are author subsidy published. Payment is via royalty (on wholesale price or royalty on retail price). Average time between acceptance of book length manuscripts and publication is two months. Simultaneous submissions accepted, and submissions accompanied by SAE will be returned. Catalogue is free on request online, www.countrybooksdirect.com/section.php?xSec=38&xTemplates=templates2/ and via email.
**Non-Fiction** Publishes General Non-fiction and Illustrated titles on the following subjects: Equestrian.

 * Publish the British Horse Society Official Books and the famous *Threshold Picture Guides*. Books cover all disciplines, Riding and Training, Dressage, Eventing, Show Jumping, Driving and Polo, Hunting, Endurance, Horse Care (covering Health, Management and Alternative Care), and Lifestyle and Young Riders.
**Submission Guidelines** Accepts query with SAE/proposal package (including, outline, sample chapter(s), publishing history, author biography) and artworks/images (send photocopies or digital files as jpegs).
**Recent Title(s)** *Homeopathy for Horses*, Tim Couzens
**Tips** Kenilworth will accept proposals, but only for horse or pony related material.

## Kenneth Mason Publications Ltd

**The Book Barn, Westbourne, Hampshire, PO10 8RS**

- 01243 377977
- 01243 379136
- info@researchdisclosure.com
- www.researchdisclosure.com

**Contact** Chairman, Kenneth Mason; Managing Director, Piers Mason
**Established** 1958
**Imprint(s)** Boatswain Press
Research Disclosure

**Insider Info** Publishes 15 titles per year. Payment is via royalties. Catalogue available online.

**Non-Fiction** Publishes General Non-fiction and Scholarly titles on the following subjects: Cooking/Foods/Nutrition, Health/Medicine, Fitness and Nutrition, Nautical.

**Submission Guidelines** Accepts query with SAE/proposal package (including outline).

**Tips** Every month we publish details of many inventions, both in our paper format *RD Journal* and also in our RD electronic database. These details are then distributed to every major patent office, and many libraries worldwide. Provide us with the disclosure text, along with any diagrams and illustrations you wish to include, in either paper copy or as an electronic file, and we'll do the rest.

## Kettillonia

**Sidlaw House, South Street, Newtyle, Angus, PH12 8UQ**

📞 01828 650615

✉ james@kettillonia.co.uk

🌐 www.kettillonia.co.uk

**Contact** James Robertson

**Established** 1999

**Fiction** Publishes Short story collections.

**Poetry** Publish a very diverse range of prose and poetry.

**Tips** Kettillonia's aim is to put 'original, adventurous, neglected and rare writing into print'. Their pamphlets are £3 each and vary tremendously in style and content.

## Kevin Mayhew Publishers

**Buxhall, Stowmarket, Suffolk, IP14 3BW**

📞 01449 737978

📞 01449 737834

✉ info@kevinmayhewltd.com

🌐 www.kevinmayhewltd.com

**Contact** Chairman/Commissioning Editor, Kevin Mayhew

**Established** 1976

**Imprint(s)** Palmtree Press

**Insider Info** Payment is via royalties. Catalogue free on request, online. Manuscript guidelines available online.

**Non-Fiction** Publishes Audio cassettes, Children's, General Non-fiction and Multimedia titles on the following subjects: Music/Dance (Sacred/Religious Music), Hymns, Religion.

**Submission Guidelines** Accepts query with SAE/proposal package (including outline, one sample chapter and SAE).

**Recent Title(s)** *Funky Flute*, Heather Hammond (Music)

**Tips** The company holds a unique position, in that its products are owned and trusted in equal measure by members of all Christian denominations. Whilst we continue to strive and pray for unity within the Church, we believe that it is possible to serve the whole Church of God - indeed many of our products enjoy broad appeal across the many streams. Please note that online submissions are not accepted, and we require a hard copy of all manuscripts, together with a one page synopsis.

## Kingfisher Publications Plc

**New Penderel House, 283–288 High Holborn, London, WC1V 7HZ**

📞 020 7903 9999

📞 020 7903 4979

🌐 www.kingfisherpub.com

**Parent Company** Houghton Mifflin Co (see entry under European & International Publishers)

**Established** 1973

**Insider Info** Catalogue available online or by email.

**Non-Fiction** Publishes Children's, Encyclopedias, Activity Books and Reference titles on the following subjects: History, Language/Literature, Nature/Environment, Religion, Science, Maths, Technology.

**Fiction** Publishes Humour, Juvenile, Picture books, Pre-school, Toddler, Gift and Children's titles.

**Poetry** Publishes Children's Poetry.

**Recent Title(s)** *British History Early Britain* Kingfisher; *Zodiac Girls Recipe for Rebellion*, Cathy Hopkins (Gift Book)

**Tips** Kingfisher is part of the American, Boston based publisher Houghton Mifflin Co. It is well know for its children's educational reference titles and picture books. Kingfisher does not accept unsolicited material.

## Kinglake Publishing

**5 George Avenue, Huddersfield, West Yorkshire, HD2 2BD**

📞 01484 535283

✉ kinglakepublishing@googlemail.com

🌐 Under construction

**Contact** Commissioning Editor, R.S. Byram (Non-Fiction); Commissioning Editor, H.L. Byram (Fiction & Educational)

**Established** 2004

**Imprint(s)** Kinglake Non-Fiction
Kinglake Religion
Kinglake Fiction

**Insider Info** Publishes 30 titles per year. Receives approximately 250 queries and 80 manuscripts per year. Five per cent of books published are from first-time authors, ten per cent of books published are from unagented authors. Five per cent of books published are author subsidy-published, based on an estimation of market reach. Payment is via royalty (on retail price), with 0.08 (per £) minimum and 0.12 (per £) maximum. Does not offer an advance. Average lead time is six months, with simultaneous submissions not accepted. Submissions accompanied by SAE will be returned. Aims to respond to queries within two days, proposals within five days and manuscripts within 14 days. Catalogue is available with an SAE, or by email. Manuscript guidelines are available by email.

**Non-Fiction** Publishes Autobiography, Biography, Booklets, Children's/Juvenile, General Non-fiction, How-to, Humour and Self-help titles on the following subjects:
 Business/Economics (General readership), Contemporary Culture (General readership), Counselling/Career, Education, Health/Medicine (Practical and Common Sense), History, Humanities, Memoirs, Nature/Environment, New Age, Nostalgia, Religion (Judaeo-Christian tradition), Spirituality, Young Adult (General and niche markets).

**Submission Guidelines** Accepts initial queries by email only (including outline and short letter).

**Fiction** Publishes Gothic, Historical, Humour, Children's, Literary, Mainstream/Contemporary, Mystery, Religious, Romance, Spiritual, Suspense and Young Adult titles.
 * Kinglake looks for quality in narrative and dialogue.

**Submission Guidelines** Accepts initial queries by email only (including outline and short letter).

**Recent Title(s)** *The Life of the Spider: The Life of the Fly*, J. Henri Fabre (Non-fiction); *The Hunting Lodge*, Max Leins (Fiction)

**Tips** Kinglake publishes books for a popular/general readership, or carefully worked out niche market. Initial queries must be by email.

## The King's England Press
**Cambertown House, Commercial Road, Goldthorpe, Rotherham, S63 9BL**
- 01484 663790
- 01484 663790
- sales@kingsengland.com
- www.kingsengland.com

**Established** 1989

**Insider Info** Submissions accompanied by SAE will be returned. Catalogue and manuscript guidelines available online.

**Non-Fiction** Publishes Anthropology/Archaeology, History, Regional and Folklore titles.

**Submission Guidelines** No unsolicited manuscripts will be accepted until 2008. Check the website for updates on this situation.

**Poetry** Publishes Children's Poetry titles.
 * Publishes the *Potty Poetry* series only (A5, 64-page books, illustrated by black and white line drawings for children).

**Submission Guidelines** No unsolicited manuscripts will be accepted until 2008.

**Recent Title(s)** *Arthur Mee and the Strength of Britain*, Maisie Robson; *Mum, the Dog's Drunk Again*, Gez Walsh

**Tips** Detailed guidelines as to how to submit manuscripts are available on the website, which will also announce when they will start accepting manuscripts again (2008 at the earliest).

## Kittiwake
**3 Glantwymyn Village Workshops, Glantwymyn, Machynlleth, Montgomereyshire, SY20 8LY**
- 01650 511314
- 01650 511314
- perrographics@btconnect.com

**Contact** Director, David Perrott (Welsh Walking Guides)

**Established** 1984

**Insider Info** Publishes six titles per year. Receives approximately two queries and six manuscripts per year. 40 per cent of books published are from first-time authors, 100 per cent of books published are from unagented authors. Payment is via royalty (on retail price), with 0.05 (per £) minimum and 0.10 (per £) maximum. Average lead time is six months, with simultaneous submissions not accepted. Submissions accompanied by SAE will be returned. Aims to respond to queries, proposals and all other enquiries within five days, and to manuscripts within four weeks. Catalogue is available with an SAE, or by email. Manuscripts guidelines are available with an SAE.

**Non-Fiction** Publishes General Non-fiction titles on the following subjects:
 Regional (Welsh), Welsh walking guides.

**Submission Guidelines** Accepts queries with SAE, and artworks/images (send photocopies, digital files as jpegs).

## Knockabout Comics

**10 Acklam Road, London, W10 5QZ**

- 020 8969 2945
- 020 8968 7614
- knockcomic@aol.com

**Contact** Editor, Carol Bennett; Editor, Tony Bennett
**Established** 1975
**Non-Fiction** Publishes Comics/Graphic novels.

## Kogan Page

**120 Pentonville Road, London, N1 9JN**

- 020 7278 0433
- 020 7837 6348
- kpinfo@kogan-page.co.uk
- www.kogan-page.co.uk

**Contact** Managing Director, Philip Kogan; Publishing Director, Pauline Goodwin; Publishing Director, Helen Kogan
**Insider Info** Publishes 130 titles per year. Catalogue and manuscript guidelines are available online.
**Non-Fiction** Publishes Reference and Technical titles on the following subjects:
 Branding, Careers, Finance, General Reference, Human Resources, Logistics, Management, Marketing, Personal Development, Personal Finance, Property, Sales, Training, Transport.
 * Kogan Page publishes titles at every level, from basic skills to high level academic and professional texts.
**Submission Guidelines** Accepts proposal package (including outline, synopsis, one sample chapter, market research and author biography).
**Recent Title(s)** *The Independent Schools Guide 2007-2008*, GABBITAS (Reference); *Profitable Marketing Communications: A Guide to Marketing Return on Investment*, Antony Young and Lucy Aitken (Marketing)
**Tips** Kogan Page is Europe's largest independent publisher of business titles, and has had a significant international presence for more than 35 years. Most of Kogan Page's books have a global readership, selling in English and foreign language editions.

## Kyle Cathie Ltd

**122 Arlington Road, London, NW1 7HP**

- 020 7692 7215
- 020 7692 7260
- general.enquiries@kyle-cathie.com
- www.kylecathie.co.uk

**Contact** Managing Director, Kyle Cathie
**Established** 1990

**Insider Info** Publishes 25 tiles per year. Receives approximately 300 queries per year. 15 per cent of books published are from first-time authos and 10 per cent are from unagented authors. Payment is via royalties (on retail price) of between 0.05 and 0.125 (per £). An advance is offered. Average lead time is six months with simultaneous submissions accepted. Aims to respond to proposals within one month and manuscripts within two months. Catalogue available online. Manuscript guidelines available online.
**Non-Fiction** Publishes Cookbooks, General Non-fiction and Illustrated titles in the following subjects:
 Cooking/Foods/Nutrition, Crafts, Gardening, Health/Medicine, Hobbies, House and Home, Spirituality.
**Submission Guidelines** Agented submissions only.
**Recent Title(s)** *The GI Counter*, Mabel Blades (Cooking/Foods/Nutrition)
**Tips** Kyle Cathie's aim is to produce the highest quality non-fiction titles. Books combine authoritative text with cutting edge design, inspirational photography and the highest possible production values. They particularly look for books which will have a long life, which contribute something new to the marketplace and which have a strong publicity angle. It is generally best to submit your work via a literary agent, as they are not able to consider all the unsolicited manuscripts they are sent.

## Ladybird Books

**80 Strand, London, WC2R 0RL**

- 020 7010 3000
- 020 7010 6060
- ladybird@uk.penguingroup.com
- www.ladybird.co.uk

**Parent Company** Penguin Group (UK)
**Insider Info** Submissions accompanied by SAE will be returned. Catalogue and manuscript guidelines are available online.
**Non-Fiction** Publishes Children's Illustrated books with an emphasis on key skills and home learning.
**Submission Guidelines** Accepts queries with SAE or submit completed manuscript and any artworks/images (send digital files as jpegs).
**Fiction** Publishes Children's and Picture book titles, including classic tales.
 * Most Ladybird story titles tend to be part of an already established series.
**Submission Guidelines** Accepts query with SAE or submit completed manuscript.
**Recent Title(s)** *Topsy and Tim - Car Games*, Jean Adamson; *Dick Whittington*, Ladybird Tales

**Tips** The well known Ladybird list covers illustrated books for Children aged 0–8 years old, with an emphasis on key skills and home learning. The list also encompasses classic children's stories and children's favourites, such as Meg and Mog, and Angelina Ballerina.

## Landmark Publishing Ltd

**Ashbourne Hall, Cockayne Avenue, Ashbourne, DE6 1EJ**

- 01335 347349
- 01335 347303
- landmark@clara.net
- www.landmarkpublishing.co.uk

**Contact** Managing Director, C.L.M. Porter
**Established** 1996
**Insider Info** Publishes 50 titles per year. Payment is via royalties. Catalogue available online.
**Non-Fiction** Publishes General Non-fiction titles on the following subjects:
History, Nature/Environment, Regional, Travel.
**Recent Title(s)** *RNLI Motor Lifeboats*, Nicholas Leach
**Tips** Publishes itinerary based travel guidebooks and local interest books.

## Laurence King Publishing

**4th Floor, 361–373 City Road, London, EC1V 1LR**

- 020 7841 6900
- 020 7841 6910
- enquiries@laurenceking.co.uk
- www.laurenceking.co.uk

**Contact** Editorial Director, Philip Cooper (Architecture, Interior Design); Senior Commissioning Editor, Jo Lightfoot (Design, Graphics); Commissioning Editor, Helen Evans (Design, Fashion)
**Insider Info** Publishes 50 titles per year. Catalogue is free on request.
**Non-Fiction** Publishes General Non-fiction and Illustrated titles on the following subjects:
Art/Architecture, Contemporary Culture, Design, Fashion.
**Tips** Laurence King publishes books for both business professionals and students, as well as for a more general readership.

## Lawrence & Wishart Ltd

**99a Wallis Road, London, E9 5LN**

- 020 8533 2506
- 020 8533 7369
- office@lwbooks.co.uk
- www.lwbooks.co.uk

**Contact** Managing Editor, Sally Davison
**Established** 1936
**Insider Info** Publish ten titles per year. Payment is via royalties. Catalogue available online.
**Non-Fiction** Publishes General Non-fiction titles on the following subjects:
Business/Economics, Education, Government/Politics, History, World Affairs.
**Submission Guidelines** Accepts query with SAE.
Submission details to: sally@lwbooks.co.uk
**Recent Title(s)** *After Blair: Politics after the New Labour Decade*, Gerry Hassan ed. (Politics)
**Tips** We started life through the merger of Martin Lawrence, the Communist Party's press and Wishart Ltd, a family owned liberal and anti-fascist publisher. Although L&W has changed in many ways, we continue to believe that serious critical thought is a crucial, but often missing part of politics. We hope you will agree that the titles we publish contribute to an understanding of the past, as well as reflecting an engagement with the present and future. An aggressively independent publisher, L&W books have a reputation for being radically political.

## Leaf Books

**GTi Suite, Valleys Innovation Centre, Navigation Park, Abercynon, RCT, CF45 4SN**

- 01443 665704
- contact@leafbooks.co.uk
- http://leafbooks.co.uk

**Insider Info** Submissions accompanied by SAE will be returned. Aims to respond to manuscripts within three weeks.
**Non-Fiction** Publishes pocket sized non-fiction.
**Submission Guidelines** No unsolicited non-fiction at present.
**Fiction** Publishes Short story collections, Novellas, Children's short stories.
* There is currently a call for submissions of novellas, no email submissions. Any other unsolicited fiction is not accepted. Check the website for details of competitions for when fiction is accepted periodically.
**Submission Guidelines** Accepts query with SAE/proposal package (including first 50 pages of the novella, double spaced, with full contact details). Send a stamped addressed postcard if you require acknowledgement of the manuscript.
**Poetry** * No unsolicited poetry at present. Check the website for details of competitions, when poetry submissions are periodically accepted.
**Recent Title(s)** *Barry's Barnet*, Gareth Rafferty; *Razzamatazz and Other Poems*, Various

**Tips** Leaf Books hold regular competitions for unpublished writers (including web publishing). Winners are often published in A5 sized anthologies and pocket sized A6 books. Entry guidelines are available on the website, as are the latest closing dates. They are generally for short stories of various genres, or poetry. Although restricted to novellas currently, future calls for submissions outside of the competitions will also be advertised on the site.

## The Learning Institute

**Overbrook Business Centre, Poolbridge Road, Blackford, Wedmore, BS28 4PA**

- 0800 781 1715
- main_index_pageUK@inst.org
- www.inst.org

**Contact** Managing Director, Kit Sadgrove

**Established** 1994

**Insider Info** Payment is via royalties. Catalogue available online. Manuscript guidelines available via SAE.

**Non-Fiction** Publishes Multimedia and Scholarly titles on the following titles:
 Education (Interior design), Garden Design and Horticulture, Writing, Complementary Therapies and Catering.
 * The Learning Institute produces vocational home-study courses for people wanting to work from home, or change their career.

**Recent Title(s)** *Diploma in Private Investigation*, Learning Institute

**Tips** Printed materials are often supported by web-based resources. All written material must work towards the courses the company run.

## Learning Matters Ltd

**33 Southernhay East, Exeter, EX1 1NX**

- 01392 215560
- 01392 215561
- info@learningmatters.co.uk
- www.learningmatters.co.uk

**Contact** Julia Morris (Education); Di Page (Social Work)

**Insider Info** Catalogue available online. Manuscript guidelines available online.

**Non-Fiction** Publishes Textbook and Scholarly titles on the following subjects:
 Counselling/Career, Education, Law, Social Service.

**Submission Guidelines** Accepts query with SAE/proposal package (including outline).
 Submission details to: editor@learningmatters.co.uk

**Recent Title(s)** *Inspiring Primary Teaching*, Denis Hayes (Educational)

**Tips** As publishers, particularly in the field of teacher training, we primarily supply books for education and social services. As a new company we are keen to talk to authors with ideas for new books. You will also be encouraged to help us with the marketing of your book. Often you will know where and how the book can be promoted better than we do, so we're pleased when authors phone us and ask whether we have made the most of every possible opportunity.

## Leckie & Leckie

**4 Queen Street, Edinburgh, EH2 1JF**

- 0131 220 6831
- 0131 225 9987
- enquiries@leckieandleckie.co.uk
- www.leckieandleckie.co.uk

**Parent Company** Huveaux

**Contact** Publishing Director, Sarah Mitchell (Secondary Education); Assistant Publisher, John MacPherson (Secondary Education)

**Established** 1989

**Insider Info** Publishes 250 titles per year. Receives approximately 30 queries and 30 manuscripts per year. Five per cent of books published are from first-time authors, 100 per cent of books published are from unagented authors. Payment is via royalty (on wholesale price). Advance offered is from £500 to £2,000. Average lead time is nine months, with simultaneous submissions accepted. Submissions accompanied by SAE will be returned. Aims to respond to queries within five days and to proposals and manuscripts within four weeks. Catalogue is free on request and available online or by email.

**Non-Fiction** Publishes Scholarly and Textbook titles on the following subjects:
 Education (Scottish specific), and Scottish Secondary and Further Education.

**Submission Guidelines** Accepts proposal package (including outline, one sample chapters, a proposal rationale, your publishing history and SAE), and artworks/images (send photocopies).
 Submission details to: john.macpherson@ leckieandleckie.co.uk

**Tips** Submissions must be specifically tailored to fit with the Scottish education system. Audiences will include Scottish secondary school teachers and students.

## Legend Press Ltd

**13a Northwold Road, London, N16 7HL**

- 020 7249 6901
- info@legendpress.co.uk

ⓦ www.legendpress.co.uk
**Contact** Managing Director, Tom Chalmers (Contemporary Fiction); Publishing Executive, Emma Howard (General Fiction)
**Established** 2005
**Insider Info** Publishes five titles per year. Receives approximately 500 queries and 300 manuscripts per year. 80 per cent of books published are from first-time authors, 80 per cent of books published are from unagented authors. Payment is via royalty (on wholesale price), with 0.08 (per £) minimum and 0.15 per cent (per £) maximum, or via royalty (on retail price), with 0.05 (per £) minimum and 0.09 (per £) maximum. Advance offered is from £1,000 to £5,000. Average lead time is six months, with simultaneous submissions accepted. Submissions will not be returned. Aims to respond to queries with five days, proposals within ten days and manuscripts withing six weeks. Catalogue is available with an A4 SAE, or by email. Manuscript guidelines are available online or by email.
**Fiction** Publishes Literary and Mainstream/Contemporary titles, as well as Short story collections (Within the Legend Short story series).
 * Legend Press publishes cutting edge contemporary fiction, both commercial and literary, for modern readers, and also a short story series.
**Submission Guidelines** Accepts proposal package (including outline, three to four sample chapters and a full synopsis).
**Recent Title(s)** *Salt & Honey*, Candi Miller (Literary fiction)
**Tips** Submissions are judged on a book by book basis, although they should generally be aimed at the mainstream, modern reader.

## Leo Cooper
**47 Church Street, Barnsley, S70 2AS**
ⓣ 01226 734639
ⓕ 01226 734478
ⓔ enquiries@pen-and-sword.co.uk
ⓦ www.pen-and-sword.co.uk
**Insider Info** Catalogue available online.
**Non-Fiction** Publishes General Non-fiction on the following subjects:
 History, Military/War.
**Submission Guidelines** Accepts query with SAE. Submission details to: editorialoffice@pen-and-sword.co.uk
**Tips** Formerly run by Jilly Cooper's husband, Leo, Pen & Sword continue to publish military history books under the Leo Cooper imprint. No unsolicited manuscripts.

## Letts Educational
**Chiswick Centre, 414 Chiswick High Road, London, W4 5TF**
ⓣ 020 8996 3333
ⓕ 0208 742 8390
ⓔ mail@lettsed.co.uk
ⓦ www.lettsed.co.uk
**Contact** Publishing Director, Wayne Davies
**Established** 1979
**Insider Info** Catalogue available online, website http://shop.letts-successzone.com/
**Non-Fiction** Publishes Textbook and Scholarly titles on the following subjects:
 Education, Revision/Study guides.
**Recent Title(s)** *Premier Quick Tests English 10-11 Years*, Letts (Study books)
**Tips** Letts Education is the UK's market leader in study and revision guides. Founded in 1979, we have helped two generations of students through their exams. Today our range of books and electronic resources are more popular than ever, and now extend to all ages from pre-school to A-Level.

## LexisNexis
**1–3 The Strand, London, WC2N 5JR**
ⓣ 020 7930 7077
ⓕ 020 7166 5799
ⓦ www.reedelsevier.com
**Parent Company** Reed Elsevier Group Plc
**Insider Info** Catalogue available online.
**Non-Fiction** Publishes General Non-fiction, Scholarly, Textbook and Multimedia titles on the following subjects:
 Law and Legal Information.
**Tips** LexisNexis is a leading provider of information and services solutions. Products and publications are aimed at a wide range of professionals in the legal, risk management, corporate, government, law enforcement, accounting and academic markets.

## LibraPharm Ltd
**29 Venture West, New Greenham Park, Newbury, RG19 6XH**
ⓣ 01635 522651
ⓕ 01635 36294
ⓔ info@librapharm.com
ⓦ www.librapharm.com
**Contact** Managing Editor, Piers Allen; Deputy Managing Editor, Joanne Nicholl; Editorial and Production Manager, Richard Powell
**Established** 1995

**Insider Info** Catalogue available online. Manuscript guidelines available online.

**Non-Fiction** Publishes Journals on the following subjects:
Health/Medicine, Science, Healthcare, Medical research.

**Submission Guidelines** Submit completed manuscript and artworks/images (digital files as jpegs).
Submission details to: rmp@rpowell.co.uk

**Recent Title(s)** *Welcome to Paediatric and Perinatal Drug Therapy*, LibrPharm (Journal)

**Tips** We are an independent publishing and communications company, offering innovative solutions to meet the information needs of professionals in the medical, pharmaceutical and biotechnology sectors. Manuscripts for publication should conform to the latest 'Aims and Scope' of the journal they are interested in. Details are available on the website.

## Libris Ltd

**26 Lady Margaret Road, London, NW5 2XL**
- 020 7482 2390
- 020 7485 2730
- libris@onetel.com
- www.librislondon.co.uk

**Contact** Director, Nicholas Jacobs; Director, S.A. Kitzinger

**Established** 1986

**Insider Info** Catalogue available online.

**Non-Fiction** Publishes Biography, General Non-fiction and Scholarly titles on the following subjects:
Language/Literature, Literary Criticism, Translation, German Studies.

**Fiction** Publishes Literary, Translation and German Literature titles.

**Poetry** Publishes Bilingual Poetry titles.

**Recent Title(s)** *In Time of Need*, Reiner Kunze and Mireille Gansel (Biography).

**Tips** Libris is a London based publisher which specialises (though not exclusively) in publishing works of and books about German literature, for an international English language readership. Libris does not have any special instructions for submissions, but is currently unable to accept any new material for consideration. Check back in the future for more details.

## The Liffey Press Ltd

**Ashbrook House, 10 Main Street, Raheny, Dublin 5, Republic of Ireland**
- 00353 1 851 1458
- 00353 1 851 1459
- info@theliffeypress.com
- www.theliffeypress.com

**Contact** Publisher, David Givens; Editorial, Brian Langan

**Established** 2001

**Insider Info** Publishes 20 titles per year. Payment is via royalties. Catalogue and manuscript guidelines available online.

**Non-Fiction** Publishes General Non-fiction and Illustrated titles on the following subjects:
Art/Architecture, Business/Economics, Contemporary Culture, Education, Government/Politics, Language/Literature, Social Sciences, World Affairs.
 * Also welcomes proposals in the areas of Irish Culture, Social Policy, Arts and Literature, Current Events, Politics, Education, Economics and related fields.

**Submission Guidelines** Accepts query with SAE/proposal package (including outline, one sample chapter, market research, your publishing history and author biography).

**Recent Title(s)** *A Guide to Dublin Bay: Mirror to the City*, John Givens

**Tips** The Liffey Press put a particular emphasis on contemporary Ireland. They will endeavour to respond promptly to all proposals received.

## The Lilliput Press Ltd

**62–63 Sitric Road, Arbour Hill, Dublin 7, Republic of Ireland**
- 00353 1 671 1647
- 00353 1 671 1233
- info@lilliputpress.ie
- www.lilliputpress.com

**Contact** Publisher/Editor in Chief, Antony Farrell (Irish Literature, History, Culture)

**Established** 1984

**Insider Info** Publishes 18 titles per year. Receives approximately 300 queries and 200 manuscripts per year. 50 per cent of books published are from first-time authors and 50 per cent of books published are from unagented authors. 10 per cent of books are author subsidy published, and these are determined by integrity of subject and source of subvention. Payment is via royalty on wholesale price, with 0.1 (per £) minimum and 0.2 (per £) maximum, or royalty on retail price with 0.05 (per £) minimum and 0.15 (per £) maximum. Advance offered is from £300–£10,000. Simultaneous submissions are accepted. Submissions accompanied by SAE will be returned. Aims to respond to queries within five days, proposals within eight days, and manuscripts within ten months. Catalogue is free on request, and available online. Author guidelines are not available, although digital work is preferred.

**Non-Fiction** Publishes Autobiography, Irish Interest, Biography, General Non-fiction, Illustrated, Reference, and Scholarly titles on the following subjects:

Art/Architecture, Contemporary Culture, History, Language/Literature, Literary Criticism, Memoirs, Nature/Environment, Philosophy, Travel, Literature.

* Authors should have a familiarity with the Lilliput list and Irish culture in general.

**Submission Guidelines** Accepts proposal package (including two sample chapters) author biography) and artworks/images.

**Fiction** Publishes Erotica and Literary fiction.

**Submission Guidelines** Accepts proposal package (including outline, two sample chapters).

**Poetry** Publishes Poetry titles, mostly with an Irish theme.

**Submission Guidelines** Submit sample poems.

**Tips** Most work published has a broadly Irish theme.

## The Lindsey Press

**Unitarian Headquarters, Essex Hall, 1–6 Essex Street, London, WC2R 3HY**

- 020 7240 2384
- 020 7240 3089
- GA@unitarian.org.uk
- www.unitarian.org.uk/lindsey_press.htm

**Contact** Publications Panel Convenor, Kate Taylor

**Insider Info** Catalogue available online.

**Non-Fiction** Publishes General Non-fiction, Multimedia and Scholarly titles on Religion.

**Recent Title(s)** *Marking the Days: a Book of Occasional Services*, Kate Taylor (ed.)

**Tips** The Lindsey Press publishes works reflecting liberal religious thought, Unitarian history, and worship material.

## Lion Hudson Plc

**Mayfield House, 256 Banbury Road, Oxford, OX2 7DH**

- 01865 302750
- 01865 302757
- enquiries@lionhudson.com
- www.lionhudson.com

**Contact** Commissioning Editor, Lois Rock (Children's Books); Commissioning Editor, Morag Reeve (Adult Books); Commissioning Editor, Carol Jones (Children's Books); Commissioning Editor, Tony Collins (Adult Books)

**Established** 1971

**Imprint(s)** Lion Children's
Candle
Monarch

**Insider Info** Publishes 160 titles per year. Receives approximately 1,000 queries and 500 manuscripts per year. Three per cent of books published are from first-time authors, 90 per cent of books published are from unagented authors. Payment is via royalty (on wholesale price) or outright purchase. Average lead time is one year, with simultaneous submissions accepted. Submissions accompanied by SAE will be returned. Aims to respond to queries within one week, proposals within two months and manuscripts within three months. Catalogue is free on request and available online. Manuscript guidelines are available online.

**Non-Fiction** Publishes Autobiography, Biography, Children's/Juvenile, General Non-fiction, Gift, Illustrated, Reference, Self-help and Textbook titles on the following subjects:

Child Guidance/Parenting, Government/Politics, History, Memoirs, Nature/Environment, Religion, Young Adult.

* All Lion Hudson books are written by people who are happy to be called Christians and reflect a Christian world view.

## Little, Brown Book Group

**Brettenham House, Lancaster Place, London, WC2E 7EN**

- 020 7911 8000
- 020 7911 8100
- juicy.books@littlebrown.co.uk
- www.littlebrown.co.uk

**Parent Company** Hachette Livre UK (see Hachette Livre entry under European & International Publishers)

**Contact** CEO and Publisher, Ursula Mackenzie

**Established** 1988

**Imprint(s)** Abacus
Atom
Little, Brown
Orbit
Sphere
Virago Press

**Insider Info** Submissions accompanied by SAE will be returned. Aims to respond to proposals within eight weeks. Catalogue available online.

**Non-Fiction** Autobiography, Biography, General Non-fiction.

* Publishes both literary and general non-fiction across its imprints.

**Submission Guidelines** Accepts query with SAE/ proposal package (including outline, three sample chapters, covering letter and SAE).

**Fiction** Publishes Mainstream/Contemporary and General fiction in most genres.

 * Publishes literary and commercial fiction across various imprints.

**Submission Guidelines** Accepts query with SAE/ proposal package (including outline, three sample chapters, covering letter and SAE).

**Recent Title(s)** *Blue Shoes and Happiness*, Alexander McCall Smith (Novel, Abacus); *The Girls*, Lori Lansens (Novel, Virago Press); *In Spite of the Gods: The Strange Rise of Modern India*, Edward Luce (Non-fiction, Little, Brown)

**Tips** Formerly known as The Time Warner Book Group, Little, Brown reverted to its original name following purchase by Hachette Livre UK. The company publishes a wide range of paperback and hardcover fiction and non-fiction across its many imprints. See individual entries for more details.

## Little, Brown

**Brettenham House, Lancaster Place, London, WC2E 7EN**

- 020 7911 8000
- 020 7911 8100
- info@littlebrown.co.uk
- www.littlebrown.co.uk

**Parent Company** Little, Brown Book Group

**Contact** Managing Director, Richard Beswick

**Insider Info** Submissions accompanied by SAE will be returned. Aims to respond to proposals within eight weeks. Catalogue available online.

**Non-Fiction** Publishes General and Literary Non-fiction in the following subject areas:
 History, Memoirs, Science, Travel.

**Submission Guidelines** Accepts query with SAE/ proposal package (including, outline, sample chapter(s), a covering letter and SAE).

**Fiction** Publishes Literary fiction.

**Submission Guidelines** Accepts query with SAE/ proposal package (including outline, sample chapter(s), a covering letter and SAE).

**Tips** Agented submissions are strongly preferred, but unagented proposals are accepted. All Little, Brown imprint books are published in hardback. Paperback versions are published by the Abacus imprint.

## Little Books Ltd

**48 Catherine Place, London, SW1E 6HL**

- 020 7792 7929

- info@littlebooks.net
- www.littlebooks.net

**Contact** Publisher, Margaret Little; Max Hamilton Little

**Established** 2003

**Imprint(s)** Max Press

**Insider Info** Catalogue available online.

**Non-Fiction** Publishes Biography and General Non-fiction titles in the following subjects:
 Cooking /Foods/Nutrition, Health/Medicine, History, Language/Literature, Nature/Environment, Travel.

**Fiction** Publishes Historical and Mainstream/ Contemporary titles.

**Recent Title(s)** *Superfeast*, Michael van Straten (Food and Nutrition)

**Tips** Little Books is a young, independent publishing company. We publish concise books to fit in your pocket, by a glittering array of contemporary, well known writers. Our philosophy is to bring books to those juggling busy lives, but still passionate about reading, who want to be entertained as well as informed, without needing to devote huge chunks of time to wading through over long tomes, or having the same book sitting on their bedside table for months on end. Each book is about something important in our lives, something that makes the world a better place. Each is individual and unique, has bite, attitude and wit. Each is written by the leading writer in their field.

## Little Tiger Press

**1 The Coda Centre, 189 Munster Road, London, SW6 6AW**

- 020 7385 6333
- 020 7385 7333
- info@littletiger.co.uk
- www.littletigerpress.com

**Parent Company** Magi Publications

**Contact** Editor, Melinda Tallier (Submissions)

**Insider Info** Aims to respond to manuscripts within two months. Catalogue and manuscript guidelines are available online.

**Fiction** Publishes Picture and Novelty Book titles for the 0–7 age group.

**Submission Guidelines** Accepts completed manuscripts by post with SAE. Manuscripts must be no longer than 750 words.

**Recent Title(s)** *Me and My Dad!*, Alison Ritchie and Alison Edgson (Picture book); *Augustus and His Smile*, Catherine Rayner (Picture book)

**Tips** Little Tiger Books focuses on contemporary and innovative books for young children (Key Stage 1) that are also fun for adults. They publish board books, picture books, character books, gift books, home learning and books suitable for use in schools and pre-schools.

## Liverpool University Press
**4 Cambridge Street, Liverpool, L69 7ZU**
- 0151 794 2231
- 0151 794 2235
- robblo@liv.ac.uk
- www.liverpool-unipress.co.uk

**Contact** Publisher, Robin Bloxsidge (Art, Architecture, Public Space and Local Studies and all Journals); Commissioning Editor, Anthony Cond (Culture, Literature, History and Social Science); Production Editor, Andrew Kirk
**Established** 1899
**Insider Info** Publishes 40 titles per year. Payment is via royalties. Catalogue available online. Manuscript guidelines available online.
**Non-Fiction** Publishes General Non-fiction, Reference, Scholarly and Technical titles in the following subjects:.
Anthropology/Archaeology, Art/Architecture, Contemporary Culture, Government/Politics, History, Language/Literature, Literary Criticism, Music/Dance, Nature/Environment, Science, Sociology, Translation, Literary Criticism, Science Fiction.
**Submission Guidelines** We would prefer to receive a proposal, rather than a completed manuscript, in the first instance. Check website for submission guidelines. Accepts query with SAE/proposal package (including outline, two sample chapters, market research, publishing history, author biography).
**Recent Title(s)** *The Angle Between Two Walls: The Fiction of J.G. Ballard*, Roger Luckhurst
**Tips** Founded in 1899 and relaunched as a limited company in 2004, Liverpool University Press (LUP) has a vigorous and distinctive publishing programme. LUP publishes academic books and journals of high quality on a wide range of subjects including history, literature, art and architecture, by authors from around the world. We are also a respected publisher of science fiction texts and Liverpool interest titles and publish the acclaimed *Public Sculpture of Britain* series. LUP publishes original peer reviewed, high quality books in the social sciences and humanities.

## Logaston Press
**Little Logaston, Woonton, Almeley, Herefordshire, HR3 6QH**
- 01544 327344
- info@logastonpress.co.uk

- www.logastonpress.co.uk
**Contact** Managing Editor, Andy Johnsom; Managing Editor, Ron Shoesmith
**Established** 1985
**Insider Info** Publishes 15 titles per year. Payment is via royalties. Catalogue available online: http://members.lycos.co.uk/simonlogaston/
**Non-Fiction** Publishes Biography, General Non-fiction and Reference titles on the following subjects:
Anthropology/Archaeology, Art/Architecture, History, Hobbies, Nature/Environment, Regional, Social Sciences, Touring/Walking guides, Folklore.
* Mostly local interest for Wales and West Midlands.
**Submission Guidelines** Query with SAE/proposal package (including outline, sample chapter(s)) and artworks/images. Essentially Logaston Press publishes books on the history, archaeology, architecture, some natural history, and guides to a region that encompasses the rural West Midlands, Central and South Wales, so your book idea should fall somewhere in those broad categories/locations.
**Recent Title(s)** The Pubs of Bromyard, Ledbury & East Herefordshire, John Eisel and Ron Shoesmith
**Tips** Logaston Press concentrate on publishing books about various subjects relating to Central and Southern Wales and the rural West Midlands, but they stray both in subject material, and geographical area from time to time.

## Loki Books
**38 Chalcot Crescent, London, NW1 8YD**
- 020 7722 6718
- all@lokibooks.vianw.co.uk
- www.lokibooks.com

**Established** 1967
**Fiction** Publishes Full-length Fiction, Short Story Collections and Drama titles in translation.
* Often publishes work with women's voices in minority languages.
**Poetry** Publishes Poetry in Translation.
**Recent Title(s)** *Cherries In The Icebox: Contemporary Hebrew Short Stories*, Marion Baraitser and Haya Hoffman (eds.)
**Tips** Founded by Marion Baraitser in 1967, Loki Books is a prize winning press that voices the unvoiced. They work with the Arts Council of England, UNESCO, and the European Jewish Publications Society, to publish the best fiction, poetry and drama, and translations. One of Loki's main concerns is to promote women writers, who are dedicated to peace and the understanding of Arab–Israeli relations.

## Lonely Planet Publications Ltd

**72–82 Rosebery Avenue, Clerkenwell, London, EC1R 4RW**

- 020 7841 9000
- 020 7841 9001
- go@lonelyplanet.co.uk
- www.lonelyplanet.com

**Contact** Editorial Head, Katherine Leck; Publishing Administrator (UK), Aaron Lamb

**Established** 1973

**Insider Info** Manuscript guidelines and catalogue available online: http://shop.lonelyplanet.com/index.cfm?affil=lpgn-index

**Non-Fiction** Publishes General Non-fiction, Illustrated books and Guidebooks on the following subjects:

Travel, Travel and Culture.

**Submission Guidelines** Accepts query with SAE/proposal package (including outline, sample chapter(s), publishing history, clips, author biography) and artworks/images.

If you are interested in becoming a guidebook writer, please send us a covering letter, your CV, and two examples of your published writing work (preferably travel related), including details on where and when they were published. Check website guidelines for further details.

Submission details to: recruitingauthors@lonelyplanet.com.au

**Recent Title(s)** *France*, 7th Edition, Nicola Williams (Travel Guide)

**Tips** Lonely Planet publishes the world's best guidebooks for independent travellers. The books are known worldwide for reliable, insightful, 'pull no punches' travel information, maps, photos, and background historical and cultural information.

## Longman

**Edinburgh Gate, Harlow, Essex, CM20 2JE**

- 01279 623623
- 01279 414130
- www.longman.co.uk

**Parent Company** Pearson Education

**Insider Info** Catalogue and manuscript guidelines are available online

**Non-Fiction** Publishes Multimedia, Reference, Scholarly and Textbook titles on the following subjects:

ELT, Primary Education (Literacy, Numeracy, Science), Secondary Education (Psychology, Sociology, Business, Economics), Language/Literature, Law, Humanities, Social Sciences.

**Submission Guidelines** Accepts proposal package (including synopsis, sample chapters, market research, your publishing history and author biography).

**Recent Title(s)** *The Pack*, Tom Pow (Teaching Guide)

**Tips** Longman, the world's oldest commercial imprint, is a leading publisher of educational materials for schools and English Language Teaching (ELT) as well as for education. Audiences include primary and secondary pupils, adult learners and students taking English exams, as well as users of dictionaries and reference titles. For students in higher education, Longman publishes textbooks for law, humanities and social sciences.

## Lorenz Books

**Hermes House, 88–89 Blackfriars Road, London, SE1 8HA**

- 020 7401 2077
- 020 7633 9499
- www.lorenzbooks.com

**Parent Company** Anness Publishing

**Contact** Chairman/Managing Director, Paul Anness; Publisher/Partner, Joanna Lorenz (Creative Issues)

**Established** 1994

**Insider Info** Publishes 140 titles each year. Catalogue available online.

**Non-Fiction** Publishes Children's/Juvenile, General Non-fiction, Gift book and Illustrated titles on the following subjects:.

Cooking/Foods/Nutrition, Crafts, Gardening, Health/Medicine, History, Nature/Environment, Recreation, Sports.

**Tips** Lorenz Books is the trade sales imprint for new hardback titles at Anness Publishing Ltd. It includes the Aquamarine list of upmarket lifestyle directories.

## Luath Press Ltd

**543/2 Castlehill, The Royal Mile, Edinburgh, Lothian, EH1 2ND**

- 0131 225 4326
- 0131 225 4324
- gavin.macdougall@luath.co.uk
- www.luath.co.uk

**Contact** Director, Gavin McDougall

**Established** 1981

**Insider Info** Publishes 30 titles per year. Receives less than 1,000 queries and less than 1,000 manuscripts per year. 10–50 per cent of books published are from first-time authors, more than 90 per cent of books published are from unagented authors. Payment is via royalty. Submissions accompanied by SAE will be returned. Catalogue is free on request and available online. Manuscript guidelines are available online.

**Non-Fiction** Publishes Autobiography, Biography, Coffee table, Cookbook, Gift, How-to, Humour, Illustrated and Reference titles on the following subjects:

Animals, Art/Architecture, Cooking/Foods/Nutrition, Creative Non-fiction, Folklore, Gardening, History, Language/Literature, Literary Criticism, Memoirs, Military/War, Music/Dance, Photography, Religion, Spirituality, Sports, Travel, Women's Issues/Studies, World Affairs, Young Adult.

 * Luath Press is committed to publishing well written books which are worth reading.

**Submission Guidelines** Accepts queries with SAE and complete manuscripts (including your publishing history, clips, author biography and SAE).

**Fiction** Publishes Mainstream/Contemporary titles.

 * Will consider well written books, which are worth reading.

**Submission Guidelines** Accepts queries with SAE and complete manuscripts (including your publishing history, clips, author biography and SAE).

**Poetry** Publishes Traditional and Contemporary poetry.

**Submission Guidelines** Accepts complete manuscripts.

**Recent Title(s)** *Wherever the Saltire Flies*, Kenny MacAskill (Non-fiction); *The Ultimate Burns Supper Book*, Clark McGinn (Non-fiction); *The Love Songs of John Knox*, Alistair Findlay (Poetry collection)

**Tips** Most, but not all of Luath Press books have a Scottish connection.

## Lund Humphries

**Gower House, Croft Road, Aldershot, Hampshire, GU11 3HR**

☎ 01252 331551

✆ 01252 344405

✉ info@lundhumphries.com

🌐 www.lundhumphries.com

**Contact** Commissioning Editor, Lucy Clark

**Insider Info** Catalogue available online. Download pdf version, or fill in the online form.

**Non-Fiction** Publishes Coffee table books, Gift books, Illustrated books, Fine Art, Decorative Arts, Architecture, Design, and Photography titles.

 * Particular areas of future interests are: publications related to UK or international exhibitions or museum collections; surveys and studies of 19th and 20th Century artists, groups of artists, or periods of art; surveys, studies and monographs in the history of design, particularly graphic design, typography and illustration; and the history and practice of printmaking and sculpture.

**Submission Guidelines** Accepts proposal package (including outline, a sample list of competitor books, publishing history, author biography, information on the intended readership and all proposed illustrations).

 For book proposals by post, do not use the main company address. Send to: Lucy Clark, Commissioning Editor, Lund Humphries, Sardinia House, 51–52 Lincoln's Inn Fields, London WC2A 3LZ (Tel: 020 74440 7530)

 Submission details to: lclark@lundhumphries.com

**Recent Title(s)** *Botanical Riches*, Richard Aitken (Botanical illustration).

**Tips** The company has been a part of Ashgate Publishing since 1999, and its publishing programme has continued to expand.

## The Lutterworth Press

**PO Box 60, Cambridge, CB1 2NT**

☎ 01223 350865

✆ 01223 366951

Email: publishing@lutterworth.com

Website: www.lutterworth.com

**Established** 1700s

**Imprint(s)** James Clarke & Co.

 Acorn Editions

**Insider Info** Catalogue and manuscript guidelines available online.

**Non-Fiction** Publishes Biography, General Non-fiction, Children's/Juvenile, Humour, Illustrated, Reference and Scholarly titles on the following subjects:

 Art/Architecture, Archaeology, Crafts, Collectables, Antiques, Education, Literature, Sports, Technology, Leisure, Theatre, Religion.

 * The Lutterworth Press specialise in adult and children's religious titles, alongside their general and scholarly non-fiction lists.

**Submission Guidelines** Accepts query with SAE/proposal package (including outline, two sample chapters and contents list).

**Fiction** Publish some children's fiction titles.

**Submission Guidelines** No submissions for children's fiction accepted.

**Recent Title(s)** *Lost People of Malplaquet*, Andrew Dalton (Children's Fiction)

**Tips** One of the UK's oldest independent publishers, founded as The Religious Tract Society to provide improving literature for young people and adults. The company ethos is still to provide high-quality publishing for children and adults with an emphasis on moral values. No manuscripts are accepted for any children's books, whether fiction of non-fiction. The press do not publish any adult fiction at all. Prospective authors are advised to thoroughly research the catalogue to ensure a book's suitability.

## Lyfrow Trelyspen

**The Roseland Institute, Gorran, St. Austell, Cornwall, PL26 6NT**

- 01726 843501
- 01726 843501
- trelispen@care4free.net

**Contact** Managing Editor, Dr. James Whetter
**Established** 1975
**Insider Info** Publishes two titles per year.
**Non-Fiction** Publishes Biography and General Non-fiction titles in the following subjects:
 History (Cornish History), Regional, Cornish Essays.
**Submission Guidelines** Accepts query with SAE/proposal package (including outline, sample chapter(s)). Accepts unsolicited submissions and ideas, providing they are of Cornish interest.
**Tips** A small press, publishing history, biographies and various essays of Cornish interest.

## M&M Baldwin

**24 High Street, Cleobury Mortimer, Kidderminster, DY14 8BY**

- 01299 270110
- mb@mbaldwin.free-online.co.uk
- www.enigmatixuk.com

**Contact** Proprietor, Dr Mark Baldwin (Waterways, Intelligence)
**Established** 1974
**Insider Info** Publishes three titles per year. Receives approximately 30 queries and 15 manuscripts per year. Ten per cent of books published are from first-time authors, 95 per cent of books published are from unagented authors. Payment is via royalty (on retail price). Average lead time is six months, with simultaneous submissions not accepted. Submissions accompanied by SAE will be returned. Aims to respond to queries, proposals and manuscripts within two days. Catalogue and manuscript guidelines are free on request.
**Non-Fiction** Publishes Biography, General Non-fiction and Reference titles on the following subjects:
 History, Marine Subjects, Military/War.
**Submission Guidelines** Accepts query with SAE and artworks/images (send photocopies).
**Recent Title(s)** *Top Secret Ultra*, Peter Calvocoressi (Military History)

## Macmillan Publishers Ltd

**Brunel Road, Houndmills, Basingstoke, Hampshire, RG21 6XS**

- fiction@macmillan.co.uk, nonfiction@macmillan.co.uk
- www.macmillan.com

**Parent Company** Verlagsgruppe Georg von Holtzbrink GmbH
**Contact** Chief Executive, Richard Charkin
**Established** 1843
**Imprint(s)** Macmillan Education (division)
 Palgrave Macmillan (division)
 Pan Macmillan (division)
**Non-Fiction** Publishes Textbooks, Reference and Scholarly titles.
**Fiction** Publishes Mainstream/Contemporary and General fiction titles.
**Tips** The Macmillan Group and its divisions cover education publishing, including English language teaching (ELT), academic publishing, including reference science, technological and medical publishing, fiction and non-fiction book publishing, and publishing services including distribution and production.
 The Macmillan website has a good deal of information about the company and its divisions, but for submission information check the relevant division site.

## Macmillan

**20 New Wharf Road, London, N1 9RR**

- 020 7014 6000
- 020 7014 6001
- fiction@macmillan.co.uk
- www.panmacmillan.com

**Parent Company** Pan Macmillan Publishers
**Insider Info** Catalogue available online.
**Non-Fiction** Publishes Biography, General Non-fiction, Illustrated books, History, Memoirs, Sports, World affairs, Politics and Current affairs.
**Submission Guidelines** Does not accept unsolicited or unagented submissions.
**Fiction** Publishes general fiction from British and international writers.
**Submission Guidelines** Will not accept unagented submissions.
**Recent Title** *Exile*, Richard North Patterson (Crime)
**Tips** New writers should try Macmillan's New Writing imprint as the Macmillan imprint does not accept any unsolicited manuscripts.
 To see an imprint catalogue, go to the Pan Macmillan website and click on imprints.

## Macmillan Children's Books

**20 New Wharf Road, London, N1 9RR**

☎ 020 7014 6000
☏ 020 7014 6001
✉ children@macmillan.co.uk
🌐 www.panmacmillan.com

**Parent Company** Pan Macmillan Publishers
**Insider Info** Catalogue available online.
**Non-Fiction** Publishes Children's/Juvenile titles.
**Submission Guidelines** Does not accept unsolicited submissions. Accepts agented submissions only.
**Fiction** Publishes Picture books, Young Adult and Children's titles.
**Submission Guidelines** Accepts agented submissions only.
**Poetry** Publishes Children's Poetry titles.
**Submission Guidelines** Accepts agented submissions only.
**Recent Title(s)** *Fairies*, Sandy Ransford (Gift); *Avalon High*, Meg Cabot (Fiction), *Scottish Poems*, chosen by John Rice (Poetry)
**Tips** Macmillan's Children's books produces a diverse and quality list of fiction and non-fiction for the ages 0–16 years.

## Macmillan Education

**Macmillan Oxford, Between Towns Road, Oxford, OX4 3PP**

☎ 01865 405700
☏ 01865 405701
✉ elt@macmillan.com, firstinitial.lastname@macmillan.com
🌐 www.macmillaneducation.com

**Parent Company** Macmillan Publishers Ltd
**Contact** Managing Director, Chris Harrison; Publisher, Sue Bale; Director of Internet Publishing, Ian Johnstone
**Insider Info** Catalogue is available online.
**Non-Fiction** Publishes Text books, Online resources, Children's/Juvenile, Reference and Scholarly titles on the following subjects:
Language/Literature, English Language teaching and Curriculum materials for schools.
**Tips** Macmillan Education operates in 40 countries, publishing school and learning materials. Most resources, both print and online, are developed in conjunction with teachers and other education professionals. Materials are always in line with the relevant curriculum. The three main areas are; Macmillan English (English language teaching), Macmillan Caribbean (books for and about the Caribbean) and Macmillan Africa (educational text books for African schools).

## Macmillan New Writing

**20 New Wharf Road, London, N1 9RR**

☎ 020 7014 6000
☏ 020 7014 6001
✉ mnwhelp@macmillan.co.uk
🌐 www.macmillannewwriting.com

**Parent Company** Pan Macmillan Publishers
**Insider Info** All books published are from first-time authors. No advances paid, instead an open ended royalty deal at a relatively high rate is offered. Aims to respond to submitted manuscripts within ten weeks. Catalogue free on request (send name and address to Catalogues at Macmillan New Writing), online and via email to: mnwcatalogue@macmillan.co.uk
**Fiction** Publishes General fiction (all genres considered).
 * Does not publish Non-fiction, Short stories, Novellas, or Children's books. Submissions must be complete novels.
**Submission Guidelines** Submit proposal package (including outline, short author biography and completed manuscript).
 Submission details to: newwriting@macmillan.co.uk
**Recent Title(s)** *Another Time and Place*, Samantha Grosser (WWII Novel/Romance)
**Tips** Macmillan New Writing is a fiction list set up specifically to attract new talent. To enable this, a streamlined publishing process has been set up. Postal or email submissions are accepted from writers who have not previously had a novel published. Please note that no correspondence will be entered into over novels that have been rejected.

## Made Simple Books

**The Boulevard, Langford Lane, Kidlington, Oxford, OX5 1GB**

☎ 01865 843000
☏ 01865 843010
✉ authorsupport@elsevier.com
🌐 www.elsevier.com/books

**Parent Company** Elsevier Ltd (Science & Technology)
**Insider Info** Authors paid by royalty. Catalogue available online. Manuscript guidelines available online.
**Non-Fiction** Publishes Text books, How-to, Reference and technical titles on Computers/Electronics.

**Submission Guidelines** Accepts query with SAE. Submit proposal package (including outline).
**Recent Title** *XML Made Simple*, Robert Henderson and Sharon Deane (Computer Programming)
**Tips** Made Simple Books publishes books and tutorial guides on basic and advanced computing, and programming. The Made Simple computing list was created for students, home enthusiasts, those taking their first steps in programming and for experienced programmers wanting to get to grips with the essentials of a new language quickly. It combines a tutorial approach, with tasks to do and easy steps using shortcuts where appropriate. Made Simple Books welcomes authors' proposals for books. The first step is to discuss the proposal with the relevant Publishing Editor. Check the website for in-depth submission guidelines and a full list of editorial contacts.

## The Maia Press
**82 Forest Road, Dalston, London, E8 3BH**
- 020 7249 3711
- 020 7683 8141
- maggie@maiapress.com
- www.maiapress.com

**Contact** Founder, Maggie Hamand; Founder, Jane Havell
**Established** 2002
**Insider Info** Publishes six titles per year. Payment is via royalties. Aims to respond to proposals and manuscripts within six weeks. Catalogue and manuscript guidelines available online.
**Fiction** Publishes Literary and Mainstream/Contemporary titles.
 * The Maia Press plans to publish works by writers from diverse backgrounds, including works in translation, giving priority to writers whose work is censored in their country of origin.
**Submission Guidelines** Accepts query with SAE/Proposal package (including outline and three sample chapters).
**Recent Title(s)** *Asboville*, Danny Rhodes (Novel)
**Tips** The Maia Press is a new publishing house, dedicated to publishing new and established authors. They only publish a small number of books per year, so submissions should be extremely targeted, according to the guidelines on the website. Do not email submissions.

## Mainstream
**Random House, 20 Vauxhall Bridge Road, London, SW1V 2SA**
- 020 7840 8400
- 020 7233 8791
- emarketing@randomhouse.co.uk
- www.randomhouse.co.uk

**Parent Company** The Random House Group Ltd
**Insider Info** Catalogue available online.
**Non-Fiction** Publishes Autobiography, Biography and General Non-fiction on the following subjects: History, Memoirs, Recreation, Sports and Drugs.
**Submission Guidelines** Submit proposal package (including outline, one sample chapter and SAE). Will accept artwork/photos (send photocopies, rather than originals).
**Recent Title** *Facing Tyson*, Ted A. Kluck; *After They Killed Our Father*, Loung Ung
**Tips** No emailed submissions. Agented submissions stand a better chance of being successful.

## Mainstream Publishing Co. (Edinburgh) Ltd
**7 Albany Street, Edinburgh, EH1 3UG**
- 0131 557 2959
- 0131 556 8720
- enquiries@mainstreampublishing.com
- www.mainstreampublishing.com

**Contact** Director, Bill Campbell; Director, Peter Mackenzie; Editorial, Ailsa Bathgate
**Established** 1978
**Insider Info** Publishes 80 titles per year. Authors paid by royalty. Catalogue and manuscript guidelines available online.
**Non-Fiction** Publishes Autobiography, Biography, Illustrated books and General Non-fiction titles on the following subjects:
 Art/Architecture, Government/Politics, Health/Medicine, History, Photography, Sports and World Affairs.
**Submission Guidelines** Accepts query with SAE. Submit proposal package (including outline and SAE).
 Submission details to: graeme.blaikie@mainstreampublishing.com
**Fiction** Publishes Mainstream/Contemporary titles.
**Submission Guidelines** Accepts query with SAE. Submit proposal package (including outline).
 Submission details to: graeme.blaikie@mainstreampublishing.com
**Recent Title** *The Deniable Agent - Undercover in Afghanistan*, Colin Berry (Autobiography)
**Tips** Mainstream publishes various biographies/autobiographies, illustrated and general non-fiction. Random House currently owns a 50 per cent share in the company. To establish how the publishing process works at Mainstream, please see the website.

## Management Books 2000 Ltd

**Forge House, Limes Road, Kemble, Cirencester, GL7 6AD**

- 01285 771441
- 01285 771055
- info@mb2000.com
- www.mb2000.com

**Contact** Publisher, Nicholas Dale-Harris

**Established** 1993

**Insider Info** Average lead time is 15 months. Catalogue available online.

**Non-Fiction** Publishes reference titles on the following subjects:
Business, Management, Self-development, Sales and Marketing.

**Submission Guidelines** Accepts proposal package (including outline, two sample chapters, your publishing history and author biography).

**Tips** Management Books publishes books for executives and managers working in the modern business world. New ideas and synopses are welcome.

## Manchester University Press

**Oxford Road, Manchester, M13 9NR**

- 0161 275 2310
- 0161 274 3346
- mup@manchester.ac.uk
- www.manchesteruniversitypress.co.uk

**Contact** Chief Executive, David Rodgers; Head of Editorial, Matthew Frost (Humanities); Commissioning Editor, Tony Mason (International Law and Economics); Commissioning Editor, Alison Welsby (History, Art History and Design)

**Established** 1904

**Insider Info** Publishes 120 titles per year. Authors paid by royalty. Catalogue free on request and available online. Manuscript guidelines available online.

**Non-Fiction** Publishes Text books, Reference and Scholarly titles on the following subjects:
Art/Architecture, Business/Economics, Government/Politics, History, Humanities, Language/Literature, Law, Literary Criticism and Media.

**Submission Guidelines** Accepts query with SAE. Submit proposal package (including outline, market research, your publishing history, author biography and SAE).
Submission details to: m.frost@manchester.ac.uk

**Recent Title** *The Changing Rules on the use of Force in International Law*, Tarcisio Gazzini (Law)

**Tips** Manchester University Press serves the international academic community, and promotes The University of Manchester by the publication of outstanding works of learning and scholarship that both reflect and enhance The University's authority and reputation. The Press was founded in 1904, primarily as an outlet to publish academic research being carried out within the Victoria University of Manchester. Today, the Press is an international concern, publishing work by authors from all over the world and selling books to a global audience. Manchester University Press offers all the advantages of a university press, including high academic standards and rigorous publishing values, along with all the benefits of a small publishing house.

## Mandrake of Oxford

**PO Box 250, Oxford, OX1 1AP**

- 01865 243671
- 01865 432929
- mandrake@mandrake.uk.net
- www.mandrake.uk.net

**Contact** Director, Mogg Morgan; Director, Kym Morgan

**Established** 1986

**Insider Info** Catalogue available online. Manuscript guidelines available online.

**Non-Fiction** Publishes Biography, General non-fiction, Illustrated and Scholarly titles on the following subjects: Alternative lifestyles, Astrology/Psychic, Contemporary culture, Philosophy, Religion, Spirituality, Crime studies and Magic/Witchcraft.

**Submission Guidelines** Accepts query with SAE. Submit proposal package (including outline, one sample chapter and SAE).

**Fiction** Publishes titles on the following subjects: Occult, Spiritual and Crime.

**Submission Guidelines** Accepts query with SAE. Submit proposal package (including outline, one sample chapter and SAE).

**Poetry** Publishes Poetry Collections.
\* Sometimes publish individual poems in a newsletter, which can be viewed by emailingmandrake-subscribe@yahoogroups.com.

**Submission Guidelines** Accepts query with SAE.

**Recent Title** *Pan's Daughter*, Nevill Drury

**Tips** Mandrake of Oxford is a specialist independent press, that are always happy to look at ideas for a new book. The publishers urge that before potential authors submit their work, they look at the catalogue, and a book in a similar category, to gauge whether a proposal fits Mandrake's list.

## Mango Publishing

**PO Box 13378, London, SE27 0ZN**

☎ 020 8480 7771

☎ 020 8480 7771

✉ info@mangoprint.com

🌐 www.mangoprint.com

**Established** 1995

**Insider Info** Catalogue available online.

**Non-Fiction** Publishes Autobiography, Biography and General Non-fiction titles in the following subjects:
Translation, Black African/Caribbean, Latin American.

**Fiction** Mainstream/Contemporary, Short story collections, Translation, Black African/Caribbean, Latin American.

**Poetry** Publishes Black African/Caribbean Poetry titles.

**Recent Title(s)** *Modernist Women Race Nation*, Giovanna Covi ed. (Literary Criticism); *Berbice to Broadstairs*, Maggie Harris (Collection)

**Tips** Mango Publishing was established in response to growing demand for a small black press, committed to promoting and publishing the work of quality first-time and established writers. They focus on publishing and promoting literary works by writers from British, Caribbean, and Latin American literary traditions. The list includes translations of important work not originally written in English such as poetry by leading contemporary authors, short and longer fiction, ranging from short story anthologies to novels and autobiographical work.

## Manson Publishing Ltd

**73 Corringham Road, London, NW11 7DL**

☎ 020 8905 5150

☎ 020 8201 9233

✉ manson@mansonpublishing.com

🌐 www.mansonpublishing.com

**Contact** Managing Director, Michael Manson

**Established** 1992

**Insider Info** Publishes ten titles per year. Payment is via royalties. Catalogue and manuscript guidelines available online.

**Non-Fiction** Publishes Scholarly, Technical, Textbook and Reference titles on the following subjects:
Health/Medicine, Science, Veterinary.

**Submission Guidelines** Accepts query with SAE. Welcomes proposals for highly illustrated books from authors in its main subject areas. Please contact Manson Publishing with an outline by email, post or fax.

Submission details to: manson@man-pub.demon.co.uk

**Recent Title(s)** *The Great Ormond Street Colour Handbook of Paediatrics and Child Health*, Stephan Strobel, Stephen D. Marks, Peter Smith, (Medical Reference)

**Tips** Manson Publishing issues books for professionals and students in medicine, veterinary medicine and the sciences. They specialise in highly illustrated books for study and reference, produced to the highest standards in full colour and at affordable prices. Subject areas covered include medicine, veterinary medicine, earth science, plant science, agriculture, and microbiology.

## Mantra Lingua

**Global House, 303 Ballards Lane, London, N12 8NP**

☎ 020 8445 5123

☎ 020 8446 7745

✉ sales@mantralingua.com

🌐 www.mantralingua.com

**Contact** Managing Director, M. Chatterji; Commissioning Editor, Henriette Barkow

**Established** 1984

**Insider Info** Aims to respond to proposals and manuscripts within two months. Catalogue available online. Manuscript guidelines available online.

**Non-Fiction** Publishes Children's, Gift book and Multimedia titles.

**Fiction** Publishes Juvenile, Multimedia, Picture books, Translation and Young Adult titles.

**Submission Guidelines** Accepts query with SAE/proposal package (including outline, sample chapter(s), or submit completed manuscript). Will accept unsolicited manuscripts and suggestions. If you feel that your writing style and manuscript are compatible with the list, send either a 250 word synopsis or your manuscript, which should be no longer than 1,200 words for picture books and 2,500 words for junior fiction.

Submission details to: mishti@mantralingua.com

**Recent Title(s)** *Fox Fables*, Dawn Casey (Children's)

**Tips** MantraLingua is a UK based publishing house that supplies bilingual resources around the world. MantraLingua is about connecting languages for children. With increased mobility of populations across the globe, e.g. Brazillians in Japan, Malis in Sweden, and Indians in Gambia, MantraLingua has developed a set of values that stems from a desire to retain distinctness, and yet encourage integration of new communities in various societies.

## Mare's Nest

**41 Addison Gardens, London, W14 0DP**

☎ 020 7603 3969

✉ maresnest@tesco.net

🌐 www.maresnest.co.uk

**Contact** Pamela Clunies-Ross

**Non-Fiction** Publishes Translations

**Fiction** Publishes Translation titles.

**Poetry** Publishes Translated Poetry titles.

**Recent Title(s)** *Between Words and Silence*, Zsuzsa Beney; *Brushstrokes of Blue*, Pall Valsson (ed.)

**Tips** Publishes English translations of Icelandic poetry and fiction as well as some Faroese fiction and Hungarian non-fiction.

## Marion Boyars Publishers Ltd

**24 Lacy Road, London, SW15 1NL**

☎ 020 8788 9522

☎ 020 8789 8122

✉ catheryn@marionboyars.com

🌐 www.marionboyars.co.uk

**Contact** Director, Catheryn Kilgarriff; Editor, Amy Christian (Non-Fiction); Editor, Rebecca Gillieron (Fiction)

**Established** 1960s

**Insider Info** Catalogue available online. Manuscript guidelines available online.

**Non-Fiction** Publishes Biography, Children's/ Juvenile, General Non-fiction and Scholarly titles on the following subjects:
Contemporary Culture, Language/Literature, Literary Criticism, Memoirs, Music/Dance, Social Sciences, Theatre.

**Submission Guidelines** Accepts query with SAE. Submit completed manuscript.
Submission details to: amy@marionboyars.com

**Fiction** Publishes Juvenile, Literary, Mainstream/ Contemporary, Translation, Black writing and Women's titles.

**Submission Guidelines** Agented submissions only. Would prefer a synopsis and sample chapter in the first instance.
Submission details to: amy@marionboyars.com

**Recent Title(s)** *Swords of Ice*, Latife Tekin (Translation/Novel)

**Tips** A literary, independent publishing house based in South West London. Renowned for being adventurous and sometimes controversial, they publish new fiction as well as non-fiction in the fields of film, music, social theory, philosophy and feminism. Marion Boyars Publishers are pleased to receive submissions for non-fiction in the areas of music, film and contemporary culture.

## Marshall Cavendish Ltd

**119 Wardour Street, London, W1F 0UW**

☎ 020 7565 6000

☎ 020 7734 6221

✉ info@marshallcavendish.co.uk

🌐 www.marshallcavendish.co.uk

**Contact** Clive Gregory

**Insider Info** Catalogue available online.

**Non-Fiction** Publishes Children's, Gift book, Partworks and General Non-fiction titles on the following subjects:
Art/Architecture, House and Home, Nature/ Environment, Science, Sex, Supernatural.

**Submission Guidelines** Accepts query with SAE.

**Recent Title(s)** *Achieve IELTS*, Louis Harrison, Caroline Cushen & Susan Hutchison (Educational)

**Tips** Marshall Cavendish is a major international publisher of books, directories, magazines and partworks. The philosophy of enriching life through knowledge transcends boundaries of geography and culture. In line with this vision, their products reach across the globe in 13 languages, and their publishing network spans Asia, Europe and the US. Their illustrated reference and non-fiction titles for schools and libraries offer materials which enhance the educational experiences of students at all levels.

## Martin Books

**Africa House, 64–78 Kingsway, London, WC2B 6AH**

☎ 020 7316 1900

☎ 020 7316 0332

✉ martinbooks@simonandschuster.co.uk

🌐 www.martinbooks.co.uk

**Parent Company** Simon & Schuster UK Ltd

**Contact** Director, Jane Copplestone; Business Development Manager, Katie Walsh; Business Development Executive, Deborah Ball

**Non-Fiction** Publishes General Non-fiction and Illustrated titles on the following subject areas:
Child Guidance/Parenting, Cooking/Foods/ Nutrition, Gardening, Lifestyle.
* Martin Books offer a bespoke publishing service to individual clients, rather than operating as a traditional commissioning publishing company. Books may be produced to a company's specifications under their own brand, or in partnership.

**Submission Guidelines** No book proposals from those looking to go down the traditional commissioning route.

**Tips** Martin Books is an imprint of Simon & Schuster and specialises in cookery book production.

## Maverick House Publishers

**Main Street, Dunshaughlin, Co. Meath, Republic of Ireland**

☎ 00353 1 824 0077

☎ 00353 1 824 1746

✉ info@maverickhouse.com

🌐 www.maverickhouse.com

**Established** 2001

**Insider Info** Aims to respond to proposals and manuscripts within eight weeks. Catalogue available online. Manuscript guidelines available online.

**Non-Fiction** Publishes Biography and General Non-fiction titles on the following subjects:

Memoirs, Sports, True Crime, Positive Living.

**Submission Guidelines** Accepts query with SAE/ proposal package (including outline, sample chapter(s), author biography).

**Recent Title(s)** *A Voice From the Grave*, Christine Holohan with Vera McHugh (True Crime)

**Tips** A dynamic, young company that produces hard hitting books that educate, stimulate and entertain. They are now the one fastest growing publisher of current affairs in the United Kingdom, Ireland and South East Asia. Firm believers that truth is stranger than fiction, so unfortunately cannot read any fiction submissions.

## Maypole Editions

**22 Mayfair Avenue, Illford, Essex, IG1 3DQ**

☎ 020 8252 3937

**Fiction** Publishes Plays.

**Poetry** Publishes Poetry titles.

* Poetry submissions are accepted for possible inclusion in anthologies. Themes usually published include social issues, ethnic minority issues, feminist themes, romance, travel and lyric rhyming verse. Generally no politics.

**Submission Guidelines** Submit sample poems. Poems should be around 30 lines.

**Tips** There could be a long delay in responding to submissions due to the volume received. Previously unpublished poets are welcome.

## McGraw-Hill Education

**McGraw-Hill House, Shoppenhangers Road, Maidenhead, Berkshire, SL6 2QL**

☎ 01628 502500

☎ 01628 770224

✉ helpme@mcgraw-hill.com

🌐 www.mcgraw-hill.co.uk

**Contact** Shona Mullen

**Established** 1909

**Imprint(s)** Open University Press

**Insider Info** Catalogue available online. Manuscript guidelines available online.

**Non-Fiction** Publishes Multimedia, Scholarly, Technical, Textbook and Reference titles on the following subjects:

Business/Economics, Computers/Electronics, Education, Engineering.

**Submissions Guidelines** McGraw-Hill Education accepts queries and proposals for scholarly books or teaching resources. Check guidelines on website for further details.

**Recent Title(s)** *Spotlight on Music*, Macmillan/ McGraw-Hill

**Tips** McGraw-Hill Education is a leading global provider of educational materials and professional information.

## Meadow Books

**35 Stonefield Way, Burgess Hill, RH15 8DW**

☎ 01444 239044

✉ meadowbooks@hotmail.com

**Contact** Managing Director, C. O'Neill

**Established** 1990

**Imprint(s)** Diggory Press

**Non-Fiction** Publishes General Non-fiction and Reference titles on the following subjects:

Spirituality, Nursing History, Nursing Photo reference books, Folklore.

**Submission Guidelines** Query with SAE. No telephone calls please.

## Meadowside Children's Books

**185 Fleet Street, London, EC4A 2HS**

☎ 0207 400 1092

☎ 0207 400 1037

✉ info@meadowsidebooks.com

🌐 www.meadowsidebooks.com

**Parent Company** DC Thomson

**Established** 2003

**Insider Info** Publishes 100 titles per year. Receives approximately 2,000 queries and 2,000 manuscripts per year. 50 per cent of books published are from first-time authors, 25 per cent of books published are from unagented authors. Payment is via royalty (on retail price). Average lead time is six months, with simultaneous submissions accepted. Submissions accompanied by SAE will be returned. Aims to respond to queries within three months. Catalogue is available with SAE, or by email. Manuscript guidelines are available online.

**Fiction** Publishes Children's and Young Adult titles.

**Submission Guidelines** Accepts proposal package (including outline, and three sample chapters).
**Poetry** Publishes Children's Poetry.
**Submission Guidelines** Accepts proposal package (including outline and three sample poems).

## Melrose Press Ltd
**St. Thomas Place, Ely, Cambridgeshire, CB7 4GG**
- 01353 646600
- 01353 646601
- info@melrosepress.co.uk
- www.melrosepress.co.uk

**Contact** Managing Director, Nicholas S. Law
**Established** 1960
**Imprint(s)** International Biographical Centre
**Insider Info** Catalogue available online.
**Non-Fiction** Publishes Biography and Reference titles.
**Recent Title(s)** *Who's Who in the 21st Century* (Directory)
**Tips** A world leader in biographical publishing, supplying biographical information to librarians, researchers and individuals worldwide, much of which is difficult to obtain elsewhere. Publishes mainly 'Who's Who' type directories, inclusion into which is voluntary (subject to merit).

## Menard Press
**8 The Oaks, Woodside Avenue, London, N12 8AR**
- 020 8446 5571
- www.menardpress.co.uk

**Established** 1969
**Insider Info** Catalogue available online.
**Non-Fiction** Publishes Autobiography, Biography, General Non-fiction and Scholarly titles on the following subjects:
Art/Architecture, History, Literary Criticism, Memoirs, Translation.
**Fiction** Publishes Literary, Mainstream/Contemporary, Short Story Collections and Translation titles.
**Poetry** Publishes Translated Poetry titles.
**Recent Title(s)** *Conversation with Goya. Signs. Bridges,* Ivo Andric; *The Stove,* Jakov Lind; *Mother's Milk,* W.G. Shepherd (Collection)
**Tips** Menard Press specialises in literary translation, mainly of poetry. In addition to its literary texts; original and translated poetry, original and translated fiction, art and literary criticism, the press has also published essays on the nuclear issue and testimonies by survivors of Nazism.

## Mentor Books
**43 Furze Road, Sandyford Industrial Estate, Dublin 18, Republic of Ireland**
- 00353 1 295 2112
- 00353 1 295 2114
- admin@mentorbooks.ie
- www.mentorbooks.ie

**Insider Info** Catalogue is available online.
**Non-Fiction** Publishes Children's, General Non-fiction, How-to, Humour, Illustrated, Textbook and Reference titles on the following subjects:
Words of Wisdom Series, Politics/Humour, True Crime, History (Irish), Trivia, Quiz, Educational titles for children (Ireland).
**Fiction** Publishes Children's titles.
**Recent Title(s)** *Words of Wisdom: Nelson Mandela,* compiled by Nicola Sedgwick (Adult Non-fiction series)

## Mercat Press Ltd
**10 Coates Crescent, Edinburgh, EH3 7AL**
- 0131 225 9774
- 0131 226 6632
- enquiries@mercatpress.com
- www.mercatpress.com

**Contact** Managing Editor, Seán Costello; Managing Editor, Tom Johnstone; Editorial and Marketing Assistant, Caroline Taylor
**Established** 1970
**Imprint(s)** Crescent Books
**Insider Info** Payment is via royalties. Aims to respond to proposals within two weeks. Catalogue free on request online and by email.
**Non-Fiction** Publishes Autobiography, Biography, and General Non-fiction titles on the following subjects:
Art/Architecture, Contemporary Culture, Hobbies, Language/Literature, Literary Criticism, Nature/Environment, Regional, Sports, Travel, Walking guides.
 * Most books are of Scottish interest.
**Submission Guidelines** Query with SAE, submit proposal package (including outline, two sample chapters and SAE).
**Fiction** Regional (Scottish interest).
**Submission Guidelines** Accepts query with SAE/proposal package (including outline, two sample chapters and SAE) sent to either Managing Editor.
**Recent Title(s)** *Edinburgh: A New Perspective,* Jason Baxter (Photography); *Bruar's Rest,* Jess Smith (Novel)
**Tips** Mercat Press is one of Scotland's leading publishers. Founded in 1970 as part of the former bookselling chain James Thin, it became an

independent company in April 2002. Mercat publishes books of predominantly Scottish interest.

## Mercia Cinema Society
**29 Blackbrook Court, Loughborough, LE11 5UA**
- 01509 218393
- mervyn.gould@virgin.net
- www.merciacinema.org.uk

**Contact** Managing Editors, Paul Smith and Mervyn Gould
**Established** 1980
**Non-Fiction** Publishes General Non-fiction and Scholarly titles on the following subjects:
 History, Regional, History of Cinema/Picture Houses.
**Submission Guidelines** Accepts query with SAE.
**Tips** A national society for the promotion and publication of research into cinema history. Declared purpose is to encourage, promote, and publish research on cinema building history (which includes theatres that have been used for bioscope and film). Always interested in well written and thoroughly researched texts on cinema exhibition.

## Mercier Press Ltd
**Mercier Press, Douglas, Cork, Republic of Ireland**
- 00353 21 489 0622
- 00353 21 489 9887
- info@mercierpress.ie
- www.mercierpress.ie

**Contact** Managing Director, Clodagh Feehan
**Established** 1944
**Imprint(s)** Marino Books
**Insider Info** Catalogue available online. Manuscript guidelines available online.
**Non-Fiction** Publishes Children's/Juvenile, General Non-fiction, Humour, Scholarly and Irish interest titles on the following subjects:
 Health/Medicine, History, Language/Literature, Regional, World Affairs.
**Submission Guidelines** Acepts query with SAE/ proposal package (including outline, sample chapter(s), author biography).
 Submission details to: publishing@mercierpress.ie
**Recent Title(s)** *Galway & The Great War*, William Henry (Irish History)
**Tips** Mercier Press is Ireland's oldest independent publishing house, based in Cork. Founded in 1944 by John and Mary Feehan, they have published books in the fields of history, folklore, art, humour, children's, drama, fiction, politics, current affairs, spirituality and religion. Today they focus mainly on history, folklore and politics, although not exclusively. Please bear in mind that they publish

mainly for the Irish market, and as such the list focuses on Irish interest non-fiction, mainly history, folklore and politics.

## Meridian Books
**40 Hadzor Road, Oldbury, West Midlands, B68 9LA**
- 0121 429 4397
- roger@bestwalks.com
- www.bestwalks.com/meridianbooks.htm

**Contact** Managing Editor, Peter Groves
**Established** 1985
**Insider Info** Publishes five titles per year. Payment is via royalties. Catalogue available online.
**Non-Fiction** Publishes General Non-fiction title on the following titles:
 Regional, Walking guides.
**Submission Guidelines** Accepts query with SAE/ proposal package (including outline and sample chapter(s)).
**Recent Title(s)** *Walks Around the Malverns*, Roy Woodcock (Walking guide)
**Tips** Small, home based business publishing regional walking guidebooks. Relevant unsolicited submissions welcomed.

## Merlin Press
**99b Wallis Road, London, E9 5LN**
- 020 8533 5800
- info@merlinpress.co.uk
- www.merlinpress.co.uk

**Contact** Editor, A.W. Zurbrugg (History, Politics); Editor, A. Howe (Environment).
**Established** 1956
**Insider Info** Publishes 15 titles per year. Receives approximately 500 queries per year. Payment is via royalty (on wholesale price). Simultaneous submissions not accepted. Submissions accompanied by SAE will be returned. Aims to respond to queries within three months. Catalogue is free on request and available online. Manuscript guidelines are free on request.
**Non-Fiction** Publishes Autobiography, Biography and Scholarly titles on the following subjects:
 Government/Politics, History, Humanities, Social Sciences, Women's Issues/Studies, World Affairs.
**Submission Guidelines** Accepts proposal package (including outline, sample chapters and SAE).
**Recent Title(s)** *Pessimism of the Intellect*, Duncan Thompson (Politics).

## Merlin Publishing

**Newmarket Hall, Cork Street, Dublin 8, Republic of Ireland**

- 00353 1 453 5866
- 00353 1 453 5930
- publishing@merlin.ie
- www.merlinwolfhound.com

**Contact** Editorial Manager, Aoife Barrett
**Established** 2000
**Imprint(s)** Wolfhound Press
**Insider Info** Publishes 15 titles per year. Catalogue available online.
**Non-Fiction** Publishes General Non-fiction, Humour, Biography and Autobiography tiles on the following subjects:
Art/Architecture, Health/Medicine, Memoirs, Music/Dance, Sports, Travel, Politics and Current Affairs, Irish Interest, Lifestyle.
**Submission Guidelines** Submissions by post or email accepted. Accepts outline, one sample chapter, author biography, SAE, list of unique selling points, artworks/images.
Submission details to: aoife@merlin.ie
**Recent Title(s)** *The Outsiders, Exposing the Secretive World of Ireland's Travellers*, Eamon Dillon
**Tips** Merlin Publishing and Wolfhound Press welcome submissions for non-fiction titles, particularly true crime, music, sports, lifestyle, politics, biography and Irish historical interest. No children's fiction or general fiction titles.

## Merlin Unwin Books

**Palmers House, 7 Corve Street, Ludlow, Shropshire, SY8 1DB**

- 01584 877456
- 01584 877457
- books@merlinunwin.co.uk
- www.merlinunwin.co.uk

**Contact** Managing Director, Karen McCall (General Countryside, Country Crafts, Natural History); Chairman, Merlin Unwin (Fishing)
**Established** 1995
**Insider Info** Publishes 12 titles per year. Receives approximately 150 queries and 50 manuscripts per year. 50 per cent of books published are from first-time authors, 95 per cent of books are from unagented authors. Payment is via net receipts. Average lead time is one year, with simultaneous submissions not accepted. Submissions accompanied by SAE will be returned. Aims to respond to queries within three days, proposals within four weeks and manuscripts within four months. Catalogue is free on request and available

online. Manuscripts guidelines are available with an SAE, or by email.
**Non-Fiction** Publishes Autobiography, Biography, Coffee table books, Cookbooks, General Non-fiction, Gift, How-to, Humour, Illustrated, Reference and Textbook titles on the following subjects:
Agriculture/Horticulture, Alternative Lifestyles, Animals, Cooking/Foods/Nutrition, Crafts, Hobbies, Memoirs, Nature/Environment, Recreation, Sports.
* All submissions must have a UK countryside angle.
**Submission Guidelines** Accepts proposal package (including outline, three sample chapters, a brief synopsis, your publishing history, author biography and SAE) and artworks/images (send photocopies).
**Tips** Merlin Unwin Books prefers to work directly with their authors, not via an agent. Merlin Unwin is prepared to offer a great deal of support to their authors, as many of the books published are written by authors who are expert in their field, but not necessarily experienced or professional writers.

## Merrell Publishers Ltd

**81 Southwark Street, London, SE1 0HX**

- 020 7928 8880
- 020 7928 1199
- mail@merrellpublishers.com
- www.merrellpublishers.com

**Contact** Publisher, Hugh Merrell; Editorial Director, Julian Honer
**Established** 1993
**Insider Info** Publishes 30 titles per year. Payment is via royalties. Catalogue free on request, online. Manuscript guidelines online.
**Non-fiction** Publishes General Non-fiction, Gift book, Illustrated and Scholarly titles on the following subjects:
Art/Architecture, Automotive, Gardening, History, House and Home, Photography, Science, Women's Issues/Studies.
**Submission Guidelines** Query with SAE, submit completed manuscript and artwork/images.
We are always happy to receive book proposals to review, and can assure you of a thorough and rapid response. Please send your proposal, with a brief covering letter, to: Julian Honer, Editorial Director, at the Head Office in London, who will also happy to discuss potential projects informally on the telephone or by email.
Submission details to: jh@merrellpublishers.com
**Recent Title(s)** *George Bellows*, Mary Sayre Haverstock (Biography/Art)
**Tips** Merrell is an independent publisher, with offices in London and New York and worldwide sales and distribution.

## Methuen Drama

**38 Soho Square, London, W1D 3HB**

- 020 7758 0200
- 020 7758 0222
- performing@acblack.com
- www.acblack.com

**Parent Company** A & C Black

**Insider Info** Catalogue available online.

**Non-Fiction** Publishes Illustrated, Reference, Technical and Anthology titles on the following subjects:
Music/Dance, Performing Arts, Classical Drama/ Plays, Screen and Cinema, Theatre Studies.

**Recent Title(s)** *Actors' Yearbook 2007*

## Methuen Publishing Limited

**11–12 Buckingham Gate, London, SW1E 6LB**

- 020 7798 1600
- 020 7828 2098/020 7233 9827
- sales@methuen.co.uk
- www.methuen.co.uk

**Contact** Managing Director, Peter Tummons

**Established** 1889

**Imprint(s)** Politico's Publishing

**Insider Info** Publishes 60 titles per year. Receives approximately 200 queries and 100 manuscripts per year. Ten per cent of books published are from first-time authors, five per cent are from unagented authors and ten per cent are author subsidy published. Catalogue is available online.

**Non-Fiction** Publishes Autobiography, Biography, Humour, Diaries, Letters, Essay, and Anthology titles on the following subjects:
Memoirs, Philosophy, Psychology , Sports , Travel, Cultural Studies, Writing Guides, Entertainment.

**Submission Guidelines** Accepts query with SAE with proposal package (including synopsis). Prefers agented submissions.

**Fiction** Publishes Literary, Short Story Collections, Drama and and Stage Play titles.

**Submission Guidelines** Accepts query with SAE with proposal package (including synopsis). Prefers agented submissions.

**Recent Title(s)** *Sailors: English Merchant Seamen 1600 - 1750*, Peter Earle; *Disturbing the Peace,* Richard Yates

**Tips** Does not encourage unagented submissions, but will accept short queries with an SAE from unagented authors. Do not send any material via email.

## Michael Joseph

**80 Strand, London, WC2R 0RL**

- 020 7010 3000
- 020 7010 6060
- customer.service@penguin.co.uk
- www.penguin.co.uk

**Parent Company** Penguin General

**Contact** Managing Director, Louise Moore; Editorial Director, Harriet Evans

**Insider Info** Catalogue is available online or by email.

**Non-Fiction** Publishes Autobiography, Biography, General Non-fiction, How-to, Illustrated and Self-help titles on the following subjects:
Celebrity Autobiography, Cookery/Foods/Nutrition, Current Affairs, History, Humour, Mind, Body and Spirit, Showbiz, Sports, Travel, Television tie-ins.

**Submission Guidelines** Agented submissions only.

**Fiction** Publishes Crime, Humour, Mainstream/ Contemporary, Romance, Suspense, Thriller and Women's Interest titles.

**Submission Guidelines** Agented submissions only.

**Recent Title(s)** *Dr Gillian McKeith's Health Food Bible*, Gillian McKeith; *31 Dream Street,* Lisa Jewell

**Tips** Michael Joseph publishes market focused popular fiction and non-fiction, and is primarily focused on top-ten best sellers from authors such as Tom Clancy, Jamie Oliver and Clive Cussler.

## Michael O'Mara Books Ltd

**9 Lion Yard, Tremadoc Road, London, SW4 7NQ**

- 020 7720 8643
- 020 7627 8953
- firstname.lastname@mombooks.com
- www.mombooks.com

**Contact** Editorial Director (Commissioning), Lindsay Davies (General Non-fiction, Biography, Humour); Director (Editorial), Toby Buchan (General Non-fiction, History, Military History)

**Established** 1985

**Imprint(s)** Buster Books (Children's)

**Insider Info** Publishes 70 titles per year. Average lead time is six months, with simultaneous submissions accepted. Submissions accompanied by SAE will be returned. Catalogue is available with an SAE. Manuscript guidelines are available online.

**Non-Fiction** Publishes Autobiography, Biography, Children's/Juvenile, General Non-fiction, Gift, How-to, Humour, Illustrated and Reference titles on the following subjects:
Animals, Contemporary Culture, Creative Non-fiction, Entertainment/Games, Health/Medicine,

History, Hobbies, Language/Literature, Memoirs, Military/War, Music/Dance, Nostalgia, Sex, Sports.
 * Michael O'Mara Books only publish commercial, mass-market non-fiction.
**Submission Guidelines** Accepts proposal package (including outline, two to three sample chapters, your publishing history, author biography and SAE) and artworks/images (send photocopies).
 Submission details to: enquiries@mombooks.com
**Poetry** Occasionally publishes humorous poetry from established authors.

## Michelin Travel Publications
**Hannay House, 39 Clarendon Road, Watford, Hertfordshire, WD17 IJA**
- 01923 205240
- 01923 205241
- Online form
- www.viamichelin.com
**Contact** J. Lewis
**Established** 1900
**Non-Fiction** Publishes General Non-fiction and Illustrated titles on the following subjects:
 Travel, Maps/Atlases.
**Tips** Travel publisher, printing maps, atlases and travel guides. Also offers an online route planning service.

## Miles Kelly Publishing Ltd
**The Bardfield Centre, Great Bardfield, Essex, CM7 4SL**
- 01371 811309
- 01371 811393
- info@mileskelly.net
- www.mileskelly.net
**Contact** Publisher, Jim Miles; Publisher, Gerard Kelly
**Established** 1996
**Imprint(s)** Miles Kelly
 Bardfield Press
**Insider Info** Publishes 100 titles per year. Catalogue available online.
**Non-Fiction** Publishes Children's, Gift book and Reference titles.
**Submission Guidelines** No unsolicited manuscripts.
**Fiction** Publishes Children's titles.
**Recent Title(s)** *World of Science*, Miles Kelly Publishing (Children's reference)
**Tips** Miles Kelly publishes children's books. Above all, the aim has been to make top quality books that are enjoyable, attractive and useful, with fresh and innovative features that appeal to a wide readership.

## Milestone Publications
**62 Murray Road, Horndean, Waterlooville, PO8 9JL**
- 023 9259 7440
- 023 9259 1975
- info@gosschinaclub.co.uk
- www.gosscrestedchina.co.uk
**Contact** Managing Director, Lynda Pine
**Established** 1967
**Insider Info** Catalogue available for a charge online and via email.
**Non-Fiction** Publishes Reference titles on the following subjects:
 Art/Architecture related to Goss and Crested china.
**Recent Title(s)** *The Price Guide to Crested China*, Nicholas Pine (Reference)
**Tips** The *Goss and Crested China Club* is the leading dealer in Goss and other crested china and is based in Horndean, Hampshire. A wide range of titles are available through Milestone Press to help you value your collection.

## Millers Dale Publications
**7 Weavers Place, Chandlers Ford, Eastleigh, Hampshire, S053 ITU**
- 023 8026 1192
- gponting@clara.net
- http://home.clara.net/gponting/index-page11.html
**Contact** Managing Editor, Gerald Ponting
**Established** 1990
**Insider Info** Catalogue available online.
**Non-Fiction** Publishes General Non-fiction and Illustrated titles on the following subjects:
 Anthropology/Archaeology, Art/Architecture, History, Regional, Hampshire history/guides.
**Submission Guidelines** Proposals for local, Hampshire based, history books are welcomed.
**Recent Title(s)** *The Chandler's Ford Story*, Barbara Hillier and Gerald Ponting (Local history)
**Tips** Millers Dale specialises in local history, particularly related to central Hampshire, and books about Gerald Ponting's historical slide presentations.

## Milo Books Ltd
**The Old Weighbridge, Station Road, Wrea Green, Lancashire, PR4 2PH**
- 01772 672900
- 01772 687727
- info@milobooks.com
- www.milobooks.com
**Contact** Publisher, Peter Walsh

**Established** 1997

**Insider Info** Publishes 12 titles per year. Receives approximately 150 manuscripts per year. 95 per cent of books published are from first-time authors, 100 per cent of books published are from unagented authors. Payment is via royalty (on retail price). Average lead time is six months, with simultaneous submissions accepted. Submissions accompanied by SAE will be returned. Aims to respond to proposals within four weeks. Catalogue is available online. Manuscript guidelines are available by email.

**Non-Fiction** Publishes Autobiography, Biography and General Non-fiction titles on the following subjects:
Contemporary Culture, History, Humanities, Law, Memoirs, Social Sciences, Sports, World Affairs.
 * Milo Books recommends that all prospective authors be familiar with their current list.

**Submission Guidelines** Accepts proposal package (including outline, two sample chapters, author biography and SAE).

# Mitchell Beazley
**2–4 Heron Quays, London, E14 4JP**
- ☎ 020 7531 8400
- ☎ 020 7531 8650
- ✉ info@mitchell-beazley.co.uk
- 🌐 www.mitchell-beazley.co.uk

**Parent Company** Octopus Publishing Group
**Contact** Publisher, David Lamb
**Imprint(s)** Miller's Antiques
**Insider Info** Catalogue available online.
**Non-Fiction** Publishes Illustrated and Reference titles on the following subjects:
Art/Architecture, Crafts, Gardening, Health/Medicine, History, Sports, Antiques, Design, Interiors, Wine, Food and Drink, Health/Wellbeing.
**Recent Title(s)** *The Wines of Chile*, Peter Richards
**Tips** Authors are often experts in their fields and include well known television personalities. Most antiques titles are published under the Miller's imprint, a leading name in antique publishing.

# Morgan Kauffman
**The Boulevard, Langford Lane, Kidlington, Oxford, OX5 1GB**
- ☎ 01865 843000
- ☎ 01865 843010
- ✉ authorsupport@elsevier.com
- 🌐 www.books.elsevier.com/uk//mk

**Parent Company** Elsevier Ltd (Science & Technology)
**Established** 1984

**Insider Info** Royalties paid. Catalogue is available online.
 Manuscript guidelines available online at: www.elsevier.com/wps/find/authors.authors/bookauthorshome
**Non-Fiction** Publishes Multimedia, Reference, Scholarly, Textbook and Technical titles on the following subjects:
 Computers/Electronics, Computer Aided Design, Software Engineering, Artificial Intelligence, Databases.
**Submission Guidelines** Accepts query with SAE/Proposal package (including outline).
**Submission Guidelines** Morgan Kaufmann welcomes authors' proposals for books. The first step is to discuss the proposal with the relevant Publishing Editor. Check the website for in-depth submission guidelines and a full list of editorial contacts.
**Recent Title(s)** *Developer's Guide to Web Application Security*, Michael Cross (Computing/Reference); *Stealing the Network: How to Own a Shadow*, Johnny Long, Timothy Mullen and Ryan Russell ('Faction' - hacking/infosec)
**Tips** Morgan Kaufmann publishes technical information resources for computer and engineering professionals. The imprint publishes books and digital material in areas such as databases, computer networking, computer systems, human computer interaction, computer graphics, multimedia information and systems, artificial intelligence, and software engineering. Publications are aimed at the research and development communities, information technology (IS/IT) managers, and students in professional degree programs.

# Morning Star
**19 Off Quay Building, Foundry Lane, Byker, Newcastle Upon Tyne, NE6 1AF**
- ☎ 0191 265 6699
- ✉ alecfinlay@yahoo.com
- 🌐 www.alecfinlay.com

**Contact** Alec Finaly
**Established** 1990
**Insider Info** Catalogue available online.
**Non-Fiction** Publishes Regional and Travel titles.
**Fiction** Publishes Regional titles.
**Poetry** Publishes Poetry titles.
 * A latest project for Morning Star is 'bookscapes', a publishing programme combining book, audio CD, DVD and the internet. This project is published under the name 'Platform Projects'.

**Recent Title(s)** Journey to the Lower World, *Marcus Coats*

**Tips** Often co-publishes innovative projects that have included pocketbooks, folios and a small press series, combining poetry and other local accounts with art in unusual ways.

## Morrigan Book Company

**Morrigan Book Company, Killala, Co. Mayo, Republic of Ireland**

- 00353 19 632555
- morriganbooks@online.ie

**Contact** Publisher, Gerry Kennedy; Editor, Gillian Brennan; Irish Language Editor, Judy-Meg Ni Chinneide

**Established** 1979

**Non-Fiction** Publishes Biography and General Non-fiction titles on the following subjects:
 History, Regional, Irish non-fiction, Irish folklore/mythology.

**Tips** Publishes general interest Irish non-fiction including history, biography and folklore. Publishes mainly to public bodies and organisations such as Foras na Gaeilge.

## Mosby

**32 Jamestown Road, Camden Town, London, NW1 7BY**

- 020 7424 4200
- 020 7482 2293
- m.ging@elsevier.com
- www.intl.elsevierhealth.com/mosby

**Parent Company** Elsevier Ltd (Health Sciences)

**Established** 1906

**Insider Info** Royalties paid. Catalogue available online. Manuscript guidelines available online.

**Non-Fiction** Publishes Booklets, Multimedia, Reference, Scholarly, Textbook, Journal and Technical titles on the following subjects:
 Education, Health/Medicine, Science, Care.

**Submission Guidelines** Online Proposal Form. Alternatively authors may contact the Publishing Director or Editor prior to submission, to discuss the proposal.
 Submission details to: c.makepeace@elsevier.com

**Recent Title(s)** *Mosby's Medical Drug Reference 2007*, Allan Ellsworth (Medical/Reference)

**Tips** Mosby specialises in medicine, nursing, allied health and veterinary medicine, and publishes a wide range of textbooks, reference books and periodicals. Mosby's suite of healthcare resources includes newsletters, videos, posters, brochures, slides, CD-ROMs, seminars and conferences.

## Motor Racing Publications

**PO Box 1318, Croydon, Surrey, CR0 5YP**

- 020 8654 2711
- 020 8407 0339
- john@mrpbooks.co.uk
- www.motorracingpublications.co.uk

**Contact** Editorial Head, John Blunsden

**Insider Info** Publishes five titles per year. Payment via royalties. Catalogue available online.

**Non-Fiction** Publishes General Non-fiction, Reference and Technical titles on the following subjects:
 Automotive, History, Hobbies, Sports.

**Submission Guidelines** Accepts query with SAE/proposal package (including outline, sample chapter(s), SAE).

**Recent Title(s)** *The British at Le Mans*, Ian Wagstaff

**Tips** A current list of more than 70 titles, from *Collector's Guides* and *MRP Autoguides*, which cover some of the world's most desirable high-performance, classic cars, to motorsports histories and biographies. Books are aimed at any motorsport or automotive enthusiast. Welcomes synopses and ideas in the specified subject areas.

## MQ Publications Ltd

**12 the Ivories, 6–8 Northampton Street, London, N1 2HY**

- 020 7359 2244
- 020 7359 1616
- mail@mqpublications.com
- www.mqpublications.com

**Contact** Publisher, Zaro Weil

**Established** 1992

**Insider Info** Publishes 70 titles per year. Catalogue free on request and available online.

**Non-Fiction** Publishes Biography, General Non-fiction, Gift book and Illustrated titles on the following subjects:
 Contemporary Culture, Cooking/Foods/Nutrition, Health/Medicine, Photography, Spirituality.

**Recent Title(s)** *Knitorama: 25 Great & Glam Things to Knit*, Rachael Matthews (Craft/Hobbies)

**Tips** MQP has become one of the UK's fastest growing and most respected publishers of illustrated non-fiction, offering beautiful books to the relatively niche craft market.

## Mudfog Press

**c/o Arts Development, The Stables, Stewart Park, The Grove, Marton, Middlesborough, TS7 8AR**

mudfog@hodgeon.demon.co.uk

www.mudfog.co.uk

**Established** 1993

**Insider Info** Submissions accompanied by SAE will be returned. Aims to respond to manuscripts within three months.

**Fiction** Publishes Short story collections.

**Submission Guidelines** Manuscript must be typed on white A4 paper, one side only, in plain font and be accompanied by full return postage. No email submissions.

**Poetry** Publishes pamphlet length and occasionally full length collections of poetry and short stories.

**Submission Guidelines** Manuscript must be typed on white A4 paper, one side only, in plain font and be accompanied by full return postage. No email submissions.

**Recent Title(s)** *Service*, Marion Husband; *Like*, Norah Hill

**Tips** Mudfog showcases writers from the Tee Valley area, only so will not accept submissions from outside this region.

## Multi-Sensory Learning Ltd

**Highgate House, Creaton, Northants, NN6 8NN**

01604 505000

01604 505001

info@msl-online.net

www.msl-online.net

**Contact** Senior Editor, Philippa Chudley

**Established** 1994

**Insider Info** Catalogue available free on request and online.

**Non-Fiction** Publishes Children's, General Non-fiction, Self-help, Textbook and Scholarly titles on Dyslexia.

**Recent Title(s)** *Teaching the Brain to Read*, Dr. Duncan Milne

**Tips** MSL has specialised in structured, multi-sensory literacy resources since 1994. Schools, colleges, learning support centres, teachers, parents and dyslexic adults have selected our extensive range of learning materials, and have been delighted with the results. Always seeking authors able to write materials for coping with, and overcoming dyslexia.

## Murdoch Books UK Ltd

**Erico House, 6th Floor, 93–99 Upper Richmond Road, London, SW15 2TG**

020 8785 5995

020 8785 5985

info@murdochbooks.co.uk

www.murdochbooks.co.uk/mbuk.htm

**Contact** CEO (AU), Juliet Rogers; Publishing Director (AU), Kay Scarlett; Publisher (AU), Will Kiester

**Imprint(s)** Pier 9

**Insider Info** Publishes 50 titles per year. Catalogue available online.

**Non-Fiction** Publishes General Non-fiction titles on the following subjects:
Cooking/Foods/Nutrition, Crafts, Gardening, Health/Medicine, Hobbies, House and Home.

**Recent Title(s)** *Nine Summers*, Rina Huber (Travel/Memoir)

**Tips** Has traditionally published high quality, predominantly illustrated non-fiction, in the leisure/lifestyle categories, particularly cooking, DIY, gardening and craft. More recently they have been extending the range to include other lifestyle categories such as health. The successful launch and development of the Pier 9 imprint will herald further growth in the general narrative non-fiction area. Has a separate email address for any submission enquiries, but unfortunately no guidelines are available on website.

## Myriad Editions

**59 Lansdowne Place, Brighton, BN3 1FL**

01273 720000

01273 720000

info@myriadeditions.com

www.myriadeditions.com

**Contact** Managing Director, Candida Lacey

**Established** 1993

**Insider Info** Catalogue available online.

**Non-Fiction** Publishes Illustrated books, Atlases and General Non-fiction titles on the following subjects:
Business/Economics, Government/Politics, Military/War, Regional, Social Sciences, Women's Issues/Studies, World Affairs.

**Fiction** Publishes Literary and Activist titles.

**Recent Title(s)** *The Atlas of Religion*, Joanne O'Brien and Martin Palmer (Atlas/World Affairs); *A Kind of Vanishing*, Lesley Thomson (Novel)

**Tips** Myriad Editions is an independent publishing house based in Brighton, UK. Founded in 1993, it has won international acclaim for its award winning *State of the World* atlas series and remains committed to mapping the most pressing issues facing the world today. These unique visual surveys of economic, political and social trends, make global issues accessible for general readers, students and professionals alike. Aim to combine clear analysis with creative graphics, in order to illustrate human development and social concerns. Myriad is now expanding its publishing programme to include edgy literary fiction, activist non fiction and documentary comic books.

## N.A.G Press
**Clerkenwell House, Clerkenwell Green, London, EC1R 0HT**
- 020 7251 2661
- 020 7490 4958
- webmistress@halebooks.com
- www.halebooks.com

**Insider Info** Catalogue free on request via email.
**Non-Fiction** Publishes specialist Horological and Gemmological titles.
**Submission Guidelines** Submit proposal package (including outline, three sample chapters, SAE).
**Tips** Book published are very niche and readers will generally be enthusiasts and collectors of gems and timepieces. No emailed submissions.

## The National Archives
**The National Archives, Kew, Richmond, Surrey, TW9 4DU**
- 020 8392 5289
- 020 8487 1974
- catherine.bradley@nationalarchives.gov.uk
- www.nationalarchives.gov.uk

**Insider Info** Publishes 20 titles per year. Catalogue and author guidelines are free on request.
**Non-Fiction** Publishes Reference, Record, Directory and Archive Material titles on History and British History.
**Recent Title(s)** *The Scotland Yard Files. Milestones in Crime Detection*, Alan Moss and Keith Skinner
**Tips** The National Archives is a government department and an executive agency under the Secretary of State for Constitutional Affairs. Book titles are primarily aimed at history enthusiasts, family history researchers and military historians. Also publishes a wealth of record keeping documentation.

## National Library of Ireland
**Kildare Street, Dublin 2, Republic of Ireland**
- 00353 1 603 0200
- 00353 1 676 6690
- info@nli.ie
- www.nli.ie

**Insider Info** Catalogue available online.
**Non-Fiction** Publishes Booklets, Illustrated books, Reference and Scholarly titles on the following subjects:
History, Irish interest.

**Recent Title(s)** *Ulysses Unbound: A Reader's Companion to James Joyce's Ulysses*, Terence Killeen (Literary criticism)
**Tips** The National Library of Ireland is a cultural institution under the aegis of the Department of Arts, Sport and Tourism. Its mission is to collect, preserve and make available, books, manuscripts and illustrative material of Irish interest.

## National Trust Books
**151 Freston Road, London, W10 6TH**
- 020 7314 1400
- 020 7314 1401
- www.anovabooks.com

**Parent Company** Anova Books Company Ltd
**Established** 2005 (became an imprint of Anova)
**Insider Info** Catalogue available online.
**Non-Fiction** Publishes Children's, Coffee table books, Cookbooks, General Non-fiction, Gift books and Illustrated titles on the following subjects: Heritage, Gardening, Craft, Cooking, Environment. Art/Architecture, Cooking/Foods/Nutrition, Gardening, History, Nature/Environment, Regional, Science, Social Sciences.
 * Books may reflect works done by the trust to preserve and protect coastline, countryside and buildings, and aim to educate people about the importance of the environment and of preserving our heritage for future generations.
**Recent Title(s)** *Arts & Crafts Needlepoint*, Beth Russell

## Natural History Museum Publishing
**Natural History Museum, Cromwell Road, London, SW7 5BD**
- 020 7942 5336
- 020 7942 6994
- publishing@nhm.ac.uk
- www.nhm.ac.uk

**Contact** Editorial Director, Trudy Brannan (Natural History/Science)
**Established** 1881
**Insider Info** Publishes eight titles per year. Receives 40 queries and 40 manuscripts per year. 50 per cent of books published are from first-time authors, 100 per cent of books published are from unagented authors. Payment is via royalty (on wholesale price) or outright purchase. Simultaneous submissions are accepted. Submissions accompanied by SAE will be returned. Aims to respond to queries and proposals within 14 days and manuscripts within 28 days. Catalogue is free on request and available by email. Manuscript guidelines are free on request.

**Non-Fiction** Publishes Coffee table, General Non-fiction, Gift, Illustrated, Reference, Scholarly and Textbook titles on the following subjects: Agriculture/Horticulture, Animals, Anthropology/Archaeology, Art/Architecture, Education, Gardening, History, Marine Subjects, Natural History, Nature/Environment, Photography, Popular Science.
**Submission Guidelines** Accepts queries with SAE.
**Recent Title(s)** *Troubled Waters*, Sarah Lazarus (Popular Science)
**Tips** Natural History Museum Publishing publishes books for a general readership, although some titles are useful for students and academics.

## The Natural History Museum Publishing Division
**Publishing, The Natural History Museum, Cromwell Road, London, SW7 5BD**
- 020 7942 5071
- 020 7942 5010
- publishing@nhm.ac.uk
- www.nhm.ac.uk/publishing

**Contact** Head of Publishing, Colin Ziegler; Editorial Manager, Trudy Brannan
**Insider Info** Catalogue available online.
**Non-Fiction** Publishes Children's/Juvenile, General Non-fiction, Reference and Scholarly titles on the following subjects: Education, History, Nature/Environment, Science. * Publish books and journals that reflect the Museum's collections, scientific work and exhibitions, with titles that vary from high-level academic books and journals, to popular science and natural history art.
**Recent Title(s)** *Natural History Museum Atlas of Bird Migration*, Jonathan Elphick (ed.)
**Tips** Most books are directly related to the museum or its contents. Separate academic and specialist titles are published in association with external publishers.

## Nature Publishing
**The Macmillan Building, 4 Crinan Street, London, N1 9XW**
- 020 7833 4000
- 020 7843 4640
- nature@nature.com, firstinitial.lastname@nature.com
- www.nature.com

**Contact** Managing Director/Publisher, Annette Thomas; Publishing Directors, David Swinbanks, Peter Collins; Senior Associate Director, Alison Mitchell; Editor in Chief, Philip Campbell (Nature Titles)
**Insider Info** Catalogue available online. Manuscript guidelines available online.
**Non-Fiction** Publishes Academic journals and online resources on the following subjects:. Health/Medicine, Nature/Environment, Science.
**Submission Guidelines** Academics should register on the website to allow the submission of their articles for particular journals.
**Tips** The scientific publishing arm of the Macmillan Group, publishing mainly journals on health, science, medicine and technology. The 'Editorial Policy' section of the website gives authors information on how to submit their original research papers for consideration for particular journals. Publications are intended for academic and professional readerships.

## Natzler Enterprises (Entertainments)
**1 Wakeford Cottages, Selden Lane, Worthing, West Sussex, BN11 2LQ**
- 01903 211785
- 01903 211519
- natzler@btinternet.com
- www.natzler.com

**Contact** Managing Editor, Paul Gordon
**Established** 1993
**Insider Info** Catalogue available online, website www.paulgordon.net/acatalog
**Non-Fiction** Publishes How-to, Multimedia and Reference titles on Magic tricks.
**Submission Guidelines** No unsolicited manuscripts, but may consider ideas.
**Tips** Publishes magic trick books and equipment.

## Nautical Data Ltd
**The Book Barn, White Chimney Row, Westbourne, Hampshire, PO10 8RS**
- 01243 389352
- 01243 379136
- enquiries@nauticaldata.com
- www.nauticaldata.com

**Contact** Managing Director, Piers Mason
**Established** 1999
**Insider Info** Publishes 20 titles per year. Payment is via royalties.
**Non-Fiction** Publishes Reference and Technical titles on the following subjects: Nautical/Sailing.
**Submission Guidelines** Accepts query with SAE/proposal package (including outline, sample chapter(s), SAE).

**Tips** Publishes books on shipping and nautical reference. Will consider project ideas and proposals but no fiction or non-nautical subjects.

## NCVO Publications

**The National Council for Voluntary Organisations, Regents Wharf, 8 All Saints Street, London, N1 9RL**

- 020 7713 6161
- 020 7713 6300
- ncvo@ncvo-vol.org.uk
- www.ncvo-vol.org.uk/publications

**Contact** CEO, Stuart Etherington; Director of Services and Development, Ben Kernigha

**Established** 1919

**Insider Info** Catalogue available free on request via email: HelpDesk@ncvo-vol.org.uk and online. No unsolicited manuscripts.

**Recent Title(s)** *The Honorary Treasurer's Handbook*, Les Jones and Tesse Akpeki

**Tips** NCVO believes passionately in the voluntary and community sector. This is a sector with the power to transform the lives of people and communities for the better. NCVO mostly publishes directories and information on management, finance and employment.

## Neate Publishing

**Hedgerows, 33 Downside Road, Winchester, SO22 5LT**

- 01962 841479
- 01962 841743
- bobbie@neatepublishing.co.uk
- www.neatepublishing.co.uk

**Contact** Managing Director, Bobbie Neate

**Established** 1999

**Insider Info** Catalogue available online.

**Non-Fiction** Publishes Children's, Textbook and Scholarly titles on Education.

**Recent Title(s)** *Body Parts*, Bobbie Neate (Education/ Reference)

**Tips** Our products are innovative and informative, specialising in non-fiction books, role play and the teaching of 'notemaking' and 'notetaking' for schools and pupils. All ideas for publishing are welcome. We specialise in primary age children and would like to hear from any potential authors. Get in touch by post. Please do not send emails with attachments, we do not open them. Particularly welcome are ideas for new role play packs.

## Neil Miller Publications

**Ormonde House, Ormonde Road, Hythe, Kent, CT21 6DW**

- neilamillerpublications@supanet.com
- www.webspawner.com/users/neilmillerpubs

**Contact** Managing Editor, Neil Miller

**Established** 1994

**Imprint(s)** Black Cat Books

**Insider Info** Manuscript guidelines are available for a cost.

**Non-Fiction** Publishes Biography, General Non-fiction and Humour titles on the following subjects: History, Memoirs, Military/War.

**Fiction** Publishes Adventure, Fantasy, Horror, Humour, Military/War, Mystery, Short story collections and Romance titles.

**Submission Guidelines** Don't submit a manuscript until you have consulted the guidelines on the website.

**Recent Title(s)** *Windjammer Landing*, Mark Carter

## Neil Wilson Publishing Ltd

**Suite Ex 8, Pentagon Centre, 44 Washington Street, Glasgow, Scotland, G3 8AZ**

- 0141 221 1117
- 0141 221 5363
- info@nwp.co.uk
- www.nwp.co.uk

**Imprint(s)** Vital Spark
In Pinn
The Angels Share
11:9

**Insider Info** Catalogue and manuscript guidelines are available online.

**Non-Fiction** Publishes Biography, General Non-fiction and Reference titles on the following subjects: General Reference, History, True Crime.

**Submission Guidelines** Submit proposal package (including outline, synopsis, one sample chapter, author biography, CV and SAE). Will accept artworks/ images.

**Recent Title(s)** *The Jacobite Dictionary*, Mary McKerracher (History)

**Tips** Neil Wilson Publishing is one of Scotland's leading independent publishers. They specialise in non-fiction and fiction of Scottish, and sometimes Irish, interest and also offer some of their specialist titles on a 'Print on Demand' basis. See imprint entries for further details.

## Nelson Thornes Ltd

**Delta Place, 27 Bath Road, Cheltenham, Gloucestershire, GL53 7TH**

- 01242 267100
- 01242 221914
- cservices@nelsonthornes.com
- http://aa.nelsonthornes.com

**Parent Company** Wolters Kluwer Group
**Contact** Managing Director, Mary O'Connor
**Established** Formed in 2000 with the merger of Thomas Nelson and Stanley Thornes publishing companies
**Insider Info** Catalogue is free on request and available online, by email to: cservices@nelsonthornes.com or by telephone, 01242 267382
**Non-Fiction** Publishes Illustrated, CD-ROM, Electronic Teaching and Learning Resource titles on the following subjects:
Education, Children's/Juvenile, Nursing, Health Sciences, Teacher Training, CPD.

## New Beacon Books Ltd

**76 Stroud Green Road, London, N4 3EN**

- 020 7272 4889
- 020 7281 4662
- newbeaconbooks@btconnect.com

**Contact** Editor in Chief, John La Rose; Managing Director, Sarah White
**Established** 1966
**Insider Info** Payment is via royalties.
**Non-Fiction** Publishes Children's, General Non-fiction, Reference and Scholarly titles on the following subjects:
Education, Government/Politics, History, Language/Literature, Black literature.
**Fiction** Publishes Black Literature titles.
**Submission Guidelines** No unsolicited material.
**Tips** New Beacon Books provides a service to individuals, academics, students, universities, libraries, schools and colleges. They specialise in books that highlight Black life in Britain and their links in Europe, the Caribbean, Africa and African America.

## New Cavendish Books

**3 Denbigh Road, London, W11 2SJ**

- 020 7229 6765
- 020 7792 0027
- sales@newcavendishbooks.co.uk
- www.newcavendishbooks.co.uk

**Established** 1973

**Insider Info** Catalogue available online, free on request.
**Non-Fiction** Publishes General Non-fiction and Reference titles on the following subjects:
Hobbies, Collecting.
**Recent Title(s)** *A Century of Deans Rag Books & Rag Dolls*
**Tips** New Cavendish Books is celebrating 30 years of dedication to publishing some of the finest books on toys, popular culture and collectibles of the 19th and 20th Centuries.

## New Holland Publishers (UK) Ltd

**Garfield House, 86–88 Edgware Road, London, W2 2EA**

- 020 7724 7773
- 020 7724 6184
- enquiries@nhpub.co.uk
- www.newhollandpublishers.com

**Contact** Managing Director, John Beaufoy; Publishing Manager, Rosemary Wilkinson; Publishing Manager, Jo Hemmings
**Established** 1956
**Insider Info** Publishes 100 titles per year. Catalogue available online.
**Non-Fiction** Publishes General Non-fiction, How-to and Reference titles on the following subjects:
Cooking/Foods/Nutrition, Crafts, Gardening, Health/Medicine, History, Hobbies, House and Home, Nature/Environment, Spirituality, Sports.
**Recent Title(s)** *The Grand Literary Cafes of Europe* (History)
**Tips** New Holland is a publishing house dedicated to the highest editorial and design standards. The publishing programme features the cream of new illustrated books from Australia, New Zealand and South Africa. With a large range of general and practical non-fiction books, New Holland have only recently begun to publish history books, and are looking to expand upon their initial success with them.

## New Hope International

**20 Werneth Avenue, Gee Cross, Hyde, Cheshire, SK14 5NL**

- 0161 351 1878
- geraldengland@yahoo.com
- www.geraldengland.co.uk

**Established** 1980
**Insider Info** Receives approximately 100 queries and 20 manuscripts per year. 100 per cent of books published are from unagented authors. Payment consists of 20 free copies plus a 50 per cent discount

on New Hope titles. Average lead time is six months, with simultaneous submissions not accepted. Submissions accompanied by SAE will be returned. Aims to respond to queries and proposals within 14 days and manuscripts within 30 days. Catalogue and manuscript guidelines are available online.

**Non-Fiction** Publishes Literary Criticism titles.

**Submission Guidelines** No new submissions are considered presently.

**Poetry** Publishes Poetry and Poetry in Translation.

**Submission Guidelines** No new submissions are considered presently.

**Recent Title(s)** *The Art of Haiku*, Gerald England ed. (Educational)

**Tip** New Hope International publishes poetry and literary criticism, including far Eastern translation, for an intelligent readership. New Hope is currently not accepting submissions.

## New Island Books
**2 Brookside, Dundrum Road, Dublin 14, Republic of Ireland**
- 00353 1 298 9937/298 3411
- 00353 1 298 2783
- thomas.cooney@newisland.ie
- www.newisland.ie

**Contact** Managing Director, Edwin Higel

**Established** 1992

**Insider Info** Catalogue free on request online.

**Non-Fiction** Publishes Autobiography, Biography, General Non-fiction, Humour and Illustrated titles on the following subjects:
 Business/Economics, Community/Public Affairs, Government/Politics, History, Humanities, World Affairs.

**Fiction** Publishes Plays and Mainstream/Contemporary titles.

**Poetry** Publishes Poetry titles.

**Recent Title(s)** *In Search of Iraq*, Richard Downes; *Not a Star*, Nick Hornby

**Tips** Also publishes the *Open Door* series of fiction novellas aimed at adults with literacy problems. *Open Door* authors are advised to avoid sentences with multiple clauses, to keep vocabulary simple, using common and straightforward words, but to allow the occasional challenging word (where useful).

## Newnes
**The Boulevard, Langford Lane, Kidlington, Oxford, OX5 1GB**
- 01865 843000
- 01865 843010
- authorsupport@elsevier.com
- www.books.elsevier.com

**Parent Company** Elsevier Ltd (Science & Technology)

**Insider Info** Royalties paid. Catalogue available online. Manuscript guidelines available online.

**Non-Fiction** Publishes Reference, Scholarly, Textbook and Technical titles on the following subjects:
 Communications, Computers/Electronics, Education, Power Engineering.

**Submission Guidelines** Accepts query with SAE/proposal package (including outline).
 Newnes welcomes authors' proposals for books. The first step is to discuss the proposal with the relevant Publishing Editor. Check the website for in-depth submission guidelines and a full list of editorial contacts.

**Recent Title(s)** *Wireless Networking Technology*, Steve Rackley (Computing/Networks)

**Tips** Newnes is a leading name in electronics and electrical engineering books, aimed at professional engineers and technicians, undergraduate and postgraduate students and electronics enthusiasts. Newnes publishes books on power engineering, telecommunications, consumer electronics, circuit design, computer engineering and embedded systems, plus vocational textbooks and the *Newnes Pocket Book* Series.

## New Playwrights' Network
**10 Station Road Industrial Estate, Colwall, Near Malvern, Herefordshire, WR13 6RN**
- 01684 540154
- 01684 540154
- simonsmith@cresselles4drama.fsbusiness.co.uk

**Contact** Publishing Director, Leslie Smith

**Fiction** Publishes Plays.

**Tips** Publishes general amateur plays of varying lengths.

## New Riders
**Edinburgh Gate, Harlow, Essex, CM20 2JE**
- 01279 623623
- 01279 414130
- www.pearsoned.co.uk/Imprints/NewRiders

**Parent Company** Pearson Education

**Insider Info** Catalogue and manuscript guidelines are available online.

**Non-Fiction** Publishes How-to, Illustrated, Multimedia and Reference titles on the following subjects:
 Graphics, Design, Creative Technology, Visual Arts.

**Submission Guidelines** Accepts proposal package (including synopsis, sample chapters, market research, your publishing history and author biography).

**Recent Title(s)** *Welcome to Oz (A Cinematic Approach to Digital Still Photography with Photoshop)*, Vincent Versace (Visual Arts)

**Tips** New Riders is a forum for leading voices in creative and information technologies. New Riders has the authors and the books that truly make a difference in professional life, from web development and design to networking and graphic design. See website for full list of submissions contacts.

## New Theatre Publications/The Playwrights' Co-operative
2 Hereford Close, Woolston, Warrington, Chesire, WA1 4HR

- 0845 331 3516
- 0845 331 3518
- info@plays4theatre.com
- www.plays4theatre.com

**Contact** Director, Ian Hornby; Director, Paul Beard
**Established** 1987
**Insider Info** Aims to respond to proposals and manuscripts within one month. Catalogue free on request, online. Manuscript guidelines available online.
**Fiction** Publishes Plays.

**Tips** New Theatre Publications is the trading name of the publishing house that is owned by members of the Co-operative. This exciting project was launched by writers Paul Beard and Ian Hornby in October 1997, following the discovery that for a number of years they, and a large number of other writers, had been systematically ripped off by a well known publishing house who were failing to pass on royalty payments. From the outset it was the intention to provide the kind of service to writers that no other publishing house offers, we constantly review our methods to keep one step ahead of all the others. We endeavour to be as open as possible in the submission and publication process, and are always looking for ways to improve. Please note that we only accept play submissions from members of the Co-operative. That's not trying to exclude anyone - we welcome all new members with open arms - but it's how we operate and how we continue to operate in financial terms.

## nferNelson
The Chiswick Centre, 414 Chiswick High Road, London, W4 5TF

- 020 8996 3333
- 020 8742 8390
- www.nfer-nelson.co.uk/

**Established** 1981
**Insider Info** Catalogue available online and by email.

**Tips** nferNelson publishes electronic and paper based tests and assessments for the educational market (largely focusing on ages up to 14 but also up to age 19), covering knowledge, understanding and progress, ability, special needs, personal development testing, and assessment.

## Nicholas Brealey Publishing
3–5 Spafield Street, Clerkenwell, London, EC1R 4QB

- 020 7239 0360
- 020 7239 0370
- sales@nicholasbrealey.com
- www.nicholasbrealey.com

**Contact** Managing Director, Nicholas Brealey
**Established** 1992
**Insider Info** Publishes 30 titles per year. Catalogue available online. Manuscript guidelines available online.
**Non-Fiction** Publishes General Non-fiction, Reference, Self-help and Technical titles on the following subjects:
 Business/Economics, Government/Politics, Health/Medicine, Psychology, Travel.
**Submission Guidelines** Accepts query with SAE/proposal package (including outline, sample chapter(s), SAE).
 Submission details to: editorial@nicholasbrealey.com

**Recent Title(s)** *50 Psychology Classics*, Tom Butler-Bowdon
**Tips** An independent publisher of innovative books in business and economics, self-help and psychology, travel writing and crossing cultures. We are a global publishing group with offices in London and Boston, which includes Intercultural Press, the premier publisher of books and training materials on cultural diversity. Nicholas Brealey Publishing welcomes fresh ideas and new insights on business and economics, intelligent self-help/popular psychology, and the increasingly significant fields of travel writing and crossing cultures. If you would like to submit a publishing proposal for consideration, please follow the guidelines on the website.

## Nick Hern Books

**The Glasshouse, 49a Goldhawk Road, London, W12 8QP**

- 020 8749 4953
- 020 8735 0250
- info@nickhernbooks.demon.co.uk
- www.nickhernbooks.co.uk

**Established** 1993

**Insider Info** Publishes 80 titles per year. Five per cent of books published are from first-time authors. Payment via royalty (on retail price). Catalogue is free on request and available online. Manuscript guidelines are available online.

**Non-Fiction** Publishes General Non-fiction and Practical titles on the following subjects: Drama, Plays, Theatre (Practical).

* Publishes books by practitioners of theatre, for practitioners of theatre, not historical/critical surveys.

**Submission Guidelines** Accepts proposal package (including outline, sample chapters, author biography and SAE).

**Fiction** Publishes Plays.

* Can only consider plays attached to significant professional productions in major theatres.

**Submission Guidelines** Submit completed manuscript.

## Nightingale Books

**Sheraton House, Castle Park, Cambridge, CB3 OAX**

- 01223 370012
- 01223 370040
- editors@pegasuspublishers.com
- www.pegasuspublishers.com

**Parent Company** Pegasus Elliot MacKenzie Publishers Ltd

**Insider Info** Catalogue and manuscript guidelines available online.

**Non-Fiction** Publishes Children's, General Non-fiction and Illustrated titles on Education.

**Submission Guidelines** Submit proposal package (including outline and two sample chapters).

**Fiction** Publishes Multimedia, Fables and Myths, Picture Books, Teenage Literature and 'Chick Lit'.

**Submission Guidelines** Submit proposal package (including two sample chapters).

**Poetry** Publishes Contemporary Poetry titles.

**Submission Guidelines** Accepts queries.

**Tips** Nightingale Books publishes children's fiction and educational resources as the children's imprint of Pegasus Elliot MacKenzie Publishers Ltd.

## NMS Enterprises Limited-Publishing

**National Museums Scotland, Chambers Street, Edinburgh, EH1 1JF**

- 0131 247 4026
- 0131 247 4012
- publishing@nms.ac.uk
- www.nms.ac.uk

**Contact** Director of Publishing, Lesley A. Taylor; Publishing Administrator, Rajeev Jose

**Established** 1987

**Insider Info** Payment is via royalties.

**Non-Fiction** Publishes Children's, General Non-fiction, Reference and Scholarly titles on the following subjects: Anthropology/Archaeology, Art/Architecture, History, Nature/Environment, Science.

**Submission Guidelines** Accepts query with SAE/proposal package (including outline, sample chapter(s) and SAE).

**Recent Title(s)** *Audubon in Edinburgh and his Scottish Associates*, John Chalmers

**Tips** Books published by National Museums Scotland reflect the range and international importance of the collections. Publications vary from full colour exhibition catalogues, to children's books, academic monographs, biography and souvenir booklets. Themes include applied art, archaeology, natural history, conservation, and Scottish history and culture. The list of titles represents collections from all our museums. Interested in proposals, but only if they concern National Museum of Scotland collections.

## No Exit Press

**PO Box 394, Harpenden, AL5 1XJ**

- 01582 761264
- 01582 7612244
- info@noexit.co.uk
- www.noexit.co.uk

**Contact** Managing Director, Ion Mills

**Fiction** Publishes Crime titles.

**Submission Guidelines** * No unsolicited material. May not return unsolicited manuscripts.

**Recent Title(s)** *Kismet*, Jacob Arjouni (Crime fiction/Urban thriller)

## Northcote House Publishers Ltd

**Horndon House, Horndon, Tavistock, Devon, PL19 9NQ**

- 01892 837171
- 01892 837272
- northcote.house@virgin.net

ⓦ www.northcotehouse.co.uk
**Contact** Publisher, Brian Hulme; General Editor, Prof. Isobel Armstrong
**Established** 1985
**Insider Info** Publishes 25 titles per year. Payment is via royalties. Catalogue available online.
**Non-Fictio. Pyam** Publishes Scholarly titles on the following subjects:
 Education, Language/Literature, Literary Criticism.
**Submission Guidelines** Accepts query with SAE/proposal package (including outline, two sample chapters, market research and SAE).
 Will not read unsolicited manuscripts but will consider well thought out proposals with sample chapters and thorough market research.
**Recent Title(s)** *Women Romantic Poets*, Anna Barbauld and Mary Robinson
**Tips** Publishes brief but rigorous critical examinations of the works of distinguished writers and schools of writing. The series embraces the best of modern literary theory and criticism, and features studies of many popular late 20th Century writers, as well as the canonical figures of literature and important literary genres.

## NorthernSky Press
**PO Box 21548, Stirling, Scotland, FK8 1YY**
ⓞ 07981 173819
ⓔ northernsky@hush.com
ⓦ www.northernskypress.co.uk
**Contact** Commissioning Editor, Sarah Young; Political Editor, Declan McCormick; Poetry Editor, Finn Brennan
**Non-Fiction** Publishes political writing.
**Submission Guidelines** Submit completed manuscript.
**Poetry** Publishes Poetry titles.
**Submission Guidelines** Submit sample poems.
**Recent Title(s)** *When the G8 Came to my Town*, Declan McCormick; *Photo-me,* Robin MacGregor
**Tips** Publishes new writing, including authors who do not come from an academic background and have no publishing history.

## Norvik Press Ltd
**LLT, University of East Anglia, Norwich, NR4 7TJ**
ⓞ 01603 593356
ⓞ 01603 250599
ⓔ norvik.press@uea.ac.uk
ⓦ www.llt.uea.ac.uk/norvik_press
**Contact** Managing Editor, Janet Garton; Managing Editor, Michael Robinson

**Insider Info** Publishes six titles per year. Payment is via royalties. Catalogue available online.
**Non-Fiction** Publishes Scholarly titles on the following subjects:
 Language/Literature, Literary Criticism, Scandinavian Literature.
**Fiction** Publishes Literary and Translation titles.
**Submission Guidelines** Query with SAE/proposal package (including outline, sample chapter(s) and SAE).
**Recent Title(s)** *Strindberg and Genre*, Michael Robinson ed. (Literary Criticism); *Days with Diam*, Svend Åge Madsen (Translated)
**Tips** Norvik Press is a publishing house based at the University of East Anglia specialising in Scandinavian literature. It also publishes the journals *Scandinavia* and *Swedish Book Review*. The press is interested in submissions within the literary criticism and history fields of Scandinavian literature.

## The Nostalgia Collection
**Silver Link Publishing Ltd, The Trundle, Ringstead Road, Kettering, Northamptonshire, NN14 4BW**
ⓞ 01832 734425
ⓞ 01832 734425
ⓔ WAdams1907@aol.com
ⓦ www.nostalgiacollection.com
**Contact** Managing Editor, Will Adams
**Established** 1985
**Imprint(s)** Silverlink
 Past and Present
 Cumha
**Insider Info** Payment is via fees. Catalogue available online.
**Non-Fiction** Publishes General Non-fiction, Illustrated, Reference and Technical titles on the following subjects:
 History, Military/War, Nature/Environment, Regional, Transportation, Rurality, Towns and Village Life, Steam Trains and Locomotives, Inland Waterways and other Rural Issues.
**Recent Title(s)** *Horton's Guide to Britain's Railways in Feature Films*, Glyn Horton
**Tips** Publishes post-war nostalgia under the Past and Present imprint; railways, road transport and maritime titles under the Silverlink imprint; and Irish interest nostalgia under the Cumha imprint.

## Nottingham University Press
**Manor Farm, Church Lane, Thrumpton, Nottingham, NG11 0AX**
ⓞ 0115 983 1011

0115 983 1003

editor@nup.com

www.nup.com

**Contact** Managing Editor, Dr. D.J.A. Cole

**Insider Info** Payment is via royalties. Catalogue available online.

**Non-Fiction** Publishes Reference and Scholarly titles on the following subjects:
 Agriculture/Horticulture, Cooking/Foods/Nutrition, Health/Medicine, Law, Social Sciences, Engineering.

**Recent Title(s)** *Managing Gut Health*, Tobias Steiner

**Tips** Nottingham University Press is a dynamic and rapidly expanding independent university press. It has gained international recognition as a publisher of high quality scientific and technical publications, particularly in the fields of animal and food science.

## nth position Press
**38 Allcroft Road, London, NW5 4NE**

020 7485 5002

020 7485 5002

val@nthposition.com

www.nthposition.com

**Contact** Editor, Val Stevenson (Politics and Fiction); Poetry Editor, Todd Swift (Poetry)

**Established** 2002

**Insider Info** Publishes four titles per year. Receives 500 queries and 500 manuscripts per year. Five per cent of books published are from first-time authors, 80 per cent of books published are from unagented authors. No payment offered as nth position is a not for profit company. Average lead time is one month, with simultaneous submissions not accepted. Submissions will not be returned. Aims to respond to queries, proposals and manuscripts within one month. Catalogue available online.

**Non-Fiction** Publishes Booklets (also in electronic format), Anthologies, e-books and pod-book titles on the following subjects:
 Creative Non-fiction, Humanities, Politics, Travel.

**Submission Guidelines** Accepts queries by email only (including author biography).

**Fiction** Publishes Literary (e-books, e-zine), and Short story titles.

**Submission Guidelines** Accepts queries by email only (including author biography).

**Poetry** Publishes Poetry and Poetry in Translation.

**Submission Guidelines** Submit two sample poems by email.

## Nyala Publishing
**4 Christian Fields, London, SW16 3JZ**

020 8764 6292

020 8764 6292

nyala.publishing@geo-group.co.uk

www.geo-group.co.uk

**Established** 1980s

**Non-Fiction** Publishes Biography, General Non-fiction titles on Travel.
 * Nyala's publishing house is small and specialised in the areas of biographies, travel and other non-fiction. No fiction or poetry. The bulk of the work that Nyala do is providing publishing services to external clients.

**Submission Guidelines** No unsolicited manuscripts. Ideas and synopses only. Only submit book ideas that meet the required criteria of biography, travel, or non-fiction.

**Tips** Nyala is part of a larger company, the Geo Group. Explore the website to get a flavour for the company as a whole.

## Oak Tree Press
**19 Rutland Street, Cork, Republic of Ireland**

00353 21 431 3855

00353 21 431 3496

info@oaktreepress.com

www.oaktreepress.com

**Contact** Managing Director, Brian O'Kane

**Established** 1991

**Insider Info** Catalogue is available online. Manuscript guidelines are available online.

**Non-Fiction** Publishes reference and technical titles on the following sbjects:
 Business/Economics, Communications, Computers/ Electronics, Law, Money/Finance and Management.

**Recent Title** *Employee Partnership in Ireland*, John O'Dowd

**Tips** As a leading business book publisher, Oak Tree Press aims to bring success to business by providing information, advice and resources to entrepreneurs and managers of SMEs, and those who support and educate them. Oak Tree Press is always interested in hearing from prospective authors, who are invited to submit book ideas and manuscripts to: info@ oaktreepress.com. The publishers are happy to discuss submissions. When putting a proposal together, please ensure you follow the guidelines on the Oak Tree Press website.

## Oberon Books Ltd
**521 Caledonian Road, London, N7 9RH**

020 7607 3637

020 7607 3629

info@oberonbooks.com

www.oberonbooks.com

**Contact** Publisher, James Hogan; Managing Director, Charles Glanville
**Insider Info** Catalogue is available online.
**Non-Fiction** Publishes Play texts (Modern and Classics), supporting material for teachers and students of the Young People's Theatre and the London Academy of Music and Dramatic Art (LAMDA). Also publishes titles on the following subjects: Dance, Opera and Theatre.
**Recent Title** *The Art of the Theatre Workshop*, Murray Melvin

## O Books
**The Bothy, Deershot Lodge, Park Lane, Ropley, Hants, SO24 0BE**
❶ 01962 773768
❶ 01962 773769
❷ john.hunt@o-books.net
❿ www.o-books.net
**Parent Company** John Hunt Publishing Ltd
**Contact** Publisher, John Hunt (MBS, Religion, History, Psychology)
**Established** 2003
**Insider Info** Publishes 80 titles per year. Receives approximately 1,000 queries and 500 manuscripts per year. 20 per cent of books published are from first-time authors, 80 per cent of books published are from unagented authors. Five per cent of books published are author subsidy published, depending on sales prospects and category of publishing. Payment is via royalty (on wholesale price), with 0.1 (per £) minimum and 0.25 (per £) maximum. Average lead time is 14 months, with simultaneous submissions not accepted. Submissions accompanied by SAE will be returned. Aims to respond to queries, proposals and manuscripts within two weeks. Catalogue and manuscript guidelines are free on request.
**Non-Fiction** Publishes Autobiography, Biography, Children's/Juvenile, General Non-fiction, Gift, How-to, Illustrated, Scholarly and Self-help titles on the following subjects:
Alternative Lifestyles, Anthropology/Archaeology, Astrology/Psychic, Business/Economics, Contemporary Culture, Health/Medicine, History, Multicultural, Nature/Environment, New Age, Philosophy, Psychology, Religion, Science, Sex, Spirituality, Women's Issues/Studies, World Affairs.
**Submission Guidelines** Accepts complete manuscripts (including outline, sample chapters, your publishing history and author biography).
**Fiction** Publishes Religious and Spiritual titles.

* O Books only publishes two or three fiction titles per year.
**Submission Guidelines** Query with SAE.

## The O'Brien Press
**12 Terenure Road East, Rathgar, Dublin 6, Republic of Ireland**
❶ 00353 1 492 3333
❶ 00353 1 492 2777
❷ books@obrien.ie
❿ www.obrien.ie
**Contact** Managing Director, Michael O'Brien; Editorial Administrator, Sarah Bredin
**Established** 1974
**Insider Info** Payment is via royalties. Aims to respond to proposals and manuscripts within eight weeks. Catalogue and manuscript guidelines available online.
**Non-Fiction** Publishes Biography, Children's/Juvenile, General Non-fiction, Humour, Illustrated and Reference titles on the following subjects: Art/Architecture, Business/Economics, Cooking/Foods/Nutrition, Crafts, Government/Politics, History, Memoirs, Music/Dance, Sports, Travel.
**Submission Guidelines** Accepts query with SAE/proposal package (including outline and two sample chapters). Will review artwork/photos as part of the manuscript package. Send photocopies.
**Fiction** Publishes Children's and Young Adult titles.
**Submission Guidelines** Accepts query with SAE/proposal package (including outline and sample chapter(s)).
**Recent Title(s)** *Castles of Ireland*, Mairéad Ashe FitzGerald; *Shamrock Sean Goes Fishing*, Brian Gogarty, (Children's)
**Tips** The O'Brien Press is Ireland's leading general publisher of both adult and children's books. Their list covers a huge range, including biography, humour, photography, history, art, fiction, politics, cookery, sport, music, memoir, true crime and travel and they are constantly expanding into new and exciting areas. The O'Brien Press publish mainly children's fiction, children's non-fiction and adult non-fiction. They generally do not publish poetry, academic works or adult fiction. They will only accept submissions/proposals/artwork via the post, email submissions will not be considered. Due to the high level of submissions they receive, unsolicited manuscripts will not be returned.

## Octagon Press Ltd
**78 York Street, London, W1H 1DP**
❶ 020 7193 6456

**☏** 020 7117 3955
**✉** admin@octagonpress.com
**🌐** www.octagonpress.com
**Contact** Managing Director, Anna Murphy
**Established** 1960
**Insider Info** Payment is via royalties. Catalogue is available online.
**Non-Fiction** Publishes Autobiography, Biography, General Non-fiction and scholarly titles on the following subjects:
History, Language/Literature, Literary Criticism, Philosophy, Translation, Travel and Folklore.
* Focuses on East/West studies.
**Submission Guidelines** Send a one page summary of the book idea.
**Poetry** Publish a small amount of translated poetry.
**Recent Title** *Travels in the Unknown East,* John Grant
**Tips** Octagon Press has built a bridge between West and East and for the past 45 years, has made available many of the greatest texts of Eastern thought, psychology and literature. The publisher's aim is to connect the Orient to the Occident, to provide accurate exposure and understanding of one tradition to the other. Concentrates on works of travel, philosophy, poetry, humanities, folklore, cultural geography and traditional psychology. No unsolicited manuscripts.

## Octopus Publishing Group
**2–4 Heron Quays, London, E14 4JP**
**☏** 020 7531 8400
**✉** info@octopus-publishing.co.uk
**🌐** www.octopus-publishing.co.uk
**Parent Company** Hachette Livre UK (see Hachette Livre entry under European & International Publishers)
**Contact** CEO, Alison Goff
**Established** Early 1970s
**Imprint(s)** Bounty Books
Cassell Illustrated
Conran Octopus
Hamlyn
Mitchell Beazley
Philip's
**Insider Info** Catalogue available online.
**Non-Fiction** Publishes General Non-fiction, Illustrated, Multimedia, Children's/Juvenile and Educational titles on the following subjects:
Food and Drink, Maps and Cartography, Antiques, General Reference, Children's, Education, Health, Style, Art, Photography.
**Recent Title(s)** *Advanced Digital Photography*, Tom Ang; *20th-century Glass*, Andy McConnell

**Tips** A major cross-platform illustrated publisher. See individual imprints for more detailed information on which imprint publishes which types of book.

## Oldcastle Books
**PO Box 394, Harpenden, AL5 1EQ**
**☏** 01582 761264
**☏** 01582 761264
**Imprint(s)** No Exit Press (Crime fiction)
Pocket Essentials (Reference)
High Stakes Publishing (Gambling)
**Non-Fiction** Publishes General Non-fiction and reference titles.
**Fiction** Publishes Suspense and Crime titles.
**Tips** See separate imprint entries for information.

## The Old Stile Press
**Catchmays Court, Llandogo, Monmouth, NP25 4TN**
**☏** 01291 689226
**☏** 01291 689226
**✉** oldstile@dircon.co.uk
**🌐** www.oldstilepress.com
**Established** 1979
**Insider Info** Publishes three titles per year. Catalogue is free on request and available online.
**Non-Fiction** Publishes Illustrated and Hand-printed Artists' titles on the following subjects:
Art/Architecture, Language/Literature.
**Poetry** Publishes Visual Poetry.
**Tips** The Old Stile Press is a small company and cannot accept any unsolicited material. They primarily work with artists and don't often respond to writer's submissions.

## The Oleander Press Ltd
**16 Orchard Street, Cambridge, CB1 1JT**
**☏** 01223 357768
**✉** editor@oleanderpress.com
**🌐** www.oleanderpress.com
**Contact** Managing Director, Dr. Jane Doyle
**Established** 1960
**Insider Info** Catalogue available online.
**Non-Fiction** Publishes General Non-fiction, Humour and Reference titles on the following subjects:
History, Language/Literature, Literary Criticism, Regional, Religion, Translation.
**Submission Guidelines** Accepts query with SAE, or via email, with proposal package (including outline and sample chapter(s)).

**Fiction** Publishes Historical, Literary and Mainstream/Contemporary titles.

**Submission Guidelines** Accepts query with SAE, or via email, with proposal package (including outline and sample chapter(s)).

**Poetry** Publishes Poetry titles.

**Submission Guidelines** Submit sample poems.

**Recent Title(s)** *A Lifetime's Reading: The World's 500 Greatest Books*, Philip Ward (Reference); *Forgotten Games*, Philip Ward (Novel)

**Tips** Titles are aimed at the discerning, erudite and sometimes eccentric reader. Oleander publishes in a wide range of fields, including cultural travel guides, arabia, local history, biography, poetry, games, classics, language and literature. Potential authors are welcome to submit their material either by email or post.

## Olympia Publishers

**78 Cannon Street, London, EC4N 6NQ**

- 020 7618 6424
- 020 7618 8001
- editors@olympiapublishers.com
- www.olympiapublishers.com

**Contact** G. Bartlett

**Insider Info** Catalogue and manuscript guidelines are available online.

**Non-Fiction** Publishes Autobiography, Biography and General Non-fiction titles on the following subjects:
Cooking/Foods/Nutrition, Education, Gardening, Government/Politics, Health/Medicine, History, Military/War, Nature/Environment, Philosophy, Psychology, Religion and Spirituality.

**Submission Guidelines** Submit query with SAE, or proposal package (including outline, sample chapter(s), your publishing history and SAE).

**Fiction** Publishes Horror, Humour, Literary, Mainstream/Contemporary, Mystery, Romance, Science Fiction and Crime titles.

**Recent Title** *Easy and Practical Food for the Vegetarian*, Jenny Carter

**Tips** Olympia Publishers aim to commission both published and unpublished authors with dynamic manuscripts whose books will explore life for a variety of people in the 21st Century. They evaluate (and consider for possible publication) manuscripts on a far ranging variety of usual and more unusual topics.

## Omnibus Press

**Music Sales Ltd, 8–9 Frith Street, London, W1D 3JB**

- 020 7434 0066
- 020 7734 2246
- chris.charlesworth@musicsales.co.uk
- www.musicsales.co.uk

**Parent Company** Music Sales Group

**Contact** Editorial Head, Chris Charlesworth

**Established** 1971

**Insider Info** Payment is via royalties.

**Non-Fiction** Publishes Audio cassettes and General Non-fiction and Multimedia titles on the following subjects:
Music/Dance

**Submission Guidelines** Submit query with SAE. Submit proposal package (including outline, sample chapter and SAE).

**Tips** Omnibus Press is a world leader in books about music, covering everything from grand opera to contemporary pop music. Titles range from highly illustrated poster books about young fashionable bands, to in-depth biographies about established artists like Ian Dury, Mick Jagger and Abba.

## Oneworld Publications

**185 Banbury Road, Oxford, OX2 7AR**

- 01865 310597
- 01865 310598
- info@oneworld-publications.com
- www.oneworld-publications.com

**Contact** Publishing Director, Juliet Mabey; Publishing Director, Novin Doostdar; Managing Director, Helen Coward

**Established** 1984

**Insider Info** Catalogue free on request online. Manuscript guidelines available online.

**Non-Fiction** Publishes Biography, General Non-fiction, Gift and Self-help titles on the following subjects:
Government/Politics, History, Philosophy, Psychology, Religion, Science.

**Submission Guidelines** Use the online submission form.

**Recent Title(s)** *Did My Genes Make Me Do It*, Avrum Stroll (Science)

**Tips** We are a leading UK publisher with a rapidly expanding reputation for excellence across a wide range of subject areas including politics, philosophy, psychology, religion, history, and popular science. Our authors are dedicated communicators and renowned experts in their fields, making our list one that provokes lively debate on exciting contemporary issues. We welcome proposals for new books in our core subject areas. If you have a project that you would like us to consider, please fill in the submissions form on our website. Please do not send complete manuscripts unless we specifically request them. We regretfully can not consider any proposals that are not on our form. Please note that we do not publish fiction, children's books, or poetry.

## Onlywomen Press

**C/O Onlywomen, 40 St. Lawrence Terrace, London, W10 5ST**

☎ 020 8354 0796

✉ onlywomenpress@btconnect.com

🌐 www.onlywomenpress.com

**Contact** Lilian Mohin

**Established** 1974

**Insider Info** Publishes four titles per year. 98 per cent of books published are from first-time authors, 100 per cent of books published are from unagented authors. Payment is via royalty (on retail price). Average lead time is one year, with simultaneous submissions not accepted. Submissions accompanied by SAE will be returned. Aims to respond to queries within one month and proposals and manuscripts within three months. Catalogue is free on request. Manuscript guidelines are available with SAE, or available online or by email.

**Non-Fiction** Publishes Biography, Booklets, Children's/Juvenile and Scholarly titles on the following subjects:
 Alternative Lifestyles, Contemporary Culture (Female), Gay/Lesbian, Language/Literature, Literary Criticism, Philosophy, Social Sciences, Sociology, Women's Issues/Studies (Lesbian feminist), Young Adult.

**Submission Guidelines** Accepts proposal package (including outline, first 60 pages, your publishing history, author biography and SAE).

**Fiction** Publishes Adventure, Fantasy, Feminist, Lesbian, Juvenile, Literary, Multicultural, Mystery, Picture books, Science Fiction, Short Story Collections and Young Adult titles.

**Submission Guidelines** Accepts proposal package (including outline, first 60 pages, your publishing history, author biography and SAE).

**Poetry** Publishes Women's Poetry.

**Submission Guidelines** Submit sample poems (also include your publishing history, author biography, SAE).

**Tips** Only accepts submissions from female authors. Priority is given to lesbian authors.

## Onstream Publications

**Currabaha, Cloghroe, Co. Cork, Republic of Ireland**

☎ 00353 21 438 5798

✉ info@onstream.ie

🌐 www.onstream.ie

**Contact** Managing Editor, Roz Crowley (Food, Wine)

**Established** 1992

**Insider Info** Publishes three titles per year. Receives 365 queries and five full manuscripts per year. 100 per cent of books published are from first-time authors, 100 per cent of books published are from unagented authors. 30 per cent of books published are author subsidy published, depending on how commercially viable the project is. Payment is via royalty (on retail price).

**Non-Fiction** Publishes General Non-fiction titles.

## Open Gate Press

**51 Achilles Road, London, NW6 1DZ**

☎ 020 7431 4391

☎ 020 7431 5129

✉ books@opengatepress.co.uk

🌐 www.opengatepress.co.uk

**Established** 1988. Incorporates Centaur Press

**Insider Info** Catalogue available online.

**Non-Fiction** Publishes Scholarly, Psychoanalysis and Politics, Philosophy, Belles Lettres, Biography and Psychology titles.

**Recent Title(s)** *Political Theory and the Psychology of the Unconscious*, Paul Roazen

## Open University Press

**McGraw-Hill Education, Shoppenhangers Road, Maidenhead, Berkshire, SL6 2QL**

☎ 01628 502500

☎ 01628 635895

✉ enquiries@openup.co.uk

🌐 www.openup.co.uk

**Contact** Senior Commissioning Editor, Rachel Gear (Social Welfare and Management); Senior Commissioning Editor, Christopher Cudmore (Media, Film and Cultural Studies, Sociology and Criminology); Senior Commissioning Editor, Mark Kavanagh (Accounting, Finance and Economics)

**Established** 1977

**Insider Info** Publishes 100 titles per year. Payment is via royalties. Catalogue available online: http://mcgraw-hill.co.uk/openup/pdf_cat.html Manuscript guidelines available online: http://mcgraw-hill.co.uk/openup/authors_proposal_guidelines.html

**Non-Fiction** Publishes General Non-fiction, Reference, Scholarly and Technical titles on the following subjects:

Counselling/Career, Education, Health/Medicine, Humanities, Social Sciences, Sociology, Media, Film and Cultural Studies.

**Submission Guidelines** Accepts query with SAE/proposal package (including outline, two sample chapters, author biography, SAE).

**Recent Title(s)** *Counselling Skill*, John McLeod

**Tips** Open University Press publishes books and resources for education, health, the social sciences, management and study skills. In 2002 Open University Press became part of McGraw-Hill Education. The majority of the books have no direct connection with Open University courses, so there is definitely scope for more general scholarly publications from established academics, or teaching resources and multimedia.

## Orbit

**Brettenham House, Lancaster Place, London, WC2E 7EN**
- 020 7911 8000
- 020 7911 8100
- orbit@twbg.co.uk
- www.orbitbooks.co.uk

**Parent Company** Little, Brown Book Group
**Contact** Publishing Director, Tim Holman
**Insider Info** Submissions accompanied by SAE will be returned. Aims to respond to proposals within 12 weeks. Catalogue available online.
**Fiction** Publishes Fantasy and Science Fiction titles.
 * Full length novels only, no short stories or poetry.
**Submission Guidelines** Accepts outline of up to 30 pages of double spaced text.
**Recent Title(s)** *Last of the Wilds*, Trudy Canavan (Fantasy).
**Tips** Orbit is the UK's leading Science Fiction and Fantasy imprint, with a market share twice that of any other publisher. Orbit does not accept emailed submissions and prefers submissions from agented writers, although will occasionally accept unsolicited material. Orbit's website is preparing to publish an online encyclopedia of science fiction which will be updated monthly and may provide useful resources for science fiction writers.

## Orchard Books

338 Euston Road
**London, NW1 3BH**
- 020 7873 6000
- 020 7873 6024
- www.wattspublishing.co.uk

**Parent Company** Hachette Children's Books (Hodder Headline)

**Insider Info** Catalogue available online.
**Fiction** Publishes Children's/Juvenile, Picture book and Young Adult titles.
**Submission Guidelines** Agented submissions only.
**Tips** Titles are aimed at encouraging children of all ages to become avid readers.

## Original Plus

**17 High Street, Maryport, Cumbria, CA15 6BQ**
- 01900 812194
- smithsssj@aol.com
- http://members.aol.com/smithsssj/index.html

**Contact** Publisher/Editor, Sam Smith (Poetry)
**Established** 1995
**Insider Info** Publishes two titles per year. Receives approximately 100 queries and 12 manuscripts per year. 50 per cent of books published are from first-time authors, 100 per cent of books published are from unagented authors. Payment is via an agreed percentage of books for resale. Average lead time is one year, with simultaneous submissions not accepted. Submissions accompanied by SAE will be returned. Aims to respond to queries within two days and proposals and manuscripts within four weeks. Manuscript guidelines available with SAE, and available online or by email.
**Non-Fiction** Publishes Language/Literature and Literary Criticism titles.
**Submission Guidelines** Accepts queries with SAE (including your publishing history) and artworks/images (send photocopies).
**Fiction** Publishes Literary fiction titles.
**Poetry** Publishes Poetry and Poetry in Translation titles.
 * Original Plus seeks poetry written about contemporary subjects in contemporary idiom, preferably poems that are not obviously religious, that do not assume a shared religious knowledge, and that do not contain religious references.
**Submission Guidelines** Submit six to ten sample poems.
**Recent Title(s)** *Yellow Torchlight and the Blues*, Emma Lee
**Tips** Original Plus also publishes *The Journal*, a literary poetry journal that is also open to single poem submissions.

## Orion Publishing Group Ltd

**Orion House, 5 Upper St Martins Lane, London, WC2H 9EA**
- 020 7240 3444
- 020 7240 4822
- www.orionbooks.co.uk

**Parent Company** Hachette Livre UK (see Hachette Livre entry under European & International Publishers)

**Contact** Chairman, Armand Nourry; Chief Executive, Peter Roche

**Established** 1992

**Imprint(s)** Everyman Classics

Orion

Gollancz

Weidenfeld & Nicholson

**Insider Info** Catalogue available online via downloadable pdf, online catalogue request form, or via email on request.

**Non-Fiction** Publishes Autobiography, Biography, Children's/Juvenile, General Non-fiction, How-to, Illustrated, Reference, Scholarly, Dictionaries and Self-help titles on the following subjects:
Child Guidance/Parenting, History, Literary Criticism, Philosophy, Religion, Sports, Drama.

**Submission Guidelines** Accepts agented submissions only.

**Fiction** Publishes Fantasy, Humour, Children's, Literary, Mainstream/Contemporary, Picture books, Science Fiction, Crime, Thriller and Classics titles.

**Submission Guidelines** Accepts agented submissions only.

**Poetry** Publish some Poetry titles.

**Recent Title(s)** *De-Stress Your Life in Seven Easy Steps*, Glen Harrold (Self-help); *The Thirteenth Tale*, Diane Setterfield; *The Open Road: Poems on Travel*, Stephen Pain

## Orion

**Orion House, 5 Upper St Martins Lane, London, WC2H 9EA**

📞 020 7240 3444

📠 020 7240 4822

🌐 www.orionbooks.co.uk

**Parent Company** Orion Publishing Group Ltd

**Contact** Managing Director, Lisa Milton; Managing Director - Orion Paperback Division, Susan Lamb

**Established**
1992

**Imprint(s)** Orion Fiction

Orion Children's Books

Orion Paperback (division)

**Insider Info** Catalogue available online, download a pdf or use online request form. Also available via email on request.

**Non-Fiction** Publishes Autobiography, Biography, Children's/Juvenile, General Non-fiction and Humour titles.

**Submission Guidelines** Accepts agented submissions only.

**Fiction** Publishes Crime and Thriller titles.

**Submission Guidelines** Accepts agented submissions only.

**Recent Titles** *Labyrinth*, Kate Mosse (Thriller)

**Tips** Founder authors of Orion's Fiction list include Ian Rankin and Maeve Binchy. Today Orion is one of the leading commercial publishers in the UK and particularly known for its crime and thriller list. Non-fiction includes memoirs and autobiography. The Orion Paperback Division was launched in 1993.

## Orion Children's Books

**Orion House, 5 Upper St Martins Lane, London, WC2H 9EA**

📞 020 7240 3444

📠 020 7240 4822

🌐 www.orionbooks.co.uk

**Parent Company** Orion

**Contact** Publisher, Fiona Kennedy

**Established** 1992

**Insider Info** Catalogue available online via request form or as a downloadable pdf.

**Non-Fiction** Publishes Children's/Juvenile, Multimedia and Illustrated titles on the following subjects:
Children's, History.

**Submission Guidelines** Accepts agented submissions only.

**Fiction** Publishes Children's, Multimedia, Picture books, Young Adult and General fiction titles.
*Children's characters include *Asterix* and *Horrid Henry*.

**Submission Guidelines** Accepts agented submissions only.

**Recent Title(s)** *Brilliant Brits: Nelson*, Richard Brassey; *Snakehead*, Ann Halam

**Tips** Orion Children's Books publishes fiction and non-fiction books for the children's and young adult markets, as well as audio and multimedia material. Orion Children's Books does not accept submissions from unknown authors unless they are submitted through a literary agent.

## Orion Paperbacks

**Orion House, 5 Upper St Martins Lane, London, WC2H 9EA**

📞 020 7240 3444

📠 020 7240 4822

🌐 www.orionbooks.co.uk

**Parent Company** Orion

**Established** 1993

**Imprint(s)** Phoenix

Everyman Classics

**Insider Info** Catalogue available online.
**Non-fiction** Publishes General Non-fiction titles on a variety of subjects.
**Submission Guidelines** Accepts agented submissions only.
**Fiction** Publishes a variety of fiction titles.
**Submission Guidelines** Accepts agented submissions only.
**Tips** All books are published in paperback. Everyman Classics' list is made up entirely of reprints.

## Orpheus Publishing House
**4 Dunsborough Park, Ripley Green, Guildford, Surrey, GU23 6AL**
✆ 01483 225777
🖷 01483 225776
✉ orpheuspubl.ho@btinternet.com
**Contact** Managing Editor, J.S. Gordon
**Established** 1996
**Insider Info** Payment is via royalty.
**Non-Fiction** Publishes General Non-fiction and Scholarly titles on the following subjects:
Philosophy, Religion, Science, Occult Science, Esotericism.
**Submission Guidelines** Accepts query with SAE and submit proposal package (including outline, three sample pages maximum and SAE).
**Tips** Publishes well grounded and serious books about occult science, esotericism and comparative philosophy/religion. Will consider well researched and argued proposals from sensible authors.

## Osprey Publishing Ltd
**Midland House, West Way, Botley, Oxford, OX2 0PH**
✆ 01865 727022
🖷 01865 727017
✉ editorial@ospreypublishing.com
🌐 www.ospreypublishing.com
**Contact** Managing Director, William Shepherd
**Established** 1969
**Insider Info** Publishes 130 titles per year. Payment by royalty. Catalogue available online.
**Non-Fiction** Publishes General Non-fiction titles on the following subjects:
History, Military/War, Aviation.
**Submission Guidelines** Accepts query with SAE and submit proposal package (including outline).
**Recent Title(s)** *Rome's Saxon Shore*, Nic Fields (Military History)
**Tips** Osprey Publishing is the world's leading publisher of illustrated military history and military aviation books. Osprey series span military history

from the ancient world to modern times. Osprey's popular series include *Men-at-Arms*, *Campaign*, *Fortress*, *New Vanguard*, *Warrior* and *Aircraft of the Ace*. Does not accept unsolicited manuscripts, but will consider carefully researched proposals.

## Oxbow Books/Aris & Phillips
**Park End Place, Oxford, OX1 1HN**
✆ 01865 241249
🖷 01865 794449
✉ oxbow@oxbowbooks.com
🌐 www.oxbowbooks.com/www.arisandphillips.com
**Contact** Publisher/Managing Director, John Hudson; Editor, Clare Litt
**Established** 1983
**Imprint(s)** Aris & Phillips
**Insider Info** Catalogue is free on request and available online.
**Non-Fiction** Publishes Scholarly titles on the following subjects:
Anthropology/Archaeology, History (Ancient and Medieval History), Classics, Egyptology, Middle Eastern, Near Eastern and Hispanic Studies.
 * Also publishes the titles of the Griffith Institute of the University of Oxford and the Australian Centre of Egyptology.
**Recent Titles** *The Luttrell Psalter: A Facsimile*, Michelle P. Brown (Medieval)
**Tips** Oxbow books is Europe's largest specialist archaeological bookseller. The publishing programme takes place under the Aris & Phillips imprint.

## Oxford University Press
**Great Clarendon Street, Oxford, OX2 6DP**
✆ 01865 556767
🖷 01865 556646
✉ webenquiry.uk@oup.com
🌐 www.oup.co.uk
**Contact** Editorial Director, Antonia Owen; Commissioning Editor, David Musson (Academic and Professional books)
**Established** 1478
**Insider Info** Publishes 6,000 titles per year. Payment is by royalties. Catalogue available online. Manuscript guidelines available online via the website.
**Non-Fiction** Publishes General Non-fiction, Reference, Scholarly, Technical and Textbook titles on the following subjects:
Anthropology/Archaeology, Business/Economics, Education, Government/Politics, Health/Medicine, History, Language/Literature, Law, Literary Criticism,

Music/Dance, Philosophy, Religion, Science and Social Sciences.

**Submission Guidelines** Accepts query with SAE/ proposal package (including outline, two sample chapters, author biography and SAE).

**Recent Title(s)** *Pathfinders: A Global History of Exploration*, Felipe Fernández-Armesto; *Peter Pan in Scarlet*, Geraldine McCaughrean (Children's Book)

**Tips** Oxford University Press (OUP) is a department of the University of Oxford. It furthers the University's objective of excellence in research, scholarship, and education by publishing worldwide. It publishes in many countries, in a variety of different languages, for all levels and across virtually the whole range of academic disciplines. With the acquisition of Blackstone Press, OUP is now one of the leading Law publishers. Please note that Oxford University Press is obliged by its charter to have all books published ratified by the University. As a rule, the press don't publish works of fiction, unless it forms part of an educational course or examination. The main criteria when evaluating a new title is its quality, and the contribution it will make to the furtherance of scholarship and education.

## Packard Publishing Ltd
**Forum House, Stirling Road, Chichester, West Sussex, PO19 2EN**
- 01243 537977
- 01243 537977
- info@packardpublishing.co.uk
- www.packardpublishing.com

**Contact** Managing Director, Clare Packard; Managing Director, Michael Packard

**Established** 1977

**Insider Info** Payment by royalties. Catalogue avaialble online.

**Non-Fiction** Publishes Biography, General Non-fiction, Reference, Scholarly and Technical titles on the following subjects:
 Agriculture/Horticulture, Art/Architecture, Education, Gardening, History, Language/Literature, Nature/Environment, Science, Translation.

**Submission Guidelines** Accepts query with SAE.

**Recent Title(s)** *Specification Writing for Garden Design*, John Heather (Gardening)

**Tips** Packard Publishing set out to be a low overhead publisher and distributor of books and journals aimed at university and professional levels, colleges and secondary schools. The company's subject specialisations are biology, especially ecology and nature conservation, land management - including agriculture, forestry and rural studies, and landscape design and its history. Packard Publishing

also produce a small amount on languages, music and general knowledge. Recent emphasis has been placed on the conservation and management of vulnerable environments, and on the restoration of damaged landscapes, on landscape architecture and garden design.

## Palgrave Macmillan
**Houndmills, Basingstoke, Hampshire, RG21 6XS**
- 01256 329242
- 01256 328339
- firstinitial.lastname@palgrave.com
- www.palgrave.com

**Parent Company** Macmillan Publishers Ltd

**Contact** Publishing Director, Margaret Hewinson (College Division); Director, Samantha Burridge (Scholarly and Reference); Publishing Director, Stephen Rutt (Economics Business and Management); Publisher, Michael Strang (History); Publisher, Alison Jones (Reference and Online Publishing); Director of Journals, David Bull.

**Established** 2000

**Insider Info** Payment by royalties. Catalogue available online and via email on request. Manuscript guidelines available online via the website.

**Non-Fiction** Publishes Biography, Reference, Scholarly, Technical, Journals, Monographs, Online publications and Textbook titles on the following subjects:
 Anthropology/Archaeology, Business/Economics, Communications, Computers/Electronics, Contemporary Culture, Counselling/Career, Education, Government/Politics, History, Language/ Literature, Law, Literary Criticism, Philosophy, Psychology , Religion, Science, Social Sciences, Sociology, Sports, Theatre and Performance, Nursing and Health, International Relations and Key Concepts.

**Submission Guidelines** Accepts proposal package (including outline, sample chapter(s), information about the book's place in the market, i.e competition and potential readership and author biography). Proposals should be sent to the relevant editors, a long list of whom are published on the website. Emailed and postal submissions are welcomed. Alternatively, use the online proposal form to structure your submission.

**Recent Titles** *The History of Havana*, Dick Cluster and Rafael Hernandez (American History); *Milton Friedman: A Biography*, Lanny Ebenstein (Biography/ Economics)

**Tips** A leading academic publisher whose authors are usually experts in their fields. Detailed author guides are downloadable from the website covering every stage, from proposals, to publicity of the finished book.

## Palladour Books
**23 Eldon Street, Southsea, Hampshire, PO5 4BS**
- 023 9282 6935
- 023 9282 6395
- jeremy.powell@ntlworld.com

**Contact** Managing Editor, Anne Powell; Managing Editor, Jeremy Powell
**Established** 1986
**Non-Fiction** Publishes Scholarly titles on the following subjects:
Literary Criticism (World War Literature).
**Fiction** Publishes Military/War, World War(s) titles.
**Poetry** Publishes Historical Poetry titles.
**Tips** Palladour Books specialise in second hand and out of print books on the literature and poetry of the first world war. They produce catalogues twice a year in May and November. Unsolicited manuscripts or proposals are not accepted.

## Pan
**20 New Wharf Road, London, N1 9RR**
- 020 7014 6000
- 020 7014 6001
- fiction@macmillan.co.uk, nonfiction@macmillan.co.uk
- www.panmacmillan.com

**Parent Company** Pan Macmillan Publishers
**Established** 1944
**Insider Info** Catalogue available online via downloadable pdf on the website.
**Non-Fiction** Publishes Biography and General Non-fiction titles on the following subjects:
Astrology/Psychic, Business/Economics, Health/Medicine, History, Memoirs, Military/War and Travel.
**Submission Guidelines** Accepts agented submissions only.
**Fiction** Publishes Mainstream/Contemporary and Popular fiction titles.
**Submission Guidelines** Accepts agented submissions only.
**Recent Titles** *Just Julie*, Julie Goodyear (Autobiography); *The Adultery Club*, Tess Stimson (Modern Fiction)
**Tips** Has a strong reputation in military history and biography, as well as other areas of non-fiction and fiction. Publishes work by new writers, but will not accept unsolicited manuscripts.

## Panacea Press Ltd
**86 North Gate, Prince Albert Road, London, NW8 7EJ**
- 020 7722 8464
- 020 7586 8187
- ebrecher@panaceapress.net
- www.panaceapress.net

**Contact** Managing Editor, Erwin Brecher
**Established** 2001
**Insider Info** Payment by royalties. Catalogue available online.
**Non-Fiction** Publishes Scholarly titles on the following subjects:
Psychology and Science.
**Submission Guidelines** Accepts query with SAE. Catalogue available online.
**Recent Title(s)** *The IQ Conspiracy*, Erwin Brecher
**Tips** Erwin Brecher formed Panacea Press Limited, to market his own books and those of other non-fiction authors. The press publishes scholarly articles related to science and psychology. Will consider academic material providing it has a wide audience and market. Approach by fax or letter, but not by telephone.

## Pan Macmillan Publishers
**20 New Wharf Road, London, N1 9RR**
- 020 7014 6000
- 020 7014 6001
- nonfiction@macmillan.co.uk
- fiction@macmillan.co.uk
- www.panmacmillan.com

**Parent Company** Macmillan Publishers Ltd
**Contact** Managing Director, David North
**Established** 1843
**Imprint(s)** Boxtree
Campbell Books
Macmillan
Macmillan Children's Books
Macmillan New Writing
Pan
Picador
Sidgwick & Jackson
Think Books
Tor
Young Picador
**Insider Info** Catalogue available online via downloadable pdf.
**Non-Fiction** Publishes Audio cassettes, Autobiography, Biography, Cookbook, General Non-fiction, Gift Books, Humour, Illustrated Books, Reference and Self-help titles on the following subjects:

Cooking/Foods/Nutrition, Entertainment/Games, Gardening, Government/Politics, Health/Medicine, History, Hobbies, Nature/Environment, Science, Sports, Travel, Poetry, Drama and Criticism and Writing.

**Submission Guidelines** Accepts agented submissions only.

**Fiction** Publishes Fantasy, Historical, Humour, Mainstream/Contemporary, Mystery, Romance, Science Fiction, Short story collections, Suspense, Sagas, Thrillers, Anthologies and General fiction titles.

**Submission Guidelines** Accepts agented submissions only.

**Recent Title(s)** *Diana Ross*, J Randy Taraborrelli (Biography); *In a Dark House*, Deborah Crombie (Crime)

**Tips** Although Pan Macmillan does not accept unsolicited/unagented manuscripts there is still a good deal of information for aspiring authors on the website. See the separate entry for the Macmillan New Writing imprint, which does accept unsolicited manuscripts, or go to:
www.macmillannewwriting.com.

## PaperBooks Ltd
**Neville House, Station Appraoch, Wendens Ambo, Essex, CB11 4LB**
- 01799 544657
- 01799 541747
- submissions@paperbooks.co.uk
- www.paperbooks.co.uk

**Contact** Keirston Clark
**Established** 2006
**Insider Info** Publishes three titles per year. Catalogue available online. Manuscript guidelines available online via the website.
**Fiction** Publishes Mainstream/Contemporary titles.
**Submission Guidelines** Accepts query with SAE and proposal package (including three sample chapters, one page synopsis, a marketing brief which details who the target reader is, a list of any authors similar in style, and any previous publishing history that may be relevant).
**Recent Title(s)** *The Angel Makers*, Jessica Gregson (Novel)
**Tips** PaperBooks is a new small independent press, dedicated to promoting and enlivening the independent book publishing world.

## Paper Tiger
**151 Freston Road, London, W10 6TH**
- 020 7314 1400

- 020 7314 1401
Website: www.anovabooks.com
**Parent Company** Anova Company Books Ltd
**Insider Info** Catalogue available online.
**Recent Title(s)** *Fabulous Women of Boris Vallejo and Julie Bell*, Boris Vallejo and Julie Bell
**Tips** Paper Tiger is a leading publisher in illustrated science fiction and fantasy art. For more information, see Anova Books Company entry.

## Paradise Press
**Unit 2, 9 Golden Square, London, W1F 9HZ**
- 020 7734 4880
- enquiries@paradisepress.org.uk
- www.paradisepress.org.uk

**Parent Company** Gay Authors Self-Publishing Society
**Established** 1995
**Insider Info** Catalogue available online. Manuscript guidelines available online via website.
**Fiction** Publishes Gay/Lesbian Short Story Collections.
**Submission Guidelines** Submit completed manuscript and SAE.
**Poetry** Publishes Gay/Lesbian Poetry titles.
**Submission Guidelines** Submit completed manuscript and SAE.
**Recent Title(s)** *Rid England of This Plague*, Rex Batten (Novel); *Slivers of Silver*, Jeffrey Doorn and Adrian Risdon eds. (Short Story Collection)
**Tips** Paradise Press is the publishing arm of Gay Authors Workshop, a collective of lesbian and gay writers. Work is only published by members of this group after a process of collective discussion and review. To submit work, first read the guidelines on the website. Current titles by new and established writers include novels, short fiction and fantasy.

## Parapress Ltd
**The Basement, 9 Frant Road, Tunbridge Wells, Kent, TN2 5SD**
- 01892 512118
- 01892 512118
- office@parapress.eclipse.co.uk
- www.parapress.co.uk

**Contact** Managing Editor, Elizabeth Imlay
**Established** 1993
**Insider Info** Publishes five titles per year. Catalogue available online.
**Non-Fiction** Publishes Autobiography, Biography, General Non-fiction and Self-help titles on the following subjects:

History, Hobbies, Literary Criticism, Military/War, Music/Dance and Nature/Environment.

**Recent Title(s)** *In Bed With The Enemy*, Aubrey Malone

**Tips** Parapress publishes general non-fiction books on military and navy, history, animals and nature, leisure, biography, autobiography and literary criticism. The press also facilitates some self-publishing, please research this option thoroughly before committing to it.

## Parthian

**The Old Surgery, Napier Street, Aberteifi, Cardigan, SA43 1ED**

☎ 01239 612059

☎ 01239 612059

✉ parthianbooks@yahoo.co.uk

🌐 www.parthianbooks.co.uk

**Contact** Publishing Director, Richard Davies (Fiction); Poetry Editor, Jasmine Donahaye (Poetry)

**Established** 1993

**Insider Info** Payment by royalties. Aims to respond to proposals and manuscripts within 12 weeks. Catalogue available online. Manuscript guidelines available online via the website.

**Fiction** Publishes Literary, Mainstream/Contemporary, Plays, Short story collections, Translation and Welsh writing in English titles.

**Submission Guidelines** Accepts query with SAE and proposal package (including outline and sample chapter(s)).

**Poetry** Publishes Welsh Poetry titles in English.

**Submission Guidelines** Submit sample poems (including 40 pages and SAE).

**Recent Title(s)** *Under The Dust*, Jordi Coca (Novel); *Things You Think I Don't Know*, Deborah Kay Davies (Short Story Collection)

**Tips** Publishes contemporary Welsh fiction, drama and poetry in English, also translations of Welsh language fiction. Has a range of new writing and are always available to read new material in the subject areas which Parthian publish.

## Paupers' Press

**37 Quayside Close, Trent Bridge, Nottingham, Nottinghamshire, NG2 3BP**

☎ 0115 986 3334

☎ 0115 986 3334

✉ books@pauperspress.com

🌐 www.pauperspress.com

**Contact** Managing Editor, Colin Stanley (Literary Criticism, Philosophy)

**Established** 1983

**Insider Info** Publishes four titles per year. Receives approximately ten queries and ten manuscripts per year. 50 per cent of books published are from first-time authors, 100 per cent of books published are from unagented authors. Payment is via royalty (on retail price), with 0.1 (per £) maximum. Average lead time is six months, with simultaneous submissions not accepted. Submissions accompanied by SAE will be returned. Aims to respond to queries and proposals within seven days, and manuscripts within 31 days. Catalogue is free on request and available online or by email.

**Non-Fiction** Publishes Booklets, Essays and Scholarly titles on the following subjects: Contemporary Culture, Humanities, Literary Criticism, Philosophy.

**Submission Guidelines** Accepts query with SAE.

**Recent Title(s)** *Ian McEwan's 'Atonement' & 'Saturday'*, Bernie C Byrnes (Literary Criticism)

**Tips** Paupers' Press is a semi-academic press and its books are written for an intelligent and scholarly readership.

## Pavilion

**151 Freston Road, London, W10 6TH**

☎ 020 7314 1400

☎ 020 7314 1401

✉ jrajasingham@anovabooks.com

🌐 www.anovabooks.com

**Parent Company** Anova Book Company Ltd

**Contact** Jeshuran Rajasingham

**Established** 1981

**Insider Info** Catalogue available online.

**Non-Fiction** Publishes Coffee table books, Cookbooks, General Non-fiction, Gift books, Illustrated books, and Reference titles on the following subjects: Cookery, Interiors, Gardening, Fairies, Popular Culture, Photography, Film and Inspirational Lifestyle books.

**Recent Title(s)** *Taking Tea With Clarice Cliff*, Leonard Griffin

**Tips** Focuses on 'glamorous' non-fiction and gift books.

## Pavilion Publishing (Brighton) Ltd

**Richmond House, Richmond Road, Brighton, East Sussex, BN2 3RL**

☎ 01273 623222

☎ 01273 625526

✉ info@pavpub.com

🌐 www.pavpub.com

**Contact** Director, Chris Parker; Director, Julie Gibson; Director, Loretta Harrison
**Established** 1987
**Insider Info** Catalogue available online.
**Non-Fiction** Publishes Reference, Health/Social Care and Training Resources titles on the following subjects:
 Counselling/Career, Health/Medicine and Social Sciences.
**Tips** Pavilion is the leading provider of social and healthcare training materials in the UK, publishing around 150 training packs, 17 journals and *Mental Health Today* magazine. As well as publishing, Pavilion organizes eight exhibitions and around 40 conferences each year for those working within the social, healthcare and housing fields. As well as publishing their own materials, Pavilion offer publishing consultancy services.

## Payne-Gallway
**Halley Court, FREEPOST (OF1771), Jordan Hill, Oxford, OX2 8EJ**
- 01865 888118
- 01865 314029
- info@payne-gallway.co.uk
- www.payne-gallway.co.uk
**Parent Company** Harcourt Education
**Contact** Editor in Chief, Pat Heathcote
**Established** 1998 (acquired by Harcourt Education in January 2005)
**Insider Info** Catalogue available as a downloadable pdf online.
**Non-Fiction** Publishes Reference, Technical and Textbook titles on the following titles:
 Computers/Electronics, IT Educational Solutions, Skills Development.
**Submission Guidelines** Accept query via email with proposal package (including outline).
**Tips** Remains an independent imprint despite being acquired by Harcourt Education. Specialises in computer and IT books, and resources for schools and colleges.

## Peachpit Press
**Edinburgh Gate, Harlow, Essex, CM20 2JE**
- 01279 623623
- 01279 414130
- www.pearsoned.co.uk/Imprints/PeachpitPress
**Parent Company** Pearson Education
**Established** 1986
**Insider Info** Catalogue and manuscripts guidelines are available online.

**Non-Fiction** Publishes Reference, Technical and Textbook titles on the following subjects:
 Web Design, Graphic Design, Web Development.
**Submission Guidelines** Accepts proposal package (including synopsis, sample chapters, market research, your publishing history and author biography).
**Recent Title(s)** *How to Wow with PowerPoint*, Scott Rekdal and Richard Harrington (Computing/Design)
**Tips** Current titles feature step by step explanations, time saving techniques, insider tips and expert advice. They are aimed at computer users of all levels. See the website for full list of submissions contacts.

## Pearson Plc
**80 Strand, London, WC2R 0RL**
- 020 7010 2314
- deborah.lincoln@pearson.com
- www.pearson.com
**Contact** Chairman (US), Glen Moreno; Chief Executive (US), Marjorie Scardino
**Established** 1844
**Imprint(s)** Financial Times Group
 Pearson Education
 Penguin Group
**Insider Info** Payment is via royalty.
**Tips** Pearson Plc is an international media company with market leading businesses in education, business information and consumer publishing. Its three main assets are Pearson Education, which is a leading educational publishing group, Penguin Group, which is one of the largest consumer publishers in the world, and the Financial Times Group, which publishes a broad range of business information and multimedia services for a growing audience of internationally minded business people. Pearson Plc is a major media company and not a stand alone publisher. All publishing submissions or enquiries must be directed at the appropriate imprint within Pearson.

## Pearson Education
**Edinburgh Gate, Harlow, Essex, CM20 2JE**
- 01279 623623
- 01279 414130
- elizabeth.kelly@pearson.com
- www.pearsoned.co.uk
**Parent Company** Pearson Plc
**Contact** CEO Pearson Education (Asia, Europe, Middle East and Africa), John Fallon; Editorial Assistant, Elizabeth Kelly
**Established** 1998

**Imprint(s)** Addison-Wesley
Allyn & Bacon
BBC Active
Benjamin Cummings
Cisco Press
FT Prentice Hall
Longman
New Riders
Peachpit Press
Pengin Longman
QUE Publishing
SAMS Publishing
Wharton
York Notes

**Insider Info** Payment is via royalties. Catalogue and manuscript guidelines are available online.

**Non-Fiction** Publishes Multimedia, Reference, Scholarly, Technical and Textbook titles on the following subjects:
Business/Economics, Education, Humanities, Language/Literature, Law, Science, Technology.

**Submission Guidelines** Accepts query with SAE or proposal package (including outline, sample chapters, market research, your publishing history author biography).

**Tips** Pearson Education is the world's leading education publisher, publishing across a wide spectrum of subjects, including business, technology, sciences, law and humanities, to an audience which ranges from primary students to professional practitioners. Pearson Education is always looking for exciting new projects to work on and new authors to work with. A project proposal can be submitted by post or email, check the website for a full list of editorial contacts and their interests. Alternatively contact one of Pearson Education's various imprints with suitable projects.

## Peepal Tree Press
**17 Kings Avenue, Leeds, LS6 1QS**
- 0113 245 1703
- contact@peepalpress.com
- www.peepaltreepress.com

**Contact** Founder and Managing Editor, Jeremy Poynting; Marketing Director, Hannah Bannister (Poetry); Editor, Kwame Dawes

**Established** 1985

**Insider Info** Publishes 15 titles per year.

**Non-Fiction** Publishes Autobiography, General Non-fiction and Academic titles.

**Fiction** Publishes Multicultural and Short story collection titles on the following subjects:
Caribbean, Black British and South Asian writing.

**Poetry** Publishes Caribbean, Black British and South Asian Poetry titles.

**Recent Title(s)** *Music for the Off-Key: Twelve Macabre Short Stories*, Courttia Newland; *First Rain*, Donna Weir-Soley

**Tips** Peepal Tree Press aims to publish books that make a difference, its primary concern is whether a book will still be alive in the future. Future plans include publishing drama titles and reissuing Caribbean classics.

## Pegasus
**Sheraton House, Castle Park, Cambridge, CB3 OAX**
- 01223 370012
- 01223 37004
- editors@pegasuspublishers.com
- www.pegasuspublishers.com

**Parent Company** Pegasus Elliot MacKenzie Publishers Ltd

**Insider Info** Catalogue available online. Manuscript guidelines available online via website.

**Non-Fiction** Publishes Biography, General Non-fiction, Reference and Scholarly titles on the following subjects:
Contemporary Culture, Education and History.

**Submission Guidelines** Accepts query with SAE.

**Fiction** Publishes Literary and Mainstream/Contemporary titles.

**Submission Guidelines** Accepts query with SAE.

**Tips** Pegasus publishes fiction, non-fiction and educational books from writers, agents and educationalists. Pegasus very rarely accepts submissions from unknown or unpublished writers, but will sometimes offer an advance for accepted work.

## Pegasus Elliot MacKenzie Publishers Ltd
**Sheraton House, Castle Park, Cambridge, CB3 OAX**
- 01223 370012
- 01223 370040
- editors@pegasuspublishers.com
- www.pegasuspublishers.com

**Contact** Senior Editor, D.W. Stern; Editor, R. Sabir

**Imprint(s)** Vanguard Press
Pegasus
Nightingale Books
Chimera

**Insider Info** Payment is via royalties. Catalogue available online. Manuscript guidelines available online via the website.

**Non-Fiction** Publishes Autobiography, Biography, Children's/Juvenile, General Non-fiction and Humour titles on the following subjects: Art/Architecture, Health/Medicine, History, Memoirs, Military/War, Music/Dance, Nature/Environment and Travel.

**Submission Guidelines** Accepts query with SAE and proposal package (including outline, two sample chapters, author biography and SAE).

**Fiction**
Publishes Erotica, Fantasy, Historical, Horror, Humour, Children's, Mainstream/Contemporary, Military/War, Romance, Science fiction, short story collections, Sports and Young Adult titles.

**Submission Guidelines** Accepts query with SAE and proposal package (including outline, two sample chapters, author biography and SAE).

**Recent Title(s)** *Understanding English Spelling*, Masha Bell (Education); *Worm In The Apple*, Terry Williams (Novel)

**Tips** Concentrates on the fiction from international writers who can bring different talents and cultural experiences to their work for both children and adults. Submissions from new writers are welcomed. The publisher works with a range of authors, including celebrities, romantic novelists and historical and other non-fiction writers. Authors may be required to contribute to production costs.

## Pen & Sword Books Ltd

**47 Church Street, Barnsely, South Yorkshire, S70 2AS**

- 01226 734555
- 01226 734438
- enquiries@pen-and-sword.co.uk
- www.pen-and-sword.co.uk

**Contact** Commissioning Editor, Peter Coles (Aviation); Commissioning Editor, Henry Wilson (Military and Maritime); Commissioning Editor, Rupert Harding (History and Local Interest)

**Imprint(s)** Leo Cooper
Wharncliffe Books

**Insider Info** Publishes 200 titles per year. Payment is via royalties. Catalogue available online.

**Fiction** Publishes Autobiography, Biography, General Non-fiction, Reference and Scholarly titles on the following subjects:
History and Military/War.

**Submission Guidelines** Accepts query with SAE or via email.

**Recent Title(s)** *The Air Battle for Malta*, James Douglas Hamilton (Military History)

**Tips** Pen & Sword Books is a leading military history publisher, specialising primarily in aviation, naval and

world war history. Also publishes books on the Napoleonic war. Unsolicited manuscripts will not be accepted. Will consider queries and proposals providing they are within the key interest areas.

## Penguin Group (UK)

**80 Strand, London, WC2R 0RL**

- 020 7010 3000
- 020 7010 6060
- customer.service@penguin.co.uk
- www.penguin.co.uk

**Parent Company** Pearson Plc

**Contact** Group Chairman and Chief Executive, John Makinson; Managing Director, Helen Fraser

**Established** 1936

**Imprint(s)** Penguin Press (division)
Penguin General (division)
Penguin Ireland
Penguin Audiobooks
ePenguin
Dorling Kindersley
Puffin
Ladybird Books
Rough Guides
Warne

**Insider Info** Publishes approximately 4,000 titles per year. Catalogue is available online.

**Non-Fiction** Publishes Autobiography, Biography, Children's/Juvenile, Cookbook, General Non-fiction, Gift, How-to, Humour, Illustrated, Reference and Self-help titles on the following subjects:
Astrology/Psychic, Business/Economics, Child Guidance/Parenting, Contemporary Culture, Cooking/Foods/Nutrition, Counselling/Career, Entertainment/Games, Government/Politics, Health/Medicine, History, Language/Literature, Law, Memoirs, Military/War, Money/Finance, Nature/Environment, Recreation, Science, Social Sciences, Sports, Travel, Film and Television Guides, Children's Tie-ins, Food and Drink Guides, Exercise and Fitness, Lifestyle and Relationships.

**Submission Guidelines** Accepts agented submissions only.

**Fiction** Publishes Children's, Picture Books, Plays, Short Story Collections, Young Adult, Crime and Thriller, Classics, General Fiction, Literary Criticism, Popular Fiction, Short Story and Anthology titles.

**Submission Guidelines** Accepts agented submissions only.

**Poetry** Publishes a wide selection of children's and adult poetry titles.

**Submission Guidelines** Accepts agented submissions only.

**Recent Title(s)** *Debbie Frank's Cosmic Ordering Guide to Life*, Love and Happiness; *The Malice Box*, Martin Langfield; *The Penguin Book of First World War Poetry*, George Walter (ed.)

**Tips** Penguin Audiobooks, including the Puffin Audiobooks imprint, publishes a diverse selection of titles from across the Penguin range on both cassette and CD. ePenguin, launched in 2001, publishes a wide range of Penguin titles, including a full selection of Penguin Classics and Rough Guides, in digital ebook format.

Penguin Group (UK) publishes roughly 4,000 titles per year across its divisions and imprints. It published 250 first-time writers in 2005. Although the Penguin Group does not accept unagented submissions, it does have some good information for would be authors on its website, including advice for aspiring adult fiction and children's fiction authors.

## Penguin General

**80 Strand, London, WC2R 0RL**

- 020 7010 3000
- 020 7010 6060
- customer.service@penguin.co.uk
- www.penguin.co.uk

**Parent Company** Penguin Group (UK)
**Contact** Managing Director, Tom Weldon
**Imprint(s)** Penguin Paperbacks
 Fig Tree
 Hamish Hamilton
 Michael Joseph
 Viking
**Insider Info** Catalogue is available online.
**Non-Fiction** Publishes Autobiography, Biography, General Non-fiction and Self-help titles on the following subjects:
 Celebrity Biography, Cookery, Comedy, Current Affairs, History, Memoir, Military History, Mind, Body and Spirit, Showbiz, Sport.
**Submission Guidelines** Accepts agented submissions only.
**Fiction** Publishes Crime, Experimental, Humour, Literary, Mainstream/Contemporary, Romance, Thriller and Women's Interest titles.
**Submission Guidelines** Accepts agented submissions only.
**Recent Title(s)** *Victoria's Wars*, Saul David (Military History); *Then We Came to the End*, Joshua Ferris (Contemporary novel)
**Tips** Covers a wide range of adult literary and popular fiction and non-fiction titles.

## Penguin Press

**80 Strand, London, WC2R 0RL**

- 020 7010 3000
- 020 7010 6060
- customer.service@penguin.co.uk
- www.penguin.co.uk

**Parent Company** Penguin Group (UK)
**Contact** Managing Director, Stefan McGrath
**Imprint(s)** Penguin Classics/Penguin Modern Classics
 Penguin Reference
 Allen Lane
**Insider Info** Catalogues are available online or by email.
**Non-Fiction** Publishes Autobiography, Biography, General Non-fiction, Illustrated and Reference titles.
 * Publishes Non-fiction under the Allen Lane and Penguin Reference imprints.
**Submission Guidelines** Accepts agented submissions only.
**Fiction** Publishes reprints of Mainstream/Contemporary, Classics and Modern Classic titles.
 * Publishes reprints of classic and modern fiction under the Penguin Classic/Penguin Modern Classics imprints.
**Submission Guidelines** Agented submissions only.
**Recent Title(s)** *Pocket Roget's Thesaurus*, George Davidson (Language/Literature); *Atlas Shrugged,* Ayn Rand (Modern Classics)
**Tips** Allen Lane, Penguin's non-fiction hardback imprint, was founded in 1967. Penguin Reference titles include *Roget's Thesaurus* and *Pears Cyclopedia* and a list of reference and dictionary titles. The Penguin Classics list was launched in 1946. The series includes over 800 titles and ranges from reprints of international classical literature through philosophy, religion, history, politics, travel and art titles. Penguin Modern Classics was relaunched in 2000, reprinting modern literature, including key works by British and American writers, and translations.

## Penguin Ireland

**25 St. Stephen's Green, Dublin 2, Republic of Ireland**

- 00 353 1 661 7695
- 00 353 1 661 7695
- info@penguin.ie
- www.penguin.ie

**Parent Company** Penguin Group (UK)
**Contact** Managing Director, Michael McLoughlin; Senior Editor, Patricia Deevy; Editor, Brendan Barrington
**Established** 2002

**Insider Info** Aims to respond to proposals within three months. Catalogue is available online.
**Non-Fiction** Publishes Autobiography, Biography and General Non-fiction titles.
**Submission Guidelines** Accepts proposal package (including outline, 20–40 sample pages and SAE).
**Fiction** Publishes Literary and Mainstream/Contemporary titles.
**Submission Guidelines** Accepts proposal package (including outline, 20–40 sample pages and SAE).
**Recent Title(s)** *Wednesday's Child*, Shane Dunphy; *Secret Diary of a Demented Housewife*, Niamh Greene
**Tips** Penguin Ireland welcomes unsolicited manuscripts and proposals. They're looking for passion and excellence from their authors, with books that are 'pitched towards that vast middle ground between popular literature and high literature,' and that get under the skin of contemporary Ireland. Accepts typewritten manuscripts only. Does not accept emailed proposals or manuscripts.

## Penguin Classics/Penguin Modern Classics
**80 Strand, London, WC2R 0RL**
☎ 020 7010 3000
🖷 020 7010 6060
✉ penguinclassics@penguin.co.uk
🌐 www.penguinclassics.co.uk
**Parent Company** Penguin Press
**Established** 1946
**Insider Info** Catalogue is available online.
**Non-Fiction** Publishes General Non-fiction titles on the following subjects:
 Art/Architecture, Government/Politics, History, Literary Criticism, Philosophy, Religion and Travel.
 * All titles are reprints of English, American, European, Classical and Non-Western Literature.
**Fiction** Publishes Literary, Classic Fiction, British and American Modern Classics titles.
 * All titles are reprints.
**Recent Title(s)** *Metamorphosis and Other Stories*, Franz Kafka (Modern Classics); *The Adventures of Tom Sawyer*, Mark Twain (Classics)
**Tips** Penguin Classics/Penguin Modern Classics do not accept submissions as they only publish reprints of classic literature.

## Penguin Longman
**Edinburgh Gate, Harlow, Essex, CM20 2JE**
☎ 01279 623623
🖷 01279 414130

🌐 www.pearsoned.co.uk/Imprints/PenguinLongman
**Parent Company** Pearson Education
**Insider Info** Catalogue and manuscript guidelines are available online.
**Non-Fiction** Publishes Reference and Textbook titles on the following subjects:
 Education, English Language Teaching (ELT), Language/Literature, Teaching Guides.
**Submission Guidelines** Accepts proposal package (including synopsis, sample chapters, market research, your publishing history and author biography).
**Recent Title(s)** *Crime Story Collection Book/CD Pack*, Sara Paretsky (Short story reader)
**Tips** Specialists in the field of English Language Teaching and reading and supplementary materials for ELT students. The Penguin Readers series publishes reading guides of classic literary and popular fiction and media tie-ins. The Penguin English Series provides teachers with guides and resources to supplement lessons. See website for ' full list of submissions contacts.

## Penguin Paperbacks
**80 Strand, London, WC2R 0RL**
☎ 020 7010 3000
🖷 020 7010 6060
✉ customer.service@penguin.co.uk
🌐 www.penguin.co.uk
**Parent Company** Penguin General
**Contact** Publishing Director, Venetia Butterfield
**Established** 1935
**Insider Info** Catalogue is available online.
**Non-Fiction** Publishes Biography, General Non-fiction and History titles.
**Submission Guidelines** Accepts agented submissions only.
**Fiction** Publishes Literary and Mainstream/Contemporary titles.
**Submission Guidelines** Accepts agented submissions only.
**Recent Title(s)** *The Autograph Man*, Zadie Smith; *The Book of Dave*, Will Self
**Tips** Penguin Paperbacks aims to bring the best writing to the widest possible audience.

## Penguin Reference
**80 Strand, London, WC2R 0RL**
☎ 020 7010 3000
🖷 020 7010 6060
✉ customer.service@penguin.co.uk
🌐 www.penguin.co.uk

**Parent Company** Penguin Press
**Insider Info** Catalogue is available online or by email.
**Non-Fiction** Publishes Illustrated and Reference titles on the following subjects:
 Dictionaries, Guidebooks, Language/Literature.
**Submission Guidelines** Accepts agented submissions only.
**Recent Title(s)** *Pocket Roget's Thesaurus*, George Davidson (Language/Literature)
**Tips** Penguin is one of the best known names in reference publishing, specialising in dictionaries and subjects as diverse as psychology, science, symbols and saints.

## Pennine Pens
**32 Windsor Road, Hebden Bridge, West Yorkshire, HX7 8LF**
☎ 01422 843724
✉ info@penninepens.co.uk
🌐 www.penninepens.co.uk
**Established** 1995
**Insider Info** Catalogue available online.
**Non-Fiction** Publishes Children's/Juvenile, General Non-fiction and Humour titles on the following subjects:
 History, Regional/Local Interest.
**Fiction** Publishes Historical, Humour, Children's and Mainstream/Contemporary titles.
**Recent Title(s)** *Some'Fine Old Ways to Save Your Life*, Simon Fletcher
**Tips** Pennine Pens started as a small press, and still publishes books, often by local authors dealing with global issues. Pennine Pens was one of the early pioneers of the e-book and mostly publishes local interest books, or books on rural life, such as walking guides.

## Pergamon Flexible Learning
**The Boulevard, Langford Lane, Kidlington, Oxford, OX5 1GB**
☎ 01865 843000
☎ 01865 843010
✉ authorsupport@elsevier.com
🌐 www.books.elsevier.com
**Parent Company** Elsevier Ltd (Science & Technology)
**Insider Info** Payment is via royalties. Catalogue and manuscript guidelines available online via the website.
**Non-Fiction** Publishes Audio cassettes, Multimedia, Reference, Scholarly, Technical and Textbook titles on the following subjects:
 Business/Economics, Counselling/Career, Education, Management Training.
**Submission Guidelines** Accepts query with SAE and proposal package including (outline).
**Recent Title(s)** *Achieving Quality Super Series (4th edition)*, ILM/Pergamon (Management Training series)
**Tips** Pergamon Flexible Learning publishes quality open learning materials for management training. The flexibility of Pergamons workbooks, CD-ROMs and cassettes make them ideal for use by individuals, colleges and trainers. They deliver bespoke programmes, as well as courses that lead to nationally recognised qualifications. Pergamon is the publishing partner of the ILM (Institute of Leadership and Management) and joint publishes the ILM Super Series, a comprehensive set of 40 open learning workbooks on key management topics. Pergamon Flexible Learning welcomes authors' proposals for books. The first step is to discuss the proposal with the relevant Publishing Editor. Check the website for in-depth submission guidelines and a full list of editorial contacts.

## Perjink Press
**8a Leopold Place, Edinburgh, EH7 5JW**
☎ 0131 478 1845
✉ djlawrenson@hotmail.com
🌐 www.dorothylawrenson.co.uk/Perjink.htm
**Contact** Dorothy Lawrenson
**Established** 2005
**Fiction** Publishes Short Story Collections.
**Poetry** Publishes Poetry Collections.
**Tips** Dorothy Lawrenson set up the press to publish her own work, and has since published two other collections in pamphlet form. It is a very small scale enterprise. Perjink Press is a member of the *Scottish Pamphlet Poetry* website.

## Persephone Books Ltd
**59 Lamb's Conduit Street, London, WC1N 3NB**
☎ 020 7242 9292
☎ 020 7242 9272
✉ info@persephonebooks.co.uk
🌐 www.persephonebooks.co.uk
**Contact** Managing Director, Nicola Beauman
**Established** 1999
**Insider Info** Publishes eight titles per year. Payment is by royalties. Catalogue is available online.
**Non-Fiction** Publishes General Non-fiction titles on the following subjects:
 Women's Issues/Studies.
 * Publishes reprints only.

**Fiction** Publishes Women's Literature titles.
 * Publishes reprints only.
**Recent Title(s)** *Plats du Jour*, Patience Gray and Primrose Boyd (Cookery)
**Tips** Persephone reprints forgotten classics by twentieth century writers, fiction and non-fiction by women, for women, and about women. The titles are chosen to appeal to busy women who rarely have time to spend in ever larger bookshops, and who would like to have access to a list of books designed to be neither too literary nor too commercial. Persephone only publishes reprinted women's literature from the mid-twentieth century. Therefore it does not print any new material or anything modern.

## Peter Collin Publishing Ltd
**38 Soho Square, London, W1D 3HB**
☎ 020 7758 0200
✆ 020 7758 0222
✉ info@petercollin.com
**Parent Company** Bloomsbury Publishing Plc
**Imprint(s)** Aspect Guides
**Insider Info** Publishes 130 titles per year. Catalogue is available online.
**Non-Fiction** Publishes General Non-fiction, Dictionaries and Reference titles on the following subjects:
 Translation, Travel, Phrasebooks and Crosswords.
**Tips** Peter Collin publishes English and bilingual dictionaries which are read by students, translators and professionals as part of a world wide audience. The imprint Aspect Guides, publishes travel guides and phrasebooks, and also crossword reference books. Peter Collin's website is generally restricted access, but details can be found on the Bloomsbury website. All queries should be directed to the Bloomsbury editorial team.

## Peter Haddock Publishing Ltd
**Pinfold Lane Industrial Estate, Bridlington, East Yorkshire, YO16 6BT**
☎ 01262 678121
✆ 01262 400043
✉ pat.hornby@phpublishing.com
🌐 www.phpublishing.co.uk
**Contact** Publisher, Pat Hornby; Creative Director, Jo Ross
**Established** 1952
**Insider Info** Catalogue and manuscript guidelines are available online via the website.
 **Non-Fiction**
 Publishes Children's/Juvenile and Multimedia titles.

**Submission Guidelines** Accepts query with SAE and only accepts submission of completed manuscripts.
**Fiction** Publishes Picture Books and Children's titles.
**Submission Guidelines** Accepts query with SAE and only accepts submission of completed manuscript.
**Tips** Peter Haddock is a publisher of children's books. Please send manuscript or ideas either via recorded delivery, addressed to the publisher, or via the online enquiry form as an attachment.

## Peter Owen Publishers
**73 Kenway Road, London, SW5 0RE**
☎ 020 7373 5628
✆ 020 7373 6760
✉ admin@peterowen.com
🌐 www.peterowen.com
**Contact** Editorial Director, Antonia Owen (Non-Fiction and Literary Fiction)
**Established** 1951
**Insider Info** Publishes 25 titles per year. Receives thousands of queries and several hundred manuscripts per year. Twenty per cent of books published are from first-time authors, 50 per cent of books published are from unagented authors. Payment via royalty (on retail price). Average lead time is one year, with simultaneous submissions accepted. Submissions accompanied with SAE will be returned. Aims to respond to queries within four weeks, proposals within six weeks and manuscripts within eight weeks. Catalogue is free on request and available online. Manuscript guidelines are available online or by email.
**Non-Fiction** Publishes Biography and General Non-fiction titles on the following subjects:
 Art/Architecture, Contemporary Culture, Entertainment/Games, History, Humanities, Language/Literature, Literary Criticism, Memoirs.
**Submission Guidelines** Accepts proposal package (including outline, one to three sample chapters, your publishing history, author biography and SAE) and artworks/images (send photocopies).
 Submission details to: antonia@peterowen.com
**Fiction** Publishes Literary Fiction and Translation titles.
 * Peter Owen only publishes four or five fiction titles per year and hardly ever publishes first novels.
**Submission Guidelines** Accepts queries with SAE or proposal package (including outline and one to three sample chapters) ideally by email.
 Submission details to: antonia@peterowen.com
**Recent Title(s)** *Wild and Fearless: The Life of Margaret Fountaine*, Natascha Scott-Stokes (Historical

Biography); *Loving Mephistopheles*, Miranda Miller (Literary Fantasy)

**Tips** Peter Owen publishes books for lovers of good quality general Non-fiction and international literary fiction. Writers should note that Peter Owen almost never publishes memoirs or fiction from unpublished authors.

## Phaidon Press Ltd

**Regents Wharf, All Saints Street, London, N1 9PA**

- 020 7843 1234
- 020 7843 1111
- enquiries@phaidon.com
- www.phaidon.com

**Contact** Group Chairman and Publisher, Richard Schlagman; Deputy Publisher, Amanda Renshaw (Photography); Managing Director, Christopher North

**Established** 1923

**Insider Info** Publishes 100 titles per year. Payment is via royalties. Catalogue available online. Manuscript guidelines available online and via the website.

**Non-Fiction** Publishes Illustrated Books, Multimedia and Reference titles on the following subjects: Art/Architecture, Photography and Design.

**Submission Guidelines** Accepts query with SAE and proposal package including (outline, sample chapter(s), Author biography, CV and SAE). Will accept artworks/images (send photocopies/digital files as jpegs).

**Recent Title(s)** *Aftermath: World Trade Center Archive*, Joel Meyerowitz (Photography)

**Tips** Phaidon Press is an international publisher of books on the visual arts, with offices in New York, London, Paris and Berlin, and distributors worldwide. The books cover everything from art, architecture, photography, design, performing arts, decorative arts, contemporary culture, fashion and film. Phaidon Press welcomes submissions for books in the following topic areas: art, architecture, photography, design and the decorative arts.

## Phaidon Press Ltd

**Regents Wharf, All Saints Street, London, N1 9PA**

- 020 7843 1000
- 020 7843 1010
- enquiries@phaidon.com
- www.phaidon.com

**Contact** Managing Director, Christopher North; Publisher, Richard Schlagman

**Established** 1923

**Insider Info** Payment is via royalties. Catalogue available online. Manuscript guidelines available online via the website.

**Non-Fiction** Publishes Children's/Juvenile, Cookbook, General Non-fiction, Illustrated Books, Multimedia and Reference titles on the following subjects: Art/Architecture, Contemporary Culture, Art History, Photography, Visual Arts/Design and Decorative Arts.

**Submission Guidelines** Accepts query with SAE and proposal package (including outline, market research, your publishing history, author biography, 20 sample images (colour copies or laser prints) and SAE). Will accept artworks/images (send photocopies/digital files as jpegs/tiffs).

**Recent Title(s)** *The Story of Art Pocket Edition*, E.H. Gombrich (Art History)

**Tips** Phaidon Press publishes high quality books on the visual arts and related subjects, and also publishes film and digital materials. Submissions welcomed for books in the following topic areas: art, architecture, photography, design and the decorative arts.

## Pharmaceutical Press

**1 Lambeth High Street, London, SE1 7JN**

- 020 7735 9141
- 020 7572 2509
- enquiries@rpsgb.org
- www.pharmpress.com

**Parent Company** RPS Publishing

**Contact** Director of Publications, Charles Fry; Publisher, Paul Weller; Senior Commissioning Editor, Christina de Bono

**Insider Info** Catalogue and author guidelines available online.

**Non-Fiction** Publishes Scholarly, Textbook, Professional Reference, Journal, Magazine and Online Resource titles on the following subjects: Pharmacy, Pharmacology, Pharmaceutical Sciences, Toxicology, Forensic Toxicology, Forensic Science.

**Submission Guidelines** Accepts proposal package (including outline, sample chapter(s), your publishing history, author biography, tentative title, estimated length, proposed date for completion, information on competing books). Will accept completed manuscripts, but prefer an initial proposal.

**Recent Title(s)** *Martindale: The complete drug reference; Clarke's Analysis of Drugs and Poisons*

**Tips** Titles are aimed at academics and professionals in the healthcare and pharmaceutical fields.

## Philip's

**111 Salusbury Road, London, NW6 6RG**

- 020 7644 6940
- 020 7644 6986
- philips@philips-maps.co.uk
- www.philips-maps.co.uk

**Parent Company** Octopus Publishing Group

**Insider Info** Catalogue is available online.

**Non-Fiction** Publish Illustrated, Reference, Maps, Atlases and Pocket Reference Guide titles on the following subjects:

History, Travel, Astronomy, Geography, Cycle Tours.

**Recent Title(s)** *Complete Guide to Stargazing*, Robin Scagell

**Tips** Most Philip's products are created from existing electronic databases that are constantly updated to record changes as they happen, producing new and foreign editions of established titles.

## Philip Wilson Publishers Limited

**109 Drysdale Street, The Timber Yard, London, N1 6ND**

- 020 7033 9900
- 020 7033 9922
- pwilson@philip-wilson.co.uk
- www.philip-wilson.co.uk

**Contact** Director, Philip Wilson (Editorial and General); Director, Slobodan Prohaska (Finance and Legal); Commissioning Editor, Anne Jackson (Editorial); Commissioning Editor, Cangy Venables (Editorial); Production Manager, Mr Norman Turpin (Production and Design); Sales Manager, Mica Ilic (Sales and Shipping)

**Established** 1977

**Insider Info** Publishes 12 titles per year. Receives 200 queries and 30 manuscripts per year. Five per cent of books published are from first-time authors, 95 per cent of books published are from unagented authors. Payment is via royalty (on wholesale price). Advance offered up to £5,000. Average lead time is nine months, with simultaneous submissions accepted. Submissions accompanied by SAE will be returned. Aims to respond to proposal within two weeks. Catalogue is free on request and available by email.

**Non-Fiction** Publishes Illustrated titles on the following subjects:

Art, Collecting, Museum Collections and Galleries.

**Submission Guidelines** Accepts proposal package (including outline and sample chapters).

**Recent Title(s)** *Kandinsky: Catalogue of Drawings*

**Tips** Submissions should be aimed at art dealers, museum experts and art historians.

## Phillimore & Co. Ltd

**Shopwyke Manor Barn, Chichester, West Sussex, PO20 2BG**

- 01243 787636
- 01243 787639
- bookshop@phillimore.co.uk
- www.phillimore.co.uk

**Contact** Managing Director, Noel Osborne

**Established** 1897

**Insider Info** Publishes 70 titles per year. Payment is via royalties. Catalogue is free on request and available online.

**Non-Fiction** Publishes General Non-fiction, How-to, Illustrated and Reference titles on the following subjects:

Local and Family History, Writing Guides.

**Recent Title(s)** *Norfolk in the Second World War*, Frank Meeres (Local History)

**Tips** Phillimore & Co. is a specialist publisher of local and family history. Potential authors or editors of new books should make contact in the early stages of their project. The company offers professional guidance on the preparation of text and illustrations, on marketing considerations, and on the submission of a synopsis and sample chapters and pictures.

## Phoenix

**5 Upper St. Martins Lane, London, WC2H 9EA**

- 020 7240 3444
- 020 7240 4822
- www.orionbooks.co.uk

**Parent Company** Orion Paperbacks (Orion Publishing Group Ltd)

**Insider Info** Catalogue available online.

**Non-Fiction** Publishes Autobiography, Biography and General Non-fiction titles.

* Publishes in paperback only.

**Submission Guidelines** Agented submissions only.

**Fiction** Publishes Mainstream/Contemporary titles.

* Publishes in paperback only.

**Submission Guidelines** Agented submissions only.

**Recent Title(s)** *Anyone Can Do It*, Duncan Bannatyne (Autobiography); *The Light of the Evening*, Edna O'Brien (Novel); *Sharp Objects*, Gillian Flynn (Novel)

**Tips** Do not accept any unsolicited submissions.

## Piatkus Books

**5 Windmill Street, London, W1T 2JA**

- 01476 541080
- 01476 541061
- info@piatkus.co.uk

ⓦ www.piatkus.co.uk

**Contact** Founder/Managing Director, Judy Piatkus; Editorial Director, Gill Bailey; Senior Commissioning Editor, Gillian Green

**Established** 1979

**Imprint(s)** Piatkus
Portrait

**Insider Info** Publishes 150 titles per year. Payment is via royalties. Aims to respond to proposals and manuscripts within 12 weeks. Catalogue and manuscript guidelines available online.

**Non-Fiction** Publishes Autobiography, Biography, General Non-fiction, Humour and Reference. titles on the following subjects:
Business/Economics, Contemporary Culture, Counselling/Career, Health/Medicine, History, Memoirs, Music/Dance, Psychology, Spirituality.

**Submission Guidelines** Accepts query/SAE with proposal package (including outline, three sample chapters, your publishing history).

**Fiction** Publishes Mainstream/Contemporary titles.

**Submission Guidelines** Accepts query/SAE with proposal package (including outline, three sample chapters, your publishing history).

**Recent Title(s)** *2012*, Daniel Pinchbeck; *How to Marry a Ghost,* Hope McIntyre (Novel)

**Tips** When submitting be sure to include details of the target market and the need for your book, information about your previous publications and credentials for writing the book.

## Piatkus

**5 Windmill Street, London, W1T 2JA**

ⓣ 01476 541080

ⓕ 01476 541061

ⓔ info@piatkus.co.uk

ⓦ www.piatkus.co.uk

**Parent Company** Piatkus Books

**Contact** Founder/Managing Director, Judy Piatkus; Editorial Director, Gill Bailey; Senior Commissioning Editor, Gillian Green

**Insider Info** Payment via royalties. Aims to respond to proposals and manuscripts within 12 weeks. Book catalogue and manuscript guidelines available online.

**Non-Fiction** Publishes General Non-fiction and Self-help titles on the following subjects:
Business/Economics, Health/Medicine, Psychology, Spirituality, Mind, Body and Spirit.

**Submission Guidelines** Accepts query with SAE, with proposal package (including outline, three sample chapters, your publishing history).

**Fiction** Publishes Mainstream/Contemporary titles.

**Submission Guidelines** Accepts query with SAE with proposal package (including outline, three sample chapters and your publishing history).

**Tips** The Piatkus imprint of Piatkus Books specialises in leading edge lifestyle titles, as well as bestselling commercial fiction.

## Picador

**20 New Wharf Road, London, N1 9RR**

ⓣ 020 7014 6000

ⓕ 020 7014 6001

ⓦ www.panmacmillan.com

**Parent Company** Pan Macmillan Publishers

**Established** 1972

**Insider Info** Catalogue available online as a downloadable pdf.

**Non-Fiction** Publishes Autobiography, Biography and General Non-fiction titles on the following subjects:
Literary, Creative Non-fiction, Memoir.

**Submission Guidelines** Accepts agented submissions only.

**Fiction** Publishes General Fiction. Mainstream/Contemporary and Literary titles.

**Submission Guidelines** Accepts agented submissions only.

**Poetry** Publishes a range of poetry titles.

**Submissions Guidelines** Accepts agented submissions only.

**Recent Title(s)** *Mother's Milk*, Edward St Aubyn; *When a Crocodile Eats the Sun,* Peter Godwin

**Tips** Picador has a particular reputation for ground breaking non-fiction, reportage, literary biography and memoir, as well as poetry. Do not send any unsolicited manuscripts.

## Pica Press

**38 Soho Square, London, W1D 3HB**

ⓣ 020 7758 0200

ⓕ 020 7758 0222

ⓔ ornithology@acblack.com

ⓦ www.acblack.com

**Parent Company** A & C Black

**Contact** Department Head, Nigel Redman; Publishing Director, Jonathan Glasspool, (Reference, Theatre and Ornithology)

**Established** 1995

**Insider Info** Catalogue available online.

**Non-Fiction** Publishes General Non-fiction, Illustrated and Reference titles on the following subjects:
Nature/Environment, Natural History, Ornithology.

**Recent Title(s)** *Stonechats - A Guide to the Genus Saxicola*, Ewan Urquhart (Ornithology)

**Tips** Pica is the sister imprint of Christopher Helm at A & C Black and publishes taxonomic and geographic bird books, field and identification guides, and general interest books on birds and nature. Pica generally publishes taxonomic bird books from recognised scientists and academics, so a background in ornithological science would be useful for any would be contributor.

## Piccadilly Press
**5 Castle Road, London, NW1 8PR**
- 020 726 74492
- 020 726 74493
- books@piccadillypress.co.uk
- www.piccadillypress.co.uk

**Contact** Publisher/Managing Director, Brenda Gardner

**Established** 1983

**Insider Info** Publishes 30 titles per year. Payment is via royalties. Catalogue and manuscript guidelines available online.

**Non-Fiction** Publishes Children's/Juvenile and General Non-fiction titles on the following subjects: Child Guidance/Parenting, Teenage Issues.

**Submission Guidelines** Accepts query with SAE with proposal package (including outline and two sample chapters). Will accept artworks/images (send photocopies).

**Fiction** Publishes Picture Book, Children's, Juvenile and Young Adult titles.

**Submission Guidelines** Accepts query with SAE with proposal package (including outline and two sample chapters).

**Recent Title(s)** *Cinnamon Girl: This Way to Paradise*, Cathy Hopkins (Novel)

**Tips** Piccadilly Press is an independent publisher, specialising in teenage fiction and non–fiction, 'tween' fiction, picture books and parenting books by highly acclaimed authors and illustrators. They publish a range of titles, but there are three strands of publishing on which they focus when commissioning new titles: picture books, teenage fiction, and teenage non-fiction. Check the website for further details.

## Pigasus Press
**13 Hazely Combe, Arreton, Isle of Wight, PO30 3AJ**
- mail@pigasuspress.co.uk
- www.pigasuspress.co.uk

**Contact** Editor, Tony Lee (Science Fiction, Fantasy, Horror)

**Established** 1989

**Insider Info** Publishes two titles per year. Simultaneous submissions are not accepted. Submissions accompanied by SAE will be returned. Aims to respond to queries within seven days, proposals within ten days, and manuscripts and all other enquiries within six months. Catalogue and manuscript guideline are available with SAE or online.

**Non-Fiction** Publishes General Non-fiction (Interviews), Profiles, Essays, Top Ten listings, Reference and Scholarly titles on the following subjects: Contemporary Culture, Entertainment/Games, Literary Criticism (Genre fiction), Science.

**Submission Guidelines** Accepts queries with SAE or completed manuscripts. Also accepts artworks/ images (send photocopies, digital files as jpegs).

**Fiction** Publishes Experimental, Fantasy (not sword and sorcery), Horror (no gore), Literary (genre content), Mystery, and Science Fiction titles.

**Submission Guidelines** Accepts queries with SAE, or completed manuscripts.

**Poetry** Publishes some contemporary genre poetry.

**Submission Guidelines** Submit six sample poems.

**Tips** Genre publisher that specialise in speculative fiction of all kinds. They also publish *Premonitions* magazine which offers further publishing possibilities.

## Pimlico
**Random House, 20 Vauxhall Bridge Road, London, SW1V 2SA**
- 020 7840 8578
- 020 7233 6117
- pimlicoeditorial@randomhouse.co.uk
- www.randomhouse.co.uk

**Parent Company** The Random House Group Ltd

**Contact** Publisher, Will Sulkin

**Insider Info** Catalogue available online.

**Non-Fiction** Publishes Biography and General Non-fiction on the following subjects: Government/Politics, History, Philosophy, Adventure.
 * Publish entirely in paperback.

**Submission Guidelines** Accepts proposal package (including outline, one sample chapter, SAE). Will accept artworks/images (send photocopies).

**Recent Title(s)** *Blitzkrieg,* Len Deighton

**Tips** Specialises in historical biographies and accounts in paperback. Strongly prefer agented submissions emailed submissions are not accepted.

## Pinwheel Limited

**Winchester House, 259–269 Old Marylebone Road, London, NW1 5XJ**

- ☎ 020 7616 7200
- ☎ 020 7616 7201
- 🌐 www.pinwheel.co.uk

**Contact** Managing Director, Andrew Flatt

**Imprint(s)** Pinwheel Children's Books
Andromeda Children's Books
Gullane Children's Books

**Insider Info** Catalogue available online.

**Non-Fiction** Publishes Children's/Juvenile, Cloth, Novelty, Gift, Illustrated, Reference, Dictionary and General Non-fiction titles on the following subjects: Baby and Child's Early Learning, Religion, Natural History.

**Submission Guidelines** Accepts entire manuscript with SAE for children's picture books (up to 800 words).

**Fiction** Publishes Children's, Picture Book and Illustrated fiction titles.

**Submission Guidelines** Accepts entire manuscript with SAE for children's picture books (up to 800 words).

**Recent Title(s)** *Amazing Earth,* Heather Maisner (Picture Book)

**Tips** Specialises entirely in children's publishing. Within the company, Pinwheel Children's imprint concentrates on packaging novelty books, and Andromeda focuses on the 3-12 year old age group with gift books. Gullane publishes the more traditional picture books, for which submissions are sought. Submissions should be addressed to: The Commissioning Editor, Gullane Children's Books. Titles submitted for consideration should be pitched at children aged seven or younger.

## Pipers' Ash Ltd

**Church Road, Christian Malford, Chippenham, Wiltshire, SN15 4BW**

- ☎ 01249 720563
- ☎ 0870 056 8916
- ✉ pipersash@supamasu.com
- 🌐 www.supamasu.com

**Contact** The Manuscript Evaluation Desk (All subjects)

**Established** 1976

**Insider Info** Publishes 15 titles per year. Receives 1,200 queries and 800 manuscripts per year. 90 per cent of books published are from first-time authors and 100 per cent are from unagented authors. Payment is via royalty (on retail price) of 0.1 (per £). No advance is offered. Average lead time is six months, with simultaneous submissions not accepted. Submissions accompanied by SAE will be returned. Aims to respond to queries within seven days, proposals within five weeks, and manuscripts within two months. Catalogue and manuscript guidelines available online.

**Non-Fiction** Publishes Autobiography, Biography, Booklets, Children's/Juvenile, Coffee Table, General Non-fiction, Gift, How-to, Scholarly, Self-help and Textbook titles on the following subjects: Creative Non-fiction, History, Humanities, Language/Literature, Marine Subjects, Memoirs, Military/War, Multicultural, Philosophy, Psychology, Recreation, Regional, Sport, Translation (well known classics), Young Adult, Science Fiction (realistic), Local Histories, Stagecraft, True Life 'Problem' Stories.
 * Potential authors should study the market, visit the website, read the guidelines, and beg, borrow or buy sample copies.

**Submission Guidelines** Accepts query with SAE or via a telephone call. Will not accept artworks/images.

**Fiction** Publishes Adventure (plausible), Historical (spirit of the age), Juvenile (realistic), Literary, Mainstream/Contemporary (appealing), Multicultural, Plays (for small drama groups), Regional (for local interest), Science Fiction (realistic), Short story collections (cohesive), Sports (true to life), Translation (well known authors), Young Adult (true to life), Contemporary Short Stories (cohesive collection), Children's and Classics titles.
 * Potential authors should study the market thoroughly.

**Submission Guidelines** Accepts query with SAE or via a telephone call.

**Poetry** Publishes poetry collections in the form of chapbooks and pamphlets.
 * Writers should make sure poems do not sound awkward when read out aloud.

**Submission Guidelines** Accepts query with SAE or via a telephone call.

**Recent Title(s)** *Nurse, Nurse!,* Lucy Samuels (True Life); *Rebecca Riotters Of Botany Bay*, Russell Roberts (Historical); *Life is a Carousel,* Dawn Stafford (Woman's Views)

**Tips** Titles aimed at a world wide readership. Visit the website and read the Piper's Ash published authors, who have set the high standards for others to follow.

## Planet

**PO Box 44, Aberystwyth, Ceredigion, SY23 3ZZ**

- ☎ 01970 611255
- ☎ 01970 611197
- ✉ planet.enquiries@planetmagazine.org.uk

ⓦ www.planetmagazine.org.uk
**Contact** Managing Editor, John Barnie
**Established** 1970
**Insider Info** Payment is via royalties. Catalogue and manuscript guidelines (for the magazine only) are available online.
**Non-fiction** Publishes Autobiography, Biography and General Non-fiction titles on the following subjects:
Art/Architecture, History, Regional, World Affairs, Welsh interest.
\* Also publishes *Planet: The Welsh Internationalist* magazine.
**Fiction** Publishes Mainstream/Contemporary, Regional, Short story collections, Translation, Welsh Fiction and World Writing titles.
**Poetry** Publishes poetry with a particular slant towards Welsh interest.
**Recent Title(s)** *The Skiffle Craze*, Mike Dewe (Music/Dance); *Wounded Wind*, Carlos Casares (Translation); *Blue*, Nigel Jenkins (Collection)
**Tips** Planet mainly focusses on the arts and current affairs magazine *Planet: The Welsh Internationalist*. It expanded in 1995 into book publishing, mostly of Welsh poetry and fiction, including short story collections, and also some translated fiction from around the world, but this is still a fairly small venture. Most articles, features and reviews in the magazine are commissioned, but if you have an idea for an article that you think might be relevant to the magazine, send a letter of enquiry with a brief synopsis.

## The Playwrights Publishing Company
**70 Nottingham Road, Burton Joyce, Nottingham, Nottinghamshire, NG14 5AL**
ⓞ 0115 931 3356
ⓔ playwrightspublishingco@yahoo.com
ⓦ www.geocities.com/playwrightspublishingco
**Contact** Partner, Tony Breeze (Drama); Partner, Elizabeth Breeze (Drama)
**Established** 1990
**Insider Info** Publish 12 titles per year. Payment is via royalty (on retail price) and performance rights. Simultaneous submissions are not accepted. Submissions accompanied by SAE will be returned. Aims to respond to queries within one day and manuscripts within four weeks. Catalogue is free on request, and available via A4 SAE, online or email. Author guidelines are free on request and available via email.
**Fiction** Publishes Plays and Drama titles.
\* A template for good scripts is *The Writer's Journey* by Christopher Vogler.

**Submission Guidelines** Accepts proposal package (including SAE, reading fee of £15 for one act, £30 for full length).
Submit completed manuscripts via email. Will not accept artwork/images.
**Recent Title(s)** *It Is Christmas After All*, Lyndon Howes (One Act Play)
**Tips** Titles aimed at general readers and drama groups. Read and digest *The Writer's Journey*.

## Plexus Publishing Ltd
**25 Mallinson Road, London, SW11 1BW**
ⓞ 020 792 44662
ⓞ 020 792 45096
ⓔ info@plexusuk.demon.co.uk
ⓦ www.plexusbooks.com
**Contact** Managing Director, Terence Porter; Editorial Director, Sandra Wake
**Established** 1973
**Insider Info** Catalogue available online.
**Non-Fiction** Publish Biography and General Non-fiction titles on the following subjects:
Contemporary Culture, Music/Dance, Film/Television, Celebrity Culture.
**Submission Guidelines** Accepts query with SAE along with the completed manuscript.
**Recent Title(s)** *Johnny Depp: A Modern Rebel*, Brian J. Robb (Biography)
**Tips** Plexus are currently updating their website and will include guidelines for authors in the future. In the meantime they will still accept unsolicited manuscripts for relevant books.

## Pluto Publishing Ltd
**345 Archway Road, London, N6 5AA**
ⓞ 020 834 82724
ⓞ 020 834 89133
ⓔ pluto@plutobooks.com
ⓦ www.plutobooks.com
**Contact** Chairman, Roger van Zwanenberg (International Studies, International Political Theory, Political Economy, Green Economics, Development Studies, Peace Studies, Middle East Studies, Irish Studies); Managing Director, Anne Beech (Current Affairs, Media Studies, Gender Studies, Anthropology, Law and Human Rights); Managing Editor, Robert Webb; Commissioning Editor, David Castle (Politics, Political Theory, History, Social Issues, Cultural Studies, Environmental Studies)
**Established** 1970
**Insider Info** Publishes 70 titles per year. Catalogue and manuscript guidelines available online.

**Non-Fiction** Publishes Scholarly titles on the following subjects:
 Anthropology/Archaeology, Contemporary Culture, Government/Politics, History, Regional, Social Sciences, World Affairs.

**Submission Guidelines** Accepts query via email, with proposal package (including outline, table of contents, two sample chapters, author biography, market research).
 Submission details to: beech@plutobooks.com, davidc@plutobooks.com, rogervz@plutobooks.com (see contacts section for areas of interest).

**Recent Title(s)** *Unravelling Gramsci*, Adam David Morton

**Tips** Pluto Press has a proud history of publishing the very best in progressive, critical thinking across politics and the social sciences. Titles are aimed at an academic audience of students and professionals in higher education worldwide. Pluto Press is always interested in receiving proposals for new books that have a sharp critical edge and an intentionally political focus.

## Pocket Books

**Africa House, 64–78 Kingsway, London, WC2B 6AH**

- 020 7316 1900
- 020 7316 0332
- enquiries@simonandschuster.co.uk
- www.simonsays.co.uk

**Parent Company** Simon and Schuster UK Ltd

**Insider Info** Catalogue available online.

**Non-Fiction** Publishes Coffee Table, General Non-fiction, Gift and Self-help titles on the following subjects:
 Health/Medicine, Spirituality, World Affairs, Television tie-ins, Current Affairs, Crime.

**Submission Guidelines** Agented submissions only.

**Fiction** Publishes Fantasy, Science Fiction, Suspense, General Mass Market Fiction and Television tie-in titles.

**Submission Guidelines** Agented submissions only.

**Recent Title(s)** *My Year Without Buying It*, Judith Levine (Non-fiction); *The Other Lover*, Sarah Jackman (General Fiction); *The Art of Star Trek*, J & G Reeves-Stevens (Television Tie-in)

**Tips** Pocket Books is Simon and Schuster's mass market fiction and non-fiction imprint. All books are published in paperback.

## Pocket Essentials

**18 Coleswood Road, Harpenden, AL5 1EQ**

- 01582 761264

- 01582 7612244
- info@pocketessentials.co.uk
- www.pocketessentials.co.uk

**Parent Company** Oldcastle Books

**Contact** Series Editor, Mel McGinnis

**Insider Info** Average lead time is five months. Catalogue and manuscript guidelines available online.

**Non-Fiction** Publishes Reference titles on the following subjects:
 Culture, Theory, Philosophy, Film, History, Literature, Science, Sport.

**Submission Guidelines** Accepts proposal package via email (including outline and samples of writing). Read the very detailed author guidelines on the website before submitting.

**Recent Title(s)** *The Indian Mutiny,* Andrew Walker; *Roget: A Biography,* Nick Rennison

**Tips** Pocket Essentials (PEs) are cultural guides packed with facts, opinion, information, critical insights, trivia, bibliographies, plot summaries, biographies and essays by experts. The largest area of publishing is on film subjects, but PEs are also published on ideas and history. A limited number are published on Television, Sport, Business, Music and Literature.

## Pocket Mountains Ltd

**6 Church Wynd, Bo'ness, West Lothian, EH51 0AN**

- 01506 500404
- info@pocketmountains.com
- www.pocketmountains.com

**Contact** Director, April Simmons; Director, Robbie Porteous

**Established** 2002

**Insider Info** Catalogue is available online. Manuscript guidelines are available online via the website.

**Non-Fiction** Publishes General Non-fiction and Reference titles on the following subjects:
 Hobbies, Nature/Environment, Regional, Sports, Travel and Hiking/Walking Guides.

**Submission Guidelines** Accepts query with SAE and proposal package (including outline, one sample chapter, author biography and SAE).

**Recent Title(s)** *Southern Highlands*, Nick Williams (Walking Guide)

**Tips** Pocket Mountains was set up by a group of outdoor enthusiasts who wanted to see books on the shelves that reflected the spirit of adventure and excitement that Scotland as an outdoors destination represents. From its roots as a mountain walking publisher, Pocket Mountains has now grown to include cycling, mountain biking and wildlife guides. Pocket Mountains is always on the lookout for new outdoor authors and welcomes ideas from non-established authors with a sound knowledge of the particular subject area, plenty of enthusiasm, and an idea that excites.

## The Policy Press
**4th Floor, Beacon House, Queens Road, Bristol, Bristol, BS8 1QU**
❶ 0117 331 4054
❶ 0117 331 4093
✉ tpp-info@bristol.ac.uk
🌐 www.policypress.org.uk
**Parent Company** University of Bristol
**Contact** Director, Alison Shaw (Social Policy); Assistant Director, Julia Mortimer (Social Work); Commissioning Editor, Philip de Bary (Social Policy, Criminology)
**Established** 1996
**Insider Info** Publishes 60 titles per year. Receives approximately 150–200, queries and 80 manuscripts per year. 15 per cent of books published are by first-time authors and 100 per cent of books published are from unagented authors. Payment is based on net receipts. Average lead time is 18 months, with simultaneous submissions accepted. Submissions accompanied by SAE will be returned. Aims to respond to queries within two days, and proposals and manuscripts within six months. Catalogue and author guidelines are free on request, and available online.
**Non-Fiction** Publishes Scholarly and Textbook titles on the following subjects:
 Community/Public Affairs, Education, Government/Politics, Health/Medicine, Social Sciences, Sociology, Women's Issues/Studies, World Affairs.
 * All publications are peer reviewed.
**Submission Guidelines** Accepts proposal package via email (including outline, sample chapter(s), your publishing history, author biography) and artworks/images (send digital files as jpegs).
 Submission details to: tpp-info@bristol.ac.uk
**Tips** Titles aimed at academics, students (all levels) and practitioners. Please follow the proposal guidelines on the website.

## Policy Studios Institute
**50 Hanson Street, London, W1W 6UP**
❶ 020 7911 7500
❶ 020 7911 7501
✉ website@psi.org.uk
🌐 www.psi.org.uk

**Contact** Director, Malcolm Rigg
**Established** 1978
**Insider Info** Catalogue and manuscript guidelines available online.
**Non-Fiction** Publishes Reference, Scholarly and Technical titles on the following subjects:
 Business/Economics, Community/Public Affairs, Contemporary Culture, Counselling/Career, Education, Government/Politics, Law, Money/Finance, Nature/Environment, Social Sciences, Transportation, World Affairs.
**Tips** PSI undertakes and publishes research studies relevant to social, economic and industrial policy. It takes a politically neutral stance on issues of public policy and has no connections with any political party, commercial interest or pressure group. Please note that PSI no longer publishes new material of its own. The remaining stock of PSI publications is handled by Central Books.

## Politico's Publishing
**11–12 Buckingham Gate, London, SW1E 6LB**
❶ 020 7798 1600
❶ 020 7828 2098/020 7233 9827
🌐 www.politicospublishing.co.uk
**Parent Company** Methuen Publishing Limited
**Contact** Chairman/Managing Director, Peter Tummons; Publishing Director, Alan Gordon-Walker
**Established** 1998 (acquired by Methuen 2003)
**Insider Info** Catalogue available online.
**Non-Fiction** Publish Autobiography, Biography, Humour, Reference, Self-help and Textbook titles on the following subjects:
 Business/Economics, Education, Government/Politics, History, Law, Military/War, Philosophy, Religion, Sociology, Travel, Communication Studies, Performing Arts, Literature, Europe, Asia.
**Submission Guidelines** Accepts query with SAE/proposal package (including synopsis). Prefers agented submissions.
**Fiction** Publishes Political Fiction titles.
**Submission Guidelines** Accepts query with SAE/proposal package (including synopsis). Prefers agented submissions.
**Recent Title(s)** *Alec Douglas-Home*, D.R. Thorpe (part of Politico's recently introduced Great Statesman series); *A Very British Coup*, Chris Mullin (Reissued Political Thriller)
**Tips** Specialists in political publishing, particularly to do with Britain, Europe, USA and the Middle East. Unagented submissions are not encouraged. No submissions by email.

## Polity Press

**65 Bridge Street, Cambridge, CB2 1UR**

- 01223 324315
- 01223 461385
- editorial@polity.co.uk
- www.polity.co.uk

**Contact** Editorial Director, Louise Knight (Politics, International Relations); Commissioning Editor, Andrea Drugan (History, Literature, Media and Culture Studies); Commissioning Editor, Emma Longstaff (Sociology); Commissioning Editor, Emma Hutchinson (All other subjects)

**Established** 1983

**Insider Info** Catalogue and author guidelines available online.

**Non-Fiction** Publishes General Non-fiction titles on the following subjects:
Anthropology/Archaeology, Government/Politics, History, Language/Literature, Literary Criticism, Philosophy, Psychology, Sex, Sociology, Women's Issues/Studies, Media and Cultural Studies.

**Submission Guidelines** Accepts query with SAE, or via email to the appropriate Commissioning Editor, with proposal package (including outline and sample chapter(s)).
Submission details to: firstname.lastname@polity.co.uk (see contacts for commissioning editors)

**Recent Title(s)** *The Chancellors' Tales - Managing the British Economy*, Howard Davies (ed.)

**Tips** Polity is a leading international publisher in the social sciences and humanities. Titles are aimed primarily at students and scholars in further and higher education. The list is particularly strong in the areas of sociology, politics, and social and political theory. They would like to hear from authors who have an idea for, or are currently writing, an academic title in the appropriate subject areas.

## Pomegranate Press

**Dolphin House, 51 St. Nicholas Lane, Lewes, Sussex, BN7 2JZ**

- 01273 470100
- 01273 470100
- pomegranatepress@aol.com
- www.pomegranate-press.co.uk

**Contact** David Arscott (Sussex Themes, Self-publishing)

**Established** 1992

**Insider Info** Publishes three titles per year. Receives approximately ten queries and six manuscripts per year. 50 per cent of books published are from first-time authors, 100 per cent are from unagented authors and 60 per cent are author subsidy published. Payment is via royalty (on retail price). Average lead time is three months. Submissions accompanied by SAE will be returned. Aims to respond to queries and manuscripts within ten days and proposals within seven days. Catalogue available via email. Manuscript guidelines available via SAE.

**Non-Fiction** Publishes General Non-fiction titles on the County of Sussex.

**Submission Guidelines** Accepts query with SAE, or via email. Will not accept artwork/images.

**Fiction** Publishes Fiction for self-publishing authors.

**Submission Guidelines** Accepts query with SAE, or via email.

**Recent Title(s)** *Sikkim Himalaya*, David Lang (Travel); *Maracas in Caracas*, David Arscott (Short Stories)

**Tips** Pomegranate are primarily a self-publishing company, although some local history books are published in the traditional manner. Research all options thoroughly.

## Poolbeg Press

**123 Grange Hill, Baldoyle Industrial Estate, Baldoyle, Dublin 13, Republic of Ireland**

- 00353 1 832 1477
- 00353 1 832 1430
- info@poolbeg.com
- www.poolbeg.com

**Contact** Publishing Director, Paula Campbell; Managing Director, Kieran Devlin

**Established** 1976

**Insider Info** Catalogue available online.

**Non-Fiction** Publishes Biography, Children's/Juvenile and General Non-fiction titles on the following subjects:
Cooking/Foods/Nutrition, Gardening, Government/Politics, Music/Dance, Regional, Religion, World Affairs.

**Fiction** Publishes Children's, Literary, Mainstream/Contemporary, Romance, Short Story Collections, Young Adult and Irish interest titles.

**Poetry** Publish Irish poetry.

**Recent Title(s)** *Exclusive*, A. O'Connor (Novel)

**Tips** Poolbeg, Ireland's premier popular fiction publishing company, publishes mainly new Irish writers.

## Portico

**151 Freston Road, London, W10 6TH**

- 020 7314 1400
- 020 7314 1401
- portico@anovabooks.com
- www.porticobooks.co.uk

**Parent Company** Anova Books Company Ltd
**Contact** Publisher, Tom Bromley
**Established** 2007
**Insider Info** Catalogue available online.
**Non-Fiction** Publishes General Non-fiction, Humour and Reference titles on the following subjects: Humour and Internet Books, Popular Culture, Reference, Sport, Narrative Non-fiction.
**Tips** Portico is Anova's new imprint for non-fiction books with a 'fresh, funny and forthright' appeal.

## Portland Press Ltd
**3rd Floor, Eagle House, 16 Procter Street, London, WC1V 6NX**
- 020 7280 4110
- 020 7280 4169
- editorial@portlandpress.com
- www.portlandpress.com

**Contact** Managing Director, Rhonda Oliver; Managing Editor, Pauline Starley; Acquisitions Editor, Roheena Anand
**Established** 1990
**Insider Info** Publishes four titles per year. Payment is via royalties. Catalogue and manuscript guidelines available online.
**Non-Fiction** Publish Reference, Scholarly and Technical titles on Biomedical Sciences.
**Submission Guidelines** Accepts query with SAE.
**Tips** Portland Press is a not for profit publisher of journals and books in the cellular and molecular life sciences. Titles are aimed largely at graduate, postgraduate and research students. The small book publishing programme falls within the biomedical sciences field, specifically the *Essays in Biochemistry* series and the Biochemical Society symposia. They do not normally accept unsolicited proposals unless they could potentially form a volume of the Essays series.

## Portobello Books ltd
**Eardley House, 4 Uxbridge Street, London, London, W8 7SY**
- 020 7908 9890
- 020 7908 9899
- mail@portobellobooks.com
- www.portobellobooks.com

**Established** 2005
**Insider Info** Publishes 20 titles per year. Catalogue is free on request.
**Non-Fiction** Publishes General Non-fiction on the following subjects: Literary, History, Anthropology, Culture.

**Submission Guidelines** Submission details to: Hannah@portobellobooks.com
**Fiction** Publish Literary Fiction and Fiction in Translation.
**Submission Guidelines** Submission details to: Hannah@portobellobooks.com
**Tips** An independent publisher that is able to take more risks with unusual or new work than is common in contemporary publishing.

## Portrait
**5 Windmill Street, London, W1T 2JA**
- 020 7631 0710
- 020 7436 7137
- info@piatkus.co.uk
- www.piatkus.co.uk

**Parent Company** Piatkus Books
**Contact** Managing Director/Publisher, Judy Piatkus
**Established** 2004
**Insider Info** Submissions accompanied by SAE will be returned. Catalogue available online.
**Non-Fiction** Publishes Autobiography, Biography and General Non-fiction titles on the following subjects: Contemporary Culture, History, Music/Dance.
**Submission Guidelines** Accepts query with SAE with proposal package (including outline, one sample chapter, the introduction).
**Recent Title(s)** *One Train Later: A Memoir,* Andy Summers
**Tips** Portrait is Piatkus' general non-fiction imprint, publishing history, memoirs, popular culture, music, humour and other subjects that appeal to the publishers and the market at the time. Emailed submissions are not accepted.

## Praxis Books
**Crossways Cottage, Walterstone, Herefordshire, HR2 0DX**
- 01873 890695
- author@rebeccatope.fsnet.co.uk
- www.rebeccatope.com/praxisbooks.asp

**Contact** Proprietor, Rebecca Smith
**Established** 1992
**Insider Info** Catalogue and manuscript guidelines available online.
**Non-Fiction** Publishes Autobiography, Children's/Juvenile and General Non-fiction titles on the following subjects: Memoirs, Philosophy, Walking Guides.
**Submission Guidelines** Accepts query with SAE.
**Fiction** Publishes Children's titles as well as Sabine Baring-Gould reprints.

**Submission Guidelines** Accepts query with SAE.
**Tips** Praxis Books is a small press mainly dedicated to the reissue of the novels of Sabine Baring-Gould. They will also occasionally consider approaches from authors. The door is never completely closed, despite limited cash flow.

## Prestel Publishing Ltd
**4 Bloomsbury Place, London, WC1A 2QA**
- 020 7323 5004
- 020 7636 8004
- sales@prestel-uk.co.uk
- www.prestel.com

**Contact** Commissioning Editor, Philippa Hurd
**Established** 1924
**Insider Info** Catalogue available online.
**Non-Fiction** Publishes Children's/Juvenile, Illustrated books and General Non-fiction titles on the following subjects:
 Art/Architecture, Contemporary Culture, Ethnic, History, Photography and Ethnology.
**Submission Guidelines** Accepts query with SAE/ proposal package (including outline, sample chapter(s) and SAE). Will accept artwork/images.
**Recent Title(s)** *The Birth of Graffiti*, Jon Naar
**Tips** With its impressive list of titles in English and German, Prestel Publishing is one of the world's leading publishers in the fields of art, architecture, photography, design, cultural history, and ethnography. Books published by Prestel range from museum guides, encyclopedic works, and monographs on artists and architects, to valuable facsimile editions and art books for children.

## Princeton University Press
**3 Market Place, Woodstock, Oxfordshire, OX20 1SY**
- 01993 814500
- 01993 814504
- admin@pupress.co.uk
- http://press.princeton.edu/

**Contact** Publishing Director - Europe, Richard Baggaley (Economics and Finance); Senior Editor, Ian Malcolm (Political Theory, Philosophy, History)
**Insider Info** Publish 200 titles per year. Simultaneous submissions accepted. Submissions will not be returned. Catalogue is free on request and available online. Manuscript guidelines are free on request and available online or via email.
**Non-Fiction** Publishes Biography, General Non-fiction, Reference, Scholarly, Technical and Textbook titles on the following subjects:
 Anthropology/Archaeology, Art/Architecture, Astrology/Psychic, Business/Economics, Education, Government/Politics, History, Humanities, Law, Literary Criticism, Marine Subjects, Military/War, Money/Finance, Multicultural, Nature/Environment, Philosophy, Psychology, Religion, Science, Social Sciences, Sociology, Translation, World Affairs.
**Submission Guidelines** Accepts proposal package (including outline, sample chapter(s), your publishing history, author biography).
**Tips** Titles aimed at university level students, as well as professional academics.

## Prion Books
**20 Mortimer Street, London, W1T 3JW**
- 020 7612 0400
- 020 7612 0401
- enquiries@carltonbooks.co.uk
- www.carltonbooks.co.uk

**Parent Company** Carlton Publishing Group
**Insider Info** Publishes four titles per year. Catalogue available online.
**Non-Fiction** Publishes Gift, Humour and Illustrated titles on the following subjects:
 Nostalgia, Photography, Entertainment, Retro Classic Anthologies.
**Submission Guidelines** Accepts proposal package (including outline, the shorter of 20 pages or two chapters).
**Recent Title(s)** *The Best of 'Girl'*, (Nostalgia); *How to Push a Perambulator,* Allison Vale and Alison Rattle (Humourous Non-fiction)
**Tips** Specialises in humour and nostalgia. Do not send full manuscripts unless via an agent.

## Profile Books
**3a Exmouth House, Pine Street, Exmouth Market, London, EC1R 0JH**
- 020 7841 6300
- 020 7833 3969
- info@profilebooks.com, firstname.lastname@profilebooks.com
- www.profilebooks.co.uk

**Contact** Managing Director, Andrew Franklin; Editor and International Rights, Penny Daniel; Editor, Daniel Crewe; Editor, Nicola Taplin
**Established** 1996
**Imprint(s)** Serpents Tail
 Profile Business
 Economist Books
**Insider Info** Publishes 60 titles per year. Payment via royalties. Catalogue available online.

**Non-Fiction** Publishes General Non-fiction and Scholarly titles on the following subjects: Business/Economics, Contemporary Culture, Government/Politics, History, Literary Criticism, Psychology, World Affairs.

**Submission Guidelines** Accepts query with SAE, or via email, with proposal package (including outline and two sample chapters) .

**Recent Title(s)** *St Pancras Station*, Simon Bradley (History)

**Tips** Most books published by Profile are submitted through literary agents. If, however, you feel that your book is in keeping with the Profile portfolio please do feel free to submit a proposal as described above, by post or email.

## Profile Business

**3a Exmouth House, Pine Street, Exmouth Market, London, EC1R 0JH**

- 020 7841 6300
- 020 7833 3969
- stephen.brough@profilebooks.com
- www.profilebooks.co.uk

**Parent Company** Profile Books

**Contact** Editor, Stephen Brough

**Insider Info** Catalogue available online.

**Non-Fiction** Publishes General Non-fiction, Reference and Scholarly titles on the following subjects: Business/Economics.

**Submission Guidelines** Accepts proposal package including (outline, two sample chapters and SAE).

**Recent Title(s)** *Battle for Barrels*, Duncan Clarke; *Family Businesses*, Peter Leach

**Tips** Most submissions are made by agents, however unsolicited proposals as described above are accepted.

## ProQuest Information and Learning Ltd

**512 The Quorm, Barnwell Road, Cambridge, CB5 8SW**

- 01223 215512
- 01223 215514
- marketing@proquest.co.uk
- www.proquest.co.uk

**Contact** General Manager, John Taylor

**Established** 1938

**Non-Fiction** Publish Reference, Scholarly and Technical titles.

**Tips** ProQuest Information and Learning provides access to information from periodicals, newspapers, out of print books, dissertations, and scholarly collections in various formats. Typically works in tandem with publishers to provide materials for academic institutions, libraries and classrooms.

## PS Avalon

**PO Box 1865, Glastonbury, Somerset, BA6 8YR**

- 01458 833864
- info@psavalon.com
- www.psavalon.com

**Contact** Director, Will Parfitt (Self-development, Poetry)

**Established** 2003

**Insider Info** Publishes four titles per year. Receives approximately 50 queries per year. 50 per cent of books published are from first-time authors, 90 per cent of books published are from unagented authors. Payment is via royalty (on retail price), with 0.1 (per £) minimum and 0.25 (per £) maximum. Average lead time is six months, with simultaneous submissions accepted. Submissions accompanied by SAE will be returned. Aims to respond to queries and proposals within seven days and manuscripts within 28 days. Catalogue is free on request and available online. Manuscript guidelines are available online.

**Non-Fiction** Publishes Autobiography, Reference, Scholarly, Self-help and Textbook titles on the following subjects: Alternative Lifestyles, Astrology/Psychic, Contemporary Culture, Counselling/Career, Creative Nonfiction, Education, Health/Medicine, New Age, Psychology, Spirituality.

   * Submissions must be of the finest quality and the author needs to be active, willing and able to promote the work.

**Submission Guidelines** Accepts query with SAE or by email, and artworks/images (send digital files as jpegs).

**Fiction** Publishes Occult, Religious and Spiritual titles.

**Submission Guidelines** Accepts query with SAE or by email.

**Poetry** * PS Avalon publishes spiritually orientated poetry but the author must be willing to give readings to promote the work.

**Submission Guidelines** Accepts query or proposal package (including two sample poems).

**Recent Title(s)** *Breaking The Spell*, Rachael Clyne (Personal Development); *The Heart's Ragged Evangelist*, Jay Ramsay (Inspirational Poetry)

**Tips** PS Avalon publishes for a general readership.

## Psychology Press

**Haines House, 21 John Street, London, WC1N 2BP**

- ☎ 020 7017 6000
- 🖨 020 7017 6701
- ⊙ Online form.
- 🌐 www.psypress.co.uk

**Parent Company** Taylor and Francis Group
**Insider Info** Catalogue and manuscript guideline are available online.
**Non-Fiction** Publishes Journals, Multimedia, Scholarly and Textbook titles on the following subjects:
 Cognitive Psychology and Cognitive Neuroscience, Developmental Psychology, Industrial Psychology, Neuropsychology, Social Psychology.
**Submission Guidelines** Uses an online form for proposal submissions. Hard copies accepted if no other option.
**Recent Title(s)** *Adulthood*, Evie Bentley; *Knowledge in Context,* Sandra Jovchelovitch
**Tips** Psychology Press publishes in all areas of psychological science. Titles must be based on psychology in the broadest sense, and be written by credible experts.

## Puffin

**80 Strand, London, WC2R 0RL**

- ☎ 020 7010 3000
- 🖨 020 7010 6060
- ⊙ customer.service@penguin.co.uk
- 🌐 www.puffin.co.uk

**Parent Company** Penguin Group (UK)
**Contact** Managing Director, Francesca Dow; Publisher and Managing Director, Rebecca McNally; Senior Editor, Fran Hammond
**Established** 1940
**Insider Info** Catalogue is available online.
**Non-Fiction** Publishes Children's/Juvenile, General Non-fiction, Gift, Illustrated and Novelty titles on the following subjects:
 Film, Popular Culture, Television tie-ins.
 * Puffin publishes non-fiction for very young readers through to teenagers.
**Submission Guidelines** Agented submissions only.
**Fiction** Publishes Children's, Humour, Mystery, Novelty, Picture, Teenage and Young Adult titles.
**Submission Guidelines** Agented submissions only.
**Poetry** * Puffin publishes collections of poetry for children and young adult readers.
**Recent Title(s)** *My Secret Unicorn: Moonlight Journey*, Lind Chapman; *Artemis Fowl and the Lost Colony*, Eoin Colfer

**Tips** Puffin is the UK's leading publisher of children's books and publishes a wide range of fiction and non-fiction for younger children through to young adult and teenage readers.

## Pulp Books

**Po Box 12171, London, N19 3HB**

- ⊙ editor@pulpfact.demon.co.uk
- 🌐 www.pulpfact.demon.co.uk

**Established** 1995
**Imprint(s)** Pulp Books
 Pulp Faction
**Insider Info** Catalogue available online.
**Non-Fiction** Publishes general non-fiction titles on the following subjects:
 Music and Dance.
**Fiction** Publishes experimental and contemporary fiction.
**Recent Title(s)** *Too Much Too Soon*, Joe Ambrose (Novel)
**Tips** Independent press Pulp Books publishes contemporary short fiction by new British authors. Authors from the United States are not considered and submissions are not accepted by email.

## Pushkin Press

**12 Chester Terrace, London, NW1 4ND**

- ☎ 020 7730 0750
- 🖨 020 7730 1341
- ⊙ books@pushkinpress.com
- 🌐 www.pushkinpress.com

**Contact** Chairman, Melissa Ulfane
**Fiction** Publishes classic and contemporary literary fiction in translation.
**Recent Title(s)** *The Fascination of Evil*, Florian Zeller (translated by Sue Dyson)
**Tips** Most publications are European translations. Publishes both full-length novels and novellas, as well as short story collections.

## QED Publishing

**226 City Road, London, EC1V 2TT**

- ☎ 020 7812 8600
- 🖨 020 7253 4370
- ⊙ qedpublishing@quarto.com
- 🌐 www.qed-publishing.co.uk

**Parent Company** The Quarto Group
**Contact** Publisher, Steve Evans; Editorial Director, Jean Coppendale; Editor, Hannah Ray
**Established** 2003
**Insider Info** Payment is via an outright fee. Catalogue free on request and available online.

**Non-Fiction** Publishes General Non-fiction, illustrated and Reference titles on the following subjects:
Children's/Juvenile, Child Guidance/Parenting, Education, History, Nature/Environment, Art and Design, ICT, Geography, Science, Maths and Literacy. *Books are specially devised to support children's curriculum learning.
**Submission Guidelines** Accepts query with SAE.
**Recent Title(s)** *Communicate Online*, Anne Rooney (Educational)
**Tips** Authors for children's educational books should be experts in their field.

## Quadrille Publishing Ltd
**5th Floor, Alhambra House, 27–31 Charing Cross Road, London, WC2H 0LS**
- 020 7839 7117
- 020 7839 7118
- enquiries@quadrille.co.uk
- www.quadrille.co.uk

**Contact** Managing Director, Alison Cathie; Editorial Director, Jane O'Shea
**Established** 1994
**Insider Info** Authors paid by royalty. Catalogue available online.
**Non-Fiction** Publishes General Non-fiction, Gift, Humour and Illustrated titles on the following subjects:
Automotive, Cooking/Food/Nutrition, Crafts, Gardening, Health/Medicine, House and Home, Nature/Environment, Photography and Spirituality.
**Recent Title(s)** *Gordon Ramsay's Sunday Lunches*, Gordon Ramsay (Cookery)
**Tips** Welcomes ideas or synopses for books but no fiction or children's books.

## Quantum Foulsham
**The Publishing House, Bennetts Close, Cippenham, Slough, Berkshire, SL1 5AP**
- 01753 526769
- 01753 535003
- marketing@foulsham.com
- www.foulsham.com

**Parent Company** Foulsham Publishers
**Insider Info** Catalogue available online.
**Non-Fiction** Publishes General Non-fiction titles on the following subjects:
Spirituality, Dreams, Angels and Healing.
**Submission Guidelines** Accepts query with proposal package (Including outline, author biography and SAE).

**Tips** Address submissions to the Editorial Department. No submissions accepted by email.

## Quartet Books
**27 Goodge Street, London, W1T 2LD**
- 020 7636 3992
- 020 7637 1866
- quartetbooks@easynet.co.uk

**Contact** Managing Director, Jeremy Beale; Publishing Director, Stella Kane
**Established** 1972
**Insider Info** Authors paid by royalty.
**Non-Fiction** Publishes Biography, General Non-fiction and Scholarly titles on the following subjects:
Contemporary Culture, Government/Politics, History, Music/Dance and Photography.
**Submission Guidelines** Accepts query with SAE including outline and two sample chapters.
**Fiction** Publishes Literary, Mainstream/Contemporary and Translations.
**Submission Guidelines** Accepts query with SAE including outline and two sample chapters.
**Tips** Synopses welcome with return postage, but no genre fiction is accepted. Submissions via email or on disk are not considered.

## The Quarto Group Inc
**226 City Road, London, EC1V 2TT**
- 020 7700 9000
- 020 7253 4437
- info@quarto.com
- www.quarto.com

**Tips** The UK based Quarto Group, which also has a presence in the US and Australia, are the owners of the UK's Apple Press, Argentum and Aurum Publishing. Co-edition publishing in the UK includes, Design Eye, EYE, Jacqui Small, Marshall Editions, QED, Quantum Publishing, Quarto Publishing, Quarto Children's Books, Qu:id, Quintessence, and Quintet Publishing. See entries for more information.

## QueenSpark Books
**49 Grand Parade, Brighton, BN2 2QA**
- 01273 571710
- 01273 571710
- info@queensparkbooks.org.uk
- www.queensparkbooks.org.uk

**Established** 1974
**Insider Info** Catalogue available online.
**Non-Fiction** Publishes Biography and General Non-fiction titles on the following subjects:
History and Regional interest.

**Recent Title(s)** *Pebble on the Beach*, Tony Diamond (Autobiography)

**Tips** QueenSpark is a Brighton based non-profit community publishing and writing organisation, publishing books about local people's lives, running creative writing groups and facilitating oral history projects. Materials are sourced mainly from associated writing groups and no unsolicited manuscripts are accepted.

## QUE Publishing
**Edinburgh Gate, Harlow, Essex, CM20 2JE**
- 01279 623623
- 01279 414130
- www.pearsoned.co.uk/Imprints/QUEPublishing

**Parent Company** Pearson Education

**Insider Info** Catalogue and manuscript guidelines are available online.

**Non-Fiction** Publishes How-to, Reference and Technical titles on the following subjects: Computers, Internet, Networking.

**Submission Guidelines** Accepts proposal package (including synopsis, sample chapters, market research, your publishing history and author biography).

**Recent Title(s)** *Absolute Beginner's Guide to Microsoft® Windows Vista®*, Shelley O'Hara and Ron Mansfield

**Tips** QUE specialises in the area of applications for computing. It is one of the largest computer book publishers in the world and sets the standard for superior tutorial reference products, covering all major computer and internet applications at every user level. See the website for full list of submissions contacts.

## Quercus Publishing Plc
**21 Bloomsbury Square, London, WC1A 2QA**
- 020 7291 7200
- 0870 730 1482
- mail@quercusbooks.co.uk
- www.quercusbooks.co.uk

**Contact** CEO/Managing Director, Mark Smith; Publishing Director, Wayne Davies; Consulting Editor, Otto Penzler (Crime Fiction)

**Established** 2004

**Imprint(s)** Quercus Editions (contract publishing) Quercus Books Limited (trade publishing)

**Insider Info** Catalogue available online.

**Non-Fiction** Publishes Biography, General Non-fiction titles on the following subjects: History, Hobbies and Science.

**Fiction** Publishes Crime and Women's fiction (trade only, no contract publishing).

**Recent Title(s)** *The Flat Tummy Book*, Denise Lewis; *The Shadow Walker*, Michael Walters (Novel)

**Tips** The business has both trade and contract publishing arms and is still largely driven by contract publishing, especially in the non-fiction areas. Their policy is to re-publish successful contract titles in trade editions, and establish a fiction list based on this trade presence.

## Quiller Publishing Ltd
**Wykey House, Wykey, Shrewsbury, Shropshire, SY4 1JA**
- 01939 261616
- 01939 261606
- info@quillerbooks.com
- www.countrybooksdirect.com

**Contact** Managing Director, Andrew Johnston (Country Sports); Editorial Director, John Beaton (Equestrian)

**Established** 2001

**Imprint(s)** Swan Hill Press Sportsman's Press Kenilworth Press

**Insider Info** Receives approximately 150 queries and 70 manuscripts per year. Ten per cent of books published are from first-time authors, 95 per cent are from unagented authors and five per cent are author subsidy published. Payment is via royalty (on wholesale price, or royalty on retail price). Average lead time is two months, with simultaneous submissions accepted. Submissions accompanied by SAE will be returned. Catalogue is free on request. Manuscript guidelines are free on request and available via email.

**Non-Fiction** Publishes Autobiography, Biography, Coffee Table books, Cookbooks, General Non-fiction, Gift, How-to, Humour, Illustrated, Reference and Technical titles on the following subjects: Agriculture/Horticulture, Animals, Cooking/Foods/Nutrition, Crafts, Gardening, Hobbies, Military/War, Nature/Environment, Sports, Travel, Country Sports and Equestrianism.

**Submission Guidelines** Accepts query with SAE, or via email with proposal package (including outline, sample chapter(s), publishing history, author biography). Will accept artworks/images (send photocopies or digital files as jpegs). Submission details to: info@quillerbooks.com

**Recent Title(s)** *Game and Fish Cookbook*, Barbara Thompson (Cookery)

**Tips** Titles aimed at country sports and equestrian enthusiasts.

## Quince books Ltd

209 Hackney Road, Shoreditch, London, E2 8JL

- ☏ 020 7033 4265
- ✉ info@quincebooks.com
- ⊕ www.quincebooks.com

**Contact** Simon Mitchell

**Insider Info** Catalogue available online.

**Non-Fiction** Publishes General non-fiction.

**Fiction** Publishes Mainstream/Contemporary and Commercial fiction titles, and works with authors to help them into print.

**Submission Guidelines** Accepts query by email only with proposal package (including outline and three sample chapters).

**Recent Title(s)** *START to Stress Less*, Vee Freir (Self-Help); *A God Named Joe*, Peter Jessop (Novel)

**Tips** Welcomes new authors. The priority is entertainment and initial interest rather than quality of writing, which can be worked on collaboratively.

## Radcliffe Publishing Ltd

18 Marcham Road, Abingdon, Oxon, OX14 1AA

- ☏ 01235 528820
- ☏ 01235 528830
- ✉ contact.us@radcliffemed.com
- ⊕ www.radcliffe-oxford.com

**Contact** Managing Director, Andrew Bax; Editorial Director, Gillian Nineham

**Established** 1987

**Insider Info** Payment is via royalties, catalogue available online

**Non-Fiction** Publishes Reference, Scholarly and Technical titles on the following subjects: Counselling/Career, Guidance, Health/Medicine, Science, General practice and health service management. In 2004 the company changed their name from Radcliffe Medical Press to Radcliffe Publishing, in order to reflect the expansion of publishing interests beyond medicine.

**Submission Guidelines** Accepts query with SAE and proposal package (including outline and two sample chapters) Will accept artwork/images. Submission details to: gnineham@radcliffemed.com

**Recent Title(s)** *Riding the Diabetes Rollercoaster*, Helen Cooper and Robert Geyer (Medical)

**Tips** Work submitted should be of a professional standard and beneficial to healthcare workers and the market in general.

## Radikal Phase Publishing House Ltd

Willow Court, Cordy Lane, Underwood, Nottinghamshire, NG16 5FD

- ☏ 01773 764288
- ☏ 01773 764282
- ✉ sales@radikalbooks.com
- ⊕ www.radikalbooks.com

**Contact** Managing Director, Philip Gardiner; Managing Director, Kevin Marks

**Established** 2001

**Insider Info** Payment is via royalties, catalogue available online.

**Non-Fiction** Publishes General Non-fiction and Technical titles on the following subjects: Religion, Science, Spirituality, Electrical engineering and Revelation.

**Submission Guidelines** Welcomes unsolicited submissions, ideally approach in writing first.

**Tips** Publishes books on radical revelations and spirituality, as well as some technical electrical books.

## The Random House Group Ltd

Random House, 20 Vauxhall Bridge Road, London, SW1V 2SA

- ☏ 020 7840 8400
- ☏ 020 7233 8719
- ✉ emarketing@randomhouse.co.uk
- ⊕ www.randomhouse.co.uk

**Parent Company** Random House Inc US (Bertelsmann AG) (see entry under European & International Publishers)

**Contact** Chief Executive, Gail Rebuck

**Imprint(s)** Arrow
 BBC Books
 Century
 Chatto & Windus
 Ebury Press
 Everyman
 Fodor
 Harvill Secker
 Hutchinson
 Jonathan Cape
 Mainstream
 Pimlico
 Rider
 Tanoshimi
 Time Out Guides Ltd
 Vermilion
 Vintage
 William Heinemann
 Yellow Jersey
 Random House Business Books
 Random House Children's Books (division)
 Transworld Publishers (division)

**Insider Info** Aims to respond to queries within 12 weeks. Catalogue is available online (to search the catalogues of individual imprints go to 'advanced search').

**Non-Fiction** Publish Autobiography, Biography, General Non-fiction and Illustrated titles on a wide variety of subjects across its imprints.

**Submission Guidelines** Accepts query with SAE/proposal package (including one sample chapter and outline). No emailed submissions.

**Fiction** Publishes Mainstream/Contemporary, Literary and Classic fiction across its imprints.

**Submission Guidelines** Accepts query with SAE/proposal package (including one sample chapter, outline). No emailed submissions.

**Poetry** Publishes a small amount of poetry per year through the Jonathan Cape list.

**Submission Guidelines** Accepts query with SAE. Submit 30–40 sample poems.

 * Poetry reading time is estimated at between two and eight weeks.

**Recent Title(s)** *According to Ruth*, Jane Feaver (Literary Fiction); *Gift Songs,* John Burnside (Poetry); *The God Delusion,* Richard Dawkins (Science)

**Tips** Random House is one of the largest general book publishing companies in the UK and has some of the world's best known authors on its lists. The Random House Group is an independently managed subsidiary of Random House Inc in the US, the trade book publishing division of Bertelsmann AG. Agented submissions are strongly preferred, but unsolicited submissions according to the above guidelines will be considered. See individual imprint entries for more information on the kinds of titles published by each imprint.

## Random House Business Books
**Random House, 20 Vauxhall Bridge Road, London, SW1V 2SA**

- 020 7840 8733
- 020 7233 6127
- emarketing@randomhouse.co.uk
- www.randomhouse.co.uk

**Parent Company** The Random House Group Ltd
**Contact** Publisher, Nigel Wilcockson
**Insider Info** Submissions accompanied by SAE will be returned. Catalogue available online.
**Non-Fiction** Publishes Reference and Scholarly titles on the following subjects:
 Business/Economics, Management, Professional Development.
**Submission Guidelines** Accepts proposal package (including outline, one sample chapter, SAE).
**Recent Title(s)** *Know-How*, Ram Charan (Advice on Careers and Achieving Success); *The Origin Of Wealth*, Eric Beinhocker

**Tips** Publish books mainly for a professional business readership. Does not accept emailed submissions.

## Random House Children's Books
**61–63 Uxbridge Road, London, W5 5SA**

- 020 8231 6800
- 020 8231 6767
- childrenseditorial@randomhouse.co.uk
- www.randomhouse.co.uk

**Parent Company** The Random House Group Ltd
**Contact** Managing Director, Philippa Dickinson
**Imprint(s)** The Bodley Head
 Corgi Children's Books
 David Fickling Books
 Doubleday Children's Books
 Hutchinson Children's Books
 Jonathan Cape Children's Books
 Red Fox
**Insider Info** Catalogue available online.
**Non-Fiction** Publishes Children's/Juvenile and Young Adult titles.
**Submission Guidelines** Accepts agented submissions only.
**Fiction** Publish Children's Fiction and Picture book titles for children from 0 to 12 plus years.
**Submission Guidelines** Agented submissions only.
**Poetry** Publish Children's Poetry.
**Submission Guidelines** Agented submissions only.
**Recent Title(s)** *Abomination*, Robert Swindell's (9-11 years Fiction); *Mole's bedtime story*, David Wood (0-5 years Fiction)
**Tips** Random House Children's Division merged with Transworld Publishers children's list in 2001, to form Random House Children's Books, and now ranks among the top five children's book publishers in the UK. Although unsolicited manuscripts are not accepted, there is some helpful submission advice on the children's division website.

## Ransom Publishing
**Rose Cottage, Howe Hill, Watlington, Oxon, OX49 5HB**

- 01491 613711
- 01491 613733
- jenny@ransom.co.uk
- www.ransom.co.uk

**Contact** Managing Director, Jenny Ertle (Literacy for ages five to adult)
**Established** 1995
**Insider Info** Publishes 50 titles per year. Receives approximately 200 queries and 150 manuscripts per year. Ten per cent of books published are from first-

time authors and 90 per cent are from unagented authors. Payment is via royalty (on retail price) with 0.1 (per £) minimum. Average lead time is six months with simultaneous submissions accepted. Submissions accompanied by SAE will be returned. Aims to respond to queries within one week, proposals within two weeks and manuscripts within two months. Catalogue and manuscript guidelines are free on request and available online.

**Non-Fiction** Publishes Children's/Juvenile titles on the following subjects:
 Education (Literacy), Young Adult (Easy Reads), Various topics suitable for Children and Young Adults.
 * Ransom specialise in books for reluctant and struggling readers and in adult literacy.

**Submission Guidelines** Accept queries via email. Will accept artworks/images (send digital files as jpegs).
 Submission details to: ransom@ransom.co.uk

**Fiction** Publishes anything suitable for reluctant and struggling readers.
 * Ransom publish very little general children's fiction. Interested primarily in books for reluctant or very poor readers, ages six up to adult.

**Submission Guidelines** Accepts queries via email. Will accept artworks/images (send digital files as jpegs).
 Submission details to: ransom@ransom.co.uk

**Recent Title(s)** *Trailblazers Series*, David Orme (Designed to encourage children to read); *Dark Man Series*, Peter Lancett (Books for young adults with low reading levels)

**Tips** Ransom titles are aimed at children and young adults who are reluctant, or struggling readers, as well as teachers of literacy and special educational needs teachers. Only submit proposals applicable to these areas of interest. Email first to see if the proposal is of interest. When sending materials always include SAE.

## Ravenhall Books
**PO Box 357, Welwyn Garden City, AL6 6WJ**
 ☎ 01707 371545
 ☎ 01707 325230
 ⊚ info@ravenhallbooks.com
 ⊛ www.ravenhallbooks.com
**Contact** Eugina North
**Insider Info** Catalogue available online.
**Non-Fiction** Publishes General Non-fiction and Scholarly titles on the following subjects:
 History, Military/War.
**Recent Title(s)** *The Inquisitor's Guide*, Bernard Gui (History)

**Tips** Ravenhall is an independent publisher specialising in historical accounts, translations and guides.

## Reader's Digest Association
**11 Westferry Circus, Canary Wharf, London, E14 4HE**
 ☎ 020 7715 8000
 ☎ 020 7715 8181
 ⊛ www.readersdigest.co.uk
**Insider Info** Catalogue available online.
**Non-Fiction** Publishes Children's/Juvenile, General Non-fiction, Humour, Illustrated and Reference titles on the following subjects:
 Cooking/Foods/Nutrition, Crafts, Gardening, Health/Medicine, History, Photography, Travel, Computing, DIY, General Knowledge.
 * Also publishes magazines, videos and CDs.
**Tips** The main editorial office for Reader's Digest is based in the US.

## Reaktion Books Ltd
**33 Great Sutton Street, London, EC1V 0DX**
 ☎ 020 7253 1071
 ☎ 020 7253 1208
 ⊚ info@reaktionbooks.co.uk
 ⊛ www.reaktionbooks.co.uk
**Contact** Managing Director, Michael R. Leaman
**Established** 1985
**Insider Info** Publishes 30 titles per year. Payment is via royalties. Catalogue available online. Manuscript guidelines available online via the website.
**Non-Fiction** Publishes General Non-fiction, Illustrated books, Reference and Scholarly titles on the following subjects:
 Art/Architecture, History, Nature/Environment, Photography, Travel, Art History, Asian Studies, Natural History and Geography.
**Submission Guidelines** Accepts query with SAE and proposal package (including outline, two sample chapters and SAE).
 Submissions to: sophie@reaktionbooks.co.uk
**Recent Title(s)** *Countering Terrorism*, Michael Chandler and Rohan Gunaratna
**Tips** Reaktion publishes non-fiction books on nature, natural history, art and architecture, asian studies, design, film, culture, history, geography, photography and travel writing. When submitting a manuscript, refer to the submission guidelines on the website.

## Reality Street Editions

**63 All Saints Street, Hastings, East Sussex, TN34 3BN**

✉ reality.street@virgin.net

🌐 www.realitystreet.co.uk

**Contact** Ken Edwards

**Established** 1993

**Fiction** Publishes Mainstream/Contemporary, and Translation titles.

**Submission Guidelines** No unsolicited manuscripts.

**Poetry** Publishes poetry titles.

 * The majority of Reality Street Editions' output is made up of poetry.

**Submission Guidelines** No unsolicited manuscripts.

**Tips** Publishing programmes are announced on the website up to two years in advance. The programme is currently full for the coming three years.

## Reardon Publishing

**Reardon Publishing, PO Box 919, Cheltenham, Glos, GL50 9AN**

☎ 01242 231800

✉ reardon@bigfoot.com

🌐 www.reardon.co.uk

**Contact** Director, Nicholas Reardon (All subjects)

**Established** 1976

**Insider Info** Publish 15 titles per year. Receives approximately 20 queries and ten manuscripts per year. 75 per cent of books published are by first-time authors, 100 per cent are by unagented authors and 50 per cent are author-subsidy published. Payment is via royalty (on retail price). Average lead time is six months with simultaneous submissions accepted. Submissions accompanied by SAE will be returned. Aims to respond to queries, proposals and manuscripts within two weeks. Catalogue available online. Manuscript guidelines available via email.

**Non-Fiction** Publish Autobiography, Biography, Booklets, Children's/Juvenile, Coffee table, Cookbook, General Non-fiction, Gift, How-to, Humour, Illustrated, Reference, Scholarly, Technical and Textbook titles on the following subjects: Animals, Anthropology/Archaeology, Communications, Education, Gardening, History, Hobbies, Language/Literature, Memoirs, Nature/Environment, Photography, Psychology, Regional, Religion, Science, Transportation, Travel, World Affairs.

**Submission Guidelines** Accepts query with SAE. Will accept artworks/images (send photocopies or digital files as jpegs).

**Fiction** Publish Adventure, Historical, Humour, Military/War, Regional, Religious, Romance and Young Adult titles.

**Submission Guidelines** Accepts query with SAE.

**Poetry** Publishes Poetry titles.

**Submission Guidelines** Accepts query with sample poems.

**Recent Title(s)** *Cheltenham in Antarctica*, David Wilson (Casebound); *Time to go Home*, A.C. Smith (Paperback); *The Vegetable Lovers Guide*, Chris Evans (Booklet)

## Red Bird Press

**Kiln Farm, Brighlingsea, Colchester, Essex, C07 0SX**

☎ 01206 303525

☎ 01206 304545

✉ info@red-bird.co.uk

🌐 www.red-bird.co.uk

**Insider Info** Catalogue available online.

**Fiction** Publishes Picture books and Children's Illustrated Fiction titles.

**Tips** Red Bird specialise in distinctive children's formats featuring 3D vision, glow in the dark, hidden pictures and other special effects. Books are often based on international licensed characters, including those from Disney, Hasbro, Mirage and Fox Kids.

## Red Fox

**61–63 Uxbridge Road, London, W5 5SA**

☎ 020 7840 8640

📠 020 7233 6058

✉ childrenseditorial@randomhouse.co.uk

🌐 www.randomhouse.co.uk/childrens

**Parent Company** Random House Children's Books

**Insider Info** Catalogue available online.

**Fiction** Publishes Picture books and Children's Fiction titles.

**Submission Guidelines** Accepts proposal package (including outline, sample chapter(s)). Accepts artworks/images (send photocopies, never originals).

**Recent Title(s)** *Jack Stalwart: The Caper of the Crown Jewels*, Elizabeth Singer Hunt; *Twinkle Tots: Max at the Seaside,* Various

**Tips** Agented submissions are strongly preferred, but unagented proposals are considered. The focus of Red Fox tends to be on illustrated books for young children.

## Reed Elsevier Group Plc

**1–3 Strand, London, WC2N 5JR**

☎ 020 7930 7077

**☎** 020 7166 5799

**⊕** www.reedelsevier.com

**Contact** CEO, Sir Crispin Davis

**Established** 1993

**Imprint(s)** Harcourt Education (division)
Elsevier Ltd (division)
LexisNexis (division)
Reed Business (division)

**Non-Fiction** Publishes General Non-fiction, CD-ROM, Multimedia, Reference and Scholarly, and Technical titles on the following subjects:
Science, Technology, Healthcare, Medicine, Law, Risk Management, Corporate, Government, Law Enforcement, Accounting, and Education.

**Tips** Reed Elsevier is a world leading publisher of information and solutions for professional users in the fields of science & medical, legal, education and business.

## Reed Business

**1–3 Strand, London, WC2N 5JR**

**☎** 020 7930 7077

**☎** 020 7166 5799

**⊕** www.reedelsevier.com

**Parent Company** Reed Elsevier Group Plc

**Non-Fiction** Publishes General Non-fiction, CD-ROM, Multimedia, Reference, Direct Scholarly, and Technical titles on the following subjects:
Business and Management.

**Tips** Titles and products are aimed at professional global business markets.

## Regency House Publishing Ltd

**Niall House, 24–26 Boulton Road, Stevenage, Hertfordshire, SG1 4QX**

**☎** 01438 314488

**☎** 01438 311303

**✉** regency-house@btconnect.com

**⊕** www.regencyhousepublishing.com

**Contact** Managing Director, Nicolette Trodd

**Established** 1991

**Insider Info** Catalogue available online.

**Non-Fiction** Publishes General Non-fiction and illustrated titles on the following subjects:
Art/Architecture, Cooking/Foods/Nutrition, Crafts, Hobbies, Nature/Environment, Regional, Sports, Transportation, Equestrianism.

**Recent Title(s)** *The Ultimate Guide to Snakes & Reptiles,* Derek Hall

**Tips** Bear in mind that Regency House produce a large list of titles for the international and co-edition markets. They also offer services as a book packager for other publishers.

## Reverb

**PO Box 615, Oxford, OX1 9AL**

**✉** mail@readreverb.com.

**⊕** www.readreverb.com

**Insider Info** Catalogue available online.

**Fiction** Publishes Mainstream/Contemporary and Literary fiction.

**Submission Guidelines** Does not accept unsolicited submissions.

**Recent Title(s)** *Ingenious' Who Needs Cleopatra? Compared to Douglas Adams,* Steve Redwood

**Tips** Reverb publishes contemporary literary fiction with an edge and has a commitment to publishing new writers (and supporting independent bookshops). Due to overwhelming demand, the imprint is not currently accepting new submissions, however the website publishes an excellent and informative Writer's Guide.

## Reynolds & Hearn Ltd

**61a Priory Road, Kew Gardens, Richmond, Surrey, TW9 3DH**

**☎** 020 8940 5198

**☎** 020 8940 7679

**✉** enquiries@rhbooks.com

**⊕** www.rhbooks.com

**Contact** Managing Director, Richard Reynolds; Editorial Director, Marcus Hearn

**Established** 1999

**Insider Info** Catalogue is available online.

**Non-Fiction** Publishes General Non-fiction titles on the following subjects:
Contemporary Culture, Film, Television and Music.

**Recent Title(s)** *21st Century Goth*, Mick Mercer

**Tips** Reynolds & Hearn specialise in media publishing, with an emphasis on subjects from the film, television and music industries.

## Richard Dennis Publications

**The Old Chapel, Shepton Beauchamp, Ilminster, Somerset, TA19 0LE**

**☎** 01460 240044

**☎** 01460 242009

**✉** books@richarddennispublications.com

**⊕** www.richarddennispublications.com

**Established** 1976

**Insider Info** Catalogue available online.

**Non-Fiction** Publishes Autobiography, Biography, Illustrated and Reference titles on the following subjects:
Art/Architecture, Hobbies, Memoirs.

* Publishes books for collectors specialising in ceramics, glass, illustration, sculpture and facsimile editions of early catalogues. The books are often unique, in that no other title is available on that subject.
**Recent Title(s)** *Memories of Life and living*, Walter Moorcroft (Memoir/Art)
**Tips** The aim of each publication is to provide as much information as possible about the history and products of a pottery, studio or artist.

## Richmond House Publishing Company Ltd
**70–76 Bell Street, Marylebone, London, NW1 6SP**
- 020 7224 9666
- 020 7224 9688
- sales@rhpco.co.uk
- www.rhpco.co.uk

**Contact** Managing Director, Gloria Gordan; Managing Director, Spencer Block
**Insider Info** Publishes three titles per year. Catalogue available online.
**Non-Fiction** Publishes Reference titles on the following subjects:
 Theatre and Entertainment Directories.
**Submission Guidelines** Accepts query with SAE.
**Recent Title(s)** *Artistes and Agents Directory* (Directory)
**Tips** Richmond House publishes directory books, and online resources for the theatre and entertainment industry. Synopses and ideas for further theatre related projects are welcome.

## Rider
**Random House, 20 Vauxhall Bridge Road, London, SW1V 2SA**
- 020 7840 8400
- 020 7840 8406
- ridereditorial@randomhouse.co.uk
- www.randomhouse.co.uk

**Parent Company** The Random House Group Ltd
**Contact** Publishing Director, Judith Kendra
**Insider Info** Catalogue available online.
**Non-Fiction** Publishes Biography and General Non-fiction titles on the following subjects:
 Astrology/Psychic, History, Memoirs, Philosophy, Psychology, Spirituality, Travel, Personal Development.
**Submission Guidelines** Accepts proposal package (including outline, one sample chapter SAE,). Will accept artworks/images (send photocopies).

**Recent Title(s)** *How to See Yourself As You Really Are*, Dalai Lama
**Tips** Agented submissions are strongly preferred. Emailed submissions are not accepted. Read the 'Rider' section of the Random House catalogue, for a detailed guide to the types of books published.

## Rigby
**Halley Court, Jordan Hill, Oxford, OX2 8EJ**
- 01865 311366
- 01865 314641
- enquiries@harcourt.co.uk
- www.harcourt.co.uk

**Parent Company** Harcourt Education
**Non-Fiction** Publishes Children's/Juvenile, Reference, Scholarly, and Textbook titles.
**Tips** Rigby publish titles that are designed to provide flexible support for teachers, and challenging materials for school pupils, mainly aged from three to twelve years.

## Rivers Oram Press
**144 Hemingford Road, London, N1 1DE**
- 020 7607 0823
- 020 7609 2776
- ro@riversoram.demon.co.uk
- www.riversoram.com

**Contact** Managing Director, Elizabeth Rivers Fidlon
**Established** 1991
**Imprint(s)** Pandora Press
**Non-Fiction** Publishes Biography, General Non-fiction, Illustrated and Reference titles on the following subjects:
 Art/Architecture, Contemporary Culture, Government/Politics, Health/Medicine, History, Photography, Sex, Social Sciences, Women's Issues/Studies, World Affairs, Media.
**Tips** Rivers Oram is a non-fiction publisher specialising in social and political sciences with a feminist slant. This is also true of its imprint, Pandora Press. Keep this in mind if submitting a proposal.

## Robert Hale Ltd
**Clerkenwell House, 45–47 Clerkenwell Green, London, EC1R 0HT**
- 020 7251 2661
- 020 7490 4958
- enquire@halebooks.com
- www.halebooks.com

**Contact** Managing Director, John Hale
**Established** 1936
**Imprint(s)** J.A.Allen

## N.A.G. Press

**Insider Info** Publish 250 titles per year. Receive approximately 3,000 queries and 1,000 manuscripts per year. 15 per cent of books published are from first-time authors and 15 per cent are from unagented authors. Five per cent of books are author subsidy published. Payment is via royalty (on retail price). Average lead time is 12 months with simultaneous submissions accepted. Aims to respond to queries within seven days, proposals within ten days, and manuscripts within two weeks. Catalogue is free on request. Manuscript guidelines are not available.

**Non-Fiction** Publishes Biography, Cookbook, General Non-fiction, Illustrated and Self-help titles on the following subjects:

Agriculture/Horticulture, Animals, Crafts, Gardening, Health/Medicine, History, Hobbies, Law, Memoirs, Mind, Body and Spirit, Military/War, Music/Dance, New Age, Photography, Regional, Spirituality, Sports Travel.

 * No specialist law, education or scientific books.
**Submission Guidelines** Accepts query with SAE/proposal package (including outline, three sample chapters). Will accept artworks/images (send photocopies).

**Fiction** Publishes Adventure, Historical, Literary, Mainstream/Contemporary, Military/War, Mystery, Regional, Romance, Suspense and Western titles.

 * No genre fiction.
**Submission Guidelines** Accepts query with SAE/proposal package (including outline, three sample chapters).

**Recent Title(s)** *English Village Architecture*, R.J. Brown; *Trails to Heaven*, Stuart Wavell

**Tips** Specialists in general hardcover fiction. Not currently accepting emailed submissions.

## Robinswood Press Ltd

**South Avenue, Stourbridge, West Midlands, DY8 3XY**

- 01384 397475
- 01384 440443
- info@robinswoodpress.com
- www.robinswoodpress.com

**Contact** Managing Editor, Chris Marshall; General Manager (sales), Tracy Cooper

**Established** 1985

**Insider Info** Publishes 15 titles per year. Payment via royalties. Catalogue and manuscript guidelines available online.

**Non-Fiction** Publishes Children's/Juvenile, General Non-fiction, Illustrated, Multimedia and Scholarly titles on the following subjects:

Child Guidance/Parenting, Education and Teacher Resources.

 * Books should contribute to a particular objective, to foster a love of reading and writing, especially where students need to overcome difficulties with words and literacy.

**Submission Guidelines** Accepts query with SAE/proposal package (including outline, one sample chapter, your publishing history, and author biography).

 Submission details to: cm@robinswoodpress.com

**Fiction** Publishes Picture books and Children's Educational titles.

**Submission Guidelines** Accepts query with SAE/proposal package (including outline, one sample chapter, your publishing history, and author biography).

 Submission details to: cm@robinswoodpress.com

**Recent Title(s)** *Left Hand Writing Skills*, Mark Stewart and Heather Stewart (Educational); *Bruno*, Guy Hallifax (Picture Book)

**Tips** Authors usually have an established reputation in some aspect of teaching or work with children. Books should fit into the Robinswood objectives of encouraging reading and writing, and helping overcome difficulties in these areas.

## Robson Books

**151 Freston Road, London, W10 6TH**

- 020 7314 1400
- 020 7314 1401
- www.anovabooks.com

**Parent Company** Anova Books Company Ltd

**Contact** Malcolm Croft

**Established** Over 30 years ago

**Insider Info** Catalogue available online.

**Non-Fiction** Publishes Autobiography, Biography, General Non-fiction, Humour and Anthology titles on the following subjects:

Memoirs, Sex, Adventure, Sports, Education, Theatre and Cinema.

**Recent Title(s)** *Pearls of Childhood*, Vera Gissing (Wartime memoir); *100 Great Poems of Love and Lust*, Dannie Abse (Anthology)

## Rockingham Press

**11 Musley Lane, Ware, Hertfordshire, SG12 7EN**

- 01920 467868
- 01920 467868
- rockpress.freeserve.co.uk
- www.rockingham-press.co.uk

**Contact** David Perman

**Established** 1991

**Insider Info** Submissions accompanied by SAE will be returned.

**Non-Fiction** Publishes Biography and General Non-fiction titles on the following subjects:
History, Memoirs and Regional interest.

**Submission Guidelines** No unsolicited manuscripts are accepted.

**Poetry** Publishes Poetry titles.

**Submission Guidelines** No unsolicited manuscripts are accepted.

**Recent Title(s)** *Ware at War 1939-1945*, Derek Armes; *Rearranging the Sky*, Frances Wilson

**Tips** Rockingham Press have little funding and a long backlog of writers whose projects are already in the pipeline. Therefore the publishers cannot accept any manuscripts from new writers at present.

## RotoVision

**Sheridan House, 112–116A Western Road, Hove, East Sussex, BN3 1DD**

📞 01273 727268

📠 01273 727269

✉ sales@rotovision.com

🌐 www.rotovision.com

**Contact** Publisher, April Sankey; Senior Project Editor, Lindy Dunlop; Project Editor, Jane Roe; Acquisitions Editor, Liz Farrelly

**Established** 1996

**Insider Info** Payment via outright purchase. Catalogue available online.

**Non-Fiction** Publishes General Non-fiction, Illustrated and Reference titles on the following subjects:
Art/Architecture, Photography, Design, Digital Media and Film and Cinema.

**Submission Guidelines** Accepts query with SAE. Will review artworks/photos as part of the manuscript package.
Submission details to: lizf@rotovision.com

**Recent Title(s)** *Mag-Art*, Charlotte Rivers

**Tips** Rotovision specialises in all aspects of design, photography and the performing arts. Book proposals must be pinned to the latest techniques and developments in film and digital media.

## Rough Guides

**80 Strand, London, WC2R 0RL**

📞 020 7010 3000

📠 020 7010 6060

✉ customer.service@penguin.co.uk

🌐 www.roughguides.com

**Parent Company** Penguin Group (UK)

**Established** 1982

**Insider Info** Catalogue is available online and by email.

**Non-Fiction** Publishes Dictionaries, Phrasebooks, General Non-fiction, Gift, Illustrated, Maps and Reference titles on the following subjects:
Contemporary Culture, History, Hobbies, Internet, Music/Dance, Pregnancy, Sports, Travel and Unexplained Phenomena.

**Submission Guidelines** Accepts proposal package (including outline, chapter breakdown, sample chapter, author biography and market research).
Submission details to: write@roughguides.com

**Recent Title(s)** *The Rough Guide to Chick Flicks*, Sam Cook (Film); *The Rough Guide to New York City*, Martin Dunford (Travel)

**Tips** Rough Guides are known for travel guides that combine a journalistic, critical approach with practical information. Rough Guides also publish reference and guidebooks on a range of other subjects including film and media, health issues, music and contemporary culture.
To apply to join their database of contributors/writers, send a CV and samples of writing with 1,000 words on any location, written in the Rough Guides style. Otherwise, submit a book proposal directly in the usual manner.

## Round Hall

**43 Fitzwilliam Place, Dublin 2, Republic of Ireland**

📞 00353 1 662 5301

✉ info@roundhall.ie

🌐 www.roundhall.ie

**Parent Company** Sweet & Maxwell Group

**Contact** Commercial Manager, Catherine Dolan (Commissioning); Editorial Manager, Martin McCann

**Established** 1980

**Insider Info** Catalogue available online.

**Non-Fiction** Publishes Reference, Journals, Periodicals, Loose leaf services, CD-ROMs, Online services, Textbooks and Scholarly titles on the following subjects: Law and Irish law and legal system.

**Recent Title(s)** *Annotated Irish Maritime Law Statutes 2000-2005*, Professor Clive Symmons; *Contract Law Nutshell*, Fergus Ryan

**Tips** Potential readership of Round Hall books include members of the judiciary, legal practitioners, academics, law students and other professionals, both in Ireland and abroad.

## Roundhouse Group

**Millstone, Limers Lane, Northam, North Devon, EX39 2RG**

☎ 01237 474474

🖷 01237 474774

✉ roundhouse.group@ukgateway.net

🌐 www.roundhouse.net

**Contact** Managing Director, Alan Goodworth

**Established** 1991

**Insider Info** Payment is via royalties.

**Non-Fiction** Publishes General Non-fiction and Reference titles on Cinema and Media.

**Submission Guidelines** Accepts query with SAE.

**Recent Title(s)** *The Films of Martin Scorsese*

**Tips** Roundhouse Group offers sales and distribution facilities to publishers across subject areas, covering information, education and entertainment books and spoken-word products at trade, reference and educational/academic level. The publisher does not accept unsolicited manuscripts or enquiries by phone.

## Routledge

**2 Park Square, Milton Park, Abingdon, Oxfordshire, OX14 4RN**

☎ 020 7017 6000

🖷 020 7017 6699

✉ jon.manley@tandf.co.uk

🌐 www.routledge.com

**Parent Company** Taylor and Francis Group

**Contact** Managing Editor, Jon Manley; Publishing Editor, Louise Glenn (Journals); Editor, Andrew Humphrys (Militay & Strategic Studies); Commissioning Editor, Samantha Grant (Sport & Leisure Studies)

**Imprint(s)** Routledge-Cavendish
Routledge Education

**Insider Info** Publishes over 1,000 titles per year. Catalogue and manuscript guidelines are available online. Routledge maintains the following series: Routledge Asian & Middle East Studies; Routledge Classics; Routledge Mental Health; Routledge Politics & International Relations; Routledge Reference; Routledge Sport & Leisure Studies; Routledge Military & Strategic Studies.

**Non-Fiction** Publishes Journals, Reference, Scholarly and Textbook titles on the following subjects: Anthropology, Art, Counselling/Guidance, Cultural Theory, Ethnic Studies, History, Leisure, Literature/Language, Mental Health, Military/War, Philosophy, Politics, Psychology, Religion, Science, Social Sciences, Sport.

**Submission Guidelines** Accepts proposal package (including outline, synopsis, one to two sample chapters, market research and CV).

**Recent Title(s)** *The International Who's Who 2007*, Routledge; *Exercise, Health & Mental Health: Emerging Relationships,* Guy E.J. Faulkner and Adrian H. Taylor (Mental Health)

**Tips** Routledge is a multi-disciplinary publisher of leading academic and reference titles. Routledge maintains a number of large dedicated lists that specialise in various subjects. Submissions should be directed towards the appropriate list/series, full editorial contacts are available on the website.

## Routledge-Cavendish

**2 Park Square, Milton Park, Abingdon, Oxford, OX14 4RN**

☎ 020 7017 6004

🖷 020 7017 6699

✉ fiona.kinnear@informa.com

🌐 www.cavendishpublishing.com

**Parent Company** Routledge (Taylor & Francis Group)

**Contact** Commissioning Editor, Fiona Kinnear; Constance Sutherland, Development Editor

**Imprint(s)** Glasshouse Press
Routledge Criminology (series)

**Insider Info** Catalogue and manuscript guidelines are available online.

**Non-Fiction** Publishes Scholarly and Technical titles on the following subjects:
Academic Law, Criminology, Law/Legal.

**Submission Guidelines** Accepts Proposal package (including outline, synopsis, one to two sample chapters, market research, and CV).

**Recent Title(s)** *Comparative Law in a Changing World*, Peter De Cruz (Law/Legal)

**Tips** Routledge-Cavendish specialises in academic law publishing, and also publishes titles on criminology under the Routledge Criminology series.

## Routledge Education

**2 Park Square, Milton Park, Abingdon, Oxford, OX14 4RN**

☎ 020 7017 6248

🖷 020 7017 6699

✉ anna.clarkson@tandf.co.uk

🌐 www.routledge.com/education

**Parent Company** Routledge (Taylor & Francis Group)

**Contact** Publisher, Anna Clarkson (Primary Education, Secondary Education, School Management and Leadership, Foundation Subjects and Classroom Issues); Senior Editor, Alison Foyle (Early Years, Childhood Studies, Special Educational Needs, Literacy); Senior Editor, Philip Mudd (Study Guides, Adult Education, Research Methods, General Books); Associate Editor, Helen Pritt (Higher Education, Further Education, e-Learning, Open and Distance Learning)

**Imprint(s)** David Fulton Publishers
Lawrence Erlbaum Associates

**Insider Info** Catalogue and manuscript guidelines are available online.

**Non-Fiction** Publishes Practical, Reference, Scholarly and Textbook titles on the following subjects:
Education (Primary, Secondary and Higher), Open and Distance Learning, Psychology, Special Needs Education, Teacher Training, Teaching Resources.

**Submission Guidelines** Accepts Proposal package (including outline, synopsis, one-two sample chapters, market research and CV).

**Recent Title(s)** *Observing, Assessing and Planning for Children in the Early Years*, Sandra Smidt (Education)

**Tips** Routledge Education publishes books for professionals in education at any level, textbooks for trainee teachers, books for classroom practitioners and research books for international academics. The Routledge Education list now includes David Fulton Publishers, and also Lawrence Erlbaum Associates.
Lawrence Erlbaum Associates is an international academic publisher of books and journals in education and psychology.

## Royal Collection Enterprises
**York House, St. James's Palace, Lonon, SW1A 1BS**
- 020 7839 1377
- 020 7839 8168
- press@royalcollection.org.uk
- www.royalcollection.org.uk/

**Contact** Publisher, Jacky Colliss Harvey; Commissioning Editor, Marie Leahy

**Established** 1993

**Insider Info** Publishes 12 titles per year. Catalogue available online at https://www.the-royal-collection.com/UK/shop/

**Non-Fiction** Publishes General Non-fiction, Gift, Illustrated and Reference titles on the following subjects:
Art/Architecture, History, Guidebooks and the Royal Family.
* Royal Collection Publications produces guidebooks, exhibition catalogues, scholarly catalogues and stand alone books on the subject matter of the collection and the royal palaces and residences.

**Recent Title(s)** *The Garden at Buckingham Palace: An Illustrated History*, Royal Collection

**Tips** All Royal Collection publications are written solely by, or in consultation with its own curators.

## Royal Irish Academy
**19 Dawson Street, Dublin 2, Republic of Ireland**
- 00353 1 676 2570
- 00353 1 676 2346
- email: publicationsria.ie
- www.ria.ie

**Established** 1787

**Insider Info** Catalogue available online.

**Non-Fiction** Publishes Reference and Scholarly titles on the following subjects:
Mathematics, Biological and Environmental Sciences, History and Archaeology.
* Also publishes journals in Irish philology and literature; the *Irish Journal of Earth Sciences* and *Irish Studies in International Affairs*.

**Recent Title(s)** *Irish Historic Towns Atlas No.15 Derry - Londonderry*, Avril Thomas

**Tips** The Academy is the largest publisher of scholarly journals in Ireland and also has an extensive list of series and monographs.

## Royal National Institute of the Blind Publications
**RNIB Corporate Publishing, 105 Judd Street, London, WC1H 9NE**
- 02073 881266
- cippub@rnib.org.uk
- www.rnib.org.uk

**Established** 1868

**Insider Info** Catalogue available online.

**Non-Fiction** Publishes Audio cassettes, General Non-fiction, Multimedia, Braille and Large Print titles on the following subjects:
Counselling/Career, Education, Health/Medicine, Hobbies, House and Home and Practical books.
* RNIB publications should help people understand and cope with sight problems, assisting them in living independent lives.

**Tips** Most titles are published in multiple formats, including braille and large print, in addition to audio cassettes and CDs. Potential readership includes parents, teachers, and health, rehabilitation and employment service professionals.

## Rudolf Steiner Press
**Hillside House, The Square, Forest Row, East Sussex, RH18 5ES**

☎ 01342 824433
🖷 01342 826437
✉ office@rudolfsteinerpress.com
🌐 www.rudolfsteinerpress.com

**Contact** Chairman, P. Martyn; Manager, S. Gulbekian

**Established** 1925

**Imprint(s)** Sophia Books

**Insider Info** Publishes 15 titles per year. Payment is via royalties. Catalogue available free on request and online.

**Non-Fiction** Publishes General Non-fiction and Scholarly titles on the following subjects:
 Education, Philosophy and Spirituality.
 * Publishes the work of Rudolf Steiner and any other related materials. Titles focus on philosophy, spirituality and the Steiner education system.

**Recent Title(s)** *The Evolution of Consciousness*, Rudolf Steiner

**Tips** Rudolf Steiner Press only publishes the works of Rudolf Steiner or directly related materials. The publisher does not accept unsolicited manuscripts.

## RYA (Royal Yachting Association)

**RYA House, Ensign Way, Hamble, Southampton, Hampshire, SO31 4YA**

☎ 023 8060 4100
🖷 023 8060 4299
✉ phil.williamsellis@rya.org.uk
🌐 www.rya.org.uk

**Contact** CEO, Rod Carr; Publications Manager, Phil Williams-Ellis

**Established** 1875

**Insider Info** Publishes ten titles per year. Payment is via royalties.

**Non-Fiction** Publishes General Non-fiction, Reference and Technical titles on the following subjects:
 Yachting, Sailing and Boating.
 * Publishes expert information on a full range of boating related subjects including training courses, handbooks, and technical and legal boating advice.

**Submission Guidelines** Accepts proposal package (including outline).

**Recent Title(s)** *RYA VHF Handbook*, Tim Bartlett

**Tips** The RYA does not accept unsolicited manuscripts, but welcomes project proposals by post or email.

## Sage Publications

**1 Oliver's Yard, 55 City Road, London, EC1Y 1SP**

☎ 020 7324 8500
🖷 020 7324 8600
✉ info@sagepub.co.uk

🌐 www.sagepub.co.uk

**Contact** Publisher, Sara Miller McCune; Managing Director, Stephen Barr; Editorial Director, Ziyad Marar

**Established** 1965

**Insider Info** Payment is via royalties. Catalogue available free on request and online. Manuscript guidelines available online.

**Non-Fiction** Publishes Textbooks, Journals, Reference and Scholarly titles on the following subjects:
 Anthropology/Archaeology, Business/Economics, Criminology, Education, Engineering, History, Humanities, Nature/Environment, Psychology, Science, Social Sciences and Sociology.
 * Publish academic textbooks, reference works and research outcomes, aimed predominantly at university level students and professionals.

**Submission Guidelines** Accepts proposal package (including outline, sample chapter(s), competing texts, a sample of your writing style, pedagogical features and author biography).

**Recent Title(s)** *Essential Social Psychology*, Richard J. Crisp and Rhiannon N. Turner

**Tips** Efforts are concentrated on providing upper level and graduate textbooks and handbooks and professional books. A full list of commissioning editors in every subject is published on the website at: www.sagepub.co.uk/editorialContacts.nav It would be useful to read the detailed proposal guidelines published on the website before submitting your manuscript.

## Saint Andrew Press

**121 George Street, Edinburgh, EH2 4YN**

☎ 0131 225 5722
🖷 0131 220 3113
✉ standrewpress@cofscotland.org.uk

**Contact** Head of Publishing, Ann Crawford

**Established** 1954

**Insider Info** Publishes 20 titles per year. Payment is via royalties.

**Non-Fiction** Publishes Children's/Juvenile, General Non-fiction and Reference titles on Religion.

**Submission Guidelines** Accepts query with SAE.

**Tips** Saint Andrew Press is owned by the Church of Scotland and publishes books on religion and general faith. Also publishes a range of reference and children's books, aimed at both local and international trade markets.

## Salariya Book Company Ltd

**Book House, 25 Marlborough Place, Brighton, BN1 1UB**

☎ 01273 603306
🖷 01273 693857
✉ salariya@salariya.com, david.salariya@salariya.com
🌐 www.salariya.com
**Contact** Director, David Salariya
**Established** 1989
**Imprint(s)** Book House
**Insider Info** Catalogue available online.
**Non-Fiction** Publishes Illustrated and Children's/ Juvenile titles.

   * Specialises in illustrated information books with a unique appeal for the younger reader. Many Salariya books are aimed at the international market and translated into multiple languages. New titles for the UK are published under the Book House imprint.
**Recent Title(s)** *Scary Creatures: Sharks*, Penny Clarke
**Tips** The publishers do not have submission guidelines as they commission the vast majority of their titles.

## Salt Publishing
**PO Box 937, Great Wilbraham, Cambridge, CB21 5JX**
☎ 01223 882220
🖷 01223 882260
✉ firstname@saltpublishing.com
🌐 www.saltpublishing.com
**Admin other Info** Directors: Linda Bennett, Chris Hamilton Emery, Linda Hamilton Emery and John Skelton; Commissioning Editor, Chris Hamilton-Emery (Poetry and Literary Studies); Commissioning Editor, Jen Hamilton-Emery (Fiction and Non-fiction); Commissioning Editor, Katherine M. Hedeen (rnunezv@kenyon.edu, Latin American Poetry); Commissioning Editor, John Kinsella (kinsellaj@ kenyon.edu, Australian and International Poetry); Commissioning Editor, Janet McAdams (mcadamsj@ kenyon.edu, Native American Writing); Commissioning Editor, Victor Rodríguez-Núñez (rnunezv@kenyon.edu, Latin American Poetry)
**Established** 1999
**Insider Info** Publishes 40 titles per year. Submissions accompanied by SAE will be returned. Aims to respond to manuscripts within seven months. Catalogue available online.
**Non-Fiction** Publishes Biography, Textbooks (From UK and US authors) and Scholarly titles on the following subjects:
  Literary Criticism and Interviews.
**Fiction** Publishes Short Story Collections.
**Submission Guidelines** Accepts Proposal package (including up to three short stories, addressed to Jen Hamilton Emery). Aims to respond to submissions within three months.

**Poetry** Publishes Poetry Collections.
**Submission Guidelines** Accepts proposal package (including six to ten sample poems, addressed to Chris Hamilton Emery). Will aim to respond to submissions within six months.
**Recent Title(s)** *Don't Start Me Talking*, Tim Allen and Andrew Duncan (eds); *The Garden*, Louis Armand; *Megalomaniac*, Shamshad Khan
**Tips** For poetry submissions, there are extensive guidelines on the website that should be read carefully. Queries about how to submit work, or advice on writing will go unanswered.

## SAMS Publishing
**Edinburgh Gate, Harlow, Essex, CM20 2JE**
☎ 01279 623623
🖷 01279 414130
🌐 www.pearsoned.co.uk/Imprints/SAMSPublishing/
**Parent Company** Pearson Education
**Insider Info** Catalogue and manuscript guidelines are available online.
**Non-Fiction** Publishes How-to, Reference and Technical titles on the following subjects:
  Computers/Electronics, Computer Programming/ Developing, Internet, Networking, System Administration.
**Submission Guidelines** Accepts proposal package (including synopsis, sample chapters, market research, your publishing history and author biography).
**Recent Title(s)** *Windows Presentation Foundation Unleashed (WPF)*, Adam Nathan (Computing)
**Tips** SAMS publishes professional reference books for programmers and developers, web developers, designers, networking and system administrators. SAMS Publishing is focused on teaching tomorrow's programmers, developers and systems administrators the skills they need to build and maintain leading edge technology, from introductory tutorials to comprehensive reference books.

## Samuel French Ltd
**52 Fitzroy Street, London, W1T 5JR**
☎ 020 7387 9373
🖷 020 7387 2161
✉ theatre@samuelfrench-london.co.uk
🌐 www.samuelfrench-london.co.uk
**Contact** Chairman, Charles R. Van Nostrand; Managing Director, Vivien Goodwin
**Established** 1830
**Insider Info** Publishes 50 titles per year. Payment is via royalties. Catalogue available online.

**Fiction** Publishes Plays.

\* Samuel French have over 2,000 published plays available, covering all genres of performing theatre including Comedies, Tragedies, Sketches and full scale Musicals. Most plays are staged prior to publication.

**Submission Guidelines** Accepts query with SAE.

**Recent Title(s)** *Tom, Dick and Harry*, Ray Cooney and Michael Cooney (Play script)

**Tips** New writers are advised to try one act plays, as these most highly demanded.

## Sangam Books Ltd

**57 London Fruit Exchange, Brushfield Street, London, E1 6EP**

📞 020 7377 6399

📠 020 7375 1230

📧 sangambks@aol.com

**Contact** Executive Director, Anthony de Souza

**Non-Fiction** Publishes General Non-fiction, Textbooks and Scholarly titles on the following subjects:

Art/Architecture, Education, Ethnic, Health/Medicine, Religion, Science, Social Sciences and Technology.

**Fiction** Publishes Literary and Mainstream/Contemporary titles.

**Tips** Sangam Books specialises in school and college textbooks and other educational publishing. They also publish fiction titles, and non-fiction titles on technology, science, medicine, India, social Sciences, art, and religion.

## Saqi Books

**26 Westbourne Grove, London, W2 5RH**

📞 020 7221 9347

📠 020 7229 7492

📧 enquiries@saqibooks.com

🌐 www.saqibooks.com

**Contact** Publisher, Andre Gaspard; Editorial Manager, Lara Frankena

**Established** 1981

**Insider Info** Publishes 20 titles per year. Payment is via royalties. Aims to respond to manuscripts within ten weeks and manuscripts within ten weeks. Catalogue available online and free on request. Manuscript guidelines available online and via the website.

**Non-Fiction** Publishes Biography, General Non-fiction, Illustrated and Scholarly titles on the following subjects:

Art/Architecture, Contemporary Culture, Cooking/Foods/Nutrition, Government/Politics, History,

Philosophy, Religion, World Affairs and Middle-East/Asia.

\* Traditionally, Saqi writers have been cutting edge and authoritative voices from North Africa and the Middle East. Lists now include writers from the Balkans, Afghanistan, Pakistan, France and the UK. All books tend to have an international cultural or political theme.

**Submission Guidelines** Accepts query with SAE/proposal package (including outline and two sample chapters). Will review artworks/photos as part of the manuscript package (send photocopies only).

**Fiction** Publishes Literary and Mainstream/Contemporary titles.

**Submission Guidelines** Accepts query with SAE/proposal package (including outline and two sample chapters).

**Recent Title(s)** *The Sunburnt Queen*, Hazel Crampton (History)

**Tips** Always keep a copy of anything submitted and never include the originals of photographs or artworks, as the publishers do not accept responsibility for loss or damage of original material. Saqi books do not accept submissions by fax, email or on disc.

## Saunders

**32 Jamestown Road, Camden Town, London, NW1 7BY**

📞 020 7424 4200

📠 020 7482 2293

📧 m.ging@elsevier.com

🌐 www.intl.elsevierhealth.com/wbs

**Parent Company** Elsevier Ltd (Health Sciences)

**Established** 1888

**Insider Info** Payment is via royalties. Catalogue available online. Manuscript guidelines available online and via the website.

**Non-Fiction** Publishes Illustrated, Multimedia, Reference, Scholarly, Textbooks and Technical titles on the following subjects:

Education, Health/Medicine, Science, Care/Nursing, Veterinary Medicine, Medical Drugs and Medical Technology.

**Submission Guidelines** Accepts submissions via the online proposal form.

Submission details to: c.makepeace@elsevier.com

**Recent Title(s)** *Pocket Essentials of Clinical Medicine - Book and PDA CD-ROM Package (4th edition)*, Anne Ballinger (Medical Reference/Electronic Media)

**Tips** Founded in 1888, Saunders publish books and multimedia specialising in health and clinical medicine, veterinary medicine, care and nursing, laboratory equipment and pharmaceuticals, amongst other medical subjects. Each title is written by experts in the field and edited to reflect the latest research. Titles are organised and indexed to enable readers to find urgent information immediately. To submit a proposal to Saunders, fill in and return a proposal form available on the website. Alternatively, authors may contact the Publishing Director or Editor prior to submission, to discuss the proposal.

## S.B. Publications
**14 Bishopstone Road, Seaford, East Sussex, BN25 2UB**
- 01323 893498
- 01323 893860
- sbpublications@tiscali.co.uk
- www.sbpublications.co.uk

**Contact** Lindsay Woods
**Established** 1987
**Insider Info** Publishes 20 titles per year. Payment s is via royalties. Catalogue available online.
**Non-Fiction** Publishes Illustrated and General Non-fiction titles on the following subjects:
 History, Hobbies, Regional, Transportation, Travel, Walking guides, Folklore and Transportation (Railway).
 * Main focus is on local and regional titles.
**Recent Title(s)** *Sussex Top Tens*, David Bathurst (Local Guide)
**Tips** S.B. Publications also offer marketing and distribution services for local authors.

## Scala Publishers
**Northburgh House, Northburgh Street, London, EC1V 0AT**
- 020 7490 9900
- 020 7336 6870
- jmckinley@scalapublishers.com
- www.scalapublishers.com

**Contact** Chairman, David Campbell; Commissioning Editor, Jenny McKinley
**Established** 1992
**Non-Fiction** Publishes General Non-fiction and Reference titles on the following subjects:
 Art/Architecture, Antiques and Museum/Gallery Guides.
**Tips** Most material published is written by the museum or gallery curators.

## Schofield & Sims Ltd
**Dogley Mill, Fenay Bridge, Huddersfield, HD8 0NQ**
- 01484 607080
- 01484 606815
- post@schofieldandsims.co.uk
- www.schofieldandsims.co.uk

**Contact** Chairman, C.N. Platts
**Established** 1901
**Insider Info** Catalogue available online and free on request.
**Non-Fiction** Publishes Multimedia, Scholarly, Textbook, Dictionaries, Posters, Educational Workbooks and Children's/Juvenile titles on the following subjects:
 Child Guidance/Parenting, Counselling/Career and Education.
**Recent Title(s)** *Understanding Maths*, Steve Mills and Hilary Koll (Textbook Series)
**Tips** Titles aimed at home tutors, schools, nurseries and playgroups. Most products are created by classroom teachers.

## Scholastic Children's Books
**Euston House, 24 Eversholt Street, London, NW1 1DB**
- 020 7756 7756
- scbenquiries@scholastic.co.uk
- www.scholastic.co.uk

**Parent Company** Scholastic Ltd
**Contact** Editorial Director, Caroline Gott (Pre-School); Editorial Director, Charlie Cousins (Non-Fiction); Editorial Director, Kristen Skidmore (Fiction)
**Imprint(s)** Hippo
 Point
 Scholastic Fiction
 Scholastic Non-Fiction
 Scholastic Press
**Insider Info** Payment is via royalties. Catalogue available online.
**Non-Fiction** Publishes Children's/Juvenile, Illustrated, Multimedia and Reference titles on the following subjects:
 Contemporary Culture, Education, History, Nature/Environment, Science, Sports and Television/Film tie-ins.
**Submission Guidelines** Accepts agented submissions only.
**Fiction** Publishes Juvenile, Picture books, Television/Film tie-ins and Young Adult titles.
**Submission Guidelines** Accepts agented submissions only.
**Recent Title(s)** *Horrible Histories: Awful Egyptians*, Terry Deary (History/Humour); *The Subtle Knife: Junior Edition*, Philip Pullman (Novel)
**Tips** Scholastic Children's Books publishes a wide range of fiction, non-fiction, picture and activity

books for children of all ages. It also publishes fiction for young adult readers, and television/film tie-ins. The Hippo imprint publishes paperback fiction for younger children. The Point imprint specialises in paperback fiction for older children and young adults, including the work of Philip Pullman. Scholastic Press is a specialist hardback imprint. Scholastic does not accept unsolicited manuscripts; most works are submitted by literary agents or are created under a contract.

## Scholastic Ltd

**Villiers House, Clarendon Avenue, Leamington Spa, CV32 5PR**
- 01926 887799
- 01926 883331
- enquiries@scholastic.co.uk
- www.scholastic.co.uk

**Parent Company** Scholastic Inc (see entry under European & International Publishers)
**Contact** Chairman and Chief Executive Officer (USA), Richard Robinson; Manging Director, Miles Stevens-Hoare (Book Fair Division and Book Clubs); Publishing Director, Anne Peel (Education).
**Established** 1920
**Imprint(s)** Scholastic Children's Books
**Non-Fiction** Publishes Children's/Juvenile, Illustrated, Multimedia, Reference and Scholarly titles on the following subjects:
 Contemporary Culture, Education, History, Nature/Environment, Science and Teaching Materials.
**Submission Guidelines** Accepts agented submissions only.
**Fiction** Publishes Children's books, Picture books and Young Adult titles.
**Submission Guidelines** Accepts agented submissions only.
**Recent Title(s)** *100 Activprimary Whiteboard Lessons Complete Set*, Scholastic (Teaching Resources); *Here Lies Arthur*, Philip Reeve (Novel)
**Tips** Scholastic Ltd publishes fiction, non-fiction and picture books for children and young adults under the Children's Division, which includes Scholastic Children's Books. The Educational Division publishes a wide range of educational and teaching material for primary school teachers, in addition to related magazines. The Direct Marketing Division handles Scholastic book fairs and the children's book clubs. Scholastic does not accept unsolicited manuscripts; most works are submitted by literary agents, or are created under a contract.

## Science Navigation Group

**Middlesex House, 34–42 Cleveland Street, London, W1T 4LB**
- 020 7323 0323
- 020 7580 1938
- info@sciencenavigation.com
- www.sciencenavigation.com

**Contact** Group Chairman, Vitek Tracz; Group Managing Director, Anne Greenwood
**Insider Info** Catalogue available online.
**Non-Fiction** Publishes Journals, Websites, Databases, Maps, Audio visuals and Multimedia, Reference, Scholarly, and Technical titles on the following subjects:
 Health/Medicine, Science and Bio-Medicine.
**Tips** Titles aimed at the professional biomedical community, as well as more general audiences. Clients include physicians, scientists, pharmaceutical companies, patients, students and the general public.

## SCM-Canterbury Press Ltd

**9–17 St Alban's Place, London, N1 0NX**
- 020 7359 8033
- 020 7359 0049
- admin@scm-canterburypress.co.uk
- www.scm-canterburypress.co.uk

**Contact** Publishing Director, Christine Smith; Senior Commissioning Editor, Barbara Laing
**Established** 1986 – SCM Press was acquired by The Canterbury Press Norwich in 1997
**Imprint(s)** Canterbury Press
 SCM Press
 Religious and Moral Education Press (RMEP)
 Epworth Press
**Insider Info** Catalogue available free on request and online.
**Non-Fiction** Publishes Autobiography, Biography, Booklets, Children's/Juvenile, General Non-fiction, Illustrated, Multimedia, Reference, Textbooks, Dictionaries, Translations, Popular Religious, Hymn books and Scholarly titles on the following subjects:
 Religion, Spirituality, Translation, Lifestyle, Contemporary Issues, History, Philosophy, Theology, Academic Theology, Poetry, Science, World Religions, and Jewish Studies.
**Submission Guidelines** Submission and manuscript information available online.
 Submission details to: barbara@scm-canterburypress.co.uk
**Recent Title(s)** *Presentations of Faith in Contemporary Detective Fiction*, Peter C. Erb (SCM Press)

**Tips** SCM Press is the UK's best known publisher of academic theology. It provides accessible and rigorous text books, reference books and other high-quality resources for students and clergy alike. Canterbury Press is a supplier of popular religious books, resources and gift stationery for the general, religious and church markets. Recent publications include high quality liturgical books, as well as general market non-fiction with a religious angle.

## Scottish Cultural Press & Scottish Children's Press

**Unit 6, Newbattle Abbey Business Park, Newbattle Road, Dalkeith, EH22 3LJ**

- 0131 660 4666
- 0131 660 4666
- info@scottishbooks.com
- www.scottishbooks.com

**Contact** Directors, Avril Gray and Brian Pugh
**Established** 1992
**Insider Info** Payment is via royalties. Aims to respond to proposals within six months. Catalogue and manuscript guidelines available online.
**Non-Fiction** Publishes Children's/Juvenile and General Non-fiction titles on the following subjects: Anthropology/Archaeology, Art/Architecture, Contemporary Culture, History, Language/Literature, Literary Criticism, Regional and Scottish Interest.
**Submission Guidelines** Accepts query with SAE/proposal package (including outline, one sample chapter, intended market and readership). Will accept artworks/images (send photocopies).
**Fiction** Publishes Children's, Literary, Mainstream/Contemporary, and Young Adult titles.
**Submission Guidelines** Accepts query with SAE/proposal package (including outline, sample chapter(s), intended market and readership). Will accept artworks/images (send photocopies).
**Poetry** Publish poetry titles.
**Recent Title(s)** *Argyll: Land of Blood and Beauty*, Mary McGrigor (Guidebook); *Moray the Dolphin's Adventure in Loch Ness*, Marit Brunskill (Picture book)
**Tips** Scottish Cultural Press is one of the foremost publishers in Scotland, specialising in quality books with a Scottish interest. Scottish Children's Press publishes quality Scottish interest books for children of all ages, from graded readers to teacher's resource books, fun and games, to young fiction. Titles are written for, about and by Scottish children and they aim to encompass Scots, English and Gaelic. As the publishers receive a great quantity of manuscripts, they recommend that prospective authors should phone first to discuss the suitability of the manuscript before sending any work.

## Scribner

**Africa House, 64–78 Kingsway, London, WC2B 6AH**

- 020 7316 1900
- 020 7316 0332
- enquiries@simonandschuster.co.uk
- www.simonsays.co.uk

**Parent Company** Simon and Schuster UK Ltd
**Established** 1999
**Non-Fiction** Publishes Biography and General Non-fiction titles on the following subjects: Contemporary Culture, Creative Non-fiction, Memoirs, Sports and Travel.
**Submission Guidelines** Accepts agented submissions only.
**Fiction** Publishes Literary titles.
**Submission Guidelines** Accepts agented submissions only.
**Recent Title(s)** *Passing For Normal*, Amy Wilensky (Non-fiction)
**Tips** Scribner is designed specifically to be Simon and Schuster's 'literary' imprint, publishing high-quality non-fiction and literary fiction.

## Scripture Union

**207–209 Queensway, Bletchley, Milton Keynes, Buckinghamshire, MK2 2EB**

- 01908 856000
- 01908 856111
- info@scriptureunion.org.uk
- www.scriptureunion.org.uk

**Contact** Publishing Director, Terry Clutterham
**Established** 1867
**Insider Info** Catalogue and manuscript guidelines available online.
**Non-Fiction** Publishes Children's/Juvenile, General Non-fiction, Multimedia, Reference and Scholarly titles on the following subjects: Religion (including Christian faith resources) and Spirituality.
**Submission Guidelines** Accepts query with SAE/proposal package (including outline and one sample chapter).
**Fiction** Publishes Juvenile, Religious (including Bible Stories) and Young Adult titles.
**Tips** Scripture Union is a non-denominational, Christ-centred international movement, working in partnership with individuals and churches across the world. Their aim is to use the Bible to inspire children, young people and adults to discover God. All books must be sympathetic to the Christian faith. Scripture Union publish very few unsolicited manuscripts.

## Seafarer Books Ltd

**102 Redwald Road, Rendlesham, Woodbridge, Suffolk, IP12 2TE**
- ☎ 01394 420789
- ☎ 01394 461314
- ✉ info@seafarerbooks.com
- 🌐 www.seafarerbooks.com

**Contact** Managing Director, Patricia Eve (Sailing Narrative)

**Established** 1998

**Insider Info** Publish four titles per year. Receives approximately 100 queries and 200 manuscripts per year. Ten per cent of books published are from first-time authors and 90 per cent are from unagented authors. Payment is via royalty (on retail price).

**Non-Fiction** Publishes Autobiography, Biography, Humour and General Non-fiction titles on the following subjects:
 Classic Sailing Narratives, Commercial Sailing, Maritime Archaeology and History, Voyaging, Guides to Practical Seamanship, Boat Building/Yacht Design, Arts, Literature.

**Fiction** Publishes General and Classic Maritime titles.

**Recent Title(s)** *Thumbnail Circumnavigation*, Paul Packwood; *Yankee Jack Sails Again*, Tony James

## Search Press

**Wellwood, North Farm Road, Tunbridge Wells, Kent, TN4 0NL**
- ☎ 01892 510850
- ☎ 01892 515903
- ✉ searchpress@searchpress.com
- 🌐 www.searchpress.com

**Contact** Editorial Director, Roz Dace (Art and Craft)

**Established** 1970

**Insider Info** Publishes 30 titles per year. Receives approximately 200 queries and 100 manuscripts per year. 50 per cent of books published are from first-time authors and 100 per cent are from unagented authors. Payment via royalty (on retail price). Simultaneous submissions are accepted and submissions accompanied with SAE will be returned. Aim to respond to queries, proposals and manuscripts within 14 days. Catalogue is free on request and available online.

**Non-Fiction** Publish How-to, Practical, Colour Illustrated and Reference titles on the following subjects:
 Art/Architecture, Crafts, Hobbies.

**Submission Guidelines** Will review artworks/images (send photocopies, transparencies, digital files as jpegs)

 Submission details to: searchpress@searchpress.com

**Recent Title(s)** *Passion for paper - Outline Stickers*, Judy Balchin (Practical how-to craft book)

**Tips** Titles aimed at hobby and professional artists and crafters. Authors are usually experts in their field and should send images of their art/craft works in the first instance.

## Seren

**57 Nolton Street, Bridgend, CF31 3AE**
- ☎ 01656 663018
- ☎ 01656 649226
- ✉ seren@seren-books.com
- 🌐 www.seren-books.com

**Contact** Chairman, Cary Archard; Managing Director, Mick Felton; Fiction Editor, Penny Thomas

**Established** 1981

**Insider Info** Publishes 25 titles per year. Payment is via royalties. Catalogue and manuscript guidelines available online.

**Non-Fiction** Publishes Biography and General Non-fiction titles on the following subjects:
 Art/Architecture, History, Language/Literature, Literary Criticism, Photography, Sports, Translation and World Affairs.

**Submission Guidelines** Accepts query with SAE/proposal package (including outline and three sample chapters).

**Fiction** Publishes Literary, Mainstream/Contemporary, Plays, Translation and Welsh writing titles.
 * Seren only publishes around five works of fiction a year.

**Submission Guidelines** Accepts query with SAE/proposal package (including outline and three sample chapters).

**Poetry** Publish Poetry titles.

**Submission Guidelines** Submit sample poems.

**Recent Title(s)** *Wales's Best One Hundred Churches*, T.J. Hughes (Architecture/Photography); *Letter to Patience*, John Haynes (Collection)

**Tips** Seren specialises in English language writing from Wales. Authors considering submitting a manuscript should be aware that fiction and poetry lists are often full at least two years in advance.

## Serendipity

**First Floor, 37–39 Victoria Road, Darlington, DL1 5SF**
- ☎ 0845 130 2434
- ✉ info@serendipitypublishers.com
- 🌐 www.serendipitypublishers.com

**Established** 2001

**Insider Info** Publishes 40 titles per year. Average lead time is six months with simultaneous submissions accepted. Submissions accompanied by SAE will be returned. Aims to respond to queries within two days and manuscripts within three weeks. Catalogue and manuscript guidelines are free on request.

**Non-Fiction** Publish Autobiography, Biography, Children's, Coffee Table, Cookery, General Non-fiction, Gift, How-to, Humour, Illustrated, Reference, Scholarly, Self-help, Technical and Textbook titles on the following subjects:
Agriculture/Horticulture, Anthropology/Archaeology, Astrology/Psychic, Automotive, Contemporary Culture, Guidance, Education, Ethnic, Government/Politics, Health/Medicine, History, Humanities, Marine Subjects, Memoirs, Military/War, Music/Dance, Nature/Environment, New Age, Nostalgia, Philosophy, Photography, Recreation, Regional, Religion, Science, Spirituality, Sports, Travel, Young Adult.

**Submission Guidelines** Accepts query with SAE, or via email. Also accepts completed manuscripts. Will accept artworks/images (send photocopies or digital files as jpegs).

**Fiction** Publish Adventure, Ethnic, Fantasy, Feminist, Historical, Horror, Humour, Children's, Literary, Mainstream/Contemporary, Military/War, Multicultural, Mystery, Occult, Picture books, Plays, Religious, Romance, Science Fiction, Short story collections, Spiritual, Sports, Suspense, Western and Young Adult titles.

**Submission Guidelines** Accepts query with SAE, or via email. Also accepts completed manuscripts.

**Poetry** Publish Poetry and Poetry in Translation.

**Submission Guidelines** Accepts query with SAE, or via email (include five sample poems). Also accepts completed manuscripts.

**Recent Title(s)** *Chamber Music Miscellany*, Tom Patterson; *No Weapon Forged*, Ron Haddow; *Lion's Tooth*, Mariegold Heron

## Serif

**47 Strahan Road, London, E3 5DA**

- 020 8981 3990
- 020 8981 3990
- stephen@serif.demon.co.uk
- www.serif.demon.co.uk

**Contact** Managing Editor, Stephen Hayward

**Established** 1993

**Insider Info** Payment is via royalties. Catalogue available online.

**Non-Fiction** Publishes General Non-fiction titles on the following subjects:
Cooking/Foods/Nutrition, History, Travel, Irish studies and African studies.

**Submission Guidelines** Accepts query with SAE.

**Fiction** Publishes Literary and Mainstream/Contemporary titles.

**Submission Guidelines** Accepts query with SAE.

**Tips** Serif welcomes ideas and proposals for publications, but does not accept unsolicited manuscripts.

## Serpent's Tail

**3a Exmouth House, Pine Street, London, EC1R OJH**

- 020 7841 6300
- info@serpentstail.com
- www.serpentstail.com

**Parent Company** Profile Books Ltd

**Established** 1987 (acquired by Profile Books in 2007)

**Insider Info** Catalogue available online.

**Non-Fiction** Publishes Autobiography, Biography, Illustrated and General Non-fiction titles on the following subjects:
Contemporary Culture, Music/Dance, Travel, Cult Books (Fiction and Non-fiction), Black Writing (Fiction and Non-fiction), Gay and Lesbian (Fiction and Non-fiction), Race, Sex/Gender, Politics/Current Affairs, Philosophy/Ideas, Cultural Criticism, World Literature (Fiction and Non-fiction).

**Submission Guidelines** Accepts agented submissions only.

**Fiction** Publishes Short Story Collections, Translation, Women's Writing, Classics, Debuts, Crime Fiction and Anthology titles.

**Submission Guidelines** Accepts agented submissions only.

**Poetry** Publishes Poetry titles.

**Submission Guidelines** Accepts agented submissions only.

**Tips** Serpent's Tail is a renowned publisher of international fiction and non-fiction, founded with a commitment to publishing authors 'neglected by the mainstream'.

## Severn House Publishers Ltd

**9–15 High Street, Sutton, Surrey, SM1 1DF**

- 020 8770 3930
- 020 8770 3850
- sales@severnhouse.com
- www.severnhouse.com

**Contact** Chairman, Edwin Buckhalter; Editorial, Amanda Stewart
**Established** 1974
**Insider Info** Publishes 150 titles per year. Payment is via royalties. Catalogue and manuscript guidelines available online.
**Fiction** Publishes Historical, Horror, Literary, Mainstream/Contemporary, Military/War, Mystery, Romance, Science Fiction, Suspense and Crime titles.
 * Severn House publishes various kinds of genre and general fiction in large and regular print sizes. Most books are hardback, aimed at fiction libraries, however some titles are produced as paperbacks.
**Submission Guidelines** Accepts agented submissions only. Will not accept unsolicited manuscripts.
**Recent Title(s)** *The Spirit of Liberty*, Ted Allbeury (Novel)
**Tips** As publications are aimed at the UK and US fiction library markets, they are unable to add authors to the list who do not have a significant background in this market.

## Shearsman Books Ltd

**58 Velwell Road, Exeter, Devon, EX4 4LD**
**☏** 01392 434511
**☏** 01392 434511
**✉** editor@shearsman.com
**�🌐** www.shearsman.com
**Contact** Publisher, Tony Frazer (Poetry)
**Established** 1981
**Insider Info** Publishes 30 titles per year. Receives 2,500 queries and 300 manuscripts per year. 15 per cent of books published are from first-time authors, 90 per cent of books published are from unagented authors. Payment is via royalty (on retail price), with 0.01 (per £) minimum and 0.02 (Per £) maximum. Average lead time is one year, with simultaneous submissions accepted. Submissions accompanied by SAE will be returned. Aims to respond to queries and proposals withing two weeks and manuscripts within four months. Catalogue and manuscript guidelines are free on request and available online or by email.
**Non-Fiction** Publishes Language/Literature and Journals/Memoir (by poets) titles.
 * Shearsman Books does not publish non-fiction other than journals and memoirs by poets, and very infrequently.
**Submission Guidelines** Accepts proposal package (including sample chapters, your publishing history, author biography and SAE).
**Poetry** * Shearsman Books publishes contemporary poetry collections and anthologies.

**Submission Guidelines** Accepts proposal package (including six to ten pages of sample poems, your publishing history, author biography and SAE).
**Recent Title(s)** *Journals*, R.F. Langley (Journals/Diaries); *Selected Poems*, Elaine Randell (Poetry)

## Sheldon Press

**36 Causton Street, London, SW1P 4ST**
**○** Online form
**🌐** www.sheldonpress.co.uk
**Parent Company** Society for Promoting Christian Knowledge
**Contact** Editor, Fiona Marshall
**Established** 1973
**Insider Info** Catalogue available online
**Non-Fiction** Publishes Self-help titles on the following subjects:
 Major Illnesses and Health, Mental Health Issues, Healthy Eating Issues, Life Challenges (Trauma and Bereavement), Life Skills, Guides for Parents and Children, Business and Work.
 * Sheldon Press is always interested in commissioning new authors and ideas, they specialise in books on medical and emotional subjects, aimed at the general reader.
**Submission Guidelines** Accepts proposal package (including outline, chapter one and introduction, author biography and market information). Send by post to the Editorial Director at the address above.
 Submission details to: director@sheldonpress.co.uk
**Recent Title(s)** *Assertiveness: Step by Step*, Windy Dryden and Daniel Constantinou

## Sheldrake Press

**188 Cavendish Road, London, SW12 0DA**
**☏** 020 8675 1767
**☏** 020 8675 7736
**✉** mail@sheldrakepress.demon.co.uk
**🌐** www.sheldrakepress.demon.co.uk
**Contact** Publisher, Simon Rigge; Assistant Editor, Nicholas Lim
**Established** 1979 (Founded as a book packager but began publishing Non-fiction titles in 1991).
**Insider Info** Catalogue available online.
**Non-Fiction** Publishes General Non-fiction and Multimedia titles on the following subjects:
 Cooking/Foods/Nutrition, History, House and Home, Travel and Stationary Books.
**Submission Guidelines** Accepts query with SAE/proposal package (including outline)
 Submission details to: jsr@sheldrakepress.demon.co.uk

**Recent Title(s)** *The Kate Greenaway First Year Baby Book*, Kate Greenaway
**Tips** Welcomes synopses for non-fiction books but will not accept any fiction titles.

## Shepheard-Walwyn (Publishers) Ltd
**Suite 604, The Chandlery, 50 Westminster Bridge Road, London, SE1 7QY**
- 020 7721 7666
- 020 7721 7667
- books@shepheard-walwyn.co.uk
- www.shepheard-walwyn.co.uk

**Contact** Managing Director, Anthony Werner
**Established** 1972
**Insider Info** Publishes five titles per year. Payment is via royalties. Catalogue available free on request and online.
**Non-Fiction** Publishes Biography, Gift, Illustrated and General Non-fiction titles on the following subjects:
 Business/Economics, Government/Politics, History, Law, Philosophy, Calligraphy, Shakespeare Studies and Scottish interest.
**Submission Guidelines** Accepts query with SAE/proposal package (including outline and author biography).
**Poetry** Publishes a variety of classic and contemporary poetry titles.
**Submission Guidelines** Accepts query with SAE.
**Recent Title(s)** *Britain's Prime Ministers*, Roger Ellis and Geoffrey Treasure
**Tips** Before submitting a proposal, visit the website to assess whether your title is suitable, then submit your synopsis and CV.

## The Shetland Times Ltd
**Gremista, Lerwick, Shetland, ZE1 0PX**
- 01595 693622
- 01595 694637
- publishing@shetland-times.co.uk
- www.shetlandtoday.co.uk

**Contact** Managing Director, June Wishart; Publications Manager, Charlotte Black
**Established** 1872
**Insider Info** Payment is via royalties. Catalogue available online.
**Non-Fiction** Publishes General Non-fiction titles on the following subjects:
 Regional, Shetland Interest.
**Recent Title(s)** *Making of the Shetland Landscape*, Susan Knox
**Tips** Much of the available literature about Shetland is printed and published by The Shetland Times,

including Shetland's only weekly magazine *The Shetland Times*, and the monthly magazine *Shetland Life*. All material is of local Shetland interest.

## Shield Publications
**PO Box 5, Low Fell, Gateshead, NE9 7YS**
- 0191 482 3222

**Contact** Managing Director, Norman Middlemiss
**Established** 1977
**Insider Info** Payment via royalties.
**Non-Fiction** Publishes Nautical and General Non-fiction titles on the following subjects:
 Hobbies, Military/War and Sports.
**Recent Title(s)** *Merchant Fleet*, Shield Books, (Series)

## Shire Publications Ltd
**Cromwell House, Church Street, Princes Risborough, Buckinghamshire, HP27 9AA**
- 01844 344301
- 01844 347080
- shire@shirebooks.co.uk
- www.shirebooks.co.uk

**Contact** General Manager, Sue Ross
**Established** 1962
**Insider Info** Publishes 25 titles per year. Payment is via royalties. Catalogue available free on request and online.
**Non-Fiction** Publishes Illustrated, Biography and General Non-fiction titles on the following subjects:
 Anthropology/Archaeology, Art/Architecture, Crafts, Ethnic, History, Hobbies, House and Home, Humanities, Photography, Regional, Transportation, Collectables and Ephemera, Regional Interest, Folklore and Legends, Egyptology and Walking.
 * It is Shire's aim to to publish authoritative, well-written and well-illustrated books, by experts on the subject, and to keep prices low.
**Submission Guidelines** Accepts query with SAE.
**Recent Title(s)** *Pub Beer Mugs and Glasses*, Hugh Rock
**Tips** Because each book is numbered within its series (except for a few miscellaneous titles), Shire books have become 'collectables' with readers seeking full sets. Prospective authors must be aware of the various Shire series' on offer.

## Short Books
**3a Exmouth House, Pine Street, Exmouth Market, London, EC1R 0JH**
- 020 7833 9429
- 020 7833 9500
- emily@shortbooks.biz

www.shortbooks.co.uk
**Contact** Editorial Director, Aurea Carpenter; Editorial Director, Rebecca Nicholson
**Established** 2000
**Insider Info** Catalogue and manuscript guidelines available online.
**Non-Fiction** Publishes Biography, Children's/Juvenile, General Non-fiction and Humour titles on the following subjects:
Education, Government/Politics, History and Teaching Resources.
* Shortbooks strives to bridge the gap between publishing and journalism. Publishes general non-fiction titles for adults and children and offers teaching resources to support classroom orientated books.
**Submission Guidelines** Accepts query with SAE/proposal package including (outline and two sample chapters). Proposals and chapters must be emailed as attachments.
**Recent Title(s)** Amo, Amas Amat... and all that, Harry Mount
**Tips** All prospective authors should bear in mind that Short Books are a small company which is inundated with book proposals and manuscripts. Prospective authors should follow the submissions policy detailed above and should not send unsolicited manuscripts. The publisher will respond to prospective authors by email.

## Sidgwick & Jackson
**20 New Wharf Road, London, N1 9RR**
020 7014 6000
020 7014 6001
fiction@macmillan.co.uk, nonfiction@macmillan.co.uk
www.panmacmillan.com
**Parent Company** Pan Macmillan Publishers
**Established** 1908
**Insider Info** Catalogue available online (downloadable pdf catalogue available on the website).
**Non-Fiction** Publishes Autobiography, Biography and General Non-fiction titles on the following subjects:
Contemporary Culture, History, Memoirs and Military/War.
**Submission Guidelines** Agented submissions only (no unsolicited manuscripts).
**Recent Title(s)** The Price of Love, Nikola T. James (Biography/Memoir)
**Tips** Sidgwick and Jackson are specialists in commercial and popular non-fiction, including high-

profile biographies, popular culture and military history. They do not publish fiction titles.

## Sigma Press
**5 Alton Road, Wilmslow, Cheshire, SK9 5DY**
01625 531035
01625 531035
info@sigmapress.co.uk
www.sigmapress.co.uk
**Contact** Senior Partner, Graham Beech (Leisure Guides, Local History)
**Established** 1980
**Insider Info** Publishes 12 titles per year. Receives approximately 100 queries and 15 manuscripts per year. 90 per cent of books published are from first-time authors and 100 per cent are from unagented authors. Payment is via royalty (on wholesale price). Average lead time is four months with simultaneous submissions not accepted. Submissions accompanied by SAE will be returned. Aims to respond to queries within two days, proposals within two weeks and manuscripts within one month. Catalogue is free on request and available online. Manuscript guidelines are free on request.
**Non-Fiction** Publish Guidebook titles on the following subjects:
Nature/Environment, Travel, UK Outdoor.
**Submission Guidelines** Accepts query with SAE, or via email. Will accept artworks/images (send digital files as jpegs).
Submission details to: info@sigmapress.co.uk
**Recent Title(s)** Peak District Natural History Walks, Chris Mitchell (Guidebook)
**Tips** Titles are aimed at walkers, or their friends and relatives.

## Simon & Schuster UK Ltd
**Africa House, 64–78 Kingsway, London, WC2B 6AH**
020 7316 1900
020 7316 0332
enquiries@simonandschuster.co.uk
www.simonsays.co.uk
**Contact** CEO/Managing Director, Ian Stewart Chapman
**Established** 1924
**Imprint(s)** Free Press
Martin Books
Pocket Books
Scribner
Simon & Schuster Children's Books (division)
**Insider Info** Catalogue available online.

**Non-Fiction** Publishes Audio cassettes, Autobiography, Biography, Children's/Juvenile, Cookbooks, General Non-fiction, Gift, Humour, Illustrated, Reference, Self-help and Media tie-in titles on the following subjects:
Alternative Lifestyles, Business/Economics, Contemporary Culture, Cooking/Foods/Nutrition, Creative Non-fiction, Government/Politics, Health/Medicine, History, Language/Literature, Memoirs, Psychology, Science, Spirituality, Sports, Translation, Travel, World Affairs and Popular Culture.
**Submission Guidelines** Accepts agented submissions only.
**Fiction** Publishes Fantasy, Historical, Horror, Humour, Juvenile, Mainstream/Contemporary, Mystery, Picture books, Romance, Science Fiction, Spiritual, Sports, Suspense, Media tie-ins and Translation titles.
**Submission Guidelines** Accepts agented submissions only.
**Recent Title(s)** *The Secret*, Rhonda Byrne (Simon and Schuster imprint); *Two Little Girls in Blue*, Mary Higgins Clark (Crime/Thriller, Pocketbooks imprint)
**Tips** Simon and Schuster has a stable of bestselling international authors. The company publishes a broad range of non-fiction and fiction, from popular bestsellers to titles from its more heavyweight Free Press imprint, a list which includes authors such as the Pulitzer Prize winning William Taubner. No unsolicited manuscripts are accepted.

## Simon & Schuster Children's Books
**Africa House, 64–78 Kingsway, London, WC2B 6AH**
- 020 7316 1900
- 020 7316 0332
- editorial.enquiries@simonandschuster.co.uk
- www.simonsays.co.uk
**Parent Company** Simon & Schuster UK Ltd
**Contact** Publishing Director, Ingrid Selberg
**Established** 1998
**Non-fiction** Publishes Children's/Juvenile, Illustrated Young Adult and Media tie-in titles.
**Submission Guidelines** Accepts agented submissions only.
**Fiction** Publishes Children's and Picture book titles.
**Submissions Guidelines** Accepts agented submissions only.
**Recent Title(s)** *Postman Pat's Wild West Rescue* (Character book); *If I had a Dragon*, Amanda Ellery (Picture book)

## Sixties Press
**89 Connaught Road, Sutton, SM1 3PJ**
- 020 8286 0419
- info@sixtiespress.co.uk, sixtiespress@blueyonder.co.uk
- www.sixtiespress.co.uk
**Contact** Publisher, Barry Tebb
**Insider Info** Catalogue available online.
**Non-Fiction** Publishes guides for, and memoirs of, the mentally ill and their carers.
**Fiction** Publishes Novels and Novellas.
**Poetry** Publishes Poetry titles.
**Tips** The website contains free samples of poetry, which the Sixties Press publish.

## Snowbooks Ltd
**120 Pentonville Road, London, N1 9JN**
- 020 7837 6482
- 020 7837 6348
- info@snowbooks.com
- www.snowbooks.com
**Contact** Director, Rob Jones; Managing Director, Emma Barnes; Publisher, James Bridle; Publisher, Anna Torborg (Memoir, Handicrafts); Publisher, Gilly Barnard
**Established** 2003
**Insider Info** Publishes ten titles per year. Payment is via royalties. Catalogue and manuscript guidelines available online.
**Non-Fiction** Publishes Biography, Illustrated and General Non-fiction titles on the following subjects:
Business/Economics, Crafts, Government/Politics, Hobbies, Memoirs, Social Sciences and Sports.
**Submission Guidelines** Accepts Proposal package (including outline, two sample chapters and author biography). Submissions must be emailed.
Submission details to: submissions@snowbooks.com
**Fiction** Publishes Mainstream/Contemporary, Short story collections, Thrillers and Women's Fiction titles.
**Submission Guidelines** Accepts proposal package (including outline and sample chapter(s)). Submissions must be emailed.
Submission details to: submissions@snowbooks.com
**Recent Title(s)** *Going Postal*, Mark Ames (Cultural study); *The Darkness Gathers*, Lisa Miscione (Novel)
**Tips** Snowbooks are happy to look at excellent works of fiction and non-fiction. The publishers will not specify particular genres as they believe it is the writing that matters, not the category. Prospective authors must email submissions straight away (there is no need to send an initial email to check if the

novel is appropriate). Postal submissions will not be accepted.

## The Society for Promoting Christian Knowledge (SPCK)
**36 Causton Street, London, SW1P 4ST**
- 020 7592 3900
- 020 7592 3939
- Online enquiry form
- www.spck.org.uk/

**Imprint(s)** Azure
Sheldon Press (see entry)

**Insider Info** Catalogue available online.

**Non-Fiction** Publishes Biography, Children's/Juvenile, Gift book, Humour, Illustrated book, Reference, Scholarly, Textbook, Commentaries; Devotional; Music Hymn Books and Self-help titles on the following subjects:
Art/Architecture, Education, History, Language/Literature, Music/Dance, Religion, Spirituality, Travel, Women's Issues/Studies, Biblical Studies, Church History, Family Life, Relationships, Comparative Religion, Liturgical Studies, Pastoral Care, Poetry.

**Submission Guidelines** Accepts proposal package (including outline and two sample chapters).
Send to Editorial Department (Submissions).

**Recent Title(s)** *For the Love of God*, Anthea Dove (Meditations for Christian Living)

**Tips** Publishes work for students and teachers of theology, lay Christians, spiritual seekers and a general readership with an interest in Christianity. SPCK produces a broad range of Christian books with a large range of topics for the general reader. Its list covers a diversity of Christian traditions from the Evangelical to the Catholic, the conservative to the liberal. Azure books explore a range of subjects and styles, from travel literature to illustrated gift books, each one with an implicit Christian understanding.

## Society of Genealogists Enterprises Ltd
**14 Charterhouse Buildings, Goswell Road, London, EC1M 7BA**
- 020 7251 8799
- 020 7250 1800
- sales@sog.org.uk
- www.sog.org.uk

**Contact** Acting Director, June Perrin

**Insider Info** Catalogue available online.

**Non-Fiction** Publishes Multimedia, Reference and Scholarly titles on Genealogy.

**Recent Title(s)** *First Steps in Family History*

**Tips** The Society of Genealogists publish research material (including books, finding aids, indexes, CDs and software) for those interested in family history and the lives of earlier generations. Any resource proposed should be designed to aid research into family history.

## Southwater
**Hermes House, 88–89 Blackfriars Road, London, SE1 8HA**
- 020 7401 2077
- 020 7633 9499
- info@anness.com
- www.annesspublishing.com

**Parent Company** Anness Publishing Ltd

**Contact** Chairman/Managing Director, Paul Anness; Publisher/Partner, Joanna Lorenz (Creative Issues)

**Established** 1999

**Insider Info** Publishes 150 titles per year. Catalogue available online.

**Non-Fiction** Publishes Children's/Juvenile, Illustrated and General Non-fiction titles on the following subjects:
Cooking/Foods/Nutrition, Crafts, Gardening, History, House and Home, Recreation, Spirituality and Sports.

**Recent Title(s)** *Meditation: Simple Steps to Peace, Well-being and Contentment*, John Hudson; *Making the Most of Annuals in the Garden*, Richard Bird; *Easter: Recipes, Gifts and Decorations*, Tessa Evelegh

**Tips** Southwater is the trade paperback imprint for Anness Publishing Ltd.

## Souvenier Press Ltd
**43 Great Russell Street, London, WC1B 3PD**
- 020 7580 9307
- 020 7580 5064
- sp.trade@ukonline.co.uk

**Contact** Managing Director, Ernest Hecht

**Imprint(s)** Condor

**Insider Info** Publishes 50 titles per year. Payment is via royalties. Catalogue available free on request and via email.

**Non-Fiction** Publishes Autobiography, Biography, Children's/Juvenile, General Non-fiction, Humour, Illustrated and Scholarly titles on the following subjects:
Anthropology/Archaeology, Art/Architecture, Astrology/Psychic, Business/Economics, Cooking/Foods/Nutrition, Crafts, Education, Gardening, Health/Medicine, History, Hobbies, Military/War, Music/Dance, Nature/Environment, Philosophy, Psychology, Religion, Sociology, Spirituality, Sports,

Women's Issues/Studies, Theatre and Magic and the Occult

**Submission Guidelines** Accepts query with SAE/ proposal package (including outline and two sample chapters).

**Fiction** Publishes Humour, Juvenile, Literary, Mainstream/Contemporary, and Crime titles.

**Submission Guidelines** Accepts query with SAE/ proposal package (including outline and two sample chapters).

**Poetry** Publishes Poetry titles.

**Submission Guidelines** Submit sample poems.

**Tips** Souvenir Press covers a wide range of academic and general non-fiction topics, specialising in spiritual and mystical titles. Fiction and poetry lists are more limited.

## Spacelink Books
**115 Hollybush Lane, Hampton, Middlesex, TW12 2QY**

- 020 8979 3148
- www.spacelink.fsworld.co.uk

**Contact** Managing Director, Lionel Beer

**Established** 1967

**Insider Info** Payment is according to contract. Catalogue available online.

**Non-Fiction** Publishes Booklets, General Non-fiction and Scholarly titles on the following subjects:
 New Age, Spirituality, UFO's and the Paranormal.

**Submission Guidelines** Accepts query with SAE.

**Tips** Spacelink is named after a UFO magazine from the 1960s/1970s and publishes general non-fiction titles on the subject of UFOs, fortean phenomena and paranormal events. Spacelink also handles distribution of a wide range of magazines and related titles. No unsolicited manuscripts are accepted, however prospective authors are encouraged to send in a synopsis.

## Special Interests Model Books
**Stanley House, 3 Fleets Lane, Poole, Dorset, BH15 3AJ**

- 01202 649930
- 01202 649950
- chrlloyd@globalnet.co.uk
- www.specialinterestmodelbooks.co.uk

**Contact** Chris Lloyd

**Insider Info** Payment is via royalties. Catalogue available online.

**Non-Fiction** Publishes General Non-fiction titles on the following subjects:

Computers/Electronics, Cooking/Foods/Nutrition, Hobbies, Transportation, Modelling/Collecting, Engineering, Wine and Beer and Engineering.
 * Specialise in hobbyist and collectables publishing.

**Recent Title(s)** *Parkflyer*, Hinrik Schulte

## Speechmark
**8 Oxford Court, St. James Road, Brackley, Northamptonshire, NN13 0XY**

- 01280 455570
- 01280 845584
- info@speechmark.net
- www.speechmark.net

**Contact** Development Manager, Karen Dewick (Speech and Language Therapy); Managing Director, Sarah Miles (Speech and Language Therapy)

**Insider Info** Publish 25 titles per year. Receive approximately 250 queries and 40 manuscripts per year. Five per cent of books published are from first-time authors and 25 per cent are from unagented authors. Payment is via royalty (on retail price) with 0.1 (per £) maximum. Average lead time is nine months with simultaneous submissions accepted. Submissions accompanied by SAE will be returned. Aims to respond to queries within seven days, proposals within six weeks, and manuscripts within six months. Catalogue is free on request and available online. Manuscript guidelines are free on request.

**Non-Fiction** Publish Professional Resources titles on the following subjects:
 Speech/Language Therapy Resources, Elderly Care Resources.

**Submission Guidelines** Accepts proposal package via post or email (including outline, one sample chapter, your publishing history, author biography, SAE). Will accept artworks/images (send photocopies).

**Recent Title(s)** *Memory Box*, Robin Dynes; *Group Games: Building Relationships*, Thorsten Boehner

**Tips** Titles aimed at health and educational professionals.

## Sphere
**Brettenham House, Lancaster Place, London, WC2E 7EN**

- 020 7911 8000
- 020 7911 8100
- info@littlebrown.co.uk
- www.littlebrown.co.uk

**Parent Company** Little, Brown Book Group

**Contact** Publishing Director, Antonia Hodgson

**Insider Info** Submissions accompanied by SAE will be returned. Aims to respond to proposals within eight weeks. Catalogue available online.
**Non-Fiction** Publishes Autobiography, Biography, Commercial Non-fiction, General Non-fiction, Memoirs and Humour titles.
**Submission Guidelines** Accepts query with SAE/proposal package (including outline, three sample chapters and covering letter). No email submissions are accepted.
**Fiction** Publishes Humour, Mainstream/Contemporary, Romance and Commercial fiction titles.
**Submission Guidelines** Accepts query with SAE/proposal package (including outline, three sample chapters and covering letter). No email submissions are accepted.
**Recent Title(s)** *Long Way Round*, Ewan McGregor and Charley Boorman; *Extreme*, Sharon Osbourne

## Spiro Press
**17–19 Rochester Row, London, SW1P 1LA**
- 0870 165 8968
- 0870 165 8989
- webenquiries@capita-ld.co.uk
**Parent Company** Capita Group
**Contact** Publisher, Susannah Lear
**Insider Info** Payment is via royalties. Catalogue available online.
**Non-Fiction** Publishes Reference and Technical titles on Business/Economics.
  * Illustrated non-fiction is not accepted.
**Submission Guidelines** Accepts query with SAE/proposal package (including outline). Submit completed manuscript.
**Tips** Spiro Press publishes general business books, guides and manuals.

## SportsBooks Ltd
**PO Box 422, Cheltenham, GL50 2YN**
- 01242 256755
- 01242 254694
- info@sportsbooks.ltd.uk
- www.sportsbooks.ltd.uk
**Contact** Chairman/Managing Director, Randall Northam
**Established** 1995
**Imprint(s)** BMM
**Insider Info** Publishes ten titles per year. Catalogue and manuscript guidelines available online.
**Non-Fiction** Publishes Biography, General Non-fiction, Practical Guides, How-to and Reference titles on a wide range of Sports.

**Submission Guidelines** Accepts query with SAE/proposal package (including outline, three sample chapters). Submissions should be sent by post. Do not send full manuscripts unless requested.
**Recent Title(s)** *Athletics 2006*, Peter Matthews

## The Sportsman's Press
**Wykey House, Wykey, Shrewsbury, Shropshire, SY4 1JA**
- 01939 261616
- 01939 261606
- admin@quillerbooks.com
- www.countrybooksdirect.com
**Insider Info** Publishes five titles per year. Ten per cent of book published are from first-time authors, 95 per cent of books published are from unagented authors and approximately five per cent of books are author subsidy published. Payment is via royalty on wholesale or retail price. Average lead time is two months. Simultaneous submissions accepted. Submissions accompanied by SAE will be returned. Catalogue free on request, online.
**Non-Fiction** General Non-fiction, Countryside pursuits.
**Submission Guidelines** Accepts proposal package (including outline, sample chapter(s), your publishing history, author biography) and artworks/images (send photocopies or digital files as jpegs). Submission details to: john@beaton.org.uk
**Tips** Postal submissions preferred.
See Quiller Publishing Ltd.

## Spy Publishing Ltd
**277–279 Chiswick High Road, London, W4 4PU**
- www.mrandmrssmith.com
**Non-Fiction** Publishes General Non-fiction titles on Travel.
**Tips** Publishes lifestyle hotel guides to European cities, the UK and Ireland.

## Stacey International
**128 Kensington Church Street, London, W8 4BH**
- 020 7221 7166
- 0207 792 9288
- enquiries@stacey-international.co.uk
- www.stacey-international.co.uk
**Contact** Chairman, Tom Stacey; Managing Director, Max Scott
**Established** 1973
**Insider Info** Catalogue available online.

**Non-Fiction** Publishes Biography, Children's/Juvenile, General Non-fiction, Illustrated and Scholarly titles on the following subjects: Anthropology/Archaeology, Cooking/Foods/Nutrition, History, Language/Literature, Memoirs, Multicultural, Nature/Environment, Photography, Religion and Travel.

 * Stacey International publish a range of books to help develop intercontinental relationships and travels. Titles range from standard illustrated reference works on the 'newer' nations of significance in today's world, to handbooks dealing with how to drive in the desert, and conversational language tuition. They also publish academic reference sources, ranging from *The Encyclopaedia of Islam* to *The Concise Dictionary of Foreign Quotations*.

**Fiction** Publish Mainstream/Contemporary titles.

**Recent Title(s)** *An A to Z of Places and Things Saudi*, Kathy Cuddihy

**Tips** Titles are orientated towards a niche readership and fulfil a specific practical use.

## Stanley Gibbons Publications
**7 Parkside, Ringwood, Ringwood, Hampshire, BH24 3SH**

- 01425 472363
- 01425 470247
- kfinney@stanleygibbons.co.uk
- www.stanleygibbons.com

**Contact** Chairman, P. Fraser; Editorial Head, H. Jeffries

**Established** 1856

**Insider Info** Publishes 20 titles per year. Payment is via royalties. Catalogue available online.

**Non-Fiction** Publishes General Non-fiction and Reference titles on the following subjects: Hobbies and Collecting (General).

 * Stanley Gibbons publishes books and reference catalogues concerning Philately (Stamp Collecting). Also publishes many international catalogues and magazines, including *Gibbons Stamp Monthly*.

**Submission Guidelines** Accepts query with SAE. Submit completed manuscript.

**Tips** Most material concerns philately, however solid proposals on other areas of collecting may be considered.

## Stenlake Publishing
**54–58 Mill Square, Catrine, Ayrshire, KA5 6RD**

- 01290 552233
- 01290 551122
- info@stenlake.co.uk
- www.stenlake.co.uk

**Contact** Managing Director, Richard Stenlake

**Established** 1997

**Insider Info** Publishes 40 titles per year. Payment is via royalties or a flat fee. Catalogue and manuscript guidelines available online.

**Non-Fiction** Publishes illustrated and General Non-fiction titles on the following subjects: Sports, Transportation (railways, aviation and canals), Local Interest and History, Towns and Suburbs, Rural areas (larger suburbs and groups of related villages) and Industry.

 * Stenlake Publishing produces books of local interest illustrated with old photographs and accompanied by an informative and interesting narrative. Proposals or ideas in the local history range will be considered.

**Submission Guidelines** Accepts query with SAE/proposal package (including outline).

**Recent Title(s)** *Bygone Scone*, Guthrie Hutton (Local History)

**Tips** Stenlake is often looking for freelance writers for commissioned works. Check the 'writers' section on their website.

## The Stinging Fly Press
**PO Box 6016, Dublin 8, Republic of Ireland**

- stingingfly@gmail.com

**Established** 2005

**Fiction** Publishes Short Story Collections.

 * Seek to promote the best in new Irish and international writing. Plans are to build up the press over the coming years, with a small number of titles.

**Poetry** Publishes Poetry titles.

**Tips** Also publishes *The Stinging Fly* magazine. Not seeking submissions.

## St. James Publishing
**Suite 213 Parkway House, Sheen Lane, East Sheen, London, SW14 8LS**

- 0870 870 8797
- 0870 870 8798
- stjamespublishing@stjamesschools.co.uk
- www.stjamespublishing.co.uk

**Contact** Managing Editors, David Smith and Linda Smith

**Established** 1995

**Insider Info** Catalogue available online.

**Non-Fiction** Publishes Textbooks, Reference and Scholarly titles on the following subjects: Education, Religion and Spirituality.

 * St. James Publishing is a registered educational charity and its publications are produced on a non-profit making basis for purchase by pupils/parents.

Any profit that may accrue through sales will be used to help fund the publication of further books.

**Recent Title(s)** *St. James Reading Scheme Level 3*, St. James Junior School English Department (Educational series)

**Tips** St. James Publishing sources most of its material internally and does not accept submissions or proposals.

## Stone Flower Ltd
**PO Box 1513, Ilford, IG1 3QU**

◉ stoneflower10622@aol.com

**Contact** Managing Editor, L.G. Norman

**Established** 1989

**Non-Fiction** Publishes Biography, General Non-fiction and Humour titles.

**Submission Guidelines** Accepts query with SAE. Submit completed manuscripts.

**Fiction** Publishes Mainstream/Contemporary titles.

**Submission Guidelines** Accepts query with SAE. Submit completed manuscripts.

**Tips** Note that Stone Flower is not interested in anthropomorphism (the attribution of human characteristics to animals).

## St. Pauls Publishing
**187 Battersea Bridge Road, London, SW11 3AS**

✆ 020 7978 4300

✆ 020 7978 4370

◉ editions@stpauls.org.uk

ⓦ www.stpauls.org.uk

**Contact** Publisher, Andrew Pudussery

**Established** 1914

**Insider Info** Publishes 30 titles per year. Catalogue available online.

**Non-Fiction** Publishes Biography, General Non-fiction and Multimedia titles on the following subjects:
Religion, Spirituality and Prayer.
* Through books, magazines, journals, film, radio, television, video and the internet, the Society of St. Paul continues the vision of its founder, James Alberione, to follow in the missionary footsteps of St. Paul the Apostle, by bringing news of Jesus Christ to the world.

**Submission Guidelines** Accepts query with SAE/proposal package (including outline). Submit completed manuscript.

**Recent Title(s)** *Plain Account of Christian Perfection*, John Wesley

**Tips** All proposals should relate to the Catholic faith.

## Straightline Publishing Ltd
**29 Main Street, Bothwell, Glasgow, G71 8RD**

✆ 01698 853000

✆ 01698 854208

◉ Online form.

ⓦ www.straightlinepublishing.com

**Contact** Director, Patrick Bellew; Editor, Colin Calder

**Established** 1989

**Insider Info** Payment is via royalties.

**Non-Fiction** Publishes Directories, General Non-fiction, Multimedia and Reference titles on the following subjects:
Business/Economics and Regional Interest.
* Straightline Publishing offers professional assistance in journalism, photography, design, print and advertising sales as a contract publisher. It also works as an independant publisher, producing newsletters, newspapers, magazines, directories, annual reports and prospectuses.

**Recent Title(s)** *Enterprising Glasgow* (Journal/Directory)

**Tips** Straightline Publishing works mainly on a contractual basis and does not accept unsolicited material.

## Stride
**4b Tremayne Close, Devoran, Cornwall, TR3 6QE**

◉ editor@stridebooks.co.uk

ⓦ www.stridebooks.co.uk

**Contact** Managing Editor, Rupert Loydell

**Established** 1982

**Insider Info** Payment is either via royalties or free copies. Catalogue and manuscript guidelines available online.

**Non-Fiction** Publishes Booklets, Magazines and Scholarly titles on the following subjects:
Literary Criticism, Music/Dance, Reviews/Interviews and Anthologies.

**Fiction** Publishes Experimental and Mainstream/Contemporary titles.
* Stride are interested in linguistically innovative as well as more traditional works, specialising in genres that re-invent the way we see the world.

**Poetry** Publishes Contemporary and Traditional Poetry titles.

**Recent Title(s)** *The Glass Cottage*, Peter Redgrove and Penelope Shuttle (Novel); *The Allotment. New Lyric Poets*, Andy Brown ed. (Collection)

**Tips** Stride expect prospective authors to have been published in reputable magazines, and to be involved in promoting their own work.

## Studymates

**PO Box 225, Abergele, Conwy County, LL18 9AY**

☎ 01745 832863

☎ 01745 826606

✉ info@studymates.co.uk

🌐 www.studymates.co.uk

**Contact** Managing Editor, Graham Lawler (Education from 14 plus to postgraduate); Senior Editor, Edward James (Writer's Guides)

**Established** 1999

**Insider Info** Publishes 20 titles per year. Receives approximately 200 queries and 50 manuscripts per year. 25 per cent of books published are from first-time authors and 95 per cent are from unagented authors. Payment is via royalty (on wholesale price) with 0.37 (per £) minimum and 0.5 (per £) maximum. Advance offered is from £150. Average lead time is 12 months with simultaneous submissions not accepted. Submissions accompanied by SAE will be returned. Aims to respond to queries within one day, proposals within five days, and manuscripts within 21 days. Catalogue is free on request, via an A5 SAE with two first class stamps, online, or via email. Manuscript guidelines free on request with an A5 SAE or email.

**Non-Fiction** Publish Scholarly and Textbook titles on the following subjects:
Agriculture/Horticulture, Business/Economics, Education, History, Humanities, Language/Literature, Literary Criticism, Marine Subjects, Military/War, Religion, Science, Social Sciences, Translation.
* All authors must be or have been recently teaching the subject of their book and have been successfully published in their genre. We also publish writer's guides.

**Submission Guidelines** Accepts query with SAE, or via email, (including author biography). Will review artworks/images (send photocopies or digital files as jpegs).
Submission details to: info@studymates.co.uk

**Recent Title(s)** *Your Masters Thesis*, Dr Alan Bond (Postgraduate)

**Tips** Titles aimed at postgraduates studying for a masters degree. Look carefully at the list and make sure you understand the type of books published. If you know the list and can see a gap, then send a letter with SAE in the first instance outlining your expertise. Do not send full manuscripts as they will be returned unopened.

## Summersdale Publishers Ltd

**46 West Street, Chichester, West Sussex, PO19 1RP**

☎ 01243 771107

☎ 01243 786300

✉ enquiries@summersdale.com

🌐 www.summersdale.com

**Contact** Commissioning Editor, Jennifer Barclay (Non Fiction)

**Established** 1990

**Insider Info** Publish 75 titles per year. Receive approximately 2,000 queries and 500 manuscripts per year. 50 per cent of books published are from first-time authors and 50 per cent are from unagented authors. Payment is via royalty (on wholesale price) or outright purchase. Average lead time is 12 months with simultaneous submissions accepted. Submissions accompanied by SAE will be returned. Aims to respond to queries and proposals within four weeks and manuscripts within 12 weeks. Catalogue available online, via email or via A4 SAE with one first class stamp. Manuscript guidelines available online.

**Non-Fiction** Publishes General Non-fiction, Gift, How-to, Humour and Self-help titles on the following subjects:
Health/Medicine, History, House and Home, Military/War, Sports, Martial Arts, Travel.
* All the latest editorial requirements are published on the website.

**Submission Guidelines** Accepts query with SAE, or via email, with proposal package (including outline, three sample chapters, your publishing history, author biography, SAE). Will review artworks/images (send digital files as jpegs).
Submission details to: submissions@summersdale.com

**Fiction** Publish Erotica and Crime titles.

**Submission Guidelines** Accepts query with SAE, or via email, with proposal package (including outline, three sample chapters). Also accepts completed manuscripts.
Submission details to: submissions@summersdale.com

**Recent Title(s)** *A Chateau of One's Own - Restoration Misadventures in France*, Sam Juneau (Travel)

**Tips** Titles aimed at a general readership. Happy to consider writers without agents.

## Summertown Publishing

**29 Grove Street, Summertown, Oxford, OX2 7JT**

☎ 01865 454130

☎ 01865 454131

✉ info@summertown.co.uk

🌐 www.summertown.co.uk

**Contact** Managing Director, Louis Garnade

**Established** 1998

**Insider Info** Catalogue available online.

**Non-Fiction** Publishes Reference, Scholarly and Textbook titles on the following subjects:
Child Guidance/Parenting, Education, Language/Literature and Teaching resources.

* Summertown Publishing is a specialist language learning publisher for professional and business English, producing textbooks and reference guides for education and business markets.

**Recent Title(s)** *Success With BULATS*, Summertown Publishing

**Tips** Summertown Publishing relies on a team of practising teachers who aim to provide solutions to the problems many teachers face in everyday classroom situations. Therefore, any proposals should be reinforced with academic experience.

## Sunflower Books

**12 Kendrick Mews, London, SW7 3HG**

- mail@sunflowerbooks.co.uk
- www.sunflowerbooks.co.uk

**Parent Company** P A Underwood Ltd

**Contact** Joint Managing Director, Patricia Underwood (Travel, Walking Guides)

**Established** 1982

**Insider Info** Publishes 12 titles per year. Receives approximately 50–60 queries per year and 20 manuscripts. 50 per cent of books published are from first-time authors and 100 per cent are from unagented authors. Payment is via royalty (on wholesale price) by arrangement. The advance offered is undisclosed. Average lead time is four months, with simultaneous submissions not accepted. Submissions accompanied by SAE will not be returned. Aims to respond to queries within three days and proposals within 14 days. Catalogue is free on request. Manuscript guidelines are available online.

**Non-Fiction** Publish Illustrated and Guidebook titles on Travel and Walking.

* All publications have to match an existing style, extent and format, therefore no unsolicited manuscripts can be accepted.

**Submission Guidelines** Accepts proposal package (including outline). Will review artworks/images (send digital files as jpegs).
Submission details to: mail@sunflowerbooks.co.uk

**Tips** Authors submitting proposals should study existing publications, check which destinations are already covered and focus on regions with which they are 100 per cent familiar - no 'armchair-researched' books will be considered.

## Superscript

**The Publishing House, 404 Robin Square, Newtown, Powys, SY16 1HP**

- 01686 610883
- drjbford@yahoo.co.uk
- www.dubsolution.org

**Contact** Prof. Ray Pahl (Social Sciences, Politics, Community); Prof. Bernard Burgoyne (Lacanian Analysis Mathematics, Logic, Philosophy); Dr. Bronwen Martin (Semiotics, Literary Fiction); Prof. Geoff Dench (Community Studies, Family); Paul Binding (Literary Fiction, Biography, Poetry); Dr. Julie Ford (Revolution, Deontology, Epistemology, Education)

**Established** 2002

**Insider Info** Publish four titles per year. Receives approximately 85 queries and ten manuscripts per year. Ten per cent of books published are from first-time authors, 100 per cent are from unagented authors and 20 per cent are author subsidy published. These are decided by a system where each title is assessed by the Editorial Board who vote on three ways forward: will not publish, will subsidy publish, or will publish traditionally. The eight members base their decision on the proposal and the comparative state of the company's and author's finances at the time the contract is negotiated. Payment is via royalty (on retail price) with 0.1 (per £) standard. Average lead time is nine months, with simultaneous submissions accepted. Submissions accompanied by SAE will be returned. Aims to respond to queries within two days, proposals within five days, and manuscripts within 21 days. Catalogue is free on request. Manuscript guidelines are available via email.

**Non-Fiction** Publish Biography, Illustrated and Scholarly titles on the following subjects:
Alternative Lifestyles, Community/Public Affairs, Contemporary Culture, Government/Politics, History, Humanities, Multicultural, Nature/Environment, Philosophy, Psychology, Religion, Social Sciences, Sociology, Spirituality and World Affairs.

* Books are para-academic in that, while not academic books, they are intended mainly for academics, students and other 'bookish' readers. All books are required to include an appropriate bibliography.

**Submission Guidelines** Accepts query with SAE, or via email, with proposal package (including outline, two sample chapters, contents page, your publishing history, author biography, SAE). Will not review artworks/images.

**Fiction** Publish Ethnic, Experimental, Historical, Literary, Mainstream/Contemporary, Multicultural,

Mystery, Science Fiction, Suspense, Political (no emotional subjectivism), Faction - 20th Century (must be 'progressive'), Spy Fiction.

  * Books should not include racism, sexism or vengeance as themes. The question must be asked of all proposals: 'What is the point of this book?'

**Submission Guidelines** Accepts query with SAE or via email.

**Poetry** Publishes Poetry titles.

**Submission Guidelines** Accepts query with SAE or via email.

**Recent Title(s)** *Last of the Guardians*, David Donnison (Biography and Autobiography); *Heads We Win*, Amy Gdala (Documentary Fiction about Surveillance)

**Tips** Titles are aimed at a readership that is university educated and/or streetwise. Potential authors should realise the company aims to spread excellent ideas, not to make writers famous or rich.

## Sussex Academic Press
**PO Box 139, Eastbourne, East Sussex, BN24 9BP**
- 01323 479220
- edit@sussex-academic.co.uk
- www.sussex-academic.co.uk

**Contact** Editorial Director, Anthony V.P. Grahame
**Established** 1994
**Imprint(s)** Alpha Press
**Insider Info** Publishes 40 titles per year. Payment is via royalties. Catalogue available free on request and online. Manuscript guidelines available online.
**Non-Fiction** Publishes Reference and Scholarly titles.

  * Publishes for the international academic community and promotes the publication of outstanding works of learning and scholarship to a global audience. Books cover all academic subject disciplines, from original research to scholarly reference. The Press continues to commission actively, and new proposals are always welcome.

**Submission Guidelines** A 'Book proposal form' can be downloaded from the Press website by clicking on the 'Authors' section.
**Recent Title(s)** *Labour and the Press*, 1972–2005 (Sean Tunney)
**Tips** All books submitted to the Press are refereed by external advisers.

## Sutton Publishing
**Phoenix Mill, Thrupp, Stroud, Gloucestershire, GL5 2BU**
- 01453 731114
- 01453 731117

- publishing@sutton-publishing.co.uk
- www.suttonpublishing.co.uk

**Contact** Managing Director, Jeremy Yates-Round; Senior Commissioning Editor, Jonathan Falconer (Military History); Senior Commissioning Editor, Christopher Feeney (General History); Senior Commissioning Editor, Simon Fletcher (Local History); Senior Commissioning Editor; Jaqueline Mitchell (Biography)
**Established** 1979
**Insider Info** Publishes 200 titles per year. Payment is via royalties. Catalogue and manuscript guidelines available online.
**Non-Fiction** Publishes Autobiography, Biography, General Non-fiction, Illustrated, Reference and Scholarly titles on the following subjects: Agriculture/Horticulture, Anthropology/Archaeology, History, Hobbies, Military/War, Photography, Regional and Transportation.

  * Publish both academic and trade titles on topics such as military, aviation, naval, transport, pre-history and modern biography. However, the company's core focus remains in 'local interest' books.

**Submission Guidelines** Accepts query with SAE/proposal package (including outline, two to three sample chapters, your publishing history and author biography).
**Recent Title(s)** *Battles for the Three Kingdoms*, John Barratt (History)
**Tips** Many of Sutton's books are illustrated and generally it is the author's responsibility to provide illustrations. Writers should investigate illustrations, cost and copyright prior to making contact. No proposals will be accepted via email.

## Swan Hill Press
**Wykey House, Wykey, Shrewsbury, Shropshire, SY4 1JA**
- 01939 261616
- 01939 261606
- admin@quillerbooks.com, john@beaton.org.uk
- www.countrybooksdirect.com

**Parent Company** Quiller Publishing Ltd
**Contact** Managing Director, Andrew Johnston; Editorial Director, John Beaton (Equestrianism)
**Insider Info** Publishes 15 titles per year. Ten per cent of books published are from first-time authors, 95 per cent are from unagented authors and approximately five per cent are author subsidy published. Payment is via royalties (on wholesale price and on retail price). Average lead time is two months with simultaneous submissions accepted. Submissions accompanied by SAE will be returned.

Catalogue available free on request, online and via email.

**Non-Fiction** Publishes Coffee table and General Non-fiction titles on the following subjects: Countryside Pursuits, Shooting and Fishing.

**Submission Guidelines** Accepts proposal package (including outline, sample chapter(s), your publishing history, author biography and SAE).

**Tips** Accepts postal submissions only. No novels or poetry titles will be considered.

## Sweet & Maxwell Group

**100 Avenue Road, Swiss Cottage, London, NW3 3PF**

☎ 020 7393 7000

✆ 020 7393 7020

✉ sweetandmaxwell.customer.services@thomson.com

🌐 www.sweetandmaxwell.co.uk

**Contact** Managing Director, Peter Lake; Editorial Manager, Linda Casbolt (Aviation, Banking, Construction, Entertainment and Media, Insurance Law); Editorial Manager, Tania Quan (Company Law/Legal, International Law, IT); Editorial Manager, Victoria Giblin (Academic)

**Established** 1799

**Imprint(s)** W. Green
Round Hall

**Insider Info** Publishes 200 titles per year. Payment is via royalties. Catalogue and manuscript guidelines available online.

**Non-Fiction** Publishes Multimedia, Reference, Scholarly and Technical titles on Law.

 * Sweet & Maxwell publishes in a variety of media for law students and legal and regulatory professionals. Products include books, journals, periodicals, looseleafs, CD-ROMs and online services. There are no plans to publish in any areas other than law and the legal system.

**Submission Guidelines** Accepts query with SAE/proposal package (including outline and author biography).

 Submission details to: firstname.lastname@thomson.com

**Recent Title(s)** *Archbold: Criminal Pleading, Evidence and Practice,* James Richardson (ed.)

**Tips** Sweet & Maxwell Group will consider proposals, but will not accept complete manuscripts with the proposal package. The website lists relevant managers and their interests to enable a more targeted submission.

## T&D Poyser

**38 Soho Square, London, W1D 3HB**

☎ 020 7758 0200

✆ 020 7758 0222

✉ ornithology@acblack.com

🌐 www.acblack.com

**Parent Company** A & C Black Publishers Ltd

**Contact** Department Head, Nigel Redman; Publishing Director, Jonathan Glasspool (Reference, Theatre and Ornithology)

**Established** 1973

**Insider Info** Catalogue available online.

**Non-Fiction** Publishes General Non-fiction, Illustrated and Reference titles on the following subjects: Nature/Environment and Natural History.

**Recent Title(s)** *The Migration Atlas*, Chris Wernham, Mike Toms, John Marchant, Jacquie Clark, Gavin Siriwardena and Stephen Baillie eds. (Ornithology)

**Tips** T & D Poyser publishes a range of ornithology and natural history titles for a general readership, specialising in ornithological atlases and natural history reference material.

## T&T Clark

**The Tower Building, 11 York Road, London, SE1 7NX**

☎ 020 7922 0880

✆ 020 7922 0881

✉ tkraft@continuumbooks.com

🌐 www.continuumbooks.com

**Parent Company** The Continuum International Publishing Group

**Contact** Associate Publisher, Thomas Kraft (Theology); Senior Editor, Haaris Naqvi (Biblical Studies and Philosophy of Religion); Editorial Assistant, Dominic Mattos

**Established** 1821

**Insider Info** Catalogue and manuscript guidelines are available online.

**Non-Fiction** Publishes Reference and Scholarly titles on the following subjects: Biblical Studies, Theology and Church History.

**Submission Guidelines** Accepts proposal package (including outline, one sample chapter, your publishing history, published clips, author biography and market research).

**Tips** In 2003, the three religious academic imprints of Sheffield Academic Press, Trinity Press International and T&T Clark were united under one imprint. Today T&T Clark represents one of the most extensive collections of religious academic books in the world.

For detailed submission guidelines, see the company website.

## Tamarind Ltd

**PO Box 52, Northwood, Middlesex, HA6 1UN**

- 020 886 68808
- 020 886 65627
- contact@tamarindbooks.co.uk
- www.tamarindbooks.co.uk

**Contact** Managing Editor, Verna Allette Wilkins

**Established** 1987

**Insider Info** Catalogue is available free on request, online, or via email to: catalogues@tamarindbooks.co.uk

**Non-Fiction** Publishes Children's and Illustrated titles on the following subjects:
Education, Ethnic and Multicultural.

**Fiction** Publishes Children's and Picture book titles.

**Recent Title(s)** *The Life of Stephen Lawrence*, Verna Allette Wilkins (Biography)

**Tips** Tamarind publishes multicultural children's books for a multicultural world. Both fiction and non-fiction, books are typically picture books with an age range of 2–12 years. Books are published for both the trade and educational markets, and scope exists for teaching reference material or classroom aids promoting a positive multicultural image.

## Tango Books Ltd

**PO Box 32595, London, W4 5YD**

- 020 8996 9970
- 020 8996 9977
- sales@tangobooks.co.uk
- www.tangobooks.co.uk

**Contact** Director, Sheri Safran (Children's Fiction, Non-Fiction)

**Established** 1982

**Insider Info** Publishes 20 titles per year. Receives approximately 500 queries and 200 manuscripts per year. 80 per cent of books published are from first-time authors and 90 per cent are from unagented authors. Payment is via royalty (on retail price) or via outright purchase. Average lead time is nine moths with simultaneous submissions accepted. Submissions accompanied by SAE will be returned. Aims to respond to queries within 14 days, proposals within 21 days and manuscripts within 30 days. Catalogue is available free on request and online. Manuscript guidelines are free on request, and available online or via email.

**Non-Fiction** Publishes Children's titles on a wide variety of subjects.

* Books must be suitable for quality novelty book publication.

**Submission Guidelines** Accepts query with SAE or via email. Will accept artworks/images (send digital files as jpegs).
Submission details to: sales@tangobooks.co.uk

**Fiction** Publishes Novelty titles.

* No poetry or rhyming stories. Strong stories are the most important element, novelty elements can be created at a later stage if the book lends itself to them.

**Submission Guidelines** Accepts query with SAE or via email. Also accepts completed manuscripts.
Submission details to: sales@tangobooks.co.uk

**Tips** Titles aimed at children aged 0–12 years, as well as schools and specialist markets (particularly in diverse and multicultural areas).

## Tanoshimi

**Random House, 20 Vauxhall Bridge Road, London, SW1V 2SA**

- 020 7840 8400
- 020 7233 8719
- info@tanoshimi.tv
- www.randomhouse.co.uk/tanoshimi

**Parent Company** The Random House Group Ltd

**Insider Info** Catalogue available online (to search the catalogues of individual imprints go to 'advanced search').

**Fiction** Publishes Illustrated Manga Fiction titles.

**Recent Title(s)** *Baselisk Volume 1*, Masaki Segawa; *Air Gear Volume 3*, Oh! Great

**Tips** Titles aimed at Manga fanatics and artists.

## Tarquin Publications

**99 Hatfield Road, St Albans, Hertfordshire, AL1 4JL**

- 01727 833866
- 0845 456 6385
- info@tarquinbooks.com
- www.tarquinbooks.com

**Contact** Managing Editor, Andrew Griffin

**Established** 1970

**Insider Info** Publishes five titles per year. Payment is via royalties. Catalogue available free on request and online.

**Non-Fiction** Publishes Multimedia and Scholarly titles on the following subjects:
Crafts, Hobbies and Paper Engineering.

* Publish a series of books about Paper Engineering, Science, Optical Illusions, Mirror Reflections, Costume and History, alongside do-it-yourself pop-

up books and collections of colourful mobiles and gift boxes.

**Submission Guidelines** Accepts query with SAE/proposal package (including outline).

**Recent Title(s)** *A Handbook of Paper Automata Mechanisms*, Walter Ruffler

**Tips** Tarquin specialise in papercraft and modelling, but will consider publishing in other areas if there is a strong connection to papercraft.

## Tartarus Press
**Coverley House, Carlton, Leyburn, North Yorkshire, DL8 4AY**
- 01969 640399
- 01969 640399
- tartarus@pavilion.co.uk
- www.tartaruspress.com

**Contact** Manager, Raymond Russell; Editor, Rosalie Parker

**Established** 1987

**Insider Info** Publishes 12 titles per year. Catalogue and manuscript guidelines available online.

**Fiction** Publishes titles on Fantasy, Gothic, Horror, Mystery, the Occult, and the Supernatural.

 * Tartarus Press is a small, independent publishing house, specialising in short stories, fiction, and reprints of classic supernatural fiction. Titles cross various genres and are often of an unusual nature, meaning that they may have been overlooked by mainstream publishers. All evoke a sense of wonder at the supernatural, in well written prose.

**Submission Guidelines** Accepts query via email with a synopsis.

**Recent Title(s)** *The Man Who Could Work Miracles*, H.G. Wells (Collection)

**Tips** Authors or editors who wish to submit a typescript should make sure that the subject matter of the book is relevant before emailing a synopsis. The manuscript, or a sample of it, may then be requested.

## Taschen UK
**5th Floor, 1 Heathcock Court, 415 Strand, London, WC2R 0NS**
- 020 7845 8585
- 020 7836 3696
- contact-uk@taschen.com
- www.taschen.com

**Insider Info** Catalogue available free on request and online.

**Non-Fiction** Publishes Autobiography, Biography, General Non-fiction and Illustrated titles on the following subjects:

Art/Architecture and Photography.

 * TASCHEN UK is an office of the German publisher TASCHEN, who publish very modern and contemporary books on artistic subjects.

**Recent Title(s)** *Peter Beard, Art Edition (No. 251-2500)*, Nejma Beard and David Fahey eds. (Art/Photography)

**Tips** Taschen's editorial offices are located in Germany at the main Taschenoffice. Any editorial queries must be sent to the main office at: Hohenzollernring 53, D–50672 Köln, Deutschland.

## Tate Publishing
**Millbank, London, SW1P 4RG**
- 020 7887 8869
- 020 788 78878
- tp.enquiries@tate.org.uk
- www.tate.org.uk/publishing/

**Contact** Publishing Director, Roger Thorpe

**Established** 1932

**Insider Info** Catalogue available online.

**Non-Fiction** Publishes General Non-fiction, Illustrated, Multimedia, Reference, Catalogues and Scholarly titles on the following subjects:
Art/Architecture and History.

 * As well as producing exhibition catalogues from exhibitions, Tate galleries also publish a number of series on different aspects of art and art history. The series are often looking for material from established academics.

**Recent Title(s)** *Jake and Dinos Chapman: Bad Art for Bad People,* Christoph Grunenberg

**Tips** Tate Publishing is one of the world's leading publishers on the visual arts, aiming to bring the best new writing on art and the highest quality reproductions to the widest possible range of readers. Authors are likely to be experts in the fields of art and art history.

## Taylor & Francis Group
**2 Park Square, Milton Park, Abingdon, Oxfordshire, OX14 4RN**
- 020 7017 6000
- 020 7017 6699
- tf.enquiries@tfinforma.com
- www.taylorandfrancis.com

**Parent Company** T&F Informa Plc

**Contact** CEO, Roger Horton

**Established** 1936

**Imprint(s)** Taylor & Francis
CRC Press
Garland Science
Psychology Press

Routledge

**Insider Info** Publishes 1,800 titles per year, and 1,000 journals per year. Catalogue and manuscript guidelines are available online.

**Non-Fiction** Publishes Multimedia, Reference, Scholarly, Technical and Textbook titles.

 * Imprints under the Taylor & Francis Group publish academic titles in a broad range of science and humanities subject areas, from Biotechnology to Ergonomics, Earth Sciences, Physical Sciences, Psychology and Social Studies.

**Submission Guidelines** Accepts proposal package (including outline, synopsis, one to two sample chapters, market research and CV).

**Tips** Taylor & Francis Group is the academic publishing division of T&F Informa Plc (formerly Informa Plc). Taylor & Francis mainly publishes at university level and readership includes researchers, students, academics and increasingly, professionals. See the individual imprint entries for more details.

## Taylor & Francis

**2 Park Square, Milton Park, Abingdon, Oxfordshire, OX14 4RN**

- 020 7017 6000
- 020 7017 6699
- tf.enquiries@tfinforma.com
- www.taylorandfrancis.com

**Parent Company** Taylor & Francis Group

**Contact** CEO, Roger Horton

**Established** 1936

**Insider Info** Catalogue and manuscript guidelines are available online.

**Non-Fiction** Publishes Multimedia, Reference, Scholarly, Technical and Textbook titles on the following subjects:
 Biotechnology, Built Environment, Engineering, Ergonomics, Geographical Information Systems, Medicine, Science.

**Submission Guidelines** Accepts proposal package (including outline, synopsis, one to two sample chapters, market research and CV).

**Recent Title(s)** *Microbial Bionanotechnology: Biological Self-Assembly Systems and Biopolymer-Based Nanostructures,* Bernd Rehm (Biotechnology)

**Tips** Taylor & Francis is best known for its scientific and reference books, they specialise in niche areas such as biotechnology and ergonomics. Taylor & Francis now includes the former imprints Martin Dunitz and Spon Press.

## Telegram Books

**26 Westbourne Grove, London, W2 5RH**

- 020 722 92911
- 020 722 97492
- info@telegrambooks.com
- www.telegrambooks.com

**Contact** Publisher, André Gaspard; Director, Mai Ghoussoub; Commissioning Editor, Rebecca O'Connor

**Established** 2005

**Insider Info** Aims to respond to proposals and manuscripts within ten weeks. Catalogue is free on request and available online or via email to catalogues@telegrambooks.com. Manuscript guidelines are available online.

**Fiction** Publishes Mainstream/Contemporary, Short story collections, Translation, and International fiction titles.

**Submission Guidelines** Accepts query with SAE, or via email, with proposal package (including outline and two sample chapters).
 Submission details to: rebecca@telegrambooks.com

**Recent Title(s)** *No Word From Gurb,* Eduardo Mendoza

**Tips** Telegram Books publish the best in new international writing, in the areas of fiction and literary memoir. Before submitting a proposal, take time to browse the website to get an idea of current tastes, which are for high quality international fiction of some sophistication. Work should match the appropriate standards and offer broad general appeal.

## Telegraph Books

**1 Canada Square, Canary Wharf, London, E14 5DT**

- 020 7538 6826
- 020 7538 6064
- support@books.telegraph.co.uk
- www.telegraphbooksdirect.co.uk

**Parent Company** Telegraph Group Ltd

**Contact** Publisher, Morven Knowles

**Established** 1920

**Insider Info** Publishes 50 titles per year. Payment is via royalties. Catalogue available online.

**Non-Fiction** Publishes Biography, General Non-fiction, Humour, Multimedia and Scholarly titles on the following subjects:
 Business/Economics, Cooking/Foods/Nutrition, Gardening, History, House and Home, Language/Literature, Law, Science, Sports, and Travel.

**Recent Title(s)** *Change in the Weather,* Philip Eden

**Tips** Telegraph Books primarily publishes books under the Telegraph newspaper name, but also offers bookselling services to other publishers. Books published at Telegraph Books will usually have some kind of link to the Telegraph newspaper.

## Templar Publishing

**Pippbrook Mill, London Road, Dorking, RH4 1JE**
- 01306 876361
- info@templarco.co.uk
- www.templarpublishing.co.uk

**Contact** Senior Editor, Dugald A. Steer
**Insider Info** Catalogue available online.
**Non-Fiction** Publishes Children's/Juvenile, Illustrated and Multimedia titles.
 * Templar publishes illustrated and interactive books for children of all ages, including the hugely successful *Ologies* series.
**Fiction** Publishes Children's, Multimedia and Picture titles.
 * Many of Templar's books have interactive elements such as puppets, pop-outs and unconventional design.
**Recent Title(s)** *Pirateology*, Dugald Steer
**Tips** Virtually all of Templar's books are highly illustrated or interactive in some way, and many are concept driven. For prospective authors, a background in art and design would be helpful.

## Temple Lodge Publishing

**Hillside House, The Square, Forest Row, East Sussex, RH18 5ES**
- 01342 824000
- 01342 824367
- office@templelodge.com
- www.templelodge.com

**Imprint(s)** Clairview Books
**Insider Info** Catalogue is available online or by email through an online form.
**Non-Fiction** Publishes Biography, Reference, Illustrated and Self-help titles on the following subjects:
 Esoteric Studies, Spirituality, Parent and Child, Mind, Body and Spirit.
**Fiction** Publishes some children's fiction.
**Recent Title(s)** *The New Experience of the Supersensible*, Jesaiah Ben-Aharon (Spiritual-Scientific); *Patter-Paws the Fox and Other Stories*, Brien Masters (Early Reader)

## Tempus Publishing Ltd

**The Mill, Brimscombe Port, Stroud, Gloucestershire, GL5 2QG**
- 01453 883300
- 01453 883233
- info@tempus-publishing.com
- www.tempus-publishing.com

**Parent Company** MPI Media
**Established** 1993
**Non-Fiction** Publishes General Non-fiction titles on Anthropology/Archaeology, Art/Architecture, Creative Non-fiction, History, Language/Literature, Recreation, Regional, Sociology, Sports, Transportation and Travel.
**Submission Guidelines** Accepts book proposals via email.
 Submission details to: submissions@tempus-publishing.com
**Tips** Tempus Publishing are specialists in local history that have branched out into other non-fiction areas, largely in historical or nostalgia genres.

## Thalamus Publishing

**4 Attorney's Walk, Bull Ring, Ludlow, Shropshire, SY8 1AA**
- 01584 874977
- 01584 872125
- sales@thalamus-books.com
- www.thalamus-books.com

**Parent Company** International Media Solutions Ltd
**Contact** Oliver Frey
**Insider Info** Catalogue available online.
**Non-Fiction** Publishes General Non-fiction, Illustrated, Reference and Scholarly titles on the following subjects:
 Art/Architecture, Entertainment/Games, History, Science, Fantasy Art, Pet Care, Aviation, Space Exploration and Knot Tying.
 * The majority of the publishing output is comprised of illustrated historical reference titles.
**Recent Title(s)** *Pirates – Predators of the Seas*, Angus Konstam with Roger Michael Kean
**Tips** Titles tend to originate from in-house interests, or are started by specific requests from foreign publishing partners.

## Thames & Hudson

**181a High Holborn, London, WC1V 7QX**
- 020 7845 5000
- 020 7845 5050
- editorial@thameshudson.co.uk
- www.thameshudson.co.uk

**Contact** Chairman, Thomas Neurath; Deputy Chairman, Constance Kaine; Managing Director, Jamie Camplin

**Established** 1949

**Insider Info** Publishes 180 titles per year. Book catalogue and manuscript guidelines available online.

**Non-Fiction** Publishes Autobiography, Biography, Coffee Table, General Non-fiction, Gift, Illustrated, Multimedia and Reference titles on the following subjects:
Anthropology/Archaeology, Art/Architecture, Contemporary Culture, Ethnic, Gardening, History, Language/Literature, Music/Dance, Nature/Environment, Philosophy, Photography, Regional, Religion, Science, Travel, Fashion, Calendars.

**Submission Guidelines** Accepts a brief proposal and CV via email (with no attachments).
Submission details to: editorial@thameshudson.co.uk

**Recent Title(s)** *Turner in his Time*, Andrew Wilton (Art)

**Tips** One of the company's best known ventures is its *World of Art* series which currently has well over 200 titles. Do not send submissions by post and do not submit fiction or children's books.

## Think Books
**Pall Mall Deposit, Barlby Road, London, W10 6BL**
- 020 8962 3020
- 020 8962 8689
- emma@thinkpublishing.co.uk
- www.think-books.com

**Parent Company** Pan Macmillan Publishers

**Contact** Publisher, Emma Jones

**Established** 1999

**Insider Info** Publishes 16 titles per year. Receives approximately 50 queries and 20 manuscripts per year. 25 per cent of books published are from first-time authors and 80 per cent of books published are from unagented authors. Payment is via outright purchase. Average lead time is two months. Submissions will not be returned. Aims to respond to queries within five days and proposals within 14 days. Catalogue is free on request, and available online. Author guidelines are not available.

**Non-Fiction** Publishes Coffee Table, General Non-fiction, Gift, Illustrated and Reference titles on the following subjects:
Animals, Cooking/Foods/Nutrition, Gardening, History, Nature/Environment, Travel.

**Submission Guidelines** Accepts proposal packages (including outline, your publishing history, author biography) and artworks/images.

Submission details to: emma@thinkpublishing.co.uk

**Recent Title(s)** *A Portrait of England; Wildlife Gardening for Everyone*

**Tips** On February 1st 2007, Think Books became an imprint of Pan Macmillan within the non-fiction division. Future books will be created in partnership between Pan Macmillan and Think Books, but will be published by Pan Macmillan. The submission guidelines in this entry were collected from Think Books before that takeover, therefore any writers interested in submitting should contact Pan Macmillan for their latest policies.

## Third Millennium Information
**2–5 Benjamin Street, London, EC1M 5QL**
- 020 7608 1800
- 020 7608 1188
- info@tmiltd.com
- www.tmiltd.com

**Contact** Managing Director, Julian Platt

**Established** 1999

**Insider Info** Publishes 15 titles per year. Payment is via royalties. Catalogue available free on request, online.

**Non-Fiction** Publishes Coffee table books, General Non-fiction, Illustrated books, Multimedia, Catalogues/Guidebooks and Magazines/Newsletters.

**Recent Title(s)** *imagine yesterday ... today*, Henrietta Van den Bergh and Helen Fickling (Photography).

**Tips** Work mainly with cultural and educational institutions in the museum, heritage and art gallery markets. Products include exceptionally beautiful illustrated books, catalogues/guidebooks, magazines/newsletters, bespoke merchandise and a variety of multimedia support activities. Mainly produces illustrated titles and multimedia for the heritage and education communities, and offers a wide range of contract publishing services. Unsolicited proposals are welcome providing they are supported by in-depth market research.

## Thoemmes Continuum
**The Tower Building, 11 York Road, London, SE1 7NX**
- 020 7922 0880
- 020 7922 0881
- evander@continuum-books.com
- www.continuumbooks.com

**Parent Company** The Continuum International Publishing Group

**Contact** Vice President and Senior Editor, Evander Lomke; Managing Editor, Merilyn Holm

**Established** 1989

**Insider Info** Catalogue and manuscript guidelines are available online.

**Non-Fiction** Publishes Bibliography, Dictionary, Encyclopedia, Reference and Scholarly titles on the following subjects:

Antiques, Biographical Dictionaries, Intellectual History, Philosophy.

**Submission Guidelines** Accepts proposal package (including outline, your publishing history, author biography and market research).

**Recent Title(s)** *Dictionary of Modern American Philosophers*, Thoemmes Continuum (Biographical Dictionary)

**Tips** Thoemmes specialises in philosophy and is well known for its biographical dictionaries. For detailed submission information and a list of editorial contacts see the company website.

## Thomas Cook Publishing
**Unit 18 Coningsby Road, Peterborough, PE3 8SB**
- 01733 416477
- 01733 416688
- publishing-sales@thomascook.com
- www.thomascookpublishing.com

**Established** 1873

**Insider Info** Publishes 165 titles per year. Payment is via outright purchase.

**Non-Fiction** Publishes General Non-Fiction and Illustrated titles on the following subjects:

Travel Guides, Holidays, Maps, Timetables, City Guides.

**Recent Title(s)** *Barcelona* (City Guide); *Out Around: London* (Guide to the Gay Scene)

## Thomson Learning Europe, Middle East and Africa (EMEA)
**High Holborn House, 50–51 Bedford Row, London, WC1R 4LR**
- 020 7067 2500
- 020 7067 2600
- Online email form
- http://hed.thomsonlearning.co.uk/

**Imprint(s)** Arden Shakespeare

**Insider Info** Catalogue available online. Proposal guidelines and manuscript preparation, as well as a list of areas where Thomson Learning are actively seeking texts, are available on the website under 'Authors'.

**Non-Fiction** Publishes Multimedia, Reference, Scholarly, Technical and Textbook titles on the following subjects:

Business, Accounting, Economics, Psychology, Hair and Beauty, Shakespeare, and other diverse areas.

**Submission Guidelines** Details on website. In the first instance email the editorial department or write to the Publishing Director at the address above.

Submission details to: tlemea.editorial@thomson.com

**Tips** Thomson EMEA publishes for academics, students and professionals in higher and further education. Thomson Learning serves secondary, post-secondary and graduate level students, teachers, librarians and learning institutions in both traditional and distance-learning environments.

## Time Out Guides Ltd
**Random House, 20 Vauxhall Bridge Road, London, SW1V 2SA**
- 020 7840 8400
- 020 7840 8791
- www.randomhouse.co.uk

**Parent Company** The Random House Group Ltd

**Insider Info** Catalogue available online.

**Non-Fiction** Publishes City guides.

**Recent Title(s)** *Time Out Paris - Eating & Drinking*, 8th Edition

**Tips** The imprint solely publishes *Time Out Guides* and no other travel writing.

See Random House Group entry for more information

## Timewell Press
**10 Porchester Terrace, London, W2 3TL**
- 0870 760 5250
- 0870 760 5250
- info@timewellpress.com
- www.timewellpress.com

**Contact** Andreas Campomar

**Insider Info** Catalogue available online.

**Non-Fiction** Publishes Autobiography, Biography and General Non-fiction titles on the following subjects:

Business/Economics, Contemporary Culture, Government/Politics, History, Regional.

**Fiction** Publishes Literary and Mainstream/Contemporary titles and Short story collections.

**Recent Title(s)** *Returning: Three Novels,* D.J. Taylor

**Tips** Timewell Press is an independent press publishing contemporary non-fiction, including autobiographies of stars such as Leslie Grantham and classic writing such as George Orwell. Timewell Press specialises in contemporary life writing and cultural writing, either concerning current affairs, or popular celebrities. Queries are welcome using the online email form on the website.

## Tindal Street Press Ltd

**217 The Custard Factory, Gibb Street, Birmingham, B9 4AA**

- 0121 773 8157
- 0121 693 5525
- info@tindalstreet.co.uk
- www.tindalstreet.co.uk

**Contact** Managing Editor, Emma Hargrave; Assistant Editor, Luke Brown; Publishing Director, Alan Mahar

**Established** 1998

**Insider Info** Publishes six titles per year. Payment is via royalties. Catalogue and manuscript guidelines available online.

**Fiction** Publishes Mainstream/Contemporary and Regional titles and Short story collections.

**Submission Guidelines** Accepts query with SAE. Submit proposal package (including outline and three sample chapters).

Submission details to: emma@tindalstreet.co.uk

**Recent Title(s)** *Kiss Me Softly, Amy Turtle*, Paul McDonald (Novel)

**Tips** Tindal Street Press provides a national and international platform for talented new writers from the English regions. Strong contemporary novels and short stories make for a varied, appealing list. Tindal Street Press publishes excellent contemporary fiction from the English regions – which means the manuscripts that interest us most have a centre of gravity outside of London and the South-East. We welcome unsolicited manuscripts, but will not consider poetry, children's, teenage, science fiction, fantasy or romance.

## Tír Eolas

**Newtownlynch, Doorus, Kinvara, Co. Galway, Republic of Ireland**

- 00353 91 637452
- 00353 91 637452
- info@tireolas.com
- www.tireolas.com

**Contact** Managing Director, Anne Korff

**Established** 1985

**Insider Info** Payment is via royalties. Catalogue available online.

**Non-Fiction** Publishes General Non-fiction and Illustrated titles on the following subjects: Anthropology/Archaeology, Contemporary Culture, History, Hobbies, Nature/Environment, Walking Guides, Irish Culture/Folklore.

**Submission Guidelines** Accepts query with SAE.

**Recent Title(s)** *The Burren Wall*, Gordon D'Arcy

**Tips** Tír Eolas is an independent publisher specialising in producing books, walking guides and maps that combine text and illustrations to an exceptionally high standard and which provide information on Irish history, archaeology, landscape, culture and tradition. The name Tír Eolas can be literally translated as 'knowledge of the land'. Tir Eolas will consider proposal submissions providing they are accompanied by high quality illustrations and are not scholarly or technical in tone.

## Titan Books

**Titan Books, 144 Southwark Street, London, SE1 0UP**

- 020 7620 0200
- 020 7803 1990
- editorial@titanemail.com
- www.titanbooks.com

**Parent Company** Titan Publishing Group

**Contact** Editorial Director, Katy Wild (Film, Television, Graphic Novels)

**Established** 1981

**Insider Info** Publishes 220 titles per year. Receives approximately 100 queries and 50 manuscripts per year. 15 per cent of books published are from first-time authors. Payment is via royalty (on retail price) or an outright purchase. Simultaneous submissions are accepted. Submissions accompanied by SAE will be returned. Aims to respond in one week to queries, one month to proposals, and three months to manuscripts. Catalogue and author guidelines are free on request.

**Non-Fiction** Publishes Coffee Table, General Non-fiction and Illustrated titles on the following subjects: Entertainment/Games, Media, Film, Television. * We only work with writers who have proven experience and contacts in the field.

**Submission Guidelines** Submit proposal package (including outline, sample chapter(s), author biography, SAE) Will not review artworks/images as part of the manuscript package.

Submission details to: editorial@titanemail.com

**Fiction** Publishes Comic Books.

**Submission Guidelines** Accepts proposal package (including outline, sample chapter(s)).

Submission details to: editorial@titanemail.com

**Recent Title(s)** *24, The Official Companion: Seasons 1 & 2*, Tara DiLullo (Television companion)

**Tips** Titles aimed at film and television fans.

## Top That! Publishing Plc

**Marine House, Tide Mill Way, Woodbridge, Suffolk, IP12 1AP**

- 01394 386651
- 01394 386011
- info@topthatpublishing.com
- www.topthatpublishing.com

**Contact** Managing Director, Barrie Henderson; Creative Director, Simon Couchman

**Established** 1999

**Imprint(s)** Top That! Kids
KUDOS
Tide Mill Press

**Insider info** Catalogue available online.

**Non-Fiction** Publishes Children's/Juvenile, General Non-fiction, Gift, Humour and Illustrated titles on the following subjects:
 Cooking/Foods/Nutrition, Crafts, Creative Non-fiction, Entertainment/Games, Hobbies, House and Home, Sex.

**Fiction** Publishes Children's and Multimedia titles and Picture books.

**Recent Title(s)** *The Country Diary of an Edwardian Lady*, Edith Holden

**Tips** Top That! Publishing Plc is an independent children's book publisher with an international reputation for producing exciting picture and novelty books that challenge and stimulate young minds. The KUDOS imprint publishes craft, entertainment, hobbies, lifestyle and gift books for the adult market. The Imagine That! imprint offers bespoke packaging services to other market leading companies. Most books in the children's ranges are highly illustrated, so it is important to send sample illustrations with any submission.

## Tor

**20 New Wharf Road, London, N1 9RR**

- 020 7014 6000
- 020 7014 6001
- fiction@macmillan.co.uk, nonfiction@macmillan.co.uk
- www.panmacmillan.com

**Parent Company** Pan Macmillan Publishers

**Established** 2003

**Insider Info** Downloadable pdf version of catalogue available online.

**Fiction** Publishes Fantasy and Science Fiction titles.

**Submission Guidelines** Agented submissions only.

**Recent Title(s)** *Polity Agent*, Neal Asher (Science Fiction)

**Tips** No unsolicited submissions. See the Pan Macmillan entry for more information.

## TownHouse Dublin

**Mountpleasant Business Centre, Mountpleasant Avenue, Ranelagh, Dublin 6, Republic of Ireland**

- 00353 1 497 2399
- 00353 1 499 5150
- books@townhouse.ie
- www.townhouse.ie

**Contact** Managing Director/Publisher, Treasa Coady; Editor, Deirdre O Neill; Editor, Marie Heaney (Non-fiction)

**Established** 1980

**Imprint(s)** Simon & Schuster/TownHouse

**Insider Info** Publishes 25 titles per year. Payment via royalties. Aims to respond to proposals and manuscripts within eight weeks. Catalogue and manuscript guidelines available online.

**Non-Fiction** Publishes Biography, General Non-fiction, Illustrated and Reference titles on the following subjects:
 Anthropology/Archaeology, Art/Architecture, Contemporary Culture, Government/Politics, Health/Medicine, History, Language/Literature, Literary Criticism, Memoirs, Music/Dance, Nature/Environment, Photography, Science, Sport, Travel, Genealogy, Irish Folklore.

**Submission Guidelines** Accepts query with SAE. Submit proposal package (including outline, three to four sample chapter(s) and author biography).

**Fiction** Publishes Literary and Mainstream/Contemporary titles.

**Submission Guidelines** Accepts query with SAE/proposal package (including outline, three to four sample chapter(s)).

**Poetry** Publish Poetry titles.

**Recent Title(s)** *Viking Age Dublin*, Ruth Johnson (History)

**Tips** TownHouse has become a leader in the production of high-quality, non-fiction, Irish interest books. The joint venture, Simon & Schuster/TownHouse, publishes fiction from both emerging and established Irish writers and is committed to the ongoing task of publishing great storytelling. Those interested in submitting manuscripts for consideration are invited to send proposals in the form of an outline in the case of non-fiction, or a synopsis in the case of fiction. A short autobiographical note and details of previous publications are also encouraged.

## Transita Ltd

**Spring Hill House, Spring Hill Road, Begbroke, OX5 1RX**

- 01865 375794

01865 379162
info@transita.co.uk
www.transita.co.uk
**Contact** Managing Director, Giles Lewis; Editorial Director, Nikki Read
**Insider Info** Catalogue is available free on request. Manuscript guidelines available online.
**Fiction** Publishes Mainstream/Contemporary titles.
**Submission Guidelines** Submit completed manuscript.
  Submission details to: nikki@transita.co.uk
**Recent Title(s)** *The Crowded Bed*, Mary Cavanagh (Novel)
**Tips** Transita books reflect the lives of mature women; contemporary women with rich and interesting stories to tell, stories that explore the truths and desires that colour their lives. Transita taps into a whole new world of fiction, publishing transformational stories that mirror the lives of women our age. They are looking for contemporary women's fiction that reflects the lives of women aged 45–75 and are seeking what is most relevant to the lives of other women out there who are facing the challenges and opportunities of the exciting, but often difficult later time of life. Please be aware that due to the high volume of submissions received, they do not acknowledge individual manuscripts.

## Transworld Publishers

**61–63 Uxbridge Road, London, W5 5SA**
020 8579 2652
020 8579 5479
info@transworld-publishers.co.uk
www.booksattransworld.co.uk
**Parent Company** The Random House Group Ltd
**Contact** Publisher, Bill Scott-Kerr
**Established** 1950
**Imprint(s)** Bantam Press
  Black Swan
  Channel 4 Books
  Corgi
  Doubleday
**Insider Info** Catalogue available online. Imprints do not have individual websites; for imprint catalogues go to 'search catalogue by imprint'.
**Non-Fiction** Publishes Autobiography, Biography, Coffee table, Cookery, General Non-fiction, Gift, How-to, Humour, Illustrated, Reference and Self-help titles on the following subjects:
  Art/Architecture, Business/Economics, Cooking/ Foods/Nutrition, Gardening, Government/Politics, Health/Medicine, History, Money/Finance, Music/ Dance, Nature/Environment, New Age, Psychology,

Religion, Science, Spirituality, Travel, Television tie-ins.
**Submission Guidelines** Agented submissions only.
**Fiction** Publishes Fantasy, Historical, Horror, Humour, Literary, Mainstream/Contemporary, Mystery, Romance, Science Fiction and Suspense titles.
**Submission Guidelines** Agented submissions only.
**Recent Title(s)** *Astrolove*, Jessica Adams; *Second Honeymoon*, Joanna Trollope
**Tips** Hardbacks are published under Doubleday or Bantam Press. Paperbacks by Black Swan, Bantam and Corgi. Absolutely no unsolicited manuscripts. Transworld Publishers also publishes books for the Eden Project, in Cornwall.

## Travel Publishing Ltd

**7a Apollo House, Calleva Park, Aldermaston, Berkshire, RG7 8TN**
0118 981 7777
0118 982 0077
info@travelpublishing.co.uk
www.travelpublishing.co.uk
**Contact** Director, Chris Day; Director, Peter Robinson
**Established** 1997
**Insider Info** Payment is via royalties. Catalogue is available free on request and online.
**Non-Fiction** Publishes Travel Guides on the following subjects:
  Cooking/Foods/Nutrition, Regional, Travel.
**Tips** Travel Publishing Ltd produce local and national travel guides covering both Britain and Ireland. The travel guides and website database detail many interesting places to visit and explore local heritage and history. They provide a wealth of information on places to stay, eat, drink and shop. The company's major series include *The Hidden Places, The Hidden Inns, Country Living Rural Guides* and *Off the Motorway*. It is best to write for one of these series, rather than writing a stand alone piece.

## Trentham Books Ltd

**Westview House, 734 London Road, Stoke on Trent, ST4 5NP**
01782 745567
01782 745553
tb@trentham-books.co.uk
www.trentham-books.co.uk
**Contact** Editorial Director, Dr. Gillian Klein; Executive Director, Barbara Wiggins
**Established** 1978

**Insider Info** Publishes 30 titles per year. Payment is via royalties. Aims to respond to proposals and manuscripts within one month. Catalogue and manuscript guidelines available online.

**Non-Fiction** Publishes Reference, Scholarly and Technical titles on the following subjects:
Education, Law, Social Sciences, Cultural/Gender Studies.

**Submission Guidelines** Accepts query with SAE. Submit proposal package (including outline, two sample chapters, publishing history and author biography). Will accept artworks/images.

**Recent Title(s)** *Another Spanner in the Works: Challenging prejudice and racism in mainly white schools*, Eleanor Knowles and Wendy Ridley

**Tips** Trentham publishes a wide range of titles, plus five professional journals, mainly in the field of education and social policy. Trenthams books are aimed at professional readers and teachers not children or parents. Trentham accepts book proposals providing they follow the guidelines from their website. All new titles must conform to Trentham's ethical stance and commitment to equality, academic rigour, and readability.

## Trident Press Ltd
**175 Piccadilly, Mayfair, London, W1J 9TB**
- 020 7491 8770
- 020 7491 8664
- admin@tridentpress.com
- www.tridentpress.com

**Contact** Managing Director, Peter Vine
**Established** 1997
**Imprint(s)** Trident Media
**Insider Info** Payment via royalties. Catalogue available online.
**Non-Fiction** Publishes general non-fiction, Illustrated, Multimedia and Reference titles on the following subjects:
Anthropology/Archaeology, Contemporary Culture, History, Nature/Environment, Photography, Translation, World Affairs, Irish Interest.
**Submission Guidelines** Accepts query with SAE.
**Fiction** Publishes Irish Interest titles.
**Recent Title(s)** *The Emirates - A Natural History*, Mohammed Al Bowardi; *Scribbles*, Mary Foyle (Collection)
**Tips** Trident Press is a London based company whose areas of special interest include wildlife, travel, lifestyle, sports, the arts, cultural and historical aspects of human development. We also publish in a wide range of languages, including French and Arabic. Trident Media is a sister company based in Ireland that handles all the pre-press work for the main press. Trident Press will not accept unsolicited submissions, but will respond to brief email or phone contact.

## Trotman & Co. Ltd
**2 The Green, Richmond, Surrey, TW9 1PL**
- 020 8486 1168
- 020 8486 1161
- enquiries@trotman.co.uk
- www.trotman.co.uk

**Contact** Managing Director, Toby Trotman; Editorial Director, Mina Patria; Commissioning Editor, Rachel Lockhart
**Established** 1970
**Insider Info** Publishes 60 titles per year. Payment is via royalties. Catalogue available online.
**Non-Fiction** Publishes General Non-fiction, Multimedia, Reference and Technical titles on the following subjects:
Business/Economics, Counselling/Career, Education, Training Courses.
**Submission Guidelines** Complete online form. Submission details to: editorial@trotman.co.uk
**Recent Title(s)** *Choosing your A levels and post-16 options*, Gary Woodward
**Tips** Trotman Publishing has been involved in publishing and distributing careers resources for over 30 years. We publish in a wide range of media – including books, photocopiable packs, videos, the internet and CD-ROMs – and cover the areas of higher education, careers information, teaching resources, employment and training. For proposals or submissions Trotman uses an electronic form which must be filled in, available on their website..

## TSO (The Stationary Office)
**Mandela Way, London, SE1 5SS**
- 020 7394 4284
- parlypubs@tso.co.uk
- www.tso.co.uk

**Parent Company** Williams Lea Holdings Plc
**Contact** Director of Parliamentary and Statutory Publishing, Richard South; Production Manager, Pete Christopher; Parliamentary and Statutory Publishing Manager, Kanta Craigen-Straughn
**Established** 1996
**Insider Info** Publishes 15,000 titles per year. Catalogue and manuscript guidelines available.
**Non-Fiction** Publishes Multimedia, Reference and Technical titles on the following subjects:
Business/Economics, Community/Public Affairs, Education, Government/Politics, Law, Nature/Environment, Transportation.

**Recent Title(s)** *UK Borders Bill: House of Commons Bill 53*, Great Britain Parliament House of Lords
**Tips** TSO is committed to delivering managed print and publishing services for our public and private sector clients. We specialise in the creation, production and distribution of information in print, online and electronic formats, including efficient, cost-effective print management and design services. We publish material sponsored by the government and other official bodies, as well as some commercial publishing in the fields of business, law, education, transportation and the environment. TSO is the largest publisher in the UK by volume, mostly of government sponsored books and reports. TSO publishes official documents and reports and does not publish general books.

## Twenty First Century Publishers Ltd
**Braunton Barn, Kiln Lane, Isfield, TN22 5UE**
☎ 01892 522802
✉ tfcp@btinternet.com
🌐 www.twentyfirstcenturypublishers.com
**Contact** Chairman, Fred Piechoczek
**Established** 2002
**Insider Info** Payment is via royalties. Catalogue and manuscripts guidelines available online.
**Fiction** Publishes Literary, Mainstream/Contemporary and Financial Thriller titles.
**Submission Guidelines** Accepts query with SAE. Submit proposal package (including outline and three sample chapters). Writers, you may send to us for review, your fictional writing in English, French or German. In the body of your email include a brief synopsis or overview and add the manuscript, or as many chapters as you wish, in a file attachment.
**Recent Title(s)** *Down to a Sunset Sea*, S. Rahman (Collection)
**Tips** TFCP concentrates on developing new authors whom we wish to bring to market. We use the latest technology to achieve publication in minimum times. We publish general fiction written thoughtfully and with insight, plot-driven original works, and knowledgeably written financial thrillers.

## Two Rivers Press
**35–39 London Street, Reading, Berkshire, RG1 4PS**
☎ 0118 966 2345
✉ tworiverspress@virgin.net
🌐 www.tworiverspress.com
**Contact** Publisher, John Froy
**Established** 1994

**Insider Info** Catalogue and manuscript guidelines available online.
**Non-Fiction** Publishes General Non-fiction and Illustrated titles on the following subjects: Local Interest (Thames Valley).
**Submission Guidelines** Accepts query with SAE. Submit proposal package (including outline and sample chapter(s)). Will accept artworks/images (send photocopies).
**Fiction** Publishes Short story collections.
**Submission Guidelines** Accepts query with SAE. Submit proposal package (including outline and sample chapter(s)).
**Poetry** Publishes poetry titles.
**Submission Guidelines** Submit six sample poems.
**Recent Title(s)** *A Thames Bestiary*, Peter Hay and Geoff Sawers, *Hearthstone*, Joseph Butler, (Collection)
**Tips** Two Rivers is a small co-operative run press. Two Rivers publishes general interest non-fiction from and about the Thames Valley area, and also poetry and prose from local writers. We are a very small press, (two part-time workers, and a number of freelancers and volunteers) and we receive funding to produce books within a well-defined remit: books about our local area, and literature (mainly poetry). Only rarely do we deviate from these areas.

## Ulric Publishing Ltd
**PO Box 55, Church Stretton, Shropshire, SY6 6WR**
☎ 01694 781354
📠 01694 781372
✉ books@ulric-publishing.com
🌐 www.ulric-publishing.com
**Contact** Director, Ulric Woodhams; Director, Elizabeth Oakes
**Established** 1992
**Insider Info** Catalogue available online.
**Non-Fiction** Publishes General Non-fiction and Illustrated titles on the following subjects: Automotive, Military/War, Transportation.
**Recent Title(s)** *Apex of Glory*, Blaine Taylor
**Tips** Ulric Publishing is a small press specialising in military and political history, automotive, classic cars, transportation and other forms of travel. Ulric does not accept any unsolicited material.

## University College of Dublin Press
**Newman House, 86 St Stephen's Green, Dublin 2, Republic of Ireland**
☎ 00353 1 716 7397
📠 00353 1 716 7211
✉ ucdpress@ucd.ie

www.ucdpress.ie
**Contact** Executive Editor, Barbara Mennell
**Insider Info** Catalogue and manuscript guidelines available online.
**Non-Fiction** Publishes Reference and Scholarly titles on the following subjects:
 Government/Politics, History, Language/Literature, Literary Criticism, Music/Dance, Nature/Environment, Science, Social Sciences, Study Guides.
**Submission Guidelines** Accepts query with SAE. Submit proposal package (including outline, three sample chapters, market research, publishing history, clips and author biography).
**Recent Title(s)** *Vision and Vacancy*, James Walton
**Tips** UCD Press is the publishing imprint of Ireland's largest university, University College Dublin. UCD Press publishes a diversity of academic titles, reflective of excellence in contemporary international scholarship. In particular, UCD Press is a market leader in research relating to historic and contemporary Ireland and is committed to enhancing further its dynamic profile in this area. UCD Press' list to date includes many titles by Irish authors and of Irish interest, but our interests are not by any means confined to Ireland. Check the website for further submission guidelines.

## University of Exeter Press
**Reed Hall, Streatham Drive, Exeter, EX4 4QR**
❶ 01392 263066
❶ 01392 263064
✉ uep@ex.ac.uk
🌐 www.exeterpress.co.uk
**Contact** Publisher, Simon Baker; Publishing Assistant, Vicky Owen
**Insider Info** Catalogue available online.
**Non-Fiction** Publishes General Non-fiction, Reference and Scholarly titles on the following subjects:
 Anthropology/Archaeology, Contemporary Culture, Education, History, Language/Literature, Literary Criticism, Multicultural, Nature/Environment, Philosophy, Regional, Religion, Social Sciences, Sociology, Translation.
**Submission Guidelines** Accepts query with SAE. Editorial enquiries, including short publishing proposals, are welcome and authors should address them to Simon Baker, Publisher.
**Recent Title(s)** *Timber Castles*, Bob Higham and Philip Barker
**Tips** The main aim of Exeter University Press is to enhance the university's academic reputation by associating its name with successful international publishing. Exeter's main subject areas are medieval

studies, classical studies, European literature, history, film history, performance studies, archaeology, landscape history and South West studies.

## University of Hertfordshire Press
**University of Hertfordshire, LRC, College Lane, Hatfield, Hertfordshire, AL10 9AB**
❶ 01707 284682
❶ 01707 284666
✉ uhpress@herts.ac.uk
🌐 www.herts.ac.uk/uhpress
**Contact** Press Manager, Jane Housham
**Established** 1992
**Imprint(s)** University of Hertfordshire Press
 Hertfordshire Publications
**Insider Info** Payment is via royalties. Catalogue and manuscript guidelines available online.
**Non-Fiction** Publishes Reference and Scholarly titles on:
 Education, History, Language/Literature, Psychology, Science, Romani Studies.
**Submission Guidelines** Accepts query with SAE. Submission details to: j.j.housham@herts.ac.uk
**Recent Title(s)** *Lilian Baylis: A Biography*, Elizabeth Schafer
**Tips** University of Hertfordshire Press is one of the leading UK university publishing houses. It publishes academic books on Romani studies, regional and local history, literature, history, sciences and psychology. The Hertfordshire Publications imprint publishes local interest and Hertfordshire history books.

## University of Plymouth Press
**Room M12, Scott Building, University of Plymouth, Drake Circus, Plymouth, Devon, PL4 8AA**
✉ phoneywill@plymouth.ac.uk
🌐 www.uppress.co.uk
**Contact** Publisher, Paul Honeywill
**Established** 2005
**Insider Info** Catalogue and manuscript guidelines available online.
**Non-Fiction** Publishes Illustrated and Multimedia titles on the following subjects:
 Art/Architecture, Music/Dance, Photography.
**Submission Guidelines** Form available online for new writers.
**Recent Title(s)** *And Stop...*, Charlotte Mutton ed. (Photography/Art)
**Tips** Publishing works that extend the intellectual reach of scholarship, while helping to define new areas of knowledge and learning. In keeping with

the University of Plymouth's mission, the Press fosters understanding and partnership between communities to enrich the cultural life of the region. See website for new author form.

## University of Wales Press
**10 Columbus Walk, Brigantine Place, Cardiff, CF10 4UP**
- 029 2049 6899
- 029 2049 6108
- press@press.wales.ac.uk
- www.uwp.co.uk

**Contact** Director, Ashley Drake (Proposals); Commissioning Editor, Sarah Lewis (Proposals); Editor, Elin Lewis; Editor, Nia Peris
**Established** 1922
**Imprint(s)** University of Wales Press
**Insider Info** Publishes 60 titles per year. Payment is via royalties. Catalogue available free on request and online. Manuscript guidelines available online.
**Non-Fiction** Publishes General Non-fiction, Scholarly and Welsh Non-fiction titles on the following subjects:
 Contemporary Culture, Government/Politics, History, Language/Literature, Law, Literary Criticism, Nature/Environment, Philosophy, Religion, Translation, Welsh Studies.
**Submission Guidelines** Accepts query with SAE. Proposal questionnaire available on website. Authors should submit a detailed proposal at an early stage, preferably before the book is written. Proposals should be structured around the proposal questionnaire (on the website). Please note that we will not give detailed consideration to your proposal until the questionnaire is received, preferably by email.
 Submission details to: s.lewis@press.wales.ac.uk
**Recent Title(s)** *Acting Wales: Stars of Stage and Screen*, Peter Stead
**Tips** The University of Wales Press now publishes nearly sixty new titles a year both in English and in Welsh, and concentrates on six main subject areas of history, political philosophy and religious studies, Welsh and Celtic studies, literary studies, European studies and Medieval studies.

## University Presses of California, Columbia & Princeton Ltd
**1 Oldlands Way, Bognor Regis, West Sussex, P022 95A**
- 01243 842165
- 01243 842167
- lois@upccp.demon.co.uk

**Non-Fiction** Publishes Reference and Scholarly titles and Textbooks on the following subjects:
 Business/Economics, Education, History, Humanities, Literary Criticism, Science.
**Submission Guidelines** Accepts query with SAE.
**Tips** UK based enquiries office for the California, Columbia and Princeton Universities. Publishes academic and reference books. The editorial departments of the three universities are based in the US at the corresponding Universities.

## Usborne Publishing Ltd
**Usborne House, 83–85 Saffron Hill, London, EC1N 8RT**
- 020 7430 2800
- 020 8636 3758
- mail@usborne.co.uk; Online form on the website
- www.usborne.co.uk

**Contact** Managing Director, Peter Usborne; Publishing Director, Jenny Tyler
**Established** 1975
**Insider Info** Publishes 250 titles per year. Payment via royalties. Aims to respond to manuscripts within six months. Catalogue and manuscript guidelines available online.
**Non-Fiction** Publishes Illustrated books, Children's/ Juvenile and Reference titles on the following subjects:
 Art/Architecture, Crafts, Entertainment/Games, Hobbies, Language/Literature, Music/Dance, Sports, Puzzle Books.
**Submission Guidelines** All unsolicited manuscripts returned unopened.
**Fiction** Publishes Children's and Early Years titles and Picture and Baby Books.
**Submission Guidelines** Submit proposal package (including outline and three sample chapters).
**Recent Title(s)** *Ancient Romans Jigsaw Book*, Struan Reid (Puzzle Book); *Farmyard Tales: Noisy Animals*, Felicity Brooks (Interactive Picture Book)
**Tips** Usborne is a major independent UK publishing company, their list includes almost every type of children's book, for babies to teenagers and covering a wide range of topics. There are books for schools and for home reading and learning. Usborne will only accept submissions for new children's fiction, not for picture books or non-fiction, as they are commissioned in-house.

## Vallentine Mitchell Publishers Ltd
**Suite 314 Premier House, 112–114 Station Road, Edgware, Middlesex, HA8 7BJ**
- 020 8952 9526

☎ 020 8952 9242
✉ info@vmbooks.com
🌐 www.vmbooks.com

**Insider Info** Publishes 30 titles per year. 80 per cent of books published are from unagented authors. Advance offered is from £250. Simultaneous submissions accepted. Submissions accompanies by SAE will be returned. Catalogue and author guidelines are free on request.

**Non-Fiction** Publishes Autobiography, Biography, Reference and Scholarly titles on the following subjects:
 Anthropology/Archaeology, Contemporary Culture, Government/Politics, History, Humanities, Literary Criticism, Memoirs, Military/War, Philosophy, Religion.
 * All titles must be of Jewish interest.

**Submission Guidelines** Accepts proposal package (including outline, sample chapter(s), your publishing history, author biography) and artworks/images.
 Submission details to: info@vmbooks.com

**Recent Title(s)** *Orthodox Judaism in Britain since 1913*, Miri Freud-Kandel (Academic)

**Tips** Make sure your book fits in with the Jewish interest of the list, and do not send in entire manuscripts.

## Vanguard Press
**Sheraton House, Castle Park, Cambridge, CB3 OAX**
☎ 01223 370012
☎ 01223 37004
✉ editors@pegasuspublishers.com
🌐 www.pegasuspublishers.com

**Parent Company** Pegasus Elliot MacKenzie Publishers Ltd

**Insider Info** Catalogue and manuscript guidelines available online.

**Non-Fiction** Publishes Autobiography, Biography and general non-fiction titles on the following subjects:
 Cooking/Foods/Nutrition, Government/Politics, History, Memoirs, Military/War, Sports, Travel, Women's Issues/Studies.

**Submission Guidelines** Accepts Proposal package (including outline, two sample chapters and SAE).

**Fiction** Publishes Adventure, Historical, Humour, Mainstream/Contemporary, Romance, Science Fiction and Crime titles.

**Submission Guidelines** Accepts proposal package (including outline, two sample chapters).

**Poetry** Publishes Poetry titles.

**Tips** Vanguard Press publishes a wide range of general interest fiction and non-fiction titles including romantic fiction, adventure, science fiction, biography, humour, history and current affairs. Vanguard Press encourages submissions from new and untested authors.

## Veritas
**7–8 Lower Abbey Street, Dublin 1, Republic of Ireland**
☎ 00353 1 878 8177
☎ 00353 1 878 6507
✉ sales@veritas.ie
🌐 www.veritas.ie

**Parent Company** Veritas Communications

**Contact** Managing Editor, Ruth Garvey; Commissioning Editor, Donna Doherty

**Established** 1969

**Insider Info** Publishes 30 titles per year. Payment via royalties. Aims to respond to proposals and manuscripts within six weeks. Catalogue and manuscript guidelines available online.

**Non-Fiction** Publishes Audio cassettes, Biography, Textbooks, Children's/Juvenile, General Non-fiction, Gift, Multimedia and Self-help titles on the following subjects:
 Child Guidance/Parenting, Health/Medicine, Philosophy, Psychology, Religion, Social Sciences, Spirituality, Christian Resources.

**Submission Guidelines** Accepts query with SAE. Submit proposal package (including outline, three sample chapters and author biography).
 Submission details to: donna.doherty@veritas.ie

**Recent Title(s)** *Epiphanies: Moments of Grace in Daily Life*, Mary Murphy

**Tips** Veritas publishes books in the following areas; theology, philosophy, spirituality, psychology, self-help, family, social issues, parish and church resources, and bible study. Our market is Christian based and is an ever growing entity. It is not restricted to the parameters of Ireland and the UK. Veritas publishes for companies and groups such as churches, schools and other organisations, and also for retail customers, including students and parents.

## Vermilion
**Random House, 20 Vauxhall Bridge Road, London, SW1V 2SA**
☎ 020 7840 8400
☎ 020 7840 8406
✉ vermilioneditorial@randomhouse.co.uk
🌐 www.randomhouse.co.uk

**Parent Company** The Random House Group Ltd

**Contact** Publishing Director, Clare Hulton

**Insider Info** Submissions accompanied by SAE will be returned. Catalogue available online.

**Non-Fiction** Publishes Autobiography, Biography, General Non-fiction and How-to titles on the following subjects:
Personal Development, Health and Diet, Parenting, Relationships.

**Submission Guidelines** Accepts Proposal package (including outline and one sample chapter). Will accept artworks/images (send photocopies).

**Recent Title(s)** *The New Contented Little Baby Book*, Gina Ford; *Sex Lives of Wives*, Holly Hollenbeck

**Tips** No emailed submissions. See Random House Group entry for more information.

## Verso Ltd
**6 Meard Street, London, W1F 0EG**

☎ 020 7437 3546

☎ 020 7734 0059

✉ enquiries@verso.co.uk

🌐 www.versobooks.com

**Contact** Managing Director, Guy Bentham

**Established** 1970

**Insider Info** Catalogue and manuscript guidelines available online.

**Non-Fiction** Publishes General Non-fiction and Scholarly titles on the following subjects:
Business/Economics, Contemporary Culture, Government/Politics, History, Philosophy, Sociology.

**Submission Guidelines** Accepts query with SAE. Submit proposal package (including outline, market research, publishing history and author biography).

**Recent Title(s)** *Pirates of the Caribbean: Axis of Hope*, Tariq Ali

**Tips** Verso is a radical publisher specialising in intelligent, critical works located at the intersection of the academic and trade markets. Verso's list of writers in English has come to include many key authors in the social sciences and humanities, with particular strength in politics, cultural studies, history, philosophy, sociology and literary criticism. Submission guidelines for Verso are available on the website. All proposals must include information on market research and target audience for the book.

## Viking
**80 Strand, London, WC2R 0RL**

☎ 020 7010 3000

☎ 020 7010 6060

✉ customer.service@penguin.co.uk

🌐 www.penguin.co.uk

**Parent Company** Penguin General

**Contact** Publisher, Venetia Butterfield

**Insider Info** Catalogue is available online.

**Non-Fiction** Publishes Biography and General Non-fiction on the following subjects:
History, Sports, Travel, Current Affairs, Belles Lettres.

**Submission Guidelines** Agented submissions only.

**Fiction** Publishes Experimental, Literary and Mainstream/Contemporary titles.

**Submission Guidelines** Agented submissions only.

**Recent Title(s)** *Home Run – Escape from Nazi Europe*, John Nicholl and Tony Rennell; *Gifted*, Nikita Lalwani (Contemporary fiction)

**Tips** Viking publishes the widest possible range of literary fiction and non-fiction. This varies from the highly literary and sometimes experimental, to more commercial titles.

## Vintage
**Random House, 20 Vauxhall Bridge Road, London, SW1V 2SA**

☎ 020 7840 8439

☎ 020 7233 6117

✉ vintageeditorial@randomhouse.co.uk

🌐 www.randomhouse.co.uk/vintage

**Parent Company** The Random House Group Ltd

**Contact** Publisher, Rachel Cugnoni

**Established** 1990

**Imprint(s)** Vintage Books
Vintage Classics
Vintage Originals

**Insider Info** Submissions accompanied by SAE will be returned. Catalogue available online.

**Non-Fiction** Publishes Autobiography, Biography, General Non-fiction, Reference and Scholarly titles on the following subjects:
Contemporary Culture, Cooking/Foods/Nutrition, Literary Criticism, Psychology, Social Sciences, Travel, Women's Issues/Studies, social history.

**Submission Guidelines** Accepts Proposal package (including outline, one sample chapter and SAE). Will accept artworks/images (send photocopies).

**Fiction** Publishes Literary and Mainstream/Contemporary titles and Classics.

**Submission Guidelines** Accepts proposal package (including outline and one sample chapter). No emailed submissions.

**Recent Title(s)** *Ameretto, Apple Cake and Artichokes*, Anna del Conte (Food writing); *Saturday*, Ian McEwan (Novel)

**Tips** Vintage publishes entirely in paperback. Vintage is at the cutting edge of contemporary fiction and non-fiction publishing. See The Random House Group entry for more information.

**353**

## Virago Press

**Brettenham House, Lancaster Place, London, WC2E 7EN**

- 020 7911 8000
- 020 7911 8100
- Virago.Press@littlebrown.co.uk
- www.virago.co.uk

**Parent Company** Little, Brown Book Group
**Contact** Publishing Director, Lennie Goodings
**Established** 1973
**Insider Info** Catalogue available online.
**Non-Fiction** Publishes Autobiography, Biography and Illustrated titles on the following subjects: Memoirs, Travel, Women's Issues/Studies.
**Submission Guidelines** Agented submissions preferred.
**Fiction** Publishes Women's Literary Fiction titles.
**Submission Guidelines** Agented submissions preferred.
**Poetry** Publish poetry by female writers.
**Submission Guidelines** Agented submissions preferred.
**Recent Title(s)** *Virginia Woolf - A Writer's Life*, Lyndall Gordon (Biography); *The Dirty Bits - For Girls*, India Knight (Anthology)
**Tips** Virago, founded by Carmen Callil, has grown into the largest women's imprint in the world and is one of the UK's most successful publishing imprints. The Virago VS list is for a new generation of Virago readers and publishes the best young female writers with an eclectic mix of subject matter and style. Virago Modern Classics incorporates a large backlist of female fiction. Virago are not currently accepting unsolicited manuscripts.

## Virgin Books Ltd

**Thames Wharf Studios, Rainville Road, London, W6 9HT**

- 020 7386 3300
- 020 7836 3360
- www.virginbooks.com

**Contact** Managing Director, K.T. Forster
**Established** 1991 (following a merger with publisher WH Allen)
**Imprint(s)** Black Lace
 Nexus
 Cheek
 Virgin
**Insider Info** Catalogue available online.
**Non-Fiction** Publishes Autobiography, Biography, Cookery, General Non-fiction, Gift, Humour, Illustrated, Multimedia, Reference and Self-help titles on the following subjects:

Animals, Business/Economics, Cooking/Foods/Nutrition, Entertainment/Games, Health/Medicine, Memoirs, Music/Dance, Nature/Environment, Sex, Sport, Food and Drink/Wine, Fitness and Exercise, Health and Beauty, Leisure Books, Mind, Body and Spirit, Paranormal, Theatre and Drama, Cult writing, Crime, Television and Film.
**Fiction** Publishes Erotica, Romance and General Adult Fiction.
**Recent Title(s)** *Max Clifford: Read All About It*, Max Clifford and Angela Levin

## Virtue Books Ltd

**Edward House, Tenter Street, Rotherham, S60 1LB**

- 01709 365005
- 01709 829982
- info@russums.co.uk
- www.russums-shop.co.uk/virtuebooks.asp

**Contact** Director, Peter E. Russum; Editorial, Karen Harrison
**Insider Info** Catalogue available free on request and online.
**Non-Fiction** Publishes General Non-fiction, How-to and Illustrated titles on the following subjects: Cooking/Foods/Nutrition.
**Tips** Virtue has over 100 years experience in the cookery book world, publishing, supplying and recommending good cookery books to professional chefs and catering schools, students, cookery shops, leading department stores, and many other retailers and wholesalers throughout the UK and around the world. Apart from a couple of historical titles, Virtue Books no longer publish and are mainly involved with distribution.

## Vital Spark

**Suite Ex 8, Pentagon Centre, 44 Washington Street, Glasgow, Scotland, G3 8AZ**

- 0141 221 1117
- 0141 221 5363
- info@nwp.co.uk
- www.nwp.co.uk

**Parent Company** Neil Wilson Publishing Ltd
**Insider Info** Catalogue and manuscript guidelines are available online.
**Non-Fiction** Publishes Illustrated Humour titles.
**Submission Guidelines** Submit proposal package (including outline, synopsis, one sample chapter, author biography, CV and SAE). Will accept artworks/images.
**Fiction** Publishes Illustrated Humour and Cartoon titles.

**Recent Title(s)** *'Away An' Ask Your Mother!': Your Scottish Father's Favourite Sayings*, Allan Morrison (Humour)

**Tips** Vital Spark is the humour imprint of Neil Wilson Publishing and will accept non-fiction humour submissions. Vital Spark mostly publishes cartoon illustrated titles, so submissions should include sample illustrations.

## Wakefield Historical Publications
**19 Pinder's Grove, Wakefield, West Yorkshire, WF1 4AH**

- 01924 372748
- kate@airtime.co.uk
- www.wakefieldhistoricalsoc.org.uk

**Parent Company** Wakefield Historical Society
**Contact** President, Kate Taylor
**Established** 1977
**Insider Info** Publishes two titles per year. Catalogue available online.
**Non-Fiction** Publishes Scholarly titles on the following subjects:
History, Regional, West Riding interest.
**Submission Guidelines** Accepts query with SAE.
**Recent Title(s)** *The Castleford Pottery*, Diane Edwards Roussel

**Tips** Wakefield Historical Publications is the publishing arm of Wakefield Historical Society and handles scholarly non-fiction of regional and historical interest, mostly about the West Riding of Yorkshire. Unsolicited proposals are welcome, but only a small amount of work is published in any given year.

## Walker Books
**87 Vauxhall Walk, London, SE11 5HJ**

- 020 7793 0909
- editorial@walker.co.uk
- www.walkerbooks.co.uk

**Contact** Publisher, Jane Winterbotham
**Established** Founded in 1978 by Sebastian Walker. In 1983 Walker became an independent company and today it is Britain's leading publisher of children's books with a list across the age range from babies to teenagers. Walker Books has sister companies in the US (Candlewick Press) and in Australia.
**Insider Info** Catalogue available online.
**Non-Fiction** Publishes Audio cassettes, Children's/Juvenile, Young adult, Gift, Illustrated and Reference titles and Big books, Board books, Character books, Novelty and Activity books on the following subjects:

Early Learning, Activity, Hobby and Craft, Biography, History, Arts, Life issues, Animals, Environment and Conservation, Feelings, Language, Football, First Concepts.
**Submission Guidelines** Agented submissions only.
**Fiction** Publishes Adventure, Humour, Children's, Young Adult and Science Fiction titles and Short story collections, Anthologies and Traditional Tales.
**Submission Guidelines** Agented submissions only.
**Poetry** Publishes Poetry titles.
**Recent Title(s)** *Cooking Up a Storm*, Susan Stem and Sam Stem (Teenage cookery); Walker character books include *Where's Wally*, *Alex Rider*, *Maisy*, and *Curious George*.

## Wallflower Press
**6a Middleton Place, Langham Street, London, W1W 7TE**

- 020 7436 9494
- 020 7690 4333
- info@wallflowerpress.co.uk
- www.wallflowerpress.co.uk

**Contact** Commissioning Editor and Editorial Director, Yoram Allon
**Established** 1999
**Insider Info** Publishes 30 titles per year. Payment is via royalties. Catalogue available online.
**Non-Fiction** Publishes General Non-fiction and Scholarly titles on the following subjects:
Contemporary Culture, Education, Film and Media Studies.
**Submission Guidelines** Accepts query by email to Yoram Allon.
Submission details to: yoram@wallflowerpress.co.uk
**Recent Title(s)** *The Unsilvered Screen: Surrealism on Film*, Graeme Harper and Rob Stone (eds.)
**Tips** Wallflower Press is an independent publishing house specialising in cinema and the moving image. They are devoted to the publication of the highest quality academic and popular literature in film, television and media studies as well as related areas of the visual arts. Contact Yoram Allon, Commissioning Editor, to discuss any ideas that you would like to propose to Wallflower Press for possible publication. You may then be invited to submit a full book proposal, for further consideration.

## The Warburg Institute
**University of London, Woburn Square, London, WC1H 0AB**

- 020 7862 8949
- 020 7862 8955

○ warburg@sas.ac.uk
Ⓦ http://warburg.sas.ac.uk/publications/
publications_index.htm

**Contact** Publications Assistant, Jenny Boyle; Editor (Warburg Journal), Jill Kraye; Editor (Warburg Journal), Elizabeth McGrath

**Insider Info** Catalogue available online.

**Non-Fiction** Publishes Scholarly titles on the following subject areas:
 Art/Architecture , History, Philosophy, Science.

**Tips** The Warburg Institute of the University of London exists principally to further the study of the classical tradition. It publishes books and journals on cultural and intellectual history, with reference to the classical tradition. The Warburg Institute also publishes its own journal. The Journal does not solicit contributions, nor can the Editors consider proposals for articles or unfinished drafts. Similarly, the Editors are obliged to pursue a stringent policy regarding submissions, which require extensive editorial input such as further research or rewriting, or creative input such as the production of print quality diagrams.

## Warne

**80 Strand, London, WC2R 0RL**
❶ 020 7010 3000
❶ 020 7010 6060
○ customer.service@penguin.co.uk
Ⓦ www.peterrabbit.com

**Parent Company** Penguin Group (UK)

**Contact** Managing Director, Sally Floyer

**Established** 1865

**Insider Info** Catalogue is available online.

**Fiction** Publishes Children's, Illustrated and Picture book titles.
 * No unagented submissions.

**Recent Title(s)** *The Tale of Peter Rabbit*, Beatrix Potter (Board book)

**Tips** Warne specialises in book based children's character properties, including the Beatrix Potter titles and other classic children's titles such as the *Flower Fairies* and *Orlando the Marmalade Cat*.

## Watling Street

**33 Hatherop, Near Cirencester, Gloucestershire, GL7 3NA**
❶ 01285 750212
○ chris.mclaren@saltwaypublishing.co.uk
Ⓦ www.flametreepublishing.co.uk

**Contact** Editorial Director, Christine Kidney (London and Local Titles)

**Established** 2000

**Insider Info** Publishes 12 titles per year. Payment is via outright purchase. Simultaneous submissions are not accepted. Submissions will not be returned. Catalogue is available online. Author guidelines are not available.

**Non-Fiction** Publishes Children's and General Non-fiction titles on the following subjects:
 Gardening, History, Nature/Environment.

**Submission Guidelines** Agented submissions only.
 Submission details to: chris.mclaren@
saltwaypublishing.co.uk

**Recent Title(s)** *London's Gardens*, Lorna Parker (Season by Season Guide to London Gardens Open to the Public)

**Tips** All unsolicited manuscripts will be returned unopened.

## The Watts Publishing Group

**338 Euston Road, London, NW1 3BH**
❶ 020 7873 6000
❶ 020 7873 6225
Ⓦ www.orchardbooks.co.uk

**Parent Company** Hachette Livre UK (see Hachette Livre entry under *European & International Publishers*)

**Established** Founded 1972

**Imprint(s)** Franklin Watts
 Orchard Books
 Cat's Whiskers

**Insider Info** Catalogue available online.

**Non-Fiction** Publishes Teacher Resources, Young Adult, Big books and Children's titles on the following subjects:
 Citizenship and PHSE, Special Needs, Religious Education, Geography - People and Environment, History through story, Social History, Science, Technology, Art, Craft and Music, Hobbies and Pets.

**Submission Guidelines** Agented submissions only.

**Fiction** Publishes Juvenile, Picture books, Gift books, Novelty books, Board books, graded Reading books and Children's classics.

**Submission Guidelines** Agented submissions only.

**Poetry** Publishes Children's Poetry titles.

**Recent Title(s)** *Sex, Puberty and All That Stuff* (age 9–16); *Faraway Farm*, Ian Whybrow

## Wayland

 338 Euston Road
**London, NW1 3BH**
❶ 020 7873 6000
❶ 020 7873 6024
Ⓦ www.wattspublishing.co.uk

**Parent Company** Hachette Children's Books (Hodder Headline)

**Established** 1972
**Insider Info** Catalogue available online.
**Non-Fiction** Publishes Children's/Juvenile and Illustrated titles, on Information and Education.
**Submission Guidelines** Agented submissions only.
**Tips** Titles must have quality educational content, and an up to date, appealing, child friendly approach to design.

## The Waywiser Press
**9 Woodstock Road, London, N4 3ET**
- 020 8374 5526
- 020 8374 5736
- waywiserpress@aol.com
- www.waywiser-press.com

**Contact** Dr. Philip Hoy (Poetry, Fiction, Memoir, Criticism)
**Established** 2001
**Imprint(s)** Between The Lines
**Insider Info** Publishes six titles per year. Receives approximately 1,000 queries and 1,000 manuscripts per year. 25 per cent of books published are from first-time authors, five per cent of books published are from unagented authors. Payment is via royalty (on retail price), with 0.08 (per £) minimum and 0.15 (Per £) maximum. Average lead time is nine months, with simultaneous submissions accepted. Submissions accompanied by SAE will be returned. Aims to respond to queries and proposals within two weeks and manuscripts within eight weeks. Catalogue and manuscript guidelines are available online.
**Non-Fiction** Publishes Autobiography, Biography, Illustrated and Scholarly titles on the following subjects:
History, Literary Criticism, Literary History, Memoirs, Poetry, Fiction.
**Submission Guidelines** Accepts proposal package (including one to two sample chapters, your publishing history, author biography and SAE), and artworks/images (send photocopies).
**Fiction** Publishes Experimental, Literary and Short story collection titles.
**Submission Guidelines** Accepts proposal package (including outline, one to two sample chapters, author biography and SAE).
**Poetry** Publishes Literary and Contemporary poetry collections.
**Submission Guidelines** Accepts complete manuscript.
**Recent Title(s)** *A Driftwood Altar*, Mark Ford (Paperback); *The Entire Animal*, Gregory Heath (Paperback); *Field Knowledge*, Morri Creech (Paperback)

**Tips** Waywiser Press titles are aimed at a general literary readership. Waywiser is currently seeking full manuscript submissions for poetry, see the website for further details.

## Websters International Publishers Ltd
**Axe & Bottle Court, 70 Newcomen Street, London, SE1 1YT**
- 020 7940 4700
- 020 7940 4701
- info@websters.co.uk
- www.websters.co.uk

**Contact** Chairman, Adrian Webster; Managing Director, Jean-Luc Barbanneau; Editorial Director, Susannah Webster; Deputy Editorial Director, Anne Lawrence; Associate Editorial Director, Fiona Holman
**Established** 1983
**Imprint(s)** Websters Multimedia
**Insider Info** Catalogue available online.
**Non-Fiction** Publishes General Non-fiction, Multimedia and Reference titles on the following subjects:
Cooking/Foods/Nutrition, Education, Health/Medicine, Travel.
**Recent Title(s)** *Oz Clarke's Bordeaux*, Oz Clarke (Cooking)
**Tips** Websters International Publishers is an independent, London based company, specialising in the creation, localisation and licensing of international reference and lifestyle content for publication in print and digital media. Websters' publishes online and digital material, mostly reference books such as *Encarta Encyclopedia*, as well as print publications.

## Weidenfeld & Nicholson
**Orion House, 5 Upper St Martins Lane, London, WC2H 9EA**
- 020 7240 3444
- 020 7240 4822
- www.orionbooks.co.uk

**Parent Company** Orion Publishing Group Ltd
**Contact** Managing Director, Malcolm Edwards; Publisher, Alan Samson
**Established** 1949
**Imprint(s)** Weidenfeld Illustrated
Weidenfeld General
Weidenfeld Fiction
Cassell Reference
**Insider Info** Catalogue available online, or via an online form.

**Non-Fiction** Publishes Autobiography, Biography, Cookbook, General Non-fiction, Gift, How-to, Illustrated, Reference, Self-help, Diaries and Letters, Television tie-ins, Dictionaries and Guide titles on the following subjects:
Child Guidance/Parenting, Cooking/Foods/ Nutrition, History, Memoirs, Military/War, Science.
**Submission Guidelines** Agented submissions only.
**Fiction** Publishes Literary, Mainstream/ Contemporary and Translation titles.
**Submission Guidelines** Agented submissions only.
**Recent Title(s)** *Princess Margaret A Life Unravelled*, Tim Heald; *Buster's Secret Diaries,* Roy Hattersley
**Tips** Weidenfeld & Nicholson publishes a range of titles under its various imprints. Weidenfeld Illustrated publishes high-quality illustrated non-fiction on subjects such as arts & craft, gardening, lifestyle and history. Weidenfeld General covers general non-fiction including military history. Weidenfeld Fiction publishes a range of literary and commercial fiction. For more information on Cassell Reference see individual entry.

## Wendy Webb Books
**9 Walnut Close, Taverham, Norwich, NR8 6YN**
- wwbuk@yahoo.co.uk
- www.webbw.freeserve.co.uk
**Contact** Wendy Webb
**Fiction** Publishes Children's fiction titles.
**Poetry** Publishes poetry titles.
 * Wendy Webb has invented a new poetry form, the 'Davidian'. Writers are encouraged to try it out.
**Tips** Contact from writers is invited by email.

## W. Green
**21 Alva Street, Edinburgh, EH2 4PS**
- 0131 225 4879
- 0131 225 2104
- wgreen.enquiries@thomson.com
- www.wgreen.co.uk
**Parent Company** Sweet & Maxwell Group
**Contact** Publisher, Jill Hyslop; Director, Gilly Grant; Head of Editorial Operations, Rebecca Standing; Commissioning Editor, Karen Fullerton
**Insider Info** Catalogue and manuscript guidelines available online.
**Non-Fiction** Publishes Textbooks, Multimedia, Reference and Scholarly titles on Law, and Scottish Law.
 * The aim of the company is to provide the Scottish legal profession with practical, quality information. Welcomes new proposals that share the same goal.

**Submission Guidelines** New writers welcome. We regularly publish first-time authors and can give advice and support where required.
Fill out the online proposal form and send it to Jill Hyslop.
Submission details to: jill.hyslop@thomson.com

## Wharncliffe Publishing
**47 Church Street, Barnsley, S70 2AS**
- 01226 734639
- 01226 734478
- editorial@wharncliffepublishing.co.uk
- www.wharncliffepublishing.co.uk
**Parent Company** Pen & Sword Books, Acredula Group
**Non-Fiction** Publishes general non-fiction titles on the following subjects:
History and Regional.
**Submission Guidelines** Accepts query with SAE.
**Tips** Publishes local history books in conjunction with Pen & Sword. No unsolicited manuscripts. Also publishes niche magazines, newspapers and business to business materials.

## Wharton School Publishing
**Edinburgh Gate, Harlow, Essex, CM20 2JE**
- 01279 623623
- 01279 414130
- gydeb@wharton.upenn.edu
- www.pearsoned.co.uk/Imprints/Wharton/
**Parent Company** Pearson Education
**Contact** Managing Director, Barbara Gyde; Chair of the Editorial Board, David C. Scmittlein; Editor, Yoram Wind
**Insider Info** Catalogue and manuscripts guidelines are available online.
**Non-Fiction** Publishes Multimedia, Reference and Scholarly titles on the following subjects:
Business, Finance, Management Practices, Policy.
**Submission Guidelines** Accepts proposal package (including synopsis, sample chapters, market research, your publishing history and author biography).
**Recent Title(s)** *Firms of Endearment: How World-Class Companies Profit from Passion and Purpose,* Jagdish Sheth, Rajendra Sisodia and David Wolfe (Business)
**Tips** Wharton publishes books and management tools in a range of formats, including print, audio and electronic titles. By publishing many of the world's leading business authors, Wharton School Publishing aims to provide practical knowledge that can be applied by business people and policy

makers, to make real change in their professional lives. See the website for full list of editorial contacts.

## Which? Books

**2 Marylebone Road, London, NW1 4DF**
- 020 7830 6000
- 020 7830 7660
- which@which.co.uk
- www.which.net

**Contact** Editorial Director, Helen Parker
**Established** 1957
**Insider Info** Publishes 30 titles per year. Payment is via royalties. Catalogue available online.
**Non-Fiction** Publishes General Non-fiction, Multimedia and Reference titles:
 Business/Economics, Cooking/Foods/Nutrition, Counselling/Career, Guidance, Education, Health/ Medicine, House and Home, Law, Money/Finance, Real Estate, Technology.
**Submission Guidelines** Accepts query with SAE.
**Recent Title(s)** *The Pension Handbook*, Which?
**Tips** Which? books are packed with independent and unbiased research, to help you make informed choices about what brand or service to buy. Which? also publishes *Which? Magazine*. Unsolicited manuscripts are not accepted, but Which? is open to queries and ideas for new topics.

## White Ladder Press

**Great Ambrook, Near Ipplepen, Devon, TQ12 5UL**
- 01803 813343
- 01803 813928
- enquiries@whiteladderpress.com
- www.whiteladderpress.com

**Contact** Publisher, Roni Jay
**Established** 2003
**Insider Info** Publishes 12 titles per year. Payment is via royalties. Catalogue and manuscript guidelines available online.
**Non-Fiction** Publishes General Non-fiction, How-to and Reference titles on the following subjects:
 Child Guidance/Parenting, Gardening, Health/ Medicine, House and Home, Miscellaneous/Practical.
**Submission Guidelines** Accepts query with SAE. Submit proposal package (including outline and market research).
**Recent Title(s)** *How Teenagers Think: An insider's guide to living with a teenager*, jellyellie
**Tips** White Ladder Press publishes practical lifestyle books with a broad appeal and a quirky angle. Our mission statement says, 'We want to teach old dogs new tricks, by presenting a new angle on everyday

living. We want to intrigue, entertain and be useful at the same time'. We're very clear about precisely what constitutes a White Ladder book. We reject plenty of our own ideas because they don't fit the bill, and we will be as brutal with you as we are with ourselves. All White Ladder titles must be quirky in some way, be practical, have plenty of obvious marketing channels outside the book trade, and must attract media interest..

## Whittet Books

**Hill Farm, Stonham Road, Cotton, Stowmarket, Suffolk, IP14 4RQ**
- 01449 781877
- 01449 781898
- annabel@whittet.dircon.co.uk
- www.whittetbooks.com

**Parent Company** A Whittet & Co Ltd
**Contact** Annabel Whittet (Natural History, Horses, Horticulture)
**Established** 1976
**Insider Info** Publishes six titles per year. 40 per cent of books published are from first-time authors and 95 per cent of books published are from unagented authors. Payment is via royalty (on retail price) with 0.1 (per £) minimum and 0.15 (per £) maximum, outright purchase is from £500. Average lead time is six months with simultaneous submissions accepted. Submissions accompanied by SAE will be returned. Aims to respond to queries in ten days, proposals in 14 days and manuscripts in eight weeks. Catalogue is free on request. Author guidelines are not available.
**Non-Fiction** Publishes General Non-fiction and Illustrated titles on the following subjects:
 Agriculture/Horticulture, Animals (Reference books, not anecdotal), Gardening, Nature/Environment (Reference books).
 * Memoirs are not published
**Submission Guidelines** Accepts query with SAE, or via email, and artworks/images (send photocopies). Submission details to: annabel@whittet.dircon.co.uk
**Recent Title(s)** *The New Hedgehog Book*, Pat Morris
**Tips** Titles are aimed at a broad, general readership.

## Whittles Publishing

**Dunbeath Mains Cottages, Dunbeath, Caithness, KW6 6EY**
- 01593 731333
- 01593 731400
- info@whittlespublishing.com
- www.whittlespublishing.com

**Contact** Publisher, Keith Whittles

**Insider Info** Payment is via royalties. Catalogue and manuscript guidelines available online.

**Non-Fiction** Publishes General Non-fiction, Reference, Scholarly and Technical titles on the following subjects:
 History, Marine Subjects, Military/War, Nature/Environment, Civil/Structural Engineering.

**Submission Guidelines** Accepts query with SAE. Submit proposal package (including outline, two sample chapter(s) and SAE).

**Recent Title(s)** *Handbook of Staircases, Escalators and Moving Walkways*, M.Y.H. Bangash

**Tips** We publish quality, well-produced and attractive books and specialise in the following subjects; geomatics, civil and structural engineering, and applied science. We are also developing new lists in specific disciplines, including engineering geomorphology and geotechnics. We are always pleased to receive ideas or proposals for new technical books within our spheres of interest, whether authors are in academia or industry. Suggestions for new non-technical books within topics such as pharology, military history, nature writing, etc. are also very welcome. An initial telephone call may prove constructive to discuss a proposal.

## Whydown Books Ltd

**Whydown Books, Sedlescombe, East Sussex, TN33 0RQ**
- 01424 870083
- 01424 870083
- readerspost@whydownbooks.com
- www.whydownbooks.com

**Contact** Editorial Head, Pamela Richards
**Established** 2002
**Insider Info** Payment via royalties. Catalogue available online.

**Non-Fiction** Publishes Biography and General Non-fiction titles on History.

**Submission Guidelines** Accepts query with SAE. Submit proposal package (including outline and publishing history).

**Fiction** Publishes Mainstream/Contemporary titles.

**Submission Guidelines** Accepts query with SAE. Submit proposal package (including outline).

**Recent Title(s)** *A Sussex Highlander: The Memoirs of Sergeant William Kenward 1767 - 1828*, Denis Kenward and Richard Nesbitt-Dufort (eds.); *Spies and Lovers*, Adrian Hill (Novel)

**Tips** We are a small independent publisher. Our raison d'etre is to publish talented new authors, who draw on first hand experience and internationally respected knowledge. We publish biography, fiction,

and general interest history books. We will accept approach by email or letter, with ideas. A writing history must also be included.

## William Heinemann

**Random House, 20 Vauxhall Bridge Road, London, SW1V 2SA**
- 020 7840 8548
- 020 7233 6127
- heinemanneditorial@randomhouse.co.uk
- www.randomhouse.co.uk

**Parent Company** The Random House Group Ltd
**Contact** Publishing Director, Ravi Mirchandani
**Insider Info** Submissions accompanied by SAE will be returned. Catalogue available online.

**Non-Fiction** Publishes General Non-fiction titles.

**Submission Guidelines** Submit proposal package (including outline, one sample chapter and SAE). Will accept artworks/images (send photocopies).

**Fiction** Publishes General, Women's fiction, Crime and Thriller titles.

**Submission Guidelines** Submit proposal package (including outline, one sample chapter and SAE).

**Recent Title(s)** *How Life Imitates Chess*, Garry Kasparov (Instructional chess book); *Beyond the Blue Hills*, Katy Flynn (Novel)

**Tips** No email submissions. Although unagented submissions are accepted, very few are ever published.

## Willow Bank Publishers Ltd

**16a Bunters Road, Wickhambrook, Newmarket, Suffolk, CB8 8XY**
- 0800 731 5258
- editorial@willowbankpublishers.co.uk
- www.willowbankpublishers.co.uk

**Contact** Christopher Sims
**Imprint(s)** Willow Books
 Derringer Books
 Butterfly Books
 Fen Books

**Insider Info** Payment is via royalties. Catalogue and manuscript guidelines available online.

**Non-Fiction** Publishes Children's/Juvenile and General Non-fiction titles.

**Submission Guidelines** Accepts query with SAE. Submit proposal package (including outline, two sample chapters and SAE).

**Fiction** Publishes Juvenile, Mainstream/Contemporary, Mystery and Crime titles.

**Submission Guidelines** Accepts query with SAE. Submit proposal package (including outline and two sample chapters).

**Recent Title(s)** *White Roads to Akyab*, James Meridew

**Tips** Willow Bank publishes general fiction and non-fiction, as well as crime fiction under thier Derringer imprint. The Butterfly Books imprint publishes children's non-fiction, fiction and poetry. The newly established Fen Books imprint is a mainstream publisher of literary fiction from authors with a proven writing history. Any book accepted by Fen Books will be funded entirely by the company and may also receive an advance. Willow Bank Publishers may choose to offer either a traditional or author-funded publishing agreement for authors whose work meets the required standard set by our publishing panel, but whose commercial viability is not quite strong enough.

## Windhorse Publications

**11 Park Road, Birmingham, B13 8AB**

- 0121 449 9191
- 0121 449 9191
- info@windhorsepublications.com
- www.windhorsepublications.com

**Contact** Commissioning Editor, Jnanasiddhi (Buddhism, Meditation)

**Established** 1972

**Insider Info** Publishes six titles per year. Receives approximately 100 queries and 50 manuscripts from writers each year. 20 per cent of books published are from first-time authors and 100 per cent of books published are from unagented authors. Payment is via royalty with 0.08 (per £) minimum and 0.1 (per £) maximum. Average lead time is 18 months with simultaneous submissions accepted. Submissions accompanied by SAE will be returned. Aims to respond to queries within 28 days, and proposals and manuscripts within three months. Catalogue is free on request, and available online or via email.

**Non-Fiction** Publishes Self-Help titles on Religion and Spirituality.

 * Windhorse are a charity, so can only accept books in the field of Buddhism and Buddhist meditation.

**Submission Guidelines** Accepts a proposal package (including outline, three sample chapters, author biography and SAE). Will not review artwork/images as part of the manuscript package.
 Submission details to: jnanasiddhi@windhorsepublications.com

**Recent Title(s)** *The Heart*, Vessantara (Paperback)

**Tips** Potential audiences are those interested in Buddhism, exploring Buddhism or practitioners of Buddhism. Also those interested in awakening and self development more generally, and in discovering a Buddhist perspective on this.

## Witan Books

**Cherry Tree House, 8 Nelson Crescent, Cotes Heath, Stafford, Staffordshire, ST21 6ST**

- 01782 791673
- witan@mail.com

**Contact** Director, Jeff Kent

**Established** 1980

**Insider Info** Publishes one title per year. Payment is via royalty (on retail price). Simultaneous submissions are accepted. Submissions accompanied by SAE will be returned. Aims to respond to queries, proposals and manuscripts within 14 days. Catalogue not available. Author guidelines available via SAE.

**Non-Fiction** Publishes Autobiography, Biography, Booklets, Coffee table, General Non-fiction, Illustrated, Reference and Scholarly titles on the following subjects:
 Alternative Lifestyles, Animals, Business/Economics, Community/Public Affairs, Creative Non-fiction, Education, Government/Politics, History, Humanities, Marine Subjects, Music/Dance, Nature/Environment, New Age, Philosophy, Recreation, Science, Social Sciences, Sociology, Spirituality, Sports, Transportation, Travel, World Affairs.

**Submission Guidelines** Accepts query with SAE or via email and artworks/images (send photocopies).
 Submission details to: witan@mail.com

**Recent Title(s)** *The Mysterious Double Sunset*, Jeff Kent (Illustrated Paperback)

**Tips** Titles are aimed at a general non-fiction market. The company began life as a self publisher, but now publishes other authors' work. Initially send just a single-sided A4 synopsis of your work, including the anticipated readership, and SAE.

## WIT Press

**Ashurst Lodge, Ashurst, Southampton, SO40 7AA**

- 023 8029 3223
- 023 8029 2853
- witpress@witpress.com
- www.witpress.com

**Contact** Chairman, Prof. Carlos Brebbia

**Established** 1980

**Insider Info** Publishes 50 titles per year. Payment is via royalties. Catalogue and manuscript guidelines are available online.

**Non-Fiction** Publishes Reference, Scholarly and Technical titles on the following subjects:
 Art/Architecture, Computers/Electronics, Science, Technology, Civil/Electrical Engineering.

**Submission Guidelines** Submission sheets are available on website.

**Recent Title(s)** *Data Mining in E-Learning*, C. Romero and S. Ventura (eds.)

**Tips** WIT Press publishes scholarly and technical scientific non-fiction including structure, engineering, biotechnology, computer systems and sustainability. All books are aimed at postgraduate level and above. To assist authors and contributors with the keying of their work to the standard required, we have made available 'Instructions for Authors' and 'Example Sheets' on our website. It is important that you use the correct set of instructions as there are four, each pertaining to a different size of book.

## Wolfhound Press

**Newmarket Hall, Cork Street, Dublin 8, Republic of Ireland**

- 00353 1 453 5866
- 00353 1 453 5930
- publishing@merlin.ie
- www.merlinwolfhound.com

**Parent Company** Merlin Publishing

**Contact** Editorial Manager, Aoife Barrett

**Established** 1974

**Insider Info** Catalogue and manuscript guidelines are available online.

**Non-Fiction** Publishes Children's/Juvenile and General Non-fiction (Irish Interest) titles.

**Submission Guidelines** Accepts proposal package (including outline, synopsis, one sample chapter, marketing information, author biography and SAE or IRC for overseas replies). Will accept artworks/images (send photocopies or digital files as jpegs). Send submissions by post or email.
 Submission details to: aoife@merlin.ie

**Fiction** Publishes the Liam O'Flaherty backlist of Irish novels and story collections.

**Recent Title(s)** *The Ancient Books of Ireland*, Michael Slavin (Irish Interest)

**Tips** Wolfhound Press has a well-known reputation for producing high quality books of Irish interest, along with a range of children's books. Wolfhound also publishes the collected fiction of Irish author Liam O'Flaherty, but will not accept any further fiction submissions.

## Wolters Kluwer (UK) Ltd

**145 London Road, Kingston upon Thames, Surrey, KT2 6SR**

- 020 8547 3333
- 020 8547 2637
- info@croner.co.uk
- www.cch.co.uk

**Established** 1948

**Non-Fiction** Publishes Multimedia, Reference and Technical titles on the following subjects:
 Business/Economics, Law, Money/Finance, Insurance, Taxation.

**Recent Title(s)** *Agriculture: An Industry Accounting and Auditing Guide*, David Missen and Grant Pilcher

**Tips** CCH is a trading name of Wolters Kluwer (UK) Limited. CCH is a leading supplier of information for accountants, tax practitioners and financial professionals, whether in practice or in business, both in the UK and globally. CCH publishes a wide variety of products – from reference books, CD-ROMs and online information services, to software packages, professional development programmes and fee protection services. CCH is an information supplier, so any publications must be on top of the latest developments and regulatory changes in the accountancy world.

## The Women's Press

**27 Goodge Street, London, W1T 2LD**

- 020 763 63992
- 020 763 71866
- sales@the-womens-press.com
- www.the-womens-press.com

**Contact** Managing Director, Stella Kane

**Established** 1978

**Imprint(s)** Women's Press Classics
 Livewire Books for Teenagers

**Insider Info** Publishes 50 titles per year. Payment is via royalties. Catalogue available online.

**Non-Fiction** Publishes Autobiography, Biography and General Non-fiction titles on the following subjects:
 Contemporary Culture, Government/Politics, Health/Medicine, History, Psychology, Sex, Women's Issues/Studies.

**Submission Guidelines** Accepts query with SAE.

**Fiction** Publishes Literary, Mainstream/Contemporary and Young Adult titles.

**Submission Guidelines** Accepts query with SAE.

**Recent Title(s)** *Perfectly Safe to Eat?*, Vicki Hird; *Those Bones Are Not My Child,* Toni Cade Bambara

**Tips** The Women's Press is dedicated to publishing incisive feminist fiction and non-fiction by outstanding women writers from all round the world. They will only publish books written by women and even then, only if there is a female protagonist (for fiction) or the book deals with women's issues (for non-fiction). A series of up-front, contemporary, issue driven works of fiction and non-fiction for young women are published in the Livewire list. A series of classic works by women are published through the Women's Press Classics list.

## Wooden Books

**The Walkmill, Cascob, Presteigne, Powys, LD8 2NT**

🖤 01547 560251

🖤 01547 560113

🖤 info@woodenbooks.com

🖤 www.woodenbooks.com

**Contact** Managing Director, John Martineau

**Established** 1996

**Insider Info** Catalogue available online.

**Non-Fiction** Publishes General Non-fiction, Illustrated and Scholarly titles on the following subjects:

Science, Spirituality, Magic, Mathematics, Folklore and Ancient Sciences.

**Recent Title(s)** *A Little History of Dragons*, Joyce Hargreaves

**Tips** Wooden Books is a series of small, beautifully produced introductions to the liberal arts, captivating scientists and artists alike. The books are produced with exquisite illustrations, superfine printing, and the finest quality recycled papers. Wooden Books is actively seeking illustrators and cartoonists to work on the Wooden Books series.

## Woodhead Publishing Ltd

**Abington Hall, Abington, Cambridge, CB21 6AH**

🖤 01223 891358

🖤 01223 893694

🖤 wp@woodheadpublishing.com

🖤 www.woodheadpublishing.com

**Contact** Editorial Director, Francis Dodds

**Established** 1989

**Insider Info** Publishes 50 titles per year. Payment is via royalties. Catalogue available free on request and online. Manuscript guidelines available online.

**Non-Fiction** Publishes Reference and Technical titles on the following subjects:

Cooking/Foods/Nutrition, Money/Finance, Science, Technology, Engineering and Construction, Environmental Technology.

**Submission Guidelines** Accepts query with SAE. Submit proposal package (including outline and two sample chapters).

**Recent Title(s)** *Shape Memory Polymers and Textiles*, Jinlian Hu

**Tips** Woodhead Publishing Limited is a leading independent international publishing company. Following initial success in the materials engineering area, Woodhead Publishing has expanded substantially and now also publishes on food science, technology and nutrition, welding and metallurgy, textile technology, environmental technology, finance, commodities and investment. Woodhead is always pleased to hear proposals from authors for new books. If there is a subject that doesn't appear in the catalogue, or you can't find the book you want, or think you could write a book, or contribute a chapter, contact the editorial staff.

## Wordsworth Editions Ltd

**8b East Street, Ware, Hertfordshire, SG12 9HJ**

🖤 01920 465167

🖤 01920 462267

🖤 dennis.hart@wordsworth-editions.com

🖤 www.wordsworth-editions.com

**Contact** Managing Director, Helen Trayler (Production, Editorial); Sales Director, Dennis Hart (Sales, Marketing, Editorial); Director, Derek Wright (Accounts, IT)

**Established** 1986

**Insider Info** Publishes 20 titles per year. Receives approximately five to ten queries and six manuscripts from writers each year. 100 per cent of books are from unagented authors. Payment is via outright purchase. Submissions accompanied by SAE will be returned. Catalogue is free on request, and available online and via email. Manuscript guidelines are not available.

**Non-Fiction** Publishes reference titles on the following subjects:

Language Dictionaries and Guides to Language, Dictionaries of History and Dates, Quotations, Drink, Medical Facts, Sexuality, Symbols, Opera and Folklore (Out of Copyright).

* Most reference works are written by specialists in their field.

**Submission Guidelines** No submissions, all work is specially commissioned. Will not review artwork/images as part of a manuscript package.

**Fiction** Publishes Gothic, Horror, Classic Fiction and Mystery titles.

* Do not publish living authors of fiction.

**Poetry** * Publish some poetry but no living authors.

**Recent Title(s)** *Book of Hymns*, Martin Manser (Reference); *The Tangled Skein*, David Stuart Davies (Mystery Fiction)

**Tips** Typical audiences are those with a general interest in fiction, and students for the reference books it publishes. Do not send in any submissions, any new non-fiction works are always commissioned, while the rest of the publishing programme is made up of reprints.

## Working White Ltd

Chancery Court, Lincolns Inn, Lincolns Road, High Wycombe, Buckinghamshire, HP12 3RE

- ☎ 01494 429318
- ☎ 01494 429317
- ✉ info@workingwhite.co.uk
- 🌐 www.workingwhite.co.uk

**Contact** Erica Filler

**Imprint(s)** Poppy Red

**Insider Info** Catalogue is available free on request and via email: sales@workingwhite.co.uk

**Non-Fiction** Publishes Children's/Juvenile and Illustrated titles.

**Fiction** Publishes Children's titles.

**Tips** Working White is an independent publisher of co-edition children's books for the international market. A Working White book offers the very best in illustration, exceptional expertise in non-fiction writing, and high-end production values for children of pre-school age through to young teenagers. Poppy Red is the sister company, which publishes and distributes the books solely in the UK. Working White children's books are always illustrated and informative, and usually have an extra 'interactive' component such as pop-up, touch and feel sections, or kit-books.

## Worple Press

12 Havelock Road, Tonbridge, Kent, TN9 IJE

- ☎ 01732 367466
- ☎ 01732 352057
- ✉ theworpleco.@aol.com
- 🌐 www.worplepress.com

**Contact** Managing Editor, Peter Carpenter; Managing Editor, Amanda Knight

**Established** 1997

**Insider Info** Publishes five titles per year. Payment is via royalties. Catalogue available free on request.

**Non-Fiction** Publishes General Non-fiction titles on Art/Architecture.

**Poetry** Publishes Poetry titles.

**Tips** Worple Press is an independent publisher of poetry and art books. They will not accept any unsolicited material.

## Wrecking Ball Press

24 Cavendish Square, Hull, East Yorkshire, HU3 1SS

- ✉ editor@wreckingballpress.com
- 🌐 www.wreckingballpress.com

**Contact** Managing Editor, Shane Rhodes

**Insider Info** Catalogue and manuscript guidelines available online.

**Fiction** Publishes Mainstream/Contemporary titles and Short story collections.

**Submission Guidelines** Submit completed manuscript.

**Poetry** Publishes poetry titles.

**Submission Guidelines** Submit complete manuscript.

**Recent Title(s)** *Daniel*, Richard Adams (Novel); *The Reater : Issue 5*, Various (Journal)

**Tips** Wrecking Ball Press is an independent press specialising in poetry and contemporary fiction. It publishes a poetry journal, *The Reater*, and specialises in 'blunt, hammered-home words'. If you wish to submit any poems or stories for inclusion in our journal *The Reater* there is a limit of six poems and two stories per person. Illustrations and photographs will also be accepted for consideration and manuscripts can also be submitted. If possible all submissions should be on a disk, as well as paper.

## Xcite Books

PO Box 26, Cardiff, CF46 9AG

- ☎ 01443 710930
- ☎ 01443 710940
- ✉ info@accentpress.co.uk
- 🌐 www.xcitebooks.moonfruit.com

**Parent Company** Accent Press

**Contact** Editor, Cathryn Cooper

**Insider Info** Catalogue is free on request, and available online. Manuscript guidelines are available via email: editor@xcitebooks.com

**Fiction** Publishes Erotica titles.

**Submission Guidelines** Email Cathryn Cooper for more information.

 Submission details to: editor@xcitebooks.com

**Poetry** Publishes erotic poetry.

**Submission Guidelines** Email Cathryn Cooper for more information.

 Submission details to: editor@xcitebooks.com

**Recent Title(s)** *Sex and Seduction: 20 Erotic Stories*, Cathryn Cooper (ed) (Short story collection); *The Last Cut*, F.M Kay (Erotic poetry)

**Tips** Short story collections are published mainly in three series; Sex and Seduction; Sex and Submission; and Sex and Satisfaction.

## The X Press

PO Box 25694, London, N17 6FP

- ☎ 020 8801 2100
- ☎ 020 8885 1322
- ✉ vibes@xpress.co.uk

**www.xpress.co.uk**
**Contact** Editorial Director, Dotun Adebayo;
Publisher, Steve Pope
**Established** 1992
**Imprint(s)** Black Classics
Nia
20/20
**Insider Info** Publishes 25 titles per year. Catalogue
available online.
**Fiction** Publishes Juvenile, Literary, Mainstream/
Contemporary and Black interest titles.
**Submission Guidelines** Submit completed
manuscript.
**Recent Title(s)** *A Chocolate Soldier*, Cyrus
Colter (Novel)
**Tips** The X Press has grown into Europe's largest
publisher of black interest books. The Nia imprint
publishes literary black fiction, 20/20 publishes
contemporary black fiction, and the Black Classics
series re-prints classic novels by black writers. The X
Press also publishes general black fiction aimed at a
younger audience, and aims to take black writing
into a new era. Prefers full manuscript submissions
rather than proposals, preferably black interest
popular fiction from black writers.

## Yale University Press (London)
**47 Bedford Square, London, WC1B 3DP**
- 020 7079 4900
- 020 7079 4901
- sales@yaleup.co.uk
- www.yalebooks.co.uk
**Established** 1961
**Insider Info** Publishes 300 titles per year. Payment is
via royalties. Catalogue available free on request
and online.
**Non-Fiction** Publishes Autobiography, Biography,
General Non-fiction, Reference and Scholarly titles
on the following subjects:
Art/Architecture , Business/Economics, Education,
Government/Politics, Health/Medicine, History,
Language/Literature, Law, Literary Criticism, Music/
Dance, Nature/Environment, Philosophy,
Psychology, Religion.
**Submission Guidelines** Accepts query with SAE.
**Recent Title(s)** *Piggy Foxy and The Sword of
Revolution: Bolshevik Self-portraits*, Alexander Vatlin
and Larisa Malashenko (eds.)
**Tips** The London office of Yale University Press was
established in 1961 as a marketing base, and in 1973
commenced publishing its own list. It has several
book series, including Yale Nota Bene paperbacks,
the Pevsner Architectural Guides, and books for the
National Gallery. Yale London publishes scholarly

books on a range of subjects, including life writing,
but always with a wide appeal that may appeal to
the general reader.

## Yellow Jersey Press
**Random House, 20 Vauxhall Bridge Road,
London, SW1V 2SA**
- 020 7840 8542
- 020 7233 6117
- yellowjerseyeditorial@randomhouse.co.uk
- www.randomhouse.co.uk
**Parent Company** The Random House Group Ltd
**Contact** Editorial Director, Tristan Jones
**Insider Info** Catalogue available online. Use
advanced search to search catalogue by imprint.
**Non-Fiction** Publishes General Non-fiction, Sports
and Leisure narratives, Television tie-ins and
Memoirs on the following subjects:
Recreation, Sports.
**Submission Guidelines** Submit proposal package
(including outline and one sample chapter and SAE).
Will accept artworks/images (send photocopies).
**Recent Title(s)** *The Accidental Angler*, Charles
Rangeley-Wilson
**Tips** No emailed submissions. Please see The
Random House Group Entry for submission
information.

## Y Lolfa Cyf
**Talybont, Ceredigion, SY24 5AP**
- 01970 832304
- 01970 832782
- ylolfa@ylolfa.com
- www.ylolfa.com
**Contact** Managing Director, Garmon Gruffudd;
Chief Editor, Lefi Gruffudd
**Established** 1967
**Imprint(s)** Dinas
**Insider Info** Publishes 50 titles per year. Payment is
via royalties. Catalogue available online.
**Non-Fiction** Publishes Biography, Children's/
Juvenile, General Non-fiction and Humour titles on
the following subjects:
Art/Architecture, Cooking/Foods/Nutrition,
Education, Government/Politics, History, Language/
Literature, Translation.
**Fiction** Publishes Mainstream/Contemporary and
Translation titles.
**Poetry** Publishes poetry titles.
**Recent Title(s)** *Tales from the Mabinogion*, Gwyn
Thomas (Children's Short stories); *Missed Chances*,
Sam Adams (Collection)

**Tips** Y Lolfa is an independent Welsh publisher specialising in fiction and non-fiction, from, or about Wales. Y Lolfa prints in both Welsh and English and also offers serves as a commercial print company. The Dinas imprint is a part-author subsidised press for unusual and non-mainstream Welsh interest books. Its aim is to produce interesting and original books, which enhance the variety of books published in Wales.

## York Notes

**Edinburgh Gate, Harlow, Essex, CM20 2JE**

- 01279 623623
- 01279 414130
- www.pearsoned.co.uk/imprints/yorknotes/

**Parent Company** Pearson Education

**Insider Info** Catalogue and manuscript guidelines are available online.

**Non-Fiction** Publishes Textbook (Study guides) titles on the following subjects:

Film, Language/Literature, Literary Criticism.

* York Notes provides three main series, catering for different ages groups: 11–14 years, 14–16 years and 16–18 years and undergraduates. Each series covers the main curriculum texts studied at that level.

**Submission Guidelines** Accepts proposal package (including synopsis, sample chapters, market research, your publishing history and author biography).

**Recent Title(s)** *When We Are Married,* A. Other (Study guide)

**Tips** York Notes publishes comprehensive literature guides to help students gain a better understanding of a curriculum text. Each title aims to help students form their own ideas and opinions, and help them to success in examinations. See the website for full list of submissions contacts.

## Young Picador

**20 New Wharf Road, London, N1 9RR**

- 020 7014 6000
- 020 7014 6001
- www.panmacmillan.com

**Parent Company** Pan Macmillan Publishers

**Established** 2002

**Insider Info** Downloadable pdf of catalogue available on line.

**Non-Fiction** Young Adult and Teenage titles.

**Submission Guidelines** Agented submissions only.

**Fiction** Publish Young Adult and Teenage titles.

**Submission Guidelines** Agented submissions only.

**Poetry** Publish a small amount of poetry.

**Submission Guidelines** Agented submissions only.

**Recent Title(s)** *Roundabout,* Rhiannon Lassiter

**Tips** Concentrates mainly on teenage fiction. The non-fiction and poetry sections of the list are extremely small. No unsolicited submissions.

## Zambezi Publishing Ltd

**PO Box 221, Plymouth, PL2 2YJ**

- 01752 367300
- 01752 350453
- info@zampub.com
- www.zampub.com

**Contact** Chair, Sasha Fenton; Managing Director, Jan Budkowski

**Established** 1999

**Imprint(s)** ESP (Exclusive Self-Publishing)

**Insider Info** Publishes 12 titles per year. Payment is via royalties. Catalogue and manuscript guidelines available online.

**Non-Fiction** Publishes General Non-fiction and Self-help titles on the following subjects:

Business/Economics, Health/Medicine, Money/Finance, Spirituality, Mind, Body and Spirit.

**Submission Guidelines** Accepts query with SAE/proposal package (including outline, one sample chapter, your publishing history, author biography, SAE).

Submission details to: sasha@zampub.com

**Recent Title(s)** *What Time were you Born?,* Sasha Fenton

**Tips** Zambezi publishes general non-fiction books. Their ESP imprint also offers 'assisted self-publishing' services and they are keen to push self-publishing as the ideal publishing method. Consider unsolicited proposals, but thorough market research is needed with every proposal.

## Zed Books Ltd

**7 Cynthia Street, London, N1 9JF**

- 020 7837 0384
- 020 7833 3960
- editorial@zedbooks.net
- www.zedbooks.co.uk

**Contact** Commissioning Editor, Ellen McKinlay (Current Affairs, Economics, African Studies, Latin American Studies); Commissioning Editor, Susannah Trefgarne (Development Studies, Gender Studies, African Studies, Middle East Studies, Asian Studies)

**Established** 1976

**Insider Info** Publishes 60 titles per year. Payment is via royalties. Catalogue available free on request, online. Manuscript guidelines available online.

**Non-Fiction** Publishes Reference, Scholarly and Technical titles on the following subjects:

Business/Economics, Government/Politics, Multicultural, Regional, Women's Issues/Studies, International Relations, Cultural/Development Studies.

**Submission Guidelines** Accepts query with SAE/proposal package (including outline, your publishing history, author biography, SAE).

Submission details to: firstname.lastname@zedbooks.net

**Recent Title(s)** *The Rise of The Global Left*, Boaventura de Sousa Santos

**Tips** Zed is an independent scholarly publishing house, catering predominantly to the needs of academics and students, and occasionally to a wider audience of activists and policy makers. They aim for books to reach the broadest possible audience, and therefore only publish those likely to have a substantial market, in hardback and paperback.

## Zoe Books Ltd
**15 Worthy Lane, Winchester, Hampshire, SO23 7AB**
- 01962 851318
- enquiries@zoebooks.co.uk
- www.zoebooks.co.uk

**Contact** Managing Director, Imogen Dawson
**Established** 1990
**Insider Info** Catalogue available online.
**Non-Fiction** Publishes Children's, Reference and Scholarly titles on Education.
**Recent Title(s)** *Clothes and Crafts*, Imogen Dawson and Philip Steele
**Tips** Publishes children's non-fiction reference and information books for schools and libraries. Zoe Books is not currently commissioning new work and will not accept any unsolicited submissions.

## Zymurgy Publishing
**Hoults Estate, Walker Road, Newcastle upon Tyne, NE6 2HL**
- 0191 276 2425
- 0191 276 2425
- martin.ellis@ablibris.com

**Contact** Chairman, Martin Ellis
**Established** 2000
**Insider Info** Payment is via royalties.
**Non-Fiction** Publishes General Non-fiction and Illustrated titles.
**Tips** Zymurgy publishes illustrated adult non-fiction on a range of subjects. Proposals welcome, but no unsolicited manuscripts.

# UK & IRISH POETRY PUBLISHERS

## Aard Press
(See entry under UK & Irish Book Publishers)

## Abbey Press
(See entry under UK & Irish Book Publishers)

## Abraxas Press
**13 Copthall Gardens, Mill Hill, London, NW7 2NG**
- poetry@abraxas.fsnet.co.uk
- www.abraxaspress.co.uk

**Insider Info** Catalogue available online.
**Poetry** Abraxas Press currently exists only to publish the work of Alan Marshfield.
**Recent Title(s)** *The Nature of Things*, Alan Marshfield

## Acair Ltd
(See entry under UK & Irish Book Publishers)

## Agenda Editions
**The Wheelwrights, Fletching Sreet, Mayfields, East Sussex, TN20 6TL**
- 01435 873703
- editor@agendapoetry.co.uk
- www.agendapoetry.co.uk

**Contact** Editor, Patricia McCarthy
**Insider Info** Catalogue available online.
**Poetry** Agenda Editions is the book publishing arm of Agenda magazine. It publishes limited editions of an individual's poems.
**Submission Guidelines** Submit six sample poems.
**Recent Title(s)** *Kurdish Poems of Love and Liberty*, Desmond O'Grady; *A Smile Between the Stones*, John Montague
**Tips** Read copies of Agenda magazine to get a feel for the types of poetry published. The editor wants less cliché ridden poetry and more well crafted and deeply felt writing. Being published in the magazine is more likely to be a step towards getting a book published than approaching the editor with an entire collection.

## Akros Publications
(See entry under UK & Irish Book Publishers)

## Alison Allison

**Double Dykes, Elm Row, Galashiels, TD1 3HT**

☎ 01896 753728

✉ alisonallisondouble@yahoo.co.uk

**Poetry** Publishes poetry books and pamphlets.

**Tips** Make contact by email for more information on current activities.

## Alma Books Ltd

(See entry under UK & Irish Book Publishers)

## Anchor Books

**Remus House, Woodston, Peterborough, PE2 9JX**

☎ 01733 898102

☎ 01733 313524

✉ anchorbooks@forwardpress.co.uk

🌐 www.forwardpress.co.uk

**Parent Company** Forward Press

**Established** 1992

**Poetry** Publishes Poetry titles.

 * Almost all material is traditional, rhymes and is family friendly. It should be uncomplicated and accessible.

**Submission Guidelines** Submit two sample poems. Submission details to: inbox@forwardpress.co.uk

**Tips** Anchor Books authors are from a variety of age ranges and backgrounds. Popular subjects tend to be those from everyday life, such as interesting anecdotes, stories and tales to give readers inspiration. Bear in mind that this imprint is very much designed to publish poetry for the whole family. The Forward Press website gives specific calls for submissions throughout the year which is an extremely useful guide for potential authors.

## Anglo-Saxon Books

(See entry under UK & Irish Book Publishers)

## Anvil Press Poetry Ltd

**Neptune House, 70 Royal Hill, London, SE10 8RF**

✉ anvil@anvilpresspoetry.com

🌐 www.anvilpresspoetry.com

**Contact** Peter Jay (Poetry, Translated poetry)

**Established** 1968

**Insider Info** Publishes 12 titles per year. Receives approximately 2,000 queries and 600 manuscripts per year. Five per cent of books published are from first-time authors and 60 per cent of books published are from unagented authors. Payment is via royalty (on retail price) with 0.07 (per £) minimum and 0.1 (per £) maximum. Advance offered is from £2,000–£5,000. Average lead time is 15 months, with simultaneous submissions accepted. Submissions accompanied by SAE will be returned. Aims to respond to queries with seven days and proposals within four weeks. Catalogue is free on request, and available online or by email.

**Poetry** Publishes book-length poetry manuscripts, or single poems in anthologies.

**Submission Guidelines** Accepts complete manuscripts by post.

**Recent Title(s)** *Things Unsaid*, Tony Connor (New and Selected Poems)

## Arrowhead Press

**70 Clifton Road, Darlington, Co. Durham, DL1 5DX**

✉ editor@arrowheadpress.co.uk, roger.collett@ntlworld.com

🌐 www.arrowheadpress.co.uk

**Contact** Managing Editor, Roger Collett; Poetry Editor, Joanna Boulter

**Established** 2001

**Insider Info** Catalogue and manuscript guidelines available online.

**Poetry** Publishes poetry in pamphlet format.

**Submission Guidelines** Accepts email queries. No unsolicited submissions.

**Recent Title(s)** *Sailing Under False Colours*, Shelly McAlister

**Tips** The editor states that it is a waste of time and money submitting to Arrowhead if you have not already been published in reputable magazines and possibly already had a pamphlet published (excluding self published works). Potential authors are recommended to make contact by email, although there is no guarantee of a quick reply due to time constraints on the editors.

## Atlantean Publishing

(See entry under UK & Irish Book Publishers)

## Atlas Press

(See entry under UK & Irish Book Publishers)

## The Barddas Society

(See entry under UK & Irish Book Publishers)

## Barque Press

**70a Cranwich Road, London, N16 5JD**

☎ 020 7502 0906

@ info@barquepress.com

@ www.barquepress.com

**Contact** Publisher, Andrea Brady; Publisher, Keston Sutherland

**Established** 1995

**Poetry** Barque Press predominantly publishes poetry titles.

 * The press is not currently accepting any new manuscripts for publication.

**Submission Guidelines** Submitted manuscripts will not be returned.

## BB Books
**Spring Bank, Longsight Road, Copster Green, Blackburn, BB1 9EU**

@ 01254 249128

**Contact** Dave Cunliffe

**Poetry** Publishes Poetry titles.

**Tips** BB Books is the publisher for poetry magazine *Global Tapestry Journal.*

## Between the Lines
(See entry under UK & Irish Book Publishers)

## Beyond the Cloister Publications
**14 Lewes Crescent, Brighton, BN2 1FH**

@ 01273 687053

@ sales@beyondthecloister.com

@ http://beyondthecloister.com

**Contact** Editor, Hugh Hellicar

**Established** 1994

**Poetry** Specialises in single poet volumes, as well as anthologies.

**Submission Guidelines** Accepts sample poems.

**Recent Title(s)** *Poems of Faith and Love*, Various; *Of Time and Small Islands*, Walter Nash

**Tips** Sample poems are welcomed by either mail or email. Please address them to the Editor.

## Big Little Poem Books
**3 Park Avenue, Melton Mowbray, Leicestershire, LE13 0JB**

@ 01664 850228

@ rmr@dmu.ac.uk

**Contact** Publisher and Editor, Robert Richardson

**Established** 1987

**Poetry** The Big Little Poem Series, a set of poems printed on cards, was discontinued in 1992. The editorial policy was to focus on consciousness of form and precision of language, and to promote effective contemporary approaches to the lyric and epigram. The book imprint may occasionally still publish.

**Tips** Submissions are limited to those poets who have already been published in the *Big Little Poem* series.

## Birlinn Ltd
(See entry under UK & Irish Book Publishers)

## Biscuit Publishing
(See entry under UK & Irish Book Publishers)

## Black Spring Press
(See entry under UK & Irish Book Publishers)

## Blackstaff Press
(See entry under UK & Irish Book Publishers)

## Bloodaxe Books
**Highgreen, Tarset, Northumberland, NE48 1RP**

@ 01434 240500

@ 01434 240505

@ editor@bloodaxebooks.com

@ www.bloodaxebooks.com

**Admin other Info** Chairman, Simon Thirsk; Editor, Neil Astley

**Established** 1978

**Insider Info** Publishes 30 titles per year. Receives approximately 5,000–6,000 queries per year. Submissions accompanied by SAE will be returned. Aims to respond to queries within four months. Catalogue available via email to: sales@bloodaxebooks.com. Manuscript guidelines available online.

**Poetry** Publish contemporary poetry titles.

 * Bloodaxe currently have a large backlog of submissions to review and may not be able to read new submissions in the short or medium term. Much of their publishing programme is already filled by authors they already publish.

**Submission Guidelines** 12 sample poems.

**Recent Title(s)** *The Bloodaxe Book of Poetry Quotations*, Dennis O'Driscoll; *Now,* Brendan Kennelly

**Tips** Bloodaxe do have a policy for publishing new writers, although they state that 'new writers' often means those that have built up extensive publishing history through literary or poetry magazines, and have a collection of poems large enough to fill a book. Do not submit a manuscript if your poetry has not already been extensively published.

## Bloomsbury Publishing Plc
(See entry under UK & Irish Book Publishers)

## Blue Butterfly Publishers
**13 Irvine Way, Inverurie, Aberdeenshire, Scotland, AB51 4ZR**
◉ blue7butterfly@which.net, marc.madhill@which.net
◍ www.madill.prodigynet.co.uk/bbp
**Insider Info** Payment is a free copy of the publication.
**Poetry** Publishes anthologies of Christian poetry, the contents largely consisting of the winning entries from annual competitions.
**Tips** Details of competitions and guidelines for the types of poetry required change with each new round, so check the website for the latest opportunities.

## Bluechrome
(See entry under UK & Irish Book Publishers)

## The Boho Press
**PO Box 109, Portishead, Bristol, BS20 7ZJ**
◉ 07092 273360
◉ 07092 273357
◉ info@bohopress.co.uk
◍ www.bohopress.co.uk
**Parent Company** Bluechrome Publishers
**Insider Info** Catalogue available online.
**Poetry** Publishes Poetry titles.
  * Boho Press are interested in Writers' Groups who may be interested in publishing an anthology. The publishers welcome emails containing an outline of the book in the first instance.
**Recent Title(s)** *Dark Corners*, Les Merton; *101 Poets for a Cornish Assembly*, Various
**Tips** Email communication is preferred over postal contact.

## Bradshaw Books
(See entry under UK & Irish Book Publishers)

## Bridge Pamphlets
**PO Box 309, Aylsham, Norwich, NR11 6LN**
◉ mail@therialto.co.uk
◍ www.therialto.co.uk
**Insider Info** Submissions accompanied by SAE will be returned. Aims to respond to proposals within ten weeks. Catalogue available online.

**Poetry** Bridge Pamphlets, associated with the *Rialto Poetry Magazine*, publishes collections in pamphlet format, from poets who are not ready for a full first collection, but deserve to be published in a single author volume.
**Submission Guidelines** Submit six sample poems.
**Recent Title(s)** *Bye for Now*, Lorraine Marnier
**Tips** Submitting poems to the magazine may be advisable to start with, rather than approaching Bridge Pamphlets with a collection that has no prior publication.

## The British Museum Press
(See entry under UK & Irish Book Publishers)

## The Brodie Press
**c/o Dept. of English, University of Bristol, 3–5 Woodland Road, Bristol, BS8 1TB**
◉ thebrodiepress@hotmail.com
◍ www.brodiepress.co.uk
**Contact** Editor, Tom Sperlinger; Editor, Hannah Sheppard
**Established** 2002
**Insider Info** Catalogue available online.
**Poetry** Publishes Poetry titles.
**Submission Guidelines** No unsolicited submissions are accepted.
**Recent Title(s)** *The Sun at Midnight*, Julie-Ann Rowell
**Tips** The Brodie Press is a not for profit organisation, staffed by volunteers. They publish new writers and established authors who wish to undertake experimental or unusual projects.

## Bullseye Publications
**5 Camptoun, North Berwick, East Lothian, Scotland, EH39 5BA**
◉ 01620 880311
◉ alancharlesgay@aol.com
**Contact** Alan Gay
**Poetry** Currently publishes the poetry of Alan Gay in book and pamphlet form.

## Calder Publications
(See entry under UK & Irish Book Publishers)

## Calder Wood Press
**1 Beachmont Court, Dunbar, East Lothian, EH42 1YF**
◉ colin.will@zen.co.uk
◍ www.calderwoodpress.co.uk

**Contact** Colin Will

**Poetry** Calder Wood Press was set up primarily to publish poetry cards, but its remit has widened and it now produces writing group anthologies, haiku collections and poetry pamphlets. It has also published a local history book and a few short story pamphlets.

**Submission Guidelines** Accepts queries.

**Recent Title(s)** *Regalia: Poems from the Quill Writing Group*, Bathgate (Various)

**Tips** If you have a project in mind that you think may be suitable for the Press, contact them with a brief query in the first instance; no unsolicited manuscripts.

## Carcanet Press Ltd
(See entry under UK & Irish Book Publishers)

## The Celtic Cross Press
(See entry under UK & Irish Book Publishers)

## Chapman Publishing
(See entry under UK & Irish Book Publishers)

## Chatto & Windus
(See entry under UK & Irish Book Publishers)

## The Cherry on the Top Press
(See entry under UK & Irish Book Publishers)

## Cinnamon Press
(See entry under UK & Irish Book Publishers)

## Clutag Press
**PO Box 154, Thame, OX9 3RQ**
- www.clutagpress.com

**Contact** Andrew McNeillie
**Established** 2000
**Insider Info** Submissions will not be returned. Catalogue is available online.
**Non-Fiction** Publishes Autobiographies, Biographies and Memoirs.
 * Only two memoirs have been published.
**Submission Guidelines** No unsolicited manuscripts.
**Poetry** Publishes pamphlet collections from well known poets, including Seamus Heany and John Fuller.

**Recent Title(s)** *Ian Niall: Part of his Life*, Andrew McNeillie; *Diehard*, Mick Imlah

**Tips** Please note that absolutely no unsolicited manuscripts will be returned, or read. If you wish to make contact please use the form on the website.

## The Collective Press
**Penlanlas Farm, Llantilio Pertholey, Y-Fenni, Gwent, NP7 7HN**
- 01873 856350
- 01873 859559
- jj@jojowales.co.uk
- www.welshwriters.com

**Contact** Coordinator, John Jones; Chief Editor, Frank Olding; Events Manager, Ric Hool; Distribution, Jane Blank
**Established** 1990
**Insider Info** Submissions accompanied by SAE will be returned.
**Poetry** Publishes poetry collections.
 * Poets are welcome from around the world and from any background.
**Submission Guidelines** Submit complete manuscript. No email submissions are accepted.
**Recent Title(s)** *Joking Apart*, Alicia Stubbersfield
**Tips** The Collective Press is a not for profit organisation and for this reason, the press appreciate it when fellow poets assist them financially by purchasing their books. They recommend that writers who are seeking publication read a few existing Collective Press titles to get a feel for what The Collective Press do. Replies to submissions may take a while due to the voluntary nature of the organisation, but manuscript submissions with enclosed SAEs should receive a reply.

## Comma Press
(See entry under UK & Irish Book Publishers)

## Crescent Moon Publishing
(See entry under UK & Irish Book Publishers)

## Dagger Press
**1 Portland Street, Worcester, WR1 2NL**
- dagger.press@tiscali.co.uk
- www.poetryworkshops.co.uk

**Contact** Editor, Brian Morse
**Poetry** Publishes thirty-two page pamphlets written by adult poets.
**Tips** The idea behind Dagger Press is to showcase poets which the publisher feels should be more

widely read. Editor, Brian Morse is himself a published children's author and poet. Three poets who have been published by Dagger have gone on to publish with larger presses.

## Dedalus Press

**13 Moyclare Road, Baldoyle, Dublin 13, Republic of Ireland**
- 00353 1 839 2034
- 0870 127 2089
- office@dedaluspress.com
- www.dedaluspress.com

**Contact** Publisher and Editor, Pat Boran (Poetry)
**Established** 1985
**Insider Info** Publishes ten titles per year. 100 per cent of books published are from unagented authors. Payment is via royalty (on retail price). Simultaneous submissions are not accepted. Submissions accompanied by SAE will be returned. Aims to respond to manuscripts within three months. Catalogue is available online. Manuscript guidelines are available online, or by email.
**Poetry** Publish a small amount of contemporary poetry collections every year.
**Submission Guidelines** Accepts query with SAE or complete manuscript (including covering letter and your publishing history).
**Recent Title(s)** *Clinging to the Myth*, Padraig J. Daly (Irish Poetry Collection)
**Tips** Dedalus Press operates a submission window system. Check their website to see when they will be accepting the next batch of submissions.

## Diehard

**91–93 Main Street, Callander, Scotland, FK17 8BQ**
- 01877 339449
- sally.king4@btopenworld.com
- www.poetryscotland.co.uk

**Contact** Editor, Sally Evans (Poetry Scotland)
**Poetry** Publishes Poetry titles as well as the poetry magazine, *Poetry Scotland*.
**Recent Title(s)** *A Man at Sea*, Gordon Mead
**Tips** Catalogue and manuscript guidelines available online. Subscribe to the *Poetry Scotland* magazine to get a feel for the types of poetry published. This will cost £5 per year and details are on the website. Do not approach Diehard if you are not currently being published by *Poetry Scotland*.

## Dionysia Press

(See entry under UK & Irish Book Publishers)

## Donut Press

**PO Box 45093, London, N4 1UZ**
- donutchops@yahoo.co.uk
- www.donutpress.co.uk

**Contact** Andy Ching
**Established** 2001
**Poetry** Publishes poetry titles.
**Recent Title(s)** *Stranded in Sub-Atomica*, Tim Turnball
**Tips** Donut Press is a small, independent publisher of poetry collections. Queries about Donut Press are invited by email.

## Dreadful Night Press

**82 Kelvin Court, Glasgow, G12 0AQ**
- 0141 339 9150
- dreadfulnight1@aol.com

**Insider Info** Booklets/Pamphlets.
**Poetry** Publishes poetry by a range of writers in both black and white, and colour booklet form.
**Recent Title(s)** *The Boy Who Came Ashore*, Alan Gay (Poetry)
**Tips** Member of the *Scottish Pamphlet Poetry* website, whose pamphlets usually have some kind of Scottish connection.

## Driftwood Publications

**5 Timms Lane, Formby, Liverpool, Merseyside, L37 9DW**
- 01704 833911
- 0151 524 0216
- janet.speedy@tesco.net

**Contact** Editor, Brian Wake (Poetry); Editor, Tony Dash (Poetry); Coordinator, Janet Speedy (Poetry)
**Established** 1972
**Insider Info** Publishes ten titles per year. Receives 750 queries and 200 manuscripts per year. 75 per cent of books published are from first-time authors, 100 per cent of books published are from unagented authors. Payment is via complimentary copies. Average lead time is nine months, with simultaneous submissions accepted. Submissions accompanied by SAE will be returned. Aims to respond to queries within two weeks, proposals within 12 weeks and manuscripts within three months. Manuscript guidelines available with SAE.
**Poetry** Publishes poetry collections and poetry in performance, ideally from unknown or neglected poets.
**Recent Title(s)** *COOEE*, Peggy Poole (Poetry)

**Tips** Driftwood is a non-profit making organisation that promotes poetry in performance and poetry publications

## Edgewell Publishing
(See entry under UK & Irish Book Publishers)

## Egg Box Publishing
(See entry under UK & Irish Book Publishers)

## Enitharmon Press
(See entry under UK & Irish Book Publishers)

## Erran Publishing
**43 Willow Road, Carlton, Nottingham, NG4 3BH**
- erranpublishing@hotmail.com
- www.poetichours.homestead.com

**Contact** Editor, Nick Clark (Poetry, Articles)
**Established** 1987
**Imprints** Poetic Hours
**Insider Info** Publishes one title per year. Receives approximately 400 queries and 400 manuscripts per year. Accepts simultaneous submissions. Submissions accompanied by SAE will be returned. Aim to respond to queries within one week and manuscripts within three weeks. Manuscript guidelines are available with SAE, and available online or by email.
**Poetry** Publishes general contemporary poetry in the *Poetic Hours Magazine*.
  * Does not publish extremist or political poetry.
**Submission Guidelines** Accepts complete manuscripts.
**Recent Title(s)** *Poetic Hours Magazine*
**Tips** Erran Publishing only publishes the *Poetic Hours Magazine*.

## Essence Press
**8 Craiglea Drive, Edinburgh, EH10 5PA**
- jaj@essencepress.co.uk
- www.essencepress.co.uk

**Contact** Editor, Julie Johnstone
**Insider Info** Submissions accompanied by SAE will be returned. Aim to respond to manuscripts within 12 weeks.
**Poetry** Publishes small hand bound poem pamphlets and poetry postcards, bookmarks and cards, taking one poem and creating an entire publication around it.
**Submission Guidelines** Submit five sample poems.

**Recent Title(s)** *Window on the Garden*, Hamish White
**Tips** The publisher will accept unsolicited submissions, although many works are commissioned. Essence Press also publishes *Island* magazine for which submissions are considered, include a brief CV. Queries will be accepted by email, but emails with unsolicited attachments will not be opened, include all information in the body of the email. The subject line of the email should be very direct; emails with vague subject lines are unlikely to be opened.

## Etruscan Books
**28 Fowler's Court, Fore Street, Buckfastleigh, TQ11 0AA**
- 01364 643128
- etruscan@macunlimited.net
- www.e-truscan.co.uk

**Contact** Nicholas Johnson
**Poetry** Publishes poetry from both UK and US poets, with distribution outlets in both countries.
**Recent Title(s)** *Time is a Fisherman*, Gael Turnball
**Tips** Etruscan also run a book club, the products of which give a good indication of the company's style.

## Everyman
(See entry under UK & Irish Book Publishers)

## Everyman Classics
(See entry under UK & Irish Book Publishers)

## Everyman's Library
(See entry under UK & Irish Book Publishers)

## Faber & Faber Ltd
(See entry under UK & Irish Book Publishers)

## Fal Publications
(See entry under UK & Irish Book Publishers)

## Five Leaves Publications
(See entry under UK & Irish Book Publishers)

## Flambard Press
(See entry under UK & Irish Book Publishers)

## Flarestack Publishing

**8 Abbot's Way, Pilton, Somerset, BA4 4BN**
☎ 01749 890019
✉ cannula.dementia@virgin.net
🌐 www.flarestack.co.uk
**Contact** Editor, Charles Johnson (Poetry)
**Established** 1995
**Insider Info** Publishes eight titles per year. Receives approximately 30 queries and 25 manuscripts per year. 60 per cent of books published are from first-time authors, 95 per cent of books published are from unagented authors. Payment is via percentage discount on sales. Simultaneous submissions are not accepted. Submissions accompanied by SAE will be returned. Aims to respond to queries and other enquiries within three weeks, proposals within one month and manuscripts within three months. Catalogue is free on request. Manuscript guidelines are free on request, and available online or by email.
**Poetry** Publishes poetry titles.
 \* Only interested in original contemporary poetry.
**Submission Guidelines** Accepts query/proposal package (including outline, six sample poems and author biography and SAE).
**Tips** Authors are advised to be bold with their submissions and to read a copy of Flarestack's poetry magazine, *Obsessed with Pipework*, to get a feel for the overall interests of the company.

## Flipped Eye Publishing Limited

(See entry under UK & Irish Book Publishers)

## Forward Press

**Remus House, Coltsfoot Drive, Woodston, Peterborough, PE2 9JX**
☎ 01733 898105
☎ 01733 898105
✉ info@forwardpress.co.uk
🌐 www.forwardpress.co.uk
**Established** 1989
**Imprint(s)** Poetry Now
 Anchor Books
 Triumph House
 Need2Know
 New Fiction
 Spotlight Poets
 Writers' Bookshop
 Pond View
**Insider Info** Average lead time is three months.
**Poetry** Publishes a wide variety of poetry titles.
 \* The website details specific calls for submissions under particular themes, these change regularly.

**Submission Guidelines** Submit two sample poems by email. Poems submitted for the monthly themes may be sent by post or email. If posting, write your name and address on each piece separately. If emailing, enter the theme name in the subject box.
**Recent Title(s)** Working Mothers - The Essential Guide, Denise Tyler (Need2Know); *Love in Ink*, Various
**Tips** Forward Press are the largest publisher of new poetry in the world. All poets published by Forward Press or any of its imprints, are automatically entered into the Top 100 Poets of the Year competition. Forward Press also publishes short stories (New Fiction imprint, launched 1992), biographies, children's titles, educational titles, general non-fiction (Pond View Books imprint), books for writers, and a series of books which address the problems/situations that ordinary people encounter in their everyday lives (Need2Know imprint).

## Four Quarters Press

**7 The Towers, Stevenage, Hertfordshire, SG1 1HE**
✉ octillion@ntlworld.com
🌐 http://homepage.ntlworld.com/chessmaster/4qp/Page_1.html
**Poetry** Publishes Poetry titles.
**Tips** Four Quarters Press produce not for profit publications (mainly poetry), for charity purposes only.

## Gairm Publications

(See entry under UK & Irish Book Publishers)

## The Galdragon Press

**2b Church Road, Stromness, Orkney, KW16 3BT**
✉ galdragonpress@ntlworld.com
🌐 http://homepage@ntlworld.com
**Contact** Anne Thomson
**Insider Info** Submissions will not be returned. Catalogue available free on request and via email. Email with your postal address for a printed list.
**Poetry** Publishes Poetry titles.
**Tips** Publishes small, hand-set, letterpress editions of poetry and some pamphlet poetry. No unsolicited manuscripts or email attachments will be accepted.

## The Gallery Press

(See entry under UK & Irish Book Publishers)

## George Ronald Publishers Ltd
(See entry under UK & Irish Book Publishers)

## Gomer Press/Gwasg Gomer
(See entry under UK & Irish Book Publishers)

## Gwasg Pantycelyn
(See entry under UK & Irish Book Publishers)

## HappenStance Press
**21 Hatton Green, Glenrothes, Scotland, KY7 4SD**
- nell@happenstancepress.com
- www.happenstancepress.com

**Contact** Helena Nelson
**Established** 2005
**Insider Info** Submissions accompanied by SAE will be returned. Aims to respond to manuscripts in two months. Catalogue and manuscript guidelines are available online.
**Poetry** Publishes poetry titles.
  * Interested in first collections from poets across the UK, but in particular those with links to Scotland.
**Submission Guidelines** Accepts unsolicited submissions along with a brief publishing history and SAE. No email submissions. Submit 8–20 sample poems.
**Recent Title(s)** *Twenty Three Poems*, Michael Mackmin
**Tips** Download for free the 'Bluffer's Guide to Getting Your Chapbook Published' and 'Dos and Don'ts' from the website, for detailed explanations as to what HappenStance Press expect from potential authors. For more information on the beginnings of the press, its aspirations and future plans, 'The HappenStance Story: Chapter One' is available for £2.50 and will give poets a good idea as to whether their work will fit into the press' lists.

## hardPressed Poetry
**Shanbally Road, Annacotty, Co. Limerick, Republic of Ireland**
- bmills@netg.ie
- www.gofree.indigo.ie/~hpp

**Contact** Billy Mews; Catherine Walsh
**Poetry** Publishes poetry titles.
  * Prefers poetry that you won't find in average bookshops.
**Tips** hardPressed has also published poetry cards, journals and anthologies in the past. There is an enquiry form on the website for more information.

## Harpercroft Publications
**Old Bank House, 24 Castle Street, Crail, KY10 3SH**
- 01333 451744

**Contact** Gordon Jarvie
**Poetry** Publishes poetry pamphlets to showcase the work of Gordon Jarvie.
**Recent Title(s)** *The Tale of the Crail Whale*, Gordon Jarvie
**Tips** Member of the *Scottish Pamphlet Poetry* website, where recent titles can also be viewed and ordered.

## Headland Publications
(See entry under UK & Irish Book Publishers)

## Headline
(See entry under UK & Irish Book Publishers)

## Hearing Eye Publications
**c/o 99 Torriano Avenue, London, NW5 2RX**
- 020 7267 2751
- hearing_eye@torriano.org
- www.hearingeye.org/zen

**Contact** John Rety
**Established** 1987
**Insider Info** Catalogue available online.
**Poetry** Publishes Poetry titles.
**Tips** Primarily publishes poetry collections, but also some other literature and have recently produced a CD of poetry readings. Attend the poetry readings at the Torriano Avenue address (check website for details) to get a flavour of their poetry, as well as browsing their catalogue.

## Heaventree Press
**Koco Building, The Arches, Spon End, Coventry, CV1 3JQ**
- 024 7671 3555
- admin@heaventreepress.com, editor@heaventreepress.com, events@heaventreepress.com
- www.heaventreepress.co.uk

**Contact** Director, Jonathan Morley; Editor, Ziqian Chan; Events Coordinator, Keisha Thompson
**Insider Info** Submissions accompanied by SAE will be returned. Catalogue available online.
**Poetry** Publishes anthologies and pamphlets of new literature.
**Submission Guidelines** Submit complete manuscript.

**Recent Title(s)** *Broadcast: New Warwick Writing*, Jeremy Treglown, ed. (Poetry)

**Tips** Heaventree is a non-profit organisation, set up by local poets to help encourage and promote arts in the Coventry area. Also publishes *Avocado* magazine.

## Hilltop Press
**4 Nowell Place, Almondbury, Huddersfield, HD5 8PD**
**Contact** Steve Sneyd
**Insider Info** Catalogue available with a SAE.
**Fiction** Publishes Fantasy, Horror and Science Fiction titles.
**Poetry** Publishes dark fantasy poetry.
**Recent Title(s)** *Medusa*, Steve Sneyd ed. (Fantasy); *Bus Stop/The Long Trip*, John Francis Haines and Dainis Bisenieks (Poetry)
**Tips** All material is in the Fantasy/Horror/Science Fiction categories. As well as by mail, a list of publications is available at www.bbr-online.com

## Hilltop Press
(See entry under UK & Irish Book Publishers)

## Honno Welsh Women's Press
(See entry under UK & Irish Book Publishers)

## Hub Editions
**Longholm, Eastbank, Wingland, Sutton Bridge, Spalding, Lincolnshire, PE12 9YS**
**Contact** Colin Blundell
**Poetry** Publishes small collections of poetry and anthologies.
**Recent Title(s)** *The Same Space*, Martin Lucas; *Im Zeichen Des Janus: Haiku Und Haibun Deutsch-Englisch (Hub Haiku)*, David Cobb

## Iron Press
(See entry under UK & Irish Book Publishers)

## Jonathan Cape
(See entry under UK & Irish Book Publishers)

## Karnak House
(See entry under UK & Irish Book Publishers)

## Katabasis
**10 St. Martin's Close, London, NW1 0HR**
☎ 020 7485 3830
✉ katabasis@katabasis.co.uk
🌐 www.katabasis.co.uk
**Contact** Dinah Livingstone
**Established** 1967
**Insider Info** Catalogue available online.
**Poetry** Publishes poetry titles.
**Submission Guidelines** No unsolicited manuscripts
**Recent Title(s)** *Collected Poems*, Anne Beresford
**Tips** Katabasis have a strong international flavour, publishing a Chilean poet, among others. They are local and international, and want down to earth poetry, that is both rooted in a particular place and history, and speaks beyond them.

## The Kates Hill Press
(See entry under UK & Irish Book Publishers)

## Kettillonia
(See entry under UK & Irish Book Publishers)

## Kingfisher Publications Plc
(See entry under UK & Irish Book Publishers)

## KT Publications
**16 Fane Close, Stamford, PE9 1HG**
☎ 01780 754193
**Contact** Kevin Troop
**Poetry** Publishes Poetry titles.
**Tips** Publishes the *Kite Modern Poetry* series as well as *The Third Half* magazine. Contact Kevin Troop for more information.

## Landfill Press
**17 Waldeck Road, Norwich, NR4 7PG**
✉ sales@landfillpress.co.uk
🌐 www.landfillpress.co.uk
**Poetry** Publishes Poetry titles.
**Recent Title(s)** *Twine*, R.F. Langley
**Tips** Publishes pocket size poem sequences. No unsolicited manuscripts.

## Lapwing Publications
**1 Ballysillan Drive, Belfast, BT14 8HQ, Northern Ireland**
☎ 028 9039 1240
☎ 028 9039 1240

○ catherine.greig1@ntlworld.com
**Contact** Dennis Greig
**Poetry** Publishes small editions of poetry collections.
**Tips** Although Lapwing started off as a not for profit organisation to serve the needs of emerging Northern Irish writers, it quickly extended its reach to the Republic of Ireland. It now publishes poets who make their home in Ireland, Irish poets who now live elsewhere, and occasionally poets who have no connection to Ireland.

## Laurel Books
**282 The Common, Holt, BA14 6QJ**
○ 01225 782874
○ mail@laurelbooks.co.uk
○ www.laurelbooks.co.uk
**Contact** Patrick Ingram
**Insider Info** Catalogue available online.
**Poetry** Publishes small poetry collections.
**Recent Title(s)** *The Deceitful Calm*, Poems by Edmund Blunden (Rennie Parker and Margi Blunden eds.)
**Tips** A small press who often commission their titles.

## Leaf Books
(See entry under UK & Irish Book Publishers)

## Leafe Press
**4 Cohen Close, Chilwell, Nottingham, NG9 6RW**
○ leafepress@hotmail.com
○ www.leafepress.com
**Poetry** Publishes pamphlets of contemporary poetry.
**Recent Title(s)** *A Strange Arrangement: New and Selected Poems*, C. J Allen
**Tips** Submissions are by invitation only. No unsolicited manuscripts.

## Libris Ltd
(See entry under UK & Irish Book Publishers)

## The Lilliput Press Ltd
(See entry under UK & Irish Book Publishers)

## Littoral Press
**38 Barringtons, 10 Sutton Road, Southend on Sea, Essex, SS2 5NA**
○ http://mysite.wanadoo-members.co.uk/mervyn_linford/press

**Contact** Mervyn Linford
**Insider Info** Publishes three titles per year.
**Poetry** Publish a small number of poetry collections a year.
**Recent Title(s)** *Bright Moon - Still Heart*, Michael Molyneux (Poetry)
**Tips** Past publications are available to order from the website, and will give an indication on the work of the press.

## Loki Books
(See entry under UK & Irish Book Publishers)

## Luath Press Ltd
(See entry under UK & Irish Book Publishers)

## Ludovic Press
**Dunadd, Lewis Crescent, Kilbarchan, PA10 2HB**
○ 01505 702906
**Poetry** Publishes Poetry titles.
**Recent Title(s)** *High Auchensale*, Jim Carruth
**Tips** Member of the *Scottish Pamphlet Poetry* website, where their publications can be ordered.

## Macmillan Children's Books
(See entry under UK & Irish Book Publishers)

## Malfunction Press
**Rose Cottage, 3 Tram Lane, Flintshire, CH7 4JB**
○ rosecot@presford.freeserve.co.uk
**Contact** Peter E. Presford
**Established** 1969
**Poetry** Publishes poetry booklets on the following subjects: Science fiction, Fantasy and Horror.
  * Publishes very infrequently.
**Submission Guidelines** Accepts email submissions.

## Mandrake of Oxford
(See entry under UK & Irish Book Publishers)

## Mango Publishing
(See entry under UK & Irish Book Publishers)

## Mare's Nest
(See entry under UK & Irish Book Publishers)

## Mariscat Press

**10 Bell Place, Edinburgh, EH3 5NT**

☎ 0131 343 1070

✉ hamish.whyte@virgin.net

**Contact** Hamish Whyte

**Poetry** Publishes poetry collections in pamphlet form.

**Recent Title(s)** *Catacoustics*, Valerie Thornton

**Tips** Member of the *Scottish Pamphlet Poetry* website, where previous publications can be ordered.

## Maypole Editions

(See entry under UK & Irish Book Publishers)

## Meadowside Children's Books

(See entry under UK & Irish Book Publishers)

## Menard Press

(See entry under UK & Irish Book Publishers)

## Mews Press

**English Department, Sheffield Hallam University, Collegiate Crescent, Sheffield, S10 2BP**

☎ 0114 225 2241

✉ s.l.earnshaw@shu.ac.uk

🌐 http://extra.shu.ac.uk/mews-press

**Contact** Dr. Steven Earnshaw

**Established** 2000

**Insider Info** Catalogue available online.

**Poetry** The press exists solely to publish poetry from students of the MA Writing course at Sheffield Hallam. No external submissions.

**Recent Title(s)** *10 Hallam Poets*, Vario

**Tips** Also produce a magazine, *Matter*, showcasing fiction, scriptwriting and poetry talent from the course.

## Michael O'Mara Books Ltd

(See entry under UK & Irish Book Publishers)

## Morning Star

(See entry under UK & Irish Book Publishers)

## Mudfog Press

(See entry under UK & Irish Book Publishers)

## New Hope International

(See entry under UK & Irish Book Publishers)

## New Island Books

(See entry under UK & Irish Book Publishers)

## Nightingale Books

(See entry under UK & Irish Book Publishers)

## NorthernSky Press

(See entry under UK & Irish Book Publishers)

## nth position Press

(See entry under UK & Irish Book Publishers)

## Object Permanence

**1st Floor, 16 Ruskin Terrace, Glasgow, G12 8DY**

✉ undigest@hotmail.com, robinpurves@yahoo.co.uk

🌐 www.objectpermanence.co.uk

**Contact** Peter Mason; Robin Purves

**Poetry** Publish pamphlet poetry collections.

**Recent Title(s)** *Being a Human Being*, Tom Leonard

**Tips** Object Permanence was once a poetry magazine and is now a small press. No unsolicited manuscripts.

## Octagon Press Ltd

(See entry under UK & Irish Book Publishers)

## Odyssey Poets

**Coleridge Cottage, Nether Stowey, Somerset, TA5 1NQ**

☎ 01278 732662

**Contact** Derrick Woolf

**Poetry** Publishes Poetry titles.

**Tips** A small press publishing poetry, prose, first collections, interim booklets and full collections.

## The Old Stile Press

(See entry under UK & Irish Book Publishers)

## The Oleander Press Ltd

(See entry under UK & Irish Book Publishers)

## The Once Orange Badge Poetry Press

**PO Box 184, South Ockendon, RM15 5WT**

☎ 01708 852827

✉ orangebadge@poetry.fsworld.co.uk

**Contact** DM Heath

**Poetry** Publishes mainly first collections in pamphlet form.

**Tips** The Press prefers enquiries and submissions via email.

## The One Time Press

**Model Farm, Linstead Magna, Halesworth, IP19 0DT**

☎ 01986 785422

🌐 www.onetimepress.com

**Contact** Peter Wells

**Poetry** Publishes Classic Poetry titles.

**Tips** The One Time Press publish fine editions of poetry by 1940s writers. No contemporary poetry will be considered.

## Onlywomen Press

(See entry under UK & Irish Book Publishers)

## Original Plus

(See entry under UK & Irish Book Publishers)

## Orion Publishing Group

(See entry under UK & Irish Book Publishers)

## The Other Press

**19 Marriot Road, London, N4 3QN**

☎ 020 7272 9023

✉ FPresley@compuserve.com

🌐 www.indigogroup.co.uk/llpp/other.html

**Poetry** Publishes Poetry titles.

**Tips** A very small poetry press based in London.

## Palladour Books

(See entry under UK & Irish Book Publishers)

## Paradise Press

(See entry under UK & Irish Book Publishers)

## Parthian

(See entry under UK & Irish Book Publishers)

## The Patchwork Press

**PO Box 109, Portishead, Bristol, BS20 7ZJ**

✉ info@patchworkpress.co.uk

🌐 www.patchworkpress.co.uk

**Contact** Editor, Beth Morgan

**Established** 2006

**Poetry** Publishes Anthologies.

**Submission Guidelines** Submit one to two sample poems. Welcomes submissions from poets who would like to be included in the Anthologies. Poems should be no longer than 32 lines long and may be posted or emailed.

**Tips** Past Anthologies have included *Poems of Love* and *My Hometown*. For up to the minute information, sign up to the newsletter via the website.

## Peepal Tree Press

(See entry under UK & Irish Book Publishers)

## Penguin Group (UK)

(See entry under UK & Irish Book Publishers)

## Perjink Press

(See entry under UK & Irish Book Publishers)

## Peterloo Poets

**The Old Chapel, Sands Lane, Calstock, Cornwall, PL18 9QX**

☎ 01822 833473

☎ 01822 833989

✉ info@peterloopoets.com

🌐 www.peterloopoets.com

**Contact** Publisher, Harry Chambers

**Established** 1976

**Insider Info** Submissions accompanied by SAE will be returned. Catalogue available online.

**Poetry** Publishes British and Irish Poetry collections.

**Submission Guidelines** Only accepts submissions periodically, please check the website for current status. Ordinarily, send a full manuscript by post, emailed submissions are not accepted.

**Recent Title(s)** Nasty, British and Short, Ann Alexander (British Poetry); *Being the Bad Guy*, John Whitworth

**Tips** Potential Peterloo authors must have had at least six poems previously published in magazines.

## Picador

(See entry under UK & Irish Book Publishers)

## Pigasus Press

(See entry under UK & Irish Book Publishers)

## Pikestaff Press

**Ellon House, Harpford, Sidmouth, Devon, EX10 0NH**

☎ 01395 568941

**Contact** Robert Robertson

**Poetry** Publish poetry collections.

**Recent Title(s)** *Green Eyes,* Adrian Blackledge

**Tips** Pikestaff is a very small press concentrating on publishing poetry collections in booklet or pamphlet form only.

## Pipers' Ash Ltd

(See entry under UK & Irish Book Publishers)

## Planet

(See entry under UK & Irish Book Publishers)

## Poems in the Waiting Room

**PO Box 488, Richmond, Surrey, YW9 4SW**

✉ pitwr@blueyonder.co.uk

🌐 www.pitwr.pwp.blueyonder.co.uk

**Contact** Editor, Michael Lee (Poetry); Joint Editor, Isobel Montgomery Campbell (Poetry); Executive Editor, Cynthia Turner Roberts (Poetry)

**Established** 1995

**Insider Info** Publishes one title per year. Receives approximately 400 queries and 1,200 manuscripts per year. Average lead time is six months, with simultaneous submissions accepted. Submissions accompanied by SAE will be returned. Aims to respond to queries within one day, proposals within two days and manuscripts within four days. Catalogue is free on request. Manuscript guidelines are available with an SAE, online or by email.

**Poetry** Publishes poetry in pamphlet form.

**Submission Guidelines** Accepts complete manuscripts.

**Recent Title(s)** *Poems in the Waiting Room,* Collected (Poetry card)

**Tips** Poems in the Waiting Room publishes poetry collections expressly for the waiting rooms of hospitals and clinics. Poems should be suitable for patients and relatives.

## Poetry Now

**Remus House, Coltsfoot Drive, Woodston, Peterborough, PE2 8JX**

☎ 01733 8998101

📠 01733 313524

✉ poetrynow@forwardpress.co.uk

🌐 www.forwardpress.co.uk

**Parent Company** Forward Press

**Contact** Steve Twelvetree

**Established** 1989

**Poetry** Publishes poetry titles with wide appeal.

**Submission Guidelines** Accepts one to two sample poems. Check the website for specific calls for submissions, particularly for themed anthologies. Send submissions via email or post.

**Tips** All work that is published by Poetry Now is considered for Forward Press poetry competitions, see the website for up to date details.

## Poetry Press Ltd

**26 Park Grove, Edgware, Middlesex, HA8 7SJ**

☎ 020 8958 6499

✉ poetrypress@yahoo.co.uk

**Contact** Commissioning Editor, Judy Karbritz (Poetry)

**Established** 2005

**Insider Info** Publishes three titles per year. Receives approximately 100 queries and 70 manuscripts per year. 100 per cent of books published are from first-time authors, 100 per cent of books published are from unagented authors. 30 per cent of books published are author subsidy published based on merit. Simultaneous submissions are accepted. Submissions accompanied by SAE will be returned. Aims to respond to queries, proposals and manuscripts within four weeks.

**Poetry** Publishes anthologies of modern and traditional poetry, often with mental health themes.

**Submission Guidelines** Accepts proposal package (including outline, author biography and three sample poems).

**Recent Title(s)** *Get Out Of My Head!,* Alison Islin (Paperback); *Pots, Pans & Poetry,* Judy Karbritz. (Hardback)

**Tips** Poetry Press titles are mainly aimed at women and sufferers of mental health problems, particularly OCD.

## Poets Anonymous

**70 Aveling Close, Purley, CR8 4DW**

✉ poets@poetsanon.org

🌐 www.poetsanon.org

**Poetry** Poets Anonymous exists to publish the individual collections and anthologies emerging from the writer's group of the same name.

## Poolbeg Press
(See entry under UK & Irish Book Publishers)

## PS Avalon
(See entry under UK & Irish Book Publishers)

## Puffin
(See entry under UK & Irish Book Publishers)

## Puppet State Press
**1 West Colinton House, 40 Woodhall Road, Edinburgh, EH13 0DU**
0131 441 9693
richard@puppetstate.com
www.puppetstate.com
**Poetry** Publishes poetry in booklet and pamphlet form.
**Tips** Member of the *Scottish Pamphlet Poetry* website.

## QQ Press
**York House, 15 Argyle Terrace, Rothesay, Isle of Bute, PA20 0BD**
**Contact** Alan Carter
**Poetry** Publishes small numbers of poetry collections and anthologies.

## Rack Press
**The Rack, Kinnerton, Presteigne, Powys, LD8 2PF**
01547 560411, 07817 424560
rackpress@britishlibrary.net
**Contact** Nicholas Murray
**Insider Info** Publishes Booklets and Pamphlets.
**Poetry** Publishes Poetry and Poetry in translation.
**Tips** Based in Wales, Rack Press has an international vision. It hopes to combine translations and versions with new work by established and new talents from all sources.

## Ragged Raven Press
**1 Lodge Farm, Snitterfield, Stratford upon Avon, Warwickshire, CV37 0LR**
01789 730320
raggedravenpress@aol.com
www.raggedraven.co.uk
**Contact** Editor, Bob Mee (Poetry); Editor, Janet Murch (Poetry)
**Established** 1998

**Insider Info** Publishes two titles per year. Receives 150 queries and 100 manuscripts per year. 100 per cent of books published are from first-time authors, 100 per cent of books published are from unagented authors. Payment is via royalty (on retail price). An advance is offered. Average lead time is nine months, with simultaneous submissions not accepted. Submissions accompanied by SAE will be returned. Catalogue is available online. Manuscript guidelines are available by email.
**Poetry** Publish poetry titles.
 * Only one or two individual collections are published each year, usually by a poet whose work has appeared in Ragged Raven's magazine, *Iota*, or through their annual anthology linked to a competition.
**Submission Guidelines** Submit six sample poems.
**Recent Title(s)** *The Invention of Butterfly*, Christopher James (Poetry collection)
**Tips** Ragged Raven also Publishes *Iota* poetry magazine and runs various poetry competitions, all of which offer publication in anthologies.

## Random House Children's Books
(See entry under UK & Irish Book Publishers)

## The Random House Group Ltd
(See entry under UK & Irish Book Publishers)

## Raunchland Publications
**26 Aldergrove, Dunfermline, KY12 8RP**
raunchland@hotmail.com
www.raunchland.co.uk
**Contact** John Mingay
**Poetry** Publish poetry titles.
 * Raunchland has two online outlets for publication as well as publishing limited edition poetry pamphlets. The first, *Eternal Anthology* requires a maximum of five short poems in any form. The second, the *Repository*, requires sequence poems or linked series.
**Submission Guidelines** Accepts between one and five sample poems. Email submissions but do not send attachments.
**Tips** No payment is made for online publication, although the poet retains all rights to their work. Read through the site to get a flavour of the different areas.

## Reality Street Editions
(See entry under UK & Irish Book Publishers)

## Reardon Publishing
(See entry under UK & Irish Book Publishers)

## Redbeck Press
**24 Airville Road, Frizinghall, Bradford, West Yorkshire, BD9 4HH**
**Contact** David Tipton.
**Poetry** Publish poetry collections.
**Tips** Redbeck are a small independent publisher who bring a few poetry collections a year. Some Redbeck poets are; Debjani Chatterjee, Barry Tebb, Michael Curtis, Terry Gifford, Jane Tipton, Tulio Mora and David Gill.

## The Red Candle Press
**1 Chatsworth Court, Outram Road, Southsea, Hampshire PO5 1RA**
**☎** 023 9275 3696
**✉** rosecottage@poetry7.fsnet.co.uk
**Established** 1970
**Insider Info** Payment is a complimentary copy. Does not accept simultaneous submissions.
**Poetry** Publishes poetry
 * The Red Candle Press only publishes the twice yearly magazine *Candelabrum*, and brings out books very occasionally. It is a formalist press, i.e. metrical and rhymed poetry has preference. It does not publish collections on behalf of authors.
**Submission Guidelines** Accepts proposal package (including outline, three to six sample poems and SAE) by post only.
**Recent Title(s)** *The Red Candle Treasury*, M.L. McCarthy (ed.)
**Tips** Red Candle's readership is people who are interested in modern formalist poetry.

## Rockingham Press
(See entry under UK & Irish Book Publishers)

## Salt Publishing
(See entry under UK & Irish Book Publishers)

## Scottish Cultural Press & Scottish Children's Press
(See entry under UK & Irish Book Publishers)

## The Seer Press
**PO Box 29313, Glasgow, G20 2AE**
**☎** 07743 307808
**✉** admin@theseerpress.com
**Poetry** Publishes Poetry titles.
**Recent Title(s)** *A Glass of Pure Water*, Suzanne Muir Scott
**Tips** Publishes poetry collections in pamphlet form. Member of the *Scottish Pamphlet Poetry* website.

## Seren
(See entry under UK & Irish Book Publishers)

## Serendipity
(See entry under UK & Irish Book Publishers)

## Serpent's Tail
(See entry under UK & Irish Book Publishers)

## Shearsman Books Ltd
(See entry under UK & Irish Book Publishers)

## Shepheard-Walwyn (Publishers) Ltd
(See entry under UK & Irish Book Publishers)

## Shoestring Press
**19 Devonshire Avenue, Beeston, Nottingham, NG9 1BS**
**☎** 0115 925 1827
**✉** info@shoestringpress.co.uk
**🌐** www.shoestringpress.co.uk
**Contact** Publisher, John Lucas
**Poetry** Publishes Poetry titles.
**Tips** Shoestring Press specialise in sequences and collections by established British poets, or poets from overseas that are unknown to a British audience. Many of the publications use layouts and visual art to enhance them.

## Sixties Press
(See entry under UK & Irish Book Publishers)

## Smith/Doorstop
**The Studio, Byram Arcade, Westgate, Huddersfield, HD1 1ND**
**☎** 01484 434840
**☎** 01484 426566
**🌐** www.poetrybusiness.co.uk
**Parent Company** The Poetry Business
**Contact** Publisher and Editor, Peter Sansom; Publisher and Editor, Janet Fisher
**Established** 1986

**Poetry** Publishes Poetry titles.

**Recent Title(s)** *Ha-Ha*, Peter Bennett; *Vanishing Trick*, Sue Butler

**Tips** Smith/Doorstop are a small independent publisher of contemporary poetry, publishing books, pamphlets and audio cassettes. They also publish the winners of *The Poetry Business* competitions (up to date details of which can be found on their website). An entry fee is charged. No email entries are accepted.

## Smokestack Books
**PO Box 408, Middlesbrough, TS5 6WA**
- 01642 813997
- info@smokestack-books.co.uk
- www.smokestack-books.co.uk

**Parent Company** Shoestring Operation
**Contact** Founder/Editor, Andy Croft (Poetry)
**Established** 2004
**Insider Info** Publishes six titles per year. Receives 40 queries and 30 manuscripts per year. 33 per cent of books published are from first-time authors, seven per cent of books published are from unagented authors. Payment consists of a standard £500 fee on publication. Average lead time is six months, with simultaneous submissions accepted. Submissions accompanied by SAE will be returned. Aims to respond to queries within two weeks and proposals and manuscripts within four weeks. Catalogue is available with an SAE and available online. Manuscript guidelines are available online.
**Poetry** Publishes new contemporary and traditional poetry.
**Submission Guidelines** Submit complete manuscript.
**Recent Title(s)** *John Lucas*, Flute Music (Paperback original)
**Tips** Smokestack champions poets who are unconventional, unfashionable, radical or left-field and who are working a long way from the metropolitan centres of cultural authority. Smokestack is interested in the world as well as the word. Smokestack believes that poetry is a part of, and not apart from society. Smokestack does not think 'difficulty' in poetry is a virtue, or that poetry is a place in which to hide. Smokestack argues that if poetry does not belong to everyone it is not poetry.

## Souvenier Press Ltd
(See entry under UK & Irish Book Publishers)

## Spectacular Diseases
**83b London Road, Peterborough, PE2 9BS**
**Contact** Paul Green
**Poetry** Publishes Poetry titles.
**Recent Title(s)** *Bird Migration in the 21st Century*, Ken Edwards
**Tips** Spectacular Diseases started as a magazine and has developed into a small poetry press. All contact must be made by post.

## The Stinging Fly Press
(See entry under UK & Irish Book Publishers)

## Stride
(See entry under UK & Irish Book Publishers)

## Superscript
(See entry under UK & Irish Book Publishers)

## Tall Lighthouse Press
**Stark Gallery, 384 Lee High Road, London, SE12 8RW**
- info@tall-lighthouse.co.uk
- www.tall-lighthouse.co.uk

**Established** 2000
**Poetry** Publishes Poetry titles.
**Recent Title(s)** *The Elephant in the Corner*, Aoife Mannix
**Tips** Tall Lighthouse is an independent literary organisation with a small publishing programme of books and pamphlets. They also organise events, workshops and readings around London and the South East, details of which are on the website.

## Tarantula Publications
**14 Vine Street, Salford, Manchester, M7 3PG**
- 0161 792 4593
- 0161 792 4593

**Contact** Sean Brody
**Poetry** Publishes Poetry titles.
**Tips** Tarantula Publications are a small publisher of poetry collections.

## Templar Poetry
**PO Box 7082, Bakewell, Derbyshire, DE45 9AF**
- 01629 582500
- info@templarpoetry.co.uk
- www.templarpoetry.co.uk

**Contact** Managing Editor, Alex McMillen

**Poetry** Publishes Poetry titles.

 \* Submissions to the press are not accepted due to time constraints, but poets looking for a route to publication are advised to enter the annual pamphlet and first collection competition. Three winners will see their small collections published in pamphlet form and will be invited to submit a full collection for publication. Other single poems will be published in an anthology. Details of each competition are available on the website.

**Recent Title(s)** *The Way I Dressed During the Revolution*, Jane Weir

**Tips** Templar Poetry aim to publish and promote the best in contemporary poetry. They will occasionally publish poets who bypass the competition, but these books are commissioned by the Editor.

## Terra Firma Press
**11 Sinclair Drive, Glasgow, G42 9PR**
**Contact** Anne Murray
**Poetry** Publishes Poetry titles.
**Recent Title(s)** *Who Cares, Writes!* Various Glasgow South Carers Writers Groups
**Tips** Terra Firma Press publishes poetry collections in pamphlet form. They are a member of the *Scottish Pamphlet Poetry* website.

## Touch the Earth Publications
**39 McKenzie Crescent, Lochgelly, Fife, KY5 9LT**
**Contact** William Hershaw
**Poetry** Publishes poetry titles.
**Recent Title(s)** *The Faerie Walk*, William Hershaw
**Tips** Publishes William Hershaw's poetry in pamphlet form. All proceeds to the CHAS (Children's Hospice Association Scotland). Member of the *Scottish Pamphlet Poetry* website.

## TownHouse Dublin
(See entry under UK & Irish Book Publishers)

## Triumph House
**Remus House, Woodston, Peterborough, PE2 9JX**
☎ 01733 898102
📠 01733 313524
✉ triumphhouse@forwardpress.co.uk
🖥 www.forwardpress.co.uk
**Parent Company** Forward Press
**Established** 1994

**Insider Info** Submissions accompanied by SAE will be returned. Catalogue available online.
**Poetry** Publishes Religious Poetry titles.
 \* Check the website for specific calls for submissions, particularly for themed anthologies.
**Submission Guidelines** Submit one to two sample poems.
 Submission details to: inbox@forwardpress.co.uk
**Tips** Triumph House is a Christian poetry imprint. Book themes are either directly about religion and faith, or cover current topics from a Christian point of view.

## Tuba Press
**Tunley Cottage, Tunley, Near Cirencester, GL7 6LW**
☎ 01285 760424
✉ peter.ellson@wanadoo.fr
**Contact** Peter Ellson; Charles Graham
**Insider Info** Accept written requests for full catalogue.
**Poetry** Publishes 20th and 21st Century Poetry and Prose titles.

## Two Rivers Press
(See entry under UK & Irish Book Publishers)

## Vane Women Press
**c/o Darlington Arts Centre, Vane Terrace, Darlington, DL3 7AX**
☎ 01325 348843
🖥 www.vanewomen.co.uk
**Poetry** Publishes poetry titles.
**Recent Title(s)** *The Spar Box*, Pippa Little
**Tips** Vane Women is a writers' collective from the North of England that also runs a small press publishing mainly poetry although they also publish some short stories. Members also perform their poetry regularly. For more information on existing writers in the collective, there are biographies and many sample poems on the website.

## Vanguard Press
(See entry under UK & Irish Book Publishers)

## Virago Press
(See entry under UK & Irish Book Publishers)

## Walker Books
(See entry under UK & Irish Book Publishers)

## Waterloo Press

**126 Furze Croft, Hove, BN3 1PF**

⊕ www.waterloopresshove.com

**Contact** Founder, Sonja Ctvrtecka; Editor, David Kendall; Editor, Andrew Duncan; Editor, Dr. David Pollard; Editor, Alan Morrison

**Poetry** Publishes Poetry titles.

**Recent Title(s)** *About Bloody Time*, Simon Jenner

**Tips** Waterloo Press is a not for profit publisher, who aim to promote regional poets to a national and international audience, and to publish established, or long neglected modern and modernist poets. There is strong editorial input from Waterloo Press' previously published poets, who recommend new poets. Also publish the poetry journal *Eratica*.

## The Watts Publishing Group

(See entry under UK & Irish Book Publishers)

## The Waywiser Press

(See entry under UK & Irish Book Publishers)

## Wendy Webb Books

(See entry under UK & Irish Book Publishers)

## West House Books

**40 Crescent Road, Sheffield, S7 1HN**

☎ 0114 258 6035

✉ info@westhousebooks.co.uk

⊕ www.westhousebooks.co.uk

**Contact** Founder, Alan Halsey; Geraldine Monk

**Established** 1994

**Insider Info** Catalogue available online.

**Poetry** Publishes poetry titles.

 * The current focus is on late modernist poetry. Pamphlets are often seen as the quickest and most effective way of publishing brand new work.

**Recent Title(s)** *The Passion of Phineas Gage & Selected Poems*, Jesse Glass

**Tips** West House involves its authors in all aspects of book production, including design and layout.

## Wild Women Press

**Flat 10, The Common, Windermere, LA23 1JH**

✉ vik@wildwomenpress.com, adam@wildwomenpress.com

⊕ www.wildwomenpress.com

**Contact** Director, Victoria Bennett; Design, Adam Clarke

**Established** 1999

**Poetry** Publishes Poetry titles.

 * Publishes unique poetry by women only, particularly writers at the start of their careers who deserve to be published.

**Submission Guidelines** Unsolicited manuscripts are not being accepted at present.

**Recent Title(s)** *Rilke Tatoo*, Gill Hands

**Tips** Wild Women Press are a not for profit collective of writers who aim to bring a 'wild' attitude to poetry publishing. As well as commissioning books, the press organises poetry events and runs competitions, details of which are on the website.

## Woodburn Press

**Kendalmere, Caledonian Road, Peebles, EH45 9DL**

**Poetry** Publishes Poetry Books/Pamphlets.

**Recent Title(s)** *Garden Party*, Gill McConnell

**Tips** Has published an award winning poetry pamphlet. Member of the *Scottish Pamphlet Poetry* website.

## Wordsworth Editions Ltd

(See entry under UK & Irish Book Publishers)

## Worple Press

(See entry under UK & Irish Book Publishers)

## Wrecking Ball Press

(See entry under UK & Irish Book Publishers)

## Xcite Books

(See entry under UK & Irish Book Publishers)

## Y Lolfa Cyf

(See entry under UK & Irish Book Publishers)

## Young Picador

(See entry under UK & Irish Book Publishers)

# UK & IRISH PACKAGERS

## Aladdin Books

**2–3 Fitroy Mews, London, W1T 6DF**

☎ 020 7383 2084

☎ 020 7388 6391

✉ alexandra.mew@aladdinbooks.co.uk

⊕ www.aladdinbooks.co.uk

**Contact** Managing Director, Charles Nicholas
**Insider Info** Founded in 1979, Aladdin Books Ltd creates highly illustrated non-fiction books for children aged from one to sixteen. The company focuses on reading schemes, and social, environmental and world issues.
**Non-fiction** Subjects covered include maths, science and technology, natural history, arts, crafts and hobbies, geography and environment, general and novelty.

## The Albion Press Ltd
**Spring Hill, Idbury, Oxfordshire, OX7 6RU**
- 01993 831094
- 01993 831982

**Contact Title** Managing Director, Emma Bradford
**Insider Info** Founded in 1984. Specialises in children's books. No unsolicited manuscripts or synopses.

## Amber Books Ltd
**Bradley's Close, 74–77 White Lion Street, London, N1 9PF**
- 020 7520 7600
- 020 7520 7606/ 7607
- editorial@amberbooks.co.uk
- www.amberbooks.co.uk

**Contact Title** Managing Director, Stasz Gynch
**Insider Info** Amber Books presents a broad range of illustrated non-fiction for adults and children.
**Non-fiction** Subjects include military history, military technology, aviation, transport, children's, combat and survival techniques, games and pastimes, music, mind, body and spirit, crime, detection and punishment, science and nature, health and medicine, social history and cookery.
**Tips** Amber Books are particularly interested in submissions on military topics, but also welcome good ideas on any non-fiction subject suitable for an illustrated book. No fiction, biography or poetry please. Send a synopsis, contents list, a sample chapter or two and a single page CV or resume to the Publishing Manager.

## BCS Publishing Ltd
**2nd Floor, Temple Court, 109 Oxford Road, Cowley, Oxford, OX4 2ER**
- 01865 770099
- 01865 770050
- bcs-publishing@dcl.pipex.com

**Contact Title** Managing Director, Steve McCurdy

**Insider Info** Produces General interest, illustrated non-fiction.

## Bender Richardson White
**PO Box 266, Uxbridge, UB9 5BD**
- 01895 832444
- 01895 835213
- lionel@brw.co.uk
- www.brw.co.uk

**Contact Title** Partner (Editorial), Lionel Bender
**Insider Info** BRW produces books for publishers around the world and develops its own projects for the international co-edition market. It specialises in illustrated non-fiction for children and adults, educational and home learning materials.

## Book Guild Publishing
**Pavilion View, 19 New Road, Brighton, East Sussex, BN1 1UF**
- 01273 720900
- 01273 723122
- info@bookguild.co.uk
- www.bookguild.co.uk

**Contact Title** Managing Director, Carol Biss; Managing Editor, Joanna Bentley
**Insider Info** Offers a variety of publishing options for authors, businesses and charities. Subjects covered are varied and include fiction, human interest, biography, history, general non-fiction and children's titles.
**Tips** Ideas and manuscripts welcome. Initially please send a synopsis, covering letter and CV. Complete manuscripts are accepted, but please enclose an SAE. Submission details on the website.

## Book Packaging and Marketing
**1 Church Street, Blakesley, Towcester, NN12 8RA**
- 01327 861300
- 01327 861300

**Contact** Martin F. Marix Evans
**Insider Info** Founded 1989. Project management for publishers and business. Illustrated adult non-fiction, specialising in military history, history and reference.

## Breslich and Foss Ltd
**Unit 2a Union Court, 20–22 Union Road, Clapham, London, SW4 6JP**
- 020 7819 3990
- 020 7819 3998

**Contact Title** Directors, Paula Breslich, K.B. Dunning

**Insider Info** Founded in 1978, Breslich and Foss are packagers of adult non-fiction, specialising in crafts, interior design, gardening, health and beauty and children's non-fiction and picture books.
**Tips** Ideas welcome, send synopses and SAE.

## The Bridgewater Book Company Ltd
**The Old Candlemakers, West Street, Lewes, East Sussex, BN7 2NZ**
- 01273 403120
- 01273 487441
- www.bridgewaterbooks.co.uk

**Contact Title** Director, Peter Bridgewater
**Insider Info** Bridgewater Books is the contract publishing arm of the Ivy Publishing Group. Illustrated books in all subject areas. Details of freelance opportunities are given on the website.

## Brown Reference Group (BRG)
**8 Chapel Place, Rivington Street, London, EC2A 3DQ**
- 020 7920 7500
- 020 7920 7501
- info@brownreference.com
- www.brownreference.com

**Contact Title** Managing Director, Sharon Hutton
**Insider Info** The Brown Reference Group (BRG) is a leading packager of high quality reference books and encyclopaedias for all age groups. The company was founded in 1995 and now has clients worldwide. BRG has produced more than 100 major reference encyclopedias and is a leading supplier of part works.

## Brown Wells and Jacobs Ltd
**Foresters Hall, 25–27 Westow Street, London, SE19 3RY**
- 020 8771 5115
- 020 8771 9994
- www.bwj.org

**Contact Title** Managing Director, Graham Brown
**Insider Info** Founded in 1978, they produce high quality non-fiction children's books, and are specialists in novelty and pop-up books.

## Cambridge Publishing Management Ltd
**Unit 2, Burr Elm Court, Main Street, Caldecote, Cambridgeshire, CB3 7NU**
- 01954 214000
- 01954 214001
- www.cambridgepm.co.uk

**Contact Title** Managing Editor, Jackie Dobbyne
**Insider Info** A creative book production company, offering a comprehensive service to publishers. Specialises in the complete project management of trade, travel, educational and ELT titles.

## Cameron and Hollis
**PO Box 1, Moffat, Dumfriesshire, DG10 9SU**
- 01683 220808
- 01683 220012
- editorial@cameronbooks.co.uk
- www.cameronbooks.co.uk

**Contact Title** Directors, Ian A. Cameron, Jill Hollis
**Insider Info** Cameron Books specialises in creating books in the fields of contemporary art, film criticism, the decorative arts, architecture, social history and the environment. They work with publishers in Britain, continental Europe and North America.

## Canopus Publishing
**27 Queen Square, Bristol, BS1 4ND**
- 0117 922 6660
- 0117 922 6660
- robin@canopusbooks.com
- www.canopusbooks.com

**Contact Title** Director, Robin Rees; Commissioning Editor, Tom Spicer; Commissioning Editor, Jim Revill
**Insider Info** A book packager, publisher and multimedia creator, launched in 1999 and specialising in science and astronomy.

## Carroll & Brown Ltd
**20 Lonsdale Road, London, NW6 6RD**
- 020 7372 0900
- 020 7372 0460
- mail@carrollandbrown.co.uk
- www.carrollandbrown.co.uk

**Contact Title** Managing Director, Amy Carroll
**Insider Info** Carroll & Brown has been a book packager for more than fifty years and has been publishing under its own imprint for more than five years. The company specialises in health, craft, mind, body and spirit and lifestyle titles for the UK and international markets.

## Cowley Hunter Publishing
**8 Belmont, Bath, BA1 5DZ**
- 01225 339999
- 01225 339995
- www.cowleyrobinson.com

**Contact Title** Publishing Director, Stewart Cowley
**Insider Info** Specialises in children's novelty and paper engineered formats.

## D & N Publishing

**Unit 3c Lowesden Business Park, Lambourn Woodlands, Hungerford, Berkshire, RG17 7RU**
- 01488 73657
- d@dnpublishing.co.uk

**Contact Title** Partners, David Price-Goodfellow, Namrita Price-Goodfellow
**Insider Info** Founded in 1991, D & N Publishing offers complete project management, including some or all of the following (depending on project), commissioning, editing, picture research, illustration and design, page layout, proofreading, indexing and printing. Each stage is managed in house, and produced on Apple Macs running the latest software. All subjects are covered, with natural history a speciality. 40–50 titles are produced per year. Clients include HarperCollins Publishers and The Crowood Press.
**Tips** No unsolicited manuscripts accepted, but there are opportunities for freelancers with a proven track record, and several years' experience (would need experience of book publishing).

## David West Children's Books

**7 Princeton Court, 55 Felsham Road, London, SW15 1AZ**
- 020 8780 3836
- 020 8780 9313
- dww@btinternet.com
- www.davidwestchildrensbooks.com

**Insider Info** Highly illustrated children's information books produced specifically for the international market and designed for translation. Subjects covered include mysteries and ancient civilisations, the animal kingdom, cinema, history, science, aviation, sports, machines, and fashion.

## Design Eye Ltd

**226 City Road, London, EC1V 2TT**
- 020 7812 8601
- 020 7253 4370
- info@designeye.co.uk
- www.quarto.com

**Contact Title** Publisher, Sue Grabham
**Insider Info** Design Eye publishes innovative interactive kit books for adults and children, often incorporating extras such as craft materials, moulded figures or working models.

## Diagram Visual Information Ltd

**195 Kentish Town Road, London, NW5 2JU**
- 020 7482 3633
- 020 7482 4932

**Contact Title** Managing Director, Bruce Robertson
**Insider Info** Founded in 1967, Diagram Visual Information Ltd is a producer of reference books for trade, library, school and academic markets.

## Eddison Sadd Editions Ltd

**St Chad's House, 148 Kings Cross Road, London, WC1X 9DH**
- 020 7837 1968
- 020 7837 2025
- reception@eddisonsadd.co.uk
- www.eddisonsadd.com

**Contact Title** Managing Director, Nick Eddison; Editorial Director, Ian Jackson
**Insider Info** Founded in 1982, Eddison Sadd is one of the world's leading co-edition packagers. The company produce non-fiction books including gift and reference books, with an emphasis on mind, body and spirit titles.
**Recent Titles** *The Druid Animal Oracle*, Philip and Stephanie Carr-Gomm

## Elm Grove Books Ltd

**Elm Grove, Henstridge, Somerset, BA8 0TQ**
- 01963 362498
- hugh@elmgrovebooks.com

**Contact Title** Directors, Hugh Elwes, Susie Elwes
**Insider Info** A children's book packager, founded in 1993.

## Focus Publishing (Sevenoaks) Ltd

**11a St Botolphs Road, Sevenoaks, Kent, TN13 3AJ**
- 01732 742456
- 01732 743381
- info@focuspublishing.co.uk
- www.focus-publishing.co.uk

**Contact Title** Publishing Director, Guy Croton
**Insider Info** Offers a complete DTP book packaging service and produces its own illustrated concepts in a range of subjects, from gardening and DIY to wine, sport and health.

## Graham Cameron Publishing & Illustration

**The Studio, 23 Holt Road, Sheringham, Norfolk, NR26 8NB**

- 01263 821333
- 01263 821334
- enquiry@graham-cameron-illustration.com
- www.graham-cameron-illustration.com

**Contact Title** Partners, Mike Graham-Cameron, Helen Graham-Cameron, Duncan Graham-Cameron
**Insider Info** Publisher and illustration agency founded in 1985.

## Haldane Mason Ltd
**PO Box 34196, London, NW10 3YB**
- 020 8459 2131
- 020 8728 1216
- info@haldanemason.com

**Contact Title** Editorial Director, Samuel Francis
**Insider Info** Founded in 1994, Haldane Mason Ltd primarily produces children's illustrated non-fiction. Their adult list is mainly mind, body and spirit titles.

## Hart McLeod Ltd
**14 Greenside, Waterbeach, Cambridge, CB5 9HP**
- 01223 861495
- 01223 862902
- inhouse@hartmcleod.co.uk
- www.hartmcleod.co.uk

**Contact Title** Partners, Graham Hart, Chris McLeod, Joanne Barker
**Insider Info** A leading supplier of editorial, design and production services in the UK. The company is at the forefront of developments in interactive publishing for UK schools. It produces around 200 titles a year.

## HL Studios Ltd
**17 Fenlock Court, Blenheim Office Park, Long Hanborough, Oxfordshire, OX29 8LN**
- 01993 881010
- 01993 882713
- info@hlstudios.eu.com
- www.hlstudios.eu.com

**Contact Title** Managing Director, Robin Hickey
**Insider Info** Founded in 1985, HL Studios Ltd specialise in educational titles and general non-fiction co-editions (e.g. travel guides, gardening, cookery) and multimedia.

## The Ilex Press Ltd
**The Old Candlemakers, West Street, Lewes, BN7 2NZ**
- 01273 487440
- 01273 487441
- name@ilex-press.com
- www.ilex-press.com

**Contact Title** Managing Director, Stephen Paul
**Insider Info** Ilex Press is a sister company to The Ivy Press Ltd. It produces titles on the digital arts, website design, graphics software and e-books.

## The Ivy Press Ltd
**The Old Candlemakers, West Street, Lewes, BN7 2NZ**
- 01273 487440
- 01273 487441
- name@ivy-press.com
- www.ivypress.co.uk

**Contact Title** Directors, Peter Bridgewater, Stephen Paul
**Insider Info** The Ivy Press Ltd is part of The Ivy Group and was founded in 1996. It produces various non-fiction illustrated titles, including those on art and design, popular culture, health and parenting, and children's titles.
**Recent Titles** *See-Through Mummies*, (Children's) John Malam; *How To Read Buildings*, Dr Elizabeth Kirk; *Literary Feasts*, Sean Brand
**Tips** Welcomes unsolicited ideas and manuscripts. Please send a synopsis and your CV, a table of contents and sample text. Project ideas should be topical and suitable for the international market.

## Julian Holland
**1st Floor, 64 High Street, Glastonbury, Somerset, BA6 9DY**
- 01458 832222
- jules@julesholland.com

**Contact Title** Proprietor, Julian Holland
**Insider Info** Julian Holland is an experienced book packager, author and photographer, specialising in travel and transport titles.
**Tips** No unsolicited manuscripts or synopses please.

## Lexus Ltd
**60 Brook Street, Glasgow, G40 2AB**
- 0141 556 0440
- 0141 556 2202
- peterterrell@lexusforlanguages.co.uk
- www.lexusforlanguages.co.uk

**Contact Title** Editorial Director, P. Terrell
**Insider Info** Founded in 1980, Lexus compiles bilingual dictionaries, phrasebooks and text books spanning 29 languages. They publish the Travelmates series and The Chinese Classroom (a beginner's course for Mandarin Chinese).

## Lionheart Books

**10 Chelmsford Square, London, NW10 3AR**

☎ 020 8459 0453

☎ 020 8451 3681

✉ Lionheart.Brw@btinternet.com

**Contact Title** Senior Partner, Lionel Bender

**Insider Info** Highly illustrated non-fiction titles for children. Specialist areas are in natural history, history and general science. Titles are generally commissioned from publishers.

## Market House Books Ltd

**2 Market House, Market Square, Aylesbury, Bucks, HP20 1TN**

☎ 01296 484911

☎ 01296 437073

✉ information@mhbref.com

🌐 www.mhbref.com

**Contact Title** Directors, Dr Alan Isaacs, Dr John Daintith, Peter Sapsed

**Insider Info** A book producer and packager specialising in reference books, with a list that ranges from small pocket dictionaries, to large multi-volume colour encyclopedias. Major reference works include the Collins *English Dictionary*, the Macmillan *Encyclopedia*, and the Grolier *Library of Women's Biographies*.

## Marshall Editions Ltd

**The Old Brewery, 6 Blundell Street, London, N7 9BH**

☎ 020 7700 6764

☎ 020 7700 4191

✉ info@marshalleditions.com

🌐 www.quarto.com

**Contact Title** Publisher, Richard Green

**Insider Info** Marshall publishes highly illustrated non-fiction books in co-edition for adults and children. These include titles on health, history, gardening, interiors, natural history and popular science.

## Mathew Price Ltd

**The Old Glove Factory, Bristol Road, Sherborne, Dorset, DT9 4HP**

☎ 01935 816010

☎ 01935 816310

✉ mathewp@mathewprice.com

🌐 www.mathewprice.com

**Contact Title** Managing Director, Mathew Price

**Insider Info** Novelty and picture books, educational titles and fiction for children up to eleven years old.

## Monkey Puzzle Media Ltd

**Gissing's Farm, Fressingfield, Eye, Suffolk, IP21 5SH**

☎ 01379 588044

☎ 01379 588055

✉ info@monkeypuzzlemedia.com

**Contact Title** Director, Roger Goddard-Coote

**Insider Info** Packager of non-fiction for trade, school, library and mass markets. Monkey Puzzle Media Ltd was founded in 1998 and creates about 80 titles a year.

## Nicola Baxter

**PO Box 215, Framingham Earl, Yelverton, Norwich, NR14 7UR**

☎ 01508 491111

**Contact Title** Proprietor and Commissioning Editor, Nicola Baxter

## Orpheus Books Ltd

**6 Church Green, Witney, Oxfordshire, OX28 4AW**

☎ 01993 774949

☎ 01993 700330

✉ info@orpheusbooks.com

🌐 www.orpheusbooks.com

**Contact Title** Executive Director, Nicholas Harris

**Insider Info** Founded in 1992, Orpheus Books are known for their unique concepts and use of die cuts, flaps and foldouts. The company list has a wide ranging subject matter, for children from three to twelve years. Orpheus also produces high quality encyclopedias and atlases.

## OutHouse Publishing

**9 Fairmount, Shalbourne, Marlborough, Wiltshire, SN8 3JQ**

☎ 01672 870350/01962 843053

☎ 01672 870350/01962 843053

✉ sales@outhousepublishing.co.uk

**Contact Title** Partners, Sue Gordon, Elizabeth Mallard-Shaw

**Insider Info** Founded in 1996, OutHouse specialises in illustrated non-fiction, with subjects including, gardening, biography, animals, walking, and British history. They offer project management; copyediting, design and layout, cartography, proofreading and indexing and can provide a full packaging service from concept to warehouse. All members of the OutHouse team are traditionally trained and highly experienced. Clients include David & Charles, The Crowood Press, New Holland Publishing and AA Publishing.

**Tips** No unsolicited ideas or manuscripts please.

### Playne Books Ltd
**Park Court Barn, Trefin, Haverfordwest, Pembrokeshire, SA62 5AU**
- 01348 837073
- 01348 837063
- playne.books@virgin.net

**Contact Title** Design and Production Director, David Playne; Editor, Gill Davies
**Insider Info** Playne Books Ltd was founded in 1987. It produces early learning titles and novelty books for young children, but also highly illustrated adult non-fiction, on a range of subjects.

### Quantum Publishing Ltd
**The Old Brewery, 6 Blundell Street, London, N7 9BH**
- 020 7700 6700
- 020 7700 4191
- quantum@quarto.com
- www.quarto.com

**Contact Title** Publisher, Isabel Leao
**Insider Info** Founded in 1995, Quantum is Quarto's specialist backlist division. It focuses on repackaging successful titles and worldwide distribution.

### Quarto Publishing plc
**The Old Brewery, 6 Blundell Street, London, N7 9BH**
- 020 7700 6700
- 020 7700 4191
- quarto@quarto.com
- www.quartobooks.com

**Contact Title** Publisher, Paul Carslake
**Insider Info** Quarto Publishing is the original co-edition list in the Quarto Group, and produces illustrated non-fiction books on art, crafts, gardening, lifestyle and reference.

### Quintet Publishing Ltd
**The Old Brewery, 6 Blundell Street, London, N7 9BH**
- 020 7700 8066
- 020 7700 4191
- quintet@quarto.com
- www.quarto.com

**Contact Title** Publisher, Gaynor Sermon
**Insider Info** Owning the copyright of its titles, Quintet Publishing Ltd (part of the Quarto Group) publishes co-edition books on a range of subjects, including sports, history and popular culture.

### Salariya Book Company Ltd
**Book House, 25 Marlborough Place, Brighton, East Sussex, BN1 1UB**
- 01273 603306
- 01273 693857
- salariya@salariya.com
- www.salariya.com

**Contact Title** Managing Director, David Salariya
**Insider Info** The Salariya Book Company is an award winning publisher specialising in illustrated information books for children. In the UK it publishes under its own imprint, Book House, which was founded in 2002. Topics include technology, science, history, earth and the environment and animals.

### Savitri Books Ltd
**25 Lisle Lane, Ely, Cambridgeshire, CB7 4AS**
- 01353 654327
- munni@savitribooks.demon.co.uk

**Contact Title** Director, Mrinalini S. Srivastava
**Insider Info** Founded in 1983 as a packager, Savitri Books Ltd commissions illustrated non-fiction, including biography, history and travel.

### Stonecastle Graphics Ltd
**Highlands Lodge, Chartway Street, Sutton Valence, ME17 3HZ**
- 01622 844414
- 01622 844414
- info@stonecastle-graphics.co.uk
- www.stonecastle-graphics.co.uk

**Contact Title** Partners, Paul Turner, Sue Pressley
**Insider Info** Complete book design, photography, editorial, illustration and packaging service. Illustrated general non-fiction is commissioned for adults and children across a range of subjects. In 2003 Stonecastle Graphics founded Touchstone Books Ltd, their own imprint, which publishes high quality, highly illustrated non-fiction adult titles. These include the award-winning *Cobra, The First 40 Years*.

### Studio Cactus Ltd
**13 Southgate Street, Winchester, Hampshire, SO23 9DZ**

- 01962 878600
- mail@studiocactus.co.uk
- www.studiocactus.co.uk

**Contact Title** Editorial Director, Damien Moore
**Insider Info** Studio Cactus, founded in 1998, produces high quality, illustrated books for international publishers including Dorling Kindersley and David & Charles. Projects range from illustrated reference to children's educational titles.
**Tips** Opportunities for designers and editorial freelancers with a proven track record.

## Tangerine Designs Ltd
**2 High Street, Freshford, Bath, BA2 7WE**
- 01225 720001
- tangerinedesign@btinternet.com

**Contact Title** Managing Director, Christine Swift
**Insider Info** Packagers and co-edition publishers of children's books, founded in 2000.

## Tony Potter Publishing Ltd
**1 Stairbridge Court, Bolney Grange Business Park, Stairbridge Lane, Bolney, West Sussex, RH17 5PA**
- 01444 232889
- 01444 232142
- info@tonypotter.com
- www.tonypotter.com

**Contact Title** Director, Tony Potter
**Insider Info** Tony Potter Publishing creates innovative paper based products and high quality books for the international co-edition market. Specialising in interactive books for children (from one to twelve years old), the company also publishes custom and own brand books for adults and children. Adult titles now come under The Teapot Press Imprint (www.teapotpress.com) and a small list is published under the Over the Moon imprint.
**Recent Titles** Land Ahoy! (Interactive information book), Duncan Crosbie (Author) Kay Dixie (Illustrator)
**Tips** Tony Potter Publishing Ltd is happy to consider unsolicited ideas (although most of their work is generated in house). Send ideas in hard copy form only and enclose an SAE.

## Toucan Books Ltd
**3rd Floor, 89 Charterhouse Street, London, EC1M 6HR**
- 020 7250 3388
- 020 7250 3123
- info@toucanbooks.co.uk
- www.toucanbooks.co.uk

**Contact Title** Director, Robert Sackville West; Managing Director, Ellen Dupont
**Insider Info** Founded by Robert Sackville West in 1985, Toucan Books has a leading reputation as a packager of illustrated reference titles. Specialising in international co-editions, Toucan commissions illustrated non-fiction for children and adults. The company client list includes Reader's Digest and the BBC.
**Recent Titles** Facts at Your Fingertips (Reader's Digest); The Kingfisher Book of Religions (Children's non-fiction)

## Tucker Slingsby Ltd
**5th Floor, Regal House, 70 London Road, Twickenham, TW1 3QS**
- 020 8744 1007
- 020 8744 0041

**Insider Info** A packager specialising in children's non-fiction, anthologies, religious and activity books. They also produce health and beauty titles for adults.

## Working Partners Ltd
**1 Albion Place, London, W6 0QT**
- 020 8748 7450
- 020 8748 7450
- enquiries@workingpartnersltd.co.uk
- www.workingpartnersltd.co.uk

**Contact Title** Managing Directors, Chris Snowdon, Charles Nettleton
**Insider Info** A creative team dedicated to the development of quality commercial fiction, contracted to supply fully edited texts. Founded in 1995, Working Partners has created some of the most recognised series in children's fiction, for example the classic Animal Ark series. Working Partners Two was founded in 2006 to create novels across most adult genres, hopefully to recreate the successes of the children's list in the adult market.
**Tips** No unsolicited manuscripts.

## Zoe Books
**15 Worthy Lane, Winchester, SO23 7AB**
- 01962 851318
- enquiries@zoebooks.co.uk
- www.zoebooks.co.uk

**Contact Title** Managing Director, Imogen Dawson
**Insider Info** Zoe Books creates and publishes quality full colour reference books, for children and young adults, and for trade and educational markets

worldwide. The company specialises in series co-editions for the school and library markets.

**Recent Titles** *The Science of Weather* series: example titles include *Drought and the Earth*, *Drought and People*, *Snow and the Earth*, *Snow and People*. Other subjects covered: Food, Clothes and Crafts, Sports, Science, Geography, History, Travel and World Habitats.

# EUROPEAN & INTERNATIONAL PUBLISHERS

## Abingdon Press
**201 Eighth Avenue South, Nashville, Tennessee, 37203, USA**
- 001 615 749 6000
- 001 615 749 6512
- www.abingdonpress.com

**Parent Company** The United Methodist Publishing House

**Contact** President/Publisher, Neil M. Alexander; Senior Editor, Robert Ratcliff; Senior Editor, Ron Kidd

**Imprint(s)** Abingdon Press

  Cokesbury

  Dimensions for Living

**Categories** Publishes Non-Fiction on the following subjects: Children's, Biography, Education, General Interest, Reference, Religion, Scholarly, Sociology, Textbook, Theology

**Insider Info** Publishes 120 titles per year. Pays 7.5 per cent royalty on retail price. Receives 3,000 queries per year. Receives 250 manuscripts per year. Does not accept simultaneous submissions. Average lead time is two years. Book catalogue available free on request.

**Submission Guidelines** Accepts unsolicited manuscripts and proposals.

**Recent Title(s)** *Ready-to-Go Missions*, Jason B. Schultz

**Tips** Abingdon also produces various multimedia products including audiobooks and computer software.

## ACER Press
**347 Camberwell Road, Camberwell, Victoria, 3124, Australia**
- 0061 3 9277 5555
- 0061 3 9277 5500
- info@acer.edu.au

- www.acer.edu.au

**Parent Company** Australian Council for Educational Research

**Contact** Chief Executive Officer, Geoff Masters; General Manager (ACER Press), Ralph Saubern

**Categories** Publishes Non-Fiction on the following subjects: Academic, Counselling, Education, Human Resources, Multimedia, Psychology, Reference, Teaching Resources

**Submission Guidelines** Accepts unsolicited manuscripts and proposals.

**Recent Title(s)** *Reasons for Living*, Marisa Crawford and Graham Rossiter

**Tips** ACER Press accepts evidence or research-based submissions as long as they are sent using the ACER Publishing Proposal Form, available on the website.

## Adams Media
**57 Littlefield Street, Avon, Massachusetts, 02322, USA**
- 001 508 427 7100
- 001 800 872 5628
- submissions@adamsmedia.com
- www.adamsmedia.com

**Parent Company** F+W Publications Inc

**Contact** Executive Publishing Director, Gary M. Krebs; Senior Editor, Jill Alexander

**Categories** Publishes Non-Fiction on the following subject areas: Self-Help, Inspiration, Women's Issues, Pop Psychology, Relationships, Business, Careers, Parenting, New Age, Gift Books, Cookbooks, How-To and Reference titles.

**Insider Info** Publishes 230 titles per year. Receives 5,000 queries and 1,500 manuscripts per year. Receives 40% of books from first-time authors. 40% of books are from unagented writers. Average lead time is 12–18 months. Accepts simultaneous submissions.

**Submission Guidelines** Accepts unsolicited manuscripts and proposals.

**Recent Title(s)** *If the Man You Love Was Abused: A Couple's Guide to Healing*, Marie H. Browne, Ph.D

**Tips** Adams will only accept proposals by post and they should include relevant market research, along with an SAE or IRC (for international submissions).

## Albert Bonniers Förlag
**PO Box 3159, S-103 63, Stockholm, Sweden**
- 0046 8 696 8620
- 0046 8 696 8369
- info@abforlag.bonnier.se
- www.albertbonniersforlag.se

**Contact** Publisher, Albert Bonnier; Editor, Åsa Ernflo; Editor, Susanna Höijer; Editor (Fiction, Poetry, Biography), Sophie SŠllström; Editor (Non-Fiction), Thomas Lundvall.

**Imprint(s)** Bonnierpocket
 Bonnier Fakta
 Bonnier Impact
 Panache

**Categories** Publishes Non-Fiction, Fiction and Children's on the following subject areas: Biography, Essays, General Interest, Literary Fiction, Mainstream Fiction, Memoir, Poetry

**Insider Info** Publishes 150 titles per year.

**Submission Guidelines** Accepts unsolicited manuscripts and proposals.

**Recent Title(s)** *Förföriskt gott*, Kristina Eriksson

**Tips** Submissions to Albert Bonniers Förlag must be directed to either the fiction or non-fiction editor, as appropriate.

## Allen & Unwin (Pty) Ltd
**PO Box 8500, St Leonards, New South Wales, 1590, Australia**
- 0061 02 8425 0100
- 0061 02 9906 2218
- frontdesk@allenandunwin.com
- www.allenandunwin.com

**Contact** Publisher, Elizabeth Weiss; Publisher (Adult Fiction), Louise Thurtell

**Imprint(s)** Arena

**Categories** Publishes Non-Fiction, Fiction, Children's on the following subjects: Academic, Biography, Business, Children's Fiction, Crime Fiction, Environment, Gender Studies, General Interest, Health, History, How-To, Humour, Literary Fiction, Mainstream Fiction, Military History, Picture Books, Practical, Scholarly, Science, Spirituality, Young Adult

**Insider Info** Publishes 220 titles per year. Responds to proposals in 10–12 weeks.

**Submission Guidelines** Accepts unsolicited manuscripts and proposals.

**Recent Title(s)** *A Field of Darkness*, Cornelia Read

**Tips** Allen & Unwin accepts submissions for their main subjects areas. For adult fiction submissions that fall outside of the main areas Louise Thurtell runs the 'Friday Pitch' where she will review any kind of submission as long as she receives it on a Friday.

## Annick Press Ltd
**15 Patricia Avenue, Toronto, Ontario, M2M 1H9, Canada**
- 001 416 221 4802
- 001 416 221 8400

- annickpress@annickpress.com
- www.annickpress.com

**Contact** Publishing Director, Rick Wilks; Associate Publisher, Colleen MacMillan.

**Categories** Publishes Non-Fiction, Fiction, Children's titles on the following subjects: Children's Fiction, Children's Non-Fiction, Picture Books, Young Adult

**Insider Info** Publishes 30 titles per year. Authors paid by royalty, with advance offered. Receives 5,000 queries and 3,000 manuscripts per year. 80–85 per cent of books are from unagented writers. 20 per cent of books are from first time authors. Aims to respond to manuscripts in three months. Average lead time is two years.

**Submission Guidelines** Accepts unsolicited manuscripts and proposals.

**Recent Title(s)** *Creature Catchers*, Lisa Smedman

**Tips** Annick Press is committed to publishing Canadian children's writers and cannot accept submissions from outside of Canada.

## Arcade Publishing
**116 John Street, Suite 2810, New York, 10038, USA**
- 001 212 475 2633
- 001 212 353 8148
- info@arcadepub.com
- www.arcadepub.com

**Contact** President/Editor-in-Chief, Richard Seaver; Publisher, Jeannette Seaver; Senior Vice President/General Manager/Senior Editor, Calvert Barksdale

**Categories** Publishes Non-Fiction and Fiction titles on the following subjects: Biography, General Interest, History, Literary Fiction, Mainstream Fiction, Memoirs, Nature, Science, Short-Story Collections, Translation, Travel

**Insider Info** Publishes 35 titles per year. Authors paid by royalty on retail price, and an advance is also offered. Authors also receive ten copies of their title. Five per cent of books published are from first-time authors. Aims to respond to manuscripts within four months. Average lead time is 18 months. Catalogue and author guidelines available free on request by sending SAE.

**Submission Guidelines** Does not accept unsolicited manuscripts or proposals.

**Recent Title(s)** *Agamemnon's Daughter*, Ismail Kadare

**Tips** Arcade publishes top-quality non-fiction and fiction, with a special interest in foreign translations. Arcade does not accept unagented submissions or proposals.

## Arnoldo Mondadori Editore S.p.A.

**via Mondadori 1, 20090, Milan, Italy**

- 0039 2 75423215
- 0039 2 75422302
- infolibri@mondadori.it
- www.mondadori.it

**Parent Company** The Mondadori Group
**Contact** Chairman, Marina Berlusconi
**Imprint(s)** Harlequin
 Mondadori Books
 Mondadori Illustrati
 Random House Mondadori

**Categories** Publishes Non-Fiction, Fiction and Children's titles on the following subjects: Autobiography, Biography, Children's Fiction, Classics, Contemporary Fiction, Education, General Interest, Literary Fiction, Local Interest, Magazines, Mainstream Fiction, Media, Professional, Tourist Guides

**Insider Info** Publishes 2,500 titles per year.
**Recent Title(s)** *Le Uova del Drago*, Pietrangelo Buttafuoco
**Tips** Mondadori are Italy's largest publisher, also publishing magazines and offering printing services. Mostly interested in contemporary adult or children's fiction and re-prints of classics.

## Ballantine Publishing Group

**1745 Broadway, 18th Floor, New York, 10019, USA**

- 001 212 782 9000
- 001 212 782 9700
- bfi@randomhouse.com
- www.randomhouse.com/rhpg

**Parent Company** Random House Inc
**Contact** President/Publisher, Gina Centrello
**Imprint(s)** Ballantine Books
 Del Rey/Lucas Books
 Fawcett
 Ivy
 One World
 Wellspring

**Categories** Publishes Non-Fiction and Fiction on the following subjects: General Interest, Health, Mainstream Fiction, Mystery, Science-Fiction/Fantasy, Western

**Insider Info** Authors paid by royalty, with advance offered.

**Submission Guidelines** Does not accept unsolicited manuscripts or proposals.
**Recent Title(s)** *Dark Prince*, David Gemmell
**Tips** Ballantine has a wide scope but generally specialises in science fiction, fantasy, westerns, and mystery novels. Ballantine does not accept any unagented submissions or proposals.

## Bantam Dell Publishing Group

**1745 Broadway, New York, 10019, USA**

- 001 212 782 9000
- 001 212 782 9700
- bdpublicity@randomhouse.com
- www.bantamdell.com

**Parent Company** Random House Inc
**Contact** Irwyn Applebaum
**Imprint(s)** Bantam Hardcover/Mass Market/Trade Paperback
 Crimeline
 Delacorte Press
 Dell, Delta, The Dial Press
 Domain, DTP, Fanfare, Island
 Spectra

**Categories** Publishes Non-Fiction and Fiction on the following subjects: General Interest, Health, Mainstream Fiction, Mystery, Science-Fiction/Fantasy, Suspense, Women's Fiction

**Insider Info** Authors paid by royalty, with advance offered. Accepts simultaneous submissions.
**Submission Guidelines** Does not accept simultaneous proposals or manuscripts.
**Recent Title(s)** *In the Country of Men*, Hisham Matar
**Tips** Bantam Dell does not accept any unagented submissions or proposals.

## Barron's Educational Series Inc

**250 Wireless Boulevard, Hauppage, New York, 11788, USA**

- 001 800 645 3476
- 001 631 434 3723
- info@barronseduc.com
- www.barronseduc.com

**Contact** Acquisitions Editor, Wayne Barr
**Categories** Publishes Non-Fiction and Children's titles on the following subjects: Art Books, Business & Finance, Children's Books, Cooking, Crafts & Hobbies, Employment/Careers, English Language Arts, Family & Health, Foreign Languages, Gift Books, History/Biography, Mind Body & Spirit, Pets, School Guides, Spanish Language, Sports & Recreation, Study Gudies, Test Preparation

**Insider Info** Publishes 300 titles per year. Pays 12–14 per cent royalty on net receipts, with advance offered. Receives 2,000 queries per year. Receives 75 per cent of books from unagented writers, and 25 per cent of books from first-time authors. Aims to respond to proposals within eight months. Accepts simultaneous submissions. Average lead time is 18 months.

**Submission Guidelines** Accepts unsolicited manuscripts and proposals.

**Recent Title(s)** *Complete French Grammar Review*, Renée White

**Tips** Barron's books usually fit within one of several different series so it is best to submit a proposal with a particular series in mind. Submissions of children's books are less likely to be successful due to the high volume of submissions.

## Berlin Verlag
**Greifswalder Strasse 207, 10405, Berlin, Germany**
- 0049 30 44 38450
- 0049 30 44 384595
- info@berlinverlag.de
- www.berlinverlag.de

**Parent Company** Bloomsbury Publishing Plc (see entry under UK & Irish Book Publishers)

**Contact** Managing Director, Kathy Rooney

**Categories** Publishes Non-Fiction, Fiction and Children's titles on the following subjects: Children's Books, Contemporary Fiction, General Interest, History, Literary Fiction, Mainstream Fiction, Translation

**Insider Info** Publishes 102 titles per year.

**Recent Title(s)** *Ruhelos*, William Boyd

**Tips** Berlin Verlag, owned by Bloomsbury Publishing Plc, is one of the leading literary publishers in Germany and focuses mainly on literary fiction for the adult market. Berlin Verlag will accept proposals in either German or English language.

## Bertelsmann
**Verlagsgruppe Random House, Neumarkter Strasse 28, 41360, Munich, Germany**
- 0049 89 41360
- 0049 89 41363333
- kundenservice@randomhouse.de
- www.randomhouse.de

**Parent Company** Random House Group

**Categories** Publishes Non-Fiction, Fiction and Children's titles on the following subjects: Biography, Children's Fiction, Contemporary Fiction, Education, General Interest, How-To, Literary Fiction, Local Interest, Mainstream Fiction, Politics, Reference, Self-Help, Travel .

**Insider Info** Average lead time is six months.

**Submission Guidelines** Accepts unsolicited manuscripts and proposals.

**Recent Title(s)** *Swamp Blooms*, Carl Hiaasens

**Tips** Bertelsmann accepts unsolicited submissions by post only, not by email.

## Bloomsbury USA
**175 Fifth Avenue, Suite 300, New York, 10010, USA**
- 001 212 307 5858
- 001 646 727 8300
- info@bloomsburyusa.com
- www.bloomsburyusa.com

**Parent Company** Bloomsbury Publishing Plc (see entry under UK & Irish Book Publishers)

**Contact** Publisher/Editorial Director, Karen Rinaldi

**Imprint(s)** Bloomsbury Adult Books
 Bloomsbury Children's Books

**Categories** Publishes Non-Fiction, Fiction and Children's titles on the following subjects: Biography, Children's Fiction, General Interest, Literary Fiction, Mainstream Fiction, Picture Books, Reference, Self-Help

**Insider Info** Authors paid by royalty, with advance offered. Simultaneous submissions accepted.

**Submission Guidelines** Accepts unsolicited manuscripts and proposals.

**Recent Title(s)** *Winterwood*, Patrick McCabe

**Tips** Bloomsbury does not accept unagented submissions to its adult division but will accept proposals for new children's fiction or non-fiction books. See website for guidelines.

## Brepols Publishers NV
**Begijnhof 67, B-2300, Turnhout, Belgium**
- 0032 14 448 020
- 0032 14 428 919
- info@brepols.net
- www.brepols.net

**Contact** General Manager, Paul De Jongh; Publishing Manager, Christophe Lebbe; Publishing Manager, Chris VandenBorre; Publishing Manager, Johan Van der Beke; Publishing Manager, Luc Jocqué; Publishing Manager, Simon Forde.

**Categories** Publishes Non-Fiction titles on the following subjects: Academic, Archaeology, Architecture, Art History, Bible Studies, Design, Electronic, Essays, Language, Linguistics, Literature, Middle Ages, Online, Religious History, Scholarly

**Recent Title(s)** *The Summa Parisiensis on the Decretum Gratiani*, T. P. McLaughlin

**Tips** Brepols specialises in publishing academic books and essays from leading scholars and also publishes electronic material.

## Cambridge University Press (US)
**32 Avenue of the Americas, New York, 10013, USA**

- 001 212 924 3900
- 001 212 691 3239
- newyork@cambridge.org
- www.cambridge.org/us

**Contact** Director, Richard L. Ziemacki

**Categories** Publishes Non-Fiction titles on the following subjects: Academic, Biography, General Interest, Higher Education, Journals, Literary Criticism, Online Products, Popular Non-Fiction, Reference, Scholarly, Textbook

**Insider Info** Authors paid by royalty, with advance offered.

**Submission Guidelines** Accepts unsolicited manuscripts and proposals.

**Recent Title(s)** *Race, Nationalism and the State in British and American Modernism*, Patricia E. Chu

**Tips** Cambridge University Press has a dedicated online service for its authors called 'authornet'. Authornet contains in-depth submission details, as well as listing the relevant editors and their fields of interest.

## Carroll & Graf Publishers Inc
**245 West 17th Street, 11th Floor, New York, 10011, USA**

- 001 212 981 9919
- 001 646 375 2571
- www.carrollandgraf.com

**Parent Company** Avalon Publishing Group

**Contact** Publisher, Will Balliett

**Categories** Publishes Non-Fiction and Fiction titles on the following subjects: Architecture, Art, Biography, Business, Companion Animals, Consumer, Current Affairs/Politics, Drama, Erotica, Film & Television, Games, Gay & Lesbian, History, Horror, Humour, Lanuage, Literary Fiction/Criticism, Legal, Memoir, Military, Mystery Fiction, Mythology, Philosophy, Poetry, Popular Culture, Reference, Science, Science Fiction, Social Science, Sports, Travel, True Crime, Women's Issues

**Submission Guidelines** Does not accept unsolicited manuscripts or proposals.

**Recent Title(s)** *Looking Good Dead*, Peter James

**Tips** Carroll & Graf does not accept unagented submissions.

## The Caxton Press
**113 Victoria Street, Christchurch, New Zealand**

- 0064 3 366 8516
- 0064 3 365 7840
- print.design@caxton.co.nz
- www.caxton.co.nz

**Contact** Managing Director, Bruce Bascand; General Manager, Peter Watson; Print and Production Manager, Murray Craig

**Categories** Publishes Non-Fiction titles on the following subjects: Art, Calendars, Craft, General Interest, History, Local Interest

**Recent Title(s)** *The Art of New Zealand Fly Fishing Calendar*

**Tips** The Caxton Press specialises in graphic design and printing, and also offers a wide range of self-publishing and printing services.

## The Charlton Press
**PO Box 820, Station Willowdale B, North York, Ontario, M2K 2R1, Canada**

- 001 416 488 1418
- 001 416 488 4656
- chpress@charltonpress.com
- www.charltonpress.com

**Contact** President, W.K. Cross

**Categories** Publishes Catalogues on Canadiana, Collectibles, Numismatics, Sports Cards.

**Recent Title(s)** *Canadian Colonial Tokens (6th Edition)*, W.K. Cross

**Tips** The Charlton Press publishes collectibles catalogues only and does not accept unsolicited submissions.

## Columbia University Press
**61 West 62nd Street, New York, 10023, USA**

- 001 212 459 0600
- 001 212 459 3678
- jc373@columbia.edu
- www.columbia.edu/cu/cup

**Contact** Associate Director/Editorial Director, Jennifer Crewe; Senior Executive Editor, Peter Dimock; Executive Editor, Lauren Dockett

**Categories** Publishes Non-Fiction and Translation titles on the following subjects: Academic, Asian Translations (Fiction/Poetry), Biography, General Interest, History, Journals, Literary Criticism, Politics, Reference, Religion, Scholarly, Science, Textbook.

**Insider Info** Authors paid by royalty, with advance offers. Aims to respond to submissions in four weeks.

**Submission Guidelines** Accepts unsolicited manuscripts and proposals.

**Recent Title(s)** *I Love Dollars*, Zhu Wen

**Tips** Columbia welcomes submissions for academic non-fiction, directed to the appropriate editor.

Columbia also publishes poetry and fiction translations from Asian language.

## The Continuum International Publishing Group

**80 Maiden Lane, Suite 704, New York, 10038, USA**
- 001 212 953 5858
- 001 212 953 5944
- info@continuum-books.com
- www.continuumbooks.com

**Contact** Editorial Director (US), David Barker; Vice President/Senior Editor, Evander Lomke; Vice President/Senior Editor, Frank Oveis

**Imprint(s)** Burns & Oates
 Continuum
 Thoemmes Continuum
 T&T Clark

**Categories** Publishes Non-Fiction on the following subjects: Academic, Biblical Studies, Education, History, Linguistics, Literature, Philosophy, Politics, Religious Studies, Theology, General Religion, Popular Culture

**Insider Info** Publishes 500 titles per year. Authors paid by royalty, with advance offered. Catalogue available free on request. Does not accept simultaneous submissions.

**Submission Guidelines** Accepts unsolicited manuscripts and proposals.

**Recent Title(s)** *On the Absence and Unknowability of God*, Andrew Louth

**Tips** Continuum only publishes in areas they are already strong in, so make sure that all submissions are in keeping with guidelines on the website.

## Cornell University Press

**Sage House, 512 East State Street, Ithaca, New York, 14850, USA**
- 001 607 277 2338
- 001 607 277 2374
- cupressinfo@cornell.edu
- www.cornellpress.cornell.edu

**Contact** Director, John G. Ackerman; Editor in Chief, Peter J. Potter

**Imprint(s)** Comstock
 ILR Press

**Categories** Publishes Non-Fiction on the following subjects: Academic, Anthropology, Asian Studies, Biological Sciences, Classics, History, Industrial Relations, Literary Criticism & Theory, Natural History, Philosophy, Politics, Scholarly, Veterinary Science, Women's Studies

**Insider Info** Publishes 150 titles per year. Authors paid by royalty, with advance offered. Accepts simultaneous submissions. Average lead time is one year.

**Submission Guidelines** Accepts unsolicited manuscripts and proposals.

**Recent Title(s)** *The Limits of Transparency*, Jacqueline Best

**Tips** Cornell welcomes academic submissions in their fields of interest, ideally addressed to the correct acquisitions editor.

## Crown Publishing Group

**1745 Broadway, New York, 10019, USA**
- 001 212 782 9000
- 001 212 782 9700
- crownbiz@randomhouse.com
- www.randomhouse.com/crown

**Parent Company** Random House Inc

**Contact** President/Publisher, Jenny Frost

**Imprint(s)** Bell Tower
 Clarkson Potter
 Crown Business/Forum
 Harmony Books
 Shaye Arehart Books
 Three Rivers Press

**Categories** Publishes Non-Fiction and Fiction titles on the following subjects: General Interest, Illustrated Books, Literary Fiction, Mainstream Fiction

**Insider Info** Authors paid by royalty with advance offered.

**Submission Guidelines** Does not accept unsolicited manuscripts or proposals.

**Recent Title(s)** *The Double Bind*, Chris Bohjalian

**Tips** Crown Publishing does not accept any unagented submissions or proposals.

## David Bateman Ltd

**Tarndale Grove, Albany Business Park, Bush Road, Albany, Auckland, 1330, New Zealand**
- 0064 9 415 7664
- 0064 9 415 8892
- bateman@bateman.co.nz
- www.bateman.co.nz

**Contact** Chairman/Publisher, David Bateman

**Categories** Publishes Non-Fiction, Fiction and Children's titles on the following subjects: Adult Books, Architecture, Art, Biography, Business, Children's Fiction, Craft, Education, General Interest, History, How-To, Literary Fiction, Local Interest,

Mainstream Fiction, Reference, Science, Self-Help, Travel, Ufology
**Recent Title(s)** *You Drive Me Crazy*, M. Esselman

## David R. Godine, Publisher Inc
**9 Hamilton Place, Boston, Massachusetts, 02108, USA**

- 001 617 451 9600
- 001 617 350 0250
- info@godine.com
- www.godine.com

**Contact** President, David Godine
**Imprint(s)** Black Sparrow Books
**Categories** Publishes Non-Fiction, Fiction and Children's books on the following subjects: Americana, Art/Architecture, Biography, Children's Books, Coffee Table Books, Cooking, Gardening, Historical Fiction, Illustrated Books, Literary Criticism, Literary Fiction, Nature, Photography, Translation, Typography
**Insider Info** Publishes 30 titles per year. Author paid by royalty on retail price. Average lead time of three years.
**Submission Guidelines** Does not accept unsolicited manuscripts or proposals.
**Recent Title(s)** *The Land of Green Ginger*, Noel Langley
**Tips** David R. Godine publishers does not accept unagented submissions.

## DAW Books Inc
**375 Hudson Street, New York, 10014, USA**

- 001 212 366 2096
- 001 212 366 2090
- daw@penguinputnam.com
- www.dawbooks.com

**Parent Company** Penguin Group (USA) Inc
**Contact** Publisher, Elizabeth R. Wollheim; Publisher, Sheila E. Gilbert; Submissions Editor, Peter Stampfel
**Categories** Publishes Fiction on the following subjects: Fantasy, Horror, Science-Fiction
**Insider Info** Publishes 80 titles per year. Aims to respond to manuscripts within three months. Does not accept simultaneous submissions.
**Submission Guidelines** Accepts unsolicited manuscripts and proposals.
**Recent Title(s)** *A Flame in Hali*, Marion Zimmer Bradley & Deborah J. Ross
**Tips** DAW Books publishes fantasy and science-fiction and welcomes submissions of first novels if they are of professional quality.

## DK Publishing Inc
**375 Hudson Street, New York, 10014, USA**

- 001 212 213 4800
- 001 212 689 4828
- info@dk.com
- www.dk.com

**Parent Company** Pearson Plc
**Contact** Publisher, Christopher Davis
**Categories** Publishes Non-Fiction and Children's titles on the following subjects: Adult Reference, Children's Reference, Disney/Pixar, Encyclopedias, Multimedia, Picture Books.
**Insider Info** Authors paid by royalty with advance offered.
**Submission Guidelines** Does not accept unsolicited manuscripts or proposals.
**Recent Title(s)** *Ultimate Visual Dictionary*, DK Publishing
**Tips** DK Publishing is a leading publisher of reference and encyclopedia books. DK does not accept unagented submissions or proposals.

## Doubleday Broadway Publishing Group
**1745 Broadway, New York, 10019, USA**

- 001 212 782 9000
- 001 212 782 9700
- ddaypub@randomhouse.com
- www.randomhouse.com/doubleday

**Parent Company** Random House Inc
**Imprint(s)** Broadway Books
 Currency
 Doubleday
 Main Street Books
 Nan A. Talese
**Categories** Publishes Non-Fiction and Fiction titles on the following subjects: Americana, Biography, Society and Culture, General Interest, Genre Fiction, Politics, Literary Fiction, Mainstream Fiction
**Insider Info** Authors paid by royalty on retail price, with advance offered. Receives thousands of manuscripts per year.
**Submission Guidelines** Does not accepts unsolicited manuscripts or proposals.
**Recent Title(s)** *Family Tree*, Barbara Delinsky
**Tips** Doubleday Broadway does not accept any unagented submissions or proposals.

## Douglas & McIntyre Publishing Group

**2323 Quebec Street, Suite 201, Vancouver, British Columbia, V5T 4S7, Canada**

- 001 604 254 7191
- 001 604 254 9099
- dm@douglas-mcintyre.com
- www.douglas-mcintyre.com

**Imprint(s)** Douglas & McIntyre
 Greystone Books

**Categories** Publishes Non-Fiction and Fiction titles on the following subjects: Architecture, Art, Canadian Interest, Celebrity Biography, Environment, Food & Drink, Health, Literary Fiction, Natural History, Popular Culture, Science, Sports

**Insider Info** Publishes 75 titles per year.

**Submission Guidelines** Accepts unsolicited manuscripts and proposals.

**Recent Title(s)** *The Chickens Fight Back*, Dr. David Waltner-Toews

**Tips** Douglas & McIntyre accepts proposals and manuscript submissions but very rarely publishes unsolicited work.

## Dover Publications Inc

**31 East 2nd Street, Mineola, New York, 11501, USA**

- 001 516 294 7000
- 001 516 873 1401
- info@doverpublications.com
- www.doverpublications.com

**Contact** Editor-in-Chief, Paul Negri; Editor (Math/Science reprints), John Grafton

**Categories** Publishes Non-Fiction and Children's titles on the following subjects: Art, Biography, Children's, Cook Book, General Interest, History, How-To, Humor, Illustrated Book, Science, Textbook

**Insider Info** Publishes 660 titles per year. Accepts simultaneous submissions.

**Submission Guidelines** Accepts unsolicited manuscripts and proposals.

**Recent Title(s)** *Creative Mind and Success*, Ernest Holmes

**Tips** Dover publishes mostly reprints. Dover will accept unsolicited proposals for non-fiction.

## The Dundurn Group

**3 Church Street, Suite 500, Toronto, Ontario, M5E 1M2, Canada**

- 001 416 214 5544
- 001 416 214 5556
- info@dundurn.com

- www.dundurn.com

**Contact** Acquisitions Editor (Fiction), Barry Jowett; Acquisitions Editor (Non-Fiction), Tony Hawke

**Imprint(s)** Boardwalk Books
 Dundurn Press
 Hounslow Press
 Simon & Pierre

**Categories** Publishes Non-Fiction and Fiction titles on the following subjects: Art Criticism, Biography, History, Illustrated Books, Literary Criticism, Literary Fiction, Politics, Popular Non-Fiction, Young Adult

**Insider Info** Pays ten percent royalty on net receipts, with advance offered. Receives 600 queries per year. 50 per cent of books come from unagented writers, and 25 per cent of books from first-time authors. Accepts simultaneous submissions. Average lead time of one year.

**Submission Guidelines** Accepts unsolicited manuscripts and proposals.

**Recent Title(s)** *Invaders from the North*, John Bell

**Tips** Dundurn does not accept submissions by email and all postal submissions must be addressed simply to the 'Acquisitions Editor' otherwise they may not get recorded in Dundurn's submission system.

## Dunmore Press Ltd

**PO Box 25083, Wellington, 6146, New Zealand**

- 0064 4 472 2705
- 0064 4 471 0604
- books@dunmore.co.nz
- www.dunmore.co.nz

**Categories** Publishes Non-Fiction titles on the following subjects: Business, Economics, Education, Environment, General Interest, Health, History, Law, Media, Politics, Society.

**Insider Info** Publishes 30 titles per year. Pays ten per cent royalty on retail price. Aims to respond to proposals within three weeks. Average lead time is three months. Authors receive ten free copies of their publication.

**Submission Guidelines** Accepts unsolicited manuscripts and proposals.

**Recent Title(s)** *Essence*, Krystine Tomaszyk

**Tips** Dunmore Press publishes New Zealand themed non-fiction only.

## ECW Press Ltd

**2120 Queen Street East, Suite 200, Toronto, Ontario, M4E 1E2, Canada**

- 001 416 694 3348
- 001 416 698 9906
- info@ecwpress.com
- www.ecwpress.com

**Contact** Publisher, Jack David; Associate Publisher, David Caron; Senior Editor, Michael Holmes; Associate Editor, Jennifer Hale

**Categories** Publishes Non-Fiction, Fiction and Poetry titles on the following subjects: Biography, Business, Creative Non-Fiction, Economics, Finance, Gay/Lesbian, General Interest, Health/Medicine, History, Literary Fiction, Memoirs, Mystery Fiction, Poetry, Politics, Regional, Sex, Short-Stories, Sports, Women's Issues/Studies, Contemporary Culture, Wicca, Gambling, Television and Movie Stars

**Insider Info** Publishes 70 titles per year. Pays 8–12 per cent royalty on net receipts, with advance offered. Receives 1,500 manuscripts per year. 30 per cent of books come from first-time authors. Aims to respond to manuscripts within four months. Accepts simultaneous submissions. Average lead time of 18 months.

**Submission Guidelines** Accepts unsolicited manuscripts and proposals.

**Recent Title(s)** *Root Bound*, Grant Budday

**Tips** ECW Press does not accept fiction or poetry submissions from writers outside of Canada.

## Editions Larousse

**21 rue de Montparnasse, F-75283, Paris, Cedex 6, France**

- 0033 1 4439 4400
- 0033 1 4439 4343
- Online form
- www.larousse.fr

**Parent Company** Hachette Livre

**Imprint(s)** Petit Larousse
Petits Classiques

**Categories** Publishes Non-Fiction and Children's titles on the following subjects: Bilingual Dictionaries, Children's, Culture, Dictionaries, Encyclopedias, General Interest, Practical, Translations, Young Adult.

**Recent Title(s)** *Balcons Fleuris*, Philippe Ferret

**Tips** Larousse is a subsidiary if Hachette-Livre and publishes practical non-fiction and dictionary books, including bilingual language dictionaries. See Hachette website for submission details.

## Egmont

**Vognmagergade 11, DK-1148, Copenhagen, K, Denmark**

- 0045 33 305550
- 0045 33 321902
- egmont@egmont.com
- www.egmont.com

**Parent Company** Egmont International Holdings A/S

**Contact** President/Chief Executive Officer, Steffen Kragh; Executive Vice President (Egmont Group)/Managing Director (Egmont Books), Tom Harald Jenssen; Editor (Aschehoug), Jeppe Markers

**Imprint(s)** Aschehoug

**Categories** Publishes Non-Fiction, Fiction and Children's titles on the following subjects: Audio Books, Children's Fiction, Education, General Interest, Literary Fiction, Mainstream Fiction

**Tips** Egmont publishes book, magazines and multimedia, and also distributes film and computer games. Egmont accepts submissions for fiction or non-fiction directed at Aschehoug publishers. See website for details.

## Elsevier Australia

**30–52 Smidmore Street, Marrickville, New South Wales, 2204, Australia**

- 0061 2 9517 8999
- 0061 2 9517 2249
- d.lee@elsevier.com
- www.elsevier.com.au

**Parent Company** Reed Elsevier Group Plc

**Contact** Publisher, Debbie Lee; Publishing Editor (Medicine, Surgery, CAM), Sophie Kaliniecki; Publishing Editor (Health Professions), Ann Crabb; Publishing Editor (Nursing & Midwifery), Meg O'Hanlon

**Imprint(s)** Balliere Tindall
Butterworth-Heinemann
Churchill Livingstone
Mosby
Saunders

**Categories** Publishes Non-Fiction on the following subjects: Academic, Health, Medicine, Psychology, Reference, Science, Technology, Textbook

**Insider Info** Author paid by royalty, with advance offered.

**Submission Guidelines** Accepts unsolicited manuscripts and proposals.

**Recent Title(s)** *Gray's Anatomy E-Dition, 41st Edition*, Standring, Ellis, Healy, Johnson, Williams

**Tips** Elsevier Australia is the leading health and science publisher for Australia and New Zealand. Eslevier Australia accepts submissions and proposals from Australian writers as well as for adaptations of international books.

## Engineers Media

**PO Box 588, 2 Ernest Place, Crows Nest, New South Wales, 1585, Australia**

● 0061 2 9438 1533
● 0061 2 9438 5934
● dgeorg@engineersmedia.com.au
● www.engineersmedia.com.au
**Parent Company** Institution of Engineers Australia
**Contact** General Manager, Bruce Roff; Managing
Editor, Dietrich Georg; Editor, Bob Jackson; Editor,
Danny Cameron ; Editor, Justin Liew
**Imprint(s)** EA Books
**Categories** Publishes Non-Fiction on the following
subjects: Construction, Engineering, Journals,
Magazines, Multimedia, Technical
**Submission Guidelines** Accepts unsolicited
manuscripts and proposals.
**Recent Title(s)** *Railway Safety Rolling Stock: Crash,
Derail, Burn*, Ian Macfarlane
**Tips** Engineers Media publishes many magazines
and journals, as well as technical books, and
submissions can be aimed exclusively at these
publications.

## F+W Publications Inc
**4700 East Galbraith Road, Cincinnati, Ohio,
45236, USA**
● 001 513 531 2690
● Online form
● www.fwpublications.com
**Contact** President, Sara Domville; Editorial Director
(Writer's Digest), Jane Friedman; Editorial Director
(North Light), Jamie Markle
**Imprint(s)** Adams Media
David & Charles
Krause Publications
Memory Makers
North Light Books
Writer's Digest Books
**Categories** Publishes Non-fiction on the following
subjects: General Interest, How-to, Antiques &
Collectibles, Art, Crafts, Equestrian, Gardening,
Sports, Automotive, Outdoors, Military, Firearms,
Writing Reference, Woodworking
**Insider Info** Authors paid by royalty with
advance offered.
**Submission Guidelines** Accepts unsolicited
manuscripts and proposals.
**Recent Title(s)** *Toddler Scrapbooks, Memory Makers;
The Weekend Artist: You Can Draw*, Lee
Hammond (Arts)
**Tips** See website or individual listings for specific
submission guidelines about the
company's imprints.

## Facts On File Inc
**132 West 31st Street, New York, 10001, USA**
● 001 212 967 8800
● 001 212 967 9196
● llikoff@factsonfile.com
● www.factsonfile.com
**Contact** Editorial Director (Science, Fashion, Natural
history), Laurie Likoff; Senior Editor (Science and
Technology, Nature, Reference), Frank Darmstadt;
Senior Editor (American History, Women's Studies,
Young Adult Reference), Nicole Bowen; Trade Editor
(Health, Pop Culture, True Crime, Sports), James
Chambers; Acquisitions Editor (Language/
Literature), Jeff Soloway
**Imprint(s)** Checkmark Books
**Categories** Publishes Non-Fiction on the following
subjects: Careers, Contemporary Culture, Education,
Education, Entertainment, Health/Medicine, History,
Language/Literature, Multicultural, Natural History,
Popular Culture, Recreation, Reference, Religion,
Sociology, Sports
**Insider Info** Publishes 150 titles per year. Pays ten
per cent royalty on retail price, with advance offered.
25 per cent of books come from unagented writers.
Accepts simultaneous submissions. Book catalogue
available free on request.
**Recent Title(s)** *Encyclopedia of the Modern World*,
William R. Keylor
**Tips** Facts On File publishes educational reference
material aimed mostly at schools and libraries.
Submissions must be directed to the
appropriate Editor.

## Fernwood Press
**PO Box 481, Simon's Town, Cape, 7995, South
Africa**
● 0027 21 786 2460
● 0027 21 786 2478
● ferpress@iafrica.com
● www.fernwoodpress.co.za
**Contact** Director, Pam Struik; Director, Pieter Struik
**Categories** Publishes Non-fiction on the following
subjects: Catalogues, Culture, History, Illustrated
Non-fiction, Local Interest, South African Non-
fiction, Travel
**Recent Title(s)** *African Basketry: Grassroots Art from
Southern Africa*, Anthony B. Cunningham and M.
Elizabeth Terry
**Tips** Fernwood specialises in illustrated non-fiction
books from or about South Africa.

## Fitzhenry & Whiteside Ltd

**195 Allstate Parkway, Markham, Ontario, L3R 4T8, Canada**

- 001 905 477 9700
- 001 905 477 9179
- godwit@fitzhenry.ca
- www.fitzhenry.ca

**Contact** President, Sharon Fitzhenry; Publisher (Children's Books), Gail Winskill; Managing Editor (Adult Books), Richard Dionne

**Imprint(s)** Fifth House
Fitzhenry & Whiteside
Stoddart Kids
Red Deer

**Categories** Publishes Non-Fiction, Poetry and Children's titles on the following subjects: Children's Books, Education, General Interest, Poetry, Social Studies, Young Adult

**Submission Guidelines** Accepts unsolicited manuscripts and proposals.

**Recent Title(s)** *A Sky Black with Crows*, Alice Walsh

**Tips** Fitzhenry & Whiteside do not accept submissions for children's books and will only accept submissions for adult trade titles by email, in the body of the email rather than as an attachment.

## Free Press

**1230 Avenue of the Americas, New York, 10020, USA**

- 001 212 698 7000
- 001 212 698 7007
- Online form
- www.simonsays.com

**Parent Company** Simon & Schuster Adult Publishing Group

**Contact** Publisher, Martha Levin; Vice President/Senior Editor (History/Serious Non-fiction), Bruce Nichols; Vice President/Senior Editor (Psychology/Spirituality/Self-help), Leslie Meredith; Vice President/Editorial Director (Self-help/Serious Non-fiction), Dominick Anfuso; Senior Editor (Literary fiction), Amy Scheibe; Senior Editor (History, Current events, Biography, Memoir), Elizabeth Stein

**Categories** Publishes Non-fiction and Fiction titles on the following subjects: Faith, General Interest, How-to, Literary fiction, Mainstream fiction, Self-help, Spirituality, Politics

**Insider Info** Publishes 85 titles per year. Authors paid by royalty, with advance offered. 15 per cent of books come from first-time authors. Average lead time of one year.

**Submission Guidelines** Does not accept unsolicited manuscripts or proposals.

**Recent Title(s)** *Born On A Blue Day: Inside the Extraordinary Mind of an Autistic Savant*, Daniel Tammet

**Tips** Despite Simon & Schuster's policy of not accepting unagented submissions, ten per cent of Free Press' publications are from unagented writers.

## The Galago Publishing Company

**PO Box 1645, Alberton, 1450, South Africa**

- 0027 11 907 2029
- 0027 11 869 0890
- lemur@mweb.co.za
- www.galago.co.za

**Contact** Managing Director, Francis Stiff; Publisher, Peter Stiff

**Categories** Publishes Non-Fiction on the following subjects: Biographies, Hunting, Local Interest, Military History, Political, South African Non-fiction

**Recent Title(s)** *The Covert War: Koevoet Operations 1979-1989*, Peter Stiff

**Tips** Galago publishes books on military history and anything relating to South Africa.

## Giunti Editore S.p.A

**Via Bolognese 165, 50139, Florence, Italy**

- 0039 55 50621
- 0039 55 5062298
- segreteriaeditoriale@giunti.it
- www.giunti.it

**Parent Company** Giunti Gruppo Editoriale

**Contact** Chairman, Sergio Giunti; Managing Director/Chief Executive Officer, Martino Montanarini; Editorial Manager, Bruno Mari

**Imprint(s)** Dami
Giunti
Giunti Demetra
Giunti Junior
Giunti Kids

**Categories** Publishes Non-Fiction, Fiction and Children's titles on the following subjects: Art, Children's Fiction, Crafts, Education, Essays, Grandi Opere, Guidebooks, History, Literary Fiction, Mainstream Fiction, Multimedia, Practical, Science, School Journals, Teaching Resources, Tourism

**Insider Info** Publishes 481 titles per year.

**Recent Title(s)** *Le Parole del Cuore*, Sabrina Carollo

**Tips** Giunti primarily publishes books and educational materials for children and students, including electronic resources.

## The Globe Pequot Press Inc

**246 Goose Lane, PO Box 480, Guilford, Connecticut, 06437, USA**

- 001 203 458 4500
- 001 203 458 4604
- info@globepequot.com
- www.globepequot.com

**Contact** President/Publisher, Linda Kennedy; Submissions Editor, Shelley Wolf

**Imprint(s)** Lyons Press

**Categories** Publishes Non-fiction titles on the following subjects: Cooking, History, Local interest, Natural History Field Guides, Nature, Outdoor Recreation Guides, Popular Western and Women's History, Regional Travel Guides, Sports, Travel

**Insider Info** Publishes 600 titles per year. Advance offered. 70 per cent of books come from unagented writers, and 30 per cent of books from first-time authors. Aims to respond to proposals within eight weeks. Accepts simultaneous submissions. Average lead time of one year.

**Submission Guidelines** Accepts unsolicited manuscripts and proposals.

**Recent Title(s)** *Allah's Bomb*, Al J. Venter

**Tips** Globe Pequot is the largest publisher of regional travel books, local interest titles and outdoor recreation guides in America. Globe Pequot welcomes proposals for travel and guide books.

## Graywolf Press

**2402 University Avenue, Suite 203, St. Paul, Minnesota, 55114, USA**

- 001 651 641 0036
- wolves@graywolfpress.org
- www.graywolfpress.org

**Contact** Director/Publisher, Fiona McCrae; Executive Editor/Art Director, Anne Czarniecki; Editorial Manager, Katie Dublinski; Poetry Editor, Jeffrey Shotts

**Categories** Publishes Non-Fiction, Fiction and Poetry titles on the following subjects: Contemporary Culture, Contemporary Poetry, Gay & Lesbian Literature, Literary Criticism, Literary Fiction, Mainstream Fiction, Memoir, Short Story Collections

**Insider Info** Publishes 25 titles per year. Royalty paid on retail price, with advance offered. Receives 3,000 queries per year. 50 per cent of books come from unagented writers and 20 per cent of books from first-time authors. Average lead time of 18 months. Catalogue available free on request.

**Submission Guidelines** Accepts unsolicited manuscripts proposals.

**Recent Title(s)** *Neck Deep and Other Predicaments*, Ander Monson

**Tips** Graywolf welcomes submissions for poetry and fiction but does not publish genre fiction. Graywolf will publish single-author collections of poetry of short-stories, as well as novels and non-fiction.

## Grove/Atlantic Inc

**841 Broadway, 4th Floor, New York, 10003, USA**

- 001 212 614 7850
- 001 212 614 7886
- info@groveatlantic.com
- www.groveatlantic.com

**Imprint(s)** Atlantic Monthly Press
 Black Cat
 Grove Press
 Atlantic Books (UK)

**Categories** Publishes Non-Fiction, Fiction and Poetry titles on the following subjects: Biography, General Interest, History, Literary Fiction, Poetry, Politics, Translation

**Insider Info** Publishes 70 titles per year. Pays 7.5–15 per cent royalty on retail price, with advance offered. 10–15 per cent of books come from first-time authors. Book catalogue available free on request.

**Submission Guidelines** Does not accept unsolicited manuscripts or proposals.

**Recent Title(s)** *Carry Me Down*, M.J. Hyland

**Tips** Grove/Atlantic does not accept unagented submissions or proposals.

## Gyldendal

**Klareboderne 3, DK-1001, Copenhagen, K, Denmark**

- 0045 33 755555
- 0045 33 755556
- gyldendal@gyldendal.dk
- www.gyldendal.dk

**Imprint(s)** Forlaget Forum
 Forlaget Fremad
 Hans Reitzels Forlag
 Høst & Sø Forlag
 Rosinante
 Samlerens Forlag

**Categories** Publishes Non-Fiction, Fiction and Children's titles on the following subjects: Art, Biography, Children's Fiction, Directories, Education, General Interest, How-To, Literary Fiction, Local Interest, Mainstream Fiction, Politics, Reference, Young Adult

**Recent Title(s)** *Al-Qaeda I Europa*, Lorenzo Vidino

**Tips** Gyldendal publishes various types of fiction and non-fiction through its many imprints. Check the individual imprint's website for possible submission guidelines.

## Hachette Livre Australia

**Level 17, 207 Kent Street, Sydney, New South Wales, 2000, Australia**

- 0061 2 8248 0800
- 0061 2 8248 0810
- auspub@hachette.com.au
- www.hha.com.au

**Parent Company** Hachette Livre Publishing Group

**Contact** Managing Director, Malcolm Edwards; Publishing Director, Fiona Hazard; Publisher, Bernadette Foley; Publisher, Vanessa Radnidge; Non-Fiction Publisher, Matthew Kelly

**Imprint(s)** Hachette Children's Books
 Hodder Headline Australia
 Little, Brown
 Orion

**Categories** Publishes Non-Fiction, Fiction and Children's titles on the following subjects: Australiana, Autobiography, Biography, Children's, Cook Books, Current Affairs, General Interest, Health, History, Humour, Lifestyle, Literary Fiction, Mainstream Fiction, Self-Help, Sport, Travel

**Insider Info** Authors paid by royalty, with advance offered. Aims to respond to proposals within three to six months.

**Submission Guidelines** Does not accept unsolicited proposals.

**Recent Title(s)** *Moths That Drink Elephants' Tears*, Matt Walker

**Tips** Hachette Livre Australia specialises in publishing Australian writers, but does not accept unagented submissions or proposals.

## Hachette Livre Publishing Group

**43 quai de Grenelle, F-75905, Paris, Cedex 15, France**

- 0033 1 4392 3000
- 0033 1 4392 3030
- info@hachette-livre.fr
- www.hachette.net

**Contact** Editor, Catherine Rouyer

**Imprint(s)** Hachette Education/Istra
 Hachette Littératures
 Hachette Pratique
 Hachette Tourisme
 Larousse
 Hachette Livre Australia

 Hachette Livre UK (including Hodder Headline Ltd; Little, Brown Book Group; Octopus Publishing Group; Orion Publishing Group; Chambers Harrap Publishers Ltd; The Watts Publishing Group)

**Categories** Publishes Non-Fiction, Fiction and Children's titles on the following subjects: Biography, Children's Fiction, Contemporary Fiction, Directories, Education, General Interest, History, How-To, Language/Literature, Literary Fiction, Local Interest, Mainstream Fiction, Politics, Practical, Reference, Science, Self-Help, Textbooks, Travel

**Insider Info** Publishes 5,000 titles per year. Authors paid by royalty, with advance offered.

**Submission Guidelines** Accepts unsolicited manuscripts and proposals.

**Recent Title(s)** *Bilan Provisoire*, Cyrille Putman

**Tips** Hachette-Livre is a major French publisher with many varied imprints. See website for editorial details and submission guidelines for each imprint. Hachette Livre UK is a division of Hachette Livre, based at the head office in France, that includes the UK imprints Hodder Headline; Octopus Publishing Group; Orion Publishing Group; Chambers Harrap Publishers Ltd; The Watts Publishing Group.

## Harcourt Inc

**525 B Street, Suite 1900, San Diego, California, 92101, USA**

- 001 619 699 6560
- 001 619 699 5555
- www.harcourtbooks.com

**Parent Company** Reed Elsevier Group Plc

**Contact** Editor in Chief, Rebecca Saletan; Managing Editor, David Hough

**Imprint(s)** Harcourt School Publishers
 Holt, Rinehart and Winston
 Harcourt Achieve
 Harcourt Trade Publishers
 Harcourt Children's Books

**Categories** Publishes Non-Fiction, Fiction and Children's titles on the following subjects: Biography, Children's, Education, General Interest, Multimedia, Reference, Technical, Textbooks

**Insider Info** Pays 6–15 per cent royalty on retail price, with advance offered.

**Submission Guidelines** Does not accept unsolicited manuscripts or proposals.

**Recent Title(s)** *B-Mother*, Maureen O'Brien

**Tips** Harcourt is a major educational and children's publisher, and will not accept unagented submissions or proposals.

## Harlequin Enterprises Ltd

**233 Broadway, Suite 1001, New York, 10279, USA**

☎ 001 212 553 4200
🌐 www.eharlequin.com
**Imprint(s)** Harlequin Books/Mills and Boon
Silhouette
Luna
Steeple Hill Books
Red Dress Ink
**Categories** Publishes Fiction titles on the following subjects: Mainstream Fiction, Romance, Women's Fiction
**Insider Info** Publishes 1,500 titles per year. Authors paid by royalty, with advance offered. Average lead time is 18 months. Aims to respond to manuscripts within three months of receipt.
**Submission Guidelines** Accepts unsolicited manuscripts and proposals.
**Recent Title(s)** *Danger Zone*, Debra Webb
**Tips** American office of Canadian publisher. Harlequin is often open to unsolicited manuscripts. Check the website for details on which imprints are currently seeking submissions.

## Harlequin Enterprises Ltd

**225 Duncan Mill Road, Don Mills, Ontario, M3B 3K9, Canada**

☎ 001 416 445 5860
☎ 001 416 445 5865
🌐 www.eharlequin.com
**Contact** President/Publisher, Donna Hayes; Vice President (Editorial), Isabel Swift
**Imprint(s)** Harlequin Books Division
Mills & Boon
**Categories** Publishes Fiction titles on the following subjects: Mainstream Fiction, Romance, Women's Fiction
**Insider Info** Publishes 1,500 titles per year. Authors paid by royalty, with advance offered. Average lead time of 18 months. Aims to respond to manuscripts within three months.
**Submission Guidelines** Accepts unsolicited manuscripts and proposals.
**Recent Title(s)** *Heart on Fire*, Charlotte Lamb
**Tips** Harlequin is Canada's largest publisher, with scores of international imprints. Harlequin supports new writers, check the website for details on which imprints are currently seeking submissions.

## HarperCollins

**10 East 53rd Street, New York, 10022, USA**

☎ 001 212 207 7000
☎ 001 212 207 7633
🌐 www.harpercollins.com
**Parent Company** News Corporation
**Contact** President, Jane Friedman
**Imprint(s)** HarperCollins Australia/New Zealand
HarperCollins Canada
HarperCollins Children's Books Group
HarperCollins General Books Group
HarperCollins UK
Zondervan
**Categories** Publishes Non-Fiction, Fiction and Children's titles on the following subjects: Academic, Business, Children's, Educational, General Interest, Genre Fiction, Mainstream Fiction, Multimedia, Professional, Religious, Spiritual
**Insider Info** Authors paid by royalty with advance offered.
**Submission Guidelines** Accepts unsolicited manuscripts and proposals.
**Recent Title(s)** *Making War to Keep Peace*, Jeane J. Kirkpatrick
**Tips** HarperCollins generally only accepts agented submissions, but the Avon imprint for romantic fiction will accept unsolicited manuscripts and has submission guidelines on the website.

## HarperCollins Canada Ltd

**2 Bloor Street East, 20th Floor, Toronto, Ontario, M4W 1A8, Canada**

☎ 001 416 975 9334
☎ 001 416 975 5223
🌐 www.harpercollins.ca
**Parent Company** News Corporation
**Contact** President, David Kent
**Imprint(s)** HarperCollins Publishers
HarperPerennial Canada
HarperTrophy Canada
Phyllis Bruce Books
**Categories** Publishes Non-Fiction, Fiction and Children's titles on the following subjects: Business, Children's, Cook Books, Educational, General Interest, Genre Fiction, Literary Fiction, Mainstream Fiction, Multimedia, Professional, Reference, Spiritual
**Insider Info** Authors paid by royalty. Advance offered.
**Submission Guidelines** Does not accept unsolicited manuscripts or proposals.
**Recent Title(s)** *Heart-Shaped Box*, Joe Hill

**Tips** HarperCollins Canada does not accept unagented submissions or proposals.

## HarperCollinsPublishers Australia

**PO Box 321, 25 Ryde Road, Pymble, New South Wales, 2073, Australia**

📞 0061 2 9952 5000

📠 0061 2 9952 5555

🌐 www.harpercollins.com.au

**Parent Company** News Corporation

**Contact** Chief Executive Officer (Australia and New Zealand), Robert Gorman; Publishing Director, Shona Martyn; Managing Editor, Belinda Yuille

**Imprint(s)** Angus & Robertson

Fourth Estate

HarperCollins/Collins

HarperSports

Harper Perennial

Voyager

**Categories** Publishes Non-Fiction, Fiction and Children's titles on the following subjects: Academic, Business, Children's, Educational, General Interest, Genre Fiction, Mainstream Fiction, Multimedia, Professional, Religious, Spiritual

**Insider Info** Authors paid by royalty with advance offered.

**Submission Guidelines** Does not accept unsolicited manuscripts or proposals.

**Recent Title(s)** *Apocalypse 2012*, Lawrence E. Joseph

**Tips** HarperCollins Australia does not accept unagented submissions or proposals.

## HarperCollinsPublishers New Zealand

**PO Box 1, 31 View Road, Glenfield, Auckland, New Zealand**

📞 0064 9 443 9400

📠 0064 9 443 9403

✉ editors@harpercollins.co.nz

🌐 www.harpercollins.co.nz

**Parent Company** News Corporation

**Contact** Chief Executive Officer (Australia and New Zealand), Robert Gorman; Managing Director, Tony Fisk; Publishing Director, Lorain Day; Commissioning Editor (Non-Fiction), Tracey Wogan

**Imprint(s)** Flamingo

HarperCollins

HarperSports

Perennial

Voyager

**Categories** Publishes Non-Fiction, Fiction and Children's titles on the following subjects: Autobiography, Biography, Business, Children's,

Cook Books, Educational, General Interest, Genre Fiction, Health, History, Literary Fiction, Mainstream Fiction, Multimedia, Professional, Reference, Spiritual, Travel, True Crime.

**Insider Info** Authors paid by royalty, with advance offered. Aims to respond to proposals within six weeks.

**Submission Guidelines** Accepts unsolicited manuscripts or proposals.

**Recent Title(s)** *Brother Odd* , Dean Koontz

**Tips** HarperCollins New Zealand does accept unsolicited submissions of non-fiction or fiction, but only from New Zealand writers.

## Harry N. Abrams Inc

**115 West 18th Street, New York, 10011, USA**

📞 001 212 206 7715

📠 001 212 519 1210

✉ submissions@abramsbooks.com

🌐 www.abramsbooks.com

**Parent Company** La Martiniere Groupe

**Contact** Chief Executive Officer, Michael Jacobs

**Imprint(s)** Abrams Books

Abrams Books for Young Readers

Abrams Image

Stewart, Tabori & Chang

**Categories** Publishes Non-Fiction and Children's titles on the following subjects: art, art history, children's books, illustrated non-fiction, picture books, scholarly

**Insider Info** Publishes 250 titles per year. Does not accept simultaneous submissions. Aims to respond to proposals within six months (if interested).

**Submission Guidelines** Accepts unsolicited manuscripts and proposals.

**Recent Title(s)** *The Adventuress*, Audrey Niffenegger

**Tips** Abrams specialises in illustrated books for the adult trade market and any sample artwork included with submissions must be in printed form rather than digital.

## Harvard University Press

**79 Garden Street, Cambridge, Massachusetts, 02138, USA**

📞 001 401 531 2800

📠 001 401 531 2801

✉ contact_hup@harvard.edu

🌐 www.hup.harvard.edu

**Contact** Editor-in-Chief, Michael Fisher

**Categories** Publishes Non-Fiction titles on the following subjects: American Literature, Economics, Education, History, History of Science, Law, Natural

Science, Philosophy, Psychology, Public Policy, Reference, Scholarly
**Insider Info** Authors paid by royalty with advance offered.
**Submission Guidelines** Accepts unsolicited manuscripts and proposals.
**Recent Title(s)** *Born In Flames*, Howard Hampton
**Tips** Harvard University Press will accept scholarly proposals in its specialist areas. See website for editorial contact details.

## H. Aschehoug & Co (W.Nygaard) AS
**Postboks 363, Sentrum, N-0102, Oslo, Norway**
☎ 0047 22 400400
☏ 0047 22 206395
✉ epost@aschehoug.no
🌐 www.aschehoug.no
**Contact** Editor, Jeppe Markers
**Imprint(s)** Forlaget Oktober AS
Kirkelig Kulturverksted AS
Universitetsforlaget AS
**Categories** Publishes non-Fiction, Fiction and Children's titles on the following subjects: Education, Fantasy, General Interest, Genre Fiction, History, Literary Fiction, Mainstream Fiction, Mystery, Practical, Romance, Science-Fiction, Teaching Resources, Textbooks, Translation
**Insider Info** Publishes 500 titles per year. Aims to respond to manuscripts within six months.
**Submission Guidelines** Accepts unsolicited manuscripts and proposals.
**Tips** Aschehoug excepts submissions in any area as long as they are directed to the correct imprint. See website for details.

## Hastings House/Daytrips Publishers
**PO Box 908, Winter Park, Florida, 32790, USA**
☎ 001 407 339 3600
☏ 001 407 339 5900
✉ hastings_daytrips@earthlink.net
🌐 www.hastingshousebooks.com
**Parent Company** Lini Llc
**Contact** Publisher, Peter Leers; Senior Travel Editor (Daytrips series), Earl Steinbicker
**Categories** Publishes Non-Fiction on the following subjects: Tourist Information, Travel, Travel Guides
**Insider Info** Publishes 20 titles per year. Pays eight–ten per cent royalty on net receipts. Receives 600 queries per year and 900 manuscripts per year. 40 per cent of books from unagented writers, and ten per cent of books from first-time authors. Average lead time of six–ten months.

**Recent Title(s)** *Daytrips Scotland & Wales*, Judith Frances Duddle
**Tips** Hastings House/Daytrips Publishers is currently focusing on the Daytrips Travel Series and is seeking material from both local and international contributors.

## Houghton Mifflin Co.
**222 Berkeley Street, Boston, Massachusetts, 02116, USA**
☎ 001 617 351 5000
🌐 www.hmco.com
**Contact** Chairman/President/Chief Executive Officer, Anthony Lucki ; Executive Vice President, Stephen Richards
**Imprint(s)** Great Source
Houghton Mifflin College Division
Houghton Mifflin School Division
Houghton Mifflin Trade and Reference Division
McDougal Littell
Riverside
**Categories** Publishes Non-Fiction, Fiction, Poetry and Children's titles on the following subjects: Biography, Children's, Education, General Interest, How-To, Literary Fiction, Reference, Self-Help, Textbooks
**Insider Info** Authors paid by royalty with advance offered. Accepts simultaneous submissions.
**Submission Guidelines** Accepts unsolicited manuscripts and proposals.
**Recent Title(s)** *The God Delusion*, Richard Dawkins
**Tips** "We are not a mass market publisher. We do practical self-help but not pop psychology. Our main focus is serious nonfiction and our audience is high end literary."

## Indiana University Press
**601 North Morton Street, Bloomington, Indiana, 47404, USA**
☎ 001 812 855 8817
☏ 001 812 855 8507
✉ iupress@indiana.edu
🌐 www.iupress.indiana.edu
**Contact** Director (Russian & East European Studies, United Nations, Jewish & Holocaust Studies, Art), Janet Rabinowitch; Editorial Director (American History, African American Studies, Bioethics, Military History, Paleontology, Philanthropy), Robert Sloan; Sponsoring Editor (African Studies, Philosophy, Religion), Dee Mortensen; Sponsoring Editor (Regional Trade, Regional Natural History, Railroads Past & Present), Linda Oblack; Sponsoring Editor (Music, Cinema, Media Studies), Jane Quinet;

Sponsoring Editor (Anthropology, Asian Studies, Middle East Studies, Political Science/International Relations, Folklore), Rebecca Tolen

**Categories** Publishes Non-Fiction and Journals on the following subjects: Academic, African, African American, Anthropology, Asian, Classical and Ancient, Cultural Studies, Gender Studies, Jewish, Middle East, Russian and East European Studies, Film, Folklore, History, Bio-ethics, Music, Paleontology, Philanthropy, Philosophy, Reference, Religion, Scholarly, Women's Studies

**Insider Info** Publishes 200 titles per year. Offers an advance. Aims to respond to proposals within four months.

**Submission Guidelines** Accepts unsolicited manuscripts and proposals.

**Recent Title(s)** *Double-wide*, Michael Martone

**Tips** Indiana University Press is the second largest public university press in America, and specialises mainly in humanities and social sciences.

## The Johns Hopkins University Press
**2715 North Charles Street, Baltimore, Maryland, 21218, USA**
- ☎ 001 410 516 6900
- ☎ 001 410 516 6968
- ✉ tcl@press.jhu.edu
- ☻ www.press.jhu.edu

**Contact** Editor-in-Chief (Mathematics, Physics, Astronomy), Trevor Lipscombe; Senior Acquisitions Editor (Clinical Medicine, Public Health, Health Policy), Wendy Harris; Senior Acquisitions Editor (American History, History of Science & Technology, Regional Books), Robert J. Brugger; Senior Acquisitions Editor (Biology & Life Sciences), Vincent J. Burke

**Categories** Publishes Non-Fiction on the following subjects: Academic, Biography, General Interest, History, Journals, Literary Criticism, Politics, Reference, Religion, Scholarly, Science, Textbook

**Insider Info** Publishes 140 titles per year. Authors paid by royalty. Average lead time is one year.

**Submission Guidelines** Accepts unsolicited manuscripts and proposals.

**Recent Title(s)** *Regime Change: U.S. Strategy through the Prism of 9/11*, Robert S. Litwak

**Tips** Johns Hopkins welcomes academic proposals providing they are sent to the correct editor. Check the website for further details.

## John Wiley & Sons Australia Ltd
**PO Box 1226, 42 McDougall Street, Milton, Queensland, 4064, Australia**
- ☎ 0061 7 3859 9755
- ☎ 0061 7 3859 9715
- ✉ brisbane@johnwiley.com.au
- ☻ www.johnwiley.com.au

**Parent Company** John Wiley & Sons Inc

**Contact** Managing Director, Peter Donoughue

**Imprint(s)** Higher Education Division
Jacaranda

**Categories** Publishes Non-Fiction and Children's titles on the following subjects: Academic, Business, Children's Education, Education, Engineering, Multimdeia, Online, Psychology, Reference, Science, Sociology, Teacher Resources, Technology, Textbook

**Insider Info** Authors paid by royalty, with advance offered.

**Submission Guidelines** Accepts unsolicited manuscripts and proposals.

**Recent Title(s)** *Financial Reporting Handbook 2007*, Keith Reilly and Jennifer Marks, eds.

**Tips** John Wiley Australia accepts submissions using a downloadable submission form. See website for further details and downloads.

## John Wiley & Sons Inc
**111 River Street, Hoboken, New Jersey, 07030, USA**
- ☎ 001 201 748 6000
- ☎ 001 201 748 6088
- ✉ info@wiley.com
- ☻ www.wiley.com

**Contact** President/Chief Executive Officer, William J. Pesce; Chairman, Peter B. Wiley

**Imprint(s)** Jossey-Bass

**Categories** Publishes Non-Fiction titles on the following subjects: Biography, Children's, Education, Health, History, Medical, Psychology, Reference, Science, Technology, Textbooks

**Insider Info** Offers an advance. Accepts simultaneous submissions.

**Submission Guidelines** Accepts unsolicited unsolicited proposals and manuscripts.

**Recent Title(s)** *Logic Modeling Methods in Program Evaluation*, Joy A. Frechtling

**Tips** John Wiley accepts unsolicited proposals and has a detailed set of submission guidelines for each division in the company, available on the website.

## Jonathan Ball Publishers
**PO Box 6836, Roggebaai, Cape Town, 8012, South Africa**
- ☎ 0027 11 622 2900
- ☎ 0027 11 622 7610
- ✉ jball@jonathanball.co.za

www.jonathanball.co.za

**Contact** Managing Director, Jonathan Ball; Publishing Director, Jeremy Boraine; Editor, Jane Rogers; Editor (Sunbird), Natanya Mulholland.

**Imprint(s)** Jonathan Ball
 Sunbird

**Categories** Publishes Non-Fiction and Fiction titles on the following subjects: Biography, History, Maps, Literary Fiction, Politics, South African Non-Fiction, Tourism, Travel

**Submission Guidelines** Accepts unsolicited manuscripts and proposals.

**Recent Title(s)** *Capitalist Nigger: The Road to Success*, Chika Onyeani

**Tips** Jonathan Ball accepts submissions from international writers but will only publish non-fiction relating to South Africa, and a limited amount of fiction.

## Juta & Company Ltd

**PO Box 14373, Lansdowne, Cape Town, 7779, South Africa**

- 0027 21 763 3500
- 0027 21 761 5861
- cserv@juta.co.za
- www.juta.co.za

**Contact** Chief Executive Officer, Lynne du Toit; Publisher (Juta Law), Chipo Chipidza; Publisher (Juta Academic), Glenda Younge

**Imprint(s)** Double Storey
 Juta Academic
 Juta Law
 Juta Learning

**Categories** Publishes Non-Fiction on the following subjects: Academic, Art, Biography, Business, Education, Health, Law, Legal Interest, Local Interest, Memoirs, Multimedia, Music, Psychology, Science, South African Non-Fiction, Spirituality, Teacher Resources, Tourism

**Recent Title(s)** *365 Ways to Change the World*, Michael Norton

**Tips** Juta specialises mainly in law and legal matters or education titles, but also publishes more mainstream South African interest titles through the Double Storey imprint.

## Kensington Publishing Corp.

**850 3rd Avenue, 16th Floor, New York, 10022, USA**

- 001 212 407 1500
- 001 212 935 0699
- jscognamiglio@kensingtonbooks.com
- www.kensingtonbooks.com

**Contact** President/CEO, Steven Zacharius; Editor-in-Chief , John Scognamiglio; Editorial Director (Romance), Kate Duffy; Editorial Director, Audrey LaFehr

**Imprint(s)** Kensington Books
 Brava Books
 Citadel Press
 Dafina Books
 Pinnacle Books
 Zebra Books

**Categories** Publishes Non-Fiction and Fiction titles on the following subjects: African-American, Biography, Gay/Lesbian, General Interest, Health, How-To, Mainstream Fiction, Mystery, Reference, Romance, Self-Help, Wiccan

**Insider Info** Publishes 600 titles per year. Pays 6–15 per cent royalty on retail price, with advance offered. Receives 5,000 queries per year and 2,000 manuscripts per year. Ten per cent of books come from first-time authors. Aims to respond to proposals within one month and manuscripts within three months. Accepts simultaneous submissions. Average lead time is one year.

**Submission Guidelines** Accepts unsolicited manuscripts and proposals.

**Recent Title(s)** *Bake Sale Murder*, Leslie Meier

**Tips** Kensington is the last major independent US publisher of trade and mass market books, and does accept submissions as long as they are addressed to the relevant editor and accompanied by an SASE. Check website for list of editors and their fields of interest.

## Key Porter Books Ltd

**6 Adelaide Street East, 10th Floor, Toronto, Ontario, M5C 1H6, Canada**

- 001 416 862 7777
- 001 416 862 2304
- info@keyporter.com
- www.keyporter.com

**Contact** Publisher, Jordan Fenn

**Imprint(s)** Key Porter Kids

**Categories** Publishes Non-Fiction and Children's titles on the following subjects: Art, Autobiography, Biography, Business, Children's, Cookbook, Gift Book, Health, History, How-To, Humor, Illustrated Books, Politics, Science, Self-Help, Translation, Travel, Young Adult

**Insider Info** Publishes 100 titles per year. Authors paid by royalty, with advance offered. Receives 1,000 queries per year and 500 manuscripts per year. Aims to respond to proposals within six months.

**Submission Guidelines** Does not accept unsolicited proposals or manuscripts.

**Recent Title(s)** *As If By Accident*, Julie Johnston

**Tips** Key Porter does not accept unagented manuscript submissions but will usually respond to proposals or queries.

## Knopf Publishing Group

**1745 Broadway, New York, 10019, USA**

- 001 212 572 2600
- 001 212 572 8700
- knopfwebmaster@randomhouse.com
- www.randomhouse.com/knopf

**Parent Company** Random House Inc

**Contact** President, Sonny Methá

**Imprint(s)** Alfred A. Knopf

Everyman's Library

Pantheon Books

Schocken Books

Vintage Anchor Publishing

**Categories** Publishes Non-Fiction, Fiction and Children's titles on the following subjects: Biography, Children's, Education, General Interest, Literary Fiction, Mainstream Fiction, Reference

**Insider Info** Authors paid by royalty with advance offered. Accepts simultaneous submissions. Catalogue available by sending SAE.

**Submission Guidelines** Does not accept unsolicited proposals or manuscripts.

**Recent Title(s)** *The California Gold Rush and the Coming of the Civil War*, Leonard L. Richards

**Tips** Knopf will not accept unagented submissions or proposals.

## Krause Publications

**700 East State Street, Iola, Wisconsin, 54990, USA**

- 001 715 445 2214
- 001 715 445 4087
- info@krause.com
- www.krause.com

**Parent Company** F+W Publications Inc

**Contact** Editorial Director, Paul Kennedy; Editor (Soft Crafts), Candy Wiza; Editor (Firearms and Knives), Derrek Sigler; Editor (Antique and Collectibles), Joe Kertzman; Editor (Transportation), John Gunnell

**Categories** Publishes Non-Fiction titles on the following subjects: Antiques & Collectibles, Crafts, Coins & Paper Money, Comics & Games, Construction, Firearms, Knives, Militaria, Old Cars, Outdoors, Records & CDs, Sports, Toys

**Insider Info** Publishes 170 titles per year. Receives 400 queries and 40 manuscripts per year. Ten per cent of books come from first-time authors, and 90 per cent of books from unagented writers. Average lead time is 18 months. Does not accept simultaneous submissions. Aims to respond to proposals and manuscripts within two months.

**Submission Guidelines** Accepts unsolicited manuscripts and proposals.

**Recent Title(s)** *The ABCs of Reloading*, Bill Chevalier

**Tips** Krause's audience consists of serious hobbyists so proposals should provide a unique contribution to the special interest. Submission guidelines available by post.

## Langenscheidt KG

**Mies van der Rohe Straße 1, 80807, Munich, Germany**

- 0049 89 360960
- 0049 89 3609 6222
- redaktion.wb@langenscheidt.de
- www.langenscheidt.de

**Parent Company** The Langenscheidt Publishing Group

**Contact** President, Andreas Langensheidt

**Imprint(s)** Axel Juncker Verlag

Berlitz

Langenscheidt Fachverlag

Mentor

Polyglott

**Categories** Publishes Non-Fiction titles on the following subjects: Atlases, Bilingual Dictionaries, Dictionaries, Encyclopedias, Language books, Road Maps, Translations, Travel Guides

**Recent Title(s)** *Amerikanisch*, Gebunden

**Tips** Langenscheidt primarily publishes dictionaries and linguistic reference materials.

## Learning Media Ltd

**PO Box 3293, Wellington, 6001, New Zealand**

- 0064 4 472 5522
- 0064 4 472 6444
- info@learningmedia.co.nz
- www.learningmedia.co.nz

**Contact** Chief Executive Officer, Gillian Candler; Manager (Sales Publishing), Michelle Kelly; Manager (Curriculum Publishing), Kirsty Farquharson; Manager (Mori Publishing), Huhana Rokx

**Categories** Publishes Non-Fiction, Fiction and Children's titles on the following subjects: Academic, Children's Fiction, Education, Language, Literacy, Multimedia, Pasifika Language, Student Resources, Teacher Resources, Translation, Young Adult.

**Insider Info** Aims to respond to proposals within 12 weeks.

**Submission Guidelines** Accepts unsolicited manuscripts/proposals.
 Submission guidelines at: www.learningmedia.co.nz/nz/online/authorsartists/writingguidelines
**Recent Title(s)** *The Legend of Pheidippides*, David Hill
**Tips** Learning Media publishes educational material for a specific region and prints in many different Pasifika languages. Learning Media recommends that submissions be written for a particular series, and are currently seeking submissions for the Tupu series in particular.

## Les Presses de la Cité
**12 avenue d'Italie, F-75627, Paris, Cedex 13 France**
- 0033 1 44 16 05 00
- 0033 1 44 16 05 05
- edito_fr_pressesdelacite@placedesediteurs.com
- www.pressesdelacite.com

**Parent Company** Editions Belfond
**Contact** Editorial Director, Jean Arcache
**Categories** Non-Fiction, Fiction, Biography, Fantasy, General Interest, Genre Fiction, History, Literary Fiction, Mainstream Fiction, Mystery, Romance, Science Fiction
**Insider Info** Responds in two months to manuscripts.
**Submission Guidelines** Accepts unsolicited manuscripts. Submissions: www.pressesdelacite.com/pressesdelacite/SITE/defaut.php
**Recent Title(s)** *Les Quarante Signes de la Pluie*, Kim Stanley Robinson
**Tips** Presses de la Cité accepts submissions by post, but not email. Enclose an SASE for return of manuscript.

## LexisNexis Canada Inc
**123 Commerce Valley Drive East, Suite 700, Markham, Ontario, L3T 7W8 Canada**
- 001 905 479 2665
- 001 905 479 2826
- info@lexisnexis.ca
- www.lexisnexis.ca

**Parent Company** LexisNexis Group
**Imprint(s)** Butterworths
 LexisNexis
 Quicklaw
**Categories** Non-Fiction, Academic, Business, Finance, Law/Legal, Multimedia, Online, Reference, Technology, Textbook.

**Insider Info** Publishes 100 titles per year. Pays 5–15 per cent royalty on wholesale price. Receives 100 per cent of its books from unagented writers. Receives 50 per cent of books from first time authors. Accepts simultaneous submissions. Publishes manuscript four months after acceptance. Book catalogue free.
**Submission Guidelines** Accepts unsolicited manuscripts/proposals.
**Recent Title(s)** *Ontario Municipal Act & Commentary, 2007 Edition*, John Mascarin and Christopher J. Williams
**Tips** LexisNexis Canada accepts submissions for law and legal material in both print and electronic formats.

## LexisNexis New Zealand
**PO Box 472, 205-207 Victoria Street, Wellington, 1, New Zealand**
- 0064 4 385 1479
- 0064 4 385 1598
- customer.service@lexisnexis.co.nz
- www.lexisnexis.co.nz

**Parent Company** LexisNexis Group
**Contact** Editorial, Helen Scott
**Categories** Non-Fiction, Academic, Business, Finance, Law/Legal, Multimedia, Online, Reference, Technology, Textbook
**Insider Info** Pays royalty. Offers advance.
**Submission Guidelines** Accepts unsolicited manuscripts/proposals.
 Submission guidelines: www.lexisnexis.co.nz/company/writeforus.asp
**Recent Title(s)** *Fair Trading: Misleading or Deceptive Conduct*, Lindsay Trotman and Debra Wilson
**Tips** LexisNexis New Zealand is always looking for submissions of law and legal related material. See website for editorial contact details.

## Llewellyn Publications
**2143 Wooddale Drive, Woodbury, Minnesota, 55125 USA**
- 001 800 843 6666
- 001 651 291 1908
- lwlpc@llewellyn.com
- www.llewellyn.com

**Parent Company** Llewellyn Worldwide Ltd
**Contact** Acquisitions Editor, Nancy J. Mostad
**Categories** Publishes Non-Fiction and Fiction titles on the following subjects: Astrology, Cooking/Foods/Nutrition, Health/Medicine, How-to, Metaphysical fiction, Multimedia, Nature, New Age, Occult, Pagan, Psychology, Self-help, Women's Issues/Studies

**Insider Info** Publishes 100 titles per year. Pays ten per cent royalty on wholesale price. 90 per cent of books come from unagented writers and 30 per cent of books from first-time authors. Accepts simultaneous submissions.

**Submission Guidelines** Accepts unsolicited manuscripts and proposals.

**Recent Title(s)** *Ascension Magick: Ritual, Myth & Healing for the New Aeon*, Christopher Penczak

**Tips** Submissions to Llewellyn should be of a practical or how-to nature, but content should remain accessible to the average reader. Manuscripts must be posted rather than emailed.

## Lonely Planet Publications
**90 Maribyrnong Street, Footscray, Victoria, 3011, Australia**
- 0061 3 8379 8000
- 0061 3 8379 8111
- talk2us@lonelyplanet.com.au
- www.lonelyplanet.com

**Contact** Director, Maureen Wheeler; Director, Tony Wheeler

**Categories** Publishes Non-fiction Tourist Guides and Travel titles.

**Insider Info** Advance offered. Accepts simultaneous submissions.

**Submission Guidelines** Accepts unsolicited manuscripts and proposals.

**Recent Title(s)** *Western Europe (8th Edition)*, Ryan Ver Berkmoes

**Tips** Lonely Planet accepts queries and submissions but read a catalogue first to get an idea of their writing style.

## Lone Pine Publishing
**10145–81 Avenue, Edmonton, Alberta, T6E 1W9, Canada**
- 001 780 433 9333
- 001 780 433 9646
- info@lonepinepublishing.com
- www.lonepinepublishing.com

**Contact** Chairman, Grant Kennedy; Managing Director, Shane Kennedy; Editorial Director, Nancy Foulds

**Imprint(s)** Ghost House Books
 Home World
 Lone Pine
 Pine Candle
 Pine Cone

**Categories** Publishes Non-Fiction titles on the following subjects: Canadian Interest, Environment, Food and Drink, Ghost Short Stories, Health, Local Interest, Natural History, Nature, Outdoors, Paranormal, Popular History, Regional Interest, Science, Travel/Tourist Guides

**Insider Info** Publishes 40 titles per year. Authors are paid by royalty, with advance offered. 95 per cent of books come from unagented writers, and 75 per cent of books from first-time authors. Does not accept simultaneous submissions. Catalogue available free on request.

**Submission Guidelines** Accepts unsolicited manuscripts and proposals.

**Recent Title(s)** *Ghost Stories of South Carolina*, A.S. Mott

**Tips** Lone Pine only publishes non-fiction books of regional interest, the exception being its Ghost House imprint, which is often interested in ghost stories as well as non-fiction.

## Macmillan South Africa
**PO Box 32484, Braamfontein, 2017, South Africa**
- 0027 11 731 3300
- 0027 11 731 3500
- info@macmillan.co.za
- www.macmillansa.co.za

**Parent Company** Boleswa

**Imprint(s)** Clever Books
 Guidelines

**Categories** Publishes Non-Fiction, Fiction and Children's titles on the following subjects: African Literature, Education, General Interest, How-To, Literacy, Mainstream Fiction, Reference, Science, Scholarly, Self-Help, Teaching Guides

**Insider Info** Authors paid by royalty, with advance offered.

**Tips** Macmillan South Africa is interested in educational non-fiction about literacy, numeracy and similar subjects. Macmillan South Africa is currently developing their website, so check back frequently for possible submission guidelines.

## Mallinson Rendel Publishers Ltd
**PO Box 9409, Level 5, 15 Courtenay Place, Wellington, New Zealand**
- 0064 4 802 5012
- 0064 4 802 5013
- publisher@mallinsonrendel.co.nz
- www.mallinsonrendel.co.nz

**Contact** Publishing Director, Ann Mallinson

**Categories** Publishes Children's titles on the following subjects: Children's Fiction, Education, Mainstream Fiction, Picture Books.

**Recent Title(s)** *Hairy Maclary's Caterwaul Caper*, Lynley Dodd

**Tips** Mallinson Rendel specialises in illustrated children's books.

## McClelland & Stewart Ltd

**75 Sherbourne Street, 5th Floor, Toronto, Ontario, M5A 2P9, Canada**

- 001 416 598 1114
- 001 416 598 7764
- editorial@mcclelland.com
- www.mcclelland.com

**Contact** Chairman/Publisher, Douglas Pepper
**Imprint(s)** Douglas Gibson Books
Emblem Editions
New Canadian Library
McClelland & Stewart
**Categories** Publishes Non-Fiction and Fiction titles on the following subjects: Art, Canadiana, General Interest, Historical Fiction, Literary Interest, Mainstream Interest, Military Interest, Nature, Photography, Short-Story Collections, Sports, Translation, Travel, Women's Issues
**Insider Info** Publishes 80 titles per year. Advance offered. Receives 1,500 queries per year. 30 per cent of books come from unagented writers, and ten per cent from first-time authors. Aims to respond to proposals within three months. Average lead time is one year.
**Recent Title(s)** *Mothers and Sons*, Colm Toibin
**Tips** McClelland does not accept unsolicited submissions or proposals.

## McGraw-Hill Professional

**2 Penn Plaza, 11th Floor, New York, 10121, USA**

- 001 609 426 5793
- 001 609 426 7917
- international_cs@mcgraw-hill.com
- www.books.mcgraw-hill.com

**Parent Company** The McGraw Hill Companies
**Contact** Publisher, Philip Ruppel; Editor in Chief, Jeffrey Krames
**Imprint(s)** McGraw-Hill Business
McGraw-Hill Medical
McGraw-Hill Education
McGraw-Hill Technical
McGraw-Hill Consumer
**Categories** Publishes Non-Fiction titles on the following subjects: How-to, Reference, Self-help, Technical, Management, Finance, Business, Careers, Health, Medicine, Education, Study Guides, Science, Engineering, Computing, Parenting, Sports, Outdoors, General Interest

**Submission Guidelines** Accepts unsolicited manuscripts and proposals.
**Recent Title(s)** *The Starbucks Experience*, Joseph Michelli
**Tips** All submissions must be as in-depth as possible and include relevant market research, including information about similar products, and a recent CV. It is advisable to send any illustrations along with the proposal and a list of potential reviewers with experience and knowledge of the subject covered.

## Melbourne University Publishing Ltd

**187 Grattan Street, Carlton, Victoria, 3053, Australia**

- 0061 3 9342 0300
- 0061 3 9342 0399
- mup-info@unimelb.edu.au
- www.mup.unimelb.edu.au

**Contact** Chairman, Robert McKay; Chief Executive Officer/Publisher, Louise Adler; Managing Editor, Felicity Edge
**Imprint(s)** Melbourne University Press
Miegunyah Press
**Categories** Publishes Non-Fiction titles on the following subjects: Aboriginal Studies, Anthropology, Archaeology, Architecture, Art, Biography, Cultural Studies, Journals, Literary Criticism, Environmental Studies, Gender Studies, Medicine, Multimedia, Natural History, Philosophy, Politics, Psychiatry, Reference, Scholarly, Science, Social Sciences
**Insider Info** Publishes 70 titles per year. Aims to respond to proposals within four months.
**Submission Guidelines** Accepts unsolicited manuscripts and proposals.
**Recent Title(s)** *Voyages to the South Seas*, Danielle Clode
**Tips** Melbourne University Press is actively seeking to expand its list of electronic publications such as CDs, databases and online resources.

## Michelle Anderson Publishing (Pty) Ltd

**PO Box 6032, Chapel Street North, South Yarra, Victoria, 3141, Australia**

- 0061 3 9826 9028
- 0061 3 9826 8552
- info@michelleandersonpublishing.com
- www.michelleandersonpublishing.com

**Categories** Publishes Non-fiction and Children's titles on the following subjects: Children's Non-fiction, Guidance, Health, Local Interest, Mind and Body, Parenting, Self-help, Spirituality, Travel

**Recent Title(s)** *Nutrition for the Brain: Feeding Your Brain for Optimum Performance*, Dr. Charles Krebs
**Tips** Michelle Anderson will accept queries, as long as an SASE is included for response.

## Michigan State University Press
**1405 South Harrison, 25 Manly Miles Building, East Lansing, Michigan, 48823, USA**
- 001 517 355 9543
- 001 517 432 2611
- msupress@msu.edu
- www.msupress.msu.edu

**Contact** Director, Fredric C. Bohm; Assistant Director and Editor in Chief, Julie L. Loehr, Acquisitions Editor, Martha A. Bates; Managing Editor (Journals Division), Margot Landa Kielhorn
**Imprint(s)** MSU Press Book Division
MSU Press Journals Division
**Categories** Publishes Non-fiction, Fiction, Poetry and Journals on the following subjects: Academic, American History, Art/Architecture, Cultural Studies, Environmental Affairs, History, Human Ecology, Literary Criticism, Literary fiction, Multicultural Studies, Native American Studies, Philosophy, Poetry, Political Sciences, Reference, Regional (Upper Midwest; Great Lakes; Canada), Rhetoric, Sciences, Scholarly, Short stories, Social Sciences, Women's Studies
**Submission Guidelines** Accepts unsolicited manuscripts and proposals.
**Recent Title(s)** *Routes of Passage*, Ruth Simms Hamilton
**Tips** MSU Press only accepts proposals, not full manuscripts, and email submissions must be included in the body of the email and not as an attached file.

## Milkweed Editions
**1011 Washington Avenue South, Suite 300, Minneapolis, Minnesota, 55415, USA**
- 001 612 332 3192
- 001 612 215 2550
- www.milkweed.org

**Contact** Editor in Chief, Daniel Slager
**Imprint(s)** Milkweeds for Young Readers
**Categories** Publishes Non-fiction, Fiction, Poetry and Children's titles on the following subjects: Children's fiction, Culture, General Interest, Literary fiction, Nature, Poetry, Social Studies, Young Adult
**Insider Info** Publishes 20 titles per year. Pays six per cent royalty on retail price, with advance offered. 70 per cent of books come from unagented writers and 30 per cent from first-time authors. Aims to respond

to manuscripts within six months. Accepts simultaneous submissions. Average lead time of 18 months.
**Submission Guidelines** Accepts unsolicited manuscripts and proposals.
**Recent Title(s)** *Water*, Bapsi Sidhwa
**Tips** Milkweed only reads poetry submissions in January and June, but non-fiction and fiction can be submitted at any time.

## Morehouse Publishing
**4775 Linglestown Road, Harrisburg, Pennsylvania, 17112, USA**
- 001 717 541 8130
- 001 717 541 8136
- nfitzgerald@cpg.org
- www.morehousepublishing.org

**Parent Company** Church Publishing Inc
**Contact** Acquisitions Editor, Nancy Fitzgerald
**Categories** Publishes Non-Fiction on the following subjects: Bible Studies, Church History, Education, Ethics, Liturgy, Marriage & Family, Multimedia, Prayer Books, Religion, Social Issues, Women's Studies.
**Insider Info** Publishes 35 titles per year. Pays ten per cent royalty on net receipts with advance offered. 50 per cent of books come from first time authors. Accepts simultaneous submissions. Average lead time is 18 months.
**Recent Title(s)** *God's Top 10*, Anne Robertson
**Tips** Morehouse Publishing focuses on books and teaching resources for a Christian readership.

## Napoleon Publishing/RendezVous Press
**178 Willowdale Avenue, Suite 201, Toronto, Ontario, M2N 4Y8, Canada**
- 001 416 730 9052
- 001 416 730 8096
- editorial@transmedia95.com
- www.rendezvouspress.com

**Contact** Editor, Allister Thompson
**Imprint(s)** Dark Star Fiction
Napoleon Publishing
RendezVous Crime
RendezVous Press
**Categories** Publishes Fiction and Children's titles on the following subjects: Canadian Literature, Children's Fiction, Contemporary Fiction, Crime Fiction, Literary Fiction, Mainstream Fiction, Mystery Fiction
**Insider Info** Publishes 20 titles per year. Receives 200 queries and 100 manuscripts per year. 80 per cent of books come from unagented writers, and 50

per cent from first-time authors. Aims to respond to manuscripts within six months. Accepts simultaneous submissions. Average lead time is 18 months.

**Submission Guidelines** Accepts unsolicited manuscripts and proposals.

**Recent Title(s)** *Lucky Strike*, Pat Wilson and Kris Wood

**Tips** Napoleon/RendezVous Press usually only accept work from Canadian writers. See the website to check which imprints are accepting submissions at any given time.

## National Archives of Australia

**PO Box 7425, Canberra Business Centre, Canberra, Australian Capital Territory, 2610, Australia**

- 0061 2 6212 3900
- 0061 2 6212 3999
- archives@naa.gov.au
- www.naa.gov.au

**Categories** Publishes Non-Fiction on the following subjects: Australian History, Biography, Catalogues, Genealogy, History, Multimedia, Reference, Teaching Resources

**Recent Title(s)** *In the Interest of National Security*, Klaus Neumann

**Tips** The National Archives mainly publishes book on Australian history, genealogy and record-keeping, but also publishes various types of multimedia material.

## NB Publisher (Pty) Ltd

**PO Box 879, Cape Town, 8000, South Africa**

- 0027 21 406 3033
- 0027 21 406 3812
- nb@nb.co.za
- www.nb.co.za

**Contact** Publisher (Non-Fiction), Danita van Romburgh

**Imprint(s)** Human & Rousseau
Kwela
Pharos
Tafelberg

**Categories** Publishes Non-Fiction, Fiction and Children's titles on the following subjects: Afrikaans Novels, Children's Fiction, Children's Non-Fiction, Cookery, Craft, Dictionaries, General Interest, Health, Literary Fiction, Local Interest, Mainstream Fiction, Picture Books, Spirituality, Young Adult

**Insider Info** Aims to respond to manuscripts within three months.

**Submission Guidelines** Accepts unsolicited manuscripts and proposals.

**Recent Title(s)** *Verkeerdespruit*, Michiel Heynes

**Tips** Accepts submissions either by post or email, providing they are sent to the correct imprint.

## NeWest Press

**201, 8540 109th Street, Edmonton, Alberta, T6G 1E6, Canada**

- 001 780 432 9427
- 001 780 433 3179
- info@newestpress.com
- www.newestpress.com

**Contact** General Manager, Amber Rider

**Categories** Publishes Non-Fiction, Fiction, Poetry and Drama titles on the following subjects: Western Canadiana, History, Literary Fiction, Mainstream Fiction, Mystery Fiction, Nature, Play Scripts, Poetry Collections, Politics

**Insider Info** Publishes 20 titles per year. Pays ten per cent royalty, with advance offered. Receives 800 manuscripts/year. 85 per cent of books come from unagented writers and 40 per cent from first-time authors. Accepts simultaneous submissions. Average lead time of two and half years.

**Submission Guidelines** Accepts unsolicited manuscripts and proposals.

**Recent Title(s)** *The Bindery*, Shane Rhodes

**Tips** NeWest Press only accepts submissions from Canadian writers.

## New York University Press

**838 Broadway, 3rd Floor, New York, 10003, USA**

- 001 212 998 2575
- 001 212 995 3833
- information@nyupress.org
- www.nyupress.org

**Contact** Director, Steve Maikowski; Editor in Chief (Literary, Cultural, and Media Studies, American History), Eric Zinner; Executive Editor (Sociology, Politics, Anthropology), Ilene Kalish; Senior Editor (Law, American History to 1900, Military History), Deborah Gershenowitz; Editor (Religion, Psychology), Jennifer Hammer

**Categories** Publishes Non-Fiction and Art titles on the following subjects: Art, Biography, Cultural and Media Studies, General Interest, History, Journals, Law, Literary Criticism, Politics, Reference, Religion, Scholarly, Textbook

**Insider Info** Publishes 100 titles per year. Pays royalty on net receipts. Receives 800–1,000 queries per year. 90 per cent of books come from unagented writers, and 30 per cent of books from first-time authors. Aims to respond to queries within four months (peer reviewed). Accepts simultaneous submissions. Average lead time of one year.

**Submission Guidelines** Accepts unsolicited manuscripts and proposals.

**Recent Title(s)** *To the Break of Dawn*, William Jelani Cobb

**Tips** New York University Press welcomes submissions in their fields of interest. Make sure submission is sent to the correct Editor.

## Norstedts Förlag
**PO Box 2052, S-103 12, Stockholm**
Sweden
- 0046 8 769 8850
- 0046 8 769 8864
- info@norstedts.se
- www.norstedt.se

**Parent Company** Norstedts Förlagsgrupp
**Contact** Publishing Chief, Ekelund Viveca; Publishing Chief, Bladh Annika; Publishing Chief, Eva Gedin; Editor in Chief, Enochsson Birgitta
**Categories** Non-Fiction, Fiction, Children's Classics, Contemporary Culture, General Interest, History, Literary Fiction, Mainstream Fiction, Swedish Fiction
**Insider Info** Publishes 100 titles per year. Responds in two months to manuscripts.
**Submission Guidelines** Accepts unsolicited manuscripts and proposals
Submissions: www.panorstedt.se/templates/Norstedts/Page.aspx?id=28829
**Recent Title(s)** *Rötter SmŠlter*, Sara Hallström
**Tips** Norstedts accepts submissions by post only, not by email. Include an SASE for return of manuscript.

## Otava Publishing Company Ltd
**Uudenmaankatu 10, SF-00120, Helsinki, Finland**
- 00358 9 19961
- 00358 9 199 6560
- name.surname@otava.fi
- www.otava.fi

**Parent Company** Otava Books and Magazines Group Ltd
**Contact** Managing Director, Antti Reenpää; Publishing Director (Otava General Literature), Leena Majander; Publishing Director (Otava Education), Jukka Vahtola
**Imprint(s)** Otava Education
Otava General Literature
**Categories** Non-Fiction, Fiction, Children's, Architecture, Art, Children's Books, Cuisine,

Dictionaries, Education, General Interest, History, Mainstream Fiction, Scholarly, Teaching Resources, Textbooks, Translation, Young Adult.
**Insider Info** Publishes 600 titles per year.
**Recent Title(s)** *Korvatunturi*, Pekka Vuori
**Tips** Otava supports new writers and has an 'open-minded, yet resolute' approach to publishing.

## The Overlook Press
**141 Wooster Street, New York, 10012, USA**
- 001 212 673 2210
- 001 212 673 2296
- sales@overlookpress.com
- www.overlookpress.com

**Parent Company** Peter Mayer Publishers Inc
**Contact** Publisher, Peter Mayer
**Imprint(s)** Ardis
Duckworth
**Categories** Publishes Non-Fiction, Fiction and Children's titles on the following subjects: Art/Architecture, Biography, Children's Books, Design, Health/Fitness, History, How-To, Lifestyle, Literary Fiction, Mainstream Fiction, Martial Arts, Picture Books, Regional (New York state), Translation
**Insider Info** Publishes 100 titles per year. Does not accept simultaneous submissions. Catalogue available free on request.
**Submission Guidelines** Does not accept unsolicited manuscripts or proposals.
**Recent Title(s)** *Thermopylae*, Paul Cartledge
**Tips** The Overlook Press does not accept unagented submissions.

## Oxford University Press (US)
**198 Madison Avenue, New York, 10016, USA**
- 001 212 726 6000
- www.oup.com/us

**Contact** Vice President/Editorial Director, Joan Bossert; President, Laura Brown
**Categories** Publishes Non-Fiction titles on the following subjects: Academic, Biography, General Interest, Higher Education, Journals, Literary Criticism, Popular Non-Fiction, Reference, Scholarly, Textbook
**Insider Info** Publishes 1,500 titles per year. Pays 0–15 per cent royalty on retail price., with advance offered. 80 per cent of books come from unagented writers, and 40 per cent from first-time authors. Aims to respond to proposals within three months. Accepts simultaneous submissions. Average lead

time of ten months. Catalogue available free on request.

**Submission Guidelines** Accepts unsolicited manuscripts and proposals.

**Recent Title(s)** *The Shock of the Old*, David Edgerton

**Tips** Oxford University Press welcomes academic proposals, but they must be sent to the correct editor. See the website for a list of editorial contacts.

## Pan Macmillan Australia Pty Ltd
**Level 25, 1 Market Street, Sydney, New South Wales, 2000, Australia**
- 0061 2 9285 9100
- 0061 2 9285 9190
- panpublishing@macmillan.com.au
- www.panmacmillan.com.au

**Contact** Publishing Director, James Fraser; Publishing Director, Roxanne Burns

**Imprint(s)** Macmillan Australia Group
 Pan Australia Group
 Picador Australia

**Categories** Publishes Non-Fiction, Fiction and Children's titles on the following subjects: Adventure, Autobiography, Biography, Children's Picture Books, Crime Fiction, Current Affairs, Fantasy, General Interest, Health, History, Horror, Humour, Literary Fiction, Mainstream Fiction, Memoir, Science Fiction, Self-Help, Thrillers, Travel, True Crime

**Insider Info** Authors paid by royalty, with advance offered. Aims to respond to proposals within 10–12 weeks.

**Submission Guidelines** Accepts unsolicited manuscripts and proposals.

**Recent Title(s)** *Size 14 is Not Fat Either*, Meg Cabot

**Tips** Pan Macmillan Australia will accept submissions for non-fiction and fiction, but is currently cutting back on their publishing programme, so unsolicited material has little chance of being accepted unless it is uniquely appealing and original.

## Paragon House
**1925 Oakcrest Avenue, Suite 7, St. Paul, Minnesota, 55113, USA**
- 001 651 644 3087
- 001 651 644 0997
- paragon@paragonhouse.com
- www.paragonhouse.com

**Parent Company** Continuum International Publishing Group Inc

**Contact** Acquisitions Editor, Rosemary Yokoi

**Imprint(s)** New Era Books
 Omega Books

**Categories** Publishes Non-Fiction titles on the following subjects: Biography, Child Guidance/Parenting, Education, Government/Politics, History, Memoirs, Multicultural, Nature, Philosophy, Reference, Religion, Science, Scholarly, Sex, Textbook, Women's Issues/Studies, World Affairs

**Insider Info** Publishes 20 titles per year. Advance offered. Receives 1,500 queries and 150 manuscripts per year. 90 per cent of books come from unagented writers and seven per cent from first-time authors. Accepts simultaneous submissions. Average lead time is one month.

**Submission Guidelines** Accepts unsolicited manuscripts and proposals.

**Tips** Paragon House accepts submission of scholarly or reference books either by post or as an email attachment. If submitting by post always include an SASE for reply.

## Paul Zsolnay Verlag GmbH
**Prinz-Eugen-Straße 30, A-1040, Vienna, Austria**
- 0043 1 5057 6610
- 0043 1 5057 66110
- info@zsolnay.at
- www.zsolnay.at

**Contact** Publisher, Michael Krÿger

**Categories** Non-Fiction, Fiction, Children's, Biography, Children's, Crime Fiction, General Interest, History, Literary Fiction, Mainstream Fiction, Poetry, Translation.

**Recent Title(s)** *Die Grÿne Schachtel*, Bogdan Bogdanovic

**Tips** Zsolnay focuses mainly on fiction submissions from new and established Austrian writers.

## Peachtree Publishers
**1700 Chattahoochee Avenue, Atlanta, Georgia, 30318, USA**
- 001 404 876 8761
- 001 404 875 2578
- hello@peachtree-online.com
- www.peachtree-online.com

**Contact** Submissions Editor, Helen Harriss

**Imprint(s)** Peachtree Children's Books

**Categories** Publishes Non-Fiction, Fiction and Children's titles on the following subjects: American South Guidebooks, Children's Fiction, Education, Health, Outdoor Pursuits, Parenting, Picture Books, Psychology, Self-Help, Young Adult

**Insider Info** Publishes 30 titles per year. Authors paid by royalty with advance offered. 75 per cent of books come from unagented writers, and 25 per cent from first-time authors. Aims to respond to manuscripts within six months. Accepts simultaneous submissions. Average lead time is one year. Catalogue available free on request – send SAE.

**Submission Guidelines** Accepts unsolicited manuscripts and proposals.

**Recent Title(s)** *Run With the Horsemen*, Ferrol Sams

**Tips** Peachtree accepts submissions for both adult and children's non-fiction, but only accepts fiction submissions for children's books.

## Pearson Education Australia

**Locked Bag 507, Unit 4, Level 3, 14 Aquatic Drive, Frenchs Forest, New South Wales, 2086, Australia**

- 0061 2 9454 2200
- 0061 2 9453 0089
- alison.green@pearsoned.com.au
- www.pearsoned.com.au

**Parent Company** Pearson Plc

**Contact** Editor inChief (Higher Education), Paul Petrulis; Senior Acquisitions Editor and Development Manager (Higher Education), Alison Green; Publisher (Professional and Vocational Education), Diane Gee-Clough; Senior Acquisitions Editor (Professional and Vocational Education), Natalie Muir

**Imprint(s)** Addison Wesley
  Allyn & Bacon
  Benjamin Cummings
  Longman
  Prentice Hall

**Categories** Publishes Non-Fiction and Children's titles on the following subjects: Academic, Children's Education, Education, Multimedia, Online, Reference, Science, Sociology, Teacher Resources, Technology, Textbook

**Insider Info** Authors paid by royalty with advance offered.

**Submission Guidelines** Accepts unsolicited manuscripts and proposals.

**Recent Title(s)** *Gaining Word Power*, Dorothy Rubin

**Tips** Pearson Education Australia accepts submissions of educational non-fiction or reference material. See website for a full list of acquisitions editors and their interests.

## Pearson Education Canada

**26 Prince Andrew Place, Toronto, Ontario, M3C 2T8, Canada**

- 001 416 447 5101
- 001 416 443 0948
- firstname.lastname@pearsoncanada.ca
- www.pearsoncanada.ca

**Parent Company** Pearson Plc

**Contact** Executive Acquisitions Editor (Accounting, Decision Science, Finance), Samantha Scully; Executive Acquisitions Editor (Anthropology, History, Linguistics, Modern Languages, Political Science), Laura Forbes; Executive Acquisitions Editor (Engineering, Science, Math, Geography, Health, Nursing), Michelle Sartor

**Imprint(s)** Addison-Wesley
  Allyn & Bacon
  Copp Clark
  Longman
  Prentice Hall

**Categories** Publishes Non-Fiction and Children's titles on the following subjects: Academic, Children's Education, Education, Multimedia, Online, Reference, Science, Sociology, Teacher Resources, Technology, Textbook

**Insider Info** Authors paid by royalty, with advance offered.

**Submission Guidelines** Accepts unsolicited manuscripts and proposals.

**Recent Title(s)** *Essentials of Pre-hospital Maternity Care*, Bonnie Urquhart-Gruenberg

**Tips** Pearson Education Canada accepts submissions of educational non-fiction or reference material. See website for a full list of acquisitions editors and their interests.

## Pearson Education New Zealand

**PO Box 102902, North Shore, North Shore City, Auckland, 0745, New Zealand**

- 0064 9 442 7400
- 0064 9 442 7401
- firstname.surname@pearsoned.co.nz
- www.pearsoned.co.nz

**Parent Company** Pearson Plc

**Contact** Publisher (Higher Education), Bronwen Nicholson; Publisher (Higher Education), Norman Mailer; Publisher (Schools), Ken Harrop

**Imprint(s)** Addison-Wesley
  Allyn & Bacon
  Benjamin Cummings
  Longman
  Prentice Hall

**Categories** Publishes Non-Fiction and Children's titles on the following subjects: Academic, Children's Education, Education, Multimedia, Online, Reference, Science, Sociology, Teacher Resources, Technology, Textbook

**Insider Info** Authors paid by royalty with advance offered.

**Submission Guidelines** Accepts unsolicited manuscripts and proposals.

**Recent Title(s)** *Society and Politics: New Zealand Social Policy*, Grant Duncan

**Tips** Pearson Education New Zealand accepts submissions of educational non-fiction or reference material. See website for a full list of acquisitions editors and their interests.

## Pearson Education South Africa
**PO Box 396, Cape Town, 8000, South Africa**
- 0027 21 532 6000
- 0027 021 532 2303
- info@pearsoned.co.za
- www.pearsoned.co.za

**Parent Company** Maskew Miller Longman
**Imprint(s)** Addison-Wesley
  Allyn & Bacon
  Benjamin Cummings
  Macmillan Lifestyle/Technical Publishing
  Maskew Miller Longman
  Prentice Hall

**Categories** Publishes Non-Fiction and Children's titles on the following subjects: Academic, Children's Education, Education, Multimedia, Online, Reference, Science, Sociology, Teacher Resources, Technology, Textbook

**Recent Title(s)** *Property*, Jackie Cameron

**Tips** Pearson Education South Africa is a subsidiary of Maskew Miller Longman, which is the countries largest educational publisher. They mainly publish educational material but also maintain a local list, including some fiction.

## Penguin Group (Australia)
**250 Camberwell Road, Camberwell, Victoria, 3124, Australia**
- 0061 3 9811 2400
- 0061 3 9811 2620
- adult.publishing@au.penguingroup.com
- www.penguin.com.au

**Parent Company** Pearson Plc
**Contact** Managing Director, Gabrielle Coyne; Publishing Director, Robert Sessions
**Imprint(s)** Penguin Books
  Lantern
  Viking

**Categories** Publishes Non-Fiction, Fiction and Children's titles on the following subjects: Children's Fiction, Contemporary Fiction, Education, General Interest, How-To, Mainstream Fiction, Reference, Self-Help.

**Insider Info** Authors paid by royalty with advance offered.

**Submission Guidelines** Does not accept unsolicited manuscripts or proposals.

**Recent Title(s)** *Jillaroo*, Rachael Treasure

**Tips** Penguin Australia does not except unagented submissions for adult non-fiction and fiction, but is occasionally open for submissions for children's books. See the website for details.

## Penguin Group (Canada)
**90 Eglinton Avenue East, Suite 700, Toronto, Ontario, M4P 2Y3, Canada**
- 001 416 925 2249
- 001 416 925 0068
- info@penguin.ca
- www.penguin.ca

**Parent Company** Pearson Plc
**Contact** President, Ed Carson
**Imprint(s)** Penguin Canada
  Puffin Canada
  Viking Canada

**Categories** Publishes Non-Fiction, Fiction and Children's titles on the following subjects: Canadian Interest, Children's Fiction, Contemporary Fiction, Education, General Interest, How-To, Mainstream Fiction, Reference, Self-Help

**Insider Info** Authors paid by royalty with advance offered.

**Submission Guidelines** Does not accept unsolicited manuscripts or proposals.

**Recent Title(s)** *Mistress of the Art of Death*, Ariana Franklin

**Tips** Penguin Canada specialises in writing about Canada, and the work of Canadian writers. Penguin Canada does not except unagented submissions or proposals.

## Penguin Group (NZ)
**67 Apollo Drive, Albany, Auckland, 10, New Zealand**
- 0064 9 442 7400
- 0064 9 442 7401
- info@penguin.co.nz
- www.penguin.co.nz

**Parent Company** Pearson Plc
**Categories** Publishes Non-Fiction, Fiction and Children's titles on the following subjects: Children's Fiction, Contemporary Fiction, Education, General Interest, How-To, Local Interest, Mainstream Fiction, Reference, Self-Help

**Insider Info** Authors paid by royalty, with advance offered. Aims to respond to queries within two months.

**Submission Guidelines** Accepts unsolicited manuscripts and proposals.
**Recent Title(s)** *Perfume*, Patrick Suskind
**Tips** Penguin New Zealand recommends submissions be directed through a literary agent but they will also accept unsolicited proposals, although the odds of them being accepted are very low.

## Penguin Group (South Africa)
**24 Sturdee Avenue, Rosebank, 2196, South Africa**
- 0027 11 327 3550
- 0027 11 327 3660
- info@za.penguingroup.com
- www.penguinbooks.co.za

**Parent Company** Pearson Plc
**Categories** Publishes Non-Fiction and Fiction titles on the following subjects: African Literature, Business, Contemporary Fiction, Current Affairs, Education, General Interest, How-To, Literary Fiction, Local Interest, Mainstream Fiction, Politics, Sports, Travel
**Insider Info** Publishes 30 titles per year. Authors paid by royalty with advance offered. Aims to respond to manuscripts within three months.
**Submission Guidelines** Accepts unsolicited manuscripts and proposals.
**Recent Title(s)** *Past Imperfect*, Emma Van der Vliet
**Tips** Penguin South Africa accepts proposals for adult non-fiction and fiction, although they warn that 'it is rare for unsolicited manuscripts or proposals to be accepted for publication.' Follow the guidelines on the website for more effective submissions.

## Penguin Group (USA) Inc
**375 Hudson Street, New York, 10014, USA**
- 001 212 366 2000
- www.penguin.com

**Parent Company** Pearson Plc
**Contact** Chief Executive Officer, David Shanks; President, Susan Petersen Kennedy; President (Books for Young Readers), Doug Whiteman
**Imprint(s)** Penguin Adult Division
 Penguin Children's Division
**Categories** Publishes Non-Fiction, Fiction and Children's titles on the following subjects:
 General Interest, Mainstream, Contemporary, How-To, Self-Help, Reference, Education, Children's
**Insider Info** Authors paid by royalty, with advance offered.

**Submission Guidelines** Does not accept unsolicited manuscripts or proposals.
**Recent Title(s)** *On Beauty*, Zadie Smith
**Tips** Penguin does not generally except unagented submissions, except for on rare occasions where one or another imprint may be seeking new titles. Penguin's website has current details of which imprints are open for submission.

## Picador
**175 Fifth Avenue, New York, 10010, USA**
- 001 646 307 5629
- 001 212 253 9627
- webmaster@picadorusa.com
- www.picadorusa.com

**Parent Company** Holtzbrinck Publishers Holdings LLC
**Categories** Publishes Non-Fiction and Fiction titles on the following subjects: Autobiography, Biography, General Interest, Literary Fiction, Mainstream Fiction, Women's Fiction
**Insider Info** Authors paid by royalty with advance offered.
**Submission Guidelines** Does not accept unsolicited manuscripts or proposals.
**Recent Title(s)** *Notes on a Scandal*, Zoë Heller
**Tips** Picador specialises in trade paperbacks and reprints. It does not accept any unagented submissions or proposals.

## Pippin Publishing Corporation
**PO Box 242, Don Mills, Ontario, M3C 2S2, Canada**
- 001 416 510 2918
- 001 416 510 3359
- cynthia@pippinpub.com
- www.pippinpub.com

**Categories** Publishes Non-Fiction titles on the following subjects: Art, Autobiography, Biography, Canadian Interest, Education, History, Humanities, Literacy, Memoir, Numeracy, Science, Teaching Resources
**Recent Title(s)** *Poetry and the Meaning of Life*, David Ian Hanauer
**Tips** Pippin Publishing is an educational publisher, and prints books written by teachers or similarly qualified academics.

## Princeton University Press
**41 William Street, Princeton, New Jersey, 08540, USA**

- ☎ 001 609 258 4900
- 🖷 001 609 258 6305
- ✉ elizabeth_byrd@pupress.princeton.edu
- 🌐 www.pup.princeton.edu

**Contact** Managing Editor, Elizabeth Byrd

**Categories** Publishes Non-Fiction titles on the following subjects: Academic, Biography, General Interest, Journals, Literary Criticism, Reference, Religion, Scholarly, Science, Textbook.

**Insider Info** Authors paid by royalty, with advance offered.

**Submission Guidelines** Accepts unsolicited manuscripts and proposals.

**Recent Title(s)** *Is Democracy Possible Here?*, Ronald Dworkin

**Tips** Submissions to Princeton require both hard-copy manuscripts and electronic forms, available on the website.

## Random House Australia Pty Ltd

**20 Alfred Street, Milsons Point, New South Wales, 2061, Australia**

- ☎ 0061 2 9954 9966
- 🖷 0061 2 9954 4562
- ✉ random@randomhouse.com.au
- 🌐 www.randomhouse.com.au

**Parent Company** Bertelsmann Book Group

**Contact** Managing Director, Margaret Seale; Head of Publishing, Jane Palfreyman

**Imprint(s)** Random House Division
Transworld Division

**Categories** Publishes Non-Fiction, Fiction and Children's titles on the following subjects: Biography, Children's Fiction, Contemporary Fiction, Education, General Interest, How-To, Literary Fiction, Local Interest, Mainstream Fiction, Reference, Self-Help, Travel

**Insider Info** Authors paid by royalty with advance offered. Aims to respond to manuscripts within nine months.

**Submission Guidelines** Accepts unsolicited manuscripts and proposals.

**Recent Title(s)** *The God Delusion*, Richard Dawkins

**Tips** Random House Australia excepts adult fiction submissions from previously published authors. It will only except submissions from new writers if they come through an agent.

## Random House Inc

**1745 Broadway, 10th Floor, New York, 10019, USA**

- ☎ 001 212 782 9000
- ✉ customerservice@randomhouse.com

- 🌐 www.randomhouse.com

**Parent Company** Bertelsmann Book Group

**Contact** See individual imprint listings for their contact details

**Imprint(s)** Ballantine Publishing Group
Bantam Dell Publishing Group
Crown Publishing Group
Doubleday Broadway Publishing Group
Knopf Publishing Group
Random House Publishing Group

**Categories** Publishes Non-Fiction, Fiction and Children's titles. See individual imprint listings.

**Insider Info** Authors paid by royalty, with advance offered.

**Submission Guidelines** Does not accept unsolicited manuscripts or proposals.

**Recent Title(s)** *Hannibal Rising*, Thomas Harris

**Tips** Random House is the world's largest English language publisher, and will not accept unagented submissions or proposals.

## Random House New Zealand

**18 Poland Road, Glenfield, Auckland, 10, New Zealand**

- ☎ 0064 9 444 7197
- 🖷 0064 9 444 7524
- ✉ editor@randomhouse.co.nz
- 🌐 www.randomhouse.co.nz

**Parent Company** Bertelsmann Book Group

**Contact** Publishing Assistant, Claire Smith

**Imprint(s)** Godwit
Random House Division

**Categories** Publishes Non-Fiction, Fiction and Children's titles on the following subjects: Art, Autobiography, Biography, Children's Picture Books, Cookery, Gardening, Health, Human Interest, Lifestyle, Literary Fiction, Local Interest, Mainstream Fiction, New Zealand Fiction, Social History, Tourism

**Insider Info** Publishes 80 titles per year. Authors paid by royalty, with advance offered.

**Submission Guidelines** Accepts unsolicited manuscripts and proposals.

**Recent Title(s)** *Shopaholic & Baby*, Sophie Kinsella

**Tips** Random House New Zealand does accept non-fiction and fiction submissions, but only of work with New Zealand based content, or from New Zealand writers.

## Random House of Canada Ltd

**1 Toronto Street, Unit 300, Toronto, Ontario, M5C 2V6, Canada**

- ☎ 001 416 364 4449
- 🖷 001 416 364 6863

🌐 www.randomhouse.ca

**Parent Company** Bertelsmann Book Group

**Contact** Chairman, John Neale

**Imprint(s)** Anchor Canada
Doubleday Canada Group
Knopf Canada
Random House Canada
Seal Books
Vintage

**Categories** Publishes Non-Fiction, Fiction and Children's titles on the following subjects: Biography, Children's Fiction, Contemporary Fiction, Education, General Interest, How-To, Literary Fiction, Local Interest, Mainstream Fiction, Reference, Self-Help, Travel

**Insider Info** Authors paid by royalty with advance offered.

**Submission Guidelines** Does not accept unsolicited manuscripts or proposals.

**Recent Title(s)** *Snow Falling on Cedars*, David Guterson

**Tips** Random House Canada does not accept unagented submissions or proposals.

## Random House South Africa
**Endulini, 5A Jubilee Road, Parktown, 2193, South Africa**

☎ 0027 11 484 3538

☎ 0027 11 484 6180

**Parent Company** Bertelsmann Book Group

**Imprint(s)** Umuzi

**Categories** Publishes Non-Fiction, Fiction and Children's titles.

**Insider Info** Authors paid by royalty with advance offered.

**Submission Guidelines** Does not accept unsolicited manuscripts or proposals.

**Tips** Random House South Africa does not accept unagented submissions or proposals.

## Reed Publishing (New Zealand) Ltd
**PO Box 34901, 39 Rawene Road, Birkenhead, Auckland 10, New Zealand**

☎ 0064 9 441 2960

☎ 0064 9 480 4999

✉ info@reed.co.nz

🌐 www.reed.co.nz

**Parent Company** Reed Elsevier Group Plc

**Contact** Managing Director, Alan Smith; Publishing Manager, Peter Janssen

**Imprint(s)** Heinemann Education
Reed Books
Reed Children's Books

**Categories** Publishes Non-Fiction and Children's titles on the following subjects: Biography, Children's Fiction, Cooking, Education, General Interest, History, Humour, Language, Mainstream Fiction, Maori Culture, New Zealand Interest, Outdoor, Picture Books, Tourism

**Submission Guidelines** Accepts unsolicited manuscripts and proposals.

**Recent Title(s)** *Business Web*, Tony Murrow

**Tips** Reed Publishing mostly publishes non-fiction of New Zealand interest and mass-market children's books. Reed publishes very little adult fiction.

## Rodale Books
**33 East Minor Street, Emmaus, Pennsylvania, 18098, USA**

☎ 001 610 967 5171

☎ 001 610 967 8963

✉ customer_service@rodale.com

🌐 www.rodale.com

**Parent Company** Rodale Book Group

**Contact** Chairman, Ardath Rodale; President and Chief Executive Officer, Steve Murphy; Vice President/Publisher (Rodale Trade Books), Liz Perl

**Categories** Publishes Non-Fiction titles on the following subjects: Cooking, Current Affairs, Gardening, General Interest, Health/Fitness, Magazines, Nature, Pet Care, Reference, Social Studies, Spirituality, Women's Studies

**Tips** Rodale is primarily a health and spirituality publisher, but also publishes topical material of global or social interest. Publishing opportunities are also available through Rodale's many magazines.

## Ronsdale Press Ltd
**3350 West 21st Avenue, Vancouver, British Columbia, V6S 1G7, Canada**

☎ 001 604 738 4688

☎ 001 604 731 4548

✉ ronsdale@shaw.ca

🌐 www.ronsdalepress.com

**Contact** Director (Fiction, Poetry, Social Commentary), Ronald B. Hatch; Managing Director (Children's Literature), Veronica Hatch

**Categories** Publishes Non-Fiction, Fiction, Poetry, Drama and Children's titles on the following subjects: Biography, Children's Literature, General Interest, Literary Fiction, Plays, Poetry, Regional History, Scholarly

**Insider Info** Publishes ten titles per year. Pays ten per cent royalty on retail price. Receives 300 queries and 800 manuscripts per year. 95 per cent of books come from unagented writers, and 60 per cent from

**423**

first-time authors. Aims to respond to manuscripts within three months. Accepts simultaneous submissions. Average lead time is six months.

**Submission Guidelines** Accepts unsolicited manuscripts and proposals.

**Recent Title(s)** *A Long Labour*, Rhodea Shandler

**Tips** As a literary publisher Ronsdale is not interested in mass-market material. Ronsdale only accepts submissions from Canadian writers.

## Routledge
**270 Madison Avenue, New York, 10016, USA**
- 001 212 216 7800
- 001 212 563 7854
- www.routledge.com

**Parent Company** Taylor and Francis LLC

**Contact** Vice President/Publisher, Mary MacInnes

**Imprint(s)** Theatre Arts Books

**Categories** Publishes Non-Fiction titles on the following subjects: Education, History, Politics, Psychology, Reference, Science, Sociology, Technology, Textbook

**Insider Info** Publishes 2,000 titles per year. Authors paid by royalty with advance offered. Nine per cent of books come from unagented writers, and ten per cent from first-time authors. Accepts simultaneous submissions. Average lead time of one year.

**Submission Guidelines** Accepts unsolicited manuscripts and proposals.

**Recent Title(s)** *Politics of Oil*, Bulent Gokay

**Tips** Routledge accepts unsolicited proposals for academic reference and educational books. The proposal must include detailed market research, including details on any relevant competitor books.

## RSVP Publishing Company Ltd
**PO Box 47–166, Ponsonby, Auckland, New Zealand**
- 0064 9 372 8480
- 0064 9 372 8480
- rsvppub@iconz.co.nz
- www.rsvp-publishing.co.nz

**Contact** Publisher, Stephen Picard; Editorial Manager, Rosie Parkes

**Categories** Publishes Non-Fiction and Fiction titles on the following subjects: Contemporary Fiction, General Interest, Local Interest, New Zealand Metaphysical Books

**Insider Info** Publishes six titles per year.

**Submission Guidelines** Accepts unsolicited manuscripts and proposals.

**Recent Title(s)** *Search for the Feathered Serpent*, Cornelius van Dorp

**Tips** RSVP primarily publish New Zealand metaphysical books but are also willing to accept other forms of innovative non-fiction or fiction.

## Rutgers University Press
**100 Joyce Kilmer Avenue, Piscataway, New Jersey, 08854, USA**
- 001 732 445 7762
- 001 732 445 7039
- lmitch@rutgers.edu
- www.rutgerspress.rutgers.edu

**Contact** Director, Marlie Wasserman ; Editor in Chief/Associate Director, Leslie Mitchner

**Categories** Publishes Non-Fiction titles on the following subjects: Academic, Biography, General Interest, History, Journals, Literary Criticism, Politics, Reference, Scholarly, Science, Textbook

**Insider Info** Publishes 90 titles per year. Pays 7.5–15 per cent royalty, with advance offered. Receives 1,500 queries and 300 manuscripts per year. 70 per cent of books come from unagented writers, and 30 per cent from first-time authors. Aims to respond to proposals within one months. Average lead time of one year. Catalogue available online or by sending SAE.

**Submission Guidelines** Accepts unsolicited manuscripts and proposals.

**Recent Title(s)** *Bridging the Divide*, Senator Edward W. Brooke

**Tips** Rutgers prefers submissions by post rather than by email, and all submissions must be addressed to the relevant editor. See website for list of editorial contacts.

## SanomaWSOY Education and Books
**PO Box 222, SF-00121, Helsinki, Finland**
- 00358 9 61681
- 00358 9 61683560
- firstname.lastname@wsoy.fi
- www.wsoy.fi

**Parent Company** Werner Söderström Corporation

**Contact** President/Chairman/COO, Hannu Syrjänen; Literary Director (General Literature), Touko Siltala

**Imprint(s)** Bertmark Media AB
General Literature
WSOYpro
WSOY Educational Corporation

**Categories** Publishes Non-Fiction, Fiction and Children's titles on the following subjects: Children's Fiction, Contemporary Fiction, Dictionaries, Directories, Education, Finnish Fiction, General

Interest, Language/Literature, Literary Fiction, Local Interest, Mainstream Fiction, Practical, Reference, Teaching Resources, Textbooks, Translated Foreign Fiction, Young Adult

**Insider Info** Publishes 800 titles per year.
**Recent Title(s)** *Huolimattomat*, Kari Hotakainen
**Tips** WSOY is one of Finland's largest book publishers, mostly specialising in educational resources for all age ranges and abilities

## Scholastic Australia Pty Ltd
**76–80 Railway Crescent, Lisarow, New South Wales, 2250, Australia**
- 0061 2 4328 3555
- 0061 2 4323 3827
- customer_service@scholastic.com.au
- www.scholastic.com.au

**Parent Company** Scholastic Inc
**Contact** General Manager (Publishing), Andrew Berkhut
**Imprint(s)** Omnibus Books
 Scholastic Australia
 Scholastic Press
**Categories** Publishes Non-Fiction, Fiction and Children's titles on the following subjects: Children's Fiction, Children's Non-Fiction, Picture Books.
**Insider Info** Authors paid by royalty with advance offered. Receives 1,000+ manuscripts per year. Aims to respond to manuscripts within three months.
**Submission Guidelines** Accepts unsolicited manuscripts and proposals.
**Tips** Scholastic Australia accepts submissions of full manuscripts for children's non-fiction, fiction and picture books from Australian writers. Scholastic Australia is also always seeking illustrators for picture books.

## Scholastic Canada Ltd
**604 King Street West, Toronto, Ontario, M5V 1E1, Canada**
- 001 416 915 3500
- 001 416 849 7912
- www.scholastic.ca

**Parent Company** Scholastic Inc
**Imprint(s)** Les Editions Scholastic
 North Winds Press
**Categories** Publishes Non-Fiction, Fiction and Children's titles, Picture Books, and Young Adult titles.
**Insider Info** Publishes 40 titles per year. Pays 5–10 per cent royalty on retail price, with advance offered. 50 per cent of books come from unagented writers, and three per cent of books from first-time authors.

Aims to respond to proposals within six months. Does not accept simultaneous submissions. Average lead time of one year. Catalogue available free with SASE.
**Recent Title(s)** *Born to Rock*, Gordan Korman
**Tips** Scholastic Canada publishes books for children and young adults, generally from Canadian authors only. To check if Scholastic Canada is open to submissions, phone their publishing status line on: 001 905 887 7323, extension 4308, or check their website.

## Scholastic Inc
**557 Broadway, New York, 10012, USA**
- 001 212 343 6100
- 001 212 343 4713
- info@scholastic.com
- www.scholastic.com

**Contact** Editorial Director, Elizabeth Szabla; Executive Editor, Kara LaReau; Senior Editor, Lauren Thompson
**Imprint(s)** Scholastic Education
 Scholastic Library Publishing
 Scholastic Media
 Scholastic Trade Books
**Categories** Publishes Non-Fiction, Fiction and Children's titles on the following subjects: Education, General Interest, Multimedia, Picture Books, Reference, Textbooks
**Insider Info** Pays royalty on retail price, with advance offered. Average lead time is two years.
**Submission Guidelines** Does not accept unsolicited manuscripts or proposals.
**Recent Title(s)** *Harry Potter and the Deathly Hallows*, J.K. Rowling
**Tips** Scholastic is major publisher of children's education and fiction books. Scholastic accepts unagented proposals for professional education books only.

## Scholastic New Zealand Ltd
**21 Lady Ruby Drive, East Tamaki, Auckland, New Zealand**
- 0064 9 274 8112
- 0064 9 274 8114
- publishing@scholastic.co.nz
- www.scholastic.co.nz

**Parent Company** Scholastic Inc
**Contact** Publishing Manager, Christine Dale
**Categories** Publishes Non-Fiction, Fiction, Children's Fiction, Children's Non-Fiction, Picture Books and Young Adult titles.

**Insider Info** Authors paid by royalty with advance offered. Aims to respond to manuscripts within three months.

**Submission Guidelines** Accepts unsolicited manuscripts and proposals.

**Tips** Scholastic New Zealand accepts submissions for their 'Survive!' and 'My Story' series from New Zealand writers. See website for guidelines.

## Scribner

**1230 Avenue of the Americas, New York, 10020, USA**

- 001 212 698 7000
- 001 212 698 7007
- Online form
- www.simonsays.com

**Parent Company** Simon & Schuster Adult Publishing Group

**Contact** Nan Graham; Sarah McGrath

**Imprint(s)** Lisa Drew Books
  Scribner Classics (reprints)
  Scribner Poetry

**Categories** Publishes Non-Fiction, Fiction and Poetry titles on the following subjects: General Interest, Literary Fiction, Mainstream Fiction, Politics, Reprints

**Insider Info** Publishes 75 titles per year. Pays 7.5–15 per cent royalty, with advance offered. Receives thousands queries per year. 20 per cent of books come from first-time authors. Accepts simultaneous submissions. Average lead time is nine months.

**Submission Guidelines** Does not accept unsolicited manuscripts or proposals.

**Recent Title(s)** *Follow the Money: How George W. Bush and the Texas Republicans Hog-Tied America*, John Anderson

**Tips** Scribner often seeks biography, but will not accept unagented submissions or proposals.

## Shuter & Shooter Publishers (Pty) Ltd

**21c Cascades Crescent, Pietermaritzburg, KwaZulu-Natal, 3201, South Africa**

- 0027 33 347 6100
- 0027 33 347 6120
- dryder@shuter.co.za
- www.shuter.co.za

**Contact** Managing Director, Dave Ryder

**Imprint(s)** Ziptales

**Categories** Publishes Non-Fiction, Fiction and Children's titles on the following subjects: Afrikaans Literature, Art, Craft, Education, General Interest, History, How-To, Literacy, Local Interest, Mainstream

Fiction, Poetry, Reference, Science, Scholarly, Teaching Guides, Textbooks

**Recent Title(s)** *NginguSosobala Mbatha*, DBZ Ntuli

**Tips** Shuter & Shooter primarily publishes Zulu fiction and poetry, as well as educational material for the whole South African region.

## Simon & Schuster Australia

**Suite 2, Lower Ground Floor, 14–16 Suakin Street, Pymble, New South Wales, 2073, Australia**

- 0061 2 9983 6600
- 0061 2 9988 4293
- info@simonandschuster.au
- www.simonsaysaustralia.com

**Parent Company** Simon & Schuster Inc

**Contact** Managing Director, Jon Attenborough

**Imprint(s)** Kangaroo Press
  Simon & Schuster Australia

**Categories** Publishes Non-Fiction, Fiction and Children's titles on the following subjects: Children's Fiction, Contemporary Fiction, Education, General Interest, How-To, Literary Fiction, Mainstream Fiction, Practical, Reference, Self-Help

**Insider Info** Authors paid by royalty with advance offered.

**Submission Guidelines** Does not accept unsolicited manuscripts or proposals.

**Recent Title(s)** *Earth User's Guide to Permaculture 2nd Edition*, Bromeliad Society of Australia

**Tips** Simon & Schuster Australia specialises in general interest non-fiction books by Australian writers. Simon & Schuster Australia does not accept submissions from unagented authors.

## Simon & Schuster Canada

**625 Cochrane Drive, Suite 600, Markham, Ontario, L3R 9R9, Canada**

- 001 905 943 9942
- 001 905 943 9026
- info@simonandschuster.ca
- www.simonsayscanada.com

**Parent Company** Simon & Schuster Inc

**Imprint(s)** Simon & Schuster
  Simon & Schuster Audio
  Simon & Schuster Books for Young Readers

**Categories** Publishes Non-Fiction, Fiction and Children's titles on the following subjects: Children's Fiction, Contemporary Fiction, Computers, Education, General Interest, How-To, Literary Fiction, Mainstream Fiction, Multimedia, Practical, Reference, Self-Help, Study Aids, Travel

**Insider Info** Authors paid by royalty with advance offered.

**Submission Guidelines** Does not accept unsolicited manuscripts or proposals.

**Recent Title(s)** *American Fascists: The Christian Right and the War On America*, Chris Hedges

**Tips** Simon & Schuster Canada does not accept submissions or proposals from unagented authors.

## Simon & Schuster Inc
**1230 Avenue of the Americas, New York, 10020, USA**
- 001 212 698 7000
- 001 212 698 7007
- Online form
- www.simonsays.com

**Parent Company** Viacom Entertainment Group

**Contact** President/Chief Executive Officer, Jack Romanos

**Imprint(s)** Simon & Schuster Adult Publishing Group
 Simon & Schuster Audio/Online
 Simon & Schuster Australia
 Simon & Schuster Canada
 Simon & Schuster Children's Publishing
 Simon & Schuster UK

**Categories** Publishes Non-Fiction, Fiction and Children's titles on the following subjects: Autobiography, Biography, Children's, Entertainment, General Interest, Genre Fiction, Mainstream Fiction, Multimedia

**Insider Info** Authors paid by royalty with advance offered.

**Submission Guidelines** Does not accept unsolicited manuscripts or proposals.

**Recent Title(s)** *Alternatives to Sex: A Novel*, Stephen McCauley

**Tips** Simon & Schuster is run alongside Paramount studios and focuses on entertainment and media. Simon & Schuster does not accept unagented submissions or proposals.

## Soho Press
**853 Broadway, New York, 10003, USA**
- 001 212 260 1900
- 001 212 260 1902
- soho@sohopress.com
- www.sohopress.com

**Contact** Editor in Chief, Laura Hruska; Editor, Katie Herman

**Imprint(s)** Soho Crime

**Categories** Publishes Non-Fiction and Fiction titles on the following subjects: Biography,

Contemporary/Modern Fiction, Contemporary Crime Fiction, Cultural History Studies, Literary Fiction

**Insider Info** Authors paid by royalty with advance offered. Accepts simultaneous submissions.

**Submission Guidelines** Accepts unsolicited manuscripts and proposals.

**Recent Title(s)** *The Collaborator of Bethlehem*, Matt Beynon Rees

**Tips** Soho Press places a high priority on publishing 'quality unsolicited materials from new writers'. Soho looks for adult literary fiction that breaks away from traditional formulas and explores new avenues.

## Springer Science+Business Media GmbH
**Heidelberger Platz 3, 14197, Berlin, Germany**
- 0049 6221 4870
- 0049 6221 487 8366
- ilka.holzinger@springer.com
- www.springer.de

**Parent Company** Springer Science+Business Media

**Contact** Managing Director, Derk Haank; Editorial Director, Ilka Holzinger.

**Categories** Non-Fiction
 Academic, Architecture, Construction, Economics, Engineering, Medicine, Reference, Science, Technology, Traffic

**Insider Info** Publishes 5,500 titles per year.

**Recent Title(s)** *Nichtmedikamentoese Pain Therapy*, G. Bernatzky

**Tips** Springer is a major global publisher of science, technology and medical material, and only publishes work from leading academics in these fields.

## Springer-Verlag GmbH
**Postfach 89, A-1201, Vienna, Austria**
- 0043 1 330 2415
- 0043 1 330 2426
- springer@springer.at
- www.springer.at

**Parent Company** Springer Science+Business Media

**Contact** Managing Director, Sven Fund; Head of Production, Franz Schaffer; Editor, Renate Eichhorn; Editor, Franziska Brugger

**Categories** Publishes Non-Fiction titles on the following subjects: Academic, Architecture, Construction, Economics, Education, Engineering, Law/Legal, Medicine, Reference, Science, Technology

**Insider Info** Publishes 220 titles per year.

**Submission Guidelines** Accepts unsolicited manuscripts and proposals.
**Recent Title(s)** *Jesus Überlistet Darwin*, H. Mühlmann
**Tips** Submissions to Springer must follow the detailed guidelines on their website.

## Stackpole Books
**5067 Ritter Road, Mechanicsburg, Pennsylvania, 17055, USA**
- 001 717 796 0411
- 001 717 796 0412
- jschnell@stackpolebooks.com
- www.stackpolebooks.com

**Contact** Acquisitions Editor (Outdoor Sports, Fly Fishing, Military Reference), Judith Schnell; Acquisitions Editor (Nature), Mark Allison; Acquisitions Editor (History), Christopher Evans; Acquisitions Editor (Regional, Travel), Kyle Weaver; Acquisitions Editor (Military, Reference), Dave Reisch
**Categories** Publishes Non-Fiction and Fiction titles on the following subjects: Fishing, History, Military/War, Mainstream Fiction, Nature, Outdoors, Pets, Recreation, Reference, Regional, Sports, Travel, Wildlife
**Insider Info** Publishes 100 titles per year. Does not accept simultaneous submissions. Average lead time of one year,
**Submission Guidelines** Accepts unsolicited manuscripts and proposals.
**Recent Title(s)** *Rails to Penn State*, Michael Bezilla and Jack Rudnicki
**Tips** Stackpole prefers queries to full submissions, along with market research and any relevant publishing history.

## Stanford University Press
**1450 Page Mill Road, Palo Alto, California, 94304, USA**
- 001 650 723 9434
- 001 650 725 3457
- info@www.sup.org
- www.sup.org

**Contact** Associate Director/Editor in Chief, Alan Harvey; Acquisitions Editor (Asian Studies, US Foreign Policy, Asian American Studies), Muriel Bell; Acquisitions Editor (Law, Political Science, Public Policy), Amanda Moran; Acquisitions Editor (Sociology, Anthropology, Education, Middle Eastern Studies), Kate Wahl; Acquisitions Editor (Economics & Organizational Studies), Margo Beth Crouppen

**Categories** Publishes Non-Fiction on the following subjects: Academic, Professional, Reference, Regional Interest, Scholarly, Textbook
**Insider Info** Offers advance. Does not accept simultaneous submissions.
**Submission Guidelines** Accepts unsolicited manuscripts and proposals.
**Recent Title(s)** *Speaking of Freedom*, Diane Enns
**Tips** Stanford University Press accepts submissions for academic and professional books, textbooks for upper-level undergraduate students, and regional interest books. All submissions must be posted, not emailed.

## St. Martin's Press
**175 Fifth Avenue, New York, 10010, USA**
- 001 212 674 5151
- 001 212 420 9314
- www.stmartins.com

**Parent Company** Holtzbrinck Publishers Holdings LLC
**Contact** President, John Sargent
**Imprint(s)** Griffin
  Minotaur
  Palgrave Macmillan
  Picador
  Thomas Dunne Books
**Categories** Publishes Non-Fiction, Fiction and Children's titles on the following subjects: Biography, Business, Children's, Cooking, Economics, Education, Fantasy, General Interest, Historical, Horror, Mainstream/Contemporary Fiction, Reference, Science-Fiction, Self-Help, Sports
**Insider Info** Publishes 1,500 titles per year. Authors paid by royalty, with advance offered.
**Submission Guidelines** Does not accept unsolicited manuscripts or proposals.
**Recent Title(s)** *Accidental Revolution: The Story of Grunge*, Kyle Anderson
**Tips** St. Martin's Press is the American arm of UK publisher Macmillan and is one of the ten largest publishers in America. St. Martin's will not accept unagented submissions or proposals.

## Struik New Holland Publishers
**PO Box 1144, Cape Town, 8000, South Africa**
- 0027 21 462 4360
- 0027 21 462 4377
- info@struik.co.za
- www.struik.co.za

**Parent Company** Johnnic Publishing Limited

**Contact** Publishing Manager (Struik Lifestyle), Linda de Villiers; Publishing Manager (Struik Natural History), Pippa Parker; Publishing Manager (Struik Travel & Tourism), Dominique le Roux; Publishing Manager (Zebra Press), Marlene Fryer; Publishing Manager (Oshun Books), Michelle Matthews; Publishing Manager (Two Dogs), Tim Richman
**Imprint(s)** Oshun
 Struik Christian Books
 Struik Lifestyle/Natural History/People, Art & Culture/Travel & Tourism
 Two Dogs
 Zebra
**Categories** Publishes Non-Fiction, Fiction and Children's titles on the following subjects: Afrikaans Literature, General Interest, Illustrated Books, Lifestyle, Local Interest, Mainstream Fiction, Memoirs, Natural History, Religion, South African Men's Literature, South African Women's Literature, Spirituality, Travel, Tourism
**Submission Guidelines** Accepts unsolicited manuscripts and proposals.
**Recent Title(s)** *Pillowbook*, Dr. Marlene Wasserman
**Tips** Struik accepts submissions for non-fiction and fiction, as long as they addressed to the correct imprint and publishing manager.

## Taschen GmbH
**Hohenzollernring 53, 50672, Cologne, Germany**
- 00 49 221 201800
- 00 49 221 254919
- contact@taschen.com
- www.taschen.com
**Contact** Editor, Dian Hanson; Editor, Eric Kroll
**Categories** Non-Fiction, Architecture, Art, Artist's Editions, Classics, Design, Film, Lifestyle, Photography, Pop Culture, Sex/Erotica
**Recent Title(s)** *Let Me In!*, Mario Testino
**Tips** Taschen is a global publisher of art and design, renowned for their stylish and often raunchy approach to publishing. Taschen also publishes various magazines.

## Tor Books
**175 Fifth Avenue, New York, 10010, USA**
- 001 212 388 0100
- 001 212 388 0191
- www.tor-forge.com
**Parent Company** Tom Doherty Associates Llc
**Imprint(s)** Forge Books
 Orb Books
 Starscape Books

 Tor Books
 Tor Teen Books
**Categories** Publishes Non-Fiction, Fiction and Children's titles on the following subjects: Autobiography, Biography, Children's Fiction, Contemporary Fantasy, Crime Fiction, Dark Fantasy, Epic Fantasy, General Interest, Genre Fiction, Graphic Novels, Historical Fiction, History, Horror, Humour, Memoir, Science, Science-Fiction, Short-Stories, Space Opera, Westerns, Young Adult
**Insider Info** Authors paid by royalty, with advance offered. Aims to respond to manuscripts within six months.
**Submission Guidelines** Accepts unsolicited manuscripts and proposals.
**Recent Title(s)** *New Spring*, Robert Jordan
**Tips** Tor publishes all types of genre fiction and maintains an open submissions policy, meaning that they will accept proposal packages from absolutely anyone. See website for further details.

## Tundra Books
**75 Sherbourne Street, 5th Floor, Toronto, Ontario, M5A 2P9, Canada**
- tundra@mcclelland.com
- www.tundrabooks.com
**Parent Company** McClelland & Stewart Ltd
**Contact** Publisher, Kathy Lowinger
**Categories** Publishes Fiction and Children's titles on the following subjects:
 Art, Children's Literature, Contemporary Fiction, Picture Books
**Submission Guidelines** Accepts unsolicited manuscripts and proposals.
**Recent Title(s)** *1, 2, 3*, Tom Slaughter
**Tips** Tundra Books does not accept many unsolicited manuscripts and will not accept art submissions at all, unless of gallery standard.

## Uitgeverij Lannoo Groep
**Kasteelstraat 97, B-8700, Tielt, Belgium**
- 0032 51 424211
- 0032 51 401152
- lannoo@lannoo.be
- www.lannoo.be
**Imprint(s)** DistriMedia nv
 Editions Racine
 LannooCampus
 Lannoo Graphics
 Uitgeverij Lannoo nv
 Uitgeverij Terra Lannoo bv
**Categories** Publishes Non-Fiction titles on the following subjects: Business, Economics, Education,

General Interest, Health, History, How-To, Local Interest, Politics, Practical, Reference, Science, Self-Help, Textbooks, Travel

**Recent Title(s)** *Als Vrouwen Beminnen*, Claire vanden Abbeele

**Tips** Lannoo is a general non-fiction publisher that specialises mainly in business and management material.

## Umuzi

**3rd Floor Safmarine House, 22 Riebeek Street, Cape Town, 8001, South Africa**

- 0027 21 410 8785
- 0027 21 410 8711
- jeanne.umuzi@randomhouse.co.za
- www.umuzi-randomhouse.co.za

**Parent Company** Random House South Africa

**Contact** Publishing Director, Annari van der Merwe; Submissions Editor, Jeanne Hromnik

**Categories** Publishes Non-Fiction, Fiction, Poetry and Children's titles on the following subjects: Afrikaans Writing, Biography, Children's Fiction, Contemporary Fiction, Education, General Interest, How-To, Literary Fiction, Local Interest, Mainstream Fiction, Reference, Self-Help, Travel

**Insider Info** Authors paid by royalty with advance offered.

**Recent Title(s)** *Playing in the Light*, Zo' Wicomb

**Tips** Umuzi is an imprint of Random House South Africa and publishes mainly in English, but also some African language translations. Umuzi accepts submissions for adult fiction and non-fiction that has a South African flavour.

## University of Alabama Press

**PO Box 870380, 20 Research Drive, Tuscaloosa, Alabama, 35487, USA**

- 001 205 348 5180
- 001 205 348 9201
- danross@uapress.ua.edu
- www.uapress.ua.edu

**Contact** Director, Daniel J.J. Ross; Senior Acquisitions Editor, Judith Knight; Acquisitions Editor (Humanities), Dan Waterman; Associate Editor (Digital and Electronic Publishing), Claire Evans; Managing Editor, Suzette Griffith

**Categories** Publishes Non-Fiction titles on the following subjects: Academic, African-American Studies, Biography, Anthropology/Archaeology, Government/Politics, History, Jewish Studies, Language/Literature, Literary Criticism, Religion, Rhetoric, Southern History, Translation

**Insider Info** Publishes 60 titles per year. Offers advance. 95 per cent of books come from unagented writers, and 70 per cent from first-time authors. Book available catalogue free on request.

**Submission Guidelines** Accepts unsolicited manuscripts and proposals.

**Recent Title(s)** *William Christenberry's Black Belt*, William Christenberry

**Tips** University of Alabama Press specialises in American South history and ethnic and religious studies, but will consider any relevant academic book for publication. Submissions must be directed to the appropriate editor, full details can be found on the website.

## University of Arkansas Press

**McIlroy House, 201 Ozark Avenue, Fayetteville, Arkansas, 72701, USA**

- 001 479 575 3246
- 001 479 575 6044
- uapress@uark.edu
- www.uapress.com

**Contact** Director and Acquisitions Editor, Lawrence J. Malley; Editorial and Production Manager, Brian King; Project Editor, Sarah White; Acquisitions Assistant, Julie Watkins; Series Editor (Poetry Series), Enid Shomer

**Imprint(s)** The University of Arkansas Press Poetry Series

**Categories** Publishes Non-Fiction and Poetry titles on the following subjects: Academic, African-American History, Arkansas & Regional Studies, Civil War Studies, Government/Politics, History, Literary Criticism, Middle East Studies, Nature, Regional, Scholarly, Southern History, Translated Fiction

**Insider Info** Publishes 20 titles per year. Royalty paid on net receipts. 95 per cent of books come from unagented writers, and 30 per cent from first-time authors. Aims to respond to proposals within three months. Average lead time of one year. Catalogue and author guidelines available free on request.

**Submission Guidelines** Accepts unsolicited manuscripts and proposals.

**Recent Title(s)** *Long Blues in A Minor*, Gerard Herzhaft

**Tips** University of Arkansas Press publishes academic books on a range of American South and social interest subjects, and also publishes an annual poetry series which is run in a similar fashion to a poetry competition. Details and instructions for submitting to the poetry series are available on the website.

## University of Chicago Press

**1427 East 60th Street, Chicago, Illinois, 60637, USA**

📞 001 773 702 7700

📠 001 773 702 9756

✉ agt@press.uchicago.edu

🌐 www.press.uchicago.edu

**Contact** Director (Books Division), Robert Lynch; Editorial Director (Humanities, Sciences), Alan G. Thomas; Editorial Director (Social Sciences, Paperback Publishing), John Tryneski; Executive Editor (Art, Architecture, Ancient Archeology, Classics, Film studies), Susan Bielstein; Executive Editor (Anthropology, Paleoanthropology, Philosophy, Psychology), T. David Brent

**Categories** Publishes Non-Fiction and Journals on the following subjects: Academic, Art/Architecture, Dictionaries, History, Humanities, Journals, Law/Legal, Multimedia, Reference, Scholarly, Science, Social Sciences

**Submission Guidelines** Accepts unsolicited manuscripts and propsals.

**Recent Title(s)** *From Counterculture to Cyberculture: Stewart Brand, the Whole Earth Network, and the Rise of Digital Utopianism*, Fred Turner

**Tips** University of Chicago Press welcomes unsolicited submissions as long as they are sent to the correct editor. Check website for full details of editorial contacts and interests. Electronic submissions are supported with 'Electronic Manuscript Preparation Guidelines for Authors', also available on the website.

## University of Illinois Press

**1325 South Oak Street, Champaign, Illinois, 61820, USA**

📞 001 217 333 0950

📠 001 217 244 8082

✉ uipress@uillinois.edu

🌐 www.press.uillinois.edu

**Contact** Director (Literature, Classics, Classical Music, Sports History), Willis Regier; Associate Director and Editor in Chief (Women's Studies, Film, African-American Studies), Joan Catapano; Acquisitions Editor (American History, Labor History, American Music, American Studies), Laurie Matheson; Poetry Editor, Laurence Lieberman

**Categories** Publishes Non-Fiction and Poetry titles on the following subjects: Academic, Americana, Animals, Biography, Cooking/Foods/Nutrition, Education, Government/Politics, History (American History), Language/Literature, Military/War, Music/Dance (American Music), Poetry, Philosophy, Reference, Regional, Scholarly, Sports, Translation, Women's Studies

**Insider Info** Publishes 150 titles per year. Pays 0–10 per cent royalty on net receipts, with advance offered. 95 per cent of books come from unagented writers and 35 per cent from first-time authors. Average lead time of one year.

**Submission Guidelines** Accepts unsolicited manuscripts and proposals.

**Recent Title(s)** *How to Think about Information*, Dan Schiller

**Tips** University of Illinois Press prefers proposals rather than full manuscript submissions, directed to the appropriate editor. UIP also publishes a poetry series which accepts submissions every February.

## University of Massachusetts Press

**PO Box 429, Amherst, Massachusetts, 01004, USA**

📞 001 413 545 2217

📠 001 413 545 1226

✉ info@umpress.umass.edu

🌐 www.umass.edu

**Contact** Director, Bruce Wilcox; Senior Editor, Clark Dougan; Managing Editor, Carol Betsch

**Categories** Publishes Non-Fiction, Fiction and Poetry titles on the following subjects: Academic, American History, Art/Architecture, Black & Ethnic Studies, Cultural Studies, History, Literary Criticism, Literary Fiction, Philosophy, Poetry, Political Sciences, Reference, Scholarly, Short-Stories, Women's Studies

**Insider Info** Publishes 40 titles per year.

**Submission Guidelines** Accepts unsolicited manuscripts and proposals.

**Recent Title(s)** *Heavier Than Air*, Nona Caspers

**Tips** The University of Massachusetts Press is rare among academic presses, in that it supports and publishes fiction and poetry. It has annual competitions; the Juniper Prize for Fiction and Poetry, and the Grace Paley Prize for short-fiction. The winning books will be published by the press.

## University of Michigan Press

**839 Greene Street, Ann Arbor, Michigan, 48104, USA**

📞 001 734 764 4388

📠 001 734 615 1540

✉ cbyks@umich.edu

🌐 www.press.umich.edu

**Contact** Director (American History), Phil Pochoda; Senior Executive Editor (American Studies, Theatre and Performance Studies, Literature), LeAnn Fields; Acquisitions Editor (Regional Interest: Michigan and

Great Lakes) , Mary Erwin; Acquisitions Editor (Music, Fiction, Classics and Archaeology, Early Modern History, German Studies), Christopher J. Hebert; Acquisitions Editor (New Media Studies, Cultural Studies), Alison MacKeen; Acquisitions Editor (Politics, Law, Economics), James F. Reische

**Imprint(s)** Sweetwater Fiction

**Categories** Publishes Non-Fiction and Fiction titles on the following subjects: American History, American Studies, Anthropology, Applied Linguistics, Classical Archaeology, Classics, Cultural Studies, Economics, English as a Second Language, Fiction, Gender Studies, German Studies, Great Lakes Regional Interest, Law, Literary Criticism and Theory, Medieval Studies, Music, Poetics, Political Science, Renaissance Studies, Theatre and Performance, Women's Studies

**Submission Guidelines** Accepts unsolicited manuscripts and proposals.

**Recent Title(s)** *How Like an Angel*, Jack Driscoll

**Tips** Apart from academic non-fiction, the University of Michigan Press also publishes literary fiction, novels and collections of short-stories that are set within the Great Lakes region.

## University of New South Wales Press

**University of New South Wales, Sydney, New South Wales, 2052, Australia**

- ☏ 0061 2 9664 0900
- 🖷 0061 2 9664 5420
- ✉ frontdesk.press@unsw.edu.au
- 🌐 www.unswpress.com.au

**Categories** Publishes Non-Fiction titles on the following subjects: Anthropology, Art, Australian Society, Biography, Cultural Studies, Journals, Environmental Studies, Medicine, Multimedia, Natural History, Philosophy, Politics, Practical Guides, Psychiatry, Reference, Scholarly, Science, Social Sciences, Teaching Resources, Textbooks

**Insider Info** Publishes 40 titles per year. Pays royalty on wholesale price.

**Submission Guidelines** Accepts unsolicited manuscripts and proposals.

**Recent Title(s)** *The Seven Deadly Sins of Obesity: How the Modern World is Making us Fat*, Jane Dixon and Dorothy Broom

**Tips** UNSW Press is a leading publisher in Australian Studies and Natural History, and many of its publications are aimed at students and teachers as teaching resources.

## University Of Queensland Press

**PO Box 6042, Staff House Road, St. Lucia, Queensland, 4067, Australia**

- ☏ 0061 7 3365 2127
- 🖷 0061 7 3365 7579
- ✉ uqp@uqp.uq.edu.au
- 🌐 www.uqp.uq.edu.au

**Categories** Publishes Non-Fiction, Fiction, Poetry and Children's titles on the following subjects: Australian History, Biography, Children's Fiction, Current Affairs, Indigenous Issues, Literary Fiction, Poetry, Politics, Social Studies, Young Adult

**Insider Info** Aims to respond to proposals within six months.

**Submission Guidelines** Accepts unsolicited manuscripts and proposals.

**Recent Title(s)** *Down to This*, Shaughnessy Bishop-Stall

**Tips** University of Queensland Press accepts unsolicited non-fiction submissions, but will only accept fiction submissions through a literary agent.

## University of Western Australia Press

**University of Western Australia, 35 Stirling Highway, Crawley, Western Australia, 6009, Australia**

- ☏ 0061 8 6488 3670
- 🖷 0061 8 6488 1027
- ✉ admin@uwapress.uwa.edu.au
- 🌐 www.uwapress.uwa.edu.au

**Contact** Director, Terri-Ann White; Publishing Manager, Janine Drakeford; Editorial Officer, Maureen de la Harpe

**Imprint(s)** Cygnet Books
Cygnet Young Fiction
Staples
Tuart House

**Categories** Publishes Non-Fiction, Fiction and Children's titles on the following subjects: Academic, Children's books, Contemporary Issues, Critical Studies, General Interest, History, Literary Studies, Maritime History, Natural History, Scholarly, Young Fiction

**Submission Guidelines** Accepts unsolicited manuscripts and proposals.

**Recent Title(s)** *The War on Democracy*, Niall Lucy and Steve Mickler

**Tips** University of Western Australia Press does not accept unsolicited manuscripts, but will accept proposals for books in the main subject areas.

## University Press of Kansas
**2502 Westbrooke Circle, Lawrence, Kansas, 66045, USA**

🕿 001 785 864 4154
🖷 001 785 864 4586
✉ upress@ku.edu
🌐 www.kansaspress.ku.edu

**Contact** Director (American Government and Public Policy, Presidential Studies, Urban Politics, Kansas and Regional Studies), Fred M. Woodward; Editor in Chief (Military History and Intelligence Studies, Law and Legal History, Political Science), Michael Briggs; Acquisitions Editor (Western History, Native American Studies, Environmental Studies, American Studies, Women's Studies), Kalyani Fernando

**Categories** Publishes Non-Fiction titles on the following subjects: Academic, American History, Cultural Studies, Government, History, Philosophy, Politcal Science, Reference, Scholarly, Social Philosophy

**Insider Info** Publishes 55 titles per year. Pays 5–15 per cent royalty on net receipts, with advance offered. Receives 600 queries per year. 98 per cent of books come from unagented writers, and 20 per cent from first-time authors. Aims to respond to proposals within one month. Does not accept simultaneous submissions. Average lead time is ten months.

**Submission Guidelines** Accepts unsolicited manuscripts and proposals.

**Recent Title(s)** *Hillary Rodham Clinton: Polarizing First Lady*, Gil Troy

**Tips** University Press of Kansas prefers proposals over submissions, and is willing to except them by email, as well as by post.

## Vanderbilt University Press
**VU Station B 351813, Nashville, Tennessee, 37235, USA**

🕿 001 615 322 3585
🖷 001 615 343 8823
✉ vupress@vanderbilt.edu
🌐 www.vanderbilt.edu/vupress

**Contact** Director, Michael Ames

**Categories** Publishes Non-Fiction titles on the following subjects: Academic, Biography, Education, General Interest, Health, Humanities, Practical, Reference, Scholarly, Social Sciences, Textbook

**Insider Info** Publishes 25 titles per year. Pays eight per cent royalty on net receipts, with advance offered. Receives 500 queries per year. 90 per cent of books come from unagented writers and 25 per cent from first-time authors. Aims to respond to proposals within two weeks. Accepts simultaneous submissions. Average lead time of ten months. Catalogue available free on request.

**Submission Guidelines** Accepts unsolicited manuscripts and proposals.

**Recent Title(s)** *Generation X Rocks*, Christine Henseler and Randolph D. Pope (eds.)

**Tips** Vanderbilt University Press looks for interdisciplinary intellectual works that 'blend scholarly and practical concerns.'

## Walker & Company
**104 Fifth Avenue, 7th Floor, New York, 10011, USA**

🕿 001 212 727 8300
🖷 001 212 727 0984
🌐 www.walkerbooks.com

**Parent Company** Bloomsbury Publishing Plc (see entry under UK & Irish Book Publishers)

**Contact** Managing Editor, Karen Rinaldi; Publisher, George Gibson

**Categories** Publishes Non-Fiction, Fiction and Children's titles on the following subjects: Biography, Business/Economics, Children's Books, Health/Medicine, History, Literary Fiction, Mystery Fiction, Nature, Picture Books, Science, Sports, Technology, Young Adult

**Insider Info** Does not accept simultaneous submissions.

**Submission Guidelines** Accepts unsolicited manuscripts and proposals.

**Recent Title(s)** *Curse of the Narrows*, Laura M. MacDonald

**Tips** Walker will consider material from new or unagented writers, but is currently only accepting submissions for children's and young adult books, particularly young adult novels and high-quality picture books.

## Warner Books
**Time & Life Building, 1271 Avenue of the Americas, New York, 10020, USA**

🕿 001 212 522 7200
🖷 001 212 522 7993
✉ info@warnerbooks.com
🌐 www.twbookmark.com

**Parent Company** Hachette Book Group USA

**Contact** Publisher, Maureen Egen; Senior Vice President/Publisher, Jamie Raab; Associate Publisher, Les Pockell; Vice President/Editorial Director (Trade Paperback), Amy Einhorn; Editorial Director (Mass Market Paperback), Beth de Guzman

**Imprint(s)** Aspect

Mysterious Press
Walk Worthy Press
Warner Business
Warner Faith
Warner Vision

**Categories** Publishes Non-Fiction, Fiction and
Children's titles on the following subjects: Biography,
Business, Children's, Cooking, Economics, Education,
Fantasy, General Interest, Historical, Horror,
Mainstream/Contemporary Fiction, Reference,
Romance, Science-Fiction, Self-Help, Sports
**Insider Info** Publishes 250 titles per year. Authors
are paid by royalty, with advance offered. Average
lead time of two years.
**Submission Guidelines** Does not accept
unsolicited manuscripts and proposals.
**Recent Title(s)** *Failing America's Faithful: How
Today's Churches Are Mixing God with Politics and
Losing Their Way*, Kathleen Kennedy Townsend
**Tips** Warner Books publishes a diverse range of
material but does not accept unagented
submissions or proposals.

## Women's Press

**180 Bloor Street West, Suite 801, Toronto,
Ontario, M5S 2V6, Canada**
☎ 001 416 929 2774
☎ 001 416 929 1926
✉ info@womenspress.ca
🌐 www.womenspress.ca
**Parent Company** Canadian Scholars' Press Inc
**Contact** Publishing Manager, Rebecca Conolly;
Editorial Director, Megan Mueller
**Categories** Publishes Non-Fiction, Fiction and
Children's titles on the following subjects:
Autobiography, Biography, Children's Literature,
Contemporary Fiction, Creative Non-Fiction, Literary
Fiction, Memoirs, Plays, Poetry, Women's Writing
**Submission Guidelines** Accepts unsolicited
manuscripts and proposals.
**Tips** Women's Press now only accepts a select few
manuscripts per year and no longer accepts any
children's material. Most Women's Press titles are
aimed at students of women's studies, gender
studies and social studies.

## Workman Publishing Co.

**225 Varick Street, New York, 10014, USA**
☎ 001 212 254 5900
☎ 001 212 254 8098
✉ info@workman.com
🌐 www.workman.com

**Contact** Editor in Chief, Susan Bolotin; Executive
Editor, Suzanne Rafer; Senior Editor, Ruth Sullivan;
Senior Editor, Margot Herrera; Senior Editor, Richard
Rosen; Senior Editor (Children's), Raquel Jaramillo
**Imprint(s)** Algonquin
Artisan
Greenwich Workshop Press
Storey
Timber
**Categories** Publishes Non-Fiction, Children's and
Calendars on the following subjects: Business, Cook
Book, Economics, General Interest, Guidance, Health,
How-To, Humour, Self-Help
**Insider Info** Publishes 40 titles per year. Authors
paid by royalty with advance offered. Receives
thousands of queries per year. Accepts simultaneous
submissions. Average lead time of one year.
**Submission Guidelines** Accepts unsolicited
manuscripts and proposals.
**Recent Title(s)** *Food to Live By*, Myra Goodman
**Tips** Workman welcomes unsolicited manuscript
submission by post only, no email submissions.
Workman also publishes various types of calendars.

## W.W. Norton & Company Inc

**500 Fifth Avenue, New York, 10110, USA**
☎ 001 212 354 5500
☎ 001 212 869 0856
✉ manuscripts@wwnorton.com
🌐 www.wwnorton.com
**Contact** Editor in Chief, Starling Lawrence; Executive
Editor, Robert Weil
**Imprint(s)** Backcountry Publication
Berkshire House Press
Countryman Press
Norton Professional Books
W.W. Norton
**Categories** Publishes Non-Fiction, Fiction and
Poetry titles on the following subjects: Agriculture/
Horticulture, Art/Architecture, Biography, Business/
Economics, Child Guidance/Parenting, Computers/
Electronics, Cooking/Foods/Nutrition, Government/
Politics, Health/Medicine, History, Hobbies,
Language/Literature, Law, Literary Fiction, Memoirs,
Music/Dance, Nature, Poetry, Photography,
Psychology, Reference, Religion, Science, Self-Help,
Sports, Translation, Travel
**Insider Info** Publishes 400 titles per year. Authors
paid by royalty, with an advance offered. Does not
accept simultaneous submissions.
**Submission Guidelines** Accepts unsolicited
manuscripts and proposals.

**Recent Title(s)** *Power, Faith, and Fantasy*, Michael B. Oren

**Tips** W.W. Norton will not accept submissions by post or as an email attachment. Submit a proposal only in the body of an email, or telephone with queries.

## Yale University Press
**302 Temple Street, New Haven, Connecticut, 06511, USA**

- 001 203 432 0960
- 001 203 432 0948
- jonathan.brent@yale.edu
- www.yale.edu/yup

**Contact** Editorial Director, Jonathan Brent; Publisher, Mary Jane Peluso ; Senior Editor, Jean E. Thomson Black; Senior Editor, John Kulka

**Categories** Publishes Non-Fiction and Poetry (Competition) titles on the following subjects: Academic, Biography, General Interest, History, Journals, Literary Criticism, Literature, Poetry, Politics, Reference, Religion, Scholarly, Science, Textbook

**Insider Info** Accepts simultaneous submissions. Book catalogue available online.

**Submission Guidelines** Accepts unsolicited manuscripts and proposals.

**Recent Title(s)** *Criticism in the Wilderness*, Geoffrey Hartman

**Tips** Aside from academic publishing, Yale University Press also runs the Yale Series of Younger Poets competition, where one previously unpublished poet can have their book published by Yale.

# MUSIC

# SHEET MUSIC

## ABRSM Publishing
**24 Portland Place, London, W1B 1LU**

- 020 7636 5400
- publishing@abrsm.ac.uk
- www.abrsmpublishing.com

**About** ABRSM produce repertoire volumes for a variety of instruments and for voice. They also publish materials used in exams, including theory papers and student textbooks.

## Bardic Edition

- 0870 950 3493
- 0870 950 3494
- info@bardic-music.com
- www.bardic-music.com

**About** Publish compositions in all genres, by a wide variety of composers.

## Boosey and Hawkes
**Aldwych House, 71–79 Aldwych, London, WC2B 4HN**

- 020 7054 7200
- www.boosey.com

**Contact** Head of Publishing
David Bray

**About** Specialists in classical music. Publish material for professionals, students and hobbyists.

## Brass Wind Publications
**4 St. Mary's Road, Manton, Oakham, Rutland, LE15 8SU**

- 01572 737210
- deliatriggel@brasswindpublications.co.uk
- www.brasswindpublications.co.uk

**About** Publishes music primarily for brass and wind instruments, and for ensembles.

## Broadbent & Dunn Ltd
**66 Nursery Lane, Dover, Kent, CT16 3EX**

- 01304 825604
- 0870 135 3567
- music@broadbent-dunn.com
- www.broadbent-dunn.com

**About** Publishes music for a variety of instruments and ensembles including strings, brass, woodwind and piano.

## Chester Music and Novello & Co.
**14–15 Berners Street, London, W1T 3LJ**

- 020 7612 7400
- 020 7612 7545
- howard.friend@musicsales.com
- www.chesternovello.com

**Contact** Managing Editor

Howard Friend

**About** Will accept unsolicited submissions. Send scores of up to three pieces, preferably with recordings, to the Managing Editor. Response time may be several months.

## Edition Peters

**Hinrichsen House, 10–12 Baches Street, London, N1 6DN**

- 020 7553 4000
- 020 7490 4921
- www.edition-peters.com

**About** Established in 1800. Publishes a wide range of compositions.

## Faber Music

**3 Queen Square, London, WC1N 3AU**

- 020 7833 7900
- 020 7833 7939
- information@fabermusic.com
- www.fabermusic.com

**About** Publishes repertory works by well known composers, but also seeks to discover new talent. Unsolicited submissions for performance and concert works are accepted by post only. Alongside the submission send your performance history, biography, recording and reviews. Unsolicited print publication submissions are rarely accepted for either scores or textbooks, check the website for details. Response is within six weeks.

## Fand Music Press

**Glenelg, 10 Avalon Close, Petersfield, GU31 4LG**

- 01730 267341
- paul@fandmusic.com
- www.fandmusic.com

**Contact** Peter Thompson

**About** First edition publisher of scores for a range of instruments, as well as educational music and CDs. The Fand Music Press also publishes fiction and non-fiction books about music, or by musicians.

## Fraser Enoch Pubilcations

**High View, Rackham Road, Amberley, West Sussex, BN18 9NR**

- 01798 831010Ê
- 01798 831010Ê
- info@fraser-enoch.com
- www.fraser-enoch.com

**About** Publishes sheet music for piano teachers.

## Good Music Publishing

**PO Box 100, Tewkesbury, GL20 7YQ**

- 01684 773883
- 01684 773884
- sales@goodmusicpublishing.co.uk
- www.goodmusicpublishing.co.uk

**About** Publishes music for a variety of instruments, and books on music.

## G. Ricordi & Co.

**20 Fulham Broadway, London, SW6 1AH**

- 020 7835 5380
- miranda.jackson@bmg.com
- www.ricordi.co.uk

**Contact** General Manager
Miranda Jackson

**About** Commissions and publishes music from in house composers. Current print focus is on choral music by living British composers.

## Guildhall School of Music

**Silk Street, Barbican, London, EC2Y 8DT**

- 020 7628 2571
- 020 7256 9438
- research@gsmd.ac.uk
- www.gsmd.ac.uk

**About** Publishes CDs and research reports with the Guildhall School Press. Also has a co-publishing arrangement with Ashgate Publishing Ltd.

## Kevin Mayhew Publishers

**Buxhall, Stowmarket, Suffolk, IP14 3PW**

- 01449 737978
- sales@kevinmayhewltd.com
- www.kevinmayhew.com

**About** Specialists in Christian music and associated products. Publishes existing recordings, books, and original recordings on its record label. Established in 1976. Hard copy submissions are accepted.

## Music Sales

**14–15 Berners Street, London, W1T 3LJ**

- 020 7612 7400
- 020 7612 7545
- www.musicsales.com

**Contact** Chairman and Managing Director
Robert Wise

**About** Publishes sheet music and other print products under its international imprints. They also handle the copyright for over 200,000 music titles. Submissions are rarely accepted but they will occasionally review manuscripts. Please send a comprehensive outline, sample pages and an assessment of market interest and placement.

## Oxford University Press
**Great Clarenden Street, Oxford, OX2 6DP**
- music.submissions.uk@oup.com
- www.oup.co.uk/music

**Contact** Kristen Thorner

**About** Publishes musical scores and books covering the professional, educational and recreational markets. They accept unsolicited and simultaneous submissions. Include a copy of the score, the text and a recording if appropriate. Responses may take several weeks.

## Stainer & Bell
**PO Box 110, Victoria House, 23 Gruneisen Road, London, N3 1DZ**
- 020 8343 3303
- 020 8343 2535
- post@stainer.co.uk
- www.stainer.co.uk

**Contact** Publishing Director
Nicholas Williams

**About** Family run business, which publishes music and musical books. Also runs an archive and hire department.

## Studio Music
**PO Box 19292, London, NW10 9WP**
- 0800 389 2484
- 020 8451 6470
- info@studio-music.co.uk
- www.studio-music.co.uk

**About** Publish music for a variety of uses, but are best known in the UK for orchestral and band music.

## United Music Publishers
- www.ump.co.uk/home2.htm

**About** Publishers of French classical sheet music and a selection of international catalogues/ They also produce a British based catalogue of works by contemporary composers.

## Universal Edition
**48 Great Marlborough Street, London, W1F 7BB**
- 020 7292 9173
- uelondon@universaledition.com
- www.universaledition.com/london

**About** Founded in 1901 in Vienna, Universal Edition has over 30,000 items in its catalogue of works. It publishes performance materials, music and literature for learners and performers.

## Warwick Music Ltd
**1 Broomfield Road, Coventry, CV5 6JW**
- 024 7671 2081
- 024 7671 2550
- sales@warwickmusic.com
- www.warwickmusic.com

**About** Publishes music for brass and wind, as well as books on music.

## Yorke Edition
**Grove Cottage, Southgate, South Creake, Norfolk, NR21 9PA**
- 01328 823501
- 01328 823502
- rodney@yorkedition.co.uk
- www.yorkedition.co.uk

**Contact** Rodney Slatford

**About** Publishes music and materials for students and children.

# MUSIC PUBLISHERS

## Big Life
**67–69 Charlton Street, London, NW1 1HY**
- 020 7554 2100
- 020 7554 2154
- firstname@biglifemanagement.com
- www.biglifemanagement.com

**About** Holds over 2,000 copyrights including artists such a Lisa Stansfield and Yazz. Manages artists such as Snow Patrol and Badly Drawn Boy.

## BMG Music Publishing
**The Fulham Centre, 20 Fulham Broadway, London, SW6 1AH**
- 020 7835 5200
- intl.coregeneral@bmg.com
- www.bmgmusicsearch.com

**Contact** Worldwide Chairman
Nicholas Firth

**About** Publishes thousands of titles including pop, Christian and classical music.

## Bucks Music

**Onward House, 11 Uxbridge Street, London, W8 7TQ**

- 020 7221 4275
- 020 7229 6893
- info@bucksmusicgroup.co.uk
- www.bucksmusicgroup.com

**About** International and independent music publisher. Demos of three to four songs on CD format should be sent by post. Queries over receipt should be directed to Catherine Joseph, cjoseph@bucksmusicgroup.com Please allow several weeks for a response.

## Carlin Music

**Iron Bridge House, 3 Bridge Approach, London, NW1 8BD**

- 020 7734 3251
- info@carlinmusic.com
- www.carlinmusic.com

**Contact** President

Freddy Bienstock

**About** Publishes a catalogue spanning a hundred years of music, including jazz, soul, blues, country, pop, dance and rock.

## Chrysalis Music Publishing

**The Chrysalis Building, 13 Bramley Road, London, W10 6SP**

- 020 7221 2213
- firstname.lastname@chrysalis.com
- www.chrysalismusic.co.uk

**Contact** A&R Manager

Alison Donald

**About** An independent publisher of music, with a particular focus on contemporary, unsigned artists. Approach the Copyright Manager, Kirsten Gilmour, or the A&R Manager's PA, Stephanie Walsh.

## EMI Music Publishing

**Publishing House, 127 Charing Cross Road, London, WC2H 0QY**

- 020 7434 2131
- 020 7434 3531
- webmaster@emimusicpub.com
- www.emimusicpub.com

**Contact** Managing Director

Guy Moot

**About** Publishes a wide range of music including two catalogues, KPM (www.playkpm.com) and

Music House (www.playmusichouse.com). No unsolicited submissions.

## Independent Music Group

**Independent House, 54 Larkshall Road, London, E4 6PD**

- 020 8523 9000
- 020 8523 8888
- firstinitialsirname@independentmusicgroup.com
- www.independentmusicgroup.com

**Contact** Chief Executive Officer

Ellis Rich

**About** Independent music publisher of thousands of pop songs and standards. Send up to four songs in CD format with a short biography. Initial enquiry can be done by phone, then follow up a submission ten days after posting with another call. Director of A&R Andy Bailey, Director of International; Catherine Kelly.

## Kobalt Music Group

**4 Valentine Place, London, SE1 8QH**

- 020 7401 5500
- 020 7401 5501
- info@kobaltmusic.com, firstname.lastname@kobaltmusic.com
- www.kobaltmusic.com

**Contact** Chief Executive Officer

Willard Ahdritz

**About** Independent and international music publisher. Clients include Gwen Stefani and Wet Wet Wet. Copyright Manager: Ed Hearsey.

## Notting Hill

**Bedford House, 8b Berkeley Gardens, London, W8 4AP**

- 020 7243 2921
- 020 7243 2894
- firstname@nottinghillmusic.com
- www.nottinghillmusic.com

**Contact** Chairman

Andy McQueen

**About** International publishers based in London and Los Angeles, they represent over 25,000 copyrights. Artists include Britney Spears and Will Smith. Managing Director; Dave Loader, Head of A&R Leo Whiteley, Royalty Manager; Liz Davey.

## Sanctuary Music Publishing

**Sanctuary House, 49–53 Sinclair Road, London, W14 0NS**

☎ 020 7602 6351
☎ 020 7603 5941
✉ musicpub@sanctuarygroup.com,
firstname.lastname@sanctuarymusicgroup.com
🌐 www.sanctuarygroup.com
**Contact** Chairman
 Bob Ayling
**About** Publishing is a growth area within the company, so a hands on approach is used to manage artists, songwriters and producers. Contact Scott van Dort, Publishing Assistant, for all general enquiries.

## Sony Music Publishing
**13 Great Marlborough Street, London, W1F 7LP**
☎ 020 7911 8868
✉ firstname_lastname@uk.sonymusic.com
🌐 www.sonyatv.com/en-uk/
**Contact** Senior Director
 Rachel Iyer
**About** Publishes a large selection of music covering a wide variety of genres. Unsolicited submissions will be accepted. Send short CDs, plus press cuttings and biography package to the A&R department, or send one MP3 file only. A response is not guaranteed,

although packages will be returned if they have an SAE. A&R Managers: Flash Taylor and James Dewar.

## Universal Music Publishing
**136–144 New Kings Road, London, SW6 4FX**
☎ 020 8752 2600
☎ 020 8752 2601
✉ ukpublishing@umusic.com
🌐 www.universalmusicpublishing.com
**Contact** Chairman and CEO (US based)
 David Renzer
**About** Owns or administers over 1,000,000 copyrights. No unsolicited submissions.

## Warner Chappell UK
**Griffin House, 161 Hammersmith Road, London, W6 8BS**
☎ 020 8563 5800
☎ 020 8563 5801
✉ webmaster@warnerchappell.com
🌐 www.warnerchappell.co.uk
**About** Large, international publisher of music in all genres.

# NEWSPAPERS & MAGAZINES

# UK & IRISH MAGAZINES

## 3D World
**30 Monmouth Street, Bath, BA1 2BW**
☎ 01225 442244
✉ jim.thacker@futurenet.co.uk
🌐 www.3dworldmag.com
**Parent Company** Future Publishing
**Editor** Jim Thacker
**Insider Info** A consumer magazine brought out every four weeks, specialising in computing. Every issue of 3D World comes with a CD packed full of 3D resources, including full software, exclusive trial and learning editions, models, textures, HDRI files, mocap data and architectural content. Present circulation is 13,503.
**Tips** 3D World is a high quality printed magazine, crammed full of news, inspiration and practical advice about 3D graphics. A strong technical knowledge base is required in every article and tutorials and 'how to' guides are the main focus of the magazine.

## 10th Muse
**33 Hartington Road, Southampton, SO14 0EW**
✉ a.jordan@surfree.co.uk
**Editor** Andrew Jordan
**Insider Info** An occasional consumer magazine, aimed at a general interest and literary audience. Aims to respond to queries and manuscripts within 12 weeks.
**Fiction** Publishes Short fiction articles.
**Submission Guidelines** Accepts queries for articles of up to 2,000 words.
**Poetry** Publishes Avant-garde and Free verse poetry.
**Submission Guidelines** Accepts queries with up to six sample poems.
**Tips** 10th Muse is a small magazine that publishes poetry, short fiction and some artwork, focusing particularly on innovative contemporary poetry. They accept poetry and fiction submissions, preferably by post with SAE.

## 247 Magazine

**Unit 29 Scott Business Park, Beacon Park Rd, Plymouth, Devon, PL2 2PB**

☎ 01752 294130
✆ 01752 564010
✉ 247@outofhand.co.uk
🌐 www.247mag.co.uk

**Parent Company** Out of Hand Ltd
**Contact** Managing Editor, Nigel Muntz
**Established** 2000

**Insider Info** A consumer magazine publication, issued monthly, covering music and lifestyle. Present circulation of 30,000. 50 per cent of the magazine is written by freelancers. Average lead time of one month. Publication is copyrighted, and a byline is given. Purchases simultaneous, electronic and regional rights. Seasonal material must be submitted two months in advance. Aims to respond to queries within a day, manuscripts and other issues within five days. Payment is on publication, via cash, with assignment expenses sometimes paid (limit agreed upon in advance). Sample copy and writer's guidelines are available free on request, online or via email. Editorial calendars are free on request.

**Non-fiction** Interested in photo features, new products and travel writing.

 * Maximum paid for assigned articles is £200. Maximum payment for unsolicited articles is £200.

**Submission Guidelines** Send query before sending submissions. Articles must be 1,000–1,500 words.
 Submission details to: 247@outofhand.co.uk

**Images** Accepts images with submission.

 * Offers no additional payment for photos accepted with manuscripts. One time rights are purchased.

**Submission Guidelines** Send images as gif/jpeg files, with captions, model releases and identification of subjects required. Send photos with submission.

**Tips** Target audience are the 18–35 year olds living in, or visiting, South West England. Includes music, lifestyle and listings guides for all suitable events taking place in the region.

## A470

**3ydd Llawr, Ty Mount Stuart, Sgwar Mount Stuart, Cardiff, CF10 5FQ**

☎ 029 2047 2266
✆ 029 2049 2930
✉ post@academi.org
🌐 www.academi.org

**Parent Company** Academi
**Editor** Peter Finch
**Established** 1998

**Insider Info** A bi-monthly literary consumer magazine aimed at a Welsh literary audience. Present circulation is 6,000. Accept queries by mail or email.

**Non-fiction** Publishes Interviews/Profiles, Reviews, General interest, News and Event listings articles.

**Submission Guidelines** Accepts queries.

**Fiction** Publishes fiction articles.

**Tips** Publishes articles in both English and Welsh. It is aimed at professional writers in Wales, and seeks the latest information and event listings for the Welsh literary scene.

## Abraxas

**57 Eastbourne Road, St. Austell, Cornwall, PL25 4SU**

✉ lordcrashingbore@btinternet.com

**Editor** Paul Newman
**Established** 1991

**Insider Info** A quarterly literary consumer magazine, aimed at a general interest literary audience. Byline is given. Accepts queries by mail or email. Writer's guidelines are available online.

**Non-fiction** Publishes Essays, Poetry articles, Features and Reviews on the following subjects: Psychology and Existentialism.

**Submission Guidelines** Accepts queries.

**Fiction** Publishes intellectual short stories.

**Submission Guidelines** Accepts queries for articles of up to 2,000 words.

**Poetry** Publishes Avant-garde, Free verse and Light verse poetry.

 * Poetry tends to be used as fillers.

**Tips** *Abraxas* incorporates the *Colin Wilson Newsletter* and publishes poetry, fiction and articles on philosophy and metaphysics. It is focused on the work of Colin Wilson, particularly scholarly articles on psychology and existentialism. Short stories are welcome as long as they are suitably intellectual, and in keeping with tone of the rest of the content.

## Action Man A.T.O.M.

**Panini House Coach and Horses Passage, The Pantiles, Tunbridge Wells, Kent, TN2 5UJ**

☎ 01892 500100
✆ 01892 500146
✉ paninicomics@panini.co.uk
🌐 www.paninicomics.co.uk

**Parent Company** Panini UK Ltd
**Editor** Ed Caruana
**Contact** Managing Editor, Alan O'Keefe
**Established** 2006

**Insider Info** A consumer magazine brought out every three weeks. The magazine is aimed at children and fans of Action Man. Present circulation is 53,000. 50 per cent of the publication is written by freelance writers. A media pack is available online.

**Tips** The magazine is specifically aimed at 6–12 year old readers and contains collectible features and fact files on the heroes, villains and hi-tech gadgets of the A.T.O.M. world, lots of innovative puzzles and high value competitions. It also has a 12 page interactive comic strip created by an award winning artist. The ethos is that a mixture of imaginative editorial, modern, urban design, and cool, aspirational heroes will attract a broad range of readers.

## Acumen

**6 The Mount, Higher Furzeham, Brixham, Devon, TQ5 8QY**

- 01803 851098
- 01803 851098
- patricia@acumen-poetry.co.uk
- www.acumen-poetry.co.uk

**Parent Company** Ember Press/Acumen Publications Ltd

**Editor** Patricia Oxley

**Insider Info** A literary consumer journal, published three times per year (in January, May and September), aimed at a general interest and literary audience. Receives approximately 10–15,000 queries per year. Aims to respond to submissions within between one and six weeks. Accepts queries by mail or email. Writer's guidelines are available online.

**Non-fiction** Publishes articles on poetry and literary criticism.

**Submission Guidelines** Accepts completed manuscript of between 1,500 and 3,500 words. No emailed submissions.

**Poetry** Publishes Avant-garde, Free verse, Light verse and Traditional poetry.
 * Buys approximately 150 poems per year.

**Submission Guidelines** Accepts sample poems. No emailed submissions.

**Tips** *Acumen* places an emphasis on publishing a wide range of poetry both in style and in its poets. Work is considered from both established and talented newcomers, on an equal basis. It publishes around 50 poems per issue as well as reviews, poetry comment, and reader feedback. Besides poetry, *Acumen* also prints articles of high quality prose on poetry or poetry related subjects. These can be literary criticism, techniques and poetics, poetry reviews, or anything similar providing they are relevant and interesting.

## Aesthetica

**PO Box 371, York, YO23 1WL**

- 01904 527560
- info@aestheticamagazine.com
- www.aestheticamagazine.com

**Editor** Cherie Federico

**Established** 2003

**Insider Info** A quarterly literary consumer magazine aimed at a general interest and literary audience. A byline is given. Accepts queries by mail or email. Writer's guidelines are available online.

**Non-fiction** Publishes articles on Poetry, Features, Reviews and General interest articles on Music and Film.

**Submission Guidelines** Accepts queries via email or post.
 Submission details to: submissions@aestheticamagazine.com

**Fiction** Publishes Prose and Mainstream fiction.
 * Payment is via contributor copy.

**Submission Guidelines** Accepts a complete manuscript of between 300 and 2,000 words via email.
 Submission details to: submissions@aestheticamagazine.com

**Poetry** Publishes Avant-garde, Free verse, Light verse and Traditional poetry.

**Submission Guidelines** Submit five sample poems.
 Submission details to: submissions@aestheticamagazine.com

**Tips** *Aesthetica* is a cultural arts magazine that publishes contemporary poetry and prose fiction, art, and articles on music and film. They do not accept postal submissions, instead send all submissions as word document attachments. Be sure to include your name and the title of your work within the email subject header.

## AFF Families Journal

**Method Publishing, Trenchard Lines, Upavon, Pewsey, Wiltshire, SN9 6BE**

- 01980 615518
- 01980 615526
- info@afj.org.uk
- www.afj.org.uk

**Parent Company** Method Publishing

**Editor** Catharine Moss

**Contact** Charlotte Eadie, Deputy Editor

**Established** 1996

**Insider Info** Quarterly magazine publication for Army families around the world. Present circulation of 64,000. Five per cent of the magazine is written by freelance writers. Submissions are published approximately three months after acceptance. Articles are written for free, as the *AFF Families Journal* is a charity. Publication is copyrighted. Editorial lead time is six weeks. Seasonal material must be submitted three months in advance. Queries accepted by mail, email, fax and telephone. Accepts simultaneous and previously published submissions. Aims to respond to queries within one day, manuscripts and other enquiries within two days. Sample copy available online or via email. Writer's guidelines available online. Editorial calendars available free on request.

**Non-fiction** Publishes articles on experiences of Army life and issues that affect Army families.

**Submission Guidelines** Articles must be 1,000–1,500 words in length.

**Images** Accepts images with submissions.
 * Does not offer payment for images.

**Submission Guidelines** Send as gif/jpeg files, including captions and identification of subjects.

**Columns** Publishes columns on 'Education', 'Army and You', 'Workplace', and 'Special Needs'.

**Fillers** Publishes letters and star letters as fillers.

**Tips** The *AFF Families Journal* is a quarterly publication that is distributed to all Army families based within the UK and across the world. The magazine is free and is funded by its advertising and is supported by the Army Families Federation, a charity that supports Army families and represents Army families. The magazine covers a range of issues that affect Army families due to their transient lifestyle, such as problems trying to access an NHS dentist, finding employment for Army spouses, housing issues, support for families who have children with special needs, separation due to soldiers' overseas deployments, problems with voting when living overseas, and disruption to children's education through constant moves. The magazine also has pages which cover life in Cyprus, Northern Ireland and Germany, where Army families are based. The magazine has a strong 'Postbag' section where letters can be published and views aired. Also offers reader giveaways.

## Agenda

**The Wheelwrights, Fletching Street, Mayfield, East Sussex, TN20 6TL**
 01435 873703
 editor@agendapoetry.co.uk
 www.agendapoetry.co.uk
**Editor** Patricia McCarthy
**Established** 1959
**Insider Info** A quarterly literary consumer journal, aimed at a general interest literary audience. Accepts queries by mail or email. Writer's guidelines available online.

**Non-fiction** Publishes articles on Poetry, Features, Book reviews, Essays and Literary Criticism articles.
 * Buys approximately 80 Non-fiction manuscripts from writers per year.

**Submission Guidelines** Accepts complete manuscript.

**Poetry** Publishes Avant-garde, Free verse, Light verse and Traditional poetry.
 * Buys approximately 200 poems per year.

**Submission Guidelines** Submit six sample poems. Avoid cliched poetry, the overly sentimental, poems with forced rhymes, and poetry that does not come from the heart.

**Tips** Sometimes publishes special issues which focus on a well-known poet alive or dead, and international issues. Each issue contains a general selection of poetry and articles including foreign language translations. Agenda aims to promote young, talented new voices, as well as previously neglected voices and work by established poets. Another of the chief aims of *Agenda* is to provide foreign language poetry to an English speaking audience.

## Aireings

**Dean Head Farm, Scotland Lane, Leeds, LS18 5HU**
**Editor** Lesley Quayle
**Established** 1980
**Insider Info** A quarterly literary consumer magazine, aimed at a general interest and literary audience.
**Non-fiction** Publishes articles on poetry.
**Poetry** Publishes Free verse and Traditional poetry.
 * Mostly women's poetry.
**Tips** *Aireings* is a small poetry magazine of 40 pages, which has no website or email address. All submissions must be sent by post with SAE in order to receive a reply.

## All Out Cricket

**Harvest Mills, Dunnington, York, YO19 5RY**
 020 7953 7473
 matt@alloutcricket.co.uk
 www.alloutcricket.co.uk
**Parent Company** Professional Cricketers Association
**Editor** Andy Afford
**Established** 2004
**Insider Info** A consumer magazine with ten issues per year, covering sports and cricket in particular. Present circulation is 30,000.

**Non-fiction** Publishes Photo features, Features and Interviews/Profiles.

**Tips** *All Out Cricket* (AOC) magazine is a contemporary lifestyle publication that gets closer to the stars of the game than any other cricket title on the market. AOC's young, lively approach to cricket is imbued with humour and irreverence, presenting a markedly less formal style than other cricket and sporting publications. It maintains a stance as a younger, more irreverent cricket magazine and looks for articles relating to the contemporary lifestyle choice of cricketers.

## Amateur Gardening
**Westover House, West Quay Road, Poole, BH15 1JG**
- 01202 440841
- 01202 440860
- amateurgardening@ipcmedia.com
- www.amateurgardening.co.uk

**Parent Company** IPC Media
**Editor** Tim Rumball
**Established** 1884
**Insider Info** A weekly consumer magazine, covering gardening topics. Present circulation of 49,681.
**Non-fiction** Publishes How-to, Features, General interest and News articles.
**Submission Guidelines** Accepts articles of up to 1,200 words.
**Images** Accepts photos with submissions.
**Tips** The editorial mix includes practical hints and tips, topical news and features and advice from the biggest names in gardening today. The magazine is looking for 'topical, practical, or newsy articles', ideally supported by colour pictures.

## Amateur Photographer
**King's Reach Tower, Stamford Street, London, SE1 9LS**
- 020 7261 5100
- 020 7261 5404
- amateurphotographer@ipcmedia.com
- www.amateurphotographer.co.uk

**Parent Company** IPC Media
**Editor** Damien Demolder
**Contact** Features Editor, Bob Aylott
**Established** 1884
**Insider Info** A weekly consumer magazine covering photography subjects. Present circulation of 26,869.
**Non-fiction** Photo features, Features, Reviews, New products and Technical articles.
**Submission Guidelines** Accepts query.
**Images** Send photos with submission.

**Tips** *Amateur Photographer* is world renowned for its authoritative and comprehensive equipment reviews. It is first for news, events, and prices, plus features on techniques, equipment tests and darkroom advice. The magazine also contains readers' pictures, profiles of professionals and advice from experts. Appeals to those interested in buying photographic equipment or wanting advice about improving their picture taking. Contact the Editor with ideas first, and remember that in general, all articles must be accompanied by photos.

## Ambit
**17 Priory Gardens, London, N6 5QY**
- 020 8340 3566
- info@ambitmagazine.co.uk
- www.ambitmagazine.co.uk

**Editor** Martin Bax
**Established** 1959
**Insider Info** A quarterly literary consumer magazine, covering literary topics. 100 per cent of the publication is written by freelancers. A byline is given. Accepts queries by mail or email. Aims to respond to queries and manuscripts within four months. Sample copy and writer's guidelines available online.
**Fiction** Publishes Humorous, Erotica, Mainstream, Experimental and Short fiction.
**Submission Guidelines** Accepts complete manuscript of up to 10,000 words. Does not accept genre fiction, horror, fantasy or science fiction unless suitably subverted. No stories about domestic boredom/bliss, school, or stories that end with 'it was all a dream'. No emailed submissions.
**Poetry** Publishes Avant-garde, Free verse, Light verse and Traditional poetry.
**Submission Guidelines** Accepts six sample poems. Does not want cliched, parochial, overly self-conscious or generalised poetry. No emailed submissions.
**Tips** *Ambit* is a popular literary magazine that prints the latest new writing; short stories, poetry, short poetry reviews and art, from new and established writers. It does not print articles, essays, interviews, memoirs or biography, and does not accept unsolicited submissions for book reviews. Ambit does not work by email and SAE must be included with any submissions.

## Ancestors Magazine
**Ruskin Avenue, Richmond, Surrey, TW9 4DU**
- 020 8392 5370
- simon.fowler@nationalarchives.gov.uk

ⓦ www.ancestorsmagazine.co.uk
**Parent Company** The National Archives
**Editor** Simon Fowler
**Established** 2001
**Insider Info** A monthly consumer magazine, covering genealogy, family history, social history (medieval to the 1950s), military history, archives and libraries. It is the monthly family history magazine of The National Archives. Present circulation of 10,000. 60 per cent of the publication is written by freelancers. It takes on average four months to publish a manuscript after acceptance. Payment is upon publication, sometimes via a contributor copy, although this is by prior agreement. A byline will be given. The publication is copyrighted and buys first UK serial rights from writers. Editorial lead time is two months and seasonal material must be submitted three months in advance. Accepts queries via mail, email, fax or phone. Aims to respond to queries and manuscripts within five days. Will not pay the expenses of writers on assignments. Sample copy and writer's guidelines are free on request.
**Non-fiction** Publishes How-to, Research (particularly tracing ancestors using particular archives or records) and Historical articles.
 * Buys approximately 60 non-fiction manuscripts per year. Pays between £50 and £180 for assigned articles. Unsolicited articles are rarely accepted.
**Submission Guidelines** Contact the Editor to discuss ideas before submission. Articles should be between 1,000 and 3,000 words. Does not publish nostalgia articles.
**Images** Accepts images with submission.
 * Negotiates payment individually. Buys one time rights.
**Submission Guidelines** Accepts gif/jpeg files with captions. State availability of photos with submission.
**Columns** Regular columns include *Off the Record,* a history column of around 700 words.
 * Buys 12 columns per year. Payment is between £30 and £50.
**Tips** Writing should be in clear, concise English and only relevant articles should be submitted. The audience of *Ancestors Magazine* is considered more 'advanced' than that of rival publications. Contact the Editor to discuss any ideas.

## Annual Bulletin of Historical Literature
**Division of History, University of Huddersfield, Queensgate, Huddersfield, HD1 3DH**
ⓞ 01484 422288
ⓞ 01484 472655

ⓔ k.laybourn@hud.ac.uk
ⓦ www.abhlo.com
**Parent Company** The Historical Association
**Editor** Keith Laybourn and Kathleen Thompson
**Established** 1916
**Insider Info** An annual literary consumer magazine covering reviews of historical books and journals. Present circulation of 1,000. A byline is given. Accepts queries by mail or email.
**Non-fiction** Publishes Essays, Features, Reviews and Historical/Nostalgic articles.
**Submission Guidelines** Accepts queries.
**Tips** The *Annual Bulletin of Historical Literature* publishes critical reviews of new historical books and journals from international scholars. They only publish academic articles from recognised history scholars.

## Anon
**67 Learmonth Grove, Edinburgh, EH4 1BL**
ⓞ 0131 332 2398
ⓔ mike@volta1.fsworld.co.uk
ⓦ www.blanko.org.uk/anon
**Editor** Mike Stocks
**Established** 2005
**Insider Info** A consumer literary journal with three issues per year, covering poetry and literature. 100 per cent of the publication is written by freelancers. A byline is given. Accepts queries by mail or email. Aims to respond to manuscripts within three months. Writer's guidelines available online.
**Non-fiction** Publishes articles on poetry.
**Submission Guidelines** Accepts queries.
**Poetry** Publishes Avant-garde, Free verse, Light verse and Traditional poetry.
 * 90 per cent of submissions to *Anon* are free verse, so formal verse submissions, or interesting hybrids, are in high demand.
**Submission Guidelines** Submit three sample poems.
**Tips** *Anon* is a poetry journal to which poems are submitted anonymously and assessed 'blind', using procedures similar to those used by poetry competitions. The selected poems are then published under their author's name. In this way *Anon* publishes any type of poetry from any type of writer, new, established or otherwise, and also prints some articles on poetry or related subjects. Please note that when submitting to *Anon*, name and address details should be included separately to the poems.

# Apollo

The International Magazine of Arts and Antiques

**20 Theobald's Road, London, WC1X 8PF**

- 020 7430 1900
- 020 7404 7386
- editorial@apollomagazine.com
- www.apollo-magazine.com

**Parent Company** The Spectator Ltd

**Editor** Michael Hall

**Established** 1925

**Insider Info** A monthly consumer magazine covering arts and antiques.

**Non-fiction** Publishes Essays, Features, Reviews, and General interest articles

**Submission Guidelines** Accepts queries for articles of up to 3,000 words.

**Tips** *Apollo* is a widely respected magazine on the fine and decorative arts. Its contributors include Martin Gayford, Gavin Stamp and Alan Powers. The publishers are most interested in research, ideally new or otherwise ground breaking, on fine arts, architecture, and antiques. A specialist knowledge would be more than useful.

# Aquarius

**Flat 4, Room B, 116 Sutherland Avenue, London, W9 2QP**

- 020 7289 4338
- www.geocities.com/eddielinden

**Editor** Eddie Linden

**Insider Info** A literary consumer magazine covering literary and poetry.

**Non-fiction** Publishes articles on poetry.

**Submission Guidelines** Accepts queries.

**Fiction** Publishes fiction articles and mainstream fiction.

**Poetry** Publishes Free verse and Traditional poetry.

**Tips** *Aquarius* is a small literary magazine that publishes prose and poetry from new and established writers. Bear in mind that although it is fairly well known in literary circles, its publication dates can be sporadic.

# AQUILA

**Studio 2, Willowfield Studios, 67a Willowfield Road, Eastbourne, East Sussex, BN22 8AP**

- 01323 431313
- 01323 731136
- office@aquila.co.uk
- www.aquila.co.uk

**Parent Company** New Leaf Publishing Limited

**Editor** Jackie Berry and Karen Lutener

**Contact** Publisher, Ron Bryant-Funnell

**Established** 1993

**Insider Info** A monthly consumer magazine for children, covering primary learning and education. Present circulation of 8,000. Sample copy is available at a cost.

**Non-fiction** Publishes Photo features, Features and General interest articles.

**Submission Guidelines** Accepts queries for articles of between 600 and 800 words.

**Fiction** Publishes Short Fiction.
 * Pays between £80 and £90 for fiction articles.

**Submission Guidelines** Accepts queries for articles of between 1,000 and 1,500 words.

**Tips** The magazine takes a non-denominational approach, and is not restricted in any way, or limited by school curriculum requirements. It aims to provide quality ideals and to encourage children to develop caring and thoughtful attitudes towards others and their environment.

# Areopagus

**48 Cornwall Road, Plympton, Plymouth, Devon, PL7 1AL**

- 0870 134 6384
- editor@areopagus.org.uk
- www.areopagus.org.uk

**Parent Company** Areopagus Publications

**Editor** Julian Barritt

**Established** 1990

**Insider Info** A quarterly consumer literary magazine, aimed at Christian writers. Byline is given. Accepts queries by mail or email. Payment may be via a contributor copy, in lieu of cash. Writer's guidelines and sample copy are available online.

**Non-fiction** Publishes How-to articles on Creative Writing and Poetry, Religious articles and Features.
 * Payment is via a contributor copy.

**Submission Guidelines** Send complete manuscript. Length should be between 300 and 1,800 words.

**Fiction** Publishes religious fiction.
 * Payment is via contributor copy.

**Submission Guidelines** Send complete manuscript. Length should be between 300 and 1,800 words.

**Poetry** Publishes Free verse and Traditional poetry.

**Submission Guidelines** Submit ten sample poems of up to 60 lines.

**Tips** *Areopagus* magazine is a special interest publication for Christian writers, which is run voluntarily by editorial teams based in both the UK and US. Due to low funding, *Areopagus* can only accept submissions from subscribers, and is therefore not interested in any unsolicited manuscripts from other sources. It is preferred that subscribers submit their work by email. All articles have a Christian basis.

## Areté

**8 New College Lane, Oxford, OX1 3BN**
- 01865 289193
- 01865 289194
- craigraine@aretemagazine.com
- www.aretemagazine.com

**Editor** Craig Raine
**Established** 1999
**Insider Info** A consumer publication with three issues per year, covering literature, poetry and fiction topics. Byline is given. Queries accepted by mail or email. Writer's guidelines available online.
**Non-fiction** Publishes articles on Poetry, Features, Interview/Profiles, Reviews and News/Reportage.
**Submission Guidelines** Accepts complete manuscript with SAE.
**Fiction** Publishes mainstream fiction and short stories.
**Poetry** Publishes Avant-garde, Free verse, Light verse and Traditional poetry.
**Tips** Focuses on poetry, fiction, reportage and book reviews. Its major emphasis is on poetry, and articles relating to poetry or poetics, many of its contributors are famous authors in their own right. *Arete* does not accept email submissions, so send work as hard copy only. All submissions must also include SAE for return or reply.

## The Art Book

**Laughton Cottage, Brickhurst Lane, Laughton, Lewes, BN8 6DD**
- 01323 811759
- 01323 811756
- ed-exec-theartbook@aah.org.uk
- www.blackwellpublishing.com/journals/artbook

**Parent Company** The Association of Art Historians
**Editor** Sue Ward
**Established** 1993
**Insider Info** A quarterly scholarly journal covering art issues. Present circulation of 9,000. Byline is given. Accepts queries by mail and email. Sample copy and writer's guidelines are available online.
**Non-fiction** Publishes articles on the history of art, architecture, design, the latest exhibitions, reviews and new media.
**Submission Guidelines** Accepts query with published clips. Articles must be 800–2,000 words.

**Tips** *The Art Book* is aimed at academics, students and anyone working with art or history, and anyone interested in new interpretations of arts histories, its contemporary provocation and visual allure, within and beyond the West. The Art Book is always looking for reviewers of the latest art history books or related subjects. All submissions for *The Art Book* must be written in a scholarly manner but with direct and accessible language and little jargon or technical terms.

## Art Monthly

**4th Floor, 28 Charing Cross Road, London, UK, WC2H 0DB**
- 020 7240 0389
- info@artmonthly.co.uk
- www.artmonthly.co.uk

**Parent Company** Britannia Art Publications
**Editor** Patricia Bickers
**Contact** Managing Editor, Letty Mooring; Deputy Editor, Ian Hunt; Editorial Assistant, Frederika Whitehead
**Established** 1976
**Insider Info** A monthly trade magazine covering contemporary visual arts, museums and galleries, curating, collecting, related book and exhibition reviews, and legal and business advice. Present circulation of 10,000. 100 per cent of the publication is written by freelance writers. Payment upon publication, with byline given. Publication is copyrighted. Queries accepted by email or phone.
**Non-fiction** Publishes exhibition reviews and features on contemporary art.
**Images** Accepts images with submission.
**Submission Guidelines** Send gif/jpeg files with captions.
**Submission Guidelines** Send photos with submission. Contact person for images is, Frederika Whitehead.
**Tips** The magazine's audience is made up of art world insiders be they students, artists, collectors, dealers or historians. It focuses on writing about art, rather than printing reproductions of art itself, therefore all freelancers require a very high level of art world knowledge. Read sample articles on the website first to check that you have sufficient background knowledge in contemporary visual art. Phone or email the Editorial Assistant to discuss any possible ideas.

## Asda Magazine

**23 Street, London, W1T 4AY**
- 020 7462 7777

☎ 020 7462 7931
✉ lucy.battersby@publicis-blueprint.co.uk
🌐 www.pubilcis-blueprint.co.uk
**Parent Company** Publicis Blueprint (Magazine Publishers) and Asda
**Editor** Helen Williams
**Contact** Features Writer, Lucy Battersby
**Established** 1999
**Insider Info** A monthly consumer magazine for the customers of Asda supermarket, covering food, drink and retail issues. Present circulation of 2,836,227.
**Non-fiction** Publishes General Interest, Interviews, Reviews and Photo Features on food, wine, new products, parenting, cookery, fashion, beauty, health and lifestyle.
**Tips** The magazine is aimed at women (mothers in particular) aged 25–44.

## Asian Times
**Unit 2, 65 Whitechapel Road, London, E1 1DU**
☎ 020 7650 2000
☎ 020 7650 2001
✉ asiantimes@ethnicmedia.co.uk
🌐 www.asiantimesonline.co.uk
**Parent Company** Ethnic Media Group
**Editor** Burhan Ahmad
**Established** 1981
**Insider Info** A weekly consumer newspaper covering news and current affairs in the Asian community. Present circulation of 28,525.
**Non-fiction** Publishes Features, Interviews/Profiles, General interest, and News/Current affairs.
**Submission Guidelines** Accepts written queries.
**Tips** For many years the *Asian Times* newspaper has been the most reliable source for creating awareness in the Asian community. The Editor is interested in relevant articles on public affairs, international issues and politics, as well as general interest and local issues affecting the British Asian community. Approach in writing with ideas before submission.

## Athletics Weekly
**83 Park Road, Peterborough, PE1 2TN**
☎ 01733 898440
☎ 01733 898441
✉ jason.henderson@athletics-weekly.co.uk
🌐 www.athleticsweekly.com
**Parent Company** Descartes Publishing
**Editor** Jason Henderson
**Established** 1945
**Insider Info** A weekly consumer magazine covering the sport of athletics. Present circulation of 14,000.

Approximately 50 per cent of the publication is written by freelance writers. It takes on average one month from acceptance of manuscript to publication. Payment upon publication, sometimes with contributor copies. A byline is given and publication is copyrighted. Editorial lead time is one week and seasonal material must be submitted one month in advance. Queries accepted by mail or email. Simultaneous submissions are accepted. Aims to respond to queries in one week, and manuscripts within one month. Expenses of writers on assignment will sometimes be paid, with a limit agreed upon in advance. Sample copy available for £3. Writer's guidelines and editorial calendars are available via email: officemanager@athletics-weekly.co.uk
**Non-fiction** Publishes athletics articles.
 * Pays £70 per 1,000 words.
**Submission Guidelines** Accepts queries.
**Images** Uses Sports Images.
 * Pays £15 per photo published.
**Submission Guidelines** Send images and captions. Contact: pictures@athletics-weekly.co.uk
**Tips** *Athletics Weekly* is a British magazine that has covered UK and international athletics for more than 60 years. It publishes every run, jump and throw of note, but also includes features, letters, fixtures and comment articles.

## Audio Visual
Communications for Business
**174 Hammersmith Rd, London, W6 7JP**
☎ 020 8267 8005
☎ 0208 267 8008
✉ peter.lloyd@haymarket.com
🌐 www.avinteractive.co.uk
**Parent Company** Haymarket
**Editor** Peter Lloyd
**Established** 1972
**Insider Info** A monthly trade magazine covering B2B communications. Present circulation of 15,000. 40 per cent of the publication is written by freelance writers. Takes on average six weeks to publish a manuscript after it is accepted. Payment is upon publication and never with contributor copies instead of cash. Kill fee for articles not published is 100 per cent. Byline is given and publication is copyrighted. Purchases all rights. Average editorial lead time is eight weeks, whilst seasonal material must be submitted three months in advance. Queries accepted by email. Aims to respond to queries and manuscripts within two months. Will sometimes pay the fees of writers on assignment with a limit agreed upon in advance. Sample copy,

**447**

editorial calendar and writer's guidelines are free on request.

**Non-fiction** Publishes Features, Interview/Profiles, Reviews, New Product, Opinion (not letters to Editor) and Personal Experience articles.

*Buys 24 non-fiction manuscripts per year. Pays £250 per 1,000 words for assigned articles. Unsolicited articles are not usually accepted.

**Submission Guidelines** Contact with synopsis, for articles of between 500 and 2,000 words. No reprints. Call Peter Lloyd to discuss in the first instance.

**Images** Uses images with articles.

*Buys all rights to images.

**Tips** The magazine is devoted to B2B communications and the use of content and technology. Research the website to gain a fuller understanding of content and issues covered.

## Australia & NZ magazine

**3–4 Riverside Court, Lower Bristol Road, Bath, Somerset, BA2 3DZ**

- 01225 786 882
- anna.scrivenger@merricksmedia.co.uk
- www.merricksmedia.co.uk

**Parent Company** Merricks Media
**Editor** Anna Scrivenger
**Contact** Deputy Editor, Kate Collyns
**Established** 2005
**Insider Info** A monthly consumer magazine covering travel, lifestyle and migration with an Australia and New Zealand region focus. Present circulation of 15,000. 30 per cent of the publication is written by freelance writers. Takes on average two months between acceptance and publication of manuscript. Payment is issued 30 days after publication. Junior writers/students may receive a free subscription instead of cash, subject to negotiation. A byline is given and publication is copyrighted. First UK serial rights, first rights, second serial (reprint) rights, and electronic rights are all purchased. Average editorial lead time is three months. Seasonal material must be submitted three months in advance. Queries accepted by mail or email. Simultaneous submissions and previously published submissions are accepted. Aims to respond to queries within one week and manuscripts within one month. Do not pay the expenses of writers on assignments. A sample copy and writer's guidelines are free on request and available via email.

**Non-fiction** Publishes Book excerpts and articles on Interiors, Recipes, Travel writing, How-to, Migration, Relocation, Property, Humour, Personal Experience, Migrant diaries, Real-life stories and Real holidays.

*Buys 40 Non-fiction manuscripts from writers per year. Pays between £200 and £300 for assigned articles and between £100 and £250 for unsolicited articles.

**Submission Guidelines** Accepts query with synopsis and intro paragraph for an article of between 1,300 and 2,000 words. Send a typed manuscript to the editor. Email submissions are preferred.

**Tips** The tone of the magazine is upbeat, friendly, with bright, lively design. Read the magazine to get an idea of its content, then email initial ideas to the Editor and they'll take it from there. Email submissions are preferred, but everything is considered.

## The Author

**84 Drayton Gardens, London, SW10 9SB**

- 020 7373 6642
- 020 7373 5768
- editor@societyofauthors.org
- www.societyofauthors.org

**Parent Company** The Society of Authors
**Editor** Andrew Taylor
**Established** 1890
**Insider Info** The quarterly journal of the Society of Authors, an organisation that serves the interests of all types of professional writers. Present circulation of 8,500. Accepts queries by mail and email.

**Non-fiction** Publishes articles and features related to Professional Writing, Reviews, and the latest news and events from the writing world.

**Submission Guidelines** *The Author* is the journal of The Society of Authors and writers must be members of the society before they can contribute anything to the journal.

**Tips** The Society of Authors itself offers various prizes and grants for professional writers.

## Autocar

**Teddington Studios, Broom Road, Teddington, Middlesex, TW11 9BE**

- 020 8267 5630
- 020 8267 5759
- autocar@haynet.com
- www.autocar.co.uk

**Parent Company** Haymarket Publishing
**Editor** Charles Hallett
**Established** 1895
**Insider Info** A weekly consumer magazine covering motoring subjects. Present circulation of 60,934. Accepts queries by mail or email.

**Non-fiction** Publishes Photo features, Features, Interviews/Profiles and Reviews.
**Submission Guidelines** Submit completed manuscript.
**Images** Send photos with submission.
**Fillers** Publishes Newsbreaks, and Hints and Tips as fillers.
**Tips** The oldest surviving car magazine in the world, dealing with all aspects of cars, motoring, and the motoring industry. The magazine is prestigious, so will be looking for articles with a strong technical understanding, but also with a friendly and approachable tone. Check previous issues for style.

## Auto Express
**30 Cleveland Street, London, W1T 4JD**
- 020 7907 6000
- 020 7907 6835
- editor@autoexpress.co.uk
- www.autoexpress.co.uk

**Parent Company** Dennis Publishing
**Editor** David Johns
**Established** 1988
**Insider Info** A weekly consumer magazine covering motoring subjects. Present circulation of 87,018. Queries accepted by email.
**Non-fiction** Publishes Photo features, Features, Interviews/Profiles, Reviews and Technical articles.
 * Pays £350 per 1,000 words for unsolicited articles.
**Submission Guidelines** Accepts queries by email for articles of up to 2,000 words. Do not send full manuscript.
**Images** Send photos with submission.
**Fillers** Publishes Newsbreaks, Hints and Tips as fillers or between 50 and 300 words.
**Tips** Specialises in car news and reviews with car specification, photos, videos rating and price. Proposals for features are welcome, but not fully-written articles. Articles will be commissioned if they are appropriate and up to the magazine's standards.

## Avantoure
 Life is a game!
**Cregmalin, Mount Ararat Road, Richmond, Surrey, TW10 6PA**
- 020 8940 7157
- publisher@avantoure.com
- www.avantoure.com

**Editor** Dan Richardson
**Contact** Publisher, Serafima Bogomolova
**Established** 2006
**Insider Info** A bi-monthly consumer interactive digital magazine. Present circulation of 11,000. 100 per cent of the publication is written by freelance writers. Takes on average one month between manuscript being accepted and its publication. Payment is upon publication, sometimes with a contributor copy by mutual agreement. A byline will be given. Publication is copyrighted and all rights are purchased. Average editorial lead time is three weeks, with seasonal material being needed four weeks in advance. Queries are accepted by mail or email. Simultaneous submissions are accepted. Aims to respond to queries within one day and manuscripts within five days. Will not pay the expenses of writers on assignments. Writer's guidelines, editorial calendars and sample copies are free on request and available online or via email.
**Non-fiction** Publishes Inspirational articles, Features, Interview/Profile, General interest, Travel and Personal experience articles.
 * Buys 50 Non-fiction manuscripts per year. Pays between $120 USD and $250 USD for assigned articles.
**Submission Guidelines** Accepts query with published clips for articles between 1,200 and 1,800 words. No reprints without a written permission from the publisher.
**Fiction** Publishes Fiction, Adventure, Historical, Science Fiction, Mystery and Fantasy fiction.
 * Buys two fiction manuscripts per year. Pays between $120 USD and $250 USD for fiction.
**Submission Guidelines** Accepts query with published clips for fiction of between 1,200 and 1,800 words. Address submissions to: Serafima Bogomolova.
**Images** Uses images with non-fiction articles.
 * Negotiates payment individually for images. Buys one-time rights.
**Submission Guidelines** Submit contact sheets, gif/jpeg files and captions. Identification of subjects is required. Send photos with submission to: Serafima Bogomolova.

## Avocado
**Koco Building, The Arches, Spon End, Coventry, CV1 3JQ**
- 024 7671 3555
- avocado@heaventreepress.com
- www.heaventreepress.co.uk/Avocado/avocado.htm

**Parent Company** The Heaventree Press
**Editor** Loveday Why
**Established** 2002
**Insider Info** A quarterly consumer journal covering literature, poetry and arts. Byline is given. Accepts queries by mail or email.

**Non-fiction** Publishes Photo features, articles on Poetry, Features, Interviews/Profiles and Literary Criticism.

**Submission Guidelines** Accepts completed manuscript of up to 1,250 words with SAE.

**Fiction** Publishes Short fiction.

**Submission Guidelines** Accepts completed manuscript of up to 1,250 words with SAE.

**Poetry** Publishes Avant-garde, Free verse, Light verse and Traditional poetry.

**Submission Guidelines** Submit sample poems of up to 40 lines with SAE.

**Images** Send photos with submission.

**Tips** *Avocado* is the literary journal of The Heaventree Press and prints new poetry, prose, fiction and artwork that is fresh, innovative and culturally aware. It seeks work that is diverse, musical, politically aware and free thinking in terms of subject matter and ideology, and that shows an understanding of writing as a craft, and contemporary art forms. Note that *Avocado* does not accept email submissions and all submissions must include SAE for reply.

## Awen

**38 Pierrot Steps, 71 Kursaal Way, Southend on Sea, Essex, SS1 2UY**

- atlanteanpublishing@hotmail.com
- www.geocities.com/dj_tyrer/awen.html

**Parent Company** Atlantean Publishing

**Editor** David-John Tyrer

**Insider Info** A literary consumer magazine, covering poetry and short fiction. Buys first UK serial rights. Accepts queries by mail or email. Previously published submissions are accepted.

**Non-fiction** Publishes articles on Poetry.

**Fiction** Publishes Flash fiction.

**Submission Guidelines** Submit complete manuscript of up to 500 words.

**Poetry** Publishes Avant-garde, Free verse, Light verse and Traditional poetry.

**Submission Guidelines** Submit poetry of up to 40 lines.

**Tips** *Awen* is a small poetry and flash-fiction magazine that prints poetry and vignette length fiction of any style or genre. Submissions to *Awen* magazine may also be considered for other titles published by Atlantean.

## Back Brain Recluse

**PO Box 625, Sheffield, S1 3GY**

- backbrainrecluse@bbr-online.com
- www.bbr-online.com/backbrainrecluse

**Parent Company** BBR Solutions Ltd

**Editor** Chris Reed

**Insider Info** A consumer literary magazine covering science fiction writing. Byline is given. Accepts queries by mail and email.

**Fiction** Publishes Science Fiction.

**Submission Guidelines** Accepts queries.

**Tips** *Back Brain Recluse* is a popular literary magazine with international standing. It publishes original science fiction writing and has built up a cult following amongst its readers. It has a policy of publishing the most experimental and uncommercial types of science fiction.

## Banipal

Magazine of Modern Arab Literature

**PO Box 22300, London, W13 8ZQ**

- 020 8569 9747
- 020 8568 8509
- editor@banipal.co.uk
- banipal.co.uk

**Parent Company** Banipal Publishing

**Editor** Margaret Obank

**Established** 1998

**Insider Info** A tri annual independent literary magazine, perfect bound, 170 x 245 mm, 160pp, covering contemporary literature from the Arab world. Present circulation of 1,200. 90 per cent of the publication is written by freelance writers. Takes on average four months from acceptance of manuscript to publication. Payment is upon publication and a byline is given. Publication is copyrighted. Accepts queries by email. Accepts previously published submissions. Aims to respond to queries within four weeks and manuscripts within three months. A sample copy is free on request. Writers guidelines and a media pack are available online.

**Non-fiction** Publishes Photo features, articles on Poetry, Features, Interviews/Profiles, Reviews and General interest articles.

**Submission Guidelines** Send completed manuscript via post or email, but do not send any email attachments.

**Fiction** Publishes Fiction in Translation from Arab writers.

**Poetry** Publishes Avant-garde, Free verse, Light verse and Traditional poetry.

**Images** Each issue is fully illustrated with author photographs, and the full colour covers feature prominent Arab artists.

**Tips** An independent literary magazine publishing contemporary authors from all over the Arab world in English translation. Publishes established and new authors in English for the first time through poems, short stories or excerpts of novels, as well as author interviews, profiles and book reviews. It is aimed at lovers of world literature, educators, professionals, academics, and all those interested in dialogue with other cultures and the relevance of cultural exchange in today's world. Please refer to the website for detailed submission methods.

## Bard

**38 Pierrot Steps, 71 Kursaal Way, Southend On Sea, Essex, SS1 2UY**

- atlanteanpublishing@hotmail.com
- www.geocities.com/dj_tyrer/bard.html

**Parent Company** Atlantean Publishing
**Editor** David-John Tyler
**Insider Info** A monthly consumer newsletter style magazine covering literature and poetry. Byline is given. Buys first UK serial rights. Accepts queries by mail or email. Previously published submissions are accepted. Writer's guidelines are available online.
**Poetry** Publishes Avant-garde, Free verse, Light verse and Traditional poetry.
**Submission Guidelines** Accepts poems of up to 40 lines.
**Tips** Bard is a flyer-style broadsheet of poetry that is provided free of charge to subscribers to Atlantean Publishing magazines. It contains short poetry from new and unpublished writers, but is a very small publication, designed to complement Atlantean's existing set of literary magazines.

## Barddas

**Pen-rhiw, 71 Ffordd Pentrepoeth, Treforys, Abertawe, SA6 6AE**

- 01792 792829
- 01792 792829
- alanllwyd@barddas.freeserve.co.uk
- www.barddas.com

**Editor** Alan Llwyd
**Established** 1976
**Insider Info** A consumer publication covering Welsh literature and poetry. Byline is given. Accepts queries by mail or email.
**Poetry** Specialises in Welsh poetry.
**Tips** Barddas is published solely in Welsh language so will only accept Welsh language submissions.

## BBC Good Food

**Room AG170, Woodlands, 80 Wood Lane, London, W12 0TT**

- 020 8433 2000
- 020 8433 3931
- goodfood@bbc.co.uk/firstname.lastname@bbc.co.uk
- www.bbcgoodfood.com

**Parent Company** BBC Worldwide
**Editor** Gillian Carter
**Contact** Editorial Assistant, Sarah Sysum
**Established** 1989
**Insider Info** A monthly consumer magazine food, drink and cooking topics. Present circulation of 350,391.
**Non-fiction** Publishes General Interest, Reviews, Features and Photo Features on food, wine and cookery.
**Tips** The magazine is aimed at food and wine enthusiasts.

## BBC Good Homes

**Woodlands, 80 Wood Lane, London, W12 0TT**

- 020 8433 2391
- 020 8433 2691
- deargoodhomes@bbc.co.uk/firstname.lastname@bbc.co.uk
- www.bbcgoodhomes.com

**Parent Company** BBC Worldwide
**Editor** Bernie Herlihy
**Contact** Home Editor, Diana Civil
**Established** 1998
**Insider Info** A monthly consumer magazine covering homes and decorating topics. Present circulation of 127,024.
**Non-fiction** Publishes General Interest Features and Photo Features on houses, style, crafts and decorating.
**Tips** The titles is aimed specifically at home owners aged 20–50.

## BBC History Magazine

(incorporating Living World)
**Tower House, Fairfax Street, Bristol, BS1 3BN**

- 0117 927 9009
- 0117 933 8032
- historymagazine@bbcmagazinesbristol.co.uk
- www.bbchistorymagazine.com

**Parent Company** BBC Worldwide Publishing
**Editor** Dave Musgrove
**Established** 2000
**Insider Info** A monthly consumer magazine, covering general history topics. Present circulation of 51,147. Accepts queries by mail or email.
**Non-fiction** Photo feature, Features, Historical/Nostalgic.

**Submission Guidelines** Accepts queries for articles between 750 and 3,000 words. Only accepts submissions from academic or expert historians/archaeologists and occasionally historically literate journalists.

**Tips** Aimed at history enthusiasts of all levels of knowledge and interest. Being a British publication, the magazine focuses particularly on British history, but its remit is worldwide. Will only consider submissions providing expert analysis and information. Features should be pegged to historical anniversaries, forthcoming books/television programmes, or current affairs topics.

## BBC Homes and Antiques
**9th Floor, Tower House, Fairfax Street, Bristol, BS1 3BN**
- 0117 927 9009
- 0117 927 9008
- angelalinforth@bbcmagazinesbristol.com
- www.homesandantiques.com

**Parent Company** BBC Worldwide/Bristol Magazines Ltd
**Editor** Angela Linforth
**Contact** Features Editor, Jan Waldron
**Established** 1993
**Insider Info** A monthly consumer magazine covering homes, antiques and lifestyle topics. Present circulation of 100,212.
**Non-fiction** Publishes General Interest Features and Photo Features on houses, heritage and antiques.
**Tips** The title is aimed specifically at antiques enthusiasts.

## BBC MindGames
**Tower House, Fairfax Street, Bristol, BS1 3BN**
- 0117 314 8775
- cavanscott@bbcmagazinesbristol.com
- www.bbcmindgames.com

**Parent Company** BBC Worldwide Publishing
**Editor** Cavan Scott
**Established** 2006
**Insider Info** A monthly consumer magazine covering mind games and puzzles.
**Non-fiction** Publishes logic games, puzzles and mind games.
**Submission Guidelines** Accepts outline queries but not entire manuscripts.
**Tips** Articles should concern 'the mind' in relation to puzzles and games. Contact the Editor with synopsis prior to submitting.

## BBC Music Magazine
**Tower House, Fairfax Street, Bristol, BS1 3BN**
- 0117 927 9009
- 0117 934 9009
- music@bbcmagazinesbristol.com
- www.bbcmusicmagazine.com

**Parent Company** BBC Worldwide Publishing
**Editor** Oliver Condy
**Established** 1992
**Insider Info** A monthly consumer magazine covering classical music topics. Present circulation of 51,272. Accepts queries by email or fax.
**Non-fiction** Publishes articles on classical music and the music industry.
**Submission Guidelines** Accepts outline ideas by email or fax, but not entire manuscripts.

## BBC Sky At Night Magazine
**Tower House, Fairfax Street, Bristol, BS1 3BN**
- 0117 927 9009
- 0117 934 9008
- inbox@skyatnightmagazine.com
- www.skyatnightmagazine.com

**Parent Company** BBC Worldwide Publishing
**Editor** Graham Southorn
**Established** 2006
**Insider Info** A monthly consumer magazine covering astronomy subjects. Accepts queries by email and phone.
**Non-fiction** Publishes articles on astronomy and related subjects.
**Submission Guidelines** Contact by phone or email with idea. Do not send in unsolicited manuscripts.
**Tips** Features contributions from world leading astronomers and writers. With articles covering the latest discoveries in astrophysics to observing guides and equipment reviews, the title is aimed at both the experienced and amateur astronomer. Articles should concern the latest in astronomical science, so a technical or academic background is necessary.

## BBC Wildlife Magazine
**Tower House, Fairfax Street, Bristol, BS1 3BN**
- 0117 927 9009
- 0117 934 9008
- wildlifemagazine@bbcmagazinesbristol.com
- www.bbcwildlifemagazine.com

**Parent Company** BBC Worldwide Publishing
**Editor** Sophie Stafford
**Established** 1963

**Insider Info** A monthly consumer magazine covering wildlife topics. Present circulation of 44,302. Accepts queries by email or phone.
**Non-fiction** Publishes Photo features, Features and General interest articles.
  * Pays between £200 and £450 for assigned articles.
**Submission Guidelines** Accepts queries by phone or email for articles of between 400 and 2,500 words.
**Tips** Most articles are illustrated with world class wildlife photography. Articles focus on the latest discoveries, views and news on wildlife, conservation and environmental issues, and trusted further information sources. The magazine is aimed at a broad readership, encompassing anyone with a passion for wildlife. Features are generally only commissioned from experts in wildlife or conservation. In-depth knowledge is essential in the first instance.

## Beat Scene

**27 Court Leet, Binley Woods, Coventry, CV3 2JQ**
- 024 7654 3604
- kev@beatscene.freeserve.co.uk
- www.beatscene.net
**Editor** Kevin Ring
**Established** 1988
**Insider Info** A consumer magazine with ten issues per year, covering the poets of the 'Beat generation'. Present circulation of 5,000.
**Non-fiction** Publishes Photo features, Essays, Poetry articles, Features, Interviews/Profiles and Reviews.
**Submission Guidelines** Accepts queries.
**Tips** *Beat Scene* is an 'information magazine' devoted to the poets of the Beat Generation, including Jack Kerouac, Allen Ginsberg and William Burroughs. The magazine does not publish and fiction or poetry, only articles or news in the relevant subject areas.

## Beautiful Weddings

**8 Hammet Street, Taunton, Somerset, TA1 1RZ**
- 01823 288344
- 01823 288239
- rachelsouthwood@giraffe-media.co.uk
- www.weddingideasmagazine.co.uk
**Parent Company** Giraffe Media Ltd
**Editor** Becky Skuse
**Established** 2006
**Insider Info** A monthly consumer magazine covering weddings and associated topics. Present circulation of 25,000. 80 per cent of the publication is written by freelance writers. Takes on average six weeks between manuscript acceptance and publication. Payment is upon publication and a byline is given. Publication is copyrighted and all rights are purchased. Editorial lead time is six weeks. Queries will be accepted by email. Simultaneous submissions and previously published submissions are accepted. Aims to respond to queries within one week. Sample copy available for £3.99.
**Non-fiction** Publishes Photo features, Real life and other Features on weddings.
**Submission Guidelines** Readers are invited to use the online form to submit their real life stories. However, this does not mean the story will be written by the reader.

## Bella

**Academic House, 24–28 Oval Road, London, NW1 7DT**
- 020 7241 8000
- 020 7241 8056
- firstname.lastname@bauer.co.uk
- www.bauer.co.uk
**Parent Company** H. Bauer Publishing
**Editor** Jayne Marsden
**Contact** Lifestyle Editor, Zoe Oliver
**Established** 1987
**Insider Info** A weekly consumer magazine covering women's lifestyle topics. Present circulation of 316,281.
**Non-fiction** Publishes General interest features, Interviews and Photo features on Real life, Fashion, Beauty, Food, Home, Competitions and Travel.
**Fiction** Publishes Short fiction of less than 1,000 words.
**Tips** The title is aimed specifically at women aged 25–54 with children.

## Birding World

**Stonerunner, Coast Road, Cley next the Sea, Holt, Norfolk, NR25 7RZ**
- 01263 740913
- 01263 741173
- steve@birdingworld.co.uk
- www.birdingworld.co.uk
**Editor** Steve Gantlett
**Established** 1987
**Insider Info** A monthly consumer magazine, covering birds and birdwatching topics. Accepts queries by mail or email. Writer's guidelines and sample copies are free on request and available with SAE.
**Non-fiction** Publishes photo features and other features on birds.

**Submission Guidelines** Accepts queries to the Editor before submitting completed manuscript.

**Images** Good quality bird photographs are always welcomed. Lesser quality photographs are also welcomed when they depict particularly rare birds.

  \* Pays between £5 and £30 per photo.

**Submission Guidelines** Accepts gif/jpeg files with captions. Send photos with submissions to the Editor, Steve Gantlett.

**Tips** Aimed at keen birdwatchers in Britain and throughout Europe, as well as North American and Worldwide birders.

## Birds

**The Lodge, Sandy, Bedfordshire, SG19 2DL**
- 01767 680551
- rob.hume@rspb.org.uk
- www.rspb.org.uk

**Parent Company** The RSPB
**Editor** Rob Hume
**Established** 1900

**Insider Info** A quarterly, members only consumer magazine, covering wild birds (not captive or pets, nor welfare of sick and injured birds), other wildlife and habitat conservation. Present circulation of 621,198. 25 per cent of the publication is written by freelance writers. Takes on average six months between acceptance of a manuscript and publication. Payment is upon publication, never with contributor copies instead of cash. A byline is given. Publication is copyrighted and all rights are purchased. Average editorial lead time is three months and seasonal material must be submitted six months in advance. Accepts queries by mail, phone or email. Aims to respond to queries and manuscripts within two weeks. Sometimes pays the expenses of writers on assignment, with a limit agreed upon in advance. Sample copies and writer's guidelines are free on request.

**Non-fiction** Publishes Photo features, Essays, Features and Personal experience articles.

  \* Payment for assigned and unsolicited articles is by negotiation.

**Submission Guidelines** Accepts query with published clips for articles between 750 and 2,000 words. Approach Rob Hume, Editor. Ideas are welcome but space limited - good writers are always required but 'RSPB led' subject matter and regular features inevitably dominate and leave little flexibility for other material. Do not send entire manuscript.

**Images** Uses images within features.

  \* Pays standard fees and buys one-time rights.

**Submission Guidelines** Identification of subjects is required, as is a statement regarding captive subjects. Send photos with submission to Picture Researcher, Lisa Fell.

**Tips** The magazine is essentially about the RSPB and what it does and why, with members' support; however, within that, evocation of wildlife experiences and features on conservation issues are also published. Articles need to be accurate and reliable but readable and enjoyable. Email or phone the Editor, with specific ideas, to discuss possibilities. There are no formal writer's guidelines but information will be given when applicable.

## Bizarre

**30 Cleveland Street, London, W1T 4JD**
- 020 7907 6000
- 020 7907 6020
- bizarre@dennis.co.uk
- www.bizarremag.com

**Parent Company** Dennis Publishing
**Editor** Alex Godfrey
**Established** 1997

**Insider Info** A monthly consumer magazine covering men's lifestyle topics. Present circulation of 65,959. Accepts queries by mail or email.

**Non-fiction** Publishes articles on events from around the world, drug culture and news, interviews with famous counter culture figures and showcases of cult directors, musicians and authors.

  \* Pays £80 per 1,000 words.

**Submission Guidelines** Accepts queries with outlines for articles of between 800 and 2,000 words. No unsolicited manuscripts.

**Images** Accepts images with submission.

  \* Pays a variable fee per photo.

**Submission Guidelines** Accepts transparencies and prints. State availability of photos with submission.

**Tips** The magazine features tend to concern unusual news on many different types of fetishistic and deviant behaviour that the mainstream media would most likely stereotype as bizarre. Does not accept unsolicited manuscripts, but does appreciate ideas for features. Study the magazine for style and content before submitting synopsis via post or email.

## Black Static

**5 Martins Lane, Witcham, Ely, CB6 2LB**
- andy@ttapress.demon.co.uk
- www.ttapress.com

**Parent Company** TTA Press

**Editor** Andy Cox

**Established** 1993

**Insider Info** A quarterly consumer magazine, covering genre fiction writing. 100 per cent of the publication is written by freelance writers. Payment is upon acceptance of manuscript. A byline is given. Accepts queries by mail or email. Writer's guidelines are available online.

**Fiction** Publishes Horror, Science Fiction, Experimental, Fantasy and Slipstream.
 * Pays £30 per 1,000 words.

**Submission Guidelines** Send complete manuscript. Does not want General fiction/Romance/etc.

**Tips** Regularly contains an exciting mix of extraordinary new fiction, stunning artwork, interesting features and provocative comment. It often transcends the genre divide between science fiction/fantasy/horror and mainstream literature. It is strongly recommended that you study the magazine before submitting as this will greatly improve your chances of acceptance. Story content often goes against the grain of 'traditional' genre writing.

## Bliss
**Panini House, Coach & Horses Passage, The Pantiles, Tunbridge Wells, TN2 5UJ**
- 01892 500100
- 01892 546666
- bliss@panini.co.uk, firstinitiallastname@panini.co.uk
- www.mybliss.co.uk

**Parent Company** Panini UK Ltd

**Editor** Leslie Sinoway

**Contact** Features Editor, Angeli Milburn; Editorial Assistant, Rebecca Davies

**Established** 1995

**Insider Info** A monthly consumer magazine covering teenage girls' lifestyle topics. Present Circulation of 151,729. A media pack is available online.

**Non-fiction** Publishes General interest features, Interviews and Photo features on Television, Real life, Fashion, Beauty, Celebrities, Health and Entertainment.

**Tips** The magazine's target audience is girls aged 12 to 18. The website gives a good idea as to the magazine's style, and has its own editorial content.

## Blithe Spirit
**12 Eliot Vale, Blackheath, London, SE3 0UW**
- 01547 528542
- 01547 520685
- www.britishhaikusociety.org

**Parent Company** British Haiku Society

**Editor** Graham High

**Established** 1990

**Insider Info** A quarterly consumer literary journal, specialising in British Haiku. Present circulation of 300. A byline is given. Queries accepted by mail. Sample copy and writer's guidelines available online.

**Non-fiction** Publishes articles on poetry (Haiku in particular), Features, Reviews and Interviews/Profiles.

**Submission Guidelines** Accepts submissions from subscribers only.

**Poetry** Publishes Haiku poetry.

**Tips** Regularly contains original poems, articles about the writing and appreciation of haiku and related forms, book reviews, letters to the editor, and announcements haiku awards and news. The editorial policy is to encourage new writing, value a diversity of approaches to haiku, and promote excellence. The magazine operates as a membership magazine, and as such, only accepts submissions from subscribers. However, non-members may be invited to contribute as featured writers.

## The Book Magazine
**PO Box 37, Southrop, Lechlade, GL7 3ZX**
- 01285 750212
- christine.kidney@thebookmagazine.co.uk
- www.thebookmagazine.co.uk

**Parent Company** The Book Magazine

**Editor** Christine Kidney

**Established** 2006

**Insider Info** A quarterly consumer magazine, covering literary and book related subjects. Present circulation 50,000. Accepts queries by mail and email.

**Non-fiction** Publishes articles, book reviews, author interviews, opinion (not letters to the Editor) and features on book-related subjects. Regular features include 'Bookworld', 'Reading Group' and 'Writer Revisited'.

**Submission Guidelines** Send query before sending submissions.

**Fiction** Publishes book excerpts and poetry.

**Tips** Articles in *The Book Magazine* are generally privately commissioned by the Editor, although they are willing to accept ideas for future articles by email.

## Books for Keeps
**1 Effingham Road, London, SE12 8NZ**
- 020 8852 4953
- 020 8318 7580

○ enquiries@booksforkeeps.co.uk
ⓦ www.booksforkeeps.co.uk
**Editor** Richard Hill
**Established** 1980
**Insider Info** A bi-monthly consumer magazine covering the children's book industry. Present circulation of 8,500. Accepts queries by mail or email. Sample copy is available online.
**Non-fiction** Publishes articles on Children's poetry, Features, Interviews/Profiles, Reviews, General interest articles and Opinions (not letters to the Editor).
**Submission Guidelines** Accepts queries.
**Fiction** Publishes some Children's fiction.
**Tips** Aimed at adults, mostly teachers, librarians and parents. It contains articles about the latest developments in children's books, interviews and reviews, excerpts and critical essays. Articles tend to be lean towards an academic and critically informative style.

## Books Ireland
**11 Newgrove Avenue, Dublin 4, Republic of Ireland**
○ 00353 1 269 2185
○ booksi@eircom.net
**Editor** Jeremy Addis
**Established** 1976
**Insider Info** A trade and consumer magazine with nine issues per year, covering Irish interest books and Irish publishing. 65 per cent of the publication is written by freelance writers. It takes on average, two months to publish a manuscript after acceptance. Payment is upon publication, and never with a sample copy instead of cash. A byline is given. Publication is copyrighted and first rights are purchased. Editorial lead time is one month. Seasonal material should be submitted six weeks in advance. Accepts queries by email. Aims to respond to queries in three days and manuscripts within two weeks. Will not pay the expenses of writers on assignments. Sample copy available for £3. Writer's guidelines are available via email.
**Non-fiction** Publishes Interviews/Profiles by prior arrangement, with people concerned with new books of Irish interest. Also publishes commissioned book reviews.
   * Buys 126 non-fiction manuscripts per year. Payment (in Euros) is agreed by arrangement for assigned articles. Does not pay for unsolicited articles.
**Submission Guidelines** Accepts queries, with published clips, for articles of between 1,000 and 3,000 words.

**Tips** Particularly interested in interviews with Irish authors and publishers.

## Book Talk
**115 Anglesea Road, Ipswich, IP1 3PJ**
○ 01473 250949
○ sblbooktalk@btinternet.com
ⓦ www.sbl.org.uk
**Parent Company** The Suffolk Book League
**Editor** Kay McElhinney
**Established** 1982
**Insider Info** A quarterly consumer newsletter covering The Sussex Book League's news and events as well as more general literature topics. Present circulation of 200.
**Non-fiction** Publishes Features, Interviews/Profiles, Reviews and News articles.
**Tips** Due to the nature of the newsletter, much of the content is sourced internally.

## Book World Magazine
**2 Caversham Street, London, SW3 4AH**
○ 020 7351 4995
○ 020 7351 4995
○ leonard.holdsworth@btopenworld.com
**Parent Company** Christchurch Publishers Ltd
**Editor** Leonard Holdsworth
**Contact** Features Editor, James Hughes
**Established** 1972
**Insider Info** A monthly trade journal covering the world of books. Present circulation of 6,000. 50 per cent of the publication is written by freelance writers. Takes on average two months between a manuscript's acceptance and its publication. Payment is upon publication, never with contributor copies instead of cash. Byline is given. Publication is copyrighted and all rights are purchased. Average editorial lead time is two months. Seasonal material should be submitted three months in advance. Accepts queries by mail, email and fax. Aims to respond to queries and manuscripts within two weeks. Does not pay the expenses of writers on assignment. Sample copy available for £2. Media pack available on request.
**Non-fiction** Publishes Essays, Features, Interviews/ Profiles and General interest articles.
   * Payment for assigned and unsolicited articles is by negotiation.
**Submission Guidelines** Accepts queries for articles of up to 5,000 words. No reprints. Contact James Hughes.
**Images** Contact James Hughes for images submissions.

**Tips** Aimed at serious book collectors, librarians and booksellers. The magazine's emphasis is on more erudite and literary books.

## Borderlines
**Nant y Brithyll, Llangynyw, Welshpool, Powys, SY21 0JS**
☎ 01938 810263
**Parent Company** Anglo-Welsh Poetry Society
**Editor** Kevin Bamford
**Established** 1986
**Insider Info** A consumer magazine with two issues per year, covering poetry and poetry related topics. Present circulation is 200. Byline is given. Accepts queries by mail or phone. Will pay the expenses of writers on assignment. Writer's guidelines and sample copy available online.
**Non-fiction** Publishes articles on poetry.
**Poetry** Publishes Avant-garde, Free verse, Haiku, Light verse and Traditional poetry.
**Tips** *Borderlines* is a long-running general literary magazine that publishes any kind of poetry from anyone, anywhere. It is open to any kind of poetry submission but the editors generally do not accept long poems.

## Brand Strategy Magazine
Strategic Thinking for Today's Marketing Professional
**50 Poland Street, London, W1F 7AX**
☎ 020 7970 4858
✉ ruth.mortimer@centaur.co.uk
🌐 www.brandstrategy.co.uk
**Parent Company** Centaur Media
**Editor** Ruth Mortimer
**Established** 2005
**Insider Info** A monthly trade magazine with a daily blog and monthly newsletter. Covers the global branding industry, advertising, marketing and new trends in the business world. Ten per cent of the publication is written by freelance writers. Takes on average one month between acceptance of manuscript, to publication. Payment is upon publication and a byline is given. Publication is copyrighted. Average editorial lead time is one month. Seasonal material must be submitted one month in advance. Accepts queries by mail or email. Writer's guidelines and sample copy are available online. Editorial calendar is not available as they do not produce forward features.
**Non-fiction** Publishes Business articles.
**Submission Guidelines** Accepts queries to Ruth Mortimer, Editor.

**Images** Accepts images with submission.
 \* Negotiates payment individually for images. Purchases all rights.
**Tips** A global marketing and business publication, whose audience is Chief Marketing Officers and other senior executives. All articles aim to help clients and agencies understand branding, trends and business philosophy in a detailed way that benefits the bottom line.

## Braquemard
**229 Hull Road, Hull, HU6 8QZ**
✉ braquemard@hotmail.com
🌐 www.braquemard.fsnet.co.uk
**Editor** David Allenby
**Insider Info** A consumer magazine with two issues per year, focusing mainly on poetry. Byline is given. Accepts queries by mail or email. Simultaneous submissions and previously published submissions are accepted. Payment may be via free contributor copies, rather than cash. Writer's guidelines are available online.
**Non-fiction** Publishes poetry articles.
**Poetry** Publishes Avant-garde, Free verse, Haiku, Light verse and Traditional poetry.
**Submission Guidelines** Accepts up to seven sample poems.
**Tips** Publishes work form new and established writers. *Braquemards'* editorial statement is, "We try to avoid politics, explicit religion, ecology and PC attitudes; we like bad taste, black humour and the sick side of human nature". Please note that at the moment the magazine is closed to submissions due to health and financial reasons. Check the website for updates on the situation.

## British Journal of Photography
The Professionals' Weekly
**Haymarket House, London, SW1Y 4RX**
☎ 020 7484 9754
✉ bjp.features@bjphoto.co.uk
🌐 www.bjp-online.com
**Parent Company** Incisive Media
**Editor** Simon Bainbridge
**Contact** Deputy Editor, Diane Smyth
**Established** 1854
**Insider Info** A weekly trade journal covering professional photography; technical reviews and issues, business matters relating to the industry, interviews with photographers, and in-depth pieces on specialist areas of the market. Present circulation of 8,000. 30 per cent of the publication is written by freelance writers. Takes on average three weeks

**457**

between the acceptance of a manuscript, to its publication. Payment is made approximately 30 days after publication and never with a free contributor copy instead of cash. Byline is given. Average editorial lead time is eight weeks. Accepts queries by email. Will not pay the expenses of writers on assignment. Writer's guidelines and editorial calendars are free on request.

**Non-fiction** Publishes Book excerpts (occasionally) How-to (only if high-end technical), Photo features (often, but unpaid), Essays, (occasionally), Features, Interviews/Profiles, (usually assigned rather than suggested), Reviews, (limited opportunities), New Product articles (two per issue), Technical articles, (freelance must have specialist knowledge), Opinions (around ten a year; writer must have some relevant position in photography), Market reports on specialist areas such as fashion, or architecture

\* Purchases 120 Non-fiction manuscripts per year. Payment is negotiable, but between approximately £150 and £1,000.

**Submission Guidelines** Accepts queries, with published clips, for articles of between 500 and 2,000 words.

**Tips** Aimed at everyone involved in the professional photography market in the UK, including photographers, picture editors, trade, students and aspiring professionals. Aims to inform them of the latest news, trends, technologies and issues in contemporary photography. They tend to find their own photographers to interview, and are more interested in ideas for specialist areas or issue-based material from freelancers. Be aware that they focus on contemporary photographers and issues and look at photography in a way that is very distinct from most other (amateur oriented) photo publications. Think about what professional photographers already assume, and what they need to learn from an article. It must be tightly focused on their needs and aspirations.

## Brittle Star
**PO Box 56108, London, E17 0AY**
- 020 8802 1507
- magazine@brittlestar.org.uk
- www.brittlestar.org.uk

**Editor** Louisa Hooper
**Established** 1999

**Insider Info** A consumer magazine with two issues per year, covering poetry and fiction. Present circulation of 200. 100 per cent of the publication is written by freelance writers. Byline is given. Accepts queries by mail or email. Aims to respond to queries

and manuscripts within six weeks. Writer's guidelines are available online.

**Non-fiction** Publishes articles on Poetry, Features, Interviews/Profiles and General interest articles.

**Submission Guidelines** Accepts queries by post with published clips.

**Fiction** Publishes Short fiction.

**Submission Guidelines** Send complete manuscript of up to 1,200 words by post.

**Poetry** Publishes Avant-garde, Free verse, Light verse and Traditional poetry.

**Submission Guidelines** Accepts up to four sample poems by post.

**Tips** *Brittle Star* is a small literary magazine which contains new poems, stories and interviews with authors. It is especially committed to giving new writers a chance to get their poetry published, but also has some space for more established writers. The magazine prefers to have submissions by post, ideally two copies. Also, authors should include a short biography of no more than 40 words, for use if the piece is selected.

## The Burlington Magazine
**14–16 Duke's Road, London, Great Britain, WC1H 9SZ**
- 020 7388 8157
- 020 7388 1230
- editorial@burlington.org.uk
- burlington.org.uk

**Editor** Richard Shone
**Contact** Editorial Assistant, Nicola Crockett
**Established** 1903

**Insider Info** An academic periodical, issued monthly. Founded in 1903 by a group of eminent art critics and historians, *The Burlington Magazine* is the world's leading monthly art periodical. 75 per cent of the publication is written by freelance writers. Submissions are published up to ten months after acceptance. Publication is copyrighted and a byline is given. Seasonal material must be submitted 12 months in advance. Accepts queries by mail and email. Accepts simultaneous submissions. Aims to respond to queries within one day and manuscripts within three months. Assignment expenses are sometimes paid (limit agreed upon in advance). Sample copy is available for £14.40. Writer's guidelines are available free on request. Editorial calendars are available via email. Media packs are available online.

**Non-fiction** Interested in Essays, Historical writing and unpublished Fine Art research of the highest quality.

**Submission Guidelines** Articles must be 1,000–5,000.

Submission details to: Editorial Assistant, Helen Oakden.

**Images** Accepts images with submission.

 * Negotiates payment for images individually.

**Submission Guidelines** State the availability of photos with submission. Send as transparencies or gif/jpeg files, with captions. Contact Editorial Assistant, Helen Oakden.

**Tips** Covering all aspects of the fine and decorative arts from ancient times to the present day, the magazine remains the most authoritative source of information on the visual arts available. We only accept contributors who have a fine arts degree at a very high level, and whose writings conclude extensive archival research.

## The Burns Chronicle

**1 Cairnsmore Road, Castle Douglas, DG7 1BN**

📞 01556 504448

📞 01556 504448

✉ admin@worldburnsclub.com

🌐 www.worldburnsclub.com

**Parent Company** The Robert Burns World Federation Ltd

**Editor** Peter J. Westwood

**Established** 1892

**Insider Info** The annual publication of The Robert Burns World Federation, which prints historical articles about Scotland and Robert Burns, as well as previously unpublished fiction and poetry from Burns and his contemporaries. *The Burns Chronicle* publishes up to date articles and news from the Burns Club, and more contemporary fiction and poetry. Present circulation of 1,200. Byline is given. Accepts queries by mail and email.

**Non-fiction** Publishes Essays, Poetry, Interviews/Profiles, General interest and Historical articles.

**Submission Guidelines** Send query before sending submissions.

**Fiction** Publishes Fiction.

**Tips** *The Burns Chronicle* generally prints articles and writing from Burns Federation members, but unsolicited submissions with new or ground breaking writing, or research on Robert Burns may be well received.

## Business Traveller

**Cardinal House, Albemarle Street, London, W1S 4TE**

📞 020 7647 6330

📞 020 7647 6331

✉ editorial@businesstraveller.com

🌐 www.businesstraveller.com

**Parent Company** Panacea Publishing International

**Editor** Tom Oley

**Established** 1976

**Insider Info** A monthly consumer magazine covering all aspects of business travel. Present circulation of 53,446. Accepts queries by mail.

**Non-fiction** Publishes features and articles on Business travel.

**Submission Guidelines** Accepts queries by post with published clips, plus CV.

**Images** State availability of photos with submission.

**Tips** Specialises in articles, features and news aimed at individual frequent, international business travellers. Submit ideas via post, but please ensure that the topic is firmly business travel only, rather than leisure.

## Cadenza

**Broadlea House, Heron Way, Hickling, Norfolk, NR12 0YQ**

✉ eds@cadenza-magazine.co.uk

🌐 www.cadenza-magazine.co.uk

**Editor** Zoe King

**Established** 2000

**Insider Info** A consumer magazine with two issues per year, focusing on poetry and short fiction. Payment is upon publication and a byline is given. Accepts queries by mail or email. Previously published submissions are accepted. Writer's guidelines are available online.

**Non-fiction** Publishes articles on poetry and all other aspects of creative writing.

**Submission Guidelines** Send complete manuscript of up to 2,000 words.

**Fiction** Publishes Mainstream and Experimental fiction.

**Submission Guidelines** Send complete manuscript pf up to 3,000 words.

**Poetry** Publishes Avant-garde, Free verse, Light verse and Traditional poetry.

**Submission Guidelines** Accepts poems of up to 40 lines. Submit to Poetry Editor, William Conelly.

**Tips** *Cadenza* is an independent literary magazine that publishes new poetry and short fiction, articles, interviews with published authors, and market information for fiction and poetry writers. It is looking for fiction writers with unique voices to produce 'crackling, vibrant work' and those who are prepared to take some risks with their writing. For poetry, *Cadenza* has in-depth submissions guidelines on their website.

## Caduceus

**9 Nine Acres, Midhurst, West Sussex, GU29 9EP**

- 01730 816799
- 01730 816799
- caduceus@caduceus.info
- www.caduceus.info

**Editor** Sarida Brown

**Established** 1987

**Insider Info** A quarterly consumer journal covering Health and Healing, Holistic Medicine, Ecology, Science and Spirituality.

**Non-fiction** Publishes Photo feature, Inspirational, Feature, Technical and General interest articles.

**Tips** *Caduceus* is an independent journal, which investigates 'critical issues ahead of mainstream media, searches out pioneers who are lighting the way for humanity, and keeps readers up to date with developments worldwide.' Tends to publish articles from academics and experienced workers from the healing and spirituality community.

## Caduta Arts Review

**23 Southgate Road, Tenterden, Kent, TN30 7BS**

- caduta@hotmail.co.uk
- www.caduta.co.uk

**Established** 2006

**Insider Info** A consumer magazine with three issues per year, covering arts subjects such as photography, painting, poetry, prose, and drama. Byline is given. Queries accepted by mail or email. Writer's guidelines are available online.

**Non-fiction** Publishes Photo feature, Poetry, and Feature articles.
 Send complete manuscript.

**Fiction** Publishes Mainstream Short fiction.

**Submission Guidelines** Send complete manuscript of up to ten pages.

**Poetry** Publishes Avant-garde, Free verse, Light verse and Traditional poetry.

**Submission Guidelines** Accepts up to six sample poems.

**Tips** A new magazine that aims to promote new and diverse talent in the arts. Accepts submissions from a wide range of arts categories, which will be published on the website as competition entries. The best selected pieces will then be printed in the magazine. Caduta does not pay for work, but offers a prize of £50 for the best selected entry.

## Cambridgeshire Agenda

**Alexander House, 1 Milton Road, Cambridge, CB4 1UY**

- 01223 309227
- 01223 309226
- editorial@thecambridgeagenda.co.uk
- www.thecambridgeagenda.co.uk

**Parent Company** Life Publishing Ltd

**Editor** Justin Coleman

**Contact** Associate Publisher, Claire Curran

**Insider Info** A monthly consumer magazine covering lifestyle topics in the Cambridgeshire area. Present circulation of 50,000. 100 per cent of the publication is written by freelance writers. Manuscripts are published four weeks after acceptance. Payment is upon acceptance. Byline given and publication is copyrighted. Editorial lead time is two months and seasonal material must be submitted two months in advance. Accepts queries by mail or email.

**Non-fiction** Publishes Beauty/Health, Fashion, Travel, Interiors and Arts features.

**Tips** All topics must be related to the Cambridgeshire area and be relevant to its residents.

## Campaign

**22 Bute Gardens, London, W6 7HN**

- campaign@haynet.com/Francesca.newland@haynet.com
- www.brandrepublic.com/campaign

**Parent Company** Haymarket Publishing

**Editor** Francesca Newland

**Established** 1968

**Insider Info** A weekly trade magazine covering the world of advertising. Present circulation of 10,309. Accepts queries by mail or email. Editorial calendar is available online.

**Non-fiction** Publishes Feature articles.

**Submission Guidelines** Accepts queries for articles of up to 2,000 words.

**Fillers** Uses newsbreaks of up to 320 words.

**Tips** Aimed at media moguls and advertising addicts, which makes it a good way to influence key opinion formers. Articles featuring insider knowledge and the latest scoops are ideal, but propose ideas in writing first, as *Campaign* is not keen on unsolicited submissions.

## Candelabrum Poetry Magazine

**1 Chatsworth Court, Outram Road, Southsea, PO5 1RA**

- rcp@poetry7.fsnet.co.uk
- www.members.tripod.com/redcandlepress

**Parent Company** Red Candle Press

**Editor** Len McCarthy

**Established** 1970

**Insider Info** A consumer poetry magazine with two issues per year. Present circulation of 900. Byline is given.

**Non-fiction** Publishes articles and features on poetry.

**Submission Guidelines** Accepts queries.

**Poetry** Publishes Haiku and Traditional poetry.

**Tips** Interested primarily in formalist poetry with traditional metrical and rhymed forms. The magazine prints articles and poems from new and established formalist poets. While *Candelabrum* specialises in formalist poetry, it doesn't disregard free verse or other forms, although they are less likely to be successful if they are submitted.

## The Cannon's Mouth

**22 Margaret Grove, Harborne, Birmingham, B17 9JH**

❶ 0121 426 6413

✉ greg@cannonpoets.co.uk

🌐 www.cannonpoets.co.uk

**Parent Company** Cannon Poets Group

**Editor** Greg Cox

**Established** 1983

**Insider Info** The quarterly journal of the Cannon Poets group. Prints new poetry and articles from subscribers and non-subscribers alike, and aims to stimulate interest in the writing of poetry and its presentation to the public. Byline is given. Queries accepted by mail and email.

**Non-fiction** Publishes Poetry and Features.

**Submission Guidelines** Send query before sending submissions.

**Poetry** Publishes Free verse, Light verse and Traditional verse.

**Tips** Cannon's Mouth now accepts submissions from non-subscribers, but the standard of poetry printed may vary, as the journal focuses on improving writing in progress through peer assessment.

## Carillon

**19 Godric Drive, Brinsworth, Rotherham, South Yorkshire, S60 5AN**

✉ editor@carillonmag.org.uk

🌐 www.carillonmag.org.uk

**Editor** Graham Rippon

**Established** 2001

**Insider Info** A consumer magazine with three issues per year (February, June, October), covering poetry, prose and literary topics. Present circulation is 100. Manuscripts are published three months after acceptance. Payment is upon publication, with contributor copies for non-subscribers instead of cash. Byline is given. Accepts queries by mail or email. Aims to respond to queries and manuscripts within two weeks. Writer's guidelines are available online.

**Non-fiction** Publishes Articles on poetry, Features and Reviews.

 * Pays between £1 and £3 for unsolicited articles (with contributor copies for non-subscribers).

**Submission Guidelines** Accepts queries.

**Fiction** Publishes Mainstream, Short fiction.

 * Pays between £1 and £3 for unsolicited articles (with contributor copies for non-subscribers).

**Submission Guidelines** Send complete manuscript of up to 1,200 words. Does not accept 'bad' language, pornography, anything socially or culturally offensive, clichéd writing or overtly political texts.

**Poetry** Publishes Free verse, Light verse and Traditional poetry.

 * Pays between £1 and £2 per poem (with contributor copies for non-subscribers).

**Submission Guidelines** Accepts poetry of up to 40 lines.

**Tips** *Carillon* magazine publishes new poetry and prose from contributors across the world, and also contains book reviews, articles on writing and reader competitions. It is an eclectic magazine and publishes newcomers and 'old hands' in both traditional and modern forms. They prefer hard copies, and will give preference to subscriber submissions.

## Carousel

 The Guide to Children's Books

**The Saturn Centre, 54–76 Bissell Street, Birmingham, B5 7HX**

❶ 0121 622 7458

❶ 0121 666 7526

✉ carousel.guide@virgin.net

🌐 www.carouselguide.co.uk

**Editor** Jenny Blanch

**Established** 1995

**Insider Info** A consumer magazine with three issues per year (March, June, October) covering children's books and stories. Present circulation of 10,000. Accepts queries by mail or email. Sample copy is available online.

**Non-fiction** Publishes Features, Interviews/Profiles, Reviews, and Opinion (not letters to the Editor).

**Tips** *Carousel* is a critical guide to the latest children's books and stories. It has a good reputation in the literary market, as a publication that offers serious and non-condescending criticism of children's books. Be aware its articles are aimed at adults, teachers and parents, rather than at children.

## Cauldron

**10 Glyn Road, Wallasey, Wirral, Merseyside, CH44 1AB**

☎ 07900 966061

☎ 0151 200 9042

✉ terence.grogan50@ntlworld.com

🌐 www.thenewcauldron.co.uk

**Editor** Terence Grogan

**Established** 1989

**Insider Info** A quarterly small press subscription magazine covering all genres of literature such as creative prose, poetry, and esoteric articles. Present circulation of 5,000. Approximately 70 per cent of the publication is written by freelance writers. Manuscripts are published six months after acceptance. Payment is upon publication, never with contributor copies in lieu of cash, with a kill fee of ten per cent for unpublished articles. Byline is sometimes given. The publication is copyrighted and first UK serial rights are purchased. Editorial lead time is three months and seasonal material should be submitted six months in advance. Accepts queries by mail, email, fax or phone. Simultaneous submissions are accepted. Aims to respond to queries within three weeks and manuscripts within six to eight weeks. Will not pay the expenses of writers on assignments. Sample copies are available for £22.50 (yearly subscription). Writer's guidelines are free on request; send a large SAE and four first class stamps.

**Non-fiction** Publish How-to, Essays, Humour, Poetry, Inspirational, Features, Reviews, Technical, General interest, Travel, Historical/Nostalgic and Personal experience articles.

**Submission Guidelines** Send complete manuscript of between 1,000 and 1,200 words. Manuscripts should be typed. Never send the original.

**Fiction** Publish Adventure, Historical, Romance, Horror, Science Fiction, Confession, Humourous, Mainstream, Slice of life vignettes, Mystery, Suspense, Western and Fantasy fiction.

**Submission Guidelines** Send complete manuscript of between 1,200 and 1,500 words.

**Poetry** Publish Avant-garde, Free verse, Haiku, Light verse and Traditional poetry.

**Submission Guidelines** Submit up to three poems, of between 12 and 30 lines.

**Fillers** Uses Anecdotes, Facts, Short humour and 'Strange but true' stories as fillers.

**Tips** Cauldron accommodates established authors, whilst seeking to provide a veritable publishing platform for fledgling writers of obvious potential as well. Before submitting a manuscript, contact the Editor via post or email, giving a brief CV and outline of work.

## Cencrastus

**Unit 1, Abbeymount Techbase, 2 Easter Road, Abbeymount, Edinburgh, EH8 8EJ**

☎ 0131 661 5687

✉ cencrastus1@hotmail.com

**Editor** Raymond Ross

**Established** 1979

**Insider Info** A consumer literary magazine covering Scottish literary topics. Present circulation of 2,000. Accepts queries by mail or email.

**Non-fiction** Publishes Essays, Poetry Articles, Features and Reviews on Scottish literature.

**Submission Guidelines** Accepts queries.

**Fiction** Publishes Scottish short fiction.

**Poetry** Publishes Scottish poetry.

**Tips** Cencrastus is a Scottish literary magazine that publishes new poetry and short fiction, articles and literary criticism, as well as line illustrations. Although it focuses on Scottish literature and arts, the magazine will also accept international submissions.

## CFUK

**105b Fidlas Road, Cardiff, CF14 0LY**

☎ 07786 988836

✉ cfuk@hotmail.co.uk

**Editor** Dylan Moore

**Insider Info** A quarterly consumer magazine covering prose, poetry and other literature. Byline is given. Accepts queries by mail and email.

**Non-fiction** Publishes Poetry and Features articles.

**Submission Guidelines** Accepts queries.

**Fiction** Publishes Mainstream fiction.

**Submission Guidelines** Send complete manuscript of up to 3,000 words.

**Poetry** Publishes Free verse and Traditional poetry.

**Tips** CFUK's aim is to provide an exciting an independent outlet for writers in Cardiff, Wales and beyond. It publishes prose, poetry and articles relating to writing. It will sometimes consider well-written articles not directly related to writing, but which are related to Cardiff or events in Cardiff.

## Chapman

Scotland's Quality Literary Magazine

**4 Broughton Place, Edinburgh, EH1 3RX**

☎ 0131 557 2207

✉ chapman-pub@blueyonder.co.uk

www.chapman-pub.co.uk

**Parent Company** Chapman Publishing Ltd.

**Editor** Joy Hendry

**Established** 1970

**Insider Info** A consumer magazine with three issues per year (April, August, December) covering the best in Scottish and international writing. Present circulation of 2,000. 95 per cent of the publication is written by freelance writers. Manuscripts are published 12 months after acceptance. Payment is upon publication and may be by contributor copies instead of cash, if the writer prefers. Byline is given. Publication is copyrighted and the magazine purchases first UK serial rights. Editorial lead time is six months. Seasonal material should be submitted six months in advance. Accepts queries by mail, email or phone. Aims to respond to queries within five days and manuscripts within three months. Does not pay the expenses of writers on assignment. A sample copy is available for £6.50 (£5.50 with SAE and four first class stamps). Writer's guidelines are free on request, send SAE with two first class stamps, or by email.

**Non-fiction** Publishes articles on Poetry, and Literary/Cultural criticism.

\* Payment for articles is by negotiation.

**Submission Guidelines** Accepts query with outline. No reprints.

**Fiction** Publishes short stories.

\* Buys 40 fiction manuscripts from writers per year. Payment is by negotiation.

**Submission Guidelines** Accepts articles of up to 5,000 words. Anything longer than 5,000 words is unlikely to be accepted. No more than two short stories per submission. Please enclose SAE for reply.

**Poetry** Publishes Avant-garde, Free verse, Haiku, Light verse and Traditional poetry.

\* Buys 500 poems per year.

**Submission Guidelines** Submit up to ten sample poems. Please enclose SAE for a reply.

**Images** Accepts images with submission.

\* Pays a varied fee per photo. Purchases one-time rights.

**Submission Guidelines** Accepts photocopies and transparencies sized 6 x 4 inches. Also accepts gif/jpeg files with captions. State availability of photos with submission.

**Tips** *Chapman* publishes the best in Scottish and international writing – new work by both well-known and new writers, and readable, enlightening critical discussion. They promote energetic ideas and approaches, always with an eye to the future. While their central commitment is to Scottish literature, *Chapman* is increasingly international, and writers the world over jostle to get into its pages. English, Scots and Gaelic appear in every issue, reflecting the linguistic diversity of Scotland. They do not accept any emailed or faxed submissions.

## Chimera

**118 Nayland Road, Mile End, Colchester, C04 5ET**

01206 751887

prose@chimeramagazine.co.uk

www.chimeramagazine.co.uk

**Contact** Poetry Editor, Robert Cole; Prose Editor, Susie Reynolds

**Established** 2004

**Insider Info** A consumer magazine with two issues per year covering new prose and poetry. Byline is given. Accepts queries by mail or email. Writer's guidelines available online.

**Non-fiction** Publishes articles on poetry and literature.

**Submission Guidelines** Accepts queries.

**Fiction** Publishes Short fiction.

\* Payment via contributor copy.

**Submission Guidelines** Send complete manuscript of up to 1,500 words.

**Poetry** Publishes Avant-garde, Free verse and Light verse poetry.

\* Payment via contributor copy.

**Tips** An award-winning small press magazine, which publishes well-written contemporary prose and poetry from both new and established writers. Chimera is open to submissions from any writer, either local or international, and often has a theme for the forthcoming issues. Check the website for further details.

## Choice

**First Floor 2 King Street, 2 King Street, Peterborouogh, PE1 1LT**

01733 555123

01733 427500

editorial@choicemag.co.uk

**Editor** Norman Wright

**Contact** Editorial Assistant, Kim Rule

**Insider Info** A monthly consumer magazine covering all aspects of retirement and retired life. Editorial lead time is eight weeks. Seasonal material should be submitted three months in advance. Accepts queries by mail, email or phone. Sample copy available for £2.70.

**Non-fiction** Publishes How-to, Interviews/Profiles, New Product, General interest, Travel and Historical/Nostalgic articles on retirement issues.

**Tips** Aimed at a readership aged over fifty.

## Church Music Quarterly

**19 The Close, Salisbury, Wiltshire, SP1 2EB**
- 01722 424848
- 01722 424849
- cmq@rscm.com
- www.rscm.com/publications/cmq.php

**Parent Company** The Royal School of Church Music
**Editor** Esther Jones
**Contact** Reviews Editor, Julian Elloway
**Established** 1977
**Insider Info** A quarterly consumer magazine covering all aspects of church music. Present circulation of 15,500. Accepts queries by email. Writer's guidelines are free on request and available via email.

**Non-fiction** Publishes Religious, Interviews/Profile, Review and General interest articles.
  * Payment for assigned articles is £60 per page (maximum).

**Submission Guidelines** Accepts queries with published clips, for articles of up to 1,400 words.
**Tips** Available exclusively to members of the RSCM, *Church Music Quarterly* offers a wide range of articles and interviews by distinguished musicians, theologians and scholars, and provides expert advice, information and inspiration for readers. Any reports, press releases, letters, classified advertisements or reviews should be sent to the Editor at least two months before publication. CMQ does not pay for unsolicited articles, only for commissioned ones.

## Church Times

**33 Upper Street, London, N1 0PN**
- 020 7359 4570
- 020 7226 3051
- news@churchtimes.co.uk/features@churchtimes.co.uk
- www.churchtimes.co.uk

**Parent Company** GJ Palmer & Sons
**Editor** Paul Handley
**Contact** News Editor, Helen Saxbee
**Established** 1863
**Insider Info** A weekly specialist religious newspaper. Present circulation of 29,000. 40 per cent of the publication is written by freelance writers. Payment is upon publication, never with contributor copies instead of cash. Byline is given. Rights are purchased by negotiation. Editorial lead time is two months. Seasonal material should be submitted six months in advance. Queries accepted by mail, email, fax, or phone. Will pay the expenses of writers on assignment. Sample copy is free on request. For an editorial calendar, request an advertising features list by email. Writer's guidelines available by email to: features@churchtimes.co.uk

**Non-fiction** Publishes Book excerpts, Photo features, Essays, Poetry, Exposé, Religious, Feature, Interviews/Profile, Travel, Historical/Nostalgic articles, as well as a travel supplement.
  * Pays between £10–£15 per 100 words for unsolicited and assigned articles.

**Submission Guidelines** Accepts query with published clips, for articles of between 1,200 and 2,000 words. Contact Allison Ward, Books Editor.
**Fiction** Publishes religious fiction.
**Submission Guidelines** Contact Books Editor, Allison Ward.
**Columns** Publishes eight columns per week.
**Submission Guidelines** Accepts query with published clips. Contact Comment Editor, Rachel Boulding.
**Tips** The *Church Times* (CT) is the UK's bestselling independent religious newspaper. It serves a largely Anglican readership and covers UK and international news, lifestyle features, faith and devotional pages, comment, books, arts, media, news from diocese and worldwide church. For features pages, it is best for a writer to write the piece first and send it on speculative basis. If CT would like to use the piece, they will inform the writer. After that it is easier to get commissioned. CT would never commission an unknown writer.

## Citizen32

**PO Box 219, Manchester, M23 9XZ**
- editor@citizen32.co.uk
- www.citizen32.co.uk

**Editor** John G.Hall
**Contact** Co-Editor, Dave Toomer
**Insider Info** A consumer literary magazine with three issues per year, covering poetry and prose. Byline is given. Accepts queries by mail or email.
**Non-fiction** Publishes articles on Poetry, Features, Interviews/Profiles, Reviews and Opinion (not letters to Editor).
**Submission Guidelines** Accepts queries.
**Fiction** Publishes Mainstream fiction.
**Poetry** Publishes Avant-garde, Free verse and Light verse poetry.
**Tips** *Citizen32* is a politically charged literary magazine that publishes contemporary poetry and prose from new and established writers, plus articles, reviews and interviews with popular authors. The magazine has a different theme for every issue, and often uses a Guest Editor, so prospective contributors must bear this in mind when

submitting. Check the website for the current theme.

## Classic & Sports Car
**Teddington Studios, Broom Road, Teddington, Middlesex, TW11 9BE**

- 020 8267 5307
- 020 8267 5318
- james.elliott@haymarket.com
- www.classicandsportscar.com

**Parent Company** Haymarket Publishing
**Editor** James Elliott
**Established** 1982
**Insider Info** A monthly consumer magazine, covering motoring and car related topics. Present circulation of 80,041. Accepts queries by email.
**Non-fiction** Publishes Photo features and Features.
 * Pays £250 per 1,000 words for unsolicited articles.
**Submission Guidelines** Send complete manuscript
**Fillers** Uses Newsbreaks.

**Tips** *Classic & Sports Car* is the market leading magazine for enthusiasts who wish to buy, maintain, restore or dream about classic cars. It combines authoritative and entertaining coverage of all types of classic cars from around the globe with unrivalled photography. When submitting feature ideas be patient as hundreds of unsolicited material is received monthly.

## The Classical Review
**The Edinburgh Building, Shaftesbury Road, Cambridge, CB2 2RU**

- 01223 326070
- 01223 325150
- journals@cambridge.org
- www.journals.cambridge.org

**Parent Company** Cambridge University Press
**Editor** Neil Hopkinson
**Established** 1886
**Insider Info** An academic journal that publishes scholarly articles on the classical civilisations, twice yearly. Present circulation is 1,800. Byline is given. Queries accepted by mail and email.
**Non-fiction** Publishes Essays, Features and Historical articles.
 * Purchases 150 manuscripts per year from freelance writers.
**Submission Guidelines** Send query before sending submissions.
**Tips** *The Classical Review* only publishes articles from leading scholars in the Classical field.

## Classic Stitches Magazine
**80 Kingsway East, Dundee, DD4 8SL**

- editorial@classicstitches.com
- www.classicstitches.com

**Parent Company** D C Thomson & Co. Ltd
**Editor** Bea Neilson
**Contact** Emil Pacholek
**Established** 1994
**Insider Info** A bi-monthly specialist hobby magazine that also appears online, covering embroidery and needlecrafts. Present circulation of 11,000. 60 per cent of the publication is written by freelance writers. Payment is upon acceptance with no kill fees. Payment is never made with contributor copies instead of cash. Byline is given. Publication is copyrighted and all rights are purchased. Editorial lead time is three months. Seasonal materials should be submitted six months in advance. Accepts queries by mail, email, fax or phone. Simultaneous submissions are accepted. Aims to respond to queries within two weeks and manuscripts within four weeks. Sometimes pays the expenses of writers on assignment (limit agreed upon in advance). Sample copy and writer's guidelines are free on request. Although they are seasonal, they do not have a calendar as such.
**Non-fiction** Publishes Book excerpts (usually stitching books), How-to (detailed stitching techniques), Features (stitching, embroidery related), Interviews/Profiles, (stitching and embroidery related) and Technical (stitching and embroidery related) articles.
 * Purchases 40 non-fiction manuscripts per year. Payment is by negotiation for assigned and unsolicited articles.
**Submission Guidelines** Accepts query with published clips for articles or between 800 and 2,000 words. No reprints. Contact Bea Neilson, Editor.
**Images** Accepts images with submission.
 * Negotiates payment individually for images. Purchases all rights.
**Submission Guidelines** Accepts contact sheets, negatives, prints and transparencies of various sizes and gif/jpeg files. Identification of subjects is required. State availability of photos with submission. Contact Sub Editor, Susan Kydd.
**Tips** The magazine is aimed at stitchers who want to explore new media and experiment. Features tend to be about designers and embroidery related exhibitions. Study the magazine and the website, it is really the only way to get to know what the magazine requires from an article.

## Closer

**Endeavour House, Shaftesbury Avenue, London, WC2H 8JG**

- 020 7437 9011
- 020 7437 8600
- closer@emap.com, firstname.lastname@ emap.com
- www.emap.com, www.closerdiets.com

**Parent Company** EMAP Plc

**Contact** Features Editor, Mel Fallowfield; Editorial Assistant, Emily Merritt

**Established** 2002

**Insider Info** A weekly consumer magazine covering women's lifestyle topics. Present circulation of 614,141.

**Non-fiction** Publishes General interest, Expose, Interviews, Reviews and Photo features on Celebrities, Fashion, Beauty, Music, Television, Film and Real-life.

**Tips** The magazine is aimed at women aged 25 to 35.

## CNN Traveller

**141–143 Shoreditch High Street, London, E1 6JE**

- 01444 475659
- dan.hayes@ink-publishing.com
- www.cnntraveller.com

**Parent Company** Ink Publishing

**Editor** Dan Hayes

**Established** 1998

**Insider Info** A bi-monthly consumer magazine covering travel journalism and holidays. Present circulation of 106,000. 50 per cent of the publication is written by freelance writers. Manuscripts are published three months after acceptance. Offers a 50 per cent kill fee for unpublished articles. Byline is given. Publication is copyrighted and all rights are purchased. Editorial lead time is six months. Seasonal material should be submitted four months in advance. Queries will be accepted by mail and fax. Will not pay the expenses of writers on assignment. Sample copy available online. Writer's guidelines are free on request.

**Non-fiction** Publishes Book excerpts and Travel articles.

 * Buys 50 non-fiction manuscripts per year.

**Submission Guidelines** Accepts queries with outline and published clips, for articles between 600 and 2,000 words.

**Images** Accepts images with submission.

 * Negotiates payment individually for images. Purchases one-time rights.

**Submission Guidelines** Accepts gif/jpeg files with captions. State availability of photos with submission.

**Columns** Purchases ten columns per year.

 * Pays between £100 and £200 per column.

**Submission Guidelines** Accepts queries with outline and published clips.

**Tips** *CNN Traveller* takes readers on a fascinating journey to some of the most intriguing and exotic places in the world, it aims to marry the best in travel journalism and photography, with the news values of CNN. The magazines takes an issues led view of travel, getting behind the headlines with articles that are guaranteed to be intriguing and thought provoking. The magazine considers work by published, professional photographers and journalists. In the first instance, email a brief synopsis of about 150 words to the Editor, giving an overview of your proposed article. Features should have a solid news, or issue led angle.

## The Coffee House

**31 Granby Street, Loughborough, Leicestershire, LE11 3DU**

- 01509 822558
- 01509 822559
- info@charnwood-arts.org.uk
- www.charnwoodarts.com

**Parent Company** Charnwood Arts

**Editor** Deborah Tyler-Bennett

**Established** 1998

**Insider Info** A poetry, prose and visual art magazine published twice yearly. Present circulation is 300. Publication is copyrighted and a byline is given. Queries accepted by mail and email.

**Non-fiction** Publishes Features and Reviews.

**Fiction** Publishes Mainstream fiction and Short stories.

**Submission Guidelines** Send complete manuscript. Articles must be 2,500 words.

**Poetry** Publishes Avant-garde poetry, Free verse, Haiku, Light verse and Traditional verse.

**Tips** *The Coffee House* serves as a literary meeting place for writers and artists of all types, and prints new poetry, prose and art from local, national and international artists. *The Coffee House* was founded primarily to serve the local arts and literature scene in Charnwood, but has outlets in New York and across the UK, and will consider submissions from further afield and even abroad. Accepts submissions of any kind of writing from ghost stories, to sonnets and villanelles.

## Coffee House Poetry

**Meirion House, Tanygrisiau, Blaenau Ffestiniog, Gwynedd, LL41 3SU**

☎ 01766 832112

✉ jan@coffeehousepoetry.co.uk

🌐 www.coffeehousepoetry.co.uk

**Parent Company** Cinnamon Press

**Editor** Jan Fortune-Wood

**Established** 2003

**Insider Info** A consumer poetry journal with three issues per year (January, May, September). Byline is given. Accepts queries by mail or email. Aims to respond to queries and manuscripts within six weeks. Writer's guidelines are available online.

**Poetry** Publishes Avant-garde, Free verse, Haiku, Light verse and Traditional poetry.

**Submission Guidelines** Accepts up to six poems, each up to 40 lines.

**Tips** A literary journal for quality contemporary poetry, which aims to provide a platform for innovative new work that has 'edge and depth'. Welcomes poetry submissions in any style, and also runs an annual competition with cash prizes, where the prize winners will also receive publication in the magazine.

## Company

**National Magazine House, 72 Broadwick Street, London, W1F 9EP**

☎ 020 7439 5000

☎ 020 7312 3797

✉ company.mail@natmags.co.uk

🌐 www.company.co.uk

**Parent Company** National Magazine Company Ltd

**Editor** Victoria White

**Contact** Features Editor, Claire Askew

**Established** 1978

**Insider Info** A monthly consumer magazine covering women's lifestyle topics. Present circulation of 264,095.

**Non-fiction** Publishes General interest, Interviews, Reviews and Photo features on Celebrities, Fashion, Beauty, Music, Television, Film and Real-life.

**Tips** The magazine is aimed at young, working women and articles must reflect this.

## CompassSport

**Glenmore House, 6 Glenmore Park, Tunbridge Wells, Kent, TN2 5NZ**

☎ 07720 952241

✉ nick@compasssport.co.uk

🌐 www.compasssport.co.uk

**Editor** Nick Barrable

**Established** 1979

**Insider Info** A bi-monthly national sports magazine covering the sport of orienteering. Present circulation of 1,600. 50 per cent of the publication is written by freelance writers. Manuscripts are published two weeks after acceptance. Contributors are not paid, although some may receive a free copy of the magazine. Byline is given. Publication is copyrighted. Editorial lead time is four weeks. Seasonal material should be submitted six weeks in advance. Accepts queries by mail, email or phone. Aims to respond to queries within one week and manuscripts within two weeks. Will not pay the expenses of writers on assignment. Sample copy available for £2. Writer's guidelines and editorial calendars available via email.

**Non-fiction** Publish features on Orienteering.

**Submission Guidelines** Send manuscripts by email.

**Images** Publish photographs and maps.

**Submission Guidelines** Email photographs or maps as digital files.

**Tips** A niche magazine for orienteering, which covers foot/trail/ski/MTBO and radio topics.

## Competitions Bulletin

**17 Greenhow Avenue, West Kirby, Wirral, Cheshire, CH48 5EL**

✉ carolebaldock@hotmail.com

**Editor** Carole Baldock

**Established** 1999

**Insider Info** A bi-monthly consumer bulletin covering news and information on literary competitions. Present circulation of 500.

**Tips** *Competitions Bulletin* provides details and other information about UK and international writing competitions. It is purely an information service for writing competitions, and does not publish articles of writing.

## Computer Arts

**30 Monmouth Street, Bath, BA1 2BW**

☎ 01225 442244

☎ 01225 732295

✉ ca.mail@futurenet.co.uk

🌐 www.computerarts.co.uk

**Parent Company** Future Publishing

**Editor** Garrick Webster

**Established** 1995

**Insider Info** A monthly consumer magazine covering computer computers and digital arts subjects. Present circulation of 19,758.

**Non-fiction** Publishes How-to, Features, Reviews, New Product and Technical articles.
**Submission Guidelines** No unsolicited manuscripts. Queries only.
**Tips** Computer Arts is the one stop shop for professional advice on creating digital art and illustrations. They won't accept unsolicited manuscripts, so approach by post or email first. Practical tips and tutorials for unusual techniques, or similar, are most useful.

## Cosmopolitan

**National Magazine House, 72 Broadwick Street, London, W1F 9EP**
- 020 7439 5000
- 020 7439 5232
- info@cosmopolitan.co.uk
- www.cosmopolitan.co.uk

**Parent Company** The National Magazine Company
**Editor** Louise Court
**Contact** Features Editor, Catherine Gray
**Established** 1886
**Insider Info** A monthly consumer magazine covering women's lifestyle and fashion topics. Present circulation of 44,2384.
**Non-fiction** Publishes Photo feature, Exposé, Features, Interviews/Profile and General interest articles.
**Tips** *Cosmopolitan* has traditionally been a women's magazine discussing such topics as sex, health, fitness and fashion. Recently the magazine is sharing their focus with men's issues as well. "Cosmo for your guy" is featured in every issue with exclusive advice for men. *Cosmopolitan* also recruit men as a part of their staff, to answer their female reader's burning questions. The magazine is always on the lookout for new writers with original and relevant ideas, and a strong voice.

## Country Homes & Interiors

**King's Reach Tower, Stamford Street, London, SE1 9LS**
- 020 7261 6434
- rhoda_parry@ipcmedia.com
- www.countryhomesandinteriors.co.uk

**Parent Company** IPC Media
**Editor** Rhoda Parry
**Contact** Features Editor, Jean Carr
**Established** 1986
**Insider Info** A monthly consumer magazine aimed at women, and covering countryside house and home topics. Present circulation of 77,771. Accepts queries by mail.

**Non-fiction** Publishes Photo features, Features and Interviews/Profiles.
 * Pays up to £250 per 1,000 words for unsolicited articles.
**Submission Guidelines** Accepts queries for articles of up to 1,200 words.
**Tips** *Country Homes & Interiors* magazine shows readers how to buy, decorate and enjoy their dream country home. They seek features on country style properties, or interviews of relevance to the target readership.

## Country Life

**King's Reach Tower, Stamford Street, London, SE1 9LS**
- 020 7261 6121
- mark_hedges@ipcmedia.com
- www.countrylife.co.uk

**Parent Company** IPC Media
**Editor** Mark Hedges
**Established** 1897
**Insider Info** A weekly consumer magazine covering countryside topics. Present circulation of 40,205.
**Non-fiction** Publishes Photo features, Features, Interviews/Profiles and General interest articles.
**Submission Guidelines** Accepts queries for articles of between 1,000 and 1,300 words.
**Tips** *Country Life* covers the pleasures and joys of rural life, as well as the concerns of rural people. It is primarily concerned with the lifestyle and concerns of landowners and other rich country dwellers, but it has many readers who do not belong to those categories. Unsolicited material is rarely accepted. The magazine seeks strong informed material, rather than amateur enthusiasm.

## The Countryman

**The Water Mill, Broughton Hall, Skipton, BD23 3AG**
- 01756 701381
- 01756 701326
- editorial@thecountryman.co.uk
- www.countrymanmagazine.co.uk

**Parent Company** Country Publications Ltd
**Editor** Bill Taylor
**Contact** Managing Editor, Paul Jackson
**Established** 1927
**Insider Info** A monthly consumer magazine covering countryside and rural issues. Present circulation of 22,793. Accepts queries by email.
**Non-fiction** Publishes Photo features, Features, Interviews/Profiles and General interest articles.
 * Pays £70 per 1,000 words for unsolicited articles.

**Submission Guidelines** Accepts queries, or complete manuscripts for articles of up to 1,200 words.

**Images** Send images with submission.

**Tips** *The Countryman* is one of the oldest, most respected countryside magazines in the world. It is read by people throughout Britain and overseas, who share its concerns for the countryside, the people who live and work in it, and its wildlife. The magazine focuses on the rural issues of today, and tomorrow, as well as including features on the people, places, history and wildlife that make the British countryside so special. Articles supplied with good quality illustrations are far more likely to be accepted.

## Countryside Tales

**14 The Park, Stow On The Wold, Cheltenham, Gloucestershire, GL54 1DX**

📞 01451 831053
✉ sales@parkpublications.co.uk
🌐 www.parkpublications.co.uk

**Parent Company** Park Publications Ltd
**Editor** David Howath
**Established** 2000
**Insider Info** A quarterly consumer magazine covering literature with a countryside theme. Byline is given. Accepts queries by mail. Writers' guidelines available online.
**Non-fiction** Publishes articles on Poetry and Features.
 * Payment is via contributor copy (plus a credit voucher for subscription).
**Submission Guidelines** Accepts queries for articles of between 400 and 1,500 words.
**Fiction** Publishes Rural/Countryside fiction.
 * Payment is via contributor copy (plus a credit voucher for subscription).
**Submission Guidelines** Send complete manuscripts for stories of up to 2,000 words.
**Poetry** Publishes Avant-garde, Free verse, Light verse and Traditional poetry.
 * Payment is via contributor copy (plus a credit voucher for subscription).
**Submission Guidelines** Accepts poetry of up to 40 lines.
**Tips** In each issue, *Countryside Tales* offers cash prizes for the best selected stories in the categories of poetry, fiction, and non-fiction.

## Crime Time

**PO Box 394, Harpenden, AL5 1XJ**
📞 01582 761264

📞 01582 712244
✉ crimetime@blueyonder.co.uk
🌐 www.crimetime.co.uk

**Parent Company** Oldcastle Books Ltd
**Editor** Barry Forshaw
**Established** 1999
**Insider Info** A bi-monthly consumer magazine covering crime fiction topics. Accepts queries by mail or email.
**Non-fiction** Publishes Features, Interviews/Profiles, Reviews and General interest articles on Crime writing.
**Submission Guidelines** Accepts queries.
**Fiction** Publishes Mystery, Suspense and Crime fiction.
**Tips** *Crime Time* is a literary magazine that publishes crime fiction stories from new and established authors, as well as articles on crime writing, film and cinema, and book reviews. It mostly publishes articles, reviews and interviews from regular contributors, rather than occasional freelancers.

## Crimewave

**5 Martins Lane, Witcham, Ely, CB6 2LB**
✉ andy@ttapress.demon.co.uk
🌐 www.ttapress.com

**Parent Company** TTA Press
**Editor** Andy Cox
**Established** 1998
**Insider Info** A quarterly consumer magazine covering new crime writing. 100 per cent of the publication is written by freelance writers. A byline is given. Accepts queries by mail. Aims to respond to queries and manuscripts within two months. Writer's guidelines available online.
**Fiction** Publishes Mystery, Suspense, Experimental and Crime fiction.
**Submission Guidelines** Send complete manuscripts. Do not send any general fiction or non-crime fiction.
**Tips** *Crimewave's* mission is to totally re-create crime fiction. They aim to publish something entirely different to whatever people have read before. They hope to help people discover a new universe of fiction in which morality is real but fluid, the story is central but skewed, and the traditions of the genre are neither dumped nor subverted, but rather viewed through fresh eyes, from a new hill. The magazine is looking for outstanding modern stories of crime, mystery and suspense, as well as borderline material which uses genre elements in a new way. It is strongly recommended that you study at least one volume of *Crimewave* before submitting.

## Critical Quarterly

**School of English, University of Exeter, Queen's Building, The Queen's Drive, Exeter, Devon, EX4 4QH**

☎ 01392 264257

☎ 01392 264361

🌐 www.criticalquarterly.com

**Parent Company** Blackwell Publishing

**Editor** Colin MacCabe

**Contact** Managing Editor, Kate Mellor; Editorial Assistant, Kate Hext

**Established** 1959

**Insider Info** A quarterly consumer literary journal covering all aspects of the arts and literature. Byline is given. Accepts queries by mail or phone. Writer's guidelines available online.

**Non-fiction** Publishes Essays, Articles on Poetry, Features, Interviews/Profiles, Reviews and Opinion (not letters to Editor) on Arts subjects.

**Submission Guidelines** Send complete manuscripts.

**Fiction** Publishes some fiction.

**Tips** *Critical Quarterly* publishes informative and scholarly criticism on all aspects of cultural studies, including literature, the arts, media, film and cinema. The journal encourages articles from both new and international writers, as well as regular contributors. It is mostly scholarly in its approach and has a detailed style guide for submissions available through the Blackwell website. Contributors must ensure that any quotations or references are accurate.

## Curlew

**Hare Cottage, Kettlesing, Harrogate, HG3 2LB**

**Editor** Jocelyn Precious

**Established** 1975

**Insider Info** A consumer magazine, covering poetry subjects.

**Non-fiction** Publishes articles on Poetry.

**Submission Guidelines** Accepts queries.

**Fiction** Publishes some fiction.

**Poetry** Publishes Free verse, Light verse and Traditional poetry.

**Images** Publishes images to accompany articles.

**Tips** *Curlew* is a small independent poetry magazine that publishes poetry of all types, as well as some fiction and articles. It is often illustrated and will accept submissions of art and graphics for inclusion in the magazine.

## Current Accounts

**16–18 Mill Lane, Horwich, Bolton, Lancashire, BL6 6AT**

☎ 01204 669858

✉ bswscribe@aol.com

🌐 http://hometown.aol.co.uk/bswscribe/myhomepage/writing.html

**Editor** Rod Riesco

**Established** 1995

**Insider Info** A semiannual creative writing magazine, covering the literary interests of the Bank Street Writer's Group. Present circulation of 70. 100 per cent of the publication is written by freelance writers. Manuscripts are published four months after acceptance. Payment is one complimentary copy. Byline is given. Publication is not copyrighted, but one time rights are bought. Editorial lead time is six months. Accepts queries by mail, email or phone. Aims to respond to queries and manuscripts within two months. Sample copy available for £3. Writer's guidelines are free on request.

**Non-fiction** Publishes articles on Poetry, Features, Essays and Reviews.

**Fiction** Publishes Short fiction.

**Submission Guidelines** Accepts queries for fiction of up to 2,000 words. No gratuitously offensive language is accepted.

**Poetry** Publishes Free verse, Light verse and Traditional poetry.

**Submission Guidelines** Accepts up to six sample poems.

**Tips** Produced by Bank Street Writers and mostly features the work of members of the group, plus contributions from others worldwide. Prefers work from subscribers to the magazine. Poetry, fiction, reviews and essays are welcome.

## Cutting Teeth

**1–2, 15 Granville Street, Glasgow, G3 7EE**

✉ info@cuttingteeth.org

🌐 www.cuttingteeth.org

**Editor** Lynne Mackenzie

**Established** 1994

**Insider Info** A consumer literary magazine with two issues per year, covering new Scottish writing. Byline is given. Accepts queries by mail or email. Writer's guidelines available online.

**Non-fiction** Publishes Articles on Poetry and Features.

**Submission Guidelines** Accepts queries.

**Fiction** Publishes Short fiction.

**Submission Guidelines** Send complete manuscripts for fiction, of up to 2,500 words.

**Poetry** Publishes Avant-garde, Free verse and Light verse poetry.

**Submission Guidelines** Accepts up to six sample poems.

**Tips** *Cutting Teeth* is a small literary magazine dedicated to promoting new Scottish writing, either from established or new Scottish writers. It publishes both poetry and prose, as well as some articles, but only accepts submissions by post. Currently redeveloping their website, check back frequently for updates.

## Cycle Sport

**Leon House, 233 High Street, Croydon, CR9 1HZ**

- 020 8726 8461
- cyclesport@ipcmedia.com
- www.cyclesport.co.uk

**Parent Company** IPC Media

**Editor** Robert Garbutt

**Contact** Deputy Editor, Nigel Wynn

**Established** 1991

**Insider Info** A monthly consumer magazine covering cycle sports subjects. Present circulation of 21,198. Accepts queries by mail and email,

**Non-fiction** Publishes Photo features and Features.
  * Pays £120 per 1,000 words for unsolicited articles.

**Submission Guidelines** Send complete manuscripts for articles between 1,500 and 2,000 words.

**Images** Send photos with submission.

**Tips** Prints comprehensive coverage of the world's leading professional events, like the Tour de France. It also has big interviews and action photography. Will consider unsolicited manuscripts, but articles with accompanying illustrations are preferred.

## Cycling Weekly

**Leon House, 233 High Street, Croydon, CR9 1HZ**

- 020 8726 8461
- cycling@ipcmedia.com
- www.cyclingweekly.co.uk

**Parent Company** IPC Media

**Editor** Robert Garbutt

**Established** 1891

**Insider Info** A weekly consumer magazine covering cycling topics. Present circulation of 26,257. Accepts queries by mail.

**Non-fiction** Publishes Features, Interviews/Profiles, Reviews, and New Product articles.
  * Purchases 60 Non-fiction manuscripts per year. Pays between £60 and £120 per 1,000 words for unsolicited articles.

**Submission Guidelines** Accepts queries or complete manuscripts of up to 2,000 words.

**Fillers** Uses Newsbreaks of up to 300 words.
  * Pays a maximum of £15 per filler.

**Tips** Britain's bestselling cycling magazine covers an mix of fitness advice, bike tests, product reviews, news and ride guides for every cyclist, as well as unrivalled coverage of the national and international racing scene. Most work is commissioned privately, but they are interested in seeing unsolicited manuscripts and ideas. Writers with a strong technical knowledge, or a background in cycle sport will have an advantage.

## Cyphers

**3 Selskar Terrace, Ranelagh, Dublin 6, Republic of Ireland**

- 00353 1 497 8866
- www.cyphersmagazine.org

**Editor** Eilean Ní Chuilleanain

**Established** 1975

**Insider Info** A consumer literary magazine covering Irish writing. Accepts queries by mail or fax.

**Non-fiction** Publishes critical articles on poetry.

**Fiction** Publishes new Irish fiction.

**Poetry** Publishes Free verse, Light verse and Traditional Irish language poetry.

**Tips** *Cyphers* is Ireland's longest running literary magazine and publishes Irish poetry - in Irish and English - and poetry in translation, as well as some prose fiction and criticism and graphic art. The major focus however, remains on Irish poetry.

## Daemon

**2/R West Bank Quadrant, Glasgow, G12 8NT**

- 0141 334 0310
- 0141 586 3027
- dharma46@hotmail.com

**Parent Company** Survivors' Poetry Scotland

**Editor** Gerry Loose

**Insider Info** A bi-monthly consumer literary magazine focusing on Scottish poetry from the survivors of abuse of various kinds.

**Tips** *Daemon* will usually only publish work from within the Survivors' Poetry Scotland group.

## Dalesman

**The Water Mill, Broughton Hall, Skipton, BD23 3AG**

- 01756 701381
- 01756 701326
- editorial@dalesman.co.uk

www.dalesman.co.uk
**Parent Company** Country Publications Ltd
**Editor** Terry Fletcher
**Established** 1939
**Insider Info** A monthly consumer magazine covering countryside pursuits in Yorkshire. Present circulation of 43,375. Accepts queries by mail, email or phone.
**Non-fiction** Publishes Photo features, Features, Interviews/Profile and Historical/Nostalgic articles on Yorkshire.
**Submission Guidelines** Accepts queries for articles of between 1,000 and 1,500 words.
**Images** Send photos with submission.
**Tips** Each issue contains stories about the people and places that make Yorkshire unique, articles on history and nature and glorious colour photographs of the stunning Yorkshire scenery. Submissions must be of specific Yorkshire interest. It is the largest local interest magazine in UK.

## Dandelion Arts Magazine

**24 Frosty Hollow, East Hunsbury, Northamptonshire, NN4 OSY**
01604 701730
01604 701730
**Editor** Joaquina Gonzales-Marina
**Insider Info** A consumer literary and arts magazine.
**Non-fiction** Publishes articles on Poetry, Features and Interviews/Profiles on Arts topics.
**Submission Guidelines** Accepts queries.
**Fiction** Publishes Short stories.
**Poetry** Publishes Free verse and Traditional poetry.
**Tips** An international magazine of arts and writing, which publishes new poetry, short stories, articles and interviews. As an arts magazine it does not solely focus on writing. Will also consider submissions from abroad.

## The Dark Horse

**c/o 3–B Blantyre Mill Road, Bothwell, South Lanarkshire, G71 8DD**
01698 850410
gjctdh@freenetname.co.uk
www.star.ac.uk/darkhorse.html
**Editor** Gerry Cambridge
**Established** 1995
**Insider Info** An international literary magazine committed to British and American poetry, published in Scotland annually. Queries are accepted by mail and email. Aims to respond to

queries and manuscripts within ten weeks. Writer's guidelines are available online.
**Submission Guidelines** Submissions should include sufficient return postage or international reply coupons and SAE if contributors wish unused submissions to be returned. Prefers to respond by email to all work submitted, and to recycle unused typescripts. Unsolicited submissions by email are not accepted. Send hard copy only in the first instance.
**Poetry** Publishes Free verse and Traditional verse.
**Tips** We publish a mix of essays, reviews, and interviews and are proud of discovering new writers and poets.

## Dark Tales

**PO Box 681, Worcester, Worcestershire, WR3 8WB**
07913 837097
sean@darktales.co.uk
darktales.co.uk
**Editor** Sean Jeffery
**Established** 2003
**Insider Info** A consumer magazine publication, issued quarterly, covering Horror, Science Fiction, Speculative Fiction and Dark Fantasy short stories. Payment is upon publication. 100 per cent of the magazine is written by freelancers. Submissions are published approximately six months after acceptance. Publication is copyrighted, and a byline is given. Publishes first UK serial rights and electronic rights. Average lead time is three months. Seasonal material must be submitted three months in advance. Queries accepted by mail and email. Aims to respond to queries within one month and manuscripts within three months. Payment is via cash and a complimentary copy. Sample copy, a 'best of' issue, is available by post for £1.50. Manuscript guidelines are available online or by email.
**Fiction** Interested in Horror (Psychological horror preferred), Science Fiction, Dark Fantasy and Speculative Fiction.
  * Buys 48 fiction manuscripts per year. Payment is £2.50 per thousand words, plus one contributor copy.
**Tips** Dark Tales is looking for well-written, entertaining speculative fiction, horror and dark fantasy stories, with believable characters and page turning plot. Think of the work of authors such as Douglas Adams, Orson Scott Card, Stephen King, Dean Koontz and Michael Marshall Smith and you're somewhere along the right lines. There must be an emotional heart to a story, no matter how dark.

## The David Jones Journal

**48 Sylvan Way, Sketty, Swansea, SA2 9JB**

- 01792 206144
- 01792 205305
- anne.price-owen@sihe.ac.uk
- www.sihe.ac.uk/davidjones/

**Parent Company** The David Jones Society
**Editor** Anne Price-Owen
**Established** 1997
**Insider Info** The annual publication of The David Jones Society. Present circulation 400.
**Non-fiction** Publishes Poetry, Features, Interviews/Profiles, Reviews and News relating to David Jones the poet.
**Submission Guidelines** Send query before sending submissions.
**Fiction** Publishes Fiction.
**Tips** Submissions should relate to the painter/poet, David Jones, his life, work and themes.

## Decanter

**Broadway House, 2–6 Fulham Broadway, London, SW6 1AA**

- 020 7261 5000
- 020 7381 5282
- editor@decanter.com
- www.decanter.com

**Parent Company** IPC Media
**Editor** Guy Woodward
**Established** 1975
**Insider Info** A monthly consumer magazine covering the world of wine. Present circulation of 35,000.
**Non-fiction** Publishes Illustrated Features on wine.
  * Pays £230 per 1,000 words for unsolicited articles.
**Submission Guidelines** Accepts articles of between 1,000 and 1,800 words by hard copy.
**Tips** *Decanter* aims to be the 'wine bible'. As Britain's leading wine magazine, it is read by both experts and enthusiasts alike in over 90 countries. The readers appreciate the authoritative editorial mix of news, interviews with leading wine personalities, regional profiles and wine recommendations. The Editor does not like email submissions, so please send feature ideas via post or fax.

## Decanto

**PO Box 3257, Littlehampton, BN16 9AF**

- masque_pub@tiscali.co.uk
- myweb.tiscali.co.uk/masquepublishing/decanto.html

**Parent Company** Masque Publishing

**Editor** Lisa Stewart
**Established** 2002
**Insider Info** A bi-monthly consumer poetry magazine. Accepts queries by mail or email. Aims to respond to queries and manuscripts within six weeks. Writer's guidelines are available online.
**Poetry** Publishes Avant-garde, Free verse, Haiku, Light verse and Traditional poetry.
**Submission Guidelines** Accepts up to six sample poems.
**Tips** *Decanto* is an independent self-funded poetry magazine, which aims to offer poets the freedom to write in whatever style they wish. It includes new poetry from new and established writers, as well as articles on poetics and reviews. The magazine will accept any kind of poetry submission, but unfortunately, being entirely self-funded, cannot offer payment or contributor copies for accepted submissions.

## Delicious

**20 Upper Ground, London, SE1 9PD**

- 020 7775 7757
- 020 7775 7705
- info@deliciousmagazine.co.uk
- www.deliciousmagazine.co.uk

**Parent Company** Seven Publishing
**Editor** Matthew Drennan
**Established** 2003
**Insider Info** A monthly consumer magazine covering cookery and kitchen topics. Present circulation of 88,096. Accepts queries by email.
**Non-fiction** Publishes Recipes and Features on Food.
**Tips** Aims to appeal to food lovers with well packaged and unusual features and food ideas. Seeks recipes, either simple or sophisticated, as well as features on food and where it comes from.

## Devon Life

**Archant House, Babbage Road, Totnes, Devon, TQ9 5JA**

- 01803 860916
- 01803 860926
- devonlife@archant.co.uk
- www.devonlife.co.uk

**Parent Company** Archant Life
**Editor** Jan Barwick
**Established** 1996
**Insider Info** A monthly consumer magazine covering lifestyle topics in the county of Devon. Present circulation of 14,152. Accepts queries by mail or email. Sample copy available online. Writer's

guidelines are free on request. Media pack is available online.

**Non-fiction** Publishes Photo features, Features, Interviews/Profiles and General interest articles.

**Submission Guidelines** Accepts queries, with published clips, for articles between 600 and 2,000 words.

**Images** Accepts Transparencies. Send photos with submission.

**Tips** *Devon Life* includes photo features, articles, regional food and drink guides, property, and general regional interest. 'It is wise to submit a synopsis that indicates why the article would appeal to *Devon Life*. Include clips and your publishing history. You can attach the complete manuscript, but there is no guarantee it will be used.'

## Dial 174

**21 Mill Road, Watlington, Norfolk, PE33 0HH**
- 01533 811949
- apoet@globalnet.co.uk
**Editor** Josephine Hemmings
**Insider Info** A quarterly consumer literary magazine.
**Non-fiction** Publishes Articles on Poetry, Features and Reviews.
**Submission Guidelines** Accepts queries.
**Fiction** Publishes Short fiction.
**Poetry** Publishes a mixture of poetry.
**Tips** *Dial 174* publishes short stories and poetry, reviews, articles on writing, news and artwork. It also runs various writing competitions, where the winners can be published in the magazine.

## Digital Camera Magazine

**30 Monmouth Street, Bath, BA1 2BW**
- 01225 442244
- 01225 732295
- editor.dcm@futurenet.co.uk
- www.dcmag.co.uk
**Parent Company** Future Publishing
**Editor** Marcus Hawkins
**Insider Info** A consumer magazine with 13 issues per year, covering digital photography topics. Present circulation of 42,276.
**Non-fiction** Publishes Photo Features and Features.
**Submission Guidelines** Accepts queries.
**Tips** The magazine uses inspirational images, expert techniques and essential tips. It also keeps up to date with the latest cameras, accessories and software. Contact the Editor with feature ideas. Technical knowledge or practical experience is necessary.

## Diplo Magazine

**156–158 Gray's Inn Road, London, WC1X 8ED**
- 020 7833 9766
- charlesb@diplo-magazine.co.uk
- www.diplo-magazine.co.uk
**Editor** Mark Hudson
**Contact** Publisher, Charles Baker
**Established** 2004
**Insider Info** A monthly consumer magazine covering international current affairs. Present circulation of 25,000. 75 per cent of the publication is written by freelance writers. Manuscript is published 30 days after acceptance. Payment may be with a contributor copy rather than cash. A Byline is given. Publication is copyrighted and all rights are purchased. Editorial lead time is seven weeks. Seasonal material should be submitted eight weeks in advance. Accepts queries by mail, email, fax or phone. Simultaneous submissions and previously published submissions are accepted. Aims to respond to queries within one day and manuscripts within four days. Sometimes pays the expenses of writers on assignment (limit agreed upon in advance). Sample copy, writer's guidelines and editorial calendar are free on request. For a media pack, contact the magazine.
**Non-fiction** Publishes Book excerpts, Photo features, Essays, Humour, Interviews/Profiles, Reviews, New Products, Technical, Opinion (not letters to the Editor), Travel and Personal experience articles.
**Submission Guidelines** Accepts queries for articles between 600 and 2,000 words. Send a tearsheet for reprints. Contact Charles Barker.
**Images** Accepts images with submission.
 * Negotiates payment individually for images. Buys one time rights.
**Submission Guidelines** Accepts contact sheets, negatives, transparencies, prints or gif/jpeg files with captions. Send photos with submission. Contact Charles Barker.
**Tips** The magazine is very graphic design centric, created for today's opinion formers and tomorrow's decision makers.

## Director

**116 Pall Mall, London, SW1Y 5ED**
- 020 7766 8950
- 020 7766 8840
- director-ed@iod.com
- www.director-magazine.co.uk
**Parent Company** Director Publications Ltd
**Editor** Joanna Higgins

**Contact** Section Editor, Amy Duff
**Established** 1947
**Insider Info** A monthly trade magazine covering business management topics. Present circulation of 58,371. 65 per cent of the publication is written by freelance writers. Manuscript is published eight weeks after acceptance. A Kill fee of 50 per cent is offered and a byline is sometimes given. Purchases all rights. Editorial lead time is 12 weeks. Seasonal material should be submitted three months in advance. Aims to respond to queries within two weeks and manuscripts within one week. Accepts queries by mail. Sample copy is free on request.
**Non-fiction** Publishes Features, Interviews/Profile and Reviews.
**Submission Guidelines** Accepts query with published clips, plus CV, for articles between 500 and 2,000 words.
**Tips** *Director's* readers are members of the prestigious UK based business organisation, the Institute of Directors (IoD). The magazine reflects the real issues and interests of this influential group, while maintaining editorial independence from the IoD. It generally only uses work from regular contributors rather than unsolicited submissions. Send a letter with feature ideas and examples of printed work to the Editor.

## Dirtbike Rider
**Victoria Street, Morecombe, Lancashire, LA4 4AG**
01524 834030
01524 423469
sean.lawless@dirtbikerider.co.uk
www.dirtbikerider.co.uk
**Parent Company** Lancaster & Morecombe Newspapers Ltd
**Editor** Sean Lawless
**Established** 1981
**Insider Info** A monthly consumer magazine covering motoring and specialising in dirtbiking. Accepts queries by email.
**Non-fiction** Publishes Features, Interviews/Profiles, Reviews, New Product and Technical articles.
**Submission Guidelines** Accepts queries for articles of up to 2,000 words.
**Tips** Publishes stories on motocross, supercross and the rest of the off-road motorcycle world. Dirtbike Rider (DBR) is distributed all over the UK and combines the month's highlights with coverage of all the key events, expert opinion, in-depth interviews with the leading lights of the off-road world, and authoritative tests of the latest machines

on the market. A high level of interest and experience in dirt bikes is essential for any article.

## Disability Arts in London (DAIL) Magazine
**20–22 Waterson Street, London, E2 8HE**
020 7739 1133
dailmagazine@gmail.com
www.ldaf.org
**Parent Company** London Disability Arts Forum (LDAF)
**Established** 1986
**Insider Info** A consumer magazine focusing on the world of disabled artists. Accepts queries by mail or email. Sample copy available online.
**Non-fiction** Publishes Photo features, Inspirational articles, Features, Interviews/Profiles and Reviews.
**Submission Guidelines** Accepts queries.
**Tips** DAIL publishes news, previews, reviews and articles about the work of disabled artists. It also prints interviews and general information about coping with disability. The magazine also runs various short fiction and poetry competitions, that are open to disabled artists and writers. Prizewinners are often published in the magazine.

## Disability Now (DN)
**6 Market Road, London, N7 9PW**
020 7619 7323
020 7619 7331
editor@disabilitynow.org.uk
www.disabilitynow.org.uk
**Parent Company** Scope
**Contact** Editorial Assistant
**Established** 1984
**Insider Info** A monthly consumer magazine covering all aspects of disability, including news, features, profiles, arts, sport, holidays and equipment. Present circulation of 20,000. 30 per cent of the publication is written by freelance writers. Payment is upon publication and never with contributor copies instead of cash. A byline is given. Publication is copyrighted. Accepts queries by mail, email, fax or phone. Will pay the expenses of writers on assignment. Sample copy, writer's guidelines and editorial calendar are free on request.
**Non-fiction** Publishes Photo features, Interviews/ Profiles, Reviews, New Product, General interest, Travel and Personal experience articles.
**Submission Guidelines** Accepts queries for articles of up to 800 words.
**Images** State availability of photos with submission. * Pays a variable fee per photo.

## Diva

**Unit M, Spectrum House, 32–34 Gordon House Road, London, NW5 1LP**

- 020 7424 7400
- 020 7424 7401
- edit@divamag.co.uk
- www.divamag.co.uk

**Parent Company** Millivres-Prowler Ltd
**Editor** Jane Czyzselska
**Established** 1994
**Insider Info** A monthly consumer magazine covering the gay and lesbian lifestyle. Accepts queries by email.
**Non-fiction** Publishes Photo features and Features of Gay and Lesbian interest.
 * Pays £10 per 100 words for unsolicited articles.
**Submission Guidelines** Accepts queries or complete manuscripts for articles of between 800 and 1,500 words.
**Images** Send photos with submission.
**Tips** *Diva* remains Europe's biggest selling lesbian magazine, offering readers information on news, entertainment, travel, music, scene, real life features and listings. The magazine welcomes unsolicited news and features, ideally supported by photographs, in keeping with the overall tone of the magazine. Check the magazine prior to submitting, for a style guide.

## Drapers

**33–39 Bowling Green Lane, London, EC1R 0DA**

- 020 7812 3765
- 020 7812 3760
- josephine.collins@emap.com
- www.drapersonline.com

**Parent Company** EMAP Retail Ltd
**Editor** Josephine Collins
**Contact** Features Editor, Lorna Hall
**Established** 1887
**Insider Info** A weekly trade journal covering fashion and clothing. Present circulation of 14,264. Accepts queries by email.
**Non-fiction** Publishes Photo features and Features.
**Submission Guidelines** Accepts queries.
**Images** Send photos with submission.
**Tips** A business editorial aimed primarily at fashion retailers. Contains articles on fashion, recruitment, current vacancies in the industry, and the latest trends. Keep in mind that this is primarily aimed at fashion retailers and is a business orientated magazine. Check previous issues for tone and content.

## Dream Catcher

**Jasmine Cottage, 4 Church Street, Market Rasen, Lincolnshire, LN8 3ET**

- 01673 844325
- paulsuther@hotmail.com

**Parent Company** Dream Catcher Books
**Editor** Paul Sutherland
**Established** 1995
**Insider Info** A consumer literary journal with two issues per year. Present circulation of 600. A byline is given.
**Non-fiction** Publishes Articles on Poetry, Features, Interviews/Profiles and Reviews.
**Submission Guidelines** Accepts queries.
**Fiction** Publishes Mainstream Short fiction.
**Submission Guidelines** Accepts queries for short fiction of up to 2,000 words.
**Poetry** Publishes Free verse and Traditional poetry.
**Tips** *Dream Catcher* is a national literary journal that publishes the latest stories, poems and artwork, as well as reviews and biographies of the new and established contributors. The magazine often has submissions from well-known authors, and is large enough to be able to accept many submissions per issue. The Editor looks for diversity in submissions and welcomes poetry, short stories, literary articles and reviews from either new, or established authors. Dream Catcher will accept longer submissions for short stories if they are of exceptional quality.

## The Drouth

**PO Box 7419, Glasgow, G5 9WB**

- 0141 554 1071
- 0141 429 1805
- thedrouth@yahoo.co.uk
- www.thedrouth.com

**Parent Company** The Drouth
**Editor** Mitchell Miller
**Established** 2001
**Insider Info** A quarterly consumer magazine offering informed critique, satire and prose and covering film and theatre. Queries accepted by mail and email. Writer's guidelines are available online.
**Non-fiction** Publishes Book excerpts, Poetry, Features and Literary criticism.
**Submission Guidelines** Send complete manuscript. Articles may be of any length.
**Fiction** Publishes Mainstream fiction, Short stories and Novellas.
**Submission Guidelines** Send complete manuscript. Submissions may be of any length.
**Poetry** Publishes Free verse and Traditional verse.

**Tips** *The Drouth* is also a forum, its format providing structure for continuing debate and dialogue. Although they have no explicit political or social agenda, each issue tends to be loosely set around an underlying satirical theme or debate. They also have a strong commitment to theatre, publishing full or extracted original plays. There is no editorial control over the views of contributors, and *The Drouth* welcomes work from a wide range of viewpoints and of any length. The editors are keen to make contact with potential writers and discuss ideas for pieces. The best way to contact them is by email.

## Earth Love
**PO Box 11219, Paisley, PA1 2WH**
⊙ earth.love@ntlworld.com
**Editor** Tracy Patrick
**Established** 2001
**Insider Info** A consumer magazine publication issued three times a year covering general interest literary subjects. A byline is given. Writer's guidelines are available online.
**Non-fiction** Interested in Photo features, Poetry, Features, Interviews/Profiles, and General interest pieces.
**Submission Guidelines** Please send complete manuscript.
**Poetry** Interested in Free verse, Light verse and Traditional poetry.
**Tips** *Earth Love* is a small poetry magazine with a conservation and nature theme. *Earth Love* is dedicated to helping the environment and all proceeds go to animal welfare and environmental charities. *Earth Love* contains poetry, articles on books, music and people, black and white photography, and articles about conservation and nature. *Earth Love* also publishes anthologies and booklets on the same theme as the magazine, and is generally seeking articles for their 'Inspirations' feature. Articles should be about conservation or nature themes, or about important people working in conservation.

## Eastern Art Report
**PO Box 13666, London, SW14 8WF**
⊙ 020 8392 1122
⊙ 020 8392 1422
⊙ info@eapgroup.com
⊛ www.eapgroup.com
**Parent Company** Eastern Art Publishing
**Contact** Managing Editor, Sajid Rizvi
**Established** 1989

**Insider Info** A consumer magazine publication issued bi-weekly, covering leisure interests and art. Present circulation of 12,500. Accepts queries by mail, email and fax. Sample copy is available free on request. Writer's guidelines and media packs are available on the website.
**Non-fiction** Interested in Reviews, Art market reports and General interest pieces.
**Submission Guidelines** Accepts query.
**Tips** *Eastern Art Report* (EAR) is an international magazine focused on the arts of Asia and Africa and the arts practised by the people of Asian and African origin in North America, Europe and elsewhere. EAR includes scholarly articles, exclusive interviews, exhibition and book reviews and news stories. Contributions to EAR are welcomed (on a wholly voluntary basis) from curators, historians, journalists and readers, provided such submissions satisfy the general guidelines on the website.

## Eastern Rainbow
**17 Farrow Road, Whaplode Drove, Spalding, PE12 0TS**
⊙ p_rance@yahoo.co.uk
⊛ http://uk.geocities.com/p_rance/pandf.htm
**Parent Company** Peace & Freedom Press
**Editor** Paul Rance
**Established** 1992
**Insider Info** A consumer magazine publication issued twice a year, which covers general interest literary subjects. Present circulation of 500. A byline is given.
**Non-fiction** Interested in Photo Features, Poetry, Features, Interviews/Profile, General interest pieces.
**Submission Guidelines** Please send complete manuscript. Articles should be a maximum of 500 words.
**Fiction** Accepts fiction pieces.
**Poetry** Accepts Free verse, Light verse and Traditional poetry.
**Submission Guidelines** Poems should have a maximum line length of 32.
**Tips** *Eastern Rainbow* is a cultural magazine, and publishes poetry and some prose, along with articles and art relating to 20th Century arts and culture. *Eastern Rainbow* accepts any kind of genre fiction, including science fiction, fantasy and horror, and often prints articles on famous 20th Century icons, such as David Bowie or George Orwell. *Eastern Rainbow* is currently only accepting submissions from subscribers and competition winners.

## East Lothian Life

**1 Beveridge Row, Belhaven, Dunbar, East Lothian, EH42 1TP**

- 01368 863593
- 01368 863593
- info@east-lothian-life.co.uk
- eastlothianlife.co.uk

**Parent Company** PJ Design
**Editor** Pauline Jaffray
**Established** 1988

**Insider Info** A consumer magazine publication issued quarterly, covering life in East Lothian. Present circulation of 3,000. Payment is upon publication. 50 per cent of the magazine is written by freelancers. Publication is copyrighted and a byline is given. Submissions are published approximately four months after publication, with an editorial lead time of 12 weeks. Seasonal material must be submitted 16 weeks in advance. Queries accepted by mail. Simultaneous submissions and previously published submissions accepted. Aims to respond to queries and manuscripts within ten days and other issues within 17 days. A sample copy and writer's guidelines are available free on request. Payment is not made with contributor copies or other premiums.

**Non-fiction** Interested in Features, General interest, Travel and Historical/Nostalgic pieces.

**Submission Guidelines** Articles should be between 650 and 1,300 words. Contact Pauline Jaffray.

**Tips** All articles must have an East Lothian slant.

## ECM

European Cosmetic Markets

**6–14 Underwood Street, London, N1 7JQ**

- 020 7549 8626
- 020 7549 8622
- ecm@wilmington.co.uk
- www.cosmeticsbusiness.com

**Parent Company** Wilmington Media
**Contact** Managing Editor, Clare Henderson; Assistant Editor, Georgina Caldwell
**Established** 1983

**Insider Info** A trade journal magazine issued monthly covering the cosmetics industry and market research. Present circulation of 500. Payment upon publication. 25 per cent of publication is written by freelancers. Submissions published approximately 30 days after acceptance with an editorial lead time of 30 days. Publication is copyrighted and a byline is sometimes given. Seasonal material must be submitted 30 days in advance. Purchases all rights. Queries accepted by email. A sample copy is available online. Editorial calendars are available free on request. Media packs are available on the website.

**Non-fiction** Publishes News and Features.

**Tips** *ECM* occupies a unique niche in the C&T industry. Its detailed market reports give the most up to date statistics, market trends and product information from France, Germany, Italy, Spain and the UK, plus columns from the US, Russia and Brazil.

## The Ecologist

**102 D Lana House Studios, 116–118 Commercial Street, London, E1 6MF**

- 020 7422 8100
- editorial@theecologist.org
- www.theecologist.org

**Parent Company** Ecosystems Ltd
**Editor** Zac Goldsmith
**Contact** Managing Editor, Jeremy Smith; Deputy Editor, Jon Hughes
**Established** 1970

**Insider Info** A monthly consumer magazine, covering science related News and Current affairs. Present circulation of 20,000. Queries accepted by email.

**Non-fiction** Publishes Social/Economic/Ecologic features and articles.

**Submission Guidelines** Send query with published clips, plus CV. Articles must be 500–3,000 words.

**Tips** For 35 years *The Ecologist* has helped set environmental and political agendas around the world by focusing on the root causes, not just the after-effects, of current events. Each month we examine the connection between a wide range of subjects. Whether it's food, war, politics, pharmaceuticals, farming, toxic chemicals, corporate fraud, mass media or supermarkets, *The Ecologist* challenges conventional thinking, and empowers readers to tackle global issues on a local scale. Any submitted work must be supported by deep and accurate scientific or political knowledge but at the same time fit in with the strong political ideology of *The Economist*.

## The Economist

**25 St. James's Street, London, SW1A 1HG**

- 020 7830 7000
- 020 7839 2968
- letters@economist.com
- www.economist.com

**Parent Company** The Economist Newspaper Ltd
**Editor** John Micklethwait
**Established** 1843

**Insider Info** A weekly consumer magazine, covering News, International affairs, Business and Finance. Present circulation 162,112. All articles published anonymously. Queries accepted by mail.

**Non-fiction** Publishes Features, Interviews/Profiles and Opinion (not letters to the Editor) on Politics/Current affairs/Economy, Science and Technology.

**Submission Guidelines** Send query before sending submissions.

**Tips** According to its contents page, its goal is to 'take part in a severe contest between intelligence, which presses forward, and an unworthy, timid ignorance obstructing our progress.' Subjects covered include international news, economics, politics, business, finance, science and technology and the arts, but not sports (though articles about the business of sports are occasionally published). The publication is targeted at the high-end 'prestige' segment of the market, and counts among its audience influential business and government decision makers. 'It is to the Radicals that *The Economist* still likes to think of itself as belonging. The extreme centre is the paper's historical position.' If submissions are as close to *The Economist's* political style as possible (prior to editing), and also have an edge of wry humour, they may have a better chance.

## Edge

### 30 Monmouth Street, Bath, BA1 2BW

- 01225 442244
- 01225 732295
- edge-online@futurenet.co.uk
- www.edge-online.co.uk

**Parent Company** Future Publishing
**Editor** Tony Mott
**Contact** 1993

**Insider Info** A consumer magazine publication issued monthly covering computing, and multi-format consoles. Present circulation of 33,597.

**Non-fiction** Interested in Features, Interviews/Profiles, Reviews, New products, and Technical pieces.

**Tips** Around the video gaming world, each and every day, things happen. Some immediately change gaming, others merely influence it, while many more are simply throwaway developments that can be entertaining, surprising or something else. *Edge* online is your guide to all of these things. *Edge* is known for its harsh editorial stance and its controversial grading of popular games. Check the magazine for style and tone before contacting the Editor with ideas.

## Edinburgh Review

### 22a Buccleuch Place, Edinburgh, EH8 9LN

- 0131 651 1415
- 0131 651 1415
- edinburgh.review@ed.ac.uk
- www.englit.ed.ac.uk/edinburghreview

**Parent Company** Centre for the History of Ideas in Scotland
**Contact** Managing editor, Brian McCabe
**Established** 1802

**Insider Info** A consumer journal publication issued three times per year, covering general interest, literary subjects. Queries accepted by mail and email. A sample copy and writer's guidelines are available online.

**Non-fiction** Interested in Reviews and Literary criticism.

**Submission Guidelines** Accepts query with published clips.

**Fiction** Interested in Novel excerpts and Short fiction pieces.

**Submission Guidelines** Please send complete manuscript. Articles should be a maximum of 3,000 words.

**Poetry** Interested in Free verse and Traditional poetry.

**Submission Guidelines** Submit a maximum of 12 poems at a time.

**Tips** Scotland's leading journal of ideas, the *Edinburgh Review* publishes essays, short fiction, poetry and reviews aimed at an educated reading public with an interest in critical thought. The journal welcomes unsolicited submissions of short fiction, novel extracts, poetry, and critical material. The *Edinburgh Review* is also keen to hear from people interested in reviewing contemporary Scottish literature and critical monographs.

## The Eildon Tree

### Library Headquarters, St. Mary's Mill, Selkirk, TD7 5EW

- 01750 724901
- artservice@scotborders.gov.uk
- www.eildontree.org.uk

**Parent Company** Scottish Borders Council
**Insider Info** A literary magazine published by the Scottish Borders Council. Queries accepted by mail and telephone.

**Non-fiction** Publishes articles and information about writing in Scotland.

**Fiction** Publishes Mainstream fiction.

**Submission Guidelines** Send query before sending submissions. Submissions should be 3,000 words in length.

**Poetry** Publishes Free verse, Light verse and Traditional verse.

**Submission Guidelines** Send query before sending submissions. Poems should be up to 40 lines in length.

**Tips** Publishes poetry and prose from writers in, or around, the Scottish Borders region, as well as some writing from further afield. Runs various themed writing competitions, which offer publication in the magazine as a prize.

## Elle

**64 North Row, London, W1K 7LL**

- 020 7150 7000
- 020 7150 7670
- www.elle.com

**Parent Company** Hachette Filipacchi Media

**Editor** Lorraine Candy

**Contact** Features Editor, Anna Pursglove

**Established** 1985

**Insider Info** A consumer magazine publication issued monthly, covering women's interests, women's lifestyle/fashion. Present circulation of 208,802. Accepts query by mail.

**Non-fiction** Interested in Exposés, Features, Interviews/Profiles, General interest pieces.

**Submission Guidelines** Articles should be between 500 and 2,000 words.

**Tips** *Elle* is the world's largest fashion magazine for the woman with a style and mind of her own. For her, fashion is self-expression, not to mention serious fun. Single and single minded, she comes to the magazine for its pitch perfect take on the trends, and stays for its thought provoking mix of culture, controversy and cool. Contact the Features Editor by post with ideas for articles, and be sure to include clippings.

## Empire

**Mappin House, 4 Winsley Street, London, W1W 8HF**

- 020 7182 8781
- 020 7182 8703
- empire@emap.com
- www.empireonline.co.uk

**Parent Company** EMAP

**Editor** Mark Dinning

**Contact** Reviews Editor, Dan Jolin

**Established** 1989

**Insider Info** A consumer magazine publication issued monthly, covering leisure interests, film and video reviews. Present circulation of 176,656.

**Non-fiction** Interested in features and reviews. * Payment for unsolicited articles is £300 per 1000 words.

**Submission Guidelines** Accepts query.

**Images** Send photos with submission.

**Tips** *Empire* is a guide to the movies, it aims to cover the world of films in a 'comprehensive, adult, intelligent, and witty package'. The majority of the magazine is devoted to mainstream cinema but it also looks at arthouse movies, as well as the technology behind television and DVD and other media forms. *Empire* does accept submissions, but it is best to contact in writing first with a synopsis and covering letter. Well-written reviews are most commonly accepted.

## Employee Benefits

**50 Poland Street, London, W1F 7AX**

- 020 7943 8060
- amanda.wilkinson@centaur.co.uk
- employeebenefits.co.uk

**Parent Company** Centaur Media

**Editor** Amanda Wilkinson

**Contact** Editorial Director, Debbie O'Donovan; Editor, Amanda Wilkinson

**Established** 1996

**Insider Info** A trade journal magazine issued monthly, covering employee benefits and human resources. Present circulation of 10,000. Payment is made upon acceptance and a byline is given. The percentage of the magazine written by freelancers varies. Queries are accepted via email.

**Tips** *Employee Benefits* is written for human resources practitioners and compensation and reward specialists.

## The Engineer

**50 Poland Street, London, W1F 7AX**

- 020 7970 4181
- 020 7970 4189
- andrew.lee@centaur.co.uk
- www.theengineer.co.uk

**Parent Company** Centaur Media

**Editor** Andrew Lee

**Contact** Features Editor, Jon Excell

**Established** 1856

**Insider Info** Fortnightly consumer magazine, covering engineering. Present circulation is 31,224. Queries accepted by mail and email.

**Non-fiction** Publishes Features, Interviews/Profiles, Technical articles and Engineering news.

**Submission Guidelines** Send query before sending submissions. Articles must be 2,000 words.

**Fillers** Publishes Newsbreaks as fillers. Maximum of 500 words in length.

**Tips** *The Engineer* provides a mixture of news, features and analysis of engineering technologies, innovations and application across industries, plus interviews with leading engineers and the latest job vacancies. There is no demand for long features but the magazine is actively seeking national freelancers, for news and specialist technology coverage.

## The English Garden

**Jubilee House, 2 Jubilee Place, London, SW3 3QT**

- 020 7751 4800
- 020 7751 4848
- englishgarden@archant.co.uk
- www.theenglishgarden.co.uk

**Parent Company** Archant Specialist

**Editor** Janine Wookey

**Contact** Deputy Editor, Jackie Bennett

**Established** 1996

**Insider Info** A monthly consumer magazine about gardening. Present circulation is 35,527. Queries accepted by mail and email.

**Non-fiction** Publishes Photo features, Features, Interviews/Profiles and Technical and How-to articles.

**Submission Guidelines** Send query before sending submissions. Articles must be 1,000–1,200 words.

**Tips** A celebration of the diverse styles that define the traditional English garden, admired and emulated around the world. Contains inspiration and design ideas to help you create the 'English' look in your own garden. Send initial synopsis of approximately 150 words with good design and planting ideas, feature proposals, or quality sets of showcase photographs to the Features Editor.

## Envoi

**44 Rudyard Road, Biddulph Moor, Stoke on Trent, ST8 7JN**

- 01782 517892

**Editor** Roger Elkin

**Established** 1957

**Insider Info** A consumer journal publication issued three times per year in February, June and October covering general interest, literary subjects. Present circulation of 800. A byline is given. Accepts queries by mail.

**Non-fiction** Interested in Poetry, features, Interviews/Profiles, Reviews, Opinion (not letters to the Editor) pieces.

**Submission Guidelines** Accepts query.

**Poetry** Interested in Avant-garde, Free verse, Light verse and Traditional poetry.

**Submission Guidelines** Submit a maximum of six poems at one time.

**Tips** *Envoi* is poetry journal that prints modern poetry from new and established writers, as well as articles on poetry, reviews, letters and competition results. All writers featured in *Envoi* will have more than poem included, so multiple submissions are necessary. *Envoi* will usually only publish work from relatively well-known or up and coming poets. *Envoi* also runs various poetry competitions in each issue, with publication as a prize.

## EOS magazine

Exploring the world of EOS photography

**The Old Barn, Ball Lane, Tackley, Kidlington, Oxon, OX5 3AG**

- 01869 331479
- editorial@eos-magazine.com
- www.eos-magazine.com

**Parent Company** Robert Scott Publishing

**Editor** Angela August

**Established** 1996

**Insider Info** A consumer magazine covering photography. The publication is issued quarterly and has a present circulation of 20,000. Payment upon acceptance. Ten per cent of the magazine is written by freelancers. Submissions are published approximately three months after acceptance with an editorial lead time of two months. Publication is copyrighted and a byline is given. Purchases first UK serial rights. Seasonal work must be submitted three months in advance. Queries are accepted via email and phone. Aims to respond to queries, manuscripts and other issues within one week. For a sample copy send SAE (32mm long by 23mm), with 4 first class stamps. Writer's guidelines and editorial calendars are free on request.

**Non-fiction** Publishes How-to and Technical articles on photography.

**Images** Accepts images with submission.

* Pays a varied fee per photo between £15 and £250. Purchases one time rights.

**Submission Guidelines** Submit gif/jpeg files with captions and model releases. Identification of subjects, camera, lens and exposure details are required. Send photos with submission. Contact Angela August.

**Tips** The magazine is dedicated to Canon EOS camera users. Articles must be technical and very specifically targeted to EOS users, and not the sort of general article you could read in other photographic press.

## Equinox
**134b Joy Lane, Whitstable, Kent, CT5 4ES**
**Editor** Barbara Dordi
**Insider Info** A consumer magazine publication published twice a year covering general interest, literary subjects.
**Poetry** Interested in contemporary poetry.
**Submissions Guidelines** Poems should have lines of no more than 40 words.
**Tips** *Equinox* is a small poetry magazine that publishes new contemporary poetry of any style. Equinox only accepts hard copy submissions, so always enclose SAE when sending work in.

## Eratica
**51 Waterloo Street, Hove, BN3 1AN**
☏ 01273 302876
🌐 www.waterloopresshove.co.uk
**Parent Company** Waterloo Press
**Editor** Alan Morrison
**Contact** Co-Editor, Simon Jenner
**Established** 2001
**Insider Info** A consumer journal publication issued semi annually, covering general interest literary subjects.
**Non-fiction** Interested in poetry, features and general interest pieces.
**Poetry** Interested in free verse, light verse and traditional poetry.
**Tips** *Eratica* poetry journal is published by Waterloo Press and prints contemporary poetry from new and established writers, as well as articles on art and music. *Erratica*'s name was formed from a crossing of 'erratic' with 'erotica' and its aim is to 'sell poetry sexily'. *Erratica* prefers to publish original, often disreputable poetry.

## Erbacce
**5 Farrell Close, Liverpool, L31 1BU**
☏ erbacce@hotmail.com
🌐 www.erbacce.com
**Editor** Andrew Taylor
**Established** 2004
**Insider Info** A consumer journal publication issued quarterly, covering general interest literary subjects.

A byline is given. Queries accepted by mail and email. A sample copy is available online.
**Non-fiction** Interested in essays, poetry, features and reviews.
**Submission Guidelines** Please send complete manuscript.
**Poetry** Interested in Avant-garde, Free verse and Light verse.
**Submission Guidelines** Submit a maximum of six poems at one time.
**Tips** *Erbacce* is a print and online literary journal, which publishes radical poetry from new and established writers, as well as articles, essays and reviews. *Erbacce* aims to 'interfere with the 'normal' and 'formal' gardens of poetry'. *Erbacce* claims that they will publish any poetry submission from anyone, so long as it is radical and non-conformist in either content or layout, even if they disagree with the content personally.

## Esquire
**National Magazine House, 72 Broadwick Street, London, W1F 9EP**
☏ 020 7439 5000
☏ 020 7437 6886
✉ esquireeditors@esquire.co.uk
🌐 www.esquire.co.uk
**Parent Company** National Magazine Company
**Editor** Jeremy Langmead
**Established** 1991
**Insider Info** A consumer magazine publication issued monthly covering men's lifestyle. Present circulation of 52,437.
**Tips** *Esquire* delivers an entertaining, sophisticated and witty read, balancing interviews, thought provoking writing and quality photography in a stylish, accessible package. *Esquire*'s target reader is the 'well educated, career-minded and successful' man of about 30 to 40 years of age.

## Essentially America
**55 Hereford Road, London, W2 5BB**
✉ marymooremason@phoenixip.com
🌐 www.essentiallyamerica.com
**Parent Company** Phoenix International Publishing
**Editor** Mary Moore Mason
**Established** 1994
**Insider Info** A consumer magazine publication issued quarterly covering travel to North America (USA, Canada, occasionally Mexico) for frequent British travellers. Present circulation of 50,000. Payment is upon publication and is not made with contributor copies or other premiums. Assignment

expenses are not paid. 90 per cent of magazine is written by freelancers. Submissions published approximately three months after acceptance with an editorial lead time of two months. Commissioning is undertaken very carefully and kill fees are very rarely required. Purchases all rights. Seasonal material must be submitted three months in advance. Accepts queries via email. Aims to respond to queries within one week. A sample copy is a available for £2.95 plus postage, which can be considerable as some issues of the magazine are more than 200 pages.

**Non-fiction** Interested in Photo features (photos are occasionally bought in to accompany articles), Humour about travel within North America, Features on Food, Drink, Film and Literary sites. Also Interviews/Profiles (occasionally publish celebrity interviews if they are destination related), Reviews (there is a book review in most issues), Travel (the majority of the publication is travel), Historical/Nostalgic (occasional features on iconic American figures such as Elvis, or Muhammad Ali, and also on great events in North American history) and Personal experience (amusing, unusual experiences in North America).

 * Receives approximately 40 manuscripts from freelancers per year. Payment for assigned and unsolicited articles is negotiated upon commission.

**Submission Guidelines** Accepts query by email. Articles should be between 500 and 2,000 words. Send a photocopy for reprint submissions.

**Images** Occasionally accepts images.

 * Pays a varied fee per photo that is negotiated on the few occasions photos are bought in. Purchases one time rights.

**Submission Guidelines** Submit gif/jpeg files with captions.

**Tips** *Essentially America* is a high quality, full colour quarterly publication exclusively covering travel to – and the lifestyle within – the USA, Canada and, to a lesser degree, Mexico. It is aimed at well-informed frequent British travellers to these destinations. Therefore our writers must be both skilled, experienced writers – although we welcome young talent – and extremely knowledgeable about North America. Potential contributors should study back issues of the magazine and then send the Editor a brief email stating in one paragraph the concept of the feature, and in a second your qualifications to write this feature.

## Essentials
**King's Reach Tower, Stamford Street, London, SE1 9LS**

- 020 7261 6970
- 0207261 5262
- essentials_feedback@ipcmedia.com
- www.essentialsmagazine.com

**Parent Company** IPC Media
**Editor** Julie Barton-Breck
**Established** 1988

**Insider Info** A consumer magazine publication issued monthly, covering women's interests, women's lifestyle/fashion. Present circulation of 74,189. Accepts query by mail.

**Non-fiction** Interested in Inspirational, Features, General interest and Personal experience pieces.

**Submission Guidelines** Accepts query. Please send complete manuscript and include SAE. Articles should be a maximum of 2,000 words.

**Tips** *Essentials* aims to give you inspiration, useful ideas and realistic advice that works for you. Whether you need to lose a lot of weight because you're worried about your health, or just drop a few pounds to look better in your bikini, we can offer the help and support you need… while you stay in control of what and when you eat. Prospective contributors should study the magazine thoroughly before submitting anything.

## Eve
**174 Hammersmith Road, London, W6 7JP**

- 020 8267 5000
- 020 8267 8222
- evemagazine@haynet.com
- www.evemagazine.co.uk

**Parent Company** Haymarket Publishing
**Editor** Sarah Cremer
**Contact** Features Editor, Linda Gray
**Established** 2000

**Insider Info** A consumer magazine publication issued monthly covering women's interests, women's lifestyle/fashion. Present circulation of 171,454. Queries accepted by mail.

**Non-fiction** Interested in Exposés, Features, Interviews/Profiles and General interest pieces.

**Submission Guidelines** Accepts query with published clips.

**Tips** *Eve* is the award winning glossy that's a must read for glamorous modern women. Stylish, intelligent and bursting with brilliant, fresh ideas. *Eve* is everything you would expect from a women's glossy and rather a lot you would not. Contact via post with ideas aimed at specific features for the magazine, and be sure to include recent examples of writing.

## Eventing

**King's Reach Tower, Stamford Street, London, SE1 9LS**

- ☎ 020 7261 6481
- ✉ julie_harding@ipcmedia.com

**Parent Company** IPC Media

**Editor** Julie Harding

**Established** 1985

**Insider Info** A consumer magazine publication issued monthly, covering equestrian interests. Present circulation of 12,000.

**Tips** The international voice and only magazine for the sport of horse trials. *Eventing* offers an insight into the world of eventing, including news, results, features, opinions and instructional articles. There are also commentaries and results from all major events, together with training features and profiles. The magazine is focused solely on the sport of horse trials and events, unrelated subjects would be covered in our sister publication, *Horse & Hound* instead.

## evo

The Thrill of Driving

**Tower Court, Irchester Road, Wollaston, Northants, NN29 7PJ**

- ☎ 020 7907 6310
- ☎ 01933 663367
- ✉ harrym@evo.co.uk
- ⊛ www.evo.co.uk

**Parent Company** Dennis Publishing

**Editor** Harrison Metcalfe

**Contact** Managing Editor, Janet Mills; Editor at Large, Richard Meaden

**Established** 1998

**Insider Info** A consumer magazine publication issued monthly covering motoring and motorcycling. Present circulation of 73,830.

**Tips** *evo* is a glossy, monthly magazine devoted exclusively to the world's fastest and most desirable cars – from affordable GTIs to 200mph super cars. With sharp, authoritative writing, the most thorough road tests yet devised, and the most compelling photography in the business, *evo*'s aim is to put the reader behind the wheel of the greatest performance cars on the market. *evo* has a definite editorial slant towards the feel of a car – the 'emotive drive' - rather than its performance, this must be reflected in submitted articles.

## Executive PA

**160-166 Borough High Street, London, SE1 1LB**

- ☎ 020 7863 3333
- ☎ 020 7173 5101
- ✉ cora.lydon@solutionspublish.co.uk
- ⊛ www.executivepa.net

**Parent Company** Solutions Publish Ltd

**Editor** Cora Lydon

**Insider Info** A trade journal magazine issued quarterly covering personal assistants – venues, office, business travel and legislation. 75 per cent of the magazine is written by freelancers. A byline is given. Seasonal material must be submitted three months in advance. Queries accepted via email. A sample copy and writer's guidelines are available via email.

## Exile

A Poetry Magazine For New Poets

**1 Armstrong Close, Hundon, Suffolk, CO10 8HD**

- ✉ exile@2from.com
- ⊛ www.2from.com/exile/poetry.htm

**Editor** Ann Elliott-Marr, John Marr

**Established** 1988

**Insider Info** A consumer magazine publication issued quarterly, covering general interest, literary subjects. A byline is given. Queries accepted by mail and email. A sample copy and writer's guidelines are available online.

**Non-fiction** Interested in Poetry Articles and Features.

**Submission Guidelines** Please send complete manuscript.

**Poetry** Interested in free verse, light verse and traditional poetry.

\* Payment for assigned poetry is with a contributor copy.

**Submission Guidelines** Poetry should have a maximum line length of 40 words.

**Tips** *Exile* is a small literary magazine that aims to encourage new poets and poetry. *Exile* prints poetry submissions, as well as some articles and writing information. Many back issues of the magazine are available as pdfs on the website. *Exile* was founded specifically to help new poets achieve publication, so submissions on any subject or in any style, from first-time writers are more than welcome.

## Families North (London)

**PO Box 14965, London, NW3 5WA**

- ☎ 020 7794 5690
- ☎ 020 7794 0951
- ✉ cathy@familiesnorth.com

www.familiesnorth.com
**Parent Company** Families Magazines Group
**Editor** Kathy Watson
**Contact** Managing Editor, Cathy Youd
**Established** 1997
**Insider Info** A consumer magazine publication issued bi-monthly, covering local life for young families. Present circulation of 19,000. Payment is not given for articles. Between zero and five per cent of the magazine is written by freelancers. Publication is not copyrighted and a byline is given. Submissions published approximately six weeks after acceptance with an editorial lead time of two months. Seasonal material should be submitted three months in advance. Queries accepted by mail, email and phone. Accepts previously published submissions. A sample copy is available free on request.
**Non-fiction** Publishes General Interest articles with a local theme.
**Tips** *Families North* is an extremely useful resource for families with young children living in North London. It provides information on all the things young parents need to know about, for example, local nurseries, children's entertainers, activities, places to go, things to do, childcare, and so on.

## Federation Magazine

**Burslem School of Art, Queen Street, Stoke on Trent, Staffordshire, ST6 3EJ**
01782 822327
fwwcp@tiscali.co.uk
www.thefwwcp.org.uk
**Parent Company** The Federation of Worker Writers & Community Publishers
**Editor** Tim Diggles
**Insider Info** A consumer magazine publication issued erratically, (often three times per year) covering general interest, literary subjects.
**Non-fiction** Interested in Poetry, Features, Interviews/Profiles, Reviews, Opinion (not letters to the Editor), News and Events pieces.
**Submission Guidelines** Accepts query.
**Fiction** Interested in Fiction pieces.
**Tips** *Federation* is the magazine of The Federation of Worker Writers & Community Publishers, which is an umbrella organisation for writers' groups and community publishers. The magazine publishes new poetry and fiction from members of the federation, and also news, events and articles of interest to the writing groups. Publication of *Federation* is erratic at best, ranging from two to four issues per year. It is best to join the federation before approaching them with any submissions.

## FHM

**Mappin House, 4 Winsley Street, London, W1W 8HF**
020 7182 8028
020 7182 8021
general@fhm.com
www.fhm.com
**Parent Company** EMAP Plc
**Editor** Anthony Noquera
**Established** 1986
**Insider Info** A consumer magazine publication issued monthly, covering men's lifestyle. Present circulation of 420,688. Accepts queries via email.
**Non-fiction** Interested in Photo features, Humour, Exposés, Features, Interviews/Profiles, General interest articles.
**Submission Guidelines** Accepts query. Articles should be between 1,200 and 2,000 words.
**Tips** 'Lads' magazine featuring the latest in men's fashion, sports, and reviews, as well as pictures of gorgeous honeys. Don't submit finished articles – a brief two line description and bullet points is more than enough, but bear in mind it is extremely unlikely that any unsolicited material will ever appear in the magazine.

## The Field

**King's Reach Tower, Stamford Street, London, SE1 9LS**
020 7261 5198
020 7261 5358
jonathan_young@ipcmedia.com
www.thefield.co.uk
**Parent Company** IPC Media
**Editor** Jonathan Young
**Established** 1853
**Insider Info** Monthly consumer magazine, covering countryside life, gun sports and hunting. Present circulation of 30,974. Queries accepted by phone. Media packs available online.
**Non-fiction** Publishes Hunting/Shooting related Photo features, Features, Interviews/Profiles, General interest and How-to articles.
**Submission Guidelines** Accepts queries and complete manuscripts.
**Tips** First launched as a country newspaper 150 years ago, *The Field* is dedicated to the celebration and preservation of Britain's countryside heritage. The monthly magazine sits at the centre of the brand, offering its dedicated readership expert writers, outstanding photographers and a dedication to country issues. Encapsulating the essence of countryside life, *The Field* is a witty,

provocative and always stimulating magazine. Rather than all countryside issues *The Field* is more or less focused on gun sports and hunting.

## Financial World

**IFS House, 4–9 Burgate Lane, Canterbury, Kent, CT1 2XJ**

☎ 01227 818605

✉ dsmith@ifslearning.com

🌐 www.financialworld.co.uk

**Parent Company** ifs School of Finance

**Editor** James Elwes

**Established** 2004

**Insider Info** A monthly management magazine, also available online, covering worldwide financial services. Present circulation of 31,569. Payment is upon acceptance and is not made with contributor copies or other premiums. Assignment expenses are not paid. 100 per cent of the magazine is written by freelancers, Submissions are published approximately two months after acceptance, with an editorial lead time of two months. Publication is copyrighted and a byline is given. Seasonal material must be submitted two months in advance. Queries are accepted by email. Simultaneous submissions are accepted. Aims to respond to queries, manuscripts and other issues within two weeks. A sample copy is available online. Writer's guidelines are available free on request, via email and online. Editorial calendars are available free on request, via email and online. Media packs are available on the website.

**Non-fiction** Interested in features on financial services topics, interview/profiles with financial services personnel and opinion (not letters to editor) on financial services topics.

**Submission Guidelines** Articles should be between 600 and 800 words. Contact Denise Smith, Online Editor and Advertising Executive.

**Tips** *Financial World,* along with its online version, is an invaluable addition to the business resources of financial services professionals. It supplies features and comment, and reveals emerging trends, across the worldwide financial services industry. Submissions, especially for the website, need to be short and punchy, and have a strict relevance to the industry. *Financial World online* is the web-based version of *Financial World*, the ifs School of Finance's management magazine.

## FIRE

**Field Cottage, Old Whitehill, Tackley, Kidlington, Oxfordshire, OX5 3AB**

☎ firejhilton@talk21.com

🌐 www.poetical.org

**Editor** Jeremy Hilton

**Established** 1997

**Insider Info** A consumer magazine publication issued twice a year and covering general interest, literary subjects. A byline is given. Accepts query by mail.

**Non-fiction** Interested in Poetry.

**Fiction** Interested in Fiction pieces.

**Poetry** Interested in Avant-garde, Free verse and Experimental poetry.

**Tips** *FIRE* is a poetry magazine that prints imaginative contemporary poetry. It aims to 'promote unpublished, unknown, and unfashionable writers, including young writers and those just starting out.' *FIRE* also actively solicits submissions from selected poets and therefore leaves little space in the magazine for work from previously published writers. *FIRE* favours inventive, experimental and alternative poetry from new writers anywhere in the world, but discourages submissions from published writers. *FIRE* prefers all correspondence in writing by post, rather than email.

## The Firing Squad

**25 Griffiths Road, West Bromwich, B71 2EH**

☎ firingsquad@purplepatchpoetry.co.uk

🌐 purplepatchpoetry.co.uk/firingsquad/

**Parent Company** Purple Patch Poetry

**Editor** Geoff Stevens

**Contact** Alex Barzdo

**Established** 1989

**Insider Info** Sister publication to *Purple Patch* magazine. Specialises in complaint or protest poetry, often of a strong and controversial nature. *The Firing Squad* is issued when the themes included are topical, and will soon be relying on the internet for publication. A byline is given. Accepts queries by mail and email.

**Poetry** Publishes Political Complaint/Protest Poetry.

**Tips** *The Firing Squad* aims to publish any political views, providing they are poetic and have some literary merit, as well as a protest element.

## First Offense

**Syringh, Stodmarsh, Canterbury, Kent, CT3 4BA**

☎ tim@firstoffense.co.uk

🌐 www.firstoffense.co.uk

**Editor** Tim Fletcher

**Insider Info** A consumer magazine publication issued annually, covering general interest, literary subjects. Present circulation of 300. A byline is given.

**Poetry** Interested in Avant-garde, Experimental and Modernist poetry.

  * No traditional poetry.

**Tips** *First Offense* is a small poetry magazine that specialises in ground breaking and inventive contemporary poetry. Modernist poetry and language based texts are good examples of the types of writing in *First Offense*. The magazine does not accept traditional forms of poetry. Submissions must be in hard copy and must include SAE, otherwise they will be rejected.

## First Time

**The Snoring Cat, 194 Downs Road, Hastings, East Sussex, TN34 2DZ**

- ☎ 01424 428855
- ☎ 01424 428855
- ✉ josephinepoetry@btinternet.com
- 🌐 www.josephineaustin.co.uk

**Editor** Josephine Austin

**Insider Info** A consumer magazine publication issued twice a year, covering general interest, literary subjects. Present circulation of 1,000. A byline is given.

**Poetry** Interested in Free verse, Light verse and Traditional poetry.

**Submissions Guidelines** Poetry should have maximum line length of 30 words.

**Tips** *First Time* is a poetry magazine that aims to encourage first time poetry writers. Generally publishes traditional and mainstream poetry on the subjects of love, the countryside and social issues. *First Time* welcomes submissions from international writers. *First Time* is geared towards helping new writers get their first poems published, and most poems are traditional in style, or otherwise mainstream, rather than experimental.

## Flight International

**Quadrant House, The Quadrant, Sutton, SM2 5AS**

- ☎ 020 8652 3842
- ☎ 020 8652 3840
- ✉ flight.international@rbi.co.uk
- 🌐 www.flightinternational.com

**Parent Company** Reed Business Information

**Editor** Murdo Morrison

**Established** 1909

**Insider Info** A trade journal magazine issued weekly, covering business travel. Present circulation of 52,000. Accepts query by phone.

**Non-fiction** Interested in Features, Interview/Profile pieces.

**Submission Guidelines** Accepts query. Send complete manuscript. Articles should be a maximum of 1,800 words.

**Tips** Every week *Flight International*'s global editorial team provides its readers with the latest technical and operational information from the defence, general aviation, business aviation, and technology and spaceflight sectors. No publication breaks as many stories or covers a wider cross-section of the aerospace industry.

  *Flight International* usually uses commissioned work only but does consider unsolicited manuscripts. Analytical, in-depth coverage is required, preferably supported by interviews.

## Focus

**14th Floor, Tower House, Fairfax Street, Bristol, BS1 3BN**

- ☎ 0117 933 8040
- ☎ 0117 934 9008
- ✉ paulparsons@bbcmagazinesbristol.com
- 🌐 www.focusmag.co.uk

**Parent Company** Origin Publishing

**Editor** Paul Parsons

**Established** 1992

**Insider Info** A consumer magazine publication issued monthly, covering men's lifestyle. Present circulation of 58,272. Accepts query via email.

**Non-fiction** Interested in Features and Technical pieces.

  * Pays £200 per 1,000 words for unsolicited articles.

**Submission Guidelines** Articles should be between 1,000 and 3,000 words.

**Tips** BBC *Focus* is a British monthly magazine about science and technology published in Bristol, by Origin Publishing. It covers all aspects of science and technology and is written for general readers as well as people with a more in-depth knowledge of science. Articles that coincide with recent BBC television programmes are often used, so peg submissions to upcoming show content.

## Fortean Times

  The World of Strange Phenomena

**PO Box 2409, London, NW5 4NP**

- ☎ 020 7907 6235
- ☎ 020 7907 6406
- ✉ david_sutton@dennis.co.uk

🌐 www.forteantimes.com
**Parent Company** Dennis Publishing
**Editor** David Sutton
**Established** 1973
**Insider Info** A consumer magazine publication issued 13 times per year, covering science fiction. Present circulation of 25,143.
**Non-fiction** Interested in Photo features, Features, General interest and News pieces.
**Submission Guidelines** Accepts query. Send complete manuscript. Articles should be between 500 and 5,000 words.
**Images** Send photos with submission.
**Tips** *Fortean Times* is a monthly magazine of news, reviews and research on strange phenomena and experiences, curiosities, prodigies and portents. Seeks 'Well-researched and referenced material on current or historical mysteries, or first hand accounts of oddities.' Approach in writing first with ideas.

## Freelance Market News
 An Essential Guide for Freelance Writers
**Sevendale House, 7 Dale Street, Manchester, M1 1JB**
☎ 0161 228 2362
📠 0161 228 3533
📧 fmn@writersbureau.com
🌐 www.freelancemarketnews.com
**Parent Company** The Writers Bureau
**Editor** Angela Cox
**Established** 1968
**Insider Info** A subscription only newsletter issued monthly covering freelance writing. Payment is upon acceptance and is not made with contributor copies, or other premiums. Assignment expenses are not paid. 25 per cent of publication is written by freelancers. Submissions published approximately three months after acceptance with an editorial leda time of three months. Publication is copyrighted and a byline is given. Purchases first UK serial rights. Seasonal material should be submitted three months in advance. Accepts queries by mail, email and fax. Aims to respond to queries, manuscripts and other issues within one month. A sample copy and writer's guidelines are available with SAE (230mm long, 160mm wide) and one first class stamp, or alternatively online. Media packs are available online.
**Non-fiction** Interested in How-to pieces on 'Improve your writing' and Features on writing for a specific market.
 * Receives approximately 12 manuscripts from freelancers per year.

**Submission Guidelines** Please send complete manuscript. Articles should be between 700 and 1,500 words. Please do no submit any previously published material. Conact Angela Cox.
**Tips** *Freelance Market News* is aimed at freelance writers of all levels and gives news, views and advice about new publications. It also publishes information on trends and developments in established markets, both in the UK and overseas.

## The Friend
**173 Euston Road, London, NW1 2BJ**
☎ 020 7663 1010
📠 020 7663 1182
📧 editorial@thefriend.org
🌐 www.thefriend.org
**Parent Company** The Friend Publications Ltd
**Editor** Judy Kirby
**Established** 1843
**Insider Info** A weekly consumer magazine, covering news and views from a Quaker perspective. Present circulation of 4,500, Byline is given. Accepts queries by mail, email and phone. Sample copy and media packs are available online.
**Non-fiction** Publishes Features and General interest articles.
**Submission Guidelines** Send query before sending submissions. Articles must be 300–1,200 words.
**Images** Send photos with submission.
**Tips** Completely independent, *The Friend* brings readers news and views from a Quaker perspective, as well as from a wide range of authors whose writings are of interest to Quakers and non-Quakers alike. There are articles in *The Friend* on issues such as peace, spirituality, Quaker belief, ecumenism and many others, as well as news of Friends from Britain and abroad. To save you wasting your time, the Editor would prefer to give you a response on an idea before you write it. Please send an outline by email or post, or give the office a ring. Judy will try and give you an answer quickly, and if she doesn't, don't be afraid to hound her.

## The Frogmore Papers
**18 Nevill Road, Lewes, East Sussex, BN7 1PF**
🌐 www.frogmorepress.co.uk
**Parent Company** The Frogmore Press
**Editor** Jeremy Page
**Established** 1983
**Insider Info** A consumer journal, issued twice a year, publishing poetry, prose and artwork from new and established authors. Byline is given. Queries accepted by mail. Sample copy is available online.

**Fiction** Publishes Fiction, Novel excerpts and Short Stories.
**Submission Guidelines** Send complete manuscript. Submissions must be 2,000 words. Will not accept anything too experimental or too traditional.
**Poetry** Publishes Free verse and Light verse. Submit a maximum of six poems. Poems must be 20–80 lines.
**Tips** *The Frogmore Papers* tries to publish work that finds a happy medium between traditional and experimental. Poetry submissions must be driven by meaning rather than form, and anything too traditional will be rejected. Prose submissions should not be too experimental, but not too traditional either.

## Frontier
The Business Magazine for Travel Retail
**Central House, 27 Park Street, Croydon, Surrey, CR0 1YD**
- 0870 049 4444
- 0870 049 4400
- marek.kolasinski@metropolis.co.uk
- www.frontiermagazine.co.uk/

**Parent Company** Metropolis Business Publishing
**Editor** Marek Kolasinski
**Established** 1983
**Insider Info** A trade journal magazine issued eight times per year covering the travel retail industry and all its related products. These include, fashion, cosmetics, accessories, wine and spirits, jewellery, electronics, etc. Present circulation of 3,921. Payment is upon acceptance and is not made with contributor copies or other premiums. Assignment expenses are not paid. 15 per cent of the publication is written by freelancers. Submissions will be published approximately one month after acceptance, with an editorial lead time of three weeks. Publication is copyrighted and a byline is given. Purchases all rights. Accepts queries by email. Aims to respond to queries within one week, manuscripts within four weeks and other issues within two weeks. Sample copy and editorial calendars are available free on request. Media packs are available on the website.
**Non-fiction** Interested in Features and Interviews/Profiles.
 * Payment for assigned and unsolicited articles is between £100 and £400.
**Submission Guidelines** Accepts query with published clips. Articles should be between 500 and 2,000 words. Please do not submit any reprint material. Contact Marek Kolasinski.

**Images** Accepts images with submission.
 * Offers no additional payment for photos accepted with a manuscript. Purchases one time rights.
**Submission Guidelines** Submit gif/jpeg files, with model releases and identification of subjects. State availability of photos with submission. Contact Marek Kolasinski.
**Tips** *Frontier* is the foremost trade publication in travel retail and the only ABC audited publication in the industry. The magazine is feature led and the articles are based on first-hand interviews with executives; be it retailers, operators, or suppliers. The writing is informational and targeted at business readers and executives around the world. There is no marketing slant to the articles and the writing itself is as objective as possible. Style is not as important as subject matter and content. If the feature is a new take on a subject, or something that has not been published yet, then it will be considered more than articles which rehash well-known subjects. Originality and quality are the key.

## Fund Manager Today
**17 Ensign House, Canary Wharf, London, E14 9XQ**
- 0870 116 2852
- 0845 638 0341
- info@clearsightmedia.co.uk
- www.clearsightmedia.co.uk

**Parent Company** Clearsight Publishing
**Contact** Managing Editor, Richard Alvin
**Established** 1996
**Insider Info** A trade journal magazine issued bi-monthly, covering global fund management and leisure/lifestyle for the cash rich. Present circulation of 8,500. Payment is upon publication and is not made with contributor copies or other premiums. Assignment expenses are sometimes paid (limit agreed upon in advance). 95 per cent of the magazine is written by freelancers. Submissions are published approximately eight weeks after acceptance, with an editorial lead time of four months. A 50 per cent kill fee is paid, although the copy is not killed. Publication is copyrighted and a byline is given. Purchases first rights and electronic rights. Accepts queries via email and fax. Accepts simultaneous submissions. Aims to respond to queries with two days, manuscripts within four days and other issues within five days. Sample copy is available free on request and online. Writer's guidelines are available via email. Editorial calendars are available free on request and via email. Media packs are available on the website.

**Non-fiction** Interested in 'Blow your bonus' features on expensive Leisure/Lifestyle pieces.
 * Pays between 35p and 65p per word for assigned articles.
**Submission Guidelines** Articles should be between 600 and 900 words. Please do not submit any reprint material.
**Images** Accepts images with submission.
 * Pays a varied fee per photo. Purchases one time rights.
**Submission Guidelines** Submit contact sheets, gif/jpeg files, captions, model releases and identification of subjects. Send photos with submission. Contact Richard Alvin.
**Tips** *Fund Manager Today* is aimed at anyone in the fund management industry around the world, or interested in either that, or similar investment fields. Potential contributors must understand the market that the magazine serves.

## Gairm
**29 Waterloo Street, Glasgow, G2 6BZ**
- 0141 221 1971
**Parent Company** Gairm Publications
**Editor** Derick Thomson
**Established** 1951
**Insider Info** A consumer magazine publication issued quarterly covering general interest, literary subjects. Present circulation of 2,000.
**Non-fiction** Interested in Poetry and Features pieces.
**Submission Guidelines** Accepts query.
**Fiction** Interested in Fiction pieces.
**Tips** *Gairm* is a Scottish Gaelic literary magazine published by one of the largest Gaelic publishing houses, Gairm Publications. It prints poetry and fiction in the Gaelic language, as well as articles about writing. *Gairm* does not have a website but Gairm Publications can be contacted for further details and submission guidelines.

## Galleries Magazine
**54 Uxbridge Road, London, W12 8LP**
- 020 8740 7020
- ed@artefact.co.uk
- www.galleries.co.uk
**Parent Company** Barrington Publications
**Editor** Andrew Aitken
**Insider Info** A consumer magazine publication issued monthly, covering general interest, literary subjects. Accepts queries by mail and email.

**Non-fiction** Interested in Photo features, Features, Interviews/Profiles, Reviews, General interest and Opinion (not letters to the Editor) pieces.
**Submission Guidelines** Accepts query.
**Tips** *Galleries Magazine* prints articles about galleries and art exhibitions in Britain, including previews of upcoming events, interviews, book and gallery reviews, opinions and features. Also has an in-depth art listings section. *Galleries* prints reviews and previews of gallery exhibitions in the UK, and would need insider or advance information of important shows nationwide.

## Gardeners' World Magazine
**Room AG 193, 80 Wood Lane, London, W12 0TT**
- 020 8433 3959
- 020 8433 3986
- gweditorial@bbc.co.uk
- www.gardenersworld.com
**Parent Company** BBC Worldwide Publishing
**Editor** Adam Pasco
**Established** 2005
**Insider Info** A consumer magazine publication issued monthly, covering home interest and gardening. Present circulation of 300,418.
**Tips** A monthly title that provides fresh ideas and clear trustworthy advice from leading television experts, including Monty Don and Alan Titchmarsh. From plants and flowers, to gardens and design, shopping ideas to practical projects, the magazine's stylish approach is an inspiration to gardeners of every ability. The magazine has many regular features, so unusual articles are more likely to succeed, ideally of a seasonal nature, or pegged to upcoming events in the gardening world.

## Gardens Illustrated
**14th Floor, Tower House, Fairfax Street, Bristol, BS1 3BN**
- 0117 314 8774
- gardens@bbcmagazinesbristol.com
- www.gardensillustrated.com
**Parent Company** BBC Worldwide Publishing
**Editor** Juliet Roberts
**Established** 1993
**Insider Info** A consumer magazine publication issued ten times per year, covering gardening. Present circulation of 23,312. Accepts queries by mail.
**Submission Guidelines** Accepts query.
**Tips** *Gardens Illustrated Magazine* is a highly respected international magazine, read in over 70 countries worldwide. Aimed at the 'discerning

gardener', *Gardens Illustrated Magazine* is a glossy, beautifully designed publication that has won widespread acclaim for its superb photography and high standards of journalism. Ideas must focus on garden design specifically, ideally with international appeal, and will be strengthened by including full colour photographs.

## Gath

**Martins Printworks, Main Street, Pittal, Berwick upon Tweed, TD15 1RS**

● 01289 306006

**Insider Info** A consumer magazine publication issued quarterly, covering general interest, literary subjects.

**Tips** *Gath* magazine is a Gaelic periodical which aims to stimulate contemporary Gaelic writing. Being a Gaelic magazine, *Gath* only accepts submissions in the Gaelic language.

## Geographical

**Circle Publishing, 2nd Floor, 83–84 George Street, Richmond, Surrey, TW9 1HE**

● 020 8332 2713

● magazine@geographical.co.uk

● www.geographical.co.uk

**Parent Company** Royal Geographic Society

**Editor** Geordie Torr

**Contact** Features Editor, Natalie Hoare

**Established** 1935

**Insider Info** A consumer magazine publication issued monthly, covering general interest, miscellaneous subjects. Present circulation of 19,692.

**Tips** Established in 1935, *Geographical* is the award-winning lively, colourful monthly magazine of the Royal Geographical Society, presenting geography in its broadest sense. It has exciting and beautifully illustrated articles on people, places, cultures, adventure, responsible travel, history, science and environmental issues. *Geographical* 'takes pride in its high quality editorial and photographic content', so all submissions must be well crafted and fully researched, supplying accompanying photographs is a must.

## Glamour

**6–8 Old Bond Street, London, WC2H 8JG**

● 020 7499 9080

● 020 7491 2551

● letters@glamourmagazine.co.uk, corrie.jackson@condenast.co.uk

● www.glamourmagazine.co.uk

**Parent Company** Conde Nast Publications Ltd

**Editor** Jo Elvin

**Contact** Features Editor, Corrie Jackson

**Established** 2001

**Insider Info** A monthly consumer magazine covering women's lifestyle topics. Present circulation of 588,539. Media pack available online: www.condenast.co.uk/mediapacks

**Non-fiction** Publishes General interest, Interviews, Reviews and Photo features on Celebrities, Fashion, Beauty, Music, Television, Film and Real-life.

**Tips** The magazine is aimed at women aged 18–35 and is published in a small, 'handbag-sized' format.

## Global Tapestry Journal

**Spring Bank, Longsight Road, Copster Green, Blackburn, Lancashire, BB1 9EU**

**Parent Company** BB Books Press

**Editor** Dave Cunliffe

**Established** 1961

**Insider Info** A consumer journal publication issued quarterly, covering general interest, literary subjects. Present circulation of 1,000. A byline is given.

**Non-fiction** Interested in Poetry, Features, Interviews/Profiles, Reviews, and Opinion (not letters to the Editor) pieces.

**Submission Guidelines** Accepts query.

**Fiction** Interested in Fiction, Mainstream, Novel excerpts and Short stories.

**Submission Guidelines** Please send complete manuscript.

**Poetry** Accepts Avant-garde, Free verse, Light verse and Traditional poetry.

**Tips** *Global Tapestry Journal* publishes global poetry and prose with a cultural orientation, as well as articles about writing, reviews, interviews, artwork and opinion columns. *Global Tapestry Journal* will publish both short and longer submissions of prose or poetry. An SAE must be enclosed with all submissions, for reply.

## Golf Monthly

**King's Reach Tower, Stamford Street, London, SE1 9LS**

● 020 7261 7237

● 020 7261 7240

● michael_harris@ipcmedia.com

● www.golf-monthly.co.uk

**Parent Company** IPC Media

**Editor** Michael Harris

**Established** 1911

**Insider Info** A consumer magazine publication issued monthly, covering golf. Present circulation of 73,775. Accepts queries by mail and email.

**Non-fiction** Interested in How-to, Features, Interviews/Profiles, Reviews, New products and General interest pieces.

**Submission Guidelines** Accepts query. Send complete manuscript. Articles should be between 1,500 and 2,000 words.

**Tips** *Golf Monthly* is an established and authoritative, yet lively and welcoming brand in a sport which continues to grow and grow. Targeted at good golfers who are regular players – and keen to get even better – *Golf Monthly* is Britain's most widely read golfing magazine. It represents the real 'voice of golf' with leading columnists, top players and unrivalled coverage of equipment and instruction. *Golf Monthly*, quite simply, is the quality brand for the golfing consumer. They are not interested in instruction articles from outside contributors – try something else such as unusual kit reviews or player profiles.

## Good Housekeeping

**National Magazine House, 72 Broadwick Street, London, W1F 9EP**

- 020 7439 5000
- 020 7439 5616
- lindsay.nicholson@natmags.co.uk
- www.goodhousekeeping.co.uk

**Parent Company** National Magazine Company
**Editor** Louise Chunn
**Contact** Features Editor, Lucy Moore
**Established** 1922

**Insider Info** A consumer magazine publication issued monthly covering women's interests and women's lifestyle/fashion. Circulation of 441,151. Accepts queries by mail.

**Non-fiction** Interested in General interest pieces.

**Submission Guidelines** Accepts query with published clips.

**Tips** *Good Housekeeping* is the UK's most popular consumer magazine for women over 35. Most work is commissioned, but send ideas via post including a synopsis of your idea, relevant cuttings in support of the idea, and examples of previously printed work.

## GQ

**Vogue House, Hanover Square, London, W1S 1JU**

- 020 7499 9080
- 020 7495 1679
- charlotte.zamani@condenast.co.uk
- www.gqmagazine.co.uk

**Parent Company** Conde Nast Publications
**Editor** Dylan Jones
**Contact** Features Director, Alex Bilmes
**Established** 1988

**Insider Info** A consumer magazine publication issued monthly covering men's lifestyle. Present circulation of 126,797. Accepts queries by mail and fax.

**Tips** *GQ* (originally called Gentlemen's Quarterly) is a monthly men's magazine which focuses on men's fashion and style. It also features articles on food, movies, fitness, sex, music, toys, and books. It is generally perceived as more upscale than 'lad mags', such as *Maxim* or *FHM*. *GQ*'s readership is older, and has more expendable income than that of other men's magazines, so any submitted ideas should be targeted accordingly and be more upmarket. Reviews of expensive high-end gadgets are popular.

## Grand Designs Magazine

**National House, 121–123 High Street, Epping, Essex, CM16 4BD**

- 01992 563422
- yasmine@granddesignsmagazine.com
- www.granddesignsmagazine.com

**Parent Company** Media 10
**Editor** Claire Barrett
**Contact** Editorial Assistant, Julie Bowyer
**Established** 2004

**Insider Info** A consumer magazine publication issued monthly covering interiors and architecture. Present circulation of 38,000. 50 per cent of the magazine is written by freelancers. Submissions are published approximately two months after acceptance, with an editorial lead time of two months. Publication is copyrighted and a byline is given. All rights are purchased. Seasonal material must be submitted approximately two months in advance. Queries accepted by mail, email and phone. Simultaneous submissions and previously published submissions are accepted. Aims to respond to queries and manuscripts within four days. Payment is upon acceptance and is not made with contributor copies, or other premiums. Assignment expenses are paid. A sample copy and writer's guidelines are available free on request. Media packs are available on the website.

**Non-fiction** Interested in How-to, Photo features Inspirational, Features, Interviews/Profiles and Technical pieces.

\* Receives approximately 50 manuscripts from freelancers per year. Payment for assigned articles is between £300 and £500. Payment for unsolicited articles is between £250 and £500.

**Submission Guidelines** Accepts email idea. Articles should be between 800 and 1,200 words. Please do not send any material for reprints. Contact Fiona Sibley.

**Images** Accepts images with submission.
 \* Negotiates payment individually. Purchases all rights.

**Submission Guidelines** State availability of photos with submission. Contact Claire Limpus.

**Tips** The readership for *Grand Designs Magazine* is 50:50 male/female ratio, of those who watch *Grand Designs* with Kevin McLeod, and those interested in home improvement. Potential contributors should contact the Deputy Editor with their idea, and then call a couple of days later to chase it up.

## Granta
**2/3 Hanover Yard, Noel Road, London, N1 8BE**
- 020 7704 9776
- 020 7704 0474
- info@granta.com
- www.granta.com

**Parent Company** Granta Publications
**Editor** Ian Jack
**Established** 1889

**Insider Info** A consumer magazine publication issued quarterly, covering new writing and documentary photography. Present circulation of 46,831. Publication is copyrighted and a byline is given. Editorial lead time is three months. Queries are accepted by mail and email. Aims to respond to manuscripts within three months. Writer's guidelines and media packs are available on the website.

**Non-fiction** Interested in Photo features, Features, Travel and Historical/Nostalgic pieces.

**Submission Guidelines** Send completed manuscript.

**Fiction** Interested in Novel excerpts and New Writing pieces.
 \* Payment for fiction is between £75 and £5,000.

**Submission Guidelines** Send complete manuscript. Please do not submit genre fiction, i.e. no romance, crime, science fiction, fantasy fiction, historical/poetry.

**Images** State availability of photos with submission. Contact Liz Jobey.

**Tips** *Granta* magazine publishes new writing, fiction, personal history, reportage and inquiring journalism, four times a year. It also publishes documentary photography. *Granta* does not have a political or literary manifesto, but it does have a belief in the power and urgency of the story, both in fiction and non-fiction, and the story's supreme ability to describe, illuminate and make real. 'The main guideline for submitting work to *Granta* is simply to read the magazine thoroughly and ask yourself honestly if you feel your piece meets our criteria. We receive many submissions every day, many of which are completely unsuitable for *Granta* (however well written).'

## Grazia
**189 Shaftesbury Avenue, London, WC2H 8JG,**
- 020 7437 9011
- 020 7520 6599
- hattie.brett@emap.com
- www.graziamagazine.co.uk

**Parent Company** EMAP Plc
**Editor** Jane Bruton
**Contact** Editorial Assistant, Hattie Brett
**Established** 2005

**Insider Info** A weekly glossy consumer magazine covering women's lifestyle topics. Present circulation of 210,200.

**Non-fiction** Publishes General interest features, Interviews and Photo features on Real life, Fashion, Beauty, Food, Home and Travel.

**Tips** The title is aimed specifically at women aged 25–45 and aims to bridge the gap between monthly glossies and weekly titles, by being Britain's first weekly glossy.

## Grow Your Own
The Best for Kitchen Gardeners
**25 Phoenix Court, Hawkins Road, Colchester, Essex, CO2 8JY**
- 01206 505979
- craig.drever@aceville.co.uk
- www.growfruitandveg.co.uk

**Parent Company** Aceville Publications
**Editor** Craig Drever
**Established** 2005

**Insider Info** A consumer magazine publication issued monthly covering growing fruit, vegetables and herbs in gardens and allotments. Present circulation of 40,000. Payment upon publication and assignment expenses are sometimes paid (limit agreed upon in advance). 50 per cent of the magazine is written by freelancers. Submissions are published approximately one month after acceptance. Publication is copyrighted and a byline is given. Seasonal material must be submitted two months in advance. Queries are accepted by mail, email, and phone. Simultaneous submissions and previously published submissions are accepted.

**493**

**Non-fiction** Interested in Book excerpts, How-to, Photo features and Technical pieces.
**Submission Guidelines** Articles should be between 400 and 2,000 words. Contact Craig Drever.
**Images** Accepts images with submission.
\* Pays a varied fee per photo.
**Submission Guidelines** Submit contact sheets, prints, gif/jpeg files. Contact Craig Drever.

## Guitarist

The Guitar Player's Bible
**30 Monmouth Street, Bath, BA1 2BW**
☎ 01225 442244
☎ 01225 732285
✉ guitarist@futurenet.co.uk
🌐 www.guitarist.co.uk
**Parent Company** Future Publishing
**Editor** Michael Leonard
**Established** 1984
**Insider Info** A magazine consumer publication issued 13 times per year, covering music, practical/playing. Present circulation of 29,152.
**Non-fiction** Publishes Photo Features, How-to an Technical articles.
**Submission Guidelines** Ideas for articles are welcome, particularly tutorial, lessons or practical techniques, so contact the Editor with a synopsis via post or email.
**Tips** *Guitarist* is the longest established guitar magazine in Europe, aimed at players who are serious about their art and craft. Each 200 plus page issue is covers exclusive gear reviews, a cover-mounted CD, in-depth interviews with guitar legends and new stars, complete tablature and backing tracks for classic tracks, and professional lessons from top tutors. An in-depth knowledge of guitar is essential for contributors.

## Guitar Techniques

**30 Monmouth Street, Bath, BA1 2BW**
☎ 01225 442244
☎ 01225 732275
✉ guitar.tech@futurenet.co.uk
🌐 www.guitar-techniques.com
**Parent Company** Future Publishing
**Editor** Neville Marten
**Insider Info** A consumer magazine publication issued monthly, covering music, practical/playing. Present circulation of 20,561.
**Tips** *Guitar Techniques* takes the UK's foremost guitar teachers and players, and transfers their finesse and passion for music into a magazine, therfore all contributors are highly skilled and experienced. The

magazine includes UK focused reports on new bands and gigs, plus kit reviews and tutorials.

## The Haiku Quarterly (HQ)

**39 Exmouth Street, Swindon, Wiltshire, SN1 3PU**
☎ 01793 523927
🌐 www.noggs.dsl.pipex.com/hq
**Parent Company** HQ Poetry Magazine
**Editor** Kevin Bailey
**Established** 1990
**Insider Info** Quarterly consumer magazine that specialises in publishing Haiku or Haiku-esque poetry from new or established writers. A byline is given. Accepts queries by mail. Aims to respond to manuscripts within six months. Sample copy is available online.
**Non-fiction** Publishes Features and Reviews.
**Submission Guidelines** Send query before sending submissions.
**Poetry** Publishes Free verse, Haiku and Light verse.
\* Payment via contributor copy for poetry.
**Tips** At least a third of every issue is given over to Haiku, the rest is filled with mainstream contemporary poetry, articles, reviews and some more experimental types of poetry. *HQ* mostly publishes work from established writers but will also accept submissions from new writers, especially experimental or developmental poetry.

## HALI

Carpet, Textile & Islamic Art
**50 Poland Street, London, W1F 7AX**
☎ 020 7970 4600
☎ 020 7578 7221
✉ hali@centaur.co.uk
🌐 hali.com
**Parent Company** Hali Publications/Centaur Media
**Editor** Ben Evans
**Contact** Managing Editor, Daniel Shaffer
**Established** 1978
**Insider Info** A special interest magazine issued bi-monthly at present, soon to return to quarterly. *HALI* covers antique and modern oriental and European carpets, tapestry, world textile art, tribal art, Asian art and Islamic art. Present circulation of 4,000. 80 per cent of magazine is written by freelancers. Payment is upon publication. Publication is copyrighted and a byline is given. Purchases one time rights and electronic rights. Average lead time is ten weeks. Seasonal material must be submitted ten weeks in advance. Queries accepted by mail, email and fax. Previously published submissions are accepted.

**Non-fiction** Publishes Features and Technical articles.

**Tips** *HALI* is a special interest magazine with a small circulation, and a loyal and very involved core readership. The magazine is mainly supported by the oriental carpet trade, but covers all aspects of the arts with textile artefacts of all kinds from all places being the starting point and unifying theme. Specialist writers need to be knowledgeable.

## Handshake
**5 Cross Farm, Station Road North, Fearnhead, Warrington, WA2 0QG**

🌐 www.waldeneast.fsnet.co.uk/handshakeinfo.htm

**Parent Company** The Eight Hand Gang
**Editor** John Francis Haines
**Insider Info** A consumer newsletter publication issued irregularly, covering general interest, literary subjects.
**Non-fiction** Interested in Poetry and Market news.
**Poetry** Interested in Science fiction poetry.
**Tips** *Handshake* is the irregular newsletter of The Eight Hand Gang, an association of UK science fiction poets. *Handshake* is one sheet of A4, a side of which contains association news and market information for science fiction poets, the other has short science fiction poetry from contributors. *Handshake* accepts submissions of science fiction poetry, providing they are short, due to the limited space available. All submissions must be accompanied by SAE.

## Harlequin
**PO Box 23392, Edinburgh, EH8 7YZ**

☎ 01506 510002
📧 columbine@harlequinmagazine.com
🌐 www.harlequinmagazine.com

**Editor** Jim Sinclair
**Established** 2001
**Insider Info** A consumer magazine publication issued three times per year covering general interest, literary subjects. Present circulation of 100.
**Poetry** Interested in Avant-garde, Free verse, Light verse, Post-modern poetry.
**Tips** *Harlequin* is a poetry magazine that combines art and poetry with a mystic, new-age theme. *Harlequin* has a very strong sense of theme and style, so it is advantageous to study back-issues of the magazine carefully, to check the suitability of your work.

## Heat
**Endeavour House, 189 Shaftesbury Avenue, London, WC2H 8JG**

☎ 020 7859 8657
☎ 020 7859 8670
📧 heat@emap.com
🌐 www.emap.com

**Parent Company** EMAP Plc
**Editor** Mark Frith
**Contact** Features Editor, Lucie Cave
**Established** 1999
**Insider Info** A weekly consumer magazine covering celebrity gossip and women's lifestyle. Present circulation of 598,623.
**Non-fiction** Publishes General interest, Expose, Reviews and Photo features on Celebrities, Fashion, Beauty, Music, Television, Film and Real-life.
**Tips** The magazine is aimed at women aged 18–40, although it also has a substantial gay male following. The publication is heavily image based and any text heavy articles tend to be celebrity interviews.

## Hello!
**Wellington House, 69–71 Upper Ground, London, SE1 9PQ**

☎ 020 7667 8700
☎ 020 7667 8716
📧 firstname.lastname@hellomagazine.com
🌐 www.hellomagazine.com

**Editor** Ronnie Whelan
**Contact** Features Editor, Juliet Herd; Features Assistant, Hayley Shedden
**Established** 1988
**Insider Info** A weekly consumer magazine covering celebrity gossip and women's lifestyle topics. Present circulation of 412,807.
**Non-fiction** Publishes General Interest Features, Interviews and Photo Features on celebrities and international royalty.
**Tips** The title is aimed specifically at women aged 25 to 44 years old.

## Hi Fi News
**10th Floor, Leon House, 233 High Street, Croydon, Surrey, CR9 1HZ**

☎ 020 8726 8311
☎ 020 8726 8397
📧 hi-finews@ipcmedia.com
🌐 www.hifinews.co.uk

**Parent Company** IPC Media
**Editor** Paul Miller; Steve Fairclough

**Contact** Managing Editor, Andrew Harrison;
Editorial Assistant, Marie Ek
**Established** 1956
**Insider Info** A consumer magazine publication
issued monthly covering high end audio equipment.
Present circulation of 15,000. 40 per cent of the
magazine is written by freelancers. It takes three
weeks from manuscript acceptance, to publication.
Publication is copyrighted and a byline is not given.
First rights are purchased. Queries will be accepted
by mail, email, fax and phone. Accepts simultaneous
submissions. Aims to respond to queries and
manuscripts within five days. Sample copy is
available free on request. Writer's guidelines are
available via email. Payment is upon publication and
writer's are not paid with contributor copies or other
premiums. Assignment expenses are sometimes
paid (limit agreed upon in advance).
**Non-fiction** Interested in Photo features, Features
Reviews, New products and Technical articles.
\* Payment is made for assigned articles on
agreement.
**Submission Guidelines** Accepts query. Articles
should be between 2,000 and 3,000 words. Please do
not submit any reprint material. Contact Marie Ek.
**Images** Send photos with submission.
**Tips** The leading audio journal in the UK. *Hi Fi News*
review, test and provide information on audio
equipment, they are passionate about all things
audio, from vintage gear to iPods. Writers should
have a passion for audio, and expert technical
knowledge. They should be dedicated to meeting
deadlines and be able to give objective views on
high-end audio kit. Love for music and sound is vital!

## History Today
**20 Old Compton Street, London, W1D 4TW**
- 020 7534 8000
- p.furtado@historytoday.com
- www.historytoday.com

**Parent Company** History Today Trust for the
Advancement of Education
**Editor** Peter Furtado
**Established** 1951
**Insider Info** A consumer magazine publication
issued monthly, covering domestic news and
current affairs. Present circulation of 27,070. Accepts
queries by mail. Please do not send any unsolicited
manuscripts.
**Non-fiction** Interested in Photo features, Features
and Historical/Nostalgic pieces.
**Submission Guidelines** Accepts query including
SAE. Articles should be a maximum of 3,500 words.

**Tips** *History Today* publishes essays on all periods,
regions and themes of history, many of them by the
world's leading scholars. All are carefully edited and
illustrated to make *History Today* a pleasurable, as
well as an informative read. The publication will only
accept freelance contributions from academic
scholars, or equivalent, concerning new
developments in history or archaeology.

## Home Cinema Choice
**30 Monmouth Street, Bath, BA1 2BW**
- 01225 224422
- 01225 732275
- www.homecinemachoice.com

**Parent Company** Future Publishing
**Editor** Steve May
**Insider Info** A consumer magazine publication
issued monthly, covering home entertainment
subjects. Present circulation of 13,542.
**Tips** *Home Cinema Choice* is the UK's best-selling
home cinema enthusiasts magazine. Every issue
features news and reviews of the latest home
cinema equipment, from amplifiers, receivers,
processors and power amps, to DVD recorders,
speakers, projectors and flat panel TVs. The
magazine also offers advice on setting up this
hardware alongside features focusing on drop dead
gorgeous home cinema installations, and reviews of
the latest DVD releases. Check regular features and
develop an article that covers unusual topics around
the magazine's interests.

## Homes & Gardens
**King's Reach Tower, Stamford Street, London,
SE1 9LS**
- 020 7261 5678
- 020 7261 6247
- homesandgardens@ipcmedia.com
- www.homesandgardens.com

**Parent Company** IPC Media
**Editor** Deborah Baker
**Contact** Managing Editor, Fiona Surfleet; Features
Editor, Helen Stone
**Established** 1919
**Insider Info** A consumer magazine publication
issued monthly, covering women's and home
interests. Present circulation of 139,017. Accepts
query by mail and email.
**Non-fiction** Interested in Photo features, Features,
Interview/Profile pieces.
**Submission Guidelines** Accepts query. Articles
should be between 900 and 1,000 words long.
**Images** Send photos with submission.

**Tips** *Homes & Gardens* celebrates the beauty of classic British style on every page. Established for over 80 years *Homes & Gardens* has always been engaging and accessible. Delivering inspirational decorating through real-life stories and beautiful photography, while at all times remaining real and relevant. It is the ultimate source book for beautiful ideas and detailed information, inspiring its readers to become their own interior designers. Most material is specially commissioned. Submissions must be supported by suitable photographs where appropriate, please include as many as possible.

## Homes Overseas Magazine

The UK's leading international property magazine
**1st floor, 1 East Poultry Avenue, West Smithfield, London, EC1A 9PT**

- ☎ 020 7002 8300
- ☎ 020 7002 8310
- ✉ info@blendoncom.com
- 🌐 www.homesoverseas.co.uk

**Parent Company** Blendon Communications Ltd
**Editor** Kate Hamilton
**Established** 1965

**Insider Info** A consumer magazine publication issued 13 times a year, covering overseas residential property. Present circulation of 50,842. 75 per cent of the magazine is written by freelancers. Submissions are published approximately three months after acceptance with an editorial lead time of two weeks. 50 per cent kill fee is paid for not published assigned manuscripts. Publication is copyrighted and all rights are purchased. Seasonal material must be submitted four weeks in advance. Accepts query by mail, email and phone. Aims to respond to queries and manuscripts within two weeks. Payment is upon publication, and is not given via contributor copies or other premiums. Assignment expenses are sometimes paid (limit agreed upon in advance), Sample copy is available with SAE. Writer's guidelines are available free on request. Limited forward features will be made available upon request. Media packs are available on the website.

**Non-fiction** Interested in How-to, Photo features, Features with generally no fewer than three property or property buying examples, Personal experience of buying overseas property, Destination (including at least three detailed property examples), Case studies (including buying process).

\* Approximately 130 Non-fiction manuscripts are purchased from freelancers each year. Assigned and unsolicited articles are paid at approximately 25p per word.

**Submission Guidelines** Accepts query with published clips. Articles should be between 1,200 and 3,000 words.

**Tips** *Homes Overseas* is positive, upbeat, objective and informative and is one of the most respected names in international residential property. The magazine offers a one stop shop of advice to potential buyers, be they holiday homers, retirees or pure investors. The readership generally falls into the ABC1 category.

## Horse & Hound

**King's Reach Tower, Stamford Street, London, SE1 9LS**

- ☎ 020 7261 6315
- ☎ 020 7261 5429
- ✉ lucy_higginson@ipcmedia.com
- 🌐 www.horseandhound.co.uk

**Parent Company** IPC Media
**Editor** Lucy Higginson
**Established** 1884

**Insider Info** A consumer magazine publication issued weekly, covering leisure interests and equestrianism. Present circulation of 71,688. Accepts queries by mail and email.

**Tips** Regarded as the 'bible' of the equestrian world, *Horse & Hound*s much respected editorial excellence makes it the number one choice for horse lovers and professionals alike. As the only equestrian weekly, *Horse & Hound* provides reportage covering all disciplines, together with the latest news and views from around the country. Specialist information is in high demand, particularly veterinary information relating to the health and care of horses.

## Horse

Inspiration for Riders
**King's Reach Tower, Stamford Street, London, SE1 9LS**

- ☎ 020 7261 5867
- ✉ joanna_pyatt@ipcmedia.com
- 🌐 www.horsemagazine.co.uk

**Parent Company** IPC Media
**Editor** Joanna Pyatt
**Established** 1997

**Insider Info** A consumer magazine publication issued monthly, covering leisure interests and equestrianism. Present circulation of 24,302.

**Non-fiction** Interested in Horse related How-to features, i.e. 'Hints and Tips', 'Techniques', 'Grooming', etc, Exposés, Interviews/Profiles and General interest articles.

**Submission Guidelines** Accepts query with published clips and a CV.

**Tips** *Horse* magazine aims to help reader get more out of their time with their horse, whether reader's ride as a hobby, or are a keen competitors looking for expert tips on how to move up to the next level. *Horse* magazine is mostly interested in articles on leading equestrian celebrities.

## Horticulture Week

**Teddington Studios, Broom Road, Teddington, Middlesex, TW11 9BE**
- 020 8267 4977
- 020 8267 4987
- kate.lowe@haymarket.com
- www.hortweek.com

**Parent Company** Haymarket Publications
**Editor** Kate Lowe
**Insider Info** A trade journal magazine issued weekly, covering horticulture. Present circulation of 8,787.

**Tips** *Horticulture Week* is the leading weekly business title for all horticulture professionals, whatever sector they work in. Each week all the latest news is published, along with in-depth analysis, uncovering the real issues that are shaping the industry. Writer's should have insider knowledge about the horticulture industry, concerning the latest developments or knowledge of related subject that is in demand.

## Hospital Doctor

**15th Floor Quadrant House, The Quadrant, Sutton, Surrey, SM2 5BR**
- 020 8652 8763
- 020 8652 8946
- hospital.doctor@rbi.co.uk
- www.hospital-doctor.net

**Parent Company** Reed Elsevier
**Insider Info** A trade journal tabloid publication issued weekly, covering NHS and private medicine for all junior, consultant and staff and associate grade hospital doctors. Present circulation of 38,800. Payment upon publication. 15 per cent of the publication is written by freelancers. Average lead time of two weeks. Publication is copyrighted and a byline is given. Seasonal material must be submitted two weeks in advance. Queries are accepted by email. Aims to respond to queries and manuscripts within three days. Sample copy is available online and via email. Writer's guidelines are available free on request and via email.

**Non-fiction** Interested in opinion (not letters to the Editor) on Medical, Financial and Political issues.

**Tips** *Hospital Doctor* provides all the clinical, political and financial news and features that busy doctors need.

## House & Garden

**Vogue House, Hanover Square, London, W1S 1JU**
- 020 7499 9080
- 020 7629 2907
- harriet.milward@condenast.co.uk
- www.houseandgarden.co.uk

**Parent Company** Condé Nast Publications
**Editor** Susan Crewe
**Established** 1947
**Insider Info** A consumer magazine publication issued monthly, covering women's and home interests. Present circulation of 140,527.

**Tips** Containing general interest articles on house and garden, along with business directories, *House & Garden* magazine supplies all the information required for any proud homeowner. Most material is produced in-house and other material will usually only come from qualified freelancers with specialised knowledge.

## House Beautiful

**National Magazine House, 72 Broadwick Street, London, W1F 9EP**
- 020 7439 5000
- 020 7439 5141
- houseb.mail@natmags.co.uk, firstname.lastname@natmags.co.uk
- www.housebeautiful.co.uk

**Parent Company** National Magazine Company
**Editor** Julia Goodwin
**Established** 1989
**Insider Info** A consumer magazine publication issued monthly covering women's home interests. Present circulation of 195,450. Queries are accepted by mail.

**Non-fiction** Interested in Photo features, Features and Interviews/Profiles.

**Submission Guidelines** Accepts queries. Please do not send any unsolicited manuscripts.

**Tips** *House Beautiful* is a popular source book of classic decorating looks, with regular and comprehensive colour scheming pages, and a wide range of shopping suggestions for those special details that make a difference. Features real reader homes from around the UK – ranging from comfortable country style, to the chic city look and provides inspiration and practical advice, whatever your decorating taste. *House Beautiful* is only looking for contributions from freelancers with specialist knowledge and examples of similar previously published articles.

## Ideal Home

**King's Reach Tower, Stamford Street, London, SE1 9LS**

- 020 7261 6474
- 020 7261 6494
- susan_rose@ipcmedia.com
- www.idealhomemagazine.co.uk

**Parent Company** IPC Media
**Editor** Susan Rose
**Established** 1920
**Insider Info** Consumer magazine publication issued monthly, covering women's and home interests. Present circulation of 237,525. Queries accepted by mail.
**Non-fiction** Interested in Photo features and Features.
**Submission Guidelines** Accepts query.
**Tips** This award winning magazine is the UK's best selling home title and has been the voice of the British homeowner for over 80 years. Its family orientated readers do their homework before embarking on projects, and are looking for inspiration to help them make the most of their homes. No magazine offers more creative ideas, decorating inspiration, real homes and expert advice on consumer issues and life at home than *Ideal Home*. Most features are privately commissioned. Check the latest trends in interior design and plan articles to work ahead of them if possible to catch the latest new, or unusual, developments.

## Illustration

**39 Elmsleigh Road, Twickenham, Middlesex, TW2 5EF**

- ruth.prickett@illustration-mag.com
- www.illustration-mag.com

**Editor** Ruth Prickett
**Established** 2004
**Insider Info** A consumer magazine publication issued quarterly covering art. Present circulation of 2,000. Queries accepted via mail and email.
**Non-fiction** Interested in Photo features, Features, Interviews/Profiles, Reviews, General interest, Historical/Nostalgic, News and events articles.
**Submission Guidelines** Accepts query.
**Tips** *Illustration* is a general magazine about art and illustration. It contains articles on artists, collectors

and collections, exhibitions, the history of art, art philosophy and any important events relating to the art world. *Illustration* often has many articles about the latest news and events in the art world, and is always seeking interesting news breaks.

## inBalance Magazine

 Health & Fitness

**50 Parkway, Welwyn Garden City, Hertfordshire, AL8 6HH**

- 01707 33900
- editor@inbalancemagazine.com
- www.inbalancemagazine.com

**Parent Company** Pintail Media Ltd
**Editor** Dave Reeder
**Contact** Managing Editor, Val Reynolds Brown; Features, Kate Campbell
**Established** 1990
**Insider Info** A consumer online magazine issued monthly via an email update, covering health and fitness. Present circulation of 2,500 email recipients. 15 per cent of the magazine is written by freelancers. Payment is not made, instead the magazine is aimed at anyone interested in widening their portfolio. Features and fiction are welcomed from first timers. Strict editorial guidelines operate and a copy of these is available on request. It takes seven days between manuscript acceptance and publication. Publication is copyrighted and a byline is given. Average lead time of six months. Seasonal material must be submitted three months in advance. Queries accepted by email. Simultaneous submissions and previously published submissions are accepted. Aims to respond to queries within two weeks and manuscripts within four weeks. Writer's may be paid with a contributor copy, via a free web link. Assignment writer's may sometimes be paid their expenses incurred whilst on an assignment (limit agreed upon in advance). Writer's guidelines are available free on request and via email. Media packs care available on the website.
**Non-fiction** Interested in Book excerpts, How-to features, Essays, Humour, Inspirational, Features, Interviews/Profiles, Reviews, New Products, Travel and Personal experience articles.
**Submission Guidelines** Accepts query. Articles should be between 250 and 5,000 words. Please do not submit material for reprints. Contact Dave Reeder.
**Fiction** Interested in Fiction, Adventure, Condensed novels, Humorous, Slice-of-life vignettes, Suspense and Novel excerpts.

**Submission Guidelines** Accepts query. Articles should be between 500 and 5,000 words. Contact Val Reynolds Brown.

**Images** Accepts images with submission.
 * No rights are purchased on photos.

**Submission Guidelines** Submit gif/jpeg files with captions and model releases. Identification of subjects is required. State availability of photos with submission. Contact Val Reynolds Brown.

**Tips** *inBalance* is an eclectic mix of information directly related to health and fitness with environmental responsibility as a strong theme. Readers are 99 per cent female, aged 25–75, and based all over UK and beyond. The readers are mainly professional, married women whose main interests are health, fitness and travel. *inBalance* had a radio programme in London that had 16,000 listeners, some of whom still receive the email update. When *inBalance* was in print it had 3,500 subscribers, many continue to receive the email update.

## In The Know
**Academic House, 24–28 Oval Road, London, NW1 7DT**
- 020 7241 8000
- intheknow@bauer.co.uk
- www.bauer.co.uk,
www.intheknowmagazine.co.uk

**Parent Company** H. Bauer Publishing
**Editor** Keith Kendrick; Commissioning Editor, Louie Matthews
**Established** 2006
**Insider Info** A weekly consumer magazine covering women's lifestyle, news and celebrity topics. Present Circulation of 107,000.
**Non-fiction** Publishes General interest features, Interviews and Photo features on Television, Real life, Current affairs, Consumer affairs, Fashion, Beauty, Celebrities, Health and Entertainment.
**Tips** *In The Know* is a relatively new venture that aims to add more international news and consumer content to the traditional woman's weekly format.

## InStyle
**King's Reach Tower, Stamford Street, London, SE1 9LS**
- 020 7261 5000
- 020 7261 6664
- firstname_lastname@instyleuk.com
- www.instyle.com

**Parent Company** IPC Media
**Editor** Trish Halpin

**Contact** Senior Features Editor, Kate O'Donnell
**Established** 2001
**Insider Info** A consumer magazine publication issued monthly, covering women's interests and women's lifestyle/fashion. Present circulation is 197,031. Accepts queries via email.
**Submission Guidelines** Accepts query.
**Tips** *InStyle* magazine is an insider's guide to the lives and lifestyles of the world's most fascinating people, offering a wealth of inspiration and ideas about beauty, fashion, home, entertaining, and charitable endeavours. Target readership is women aged 25–44. Ideas for features or articles aimed at their target audience are welcome.

## Interlude
**Limehouse Town Hall, 646 Commercial Road, London, E14 7HA**
- submissions@interludemagazine.co.uk
- www.interludemagazine.co.uk

**Editor** Francesca Ricci; Helen Nodding; Becky Philp
**Insider Info** A consumer magazine publication, covering general interest, literary subjects. Queries accepted by mail and email. Sample copy is available online.
**Non-fiction** Interested in Poetry, Features and Visual art pieces.
**Submission Guidelines** Submit complete manuscript.
**Fiction** Interested in Fiction pieces.
**Tips** *Interlude* is a multi-disciplinary magazine, which publishes poetry, fiction, visual art, and anything in between. Each page is designed and formatted by the contributor of the work appearing on it. *Interlude*'s editors take a back seat on the design process, making it very much a 'writers magazine'. *Interlude* has no particular theme and will accept any type of submission, but content in the magazine does tend to be very visually or conceptually driven.

## The Interpreter's House
**19 The Paddox, Oxford, OX2 7PN**
- www.interpretershouse.org.uk

**Editor** Merryn Williams
**Established** 1996
**Insider Info** A consumer magazine, issued three times a year, covering poetry and prose. Present circulation of 350. A byline is given. Sample copy is available online.
**Fiction** Publishes Mainstream Fiction, Mystery and Short stories.

**Submission Guidelines** Send complete manuscript.

**Poetry** Publishes Free verse, Light verse and Traditional Poetry.

**Tips** *The Interpreter's House* is a poetry and prose magazine, which prints writing that blends mystery and simplicity. Each issue contains new short stories and poems from contributors, as well as various writing competitions. Any poems that are published in the magazine may also appear on the website and be submitted for the Forward Prize.

## Interzone

**5 Martins Lane, Witcham, Ely, CB6 2LB**

🆔 andy@ttapress.demon.co.uk

🌐 www.ttapress.com

**Parent Company** TTA Press

**Editor** Andy Cox

**Established** 1982

**Insider Info** A consumer magazine publication issued bi-monthly, covering new and genre writing. Present circulation is 10,000. A byline is given. Queries are accepted by mail and email. Writer's guidelines are available online.

**Non-fiction** Interested in Interviews/Profiles and Reviews.

**Submission Guidelines** Accepts query. Send complete manuscript.

**Fiction** Interested in Science fiction and Fantasy pieces.

  \* Payment is £30 per 1000 words.

**Submission Guidelines** Accepts query. Send complete manuscript of a maximum of 1,500 words.

**Tips** *Interzone* has published short stories by many of the big names in the fantasy and science fiction fields, from Brian Aldiss and J.G. Ballard, to Ian Watson and Gene Wolfe, but its particular strength has been in the nurturing of newer writers. Unsolicited manuscripts are welcome 'from writers who have a knowledge of the magazine and its contents'. *Interzone* is an established magazine and submitted stories must fit into its preferred style. *Interzone* only excepts email submissions during certain months, so make sure you check the details on the submissions section of the website.

## Iota

**1 Lodge Farm, Snitterfield, Stratford upon Avon, Warwickshire, CV37 0LR**

☎ 01789 730320

🆔 iotapoetry@aol.com

🌐 www.iotapoetry.co.uk

**Parent Company** Ragged Raven Press

**Editor** Bob Mee

**Contact** Co-Editor, Janet Murch

**Established** 1987

**Insider Info** A consumer magazine publication issued quarterly, covering general interest, literary subjects. Present circulation is 300. A byline is given. Queries by mail are accepted and previously published submissions are accepted.

**Non-fiction** Interested in Poetry and Review articles.

**Poetry** Interested in Free verse, Light verse and Traditional poetry.

**Submission Guidelines** Maximum of six poems to be submitted at a time.

**Tips** *Iota* publishes poetry from new and established authors, along with poetry reviews and profiles. *Iota* prefers submissions of poetry by post, but will accept submissions by email as well, providing that the poetry is printed in the body text of the email, rather than saved as an attachment.

## Irish Pages

A Journal of Contemporary Writing

**The Linen Hall Library, 17 Donegall Square North, Belfast, BT1 5GB Northern Ireland**

🆔 irishpages@yahoo.co.uk

🌐 www.irishpages.org

**Parent Company** Irish Pages

**Editor** Chris Agee

**Contact** Managing Editor, Sean Mac Aindreasa; Irish Language Editor, Cathal Ó Searcaigh

**Established** 2002

**Insider Info** A consumer journal publication issued twice a year, covering general interest, literary subjects. A byline is given.

**Non-fiction** Interested in Photo features, Poetry, Features, Interviews/Profiles, General interest and Travel pieces.

**Submission Guidelines** Accepts query.

**Fiction** Interested in Fiction, Mainstream and Irish language pieces.

**Submission Guidelines** Send complete manuscript.

**Poetry** Interested in Free verse, Light verse and Traditional poetry.

**Submission Guidelines** A maximum of six poems to be submitted at a time.

**Tips** *Irish Pages* is a literary journal, based in Belfast, that publishes English and Irish fiction and poetry, articles, photography features, and general Irish interest articles. *Irish Pages* likes to remain unbiased in its editorial policy and will be as likely to accept submissions from unknown, unsupported authors, as it is from popular writers, or writing organisations.

## Island

**8 Craiglea Drive, Edinburgh, EH10 5PA**

✉ jaj@essencepress.co.uk

🌐 www.essencepress.co.uk

**Parent Company** Essence Press

**Editor** Julie Johnstone

**Established** 1999

**Insider Info** A consumer magazine publication issued twice a year, covering general interest, literary subjects. Circulation of 200. A byline is given. Queries accepted by mail and email. Aims to respond to queries and manuscripts within 12 weeks. Writers are always paid with contributor copies or other premiums. Writer's guidelines and editorial calendars are available online.

**Non-fiction** Interested in Essays, Poetry and Features pieces.

**Submission Guidelines** Accepts query.

**Fiction** Interested in Fiction, Mainstream and Short stories.

**Submission Guidelines** Submit complete manuscript.

**Poetry** Interested in Avant-garde, Free verse, Light verse, Traditional, Concrete poetry and Prose poems.

**Tips** *Island* is a literary magazine that provides a 'distinctive space for new writing inspired by nature, that explores our place within the natural world.' *Island* publishes poetry, prose poems, concrete poetry, essays and non-fiction fragments. The Editor of *Island* has a preference for work that uses the landscape of the page creatively. Also note that although unsolicited submissions are welcome, most content for *Island* is commissioned directly by the Editor.

## Is This Music?

**PO Box 13516, Linlithgow, EH49 6WB**

☎ 01506 840063

✉ editor@isthismusic.com

🌐 www.isthismusic.com

**Editor** Stuart McHugh

**Established** 2002

**Insider Info** A consumer magazine publication issued bi-monthly, covering music in Scotland.

**Non-fiction** Interested in Photo features, Features, Interviews/Profiles, Reviews, General interest articles.

**Submission Guidelines** Accepts query.

**Tips** *Is This Music?* is an independent contemporary music magazine dedicated to reporting on, and supporting, the music scene all over Scotland. Contains reviews, articles, photo features, interviews and profiles. *Is This Music?* runs lots of news and review articles on all aspects of the Scottish music scene, including smaller groups and gigs, and unsigned artists.

## Italy Magazine

**Middle Farm, Middle Farm Way, Dorchester, Dorset, DT1 3RS**

☎ 01305 266360

☎ 01305 262760

✉ editor@italymag.co.uk

🌐 www.italymag.co.uk

**Parent Company** Poundbury Publishing

**Editor** Melissa Ormiston

**Established** 2001

**Insider Info** A monthly consumer magazine, covering all things Italian. It is the bestselling glossy magazine about Italy published in the UK. Present circulation of 20,000. 80 per cent of the publication is written by freelance writers. Submissions are published up to six months after acceptance. Payment is upon publication. Writers may be paid with advertising space if they prefer. Publication is copyrighted. A byline is given. Purchases first UK serial rights, second serial (reprint) rights and electronic rights. Editorial lead time is three months and seasonal material must be submitted six months in advance. Queries are accepted by email. Aims to respond to queries within one week, and manuscripts within four weeks. Will not pay the expenses of writers on assignment. Sample copy and media pack available online. Writer's guidelines available via email.

**Non-fiction** Interested in Photo features, Features, and Travel pieces. Publish special supplements bi-monthly, which focus on Italian themes such as Winter holidays, Language courses. Also publish a weddings magazine four times a year, that is distributed with the magazine.

 \* Payment for assigned articles is between £60 and £300.

**Submission Guidelines** Accepts email synopsis for articles of between 500 and 1,500 words. Of particular interest are tutorial, lessons or practical techniques. Images must also be sent to the Art Editor to check before any submission is made. Does not accept reprints. Contact Melissa Ormiston, Editor.

**Images** Accepts images with submission.

 \* Payment for two images are included in the text fee and then additional images are paid at £35 each. Buys one time rights.

**Submission Guidelines** Submit gif/jpeg files and captions. Identification of subjects is required. Send photos with submission. Contact Art Editor, Paul Tutill.

**Tips** *Italy Magazine* was the first glossy lifestyle magazine about the country on general sale in the UK and to this day remains the market leader. Readers come from mainly the UK and USA, with subscriptions to the magazine from all over the world. The magazine covers all aspects of Italian life: food, wine, sport, fashion, house interiors, gardens, arts, culture, holidays, destination guides and property. There are also popular case studies and business pages. Once writers have heard back about their submission (which could take several weeks) and the Editor likes the idea, they will be asked to send images to accompany the feature to be checked by the Art Editor. Due to the overwhelming number of submissions, the whole process could take up to three months.

## Jewish Chronicle

**25 Furnival Street, London, EC4A 1JT**

- ☎ 020 7415 1500
- ☎ 020 7405 9040
- ✉ editorial@thejc.com
- 🌐 www.thejc.com

**Parent Company** Kessler Foundation
**Editor** David Rowan
**Contact** Features Editor, Gerald Jacobs
**Established** 1841
**Insider Info** Consumer newspaper publication issued covering general interest religion. Present circulation of 34,492. Queries accepted by mail.
**Non-fiction** Interested in Religious, Features pieces.
**Submission Guidelines** Accepts query. Articles should be a maximum of 1,500 words.
**Tips** The world's oldest and most influential Jewish newspaper, the London based *Jewish Chronicle* has a 164 year history of editorial independence. Its news and opinion pages reflect the entire spectrum of Jewish religious, social and political thought, from left to right, orthodox to secular. The arts and lifestyle coverage includes film, theatre, travel, cookery and youth, and singles events. News articles are appreciated, especially when linked to upcoming community events.

## Jewish Quarterly

**PO Box 37645, London, NW7 1WB**

- ☎ 020 8830 5367
- ✉ editor@jewquart.freeserve.co.uk
- 🌐 www.jewishquarterly.org

**Editor** Matthew Reisz
**Established** 1953
**Insider Info** A consumer magazine publication issued quarterly covering general interest, literary topics. Present circulation of 2,000. A byline is given. Queries accepted by mail and email.
**Non-fiction** Interested in Religious, Features, Interviews/Profiles, Reviews, General interest and Opinion (not letters to the Editor) pieces.
**Submission Guidelines** Accepts query.
**Fiction** Interested in Fiction, Mainstream Jewish fiction and Religious Jewish fiction pieces.
**Submission Guidelines** Accepts query.
**Tips** *Jewish Quarterly* publishes news, reviews, interviews and articles from the Jewish community, as well as new Jewish fiction. *Jewish Quarterly* holds an annual writing competition called the 'Wingate Literary Prize' which is Britain's only major literary award for Jewish interest books. The prize recognizes work that stimulates an interest in, and awareness of themes of Jewish concern, among a wider reading public and offers a prize of £5,000, along with publication in the *Jewish Quarterly*.

## The Journal

**17 High Street, Maryport, Cumbria, CA15 6BQ**

- ☎ 01900 812194
- ✉ smithsssj@aol.com
- 🌐 http://members.aol.com/smithsssj/index.html

**Parent Company** Original Plus
**Editor** Sam Smith
**Established** 1994
**Insider Info** Poetry magazine, issued three times a year. Present circulation of 150. 100 per cent of the publication is written by freelance writers. Submissions are published approximately five months after acceptance. Contributors receive a complimentary copy of the magazine as payment. Publication is copyrighted and a byline is given. Acquires first UK serial rights on accepted submissions. Editorial lead time is five months. Queries accepted by mail and email. Accepts simultaneous and previously published submissions. Aims to respond to queries and manuscripts within three weeks. Assignment expenses are not paid. Sample copy is available for 1.50. Writer's guidelines are available free on request.
**Non-fiction** Publishes Poetry (original or translations), Reviews of poetry collections and articles on the poetry scene. The Journal does not have special issues.
  \* Payment for unsolicited manuscripts is a complimentary copy of the magazine.
**Submission Guidelines** Send complete, typed manuscript to the Editor, Sam Smith. Submissions must be 1,000 words.
**Fictions** Publishes Mainstream fiction.

**Submission Guidelines** Send complete manuscript.

**Poetry** Publishes Free verse, Haiku, Traditional and Avant-garde poetry and Translations.

**Submission Guidelines** Submit a maximum of six poems. There is no limit on line length. Will not accept end rhyming poems or anything with religious content.

**Tips** Editorial policy is to try to publish poems written with thought as to what the poem is saying, and to how it is being said. Also welcomed are poems that can travel, that can cross boundaries and do not assume in their readers a shared knowledge, or a shared set of beliefs. Aside from poetry and prose submissions *The Journal* is also interested in interviews with poets, reviews, and appraisals of the current poetry scene.

## Journal of Hellenic Studies
**Senate House, Malet Street, London, WC1E 7HU**
- 020 7862 8730
- 020 7862 8731
- office@hellenicsociety.org.uk
- www.hellenicsociety.org.uk

**Parent Company** The Society for the Promotion of Hellenic Studies

**Editor** Angus Bowie

**Established** 1880

**Insider Info** A trade journal published annually, covering general interest, literary subjects, Present circulation of 3,500. A byline is given. Queries accepted by mail and email. Writer's guidelines are available online.

**Non-fiction** Interested in Features, Reviews, Technical and Historical/Nostalgic pieces.

**Submission Guidelines** Please send complete manuscript.

**Tips** The *Journal of Hellenic Studies* is an academic journal that publishes articles on the research and study of Greek language, literature, art and history. It also prints reviews of books relating to Hellenic studies. The *Journal of Hellenic Studies* will only consider article submissions from recognised scholars in the field of Hellenic studies, and then only if they follow the detailed guidelines on the website.

## KAL
**57 Poland Street, London, W1F 7NW**
- 020 7439 9100
- 020 7439 9101
- media@arberrypink.co.uk
- www.kalmagazine.com

**Parent Company** Arberry Pink Ltd

**Editor** Laura Sheed

**Established** 1994

**Insider Info** Student and graduate careers/recruitment magazine and online publication issued bi anually, covering career opportunities for black and minority ethnic students and graduates. Present circulation of 10,000. 75 per cent of the publication is written by freelancers. Material is provided through work experience and free contributions. Publication is copyrighted and a byline is given. Purchases all rights. Editorial lead time is four weeks. Queries accepted by mail and email. Aims to respond to queries within three days, manuscripts within one week and other issues within three days. A sample copy is available for a cost of £3, online and via email. Writer's guidelines are available free on request, online and via email.

**Non-fiction** Interested in How-to, Photo feature, Essays, Humour, Poetry, Exposé, Inspirational, Features, Interviews/Profiles, Reviews, New products, General interest, Opinion (not letters to the Editor), Travel, Historical/Nostalgic and Personal experience pieces.

**Submission Guidelines** Articles should be between 400 and 1,200 words.

**Tips** A contemporary careers magazine written to inspire and inform students and graduates from ethnic minority backgrounds. Written by students, for students.

## Keystone
**53 Arcadia Court, 45 Old Castle Street, London, E1 7NY**
- 020 7375 0258
- info@pennedinthemargins.co.uk
- www.pennedinthemargins.co.uk

**Parent Company** Penned in the Margins

**Editor** Tom Chivers

**Insider Info** A consumer magazine publication covering general interest, literary subjects. Queries accepted by mail and email.

**Tips** *Keystone* is an eclectic literary magazine that publishes contemporary and visual poetry from both known and unknown writers. *Keystone* is currently dormant and not accepting any further submissions. Check the website frequently for new developments.

## Koi
Britain's bestselling Koi magazine
**Tower House, Fairfax Street, Bristol, Bristol, BS1 3BN**

☎ 0117 927 9009
🖷 0117 934 9008
✉ hilaryclapham@originpublishing.co.uk
🌐 www.koimag.co.uk
**Parent Company** Origin Publishing
**Editor** Hilary Clapham
**Established** 1999
**Insider Info** A consumer magazine publication issued every four weeks, covering the Koi keeping hobby, including Koi health and pond construction. Present circulation is 15,000. 80 per cent of publication is written by freelancers. Submissions are published approximately two months after acceptance, with an editorial lead time of three months. A byline is given. Seasonal material must be submitted three months in advance. Queries are accepted by email and phone. Payment is not made with contributor copies or other premiums. A sample copy and writer's guidelines are available free on request.
**Non-fiction** Interested in How-to, Practical, Photo features, Interviews/Profiles, Reviews, New products, Press releases, Opinion (not letters to the Editor) and Personal experience pieces.
**Images** Accepts images with submission.
  * Negotiates payment individually for images.
**Submission Guidelines** Submit transparencies, print or gif/jpeg files. Contact Hilary Clapham.
**Tips** The magazine is aimed at every kind of hobbyist, from the beginner to the more advanced.

## Krax

**63 Dixon Lane, Leeds, LS12 4RR**
**Editor** Andy Robson
**Established** 1971
**Insider Info** A consumer magazine publication issued annually, covering general interest, literary subjects. Present circulation of 400. A byline is given. Payment is always made with contributor copies or other premiums.
**Non-fiction** Interested in Poetry.
**Submission Guidelines** Submit query.
**Fiction** Interested in Fiction and Short fiction pieces.
**Submission Guidelines** Send complete manuscript.
**Poetry** Interested in Contemporary poetry.
**Tips** Krax is a literary magazine that publishes contemporary poetry, prose and artwork. Krax's contents are generally whimsical or humorous in nature. Krax often has a large amount of submissions, so publication of accepted stories can often take a long time.

## The Lady

**39–40 Bedford Street, London, WC2E 9ER**
☎ 020 7379 4717
🖷 020 7379 4620
✉ editors@lady.co.uk
🌐 www.lady.co.uk
**Editor** Arline Usden
**Established** 1885
**Insider Info** A weekly consumer magazine, covering women's interests. Present circulation of 34,302. Queries accepted by mail.
**Non-fiction** Publishes Photo features, Features, General interest, Travel and How-to articles.
**Submission Guidelines** Accepts queries and completed manuscripts. Articles should be 1,200 words.
**Images** State availability of photos with submission.
**Tips** The Lady contains a fascinating range of features, on subjects including culture, travel, interviews, gardening, art and antiques, books, finance and history, as well as fashion, cookery and beauty, always presented with the taste and quality that The Lady readers have come to expect. Ideally looking for well-researched pieces on local or foreign travel, historical subjects, or events. The magazine has regular staff writer features, so ensure submissions do not cover any of these areas.

## Lallans

**Blackford Lodge, Blackford, Perthshire, PH4 1QP**
☎ 01764 682315
🖷 01764 682465
✉ mail@lallans.co.uk
🌐 www.lallans.co.uk
**Parent Company** The Scots Language Society
**Editor** John Law
**Established** 1972
**Insider Info** Semi annual consumer journal for the general interest literary market.
**Non-fiction** Publishes Features, Reviews and General interest articles.
**Submission Guidelines** Queries accepted by mail and email.
**Fiction** Publishes Short stories. Writers should query before any submission.
**Poetry** Publishes Free verse and Traditional poetry.
**Tips** Lallans is the literature journal of the Scots Language Society, and includes poetry, short fiction, reviews and articles printed in the Scottish dialect. Lallans welcomes short story and poetry submissions, providing they are written in Scottish dialect.

## Lamport Court

**63 Lamport Court, Manchester, M1 7EG**

🌐 lamportcourt.blogspot.com/

**Established** 2004

**Insider Info** Semi annual consumer magazine for the general interest literary market. A byline will be given. Accepts queries by mail.

**Poetry** Publishes Poetry

**Fiction** Publishes Fiction.

**Tips** *Lamport Court* is a small literary magazine that publishes new poetry, fiction and artworks. *Lamport Court* offers an established community forum in support of its print magazine, where writers and contributors can get valuable support and feedback from their peers.

## Land Rover World

**Leon House, 233 High Street, Croydon, CR9 1HZ**

☎ 020 8726 8000

🖷 020 8726 8296

✉ landroverworld@ipcmedia.com/john_carroll@ipcmedia.com

🌐 www.landroverworld.co.uk

**Parent Company** IPC Media

**Editor** John Carroll

**Established** 1993

**Insider Info** Monthly consumer magazine covering motoring, motorcycling and motoring 4x4. Present circulation of 30,000. Queries accepted by mail and email. Media packs available at: www.ipcmedia.com/magazines/landroverworld/

**Non-fiction** Publishes Photo features, Features, Reviews, New product and Technical articles.

**Submission Guidelines** Accepts queries. Send complete manuscript.

**Images** Send photos with submission.

**Tips** *Land Rover World* is inspirational, informed, authoritative, friendly and hands on. Since launch, it has become a highly respected title in the industry with a growing circulation among enthusiasts and professionals. It is regarded as essential reading by those within the scene, with features on rare and unusual Land Rovers, travel stories from around the world, unparalleled technical advice and comprehensive clubs coverage. Include high quality illustrations in support of any submissions.

## Language Travel Magazine

**11–15 Emerald Street, London, WC1N 3QL**

☎ 020 7440 4020

🖷 020 7440 4033

✉ mail@hothousemedia.com

🌐 www.hothousemedia.com

**Parent Company** Hothouse Media

**Editor** Amy Baker

**Established** 1991

**Insider Info** A monthly B2B magazine, covering education and travel. Present circulation is 12,000. Queries accepted by email. Media packs available on the website.

**Tips** *Language Travel Magazine* is the only B2B publication written for, and read by, students, recruiters and educational consultants in over 100 countries every month.

## Leisure Report

**Broadfield House, Broadfield Park, Crawley, Sussex, RH11 9RT**

☎ 01293 846500

✉ duncan.rowe@william-reed.co.uk

🌐 www.wr-bi.com

**Parent Company** William Reed

**Editor** Duncan Rowe

**Established** 2000

**Insider Info** A monthly journal covering the business aspects of the UK leisure sector; health and fitness, betting and gaming, tourism, entertainment, attractions, cinema, tenpin, food etc. Present circulation is approximately 450. Ten per cent of the publication is written by freelance writers. Takes one week to publish manuscripts after acceptance. Payment on publication. Kill fee for assigned manuscripts not published is negotiable. A byline is given and simultaneous rights are purchased. Editorial lead time is five weeks. Seasonal material must be submitted one month in advance. Queries are accepted via email. Aims to report back on queries within three days. No payment other than cash. Payment of assignment expenses will occasionally be made. Sample copy and writer's guidelines are free on request. Don't carry advertising, or compile a 'Forward Features' list. Editorial decides monthly which features to run, based on what is newsworthy. Will always listen to relevant ideas for submission. Media packs available online.

**Non-fiction** Articles include, Book excerpts, Interviews/Profiles, New products and Technical pieces, all of which are linked to the UK leisure market.

\* Negotiable payment for assigned articles.

**Submission Guidelines** Accepts queries from writers. Articles should be a 1,300 words minimum, 2,500 words maximum. No reprints accepted.

**Tips** High level readership, which requires in-depth sector and business knowledge. We consider ourselves the 'FT' of the UK leisure sector. You should have a strong understanding of current events and trends in the UK leisure market, and use this knowledge in your work.

## The Liberal
**208–210a High Road, London, N2 9AY**
- 020 8444 5413
- 020 8444 1944
- editor@theliberal.co.uk
- www.theliberal.co.uk

**Editor** Ben Ramm
**Established** 2004
**Insider Info** A consumer magazine, issued every two months, covering literary/political subjects. Present circulation of 35,000. Queries accepted by mail and email.
**Non-fiction** Publishes Photo features, Features, Interviews/Profiles, Reviews, Opinion (not letters to the Editor) and Travel articles.
**Submission Guidelines** Send query before sending submission.
**Fiction** Publishes Fiction.
**Poetry** Publishes Poetry.
**Tips** *The Liberal* is a literary political magazine that publishes newsy articles, interviews, book reviews and some fiction and art. *The Liberal* is currently in the process of re-launching their website. Check the website in the future for updated submission guidelines.

## Linkway Magazine
**The Shieling, The Links, Burry Port, Carmarthenshire, SA16 0HU**
- 01554 834486
- 01554 834486

**Editor** Fay Davies
**Established** 1999
**Insider Info** Consumer magazine covering literary general interest. A byline is given. Accepts queries by mail. Sample copy is available via SAE (include two first class stamps).
**Non-fiction** Articles include Poetry and Features about Creative writing.
**Submission Guidelines** Accepts queries.
**Fiction** Articles include Mainstream and Short fiction.
**Poetry** Articles include Free verse, Light verse and Traditional poetry.
**Tips** *Linkway Magazine* publishes new short stories, poetry and articles on creative writing for a general

readership. *Linkway* runs various writing competitions, offering publication in the magazine as prizes. Also accepts unsolicited submissions, but it is advisable to read the magazine first to ensure suitability.

## Linux Format
(DVD Edition)
**30 Monmouth Street, Bath, BA1 2BW**
- 01225 442244
- 01225 732275
- lfx.letters@futurenet.co.uk, nick.veitch@futurenet.co.uk
- www.linuxformat.co.uk

**Parent Company** Future Publishing
**Editor** Nick Veitch
**Established** 2000
**Insider Info** Consumer magazine publishing 13 issues per year, covering miscellaneous computing. Present circulation is 26,700. Accepts queries by mail and email. Sample copy is available via website. Writer's guidelines available at: paul.hudson@futurenet.co.uk
**Non-fiction** Publishes articles on How-to, Features, Reviews, Technical and New Products. Contact Paul Hudson.
**Submission Guidelines** Accepts queries, submission guidelines online.
**Tips** Your complete guide to the world of Linux. Whether you've just discovered Linux, or you're a full-time guru, *Linux Format* has everything you need to make the most of your OS. *Linux Format* actively encourages submissions from freelancers that know their subject. Check out their website for full submission guidelines.

## The List
**14 High Street, Edinburgh, EH1 1TE**
- 0131 550 3050
- 0131 557 8500
- mail@list.co.uk
- www.list.co.uk

**Editor** Claire Prentice
**Established** 1985
**Insider Info** A fortnightly consumer magazine, covering arts and entertainment listings in Glasgow and Edinburgh. Present circulation of 11,141. 25 per cent of the magazine is written by freelance writers. Submissions are published approximately two weeks after acceptance. Payment is made on publication of material. Publication is copyrighted and a byline is given. Kill fee for articles not

published is 100 per cent of the original fee. Purchases first rights and second serial (reprint) rights. Editorial lead time is one month. Seasonal material must be submitted one month in advance. Queries accepted by mail and email. Accepts simultaneous submissions. Assignment expenses sometimes paid (limit agreed upon in advance). Media packs available online.

**Non-fiction** Publishes Interviews/Profiles, Opinion (not letters to the editor) and Travel articles.

**Submission Guidelines** Send query with published clips. Articles must be 300 words.

**Columns** Publishes Reviews (50–650 words), Book Reviews (150 words), Comic Reviews (100 words), Television/Video Reviews (100 words) and Record Reviews (100 words).

  * Payment for columns is between £10 and £35.

**Submission Guidelines** Query with published clips.

**Tips** *The List* was originally founded to publicise and promote the wide range of arts and entertainment taking place throughout the year in Glasgow and Edinburgh, and to publish a general interest magazine of quality in Scotland. The company now produces a series of additional titles and supplements and is at the forefront of gathering and collating events information for a wide variety of publications, organisations and new media. *The List* is pitched at educated 18–35 year olds. Any articles or features that are included in each issue usually preview forthcoming events in greater detail.

## Literary Review

**44 Lexington Street, London, W1F OLW**

- ☎ 020 7437 9392
- ☎ 020 7734 1844
- ✉ editorial@literaryreview.co.uk
- 🌐 www.literaryreview.co.uk

**Editor** Nancy Sladek

**Established** 1979

**Insider Info** A monthly consumer journal covering literary general interest. Circulation is presently 15,000. Accepts queries by mail and email.

**Non-fiction** Publishes Features, Interviews/Profiles, and Reviews.

**Submission Guidelines** Accepts queries.

**Tips** *The Literary Review* publishes reviews of the best new books, along with author interviews and articles about writing. *The Literary Review* aims to be an 'intelligent literary magazine for people who love reading, but hate academic and intellectual jargon.' *The Literary Review* prints informative reviews of the latest book releases, but tries to keep jargon and academic styles to a minimum. Reviews are usually sourced from professional authors rather than critics.

## Loaded

**King's Reach Tower, Stamford Street, London, SE1 9LS**

- ☎ 020 7261 5562
- ☎ 020 7261 5557
- ✉ firstname_lastname@ipcmedia.com
- 🌐 www.loaded.co.uk

**Parent Company** IPC Media

**Editor** Martin Daubney

**Contact** Features Editor and Commissioning Editor, Andy Sherwood

**Established** 1994

**Insider Info** A monthly consumer magazine covering men's lifestyle topics. Present circulation of 162,554.

**Non-fiction** Publishes General interest, Interviews, Reviews and Photo features on Celebrities, Fashion, Sport, Humour, Sex, Music, Television, Film and Real-life.

**Tips** The magazine is aimed at young men aged 18–30 and can contain some adult content.

## The London Magazine

A Review of Literature and the Arts

**70 Wargrave Avenue, Stamford Hill, London, N15 6UB**

- ☎ 020 8802 6686
- ☎ 020 8994 1713
- ✉ editor@thelondonmagazine.net
- 🌐 www.thelondonmagazine.net

**Editor** Sebastian Barker

**Established** 1732

**Insider Info** A consumer magazine, published every two months, covering poetry, fiction, features about all the arts, and critical reviews of literature and the arts. Present circulation of 1,200. 100 per cent of the magazine is written by freelance writers. Submissions are published approximately three months after acceptance. Payment is made on publication of material. Copyright is held by contributors. Queries are accepted by mail. Aims to respond to manuscripts within six weeks. Sample copy, writer's guidelines and editorial calendars are available online.

**Non-fiction** Publishes Photo features, Essays, Humour, Exposé, Features, Interviews/Profiles, Reviews and General interest, Travel, Historical, Inspirational and Religious articles, as well as pieces on Music, Film, Satire, Science, Painting, Dance, Archaeology, Drama, Translation, Sculpture and Biography. No special issues.

* Purchases 18 Non-fiction manuscripts from freelance writers per year. Payment for articles is between £30 and £175.

**Submission Guidelines** Send complete manuscript. Articles must be 250–5,000 words. Submissions must be of high quality.

Submission details to: Sebastian Barker, Editor.

**Fiction** Publishes Adventure, Erotica, Fantasy, Historical, Humorous, Mainstream, Ethnic and Experimental fiction.

Purchases 18 fiction manuscripts per year. Payment is between £50 and £75.

**Submission Guidelines** Send complete manuscript. Submissions must be 250–5,000 words. Will not accept fiction that lacks literary merit.

Submission details to: Editor, Sebastian Barker.

**Poetry** Publishes Free verse, Haiku, Light verse, Avant-garde and Traditional poetry.

* Purchases 100 poems per year. Payment for poetry is between £30 and £175.

**Submission Guidelines** Submit a maximum of six poems. Poems should be 10–4500 lines in length. Poetry must be of quality.

Submission details to: Sebastian Barker, Editor.

**Images** Accepts images with submission.

* Varied fee per photo. Rights stay with photographer.

**Submission Guidelines** Send Transparencies, Prints or gif/jpeg files with submission.

**Tips** Committed to established, young, and unknown talents – writers, artists, and critics – from all backgrounds around the world. Writers should send in well-produced manuscripts with SAE or International Reply Coupon (IRC) if abroad. The SAE or IRC must cover return postage for a reply only, or for return of the manuscript, whichever is applicable.

## London Review of Books

**28 Little Russell Street, London, WC1A 2HN**

- 020 7209 1101
- 020 7209 1102
- edit@lrb.co.uk
- www.lrb.co.uk

**Parent Company** LRB Ltd
**Editor** Mary-Kay Wilmers
**Contact** Deputy Editor, Jean McNichol
**Established** 1979
**Insider Info** Bi-weekly consumer journal covering literary general interest. Present circulation of 43,500. A byline is given. Accepts queries by mail and email.
**Non-fiction** Publishes Essays, Features, Interviews/ Profiles and Reviews.
**Submission Guidelines** Queries accepted.

**Tips** *The London Review of Books* is an old fashioned literary journal, that publishes critical essays from leading writers and critics, as well as interviews and the latest book reviews. Sources most of its content from regular contributing editors, including leading writers and literary critics.

## Look

**Kings Reach Tower, Stamford Street, London, SE1 9LS**

- 020 7261 5000
- 020 7261 5008
- look.editorial@ipcmedia.com
- www.look.co.uk

**Parent Company** IPC Media
**Editor** Alison Hall
**Contact** Features Editor, Zoe Oliver; Managing Editor, Duncan Baizley
**Established** 2007
**Insider Info** A weekly consumer magazine covering women's lifestyle and celebrity topics. A preview sample of an issue is available online.
**Non-fiction** Publishes General interest features, Interviews and Photo features on Celebrities, Real life, Fashion and Beauty.
**Tips** The title is aimed specifically at women aged 18 to 30. Its main focus is celebrity gossip and style advice for young women.

## MacFormat

**30 Monmouth Street, Bath, BA1 2BW**

- 01225 442244
- 01225 732275
- graham.barlow@futurenet.co.uk
- www.macformat.co.uk

**Parent Company** Future Publishing
**Editor** Graham Barlow
**Insider Info** Monthly consumer magazine covering Mac computing. Present circulation of 18,722.
**Tips** *MacFormat* is the No.1 selling consumer Mac magazine, full of practical, authoritative and passionate advice. To make sure you get more from your Mac, the magazine includes a DVD packed with full programs, the latest demos and updates each month. It doesn't just deal with Mac computers, it also handles all Mac/Apple accessories including iPods and iPod related gadgets. It also deals with music and the downloading of music for use on Macs and iPods.

## MacUser

**30 Cleveland Street, London, W1T 4JD**

☎ 020 7907 6000

✉ mailbox@macuser.co.uk

🌐 www.macuser.co.uk

**Parent Company** Dennis Publishing

**Editor** Nik Rawlinson

**Established** 1985

**Insider Info** A fortnightly consumer magazine covering Mac computing. Present circulation of 18,900.

**Non-fiction** Publishes How-to, Feature and Technical Articles.

**Tips** *MacUser* is a magazine focused at the professional and creative markets with its core readers working in graphics, design and publishing, video and audio. With in-house testing, *MacUser*'s reviews are rigorous and extensive, making it the 'must read' for all Mac users and strategic purchasers within the UK. The magazine also features many articles completely unrelated to Mac computers, such as the latest gadget trends, or news from the electronic industry. As long as it is Mac compatible, for example the latest digital video camcorder, then it is possible to write a feature about it.

## Magma

**43 Keslake Road, London, NW6 6DH**

☎ 020 7975 5236

☎ 020 8980 6533

✉ magmapoetry@ntlworld.com

🌐 www.magmapoetry.com

**Editor** David Boll

**Contact** Editor, David Boll

**Established** 1994

**Insider Info** Consumer magazine publishing three issues per year (Spring, Autumn, Winter). Covers literary general interest. Present circulation of 700. 100 per cent of the publication is written by freelance writers. Accepts queries by mail and email. Sample copy is available online: www.magmapoetry.com/submission.php, or contributions@magmapoetry.com

**Non-fiction** Publishes articles on Poetry, Features, Interviews/Profiles and Reviews.

**Submission Guidelines** Accepts queries.

**Poetry** Publishes Free verse, Light verse and Traditional poetry. No more than six poems to be submitted at one time.

**Tips** *Magma* is a literary magazine that prints poetry and articles about poetry, as well as a range of features, reviews and interviews. It is run by a group of editors who take turns to edit the magazine.

Magma looks for well-crafted poems 'which give a direct sense of what it is to live today - honest about feelings, alert about world, sometimes funny.' Magma accepts email submissions, but prefers that poems are embedded in the body of the text rather than attached separately.

## Marie Claire

**King's Reach Tower, Stamford Street, London, SE1 9LS**

☎ 020 7261 5240

✉ marieclaire@ipcmedia.com

🌐 www.marieclaire.co.uk

**Parent Company** IPC Media

**Editor** Marie O'Riordan

**Contact** Deputy Editor, Vanessa Thompson

**Established** 1988

**Insider Info** Monthly consumer magazine covering women's interests, lifestyle and fashion. Present circulation is 331,000. Queries by mail and email.

**Non-fiction** Publishes Features and Articles on General interest, Fashion and Health.

**Submission Guidelines** Accepts queries with published clips. No unsolicited manuscripts.

**Tips** *Marie Claire* is a worldwide icon; with editions in 25 countries, it epitomises style and substance. Its fashion and beauty features embrace everything from catwalk to high street and feature content that reflects both the fun and more serious sides of its readers' personality. A true leader, *Marie Claire* sets the pace in the fashion monthly sector. Any feature ideas must be submitted to the Features Editor and must also include samples of previous printed work.

## Marketing Week

**St. Giles House, 50 Poland Street, London, W1F 7AX**

☎ 020 7970 6328

☎ 020 7970 6721

✉ stuart.smith@centaur.co.uk

🌐 www.marketingweek.co.uk

**Parent Company** Centaur Communications

**Editor** Stuart Smith

**Contact** Features Editor, Daney Parker

**Established** 1978

**Insider Info** Weekly trade journal magazine, covering marketing. Present circulation is 39,000. Accepts queries by mail and email.

**Non-fiction** Publishes Features, Interviews/Profiles and News/Analysis.

\* Pays £200 per 1,000 words.

**Submission Guidelines** Accepts queries. Send complete manuscript of 1,000 words minimum and 2,000 words maximum.

**Tips** *Marketing Week* is the UK's leading magazine for professionals working in marketing, marketing services and media. Its respected and authoritative editorial team provide a unique blend of exclusive news on new product launches, major shifts in brand strategies, account moves and people and appointments and departures. However, *Marketing Week* is more than just news. We go behind the scenes and offer insightful analyses on today's most significant stories. We deliver expert comment, invaluable weekly insights into current and future trends and educational features across all sectors and disciplines. We also publish a range of useful supplements and yearbooks, from design, market research, conferences and exhibitions, through to search marketing. As the magazine is aimed at marketing management any article submissions must include relevant data and statistical analysis.

# Markings
**44 High Street, Gatehouse of Fleet, Dumfries and Galloway, DG7 2HP**
- 01557 814196
- 01557 332339
- johnhudson@markings.org.uk
- www.markings.org.uk

**Parent Company** The Bakehouse
**Editor** John Hudson
**Established** 1995
**Insider Info** Bi-annual consumer magazine covering literary general interest.
**Non-fiction** Publishes Poetry and Literary criticism.
**Submission Guidelines** Send complete manuscript.
**Fiction** Publishes Short story and Mainstream fiction.
Send complete manuscript.
**Poetry** Publishes free verse and traditional poetry.
**Tips** *Markings* is a bi-annual arts magazine in its eleventh year offering a synergy between the written word and performance, and is now one of Scotland's most popular literary magazines. *Markings* prints poetry, fiction, artwork and literary criticism. *Markings* invites unsolicited submissions of poetry, fiction, artwork and criticism. Submissions in any language are welcome, providing they are accompanied by either an English or Scots translation.

# Matchbox
**87 Thornton Road, Fallowfield, Manchester, M14 7NT**
- matchbox@matchbox.org.uk
- www.matchbox.org.uk

**Editor** James Davies
**Insider Info** Consumer publication in the 'Matchbox' format, publishing three editions per year and covering literary general interest.
**Tips** Each *Matchbox* publication consists of a decorated matchbox (a real matchbox) containing selected poetry by a single writer, usually well-established, and a free gift. They are available from certain shops in Manchester, as well as from the *Matchbox* website. *Matchbox* issues are always dedicated to selected well-known writers and therefore *Matchbox* does not accept submissions of any kind, although general queries are welcome by email.

# Maxim
**30 Cleveland Street, London, W1T 4JD**
- 020 7907 6410
- 020 7907 6439
- editorial@maxim-magazine.co.uk, derek_harbinson@dennis.co.uk
- www.maxim-magazine.co.uk

**Parent Company** Dennis Publishing
**Editor** Derek Harbinson
**Established** 1995
**Insider Info** Monthly consumer magazine covering men's lifestyle. Present circulation is 146,000. Accepts queries by mail.
**Non-fiction** Publishes Features, Interview/Profile, Reviews and Travel.
**Submission Guidelines** Accepts query with published clips of 1,500 words minimum and 2,500 words maximum.
**Tips** *Maxim* addresses the real life needs of intelligent, professional men in an entertaining as well as informative way. We set out to reach men in their late 20s rather than out and out 'lads', producing a magazine that readers can grow into rather than out of. Research confirms that our mean average age is on target at 28. *Maxim* is aimed at the mid to late twenties man so articles should be written accordingly.

# Media Week
**174 Hammersmith Road, London, W6 7JP**
- 020 8267 8032
- 020 82678020

⊙ mwnewsdesk@haynet.com, steve.barrett@ haymarket.com

⦿ www.mediaweek.co.uk

**Parent Company** Haymarket Publishing

**Editor** Steve Barrett

**Contact** Features Editor, Julia Martin

**Established** 1985

**Insider Info** Weekly trade journal magazine covering advertising. Present circulation is 19,300. Accepts queries by mail and email.

**Tips** In short, *Media Week* is not only the best place to find out what's hot and what's happening in media, it's the *only* place that is dedicated to telling media's big stories. *Media Week* is a trade journal and so any submitted articles will be expected to contain relevant information and statistical analysis.

## Metal Hammer

**1 Balcombe Street, London, NW1 6NA**

⊙ 0870 444 8649

⊙ jamie.hibbard@futurenet.co.uk

⦿ www.metalhammer.co.uk

**Parent Company** Future Publishing

**Editor** Jamie Hibbard

**Contact** Managing Editor, Alex Burrows

**Established** 1983

**Insider Info** Monthly consumer magazine covering rock music. Present circulation is 45,400.

**Non-fiction** Publishes Features, Interviews/Profile, Reviews, Gig reports and Alternative lifestyle features.

**Tips** Britain's only monthly music magazine which covers both traditional and contemporary metal bands, hardcore, gothic rock, punk and alternative. We report on the burgeoning British scene as well as all the latest bands Stateside, and around the world. Most reviews and interview material is commissioned from regular contributors or staff, so focus on alternative lifestyle features, or possibly local interest articles.

## Military Modelling

**Berwick House, 8–10 Knoll Rise, Orpington, Kent, BR8 0PS**

⊙ 01689 899200

⊙ 01689 899240

⊙ editor@militarymodelling.com

⦿ www.militarymodelling.com

**Editor** Ken Jones

**Established** 1970

**Insider Info** Monthly consumer magazine covering military model collecting.

**Non-fiction** Publishes Feature and Photo Features about Collecting/Modelling.

**Submission Guidelines** Submissions should be 2,000 words maximum.

**Tips** The award winning military modelling magazine, now in its 31st year of continuous publication. Written by leading experts, many of whom are well known modellers in their own right, *Military Modelling* continues to be the top mainstream publication for the military modeller. Articles should contain both illustrations and historical context in support of the models in question.

## Miniature Wargames

**Suite 13, Wessex House,, St. Leonard's Road,, Bournemouth, Dorset, BH8 8QS**

⊙ 01202 297344

⊙ 01202 297345

⊙ iain@miniwargames.com

⦿ www.miniwargames.com

**Parent Company** Pireme Publishing Ltd

**Editor** Iain Dickie

**Established** 1983

**Insider Info** Monthly consumer magazine covering gaming military history from all periods of history and all theatres of the world. Present circulation is 10,000. 80 per cent of the publication written by freelancers. Manuscripts are published four months after acceptance. Payment is on publication and no payment other than cash is offered. Expenses are paid sometimes (limit agreed upon in advance). A byline is given and publication copyrighted. First UK serial rights are purchased. Editorial lead time is seven weeks. Seasonal material should be submitted three months in advance. Accepts queries by mail and email. Aim to respond to queries and manuscripts within two weeks, and anything else within three days. Sample copy available for cost of £4.10. Writer's guidelines are free on request via email, media packs are available on request. Editorial calendar not available.

**Non-fiction** Publishes articles about New products (figures and rule reviews), Gaming and Tactical issues, Translating military history into a tabletop game, and Wargaming (battle game reports). * 60+ Non-fiction manuscripts per year are bought from freelancers. Pays £20 per published page.

**Submission Guidelines** Send complete manuscripts between 1,700 and 5,400 words. No reprints accepted.

**Fiction** Publishes articles covering Historical, Science fiction, Western and Fantasy.

**Images** Accepts images with submission.

* Negotiates payment individually and purchases one time rights.

**Submission Guidelines** Reviews gif/jpeg files; identification of subjects is required. State availability of photos with submission.

**Columns** Columns featured include Book, Figure and Gaming reviews, each an average of 150 words.

* 120 columns bought every year for £10 each. Accepts queries.

**Fillers** Publishes jokes, to be illustrated by the cartoonist, and letters.

**Tips** The articles convert an historical scenario into a tabletop game. At least half of any articles should be on gaming rather than history. Phone or email queries first.

## MiniWorld Magazine

**King's Reach Tower, Stamford Street, London, SE1 9LS**

📞 020 8726 8357

✉ monty_watkins@ipcmedia.com, miniworld@ipcmedia.com

🌐 www.miniworld.co.uk

**Parent Company** IPC Media

**Editor** Monty Watkins

**Established** 1991

**Insider Info** Monthly consumer magazine covering general motoring and motorcycling. Present circulation is 37,000. Accepts queries by mail and email.

**Non-fiction** Publishes Features, Interviews/Profiles, Technical and General interest articles.

**Submission Guidelines** Accepts queries.

**Tips** Dedicated to the 'car of the century', *MiniWorld* covers the scene worldwide - from driving, tuning, servicing, rebuilding and rallying, it provides the reader with everything they need to know about enjoying this great vehicle. *MiniWorld* also brings the magazine content to life with its annual event, The MiniWorld Show. Ideal articles should cover unusual mini's owned by the reader; a review and full details of the work carried out on the car would be ideal.

## Model Collector

**Leon House, 233 High street, Croydon, CR9 1HZ**

📞 020 8726 8000

✉ lindsey_amrani@ipcmedia.com

🌐 www.modelcollector.co.uk

**Parent Company** IPC Media

**Editor** Lindsey Amrani

**Established** 1987

**Insider Info** Consumer magazine publishing 13 issues per year, covering collecting. Present circulation of 13,000. Media packs available via: www.ipcmedia.com/magazines/modelcollector/

**Non-fiction** Publishes New product and Historical/Nostalgic articles.

**Submission Guidelines** Queries accepted.

**Images** State availability of photos with submission.

**Tips** Every month *Model Collector* is packed with news, reviews, special reports, features, interviews, and details of forthcoming events and dates for your diary, as well as exclusive reader offers and fantastic competitions. Contact the Editor with ideas for articles, particularly historical pieces about particular models or ranges.

## Modern Poetry in Translation

**The Queens College, Oxford, OX1 4AW**

📞 01865 244701

✉ see online form

🌐 www.mptmagazine.com

**Editor** David Constantine

**Contact** Co-Editor, Helen Constantine

**Established** 1966

**Insider Info** Consumer magazine published twice a year concerning literary general interest. Accepts queries by mail. Writer's guidelines are available online.

**Non-fiction** Publishes Essays and Poetry.

**Submission Guidelines** Send complete manuscript.

**Poetry** Publishes Free verse, Light verse, Traditional poetry and Translation.

**Tips** Modern Poetry in Translation *(MPT)* is an international magazine that specialises in the translation of poetry into English. *MPT* prints the latest translated foreign language poetry, as well as articles on poetry and poets, and articles on translation. *MPT* will accept submissions of good translated poetry from anywhere in the world, as well as poems and short essays that 'address such characteristic signs of our times as exile, the movement of peoples, the search for asylum, the speaking of languages outside their native home'.

## Money Marketing

**St. Giles House, 50 Poland Street, London, W1T 3QN**

📞 020 7970 4000

📞 020 7943 8097

🌐 www.moneymarketing.co.uk

**Parent Company** Centaur Communications

**Editor** John Lappin

**Established** 1985

**Insider Info** Weekly trade newspaper journal, covering finance and investment. Present circulation of 33,000. Accepts queries by mail, fax and phone.

**Non-fiction** Publishes Features, Interviews/Profiles and Technical articles.

**Submission Guidelines** Articles should be 900 words minimum.

**Tips** *Money Marketing* is the number one weekly newspaper for the Independent Financial Adviser (IFA). With the most respected journalists in the business, the major news stories break first in *Money Marketing* and with an unrivalled understanding of the market issues and product analysis, *Money Marketing* provides a complete information source and so captures a quality IFA reader audience. As it is a business journal, subjects covered must be breaking news/latest developments, and articles must contain a degree of in-depth knowledge and factual analysis.

## Monkey Kettle

**PO Box 4616, Kiln Farm, Milton Keynes, MK12 6XZ**

◉ monkeykettle@hotmail.com
◉ www.monkeykettle.co.uk

**Editor** Matthew Michael Taylor

**Established** 1998

**Insider Info** Consumer magazine published three timer a year, concerning literary general interest. Present circulation is 100. 100 per cent of the publication is written by freelancers. Accepts queries by email.

**Non-fiction** Publishes Poetry, Features, Interviews/Profiles and Reviews.

**Submission Guidelines** Accepts queries.

**Fiction** Publishes Mainstream fiction and Short stories. Send complete manuscript of 2,000 words maximum.

**Poetry** Publishes Free verse, Light verse and Traditional poetry. A maximum of ten poems may be submitted at one time.

**Tips** *Monkey Kettle* is a small, black and white printed poetry and fiction magazine. It contains new poetry and short stories from contributors and also has a website that runs news stories, interviews and articles related to writing. *Monkey Kettle* doesn't have any concrete submission guidelines, and are willing to consider anything, but the preference is for the funny, surreal, dark, poignant or political.

## Monomyth

**38 Pierrot Steps, 71 Kursaal Way, Southend on Sea, Essex, SS1 2UY**

◉ atlanteanpublishing@hotmail.com
◉ www.geocities.com/dj_tyrer/monomyth.html

**Parent Company** Atlantean Publishing

**Editor** David-John Tyrer

**Insider Info** Quarterly consumer magazine covering literary general interest. A byline is given. First UK serial rights are bought. Accepts queries by mail and email. Accepts previously published submissions. Writer's guidelines available online.

**Non-fiction** Publishes Poetry and General interest writing.

**Submission Guidelines** Send complete manuscript.

**Fiction** Publishes Mainstream fiction and Short fiction. Send complete manuscript.

**Poetry** Publishes Avant-garde, Free verse, Light verse and Traditional poetry.

**Tips** *Monomyth* is a quarterly literary magazine from Atlantean Publishing that specialises in printing longer short fiction and poetry. Welcomes new and unpublished writers, and will print stories in any genre or style. Also prints articles on fiction or poetry writing. Will consider longer unsolicited manuscripts for fiction or poetry in any genre or style. Submissions to *Monomyth* will also be considered for Atlantean's other literary publications.

## More!

**Endeavour House, 189 Shaftesbury Avenue, London, WC2H 8JG**

◉ 020 7208 3165
◉ 020 7379 4936
◉ more.letters@emap.com, firstname.lastname@emap.com
◉ www.moremagazine.co.uk

**Parent Company** EMAP Plc

**Editor** Lisa Smosarski

**Contact** Features Editor, Susan Riley; Acting Editorial Assistant, Helen Brown

**Established** 1988

**Insider Info** A fortnightly consumer magazine covering young women's lifestyle and celebrity topics. Present Circulation of 271,629.

**Non-fiction** Publishes General interest features, Interviews and Photo features on Television, Real life, Fashion, Sex, Beauty, Celebrities, Health and Entertainment.

**Tips** The magazine's target audience is girls aged 18-25, the style and content bridges a gap between teenage magazines and the classic women's glossies. The website gives a good idea as to the magazine's content.

## Mortgage Finance Gazette

**36–41 Arnold House, Holywell Lane, London, EC2A 3SF**

☏ 020 7827 5454

☏ 020 7827 0567

✉ jatkin@ccplcemail.co.uk

🌐 www.mfgonline.co.uk

**Parent Company** Charterhouse Communications

**Editor** Joanne Atkin

**Established** 1869

**Insider Info** Monthly trade journal magazine covering the mortgage lending industry. Present circulation of 5,000. Ten percent of the publication is written by freelancers. Takes five weeks to publish a manuscript after acceptance. Payment is on publication and a byline is given. Publication is copyrighted and all rights are purchased. Editorial lead time is three months. Queries accepted by mail, email and phone. Expenses will not be paid. Sample copy and editorial calendar available free on request. Media pack available online.

**Submission Guidelines** Manuscripts should be between 1,500 and 2,000 words.

**Images** Accepts images with submission.
 * Offers no additional payment for photos accepted with manuscript.

**Tips** Aimed at mortgage lenders and associated industries such as legal, insurance, and IT.

## Motor Boat & Yachting

**King's Reach Tower, Stamford Street, London, SE1 9LS**

☏ 020 7261 5333

☏ 020 7261 5419

✉ mby@ipcmedia.com

🌐 www.mby.com

**Parent Company** IPC Media

**Editor** Hugo Andreae

**Established** 1904

**Insider Info** Monthly consumer magazine covering boating leisure interests. Present circulation of 17,000. Accepts queries by mail and email. Media pack available at: www.ipcmedia.com/magazines/mby/

**Non-fiction** Publishes Features, Interviews/Profile, Reviews, New products, General interest and Sea-faring/Nautical articles.
 * Pays average of £100 per 1,000 words.

**Submission Guidelines** Send complete manuscript of 3,000 words maximum.

**Tips** Now in its 100th year, *Motor Boat & Yachting (MBY)* is Europe's premier motor cruising magazine.

*MBY*'s boat tests are acknowledged as the most authoritative in the business and its technical coverage is without equal. In addition, no other publication offers so many motorboats for sale. Core editorial coverage focuses on boats up to 80ft, while four times a year *MBY* also carries 'Custom Yachting', a special focus on 80ft plus boats. Although a good deal of technical knowledge is useful, will accept articles on general (sea-faring) interest, as well as specialist motor boating subjects.

## Motor Boats Monthly

**King's Reach Tower, Stamford Street, London, SE1 9LS**

☏ 020 7261 7256

☏ 020 7261 7900

✉ mbm@ipcmedia.com/simon_collis@ipcmedia.com

🌐 www.mbmclub.com

**Parent Company** IPC Media

**Editor** Simon Collis

**Established** 1982

**Insider Info** Monthly consumer magazine covering motorboats. Present circulation of 16,000. 30 per cent of publication written by freelancers. Payment is upon publication and only in cash. Expenses are paid sometimes (limit agreed upon in advance). A byline is given and publication is copyrighted. Accepts queries by mail and email. Accepts simultaneous and previously published submissions. Aims to respond to queries and manuscripts within one day. A sample copy is free on request via email and website. Writer's guidelines available free on request via email.

**Non-fiction** Publishes Humour, Features, Interviews/Profiles, New products, Travel, Historical/Nostalgic and Personal experience articles.

**Submission Guidelines** Contact Claire Frew, Editorial Assistant.

**Images** Accepts images with submission.
 * Pays varied fee per photo.

**Submission Guidelines** Reviews contact sheets, transparencies, gif/jpeg files with identification of subjects required. Send photos with submission to Editorial Assistant, Claire Frew.

**Tips** The UK's hardest-hitting and favourite motorboating magazine, *MBM* is firmly focused on practical motor cruising. With editorial coverage ranging from the booming RIB and sports boat markets right up to 40-foot cruisers and beyond, *MBM*'s comprehensive range of new and secondhand tests ensure that readers are always equipped with the very best buying information. Often includes anecdotal stories pertaining to motor boating, so travel writers may have an edge. Ideally submissions should also include relevant photos/illustrations.

## Motorcaravan & Motorhome Monthly
**PO Box 88, Tiverton, Devon, EX16 7ZN**
- 01778 391181
- mmmeditor@warnersgroup.co.uk
- www.mmmonline.co.uk
**Parent Company** Warners Group Publications
**Editor** Mike Jago/Jane Jago
**Established** 1966
**Insider Info** Monthly consumer magazine covering motoring and motorcycling caravanning. Present circulation of 33,379. Accepts queries by mail.
**Non-fiction** Publishes Features, Technical and Travel articles.
**Submission Guidelines** Accepts Queries. Manuscripts should be 2,000 words, maximum.
**Tips** *Motorcaravan & Motorhome Monthly* - the best selling motorhome magazine for 40 years! If you want to know what is really going on in the world of motorcaravans and motorcaravanning, then there's only one place to look. Contact the Editor with relevant ideas.

## Motor Caravan
**King's Reach Tower, Stamford Street, London, SE1 9LS**
- 020 8726 8248
- 020 8726 8299
- helen_avery@ipcmedia.com
- www.motorcaravanmagazine.co.uk
**Parent Company** IPC Media
**Editor** Helen Avery
**Established** 1986
**Insider Info** Monthly consumer magazine covering motoring and motorcycling caravanning. Present circulation of 15,000. Accepts queries by email and phone. Media packs available at: www.ipcmedia.com/magazines/motorcaravan/
**Non-fiction** Publishes Photo features, Features, and Travel articles.
   * Pays £60 per page.
**Submission Guidelines** £2,500 words maximum.
**Tips** *Motor Caravan* is full of great ideas about where to go in your motorhome, expert advice to keep trips fun and practical advice on vans and kit. With the best vehicle testers in the business, *Motor Caravan* offers unrivalled guidance on buying new and used motorhomes. Mostly interested in holiday reports, interesting or unusual caravans, and

practical caravanning features. Phone or email the Editor to outline ideas.

## Moving Worlds
**School of English, University of Leeds, Leeds, LS2 9JT**
- mworlds@leeds.ac.uk
- www.movingworlds.net
**Editor** Shirley Chew
**Contact** Susan Burns
**Insider Info** Bi-annual consumer journal covering literary general interest. Accepts queries by mail and email.
**Non-fiction** Publishes Essays, Poetry and Features.
**Submission Guidelines** Send complete manuscript.
**Fiction** Publishes Fiction.
**Tips** *Moving Worlds* is an international literary journal that publishes creative, critical, literary and visual texts. Encourages submission from new writers especially, from any cultural background and aims to be as diverse as possible with its content. Publishes a wide range of material and is looking for scholarly critical work from international writers, as much as fiction or poetry.

## Mslexia
**PO Box 656, Newcastle upon Tyne, NE99 1PZ**
- 0191 261 6656
- 0191 261 6636
- postbag@mslexia.demon.co.uk, daneet@mslexia.demon.co.uk
- www.mslexia.co.uk
**Parent Company** Mslexia Publications Ltd
**Editor** Daneet Steffens
**Established** 1999
**Insider Info** Quarterly consumer magazine covering literary general interest. Present circulation of 20,000. 60 per cent of the publication is written by freelancers. Payment is on publication. There is a 50 per cent kill fee for assigned manuscripts not published. A byline is given. Editorial lead time is three months. Seasonal material must be submitted three months in advance. Accepts queries by mail, email and phone. Accepts simultaneous submissions; aims to report back on manuscripts within three months. Sample copy free on request online. Writer's guidelines, editorial calendar and media pack available online.
**Non-fiction** Publishes How-to, Interviews/Profiles, Opinion (not letters to the Editor) and Personal experience articles.

\* 40 manuscripts are bought from freelance writers every year.

**Submission Guidelines** Accepts query with published clips. Articles should be between 500 and 2,000 words.

**Fiction** Publishes Mainstream and Literary fiction.
 \* 30 manuscripts are bought from freelance writers per year. Will pay £15 per 1,000 words.

**Submission Guidelines** Send complete manuscript, which should be between 50 and 3,000 words.

**Poetry** Publishes Avant-garde, Free verse, Haiku and Traditional poetry.
 \* 40 poems are bought per year. Pays £25 per poem.

**Submission Guidelines** Submit a maximum of four poems at once.

**Columns** Uses columns in the publication.
 \* 12 columns bought per year.

**Submission Guidelines** Accepts query with published clips.

**Tips** *Mslexia* is a national magazine for woman writers, it prints a substantial section of poetry and prose by published and unpublished authors. *Mslexia* is read by top authors and absolute beginners. A quarterly masterclass in the business and psychology of writing, it's the essential magazine for women who write. Welcomes submissions for every part of the magazine. The editors commission work by prominent authors and artists, as well as talented newcomers and aim to publish some new voices in every copy of the magazine. The majority of readers live in the UK, so any feature pitches should be aware of this. Also, please note that they only accept email submissions from overseas writers.

## Musical Opinion
**2 Princes Rd, St. Leonards on Sea, East Sussex, TN37 6RS**
- 01424 715167
- 01424 712214
- musicalopinion2@aol.com
- www.musicalopinion.com

**Editor** Denby Richards

**Contact** Managing Editor, Judith Monk

**Established** 1877

**Insider Info** Bi-monthly consumer magazine covering musical opinion. A specialist magazine for classical music lovers, which offers many years of expertise in presenting in-depth information for concerts, operas, festivals, instruments and musical education to name but a few. Present circulation of 8,500. 50 per cent is written by freelancers. Takes three months to publish a manuscript after acceptance. Payment is on publication. A byline is given and publication is copyrighted. There is an editorial lead time of six weeks. Seasonal material should be submitted eight weeks in advance. Accepts queries by email. Aims to respond to queries within two weeks. Expenses are not paid. Sample copy available for cost of £5.50. Writer's guidelines available by email.

**Non-fiction** Publishes Features and Interviews/Profiles (well written and relevant to the field).

**Submission Guidelines** Accepts queries; contact Judith Monk, Managing Editor.

**Tips** *Musical Opinion* was established in 1877 and is celebrating its 130th anniversary this year. With a strong and loyal following of all age groups in the UK and abroad, it reaches over 38 countries. It is read by musicians, teachers, students, artist management agents, concert hall managers and many professionals in the music world.

## myBOOKSmag
**4 Froxfield Close, Winchester, SO22 6JW**
- 01962 620320
- guy@newbooksmag.com
- www.newbooksmag.com

**Parent Company** New Books

**Editor** Guy Pringle

**Established** 2002

**Insider Info** Quarterly consumer magazine covering literary general interest. Present circulation is 5,000.

**Non-fiction** Publishes Photo features, Features, Interviews/Profiles and Reviews.

**Submission Guidelines** Accepts queries.

**Fiction** Publishes Fiction and Children's book excerpts. Accepts queries.

**Tips** *myBOOKSmag* is a literary magazine aimed at five to seven year olds. It contains extracts from children's books, as well as activities, author and illustrator information, reviews and directories. Often requires lots of reviews of current children's books, especially with a seasonal theme.

## My Weekly
**80 Kingsway East, Dundee, DD4 8SL**
- 01382 223131
- 01382 452491
- myweekly@dcthomson.co.uk, shampton@dcthomson.co.uk

**Parent Company** D.C. Thomson & Co Ltd

**Editor** Sally Hampton

**Established** 1910

**Insider Info** Weekly consumer magazine covering women's interests. Present circulation of 199,000.

Seasonal material should be submitted three months in advance. Accepts queries by mail and email. Writer's guidelines free on request by email.

**Non-fiction** Publishes Humour, Historical/Nostalgic, Serialised novels and Seasonal articles.

**Submission Guidelines** Send complete manuscript, between 1,500 and 4,000 words.

**Fiction** Publishes fiction.

**Tips** *My Weekly* is the magazine for women who love good reading. Prints fiction stories, great food and cookery, inspirational real-life articles, all the latest fashion, beauty and shopping news plus travel and finance features. *My Weekly* is aimed at 'young' women of all ages; stories deal with real, down to earth themes that are related to the lives of readers.

## Nasty Piece of Work

**20 Drum Mead, Petersfield, Hampshire, GU32 3AQ**

**Editor** David Green

**Insider Info** Quarterly consumer magazine covering literary general interest.

**Fiction** Publishes Horror.

**Tips** A quarterly genre magazine, dedicated to publishing horror fiction and poetry. The content is often extreme in nature, even by typical horror fiction standards. The stories and poetry are often extremely graphic or violent, and otherwise controversial, but must still be considered intelligent contemporary horror.

## The Naturalist

**Department of Environmental Science, University of Bradford, Bradford, Yorkshire, BD7 1DP**

- 01274 234212
- 01274 234231
- m.r.d.seaward@bradford.ac.uk

**Parent Company** Yorkshire Naturalists' Union

**Editor** Professor Mark R. D. Seaward

**Established** 1876

**Insider Info** Quarterly scientific journal, covering biological sciences and natural history, particularly relating to the North of England. Present circulation of 1,000. Features peer reviewed articles for an amateur and professional scientific readership. Submissions are published approximately ten weeks after acceptance. No payment is made for submissions. Publication is copyrighted and queries are accepted by mail, email, fax and telephone. Aims to respond to queries with one week, and manuscripts within four weeks. Assignment

expenses are not paid. Sample copy is available on receipt of SAE (230mm x 160mm). Writer's guidelines are available free on request.

**Non-fiction** Publishes articles on Natural History and Biological sciences.

## Nature

**The Macmillan Building, 4–6 Crinan Street, London, N1 9XW**

- 020 7833 4000
- 020 7843 4596
- nature@nature.com
- www.nature.com/nature

**Parent Company** Nature Publishing Group

**Editor** Phillip Campbell

**Established** 1869

**Insider Info** Weekly trade journal, covering science news and current affairs. Present circulation of 65,000. Byline is given. Publication is copyrighted. Aims to respond to queries and manuscripts within one week. Writer's guidelines are available online.

**Non-fiction** Publishes Technical and Science/Research articles.

**Submission Guidelines** Accepts queries. Send complete manuscript.

**Images** Send photos with submission.

**Tips** *Nature* is one of the oldest scientific journals. Although most scientific journals are now highly specialised, *Nature* is idiosyncratic in still publishing original research articles across a wide range of scientific fields. In most fields of scientific research, many of the most important new advances each year are published as articles or letters. Articles must be considered ground breaking as well as being scientifically relevant and contemporary. They must also be from a specialist with an advanced knowledge of their field.

## The Nautical Magazine

**4–10 Darnley Street, Glasgow, G41 2SD**

- 0141 429 1234
- 0141 420 1694
- info@skipper.co.uk
- www.skipper.co.uk

**Parent Company** Brown, Son & Ferguson Ltd

**Editor** Leslie Ingram-Brown

**Established** 1832

**Insider Info** Monthly consumer journal covering Nnautical and maritime interest. Present circulation is 800. 100 per cent of the publication is written by freelance writers. Submissions are published up to three months after acceptance. Payment is on publication. Publication is copyrighted and first rights are purchased. Average lead time is four weeks. Seasonal material must be submitted three months in advance. Queries accepted by mail, email and fax. Accepts simultaneous submissions. Aims to respond to queries and manuscripts within four weeks. Sample copy, manuscript guidelines and editorial calendars are free on request. Media pack is available online.

**Non-fiction** Interested in Features, Reviews of nautical books, Technical, General interest, Historical/Nostalgic and Personal experience articles.
 * Purchase approximately 200 Non-fiction manuscripts per year.

**Submission Guidelines** Accepts complete manuscripts of between 100 and 1,000 words. Does not publish reprints.

**Fiction** Publishes Historical and Nautical short fiction.
 * Purchases 50 fiction manuscripts per year.

**Submission Guidelines** Accepts complete manuscripts.

**Fillers** Publishes Facts, Newsbreaks and Letters of up to 500 words.

**Tips** *The Nautical Magazine* is aimed at anyone interested in nautical or maritime subjects. Articles can be technical or general interest in tone.

## Neon Highway
### 37 Grinshill Close, Liverpool, L8 8LD
0151 727 5129
poetshideout@yahoo.com
www.neonhighway.co.uk
**Editor** Alice Lenkiewicz
**Established** 2002
**Insider Info** Annual consumer magazine covering literary general interest. Byline is given.
**Poetry** Publishes Avant-garde, Free verse, Light verse and Experimental poetry.
**Tips** *Neon Highway* publishes original and experimental poetry and also organises public poetry reading events in the North West. It commissions all poetry content ,and does not accept unsolicited submissions.

## .net
### 30 Monmouth Street, Bath, BA1 2BW
01225 442244
01225 732295
mailus@netmag.co.uk
www.netmag.co.uk
**Parent Company** Future Publishing
**Editor** Dan Oliver
**Established** 1994

**Insider Info** Monthly consumer magazine covering internet computing. Present circulation of 14,000. Accepts queries by mail and email.
**Non-fiction** Publishes Features and Technical articles.
**Submission Guidelines** Send complete manuscript between 1,000 and 3,000 words.
**Tips** *.net* delivers cutting edge practical advice on the full range of topics essential for today's web builders; design, development, sales, marketing, usability and accessibility, information architecture, security, copywriting, advertising and more. It is read by people who are serious about the commercial application of the internet. *.net* is a professional magazine read by 'people who are serious about the commercial application of the internet.' Therefore an amount of technical or business expertise relating to the internet is invaluable.

## Never Bury Poetry
### The Met, Market Street, Bury, Lancashire, BL9 0BW
n.b.poetry@zen.co.uk
www.nbpoetry.care4free.net/index.htm
**Editor** Jean Tarry
**Established** 1989
**Insider Info** Quarterly consumer magazine covering literary general interest. Present circulation of 100. A byline is given. Accepts queries by mail.
**Poetry** Publishes Free verse, Light verse and Traditional poetry.
**Submission Guidelines** Accepts queries.
**Tips** *Never Bury Poetry* is a small magazine, which publishes new poetry from contributors. Each issue of the magazine has a specific theme. All submissions must be in line with the theme of the issue. Upcoming themes are announced in each issue, but not announced on the website. Also, note that email submissions are not accepted.

## newBOOKS
### 4 Froxfield Close, Winchester, SO22 6JW
01962 620320
guy@newbooksmag.com
www.newbooksmag.com
**Editor** Guy Pringle
**Established** 2000
**Insider Info** Bi-monthly consumer magazine covering literary topics for readers and writers' groups. Present circulation of 17,000. Accepts queries by mail and email. Sample copy free on request, online.

**Non-fiction** Publishes Features, Interviews/Profiles, Reviews, General interest and News articles.
**Submission Guidelines** Accepts queries.
**Fiction** Publishes Fiction.
**Tips** *newBOOKS* has in-depth interviews with the latest authors, book related articles and insider knowledge. It also offers the opportunity to apply for free books to read. Interested in any genre or type of book, *newBOOKS* is always seeking reviews of the latest releases.

## The New Cauldron

**10 Glyn Road, Wirral, CH44 1AB**
- 07775 645497
- 0151 200 9402
- terence.grogan50@ntlworld.com
- www.thenewcauldron.co.uk

**Editor** Terence Grogan
**Insider Info** Quarterly consumer magazine covering literature. Byline is given. Accepts queries by mail and email.
**Non-fiction** Interested in Features and Articles on Prose and Poetry writing.
**Submission Guidelines** Accepts queries for articles up to 1,000 words.
**Fiction** Publishes Short fiction.
**Submission Guidelines** Accepts complete manuscripts up to 1,500 words.
**Poetry** Publishes Contemporary, Free verse, Light verse and Traditional poetry.
**Submission Guidelines** Submit poems up to 30 lines in length.
**Tips** *The New Cauldron* is an international small press magazine that publishes poetry and fiction, letters, articles and special features for readers and writers. *The New Cauldron* also runs various writing competitions and challenges, and offers a critiquing service to subscribers. *The New Cauldron* aims to encourage submissions from new, unpublished writers, but will give priority to subscribers.

## New Day

Working towards a world without leprosy
**Goldhay Way, Orton Goldhay, Peterborough, Cambridgeshire PE2 5GZ**
- 01733 370505
- 01733 404880
- post@tlmew.org.uk
- www.leprosymission.org.uk

**Parent Company** The Leprosy Mission
**Editor** Karen du Plessis
**Contact** Managing Editor, Jean Jones; Communications Officer, Karen du Plessis

**Established** 1896
**Insider Info** A free charity magazine with two issues per year. It covers The Leprosy Mission's work to eradicate the causes and consequences of leprosy, and looks at healthcare, fighting stigma and poverty. Present circulation of 150,000. A byline is given. Editorial time is 13 weeks. Seasonal material should be submitted 13 weeks in advance. Accepts queries by mail, email, fax or phone. Accepts previously published submissions. Aims to respond to queries within five days and manuscripts within four months. Will not pay the expenses of writers on assignments. Sample copy is free on request and available online or by email. Writer's guidelines and editorial calendars are available via email.
**Non-fiction** Publishes Features with a focus on leprosy.
**Submission Guidelines** Accepts queries for articles of between 350 and 850 words. No reprints. Contact Karen du Plessis, Communications Officer.
**Images** Accepts images with submission.
 * Pays a variable fee per photo up to a maximum of £100. Buys one time rights.
**Submission Guidelines** Accepts gif/jpeg files and identification of subjects is required. Send photos with submission to Communications Officer, Karen du Plessis.
**Tips** *New Day* is a free magazine mailed twice a year to supporters in England, Wales, the Channel Islands and the Isle of Man. It covers The Leprosy Mission's work around the world with people affected by leprosy. The Leprosy Mission is a Christian charity but helps people from all faiths and their supporters come from a wide cross section of society. Email to ask what kind of article is needed. The magazine does not pay for submissions

## New Internationalist

**55 Rectory Road, Oxford, OX4 1BW**
- 01865 728181
- 01865 793152
- ni@newint.org
- www.newint.org

**Parent Company** New Internationalist Trust
**Editor** Vanessa Baird/David Ransom/Katharine Ainger/Dinyar Godrej
**Established** 1973
**Insider Info** A monthly consumer magazine covering international news and current affairs. Present circulation of 75,000. Accepts queries by mail or email. Writer's guidelines, editorial calendar and media pack available online.
**Non-fiction** Publishes Features, Opinion (not letters to the Editor) and World affairs/Politics articles.

\* Pays £80 per 1000 words for unsolicited articles
**Submission Guidelines** Send complete manuscript.
**Tips** The *New Internationalist* is renowned for its radical, campaigning stance on a range of world issues, from the cynical marketing of baby milk in the majority world, to human rights in Burma. Please note that the format of the *New Internationalist* magazine always has the main body of the magazine dedicated to the theme of the month. This means that in general, all pieces are commissioned for that particular theme. However, if you have a local perspective on a social event that occurred recently (e.g. a rally, protest, or other significant social change event) perhaps it may be suitable for the 'NI Special Features' section of their website. If so, email the editorial team with your suggestion.

# New Nation
**Unit 2, 65 Whitechapel Road, London, E1 1DU**
- 020 7650 2000
- 020 7650 2001
- general@ethnicmedia.co.uk
- www.newnation.co.uk

**Parent Company** Ethnic Media Group
**Editor** Michael Eboda
**Established** 1996
**Insider Info** Weekly consumer magazine covering News and Current Affairs. Present circulation is 21,630. Accepts queries by mail.
**Non-fiction** Interested in General interest and Political articles.
**Submission Guidelines** Accepts queries in the first instance.
**Tips** *New Nation* has become Britain's most popular black weekly magazine since its launch in 1996. Aimed at young, educated black Britons and the wider African and Caribbean communities, *New Nation* features a vibrant mix of news, sport, social and political issues, recruitment and contact pages. Relevant current affairs, especially local interest pieces, are appreciated.

# New Scientist
**8th Floor, Lacon House, 84 Theobalds Road, London, WC1X 8NS**
- 020 8652 3500
- 020 7611 1200
- www.newscientist.com

**Parent Company** Reed Business Information Ltd
**Editor** Jeremy Webb
**Established** 1956

**Insider Info** Weekly consumer magazine covering scientific news and current affairs. Present circulation is 176,000. Accepts queries by email.
**Non-fiction** Interested in Photo features, Features and Technical articles.
**Submission Guidelines** Accepts queries in the first instance.
**Tips** *New Scientist* keeps its readers up to date with the latest science and technology news from around the world. Although *New Scientist* rarely uses unsolicited work, they do run an internship program for any budding scientific journalists, which can lead to publication in the magazine. Further details can be found on their website.

# New Statesman
**3rd Floor, 52 Grosvenor Gardens, London, SW1W 0AU**
- 020 7730 3444
- 020 7259 0181
- sue@newstatesman.co.uk
- www.newstatesman.co.uk

**Editor** John Kampfner
**Contact** Deputy Editor, Sue Matthias
**Established** 1913
**Insider Info** Weekly consumer magazine covering news and current affairs. Present circulation is 25,505. Accepts queries by mail.
**Non-fiction** Interested in Features, Interviews/ Profiles, Reviews and General interest articles.
**Submission Guidelines** Accepts queries (including SAE).
**Tips** The *New Statesman* is a British left of centre political magazine published weekly in London. The magazine is committed to 'development, human rights and the environment, global issues the mainstream press often ignores'. *New Statesman* has a very well defined writing style and also a political bias. Be aware of these things before submitting.

# New Stitches
**Well Oast, Brenley Lane, Faversham, Kent, ME13 9LY**
- 01227 750215
- 01227 750813
- janice@ccpuk.co.uk
- www.newstitches.co.uk

**Parent Company** Creative Crafts Publishing
**Editor** Janice Broadstock
**Established** 1992
**Insider Info** A consumer magazine publication issued monthly. Present circulation of 25,000. Payment is upon publication. 30 per cent of

thepublication is written by freelancers. Submissions are published approximately one month after acceptance, with an editorial lead time of two months. Publication is copyrighted and first UK serial rights are purchased. Seasonal material must be submitted two months in advance. Accepts queries by mail, email and fax. Aims to respond to queries within two days.

**Non-fiction** Publishes How-to, Technical and General interest articles on needlecraft.

**Tips** *New Stitches* is aimed at the discerning embroiderer with emphasis on high quality designs covering cross stitch, hardanger, blackwork and many other embroidery techniques.

## New Welsh Review
**PO Box 170, Aberystwyth, Ceredigion, SY23 1WZ**
- 01970 628410
- editor@newwelshreview.com
- www.newwelshreview.com

**Editor** Francesca Rhydderch
**Established** 1988
**Insider Info** A quarterly consumer literary journal focusing Welsh writing in English. Present circulation of 3,500. Payment is upon publication. A byline is given. Queries are accepted by mail or email. Aims to respond to queries and manuscripts within three months. Writer's guidelines are available online.

**Non-fiction** Publishes articles on Poetry, Features, Interview/Profiles, Reviews and General interest articles relating to the Welsh literary scene.
 * Pays between £100 and £150 for unsolicited articles.

**Submission Guidelines** Accepts queries with outlines.

**Fiction** Publishes Short stories.
 * Pays between £60 and £75 for fiction.

**Submission Guidelines** Submit complete manuscript by post.

**Poetry** Publishes Free verse, Light verse and Traditional poetry.
 * Pays £25 maximum for poems.

**Tips** The *New Welsh Review* maintains a cosmopolitan outlook to appeal to international markets. It accepts postal submissions for poetry and fiction, but most non-fiction articles are commissioned privately, so only submit a query for these. The magazine is always looking for freelance reviewers, either send a CV or check the website for further detail.

## New Woman
**Endeavour House, 189 Shaftesbury Avenue, London, WC2H 8JG**
- 020 7437 9011
- 020 7208 3585
- firstname.lastname@emap.com
- www.newwoman.co.uk

**Parent Company** EMAP Plc
**Contact** Deputy Editor, Amanda Astill; Editorial Assistant, Nina Baglin
**Established** 1988
**Insider Info** A monthly consumer magazine covering women's lifestyle topics. Present circulation of 231,785.

**Non-fiction** Publishes General Interest Features, Interviews, Reviews and Photo Features on Celebrities, Entertainment, Fashion, Beauty, Health, Work, Travel and Real life.

**Submission Guidelines** Accepts queries for articles of up to 2,000 words. No fiction.

**Tips** Rarely but occasionally accepts articles from freelancers. The magazine is aimed at women between 23 and 37 years old.

## The New Writer
**PO Box 60, Cranbrook, Kent, TN17 2ZR**
- 01580 212626
- 01580 212041
- editor@thenewwriter.com
- www.thenewwriter.com

**Editor** Suzanne Ruthven
**Established** 1996
**Insider Info** Bi-monthly trade journal covering literature and creative writing. Present circulation is 3,000. 80 per cent of the publication is written by freelance writers. Submissions published approximately four months after acceptance. Payment is on publication. A byline is given. Publication is copyrighted and first UK serial rights are purchased. Average lead time is four months. Accepts queries by mail and email. Aims to respond to queries within three weeks and manuscripts within six months. Sometimes pays writer's with contributor copies. Sample copy is available with SAE. Manuscript guidelines are free on request. Media pack is available by email.

**Non-fiction** Interested in How-to (Creative Writing), Features, Interviews/Profiles and Articles on poetry and prose writing.
 * Payment for non-fiction is £20 per 1,000 words.

**Submission Guidelines** Accepts complete manuscript of between 500 and 2,000 words.

**Fiction** Publishes Mainstream Short fiction.

\* Accepts fiction submissions from prizewinners or subscribers only.

**Submission Guidelines** Accepts complete manuscript up to 4,000 words.

**Poetry** Publishes Contemporary, Free verse and Traditional poetry.

**Submission Guidelines** Submit up to five poems. Do not submit therapeutic/confessional poetry, or poems that meander without rhyme or reason.

**Tips** *The New Writer* is a forward looking magazine with a range of expert contributors. Every issue contains original short stories, a showcase for new poetry, articles, book reviews, market information, news and readers' views. *The New Writer* accepts article and poetry submissions, but only accepts fiction submissions from prizewinners or subscribers. All submissions should be posted to the Editor.

## New Writing Scotland
**9 University Gardens, University of Glasgow, Glasgow, Strathclyde, G12 8QH**
- 0141 330 5309
- 0141 330 5309
- nws@asls.org.uk
- www.asls.org.uk

**Parent Company** ASLS
**Editor** Liz Niven and Brian Whittingham
**Contact** Managing Editor, Duncan Jones
**Established** 1982

**Insider Info** An annual anthology of short fiction, poetry and other creative prose, written in any of the languages of Scotland. Present circulation of 600. 100 per cent of the publication is written by freelance writers. Manuscripts are published six months after acceptance. Payment is upon publication and never with contributor copies instead of cash. A byline is given. Purchases first serial rights, and copyright reverts to the individual authors after publication. Accepts queries by mail, email, fax or phone. Aims to respond to queries within two months and manuscripts within six months. A sample copy is available for cost. Writer's guidelines are free on request and available online.

**Fiction** Publishes Adventure, Historical, Romance, Horror, Science Fiction, Confession, Humourous, Erotica, Mainstream, Slice of life vignettes, Ethnic, Mystery, Suspense, Experimental, Novel excerpts, Western, Fantasy, and Religious fiction.

\* Purchases 50 fiction manuscripts per year. Pays £20 per published page.

**Submission Guidelines** Send complete manuscripts for fiction of up to, 3,500 words. No previously published material. Contact Managing Editor, Duncan Jones.

**Poetry** Publishes Avant-garde, Free verse, Haiku, Light verse, Traditional and Concrete poetry.

\* Purchases 40 poems per year. Pays £20 per published page

**Submission Guidelines** Accepts up to four sample poems. No previously published material. Contact Managing Editor, Duncan Jones.

**Tips** *New Writing Scotland* publishes new short fiction and poetry, in any of the languages of Scotland, from writers resident in Scotland or Scots by birth, upbringing or inclination. Style and subject matter are unimportant, the quality of writing is what counts. There is no need to be consciously Scottish, nor any penalty for being so.

## NME
(New Musical Express)
**King's Reach Tower, Stamford Street, London, SE1 9LS**
- 020 7261 6472
- 020 7261 5185
- conor_mcnicholas@ipcmedia.com
- www.nme.com

**Parent Company** IPC Media
**Editor** Conor McNicholas
**Established** 1952

**Insider Info** A weekly consumer magazine covering the world of rock and alternative music. Present circulation of 74,206. Accepts queries by mail. Media pack available online.

**Non-fiction** Publishes Features, Interviews/Profiles and Reviews.

**Submission Guidelines** Accepts queries
**Tips** *NME* is the biggest selling and most respected music weekly in the world. Freelancers are often used, but usually for reviews first and foremost.

## The North
**The Studio, Byram Arcade, Westgate, Huddersfield, HD1 1ND**
- 01484 434840
- 01484 426566
- www.poetrybusiness.co.uk

**Parent Company** The Poetry Business Ltd
**Editor** Peter Sansom
**Contact** Co-Editor, Janet Fisher
**Established** 1986

**Insider Info** A consumer magazine, with two issues per year, covering contemporary poetry. Present circulation is 500. Payment on publication. A byline is given. Accepts queries by mail. Aims to respond to queries and manuscripts within six weeks. Manuscript guidelines are available online.

**523**

**Non-fiction** Interested in Essays, Features, Interviews/Profiles and Reviews.
**Submission Guidelines** Accepts queries in the first instance.
**Poetry** Publishes Contemporary poetry.
**Submission Guidelines** Submit up to six poems.
**Tips** *The North* is an independent magazine that publishes contemporary poetry from new and established writers, book reviews, critical articles, interviews and autobiographies, criticism and guides. *The North* accepts submissions for contemporary poetry in any style, as long as they are sent by post. Also, *The North* is always seeking synopses for good critical articles and reviews concerning contemporary poetry.

## North West Business Insider
**Boulton House, 17–21 Chorlton Street, Manchester, M1 3HY**
- 0161 907 9711
- 0161 236 9862
- insider@newsco.com
- www.insidermagazine.co.uk

**Parent Company** Insider Media
**Editor** Michael Taylor
**Contact** Deputy Editor, Lisa Miles
**Established** 1991
**Insider Info** A monthly regional business magazine covering business issues in the North West of England. Present circulation of 20,000. 50 per cent of the publication is written by freelance writers. Manuscripts are published one month after acceptance. Payment is upon publication. A byline is given. Publication is copyrighted and all rights are purchased. Editorial lead time is one month. Seasonal material should be submitted one month in advance. Queries are accepted by email. Sample copy, media pack and editorial calendar available online. Writer's guidelines are free on request.
**Non-fiction** Publishes Feature articles on business topics.
**Tips** Insider is aimed at business owners and company directors. The editors recommend reading the magazine and understanding the target audience, before submitting original ideas they won't have thought of.

## Northwords Now
**28 Drummond Circus, Inverness, IV2 4QF**
- 01463 231758
- rhoda8@btopenworld.com

**Editor** Rhoda Michael
**Established** 2005

**Insider Info** A quarterly consumer literary magazine. Accepts queries by mail or email.
**Fiction** Publishes Short stories.
**Submission Guidelines** Send complete manuscript by post.
**Poetry** Publishes Free verse and Traditional poetry.
**Tips** *Northwords Now* is the literary magazine of the north. It publishes new fiction and poetry from new and established writers, including younger writers (17–25 years). Accepts poetry and fiction submissions by post, and must only be in English, Gaelic, or other local dialects.

## Notes & Queries
**Pembroke College, Oxford, OX1 1DW**
- 01865 276463
- notes.queries@oup.com
- http://nq.oxfordjournals.org/

**Parent Company** Oxford University Press
**Editor** L. Glenn Black, J. Bernard O'Donoghue
**Established** 1849
**Insider Info** A quarterly consumer literary journal. Present circulation of 1,475. A byline is given. Queries accepted by mail and email. Writer's guidelines are available online.
**Non-fiction** Publishes Features, Reviews and Letters/Queries on literary subjects.
**Submission Guidelines** Accepts complete manuscripts.
**Tips** *Notes & Queries* is a literary journal that aims to answer readers queries about various language and literature subjects. Each issue focuses on works of a specific period and prints factual notes, book reviews, readers queries and replies. The articles published are often quite short, and any submission should be as factually informative as possible, rather than speculative.

## Now
**King's Reach Tower, Stamford Street, London, SE1 9LS**
- 020 7261 6274
- 020 7261 6789
- karen_cross@ipcmedia.com
- www.nowmagazine.co.uk

**Parent Company** IPC Media
**Contact** Assistant Editor, Karen Cross
**Established** 1996
**Insider Info** A weekly consumer magazine covering celebrity gossip and women's lifestyle. Present circulation of 539,902.
**Non-fiction** Publishes Exposé, General interest and Celebrity Culture articles.

**Tips** *Now's* target readership is, 'Young, independent urbanites with a high disposable income, aged between 16 and 34'. Write a celebrity article aimed at this audience, but contact the Editor first with a synopsis.

## Nursery World

**Admiral House, 66–68 East Smithfield, London, E1W 1BX**

☎ 020 7782 3120

☎ 020 7782 3131

✉ liz.roberts@nurseryworld.co.uk

🌐 www.nurseryworld.co.uk

**Parent Company** TSL Education Ltd

**Editor** Liz Roberts

**Insider Info** A weekly trade magazine covering nursery level education. Present circulation of 23,784. Accepts queries by mail or email.

**Non-fiction** Publishes How-to, Features and Childcare articles.

**Submission Guidelines** Send complete manuscript for articles of between 800 and 1,300 words.

**Images** Send photos with submission.

**Tips** The leading magazine for early years and childcare practitioners, publishing an extensive range of free supplements and specials, offering in-depth coverage in specific areas of the early years and childcare sector. Guides for managers and practitioners, all written by early years experts, provide clear, accessible information and advice on key issues such as behaviour, additional learning needs, planning, working with under threes and nursery food. Articles should be as practical and informal as possible, so an academic or practical background in early years studies would be useful. Include any relevant photographs.

## Nursing Times

**Greater London House, Hampstead Road, London, NW1 7EJ**

☎ 020 7874 0502

☎ 020 7874 0505

✉ nt@emap.com

🌐 www.nursingtimes.net

**Parent Company** EMAP Healthcare

**Editor** Rachel Downey

**Established** 1905

**Insider Info** A weekly trade magazine focussing on nursing topics. Present circulation of 63,833. Accepts queries by mail.

**Non-fiction** Publishes How-to, Feature and Technical articles.

**Submission Guidelines** Accepts completed manuscripts.

**Tips** The UK's best selling weekly magazine for nurses, publishing news, clinical features and educational material. *Nursing Times* makes ready use of unsolicited content but it is a trade orientated publication, so expert clinical knowledge and insider knowledge of the nursing industry and new developments is essential.

## Nuts

**King's Reach Tower, Stamford Street, London, SE1 9LS**

☎ 020 7261 5660

☎ 020 7261 5480

✉ nutsmagazine@ipcmedia.com

🌐 www.nuts.co.uk

**Parent Company** IPC Media

**Editor** Dominic Smith

**Established** 2004

**Insider Info** A weekly consumer magazine covering young men's lifestyle topics. Present circulation of 304,785. Accepts queries by email.

**Non-fiction** Publishes Photo features, Humour, Exposé, Features, Interviews/Profiles, Reviews and General interest articles.

**Submission Guidelines** Accepts queries.

**Tips** The magazine's mix of humour, sport, news, television, women and true stories is aimed a target readership of 16–45 year old men. Will not accept fashion, health, or grooming articles.

## Obsessed With Pipework

**8 Abbot's Way, Pilton, Somerset, BA4 4BN**

☎ 01749 890019

✉ cannula.dementia@virgin.net

🌐 www.flarestack.co.uk/obsessedwithpipework.htm

**Parent Company** Flarestack Publishing

**Editor** Charles Johnson

**Established** 1997

**Insider Info** A quarterly consumer literary magazine focusing on poetry. Accepts queries by mail or email.

**Poetry** Publishes Avant-garde, Free verse and Light verse poetry.

**Tips** *Obsessed With Pipework* publishes new poetry from both new and established writer. They tend to prefer modern, non-conformist poetry, which takes risks and attempts to 'make it new'. They do not want safe poems that are about what the author knows. They want poems in which the author tries to write about something new to themselves.

## Occupational Health Journal

**Quadrant House, The Quadrant, Sutton, Surrey, SM2 5AS**

- 020 8652 4669
- 020 8652 8805
- OH.Editor@rbi.co.uk, noel.oreilly@rbi.co.uk
- www.ohmagazine.co.uk

**Parent Company** Reed Business Information

**Editor** Noel O'Reilly

**Contact** Managing Editor, Rob Willock

**Insider Info** A monthly trade magazine covering aspects of occupational health. Present circulation of 5,000. 50 per cent of the publication is written by freelance writers. Manuscripts are published eight months after acceptance. Payment is upon publication, never with contributor copies instead of cash, with no formal kill fee offered. The expenses of writers on assignments will sometimes be paid (limit agreed upon in advance). A byline is given. Publication is copyrighted and all rights are purchased. Editorial lead time is three months. Seasonal material should be submitted four months in advance. Queries are accepted by mail, email or phone. Sample copies are available for £99 per year. Writer's guidelines and editorial calendar are free on request.

**Non-fiction** Publishes Features and Technical articles.

**Submission Guidelines** Accepts queries with published clips, for articles of between 700 and 2,200 words.

**Tips** The magazine is read by occupational health nurse practitioners and others with responsibility for health at work. It covers workplace health and well-being issues for a professional audience.

## Official Xbox 360

**1 Balcombe Street, London, NW1 6NW**

- 01225 442244
- 01225 732285
- oxmspiff@futurenet.co.uk
- www.oxm.co.uk

**Parent Company** Future Publishing

**Editor** Steve Brown

**Contact** Features Editor, Gary Cutlack

**Insider Info** A monthly consumer magazine focusing on the Xbox games console. Present circulation of 42,680.

**Non-fiction** Publishes Features and Technical articles directly relating to the Xbox, its capabilities and its games.

**Tips** The magazine is linked to a playable demo disc and website. Game coverage is done internally by staff writers, but there is scope for detailed articles concerning Xbox 360's external capabilities as a media centre. Hardware reviews and pieces on unusual console uses would be the most likely to succeed.

## OK!

**10 Lower Thames Street, London, EC3R 6EN,**

- 0871 434 1010
- firstname.lastname@express.co.uk
- www.ok-magazine.com

**Parent Company** Northern & Shell Plc

**Editor** Lisa Byrne

**Contact** Deputy Editor, Julia Davis

**Established** 1923

**Insider Info** A weekly consumer magazine covering celebrity gossip and women's lifestyle topics. Present circulation of 624,091.

**Non-fiction** Publishes General interest features, Interviews and Photo features on Celebrities.

**Tips** The title is aimed specifically at women, articles tend to be aspirational and based around the rich and famous. Also includes the sister magazine, *Hot Stars.*

## The Oldie

**65 Newman Street, London, W1T 3EG**

- 020 7436 8801
- 020 7436 8804
- theoldie@theoldie.co.uk
- www.theoldie.co.uk

**Parent Company** Oldie Publications Ltd

**Editor** Richard Ingrams

**Established** 1992

**Insider Info** Monthly consumer magazine covering news, current affairs and lifestyle. Present circulation is 23,412. Accepts queries by mail and email. Sample copy is free on request and available by email. Manuscript guidelines are available online.

**Non-fiction** Interested in Humour and General interest articles.

**Submission Guidelines** Accepts complete manuscripts (including SAE) of between 600 to 1,800 words.

**Tips** *The Oldie* is a tongue in cheek, general interest news and lifestyle magazine, aimed at the older generation. The magazine will not commission articles from ideas or treatments, so always send them completed articles for consideration. Detailed submission guidelines are available on their website.

## Olive

**80 Wood Lane, London, W12 0TT**

☎ 020 8433 1828

✉ letters@olivemag.co.uk

🌐 www.olivemagazine.co.uk

**Parent Company** BBC Worldwide Publishing Ltd

**Editor** Christine Haynes

**Contact** Features Editor, Jenny McIvor

**Established** 2003

**Insider Info** A monthly consumer magazine covering cookery and kitchen topics. Present circulation of 66,014.

**Non-fiction** Publishes Photo features and Features on food and cooking.

**Tips** Olive generally only uses regular freelancers for its features. It is impossible for them to respond to all the proposals that they receive.

## The Once Orange Badge Poetry Supplement

**PO Box 184, South Ockendon, Essex, RM15 5WT**

☎ 01708 852827

✉ onceorangebadge@poetry.fsworld.co.uk

**Editor** D. Martyn Heath

**Established** 2003

**Insider Info** A consumer supplement, with two issues per year, covering poetry. A byline is given. Accepts queries by mail and email. Sample copy is free on request, or available by email.

**Poetry** Publishes Contemporary, Free verse, Light verse and Traditional poetry.

**Tips** *The Once Orange Badge Poetry Supplement* is a free supplement for everyone who has been touched by disability in some way, or at some time. It prints modern poetry of any style or type. Send submissions with SAE to ensure reply. The supplement is usually seeking regular contributors rather than single submissions, so there is plenty of scope for multiple publications.

## Open Wide Magazine

**The Flat, Yew Tree Farm, Sealand Road, Chester, CH1 6BS**

✉ contact@openwidemagazine.co.uk

🌐 www.openwidemagazine.co.uk

**Parent Company** Open Wide Books

**Editor** Elizabeth Roberts

**Contact** Managing Editor, James Quinton

**Established** 2001

**Insider Info** A quarterly consumer literary magazine showcasing new poetry and prose. Present circulation of 1,000. 100 per cent of the publication is written by freelance contributors. Manuscripts are published four months after acceptance. A byline is given. Publication is copyrighted and first UK serial rights are purchased. Editorial lead time is three months, seasonal material should be submitted nine months in advance. Queries are accepted by email. Simultaneous submissions are accepted. Aims to respond to queries and manuscripts within one month. Will not pay the expenses of writers on assignment. A sample copy is available for £4/$9. Writer's guidelines are free on request and available online or via email. Editorial calendar is available via email.

**Non-fiction** Publishes Literary features and Reviews.

**Submission Guidelines** Accepts queries with published clips. No reprints.
 Email: submissions@openwidemagazine.co.uk

**Fiction** Publishes Short fiction.

**Submission Guidelines** Accepts completed manuscripts for stories of between 500 and 2,500 words.
 Email submission as a word attachment to: submissions@openwidemagazine.co.uk

**Poetry** Publishes a mixture of Poetry forms.

**Submission Guidelines** Accepts any length of poetry.
 Email submission as a word attachment to: submissions@openwidemagazine.co.uk

**Tips** Welcomes submissions from new writers. Makes no payment to any contributors. Tends to favour submissions that go against literary traditions.

## Orbis

Quarterly International Literary Journal

**17 Greenhow Avenue, West Kirby, Wirral, CH48 5EL**

☎ 0151 625 1446

✉ carolebaldock@hotmail.com

🌐 www.poetrymagazines.org.uk

**Editor** Carole Baldock

**Established** 1969

**Insider Info** A quarterly literary journal with 84 pages of news, reviews, views, letters, features, prose and quite a lot of poetry. 100 per cent of the publication is written by freelance writers. Manuscripts are published three months after acceptance. Payment is via a Readers' Award of £50, plus £50 for four runners up. All contributors are paid with contributor copies. A byline is given. Contributors retain copyright, but the magazine purchases first UK serial rights. Editorial lead time is three months and seasonal material should be submitted six months in advance. Accepts queries by mail, email or phone. Simultaneous submissions are accepted. Aims to respond to queries within seven days and manuscripts within 14 days. Will not pay the expenses of writers on assignment. Sample copy available for £4 or £15 for four, send SAE. Writer's guidelines available, with SAE, or online, or via email.

**Non-fiction** Publishes Book excerpts, How-to, Essays, Humour, Inspirational articles, Features, Interviews/Profiles and Reviews.

\* Purchases eight non-fiction manuscripts per year.

**Submission Guidelines** Accepts queries with outline and published clips for articles of between 500 and 1,000 words. No reprints. Contact Carole Baldock, Editor or Nessa O'Mahony, Reviews Editor (for reviews only).

**Fiction** Publishes Adventure, Historical, Romance, Condensed novels, Horror, Science Fiction, Humourous, Mainstream, Ethnic, Mystery, Suspense, Experimental, Novel excerpts and Fantasy fiction.

\* Buys 12 fiction manuscripts per year.

**Submission Guidelines** Send complete manuscripts for stories of between 500 and 1,000 words.

**Poetry** Publishes Avant-garde, Free verse, Haiku, Light verse, Traditional and Rhyming poetry.

\* Purchases 200 poems per year.

**Submission Guidelines** Accepts up to four sample poems.

**Tips** Besides poems (and occasionally upbeat doesn't come amiss), *Orbis* welcomes prose, 500 to 1,000 words, suggestions for cover artwork and features, e.g. the 'Past Master Section'. Do not send in the entire manuscript for non-fiction before discussing the idea first. The Editor has been involved for some time with social inclusion projects and encouraging access to the arts, for example, the South Asian Showcase for Liverpool. She is interested in work from all such communities, especially young people, under 20s and 20 somethings. Also, women writers, because although magazine subscriptions are around 50 per cent each, male and female, submissions are still a good third less than those from men. Writers are recommended to study the guidelines, and stick to them. Always enclose SAE, with sufficient postage.

## Orient Express

The Best of Contemporary Writing

**Wythgreen House, Coleshill, Swindon, SN6 7PS**

- oemagazine@yahoo.co.uk
- www.writersartists.net/oexpress/orientex.htm

**Editor** Fiona Sampson

**Established** 2002

**Insider Info** A consumer book length journal with two issues per year, covering European literature. Queries accepted by mail or email.

**Non-fiction** Publishes Essays, Articles on Poetry and Features.

**Fiction** Publishes Short fiction.

**Tips** *Orient Express* specialises in publishing literature, both fiction and non-fiction, from the entire European region. The magazine is particularly interested in submissions from the European enlargement area, with countries such as Croatia, Lithuania and Ukraine.

## The Orphan Leaf Review

**26 Grove Park Terrace, Bristol, BS16 2BN**

- orphanleaf@jpwallis.co.uk
- www.jpwallis.co.uk/orphanleaf/index.htm

**Parent Company** The Orphan Leaf

**Editor** James Paul Wallis

**Established** 2004

**Insider Info** A consumer magazine, with two issues per year, covering literature. A byline is given. Accepts queries by mail and email. Manuscript guidelines are available online.

**Non-fiction** Interested in 'Orphan Leaf' non-fiction as well as Author information and Interviews/ Profiles.

**Fiction** Publishes 'Orphan Leaf' fiction.

**Tips** An orphan leaf is a single page of text taken from within a longer work, such as a novel, which may or may not exist. *The Orphan Leaf Review* publishes these orphan leaves from international writers. Each magazine consists of the leaves, which are each individual, often being printed in different styles and on different paper, and information about their authors. *The Orphan Leaf Review* has very detailed submission guidelines on their website, including a template for submissions. Leaves can be in any style, or 'from' any type of book, as long as they test the boundaries of the genre.

## OS Magazine

Office Secretary

**15 Grangers Place, Witney, Oxfordshire, OX28 4BS**

- 01993 775545
- 01993 778884
- paul.ormond@peeblesmedia.com
- www.peeblesmedia.com

**Parent Company** Peebles Media

**Editor** Michelle Crawley

**Contact** Managing Editor, Mike Travers; Sponsorship and Promotions Manager, Paul Ormond

**Established** 1976

**Insider Info** A bi-monthly trade magazine aimed at secretaries. Present circulation of 25,000. Ten per cent of the publication is written by freelance writers. Payment is upon acceptance and a byline is given. Simultaneous submissions are accepted. A sample copy is free on request.

**Non-fiction** Publishes Feature and News articles on office and secretarial topics.

**Tips** *OS Magazine* is aimed at PAs, office managers, and senior and executive secretaries.

## Other Poetry
**29 Western Hill, Durham, DH1 4RL**

- editors@otherpoetry.com
- www.otherpoetry.com

**Editor** Michael Standen
**Established** 1979

**Insider Info** A consumer literary magazine with three issues per year, focusing mainly on poetry. Present circulation of 250. 100 per cent of the publication is written by freelance writers. A byline is given. Queries are accepted by mail or email. Aims to respond to queries and manuscripts within six weeks. Sample copy available, send SAE with three first class stamps.

**Non-fiction** Publishes articles on Poetry.

**Poetry** Publishes Avant-garde, Free verse, Light verse and Traditional poetry.

**Submission Guidelines** Accepts up to six sample poems.

**Tips** *Other Poetry* is a small magazine that publishes 'good poetry in all its forms'. It prints any kind of poetry, from any kind of writer and its main aim is to publish those poems which do not conform to modern trends. They request that SAEs be included with every postal submission.

## Panda Poetry
**46 First Avenue, Clase, Swansea, SA6 7LL**

- poet_077@lineone.net
- http://website.lineone.net/~poet_077/newpage.html

**Editor** Esmond Jones
**Established** 2000

**Insider Info** A consumer magazine, published quarterly, covering general literary interest.

**Poetry** Publishes Free verse, Light verse and Traditional poetry.

**Tips** *Panda* is a small magazine that publishes general, mainstream poetry from new writers. Panda will accept submissions of any type of poetry, either by post or email.

## Park Home & Holiday Caravan
**King's Reach Tower, Stamford Street, London, SE1 9LS**

- 020 8726 8252
- em_bartlett@ipcmedia.com
- www.phhc.co.uk

**Parent Company** IPC Media
**Editor** Emma Bartlett
**Established** 1960

**Insider Info** A consumer magazine, publishing 13 issues per year. Covers Motoring. Motorcycling and Caravanning.

**Non-fiction** Publishes Features, Reviews, New Product and Technical articles.

**Submission Guidelines** Send complete manuscripts.

**Tips** *Park Home & Holiday Caravan* are the UK's definitive guide for those who own, or are planning to buy, a park or leisure holiday home. Covers everything you need to know to discover this new way of life, from reviews of the best parks, and legal advice, to essential buying tips. The magazine is published every four weeks. They will take anything directly, so there will be a higher than average volume of submissions. To be more noticeable than other submissions, writers should focus on style, more than content. Any 'hooks', such as specialist, or insider knowledge would also be helpful in the long run.

## Parking Review
**Quadrant House, 250 Kennington Lane, London, SE11 5RD**

- 0845 270 7871
- ed.pr@landor.co.uk
- www.landor.co.uk/parkingreview

**Parent Company** Landor Publishing
**Editor** Mark Moran
**Established** 1989

**Insider Info** A trade magazine, published monthly and covering motoring and motorcycling parking issues.

**Tips** *Parking Review* offers unique news, and features coverage of the on-street and off-street parking sectors. It is the place to get the latest information on management, policy, legal and technical issues in the parking world. The magazine also runs the popular and sought after 'British Parking Awards', which are announced each February. Article submissions would have to contain a good deal of industry related knowledge, although there is scope for more humanised articles to run alongside the 'Special Focus' section.

## Passion

**PO Box 393, Maidstone, Kent, ME14 5XU**

☎ 01622 729593

✉ cresmopub@yahoo.co.uk

🌐 www.crescentmoon.org.uk

**Parent Company** Crescent Moon Publishing

**Editor** Jeremy Robinson

**Established** 1994

**Insider Info** A consumer magazine, published quarterly and covering general literary interest. Present circulation is 200. Byline is given. Accepts queries by mail and email. Writer's guidelines available online.

**Non-fiction** Publishes Essays, Poetry, Features, Reviews and Opinion (excluding letters to the Editor).

**Submission Guidelines** Accepts Query.

**Fiction** Publishes Mainstream fiction. Accepts query.

**Poetry** Publishes Avant-garde, Free verse and Light verse.

**Submission Guidelines** A maximum of six poems are to be submitted at one time.

**Tips** *Passion* is a literary magazine that publishes new poetry and fiction, reviews, essays on fine art and cultural studies, articles on the media and politics and literary criticism from around the world. Passion publishes work from both new and established writers, and is dedicated to passionate and emotional writing. Passion is looking for submissions of book reviews on a wide range of subjects, critical essays on politics, philosophy, ideologies and media and submissions of fiction of poetry. Check the website for further details and full submission guidelines.

## PC Advisor

**99 Gray's Inn Road, London, WC1X 8TY**

☎ 020 7071 3658

📠 020 7071 3658

✉ letters@pcadvisor.co.uk

🌐 www.pcadvisor.co.uk

**Parent Company** International Data Group

**Editor** Paul Trotter

**Contact** Features Editor, Rosemary Haworth

**Established** 1995

**Insider Info** A consumer magazine, published monthly and covering computing and business. Current circulation of 67,059. Accepts queries by mail and email.

**Non-fiction** Publishes How-to, Features, Interviews/ Profiles, New Product and Technical articles.
  * Will pay £200 per 1,000 words for unsolicited articles.

**Submission Guidelines** Accepts Query. Always send complete manuscript. Articles must be between 1,500 and 3,000 words.

**Images** Send photos with submission.

**Tips** *PC Advisor* delivers expert advice you can trust to business and home PC users who want to buy the best value equipment and make the most out of the equipment they already own. First published in 1995 by IDG, the world's leading IT publisher, *PC Advisor* has built a considerable reputation for offering comprehensive and impartial buying advice, informed and easy to understand tutorials and workshops, as well as ground breaking coverage of service related issues. Articles pegged on upcoming releases, i.e. reviews, comparisons and tutorials, are least in demand. There may be scope for more practical advice, such as articles on physical computer repair.

## PC Answers

**30 Monmouth Street, Bath, BA1 2BW**

☎ 01225 442244

📠 01225 732295

✉ pca.experts@futurenet.co.uk

🌐 www.pcanswers.co.uk

**Parent Company** Future Publishing

**Editor** Simon Pickstock

**Established** 1991

**Insider Info** A consumer magazine, publishing 13 issues per year, covering computing and PC leisure. Current circulation is 25,564.

**Non-fiction** Publishes How-to, Features, Reviews, New Product and Technical articles.

**Submission Guidelines** Maximum length for articles is 2,500 words.

**Tips** *PC Answers* targets an audience of dedicated PC enthusiasts with the best advice to help them get more out of their PC. The aim of *PC Answers* is to provide help and guide readers through the minefield of computing. The magazine contains practical articles and 'how-to advice' and most articles are system or software based. There may be scope for pieces on computer DIY, i.e. articles on the physical repair or upgrading of damaged or flagging computers.

## PC Format

**30 Monmouth Street, Bath, BA1 2BW**

☎ 01225 442244

📠 01225 732295

✉ pcfmail@futurenet.co.uk

🌐 www.pcformat.co.uk

**Parent Company** Future Publishing

**Editor** Adam Evans
**Contact** Deputy Editor, Ian Dexter
**Established** 1991
**Insider Info** A consumer magazine, issued four weekly, covering computing and PC leisure. Current circulation is 30,488.
**Non-fiction** Publishes Features, Interviews/Profiles and Technical articles.
**Submission Guidelines** Accepts queries.
**Tips** *PC Format (PCF)* is a computer magazine which includes articles about games, entertainment and how to get the most out of the platform. Despite the occasional mention of alternatives, *PC Format* takes the term 'PC' to mean a Microsoft Windows based computer. Aimed at a reader with an average age of around 30, *PCF* is far more irreverent and opinionated than its competition, edging it towards being a lifestyle magazine, as well as a computing one. It is open to ideas but does not like unsolicited work. Contact by phone, email, or writing, prior to sending anything in.

## Pennine Ink
**The Gallery, Yorke Street, Haslingden, BB11 1HD**
- 01282 703657
- sheridans@casanostra.p3online.net
**Parent Company** Mid Pennine Arts
**Editor** Laura Sheridan
**Established** 1983
**Insider Info** An annual consumer magazine covering general literary interest. Current circulation of 400.
**Non-fiction** Publishes Poetry Articles, Features and Reviews.
**Submission Guidelines** Accepts queries.
**Poetry** Publishes Avant-garde, Free verse, Light verse and Traditional poetry.
 * Purchases 50 poems per year.
**Submission Guidelines** Maximum length for poems is 40 lines.
**Tips** *Pennine Ink* magazine publishes contemporary poetry and related articles, usually featuring work from workshops held at the Mid Pennine Arts Gallery. *Pennine Ink* is in the process of developing a website which will include submission details for the magazine. Until then *Pennine Ink* is willing to accept submission for any type of modern poetry and also some short fiction.

## Pennine Platform
**Frizingley Hall, Frizinghall Road, Bradford, BD9 4LD**
- 01274 541015

- nicholas.bielby@virgin.net
- www.pennineplatform.co.uk
**Editor** Nicholas Bielby
**Established** 1973
**Insider Info** A twice-yearly consumer magazine covering general literary interest. Present circulation of 300. 100 per cent of the publication is written by freelance writers. A byline is given. Accepts queries by mail.
**Non-fiction** Publishes Poetry Articles, Features and Reviews.
**Submission Guidelines** Accepts queries.
**Poetry** Publishes Light verse and Traditional poetry.
**Tips** *Pennine Platform* is a long running independent literary magazine that publishes new poetry, book reviews and articles. It is supported by the Leeds Philosophical and Literary Society. *Pennine Platform* prefers traditionally influenced poetry over 'free verse' and the Editor will respond with feedback to every submission sent. Therefore, response and publication times can often be quite long. Include SAE with your submission.

## Pensions World
**Tolley House, 2 Addiscombe Road, Croydon, CR9 5AF**
- 020 8686 9141
- 020 8212 1970
- stephanie.hawthorne@lexisnexis.co.uk
- www.pensionsworld.co.uk
**Parent Company** Tolley Publishing
**Editor** Stephanie Hawthorne
**Established** 1972
**Insider Info** A monthly trade magazine, covering finance and investment. Current circulation is 7,372.
**Tips** *Pensions World* is the leading monthly magazine for pensions professionals, published by Butterworths Tolley. By arrangement it is distributed to all members of the NAPF (National Association of Pension Funds). *Pensions World* does not take any unsolicited work, so the best method of approach is to email them with a synopsis, along with CV and any relevant examples of previous work. A degree of expertise in the field would be an advantage.

## People Management
**17–18 Britton Street, London, EC1M 5TP**
- 020 7324 2729
- 020 7324 2791
- editorial@peoplemanagement.co.uk
- www.peoplemanagement.co.uk
**Parent Company** Chartered Institute of Personnel and Development

**Editor** Steve Crabb

**Contact** Managing Editor, Rima Evans; Commissioning Editor, Claire Warren

**Established** 1995

**Insider Info** A bi-weekly trade magazine, covering personnel management. Current circulation of 124,964. Editorial lead time is two months. Accepts queries by email and phone. Writer's guidelines available online.

**Non-fiction** Publishes How-to and General interest articles.

**Submission Guidelines** Accepts query (include published clips and author biography) Articles must be between 1,000 and 2,500 words.

**Columns** Publishes the following columns: Indicator (business-related research/analysis slant, maximum 400 words), Learning centre/Viewpoint (training and development matters/opinions slant, 350–600 words), Research (academic research slant, maximum 500 words), Troubleshooter (problems/solution slant, 350–400 words).

**Submission Guidelines** Accepts query with published clips.

**Tips** *People Management* publishes articles on all aspects of managing and developing people at work. It is the official magazine of the Chartered Institute of Personnel and Development, with a fortnightly circulation of more than 120,000 copies - by far the largest in its field. They publish articles about best practice and leading edge ideas and act as a forum for debate on topical issues. They do not normally accept articles that have been published elsewhere, that promote a particular product or service, or are purely promotional copy for the organisation involved. In the first instance, it is useful for the editors to receive a summary of your ideas for an article. Proposals should be no longer than two pages.

## Personal Computer World

**Tower House, Sovereign Park, Market Harborough, Leicester, LE16 9EF**

- 01858 438881
- 01858 468969
- letters@pcw.co.uk
- www.pcw.co.uk

**Parent Company** VNU Business Publications Ltd

**Editor** Dillan Ambrust

**Contact** Deputy Editor, Kelvyn Taylor

**Established** 1979

**Insider Info** A monthly consumer magazine, covering computing and PC business. Current circulation of 76,020.

**Tips** *Personal Computer World* is the UK's longest running, and best established monthly consumer PC magazine, providing cutting edge news, insight and advice on the best computer technology available today. For over 27 years the magazine has been at the forefront of technology publishing, providing balanced and incisive editorial to its audience of technology enthusiasts and IT business professionals. *Personal Computer World*'s editorial is respected for its 'accuracy, impartiality and insight.' Therefore any article submitted must be thorough and accurate in its reporting or analysis, and must also remain unbiased as far as possible.

## The Pharmaceutical Journal

**1 Lambeth High Street, London, SE1 7JN**

- 020 7572 2414
- 020 7572 2405
- editor@pharmj.org.uk
- www.pjonline.com

**Parent Company** RPS Publishing

**Editor** Olivia Timbs

**Contact** Managing Editor, Graeme Smith; News Editor, Harriet Adcock

**Established** 1841

**Insider Info** Weekly trade journal covering pharmaceutical subjects and trade information. Present circulation is 50,981. One per cent of the publication is written by freelance writers. Submissions are published up to two months after acceptance. Payment is on publication and sometimes pays by contributor copies. The expenses of writers on assignment are sometimes paid (limit agreed upon in advance). A byline is given for features only. Publication is copyrighted. Average lead time is two days. Accepts queries by mail, email, fax and telephone. Aims to respond to queries within two days and manuscripts within six days. Sample copy is free on request and available online. Manuscript guidelines are available online.

**Non-fiction** Interested in Pharmacy related Features, New Product reviews and News features.
 * Payment for assigned articles is £0.0955 per word. Payment for unsolicited articles is £0.04775 per word.

**Images** Accepts images with submission.
 * Negotiates payment individually.

**Submission Guidelines** Send contact sheets, negatives, transparencies, prints or gif/jpeg files with captions, model releases and identification of subjects to News Editor, Harriet Adcock. State the availability of photos with submission.

**Columns** Publishes News and Broad spectrum columns.

**Tips** *The Pharmaceutical Journal* is the official journal of the Royal Pharmaceutical Society of Great Britain. Founded in 1841, it has been published weekly since 1870. It publishes articles and insider information from professionals within the pharmaceutical industries.

## Pick Me Up

**Kings Reach Tower, Stamford Street, London, SE1 9LS**

- 020 7261 5000
- 020 7261 5765
- pickmeup@ipcmedia.com
- www.pickmeupmagazine.com

**Parent Company** IPC
**Editor** June Smith-Shepphard
**Contact** Features Editor, Heather Bishop
**Established** 2005

**Insider Info** A weekly consumer magazine covering real life stories and women's lifestyle topics. Present Circulation of 424,410. Media pack is available online.
**Non-fiction** Publishes General Interest Features, Interviews and Photo Features on Television, Real life, Fashion, Home, Food, Cookery and Beauty.
**Tips** The magazine's main focus is on real life experiences and its editorial style is described as bringing the feel of a celebrity weekly to the real life market. Its tone aims to be that of a 'girl's night out'. Readers are invited to tell their true stories and offer their tips for sums of money, however it is likely that the piece will be ghost-written.

## Pilot

**The Mill, Bearwalden Business Park, Saffron Walden, CB11 4GB**

- 01799 544200
- 01799 544201
- nick.bloom@pilotweb.aero
- www.pilotweb.co.uk

**Parent Company** Archant Specialist
**Editor** Nick Bloom
**Established** 1968

**Insider Info** A monthly consumer magazine, covering aviation. Current circulation of 19,811. Will pay on publication and all rights are purchased. Byline given and the publication is copyrighted. Accepts queries via mail and email. Writer's guidelines available online.
**Non-fiction** Publishes How-to, Photo Features, Interviews/Profiles, Technical, Travel and Private aviation based articles.
  * Pays between £150 and £400, or more for longer features.

**Submission Guidelines** Send complete manuscript (including SAE). Maximum length of 1,200 words.
**Images** Accepts images with submission.
  * Will pay a varied fee per photo and will purchase all rights.
**Submission Guidelines** Reviews prints, gif/jpeg files, and captions. Send photos with submission.
**Tips** *Pilot* has been published for more than 35 years and has won more awards for the quality and authority of its journalism than any other UK flying magazine. The magazine and the website work together to offer an enhanced and interactive service to *Pilot* readers and subscribers. Submit a straightforward account, preferably on a subject of widespread, rather than purely personal, interest. Humour is particularly welcome. See the website for submission guidelines.

## Planet - The New Welsh Internationalist

**PO Box 44, Aberystwyth, Ceredigion, SY23 3ZZ**

- 01970 611255
- 01970 611197
- planet.enquiries@planetmagazine.org.uk
- www.planetmagazine.org.uk

**Editor** Helle Michelsen
**Established** 1970

**Insider Info** A bi-monthly consumer publication, covering general literary interest. Current circulation of 1,500. Will pay on publication. Sample copies available, costing £4. Writer's guidelines available online. Will accept queries by mail, or via email to: helle.michelsen@planetmagazine.org.uk
**Fiction** Publishes mainstream fiction.
  * Will pay £50 per 1,000 words.
**Submission Guidelines** Accepts queries. Word length for articles should be between 1,500 and 4,000 words. Will not consider magical realism, horror or science fiction.
**Poetry** Publishes Traditional poetry.
**Tips** *Planet* covers the arts, culture and politics in Wales and beyond. In addition to features on, and interviews with contemporary Welsh artists and writers, it includes political analysis, both of Welsh affairs and international issues. *Planet* also prints several poems and one short story in every issue of the magazine. They do not look for fiction which necessarily has a 'Welsh' connection, which some writers assume from our title. *Planet* says; 'We try to publish a broad range of fiction and our main criterion is quality.'

## PN Review

4th Floor, Alliance House, Cross Street, Manchester, M2 7AP

- ☎ 0161 834 8730
- ✆ 0161 832 0084
- ✉ info@carcanet.co.uk
- 🌐 www.pnreview.co.uk

**Parent Company** Carcanet Press Ltd

**Editor** Michael Schmidt

**Established** 1973

**Insider Info** A bi-monthly consumer magazine, covering general literary interest. Bylines are given. Accepts queries by mail. Writer's guidelines available online.

**Non-fiction** Publishes Poetry, Features, Interviews/Profiles, Reviews and Opinion articles (excluding letters to the Editor).

**Submission Guidelines** Accepts queries.

**Poetry** Publishes Avant-garde, Free verse and Light verse Poetry.

**Tips** *PN Review* is a major literary magazine and publishes new poetry, prose, book reviews, articles on writing, interviews and features. *PN Review* has an international focus and is a champion of modernist and experimental writing. *PN Review* does not publish short stories or any non-poetry related articles, and is not considering fiction in English, or in translation at the moment. Proposals for poetry submission must be posted rather than emailed.

## Poetic Hours

43 Willow Road, Carlton, Nottingham, NG4 3BH

- ✉ erranpublishing@hotmail.com
- 🌐 www.poetichours.homestead.com

**Parent Company** Erran Publishing

**Editor** Nick Clark

**Insider Info** A twice-yearly consumer magazine, covering general literary interest. A byline is given. Accepts queries by email.

**Non-fiction** Publishes Poetry titles.

**Poetry** Publishes Free verse, Light verse and Traditional articles.

**Submission Guidelines** Maximum of four poems to be submitted at any one time.

**Tips** *Poetic Hours* is a small, not for profit poetry magazine that donates all of its proceeds to charity. Its main aims are firstly, to raise money for charity, and secondly, to provide an opening for amateur poets to publish their work. The magazine is for charity, so contributors can donate their poetry on a 'single use' basis but will not be paid. *Poetic Hours* will not accept any work that attacks the position of any other person, group or belief.

## The Poetry Church

PO Box 438, Shrewsbury, SY3 0WN

- ☎ 01743 872177
- ✆ 01743 872177
- ✉ john@waddysweb.freeuk.com
- 🌐 www.waddysweb.freeuk.com

**Parent Company** Feather Books

**Editor** John Waddington Feather

**Established** 1995

**Insider Info** Quarterly consumer magazine covering poetry.

**Non-fiction** Interested in Religious and poetry related articles.

**Submission Guidelines** Accepts queries in the first instance.

**Poetry** Publishes Free verse, Light verse and Traditional religious poetry.

**Tips** *The Poetry Church* is a religious poetry magazine that prints new poetry and articles with a Christian slant. *The Poetry Church* generally only accepts manuscripts from subscribers, and offers no payment for contributions.

## Poetry Combination Module

196 High Road, London, N22 8HH

- ✉ page84direct@yahoo.co.uk
- 🌐 www.geocities.com/andyfloydplease

**Parent Company** P.E.F Productions

**Editor** Mr. Pef

**Contact** Managing Editor, Andy Floyd

**Established** 1999

**Insider Info** A poetry magazine in A5 format, publishing Winter, Spring and Autumn Issues. Publishes articles on poetry, anti-poetry, art and artwork. 100 per cent of the magazine is written by freelance writers. Lead time is approximately five months. The magazine does not offer payment, but sends writers two free issues which are printable online. Bylines are given and the magazine is copyrighted. Seasonal material must be submitted five days in advance. Accepts queries by mail and email, and will accept simultaneous submissions and previously published submissions. Aims to report back to queries within five weeks. Writer's guidelines are available free on request, with SAE, or online. Writer's guidelines and editorial guidelines are also available online.

**Non-fiction** Publishes Photo features, Humour, Poetry, Personal experience, Anti-poetry, Aphorism and Graphic Art articles, as well as Cartoons. Forthcoming issues for which freelance material will be needed in the next few months are *PCM* 27 (The Family Issue), poetry on Family Matters, *PCM 28* (The

British Shorthair Issue) – poetry on British Shorthair (cat breed), Cats, Hair and Hairy matters and for *PCM 29*, Poetry on Benignant Issues. Aphorism on topics is also welcome.

**Submission Guidelines** Send a sample of work via email.

**Fiction** Publishes Adventure, Historical, Romance, Humorous, Mainstream, Ethnic, Mystery, Suspense, Experimental, Fantasy, Societal and Environmental fiction.

**Poetry** Publishes Avant-garde, Free verse, Light verse and Traditional Poetry.

**Images** Accepts images with submission.
 * Will not offer payment for photos accepted.

**Fillers** Publishes Anecdotes, Facts, Jokes (to be illustrated by a cartoonist), Short humour, Hints and Tips and Strange but true fillers.

**Tips** Include the words 'PCM Submission' in email message. Clearly state the writer and where you live (e.g. London) after each poem.

## Poetry Cornwall
**1 Station Hill, Redruth, Cornwall, TR15 2PP**
- poetrycornwall@yahoo.com
- www.poetrycornwall.freeservers.com

**Editor** Les Merton
**Established** 2002

**Insider Info** A consumer magazine, publishing three times per year, covering general literary interest. A byline is given. Accepts queries by mail and email. Sample cover available, with SAE and two first class stamps. Writer's guidelines available online.

**Non-fiction** Publishes Poetry Articles and Features.

**Submission Guidelines** Accepts queries.

**Poetry** Accepts Free verse, Traditional and Translation/Dialect Poetry.

**Submission Guidelines** A maximum of three poems can be submitted at one time, and poems must be a maximum of 36 lines.

**Tips** *Poetry Cornwall* publishes new and established poets from around the world, as well as poetry in various dialects including Cornish, Devonish, Norfolk and Jamaican. Subscribers are allowed to send poetry submissions by email. Non-subscribers must use standard post and include SAE. Apart from poetry, the magazine is also interested in short articles on related subjects.

## Poetry Express
**Diorama Arts Centre, 34 Osnaburgh Street, London, NW1 3ND**
- 020 7916 5317
- survivor@survivorspoetry.org.uk

**Parent Company** Survivor's Poetry Group
**Established** 1997

**Insider Info** A consumer newsletter, issued quarterly and covering general literary interest. Current circulation of 2,500. Byline is given. Accepts query by mail and email. Will always pay writers with a contributor copy.

**Non-fiction** Publishes Poetry, General interest, News/Events, and News/Events related to the Survivor's Group.

**Submission Guidelines** Accepts Query.

**Fiction** Publishes Fiction.

**Poetry** Publishes Avant-garde, Free verse, Light verse and Traditional titles. Maximum of four poems to be submitted at one time.

**Tips** The Survivor's Poetry Group is an arts charity dedicated to promoting poetry by, and for survivors of mental distress. The *Poetry Express* is the quarterly newsletter of the group and publishes the latest news and events concerning the group as well as new poetry and prose articles of interest to survivors. The *Poetry Express* is the newsletter of the Survivor's Group, and any submissions must be of interest to survivors of mental distress.

## Poetry Ireland Review
**2 Prouds Lane, St. Stephen's Green, Dublin 2, Republic of Ireland**
- 00353 1 478 9974
- 00353 1 478 0205
- poetry@iol.ie
- www.poetryireland.ie

**Parent Company** Poetry Ireland/Éigse Éireann
**Editor** Peter Sirr

**Insider Info** A quarterly consumer journal, covering general literary interest. A byline is given. Accepts queries by mail and email. Reports back on queries and manuscripts within six months. Writer's guidelines available online.

**Non-fiction** Publishes Poetry, Features and Reviews.
 * Maximum pay for assigned and unsolicited articles is €50, plus one contributor copy.

**Submission Guidelines** Accepts queries.

**Poetry** Publishes Avant-garde, Free verse, Light verse and Traditional poetry.
 * Maximum pay for poems is €32, plus one contributor copy.

**Submission Guidelines** Maximum of six poems to be submitted at one time. Poems advocating sexism or racism will not be accepted.

**Tips** *Poetry Ireland Review* publishes poetry from new and established writers from both Ireland and abroad. In order to keep the review progressive, a new editor is appointed every four issues. Articles and reviews are mostly commissioned privately but the Editor will accept unsolicited proposals for articles, not full manuscripts.

## Poetry London

**1a Jewel Road, London, E17 4QU**

- 020 8521 0776
- 020 8521 0776
- editors@poetrylondon.co.uk
- www.poetrylondon.co.uk

**Editor** Maurice Riordan

**Established** 1988

**Insider Info** A consumer journal, publishing three issues per year (March, June, October) and covering general literary interest, particularly poetry. Current circulation of 800. A byline is given. Accepts queries by mail and email. Aims to report back on queries and manuscripts within two months.

**Non-fiction** Publishes Poetry, Features, Interviews/Profiles, Reviews and News/Event listings.

**Submission Guidelines** Accepts Query.

**Poetry** Publishes Avant-garde, Free verse, Light verse and Traditional poetry.

**Tips** *Poetry London* publishes new poetry from new and established writers, as well as selected poetry from competition winners. It also publishes a wide range of event listings, reviews, feature articles, interviews and general information from the poetry world. Submissions for poetry and reviews must be directed to different addresses (see the website for details). *Poetry London* will often print translated poetry, as well as the regular submissions.

## Poetry Monthly

**39 Cavendish Road, Long Eaton, Nottingham, NG10 4HY**

- 0115 946 1267
- poetrymonthly@btinternet.com
- www.poetrymonthly.com

**Parent Company** Poetry Monthly Press and Graphics

**Editor** Martin Holroyd

**Established** 1996

**Insider Info** Publishes a monthly consumer magazine, covering general literary interest. Current circulation of 200. Bylines are given. Accepts queries by mail and email. Payment is via a contributor copy. Writer's guidelines are available online.

**Non-fiction** Publishes Poetry, Features and Artwork/Illustration.

**Submission Guidelines** Accepts queries.

**Poetry** Publishes Avant-garde, Free verse, Light verse and Traditional Poetry.

* Payment for poetry is via a contributor copy.

**Tips** *Poetry Monthly* is a small magazine that prints new poetry from contributors, as well as some short articles on related subjects, and where space allows, line illustrations and art. *Poetry Monthly* takes submissions of new poetry in any form or style, and will accept submissions by email. Postal submissions must be accompanied by SAE for a reply.

## Poetry Nottingham

**11 Orkney Close, Stenson Fields, Derbyshire, DE24 3LW**

- info@nottinghampoetrysociety.co.uk
- http://jeremyrduffield.members.beeb.net/index.html

**Parent Company** Nottingham Poetry Society

**Editor** Adrian Buckner

**Established** 1947

**Insider Info** A quarterly consumer magazine, covering the interests of the Nottingham Poetry Society. Current circulation of 250. Bylines are given. Accepts query via mail or email.

**Non-fiction** Publishes Poetry Articles, Features and Reviews.

**Submission Guidelines** Accepts queries.

**Poetry** Publishes Avant garde, Free verse, Light verse and Traditional titles.

**Submission Guidelines** Accepts postal submissions accompanied by SAE.

**Tips** *Poetry Nottingham* publishes new poetry, articles and reviews and has an international outlook, accepting submissions from anywhere in the world. The magazine is based in Nottingham, but will accept submissions from international writers.

## Poetry Now

**Remus House, Woodston, Peterborough, PE2 9JX**

- 01733 898101
- 01733 313524
- poetrynow@forwardpress.co.uk
- www.forwardpress.co.uk

**Parent Company** Forward Press

**Editor** Heather Killingray

**Established** 1989

**Insider Info** Consumer monthly magazine, covering general literary and poetry interests. Bylines are given. Accepts query via mail and email.

**Non-fiction** Publishes poetry.

**Submission Guidelines** Accepts queries.

**Poetry** Publishes Avant-garde, Free verse, Light verse and Traditional poetry.

**Tips** *Poetry Now* aims to publish poetry for the simple pleasure of reading, rather than for academic reasons, and actively supports new writers that wish to see their work in print. It prints poetry of any style or form, as long as it is relevant to everyday life. *Poetry Now* also publishes books and anthologies to place new writers alongside established writers. The magazine has a different theme each month for poetry submissions, as well as regular features and competitions. The theme of the month can be found on the website, but the magazine also offers a monthly email, which details the theme and all relevant submission guidelines for the forthcoming issue.

## Poetry Review
### 22 Betterton Street, London, WC2H 9BX
- 020 7420 9880
- 020 7240 4818
- poetryreview@poetrysociety.org.uk
- www.poetrysociety.org.uk

**Parent Company** The Poetry Society
**Editor** Fiona Sampson
**Established** 1912
**Insider Info** Publishes a quarterly consumer journal, covering general literary interest. Current circulation of 4,000. A byline is given. Accepts query via mail and email. Writer's guidelines are available online.
**Non-fiction** Publishes Poetry, Features and Reviews.
**Submission Guidelines** Accepts queries.
**Poetry** Publishes Avant-garde, Free verse, Light verse and Traditional titles.
**Submission Guidelines** A maximum of six poems can be submitted at one time.
**Tips** *The Poetry Review* prints articles and reviews of the latest poetry. Its aim is to help poets and poetry thrive in Britain today. *The Poetry Review* is very popular and receives between 30,000 to 50,000 poetry submissions every year, but prints only 200 at most. However, the *Review* does support new poets and actively encourages submissions from first-time writers.

## Poetry Scotland
### 91–93 Main Street, Callander, FK17 8BQ
- sally.king4@btinternet.com
- www.poetryscotland.co.uk

**Parent Company** Diehard Publishers
**Editor** Sally Evans
**Insider Info** A quarterly consumer poetry broadsheet, publishing nothing but new poetry, from new and established writers. Accepts query by mail and email.

**Poetry** Publishes Avant-garde, Free verse, Light verse and Traditional Poetry.
**Tips** *Poetry Scotland* generally runs a Scottish theme for submissions, but will also accept submissions from, or about, other places.

## Poetry Wales
### 57 Nolton Street, Bridgend, CF31 3AE
- 01656 663018
- 01656 649226
- poetrywales@seren-books.com
- www.poetrywales.co.uk

**Editor** Robert Minhinnick
**Established** 1965
**Insider Info** A quarterly consumer magazine, covering general literary interest. Current circulation is 800. Byline is given. Accepts queries via mail or email.
**Non-fiction** Publishes Poetry Articles, Features and Reviews.
**Submission Guidelines** Accepts queries.
**Poetry** Publishes Avant-garde, Free verse, Light verse and Traditional poetry.
**Tips** *Poetry Wales* is a literary magazine that publishes the best new poetry from both Wales and abroad. *Poetry Wales* supports new poetry and publishes work from new and established writers. *Poetry Wales* accepts poetry submissions from international writers, but one of its main aims is to help new writers in Welsh achieve publication.

## Poet's Letter Magazine
### 75 Cannon Street, London, EC4N 5BN
- 020 7556 7052
- 020 7556 7511
- editor@poetsletter.com
- www.poetsletter.com

**Editor** Munayem Mayenin
**Established** 2006
**Insider Info** A monthly consumer magazine, covering general literary and poetry interest. Current circulation of 90,000. Byline s given. Accepts queries via mail and email.
**Non-fiction** Publishes Photo features, Poetry, Religious, Features, Interviews/Profiles, Reviews, General Interest and Travel articles.
**Submission Guidelines** Send complete manuscripts.
**Fiction** Publishes Mainstream Short fiction.
**Submission Guidelines** Send complete manuscripts.
**Poetry** Publishes Free verse, Light verse and Traditional poetry.

**Submission Guidelines** A maximum of three poems can be submitted at one time.

**Tips** *Poet's Letter Magazine* is a general interest international literary magazine, based in London, which specialises in articles on politics, poetry, prose, world culture and sciences, and all kinds of literature. *Poet's Letter* accepts submissions for poetry, short stories, novel excerpts, book reviews, interviews and articles on philosophy, psychology, sociology, politics and the arts.

## Porsche Post

**Cornbury House, Cotswold Business Village, London Road, Moreton in Marsh, Gloucestershire, GL56 0JQ**
- 01608 652911
- 01608 652944
- publications@porscheclubgb.com
- www.porscheclubgb.com

**Parent Company** Porsche Club GB
**Editor** Stephen Mummery
**Established** 1962
**Insider Info** A monthly consumer magazine, about Porsche cars. Present circulation of 16,000. Ten to twenty percent of the magazine is written by freelance writers. Payment is on publication. A byline is given and the publication is copyrighted. Purchases first UK serial rights on accepted material. Accepts queries by mail, email and phone. Will accept previously published submissions. A sample copy is free on request.
**Non-fiction** Publishes articles about Porsche and related topics.

## Portfolio

**43 Candlemaker Row, Edinburgh, EH1 2QB**
- 0131 220 1911
- 0131 226 4287
- info@portfoliocatalogue.com
- www.portfoliocatalogue.com

**Editor** Gloria Chalmers
**Insider Info** A consumer magazine, publishing two issues per year (June and December), covering photography. Accepts queries via mail and email.
**Non-fiction** Publishes Photo features, Essays, Features, Interviews/Profiles, Reviews, Technical and General interest articles.
**Submission Guidelines** Send complete manuscript.
**Tips** *Portfolio* is an art magazine with very high production values. It publishes innovative photographic art from established artists, as well as articles and essays on photography and visual arts,

and a series of portfolios by up and coming artists. *Portfolio* is a visual arts magazine only, and as such only accepts submissions of visual art. Portfolio is especially keen to see proposals from new artists with a ready portfolio of work that might be suitable for the magazine.

## Portuguese Studies

**1 Carlton House Terrace, London, SW1Y 5DB**
- 020 7848 2507
- 020 7848 2787
- portuguese@mhra.org.uk
- www.mhra.org.uk/Publications/Journals/Portuguese.html

**Parent Company** Modern Humanities Research Association
**Editor** David Treece
**Established** 1985
**Insider Info** A consumer journal, publishing two issues per year, covering Portuguese studies. Byline is given.
**Non-fiction** Publishes Photo features, Features, Technical and Historical/Nostalgic articles.
**Submission Guidelines** Send complete manuscripts.
**Tips** *Portuguese Studies* is an academic journal dedicated to research on the culture and history of Portuguese society. It welcomes scholarly contributions on all aspects of the literature, culture and history of the Portuguese societies.

## Practical Boat Owner

**Westover House, West Quay Road, Poole, BH15 1JG**
- 01202 440820
- 01202 440860
- pbo@ipcmedia.com
- www.pbo.co.uk

**Parent Company** IPC Media
**Editor** Sarah Norbury
**Contact** Managing Editor, Andrew Simpson; News Editor/Features Writer, Alison Wood
**Established** 1967
**Insider Info** A monthly consumer magazine, covering boating. Present circulation of 50,013. Accepts query via mail and email.
**Non-fiction** Publishes How-to, Photo features, Features, Interviews/Profiles, Reviews, New Product and Technical articles.
**Submission Guidelines** Accepts query with SAE and synopsis
**Tips** *Practical Boat Owner (PBO)* is Britain's biggest selling boating magazine and a brand that readers

really trust. A source of useful and helpful information for boat owners, both power and sail, it helps them get the most from their chosen leisure activity. Its affluent, but practically minded consumers, find *PBO* is a forum for interacting with like minded individuals. It is interested in hard facts about gear, equipment, pilotage and renovation from experienced yachtsman.

## Practical Caravan

**Teddington Studios, Broom Road, Teddington, TW11 9BE**

- 020 8267 5629
- 020 8267 5725
- practical.caravan@haynet.com
- www.practicalcaravan.com

**Parent Company** Haymarket Publishing
**Editor** David Motton
**Established** 1967
**Insider Info** A monthly consumer magazine, covering caravanning. Present circulation of 44,062. Accepts query via mail and email.
**Non-fiction** Publishes Photo features, Features, Reviews and Technical articles.
**Submission Guidelines** Send complete manuscript. Maximum length for articles is 2,000 words.
**Images** Send photos with submission.
**Tips** The magazine is a complete A-Z guide to caravanning, with every issue providing readers with a great guide on what to buy, where to go and how to get the most from their hobby. The varied content, in-depth tests and 'Great Escape' holiday features ensures there is always something that will appeal to every caravanning holidaymaker. Article submissions must be relevant to the caravanning hobby and must include a good depth of detail, but must also be written in a chatty and friendly manner. The inclusion of photos is essential.

## Practical Parenting

**King's Reach Tower, Stamford Street, London, SE1 9LS**

- 020 7261 5058
- 020 7261 6542
- susie_boon@ipcmedia.com
- www.practicalparenting.co.uk

**Parent Company** IPC Media
**Editor** Susie Boon
**Contact** Features Assistant, Cassandra Roberts
**Established** 1987
**Insider Info** A monthly consumer magazine, covering parenthood. Present circulation of 43,465.

Accepts query via mail and email. Media packs available online.
**Non-fiction** Publishes How-to, Features and Parenting/Childcare articles.
**Submission Guidelines** Accepts query with complete manuscript. Articles must be between 750 and 3,000 words.
**Tips** Readers are devoted to their magazine because *Practical Parenting* is committed to the most important issues in their lives - pregnancy, birth, babies, toddlers and pre-schoolers. Aimed at pregnant women, and mums with children aged 0-5, *Practical Parenting* delivers friendly, expert advice on all aspects of raising healthy, happy babies and young children, helping each reader make the best decisions for their family. It is interested in long feature articles or shorter viewpoint pieces, written in the existing style of the magazine.

## Prediction

**King's Reach Tower, Stamford Street, London, SE1 9LS**

- 020 8726 8255
- Marion_williamson@ipcmedia.com, predictionfeatures@ipcmedia.com
- www.predictionmagazine.com

**Parent Company** IPC Media
**Editor** Marion Williamson
**Established** 1936
**Insider Info** A monthly consumer magazine, covering astrology. Present circulation of 14,326. Average lead time is four months and payment is on publication. A byline is given and the publication is copyrighted. All rights are purchased on accepted material. Seasonal material must be submitted four months in advance. Accepts queries via mail or email. Aims to report back on manuscripts within six weeks. Writer's guidelines available with SAE, or online. Media packs available online.
**Non-fiction** Publishes Features, General interest, Astrology and Mind/Body/Spirit articles.
**Submission Guidelines** Accepts query with complete manuscript. Maximum length for articles is 3,000 words.
**Tips** Prediction is Britain's original mind, body and spirit magazine and contains information on angels, the meaning of dreams, the tarot, holistic healing and more. In addition, its comprehensive 18 page astrology section gives an insight in what might happen in your month ahead. Articles should be aimed at benefiting women, and should be optimistic, light, practical or problem solving, with a humorous tone where it suits. Articles must be

written in the second person if possible, as the magazine likes to talk to its readers directly.

## Premonitions

**13 Hazely Combe, Arreton, Isle of Wight, PO30 3AJ**

☎ 01983 865668

✉ mail@pigasuspress.co.uk

🌐 www.pigasuspress.co.uk

**Parent Company** Pigasus Press

**Editor** Tony Lee

**Established** 1992

**Insider Info** An annual consumer magazine, covering science fiction, fantasy and horror. 100 per cent of the magazine is written by freelance writers. Average lead time is eighteen months. Payment is on publication. A byline is given and the publication is copyrighted. Purchases first UK serial rights on accepted material. Accepts query by mail and email. Aims to report back on queries within two weeks and manuscripts within six weeks. The company does not pay with contributor copies, or other premiums and will pay the expenses of the writer on assignment. A sample copy and writer's guidelines are available to order from the website.

**Fiction** Publishes Fiction, Horror, Science Fiction and Fantasy articles.

 * Purchases twelve manuscripts per year. Will pay £5 per 1,000 words, plus one contributor copy.

**Submission Guidelines** Send complete manuscript. Special instructions are as follows; for horror writing, there must be no serial killers, mystery writing must have science fiction content and fantasy writing must contain no sorcery.

**Poetry** Publishes Avant-garde, Free verse, Light verse and Science fiction poetry.

**Submission Guidelines** A maximum of six poems can be submitted at one time and poems must be between five and 100 lines. Is not interested in non-genre poetry.

**Tips** *Premonitions* is genre writing magazine that publishes horror, fantasy and science fiction short stories, genre poetry and artwork. Also publishes graphic poetry, in a graphic novel style. The main aim of *Premonitions* is to bridge the British horror and science fiction fields, without compromising the quality of the writing.

## Presence

**90d Fishergate Hill, Preston, PR1 8JD**

✉ martin.lucas2@btinternet.com

🌐 freespace.virgin.net/haiku.presence/index.html

**Parent Company** Haiku Presence Group

**Editor** Martin Lucas

**Insider Info** A consumer magazine, publishing three issues per year, covering literary interest. A byline is given. Accepts query by mail and email. Writer's guidelines available online.

**Non-fiction** Publishes Poetry Articles, Features, Reviews and News/Events articles.

**Submission Guidelines** Send complete manuscript.

**Poetry** Publishes Haiku Poetry. A maximum of 12 poems can be published at one time.

**Tips** *Presence* is a specialist poetry magazine that publishes Haiku poetry in all its forms, including Haiku, Senryu, Tanka, Renga/Renku and related poetry. Also publishes Haibun (Haiku Prose), articles, news, events information and book reviews on the subject of Haiku. *Presence* accepts submissions either by post or email, but due to limited space will only consider submissions from subscribers or contributors who have bought the previous issue of the magazine.

## Pretext

**School of Literature and Creative Writing, University of East Anglia, Norwich, Norfolk, NR4 7TJ**

☎ 01603 592783

☎ 01603 507728

✉ info@penandinc.co.uk

🌐 www.penandinc.co.uk

**Parent Company** Pen & Inc Press

**Editor** Katri Skala

**Established** 1999

**Insider Info** A consumer magazine, publishing two issues per year and covering general literary interest. Current circulation of 800. A byline is given. Accepts queries via mail and email, and reports back on queries and manuscripts within two months. Writer's guidelines available online.

**Non-fiction** Publishes Essays, Poetry Articles and Features.

**Submission Guidelines** Accepts Query.

**Fiction** Publishes Fiction, Mainstream and Short stories.

 * Will pay a maximum of £50 for fiction.

**Submission Guidelines** Send complete manuscript. Maximum word length for articles is 6,000 words.

**Poetry** Publishes Avant-garde, Free verse and Light verse poetry.

**Submission Guidelines** A maximum of five poems can be submitted at one time.

**Tips** *Pretext* is an international literary magazine that publishes new fiction, poetry and literary essays from new and established writers. The magazine prefers submissions by post with SAE. The magazine aims to encourage new writers by championing the best of contemporary literature and opening new channels for short stories.

## Prima

**National Magazine House, 72 Broadwick Street, London, W1F 9EP**

- 020 7312 4114
- 020 7439 4100
- prima@natmags.co.uk, firstname.lastname@natmags.co.uk
- www.primamagzine.co.uk

**Parent Company** National Magazine Company Ltd
**Editor** Marie Fahey
**Contact** Features Editor, Carrie Buckle
**Established** 1986
**Insider Info** A monthly consumer magazine covering women's lifestyle topics. Present Circulation of 315,149. Media pack available online.
**Non-fiction** Publishes General Interest Features, Interviews and Photo Features on Television, Real life, Fashion, Beauty, Craft, Celebrities, Food, Cookery, Travel, Home, Health and Entertainment.
**Tips** Aimed at women aged 25–45 with a warm, supportive tone, and what is described as a 'modern' point of view.

## Product

**PO Box 23071, Edinburgh, EH7 5GT**

- 0141 332 3738
- 0141 332 3738
- info@productmagazine.co.uk
- www.productmagazine.co.uk

**Parent Company** Red Herring Arts and Media Ltd
**Editor** Chris Small
**Established** 1999
**Insider Info** A quarterly consumer magazine, covering literary interests.
**Non-fiction** Publishes Photo features, Poetry, Features, General interest, Opinion (excluding letters to the Editor) and Literary Criticism articles.
**Fiction** Publishes Mainstream Short stories.
**Submission Guidelines** Accepts Query.
**Poetry** Publishes Free verse and Traditional poetry.
**Tips** *Product* is an independent magazine established in 1999 to promote the work of Scottish writers and artists. It covers ground breaking ideas missed by the mainstream media. A stylishly designed quarterly, *Product* delivers intelligent, compelling writing about music, film, art and books. *Product* accept submissions for fiction and poetry, as well as feature articles about counter-culture, or other ideas and events.

## Professional Electrician

The Business Magazine for the Electrical Trade

**Regal House, Regal Way, Watford, Hertfordshire, WD24 4YF**

- 01923 237799
- 01923 246901
- pe@hamerville.co.uk
- www.hamerville.co.uk

**Parent Company** Hamerville Magazines
**Editor** Jonathan Cole
**Contact** Managing Editor, Terry Smith; Editor, Jonathan Cole
**Established** 1984
**Insider Info** A monthly trade magazine. Present circulation of 60,000. Five per cent of the publication is written by freelance writers. Will pay on publication. A byline is sometimes given. Editorial lead time is two months. Accepts queries by mail, and editorial catalogues are free on request.

## Prospect

**2 Bloomsbury Place, London, WC1A 2QA**

- 020 7255 1281
- 020 7255 1279
- editorial@prospect-magazine.co.uk
- www.prospect-magazine.co.uk

**Parent Company** Prospect Publishing
**Editor** David Goodhart
**Contact** Editorial Assistant, Tom Chatfield
**Established** 1995
**Insider Info** A monthly consumer magazine, covering domestic news and current affairs, with a current circulation of 24,700. Will pay up to six weeks after publication. The publication will sometimes pay pay the expenses of writers on assignment (limit agreed upon in advance). A byline is given and the magazine is copyrighted. Will accept simultaneous submissions and aims to report on manuscripts within three months. Accepts query by mail, fax and email. For writer's guidelines or email queries, email: submissions@prospect-magazine.co.uk
**Non-fiction** Publishes Book excerpts, Essays, Humour, Exposé, Features, Interviews/Profiles, Reviews, General interest, Opinion (excluding letters to the Editor) and Personal experience articles.
**Submission Guidelines** Contact Tom Chatfield, Editorial Assistant for submission guidelines. Accepts query. Send a complete manuscript. Articles should be between 3,000 and 6,000 words.
**Fiction** Publishes Short Fiction.

**Tips** *Prospect* has acquired a reputation as the most intelligent magazine of current affairs and cultural debate in Britain. Both challenging and entertaining, the magazine seeks to make complex ideas accessible and enjoyable by commissioning the best writers and packaging their work in a well designed and illustrated monthly. *Prospect* aims to be 'more readable than the Economist, more relevant than the Spectator, more romantic than the New Statesman.' The short story content is generally specially commissioned from well-known authors such as Margaret Atwood, Michel Faber and Ali Smith, therefore the fiction side of the magazine can be very tough get in to.

## Pulsar Poetry Magazine

**34 Lineacre, Grange Park, Swindon, Wiltshire, SN5 6DA**

✉ pulsar.ed@btopenworld.com

**Editor** David Pike

**Established** 1994

**Insider Info** A consumer magazine, publishing two issues per year (in March and September) and covering general literary interest. Present circulation of 400. A byline is given. Accepts queries via mail and email.

**Non-fiction** Publishes Poetry, Features and Reviews.

**Submission Guidelines** Accepts Query.

**Poetry** Publishes Avant-garde, Free verse, Light verse and Traditional poetry.

\* Will pay for assigned poetry with a contributor copy.

**Submission Guidelines** A maximum of six poems can be submitted at any one time.

**Tips** *Pulsar* is a small literary magazine that publishes new poetry from anyone and anywhere in the world. It also prints book and event reviews and is often fully illustrated. *Pulsar* looks for well-written poetry submissions, which are 'thought provoking and hard-hitting poems which have something interesting to say.'

## Pulse

**Ludgate House, 245 Blackfriars Road, London, SE1 9UY**

✆ 020 7921 8102

✆ 020 7921 8133

✉ pulse@cmpmedica.com

🌐 www.pulse-i.co.uk

**Parent Company** CMPMedica

**Editor** Jo Haynes

**Contact** Publisher, Phil Johnson; News Editor, John Robinson

**Insider Info** A weekly consumer newspaper, covering medical information. Present circulation is 41,000. Two per cent of the publication is written by freelance writers. Will take up to 12 months to publish a manuscript after it has been accepted. Will pay on publication, sometimes pays the expenses of writers on assignment (limit agreed upon in advance). A byline is given and the publication is copyrighted. Will purchase all rights on accepted material. Editorial lead time is six months and seasonal material must be submitted six months in advance. Accepts queries by mail, email, fax and phone. Simultaneous submissions and previously published submissions will be accepted. Sample copies and writer's guidelines are available free on request. For an editorial calender, contact Julia Mcnamara on 020 7921 8120.

**Non-fiction** Publishes Photo features, Inspirational, Features, Interviews/Profiles, Reviews, Technical, General interest and Personal experience articles.

**Submission Guidelines** Contact John Robinson, News Editor, for more information.

**Images** Contact Picture Editor, Marie-Louise Collard for photos.

\* Negotiates payment individually on photos and all rights will be purchased.

**Tips** *Pulse* is the leading GPs' newspaper.

## Purple Patch

**25 Griffiths Road, West Bromwich, B71 2EH**

✉ geoff@purplepatchpoetry.co.uk

🌐 www.purplepatchpoetry.co.uk

**Editor** Geoff Stevens

**Established** 1976

**Insider Info** A consumer magazine, publishing three issues per year, and covering literary and poetry interests. A byline is given. Accepts queries via mail and email.

**Poetry** Publishes Avant-garde, Free verse, Haiku, Light verse and Traditional poetry.

**Tips** *Purple Patch* is a long running literary magazine that publishes open submission of any kind of poetry from anyone, anywhere in the world. *Purple Patch* usually accepts open submissions of any kind of poetry, but will occasionally have a themed issue, which would be announced in the previous issue.

## Quattrocento

**'Bodnant', 10 Llwynnon Gardens, Llandudno, Conwy, LL30 2HP**

✉ peter@quattrocento.co.uk

🌐 www.quattrocento.co.uk

**Editor** Malcolm Bradley

**Established** 2004

**Insider Info** A consumer magazine, publishing two issues per year (April and October), covering poetry and the arts. 100 per cent of the publication is written by freelance writers. A byline is given. Accepts queries via mail and email. Writer's guidelines available online and free on request. Sample copies and editorial calenders available free on request.

**Non-fiction** Publishes Photo features, Essays and Poetry.

**Submission Guidelines** Send complete manuscript. Articles should be between 2,000 and 3,000 words.

**Fiction** Publishes Mainstream fiction. Send complete manuscript.

**Submission Guidelines** Short stories must be a maximum of 3,000 words. For fiction, contact Editor, Malcolm Bradley.

**Poetry** Publishes Avant-garde, Free verse, Light verse, Experimental, Haiku and Traditional poetry.
 * Will pay for assigned poetry with a contributor copy.

**Submission Guidelines** Poems should be a maximum of 150 lines. For poetry, contact Editor, Malcolm Bradley.

**Tips** *Quattrocento* is Welsh literary magazine with an international readership. The magazine publishes poetry and prose writing with a particular interest in supporting new writers and experimental writing. *Quattrocento* also publishes essays, memoirs and photography. The magazine is is keen to receive submissions of risk taking, experimental poetry, providing they are artistically successful and are suitable for small-press production.

## Quid

**70a Cranwich Road, London, N16 5JD**

- 020 7502 0906
- info@barquepress.com
- www.barquepress.com

**Parent Company** Barque Press
**Editor** Dr. Keston Sutherland
**Established** 1995

**Insider Info** A consumer journal, covering literary interest. Frequency of publication varies. A byline is given. Accepts queries via mail and email.

**Non-fiction** Publishes Essays, Poetry, Features, Reviews and Opinion articles (excluding letters to the Editor).

**Submission Guidelines** Accepts queries.

**Poetry** Publishes Avant-garde, Free verse and Light verse poetry.

**Tips** *Quid* is an occasional journal that publishes poetry, criticism, opinions, reviews and articles on poetics and writing. *Quid* has a largely modernist/post-modernist outlook. The magazine is not currently accepting unsolicited submissions and most content is sourced internally.

## The Quiet Feather

**St. Mary's Cottage, Church Street, Dalton in Furness, Cumbria, LA15 8BA**

- editors@thequietfeather.co.uk
- www.thequietfeather.co.uk

**Editor** Dominic Hall

**Insider Info** A consumer magazine covering literature. A byline is given. Accepts queries by mail and email. Manuscript guidelines are available online.

**Non-fiction** Interested in Photo features, Features, Interviews/Profiles, Reviews, Opinion and General interest articles on poetry and prose.

**Submission Guidelines** Accepts complete manuscripts of up to 1,500 words.

**Fiction** Publishes Mainstream short fiction.

**Poetry** Publishes Contemporary, Avant-garde, Free verse and Light verse poetry.

**Images** Send photos with submission, including captions.

**Tips** *The Quiet Feather* is an eclectic literary magazine that, as well as publishing new poetry and prose, also prints various articles and features on practically anything including music, local interest and activities so long as it is well-written, interesting and informative. The magazine is always looking for photographers, cartoonists and illustrators to tell their stories in pictures, but is often unable to reply directly to all submissions.

## Racecar Engineering

**King's Reach Tower, Stamford Street, London, SE1 9LS**

- 020 8726 8362
- racecar@ipcmedia.com
- www.racecar-engineering.com

**Parent Company** IPC Media
**Editor** Charles Armstrong-Wilson
**Established** 1990

**Insider Info** A monthly consumer magazine, covering motoring sports. Present circulation of 22,000.

**Non-fiction** Publishes Reviews, New Product and Technical articles.

**Submission Guidelines** Maximum length for articles is 3,000 words. Contact by phone or email to discuss ideas.

**Tips** Each month *Racecar Engineering* brings the best possible insight into all forms of the rapidly changing world of motorsport engineering. It aims to keep pace with the latest technologies and expand the readers' knowledge of racecar design and operation. Articles must contain specialist or insider knowledge about racecar engineering only, no road cars.

## Radio Times

**Room A1179, 80 Woodlane, London, W12 0TT**
- 020 8433 3400
- 020 8433 3160
- radio.times@bbc.co.uk
- www.radiotimes.com

**Parent Company** BBC Worldwide
**Editor** Gill Hudson
**Contact** Features Editor, Kim Newson
**Established** 1923
**Insider Info** A weekly consumer magazine covering televsion and radio listings and related topics. Present circulation of 1,082,338.
**Non-fiction** Publishes General interest features and Photo features on current happenings in television and radio programmes, as well as other media.
**Submission Guidelines** Query with ideas for feature articles of around 600–2,500 words. Do not send entire manuscript.

## Railway Gazette International

**Quadrant House, Sutton, SM2 5AS**
- 020 8652 8608
- 020 8652 3738
- railway.gazette@rbl.co.uk
- www.railwaygazette.com

**Parent Company** Reed Business Information
**Editor** Chris Jackson
**Established** 1835
**Insider Info** A monthly trade magazine, covering railways. Present circulation is 9,752. Accepts queries via mail or phone.
**Non-fiction** Publishes Photo features, Features, Technical and General interest articles.
**Submission Guidelines** Accepts Query.
**Images** Send photos with submission.
**Tips** *Railway Gazette International* is a monthly business journal covering the railway, metro, light rail, and tram industries worldwide. Features a mix of technical, commercial and geographical feature articles, plus the regular monthly news pages,

covering developments in all aspects of the rail industry, including infrastructure, operations, rolling stock and signalling. Articles of a practical or technical nature are required, rather than 'material for railway enthusiast publications.' Write a letter, or phone to discuss ideas before submitting material

## The Railway Magazine

**King's Reach Tower, Stamford Street, London, SE1 9LS**
- 020 7261 5821
- 020 7261 5269
- nick_pigott@ipcmedia.com
- www.railwaymagazine.co.uk

**Parent Company** IPC Media
**Editor** Nick Pigott
**Established** 1897
**Insider Info** Monthly consumer magazine covering railways. Present circulation is 30,783. Accepts queries by mail and email.
**Non-fiction** Interested in Photo features, Interviews/Profiles, Technical, General interest and Historical/Nostalgic articles.
**Submission Guidelines** Accepts complete manuscripts up to 2,000 words.
**Tips** *The Railway Magazine* is a clear and trusted voice for the railway community, covering all aspects of the scene from steam through to modern rail developments. It seeks articles, ideally with photos, covering modern railways, or steam preservation and railway history.

## Rain Dog

**PO Box 68, Manchester, M19 2XD**
- rd_poetry@yahoo.com
- www.panshinepress.co.uk

**Parent Company** Panshine Press
**Editor** Suzanne Batty, Jan Whalen
**Established** 2000
**Insider Info** A consumer magazine, publishing two issues per year and covering literary interest. 100 per cent of the publication is written by freelance writers. A byline is given. Accepts query via mail and email. Writer's guidelines are available online.
**Poetry** Publishes Avant-garde, Free verse, Light verse and Traditlonal poetry.
  * Will pay for assigned poetry with a contributor copy.
**Submission Guidelines** A maximum of five poems can be submitted at one time.
**Tips** *Rain Dog* is a creative writing magazine that publishes contemporary poetry from both new and established writers. *Rain Dog* offers book vouchers as

prizes for the top selected poems each issue. The magazine welcomes submissions of poetry that are exciting, moving, inspiring or honest, and in particular are looking for submissions from women poets whom they feel to be generally under-represented in the small press poetry world.

## Rare Book Review

**24 Maddox Street, London, W1S 1PP**
- 020 7495 9499
- 020 7529 4229
- editor@rarebookreview.com
- www.rarebookreview.com

**Parent Company** Countrywide Editions Ltd
**Editor** Jeff Hudson
**Established** 1974
**Insider Info** A bimonthly trade journal covering literary interest. Accepts queries via mail and email.
**Non-fiction** Publishes Photo features, Features, Interviews/Profiles, Reviews and General interest and Historical/Nostalgic articles.
**Submission Guidelines** Accepts queries.
**Tips** *Rare Book Review* is the world's leading magazine for all those who love, collect, or deal in, rare and valuable books. It covers printed items of all kinds, with the proviso that they should be rare and sought after. The magazine contains interviews with distinguished collectors, surveys of important collections, both public and private, and profiles of important authors, illustrators and publishers. *Rare Book Review* is truly international in scope, and the magazine plans to increase coverage of the book collecting scene in Europe, Asia and the United States. Articles about collections, or collectors abroad would be well received.

## Raw Edge

**PO Box 4867, Birmingham, B3 3HD**
- raw_edgemag@yahoo.co.uk
- www.lit-net.org/remhp.htm

**Parent Company** The Moving Finger Press
**Editor** Dave Reeves
**Established** 1995
**Insider Info** A consumer magazine, publishing two issues per year and covering literary interests. A byline is given. Accepts queries via mail and email. Sample copy available online.
**Non-fiction** Publishes Poetry, Features, Interviews/Profiles, Reviews and News articles.
**Submission Guidelines** Accepts queries.
**Fiction** Publishes Mainstream fiction.
**Poetry** Publishes Avant-garde, Free verse, Light verse and Traditional poetry.

**Tips** *Raw Edge* is a free literary magazine for the West Midlands region. It publishes the best new poetry and prose from the region, as well as news, interviews, reviews and information for writers in the West Midlands area. *Raw Edge* is distributed through libraries and arts outlets, as well as by post, for the West Midlands area. As such it only excepts submissions from writers in the West Midlands area.

## Raw Vision

International Journal of Outsider Art
**1 Watford Road, Radlett, Hertfordshire, WD7 8LA**
- 01923 856644
- 01923 859897
- info@rawvision.com
- rawvision.com

**Parent Company** Raw Vision Ltd
**Editor** John Maizels
**Insider Info** A quarterly magazine, covering outsider art, visionary art and contemporary folk art. Present circulation is 10,000. 50 per cent of the publication is written by freelance writers. Editorial lead time is three months and seasonal material must be submitted two months in advance. Will pay on publication. A byline is given and the publication is not copyrighted. Will buy one time rights on accepted material. Accepts queries via mail, email, fax, and phone. Simultaneous submissions and previously published submissions will be accepted. Aims to report back on queries within two weeks, on manuscripts within one months. Sample copies available with SAE, and writer's guidelines available free on request and via email. Editorial calendars are available via email.

## The Reader

**19 Abercromby Square, Liverpool, L69 7ZG**
- 0151 794 2830
- readers@liv.ac.uk
- www.thereader.co.uk

**Editor** Jane Davis
**Established** 1997
**Insider Info** Quarterly consumer magazine covering poetry and literature. Byline is given. Accepts queries by mail and email. Manuscript guidelines are available online.
**Non-fiction** Interested in Literary Essays, Features, Interviews/Profiles, Reviews and articles on poetry and prose.
**Submission Guidelines** Accepts complete manuscript of between 1,500 and 4,000 words by post only.
**Fiction** Publishes Mainstream short fiction.

**Submission Guidelines** Accepts complete manuscript of between 2,000 and 2,500 words by post only.

**Poetry** Publishes Contemporary, Free verse, Light verse and Traditional poetry.

**Tips** *The Reader* publishes some new poetry and short fiction, along with book reviews, interviews and articles on writers, writing, and reading. *The Reader* welcomes submissions for short fiction and poetry, as well as for non-fiction articles. Submissions for short fiction greatly outnumber those of non-fiction, despite only making up 25 per cent of the magazine.

## Read The Music

25 Griffiths Road

**West Bromwich, B71 2EH**

☎ 0121 556 9304

✉ admin@poetrywednesbury.co.uk

🌐 www.poetrywednesbury.co.uk

**Parent Company** Poetry Wednesbury

**Editor** Brendan Hawthorne

**Insider Info** A consumer magazine, covering literary interest.

**Poetry** Publishes Free verse, Light verse and Traditional poetry.

**Tips** *Read The Music* publishes poetry submissions inspired by music and its influences. The magazine is always looking for submissions of music themed poetry to be sent in by post, with SAE attached.

## Real Business Magazine

**198 King's Road, London, SW3 5XP**

☎ 020 7368 7189

✉ editors@realbusiness.co.uk

🌐 www.realbusiness.co.uk

**Parent Company** Caspian Publishing

**Contact** Managing Editor, Kate Pritchard, Deputy Editor, Charles Orton-Jones

**Established** 1997

**Insider Info** A B2B monthly magazine, covering entrepreneurs and fast-growth SMEs. Ten per cent of the publication is written by freelance writers. A byline is given and the publication is copyrighted. Accepts queries via email and phone. Sample copies and writer's guidelines are available free on request.

**Non-fiction** Publishes How-to, Interviews/Profiles and Opinion articles (excluding letters to the Editor).

**Submission Guidelines** Contact Online Editor, Dan Matthews, for information.

**Images** State availability of photos with submission. Contact Art Director, Erroll Jones for photos.

## The Reater

**24 Cavendish Square, Hull, East Yorkshire, HU3 1SS**

☎ 01430 424346

✉ editor@wreckingballpress.com

🌐 www.wreckingballpress.com/html/reater.php

**Parent Company** Wrecking Ball Press

**Editor** Shane Rhodes

**Established** 1997

**Insider Info** Annual consumer magazine covering contemporary poetry, prose and photography. Present circulation is 800. Byline is given. Accepts queries by mail and email.

**Non-fiction** Interested in Features and articles on poetry and literature..

**Submission Guidelines** Accepts queries in the first instance.

**Fiction** Publishes Contemporary short fiction.

**Poetry** Publishes Contemporary, Avant-garde, Free verse and Light verse poetry.

**Submission Guidelines** Submit up to six poems.

**Tips** *The Reater* publishes new poetry and prose, primarily from Yorkshire writers, but also from further afield. The magazine also prints illustrations and photographs. *The Reater's* editorial stance is as follows: 'Strictly no flowers, just blunt hammered-home words.' Submissions should be hard-hitting and direct.

## Record Collector

Serious About Music

**Room 101, The Perfume Factory, 140 Wales Farm Road, London, W3 6UG**

☎ 0870 732 8080

☎ 0870 737 6060

✉ alan.lewis@metropolis.co.uk

🌐 www.recordcollectormag.com

**Parent Company** Diamond Publishing Ltd

**Editor** Alan Lewis

**Established** 1979

**Insider Info** A monthly consumer magazine, covering popular music from 1950 to the present, especially focusing on classic, rare and reissued records. Present circulation is over 30,000. *Record Collector* is the longest established monthly music magazine in the UK and is respected worldwide by serious collectors of popular music across all genres. 80 per cent of the publication is written by freelance writers. Editorial lead time is one month and seasonal material must be submitted two months in advance. Will pay on publication and the kill fee for for assigned manuscripts not published is 50 per cent. A byline is given and the publication is copyrighted. Will purchase all rights on accepted material. Accepts queries via email. Simultaneous submissions and previously published submissions will be accepted. Aims to report back on queries within two days and manuscripts within one week. The publication will not pay writers with contributor copies or other premiums other than a cash payment. They will sometimes pay the advances of writers on assignment (limit agreed upon in advance). They send out sample copies to selected contacts via email. Writer's guidelines and editorial calenders available via email. Media packs available on www.recordcollectormag.com

**Non-fiction** Publishes Book excerpts, How-to, Essays, Humour, Features, Interviews/Profiles, Reviews, New Product, Technical, Opinion (excluding letters to the Editor), Personal experience, Illustrated discographies articles, and items about rare records and interesting sales of records on eBay.

\* Purchases 100 non-fiction articles from freelance writers every year. Will pay between £50 and £1,000 for assigned articles and approximately 8p per word for unsolicited articles.

**Submission Guidelines** Accepts Query (including published clips). Articles can be up to 10,000 words in length (send photocopies). Contact Alan Lewis, Editor, for more information.

**Images** Accepts images with submission.

\* Will negotiate payment individually and will purchase one-time rights on photos.

**Submission Guidelines** Reviews gif/jpeg files and requires identification of subjects. Freelancers must state availability of photos with submission. Contact Editor, Alan Lewis, for more information.

**Columns** Regularly publishes reviews of CDs, DVDs and books.

\* Purchases 2,000 columns per year and pays between £10 and £50.

**Submission Guidelines** Accepts query (including published clips). Contact Reviews Editor, Jason Draper for columns.

**Tips** *Record Collector* covers popular music of all genres from 1950 to the present. In particular it celebrates collectable, rare and classic records with in-depth interviews, discographies and the world's biggest coverage of reissued albums on CD, vinyl and download.

## Red
**64 North Row, London, W1K 7LL**
- 020 7150 7641
- 020 7150 7684
- gabriellenathan@hf-uk.com
- www.redmagazine.co.uk

**Parent Company** Hachette Filipacchi
**Editor** Sam Baker
**Contact** Features Assistant, Gabrielle Nathan
**Established** 1998

**Insider Info** A monthly consumer magazine covering women's interests, lifestyle and fashion. Present circulation of 221,940. Accepts queries via mail.

**Non-fiction** Publishes Humour, Features and Interviews/Profile articles.

**Submission Guidelines** Send complete manuscript. Maximum length for articles is 1,500 words.

**Images** Send photos with submission.

**Tips** *Red* is a gorgeous, luxurious and, above all, relevant read for today's thirty-something women, who live real lives in fabulous shoes. Articles for *Red* must be written in a witty and intelligent manner. Aims at stylish and independent readers with a youthful spirit.

## Redline
**30 Monmouth Street, Bath, BS1 2BW**
- 01225 442244
- redline@futurenet.co.uk
- www.redlinemag.com

**Parent Company** Future Publishing Ltd
**Editor** Dan Lewis

**Insider Info** A four-weekly consumer magazine, covering tuned/modified performance cars. 40 per cent of the publication is written by freelance writers. Editorial lead time is four months and seasonal material must be submitted four months in advance. Will pay on publication. A byline is given and the magazine is copyrighted. Rights purchased can be negotiated. Accepts query via mail and email.

## The Red Wheelbarrow
**School of English, University of St Andrews, Castle House, The Scores, St Andrews, Fife, KY16 9AL**
- 01334 462666
- redwheelbarrow@st-and.ac.uk
- www.st-andrews.ac.uk/~www_se/ redwheelbarrow/index.html

**Established** 1999

**Insider Info** A consumer magazine, with two issues per year, covering literature. Byline is given. Accepts queries by mail and email.

**Non-fiction** Interested in Literary Essays, Features, Opinion and articles on poetry.

**Submission Guidelines** Accepts queries in the first instance.

**Poetry** Publishes Contemporary, Free verse, Light verse and Traditional poetry.

**Tips** *The Red Wheelbarrow* publishes poetry and opinion from both amateur and professional writers, as well as articles, essays and writing related to poetry. *The Red Wheelbarrow* is looking for international submissions, either of contemporary poetry or related non-fiction.

## reFRESH Magazine
**22a Iliffe Yard, Kennington, London, SE17 3QA**
- 020 7277 4517
- 020 7703 8718
- david@wildpublishing.com
- www.refreshmag.co.uk

**Parent Company** Wild Publishing Limited
**Editor** David Tickner
**Contact** Editorial Assistant, Jolee Wakefield
**Established** 2002

**Insider Info** A bi-monthly consumer magazine, covering gay lifestyle – culture, arts, fashion, style, travel, homes and interiors, general features, business and topical issues. Present circulation of 40,000. 65 per cent of the publication is written by freelance writers. A manuscript will be published six months after it is accepted. Payment will be on publication and kill fee for assigned manuscripts not used is 50 per cent. A byline is given and the publication is copyrighted. Will purchase first rights on accepted material. Editorial lead time is eight weeks and seasonal material must be submitted ten months in advance of publication. Accepts queries via mail and email. Simultaneous submissions will be accepted. Will aim to report on queries, manuscripts and any other information within four days. The publication will not pay writers with contributor copies or other premiums other than a cash payment. They will sometimes pay the expenses of a writer on assignment (limit agreed upon in advance). Sample copies available with SAE (envelope must be 340mm length and 240mm width, and postage cost will be £3). Writer's guidelines and editorial catalogues are available free on request and media packs are available on: www.refreshmag.co.uk

**Non-fiction** Publishes How-to, Photo features, Exposé, Features, Interviews/Profiles, Reviews, General interest, Opinion (excluding letters to the Editor) and Travel articles.

\* Will pay a minimum of £200 for assigned articles.

**Submission Guidelines** Articles must be between 500 and 1,500 words in length. Contact Editor in Chief, David Tickner, for more information.

**Images** Accepts images with submission.

\* Offers no additional payment for photos accepted with manuscripts. Will negotiate payment individually, depending on the situation.

**Submission Guidelines** Requires captions and model releases and freelancers must state availability of photos with submission. Contact Editor in Chief, David Tickner for photos.

**Tips** Presented in a coffee table style format, *reFRESH* is the only gay lifestyle magazine on the newsstand that does not contain any adult content. The magazine's core audience ranges from 18 to 55.

## Resurgence
**Ford House, Hartland, Bideford, Devon, EX39 6EE**
- 01237 441293
- 01237 441203
- editorial@resurgence.org
- www.resurgence.org

**Editor** Satish Kumar
**Contact** Co-Editor, Lorna Howarth
**Established** 1966

**Insider Info** A bi-monthly consumer magazine, covering literary interest. Present circulation of 30,000. Accepts queries via mail and email. Aims to report back on queries and manuscripts within one month. Writer's guidelines available online.

**Non-fiction** Publishes Photo features, Essays, Humour, Poetry, Features, Interviews/Profiles, Reviews, General interest, Opinion (excluding letters to the Editor), Travel and Historical/Nostalgic articles.

**Submission Guidelines** Accepts queries.

**Poetry** Publishes Free verse, Light verse and Traditional poetry.

**Tips** *Resurgence* is an informative magazine that publishes articles on ecology, the environment, the arts and spirituality. The magazine also prints social commentaries and political articles, humour and more general articles from writers. *Resurgence* has a regular poetry page, and welcomes submissions of poetry that are in keeping with the style and content of the magazine in general.

## Retail Jeweller
**33–39 Bowling Green Lane, London, EC1R 0TD**
- 020 7812 3725
- 020 7812 3720
- jenni.middleton@emap.com
- retail-jeweller.com

**Parent Company** Emap
**Contact** Deputy Editor, Marie Dill
**Established** 1965

**Insider Info** A monthly trade magazine, covering jewellery and watches. Present circulation of 5,000. 30 per cent of the publication is written by freelance writers. Manuscripts will be published two months after they are accepted. Payment on publication. A byline is sometimes given and the publication is copyrighted. All rights will be purchased on accepted material. Editorial lead time is four months and seasonal material must be submitted three months before it is published. Accepts queries by mail, phone, fax and email to rj@fashion.emap.co.uk. Simultaneous submissions will be accepted. Aims to report back to queries within one week, and manuscripts within two weeks. Sample copies are free on request and they do not have written writer's guidelines. Editorial calendars are on a person-by-person basis.

**Non-fiction** Publishes How-to, Features, Interviews/Profiles, Reviews and New Product articles.

**Tips** *Retail Jeweller* is a monthly B2B magazine published by Emap for retailers in the jewellery and watch industry. Its mission is to help retailers sell more watches and jewellery.

## Retail Week

### 33–39 Bowling Green Lane, London, EC1R 0DA

- ☏ 020 7320 3505
- ☏ 020 7520 3519
- ✉ tim.danaher@emap.com
- ⊕ www.retail-week.com

**Parent Company** EMAP Retail

**Editor** Tim Danaher

**Contact** Acting Features Editor, Charlotte Dennis-Jones

**Established** 1988

**Insider Info** A weekly trade magazine on retailing, with a present circulation of 10,683.

**Non-fiction** Publishes Features and Business news.

**Submission Guidelines** Maximum length for articles is 1,000 words.

**Images** Send photos with submission.

**Tips** *Retail Week* is the market leading publication for the UK retail sector. Delivering exclusive news, market data, comment and analysis on the issues that matter to retailers, it is a must read for anyone working in the sector. *Retail Week* is very clearly focused on the marketing and retail management industry, and therefore insider or specialist knowledge is definitely required in any submitted article.

## Reveal

### National Magazine House, 33 Broadwick Street, London, W1F 0DQ

- ☏ 020 7339 4534
- ☏ 020 7339 4529
- ✉ jennifer.dunkerley@acp-natmag.co.uk
- ⊕ www.natmags.co.uk

**Parent Company** National Magazine Company Ltd

**Editor** Michael Butcher

**Contact** Editorial Assistant/Work Experience Liason, Jennifer Dunkerley

**Established** 2004

**Insider Info** A weekly consumer magazine covering celebrity gossip and women's lifestyle topics. Present Circulation of 345,508. Media pack is available online.

**Non-fiction** Publishes General Interest Features, Exposes, Interviews and Photo Features on Celebrities, Television, Real life, Fashion, Home, Food, Cookery and Beauty.

**Tips** The title is aimed specifically at women between 25 and 45, although the readership can be younger. Most lead articles relate directly to celebrity interviews and gossip. Articles should be instantly involving, and suitable for the intended readership.

## The Review

### 4 Algar House, Webber Row, London, SE1 8QT

- ☏ 020 7261 1134
- ✉ editor@thereview.freeserve.co.uk
- ⊕ www.thereview.freeserve.co.uk

**Editor** Raúl Peschiera

**Established** 1995

**Insider Info** Annual consumer magazine contemporary poetry and literature. Byline is given. Accepts queries by mail and email.

**Non-fiction** Interested in Features, Interviews/Profiles, Reviews and articles on poetry and literature.

**Submission Guidelines** Accepts query in the first instance.

**Fiction** Publishes Contemporary short fiction.

**Poetry** Publishes Contemporary and Translated poetry.

**Tips** *The Review* was originally based in America and Canada, but moved to the UK following publication of its fourth issue. *The Review* publishes the best international poetry, fiction, reviews, interviews and translations. *The Review* is based in London, but will accept submissions from anywhere in the world and is especially interested in literary translations and contemporary poetry.

## The Rialto

**PO Box 309, Aylsham, Norwich, NR11 6LN**

- 01603 666455
- mail@therialto.co.uk
- www.therialto.co.uk

**Editor** Michael Mackmin

**Established** 1984

**Insider Info** A consumer magazine, with three issues per year, covering contemporary poetry. Present circulation is 1,500. Byline is given. Accepts queries by mail and email. Aims to respond to queries and manuscripts within ten weeks. Manuscript guidelines are available online.

**Non-fiction** Interested in Features, Reviews and articles on Poetry.

**Poetry** Publishes Contemporary, Avant-garde, Free verse, Light verse and Traditional poetry.

**Submission Guidelines** Submit up to six poems.

**Tips** *The Rialto* is a respected literary magazine that publishes the best contemporary poetry from new or established writers, as well as some literary articles and reviews. *The Rialto* receives many poetry submissions every week and it can take some time for a reply to be sent. At present *The Rialto* commissions all article and review content internally, and is only accepting unsolicited submissions for poetry.

## Rugby World

**King's Reach Tower, Stamford Street, London, SE1 9LS**

- 020 7261 6810
- 020 7261 5419
- paul_morgan@ipcmedia.com
- www.rugbyworld.com

**Parent Company** IPC Media

**Editor** Paul Morgan

**Established** 1960

**Insider Info** A monthly consumer magazine, covering rugby. Present circulation of 45,244. Accepts query via mail and phone and media packs available on www.ipcmedia.com/magazines/rugby/

**Non-fiction** Publishes Features on rugby.
 * Will pay a maximum of £120 for unsolicited articles.

**Submission Guidelines** Accepts query. Send complete manuscript. Maximum length for articles is 1,200 words.

**Images** Send photos with submission.

**Tips** *Rugby World* is the voice of global rugby and the biggest selling rugby magazine anywhere. Building on its standing within the rugby community, the brand offers a comprehensive round up of rugby action, results and fixtures as well as dynamic photography. *Rugby World* has also ventured online with a successful website. Find unusual rugby based subjects for articles, rather than just match reports, etc. Quality photographs are also essential.

## Runner's World

**33 Broadwick Street, London, W1F 0DQ**

- 020 7339 4400
- 020 7339 4220
- editor@runnersworld.co.uk
- www.runnersworld.co.uk

**Parent Company** Rodale Press

**Editor** Andy Dixon

**Established** 1979

**Insider Info** A monthly consumer magazine covering athletics. Present circulation is 83,527. Accepts queries by mail.

**Non-fiction** Publishes Features, Interviews/Profiles, Reviews, New Products and Running articles.

**Submission Guidelines** Accepts query with complete manuscript.

**Tips** *Runner's World* is the UK's largest running magazine. Is seeking articles on famous non-sportspeople who run, personal running articles, or 'off-beat travel articles'.

## Sable

**PO Box 33504, London, E9 7YE**

- 020 8985 9419
- editorial@sablelitmag.org
- www.sablelitmag.org

**Parent Company** S.A.K.S. Media

**Editor** Dorothea Smartt

**Contact** Kadija Sesay

**Established** 2000

**Insider Info** A quarterly consumer magazine, covering literary interests. A byline is given. Accepts query by mail and email. Writer's guidelines and sample copy available online.

**Non-fiction** Publishes Poetry Articles, Features, Interviews/Profiles and Reviews.

**Submission Guidelines** Send complete manuscript. Maximum length for articles is 3,000 words.

**Fiction** Publishes Mainstream fiction and novel excerpts.

**Submission Guidelines** Accepts query. Maximum length for articles is 5,000 words.

**Poetry** Publishes Free verse, Light verse and Traditional poetry. A maximum of 15 poems can be submitted at one time.

**Tips** *Sable* is a literary magazine for writers of colour and publishes new fiction and poetry, including translations, as well as articles, interviews, reviews and information. *Sable* is not currently accepting submissions for fiction but they are looking for poetry submissions, reviews and essays on historical or contemporary aspects of literature or culture. Check the guidelines on the website for further details.

## Saga Magazine
**Enbrook Park, Folkestone, CT20 3SE**
- 01303 771523
- 01303 776699
- editor@saga.co.uk
- www.saga.co.uk/magazine

**Parent Company** Saga Publishing Ltd
**Editor** Emma Soames
**Established** 1984

**Insider Info** A monthly consumer magazine, covering retirement, with a present circulation of 610,771.

**Submission Guidelines** Articles must be between 1,000 and 1,200 words.

**Non-fiction** Publishes General interest non-fiction article aimed at older peoples.

**Tips** *Saga Magazine* sets out to celebrate the role of older people in society, reflecting their achievements, promoting their skills, protecting their interests and campaigning on their behalf. Most material is commissioned in-house. Exclusive celebrity interviews with a warm, personal approach are well received, if relevant, ideally with photos.

## Sailing Today
**4 Chapel Road, Bath, BA1 1HN**
- 01489 580836
- 01489 482748
- john.goode@sailingtoday.co.uk
- www.sailingtoday.co.uk

**Parent Company** Boat International Group
**Editor** John Goode
**Established** 1997

**Insider Info** A monthly consumer magazine, covering watersports. Accepts queries via email and phone. Writer's guidelines available online.

**Non-fiction** Publishes Photo features, Features, Reviews, New Product, Technical and Travel articles.

**Submission Guidelines** Accepts queries.

**Tips** *Sailing Today* is Britain's youngest mainstream yachting magazine, it has a distinctly forward looking and independent approach, which appeals to today's busy boat owners. Articles cover relevant,

up to date information in a concise, authoritative, yet entertaining way. The magazine would like to hear from writers who would like to share how they tackled a practical maintenance or upgrade project, have an interesting account of cruising their own boat (even if it's a small one), or an out of the ordinary tale to tell about their charter/flotilla trip.

## Sainsbury's Magazine
**Sea Containers House, 20 Upper Ground, London, SE1 9PD**
- 020 7633 0266
- 020 7401 9423
- edit@7publishing.co.uk
- www.sainsburysmagazine.co.uk

**Parent Company** Seven Publishing and Sainsburys
**Editor** Sue Robinson
**Contact** Deputy Editor, Gillian Rhys
**Established** 1993

**Insider Info** A monthly consumer magazine for the customers of Sainsbury's supermarket, covering food, drink and retails issues. Present circulation of 357,883.

**Non-fiction** Publishes General Interest, Interviews, Reviews and Photo features on Food, Wine, New products, Parenting, Cookery, Fashion, Beauty, Health and Lifestyle.

**Tips** The magazine's readership is split roughly 70:30, women to men. A large proportion of these readers are women aged 35–44. The editorial content of the magazine is split evenly between food and drink articles and lifestyle articles.

## Saltire Magazine
**9 Fountain Close, 22 High Street, Edinburgh, EH1 1TF**
- 0131 556 1836
- saltire@saltiresociety.org.uk
- www.saltiresociety.org.uk

**Parent Company** The Saltire Society
**Editor** Michael Hance
**Contact** A consumer magazine, publishing two issues per year, covering literary interest.

**Non-fiction** Publishes Features, General interest and Opinion articles (excluding letters to the Editor).

**Tips** *Saltire magazine* is published by The Saltire Society to encourage debate and discussion about cultural issues. *Saltire* does not publish any fiction or poetry, only the latest news, views and interviews from the Saltire Society.

## Saw
Poetry with an Edge
**4 Masefield Avenue, Barnstaple, Devon, EX31 1QJ**

☎ 01271 342999

✉ sawpoems@btinternet.com

🌐 myspace.com/sawinghorse

**Parent Company** Bally Who? Press
**Editor** Colin Shaddick
**Contact** Editor, Colin Shaddick
**Established** 2005

**Insider Info** A consumer magazine, publishing two issues per year (April and September) and covering literary agents. A byline is given. Accepts queries by mail and email. Present circulation is over 150. *Saw* will endeavour to relate to what is going on in the world today, and will not step back when it comes to publishing work that tackles difficult issues. Takes an average of three months to publish a manuscript after it has been accepted. Pays with free copy. A byline is sometimes given and the publication is copyrighted. Editorial lead time is one month and seasonal material must be submitted one month before it is published. Simultaneous submissions will be accepted. Aims to report back on queries within one week and manuscripts within one month. Will always pay writers with contributor copies. The publication will not pay the expenses of writers on assignments. A sample copy is available for £4, with A5 SAE and two first class stamps. Writer's guidelines available online, via email and with SAE (220mm in length and 110mm in length).

**Poetry** Publishes Avant-garde, Free verse and Haiku poetry, that expands the arena of confinement.

**Submission Guidelines** Send a maximum of six poems at one time. Send typed manuscript by post or via email.

**Tips** *Saw* magazine prints contemporary poetry from new and established writers. It goes against traditional poetry magazines and happily engages with raw, emotional social commentary. Poetry for *Saw* should comment on contemporary social issues, including the 'e-driven metamorphosis' of the English language.

## Scarlet
The Magazine that Turns Women On
**9 Rickett Street, Fulham, London, SW6 1RU**

☎ 020 7835 5554

✉ sarah@helixmedia.co.uk

🌐 www.scarletmagazine.co.uk

**Parent Company** Scarlet Publishing
**Editor** Sarah Hedley

**Contact** Assistant Editor, Linda McCormick
**Established** 2003

**Insider Info** A monthly consumer magazine, with a present circulation of 40,000. 70 per cent of the the publication is written by freelance writers. It takes one month to publish a manuscript after it has been accepted. Payment occurs 30 days after publication and kill fee is 50 per cent. A byline is given and the publication is copyrighted. All rights will be purchased on accepted material. Editorial lead time is two months and seasonal material must be submitted two months in advance. Accepts queries via mail, email and phone. Simultaneous submissions will be accepted. Aims to report back on queries within two months. Sample copies are available at £2.50 per issue. Writer's guidelines are available free on request. Editorial calenders are available for cost and media packs are available at: www.scarletmagazine/co.uk

**Non-fiction** Publishes How-to, Photo features, Humour, Exposé, Inspirational, Features, Interview/Profile, New Product, General interest, Opinion (excluding letters to the Editor), Historical/Nostalgic and Personal experience articles.

**Submission Guidelines** Contact Assistant Editor, Linda McCormick, for more information.

**Fiction** Publishes Fiction and Erotica. Contact Deputy Editor, Alyson Fixter, for fiction.

**Tips** *Scarlet* is a middle-shelf glossy magazine aimed at women aged 20 to 40.

## Scheherazade
**14 Queens Park Rise, Brighton, BN2 9ZF**

✉ editor@schez.co.uk

🌐 www.schez.co.uk

**Parent Company** Scheherazade
**Contact** Elizabeth Counihan

**Insider Info** A consumer magazine publication, issued three times per year.

**Non-fiction** Publishes General Interest articles and Literary Reviews.

**Submission Guidelines** Accepts query by mail and email.

**Fiction** Interested in reviewing and publishing Horror, Science Fiction, Fantasy and Gothic Romance short stories.

**Submission Guidelines** Send complete manuscript.

**Tips** *Scheherazade* is a literary magazine that publishes Fantasy, Science Fiction and Gothic Romance short stories. Look at the website for news and developments.

## Scintilla

**Little Wentwood Farm, Llantrisant, Usk, NP5 1ND**

- anne.cluysenaar@virgin.net
- www.cf.ac.uk/encap/scintilla

**Parent Company** Usk Valley Vaughan Association (UVVA)

**Editor** Dr. Peter Thomas

**Contact** Editor, Anne Cluysenaar

**Established** 1995

**Insider Info** A consumer journal publication, issued annually, covering general literary interest. Byline is given.

**Non-fiction** Publishes Essays on themes related to the Breconshire writers Henry and Thomas Vaughan.

**Submission Guidelines** Accepts queries.

**Fiction** Publishes Poetry, Prose Fiction, Drama and on themes related to the Breconshire writers Henry and Thomas Vaughan.

**Tips** Articles in *Scintilla* engage in some way with Henry and Thomas Vaughan, famous for poetry, medical practice and alchemy.

## Scotland in Trust

Membership Magazine of The National Trust for Scotland

**91 East London Street, Edinburgh, Midlothian, EH7 4BQ**

- 0131 556 2220
- 0131 556 3300
- editor@scotlandintrust.co.uk
- www.scotlandintrust.co.uk

**Parent Company** CMYK Design

**Contact** Iain Gale

**Established** 2002

**Insider Info** A membership magazine publication, issued three times a year, covering historical, conservation and wildlife issues surrounding the National Trust for Scotland. Present circulation is 158,378. 70 per cent of the magazine is written by freelance writers. Average lead time is one month and payment is on publication. The kill fee for manuscripts not published is 50 per cent of original fee. It takes two months to publish a manuscript once it is accepted. Publication is copyrighted, and a byline is given. Purchases one-time rights. Seasonal material must be submitted three months in advance. Accepts queries by mail and email, and aims to respond to queries within five days. Assignment expenses are sometimes paid (limit agreed upon in advance). Sample copy is available with SAE (320mm x 230mm and three first class stamps), and writer's guidelines and editorial calendars are available via email request.

**Non-fiction** Interested in New Products and publishes features and General interest, Opinion (not letters to the Editor), Travel and Historical/Nostalgic articles.

**Submission Guidelines** Query with published clips. Does not accept unsolicited manuscripts.

**Images** Accepts images with submission.
 * Negotiates payment individually. One time rights purchased.

**Submission Guidelines** Send photos with submission to Art Director, Neil Braidwood and supply captions and identify subjects.

**Tips** The magazine is sent by direct mail to households with members of The National Trust for Scotland, Scotland's leading conservation charity. With a circulation of 158,000 throughout the world, the readership is very broad and aged from early 20s to over 100. Research shows that the readership enjoys taking holidays at home and abroad, gardening, wine, theatre and visiting museums and galleries. Readers are also moving with the times, 55 per cent regularly use a personal computer and 42 per cent regularly use the internet. Above all, and as a common denominator, readers have an interest in, or passion for, Scotland – heritage, gardens, buildings, countryside and culture.

## Scottish Home & Country

**42 Heriot Row, Edinburgh, EH3 6ES**

- 0131 225 1724
- 0131 225 8129
- magazine@swri.demon.co.uk
- www.swri.org.uk

**Parent Company** Scottish Women's Rural Institutes

**Editor** Liz Ferguson

**Contact** 1924

**Insider Info** A voluntary organisation magazine publication issued monthly, covering issues faced by members of Scottish Women's Rural Institutes. Present circulation of 10,000. Payment upon publication. 50 percent of magazine is written by freelancers. A byline is given. Editorial lead time is four weeks. Accepts query by mail, email, fax and phone. Aims to respond to queries, manuscripts and other issues within one week. Payment is not made with contributor copies or other premiums. Assignment expenses are not paid. Sample copy and writer's guidelines are free on request.

**Non-fiction** Interested in Humour, Inspirational, Features, Interview/Profile, General interest, Opinion (not letters to the Editor), Travel, Historical/Nostalgic, Personal experience, Health, Cookery, Crafts, Rural issues, Women's issues.

\* Receives approximately 50 manuscripts per year. Pays between £20 and £60 for unsolicited articles.

**Submission Guidelines** Please send complete manuscript. Articles should be between 500 and 1,000 words. Contact Liz Ferguson.

**Images** Accepts images with submission.

\* Pays a varied fee per photo. Purchases one-time rights.

**Submission Guidelines** Submit transparencies, prints, gif/jpeg files. Send photos with submission. Contact Liz Ferguson.

**Fillers** Interested in Facts, Short humour, Hints and tips and Strange but true pieces.

**Tips** Readership is mainly women, aged 50 and upwards, who live largely in rural Scotland. Features cover cookery, travel, rural issues, women's issues, health, crafts, general interest. Illustrated articles always have an advantage, as do seasonal features.

## Screen International

The International Voice Of The Film Business

**33–39 Bowling Green Lane, London, EC1R 0DA**

- 020 7505 8000
- michael.gubbins@emap.com
- www.screendaily.com

**Parent Company** EMAP Plc

**Contact** Michael Gubbins

**Established** 1976

**Insider Info** A trade journal magazine, issued weekly, covering the film industry. Present circulation is 8,000. 60 per cent of the magazine is written by freelancers. It takes three months to publish a manuscript after it is accepted. Payment is upon publication. 30 per cent kill fee (of original fee) for manuscripts not published. Publication is copyrighted, and a byline given. Purchases first UK serial rights, first rights, second serial (reprint) rights and electronic rights. Average lead time is three weeks. Seasonal material must be submitted four weeks in advance. Accepts queries by mail, email, fax and phone. Accepts simultaneous submissions. Aims to respond to queries within one day and manuscripts within three days. Never pays writers with contributor copies or other premiums. Payment is via cash, with assignment expenses sometimes paid (limit agreed upon in advance). Writer's guidelines and editorial calendars are free on request. Sample copy is available with SAE.

**Non-fiction** Publishes Book excerpts, Features, Interviews/Profiles and Technical articles, and articles on new products.

\* Minimum payment for assigned and unsolicited articles is £250 per 1,000 words.

**Submission Guidelines** Articles must be 250–3,000 words.

**Images** Accepts images with submission.

\* *Screen International* negotiates payment individually. One-time rights purchased.

**Submission Guidelines** Send images as gif/jpeg files, with captions, and identification of subjects to Art Editor, Alan Bingle.

**Tips** Target audience is anyone involved in the international film business, who has special interest in any area of the film industry, and that travels globally.

## ScriptWriter Magazine

**2 Elliott Square, London, NW3 3SU**

- 020 7586 4853
- 020 7284 0442
- julian@scriptwritermagazine.com
- www.scriptwritermagazine.com

**Parent Company** Scriptease Ltd

**Contact** Julian Friedmann

**Established** 2001

**Insider Info** A creative writing, craft skills magazine, issued bi-monthly, covering scriptwriting and script development, and film and television from a creative point of view. A magazine for professional scriptwriters, or those wanting to be professional. Also relevant to script editors, development executives, producers and directors - anyone who works with writers. Present circulation of 5,000. 50 per cent of the magazine is written by freelancers. Manuscripts are published within eight weeks of being accepted. Payment is on publication. Publication is copyrighted, and a byline given. Purchases one time rights (sometimes repeated). Average lead time of ten weeks. Seasonal material must be submitted eight weeks in advance. Accepts queries by mail, email and fax. Aims to respond to queries and manuscripts within two weeks. Sometimes pays writers with contributor copies or other premium other than cash if contributor asks. Assignment expenses sometimes paid (limit agreed upon in advance). Sample copy available: £7 per copy; £36 for subscription of six issues. Writer's guidelines are available via email on request.

**Non-fiction** Publishes Book excerpts, How-to and Humour articles, Features, Interviews/Profiles, Opinion (not letters to the Editor), and an Annual on audiences - demographic and psychological profile and analysis of who watches what.

\* Buys 50 manuscripts from freelancers each year. Pays £20 per 1,000 words (it is a non-profit making magazine) for both assigned and unsolicited articles.

**Submission Guidelines** Accepts query with published clips. Send complete manuscript. Submit 1,500 words (two page articles) and 4,000 words for (five page articles).

**Images** Accepts images with submission.

 * Offers no additional payment for photos accepted with the manuscript.

### Columns

Publishes a Humorous column about being a writer.

 * Pays £20 per 1,000 words.

**Submission Guidelines** Accepts query with published clips. Send complete manuscript.

**Tips** A pragmatic magazine about how professional writers work; useful to beginners but not specifically for beginners. Read the magazine first (important – some information can be found on our website). Send an example of writing together with a proposal for an article.

## Seam

**PO Box 1051, Sawston, Cambridge, CB22 3WT**

 seam.magazine@googlemail.com

 www.seampoetry.co.uk

**Editor** Anne Berkeley, Frank Dullaghan

**Established** 1994

**Insider Info** A consumer magazine publication, issued twice yearly, covering general literary interest. A byline is given. Accepts queries by mail and email. Writer's guidelines are available online.

**Non-fiction** Publishes Poetry, Features, Interviews/Profiles and Reviews.

**Submission Guidelines** Send query before sending submissions.

**Poetry** Publishes Avant-garde, Free Verse and Light Verse.

**Tips** Seam publishes the latest contemporary poetry from new and established writers, along with reviews, interviews and essays. Seam is interested in exploration and experimental poetry, as well as translated literature. Seam does not accept email submission, and will only accept proposals for essays not full manuscripts.

## SelfBuild & Design

**151 Station Street, Burton on Trent, DE14 1BG**

 01584 841417

 01584 841417

 ross.stokes@sbdonline.co.uk

 www.selfbuildanddesign.com

**Parent Company** Waterways World Ltd

**Contact** Ross Stokes

**Established** 1997

**Insider Info** A consumer magazine publication, issued monthly, covering home DIY. Accepts queries by email.

**Non-fiction** Interested in How-to, Photo and Technical features and articles.

 * Pays £100–£200 per 1000 words.

**Submission Guidelines** Send complete manuscript.

**Tips** SelfBuild & Design is the monthly magazine for home builders and renovators. From starting out to topping out, SelfBuild & Design has articles and information to guide readers through building their own dream home. Welcomes tips and advice from readers wanting to share their knowledge, and articles from people nearing completion of their home. Email article and details to the Editor.

## The Sentinel Quarterly

The Journal of African and World Literature

**60 Titmuss Avenue, London, SE28 8DJ**

 0870 127 1967

 07812 755751

 thequarterly@sentinelpoetry.org.uk

 www.sentinelpoetry.org.uk

**Parent Company** Sentinel Poetry Movement

**Editor** Afam Akeh

**Established** 2004

**Insider Info** Quarterly literary journal covering poetry and short fiction. Byline is given. Accepts queries by mail and email. Aims to respond to queries and manuscripts within eight weeks. Manuscript guidelines are available online.

**Non-fiction** Interested in Essays, Features, Interviews/Profiles, Literary Criticism, Reviews and articles on poetry and literature.

 * Payment is via a contributor copy.

**Submission Guidelines** Accepts complete manuscripts of up to 8,000 words.

**Fiction** Publishes short fiction.

**Poetry** Publishes Contemporary, Avant-garde, Free verse, Light verse and Traditional poetry.

**Submission Guidelines** Submit up to six poems of 40 lines in length.

**Tips** The Sentinel Quarterly is the literary journal of The Sentinel Poetry Movement and publishes poetry and short fiction, reviews, critical essays and articles on all literary genres. The Sentinel has a sister website, which is independent from the printed journal. The Sentinel publishes work from any background, but its main focus is on literature of the African diaspora.

## Seventh Quarry
The Swansea Poetry Quarterly

**Dan-y-bryn, 74 Cwm Level Road, Brynhyfryd, Swansea, SA5 9DY**

**Editor** Peter Thabit Jones

**Insider Info** A consumer magazine publication, covering poetry and prose interests.

**Tips** *Seventh Quarry* is an established literary magazine in Swansea that publishes poetry and new writing, mainly from Swansea but also from outside the area. The magazine often organizes poetry readings and events in the Swansea area in conjunction with the local arts councils. Contact the Editor for submission details.

## SFX

**30 Monmouth Street, Bath, BA1 2BW**

☎ 01225 442244
☎ 01225 822793
✉ sfx@futurenet.co.uk
🌐 www.sfx.co.uk

**Parent Company** Future Publishing
**Contact** Dave Bradley
**Established** 1995

**Insider Info** A consumer magazine publication, issued monthly, covering science fiction. Present circulation is 34,606. Payment is on acceptance.

**Non-fiction** Publishes General and Technical articles.

**Submission Guidelines** Email a CV and samples of work for consideration (word documents are best).

**Tips** *SFX* is a science fiction and fantasy magazine based in Britain, and published by Future Publishing. It's the market leader in the genre magazine arena, and has been running since 1995. It covers all aspects of science fiction and fantasy, including television, films, DVDs, books, comics, games, collectables and more. *SFX* generally do not accept speculative submissions.

## She

**National Magazine House, 72 Broadwick Street, London, W1F 9EP**

☎ 020 7439 5000
☎ 020 7437 6886
✉ editor@shemagazine.co.uk
🌐 www.she.co.uk

**Parent Company** National Magazine Company
**Contact** Sian Rees
**Established** 1955

**Insider Info** A consumer magazine publication, issued monthly, covering women's interests and women's lifestyle/fashion. Present circulation of 146,001. Accepts queries by mail and email.

**Non-fiction** Publishes Features and General Interest, Childcare and Health articles.

**Submission Guidelines** Send query before sending submissions. Articles should be a maximum of 1,200 words.

**Tips** *She* magazine is a guide to modern living; answering life questions and discussing home, fashion, beauty and health issues. Readers are defined by their underlying subscription to middle class values, and are educated women. Whether or not she has opted for children, the reader has moved into a settled life pattern and is affluent enough to afford the time to think about herself.

## Shearsman

**58 Velwell Road, Exeter, Devon, EX4 4LD**

☎ 01392 434511
☎ 01392 434511
✉ editor@shearsman.com
🌐 www.shearsman.com

**Parent Company** Shearsman Books Ltd
**Editor** Tony Frazer
**Established** 1981

**Insider Info** A consumer magazine publication, issued twice yearly, covering general literary interest, Publication is copyrighted. Accepts queries by mail and email. Writer's guidelines available online.

**Non-fiction** Publishes Poetry features.

**Submission Guidelines** Send query before sending submissions.

**Fiction** Publishes Prose fiction.

**Poetry** Publishes Avant-garde, Free verse and Light verse poetry.

**Tips** *Shearsman* publishes contemporary modernist poetry and some prose fiction. *Shearsman* also offers a pdf version of the magazine, available for download from the website. *Shearsman* operates a 'reading window' system for dealing with submissions, whereby there will be a two month 'window' for each issue, when writers can submit their manuscripts. Details of the reading windows are on the website.

## Sherlock

**31 Matthew Lane, Meltham, West Yorkshire, HD9 5JS**

☎ 01484 854576
✉ overdale@btinternet.com
🌐 www.sherlockholmes.com

**Contact** Atlas Publishing Ltd
**Editor** Teddy Hayes

**Established** 1991

**Insider Info** A consumer magazine, issued every two months, specialising in anything to do with Sherlock Holmes, including articles and reviews related to the latest crime fiction. Also publishes short crime fiction from contributors. Present circulation of 4,800. Byline is given. Queries accepted by mail and email. Writer's guidelines are available online.

**Non-fiction** Publishes Features, Interviews/Profiles, Reviews, Historical/Nostalgic articles.

**Submission Guidelines** Send query with published clips. Article submissions should be either 900, 1,800 or 2,400 words.

**Fiction** Publishes Crime/Detective fiction.

**Submission Guidelines** Send query with published clips. Submissions must be 6,000–7000 words, and be about a detective solving crimes.

**Tips** *Sherlock* has fairly stringent submission guidelines on the website.

## Shoot Monthly

**King's Reach Tower, Stamford Street, London, SE1 9LS**

- 020 7261 6287
- 020 7261 6019
- shoot@ipcmedia.com
- www.shoot.co.uk

**Parent Company** IPC Media

**Editor** Colin Mitchell

**Established** 1969

**Insider Info** A consumer magazine publication, issued monthly, covering football for young people. Present circulation of 28,505. Accepts queries by mail and email.

**Non-fiction** Interested in Photo features and Football articles.

**Submission Guidelines** Send query before sending submissions. Articles must be 500–2,000 words.

**Images** Send photos with submission.

**Tips** *Shoot Monthly* contains exclusive interviews, news and facts and the inside track on the biggest stars and clubs in UK football. *Shoot Monthly* is one of the most familiar brands in the British game giving readers, both younger and older, unrivalled access to the top names in soccer in the UK. Every month it offers a unique insight into the changing face of football, wrapped up in an informative and entertaining editorial package. Features must be hard hitting, topical and off beat. Aim for something relevant, but that is not usually covered in the magazine.

## Simply Knitting

It's easy when you know how!

**30 Monmouth Street, Bath, BA1 2BW**

- 01225 442244
- 01225 822793
- simplyknitting@futurenet.co.uk
- www.simplyknitting.co.uk

**Parent Company** Future Publishing

**Editor** Debora Bradley

**Contact** Editor, Debora Bradley

**Established** 2005

**Insider Info** A monthly consumer magazine covering knitting. Present circulation of 24,485. Ten per cent of the magazine is written by freelance writers. Submissions are published approximately six months after acceptance. Payment is made on publication of material. Kill fee for commissioned articles that are not published is 50 per cent of original fee. Publication is copyrighted and a byline is given. Purchases all rights. Editorial lead time is six weeks. Seasonal material must be submitted six months in advance. Queries accepted by mail and email to debora.bradley@futurenet.co.uk. Aims to respond to queries within one week and manuscripts within three months. If writers submit features which are to do with their own business, then the publicity is considered to be the 'fee'. Assignment expenses are sometimes paid (limit agreed upon in advance). Editorial calendars are available free on request. Media packs are available by email: amanda.haughey@futurenet.co.uk

**Non-fiction** Publishes Features and Photo Features.

**Submission Guidelines** Send query before sending submissions. Articles must be 300–1,000 words. No reprints.

**Tips** The magazine covers the best new products, interviews, club news, competitions and technical advice. *Simply Knitting* has the most stylish new designs, and famous names on the UK knitting scene. The audience is largely female, with an average age of 48 and are dedicated enthusiasts. Writing, or submitted knitwear designs should reflect the gender and age of reader, recognising there are readers from 8 to 80. The tone should be friendly and non-patronising, and knitwear design must be modern, but mainstream.

## Skald

**6 Hill Street, Menai Bridge, Anglesey, LL59 5AG**

- 01248 716343
- editors@skald.co.uk
- www.skald.co.uk

**Editor** Zoe Skoulding

**557**

**Contact** Co-Editor, Ian Davidson
**Established** 1994
**Insider Info** A consumer magazine, with two issues per year, covering literature. Byline is given. Accepts queries by mail and email.
**Non-fiction** Interested in Photo features and Literary articles.
**Submission Guidelines** Accepts queries in the first instance.
**Fiction** Publishes Short fiction.
**Poetry** Publishes Contemporary, Avant-garde, Free verse and Light verse poetry.
**Tips** *Skald* is a small magazine that publishes new poetry and short fiction, as well as some visual art in black and white. *Skald* prints work in both the English and Welsh language. A wide range of poetry is published, including experimental work, the magazine is interested in representing both local and international writers.

## Slim at Home

No gyms, no meetings, no problem
**25 Phoenix Court, Hawkins Road, Colchester, Essex, CO2 8JY**
- 01206 505987
- rachel@aceville.co.uk
**Parent Company** Aceville Publications Ltd
**Contact** Rachel Callen
**Established** 2007
**Insider Info** A consumer publication magazine, issued monthly, covering weight loss. Present circulation of 100,000. Zero to ten per cent of articles are written by freelancers. Manuscripts are published two months after they are accepted. Payment is on publication. A byline is sometimes given. Publication is copyrighted. Average lead time of one month. Seasonal material must be submitted two months in advance. Accepts queries by email and phone. Does not pay the expenses of writers on assignment.
**Non-fiction** Publishes Features and Photo Features on slimming.
 * Buys two to three manuscripts from freelancers per year.
**Submission Guidelines** Send query with published clips before sending submissions.
**Images** Send photos with submission.
 * Negotiates payment for individual photos.
**Tips** *Slim at Home* is an exciting new slimming magazine for independent women who want to lose weight their own way. It is packed with focused articles, motivation, psychology, recipes and the tools to help readers shed pounds safely.

## Smallholder

**3 Falmouth Business Park, Bickland Water Road, Falmouth, Cornwall, TR11 4SZ**
- 01354 741538
- 01354 741182
- liz.wright1@btconnect.com
- www.smallholder.co.uk
**Parent Company** Newsquest Plc
**Editor** Liz Wright
**Contact** Managing Editor, Terry Lambert
**Established** 1975
**Insider Info** Monthly consumer magazine covering agriculture, farming and smallholdings. Present circulation is 20,000. 75 per cent of the publication is written by freelance writers. Submissions published up to eight weeks after acceptance. Payment on publication. Byline is given. Publication is copyrighted. Purchases first UK serial rights. Average lead time is two months. Seasonal material must be submitted three months in advance. Accepts queries by email. Aims to respond to queries within one week and manuscripts within four months. Sample copy, manuscript guidelines and editorial calendar are free on request.
**Non-fiction** Interested in Book excerpts, How-to, Photo features, Inspirational, Features, Interviews/Profiles, Reviews, New Products, Technical, Opinion and Travel articles.
**Submission Guidelines** Accepts queries for articles of between 500 and 2,000 words.
**Images** Accepts images with submission.
 * Negotiates payment individually for photos.
**Submission Guidelines** State availability of photos with submission. Include contact sheets, captions and identification of subjects.
**Tips** *Smallholder* is a practical magazine for smallholders in country or town situations.

## Smiths Knoll

**Goldings, Goldings Lane, Leiston, Suffolk, IP16 4EB**
- 01728 830631
- michael.laskey@ukonline.co.uk
**Editor** Michael Laskey
**Contact** Co-Editor, Joanna Cutts
**Established** 1991
**Insider Info** A consumer magazine, with three issues per year covering poetry. Present circulation is 500. Submissions are published up to four months after acceptance. Payment is on publication. A byline is given. Accepts queries by mail and email. Aims to respond to queries and manuscripts within two weeks.

**Poetry** Publishes Contemporary, Avant-garde, Free verse, Light verse and Traditional poetry.

**Tips** *Smiths Knoll* is a small magazine with high production values that publishes any type of poetry from new and established writers. Roughly 40 per cent of the poetry in each issue is from new contributors, and the magazine has a history of nurturing new poets. *Smiths Knoll* will give critical feedback on any submission that interests them, they also offer weekend writing courses for subscribers.

## Smoke

**Liver House, 96 Bold Street, Liverpool, L1 4HY**
- 0151 709 3688
- 0151 707 8722
- windows@windowsproject.demon.co.uk
- www.windowsproject.demon.co.uk

**Parent Company** The Windows Projects Trust
**Editor** Dave Ward
**Contact** Co-Editor, Dave Calder
**Established** 1974

**Insider Info** A consumer magazine, with two issues per year, covering poetry. Present circulation is 700. Byline is given. Accepts queries by mail and email. Sample copy is available online.

**Poetry** Publishes Contemporary, Avant-garde, Free verse, Light verse and Traditional poetry.

**Tips** *Smoke* magazine publishes new poetry, artwork and some short fiction. Although not aimed at young readers, *Smoke* is published by The Windows Project which is a charity that aims to help children get involved with poetry. *Smoke* accepts submissions of any kinds of poetry, usually contemporary poems aimed at an adult readership.

## Solicitors Journal

**Paulton House, 8 Shepherdess Walk, London, E15 4DD**
- 020 7566 5757
- 020 7566 8238
- clientservices@solicitorsjournal.co.uk
- www.solicitorsjournal.com

**Parent Company** Waterlow Legal & Regulatory Ltd
**Editor** Jean-Yves Gilg
**Established** 1856

**Insider Info** Weekly trade journal covering the legal trade. Present circulation is 5,000.

**Tips** *Solicitors Journal* is a leading weekly magazine for the legal profession providing news, analysis, topical comments and practical articles about the legal trade.

## Sol Magazine

**PO Box 5828, Southend on Sea, SS1 9FA**
- solmag@solpubs.freeserve.co.uk
- www.solpubs.freeserve.co.uk/solmagazine.htm

**Parent Company** Sol Publications
**Editor** Malcolm E. Wright
**Established** 1969

**Insider Info** A consumer magazine, with two issues per year, covering poetry and fiction. Byline is given. Accepts queries by mail and email. Manuscript guidelines are available online.

**Non-fiction** Interested in Features, Reviews and articles on poetry and prose writing.

**Submission Guidelines** Accepts queries in the first instance.

**Fiction** Publishes Short fiction.

\* Contributors receive one year's free subscription to the magazine.

**Submission Guidelines** Accepts complete manuscripts of between 500 and 5,000 words.

**Poetry** Publishes Contemporary, Free verse, Light verse and Traditional poetry.

**Submission Guidelines** Submit up to six poems.

**Tips** *Sol Magazine* publishes short stories, poetry, book reviews and articles about literature, music and philosophy. *Sol* publishes any kind of poetry or fiction as long as they are original. Longer works of fiction may be considered for individual publication as a booklet, instead of in the magazine.

## Solo Survivors

**37 Micklehill Drive, Shirley, Solihull, West Midlands, B90 2PU**
- 0121 743 4381
- johnalanhirst@ukonline.co.uk
- www.johnalanhirst.com/solo_survivors_mag.shtml

**Parent Company** Survivor's Poetry Group
**Editor** John Hirst
**Established** 2002

**Insider Info** Quarterly consumer magazine covering poetry and fiction. Byline is given. Accepts queries by mail and email. Manuscript guidelines are available online.

**Non-fiction** Interested in Features, Interviews/Profiles, Opinion, Self-Help and Poetry articles.

**Submission Guidelines** Accepts complete manuscript.

**Fiction** Publishes Short fiction.

**Poetry** Publishes Contemporary, Free verse, Light verse and Traditional poetry.

**Submission Guidelines** Submit up to three poems of 30 lines in length.

**Tips** *Solo Survivors* is a small magazine published in accordance with the Survivor's Poetry Group, a group for survivors of mental or physical distress. The magazine focuses on publishing poetry from new and established contributors, and also prints short fiction, self-help articles, artwork and a 'guest poet' slot. *Solo Survivors* will accept any kind of submission, including self-help articles, but will focus mostly on poetry. Submissions should ideally come from members of the Survivor's Group.

## Somerfield Magazine
**The Mill House, Redcliff Backs, Bristol, BS1 6LY**
- 0117 989 7800
- hsmith@rarepublishing.co.uk

**Parent Company** PSP Rare
**Editor** Hannah Smith
**Insider Info** Monthly consumer magazine covering customer information and products for Somerfield Stores. Present circulation is 1,092,935. Ten per cent of the publication is written by freelance writers. Payment is on publication. Publication is copyrighted and the publisher purchases all rights. Average lead time is four months. Seasonal material must be submitted four weeks in advance. Accepts queries by email.
**Non-fiction** Publishes General Interest articles and Photo features.
**Tips** Customer magazine free to Somerfield shoppers, deals mainly with food and food related issues, but also health and lifestyle.

## South
**PO Box 5369, Poole, Dorset, BH14 0XN**
- south@martinblyth.co.uk

**Editor** Martin Blyth
**Established** 1990
**Insider Info** A consumer magazine, with two issues per year, covering literature and writing. Present circulation is 350. Byline is given.
**Non-fiction** Interested in Features, Book Reviews and articles on poetry and prose.
**Fiction** Publishes Short fiction.
**Poetry** Publishes Contemporary, Free verse, Light verse and Traditional poetry.
**Tips** *South* is a literary magazine that focuses on writers and work from the southern counties of England, including Berkshire, Dorset, Hampshire and Sussex. *South* has a 'rolling editorial' where each issue has a new editor, or editorial team. This allows *South* to use a completely anonymous selection process and give every contributor the same chance of publication.

## Spanner
**14 Hopton Road, Hereford, HR1 1BE**
- kaa45@dial.pipex.com
- www.shadoof.net/spanner

**Editor** Allen Fisher
**Insider Info** A consumer magazine, publishing three issues per year, covering literary interests.
**Tips** *Spanner* is a literary magazine that focuses on specific authors or subjects in each issue. The magazine publishes examples and reproductions of the work in question, and articles about the subject. *Spanner* does not accept contributions in any form.

## The Spectator
**56 Doughty Street, London, WC1N 2LL**
- 020 7405 1706
- 020 7242 0603
- editor@spectator.co.uk
- www.spectator.co.uk

**Parent Company** The Spectator Ltd
**Editor** Matthew d'Ancona
**Established** 1828
**Insider Info** Weekly consumer magazine covering news and current affairs. Present circulation is 70,090. Accepts queries by mail and email.
**Non-fiction** Interested in Book excerpts, Essays, Features, Interviews/Profiles, Reviews and General interest articles on Current affairs, News and Politics.
**Submission Guidelines** Accepts complete manuscripts.
**Tips** *The Spectator* was established in 1828, and is the oldest continuously published magazine in the English language. Controversy is important to *The Spectator*, so submissions should cover breaking, or forthcoming current affairs that will cause a stir. The quality of writing is also of high priority, so ensure your article is submitted in clear, elegant prose.

## Stamp Lover
**107 Charterhouse Street, London, EC1M 6PT**
- 020 7490 9610
- nps@ukphilately.org.uk
- www.ukphilately.org.uk/nps

**Parent Company** The National Philatelic Society
**Editor** D. Alford
**Established** 1908
**Insider Info** Bi-monthly society journal covering stamp collecting and history. Present circulation is 700. Submissions are published up to three months after acceptance. No payment is offered for contributions. Byline is given. Publication is copyrighted. Average lead time is one month.

Seasonal material must be submitted two months in advance. Accepts queries by mail.

**Non-fiction** Publishes General articles on stamps.

**Tips** *Stamp Lover* is the journal of the National Philatelic Society and covers all aspects of stamp collecting, including history, collection reviews, and markets.

## Stand Magazine

**School of English, Leeds University, Leeds, LS2 9JT**

- ☎ 0113 233 4794
- 🖷 0113 233 2791
- ✉ stand@leeds.ac.uk
- 🌐 www.standmagazine.org

**Editor** John Whale

**Contact** Managing Editor, Jon Glover

**Established** 1952

**Insider Info** Quarterly consumer magazine covering literature. Payment is on publication. Accepts queries by mail. Manuscript guidelines are available online.

**Fiction** Publishes Mainstream and Literary short fiction.

  \* Payments is £20 for the first 1,000 words, £5 for additional words.

**Submission Guidelines** Accepts complete manuscripts.

**Poetry** Publishes Traditional poetry.

**Tips** *Stand* publishes poetry, prose and various literary articles. *Stand* can only consider previously unpublished material, including that sent in by literary agents. Manuscripts should be accompanied by SAE. Please note that email submissions are not accepted.

## Staple

**74 Rangeley Road, Walkley, Sheffield, S6 5DW**

- ☎ 0114 233 6946
- 🖷 0870 054 7400
- ✉ e.barrett@shu.ac.uk

**Editor** Elizabeth Barrett

**Contact** Co-Editor, Ann Atkinson

**Established** 1983

**Insider Info** A consumer magazine, with three issues per year (March, July, November), covering literature. Byline is given. Accepts queries by mail and email.

**Fiction** Publishes Contemporary and Experimental short fiction.

**Poetry** Publishes Contemporary, Avant-garde and Free verse poetry.

**Tips** *Staple* is a small press magazine that publishes contemporary, often experimental, poetry, and short stories which are more likely to subvert the norms of fiction narratives, rather than to conform. *Staple* looks for submissions from abroad, as well as in the UK. *Staple* is proud of its small press heritage and always looks for submissions with an independent spirit, experimental stories and poems that work against the accepted norm.

## The Stinging Fly

Dublin's Literary Magazine

**PO Box 6016, Dublin 8, Republic of Ireland**

- ✉ stingingfly@gmail.com
- 🌐 www.stingingfly.org

**Parent Company** The Stinging Fly Press

**Editor** Declan Meade

**Contact** Poetry Editor, Eabhan Ní Shúileabháin

**Established** 1997

**Insider Info** A consumer literary magazine, with three issues per year, covering Irish and international literature. Byline is given. Accepts queries by mail and email. Manuscript guidelines are available online.

**Non-fiction** Interested in Features, Reviews and articles on Poetry and Literature.

**Submission Guidelines** Accepts queries in the first instance.

**Fiction** Publish Mainstream and Contemporary Short fiction.

  \* Payment is two contributor copies.

**Submission Guidelines** Accepts complete manuscripts of up to 3,000 words.

**Poetry** Publishes Contemporary, Avant-garde, Free verse, Light verse and Traditional poetry.

**Tips** *The Stinging Fly* is an Irish literary magazine that publishes short fiction, poetry and book reviews. The magazine welcomes submissions from Irish and international writers and has a particular interest in new writers and promoting the short story form. *The Stinging Fly* operates a 'reading window', so submissions will only be accepted during the first three months of the year.

## Streetfighters

**19th Floor, 1 Canada Square, Canary Wharf, London, E14 5AP**

- ☎ 020 7772 8585
- ✉ dave.manning@oceanmedia.co.uk
- 🌐 www.streetfightersmag.com

**Parent Company** Ocean Media

**Editor** Dave Manning

**Contact** Managing Editor, Stu Garland

**Established** 1991
**Insider Info** Monthly consumer magazine covering motorcycle riding and modification. Present circulation is 25,000. 50 per cent of the publication is written by freelance writers. Submissions are published up to six weeks after acceptance. Payment is on publication and the publication will be copyrighted. Average lead time is six weeks and seasonal material must be submitted six weeks in advance. Accepts queries by mail, email and fax. Simultaneous submissions are accepted, as are previously published submissions. Aims to respond to queries within two days and manuscripts within ten days.
**Non-fiction** Interested in How-to, Motorcycle modification, Photo features, Humour, Inspirational, Features, Interviews/Profiles, New Product Reviews, Technical and Personal experience articles.
**Submission Guidelines** Accepts manuscripts of between 800 and 3,000 words.

## Sugar
**64 North Row, London, W1K 7LL**
- 020 7150 7087
- 020 7150 7678
- sugarreaders@sugarmagazine.co.uk
- www.sugarmagazine.co.uk
**Parent Company** Hacette Filipacchi
**Editor** Annabel Brog
**Contact** Features Editor, Diane Leeming
**Established** 1994
**Insider Info** A monthly consumer magazine for teenage girls. Present circulation of 200,187. Queries accepted by mail.
**Tips** The magazine's content concentrates mainly on the opposite sex, fashion, celebrities, and real stories about teenagers. *Sugar* helps solve 'female' issues by publishing articles that offer helpful advice. *Sugar* seeks real life stories, but also practical articles of help dealing with teenage issues. Experience as either a guidance counsellor, or a previously troubled teenager, would add to any article idea.

## SuperBike
**King's Reach Tower, Stamford Street, London, SE1 9LS**
- 020 8726 8445
- kenny_pryde@ipcmedia.com
- www.superbike.co.uk
**Contact** IPC Media
**Editor** Kenny Pryde
**Established** 1977

**Insider Info** A monthly consumer magazine covering motoring and motorcycling. Present circulation of 54,642. Queries accepted by mail and email.
**Non-fiction** Publishes Features, Reviews, New Product and Technical articles.
**Submission Guidelines** Accepts queries and complete manuscripts.
**Tips** Britain's best selling sports bike magazine. Focuses on serious testing, technical features and in-depth bike reviews. Mostly focuses on road testing of high performance bikes, or technical features, so any expertise in these areas – especially technical bike maintenance/modification – would be favourable.

## The Tabla Book of New Verse
**Department of English, University of Bristol, 3–5 Woodland Road, Bristol, BS8 1TB**
- stephen.james@bristol.ac.uk
- www.bris.ac.uk/tabla
**Editor** Stephen James
**Insider Info** Annual literary anthology covering verse poetry.
**Non-fiction** Interested in Essays, Features and articles on Poetry.
**Poetry** Publishes all forms of verse poetry.
**Tips** *The Tabla Book of New Verse*, formerly known as Tabla, is an annual anthology of high quality verse poetry from established writers and former contributors. New contributors can only be published in the Tabla anthology by going through the annual writing competition.

## Take A Break
**Academic House, 24–28 Oval Road, London, NW1 7DT**
- 020 7241 8000
- 020 7241 8052
- tab.features@bauer.co.uk
- www.bauer.co.uk
**Parent Company** H. Bauer Publishing
**Editor** John Dale
**Contact** Fiction Editor, Norah McGrath
**Established** 1990
**Insider Info** A weekly consumer magazine covering women's lifestyle topics. Present circulation of 1,027,013.
**Non-fiction** Publishes General interest features, Interviews and Photo Features on Real life, Fashion, Beauty, Food, Home, Travel and Competitions.
**Fiction** Publishes Women's short fiction.

**Tips** The title is aimed specifically at women aged 25–55 with children. It has been the UK's biggest selling women's weekly for more than 14 years.

## Taliesin

**Ty Mount Stuart, Sgwâr Mount Stuart, Cardiff, CF10 5FQ**

- 029 2047 2266
- 029 2049 2930
- taliesin@academi.org
- www.academi.org/taliesin

**Parent Company** Yr Academi Gymreig

**Editor** Manon Rhys

**Established** 1959

**Insider Info** Welsh language literary journal, published three times per year (March, July, December) by the Academi, which is the Welsh National Literature Promotion Agency and Society for Authors. Present circulation of 1,000. Queries accepted by mail and email.

**Non-fiction** Publishes Features, Interviews/Profiles and Reviews on all subjects to do with Welsh Literature.

**Fiction** Publishes Fiction.

**Tips** *Taliesin* is written purely in the Welsh language and will only accept submissions related to Welsh literature.

## Tatler

**Vogue House, Hanover Square, London, W1S 1JU**

- 020 7499 9080
- 020 7493 1641
- fiona.kent@condenast.co.uk
- www.tatler.co.uk

**Parent Company** Condé Nast Publications Ltd

**Editor** Geordie Greig

**Established** 1707

**Insider Info** A monthly consumer magazine, covering contemporary British society/lifestyle/fashion. Present circulation of 88,920. Queries accepted by mail.

**Non-fiction** Publishes Features, Interviews/Profiles and General interest articles.

**Submission Guidelines** Send query with published clips and CV.

**Tips** Carries articles on a broad number of topics, but its primary focus is on social trends amongst the very wealthy and aristocratic. Previous Editor Geordie Greig said that reading *Tatler* should be 'like a fabulous journey in an incredible sports car...you can go fast, you can go round the bend, you can go a bit mad, you can have pretty girls in it, you can

stop at stately homes, as well as go round to Monte Carlo. It should be a journey of speed and surprises.' Remember this when submitting your details.

## Taxation

**2 Addiscombe Road, Croydon, Surrey, CR9 5AF**

- 020 8212 1949
- 020 8212 1970
- mike.truman@lexisnexis.co.uk
- www.taxation.co.uk

**Parent Company** LexisNexis

**Editor** Mike Truman

**Contact** Feature Editor, Allison Plager

**Established** 1927

**Insider Info** A weekly trade journal covering accountancy. Present circulation of 8,317. Queries accepted by mail and email.

**Non-fiction** Publishes Technical and Legal articles on Taxation.

  * Payment for unsolicited articles is £100 per 800 words.

**Submission Guidelines** Accepts queries and complete manuscripts. Articles must be 2,000 words.

**Tips** *Taxation* is the leading authority on tax law, practice and administration. The magazine provides its readership with news and comment on legal decisions for all those engaged in tax work, as well as information on changes in legislation, and items affecting tax practice. There are practical solutions to problems, lively debate, and commentary from leading experts every week. Professional expertise in tax law or similar is a pre-requisite for submissions. Articles, ideally about upcoming changes in UK tax law, should examine the legal issues thoroughly and also present solutions to any problems.

## tBkmag

**4 Froxfield Close, Winchester, SO22 6JW**

- 01962 620320
- www.newbooksmag.com

**Parent Company** New Books

**Editor** Guy Pringle

**Insider Info** A quarterly book magazine for pre-teenage readers (the sister publication of *myBOOKSmag*). Present circulation of 10,000.

**Non-fiction** Publishes Features, Interviews/Profiles, Reviews, General interest articles and Event news.

**Submission Guidelines** Send query before submitting.

**Fiction** Publishes Fiction and Book excerpts.

**Submission Guidelines** Send query before submitting.

**Tips** Publishes book reviews, information on children's and young adult books, book excerpts, interviews, and reports on events for young readers. *tBkmag* often requires lots of reviews and book excerpts from the latest children's and young person's books.

## Tears in the Fence
**38 Hod View, Stourpaine, Blandford Forum, Dorset, DT11 8TN**
- 01258 456803
- 01258 454026
- editors@tearsinthefence.co.uk
- www.tearsinthefence.co.uk

**Editor** David Caddy
**Contact** Associate Editor, Sarah Hopkins
**Established** 1984
**Insider Info** An international literary journal, published three times a year, covering poetry, fiction, translations, reviews and essays from new and established writers around the world. 100 per cent of the publication is written by freelance writers. Byline is given. Queries are accepted by mail and email. Sample copy is available online.
**Non-fiction** Publishes Features and Reviews.
**Submission Guidelines** Send query before submitting.
**Fiction** Publishes Mainstream and Experimental fiction.
**Submission Guidelines** Send complete manuscript. Submissions must be 100–25,000 words.
**Poetry** Publishes Free verse, Light verse and Avant-garde Poetry.
**Tips** *Tears in the Fence* focuses on political and socio-economic themes and is keen to keep up to date with the latest trends in world poetry. *Tears in the Fence* does not have a set theme for poetry and fiction submissions, but is looking for work that is unexpected and takes the reader on a journey. Submissions by post only, including SAE.

## Tesco: The Magazine
**Pegasus House, 37–43 Sackville Street, London, W1S 3EH**
- 020 7534 2400
- 020 7534 2555
- emma.oliver@cedarcom.co.uk
- www.tescomagazine.co.uk

**Parent Company** Cedar (Magazine Publishers) and Tesco
**Editor** Dawn Alford
**Contact** Editorial Assistant, Emma Oliver
**Established** 1993

**Insider Info** A bi-monthly consumer magazine for the customers of Tesco supermarket, covering food, drink and retail issues. Present circulation of 2,494,330.
**Non-fiction** Publishes General Interest, Interviews, Reviews and Photo Features on Food, Wine, New products, Parenting, Cookery, Fashion, Beauty, Health and Lifestyle.
**Tips** The magazine is aimed at women aged 25 to 45. The editorial content of the magazine accounts for roughly 70 per cent, the rest is advertising.

## Textualities
**8 Lauriston Street, Edinburgh, EH3 9EU**
- 0131 228 4837
- 0131 228 4837
- the.editor@textualities.net
- www.textualities.net

**Contact** Textualities
**Editor** Jennie Renton
**Insider Info** The annual printed journal of Textualities.net, an online literature and writing magazine.
**Non-fiction** Publishes Interviews/Profiles, Literary Criticism, Bibliography and General interest articles.
**Submission Guidelines** Send complete manuscript.
**Fiction** Publishes Mainstream fiction.
**Poetry** Publishes Free verse and Traditional poetry.
**Tips** The journal includes new fiction and poetry, literary criticism, interviews and bibliography. To submit an article to textualities.net or *Textualities* print edition, email the Editor with your proposal. All submitted articles must relate in some way to books and writing.

## That's Life!
**24–28 Oval Road, London, NW1 7DT**
- 020 7241 8000
- 020 7241 8008
- jo.checkley@bauer.co.uk
- www.bauer.co.uk/website/thatslife.cfm

**Parent Company** H. Bauer Publishing
**Editor** Jo Checkley
**Established** 1995
**Insider Info** A weekly consumer magazine, covering women's interests. Present circulation of 490,220. Seasonal material must be submitted three months in advance. Queries accepted by mail and email. Aims to respond to manuscripts with six weeks. Writer's guidelines are available free on request and by email.

**Fiction** Publishes Romance, Humorous and Mainstream fiction.
 \* Maximum payment for accepted submissions is £400.
**Submission Guidelines** Send complete manuscript. Submissions must be 700 words. Will not accept straightforward romance, historical, science fiction, animal or children's stories. No stories about gratuitous violence or sex crimes.
**Tips** *That's Life!* prints real life stories combined with classic women's weekly editorial and a real sense of humour. Its unique mix of sassy, gritty and involved editorial, ensure that *That's Life!* has the highest reader loyalty in the market and is the most thoroughly read magazine in the UK. Stories should have a strong plot and a good twist. A sexy relationship/scene can feature strongly, but isn't essential – the plot twist is much more important. The writing should be chronological and fast moving, with a maximum of four characters.

## This Is...

**PO Box 16185, Writing Space Publications, London, NW1 8ZH**

- writingspace@btinternet.com
- www.btinternet.com/~writingspace/thisis/

**Parent Company** Writing Space Publications
**Editor** Carol Cornish
**Insider Info** Quarterly consumer literary magazine covering short fiction and poetry. Byline is given. Accepts queries by mail and email. Manuscript guidelines are available online.
**Non-fiction** Interested in Features and Articles on poetry.
**Submission Guidelines** Accepts queries in the first instance.
**Fiction** Publishes Mainstream and Experimental short fiction and works in progress.
**Submission Guidelines** Accepts complete manuscripts.
**Poetry** Publishes Avant-garde, Contemporary and Free verse poetry.
**Tips** *This Is...* publishes short stories, poetry, and works in progress, as well as black and white photography and illustrations. *This Is...* looks for extreme writing with a 'sharp cutting edge', that is non-conformist and will force a reaction from the reader. The magazine has a theme for every issue and submissions must be written with the theme in my mind. Forthcoming themes will be detailed on the website, along with submission guidelines.

## Time

**Brettenham House, Lancaster Place, London, WC2E 7TL**

- 020 7499 4080
- edit_office@timemagazine.com
- www.timeeurope.com

**Parent Company** Time Inc
**Editor** Eric Pooley
**Established** 1923
**Insider Info** Weekly consumer magazine covering international news and current affairs. Present circulation is 142,314.
**Tips** *Time* is one of the world's best know news publications, and has set the standard for leadership, authenticity and authoritative journalism since 1923. *Time* has very little opportunity for freelance work, as nearly all of its material is produced internally in its various international bureaus.

## Time Out London

**Universal House, 251 Tottenham Court Road, London, W1T 7AB**

- 020 7813 3000
- 020 7323 3438
- editorial@timeout.com
- www.timeout.com

**Parent Company** Time Out Group Ltd
**Editor** Gordon Thomson
**Contact** Features Editor, Jessica Cargill Thompson
**Established** 1968
**Insider Info** Weekly consumer magazine covering consumer lifestyle and culture in London. Present circulation is 92,233. Accepts queries by mail.
**Non-fiction** Interested in Interviews/Profiles, Reviews and General interest articles on London entertainment and events listings.
**Submission Guidelines** Accepts proposals for articles up to 2,000 words in length.
**Tips** *Time Out London* is the Time Out Group's flagship publication. It was the first listings magazine to cover all aspects of cultural and consumer life in London. *Time Out London* is always looking for ideas for relevant articles, ideally a detailed local knowledge of the entertainment scene is required.

## The Times Educational Supplement

**Admiral House, 66–68 East Smithfield, London, E1W 1BX**

- 020 7782 3000
- 020 7782 3200
- editor@tes.co.uk
- www.tes.co.uk

**Parent Company** TSL Education Ltd
**Editor** Bob Doe
**Established** 1910
**Insider Info** Weekly consumer magazine covering education. Present circulation is 76,645. Accepts queries by mail.
**Non-fiction** Interested in Features, Reviews and General interest articles on Education.
**Submission Guidelines** Accepts queries (including published clips and CV) for articles of between 1,000 to 2,000 words.
**Tips** *The Times Educational Supplement* is Britain's leading publication covering the world of primary, secondary and further education, as well as the market leader for teaching job vacancies. Specialist knowledge in the teaching industry is required for all submissions, but humour is also important.

## The Times Educational Supplement Scotland

**Scott House, 10 South St. Andrew Street, Edinburgh, EH2 2AZ**
- 0131 557 1133
- 0131 558 1155
- scoted@tes.co.uk
- www.tes.co.uk/scotland

**Parent Company** TSL Education Ltd
**Editor** Neil Munro
**Established** 1965
**Insider Info** Weekly consumer magazine covering Scottish education. Present circulation is 6,528 Accepts queries by mail.
**Non-fiction** Interested in Features, Interviews/ Profiles and Technical or General interest articles on Scottish education.
**Submission Guidelines** Accepts queries (including published clips and CV) for articles of between 1,000 to 2,000 words.
**Tips** *The Times Educational Supplement Scotland* is the sister magazine to *The Times Educational Supplement*. It covers the world of primary, secondary and further education in Scotland, and is the market leader for Scottish teaching job vacancies. Specialist knowledge in the teaching industry is required for all submissions, but humour is also important.

## The Times Literary Supplement

**Admiral House, 66–68 East Smithfield, London, E1W 1BX**
- 020 7782 3000
- 020 7782 3100
- letters@the-tls.co.uk

- www.the-tls.co.uk

**Parent Company** TSL Education Ltd
**Editor** Peter Stothard
**Established** 1902
**Insider Info** Weekly consumer literary magazine covering literature, literary criticism and literary markets. Present circulation is 34,373. Accepts queries by mail.
**Non-fiction** Interested in Book excerpts, Essays, Features, Reviews and articles on poetry and literature.
**Submission Guidelines** Accepts queries in the first instance.
**Tips** Since 1902, *The Times Literary Supplement* has followed the work of the twentieth century's leading writers and thinkers. *The Times Literary Supplement* covers developments in literature, politics, scholarship and the arts. It will consider poems, literary discoveries and current affairs articles for publication.

## Top Santé Health & Beauty

**Greater London House, Hampstead Road, London, NW1 7EJ**
- 020 7874 0200
- 020 7391 3333
- firstname.lastname@emap.com
- www.emap.co.uk

**Parent Company** EMAP Plc
**Editor** Lauren Libbert
**Contact** Acting Features Editor, Beth Gibbons; Editorial Assistant, Alex Rees
**Established** 1993
**Insider Info** A monthly consumer magazine covering health and beauty topics. Present circulation of 117,968.
**Non-fiction** Publishes General interest features, and Photo features on Health, Fitness and Beauty.
**Tips** Aimed at women of all ages. As well as general health and beauty features, the magazine also publishes details of medical reports and specific health issues.

## Total Film

**2 Balcombe Street, London, NW1 6NW**
- 020 7042 4833
- 020 7317 2642
- totalfilmonline@futurenet.co.uk
- www.totalfilm.com

**Parent Company** Future Publishing
**Editor** Nev Pierce
**Contact** Managing Editor, Aubrey Day; Associate Editor (Creative), Andy Lowe

**Established** 1996

**Insider Info** Monthly consumer magazine covering film and video reviews. Present circulation is 91,000. Payment is on acceptance.

**Non-fiction** Interested in Features, Reviews and General interest articles on film.

**Submission Guidelines** Accepts queries in the first instance.

**Tips** *Total Film* covers all the latest releases, exclusive news and DVD reviews, plus interviews, features and competitions. Short review material will be published, but longer features are generally privately commissioned.

## Total Guitar

**30 Monmouth Street, Bath, BA1 2BW**

- 01225 442244
- 01225 73253
- totalguitar@futurenet.co.uk
- www.totalguitar.co.uk

**Parent Company** Future Publishing

**Editor** Stephen Lawson

**Insider Info** Monthly consumer magazine covering practical guitar playing and reviews. Present circulation is 52,183.

**Tips** *Total Guitar* is a comprehensive guide for guitarists and guitar enthusiasts of all abilities. It features product reviews, artist profiles and interviews as well as techniques and tutorial pages. It is Europe's best selling guitar magazine. *Total Guitar* is aimed at novice guitar players, and therefore has more tutorial content than features.

## Traction

**The Maltings, West Street, Bourne, Lincolnshire, PE10 9PH**

- 01778 391160
- 01778 425437
- davidb@warnersgroup.co.uk
- www.traction.co.uk

**Parent Company** Warners Group Publications

**Contact** Managing Editor, David Brown

**Established** 1993

**Insider Info** Monthly consumer magazine covering diesel and electric railway nostalgia. Present circulation is 8,000. 90 per cent of the publication is written by freelance writers. Manuscripts are published 14 days after acceptance. Payment is on publication and a byline is given. Publication is not copyrighted and first UK serial rights will be purchased. Average lead time is two days. Seasonal material must be submitted one month in advance. Accepts queries by mail and email. Aims to respond to queries within two weeks and manuscripts within five weeks. Sample copy and manuscript guidelines are free on request.

**Non-fiction** Interested in Photo features, Features, Reviews and Technical articles.

 * Purchases over 100 manuscripts per year. Payment is £50 per published page.

**Submission Guidelines** Accepts complete manuscripts of between 750 and 8,500 words. Does not publish reprints. Send submissions to Managing Editor, David Brown.

**Images** Accepts images with submission.

 * Payment varies from between £15 to £50 per photo. Purchases one time rights.

**Submission Guidelines** Send transparencies, prints or gif/jpeg files, with captions and identification of subjects to, Managing Editor, David Brown. Send photos with submissions.

**Tips** *Traction* is the only monthly publication devoted to classic diesel and electric trains past and present. Ideas for potential articles can be sent to the Managing Editor for approval. Submissions require a good knowledge of railway operation and/or enthusiasm.

## Translation and Literature

**Edinburgh University Press Ltd, 22 George Square, Edinburgh, EH8 9LF**

- 0131 650 4218
- 0131 662 0053
- editorial@eup.ed.ac.uk
- www.eup.ed.ac.uk/journals

**Parent Company** Edinburgh University Press Ltd

**Editor** Stuart Gillespie

**Established** 1992

**Insider Info** A consumer literary Journal, with two issues per year, covering literary translation. Present circulation is 500.

**Non-fiction** Interested in Essays, Features, Technical, Opinion and Historical/Nostalgic articles.

**Submission Guidelines** Accepts queries in the first instance.

**Tips** *Translation and Literature* is an academic journal that prints articles on translations of classic texts into English language, translation theory and techniques, and the history of translation in literature. *Translation and Literature* will consider articles on any theme related to translation in literature, but they must be from established academics in the field.

## Traveller Magazine

**Traveller/Wexas, 45–49 Brompton Road, London, SW3 1DE**

**☎** 020 7589 0500
**🖷** 020 7581 8476
**✉** traveller@wexas.com, duncanmills@wexas.com
**🌐** www.traveller.org.uk
**Parent Company** Wexas Ltd
**Editor** Amy Sohanpaul
**Contact** Deputy Editor, Duncan Mills
**Established** 1970
**Insider Info** Quarterly consumer magazine covering travel. Present circulation is 30,000. 50 per cent of the publication is written by freelance writers. Submissions are published up to three months after acceptance. Payment is on publication and a byline is given. Publication is copyrighted and one time rights are purchased. Average lead time is three months. Seasonal material must be submitted four months in advance. Accepts queries by mail, email, fax and telephone. Manuscript guidelines are free on request and available online or by email.
**Non-fiction** Interested in Features, Travel and Personal experience articles.
 * Pay for unsolicited articles ranges from £100 to £200.
**Submission Guidelines** Accepts manuscripts of between 800 and 1,000 words.
**Images** Accepts images with submission.
 * Negotiates payment individually. Purchases one time rights.
**Submission Guidelines** Send contact sheets, transparencies and gif/jpeg files, to Deputy Editor, Duncan Mills. Send images with submissions.
**Tips** *Traveller* is the UK's oldest travel magazine and reports on the real experience of travelling the world, especially to 'off the beaten track' destinations.

## Tremblestone
**Stowford House, 43 Seymour Avenue, St. Judes, Plymouth, PL4 8RB**
**🌐** www.tremblestone.co.uk
**Editor** Kenny Knight
**Established** 1999
**Insider Info** A literary journal covering contemporary poetry as well as literature reviews. Byline is given. Accepts queries by mail. Aims to respond to queries and manuscripts within two months.
**Non-fiction** Interested in articles on Poetry and Literary reviews.
**Submission Guidelines** Accepts queries in the first instance.
**Poetry** Publishes Contemporary, Avant-garde, Free verse and Light verse poetry.

**Submission Guidelines** Submit up to six poems at a time.
**Tips** *Tremblestone* is a literary journal with an international outlook, which publishes new contemporary poetry, as well as book and magazine reviews. It is open to 'surprising' poetry and is looking for the more unusual side of contemporary poetry, including submissions from abroad.

## The Ugly Tree
**6 Chiffon Way, Trinity, Greater Manchester, M3 6AB**
**✉** paul@mucusart.co.uk
**🌐** www.mucusart.co.uk, theuglytree.htm
**Parent Company** Mucusart Publications
**Editor** Paul Neads
**Insider Info** A consumer magazine, with three issues per year (February, June, October), covering print and performance poetry. Byline is given. Accepts queries by mail and email. Manuscript guidelines are available online.
**Non-fiction** Interested in articles on Poetry and Reviews.
**Submission Guidelines** Accepts queries in the first instance.
**Poetry** Publishes Contemporary, Avant-garde, Free verse, Light verse and Spoken/Performance poetry.
**Submission Guidelines** Submit up to five poems of 40 lines in length.
**Tips** *The Ugly Tree* is a small poetry magazine published by Mucasart Publications. It specialises in the relationship of spoken and performance poetry with the printed page, but will often publish any type or style of poetry. *The Ugly Tree* also prints some reviews and articles related to poetry. They also run poetry writing competitions that offer cash prizes, as well as publication in the magazine.

## Ulster Grocer
**5b Edgewater Business Park, Edgewater Road, Belfast Harbour Estate, Belfast, Antrim, BT3 9JQ, Northern Ireland**
**☎** 028 9078 3200
**🖷** 028 9078 3210
**✉** kathyj@writenow.prestel.co.uk
**🌐** www.greerpublications.com
**Parent Company** Greer Publications
**Editor** Kathy Jensen
**Established** 1972
**Insider Info** Monthly trade journal covering issues relevant to the grocery retail trade in Northern Ireland. Present circulation is 4,849. Five per cent of the publication is written by freelance writers.

Submissions are published up to four weeks after acceptance. Payment completed 30 days after publication. Publication is copyrighted. Average lead time is four weeks. Seasonal material must be submitted four weeks in advances. Accepts queries by email. Aims to respond to queries within five days and manuscripts within seven days. Sometimes pays expenses of writers on assignment (limit agreed upon in advance). Sample copy is free on request. Editorial calendar and manuscript guidelines are free on request and available by email. Media pack is available online.

**Non-fiction** Interested in Photo features (Relevant news stories), Features, Interviews/Profiles, Technical and relevant General interest articles.

* Freelance articles are by commission only. Fee is by agreement beforehand.

**Submission Guidelines** Accepts queries in the first instance. Articles are between 700 and 2,000 words.

**Tips** *Ulster Grocer* is ABC audited and is distributed to multiple, symbol and independent retailers; confectionery, tobacconists and newsagents, buyers, wholesalers, FMCG manufacturers, agents and distributors, and others involved in the grocery trade. *Ulster Grocer* is the key medium to reach the highly successful and extremely buoyant independent retail sector, which continues to account for a significant share of overall Northern Irish grocery spend.

## Uncut
Music and Movies With Something To Say
**25th Floor, King's Reach Tower, Stamford Street, London, SE1 9LS**
- 020 7261 6992
- 020 7261 5573
- farah_ishaq@ipcmedia.com
- www.uncut.co.uk

**Parent Company** IPC Media
**Editor** Allan Jones
**Insider Info** Monthly consumer magazine covering music and film. Present circulation is 93,000. 75 per cent of the publication is written by freelance writers. Payment is on publication. The kill fee for assigned manuscripts not published is between 50 and 100 per cent. Byline is given. Publication is copyrighted and all rights are purchased. Aims to respond to queries within two months and manuscripts within three months. Accepts queries by mail and email. Manuscript guidelines are free on request.

**Non-fiction** Interested in Features, Interviews and Reviews.

**Images** Accepts images with submission.

* Negotiates payment individually. Purchases one time rights.

**Submission Guidelines** Send images (contact sheets, negatives, transparencies, prints, gif/jpeg files) to Picture Editor, May Starey. State availability of photos with your submission.

## Understanding
**20a Montgomery Street, Edinburgh, EH7 5JS**
- 0131 478 0680
- 0131 478 0680

**Parent Company** Dionysia Press
**Editor** Denise Smith
**Established** 1989
**Insider Info** Annual consumer literary magazine covering new poetry, prose and drama. Present circulation is 500.

**Non-fiction** Interested in Essays, Literary Articles, Features and Reviews.

**Submission Guidelines** Accepts queries in the first instance.

**Fiction** Publishes short fiction and plays.
**Poetry** Publishes Contemporary and Traditional poetry.

**Tips** *Understanding* is a yearly literary magazine that publishes new poetry and short fiction, play excerpts, reviews, articles and some literary criticism. *Understanding* accepts submissions for general poetry and short fiction, as well as more academic submissions of literary criticism, ideally by post with SAE.

## Urthona
**9a Auckland Road, Cambridge, CB5 8DW**
- 01223 309470
- 01223 868601
- urthonamag@onetel.com
- www.urthona.com

**Parent Company** FWBO Arts
**Established** 1992
**Insider Info** A consumer magazine, with two issues per year, covering international Buddhist arts and culture. Present circulation is 1,100. Accepts queries by mail and email.

**Non-fiction** Interested in Features, Interviews/ Profiles and Reviews.

**Tips** *Urthona* is a Buddhist arts and world culture magazine, publishing articles on the arts, including interviews with artists, historical articles, reviews and events news. In particular *Urthona* often publishes Buddhist readings, and interpretations of famous artists or literary works.

## Utility Week

**Quadrant House, The Quadrant, Sutton, Surrey, SM2 5AS**

☎ 020 8652 8678
🖷 020 8652 8906
✉ steve.hobson@rbi.co.uk
🌐 www.utilityweek.co.uk
**Parent Company** RBI
**Editor** Steve Hobson
**Established** 1994

**Insider Info** Weekly trade journal covering business issues relating to UK utilities (gas, water and electricity). Present circulation is 4,000. 25 per cent of the publication is written by freelance writers. Submissions are published up to six weeks after acceptance. Payment is on acceptance. A byline is given. Publication is copyrighted and all rights are purchased. Average lead time is six weeks. Accepts queries by email and telephone. Simultaneous submissions will be accepted. Aims to respond to queries and manuscripts within one week. Sometimes pays the expenses of writers on assignment. Sample copy, editorial calendars and manuscript guidelines are free on request. Media pack is available online.

**Non-fiction** Interested in Features, New Product reviews and Technical articles.
 * Payment is £220 per 1,000 words.
**Submission Guidelines** Accepts manuscripts of between 800 and 1,500 words.
**Images** Accepts images with submission.
 * Payment varies per photo. Purchases all rights.
**Submission Guidelines** Include captions, model releases and identification of subjects. State availability of photos with submission.
**Tips** *Utility Week* is aimed at managers and directors working for UK utilities companies. Major issues covered include regulation, competitive environment, customer service and asset management. Queries by phone call are preferred.

## Vanity Fair

**Vogue House, Hanover Square, London, W1S 1JU**

☎ 020 7499 9080
🖷 020 7493 1962
🌐 www.vanityfair.com
**Parent Company** Conde Nast Publications
**Editor** Henry Porter
**Established** 1914

**Insider Info** Monthly consumer magazine covering women's interests, lifestyle and fashion. Present circulation is 97,414. Editorial calendars and media pack are available online.

**Tips** *Vanity Fair* is an intellectual and visually orientated magazine that aims to cover the people, places, and ideas that are defining modern culture. *Vanity Fair* does not accept unsolicited manuscripts and commissions all work internally.

## Variant

**1/2 189b Maryhill Road, Glasgow, G20 7XJ**

☎ 0141 333 9522
🖷 0141 333 9522
✉ variantmag@btinternet.com
🌐 www.variant.org.uk
**Editor** Leigh French
**Established** 1996

**Insider Info** A consumer literary magazine, with three issues per year (February, June, October), covering Literature, Arts and Culture. Present circulation is 15,000. Accepts queries by mail and email. Sometimes pays writers with contributor copies. Media pack and manuscript guidelines are available online.

**Non-fiction** Interested in Features, Interviews/ Profiles, Reviews and General interest articles.
**Submission Guidelines** Accepts queries of between 750 and 4,000 words.

**Tips** Based in Glasgow and Belfast, *Variant* is the UK and Ireland's only free international arts and culture magazine. *Variant* welcomes contributions in the form of news, previews, articles, interviews, polemical pieces and artists pages. It aims to include writing which is constructive and thought provoking, and which provides a context in which younger writers can find a platform for their work.

## Vertigo

**4th Floor, 26 Shacklewell Lane, London, E8 2EZ**

☎ 020 7690 0124
✉ editor@vertigomagazine.co.uk
🌐 www.vertigomagazine.co.uk
**Editor** Holly Aylett
**Contact** Co-Editor, Gareth Evans
**Established** 1994

**Insider Info** Quarterly consumer magazine covering independent film and media. Present circulation is 7,000. Accepts queries by mail and email. Manuscript guidelines are available by email.

**Non-fiction** Publishes Essays, Features, Interviews/ Profiles, Reviews and Opinions.
**Submission Guidelines** Accepts queries in the first instance.

**Tips** *Vertigo* magazine is published as both a print and online magazine, and publishes articles, interviews and critical debate about independent and artists' filmmaking. Vertigo encourages submission of articles on a voluntary basis. Email the Editor for full submission guidelines.

## Village

Ireland's weekly current affairs magazine
**44 Westland Row, Dublin 2, Republic of Ireland**
- 00353 1 642 5050
- 00353 1 642 5001
- editor@villagemagazine.ie
- www.village.ie

**Parent Company** Village Communications Ltd
**Editor** Vincent Browne
**Established** 2004
**Insider Info** Weekly consumer magazine covering current affairs, including politics, media, arts, books and technology. Present circulation is 9,467. 30 per cent of the publication is written by freelance writers. Submissions are published up to one week after acceptance. Payment is completed 30 days after publication. A byline is given. Publication is copyrighted and first rights are purchased. Average lead time is three days. Seasonal material must be submitted 14 days in advance. Accepts queries by email. Simultaneous submissions will be accepted. Aims to respond to queries and manuscripts within three days. Sometimes pays expenses of writers on assignment (limit agreed upon in advance). Sample copy and editorial calendars are available online. Manuscript guidelines are free on request.
**Non-fiction** Publishes Book excerpts (non-fiction), Photo features (related to social issues), Exposés, Religious pieces, Features, Interviews/Profiles, General interest and Historical/Nostalgic articles.
 * Payment is from €100 to €400.
**Submission Guidelines** Accepts complete manuscripts of between 500 and 2,000 words. Does not publish reprints.
**Images** Accepts images with submissions.
 * Offers no additional payment for photos accepted with manuscripts. Purchases one time rights.
**Submission Guidelines** Send contact sheets and gif/jpeg files, with captions, to News Editor, John Byrne.
**Tips** *Village* has a left of centre political viewpoint and all submissions must be written accordingly.

## Viz

**30 Cleveland Street, London, W1T 4JD**
- 020 7907 6000
- 020 7907 6020
- viz@viz.co.uk
- www.viz.co.uk

**Parent Company** Dennis Publishing
**Editor** Simon Donald
**Established** 1979
**Insider Info** A consumer magazine, with ten issues per year, covering adult humour, satire and cartoons. Present circulation is 112,288.
**Tips** *Viz* is an adult comic with recurring characters such as 'the Fat Slags', 'Roger Mellie' and 'Sid the Sexist'. *Viz* tends to contain lewd contain and explicit language. It is mostly an illustrated comic and there is little scope for written contribution, but a high quality satirical article or spoof newspaper feature may be considered.

## Vogue

**Vogue House, Hanover Square, London, W1S 1JU**
- 020 7499 9080
- 020 7408 0559
- voguemagazine@condenast.co.uk
- www.vogue.co.uk

**Parent Company** Condé Nast Publications
**Editor** Alexandra Shulman
**Contact** Features Assistant, Aimee Farrell
**Established** 1916
**Insider Info** Monthly consumer magazine covering women's Interests, lifestyle and fashion. Present circulation is 216,218.
**Tips** *Vogue* is a fashion and lifestyle magazine published in several countries around the world. *Vogue Paris* and *Vogue Italia* are possibly the most influential magazines of the modern fashion world. *Vogue* tends to use commissioned work, or submissions from well-known writers only, so good internal contacts are important. It's best to focus on upmarket general interest such as highbrow art and literary articles, as well as reviews, home interest, and cuisine.

## Walk

**2nd Floor, Camelford House, 87–90 Albert Embankment, London, SE1 7TW**
- 020 7339 8500
- 020 7339 8501
- chriso@ramblers.org.uk
- www.ramblers.org.uk

**Parent Company** The Ramblers' Association
**Editor** Chris Ord
**Established** 2003

**Insider Info** Quarterly consumer magazine covering camping, walking, climbing and outdoor interests. Present circulation is 107,050. Payment is on publication. Average lead time is six months. Accepts queries by mail. Sample copy is available with SAE. Manuscript guidelines are free on request or available by email.

**Non-fiction** Interested in Photo features, Features and Travel articles.

**Submission Guidelines** Accepts queries of between 500 and 800 words, with published clips.

**Images** Accepts images with submissions.

\* Negotiates payment individually.

**Submission Guidelines** Send photos with captions

**Tips** Formerly known as The Rambler, *Walk* contains stunning photography and design, engaging issues based articles, editorial opinion, reviews, competitions and inspirational walking guides. Articles are normally written in-house. Feature articles should promote an interest in walking, but should not just profile a location. Articles should describe why a particular walk is special to the writer.

## Wallpaper*

**Brettenham House, Lancaster Place, London, WC2E 7TL**

☎ 020 7322 1177

🖷 020 7322 1171

✉ editor@wallpaper.com

🌐 www.wallpaper.com

**Parent Company** IPC Media

**Editor** Tony Chambers

**Established** 1996

**Insider Info** A consumer magazine, with ten issues per year, covering contemporary interior design and lifestyle. Present circulation is 110,246.

**Tips** *Wallpaper** has championed the best new design for the past decade and continues to be the most authoritative voice on contemporary design and lifestyle in publishing today. *Wallpaper** prides itself on having 'consistently been one of the most influential design magazines, as well as the most beautiful.' Therefore any submitted articles or ideas must be well-designed and attractive, as well as being on the cutting edge of the latest trends on design.

## Wasafiri

The Magazine Of International Contemporary Writing

**The Open University, 1–11 Hawley Crescent, Camden Town, London, NW1 8NP**

☎ 020 7556 6110

☎ 020 7556 6187

✉ wasafiri@open.ac.uk

🌐 www.wasafiri.org

**Editor** Susheila Nasta

**Contact** Editorial Manager, Teresa Palmiero

**Established** 1984

**Insider Info** A consumer magazine, with three issues per year (March, July, November), covering all aspects of international writing. Present circulation is 6,000. Byline is given. Accepts queries by mail and email. Manuscript guidelines are available online.

**Non-fiction** Interested in Poetry and Prose articles, Features, Interviews/Profiles and Reviews.

**Submission Guidelines** Accepts complete manuscripts of between 1,000 and 2,500 words.

**Fiction** Publishes International fiction and Translated/Foreign language fiction.

**Submission Guidelines** Accepts complete manuscripts of between 5,000 and 6,000 words.

**Poetry** Publishes International poetry.

**Tips** *Wasafiri* is a literary magazine that focuses on writing as a 'form of cultural travelling'. It prints contemporary international literature, both fiction and poetry, and also various articles on contemporary art and book reviews. When submitting to *Wasafiri* it is required to include two hard copies, one for reference, and also an electronic submission. *Wasafiri's* website has a very extensive style guide for article submissions.

## Waterstone's Books Quarterly

**Capital Court, Capital Interchange Way, Brentford, TW8 0EX**

☎ 020 8742 3800

🖷 020 8742 0215

✉ ed.wood@squareonegroup.co.uk

🌐 www.squareonegroup.co.uk

**Parent Company** Square One Group

**Editor** Ed Wood

**Established** 2001

**Insider Info** Quarterly consumer magazine covering new books and literary markets at Waterstone's the retailer. Present circulation is 150,000.

**Non-fiction** Publishes Book excerpts, Features, Interviews/Profiles and Reviews.

**Tips** *Waterstone's Books Quarterly* is published to promote new book releases and unknown authors to Waterstone's customer base. The magazine prints book reviews, interviews and articles about the latest developments in the book trade. The majority of content in *Waterstone's Books Quarterly* is made up of reviews of the latest books, many of which are commissioned from freelance writers.

## Waterways World

**151 Station Street, Burton on Trent, Staffordshire, DE14 1BG**

☎ 01283 742951
☎ 01283 742957
✉ richard.fairhurst@wwonline.co.uk

**Editor** Richard Fairhurst
**Established** 1972

**Insider Info** Monthly consumer magazine covering boating and UK waterways. Present circulation is 16,782. Payment is on publication. Average lead time is two months. Accepts queries by mail and email. Manuscript guidelines are free on request or available by email.

**Non-fiction** Interested in Photo features and General interest articles.

**Submission Guidelines** Accepts complete manuscripts.

**Images** Accepts images with submissions.

**Submission Guidelines** Send transparencies.

**Tips** *Waterways World* is a monthly magazine covering news, photographs and illustrated articles on all aspects of inland waterways in Britain, and also on limited aspects of waterways abroad. *Waterways World is* interested in all canals and navigable rivers, whether operational or derelict, and suggested topics for feature articles include waterways, boats and boating, waterway history and current waterway affairs.

## Web User

**King's Reach Tower, Stamford Street, London, SE1 9LS**

☎ 020 7261 7330
☎ 020 7261 7878
✉ editor@web-user.co.uk
🌐 www.webuser.co.uk

**Parent Company** IPC Media
**Editor** Claire Woffenden
**Established** 2001

**Insider Info** Bi-weekly consumer magazine covering computing and the internet. Present circulation is 31,886. Accepts queries by mail and email. Media pack is available online.

**Tips** *Web User* publishes articles on the best of the net, helping the internet consumer have a more interesting time online. *Web User* is approved by the 'Plain English Campaign' which means that they keep technical jargon to a minimum. Articles must be informative, but clear and easy to read and understand.

## The Weekly News

**2 Albert Square, Dundee, Tayside, DD1 9QJ**

☎ 01382 223131
☎ 01382 201390
✉ dburness@dcthomson.co.uk
🌐 www.dcthomson.co.uk

**Parent Company** DC Thomson & Co. Ltd
**Editor** David Burness
**Contact** Deputy Editor, Rod Cameron
**Established** 1855

**Insider Info** Weekly consumer newspaper covering news, culture and lifestyle. Present circulation is 83,633. Five per cent of the publication is written by freelance writers. Payment is on acceptance and a byline is given. Publication is copyrighted, with first UK serial rights purchased. Average lead time is two weeks. Seasonal material should be submitted four weeks in advance. Accepts queries by mail and email. Aims to respond to queries within five days and manuscripts within two weeks. Sample copy and manuscript guidelines are free on request. Media pack is available online.

**Non-fiction** Interested in Photo features and Personal experience (first person style).
 * Purchases approximately 200 non-fiction manuscripts per year. Payment is by arrangement.

**Submission Guidelines** Accepts complete manuscripts of up to 1,200 words. Send submissions to Deputy Editor, Rod Cameron.

**Fiction** Publishes Adventure, Humorous, Mainstream, Mystery and Suspense short fiction.
 * Purchases approximately 50 fiction manuscripts per year. Payment is by arrangement.

**Submission Guidelines** Accepts complete manuscripts of between 600 to 1,200 words. Send submissions to Fiction Editor, Jill Finlay.

**Tips** *The Weekly News* targets both men and women, mainly in the 50 plus age group. There is a wide mix of subject matter, including real-life human interest, celebrity interviews, health, leisure (including travel and gardening), royalty, fiction and sport. Fiction submissions must be general interest rather than overly romantic, and must appeal to both sexes.

## Welsh Country

**Aberbanc, Llandysul, Ceredigion, SA44 5NP**

☎ 01559 372010
☎ 01559 371995
✉ kath@welshcountry.co.uk
🌐 www.welshcountry.co.uk

**Parent Company** Equine Marketing Ltd
**Editor** Kath Rhodes
**Established** 2004

**Insider Info** Bi-monthly consumer magazine covering Welsh interest subjects. Present circulation is 19,408. 20 per cent of the publication is written by freelance writers. Submissions are published approximately three months after acceptance. Payment is on publication Sometimes the expenses of writers on assignment are paid (limit agreed upon in advance). Publication is copyrighted and one time rights are purchased. A byline is sometimes given. Average lead time is two months, seasonal material must be submitted four months in advance. Accepts queries by email and telephone. Aims to respond to queries within five days and manuscripts within three months. Sample copy is available for £2.95. Editorial calendars are available by email. Media pack is available online.

**Non-fiction** Interested in Photo features, Poetry Articles, Features and Historical/Nostalgic articles.
 * All articles must be of Welsh interest.

**Submission Guidelines** Accepts queries of between 700 and 2,000 words by email, with published clips.

**Images** Accepts images with submission.
 * Purchases one time rights. Offers no additional payment for photos accepted with manuscripts.

**Submission Guidelines** Send gif/jpeg files with captions and credit name to the Artistic Designer, Abi Thrift.

**Columns** Publishes Motoring and Wine columns, depending on advertising, of 600 words each.
 * Buys approximately eight column pieces per year.

**Fillers** Publishes Letters and Star letters.

**Tips** *Welsh Country* covers an eclectic mix of articles about Welsh culture, interests and general information about Wales. *Welsh Country* sources much of its material from a pool of regular freelancers.

## Weyfarers
**1 Mountside, Guildford, Surrey, GU2 4JD**
- admin@weyfarers.com
- www.weyfarers.com

**Parent Company** Guildford Poets Press
**Editor** Martin Jones, Stella Stocker, Jeffery Wheatley
**Established** 1972

**Insider Info** A consumer magazine, with three issues per year, covering contemporary and traditional international poetry. A byline is given. Accepts queries by mail.

**Non-fiction** Interested in articles on International poetry and Literary reviews.

**Poetry** Publishes International, Contemporary, Free verse, Light verse and Traditional poetry.
 * Payment is by contributor copies.

**Submission Guidelines** Accepts queries by email only.

**Tips** *Weyfarers* is an international poetry magazine, which publishes modern and traditional poetry from new and established writers, including translations of foreign language poetry. The magazine also prints book and magazine reviews. *Weyfarers* does not accept submission by email. All submissions must be posted and include SAE for reply.

## What Hi-FI? Sound & Vision
**Teddington Studios, Broom Road, Teddington, Middlesex, TW11 9BE**
- 020 8267 5000
- 020 8267 5019
- whathifi@haynet.com
- www.whathifi.com

**Parent Company** Haymarket Publishing
**Editor** Claire Newsome
**Established** 1976

**Insider Info** A consumer magazine, published 13 times per year, covering hi-fi and home cinema equipment and markets. Present circulation is 62,459.

**Tips** *What Hi-Fi? Sound & Vision* is the world's leading independent guide to buying and owning hi-fi and home cinema products. Freelance writing for reviews is no longer accepted, but they will consider ideas for general or specific features on hi-fi or home cinema.

## Which Caravan
**The Maltings, West Street, Bourne, Lincolnshire, PE10 9NS**
- 01778 391000
- marks@warnersgroup.co.uk
- www.whichcaravan.co.uk

**Parent Company** Warners Group Publications
**Editor** Mark Sutcliffe
**Established** 1987

**Insider Info** Monthly consumer magazine covering new and used caravans. Present circulation is 9,000. 70 per cent of the publication is written by freelance writers. Payment is on publication. Byline given. Publication is copyrighted and all rights are purchased. Accepts queries by mail and email.

**Non-fiction** Publishes Features and Reviews.

**Tips** *Which Caravan* is the only magazine dedicated solely to reviewing and rating new and used caravans in the UK.

## Which Kit Car?

**10 Church Lane, Rotherfield Peppard, Henley on Thames, Oxfordshire**

- 01491 628508
- ian@performancepublishing.co.uk
- www.whichkitcar.com

**Parent Company** Performance Publishing Ltd
**Editor** Ian Stent
**Established** 1986

**Insider Info** Monthly consumer magazine covering the UK kit car market. Present circulation is 6,000. Five per cent of the publication is written by freelance writers. Payment is on publication. A byline is sometimes given. Publication is copyrighted and first UK serial rights are purchased. Average lead time is one month. Seasonal material must be submitted two months in advance. Accepts queries by mail, email, or by telephone. Aims to respond to queries within one week and manuscripts within two weeks. Sample copy is available for £3.95. Manuscript guidelines and editorial calendars are available by email.

## The Wolf

**April Heights, Fagnal Lane, Winchmore Hill, Amersham, HP7 0PG**

- editor@wolfmagazine.co.uk
- www.wolfmagazine.co.uk

**Editor** James Byrne
**Established** 2002

**Insider Info** A consumer literary magazine with three issues per year, covering contemporary poetry and photography. A byline is given. Accepts queries by mail and email. Manuscript guidelines are available online.

**Non-fiction** Interested in Photo features, Essays (on poetry subjects), Interviews/Profiles and Reviews.
**Submission Guidelines** Accepts queries in the first instance, for articles between 500 and 1,500 words.
**Poetry** Publishes contemporary, Avant-garde, Free verse and Light verse poetry.
**Submission Guidelines** Submit up to five poems.
**Images** Send photos with submission.
**Tips** *The Wolf* is a literary magazine that publishes interviews with leading contemporary poets as well as poetry from contributors and the latest in contemporary photography. *The Wolf* is open to submissions of contemporary poetry from new and established authors, however, it is a relatively new, self-funded magazine and so cannot offer any payment or contributor copies for accepted contributions.

## Woman & Home

**King's Reach Tower, Stamford Street, London, SE1 9LS**

- 020 7261 5176
- 020 7261 7346
- sue_james@ipcmedia.com
- www.womanandhome.com

**Parent Company** IPC Media
**Editor** Sue James
**Established** 1926

**Insider Info** Monthly consumer magazine covering women's lifestyle and fashion. Present circulation is 325,223. Accepts queries by mail.
**Non-fiction** Interested in General interest articles on Home and Garden, Health, Beauty and Fashion.
**Submission Guidelines** Accepts queries of between 3,000 and 4,500 words, including SAE.
**Fiction** Publishes Short Stories.
**Tips** *Woman & Home* magazine presents a stylish mix of content, reflecting the way women live and work today. There is not much scope for freelance work, as most material is specially commissioned.

## Woman Alive

**Garcia Estate, Canterbury Road, Worthing, West Sussex, BN13 1BW**

- 01903 264556
- 01903 821081
- womanalive@cpo.org.uk
- www.womanalive.co.uk

**Parent Company** Christian Publishing & Outreach
**Editor** Jackie Stead
**Contact** Editor, Russ Bravo
**Established** 1982

**Insider Info** Monthly consumer magazine covering Christian women's issues. Present circulation is 10,000. 65 per cent of the publication is written by freelance writers. Payment on is publication and a byline given. Purchases first UK serial rights. Average lead time is three months. Seasonal material must be submitted three months on advance. Accepts queries by mail and email. Accepts simultaneous submissions. Aims to respond to queries within three days and manuscripts within seven days. Sometimes pays writers with contributor copies for promotional reasons. Sometimes pays the expenses of writers on assignment (limit agreed upon in advance). Sample copy is available for £2.20. Manuscript guidelines are available with SAE, or by email.
**Non-fiction** Interested in How-to, Inspirational, Religious, Features, Interviews/Profiles, New Product, General interest and Personal experience articles.

* Payment for assigned articles ranges from £70 to £125.

**Submission Guidelines** Accepts complete manuscripts of between 750 and 1,600 words.

**Tips** The majority of *Woman Alive* readers are aged between 35 and 50.

## Woman's Weekly

**King's Reach Tower, Stamford Street, London, SE1 9LS**

- 0870 444 5000
- 020 7261 6322
- womansweeklypostbag@ipcmedia.com
- www.ipcmedia.com

**Parent Company** IPC Media

**Editor** Sheena Harvey

**Contact** Fiction Editor, Gaynor Davies; Features Editor, Sue Pilkington

**Established** 1993

**Insider Info** A weekly consumer magazine covering women's lifestyle and hobby topics. Present circulation of 387,098. Media pack available online.

**Non-fiction** Publishes General Interest Features, Practical Articles and Photo Features on Crafts, Food, Cookery, Fashion, Lifestyle and Leisure.

**Fiction** Publishes Women's Short Fiction, including several fiction special editions. Contact the Fiction Editor for more details.

**Tips** Aimed at mature women, the average age of the reader is 55. The magazine takes a practical stance on many issues, designed to have a real impact on women's lives, particularly domestically.

## World Soccer

**King's Reach Tower, Stamford Street, London, SE1 9LS**

- 020 7261 5737
- 020 7261 7474
- jamie_rainbow@ipcmedia.com
- www.worldsoccer.com

**Parent Company** IPC Media

**Editor** Jamie Rainbow

**Established** 1960

**Insider Info** Monthly consumer magazine covering international football. Present circulation is 45,497. Accepts queries by email.

**Non-fiction** Interested in articles on General interest (football) and Football culture.

**Submission Guidelines** Accepts complete manuscripts of between 600 and 2,000 words.

**Tips** The best writers, analytical features and the ability to deliver the inside track on domestic and world football have made *World Soccer* the

unrivalled authority on the game of soccer around the world. *World Soccer* is very much focused on international football, and is aimed at an adult audience only.

## Writers' Forum

**PO Box 3229, Bournemouth, BH1 1ZS**

- 01202 589828
- 01202 587758
- editorial@writers-forum.com
- www.writers-forum.com

**Parent Company** Writers International Ltd

**Editor** John Jenkins

**Established** 1995

**Insider Info** Monthly consumer literary magazine covering short stories, magazine features, novels, plays, film scripts and poetry. Present circulation is 25,000.

**Non-fiction** Interested in How-to (craft of writing) articles.

**Submission Guidelines** Accepts queries between 800 and 1,500 words.

**Tips** *Writers' Forum* is dedicated to providing encouragement and inspiration to those who want to write and see their work published. *Writers' Forum* runs both a poetry and short fiction competition every issue and offers cash prizes for each. The majority of writing published in the magazine is from competitions.

## Writers' News

**5th Floor, 31–32 Park Row, Leeds, LS1 5JD**

- 0113 200 2929
- 0113 200 2928
- jonathan.telfer@writersnews.co.uk
- www.writersnews.co.uk

**Parent Company** Warners Group Publications

**Editor** Jonathan Telfer

**Established** 1989

**Insider Info** Monthly literary journal covering all the latest news, insider information, market leads and research from the world of writing, as well as directory listings and help columns. Payment is on publication and a byline given. Accepts queries by mail or email. Manuscript guidelines are available online.

**Non-fiction** Interested In Exposé, Features, Interviews/Profiles, Reviews, Personal experience and News articles.

**Submission Guidelines** Accepts query in the first instance.

**Tips** *Writers' News* is a guide to what's going on in the world of writing. *Writers' News* is mostly interested in articles and market news reports, but also runs writing competitions, which offer cash prizes and publication in the magazine.

## Writing Magazine
**5th Floor, 31–32 Park Row, Leeds, LS1 5JD**

☎ 0113 200 2929

☎ 0113 200 2928

✉ derek.hudson@writersnews.co.uk

🌐 www.writersnews.co.uk

**Parent Company** Warners Group Publications
**Editor** Derek Hudson
**Established** 1992
**Insider Info** Monthly literary journal covering every genre of writing with regular how-to guides, columns, interviews and articles. Payment on publication. Byline is given. Accepts queries by mail and email. Manuscript guidelines are available online.
**Non-fiction** Interested in How-to articles, Features, Interviews/Profiles and Reviews.
**Submission Guidelines** Accepts queries in the first instance.
**Fiction** Publishes Adventure, Historical, Romance, Horror, Science Fiction, Confession, Humorous, Erotica, Mainstream, Ethnic, Mystery, Suspense, Experimental, Western, Fantasy and Religious short stories.
 * Only publishes fiction from competition winners.
**Poetry** Publishes Avant-garde, Contemporary, Free verse, Light verse and Traditional poetry.
 * Only publishes poetry from competition winners.
**Tips** *Writing Magazine* is the sister publication to *Writers' News* and covers every genre of writing, both prose and poetry. *Writing Magazine* runs runs various writing competitions with the winners being published in the magazine. Always contact with a proposal first, rather than submitting an unsolicited article.

## X Magazine
**PO Box 43771, London, W14 8ZY**

☎ 0845 430 9517

☎ 0845 430 9518

✉ submissions@x-bout.com

🌐 www.flippedeye.net/xmag

**Parent Company** Flipped Eye Press
**Editor** Sally Strong
**Established** 2002
**Insider Info** A consumer literary magazine covering poetry and fiction, experimental writing, interviews, feature articles and competition listings. 100 per cent of the publication is written by freelance writers. Byline is given. Accepts queries by mail and email. Manuscript guidelines are available online.
**Non-fiction** Interested in Cover Art, Features, Interviews/Profiles and Reviews.
**Fiction** Publishes Contemporary and Experimental short fiction.
**Submission Guidelines** Accepts completed manuscripts of no more than 5,000 words.
**Poetry** Publishes Avant-garde, Contemporary, Free verse and Light verse.
**Submission Guidelines** Submit a maximum of five poems.
**Tips** *X Magazine* only considers submissions from live performance writers who read their work in public at least once every other month, and prefers to take submissions from writers' groups, or regular events, in order to feature a few writers from one group/event at a time. They only accepts submissions by email, and then only during reading periods in February, May, August and November. Work submitted outside of these months is likely to be deleted unread.

## Yachting World
**King's Reach Tower, Stamford Street, London, SE1 9LS**

☎ 020 7261 6800

☎ 020 7261 6818

✉ yachting_world@ipcmedia.com

🌐 www.yachtingworld.com

**Parent Company** IPC Media Ltd
**Editor** Andrew Bray
**Contact** Deputy Editor, David Glenn
**Established** 1894
**Insider Info** Monthly consumer magazine covering yachting, blue water cruising, global sailing epics, international yacht racing, super yachting, international events and charters. Present circulation is 29,152. Accepts queries by mail and email. Manuscript guidelines are free on request and available by email to: andrew_bray@ipcmedia.com
**Non-fiction** Interested in Photo features, Features, Reviews and Technical articles.
**Submission Guidelines** Accepts queries with published clips, or completed manuscripts of between 2,500 and 3,000 words.
**Tips** *Yachting World* is the world's oldest sailing magazine. Over 50 per cent of the circulation is outside of the UK. The editorial emphasis is on quality of writing, photography, and the topics covered.

## Yachts and Yachting

**196 Eastern Esplanade, Southend on Sea, Essex, SS1 3AB**

☎ 01702 582245
☎ 01702 588434
✉ gael@yachtsandyachting.com
🌐 www.yachtsandyachting.com
**Parent Company** Yachts and Yachting Ltd
**Editor** Gael Pawson
**Established** 1947
**Insider Info** A bi-weekly consumer magazine that covers all aspects of yachting, from sport and race meets, to buying and restoring boats. Accepts queries by mail or email.
**Non-fiction** Interested in How-to, New Product, General interest and Personal experience articles related to Yachting.
**Submission Guidelines** Accepts queries and completed manuscript submissions.
**Tips** *Yachts and Yachting* will accept submissions of short, technically correct articles.

## The Yellow Crane

**20 Princes Court, The Walk, Roath, Cardiff, CF24 3AU**

**Editor** Jonathan Brookes
**Insider Info** A consumer literary magazine covering Welsh poetry.
**Poetry** Publishes Contemporary, Free verse, Light verse and Traditional poetry from Welsh and International writers.
**Submission Guidelines** Accepts complete manuscripts by post.
**Tips** *The Yellow Crane* is a Welsh literary magazine that publishes mainstream poetry from new and established writers. *The Yellow Crane* is based in South Wales, but will accept poetry submissions from outside the region as well, including from international writers.

## Yorkshire Women's Life Magazine

**PO Box 113, Leeds, West Yorkshire, LS8 2WX**

✉ ywlmagenquiries@btinternet.com
🌐 www.yorkshirewomenslife.co.uk
**Editor** Dawn-Maria France
**Contact** Editorial Assistant, India Jones
**Established** 2001
**Insider Info** A consumer magazine, published three time per year. Covers women's lifestyle, news, art and fashion. Present circulation is 15,000. Ten per cent of the magazine is written by freelance writers. Submissions are published approximately two

months after acceptance, payment is on publication. Byline is given and publication is copyrighted. Average lead time is four months and seasonal material must be submitted four months in advance. Accepts queries by mail or email. Accepts simultaneous submissions. Aims to respond to queries and manuscripts within two months. Sample copy is available for £9.25. Manuscript guidelines and editorial calendars are available with SAE and two first-class stamps.
**Non-fiction** Interested in Interviews/Profiles, Reviews of new Beauty and Lifestyle products, and articles on Personal experience.
 * Payment for articles is negotiable.
**Submission Guidelines** Accepts queries with published clips for articles between 180 and 250 words. Does not publish reprints.
**Fillers** Interested in Jokes (to be illustrated by cartoonist) and Newsbreak fillers between 55 and 80 words.
 * Payment for fillers is negotiable.
**Tips** *Yorkshire Women's Life* is an independent, handbag sized women's magazine aimed at career minded women; managers and working professional women. *Yorkshire Women's Life* works with subscribers in order to get their work on the pages of the title, wherever possible.

## Young People Now

**174 Hammersmith Road, London, W6 7JP**

☎ 020 8267 4793
☎ 020 8267 4728
✉ ypn.editorial@haynet.com
🌐 www.ypnmagazine.com
**Parent Company** Haymarket Publishing
**Editor** Ravi Chandiramani
**Contact** Features Editor, Andy Hillier
**Established** 1989
**Insider Info** Weekly trade journal covering social services and welfare for young people. Present circulation is 14,688.
**Tips** *Young People Now* is the only weekly title for those who work with young people between the ages of 11 to 25. It is an industry publication, so a specialist knowledge in the field of child care/youth guidance is essential for contributors.

## Zest

**National Magazine House, 72 Broadwick Street, London, W1F 9EP**

☎ 020 7439 5000
☎ 020 7437 6886
✉ zest.mail@natmags.co.uk

ⓦ www.zest.co.uk

**Parent Company** National Magazine Company

**Editor** Alison Pylkkanen

**Contact** Features Assistant, Zoe McDonald

**Established** 1994

**Insider Info** A monthly consumer magazine covering women's interests, health, beauty, diet and fitness. Present circulation of 98,347.

**Non-fiction** Publishes General interest articles aimed at women's lifestyle.

**Fiction** Publishes Short stories and articles of 50–2,000 words in length.

**Tips** *Zest* is targeted firmly at a female readership, and any story or article submissions must be written with this in mind, as well as being generally uplifting in tone.

## Zoo

**Mappin House, Winsley Street, London, W1W 8HF**

ⓞ 020 7295 8355

ⓞ 020 7182 8300

ⓔ info@zooweekly.co.uk, firstname.lastname@emap.com

ⓦ www.zooweekly.co.uk

**Parent Company** EMAP Plc

**Editor** Ben Todd

**Contact** Editorial Assistant, Jo Usmar; Features Editor, Matt Mason

**Established** 2004

**Insider Info** A weekly consumer magazine covering men's lifestyle topics. Present circulation of 204,564.

**Non-fiction** Publishes General Interest, Interviews, Reviews and Photo features on Celebrities, Fashion, Sport, Humour, Sex, Music, Television, Film and Real-life.

**Tips** The magazine is aimed at young men aged 16–30 and may contain mild adult content.

# UK & IRISH NATIONAL NEWSPAPERS

## The Business

Sir David and Sir Frederick Barclay

**292 Vauxhall Bridge Road, London, SW1V 1SS**

ⓞ 020 7961 0000

ⓞ 020 7961 0101

ⓔ newsdesk@thebusiness.press.net

ⓦ www.thebusinessonline.com

**Contact** Editor, Ian Watson; Editor in Chief, Andrew Neil

**Insider Info** A Sunday national newspaper which focuses on different aspects of business. Launched in 1998, it has a circulation of 136,620. Aimed primarily at business people and entrepreneurs aged 35 plus and working in London. Contact the relevant editor with ideas. Do not send unsolicited articles. Publishes a mixture of short news stories of 200 plus words and features, which are considerably longer. Payment varies from job to job.

**Tips** Browse their website for a breakdown of topics and features that *The Business* consider topical business news.

## Daily Express

Northern & Shell Media/Richard Desmond

**The Northern & Shell Building, 10 Lower Thames Street, London, EC3R 6EN**

ⓞ 0871 434 1010

ⓔ news.desk@express.co.uk

ⓦ www.express.co.uk

**Contact** Editor, Peter Hill; City Editor, Stephen Kahn; Deputy Editor, Hugh Whittlow; Diary Editor, Kathryn Spencer; Environment Editor, John Ingham; Features Editor, Greg Swift; News Editor, Heather Preen; Political Editor, Bill Bradshaw

**Insider Info** A daily tabloid, established in 1900. National and international news is covered, along with features on business and finance, entertainment and sport. Circulation of around 773,768. For features, write to the relevant department editor with an outline. There are quick links on the website to send ideas in. If you have a news story, call 0871 202982. Publishes features and news stories. Also publishes feature articles in its supplements. If you have a photograph relevant to a news story, call 0871 520 7171. Send mobile phone pictures by texting EXPRESS to 07843 500911. Email to expresspix@express.co.uk

**Tips** Although ideas are welcome, be aware that at a national newspaper, outlines from unknown writers will stand little chance of being commissioned.

## Daily Mail

Associated Newspapers/Lord Rothermere

**Northcliffe House, 2 Derry Street, London, W8 5TT**

ⓞ 020 7938 6000

ⓞ 020 7937 3251

ⓔ news@dailymail.co.uk

ⓦ www.dailymail.co.uk

**Contact** Editor, Paul Dacre; City Editor, Alex Brummer; Diary Editor, Richard Kay; Literary Editor,

Jane Mays; Money Editor, Tony Hazel; Political Editor, David Hughes; Political Editor, Heather McGlone

**Insider Info** Established in 1896, the Daily Mail now has a circulation of over two million. Its readership is primarily ABC1. Produced from Monday to Saturday. Phone or email with exclusive news. Most other material is written by known freelancers, or in-house staff. Publishes breaking news stories. There are regular columns on sport, showbiz, health, travel and money. Photographs relating to current news stories are welcome.

**Tips** The *Daily Mail* has a large readership and often takes a very particular stance on issues. Read several copies of the paper to get an idea of its style.

## Daily Mirror

Trinity Mirror plc

**1 Canada Square, Canary Wharf, London, E14 5AP**

- 020 7293 3000
- 020 7293 3409
- mirrornews@mirror.co.uk
- www.mirror.co.uk

**Contact** Editor, Richard Wallace; Business Editor, Clinton Manning; News Editor, Anthony Harwood

**Insider Info** Tabloid founded in 1903. Covers national and international news stories, with particular emphasis on entertainment, showbiz and sport. Publishes from Monday to Saturday. For current news stories, call 0800 282591. Call the 3am pages on 020 7293 3950 for showbiz stories. Unknown feature writers are unlikely to be published. Regularly features celebrity and gossip columns. For general news pictures email, picturedesk@mirror.co.uk

**Tips** The news stories can be heavily influenced by celebrity stories. Known tabloid freelancers stand a much better chance of being published than new writers.

## Daily Record

Trinity Mirror plc

**1 Central Quay, Glasgow, G3 8DA**

- 0141 309 3000
- 0141 309 3340
- reporters@dailyrecord.co.uk
- www.record-mail.co.uk

**Contact** Editor, Bruce Waddell; News Editor, Tom Hamilton; Features Editor, Melanie Harvey

**Insider Info** A Scottish tabloid, established in 1895. Circulation is around 407,212. It publishes from Monday to Saturday. Publishes some freelance material. Publishes a mixture of news and features.

**Tips** Articles of Scottish relevance are of particular interest.

## Daily Sport

Sport Newspapers

**19 Great Ancoats Street, Manchester, M60 4BT**

- 0161 236 4466
- 0161 236 4535
- www.dailysport.co.uk

**Contact** Editor, David Beevers; Editor in Chief, Tony Livesey; News Editor, Jane Field

**Insider Info** A daily tabloid, established in 1986 alongside its sister title, *The Sunday Sport*. The content tends to centre around female celebrities and models, humour and scandal. Circulation of around 300,000. Unsolicited material, which is relevant to the style of the paper will be accepted. Publishes fairly short articles, both news and features, often less than 1,000 words.

**Tips** The content and style of the paper is very specifically aimed at young men, so check the suitability of your work before submission.

## Daily Star

Northern & Shell Media/Richard Desmond

**The Northern & Shell Building, 10 Lower Thames Street, London, EC3R 6EN**

- 0871 434 1010
- news@dailystar.co.uk
- www.dailystar.co.uk

**Contact** Editor, Dawn Neesom; Deputy Editor, Jim Mansell

**Insider Info** Established in 1978, the *Daily Star* is published from Monday to Saturday. Stories tend to revolve around celebrities, sport, news and gossip. Circulation of around 750,374. Freelance payment can range from less than £100 for short articles, to upwards of £500 for double page spreads. Even more is paid for leading exclusives. Publishes big news exclusives, often celebrity interviews. The stance of the newspaper leans towards right wing. Publishes picture features.

**Tips** The content and style of the paper is very specifically aimed at young men, so check the suitability of your work before submission.

## Daily Star Sunday

Northern & Shell Media/Richard Desmond

**The Northern & Shell Building, 10 Lower Thames Street, London, EC3R 6EN**

- 0871 434 1010
- 0871 434 2941

@ news@dailystar.co.uk

@ www.dailystarsunday.co.uk

**Contact** Editor, Gareth Morgan; News Editor, Michael Booker

**Insider Info** Similar to the *Daily Star*, it is aimed at a young male readership. It offers sports, quirky stories and celebrity gossip. There are opportunities for freelance workers.

**Tips** Aim articles specifically towards the target audience.

## The Daily Telegraph
Sir David and Sir Frederick Barclay

**111 Buckingham Palace Road, London, SW1W 0DT**

@ 020 7538 5000

@ 020 7513 2506

@ dtnews@telegraph.co.uk

@ www.telegraph.co.uk

**Contact** Editor, Will Lewis; Deputy Editor, Ian MacGregor; Editor at Large, Jeff Randall; Assistant Editor, Andrew Pierce

**Insider Info** A broadsheet, containing in-depth national and international news, political and financial coverage, social issues, media, IT, jobs, travel, sport, arts and entertainment. Publication is from Monday to Saturday. The paper was founded in 1855, and now has a circulation of 899,493. The *Sunday Telegraph* is its sister newspaper. Articles on a wide range of subjects are considered. You need to show a very good understanding in the field you write about. However, few outside contributors are ever published.

**Tips** Make sure you are well informed about the area you are writing about.

## The Financial Times
Pearson PLC

**1 Southwark Bridge, London, SE1 9HL**

@ 020 7873 3000

@ 020 7873 3076

@ news.desk@ft.com

@ www.ft.com

**Contact** Editor, Lionel Barber; Consumer Industries Editor, Richard Tomkins

**Insider Info** Founded in 1888, *The Financial Times* is a broadsheet newspaper providing UK and international coverage of finance and business news. It also includes features on IT, national and international news, sport and entertainment. Readers tend to be high achievers in business and politics. Circulation of around 437,720. Accepts articles of financial, commercial, industrial and economic interest.

**Tips** It is worth bearing in mind they get less unsolicited contributions than any other national newspaper.

## The Guardian
The Scott Trust

**119 Farringdon Road, London, EC1R 3ER**

@ 020 7278 2332

@ 020 7837 2114

@ home@guardian.co.uk

@ www.guardian.co.uk

**Contact** Editor, Alan Rusbridger; Deputy Saturday Editor, Charlie English; Literary Editor, Claire Armitstead; Health Editor, Sarah Boseley; Deputy Travel Editor, Isabel Choat; Arts Editor, Melissa Denes

**Insider Info** *The Guardian* was founded in 1821. Published from Monday to Friday, it has a circulation of 365,635. Because of the specialised pages, freelancers have greater opportunities to get their work published. Work must be emailed in to the paper. Payment is from £271.05 per 1,000 words, unless special arrangements are made. News and feature pictures.

**Tips** For the best chance for your work to be chosen, research their specialised pages thoroughly. There is a freelance guide on their website with the necessary information.

## The Herald
Gannet UK Ltd

**200 Renfield Street, Glasgow, G2 3PR**

@ 0141 302 7000

@ 0141 302 7007

@ www.theherald.co.uk

**Contact** Editor, Charles McGhee

**Insider Info** Quality broadsheet, focused on Scottish news, with a mainly ABC1 readership. Circulation is 69,873.

## The Independent
Independent Newspapers

**Independent House, 191 Marsh Wall, London, E14 9RS**

@ 020 7005 2000

@ 020 7005 2999

@ newsdes@independent.co.uk

@ www.independent.co.uk

**Contact** Editor, Simon Kelnor; Features Editor, Ian Irvine; Deputy Political Editor, Chris Brown; Foreign Editor, Leonard Doyle; Media Editor, Ian Burrell;

Science Editor, Steve Conner; Picture Editor,
Lyn Cullen

**Insider Info** 1,300,000 readers. The paper is mainly
aimed at an intelligent ABC1 readership. Likes to
focus on the arts and culture. Appears to encourage
freelance contributions. However, a fee will not
always be paid for published work. Has regular
features on the arts, lifestyle, motoring, education
and book reviews.

**Tips** *The Independent* likes to receive work in hard
copy form. Further information for freelance writers
is on the website.

## The Independent on Sunday

Independent Newspapers

**Independent House, 191 Marsh Wall, London,
E14 9RS**

- 020 7005 2000
- 020 7005 2999
- www.independent.co.uk

**Contact** Editor, Tristan Davies; News Editor, Andy
Malone; Sports Editor, Simon Redfern; Literary Editor,
Suzi Feay; Arts Editor, Ian Irvine

**About** Quality Sunday paper, similar readership to
*The Independent*.

**Tips** *The Independent on Sunday* like to receive work
in hard copy form. Further information for freelance
writers is on the website.

## Irish Daily Star

Independent News and Media/Express
Newspapers Ltd

**Star House, 62a Terenure Road North, Dublin
6W, Republic of Ireland**

- 00353 1 490 1228
- 00353 1 490 2193
- info@therstar.ie
- www.thestar.ie

**Contact** Editor, Gerard Colleran

**Insider Info** A sports based paper, aimed at young
male readers. Call 00353 1 490 1228, if you
have a story.

**Tips** When writing, bear in mind the large male
readership of the paper.

## Irish Examiner

Thomas Crosbie Holdings

**The Irish Examiner, City Quarter, Lapps Quay,
Cork**

- 00353 21 427 2722
- 00353 21 427 5477
- name.surname@examiner.ie

- www.irishexaminer.com

**Contact** Editor, Tim Vaughn; Sports Editor, Tony
Leen; News Editor, John O'Mahony; Features Editor,
Joe Dermody

**Insider Info** A broadsheet with 259,000 adult
readers in Ireland. Covers national and international
news. In-depth coverage of sport, but also has
regular features on politics, health, business, finance,
and general topics of interest.

**Tips** Any correspondence should be via email.

## Irish Independent

**Independent House, 27–32 Talbot Street, Dublin
1, Republic of Ireland**

- 00353 1 705 5333
- 00353 1 872 0304
- info@independent.ie/independent.letters@
independent.ie
- www.independent.ie

**Contact** Editor, Gerard O'Regan; Business Editor,
Richard Curran; Deputy Editor, Michael Wolsey;
Features Editor, Peter Carvosso

**Insider Info** Focuses on topical news.

**Tips** Letters can be sent to the editor, via
independent.letters@independent.ie

## Irish Mail on Sunday

**Associated Newspapers Ltd, Embassy House,
Ballsbridge, Dublin 4, Republic of Ireland**

- 00353 1 637 5800
- 00353 1 637 5880
- news@irelandonsunday.com

**Contact** Editor, Paul Drury; Assistant Editor,
John Cooper

## Irish Times

**11–15 D'Olier Street, Dublin 2, Republic of
Ireland**

- 00353 1 675 8000
- 00353 1 675 8035
- www.ireland.com

**Contact** Editor, Geraldine Kennedy; Features Editor,
Sheila Wayman; News Editor, Miriam Donohoe;
Literary Editor, Caroline Walsh

## Mail on Sunday

Associated Newspapers/Lord Rothermere

**Northcliffe House, 2 Derry Street, London,
W8 5TS**

- 020 7938 6000

○ 020 7937 3829

○ news@mailonsunday.co.uk

○ www.mailonsunday.co.uk

**Contact** Editor, Peter Wright; News Editor, David Dillon; Features Editor, James Sian; Letters Editor, Dominic Connolly; Literary Editor, Susanna Gross

**Insider Info** Has a readership of 2,241,752. Deals with news media and current affairs. Feature writers are frequently used. Recurring features on travel, women's interest, health and entertainment. Has a colour supplement called *You*.

**Tips** Take advantage of any knowledge you have on their regular features.

## Morning Star

People's Press Printing Society

**William Rust House, 52 Beachy Road, London, E3 2NS**

○ 020 8510 0815

○ 020 8986 5694

○ newsed@peoples-press.com

○ www.morningstaronline.co.uk

**Contact** Editor, John Haylett; Features Editor, Richard Bagley; News Editor, Daniel Coysh; Arts Editor, Katie Gilmore; Sports Editor, Mark Barber

**Insider Info** Circulation is around 25,000. A socialist paper aimed at Labour supporters. There are opportunities for freelance writers, but to be considered stories need to take a left wing stance. Focuses on current affairs, politics and the Labour Party.

**Tips** Remember to take in to account the left wing views of the readership.

## News of the World

News International Plc

**1 Virginia Street, London, E98 1NW**

○ 020 7782 4000

○ 020 7583 9504

○ newsed@notw.co.uk

○ www.newsoftheworld.co.uk

**Contact** News Editor, Matt Nixon; Sunday Editor, Louise Oswald; Political Editor, Ian Kirby; Showbiz Editor, Rachel Richardson; Features Editor, Douglas Wight

**Insider Info** Circulation of 3,380,746. The paper was first published in 1843. It covers news, media and current affairs. Celebrity exposés are appreciated. Payment for stories varies according to importance and the position printed in the paper. Has regular celebrity gossip columns in their *Sunday* magazine. Photographs are welcome.

**Tips** Stories from outside the paper are welcome, but bear in mind the target audience enjoys celebrity gossip and breaking news. For more information on how to sell a story, see the website.

## The Observer

Guardian Newspapers Ltd

**3–7 Herbal Hill, London, EC15 5EJ**

○ 020 7278 2332

○ 020 7837 7817

○ reader@observer.co.uk

○ www.observer.co.uk

**Contact** Editor, Roger Alton; Arts Editor, Sarah Donaldson; Business Editor, Richard Wachman; Literary Editor, Robert McCrum

**Insider Info** The longest running Sunday national. Focuses in-depth on national and international news. It has a large readership of working women. Unusual for the paper to except freelance work. Includes special interest supplements, such as *Observer Food Monthly*, *Observer Women*, *Observer Sport Monthly*.

**Tips** Expertise in any of the supplement subjects will be an advantage.

## The People

Trinity Mirror plc

**1 Canada Square, Canary Wharf, London, E14 5AP**

○ 020 7293 3000

○ 020 7293 3571

○ peoplenews@mgn.co.uk

○ www.people.co.uk

**Contact** Editor, Mark Thomas; Deputy Editor, Ben Procter; Features Editor, Chris Bucktin; Investigations Editor, Roger Insall; Sports Editor, Lee Horton; Political Editor, Nigel Nelson

**Insider Info** Focuses on exclusives and celebrity stories. Uses investigative journalism. If you have a story, call 020 7293 3202. Has in-depth sports features. Stories can fetch high prices. Exclusives very welcome. Photographs are welcome, either send to pictures@people.co.uk, or ring 020 7293 3901.

**Tips** It is worth bearing in mind that popular stories are based around high profile celebrity gossip. Advice on selling stories can be found on the website.

## Scotland on Sunday

Scotsman Publications Ltd

**Barclay House, 108 Holyrood Road, Edinburgh, EH8 8AS**

○ 0131 620 8620
○ 0131 020 8491
○ newssos@scotlandonsunday.com
**Contact** Deputy Editor, Tim Little; Business Editor, Terry Murden; Travel Editor, Clair Trodden
**Insider Info** A popular Sunday broadsheet, which was first published in 1988. Features national and international news, and current affairs. To contact individual editors, use firstinitiallastame@scotsman.com. Articles appear on politics, finance, business and health. Has regular features such as reviews.
**Tips** The paper is aimed at a fairly intellectual reader. Scottish related work is welcome.

## The Scotsman
Scotsman Publications Ltd
**Barclay House, 108 Holyrood Road, Edinburgh, EH8 8AS**
○ 0131 620 8620
○ 0131 620 8616
○ newsdesk_ts@scotsman.com
**Contact** Editor, Mike Gilson; Assistant Editor, Lee David; Features Editor, Jackie Hunter; Business Editor, Nick Bevens; Foreign Editor, Rob Corbridge; Arts Editor, Andrew Eaton; News Editor, James Hall
**Insider Info** A quality paper focusing on news and current affairs. Established in 1817. There is a better chance of freelance work being published, than at other, similar papers. Regular articles on education, business, sport, and UK news, as well as Scottish news.
**Tips** Stories on topical issues are appreciated.

## Star Sunday
Independent News and Media/Express Newspapers Ltd
**Star House, 62a Terenure Road North, Dublin 6W, Republic of Ireland**
○ 00353 1 490 1228
○ 00353 1 490 1538
○ news.sunday@thestar.ie
○ www.thestar.ie
**Contact** Editor, Des Gibson
**Insider Info** Sports-based Sunday paper, aimed predominantly at young male readers.

## The Sun
News International plc
**1 Virginia Street, London, E1 9XP**
○ 020 7782 4000
○ 020 7782 4095
○ news@thesun.co.uk
○ www.thesun.co.uk
**Contact** Editor, Rebekah Wade; Deputy Editor, Fergus Shanahan; News Editor, Chris Pharo; Business Editor, Ian King; Features Editor, Ben Jackson; Women's Editor, Sally Brook
**Insider Info** Daily paper focusing on celebrity culture and popular news. The readership is fairly young. Freelance ideas and stories are accepted. Exposés can be highly paid. Large sports section and regular 'Page 3' feature aimed at male readers.
**Tips** Look for investigative journalism pieces. The links to send in a story are on the website.

## The Sunday Business Post
**80 Harcourt Street, Dublin 2, Republic of Ireland**
○ 00353 1 602 6000
○ 00353 1 679 6496/679 6498
○ sbpost@iol.ie
○ www.thepost.ie
**Contact** Editor, Cliff Taylor
**Insider Info** Sunday newspaper focusing on financial, political and economical news. Readership is largely those involved in making key business decisions. Freelance work is considered. Features articles on motoring and computers.
**Tips** It is important to show a good understanding of the area you choose to write about.

## Sunday Express
Northern & Shell Media/Richard Desmond
**10 Lower Thames Street, London, EC4R 6EN**
○ 0871 434 1010
○ 0871 434 7300
○ newsdesk@express.com
○ www.express.co.uk
**Contact** Editor, Martin Townsend; Assistant Editor, Jim Murrey; News Editor, Stephen Rigley; Business Editor, Lawrie Holmes; Political Editor, Jason Groves; Arts Editor, Rachel James
**Insider Info** Tabloid-style Sunday paper. Likes to feature stories on celebrities. To contact individual editors, use the email address, firstname.lastname@express.com. Regularly features celebrity exclusives and gossip columns.
**Tips** You will find links to sell stories through website. They are interested in fresh spins on popular culture and exposes. An investigative style of journalism is popular with the *Sunday Express*.

## Sunday Herald

Newsquest

**200 Renfield Street, Glasgow, G2 3QB**

☎ 0141 302 7800

☏ 0141 302 7815

✉ news@sundayherald.com

🌐 www.sundayherald.com

**Contact** Editor, Richard Walker; Deputy Editor, David Milne; Business Editor, Ken Symon; Political Editor, Paul Hutcheon; Sports Editor, Stephen Penham; Magazine Editor, Jane Wright; News Editor, Charlene Sweeney

**Insider Info** An award winning independent newspaper. Features national and international news. Favours stories of Scottish interest.

**Tips** The links to specific contacts are on the website.

## Sunday Independent

**27–32 Talbot Street, Dublin 1, Republic of Ireland**

☎ 00353 1 705 5333

☏ 00353 1 872 0304

✉ info@independent.ie, independent.letters@independent.ie

🌐 www.independent.ie

**Contact** Editor, Aengus Fanning; Business Editor, Shane Ross

**Insider Info** Popular Irish Sunday newspaper. Freelance work is considered. Published in five sections: News, Sport, Business, Property, and Living.

## Sunday Mail

Trinity Mirror plc

**1 Central Quay, Glasgow, G3 8DA**

☎ 0141 309 3000

✉ mailbox@sundaymail.co.uk

🌐 www.sundaymail.co.uk

**Contact** Editor, Allan Rennie; News Editor, Brendan McGinty; Deputy Editor, Jim Wilson; Showbiz Editor, Billy Sloan; Sports Editor, George Cheyne

**Insider Info** Scottish Sunday tabloid, which combines news, showbiz and current affairs. Contact individual editors by email using initial.lastname@sundaymail.co.uk. Payment for exclusives can be generous. Publishes a mixture of news and features. Has a supplement magazine called *7-Days*, edited by Liz Cowan.

**Tips** Exclusives, or articles of Scottish relevance are favoured.

## Sunday Mirror

Trinity Mirror plc

**1 Canada Square, Canary Wharf, London, E14 5AP**

☎ 020 7293 3000

☏ 020 7293 3939

✉ scoops@sundaymirror.co.uk

🌐 www.sundaymirror.co.uk

**Contact** Editor, Tina Weaver; Associate Editor, Nick Buckley; Deputy Editor, James Scott; News Editor, James Saville; Features Editor, Jill Main; Sports Editor, David Walker; Political Editor, Vincent Moss

**Insider Info** Sunday tabloid, which likes to cover big news scoops. To sell a story, call 0800 282591. Tip-offs and freelance work on exclusives can be highly paid. Articles on breaking news, entertainment, current affairs and sports. For sports stories, email sports@sundaymail.co.uk. Photograph exclusives are welcome. Photographs can be sent to 07921 688476.

**Tips** Stories are only welcome if they fit in with the style of the newspaper. A good knowledge of the paper and their readership is essential.

## Sunday Post

D.C Thompson & Co. Ltd

**144 Port Dundas Road, Glasgow, G4 0HZ**

☎ 0141 332 9933

☏ 0141 331 1595

✉ newsdesk@sundaypost.com

🌐 www.sundaypost.com

**Contact** Editor, David Pollington; News Editor, Colin Grant; Sports Editor, David Walker

**Insider Info** A Sunday paper, which focuses on news and topical interests. Freelance writers are considered. Articles include those on health and sport. A pull out magazine is also available.

**Tips** In order to be considered, you need to be highly knowledgeable about the subject you are writing about.

## Sunday Telegraph

Press Holdings Ltd

**111 Buckingham Palace Road, London, SW1W 0DT**

☎ 020 7931 2000

☏ 020 7513 2504

✉ stnews@telegraph.co.uk

🌐 www.telegraph.co.uk

**Contact** Editor, Patience Wheatcroft; Deputy Editor, Ian Martin; News Editor, Tim Wodward; Political

Editor, Patrick Hennessy; Literary Editor, Michael Prodger; Sports Editor, Jon Ryan

**Insider Info** Traditional quality broadsheet. Tends to have a slightly older readership. Freelance work is considered. Features about politics, national and international news, lifestyle and sports. Produces colour supplements.

**Tips** In order to be considered, you need to be highly knowledgeable on the subject you are writing about.

## The Sunday Times

News International Plc

**1 Virginia Street, London, E98 1ST**

☎ 020 7782 5000

☎ 020 7782 5731

✉ newsdesk@Sunday-times.co.uk

🌐 www.sunday-times.co.uk

**Contact** Editor, John Whitrow; Deputy Editor, Sian Griffiths; News Editor, Charles Hymas; Business Editor, John Waples; Political Editor, David Cracknell; Culture Editor, Helen Hawkins; Sports Editor, Alex Butler

**Insider Info** Quality broadsheet known for its investigative journalism and rebellious stance on issues. Aimed at an educated readership. Exclusives can reach high prices. Has a colour supplement containing lifestyle features.

**Tips** You will need an in-depth knowledge of your subject matter.

## The Sunday Times Scotland

News International plc

**124 Portman Street, Kinning Park, Glasgow, G41 1EJ**

☎ 0141 420 5100

☎ 0141 420 5262

✉ scotland@sundaytimes.co.uk

🌐 www.timesonline.co.uk

**Contact** Editor, Carlos Alba; Deputy Editor, Camillo Fracassini; Features Editor, Mike Wade; Business Editor, John Penman

**Insider Info** Scottish national broadsheet.

## The Times

News International plc

**1 Pennington Street, London, E98 1TT**

☎ 020 7782 5000

☎ 020 7782 5988

✉ home.news@thetimes.co.uk

🌐 www.thetimes.co.uk

**Contact** Editor, Robert Thompson; Deputy Editor, Ben Preston; Features Editor, Micheal Harvey; Business Editor, James Harding; Saturday Editor, George Brock; Arts Editor, Alex O'Connell; Overseas Editor, James Harding

**Insider Info** A broadsheet for 200 years, it recently switched to a more compact size in order to appeal to a younger audience. Readership consists largely of professionals. *The Times* is considered to have a right wing stance, but it has supported New Labour. All contact to be addressed to relevant desks, firstname.lastname@thetimes.co.uk. Has in-depth articles on national and international news, sport, finance and lifestyle.

**Tips** Take into account the paper's desire to appeal to a younger audience.

## Wales on Sunday

**Thompson House, Havelock Street, Cardiff, CF10 1XR**

☎ 029 2058 3733

☎ 029 2058 3725

✉ wosmail@wme.co.uk

🌐 www.icwales.co.uk

**Contact** Editor, Tim Gordon; Deputy Editor, Wayne Davies; News Editor, Laura Kemp; Features Editor, Rachel Mainwaring; Picture Editor, Rob Watkins

**Insider Info** National Welsh Sunday newspaper, with a circulation of around 44,591. To contact the paper with a story, call 029 2058 3733. Covers news sports and entertainment, mainly of Welsh importance.

**Tips** Welsh interest stories are preferable.

# UK & IRISH LOCAL NEWSPAPERS

## The Argus

**Argus House, Crowhurst Road, Hollingbury, Brighton, BN1 8AR**

☎ 01273 544544

☎ 01273 505703

✉ news@theargus.co.uk

🌐 www.theargus.co.uk

**Contact** Editor, Micheal Beard; News Editor, Melanie Downing

**Insider Info** Articles: Features on local homes, business, cars and lifestyle.

## The Bath Chronicle

Northcliffe Newspaper Group

**Windsor House, Windsor Bridge, Bath, Somerset, BA2 3AU**

- 01225 322322
- 01225 322291
- news@bathchron.co.uk
- www.bathchronicle.co.uk

**Contact** Editor, Sam Holliday; News Editor, Paul Wiltshire; Features Editor, Georgette McCready; Picture Editor, Kevin Bates; Sports Editor, Julie Riegal
**Insider Info** Established 1760.
**Tips** News and stories of local interest are very much favoured.

## Belfast Telegraph

Independent News and Media

**124–144 Royal Avenue, Belfast, BT1 1EB, Northern Ireland**

- 028 9026 4000
- 028 9055 4507
- newseditor@belfasttelegraph.co.uk
- www.belfasttelegraph.co.uk

**Contact** Editor, Martin Lindsay; News Editor, Henry Ronan; Deputy Editor, Paul Connelly; Business Editor, Nigel Tilson; Sports Editor, Steven Beacom
**Insider Info** A widely read daily paper, covering local, national and international news. Freelance work is considered. Has a wide ranging editorial coverage. Regular features appear on recruitment, property, motoring and business. For the *Community Telegraph*, focusing on localised news and events contact, victoriasloss@belfasttelegraph.co.uk.
**Tips** Ideally work should be connected with Northern Ireland.

## Birmingham Mail

**PO Box 78, Weaman Street, Birmingham, B4 6AY**

- 0121 236 3366
- 0121 233 0271
- www.icbirmingham.co.uk

**Contact** Editor, Steve Dyson; Head of News, Andy Richards; Deputy Editor, Carole Cole; Business Editor, Jon Griffin; Picture Editor, Steve Murphy
**Insider Info** Established in 1870. Contact the editor, steve_dyson@mrn.co.uk

## The Birmingham Post

**PO Box 78, Weaman Street, Birmingham, B4 6AY**

- 0121 236 3366
- 0121 625 1105
- postnewsdesk@mrn.co.uk
- www.icbirmingham.icnetwork.co.uk/birminghampost/

**Contact** Editor, Marc Reeves; News Editor, Mo Ilyas
**Insider Info** Quality paper covering news in the Midlands. Features on business and industry.
**Tips** An in-depth knowledge of subject you choose to write about is required.

## Blackpool Gazette

Blackpool Gazette and Herald Ltd

**Avroe House, Avroe Crescent, Blackpool Business Park, Squires Gate, Blackpool, Lancashire, FY4 2DP**

- 01253 361842
- editorial@blackpoolgazette.co.uk
- www.blackpooltoday.co.uk

**Contact** Editor, David Helliwell
**Insider Info** Covers local news, sport and entertainment. The links to email the appropriate editors are on website.
Photos: Photographs are accepted.

## Bolton News

**Newspaper House, Churchgate, Bolton, Lancashire, BL1 1DE**

- 01204 522345
- 01204 365068
- newsdesk@theboltonnews.co.uk
- www.thisisbolton.co.uk

**Contact** Editor, Steve Hughes; News Editor, James Higgins; Features Editor, Andrew Mosley; Picture Editor, Richard Rollon
**Insider Info** Established 1867. Contact the relevant editor with a story. Has pages on business, leisure, homes and jobs.

## Bristol Evening Post

**Temple Way, Bristol, Somerset, BS99 7HD**

- 0117 934 3000
- 0117 934 3575
- epnews@bepp.co.uk
- www.thisisbristol.co.uk

**Contact** Editor, Mike Norton; News Editor, Rob Perkins
**Insider Info** Established 1932.

## Burton Mail

Staffordshire Newspapers Ltd

**65–68 High Street, Burton on Trent, DE14 1LE**

- 01283 512345

**☎** 01283 515351
**✉** editorial@burtonmail.co.uk
**✇** www.burtonmail.co.uk
**Contact** Editor, Paul Headline; News Editor, Steve Doohan; Features Editor, Louise Elliot; Business Editor, Jonathan Horsfall; Picture Editor, Neil Barker
**Insider Info** Daily paper, with a circulation of 15,665.
 Articles: Has features on jobs, property and motors as well as entertainment and lifestyle.

## Cambridge Evening News
 Cambridge Newspapers Ltd
**Winshio Road, Milton, Cambridge, CB4 6PP**
**☎** 01223 434434
**☎** 01223 434415
**✉** newsdesk@cambridge-news.co.uk
**✇** www.cambridge-news.co.uk
**Contact** Editor, Murrey Morse; News Editor, John Deex; Features Editor, Paul Kirkley; Business Editor, Jenny Chapman; Sports Editor, Chris Gill; Picture Editor, Dave Harwood
**Insider Info** Covers local news, sports and entertainment.
 Articles: Magazine supplements include, *Style* magazine and *Our Time* magazine. Magazine Editor, 01223 434409.

## Camden New Journal
 New Journal Enterprises
**40 Camden Road, Camden Town, London, NW1 9DR**
**☎** 020 7419 9000
**☎** 020 7209 1322
**✉** editorial@camdennewjournal.co.uk
**✇** www.thecnj.com
**Contact** Editor, Eric Gordon; Deputy Editor, Andrew Johnson
**Insider Info** A free, independent newspaper covering the London Borough of Camden, borne out of a strike in the 1980s.
 Articles cover local and national news, health, events and sport.
**Tips** The newspaper is known for its investigative journalism and high news content, both local and national.

## Chester Chronicle
 Trinity Mirror Cheshire
**Chronicle House, Commonhall Street, Chester, Cheshire, CH1 2AA**
**☎** 01244 340151
**☎** 01244 606498

**✉** newsroom@cheshirenews.co.uk, firstname.lastname@cheshirenews.co.uk
**✇** www.iccheshireonline.co.uk
**Contact** Editor, Eric Langton; Deputy Editor, Michael Green; Picture Editor, Haydn Inall; Sports Editor, David Triggs
**Insider Info** Established in 1775. There are localised versions of the paper for separate areas, these include: *Chester City and Country* editions, and *Chronicles* for Wirral, Frodsham and Helsby, Deeside, Flint and Holywell and Mold and Buckley.
 Articles: Articles include local news, sport and events. *The Guide*, a supplement, contains features on arts and entertainment.

## Chronicle and Echo (Northampton)
 Northamptonshire Newspapers Ltd
**Upper Mounts, Northampton, DE1 3HR**
**☎** 01604 467000
**☎** 01604 467190
**✉** editor@northantsnews.co.uk
**✇** www.northamptonchron.co.uk
**Contact** Editor, Mark Edwards; News Editor, Richard Edmonson; Deputy Editor, Graham Tebbutt; Picture Editor, Tracey Chambers; Literary Editor, Vaughan Tucker
**Insider Info** Established in 1931.
 Articles: Supplements include *Sport on Monday*, *Term Time*, *Property Today*, *Jobs Today*, *The Guide* and *Weekend Life*.
 Photos: Email photographs to, editor@ northantsnews.co.uk

## The Citizen
**6–8 The Oxbode, Gloucester, GL1 1R5**
**☎** 01452 420621
**☎** 01452 420664
**✉** citizen.news@glosmedia.co.uk
**✇** www.thisisgloucestershire.co.uk
**Contact** Editor, Ian Mean
**Insider Info** A daily paper which covers the western side of Gloucester.

## Cornish Guardian Series
 Cornwall and Devon Media Ltd
**30 Fore Street, Bodmin, Cornwall, PL31 2HQ**
**☎** 01276 76815
**☎** 01726 69694
**✉** cgedit@c-dm.co.uk, cgsport@c-dm.co.uk, firstinitiallastmane@c-dm.co.uk
**✇** www.thisiscornwall.co.uk

**Contact** Editor, Jeremy Ridge; Community Editor, Richard Whitehouse; Community Editor, Sarah Carey; Book Review/Local News Editor, Julia Bryan
**Insider Info** Established in 1901. Publishes eight weekly editions, including St. Austell, Newquay, Lostwithiel and Fowey, Bodmin, Wadebridge, Camelford, Launceston and Bude, and Liskeard. Combined circulation is around 37,332. Email the news or sports desk with stories.
  Articles focus on local and regional news, sport and features.
**Tips** For contact details of individual local editions, visit the website. Bear in mind that a majority of the readership will live in rural or semi-rural locations.

## The Courier and Advertiser
  D.C Thompson and Co. Ltd
**80 Kingsway East, Dundee, DD4 8SL**
- 01382 223131
- 01382 454590
- courier@dcthompson.co.uk
- www.thecourier.co.uk
**Contact** Editor, Bill Hutcheon; Deputy Editor, Jim Allison; News Editor, Arliss Rhind; Features Editor, Catriona McInnes; Sports Editor, Graeme Dey
**Insider Info** Covers local news and sport across Tayside and Fife.
  Articles: Regular feature pages on health, fashion, motors and art.

## Coventry Evening Telegraph
**Corporation Street, Coventry, CV1 1FP**
- 024 7663 3633
- 024 7655 0869
- news@coventry-telegraph.co.uk
- www.go2coventry.co.uk
**Contact** Editor, Alan Kirby
**Insider Info** Local tabloid paper.
  Articles: Supplements include *What's On*, a weekly entertainment guide.

## Daily Echo
**Richmond Hill, Bournemouth, Dorset, BH2 6HH**
- 01202 5546001
- 01202 551246
- newsdesk@bournemouthecho.co.uk
- www.thisisbournemouth.co.uk
**Contact** Editor, Neal Butterworth; Features Editor, Kevin Nash
**Insider Info** Circulation of 34,324. Freelance news and feature articles are considered.

## Derby Evening Telegraph
  Northcliffe Newspaper Group
**Northcliffe House, Meadow Road, Derby, DE1 2DW**
- 01332 291111
- newsdesk@derbytelegraph.co.uk
- www.thisisderbyshire.co.uk
**Contact** Editor, Steve Hill; Deputy Editor, Neil White; News Editor, Cheryl Hague; Features Editor, Jill Gallone; Political Editor, Paul Watson
**Insider Info** Circulation of around 47,406. Contact an individual using this formula, firstinitiallastname@derbytelegraph.co.uk

## Dorset Echo
**Newscom, Fleet House, Weymouth, Dorset, DT4 9XD**
- 01305 830930
- 01305 830956
- newsdesk@dorsetecho.co.uk
- www.dorsetecho.co.uk
**Contact** Editor, David Murdock; News Editor, Paul Thomas; Features Editor, Diarmuid MacDonagh; Picture Editor, Geoff Moore; Sports Editor, Nigel Dean
**Insider Info** Evening paper. Contact the news desk on 01305 830999 if you have a story.

## Dundee Evening Telegraph and Post
  D.C Thompson and Co. Ltd
**80 Kingsway East, Dundee, DD4 8SL**
- 01382 223131
- 01382 454590
- newsdesk@eveningtelegraph.co.uk
- www.eveningtelegraph.co.uk
**Contact** Editor, Gordon Wishart; Deputy/Features Editor, Philip Smith; News Editor, Elaine Harrison; Sports Editor, Ian Duncan
**Insider Info** Local news and sport coverage for Tayside, Dundee and Fife.

## East Anglian Daily Times
**Press House, 30 Lower Brook Street, Ipswich, IP4 1AN**
- 01473 230023
- 01473 324776
- news@eadt.co.uk
- www.eadt.co.uk
**Contact** Editor, Terry Hunt; Business/Agricultural Editor, Duncan Brodie; Features Editor, Julian Ford;

News Editor, Brad Jones; Political Editor, Graham Dines

**Insider Info** Founded in 1884, it covers full range of local, national, and international news and sport.
Insider info: News stories should be sent to the news desk via email, or text to 84070 starting the message with EADT.
Articles: Regular lifestyle and entertainment supplements.
Photos: Photographs are considered.
**Tips** Local interest stories are well received.

## Eastern Daily Press
Archant Regional
**Prospect House, Rouen Road, Norwich, NR1 1RE**
❶ 01603 628311
❶ 01603 612930
✉ edpnewsdesk@archant.co.uk
🌐 www.edp24.co.uk
**Contact** Editor, Peter Franzen OBE
**Insider Info** A daily paper, which likes to centre on the local community.
Articles: Covers news, business, lifestyle and entertainment.
**Tips** Information on getting started in journalism is on the website, which has good key advice.

## The Echo
**Newspaper House, Chester Hall Lane, Basildon, Essex, SS14 3BL**
❶ 0844 477 4512
❶ 0844 477 4286
✉ echonews@nqe.com
🌐 www.echo-news.co.uk
**Contact** Editor, Martin McNeill; Features Editor, Claire Borley; Sports Editor, Paul Alton
**Insider Info** Daily paper. Founded in 1969.

## Evening Chronicle
Trinity Mirror Plc
**Groat Market, Newcastle upon Tyne, NE1 1ED**
❶ 0191 232 7500
❶ 0191 232 2256
✉ ec.news@ncjmedia.co.uk
🌐 www.icnewcastle.co.uk
**Contact** Editor, Paul Robertson; News Editor, James Marley; Features Editor, Jennifer Bradbury; Picture Editor, Rod Wilson; Sports Editor, Paul New; Political Editor, Peter Young
**Insider Info** Covers a mix of local news, sport and entertainment.

## Evening Courier
**PO Box 19, Kings Cross Street, Halifax, HX1 2SF**
❶ 01422 260200
❶ 01422 260341
✉ newsdesk@halifaxcourier.co.uk
🌐 www.halifaxcourier.co.uk
**Contact** Editor, John Furbisher; News Editor, Geoff Fox
**Insider Info** Founded in 1937.
Articles: Guides to local entertainment and events.
**Tips** Local interest stories are considered.

## Evening Echo (Cork)
Evening Echo Publications Ltd
**1–6 Academy Street, Cork, Republic of Ireland**
❶ 00353 21 427 2722
❶ 00353 21 480 2135
✉ firstname.lastname@eecho.ie
🌐 www.eveningecho.ie
**Contact** Editor, Maurice Gubbins; News Editor, Emma Connolly; Features Editor, John Dolan; Sports Editor, Eamon Murphey; Pictures Editor, Brian Lougheed
**Insider Info** Covers in-depth local news, national news and sports.
Articles: Regular features on local community news.
**Tips** Individual contact details can be found on the website.

## Evening Express
Scotsman Publications Ltd
**PO Box 43, Lang Stracht, Mastrick, Aberdeen, AB15 6DF**
❶ 01224 690222
❶ 01224 699575
✉ ee.news@ajl.co.uk
🌐 www.thisisaberdeen.co.uk
**Contact** Editor, Damien Bates; Deputy Editor, Richard Prest; News Editor, Louise Redvers; Picture Editor, Alan Paterson; Sports Editor, Charlie Allen
**Insider Info** Covers local, national and international news. If you have a news story, call 01224 344150. Additional contacts are on the website.

## Evening Gazette
Trinity Mirror Plc
**Borough Road, Middlesbrough, TS1 3AZ**
❶ 01642 245401
❶ 01642 232014
✉ newsdesk@eveninggazette.co.uk
🌐 www.gazettelive.co.uk

**Contact** Editor, Darren Thwaites; News Editor, Jim Horsley; Sports Editor, Philip Tallentire
**Insider Info** Popular daily paper providing coverage for the Tees Valley area. Freelance work is considered.
**Tips** Work of local interest is popular.

## Evening Gazette (Colchester)
Newsquest Ltd
**43 North Hill, Colchester, Essex, CO1 1TZ**
☎ 01206 506000
🖷 01206 508274
✉ gazette_newsdesk@nqe.com,firstname.lastname@nqe.com
🌐 www.gazette-news.co.uk
**Contact** Editor, Irene Kettle; Group News Editor, Sally Teatheredge; Head of Features, Iris Clapp; Deputy News Editor, Wendy Brading
**Insider Info** Established in 1970. A paid for local paper, with a circulation of around 24,000. Articles cover regional news, current affairs and features, as well as entertainment and sport.

## Evening Herald
Independent News and Media
**27–32 Talbot Street, Dublin 1, Republic of Ireland**
🌐 www.evening-herald.ie

## Evening Herald (Plymouth)
Northcliffe Newspaper Group
**17 Brest Road, Derriford Business Park, Plymouth, Devon, PL6 5AA**
☎ 01752 765500
🖷 01752 765527
✉ newsdesk@eveningherald.co.uk
🌐 www.thisisplymouth.co.uk
**Contact** Editor, Bill Martin; News Editor, James Garnett
**Insider Info** Local interest stories are considered.

## Evening News
Archant Ltd
**Prospect House, Rouen Road, Norwich, NR1 1RE**
☎ 01603 628311
🖷 01603 219060
✉ eveningnews@archant.co.uk
🌐 www.eveningnews24.co.uk
**Contact** Editor, David Bourn; Deputy Editor, Tim Williams; News Editor, Tim Hawkins; Features Editor, Derek James; Picture Editor, Nolan Lincoln

**Insider Info** Combines a mix of news and information on the local area. If you have a story call the News Editor on 01603 772443.
**Tips** Interested in stories about local communities or individuals.

## Evening News (Edinburgh)
**108 Holyrood Road, Edingburgh, EH8 8AS**
☎ 0131 620 8620
🖷 0131 620 8696
✉ news_en@scotsman.com
🌐 www.edinburghnews.co.uk
**Contact** Editor, John McLellan; News Editor, Euan McGrory; Picture Editor, Roger Johnathan; Business Editor, Jim Stanton; Sports Editor, Graham Lindsay
**Insider Info** Covers local, national, and international news.
 Articles: Regular features on business, health, politics and entertainment.

## Evening News (Scarborough)
**17–23 Aberdeen Walk, Scarborough, Yorkshire, YO11 1BB**
☎ 01723 383817
✉ newsdesk@yrnltd.co.uk
🌐 www.scarborougheveningnews.co.uk
**Contact** Editor, Ed Asquith

## Evening Standard
Associated Newspapers Ltd
**Northcliffe House, 2 Derry Street, London, W8 5EE**
☎ 020 7938 6000
✉ news@standard.co.uk
🌐 www.thisislondon.co.uk
**Contact** Editor, Veronica Wadley; News Editor, Hugh Dougherty; Features Editor, Simon Davis; Picture Editor, David Olfield; Sports Editor, Martin Chilton; Arts Editor, Fiona Hughs
**Insider Info** Tabloid sized paper delivering people in London coverage of city news, sport and lifestyle. National and international news is also covered.
 Articles: Has regular guides to what's on in London, arts and reviews. Weekly colour supplements are *ES Magazine* and *Homes and Property*.
**Tips** Good chances of getting published if the work is of local importance.

## Express & Echo
**Heron Road, Sowton, Exeter, Devon, EX2 7NF**
☎ 01392 442211

● 01392 442294/442287
◉ echonews@expressandecho.co.uk
◉ www.thisisexeter.co.uk
**Contact** Editor, Marc Astley; News Editor, Sue Kemp; Picture Editor, James Millar; Features Editor, Lynne Turner; Content Editor, Patrick Phelvin
**Insider Info** Daily paper covering local news and sport for Exeter and the surrounding areas.
 Articles: Regular supplements on property, jobs, business and motoring.

## Express & Star
**51–53 Queen Street, Wolverhampton, WV1 1ES**
● 01902 313131
● 01902 319721
◉ newsdesk@expressandstar.co.uk
◉ www.expressandstar.co.uk
**Contact** Editor, Adrian Faber; Deputy Editor, Keith Harrison; Features/Lifestyle Editor, Emma Farmer
**Insider Info** Founded in the 1880s. The *Express and Star* is the biggest selling regional evening newspaper.
 Articles: Covers local news and events.
 Photos: Send Photographs to, internet@expressandstar.co.uk

## Glasgow Evening Times
**200 Renfield Street, Glasgow, G2 3PR**
● 0141 302 7000
● 0141 302 6600
◉ times@eveningtimes.co.uk
◉ www.eveningstar.co.uk
**Contact** Editor, Donald Martin; News Editor, Hugh Boag
**Insider Info** One of Scotland's best selling newspapers. It provides in-depth coverage of local news and sport.

## Gloucestershire Echo
**1 Clarence Parade, Cheltenham, Gloucestershire, GL50 3NY**
● 01242 271900
● 01242 271848
◉ editor@glosecho.co.uk
◉ www.thisisgloucestershire.co.uk
**Contact** Editor, Anita Syvret; Features Editor, Tanya Gedhill
**Insider Info** Established in 1873.
**Tips** Local stories are considered.

## Grimsby Telegraph
**80 Cleethorp Road, Grimsby, Lincolnshire, DN31 3EH**
● 01472 360360
● 01472 372257
◉ newsdesk@grimsbytelegraph.co.uk
◉ www.thisisgrimsby.co.uk
**Contact** Editor, Michelle Lalor; News Editor, Lucy Wood
**Insider Info** Established in 1897.

## Guernsey Press and Star
**PO Box 57, Braye Road, Guernsey, Vale, GY1 3BW**
● 01481 240240
● 01481 240235
◉ newsroom@guernsey-press.co.uk
◉ www.guernseypress.co.uk
**Contact** Editor, Richard Digard; News Editor, Paul Baker; Features Editor, Di Digard; Sports Editor, Robert Batiste
**Insider Info** A popular tabloid paper, which covers local news and sport. The main readership is aged between 35 to 64. Letters and commentaries about local issues are invited.
 Articles: Has in-depth coverage of local financial and commercial news. Supplements include, motoring, property, finance, personal finance, leisure, boating and Christmas specials.

## Hartlepool Mail
 Johnston Press
**New Clarence House, Wesley Square, Hartlepool, TS24 8BX**
● 01429 239333
● 01429 869024
◉ mail.news@north-eastpress.co.uk
◉ www.hartlepooltoday.co.uk
**Contact** Editor, Joy Yates; Deputy Editor, Brian Nuttney; News Editor, Peter McCusker; Sports Editor, Roy Kelly
**Insider Info** Founded in 1849. Delivers local news and sport to Hartlepool and the surrounding area. Contact links can be found on the website.

## Herald Express
**Harmsworth House, Barton Hill Road, Torquay, Devon, TQ2 8JN**
● 01803 676223
● 01803 676228
◉ newsdesk@heraldexpress.co.uk

● www.thisissouthdevon.co.uk

**Contact** Editor, Andy Phelan; Sports Editor, Chris Clarke

**Insider Info** Circulation of around 25,971. The paper covers local news and sport for Torquay and surrounding areas.

**Tips** Interested in work that reflects the life of the local communities.

## The Huddersfield Daily Examiner

**PO Box A29, Queen Street South, Huddersfield, HD1 2DT**

● 01484 430000

● 01484 437789

● editorial@examiner.co.uk

● www.examiner.co.uk

**Contact** Editor, Roy Wright; News/Picture Editor, Neil Atkinson

**Insider Info** First published in 1871.

## Hull Daily Mail

**Blundells Corner, Beverly Road, Hull, HU3 1XS**

● 01482 327111

● 01482 315353

● news@hdmp.co.uk

● www.thisishullandeastriding.co.uk

**Contact** Editor, John Meehan; News Editor, Paul Baxter

**Insider Info** Local sport and news for Hull and the surrounding areas.

## Inverness Courier

**New Century House, Stadium Road, Inverness, IV1 1FF**

● 01463 233059

● 01463 243439

● editorial@inverness-courier.co.uk

● www.inverness-courier.co.uk

**Contact** Editor, Robert Taylor; News Editor, Olivia Bell

**Insider Info** Local paper covering much of the Highlands.

**Tips** Welcome stories of local public interest, current or historical.

## Irish News

Irish News Ltd

**113–117 Donegall Street, Belfast, BT1 2GE, Northern Ireland**

● 028 9032 2226

● 028 9033 7505

● newsdesk@irishnews.com

● www.irishnews.com

**Contact** Editor, Noel Doran; Features Editor, Joanna Branif; News Editor, Billy Foley; Business Editor, Gary McDonald; Picture Editor, Ann McManus; Sports Editor, Thomas Hawkins

**Insider Info** Regarded as a quality paper, it covers local and national news and sport. Founded in 1891. Insider info: Freelance work is considered. Articles: Has in-depth coverage of Gaelic sport. Supplements include, *Jobs on Thursday*, *Scene*, *Business Insight*, *Women Talk*, *Weekend* and *Drive*.

**Tips** Work should be sent to the appropriate department, details are on the website.

## Jersey Evening Post

**PO Box 582, Five Oaks, Jersey, St Savior, JE4 8XQ**

● 01534 611611

● 01534 611622

● editorial@jerseyeveningpost.com

● www.thisisjersey.com

**Contact** Editor, Chris Bright; Features Editor, Carl Walker; Business Editor, Christine Herbert; Sports Editor, Ron Felton; Pictures Editor, Peter Mourant

**Insider Info** Established in 1890, the Jersey Evening Post has 73 per cent of Jersey's adult readership. Articles: Regular features include, property, business, food and drink, farming and careers.

## The Journal

**Groat Market, Newcastle upon Tyne, NE1 1ED**

● 0191 232 7500

● 0191 201 6044

● jnl.newsdesk@ncjmedia.co.uk

● www.icnewcastle.co.uk

**Insider Info** Correspondence is welcomed, email the editor, letters@nwemail.co.uk Articles: Regular articles on local jobs, property and entertainment.

## Kent Messenger

Kent Messenger Group

**6–7 Middle Road, Maidstone, ME14 1TG**

● 01622 695666

● 01622 757227

● messengernews@thekmgroup.co.uk

● www.kentonline.co.uk

**Contact** Editor, Bob Bounds; Business Editor, Trevor Sturgess; News Editor, Nikki White; Political Editor, Paul Francis; Travel Editor, Dave Barlow

**Insider Info** Circulation of 110,182.

## Lancashire Evening Post

**Oliver's Olace, Eastway, Fulwood, Preston, Lancashire, PR2 9NZ**

- 01772 254841
- 01772 204941
- lep.newsdesk@lep.co.uk
- www.lep.co.uk

**Contact** Editor, Simon Reynolds; Features Editor, Peter Richardson; Sports Editor, Peter Storey

**Insider Info** Covers local news, sport and entertainment for Lancashire.

## Lancashire Evening Telegraph

**Newspaper House, High Street, Blackburn, Lancashire, BB1 1HT**

- 01254 678678
- 01254 680429
- let.editorial@lancashire.newsquest.co.uk
- www.thisislancashire.co.uk

**Contact** Editor, Kevin Young; Deputy Editor, Alan Simpson; Features Editor, John Anson; Picture Editor, Neil Johnson; Sports Editor, Paul Plunkett

**Insider Info** Well established tabloid, which provides local and national news to East Lancashire.

**Tips** Local news is favoured.

## The Leicester Mercury

Northcliffe Newspaper Group

**St. George Street, Leicester, LE1 9FQ**

- 0116 251 2512
- 0116 253 0645
- newsdesk@leicestermercury.co.uk
- www.thisisleicestershire.co.uk

**Contact** Editor, Nick Carter; News Editor, Mark Charlton; Features Editor, Alex Dawson

**Insider Info** Covers local news, sports and entertainment. If you have a story, email the news desk.

**Tips** Good contact links on the web page.

## Lincolnshire Echo

**Brayford Wharf East, Lincoln, Lincolnshire, LN5 7AT**

- 01522 820000
- 01522 804493
- news@lincolnshireecho.co.uk
- www.thisislincolnshire.co.uk

**Contact** Editor, Jon Grubb; News Editor, Mel West; Features Editor, Sarah Overton; Sports Editor, Jo Halpin; Deputy Editor, Martin Mammett

**Insider Info** Circulation of 25,560.

**Tips** The specific target areas for this newspaper, as well as Scunthorpe itself, are Barton upon Humber, Brigg, Epworth, Crowle and Messingham.

## Liverpool Daily Post

**PO Box 48, Old Hall Street, Liverpool, L69 3EB**

- 0151 227 2000
- 0151 472 2474
- andykelly@dailypost.co.uk
- www.liverpooldailypost.co.uk

**Contact** Editor, Mark Thomas; News Editor, Andrew Kelly; Picture Editor, Stephen Shakeshaft; Sports Editor, Richard William

**Insider Info** Covers local news and sport.
Articles: Regular features on local lifestyle and entertainment.

## Liverpool Echo

**PO Box 48, Old Hall Street, Liverpool, L69 3EB**

- 0151 227 2000
- 0151 272 2474
- www.icliverpool.co.uk

**Contact** Editor, Alistair Machray; News Editor, Alison Gow; Picture Editor, Stephen Shakeshaft; Arts Editor, Joe Riley; Sports Editor, John Thompson

**Insider Info** Popular local paper consisting of local news and sport. Circulation is around 121,517. Contact the editor on 0151 472 2507, but send ideas in writing first.

## Manchester Evening News

**1 Scott Place, Hardman Street, Manchester, M3 3RN**

- 0161 832 7200
- 0161 834 3814
- newsdesk@men-news.co.uk
- www.manchesteronline.co.uk

**Contact** Editor, News Editor; Sarah Lester, Features Editor; Deanna Delamotta, Showbiz Editor; Diane Bourne, Picture Editor; John Jaffay

**Insider Info** A leading regional paper with over half its readers between the ages of 15 to 44. Stories can be sent to the appropriate email addresses. These can all be found on the website.

Articles: Regular features such as: *Property World*, *Lifestyle*, *Go*, *Go Family* and *Business*. Articles should really be no more than 1,000 words.

## Medway Messenger

**Medway House, Ginsbury Close, Sir Thomas Longley Lane, Strood, Kent, ME2 2DU**

● 01634 227834

● 01634 715256

✉ medwaymessenger@thekmgroup.co.uk

🌐 www.kentonline.co.uk

**Contact** Editor, Bob Dimond; News Editor, Sarah Clarke; Picture Editor, Barry Hollis

**Insider Info** A twice weekly paper, which publishes local news and sport.

## News Letter
### Metro Building, Portadown, Belfast, Northern Ireland

● 028 9089 7700

● 028 3839 3941

✉ newsdesk@newsletter.co.uk

🌐 www.newsletter.co.uk

**Contact** Editor, Darwin Templeton; News Editor, Steven Moore; Business Editor, Adrienne McGill; Political Editor, Stephen Dempster; Sports Editor, Brian Millar; Arts Editor, Philip Crossey

**Insider Info** A well established paper which has been in publication since 1737. Covers national and international news. The paper can be approached with ideas and comments through its website. Articles: Regular colour supplements. Features include, lifestyle, motoring and health.

## The News (Portsmouth)
### The News Centre, Hilsea, Portsmouth, PO2 9SX

● 023 9266 4488

● 023 9267 6363

✉ newsdesk@thenews.co.uk

🌐 www.thenews.co.uk

**Contact** Editor, Mike Gilson; Business Editor, Jeremy Dunning; Features Editor, Graeme Patfield

**Insider Info** A daily tabloid established in 1877. The paper appeals to the cross section of the community. It has in-depth coverage of local news.

**Tips** Changed from broadsheet to tabloid recently, in order to appeal to a younger audience.

## The Northern Echo
### PO Box 14, Priestgate, Darlington, Co. Durham, DL1 1NF

● 01325 381313

● 01325 380539

✉ echo@nne.co.uk

🌐 www.thisisthenortheast.co.uk

**Contact** Editor, Peter Barron; News Editor, Nigel Burton; Deputy Editor, Chris Lloyd; Business Editor, Kate Bowman; Sports Editor, Nick Loughlin

## North-West Evening Mail
### Newspaper House, Abbey Road, Barrow in Furness, LA14 5QS

● 01229 821835

● 01229 840164

✉ news@nwemail.co.uk

🌐 www.nwemail.co.uk

**Contact** Editor, Steve Brauner; News Editor, Jon Townsend; Features Editor, Peter Leach; Sports Editor, Frank Cassidy

**Insider Info** Covers sport and news for the North East region of England. Stories welcome, contact the news desk.

**Tips** The paper likes stories relevant to the local area area.

## Nottingham Evening Post
Northcliffe Newspaper Group
### Castle Wharf House, Nottingham, NG1 7EU

● 0115 948 2000

● 0115 964 4032

✉ newsdesk@nottinghameveningpost.co.uk

🌐 www.thisisnottingham.co.uk

**Contact** Editor, Malcolm Pheby; News Editor, Steven Fletcher

**Insider Info** Founded in 1778, the paper now has a circulation of 65,623. Send stories or ideas to the news desk.

**Tips** Focus on local interests.

## Oldham Evening Chronicle
### PO Box 47, Union Street, Oldham, Lancashire, OL1 1EQ

● 0161 633 2121

● 0161 652 2111

✉ news@oldham-chronicle.co.uk

🌐 www.oldham-chronicle.co.uk

**Contact** Editor, Jim Williams; News Editor, Mike Attenborough; Deputy Editor, David Whaley; Business Editor, Martyn Torr; Picture Editor, Vincent Brown

**Insider Info** Family owned newspaper, covering news in Oldham.

**Tips** Local news articles are most popular with their readership.

## Oxford Mail
### Newspaper House, Osney Mead, Oxford, OX2 0EJ

● 01865 425262

● 01865 425554

○ nqonews@nqo.com

ⓦ www.thisisoxfordshire.co.uk

**Contact** Editor, Simon O'Neil; News Editor, Jason Collie

**Insider Info** Daily paper.

## Paisley Daily Express

Scottish and Universal Newspapers Ltd

**14 New Street, Paisley, Renfrewshire, PA1 1YA**

❶ 0141 887 7911

❶ 0141 887 6254

○ pde@s-un.co.uk

ⓦ www.insidescotland.co.uk

**Contact** News/Features Editor, Anne Dalrymple

**Insider Info** Local coverage of news, sports and features. Freelance material is considered.

**Tips** Only considered if work is about local interests, or communities.

## Peterborough Evening Telegraph

**57 Priestgate, Peterborough, PE1 1JW**

❶ 01733 555111

❶ 01733 313417

○ news@peterboroughtoday.co.uk

ⓦ www.peterboroughtoday.co.uk

**Contact** Editor, Rebecca Stephens; News Editor, Rose Taylor; Features Editor, Jemma Walton; Picture Editor, Rowland Hobson; Sports Editor, Bob French

**Insider Info** Peterborough's number one newspaper, covers local news, sport and community. To contact with a story, call 01733 588713 or send an email. Email formula is, firstname.lastname@peterboroughtoday.co.uk

Photos: Photographs are welcome.

## The Press

**PO Box 29, 76–86 Walmgate, York, Yorkshire, YO1 9YN**

❶ 01904 653051

❶ 01904 612853

○ newsdesk@ycp.co.uk, features@ycp.co.uk, ron.godfrey@ycp.co.uk

ⓦ www.thisisyork.co.uk

**Contact** Editor, Kevin Booth; Business Editor, Ron Godfrey

**Insider Info** Covers a large area of North and East Yorkshire, based around York. Known as a campaigning, community newspaper. Strong coverage of business and commerce in York, as well as around North and East Yorkshire. For business ideas, contact the Business Editor.

Photos: For photographs, contact the picture desk at photographers@ycp.co.uk

**Tips** Readers letters are always welcome, but those under 300 words are more likely to be published. Email letters@ycp.co.uk and include your full postal address.

## The Press and Journal

D.C Thompson and Co. Ltd

**Lang Stracht, Aberdeen, AB15 6DF**

❶ 01224 343311

❶ 01224 663575

○ pj-editor@ajl.co.uk

ⓦ www.thisisnorthscotland.co.uk

**Contact** Editor

**Insider Info** Circulation is across a large area of North Scotland.

Articles: Monthly supplements, *Your Car*, *Your Job*, *Your Home*. Weekly lifestyle magazine, *Your Life*.

**Tips** Interesting quirky local stories or ideas are well received.

## Reading Evening Post

**8 Tessa Road, Reading, Berkshire, RG1 8NS**

❶ 0118 918 3000

❶ 0118 959 9363

○ editorial@reading-epost.co.uk

ⓦ www.getreading.co.uk

**Contact** Editor, Andy Murril; News Editor, Lucy Allen; Features Editor, Maria Brunsdun; Picture Editor, Steve Templeton; Sports Editor, Dave Wright

**Insider Info** The only daily paper to cover Reading and the surrounding areas. Very much a community paper.

Articles: Special features include business, community, entertainment, recruitment, motoring and sport.

**Tips** Local life makes up the main content of the paper.

## The Scottish Sun

**124 Portman Street, Kinning Park, Glasgow, G41 1EJ**

❶ 0141 420 5200

❶ 0141 4205248

○ scottish-sun@the-sun.co.uk

**Contact** Editor, David Dinsmore; News Editor, Alan Muir; Features Editor, David Reynolds; Picture Editor, Mark Sweeny; Sports Editor, Andy Swinburne

**Insider Info** A tabloid paper aimed at a young demographic. It publishes showbiz news and exposes, as well as current affairs.
Photos: Photographs are welcome.

## Scunthorpe Telegraph
**4–5 Park Square, Laneham Street, Scunthorpe, DN15 6JH**
- 01724 273273
- 01724 273101
- newsdesk@scunthorpetelegraph.co.uk, firstname.lastname@scunthorpetelegraph.co.uk
- www.thisisscunthorpe.co.uk

**Contact** Editor, Jane Manning; News Editor, Vicky Cottam; Features Editor, Christopher Horan; Sports Editor, Bob Steels
**Insider Info** A paid for local newspaper covering the Scunthorpe area. Its circulation is just under 21,000. Publishes six days a week. For news stories relating to the Scunthorpe area, email the news desk.
Photos: For photographs, email pictures@grimsbytelegraph.co.uk

## The Sentinel
**Sentinel House, Forge Lane, Staffordshire, Stoke on Trent, ST1 5SS**
- 01782 602525
- 01732 201167
- newsdesk@thesentinel.co.uk
- www.thesentinel.co.uk

**Contact** Editor, Mike Sassi; News Editor, Rob Cotterill; Deputy Editor, Richard Bowyer
**Insider Info** News, sport and entertainment in the local area.
Articles: Sentinel Sunday articles are not restricted in length. The editor is Steven Houghton.

## Sheffield Star
**York Street, Sheffield, S1 1PU**
- 0114 276 7676
- 0114 272 5978
- starnews@sheffieldnewspapers.co.uk
- www.sheffieldtoday.co.uk

**Contact** Editor, Alan Powell; Features Editor, Martin Smith
**Insider Info** First published in 1870.
Articles: Regular features on entertainment.
**Tips** Local community interests are favoured.

## Shropshire Star
**Ketley, Telford, TF1 5HU**
- 01952 242424
- 01952 254605
- newsroom@shropshirestar.co.uk
- www.shropshirestar.co.uk

**Contact** Editor, Sarah Jane Smith; News Editor, John Simmock; Picture Editor, Paul Morstatt; Sports Editor, Dave Ballinger; Arts Editor, Sharon Walters
**Insider Info** Evening paper which covers Shropshire and Mid Wales. Fiction work is not accepted.
Articles: Regular features on business, lifestyle, community, motors and jobs.

## Somerset Guardian Series
Western Newspapers Ltd
**Windsor House, Windsor Bridge, Bath, BA2 3AU**
- 01225 322322
- 01225 322292
- editor@somersetguardian.co.uk, firstinitial.lastname@westnews.co.uk
- www.somersetguardian.co.uk

**Contact** Editor, Sam Holliday; Assistant Editor, Stephanie Feldwicke; Sports Editor, Nick Gregory
**Insider Info** A series of local paid for, weekly newspapers for the Somerset area. These include, the *Warminster and Westbury Standard*, *The Somerset Guardian* and the *Frome and Somerset Standard*. The combined circulation of these papers is up to 20,000.
Articles: Articles tend to focus on regional and local news, and sport.
**Tips** The newspapers' have a high rural and semi-rural readership.

## Southend Echo
Newsquest Ltd
**Newspaper House, Chester Hall Lane, Basildon, Essex, SS14 3BL**
- 0844 477 4512
- 0844 477 4286
- echonews@nqe.com, firstname.lastname@nqe.com
- www.echo-news.co.uk

**Contact** Editor, Martin McNeill; Assistant Editor, Chris Hatton; Sports Editor, Paul Alton; Picture Editor, Nick Ansell
**Insider Info** Part of the Echo group of newspapers covering Essex. A paid for local paper for Southend previously known as the *Southend Evening Echo*. Circulation of just under 20,000. Email or call the news desk with stories.

Articles: Articles focus on local news, sport and events.

## The Southern Daily Echo
**Newspaper House, Test Lane, Redbridge, Southampton, SO16 9JX**
- 023 8042 4777
- 023 8042 4545
- newsdesk@soton-echo.co.uk
- www.dailyecho.co.uk

**Contact** Editor, Ian Murrey; News Editor, Gordon Sutter; Features Editor, Andy Bissell; Picture Editor, Paul Collins; Sports Editor, Simon Carter
**Insider Info** Popular daily newspaper. Outsider writers are rarely used, but they will be considered.
Articles: Weekend magazine, containing features on lifestyle, fashion, entertainment and food.

## South Wales Argus
**Cardiff Road, Maesglas, Newport, Gwent, NP20 3QN**
- 01633 772229
- 01633 777202
- newsdesk@gwent-wales.co.uk
- www.southwalesargus.co.uk

**Contact** Editor, Gerry Keighley
**Insider Info** Covers news and sport, in and around the Gwent area.

## South Wales Echo
**Thomson House, Havelock Street, Cardiff, CF10 1XR**
- 029 2058 3583
- 029 2058 3624
- echo.newsdesk@wme.co.uk
- www.icwales.co.uk

**Contact** Editor, Richard Williams; Head of News, Cathy Owens
**Insider Info** Covers news, sport, features and entertainment. Outside work or input is considered.

## South Wales Evening Post
**PO Box 14, Adelaide Street, Swansea, SA1 1QT**
- 01792 510000
- 01792 514697
- postbox@swwp.co.uk
- www.thisissouthwales.co.uk

**Contact** Editor, Spencer Feeney; News Editor, Peter Slee
**Insider Info** Founded in 1897.

Articles: Regular features on health, business, property and the environment.

## Sunday Independent
**Webbs House, Tindle Suite, Liskeard, Cornwall, PU4 6AH**
- 01579 342174
- newsdesk@sundayindependent.co.uk

**Contact** Editor, John Noble

## Sunday Life
**124 Royal Avenue, Belfast, BT1 1EB, Northern Ireland**
- 028 9026 4000
- 028 9055 4507
- m.hill@belfasttelegraph.co.uk
- www.sundaylife.co.uk

**Contact** Editor, Jim Flanagan; News Editor, Martin Hill; Features Editor, Audrey Watson; Sports Editor, Jim Gracey; Pictures Editor, Mark McCormack

## Sunday Mercury
**PO Box 78, Weaman Street, Birmingham, B4 6AY**
- 0121 234 5567
- 0121 234 5877
- sundaymercury@mrn.co.uk
- www.sundaymercury.co.uk

**Contact** Editor, David Brookes; News Editor, Tony Larner; Deputy Editor, Paul Cole; Picture Editor, Adam Fradgley
**Insider Info** Sunday tabloid focusing on exclusive news, sport and entertainment.
**Tips** Keen on investigative writing.

## Sunday Sun
Trinity Mirror Plc
**Groat Market, Newcastle upon Tyne, NE1 1ED**
- 0191 201 6201
- 0191 201 6180
- scoop.sundaysun@ncjmedia.co.uk
- www.sundaysun.co.uk

**Contact** Editor, Colin Patterson; Deputy Editor, Ken Oxley; News Editor, Mike Kelly; Sports Editor, Neil Farrington; Travel Editor, Roger Domeneghetti
**Insider Info** Sunday tabloid founded in 1919. It covers local news and sport, as well as international news. Contact the editor on 0191 201 6299.
**Tips** Local interest stories are favoured.

## The Sunday Tribune

Tribune Publications Plc

**15 Lower Baggot Street, Dublin 2, Republic of Ireland**

- 00353 1 661 5555
- 00353 1 661 5302
- newsdesk@tribune.ie
- www.tribune.ie

**Contact** Editor, Noirin Hegarty; Magazine Editor, Fionnuala McCarthy

**Insider Info** Sunday paper covering local and international news. Where possible contact the editor via email, nhegarty@tribune.ie

Articles: *The Tribune Review* includes articles on books, health, jobs, motoring and finance. *The Tribune Magazine* contains features on fashion and lifestyle.

## Sunderland Echo

**Echo House, Pennywell, Sunderland, SR4 9ER**

- 0191 501 5800
- 0191 534 5975
- echo.news2northeast-press.co.uk
- www.sunderlandtoday.co.uk

**Contact** Deputy Editor, Richard Ord; News Editor, Gavin Foster; Features Editor, Paul Taylor; Sports Editor, Neil Watson

**Insider Info** Founded in 1873. Covers local news, sport and entertainment.

Articles: Regular columns on cooking, lifestyle, and local community issues.

## Swindon Advertiser

**100 Victoria Road, Old Town, Swindon, Wiltshire, SN1 3BE**

- 01793 528144
- 01793 542434
- newsdesk@neswilts.co.uk
- www.swindonadvertiser.co.uk

**Contact** Editor, Mark Waldron; Features Editor, Jaine Blackman; Business Editor, Leigh Robinson; Picture Editor, Dave Evans; Sports Editor, Steve Butt

**Insider Info** Established in 1854.

**Tips** Only local interest stories are considered.

## Telegraph & Argus

**Hall Ings, Bradford, Yorkshire, BD1 1JR**

- 01274 729511
- 01274 723634
- newsdesk@bradford.newsquest.co.uk
- www.thisisbradford.co.uk

**Contact** Editor, Perry Austin-Clarke; Sports Editor, Blake Richardson

**Insider Info** Award winning tabloid, with over 113,232 readers. Approach the editor with ideas, on 01274 729511.

## Western Daily Press

**Bristol Evening Post and Press Ltd, Temple Way, Bristol, BS99 7HD**

- 0117 934 3000
- 0117 934 3575
- wdnews@bepp.co.uk
- www.westpress.co.uk

**Contact** Editor, Andy Wright; Features Editor, David Webb; News Editor, Cathy Ellis; Business Editor, Robert Buckland; Sports Editor, Steve Mellen

**Insider Info** Established 1858.

Articles: Regular features on education, finance, business and industry.

## The Western Mail

**The News Centre, Havelock Street, Cardiff, CF10 1XR**

- 029 2058 3654
- 029 2058 3652
- newsdesk@wme.co.uk
- www.icwales.co.uk

**Contact** Editor, Alun Edmunds; News Editor, Paul Carey

**Insider Info** Established in 1869. Freelance work is considered, but the value of articles may vary.

**Tips** Local interest stories are preferred.

## Western Morning News

Northcliffe Newspaper Group

**17 Brest Road, Derriford Business Park, Plymouth, Devon, PL6 5AA**

- 01752 765538
- 01752 765535
- wmnnewsdesk@westernmorningnews.co.uk
- www.westernmorningnews.co.uk

**Contact** Editor, Alan Qualtrough; Features Editor, Sue Carol

**Insider Info** Coverage of local, national and international news for Devon, Cornwall, West Somerset and West Dorset. Unsolicited work is welcome.

**Tips** Local news and features are favoured.

## Wigan Evening Post

Lancashire Publications Ltd
**Martland Mill, Martland Mill Lane, Wigan,
WN5 0LX**
- 01942 228000
- 01942 221223
- fistname.lastname@lancspublications.co.uk
- www.wigantoday.net

**Contact** Editor, Simon Reynolds; Head of Content,
Gillian Gray; Features Editor, Peter Richardson; Sports
Editor, Peter Storey

**Insider Info** Established in the 1950s, it is circulated
six nights a week to the Wigan area. Formerly the
Wigan Post and Chronicle.
Articles: Features news, sport, competitions,
entertainment and gossip.
Columns: Regular columns include Talking Sport,
Music Scene and Charles Graham.

## Worcester News

**Berrows House, Hylton Road, Worcester,
Worcestershire, WR2 5JX**
- 01905 742244
- 01905 748200
- wenedit@thisisworcester.co.uk
- www.worcesternews.co.uk

**Contact** Editor, Stewart Gilbert; Features Editor,
David Chapman

**Insider Info** First published in 1937. Outside
contributions are considered.
Articles: Local and national news articles.

## Yorkshire Evening Post

**PO Box 168, Wellington Street, Leeds, Yorkshire,
LS1 1RF**
- 0113 243 2701
- 0113 238 8535
- eped@ypn.co.uk
- www.ypn.co.uk

**Contact** Editor, Paul Napier; Features Editor, Jayne
Dawson; Sports Editor, Phil Rostron; Business Editor,
Nigel Scott; Picture Editor, Andy Manning

**Insider Info** First published in 1890.

## Yorkshire Post

**PO Box 168, Wellington Street, Leeds, Yorkshire,
LS1 1RF**
- 0113 243 2701
- 0113 238 8535
- yp.newsdesk@ypn.co.uk
- www.yorkshireposttoday.co.uk

**Contact** Editor, Peter Charlton; News Editor, Hannah
Start; Picture Editor, Ian Day; Features Editor, Sarah
Freeman; Magazine Editor, Mick Hickling

**Insider Info** First published in 1734.
Articles: Weekly Yorkshire Post Magazine.

# WEB PUBLISHING

# PODCASTING

## Audemos

**PO Box 5026, Brighton, BN50 9LE**
- 0870 803 0013
- listen@audemos.co.uk
- www.audemos.co.uk

**About** Provides all services to produce and publish
podcasts, including brand led content, production
and licensing issues. Past clients include
Heineken and HMV.

## Audio for the Web

- 020 7033 3724
- info@audiofortheweb.com
- www.audiofortheweb.com

**About** Provide all the services needed to create a
podcast. They also run training sessions in areas such
as scriptwriting, interview techniques and audio
production.

## British Podcasting Corporation

- 020 8340 9419
- mail@britishpodcastingcorporation.com
- www.britishpodcastingcorporation.com

**About** Create custom podcasts for clients.

## Direct Recordings

- 0845 226 8591
- enquiries@directrecordings.co.uk, firstname@
directrecordings.co.uk
- www.directrecordings.co.uk

**Contact** Managing Director

Ben Marshall
Design Manager
Rachel Hartley
Project Coordinators
Jack Chetwynd, Matt Chugg
**About** Provide all the services necessary to create a podcast. Current clients include many live music acts.

## Media on Demand
**Media House, 9–15 Weyhill, Haslemere, Surrey, GU27 1BZ**
- 01428 656637
- 01428 656681
- info@mediaondemand.net
- www.mediaondemand.net
**About** Established in 1984. Provide webcasting and podcasting services.

## Mosaic Publicity
**11 St. Peter's Court, St. Peter's Street, Colchester, CO1 1WD**
- 01206 548100
- 01206 548200
- training@mosaicpublicity.co.uk
- www.podcast-training.co.uk
**About** Runs training courses on using podcasts for marketing and PR campaigns.

## Pod Bean
- www.podbean.com
**About** Publishes podcasts from pre-created audio files.

## Podcast Blaster
- info@podcastblaster.com
- www.podcastblaster.com
**About** Provides a complete package for podcasting, includes a manual, recording software, sound files and web resources for music. The website includes information on the history of podcasting, making money from it and a top tips forum.

## The Podcast Brewery
- hello@podcastbrewery.com
- www.podcastbrewery.com
**About** Produces and publishes podcasts, primarily for record labels who wish to promote new artists.

## Podcast Directory
- info@podcastdirectory.com
- www.podcastdirectory.com
**About** Searchable directory of international podcasts. Also provides help and tips on setting one up.

## Podcast Generation
- info@podcastgeneration.com, firstname.lastname@podcastgeneration.com
- www.podcastgeneration.com
**Contact** Creative Director
Darren Michael
Technical Director
Andrew Buonocore
**About** Provide a full range of services, including content creation, production and serving. Also sell a small selection of music for podcasts through their website.

## Podcast Matters
- 0141 616 3152
- podcastmatters@designmattersgroup.com
- www.podcastmatters.co.uk
**About** Provides all services for podcasting, including scripting, editing, design and publication.

## Podcast Voices
**54–55 Margaret Street, London, W1W 8SQ**
- 020 7291 0775
- info@podcastvoices.com
- www.podcastvoices.com
**About** Established in 2005. Provides a range of services, from scripting and providing actors, to hosting and marketing the podcast.

## Podooch
- www.podooch.com
**About** Facilitates podcast publishing, by managing audio/video content and making it iTunes ready. Also offer a free personal website.

## Spoken
**Unit 2K St. Mark's Industrial Estate, 439 North Woolwich Road, Silvertown, London, E16 2BS**
- 020 7511 7746
- 020 7511 1389
- firstname.lastname@spoken-podcast.co.uk
- www.spoken-podcast.com
**Contact** Tony Lynch

Rebecca Snook

**About** Provide services for corporate podcasts, including scripting, professional voices, marketing, and compatibility with Apple and iTunes.

## Wells Park

**Kemble Road, Forest Hill, London, SE23 2DJ**

- 0845 108 1654
- 0870 762 6057
- nick@wellspark.co.uk
- www.wellspark.co.uk

**About** Provide all services for a podcast Also sell, or rent kits to enable you to do it yourself. Clients include Lonely Planet and Microsoft.

# BLOGGING

## SOFTWARE AND HOSTS

### Blog
- www.blog.co.uk

**About** Free blog hosting.

### Blogger
- www.blogger.com

**About** Free application allows you to create a blog and potentially earn money from pay per click advertising.

### Blog Rig
- www.blogrig.com

**About** Free blogs with more than 30 templates.

### Brit-Journal
- www.brit-journal.com

**About** Offers free blogging accounts to become part of the brit-journal community.

### Daypop
- www.daypop.com

**About** A search engine for information sites, including blogs. Submit the URL for your blog and providing the site is constantly updated, Daypop will list it.

### Ebay blogs
- http://blogs.ebay.co.uk

**About** Community of blogs hosted by the auction site.

### Google Adsense
- www.google.com/adsense

**About** A way of using your blog to earn money from advertising. The scheme is free to join, but potential members must apply to be accepted.

### Live Journal
- www.livejournal.com

**About** Large community of free and paid for blogging accounts.

### MySpace
- www.myspace.com

**About** A free web page that can be used as a blog, as well as an online photo album and for sending and receiving messages.

### Orble
- www.orble.com

**About** Free blogging account.

### Real Life Log
- www.reallifelog.com

**About** Free blogs, also offers video content.

### Selectablog
- www.selectablog.com

**About** Free blogging accounts. Also offer the option of paid for accounts with no advertising and extra facilities.

### Squarespace
- www.squarespace.com

**About** Offer a range of services including website publishing and blogging, for a fee.

### Technorati
- www.technorati.com

**About** A search engine for blogs. Users submit their URL and Technorati indexes the blogs, allowing people to search by particular criteria. This way targeted visitors are sent to each URL.

## World Nomads
🌐 www.worldnomads.com
**About** Free travel blogs.

# WRITER'S BLOGS

## Author's Blogs
🌐 www.authorsblogs.com
**About** An extensive directory of blogs from published and aspiring writers. There is also the opportunity to add your own blog to the list.

## BookBlog
🌐 www.bookseller.com
**About** An interactive news blog from the publishing industry journal and website.

## Book Slut
🌐 www.bookslut.com/blog
**About** A US blog, regularly updated, that charts gossip and news from the world of books and publishing.

## Grumpy Old Book Man
🌐 http://grumpyoldbookman.blogspot.com
**About** An amusing and interesting look at books and the publishing industry from Michael Allen.

## In Search of Adam
🌐 www.insearchofadam.blogspot.com
**About** Caroline Smailes' blog. Caroline is the author of In Search of Adam, published by The Friday Press. An example of a blog that attracted the attention of a publisher, who went on to publish it as a novel.

## The Internet Writing Journal
🌐 www.internetwritingjournal.com/authorblogs
**About** A directory of blogs by authors and writers, including group blogs.

## John Baker's Blog
📧 john@johnbakersblog.co.uk
🌐 http://johnbakersblog.co.uk
**About** The diary of a writer, focuses on the writing process and his day to day life.

## The Knight Agency
🌐 http://knightagency.blogspot.com
**About** A blog written by agents at this US literary agency.

## Me and My Big Mouth
🌐 www.thefridayproject.co.uk/pack
**About** Scott Pack, Commercial Director of The Friday Project publishing company, writes a blog on his life within the publishing industry.

## Organ Grinder
🌐 http://blogs.guardian.co.uk/organgrinder
**About** A media blog by the Guardian, covers media news and opinion.

## The Publishing Contrarian
🌐 www.thepublishingcontrarian.com
**About** Written by 'The Wicked Witch of Publishing', Lynne W. Scanlon, a US publisher, author and editor. A humorous blog about the publishing industry worldwide.

## Random Acts of Reality
🌐 http://randomreality.blogware.com
**About** A blog by Tom Reynolds, an Emergency Medical Technician (E.M.T), working for the London Ambulance Service. His blog about his work was turned into a book; Blood, Sweat and Tea and published by The Friday Project.

## Ready Steady Book
🌐 www.readysteadybook.com
**About** A book review blog.

## Screenwriting Life
🌐 www.screenwritinglife.com
**About** Written by a screenwriter in Los Angeles. He charts his life, work, upcoming projects and looks at the screenwriting profession in general.

These listings include all of the household names in national, local and commercial television and radio, many production companies and digital satellite and cable companies. Although opportunities for writers may be limited in some cases, these listings reflect the sheer scale of opportunity for writing within these media, with local radio being particularly invaluable for both the published author's publicity, and for the uncommissioned writer to pitch to. As ever, look on the companies' websites for further information, and to keep up to date with any specific campaigns they may be running.

## THE BBC

The BBC as a whole is split into five areas: Radio and Music; Drama, Entertainment and Children's; Factual and Learning; Sport; and News. All information on commissioning in each of these areas can be found at: www.bbc.co.uk/commissioning Proposals from members of the public to BBC national programming may only be submitted in these three areas: Drama and comedy scripts, via Writers Room (see entry); Entertainment formats, including quiz and game shows, sent to: Format Entertainment Development Team, Room 4010, BBC Television Centre; and Factual entertainment treatments sent to: Factual Entertainment Development, Room 4010 BBC Television Centre. All other areas of programming are commissioned through independent production companies. Submissions for these must be made through the RAP system. For access, contact Gerardina Carbone on 020 7765 4901. BBC local programming may be interested in ideas with a regional flavour.

### The BBC
**BBC Television Centre, Wood Lane, London, W12 7RJ**
- 020 8743 8000
- firstname.lastname@bbc.co.uk
- www.bbc.co.uk

**Contact Title** Director General
Mark Thompson
Deputy Director General
Mark Byford
Director, BBC Vision
Jana Bennett
Director of Sport
Roger Mosey
Director of BBC Future Media and Technology
Ashley Highfield

Creative Director
Alan Yentob

## BBC TV CHANNELS

### BBC One
**BBC Television Centre, Wood Lane, London, W12 7RJ**
- 020 8576 8000
- firstname.lastname@bbc.co.uk
- www.bbc.co.uk/bbcone

**Contact** Controller, BBC One, Peter Fincham
**About** A terrestrial channel that aims to be the favourite channel for most people, most of the time. It broadcasts flagship events such as Live 8, weddings and funerals, as well as a mix of comedy, drama and entertainment. There are also slots for historical, factual, educational and learning programming as well as regular news and sport. BBC One is regarded as the shop window to all other BBC channels and its audience is massively wide ranging. Recent programmes: Friday Night with Jonathan Ross; Doctor Who, Panorama.

### BBC Two
**BBC Television Centre, Wood Lane, London, W12 7RJ**
- 020 8576 8000
- firstname.lastname@bbc.co.uk
- www.bbc.co.uk/bbctwo

**Contact** Controller, BBC Two, Roly Keating
**About** A terrestrial channel that aims to broadcast entertaining programmes with depth and substance. Factual programmes are the core of the schedules, although drama is present, along with documentary and light entertainment formats. The

channel's audience is broad but tends towards an older audience of 35–54.

Recent programmes: Never Mind the Buzzcocks; Coast; Dragon's Den.

## BBC Three

**BBC Television Centre, Wood Lane, London, W12 7RJ**

☎ 020 8576 8000

✉ firstname.lastname@bbc.co.uk

🌐 www.bbc.co.uk/bbcthree

**Contact** Controller, BBC Three and News Editor, Julian Bellamy; Head of Programming, Damien Kavangh

**About** A digital channel with mixed programming aimed at a young audience, mainly 25–30 year olds. It often acts as a laboratory for BBC One and Two in its comedy and entertainment content. The channel also broadcasts drama, current affairs and factual programming and incorporates repeats from BBC One and Two. The tone of the channel is fun, cheeky and unconventional, whilst remaining appealing to a wider audience.

Recent programmes: Torchwood; House of Tiny Tearaways; I'm With Stupid.

## BBC Four

**BBC Television Centre, Wood Lane, London, W12 7RJ**

☎ 020 8576 8000

✉ firstname.lastname@bbc.co.uk

🌐 www.bbc.co.uk/bbcfour

**Contact** Controller, BBC Four, Janice Hadlow; Channel Executive and News Editor, Mark Bell

**About** A digital channel that aims to be a place to think, 'unashamedly intelligent' and to provide an alternative to the mainstream channels. The content will begin to move towards more series based programming, rather than the current one offs, seasons and theme nights. It will still retain the diversity of the programming. The channel's audience is not distinguished by age, but rather by the fact that television is likely to compete with radio, print journalism and other interests. This attitude means television watching must be time well spent, so these viewers need authoritative and sharp content.

Recent programmes: Never Mind the Full Stops; The Quatermass Experiment; Folk Britannia.

## BBC News 24

**BBC Television Centre, Wood Lane, London, W12 7RJ**

☎ 020 8576 8000

✉ firstname.lastname@bbc.co.uk

🌐 www.bbc.co.uk/bbcnews24

**Contact** Controller, BBC News 24, Kevin Backhurst

**About** A 24 hour digital news and weather channel.

## BBC Parliament

**4 Millbank, London, SW1P 3JA**

☎ 0870 010 0123

✉ parliament@bbc.co.uk

🌐 www.bbc.co.uk/bbcparliament

**About** A 24 hour digital channel dedicated to political coverage, supplemented by live footage from The Houses of Parliament.

## BBC World

**BBC Television Centre, Wood Lane, London, W12 7RJ**

☎ 020 8576 8000

✉ firstname.lastname@bbc.co.uk

🌐 www.bbcworld.com

**Contact** News Editor, Eleanor Montague

**About** A commercially funded 24 hour news channel, which broadcasts around the world from its base in London.

## CBBC Channel

**BBC Television Centre, Wood Lane, London, W12 7RJ**

☎ 020 8576 8000

✉ firstname.lastname@bbc.co.uk

🌐 www.bbc.co.uk/cbbc

**Contact** Controller, BBC Childrens, Richard Deverell; Creative Director, CBBC, Anne Gilchrist; Head of Entertainment, Joe Godwin; Head of Drama, John East; News Editor, Cathy Derrick

**About** A digital channel aimed primarily at children aged 6–12, aiming to offer children a breadth of multi platform content. The channel runs from 7am–7pm but its output is also broadcast on BBC One and Two at peak times. Programming includes drama, animation, comedy, news, factual programming and events.

Recent programmes: Johnny and the Bomb; TMI; Smile.

## Cbeebies Channel

**BBC Television Centre, Wood Lane, London, W12 7RJ**

☎ 020 8576 8000

✉ firstname.lastname@bbc.co.uk

🌐 www.bbc.co.uk/cbeebies

**Contact** Controller, BBC Children's, Richard Deverell; Creative Director, Cbeebies, Michael Carrington; Producer and News Editor, Angela Young

**About** A digital channel aimed at pre-school children. Cbeebies is designed to be a brand, rather than simply a channel and as such offers content across many media platforms. The channel airs from 6am–7pm and content is sometimes simultaneously broadcast on BBC Two. Content should inspire play, creativity and imagination.

Recent programmes: Bob the Builder; Fireman Sam; Jackanory Junior.

# BBC RADIO & MUSIC STATIONS

BBC Radio and Music is responsible for commissioning content for all national BBC analogue and digital radio stations. It also deals with much of the music and dance content on BBC television channels, as well as music content on the BBC World Service. Radio entertainment is one of the few areas that will accept unsolicited proposals from writers not already attached to a production company. www.bbc.co.uk/writersroom/writing/submissions_other_radioents for submission guidelines.

## BBC Radio and Music

**BBC Broadcasting House, Portland Place, London, W1A 1AA**

☎ 020 7580 4468

✉ firstname.lastname@bbc.co.uk

**Contact** Director of BBC Radio and Music, Jenny Abramsky CBE; Head of Compliance, Susan Binney; Finance Director, Jo Brindley; (Acting) Head of Rights and Business, Radio and Music, and Head of Talent Rights Group, Simon Hayward-Tapp; Head of Press and Publicity, Sue Lynas; Head of Radio Drama, Alison Hindell; Head of Radio Entertainment, Paul Schlesinger; Head of BBC Radio News, Stephen Mitchell; Head of Radio Current Affairs, Gwyneth Williams; Head of BBC Radio Sport, Gordon Turnball

## BBC 1Xtra

**BBC Broadcasting House, Portland Place, London, W1A 1AA**

☎ 020 7580 4468

✉ firstname.lastname@bbc.co.uk

🌐 www.bbc.co.uk/1xtra

**Contact** Controller, 1Xtra, Andy Parfitt; Managing Editor, Tarrant Streele; Commissioning Editor, Documentaries, Russell Crewe; News Editor, Angela Clark

**About** A digital station whose target audience is 16–24 year old fans of black music. Development priorities can be viewed at www.bbc.co.uk/commissioning, most content is made in house although documentaries are made by a combination of freelancers, in house producers and independent production companies. Documentaries are preferred in the first person narrative and must be of direct relevance to the target audience. Commissioning rounds take place through the year, but a short synopsis may be submitted to Russell Crewe on 020 7765 5551 or by email, as an initial query before submitting through the RAP system.

Recent programmes: *Friday Night Mixtape; Uptown Anthems*

## BBC Radio Five Live

**BBC Broadcasting House, Portland Place, London, W1A 1AA**

☎ 020 7580 4468

✉ firstname.lastname@bbc.co.uk

🌐 www.bbc.co.uk/fivelive

**Contact** Controller, Five Live, Bob Shennan; Commissioning Editor, Moz Dee; Head of News, Matt Morris; News Editor, Robin Britten

**About** Five Live is a 24 hour rolling sports and news service, and much of the content is live. There are no formal commissioning rounds, however treatments will be looked at throughout the year. Submissions to Moz Dee by email or phone, 020 8624 8948.

Recent programmes: *Sports week; Wake Up to Money*

## BBC 6 Music

**BBC Broadcasting House, Portland Place, London, W1A 1AA**

☎ 020 7580 4468

✉ firstname.lastname@bbc.co.uk

🌐 www.bbc.co.uk/6music

**Contact Title** Controller, 6 Music, Lesley Douglas; Head of Programmes, Ric Blaxill; Managing Editor and News Editor, Antony Bellekom

**About** A digital radio station aimed at 25–44 year old music fans. Strands that are open for independent production companies are announced on the www.bbc.co.uk/commissioning in the 6 Music section.

Recent programmes: *6 Mix*; *The Dream Ticket*

## BBC 7

**BBC Broadcasting House, Portland Place, London, W1A 1AA**

- 020 7580 4468
- firstname.lastname@bbc.co.uk
- www.bbc.co.uk/bbc7

**Contact** Controller, BBC 7, Mark Damazer; Head of Programmes and News Editor, Mary Kalemkerian; Programme Controller, Mark Damazer

**About** A digital radio station for comedy and drama. Commissions through BBC Writer's Room website.

Recent programmes: *Lee and Herring's Fist of Fun*; *Little Dorrit*

## BBC Asian Network

**The Mailbox, Birmingham, B1 1RF**

- 0121 567 6767
- firstname.lastname@bbc.co.uk
- www.bbc.co.uk/asiannetwork

**Contact** Controller, Asian Network, Bob Shennan; Head of Asian Network, Vijay Sharma; Network Manager, Michael Hill; Head of News, Husain Husaini; News Editor, Neerja Sood; Head of Music, Mark Strippel

**About** The target audience is British Asians under 35, in major cities and towns throughout the UK. Approximately 10 per cent of content is commissioned from independent producers. Music and journalism is predominantly Asian with an 'urban' feel. Details of specific commissioning rounds are posted on www.bbc.co.uk/commissioning in the Asian Network section. Short synopses may be also be submitted to Michael Hill by email or phone; 020 8624 8945, before submitting through the RAP system.

Recent programmes: *Silver Street*; *The Hype Show*

## BBC Radio 1

**BBC Broadcasting House, Portland Place, London, W1A 1AA**

- 020 7580 4468
- firstname.lastname@bbc.co.uk
- www.bbc.co.uk/radio1

**Contact Title** Controller, Radio 1, Andy Parfitt; Head of Programmes, Ben Cooper; Executive Producer, Speech and Campaigns, Sam Steele

News Editor and Head of Music, George Ergatoudis

**About** Radio 1 mostly broadcasts long running strands, which are commissioned by Ben Cooper. All documentaries are commissioned by Sam Steele and enquiries from independent production companies or established programme makers about submitting documentary ideas should be directed to her, by email or phone, 020 7765 3827. Commissioning rounds for this are usually twice yearly, the current one being for March–September 2007 and beyond. Commissioning briefs are downloadable from the www.bbc.co.uk/commissioning

Recent programmes: *The Chart Show*; *The Chris Moyles Show*

## BBC Radio 2

**BBC Broadcasting House, Portland Place, London, W1A 1AA**

- 020 7580 4468
- firstname.lastname@bbc.co.uk
- www.bbc.co.uk/radio2

**Contact** Controller, Radio 2, Lesley Douglas; Head Live Music, Events and Talent, Lewis Carnie; Editor, Planning and Station Sound, Robert Gallacher; Manager, Commissions and Schedules, Julian Grundy

**About** Radio 2 mostly consists of long running strands, however commissioning rounds take place twice yearly for additional content and are open to submissions from independent producers or production companies. Initial enquiries about submissions should be directed by email, or phone to Robert Gallacher, 020 7765 4373, or Lewis Carnie. Development priorities can be viewed at www.bbc.co.uk/commissioning

Recent programmes: *All Singing All Dancing*; *Best of Jazz*

## BBC Radio 3

**BBC Broadcasting House, Portland Place, London, W1A 1AA**

- 020 7580 4468
- firstname.lastname@bbc.co.uk
- www.bbc.co.uk/radio3

**Contact** Controller, Radio 3, Roger Wright; Head of Speech Programming and Presentation, Abigail Appleton; Commissions and Schedules Manager, David Ireland; Music Editors, Edward Blakeman, Tony

Cheevers, Adam Gatehouse, Andrew Kurowski, Edwina Wolstencroft

**About** Radio 3 is aimed at listeners of any age and its current priorities are classical music, jazz, drama, world music and speech programmes. As well as broadcasting long-running strands, Radio 3 holds commissioning rounds for both drama and non-drama content. These usually open in April to May, for the following year. Details of these rounds are on www.bbc.co.uk/commissioning, initial enquiries should be directed to David Ireland by email or phone, 020 7765 4943.

 Recent programmes: *Between the Ears; British Composer Awards*

## BBC Radio 4

**BBC Broadcasting House, Portland Place, London, W1A 1AA**

☎ 020 7580 4468

✉ firstname.lastname@bbc.co.uk

🌐 www.bbc.co.uk/radio4

**Contact** Controller, Radio 4, Mark Damazer; Commissioning Editor, Comedy and Entertainment, Caroline Raphael; Commissioning Editor, Specialist Factual Programmes, Andrew Caspari; Commissioning Editor, General Factual Programmes, Jane Ellison; Commissioning Editor, Drama, Jeremy Howe; Creative Director, New Writing, Kate Rowland

**About** Radio 4 do not accept any proposals, unless through an in house production department, or a registered independent production company. Submission forms are downloadable from www.bbc.co.uk/commissioning, in the Radio 4 section.

 Recent programmes: *21 Conversations with a Hairdresser; Woman's Hour*

## BBC World Service

**Bush House, London, WC2B 4PH**

☎ 020 7240 3456

☎ 020 7557 1900

✉ firstname.lastname@bbc.co.uk

🌐 www.bbc.co.uk/worldservice

**Contact** Director, World Service, Nigel Chapman; Editor, News and Current affairs, Liliane Landor; News Editor, Peter Burdin; Business Editor, Martin Webber

**About** The World Service commissions a wide range of content through its 'Invitation to Bid' scheme, details of which come out in May/June each year. The invitation to bid gets automatically sent to a list of suppliers. If you wish to join this list, contact Karen Howe by email or post (Room 828).

# BBC REGIONAL & LOCAL RADIO STATIONS

There are 40 BBC radio stations throughout the UK, some transmitting on AM and some on FM. They are mainly news and sport based, however some transmit other content relevant to their area.

## BBC Coventry and Warwickshire

**Priory Place, Coventry, CV1 5SQ**

☎ 024 7655 1000

✉ firstname.lastname@bbc.co.uk, coventry@bbc.co.uk, warwickshire@bbc.co.uk

🌐 www.bbc.co.uk/coventry/local_radio

**Contact** Editor, David Clargo; Assistant Editor, Duncan Jones; News Editor, Paul Marriott; Rugby Correspondent, Sue Curtis

**About** First came on air in 1990 under the name CWR. Broadcasts on 94.8, 104 and 103.7 FM and DAB digital radio.

## BBC Essex

**PO Box 765, Chelmsford, CM2 9XB**

☎ 01245 616000

☎ 01245 492983

✉ firstname.lastname@bbc.co.uk, essex@bbc.co.uk

🌐 www.bbc.co.uk/essex

**Contact** Managing Editor, Margaret Hyde; Head of Music, Steve Scruton; Programme Editor, Tim Gillet

**About** Broadcasts on 103.5 and 95.3 FM and DAB digital radio.

## BBC Guernsey

**Broadcasting House, Bulwer Avenue, St. Sampson's, Guernsey, GY2 4LA**

☎ 01481 200600

☎ 01481 200361

✉ firstname.lastname@bbc.co.uk,

🌐 www.bbc.co.uk/guernsey

**Contact** Managing Editor, David Martin; Assistant Editor, Kay Langlois

**About** First came on air in 1982. Broadcasts on 93.2 and 99 FM, and 1116 MW.

## BBC Hereford & Worcester

**Hylton Road, Worcester, WR2 5WW**

☎ 01905 748485

☎ 01905 748446

✉ firstname.lastname@bbc.co.uk, bbchw@bbc.co.uk

🌐 www.bbc.co.uk/herefordworcester

**Contact** Managing Editor, James Coghill; Assistant Editor, Mark Hellings; Head of Music, Max Thomas; News Editor, Joe Baldwin; Sports Editor, Trevor Owens

**About** Also based at 43 Broad Street, Hereford, HR4 9HH. Broadcasts on 104, 104.4, 104.6 and 94.7 FM and 738 and 1584 MW.

## BBC London
**PO Box 94.9, Marylebone High Street, London, W1A 6FL**

☎ 020 7224 2424

☎ 020 7224 2424

✉ firstname.lastname@bbc.co.uk, yourlondon@bbc.co.uk

🌐 www.bbc.co.uk/london

**Contact** Managing Editor, David Robey; News Editor, Lorraine Maguire; Sports Editor, Pete Stevens

**About** Covers Greater London and the Home Counties. Broadcasts on 94.9 FM and DAB digital radio.

## BBC Radio Berkshire
**PO Box 104.4, Reading, RG4 8FH**

☎ 0845 900 1044/0118 946 4200

☎ 0118 946 4555

✉ firstname.lastname@bbc.co.uk, radio.berkshire.news@bbc.co.uk

🌐 www.bbc.co.uk/berkshire

**Contact** Station Manager, Lizz Loxam; News Editor, Patrick O'Hagan; Sports Editor, Joel Hufford

**About** Broadcasts on 104.1, 104.4, 95.4 and 94.6 FM, DAB digital radio and online.

## BBC Radio Bristol
**PO Box 194, Bristol, BS99 7QT**

☎ 0117 974 1111

☎ 0117 923 8323

✉ firstname.lastname@bbc.co.uk, radio.bristol@bbc.co.uk

🌐 www.bbc.co.uk/bristol

**Contact** Station Manager, Tim Pemberton; News Editor, Charlotte Callen; Sports Editor, Geoff Twentyman

**About** Broadcasts on 95.5 and 94.9 FM and 1548 AM and DAB digital radio.

## BBC Radio Cambridegshire
**104 Hills Road, Cambridge, CB2 1LD**

☎ 01223 259696

☎ 01223 460832

✉ firstname.lastname@bbc.co.uk, cambs@bbc.co.uk

🌐 www.bbc.co.uk/cambridge

**Contact** Managing Editor, Jason Horton; Assistant Editor, Alison Dawes; News Editor, Harry Beer; Sport Editor, Tom Williams; Trustline Producer, Jan Reynolds; CSV Action Desk Producer, Pamela Mungroo

**About** Broadcasts on 96 and 95.7 FM and DAB digital radio. First came on air in 1982.

## BBC Radio Cleveland
**PO Box 95FM, Broadcasting House, Newport Road, Middlesborough, TS1 5DG**

☎ 01642 225211

☎ 01642 211356

✉ firstname.lastname@bbc.co.uk, cleveland.studios@bbc.co.uk, cleveland.programmes@bbc.co.uk, cleveland.news@bbc.co.uk

🌐 www.bbc.co.uk/tees/local_radio

**Contact** Managing Editor, Peter Cook; Head of Programmes, Will Davies; News Editor, Peter Harris; Sport Editor, Paul Addison

**About** Covers Teesside, County Durham and North Yorkshire. Broadcasts on 95 FM and DAB digital radio.

## BBC Radio Cornwall
**Phoenix Wharf, Truro, TR1 1UA**

☎ 01872 275421

✉ firstname.lastname@bbc.co.uk, radio.cornwall@bbc.co.uk

🌐 www.bbc.co.uk/radiocornwall

**Contact** Editor, Pauline Causey; Assistant Editor, Daphne Skinnard; News Editor, Ed Goodridge; Sports Editor, Matt Sandoz

**About** Covers Cornwall and the Isle of Scilly. Broadcasts on 103.9 and 95.2 FM and DAB digital radio.

## BBC Radio Cumbria
**Annetwell Street, Carlisle, CA3 8BB**

☎ 01228 592444

☎ 01228 511195

✉ firstname.lastname@bbc.co.uk,

🌐 www.bbc.co.uk/cumbria

**Contact** Managing Editor, Nigel Dyson; News Editor, Neil Smith; Assistant Editor, Graham Moss

**About** Broadcasts on 95.6, 96.1 and 104.1 FM and DAB digital radio.

## BBC Radio Cymru
**Broadcasting House, Llandaff, Cardiff, CF5 2YQ**
- 029 2032 2018
- 029 2032 2473
- radio.cymru@bbc.co.uk
- www.bbc.co.uk/cymru/radiocymru

**Contact** Deputy Editor, Orwain Arfon Williams; News Editor, Bethan Roberts; Political Editor, Ashok Ahir

**About** A Welsh language station. Broadcasts a daily soap, Rhydeglwys and other drama and comedy as well as music, news, sport and features.

## BBC Radio Derby
**PO Box 104.5, St. Helen's Street, Derby, DE1 3HL**
- 01332 361111
- 01332 290794
- firstname.lastname@bbc.co.uk, radio.derby@bbc.co.uk
- www.bbc.co.uk/derby

**Contact** Editor, Simon Cornes; News and Sports Editor, John Atkin

**About** Broadcasts on 104.5, 95.3 and 96 FM and 1116 AM.

## BBC Radio Devon
**Broadcasting House, Seymour Road, Plymouth, PL3 5YQ**
- 01752 260323
- 01752 234564
- firstname.lastname@bbc.co.uk, radio.devon@bbc.co.uk
- www.bbc.co.uk/devon

**Contact** Managing Editor, Robert Wallace; Head of Programmes, Ian Timms; News Editor, Emma Clements; Sports Editor, Richard Green

**About** Also based at Walnut Gardens, St. David's Hill, Exeter, EX4 4DB. First came on air in 1983. Broadcasts on 103.4, 94.8, 95.7 and 95.8 FM and various AM frequencies around the county.

## BBC Radio Foyle
**8 Northland Road, Londonderry, Northern Ireland, BT48 7GD**
- 028 7137 8600
- 028 7137 8666
- firstname.lastname@bbc.co.uk, radio.foyle@bbc.co.uk

- www.bbc.co.uk/northernireland/radiofoyle

**Contact** Managing Editor, Paul McCauley; Head of News, Eimear O'Callaghan

**About** Broadcasts on 93.1 FM and 792 MW. Some programmes are transmitted simultaneously on BBC Radio Ulster.

## BBC Radio Gloucestershire
**London Road, Gloucester, GL1 1SW**
- 01452 308585
- 01452 309491
- firstname.lastname@bbc.co.uk, radio.gloucestershire@bbc.co.uk
- www.bbc.co.uk/radiogloucestershire

**Contact** Managing Editor, Mark Hurrell; News Editor, Graham Day; Sports Editor, Ian Randall

**About** Broadcasts on 104.7, 95 and 95.8 FM and 1413 AM.

## BBC Radio Humberside
**Queen's Court, Queen's Gardens, Hull, HU1 3RH**
- 01482 3233232
- 01482 621403
- firstname.lastname@bbc.co.uk, radio.humberside@bbc.co.uk
- www.bbc.co.uk/radiohumberside

**Contact** Managing Editor, Derrick McGill; Head of Programmes, Carl Wheatley; News Editor, Kate Slade; Sports Editor, David Burns

**About** First came on air in 1971. Broadcast on 95.9 FM and DAB digital radio.

## BBC Radio Jersey
**18 & 21 Parade Road, St. Helier, Jersey, JE2 3PL**
- 01534 870000
- 01534 732569
- firstname.lastname@bbc.co.uk, radiojersey@bbc.co.uk
- www.bbc.co.uk/jersey

**Contact** Managing Editor, Denzil Dudley; Assistant Editor, Matthew Price; News Editor, Hamish Marret-Crosby; Editor, Denzil Dudley

**About** Broadcasts on 88.8 FM.

## BBC Radio Kent
**The Great Hall, Mount Pleasant Road, Tunbridge Wells, TN1 1QQ**
- 01892 670000
- 01892 549118
- firstname.lastname@bbc.co.uk, radio.kent@bbc.co.uk

ⓦ www.bbc.co.uk/kent

**Contact** Managing Editor, Paul Leaper; Assistant Editor, Will Roffey; News Editor, Simon Long-Price; Sport Editor, Matt Davison

**About** Broadcasts on 96.7, 104.2, 97.6 FM and DAB digital radio.

## BBC Radio Lancashire
**20–26 Darwen Street, Blackburn, BB2 2EA**
ⓞ 01254 262411
ⓔ firstname.lastname@bbc.co.uk,
ⓦ www.bbc.co.uk/lancashire

**Contact** Editor, John Clayton; Head of Programming, Alison Brown; News Editor, Chris Rider; Sports Editor, Gary Hickson

**About** Broadcasts on 103.9, 95.5 and 104.5 FM and DAB digital radio.

## BBC Radio Leeds
**2 St. Peter's Square, Leeds, LS9 8AH**
ⓞ 0113 244 2131
ⓞ 0113 224 7316
ⓔ firstname.lastname@bbc.co.uk, radioleeds@bbc.co.uk
ⓦ www.bbc.co.uk/radioleeds

**Contact** Managing Editor, Phil Roberts; Assistant Editor and News Editor, Phil Squire; Sports Editor, Derm Tanner

**About** Broadcasts on 92.4 and 95.3 FM, 774 AM and DAB digital radio. Covers most of West Yorkshire.

## BBC Radio Leicester
**9 St. Nicholas Place, Leicester, LE1 5LB**
ⓞ 0116 251 6688
ⓞ 0116 251 1463
ⓔ firstname.lastname@bbc.co.uk, radioleicester@bbc.co.uk
ⓦ www.bbc.co.uk/leicester

**Contact** Managing Editor, Kate Squire; News Editor, Lucy Collins

**About** Britain's first local radio station. Broadcasts on 104.9 FM and DAB digital radio.

## BBC Radio Lincolnshire
**PO Box 219, Newport, Lincoln, LN1 3XY**
ⓞ 01522 511411
ⓞ 01522 511058
ⓔ firstname.lastname@bbc.co.uk, radio.lincolnshire@bbc.co.uk
ⓦ www.bbc.co.uk/radiolincolnshire

**Contact** Managing Editor, Charlie Partridge; Assistant Editor, Andy Farrant; News Editor, Maggie Curtis; Sports Editor, Michael Hortin

**About** Broadcasts on 94.9 and 104.7 FM, 1368 AM and DAB digital radio.

## BBC Radio Manchester
**PO Box 951, Oxford Road, Manchester, M60 1SD**
ⓞ 0161 200 2000
ⓞ 0161 228 6110
ⓔ firstname.lastname@bbc.co.uk, radio.manchester@bbc.co.uk
ⓦ www.bbc.co.uk/manchester

**Contact** Managing Editor, John Ryan; Head of Programmes, Lawrence Mann; News Editor, Mark Elliott; Sports Editor, Andy Buckley

**About** First aired in 1970. Covers the Greater Manchester area. Broadcasts on 95.1 FM and DAB digital radio.

## BBC Radio Merseyside
**55 Paradise Street, Liverpool, L1 3BP**
ⓞ 0151 708 5500
ⓞ 0151 794 0988
ⓔ firstname.lastname@bbc.co.uk, radio.merseyside@bbc.co.uk
ⓦ www.bbc.co.uk/radiomerseyside

**Contact** Editor, Mick Ord; News Editor, Andy Ball; Arts Editor, Angela Heslop; Sports Editor, Ian Kennedy

**About** Broadcasts on 95.8 FM and 1485 AM.

## BBC Radio nan Gaidheal
**Rosebank, Church Street, Stornoway, Isle of Lewis, HS1 2LS**
ⓞ 01851 705000
ⓔ firstname.lastname@bbc.co.uk
ⓦ www.bbc.co.uk/scotland/alba

**Contact** Editor, Marion Mackinnon

**About** A Gaelic language service.

## BBC Radio Newcastle
**Broadcasting Centre, Barrack Road, Newcastle upon Tyne, NE99 1RN**
ⓞ 0191 232 4141
ⓔ firstname.lastname@bbc.co.uk, radionewcastle.news@bbc.co.uk
ⓦ www.bbc.co.uk/tyne, www.bbc.co.uk/wear

**Contact** Managing Editor, Graham Moss; Assistant Managing Editor, Doug Morris; News Editor, Rik Martin; Editor, Andrew Robson

**About** First aired in 1971. Broadcasts on 95.4 FM and DAB digital radio.

## BBC Radio Norfolk
**The Forum, Millennium Plain, Norwich, NR2 1BH**
- 01603 617411
- 01603 633692
- firstname.lastname@bbc.co.uk, radionorfolk@bbc.co.uk
- www.bbc.co.uk/radionorfolk

**Contact** Managing Editor, David Clayton; Assistant Editor, Graham Barnard; News Editor, Sarah Kings; Sports Editor, Matthew Gudgin
**About** Broadcasts on 95.1, 95.6 and 104.4 FM and DAB digital radio.

## BBC Radio Northampton
**Broadcasting House, Abington Street, Northampton, NN1 2BH**
- 01604 239100
- 01604 230709
- firstname.lastname@bbc.co.uk, northampton@bbc.co.uk
- www.bbc.co.uk/northampton

**Contact** Editor, Laura Moss; Assistant Editor, Louise Daw; Sports Editor, Geoff Doyle
**About** Broadcasts on 104.2 and 103.6 FM.

## BBC Radio Nottingham
**London Road, Nottingham, NG2 4UU**
- 0115 955 0500
- 0115 902 1983
- firstname.lastname@bbc.co.uk, radio.nottingham@bbc.co.uk
- www.bbc.co.uk/radionottingham

**Contact** News Editor, Aeneas Rotsos; Sports Editor, Colin Fray
**About** Broadcasts on 95.5 and 103.8 FM and DAB digital radio.

## BBC Radio Orkney
**Castle Street, Kirkwall, KW15 1DF**
- 01856 873939
- 01856 872908
- firstname.lastname@bbc.co.uk, radio.orkney@bbc.co.uk
- www.bbc.co.uk/radioorkney

**Contact** Editor and News Editor, John Ferguson
**About** A BBC community radio station. All content is produced in the Orkney Islands.

## BBC Radio Oxford
**269 Banbury Road, Oxford, OX2 7DW**
- 0845 931 1444
- 0845 931 1555
- firstname.lastname@bbc.co.uk, oxford@bbc.co.uk
- www.bbc.co.uk/oxford

**Contact** Executive Editor, Steve Taschini; Assistant Editor, Will Banks; Sports Editor, Jerome Sale
**About** Formerly known as BBC Thames Valley and BBC Radio Berkshire. Broadcasts on 95.2 FM.

## BBC Radio Scotland
**BBC Broadcasting House, Queen Margaret Drive, Glasgow, GL12 8DG**
- 0141 339 8844
- firstname.lastname@bbc.co.uk
- www.bbc.co.uk/scotland

**Contact** Head of BBC Radio Scotland, Jeff Zycinski; Head of Programming, Maggie Cunningham; Art Editor, Pauline McLean; Editor of Radio Drama, Bruce Young
**About** Broadcasts throughout Scotland on 92.4–94.7 FM and 810 MW (585 Dumfries).

## BBC Radio Scotland (Aberdeen)
**Beechgrove Terrace, Beechgrove House, Aberdeen, AB15 5ZT**
- 01224 384888
- news.aberdeen@bbc.co.uk
- www.bbc.co.uk/scotland

**Contact** Head of Programmes, Andrew Jones; Head of News, Sandy Bremner; Radio Bulletin Editor, Fiona Stalker
**About** Broadcasts new bulletins across the North East of Scotland on BBC Radio Scotland.

## BBC Radio Scotland (Dumfries)
**Elmbank, Lover's Walk, Dumfries, DG1 1NZ**
- 01387 268008
- 01387 252568
- firstname.lastname@bbc.co.uk, dumfries@bbc.co.uk
- www.bbc.co.uk/scotland

**Contact** Senior Broadcast Journalist, Sports and News Editor, Willie Johnston
**About** Mainly news bulletins, which are broadcast four times a day on BBC Radio Scotland.

## BBC Radio Scotland (Inverness)
**7 Culduthel Road, Inverness, IV2A 4AD**
- 01463 720720

● inverness.news@bbc.co.uk
● www.bbc.co.uk/scotland
**Contact** News Editor, Craig Swan; Sports Editor, Charles Bannerman
**About** Mainly news bulletins, which are broadcast four times a day, on BBC Radio Scotland.

## BBC Radio Scotland (Selkirk)
**Unit 1, Ettrick Riverside, Dunsdale Road, Selkirk, TD7 5EB**
● 01750 724567
● 01750 724555
● firstname.lastname@bbc.co.uk, selkirk@bbc.co.uk
● www.bbc.co.uk/scotland
**Contact** Senior Broadcaster and News Editor, Cameron Battle; Sports Editor, Grahame MacGregor
**About** Mainly news bulletins, which are broadcast four times a day, on BBC Radio Scotland.

## BBC Radio Sheffield
**54 Shoreham Street, Sheffield, S1 4RS**
● 0114 273 1177
● 0114 267 5454
● firstname.lastname@bbc.co.uk, radio.sheffield@bbc.co.uk
● www.bbc.co.uk/southyorkshire
**Contact** Managing Editor, Gary Keown; Head of News, Mark Woodcock; Sports Editor, Paul Walker

## BBC Radio Shetland
**Pitt Lane, Lerwick, ZE1 0DW**
● 01595 694747
● 01595 694307
● firstname.lastname@bbc.co.uk, radio.shetland@bbc.co.uk
● www.bbc.co.uk/scotland
**Contact** News and Sports Editor, Caroline Moyes
**About** Broadcasts regular news bulletins and programmes such as Good Evening Shetland.

## BBC Radio Shropshire
**2–4 Boscobel Drive, Shrewsbury, SY1 3TT**
● 01743 248484
● 01743 237018
● firstname.lastname@bbc.co.uk, radio.shropshire@bbc.co.uk
● www.bbc.co.uk/shropshire
**Contact** Managing Editor, Tim Beech; News and Environment Editor, Sharon Simcock
**About** Broadcasts on 96 FM and DAB digital radio. First came on air in 1985.

## BBC Radio Solent
**Broadcasting House, Havelock Road, Southampton, SO14 7PW**
● 023 8063 2811
● 023 8033 9648
● firstname.lastname@bbc.co.uk, radio.solent@bbc.co.uk
● www.bbc.co.uk/radiosolent
**Contact** Managing Editor, Mia Costello
**About** Broadcasts on 96.1 and 103.8 FM and DAB digital radio.

## BBC Radio Stoke
**Cheapside, Hanley, Stoke on Trent, ST1 1JJ**
● 01782 208080
● 01782 289115
● firstname.lastname@bbc.co.uk, radio.stoke@bbc.co.uk
● www.bbc.co.uk/radiostoke
**Contact** Managing Editor, Sue Owen; Programme Organiser, Mary Fox; News Editor, James O' Hara; Sports Editor, Graham McGarry
**About** First came on air in 1968. Broadcasts on 64.6 and 104.1 FM and DAB digital radio.

## BBC Radio Suffolk
**Broadcasting House, St. Matthew's Street, Ipswich, IP1 3EP**
● 01473 250000
● 01473 210887
● firstname.lastname@bbc.co.uk, radiosuffolk@bbc.co.uk
● www.bbc.co.uk/radiosuffolk
**Contact** Managing Editor, Gerald Main; News Editor, Lis Henderson; Sports Editor, Mark Matthews
**About** Broadcasts on 95.5, 95.9, 103.9 and 104.6 FM. Email the Editor with any local programme ideas or queries.

## BBC Radio Swindon
**BBC Broadcasting House, Prospect Place, Swindon, SN1 3RW**
● 01793 513626
● 01793 513650
● firstname.lastname@bbc.co.uk, radio.swindon@bbc.co.uk
● www.bbc.co.uk/wiltshire/local_radio/radio_swindon
**Contact** Managing Editor, Tony Worgan; News Editor, Jillian Moody

**About** Broadcasts on 103.6 FM and DAB digital radio.

## BBC Radio Ulster
**Broadcasting House, Ormeau Avenue, Belfast, Northern Ireland, BT2 8HQ**
- 028 9033 8000
- firstname.lastname@bbc.co.uk,
- www.bbc.co.uk/northernireland/radioulster

**Contact** Controller, Peter Johnston; Head of News, Andrew Colman; News Editor, Kathleen Carragher; Art and Entertainment Editor, Maggie Taggart; Sports Editor, Edward Smith

**About** Broadcasts on 92–95 FM.

## BBC Radio Wales
**Broadcasting House, Llandaff, Cardiff, CF5 2YQ**
- 029 2032 2000
- 029 2032 2674
- firstname.lastname@bbc.co.uk, radio.wales@bbc.co.uk
- www.bbc.co.uk/radiowales

**Contact** Editor, Sali Collins; Editor, Ruth Sally; Head of News, Mark O'Callaghan

**About** Broadcasts 19 hours a day in the English language, for an audience living west of Offa's Dyke.

## BBC Radio Wiltshire
**BBC Broadcasting House, Prospect Place, Swindon, SN1 3RW**
- 01793 513626
- 01793 513650
- firstname.lastname@bbc.co.uk, radio.wiltshire@bbc.co.uk
- www.bbc.co.uk/wiltshire

**Contact** Managing Editor, Tony Worgan; News Editor, Kirsty Ward; Sports Editor, Ed Hadwin

**About** Closely linked with BBC Radio Swindon. Broadcasts on 103.5, 104.3 and 104.9 FM and DAB digital radio.

## BBC Radio York
**20 Bootham Row, York, YO30 7BR**
- 01904 641351
- 01904 610937
- firstname.lastname@bbc.co.uk, radio.york@bbc.co.uk
- www.bbc.co.uk/northyorkshire

**Contact** Managing Editor, Matt Youdale; News Editor, Anna Evans

**About** Broadcasts on 103.7, 104.3 and 95.5 FM.

## BBC Somerset Sound
**Broadcasting House, Park Street, Taunton, TA1 4DA**
- 01823 348920
- 01823 332539
- firstname.lastname@bbc.co.uk, somerset.sound@bbc.co.uk
- www.bbc.co.uk/somerset

**Contact** Managing Editor and News Editor, Simon Clifford

**About** Broadcasts on 1566 AM across Somerset.

## BBC Southern Counties Radio
**Broadcasting House, 40–42 Queen's Road, Brighton, BN1 3XB**
- 01273 320400/01483 306306
- firstname.lastname@bbc.co.uk, southern.counties.radio@bbc.co.uk
- www.bbc.co.uk/southerncounties

**Contact** Managing Editor, Nicci Holliday; Programme Editor, Mark Carter; Sports Editor, Tim Durrans

**About** Also has a base at Broadcasting Centre, Guildford, GU2 7AP. Broadcasts on 104-104.8 and 95-95.3 FM and DAB digital radio.

## BBC Three Counties Radio
**1 Hastings Street, Luton, LU1 5XL**
- 01582 637400
- 01582 401467
- firstname.lastname@bbc.co.uk, threecounties@bbc.co.uk
- www.bbc.co.uk/threecounties

**Contact** Station Editor, Angus Moorat; Sports Editor, Simon Oxley

**About** Covers Bedfordshire, Hertfordshire and Buckinghamshire. Broadcasts on 90.4, 92.1, 94.7, 95.5, 98, 103.8 and 104.5 FM.

## BBC WM
**The Mailbox, Birmingham, B1 1RF**
- 0845 300 9956
- 0121 567 6025
- firstname.lastname@bbc.co.uk, bbcwm@bbc.co.uk
- www.bbc.co.uk/radiowm

**Contact** Managing Editor and News Editor, Keith Beech; News Editor, Chris Kowalik

**About** Broadcasts on 95.6 FM and DAB digital radio. Covers the West Midlands, South Staffordshire and North Worcestershire.

# BBC DRAMA, ENTERTAINMENT & CHILDREN'S

BBC Drama, Entertainment and Children's is responsible for commissioning content in these areas, across television, radio and film.

## BBC Drama, Entertainment and Children's
**BBC Television Centre, Wood Lane, London, W12 7RJ**
- 020 8743 8000
- firstname.lastname@bbc.co.uk

**Contact** Director, Drama Production, Nicolas Brown; Creative Director, Drama, Sally Woodward Gentle; Controller, In House Drama, John Yorke; Controller, BBC Fiction, BBC Vision, Jane Tranter; Controller, Entertainment Group, BBC Vision Studios, Jon Beazley; Creative Director, Entertainment Production, BBC Vision Studios, Karen Smith; Executive Producer, *EastEnders*, Kate Harwood; Controller, BBC Children's, Richard Deverell

## BBC Comedy
**BBC Television Centre, Wood Lane, London, W12 7RJ**
- 020 8743 8000
- firstname.lastname@bbc.co.uk
- www.bbc.co.uk/comedy

**Contact** Controller of Comedy Commissioning, Lucy Lumsden; Executive Editors, Cheryl Taylor, Simon Wilson, John Rolph; Development Coordinator, Comedy, Michael Buchanan-Dunne; Comedy contact, Scotland, Alan Tyler; Comedy contact, Northern Ireland, Mike Edgar; Comedy contact, Wales, Gareth Gwenlan

**About** Responsible for commissioning comedy (sitcom and sketch) across all BBC channels. Check www.bbc.co.uk/commissioning for current development focus. Lucy Lumsden is on maternity leave until May 2007, Acting Controller until then is Cheryl Taylor. Proposals from independent producers may be submitted at any time. For the London team, contact Michael Buchanan-Dunne. For the nations and regions, approach the relevant comedy/entertainment contact.
 Recent programmes: *Extras; Little Miss Jocelyn*.

## BBC Daytime
**BBC Television Centre, Wood Lane, London, W12 7RJ**
- 020 8743 8000
- firstname.lastname@bbc.co.uk

**Contact** Controller of Daytime, Jay Hunt; Executive Producer (Independent Producers), Alison Kirkham; Commissioning Editor, Entertainment and Out of London, Sumi Coonock; Executive Editor, Lindsay Bradbury

**About** Commissioning covers daytime drama, entertainment and factual entertainment. Development priorities can be viewed at www.bbc.co.uk/commissioning Proposals from outside of London go to Sumi Connock. All other proposals go to Lindsay Bradbury. Proposals from independent producers may be submitted at any time.
 Recent programmes: *Don't Get Done, Get Dom; Hands on Nature*.

## BBC Drama
**BBC Television Centre, Wood Lane, London, W12 7RJ**
- 020 8743 8000
- firstname.lastname@bbc.co.uk
- www.bbc.co.uk/drama

**Contact** Head of Series and Serials, Kate Harwood; Head of Drama Serials, Laura Mackie; Head of Independent Drama, Lucy Richer; Head of Drama, BBC Wales and Head of Drama Commissioning, Julie Gardner; Head of Drama, BBC Northern Ireland, Patrick Spence

**About** Check www.bbc.co.uk/commissioning for latest development priorities. Proposals may be submitted from independent producers at any time to the Editorial heads: Julie Gardner; Sarah Brandist; Polly Hill; Patrick Spence; and Anne Mensah. There are three possible outcomes to a submission: input into paid development; unpaid development; or rejected. This will be announced within four weeks.
 Recent programmes: *Spooks; Robin Hood*.

## BBC Entertainment
**BBC Television Centre, Wood Lane, London, W12 7RJ**
- 020 8743 8000
- firstname.lastname@bbc.co.uk
- www.bbc.co.uk/entertainment

**Contact** Controller, BBC Entertainment, Multi-Platform Commissioning, Elaine Bedell; Executive Editors, Jo Wallace, Katie Taylor, Suzanne Gilfillan;

Executive Producers (Independent Producers), Gilly Hall; Development Coordinator, Pinki Chambers; Entertainment contact, Scotland, Alan Tyler; Entertainment contact, Northern Ireland, Mike Edgar; Entertainment contact, Wales, David Jackson; Head of Genre Management, Claire Evans

**About** Responsible for commissioning entertainment formats, light entertainment, quizzes and panel shows and entertainment/celebrity documentaries. Check www.bbc.co.uk/commissioning for the latest development priorities. Independent producers/companies wishing to submit proposals may do so at any time. For nationwide proposals, contact Pinki Chambers and for the nations and regions, submit via the contact for that area. A decision will be made within six weeks of receipt.

Recent programmes: *Strictly Come Dancing; Friday Night with Jonathan Ross.*

## BBC Films

**Grafton House, 379–381 Euston Road, London, NW1 3AU**

- 020 7765 0251
- 020 7765 0278
- www.bbc.co.uk/bbcfilms

**Contact** Head of BBC Films, David Thompson; Development Editor, Beth Richards

**About** The feature film arm of the BBC. No unsolicited scripts. Submit via Writers Room, www.bbc.co.uk/writersroom. Independent producers may submit scripts by post to Beth Richards.

Recent programmes: *Billy Elliot; Miss Potter.*

## BBC Writers Room

**Grafton House, 379–381 Euston Road, London, NW1 3AU**

- writersroom@bbc.co.uk
- www.bbc.co.uk/writersroom

**Contact** Creative Director, New Writing, Kate Rowland; Development Manager, Paul Ashton

**About** A route for the public to submit scripts for radio drama, television series, serial and factual drama, CBBC, television/radio comedy, fictionlab, animation, film, blast, new media, film network and specialist factual. There are detailed guidelines online about what to submit and what not to submit, as well as links to other BBC departments (very few) that will also accept unsolicited material from the public. Send hard copies only, addressed to the Development Editor, with an SAE. Read all guidelines thoroughly before submitting.

## CBBC

**BBC Television Centre, Wood Lane, London, W12 7RJ**

- 020 8743 8000
- firstname.lastname@bbc.co.uk, cbbcanimation.submissions@bbc.co.uk
- www.bbc.co.uk/cbbc

**Contact** CBBC Creative Director, Anne Gilchrist; Head of CBBC Drama and Animation, Jon East; Head of CBBC Co productions and Acquisitions, Jesse Cleverly

**About** Aimed at children and young people, CBBC runs two commissioning rounds a year. Details of closing dates are posted on www.bbc.co.uk/commissioning it is a self commissioning, self scheduling department. Independent producers may submit proposals to Anne Gilchrist, or Jon East for drama. Acquisitions and animation enquiries should be directed to Jesse Cleverly. A final decision will be given no longer than 20 weeks after receipt of the proposal. Children's drama is one of a few departments that accept unsolicited proposals from writers. See www.bbc.co.uk/writersroom/writing/submissions_other_childrens for submission guidelines.

Recent programmes: *Grange Hill; Blue Peter.*

## CBeebies

**BBC Television Centre, Wood Lane, London, W12 7RJ**

- 020 8743 8000
- firstname.lastname@bbc.co.uk
- www.bbc.co.uk/cbeebies

**Contact Title** Cbeebies Creative Director, Michael Carrington; Head of Cbeebies Acquisitions and Animation, Kay Benbow

**About** Aimed at a very young audience, content includes entertainment, drama, comedy and factual programming. Cbeebies run two commissioning rounds a year, details of which appear on www.bbc.co.uk/commissioning Independent producers may send proposals in to Michael Carrington, or direct animation or acquisition enquiries to Kay Benbow. Replies to proposals should be within five weeks. The department is one of few that still accept unsolicited proposals from writers themselves.

For submission guidelines see: www.bbc.co.uk/writersroom/writing/submissions_other_cbeebies Recent programmes: *Tweenies; Teletubbies*

# BBC FACTUAL & LEARNING

The Factual and Learning division is responsible for content across many platforms including television, radio and interactive. The academic revision guides such as GSCE Bitesize, are part of its remit, as well as campaigns and technology awareness.

## BBC Factual and Learning

BBC Television Centre, Wood Lane, London, W12 7RJ

☎ 020 8743 8000

✉ firstname.lastname@bbc.co.uk

**Contact** Controller, Knowledge, BBC Vision, Glenwyn Benson

## BBC Arts, Music, Performance and Religion

BBC Television Centre, Wood Lane, London, W12 7RJ

☎ 020 8743 8000

✉ firstname.lastname@bbc.co.uk, arts.proposals@bbc.co.uk

**Contact** Commissioning Editor, Adam Kemp; Executive Producer (Independents), Jaquie Hughes; Factual and CA Network and Commissions, Northern Ireland, Jeremy Adams; Head of Factual Programmes, Scotland, Andrea Miller; Series Producer, Imagine, Janet Lee; Series Editor, Arena, Anthony Wall; Executive Producer, BBC Religion & Ethics (Songs of Praise), Hugh Faupel; Religion, Northern Ireland, Bert Tosh; Arts, Northern Ireland, Mike Edgar; Music, Northern Ireland, Declan McGovern

**About** Commissions across all media platforms, in the areas of arts, music and religion. The aim is to produce programming with depth, ambition and style. Development priorities are posted on www.bbc.co.uk/commissioning for each commissioning round. Independent proposals should be sent to Adam Kemp, preferably by email, or by post to: Room 6051, BBC Television Centre. Strand proposals may be sent straight to the strand editor or producer, and proposals from the nations may be sent directly to the relevant contact. An initial decision is made within 6 weeks.

Recent programmes: *Songs of Praise*, BBC1.

## BBC Documentaries

BBC Television Centre, Wood Lane, London, W12 7RJ

☎ 020 8743 8000

✉ firstname.lastname@bbc.co.uk, docs.proposals@bbc.co.uk

**Contact** Commissioning Editor, Richard Klein; Executive Producer (Independents), Charlotte Moore, Ben Gale (BBC3), Maxine Wilson, Emma Willis; Documentary contact, Northern Ireland, TBA; Head of Factual Programmes, Scotland, Andrea Miller; Head of Factual Programmes, Wales, Adrian Davies; Commissioning Editor, Documentaries (One Life), Todd Austin; Commissioning Editor, Storyville, Nick Fraser

**About** Commissions documentaries across all content platforms as singles or series. Development priorities are posted on www.bbc.co.uk/commissioning, independent proposals should be sent to Richard Klein preferably by email, or by post to: Room 6060, BBC Television Centre. Strand ideas may be sent direct to the editor or producer of the strand. For One Life documentaries, send a one page proposal including possible producers or directors to Todd Austin, preferably by email, onelife.documentaries@bbc.co.uk, or by post to: Room 5503, BBC White City, Wood Lane, London, W12 7TS. To speak with Todd, call 020 8752 6608 or fax 020 8752 6117. One Life films must reflect contemporary British Life. For the Storyville strand, send proposals to Nick Fraser, preferably by email to, storyville@bbc.co.uk or by post to: Room 202, 1 Mortimer Street, London, W1T 3JA. To speak with Nick Fraser call 020 7765 5211 or fax 020 7765 5210. Proposals from the nations may be sent directly to the contact in that country. An initial decision is available in six weeks.

Recent programmes: *The Armstrongs*, BBC2.

## BBC Features and Factual Entertainment

BBC Television Centre, Wood Lane, London, W12 7RJ

☎ 020 8743 8000

✉ firstname.lastname@bbc.co.uk,features.proposals@bbc.co.uk

**Contact** Commissioning Editor, Features and Factual Entertainment, Elaine Bedell; Executive Producers (Independents), Mirella Breda, Ben Gale (BBC3); Factual and CA Network Commissions, Northern Ireland, Jeremy Adams; Head of Programme Production, Northern Ireland, Mike Edgar; Head of Factual Programmes, Wales, Adrian

Davies; Head of Factual Programmes, Scotland, Andrea Miller

**About** Feature and factual entertainment, commissions all video content across television, radio, mobile, interactive and 'red button' platforms. Deals with the 'lighter' side of factual programming. Development priorities are updated for every commissioning round on www.bbc.co.uk/commissioning, proposals from independent production companies should be sent to, Elaine Bedell, preferably by email, or by post to: Room 6060, BBC Television Centre. An announcement from the website will let the public know if they are accepting proposals not linked to production companies. Independent producers in the nations may submit to the relevant contact in their area. An initial decision should be available within six weeks.

Recent programmes: *What Not to Wear,* BBC1.

## BBC Specialist Factual

**BBC Television Centre, Wood Lane, London, W12 7RJ**

**☏** 020 8743 8000

**✉** firstname.lastname@bbc.co.uk, specfact.proposals@bbc.co.uk

**Contact** Commissioning Editor, Emma Swain; Executive Producer (Independents), Martin Davidson; Factual and CA Network and Commissions, Northern Ireland, Jeremy Adams; Head of Factual Programmes, BBC Wales, Adrian Davies; Creative Director, Specialist Factual, Scotland, Neil McDonald; Editor, Horizon, Andrew Cohen; Executive Producer, Money Programme, Clive Edwards; Editor, Timewatch, John Farren; Executive Editor, Wild, Vyv Simson; Series Editor, Natural World, Tim Martin

**About** Commissions across all media platforms, in the areas of science, history, business and natural history. Detailed development plans and editorial needs are posted on www.bbc.co.uk/commissioning, independent proposals should be sent to Emma Swain, preferably by email, or by post to: Room 6051, BBC Television Centre. Independent proposals for specific strands may be sent directly to the strand editor, and independent proposals from the nations may be sent straight to the appropriate contact. An initial decision will be made within six weeks.

Recent programmes: *The Real Hustle,* BBC3.

# BBC NEWS

BBC News is responsible for national daily news, business, political and current affairs programmes on BBC television and radio. It also produces the continuous news channels BBC News 24, BBC Parliament, BBC World, interactive services, Ceefax and the BBC News website.

## BBC News

**BBC Television Centre, Wood Lane, London, W12 7RJ**

**☏** 020 8743 8000

**✉** firstname.lastname@bbc.co.uk

**⊕** www.bbc.co.uk/news

**Contact** Director, News, Helen Boaden; Head of Radio News, Stephen Mitchell; Head of Television News, Peter Horrocks; Deputy Director of News and Controller, News Production, Adrian Van Klaveren; Head of Political Programmes, Sue Inglish; Economics Editor, Evan Davis; Editor, Economics and Business Centre, Daniel Dodd; Controller, Editorial Policy, David Jordan; Political Editor, Nick Robinson; Head of BBC News gathering, Francesca Unsworth

## BBC Current Affairs and Investigations

**BBC White City, 201 Wood Lane, London, W12 7TS**

**✉** firstname.lastname@bbc.co.uk, curraffairs.proposals@bbc.co.uk

**Contact** Commissioning Editor, George Entwistle; Executive Producers (Independents), Eamon Hardy, Lucy Hetherington; Head of Programme Production, Northern Ireland, Mike Edgar; Head of Factual Programmes, Scotland, Andrea Miller; Head of Factual Programmes, Wales, Adrian Davies; Editor, Panorama, Sandy Smith; Editor, This World, Karen O'Connor; Executive Editor, Network Current Affairs, Manchester (Real Story), Dave Stanford

**About** Commissions across all platforms, aiming to open viewers' eyes to world issues. Development priorities are updated on www.bbc.co.uk/commissioning independent proposals should be sent to George Entwistle preferably by email, or by post to: Room 1172, BBC White City. Strand proposals may be sent directly to the strand editor and proposals from the nations may be sent to the relevant contact in that country. An initial decision will be made within six weeks.

Recent programmes: Who Do You Think You Are, BBC1.

## BBC News Interactive
**BBC Television Centre, Wood Lane, London, W12 7RJ**
- 020 8576 8000
- firstname.lastname@bbc.co.uk
- www.bbc.co.uk/news

**Contact** Editor, BBC News Website, Steve Hermann; Deputy Editor, BBC News Website, Paul Brannan; Editor, Interactivity, Vicky Taylor; UK Editor, BBC News website, Gary Duffy; World editor, BBC News website, Adam Curtis

**About** Covers interactive mediums, including websites and Ceefax.

## BBC Radio News Programmes
**BBC Television Centre, Wood Lane, London, W12 7RJ**
- 020 8743 8000
- firstname.lastname@bbc.co.uk

**Contact** Editor, Today, Kevin Marsh; Editor, World at One and The World This Weekend, Colin Hancock; Editor, PM and Broadcasting House, Peter Rippon

**About** Covers all news content on analogue and digital radio stations.
Recent programmes: *The Today Programme,* Radio 4.

## BBC Television News Programmes
**BBC Television Centre, Wood Lane, London, W12 7RJ**
- 020 8743 8000
- firstname.lastname@bbc.co.uk
- www.bbc.co.uk/news

**Contact** Editor, Daytime News, Amanda Farnsworth; Editor, Newsnight, Peter Barron; Political Editor, Newsnight, Martha Kearney; Newsnight Science Editor, Susan Watts; Editor, Sunday AM, Barney Jones; Editor, Breakfast, David Kermode; Controller, BBC Parliament, Peter Knowles; Controller, News 24, Kevin Bakhurst; Editorial Director, BBC News 24, Mark Popescu

**About** Covers all news content on terrestrial and digital television channels.
Recent programmes: *The One O'Clock News,* BBC1.

# BBC SPORT

## BBC Sport
**BBC Television Centre, Wood Lane, London, W12 7RJ**
- 020 8576 8000
- firstname.lastname@bbc.co.uk
- www.bbc.co.uk/sport

**Contact** Director of Sport, Roger Mosey; Head of Major Events, BBC Sport, Dave Gordon; Editor, BBC Sport Interactive, Ben Gallop; Head of Radio Sport, Gordon Turnbull; Sports Editor, Interactive, Alex Gubbay; Head of BBC Football, Neil Sloane

**About** Responsible for sports coverage across the full range of BBC media platforms.
Recent programmes: *Match of the Day,* BBC1.

# BBC NATIONS & REGIONS

This sector of the BBC is responsible for a large proportion of the corporation's output across television and radio. BBC Scotland, Northern Ireland and Wales produce content for their national networks, while the 12 BBC regions produce regular news and current affairs programming for television and local radio. National and regional BBC websites are also part of the remit.

## BBC Nations and Regions
**BBC Media Centre, 201 Wood Lane, London, W12 7TQ**
- 020 8743 8000
- firstname.lastname@bbc.co.uk

**Contact** Director, Nations and Regions, Pat Loughrey; Controller, English Regions, Andy Griffee

## BBC Birmingham
**The Mailbox, Birmingham, B1 1RF**
- 0121 567 6767
- 0121 567 6875
- firstname.lastname@bbc.co.uk
- www.bbc.co.uk/birmingham

**Contact** Head of Regional and Local Programmes, David Holdsworth; Head of Studio, Factual and Learning, Birmingham, Tessa Finch

**About** BBC Birmingham's main headquarters contains the Documentaries and Contemporary Factual Department. They produce content for all

BBC channels. It also acts as the headquarters for all BBC regions.
 Recent programmes: *To Buy or Not to Buy; Gardener's World.*

## BBC Birmingham Drama Village
**Archibald House, 1059 Bristol Road, Selly Oak, Birmingham, B29 6LT**
☎ 0121 567 7350
**About** BBC Drama Village is based on the Selly Oak campus of the University of Birmingham and is used as a set for BBC dramas.
 Recent programmes: *Dalziel and Pascoe; Doctors; The Afternoon Play.*

## BBC Bristol Natural History Unit
**BBC Broadcasting House, White Ladies Road, Bristol, BS28 2LR**
☎ 0117 973 2211
✉ firstname.lastname@bbc.co.uk
🌐 www.bbc.co.uk/bristol
**Contact** Head of Programmes, Leisure and Factual Entertainment, Tom Archer; Head of Natural History Unit, Neil Nightingale
**About** Home of the BBC's Natural History Unit, producing programmes for all major BBC channels.
 Recent programmes: *The Really Wild Show; Blue Planet.*

## BBC East
**The Forum, Millennium Plain, Norwich, NR2 1AW**
☎ 01603 284700
☎ 01603 284399
✉ firstname.lastname@bbc.co.uk
🌐 www.bbc.co.uk/norfolk
**Contact** Head of Regional Programming, Tim Bishop; Planning and News Editor, Jackie Leggett

## BBC East Midlands
**East Midlands Broadcasting Centre, London Road, Nottingham, NG2 4UU**
☎ 0115 955 0500
✉ firstname.lastname@bbc.co.uk
🌐 www.bbc.co.uk/nottingham
**Contact** Head of Regional Programming, Aziz Rashid; TV and News Editor, Emma Agnew; Assistant Editor, Kevin Hill

## BBC London
**35 Marylebone High Street, London, W1U 4QA**
☎ 020 7224 2424

✉ firstname.lastname@bbc.co.uk
🌐 www.bbc.co.uk/london
**Contact** Head of BBC London, Michael MacFarlane; Head of News and Sport, Pete Stevens; Assistant Editor, Duncan Williamson
**About** Responsible for BBC London News, BBC London 94.9FM and the BBC London website.

## BBC North East & Cumbria
**Broadcasting Centre, Barrack Road, Newcastle upon Tyne, NE99 2NE**
☎ 0191 232 1313
✉ firstname.lastname@bbc.co.uk
**Contact** Head of Local and Regional Programmes, Wendy Pilmer; TV Editor, Andy Cooper; News Editor, John Lawrence; Sports Editor, Jeff Brown

## BBC Northern Ireland
**BBC Broadcasting House, Ormeau Avenue, Belfast, Northern Ireland, BT2 8QH**
☎ 028 9033 8000
✉ fistname.lastname@bbc.co.uk
🌐 www.bbc.co.uk/northernireland
**Contact** Controller, BBC Northern Ireland, Peter Johnstone; Head of Arts and Entertainment, Mike Edgar; Head of Programmes, Ailsa Orr; Head of Drama, Patrick Spence; News Editor, Tom Coulter
**About** Produces a wide variety of content for both main BBC platforms and regional channels. Programming includes drama, documentaries, current affairs, news, sports and entertainment, often relating to Irish and Ulster Scots. Scripts for dramas, via agents only, may be sent to: Susan Carson, Programme Development Executive (Television), or Anne Simpson, Manager (Radio), Radio Drama, BBC Northern Ireland Drama, Room 3.07, Blackstaff House, Great Victoria Street, Belfast, BT2 7BB. Alternatively email, tvdrama.ni@bbc.co.uk The latest writing opportunities and competitions are posted on the website.

## BBC North West
**New Broadcasting House, Oxford Road, Manchester, M60 1SJ**
☎ 0161 200 2020
✉ firstname.lastname@bbc.co.uk
**Contact** Head of Local and Regional Programming, Leo Devlne; News Assistant Editor, Jim Clarke

## BBC Scotland

**BBC Broadcasting House, Queen Margaret Drive, Glasgow, G12 8DG**

☎ 0141 339 8844

✉ firstname.lastname@bbc.co.uk

🌐 www.bbc.co.uk/scotland

**Contact** Controller, BBC Scotland, Ken MacQuarrie; Head of New Media, Learning and Communities, BBC Scotland, Julie Adair; Commissioning Editor, Television, BBC Scotland, Ewan Angus; Head of Programmes and Services, BBC Scotland, Maggie Cunningham; Editor, BBC Scotland News Interactive (News Online and Ceefax), Mark Coyle; Editor, Features and Religion, BBC Scotland, Jane Fowler; Head of News and Current Affairs, Atholl Duncan; Arts Editor, May Miller; Head of Drama, BBC Scotland, Anne Mensah; Head of Factual, BBC Scotland, Andrea Miller; Head of Gaelic, BBC Scotland, Margaret Mary Murray

**About** One of the largest production centres outside of London. Produces a variety of content for both regional (BBC One and Two Scotland) and nationwide networks. These include drama, entertainment formats, current affairs, news, sports, documentary, arts, religion and music. There are several production centres in Scotland other than the headquarters. The BBC Scotland website announces any competitions, or calls for writing submissions from the public although these are rare.

## BBC South

**Broadcasting House, Havelock Road, Southampton, SO14 7PU**

☎ 023 8022 6201

✉ firstname.lastname@bbc.co.uk

**Contact** Head of Local and Regional Programming, Eve Turner; News Editor, Liesel Smith; TV Editor, Lee Desty; Sports Editor, Roger Johnson

**About** Responsible for BBC Radio Berkshire, BBC Radio Oxford, BBC South TV, BBC Radio Solent and all online content across the region.

## BBC South East

**The Great Hall, Mount Pleasant Road, Tunbridge Wells, TN1 1QQ**

☎ 01892 670000

✉ firstname.lastname@bbc.co.uk

**Contact** Head of Local and Regional Programming, Mike Hapgood; Sports Editor, Neil Bell

**About** Covers BBC South East (Television), BBC Radio Kent and BBC Southern Counties Radio.

## BBC South West

**Broadcasting House, Seymour Road, Mannamead, Plymouth, PL3 5BD**

☎ 01752 229201

✉ firstname.lastname@bbc.co.uk

**Contact** Head of BBC South West, John Lilley; News Editor, Simon Read; Political Editor, Chris Rogers

**About** Responsible for BBC South West TV, BBC Spotlight, Inside Out, The Politics Show South West, BBC Radio Devon, BBC Radio Cornwall, BBC Radio Guernsey, BBC Radio Jersey and all regional websites.

## BBC Wales

**Broadcasting House, Llandaf, CF5 2YQ**

☎ 029 2032 2000

☎ 029 2055 2973

✉ firstname.lastname@bbc.co.uk

🌐 www.bbc.co.uk/wales

**Contact** Controller, BBC Wales, Menna Richards; Head of Programmes (English), Clare Hudson; Head of Programmes (Welsh and New Media), Keith Jones; Head of Broadcast Development, Cathryn Allen; Head of News and Current Affairs, Mark O'Callaghan; Head of Sport, Nigel Walker; Head of Comedy, Gareth Gwenlan; Head of Music, David Jackson

**About** Provides content in both Welsh and English for a wide range of platforms including regional Welsh channels BBC One and Two Wales, BBC2W and S4C, as well as mainstream BBC channels. There are detailed guidelines on commissioning at: www.bbc.co.uk/wales/info/commissioning, however this mainly applies to independent production companies or in house producers. The BBC Wales writers unit undertakes to read unsolicited scripts and give brief feedback on them. In rare cases this may lead to script development opportunities. For more information, visit: www.bbc.co.uk/wales/info/commissioning/content/writers or email writerswales@bbc.co.uk

## BBC West

**BBC Broadcasting House, White Ladies Road, Bristol, BS28 2LR**

☎ 0117 973 2211

✉ firstname.lastname@bbc.co.uk

🌐 www.bbc.co.uk/bristol

**Contact** Head of Local and Regional Programmes, Roger Farrant; News Editor, Caroline Le Marachel

**About** The West region broadly covers Bristol, Wiltshire, Somerset and Gloucestershire.

Recent programmes: BBC Points West; Inside Out West.

## BBC Yorkshire

**Broadcasting Centre, 2 St. Peter's Square, Leeds, LS9 8AH**

☎ 0113 244 1188

✉ firstname.lastname@bbc.co.uk

**Contact** Head of BBC Yorkshire, Helen Thomas

# BBC WORLDWIDE

BBC Worldwide Ltd is a subsidiary of the BBC, dealing with the BBC's commercial activities. Its seven areas of business are: television channels; television sales; content and production; magazines; digital media; home entertainment; and children's.

## BBC Worldwide

**Woodlands, 80 Wood Lane, London, W12 0TT**

☎ 020 8433 2000

☎ 020 8433 2000

🌐 www.bbcworldwide.com

**Contact** Chief Executive, John Smith; Managing Director, Global Channels, Darren Childs; Director of Business Affairs, Sarah Cooper; Director of Content and Production, Wayne Garvie; Managing Director, Digital Media and Director, Strategy and Business Development, David Moody; Managing Director, BBC Magazines, Peter Phippen; Managing Director, Home Entertainment, Chris Weller; Managing Director, Global Television Sales and Managing Director, Children's, Mark Young

# UK & IRISH TV COMPANIES

# COMMERCIAL NATIONAL TV

## Channel 4

**124 Horseferry Road, London, SW1P 2TX**

☎ 020 7396 4444

☎ 020 7306 8356

🌐 www.channel4.com

**Contact** Director of Television, Kevin Lygo; Controller – Broadcasting, Rosemary Newell

**About** Channel 4 first broadcast in 1981. It now broadcasts across the UK, except to parts of Wales covered by S4C. It is a free to air, public service channel, funded entirely by advertising revenue and sponsorship. Along with Channel 4 itself, there are also the free digital channels, E4 (teenage/young adult audiences), More4 (a lifestyle and current affairs channel for older audiences), FilmFour (independent, contemporary cinema) and the broadband service FourDocs.

All content is commissioned through independent production companies or producers. For up to date names and contact details of the entire Channel 4 commissioning structure, visit www.channel4.com/corporate/4producers where there are downloadable documents. For opportunities to showcase your talent to the channel, visit the website, where you will find details of schemes, competitions and opportunities for members of the public. www.channel4.com/corporate/4talent

## Five

**22 Long Acre, London, WC2E 9LY**

☎ 020 7550 5555/0845 705 0505

☎ 020 7550 5554

✉ customerservices@five.tv

🌐 www.five.tv

**Contact** Chief Executive, Jane Lighting; Managing Director of Content, Lisa Opie

**About** Five is the final terrestrial free to view channel, which launched in 1997. For details of submitting programme ideas (mainly for independent producers/companies) visit www.five.tv/aboutfive/producersnotes The site contains controller level contacts and development priorities in all areas of programming. Each controller specifies how to submit ideas in their area. Response time is around four weeks.

## GMTV

**London Television Centre, Upper Ground, London, SE1 9TT**

☎ 020 7827 7000

☎ 020 7827 7249

✉ firstname.surname@gmtv.co.uk

🌐 www.gm.tv

**Contact Title** Managing Director, Paul Corley; Director of Programmes, Peter McHugh; Managing Editor, John Scammell; Editor, Martin Frizell

**About** GMTV owns ITV1's breakfast franchise and has been broadcasting since 1993. Owned by ITV Plc and Disney. GMTV2 is broadcast on ITV2, the network's digital channel. Programming is a mixture of news, sports, entertainment, current affairs, travel and lifestyle.

## ITN

**200 Grays Inn Road, London, W1CX 8XZ**

- 020 7833 3000
- 020 7430 4868
- itvplanning@itn.co.uk (ITN News), newsdesk@itvlondon.com (ITN London News), c4home@itn.co.uk (C4 News)
- www.itn.co.uk

**Contact** Chief Executive, Mark Wood; Editor in Chief, ITV News, David Mannion; Editor, ITV News, Deborah Turness; Head of ITN Factual, Philip Armstrong-Dampier; Editor, Channel 4 News, Jim Gray

**About** ITN is made up of five business areas; ITN News, ITN Source, ITN On, ITN Factual and Visual Voodoo.

ITN News produces the ITV News, Channel 4 News, More 4 News, London Tonight and International distributing news worldwide. ITN Source is a large moving image library. ITN On delivers content via mobile, radio and broadband. ITN Factual is a production house and Visual Voodoo, is another production company under the ITN umbrella.

## ITV Network

**200 Grays Inn Road, London, WC1X 8HF**

- 020 7843 8000
- 020 7843 8158
- info@itv.com, firstname.lastname@itv.com
- www.itv.com

**Contact** Director of Television, Simon Shaps; Director of Programme Strategy, David Bergg; Director of Factual and Daytime, Alison Sharman; Director of Drama, Nick Elliott; Director of Entertainment and Comedy, Paul Jackson

**About** ITV is Britain's most watched commercial television channel; it broadcasts across 15 regional licences and has three digital channels; ITV2, ITV3 and ITV4. At least 25 per cent of the output is commissioned through independent producers and production companies. For details on the procedure, visit the 'producer's page' on the ITV website.

## Radio Telef's Éireann (RTÉ)

**Donnybrook, Dublin 4, Republic of Ireland**

- 00353 1 208 3111
- 00353 1 208 3080
- info@rte.ie
- www.rte.ie

**Contact** Director General, Cathal Goan; Managing Director, Television, Noel Curran; Managing Director, Radio, Adrian Moynes; Managing Director, News and Current Affairs, Ed Mulhall; Managing Director, Publishing, Muirne Laffan

**About** Ireland's public service broadcaster, which outputs content on television, radio and the internet. For full details on commissioning for independent producers, including commissioning rounds and contact details visit the website.

## S4C

**Parc Ty Glas, Llanishen, Cardiff, CF14 5DU**

- 029 2074 7444
- 029 2075 4444
- s4c@s4c.co.uk
- www.s4c.co.uk

**Contact Title** Chief Executive, Iona Jones; Director of Commissioning, Rhian Gibson

**About** Currently a channel broadcast in Wales, in place of Channel 4. As such, rescheduled Channel 4 content makes up some of the programming, as do outputs from ITV Wales and the BBC. The majority of programmes are commissioned from independent producers. In 2009, at the time of the digital switchover, S4C will cease showing Channel 4 programmes, as Channel 4 will then be available in Wales. To contact Rhian Gibson, Director of Commissioning, approach Gwerfyl Griffiths at rhaglennide@s4c.co.uk, or on 029 2074 1422. For details on the commissioning procedures for independent producers, visit www.s4c.co.uk/production

# COMMERCIAL REGIONAL TV

## Channel Television Ltd

**Television Centre, La Pouquelaye, St. Helier, Jersey, JE1 3ZD**

- 01534 816816
- 01534 241889
- broadcast@channeltv.co.uk
- www.channeltv.co.uk

**Contact** Managing Director, Michael Lucas; Executive Chairman, Michael Desmond; Managing Director (Enterprise Division), Rowan O'Sullivan; Director of Programmes, Karen Rankine; Director of Resources and Transmission, Kevin Banner
**About** The smallest ITV regional company, which only broadcasts in the Channel Islands. Launched in 1962, it produces five hours and thirty eight minutes of regional programming per week.

## ITV Anglia
**Anglia Television, Rose Lane, Anglia House, Norwich, NR1 3JG**
- 01603 615151
- 01603 631032
- anglianews@itv.com (East region), mystory@angliatv.com (West region), firstname.lastname@itv.com
- www.itvregions.com/anglia

**Contact** Managing Director, Neil Thompson
**About** First broadcast in 1959, now one of the largest ITV regional stations. Also incorporates Anglia Factual, a production house which makes content for UK and US audiences, and Commercial Breaks, an advertisement production house.

## ITV Border
**The Television Centre, Carlisle, CA1 3NT**
- 01228 525101
- 01228 541384
- btvnews@itv.com (newroom only)
- www.itvregions.com/border

**Contact** Managing Director, Paddy Murrall
**About** ITV Border encompasses three different cultures; English, Scottish and Manx. It broadcasts across the region surrounding the England/Scotland border.

## ITV Central
**Gas Street, Birmingham, B1 2JT**
- 0870 600 6766
- 0121 634 4898
- centralnews@itv.com (news desk only), firstname.lastname@itv.com
- www.itvregions.com/central

**Contact** Managing Director, Ian Squires
**About** ITV Central covers a large area, stretching from the Welsh border, to the Peak District and down to the Home Counties. It is divided into three sub regions, West, South and East. Each has its own news service. News for the West is based at the administrative headquarters in Birmingham, East is based in Nottingham and South is in Abingdon near Oxford.

## ITV Granada
**Quay Street, Manchester, M60 9EA**
- 0161 832 7211
- 0161 953 0283
- granada.reports@itv.com (newsdesk), firstname.lastname@itv.com
- www.itvregions.com/granada

**About** Established in 1959, Granada is the longest running ITV regional station. As well as regional programming covering the North West of England and North Wales, its studios produce national content, such as Coronation Street and A Question of Sport.

## ITV London
**London Television Centre, Upper Ground, London, SE1 9LT**
- 020 7261 8162
- 020 7261 8163
- newsdesk@itvlondon.com, firstname.lastname@itv.com
- www.itvregions.com/london

**Contact** Managing Director, Christy Swords
**About** Formerly LWT and Carlton, ITV London was formed in 2004. Broadcasts to the Greater London Area.

## ITV Meridian & Thames Valley
**Forum One, Solent Business Park, Whiteley, PO15 7PA**
- 01489 442000
- 01489 442200
- Newsdesks, yournews@itv.com (Kent, East Sussex, South Essex), thamesvalley@itv.com (Thames Valley, North Hampshire, Wiltshire, Surrey, Oxfordshire, Berkshire and Bucks), meridiannewssouth@itv.com (South Hampshire and the Isle of Wight, East Dorset and West Sussex). firstname.lastname@itv.com
- www.itvlocal.tv

**Contact** Managing Director, Lindsay Charlton
**About** Covers the region along the south coast, from Weymouth to Southend on Sea, as well as stretching up to the Thames Valley area. The area is split into three, with each having a separate news bulletin.

## ITV Tyne Tees
**Television House, The Watermark, Gateshead, NE11 9SZ**
- ☎ 0191 404 8700
- 🖷 0191 404 8710
- ✉ Newsdesks, news@tynetees.tv (Newcastle), newstoday@tynetees.tv (Gateshead). Firstname.lastname@itv.com
- 🌐 www.itvregions.com/Tyne_Tees

**Contact** Managing Director and Controller of Programmes, Graeme Thompson; Head of New Media, Malcolm Wright

**About** Covers the North East of England and North Yorkshire. Tyne Tees Television is now part of the Granada group of companies.

## ITV Wales
**The Television Centre, Culverhouse Cross, Cardiff, CF5 6XJ**
- ☎ 029 2059 0590
- 🖷 029 2059 7183
- ✉ info@itvwales.com, wtw@itvwales.com (current affairs), news@itvwales.com (news), firstname.lastname@itvwales.com
- 🌐 www.itvregions.com/wales

**Contact** Managing Director and Controller of Programmes, Elis Owen; Head of News, John Williams; Carmarthen Office, Giles Smith; Colwyn Bay Office, Carole Green, Ian Lang; Newtown Office, Rob Shelley; Wrexham Office, Paul Mewies

**About** Formerly HTV Wales, ITV Wales now broadcasts nine and a half hours of regional programming per week for Welsh viewers. There are several regional centres across Wales. Programming is a mix of news, current affairs, features, comedy and music.

## ITV West
**The Television Centre, Bath Road, Bristol, BS4 3HG**
- ☎ 0117 972 2722
- 🖷 0117 971 7685
- ✉ itvwestnews@itv.com (news), firstname.lastname@itv.com
- 🌐 www.itvregions.com/west

**Contact** Managing Director, Mark Haskell; Director of Programmes, Jane McCloskey

**About** Formerly HTV, ITV West now broadcasts seven hours per week of regional programming for the West of England.

## ITV Westcountry
**Langage Science Park, Western Wood Way, Plymouth, PL7 5BQ**
- ☎ 01752 333333
- 🖷 01752 333444
- ✉ news@westcountry.co.uk (news), firstname.lastname@itv.com
- 🌐 www.itvregions.com/westcountry

**Contact** Managing Director, Mark Haskell; Director of Programmes, Jane McCloskey

**About** Based in Plymouth, but with regional offices in Exeter, Weymouth, Taunton, Barnstaple, Truro and Penzance. ITV Westcountry broadcasts to Cornwall and Devon, as well as much of Somerset and Dorset.

## ITV Yorkshire
**The Television Centre, Leeds, LS3 1JS**
- ☎ 0113 243 8283
- 🖷 0113 244 5107
- ✉ calendar@yorkshiretv.com (newsdesk)
- 🌐 www.itvregions.com/yorkshire

**Contact** Managing Director, David Croft; Controller of Drama, Keith Richardson

**About** Established in 1968, ITV Yorkshire is now one of the biggest ITV regional companies. Broadcasts a mixture of programming, including 'Calendar News' bulletins. As well as local programming, ITV Yorkshire also produces drama and entertainment shows such as A Touch of Frost and Countdown.

## STV
**Pacific Quay, Glasgow, G51 1PQ**
- ☎ 0141 300 3300
- 🌐 www.stv.co.uk

**Contact** Managing Director, Bobby Hain; Deputy Managing Director, Derrick Thompson

**About** STV, owned by SMG, holds the current licence for Northern and Southern Scotland. There are separate news bulletins for the Scottish regions along with fifteen hours of other regional programming for Scotland. SMG also owns Ginger Productions.

## UTV
**Havelock House, Ormeau Road, Belfast, Northern Ireland, BT7 1EB**
- ☎ 028 9032 8122
- 🖷 028 9024 6695
- ✉ info@u.tv
- 🌐 www.u.tv

**Contact** Group Chief Executive, John McCann; Head of Television, Michael Wilson; Managing Director (UTV Radio Great Britain), Scott Taunton; Managing Director (UTV Radio Ireland), Ronan McManamy; Head of News, Current Affairs & Sports, Rob Morrison
**About** UTV broadcasts across television, radio and new media. It covers Northern Ireland and around 70 per cent of the Republic of Ireland. UTV is part of the ITV network.

# DIGITAL, SATELLITE AND CABLE

## ABC1
**Chiswick Park, Building 12, 566 Chiswick High Road, London, W4 5AN**
☎ 0870 880 7080
✉ feedback@abc1tv.co.uk
🌐 www.abc1tv.co.uk
**About** A Walt Disney owned channel, broadcasting for 12 hours a day on freeview and 24 hours a day on cable and satellite. Programming is mainly US comedy drama.

## Alpha ETC Punjabi
**Belvue Business Centre, Belvue Road, Northolt, UB5 5QQ**
☎ 020 8839 4000
☎ 020 8841 9550
✉ firstname.lastname@zeetv.co.uk
🌐 www.zeetv.co.uk
**Contact** News Editor, Sumant Dahl; Communications Manager, Kevin Rego
**About** A Punjabi language channel, which broadcasts a mixture of entertainment, drama and music.

## Animal Planet
**Discovery House, Chiswick Park, Building 2, 566 Chiswick High Road, W4 5YB**
☎ 020 8811 4422 (Press)
🌐 www.animalplanet.co.uk
**Contact** News Editor and Press Officer, Delyth Hughes
**About** A sister channel to the Discovery Channel. Programming centres on wildlife. For submissions from independent producers visit http://producers.discovery.com and register.

## Artsworld
**New Horizons Court 1, Grant Way, Isleworth, TW7 5QD**
☎ 0870 590 0700
✉ firstname.lastname@bskyb.com, tv@artsworld.com
🌐 www.artsworld.com
**Contact** Press Enquiries, Alyssa Bonic
**About** A digital channel dedicated to the arts, featuring live performances, documentaries and films.

## At The Races
**Customer Services, James House, 18–21 Horsham Street, London, N1 6DR**
✉ firstname.lastname@attheraces.com
🌐 www.attheraces.com
**Contact** International Director, Nigel Roddis; News Editor & Office Manager, Julie Phelps
**About** Horse racing channel, showing many live races and related shows.

## Avago
**Yoo Media Gaming Studios, 6 & 7 Prince Court, Wapping Lane, London, E1W 2DA**
✉ kelly.hobbs@yoomedia.com
🌐 www.yoomedia.com
**About** Interactive digital betting channel.

## B4
**37 Harwood Road, London, SW6 4QP**
☎ 020 7371 5999
☎ 020 7384 2026
🌐 www.b4.tv
**Contact** Chief Executive, Gail Screene; Head of Music, Sarah Gaughan
**About** New music channel, owned by Chart Show Television.

## B4U Music & Movies
**19 Heather Park Drive, Transputec House, Wembley, Middlesex, HA0 1SS**
☎ 020 8795 7171
☎ 020 8795 7181
✉ enquiries@b4unetwork.com, firstname@b4unetwork.com
🌐 www.b4utv.com
**Contact** Chief Executive, Sunil Rohra; News Editor, Kevin Rego
**About** B4U, a leading Bollywood network, launched B4U Music and B4U Movies in the UK, in 1999.

## The Baby Channel

**1st Floor, Bentima House, 168–172 Old Street, London, EC1V 9BP**

- ☎ 0870 787 7351
- ✉ info@babychanneltv.com
- 🌐 www.babychanneltv.com

**Contact** Chief Executive, Leon Hawthorne

**About** A digital channel aimed at pregnant women and parents of children under five years old. Topics for programmes include pregnancy, child health, early learning, first aid, safety and cooking for children.

## Bangla TV

**Warton House, 150 High Street, London, E15 2NE**

- ☎ 0870 005 6778
- ☎ 0907 147 2220
- ✉ news@banglatv.co.uk
- 🌐 www.banglatv.co.uk

**Contact** News Editor, Feroze Kahn

**About** A digital channel aimed at Bengali speaking audiences. Broadcasts entertainment, news and current affairs programmes.

## BEN (Bright Entertainment Network)

**25 Ashley Road, London, N17 9LJ**

- ☎ 020 8808 8800
- ✉ info@bentelevision.com
- 🌐 www.bentelevision.com

**Contact** Director, Alistair Prince

**About** A British channel aimed at expatriate Africans living in Europe. It broadcasts home grown programming, Nollywood films and several hours of programming from African Independent Television. Free to air on sky digital.

## Bid TV

**Sit Up House, 179–181 The Vale, London, W3 7RW**

- ☎ 020 8600 9700
- ☎ 020 8746 0299
- 🌐 www.bid.tv

**Contact Title** Chief Executive

**About** An auction shopping channel, owned by Sit Up TV.

## Big Game TV

**PO Box 5372, London, W1A 8WN**

- ☎ 020 7432 7300
- ✉ Info@biggametelevision.com
- 🌐 www.biggame.tv

**About** A digital television quiz channel.

## Biography Channel

**Grant Way, Isleworth, TW7 5QD**

- ☎ 0870 240 3000
- ☎ 0870 240 3060
- 🌐 www.thebiographychannel.co.uk

**Contact** Managing Director, Geoff Metzger; Head of Programming, Richard Melman; Head of New Media, Emily Lloyd; Head of On Air, Richard Morgan; Head of Marketing, Nicki Harris; New Media Editor, Simon Clarke

**About** A digital channel featuring the latest showbiz news, profiles and biographical movies.

## Bliss

**37 Harwood Road, London, SW6 4QP**

- ☎ 020 7371 5999
- ☎ 020 7384 2026
- 🌐 www.bliss.tv

**Contact** Chief Executive, Gail Screene; Head of Music, Sarah Gaughan

**About** A continuous music channel.

## Bloomberg

**City Gate House, 39–45 Finsbury Square, London, EC2A 1PQ**

- ☎ 020 7330 7797
- ✉ newsalert@bloomberg.net
- 🌐 www.bloomberg.com

**Contact** News Editor, Laura Chapman

**About** A 24 hour digital channel with a multi screen format. Bloomberg delivers news, data, financial market updates and weather reports.

## Boomerang

**Turner House, 16 Great Marlborough Street, London, W1W 8HF**

- ☎ 020 7693 1000
- ☎ 020 7693 1001
- 🌐 www.boomerangtv.co.uk

**About** A 24 hour cartoon channel, it broadcasts mainly from Warner Brothers and Hanna-Barbera archives.

## The Box

**Mappin House, 4 Winsley Street, London, W1W 8HF**

- ☎ 020 7182 8000

@ firstname.lastname@emap.com,tvfeedbackmusic@
emap.com

@ www.thebox.co.uk

**Contact** Brand and Communications Director, Vikki
Timmons; Commercial Manager, Katie Teesdale;
Head of TV Radio Sponsorship and Promotions,
Darren Kahn; Head of Press and PR Emap Radio,
Maureen Corish; Programme Director, David Young

**About** A 24 hour viewer requested music channel.

## Bravo
**160 Great Portland Street, London, W1W 5QA**

@ 0870 043 4029

@ enquiries@bravo.co.uk

@ www.bravo.co.uk

**Contact** Commissioning Editor, Steve Jones

**About** An entertainment channel aimed at men
aged 16–44. Programming includes crime
documentaries, factual entertainment, comedy and
drama. Submissions are only accepted from
independent production companies, for
commissioning needs, visit www.flextech.co.uk/
commissioning/bravo

## British Eurosport (1&2)
**Eurosport TV, Heathrow West Business Park,
Heron Drive, Langley, SL3 8XP**

@ 020 7468 7777

@ ukcomms@eurosport.com, ukfeedback@
eurosport.com (internet editors)

@ www.eurosport.co.uk

**Contact** Director, David Kerr; Managing Editor,
Adam Marshall; News Editor, Louise Moss

**About** Live and recorded sports programming.

## BSkyB
**Grant Way, Isleworth, TW7 5QD**

@ 0870 240 3000

@ 0870 240 3060

@ www.sky.com

**Contact** Chief Executive, James Murdoch

**About** The UK's biggest digital provider. Also
broadcasts a number of Sky channels.

## Cartoon Network
**Turner House, 16 Great Marlborough Street,
London, W1W 8HF**

@ 020 7693 1000

@ 020 7693 1001

@ www.cartoon-network.co.uk

**About** A cartoon channel owned by Turner
Entertainment, a division of Time Warner.

## Celtic TV
**4th Floor, 8 Waterloo Place, London, SW1Y 4BE**

@ 020 7766 8484

@ 020 7766 8485

@ helena@setanta.com

@ http://gb.setanta.com

**Contact** Contact, Helena O'Sullivan

**About** A paid for digital channel on Celtic
Football Club.

## Challenge
**160 Great Portland Street, London, W1W 5QA**

@ 0870 043 4030

@ enquiries@challenge.co.uk

@ www.challenge.co.uk

**Contact** Editor, Kate Barnes; News Editor, Jakki Lewis

**About** A gameshow and quiz channel, with both
repeats and original broadcasting. For
commissioning needs, visit www.flextech.co.uk/
commissioning/challenge, all proposals must come
via independent production companies.

## Channel U
**Video Interactive Television, Studio 4, 3 Lever
Street, London, EC1V 3QU**

@ 020 7054 9010

@ 020 7054 9011

@ info@vitv.co.uk, production@vitv.co.uk

@ www.channelu.tv

**Contact** Director, Darren Platt; News Editor,
Nick Dereka

**About** An urban music video channel. Video
submissions by post only, with a £20 fee to cover
administrative costs. Read the submissions section
on the website for full guidelines.

## Chart Show TV
**37 Harwood Road, London, SW6 4QP**

@ 020 7371 5999

@ 020 7384 2026

@ info@chartshow.tv

@ www.chartshow.tv

**About** Chart music video channel.

## Chelsea TV
**Stamford Bridge, Fulham Road, London,
SW6 1HS**

@ 020 7915 1980

☎ 020 7915 2902
🌐 www.chelseafc.com
**About** Programming centering on Chelsea football club, mainly previous matches and features.

## Classic FM TV
**Open Access Music Group Ltd, 30 Leicester Square, London, WC2H 7LA**
☎ 020 7343 9000
✉ classicfmtv@classicfm.com
🌐 www.classicfm.co.uk
**Contact** Managing Director, Darren Henley
**About** 24 hour classical music channel.

## CNBC Europe
**10 Fleet Place, London, EC4M 7QS**
☎ 020 7653 9300
☎ 020 7653 9488
🌐 www.cnbceurope.com
**About** The leading pan European business and financial television channel. Real time coverage of financial markets and international business news.

## CNN International
**Turner House, 16 Great Marlborough Street, London, W1W 8HF**
☎ 020 7693 0786
☎ 020 7693 0788
🌐 www.europe.cnn.com
**Contact** International Managing Editor (CNN Europe), Nick Wrenn
**About** An international news channel.

## Community Channel
**3–7 Euston Centre, Regent's Place, London, NW1 3JG**
☎ 0870 850 5500
✉ info@communitychannel.org
🌐 www.communitychannel.org
**About** A 24 hour channel dedicated to highlighting issues from both local and international communities, as well as the voluntary and charitable sectors. It broadcasts original shows, repeats from terrestrial television, and showcases the work of new directors and community programme makers. The Film Makers' Guide on the website details how to submit your film to the channel.

## Create and Craft
**Ideal Home House, Newark Road, Peterborough, Cambridgeshire, PE1 5WG**

☎ 0870 077 7002
☎ 0870 078 0739
🌐 www.createandcraft.com
**About** A demonstration and shopping channel entirely about crafts.

## Dating Channel
**130 City Road, London, EC1V 2NW**
☎ 020 7748 1500
✉ info@thedatingchannel.com
🌐 www.thedatingchannel.com
**About** An interactive dating channel.

## Discovery Channel
**Discovery House, Chiswick Park Building 2, 566 Chiswick High Road, London, W4 5YB**
☎ 020 811 3000
☎ 020 8811 3100
✉ firstname_lastname@discovery-europe.com
🌐 www.discoverychannel.co.uk
**About** Broadcasts programmes on technological and natural knowledge, and investigations. Programme ideas should be registered at http://producers.discovery.com or sent to 'The Commissioning Editor, Commissioning Department'.

## Discovery Civilisation
**Discovery House, Chiswick Park Building 3, 566 Chiswick High Road, London, W4 5YB**
☎ 020 811 3000
☎ 020 8811 3100
✉ firstname_lastname@discovery-europe.com
🌐 www.discoverycivilisation.co.uk
**Contact** News Editor and Press Officer, Kate Buddle
**About** Documentaries and features about people and events that have shaped civilisation. Programme ideas should be registered at http://producers.discovery.com or sent to 'The Commissioning Editor, Commissioning Department'.

## Discovery Home and Health
**Discovery House, Chiswick Park Building 3, 566 Chiswick High Road, London, W4 5YB**
☎ 020 811 3000
☎ 020 8811 3100
✉ firstname_lastname@discovery-europe.com
🌐 www.homeandhealthtv.co.uk
**About** Programming on health and lifestyle. Programme ideas should be registered at http://producers.discovery.com or sent to 'The Commissioning Editor, Commissioning Department'.

## Discovery Kids

**Discovery House, Chiswick Park Building 3, 566 Chiswick High Road, London, W4 5YB**

- 020 811 3000
- 020 8811 3100
- firstname_lastname@discovery-europe.com
- www.discoverykids.co.uk

**Contact** News Editor and Press Officer, Caroline Watt

**About** Television, which encourages children to 'find out' and 'discover', whilst having fun. It is a broadly educational channel. Programme ideas should be registered at http://producers.discovery.com or sent to 'The Commissioning Editor, Commissioning Department'.

## Discovery Real Time

**Discovery House, Chiswick Park Building 3, 566 Chiswick High Road, London, W4 5YB**

- 020 811 3000
- 020 8811 3100
- firstname_lastname@discovery-europe.com
- www.realtimetv.co.uk

**Contact** News Editor and Press Officer, Caroline Watt

**About** Programming about property, DIY, mechanics and fishing. Programme ideas should be registered at http://producers.discovery.com or sent to 'The Commissioning Editor, Commissioning Department'.

## Discovery Science

**Discovery House, Chiswick Park Building 3, 566 Chiswick High Road, London, W4 5YB**

- 020 811 3000
- 020 8811 3100
- firstname_lastname@discovery-europe.com
- www.discoveryscience.co.uk

**Contact** News Editor and Press Officer, Kate Buddle

**About** Broadcasts programmes based around scientific knowledge and investigations. Programme ideas should be registered at http://producers.discovery.com or sent to 'The Commissioning Editor, Commissioning Department'.

## Discovery Travel and Living

**Discovery House, Chiswick Park Building 3, 566 Chiswick High Road, London, W4 5YB**

- 020 811 3000
- 020 8811 3100
- firstname_lastname@discovery-europe.com
- www.travelandliving.co.uk

**Contact** News Editor and Press Officer, Caroline Watt

**About** Programmes aimed at discovering exotic and interesting places to visit and live. Programme ideas should be registered at http://producers.discovery.com or sent to 'The Commissioning Editor, Commissioning Department'.

## Discovery Wings

**Discovery House, Chiswick Park Building 3, 566 Chiswick High Road, London, W4 5YB**

- 020 811 3000
- 020 8811 3100
- firstname_lastname@discovery-europe.com
- www.discoverywings.co.uk

**Contact** News Editor and Press Officer, Kate Buddle

**About** A channel about aviation, space and transportation. Programme ideas should be registered at http://producers.discovery.com or sent to 'The Commissioning Editor, Commissioning Department'.

## Disney Channel

**Building 12, 2nd Floor, 566 Chiswick High Road, London, W4 5AN**

- 0870 880 7080
- studio@disneychannel.co.uk
- www.disneychannel.co.uk

**Contact** Managing Director (Disney TV Europe), John Hardie; Executive Producer, Steve Wynne

**About** Live action shows, animations and original films make up the content for this children's channel.

## Disney Cinemagic

**Building 12, 2rd Floor, 566 Chiswick High Road, London, W4 5AN**

- 0870 880 7080
- studio@disneychannel.co.uk
- www.disney.co.uk/DisneyChannel/cinemagic

**Contact** Managing Director (Disney TV Europe), John Hardie

**About** Broadcasts live action and animated Disney films.

## DM Digital

**33–35 Turner Street, Manchester, M4 1DW**

- 0161 795 4844
- http://dmdigitaltv.co.uk

**Contact** Chairman, Dr Liaqat Malik; Head of Music, Irfan Malik
**About** A 24 hour business and general entertainment channel, available via cable and satellite in the UK, Europe, Middle East, Africa and Asia.

## DM Islam
### 33–35 Turner Street, Manchester, M4 1DW
- 0161 795 4844
- http://dmdigitaltv.co.uk

**Contact** Chairman, Dr Liaqat Malik; Head of Music, Irfan Malik
**About** An Islamic channel broadcasting in Urdu, Punjabi, English, Arabic, Sindhi, Kashmiri and Pushto languages.

## E!
### 141 Wardour Street, London, W1F 0UT
- 020 7297 5050
- 020 7297 5060
- www.eonline.com

**About** Showbiz and entertainment programming, mainly from the US.

## E4
### 124 Horseferry Road, London, SW1P 2TX
- 020 7396 4444
- www.channel4.com/e4

**Contact** Head of E4, Danny Cohen; Editor, Ruby Kuraishe
**About** A digital station from Channel 4, which screens repeats from terrestrial television, as well as the original programming and first broadcasts of US programmes. For all commissioning details for independent producers, visit www.channel4.com/corporate/4producers

## eeZee TV
### Regis Road, Kentish Town, London, NW5 3EG
- 0870 128 7288
- 0870 122 0210
- service.centre@eezeetv.com, press@eezeetv.com, firstname@eeztv.com
- www.eezeetv.com

**Contact** New Media Editor, Max Way
**About** A shopping channel with next day delivery.

## Extreme Sports Channel
### 19 Bolsover Street, London, W1W 5NA
- 020 7244 1000

- 020 7244 0101
- info@extremesportschannel.com, jdubern@chellomedia.com

## Fame TV
### PO Box 249, Radlett, WD7 0DH
- 01923 857004
- fame@fametv.com
- www.fametv.com

**Contact** Development Producer, John Hayes
**About** A viewer generated content channel. Clips, pictures, texts and shorts are uploaded, via email or SMS. There is a charge for uploading.

## Fashion Music TV
### 118–120 Great Tichfield Street, London, W1W 6SS
- 020 7436 8858
- 020 7436 8814
- info@fashionmusic.tv
- www.fashionmusic.tv

**About** Due to launch in 2007. A mixture of music, fashion, lifestyle, art and entertainment. Heavy links with sponsors and advertisers.

## FilmFour
### 124 Horseferry Road, London, SW1P 2TX
- 020 7396 4444
- 020 7244 0101
- editorialissues@filmfour.com, firstinitiallastname@channel4.com
- www.filmfour.co.uk

**Contact** Director of Acquisitions and Film Four, Jeff Ford; News Editor & Press Office, Steve Pinder
**About** A digital channel, owned by Channel 4. It broadcasts contemporary and independent films.

## Five Life
### 22 Long Acre, London, WC2E 9LY
- 020 7550 5555/0845 705 0505
- 020 7550 5554
- customerservices@five.tv
- www.five.tv/life

**Contact** Controller, Nick Thorogood
**About** Broadcasts children's programs, films, drama, soaps, and lifestyle shows geared toward women. Sister channel of Five.

## Five US
### 22 Long Acre, London, WC2E 9LY
- 020 7550 5555/0845 705 0505

202 7550 5554
customerservices@five.tv
www.five.tv/us
**Contact** Controller, Nick Thorogood
**About** Broadcasts drama, comedy, films, sports and youth programming from the US. Sister channel of Five.

## Fizz

**Video Interactive Television, Studio 4, 3 Lever Street, London, EC1V 3QU**
020 7054 9010
020 7054 9011
**Contact** Director, Darren Platt; News Editor, Nick Dereka
**About** Music video channel.

## Flaunt

**Grant Way, Isleworth, TW7 5QD**
0870 240 3000
www.flaunt.tv
**Contact** Chief Executive, Gail Screene; Head of Music, Sarah Gaughan
**About** A gay channel, broadcasting music videos.

## FTN

**160 Great Portland Street, London, W1W 5QA**
0870 043 4141
enquiries@ftn.tv, firstname_lastname@flextech.co.uk
www.ftn.tv
**Contact** Programme Editor, Hannah Barnes
**About** A free to air entertainment channel, owned by Flextech. The channel broadcasts programmes from LivingTV, Bravo, Trouble and Challenge, as well as some original programming. Airs from 6pm to 6am. For commissioning needs visit www.flextech.co.uk/commissioning/ftn all proposals via in independent production company.

## FX

**Unit 2.5, Shepherd's Studios, Richmond Way, London, W14 0DQ**
020 7751 7602
020 7751 7601
www.fxuk.com
**About** A drama and comedy channel, with much of its content from the US network, Fox.

## Gala TV

**New Castle House, Castle Boulevard, Nottingham, NG7 1FT**
0800 294 7294
01483 747097
customer.services@galabingo.co.uk
www.galatv.co.uk
**About** An interactive live bingo and gaming channel.

## Gay Date TV

**Room 101, Coppergate House, 16 Brune Street, London, E1 7NJ**
020 7748 1500
020 7748 1501
www.gaydatetv.co.uk
**About** A gay dating channel.

## Gems.TV & Gems.TV2

**PO Box 12916, Redditch, Worcestershire, B97 9BT**
01527 406100
01527 406128
customercare@gemstv.com
www.gemstv.co.uk
**About** A gem set jewellery shopping channel.

## Get Lucky TV

**c/o Bentinck House, 3–8 Bolsover Street, London, W1W 6AB**
020 7190 0300
020 7190 0301
www.getlucky.tv
**About** An interactive gaming channel.

## The God Channel

**Angel House, Borough Road, Sunderland, SR1 1HW**
0191 568 0800
0191 568 0808
info@god.tv, firstinitiallastname@god.tv
www.god.tv
**Contact** Regional Director for UK and Ireland, Chris Cole; News Editor & Communications Officer, Alastair Gibson; Head of Production, Graeme Spencer
**About** A digital channel broadcasting religious programmes.

## The Golf Channel UK

**Martland Park, Challenge Way, Wigan, Lancashire, WN5 0LD**

- 01942 210989
- 01942 210997
- press@golftvinfo.co.uk (press only)
- www.thegolfchanneluk.com

**About** Golf tournaments and features.

## Golf TV Pro Shop

**Challenge Way, Martland Hill Industrial Estate, Wigan, WN5 0LD**

- 01942 214215
- 01942 210997
- firstname.lastname@golftvgroup.com
- www.golftvproshop.com

**Contact** Senior Vice President, Lee Kenny

**About** A golf equipment shopping channel, broadcasts daily.

## Hallmark Channel

**234a Kings Road, London, SW3 5UA**

- 020 7368 9100
- www.hallmarkchannel.com

**Contact** Managing Director, Rosie Hill-Davies

**About** Broadcasts both films, comedy and drama series. Films are always acquired through major production companies, although if scripts are sent directly to Hallmark from individuals or smaller production companies, they will endeavour to pass them on to suitable larger organisations.

## Hellenic TV

**50 Clarendon Road, London, N8 0DJ**

- 020 8292 7037
- 020 8292 7042
- info@hellenictv.net, konstantinos@hellenictv.net (submissions queries)
- www.hellenictv.net

**Contact** Manager, Myroula Fellas

**About** A Greek language channel broadcasting 24 hours a day. Email Greek language programme ideas to the team.

## History Channel

**Grant Way, Isleworth, TW7 5QD**

- 020 7941 5194
- 020 7941 5187
- feedback@thehistorychannel.co.uk, firstname.lastname@bskyb.com
- www.thehistorychannel.co.uk

**Contact** Channel Director, Richard Melman; News Editor and PR Manager, Joannna Mitchell

**About** Historical programming, mainly documentaries and features.

## The Hits

**Mappin House, 4 Winsley Street, London, W1W 8HF**

- 020 7182 8000
- firstname.lastname@emap.com,tvfeedbackmusic@emap.com
- www.emap.com

**Contact** Brand and Communications Director, Vikki Timmons; Commercial Manager, Katie Teesdale; Head of TV Radio Sponsorship and Promotions, Darren Kahn; Head of Press and PR Emap Radio, Maureen Corish; Director of Music, Simon Sadler; Programme Controller, Phil Poole

**About** 24 hour music video channel.

## Hollywood Classics Network

**PO Box 7777, Brixworth, Northamptonshire, NN6 9YJ**

- 01604 882581
- shaneknock@hollywoodclassics.co.uk
- www.openaccess.tv

**About** A free to air film and comedy channel, with a large archive of classic US content.

## Home Abroad.TV

**Unit 318 The Plaza, 535 Kings Road, London, SW10 0SZ**

- 020 7349 5536
- 020 7352 8332
- mike@homeabroad.tv, info@omeabroad.tv

**Contact** Managing Director, Michael De Vere; Head of Sales, Jon Waters; Technical Advisor, Sass Jahani

**About** Opportunities for property companies to script and broadcast programmes about buying properties abroad. Broadcasts 24 hours a day.

## Hometime TV

**32 Ludgate Hill, Birmingham, B3 1EH**

- 0121 200 2444
- 0121 200 3002
- info@hometimetv.com
- www.hometimetv.com

**About** A channel for estate agents and property sellers to market their properties. It broadcasts some features and studio based programmes, all of which are property related.

## Horse & Country TV

**Barley Hollow, Bennett End, Radnage, High Wycombe, HP14 4EE**

- 01494 485959
- 01494 485858
- nick@horseandcountry.tv
- www.horseandcountry.tv

**Contact** Director of Programming, Nicholas Ludlow; New Media and Marketing Director, Clive Hetherington; Channel Controller, Dominic Matterson

**About** An online television channel due to launch on digital television in 2007. It currently has six categories on its online service, 'British Heritage', 'Rural Living', 'Equestrian', 'Animals and Wildlife', 'Rural Business' and 'Sports and Pastimes'.

## iBuy TV

**Unit 1a Hogarth Business Park, Burlington Lane, Chiswick, W4 2TJ**

- 020 8233 6966
- 020 8233 6901
- info@ibuy.tv
- www.ibuy.tv

**About** Teleshopping channel.

## Ideal Vitality Channel

**Ideal Home House, Newark Road, Peterborough, PE1 5WG**

- 0870 077 7002
- 0870 077 7003
- customerservices@idealshoppingdirect.co.uk
- www.idealvitality.tv

**About** Shopping channel.

## Ideal World

**Ideal Home House, Newark Road, Peterborough, PE1 5WG**

- 0870 077 7002
- 0870 070 0803
- customerservices@idealshoppingdirect.co.uk
- www.idealworld.tv

**About** Shopping channel.

## Information TV

**1 Stephen Street, London, W1T 1AL**

- 020 7691 6302
- 020 7691 5089
- fred.perkins@information.tv
- www.information.tv

**Contact** Chief Executive, Fred Perkins; Production Manager, Paul Nicholson

**About** A digital channel providing access to broadcast television, for organisations who wish to reach specific target audiences. Programming includes content from government departments, public bodies, public service institutions, and from would be broadcasters in small, regularly scheduled programmes in ÔMicro Channels', which they control.

## iPlay

**Communications House, Station Court, Station Road, Great Shelford, Cambridge, CB2 5LR**

- 01223 551000
- 01223 841491
- sales@transactgroup.net, nick.vale@transactgroup.net
- www.transactgroup.net

**Contact** Contact, Nick Vale

**About** An interactive games and quiz channel.

## Islam Channel

**14 Bonhill Street, London, EC2A 4BX**

- 020 7374 4511
- 020 7374 4602
- pr@islamchannel.tv
- www.islamchannel.tv

**About** An English digital channel broadcasting internationally. Programming aims to represent and reinforce true Islamic values.

## iSports TV

**Television Gaming Group, 6–7 Princes Court, Wapping Lane, London, E1W 2DA**

- 020 7942 7942
- www.isports.tv

**About** Mainly horse racing, with some opportunities to place bets digitally.

## ITV2

**200 Grays Inn Road, London, WC1X 8HF**

- 020 7843 8140
- 020 7843 8432
- itv2@itv.com, firstname.lastname@itv.com
- www.itv.com/itv2

**Contact** Controller, Zai Bennett; News Editor, Emma Harvey; Director, Jonathan Lewis

**About** A younger, entertainment based sister channel to ITV1. Broadcasts drama, comedy, sport, films and events including original commissions, high profile ITV1 programming and brand extensions of ITV1 shows. At least 25 per cent of the output is commissioned through independent producers and production companies. For details on the procedure, visit the 'producer's page' on the ITV website.

## ITV3

**200 Grays Inn Road, London, WC1X 8HF**
- 020 7843 8140
- 020 7843 8432
- firstname.lastname@itv.com
- www.itv.com/itv3

**Contact** Channel Editor, Emma Tennant; General Manager, Sarah Rose; Director, Jonathan Lewis
**About** Broadcasts the best of ITV drama, with programmes from ITV1 and ITV2. At least 25 per cent of the output is commissioned through independent producers and production companies. For details on the procedure, visit the 'producer's page' on the ITV website.

## ITV4

**200 Grays Inn Road, London, WC1X 8HF**
- 020 7843 8140
- 020 7843 8432
- www.itv.com/itv4

**Contact** Controller, David Fewings
**About** Broadcasts programmes from 6pm each day. These include live sport and new cutting edge drama. At least 25 per cent of the output is commissioned through independent producers and production companies. For details on the procedure, visit the 'producer's page' on the ITV website.

## ITV Play

**PO Box 49756, London, WC1X 8WN**
- 0845 014 7529/ 020 7843 8276
- 020 7843 8157
- itvplay@itv.com
- http://play.itv.com

**About** An interactive game and quiz channel.

## Jetix

**Building 12, 2nd Floor, 566 Chiswick High Road, London, W4 5AN**
- webmaster_uk@jetixeurope.net
- www.jetix.co.uk

**Contact** UK Managing Director, Boel Ferguson

**About** Digital channel dedicated to children's programming. The Walt Disney Company owns a 75 per cent share.

## The Jewellery Channel

**Teddington Studios, Broom Road, Middlesex, TW11 9NT**
- 0844 412 2222
- www.thejewellerychannel.tv

**About** A digital shopping channel for jewellery.

## Just Fabulous TV

**Tower Bridge Business Complex, 100 Clements Road, London, SE16 4DG**
- 020 7237 2707
- 020 7237 2717
- info@justfaboulostv.com, press@justfaboulostv.com
- www.justfabulousgroup.com

**Contact** Contact, Mamun Uddin
**About** An urban entertainment and lifestyle channel.

## Kerrang

**Mappin House, 4 Winsley Street, London, W1W 8HF**
- 020 7436 1515
- 020 7376 1313
- tvfeedback@kerrang.com, firstname.lastname@emap.com
- www.kerrang.com

**Contact** Brand and Communications Director, Vikki Timmons; Commercial Manager, Katie Teesdale; Head of TV Radio Sponsorship and Promotions, Darren Kahn; Head of Press and PR Emap Radio, Maureen Corish; Programme Director, David Young; Music Editor, Simon Sadler
**About** A music video channel focused on rock and alternative music.

## Kiss TV

**Mappin House, 4 Winsley Street, London, W1W 8HF**
- 020 7182 8000
- firstname.lastname@emap.com, tvfeedbackmusic@emap.com
- www.totalkiss.com

**Contact** Brand and Communications Director, Vikki Timmons; Commercial Manager, Katie Teesdale; Head of TV Radio Sponsorship and Promotions, Darren Kahn; Head of Press and PR Emap Radio,

Maureen Corish; News Editor and Programme Director, David Young

**About** A commercial music television channel owned by Emap. It plays mainstream urban music and is based on the format of the London radio station Kiss 100.

## Konta Music

**9 Ilex Close, Hampton Hargate, PE7 8AD**

- 0845 051 9998/0798 557 3864
- 0871 666 3074
- info@kontamtv.com
- www.kontamtv.com

**About** A channel combining a mix of programmes, including cultural heritage, news, current affairs, folk music, chat shows,and comedy. Aimed at African and Caribbean audiences in Europe and across the world. To submit music videos, download the form from the website.

## Legal TV

**Unit 3 Avenue Road, Aston, Birmingham, B6 4DY**

- 0121 380 1050
- 0121 359 8839
- info@legaltv.co.uk
- www.legaltv.co.uk

**Contact** Production Manager, Simon Harland

**About** A digital channel featuring fiction and non-fiction legal programmes, designed to inform viewers about the legal system.

## Life TV

**Maidstone Studios, New Cut Road, Maidstone, Kent, ME14 5NZ**

- 01622 684444
- 01622 684445
- info@lifetv.org.uk
- www.lifetv.org.uk

**Contact** Chairman, James Braithwaite; General Manager, Jenny Taylor

**About** A digital channel combining drama, entertainmnet and factual formats.

## Living TV

**160 Great Portland Street, London, W1W 5QA**

- 0870 043 4028
- enquiries@livingtv.co.uk, firstname_lastname@flextech.co.uk
- www.livingtv.co.uk

**Contact** Channel Controller, Richard Woolfe; Director of Programmes, Claudia Rosencrantz;

Commissioning Editor, Steve Regan; News Editor, Judy Wells

**About** Broadcasts a mixture of high end factual entertainment, premiere dramas, groundbreaking comedy, pre school programmes and reality television. All programme ideas must be submitted via an independent production company. For commissioning needs, visit www.flextech.co.uk/commissioning/livingtv

## Loveworld

**10 Henley Road, Standard Industrial Estate, Woolwich, Docklands, E16 2ES**

**About** A 24 hour digital channel broadcasting Christian faith based programmes.

## Magic

**Mappin House, 4 Winsley Street, London, W1W 8HF**

- 020 7436 1515
- 020 7376 1313
- tvfeedbackmusic@emap.com
- www.magic.fm

**Contact Title** Managing Director, Magic, Andria Vidler; Brand and Communications Director, Vikki Timmons; Commercial Manager, Katie Teesdale; Head of TV Radio Sponsorship and Promotions, Darren Kahn; Head of Press and PR Emap Radio, Maureen Corish; Music and Programme Director, Simon Sadler; Programme Controller, Phil Poole

**About** A music video channel which broadcasts classic pop hits. Also a radio station, Magic FM.

## MATV

**Combine House, 7 Woodboy Street, Leicester, LE1 3NJ**

- 0116 253 2288
- 0116 253 8900
- info@matv.co.uk, localprograme@matv.co.uk
- www.matv.co.uk

**Contact** Chief Executive, Vinod Popat; News Editor, Sandi Shidhu

**About** A free to air 'sixth terrestrial channel' available to over 180,000 homes in Leicestershire. Also available as a digital channel. Aimed at the Asian market, the channel has links with Bollywood and Indian broadcaster SAB. Programmes include drama, current affairs, comedy, cookery and local interest.

## Max TV

**Brooms Road, Stone Business Park, Stone, Staffordshire, ST15 0DG**

- 0845 070 2571
- support@max.tv
- www.max.tv

**About** A shopping channel dedicated to video game accessories and innovative gadgets.

## Men and Motors

**200 Grays Inn Road, London, WC1X 8HF**

- 020 7843 8392 (press)
- men@itv.com, firstname.lastname@itv.com
- www.menandmotors.co.uk

**Contact** Press Officer and News Editor, Mirinda Dawkins; Commissioning Editor, Joe Talbot

**About** A mixture of adult programming, factual, and motor sports content, heavily targeted towards men.

## More4

**124 Horseferry Road, London, SW1P 2TX**

- 020 7306 3636
- 020 7340 9733
- firstinitiallastname@channel4.co.uk,
- www.channel4.com

**Contact** Head of More4, Peter Dale; Editor, Katie Speight; Editorial Manager, Peter Wildash

**About** A digital channel from Channel 4, it broadcasts repeated Channel 4 content and other lifestyle programming. Aimed at a middle aged audience.

## Movies4Men and Movies4Men2

**Dolphin Broadcasting Services Ltd, 3rd Floor, 114 St. Martin's Lane, London, WC2N 4BE**

- 0207 420 8290
- info@dolphintv.com, press@dolphintv.com
- www.movies4men.co.uk

**About** Two digital film channels aimed specifically at men. Movies4Men broadcasts classic western, war, film noir and detective films. Movies4Men2 broadcasts more contemporary films, such as gangster, drama and martial arts movies.

## Movies 24 & More 24

**234a Kings Road, London, SW3 5UA**

- 020 7368 9100
- 020 7368 9101
- www.tvmovies24.com

**About** A channel totally dedicated to made for television films. More 24 is the same channel, but

with programmes running two hours later. They do not produce films however, so do not submit scripts to them.

## MTV

**180 Oxford Street, London, W1D 1DS**

- 020 7478 6000
- 020 7478 6007
- contact@mtvne.com
- www.mtv.co.uk

**Contact** Managing Director, MTV UK and Ireland, Michiel Bakker; VP MTV Channels, Michael Barry; Executive Producer and News Editor, Lisa Stokoe

**About** A music television channel broadcasting music videos, documentaries, comedy and celebrity related programming. Also broadcasts live studio programmes.

## MTV2

**180 Oxford Street, London, W1D 1DS**

- 020 7478 6000
- 020 7478 6007
- contact@mtvne.com
- www.mtv.co.uk/channel/mtv2

**Contact** Managing Director, MTV UK and Ireland, Michiel Bakker; VP MTV Channels, Michael Barry; Executive Producer, Jamie Rae; News Editor, Joleen Moore

**About** A music television channel focused around new and alternative music.

## MTV Base

**180 Oxford Street, London, W1D 1DS**

- 020 7478 6000
- 020 7478 6007
- contact@mtvne.com
- www.mtv.co.uk/mtvbase

**Contact** Managing Director, MTV UK and Ireland, Michiel Bakker; VP MTV Channels, Michael Barry

**About** A music television channel focused on urban music.

## MTV Dance

**180 Oxford Street, London, W1D 1DS**

- 020 7478 6000
- 020 7478 6007
- contact@mtvne.com, lastname.firstname@mtvne.com
- www.mtv.co.uk/channel/mtvdance

**Contact** Managing Director, MTV UK and Ireland, Michiel Bakker; VP MTV Channels, Michael Barry; News Editor and Press Officer, Zoe Stafford
**About** A music television channel focused on dance music.

## MTV Flux
**180 Oxford Street, London, W1D 1DS**
- 020 7478 6000
- 020 7478 6007
- contact@mtvne.com
- www.mtv.co.uk/channel/flux

**Contact** Managing Director, MTV UK and Ireland, Michiel Bakker; VP MTV Channels, Michael Barry; Controller of Programmes, Steve Shannon
**About** A music video channel that allows viewers to publish messages and video content, via mobile phone or the internet. These then play alongside music videos of the viewers' choice.

## MTV Hits
**180 Oxford Street, London, W1D 1DS**
- 020 7478 6000
- 020 7478 6007
- contact@mtvne.com
- www.mtv.co.uk/hits

**Contact** Managing Director, MTV UK and Ireland, Michiel Bakker; VP MTV Channels, Michael Barry
**About** A chart music channel. Features requests, competitions, features, a forum and charts.

## MUTV
**274 Deansgate, Manchester, M3 4JB**
- 0161 868 8435
- 0161 868 8848
- sameer.pabari@manutd.co.uk
- www.manutd.com/mutv

**Contact** Contact, Sameer Pabari
**About** A digital channel broadcasting matches, news and features about Manchester United Football Club.

## National Geographic Channel
**4th Floor, Shepherds Building East, Richmond Way, W14 0DQ**
- 020 7751 7681
- 020 7751 7699
- natgeoweb@bskyb.com
- www.nationalgeographic.co.uk

**Contact** News Editor, Emma Murphy; News Editor, Luigia Minichiello

**About** A wildlife and nature channel normally included in the free packages by most digital television providers. All commissioning for the channel is done electronically through the website, www.ngcideas.com

## National Geographic Wild
**3rd Floor, Shepherds Building East, Richmond Way, W14 0DQ**
- natgeoweb@bskyb.com
- www.nationalgeographic.co.uk

**About** A sister channel to the National Geographic Channel, launched in March 2007, in place of Adventure One. Content comes from co productions and international acquisitions and is mainly related to wildlife and nature. The National Geographic channels have gone paper free; so all commissioning is done through www.ngcideas.com, where interested parties can register their ideas.

## Nepali TV
**Westec House, Westgate, Ealing, London, W5 1YY**
- 020 8728 6470
- 020 8728 6479
- info@nepalitv.com, bijaya@nepalitv.com
- www.nepalitv.com

**Contact** Contact, Bijaya Thapa
**About** A Nepalese satellite channel broadcasting the latest news, current affairs, films, music and television series from Nepal, to over 58 countries.

## New You
**DMA Media Ltd, 6th Floor, 33 Margaret Street, London, W1G 0JD**
- 020 7612 0120
- rbeynon@dma-media.com
- www.dma-media.com/tvchannels/newyou

**About** An on demand digital channel broadcasting diet, fitness and lifestyle programming. Produces mini programmes for IPTV, cable, mobile and broadband television.

## Nick Jr.
**15–18 Rathbone Place, London, W1T 1HU**
- 020 7462 1000
- 020 7462 1030
- howard.litton@nickelodeon.co.uk
- www.nickjr.co.uk/primary/nickjr.aspx

**Contact** Director of Channels, Howard Litton; News Editor, Louise Condon
**About** A digital channel for pre school children, which aims to combine entertainment with learning and development. Much of the programming is produced in collaboration with child development experts.

### Nickleodeon
**15–18 Rathbone Place, London, W1T 1HU**
- 020 7462 1000
- 020 7462 1030
- howard.litton@nickelodeon.co.uk
- www.nicktv.co.uk

**Contact** Director of Channels, Howard Litton; News Editor, Louise Condon
**About** A digital channel for children, broadcasting a mixture of live studio programmes, comedy dramas and animations.

### Nicktoons
**15–18 Rathbone Place, London, W1T 1HU**
- 020 7462 1000
- 020 7462 1030
- howard.litton@nickelodeon.co.uk
- www.nick.co.uk/nicktoons

**Contact** Director of Channels, Howard Litton
**About** A digital channel for children broadcasting entirely animated shows.

### Nollywood Movies
**40 Bowling Green Lane, Clerkenwell, London, EC1R 0NE**
- 020 7837 7888
- 020 7837 7612
- info@zenithfilms.co.uk

**Contact** Head of Sales and Marketing, Zenith Films, Alfred Soroh
**About** Launched in 2007, a digital channel dedicated to the third largest film industry in the world, Nigeria's Nollywood.

### Noor TV
**14 Victoria Road, Aston, Birmingham, B6 5HA**
- 0121 551 5700
- 0121 551 5700
- info@noortv.co.uk
- www.noortv.co.uk

**Contact** Contact, Tahir Riaz

**About** Due to launch in 2007, Noor TV is an Islamic channel, dedicated to promoting 'love and harmony' amongst people and communities.

### Open View
**6 Hoxton Square, London, N1 6NU**
- 020 7012 1200
- 020 7729 9540
- info@openaccess.tv, freelancers@openaccess.tv
- www.openaccess.tv

**Contact** Channel Manager, Matthew Andrew
**About** A digital channel broadcasting at Friday 11.30pm and Sunday 7.00pm, where freelance film makers may submit their films for broadcast and peers can vote for their favourite via a forum. The channel is due to become interactive, whereby viewers will also be able to vote on the films. It acts as a competition and showcase channel. Freelancers should download an application form from the website to join the database.

### Overseas Property TV
**Church Studios, 50 Church Road, London, NW10 9PY**
- 020 8965 6694
- 020 8181 4542
- wendy@macanthonyrealty.com

**Contact** Contact, Wendy MacAnthony
**About** A digital channel to showcasing properties to buy abroad.

### Paramount Comedy
**180 Oxford Street, London, W1D 1DS**
- 020 7478 5300
- 020 7478 5446
- press@paramountcomedy.com, firstname.lastname@paramountcomedy.com
- www.paramountcomedy.com

**Contact** Head of Programming and Development, Sarah Mahoney; Press Contact, Zoe Diver
**About** A digital channel, broadcasting mainly US comedy series with a few British re-runs. Also produces some original comedy content with Five.

### Passion TV
**2nd Floor, Unit 28, 34 Bowater Road, Woolwich, London, SE18 5TF**
- 020 8855 5010
- 020 8855 5949
- info@passiontv.co.uk
- www.passiontv.co.uk

**About** A digital channel aimed at meeting the audience needs of British Afro Caribbeans. It seeks to broadcast challenging, thought provoking programming, on difficult and taboo issues. To volunteer to help with the running of the channel, from production, to press and marketing, as well as being involved in creative ideas, email smakinde@ passiontv.co.uk

## Performance Channel

**4 Farleigh Court, Old Weston Road, Flax Bourton, Bristol, BS48 1UL**
- 01275 463931
- 01275 464070
- firstname.lastname@eicom.co.uk
- www.performance-channel.com

**Contact** Contact, Cleveland Salmon; Content Manager & News Editor, Matthew Clements
**About** A digital channel, broadcasting rock, pop, jazz, easy listening, opera and classical music, as well as shows on acting techniques through interviews with well known actors.

## Pitch TV

**13 Station Road, Finchley, London, N3 2SB**
- 0871 225 3946
- 020 8438 6445
- customerservice@pitchwell.com
- www.pitchwell.com

**About** A digital shopping channel where products are demonstrated by experts, not presenters.

## Playhouse Disney

**Building 12, 2nd Floor, 566 Chiswick High Road, London, W4 5AN**
- 0870 880 7080
- studio@disneychannel.co.uk
- www.disney.co.uk/disneychannel/playhouse

**Contact** Managing Director, Disney TV Europe, John Hardie; Channel Manager, Jonathan Boseley
**About** Disney programmes for younger children.

## Play Jam

**5 Old Street, London, EC1V 9HL**
- 020 7250 1244
- firstinitiallastname@playjam.com
- www.playjam.com

**Contact** Channel Head, Jeff Zie; Head of Operations, Matt Wilson; Executive Producer, Graham Sidwell
**About** An interactive digital games channel.

## The Poker Channel

**Queen's Wharf, Queen Caroline Street, London, W6 9RJ**
- 020 8600 2698
- 020 8600 2501
- info@thepokerchannel.co.uk, firstname.lastname@ thepokerchannel.co.uk
- www.pokerchannel.co.uk

**Contact** Chief Executive, Crispin Nieboer; Commercial Director, Chris White; Viewer Enquiries and Programme Pitches, Angus Gairdner; Website Enquiries, Joshua Thomas; Head of Programming, James Hopkins
**About** Live programmes and features dedicated to poker.

## Pokerzone

**Northumberland House, 155–157 Great Portland Street, London, W1W 6QP**
- 020 7942 7942
- 020 7942 7943
- www.pokerzone.tv

**Contact** Managing Director, Jim Sibcy; Creative Director, Sam Ormas
**About** Casino and poker programming.

## Pop

**37 Harwood Road, London, SW6 4QP**
- 020 7371 5999
- 020 7736 6462
- rorry@popclub.tv
- www.popclub.tv

**Contact** Music Contact, Matt Howes; Press Officer, Francesca Newington
**About** A mixture of cartoons and pop music for children.

## Price Busters TV

**Gear House, Unit A, Camberley Court, Blenheim Industrial Estate, Bulwell, Nottingham, NG6 8GE**
- 0115 849 4500
- 0115 875 4105
- customer.service@pricebusters.tv
- www.pricebusters.tv

**About** A digital shopping channel.

## Price Drop TV

**Sit Up House, 179–181 The Vale, London, W3 7RW**
- 020 8600 9700
- 020 8746 0299

◍ www.price-drop.tv

**Contact** Chief Executive, Ian Percival

**About** An auction shopping channel where the price drops until the product is sold out. Owned by Sit Up TV.

## Prime TV

**Crown House, North Circular Road, London, NW10 7PN**

☏ 020 8965 0333

☏ 020 8965 5723

◉ info@ptv-prime.tv

◍ www.primetv.tv

**Contact** Managing Director, Haroon Kahn; News Editor and Adminstrator, Ali Raza

**About** A Pakistani family entertainment channel, broadcasting a mixture of religious, music, current affairs and entertainment programmes.

## Propeller

**46 The Calls, Leeds, LS2 7EY,**

☏ 0113 236 8240

◉ filmfirst@propellertv.co.uk (independents), redcarpet@propellertv.co.uk (students)

◍ www.propellertv.co.uk

**About** Working with the Skills Set organisation and wholly owned by the Grimsby Institute, Propeller is a digital channel set up to showcase new talent in film and television. The scheme 'Red Carpet' is an arena for students to air their work and 'Film First' is for independents and community groups to display their shorts or feature films. The channel also broadcasts news programmes and industry features. To submit content, visit the website and read through the online PDF files before sending films by post to either John Offord (Film First), or Dawn Simpson (Red Carpet). Films must have a minimum technical specification but Propeller is always looking for new approaches to animation, comedy, drama, music and documentary making.

## Psychic TV

**16 Hanover Square, Mayfair, London, W1S 1HT**

☏ 020 7408 9475

☏ 020 7408 9414

◍ www.psychic-tv.com

**Contact** Contact, Steve Fishwick

**About** A live phone in channel for psychic readings.

## The Pub Channel

**Grant Way, Isleworth, TW7 5QD**

☏ 020 7705 3000

☏ 020 7941 5123

◉ generalenquiries@pubchannel.com, firstname.lastname@bskyb.com

◍ www.pubchannel.com

**Contact** Head of Editorial, New Media, Kate Oppenheim; Assistant Producer, Alison Clarke

**About** A digital channel aimed at the pub trade, it shows a mixture of features, entertainment and documentaries about the licensing industry.

## Q

**Mappin House, 4 Winsley Street, London, W1W 8HF**

☏ 0845 053 1052

◉ QTV@Q4music.comÊ

◍ www.q4music.com

**Contact** Brand and Communications Director, Vikki Timmons; Commercial Manager, Katie Teesdale; Head of TV Radio Sponsorship and Promotions, Darren Kahn; Head of Press and PR Emap Radio, Maureen Corish; Music and Programme Director, Simon Sadler; Programme Controller, Phil Poole

**About** A music video channel linked with Q magazine.

## Quiz Nation

**6–7 Princes Court, Wapping Lane, London, EW1 2DA**

☏ 020 7942 7942

◉ customer.services@quiznation.tv

◍ www.quiznation.tv

**About** An interactive quiz channel.

## QVC

**Marco Polo House, Chelsea Bridge, 346 Queenstown Road, London, SW8 4NQ**

☏ 020 7705 5600

☏ 020 7705 5607

◍ www.qvcuk.com

**About** A digital shopping channel.

## Racing UK

**4th Floor, 8 Waterloo Place, London, SW1Y 4BE**

☏ 020 7766 8484

☏ 020 7766 8485

◉ helena@setanta.com

◍ http://gb.setanta.com

**Contact** Executive Assistant, Zenia Wright

**About** A horse racing channel, showing over 600 live horse races throughout the year. It is a paid for digital channel.

## Racing World
**4th Floor, 8 Waterloo Place, London, SW1Y 4BE**
- 020 7766 8484
- 020 7766 8485
- helena@setanta.com
- http://gb.setanta.com

**Contact** Contact, Helena O'Sullivan
**About** The sister channel to Racing UK, broadcasting programming from the world of US Horse Racing.

## Raj TV
**150–152 Wharfside Street, The Mailbox, Birmingham, B1 1RQ**
- 0121 632 1011
- 0121 632 1482
- info@raj.tv
- www.raj.tv

**Contact** Contact, Iris Farley
**About** A free to air digital channel aimed at 16–35 year olds, due to re-launch with a new image in 2007.

## Rangers TV
**4th Floor, 8 Waterloo Place, London, SW1Y 4BE**
- 020 7766 8484
- 020 7766 8485
- helena@setanta.com
- http://gb.setanta.com

**Contact** Contact, Helena O'Sullivan
**About** A paid for digital channel about Glasgow Rangers Football Club.

## Rapture
**79 Brewer Street, London, W1F 9UU**
- 020 7734 2323
- info@rapturetv.com
- www.rapturetv.com

**Contact** Managing Director, David Henry; Head of Programming, Rebecca Knapp
**About** A general entertainment digital channel which broadcasts gaming, music and current affairs shows.

## Real Estate TV
**3rd Floor, 1–6 Falconberg Court, London, W1D 3AB**
- 020 7440 1070
- 020 7440 1077
- info@realestatetv.tv, mark@realestatetv.tv
- www.realestatetv.tv

**Contact** Head of Channels, Mark Dodd
**About** A digital channel broadcasting property programmes from the UK and abroad, as well as commissioned programmes. It also broadcasts long advertisements for estate agents and property developers.

## Revelation TV
**117a Cleveland Street, London, W1T 6PX**
- 020 7631 4446
- 020 7631 0751
- info@revelationtv.com
- www.revelationtv.com

**Contact** Founders, Lesley and Howard Conder; Operations Manager & News Editor, William George
**About** A Christian television channel.

## Sci Fi UK
**Oxford House, 76 Oxford Street, London, W1D 1BS**
- 020 7307 6600
- 020 7307 6695
- scifipressoffice@nbcuni.com, firstname.lastname@ncbuni.com
- www.scifiuk.com

**Contact** Head of Press, Dan Winter
**About** A digital channel dedicated entirely to Sci Fi content.

## Screenshop
**Sit Up House, 179-181 The Vale, London, W3 7RW**
- 020 8600 9700
- 020 8746 0299
- www.screenshop.co.uk

**Contact** Chief Executive, Ian Percival
**About** A shopping channel owned by Sit Up TV.

## Scuzz
**37 Harwood Road, London, SW6 4QP**
- 020 7371 5999
- 020 7736 6462
- moshpit@scuzz.tv
- www.scuzz.tv

**Contact** Chief Executive, Gail Screene; Head of Music, Sarah Gaughan

**About** A music channel based around rock and indie music.

## See TV
**Maidstone Studios, New Cut Road, Vinters Park, Maidstone, ME14 5NZ**
- 01622 684444
- 01682 684445
- info@seetv.tv
- www.seetv.tv

**Contact** Director of Programmes, Bruce Vigar
**About** A Southeast regional digital channel. It broadcasts entertainment, current affairs and local events to people in the region.

## Setanta Golf
**4th Floor, 8 Waterloo Place, London, SW1Y 4BE**
- 020 7766 8484
- 020 7766 8485
- helena@setanta.com
- http://gb.setanta.com

**Contact** News Editor and Managing Director, Leonard Ryan; Programme Officer, Siobhan Persse
**About** Paid for golf channel.

## Setanta Ireland
**4th Floor, 8 Waterloo Place, London, SW1Y 4BE**
- 020 7766 8484
- 020 7766 8485
- helena@setanta.com
- http://gb.setanta.com

**Contact** News Editor and Managing Director, Leonard Ryan
**About** A paid for digital channel broadcasting Irish sports, including football and rugby. Also broadcasts a daily magazine show, 'The Hub'.

## Setanta Sports 1 & 2
**4th Floor, 8 Waterloo Place, London, SW1Y 4BE**
- 020 7766 8484
- 020 7766 8485
- helena@setanta.com
- http://gb.setanta.com

**Contact** News Editor and Managing Director, Leonard Ryan
**About** Paid for digital sports channels. Setanta Sports 1 shows SPL matches and Setanta Sports 2 broadcasts European league football matches.

## Simply Ideas
**1st Floor, Bentima House, 168-172 Old Street, London, EC1V 9BP**
- 020 8104 0493
- 020 8104 0494
- info@simplymedia.tv
- www.simplymedia.tv

**Contact** Chief Executive, Henry Scott
**About** A 24 hour digital shopping channel.

## Simply Shopping TV
**1st Floor, Bentima House, 168-172 Old Street, London, EC1V 9BP**
- 020 8104 0493
- 020 8104 0494
- info@simplymedia.tv
- www.simplymedia.tv

**About** A 24 hour digital shopping channel.

## Sit Up TV
**Sit Up House, 179–181 The Vale, London, W3 7RW**
- 020 8600 9700
- 020 8746 0299
- www.sit-up.tv

**Contact** Chief Executive, Ian Percival
**About** TV retail channels, including Bid TV, Price Drop TV, Speed Auction TV and Screenshop TV.

## Sky Bet
**Grant Way, Isleworth, TW7 5QD**
- 0800 0724 777
- 01423 720578
- firstname.lastname@skybet.com
- www.skybet.com

**Contact** Entertainment Consultant, Helen Jacobs; PR Coordinator, Tim Reynolds
**About** An interactive betting channel.

## Sky Box Office
**Grant Way, Isleworth, TW7 5QD**
- 0870 240 3000
- 0870 240 3060
- www.skymovies.com

**About** A pay per view film service.

## Sky Movies 1-10
**Grant Way, Isleworth, TW7 5QD**
- 0870 240 3000
- 0870 240 3060

www.skymovies.com
**About** Continuous films across ten channels.

## Sky Movies Cinema
**Grant Way, Isleworth, TW7 5QD**
0870 240 3000
0870 240 3060
www.skymovies.com
**About** Film repeats.

## Sky News
**Grant Way, Isleworth, TW7 5QD**
0870 240 3000
0870 240 3060
news.plan@bskyb.com
www.skynews.co.uk
**Contact** Viewer's Editor, Paul Bromley; Head of News, Nick Pollard; Deputy Head of News, Simon Cole; Deputy News Editor, Victoria Bird; Head of Home News, Phil Wardman; Head of Foreign News, Adrian Wells
**About** Continuous news coverage.

## Sky One
**Grant Way, Isleworth, TW7 5QD**
0870 240 3000
0870 240 3060
www.skyone.co.uk
**Contact** Head of Sky 1, 2 and 3, Richard Woolfe; Commissioning Editor, Specialist Factual and Factual Entertainment, Emma Read; Commissioning Editor, Entertainment, Andrea Hamilton; Commissioning Editor, Drama, Elaine Pyke; Commissioning Editor, Features, Sky 1, 2 and 3, Donna Taberer; Commissioning Editor, Factual, Andrew O'Connell; Commissioning Editor, Entertainment and Factual Entertainment, Steve Jones
**About** The UK's leading non-terrestrial channel, broadcasting a mixture of drama, factual and entertainment programming. For independent production companies, all details of commissioning routes can be found at www.skyone.co.uk/ commissioning, where the specific needs of individual commissioning editors are displayed.

## Sky Sports 1, 2, 3 & Extra
**Grant Way, Isleworth, TW7 5QD**
0870 240 3000
0870 240 3060
www.skysports.co.uk
**Contact** Managing Director, Vic Wakeling

**About** Broadcasts news, features and live action from a wide variety of international sports. Some pay per view programming.

## Sky Sports News
**Grant Way, Isleworth, TW7 5QD**
0870 240 3000
0870 240 3060
snn-planning@bskyb.com
www.skysports.co.uk
**Contact** Managing Director, Vic Wakeling; News Editor, Nick Seymour
**About** A digital channel showing only sports news.

## Sky Three
**Grant Way, Isleworth, TW7 5QD**
0870 240 3000
0870 240 3060
www.skyone.co.uk/skythree
**Contact** Head of Sky 1, 2 and 5, Richard Woolfe
**About** Sky's first freeview digital entertainment channel. It showcases programming from Sky One, Sky Travel, and Artsworld. It also broadcasts news and reviews from Sky Movies and Sky Sports.

## Sky Travel, Sky Travel+1, Sky Travel Extra & Sky Travel Shop
**Grant Way, Isleworth, TW7 5QD**
0870 240 3000
0870 240 3060
firstname.lastname@bskyb.com
www.skytravel.com
**Contact** Head of Communications, Andrea Weselby; Channel Manager, Barbara Gibbons
**About** Sky Travel Shop is a 24/7 interactive holiday shop channel. Sky Travel and Sky Travel Extra are travel related entertainment channels, featuring a wide range of programming formats.

## Sky Two
**Grant Way, Isleworth, TW7 5QD**
0870 240 3000
0870 240 3060
www.skyone.co.uk
**Contact** Head of Sky 1, 2 and 4, Richard Woolfe
**About** Sister channel of Sky One, it broadcasts the same content at alternative times.

## Sky Vegas Live
**Grant Way, Isleworth, TW7 5QD**
0870 240 3000

- 0870 240 3060
- www.skyvegas.com

**About** A Las Vegas casino style gambling channel.

## Smash Hits

**Mappin House, 4 Winsley Street, London, W1W 8HF**

- 020 7436 1515
- 020 7376 1313
- firstname.lastname@emap.com
- www.smashhits-tv.co.uk

**Contact** Brand and Communications Director, Vikki Timmons; Commercial Manager, Katie Teesdale; Head of TV Radio Sponsorship and Promotions, Darren Kahn; Head of Press and PR Emap Radio, Maureen Corish; Director of Music, Simon Sadler; Programme Controller, Phil Poole; Programme Director, David Young

**About** A pop music video channel.

## Solent TV

**Media Centre, Newport, Isle of Wight, PO30 5HE**

- 01983 522344
- contact@solent.tv, news@solent.tv, sport@solent.tv
- www.solent.tv

**Contact** Director of Broadcasting, Paul Topping; Sports Editor, Cameron Bowles

**About** The first not for profit local television station in the UK. Broadcasts news, current affairs and other programmes of local interest to the Isle of Wight.

## Speed Auction

**Sit Up House, 179-181 The Vale, London, W3 7RW**

- 020 8600 9700
- 020 8746 0299
- www.speedauction.tv

**Contact** Chief Executive, Ian Percival

**About** An auction shopping channel owned by Sit Up TV.

## Sumo TV

**148–150 Great Portland Street, London, W1W 6QD**

- 020 7190 0300
- 020 7190 0350
- www.sumo.tv

**About** A digital and online channel broadcasting short clips, often uploaded by viewers. Users can earn money each time their clip is broadcast or downloaded.

## Sunrise TV

**Sunrise House, Merrick Road, Southall, Middlesex, UB2 4AU**

- 020 8843 5353
- 020 8813 9700
- reception@sunriseradio.com
- www.sunriseradio.com

**Contact** Contact, Avrind Audit

**About** The audio visual arm of Sunrise Radio, a station aimed at Britain's Asian community.

## Superstore TV

**1st Floor, Bentima House, 168–172 Old Street, London, EC1V 9BP**

- 020 7608 8650
- 020 7608 8651
- info@simplymedia.tv, ed@superstore.tv
- www.superstore.tv

**About** A digital shopping channel.

## TCM

**Turner House, 16 Great Marlborough Street, London, W1F 7HS**

- 020 7693 1000
- 020 7693 1001
- tcmmailuk@turner.com
- http://tcmonline.co.uk

**About** A 24 hour digital channel broadcasting 20th Century Hollywood films, from classics to more contemporary pieces. Also runs an annual short film competition in association with the London Film Festival.

## TCM 2

**Turner House, 16 Great Marlborough Street, London, W1F 7HS**

- 020 7693 1000
- 020 7693 1001
- tcmmailuk@turner.com
- www.tcm2.co.uk

**Contact** News Editor, Ann Rosen

**About** A sister channel to TCM, which broadcasts from 7pm–3am. It concentrates on core films and shows the same films every night for a week. Programmes change on Sundays.

## Teachers' TV
**16–19 Berners Street, London, W1T 3LN**
- 020 7182 7430
- 020 7580 3656
- firstname.lastname@teachers.tv, summary@teachers.tv (submissions), news@teachers.tv (urgent news)
- www.teachers.tv

**Contact** Joint Head of Programmes, Paul Ashton; Joint Head of Programmes, David Libbert; Head of Scheduling and Acquisitions, Alison Martin; Head of Transmission and Presentation, John Logan

**About** A digital satellite and web based channel aimed at teachers and those in the education industry. Programming includes features from inside the classroom and is designed to help improve teaching throughout the country. Programme ideas are best submitted through a teaching or educational organisation, e.g. DfES. Most of these organisations will have a nominated person who deals with the channel and it is recommended that you go through them. Individuals may approach the channel directly but are less likely to receive a response. Do not send full programmes, only a brief proposal. There are three commissioning rounds per year: March, June and November, with a deadline two months before each one. Programmes usually take six to nine months between commissioning and broadcast, so if a piece is directly related to current news, use the 'news' email address.

## Teletext Holidays
**Building 10 Chiswick Park, 566 Chiswick High Road, London, W4 5TS**
- 0870 731 3000
- 0870 731 3001
- webmaster@teletext.co.uk
- www.teletextholidays.co.uk

**About** A holiday shopping channel.

## TG4
**Baile na hAbhann, Co. na Gaillimhe, Republic of Ireland**
- 00353 91 505050
- 00353 91 505021
- eolas@tg4.ie, firstname.lastname@tg4.ie
- www.tg4.ie

**Contact** Director of Television, Alan Esslemont; Commissioning Editor, Proinsias Ni Ghrainne; Commissioning Editor, Maire Ni Chonlain

**About** An Irish digital channel celebrating Irish storytelling, sport, music, drama and culture.

Programmes are often in the Irish language. For submission information, visit www.tg4.ie/Bearla/Fais/fais Submissions from independent companies are invited for documentaries, music, comedy, drama, soaps, lifestyle and travel. All submissions must be via the form, downloadable from the website.

## Tiny Pop
**37 Harwood Road, London, SW6 4QP**
- 020 7371 5999
- 020 7736 6462
- firstname@popclub.tv
- www.popclub.tv

**Contact** Music Contact, Matt Howes; Press Officer, Francesca Newington

**About** A mixture of cartoons and pop music for very young children. Formerly Pop Plus.

## TMF
**17–29 Hawley Crescent, London, NW1 8TT**
- 020 7284 7777
- 020 7284 6466
- lastname.firstname@mtvne.com
- www.mtv.co.uk/tmf

**Contact** Controller of Programmes, Michael Barry; Programme Director, Jed Mahoney

**About** A digital music channel broadcasting music videos, entertainment and features on popular music.

## Travel Channel
**64 Newman Street, London, W1T 3EF**
- 020 7636 5401
- 020 7636 6424
- enquiries@travelchannel.co.uk, firstname@travelchannel.co.uk
- www.travelchannel.co.uk

**Contact** Press Contact and Head of Research, Petra Shepherd

**About** A digital channel broadcasting travel and holiday features from around the world.

## Trouble
**160 Great Portland Street, London, W1W 5QA**
- 020 7299 5000
- 020 7299 5516
- firstname_lastname@flextech.co.uk
- www.trouble.co.uk

**Contact** Director of Programmes, Jonathan Webb; Channel Editor, Celia Taylor; News Editor and PR Manager, Jakki Lewis
**About** A children's digital channel broadcasting mainly US children's and teenage drama and comedies.

## TWC Fight!
**114 St. Martin's Lane, London, WC2N 4BE**
- 020 7420 8290
- 020 7420 8299
- press@twcfight.com
- www.twcfight.com

**Contact** Managing Director, David Goffin; Director of Programmes, Sean Herbert
**About** A digital channel broadcasting professional wrestling.

## UKTV Bright Ideas
**2nd Floor, 160 Great Portland Street, London, W1W 5QA**
- 020 7299 5000
- 020 7299 5412
- firstname.lastname@uktv.co.uk
- www.ukbrightideas.tv

**Contact** News Editor and PR Manager, Tamsin Zietsman
**About** A digital channel broadcasting lifestyle programmes made in the UK, specifically for a UK audience.

## UKTV Documentary
**2nd Floor, 160 Great Portland Street, London, W1W 5QA**
- 020 7299 5000
- 020 7299 5412
- firstname.lastname@uktv.co.uk
- www.uktvdocumentary.co.uk

**Contact** News Editor and Press Officer, Chris Masters
**About** A digital channel broadcasting documentaries on a variety of topics. Also has occasional themed days and evenings.

## UKTV Drama
**2nd Floor, 160 Great Portland Street, London, W1W 5QA**
- 020 7299 5000
- 020 7299 5412
- firstname.lastname@uktv.co.uk
- www.uktvdrama.co.uk

**Contact** News Editor and PR Manager, Zoe Clapp

**About** A digital channel broadcasting drama and films, mainly archive content.

## UKTV Food
**2nd Floor, 160 Great Portland Street, London, W1W 5QA**
- 020 7299 5000
- 020 7299 5412
- firstname.lastname@uktv.co.uk
- www.ukfood.tv

**Contact** News Editor and PR Manager, Tamsin Zietsman
**About** A digital channel focused entirely on food and cooking. It shows a mixture of archive and original programming, including magazine style shows.

## UKTV G2
**2nd Floor, 160 Great Portland Street, London, W1W 5QA**
- 020 7299 5000
- 020 7299 5412
- firstname.lastname@uktv.co.uk
- www.uktvg2.co.uk

**Contact** News Editor and PR Manager, Zoe Clapp
**About** A digital channel broadcasting contemporary entertainment, often with a satirical edge. Mostly archive content.

## UKTV Gold
**2nd Floor, 160 Great Portland Street, London, W1W 5QA**
- 020 7299 5000
- 020 7299 5412
- firstname.lastname@uktv.co.uk
- www.uktvgold.co.uk

**About** A digital channel broadcasting comedy and entertainment, mainly from the archives of terrestrial television channels.

## UKTV History
**2nd Floor, 160 Great Portland Street, London, W1W 5QA**
- 020 7299 5000
- 020 7299 5412
- firstname.lastname@uktv.co.uk
- www.ukhistory.tv

**Contact** News Editor and Press Officer, Chris Masters
**About** A digital history channel broadcasting a mixture of newly commissioned and archive programmes.

## UKTV People

**2nd Floor, 160 Great Portland Street, London, W1W 5QA**

- 020 7299 5000
- 020 7299 5412
- firstname.lastname@uktv.co.uk
- www.uktvpeople.co.uk

**Contact** News Editor and Press Officer, Chris Masters

**About** A digital channel specialising in real life stories. Programming includes a range of docusoaps.

## UKTV Style

**2nd Floor, 160 Great Portland Street, London, W1W 5QA**

- 020 7299 5000
- 020 7299 5412
- firstname.lastname@uktv.co.uk
- www.ukstyle.tv

**Contact** News Editor and PR Manager, Tamsin Zietsman

**About** A digital lifestyle channel broadcasting programmes from the UK and US. Subjects include homes, property, fashion, makeovers and self improvement.

## UKTV Style Gardens

**2nd Floor, 160 Great Portland Street, London, W1W 5QA**

- 020 7299 5000
- 020 7299 5412
- firstname.lastname@uktv.co.uk
- www.uktvstylegardens.co.uk

**Contact** News Editor and PR Manager, Tamsin Zietsman

**About** A digital channel, which specialises in gardening, it broadcasts mainly archive programmes.

## The Vault

**37 Harwood Road, London, SW6 4QP**

- 020 7371 5999
- 020 7384 2026
- info@chartshow.tv
- www.thevault.tv

**Contact** Chief Executive, Gail Screene; Head of Music, Sarah Gaughan

**About** A music video channel broadcasting music mainly from the 70s, 80s and 90s.

## Vector 24/7 & Shop Plus

**Orchard Lea, Winkfield Lane, Windsor, SL4 4RU**

- 01344 887436
- 01344 887409
- www.vectordirect.tv

**Contact** Media Contact, Paul Howland

**About** Two digital TV shopping channels.

## VH1

**17–29 Hawley Crescent, London, NW1 8TT**

- 020 7284 7777
- 020 7284 6466
- lastname.firstname@mtvne.com
- www.mtv.co.uk/channel/vh1

**Contact** Controller of Programmes, Steve Shannon; News Editor & Publicity, Mandy Hershon

**About** A music video channel broadcasting features, documentaries and popular music.

## VH1 Classic

**17–29 Hawley Crescent, London, NW1 8TT**

- 020 7284 7777
- 020 7284 6466
- lastname.firstname@mtvne.com
- www.mtv.co.uk/channel/vh1

**Contact** Controller of Programmes, Steve Shannon; News Editor & Publicity, Mandy Hershon

**About** A music video channel broadcasting features and music tracks aimed at 30–45 year olds.

## Wedding TV

**44 Clipstone Street, London, W1W 5JT**

- 020 7255 6240
- 020 7255 6241
- info@weddingtv.com
- www.weddingtv.com

**Contact** Programming Director, Tony Prince

**About** A digital channel based entirely around weddings. Broadcasts a mixture of entertainment, documentaries, reality television and gameshows.

## Yes661

**Harper Road, Sharston, Manchester, M22 4RG**

- 0161 947 2580
- 0161 947 2581
- david@masterchemicals.co.uk
- www.yes661.com

**Contact** Contact, David Ades

**About** A digital shopping channel run by Master Chemicals (Leeds).

## Zee Cinema

**Unit 8 Belvue Business Centre, Belvue Road, Northolt, UB5 5QQ**

- 020 8839 4000
- 020 8841 6123
- firstname.lastname@zeetv.co.uk
- www.zeetelevision.com

**Contact** News Editor, Sangraam Marathe
**About** A digital channel focusing on Asian cinema.

## Zee Music

**Unit 8 Belvue Business Centre, Belvue Road, Northolt, UB5 5QQ**

- 020 8839 4000
- 020 8841 6123
- firstname.lastname@zeetv.co.uk
- www.zeetelevision.com

**Contact** News Editor, Sangraam Marathe
**About** A digital channel featuring Asian music programming.

## Zee TV

**Unit 8 Belvue Business Centre, Belvue Road, Northolt, UB5 5QQ**

- 020 8839 4000
- 020 8841 6123
- firstname.lastname@zeetv.co.uk
- www.zeetelevision.com

**Contact** Controller of Programmes, Shaney Burney; News Editor, Sangraam Marathe
**About** A digital channel aimed at an Asian audience. Broadcasts entertainment, news, drama and music.

## Zone Club

**105–109 Salisbury Road, London, NW6 6RG**

- 020 7328 8808
- 020 7624 3652
- firstname.lastname@zonevision.com
- www.zonereality.tv

**Contact** Press Contact, George Hills
**About** A digital lifestyle television channel broadcasting dramas, chat, DIY and documentaries. Aimed at women viewers.

## Zone Horror

**105–109 Salisbury Road, London, NW6 6RG**

- 020 7328 8808
- 020 7624 3652
- firstname.lastname@zonevision.com
- www.zonereality.tv

**Contact** Press Contact, George Hills
**About** A digital channel dedicated to horror films, and features about the making of them.

## Zone Reality

**105–109 Salisbury Road, London, NW6 6RG**

- 020 7328 8808
- 020 7624 3652
- firstname.lastname@zonevision.com
- www.zonereality.tv

**Contact** Press Contact, George Hills
**About** A 24 hour digital channel dedicated entirely to reality television.

# UK & IRISH NATIONAL RADIO

## Capital Life

**30 Leicester Square, London, WC2H 7LA**

- 020 7766 6000
- 020 7766 6601
- firstname.lastname@qcapmedia.com
- www.ukcapitallife.com

**Contact** Programme Director, Kevin Palmer
**About** A national digital radio station broadcasting a mixture of classic and contemporary pop music for listeners aged 25 plus.

## Classic FM

**30 Leicester Square, London, WC2H 7LA**

- 020 7343 9000
- 020 7766 6100
- firstname.lastname@classicfm.com
- www.classicfm.com

**Contact** Station Manager, Darren Henley; News Manager, Ann-Marie Minhall
**About** A national station which is available on analogue and digital radios. It broadcasts classical music, features, interviews and news programmes.

## Core

**Gcap Media, PO Box 2000, Bristol, BS99 7SN**

- 0117 984 3200
- fresh@corefreshhits.com
- www.corefreshhits.com

**Contact** Station Manager, Bern Leckie
**About** Part of the Digital One network. A digital radio station broadcasting contemporary pop music and news, for a young adult audience.

## Digital One
**7 Swallow Place, London, W1B 2AG**
- 020 7288 4600
- 020 7288 4601
- info@digitalone.co.uk
- www.digitalone.co.uk

**About** The UK's largest digital radio multiplex operator. Stations include Classic FM, Capital Life, Virgin Radio, Core, TalkSport, Rock, One Word and theJazz.

## Newstalk
**Warrington House, Mount Street Crescent, Dublin 2, Republic of Ireland**
- 00353 1 6445100
- 00353 1 6611602
- info@newstalk.ie
- www.newstalk.ie

**Contact** Station Editor, Garett Harte; News Director, John Keogh; Sports Editor, Jerry O'Sullivan
**About** A national station for Ireland, which broadcasts a variety of programmes; mainly news, sport, discussion and entertainment.

## OneWord Radio
**50 Lisson Street, London, NW1 5DF**
- 020 7453 1600
- 020 7723 6132
- firstname.lastname@oneword.co.uk
- www.oneword.co.uk

**Contact** Managing Director and News Editor, Simon Blackmore
**About** A national digital radio station, broadcasting a mixture of features on books, comedy, drama and discussion. Part of the Digital One network. There is currently no budget for producing new shows and therefore scripts are not being accepted.

## Planet Rock
**30 Leicester Square, London, WC2H 7LA**
- 020 7054 8000
- firstname@planetrock.com
- www.planetrock.com

**Contact** Executive Producer, Trevor White; Marketing Manager, Jon Norman

**About** A national digital radio station, part of the Digital One network. Broadcasts rock music mainly from the 60s, 70s and 80s, as well as live music, interviews and features on rock music.

## RTÉ 2FM
**Donnybrook, Dublin 4, Republic of Ireland**
- www.rte.ie/2fm

**About** A national public service radio station for Ireland, broadcasting a variety of music and entertainment features.

## RTÉ Lyric FM
**Cornmarket Square, Limerick, Republic of Ireland**
- 00353 61 207300
- 00353 61 207390
- lyric@rte.ie
- www.rte.ie/lyricfm

**About** A national public service radio station for Ireland, it broadcasts a mixture of programmes on opera, musicals, jazz, new music, arts and the theatre.

## RTÉ Radio 1
**Donnybrook, Dublin 4, Republic of Ireland**
- 00353 1 208 3111
- radio1@rte.ie
- www.rte.ie/radio1

**Contact** Head of Radio, Adrian Moynes; Head of RTÉ Radio 1, Anna Leddy
**About** A national public service broadcast radio station for Ireland. A mixture of news, current affairs, drama, music, entertainment features and arts.

## RTÉ Raidió na Gaeltachta
**Casla, Conamara, Co. na Gaillimhe, Republic of Ireland**
- 00353 91 506677
- 00353 91 506666
- rnag@rte.ie
- www.rte.ie/rnag

**About** An Irish language radio station, with regional headquarters.

## talkSport
**18 Hatfields, London, SE1 8DJ**
- 020 7959 7800
- 020 7959 7806
- firstinitiallastname@talksport.co.uk
- www2.talksport.net/index.asp

**Contact** Programme Manager, Matt Smith;
Programme Director, Bill Ridley; Sports Editor,
Andrew McKenna
**About** Part of the Digital One network. A talk based
radio station concentrating mainly on sports
programmes, but also broadcasting news, current
affairs and entertainment content.

## theJazz
**30 Leicester Square, London, WC2H 7LA**
- 020 7054 9000
- 020 7344 2703
- www.thejazz.com

**Contact** Station Manager, Darren Henley
**About** A national digital radio station, part of the
Digital One network and sister station to Classic FM.
Broadcasts jazz music and features.

## Today FM
**124 Upper Abbey Street, Dublin 1, Republic of
Ireland**
- 00353 1 804 9000
- www.todayfm.com

**About** Ireland's main independent national
radio station.

## Virgin Radio
**1 Golden Square, London, W1F 9DJ**
- 020 7434 1215
- 020 7434 1197
- newsroom@virginradio.co.uk, firstname.lastname@
virginradio.co.uk
- www.virginradio.co.uk

**Contact** Programme Director, Paul Jackson; Head of
News, Andrew Bailey; Head of Music, James Curran;
Head of Sport, Dominic Johnson
**About** First broadcast in 1993. An analogue and
digital station playing contemporary music, along
with classic rock and pop music. Part of the Digital
One network.

# COMMERCIAL UK & IRISH LOCAL RADIO

## 98FM
**South Block, The Malthouse, Grand Canal Quay,
Dublin 2, Republic of Ireland**
- 00353 1 439 8800
- 00353 1 670 8969
- dublinnewscentre@98fm.ie
- www.98fm.ie

**Contact** Managing Director, Ciaran Davis
**About** A station for Dublin and the surrounding
area, broadcasting mainly music programming.

## Capital Radio
**30 Leicester Square, London, WC2H 7LA**
- 020 7766 6155
- 020 7766 6012
- newsdesk@capitalradio.com, firstname.lastname@
capitalradio.com
- www.capitalradio.com

**Contact** Music and Film Editor, Sarah Ward;
Entertainment Reporter, Jodie Ross
**About** A London station broadcasting a mixture of
popular music, celebrity features and news.

## Central FM
**201–203 High Street, Falkirk, FK1 1DU**
- 01324 611164
- 01324 611168
- news@centralfm.co.uk
- www.centralfm.co.uk

**Contact** Controller of Programmes, Tom Bell; Sports
Editor, Tadek Kopszywa
**About** Broadcasts to central Scotland on the FM
wavelength. Programmes include music, sports,
news and local events and information.

## Clare FM
**Abbeyfield Centre, Francis Street, Ennis, Co.
Clare, Republic of Ireland**
- 00353 65 682 8888
- 00353 65 682 3366
- info@clarefm.ie
- www.clarefm.ie

**Contact** Managing Director, Liam O'Shea; News
Editor, John Cooke
**About** A station broadcasting to County Clare and
the surrounding areas. A mixture of music,
news and talk.

## Clyde 1

**Clydebank Business Park, Clydebank, G81 2RX**

☎ 0141 565 2200
☎ 0141 565 2265
✉ clydenews@radioclyde.com
🌐 www.clyde1.com

**Contact** Managing Director, Paul Cooney; Head of News and Sport, Russel Walker

**About** A Glasgow radio station aimed at older teens and young adults. Broadcasts a mixture of music, news, sport, competitions and entertainment features. Most content is produced in house or commissioned by invitation.

## Clyde 2

**Clydebank Business Park, Clydebank, G81 2RX**

☎ 0141 565 2200
☎ 0141 565 2265
✉ clydenews@radioclyde.com
🌐 www.clyde2.com

**Contact** Head of News and Sport, Russel Walker

**About** A sister station to Clyde 1, it is aimed at an older audience of 35 plus. Programmes include music, news, sport and competitions. Most content is produced in house or commissioned by invitation.

## Cork's 96 FM & 103 FM

**Broadcasting House, Patrick's Place, Cork**

✉ info@96fm.ie, news@96fm.ie
🌐 www.96fm.ie

**About** A station for Cork, broadcasting mainly music and light entertainment features.

## Downtown Radio

**Newtownards, Co. Down, Northern Ireland, BT23 4ES**

☎ 028 9181 5555
☎ 028 9181 7878
✉ news@downtown.co.uk, programmes@downtown.co.uk
🌐 www.downtown.co.uk

**Contact** Managing Director, David Sloan; Features Coordinator, Florence Ambrose; Head of Music, Eddie West

**About** A radio station for Northern Ireland, which broadcasts music, news, sport and entertainment features. The station runs an annual short story competition for previously unpublished work. Entrants must live in the Downtown area. The prize is £250 in cash and £100 in gift vouchers. There are four categories. For details of closing dates and categories, go to www.downtown.co.uk/article.asp?id=170750

## Dublin's Q102

**Glengeary Office Park, Glengeary, Co. Dublin, Republic of Ireland**

☎ 00353 1 662 1022
☎ 00353 1 662 9974
✉ comments@q102.ie, news@q102.ie, admin@q102.ie
🌐 www.q102.ie

**About** A station for the Dublin area, broadcasting mainly music and news, it is aimed at a 30 plus audience.

## Forth 1

**Forth House, Forth Street, Edinburgh, EH1 3LE**

☎ 0131 557 1005
☎ 0131 557 8489
✉ forth-news@radioforth.com, firstname.lastname@radioforth.com
🌐 www.forthone.com

**Contact** Managing Director, Adam Finlay; Programme Director, Luke McCullough; Head of News, Paul Robertson

**About** A Scottish radio station aimed at young adults. Broadcasts music, news, sport and entertainment features.

## Forth 2

**Forth House, Forth Street, Edinburgh, EH1 3LE**

☎ 0131 557 1005
☎ 0131 557 8489
✉ forth-news@srh.co.uk, firstname.lastname@radioforth.com
🌐 www.forth2.com

**Contact** Head of News, Paul Robertson; Sports Editor, Mark Donaldson

**About** A sister station to Forth 1, aimed at a slightly older audience aged 35 plus. Content includes music, sport and a range of interesting features relevant to the people of Scotland.

## Heart FM

**1 The Square, 111 Broad Street, Birmingham, B15 1AS**

☎ 0121 695 0000
☎ 0121 696 1007
✉ news@heartfm.co.uk
🌐 www.heartfm.co.uk

**Contact** Managing Director, Anita Wright; News Editor, Dave McMullen
**About** A regional West Midlands station with a newer sister station in London. Broadcasts female friendly music, news and entertainment features.

## Isle of Wight Radio
**8 Dondor Park, Newport, PO30 5XE**
☎ 01983 821777
📠 01983 821690
✉ news@iwradio.co.uk, firstname.lastname@iwradio.co.uk
🌐 www.iwradio.co.uk
**Contact** Station Manager, Any Stroud; Controller of Programmes, Tom Stroud
**About** A station for the Isle of Wight that also reaches parts of Hampshire, Dorset and Sussex. The audience is primarily middle aged, and programmes are a mixture of music, news, sport and general entertainment and community features.

## KCLR 96 FM
**Exchequer House, Potato Market, Carlow, Republic of Ireland**
☎ 00353 59 913 9696
📠 00353 59 913 9712
✉ programmecoordinator@kclr96fm.com, news@kclr96fm.com
🌐 www.kclr96fm.com
**Contact** Programme Coordinator, Mags Murphy
**About** A station broadcasting to Kilkenny Carlow. Content is a mixture of music, news, sport and local community features. For any news, documentary or local feature enquiries, contact Mags Murphy.

## KMfm
**Express House, 34–36 North Street, Ashford, TN24 8JR**
☎ 01233 623232
✉ news@kmfm.co.uk
🌐 www.kmfm.co.uk
**About** A group of local station for Kent, with the head office in Ashford and other studios in Medway, Canterbury, Thanet, Folkestone and West Kent. Broadcasts local news and sport, as well as music and general entertainment features.

## LBC
**The Chrysalis Building, 13 Bramley Road, London, W10 6SP**
☎ 020 7314 7300
☎ 020 7314 7317
✉ newsroom@lbc.com, firstname.lastname@lbc.co.uk
🌐 www.lbc.co.uk
**Contact** Managing Director, David Lloyd; Programme Controller, Scott Salder; Editorial Director (News), Jonathan Richards
**About** Broadcasts news, current affairs and features for London. Submit interesting news stories through the online form.

## LMFM
**Rathmullan Road, Drogheda, Co. Louth, Republic of Ireland**
☎ 00353 1850 715958
📠 00353 41 983 2957
🌐 www.lmfm.ie
**Contact** Production, Maria Harman
**About** The largest local radio station for Ireland outside of Dublin and Cork. Broadcasts to Counties Meath and Louth. A mix of music, news and local programmes.

## Midlands 103
**The Mall, William Street, Tullamore, Co. Offaly, Republic of Ireland**
☎ 00353 57 935 1333
📠 00353 57 935 2444
✉ firstname@midlandsradio.fm
🌐 www.midlandsradio.fm
**Contact** Managing Director, Albert FitzGerald; Director of Programming, Will Faulkner
**About** A radio service broadcasting to Counties Laois, Offaly and Westmeath. A mixture of news, music and local events.

## NorthSound One
**Abbotswell Road, West Tullos, Aberdeen, AB12 3AJ**
☎ 01224 337002
📠 01224 633282
✉ news@northsound.co.uk
🌐 www.northsound1.com
**Contact** Managing Director, Ken Massie; Programme Director, Chris Thompson; Head of News, Neil Metcalfe; Sports Editor, David Ridd
**About** A station for Aberdeen and the surrounding area, aimed at teenagers and young adults. Broadcasts a mixture of contemporary music, news, sport and entertainment.

## NorthSound Two

**Abbotswell Road, West Tullos, Aberdeen, AB12 3AJ**

📞 01224 337000
📠 01224 633282
✉ news@northsound.co.uk
🌐 www.northsound2.com

**Contact** Managing Director, Ken Massie; Programme Director, Chris Thompson; Head of News, Neil Metcalfe; Sports Editor, David Ridd

**About** A sister station of NorthSound One, aimed an older audience of over 30s. Broadcasts music, news and general interest features. Also features live local sport.

## Premier Christian Radio

**22 Chapter Street, London, SW1P 4NP**

📞 020 7316 1338
📠 020 7316 1371
✉ firstname.lastname@premier.org.uk
🌐 www.premier.org.uk

**Contact** Chief Executive, Peter Kerridge; Programme Controller, Charmaine Noble-McLean; News Editor, Victoria Lawrence

**About** A Christian station broadcasting to the London area, featuring music and speech in a Christian vein. The station is run by a team of volunteers. Contact eventsteam@premier.org.uk to find out more information.

## Radio Kerry

**Maine Street, Tralee, Co. Kerry, Republic of Ireland**

📞 00353 66 712 3666
🌐 www.radiokerry.ie

**About** A station broadcasting throughout County Kerry. A mixture of discussion, features, news and music.

## Radio XL

**KMS House, Bradford Street, Birmingham, B12 0JD**

📞 0121 753 5353
📠 0121 753 3111
✉ news@radioxl.net, info@radioxl.net,
🌐 www.radioxl.net

**Contact** Managing Director, Arun Bajaj

**About** A West Midlands radio station aimed at the Asian community. A major audience group is young people ages 15 plus. Programmes are broadcast mainly in Hindi and English. Specialist programmes

are in other languages such as Urdu, Gujarati, Punjabi and Bengali.

## Real Radio Scotland

**PO Box 101, Unit 1130, Parkway Court, Glasgow, G69 6GA**

📞 0141 781 1011
📠 0141 781 1112
🌐 www.realradiofm.com

**About** A station for Scotland, which broadcasts phone-ins, discussions, news, sport and music.

## Real Radio Wales

**1 Ty Nant Court, Morganstown, Cardiff, CF15 8YF**

📞 029 2031 5100
📠 029 2031 5150
🌐 www.realradiofm.com

**Contact** Managing Director, Billy Andersen; Programme Director, Jay Crawford

**About** A station for Wales, which broadcasts phone-ins, discussions, news, sport and music.

## Real Radio Yorkshire

**1 Sterling Court, Capitol Business Park, Wakefield, WF3 1EL**

📞 0113 238 1114
📠 0113 238 1191
🌐 www.realradiofm.com

**Contact** Programme Director, Terry Underhill

**About** A station for Yorkshire, which broadcasts phone-ins, discussions, news, sport and music.

## Sabras Radio

**Radio House, 63 Melton Road, Leicester, LE4 6PN**

📞 0116 261 0666
📠 0116 266 7776
✉ studio@sabrasradio.com, sales@sabrasradio.com, firstname@sabrasradio.com
🌐 www.sabrasradio.com

**Contact** Managing Director, Don Kotak

**About** An Asian radio station broadcasting to Greater London, parts of the South and South East and to the East Midlands. Programmes are a mixture of music, news and discussion.

## Saga FM

**3rd Floor Crown House, 123 Hagley Road, Birmingham, B16 8LD**

📞 0121 452 1057
📠 0121 452 3222

www.saga.co.uk

**About** A radio station broadcasting to the West Midlands and aimed exclusively at over 50s. Programmes are a mixture of music, news, features and talk shows. The station has many resident experts for a variety of topics.

## Shannonside FM

**Mastertech Business Park, Athlone Road, Co. Longford, Republic of Ireland**

00353 1850 796796

00353 87 120 0900

info@shannonside.ie, news@shannonside.ie

www.shannonside.ie

**Contact** Head of Programmes, Jon Finnegan; Head of News, Ann Norris; Head of Sport, John Lynch

**About** A station broadcasting to Counties Longford, Roscommon, South Leitrim, Cavan and Monaghan. There is a strong bias towards speech based programming, with news, community events and sport, although there is some music programming.

## Spectrum Radio

**International Radio Centre, 4 Ingate Place, Battersea, London, SW8 3NS**

020 7627 4433

020 7627 3409

enquiries@spectrumradio.net

www.spectrumradio.net

**Contact** General Manager, Paul Hogan

**About** A radio station aimed at London and the South East's ethnic population. It broadcasts a variety of programmes for the different nationalities and ethnicities living in the UK. Content includes music, news and features.

## Spire FM

**City Hall Studios, Malthouse Lane, Salisbury, SP2 7QQ**

01722 416644

01722 416688

news@spirefm.co.uk

www.spirefm.co.uk

**Contact** Station Manager, Karen Boseley; Programme Controller, Stuart McGinley

**About** A station for Salisbury and the surrounding areas in Wiltshire and parts of Hampshire. Broadcasts a mixture of music, news and sport.

## Sunrise Radio (Yorkshire)

**Sunrise House, 30 Chapel Street, Little Germany, Bradford, BD1 5DN**

01274 735043

01274 728534

news@sunriseradio.fm, info@sunriseradio.fm

www.sunriseradio.fm

**Contact** Chief Executive, Usha Parmar; News Editor, Gail Papworth

**About** A radio station aimed at Yorkshire's Asian community. Broadcasts a mixture of music, news and information features.

## Swansea Sound

**Victoria Road, Gowerton, Swansea, SA4 3AB**

01792 511170

01792 897115

newsroom@swanseasound.co.uk, reception@swanseasound.co.uk, firstname.lastname@swanseasound.co.uk

www.swanseasound.co.uk

**Contact** Managing Director, Carrie Moseley; Head of News, Emma Thomas; Sports Editor, Wyn Evans

**About** An AM frequency station for Swansea and South Wales, it broadcasts a mixture of music, news and regional programming.

## Talk 107

**9 South Gyle Crescent, Edinburgh Park, Edinburgh, EH12 9EB**

0131 316 3106

0131 316 3136

news@talk107.co.uk, studio@talk107.co.uk

www.talk107.co.uk

**Contact** Programme Director, Mike Graham; News Editor, Gwen Lawrie

**About** A station broadcasting to Edinburgh, Fife and the Lothians. Content includes local news, opinions and discussion, and sport.

## The Wave

**Victoria Road, Gowerton, Swansea, SA4 3AB**

01792 511964

01792 897115

news@thewave.co.uk, firstname.lastname@thewave.co.uk, reception@thewave.co.uk

www.thewave.co.uk

**Contact** Programme Manager, Steve Barnes; Head of News, Emma Thomas

**About** An FM sister station to Swansea Sound, broadcasting mainly popular music, as well as local news for Swansea and the surrounding areas.

## 12 Yard Productions
**10 Livonia Street, London, W1F 8AF**
- 020 7432 2929
- 020 7439 2037
- contact@12yardproductions.com
- www.12yard.com

**Established** 2001

**Insider Info** Produces television shows, mainly quiz show formats and innovative factual entertainment. Recent productions include *Eggheads* for BBC2 and *Without Prejudice* for Channel 4.

**Tips** The company run a creative trainee scheme for those interested in developing programme ideas. Contact trainees@12yard.com, for details.

## Aardman Animations
**Gas Ferry Road, Bristol, BS1 6UN**
- 0117 984 8485
- 0117 984 8486

**Contact** Creative Director, Features, Peter Lord

**Established** 1972

**Insider Info** Produces material for film and television. Specialists in animation, traditionally using models but more recently using CGI. Well-known characters include Wallace and Gromit and Angry Kid. Will not accept previously published material. Submissions will not be returned.

**Tips** No unsolicited manuscripts.

## Above the Title
**Level 2, 10–11 St. George's mews, London, NW1 8XE**
- 020 7916 1984
- 020 7722 5706
- mail@abovethetitle.com
- www.abovethetitle.com

**Contact** Head of Development, Jo Wheeler

**Insider Info** Productions include radio programming on music, the arts, comedy, drama, and factual subjects. BBC Radios 2 and 4 are frequent recipients of the shows. Submissions accompanied by SAE will be returned. Catalogue available online.

**Submission Guidelines** Send a one paragraph synopsis to Jo Wheeler. Email or postal submissions accepted.

**Tips** Read the extensive back catalogue of productions on the website and note where each show was broadcast, for an idea of style and potential audience groups.

## Absolutely Productions
**Unit 19, 77 Beak Street, London, W1F 9BD**
- 020 7644 5575
- www.absolutely.biz

**Established** 1988

**Insider Info** Produces programming for national television and radio stations, particularly comedy and drama. Recent productions include *Historyville* for Channel 4 and Baggage for Radio 4. Catalogue available online.

**Tips** No unsolicited manuscripts.

## Abstract Images
**117 Willoughby House, Barbican, London, EC2Y 8BL**
- 020 7638 5123
- productions@abstract-images.co.uk

**Insider Info** A producer of factual and dramatic programmes for television. Includes some Christian programmes.

**Tips** Contact the company by email for more information on submitting scripts. If in doubt, send a synopsis and your contact details.

## Acacia Productions
**80 Weston Park, London, N8 9TB**
- 020 8341 9392
- 020 8341 4879
- em@acaciaproductions.co.uk/projects@acaciaproductions.co.uk
- www.acaciaproductions.co.uk

**Contact** Managing Director, J. Edward Milner

**Established** 1984

**Insider Info** Produces material for television and Video and DVD (non-broadcast). Produces documentaries and features, predominantly on environmental and third world issues, as well as current affairs in general. Broadcast outlets have included the BBC.

**Tips** No unsolicited manuscripts.

## ACP Television & Crosshands Ltd
**Crosshands, Ludlow, Shropshire, SY8 3AR**
- 01584 890893
- 01584 890893
- webmaster@acptv.com
- www.acptv.com

**Contact** Richard Uridge

**Insider Info** A producer of television and radio documentaries. Work has previously been broadcast on satellite channels such as UKTV Style.

**Tips** Contact Richard Uridge for more information on the company. Does not produce drama or other fictional programming.

## Acrobat Television

**107 Wellington Road North, Stockport, Cheshire, SK4 2LP**

- 0161 477 9090
- 0161 477 9191
- info@acrobat-tv.co.uk
- www.acrobat-tv.co.uk

**Established** 1986

**Insider Info** Provides production services both for broadcast TV and corporate videos. Specialises in sports and action filming. Also draws from an extensive footage library.

**Tips** No unsolicited manuscripts.

## Actaeon Films

**49 Blenheim Gardens, London, NW2 4NR**

- 020 8830 7990
- 0870 134 7980
- info@actaeonfilms.com
- www.actaeonfilms.com

**Contact** Founder, Daniel Cormack

**Established** 2004

**Insider Info** Produces material for film, the web and new media e.g. mobile phones and 3G. Produces feature length and short films with typically commercial elements that are given a new, innovative twist. A recent example of a feature film is *Amelia and Michael*, in association with Fortune films and starring Anthony Head. Submissions accompanied by SAE will be returned. Aims to respond to submissions within one month.

**Tips** A young company who are interested in new writing but will not necessarily be able to respond in full to all unsolicited manuscripts.

## All3Media

**87–91 Newman Street, London, W1T 3EY**

- 020 7907 0177
- 020 7907 0199
- information@all3media.com
- www.all3media.com

**Contact** Creative Director, David Liddiment

**Established** 2003

**Insider Info** Produces material for film and television. All3Media group encompasses a range of production companies: ARG; Bentley Productions; Cactus TV; Company Pictures; IdtV Productions; Lion Television; Lime Pictures; North One Television and Pacific Pictures. Among them they produce high-profile programming nationally and internationally.

**Tips** All3Media's output is varied depending on the subsidiary company involved. Visit each company's section of the website for further details but be aware that much of the programming is commercially very high-profile. Examples include *Midsomer Murders* and *Richard and Judy*.

## All Out Films

**50 Copperas Street, Manchester, M4 1HS**

- 0161 834 9955
- 0161 834 6978
- mail@allout.co.uk/firstname.lastname@allout.co.uk
- www.allout.co.uk

**Contact** Founders, David Cook, David Prosser and Nigel Wrench

**Insider Info** Produces news, factual features, documentaries and current affairs programming, predominantly for BBC radio. Catalogue available online.

**Submission Guidelines** Accepts query with synopsis.

**Tips** No unsolicited full manuscripts. Bear in mind that productions are usually commissioned for broadcast on BBC radio stations and their various audiences.

## Angel Eye Media

**9 Rudolf Place, Miles Street, London, SW8 1RP**

- 0845 230 0062
- 0845 230 9562
- ideas@angeleye.co.uk
- www.angeleye.co.uk

**Contact** Creative Director, John O'Callaghan

**Insider Info** Produces material for film, television, radio, the web and new media. Produces programming for various media platforms including comedy, entertainment, documentary, education and drama. Clients have included the BBC, Channel 4, Channel Five and numerous corporate clients. Submissions will not be returned.

**Submission Guidelines** Email submissions only. Send proposal as an attachment.

**Tips** Read the 'Ideas' page on the website carefully before submitting treatments.

## Anglo-Fortunato Films Ltd

**170 Popes Lane, London, W5 4NJ**

- 020 8932 7676
- 020 8932 7491

**Contact** Luciano Celentino

**Insider Info** Produces material for film and television. Genres worked with tend to be dramas, both action thriller and comedy.

**Tips** No unsolicited manuscripts.

## Arlington Productions Ltd

**Cippenham Court, Cippenham Lane, Cippenham, Slough, SL1 5AU**

- 01753 516767
- 01753 691785

**Insider Info** Produces dramas and documentaries for television audiences.

**Submission Guidelines** Agented submissions only.

**Tips** Arlington do commission new writers but will no accept unsolicited scripts. Approach agents in the first instance.

## Art & Training Films Ltd

**PO Box 3549, Stratford Upon Avon, CV37 6ZJ**

- andrew.haynes@aft.org.uk
- www.atf.org.uk

**Contact** Andrew Haynes

**Insider Info** Produces material for film and television and video content for theatre productions. Previous output has included history documentaries, corporate training videos and short films. Projects in development include a sitcom and a dramatic adaption of a novel.

**Tips** Agented submissions only.

## Art and Adventure Ltd

**5 Darling Road, London, SE4 1YQ**

- 020 8692 0145
- 020 8692 0145
- roger@artandadventure.org
- www.artandadventure.org

**Contact** Creative Director, Roger Elsgood

**Established** 1996

**Insider Info** Produces material for film, radio and the web. Produces broadcast content for national and international audiences. Credits Include *King Trash* for BBC Radio 4 and *Between The Ears* for BBC Radio 3. Works with about 30 writers per year. Purchases all rights on accepted material. Will accept previously published material. Aims to respond to queries within two weeks and submissions within

one month. Payment via outright purchase. Catalogue available by email.

**Submission Guidelines** Produces films and CDs. Accepts query with synopsis and CV.

**Tips** Needs good, relevant, drama scripts for BBC Radio 4. Writers should know BBC Audio commissioning schedule requirements, published at www.bbc.co.uk/commissioning.

## Ashford Entertainment

**20 The Chase, Coulsdon, CR5 2EG**

- 020 8660 9609
- 0870 116 4142
- info@ashford-entertainment.co.uk
- www.ashford-entertainment.co.uk

**Contact** Founder, Frazer Ashford

**Established** 1996

**Insider Info** Produces dramatic film and television programming as well as documentaries. Much output has been broadcast on satellite channels and some on terrestrial television. Recent examples include *Serial Killers* for The Crime Network Channel. Submissions accompanied by an SAE will be returned. Aims to respond to queries within four weeks.

**Submission Guidelines** Accepts query with synopsis.

**Tips** Submit succinct documentary treatments by post.

## Athena Media

**Digital Depot, Digital Hub, Thomas Street, Dublin 8**

- 00353 1488 5850
- info@athenamedia.ie
- www.athenamedia.ie

**Contact** Helen Shaw

**Established** 2003

**Insider Info** Produces radio and television documentaries, as well as multimedia projects for various broadcast and corporate clients such as *The Irish Times* and SABC (South African Broadcast Commission).

**Tips** Does not produce drama. A major broadcast client is BBC Radio 4. Non-broadcast clients are very varied and range from publishers, to newspapers, to health agencies. Recent projects include an audiovisual awareness video for the Crisis Pregnancy Agency. The aim of the company is to add value to other businesses or organisations through digital products.

## At IT Productions Ltd

**68 Salisbury Road, London, NW6 6NU**

- 020 8964 2122
- 020 8964 2133
- enquiries@atitproductions.com
- www.atitproductions.com

**Contact** Director of Programmes, Tamsin Summers

**Established** 1997

**Insider Info** Producers of television programmes for Channel 4, Channel Five, BBC, ITV and Sky One and the US channels TLC and The Discovery Channel. Genres include documentaries, travel, pop music, films, quiz shows and children's television. An example of current output is the teenage brand, *T4*, currently showing on Channel 4.

**Tips** For a feel of the style and production values of the company, view the digital showreel available on the website.

## Attaboy TV

**Unit 1, 23a Blue Anchor Lane, London, SE16 3UL**

- 020 7740 3000
- 020 7740 3008
- info@attaboytv.com
- www.attaboytv.com

**Contact** Directors, Michael Wood and Daniel Allum

**Established** 1997

**Insider Info** Produces factual entertainment series and documentaries as well as interactive programmes and commercials. Credits include *Road Movies* for Channel 4 and *The High Road* for Carlton.

**Submission Guidelines** Individuals and companies are welcome to make contact with programme ideas.

**Tips** Ideas should be able to entertain a large television audience on terrestrial or satellite television and must be factual. No drama.

## Baby Cow Productions Ltd

**77 Oxford Street, London, W1D 2ES**

- 020 7399 1267
- 020 7399 1262

**Established** 1999

**Insider Info** Founded by Steve Coogan and Henry Normal. Produces comedy programming for a range of UK and international broadcasters, including the BBC and ITV. The company have recently added Baby Cow Radio, Films and Animations to their profile, producing comedy output in these genres. A recent example of a Baby Cow Film production is *A Cock and Bull Story*, starring Steve Coogan.

Submissions accompanied by SAE will be returned. Catalogue available online.

**Submission Guidelines** Accepts query with synopsis. Include a ten page sample and a DVD or VHS sample if possible. Send by post or email to john@babycow.co.uk.

**Tips** Work should be cutting-edge comedy with widespread broadcast potential. A dedicated team will look at all unsolicited manuscripts but there may be delays in response due to the volume of material received.

## Beckmann International

**Milntown Lodge, Lezayre Road, Ramsey, Isle of Man, IM8 2TG**

- 01624 816585
- 01624 816589
- sales@beckmanngroup.co.uk, firstinitiallastname@beckmanngroup.co.uk
- www.beckmanngroup.co.uk

**Contact** Managing Director, Jo White

**Established** 1983

**Insider Info** Distributors of factual documentary programming for a variety of television broadcasters and DVD/VHS output. Catalogue available online.

**Tips** For producers of documentaries and factual programming, fill in the online submissions form to apply for distribution through Beckmann.

## Big Heart Media

**Flat 4, 6 Pear Tree Court, London, EC1R 0DW**

- 020 7608 0352
- 020 7250 1138
- info@bigheartmedia.com
- www.bigheartmedia.com

**Contact** Director of Programmes, Colin Izod

**Established** 1998

**Insider Info** Producers of educational, factual and dramatic programming for television, radio and the web. Clients include the BBC, Pearson Education, Teacher's TV and Channel 4.

**Submission Guidelines** Accepts query with synopsis by email only. No unsolicited manuscripts.

**Tips** Although the full catalogue is not available on the website, samples and clips of work across all media platforms give a sense of the style and content of the company's productions.

## Big Umbrella Media

**The Oracle Building, Blythe Valley Park, Solihull, B90 8AD**

- 0121 506 9620

**☎** 0121 506 9621

**✉** production@bigumbrellamedia.co.uk

**🌐** www.bigumbrellamedia.co.uk

**Contact** Head of Development (Broadcast),
Claire Campbell

**Established** 1998

**Insider Info** Develops and produces formats, one-offs and series for UK and international television broadcasters. Focuses on factual entertainment and documentaries.

**Submission Guidelines** Agented submissions welcome, as are collaborative ideas from other production companies.

**Tips** Check the broadcast news section of the website for upcoming projects and chances to become involved in programmes.

## Bona Broadcasting Ltd
**Media Suite 1, 43 Cavalry Park Drive, Edinburgh, EH15 3QG**

**☎** 0131 661 7550

**☎** 0131 661 7558

**✉** enquiries@bonabroadcasting.com

**🌐** www.bonabroadcasting.com

**Contact** Director, Turan Ali

**Insider Info** Produces material for film, television and Radio. Producers of drama, comedy, magazine shows and documentary output for clients such as the BBC.

**Submission Guidelines** Send a one-paragraph synopsis to ideas@bonabroadcasting.com.

**Tips** No unsolicited manuscripts. Individuals whose ideas are commissioned and who have the appropriate professional experience will be guaranteed a role on the production team.

## Brook Lapping Productions
**6 Anglers Lane, London, NW5 3DG**

**☎** 020 7428 3100

**☎** 020 7284 0626

**✉** info@brooklapping.com

**🌐** www.brooklapping.com

**Contact** Lesley Calmels

**Established** 1982

**Insider Info** A producer of current affairs television and radio programming for broadcasters such as BBC, ITV, Channel 4 and international broadcasters.

**Tips** The website section on past productions gives a flavour of the high-profile nature of previous programmes. These include T*he Real Bad Girls* for ITV1 and *Geldof in Africa* for BBC1.

## Cactus TV
**373 Kennington Road, London, SE11 4PS**

**☎** 020 7091 4900

**☎** 20 7091 4901

**✉** touch.us@cactustv.co.uk

**🌐** www.cactustv.co.uk

**Contact** Managing Directors, Amanda Ross and Simon Ross

**Established** 1994

**Insider Info** Produces popular light entertainment programmes for television. Catalogue available online.

**Tips** Check the online catalogue for the nature of programmes produced. Recent examples include *Richard and Judy* for Channel 4 and *Saturday Kitchen* for the BBC. Does not make drama or other fictional television.

## Caledonia TV
**147 Bath Street, Glasgow, G2 4SQ**

**☎** 0141 564 9100

**☎** 0141 564 9200

**✉** info@caledonia.tv/lcumming@caledonia.tv

**🌐** www.caledonia.tv

**Contact** Head of Development, Linda Cummings

**Established** 1992

**Insider Info** Producers of documentaries, factual entertainment formats and and children's programmes for television. Subjects include history, science, current affairs, arts and education.

**Tips** Proposals welcome from experienced producers, directors or researchers of factual programming. No drama scripts.

## Calon Ltd
**3 Mount Stuart Square, Butetown, Cardiff, CF10 5EE**

**☎** 029 2048 8400

**☎** 029 2048 5962

**✉** enquiries@calon.tv

**🌐** www.calon.tv

**Contact** Head of Development, Andrew Offiler

**Insider Info** Produces material for television – live action and animated drama and entertainment for children.

**Submission Guidelines** Accepts query with synopsis. No unsolicited manuscripts.

**Tips** Formerly Siriol Productions, the focus has traditionally been on animated series such as *SuperTed* and *Hilltop Hospital*. Calon is now moving into live action programming. View clips in the production section of their website for programmes in development.

## Campbell Davison Media
**110 Gloucester Avenue, London, NW1 8JA**
- 020 7209 3740
- 020 7209 3743
- clare@campbelldavison.com
- www.campbelldavison.com

**Contact** Clare Davison
**Established** 1991
**Insider Info** Produces news, features, live sport, documentaries and entertainment programming for the BBC and commercial radio and television. Credits include *606* and *The Rumour Mill* for BBC Radio Five Live. Catalogue available.
**Tips** All programming is factually based. Radio productions are much more prevalent than television programmes. Much of the live radio has a sports topic but the documentaries for BBC Radio 4 are more varied in terms of themes. For BBC commissioning information that Campbell Davison will use themselves, see www.bbc.co.uk/ commissioning.

## Carbon Princess
**Princess Studios, 3rd Floor Whiteleys, 151 Queensway, London, W2 4SB**
- 020 7985 1985
- 020 7985 9451
- the.mikes@carbonhq.com
- www.carbonhq.com

**Contact** Mike Christie and Mike Smith
**Established** 2004
**Insider Info** Works with Princess TV. Produces television documentaries and material for film. Credits include *Body Talk* and *Jump London*, both for Channel 4.
**Tips** For editorial queries, contact either of the 'Mikes' by email. Be aware that the main broadcast route so far for Carbon Princess has been Channel 4, typically an 8pm weekday slot.

## Carnival (Films & Theatre) Ltd
**47 Marylebone Lane, London, W1U 2NT**
- 020 7317 1370
- 020 7317 1380
- info@carnival-films.co.uk/ firstname.lastname@ carnival-films.co.uk
- www.carnival-films.co.uk

**Contact** Managing Directors, Gareth Neame
**Established** 1978

**Insider Info** Producers of popular drama for theatre, television and film. Productions are commissioned by all major terrestrial UK networks and feature films have been nominated for awards such as Oscars and BAFTAs. Recent output includes *Hotel Babylon* for BBC1 and *Rosemary and Thyme* for ITV1.
**Tips** No unsolicited manuscripts. Although Carnival are committed to new writing, connections are made through known drama commissioners.

## Cartwn Cymru
**32 Wordsworth Avenue, Roath, Cardiff, CF24 3FR**
- 029 2046 3556/07771 6404000
- production@cartwn-cymru.com

**Contact** Producer, Naomi Jones
**Insider Info** An animation production company producing both drawn and 3D animation for film and television.
**Tips** Contact Naomi Jones for more information on this company. Previous productions include Welsh animations such as *Otherworld*, written by Martin Lamb and Penelope Middelboe.

## Celador Films
**39 Long Acre, London, WC2E 9LG**
- 020 7845 6988
- 020 7845 6979
- www.celadorfilms.com

**Contact** Head of Development, Ivana MacKinnon
**Insider Info** Produces commercial feature films. Previous productions include *The Descent* and *Separate Lies*.
**Submission Guidelines** Agented submissions only.
**Tips** Films produced by Celador must be commercially viable and commissions are usually made through script agents or collaborations with other production companies.

## Celador Productions
**39 Long Acre, London, WC2E 9LG**
- 020 7845 6988
- 020 7845 6979
- www.celadorproductions.com

**Contact** Director of Production, Heather Hampson
**Established** 1983
**Insider Info** Produces quizzes, comedy, drama, factual entertainment and daytime game shows for television, as well as radio. Output includes *Who Wants to be a Millionaire* for ITV 1 and commissions for BBC Radio 2 and 4. Submissions accompanied by SAE will be returned.

**Submission Guidelines** Accepts unsolicited submissions for radio programmes only. Post to Liz Anstee, Head of Radio.

**Tips** No unsolicited manuscripts for television formats.

## Celtic Films

**Lodge House, 69 Beaufort Street, London, SW3 5AH**

- 020 7351 0909
- 020 7351 4139
- info@celticfilms.co.uk
- www.celticfilms.co.uk

**Contact** Director, Muir Sutherland

**Established** 1986

**Insider Info** Specialist producers of television drama and feature films. Well known productions include *Sharpe* for the BBC and *Hornblower* for ITV. Submissions accompanied by SAE will be returned.

**Submission Guidelines** Read submissions guidelines and agreement documents, downloadable from the website, before submitting.

**Tips** Unsolicited material is welcome but bear in mind that the company produces mainly one-off drama features or drama series. For series, prepare a pilot episode.

## Chameleon TV

**Great Minster House, Lister Hill, Horsforth, Leeds, LS18 5DL**

- 0113 205 0040
- 0113 281 9454
- firstname@chameleontv.com
- www.chameleontv.com

**Contact** Head of Production, Richard Everiss

**Insider Info** Produces television documentaries, current affairs, drama and factual programmes for broadcasters such as the BBC and Channel 4. Previous subject matters have included docusoaps, religion, arts and wildlife.

**Tips** Agented submissions only, although new writing submitted this way is welcome.

## Charles Dunstan Communications

**42 Wolseley Gardens, London, W4 3LS**

- 020 8994 2328
- 020 8994 2328

**Insider Info** Produces material for film, television and corporate video – mainly factual material for documentaries.

**Tips** No unsolicited manuscripts.

## Children's Film and Television Foundation

**Ealing Sudios, Ealing Green, London, W5 5EP**

- 07887 573479
- info@cftf.org.uk
- www.cftf.org.uk

**Contact** Chief Executive, Anna Home

**Established** 1951

**Insider Info** Has produced films and television content for children such as *The Borrowers* and *The Queen's Nose*, both for the BBC. The production archive is administered by Granada International.

**Tips** The most recent source of funding has stopped, therefore the Foundation are no longer undertaking new projects.

## Cinécosse

**Lethenty Mill, Inverurie, AB51 0HQ**

- 01467 670707
- 01467 670071
- info@cinecosse.co.uk, admin@cinecosse.co.uk
- www.cinecosse.co.uk

**Established** 1978

**Insider Info** Produces corporate videos, educational training packs and some documentaries and features for television broadcast. Also undertakes graphic design projects, media training and a range of other services.

**Tips** No unsolicited manuscripts.

## Classic Arts

**The Old Rectory, Hampton Lovett, Droitwich, Worcestershire, WR9 0LY**

- 01299 851563
- 01299 851728
- wendy@classicarts.co.uk
- www.classicarts.co.uk

**Contact** Executive Director, Wendy Thompson

**Established** 1993

**Insider Info** Producers of music and arts programmes, mainly for BBC Radio. Content is live music, as well as documentary style programmes.

**Tips** Specialists in classical music. Major broadcast routes are BBC Radio 3 for music and BBC Radio 4 for speech based programming. Their commissioning needs can be found at www.bbc.co.uk/commissioning

## Collingwood O'Hare Entertainment

**10–14 Crown Street, London, W3 8SB**

- 020 8993 3666

- 020 8993 9595
- info@crownstreet.co.uk
- www.collingwoodohare.com

**Contact** Head of Development, Helen Stoud
**Established** 1988
**Insider Info** A leading animation studio for children's television. Productions include *The Magic Key* for BBC and *Pond Life* for Channel 4.
**Tips** No unsolicited submissions, but they are interested in new writing. This will normally be sourced through industry contacts or agents.

## The Comedy Unit
**Glasgow Media Park, Craigmont Street, Glasgow, G20 9BT**
- 0141 305 6666
- 0141 305 6600
- info@comedyunit.co.uk
- www.comedyunit.co.uk

**Contact** Marketing and Talent Manager, Claire Hancock
**Established** 1996
**Insider Info** The Comedy Unit produce comedy programmes for network and satellite television, radio and websites. Credits include *Chewin' the Fat* and *Rab C. Nesbitt*. The company works with 20 to 50 writers and performers per year and will accept previously published material. Submissions accompanied by SAE will be returned, although they will not send a catalogue to writers on request.. The company aim to report on queries within two days and submissions within 25 days. Payment is in accordance with industry standards.
**Submission Guidelines** Submit completed script.
**Tips** Email or postal submissions are welcome (email: scripts@comedyunit.co.uk). Scripts themselves should be emailed as an attachment.

## Company Pictures
**Suffolk House, 1–8 Whitfield Place, London, W1T 5JU**
- 020 7380 3900
- 020 7380 1166
- enquiries@companypictures.co.uk
- www.companypictures.co.uk

**Contact** Managing Directors, George Faber and Charles Pattinson
**Established** 1998
**Insider Info** Produces television drama series and features, as well as some feature films. Productions include Jimmy McGovern's *The Lakes* for BBC 1 and *Wild at Heart* for ITV 1.
**Submission Guidelines** Agented submissions only.

**Tips** For those writers that do have agents, be aware that the television drama produced by Company is often for prime time terrestrial television and must have widespread appeal. The feature films are relatively less high profile.

## Cosgrove Hall Films
**8 Albany Road, Chorlton cum Hardy, Manchester, M21 0AW**
- 0161 882 2500
- 0161 882 2555
- animation@cosgrovehall.com
- www.cosgrovehall.com

**Contact** Managing Director, Anthony Utley
**Established** 1976
**Insider Info** Specialists in animation of all kinds for film and television. Develops mainly children's programmes, although animation for adults is also produced.
**Tips** Cosgrove Hall has produced both series, such as *Andy Pandy* for CBeebies and feature films such as *Roald Dahl's BFG*. Co-productions are becoming increasingly popular, as are series that have an international saleability without alienating British audiences.

## The Creative Partnership
**13 Bateman Street, London, W1D 3AF**
- 020 7439 7762
- 020 7437 1467
- firstname.lastname@thecreativepartnership.co.uk
- www.thecreativepartnership.co.uk

**Contact** Creative Directors, Chris Fowler and Mike Devery
**Insider Info** The Creative Partnership are a film marketing agency who write campaigns to go alongside both feature films and television projects.
**Tips** Experienced writers interested in writing marketing copy and campaigns for films and television should submit their CVs.

## CSA Word
**6a Archway Mews, 241a Putney Bridge Road, London, SW15 2PE**
- 020 8871 0220
- 020 8877 0712
- info@csaword.co.uk, firstname@csaword.co.uk
- www.csaword.co.uk

**Contact** Commissioning Editor, Victoria Wood
**Established** 1989
**Insider Info** Produces radio drama series for the BBC as well as making audio books.

**Submission Guidelines** Post or email submissions.
**Tips** The audiences for radio dramas are exclusively
BBC Radio 2 and 4, therefore it is a good idea to
research these stations thoroughly.

## Cutting Edge Productions
**27 Erpingham Road, London, SW15 1BE**
- 020 8780 1476
- 020 8780 0102
- juliannorridge@btconnect.com
**Contact** Director, Julian Norridge
**Insider Info** Produces television documentaries as
well as some corporate videos.
**Submission Guidelines** No unsolicited
submissions.
**Tips** The company has no official website. Contact
Julian Norridge for the latest information.
Documentary ideas are usually commissioned
directly through existing contacts.

## Darrall MacQueen
**17 Park Street, Borough Market, London,
SE1 9AB**
- 020 7407 2322
- info@darrallmacqueen.com
- www.darrallmacqueen.com
**Contact** Development, Maddy Darrall
**Insider Info** Produces material for television, the
web, mobiles and interactive media. A large
independent producer of children's television. Third
largest supplier of programmes for the BBC.
**Tips** Produces both presenter led live shows, as well
as original children's drama series for CBBC. For the
BBC children's commissioning needs, visit:
www.bbc.co.uk/commissioning

## Diverse Production
**6 Gorleston Street, London, W14 8XS**
- 020 7603 4567
- 020 7603 2148
- www.diverse.tv
**Contact** Creative Director, Roy Ackerman
**Insider Info** Produces factual television and drama
documentary for major broadcasters. Much of the
output is for prime time slots in terrestrial television
channels. Subject matters include religion, the arts,
current affairs and investigative journalism. Previous
productions include *Beyond Boundaries: The African
Challenge* for BBC 2 and *Who You Callin' a Nigger?*,
which was nominated for a Bafta. Catalogue
available online.
**Tips** Strictly no unsolicited manuscripts.

## DMS Films
**89 Sevington Road, London, NW4 3RU**
- 020 8203 5540
- 0870 762 5871
- danny@dmsfilms.co.uk
- www.dmsfilms.co.uk
**Contact** Daniel M. San
**Insider Info** Produces feature films, shorts, retail
video films and television content including
documentaries. A recent project is the British
teenage comedy *Popcorn*.
**Submission Guidelines** Post or email a short
synopsis only to begin with.
**Tips** No unsolicited manuscripts. Read the 'credits'
section of the website to view the full breadth of
projects undertaken by DMS films.

## DoubleBand Films
**3 Crescent Gardens, Belfast, BT7 1NS Northern
Ireland**
- 028 90 24 3331
- 028 90 23 6980
- firstinitiallastname@doublebandfilms.com
- www.doublebandfilms.com
**Contact** Directors, Michael Hewitt and
Dermot Lavery
**Established** 1985
**Insider Info** A producer of documentaries, mainly
on sports, medical and social topics. Also produces
occasional drama features. Credits include *George
Best's Body* for Channel 4 and *Unfinished Business*
for the BBC.
**Tips** The company's back catalogue is available
online, which shows the types of documentaries
previously made. Their three major clients are the
BBC, Channel 4 and RTE.

## Eagle & Eagle Production
**15 Marlborough Road, London, W4 4EU**
- 020 8995 1884
- 020 8995 5648
- producer@eagletv.co.uk
- www.eagletv.co.uk
**Contact** Producers, Robert Eagle and Catharine
Alen-Buckley
**Insider Info** Produces documentaries, drama and
educational programming, mainly for terrestrial and
satellite TV channels. Previous credits include *The
Nuclear Boy Scout* for Channel 4 and *Robo Sapiens* for
The Discovery networks.
**Tips** New projects in the pipeline include a dramatic
adaption of a novel. Much of the output remains

factual though, often with scientific, environmental or social history topics.

## Ecosse Films
**Brigade House, 8 Parsons Green, London, SW6 4TN**
- 020 7371 0290
- 020 7736 3436
- info@ecossefilms.com
- www.ecossefilms.com

**Contact** Managing Director and Executive Producer, Douglas Rae

**Insider Info** Produces television dramas and feature films. Recent productions include the feature film *Becoming Jane*, written by Kevin Hood and Sarah Williams, and an adaption of Thomas Hardy's *Under the Greenwood Tree* for ITV1. Catalogue available online.

**Tips** Agented submissions only, no unsolicited manuscripts.

## The Elstree Company
**Shepperton Studios, Building 20 Studios Road, Shepperton, TW17 0QD**
- 01932 592680
- 01932 592682
- enquiries@elsprod.com
- www.elsprod.com

**Contact** Producer, Greg Smith

**Insider Info** The Elstree Company produce entertainment, drama and factual programming for television, as well as theatre productions. Catalogue available online.

**Tips** Clients tend to include many satellite channels such as TNT and Hallmark, as well as terrestrial television. Formats include full length television films, documentaries, sit-coms and dramatic adaptions of well known novels.

## Endemol UK
**Shepherd's Building Central, Charechrost Way, London, W14 0EE**
- 0870 333 1700
- 0870 333 1800
- info@endemoluk.com
- www.endemoluk.com

**Contact** Creative Director, Richard Osman

**Insider Info** Produces material for television and the web and produces digital content. A leading producer of factual and entertainment formats for television including *Big Brother* for Channel 4 and *Restoration Village* for BBC 2. Endemol UK companies include Brighter Pictures, Cheetah Television, Endemol Gaming, Endemol Mobile, Hawkshead, Initial, Showrunner, Victoria Real, Zeppotron.

**Tips** Endemol's productions are largely very high profile. Unlikely to commission unsolicited manuscripts. Do not tend to produce straight drama, although the Endemol company Zeppotron does produce comedy programming.

## Fairline Productions
**15 Royal Terrace, Glasgow, G3 7NY**
- 0141 331 0077
- 0141 331 0066
- team@fairlineproductions.com
- www.fairlineproductions.com

**Insider Info** A producer of corporate and broadcast television. Credits include *Fishing Road Trip USA* and video content for The Institute of Customer Service and Budweiser. An extended showreel of Fairline Productions' work can be ordered from the website.

**Tips** No unsolicited manuscripts.

## Farnham Film Company
**34 Burnt Hill Road, Lower Bourne, Farnham, GU10 3LZ**
- 01252 710 313
- 01252 725855
- info@farnfilm.com
- www.farnfilm.com

**Contact** Company Directors, Ian Lewis and Melloney Roffe

**Established** 1985

**Insider Info** Producers of television programmes and occasional low budget feature films. Credits include *Gumdrop*, an animated children's series, and *Cafes of Europe*, a factual series. Submissions accompanied by SAE will be returned.

**Submission Guidelines** For feature films, submit full scripts. For series, submit one or two episodes (not the first) and a further six or so outlines. No email submissions.

**Tips** Particular needs are for feature films and children's television scripts including drama, comedy, animation and factual (but not game shows). Any children's ideas should have series potential. No unpublished or self-published novels, handwritten scripts or short films.

## Feelgood Fiction Ltd
**49 Goldhawk Road, London, W12 8QP**
- 020 8746 2535
- 020 8740 6177

- feelgood@feelgoodfiction.co.uk
- www.feelgoodfiction.co.uk

**Contact** Managing Directors, Philip Clarke and Lawrence Bowen
**Established** 1996
**Insider Info** Producers of film and television comedy and drama. Credits include *Hello Girls*, a comedy series for BBC 1 and *The English Harem*, a feature length drama for ITV 1.
**Tips** Feelgood Fiction also has a feature film arm, Feelgood Films, which has produced the film *Miranda*. The company as a whole are committed to developing new writers and many of their projects, although high profile, are the first credits of the writers. A list of the new writers they are currently working with is published on the website.

## Festival Productions
**PO Box 70, Brighton, BN1 1YJ**
- 01273 669595
- 01273 669596
- info@festivalradio.com
- www.festivalradio.com

**Contact** Director, Steve Strak
**Established** 1989
**Insider Info** Produces drama features and series as well as documentaries, mainly for BBC Radio. Also creates music based programming for commercial radio stations.
**Tips** The writing opportunities are likely to come in the dramas and documentaries which are almost entirely made for BBC Radio 3 and 4. For their programme needs see: www.bbc.co.uk/commissioning

## Film and General Productions Ltd
**4 Bradbrook House, Studio Place, London, SW1X 8EL**
- 020 7235 4495
- 020 7245 9853
- cparsons@filmgen.co.uk

**Contact** Producer, Clive Parsons
**Established** 1971
**Insider Info** Produces film and television drama for general audiences and children. Credits include *The Queen's Nose* for the BBC and the Feature Film *Tea with Mussolini*. Works with three scripts and writers per year and purchases film and television rights on accepted material. Will accept previously published material and submissions accompanied by SAE will be accepted. Aims to respond to queries within three days and submissions within two weeks. Writers will be paid for their work in accordance with

industry standards. Will not send a catalogue to a writer on request.
**Submission Guidelines** Accepts query with synopsis.
**Tips** Do not send full scripts without querying first.

## The First Film Company Ltd
**3 Bourlet Close, London, W1W 7BQ**
- 020 7436 9490
- 020 7637 1290
- info@firstfilmcompany.com
- www.firstfilmcompany.com

**Contact** Producers, Robert Randall-Cutler and Robert Cheeck
**Established** 1984
**Insider Info** The First Film Company produce UK feature films for cinema and television.
**Tips** Accepts agented submissions only.

## First Writes Radio
**Lime Kiln Cottage, High Starlings, Banham, Norwich, NR16 2BS**
- 01953 888525
- 01953 888974
- info@firstwrites.co.uk
- www.first-writes.co.uk

**Contact** Executive Producer, Richard Blake
**Established** 1995
**Insider Info** First Writes are a specialist radio drama producer for BBC Radio 2 and 4. Credits include *The Wonderful Adventures of Mrs Mary Seacole in Many Lands* and *Merely Players*.
**Tips** First Writes are unlikely to be able to develop first time writers. Productions are generally made with particular attention paid to careful casting and highlighting the atmospheric nature of the piece. Audiences are that of BBC Radio 2 and 4.

## Flashback Television Ltd
**9–11 Bowling Green Lane, London, EC1 0BG**
- 020 7490 8996
- 020 7490 5610
- mailbox@flashbacktv.co.uk
- www.flashbacktelevision.com

**Contact** Creative Director, David Edgar
**Established** 1982
**Insider Info** Producers of factual entertainment television programmes for broadcasters both in the UK and internationally. Clients include the BBC, Channel 4 and The Discovery network. They have recently branched out into drama for the first time.

**Tips** An extensive list of current and past productions is published on the website, and gives an idea of the scope of Flashback. Recent credits include *Nigella's Christmas Kitchen* for the BBC, and *Weaponology* for The Discovery Military Channel.

## Focus Films Ltd
**The Rotunda Studio, Rear of 116–118 Finchley Road, London, NW3 5HT**
- 020 7435 9004
- 020 7431 3562
- focus@focusfilms.co.uk, firstname@focusfilms.co.uk
- www.focusfilms.co.uk

**Contact** Head of Development, Malcolm Kohll
**Established** 1982
**Insider Info** Focus Films are a feature film production company, that also finance and develop films in collaboration with other production companies. Credits include *The Bone Snatcher* and *51st State*.
**Tips** No unsolicited manuscripts will be accepted. Agents of writers should email Malcolm Kohll at: malcolm@focusfilms.co.uk with script ideas. The company is in the process of setting up Chilla Productions, an imprint created to make low-budget (under $5 million) thriller films.

## Fox Television Studios UK
**Lamb House, Church Street, London, Greater London, W4 2PD**
- 020 8995 8255
- 020 8995 8456
- info@foxtvstudios.co.uk
- www.foxtvstudios.co.uk

**Contact** Office Manager, Caroline Christierson
**Established** 2001
**Insider Info** Fox Television Studios produce television programming for a wide, general audience (both terrestrial and satellite channels). Accepts previously published material, and submissions accompanied by SAE will be returned. Aims to report on queries and submissions within two weeks. Will not send a catalogue to writers on request. Writers are paid for their work in accordance with industry standards.
**Submission Guidelines** Produces tapes and cassettes. Accepts query with synopsis.
**Tips** Do not send entire scripts unless invited after querying.

## Free@last TV
**2nd Floor, 47 Farringdon Road, London, EC1M 3JB**
- 020 7242 4333
- 020 7 242 7910
- info@freeatlasttv.co.uk
- www.freeatlasttv.co.uk

**Established** 2000
**Insider Info** Producers of mainly factual television programming, including music-based programmes, documentaries and reality formats. Recent credits include *Who Wants to be a Centrefold* for Channel Five and *Spandau Ballet Live* for ITV 1.
**Submission Guidelines** Accepts query with synopsis. Send ideas by email only.
**Tips** Much of the programming tends to focus on celebrity, music and light entertainment. Clients include ITV 1, 3 and 4, Channel 4, Channel Five and The Sci Fi Channel.

## FreMantle media Ltd
**1 Stephen Street, London, W1T 1AL**
- 020 7691 6000
- 020 7691 6100
- www.fremantlemedia.com

**Contact** CEO, Tony Cohen
**Established** 1993
**Insider Info** Formerly Pearson Television, FreMantle are Major producers of prime time television drama, serial drama, entertainment and factual entertainment programmes. Companies under the Fremantle umbrella include, UFA, Blu, teamWorx, talkbackThames, Grundy, Blue Circle and Crackerjack.
**Tips** Many productions have been big-budget, international successes and include *X Factor* and *American Idol*. Dramas include *The Bill* and *Neighbours*. Shows generally have an international appeal and need to be commercially successful.

## Fulcrum TV
**3rd Floor Bramah House, 65–71 Bermondsey Street, London, SE1 3XF**
- 020 7939 3160
- 020 7403 2260
- team@fulcrumtv.com
- www.fulcrumtv.com

**Contact** Head of Production, Martin Long
**Insider Info** Produce factual television programming, including light entertainment, investigative journalism and programmes to mark major events. Subjects include history, politics, archaeology and memoirs. Credits include *The*

*Sixties: The Beatles Decade* for UKTV History and *Revealed: When M&S Lost its Billions* for Channel Five.
**Tips** Work in both live action and animation formats. Part of the company's ethos is to bring new ideas and talent to the screen, they are committed to finding new funding streams in order to do so.

## Gaia Communications
**20 Pevensey Road, Eastbourne, East Sussex, BN21 3HP**
- 01323 727183
- 01323 734809
- production@gaiacommunications.co.uk
- www.gaiacommunications.co.uk

**Contact** Directors, Robert Armstrong and Loni von Gruner
**Insider Info** Produces tourist and local heritage television programmes, as well as a range of videos and audio books on holistic subjects.
**Submission Guidelines** Produces videotapes, DVDs and audio books.
**Tips** Gaia are specialists in the South East Counties. Previous projects have included writers' views and musings on their surroundings, in a narrated documentary format.

## Ginger Productions
**1st Floor 3 Waterhouse Square, 138–142 Holborn, London, EC1N 2NY**
- 020 7882 1020
- 020 7882 1040
- production@ginger.com
- www.ginger.tv

**Contact** Creative Directors, Ed Stobart and Stephen Joel
**Insider Info** Produces factual entertainment and light entertainment television formats. Credits include *Jack Osbourne: Adrenaline Junkie* and *Kelly Osbourne: Turning Japanese*. Owned by SMG productions.
**Tips** Ginger's style tends to be light hearted, humorous and aimed at a fairly young teenage/adult audience.

## Goldcrest Films
**65–66 Dean Street, London, W1D 4PL**
- 020 7437 8696
- 020 7437 4448
- mailbox@goldcrestfilms.com, firstinitiallastname@goldcrestfilms.com
- www.goldcrestfilms.com

**Contact** Director of Acquisitions and Development, Seth Carmichael
**Established** 1977
**Insider Info** Goldcrest finances, produces and distributes feature films.
**Submission Guidelines** Accepts agented submissions only.
**Tips** The Goldcrest Finishing Fund is a source of funding to help independent films reach completion. Films must have most of the funding in place and can be either in development, production or post production. Contact Seth Carmichael for further details of this opportunity.

## The Good Film Company Ltd
**The Studio, 5–6 Eton Garages, Lambolle Place, London, NW3 4PE**
- 020 7794 6222
- 020 7794 4651
- info@goodfilms.co.uk
- www.goodfilms.co.uk

**Contact** Producers, Yanina Barry and Maino Saikawafilm (Video and Multimedia Production)
**Established** 1988
**Insider Info** The Good Film Company produce film, video and multimedia pieces, including documentaries, music videos and commercials. Credits include *Kishidan Pop Video* and *A conversation with Jim Broadbent, Lindsay Duncan & Tom Hooper* for Home Box Office Creative Services, New York.
**Tips** No unsolicited manuscripts.

## Green Umbrella
**59 Cotham Hill, Stoke Bishop, Bristol, BS6 6JR**
- 01179 064336
- 01179 237003
- postmaster@umbrella.co.uk
- www.umbrella.co.uk

**Contact** Managing Director, Nigel Ashcroft
**Established** 1991
**Insider Info** Green Umbrella originally produced science and natural history television programmes. The company has since moved into other areas, including lifestyle, history and earth sciences. Credits include *Dirty Weekend* for ITV and *Escape From Berlin* for Discovery. Submission accompanied by SAE will be returned.
**Tips** Material submitted must directly relate to the company's specialist subject areas, in particular science, including wildlife, and natural history.

## Greenwich Village Productions & Fiction Factory

**14 Greenwich Street, London, SE10 9BJ**

- 020 8853 5100
- 020 8293 3001
- gvproductions@fictionfactory.co.uk, radio@fictionfactory.co.uk
- www.fictionfactory.co.uk

**Insider Info** GVT produces television documentaries and short films. Recent productions include *Poems in the Picture 2: Adlestrop* (poems by Edward Thomas put to visuals and music). Fiction Factory supplies radio and television productions for the BBC.

**Submission Guidelines** Accepts postal submissions of radio scripts by established writers, or through agents.

**Tips** Although Greenwich Village and Fiction Factory will only read scripts by experienced writers, they employ the services of Brian Miller Script Reading to deal with unsolicited manuscripts from new writers. Brian can be contacted via email (brianmiller19@yahoo.co.uk). There is a fee for this service and the company are currently only accepting radio scripts (no television or stage work will be accepted).

## Hattrick Productions Ltd

**10 Livonia Street, London, W1F 8AF**

- 020 7434 2451
- 020 7287 9791
- info@hattrick.com
- www.hattrick.com

**Contact** Managing Director, Jimmy Mulville
**Established** 1986

**Insider Info** Produce mainstream comedy, drama and entertainment for most major television broadcasters. Recent credits include *Have I Got News for You* and *Room 101* for the BBC, and the film drama *In Denial of Murder*.

**Submission Guidelines** Accepts agented submissions only.

**Tips** No unsolicited manuscripts will be accepted.

## Heavy Entertainment

**111 Wardour Street, London, W1F 0UH**

- 020 7494 1000
- 020 7494 1100
- info@heavy-entertainment.com
- www.heavy-entertainment.com

**Contact** Directors, David Roper and David Nougarede
**Established** 1992

**Insider Info** Heavy Entertainment produce material for television, radio, websites, videos, DVDs and CD-ROMs. They produce corporate videos and news releases, as well as programmes for broadcast radio. They also produce radio advertising and audio books. Programmes range from high end documentaries, to light entertainment formats and quizzes.

**Tips** In terms of broadcast radio, Heavy Entertainment work with all BBC stations, meaning their content and formats are extremely varied. Drama productions are likely to be limited to BBC Radio 4.

## Heritage Theatre Ltd

**Unit 1, 8 Clanricarde Gardens,, London, W2 4NA**

- 020 7243 2750
- 020 7792 8584
- rm@heritagetheatre.com
- heritagetheatre.com

**Contact** Managing Director, Robert Marshall
**Established** 2000

**Insider Info** Heritage produce material for television, DVD production and distribution. The company produce programmes for lovers of great live theatre productions, arts and theatre viewers, teachers and students. Aims to report on queries within two days. Purchases rights on broadcast and DVD distribution of live production. Will accept previously published material and submissions accompanied by SAE will be returned. Payment is via royalty. Catalogue available with SAE, or online or via email.

**Submission Guidelines** Produces videotapes and DVD. Heritage do not work from a script, but from live productions.

**Tips** Heritage produce recordings of important live stage productions for distribution to broadcasters and on their DVD label. They do not accept submissions from writers.

## Hourglass Productions

**27 Princes Road, Wimbledon, London, SW19 8RA**

- 020 8540 8786
- 020 8543 8396
- productions@hourglass.co.uk
- www.hourglass.co.uk

**Contact** Director, Martin Chilcott
**Established** 1984

**Insider Info** Produces documentaries and factual features for film and television on scientific, educational and current affairs subjects. Clients include the BBC, Channel 4 and The Discovery

Network. Past productions include *Fruity Stories* for Channel 4 and an episode of *Horizon* for BBC 2.

**Tips** Recent production styles have included the use of technology to explain or investigate detailed subjects, such as medical or environmental matters. The programmes tend to offer an air of authority on important issues.

## Icon Films

**10 Redland Terrace, Bristol, BS6 6TD**

- 0117 924 8535
- 0117 974 4971
- info@iconfilms.co.uk
- www.iconfilms.co.uk

**Contact** Creative Directors, Harry Marshall

**Insider Info** Producers of documentaries for UK and international television. Specialist subjects include natural history (particularly the Indian subcontinent), history, science, travel, anthropology and religion. Recent productions include *Nick Baker's Weird Creatures* for Animal Planet and *Tiger Diaries* for the BBC.

**Submission Guidelines** Accepts query with synopsis.

**Tips** Ideas must be documentaries, broadly within the subject areas that Icon are familiar with. Possible broadcast outlets include the BBC, Channel 4 and the Discovery network of channels.

## Ignition Films

**1 Wickham Court, Bristol, BS16 1DQ**

- 0117 958 3087
- 0117 965 7674
- alison@ignitionfilms.org, terry@ignitionfilms.org
- www.ignitionfilms.org

**Contact** Alison Sterling

**Established** 1999

**Insider Info** Ignition Films are producers of TV, cinema, internet, home DVD and digital installations. They are specialists in high definition television and programmes produced include feature films, drama and documentaries. Credits include *Botanical Wonders* for ITV and the feature film *Human Remains*.

**Submission Guidelines** Accepts agented submissions only.

**Tips** Although unsolicited scripts are not accepted, Ignition have a commitment to new writing, particularly from South West based writers. A feature film has been commissioned from the winner of a South West Script Award.

## Illuminations

**19–20 Rheidol Mews, Rheidol Terrace, London, N1 8NU**

- 020 7288 8400
- 020 7359 1151
- firstname@illuminationsmedia.co.uk
- www.illuminationsmedia.co.uk

**Contact** Head of Production, Seb Grant

**Established** 1982

**Insider Info** Illuminations produce material for television, websites, video and DVD. Television and multimedia programming is in the fields of the arts, culture, science and innovation. Clients include the BBC, Channel 4, Channel Five, and Artsworld. Catalogue available online.

**Tips** Programmes are not only made for broadcast television, but for corporate clients, educational institutions and arts organisations. They usually have an arts or cultural theme at their core.

## Imari Entertainment

**PO Box 158, Beaconsfield, Buckinghamshire, HP9 1AY**

- 01494 677147
- 01494 677147
- info@imarientertainment.com
- www.imarientertainment.com

**Established** 1999

**Insider Info** Mainly known for corporate video production, Imari has also developed and produced content for presentation to television commissioning editors. Areas include light entertainment, documentaries, sit-coms, and children's and adult's drama.

**Tips** The corporate side of the business is the most developed and unsolicited manuscripts for television pilots are unlikely to be taken on. A recent television project, children's drama *Operation Fox*, was developed in conjunction with a local published writer.

## Isis Productions

**106 Hammersmith Grove, London, W6 7HB**

- 020 8748 3042
- 020 8748 3046
- isis@isis-productions.com
- www.isisproductions.co.uk

**Contact** Directors, Nick de Grunwald and Jamie Rugge-Price

**Established** 1991

**Insider Info** Produces mainly documentary and factual entertainment television programmes, largely centred on music. Programmes have been shown on ITV 1, Channel Five and the BBC.

**Tips** A popular style of programming has been biography type documentaries on particular musical artists with a colourful life story.

### ITV Productions (Granada)
**The London Television Centre, Upper Ground, London, SE1 9LT**

- 020 7620 1620
- www.granadamedia.com

**Contact** Directors, John Whiston

**Insider Info** Produces a wide range of television programming, including drama, children's, arts, factual, entertainment, sport, daytime and lifestyle content. Acts as the main provider of content for the ITV channels but also produces programming for the BBC, Channel 4, Sky One, Channel Five and many satellite channels.

**Tips** Much of the content is made up of entertainment formats, factual programming, drama and comedy series and dramatic adaptions of established novels, such as those of Agatha Christie. Although original drama is produced, there is unlikely to be any opportunities for unknown writers.

### IWC
**St. George's Studio, 93–97 St George's Road, Glasgow, G3 6JA**

- 0141 353 3222
- mailglasgow@iwcmedia.co.uk
- www.iwcmedia.co.uk

**Contact** Head of Production, Jonathan Warne

**Insider Info** Owned by the RDF Media group, IWC produces prime time television programming including drama, documentaries, history, reality TV and features. Credits include *Relocation Relocation* for Channel 4 and the US series *Survival of the Richest*.

**Tips** Writers with an established record but no prime time television credits may apply to the 'Coming Up' scheme, in association with Channel 4. Eight winners get a 30 minutes slot on Channel 4 for a piece of drama and £3,000. Submission guidelines are on the website, where details will appear each year for the annual scheme. Multicultural and regional film makers are particularly encouraged to apply. The scheme is not for complete beginners.

### JAM Pictures and Jane Walmsley Productions
**8 Hanover Street, London, W1S 1YE**

- 020 7290 2676
- 020 7256 6818
- producers@jampix.com

**Contact** Producer, Jane Walmsley

**Insider Info** JAM pictures produces drama for various media, including television films, feature films and some theatre pieces. Jane Walmsley Productions produces features and documentaries mainly for broadcast television.

**Submission Guidelines** Accepts query with synopsis.

**Tips** Do not send the full scripts in the first instance. A writing CV, or a list of credits will help in establishing your quality and experience.

### Jane Marshall Productions
**The Coach House, Westhill Road, Blackdown, Leamington Spa, CV32 6RA**

- 01926 831680
- jane@jmproductions.freeserve.co.uk

**Contact** Jane Marshall

**Insider Info** Produces radio programmes from book readings. Will accept previously published material.

**Tips** Readings must be taken from formally published books.

### Justice Entertainment
**PO Box 4377, London, W1A 5SX**

- 020 7467 5450
- 020 7467 5451
- info@timwestwood.com
- www.timwestwood.com

**Contact** CEO, Tim Westwood

**Insider Info** Produces programmes for BBC Radio 1 specialising in black and urban music. Credit include the Radio 1 Rap show, *In New Music We Trust* show and *Reggae Dancehall*.

**Tips** No unsolicited manuscripts will be accepted.

### Keo Films
**101 St. John Street, London, EC1M 4AS**

- 020 7490 3580
- 020 7490 8419
- keo@keofilms.com
- www.keofilms.com

**Contact** Head of Development, Jaimie D'Cruz

**Insider Info** Keo Films produce material for television, websites and digital output. They are producers of light entertainment formats, documentaries and interactive content for a variety of media. Credits include *Save Lullingstone Castle* for BBC2 and *Hip Hop Candy* for MTV.

**Submission Guidelines** Accepts query with synopsis, via email only. Mark emails 'Development'.

**Tips** No unsolicited manuscripts will be accepted. A major area of business for the company is producing documentaries, both features and series, to be broadcast on Channel 4.

## Kingfisher Television

**Martindale House, The Green, Ruddington, Nottingham, NG11 6HH**

- 0115 945 6581
- info@kingfishertv.co.uk
- www.kingfishertv.co.uk

**Contact** Managing Director, Tony Francis

**Established** 1988

**Insider Info** Produces factual content for television broadcast outlets, such as the BBC, ITV, Channel 4, Animal Planet and Discovery. Subjects have included sports, the environment and wildlife. Recent productions include the rural series *Tales from the Country* for the BBC and *Safari Park* for ITV.

**Tips** Email or post ideas for programmes or features, bearing in mind the topics and styles of programme previously worked with. View the website for examples, as well as upcoming programmes.

## Kudos Film and Television

**12–14 Amwell Street, London, EC1R 1UQ**

- 020 7812 3270
- 020 7812 3271
- info@kudosfilmandtv.com
- www.kudosfilmandtv.com

**Contact** Managing Directors, Stephen Garrett and Jane Featherstone

**Established** 1992

**Insider Info** Producers of drama and documentaries for television and feature films. Recent productions include *Spooks* for BBC1 and the feature films *Pure* and *Among Giants*.

**Submission Guidelines** Accepts agented submissions only.

**Tips** No unsolicited manuscripts will be accepted. For those writers with agents, view the production archive to get a feel for previous productions. Their style tends to be sharp and edgy, yet deals with both controversial subject matters as well as lighter entertainment.

## Ladbroke Radio (Electric Airwaves)

**Essel House, 29 Foley Street, London, W1W 7JW**

- 020 7323 2770
- 020 7079 2080
- neil@electricairwaves.com
- www.electricairwaves.com

**Contact** Managing Director, Andrew Caesar-Gordon

**Insider Info** Ladbroke is an independent radio production company, producing content for the BBC and Channel 4 radio. They also cater for corporate clients.

**Tips** Ladbroke Radio, owned by Electric Airwaves, was the first independent radio production company to be commissioned by the BBC and continue to work within the BBC's commissioning needs.

## Lagan Pictures Ltd

**21 Tullaghbrow, Tullaghgarley, Ballymena, BT42 2LY Northern Ireland**

- 028 2563 9479
- 028 2563 9479
- laganpictures@tullaghbrow.freeserve.co.uk

**Contact** Producer, Stephen Butcher

**Insider Info** Producers of factual, drama and corporate programming for film and television. Credits include *A Force Under Fire* for Ulster TV.

**Submission Guidelines** Accepts query with synopsis.

**Tips** Writers from Northern Ireland, or pieces to do with the region are of particular interest.

## Landseer Films

**140 Royal College Street, London, NW1 0TA**

- 020 7485 7333
- mail@landseerfilms.com, db@landseerfilms.com, ken@landseerfilms.com
- www.landseerfilms.com

**Contact** Directors, Derek Bailey and Ken Howard

**Established** 1977

**Insider Info** Producers of television broadcasts, including dance, drama, children's television, opera, documentaries and music. Programmes are regularly made for prime time slots across international networks. Credits include *Ballet Boyz* for Channel 4 and *The Double Life of Alan Ayckbourn* for the BBC. Catalogue available online.

**Tips** Potential writers should bear in mind the heavy bias towards culture and arts based programming. View the website for a full list of productions.

## Leopard Films

**1–3 St Peters Street, Islington, London, N1 8JD**

**☎** 0870 420 4232

**☎** 0870 443 6099

**✉** enquiry@leopardfilms.com, firstnamelastname@leopardfilms.com

**🌐** www.leopardfilms.com

**Contact** Head of Programmes, Bernard Periatambee

**Insider Info** Produces a broad range of programming for major terrestrial and satellite television channels across the world. Productions range from drama and to documentary, to light entertainment series. Credits include *Farm of Fussy Eaters* for UKTV Style and *Body Building Pensioners* for BBC 1's One Life series. A sister company of Leopard Films USA.

**Tips** No unsolicited manuscripts will be accepted.

## Libra Television

**4th Floor, 22 Lever Street, The Northern Quarter, Manchester, M1 1EA**

**☎** 0161 236 5599

**☎** 0161 236 6877

**✉** hq@libratelevision.com

**🌐** www.libratelevision.com

**Contact** Manging Directors, Louise Lynch and Madeline Wiltshire

**Established** 1999

**Insider Info** Producers of children's television and educational programming. Credits include *Sci-Busters* for Discovery Kids and *How To Be A Bully* for the BBC education department.

**Tips** Broadcast outlets include Teacher's TV, the BBC, Discovery Kids, 4Learning, Channel 4 and CITV. People wishing to work or gain experience with children's television production should research the company carefully before sending their CV to the Managing Directors.

## Lilyville Screen Entertainment Ltd

**7 Lilyville Road, Fulham, London, SW6 5DP**

**☎** 020 7471 8989

**✉** tony.cash@btclick.com

**Contact** Managing Director, Tony Cash

**Established** 1983

**Insider Info** Produces television and radio dramas and documentaries for a general audience. Credits include *Poetry in Motion* for Channel 4 and *Landscape and Memory* for the BBC. Accepts previously published material and submissions accompanied by SAE will be returned. Aims to report on queries and submissions within two weeks.

Payment will be in accordance with industry standards. Will not send a catalogue to a writer on request.

**Submission Guidelines** Accepts query with synopsis.

**Tips** Lilyville is currently looking for religious, arts, music and historical documentaries as well as dramas.

## Lime Pictures

**Campus Manor, Childwall Abbey Road, Childwall, Liverpool, L16 OJP**

**☎** 0151 722 9122

**☎** 0151 722 1969

**🌐** www.limepictures.com

**Contact** Creative Director, Tony Wood

**Established** 1982

**Insider Info** Formerly known as Mersey TV, Lime Pictures produce drama content for broadcast television. Long running productions include *Grange Hill* for BBC1 and *Hollyoaks* for Channel 4. Newer developments include *Bonkers* for ITV1.

**Tips** Much of Lime Pictures' output is made up of long running series and its newer drama developments are high profile ones for prime time terrestrial television. Unsolicited scripts are unlikely to be taken further within this environment.

## Lion Television

**Lion House, 26 Paddenswick Road, London, W6 0UB**

**☎** 020 8846 2000

**☎** 020 8846 2001

**🌐** www.liontv.co.uk

**Contact** Head of Production, Patsy Blades

**Established** 1997

**Insider Info** Produces documentaries, entertainment, factual and history programming for most major television broadcasters in the UK and US. Credits include *Ape to Man* for The History Channel and *Whose Wedding Is It Anyway?* for the BBC.

**Submission Guidelines** Accepts query with synopsis, via email (ideas@liontv.co.uk).

**Tips** Explore the website to get an idea of the breadth of past projects undertaken by Lion. Detailed information on brand new commissions are also published.

## Little Bird

**9 Grafton Mews, London, W1T 5HZ**

**☎** 020 7380 3980

**☎** 020 7380 3981

- info@littlebird.ie
- www.littlebird.ie

**Contact** Chairmen, James Marshall and Jonathan Cavendish

**Established** 1982

**Insider Info** An independent producer of television and film with offices in Dublin, London and Johannesburg. Credits include *Bridget Jones' Diary* and *Bridget Jones: The Edge of Reason*, both in association with Working Title Films. Submissions accompanied by SAE will not be returned.

**Tips** Unsolicited scripts are not accepted and will not be read. The company state that they a free to use any ideas or material contained in unsolicited communications they receive from the public.


## Loftus Productions Ltd

**2a Aldine Street, Shepherd's Bush, London, W12 8AN**

- 020 8740 4666
- 020 8740 4777
- ask@loftusproductions.co.uk
- www.loftusproductions.co.uk

**Contact** Producer, Nigel Acheson

**Established** 1996

**Insider Info** Radio, Produces documentaries and features for radio. Credits include *Fabulous Fables* for BBC Radio 4 and *The Big Question: Who Needs Migrant Workers?* for the BBC World Service.

**Submission Guidelines** Accepts query with synopsis, via email.

**Tips** A major broadcast outlet for radio productions is BBC Radio 4. Check the BBC website, www.bbc.co.uk/commissioning for commissioning needs. Loftus are also interested in developing scripts already commissioned for the station.


## London Scientific Films Ltd

**Dassels House, Dassels, Braughing, Ware, Hertfordshire, SG11 2RW**

- 01763 289905
- lsf@londonscientificfilms.co.uk
- www.londonscientificfilms.co.uk

**Contact** Mike Vockburn

**Insider Info** Producers of integrated media output on scientific and medical subjects.

**Tips** No unsolicited manuscripts will be accepted.


## Lupus Films

**Studio 212, Black Bull Yard, 24–28 Hatton Wall, London, EC1N 8JH**

- 020 7419 0997
- 020 7404 9474
- info@lupusfilms.net
- www.lupusfilms.net

**Contact** Directors, Camilla Deakin and Ruth Fielding

**Established** 2002

**Insider Info** Lupus Films produce animated features, shorts, and series, mainly for television. They work with puppetry and 2D techniques. Credits include *Combat Club* for Channel Five and *Meerkats Luuvies* for UKTV Documentaries.

**Tips** The vast majority of programming is aimed at young children and families. New projects in development are published on the website and give an idea as to current priorities.


## Malone Gill Productions Ltd

**27 Campden Hill Road, London, SE21 8BN**

- 020 7937 0557
- 020 7376 1727
- malonegill@aol.com

**Contact** Producer, Georgina Denison

**Established** 1978

**Insider Info** A production company making documentaries and drama for television. Credits include *The Feast of Christmas* for Channel 4 and *Highlanders* for ITV.

**Submission Guidelines** Accepts query with synopsis.

**Tips** Approach in writing for more information on the company and its future projects.


## Marchmont Films

**24 Three Cups Yard, Sandland Street, London, WC1R 4PZ**

- office@marchmontfilms.com
- www.marchmontfilms.com

**Contact** Executive Producer, Mark Tuffey

**Insider Info** Film, Television, Producers of short films and features. Credits include Andrew Cussens' *Out in the Cold* and Terry Newman's *The Green Wave*.

**Submission Guidelines** Use the online form to submit script ideas. Specific deadlines are published on the site.

**Tips** Within the specified calls for submissions, Marchmont are keen to hear from both new and established writers of short and feature length drama. Productions tend to be low budget, but are not restricted to any particular genres.


## Maverick TV

**Progress Works, Heath Mill Lane, Birmingham, B9 4AL**

0121 771 1812

0121 771 1550

mail@mavericktv.co.uk, firstinitial.lastname@mavericktv.co.uk

www.mavericktv.co.uk

**Contact** Head of Development, Kelly Frankel

**Established** 1994

**Insider Info** Producers of broadcast television, digital media and printed books for television, DVD and websites. Credits include *10 Years Younger* for Channel 4, *Ghetto Britain - 30 Years of Race* for More 4 and *Working The Sea* for BBC 1.

**Submission Guidelines** Accepts query with synopsis. Email queries relating to factual, entertainment or documentary programmes, websites or books. No unsolicited scripts for drama or unagented submissions will be considered.

**Tips** Bear in mind that Maverick produce television, websites and books, and they welcome project ideas that combine all three medias.

## Maya Vision International
**6 Kinghorn Street, London, EC1A 7HW**

020 7796 4842

020 7796 4580

info@mayavisionint.com

www.mayavisionint.com

**Contact** Producer and Director, Rebecca Dobbs

**Established** 1982

**Insider Info** Producers of history documentaries, and other factual programming for film and television, including archaeology, the arts and current affairs. Maya Vision International also produce low budget features films and experimental dramas.

**Tips** No unsolicited manuscripts will be accepted.

## Melendez Films
**Julia House, 44 Newman Street, London, W1T 1QD**

020 7323 5273

020 7323 5373

stevemelendez@billmelendez.tv

www.billmelendez.tv

**Contact** Steve Melendez

**Established** 1963

**Insider Info** Melendez Films produce material for film and television, it is also the London office of Bill Melendez, an American animator. The company as a whole produces television series and commercials. Credits include *Babar*, *The Lion, The Witch and The Wardrobe* and numerous *Snoopy* and *Charlie Brown*

series and specials. Submissions accompanied by SAE will be accepted.

**Submission Guidelines** Accepts query with synopsis.

**Tips** All programming is aimed at children and often has a strong American feel, due to the organisation of the company.

## Mendoza
**3–5 Barrett Street, London, W1U 1AY**

020 7935 4674

020 7935 4417

office@mendozafilms.com

www.mendozafilms.com

**Contact** Executive Producer, Debby Mendoza

**Insider Info** Mendoza are a production company specialising in television commercials, producing material for film and television. They also produce title sequences and are moving into the development of feature films, comedies in particular. Submissions accompanied by SAE will be returned.

**Submission Guidelines** Submit completed manuscript, enclosing SAE.

**Tips** Only send comedy scripts that may be suitable for future development. The company's main business remains the production of television commercials.

## Mentorn
**43 Whitfield Street, London, W1P 6TG**

020 7258 6800

020 7258 6888

factual@mentorn.tv, entertainment@mentorn.tv, currentaffairs@mentorn.tv

www.mentorn.co.uk

**Established** 1985

**Insider Info** Producers of drama, current affairs, factual and entertainment programming for major television broadcasters in the UK and internationally. Past productions include the political dramatisations, *A Very Social Secretary* and *The Government Inspector* as well as the documentary *The Boy Who Gave Birth to His Twin* and ITV's entertainment show *Take My Mother-in-Law*.

**Submission Guidelines** Accepts query with synopsis. Email the relevant department (factual, entertainment or current affairs).

**Tips** Mentorn's output is extremely varied in style and content. The company recommend that ideas are focused on either factual, entertainment or current affairs categories; in order to help direct them to to the right person within the company. Explore the website for past programmes that fall within these three categories to help guide your submission.

## Mint Productions
**205 Lower Rathmines Road, Dublin 6, Republic of Ireland**
- 00353 1 491 3333
- 00353 1 491 3334
- info@mint.ie
- www.mint.ie

**Contact** Head of Development, Paula Williams
**Insider Info** Producers of documentaries for UK and Irish Television. Productions include *Maybe Baby* for RTE and *De Lorean* for the BBC.
**Tips** Mint Productions are specialists in historical and observational documentaries.

## Moonstone Films
**5 Linkenholt Mansions, Stamford Brook Avenue, London, W6 0YA**
- 020 8846 8511
- 0870 005 6839
- info@moonstonefilms.co.uk
- www.moonstonefilms.co.uk

**Contact** Executive Producer, Tony Stark
**Insider Info** Produces documentaries for television, both in historical and investigative, presenter led formats. Credits include *Arafat Investigated* for BBC 2 and *Under Pressure* for Channel 4. Submissions accompanied by SAE will be returned.
**Submission Guidelines** Accepts unsolicited manuscripts.
**Tips** Documentary ideas should fall into the very broad remits of 'current affairs' or 'historical'.

## Mute Marmalade
**23 Prince Albert Rd, London, NW1 7ST**
- 020 7449 2552
- 020 7449 2662
- info@mutemarmalade.com
- www.mutemarmalade.com

**Contact** Jonathan Bentata
**Insider Info** Mute Marmalade are producers of films including *Black Soles* and *Making Mistakes*. Will report on queries within one week. Catalogue available onine.
**Submission Guidelines** Produce films (35mm). Send a beat sheet (short sentences arranged in columns that break down a screenplay to its narrative core), a one page synopsis and a signed submissions sheet, available from the website.

**Tips** See the website for an example of a beat sheet for *Notting Hill*, as an example of how yours should be laid out. Do not send full manuscript. Selected writers who submit will win a paid for course at The Script Factory.

## Neon
**Studio 2, 19 Marine Crescent, Glasgow, G51 1HD**
- 0141 429 6366
- 0141 429 6377
- mail@go2neon.com
- www.go2neon.com

**Contact** Managing Directors, Stephanie Poradge and Robert Noakes
**Established** 1995
**Insider Info** Neon produce material for film and radio. They are producers of weekly programmes, short series, stand alone features and music videos. Specialist areas include drama, arts and music and documentary production. The company also runs a record label and a music publishing business.
**Submission Guidelines** Query first, before sending any manuscripts.
**Tips** Much of the radio output in particular is for BBC Scotland's regional stations, as well as BBC national stations. Content with a Scottish connection has featured heavily in their back catalogue.

## Nexus Productions Ltd
**113–114 Shoreditch High Street, London, E1 6JN**
- 020 7749 7500
- 020 7749 7501
- info@nexusproductions.com
- www.nexusproductions.com

**Established** 1997
**Insider Info** Nexus produce animated content for television commercials, programmes, music videos and films. Work with 2D, 3D, puppetry, live-action and flash techniques.
**Tips** Nexus work with creative professionals, including writers from all over the world. The main bulk of its output is television commercials and music videos, therefore animated features or films are unlikely to be accepted at this particular company.

## Noel Gay Television
**19 Denmark Street, London, WC2H 8NA**
- 020 7836 3941
- info@noelgay.com
- www.noelgay.com

**Established** 1987

**Insider Info** Producers of comedy, entertainment and drama formats for television. Credits include Rob Grant and Doug Naylor's *Red Dwarf*.
**Submission Guidelines** Accepts query with synopsis.
**Tips** Strictly no unsolicited manuscripts will be accepted.

## Number 9 Films
**Linton House, 24 Wells Street, London, W1T 3PH**
☎ 020 7323 4060
✆ 020 7323 0456
✉ info@number9films.co.uk
**Contact** Stephen Wooley and Elizabeth Karlsen
**Established** 2002
**Insider Info** Number 9 are producers of feature films including *Stoned* and *Breakfast on Pluto*. The company recently entered a funding agreement with the UK Film Council, Film 4, Intandem Films and the Irish Film Board; one of several partnerships designed to build the profile of British cinema.
**Tips** No unsolicited manuscripts will be accepted.

## Odyssey Productions Ltd
**72 Tay Street, Newport on Tay, DD6 8AP**
☎ 01382 542070
✆ 01382 542070
✉ billykay@sol.co.uk
🌐 www.sol.co.uk/b/billykay
**Contact** Directors, Billy Kay and Maria João Kay
**Established** 1994
**Insider Info** Odyssey produces radio features as well as corporate audiovisual packages. Previous productions have been broadcast on BBC Radio 2 and 4 as well as BBC Radio Scotland.
**Submission Guidelines** Accepts query with synopsis.
**Tips** Many past productions have had a Scottish theme, including At *Hame Wi' Burns*, where people from Ayrshire talk about the poet Burns and *We'll Support You Evermore*, based around support for the Scottish national football team.

## Omnivision
**Pinewood Studios, Iver Heath, Buckinghamshire, SL0 0NH**
☎ 01753 656329
✆ 01753 631146
✉ info@omnivision.co.uk, firstname@omnivision.co.uk
🌐 www.omnivision.co.uk
**Contact** Senior Editor, Nick Long

**Insider Info** Omnivision produce material for television, video and DVDs. This includes broadcast and corporate television productions, including documentaries, news, current affairs, sports and outside broadcasts.
**Submission Guidelines** Accepts query with synopsis. Email programme ideas or fill in the online contact form, including your full contact details.
**Tips** In terms of ideas for broadcast television, the areas to aim for are; documentary, news, features and lifestyle programmes.

## Orlando Media
**Up the Steps, Little Tew, Chipping Norton, Oxfordshire, OX7 4JB**
☎ 01608 683218
✆ 01608 683364
✉ info@orlandomedia.co.uk
🌐 www.orlandodigital.co.uk
**Contact** Creative Director, Mike Tomlinson
**Insider Info** Orlando Media produce material for television, web and digital media, including factual programming for broadcast TV and video. Subject areas include science, nature and technology. Credits include *The Planets* for BBC and *Peak Performance* for the ITV network.
**Tips** The Creative Director, Mike Tomlinson, also acts as a writer for much of the programming. Therefore proposals from other writers are usually with a view to collaborating.

## Oxford Scientific (OSF)
**Network House, Station Yard, Thame, Oxfordshire, OX9 3UH**
☎ 01844 262370
✆ 01844 262380
✉ uksales@osf.co.uk
🌐 www.osf.co.uk
**Insider Info** Oxford Scientific have a large image library (still and moving) on worldwide wildlife. Images are sold on for television and film production.
**Tips** If you have existing footage or photography, there is information on the website as to how to submit your images to the library.

## Parallax Independent Ltd
**7 Denmark Street, London, WC2H 8LZ**
☎ 020 7836 1478
✆ 020 7497 8062
🌐 www.parallaxindependent.co.uk

**Insider Info** FA co-operative of producers and directors of feature films, short films and documentaries for television. Credits include *The Navigators* and *Bread and Roses*.

**Tips** Parallax state they have 'an open door policy' for new writers and directors. Current members include film makers Les Blair and Sarah Curtis.

## Passion Pictures
**3rd Floor, 33–34 Rathbone PLace, London, W1T 1JN**
- 020 7323 9933
- 020 7323 9030
- info@passion-pictures.com
- www.passion-pictures.com

**Contact** Associate Producer, Andrew Ruhemann

**Insider Info** Produces material for film and television, including animated and live action work for feature films, short films, music videos and commercials. Credits include the animated pop band *Gorillaz* and the Domestos 'Multiplication' advert.

**Tips** Although the company is best known for its animation, particularly in music videos and advertisements, it has recently developed some award winning documentaries for broadcast television. A list of development projects are published on the website give an idea of where the company might be heading.

## Pathé Productions Ltd
**Kent House, 14–17 Market Place, Great Titchfield Street, London, W1W 8AR**
- 020 7323 5151
- 020 7631 3568
- www.pathe.co.uk

**Insider Info** A feature film production and distribution company. Recent production credits include *The Queen* and *Big Nothing*.

**Submission Guidelines** Agented submissions or proposals from independent production companies only.

**Tips** Pathé's output is extremely varied in genre and subject matter. Its own productions are reasonably high profile, and normally achieve a general cinema release.

## Pennine Productions
**Kilmagadwood Cottage, Scotlandwell, Kinross, KY13 9HY**
- 01560 472247
- firstname@pennine.biz

- www.pennine.biz

**Contact** Producers, Mark Whitaker, Clare Jenkins, Janet Graves and Mike Hally

**Established** 2000

**Insider Info** Producers for BBC Radio. Programmes include documentaries, features and readings.

**Submission Guidelines** Accepts queries with a brief email summarising the idea.

**Tips** No unsolicited manuscripts will be accepted. Be aware that BBC Radio listeners will be the eventual audience. Programmes that deal with stories from interesting, worldwide locations are preferred.

## Photoplay Productions Ltd
**21 Princess Road, London, NW1 8JR**
- 020 7722 2500
- 020 7722 6662
- info@photoplay.co.uk
- www.photoplay.co.uk

**Contact** Patrick Stanbury

**Insider Info** Producers of documentaries and restorers of silent films and theatrical work for film and television. Past work has been broadcast on Channel 4. Credits include *The Iron Mask* and *The Phantom of The Phantom of the Opera*.

**Submission Guidelines** No unsolicited manuscripts will be accepted.

**Tips** Due to the nature of work undertaken by Photoplay, works are written, developed or restored in-house.

## Picardy Media & Communication
**1 Park Circus, Glasgow, G3 6AX**
- 0141 333 5554
- 0141 332 6002
- info@picardy.co.uk, firstinitiallastname@picardy.co.uk
- www.picardy.co.uk

**Contact** Melissa Todd, Bill Fairweather, Sharon Fullarton, John Rocchiccioli

**Established** 1993

**Insider Info** Produces material for television, websites, interactive CDs and DVDs, including screen-based projects, mainly for corporate clients. Areas of expertise include sales and marketing, health and safety, HR, and training and communications.

**Submission Guidelines** Accepts queries via direct email to a staff member.

**Tips** A show reel is published on the website from which writers can get a sense of the projects undertaken. The aim from the output is to entertain people whilst training, educating or informing them in some way, according to the needs of the client.

## Picture Palace Films
**13 Egbert Street, London, NW1 8LJ**

☏ 020 7586 8763

☏ 020 7586 9048

✉ info@picturepalace.com

🌐 www.picturepalace.com

**Contact** Managing Director, Malcolm Craddock

**Established** 1972

**Insider Info** Produces material for a UK adult audience for film and television. The London base, headed by Malcolm Craddock, produces television drama such as *Sharpe's Challenge* and *Frances Tuesday* for ITV. Picture Palace North, the Manchester base headed by Alex Usbourne, produces controversial films and dramas set in the north, such as *F\*\*\*ing Sheffield* and *Large*. The company purchases three to five scripts per year and works with three to five writers accordingly. They purchases all rights on accepted material. Picture Palace will accept previously published material and submissions accompanied by SAE will be returned. They aim to report on queries within two weeks and submissions within six weeks and will not send a catalogue to a writer on request. Writers are paid for their work in accordance with industry standards.

**Submission Guidelines** Produces films (16 or 35mm) and videotapes (in digibeta format). Accepts query with synopsis.

**Tips** Bear in mind that although the broadcast drama is fairly high profile, the feature film productions tend to be low budget and deal with difficult, gritty subjects.

## Pier Productions
**Lower Ground Floor, 1 Marlborough Place, Brighton, BN1 1TU**

☏ 01273 691401

☏ 01273 693658

✉ pierprod@mistral.co.uk

**Contact** Managing Director, Peter Hoare

**Insider Info** Produce drama and documentaries for film, television and radio (particularly prevalent in radio). Credits include Neville Smith's *Dear Doctor Goebbels* for BBC Radio 4.

**Tips** For radio drama scripts, BBC Radio 4 is the most likely commissioner of Pier's work.

## Plantaganet Fillms Ltd
**Ard-Daraich Studio B, Ardgour, Near Fort William, PH33 7AB**

☏ 01588 841384

☏ 01855 841384

✉ plantaganetfilms@aol.com

**Contact** Norrie Maclaren

**Established** 1949

**Insider Info** Produces factual and drama programming for broadcast television and film. Credits include episodes of *Dispatches* for Channel 4.

**Tips** Contact Norrie Maclaren for more information on how to submit manuscripts. Will potentially work with new writing.

## Portobello Pictures
**Eardley House, 4 Uxbridge Street, London, W8 7SY**

☏ 020 7908 9890

☏ 020 7908 9899

✉ mail@portobellopictures.com

🌐 www.portobellopictures.com

**Established** 1987

**Insider Info** Producers of feature films and television dramas. Credits include the film *Birthday Girl* and the long running series *Dalziel and Pascoe* for ITV. The company has also moved into theatre productions.

**Tips** The company state that as well as developing film and television projects with established writers, they are keen to develop new talent. In 2006 they set up a base in South Africa and have begun producing new drama using South African writers, stories and actors. This is part of a commitment to bring the country's creative output onto an international level.

## Pozzitive Television
**Paramount House, 162–170 Wardour Street, London, W1F 8AB**

☏ 020 7734 3258

☏ 020 7437 3130

✉ david@pozzitive.co.uk

**Contact** David Tyler

**Insider Info** Produce comedy and entertainment for major radio and television broadcasters including the BBC. Productions include *Dinnerladies* for BBC 1 and *The Very World of Milton Jones* for Radio 4.

**Submission Guidelines** Submit completed manuscript. Accepts postal submissions only, no email submissions will be considered.

**Tips** Pozzitive focuses strongly on comedy. The BBC is a regular client and it may be useful to bear in mind their commissioning strategies, published at: www.bbc.co.uk/commissioning

## Praxis Films Ltd
**Unit 3N Leroy House, 436 Essex Road, London, N1 3QP**
- 020 7682 1865
- 020 7682 1868
- info@praxisfilms.co.uk
- www.praxisfilms.co.uk

**Contact** Tony Cook
**Established** 1985
**Insider Info** Produces documentaries, current affairs and factual programming for broadcast TV. Also produces material for videos, DVDs and CDS, including non broadcast products, such as educational and training titles.
**Tips** Praxis offer training in various areas of media production. For those interested in the styles of their production output and writers they have previously worked with, credits are published on the website.

## Princess Productions
**Whiteley's Centre, 151 Queensway, London, W2 4SB**
- 020 7985 1985
- 020 7985 1986
- formatsales@princeestv.com
- www.princesstv.com

**Established** 1996
**Insider Info** Produces entertainment programming for UK television broadcasters. Recent credits include *The Friday Night Project* for Channel 4 and *The Real little Britain* for BBC 3 (produced by sister company Carbon Princess). Catalogue available online.
**Tips** Formats tend to be light entertainment, with a satirical or comedic edge. View the catalogue published online for more details.

## Promenade Enterprises Ltd
**6 Russell Grove, London, SW9 6HS**
- 020 7582 9354
- 020 7564 3026
- nnewton@promenadeproductions.com
- www.promenadeproductions.com

**Contact** Director, Nicholas Newton
**Established** 1994
**Insider Info** Producers of drama, primarily for BBC Radio but also for television and theatre. Previous radio productions include *Afternoon Romancers* and *The Pickwick Papers*.

**Submission Guidelines** Agented submissions only will be accepted.
**Tips** No unsolicited manuscripts will be considered. For those with agents, BBC Radio 4 is a regular broadcaster of productions from Promenade, both for new writing and adaptions of established books and plays.

## Prospect Pictures
**13 Wandsworth Plain, London, SW18 1ET**
- 020 7636 1234
- 020 7636 1236
- info@prospect-uk.com
- www.prospect-uk.com

**Contact** Managing Director, Liam Hamilton
**Insider Info** Produce lifestyle television programming, as well as factual entertainment and entertainment formats. Credits include *Saturday Cooks* and *Call Me A Cabbie*. Catalogue available online.
**Tips** Light entertainment programmes dealing with food and cooking are a particular speciality of Prospect, although programmes are also produced on a wide range of other topics including sport, music, comedy, gardening, health and travel.

## Raw Charm
**Ty Cefn, Rectory Road, Cardiff, CF5 1QL**
- 029 2064 1511
- 029 2066 8220
- enquiries@rawcharm.tv, ian@rawcharm.co.uk
- www.rawcharm.tv

**Contact** Development Producer, Ian Brown
**Established** 1990
**Insider Info** Producers of factual programming for broadcast television and radio, both national and regional. Credits include *Raw Stories* for BBC Wales and *Bad Boys* for Channel Five.
**Tips** Currently seeking international collaborations and co-productions. A particular area of interest to the development producer is programming for digital and satellite channels.

## RDF Television
**The Gloucester Building, Kensington Village, Avnmore Road, London, W14 8RF**
- 020 7013 4000
- 020 7013 4001
- contactus@rdftelevision.com
- www.rdftelevision.com

**Contact** Head of Production, Jane Wilson
**Established** 1993

**Insider Info** The largest television company within the RDF Media Group. Produces a wide range of television programmes including entertainment formats, reality TV, documentaries and features. Credits include *Rock School* for Channel 4 and *Oz & James's Big Wine Adventure* for BBC 2. Catalogue available online.

**Tips** No unsolicited showreels will be accepted. The programmes produced at RDF are high profile, prime time entertainment shows and unsolicited manuscripts are unlikely to be taken further.

## Red Kite Animations
**89 Giles Street, Edinburgh, EH6 6BZ**
- 0131 554 0060
- 0131 553 6007
- info@redkite-animations.com
- www.redkite-animation.com

**Contact** Managing Director, Ken Anderson
**Established** 1997
**Insider Info** Produces animated content for broadcast television and film in the UK and internationally, as well as commercials. Clients include the BBC, S4C, Cartoon Network US and Disney Japan. Previous productions include *Wilf*, *The Witch's Dog* and *Benjamin Bear*.
**Submission Guidelines** No unsolicited showreels will be considered.
**Tips** Red Kite run workshops in animation throughout Scotland. For more information, emai:l studio@redkite-animation.com

## Redweather Productions
**Easton Business Centre, Felix Road, Bristol, BS5 0HE**
- 01179 415854
- enquiries@redweather.co.uk
- www.redweather.co.uk

**Insider Info** Produce short series and feature documentaries for broadcast television, as well as creating corporate videos, CD-ROMs and DVDs.
**Tips** Any ideas that are designed for broadcast television should be within the specialisms of the arts and the politics of disability. Recent productions can be viewed on the website and include *Old School Ties* for BBC2 and *The Real Helen Killer* for Channel 4.

## RS Productions
**191 Trewhitt Road, Heaton, Newcastle upon Tyne, NE6 5DY**
- 0191 224 4301
- info@rsproductions.co.uk
- www.rsproductions.co.uk

**Contact** Managing Director and Producer, Mark Lavender
**Established** 1993
**Insider Info** RS Producers produce material for film, television, websites and new media. They produce documentaries and factual programmes, as well as feature films. Co-productions are developing with companies from the UK, USA, Germany, Denmark and Hungary. Submissions accompanied by SAE will be returned.
**Submission Guidelines** For television proposals, send a one or two page synopsis with any relevant background information. For feature films, send a one or two page synopsis with details of where the films has been sent before, and what the response was, and an author biography. No unsolicited manuscripts will be accepted, unless from agents, publishers or lawyers.
**Tips** Ideas should be fresh and original. Be aware that hard copy materials will not be returned.

## Ruth Evans Productions Ltd
**4 Offlands Cottages, Moulsford, Oxon, OX10 9HP**
- 01491 651331
- ruth@ruthevans.com

**Contact** Ruth Evans
**Established** 2002
**Insider Info** An independent radio producer. Programmes include factual features and documentaries.
**Tips** Main clients are BBC Radio 4 and BBC World Service. For more information on their programming needs see: www.bbc.co.uk/commissioning

## Scala Productions
**4th Floor Portland House, 4 Great Portland Street, London, W1W 8QJ**
- 020 7612 0060
- 020 7612 0031
- scalaprods@aol.com

**Contact** Chairman and Director, Nik Powell
**Established** 1983
**Insider Info** Previously known as Palace Productions, Scala are producers of feature films including *Little Voice* and *Ladies in Lavender*.
**Tips** There is often a strong British theme in Scala films; many have starred well known British actors and have been set in Britain.

## Scope Productions Ltd

**180 West Regent Street, Glasgow, G2 4RW**

- 0141 332 7720
- 0141 332 1049
- laurakingwell@scopeproductions.co.uk
- www.scopeproductions.co.uk

**Established** 1984

**Insider Info** Scope are producers of corporate videos, DVDs and multimedia projects. They also create some broadcast documentaries and televisioncommercials.

**Tips** Bear in mind a major part of the business is corporate work. No full length dramas will be considered.

## Screen First Ltd

**The Studios, Funnells Farm, Down Street, Nutley, TN22 3LG**

- 01825 712034
- 01825 713511
- paul.madden@virgin.net

**Contact** Paul Madden

**Insider Info** Produces children's animations, dramas and documentaries for broadcast television. Credits include Raymond Briggs' *Ivor the Invisible* for Channel 4.

**Tips** No unsolicited manuscripts will be accepted.

## Screenhouse Productions

**Chapel Allerton House, 114 Harrogate Road, Leeds, LS7 4NY**

- 0113 266 8881
- 0113 266 8882
- info@screenhouse.co.uk, paul.bader@screenhouse.co.uk
- www.screenhouse.co.uk

**Contact** Creative Director, Paul Badder

**Established** 1991

**Insider Info** Producers of science and history television programmes and websites. Also produce props and machinery for scientific television content. Credits include *Hart-Davis on History* for the BBC.

**Submission Guidelines** Accepts query with synopsis, Contact Paul Badden with ideas.

**Tips** Screenhouse goes beyond television production to develop projects with websites, books, props and events. Much of the content is conceived and developed in-house, therefore unsolicited ideas are unlikely to be taken further. Keep ideas within science or history topic areas.

## Screen Projex

**13 Manette Street, London, W1D 4AW**

- 020 7287 1170
- 020 7287 1123
- info@screenprojex.com
- www.screenprojex.com

**Contact** Managing Director, Julia Vickers

**Insider Info** Screen Projex are a distribution company created to acquire and promote independent British films. Their portfolio includes Simon Rumley's *Club Le Monde* and *Holding On*, produced by Altered Perceptions.

**Tips** Accept finished films only, from British producers. Any genre will be considered as long as it has an engaging narrative and strong production values.

## Screen Ventures

**49 Goodge Street, London, W1T 1TE**

- 020 7580 7448
- 020 7631 1265
- info@screenventures.com
- www.screenventures.com

**Contact** Development Producer, Naima Mould

**Established** 1978

**Insider Info** Screen Ventures produces, markets and sells TV programmes and films. In-house production credits include *Mojo Working: The Making of Modern Music* for Channel 4 and *The South Bank Show* for ITV.

**Tips** Incoming scripts and ideas are assessed initially by Naima Mould.

## September Films

**Glen House, 22 Glenthorne Road, London, W6 0NG**

- 020 8563 9393
- 020 8741 7214
- september@septemberfilms.com
- www.septemberfilms.com

**Contact** Director of Programmes, Peter Davey

**Established** 1992

**Insider Info** Produces factual entertainment, features, reality programming and entertainment formats for broadcast television. Recent credits include *Beauty and the Geek* for Channel 4 and E4, and *Celebrity Bodies* for Trouble UK. The company is now branching out into feature films.

**Tips** Productions are often aimed at both the UK and US market. The majority of September's output remains focused on popular light entertainment and dramatic writing is largely restricted to a small list of television dramas and feature films.

## Shell Like

**81 Whitfield Street, London, W1T 4HG**

☎ 020 7255 5203

✉ richard@shelllike.com

🌐 www.shelllike.com

**Contact** Production Assistant, Richard Donaghue

**Insider Info** Producers of radio material, particularly commercials. Clients include Toyota and Breakthrough Breast Cancer.

**Tips** Send all ideas by email to Richard Donaghue.

## Sianco Cyf

**36 Y Maes, Caernarfon, LL55 2NN**

☎ 01286 676100

☎ 01286 677616

✉ www.sianco.tv

🌐 post@sianco.tv

**Contact** Managing Director, Siân Teifi

**Insider Info** Specialises in children's television programming but also produces adult entertainment, factual and documentary programmes.

**Tips** No unsolicited manuscripts will be accepted.

## Silent Sound Films Ltd

**Cambridge Court, Cambridge Road, Frinton on Sea, CO13 9HN**

☎ 01255 676381

☎ 01255 676381

✉ thj@silentsoundfilms.co.uk

🌐 www.silentsoundfilms.co.uk

**Contact** Managing Director, Timothy Foster

**Established** 1997

**Insider Info** Silent Sound Films are producers of films and musical scores for silent films. They also aim to develop the awareness of the arts through documentaries. Does not accept previously publishes material. Aims to respond to queries within two weeks and submissions within two months. Writers are paid in accordance with WGA standards or the UK 'pact' agreement, if it is a British production.

**Submission Guidelines** Produces material for films (35mm). Accepts query with synopsis by email only (including a one-page synopsis, eight pages of scenario and a writer biography). No images, complete plays or other large attachments will be accepted.

**Tips** Silent Sound Films are interested in excellent writing (specifically musicals, art house and stage plays) with well-developed plot themes and original characters. They seek material that may well include

a good 'pitchable idea' but also one that goes a lot deeper. No US based films, or storylines based around American characters will be accepted, to avoid being in competition with successful American 'arthouse' productions.

## Skyline Productions

**10 Scotland Street, Edinburgh, EH3 6PS**

☎ 0131 557 4580

☎ 0131 556 4377

✉ admin@skyline.uk.com

🌐 www.skyline.uk.com

**Contact** Leslie Hills

**Established** 1974

**Insider Info** Skyline produces features films, documentaries, music, arts and comedy programming for television. Broadcasters worked with include major UK terrestrial channels and stations across Europe and the US. Credits include *Women in Black* and *Rivers and Tides*. Skyline Films, based in London, concentrates solely on feature films and can be reached on 020 7463 2150.

**Tips** For enquiries about projects past, present and future, email Leslie Hill at leslie@skyline.uk.com

## SMG Productions

**Pacific Quay, Glasgow, G51 1PQ**

☎ 0141 300 3000

✉ website@smgproductions.tv

🌐 www.smgproductions.tv

**Contact** Managing Director, Elizabeth Partyka

**Insider Info** Produces adult and children's television programming, including drama, documentaries, factual entertainment and entertainment formats. Credits include *Taggart* for ITV1 and *Club Reps*. SMG Productions also incorporates Ginger Productions.

**Tips** SMG's range of programming is varied in style, however most output is broadcast on major terrestrial and satellite channels, often in prime time slots. Unsolicited manuscripts from new writers are unlikely to be picked up, due to the high profile needed for the shows.

## Smooth Operations

**PO Box 286, Cambridge, CB1 7XW**

☎ 01223 244544

☎ 01223 244384

✉ info@smoothoperations.com,firstname.lastname@bbc.co.uk

🌐 www.smoothoperations.com

**Contact** Nick Barraclough

**Insider Info** Smooth Operations are producers of music programming and content for BBC television and radio. Credits include *The Mark Radcliffe Show* for BBC Radio 2 and *Did I Shave My Legs For This? - Feminism in Country Music* for BBC Radio 4. They also operate from a base in Oldham, headed up by John Leonard. Catalogue available online.

**Tips** All content is for BBC television and radio and music is the sole focus of all productions.

## Somethin Else

**Units 1–4, 1a Old Nichol Street, London, E2 7HR**

☎ 020 7613 3211

☎ 020 7739 9799

✉ info@somethinelse.com

🌐 www.somethinelse.com

**Contact** Creative Director, Jez Nelson

**Insider Info** Somethin Else is the largest UK independent radio producer and also produces television entertainment formats. As well as television and radio, content is made for interactive media such as the web, games and mobile television. Credits include *Buzz* for Playstation 2 and *MyTv: Homegrown* for Trouble.

**Submission Guidelines** Accepts query with synopsis. Send ideas by post.

**Tips** Much of the content produced across all media is based around light entertainment, music and pop culture. For more information on the various media output contact: samb@somethinelse.com for radio, leo.burley@somethinelse.com for television and simon.hopkins@somethinelse.com for interactive.

## So Television

**18 Hatfields, London, SE1 8GN**

☎ 020 7960 2000

☎ 020 7960 2095

✉ info@sotelevision.co.uk

🌐 www.sotelevision.co.uk

**Contact** Founders, Graham Norton and Graham Stuart

**Established** 2000

**Insider Info** So Television also incorporates So Radio and produces entertainment formats for broadcast television. Credits include *The Graham Norton Show* for the BBC and *Nortonland* for Challenge.

**Tips** No unsolicited manuscripts will be accepted.

## Soundplay

**17 Gleneagles Drive, Henbury, Bristol, BS10 7PS**

☎ 07818 271659

✉ enquiries@soundplay.co.uk

🌐 www.soundplay.co.uk

**Contact** Shaun MacLoughlin, Tom Bennett, Vanessa Dodd

**Established** 1998

**Insider Info** Soundplays are producers of radio dramas, podcasts and features. Soundplay aim to bring attention to the media through working with schools, community groups and prison groups. Productions include *Brave Georgina* by Matthew Friday and in *In Search of the Picturesque*. Most output is designed to be broadcast across the internet. Catalogue available online.

**Tips** Bear in mind that Soundplay do not produce radio for broadcast. They undertake community projects, often culminating in radio productions that can be listened to through their website. Information on upcoming projects will be published on their website, where there is also a discussion board.

## Specific Films

**25 Rathbone Street, London, W1T 1NQ**

☎ 020 7580 7476

☎ 020 7494 2676

✉ info@specificfilms.com

**Contact** Managing Director, Michael Hamlyn

**Established** 1991

**Insider Info** Producer of feature films and material for television. Credits include *The Adventures of Priscilla* and *Queen of the Desert*.

**Tips** Specific Films also produce music videos for very high profile artists.

## Spice Factory UK

**14 Regent Hill, Brighton, BN1 3ED**

☎ 01273 739182

☎ 01273 749122

✉ info@spicefactory.co.uk

🌐 www.spicefactory.co.uk

**Contact** Head of Development, Lucy Shuttleworth

**Established** 1995

**Insider Info** Produces feature films. Credits include *Perfect Creature* and *The Merchant of Venice*.

**Submission Guidelines** No unsolicited manuscripts will be accepted.

**Tips** Despite not receiving any unsolicited material, Spice Factory's development department are active in seeking new writing talent and do employ script readers. Previous features have come about after the successful production of short films from new writers.

## Spire Films

**7 High Street, Kidlington, Oxford, OX5 2DH**

☎ 01865 371979

☎ 01865 371962

✉ proposals@spirefilms.co.uk

🌐 www.spirefilms.co.uk

**Contact** Head of Development, Bernadette O'Farrell

**Established** 1997

**Insider Info** Produces factual Television programming for terrestrial and satellite channels in the UK and the US. Subjects include history, the arts, leisure and entertainment. Productions include *Delia's How to Cook* for the BBC and *The Worst Jobs in History* for Channel 4 and Discovery.

**Submission Guidelines** Accepts query with synopsis, via email.

**Tips** Spire Films do not produce any drama.

## Stampede Limited

**The Hat Factory, 65–67 Bute Street, Luton, Bedfordshire, LU1 2EY**

☎ 01582 727330

☎ 01582 726910

✉ mike@stampede.co.uk

🌐 www.stampede.co.uk

**Contact** Managing Director, Mike Chamberlain

**Established** 1996

**Insider Info** Stampede Limited produce film and television documentaries for a wide British and international audience. Credits include *Tantric Yogi* for Channel 4. Purchases first rights on accepted material. Will accept previously published material and submissions accompanied by SAE will be returned. Will aim to report on queries within two weeks and submissions within five weeks. Payment will be in accordance with industry standards. Catalogue available online or via email.

**Submission Guidelines** Accepts queries.

**Tips** Stampede Limited produce documentaries only. Work should be challenging, and go beyond being formulaic.

## Stirling Film and Television Productions Ltd

**137 University Street, Belfast, BT7 1HP Northern Ireland**

☎ 028 9033 3848

☎ 028 9043 8644

✉ anne@stirlingtelevision.co.uk

🌐 www.stirlingtelevision.co.uk

**Contact** Anne Stirling

**Established** 1994

**Insider Info** Produces factual programming for broadcast television. Clients include BBC, Channel 4, Five, Discovery and RTE. Stirling work across a range of subject areas, although their specialism is in Irish music and dance.

**Tips** A major broadcast outlet for Stirling is the Irish station RTE. Much of the content for this station has a specifically Irish theme, subject or feel.

## Straight Forward Film and Productions Ltd

**Building 2, Lesley Office Park, 393 Holywood Road, Belfast, BT4 2LS Northern Ireland**

☎ 028 9065 1010

☎ 028 9065 1012

✉ enquiries@straightforwardltd.co.uk, firstname@straightforwardltd.co.uk

🌐 www.straightforwardltd.co.uk

**Contact** Head of Production, Joy Hines

**Established** 1992

**Insider Info** Produces factual television programmes for broadcasters including BBC Northern Ireland, Ulster Television, RTE, TG4, Channel 4, Five, Living, PBS (US) and NHK (Japan). Subject matters covered include news and current affairs, light entertainment, arts, sport, history and lifestyle. Catalogue available online.

**Tips** The company state that they are always looking out for new talent and ideas, and use freelancers along with their core staff frequently.

## Sunset+Vine Productions

**30 Sackville Street, London, W1S 3DY**

☎ 020 7478 7300

☎ 020 7478 7403

✉ reception@sunsetvine.co.uk

🌐 www.sunsetvine.co.uk

**Established** 1983

**Insider Info** Produces sports television programming, including both live coverage and features for major broadcasters and entertainment formats. Credits include *The Tour de France* for ITV and *Showbiz Poker* for Challenge.

**Tips** No unsolicited manuscripts will be considered. Accepts commissions only.

## Table Top Productions

**1 The Orchard, Chiswick, London, W4 1JZ**

☎ 020 8742 0507

☎ 020 8742 0507

✉ top@tabletopproductions.com

🌐 www.tabletopproductions.com

**Contact** Production Manager, Ben Berry
**Established** 1989
**Insider Info** Producers of feature films and drama for television. Film credits include *The Breadwinner* and *Dirty Tricks*.
**Tips** No unsolicited manuscripts will be accepted.

## Talent Television
**Lion House, 72–75 Red Lion Street, London, WC1R 4NA**
- 020 7421 7800
- 020 7421 7811
- entertainment@talenttv.com
- www.talenttv.com

**Contact** Creative Director, John Kaye-Cooper
**Established** 2002
**Insider Info** Produces entertainment and factual television programmes for UK and international broadcasters. Credits include *Test the Nation* for the BBC and *Man With 80 Wives* for Channel 4.
**Tips** No drama or fictional output will be accepted. A full back catalogue is published on the website.

## Talisman Films Ltd
**5 Addison Place, London, W11 4RJ**
- 020 7603 7474
- 020 7602 7422
- email@talismanfilms.com
- www.writewords.org.uk

**Contact** Director of Programmes, Richard Jackson
**Established** 1991
**Insider Info** Creates screenplays for film and television dramas. Credits include *Complicity* and *The Secret Adventures of Jules Verne*.
**Tips** Synopses should be sent via agents. No unsolicited manuscripts will be accepted.

## talkbackThames
**20–21 Newman Street, London, W1T 1PG**
- 020 7861 8000
- 020 7861 8001
- reception@talkbackthames.tv
- www.talkbackthames.tv

**Contact** Director of Production, Joanna Beresford
**Established** 2003
**Insider Info** TalkbackThames is the UK arm of Fremantle Media. The company produce drama, comedy, entertainment, features, documentaries and factual entertainment programming for major television broadcasters. Credits include Stephen Poliakoff's *The Lost Prince* and *The Green Wing*.

**Tips** Shows are very high profile and often fill prime time slots on national TV channels. Strictly no unsolicited comedy manuscripts.

## Talking Heads Productions
**2–4 Noel Street, London, W1F 8GB**
- 020 729 27575
- 020 7292 7576
- johnsachs@talkingheadsproductions.com
- www.talkingheadsproductions.com

**Contact** John Sachs
**Established** 1992
**Insider Info** Talking Heads Productions historically produced trailers and commercials for corporate clients and now project manages films and television projects. Credits include management of aspects of *The Merchant of Venice*.
**Tips** Contact John Sachs by email for more information on possible projects.

## Tandem TV
**Charleston House, 13 High Street, Hemel Hempstead, HP1 3AA**
- 01442 261576
- 01442 219250
- info@tandemtv.com
- www.tandemtv.com

**Insider Info** Produces content for corporate and broadcast television. Specialisms in the corporate area are in construction, civil engineering, tunnelling and charities. Tandem deal with both factual and dramatic content.
**Tips** Tandem provide services to help people or companies achieve their audiovisual projects. Contact them for more details on the services provided, from scripting to foreign versions, and to get more information on pricing.

## Taylor Made Broadcasts
**3B Cromwell Park, Chipping Norton, OX7 5SR**
- 01608 646444
- 01608 646461
- post@tmtv.co.uk

**Contact** Trevor Taylor
**Insider Info** Taylor Made produce broadcast and corporate television, video and radio material, specialising in documentaries and factual programmes.
**Tips** No unsolicited manuscripts will be accepted.

## Telemagination

**Royalty House, 72–74 Dean Street, London, W1D 3SG**

- 020 7434 1551
- 020 7434 3344
- mail@tmation.co.uk
- www.telemagination.co.uk

**Contact** Managing Director, Beth Parker
**Established** 1983
**Insider Info** Telemagination is a 2D animation studio, mainly producing content for children's television and occasionally producing feature films. Credits include *Heidi* (feature film) and *The Cramp Twins II* (series).
**Tips** Programmes tend to be aimed specifically at young children. View the filmography on the website for examples.

## Television Junction

**Waterside House, 46 Gas Street, Birmingham, B1 2JT**

- 0121 248 4466
- 0121 248 4477
- info@televisionjunction.co.uk
- www.televisionjunction.co.uk

**Contact** Managing Directors, Yvonne Davies and Paul Davies
**Established** 1997
**Insider Info** Produces material for television, websites, DVD, CD-ROM and print, including educational programming for television. Credits include *What's So Good About Jacqueline Wilson?* for Channel 4.
**Submission Guidelines** Television Junction is happy to receive and review programme ideas.
**Tips** Programmes should be educational and productions include documentaries, animation, drama, training films and corporate videos. Two main broadcast routes are Teachers' TV and Channel 4 daytime.

## Tern Television Productions Ltd

**73 Crown Street, Aberdeen, AB11 6EX**

- 01224 211123
- 01224 211199
- aberdeen@terntv.com
- www.terntv.com

**Contact** Managing Directors, David Strachan and Gwyneth Hardy
**Insider Info** Produces mainly factual content for broadcast television. Clients include The BBC, ITV, Channel 4 and UKTV. Credits include *The Spa Of*

*Embarrassing Illnesses* for UKTV Style and *The Greenmount Garden* for BBC Northern Ireland. Also has an office in Glasgow and Belfast.
**Tips** Tern Television produce both regional (for BBC regional channels) and national programming. An overarching theme is 'lifestyle'. Potential writers should explore the back catalogue for a feel of previous style and subject matter.

## Testbed

**Fifth Floor, 14–16 Great Portland Street, London, W1W 8QW**

- 020 7436 0555
- 020 7436 2800
- mail@testbed.co.uk
- www.testbed.co.uk

**Contact** Directors, Nick Baker and Viv Black
**Established** 1992
**Insider Info** Testbed are an independent radio production company specialising in factual programmes, including documentaries, entertainment features and audience participation shows. Credits include *Ha Ha Mathematics* and *The Joy Of Gibberish* for BBC Radio 4.
**Submission Guidelines** Accepts query with synopsis.
**Tips** BBC Radio 4 is the main commissioner of Testbed programmes. Read the archive productions on the site to get a flavour of previous content.

## Testimony Films

**12 Great George Street, Bristol, BS1 5RH**

- 0117 925 8589
- steve.humphries@testimonyfilms
- www.testimonyfilms.com

**Contact** Executive Producer, Producer and Director, Steve Humphreys
**Established** 1992
**Insider Info** Producers of social history and life story programmes for television. Credits include *The Affair* and *Britain's Boy Soldiers* for Channel 4's 'Secret History' series and *Bad Boys of the Blitz* for Channel Five.
**Submission Guidelines** Fill in the online form in the 'Tell us your Story' link on the website. All programme ideas are read.
**Tips** Ideas should be based around biographies, autobiographies or historical topics in general. Sex histories have recently been particularly successful.

## Tiger Aspect Productions

**7 Soho Street, London, W1D 3DQ**

- 020 7434 6700
- 020 7434 1798
- general@tigeraspect.co.uk
- www.tigeraspect.co.uk

**Contact** Managing Director, Andrew Zein

**Insider Info** Producers of comedy, drama, entertainment, factual, animation and wildlife programming for television, alongside feature films. Credits include *Fat Friends* for ITV1 and *The Vicar of Dibley* for BBC1.

**Submission Guidelines** Accepts agented submissions only.

**Tips** No unsolicited manuscripts, programme ideas or showreels will be considered.

## Torpedo Ltd

**Llantrisant House, Llantrisant, Cardiff, CF72 8BS**

- 01443 231989
- 01443 231664
- info@torpedoltd.co.uk, firstname.lastname'torpedoltd.co.uk
- www.torpedoltd.co.uk

**Contact** Ceri Wyn Richards

**Insider Info** Produce factual entertainment and documentaries for radio and television, for a variety of clients including the BBC, ITV and S4C.

**Tips** Much of the TV production in particular has been made for broadcast on regional Welsh stations, and has consisted of documentaries with a strong Welsh element.

## Touch Productions

**18 Queen Street, Bath, BA1 2HN**

- 01225 484666
- 01225 483620
- ideas@touchproductions.co.uk, firstname@touchproductions.co.uk
- www.touchproductions.co.uk

**Contact** Creative Director and Executive Producer, Malcolm Brinkworth

**Insider Info** Touch produce factual content for broadcast television. Subjects include science, history, current affairs, documentaries, medicine, social history and the arts. Styles range from landmark features to Saturday night entertainment formats. Credits include *Brit School* for CBBC and *Parish in the Sun* for ITV1.

**Submission Guidelines** Accepts query with synopsis (email a one page proposal).

**Tips** Touch productions welcomes ideas for features or series.

## TransAtlantic Films

**Studio 1, 3 Brackenbury Road, London, W6 0BE**

- 020 8735 0505
- 020 8735 0605
- mail@transatlanticfilms.com
- www.transatlanticfilms.com

**Contact** Managing Director, Corisande Albert

**Established** 1968

**Insider Info** Produce television documentaries and series, particularly in the areas of travel, music, the arts, science and history. Catalogue available online.

**Tips** No unsolicited scripts will be accepted.

## TV Choice

**PO Box 597, Bromley, Kent, BR2 0YB**

- 020 8464 7402
- 020 8464 7845
- tvchoice@aol.com
- www.tvchoice.uk.com

**Contact** Norman Thomas

**Established** 1982

**Insider Info** Produces material for television, video and DVD. The company produces and distributes educational films for school, libraries, colleges and universities.

**Submission Guidelines** Accepts query with synopsis.

**Tips** The productions and distribution library are not primarily for broadcast, but rather for publishing on removable media. Subject matters are wide ranging, but are always educational.

## Twentieth Century Fox Productions Ltd

**Twentieth Century House, 31–32 Soho Square, London, W1D 3AP**

- 020 7437 7766
- 020 7434 2170
- www.fox.co.uk

**Insider Info** The UK arm of the US feature film company. Credits include *The History Boys* and *The Last King of Scotland*.

**Submission Guidelines** Accepts agented submissions only.

**Tips** No unsolicited manuscripts, treatments or ideas will be accepted.

## TwoFour Productions Ltd

**TwoFour Studios, Estover, Plymouth, PL6 7RG**

☎ 01752 727400

🖷 01752 727450

✉ enq@twofour.co.uk

🌐 www.twofour.co.uk

**Contact** Creative Director and Executive Producer, Stuart Murphy

**Established** 1987

**Insider Info** TwoFour produce factual entertainment for UK and international terrestrial and satellite television channels. Credits include *Martin Shaw: Aviators* for Discovery Real Time and *Agatha Christie's Garden* for ITV1.

**Tips** Although TwoFour is predominantly known for factual and light entertainment, it has recently opened a new drama department and plans to expand its studio space in Plymouth to accommodate the filming of new drama features and series. This department is headed by Jo Wright.

## UBA Ltd

**21 Alderville Road, London, SW6 2EE**

☎ 01984 623619

🖷 01984 623733

✉ peterjshaw@btinternet.com

**Contact** Peter Shaw, Joanna Shaw

**Insider Info** UBA produce feature films with an international flavour. Credits include *Turtle Diary* and *Castaway*.

**Tips** UBA will considers new writers. Films should have appeal to an international market.

## UBC Media Group

**50 Lisson Street, London, NW1 5DF**

☎ 020 7453 1600

🖷 020 7723 6132

✉ info1@ubcmedia.com

🌐 www.ubcmedia.com

**Insider Info** UBC Media own the radio stations Classic Gold Digital and One Word Radio. They also produce content for many UK commercial radio stations as well as the BBC. The group encompasses Unique and Smooth Operations production companies. Programming ranges from factual entertainment to documentaries, specialist music shows and comedy.

**Tips** UBC do not tend to produce straight drama. Most content is factual and varies depending on the radio audience, which in UBC's case stretches across both commercial and public service broadcasters.

## Vera Productions

**66–68 Margaret STreet, London, W1W 8SR**

☎ 020 7436 6116

🖷 020 7436 6117

**Contact** Vivienne Clore, Geoff Atkinson

**Established** 1994

**Insider Info** Vera produce television comedy. Credits include *Bremner, Bird and Fortune*. A recent link up with Hanrahan Media means a move towards documentary making alongside the comedy.

**Tips** Vera Productions have recently been working on developing a successful sit-com type show, particularly for ITV1. As well as traditional broadcasting, Vera also explore viral methods such as internet publishing and podcasting.

## VIP Broadcasting

**8 Banbury Way, Epsom, KT17 4JP**

☎ 01372 721196

🖷 01372 726697

✉ info@vipbroadcasting.co.uk

🌐 www.vipbroadcasting.co.uk

**Contact** Chris Vezey

**Established** 1998

**Insider Info** Produces features, series and concerts for radio broadcasters.

**Submission Guidelines** Accepts query with synopsis.

**Tips** No unsolicited manuscripts will be accepted. Programmes are mainly music based. VIP also publish CDs (both live recordings and information based productions).

## Waddell Media

**Strand Studios, 5–7 Shore Road, Holywood, County Down, BT18 9HX Northern Ireland**

☎ 028 9042 7646

🖷 028 9042 7922

✉ info@waddellmedia.com, davidc@waddellmedia.com

🌐 www.waddellmedia.com

**Contact** Head of Development, David Cumming

**Established** 1988

**Insider Info** Waddell media produce factual and documentary programming for broadcast television. Subjects include lifestyle, leisure, entertainment and music. Credits include *Futureweapons* for Discovery US and *Looking for Love* for BBC Northern Ireland.

**Tips** Waddell Media do not produce any drama. Waddel's market includes the US, as well as the UK and its regions.

## Wag TV

2D Leroy House, 436 Essex Road, London,
N1 3QP

- 020 7688 1711
- 020 7688 1702
- info@wagtv.com
- www.wagtv.com

**Contact** Head of Development, Eliya Arman

**Insider Info** WAG TV produce factual television programmes and documentaries across a range of subjects. Clients include the BBC, Channel 4, Channel Five, Discovery Networks and PBS.

**Tips** Copies of past productions are available from the website and will give a feel for previously successful styles and subject matters.

## Wall to Wall

8–9 Spring Place, Kentish Town, London,
NW5 3ER

- 020 7485 7424
- 020 7267 5292
- mail@walltowall.co.uk, development@walltowall.co.uk
- www.walltowall.co.uk

**Contact** Head of Development, Gavin Rota

**Insider Info** Produces factual and drama programming for broadcast television. Credits include *Who Do You Think You Are* for the BBC. Submissions accompanied by SAE will not be returned. Catalogue available online.

**Submission Guidelines** Accepts queries by email or through an agent first.

**Tips** No unsolicited manuscripts will be accepted, read or stored. Most development is done using in-house writers.

## Walsh Bros.

4 The Heights, London, SE7 8JH

- 020 8858 6870
- development@walshbros.co.uk
- www.walshbros.co.uk

**Contact** John Walsh, David Walsh

**Insider Info** Produce high-end documentaries, television drama and feature films. Credits include *Headhunting The Homeless* for the BBC and the feature film *The Sleeper*.

**Submission Guidelines** Accepts query via email.

**Tips** Particular needs for submissions are published on the website. Priorities for 2007/8 are contemporary teenage drama and contemporary British science fiction.

## Walt Disney Company Ltd

3 Queen Caroline Street, London, W6 9PE

- 020 8222 1000
- 020 8222 2795
- customer.support.london@disney.co.uk
- www.disney.co.uk

**Insider Info** The London offices of the Disney Corporation, producing live action and animated feature films and television, primarily for children and families.

**Submission Guidelines** No unsolicited manuscripts.

**Tips** All Disney's commissioning takes place in the US Office and is through script and film agents only.

## Warner Bros.

Warner House, 98 Theobald's Road, London,
WC1X 8WB

- 020 7984 5000
- www.warnerbros.co.uk

**Insider Info** The UK office of the major US production company. Produce feature films and television series, including *The Polar Express* and *Friends*.

**Tips** Accepts agented writers only.

## Whistledown Productions Ltd

66 Southwark Bridge Road, London, SE1 0AS

- 020 7922 1120
- 020 7261 0939
- info@whistledown.net
- www.whistledown.net

**Established** 1998

**Insider Info** Produces features, documentaries, podcasts and adverts for radio. Credits include *Churchill Confidential* and *Down at the Docks* for BBC Radio 4.

**Submission Guidelines** Accepts queries.

**Tips** No unsolicited manuscripts will be accepted without prior arrangement. The main broadcast route for Whistledown Productions is BBC Radio 4.

## Wild Rover Productions

112–114 Lisburn Road, Belfast, BT9 6AH
Northern Ireland

- 028 9050 0980
- 028 9050 0970
- enquiries@wild-rover.com
- www.wild-rover.com

**Contact** Head of Development, John Fitzgerald

**Insider Info** Produces factual, comedy and entertainment programmes for broadcast television. Credits include *Just for Laughs* for BBC1 and *Nolan Live* for UTV.

**Tips** Previous programmes have included documentaries and live shows specifically relevant to Northern Ireland, as well as entertainment shows with an international appeal.

## Wise Buddah

**74 Great Titchfield Street, London, W1W 7QP**

- 020 7307 1600
- 020 7307 1602
- info@wisebuddah.com, firstname.lastname@ wisebuddah.com
- www.wisebuddah.com

**Contact** Paul Plant, Mark Goodier

**Established** 1994

**Insider Info** Produces radio programmes, as well as providing post production facilities, talent management, and jingles and music remix production facilities. Productions include *The Johnnie Walker Show* for BBC Radio 2 and *Send In The Clones* for BBC Radio 4.

## Working Title Films

**Oxford House, 76 Oxford Street, London, W1D 1BS**

- 020 7307 3000
- 020 7307 3001
- www.workingtitlefilms.com

**Contact** Chairmen, Tim Bevan and Eric Fellner

**Insider Info** Produces feature films and drama, family entertainment and comedy for television. Credits include the films *Pride and Prejudice* and *Nanny McPhee*, as well as the TV series *Randall and Hopkirk* and *The Borrowers*.

**Tips** No unsolicited manuscripts will be accepted.

## World Productions Limited

**16 Dufours Place, London, United Kingdom, W1F 7SP**

- 020 7734 3536
- 020 7758 7000
- fenella@world-productions.com
- www.world-productions.com

**Contact** Development Coordinator, Fenella Watkinson

**Established** 1990

**Insider Info** Produce British television drama. Recent credits include *Rough Diamond* for BBC1 and *Goldplated* for Channel 4. Purchases around 100 hours of scripts per year and purchases all rights on accepted material. Will accept previously published material and submissions accompanied with SAE will be returned. Catalogue available online.

**Tips** World Productions produce drama for all of the main UK television broadcasters. For information on submitting scripts, email Fenella Watkinson directly.

## Wortman UK/Polestar

**48 Chiswick Staithe, Hounslow, London, W4 3TP**

- 020 8994 8886
- nevillewortman@beeb.net

**Contact** Producer Development, Neville Wortman

**Established** 1989

**Insider Info** Film and Television. Produces drama, entertainment, documentaries and corporate content for mainstream audiences.

**Submission Guidelines** For films, submit resume, writing samples and include a short example of dialogue.

**Tips** We always look ahead and don't follow current trends.

## WT2

**Oxford House, 76 Oxford Street, London, W1D 1BS**

- 020 7307 3000
- 020 7307 3004
- www.workingtitlefilms.com

**Insider Info** A sister company of Working Title films, developing lower budget feature films. Credits include *Billy Elliot* and *Shaun of the Dead*.

**Tips** No unsolicited manuscripts.

Our listings reveal the remarkable diversity of UK and Irish theatres and theatrical production companies. They range from the mainstream to niche, with opportunities for writers at many levels. We have provided guidelines where we have been able to, but many of them have websites that are sources of further information and background material that you should check. Some have very specific requirements and, as ever, you should read carefully before submitting.

## 7:84 Theatre Company Scotland

**333 Woodlands Road, Glasgow, G3 6NG**
- 0141 334 6686
- 0141 334 3369
- admin@784theatre.com/ firstname@784theatre.com
- www.784theatre.com

**Artistic/Editorial Director** Lorenzo Mele
**Established** 1970
**Insider Info** A prominent Scottish touring company whose focus is on political theatre and its ability to affect policy making decisions. Performances are hosted at theatres and other arts venues throughout Scotland.
**Submission Guidelines** No unsolicited manuscripts.
**Tips** Although 7:84 cannot accept scripts from new writers, it does take part in Fuse, a national script search project in association with Playwrights' Studio, Scotland and NTS Workshop. For more information on submitting your script to Fuse, visit www.playwrightsstudio.co.uk/fuse.

## Abbey Theatre

**26 Lower Abbey Street, Dublin 1, Republic of Ireland**
- 00353 1 8872000
- 00353 1 8729177
- info@abbeytheatre.ie/ firstnamelastname@abbeytheatre.ie
- www.abbeytheatre.ie

**Artistic/Editorial Director** Fiach Mac Conghail
**Contact** Literary Assistant, Aoife Habenicht
**Established** 1904
**Insider Info** Also known as the National Theatre of Ireland.
**Submission Guidelines** Submit complete script but do not write your name on the script itself, only on the covering letter, which should include contact details, background information on the play and your writing experience to date. Submissions accompanied by SAE will be returned. There is no particular style of genre of writing needed, only original, theatrical scripts. Will not accept television or radio scripts, previously published or produced plays, handwritten or emailed scripts, or incomplete scripts.
**Tips** Presently concentrating on Irish writing therefore writers must be from Ireland. Check the website for changes to this policy.

## Actual Theatre

**25 Hamilton Drive, Glasgow, G12 8DN**
- 0141 339 0654
- 0141 339 0654
- ramshorn.theatre@strath.ac.uk

**Artistic/Editorial Director** Susan Triesman
**Established** 1980
**Insider Info** Previous plays have been produced in conjunction with the Ramshorn Theatre at the University of Strathclyde.
**Tips** Past productions have tackled difficult and sensitive subject areas.

## Almeida Theatre

**Almeida Theatre, Almeida Street, London, N1 1TA**
- 020 7288 4900
- 020 7288 4901
- info@almeida.co.uk
- www.almeida.co.uk

**Artistic/Editorial Director** Michael Attenborough
**Established** 1837
**Insider Info** A theatre that produces classic British, Irish and international plays, as well as newly commissioned material. Also hosts an annual opera season. The theatre has a distinctive rounded back wall.
**Submission Guidelines** No unsolicited scripts.
**Tips** Freelance directors and assistant directors and actors are used for various productions. Queries about upcoming vacancies accepted by email.

## ATC (Actors Touring Company)

**Malvern House, 15–16 Nassau Street, London, W1W 7AB**

- 020 7580 7723
- 020 7580 7724
- info@atc-online.com
- www.atc-online.com

**Artistic/Editorial Director** Gordon Anderson
**Established** 1980
**Insider Info** The ATC is a company that produces and tours innovative new work from both the UK and abroad. Plays are performed in small theatres throughout the country.
**Tips** ATC place great importance on adaptions and translations of international plays, as well as innovative pieces from the UK, and have forged links with companies and playwrights from other countries.

## Belgrade Theatre
**Belgrade Square, Coventry, CV1 1GS**
- 024 7625 6431
- admin@belgrade.co.uk
- www.belgrade.co.uk

**Artistic/Editorial Director** Hamish Glen
**Established** 1958
**Insider Info** Since opening, the Belgrade has produced more than 800 shows including musicals, comedies and drama seen by over four million people.
**Tips** The Belgrade is currently closed for re-development. Check website for details of re-opening.

## Bill Kenwright Ltd
**BKL House, 106 Harrow Road, London, W2 1RR**
- 020 7446 6200
- 020 7446 6222
- www.kenwright.com

**Artistic/Editorial Director** Bill Kenwright
**Insider Info** The UK's largest independent theatre production company, producing major plays and musicals for the West End, Broadway and touring companies.
**Submission Guidelines** Submit script and covering letter by post. Submissions accompanied by an SAE will be returned.
**Tips** Most of the plays produced are by established writers and past productions include hits such as Willy Russel's *Blood Brothers*. Unsolicited scripts are unlikely to be commissioned.

## Birmingham Repertory Theatre
**Broad Street, Birmingham, B1 2EP**
- 0121 245 2000

- info@birmingham-rep.co.uk
- www.birmingham-rep.co.uk

**Artistic/Editorial Director** Rachel Kavanaugh
**Established** 1913
**Insider Info** The Rep has produced many new UK and foreign plays and many have transferred to London theatres. An emphasis is placed upon encouraging a young audience and this is helped by 'Transmissions', a young writers' festival, 'The Young Rep' youth theatre and 'Page to Stage', a project during which young people can experience the processes involved in producing a new play.
**Submission Guidelines** No unsolicited scripts.
**Tips** Although the theatre no longer accepts unsolicited scripts, scripts will be read as part of the 'attachment' scheme with the aim of developing new pieces for production by the company and to give the writer creative support. First-time writers are eligible, as are established writers who want to develop a brand new play with no pressure. For more information, contact the literary department on 0121 245 2045.

## Bootleg Theatre Company
**23 Burgess Green, Bishopdown, Salisbury, Wiltshire, SP1 3EL**
- 01722 421476
- colin281@btinternet.com
- under construction

**Artistic/Editorial Director** Colin Burden
**Contact** Colin Burden
**Established** 1991
**Insider Info** Bootleg Theatre Company produces new writing with socially relevant themes for as wide an audience as possible. Produces two professional small scale productions per year, which tour briefly before running on the London Fringe. Aims to respond to manuscript submissions within four weeks. Obtains sole performing rights during the time of production on accepted manuscripts. Payment for accepted manuscripts is a minimum of £500. The maximum depends on funding but can be the Arts Council recommendation payment.
**Submission Guidelines** Submit complete manuscript. Submissions accompanied by SAE will be returned. Usually produces comedy dramas in the vein of Barrie Keeffe, Tony Marchant etc., which are between 60 and 100 minutes in length. They are simple yet effective with fairly minimalistic staging and no more than four cast members. Will not consider any physical theatre, Greek-style tragedy or Agatha Christie-style pieces with large casts.
**Tips** Bootleg avoids predictable new work that does not challenge an audience or provoke any thought

whatsoever. It produces pieces thoughtful as well as entertaining.

## Borderline Theatre Company
**North Harbour Street, Ayr, KA8 8AA**
- 01292 281010
- enquiries@borderlinetheatre.co.uk/ firstname@borderlinetheatre.co.uk
- www.borderlinetheatre.co.uk

**Contact** Producer, Eddie Jackson
**Established** 1974
**Insider Info** One of Scotland's oldest touring companies. Also runs a Lifelong Learning Programme and over 1,400 drama workshops each year in schools and within local communities.
**Submission Guidelines** Recent plays include *Passing Places*, Stephen Greenhorn; *Good Things*, Liz Lochhead; *Dead Funny* by Terry Johnson
**Tips** As well as the adult touring company, Borderline are also involved in youth theatre, and work with new plays. Contact emma@borderlinetheatre.co.uk for more details on the youth theatre in general.

## Bristol Old Vic Theatre
**King Street, Bristol, BS1 4ED**
- 0117 949 3993
- 0117 949 3996
- admin@bristol-old-vic.co.uk/firstinitiallastname@bristol-old-vic.co.uk
- www.bristol-old-vic.co.uk

**Artistic/Editorial Director** Simon Reade
**Contact** Assistant to the Directors, Jane Totney
**Established** 1776
**Insider Info** The Main House theatre is set in a Georgian auditorium and is the oldest continuously working theatre in the country. The Studio is a smaller space in the same complex.
**Submission Guidelines** Submit query to Jane Totney.
**Tips** The theatre are keen on commissioning new work for the Main House and Studio, as well as for a basement space they have available for development of new pieces. Be aware however, that there is no formal script reading service and it is not exclusively new work that they produce.

## Bruce James Productions
**68 St. George's Park Avenue, Westcliff-on-Sea, Essex, SS0 9UD**
- 01702 335970
- info@brucejamesproductions.co.uk

- www.brucejamesproductions.co.uk

**Artistic/Editorial Director** Bruce James
**Established** 1995
**Insider Info** The company has produced over 100 musicals, comedies, thrillers, dramas and pantomimes for a number of venues across the country.
**Tips** Already has an extensive portfolio of shows – see website for details.

## Bush Theatre
**Bush Theatre, Shepherd's Bush Green, London, W12 8QD**
- 020 7602 3703
- 020 7602 7614
- info@bushtheatre.co.uk, production@bushtheatre.co.uk
- www.bushtheatre.co.uk

**Artistic/Editorial Director** Fiona Clark
**Contact** Literary Manager, Abigail Gonda
**Established** 1972
**Insider Info** A London theatre that both commissions pieces and hosts guest productions throughout the year. Produces eight plays per year. Aims to respond to manuscript submissions within four months.
**Submission Guidelines** Send full manuscript of plays, which are at least 80 minutes in length, by post. Also include a short covering letter and an email address. Submissions accompanied by an SAE will be returned.
**Tips** Out of the eight new plays produced per year, around five or six of these are commissioned from new writers through the script reading service. This is a tiny proportion of the 1,000s of scripts received, but the reading team will attempt to give some feedback to each writer that submits their work, even if they are unsuccessful.

## The Byre Theatre of St. Andrews
**Abbey Street, St. Andrews, KY16 9LA**
- 01334 476288
- 01334 475370
- firstname.lastname@byretheatre.com /enquiries@byetheatre.com
- www.byretheatre.com

**Artistic/Editorial Director** Stephen Wrentmore
**Established** 1933
**Insider Info** The theatre puts on a programme of drama, dance and music. It also runs an active education programme, including groups and projects for the young and old.

**Tips** The theatre runs a playwrights group, 'Byrewriters'. This is a good source of support for and development of new writing and group members have gone on to be successful playwrights and screenwriters. For more information on joining this group, telephone or write to Elsie Lindsay.

## Cheeky Maggot Productions

**PO Box 273, 2–3 Bedford Street, London, WC2E 9HH**

- ◉ info@cheekymaggot.co.uk
- ◍ www.cheekymaggot.co.uk

**Artistic/Editorial Director** Amber Agar
**Established** 2002
**Insider Info** Cheeky Maggot's aim is to support new writing talent for stage and screen, including the development of first-time writers. Writers who come from minority groups and those who write about subjects that are not typically dealt with in mainstream theatre and film are welcomed. Plays have been performed at the Hampstead Theatre and The Soho Theatre.
**Submission Guidelines** Submit CV, a description of what you want to work on (new play, workshop, rewrites etc) and full script if applicable, to: writers@cheekymaggot.co.uk
 Produces plays with an edge, a passion and a message that will stimulate an audience. This includes politically or socially aware works. The maximum cast number is usually eight. Prefers not to see previously performed work, although rewrites are considered.
**Tips** No postal submissions. Actors and directors are also invited to join the company. The company has recently branched out into film development after concentrating mainly on theatre since 2002.

## Chichester Festival Theatre

**Oaklands Park, Chichester, West Sussex, PO19 6AP**

- ◉ 01243 354951
- ◑ 01244 354953
- ◉ admin@cft.org.uk
- ◍ www.cft.org.uk

**Artistic/Editorial Director** Jonathan Church
**Established** 1962
**Insider Info** The theatre presents major productions for audiences both from the UK and internationally. A highlight of the theatre's programme is the Summer Festival, which runs from April to September and showcases both new and classic pieces of theatre. The smaller Minerva Theatre is a later addition to the theatre in a separate building.

**Tips** Each month, the website publishes an interview with a key member of the theatre's staff. This can be a good source of information on future plans and directions for the theatre. Writers may also email: marketing@cft.org.uk with a review of one of the shows, (250 words maximum). Those selected will gain free entry to a future show and the review published on the website. The subject line for this email should read 'Community Critic'.

## Citizens Theatre

**119 Gorbals Street, Glasgow, G5 9DS**

- ◉ 0141 429 5561
- ◑ 0141 429 7374
- ◉ info@citz.co.uk
- ◍ www.citz.co.uk

**Artistic/Editorial Director** Jeremy Raison
**Established** 1943
**Insider Info** Citizens' Theatre is both a company and a theatre building. As well as the 600 seat Citizens' Theatre, there are the Circle Studio, which seats 120 and the Stalls Studio, seating 60. The company largely focuses on classic plays, both British and international, and has presented 288 productions since it began.
**Tips** Anyone wishing to become involved in the Citizens' Community Company, an amateur theatre group, should contact Martin Travers by email: martin@citz.co.uk

## Clwyd Theatr Cymru

**Mold, Flintshire, CH7 1YA**

- ◉ 01352 756331
- ◑ 01352 701558
- ◉ admin@clwyd-theatr-cymru.co.uk
- ◍ www.clwyd-theatr-cymru.co.uk

**Artistic/Editorial Director** Terry Hands
**Established** 1976
**Insider Info** The theatre is Wales' most prominent drama production outlet, and houses a production company that tours throughout Wales and the UK, performing mainly in English, but also in Welsh. The Theatre for Young People department uses the same performers, technicians and creative staff when developing productions as the main company does. Hosts drama, dance, music and a community festival in the summer.
**Submission Guidelines** Plays are a mixture of classics, contemporary pieces and new writing.
**Tips** Plays from Welsh writers, or about Wales, are of particular interest.

## The Coliseum Theatre

**Fairbottom Street, Oldham, OL1 3SW**

- 0161 624 1731
- 0161 624 2829
- annelouisejones@coliseum.org.uk
- www.coliseum.org.uk

**Artistic/Editorial Director** Kevin Shaw

**Contact** Anne Louise Jones

**Insider Info** The Coliseum Theatre hosts touring productions and commissions new work. Aims to respond back to writers within four months.

**Submission Guidelines** Submit complete script, typed on single-sided A4 sheets (including a synopsis and a list of casting requirements). Submissions accompanied with SAE will be returned.

**Tips** The Coliseum runs playwrights courses, and workshops as well as industry sessions and playwrighting competitions. Check the website for details, or email: insideout@coliseum.org.uk

## Compass Theatre Company

**St. Jude's Parish Hall, 175 Gibraltar Street, Sheffield, S3 8UA**

- 0114 275 5328
- 0114 278 6931
- firstname@compasstheatrecompany.com
- www.compasstheatrecompany.com

**Artistic/Editorial Director** Neil Sissons

**Established** 1981

**Insider Info** A touring company mainly focused on performing classical, modern theatre that already has a classic status, and classic children's plays.

**Tips** Although the company are mainly dedicated to producing established plays, part of their artistic policy is to develop some new work that fits well with their classical focus.

## Concordance

**Finborough Theatre, 118 Finborough Road, London, SW10 9ED**

- admin@concordance.org.uk
- www.concordance.org.uk

**Artistic/Editorial Director** Neil McPherson

**Contact** Literary Manager, Alexandra Wood

**Established** 1981

**Insider Info** Theatrical production company resident at the Finborough Theatre, London. Produces six plays per year, which are performed at the Finborough Theatre. Aims to respond to manuscript submissions within three months. Rights obtained on accepted manuscripts are negotiable. Payment is via royalty.

**Submission Guidelines** Read the Literary Policy at www.finboroughtheatre.co.uk Submissions accompanied by SAE will be returned. Produces plays with political and social themes, musical theatre and adaptations of novels. Will not consider adaptations of famous novels and on any literary figure prior to 1850.

**Tips** Read the Literary Policy available online carefully.

## Contact Theatre Company

**Oxford Road, Manchester, M15 6JA**

- 0161 274 3434
- 0161 274 0640
- info@contact-theatre.org.uk
- www.contact-theatre.org

**Artistic/Editorial Director** John E. McGrath

**Contact** Punam Ramchurn

**Insider Info** An innovative theatre comprising: Space 1, a 350 seat theatre; Space 2, an 80 seat studio; and Space 3, a rehearsal, workshop and performance space. Performances are also put on in the lounge/bar area. Most audiences and participants are aged between 13 and 30, although all ages are welcome. Participation and community outreach is a major part of the theatre's work. Payment for full commissions is in accordance with the Writers' Guild of Great Britain rates.

**Submission Guidelines** Submit an outline summary, a sample of work and background information on the writer(s) in the form of a covering letter to RAW@contact-theatre.org.uk or by post. RAW (Rythym and Words) is the theatre's new writing scheme. It commissions, to various stages, not only full plays but poetry, rap, dance and visual arts pieces. Anyone with a performance idea that could work in a theatre, whatever its form, is welcome to get in touch.

**Tips** RAW guidelines are available to download from the website. Ideas go through initial script development (Seed Commission), then onto 'Flip the Script' night, whereby actors perform a small section of the play to a live audience who vote for their favourite. The next stage is a development workshop (this can be the first stage for some ideas). Ideas that are deemed ready are then considered for a full commission.

## Crucible Theatre

**55 Norfolk Street, Sheffield, S1 1DA**

- 0114 249 5999

☎ 0114 249 6003
🌐 www.sheffieldtheatres.co.uk
**Artistic/Editorial Director** Samuel West
**Contact** Literary Associate, Matthew Byam Shaw
**Established** 1971
**Insider Info** The Crucible is the main venue in the Sheffield Theatres group for producing theatre works. It also hosts touring productions and famously, the annual World Snooker Championships.
**Submission Guidelines** Productions tend to use minimal scenery, so as not to block audience views.
**Tips** Although few unsolicited scripts are commissioned for the Crucible, the position of Literary Associate is designed to source and read new scripts and pass promising works on to the Associate Director.

## CV Productions
**Hampden House, 2 Weymouth Street, London, W1N 3FD**
☎ 020 7636 4343
☎ 020 7636 2323
✉ info@cvtheatre.co.uk
🌐 www.cvtheatre.co.uk
**Artistic/Editorial Director** Charles Vance
**Established** 1960
**Insider Info** Presents quality productions in theatres throughout the UK, including adaptations, classic drama and weekly repertory, musicals and pantomime.
**Tips** Very rarely commissions new works.

## Derby Playhouse
**Eagle Centre, Theatre Walk, Derby, DE1 2NF**
☎ 01332 363275
☎ 01332 547200
✉ info@derbyplayhouse.co.uk
🌐 www.derbyplayhouse.co.uk
**Artistic/Editorial Director** Stephen Edwards and Karen Louise Hebden
**Established** 1975
**Insider Info** Produces new and classic plays. Recent productions include *The Importance of Being Earnest* and *Merrily We Roll Along*. The theatre has a strong reputation outside of the UK.
**Tips** No longer able to accept unsolicited scripts.

## Druid Theatre Company
**Flood Street, Galway, Republic of Ireland**
☎ 00353 91 568660
☎ 00353 91 568660
✉ info@druidtheatre.com
🌐 www.druidtheatre.com
**Artistic/Editorial Director** Garry Hynes
**Contact** New Writing Manager, Thomas Conway
**Established** 1975
**Insider Info** Druid was the first professional theatre company in Ireland outside Dublin. Productions are performed at its home theatre in Galway, as well as being toured nationally and internationally.
**Submission Guidelines** Submit complete manuscript, with a covering letter. All pages should be A4, single-sided, numbered and bound. Postal submissions only. Submissions accompanied by SAE will be returned. Will not accept plays that have been professionally produced before, or unfinished plays. Cannot produce one act plays, children's plays or musicals, although they can be considered as an introduction to a writer's work.
**Tips** Although Druid is committed to nurturing new Irish writing, writers from any location are welcome to submit their scripts. Those submitting from outside Ireland must include International Reply Coupons if the manuscript is to be returned.

## The Dukes
**Moor Lane, Lancaster, LA1 1QE**
☎ 01524 598505
✉ info@dukes-lancaster.org
🌐 www.dukes-lancaster.org
**Artistic/Editorial Director** Ian Hastings
**Contact** Theatre Secretary, Jacqui Wilson
**Established** 1971
**Insider Info** The Dukes is a producing theatre and independent theatre with an integrated programme of participatory activities. The company produces approximately six plays per year. There are five professional productions at The Dukes, and one site specific production at Williamson Park, Lancaster. Plays for, and by young people are presented, specifically at DT3, a dedicated space for this work. Payment is via royalties (eight per cent).
**Submission Guidelines** Accepts query and synopsis.

## Dundee Repertory Theatre
**Tay Square, Dundee, DD1 1PB**
☎ 01382 227684
☎ 01382 228609
✉ enquiries@dundeereptheatre.co.uk
🌐 www.dundeereptheatre.co.uk
**Artistic/Editorial Director** James Brining and Dominic Hill
**Established** 1939

**Insider Info** The Rep acts as a production house, producing around six new plays a year, as well as receiving touring productions. Works range from drama and comedy to dance.

**Tips** The Rep also commissions new works and seeks to translate and adapt classical texts, giving them relevance to Scotland today.

## Eastern Angels Theatre Company

**Sir John Mills Theatre, Gatacre Road, Ipswich, Suffolk, IP1 2LQ**

- 01473 218202
- box1@eaternangels.co.uk, firstname@easternangels.co.uk
- www.easternangles.co.uk

**Artistic/Editorial Director** Ivan Cutting

**Insider Info** Produces new plays, mostly with a direct link to East Anglia, either through the writer or subject matter. Plays are performed in theatres throughout the East of England, as well as other venues that can be adapted for the purposes of individual plays.

**Tips** Eastern Angels focus exclusively on new writing and welcome script submissions, but bear in mind the necessary connection to East Anglia and the types of rural venues that plays are likely to be performed in.

## English Touring Theatre

**25 Short Street, London, SE1 8LJ**

- 020 7450 1990
- 020 7450 1991
- admin@ett.org.uk, firstinitiallastname@ett.org.uk
- www.ett.org.uk

**Artistic/Editorial Director** Stephen Unwin

**Established** 1993

**Insider Info** The company usually spends a part of each season in London, as well as touring the rest of the country. It has a repertoire of around 40 productions of both European classics and new works. Plays are usually performed in medium-sized theatres throughout the UK.

**Submission Guidelines** No unsolicited submissions.

**Tips** Although the company do not accept scripts, they do offer some work experience places and a fast track professional development programme, for black, Asian and minority ethnic trainee arts managers.

## Everyman Theatre

**Regent Street, Cheltenham, GL50 1HQ**

- 01242 512515
- 01242 224305
- admin@everymantheatre.org.uk
- www.everymantheatre.org.uk

**Artistic/Editorial Director** Sue Colverd

**Established** 1891

**Insider Info** Produces and hosts ballet, opera, drama, dance, comedy, musical performances and Christmas pantomimes. As well as the main theatre seating 684, there is also space for 66 people in The Other Space studio theatre, a flexible performance space.

**Tips** Everyman Reachout is a community scheme designed to involve the young, through youth theatre, right through to older people with the lifelong learning scheme. Part of Reachout's remit is to work with and develop new writers. For more information on any Reachout scheme, contact: reachout@everymantheatre.org.uk

## Finborough Theatre

**118 Finborough Road, LondonSW10 9ED**

- admin@finboroughtheatre.co.uk
- www.finboroughtheatre.co.uk

**Artistic/Editorial Director** Neil McPherson

**Contact** Literary Manager, Alexandra Wood

**Established** 1980

**Insider Info** One of London's leading off West End venues, well known for new writing. Produces 15 plays per year, which are performed at the Finborough Theatre. A number transfer to other theatres including those in the West End. Aims to respond to manuscript submissions within three months. Rights obtained on commissioned plays are negotiable. Payment is via royalty.

**Submission Guidelines** Please read and submit according to the 'Literary Policy' on website. Submissions accompanied by SAE will be returned. Produces new plays, usually on political and social themes. See website for details of what will not be accepted, including plays about the relationships or emotional problems of twenty-somethings and historical and biographical plays set before 1850.

**Tips** Strongly prefers plays that can only be produced for the stage, and are not just television or radio scripts by any other name. Please read the 'Literary Policy' on the website.

## Focus Theatre Company
**School House, Down Hatherley, Gloucester, GL2 9QB**

☎ 01452 731099

✉ info@focustheatre.co.uk

🌐 www.focustheatre.co.uk

**Artistic/Editorial Director** Sheila Mander

**Insider Info** A company of young people who produce and perform mainly musical theatre at a range of venues.

**Tips** The website lists the existing portfolio of shows and songs.

## Full Circle Theatre Company
**16 Hagden Lane, Watford, Hertfordshire, WD18 0HE**

☎ 01923 499 549

✉ info@fullcircletheatre.co.uk, scripts@fullcircletheatre.co.uk

🌐 www.fullcircletheatre.co.uk

**Established** 2002

**Insider Info** Produces an entire show from script to production. Encourages new writing and the philosophy is to involve members in all aspects of the creative process. Also runs workshops in theatre production and writing skills. Produces two plays per year. Previous performance venues have included the Harrow Arts Centre. Copyright remains with the author. Writers are not paid, but are given full acknowledgement.

**Submission Guidelines** Submit complete manuscript. All material must be typed. Include contact details on a separate page. Scripts can be in any genre and of any style. One act plays running from 30 to 45 minutes, and short plays which can range from 5 to 20 minutes are considered. Will not accept previously published plays.

**Tips** Any number of scripts can be submitted by one writer at any time. Those interested in volunteering to become involved in any aspect of the productions are advised to make contact by email.

## Gate Theatre Company
**11 Pembridge Road, London, W11 3HQ**

☎ 020 7229 5387

☎ 020 7221 6055

✉ gate@gatetheatre.co.uk

🌐 www.gatetheatre.co.uk

**Artistic/Editorial Director** Thea Sharrock

**Contact** Literary Manager, Claire Lovett

**Established** 1979

**Insider Info** The Gate is London's only theatre dedicated to producing international work on a British stage. It has a capacity of around 70.

**Submission Guidelines** Submit complete manuscript. Submissions accompanied by SAE will be returned. Produces English language plays from non-British writers, including those from North America, Canada, New Zealand, Australia and the Republic of Ireland. Also seeks plays from any country, translated from any language. Will not accept plays by British writers, except foreign adaptions.

**Tips** Particular attention is paid to lesser known plays in translation. Rights for translation and adaption must be checked thoroughly. Details are usually found within the publication of the play.

## Graeae Theatre Company
**LVS Resource Centre, 356 Holloway Road, London, N7 6PA**

☎ 020 7700 2455

☎ 020 7609 7324

✉ info@graeae.org

🌐 www.graeae.org

**Artistic/Editorial Director** Jenny Sealey

**Established** 1980

**Insider Info** A theatre company staffed and run by disabled people. Productions are a mixture of new interpretations of established plays and newly commissioned pieces. Produces one to three plays per year.

**Submission Guidelines** Submit complete manuscript. Submissions accompanied by SAE will be returned. Plays must suitable for disabled performers.

**Tips** Only interested in plays in English from disabled writers. Although unsolicited scripts are welcomed, there is no official reading service and most plays are commissioned based on previous writing credits.

## Hampstead Theatre
**Eton Avenue, Swiss Cottage, London, NW3 3EU**

☎ 020 7449 4200

☎ 020 7449 4201

✉ info@hampsteadtheatre.com, literary@hampsteadtheatre.com

🌐 www.hampsteadtheatre.com

**Artistic/Editorial Director** Anthony Clark

**Contact** Literary & Education Assistant, Holly Hughes

**Insider Info** Aims to be a leading theatre for new writing. Rarely produces previously performed plays unless there is a good enough artistic reason to do so. Presents both British and international work. The main auditorium seats 325.

**Submission Guidelines** Submit complete manuscript. Include a short synopsis and covering letter as well as an equal opportunities form, available from the website. All pages must be typed, double spaced and A4-sized. Submissions accompanied by SAE will be returned. Will not accept musicals or genre plays.

**Tips** The theatre is unlikely to produce a play that has been performed before, even at a fringe venue (although it is still worth sending, as an example of your work). All writers who submit work will be given feedback but this is limited to once per play. Only writers who are being developed will be given further assistance, therefore submitting a play before it is ready is unadvisable.

## Harrogate Theatre
**Oxford Street, Harrogate, HG1 1QF**
- 01423 502710
- 01423 563205
- info@harrogatetheatre.co.uk, firstname.lastname@harrogatetheatre.co.uk
- www.harrogatetheatre.co.uk

**Established** 1900

**Insider Info** The theatre and company focus on high quality professional productions alongside community and outreach work.

**Tips** In partnership with Marcus Romer, the Artistic Director of Pilot Theatre, Harrogate Theatre is developing a scheme called 'The Academy', which will seek to undertake the commissioning of new projects by working with writers, directors, artists and actors. The Academy will focus on unestablished people and equip them with the skills to develop alongside established professionals. For further information on The Academy, contact the theatre.

## Headlong Theatre
**12 Mercer Street, London, WC2H 9QD**
- 020 7438 9940
- 020 7438 9941
- info@headlongtheatre.co.uk
- www.headlongtheatre.co.uk

**Artistic/Editorial Director** Rupert Goold

**Insider Info** A touring company interested in exploring new and established writers. The Headlong likes to commission new work from a wide range of sources. Previously known as the Oxford Stage Company.

**Tips** No unsolicited submissions due to the lack of a dedicated literary department.

## Hiss and Boo Theatre Company
**1 Nyes Hill, Wineham Lane, Bolney, RH17 5SD**
- 01444 881707
- 01444 882057
- ian@hissboo.co.uk
- www.hissboo.co.uk

**Artistic/Editorial Director** Ian Liston

**Established** 1977

**Insider Info** A company specialising in music hall, pantomimes, children's theatre, light entertainment and variety. Also provide corporate entertainment and has had some success overseas. Productions are performed in theatres and other venues of all sizes across the UK and abroad. Some productions have been housed in the West End.

**Submission Guidelines** Accepts query and synopsis by post only (no phone calls). Submissions accompanied by SAE will be returned. Interested in fresh approaches to pantomimes, comedies, thrillers, compilation musicals, children's theatre and revue-style shows.

**Tips** Hiss Boo do not usually have the resources to develop new projects, but will read synopses of suitable pieces as detailed above.

## Hull Truck Theatre Company
**Spring Street, Hull, HU2 8RW**
- 01482 224800
- 01482 581182
- admin@hulltruck.co.uk, literary@hulltruck.co.uk
- www.hulltruck.co.uk

**Artistic/Editorial Director** John Godber and Gareth Tudor Price

**Contact** Literary Development Manager, Steven Jon Atkinson

**Established** 1971

**Insider Info** One of only six producing theatres in Yorkshire, committed to producing popular and accessible plays. In the past, the works of John Godber have dominated the theatre's programmes.

**Submission Guidelines** Submit complete manuscript. Script must be bound and typed in single spacing on A4 paper. Also include a covering letter and a half page synopsis. Submissions accompanied by SAE will be returned.

**Tips** As well as the opportunity to submit unsolicited scripts, Hull Truck also offer the PlayWrite scheme, a 10 week course during which students will be encouraged to write a play whilst learning about the craft. Application details and the latest course dates are available on the website. The course is free of charge with the exception of a small admin fee.

## Kali Theatre Company
**18 Rupert Street, London, W1D 6DE**
- 020 7494 9100
- info@kalitheatre.co.uk
- www.kalitheatre.co.uk

**Artistic/Editorial Director** Janet Steele
**Established** 1995
**Insider Info** A company focusing on the writing of Asian women, seeking to give them a voice and to tackle difficult subjects. Presents full touring productions.
**Tips** Kali Shorts is a programme that seeks first-time Asian women writers and gives those chosen the chance to go through basic script development, workshops and produce a short piece of their script for audience feedback. Kali Features gives those successful in Kali shorts further one toone support, working towards a public reading at the Soho Theatre and Writers Centre. For more information on these schemes, sign up for the newsletter and state that you are a writer.

## Kings Head Theatre
**115 Upper Street, London, N1 1QN**
- 020 7226 8561
- 020 7226 8507
- www.kingsheadtheatre.org

**Artistic/Editorial Director** Stephanie Sinclaire and Ann Pinnington
**Insider Info** One of London's oldest fringe theatres. Produces new works, musicals, classic plays, British contemporary pieces and revues. Performance venue is situated above a bar.
**Submission Guidelines** No unsolicited scripts.
**Tips** Although it does not accept unsolicited manuscripts, the King's Head runs a 'Trainee Assistant Director Programme' and an 'Intern programme'. Details are on the website.

## Leicester Haymarket Theatre
**Belgrave Gate, Leicester, LE1 3YQ**
- 0116 253 0021
- 0116 251 3310
- enquiries@lhtheatre.co.uk
- www.lhtheatre.co.uk

**Artistic/Editorial Director** Paul Kerryson
**Insider Info** The theatre will shortly change locations to a brand new building in Rutland Street –

see the website for details. Performances include original works and established plays and the theatre has a strong educational programme.
**Tips** For 16–25 year olds, Young Blood gives potential scriptwriters, aspiring actors and production staff the chance to develop their skills as part of a company. Contact developingtalent@lhtheatre.co.uk to apply. 'In Residence' is a bursary scheme for writers from the Leicester area to experiment and develop their ideas over six months.

## Library Theatre Company
**St. Peters Square, Manchester, M2 5PD**
- 0161 234 1920
- 0161 228 6481
- ltc@libraries.manchester.gov.uk
- www.librarytheatre.com

**Artistic/Editorial Director** Chris Honer
**Established** 1934
**Insider Info** Produces modern classics, contemporary work and children's theatre.
**Tips** The theatre is a producing theatre and commissions many new plays, although rarely from unsolicited manuscripts.

## Liverpool Everyman and Playhouse
**13 Hope Street, Liverpool, L1 9BH**
- 0151 708 3700
- 0151 708 3701
- info@everymanplayhouse.com
- www.everymanplayhouse.com

**Artistic/Editorial Director** Gemma Bodinetz
**Contact** Literary Manager, Suzanne Bell
**Established** 1964
**Insider Info** A producing theatre with a strong new writing element. Aims to respond to manuscript submissions within three months.
**Submission Guidelines** Submit complete manuscript. All pages must be typed on A4 paper and numbered. Include covering letter, a title page and a list of characters. Submissions accompanied by SAE will be returned. There are no set styles, subjects or genre for plays, but the theatre look for writers who have a genuine passion for storytelling and a willingness to learn, develop and challenge themselves.
**Tips** No email or faxed scripts. All scripts received with incorrect return postage will be recycled.

## Live Theatre Company
**7–8 Trinity Chare, Newcastle Upon Tyne, NE1 3DF**

- ☎ 0191 261 2694
- 🖷 0191 232 2224
- ✉ info@live.org.uk
- 🌐 www.live.org.uk

**Artistic/Editorial Director** Max Roberts
**Contact** Administrator, Degna Stone
**Established** 1973

**Insider Info** A theatre company based in a small venue in Newcastle, whose main emphasis is on developing and performing new writing. Works in radio, television and film, as well as theatre. Offers a free script reading service to encourage new writing. Aims to respond to manuscript submissions within two months.

**Submission Guidelines** Submit complete manuscript. Send two copies, double-spaced on A4 paper, loosely bound. Include a covering letter, a title page and a list of characters. Number all pages and include all contact details on the first page. Submissions will not be returned. Will not accept handwritten manuscripts, email submissions, incomplete scripts, synopses, pantomimes, autobiographies, novels or poetry.

**Tips** As well as the script reading service in which work is read by a specialist reader and possibly the artistic director, Live Theatre run a scheme called 'Short Cut'. Email a five minute play or excerpt along with contact details, a synopsis and a character list to degna@live.org.uk and it will be posted on the website for peer review and discussion. The scheme is designed for writers in the Newcastle/North East region to gain support and constructive feedback.

## London Bubble Theatre Company
**5 Elephant Lane, London, SE16 4JD**
- ☎ 020 7237 4434
- 🖷 020 7231 2366
- ✉ admin@londonbubble.org.uk
- 🌐 www.londonbubble.org.uk

**Artistic/Editorial Director** Jonathon Petherbridge
**Insider Info** The company exists to promote theatre arts to both existing fans and first-time theatre goers. Particular emphasis is placed on involving those for whom theatre is not usually accessible because of financial, cultural or geographical barriers. Produces one to five plays per year. Pieces are performed in small theatres and other venues around London.
**Tips** London Bubble like to tackle subjects that challenge bigotry and celebrate diversity, whilst remaining accessible and open to those unfamiliar with theatre and the arts.

## Lyric Hammersmith
**Lyric Square, King Street, London, W6 0QL**
- ☎ 020 7494 5840
- 🖷 020 8741 5965
- ✉ enquiries@lyric.co.uk
- 🌐 www.lyric.co.uk

**Artistic/Editorial Director** David Farr
**Insider Info** The Lyric's main, traditional auditorium seats 550 whilst The Lyric Studio is a 100 seat 'black box'. The theatre both produces and receives pieces from Britain and abroad.
**Tips** Productions made in-house are very rarely the result of unsolicited scripts. New pieces are far more likely to come out of an ongoing relationship with a promising writer.

## M6 Theatre Company
**Hamer C.P. School, Albert Royds Street, Rochdale, Lancashire, OL16 2SU**
- ☎ 01706 355898
- 🖷 01706 712601
- ✉ info@m6theatre.co.uk
- 🌐 www.m6theatre.co.uk

**Artistic/Editorial Director** Dot Wood
**Insider Info** A touring company, designed to encourage the development of theatre for young people. Tours schools, community centres and arts centres, mainly in the North West.
**Tips** The audiences of M6's productions range from very young children to teenagers.

## mac
**Cannon Hill Park, Birmingham, B12 9QH**
- ☎ 0121 440 3838
- 🖷 0121 446 4372
- ✉ info@mac-birmingham.org.uk
- 🌐 www.macarts.co.uk

**Artistic/Editorial Director** Dorothy Wilson
**Established** 1963

**Insider Info** An arts centre offering a wide range of activities and performances, including live theatre, literary events and children's shows. Spaces include a theatre, cinemas and a variety of other creative studios.
**Tips** mac Productions is the centre's in-house production company. Opportunities to become involved will be advertised on the website.

## Mercury Theatre
**Balkerne Gate, Colchester, Essex, CO1 1PT**
- ☎ 01206 577006

☎ 01206 769607
✉ info@mercurytheatre.co.uk
🌐 mercurytheatre.co.uk

**Artistic/Editorial Director** Dee Evans
**Contact** Administration Assistant, Sam Leppard
**Established** 1972
**Insider Info** The Mercury Theatre Company is a highly respected ensemble company producing classic plays and working extensively in the community. Its work is at the heart of the Mercury's single objective: to inspire, engage and entertain through theatre. Although it focuses predominantly on classic work, there is some scope for producing new writing. Professional productions take place in Mercury's main house or studio theatre. On occasion these productions may subsequently tour.
**Submission Guidelines** Submit complete manuscript. Manuscripts accompanied by SAE will be returned. Mercury are interested in plays that at some level address significant contemporary questions. Although there are opportunities for new work to be staged in Mercury's main house, it is more likely to consider work that is suitable for its Studio Theatre. The website displays Mercury's current season, which should give an idea of the kind of work produced. Although Mercury are fond of farce and light hearted drama, this type of work is generally brought in from commercial producers.

## Michael Codron Plays
**Aldwych Theatre Offices, Aldwych, London, WC2B 4DF**
☎ 020 7240 8291
☎ 020 7240 8467

**Artistic/Editorial Director** Michael Codron
**Insider Info** A renowned theatre producer, whose company also manages the Aldwych Theatre in London. Not all plays are performed at the Adlwych; many are performed at other venues throughout London and are toured throughout the UK.
**Tips** Plays produced tend to be larger productions and are usually straight dramas rather than musicals.

## Moral Support
**Studio 2 Greville House, 35 Greville Street, London, EC1N 8TB**
☎ 020 7430 9324
✉ moralsupportadmin@gmail.com
🌐 www.moralsupport.org.uk

**Artistic/Editorial Director** Elizabeth Barber
**Established** 1993
**Insider Info** Moral Support are a multimedia performance company, which also run an education programme. Performances are usually staged in fringe theatres and other small arts venues across London and the UK.
**Tips** All productions are innovative and make use of various media elements. Previous performances have included visual art, dance, sign language and electronic music.

## Neal Street Productions
**1st Floor, 26–28 Neal Street, London, WC2H 9QQ**
☎ 020 7240 8890
☎ 020 7240 7099
✉ post@nealstreetproductions.com
🌐 www.nealstreetproductions.com

**Artistic/Editorial Director** Caro Newling
**Insider Info** Neal Street are a large scale independent theatre and film production company set up by Sam Mendes, Pippa Harris and Caro Newling. Performances take place in a range of venues, from Broadway to major UK theatres. Productions in the pipeline include *Shrek: The Musical*.
**Submission Guidelines** Submissions accompanied by SAE will be returned.
**Tips** For legal reasons, unsolicited submissions will not be accepted. All scripts will be returned unread.

## Net Curtains Theatre Company
**The Bath House, 96 Dean Street, London, W1D 3TD**
☎ 07968 564687
✉ claire@netcurtains.org, newplays@netcurtains.org
🌐 www.netcurtains.org

**Artistic/Editorial Director** Claire Farrington
**Contact** Lorraine Coady
**Established** 2001
**Insider Info** Net Curtains are a company of actors that produce and develop new writing for the theatre. They produce appropriately two to three plays per year. The company mainly perform in small theatres and other arts venues around London.
**Submission Guidelines** Submit complete manuscript by post (including synopsis and SAE). Submissions accompanied by SAE will be returned. There are no specific styles or genres required, however pieces on social issues that capture the imagination of the company are preferred.
**Tips** The company meet once a week to review scripts that have either been commissioned or submitted. They also welcome applications from workshop leaders and directors who are interested in working in partnership with them. Email for further details.

## Newpalm Productions

**20 Cavendish Avenue, London, N3 3QN**

☎ 020 8349 0802

☏ 020 8346 8257

**Artistic/Editorial Director** John Newman

**Established** 1970

**Insider Info** Newpalm Productions is a production company that has produced hundreds of touring productions for the UK (including the West End) and internationally. Previous shows have included *The Blue Angel* and *Peter Pan – The Musical*, both in the West End.

**Tips** Newpalm Production very rarely produces new writing, although new pieces have been produced in the past.

## New Perspectives Theatre Company

**Park Lane Business Centre, Park Lane, Basford, Nottingham, NG6 0DW**

☎ 01623 635225

☏ 01623 635240

✉ info@newperspectives.co.uk/firstnamelastname@newperspectives.co.uk

🌐 www.newperspectives.co.uk

**Artistic/Editorial Director** Daniel Buckroyd

**Insider Info** New Perspectives is a touring company that aims to bring theatre to new and existing audiences around the villages, market towns and more prominent venues. Three to four plays are produced per year.

**Tips** The company offer trainee schemes and other opportunities to get involved. Subscribe to the e-newsletter for news on the latest commissions and opportunities for new talent.

## The New Theatre

**43 East Essex Street, Temple Bar, Dublin 2, Republic of Ireland**

☎ 00353 1 670 3361

✉ info@thenewtheatre.com

🌐 www.thenewtheatre.com

**Insider Info** The New Theatre presents and produces new work, established plays and other theatre mainly dealing with Irish social issues. It is also available to youth theatre companies and can offer them the chance to work with theatre professionals.

**Tips** Prospective writers must bear in mind the Irish slant on most new work produced. The theatre has recently undergone extensive refurbishment but is due to re-open in 2007.

## The New Vic Theatre

**Eturia Road, Newcastle under Lyme, ST5 0JG**

☎ 01782 717954

☏ 01782 712885

✉ admin@newvictheatre.org.uk

🌐 www.newvictheatre.org.uk

**Artistic/Editorial Director** Theresa Heskins

**Established** 1986

**Insider Info** The New Vic is Staffordshire's regional producing theatre. It also tours productions and receives a number of shows and exhibitions. Ten new plays are produced per year.

**Submission Guidelines** Submissions accompanied by SAE will be returned.

**Tips** Most new plays are produced through commissions and there is no official script reading service for writers unknown to the theatre.

## The New Wolsey Theatre

**Civic Drive, Ipswich, Suffolk, IP1 2AS**

☎ 01473 295911

☏ 01473 295910

✉ info@wolseytheatre.co.uk, ekidd@wolseytheatre.co.uk

🌐 www.wolseytheatre.co.uk

**Artistic/Editorial Director** Peter Rowe

**Established** 2001

**Insider Info** After the closure of the original Wolsey Theatre, The New Wolsey opened in 2001. The main theatre seats 400 and hosts in-house productions, as well as those from touring companies. Performances include drama, music, comedy, poetry, dance and children's shows.

**Tips** For playwrights wishing to develop their scripts, the theatre runs a variety of workshops and competitions.

## NITRO

**6 Brewery Road, London, N7 9NH**

☎ 020 7609 1331

☏ 020 7609 1221

✉ info@nitro.co.uk

🌐 www.nitro.co.uk

**Artistic/Editorial Director** Felix Cross

**Established** 1978

**Insider Info** Previously known as The Black Theatre Cooperative, Nitro is Europe's oldest black theatre company and produces mainly musical theatre from new black writers.

**Tips** New writing should reflect the experiences of black people in contemporary society.

## Northcott Theatre

**Stocker Road, Exeter, Devon, EX4 4QB**

- 01392 223999
- 01392 223996
- www.northcott-theatre.co.uk

**Artistic/Editorial Director** Ben Crocker

**Established** 1967

**Insider Info** Northcott Theatre is the South West's leading producing theatre, opening around 44 weeks per year. The theatre also hosts a limited number of touring productions. Produces approximately ten productions per year.

**Tips** The Northcott is closing for refurbishment for most of 2007, therefore will not be putting on any productions, with the exception of summer shows in outdoor venues. Email marketing@northcott-theatre.co.uk to sign up for a newsletter and keep updated with the news surrounding future programmes.

## Northern Stage

**Barras Bridge, Newcastle upon Tyne, NE1 7RH**

- 0191 230 5151
- info@northernstage.co.uk
- www.northernstage.co.uk

**Artistic/Editorial Director** Erica Whyman

**Insider Info** Northern Stage is the largest producing theatre company in the North East. They also tour throughout the UK and Europe and seek to continue forging links with theatre groups in South Africa.

**Tips** The theatre's audience is very varied. Past shows have included modern dance, Shakespeare, children's theatre, musicals, comedy, poetry and international drama.

## Northumberland Theatre Company (NTC)

**The Playhouse, Bondgate Without, Alnwick, NE66 1PQ**

- 01665 602586
- 01665 605837
- admin@ntc-touringtheatre.co.uk
- www.ntc-touringtheatre.co.uk

**Artistic/Editorial Director** Gillian Hambleton

**Established** 1978

**Insider Info** NTC is a professional small scale touring company that aims to provide theatre to rural areas, where access to live performance is scarce.

**Tips** Unsolicited scripts are unlikely to be commissioned. However, this contact may lead to a future relationship in the case of promising writers.

## Norwich Puppet Theatre

**St James, Whitfriars, Norwich, Norfolk, NR3 1TN**

- 01603 615564
- 01603 617578
- info@puppettheatre.co.uk
- puppettheatre.co.uk

**Artistic/Editorial Director** Artistic Director, Luis Boy

**Contact** Artistic Director, Luis Boy

**Established** 1980

**Insider Info** Norwich Puppet Theatre produces puppetry and theatre of animation, primarily for a family centred audience. The touring company performs at their home base in Norwich and also to schools, venues in the UK and festivals abroad. The aims of the company are to develop the art form of puppetry/theatre of animation artistically, and to wider audiences. If they are selected to go to festivals, productions can travel through Europe and beyond. The company produce one play per year and aim to report back to writers within four weeks. Most NPT productions are created in a workshop environment, so often a script is the starting point from which the production will be created. The rights agreement and subsequent payment will depend on the resulting production and payment will be via royalties (three per cent).

**Submission Guidelines** Accepts query and synopsis. Submissions accompanied by SAE will be returned.

## Nottingham Playhouse

**Wellington Circus, Nottingham, NG1 5AF**

- 0115 947 4361
- 0115 947 5759
- www.nottinghamplayhouse.co.uk

**Artistic/Editorial Director** Giles Croft

**Contact** Literary Manager, Sarah Françoise

**Insider Info** Nottingham Playhouse is a 750 seat theatre, which opened in 1963. They produce new pieces, as well as receiving productions and touring.

**Tips** Nottingham Playhouse is part of the Theatre Writing Partnership scheme, along with Derby Playhouse, Leicester Haymarket, New Perspectives and Royal and Derngate Theatres, Northampton. The scheme is designed to develop new theatre writing in the region. For more information, visit www.theatrewritingpartnership.com

## Nottingham Playhouse Roundabout

**Wellington Circus, Nottingham, NG1 5AF**

- 0115 947 4361
- 0115 947 5759

ⓦ www.nottinghamplayhouse.co.uk
**Established** 1973
**Insider Info** Nottingham Playhouse Roundabout is a theatre in education company, working as part of Nottingham Playhouse Theatre. It produces plays and workshops for children and young people and training and support for teachers. They mainly work within schools, colleges, universities, community and youth groups, small theatre venues, conferences and festivals around Nottingham, although they occasionally tour around the UK and internationally.
**Tips** For more information for new writers, visit the Theatre Writing Partnership, www.theatrewritingpartnership.com, of which the Roundabout Theatre company are members. Bear in mind that scripts must have an educational value and be aimed at children.

## Nuffield Theatre
**University Road, Southampton, SO17 1TR**
ⓞ 023 8031 5500
ⓞ 023 8031 5511
ⓔ info@nuffieldtheatre.co.uk
ⓦ www.nuffieldtheatre.co.uk
**Artistic/Editorial Director** Patrick Sandford
**Established** 1964
**Insider Info** The Nuffield theatre produces plays for adults and children in the main house and studio. It also tours nationally and internationally to theatres, schools and other arts venues. Productions include new writing and classics.
**Tips** New writers wishing to work with the theatre are invited to apply for The Nuffield Theatre Writers' Group, which meets fortnightly on Thursday evenings. Each cycle runs for two years and members produce a ten minute play, a 40 minute radio play and a full length piece for the theatre. For details for the next round of applications email: alison.thurley@nuffieldtheatre.co.uk

## Octagon Theatre
**Howell Croft South, Bolton, BL1 1SB**
ⓞ 01204 529407
ⓞ 01204 556502
ⓔ info@octagonbolton.co.uk
ⓦ www.octagonbolton.co.uk
**Artistic/Editorial Director** Mark Babych
**Established** 1967
**Insider Info** Octagon Theatre is a production and receiving theatre company with two seasons of shows per year; January to July and September to

January. Shows include musical theatre, classic drama, contemporary classics and comedies.
**Tips** There are many community and education projects linked with the theatre that can help develop script writing skills, as well as an established youth theatre. There is no literary department and therefore they have no official reading scheme for unsolicited scripts.

## Old Red Lion Theatre
**418 St. John Street, London, EC1V 4NJ**
ⓞ 020 7833 3053
ⓦ www.oldredliontheatre.co.uk
**Artistic/Editorial Director** Helen Devine
**Established** 1979
**Insider Info** The Old Red Lion theatre is mainly a receiving theatre for innovative and contemporary work.
**Tips** Theatre companies that are producing new writing and interested in hiring the venue should post a script to the Artistic Director, including some information about the company and a production proposal.

## Operating Theatre Company
**22 Burghley Road, Kentish Town, London, NW5 1UE**
ⓞ 020 7419 2476
ⓞ 020 7419 2476
ⓔ info@operating-theatre.co.uk
ⓦ operating-theatre.co.uk
**Artistic/Editorial Director** Ken Christiansen
**Contact** Literary Manager, Mali Tudno Jones
**Established** 2002
**Insider Info** Operating Theatre Company is a new writing theatre network. The company offers opportunities and developmental training to all manner of writers. From established names through to novices and first-time playwrights, they provide dramaturgical services and run regular workshops to improve skills and test ideas. Since 2002 the company has strived to generate the sharpest and most original new writing in the UK, and has created a community of enthusiastic and busy artists. Approximately 14 plays aimed at all audiences are produced every year, at various venues. The company aims to respond to writers within six weeks. No rights are obtained on accepted manuscripts and payment is via outright purchase (minimum £1,500, maximum £6,000).
**Submission Guidelines** Submissions accompanied by SAE will be returned. Email copies are preferred on request. Plays produced focus upon new writing

and there are no limitations in terms of cast, props or staging.

## Orange Tree Theatre
**1 Clarence Street, Richmond, Surrey, TW9 2SA**
- 020 8940 0141
- 020 8332 0369
- admin@orange-tree.demon.co.uk
- www.orangetreetheatre.co.uk

**Artistic/Editorial Director** Sam Walters
**Established** 1971
**Insider Info** Orange Tree Theatre is an off West End theatre, in the round, producing new plays, adaptions, foreign pieces and musicals.
**Submission Guidelines** No unsolicited manuscripts will be accepted. Send an initial query before submitting material.
**Tips** All productions must be suitable for a theatre in the round.

## Out of Joint
**7 Thane Works, Thane Villas, London, N7 7NU**
- 020 7609 0207
- 020 7609 0203
- ojo@outofjoint.co.uk
- www.outofjoint.co.uk

**Artistic/Editorial Director** Max Stafford-Clark
**Contact** Literary Manager, Alex Roberts
**Insider Info** Out of Joint is a national and international touring company focused on the development and production of new writing. The company performs in various venues throughout the UK and abroad. Frequent venues include the Royal Court and the National Theatre. They will aim to report back to writers within three months.
**Submission Guidelines** Submit complete manuscript. Postal submissions only will be accepted and submissions accompanied by SAE will be returned.
**Tips** View www.outofjoint.co.uk/education/readinglist for an extensive list of writers that Out of Joint have previously worked with.

## Ovation Theatres
**117 Hampstead Road, London, NW1 3EF**
- 020 7837 2342
- 020 7380 0404
- events@ovationproductions.com
- www.ovationtheatres.com

**Established** 1985
**Insider Info** Ovation Theatres is the company responsible for running Upstairs at the Gatehouse, a 140 seat fringe theatre in Highgate, North London. It also stages productions for events such as the Edinburgh Fringe festival.
**Tips** Upstairs at the Gatehouse's artistic policy is to encourage new writers and directors. They will give preference to the hire of theatre space for theatre companies who wish to revive established plays.

## Paines Plough
**4th Floor 43 Aldwych, London, WC2B 4DN**
- 020 7240 4533
- 020 7240 4534
- office@painesplough.com, firstname@painesplough.com
- www.painesplough.com

**Artistic/Editorial Director** Roxana Silbert
**Contact** Literary Manager, Pippa Ellis
**Insider Info** Paines Plough is a touring company, specialising in developing new and contemporary writers and the production of their work. They also offer a script reading service. Aims to respond to writers within three months.
**Submission Guidelines** Submit complete manuscript. Postal submissions only will be accepted. Submissions accompanied by SAE will be returned. Will not accept musicals, pantomimes, TIE plays or performance art pieces, or any scripts from writers outside the UK.
**Tips** Other than the script reading facility, Paines Plough offer other services to new writers such as 'Wild Lunches' where 45 minute scripts are developed in conjunction with the theatre and then performed to the public. Check their website for other upcoming calls for submissions and competitions.

## Perth Theatre and Horsecross
**185 High Street, Perthshire, PH1 5UW**
- 0845 612 6324
- 01738 624576
- info@horsecross.co.uk, firstinoitiallastname@horsecross.co.uk
- www.horsecross.co.uk

**Artistic/Editorial Director** Ian Grieve
**Insider Info** The theatre hosts performances produced by Horsecross, an organisation borne out of the Perth Theatre. Horsecross produce a varied programme of theatre, dance, drama, comedy and music in this and other venues.
**Tips** 'Horsecross' is the brand name for the Perth Concert Hall, the Perth Theatre, Horsecross conferences and Horsecross events. As a brand, they place great emphasis on new technologies and

experimental performances, as represented by Threshold, the new media digital art exhibition space in Perth Concert Hall foyer.

## Polka Theatre for Children
**240 The Broadway, Wimbledon, London, SW19 1SB**

- 020 8545 8320
- 020 8545 8365
- admin@polkatheatre.com, richardmashannon@polkatheatre.com
- www.polkatheatre.com

**Artistic/Editorial Director** Jonathan Lloyd
**Contact** Associate Director, New Writing, Richard Shannon
**Established** 1967
**Insider Info** The Polka Theatre is a specialist theatre for young people and children, exploring new writing and classics. It is a registered charity, open to a local and international audience.
**Submission Guidelines** Submit a five page sample and a synopsis in the first instance, then a full script may be requested. Submissions accompanied with an SAE will be returned.
**Tips** There are extremely detailed guidelines on the website as to what makes a good piece of children's theatre. The theatre also runs the scheme, 'Playgrounding', through which writers can develop through workshops, one to one sessions and mentoring. For further details of the scheme and how to apply, email: frauke@polkatheatre.com

## Popular Productions Ltd
**6a Palace Gates Road, London, N22 7BN**

- 020 8365 8522
- info@popularproductions.co.uk, firstinitiallastinitial@popularproductions.co.uk
- www.popularproductions.co.uk

**Artistic/Editorial Director** John Payton and Lucy Blakeman
**Insider Info** The company produces a range of theatre, from musical comedies to straight drama and thrillers. Recent productions have included *Teechers* by John Godber and *Look Back in Anger* by John Osbourne, at the Madinat Theatre in Dubai. Most plays are performed at prominent theatrical venues across the world.
**Tips** Although the company tend to put on well established, popular works, they state that new writing is something that they develop alongside their more commercial shows.

## Proteus Theatre Company
**Queen Mary's College, Cliddesden Road, Basingstoke, Hampshire, RG21 3HF**

- 01256 354541
- 01256 356186
- info@proteustheatre.com
- www.proteustheatre.com

**Artistic/Editorial Director** Mary Swan
**Established** 1979
**Insider Info** Proteus is a touring company with an audience across the South East of England, producing approximately three plays per year.. Many shows are inter-disciplinary, including photography, film, dance, music and visual arts. Touring venues are mainly village halls and community spaces.
**Submission Guidelines** No unsolicited manuscripts will be accepted. Proposals must include a synopsis, cast breakdown and a CV. A cast of approximately four actors is normally employed, although there can be more than four characters in the play.
**Tips** The subject matter of the plays must appeal to families.

## Queen's Theatre
**Billet Lane, Hornchurch, RM11 1QT**

- 01708 462362
- 01708 462363
- info@queens-theatre.co.uk
- www.queens-theatre.co.uk

**Artistic/Editorial Director** Bob Carlton
**Established** 1953
**Insider Info** Queens is a producing theatre for Essex and Outer London. The main theatre seats 503 people.
**Submission Guidelines** Accepts submissions via query and synopsis. No unsolicited scripts will be considered. Queen's Theatre produces a mixture of musical theatre, comedy and straight drama.
**Tips** The theatre runs an established new writing programme, including an awards scheme, a playwright's festival, a writers' group and playwriting courses. Details and dates of events are advertised on the website.

## The Questor's Theatre
**Mattock Lane, Ealing, London, W5 5BQ**

- 020 8567 0011
- editor@questors.org.uk
- www.questors.org.uk

**Artistic/Editorial Director** Peter Field
**Established** 1929

**Insider Info** The Questor is Europe's largest community theatre, producing both classic theatre and new writing, as well as reviving little known plays. The complex has a 400 seat main theatre and a 100 seat studio space.

**Submission Guidelines** Recent productions include JM Barrie's *Peter Pan* and Shakespeare's *As You Like It*.

**Tips** No unsolicited manuscripts will be accepted.

## Quicksilver Theatre
**4 Enfield Road, London, N1 5AZ**
- 020 7241 2942
- 020 7254 3119
- talktous@quicksilvertheatre.org
- www.quicksilvertheatre.org

**Artistic/Editorial Director** Guy Holland and Carey English

**Established** 1977

**Insider Info** Quicksilver is a touring company specialising in new writing for children. An emphasis is placed on bold visual style and strong narratives, to produce exciting and educational theatre for young audiences.

**Tips** Quicksilver usually split their audience into two groups; three to five year olds who like small productions in intimate venues, based on things that matter to their lives; and older children who require challenging plays with thought provoking storylines.

## The Ramshorn Theatre
**University of Strathclyde Drama Centre, 98 Ingram Street, Glasgow, G1 1ES**
- 0141 552 3489
- 0141 553 2036
- ramshorn.theatre@strath.ac.uk
- www.strath.ac.uk/culture/ramshorn

**Artistic/Editorial Director** Susan Triesman

**Established** 1992

**Insider Info** The Ramshorn Theatre is based around an 80 seater studio space with a movable seating system. It has an very close relationship with the Strathclyde Theatre Group.

**Tips** The Ramshorn New Playwrights Initiative encourages new playwriting through readings, courses and productions. The idea is to give a voice to those writers not normally heard in Scottish Theatre. Contact the theatre for details on how to become involved.

## The Really Useful Group Ltd
**22 Tower Street, London, WC2H 9TW**
- 020 7240 0880
- 020 7240 1204
- Online_Team@reallyuseful.co.uk
- www.reallyuseful.com

**Artistic/Editorial Director** Andrew Lloyd Webber

**Established** 1977

**Insider Info** The Really Useful Group is an international entertainment company whose activities include theatre, film, television, video and concert productions, merchandising, records and music publishing., Performances are usually for the West End, or Broadway initially and have resulting tours.

**Submission Guidelines** Theatre productions tend to be large scale musical productions or dramas. Recent productions include *The Sound of Music* and *The Woman in White*.

**Tips** The programme is already planned for the next three years. No unsolicited manuscripts will be accepted and all scripts will be returned unopened.

## Real People Theatre Company
**37 Curlew Glebe, Dunnington, York, YO19 5PQ**
- 01904 488870
- realpeople@totalserve.co.uk
- http://web.onetel.com/~susieann

**Artistic/Editorial Director** Sue Lister

**Established** 1999

**Insider Info** Real People Theatre Company is a touring company of women.

**Tips** Contact Sue Lister for details of current and future work. Writing and productions are by women only.

## Red Ladder Theatre Company
**3 St. Peter's Buildings, York Street, Leeds, LS9 1AJ**
- 0113 245 5311
- 0113 245 5351
- firstname@redladder.co.uk
- www.redladder.co.uk

**Artistic/Editorial Director** Rod Dixon

**Established** 1969

**Insider Info** The company produces approximately three performances per year and aims to produce high quality theatre, new writing and educational works. Performances tend to take place in small community venues, youth clubs and small-scale theatres, where theatre is not normally available to young people. Aims to respond back to writers within six months and offers ITC/Equity writer's contract rights on accepted manuscripts.

**Submission Guidelines** Accepts query and synopsis. Produces plays one hour in length for a cast of no more than five actors. The work produced connects with a youth audience that both challenges them and offers them new insights. The company considers a range of styles and seeks originality. No single issue dramas will be considered.

**Tips** Upcoming trends to be aware of include the uses of new technologies in production (DVD, video projection), which appeal to sophisticated young audiences. The company request that full length plays are not submitted and that prospective writers get in contact before submitting any material, with details about yourself, why you would like to write for Red Ladder and any ideas you have. For young people aged 18–25 who want to become involved in the company in any capacity, email Leyla Asadi for more information. For young, Northern Asian people who wish to attend drama workshops in Bradford as part of Red Ladder's ATC (Asian Theatre School), email Madani Younis.

## Red Shift Theatre Company
**TRG2 Trowbridge House, 108 Weston Street, London, SE1 3QB**
- 020 7378 9787
- 020 7378 9789
- mail@redshifttheatreco.co.uk, firstname@redshifttheatre.co.uk
- www.redshifttheatreco.co.uk

**Artistic/Editorial Director** Jonathon Holloway
**Established** 1982
**Insider Info** The Red Shift Theatre Company is a touring company. It was founded to bring accessible story based theatre, making use of their actors as physical beings and specially designed objects to produce unusual performances. Produces one or two performances per year. Performances usually take place in unusual venues, both rural and urban, throughout the UK.

**Submission Guidelines** No unsolicited scripts will be accepted. The company produce adaptions of classic works, in addition to some new writing.

**Tips** Although Red Shift do not read unsolicited scripts, they do have occasional placements for directing and administration staff for particular productions. Visit the jobs section of the website for details.

## Ridiculusmus
**BAC, Lavender Hill, London, SW11 5TN**
- 020 7223 9959
- 020 7978 5207
- enquiries@ridiculusmus.com
- www.ridiculusmus.com

**Artistic/Editorial Director** David Hough and John Woods
**Established** 1992
**Insider Info** Ridiculusmus is a touring company that produces new plays and adaptions.

**Submission Guidelines** Plays tend to be produced spontaneously rather than to adhere to an artistic policy.

**Tips** The company is currently run by only two people, and therefore will not accept unsolicited scripts.

## Robert Fox Ltd
**6 Beauchamp Place, London, SW3 1NG**
- 020 7584 6855
- 020 7225 1638
- info@robertfoxltd.com
- www.robertfoxlimited.com

**Artistic/Editorial Director** Robert Fox
**Established** 1980
**Insider Info** Robert Fox is a producer of high profile theatre and films. Stage productions are mainly for the West End. Recent venues have included the Theatre Royal, Haymarket and the Wyndhams Theatre.

**Submission Guidelines** Either fill out the online form, or send a one page synopsis by mail. No full manuscripts will be accepted, Plays must appeal to audiences in the West End, on Broadway and at other major receiving theatres throughout the UK, the US and Australia.

**Tips** Read through the extensive list of previous productions on the website to check that your work is on a similar scale.

## Royal Court Theatre
**Sloane Square, London, SW1W 8AS**
- 020 6565 5050
- 020 7565 5002
- info@royalcourttheatre.com
- www.royaltheatre.com

**Artistic/Editorial Director** Domonic Cooke
**Established** 1956
**Insider Info** Royal Court Theatre is a leading national theatre company focussed on new writing from the UK and abroad. The theatre has strong links

with many countries across the world and runs a very active international education programme. As well as at its home in London, productions are staged in the US and Australia.

**Submission Guidelines** Submit complete manuscript, by mail only, addressed to the Literary Department (including a half page synopsis and SAE). Strictly no email or fax submissions will be accepted. Submissions accompanied with SAE will be returned.

**Tips** The theatre also runs a Young Writer's Programme for people aged 13–25 who want to become involved in contemporary drama production. The scheme involves courses, workshops and much more and young people are welcome to submit their scripts for feedback. For more information, contact: ywp@royalcourttheatre.com

## Royal Exchange Theatre Company
**St. Ann's Square, Manchester, M2 7DH**
- 0161 615 6709
- 0161 832 0881
- marketing@royalexchange.co.uk, firstname.lastname@royalexchange.co.uk
- www.royalexchange.co.uk

**Artistic/Editorial Director** Braham Murray and Greg Hersov
**Established** 1976

**Insider Info** The Royal Exchange Theatre Company is committed to developing and producing new writing. Since the opening of a 90 seat studio in 2002, performances have included international pieces, commissions by writers from the North West and plays for young people.

**Tips** In recent years, writers have been invited to enter the Bruntwood Playwrighting Competition as a way of submitting scripts to the theatre. They have also been offered the opportunity to propose short pieces for performance in summer festivals. Check the website for ongoing schemes such as this, as the theatre is dedicated to new writing.

## Royal Lyceum Theatre Company
**Grindlay Street, Edinburgh, EH3 9AX**
- 0131 248 4800
- 0131 228 3955
- info@lyceum.org.uk
- www.lyceum.org.uk

**Artistic/Editorial Director** Mark Thomson
**Established** 1965

**Insider Info** The Royal Lyceum Theatre Company produces classic British and international plays. They

are also keen on developing new writing, particularly by Scottish writers. The theatre itself has a well developed range of educational programmes.

**Tips** New Scottish writing is always of interest, but there is no official script reading policy in place.

## Royal National Theatre
**South Bank, London, SE1 9PX**
- 020 7452 3333
- 020 7452 3344
- info@nationaltheatre.org.uk
- www.nationaltheatre.org.uk

**Artistic/Editorial Director** Nicholas Hytner
**Contact** Literary Manager, Jack Bradley
**Established** 1963

**Insider Info** The National Theatre's complex houses three theatres and has up to eight productions in repertory at any one time. As well as productions, the theatre offers other events and services, including short early evening performances, children's and educational work, exhibitions, live music and outdoor events.

**Submission Guidelines** The theatre will accept postal submissions only of entire scripts. Submissions accompanied by SAE will be returned.

**Tips** Although the National Theatre is dedicated to producing new writing, the pieces are usually directly commissioned. They do state however, that unsolicited scripts will get read and responded to individually, although there may a be a delay due to the sheer volume of scripts received.

## Royal Shakespeare Company
**Waterside, Stratford upon Avon, CV37 6BB**
- 01789 403444
- www.rsc.org.uk

**Artistic/Editorial Director** Michael Boyd
**Insider Info** The Royal Shakespeare Company is a national theatre company who perform both at home in Stratford upon Avon and in venues throughout the UK. Productions include the works of Shakespeare, other classic English plays, and new writing.

**Tips** The vast majority of productions are Shakespeare plays and although the RSC do produce some new plays, these are usually directly commissioned by well known writers.

## Salisbury Playhouse
**Malthouse Lane, Salisbury, Wiltshire, SP2 7RA**
- 01722 320117
- 01722 421991

○ info@salisburyplayhouse.com
○ www.salisburyplayhouse.com
**Artistic/Editorial Director** Joanna Read
**Insider Info** Salisbury Playhouse is a producing theatre for audiences in Salisbury, Wiltshire, Hampshire and Dorset. The company aims for a mixture of local, national and international theatre and stages both new and classic productions.
**Tips** Co-productions are an emerging trend in the theatre's output, including collaborations with the Young Vic and the Chester Gateway. Plays staged at the Playhouse need to appeal to a largely semi-rural audience.

## SgriptCymru
**Chapter, Market Road, Canton, Cardiff, CF5 1QE**
○ 029 2023 6650
○ 029 2023 6651
○ sgriptcymru@sgriptcymru.com
○ www.sgriptcymru.com
**Artistic/Editorial Director** Simon Harris
**Contact** Literary Manager, Arwel Gruffydd
**Established** 2000
**Insider Info** SgriptCymru is Wales' national company for contemporary theatre, dedicated to developing new writing. Plays are produced in both Welsh and English.
**Submission Guidelines** Submit complete manuscript. All pages should be single sided, typed, loosely bound and accompanied by SAE. No email submissions will be accepted. Submissions accompanied by SAE will be returned. No film, television or radio scripts will be accepted.
**Tips** Writers must either be Welsh or living in Wales. Although Welsh themes are important, scripts do not have to reflect these directly and the writer's Welsh connection is more important than the story's. Plays should be broadly placed in the contemporary drama genre.

## Shared Experience
**The Soho Laundry, 9 Dufour's Place, London, W1F 7SJ**
○ 020 7434 9248
○ 020 7287 8763
○ admin@sharedexperience.org.uk
○ www.sharedexperience.org.uk
**Artistic/Editorial Director** Nancy Meckler and Polly Teale
**Established** 1975
**Insider Info** Shared experience is a touring company whose aim is to explore the physical and emotional relationship between the actor and the audience.
**Submission Guidelines** No unsolicited manuscripts will be accepted. Recent productions have included Diane Samuels' *Kindertransport*.
**Tips** Shared Experience are not a new writing company and although they produce some new adaptions, these are always directly commissioned.

## Sherman Theatre Company
**Senghennydd Road, Cardiff, CF24 4YE**
○ 029 2064 6901
○ 029 2064 6902
○ admin@shermantheatre.demon.co.uk
○ www.shermantheatre.co.uk
**Artistic/Editorial Director** Phil Clark
**Contact** Dinos Aristidou
**Insider Info** The Sherman Theatre Company houses a producing and receiving theatre, a touring company, and a well developed youth theatre. Performances are primarily aimed at young audiences. Plays are performed at the Sherman theatre and toured nationally and internationally.
**Tips** Script Slam is a monthly event at which four new young writers can present a 15 minute piece of their scripts and the audience vote for the piece they want to see developed. Submit 10–20 pages of script (either a full play or a sample) for up to eight actors, to Dinos Aristidou. Script Slam leaflets are also available from the theatre.

## Show of Strength
**74 Chessel Street, Bedminster, Bristol, BS3 3DN**
○ 0117 902 0235
○ 0117 902 0196
○ info@showofstrength.org.uk
○ www.showofstrength.org.uk
**Artistic/Editorial Director** Sheila Hannon
**Established** 1986
**Insider Info** Show of Strength is a company that focuses on contemporary drama in unusual spaces, from conventional theatres to railway stations. The company is mainly based in the South West England.
**Tips** Recent productions have included short pieces on railway platforms at commuter times, demonstrating the innovative nature of the company. Staffing and time issues mean there may be a long delay in reading any unsolicited scripts.

## Soho Theatre

**21 Dean Street, London, W1D 3NE**

- 020 7287 5060
- 020 7287 5061
- writers@sohotheatre.com
- www.sohotheatre.com

**Artistic/Editorial Director** Lisa Goldman
**Contact** Literary Assistant, Rachel Taylor
**Established** 1969

**Insider Info** Soho Theatre is a London producing theatre whose productions include drama, comedy and cabaret, appealing to a wide ranging audience. The theatre has a well developed new writing programme. Aims to report back to writers within three months.

**Submission Guidelines** Submit complete manuscript (including a brief covering letter and an SAE). No email submissions will be accepted. Submissions accompanied by SAE will be returned. No excerpts, incomplete scripts, pieces for radio, TV or film, novels, or poetry that is not specifically for performance will be considered.

**Tips** As well as the script reading service, the theatre's new writing programme offers writing attachments, competitions, awards and seed commissions, all open to new playwrights. Visit the website for full details.

## Solent People's Theatre

**Bedhampton Arts Centre, Bedhampton Road, Havant, PO9 3ET**

- 023 9242 3399
- 023 9242 3401
- James@solentpeoplestheatre.com
- www.solentpeoplestheatre.com

**Established** 1976

**Insider Info** Solent People's Company is a touring company that aims not only to entertain audiences, but to forge communities through cultural participation.

**Submission Guidelines** An example of the theatre's work is the current three year project, 'Critical Engagement' that aims to encourage participation in democracy, especially by young people. Performances include a short piece of drama followed by the use of electronic voting systems and democratic discussion.

**Tips** Bear in mind the theatre's aim to engage people and communities in wider social issues that directly affect them.

## Sphinx Theatre Company

**25 Short Street, London, SE1 8LJ**

- 020 7401 9993
- 020 7401 9995
- info@sphinxtheatre.co.uk, firstnamelastname@sphinxtheatre.co.uk
- www.sphinxtheatre.co.uk

**Artistic/Editorial Director** Sue Parrish
**Established** 1973

**Insider Info** The Sphinx Theatre Company is touring company focused on women's experiences. Writers and directors are predominantly women, although men are involved as actors and other collaborators. The company usually tours small or mid-sized venues throughout the UK and sometimes internationally.

**Submission Guidelines** Submit complete manuscript (hard copies only, including SAE) addressed to the Artistic Director. Submission accompanied by SAE will be returned.

**Tips** Writers are advised to contact the Artistic Director before submitting a script, to establish if there is any initial interest. Productions are predominantly written by women, but men are invited to submit scripts for the Brave New Roles scriptwriting award, details of which will appear on the website.

## Steven Joseph Theatre

**Westborough, Scarborough, YO11 1JW**

- 01723 370540
- 01723 360506
- enquiries@sjt.uk.com
- www.sjt.uk.com

**Artistic/Editorial Director** Alan Ayckbourn
**Established** 1955

**Insider Info** The Steven Joseph Theatre as it exists now, was opened in 1996. It houses The Round, a 404 seat auditorium, and The McCarthy, a 165 seat end stage. Most resources are put into first productions of new plays. Produces appropriately ten plays per year.

**Submission Guidelines** Many of the plays produced are the work of Alan Ayckbourn, however a new writing programme does exist to ensure other writers are given opportunities.

**Tips** No unsolicited submissions will be accepted until May 2007 at the earliest. Check the website for further details after this date. In usual circumstances, scripts will be read and assessed by a team of readers. It is rare for an unsolicited script to be produced but it can be a way of starting a relationship with the theatre.

## Tabard Theatre

**2 Bath Road, London, W4 1LW**
- 020 8995 6035
- info@tabardtheatre.co.uk
- www.tabardtheatre.co.uk

**Established** 1985

**Insider Info** Located above a pub, the theatre has traditionally been known for new writing, but now has a broader programme of entertainment and theatre.

**Tips** New writing is less of a focus for the theatre now, as it becomes a more prominent receiving venue.

## TEG Productions

**11–15 Betterton Streer, London, WC2H 9BP**
- 020 7379 1066
- info@tegproductions.com
- www.jeremymeadow.com

**Artistic/Editorial Director** Jeremy Meadow

**Established** 1997

**Insider Info** TEG productions is a producer of large scale musicals and straight theatre.

**Submission Guidelines** Recent productions include Alan Plater's *Blonde Bombshells of 1944* at the Hampstead Theatre and Bolton Octagon.

**Tips** TEG Productions only produces plays with huge commercial potential, and is not likely to commission unknown writers.

## Theatre Absolute

**57–61 Corporation Street, Coventry, CV1 1GQ**
- 024 7625 7380
- 024 7655 0680
- firstname@theatreabsolute.co.uk
- www.theatreabsolute.co.uk

**Artistic/Editorial Director** Chris O'Connell

**Established** 1992

**Insider Info** Theatre Absolute is a touring company dedicated to developing and producing new writing. Performance venues tend to be small and mid-sized theatres and arts centres across the UK.

**Submission Guidelines** Submit complete manuscript.

**Tips** Plays are invited for submission to The Writing House, a scheme whereby plays are given real, in-depth development over a long period, with no time or commissioning pressures. An example of a play developed in this way is Chris O'Connell's *Street Trilogy*.

## Theatre Centre

**Shoreditch Town Hall, 380 Old Street, London, EC1V 9LT**
- 020 7729 3066
- 020 7739 9741
- admin@theatre-centre.co.uk
- www.theatre-centre.co.uk

**Artistic/Editorial Director** Rosamunde Hutt

**Established** 1953

**Insider Info** Theatre Centre is a touring company that aims to produce exciting new theatre for young people. The company produces approximately four new productions per year. Performance sites include schools, theatres and other arts venues that are accessible for young people.

**Submission Guidelines** An example of a recent production is Sarah Woods' *Walking on Water*, a piece about exclusion using playground games, music and strong visuals to convey a message.

**Tips** The company has a strong new writing policy. As part of its equal opportunities philosophy, new writing from women, Black, Asian, gay, disabled and young people is welcomed. The theatre current commissions plays by firstly approaching writers of whom they have been made aware.

## Theatre of Comedy Company

**210 Shaftesbury Avenue, London, WC2H 8DP**
- 020 7379 3345
- 020 7836 8181

**Insider Info** The Theatre of Comedy Company produces new comedy and adapts established and classic works.

**Tips** The company reviews scripts for film and TV as well as theatre. All submissions must be comedic in the broadest sense.

## The Theatre Royal and Drum Theatre

**Royal Parade, Plymouth, PL1 2TR**
- 01752 230347
- 01752 230347
- info@theatreroyal.com
- www.theatreroyal.com

**Artistic/Editorial Director** Simon Stokes

**Insider Info** A producing and receiving theatre with two auditoriums. The main theatre seats between 787 and 1,315 with its adjustable seating and the Drum seats 200. Presents a mixture of musical theatre and drama by local, national and international companies.

**Submission Guidelines** No unsolicited manuscripts will be accepted.

**Tips** Although the theatre does produce original material, this is normally commissioned via known agents or scriptwriters' societies.

## Theatre Royal Stratford East
**Gerry Raffles Square, London, E15 1BN**
- 020 8279 1104
- 020 8534 8381
- theatreroyal@stratfordeast.com, writers@stratfordeast.com
- www.stratfordeast.com

**Artistic/Editorial Director** Kerry Michael
**Contact** New Writing Project Manager, Sita Ramamurthy
**Established** 1884
**Insider Info** Located in a very culturally mixed community, the theatre is committed to developing new writing that reflects and appeals to a diverse audience.
**Submission Guidelines** No unsolicited manuscripts will be accepted (including a synopsis, ten page sample and a short writer's biography).
**Tips** Be very aware of the local community and potential audience, as the area contains very deprived communities and is extremely culturally diverse. Plays that bring out these themes through drama are welcomed, although quality pieces on a variety of other themes will also be considered. Check the website for up to date details of courses and workshops that a regularly offered.

## Theatre Royal Windsor
**Windsor, SL4 1PS**
- 01753 863444
- 01753 831673
- info@theatreroyalwindsor.co.uk
- www.theatreroyalwindsor.co.uk

**Artistic/Editorial Director** Bill Kenwright
**Established** 1793
**Insider Info** The Theatre Roual Windsor is a producing theatre, whose productions include classics, drama, comedy, pantomime and new work.
**Tips** The theatre has produced several plays that have been transferred to the West End. Productions tend to be reasonably commercial and comedies, thrillers and dramas are most popular.

## Theatre Workshop
**34 Hamilton Place, Edinburgh, EH3 5AX**
- 0131 225 7942
- 0131 220 0112
- firstinitiallastname@twe.org.uk
- www.theatre-workshop.com

**Artistic/Editorial Director** Robert Rae
**Established** 1965
**Insider Info** Theatre Workshop is a producing theatre that includes disabled actors in its main productions, paying special attention to access and inclusion issues. The theatre itself seats 155.
**Tips** Theatre Workshop regularly commissions new writing. As the theatre is located in Scotland, Scottish writers or pieces relevant to modern Scottish life are popular. Scripts should take into account that actors and others involved may be disabled, as well as able bodied. The theatre enjoys working with organisations of minority groups.

## The Torch Theatre
**St. Peter's Road, Milford Haven, Pembrokeshire, SA73 2BU**
- 01646 694192
- 01646 698919
- info@torchtheatre.co.uk
- www.torchtheatre.co.uk

**Artistic/Editorial Director** Peter Doran
**Established** 1977
**Insider Info** The Torch Theatre produces pieces for in-house performances and touring. Recent productions include the farce piece *Noises Off.*
**Tips** The Torch Theatre is a registered charity and is unlikely to have the funding to produce work from new writers. However, this does not mean that scripts will not be read, time permitting.

## Traverse Theatre
**Cambridge Street, Edinburgh, EH1 2ED**
- 0131 228 3223
- firstname.lastname@traversetheatre.co.uk
- www.traversetheatre.co.uk

**Artistic/Editorial Director** Philip Howard
**Contact** Literary Assistant, Louise Stephens
**Established** 1963
**Insider Info** Scotland's theatre of new writing, with two performance spaces; a 100 seater and a 250 seater. Produces six plays per year. Aims to respond to manuscript submissions within six months. Only retains rights on play texts at the point at which they are produced, unless they are commissioned scripts.
**Submission Guidelines** Submit complete manuscript. Submissions accompanied by SAE will be returned. Focuses on producing contemporary Scottish plays, plays by writers based in Scotland and plays with a strong and clear connection to Scottish culture.

**Tips** Produces some international work but rarely from unsolicited sources.

## Trestle Theatre Company
**Trestle Arts Base, Russet Drive, St. Albans, AL4 0JQ**
- 01727 850950
- 01727 855558
- admin@trestle.org.uk, firstname@trestle.org.uk
- www.trestle.org.uk

**Artistic/Editorial Director** Emily Gray
**Established** 1981
**Insider Info** A touring company producing storytelling, mask-based theatre from its Hertfordshire base. Offers a range of educational and community drama activities. Produces two to three plays per year. Performances take place at a variety of venues including small and medium sized theatres and arts centres across the UK.
**Submission Guidelines** A recent production was *Little India*, a reworking of *Shakuntala*, involving the physicalities of martial arts, rhythmic patterns and hand gestures. Unsolicited scripts are unlikely to be accepted.

## Tricycle Theatre
**269 Kilburn High Road, London, NW6 7JR**
- 020 7372 6611
- 020 7328 0795
- info@tricycle.co.uk
- www.tricycle.co.uk

**Artistic/Editorial Director** Nicholas Kent
**Established** 1980
**Insider Info** A theatre, cinema and exhibition centre within a culturally diverse community.
**Submission Guidelines** Submissions accompanied by SAE will be returned.
**Tips** The local community includes such diverse cultural groups as Irish, Afro-Caribbean, Jewish and Asian, and the choice of writers and writing tends to reflect this. A fee may be charged for unsolicited scripts. Please phone or email for details.

## Tron Theatre Company
**63 Trongate, Glasgow, G1 5HB**
- 0141 552 3748
- 0141 552 6657
- firstname.lastname@tron.co.uk
- www.tron.co.uk

**Artistic/Editorial Director** Gregory Thompson
**Established** 1981

**Insider Info** A producing and receiving theatre committed to producing new work from Scottish writers, as well as hosting drama, music and comedy events. Although the theatre itself houses most of the home grown productions, some pieces are toured internationally.
**Tips** No unsolicited manuscripts.

## Unicorn Theatre
**147 Tooley Street, More London, London, SE1 2HZ**
- 020 7645 0500
- 020 7645 0550
- stagedoor@unicorntheatre.com
- www.unicorntheatre.com

**Artistic/Editorial Director** Tony Graham
**Contact** Assistant to the Artistic Team, Rhona Foulis
**Established** 1947
**Insider Info** Professional theatre, producing and programming work for a young and family audience. Produces four plays per year, which are performed at the Unicorn Theatre, London. Aims to respond to manuscript submissions within one month.
**Submission Guidelines** Please email artistic@unicorntheatre.com for information on the way in which we work with writers, Submissions accompanied by SAE will be returned. Produces theatre for children/family audiences, with a maximum cast of eight.

## Warehouse Theatre
**Dingwall Road, Croydon, CR0 2NF**
- 020 8681 1257
- info@warehousetheatre.co.uk, firstname@warehousetheatre.co.uk
- www.warehousetheatre.co.uk

**Artistic/Editorial Director** Ted Craig
**Contact** Festival Administrator, Rose Marie Vernon
**Established** 1977
**Insider Info** A producing theatre focused on new writing. The theatre itself seats around 100. Also runs the annual International Playwriting Festival.
**Submission Guidelines** Read the guidelines on the website for information on how to submit plays for the International Playwriting Festival and to download an application form. Postal submissions only.
**Tips** The best way to submit a script is via the festival (see above). Entries must not have been published or performed before (amateur productions notwithstanding), but may be translations. Full length plays only, on any topic. Firstly the judges select the shortlist of ten plays, then four of these

plays are selected to be performed during the festival itself. Full details are published on the website, or contact rose@warehousetheatre.co.uk

## Watford Palace Theatre
**Clarendon Road, Watford, WD17 1JZ**
- 01923 235455
- 01923 819664
- enquiries@watfordpalacetheatre.co.uk
- www.watfordtheatre.co.uk

**Artistic/Editorial Director** Brigid Larmour
**Established** 1908
**Insider Info** A regional producing theatre presenting modern works, comedy, adaptations, classics, and pantomimes. Also acts as a receiving theatre to touring productions.
**Submission Guidelines** Although unsolicited scripts will be read, writers are advised to send a synopsis in the first instance. Submissions accompanied by SAE will be returned.
**Tips** The theatre runs a playwright's group, WPT Playwrights, designed to provide script development and support. Group plays are sometimes performed at the theatre. Contact Katy Silverton at the theatre for more information. There is a separate group for young playwrights.

## West Yorkshire Playhouse
**Playhouse Square, Leeds, LS2 7UP**
- 0113 213 7800
- 0113 213 7250
- info@wyp.org.uk, firstname.lastname@wyp.org.uk
- www.yph.org.uk

**Artistic/Editorial Director** Ian Brown
**Contact** Literary Manager, Alex Chisholm
**Established** 1990
**Insider Info** A community producing theatre comprising of 750 seat Quarry Theatre, and the Courtyard Theatre, which seats 350. Has a strong new writing emphasis.
**Submission Guidelines** Only send the first ten pages in the first instance – promising scripts will be requested in full. Address to Alex Chisholm. Submissions accompanied by SAE will be returned. Productions include classic British and international drama, contemporary work, and new plays with particular focus on writers from the North of England.
**Tips** As well as the script reading service, the Playhouse offer a range of schemes designed to foster new writing, including performances of developing plays with after show discussions,

workshops and the chance to apply for script development grants.

## Whirligig Theatre
**14 Belvedere Drive, Wimbledon, London, SW19 7BY**
- 020 8947 1732
- 020 8947 1732
- whirligig-theatre@virgin.net
- www.davidwood.org.uk

**Artistic/Editorial Director** David Wood
**Insider Info** Occasionally produces theatre for young children, both from new writing and adaptions of existing plays and children's books. Performance venues range from primary schools to theatres.
**Tips** David Wood's back catalogue of plays is available on his website. He also answers script queries from new writers through a forum on the site.

## White Bear Theatre Club
**138 Kennington Park Road, London, SE11 4DJ**
- 020 7793 9193
- 020 7793 9193
- www.whitebeartheatre.co.uk

**Artistic/Editorial Director** Mike Kingsbury
**Insider Info** A company producing new writing and reviving classic plays. Recently had productions transferred to the West End.
**Tips** Scripts should fit with the contemporary, risk-taking ethos of the company. View the recent productions on the website, as well as the website of their associated company, Box of Tricks, at www.boxoftrickstheatre.co.uk

## York Theatre Royal
**St. Leonard's Place, York, YO1 7HD**
- 01904 658162
- 01904 550164
- www.yorktheatreroyal.co.uk

**Artistic/Editorial Director** Damien Cruden
**Established** 1744
**Insider Info** A primarily receiving theatre, presenting drama and musical theatre, including West End shows.
**Tips** The theatre runs youth projects and community education projects. There is no official new writing scheme.

## The Young Vic
**66 The Cut, London, SE1 8LZ**

- 020 7922 2800
- 200 7922 2802
- info@youngvic.org, firstnamelastname@youngvic.org
- www.youngvic.org

**Artistic/Editorial Director** David Lan
**Established** 1970
**Insider Info** A leading theatre for young talent, particularly directors. These productions are presented alongside those by more established artists. Recent productions include Thomas Otway's *The Soldier's Fortune* and Debbie Tucker's *Generations*.
**Tips** There are extensive opportunities for young people and adults to become involved with the theatre in many capacities. Visit the website for details of schemes such as work experience and training projects. The productions tend to be fairly high profile, so unsolicited scripts are unlikely to be commissioned.

## Y Touring Theatre Company
**One KX, 120 Cromer Street, London, WC1H 8BS**

- 020 7520 3090
- 020 7520 3099
- info@ytouring.org.uk, firstinitial.lastname@ytouring.org.uk
- www.ytouring.org.uk

**Artistic/Editorial Director** Nigel Townsend
**Contact** General Manager, Michael White
**Established** 1989
**Insider Info** The touring theatre arm of the YMCA, which aims to explore issues that are pertinent for young people in contemporary society. Many productions deal with difficult subjects. Recently, the company has moved into performances for adults.
**Submission Guidelines** Submit complete manuscript. Include a CV and covering letter. Email or postal submissions accepted.
**Tips** The company advise that responses to scripts may be subject to lengthy delays due to time and staffing constraints. It is also recommended that writers join the mailing list, so they can be kept up to date with productions in their area.

## Yvonne Arnaud Theatre
**Millbrook, Guildford, Surrey, GU1 3UX**

- 01483 440077
- 01483 564071
- yat@yvonne-arnaud.co.uk
- www.yvonne-arnaud.co.uk

**Artistic/Editorial Director** James Barber
**Established** 1965
**Insider Info** A theatre complex with a main stage hosting pantomimes, touring productions and plays commissioned in-house, and the smaller Mill Studio showcasing smaller, experimental productions and dance shows.
**Tips** The website details the many community projects and courses that those interested in the theatre may become involved in, including production groups, outreach projects and classes.

Literary agencies are usually specific about how you should contact them and what they accept as submissions. Many do not accept contact by email. Read the article by Mandy Little of Watson, Little in the front section of this book to discover more about the way agents work. Editorial consultancies covers a wide range of companies and individuals who help writers with editing, proofing, project management and so forth. Book packagers are listed separately in the Publishers section of the book.

## UK & IRISH LITERARY AGENTS

### A & B Personal Management Ltd
**Suite 330 Linen Hall, 162–168 Regent Street, London, W1B 5TD**
- 020 7434 4262
- 020 7038 3699
- billellis@aandb.co.uk

**Contact** R. W. Ellis
**Established** 1982
**Insider Info** Currently handles non-fiction books, novels, TV scripts, movie scripts, stage plays, episodic dramas and sitcoms. Manuscripts returned with SAE. Commission rates of 12.5 per cent for domestic sales, 15 per cent for foreign sales, 12.5 per cent for film sales. Reading fee charged for full length book manuscripts.
**Tips** Enquire about fees before submitting manuscript. No unsolicited manuscripts considered.

### Abner Stein
**10 Roland Gardens, London, SW7 3PH**
- 020 7373 0456
- 020 7370 6316

**Contact** Abner Stein
**Established** 1971
**Insider Info** Not currently seeking new clients. Handles non-fiction books and novels. Submissions by query letter first. Commission rates of ten per cent for domestic sales, 20 per cent for foreign sales.
**Tips** Represents mainly US authors and agents.

### The Agency (London) Ltd
**24 Pottery Lane, London, W11 4LZ**
- 020 7727 1346
- 020 7727 9037
- info@the agency .co.uk
- www.theagency.co.uk

**Contact** Directors, Hilary Delamere & Katie Haines (Children's authors/illustrators, Publishing/media

rights); Anna Cameron & Stephanie Hul (Legal & Business Affairs); Monica Epega (Accounts); Natalicio Blackman (Royalty Management); Stephen Durbridge, Leah Schmidt, Julia Kreitman, Bathan Evans and Norman North (Executives)
**Established** 1995
**Insider Info** Currently handles writers and authors for TV, film, theatre and radio as well as directors, producers and composers. Seeking both new and established writers in the areas of TV scripts, film scripts, stage plays, radio scripts and fiction. Proposals returned if accompanied by SAE. Obtains new clients through queries and submissions. Commission rates of ten per cent for domestic sales with foreign sale commission by arrangement. Do not charge a reading fee.
**Fiction** Will consider children's fiction.
**Scripts** Will consider film, TV, radio and theatre scripts.
**Submission Guidelines** Send a query letter with SAE.
**Recent Sale(s)** *Bonkers*, Sally Wainwright (Lime Pictures); *Instinct*, Lizzie Mickery (Tightrope); *Lilies*, Heidi Thomas (World Productions); *Wild at Heart*, Ashley Pharoah (Company TV)
**Client(s)** Steve Barlow, Janet Burchett, Alan Durant, Amanda Swift, Fiona Dunbar, Michael Bond, Heather Dyer, Tom Macrae, Andrew Norris, Malorie Blackman, Neil Arksey.
**Tips** Adult fiction is accepted from existing clients only. Will not accept unsolicited manuscripts.

### Alan Brodie Representation Ltd
**6th Floor Fairgate House, 78 New Oxford Street, London, WC1A 1HB**
- 020 7079 7990
- 020 7079 7999
- info@alanbrodie.com
- www.alanbrodie.com

AGENCIES & CONSULTANCIES

LISTINGS

**Contact** Managing Director (and Agent), Alan Brodie; Director (and Agent), Sarah McNair; Director, Alison Lee (Finance); Agent, Lisa Foster (New Writing); PA to Alan Brodie, Harriet Pennington Legh (Amateur Licensing)

**Established** 1989

**Insider Info** Specialises in TV, film, stage plays & radio. Seeking both new and established writers for TV scripts, movie scripts, stage plays and radio scripts. Queries responded to within three months. Manuscripts returned only if accompanied by SAE. No reading fee charged. Clients usually obtained through recommendation. Commission rates of ten per cent for domestic sales, 15 per cent for foreign sales.

**Scripts** Will consider TV, film, stage play and radio scripts.

**Submission Guidelines** Accepts query letter with SAE and biography.

* No book proposals considered.

**Recent Sale(s)** *Leaves,* Lucy Caldwell; *King of Hearts,* Alistair Beaton; *Kinky Boots,* Tim Firth; *The Black Watch,* Gregory Burke.

**Clients** Paul Mendelson, Penny Black, Roger Crane, John Godber, Tom McGrath, Gordon Steel, Malcolm McGee, C. P.Taylor, Sharon Foster, Nell Dunn, Alistair McGowan, Moby Pomerance, James Stock, Mark Tuohy, Morna Regan, Bill Morrison, Michael Wilcox, Abi Zakarian, Thornton Wilder, Corin Redgrave, Bertolt Brecht.

**Tips** Initial contact must include a recommendation from an industry professional. No unsolicited manuscripts accepted.

## Alexandra Nye

'Craigower', 6 Kinnoull Avenue, Dunblane, Perthshire, FK15 9JG

01786 825114

**Contact** Director, Alexandra Nye

**Established** 1991

**Insider Info** Actively seeking clients. Currently handles fiction and non-fiction books and novels. Submissions accompanied by SAE will be returned. Clients usually obtained through queries/submissions. Commission rates of ten per cent for domestic sales, 20 per cent for foreign sales. Reading fee will be charged for a detailed report on manuscripts.

**Fiction** Will consider general and literary fiction.

**Non-fiction** Will consider biography/autobiography and history.

**Submission Guidelines** Accepts query with SAE and synopsis.

*No telephone enquiries. Poetry or plays not considered.

**Client(s)** Dr. Tom Gallagher, Harry Mehta.

**Tips** The agency is known for its interest in Scottish history and literary fiction.

## A. M. Heath

6 Warwick Court, London, WC1R 5DJ

020 7242 2811

020 7242 2711

www.amheath.com

**Contact** Bill Hamilton, (Literary and commercial fiction and non-fiction); Sara Fisher (Translation rights, client representation); Sarah Molloy (Children's writers); Victoria Hobbs (Literary and commercial fiction and non-fiction); Euan Thorneycroft (Literary and commercial fiction and non-fiction)

**Established** 1919

**Insider Info** Actively seeking clients. Currently handles non-fiction books, juvenile books and novels. Aims to respond within four months. Proposals returned if accompanied by SAE. Commission rates of 15 per cent for domestic sales, 20 per cent for foreign sales, 15 per cent for film sales. No reading fee charged.

**Fiction** Will consider literary, commercial and children's fiction

**Non-fiction** Will consider biography/autobiography, history.

**Submission Guidelines** Send query letter with SAE, synopsis and three sample chapters. Submission should be double spaced on single-sided A4 paper.

**Client(s)** Christopher Andrew, Rosemary Ashton and William Horwood.

**Tips** No young children's fiction, scripts or poetry accepted. No manuscripts or queries accepted by email.

## The Ampersand Agency

Ryman's Cottages, Little Tew, Chipping Norton, Oxfordshire, OX7 4JJ

01608 683677/683898

01608 683449

peter@theampersandagency.co.uk

www.theampersandagency.co.uk

**Contact** Peter Buckman (All types of submissions); Anne-Marie Doulton (Literary fiction, Women's fiction); Peter Janson-Smith (Crime, Historical fiction)

**Established** 2003

**Insider Info** Seeking both new and established writers. Considers non-fiction books, juvenile books, novels, fiction and novellas. Represents more than

35 clients, 85 per cent of whom are new or previously unpublished writers. Will consider simultaneous submissions. Aims to respond to queries within two weeks and manuscripts within four weeks. Unsuccessful proposals will be returned with SAE. The Ampersand Agency obtains new clients through recommendations from others and through queries and submissions. Will also sometimes approach writers with ideas. Has sold 14 book projects in the past year. Commission rates of 10–15 per cent for domestic sales, 20 per cent for foreign sales and 15 per cent for film sales. Offers a written contract that may be terminated at any time. Does not charge a reading fee or offer a criticism service.

 * The agency specialises in good story-telling, whether in fiction or non-fiction, and is made distinct by its candour and rapid responses. Before becoming an agent, Peter Buckman was a publisher and then a full-time writer, Anne-Marie Doulton was an editor and a literary scout and Peter Janson-Smith ran his own agency.

**Non-fiction** Will consider Biography/autobiography, Cooking/food/nutrition, Education, History, How-to, Humour, Juvenile, Language/literature/criticism, Memoirs, Music/dance/theatre/film, Popular culture, True crime/investigative and Women's issues/women's non-fiction.

**Fiction** Will consider Action/adventure, Confessional, Detective/police/crime, Experimental, Family saga, Historical, Humour/satire, Juvenile, Literary, Mainstream, Mystery, Romance, Thriller/espionage, Women's/chick lit and Young adult fiction.

**Scripts** Only handles scripts from existing book author clients.

**Submission Guidelines** Send query letter with outline, one or two sample chapters and author biography. Also accept queries via email. Are actively seeking good stories, commercial and literary fiction and non-fiction, for adults and young people. Does not want poetry, science fiction, fantasy or political satires set in the future.

**Recent Sale(s)** *The Night Climbers,* Ivo Stourton (Doubleday); *Sacrifice,* S J Bolton (Bantam); *Olaf the Viking,* Martin Smith (Oxford); *The Adversary,* Michael Walters (Quercus)

**Client(s)** Druin Burch, Anna Crosbie, Andrew Cullen, Vanessa Curtis, Will Davis, Catherine Deveney, Cora Harrison, Georgette Heyer, Michael Hutchinson, Derek Keilty, Beryl Kingston, Miriam Morrison, Philip Purser, Paul Smith, Vikas Swarup, Nick Van Bloss, Helen Wilkinson

## Andrew Lownie Literary Agency Ltd
**36 Great Smith St, London, SW1P 3BU**
- 020 7222 7574
- 020 7222 7576
- lownie@globalnet.co.uk
- www.andrewlownie.co.uk

**Contact** Managing Director, Andrew Lownie (history and biography)

**Established** 1988

**Insider Info** Actively seeking clients. Currently handles non-fiction books. Approximately 150 clients of which 20 per cent are new or unpublished writers. Simultaneous submissions accepted. Aims to respond to queries within two days and proposals within 14 days. Submissions accompanied by an SAE will be returned. Clients usually acquired through recommendation or queries/submissions. 32 books sold in the last year. Commission rates of 15 per cent for domestic sales, 15 per cent for foreign sales and 15 per cent for film sales. Written contract offered.

 * The agency specialises in non-fiction, in particular history and biography. All clients are handled by Andrew Lownie. Prior to becoming an agent, Andrew Lownie was a journalist, bookseller, publisher, writer and law student.

**Non-fiction** Will consider biography/autobiography, child guidance/parenting, current affairs, history, humour, memoirs, military/war, true crime/investigative.

**Submission Guidelines** Send proposal with SAE, synopsis, one sample chapter and biography.

**Recent Sale(s)** *Damaged,* Cathy Glass (Harper Collins); three book thriller deal, Duncan Falconer (Little, Brown); *Derek,* Adam Ockelford (Hutchinson); *The Last Day,* Nicholas Best (Orion)

**Client(s)** Richard Aldrich, Juliet Barker, Joyce Cary Estate, Roger Crowley, Tom Devine, Patrick Dillon, Peter Forbes, Laurence Gardner, Timothy Good, David Hasselhoff, Lawrence James, Damien Lewis, Julian Maclaren-Ross Estate, Peter Padfield, Tom Pocock, David Roberts, Norman Rose, Michael Schuster, David Stafford, Daniel Tammet, Peter Thompson, Christopher Warwick, Adrian Weale, Christian Wolmar, Simon Young, Charlotte Zeepvat.

**Tips** Seeking published writers, journalists, young academics and celebrities. No fiction considered.

## Andrew Mann Ltd
**1 Old Compton Street, London, W1D 5JA**
- 020 7734 4751
- 020 7287 9264
- manscript@onetel.com

**Contact** Anne Dewe; Tina Betts; Sacha Elliot

**Established** 1975

**Insider Info** Actively seeking clients. Considers non-fiction books, juvenile books, novels, TV scripts, movie scripts and stage plays. Submissions accompanied by an SAE will be returned. Clients usually acquired through queries/submissions. Commission rates of 15 per cent for domestic sales, 20 per cent for foreign sales. No reading fees charged.

**Non-fiction** Will consider general non-fiction.

**Fiction** Will consider children's and adult fiction.

**Scripts** Will consider scripts for film, TV and radio plays.

**Submission Guidelines** Send submissions with SAE, synopsis and three sample chapters. Queries accepted by email. No poetry considered.

**Tips** Manuscripts sent by email will not be accepted, send a synopsis only. Unsolicited manuscripts will only be accepted with an accompanying letter.

## Andrew Nurnberg Associates Ltd
**Clerkenwell House, 45–47 Clerkenwell Green, London, EC1R 0QX**
- 020 7417 8800
- 020 7417 8812
- all@nurnberg.co.uk

**Contact** Director, Andrew Nurnberg

**Established** 1970s

**Insider Info** Seeking both new and established writers. Considers non-fiction books and novels. Clients usually acquired through queries/submissions. Commission rates of 15 per cent for domestic sales and 20 per cent for foreign sales.

**Non-fiction** Will consider general non-fiction.

**Fiction** Will consider novels.

**Tips** Represents established authors and agents. Specialises in foreign rights.

## Annette Green Authors' Agency
**1 East Cliff Road, Tunbridge Wells, Kent, TN4 9AD**
- 01892 514275
- 01892 518124
- annettegreen@aol.com
- www.annettegreenagency.co.uk

**Contact** Annette Green, David Smith

**Established** 1998

**Insider Info** Actively seeking clients. Considers non-fiction books, juvenile books and novels. Simultaneous submissions accepted. Aims to respond to queries/proposals within four weeks. Submissions accompanied by SAE will be returned. Clients usually acquired through queries/

submissions. Commission rates of 15 per cent for domestic sales and 20 per cent for foreign sales. No reading fee charged.

\* Annette Green established her own literary agency in 1998 after working at A.M. Heath & Co. Ltd. for several years. David Smith joined as a partner in 2001.

**Non-fiction** Will consider biography/autobiography, current affairs, history, juvenile, music, dance, theatre, film, popular culture and science/technology.

**Fiction** Will consider novels.

**Submission Guidelines** Send query letter with SAE, synopsis and 5–10,000 words of the opening chapters. No dramatic scripts, poetry, science fiction or fantasy considered.

**Recent Sale(s)** *Rage*, Simon Conway; *All American Girl*, Meg Cabot; *Mother's Day*, Kirsty Scott; *The Dust Diaries*, Owen Sheers

**Client(s)** Fiona Gibson, Justin Hill, J.B.Aspinall, Ian Marchant, Anvar Khan, Bernadette Strachan

**Tips** Specialises in discovering new exciting talent.

## Anthony Sheil in association with Gillon Aitken Associates
**18–21 Cavaye Place, London, SW10 9PT**
- 020 7373 8672
- 020 7373 6002
- anthony@gillonaitken.co.uk
- www.gillonaitkenassociates.co.uk

**Contact** Anthony Sheil

**Established** 1998

**Insider Info** Actively seeking clients. Considers non-fiction books and novels. Aims to respond to queries/proposals within eight weeks. Submissions accompanied by SAE will be returned. Clients usually acquired through queries/submissions. Commission rates of ten per cent for domestic sales and 20 per cent for foreign sales. No reading fee charged.

\* Anthony Sheil became an independent agent in association with Gillon Aitken Associates in 1998, after running Anthony Sheil Associates and being Chairman of Sheil Land Associates.

**Non-fiction** Will consider general non-fiction.

**Fiction** Will consider novels.

**Submission Guidelines** Send query letter with SAE, synopsis and sample chapters consisting of the first 30 pages of continuous text. Submission should be double spaced, single-sided A4.

**Recent Sale(s)** *My Hungry Hell*, Kate Chisholm; *Salad*, Jemma Kennedy; *Snitch*, Katherine Beck; *Bringing the House Down*, David Profumo

**Client(s)** Caroline Alexander, John Fowles, Josephine Cox, John Keegan.

**Tips** Qualifications must be included when submitting non-fiction.

## Antony Harwood Ltd

**103 Walton Street, Oxford, OX2 6EB**

☎ 01865 559615

☎ 01865 310660

✉ mail@antonyharwood.com

🌐 www.antonyharwood.com

**Contact** Antony Harwood, James MacDonald Lockhart

**Established** 2000

**Insider Info** Actively seeking clients. Considers non-fiction books and novels. Submissions accompanied by SAE will be returned. Clients usually acquired through queries/submissions. No reading fee charged.

 * Before establishing the agency in 2000, Antony Harwood began in publishing at Chatto & Windus in 1978, then became an agent at Gillon Aitken. In 1990 he joined the Curtis Brown Group as a director, before returning for a period to Gillon Aitken. James MacDonald Lockhart was with Hodder Headline before going to Gillon Aitken in 1998. Two years later he joined Antony Harwood to set up their own independent agency.

**Non-fiction** Will consider all genres except books for young children.

**Fiction** Will consider all genres except books for young children.

**Submission Guidelines** Send query letter with SAE, synopsis and three sample chapters. Queries accepted by email. No material for children under ten. Screenwriting or poetry considered.

**Recent Sale(s)** *Kissing Toads*, Jemma Harvey; *Divine Concepts of Physical Beauty*, Michael Bracewell; *Learning to Swim*, Clare Chambers; *Day*, A.L. Kennedy.

**Client(s)** Douglas Kennedy, Malcolm Knox, Deborah Levy, Roger Levy, Mark Lynas.

## Anubis Literary Agency

**6 Birdhaven Close, Lighthorne, Warwick, CV35 0BE**

☎ 01926 642588

☎ 01926 642588

**Contact** Steve Calcutt

**Established** 1994

**Insider Info** Specialise in fiction. Submissions accompanied by SAE will be returned. Commission rates of 15 per cent for domestic sales, 20 per cent for foreign sales. No reading fee charged.

**Fiction** Will consider fantasy, horror and science fiction.

**Submission Guidelines** Send submission with SAE, one-page synopsis and first 50 pages only. No queries accepted by telephone.

**Tips** No manuscripts accepted other than fiction in the above categories.

## A.P. Watt Ltd

**20 John Street, London, WC1N 2DR**

☎ 020 7405 6774

☎ 020 7831 2154

✉ apw@apwatt.co.uk

🌐 www.apwatt.co.uk

**Contact** Caradoc King, Derek Johns, Georgia Garrett (literary fiction, general non-fiction, narrative non-fiction and children's authors); Linda Shaughnessy (translation rights, literary estates); Natasha Fairweather (non-fiction, young novelists); Sheila Crowley (women's commercial fiction, thrillers, children's fiction and mass market non-fiction); Kevin Conroy Scott, Christine Glover (scripts, screenplays and playwriting)

**Established** 1875

**Insider Info** Actively seeking clients. Considers non-fiction books, juvenile books, novels, TV scripts, movie scripts, stage plays. Unsuccessful submissions discarded. Commission rates of 15 per cent for domestic sales, 20 per cent for foreign sales. No reading fee charged.

**Non-fiction** Will consider general non-fiction.

**Fiction** Will consider literary, commercial and children's fiction.

**Scripts** Will consider TV and film scripts and stage plays.

**Submission Guidelines** Send query letter. No poetry considered.

**Recent Sale(s)** *The Testament of Gideon Mack*, James Robertson; *On Beauty*, Zadie Smith

**Client(s)** Tony Parsons, Dame Ellen MacArthur, Rudyard Kipling, John Creed, Michael Innes and Camille Griffin.

**Tips** No unsolicited manuscripts accepted. No responsibility accepted for submitted materials.

## Artellus Ltd

**30 Dorset House, Gloucester Place, London, NW1 5AD**

☎ 020 7935 6972

☎ 020 7487 5975

🌐 www.artellusltd.co.uk

**Contact** Chairperson/Agent/Consultant, Gabriele Pantucci; Director/Agent, Leslie Gardner (film rights);

Associate Agent/Company Secretary, Darryl Samaraweera (foreign and theatrical rights); Associate Agent/Administrator/Picture Researcher, Liz Mallett

**Established** 1986

**Insider Info** Actively seeking clients. Considers non-fiction books, scholarly books, textbooks, juvenile books, novels, novellas. Submissions accompanied by SAE will be returned. Clients usually acquired through recommendation or queries/submissions. Commission rate of ten per cent for domestic sales, 15 per cent for foreign sales. Fee charged for a selective reading service, by invitation.

**Non-fiction** Will consider art/architecture/design, biography/autobiography, current affairs, ethnic/cultural interests, history, military/war, popular culture, science/technology, fashion and celebrity.

**Fiction** Will consider detective/police/crime, fantasy, literary and science fiction.

**Submission Guidelines** Send query letter with SAE, synopsis, three sample chapters and a biography. No film or TV scripts considered.

**Recent Sale(s)** *Untouchables*, Michael Gillard & Laurie Flynn; *Critique of Criminal Reason*, Michael Gregorio; *Culture & Prosperity*, John Kay; *London High*, Herbert L.Wright

**Client(s)** Anthony Burgess, Lois McMaster Bujold, Sir John Pope-Hennessy, Roger Lewis, Martin van Creveld, Robert Hazen, Robert Gallo, Salma Samar Damluji.

**Tips** The agency has a worldwide client list, and is established in the handling of all exploitation of book rights through to periodicals, film, TV and radio. Enquire thoroughly about the reading fee before submitting.

## Author Literary Agents

**53 Talbot Road, Highgate, London, London, N64QX**
☎ 020 8341 0442
☎ 020 8341 0442
✉ agile@authors.co.uk

**Contact** John Havergal

**Established** 1997

**Insider Info** Actively seeking clients. Considers non-fiction books, juvenile books, novels, TV scripts, movie scripts, animation and thrillers. Prefers to receive exclusive submissions. Aims to respond to queries within seven days. Submissions accompanied by SAE will be returned. Clients usually acquired through recommendation or queries/submissions. Does not charge reading fee.

**Non-fiction** Will consider agriculture/horticulture, animals, anthropology/archaeology, art/

architecture/design, biography/autobiography, business, child guidance/parenting, computers/electronics, cooking/food/nutrition, crafts/hobbies, education, history, psychology, humour, interior design/decorating, language/literature/criticism, money/finance/economics, music/dance/theatre/film, nature/environment, religious/inspirational, science/technology, sociology and true crime/investigative.

**Fiction** Will consider action/adventure, confessional, detective/police/crime, experimental, family saga, fantasy, historical, juvenile, literary, mainstream, mystery, picture book, religious/inspirational, romance, science fiction, thriller/espionage and young adult.

**Scripts** Will consider action/adventure, biography/autobiography, cartoon/animation, contemporary issues, detective/police/crime, experimental and family saga.

**Submission Guidelines** Send query letter with SAE, outline, synopsis, biography and first chapter. Queries accepted by fax, email and telephone.

## Barbara Levy Literary Agency

**64 Greenhill, Hampstead High Street, London, NW3 5TZ**
☎ 020 7435 9046
☎ 020 7431 2063

**Contact** Director, Barbara Levy; Associate and Solicitor, John Selby

**Established** 1986

**Insider Info** Actively seeking clients. Considers non-fiction books and novels. Unsuccessful proposals will be returned if accompanied by SAE. Obtains new clients by queries and submissions. Commission rates of ten per cent for domestic sales with rates for foreign sales by arrangement. Do not charge a reading fee.

**Non-fiction** Will consider general non-fiction books.

**Fiction** Will consider general fiction, mainly full length novels.

**Submission Guidelines** Send query letter with synopsis and SAE.

**Tips** Do not send entire manuscripts.

## Barrie James Literary Agency

**Rivendell, Kingsgate, Torquay, Devon, TQ2 8QA**
☎ 01803 326617
✉ mail@newauthors.org.uk
🌐 www.newauthors.org.uk

**Contact** Barrie James

**Established** 1997

Insider Info Actively seeking clients. Considers novels, non-fiction books and poetry. Will consider simultaneous submissions. Unsuccessful proposals will be returned if accompanied by SAE. Obtains new clients through queries and submissions.

**Non-fiction** Will consider general non-fiction.

**Fiction** Will consider general fiction and poetry.

**Submission Guidelines** Accepts query letter with SAE or queries via email.

**Tips** Operates a website for new authors to display their work. See website for full submission guidelines, costs and new author listings but research costs and benefits thoroughly before committing.

## The Bell Lomax Agency

**James House, 1 Babmaes Street, London, SW1Y 6HF**

☎ 020 7930 4447

☎ 020 7925 0118

✉ agency@bell-lomax.co.uk

**Contact** Executives, Eddie Bell, Pat Lomax, Paul Moreton, June Bell

**Established** 2000

**Insider Info** Actively seeking clients. Considers non-fiction books, juvenile books and novels. Unsuccessful proposals are returned with SAE. Obtains new clients through queries and submissions. Does not charge a reading fee.

**Non-fiction** Considers Biography/autobiography, Business, Juvenile and Sports non-fiction titles.

**Fiction** Considers general and children's fiction.

**Submission Guidelines** Send query letter. Will not accept scripts.

**Tips** Do not send any manuscripts before approaching with a query letter.

## Bill McLean Personal Management Ltd

**23b Deodar Road, London, SW15 2NP**

☎ 020 8789 8191

**Contact** Bill McLean

**Established** 1972

**Insider Info** Seeking both new and established writers. Considers TV scripts, film scripts, stage plays and radio scripts. Unsuccessful proposals will be returned if accompanied by SAE. Obtains new clients through queries and submissions. Commission rates of ten per cent for domestic sales. Does not charge a reading fee.

**Scripts** Considers a variety of scripts for Tv, film, radio and theatre.

**Submission Guidelines** Send query letter with SAE or query over the phone. Does not accept any books.

**Tips** Will not accept any unsolicited manuscripts.

## Blake Friedmann Literary, Film & TV Agency

**122 Arlington Road, London, NW1 7HP**

☎ 020 7284 0408

☎ 020 7284 0442

✉ firstname@blakefriedmann.co.uk

🌐 www.blakefriedmann.co.uk

**Contact** Carole Blake (Books); Julian Friedmann (Film/TV); Conrad Williams (Original Scripts/Radio); Isobel Dixon (Books)

**Established** 1977

**Insider Info** Actively seeking clients. Considers non-fiction books, novels, TV scripts, short story collections, film scripts, and radio scripts. Unsuccessful proposals will be returned if accompanied by SAE. Obtains new clients through queries and submissions. Commission rates of 15 per cent for domestic sales and 20 per cent for foreign sales. Does not charge a reading fee.

\* Specialises in film and TV rights.

**Non-fiction** Considers biography/autobiography, investigative and travel titles.

**Fiction** Considers general fiction, genre fiction, literary and commercial titles.

**Scripts** Considers scripts for TV, film and radio.

**Submission Guidelines** Send query letter with a synopsis and two sample chapters. Do not send any science fiction or poetry.

**Client(s)** Jane Asher, Elizabeth Chadwick, Maeve Haran, Ken Hom, Craig Russell, Peter James.

**Tips** Short stories are only accepted from existing clients. Caters for a large overseas market. Fiction from genre to literary in all ranges are accepted.

## Blanche Marvin

**21a St. John's Wood High Street, London, NW8 7NG**

☎ 020 7722 2313

☎ 020 7722 2313

🌐 www.blanchemarvin.com

**Contact** Blanche Marvin

**Insider Info** Seeking both new and established writers. Considers TV scripts and stage plays. Unsuccessful proposals will be returned with SAE. Obtains new clients through queries and submissions. Does not charge a reading fee.

* Blanche Marvin is a renowned theatre critic. The agency specialises in theatre scripts and performance rights.

**Scripts** Considers mainly theatre scripts.

**Submission Guidelines** Send a query letter with an outline and SAE.

**Client(s)** Christopher Bond.

## BookBlast Ltd

**PO Box 20184, London, W10 5AU**

- 020 8968 3089
- 020 8932 4087
- gen@bookblast.com
- www.bookblast.com

**Contact** Georgia de Chamberet

**Established** 1997

**Insider Info** Actively seeking clients. Considers non-fiction books and novels. Unsuccessful proposals will be returned if accompanied by SAE. Obtains new clients through queries and submissions as well as initiating in-house projects. Commission rates of 12 per cent for domestic sales and 20 per cent for foreign sales.

* Before founding BookBlast Ltd., Georgia de Chamberet was an editor at Quartet Books.

**Non-fiction** Considers literary non-fiction, memoir, travel, popular culture and multicultural writing.

**Fiction** Considers literary and mainstream adult fiction.

**Submission Guidelines** Send query letter. Does not accept scripts, horror, crime, science fiction and fantasy, poetry, children's books, health, cookery, gardening, short stories or articles.

**Recent Sale(s)** *Britain's Slave Trade,* S.I.Martin; *Daybreak & Darkness,* Rupert Bogarde; *The Demented Dance,* Mounsi; *The Mad Mosaic,* Gael Elton Mato

**Client(s)** Luis Dominques, Christopher Ruhn, Jamika Ajalon

**Tips** Always write before sending any manuscripts. Email enquiries are accepted as body text only.

## The Book Bureau Literary Agency

**7 Duncairn Avenue, Bray, Co.Wicklow, Republic of Ireland**

- 00353 01 2764996
- 00353 01 2764834
- thebookbureau@oceanfree.net

**Contact** Geraldine Nichol

**Insider Info** Actively seeking clients. Considers novels. Unsuccessful proposals will be returned if accompanied by SAE, Obtains new clients through queries and submissions. Commission rates of ten

per cent on domestic sales and 20 per cent on foreign sales. Does not charge a reading fee.

**Fiction** Consider Literary, Thriller/espionage, Women's/chick lit and General commercial fiction.

**Submission Guidelines** Send query letter with a synopsis, three–five sample chapters and SAE. Does not accept science fiction, horror, poetry or children's titles.

**Tips** Writers may usually expect a prompt response to proposals and may be offered editorial support.

## Brie Burkeman

**14 Neville Court, Abbey Road, London, NW8 9DD**

- 0870 199 5002
- 0870 199 1029
- brie.burkeman@mail.com

**Contact** Isabel White

**Established** 2000

**Insider Info** Seeking both new and established writers. Considers non-fiction books, novels, TV scripts, movie scripts, and stage plays. Prefers to receive exclusive submissions. Unsuccessful proposals will be returned with SAE. Obtains new clients through recommendations from others, queries and submissions. Does not charge a reading fee or offer a criticism service.

**Non-fiction** Considers Anthropology/archaeology, Biography/autobiography, Cooking/food/nutrition, History, Memoirs, Popular culture and True crime/investigative non-fiction.

**Fiction** Considers Action/adventure, Detective/police/crime, Ethnic, Historical, Horror, Literary, Mainstream, Mystery, Thriller/espionage and Young adult fiction.

**Scripts** Considers Action/adventure, Comedy, Contemporary issues, Detective/police/crime and Ethnic scripts.

**Submission Guidelines** Send query letter with an outline, sample chapters and author biography. Do not send any poetry, musicals, text books or academic titles.

## Bryan Drew Ltd

**Quadrant House, 80–82 Regent Street, London, W1B 5AU**

- 020 7437 2293
- 020 7437 0561
- bryan@bryandrewltd.com

**Contact** Literary Manager, Bryan Drew

**Established** 1962

**Insider Info** Seeking both new and established writers. Considers non-fiction books, novels, TV scripts, movie scripts, and stage plays. Unsuccessful proposals will be returned if accompanied by SAE. Obtains new clients through queries and submissions. Commission rates of 12.5 per cent for domestic sales and 15 per cent for foreign sales. Does not charge a reading fee.

**Non-fiction** Considers Biography/autobiography titles.

**Fiction** Considers Thriller/espionage and General fiction titles.

**Scripts** Considers scripts for TV, film and theatre.

**Submission Guidelines** Send query letter with synopsis, two–three sample chapters and SASE.

**Tips** An SAE is essential.

## The Buckman Agency

**Ryman's Cottages, Little Trew, OX7 4JJ**

- 01608 683677
- 01608 683449
- r.buckman@talk21.com/j.buckman@talk21.com

**Contact** Rosie Buckman, Jessica Buckman

**Established** Early 1970s

**Insider Info** Seeking mostly established writers through referrals. Commission rates of 20 per cent for domestic and foreign sales.

   * Specialises in foreign rights.

**Tips** Represents established authors and agents from the UK and USA.

## Campbell, Thomson & McLaughlin Ltd

**11–12 Dover Street, London, W1S 4LJ**

- 020 7399 2808/2800
- 020 7399 2801
- submissions@ctmcl.co.uk

**Contact** Charlotte Bruton

**Established** 1931

**Insider Info** Seeking both new and established writers. Considers non-fiction books and novels. Unsuccessful proposals will be returned if accompanied by SAE. Obtains new clients through queries and submissions. Commission rates of ten per cent for domestic sales and up to 20 per cent for foreign sales. Does not charge a reading fee.

**Non-fiction** Considers general non-fiction.

**Fiction** Considers general fiction.

**Submission Guidelines** Send query letter with SAE or query via email. Do not send scripts, poetry or children's titles.

**Tips** Do not send entire manuscript before sending a query letter.

## Capel & Land Ltd

**29 Wardour Street, London, W1D 6PS**

- 020 7734 2414
- 020 7734 8101
- georgina@capelland.co.uk
- www.capelland.com

**Contact** Director, Georgina Capel (Literary); Director, Anita Land (TV & Radio); Yvonne Anderson (Corporate, Film & TV rights, TV and Radio); Phillipa Brewster, (Literary); Abi Fellows, (Literary)

**Established** 2000

**Insider Info** Actively seeking clients. Considers non-fiction books, novels, TV scripts and film scripts. Obtain new clients through queries and submissions. Commission rates of 15 per cent for domestic and foreign sales. Does not charge a reading fee.

**Non-fiction** Considers biography/autobiography, general non-fiction and History titles.

**Fiction** Considers general and literary fiction.

**Scripts** Considers film and TV scripts.

**Submission Guidelines** Send query letter with a synopsis, three sample chapters and SAE.

**Recent Sale(s)** *She May Not Leave,* Fay Weldon; *Queen of Beasts,* Colleen McCullough; *First Time Parent,* Lucy Atkins; *In Search of Sweden,* Andrew Brown

**Client(s)** Kohn Bew, Matthew Dennison, Julie Burchill, Andrew Greig, Liz Jones, Dr.Tristram Hunt, Stella Rimington, Jeremy Paxman.

**Tips** In some instances revision to proposals or manuscripts may be suggested.

## Caroline Davidson Literary Agency

**5 Queen Anne's Gardens, London, W4 1TU**

- 020 8995 5768
- 020 8994 2770
- caroline@cdla.co.uk
- www.cdla.co.uk

**Contact** Founder, Caroline Davidson

**Established** 1988

**Insider Info** Actively seeking clients. Considers non-fiction books and novels. Represents around 30 clients. Aims to respond to queries and proposals with four weeks. Obtains new clients through queries and submissions. Commission rates of 12.5 per cent for domestic sales and foreign sales (20 per cent for foreign sales if sub-agents are involved). Does not charge a reading fee.

   * Caroline Davidson was has been a journalist for Reuters in London and BBC television in the USA, having wide experience of the international market.

She has been the author of five books including *A Woman's Work is Never Done.*

**Non-fiction** Considers Agriculture/horticulture, Animals, Art/architecture/design, Biography/autobiography, Health/medicine, History, Nature/environment and Science/technology titles.

**Fiction** Considers literary fiction.

**Submission Guidelines** Send query letter with a synopsis, the first 50 pages for fiction writing, author biography and SAE. Do not send fantasy, thrillers, crime, occult, children's, scripts or poetry titles.

**Recent Sale(s)** *The Light Revolution,* Richard Hobday; *Champagne & Shambles,* Catherine Beale; *The Islamist,* Ed Husain; *Re-Think,* Andrew May Barlow

**Client(s)** Perter Barham, Nigel Barlow, Emma Donoghue, Paul Luff, Malachi McIntosh, Simon Unwin, Helena Whitbread.

**Tips** A CV must accompany the preliminary letter and submission. The agency will endeavour to reply to submissions as quickly as possible. No response will be given to submissions by fax or e-mail.

---

## Caroline Sheldon Literary Agency

**Thorley Manor Farm, 70–75 Cowcross Street, London EC1M 6EJ/Thorley, Yarmouth, PO41 0SJ**

- 01983 760205
- carolinesheldon@carolinesheldon.co.uk/ pennyholroyde@carolinesheldon.co.uk
- www.carolinesheldon.co.uk

**Contact** Caroline Sheldon, Penny Holroyde

**Established** 1985

**Insider Info** Actively seeking clients. Considers non-fiction books, juvenile books and novels. Aims to respond to proposals within four weeks. Unsuccessful proposals will be returned with SAE. Obtains new clients through queries and submissions.Commission rates of 10–15 per cent for domestic sales and 20 per cent for foreign sales. Does not charge a reading fee.

*Before establishing her agency, Caroline Sheldon was a publisher at Hutchinson/Arrow, specialising in women's and children's books. Penny Holroyde has worked at Walker Books and as a rights director for Candlewick Press in the USA. She joined Caroline Sheldon in 2004.

**Non-fiction** Considers Memoirs and Human Interest titles.

**Fiction** Considers adult's and children's fiction.

**Submission Guidelines** Send query letter with a synopsis, three sample chapters and SAE. Pages should be double-spaced and single-sided A4. No staples or bound manuscripts. Do not send scripts.

**Tips** All submissions to be sent to the Thorley Manor Farm address, and a letter giving ambitions and future aspirations should be included. Submissions will not be accepted by e-mail.

---

## Casarotto Ramsay & Associates Ltd

**Waverley House, 7–12 Noel Street, London, W1F 8GQ**

- 020 7287 4450
- 020 7287 9128
- info@casarotto.co.uk
- www.casarotto.co.uk

**Contact** Jenne Casarotto (Film and TV, Represents writers and directors); Tom Erhardt (Theatrical); Mel Kenyon, (Theatrical); Ruth Arnaud (Amateurs and Stock Rights)

**Established** 1989

**Insider Info** Actively seeking clients. Considers TV scripts, movie scripts, stage plays and radio scripts. Unsuccessful proposals will be returned if accompanied by SAE. Obtains new clients through queries and submissions. Commission rates of ten per cent for domestic sales. Does not charge a reading fee.

**Scripts** Considers scripts for film, TV, radio and stage.

**Submission Guidelines** Send query letter with SAE.

**Client(s)** J.G.Ballard, Howard Brenton, Simon Callow, Caryl Churchill, David Hare, Nick Hornby, Bob Hoskins, Terry Jones, Dominic Minghella, Frank McGuinness, Ian Hislop, Nick Newman.

**Tips** Do not send any book manuscripts, only scripts. A preliminary letter is essential.

---

## Cat Ledger Literary Agency

**20–21 Newman Street, London, W1T 1PG**

- 020 7861 8226
- 020 7861 8001

**Contact** Cat Ledger

**Insider Info** Seeking both new and established writers. Considers non-fiction books and novels. Unsuccessful proposals will be returned with SAE.

**Non-fiction** Considers Biography/autobiography, Government/politics/law, Humour, Music/dance/theatre/film, Sports, True crime/investigative, The Arts, Lifestyle, Travel, Academia and Journalism titles

**Fiction** Considers General adult fiction.

**Submission Guidelines** Send query letter with SAE. Do not send poetry, science fiction, fantasy, romance, scripts or children's titles.

**Tips** Mostly deals with non-fiction titles.

---

## Cecily Ware Literary Agents

**19C John Spencer Square, London, N1 2LZ**

- 020 7359 3787

- ☎ 020 7226 9828
- ✉ info@cecilyware.com

**Contact** Cecily Ware, Warren Sherman, Gilly Schuster,

**Established** 1972

**Insider Info** Seeking both new and established writers. Considers TV scripts and film scripts. Unsuccessful proposals are returned if accompanied by SAE. Obtains new clients through queries and submissions. Commission rates of ten per cent for domestic sales and 10–20 per cent for foreign sales. Does not charge a reading fee.

**Scripts** Considers Comedy, Family saga, Adaptations, drama, series/serials, and children's scripts.

**Submission Guidelines** Send query letter with SAE.

**Tips** Never send entire manuscript unless requested.

## Celia Catchpole

**56 Gilpin Avenue, London, SW14 8QY**

- ☎ 020 8255 7755
- 🌐 www.celiacatchpole.co.uk

**Contact** Celia Catchpole

**Established** 1996

**Insider Info** Seeking both new and established writers. Considers Juvenile books and novels. Simultaneous submissions are accepted. Unsuccessful proposals will be returned if accompanied by SAE. Obtains new clients through queries and submissions. Commission rates of ten per cent for domestic sales (15 per cent for illustrators) and 20 per cent on foreign sales.

  * Specialises in children's authors and illustrators.

**Fiction** Considers Juvenile and Children's Picture book titles.

**Submission Guidelines** Send query letter with SAE. Do not accept scripts or poetry.

**Recent Sale(s)** *Muck It Up!,* Jane Clark and Trevor Duncan (HarperCollins); *Swallowcliffe Hall* series, Jennie Walters (Simon & Schuster); *'Varjak Paw'* series, S.F.Said (David Fickling Books); *Tabitha's Terrifically Tough Tooth,* Charlotte Middleton (Gullane Children's Books)

**Client(s)** Josephine Poole, Hannah Webb, Polly Dunbar, Mick Gowar, Malachy Doyle, Fernando Vilela, Daniel Postgate, Jane Simmons, Trish Phillips, Tim Hopgood, Joseph Theobald, Pedro De Alcantara, Rob Childs, Sandra Ann Horn, Lucy Micklethwait, Julia Rawlinson, Sean Taylor, Peter Utton.

**Tips** Does not accept unsolicited manuscripts.

## Chapman & Vincent

**The Mount, Sun Hill, Royston, Hertfordshire, SG8 9AT**

- ☎ 01763 245005
- ☎ 01763 243033
- ✉ info@chapmanvincent.co.uk

**Contact** Directors, Jennifer Chapman and Gilly Vincent

**Established** 1992

**Insider Info** Seeking mostly established writers through referrals. Consider non-fiction books and novels. Simultaneous submissions are accepted. Unsuccessful proposals will be returned with SAE. Obtains new clients through recommendations from others as well as queries and submissions. Commission rates of 15 per cent for domestic sales and 20 per cent for foreign sales. Do not charge a reading fee.

**Non-fiction** Considers General non-fiction titles.

**Fiction** Considers upmarket adult fiction titles.

**Submission Guidelines** Send query letter with two sample chapters and SAE. No thrillers, adventure, poetry, scripts or children's books.

**Client(s)** George Carter, Leslie Geddes-Brown, Rowley Leigh, Eve Pollard.

**Tips** The agency does not accept telephone calls, or any proposals by fax or e-mail.

## Christine Green Authors' Agent

**6 Whitehorse Mews, Westminster Bridge Road, London, SE1 7QD**

- ☎ 020 7401 8844
- ☎ 020 7401 8860
- ✉ info@christinegreen.co.uk
- 🌐 www.christinegreen.co.uk

**Contact** Christine Green

**Established** 1984

**Insider Info** Actively seeking clients. Considers non-fiction books and novels. Prefers to receive exclusive submissions. Aims to respond to queries and proposals within four weeks. Unsuccessful proposals will be returned with SAE. Obtains new clients through queries and submissions. Commission rates of 10 per cent for domestic sales and 20 per cent for foreign sales. Does not charge a reading fee.

**Non-fiction** Considers General non-fiction titles.

**Fiction** Considers General fiction titles.

**Submission Guidelines** Send a query letter with the first three chapters, a synopsis and SAE. Pages should be double-spaced, single sided, numbered and A4 in size. Do not send scripts, science fiction, fantasy, children's books or poetry.

**Recent Sale(s)** *Whitethorn Woods,* Maeve Binchy; *Harlequin's Daughter,* Mary Joyce; *A Literary Woman,* Mary Beckett; *Sundowners,* Lesley Lokko
**Client(s)** Lyn Andrews, Ita Daly, Winston Fletcher, Sylvian Hamilton, Marilyn Heward Mills.

## The Christopher Little Literary Agency

**10 Eel Brook Studios, 125 Moore Park Road, London, SW6 4PS**
☎ 020 7736 4455
☎ 020 7736 4490
✉ info@christopherlittle.net
🌐 www.christopherlittle.net
**Contact** Christopher Little
**Established** 1979
**Insider Info** Actively seeking clients. Considers non-fiction books, novels, Juvenile books, TV scripts and movie scripts. Aims to respond to queries and manuscripts within six weeks. Unsuccessful proposals will be returned with SAE. Obtains new clients through queries and submissions. Commission rates of 15 per cent for domestic sales, and 20 per cent for foreign sales and film rights. Does not charge a reading fee.
**Non-fiction** Considers mainstream and literary non-fiction.
**Fiction** Considers mainstream and literary full length fiction.
**Scripts** Mainly considers scripts from existing clients only.
**Submission Guidelines** Send query letter with synopsis, three sample chapters and SAE. Pages should be double-spaced, single-sided and A4 sized. No poetry, plays, science fiction, illustrated material, fantasy, textbooks or short stories.
**Recent Sale(s)** *Dark Fores* series, Steve Barlow and Steve Skidmore; *Harry Potter* series, J.K.Rowling; *Man on Fire,* A.J.Quinnell; *The Kingdom of the Frosty Mountain,* Angela Woolfe.
**Client(s)** Paul Bajoria, AJ Butcher, Janet Gleeson, Gorillaz, Christopher Hale, Pete Howells, Carol Hughes, Ge.Sir Mike Jackson, Lauren Liebenberg, Alistair MacNeill, Christopher Matthew, Robert Mawson, Haydn Middleton, Shiromi Pinto, Robert Radcliffe, Dr.Nicholas Reeves, Darren Shan, Darren O'Shaughnessy, Wladyslaw Szpilman, Shayne Ward, Pip Vaughn-Hughes, John Watson, Anne Zouroudi.
**Tips** The agency also handles merchandising, in-house legal matters, contract affairs, royalties and accounting for their clients and offer a high level of personal, hands on representation.

## Conville & Walsh Ltd.

**2 Ganton Street, London, W1F 7QL**
☎ 020 7287 3030
☎ 020 7287 4545
✉ firstname@convilleandwalsh.com
**Contact** Director, Clare Conville; Director, Patrick Walsh (Book rights); Director, Peter Tallack (Popular Science)
**Established** 2000
**Insider Info** Seeking both new and established writers. Considers Non-fiction books, Juvenile books and Novels. Unsuccessful proposals will be returned if accompanied by SAE. Obtains new clients through queries and submissions. Commission rates of 15 per cent for domestic sales and 20 per cent for foreign sales. Does not charge reading fees.
**Non-fiction** Considers History, Juvenile, Science/technology and Journalism titles.
**Fiction** Considers Juvenile, Literary and Commercial fiction.
**Submission Guidelines** Accepts query letter with a synopsis, three sample chapters and SAE. No scripts, short stories or poetry.
**Client(s)** John Burningham, Helen Castor, Mike Dash, Professor John Emsley, Dermot Healy, Manjit Kumar, Patrick Redmond.
**Tips** Has an interest in first-time novelists.

## Coombs Moylett Literary Agency

**3 Askew Road, London, W12 9AA**
☎ 020 8740 0454
☎ 020 8354 3065
**Contact** Lisa Moylett
**Insider Info** Seeking both new and established writers. Considers non-fiction books and novels. Aims to respond to queries and proposals within one week. Unsuccessful proposals will be returned if accompanied by SAE. Obtains new clients through queries and submissions. Commission rates of 15 per cent for domestic sales, foreign sales and film rights. Does not charge a reading fee.
**Non-fiction** Considers Biography/autobiography, Current affairs and History titles.
**Fiction** Considers Detective/police/crime, Literary, Thriller/espionage, Women's/chick lit and Contemporary fiction.
**Submission Guidelines** Send query letter with SAE, synopsis and three sample chapters.
**Tips** The agency is known for quickly responding to submissions. No electronic submissions.

## Crawford & Pearlstine Associates Ltd

**31 Ashley Gardens, Ambrosden Avenue, London, SW1P 1QE**

- 0845 262 4212
- 0845 262 5546

**Contact** Jamie Crawford, Maggie Pearlstine
**Established** 1989
**Insider Info** Seeking both new and established writers. Considers non-fiction books and novels. Commission rates are variable for domestic sales and 20 per cent for foreign sales and film rights. Do not charge reading fee.
**Non-fiction** Considers Biography/autobiography, Current affairs, Health/medicine, History, Sports and General non-fiction titles.
**Fiction** Considers General fiction.
**Submission Guidelines** Send query letter with SAE and sample chapters. No poetry, science fiction, short stories, horror, scripts or children's books.
**Tips** No fax or e-mail submissions and no submissions from outside the UK.

## Curtis Brown Group Ltd.

**Haymarket House, 28–29 Haymarket, London, SW1 4SP**

- 020 7393 4400
- 020 7393 4400
- cb@curtisbrown.co.uk
- www.curtisbrown.co.uk

**Contact** Ceo. Jonathan Lloyd (Fiction, Autobiographies); MD, Jonny Geller (Book Division); Gordon Wise, (History, Lifestyle, Literary estate of Winston Churchill); Camilla Hornby/Vivienne Schuster (Non-fiction, Literary estates, Literary Commercial fiction, Biographies, Memoirs, History and travel); Elizabeth Sheinkman/Janice Swanson (Debut Novelists, Journalism, Memoirs, Culture and History, Children's Authors, Author Illustrators, Literary estates)
**Established** 1899
**Insider Info** Actively seeking clients. Considers non-fiction books, juvenile books, novels, TV scripts, movie scripts, stage plays, multimedia and radio scripts. Simultaneous submissions are accepted. Aims to respond to queries and proposals within eight weeks. Unsuccessful proposals are returned if accompanied by SAE. Obtains new clients by queries and submissions. Does not charge a reading fee.
   * Jonathan Lloyd was with HarperCollins before joining the Curtis Brown Group Ltd. in 1994. He was also President of the Association of Author's Agents (AAA) from 1999–2002. Jonny Geller originally trained as a actor, but joined the group in 1993 as a book agent. He is also author of *Yes, but it is Good for the Jews*.
**Non-fiction** Considers Biography/autobiography, History, Humour, Memoirs and Popular culture titles.
**Fiction** Considers Humour/satire, Literary and Women's/chick lit titles.
**Scripts** Considers scripts for TV, radio, film amd theatre.
**Submission Guidelines** Send query letter with SAE a synopsis and three sample chapters. Pages should be double-spaced, single-sided and A4 sized.
**Recent Sale(s)** *Liar's Landscape,* Malcolm Bradbury; *The House by the Thames,* Gillian Tindall; *Fat,* Rob Grant; *Ollie,* Stephen Venables.
**Client(s)** Jake Arnott, Barbara Davies, Jane Fallon, Jane Harris, David Hewson, F.E.Higgins, Cathy Kelly, Marion Keyes, Josie Lloyd, Emlyn Rees, David Mitchell, Christopher Skidmore.
**Tips** When submitting sample chapters make sure your name, contact number and e-mail address are clearly written on the cover. No stapled, bound, or e-mailed manuscripts.

## Darley Anderson Literary, TV and Film Agency

**Estelle House, 11 Eustace Road, London, SW6 1JB**

- 020 7385 6652
- 020 7386 5571
- enquiries@darleyanderson.com
- www.darleyanderson.com

**Contact** Darley Anderson (Crime and thrillers); Julia Churchill (Children's books); Lucie Whitehouse (Women's fiction); Zoe King (Non-fiction)
**Established** 1988
**Insider Info** Actively seeking clients. Considers non-fiction books, juvenile books, novels, TV scripts and movie scripts. 95 per cent of clients are new or previously unpublished writers. Simultaneous submissions are accepted. Aims to respond to queries, proposals and manuscripts within one month. Unsuccessful proposals will be returned if accompanied by SAE. Obtains new clients through recommendations from others, queries and submissions.
**Non-fiction** Considers Animals, Biography/autobiography, Child guidance/parenting, Cooking/food/nutrition, Juvenile, Memoirs, Money/finance/economics, Popular culture, Religious/inspirational, Self-help/personal improvement and Sports titles.
**Fiction** Considers Action/adventure, Confessional, Detective/police/crime, Erotica, Ethnic, Family saga, Fantasy, Gay/lesbian, Glitz, Historical, Horror, Juvenile, Mainstream, Mystery, Picture book, Psychic/

supernatural, Regional, Religious/inspirational, Romance, Science fiction, Sports, Thriller/espionage, Women's/chick lit and Young adult titles.

**Scripts** Considers Action/adventure, Biography/autobiography, Cartoon/animation, Comedy, Contemporary issues, Detective/police/crime, Ethnic, Sitcom and Family saga scripts.

**Submission Guidelines** Send query letter with SAE, Synopsis and the first three chapters. Also accepts queries by email or phone.

## David Grossman Literary Agency Ltd
**118b Holland Park Avenue, London, W11 4UA**
- 020 7221 2770
- 020 7221 1445

**Established** 1976

**Insider Info** Actively seeking clients. Considers novels. Simultaneous submissions are accepted. Unsuccessful manuscripts are returned if accompanied by SAE. Obtains new clients through queries and submissions. Commission rates are variable for domestic sales and 20 per cent for foreign sales. Do not charge a reading fee.

**Fiction** Considers literary and general fiction.

**Submission Guidelines** Send query letter with SAE, synopsis and the first 50 pages. No poetry, textbooks or scripts.

**Tips** No faxes or e-mailed submissions will be accepted. Debut novelists' well written, original works will be considered.

## David Higham Associates Ltd
**5–8 Lower John Street, Golden Square, London, W1F 9HA**
- 020 7434 5900
- 020 7437 1072
- dha@davidhigham.co.uk
- www.davidhigham.co.uk

**Contact** Anthony Goff, Alice Wilson, Bruce Hunter, Anthony Goff, Lizzy Kremer, Veronique Baxter (Fiction, Non-fiction, Children); Caroline Walsh (Fiction, Children, Illustrators); Georgia Glover, Jacqueline Korn (Fiction, Non-fiction); Gemma Hirst, Jessica Cooper, Nicky Lund (Script Writing and Drama); Ania Corless (Translation)

**Established** 1935

**Insider Info** Seeking both new and established writers. Considers non-fiction, fiction, film scripts, TV scripts, stage plays and Children's books. Simultaneous submissions are accepted. Unsuccessful proposals will be returned with SAE. Obtains new clients through recommendations from others, queries and submissions. Commission

rates of 15 per cent for domestic sales, 20 per cent for foreign sales and 15 per cent for film rights (scripts ten per cent). Offers a written contract until it is terminated by either party. Does not charge a reading fee or offer a criticism service.

**Non-fiction** Considers general non-fiction titles.

**Fiction** Considers adult's and children's fiction.

**Scripts** Considers scripts for film, TV and theatre.

**Submission Guidelines** Send query letter with SAE, outline, synopsis, three sample chapters and an author biography. The agency is actively seeking good commercial and literary fiction, and general non-fiction.

**Tips** Postal submissions only.

## David O'Leary Literary Agency
**10 Lansdowne Court, Lansdowne Rise, London, W11 2NR**
- 020 7229 1623
- 020 7229 1623
- d.o'leary@virgin.net

**Contact** David O'Leary

**Established** 1988

**Insider Info** Seeking both new and established writers. Considers non-fiction books and novels. Simultaneous submissions are accepted. Unsuccessful proposals will be returned if accompanied by SAE. Obtains new clients through queries and submissions. Commission rates of ten per cent for domestic and foreign sales. Does not charge a reading fee.

**Non-fiction** Considers History and Popular science titles.

**Fiction** Considers Literary and Thriller/espionage fiction titles.

**Submission Guidelines** Send query letter with SAE and outline proposal. Also accepts queries by email and phone. No science fiction or poetry.

**Client(s)** Nick Kochan, Jim Lusby, Derek Malcolm, Ken Russell.

**Tips** The agency are happy to discuss proposals, but do not accept unsolicited manuscripts.

## Deborah Owen Ltd
**78 Narrow Street, London, E14 8BP**
- 020 7987 5119/5441
- 020 7538 4004

**Contact** Deborah Owen

**Established** 1971

**Insider Info** Not currently seeking new clients. Represents non-fiction books.

 * A small agency which represents two authors only.

**Client(s)** Delia Smith, Amos Oz.

## The Dench Arnold Agency

**10 Newburgh Street, London, W1F 7RN**

- 020 7437 4551
- 020 7439 1355
- contact@den* denmarcharnold.co.uk
- www.denmarcharnold.co.uk

**Contact** Elizabeth Dench, Michelle Arnold, Matthew Dench, Fiona Grant, Dariella Malde

**Established** 1972

**Insider Info** Seeking both new and established writers. Considers TV scripts, movie scripts, non-fiction and fiction. Unsuccessful proposals will be returned if accompanied by SAE. Obtains new clients through queries and submissions. Commission rates of 10–15 per cent on domestic sales.

**Non-fiction** Considers General non-fiction titles.

**Fiction** Considers General fiction titles.

**Scripts** Considers scripts for TV and film.

**Submission Guidelines** Send query letter with SAE, author biography and a sample of work for scripts.

## DGA Ltd

**55 Monmouth Street, London, WC2H 9DG**

- 020 7240 9992
- 020 7395 6110
- assistant@davidgodwinassociates.co.uk
- www.davidgodwinassociates.co.uk

**Contact** Director, David Godwin; Director, Heather Godwin; Sophie Hoult (Permissions, Interviews, Publicity); Cathryn Summerhayes (UK, USA, translation audio rights, client enquiries); Kirsty McLachan (Film/TV rights)

**Established** 1995

**Insider Info** Considers non-fiction books and novels. Aims to respond to queries within three weeks. Unsuccessful proposals will be returned if accompanied by SAE.

  * Specialises in film and TV rights worldwide.

**Non-fiction** General non-fiction.

**Fiction** Considers Literary fiction.

**Submission Guidelines** Send query letter with SAE, synopsis, three sample chapters and an author biography. No science fiction, autobiographical, graphic/illustrated novels or children's titles.

**Client(s)** Diane Atkinson, Arundhati Roy, Aiden Hartley, Jim Crace, Michael Pye, Simon Armitage, Ronan Bennett, William Dalrymple, Joe Lovejoy, Clare Tomalin, Donald Sassoon, Ben Rice, Alan Warner.

**Tips** No e-mail submissions from new writers.

## Diane Banks Associates

**PO Box 53930, London, SW15 6YS**

- 020 8785 1086
- 020 8785 1086
- submissions@dianebanks.co.uk

**Contact** Diane Banks

**Established** 2006

**Insider Info** Seeking both new and established writers. Considers non-fiction books and novels. Simultaneous submissions will be accepted. Aims to respond to queries within two weeks. Obtains new clients through queries and submissions. Commission rates of 15 per cent for domestic sales and 20 per cent for foreign sales. Does not charge a reading fee.

**Non-fiction** Considers Biography/autobiography, Health/medicine, History, Psychology, Memoirs, Self-help/personal improvement, Popular science, Fashion and Beauty titles.

**Fiction** Consider Detective/police/crime, Literary, Thriller/espionage and Women's/chick lit titles.

**Submission Guidelines** Send a synopsis, two–three sample chapters, and an author biography. Also accepts queries by email. No short stories, poetry, scripts, academic, science fiction or children's titles.

**Tips** Initial contact should be made by e-mail. Will suggest any revisions on manuscripts that have been requested.

## Dinah Wiener Ltd

**12 Cornwall Grove, London, W4 2LB**

- 020 8994 6011
- 020 8994 6044

**Contact** Dinah Wiener

**Established** 1985

**Insider Info** Actively seeking clients. Considers non-fiction books and novels. Simultaneous submissions are accepted. Unsuccessful submissions will be returned with SAE. Obtains new clients through queries and submissions. Commission rates of 15 per cent for domestic sales and 20 per cent for foreign sales.

**Non-fiction** Considers Biography/autobiography, Cooking/food/nutrition, Popular culture, Science/technology and Lifestyle titles.

**Fiction** Considers general fiction titles.

**Submission Guidelines** Send query letter, SAE, two sample chapters and a CV giving information on past work and future plans. No scripts, poetry or children's books.

**Tips** All submitted manuscripts must be double-spaced, single-sided and A4 sized.

## Don Baker Associates

**25 Eley Drive, Rottingdean, East Sussex, BN2 7FH**
- 01273 386842
- 01273 386842

**Contact** Director, Donald Baker; Director, Katy Quayle
**Established** 1996
**Insider Info** Seeking both new and established writers. Considers TV scripts, movie scripts and stage plays. Simultaneous submissions are accepted. Obtains new clients through queries and submissions. Commission rates of 12.5 per cent for domestic sales and 15 for foreign sales. Does not charge a reading fee.
**Scripts** Considers Fiction scripts for TV, film and stage.
**Submission Guidelines** Send a query letter with SAE.
**Tips** No unsolicited submissions.

## Dorian Literary Agency (DLA)

**Upper Thornehill, 27 Church Road, St.Marychurch, Torquay, Devon, TQ1 4QY**
- 01803 312095
- 01803 312095

**Contact** Proprietor, Dorothy Lumley
**Established** 1986
**Insider Info** Actively seeking clients. Considers non-fiction and novels. esSimultaneous submissions are accepted. Unsuccessful proposals will be returned if accompanied by SAE. Obtains new clients through queries and submissions. Commission rates are variable for domestic sales and 15 per cent for foreign sales. Do not charge a reading fee.
**Non-fiction** Considers Popular culture titles.
**Fiction** Considers Detective/police/crime, Family saga, Fantasy, Historical, Horror, Romance, Science fiction, Thriller/espionage and Women's/chick lit titles.
**Submission Guidelines** Send query letter with SAE, synopsis and three sample chapters. No poetry, drama or children's books for under 10 years.
**Client(s)** Gillian Bradshaw, Brian Lumley, Rosemary Rowe, Lyndon Stacey.
**Tips** No enquiries via telephone, or manuscripts via email or fax.

## Dorie Simmonds Agency

**Riverbank House, 1 Putney Bridge Approach, London, SW6 3JD**
- 020 7736 0002
- dhsimmonds@aol.com

**Contact** Dorie Simmonds
**Insider Info** Seeking both new and established writers. Considers non-fiction books, scholarly books and children's books. Unsuccessful proposals will be returned if accompanied by SAE. Obtains new clients through queries and submissions. Commission rates of 15 per cent for foreign and domestic sales. Does not charge a reading fee.
**Non-fiction** Considers Biography/autobiography, History, Juvenile, Academic, and Commercial non-fiction titles.
**Fiction** Considers Historical, Children's, Women's/chick lit, General and Commercial fiction titles.
**Submission Guidelines** Send a query letter with SAE, synopsis and two-three sample chapters. Include any publishing history in the letter.
**Tips** Authors of non-fiction are to submit only an outline with the preliminary letter.

## Duncan McAra

**28 Beresford Gardens, Edinburgh, EH5 3ES**
- 0131 552 1558
- 0131 552 1558
- duncanmcara@hotmail.com

**Contact** Duncan McAra
**Established** 1988
**Insider Info** Actively seeking clients. Considers non-fiction books and novels. Commission rates of ten per cent on domestic sales and 20 per cent on foreign sales. Does not charge a reading fee.
**Non-fiction** Considers Anthropology/archaeology, Art/architecture/design, Biography/autobiography, Military/war, Travel, local, Scottish and Academic titles.
**Fiction** Considers literary fiction.
**Submission Guidelines** Send query letter with SAE, synopsis, and sample chapters.

## Eddison Pearson Ltd

**West Hill House, 6 Swains Lane, London, N6 6QS**
- 020 7700 7763
- 020 7700 7866
- info@eddisonpearson.com

**Contact** Clare Pearson
**Established** 1996
**Insider Info** Considers non-fiction books, poetry, children's books, and novels. Simultaneous submissions are accepted. Aims to respond to queries and proposals within four weeks. Unsuccessful proposals will be returned with SAE. Obtains new clients through queries and submissions. Commission rates of 10 per cent for

domestic sales and 15–20 per cent for foreign sales. Does not charge a reading fee.

**Non-fiction** Considers literary and general non-fiction.

**Fiction** Considers literary and children's fiction.

**Submission Guidelines** Send query letter with SAE and outline.

**Client(s)** Valerie Bloom, Sue Heap, Robert Muchamore

**Tips** Query by email for up-to-date submission guidelines. The agency endeavours to reply promptly to all submissions.

## Ed Victor Ltd
**6 Bayley Street, Bedford Square, London, WC1B 3HE**

🕿 020 7304 4100

🕿 020 7304 4111

**Contact** Executive Chairman, Ed Victor; Director, Sophie Hicks; Director, Margaret Phillips

**Established** 1976

**Insider Info** Actively seeking clients. Considers non-fiction books, children's books and novels. Simultaneous submissions will be accepted. Unsuccessful proposals will be returned with SAE. Obtains new clients through queries and submissions. Commission rates of 15 per cent on domestic and foreign sales. Does not charge reading fees.

**Non-fiction** Considers general non-fiction.

**Fiction** Considers Action/adventure, Children's, Mystery, Romance, Thriller/espionage and Women's/chick lit titles.

**Submission Guidelines** Send query letter with SAE and synopsis. No scripts, academic or poetry titles.

**Client(s)** John Banville, Herbie Brennan, Eoin Colfer, Frederick Forsyth, A. A.Gill, Josephine Hart, Jack Higgins, Nigella Lawson, Kathy Lette, Allan Mallinson, Andrew Marr, Janet Street-Porter.

**Tips** All manuscripts must be submitted by post. The agency also represents the estates of Douglas Adams, Raymond Chandler, Dame Iris Murdoch, Sir Stephen Spender and Irving Wallace.

## Edwards Fuglewicz
**49 Great Ormond Street, London, WC1N 3HZ**

🕿 020 7405 6725

🕿 020 7405 6726

**Contact** Partners, Ros Edwards/Helenca Fuglewiscz

**Established** 1996

**Insider Info** Actively seeking clients. Considers non-fiction books, novels, and scholarly books. Simultaneous submissions are accepted.

Unsuccessful submissions will be returned if accompanied by SAE. Obtains new clients through queries and submissions. Commission rates of 15 per cent on domestic sales and 20 per cent on foreign sales. Does not charge a reading fee.

**Non-fiction** Considers Biography/autobiography, History and Popular culture titles.

**Fiction** Considers literary and commercial fiction.

**Submission Guidelines** Send query letter with SAE, three sample chapters and a brief CV. No science fiction, fantasy, horror or scripts.

**Tips** No unsolicited submissions or electronic manuscripts.

## Elaine Steel
**110 Gloucester Avenue, London, NW1 8HX**

🕿 020 8348 0918

🕿 020 8341 9807

✉ ecmsteel@aol.com

**Contact** Elaine Steel

**Established** 1986

**Insider Info** Seeking both new and established writers. Considers non-fiction books, novels, TV scripts, movie scripts and stage plays. Unsuccessful proposals will be returned if accompanied by SAE. Obtains new clients through queries and submissions. Commission rates of ten per cent for domestic sales and 20 per cent for foreign sales.

**Non-fiction** Considers General non-fiction.

**Fiction** Considers General fiction.

**Scripts** Considers scripts for film, TV and theatre.

**Submission Guidelines** Send query letter with SAE. No academic or technical titles.

**Tips** First contact by telephone preferred.

## Elisabeth Wilson
**24 Thornhill Square, London, N1 1BQ**

🕿 020 7609 6045

**Established** 1979

**Insider Info** Seeking both new and established writers. Considers non-fiction and illustrated books. Simultaneous submissions are accepted. Unsuccessful proposals will be returned if accompanied by SAE. Obtains new clients through queries and submissions.

**Non-fiction** Considers illustrated non-fiction.

**Submission Guidelines** Send query letter with SAE. No children's titles.

**Tips** Mainly acts as a rights agent and consultant rather than as a traditional agent.

## Elizabeth Roy Literary Agency

White Cottage, Greatford, Nr. Stamford,
Lincolnshire, PE9 4PR

**☎** 01778 560672

**☏** 01778 560672

**Established** 1990

**Insider Info** Seeking both new and established writers. Considers non-fiction books, children's books and novels. Simultaneous submissions are accepted. Unsuccessful proposals will be returned if accompanied by SAE. Obtains new clients through queries and submissions. Commission rates of 15 per cent for domestic sales and 20 per cent on foreign sales. Does not charge a reading fee.

 * Specialises in children's books, both writers and illustrators.

**Non-fiction** Considers children's non-fiction titles.

**Fiction** Considers children's and picture book fiction titles.

**Submission Guidelines** Send query letter with SAE, synopsis and two–three sample chapters.

**Tips** Writers should declare all agents and publishers the proposal has already been submitted to.

## Elspeth Cochrane Personal Management

16 Old Town, Clapham, London, SW4 0JY

**☎** 020 7819 6256

**☏** 020 7819 4297

**✉** elspeth@elspethcochrane.co.uk

**Contact** Elspeth Cochrane

**Established** 1960

**Insider Info** Actively seeking clients. Considers non-fiction books, novels, TV scripts, movie scripts, stage plays, and radio scripts. Obtains new clients through queries and submissions. Commission rates are variable on domestic sales. Does not charge a reading fee.

**Non-fiction** Considers Biography/Autobiography and General non-fiction titles.

**Fiction** Considers general adult's fiction titles.

**Scripts** Considers scripts for film, TV, radio and theatre.

**Submission Guidelines** Send query letter with SAE and synopsis. Telephone in first instance before submitting any proposal. No self-help, memoirs, poetry or children's fiction.

**Client(s)** Alex Jones, Dominic Leyton, Royce Ryton, F. E. Smith, Robert Tannitch

## Eric Glass Ltd

25 Ladbroke Crescent, London, W11 1PS

**☎** 020 7229 9500

**☏** 020 7229 6220

**✉** eglassltd@aol.com

**Contact** Janet Glass

**Established** 1932

**Insider Info** Actively seeking clients. Considers non-fiction books, novels, TV scripts, movie scripts, stage plays and radio scripts. Simultaneous submissions are accepted. Unsuccessful proposals will be returned if accompanied by SAE. Obtains new clients through queries and submissions. Commission rates of 15 per cent for domestic sales and 20 per cent for foreign sales. Does not charge a reading fee.

**Non-fiction** Considers General non-fiction.

**Fiction** Considers General fiction.

**Scripts** Considers scripts for TV, film, radio and theatre.

**Submission Guidelines** Send query letter with SAE and the entire manuscript if requested. No short stories, poetry or children's titles.

**Client(s)** Herbert Appleman, Henry Fleet, Alan Melville

**Tips** No unsolicited manuscripts.

## Eunice McMullen Children's Literary Agent Ltd

Low Ibbotsholme Cottage, Off Bridge Lane, Troutbeck Bridge, Windemere, Cumbria, LA23 1HU

**☎** 01539 448551

**☏** 01539 442289

**✉** eunicemcmullen@totalise.co.uk

**🌐** www.eunicemcmullen.co.uk

**Contact** Director, Eunice McMullen

**Established** 1992

**Insider Info** Actively seeking clients. Considers Children's books and novels. Unsuccessful proposals will be returned if accompanied by SAE. Obtains new clients through queries and submissions. Commission rates of ten per cent on domestic sales and 15 per cent on foreign sales.

 * Eunice had worked in publishing, including for the Puffin imprint of Penguin, before beginning work as an agent. In 1992 she established her own agency.

**Non-fiction** Considers children's titles.

**Fiction** Considers Children's and Picture book titles.

**Submission Guidelines** Query via phone.

**Recent Sale(s)** *Septimus Heap Book 1 'Magyk'*, Angie Sage.

**Client(s)** Wayne Anderson, Sam Childs, Ross Collins, Charles Fuge, Gillian Shields, Susan Winter.

**Tips** Telephone enquiries only before submission, no unsolicited manuscripts.

## Eve White
**1a High Street, Kintbury, Berkshire, RG179TJ**
- 01488 657656
- 01488 657656
- evewhite@btinternet.com
- www.evewhite.co.uk

**Contact** Eve White
**Established** 2003

**Insider Info** Seeking both new and established writers. Considers non-fiction books, children's books and novels. Represents 90 clients, 30 of whom are new or previously unpublished writers. Prefers to receive exclusive submissions. Aims to respond to manuscripts within two months. Unsuccessful proposals will be returned if accompanied by SAE. Obtains new clients through recommendations from others, queries and submissions. Commission rates of 15 per cent on domestic sales and 20 per cent on foreign sales and film rights. Offers a written contract until terminated by either party with 60 days notice. Does not charge a reading fee or offer a criticism service. They will sometimes suggest a literary consultancy or a specific editor where work looks promising but not right for them at the time. Writers may be charged for printing manuscripts and for overseas postage.

    * Eve White has a degree in Education (with English and Drama). She worked as a teacher and then as a writer, director and actress in theatre and television. The agency is friendly and efficient and prides itself on keeping clients well informed at each stage of the publishing process. Also loves to get involved in the PR side of an author's career.

**Non-fiction** Considers Biography/autobiography, Child guidance/parenting, Cooking/food/nutrition, Current affairs, How-to, Humour, Memoirs, Music/dance/theatre/film, Popular culture, Self-help/personal improvement and Sports titles.

**Fiction** Considers Action/adventure, Confessional, Detective/police/crime, Ethnic, Historical, Humour/satire, Children's, Literary, Mainstream, Mystery, Picture book, Romance, Sports, Thriller/espionage, Women's/chick lit and Young adult titles.

**Submission Guidelines** Send query letter with SAE, synopsis, sample chapters and an author biography. No poetry and no email submissions.

**Tips** Clearly mark submissions 'Children's' or 'Adult'.

## Faith Evans Associates
**27 Park Avenue North, London, N8 7RU**
- 020 8340 9920
- 020 8340 9410

**Contact** Faith Evans
**Established** 1987

**Insider Info** Actively seeking clients. Currently handles non-fiction books and novels. Considers non-fiction and fiction. Obtains commissions through recommendations from others. Commission rates of 15 per cent for domestic sales and 20 per cent for foreign sales.

**Non-fiction** Considers general non-fiction titles
**Fiction** Considers general fiction titles.

**Submission Guidelines** Does not accept scripts.

**Client(s)** Melissa Benn, Shyam Bhatia, Cherie Booth, Carolyn Cassady, Caroline Conran, Alicia Foster, Helena Kennedy, Seumas Milne, Jim Kelly.

**Tips** Does not accept telephone queries. Manuscripts are only accepted by recommendation.

## Felicity Bryan Literary Agency
**2a North Parade, Banbury Road, Oxford, Oxon, OX2 6LX**
- 01865 513816
- 01865 310055
- agency@felicitybryan.com
- www.felicitybryan.com

**Established** 1988

**Insider Info** Seeking both new and established writers. Currently handles non-fiction books and novels. Considers non-fiction, fiction, and children's books. Simultaneous submissions are accepted. Aims to respond to queries and manuscripts within eight weeks. Unsuccessful proposals are returned if accompanied by SAE. Obtains new clients through recommendations from others and queries/submissions. Written contract offered. Does not charge a reading fee. Does not offer a criticism service.

**Non-fiction** Considers biography/autobiography, history and popular culture titles.

**Fiction** Considers detective/police/crime, children's, literary, mystery, thriller/espionage and women's/chick lit titles.

**Submission Guidelines** Send query letter with SAE, outline, synopsis, sample chapters, biography and a proposal. Does not accept poetry, film, TV and play scripts, science fiction, fantasy, light romance or how-to books.

**Client(s)** Authors include Roy Strong, John Julius Norwich, A. C. Grayling, Meg Rosoff, Iain Pears, Miriam Stoppard, Karen Armstrong, John Dickie,

Simon Blackburn, Katherine Langrish, Eleanor Updale, Matthew Skelton and James Naughtie. **Tips** Does not accepts authors from North America for practical reasons.

## Felix De Wolfe
**Kingsway House, 103 Kingsway, London, WC2B 6QX**
- 020 7242 5066
- 020 7242 8119
- www.felixdewolfe.com

**Insider Info** Seeking both new and established writers. Currently handles non-fiction books, novels, TV scripts, movie scripts, stage plays and sound broadcasting scripts. Considers non-fiction, fiction, film scripts, TV scripts, stage plays and sound broadcasting. Obtains new clients by queries/submissions. Commission rates of 10–15 per cent for domestic sales and 20 per cent for foreign sales. Does not charge a reading fee.
**Non-fiction** Considers general non-fiction.
**Fiction** Considers general fiction.
**Scripts** Considers general scripts.
**Tips** Approach first by telephone.

## Film Rights Ltd
**Mezzanine, Quadrant House, 80–82 Regent Street, London, W1B 5AU**
- 020 7734 9911
- 020 7734 0044
- information@film rights.ltd.uk
- www.filmrights.ltd.uk

**Contact** Director, Brendan Davis; Director, Joan Potts
**Established** 1932
**Insider Info** Seeking both new and established writers. Currently handles TV scripts, movie scripts, stage plays, radio broadcasting. Considers non-fiction, fiction, film scripts, TV scripts, stage plays, radio broadcasting. Unsuccessful proposals are returned if accompanied by SAE. Obtains new clients by queries/submissions. Commission rate of ten per cent for domestic sales and 15 per cent for foreign sales. No reading fee.
**Non-fiction** Considers general non-fiction..
**Fiction** Considers general fiction
**Scripts** Considers general scripts.
**Submission Guidelines** Send query letter with SAE.
**Tips** Works in association with Laurence Fitch Ltd.

## Fox & Howard Literary Agency
**4 Bramerton Street, London, SW3 5JX**
- 020 7352 8691
- 020 7352 8691

**Contact** Chelsey Fox; Charlotte Howard
**Established** 1992
**Insider Info** Actively seeking clients. Currently handles non-fiction books. Unsuccessful proposals are returned if accompanied by SAE. Obtains new clients by queries and submissions. Commission rates of 15 per cent for domestic sales and 20 per cent for foreign sales. Does not charge a reading fee.
**Non-fiction** Considers Agriculture/horticulture, biography/autobiography, health/medicine, popular culture, self-help/personal improvement, academia, mind body & spirit and lifestyle titles.
**Submission Guidelines** Send query letter with SAE and a synopsis.
**Tips** Please do not send any unsolicited manuscripts.

## Frances Kelly
**111 Clifton Road, Kingston-upon-Thames, Surrey, KT2 6PL**
- 020 8549 7830
- 020 8547 0051

**Contact** Frances Kelly
**Established** 1978
**Insider Info** Actively seeking clients. Currently handles non-fiction, and illustrated books. Considers non-fiction. Unsuccessful proposals are returned if accompanied by SAE. Obtains new clients with queries/submissions. Commission rates of ten per cent for domestic sales and 20 per cent for foreign sales. Does not charge a reading fee.
**Non-fiction** Considers art/architecture/design, biography/autobiography, business, cooking/food/ nutrition, health/medicine, history, money/finance/ economics, self-help/personal improvement, academia, therapeutic and lifestyle titles.
**Submission Guidelines** Send query letter with SAE, synopsis and a biography. Does not accept scripts except from existing clients.
**Tips** Please do not send any unsolicited manuscripts.

## Fraser Ross Associates
**6 Wellington Place, Edinburgh, EH6 7EQ**
- 0131 657 4412/0131 553 2759
- kjross@tiscali.co.uk/linsey.fraser@tiscali.co.uk
- www.fraserross.co.uk

**Contact** Linsey Fraser; Kathryn Ross

**Established** 2002

**Insider Info** Actively seeking clients. Currently handles children's books, and novels. Considers fiction and juvenile books. Unsuccessful proposals are returned if accompanied by SAE. Obtains new clients by queries/submissions. Commission rates of ten per cent for domestic sales and 20 per cent for foreign sales. Does not charge a reading fee.

\* Both partners had careers in readership development, book-selling and teaching before establishing their own agency, and they also ran the Scottish Book Trust from 1991–2002. They have been judges on panels for such prizes as the Whitbread and Fidler, and have addressed conferences on readership development worldwide. Presently they run the Pushkin Prizes, are National Co-ordinators for the Scottish Executive's Read Together initiative and administer the Blue Peter Awards.

**Fiction** Considers children's and picture books.

**Submission Guidelines** Send query letter with SAE, synopsis, three sample chapters and a biography. Pages should be one-sided, double-spaced, numbered pages and A4 sized. Please do not send any unfinished work.

**Client(s)** Gill Arbuthnott, Erica Blaney, John Cresswell, Samantha David, Vivian French, Chris Higgins, Liz MacWhirter, Jack McLean, Jan and Tony Payne, Jamie Rix and Linda Strachan. Illustrators: Jo Allen, Tony Bibby, Chris Fisher, Mark Jobe and Julie Lacome.

**Tips** When submitting picture books send complete manuscript for illustrators, two–three samples of artwork (colour and black & white), plus a rough storyboard of sketches with complete story. If acknowledgement is required of submitted material a paid reply postcard must be included with manuscript.

## Futerman, Rose & Associates (FRA)
**17 Deanhill Road, London, SW14 7DQ**
- 020 8255 7755
- 020 8286 4860
- guy@futermanrose.co.uk(generalenquiries)/betty@futermanrose.co.uk (fiction submissions)
- www.futermanrose.co.uk

**Contact** Partner, Guy Rose (non-fiction, auto/biographical, film, TV, client & business development); Betty Schwartz (commercial and literary fiction); Barnaby Fisher-Turner (Screenplays and TV); Alexandra Green (teenage fiction)

**Established** 1984

**Insider Info** Actively seeking clients. Currently handles non-fiction books, novels, TV scripts and movie scripts. Considers non-fiction, fiction, film scripts and TV scripts. Unsuccessful proposals are returned with SAE. Obtains new clients by queries and submissions. Commission rates of ten per cent for domestic sales and 20 per cent for foreign sales. Does not charge a reading fee.

**Non-fiction** Considers biography/autobiography titles.

**Fiction** Considers women's/chick lit and young adult titles.

**Scripts** Considers general scripts

**Submission Guidelines** Send query letter with SAE, synopsis, three sample chapters and a biography. Does not accept science fiction, poetry, young children's or textbooks.

**Recent Sale(s)** *Diary of a Facelift*, Toyah Wilcox; *My Now or Never Diary*, Liz Rettig; *Infernal Child 'World Without Love'*, Erin Pizzey; *The Kennedys & Cuba*, Mark White

**Client(s)** Paul Hendy, Ciaran O'Keeffe, Sue Lenier, David Brett, Susan George, Stephen Griffin, Yvette Fielding, Iain Duncan Smith, Paul Marx and Philip Dart.

**Tips** The agency are especially interested in political, music and show business autobiographies.

## Gillon Aitken Associates
**18–21 Cavaye Place, London, SW10 9PT**
- 020 7373 8672
- 020 7373 6002
- recep@gillonaitken.co.uk
- www.gillonaitkenassociates.co.uk

**Contact** Gillon Aitken; Clare Alexander (new fiction writers, history, biography, memoir and science); Kate Shaw (literary and popular fiction for adults and children's authors); Lesley Thorne (screenplays, literary fiction, crime thrillers, memoir, travelogue/adventure, biography and popular culture)

**Established** 1977

**Insider Info** Actively seeking clients. Currently handles non-fiction books, novels, TV scripts, movie scripts. Considers non-fiction, fiction, children's books, film scripts and TV scripts. Aims to respond to queries and proposals within eight weeks. Unsuccessful submissions are returned with SAE. Commission rates are ten per cent for domestic sales, 20 per cent for foreign sales and ten per cent for film sales. Doe not charge a reading fee.

\* The agents have mainly come from publishing and editorial backgrounds.

**Non-fiction** Considers biography/autobiography, history, memoirs, popular culture, science/technology and travel books.

**Fiction** Consider general fiction titles.

**Scripts** Considers general scripts.

**Submission Guidelines** Send query letter with outline, biography and a 30-page sample of writing. All pages should be single-sided and double-spaced.
**Client(s)** Sebastian Faulks, Helen Fielding, Nicholas Stargardt and Andrew Wilson.
**Tips** Unable to answer queries by email. Postal queries and submissions only. A list of writing credits (in any genre) would be useful to include with the submission.

## Graham Maw Literary Agency
**16 De Beauvoir Square, London, N1 4LD**
- 020 7812 9937
- enquiries@grahammawagency.com
- www.grahammawagency.com

**Contact** Jane Graham Maw; Jennifer Christie
**Established** 2005
**Insider Info** Seeking mostly established writers through referrals. Currently handles non-fiction books, TV tie-ins and web-to-book projects. Considers non-fiction books. Obtains new clients through recommendations from others. Commission rates of 15 per cent for domestic sales and 20 per cent for foreign sales. No reading fee.
**Non-fiction** Considers biography/autobiography, business, child guidance/parenting, health/medicine, history, psychology, memoirs, popular culture, lifestyle, mind, body and spirit titles.
**Submission Guidelines** Any authorised submissions should include a one-page summary and a paragraph on the content of each chapter, the qualification one has for writing upon the subject, ideas for promotion of the material, plus full contact details. Does not accept fiction, children's or poetry titles.
**Tips** Please do not send any unsolicited manuscripts by post. The agency prefers to work with existing authors and by recommendation only.

## Greene & Heaton Ltd.
**37 Goldhawk Road, London, W12 8QQ**
- 020 8749 0315
- 020 8749 0318
- info@greeneheaton.co.uk
- www.greeneheaton.co.uk

**Contact** Director, Carol Heaton (Authors); Judith Murray (Authors); Antony Topping (Authors); Nick Harrop (Authors); Linda Davis (Children's Authors); Ellie Glason (Translations and Subsidiary rights); Will Francis (Authors)
**Established** 1963
**Insider Info** Actively seeking clients. Currently handles non-fiction books, children's books, novels.

Considers non-fiction, fiction and children's books. Simultaneous submissions are accepted. Aims to respond to queries and proposals within six weeks. Unsuccessful submissions returned with SAE. Obtains new clients by queries and submissions. Commission rates of 10–15 per cent for domestic sales and 20 per cent for foreign sales. No reading fee.
**Non-fiction** Considers Agriculture/Horticulture, History, Humour, Children's, Science/Technology, Travel and General Non-fiction titles.
**Fiction** Considers Children's and General fiction titles.
**Submission Guidelines** Send query letter with SAE, synopsis and three sample chapters. Does not accept scripts.
**Recent Sale(s)** *Urban Sanctuaries*, Stephen Anderton; *How to be Cool*, Will Smith; *Unknown Soldiers*, Matthew Carr; *Voyaging the Pacific*, Miles Hordern
**Client(s)** Michael Frayn, P.D. James, William Shawcross, Mark Barrowcliffe, Bill Bryson, Hugh Fearnley-Whittingstall, C.J.Sansom, Marcus du Sautoy, Sarah Waters, Kathryn Hymen, Tom Ryan, Russell Davis and Tabitha Suzuma.
**Tips** The agency has a very diverse list of clientele, handling all types of fiction and non-fiction.

## Gregory & Company Authors' Agents
**3 Barb Mews, London, W6 7PA**
- 020 7610 4676
- 020 7610 4686
- info@gregoryandcompany.co.uk (general enquiries)
- www.gregoryandcompany.co.uk

**Contact** Jane Gregory (Director); Emma Dunford (Editorial); Claire Morris (Rights)
**Established** 1987
**Insider Info** Actively seeking clients. Currently handles non-fiction books and novels. Accepts simultaneous submissions. Unsuccessful manuscripts will bee returned if accompanied by SAE. Clients usually obtained through queries and submissions. Commission of 15 per cent for domestic sales, 20 per cent for foreign sales. Does not charge a reading fee.
**Non-fiction** Will consider biography/autobiography and general non-fiction.
**Fiction** Will consider detective/police/crime, family saga, historical, literary and thriller/espionage.
**Submission Guidelines** Authors should include query letter, SAE, synopsis and three sample chapters as double-spaced, one-sided A4. Accepts queries by email. No chick lit., children's, science

fiction, fantasy, poetry, short stories or scripts considered.

**Recent Sales** *Come Away With Me,* Sarah MacDonald; *Killer Tune,* Dreda Say Mitchell, *Absolute Power,* Mark Tavener; *Angels Alone,* Natasha Cooper.

**Clients** Julian Thompson, John Ryan, Eileen Dewhurst, Betty Boothroyd, Jo Bannister, Minette Walters, Robert Barnard, Gladys Mitchell, Sarah Diamond, Val McDermid

**Tips** If submission is by email, send a brief letter with a synopsis, but no more than ten pages. When entering the book title also write 'Submission' in subject line. Do not send an entire manuscript without prior authorisation.

## Gunn Media Associates

**8 Lower James street, London, W1F 9EL**

- ali@gunnmedia.co.uk

**Contact** Ali Gunn

**Established** 2005

**Insider Info** Seeking both new and established writers. Considers non-fiction books and novels. Simultaneous submissions are accepted. Unsuccessful proposals will be returned with SAE. Obtains new clients through queries and submissions. Commission rates of 15 per cent on domestic sales and 20 per cent on foreign sales. Does not charge reading fees.

**Non-fiction** Considers commercial non-fiction.

**Fiction** Considers commercial fiction.

**Submission Guidelines** Send a query letter with SAE, synopsis and two–three sample chapters. No scripts.

**Tips** Unsolicited proposals are welcome by post only.

## Henser Literary Agency

**174 Pennant Road, Llanelli, Wales, SA4 8HN**

- 01554 753520
- henserliteraryagency@btopenworld.com

**Contact** Steve Henser

**Established** 2002

**Insider Info** Seeking both new and established writers. Considers novels, TV scripts, movie scripts, stage plays and radio scripts. Simultaneous submissions are accepted. Obtains new clients through queries and submissions. Commission rates of 15 per cent on domestic sales and 20 per cent on foreign sales.

**Fiction** Considers Fantasy, Literary, Mainstream, Mystery and Science fiction titles.

**Scripts** Considers scripts for TV, film, radio and theatre.

**Submission Guidelines** Send query letter with SAE and synopsis. No horror.

**Tips** Does not accept unsolicited manuscripts.

## HHB Agency Ltd

**6 Warwick Court, London, WC1R 5DJ**

- 020 7405 5525
- heather@hhbagency.com
- www.hhbagency.com

**Contact** Heather Holden-Brown

**Established** 2005

**Insider Info** Actively seeking clients. Considers non-fiction books and novels. Simultaneous submissions are accepted. Unsuccessful proposals will be returned if accompanied by SAE. Obtains new clients through queries and submissions. Commission rates of 15 per cent on domestic sales. Does not charge reading fees.

**Non-fiction** Considers Biography/Autobiography, Business, Cooking/Food/Nutrition, Current affairs, Government/Politics/Law, History, Memoirs, and Journalism titles.

**Fiction** Considers Detective/police/crime, Historical and Women's/'Chick lit' titles.

**Submission Guidelines** Send query letter with SAE, synopsis and three sample chapters.

**Recent Sale(s)** *Loose Cannon,* Malcolm Brahant; *Catch Me Before I Fall,* Rosie Child and Diane Taylor

**Client(s)** Tom Pugh

**Tips** HHB are a new agency looking for bright and exciting talent.

## ICM Books

**4–6 Soho Square, London, W1D 3PZ**

- 020 7432 0800
- 020 7432 0808
- icmbookslondon@icmtalent.com
- www.icmtalent.com

**Contact** Kate Jones, Margaret Halton

**Insider Info** Seeking both new and established writers. Considers non-fiction books and novels. Unsuccessful proposals will be returned with SAE. Obtains new clients through queries and submissions. Does not charge reading fees.

**Non-fiction** Considers General non-fiction and Journalism titles.

**Fiction** Considers General Commercial fiction titles.

**Submission Guidelines** Send query letter with SAE.

**Tips** No unsolicited manuscripts.

## IMG UK Ltd

**McCormack House, Burlington Lane, London, W4 2TH**

☎ 020 8233 5300

🖷 020 8233 5301

🌐 www.imgworld.com

**Contact** Joint CEOs, Bob Kain and Alastair Johnston

**Insider Info** Considers non-fiction books and celebrity and sports related material. Unsuccessful proposals will be returned with SAE. Obtains new clients through queries and submissions. Commission rates of 15 per cent for domestic sales and 20–25 per cent for foreign sales. Do not charge reading fees.

 * IMG are a specialist sports and entertainment media company.

**Non-fiction** Consider Music, Dance, Theatre, Film, Sports and Celebrity titles.

**Submission Guidelines** Send query letter with SAE.

**Tips** Represents television properties, celebrities, entertainers, artists, musicians, sports personalities, organisations and events, as well as writers.

## The Inspira Group

**5 Bradley Road, Enfield, Middlesex, EN3 6ES**

☎ 020 8292 5163

🖷 0870 139 3057

📧 darin@theinspiragroup.com

🌐 www.theinspiragroup.com

**Contact** Darin Jewell

**Established** 2001

**Insider Info** Seeking both new and established writers. Considers non-fiction books, children's books, novels, general fiction and short story collections. Represents 18 clients, 50 per cent of whom are new and previously unpublished writers. Simultaneous submissions are accepted. Aims to respond to queries within three days and manuscripts within 14 days. Unsuccessful proposals will be returned with SAE. Obtains clients through recommendations from others, queries and submissions. Has sold nine books within the last year. Commission rates of 15 per cent on domestic and foreign sales. Offers a written contract until terminated by either party with 30 days notice. Does not charge a reading fee or offer a criticism service.

 * Darin pursued his doctoral research at Cambridge in England before becoming an agent. He likes to work with talented writers, whether they be first-time authors or previously published authors.

**Non-fiction** Considers all types of non-fiction.

**Fiction** Considers all types of fiction.

**Submission Guidelines** Send query letter, with SAE, entire manuscript, synopsis and an author biography. Initial queries are invited by email or phone. Actively seeking talented writers who have a passion for writing. No poetry, biographies or anthologies.

**Recent Sale(s)** *Teach Your Children to Read and Write,* Dominic Wyse (Pearson Education); *Broken Glass,* C.W. Reed Robert Hale Publishing); *So You're 40, 50, 60,* Mike Haskins and Clive Whichelow (Summersdale Publishing); *Two Nuns in a Bath,* Steve Arnott and Mike Haskins (Carlton Books)

**Client(s)** A list of the authors the group represents can be found online.

## Intercontinental Literary Agency

**Centric House, 390–391 Strand, London, WC2R 0LT**

☎ 020 7379 6611

🖷 020 7240 4724

📧 ila@ila-agency.co.uk

🌐 www.ila-agency.co.uk

**Contact** Nicki Kennedy (Rights in France, Germany, Italy, Spain and Japan); Sam Edenborough, (Rights in Denmark, Finland, Sweden, Norway, Holland, Greece, Iceland, Portugal and Brazil); Mary Esdaile (Arabic and Indonesian rights, works with co-agents in Bulgaria, Hungary, Lithuania, Romania, Estonia, Croatia, the Czech Republic, Latvia, Serbia, Slovakia, Slovenia, Turkey, China, Korea, Thailand and Israel); Tessa Girvan (Rights for Children's and Young Adult titles Worldwide, including work with co-agents in Poland and Russia)

**Established** 1965

**Insider Info** Considers non-fiction, fiction, children's books and young adult titles. Works with other agents and publishers exclusively.

 * Specialises in translation rights for authors from Britain, USA and Australia.

**Client(s)** Elyse Cheney Literary Associates, Lucas Alexander Whitley Ltd, Luigi Bonomi Associates, Mulcahy & Viney Ltd, PDF, Turnbull Agency (John Irving), Wade & Doherty Literary Agency

**Tips** Does not deal directly with writers, only other agents and publishers.

## International Scripts

**1a Kidbrooke Park Road, London, SE3 0LR**

☎ 020 8319 8666

🖷 020 8319 0801

📧 internationalscripts@btinternet.com

**Contact** H.P.Tanner, J.Lawson

**Established** 1979

**Insider Info** Actively seeking clients. Considers non-fiction books, novels, televison scripts and movie scripts. Simultaneous submissions are accepted. Unsuccessful proposals will be returned with SAE. Obtains new clients through queries and submissions. Commission rates of 15 per cent on domestic sales and 20 per cent on foreign sales. May charge reading fees.

**Non-fiction** Considers Biography/Autobiography, Business and General non-fiction titles.

**Fiction** Considers Detective/Police/Crime, Women's/'Chick lit' and General Contemporary fiction titles.

**Scripts** Considers scripts for television and film.

**Submission Guidelines** Send query letter with SAE. No short stories, poetry or articles.

**Client(s)** Jane Adams, Ashleigh Bingham, Dr. James Fleming, Trevor Lummis, Chris Pascoe, Anne Spencer

**Tips** If a full manuscript is requested, an editorial financial contribution may be required along with SAE.

## Jane Conway-Gordon Ltd
**1 Old Compton Street, London, W1D 5JA**

☎ 020 7494 0148

✆ 020 7287 9264

**Contact** Jane Conway-Gordon

**Established** 1982

**Insider Info** Actively seeking clients. Currently handles general fiction and non-fiction books and novels. Accepts simultaneous submissions. Manuscripts returned with SAE. Clients usually obtained through queries/submissions. Commission rate of 15 per cent for domestic sales, 20 per cent for foreign sales. No reading fee charged.

**Submission Guidelines** Authors should include query letter and SAE with submissions. No Short stories, Poetry, Science fiction or Children's books considered.

**Tips** The agency is represented worldwide.

## Jane Judd Literary Agency
**18 Belitha Villas, London, N1 1PD**

☎ 020 7607 0273

✆ 020 7607 0623

**Contact** Jane Judd

**Established** 1986

**Insider Info** Actively seeking clients. Currently handles non-fiction books and novels. Accepts simultaneous submissions. Manuscripts returned with SAE. Clients usually obtained through queries/submissions. Commission rates of ten per cent for

domestic sales, 20 per cent for foreign sales. No reading fee charged.

**Non-fiction** Will consider Biography/Autobiography, Health/Medicine, Humour, Travel, Lifestyle and General.

**Fiction** Will consider Detective/Police/Crime, Thriller/Espionage, Women's/'Chick lit' and literary fiction.

**Submission Guidelines** Authors should include query letter, SAE, synopsis, one sample chapter and complete contact details and email address with their submission. No academia, scripts, DIY or gardening considered.

## Janet Fillingham Associates
**52 Lowther Road, London, SW13 9NU**

☎ 020 8748 5594

✆ 020 8748 7374

✉ info@janetfillingham.com

🌐 www.janetfillingham.com

**Contact** Director, Janet Fillingham

**Established** 1992

**Insider Info** Seeking mostly established writers through referrals. Currently handles TV scripts, movie scripts and stage plays. Clients usually obtained through recommendations from others. Commission rates of ten per cent for domestic sales, 15–20 per cent for foreign sales.

**Recent Sales** *Bye Bye Harry*, Graham Alborough; *Casualty*, Ray Brooking; *Doctors*, Michael Chappell & Richard Stevens;*Dream Team*, Eddy Marshall

**Clients** Esther May Campbell, Clive Endersby, Nick Gleaves, Christopher Green, Steve Griffiths, Charles McKeown, Dale Overton, Tina Pepler, Allan Plenderleith, Robert Rigby, Robert Rohrer, Frances Tomelty

**Tips** First contact must be by email with only CV and contact details. No unsolicited manuscripts accepted, as the agency prefers to work via referrals and recommendations.

## Jane Turnbull
**58 Elgin Cresent, London W11 2JJ, Mailing address: Barn Cottage, Veryan, Truro TR2 5QA**

☎ 020 7727 9409/01872 501317

✉ jane.turnbull@btinternet.com

**Contact** Jane Turnbull

**Established** 1986

**Insider Info** Actively seeking clients. Currently handles non-fiction books and novels. Manuscripts returned with SAE. Clients usually obtained through queries/submissions. Commissions rates of ten per cent for domestic sales, 20 per cent for foreign sales. Does not charge reading fee.

**Non-fiction** Will consider Biography/Autobiography, Current affairs, Health/Medicine, History, Lifestyle and Diet.

**Submission Guidelines** Authors should include query letter and SAE with submissions. No romantic, sagas or science fiction considered.

**Tips** No unsolicited manuscripts.

## Janklow & Nesbit (UK) Ltd
**33 Drayson Mews, London, W8 4LY**
- 020 7376 2733
- 020 7376 2915
- queries@janklow.co.uk

**Contact** Tif Loehnis, Claire Paterson, Jenny McVeigh

**Established** 2000

**Insider Info** Seeking both new and established writers. Currently handles non-fiction books, scholarly books and novels. Accepts simultaneous submissions. Manuscripts returned with SAE. Does not charge reading or office fees, or a criticism service. Does not refer to editing service.

**Submission Guidelines** Authors should include query letter, SAE, outline, synopsis, three sample chapters, author biography and proposal with submissions. Actively seeking fiction and non-fiction; commercial and literary. Email submissions are not accepted.

## Jeffrey Simmons
**15 Penn House, Mallory Street, London, NW8 8SX**
- 020 7224 8917
- jasimmons@btconnect.com

**Contact** Jeffrey Simmons

**Insider Info** Actively seeking clients. Currently handles non-fiction books and novels. Accepts simultaneous submissions. Manuscripts returned with SAE. Clients usually obtained through queries/submissions. Commission rate is ten per cent for domestic sales, 15 percent for foreign sales. Does not charge a reading fee.

**Non-fiction** Will consider Biography/Autobiography, Current affairs, Government/Politics/Law, History, Sports, True crime/Investigative, Academia, Parapsychology, Quality commercial, and the Arts.

**Fiction** Will consider quality commercial fiction.

**Submission Guidelines** Authors should include query letter, SAF, synopsis, two or three sample chapters, author biography, brief publishing history including list of manuscripts with submission. No

hobbies, science fiction, fantasy, horror, children's, cookery or gardening considered.

**Tips** Genuinely interested in new, young exciting writers. Will suggest revisions. Include any publishing history and a list of agents/publishers that the manuscript has been submitted to.

## Jennifer Luithlen Agency
**88 Holmfield, Leicester, LE2 1SB**
- 0116 273 8863
- 0116 273 5697

**Contact** Jennifer Luithlen, Agent; Penny Luithlen, Agent

**Established** 1986

**Insider Info** Not currently seeking new clients. Currently handles juvenile books and fiction. Commission rate is 15 per cent for domestic sales, 20 per cent for foreign sales.

**Fiction** Will consider Detective/Police/Crime, Family saga, Historical, Juvenile, Literary and General.

**Tips** No unsolicited manuscripts.

## Jenny Brown Associates
**33 Argyle Place, Edinburgh, EH9 1JT**
- 0131 229 5334
- 0131 229 6695
- jenny-brown@blueyonder.co.uk
- www.jennybrownassociates.com

**Contact** Jenny Brown (represents writers of literary fiction & non-fiction); Mark Stanton (non-fiction - sports/music); Allan Guthrie; Lucy Juckes (writers & illustrators for children's books)

**Established** 2002

**Insider Info** Actively seeking clients. Currently handles non-fiction books, juvenile books and novels. Before establishing the agency, Jenny Brown was formerly Director of the Edinburgh International Book Festival and Head of Literature at the Scottish Arts Council. Accepts simultaneous submissions. Aims to respond to queries/proposals withing six weeks. Manuscripts returned with SAE. Clients usually obtained through queries/submissions. Commissions rate of 12.5 per cent for domestic sales, 20 per cent for foreign sales. Does not charge reading fee.

**Non-fiction** Considers Biography/Autobiography, History, Music/Dance/Theatre/Film, Popular culture and Sports.

**Fiction** Considers Detective/Police/Crime, Juvenile and Literary.

**Submission Guidelines** Authors should include SAE, synopsis, sample chapters, author biography, one page synopsis and brief CV with submission, which should be double-spaced, one-sided A4, of 25 pages only. No poetry, science fiction, fantasy, sagas or academia considered.

**Recent Sale** *Two Way Split*, Allan Guthrie; *Vanessa & Virginia*, Susan Sellers; *Just Take Charlie*, Kim Elliott; *Meet Me Under the Westway*, Stephen Thompson

**Clients** Lin Anderson, Richard Blandford, Linda Cracknell, David White, Patrick Lambe, Esther Woolfson, Dennis O'Donnell, Erica Munro, Alex Gray, Diana Hendry, David Barnes, Catherine De Courcy, Neil Drysdale, Guy Kennaway, Richard Moore, Aidan Smith

**Tips** Any non-fiction manuscripts should be accompanied by ideas for possible promotion and outlets, plus any notes on comparable or competing literature.

## Jill Foster Ltd

**9 Barb Mews, Brook Green, London, W6 7PA**

☎ 020 7602 1263

☏ 020 7602 9336

✉ agents@jfagency.com

**Contact** Jill Foster, Alison Finch, Simon Williamson, Dominic Lord, Gary Wild

**Established** 1976

**Insider Info** Actively seeking clients. Currently handles television scripts, movie scripts, stage plays and fiction. Accepts simultaneous submissions. Clients usually obtained through queries/ submissions. Commission rate of 12.5 per cent for domestic sales, 15 per cent for foreign sales. Does not charge reading fee.

**Submission Guidelines** Authors should include query letter with submission. No books, poetry or short stories considered.

**Tips** No submissions by email. A preliminary letter is essential in the first instance.

## JMLA

**The Basement, 94 Goldhurst Terrace, London, NW6 3HS**

☎ 020 7372 8422/3140

☏ 020 7372 8423

**Contact** Managing Director, Judy Martin

**Established** 1990

**Insider Info** Actively seeking clients. Currently handles non-fiction books. Manuscripts returned with SAE. Clients usually obtained through queries/ submissions Commission rate of 15 per cent for domestic sales, 20 per cent for foreign sales. Does not charge reading fee.

**Non-fiction** Will consider Biography/ Autobiography, Jazz origins/History/American, Art/ Surrealism.

**Submission Guidelines** Authors should include query letter, SAE, synopsis, two to three sample chapters, and publishing history with submission. No cookery, gardening, poetry or children's considered.

**Tips** Specialises in jazz material.

## J.M.Thurley Management

**Archery House, 33 Archery Square, Walmer, Deal, Kent, CT14 7JA**

☎ 01304 371421

☏ 01304 371416

✉ JMThurley@aol.com

**Contact** Jon Thurley

**Established** 1976

**Insider Info** Seeking both new and established writers. Currently handling novels, television scripts, movie scripts and fiction. Accepts simultaneous submissions. Manuscripts returned with SAE. Clients usually obtained through queries/submissions. Commission of 15 per cent for domestic sales, 20 per cent for trade sales. Does not charge a reading fee.

**Fiction** Will consider literary and commercial fiction.

**Scripts** Will consider general/commercial scripts.

**Submission Guidelines** Authors should include query letter and SAE with submissions. No short stories, poetry, articles, fantasy or play scripts considered.

**Tips** The agency provides editorial and creative assistance to new, exciting writers and constructive revision advice to authorised manuscripts that are rejected.

## John Pawsey

**60 High Street, Tarring, Worthing, Essex, BN14 7NR**

☎ 01903 205167

☏ 01903 205167

**Contact** John Pawsey

**Established** 1981

**Insider Info** Actively seeking clients. Currently handles non-fiction books and novels. Accepts simultaneous submissions. Manuscript return with SAE. Clients usually obtained through queries/ submissions. Commission for domestic and foreign sales variable. Does not charge a reading fee.

**Non-fiction** Will consider Art/Architecture/Design, Biography/Autobiography, Business, Current affairs, Ethnic/Cultural interests, Music/Dance/Theatre/Film, Popular culture, Sports, Lifestyle, Travel and Politics.

**Fiction** Will consider Detective/Police/Crime, Mystery and Thriller/Espionage.

**Submission Guidelines** Authors should submit query letter, SAE, synopsis and three sample chapters with submission. No science fiction, fantasy, horror, poetry, children's, short stories, journalism, scripts or drama considered.

**Clients** Jennie Bond, David Ashforth, William Fotheringham, Don Hale, Patricia Hall, Dr. David Lewis, Anne Mustoe

**Tips** Has a strong list of established clients, but is always looking to meeting bright new talent.

## Johnson & Alcock Ltd
**Clerkenwell House, 45–47 Clerkenwell Green, London, EC1R 0HT**
- 020 7251 0125
- 020 7251 2172
- info@johnsonandalcock.co.uk

**Contact** Michael Alcock, Anna Power, Andrew Hewson, Merel Reinink
**Established** 1956
**Insider Info** Actively seeking clients. Currently handles nonfiction books, juvenile books and novels. Accepts simultaneous submissions. Manuscripts returned with SAE. Clients usually obtained through queries/submissions. Commission of 15 per cent on domestic sales, 20 per cent on foreign sales. Does not charge a reading fee.
**Non-fiction** Will consider Biography/Autobiography, Current affairs, Health/Medicine, History, Memoirs, Self-help/Personal improvement and Lifestyle.
**Fiction** Will consider Juvenile, Literary and Commercial fiction.
**Submission Guidelines** Authors should include query letter, SAE, synopsis and author biography with submissions. Include details of media/writing experience. No scripts, poetry, science fiction, academia or technical writing considered.
**Tips** No unsolicited manuscripts, but fiction writers may submit the first three chapters with first contact. No email submissions.

## John Welch, Literary Consultant & Agent
**Mill Cottage, Calf Lane, Chipping Camden, GL55 6JQ**
- 01387 840237
- 01386 840568

**Contact** John Welch
**Established** 1992

**Insider Info** Not currently seeking new clients. Currently handles non-fiction books. Commission of ten per cent on domestic sales.
**Non-fiction** Will consider Biography/Autobiography, History, Military/War, Sports, Aviation and Naval History and Travel.
**Submission Guidelines** Authors should submit query letter and SAE with submissions. No fiction, poetry, scripts or children's writing considered.
**Tips** No unsolicited manuscripts. No new authors considered at this time.

## Jonathan Clowes Ltd
**10 Iron Bridge Road, Bridge Approach, London, NW1 8BD**
- 020 7722 7674
- 020 7722 7677

**Contact** Jonathan Clowes
**Established** 1960
**Insider Info** Actively seeking clients. Currently handles non-fiction books, novels, television scripts, movie scripts, and stage plays. Manuscripts returned with SAE. Clients usually obtained through recommendations from others and queries/submissions. Commission rate of 15 per cent for domestic sales, variable for foreign sales. No reading fee charged.
**Fiction** Will consider literary fiction.
**Scripts** Will consider comedy.
**Submission Guidelines** Authors should include query letter and SAE with submissions. No textbooks or children's considered.
**Tips** No unsolicited manuscripts.

## Jonathan Williams Literary Agency
**Rosney Mews, Upper Glenageary Road, Glenageary, Co. Dublin, Republic of Ireland**
- 00353 1 280 3482
- 00353 1 280 3482

**Contact** Director, Jonathan Williams
**Established** 1981
**Insider Info** Seeking both new and established writers. Currently handles non-fiction books and novels. Manuscripts returned with SAE. Clients usually obtained through queries/submissions. Commission rate of 10 per cent on domestic sales. Does not charge reading fee (see Tips).
**Non-fiction** Considers general non-fiction.
**Fiction** Considers general fiction.
**Submission Guidelines** Authors should include query letter, SAE, synopsis and two to three sample chapters.

**Tips** Reading fees will be charged if a quick response is required. No UK stamps, only IRCs.

## Josef Weinberger Plays

**12–14 Mortimer Street, London, W1T 3JJ**

- 020 7580 2827
- 020 7436 9616
- general.info@jwmail.co.uk
- www.josef-weinberger.com

**Contact** Michael Callahan, (Stage Licensing (Plays) Professional); John Schofield, Sally Irwin, Sean Gray (Stage Licensing (Musicals) Professional); Lewis Mitchell (Concert & Educational Music Promotion); Rupert Sharp, Ian Reeder, Emma Dolan, Caroline Moore (Stage Licensing (Musicals & Plays) Amateur); Stephanie Parker (Perusal Requests - Amateur)

**Established** 1938

**Insider Info** Actively seeking clients. Currently handles stage plays, ballet, musicals and operas and operettas. Accepts simultaneous submissions. Clients usually obtained through queries/submissions.

**Submission Guidelines** Submit query letter.

**Tips** The agency specialises in stage plays on an international scale. No unsolicited manuscripts.

## Judith Chilcote Agency

**8 Wentworth Mansions, Keats Grove, London, NW3 2RL**

- 020 7794 3717
- judybks@aol.com

**Contact** Judith Chilcote

**Established** 1990

**Insider Info** Actively seeking clients. Currently handles non-fiction books and novels. Accepts simultaneous submissions. Manuscripts returned with SAE. Clients usually obtained through queries/submissions. Does not charge a reading fee.

**Non-fiction** Will consider Art/Architecture/Design, Biography/Autobiography, Cooking/Food/Nutrition, Current affairs, Health/Medicine, Psychology, Popular culture, Self-help/Personal improvement, Sports and Lifestyle.

**Fiction** Will consider commercial fiction.

**Submission Guidelines** Authors should include query letter, SAE, three sample chapters and biography with submission. No poetry, scripts, short stories, academia or children's considered.

**Tips** A CV is essential with submissions. The agency is interested in cinema/television tie-ins for its clients.

## Judith Murdoch Literary Agency

**19 Chalcot Square, London, NW1 8YA**

- 020 7722 7674

**Contact** Judith Murdoch

**Established** 1993

**Insider Info** Clients usually obtained through queries/submissions Commission rate of 15 per cent for domestic sales, 20 per cent for foreign sales. Does not charge a reading fee.

**Fiction** Will consider Literary, Women's/'Chick lit' and General fiction.

**Submission Guidelines** Author should include query letter, SAE, synopsis and two sample chapters with submission. No thrillers, poetry, science fiction, fantasy, short stories or children's considered.

**Tips** No telephone approaches.

## Judy Daish Associates Ltd

**2 St. Charles Place, London, W10 6EG**

- 020 8964 8811
- 020 8964 8966

**Contact** Judy Daish, Howard Gooding, Tracey Elliston

**Established** 1978

**Insider Info** Actively seeking clients. Currently handling television scripts, movie scripts, stage plays and radio scripts. Accepts simultaneous submissions. Manuscripts returned with SAE. Clients usually obtained through queries/submissions. Commission rated on domestic and foreign sales by negotiation. Does not charge a reading fee.

**Submission Guidelines** Authors should submit query letter. No books considered.

**Tips** No unsolicited manuscripts.

## Juliet Burton Literary Agency

**2 Clifton Avenue, London, W12 9DR**

- 020 8762 0148
- 020 8743 8765
- juliet.burton@btinternet.com

**Contact** Juliet Burton

**Established** 1999

**Insider Info** Seeking both new and established writers. Currently handles non-fiction books and novels. Manuscripts returned with SAE. Clients usually obtained through queries/submissions. Commission rate of 15 per cent for domestic sales, 20 per cent for foreign sales. Does not charge a reading fee.

**Non-fiction** Will consider True crime/Investigative.

**Fiction** Will consider Detective/Police/Crime and Women's/'Chick lit'.

**Submission Guidelines** Authors should include query letter, SAE, synopsis and two to three sample chapters with submission. No scripts, academia, poetry or articles considered.

**Tips** No unsolicited or emailed manuscripts.

## Juri Gabriel

**35 Camberwell Grove, London, SE5 8JA**

- 020 7703 6186
- 020 7703 6186

**Contact** Juri Gabriel

**Insider Info** Actively seeking clients. Currently handles non-fiction books and novels. Juri Gabriel worked in television for many years and is the author of several books. He is also chairman of Dedalus publishers. Simultaneous submissions accepted. Manuscripts returned with SAE. Clients usually obtained through queries/submissions. Commission rate of ten percent for domestic sales, 20 per cent for foreign sales. Does not charge a reading fee.

**Fiction** Will consider literary fiction.

**Submission Guidelines** Authors should include query letter, SAE, three sample chapters, biography and written query with submissions. No poetry, short stories, articles or children's considered.

**Clients** Maurice Caldera, Diana Constance, Miriam Dunne, Richard Mankiewicz, Karina Mellinger, Dr. Terence White

**Tips** Agency handles mainly established clients and insists on a high quality of manuscript. Much work consists of television, film and radio rights.

## Kate Hordern Literary Agency

**18 Mortimer Road, Clifton, Bristol, BS8 4EY**

- 01179 239368
- 01179 731941
- katehordern@blueyonder.co.uk

**Contact** Kate Hordern

**Established** 1999

**Insider Info** Actively seeking clients. Currently considers Non-fiction books and Novels. Considers Non-fiction and Fiction. Will consider simultaneous submissions and unsuccessful proposals will be returned with SAE. Obtain new clients via queries/submissions. Commission rates of 15 per cent by domestic sales and 20 per cent by foreign sales. No reading fee.

**Non-fiction** Will consider quality general non-fiction titles.

**Fiction** Will consider quality general fiction titles.

**Submission Guidelines** Send proposal package with query letter, SAE and synopsis.

**Tips** Sample chapters for fiction upon request only. For non-fiction first contact, submit only a proposal and chapter breakdown. No unsolicited manuscripts will be accepted.

## Knight Features (Peter Knight Agency)

**20 Crescent Grove, London, SW4 7AH**

- 020 7622 1467
- 020 7622 1522
- peter@knightfeatures.co.uk
- www.knightfeatures.co.uk

**Contact** Director, Peter Knight; Associate, Andrew Knight; Associate, Gaby Martin; Associate, Samantha Ferris

**Established** 1985

**Insider Info** Actively seeking clients. Will consider Non-fiction and Syndicated material. Will consider simultaneous submissions and unsuccessful proposals will be returned with SAE. Obtains new clients via queries/submissions.

**Non-fiction** Will consider Biography/Autobiography, Business, History, Humour, Motor sport, Puzzles, Academic and Wellbeing titles.

**Fiction** Will consider Cartoons/Comics titles.

**Submission Guidelines** Send proposal package with query letter, SAE, synopsis and author biography. Will not consider Science Fiction, Poetry or Cookery titles.

**Client(s)** Simon Shuker, Frank Dickens, Gray Jolliffe, Angus Mcgill, Chris Maslanka, Barbara Minto

**Tips** No emailed or unsolicited submissions will be accepted.

## Laura Morris Literary Agency

**21 Highshore Road, London, SE15 5AA**

- 020 7732 0153
- 020 7732 9022
- laura.morris@btconnect.com

**Contact** Laura Morris

**Established** 1998

**Insider Info** Actively seeking clients. Currently handles Non-fiction books and Novels. Will consider Non-fiction and Fiction. Will consider simultaneous submissions and unsuccessful proposals will be returned with SAE. Obtains new clients via queries/submissions. Commission rates of ten per cent by domestic sales and 20 per cent by foreign sales. No reading fee.

**Non-fiction** Will consider Biography/Autobiography, Cooking/Food/Nutrition, Ethnic/Cultural interests, Humour, Popular culture and Film/Media studies titles.

**Fiction** Will consider Literary titles.

**Submission Guidelines** Send proposal package with query letter and SAE. No children's books will be considered.

**Tips** No unsolicited manuscripts will be accepted.

## Laurence Fitch Ltd

**Mezzanine, Quadrant House, 80–82 Regent Street, London, W1B 5AU**

☎ 020 7734 9911

☎ 020 7734 0044

✉ information@laurencefitch.com

🌐 www.laurencefitch.com

**Contact** Director, Brendan Davis

**Established** 1952

**Insider Info** Actively seeking clients. Currently handles Television scripts, Movie scripts, Stage plays and Radio Scripts. Will consider Juvenile books, Film scripts, Television scripts, Stage plays and Radio scripts. Will consider simultaneous submissions. Unsuccessful proposals will be returned with SAE. Obtains new clients via queries/submissions. Commission rates of ten per cent by domestic sales and 15 per cent by foreign sales. Does not charge a reading fee.

**Fiction** Will consider Horror, Children's and General fiction titles.

**Scripts** Will consider General and Horror scripts.

**Submission Guidelines** Send proposal package with query letter, SAE, synopsis, sample chapters and three sample scenes/screens.

**Recent Sale(s)** *I Capture the Castle*, Dodie Smith; *Dracula*; *101 Dalmations/102 Dalmations*; *Dry Rot*, John Chapman

**Client(s)** Dave Freeman, Ray Cooney, Walter Greenwood, Ronald Gow, Edward Taylor, John Graham

**Tips** No unsolicited manuscripts will be accepted. The agency works in association with Film Rights Ltd.

## Lavinia Trevor

**The Glasshouse, 49a Goldhawk Road, London, W12 8QP**

☎ 020 8749 8481

☎ 020 8749 7377

**Contact** Lavinia Trevor

**Established** 1993

**Insider Info** Actively seeking clients. Currently handles Novels and General titles. Will consider Non-fiction and Fiction titles. Will consider simultaneous submissions. Unsuccessful proposals will be returned with SAE. Obtains clients via queries/Submissions. Commissions paid for domestic and foreign sales by agreement. Does not charge a reading fee.

**Non-fiction** Will consider Popular Science titles.

**Fiction** Will consider Literary and General and Commercial titles.

**Submission Guidelines** Send proposal package with query letter, SAE, synopsis, sample chapters, brief biography and the first 50–60 pages only. No scripts, Poetry, Science fiction, Fantasy, Academia, Technical or Children's titles will be considered.

**Tips** Concentrating mainly on literary and commercial fiction/non-fiction.

## LAW Ltd

**14 Vernon Street, London, W14 0RJ**

☎ 020 7471 7900

☎ 020 7471 7910

🌐 www.lawagency.co.uk

**Contact** Mark Lucas, Julian Alexander, Araminta Whiteley (Fiction and Non-fiction); Lucinda Cook (Translation rights and Literary estates); Philippa Milnes-Smith (Children's and Young adults); Alice Saunders, (Audio rights and Speaker engagements)

**Established** 1996

**Insider Info** Actively seeking clients. Currently handles Non-fiction books, Children's books and Novels. Will consider Non-fiction, Fiction and Children's books. Will consider simultaneous submissions. Aims to respond to queries/proposals within eight weeks. Unsuccessful proposals will be returned with SAE. Obtains new clients via queries/submissions. Commission rates are 15 per cent by domestic sales and 20 per cent by domestic sales. No reading fee.

**Non-fiction** Will consider Commercial non-fiction.

**Fiction** Will consider Children's, Literary and Young Adult.

**Submission Guidelines** Send proposal package with query letter, SAE, synopsis, and two sample chapters or up to 30 pages in single-sided, double-spaced A4 format. No scripts, poetry or textbooks will be accepted.

**Recent Sale(s)** *The Demon Headmaster*, Gillian Cross; *A Profound Secret*, Josceline Dimbleby; *'A Time to Die' The Kursk Disaster*, Robert Moore; *Eleanor of Aquitaine*, Alison Weir

**Client(s)** John Sergeant, Nigel Slater, Andy McNab, Livi Michael

**Tips** The agency may take longer than specified to reply to submissions during a busy period, and will not accept international reply coupons. Submissions by email, fax or disk will not be accepted.

## Limelight Management

**33 Newman Street, London, W1T 1PY**

☎ 020 7637 2529

☎ 020 7637 2538

✉ info@limelightmanagement.com/submissions@limelightmanagement.com

🌐 www.limelightmanagement.com

**Contact** Managing Director and Literary Agent, Fiona Lindsay; Partner and Agent, Linda Shanks

**Established** 1991

**Insider Info** The company's speciality is celebrity management and literary agency. Actively seeking clients. Currently handles Non-fiction books and Novels and will consider Non-fiction and Novellas. Will consider simultaneous submissions. Obtains new clients via queries/submissions. Commission rate is 15 per cent by domestic sales and 20 per cent by foreign sales. No reading fee.

**Non-fiction** Will consider Agriculture/Horticulture, Business, Cooking/Food/Nutrition, Health/Medicine, Interior design/Decorating, Lifestyle and Beauty.

**Fiction** Will consider Women's/'Chick lit'.

**Submission Guidelines** Send proposal package with query letter and proposal. Accepts queries by email.

**Client(s)** Paul Gaylor, Alastair Hendy, Orlando Murrin, Jo Glanville-Blackburn, Fumi Odulate, Fay Goodman, Richard Koch, Jill Billington, Barbara Griggs, Pat Chapman, Ariana Bundy

**Tips** The agency will respond only if interested in the proposal email. They will not accept large attachments, and if any are received they are automatically deleted. Currently there is an interest in women's fiction.

## Lisa Eveleigh Literary Agency

**c/o Pollinger Ltd, 9 Staple Inn, London, WC1V 7QH**

☎ 020 7404 0342

☎ 020 7242 5737

✉ lisaeveleigh@dial.pipex.com

**Contact** Lisa Eveleigh

**Established** 1996

**Insider Info** Actively seeking clients. Currently handles Non-fiction books and Juvenile books. Will consider Novels, Non-fiction, Fiction and Children's books. Unsuccessful submissions will be returned with SAE. Obtains new clients via queries/submissions. Commission rate is 15 per cent by domestic sales and 20 per cent by foreign sales. Does not charge a reading fee.

**Non-fiction** Will consider Biography/Autobiography, Health/Medicine, Commercial non-fiction and Astrology titles.

**Fiction** Will consider Children's, Literary, Young Adult and Commercial fiction titles.

**Submission Guidelines** Send proposal package with query letter, SAE, synopsis, two to three sample chapters, author biography. Accepts queries by email. No Scripts, Children's picture books, Horror, Science Fiction or Poetry titles will be accepted.

**Tips** Send preliminary letter only via email (no manuscripts).

## The Lisa Richards Agency

**108 Upper Leeseon Street, Dublin 4, Republic of Ireland**

☎ 00353 1 6375000

☎ 00353 1 6671256

✉ info@lisarichards.ie

🌐 www.lisarichards.ie

**Contact** Chairman, Alan Cook; MD, Lisa Cook, Directors, Richard Cook, Miranda Pheifer, Fergus Cronin, Patrick Sutton; Actors' Agents, Lisa Cook, Richard Cook, Jonathan Shankey, Lorraine Cummins; Comedy Agents, Caroline Lee, Christine Dwyer; Literary Agent, Faith O'Grady, Voice Overs and Corporate Bookings, Eavan Kenny

**Established** 1989

**Insider Info** Seeking both new and established writers. Currently handles Non-fiction books, Novels, Television scripts, Movie scripts and Stage plays. Will consider Non-fiction, Fiction, Film scripts, Television scripts and Stage plays. Unsuccessful proposals will be returned with SAE. Obtains new clients via queries/submissions. Commission rates are 10–15 per cent by domestic sales, 20 per cent by foreign sales and 15 per cent by film sales. Does not charge a reading fee.

**Non-fiction** Will consider Biography/Autobiography, Current affairs, Government/Politics/Law, History, Memoirs, Popular culture and Travel titles.

**Fiction** Will consider General fiction titles.

**Scripts** Will consider Comedy and General scripts.

**Submission Guidelines** Send proposal packs with query letter, SAE, synopsis and two to three sample chapters.

**Client(s)** Denise Deegan, Arlene Hunt, Roisin Ingle, Declan Lynch, Jennifer MacCann, Sarah O'Brien, Kevin Rafter

**Tips** Non-fiction submissions should include a detailed proposal and one sample chapter only. For stage/screen scripts, send a treatment with first act.

## London Independent Books

**26 Chalcot Crescent, London, NW1 8YD**

☎ 020 7706 0486

🖷 020 7724 3122

**Contact** Carolyn Whitaker

**Established** 1971

**Insider Info** Actively seeking clients. Currently handles Non-fiction books and Novels. Will consider Non-fiction and Fiction titles. Simultaneous submissions will be accepted. Unsuccessful proposals will be returned with SAE. Obtains new clients via queries/submissions. No reading fee.

**Non-fiction** Will consider Travelogues.

**Fiction** Will consider Fantasy, Young Adult and Commercial fiction.

**Submission Guidelines** Send proposal package with query letter, SAE, synopsis, two sample chapters or up to 30 pages. No young children's or computer books.

**Tips** The agent will suggest revision and offer constructive criticism.

## Lorella Belli Literary Agency (LBLA)

**54 Hartford House, 35 Tavistock Crescent, Notting Hill, London, W11 1AY**

☎ 020 7727 8547

🖷 0870 787 4194

✉ info@lorellabelliagency.com

🌐 www.lorellabelliagency.com

**Contact** Lorella Belli

**Established** 2002

**Insider Info** Young dynamic and successful small agency seeking both new and established writers. Lorella Belli worked professionally for publishers and other literary agencies prior to LBLA. Currently handles non-fiction books and novels. Aims to respond to queries/proposals within one week and manuscripts within one month. Manuscripts will be returned with SAE. Clients are usually obtained through recommendations from others, queries/submissions and conferences. Commission rate of 15 per cent for domestic sales, 20 per cent for foreign sales and 20 per cent for film sales. Offers written contract that is binding until terminated by either party, 60 days notice must be given to terminate. No reading fee charged or criticism service offered.

**Non-fiction** Will consider animals, art/architecture/design, biography/autobiography, business, child guidance/parenting, cooking/food/nutrition, current affairs, ethnic/cultural interests, gay/lesbian issues, government/politics/law, history, how-to, humour, interior design/decorating, memoirs, military/war, money/finance/economics, music/dance/theatre/film, nature/environment, popular culture, science/technology, self-help/personal improvement, sociology, sports, true crime/investigative and women's issues/women's studies.

**Fiction** Will consider action/adventure, confessional, detective/police/crime, erotica, ethnic, experimental, family saga, feminist, gay/lesbian, glitz, historical, humour/satire, literary, mainstream, mystery, psychic/supernatural, romance, sports, thriller/espionage and women's/'chick lit'.

**Submission Guidelines** Authors should include query letter, SAE, outline, synopsis, sample chapters (initial three for fiction, two for non-fiction), biography and proposal with submission. Accepts queries by fax, email, and phone. Actively seeking first novelists, journalists, international and multicultural writing, non-fiction proposals, books on Italy/with an Italian connection. Do not accept children's and juvenile books, fantasy and science fiction, poetry, scripts, plays, academic books and short stories.

**Recent Sales** *The Fabulous Mum's Handbook*, Grace Saunders (Random House (Century)); *Baby Proof*, Emily Giffin (Orion); B*ehind Every Great Woman There is a Fabulous Gay Man*, Dave Singleton, (Transworld (Corgi)); *Black Bodies & Quantum Cats*, Jennifer Ouellette (Oneworld)

**Clients** Michael Bess, Zoe Bran, Sean Bidder, Annalisa Coppolaro-Nowell, Dario Fo, Emily Giffin, Rick Mofina, Paul Martin, Nisha Minhas, Alanna Mitchell, Angela Murrills, Jennifer Ouellette, Robert Ray, Grace Saunders, Dave Singleton, Rupert Steiner, Diana Winston. We also represent a number of US, Canadian, Australian and European agencies in the UK.

## Louise Greenberg Books Ltd

**The End House, Church Crescent, London, N3 1BG**

☎ 020 8349 1179

🖷 020 8343 4559

✉ louisegreenberg@msn.com

**Contact** Louise Greenberg,

**Established** 1997

**Insider Info** Actively seeking clients. Currently handles non-fiction books and novels. Manuscripts returned with SAE. Clients usually obtained through queries/submissions. Commission rate of 15 per cent for domestic sales, 20 per cent for foreign sales. No reading fee charged.

**Non-fiction** Will consider serious non-fiction.

**Fiction** Will consider literary fiction.

**Submission Guidelines** Author should submit query letter, SAE and three sample chapters with submissions.

**Tips** No telephone enquiries.

## Lucy Luck Associates

**20 Cowper Road, London, W3 6PZ**

☎ 020 8992 6142

✉ lucy@lucyluck.com

🌐 www.lucyluck.com

**Contact** Lucy Luck

**Established** 2006

**Insider Info** Lucy Luck has worked in agenting since 1997 and specialises in edgy, thoughtful literary fiction and quirky, narrative non-fiction. We work with young writers to establish a writing career, in the first instance forming a relationship with a publisher but then working on related areas such as journalism. The agency has experience in working with authors from first-time novelists to established writers. Our strength is our commitment to personal relationships and a belief that books matter. Seeking both new and established writers. Currently handles non-fiction books, novels, novellas and short story collections. Currently represent 20 clients, 50 per cent of which are new/previously unpublished writers. Accepts simultaneous submissions. Aims to respond to queries/proposal and manuscripts within three months. Manuscript returned with SAE. Clients usually obtained through recommendations from others. Ten titles sold in the last year. 60 days notice required to terminate contract. No reading or office fees charged. Criticism service offered.

**Non-fiction** Will consider biography/autobiography, current affairs, history, popular culture and sports.

**Fiction** Will consider action/adventure, detective/police/crime, historical, literary, mystery, thriller/espionage and young adult fiction.

**Submission Guidelines** Authors should include query letter, SAE, sample chapters and biography with submission. Accept queries by email. Actively seeking writers of ability, both fiction and non-fiction, who are looking to build a career through their writing. Illustrated books or one-off books, anything too technical or academic, or anything too derivative will not be considered.

**Recent Sales** *The Ossians,* Doug Johnstone (Penguin); *The Years of the Locust*, Jon Hotten (Yellow Jersey); *How Low Can You Go?*, Tom Chesshyre (Hodder); *Play Britannia*, Iain Simons (Snowbooks)

**Clients** Ewan Morrison, Philip O Ceallaigh, Lorelei Matthias, J. A. Henderson, Catherine O'Flynn

**Tips** There is a secure online form to use for submissions.

## Luigi Bonomi Associates Ltd

**91 Great Russell Street, London, WC1B 3PS**

☎ 020 7637 1234

☎ 020 7637 2111

✉ info@bonomiassociates.co.uk

**Contact** Luigi Bonomi, Amanda Preston

**Established** 2005

**Insider Info** Actively seeking clients. currently handles non-fiction books and novels. Manuscripts are returned with SAE. Clients usually obtained through queries/submissions. Commission rate of 15 per cent for domestic sales, 20 per cent for foreign sales and 15 per cent for film sales. No reading fee charged.

**Non-fiction** Will consider agriculture/horticulture, child guidance/parenting, cooking/food/nutrition, health/medicine, history, science/technology, sports, mind body and spirit, lifestyle and journalism.

**Fiction** Will consider detective/police/crime, literary, thriller/espionage, women's/'chick lit' and young adult fiction.

**Submission Guidelines** Authors should submit query letter, SAE, synopsis and three sample chapters with submission. No poetry science fiction, fantasy, scripts or children's will be considered.

**Clients** James Barrington, John Humphreys, Nick Foulkes, Eamonn Holmes, James May, Richard Madeley and Judy Finnigan, Esther Rantzen, Professor Bryan Sykes, Alan Titchmarsh, Kim Woodburn and Aggie MacKenzie, Sir Terry Wogan

**Tips** Interested in new authors and television tie-ins.

## Lutyens and Rubinstein

**231 Westbourne Park Road, London, W11 1EB**

✉ firstname@lutyensrubinstein.co.uk

**Contact** Susannah Godman

**Established** 1991

**Insider Info** Currently handles non-fiction books, juvenile books and novels. Accepts simultaneous submissions. Aims to respond to queries/proposals and within six week. Manuscripts returned with SAE.

**Submission Guidelines** Authors should include query letter, SAE, synopsis and sample chapters with submissions. Queries accepted by email.

## Magaret Hanbury Literary Agency

**27 Walcot Square, London, SE11 4UB**

☎ 020 7735 7680

☎ 020 7793 0316

**Contact** Margaret Hanbury
**Established** 1983
**Insider Info** Actively seeking clients. Currently handles novels and fiction. Proposals returned if accompanied by SAE. Commission rates of 15 per cent for domestic sales and 20 per cent for foreign sales.
**Fiction** Considers literary fiction.
**Submission Guidelines** Send query, including SAE, before sending submission. Will not accept scripts, children's fiction, poetry, fantasy or horror.
**Client(s)** George Alagiah, J.G.Ballard, Simon Callow, Judith Lennox
**Tips** No unsolicited manuscripts.

## Maggie Noach Literary Agency
**22 Dorville Crescent, London, W6 0HJ**
☎ 020 8748 2926
☎ 020 8748 8057
✉ m-noach@dircon.co.uk
**Established** 1982
**Insider Info** Actively seeking clients. Considers children's books, novels, non-fiction and fiction. Prefers to receive exclusive submissions. Proposals accompanied by SAE will be returned. Commission rates of 15 per cent for domestic sales and 20 per cent for foreign sales. Does not charge a reading fee.
**Non-fiction** Will consider biography/autobiography, history and travel.
**Fiction** Will consider children's and young adult fiction.
**Submission Guidelines** Send proposal package with SAE, synopsis and two or three sample chapters. Will not accept manuscripts for very young children or any illustrated books for children. Will not accept scientific, academia or specialist non-fiction, poetry, short stories or plays.
**Tips** No fax or emailed submissions – they will be deleted unopened.

## Manuscript ReSearch
**PO Box 33, Bicester, Oxfordshire, OX26 4ZZ**
☎ 01869 322552
**Contact** Graham Jenkins
**Insider Info** Seeking both new and established writers. Currently handles television scripts, film scripts and fiction. Proposals accompanied by an SAE will be returned.
**Scripts** Considers general television/film scripts.
**Submission Guidelines** Send a query letter, including SAE.
**Tips** Only interested in books from existing clients.

## Marianne Gunn O'Connor Literary Agency
**Morrison Chambers, Suite 17, 32 Nassau Street, Dublin 2, Republic of Ireland**
✉ magoclitagency@eircom.net
**Contact** Marianne Gunn O'Connor
**Established** 1996
**Insider Info** Seeking both new and established writers. Currently handles non-fiction books, children's books, novels and fiction. Proposals accompanied by SAE will be returned. Commission rates are 15 per cent for domestic sales, 20 per cent for foreign sales and 20 per cent for films.
**Non-fiction** Will consider biography/autobiography and commercial non-fiction.
**Fiction** Will consider children's, literary and commercial fiction.
**Submission Guidelines** Send proposal package including a brief synopsis and two or three sample chapters.
**Tips** No unsolicited manuscripts.

## Marjacq Scripts Ltd
**34 Devonshire Place, London, W1G 6JW**
☎ 020 7935 9499
☎ 020 7935 9115
✉ enquiries@marjacq.com
🌐 www.marjacq.com
**Contact** CEO, Jacqui Lyons; Literary Agent, Philip Patterson; Film and TV Agent, Luke Speed
**Established** 1974
**Insider Info** Actively seeking clients. Currently handles non-fiction books, novels, fiction, television scripts, radio scripts, film scripts. Will consider simultaneous submissions. Aims to respond to queries/proposals within six weeks. Commission rates are 10 per cent for domestic sales and 20 per cent for foreign sales. Does not charge a reading fee.
**Non-fiction** Will consider biography/autobiography, health/medicine, history, children's, sports and travel titles.
**Fiction** Will consider detective/police/crime, horror, children's, literary, science fiction, thriller/espionage, women's/'chick lit' and commercial fiction.
**Submission Guidelines** Send proposal package with synopsis and three sample chapters (typed, single-side and double-spaced on A4 paper). Will not accept stage plays or poetry. For screenplay submissions send a letter, your CV and a sample film/showreel. DVDs and VHS tapes are both acceptable.

**Recent Sale(s)** *A Child's Game*, John Connor; *The Bad Apple*, Rosie Goodwin; *You Ain't Seen Nothing Yet*, Bob Cotton; *Babies for Beginners*, Ros Jay

**Client(s)** Anita Anderson, Bill Brown, David Evans and Scott Michaels, James Follett, Ian Pryor, Richard Templar, Stuart Macbride, Jeannie Johnson

**Tips** Will not accept handwritten/illegible material or queries without submission. Submissions are usually shredded. The agency does not discuss manuscripts unless the author becomes a client.

## The Marsh Agency Ltd
**11–12 Dover Street, London, W1S 4LJ**
- 020 7399 2800
- 020 7399 2801
- submissions@marsh-agency.co.uk
- www.marsh-agency.co.uk

**Contact** Managing Director, Paul Marsh (serious non-fiction, literary fiction, client development, business development and client account management); Rights Director, Camilla Ferrier; Agent, Geraldine Cooke; Agent, Jessica Woollard; Agent, Leyla Moghadam (English language sales)

**Established** 1994

**Insider Info** Seeking both new and established writers. Currently handles non-fiction, children's books, novels, fiction and short story collections. Proposals accompanied by SAE will be returned. Commission rates are 15 per cent for domestic sales and 20 per cent for foreign sales.

　* Paul Marsh worked for Anthony Sheil Associates Ltd, from 1977 and became their Foreign Rights Director in 1979. He left in 1993 and went on to establish The Marsh Agency in 1994 with his wife. Camilla Ferrier worked for HarperCollins prior to joining the agency in 2002, and Geraldine Cooke was an Editor for many years at Penguin before joining in 2004. She also founded the Headline Review List. Jessica Woollard was a Director for Toby Eady Associates before joining the agency in 2006, and Leyla Moghadam worked for some time at the European Commission. Leyla is multi-lingual, speaking English, German, French & Farsi.

**Non-fiction** Will consider Biography/Autobiography, Business, Child guidance/Parenting, Current affairs, Ethnic/Cultural interests, Health/Medicine, History, Psychology, Humour, Children's, Memoirs, Nature/Environment, Popular culture, Religious/Inspirational, Self-help/Personal improvement, Anthologies, Commercial Non-fiction, Travel, Philosophy, Popular science and Quiz titles.

**Fiction** Will consider Action/Adventure, Detective/Police/Crime, Fantasy, Historical, Children's, Literary, Mystery, Romance, Science fiction, Thriller/Espionage and Young Adult titles.

**Submission Guidelines** Send proposal package with SAE, synopsis, three sample chapters and author biography (double-spaced, numbered A4 pages). Accepts queries by email. Will not accept scripts, poetry or children's picture books.

**Recent Sale(s)** *Undersea Prisoner*, Duncan Falconer; *Spartacus: The Man & the Myth*, M.J.Trow; *Who Really Matters*, Art Kleiner; *The Mother in Law*, Eve Makis

**Client(s)** Monica Ali, Kate Atkinson, Jonathan Safran Foer, Meg Cabot, Toby Litt, Vikram Seth, Bill Bryson

**Tips** When submitting manuscripts print your name, address and contact number on the front, and your name and the title on all pages.

## Mary Clemmy Literary Agency
**6 Dunollie Road, London, NW5 2XP**
- 020 7267 12990
- 020 7482 7360

**Contact** Mary Clemmy

**Established** 1992

**Insider Info** Actively seeking both new and established clients. Currently handles general non-fiction and fiction titles. Proposals returned with SAE. Commission rates of 10 per cent for domestic sales and 20 per cent for foreign sales. Usually obtains new clients through queries and submissions. Does not charge a reading fee.

**Non-fiction** Will consider General Non-fiction titles.

**Fiction** Will consider General fiction titles.

**Submission Guidelines** Accepts proposal package with query letter, SAE and outline.

**Tips** Accepts scripts from existing clients only. Does not deal with science fiction, fantasy or children's titles.

## MayerBenham Ltd
**55 Athenlay Road, London, SE15 3EN**
- 020 7277 8560
- 020 7277 8560
- simon@mayerbenham.co.uk

**Contact** Director and Agent, Simon Benham; Director, Agent and Film Rights, Jo Mayer

**Established** 2002

**Insider Info** Actively seeking both new and established clients. Deals with general non-fiction titles. Unwanted material will be returned with SAE. New clients are usually obtained through queries and submissions. Commission rates of 10 per cent for domestic sales. Does not charge a reading fee.

**Non-fiction** Will consider Business, History, Humour, Popular Culture and Music titles.

**Submission Guidelines** Accepts submission with query letter and SAE.

**Tips** Will not accept unsolicited manuscripts. MayerBenham may suggest revisions to manuscripts.

## MBA Literary Agents Ltd

**62 Grafton Way, London, W1T 5DW**

☎ 020 7387 2076

☎ 020 7387 2042

✉ firstname@mbalit.co.uk

🌐 www.mbalit.co.ukthe shar

**Contact** Managing Director and Literary Agent, Diana Tyler; Director, John Richard Parker (Fiction/Non-fiction, Science Fiction and Fantasy); Director, Meg Davis (Scriptwriters/Authors all genres); Director, Laura Longrigg (Fiction/Non-fiction); David Riding and Jean Kitson (Film, Television, Theatre, Radio Scripts)

**Established** 1971

**Insider Info** Actively seeking clients. Deals with non-fiction, novels, television scripts, film scripts, stage plays, radio scripts and fiction titles. Will consider simultaneous submissions. Unwanted material will be returned with SAE. New clients are usually obtained through queries and submissions. Commission rates of 15 per cent for domestic sales, 20 per cent for foreign sales and 10–20 per cent for firm sales.

**Non-fiction** Will consider Biography/Autobiography, History, Memoirs, Popular Culture, Self-help/Personal Improvement and Travel titles.

**Fiction** Will consider Fantasy, Literary and Science Fiction titles.

**Submission Guidelines** Accepts proposal package with query letter, SAE and three sample chapters.

**Recent Sale(s)** *The Tenderness of Wolves*, Stef Penney; *Warprize*, Elizabeth Vaughan; *Hideous Absinthe*, Jad Adams; *A Fete Worse than Death*, Iain Aitch

**Client(s)** Robert Jones, Nick Angel, Dr Mark Atkinson, Anila Baig, Rob Bailey and Ed Hurst, Christopher Bird, Vivienne Bolton, Audrey and Sophie Boss, Martin Buckley, Debbie cash, Vic Darkwood, Sarah Ash, Michael Cobley, Murray Davis, Alan Dunn

**Tips** Check the agency website before submitting a manuscript to a specific agent.

## McKernan Agency

**5 Gayfield Square, Edinburgh, EH1 3NW**

☎ 0131 557 1771

✉ maggie@mckernanagency.co.uk

🌐 www.mckernanagency.co.uk

**Contact** Maggie McKernan (Editing fiction)

**Established** 2005

**Insider Info** A small agency, therefore clients receive very individual attention. During Maggie McKernan's career she edited many prize winning authors, including Jim Crace, Ben Okri, Vikram Seth - and many others, and she brings the benefit of her editorial experience and skill to her work as an agent. Actively seeking both new and established clients. Deals with non-fiction, children's books, fiction and anthologies. Currently working with 17 clients, 50 per cent of whom are previously unpublished writers. Accepts queries by email. Will accept simultaneous submissions. Aims to respond to queries and proposals within two weeks and manuscripts within four weeks. Will return unwanted material with SAE. Usually obtains new clients through recommendations from others, queries and submissions.

**Non-fiction** Will consider Agriculture/Horticulture, Animals, Anthropology/Archaeology, Art/Architecture/Design, Biography/Autobiography, Cooking/Food/Nutrition, Crafts/Hobbies, Current Affairs, Ethnic/Cultural Interests, Gay/Lesbian Issues, Government/Politics/Law, History, Psychology, Humour, Interior Design/Decorating, Children's, Language/Literature/Criticism, Memoirs, Military/War, Music/Dance/Theatre/Film, Nature/Environment, Photography, Popular Culture, Religious/Inspirational, Science/Technology, Sociology, Translations, True Crime/Investigative, Women's Issues/Women's Studies.

**Fiction** Action/Adventure, Confessional, Detective/Police/Crime, Ethnic, Experimental, Family Saga, Fantasy, Feminist, Gay/Lesbian, Glitz, Historical, Horror, Humour/Satire, Children's, Literary, Mainstream, Mystery, Psychic/Supernatural, Regional, Religious/Inspirational, Romance, Thriller/Espionage, Women's/'Chick Lit', Young Adult.

**Submission Guidelines** Accepts proposal package including query letter, SAE, outline, three sample chapters, author biography and proposal. Accepts queries by email.

 * Seeking novels of all kinds, both commercial and literary, quality non-fiction, biography and history.

## Merric Davidson Literary Agency

**12 Priors Heath, Goudhurst, Cranbrook, Kent, TN17 2RE**

☎ 01580 212041

☎ 01580 212041

✉ md@mdla.co.uk

🌐 www.mdla.co.uk

**Contact** Merric Davidson

**Insider Info** Actively seeking both new and established clients. Deals with children's books, novels, fiction. Will consider simultaneous submissions. Will return unwanted material with SAE. Usually obtains new clients through queries and submissions.
**Fiction** Will consider Children's and Modern Contemporary fiction titles.
**Submission Guidelines** Accepts proposal package with query letter, SAE, synopsis, author biography.
 * Will not accept short stories, academia or scripts.
**Tips** The agency is part of MBA Literary Agent Ltd. Will not accept unsolicited manuscripts.

## Mic Cheetham Literary Agency
**11–12 Dover Street, London, W1S 4LJ**
- 020 7495 2002
- 020 7399 2801
- www.miccheetham.com
**Contact** Director, Mic Cheetham
**Established** 1994
**Insider Info** Actively seeking both new and established clients. Deals with fiction titles. Unwanted material will be returned with SAE. Obtains new clients mostly through queries and submissions. Commission rates of 10–15 per cent for domestic sales, 10–15 per cent for foreign sales and 10–20 per cent for film sales. Does not charge a reading fee.
**Fiction** Will consider General fiction titles.
**Submission Guidelines** Accepts proposal with SAE, one page synopsis, three sample chapters. If submitting children's books of 500 words or under, then send entire manuscript. Will not accept poetry or illustrated books.
**Tips** Will not accept entire scripts, except from existing clients.

## Michael Motley Ltd
**The Old Vicarage, Tredington, Tewkesbury, Gloucestershire, GL20 7BP**
- 01684 276390
- 01684 297355
**Contact** Michael Motley
**Established** 1973
**Insider Info** Seeking mostly established writers through referrals. Currently handles fiction. Commission rate of 10 per cent for domestic sales, 15 per cent for foreign sales. Does not charge a reading fee.
**Submission Guidelines** No science fiction, poetry, horror, short stories or journalism will be considered.

**Tips** All submissions by referral. No unsolicited manuscripts.

## Micheline Steinberg Associates
**104 Great Portland Street, London, W1W 6PE**
- 020 7631 1310
- info@steinplays.com
- www.steinplays.com
**Contact** Agent, Micheline Steinberg; Agent, Matt Connell; Assistant, Helen MacAuley
**Established** 1985
**Insider Info** Actively seeking clients. Currently handles television scripts, movie scripts, stage plays, radio scripts, animation, soap opera, mini series. Manuscript returned with SAE. Clients usually obtained through recommendations from others and queries/submissions. Commission rate of ten per cent for domestic sales, 15-20 per cent for foreign sales. Does not charge a reading fees.
**Scripts** Will consider all areas.
**Submission Guidelines** Include SAE.
**Recent Sales** *Chasing the Moment*, Jack Shepherd; *Walking on Water*, Sarah Woods; *Kindertransport*, Diane Samuels; *The May Queen*, Stephen Starkey
**Clients** Ed Harris, Tim Green, Matt Evans, Polly Wiseman, David Hermanstein, Jennifer Farmer
**Tips** Contact by email for submission details. Specialises in stage, television, film and radio plays, and animation.

## Michelle Kass Associates
**85 Charing Cross Road, London, WC2H 0AA**
- 020 7439 1624
- 020 7734 3394
- office@michellekass.co.uk
**Contact** Michelle Kass
**Established** 1991
**Insider Info** Seeking both new and established writers. Currently handles movie scripts - fiction. Clients usually obtained through queries/submissions. Commission rate of ten per cent for domestic sales, 15-20 per cent for foreign sales. Does not charge a reading fee.
**Scripts** Will consider Drama and Literary fiction.
**Tips** Contact by telephone before submitting manuscripts. No unsolicited manuscripts.

## Mulcahy and Viney Ltd
**15 Canning Passage, Kensington, London, W8 5AA**
- ivanmulcahy@mvagency.com
- www.mvagency.com

**Contact** Ivan Mulcahy, Charlie Viney, Jonathan Conway

**Established** 2002

**Insider Info** Seeking both new and established writers. Currently handles non-fiction books, novels and children's books, representing 72 clients. The agents' backgrounds include periods in journalism, publishing, printing, business and research. Accepts simultaneous submissions. Unwanted material discarded. Does not charge a reading fee.

**Non-fiction** Will consider Biography/Autobiography, Cooking/Food/Nutrition, History and Politics.

**Submission Guidelines** With their submission, authors should include query letter, outline, synopsis, sample chapters, biography and a summary of competitor books in the market.

**Recent Sales** *Bedlam - London and Madness*, Catharine Arnold (Simon & Schuster UK); *In the Line of Fire*, Tony Allan (Usborn); *The Sacred Bones*, Michael Byrnes (HarperCollins); *Beau Brummel - The Rise and Fall of London's First Celebrity*, Ian Kelly (Hodder & Stoughton)

**Clients** Michelle Dewberry, Roisin McAuley, David Hencke, Shrabani Basu

**Tips** Unsolicited adult non-fiction proposals only. No email queries, post only. Unsolicited fiction proposals or children's books must be by previously published writers.

## The Narrow Road Company
**182 Brighton Road, Coulsden, Surrey, CR2 2NF**
- 020 8763 9695
- 020 8763 9329
- narrowroad@freeuk.com
- www.narrowroad.co.uk

**Insider Info** Actively seeking clients. Currently handles television scripts, stage plays, radio scripts - non-fiction and fiction. Accepts simultaneous submissions. Manuscripts returned with SAE. Clients usually obtained through queries/submissions.

**Scripts** Will consider General scripts.

**Submission Guidelines** Authors should include query letter, SAE and biography. No novels or poetry considered.

## Paterson Marsh Ltd
**11–12 Dover Street, London, W1S 4LJ**
- 020 7399 2800
- 020 7399 2801
- submission@patersonmarsh.co.uk
- www.patersonmarsh.co.uk

**Contact** Mark Paterson, Stephanie Ebdon

**Established** 1961

**Insider Info** Representing the world rights for estates, authors and publishers with specialization in psychoanalysis, psychotherapy and related subjects. Seeking both new and established writers. Currently handles nonfiction books. Manuscripts returned with SAE. Clients usually obtained through queries/submissions. Commission rate is 20 per cent for domestic and foreign sales. No reading fee charged.

**Non-fiction** Will consider Child guidance/Parenting, Education, Health/Medicine, History, Psychology and Neuro-science.

**Submission Guidelines** Authors should include query letter, SAE, synopsis and sample chapters with submission. No fiction, poetry, children's, scripts, articles or short stories considered.

**Recent Sales** *The Deeds of Jutes*, Professor Hugh Brogan; *The Parent's Handbook*, Audrey Sandbank; *Treat It Gentle*, Sidney Bechet; *Natural Energy*, Professor Basant K. Puri

**Clients** The estates of Anna Freud, Sigmund Freud, Sandor Ferenczi, Donald Winnicott, Michael Ballint, Wilfred R.Bion

**Tips** Articles are only accepted for existing clients.

## Peake Associates
**14 Grafton Crescent, London, NW1 8SL**
- 020 7482 0609
- 0870 141 0447
- tony@tonypeake.com
- www.tonypeake.com

**Contact** Tony Peake

**Insider Info** Not currently seeking new clients. Currently handles non-fiction books, poetry and novels, television scripts and movie scripts. Tony has spent time as a theatre production manager, model, actor and film distributor.

**Clients** Johnathon Coe, Steven Kelly, David Reynolds, Alison Fell

**Tips** Absolutely no unsolicited manuscripts or proposals.

## PFD (Peters, Fraser & Dunlop)
**Drury House, 34–43 Russell Street, London, WC2B 5HA**
- 020 7344 1000
- 020 7836 9539/7836 9541
- postmaster@pfd.co.uk
- www.pfd.co.uk

**Contact** Joint Chairmen, Maureen Vincent, St. John Donald; Books, Caroline Dawnay, Michael Sissons, Pat Kavanagh, Charles Walker, Robert Kirby, Simon Trewin, James Gill, Anna Webber; Children's Books,

Rosemary Canter; Film/Television/Theatre Agents, Natasha Galloway, Antony Jones, Tim Corrie, Charles Walker, St. John Donald, Rose Cobbe, Jago Irwin, Hannah Begbie

**Insider Info** Currently handles non-fiction books, novels, television scripts and movie scripts. Will consider all genres of work. Prefers to receive exclusive submissions. Commission rates of ten per cent for domestic sales, and 20 for foreign sales.

**Non-fiction** Will consider all genres.

**Fiction** Will consider all genres.

**Scripts** Will consider all genres.

**Submission Guidelines** Send query letter, SASE, synopsis, two to three sample chapters and author biography. Submission should be double-spaced, on single-sided A4. Do not bind or staple. Include a brief CV.

**Recent Sale(s)** *Enemy Within*, Paul Adam, *Second Honeymoon*, Joanna Trollope, *Untold Stories*, Alan Bennett, *Stars are Stars*, Kevin Sampson

**Client(s)** Sandy Gall CBE, Mary Alexander, Paul Arnott, Hilaire Belloc (Estate), Michael Collins, Lucy Diamond, Ewan McGregor, Rick Parfitt, Richard Pitman, Robery Uhlig, Ann Widdecombe, Barbara Vine, Clive james, Rt. Hon. William Hague MP

**Tips** The agency have a vast worldwide client list. Writers of non-fiction, children's books, scripts and illustrators should visit the website before submitting material, as details may vary.

## Pollinger Ltd

**9 Staple Inn, London, WC1V 7QH**

- 020 7404 0342
- 020 7242 5737
- info@pollingerltd.com
- www.pollingerltd.com

**Contact** Managing Director/Agent, Lesley Pollinger; Agent, Joanna Devereux; Agent, Tim Bates; Consultant, Leigh Pollinger; Consultant, Joan Deitch

**Established** 1935

**Insider Info** Currently handles non-fiction books, juvenile books, novels, television scripts and movie scripts. The agency has always been a family business. Manuscripts will be returned with SAE. Clients usually obtained through queries/ submissions. Commission rate of 15 per cent for domestic sales, 20 per cent for foreign sales.

**Non-fiction** Will consider most subjects including Juvenile and Photography.

**Fiction** Will consider all genres.

**Scripts** Will consider all genres.

**Submission Guidelines** Authors should include query letter, SAE, synopsis, three sample chapters and biography with submissions, which should be in

black type, double-spaced, one-sided A4. No poetry or academia considered.

**Recent Sales** *The Lost People of Malplaquet*, Andrew Dalton, *Lila*, Robert M. Pirsig; *The Legend of Bass Reeves*, Gary Paulsen; *God's Cop*, Michael Litchfield

**Cliens** Max Allen, Peter Clover, Michael Coleman, Laura Denham, Teresa Driscoll, Jacqui Farley, Catherine Fisher, Helen Macgee, Anne Miller, Gareth Owen, Roger Forsdyke, Philip Cross, Bruce Hobson, Alan Wilkinson, Peter Walker, Mark Stay, Robert Sellers

**Tips** No manuscripts by email or fax.

## Puttick Agency

**46 Brookfield Mansions, Highgate West Hill, London, N6 6AT**

- 020 8340 6383
- 0870 751 8098
- enquiries@puttick.com
- www.puttick.com

**Contact** Elizabeth Puttick, Robin Puttick

**Established** 1995

**Insider Info** Seeking both new and established writers. Currently handles non-fiction books and television tie-ins. Accepts simultaneous submissions. Proposals returned if accompanied by SAE. Obtains new clients by queries or submissions. Commission rates of 15 per cent for domestic sales and 20 per cent for foreign sales. No reading fee.

 * Elizabeth Puttick has vast experience in publishing, including time as an Editorial Director for HarperCollins. She has also written two books and many articles. Robin Puttick has worked in adult education and training, IT management and programming, and international sales.

**Non-fiction** Will consider Animals, Anthropology/ Archaeology, Art/Architecture/Design, Biography/ Autobiography, Business, Child guidance/Parenting, Cooking/Food/Nutrition, Current affairs, Government/Politics/Law, Health/Medicine, History, Psychology, Humour, Memoirs, Nature/Environment, Popular culture, Science/Technology, Self-help/ Personal improvement, Women's issues/Women's studies, Beauty, Lifestyle, Illustrated, Narrative, Philosophy, Relationships, Travel, Shamanism and Mind Body and Spirit titles.

**Scripts** Will consider Television tie-ins.

**Submission Guidelines** Send query letter with SAE, synopsis and two to three sample chapters by post or email. No fiction, children's books, poetry, drama or scripts considered.

**Recent Sale(s)** *The Money Diet*, Martin Lewis; *Everything I Know I Learned From TV*, Mark Rowlands; *Once-a-Week Workout*, Mark Anthony

**Client(s)** Al Avlicino, Karen Bali, Cornel Chin, Nicki Defago, Mike Fisher, Sue Kay, Bonnie Macmillan, Sarah Modlock, Steve Nobel, Emma Restall-Or, Ed & Deb Shapiro, Margot Sutherland, Lorraine Thomas, John Timperley, William Young

**Tips** Puttick Agency specialises in non-fiction and televsion tie-ins and prefers email contact in the first instance.

## PVA Management
**Hallow Park, Worcester, WR2 6PG**

- 01905 640663
- 01905 641842
- books@pva.co.uk

**Contact** Managing Director, Paul Vaughan
**Established** 1978

**Insider Info** Actively seeking clients. Currently handles non-fiction books. Accepts simultaneous submissions. Obtains new clients by queries or submissions. Commission rates of 15 per cent for domestic sales and 20 per cent for foreign sales.
**Non-fiction** Will consider General non-fiction titles.
**Submission Guidelines** Send proposal package with SAE, synopsis and three sample chapters.
**Tips** PVA Management handles non-fiction only.

## Real Creatives Worldwide
**14 Dean Street, London, W1D 3RS**

- 020 7437 4188
- malcolm.rasala@realcreatives.com

**Contact** Malcolm Rasala, Mark Maco.
**Established** 1984

**Insider Info** Seeking both new and established writers. Currently handles television and film scripts. Obtains new clients by queries or submissions. Charges reading fee of £125.
**Scripts** Will consider Drama, Technology, Science and General Entertainment scripts.
**Submission Guidelines** Send query letter with SAE, or by email.
**Tips** Real Creatives Worldwide Specialises in film and TV scripts. The initial contact should request a writer's submission agreement. The agency also has a production interest.

## Rebecca Winfield Literary Agency
**84 Cowper Road, London, W7 1EJ**

- 020 8567 6738
- rebecca.winfield@btopenworld.com

**Contact** Proprietor, Rebecca Winfield
**Established** 2003

**Insider Info** Actively seeking clients. Currently handles non-fiction books and fiction novels. Accepts simultaneous submissions. Proposals will be returned if accompanied by SAE. Obtains new clients by queries or submissions. Commission rates of 15 per cent for domestic sales and 20 per cent for foreign sales. Does not charge a reading fee.
**Non-fiction** Will consider Ethnic/Cultural interests, History, Memoirs, Popular culture, Sociology, Political and Popular Science titles.
**Fiction** Will consider Literary fiction.
**Submission Guidelines** Send query letter with SAE, three sample chapters and publishing history. No science fiction, fantasy, children's books, poetry or scripts.
**Tips** Rebecca Winfield Literary Agency will not accept submissions by email.

## Redhammer Management Ltd
**186 Bickenhall Mansions, London, W1U 6BX**

- 020 7224 1748
- 020 7224 1802
- info@redhammer.info
- www.redhammer.info

**Contact** Managing Director, Peter Cox
**Insider Info** Seeking both new and established writers. Currently handles non-fiction books, fiction novels, children's books, television scripts and film scripts. Accepts simultaneous submissions. Aims to respond to queries, proposals and manuscripts within six weeks. Proposals will be returned if accompanied by SAE. Obtains new clients by queries or submissions. Commission rates of 17.5 per cent for domestic sales and 20 per cent for foreign sales. Does not charge a reading fee.
**Non-fiction** Will consider Biography/Autobiography, Business, Current affairs, Gay/Lesbian issues, Government/Politics/Law, Health/Medicine, History, Psychology, How-to, Humour, Language/Literature/Criticism, Memoirs, Military/War, Money/Finance/Economics, Music/Dance/Theatre/Film, Nature/Environment, Popular culture, Religious/Inspirational, Science/Technology, Self-help/Personal improvement, Sociology, Sports and True crime/Investigative titles.
**Fiction** Will consider Action/Adventure, Erotica, Family saga, Feminist, Gay/Lesbian, Historical, Horror, Humour/Satire, Juvenile, Literary, Mystery, Romance, Science fiction, Sports, Thriller/Espionage, Women's/ 'Chick lit', Young Adult and Mainstream/Contemporary fiction.
**Scripts** Will consider Action/Adventure, Biography/Autobiography, Comedy, Contemporary issues, Detective/Police/Crime, Fantasy, Glitz, Historical,

Juvenile, Mainstream/Contemporary, Mystery/
Suspense, Romantic comedy/Drama, Science fiction
and Thriller scripts.

**Recent Sale(s)** *The F2 Diet,* Audrey Eyton; *Chronicles
of Ancient Darkness,* Michelle Paver (series)

**Client(s)** Martin Bell, Nicholas Booth, Brian Clegg,
Joe Donnelly, Amanda Lees, Carole Stone,
Justin Wintle

**Tips** Redhammer Management only accepts
submissions from previously published writers. A
limited number of unpublished writers may be
approached by the agency through Litopia Writers'
Colony, an internet writing community,
www.litopia.com

## Richard Hatton Ltd
**29 Roehampton Gate, London, SW15 5JR**
- 020 8876 6699

**Contact** Richard Hatton

**Insider Info** Seeking both new and established
writers. Currently handles television scripts, film
scripts and radio scripts. Proposal will be returned if
accompanied by SAE. Obtains new clients by queries
or submissions.

**Scripts** Will consider Film, Television and
Radio scripts.

**Submission Guidelines** Send query letter with SAE.

**Tips** Richard Hatton does not accept unsolicited
manuscripts.

## Robert Dudley Agency
**8 Abbotstone Road, London, SW15 1QR**
- 020 8788 0938
- 020 8780 3586
- rdudley@btinternet.com
- www.robertdudleyagency.co.uk

**Contact** Proprietor, Robert Dudlley.

**Established** 2000

**Insider Info** Seeking both new and established
writers. Currently handles non-fiction books. 60 per
cent of their clients are new or previously
unpublished authors. Proposals will be returned if
accompanied by SAE. Obtains new clients by queries
or submissions. Commission rates of 15 per cent for
domestic sales, 15 per cent for foreign sales and 15-
20 per cent for film sales. Does not charge a reading
fee. reading fee.

**Non-fiction** Will consider Biography/
Autobiography, Business, Current affairs, Health/
Medicine, History, Memoirs, Military/War and
Sports titles.

**Submission Guidelines** Send proposal package
with SAE, synopsis, three sample chapters and

author biography. No film or television scripts unless
derived from book sales.

**Recent Sale(s)** *After the Holocaust,* Eva Kolinsky
(Pimlico); *F1 Made in Britain,* Clive Couldwell (Virgin);
*Matchday - What Makes Saturday Special?,* Chris
Green (Highdown)

**Client(s)** Robert Ashton, Ian Baxter, Professor Paul
Cornish, Jim Drury, Paul Gannon, Solomom Hughes,
Duncan Martin, Ian Pont, Rosy Thornton,
David Tweedie

**Tips** When submitting to Robert Dudley, keep the
synopsis and author biography fairly brief.

## Robert Smith Literary Agency Ltd
**12 Bridge Wharf, 156 Caledonian Road, London,
N1 9UU**
- 020 7278 2444
- 020 7833 5680
- robertsmith.literaryagency@virgin.net

**Contact** Robert Smith

**Established** 1997

**Insider Info** Actively seeking clients. Currently
handles non-fiction books. Obtains new clients by
queries or submissions. Commission rates of 15 per
cent for domestic sales and 20 per cent for foreign
sales. Does not charge a reading fee.

**Non-fiction** Will consider Art/Architecture/Design,
Biography/Autobiography, Cooking/Food/Nutrition,
Health/Medicine, True crime/Investigative, Lifestyle
and Entertainment titles.

**Submission Guidelines** Send proposal package
including synopsis. No fiction, scripts, poetry or
children's books considered.

**Client(s)** Kate Adie, Martin Allen, Amanda Barrie,
Kevin Booth, Stewart Evans, Neil & Christine
Hamilton, Judy Huxtable

**Tips** Robert Smith does not accept unsolicited
manuscripts, but will suggest revisions if needed in
the cases where full manuscripts are requested.

## Robinson Literary Agency Ltd
**Block A511, The Jam Factory, 27 Green Walk,
London, SE11 4TT**
- 020 7096 1460
- 020 7245 6326
- info@rlabooks.co.uk

**Contact** Managing Director, Peter Robinson

**Established** 2005

**Insider Info** Seeking both new and established
writers. Currently handles non-fiction books, fiction
novels and documentary scripts. Commission rates
vary for domestic sales and are 20 per cent for
foreign sales. Does not charge a reading fee.

**Non-fiction** Will consider Popular culture and General Non-fiction titles.
**Fiction** Will consider General Mainstream/ Contemporary fiction.
**Scripts** Will consider scripts for Documentaries.
**Submission Guidelines** Send query letter with SAE.
**Tips** Robinson Literary Agency will suggest revisions for any submitted work.

## Rochelle Stevens & Co.
**2 Terretts Place, Upper Street, London, N1 1QZ**
- 020 7359 3900
- 020 7354 5729
- info@rochellestevens.com

**Contact** Founder, Rochelle Stevens; Frances Arnold, Lucy Fawcett
**Established** 1984
**Insider Info** Actively seeking clients. Currently handles television scripts, film scripts, stage plays and radio scripts. Obtains new clients by queries or submissions. Commission rates of ten per cent for domestic sales and 15 per cent for foreign sales. Does not charge a reading fee.
**Scripts** Will consider Television, Film and Radio scripts, as well as Drama and Stage plays.
**Submission Guidelines** Send query letter with SAE and author biography.
**Tips** Rochelle Stevens & Co. does not accept unsolicited manuscripts.

## The Rod Hall Agency
**6th Floor, Fairgate House, London, WC1A 1HB**
- 020 7079 7987
- 020 7079 7988
- office@rodhallagency.com
- www.rodhallagency.com

**Contact** Company Director, Charlotte Mann; Tanya Tillet (Submissions, Amateur & Play leasings, Foreign rights, General enquiries)
**Established** 1997
**Insider Info** Not currently seeking new clients. Currently handles television scripts, film scripts, stage plays and radio scripts. Does not accept simultaneous submissions. Proposals returned if accompanied by SAE. Obtains new clients by queries or submissions. Commission rates of ten per cent for domestic sales and 15 per cent for foreign sales. No reading fee.
   * Charlotte Mann has worked extensively in theatre, whilst Tanya Tillet's experience lies in film and television development and production.
**Scripts** Will consider most categories of scripts.

**Submission Guidelines** Send query with SAE, outline, author biography and CV. No writing partnerships or soap writers considered.
**Recent Sale(s)** *Driving Lessons,* Jeremy Brock; *Men Behaving Badly,* Simon Nye; *Flush,* David Dipper
**Client(s)** Sean Buckley, Clare Duffy, Tom Farrelly, Patrick Gale, Bettina Gracias, Mike Packer, Mike Wheatley
**Tips** The Rod Hall Agency is only interested in career writers who also direct. The agency will sometimes sell books for existing clients or very talented new clients.

## Roger Hancock Ltd
**4 Water Lane, London, NW1 8NZ**
- 020 7267 4418
- 020 7267 0705
- info@rogerhancock.com
- www.rogerhancock.com

**Established** 1960
**Insider Info** Actively seeking clients. Currently handles television and film scripts. Obtains new clients by queries or submissions. Commission rates of ten per cent for domestic sales and 15 per cent for foreign sales.
**Scripts** Will consider Comedy, Drama and Light entertainment scripts.
**Tips** Roger Hancock specialises in comedy, drama and light entertainment. First contact should be by telephone.

## Rogers, Coleridge & White Ltd
**20 Powis Mews, London, W11 1JN**
- 020 7221 3717
- 020 7229 9084
- info@rcwlitagency.co.uk
- www.rcwlitagency.co.uk

**Contact** Deborah Rogers (Illustrated, Children's); Gill Coleridge (Illustrated, Children's); Pat White (Illustrated, Children's); Peter Straus (Fiction, Biography, Current Affairs, Narrative, History); David Miller (Fiction, Biography, Current Affairs, Narrative, History); Zoe Waldie (Fiction, Biography, Current Affairs, Narrative, History); Laurence Laluyaux (Foreign Rights); Stephen Edwards (Foreign Rights)
**Established** 1987
**Insider Info** Seeking both new and established writers. Currently handles non-fiction books, fiction novels and children's books. Aims to respond to queries and proposals within eight weeks. Proposals will be returned if accompanied by SAE. Obtains new clients by recommendation, conferences and queries or submissions. Commission rates of 15 per

**761**

cent for domestic sales and 20 per cent for foreign sales.

 * Prior to opening the agency Deborah Rogers was an agent for Peter Janson-Smith. She worked at Sidgwick & Jackson, Chatto Windus and Anthony Sheil Associates. Pat White was an editor and rights director for Simon Schuster. Peter Straus worked at Hodder & Stroughton, Hamish Hamilton and Macmillan. David Miller worked as Deborah Rogers' assistant and was treasurer of the AAA. Zoe Waldie worked with Carole Smith.

**Non-fiction** Will consider Biography/ Autobiography, Cooking/Food/Nutrition, Current affairs, History, Humour, Sports and Satirical titles.
**Fiction** Will consider most categories of fiction.
**Submission Guidelines** Send proposal package with SAE, synopsis, three sample chapters and author biography. No plays, screenplays, technical or educational books considered.
**Recent Sale(s)** *Where They Were Missed,* Lucy Caldwell (Viking); *Theft: A Love Story,* Peter Carey (Faber & Faber); *Nefertiti,* Nick Drake (Transworld)
**Tips** Rogers, Coleridge & White does not accept submissions by fax or email.

## Rosemary Sandberg Ltd
**6b Bayley Street, London, N4 2EE**
- 020 7304 4110
- 020 7304 4109
- rosemary@sandberg.demon.co.uk
**Contact** Director, Rosemary Sandberg
**Established** 1991
**Insider Info** Not currently seeking new clients. Currently handles children's books and fiction.
**Fiction** Will consider Children's fiction, Picture books and Children's illustrated titles.
**Tips** Rosemary Sandberg's client list is full at present, and the agency is not currently accepting unsolicited submissions of any kind.

## Rosica Colin Ltd
**1 Clareville Grove Mews, London, SW7 5AH**
- 020 7370 1080
- 020 7244 6441
**Contact** Director, Joanna Marston
**Established** 1949
**Insider Info** Actively seeking clients. Currently handles television scripts, film scripts, stage plays and radio scripts. Aims to respond to queries and proposals within four months. Proposals will be returned if accompanied by SAE. Obtains new clients by queries or submissions. commission rates of ten

per cent for domestic sales and 10–20 per cent for foreign sales. Does not charge a reading fee.
**Scripts** Will consider Television, Film and Radio scripts, as well as Stage plays.
**Submission Guidelines** Send query letter with SAE and synopsis.
**Tips** Covering letter should include details of any previous writing credits, and whether the manuscript has been submitted previously to any other agents or publishers.

## Rupert Crew Ltd
**1a King's Mews, London, WC1N 2JA**
- 020 7242 8586
- 020 7831 7914
- info@rupertcrew.co.uk
- www.rupertcrew.co.uk
**Contact** Director, Doreen Montgomery; Director, Caroline Montgomery (Fiction)
**Established** 1937
**Insider Info** Actively seeking clients. Currently handles non-fiction books fiction novels. Proposals will be returned if accompanied by SAE. Obtains new clients by queries or submissions. Commission rates of 15 per cent for domestic sales and 20 per cent for foreign sales. Does not charge a reading fee.
**Non-fiction** Will consider Biography/ Autobiography, Cooking/Food/Nutrition, Health/ Medicine, History, Memoirs, Popular culture, True crime/Investigative, Mind body and spirit, Travel and Natural history titles.
**Fiction** Will consider Detective/Police/Crime, Literary, Thriller/Espionage, Women's/'Chick lit' and Young Adult fiction.
**Submission Guidelines** Accepts query letter with SAE. No scripts, poetry, short stories, journalism, science fiction or fantasy considered.
**Client(s)** Represents the estates of Sir Cecil Beaton, Patience Strong & Dame Barbara Cartland
**Tips** Rupert Crew independently acts as a publisher/ consultant for various literary estates.

## Rupert Heath Literary Agency
**177a Old Winton Road, Andover, SP10 2DR**
- 020 7788 7807
- 020 7691 9331
- emailagency@rupertheath.com
**Contact** Rupert Heath
**Established** 2000
**Insider Info** Actively seeking clients. Currently handles non-fiction books and fiction novels. Accepts simultaneous submissions. Proposals will be returned if accompanied by SAE. Obtains new clients

by queries or submissions. Commission rates of 15 per cent for domestic sales and 20 per cent for foreign sales. No reading fee.

**Non-fiction** Will consider Biography/ Autobiography, Current affairs, History, Popular culture, Popular science and Arts titles.

**Fiction** Will consider General Mainstream/ Contemporary fiction.

**Submission Guidelines** Send query letter with SAE and one sample chapter by email. No poetry or scripts considered.

**Tips** Rupert Heath prefers to receive submissions by email.

## Sarah Manson Literary Agent

**6 Totnes Walk, London, N2 0AD**

☎ 020 8442 0396

✉ info@sarahmanson.com

🌐 www.sarahmanson.com

**Contact** Sarah Manson

**Established** 2002

**Insider Info** Currently handles children's fiction books. Does not accept simultaneous submissions. Does not charge a reading fee.

**Fiction** Will consider Children's fiction, Children's Picture books and Young Adult titles.

**Submission Guidelines** Send proposal package with SAE, synopsis, three sample chapters and author biography.

**Tips** Sarah Manson primarily deals with children's fiction and picture books, and prefers exclusive submissions.

## Sayle Screen Ltd

**11 Jubilee Place, London, SW3 3TD**

☎ 020 7823 3883

☎ 020 7823 3363

✉ info@saylescreen.com

🌐 www.saylescreen.com

**Contact** Toby Moorcroft, Jane Villiers, Matthew Bates

**Established** 1952

**Insider Info** Seeking both new and established writers. Currently handles television scripts and film scripts. Aims to respond to queries, proposals and manuscripts within three months. Proposals will be returned if accompanied by SAE. Obtains new clients by recommendation. Commission rates of ten per cent for domestic sales and 15 per cent for foreign sales. Does not charge a reading fee.

**Scripts** Will consider Action/Adventure, Comedy, Contemporary issues, Detective/Police/Crime, Ethnic, Experimental, Fantasy, Glitz, Historical,

Juvenile, Mainstream/Contemporary, Mystery/ Suspense, Romantic comedy/Drama, Science fiction and Thriller titles.

**Submission Guidelines** Send query letter with SAE, synopsis, and author biography.

**Tips** Sayle Screen does not accept submissions by email.

## Scott Ferris Associates

**Brynfield, Reynoldston, Swansea, SA3 1AE**

☎ 01792 390009

✉ scottferris@macunlimited.net

**Contact** Gloria Ferris, Rivers Scott.

**Established** 1981

**Insider Info** Currently handles non-fiction books and fiction novels. Commission rates of 15 per cent for domestic sales and 20 per cent for foreign sales. Charges an arranged reading fee.

**Non-fiction** Will consider General non-fiction titles.

**Fiction** Will consider General fiction.

**Submission Guidelines** Send query letter with SAE.

**Tips** Scott Ferris does not accept unsolicited manuscripts.

## The Sharland Organisation Ltd

**The Manor House, Manor Street, Raunds, Northamptonshire, NN9 6JW**

☎ 01933 626600

☎ 01933 624860

✉ tsoshar@aol.com

🌐 www.sharlandorganisation.co.uk

**Contact** Managing Director, Mike Sharland; Director, Alice Sharland

**Established** 1988

**Insider Info** Seeking both new and established writers. Currently handles television scripts, film scripts, stage plays and radio scripts. Does not accept simultaneous submissions. Proposals will be returned if accompanied by SAE. Obtains new clients by queries or submissions. Commission rates of 15 per cent for domestic sales and 20 per cent for foreign sales. Does not charge a reading fee.

**Scripts** Will consider most categories of script writing, including Documentary, Soap opera and Mini-series.

**Submission Guidelines** End your query letter with SAE. No scientific, technical or poetry titles considered.

**Tips** The Sharland Organisation works in conjunction with overseas agents and specialises in international rights.

## Sheila Ableman Literary Agency

**3rd Floor, Lymehouse Studios, 38 Georgiana Street, London, NW1 0ED**

- 020 7485 3409
- sheila@sheilaableman.co.uk

**Contact** Sheila Ableman

**Established** 1999

**Insider Info** Not currently seeking new clients. Currently handles non-fiction books. Proposals will be returned if accompanied by SAE. Obtains new clients by queries or submissions. Commission rates of 15 per cent for domestic sales and 20 per cent for foreign sales.

**Non-fiction** Will consider Biography/Autobiography, Cooking/Food/Nutrition, History, Science/Technology, the Arts and Academia titles.

**Submission Guidelines** Send query letter with SAE, three sample chapters, author biography and publishing history. No gardening, sports, poetry or children's titles considered.

**Tips** Sheila Ableman Literary Agency is primarily interested in television tie-ins, and specialises in ghost-writing.

## Sheil Land Associates Ltd

**52 Doughty Street, London, WC1N 2LS**

- 020 7405 9351
- 020 7831 2127
- info@sheilland.co.uk

**Contact** Sonia Land; Vivien Green; Ben Mason; Emily Hayward (Film, Theatre and Television); Sopie Janson (Film, Theatre and Television); Gaia Banks (Foreign Rights)

**Established** 1962

**Insider Info** Seeking both new and established writers. Currently handles non-fiction books, fiction novels, television scripts, film scripts and stage plays. Proposals will be returned if accompanied by SAE. Obtains new clients by queries or submissions. Commission rates of 15 per cent for domestic sales and 20 per cent for foreign sales. Does not charge a reading fee.

**Non-fiction** Will consider Agriculture/Horticulture, Biography/Autobiography, Cooking/Food/Nutrition, Government/Politics/Law, History, Humour, Military/War and Travel titles.

**Fiction** Will consider Drama, Detective/Police/Crime, Literary, Romance and Thriller/Espionage fiction.

**Submission Guidelines** Send proposal package with SAE, synopsis, two to three sample chapters and author biography. No science fiction, fantasy children's or poetry considered.

**Client(s)** Peter Ackroyd, Hugh Bicheno, Melvyn Bragg, David Cohen, Anna del Conte, Seamus Dean, Bonnie Greer, Susan Hill, Richard Holmes, HRH The Prince of Wales, Mark Irving, Richard Mabey

**Tips** Sheil Land Associates welcomes new writers and aims to help in the development of their careers.

## Shelley Power Literary Agency

**13 rue du Pre Saint Gervais, Paris, 75019**

- 0033 1 42 38 36 49
- 0033 1 40 40 70 08
- shelley.power@wanadoo.fr

**Contact** Shelley Power

**Established** 1977

**Insider Info** Seeking both new and established writers. Currently handles non-fiction books and fiction novels. Currently represents 35 clients. Does not accept simultaneous submissions. Aims to respond to queries and proposals within one week, and manuscripts within three weeks. Proposals will be returned if accompanied by SAE. Obtains new clients by recommendation and by queries or submissions. Commission rates of ten per cent for domestic sales, 19 per cent for foreign sales and 19 per cent for film sales. Offers an open-ended written contract with 60 days notice for termination. Does not charge a reading fee.

**Non-fiction** Will consider Anthropology/Archaeology, Art/Architecture/Design, Biography/Autobiography, Business, Current affairs, Health/Medicine, Psychology, How-to, Memoirs, Popular culture, Self-help/Personal improvement, True crime/Investigative and Women's issues/Women's studies titles.

**Fiction** Will consider Detective/Police/Crime, Family saga, Feminist, Glitz, Historical, Literary, Mainstream, Thriller/Espionage and Women's/'Chick lit' fiction.

**Submission Guidelines** Send query letter with SAE, outline, three sample chapters and author biography by email. No children's books, poetry, plays, scripts, short stories, science fiction, or fantasy considered.

**Tips** Shelley Power works with English and French clients, but is mainly based in France.

## Shirley Stewart Literary Agency

**3rd Floor, 21 Denmark Street, London, WC2H 8NA**

- 020 7836 4440
- 020 7836 3482

**Contact** Director, Shirley Stewart (Literary)

**Established** 1993

**Insider Info** Actively seeking clients. Currently handles non-fiction books and fiction novels. Proposals will be returned if accompanied by SAE. Obtains new clients by queries or submissions. Commission rates of 10–15 per cent for domestic sales and 20 per cent for foreign sales. No reading fee.

**Non-fiction** Will consider General Non-fiction titles.

**Fiction** Will consider Literary fiction.

**Submission Guidelines** Send query letter with SAE, synopsis and three sample chapters. No scripts, poetry, science fiction, fantasy or children's titles.

**Tips** Shirley Stewart Literary Agency does not accept submissions by fax or disk.

## Sinclair-Stevenson
**3 South Terrace, London, SW7 2TB**
- 020 7581 2550
- 020 7581 2550

**Contact** Director, Christopher Sinclair-Stevenson; Director, Deborah Sinclair-Stevenson

**Established** 1995

**Insider Info** Seeking both new and established writers. Currently handles non-fiction books fiction novels. Accepts simultaneous submissions. Proposals will be returned if accompanied by SAE. Obtains new clients by queries or submissions. Commission rates of ten per cent for domestic sales and 15 per cent for foreign sales. No reading fee.

**Non-fiction** Will consider Biography/ Autobiography, Current affairs, History, Popular culture, Travel and Arts titles.

**Fiction** Will consider General fiction.

**Submission Guidelines** Send query letter with SAE and synopsis. No science fiction, fantasy, academia, scripts or children's titles.

**Tips** Sinclair-Stevenson also handles estates and will suggest revisions on authorised submissions.

## The Standen Literary Agency
**41b Endymion Road, London N4 1EQ, London**
- 020 8444 1641
- 020 8444 1641
- info@standenliteraryagency.com
- www.standenliteraryagency.com

**Contact** Yasmin Standen

**Established** 2004

**Insider Info** Not currently seeking new clients. Currently handles non-fiction books, fiction novels and children's books. Aims to respond to queries and proposals within four months. Proposals will be returned if accompanied by SAE. Obtains new clients by queries or submissions. Commission rates of 15

per cent for domestic sales and 20 per cent for foreign sales. No reading fee.

**Non-fiction** Will consider General interest and Children's titles.

**Fiction** Will consider Literary and Children's fiction.

**Submission Guidelines** In general, send query letter with SAE, synopsis and three sample chapters. For children's books of 500 words or less send the entire manuscripts. No Illustrated or science fiction titles or scripts considered.

**Recent Sale(s)** *Elgar's Breakfast*, J.Y.Bee; *Taffy*, J.Y.Bee

**Client(s)** Kara Kane, Zoe Marriott, Andrew Murray

**Tips** Does not accept submissions by recorded/ special delivery or electronic submissions of any form. Please advise us if your manuscript has been submitted to other agents. Overseas submissions will not be returned, but include an email address for response.

## Sunflower Literary Agency
**106 Mansfield Drive, Redhill, RH1 3JN**
- submission@sunflowerliteraryagency.com
- www.sunflowerliteraryagency.com

**Contact** David Sherriff (Submissions and Correspondance); Senior Editor and Agent, Phillip Adams (Action, Psychological and Techno-thrillers); Mrs Stone (Literary Novels and Social Satire).

**Established** 2003

**Insider Info** Seeking both new and established writers. Currently handles fiction novels. Does not accept simultaneous submissions. Proposals will be returned if accompanied by SAE. Obtains new clients by queries or submissions. Commission rates are variable.

**Fiction** Will consider Detective/Police/Crime, Literary, Thriller/Espionage, Psychological/Techno thrillers and Satirical fiction.

**Submission Guidelines** Send query letter with SAE by email. No scripts, romance, 'who done it' or spirit world titles considered.

**Tips** See website for submission process, as the agency practises very strict submission rules. Sunflower is interested in new authors or established authors who are changing genre. Sunflower does not accept unsolicited manuscripts and is usually closed to all submissions in January and February.

## The Susie Adams Agency
**PO Box 3820, Bath, BA2 4WY**
- 01225 445777
- susieara@aol.com

**Contact** Susie Adams

**Established** 1998
**Insider Info** Seeking both new and established writers.
**Tips** The Susie Adams agency is a rights consultancy and subsidiary rights agent. Handles literary agents, packagers and publishers.

## The Susijn Agency Ltd

**3rd Floor, 64 Great Titchfield Street, London, W1W 7QH**

- 📞 020 7580 6341
- 📠 020 7580 8626
- ✉ info@thesusijnagency.com
- 🌐 www.thesusijnagency.com

**Contact** Founder & Agent, Laura Susijn; Agent, Nicola Barr.
**Established** 1998
**Insider Info** Actively seeking clients. Currently handles non-fiction books and fiction novels. Aims to respond to queries and proposals within eight weeks. Proposals will be returned if accompanied by SAE. Obtains new clients by queries or submissions. Commission rates of 15 per cent for domestic sales, 20 per cent for foreign sales and 15 per cent for film sales. Does not charge a reading fee.
**Non-fiction** Will consider Ethnic/Cultural interest and General Non-fiction titles.
**Fiction** Will consider Literary fiction.
**Submission Guidelines** Send proposal package with SAE, synopsis and two sample chapters. No self-help, romance, sagas, science fiction, fantasy, computer, business, military, screenplay, children's or illustrated titles.
**Client(s)** Peter Ackroyd, Jose Luis Correa, Bi Feiyu, Paul Gogarty, Kolton Lee, Christine Leunens, Adam Zameenzad, Tessa De Loo, Jeffrey Moore, Tor Norretranders, Mineke Schipper, Shimon Tzabar, Alex Wheatle, Henk Van Woerden
**Tips** The Susijn Agency are specialists in English and foreign language world rights and are interested in authors from various cultures with cross-cultural themes. Does not accept submissions by email, but include an email address with manuscripts for a quick reply.

## Talent Media Group t/a ICM

**Oxford House, 76 Oxford Street, London, W1D 1BS**

- 📞 020 7636 6565
- 📠 020 7323 0101
- ✉ writers@icmlondon.co.uk

**Contact** Director, Lyndsey Posner; Director, Sally Long-Innes; Director and Agent, Duncan Heath;

Director and Agent, Susan Rodgers; Director and Agent, Paul Lyon-Maris; Jessica Sykes, Catherine King, Greg Hunt, Hugo Young, Michael McCoy
**Insider Info** Seeking both new and established writers. Currently handles television scripts, film scripts, stage plays and radio scripts. Commission rates of ten per cent for domestic sales, and ten per cent for foreign sales.
**Scripts** Will consider general scripts for Television, Film and Radio, as well as stage plays.

## Tamar Karat Literary Agency

**56 Priory Road, London, N8 7EX**

- 📞 020 8340 6460
- ✉ tamar.karat.agent@btinternet.com

**Contact** Tamar Karat
**Insider Info** Actively seeking clients. Currently handles non-fiction books and fiction novels. Accepts simultaneous submissions. Proposal will be returned if accompanied by SAE. Obtains new clients by queries or submissions. Commission rats of 15 per cent for domestic sales, and 20 per cent for foreign sales.
**Non-fiction** Will consider Biography/Autobiography, Government/Politics/Law, History, Sociology, Travel and Leisure titles.
**Fiction** Will consider Literary fiction.
**Submission Guidelines** Send proposal package with SAE, synopsis and two to three sample chapters. No science fiction, academia, poetry, horror, military or children's titles considered.
**Tips** Tamar Karat does not accept submissions by email, but include an email address with manuscripts for a quick reply.

## Tanja Howarth Literary Agency

**19 New Row, London, WC2N 4LA**

- 📞 020 7240 5553
- 📠 020 7379 0969
- ✉ tanja.howarth@btinternet.com

**Established** 1970
**Insider Info** Actively seeking clients. Currently handles fiction novels. Accepts simultaneous submissions. Proposals will be returned if accompanied by SAE. Commission rates of 15 per cent for domestic sales, and 20 per cent for foreign sales. Does not charge a reading fee.
**Fiction** Will consider General fiction.
**Submission Guidelines** Send query letter with SAE. No scripts, poetry or children's titles considered.
**Tips** Tanja Howarth specialise in German translation rights. Does not accept unsolicited manuscripts.

## The Tennyson Agency

**10 Cleveland Avenue, London, SW20 9EW**

☎ 020 8543 5939

✉ submissions@tenagy.co.uk

🌐 www.tenagy.co.uk

**Contact** Christopher Oxford (Film, Theatre and TV scripts); Adam Sheldon (Arts and Humanities); Jane Hutchinson

**Established** 2001

**Insider Info** Seeking both new and established writers. Currently handles non-fiction fiction, television scripts, film scripts, stage plays and radio scripts. Aims to respond to queries and proposals within 28 days. Proposals will be returned if accompanied by SAE. Obtains new clients by queries or submissions. Commission rates of 12.5 to 15 per cent for domestic sales, 17.5 to 20 per cent for foreign sales, and 15-20 per cent for film sales. Does not charge a reading fee.

**Non-fiction** Will consider Popular culture, Arts and Humanities titles.

**Fiction** Will consider General fiction.

**Scripts** Will consider Television, Film and Radio scripts, as well as stage plays.

**Submission Guidelines** Send proposal package with SAE, full synopsis, author biography and details of any previously published work. No poetry, short stories, science fiction, fantasy or children's titles will be considered.

**Recent Sale(s)** *Billy's Day Out,* Anthony Mann; *Helen's Story,* Ken Ross; *Lighthouse,* Graeme Scarfe; *The Hammer,* Jonathan Holloway

**Client(s)** Vivienne Allen, Tony Bagley, Kristina Bedford, Alastair Cording, Caroline Coxon, Iain Grant, Philip Hurd-Wood, Joanna Leigh, Steve MacGregor, John Ryan, Walter Saunders, Diane Speakman, Diana Ward and the estate of Julian Howell

**Tips** The Tennyson Agency specialises in scripts for television, film, theatre, radio and related material. Include an email address with any submission for a swift response.

## Teresa Chris Literary Agency

**43 Musard Road, London, W6 8NR**

☎ 020 7386 0633

**Contact** Director, Teresa Chris

**Established** 1988

**Insider Info** Actively seeking clients. Currently handles non-fiction books and fiction novels. Accepts simultaneous submissions. Proposals will be returned if accompanied by SAE. Obtains new clients by queries or submissions. Commission rates of 10 per cent for domestic sales and 20 per cent for foreign sales. Does not charge a reading fee.

**Non-fiction** Will consider Agriculture/Horticulture, Biography/Autobiography, Cooking/Food/Nutrition, Health/Medicine, History, Popular culture, Sports, True crime/Investigative, Women's issues/Women's studies, Lifestyle, and Fitness titles.

**Fiction** Will consider Detective/Police/Crime, Literary and Women's/'Chick lit' fiction.

**Submission Guidelines** Send query letter with SAE, synopsis and two to three sample chapters. No scripts, poetry, academia, short stories or genre fiction considered.

**Tips** Teresa Chris Literary Agency welcomes unsolicited manuscripts.

## Toby Eady Associates

**3rd Floor, 9 Orme Court, London, W2 4RL**

☎ 020 7792 0092

☎ 020 7792 0879

✉ toby@tobyeady.demon.co.uk

🌐 www.tobyeadyassociates.co.uk

**Contact** Toby Eady (China, the Middle East, Africa, and Politics of a Swiftian Nature); Laetitia Rutherford (Fiction/Non-fiction Worldwide).

**Established** 1968

**Insider Info** Seeking both new and established writers. Currently handles non-fiction books, fiction, novels, novellas, short story collections and anthologies. Proposals will be returned if accompanied by SAE. Obtains new clients from recommendation, conferences and queries or submissions. Commission rates of 15 per cent for domestic sales and 20 for foreign sales. Written contract is offered, with three months notice required for termination.

 * Attends the City Literature Writer's Festival, in Winchester.

**Non-fiction** Will consider Art/Architecture/Design, Cooking/Food/Nutrition, Current affairs, Ethnic/Cultural interests, Government/Politics/Law, Health/Medicine, History, Memoirs and Popular culture titles.

**Fiction** Will consider Action/Adventure, Confessional, Historical, Literary, Mainstream and Contemporary fiction.

**Submission Guidelines** Send proposal package with SAE, outline, synopsis, two sample chapters and author biography. No poetry, children's books or screenplays considered.

**Recent Sale(s)** *My Name is Salma,* Fadia Faqir (Doubleday); *Speaking to the Heart,* Sister Wendy Beckett (Constable & Robinson); *February Flowers,* Fan Wu (Picador, Asia)

**Client(s)** Bernard Cornwell, Chris Cleave, Rana Dasgupta, Julia Lovell, Rachel Sieffert

**Tips** Top quality research is essential in any submitted material.

## TV Writers Ltd
**74 The Drive, Fulham Road, London, SW6 6JH**
☎ 020 7371 8474
☎ 0207371 8474
✉ tvwriters@gmail.com
**Contact** Company Director, Marie-Louise Hogan
**Established** 2005
**Insider Info** Seeking both new and established writers. Currently handles television scripts, film scripts and radio scripts. Will consider simultaneous submissions. Proposals will be returned if accompanied by SAE. Obtains new clients by queries or submissions. Commission rates of 10-15 per cent for domestic sales. Does not charge a reading fee.
**Scripts** Will consider Comedy, Drama and Factual scripts.
**Submission Guidelines** Send query letter with SAE.
**Client(s)** Ali Crockatt, Lee Stuart Evans, Jez Stevenson
**Tips** TV Writers will only accept book manuscripts from its existing clients.

## Uli Rushby-Smith Literary Agency
**72 Plimsoll Road, London, WN4 2EE**
☎ 020 7354 2718
☎ 020 7354 2718
**Contact** Uli Rushby-Smith
**Established** 1993
**Insider Info** Seeking both new and established writers. Currently handles non-fiction books, fiction, novels and children's books. Will consider simultaneous submissions. Proposals will be returned if accompanied by SAE. Commission rates of 15 per cent for domestic sales and 20 per cent for foreign sales. Does not charge a reading fee.
**Non-fiction** Will consider General Non-fiction and Children's titles.
**Fiction** Will consider Literary, General and Commercial fiction.
**Submission Guidelines** Send query letter with SAE, outline and two to three sample chapters. No scripts or poetry considered.
**Tips** Uli Rushby-Smith does not accept submissions on disk.

## United Authors Ltd
**11–15 Betterton Street, London, WC2H 9BP**
☎ 020 7470 8886
☎ 020 7470 8887
✉ editorial@unitedauthors.co.uk
**Established** 1998
**Insider Info** Seeking both new and established writers. Currently handles non-fiction, fiction and children's books. Will consider simultaneous submissions. Proposals will be returned if accompanied by SAE. Obtains new clients by queries or submissions. Commission rates of 12 per cent for domestic sales, 20 per cent for foreign sales and 15–20 per cent for film (and radio) sales. Does not charge a reading fee.
**Non-fiction** Will consider Biography/Autobiography, Children's, General Non-fiction and Travel titles.
**Fiction** Will consider General fiction, Novels and Children's fiction.
**Submission Guidelines** Send query letter with SAE.
**Client(s)** Terence Brady, Peter Willet, Charlotte Bingham, The estate of John Bingham
**Tips** Will suggest revision on any solicited manuscripts.

## Valerie Hoskins Associates Ltd
**20 Charlotte street, London, W1T 2NA**
☎ 020 7637 4490
☎ 020 7637 4493
✉ vha@vhassociates.co.uk
**Contact** Valerie Hoskins, Rebecca Watson
**Established** 1983
**Insider Info** Seeking both new and established writers. Currently handles television scripts, film scripts, radio scripts and animation and non-fiction. Will consider simultaneous submissions. Proposals will be returned if accompanied by SAE. Obtains new clients by queries or submissions. Commission rates of 12.5 per cent for domestic sales, and 20 per cent for foreign sales. Does not charge a reading fee.
**Scripts** Will consider General scripts, Radio scripts and Animation.
**Submission Guidelines** Send query letter with SAE.
**Tips** Valerie Hoskins specializes in feature films, television and animation. Does not accept unsolicited manuscripts.

## Vanessa Holt Ltd
**59 Crescent Road, Leigh on Sea, Essex, SS9 2PF**
☎ 01702 473787
☎ 01702 471890

○ vanessa@holtlimited.freeserve.co.uk
**Contact** Director, Vanessa Holt
**Established** 1989
**Insider Info** Actively seeking clients. Currently handles non-fiction books, fiction, novels, and children's books. Will consider simultaneous submissions. Proposals will be returned if accompanied by SAE. Obtains new clients by queries or submissions. Commission rates of 15 per cent for domestic sales, 20 per cent for foreign sales and 15 per cent for film sales. Does not charge a reading fee.
**Non-fiction** Will consider General Non-fiction and Children's titles.
**Fiction** Will consider Detective/Police/Crime, Children's, Literary, Young Adult and General fiction.
**Submission Guidelines** Send query letter with SAE. No children's illustrated books, scripts, poetry, academia or technical books considered.
**Tips** Vanessa Holt is interested in books with potential film, television or radio tie-ins. Does not accept unsolicited manuscripts.

## Wade & Doherty Literary Agency Ltd
**33 Cormorant Lodge, Thomas More Street, London, E1W 1AU**
☎ 020 7488 4171
🖷 020 7488 4172
○ rw@rwla.com
🌐 www.rwla.com
**Contact** Robin Wade (General Fiction, Non-fiction and Children's Books); Broo Doherty (General Fiction, Non-Fiction, Commercial Women's Fiction and Crime Novels)
**Established** 2001
**Insider Info** Actively seeking clients. Currently handles non-fiction books, scholarly books, fiction, novels, children's books and anthologies. Currently represents 31 clients, 50 per cent of whom are new or previously unpublished writers. Will consider simultaneous submissions. Aims to respond to queries and proposals within seven days, and manuscripts within 30 days. Proposals returned if accompanied by SAE. Obtains new clients by recommendation, conferences and queries or submissions. Has sold 21 titles in the past year. Commission rates of ten per cent for domestic sales, 20 per cent for foreign sales and 20 for film sales. Written contract offered for extent of publishing, with 30 days notice required for termination. Does not charge a reading fee, and does not offer a criticism service.
 * Attends the annual Crime Writers Association conference, in Harrogate, and the Romantic Novelists Association conference, in London.

**Non-fiction** Will consider Anthropology/ Archaeology, Biography/Autobiography, Business, Cooking/Food/Nutrition, Current affairs, Government/Politics/Law, History, How-to, Humour, Children's, Memoirs, Military/War, Nature/ Environment, Popular culture, Science/Technology, Self-help/Personal improvement, Sports and True crime titles.
**Fiction** Will consider Action/Adventure, Confessional, Detective/Police/Crime, Erotica, Ethnic, Experimental, Family saga, Fantasy, Feminist, Gay/ Lesbian, Glitz, Historical, Horror, Humour/Satire, Children's, Literary, Mainstream, Mystery, Picture book, Psychic/Supernatural, Regional, Religious/ Inspirational, Romance, Science fiction, Sports, Thriller/Espionage, Women's/'Chick lit' and Young Adult fiction.
**Submission Guidelines** Send proposal package with synopsis, author biography and first 10,000 words of sample material by email.
**Recent Sale(s)** *The Solitude of Thomas Cave,* Georgina Harding (Bloomsbury); *Dragon Horse,* Peter Ward (Random House Children's Books); *The Hunt for Atlantis,* Andy McDermott (Headline); *Love Out of Season,* Ray Connolly (Quercus)
**Client(s)** Philippa Ashley, Marion Husband, Caroline Kington, Ray Connolly, Georgina Harding, Helen Oyeyemi, Lance Price, Rachel Trezise, Caroline Carver, Angela Dracup, Steve Hague, Eve Isherwood, Andy McDermott, Paul Johnston, Louise Cooper, Kimberly Greene, Adam Guillain, Steve Alton, Andrea Shavick, Peter Ward, Sameem Ali, Alison Bruce, Steuart Campbell, Sheila Hardy, Neil Hegarty, Brenda James, Prof. W.D. Rubinstein, Mike Newlands, Lance Price, Ewen Southby-Tailyour, Ayowa Taylor

## Watson, Little Ltd
**Lymehouse Studios, 38 Georgiana Street, London, NW1 0EB**
☎ 020 7486 5935
🖷 020 7486 6051
○ office@watsonlittle.com
🌐 www.watsonlittle.com
**Contact** Managing Director, Mandy Little; Senior Agent, James Willis; Literary Agent, Isabel Atherton (Young Authors)
**Insider Info** Actively seeking clients. Currently handles non-fiction books, fiction, novels and children's books. Will consider simultaneous submissions. Proposals returned if accompanied by SAE. Obtains new clients by queries or submissions. Commission rates of 15 per cent for domestic sales, 20 per cent for foreign sales and 15 per cent for film sales. Does not charge a reading fee.

**Non-fiction** Will consider Biography/ Autobiography, Business, Cooking/Food/Nutrition, Health/Medicine, History, Psychology, Children's, Popular culture, Science/Technology, Self-help/ Personal improvement, True crime/Investigative, Women's issues/Women's studies, Lifestyle and Arts and craft titles.

**Fiction** Will consider Detective/Crime, Historical, Children's, Literary, Women's/'Chick lit' and Young Adult fiction.

**Submission Guidelines** Send query letter with SAE and synopsis. No scripts, poetry, short stories or pure academia considered.

**Recent Sale(s)** *A Plum in Your Mouth,* Andrew Taylor (Harper Collins); *Fat Dog Thin,* David Alderton (Hamlyn); *Maddigan's Fantasia,* Margaret Mahy (Faber & Faber); *Just Another Day,* Adam Hart-Davis (Orion)

**Client(s)** Helen Armstrong, Adrian Bloom, Robin Cohen, Mark Hanson, Deborah Jaffe, Michael Jordan, Alice Muir, Ian Palmer, Mark Ronan, Rosie swale, Edward craig, Robert Giddings, Mukul Patel, Stewart Ross, Wayne Talbot, Henning Wehn, Duncan Cameron, Nicola Hill, Ann Kramer, Karen Saunders, Jane Wright

**Tips** Watson, Little does not accept email queries or full-length unsolicited manuscripts. The agency also represents illustrators.

## William Morris Agency (UK) Ltd
**52–53 Poland Street, London, W1F 7LX**
- 020 7534 6900
- www.wma.com

**Contact** Managing Director, Caroline Michel
**Established** 1965
**Insider Info** Seeking both new and established writers. Currently handles non-fiction books, fiction, novels, television scripts and film scripts. Will consider simultaneous submissions. Proposals returned if accompanied by SAE. Obtains new clients by queries or submissions. Commission rates of 15 per cent for domestic sales, 20 per cent for foreign sales, and ten per cent for film sales. Does not charge a reading fee.

**Non-fiction** Will consider General non-fiction.
**Fiction** Will consider General fiction and novels.
**Scripts** Will consider Television and Film scripts.
**Submission Guidelines** Send query letter with SAE, synopsis and up to 50 sample pages.

**Tips** William Morris has worldwide offices and represents both entertainment talent and literary clients. Contact by telephone first for television or film scripts.

## The Wylie Agency (UK) Ltd
**17 Bedford Square, London, WC1B 3JA**
- 020 7908 5900
- 020 7908 5901
- mail@wylieagency.co.uk
- www.wylieagency.com

**Contact** President, Andrew Wylie
**Established** 1996
**Insider Info** Seeking both new and established writers. Currently handles fiction novels. Consider simultaneous submissions. Proposals returned if accompanied by SAE. Obtains new clients by queries or submissions. Commission rates of ten per cent for domestic sales, and between 15 and 20 per cent for foreign sales. Does not charge a reading fee.

**Fiction** Will consider Novels and General fiction.
**Submission Guidelines** Send query letter with SAE, or query by email. No scripts or children's fiction considered.

**Client(s)** Ken Adam, Arthur Allen, Martin Amis, Laurie Anderson, Matt Bai, Philip Bobbitt, Patricia Bosworth, Paul Collier, Ian Frazier, Al Gore, Tipper Gore, Dennis Hopper, Michael Kantor, Annie Leibovitz, Norman Mailer, Jon McGregor, Louis Menand, Miyuki Miyabe, Thom Mount, Michael O'Brien, Paul Preston, Lou Reed, Salman Rushdie, Jeffrey D.Sachs, Robert Schlesinger

**Tips** The Wylie Agency does not accept unsolicited manuscripts.

## Zebra Agency
**Broadland House, 1 Broadland, Shevington, Lancashire, WN6 8DH**
- 07949 584758
- admin@zebraagency.co.uk
- www.zebraagency.co.uk

**Insider Info** Seeking mostly established writers through referrals. Currently handles non-fiction books, novels, television scripts, movie scripts, stage plays and radio scripts. Considers simultaneous submissions. Obtains new clients by queries or submissions.

**Tips** Zebra Agency only represents professional writers.

## 1st Call Editorial

**19 Albermarle Road, Gorleston on Sea, Norfolk, NR31 7AR**

- 01493 444556
- 01493 444556
- admin@1stcalleditorial.com
- www.1stcalleditorial.com

**About** On screen proofreading and copyediting from Eldo Barkhuizen, an advanced member of the SFEP.

## Adventures in Fiction

**14 Grosvenor Avenue, London, N5 2NR**

- 020 7354 2598
- enquiries@adventuresinfiction.co.uk
- www.adventuresinfiction.co.uk

**About** A consultancy that can offer appraisal services for individual manuscripts, or an ongoing 'mentoring' service through the writing process.

## Andrew Croft

- 01403 864518
- croftsa@aol.com
- www.andrewcrofts.com

**About** A professional, best selling ghost writer, dealing in fiction and non-fiction.

## Anne Barclay Enterprises

**The Old Farmhouse, Hexworthy, Yelverton, Devon, PL20 6SD**

- 01364 631405
- 01364 631112
- amb@theswiftgroup.co.uk
- www.theswiftgroup.co.uk

**About** Provides editorial services to both published and non-published authors and publishers. Packages include ghost writing, editing, copyediting and assessment of manuscripts.

## Book Production Consultants

**25–27 High Street, Chesterton, Cambridge, CB4 1ND**

- 01223 352790
- 01223 460718
- tl@bpccam.co.uk
- www.bpccam.co.uk

**About** Businesses are taken through the complete publishing processes including writing, editing, production and distribution. Books, manuals, catalogues, leaflets, electronic publishing and reports are all dealt with.

## BookType

**17 Yeoford Meadows, Yeoford, Crediton, Devon, EX17 5PW**

- 01363 84352
- info@booktype.co.uk
- www.booktype.co.uk

**About** A typesetting service for publishers, as well as manuscript preparation and word processing services for writers.

## Brackley Proofreading Services

**PO Box 5920, Brackley, Northamptonshire, NN13 6YB**

- 01280 703355
- brackleyproof@lineone.net

**About** Proofreading services from John Skermer.

## Cambridge Publishing Management

**Unit 2, Burr Elm Court, Main Street, Caldecote, CB3 7NU**

- 01954 214000
- 01954 214002
- j.dobbyne@cambridgepm.co.uk
- www.cambridgepm.co.uk

**About** Provides full editing and production services for publishers of business, educational, travel, and illustrated non-fiction titles.

## Chapter One Promotions

**PO Box 43667, London, SE22 9XU**

- 0845 456 5364
- info@chapteronepromotions.com
- www.chapteronepromotions.com

**About** Poetry and fiction critique services, as well as proofreading. The team of industry professionals also run workshops.

## Christine Foley Secretarial Services

**Glynedwydd, Login, Whitland, Carmarthenshire, SA34 0TN**

- 01994 448414
- 01994 448414
- foley@glyndedwydd.freeserve.co.uk

**About** A secretarial service which includes the copy typing, or audio typing of manuscripts.

## Christopher Pick

**41 Chestnut Road, London, SE27 9EZ**

- 020 8761 2585
- christopher@the-picks.co.uk

**About** Writer of promotional material, as well as fiction, non-fiction and children's books. Editorial, or ghost writing services are provided. Member of the Society of Authors.

## College on the Net

**81 Warwick Road, Sutton, Surrey, SM1 4BL**

- 020 8642 1063
- 07092 194837
- info@college-on-the-net.co.uk
- www.college-on-the-net.co.uk

**About** Offer an author's appraisal service, where specialists will provide various levels of critique on either a sample, or a whole manuscript. Clients may use the service as an ongoing course, or as a one off. They deal with novels, short stories, poetry, journalism, writing for children and scriptwriting.

## Cornerstones

**Milk Studios, 34 Southern Row, London, W10 5AN**

- 020 8968 0777
- 020 8969 8677
- helen@cornerstones.co.uk
- www.cornerstones.co.uk

**About** Produce reports on adult and children's fiction and non-fiction. They work with over 60 editors, who occasionally scout for literary agents. There are also 'teach yourself' workshops on self editing.

## Creative Plus Publishing

**2nd Floor, 151 High Street, Billericay, Essex, CM12 9AB**

- 01277 633005
- 01277 633003
- mail@creative-plus.co.uk
- www.creative-plus.co.uk

**About** Editorial and design services offered for books, part works and magazines. They are specialists in crafts, home and garden, cookery, art, literature, children's books and adaptations.

## The Cutting Edge

**Archery House, 33 Archery Square, Deal, Kent, CT14 7JA**

- 01304 371721
- 01304 371416
- jmthurley@aol.com
- www.thecuttingedge.biz

**About** Offer many services, including manuscript assessment, editorial input, constructive criticism and creative advice, re-writing, presentation for the market, and contractual and business advice.

## David Price

**Acupunctuation Ltd, 4 Harbidges Lane, Long Buckby, Northampton, NN6 7QL**

- 01327 844119
- 01327 844119
- waywithwords@fireflyuk.net
- www.waywithwords.co.uk

**About** Proofreading and editing services available, particularly in the areas of travel, dance, arts, popular culture and European history.

## David Winpenny Public Relations Ltd

**Victoria Villa, Princess Road, Ripon, North Yorkshire, HG4 1HW**

- 01765 607641
- 01765 608320
- david@winpennypr.co.uk
- www.winpennypr.co.uk

**About** A public relations and media agency that provides editorial services including ghost writing, feature writing, copyediting and proofreading.

## Duncan McAra

**28 Beresford Gardens, Edinburgh, EH5 3ES**

- 0131 552 1558
- 0131 552 1558
- duncanmcara@hotmail.com

**About** Provides a full range of editorial services for publishers, and other businesses and institutions. These include editing, re-writing, copyediting and proofreading. Specialises in Scottish literature, art, architecture, travel, military history and archaeology. Also acts as a literary agent.

## Editorial Solutions
**537 Antrim Road, Belfast, Northern Ireland, BT15 3BU**

- 028 9077 2300
- info@editorialsolutions.com
- www.editorialsolutions.com

**About** Writing and editing services, primarily for business documents, marketing and public relations material, and websites. Packages include copywriting, copyediting, proofreading, page design and complete project management.

## First Editing
- questions@firstediting.com
- www.firstediting.com

**About** US based editing service, which will edit anything from a full length manuscript to a business speech. A team of professional editors reviews all documents. They offer an initial free sample, email them part of your writing and they will proofread, revise, and edit a small section of it and provide you with a precise price quote.

## First Edition Translations
**6 Wellington Court, Wellington Street, Cambridge, CB1 1HZ**

- 01223 356733
- 01223 321488
- info@firstedit.co.uk
- www.firstedit.co.uk

**About** A translations service for books of all kinds. Proofreading, copyediting, and typesetting are also offered, as is Americanisation and indexing.

## Fish Publishing
**Durras, Bantry, Co. Cork, Republic of Ireland**

- kgould@fishpublishing.com
- www.fishpublishing.com

**About** An editorial consultancy service run by Katie Gould, to provide detailed critiques for novel writers. No electronic submissions at present.

## Florence Productions
**Stoodleigh Court, Stoodleigh, Devon, EX16 9PN**

- 01398 351556
- 01398 351388
- info@florenceproduction.co.uk
- www.florenceproduction.co.uk

**About** An out of house, desk editing and typesetting service for publishers. Individual services

can be provided, or they can project manage the entire process.

## Good Writing Matters
**2 The Island, Thames Ditton, Surrey, KT7 0SH**

- 020 8339 0945
- 020 8339 0945
- mruswords@aol.com
- www.good-writing-matters.co.uk

**About** Provides copyediting and proofreading services for businesses and individual clients. Also run a small publishing imprint, Riverside Press.

## Hans Zell Publishing
**Glais Bheinn, Lochcarron, Ross-shire, IV54 8YB**

- 01520 722951
- 01520 722953
- hanszell@hanszell.co.uk
- www.hanszell.co.uk

**About** Academic, reference, and journal publishing management is offered, as are marketing and training services for businesses and individuals. Specialists in providing internet training for publishers in developing countries in the third world, particularly Africa.

## The Hilary Johnson Authors' Advisory Service
**1 Beechwood Court, Syderstone, Norfolk, PE31 8TR**

- 01485 578594
- 01486 578594
- enquiries@hilaryjohnson.com
- www.hilaryjohnson.demon.co.uk

**About** Offers various editorial services for all types of manuscript, including screenplays, novels and short stories of all genres, as well as advice on submitting to agents and publishers. Acts as a scout for an unnamed literary agency.

## IB Editorial Services
**16 Hipkin Road, Dersingham, Near Kings Lynn, Norfolk, PE31 6XX**

- 01485 543746
- 01486 543746
- boston@ibss.fsnet.co.uk
- www.ibedit.fsnet.co.uk

**About** Editorial services offered by Irene Boston. Copyediting, proofreading, indexing and technical writing are among the packages. Assistance is also provided for students and academics with reports and theses.

## Indexing Specialists (UK) Ltd
**Regent House, Hove Street, Hove, East Sussex, BN3 2DW**
- 01273 738299
- 01273 323309
- richardr@indexing.co.uk
- www.indexing.co.uk

**About** Specialist, comprehensive indexing services, as well as copyediting, conference document management, and website management.

## Jacqui Bennett Writers Bureau
**87 Home Orchard, Yate, South Gloucestershire, BS37 5XH**
- 01454 324717
- jenny@jbwb.co.uk
- www.jbwb.co.uk

**About** Can either read and critique a sample of work, or edit a full manuscript. Fees vary depending on the service required and length of the manuscript. Clients have a choice of three editors, their biographies are on the website.

## Jan Hanley Manuscript Appraisal Service
- 01903 235508
- jan.henley@ntlworld.com
- www.annacheska.co.uk

**About** Published writer Jan Henley (Anna Cheska) offers a personal manuscript appraisal service with links to a leading literary agent.

## Jeremy Lockyer
- jeremy@jeremylockyer.co.uk
- www.jeremylockyer.co.uk

**About** A freelancer, providing proofreading, editing, re-writing and photography services for writers and publishers.

## Linda Acaster
- lindaacaster@yahoo.co.uk
- www.linda.acaster.btinternet.co.uk

**About** Work is reviewed by a published writer, and former tutor at the Arvon Foundation, and the Open College of Arts. Detailed feedback is given on works in progress, but no poetry or television scripts.

## The Literary Consultancy
**Diorama Arts, No 1 Euston Centre, London, NW1 3JG**
- 020 7813 4330
- info@literaryconsultancy.co.uk
- www.literaryconsultancy.co.uk

**About** Fiction, non-fiction, autobiography and children's books are critiqued, as are film, television, theatre and radio scripts, and poetry. They scout for leading agencies.

## New Writers Consultancy
**35a Lower Park Road, Brightlingsea, Colchester, Essex, CO7 0JX**
- 01206 303607
- submissions@new-writers-consultancy.com

**About** Offers a variety of packages including appraisals, critiques and editing. Services are provided by Diana Hayden, an ex BBC worker, editor and proofreader, and Karen Scott, a published author. Submissions accepted by post or email.

## Nyala Publishing (Geo Group)
**4 Christian Fields, London, SW16 3JZ**
- 020 8764 6292
- 020 8764 6292
- nyala.publishing@geo-group.co.uk
- www.geo-group.co.uk

**About** Offer a range of services including copyediting, proofreading, manuscript appraisal and research. Promotional material can also be designed and produced.

## Oxford Designers and Illustrators
**Aristotle House, Aristotle Lane, Oxford, OX2 6TR**
- 01865 512331
- 01865 512408
- pete@odi-design.co.uk
- www.o-d-i.com

**About** Project management service dealing with design, illustration and typesetting of materials, including books. A specialist area is illustrated educational texts.

## Oxford Literary Consultancy
**35 Howard Street, Oxford, OX4 3AY**
- 01865 725786
- admin@oxfordwriters.com
- www.oxfordwriters.com

**About** Produce reader's reports on fiction, non-fiction, scripts and poetry. Also offer proof reading and copyediting services as well as acting as a scout for leading agents.

## Reading and Righting
**618b Finchley Road, London, NW11 7RR**
- 020 8455 4564
- 020 8455 4564
- lambhorn@tiscali.co.uk
- http://readingandrighting.netfirms.com

**About** A manuscript reading and assessment service, as well as advice on agents and publishers. Fiction, plays, screenplays and non-fiction are dealt with. Specialist interests include the performing arts, popular culture, psychotherapy, social issues and current affairs. One to one follow up tuition can also be provided. Other services include consultations and complete manuscript editing, as well as workshops and lectures.

## Real Writers
**PO Box 170, Chesterfield, Derbyshire, S40 1FE**
- info@real-writers.com
- www.real-writers.com

**About** Offer a manuscript appraisal service by correspondence, on either a one off, or an ongoing basis. Readers are specialists in fiction, poetry, journalism, writing for children and scriptwriting. Also run a short story competition and run workshops on request.

## Sandhurst Editorial Consultants
**36 Albion Road, Sandhurst, Berkshire, GU47 9BP**
- 01252 877645
- mail@sand-con.demon.co.uk
- www.sand-con.demon.co.uk

**About** Editorial services for both writers and publishers. Packages include manuscript appraisal, proofreading, copyediting, writing, re-writing and if desired, complete project management.

## Sarah Sutton Consulting
**PO Box 134, Shaftesbury, Dorset, SP7 8HB**
- 01747 850100
- info@sarahsutton.co.uk
- www.sarahsutton.co.uk

**About** Offers freelance editorial services to publishers, as well as being a writer specialising in business, lifestyle, parenting, and television tie ins.

## Script Centre
**13 Wingfield Street, London, SE15 4LN**
- 020 7358 8216
- info@scriptcentre.co.uk
- www.scriptcentre.co.uk

**About** Offers either initial comments, standard feedback, or an extensive report on scripts for film, television, radio or theatre.

## Small Print
**The Old School House, 74 High Street, Swavesey, Cambridge, CB4 5QU**
- 01954 231713
- 01954 205061
- info@smallprint.co.uk
- www.smallprint.co.uk

**About** Project management packages for publishers, including commissioning writers and illustrators, translations, research, proofreading, copyediting, page design and layout. Specialists in non-fiction, particularly foreign language course books, training materials, guidebooks, dictionaries, and audio packages. Print, online and audio visual media are all dealt with.

## Special Edition Pre-Press Services
**2 Caledonian Wharf, London, E14 3EW**
- 020 7987 9600
- c.orde@btinternet.com
- www.special-edition.co.uk

**About** Provide a range of services including editing and proofreading, typesetting and design, and services for self publishers. Works with both individual and corporate clients.

## S. Ribeiro, Literary Consultant
**42 West Heath Court, North End Road, London, NW11 7RR**
- 020 8458 9082
- sribeiroeditor@aol.com

**About** Freelance services include copywriting, particularly public relations and jacket information, editing to publication standards and detailed manuscript appraisal. Works with writers, small presses and self published writers.

## Storytracks
**16 St. Briac Way, Exmouth, Devon, EX8 5RN**
- 01395 279659
- margaret@jamesk.freeserve.co.uk
- www.storytracks.net

**About** Provide manuscript appraisal services on fiction, non-fiction and writing for children, but not poetry. Also offer a ghost writing service, can run workshops, and may act as a scout for a literary agency.

## Susan Wallace
**PO Box 95, Liverpool, L17 8WY**
☎ 0151 233 3689
✉ susanwallace@blueyonder.co.uk
🌐 www.susanwallace.co.uk
**About** A freelance feature writer, columnist and psychology expert, who provides copyediting and other editorial services.

## Welsh Books Council
**Castell Brychan, Aberystwyth, Ceredigion, SY23 2JB**
☎ 01970 624151
☎ 01970 635385
✉ eleri.huws@wbc.org.uk
🌐 www.cllc.org.uk/serv_editing
**About** A free of charge reader's report can be produced on a partial or complete manuscript. Open to writers in Wales only. Advice on getting published may also be sought. Contact Eleri Huws, Senior Editorial Officer.

## Whitaker's Literary Consultancy
✉ whitakersliteraryconsultancy@fsmail.net
🌐 www.whitakersliteraryconsultancy.co.uk/
**About** Offers freelance copyediting, proofreading and appraisal services for all UK & English language publishers, editors and authors (published and unpublished).

## WordsRU
**Uplands, Shipham Lane, Winscombe, Somerset, BS25 1PX**
☎ 07789 495922
🌐 www.wordsru.com
**About** Proofreading and editing services across a wide range of texts including novels, articles, screenplays, business and academic documents, application forms, letters and many more.

## Writers' Workshop
**Pritchard's Cottage, Steeple Barton, Oxfordshire, OX25 4QP**
☎ 01869 347550
✉ enquiries@writersworkshop.co.uk

🌐 www.writersworkshop.co.uk
**About** The team will appraise manuscript and produce reports, as well as entering into dialogue over the findings of the appraisal. Most types of manuscript are dealt with, including fiction, poetry, scripts and writing for children. The editors are a team of writers themselves, many of whom are published. Check the website to view their credentials.

## The Writing Coach
🌐 www.thewritingcoach.co.uk
**About** Run by published writer Jacqui Lofthouse. Provides either a reader's report or a full critique of both fiction and non-fiction. No poetry of screenplays, although recommendations of other consultants in these areas are available. Jacqui is the sole editor.

## Writing Literary Consultants
**Neville House, Station Approach, Wendens Ambo, Essex, CB11 4LB**
☎ 01799 544659
✉ info@writing.co.uk
🌐 www.writing.co.uk
**About** Provide a range of services, from assisting with approaching publishers, to manuscript appraisals. Books, poetry, screenplays and even illustrations are dealt with. They also act as scouts for leading literary agents.

# ORGANISATIONS, GROUPS & CLUBS

We have included a wide range of companies and bodies (both public and private) in organisations. If you are seeking a professional writer's group to join, for example, this is where you should look. This is where you will also find campaigning groups, charities, and the official bodies that work on behalf of writers and publishers. Writer's groups tend to come and go, so always check before you turn up to your first meeting.

# ORGANISATIONS

## ABC

ⓦ www.abc.org.uk

**Contact** Chief Executive, Chris Boyd

**About** ABC (the Audit Bureau of Circulation) is the UK's leading source of information and statistics for newspapers, magazines and periodicals. Use its website to learn such things as what are the bestselling magazines. ABC is an independent not-for-profit organisation.

## Academi

**Main Office: 3rd floor, Mount Stewart House, Mount Stuart Square, Cardiff, CF10 5FQ**

ⓞ 029 2047 2266

ⓞ 029 2049 2930

ⓦ www.academi.org

**Contact** Chief Executive, Peter Finch

**About** The Academi is the Welsh National Literature Promotion Agency and Society for Authors. It works to promote the literature of Wales both in Wales and elsewhere. It hosts literary events and competitions, including the Cardiff International Poetry Competition and the Wales Book of the Year awards. It also provides bursaries and grants.

## ALCS

**Marlborough Court, 14–18 Holborn, London, EC1N 2LE**

ⓞ 020 7395 0600

ⓞ 020 7395 0660

ⓞ alcs@alcs.co.uk

ⓦ www.alcs.co.uk

**Contact** Manager, Member Services Department, Collette Scourse

**About** ALCS (the Author's Licensing and Collecting Society) aims to ensure that writers are fairly compensated for any works that are copied, broadcast or recorded, particularly with regard to secondary rights in such usage as photocopying, repeat broadcasts and digital use. It distributes millions of pounds to authors every year. It is also an internationally-known centre of expertise on copyright generally.

## Alliance of Literary Societies

**22 Belmont Grove, Havant, Hants, PO9 3PU**

ⓞ 023 9247 5855

ⓞ 0870 056 0330

ⓞ rosemary@sndc.demon.co.uk

ⓦ www.sndc.demon.co.uk

**Contact** President, Aeronwy Thomas; Secretary, Rosemary Culley

**About** The Society was founded in 1973 so that by joining forces various individual literary societies would have more clout. It now has over 100 literary societies under its umbrella. Links to all of these are on its website, making this a valuable research tool in itself.

## ALPSP

**Blenheim House, 120 Church Street, Brighton, BN1 1AU**

ⓞ 082 7709 188

ⓞ 082 7709 188

ⓦ www.alpsp.org.uk

**Contact** Chief Executive, Ian Russell; Administrative Assistant, Diane French

**About** ALPSP (the Association of Learned and Professional Society Publishers) is the international trade association for not-for-profit publishers and those who work with them. Its primary interest for writers is as a source of news and information about this sector of the publishing world.

## An Comunn Gàidhealach

**109 Church Street, Inverness, IV1 1EY**

ⓞ 01463 231226

ⓞ 01463 715557

info@ancomunn.co.uk
www.ancomunn.co.uk
**Contact** Chief Executive, Calum Iain MacLeod
**About** The aims of the Association are to support and develop all aspects of the Gaelic language, culture, history and heritage at local, national and international levels.

## Apples & Snakes
info@applesandsnakes.org
www.applesandsnakes.org
**Contact** Director, Geraldine Collinge; Administration Assistant, Chikodi Nwaiwu; see website for regional co-ordinators
**About** Apples & Snakes is a poetry performance organisation covering all of England. It focuses on working with emerging artists and commissions and produces new work. It regularly curates, hosts and acts as a partner to facilitate and promote performance poetry through live events. With education at the core of its mission, it works with schools, prisons, libraries and more to use performance poetry to develop literacy and communication skills, motivation and self-esteem.

## ASLIB
**Holywell Centre, 1 Phipp Street, London, EC2A 4PS**
020 7613 3031
020 7613 5080
aslib@aslib.com
www.aslib.co.uk
**About** The Association for Information Management will be of interest primarily to writers and information specialists who are seeking knowledge about managing information in large and corporate environments. One of its roles is to represent and lobby for the interests of the information sector on matters which are of national and international importance varying from copyright and data protection to the role of scientific journals. The website, marred by irritating animated graphics, contains much of practical use. See also www.managinginformation.com

## ASLS
**c/o Department of Scottish History, University of Glasgow, 9, University Gardens, Glasgow, G12 8QH**
0141 330 5309
0141 330 5309
www.asls.org.uk

**Contact** General Manager, Duncan Jones
**About** ASLAS (The Association for Scottish Literary Studies) aims to promote the study, teaching and writing of Scottish literature, and to further the study of the languages of Scotland. To that end, it publishes various collections of Scottish writing and poetry, and also publishes the International Journal of Scottish Literature.

## Association of Authors Agents
aaa@johnsonandalcock.co.uk
www.agentsassoc.co.uk
**Contact** Secretary, Anna Power
**About** The Association exists to provide a forum for member agents to discuss industry matters, to represent the interests of agents and their clients and to uphold a code of good practice. The majority of established agencies in the UK belong. Most writers will never need to have direct contact with the Association, but all receive indirect benefits.

## Association of British Science Writers
0870 770 3361
absw@absw.org.uk
www.absw.org.uk
**About** The ABSW exists to help those who write about science and technology, and to improve the standard of science journalism in the UK. If you are a science writer you will probably consider joining the association as doing so will help you obtain work. The ABSW Science Writers' Awards seek to set standards of excellence in science writing across eight categories.

## Association of Christian Writers
www.christianwriters.org.uk
**About** The vision of the Association of Christian Writers is to see quality writing in every area of the media, whether it be overtly Christian or shaped by a Christian perspective, reaching the widest possible range of people throughout the United Kingdom and beyond.

## Association of Freelance Editors, Proofreaders & Indexers (Ireland)
00353 2952194
00353 2952300
brenda@ohanlonmediaservices.com
www.afepi.ie
**Contact** Brenda O'Hanlon

**About** The Irish Association of Freelance Editors, Proofreaders and Indexers was established to provide information to publishers on freelancers working in this field and to protect the interests of those freelancers. All members are expected to have professional experience.

## The Association of Learned and Professional Society Publishers

☎ 01827 709188
☎ 01827 709188
🌐 www.alpsp.org

**Contact** Chief Executive, Ian Russell; Administrative Assistant, Diane French

**About** The Association of Learned and Professional Society Publishers (ALPSP) is the international trade association for not-for-profit publishers and those who work with them. It provides information, education, representation, cooperative initiatives and guidelines for good practice.

## The Audiobook Publishing Association

☎ 07971 280788.
✉ charlotte.mccandlish@ntlworld.com
🌐 www.theapa.net

**Contact** Chair, Jo Forshaw; Administrator, Charlotte McCandish

**About** The APA is the UK trade association for the audiobook industry with membership open to all those involved in the publishing of spoken word audio, including, among others, publishers, producers, abridgers, agents, actors and studios.

## The Bibliographical Society

**c/o Institute of English Studies, University of London, Senate House, Malet Street, London, WC1E 7HU**

✉ Secretary@BibSoc.org.uk
🌐 www.bibsoc.org.uk

**Contact** Hon. Secretary, Meg Ford

**About** The Bibliographical Society deals with the study of the book and its history. Its objectives are to promote and encourage study and research in the fields of historical, analytical, descriptive and textual bibliography, and the history of printing, publishing, bookselling, bookbinding and collecting.To this end it holds meetings at which papers are read and discussed; publishes its journal (The Library) and books concerned with bibliography; maintains a bibliographical library; and from time to time awards a medal for services to bibliography. It

supports bibliographical research by awarding grants and bursaries. Full details of meetings are on the website.

## Book Marketing Ltd

🌐 www.bookmarketing.co.uk

**About** BML is the UK's premier source of information and research on the book industry, undertaking a wide range of research projects, and publishing a variety of market research. It is best known for its *Books and the Consumer* survey, accessed on subscription via its website.

## The Bookseller

**Endeavour House, 189 Shaftesbury Avenue, London, WC2H 8TJ**

☎ 020 7420 6006
✉ firstname.secondname@bookseller.co.uk
🌐 www.thebookseller.com

**Contact** Editor-in-chief, Neill Denny

**About** The Bookseller is the UK's leading journal for book publishing professionals, covering every aspect of the book publishing industry. It's read for its news, for its statistics on the industry, and for its in-depth articles.

## The Booksellers Association

**The Booksellers Association, Minster House, 272 Vauxhall Bridge Road, London, SW1V 1BA**

☎ 020 7802 0802
☎ 020 7802 0803
✉ mail@booksellers.org.uk
🌐 www.booksellers.org.uk

**Contact** Chief Executive, Tim Godfray

**About** The Booksellers Association represents over 95 per cent of booksellers in the UK and Ireland. Its website will be of interest to writers for its overall information about the book and publishing industry, and for its statistical information on numbers of book published, etc.

## Booktribes

🌐 www.booktribes.com

**About** Booktribes is genuinely innovative: it is an online community for book lovers where they can share their passion for books they already know, and discover books that they don't know through recommendation. Any book could appear on Booktribes, so its potential is enormous. New and exciting.

## Booktrust

Book House, 45 East Hill, London, SW18 2QZ

- ☎ 020 8516 2977
- 🖷 020 8516 2978
- ✉ query@booktrust.org.uk
- 🌐 www.booktrust.org.uk

**About** Booktrust is an independent national charity that encourages people of all ages and cultures to discover and enjoy reading. It administers seven book prizes, including the Orange Prize for Fiction. It has many ongoing projects that promote reading, including the Children's Laureate.

## BRAD

- ☎ 020 7505 8455
- 🖷 020 7505 8201
- ✉ info@brad.co.uk
- 🌐 www.brad.co.uk

**About** BRAD is available in both print and online versions, and is one of the UK's leading media databases, covering newspapers,consumer and business press, radio, TV and new media.

## BRAW

Scottish Book Trust, Sandeman House, Trunks Close, 55 High Street, Edinburgh, EH1 1SR

- ☎ 0131 524 0160
- 🖷 0131 524 0161
- ✉ info@braw.org.uk
- 🌐 www.braw.org.uk

**About** BRAW (Books, Reading and Writing) is an initiative of the Scottish Book Trust that promotes Scottish books and their reading. Its website is an excellent resource for anyone interested in Scottish Children's books.

## The British Academy

10 Carlton House Terrace, London, SW1Y 5AH

- ☎ 020 7969 5200
- 🖷 020 7969 5300
- ✉ chiefexec@britac.ac.uk
- 🌐 www.britac.ac.uk

**Contact** Chief Executive, Dr. R. Jackson

**About** The British Academy is the national academy for the humanities and the social sciences. It represents the interests of scholarship nationally and internationally and promotes and supports research. It seeks to make research and scholarship more widely understood and appreciated. It awards eight medals and prizes in specialist areas of learning and research.

## The British Academy of Composers and Songwriters

26 Berners Street, London, W1T 3LR

- ☎ 020 7636 2929
- 🖷 020 7636 2212
- 🌐 www.britishacademy.com

**Contact** CEO, Chris Green; Membership enquiries, Fran Matthews

**About** The 'voice' of all UK composers and songwriters, the BAC&S campaigns to protect the value of copyright and to create a better environment in which music writers can flourish.It is the home of the prestigious Ivor Novello and British Composer Awards celebrating excellence in contemporary songwriting and composing.

## British Association of Communicators in Business

Suite GA2, Oak House, Woodlands Business Park, Linford Wood, Milton Keynes, MK14 6EY

- ☎ 01908 313755
- 🖷 01908 313661
- ✉ enquiries@cib.uk.com
- 🌐 www.cib.uk.com

**Contact** Secretary General, Kathie Jones; Administrator, Brenda Scott

**About** The British Association of Communicators in Business (CiB) is a professional body for in-house, freelance and agency staff involved in internal and corporate communications.

## The British Association of Journalists

89 Fleet Street, London, EC4Y 1DH

- ☎ 020 7353 3003
- 🖷 020 7353 2310
- 🌐 www.bajunion.org.uk
- 🌐 www.bajunion.org.uk

**Contact** General Secretary, Steve Turner

**About** A union for journalists which seeks to protect and improve pay, conditions, pensions and fees for its members. It seeks to defend and promote freedom of information

## The British Comparative Literature Association

Department of French Studies, University of Manchester, Oxford Road, Manchester, M13 9PL

- 🌐 www.bcla.org

**Contact** Secretary, Penny Brown

**About** The British Comparative Literature Association (BCLA), aims to promote the scholarly study of literature without confinement to national and linguistic boundaries, and in relation to other disciplines. The BCLA's primary interests are in literature, the contexts of literature and the interaction between literatures. It is primarily an academic organisation, one of its aims being to foster and make possible links between people involved in similar research areas.

## The British Copyright Council
**29–33 Berners Street, London, W1T 3AB**
- 01986 788 122
- 01986 788 847
- secretary@britishcopyright.org
- www.britishcopyright.org

**Contact** President of Honour, Maureen Duffy, FRSL
**About** The British Copyright Council is an umbrella organisation bringing together organisations which represent those who create, or hold rights in literary, dramatic, musical and artistic works and those who perform such works. It functions principally as a liaison committee for its member associations, providing them with a forum for the discussion of matters of copyright interest.

## The British Council
**10 Spring Gardens, London, SW1A 2BN**
- 0161 957 7755
- 0161 957 7762
- general.enquiries@britishcouncil.org
- www.britishcouncil.org

**Contact** Director General, Sir David Green
**About** The British Council is the UK's international organisation for educational opportunities and cultural relations. Its purpose is to build mutually beneficial relationships between people in the UK and other countries and to increase appreciation of the UK's creative ideas and achievements. For writers, this might mean your book or ideas being promoted, perhaps in one of the Council's exhibitions or publications, or in one of its libraries. See the website for details.

## The British Fantasy Society
**36 Town End, Cheadle, Staffs, ST10 1PF**
- www.britishfantasysociety.org.uk

**Contact** President, Ramsey Campbell; Secretary, Vicky Cook
**About** The British Fantasy Society exists to promote and enjoy the genres of fantasy, science fiction and horror in all its forms. It has an active and

enthusiastic membership, and it awards are well-respected.

## British Guild of Beer Writers
**Lee Farm, Winsford, Somerset, TA24 7HX**
- 01643 851469
- tierneyjones@btinternet.com
- www.beerwriters.co.uk

**Contact** Chair, Tim Hampson; Secretary, Adrian Tierney-Jones
**About** The Guild promotes good writing about beer. Its 130 members cover every aspect of beer, from making to drinking; their details can be found on the website.

## British Guild of Travel Writers
**51b Askew Crescent, London, W12 9DN**
- 020 8749 1128
- 020 8749 1128
- www.bgtw.org

**Contact** Chairman, Mary Anne Evans
**About** The Guild is an association of nearly 300 writers, editors, photographers, producers, radio and television presenters involved in the world of travel. Its Yearbook – available via the website – is an invaluable tool for all involved in travel writing and travel publishing.

## The British Haiku Society
**38 Wayside Avenue, Hornchurch, Essex, RM12 4LL**
- www.haikusoc.ndo.co.uk

**Contact** Membership Secretary, Stanley Pelter
**About** The BHS seeks to promote and encourage haiku in as many ways and in as many places as possible, including in education. The society has a journal which members can contribute to, and it has several prizes for haiku. Its 300 members are linked to similar organisations throughout the world.

## British Society of Magazine Editors
**Gill Branston & Associates, 137 Hale Lane, Edgware, Middlesex, HA8 9QP**
- 020 8906 4664
- admin@bsme.com
- www.bsme.com

**Contact** Chair, Jane Bruton; Administrator/Contact, Gill Branston
**About** The BSME aims to represent the needs and views of all UK magazine editors, and enhance their status, acting as a voice for the industry.

## Broadcasting Press Guild

☎ 01483 764895
☎ 01483 765882
🌐 www.broadcastingpressguild.org
**Contact** Chair, Conor Dignam; Membership Secretary, Richard Last
**About** The Broadcasting Press Guild is an association of journalists who specialise in writing and broadcasting about television, radio and the media generally. Membership is by invitation only.

## Campaign for Press & Broadcasting Freedom

**2nd Floor, Vi and Garner Smith House, 23 Orford Road, Walthamstow, London E17 9NL**
☎ 0208 521 5932
✉ freepress@cpbf.org.uk
🌐 www.cpbf.org.uk
**Contact** National Organiser, Barry White
**About** The CPBF campaigns to defend the principles of public service broadcasting and to argue for democratically accountable forms of broadcasting regulation which actively promote and encourage high programme standards and genuine cultural diversity.

## Career Writers' Association

✉ ann@ann50.freeserve.co.uk
🌐 www.careerswriters.co.uk
**About** The CWA attracts professionals who work in careers writing. Membership is only open to writers with an established reputation for providing objective and up-to-date careers information. Many draw on expertise gained as specialist information providers in careers services, as employment researchers, or as careers consultants to the national press. The CWA believes that providing thoroughly researched, accurate and up-to-date information is essential to help individuals of all ages make informed choices of courses and careers.

## Centreprise Literature Development Project

**136–138 Kingsland High Street, London, E8 2NS**
☎ 020 7249 6572
✉ literature@centreprisetrust.org
🌐 www.centrepriseliterature.com
**Contact** Development Coordinator, Eva Lewin; Managing Editor, Calabash, Sharon Duggal
**About** Centreprise Literature is an arts development agency for the promotion of access to and enjoyment of literature in all its forms, through local and community based initiatives. Centreprise Literature serves north and north east London with two parallel programmes of work. Its core programme focuses on providing a through-line of support for writers by offering courses, specialist groups, and one-to-one support. Its magazine, Calabash, has a high reputation, focusing on Black and Asian literature. It runs the Hackney Word Festival.

## Chartered Institute of Journalists

**2 Dock Offices, Surrey Quays Road, London, SE16 2XU**
☎ 020 7252 1187
☎ 020 7232 230
✉ memberservices@cioj.co.uk
🌐 www.cioj.co.uk
**Contact** President, Sangita Shah
**About** The Chartered Institute of Journalists combines the role of professional society with that of a trade union – known as the IoJ (TU). The Institute's union section protects its members' interests in the workplace and campaigns for better conditions for working journalists. The Institute's professional side is concerned with the standards and ethics of the media, the protection of journalistic freedom, training and administers the Institute's many charities.

## CILIP

**7 Ridgmount Street, London, WC1E 7AE**
☎ 020 7255 0500
☎ 020 7255 0501
✉ info@cilip.org.uk
🌐 www.cilip.org.uk
**Contact** Chief Executive, Bob McKee; Administrator, Dorothy Josem
**About** CILIP (the Chartered Institute of Library and Information Professionals) is the leading professional body for librarians, information specialists and knowledge managers.

## Circle of Wine Writers

**c/o Scots Firs, 70 Joiners Lane, Chalfont St Peter, Buckinghamshire, SL9 0AU**
☎ 01753 882320
☎ 01753 882320
✉ administrator@winewriters.org
🌐 www.winewriters.org
**Contact** President, Steven Spurrier; Circle administrator, Andrea Warren

**About** The Circle of Wine Writers is an association of authors, broadcasters, journalists, photographers and lecturers who are professionally engaged in communicating about wines and spirits. It aims to improve the standard of communication about wines, spirits and beers, and to contribute to the growing knowledge and interest in wine.

## CLA
**Saffron House, 6–10 Kirby Street, London, EC1N 8TS**
- 020 7400 3100
- 020 7400 310
- cla@cla.co.uk
- www.cla.co.uk

**Contact** Chief executive and company secretary, Peter F Shepherd

**About** The CLA (Copyright Licensing Agency) is the pivotal organisation in the UK for the licensing of re-use, reproduction and copying of copyrighted materials in books, journals, magazines and periodicals. It pays authors and publishers for such use through ALCS, DACS and PLS (see relevant entries). The CLA's excellent website explains its various roles in depth, and has a valuable section on copyright that will be of use to all writers.

## Classical Association
**Senate House, Malet St, London, WC1E 7HU**
- 020 7862 8706
- 020 7255 2297
- office@classicalassociation.org
- www.classicalassociation.org

**Contact** Secretary, Mrs Clare Roberts

**About** The Classical Association is the largest classical organisation in Great Britain. It has a worldwide membership, and unites the interests of all who value the study of the languages, literature and civilisation of ancient Greece and Rome.The CA website has a database of all classicists in UK universities.

## Cle
**25 Denzille Lane, Dublin 2**
- 00353 16394868
- info@publishingireland.com
- www.publishingireland.com

**Contact** President, Tony Farmar; Treasurer, Marie Maguire

**About** Cumann Leabharfhoilsitheoiri Eireann, the Irish Book Publisher's Association, is a cross-border organisation representing all the publishers in Ireland. Its website is useful for writers as it provides information and links to Irish publishers, agents and publishing freelancers, and information about copyright and other issues.

## Crime Writer's Association
- 07780 693144 press only
- info@thecwa.co.uk
- www.thecwa.co.uk

**Contact** Chair, Robert Richardson; Membership Secretary, Rebecca Tope

**About** The Crime Writer's Association has over 450 members, all of them with at least one published book with a crime theme to their name, the minimum qualification for membership.It is best known for its 'Dagger' awards.

## The Critics Circle
**1, The Firs, 162 Longlands Road, Sidcup, Kent, DA15 7LG**
- dsilvestercarr@compuserve.com
- www.criticscircle.org.uk

**Contact** President, Marianne Gray; Hon. Secretary, Denise Silvester-Carr

**About** The Critics Circle aims to promote the art of criticism, to uphold its integrity in practice, to foster and safeguard members' professional interests, to provide opportunities to meet, and to support the advancement of the arts. Membership is by invitation of the Circle only. It give awards in three categories each year, Dance, Drama and Film, as well as the prestigious Critics Circle Annual Award.

## Data Publishers Association
**Queens House, 28 Kingsway, London, WC2B 6JR**
- 020 7405 0836
- 020 7404 4167
- christine@dpa.org.uk
- www.dpa.org.uk

**Contact** Head of DPA, Christine Scott

**About** The Data Publishers Association (DPA) is the industry body representing data and directory publishers in the UK. Its role is to protect and promote the interests of the industry, both in print and electronic media.

## Digital Content Forum
**c/o ELSPA, 167 Wardour Street, London, W1F 8WL**
- 0207 534 0589
- Info@dcf.org.uk

ⓦ www.dcf.org.uk

**Contact** Chair, Paul Jackson; Policy & Communications Manager, Simon Sauntson

**About** The DCF's own mission statement says:' The DCF forms a two-way conduit between industry and government to gather views and input into policy-making processes. It goes further to broker relationships, develop shared knowledge and undertake activities to promote innovation and excellence in the content sector.' For writers, its main use will probably be the news, reports and information on all aspects of digital content on its website.The site also has useful links to official bodies and quangos.

## EBU

**L'Ancienne-Route 17A, CH-1218 Grand-Saconnex, Switzerland**

ⓞ 00 41 (0) 22 717 2111

ⓕ 00 41 (0) 22 747 4000

ⓔ ebu@ebu.ch

ⓦ www.ebu.ch

**Contact** Secretary General, Jean Réveillon; Head of Brussels Office, Jacques Briquemont

**About** The European Broadcasting Union (EBU) is the largest professional association of national broadcasters in the world. Working on behalf of its Members in the European area, it negotiates broadcasting rights for major sports events, operates the Eurovision and Euroradio networks, organizes programme exchanges, stimulates and coordinates co-productions, and provides a full range of other operational, commercial, technical, legal and strategic services.

## English Association

**University of Leicester, University Road, Leicester, LE1 7RH, UK**

ⓞ 0116 252 3982

ⓕ 0116 252 2301

ⓔ engassoc@leicester.ac.uk

ⓦ www.le.ac.uk/engassoc/index.html

**Contact** President, Professor Elaine Treharne; Chief Executive, Helen Lucas

**About** The aim of the English Association is to further knowledge, understanding and enjoyment of the English language and its literatures and to foster good practice in its teaching and learning at all levels. Based at the University of Leicester, the Association awards four prizes a year in specialist areas, and organizes and participates in academic conferences.

## English Pen

**6–8 Amwell Street, London, EC1R 1UQ**

ⓞ 020 7713 0023

ⓕ 020 7837 7838

ⓦ www.englishpen.org

**Contact** President, Dr. Alastair Niven; Office and Events Manager, Alice O'Hanlon

**About** English Pen exists to work with and fight for the rights of writers throughout the world who are persecuted or imprisoned because of their writing. It fights for freedom of speech and expression everywhere.

## English Speaking Union

**Dartmouth House, 37 Charles Street, London, W1J 5ED**

ⓞ 020 7529 1550

ⓕ 020 7495 6108

ⓔ esu@esu.org

ⓦ www.esu.org

**Contact** Director-General, Valerie Mitchell; Communications Officer, Norma Reid

**About** The English-Speaking Union is an international educational charity founded in 1918 to promote "international understanding and friendship through the use of the English language." With almost 40 branches in the UK, and over 50 international branches in countries in every part of the world, the ESU's mission is to bring people together and share their experiences. It is this network that writers may find of value.

## Fabian Society

**11 Dartmouth Street, London, SW1H 9BN**

ⓞ 020 7227 4900

ⓕ 020 7976 715

ⓔ info@fabian-society.org.uk

ⓦ www.fabian-society.org.uk

**Contact** Office Manager, Claire Willgress; Editorial Director, Tom Hampson

**About** The Fabian Society plays an important role in the development of political ideas and public policy on the left of centre. Analysing the challenges facing the UK and the rest of the industrialised world in a changing society and global economy, the Society's programme aims to explore the political ideas and the policy reforms which will define progressive politics in the new century.The Society is a democratically-constituted membership organisation. It is affiliated to the Labour Party but is editorially and organisationally independent. Through its publications, seminars and conferences, the Society provides an arena for open-minded public debate.

## FACT

**7 Victory Business Centre, Worton Road, Isleworth, Middlesex, TW7 6DB**

☎ 020 8568 6646

✆ 020 8560 6364

✉ contact@fact-uk.org.uk

🌐 www.fact-uk.org.uk

**About** The Federation Against Copyright Theft is the leading UK representative trade body committed to protecting the interests of the industry in the fight against pirate film and DVDs and the increasing threat from online piracy.

## Fellowship of Authors and Artists

**PO Box 158, Hertford, SG13 8FA**

☎ 0870 747 2514

✆ 0870 116 3398

🌐 www.author-fellowship.co.uk

**Contact** Graham Irwin

**About** The stated aims of the Fellowship are to promote and encourage the use of writing and all art forms as a means of therapy and self-healing; see website for further details.

## The Folklore Society

**The Warburg Institute, Woburn Square, London, WC1H 0AB**

☎ 020 7862 8564

✉ susanvass@hotmail.com

🌐 www.folklore-society.com

**Contact** Administrator, Mrs Susan Vass

**About** The Folklore Society's interest and expertise covers topics such as traditional music, song, dance and drama, narrative, arts and crafts, customs and belief. It is also interested in popular religion, traditional and regional food, folk medicine, children's folklore, traditional sayings, proverbs rhymes and jingles. Its aims are to foster folklore research and recording worldwide, and to make the results of such study available to all, whether members of the Society or not. The Society's journal, *Folklore*, is excellent, and the links to other folklore sites on its website are essential for anyone interested in this area of research.

## The Football Writers' Association

🌐 www.footballwriters.co.uk

**About** Membership of this organisation is by invitation only for working journalists who are accredited football correspondents for newspapers and agencies. Contact via the website.

## Garden Writer's Guild

**c/o The Institute of Horticulture, 14–15 Belgrave Square, London, SW1X 8PS**

☎ 020 7245 6943

✆ 020 7245 6943

✉ info@gardenwriters.co.uk

🌐 www.gardenwriters.co.uk

**Contact** Membership Administator, Erin Taylor

**About** The Garden Writer's Guild's aims are to raise the quality of garden writing, photography and broadcasting, and keep members up-to-date with what's going on in the world of gardening and horticulture. Its awards, presented at an annual lunch, are the most prestigious in the UK's gardening world.

## Guild of Agricultural Journalists

**c/o Woodcote Communications, 14 Clarice Way, Wallington, Surrey, SM6 9LD**

☎ 020 8669 0686

✆ 020 8669 3678

✉ lindym@woodcote-communications.co.uk

🌐 www.gaj.org.uk

**Contact** General Secretary, Don Gomery; Membership Secretary, Lindy Margach

**About** The Guild of Agricultural Journalists represents more than 500 journalists and media specialists working in the agricultural industry. Members range from agricultural and environmental correspondents to specialists writing for industry magazines, plus the PR and marketing managers of companies and organisations supporting British agriculture.

## Guild of Food Writers

**255 Kent House Road, Beckenham, Kent, BR3 1JQ**

☎ 020 8659 0422

✉ guild@gfw.co.uk

🌐 www.gfw.co.uk

**Contact** Administrator, Jonathan Woods

**About** The Guild represents professional food writers and broadcasters in the UK. It has over 350

authors, columnists, freelance journalists and broadcasters amongst its members.

## Guild of Health Writers
**Dale Lodge, 88 Wensleydale Road, Hampton, Middlesex, TW12 2LX**
- 020 8941 2977
- admin@healthwriters.com
- www.healthwriters.com

**Contact** Chair, Simon Crompton; Hon Sec, Lisa Melton

**About** The Guild of Health Writers is a national, independent membership organisation representing Britain's leading health journalists and writers. It was founded to encourage the provision of readable and accurate health information to the public. Members write on every aspect of health and well-being, from innovative medical science to complementary therapies and lifestyle issues. Membership of the Guild brings access to training, networking opportunities and a forum for balanced debate.

## Guild of Motoring Writers
**39 Beswick Avenue, Bournemouth, BH10 4EY**
- 01202 518808
- 01202 518808
- chris@whizzco.freeserve.co.uk
- www.guildofmotoringwriters.co.uk

**Contact** General Secretary, Patricia Lodge

**About** The Guild is the UK's professional body for motoring journalists. It has over 400 members, including daily and regional newspaper correspondents, magazine writers, book publishers, photographers, and radio and television broadcasters.

## Harleian Society
**College of Arms, Queen Victoria Street, London, EC4V 4BT**
- info@harleian.co.uk
- www.harleian.co.uk

**Contact** Chair, Thomas Woodcock; Hon Sec, Timothy Duke

**About** The Society's official objects are "the transcribing, printing and publishing of the heraldic visitations of counties, parish registers or any manuscripts relating to genealogy, family history and heraldry". The Society is unable to provide any services, apart from the sale of volumes either by annual subscription or individual purchase. It cannot

help with research queries. You may be able to find what you require from its links page.

## Historical Novel Society
- richard@historicalnovelsociety.org
- www.historicalnovelsociety.org

**Contact** Founder/Publisher, Richard Lee

**About** The Society promotes all aspects of historical fiction, providing support and opportunities for new writers, information for students, booksellers, and librarians, and a community for authors, readers, agents and publishers.

## HoldtheFrontPage
**Ground Floor, East Point, Cardinal Square, 10 Nottingham Road, Derby, DE1 3QT**
- 0116 227 3122 or 0116 227 3121
- pastill@nep.co.uk
- www.holdthefrontpage.co.uk

**Contact** Publisher, Patrick Astill; Reporter, Nikki Sargeson

**About** This is a website for journalists and journalism students. For those who are are working, or want to work, in the regional press, this is a place to find out more about the industry. It offers news stories about what is happening in the regional press, information on campaigning journalism and updates on breaking news. It has full details of job vacancies in the industry.

## Horror Writers Association UK
- hwa@horror.org
- www.horror.org/UK

**About** The Horror Writers Association UK is the UK chapter of the Horror Writers Association, a worldwide organisation of writers and publishing professionals. The Society is dedicated to the pursuit of professional conduct within the industry and to creating quality horror literature. Please note that the email contact given is to the HWA central US site.

## Institute of Copywriting
**Overbrook Business Centre, Poolbridge Road, Blackford, Wedmore, Somerset, BS28 4PA**
- 0800 781 1715
- 01934 713492
- copy@inst.org
- www.inst.org/copy

**About** The Institute acts as a community for copywriters, providing a membership base, courses, a database of copywriters, and advice on copywriting.

## The Institute of Linguists

**Saxon House, 48 Southwark Street, London, SE1 1UN**
- 020 7940 3100
- 020 7940 3101
- info@iol.org.uk
- www.iol.org.uk

**Contact** Chief Executive, John Hammond
**About** The Chartered Institute of Linguists serves the interests of professional linguists throughout the world and acts as a language assessment and accredited awarding body. It aims to promote the learning and use of modern languages, improve the status of all professional linguists, establish and maintain high standards of work, serve the interests of all linguists and ensure professional standards among language practitioners through its code of conduct.

## The Institute of Translators & Interpreting

**Fortuna House, South Fifth Street, Milton Keynes, MK9 2EU**
- 01908 325250
- 01908 325259
- info@iti.org.uk
- www.iti.org.uk

**About** The ITI is the only independent professional association of practising translators and interpreters in the United Kingdom. It is one of the primary sources of information on these services to government, industry, the media and the general public. With its aim of promoting the highest standards in the profession, ITI serves as a meeting place for all those who understand the importance of translation and interpreting to the economy and society, particularly with the expansion of a single European market of over forty languages and the growth of worldwide communications. ITI offers guidance to those entering the profession and advice not only to those who offer language services but also to their customers.

## International Publishers Association

**3 avenue de Miremont, 1206 Geneva, Switzerland**
- 00 41 22 346 3018
- 00 41 22 347 5717
- secretariat@ipa-uie.org
- www.ipa-uie.org

**Contact** Secretary General, Jens Bammel; Director, Freedom to Publish, Alexis Krikorian
**About** The IPA's aims are to uphold and defend the right of publishers to publish and distribute the works of the mind in complete freedom. It promotes and protects the principles of copyright, and works to overcome illiteracy, lack of books and of other education materials. It has links to many other publishing organisations and international governing bodies and governments. Writers wil find its website links useful in research.

## The Irish Copyright Licensing Agency

**25 Denzille Lane, Dublin 2**
- 00353 1 662 4211
- 00353 1 662 4213
- info@icla.ie
- www.icla.ie

**About** The ICLA licenses the copying of extracts from books, journals and magazines protected by copyright and published in the UK and 17 other countries.

## Irish Playwrights and Screenwriters Guild

**Art House, Curved Street, Temple Bar, Dublin 2**
- 00353 1 670 9970
- info@script.ie
- www.script.ie

**Contact** Chair, Sean Moffatt; Chief Executive, David Kavanagh
**About** The Irish Playwrights and Screenwriters Guild is the representative body in Ireland for writers for the stage and screen.

## Irish Translators' Association

**19 Parnell Square, Dublin 1**
- 00353 1 8721302
- 00353 1 8726282
- itiasecretary@eircom.net
- www.translatorsassociation.ie

**Contact** Chairperson, Annette Schiller
**About** The Irish Translators and Interpreters Association (Cumann Aistritheoir' agus Teangair' na hÉireann) represents the interests of translators and interpreters in Ireland. It aims to promote the highest professional and ethical standards in translation and interpreting.

## Irish Writers' Union
**19 Parnell Square, Dublin 1**
☎ 00353 01 8721302
🌐 www.ireland-writers.com
**About** The Irish Writers' Union represents the interests of all Irish writers, whether they were born in Ireland or elsewhere. Writers who are Irish by attachment, inclination, or persuasion, are welcome to join.

## literaturetraining
**PO Box 23595, Edinburgh, EH6 7YX**
☎ 0131 553 2210/0131 476 4039
📧 info@literaturetraining.com
🌐 www.literaturetraining.com
**Contact** Director, Philippa Johnston; Information Manager, Amanda Liddle
**About** literaturetraining is the UK's only dedicated provider of free information and advice on professional development for the literature sector. Its aim is to help writers and literature professionals at every stage of their career to invest in themselves and their professional development so that they can realise their full potential. Writers and those involved in some way with creating or supporting new writing and literature will find information on training and professional development opportunities on the website. If advice is needed on how to move forward professionally, literaturetraining can offer various forms of help.

## Mechanical-Copyright Protection Society Ltd
**MCPS-PRS Alliance, Copyright House, 29–33 Berners Street, London, W1T 3AB**
☎ 020 7306 4848
☎ 020 8696 5117
📧 publisherquery@mcps-prs-alliance.co.uk
🌐 www.mcps.co.uk
**About** The Mechanical-Copyright Protection Society (MCPS) is a not-for-profit organisation which currently represents over 18,000 composers, songwriters and music publishers. Its essential function is to collect and distribute royalties. It acts on behalf of its members by negotiating agreements with those who wish to record and distribute product containing copyright musical works and collecting licence fees for this use. The money is subsequently distributed to its members as mechanical royalties. Also see the Performing Rights Society.

## The Media Society
**66 Lincoln's Inn Fields, London WC2A 3LH**
📧 dorothy@themediasociety.co.uk
🌐 www.themediasociety.co.uk
**Contact** President, Geraldine Sharpe-Newton; Administrator, Dorothy Josem
**About** The Media Society stands for freedom of expression and the encouragement of high standards in journalism. It is unique in bringing together people working in all branches of the media – radio and television production and broadcasting, newspapers and magazines, new media, academia and media law. Its membership includes senior figures and those at the beginning of their careers.

## Mediawatch-UK
**3 Willow House, Kennington Road, Ashford, Kent, TN24 0NR**
☎ 01233 633936
📧 info@mediawatchuk.org
🌐 www.mediawatchuk.org
**Contact** Director, John Beyer
**About** Founded by the late Mary Whitehouse, MediaWatch UK provides an independent voice for those concerned about issues of taste and decency in the media. It publishes newsletters and reports on the portrayal of violence, bad language and sexual conduct, briefings on film classification, content regulation and the public interest.

## Medical Journalist's Association
**Red Door Communications, The Limes, 123 Mortlake High Street, London, SW14 8SN**
🌐 www.mja-uk.org
**Contact** Membership Secretary, Rachel Vrettos
**About** The MJA exists to support and encourage its members and enable them to work efficiently and at high levels of accuracy. More than 400 of the UK's medical and health journalists belong to the MJA, making its website a point of contact for anyone wanting to employ a writer with specific expertise, or alert medical journalists to events or achievements that deserve publicity.

## Music Publishers' Association
**6th Floor, British Music House, 26 Berners Street, London, W1T 3LR**
☎ 020 7580 0126
☎ 020 7637 3929
📧 info@mpaonline.org.uk

www.mpaonline.org.uk
**Contact** Chief Executive, Stephen Navin; Administrator/PA, Gina Clarke
**About** The Music Publishers Association (MPA) looks after the interest of all music publishers based or working in the UK and exists to safeguard and improve the business and legal environment within which its members are operating.

## National Association for Literature Development
**PO Box 23799, Edinburgh, EH7 5LE**
0131 652 1871/020 7272 8386
admin@nald.org
www.nald.org
**Contact** Director, Melanie Abrahams; Administrator, Claire Wingfield
**About** NALD is the UK's largest membership organisation for literature professionals. It is the only national body for all those involved in developing writers, readers and literature audiences. It exists so that literature professionals can communicate with each other.

## National Association of Press Agencies
**41 Lansdowne Crescent, Leamington Spa, Warwickshire, CV32 4PR**
0870 609 1935
secretariat@napa.org.uk
www.napa.org.uk
**About** NAPA is an umbrella organization covering press agencies throughout the UK. It members adhere to a code of conduct. Its website provides links by region and field of interest for those who may wish to contact them with a story.

## National Association of Writers in Education
**Box 1, Sheriff Hutton, York, YO60 7YU**
01653 618429
paul@nawe.co.uk
www.nawe.co.uk
**Contact** Director, Paul Munden
**About** The National Association of Writers in Education seeks to support those working in writing related occupations throughout both formal and informal education. The writing can cover any form, area or genre. The website provides extensive information and links for all interested in this field, including a database of funding opportunities, and,

as part of its Higher Education Network, a list of all writing courses in UK HE.

## National Centre for Research in Childern's Literature
**Roehampton University, Froebel College, London, SW15 5PJ**
020 8392 3008
0181 392 3819
NCRCL@roehampton.ac.uk
www.ncrcl.ac.uk
**About** A research centre within the School of Arts at Roehampton University, the NCRCL works to research the whole area of children's literature. It has PhD students, runs an MA, and holds conferences. Writers will find the links on its website of use.

## National Literary Trust
**Swire House, 59 Buckingham Gate, London, SW1E 6AJ**
020 7828 2435
020 7931 9986
contact@literacytrust.org.uk
www.literacytrust.org.uk
**Contact** Director, Jonathan Douglas; Trust Administrator, Jacky Taylor
**About** The National Literacy Trust is dedicated to building a literate nation. Among its campaigns to this end are: Reading Is Fundamental, UK, the National Reading Campaign, Talk To Your Baby, Reading The Game, Reading Connects, and the Vital Link. Results of research into specific areas of concern to do with literacy can be found on the website. The site also provides a rich range of resources to help with reading, and it also links to many other organisations.

## National Union of Journalists
**Headland House, 308–312 Gray's Inn Road, London, WC1X 8DP**
020 7278 7916
020 7837 8143
info@nuj.org.uk
www.nuj.org.uk
**Contact** General Secretary, Jeremy Dear; See website for extensive contact details in regions and sectors
**About** The NUJ has been Britain and Ireland's leading trades union for journalists of all sorts since 1907. Members cover the whole range of editorial work – staff and freelance, writers and reporters, editors and sub-editors, photographers and

illustrators, working in broadcasting, newspapers, magazines, books, on the internet and in public relations.

## The Newspaper Society

St. Andrew's House, 18–20 St. Andrew Street, London, EC4A 3AY

- ☎ 020 7632 7400
- 🖷 020 7632 7401
- ✉ ns@newspapersoc.org.uk
- 🌐 www.newspapersoc.org.uk

**Contact** Director, David Newell

**About** The Newspaper Society represents and promotes the interests of Britain's regional and local press, who between them own over 1,300 daily and weekly, paid-for and free newspaper titles. It was founded in 1836 and is believed to be the oldest publishers' association in the world. Its services are split into three broad areas: lobbying, marketing and communications. It provides legal advice and lobbying services to regional newspaper publishers and their staff, and also to the national newspaper, magazine and distribution industries. It promotes the regional press as a medium to national advertisers and agencies. It holds a series of conferences and seminars and runs the annual Local Newspaper Week.

## New Writing North

Culture Lab, Grand Assembly Rooms, Newcastle University, King's Walk, Newcastle upon Tyne, NE1 7RU

- ☎ 0191 222 1332
- 🖷 0191 222 1372
- ✉ mail@newwritingnorth.com
- 🌐 www.newwritingnorth.com

**About** New Writing North is the writing development agency for the north east of England (the area covered by Arts Council England North East). It aims to create an environment in the north east in which new writing in all genres can flourish and develop. It merges individual development work with writers across all media with educational work and the production of creative projects. It works with writers from different genres and forms to develop career opportunities, new commissions, projects, residencies, publications and live events. NWN manage the Northern Writers' Awards and the Northern Rock Foundation Writer's Award (currently the largest literary award in the UK) and supports writers at all stages of their careers by mentoring and by the creation of professional development training initiatives and projects.

## New Writing South

9 Jew Street, Brighton, East Sussex, BN1 1UT

- ☎ 01273 735353
- ✉ enquiries@newwritingsouth.com
- 🌐 www.newwritingsouth.com

**About** A writing organisation open to all creative writers in the South East of England, and for those seeking creative writers and for other creative writing agencies including all producers of dramatic writing.

## Outdoor Writers' Guild

PO Box 520, Bamber Bridge, Preston, Lancashire, PR5 8LF

- ☎ 01772 321243
- 🖷 0870 137 8888
- ✉ secretary@owg.org.uk
- 🌐 www.owg.org.uk

**About** The Outdoor Writers' Guild is open to writers, journalists, photographers, illustrators, broadcasters, film-makers, artists, publishers and editors who are actively and professionally involved in sustainable activities in any outdoor setting. The Guild is an important link between the outdoor trade and the public, and offers a wide range of services to meet the needs of editors, publishers, public relations companies and picture researchers.

## PACT

Procter House, 1 Procter Street, Holborn, London, WC1V 6DW

- ☎ 020 7067 4367
- ✉ enquiries@pact.co.uk
- 🌐 www.pact.co.uk

**Contact** Chief Executive, John McVay; Receptionist/ Administrator, Hayley McClelland

**About** Pact is the UK trade association that represents and promotes the commercial interests of independent feature film, television, animation and interactive media companies.It negotiates terms of trade with all public service broadcasters in the UK and supports members in their business dealings with cable and satellite channels.

## Performing Rights Society

Copyright House, 29–33 Berners Street, London, W1T 3AB

- ☎ General queries: 020 7580 5544/ Queries from writers: 020 7306 4801
- ✉ writerquery@mcps-prs-alliance.co.uk
- 🌐 www.prs.co.uk

**About** PRS is known as a 'collecting society' because its primary role is collecting royalties from music users in the UK who every day publicly perform, broadcast and include music in cable production services. PRS also collects royalties from around the world for its members through reciprocal agreements with collecting societies overseas. PRS collects the royalties by issuing a licence to the music user (usually charged on an annual basis). In order to then make royalty payments to its members, PRS needs to know what music is being played. Major users, such as the BBC and large concert venues, give PRS detailed reports of the music they play. For many other venues including commercial discos, clubs and pubs, PRS sends researchers to obtain first-hand information. PRS is a non-profit making organisation. It works in close alliance with the MCPS- see entry.

## Periodical Publishers Association
**Queens House, 28 Kingsway, London, WC2B 6JR**
- 020 7404 4166
- 020 7404 4167
- www.ppa.co.uk

**Contact** Chief executive, Ian Locks; Chief Executive PPA Ireland, Grace Aungier

**About** The Periodical Publishers Association (PPA) is the organisation for magazine and professional media publishers in the UK. PPA's role is to promote and protect the interests of the industry in general, and member companies in particular.

## The Personal Managers' Association Ltd
**1 Summer Road, East Molesey, Surrey, KT8 9LX**
- 020 8398 9796
- 020 8398 9796
- www.thepma.com

**About** The PMA is the professional association of agents representing UK based actors, writers, producers, directors, designers and technicians in the film, television and theatre industries.

## Player-Playwrights
- 020 8883 0371
- P-P@dial.pipex.com
- www.groups.msn.com/PlayerPlaywrights

**About** An networking group where actual and aspiring playwrights discuss their work, and where links are made to potential producers, and to actors. Meetings take place at the Horse and Groom, Great

Portland St, London, W1; see website for more details.

## Press Complaints Commission
**Halton House, 20–23 Holborn, London, EC1N 2ID**
- 020 7831 0022
- complaints@pcc.org.uk
- www.pcc.org.uk

**About** If you have a complaint about a newspaper or magazine in the UK, this is the place register that complaint. Visit the website to learn more.

## Public Lending Right
**Richard House, Sorbonne Close, Stockton-on-Tees, TS17 6DA**
- 01642 604699
- 01642 615641
- www.plr.uk.com

**About** Under the United Kingdom's PLR Scheme authors receive payments from government funds for the free borrowing of their books from public libraries. To qualify for payment, authors must apply to register their books with the PLR organisation. Payments are made annually on the basis of loans data collected from a sample of public libraries in the UK. All authors can benefit from this; indeed, books that may not necessarily have been successes in the high street might earn pleasant fees from library borrowing over time. Most writers would be advised to register their titles for PLR.

## The Publishers Association
**29b Montague Street, London, WC1B 5BW**
- 020 7691 9191
- 020 7691 9199
- mail@publishers.org.uk
- www.publishers.org.uk

**About** The Publishers Association is the leading organisation working on behalf of book, journal and electronic publishers based in the UK. It brings publishers together to discuss the issues facing the industry and to definite the practical policies which will drive lobbying and campaigns in the UK and internationally. The aim of The Publishers Association is to ensure a secure future for the UK publishing industry.

## Publishers Licensing Society Ltd
**37–41 Gower Street, London, WC1E 6HH**
- 020 7299 7730
- 020 7299 7780

○ pls@pls.org.uk
🌐 www.pls.org.uk
**Contact** Chief Executive, Dr Alicia Wise;
Communications & Administration Officer,
Imogen Forbes.
**About** Together with ALCS and CLA (see entries)
PLS manages the collective licensing of reprography
in the UK. To do this, PLS needs agreement from
publisher rights owners to authorize CLA to operate
its licensing schemes. These non-exclusive licences
allow PLS to include those mandating publishers'
works in the repertoire offered to licensees by CLA.
CLA offers licences to institutions and individuals
who want to photocopy parts of copyright works.
The money collected from these licences, after
deduction of costs, is shared between PLS and ALCS
(artists also get a share through DACS). These
societies then have a responsibility for distributing
that share fairly to their rights owner members. CLA
licenses educational, business and government
sectors to copy parts of works. Most of the licences
are blanket licences. Users pay an annual fee
determined on the basis of the number of full time
equivalent students, or employees, in the
organisation.

## Publisher's Publicity Circle
**65 Airedale Avenue, London, W4 2NN**
☎ 020 8994 1881
○ ppc-@lineone.net
🌐 www.publisherspublicitycircle.co.uk
**About** The Publisher's Publicity Circle exists to
enable all book publicists from publishing houses
and freelance PR agencies to gather and share
information on a regular basis. Monthly meetings are
held in central London to provide a forum for press
journalists, television and radio researchers and
producers to meet publicists collectively.
Representatives from the media are invited to speak
about the ways in which they can feature authors
and their books, and how book publicists can most
effectively provide relevant information and
material. The PPC website has a directory of
publicists, both in publishing house and freelance.

## Publishing Scotland
(See Scottish Publishers Association)

## The Radio Academy
**5 Market Place, London, W1W 8AE**
☎ 020 7255 2010
○ trevor@radioacademy.org

🌐 www.radioacademy.org
**Contact** Director, Trevor Dann
**About** The Radio Academy is dedicated to the
encouragement, recognition and promotion of
excellence in UK broadcasting and audio
production. It represents the radio industry to
outside bodies including the government and offers
neutral ground where everyone from the national
networks to individual podcasters is encouraged to
discuss the broadcasting, production, marketing and
promotion of radio and audio.

## The Romantic Novelists' Association
Email: The New Cavendish Club, 44 Great
Cumberland Place, London, W1H 8BS
🌐 www.rna-uk.org
**Contact** President, Diane Pearson; Hon Sec,
Eileen Ramsay
**About** The RNA works to enhance and promote the
various types of romantic and historical fiction, to
encourage good writing in all its many varieties, to
learn more about the craft and help readers enjoy it.
Membership of the association now stands at almost
700. A scheme for appraisal of manuscripts (see
website), is an important element in helping
unpublished writers to achieve first publication. See
the RNA website for details, dates and contact
information.

## The Royal Literary Fund
**3 Johnson's Court, off Fleet Street, London,
EC4A 3EA**
☎ 020 7353 7159
○ egunnrlf@globalnet.co.uk
🌐 www.rlf.org.uk
**Contact** General Secretary, Eileen Gunn
**About** The Royal Literary Fund is a benevolent fund
for professional published authors in financial
difficulties. It has been continuously helping authors
since it was set up in 1790. It is funded by bequests
and donations from writers who wish to help other
writers. Its committee members come from all walks
of literary life and include novelists, biographers,
poets, publishers, lawyers and agents. Help is given
to writers in many different situations where
personal or professional setbacks have resulted in
loss of income. Pensions are considered for older
writers who have seen their earnings decrease. The
RLF also runs a Fellowship scheme for writers in
partnership with British universities and colleges.
Writers are appointed as Fellows based on their
literary merit and aptitude for the role, and
irrespective of their financial circumstances. Of

special interest to all involved in writing in HE is *Writing Matters*, the RLF Report on Student Writing in Higher Education. It examines the difficulties many students face in writing effectively and proposes a range of measures to address these. The report argues that much greater attention should be paid to helping students adjust to the demands of writing at university and that writing development is a key factor for progress in the HE sector.

## The Royal Society of Literature
**The Strand, London, WC2R 1LA**

- 020 7845 4676
- info@rslit.org
- www.rslit.org

**Contact** President, Michael Holroyd; Secretary, Maggie Fergusson

**About** The Royal Society of Literature is entirely devoted to the promotion and enjoyment of excellence in British writing. Founded in 1820, past and present Fellows (who are elected) include some of the most eminent names in British literature. Membership is open to all. Regular meetings with speakers from the world of literature are held at Somerset House; members of the public welcome. See website for details. The society has major annual awards for both fiction and non-fiction. It supports the work of writers in many ways, including campaigning for libraries to remain providers of good books above all else, and to keep English literature at the heart of the learning curriculum.

## Royal Television Society
**5th Floor, Kildare House, 3 Dorset Rise, London, EC4Y 8EN**

- 020 7822 2810
- 020 7822 2811
- info@rts.org.uk
- www.rts.org.uk

**Contact** Chief Executive, Simon Albury; Office Administrator/Receptionist, Tasha Sutherland

**About** With a veritable who's-who in television names and personalities associated with it, the RTS is influential and respected. It is a forum for discussion and debate on all aspects of the television community. With a full calendar of events, dinners, meetings, talks, awards and ceremonies, it gives its full members and patrons opportunities to communicate and learn. Members receive the monthly magazine *Television*.

## Science Fiction Foundation
**75 Rosslyn Avenue, Harold Wood, Essex, RM3 0RG**

- www.sf-foundation.org

**Contact** Roger Robinson

**About** The aim of the SFF is to promote science fiction and bring together those who read, write, study, teach, research or archive science fiction in Britain and the rest of the world. It also supports science fiction at conventions, at conferences and at other events which bring those interested in science fiction together. The four main objectives of the SFF are: to provide research facilities for anyone wishing to study science fiction; to investigate and promote the usefulness of science fiction in education; to disseminate information about science fiction; and to promote a discriminating understanding of the nature of science fiction. Its main activities include publication of the journal Foundation: the international review of science fiction, and supporting the research library The Science Fiction Foundation Collection at the University of Liverpool.

## Scottish Book Trust
**Sandeman House, Trunk's Close, 55 High Street, Edinburgh, EH1 1SR**

- 0131 524 0160
- 0131 524 0161
- info@scottishbooktrust.com
- www.scottishbooktrust.com

**Contact** CEO Marc Lambert; General Manager, Jeanette Harris

**About** Scottish Book Trust is Scotland's national agency for reading and writing. It promotes reading and books. Under its umbrella is Live Literature Scotland, a national initiative that enables Scottish citizens to engage with the nation's authors, playwrights, poets, storytellers and illustrators. It is the only writer bursary scheme of its kind in the UK, subsidising the cost of 1,200 community visits by writers in all areas of Scotland, and is extremely popular. More than 500 writers who are available to conduct readings and literary events in Scotland are listed and searchable on the SBT database.

## Scottish Newspaper Publishers Association
**48 Palmerston Places, Edinburgh, EH12 5DE**

- 0131 220 4353
- 0131 220 4344
- info@snpa.org.uk
- www.snpa.org.uk

**About** The Scottish Newspaper Publishers Association (SNPA) is the trade association representing publishers of 100 weekly and bi-weekly newspapers, and a further 30 free distribution newspapers. Its website is particularly useful for links to Scottish local paper groups.

## Scottish Publishers Association aka Publishing Scotland

**Scottish Book Centre, 137 Dundee Street, Edinburgh, EH11 1BG**

- 0131 228 6866
- 0131 228 3220
- info@scottishbooks.org
- www.scottishbooks.org

**Contact** Director, Lorraine Fannin; Information and Professional Development, Katherine Naish

**About** Publishing Scotland, previously The Scottish Publishers Association, is a trade association of almost 80 Scottish publishers. It is the voice and the network for publishing in Scotland. It works to help its members with the marketing of their books to the widest possible readership within the UK and overseas. On members' behalf, it attends many national and international book fairs and exhibitions. It also co-ordinates bookshop and library promotions, and other marketing initiatives.

## Scottish Screen

**249 West George Street, Glasgow, G2 4QE**

- 0845 300 7300
- info@scottishscreen.com
- www.scottishscreen.com

**Contact** Chief Executive, Ken Hay

**About** Scottish Screen is the national screen agency for Scotland with responsibility for developing all aspects of screen culture and industry across the country. Its work includes: production company growth; short and feature film development and production; freelancer and company skills development; experimental, alternative and interactive digital screen content, formats and platforms; the development and production of television drama pilots; and audience and market development and distribution initiatives.

## SfEP

**Riverbank House, 1 Putney Bridge Approach, Fulham, London, SW6 3JD**

- 020 7736 3278
- 020 7736 3318
- administration@sfep.org.uk

- www.sfep.org.uk

**Contact** Honorary president, Judith Butcher

**About** The Society for Editors and Proofreaders (SfEP) is a professional organisation for editors and proofreaders. Its aims are to promote high editorial standards and to achieve recognition of the professional status of its members and associates.

## The Society for Theatre Research

**c/o The Theatre Museum, 1E Tavistock Street, London, WC2E 7PR**

- e.cottis@btinternet.com
- www.str.org.uk

**Contact** Eileen Cottis

**About** The Society for Theatre Research provides a meeting point for all those interested in the history and technique of the British theatre. It acts as an advisory body on theatrical matters and puts on occasional Study Days on particular aspects of theatre, publishes new books and reprints texts chosen to illustrate aspects of theatre history (members receive a free book every year), awards research grants to encourage work on theatrical subjects, especially those connected with live theatre, and awards an annual theatre book prize for original research into any aspect of the history and technique of the British theatre. It also distributes *Theatre Notebook*, an illustrated journal devoted to the history and technique of the British theatre, hosts lectures in London on topics of theatrical interest, and holds an annual festival in memory of William Poel.

## The Society of Authors

**The Society of Authors, 84 Drayton Gardens, London, SW10 9SB**

- 020 7373 6642
- 020 7373 5768
- info@societyofauthors.org
- www.societyofauthors.org

**Contact** Chair, Tracy Chevalier; General Secretary, Mark Le Fanu

**About** Grants for previously published writers who are British by birth and under the age of 40, to benefit them in research and travel. Work must contribute to the greater understanding of existing social and economic organisation' and fiction is included. The twice-yearly grants, awarded in April and September, are normally between £1,000 and £2,000 and rarely exceed £4,000. Authors must submit: a copy of their latest published book; a brief history of their writing career; details of their current work; size of advance (if any); names of publishers already approached or working with; overall financial position and why the grant is needed; details of past grants; confirmation of their eligibility to enter; and copies of past reviews (if any). Full application details are available on the website. See entries under Bursaries, Fellowships and Grants and Competitions and Prizes for more information.

## The Society of Authors in Scotland

**About** See website of Society of Authors, under Subsidiary Groups (details above).

## Society of Children's Book Writers and Illustrators

UK Membership Coordinator, Sue Hyams, 56 Ackroyd Road, Forest Hill, London, SE23 1DL

- membership@britishscbwi.org, info@britishscbwi.org
- www.britishscbwi.org

**Contact** Regional Advisor, Natascha Biebow

**About** The British arm of the Society of Children's Book Writers and Illustrators is part of an international organization offering a variety of services to people who write, illustrate, or share an interest in children's literature. SCBWI acts as a network for the exchange of knowledge between writers, illustrators, editors, publishers, agents, librarians, educators, booksellers and others involved with literature for young people. There are currently more than 12,000 members worldwide, in over 70 regions, making it the largest children's writing organization in the world. The British SCBWI offers members support, information and education at a local level. See website for local regional contacts.

## The Society of Civil and Public Service Writers

c/o Membership Secretary, 17 The Green, Corby Glen, Grantham, NG33 4NP

- joan@lewis5634.fsnet.co.uk
- www.scpsw.co.uk

**Contact** Chair, Terry Rickson; Membership Secretary, Joan M Lewis

**About** The society encourages authorship by present and past members of the Civil Service, Armed Forces and certain other public service bodies. It also provides opportunities for social and cultural activities. There is an annual Poetry Weekend at Birmingham University and the society supports and encourages writers' weekend meetings in any part of the country.

## Society of Editors

University Centre, Granta Place, Mill Lane, Cambridge, CB2 1RU

- 01223 304080
- 01223 304090
- info@societyofeditors.org
- www.societyofeditors.co.uk

**Contact** Executive Director and Company Secretary, Bob Satchwell

**About** The society campaigns and lobbies to fight for media freedom. It has more than 400 members made up of editors, managing editors, editorial directors, training editors, editors-in-chief and deputy editors in national, regional and local newspapers, magazines, radio, television and new media, lawyers and academics in journalism education. Its values are: the promotion of press and broadcasting freedom and the public's right to know; the universal right to freedom of expression; the vitality of the news media in a democratic society; the commitment to high editorial standards. The society influences debate on press and broadcasting freedom, ethics and the culture and business of news media.

## Society of Indexers

Woodbourn Business Centre, 10 Jessell Street, Sheffield, S9 3HY

- 0114 244 9561
- 0114 244 9563
- info@indexers.org.uk
- www.indexers.org.uk

**Contact** Chair, Sue Lightfoot; Secretary, Judith Menes

**About** The Society exists to promote indexing, the quality of indexes and the profession of indexing. Its website contains a wealth of information for indexers, and, as one would expect, is very easy to navigate.

## The Society of Medical Writers

- irene.ranner@talk21.com
- www.somw.org.uk

**Contact** Chair, Professor Brian McGuinness; Secretary, Mrs Irene Ranner

**About** Membership of the Society of Medical Writers is open to anyone who publishes or aspires to publish written work of whatever nature – fact or fiction, prose or poetry. It is intended that the association should be enjoyable, stimulating and educational so that writing from medical practice, including general practice is improved and encouraged. See the website for various committee, activity and competition names, contacts and addresses.

## Society of Women Writers & Journalists

ⓦ www.swwj.co.uk
**Contact** Membership Secretary, Wendy Hughes
**About** The aims of the SWWJ include the encouragement of literary achievement, the upholding of professional standards, and social contact with fellow writers and others in the field, including editors, publishers, broadcasters, and agents. It is an international association, and is affiliated to women's associations across the world. See the website for regional contacts and activities. Many of the London meetings are held at The New Cavendish Club, 44 Great Cumberland Place, London W1.

## Society of Young Publishers

**c/o The Bookseller, Endeavour House, 189 Shaftesbury Avenue, London, WC2H 8TJ**
ⓔ membersec@thesyp.org.uk
ⓦ www.thesyp.org.uk
**Contact** Chair, Doug Wallace; Membership Secretary, Claire Morrison
**About** The Society of Young Publishers is open to anyone in publishing or a related trade (in any capacity) – or who is hoping to be soon. Anyone interested or working in the publishing industry is welcome to join. The only exception is that those who have been in the industry for more than ten years are not able to stand on the committee. There are two branches – in London and Oxford. Both branches have regular events and meetings, and both are run by volunteers.

## Sports Journalists' Association of Great Britain

**c/o Start2Finish Event Management, Unit 92, Capital Business Centre, 22 Carlton Road, Surrey, CR2 0BS**
ⓣ 020 8916 2234
ⓣ 020 8916 2235
ⓔ stevenwdownes@btinternet.com
ⓦ www.sportsjournalists.co.uk
**Contact** Chairman, Barry Newcombe; Secretary, Steven Downes
**About** The SJA is an association for British-based professional sports journalists, whether writers or photographers, editors or broadcasters.

## The Translators Association

(See The Society of Authors)

## VLV

**101 King's Drive, Gravesend, Kent, DA12 5BQ**
ⓣ 01474 352835
ⓣ 01474 351112
ⓔ info@vlv.org.uk
ⓦ www.vlv.org.uk
**Contact** Executive Director, Peter Blackman; Membership Secretary, Sue Washbrook
**About** Voice of the Listener & Viewer (VLV) represents the citizen and consumer interest in broadcasting and works for quality and diversity in British broadcasting. It campaigns for high quality radio and television programmes, and in particular for the principles of public service broadcasting. It is influential, and attracts big names as speakers and contributors to its conferences and events. It represents the interests of listeners, viewers, citizens and consumers and works to keep listeners and viewers informed about current developments in British broadcasting. These include proposed new legislation, public consultation on broadcasting policy and the likely impact of digital technology.

## WATCH

**c/o University of Reading Library, PO Box 223, Whiteknights, Reading, RG6 6AE**
ⓣ 0118 931 8783
ⓔ D.C.Sutton@reading.ac.uk
ⓦ www.watch-file.com
**Contact** Director of Research Projects, David Sutton
**About** WATCH is an online database of authors and artists that enables users to search for contact details of rights holders. This is primarily of use when looking for contacts of those holding or administering the rights of deceased persons. Searches are free. The database is managed jointly by the University of Reading and by the University of Texas.

## Welsh Books Council

**Castell Brychan, Aberystwyth, Ceredigion, SY23 2JB**
ⓣ 01970 624151
ⓣ 01970 625385
ⓔ castellbrychan@wbc.org.uk
ⓦ www.wbc.org.uk
**Contact** Director, Gwerfyl Pierce Jones

**About** The Welsh Books Council is a national body, funded by the Welsh Assembly Government, which provides a focus for the publishing industry in Wales. It provides a number of specialist services (in the fields of editing, design, marketing and distribution) with a view to improving standards of book production and publication in both Welsh and English. For writers, its main interest may be that it aims to assist and support them by providing services and by awarding grants/commissions which are channelled through publishers. See the website for further details.

## Women in Publishing

- info@wipub.org.uk
- www.wipub.org.uk

**Contact** Membership, Janey Burton; for regional contacts see website

**About** Women in Publishing works to promote the status of women working in publishing and related trades by helping them to develop their careers. Its aims are to provide a forum for the discussion of ideas, trends and subjects of interest to women in the publishing trades, to encourage networking and mutual support, to provide opportunities for sharing information and expertise, to support and publicise women's achievements and successes, and to promote the status of women within publishing.Monthly meetings are a key part of what WiP does. See website for location of monthly meetings.

## Women Writers Network

- www.womenwriters.org.uk

**About** WWN is a networking group for professional women writers.Most are freelance, some are salaried, and together they represent a wide range of writing interests. WWN not a writers' circle but a group formed to help women further their professional development. NB: Meeting venue is Conway Hall, 25 Red Lion Square, Holborn, London WC1 (2nd Monday of the month – see website for details).

## Writernet

**Cabin V, Clarendon Buildings, 25 Horsell Road, London, N5 1XL**

- 020 7609 7474
- 020 7609 7557
- www.writernet.co.uk

**Contact** Chair, Bonnie Greer

**About** Writernet provides writers for all forms of live and recorded performance with a range of services

which enable them to pursue their careers better. It also provides a wide range of producers who employ writers with the opportunity to make more informed choices to meet their needs. It is a national, not-for-profit organisation operating strategically across four areas – professional development, international work, cultural diversity and third sector: co-producing, publishing, providing information, advice and guidance, dramaturgical and other development support.

## Writers Advice Centre for Children's Books

**16 Smiths Yard, Summerley Street, London, SW18 4HR**

- 07979 905353
- Info@writersadvice.co.uk
- www.writersadvice.co.uk

**Contact** Editorial Director, Louise Jordan

**About** A literary consultancy service offering professional editorial & marketing advice to new and published children's writers, on a fee basis. The Writers' Advice Centre for Children's Books is the only manuscript agency in the UK specialising solely in children's publishing. Its manuscript assessment service provides new, and published, children's writers with critical feedback that can increase chances of publication. The Writers' Advice Centre is open to everyone writing for children whether they be complete beginners or already published authors. It will look at all types of writing for children. This could include picture books, early readers, short stories, novels for older children, non-fiction and poetry.

## The Writers' Guild of Great Britain

**15 Britannia Street, London, WC1X 9JN**

- 020 7833 0777
- 020 7833 0777
- admin@writersguild.org.uk
- www.writersguild.org.uk

**Contact** President, David Nobbs; Chair, Katharine Way; General Secretary, Bernie Corbett; Deputy General Secretary, Anne Hogben; Assistant General Secretary, Naomi MacDonald

**About** The Writers' Guild of Great Britain is the trade union representing writers in TV, radio, theatre, books, poetry, film and video games. In TV, film, radio and theatre, the Guild is the recognised body for negotiating minimum terms and practice agreements for writers. It campaigns and lobbies on behalf of all writers, and is influential up to government level. Its voice is listened to and its views are respected. Any writer who has received payment under a contract in terms at or above the Writers' Guild minimum terms for at least one piece of work is entitled to become a full member.

## Yachting Journalists Association
**Harefield Farm, Hogbens Hill, Selling, Faversham, Kent, ME13 9QZ**
☎ 01227 752815
☎ 01227 752815
✉ sec@yja.co.uk
🌐 www.yja.co.uk
**Contact** Chair, Bob Fisher; Honorary Treasurer and Membership Secretary, Amanda Fisher
**About** The aims of the Yachting Journalists' Association are to promote greater awareness of a wide range of leisure boating activities through the professional services offered by its members.

# WRITER'S GROUPS

## 4Words Media Group/ Interchange4Words
**Bradford, West Yorkshire and online**
✉ joedot@blueyonder.co.uk
🌐 http://uk.groups.yahoo.com/group/hear4words
**Contact** Joe Ogden
**Meeting Time** Online 24/7 and occasionally on Fridays in Bradford
**About** What started as the Interchange Writers' Network has now become the 4Words Media Group, an online writing community. New members are welcome as long as they have internet access. They should contact Joe Ogden by email. The group mainly deals with poetry, writing, plays and screenplays, although they can put you in contact with other groups in and around the Bradford area. Other sites to look at include ether blog at www.blogcharm.com/interchange4words, their MySpace at www.myspace.com/4wordsmedia and the irdaio at www.live365.com/stations/306906. There are no fees.

## Aberdeen Writers' Circle
**Aberdeen Arts Centre, 33 King Street, Aberdeen, AB24 5AA**
✉ awcwrite@aol.com
**Contact** Moira Brown
**Meeting Time** 10am–12pm, every Wednesday
**About** New members are welcome, either make contact or go along. Meetings take the form of readings and constructive feedback. There are sometimes written exercises, guest speakers and workshops throughout the year. Fees are £2 per meeting.

## Anderida Writers
**York House Hotel, Royal Parade, Eastbourne, East Sussex**
☎ 01323 640483
✉ ann@jaapann.freeserve.co.uk
**Contact** Mrs. Ann Botha
7 Fraser Avenue
Eastbourne
East Sussex
BN23 6BB
**Meeting Time** 8pm, first Tuesday of each month
**About** New members are welcome; please contact Ann Botha for details. All types of writing are covered and members are encouraged to eventually produce a piece of publishable standard work. Current members are both published and unpublished. The group holds an annual short story competition and a Christmas dinner. Fees are £15 per annum, but new members attend first as a guest with a fee of £1.50.

## Ashburton Writers' Group
**Members' homes, Ashburton area**
☎ 01364 653177 (Jean Clegg)
✉ ianroyce@tesco.net
**Contact** Ian Chamberlain
**Meeting Time** 9.30am, alternate Tuesdays
**About** New members welcome. The informal meetings, based on a set theme and led by different members each week, include an hour of actual writing, followed by critiques of previously circulated members' work. A range of writing is covered, from biography, to journalism, to historical writing and current members include award winning poets. There are no fees.

## Ayr Writers' Club

Prestwick Community Centre, 25 Caerlaverlock Road, Prestwick, Ayrshire, KA9 1HP

☎ 01294 214641
✉ toclearcom@aol.com
🌐 www.ayrwritersclub.co.uk

**Contact** Catherine Lang

**Meeting Time** 7.30–9.30pm, Wednesday evenings

**About** New members over the age of 16 are welcome. Either make contact or go to a meeting. Meetings are workshops, informal club nights, or based around guest speakers. The group also runs competitions, which are judged by guest speakers. Check the website for up to date programmes. Fees are £20 per annum or £10 per annum for postal membership. Non-members may attend twice for free before joining.

## Ballymena Writers' Group

The Showgrounds, Warden Street, Ballymena, Northern Ireland, BT43 7DR

☎ 028 2564 3904
✉ r.doherty2@ukonline.co.uk (Rita Doherty, secretary)

**Contact** Mary Higgins

**Meeting Time** 7.30pm–9.30pm, every Monday

**About** New members are welcome, the only requirement is an interest in writing. There is full disabled access. The group has tutors that cover every genre of writing.

## Bank Street Writers

Venue in the centre of Bolton

☎ 01204 669858
✉ bswscribe@aol.com
🌐 http://hometown.aol.co.uk/bswscribe/myhomepage/writing.html

**Contact** Rod Riesco
16–18 Mill Lane
Horwich
Bolton
BL6 6AT

**Meeting Time** Monthly, first Wednesday

**About** New members of any level and experience are welcome. Covers all types of writing including fiction, non-fiction, poetry and drama. The group also produces a magazine, "Current Accounts" and runs a writing competition. Fees are £10 per annum but new members are welcome to attend for free on a trial basis.

## Basingstoke Writers' Circle

United Reform Church, London Road, Basingstoke, Hampshire

☎ 01256 326453
🌐 www.communigate.co.uk/hants/bwc/

**Meeting Time** 8pm–10pm, fourth Tuesday of each month

**About** New members welcome, but are recommended to make contact to confirm the venue first. All levels of experience are catered for and meeting structures vary from week to week. Fees are £2.50 per meeting and £10 per annum, but new members can try the group for free before committing.

## Battersea Writers' Group

Family Room, Battersea Arts Centre, Lavender Hill, London, SW11 5TN

✉ jasonyoung72@yahoo.com
🌐 http://thebatterseawritersgroup.blogspot.com/

**Contact** Jason Young

**Meeting Time** 7.30pm, one Wednesday a month

**About** An informal forum to workshop new material. Contact Jason Young for details.

## The Birmingham Writers

Birmingham Central Library, Chamberlain Square, Birmingham, B3 3HQ

☎ 0121 711 2166
✉ isabella.self@bluyonder.co.uk
🌐 www.scorpiopsc.pwp.blueyonder.co.uk/bw/

**Meeting Time** 6pm–8pm, first and third Wednesdays of each month (excluding August)

**About** New members should call or email for more details. The group organise a structured programme of meetings for the year including themes, competitions and workshops. Members have the opportunity to receive feedback on their work. Fees are £1 each for the first two sessions and if accepted, an undisclosed annual membership fee.

## Blackheath Poetry Society

Members' homes, Blackheath, London SE3

☎ 020 8852 9608
✉ gps5@tutor.open.ac.uk
🌐 http://pages.britishlibrary.net/gill.stoker/bps.htm

**Contact** Gill Stoker
38 Lee Road
London
SE3 9RU

**Meeting Time** Second Monday of every other month

**About** New members welcome, please call, or email Gill Stoker. The group is mainly based around poetry appreciation rather than creative writing, although members do write their own pieces. A theme is usually set for the evening and poetry read and discussed. There are no fees, but a small contribution is required towards the cost of refreshments.

## Brentwood Writers' Circle
**Fairview Room, Ursuline High School, Queen's Road, Brentwood, Essex**
☎ 01277 226840
✉ ena.love@tiscali.co.uk
**Contact** Ena Olve
Farringford
1 Delta Road
Hutton
Brentwood
CM13 1NG
**Meeting Time** 2.30–4.30pm, first Saturday of the month

**About** New members are welcome but there may be a waiting list as membership is restricted to 60. Applications should be made to the secretary, Ena Love. All genres of writing are covered, except poetry. Alternate meetings involve guest speakers. Most other meetings are workshops, with a special writers day taking place on the first Saturday in June 2007 where Colin Dexter will be the guest. The December meeting is a Christmas party and an awards ceremony.

## Bridgend Writers Circle
**Coed Parc, Library Headquarters, Park Street, Bridgend**
✉ kirsten@barrettpianos.co.uk
**Contact** Kirsten Barrett
**Meeting Time** 7.15pm, second Friday of each month

**About** New members are welcome. Any type of creative writing and level of experience are covered as the group is not tutored, but it is designed to be stimulating. Fees are £6 per year, but new members may attend for free initially.

## Bridgnorth Writers' Group
**Cinnamon Coffee and Meeting Place, Cartway, Bridgnorth, WV16 4EG**
☎ 01746 761246
✉ phelps_jeff@tiscali.co.uk

**Contact** Jeff Phelps
18 Pineway
Bridgnorth
Shropshire
WV15 5DT
**Meeting Time** 7.30pm–10pm, third Tuesday of each month

**About** New members welcome, any level of experience. Current members range from published writers to hobbyists, to beginners. Writing tends to be poetry, short stories, plays and novels, although other types of writing are encouraged and welcomed. Meetings are usually based around reading of members' work and feedback, but there is no obligation to read or write anything every month. The group organises occasional social events and encourages the sharing of work and experiences with other writers' groups in the area. Fees are either £15 per annum or £2 per session and the first visit is free.

## Brighton Nightwriters
**The Pub With No Name, 58 Southover Street, Brighton, BN2 2UF**
☎ 01273 505642
**Contact** Tim Shelton-Jones
**Meeting Time** 7.30pm every Wednesday

**About** New members welcome, just turn up to a meeting, or call for details. All types of writing covered. A friendly, informal group with both regular and irregular members.

## Bristol Writers' Group
**Members' homes, Bristol**
✉ enquiries@bristolwritersgroup.org
🌐 www.bristolwritersgroup.org
**Contact** Louise Gethin
**Meeting Time** 7.30pm–9.30pm every Wednesday

**About** Predominantly a fiction writing group, although sometimes members bring travel writing, poetry or scripts. Meetings are focused around one piece of a member's work, which is emailed around in advance, on a rota basis. The group also organises social events. There are no fees.

## Bute Writers
**Orissor House, Craigmore Road, Rothesay, Isle of Bute**
✉ secy@butewriters.org
🌐 www.butewriters.org
**Contact** Jenny Campbell
**Meeting Time** 7.30pm every second Wednesday

**About** Meetings usually take the form of business meetings, a pre-assigned project or assignment or a workshop. The group also arranges visits and guest speakers and welcomes contact with other writers' groups.

## Café Writers

**Jurnet's Bar, Wensum Lodge, King Street, Norwich**

- richard@cafewriters.org.uk
- www.cafewriters.org.uk

**Meeting Time** 7.15pm, second Monday of each month

**About** The main meeting is based around reading of poetry; however there are two off shoot writers groups, one for poetry and one for other writing. The poetry group meets 7.30pm-9.30pm every other Monday. Contact dstreet@streetview.co.uk for details. The Voices Writers meet on the first and third Tuesdays of each month, in the BBC Voices room, first Floor of The Forum, Norwich. Contact Nic Rigby, nic.rigby@bbc.co.uk, for details. Please make contact before turning up, as groups may be full or venues may have changed.

## Cannon Poets

**Midland Arts Centre, Cannon Hill, Birmingham, B12 9QH**

- info@cannonpoets.co.uk
- www.cannonpoets.co.uk

**Contact** Martin Underwood
c/o 22 Margaret Grove
Harbourne
Birmingham
B17 9JH

**Meeting Time** 2pm, Sundays, monthly

**About** Group revolves around poetry workshops run by members, or visitors. Members can be published in the quarterly journal, Cannon's Mouth, which can be subscribed to for £10.50 per annum. The group also runs poetry competitions. Full membership (group and journal) is £30 per annum, £20 for concessions, and families may pay the cost of two adults less the cost of one subscription to the journal. Associate membership is £15 and meeting attendance is £3 or £2 for concessions.

## Cardiff Writers' Circle

**62 Park Place, Cardiff, CF10 3AS**

- niva@nivapete.freeserve.co.uk

**Meeting Time** 7pm every Monday (term time only)

**About** New writers of all genres welcome. The aim of the group is to promote good writing for publication and members are published writers as well as beginners. Membership costs £10 per annum, plus £1.50 for each meeting attended (hot drink included). The group holds three annual competitions for articles, poetry and short stories, with professional adjudicators.

## Caron Writers

**Argoed Hall Studio, Tregaron, Ceredigion, Wales, SY25 6JR**

- 01974 298070
- john.wilson@virgin.net
- www.argoedebooks.com

**Contact** John Wilson

**Meeting Time** 2pm-4pm every second Sunday

**About** Welcomes new writers of any genre. Fees are £25 to join for the first year, and £15 per year thereafter.

## Cheltenham Writers' Circle

**Parmoor House, 13 Lypiatt Terrace, Lypiatt Road, Cheltenham, GL50 2SX**

- 01242 528744
- susan@kay-holloway.freeserve.co.uk

**Contact** Susan Holloway
6 St. Edwards Walk
Cheltenham
GL53 7RS

**Meeting Time** 7.30pm-10pm, first and third Mondays of each month

**About** New members are welcome and can simply turn up, or make prior contact if they wish. The circle covers all genres of writing at all levels of experience and most meetings provide the chance to present work and receive constructive feedback. Occasionally there will be a guest speaker, a workshop or an outing. Fees are £12 a year, plus £1 for each meeting attended. New members may attend one meeting for free and another at £1 before committing to the annual fee.

## Chirk Writers' Circle

**The Bungalow, Church of the Sacred Heart, Station Road, Chirk, Wrexham, Wales**

- 01691 777390
- melodyrobinson@btinternet.com

**Contact** Melody Robinson

**Meeting Time** 10am-12pm, first Wednesday of every month

**About** New members welcome, apply by phone to the secretary. The group deals with all types of writing and levels of experience. Each meeting has a tutor and the group arranges outings to the theatre, workshops and participates in local events. Fees are £3 and £2 for concessions.

## Deal Writers
**Dealability, 45 Victoria Road, Deal, Kent, CT14 7AY**
☎ 01304 360228
✉ john.spooner01@virgin.net
🌐 www.dealwriters.org.uk
**Contact** John Spooner
c/o 25 Church Path
Deal
Kent
CT14 9TH
**Meeting Time** First Thursday of each month
**About** New members are welcome to turn up, or contact the Chair, John Spooner. Meetings usually alternate between guest speakers and critique of members' work. Fees are £15 per annum to cover the expenses of guest speakers, plus £1 each month for the room hire.

## The Deeside Writers
**Burnett Arms Hotel, Banchory, Scotland**
☎ 01330 850691
✉ mslaven@aol.com
**Contact** Marion Slaven
Adendale
Strachan
Aberdeenshire
AB31 6NP
**Meeting Time** 10am–12pm and 7.30pm–9.30pm (alternate weeks) every Thursday during term time
**About** New members of any age and any level of experience are welcome. People can go to the morning, evening or both sessions, depending on their availability. Current members include poets, budding novelists and those who submit articles for publication. Fees are £10 per annum, plus £2 per session which includes hot drinks.

## Denny Writers
**Community Education Centre, 40 Duke Street, Denny, FK6 6NW**
☎ 01324 504260
✉ jimturpie@hotmail.com
🌐 www.fdacc.org.uk/dennywriters.htm
**Contact** Jim Turpie

**Meeting Time** 1.30pm–2.45pm, every Thursday
**About** New members welcome. Group includes hobby writers and professionals of all ages and genders, working under the guidance of a tutor.

## Dereham & District Writers' Group
**Members' homes**
☎ 01362 850433
✉ william.english@virgin.net
**Contact** William English
Wisteria Cottage
South Green
Mattishall
Norfolk
NR20 3JZ
**Meeting Time** 7.30pm–9.30pm
**About** New members are welcome, numbers permitting. Please contact William English in the first instance. The group deals mainly with fiction in all genres, although there is flexibility if a poet joins. The group works to a four week cycle: week one is submissions for review; week two is writing exercises; week three is short story writing; and week four is the review session where members critique the submitted work based on rough guidelines. The group roughly follows the academic terms and costs £2 per meeting, saved by the treasurer for an end of term meal.

## Devizes Writers' Group
**The Crown Centre, St. John's Street, Devizes**
✉ Email form on the website
**Meeting Time** 7.30pm, fourth Tuesday of each month
**About** The group is very informal, with some on the spot writing and some 'homework' on a pre-allocated theme. There is an email form on the website for contact.

## Elham Valley Writers' Group
**St Mary's Church Hall, Elham, Kent**
✉ friends@gabrielle.tv
**Contact** Marianne McKinnon
6 Hog Green
Elham
Canterbury
Kent
CT4 6TU
**Meeting Time** 2pm–4.30pm every second Wednesday
**About** Run by published writer Marianne McKinnon. New members welcome, as is any type of writing,

although Marianne's work is mainly fiction, autobiography, short stories and articles. Sessions involve both mutual critique and an element of teaching from Marianne for those that want it. The first session is free and the fees are £5.50 per month (two sessions) thereafter.

## Fire River Poets
**Private houses in Taunton and Somerset**
**☎** 01823 252486
**✉** enquiry@fireriverpoets.org.uk
**⊛** www.fireriverpoets.org.uk
**Contact** John Wilson
 2 Deane View
 Bishop's Hull Road
 Bishop's Hull
 Taunton
 TA1 5EG
**Meeting Time** Monthly, no fixed venue
**About** New members are always welcome, but as the meeting places are private houses there are sometimes limits to group size. Prospective members should approach John Wilson with a sample of their work. The group is restricted to practising poets only, and beginners are referred to local writing courses. Meetings usually focus around reading and criticising poetry from other members, however consideration is sometimes given to other published poets and once every few months meetings take the form of a workshop where poetry is written in class to a given specification. Members pay £2 per meeting.

## Free Spirit Writers
**40 Burstall Hill, Bridlington, East Yorkshire, YO16 7GA**
**✉** freespiritwriters@tesco.net
**⊛** www.freespiritwriters.me.uk
**Contact** Mike and Diane Wilson
**About** Freespirit Writers is an informal group consisting of husband and wife Mike and Diane Wilson. They are not seeking new members, although anyone interested in their extensive catalogue of poetry, novels, dramas and numerous other projects should contact them, or visit their website. Mike and Diane are available to give talks and workshops on their historical novels and dramas and have in the past worked within schools.

## The Glass Mountain Writers
**Crystal Peaks Library, 1–3 Peak Square, Crystal Peaks Complex, Waterthorpe, Sheffield S20 7PH**
**☎** 0114 293 0612/3
**☎** 0114 293 0611
**✉** crystalpeaks.library@sheffield.gov.uk
**Contact** John Gosnell/Margaret Lambert
**Meeting Time** 2pm–3.30pm, every Thursday
**About** New members welcome, either turn up, or phone in advance. Covers every type of writing, including fiction, song writing, poetry and plays. Meetings are usually based around listening and commenting on members' work and set exercises, although there are occasional workshops and visiting writers. Fees are 50 pence to cover tea, coffee and biscuits.

## Havering Writers' Circle
**Fairkytes Arts Centre, 53 Billet Lane, Hornchurch, Essex, RM11 1AX**
**☎** 01708 341578
**☎** 01708 341578
**✉** johnfarley@ntlworld.com
**Contact** John Farley
 44 Avenue Road
 Harold Wood
 Romford
 Essex
 RM3 0SU
**Meeting Time** 7.30pm–10pm, first Monday of each month
**About** New members are welcome and should contact John Farley. Membership costs £25 per annum, concessions £20. Consists of published and unpublished writers, mainly of prose (little poetry).

## Hertsmere Writers' Circle
**Bushey Grove Leisure Centre, Aldenham Road, Bushey, Hertfordshire, WD23 2TD**
**☎** 01923 247329/01923 470140
**✉** srilekharach@ho
**Contact** Coordinator/Assistant Coordinator
**Meeting Time** 1pm–3pm every Wednesday
**About** Welcomes new members, particularly poets, novelists and short story writers of all genres. Please phone or email the Coordinator or Assistant Coordinator. As well as opportunities to give and receive constructive feedback on your writing, the circle also runs brief workshops and organise set projects designed to encourage creativity. Members are required to take an active part.

## Hornsea Writers
**The Bowls Club, Atwick Road, Hornsea, East Yorkshire**

○ lindaacaster@yahoo.co.uk
**Contact** Linda Acaster
**Meeting Time** 7.30pm every Wednesday
**About** New members welcome if they're willing to accept constructive criticism. Full disabled access. All prose writing is covered, including short fiction and novels, scripts, non-fiction and memoirs. No poetry. The group is geared towards writers with a professional attitude towards honing their skills. Most members are published and the emphasis is on gaining feedback on individual pieces, not on group projects.

## Identity Workshop
**6 Mount Street, Manchester, M2 5NS**
○ 0161 832 3777
○ 0161 832 2929
○ cultureword@commonword.org.uk
◉ www.commonword.org.uk
**Contact** Pete Kalu
**Meeting Time** 7pm–9pm, every Wednesday
**About** New members welcome. The group is for Asian, African Caribbean and Chinese writers of all levels. Contact Commonword for further details.

## Irish Writers' Centre
**19 Parnell Square, Dublin 1, Republic of Ireland**
○ 00353 1 872 1302
○ 00353 1 872 6282
○ akudryavitsky@hotmail.com
◉ www.writerscentre.ie
**Contact** Anthony Anatoly Kudryavitsky
**Meeting Time** Monthly or fortnightly
**About** A new writers group at the writers' centre aimed at refugees, asylum seekers, migrant workers and members of other language communities in the Dublin area. Its function will be to develop writing skills and creativity in these categories of people, introduce them to Irish literature and encourage their wider participation in local cultural activities. No fee. Please contact tutor Anthony Anatoly Kudryavitsky for more information.

## Johnstone Writers' Group
**Johnstone Central Library, Ludovic Square, Johnstone, Renfrewshire**
○ 07896 290418
○ ihunter24601@hotmail.com
◉ www.johnstonewritersgroup.com
**Contact** Ian Hunter
**Meeting Time** 7pm–8.45pm, every Thursday

**About** Potential members should contact Ian Hunter, Chair. The group is over 20 years old and has around 18 members, some of whom are published. Everything from poetry to novels is covered. The group also has its own publishing imprint, Ludovic Press, which publishes members' poetry and books. There are special events, around once a month which include visiting writers. There are no fees.

## Kent and Sussex Poetry Society
**The Camden Centre, Market Square, Tunbridge Wells, Kent, TN1 2SW**
○ info@kentandsussexpoetrysociety.org
◉ www.kentandsussexpoetrysociety.org
**Contact** Keith Francis
Broomhill
Benenden
Kent
TN17 4JT
**Meeting Time** 8pm, Tuesdays, two per month
**About** New members are welcome, email for details. Poetry only. The group holds two meetings a month with readings, special guests and workshops. There is an annual fee of £15. Non-members may attend the meetings for £3 (£2 concessions). The society also runs a competition, extra workshops and organises a retreat.

## King's Lynn Writers' Circle
**The Friend's Meeting House, 38 Bridge Street, King's Lynn, Norfolk**
○ 01760 755993
○ enquiries@lynnwriters.org.uk
◉ www.lynnwriters.org.uk
**Contact** Chris Gutteridge
54 Foxes Meadow
Castle Acre
King's Lynn
PE32 2AS
**Meeting Time** 7.30pm, second Thursday of each month
**About** New members welcome, either contact Chris Gutteridge or come along to a meeting. All types of writing covered. The group also runs an annual international competition, details of which are on the website.

## Lampeter Writers' Group
**Lecture Room 7, Canterbury Building, University of Wales, Lampeter**
○ k.miles@lamp.ac.uk, gillian@gillianclarke.co.uk
**Contact** Gillian Clarke (contact via Kathy Miles)

c/o Library, University of Wales, Lampeter
Lampeter
Ceredigion
SA48 7ED
**Meeting Time** 7pm–9pm (contact for days, term time only)
**About** New members are welcome to attend at any time. All forms of writing are covered, but the main emphasis is on poetry. There is a charge of £20 per term, however students at the university may attend for free.

## Llantrisant Ready Writers
**8 Davids Court, Pontyclun, Mid Glamorgan, CF72 9AY**
☎ 01443 239868
✉ readywritersllan@aol.com
**Contact** Judith Sly
c/o Library, University of Wales, Lampeter
Lampeter
Ceredigion
SA48 7ED
**Meeting Time** 7.30pm, second Thursday of each month
**About** New members welcome, please apply by post, phone or email. Any types of creative writing are covered as long as they do not conflict with the Christian ethos of the group. The group normally publish a twice yearly magazine and organise an annual gathering with other Christian writers' groups where they invite a guest speaker and enjoy a three course lunch, for no more than £14 inclusive. Fees are currently £16 per year.

## Lucht Focail Irish Writer's Group
**Leeds Irish Centre, York Road, Leeds, LS9 9NT**
☎ 0113 242 9765
✉ bill.fitzsimons@lfha.co.uk
**Contact** Bill Fitzsimons
32 Alexandra Grove
Hyde Park
Leeds
LS6 1QX
**Meeting Time** 8pm, second and fourth Thursday of each month
**About** New members welcome, any level of experience. Either come along for a taster session, or contact Bill Fitzsimons. The group is principally poetry, but prose is encouraged too. Work tends to reflect the ethnic background of members, which is mostly Irish, but not exclusively so. No fees.

## Marsh Ink Writers' Group
**Southlands Comprehensive School, Station Road, New Romney, Kent**
☎ 01797 366621
✉ bridget@fowkes16.fsnet.co.uk
**Contact** Bridget Fowkes
**Meeting Time** 7.30pm–9.30pm, two Wednsdays a month during term time
**About** New members are welcome, either contact Bridget Fowkes or simply turn up. Covers all types of fiction and non-fiction writing. The group's president is novelist Pamela Oldfield. It has frequent guest speakers and runs workshops. Previous guests have included Jane Wenham-Jones and Simon Brett. Fees are £12 per year, plus £1 per meeting, £1.50 when a guest speaker is present and £3 for non-members. The first meeting is free for prospective new members.

## Mayo Writers' Block
**Venues in Claremorris, Republic of Ireland**
☎ 00353 87 984 3900
✉ info@mayowriters.org
🌐 http://mayowriters.org
**Meeting Time** Second and fourth Wednesday of the month
**About** New members welcome, please contact by phone or email. The group aims to encourage creative writing of all kinds and its members range for beginners, to those who have more experience.

## Medway Mermaids
**The Sunlight Centre, 105 Richmond Road, Gillingham, Kent, ME7 1LX**
✉ medwaymermaids@yahoo.co.uk
🌐 www.medwaymermaids.btik.com
**Contact** Chair
**Meeting Time** 7.30pm–9.30pm, one Monday a month
**About** Welcomes new members, who must apply with a sample of their writing to be reviewed by the group. Will also meet prospective members for an informal chat. All types of writing are covered including poetry, prose, factual and plays. Fees are £18 pa or £9 for six months. Members need to attend regularly and be prepared to comment on the work of others.

## New Edinburgh Writers
**Fountainbridge Library, Dundee Street, Edinburgh, Scotland**

**☎** 0131 466 2384
**✉** edinnick272hotmail.com
**🌐** www.newedinburghwriters.pwp.
blueyonder.co.uk
**Contact** Nick Morrison
7/4 Weir Court
3 Sighthill Bank
Edinburgh
EH11 4BB
**Meeting Time** 6pm–7.45pm every Wednesday
**About** New members welcome, although numbers
are limited by room size. Most current members are
writers of poetry and short stories, although novels
and screenplays are also familiar to some members.
The meetings usually consist of members reading
their work and receiving feedback, the aim of which,
is to get work to competition standard. Fees are £2
per month which covers refreshments,
competitions, trips out and magazines.

## North Camden and Belsize Writers' Group

**Members' homes**
**✉** simeon.shoul@virgin.net
**Contact** Simeon Shoul
**Meeting Time** Approximately once every four
weeks, each member hosts in turn
**About** New members should make initial contact by
email. Please be aware that there is often a waiting
list. Covers fiction only, but all genres welcome.
There are no fees charged.

## Northern Gay Writers

**6 Mount Street, Manchester, M2 5NS**
**☎** 0161 832 3777
**☎** 0161 832 2929
**✉** cathy@commonword.org.uk
**🌐** www.commonword.org.uk
**Meeting Time** 2pm–4pm, Saturdays
**About** Open to lesbian, gay and bisexual writers.
Contact for details of meeting dates.

## Northwest Highland Writers

**Durness Village Hall/Scourie Village Hall/
Lochinver Community Room/ Ullapool Ceilidh
Place**
**☎** 01571 844020/07734 235704
**✉** hag@worldforests.org
**Contact** Mandy Haggith
95 Achmelvich
Lochinver
Sutherland

Scotland
IV27 4JB
**Meeting Time** second Saturday of each month,
venues rotate
**About** New members welcome; either get in touch
or go along to a meeting. Any creative writing is
covered, however the members must live in
Northwest Sutherland or Wester Ross. Fees are £5
per annum, plus £1 per meeting to cover the cost of
the venue.

## Octoprose

**Various locations around Guildford**
**☎** 01428 606152
**✉** steadyone@nations.fsnet.co.uk
**Contact** Dan Franklin
5 Rockdale Drive
Grayshott
Hindhead
Surrey
GU26 6UB
**Meeting Time** Every other Thursday, term time only
**About** New members are welcome, contact Dan
Franklin for more information. All types of writing are
covered, although they currently do not deal with a
lot of poetry. Fees are £3.50 per meeting, which
covers room hire and refreshments, with any excess
going towards group meals out.

## The Original Writers' Group

**Garfield Community Centre, 64 Garfield Road,
London, SW11 5PN**
**✉** info@theoriginalwriter.com
**🌐** www.theoriginalwriter.com
**Contact** Rupert Davies-Cooke
**Meeting Time** 7pm–9pm every second and
fourth Wednesday
**About** New members are welcome, even if they
have no writing to share. Each writer usually gets ten
minutes of reading time, followed by ten minutes of
criticism. Fees are £2 per session.

## Ormskirk Writers and Literary Society (OWLS)

**Art & Community Centre, St. Helens Road,
Ormskirk, L39 4QR**
**☎** 01695 571748
**✉** ikargar@tiscali.co.uk
**Contact** Ishbel Kargar
**Meeting Time** 7.30pm–10pm, first and third
Tuesday of each month

**About** New members welcome. Covers stories, plays, sketches, verse and other types of writing. Members suggest topics for meetings including manuscript readings, writing workshops, competitions and guest speakers. Fees are £20 per annum, but new members may attend three sessions for free.

## Penicuik Writers' Group
**TBA 2007**
- 0131 440 1051/07811 991781
- davidcpurdie@aol.com
- www.tyne-esk-writers.com

**Contact** David Purdie
12 Mayburn Vale
Loanhead
Midlothian
EH20 9HH

**Meeting Time** TBA

**About** New members welcome, just turn up to the meetings. All types of creative writing covered, no fees.

## Pennine Ink Writers' Workshop
**The Woodman Inn, Burnley, Lancashire**
- sheridansand1@yahoo.co.uk

**Contact** Laura Sheridan
Mid Pennine Arts
The Gallery
Yorke Street
Burnley
Lancashire

**Meeting Time** 8pm–10pm every Monday

**About** New members are always welcome, as long as they are willing to listen to constructive criticism, please contact Laura Sheridan. Covers all types of writing. Fees are £1 per session.

## The Pennine Poets Group
**Private homes in West Yorkshire**
- www.penninepoets.co.uk

**About** Welcomes new members, first point of contact should be through the website. Please check the site for up to date details of meetings and who to contact. Poetry is the main focus of the group and readings to music are held regularly. The group also takes part in literary festivals and is associated with the journal 'Pennine Platform'. Their small press, 'Pennine Poets Publications', also occasionally publishes members' work and anthologies have just been published by Fighting Cock Press.

## Phrase Writers
**Hillingdon Park Baptist Church, Hercies Road, Hillingdon, Uxbridge, UB10 9LS**
- vivienhampshire@btinternet.com

**Contact** Vivien Hampshire
2 Narborough Close
Ickenham
Uxbridge
Middlesex
UB10 8TN

**Meeting Time** 1pm–3pm on alternate Thursdays

**About** Not actively seeking new members, so please do not turn up unannounced, however the group welcome enquiries from suitable local writers of all abilities. Current members are mainly over retirement age and writing fiction, some non-fiction and plays. The group is involved with the Talking Newspapers for the Blind and also write, act and produce plays for a local blind audience. Fees are payable annually or monthly, equivalent to £2.50 per meeting.

## Plymouth Writers' Circle
**Plymstock Community Centre, Plymstock, Plymouth, Devon**
- 01752 491616
- edward.cartner@lineone.net

**Contact** Edward Cartner
66 Mount Batten Way
Plymstock
Plymouth
PL9 9EB

**Meeting Time** 7.30pm–9.30pm, every Tuesday

**About** New members from all backgrounds and levels of experience are welcome, just turn up on the night. Current members range from published writers to beginners. The group covers all types of fiction and non-fiction. The group does not adopt a teaching style and members can take what they want from the informal, friendly meetings. The group also stage an annual short story and verse competition. Fees are £1 per session.

## The Poetry Society of Cheltenham
**A venue in Montpellier, Cheltenham**
- 01242 515595
- rturner@asvr.freeserve.co.uk

**Contact** Roger Turner

**Meeting Time** Last Tuesday of each month

**About** New poets are welcome and should contact Roger Turner (Chair) or Michael Newman (01242 675028). You will be asked to send a sample of writing to ensure a match of expectations. There is also a reading group that meets on the third Thursday of the month to read and discuss poetry.

## Porthcawl Ready Writers
**12 Hawkhurst Court, Porthcawl, Wales, CF36 3NU**
☏ 01656 783873
✉ jopalewis@aol.com
**Contact** Pauline Lewis
c/o Library, University of Wales, Lampeter
Lampeter
Ceredigion
SA48 7ED
**Meeting Time** 7.30pm, first Tuesday of each month
**About** New members welcome, but please make contact first. The writing covered is mostly Christian and devotional, although all types are possible. The group joins other Christian writers groups for an annual day with a guest speaker, around £14 for the day.

## Portway Writers
**Adult Learning and Leisure Centre, Portway Annexe, Portway, Wells**
☏ 01749 676441
✉ jmthom@tiscali.co.uk
**Contact** Judith Thomas
11 Chapman's Close
Wookey
Wells
BA5 1LU
**Meeting Time** 10.30am–12.30pm, Tuesdays
**About** New members should contact Judith Thomas in the first instance, but will have to enrol at the leisure centre by phone. Beginners are welcome and the building has full disabled access. The group is a tutored class, as well as a writers' circle. Poetry, prose and drama writing are covered at the moment, although any other genres could be catered for. There are several social events and members also take part in the Bath Festival in March.

## Rathmine Writers' Workshop
**Christ Church, Rathgar, Republic of Ireland**
☏ 00353 86 402 5578
✉ info@rathmineswritersworkshop.com
🌐 www.rathmineswritersworkshop.com
**Contact** James Conway
**Meeting Time** 7.30pm–10pm, every other Thursday
**About** The focus is around readings of members' work and group feedback. Members currently write

both poetry and prose, however there are additional prose only meetings every third Monday. Fees are €5 per person, €3 for concessions.

## Redcar Writers
**Redcar Central Library, Coatham Road, Redcar, TS10 1RP**
☏ 01642 478699
✉ writers@redpark.co.uk
🌐 www.communigate.co.uk/ne/redcarwritersgroup
**Contact** Brian Morton
33 Park Avenue
Redcar
TS10 3LW
**Meeting Time** 7.15pm–9pm every second Monday
**About** New members are welcome and there are no fees. Current members are writers of poetry, short stories, plays and novels. Also hold an annual competition for poetry and short stories, usually launched in January or February with a closing date at the end of July.

## Redwell Writers
**Church House, Church Street, off Redwell Street, Norwich**
✉ elasticpress@elasticpress.com
**Contact** Andrew Hook
85 Gertrude Road
Norwich
NR3 4SG
**Meeting Time** 7pm–9pm every Wednesday
**About** New members welcome, apply by email in the first instance. The group covers short story and novel writing of any genre, but not poetry. The fees are £5 per meeting.

## Salisbury Writers
**The United Reformed Church, Fisherton Street, Salisbury, Dorset**
☏ 01980 629440
✉ susandown@aol.com
**Contact** Susan Down
4 Rosedale
Cholderton Road
Newton Toney
Salisbury
SP4 0EU
**Meeting Time** 7pm–9pm, first Thursday of every month
**About** New members welcome, with any level of experience. Current interests include poetry, short stories, novels, crime, romance and biography. The

group also have a 'buddy system' for members to exchange longer pieces of work outside of the group. This is usually a pair that has found each other's comments helpful. Fees are £3 per session, plus £28 per annum.

## Scarborough Writers' Circle
**Allatt House, West Parade Road, Scarborough, YO12 5ED**
☎ 01723 30535
✉ carol@newby.btinternet.com
**Contact** Carol Stockill
16 Fieldstead Crescent
Newby
Scarborough
North Yorkshire
YO12 6TH
**Meeting Time** 7.30pm every other Tuesday
**About** New members are welcome and can attend meetings as guests. Anyone wishing to join must submit a piece of writing to the president. The group encourages and shares all kinds of writing. Fees are £18 per annum, plus £1 per meeting. Guests can pay £3 per meeting.

## Speakeasy, Milton Keynes Writers' Group
**The Quaker Centre, 1 Oakley Gardens, Downhead Park, Milton Keynes**
☎ 01908 663860
✉ speakeasy@writerbrock.co.uk
🌐 www.mkweb.co.uk/speakeasy
**Contact** Martin Brocklebank
46 Wealdstone Place
Springfield
Milton Keynes
MK6 3JG
**Meeting Time** 8pm–10.15pm, first Friday of each month
**About** New members are welcome to turn up and introduce themselves at any meeting. All genres of writing are covered, but members must write in English. Fees will be around £4 per session and £6 for a visiting guest night.

## Stortford Scribblers
**Apton Road Day Centre, Apton Road, Bishop's Stortford, Hertfordshire**
☎ 01279 503582
✉ leo@applecroft.freeserve.co.uk
**Contact** Lesley Mace
29 Zambesi Road

Bishop's Stortford
Hertfordshire
CM23 3JR
**Meeting Time** 8pm, every other Thursday
**About** New members welcome. Either make contact or turn up to a meeting. Any type of writing in any genre is also welcome. Fees are £12 per annum, plus £3 per meeting.

## Stort Valley Writers Group
**Members' homes, Essex**
☎ 01376 551379
✉ liberato@talktalk.net
**Contact** Maureen Blundell
16 Middle King
Braintree
Essex
CM7 3XY
**Meeting Time** Every second Monday
**About** New members welcome, please contact Maureen Blundell for information. Fiction, autobiography, poetry and article writing are covered. Members are encouraged to read their work and receive feedback from the group, but this is not compulsory. Trips are organised around once a year, as well as an annual Christmas dinner that is not always at Christmas. Fees are 50 pence per session.

## Sutton Writers
**Civic Offices, St. Nicholas Way, Sutton, SM1 1EA**
✉ teresa.tipping@tesco.net
🌐 www.suttonwriters.info
**Contact** Teresa Tipping
24 Twickenham Close
Beddington
Croydon CR0 4SZ
**Meeting Time** 7.30pm–10pm, second Friday of each month
**About** New members are welcome, either to attend meetings month by month, or to become a full member. All types of creative writing are covered, including poetry, articles, short stories, writing for children and novels. Various workshops for full members are run in members' homes. Any level of experience is welcome, whether writing for pleasure or for profit. Fees for full members are £18 per annum, which entitles them to free meetings, workshops in house competitions and copies of the newsletter. Members who cannot attend the meetings but wish to enter competitions and receive the newsletter are charged £9 per annum.

Visitors are charged £3 per meeting but may apply to become full members.

## Tenbury Writers' Group

**Tenbury Library, 24 Teme Street, Tenbury Wells, Worcestershire, WR15 8AA**
☎ 01584 810493
✉ sallytenbury@yahoo.com
**Contact** Sally Matthews
**Meeting Time** 7.30pm, second Tuesday of each month
**About** All types of writing are tried and reviewed. Current members range from 16–70 so anyone is welcome to make contact. There are no fees except for coffee at 50 pence.

## Thames Valley Writers' Circle

**St. Joseph's Church Hall, Berkshire Drive, Tilehurst, Reading, RG31 5JJ**
✉ sawdonsmith@hotmail.com
🌐 www.thamesvalleywriterscircle.org
**Contact** Dick Sawdon Smith
**Meeting Time** 7.30pm–9.30pm every Tuesday
**About** New members are welcome. Novels, articles, short stories and poetry are all covered. Meetings usually revolve around constructive feedback after members' readings of the work. Longer work may be dissected before the meeting. The group also organises workshops, outings and guest speakers, a notable past guest speaker being Colin Dexter. Fees are £3 per session, or £2 for concessions.

## Toddington Poetry Society

**Hightown Community Centre, Concorde Street, Luton, Bedfordshire**
☎ 01234 822230
✉ toddington.poetry@tiscali.co.uk
🌐 www.toddingtonpoetrysociety.co.uk
**Contact** Peter Stileman
**Meeting Time** 8pm, second and fourth Tuesdays of each month
**About** New members welcome. Either turn up or make contact. Focused entirely on poetry, with either guest speakers (previous guests have included Andrew Motion and Roger McGough) or more informal evenings.

## The T Party Writers' Group

**A pub in Central London**
☎ 020 8773 3566
✉ enquiries@t-party.org.uk
🌐 www.t-party.org.uk
**Contact** Sara Townsend
8 Wrythe Green
Carshalton
Surrey
SM5 2QR
**Meeting Time** Monthly, Saturday afternoons
**About** Specialist group in science fiction, fantasy and horror only. New members welcome, please make email contact in the first instance and explore the website. Members should have had something published prior to joining, as the group is serious and professional in its criticisms of work and not suitable for beginners. New members are advised to sit in on a couple of meetings first, before committing to join. Special guest speaker events are run alongside the monthly meetings, with input from writers, editors and agents. Fees are £10 per annum.

## The University of Liverpool Creative Writing Society for Lifelong Learning

**Room 102, The Alastair Pilkington Building, University of Liverpool, Liverpool**
☎ 0151 291 6942
✉ thomas.mcbride2@btopenworld.com
**Contact** Tommy McBride
**Meeting Time** 7pm–9pm every Monday
**About** New members welcome, any level of experience. The group is informal and friendly and meets to discuss the theory and practice of creative writing. All genres of creative writing are covered and members can bring their work to be criticised. Each week a theme is put forward to offer the writers a challenge, but this aspect, as with all aspects of the group, is entirely optional.

## Ver Poets

**St. Michael's Church Hall, St. Michael's Street, St. Albans, Hertfordshire**
☎ 01727 864898
✉ daphne.schiller@virgin.net
🌐 www.verpoets.org.uk
**Contact** Daphne Schiller
15 Brampton Road
St. Albans
Hertfordshire
AL1 4PP
**Meeting Time** 8pm, monthly on a Friday
**About** Membership enquiries welcome from people with a love of poetry. Day workshops for members only are held fortnightly in members' homes, although anyone can attend the evening meetings.

The group runs two members' competitions, as well as an annual open competition. One for 15–19 year olds is planned for 2007. Fees are £3 per meeting for non-members and £2 for members.

## Verulam' Writers Circle
**St. Michael's Church Hall, St. Albans, and, The Goat Pub, St. Albans**
☎ 07713 515868
✉ info@verulamwriterscircle.org.uk
🌐 www.verulamwriterscircle.org.uk
**Contact** Kevin
**Meeting Time** 8pm (see website for programme)
**About** The group holds regular manuscript evenings, workshops and meetings at both venues. Writers of any level of experience and any type of writing are welcome. The group run competitions and have a very active and full website. Fees are £30 per year for membership but guests can 'pay as you go' for £3 per meeting or £5 for a guest speaker. Manuscript evenings at The Goat pub are £1 for members and non-members.

## Walsall Writers' Circle
**Park Hall Community School, Park Hall Road, Walsall**
☎ 01922 458595
✉ walsallwriterscircle@mereed.co.uk
🌐 www.wwc.mereed.co.uk
**Contact** Mrs A. R. Reed
 17 Highfield Way
 Aldridge
 Walsall
 WS9 8XF
**Meeting Time** 7.30pm, second Thursday of each month (except August)
**About** New members welcome of any level of experience. The meetings are varied and can be based around members' manuscripts, workshops, special events and competitions. Fees are £6 per annum. Postal members and families may subscribe for £9 per annum. Visitors pay £1 that can be refunded if they join.

## Watford Writers
**Cha Cha Cha Café, Cassiobury Park, Cassiobury Park Avenue, Watford, Hertfordshire**
☎ 01923 227054
✉ watfordwriters@gmail.com
🌐 www.watfordwriters.co.uk
**Contact** Lynne Motijoane
 2 Howard Close

 Watford
 WD24 5JB
**Meeting Time** 7.30pm–9.30pm every Monday
**About** New members should contact Lynne Motijoane. The group organises guest speakers, workshops and manuscript evenings. Fees are £3 per session.

## Western Writers' Centre
**34 Nun's Island, Galway, Republic of Ireland**
☎ 00353 91 533595
✉ fred@twwc.ie
🌐 www.twwc.ie
**Meeting Time** 2pm every Wednesday or Thursday
**About** The centre runs a 'Diverse Writers Group' which is free of charge, as well as a general writers group on a Wednesday, also at 2pm.

## West Sussex Writers' Club
**The Pavillion, Field Place, The Boulevard, Worthing**
☎ 01273 701235
**Contact** Heather Reay
 131 Bevendan Crescent
 Brighton
 BN2 4RE
**Meeting Time** 7.30pm, second Thursday of each month
**About** New members welcome of any level of experience. The group covers every genre of writing from scriptwriting, to journalism to novels to non-fiction. There is a guest speaker each month, and the group runs various workshops and competitions. It is a large group, with over 130 members.

## Wimpole Street Writers
**Wimpole Street, Westminster, London, NW1**
☎ 020 7486 6128
✉ jschary@aol.com
🌐 www.wimpolestreetwriters.com
**Contact** Jill Robinson
**Meeting Time** 6.30pm–9.30pm, every Tuesday and Thursday
**About** New members who are committed to writing are welcome, subject to space, and are advised to contact Jill Robinson for an informal interview. Workshops are held in Jill's dining room where she makes dinner for the writers. The group covers fiction, non-fiction, memoirs, plays, screenplays and poetry. An annual literary event is also held in January where members read their work to invited members of the press. Jill is also involved

in meeting with agents and publishers. Fees are £35 per session (including dinner).

## Wirral Writers
**Bebington Civic Centre, Joseph Meyer Rooms, Civic Way, Bebington, Wirral, CH63 7PN**
- 01352 750708
- clang5454@aol.com
- www.communigate.co.uk/chesh/wirralwritersgroup/

**Contact** Cheryl Lang
8 Llys Gwynant
Bryn Road, Byn y Baal
Mold
Flintshire
CH7 6NL

**Meeting Time** 7.30pm–10pm, first and third Fridays of each month
**About** New members welcome. Either go along, or contact beforehand for an informal chat. Members range from beginners to the more experienced and all types of writing are encouraged. Meetings are usually informal feedback sessions and throughout the year the group hold competitions, workshops and special discussions. They also occasionally organise social meals or walks. Fees are £20 per annum, but new members can trial before they commit.

## Woking Writer's Circle
**Strollers, The Generation Centre, Goldsworth Park Centre, Woking, Surrey**
- info@wokingwriterscircle.org.uk
- www.wokingwriterscircle.org.uk

**Contact** Sharyn Owen
**Meeting Time** 7.30pm–10pm, third Thursday of each month
**About** The group is for people who write for pleasure but would also like to be published. Current members are very mixed in terms of age, gender and ethnic background. The main focus of each meeting is to receive constructive feedback on your work, although there are sometimes exercises and 'homework' set. The group also runs an informal breakfast meeting on the first Sunday of each month, at 10am in the Continental Cafe, Goldsworth Road, Woking. Fees are £20 per annum, although new members can attend twice for free.

## Womanswrite
**6 Mount Street, Manchester, M2 5NS**
- 0161 832 3777
- 0161 832 2929
- cathy@commonword.org.uk
- www.commonword.org.uk

**Meeting Time** 11am–1pm every Tuesday
**About** Open to women to meet and discuss different aspects of writing and publishing every week. Sometimes use practical exercises to stimulate creativity.

## Wood Green Group
**Wood Green Library, High Road, Wood Green, London, N22 6XD**
- richardtyronejones@hotmail.com
- www.wforw.org.uk

**Contact** Richard Jones
**Meeting Time** 11am–1pm every Saturday
**About** This group is an offshoot of Word for Word (see their entries).

## Worcester Writers' Circle
**Dancox House Club Room, St. Clements Close, St. John's, Worcester**
- 01905 619062
- www.fortroyal.org.uk/writerscircle/4.html

**Contact** Sue Round
**Meeting Time** 7.30pm–9.30pm, every other Tuesday
**About** New members welcome. For more information contact Susan Round. Meetings usually consist of readings, feedback and discussions. Current members range from hobbyists to published writers.

## Word for Word Novel Writing Group
**Hornsea Library, Haringey Park, Crouch End, London, N8 9JA**
- info@wforw.org.uk
- www.wforw.org.uk

**Meeting Time** 3.15pm–5.15pm alternate Wednesdays
**About** New members welcome, numbers permitting. Please make contact in the first instance. Writers of every kind are welcome as long as they are beginning, or working on a novel, and are committed to participating in feedback sessions.

## Word for Word Poetry Group
**Hornsea Library, Haringey Park, Crouch End, London, N8 9JA**
- poetic@btinternet.com
- www.wforw.org.uk

**Contact** Laurence Scott
**Meeting Time** 1pm–3pm every Wednesday during term time
**About** New members welcome, contact tutor and published poet, Laurence Scott. Designed for beginning and improving poets. Fees range from £4–£6 per meeting, the first meeting is free.

## Word Weavers
**South Moor Branch Library, and, Oxhill Workingmen's Club, Stanley, County Durham**
◍ www.wordweavers.org.uk
**Contact** Marjorie Briggs
**Meeting Time** 6pm–8pm, first Thursday of each month-library. Every other Thursday 7pm–9pm (Working Men's Club)
**About** New members welcome, visit website for details. Small, friendly group.

## WordWrights
**The Abbey Room, Titchfield Communtiy Centre, Mill Street, Titchfield, Hampshire**
☎ 01329 846480
◎ liza.look@btinternet.com
**Contact** Rosa Johnson
Little Oak
293a Titchfield Road
Titchfield
Hampshire
PO14 3ER
**Meeting Time** 1.30pm, first and third Thursday of every month
**About** New members welcome as long as the maximum limit of 22 members isn't exceeded. Please call Rosa Johnson in the first instance. Most types of writing are covered and members are expected to take part in giving mutual support. The group does not organise its own special events but does help with other community projects. Fees are £10 per annum, plus £1.50 per meeting.

## Wrekin Writers
**Wrekin Housing Trust Offices, Colliers Way, Old Park, Telford, TF3 4AW**
◎ admin@wrekinwriters.co.uk
◍ www.wrekinwriters.co.uk
**Meeting Time** 10am–12pm, third Saturday of each month
**About** Welcomes new members. "Just come along to any meeting and try us out for a few months to see if you like us." Covers all types of novels, poetry, short stories and articles. Runs an open writing

workshop in October each year, in conjunction with Wellington Literary Festival, as well as an annual retreat.

## Writability
**Carnegie Library, Main Street, Ayr, Scotland**
◎ webmaster@writability.co.uk
◍ http://mysite.wanadoo-members.co.uk/Writability/
**Meeting Time** 7pm–9pm, Mondays from October–May
**About** A readers and writers group, with a strong emphasis on books and writing book reviews. Able bodied and disabled members are welcome. Run by Writeability, an educational charity.

## Write Now
**Permanent venue in Bury St. Edmonds**
☎ 01284 767734
◎ george@wickerswork.co.uk
◍ www.wickerswork.co.uk/writenow/home.html
**Meeting Time** 7.30pm–10pm every other Tuesday
**About** New members can be nominated by existing members or make contact directly. They must have approval from all members before joining. Meetings are very structured and focused around a set theme. Writers are expected to fully participate and clear guidelines are available on the website. Fees are £2 per meeting.

## Writers Against Writing
**Various locations around Edinburgh**
◎ writersagainstwriting@yahoo.co.uk
◍ www.writersagainstwriting.co.uk
**Meeting Time** Irregular meetings
**About** New members are always welcome, email for details. The group is mainly web based and face to face meetings are irregular and sporadic. The group's ethic is strongly against writing to get published, or writing within constraints. It encourages not for profit writing that will never be bought or sold. Prose is the main focus although there is occasional poetry.

## Writers' Meet
**Clevedon Community Centre, Princes Hall, Sunhill Park, Clevedon**
☎ 01275 873452/07929078822
◎ snake@ukgateway.net
**Contact** David Robinson

**Meeting Time** 10.30am–12.30pm, every second Thursday
**About** Potential new members should phone or email in the first instance. They should be currently engaged in writing, and producing results in any genre. The group's primary function is help and support although they also organise member led workshops and regular guest speakers.

## Writers of our Age
**Various venues around Brockley, South East London**
- 07748 185325
- pjbruce@ukonline.co.uk
**Contact** Pamela Bruce
**Meeting Time** Fortnightly
**About** New members welcome. Call or email for details of the next meeting. The group deals with all types of fiction, but primarily novels of any genre. Once a year the group organises a weekend away.

## York Writers
**Guppy's Enterprise Club, 17 Nunnery Lane, York, YO23 1AB**
- clintwastling@aol.com
**Contact** Clint Wastling
**Meeting Time** 8pm, alternate Wednesdays
**About** Meetings vary between workshops (held at a private venue; contact for details) and meetings, which are usually with a speaker, a discussion, or readings. All types of creative writing are covered. Entry to the club is £2.40 for guests, but the writers group itself is free for two meetings. After this, membership is £15 per annum, or £8 for under 21s; club entry for members is £1.90.

# BOOK CLUBS

## Artists' Choice
**Artists' Choice Ltd, PO Box 3, Huntingdon, Cambridgeshire, PE28 0QX**
- 01832 710201
- 01832 710488
- www.artists-choice.co.uk
**About** An independent book club for practicing artists with a quarterly magazine.

## Baker Books
**Manfield Park, Cranleigh, Surrey, GU6 8NU**
- 01483 267888
- 01483 267409
- bakerbooks@dial.pipex.com
- www.bakerbooks.co.uk
**About** An independent school book club, for children aged between three and thirteen.

## BCA
**Greater London House, Hampstead Road, London, NW1 7TZ**
- 0870 165 0200
- 0870 165 0222
- e-support@booksdirect.co.uk
- www.bca.co.uk
**About** BCA is a wholly owned subsidiary of Bertelsmann. Its clubs include: World Books; Mango; World of Mystery and Thriller; History Guild; Ancient History; Arts; Fantasy and Science Fiction; Railway; Books for Children; Military and Aviation; Escape Fiction; Quality Paperbacks Direct (QPD) and The Softback Preview (TSP).

## Bilbiophile
**5 Thomas Road, London, E14 7BN**
- 020 7515 9222
- 020 7538 4115
- customercare@bibliophilebooks.com
- orders@bibliophilebooks.com
**Contact** Anne Quigley
**About** A discount postal club with around 4,000 titles available, in a wide range of genres. Request the free catalogue, or order directly from the website.

## The Book People Ltd
**Catteshall Manor, Catteshall Lane, Godalming, Surrey, GU7 1UU**
- 01483 861144
- 01483 861256
- feedback@thebookpeople.co.uk
- www.thebookpeople.co.uk
**About** Not a traditional book club, as there is no obligation to buy more than once. Members can receive a free monthly catalogue.

## Cygnus Book Club

PO Box 15, Llandeilo, Carmarthenshire, SA19 6YX

- 01550 777701
- 01550 777569
- enquiries@cygnus-books.co.uk
- www.cygnus-books.co.uk

**About** A book club catering for those interested in mind, body and spirit products. They also publish a monthly magazine.

## David Arscott's Sussex Book Club

Dolphin House, 51 St. Nicholas Lane, Lewes, BN7 2JZ

- 01273 470100
- 01273 470100
- sussexbooks@aol.com

**Contact** David Arscott

**About** Caters for those interested in books on Sussex and Sussex life.

## The Folio Society

44 Eagle Street, London, WC1R 4FS

- 020 7400 4222
- 020 7400 4242
- www.foliosociety.com

**About** Catering for those interested in classic literature.

## Letterbox Library

71–73 Allen Road, London, N16 8RY

- 020 7503 4801
- 020 7503 4800
- info@letterboxlibrary.com
- www.letterboxlibrary.com

**About** A not for profit workers cooperative, which specialises in multicultural, non-sexist, children's books.

## The Poetry Book Society

4th Floor, Tavistock Place, London, WC1H 9RA

- 020 8870 8403
- 020 8870 0865
- info@poetrybooks.co.uk
- www.poetrybooks.co.uk

**About** A poetry book club, which also has a children's poetry book club and a niche online poetry store.

## Readers' Union

Brunel House, Forde Close, Newton Abbot, Devon, TQ12 4PU

- 01626 323200
- 01626 323318
- comments@readersunion.co.uk
- www.readersunion.co.uk

**About** Runs ten different clubs including: The Craft Club; Needlecrafts with Cross Stitch; Gardeners' Book Society; Country Sports Book Club; Anglers' Book Club; Painting for Pleasure; Craftsman's Book Club; The Equestrian Book Society; Photographers' Book Club and Puzzles Plus.

## Red House

PO Box 142, Bangor, Wales, LL57 4ZP

- 0870 191 9980
- 0870 607 7720
- feedback@redhouse.co.uk
- www.redhouse.co.uk

**About** Red House isn't a traditional book club as there is no obligation to buy. It sells children's books through a free monthly catalogue.

## Scholastic Book Clubs

Windrush Park, Range Road, Witney, Oxfordshire, OX29 0YZ

- 01993 893456
- 01993 776813
- sbcenquiries@scholastic.co.uk
- www.scholastic.co.uk

**About** Five age specific school book clubs for children.

## Writers' Bookshelf

Writers' News, 1st Floor Victoria House, 143–145 The Headrow, Leeds, LS1 5RL

- 0113 200 2929
- 0113 200 2928
- castlehills@yorkshirebooks.com
- www.writersnews.co.uk

**About** Writers' News magazine compiles a selection of books for writers.

# RESOURCES

Even in the age of the internet, bricks and mortar libraries remain a vital and superb resource, which writers should use and support. We have included here details of the major reference and specialist libraries, as well as links to local and general libraries via the internet, and links to online library and archive resources. Note that some of the reference and specialist libraries are not open to non-members, or are open only on application.

## REFERENCE & SPECIALIST LIBRARIES

### The Ancell Library
**King Charles Street, London, SW1A 2AH**
- 020 7008 3925
- 020 7008 3270
- library.enquiries@fco.gov.uk
- www.fco.gov.uk

**About** The Ancell Library has a collection of books, journals, pamphlets and papers on international affairs, diplomacy, defence and security issues, countries and regions, political, parliamentary, maps and geographical information. The historical collection includes material of the former Foreign Office, Colonial Office and Commonwealth Relations Office and includes many rare volumes and early works on travel. Much of the historical collection is in the process of being transferred to another institution - see the website for details.

Although it is primarily a resource for Foreign and Commonwealth Office (FCO) staff, access to The Ancell Library is available to the general public, if publications are not available elsewhere. An application form must be submitted by post. See the website for further details.

### Armitt Gallery, Museum and Library
**Rydal Road, Ambleside, Cumbria, LA22 9BL**
- 01539 431212
- 01539 431313
- info@armitt.com
- www.armitt.com

**About** The Armitt Museum and Library houses a collection of art, archaeology, archives, books, geology and photography. There is also a local history collection, which includes over 400 water colours by Beatrix Potter. The library has over 10,000 titles relating to the Lake District and the people who lived, worked and visited there, plus an extensive collection of early guidebooks.

### Atheneum Liverpool
**Church Alley, Liverpool, L1 3DD**
- 0151 709 7770
- 0151 709 7770
- library@theathenaeum.org.uk
- www.theathenaeum.org.uk

**About** Liverpool's renowned Athenaeum Library, founded in 1797, is one of the most important regional history resources in the country. The collection is particularly strong in classical and other literature, and theology, history, biography and travel. The local history section includes manuscripts, maps, playbills, prints and drawings. There are also books from the library of William Roscoe, 17th Century grammars of South American Indian languages, and 18th Century plays. Other collections include bound volumes of economic pamphlets and local directories. See the website for access details for non-members.

### Barbican Library
**Barbican Centre, Silk Street, London, EC2Y 8DS**
- 020 7638 0569
- 020 7638 2249
- www.cityoflondon.gov.uk

**About** The largest of the City of London's public lending libraries, the Barbican Library has specialist sections on conservation, crime fiction, finance, the history of London, natural resources and socialism. The Barbican Music Library has one of the largest recorded music collections in London that is available to the public.

### Bath Royal Literary and Scientific Institution
**6–18 Queen Square, Bath, BA1 2HN**
- 01225 312084
- 01225 442460
- enquiries@brlsi.org

@ www.brlsi.org

**About** The Bath Royal Literary and Scientific Institution (BRLSI) was founded in 1824. Its antiquarian library now contains over 7,000 volumes, notably from the Jenyns and Broome natural history libraries. Smaller collections cover local history, theology, travel and government. Archives contain bound volumes of letters from eminent naturalists and scientists, including Charles Darwin, Sir Joseph Hooker and Professor J.S.Henslow. Open to members (new members welcome) and to researchers by appointment. There are frequent lectures, special events and exhibitions, specialist discussion groups on literature, science and the arts and scientific demonstrations for young people.

## BFI National Library
**21 Stephen Street, London, W1T 1LN**
@ 020 7255 1444
@ 020 7436 2338
@ library@bfi.org.uk
@ www.bfi.org.uk

**About** Holding the world's largest collection of film and television information, the BFI National Library is a major national research collection of documentation and information on film and television. The library specialises in British film and television, but it also has international scope. There is an online catalogue.

## Birmingham and Midland Institute
**9 Margaret Street, Birmingham, B3 3BS**
@ 0121 236 3591
@ 0121 212 4577
@ admin@bmi.org.uk
@ www.bmi.org.uk

**About** Private lending library for Institute members, a few of the local history books can be purchased as copies on a CD. Specialises in humanities.

## Birmingham Library Services
**Central Library, Chamberlain Square, Birmingham, B3 3HQ**
@ 0121 393 4511
@ 0121 233 4458
@ central.library@birmingham.gov.uk
@ www.birmingham.gov.uk/libraries

**About** Birmingham Central Library holds one of the national collections of photography. Materials held include prints, lantern slides and books illustrated with photographic prints. There are also numerous other special collections, including the Buffalo Bill collection, about the American showman who brought his Wild West Show to Birmingham in 1900.

## Bishopsgate Institute Reference Library
**230 Bishopsgate, London, EC2M 4QH**
@ 020 7392 9270
@ 020 7392 9275
@ library@bishopsgate.org.uk
@ www.bishopsgate.org.uk

**About** Free public access to world renowned collections on London, Labour, Freethought and Cooperation. Collections are a focal point for research into the history and topography of London, in particular the East End, and the Freethought, early Labour, and Cooperative movements. The extensive London history section includes the personal library and papers of George Howell; publications and papers of George Jacob Holyoake; Raphael Samuel archive and the London Cooperative Society collection. In addition, the Library holds research materials for local and family historians, general reference materials and current national and local newspapers.

## British Architectural Library
**Royal Institute of British Architects, 66 Portland Place, London, W1B 1AD**
@ 020 5480 5533
@ 020 7631 1802
@ info@inst.riba.org
@ www.architecture.com

**About** The largest and most comprehensive resource in Britain for research and information on all aspects of architecture. The British Architectural Library is one of the most outstanding institutions of its kind in the world. The library collections (close to four million objects) include books, periodicals, manuscripts, archives, drawings, photographs, models, paintings, medals and artefacts. Books, periodicals and photographs are held at the Royal Institute of British Architects (RIBA) headquarters, and drawings and archives are located at the Victoria and Albert Museum (V&A). Library services include a cutting edge information centre, available to both the public and RIBA members.

## The British Library
**St. Pancras, 96 Euston Road, London, NW1 2DB**
@ 0870 444 1500 (Main switchboard)
@ visitor-services@bl.uk
@ www.bl.uk

**About** One of the world's greatest libraries, the British Library is the national library of the United Kingdom. Treasures include the Magna Carta, Lindisfarne Gospels and Leonardo da Vinci's notebook. The British Library serves business and industry, researchers, students and academics in the UK and worldwide. The collection includes 150 million items in most known languages, with three million new items being incorporated each year. There is space at the library for over 1,200 readers. Collections include; Americas, Asia, Pacific & Africa, East European, Modern British, Modern Irish, and West European. There are also collections on early printed manuscripts, maps, music, newspapers, patents, trademarks and designs. Alongside this, there are also reports, conferences and theses, philatelic, science technology and the business and sound archive.

## British Library, Newspapers
**Colindale Avenue, London, NW9 5HE**
- 020 7412 7353
- 020 7412 7379
- newspaper@bl.uk
- www.bl.uk

**About** British Library Newspapers contains the national archive collection of British and overseas newspapers. The collection also includes popular magazines and periodicals and is available in hard copy, microform or CD-Rom. The library has over 52,000 newspaper and periodical titles within its web catalogue. There is an online search function for selected issues of London's Daily News, The News of the World, The Weekly Dispatch and The Manchester Guardian.

## British Organ Archive
**Birmingham Central Library (Archives Department), Birmingham, B3 3HQ**
- 0121 303 4217

**About** Material held at the library is mainly the property of the British Institute of Organ Studies. The collections held relate to all aspects of these instruments, their history and conservation.

## Bromley House Library/The Nottingham Subscription Library
**Bromley House, Angel Row, Nottingham, NG1 6HL**
- 0115 947 3134

**About** Founded in 1816, the Nottingham Subscription Library collection has approximately 35,000 books. These include local history, many topographical works and a wide selection of 19th and early 20th Century novels. In recent years the collection's emphasis has been on biographies, travel books and new novels.

## CAA Library and Information Centre
**Aviation house, Gatwick Airport South, Gatwick, RH6 0YR**
- 01293 573725
- 01293 573181
- infoservices@caa.co.uk
- www.caa.co.uk

**About** The CAA Library and Information Centre is open to the public and contains a collection of books, reports, directories, statistics, videos, and periodicals on most aspects of civil aviation and related subjects.

## The Caird Library, National Maritime Museum
**Park Row, Greenwich, London, E10 9NF**
- 020 8312 6516 (e-library/General enquiries); 020 8312 6528/6673 (library); 020 8312 6691/6669 (Manuscripts); 020 8312 6757 (Charts and maps)
- library@nmm.ac.uk
- www.nmm.ac.uk

**About** Named after the Museum's principal founder and benefactor, Sir James Caird, the National Maritime Museum Library holds over 100,000 books, 20,000 pamphlets, 20,000 bound periodicals and 8,000 rare books, dating from 1474 to 1850. The Library's contents cover every aspect of maritime history, including emigration, navigation, piracy, and astronomy, shipping companies, shipwrecks, biographies, the two world wars and the merchant and royal navy. There are special collections for researching family history, merchant shipping and warships. The manuscripts collection is the largest and most important dedicated archive for the study of maritime history in the world. The library is open to anyone over 18 years of age with a research query. There is an online catalogue and on site e-library.

## Catholic Central Library
**St. Michael's Abbey, Farnborough Road, Farnborough, GU14 7NQ**
- 01252 543818
- library@catholic-library.org.uk
- www.catholic-library.org.uk

**About** The Catholic Central Library has 65,000 books and periodicals, including subjects on theology, spirituality, biography and history (including Catholic Family History).

## Chetham's Library
**Long Millgate, Manchester, M3 1SB**
- 0161 834 7961
- 0161 839 5797
- librarian@chethams.org.uk
- www.chethams.org.uk

**About** Founded in 1653, Chetham's Library is the oldest public library in the English speaking world. The library holds more than 100,000 volumes of printed books, of which 60,000 were published before 1851. It houses renowned collections of 16th and 17th Century printed works, periodicals and journals, and a wide ranging collection of images and photographs. Specialises in the history of northwest of England.

## City Business Library
**1 Brewers' Hall Garden (off Aldermanbury Square), London, EC2V 5BX**
- 020 7332 1812
- 020 7332 1847
- www.cityoflondon.gov.uk

**About** One of the leading business information libraries in the UK, with a major collection of sources of business information including market research, and UK and international directories, in both print and electronic format. No membership required - email enquiry service is via an online form on the website.

## Commonwealth Secretariat Library
**Marlborough House, Pall Mall, London, SW1 5HX**
- 020 7747 6253
- 020 7747 6168
- library@commonwealth.int
- www.thecommonwealth.org

**About** The Commonwealth Secretariat is the main intergovernmental agency of the Commonwealth. The Library has a collection of documentation covering a subject range that includes politics and international relations, economics, education, health, gender, environment, science and technology, and management. Much of the collection consists of government publications, conference reports, discussion and working papers and a wide range of publications from international organisations. Most of the materials have been published within the last ten years. The library is also the official repository for the Secretariat's own publications and holds more than 3,000 separate items. Open to members of the public by prior appointment.

## Copac
- www.copac.ac.uk

**About** Free access to merged online catalogues of 24 major research libraries in the UK and Ireland.

## The Devon and Exeter Institution Library
**7 The Close, Exeter, Devon, EX1 1EZ**
- 01392 251017
- info@devonandexeterinstitution.org.uk
- www.devonandexeterinstitution.org.uk

**About** The Devon and Exeter Institution is an independent subscription library founded in 1813. The Library collections, of around 34,000 volumes, are included on the University of Exeter's Library catalogue. They are particularly strong in West Country materials, and 18th and 19th Century books. For access please contact the institution.

## Directory of Local Councils
- www.direct.gov.uk/en/Dl1/Directories/Localcouncils/index.htm

**About** Lists local councils by region. Find public library information from the local authority website (to find the relevant local authority use the searchable database www.ordnancesurvey.co.uk/oswebsite/freefun/didyouknow/).

## Dr William's Library
**14 Gordon Square, London, WC1H 0AG**
- 020 7387 3727
- 020 7388 1142
- enquiries@dwlib.co.uk

**About** Dr William's Library is primarily a theological library, although collections also include philosophy, history and literature. The library has a large collection of Byzantine history and culture, and considerable holdings of pre 19th Century works relating to English Nonconformity.

## Family Records Centre
**1 Myddelton Street, Islington, London, EC1R 1UW**
- 020 8392 5300
- enquiry@nationalarchives.gov.uk
- www.familyrecords.gov.uk

**About** The Family Records Office is part of The National Archive. It holds census records, records of births, marriages & deaths, adoptions, religious records, wills, immigration, emigration, and military records.

## French Institute Library (Institut Français)
**17 Queensberry Place, London, SW7 2DT**
- 020 7073 1354
- 020 7073 1355
- library@ambafrance.org.uk
- www.institut-francais.org.uk

**About** The French Institute Library has wide and varied documentation on all aspects of France, especially the works of French and French speaking authors. There are books, comics, CD, videos and DVDs, CD-ROMs, talking books, French newspapers and periodicals, press cutting files, archival audio material, specialist resources for French language learners and a children's library. Loans are restricted to members, but the library is open to the general public for reference.

## Goethe Institute Library
**50 Princes Gate, Exhibition Road, London, SW7 2PH**
- 020 7596 4044
- 020 7594 0230
- library@london-goethe.org
- www.goethe.de/london

**About** The German Cultural Centre library has an up to date collection of German language books, English translations, reference works and dictionaries. There are also German newspapers and journals, databases and language resources. The library houses specialist collections on contemporary literature, film and theatre, fine arts and photography.

## The Guildford Institute of the University of Surrey
**Ward Street, Guildford, Surrey, GU1 4LH**
- 01483 562142
- 01483 451034
- c.miles@surrey.ac.uk

**About** The Institute (originally the Guildford Mechanics Institute) was founded in 1834. It holds 3,000 volumes, of which nearly 2,000 pre-date the First World War. They hold up to date fiction, and non-fiction, plus newspapers and periodicals. Books, photographs, prints and drawings are held, which relate to the history, people, antiquities and topography of Guildford and the county of Surrey. Appointments should be made in advance. The Surrey History Service holds the institutional archive.

## Guildhall Library
**Aldermanbury, London, EC2P 7HH**
- Printed books: 020 7332 1868/020 7332 1870; Manuscripts: 020 7332 1862/020 7332 1863; Prints and Maps: 020 7332 1839
- printedbooks.guildhall@cityoflondon.gov.uk, manuscripts.guildhall@cityoflondon.gov.uk, prints&maps@cityoflondon.gov.uk
- www.cityoflondon.gov.uk

**About** A major public reference library, founded in the early 15th Century, and specialising in the history of London, especially the City. Specialist collections in the printed books department include; the Gardeners' Company Collection (historic books on gardening), the Fletchers' Company Collection (archery), the Gresham College Collection (17th and 18th Century music, and early travel and exploration), the Cock Collection (material on Sir Thomas More), the Charles Lamb Society Collection, the Chapman Bequest (19th Century plays), the Hamilton Bequest (18th and 19th Century plays), and the Pepys Collection. There are also collections on marine history, clocks and clockmakers, wine and food, English law and business. The Print Room is a source of historic pictures and maps of Greater London and is used by picture researchers, architectural historians, family historians and art historians. The Manuscripts section is the local record office for the City of London and includes the archives of about 80 of the City livery companies. Holdings date from the 11th Century.

## HERO (Higher Education Research Organisation)
- www.hero.ac.uk

**About** HERO is the official gateway to universities, colleges and research organisations in the UK. It links to the online library catalogues of higher education institutions (see reference and subject resources).

## Highgate Literary and Scientific Institution Library
**11 South Grove, Highgate, London, N6 6BS**
- 020 8340 3343
- 020 8340 5632
- admin@hlsi.net
- www.hlsi.net

**About** Established in 1839, The Highgate Literary and Scientific Institution Library has extensive local archives and special collections on London, and local poets Coleridge and Betjeman There is also a general fiction and non-fiction section and a children's section.

## Imperial College and Science Museum Libraries
**Imperial College Road, South Kensington, London, SW7 5NH**
- 020 7942 4242
- 020 7942 4243
- smlinfo@nmsi.ac.uk
- www.sciencemuseum.org.uk/library

**About** Founded in 1883 the Science Museum Library is a research library for the history and public understanding of the physical sciences and all branches of engineering. Since 1992 it has been linked with the Central Library of Imperial College London, which is open to all for reference use. The collection of rare books includes major classics in the history of science and technology. There are sections on astronomy, biology, chemistry, physics, medicine and engineering. More general works on history and languages, and accounts of voyages of discovery are also housed.

## The Imperial War Museum
**Lambeth Road, London, SE1 6HZ**
- 020 7416 5342
- 020 7416 5374
- books@iwm.org.uk
- http://collections.iwm.org.uk

**About** Books, pamphlets, periodicals, maps, technical drawings, propaganda leaflets, song sheets and army forms are among the items that can be viewed in the Reading Room of the Imperial War Museum, a major national gallery and archive. Open to any member of the public.

## Innerpeffray Library
**Innerpeffray, by Crieff, Perthshire, PH7 3RF**
- 01764 652819
- library@innerpeff.fsnet.co.uk

**About** The collection at Innerpeffray Library was founded before 1680 and includes some 3,000 titles printed between 1502 and 1799, specialising in religious titles and contains many rare works. There are 1,400 items in the rest of the collection, printed after 1799. The library is open to the general public (there is a small admission charge).

## Institute of Commonwealth Studies
**28 Russell Square, London, WC1B 5DS**
- 020 7862 8844
- 020 7862 8820
- http://commonwealth.sas.ac.uk

**About** A major resource on the Commonwealth and its member states. Subjects include history, politics and international relations, agriculture, education, the environment and social questions. They specialise in providing material that is unavailable elsewhere in the UK.

## The Institute of Contemporary History and Wiener Library
**4 Devonshire Street, London, W1W 5BH**
- 020 7636 7247
- 020 7436 6428
- info@wienerlibrary.co.uk web
- www.wienerlibrary.co.uk

**About** Founded in 1933, The Wiener Library is the world's oldest Holocaust memorial institution. Its multi-language collections are of material related to the Holocaust, its causes and legacies. There are collections on modern Central European Jewish history, the rise and fall of Nazi Germany, war crimes and war crimes trials. The library has holdings of approximately 50,000 items. Open to the general public, but users must bring identification, and undergraduate students need a letter of introduction from their tutor. Only members of the library may borrow books.

## The Institute of Historical Research
**Senate House, Malet Street, London, WC1E 7HU**
- 020 7862 8760
- 020 7862 8762
- ihrlibrary@sas.ac.uk
- www.history.ac.uk/library

**About** The best open access collection of printed historical sources in the United Kingdom, the Institute of Historical Research holds around 169,000 items. Central to the collection are primary sources for the medieval and modern history of the British Isles and Western Europe, the history of North and South America, international relations and war. There is also a large collection of the most essential historical periodicals, microforms and electronic resources. Most of the holdings are open access; membership is free for staff and postgraduate students of all UK and EU universities.

## Ipswich Institute Reading Room and Library

**15 Tavern Street, Ipswich, Suffolk, IP1 3AA**

☎ 01473 253992

**About** The library of the Ipswich Institute has around 9,000 books, including an impressive collection of books of local interest.

## Italian Institute, Eugenio Montale Library

**39 Belgrave Square, London, SW1X 8NX**

☎ 020 7296 4425

☎ 020 7235 4618

✉ icilondon@esteri.it

🌐 www.italcultur.org.uk

**About** The Eugenio Montale Library is open to the general public and has around 25,000 books in Italian, with a large reference section on Italian culture and history. Major Italian newspapers are delivered to the Institute daily.

## Kew Library

**The Library & Archives, Royal Botanic Gardens, Kew, Surrey, TW9 3AE**

☎ 020 8332 5414

☎ 020 8332 5430

✉ library@kew.org

🌐 www.rbgkew.org.uk/library

**About** One of the most important botanical reference sources in the world, the library at Kew is open to researchers by appointment, although a written application (by fax, email or letter) is usually required. The library and archives contain more than half a million items, including books, botanical illustrations, photographs, letters and manuscripts.

## Lambeth Palace Library

**Lambeth Palace, London, SE1 7JU**

☎ 020 7898 1400

☎ 020 7928 7932

✉ lpl.staff@c-of-e.org.uk

🌐 www.lambethpalacelibrary.org

**About** Lambeth Palace Library is one of Britain's oldest public libraries, it is the historic library of the Archbishops of Canterbury and the principal library and record office for the history of the Church of England. Specialising in ecclesiastical history, collections include the history of art and architecture, and colonial and commonwealth history. The library is also a resource for local history and genealogy, and many aspects of English social,

political and economic history. Founded in 1610, it contains an immense quantity of important historical books and documents. It houses over 4,600 manuscripts and almost 200,000 printed books with around 30,000 items printed before 1700. In 1996 the Library acquired the Sion College collection of books and manuscripts. Those wishing to use the library must obtain a readers' ticket, further details are given on the website.

## The Langholm Library

**3 Walter Street, Langholm, Dumfriesshire, DG13 0AX**

**About** The Langholm Library was founded in 1800 and in 1834 it received a substantial bequest in the will of Thomas Telford, the engineer. In 1853 it absorbed the Langholm Trades Library. The collection consists of 5,000 books, representing stock typical of a Scottish community library at the turn of the century.

## The Leeds Library

**18 Commercial Street, Leeds, LS1 6AL**

☎ 0113 245 3071

☎ 0113 245 1191

✉ enquiries@leedslibrary.co.uk

**About** The Leeds Library, the oldest surviving proprietary subscription library in the UK, has a stock of over 135,000 books. The library is particularly strong in travel, biography, history and literature. Special collections include Civil war pamphlets and Reformation tracts. Open to members only, researchers require a letter of reference from an appropriate institution or a professional person, and should make a prior appointment.

## Library of the Religious Society of Friends

**Friends House, 173–177 Euston Road, London, NW1 2BJ**

☎ 020 7663 1135

☎ 020 7663 1001

✉ Online contact form on the website

🌐 www.quaker.org.uk

**About** The library holds one of the most important collections relating to Quakers in the world. Founded in 1673, the collection covers Quaker history and thought. It has collections relating to areas in which Quakers have been active, including peace, anti-slavery, and relief work. There is a unique collection of 17th Century pamphlets, which include anti-Quaker material. Quakers and non-Quakers from all around the world use the Library, you must register on your first visit.

## Linen Hall Library
**17 Donegall Square North, Belfast, BT1 5GB, Northern Ireland**
- 028 9032 1707
- 028 9043 8586
- info@linenhall.com
- www.linenhall.com

**About** Founded in 1788, Belfast's Linen Hall Library is renowned for its unparalleled Irish and Local Studies Collection including the Northern Ireland Political Collection. Also a noted theatre and performing arts archive, a significant genealogy and heraldry collection and one of the largest collections of Burnsiana outside Scotland.

## The Literary and Philosophical Society of Newcastle upon Tyne
**23 Westgate Road, Newcastle upon Tyne, NE1 1SE**
- 0191 232 0192
- 0191 261 4494
- library@litandphil.org.uk
- www.litandphil.org.uk

**About** The Literary & Philosophical Society, founded in 1793 as a learned society, took on the role of a university in the city. It is the largest independent library outside of London, housing over 150,000 books (including many rare items). Alongside the wide selection of current fiction and non-fiction, are historical collections covering every field of interest. Specialist areas include 19th Century science and technology, exploration and travel, history, biography, literature, music and local history. The music library is unequalled in the North of England. Non-members should apply to the Librarian.

## The London Library
**14 St. James's Square, London, SW1Y 4LG**
- 020 7930 7705
- 020 7766 4766
- enquiries@londonlibrary.co.uk
- www.londonlibrary.co.uk

**About** Founded by Thomas Carlyle in 1841, The London Library was set up with the aim of advancing education, learning and knowledge. It is now the largest independent lending library in the world, serving readers, writers, researchers and scholars. There are over one million volumes in the collection, covering every aspect of the humanities,

in all major (and many minor) European languages, dating from the 16th Century, to the present. The library specialises in history, literature, biography, art, religion, bibliography and travel and topography. Over 95 per cent of the collection is housed on open access shelves, and over 97 per cent is available for loan. Membership is open to all; temporary reference tickets are also available.

## London Metropolitan Archives, Library Services
**40 Northampton Road, Clerkenwell, London, EC1R 0HB**
- 020 7332 3820
- 020 7833 9136
- ask.lma@cityoflondon.gov.uk
- www.cityoflondon.gov.uk

**About** London Metropolitan Archives (LMA) is the largest local authority record office in the UK. Material dates from 1067 to 2006 and is part of the History of London Collection. The City of London archive is one of the oldest, most complete, and wide ranging civic archives in the world. Collections include topics that range from the built environment, education, justice, migration and settlement, to social activities. Downloadable factsheets on a wide range of topics are available from the website.

## Marsh's Library
**St. Patrick's Close, Dublin 8, Republic of Ireland**
- 00353 1 454 3511
- 00353 1 454 3511
- keeper@marshlibrary.ie
- www.marshlibrary.ie

**About** Built in 1701 by Archbishop Narcissus Marsh, Marsh's Library was the first public library in Ireland. It is housed in one of the few 18th Century buildings in Dublin that is still used for its original purpose, and is a fine example of a 17th Century scholar's library. The library houses four main collections, many of which are still kept on the shelves allocated to them when the library first opened. The main collections consist of 25,000 books relating to the 16th, 17th and the early part of the 18th Centuries. Works include liturgical works, missals, breviaries, books of hours of the sarum use, bibles printed in almost every language, theology and religious controversy. There are also collections on medicine, law, science, travel, navigation, mathematics, music, surveying and classical literature. A separate room is reserved for books and periodicals relating to Irish history printed in the last hundred years. The most important collection is the library of Edward Stillingfleet (1635-1699) who was Bishop of Worcester. Stillingfleet's library of nearly 10,000 books was regarded as the finest private library in England, in the later part of the 17th Century. Students and scholars are admitted free, but there is a charge for visitors.

## The Mitchell

**North Street, Glasgow, G37DN**

- 0141 287 2999
- 0141 287 2815
- lil@cls.glasgow.gov.uk
- www.glasgow.gov.uk

**About** Glasgow's famous Mitchell Library opened in 1877; it is one of Europe's largest public reference libraries. From its earliest years it established two main collections, the Scottish Poetry Collection and the Glasgow Collection. The library holds the world's largest Robert Burns collection and the Jeffrey Library, which contains illustrated volumes on travel, literature, art, architecture and natural history, including the extremely valuable Birds of America series of prints, by J.J. Audubon. The Baillie's Institution Library is also housed in the Mitchell (Baillie was an early pioneer of 'adult education'), as is the Henry Dyer Collection, which includes unique Japanese scrolls and albums acquired by the Glasgow engineer and educationalist.

## The Morrab Library

**Morrab House, Morrab Gardens, Penzance, Cornwall, TR18 4DA**

- 01736 364474
- morrablibrary@hotmail.co.uk
- www.morrablibrary.co.uk

**About** The Morrab Library, founded in 1818, is the sixth largest independent library in the country with more than 40,000 volumes. It is strong in literature, history, biography, antiquities, topography and travel and religion. The Jenner Room houses an extensive Cornish collection and holdings on other Celtic countries. There is also a collection of 3,000 Napoleonic memorabilia, described as "the only great Napoleonic collection in the world". The library's photographic archive has a catalogue of over 10,000 prints and negatives of antiquities, places, people and events in West Cornwall. It has recently acquired a further 15,000 transparencies of buildings, industrial archaeology and related interests.

## Museum of the History of Science

**Old Ashmolean Building, Broad Street, Oxford, OX1 3AZ**

- 01865 277278
- 01865 277288
- library@mhs.ox.ac.uk
- www.mhs.ox.ac.uk/

**About** The Museum library holds approximately 20,000 items with a main theme of scientific instruments. However, it also has strong collections in other fields, including zoology, botany, the medical sciences, Oxford science and the history of museums. The library holds rare early pamphlets and runs of old scientific periodicals. Dating from 1476, antiquarian material predominates; some modern reference works, historical monographs, and relevant history of science journals supplement this. The library also manages the Museum's important collections of printed ephemera, prints, photographs, and manuscripts. Mainly a research and reference source for academics, researchers and students, but the library welcomes members of the public with an interest in its collections (by prior appointment). An online catalogue is also available.

## The National Archives

**Ruskin Avenue, Kew, Richmond, Surrey, TW9 4DU**

- 020 8876 3444
- Online contact form on the website
- www.nationalarchives.gov.uk

**About** The National Archives is the official archive for England, Wales and the central UK government. It holds 900 years of history from the Domesday Book, to the most recent government papers. The collection covers the British Isles, territories that formed the British Empire and the countries of the Commonwealth. There is also a museum, which is free of charge. There is an online catalogue and certain documents are downloadable.

## The National Archives (Ireland)

**Bishop Street, Dublin 8, Republic of Ireland**

- 00353 1 407 2300
- 00353 1 407 2333
- mail@nationalarchives.ie
- www.nationalarchives.ie

**About** The Irish National Archives holds the records of the modern Irish state and documents its historical evolution. It holds many of the records relevant to Irish genealogy and local history.

## National Art Library

**V&A South Kensington, Cromwell Road, London, SW7 2RL**

- 020 7942 2400
- 020 7942 2401
- nal.enquiries@vam.ac.uk
- www.vam.ac.uk/nal/

**About** Major public reference library for the fine and decorative arts. Material must be consulted in one of the libraries' reading rooms.

## National Library for the Blind

- www.nlb-online.org

**About** The National Library for the Blind is a leading agency in the provision of library and information services for visually impaired people. The library holds Europe's largest collection of Braille and Moon books, and provides a free postal library service to blind and partially sighted people worldwide. It also has a large collection of Braille music scores, giant print books, e-resources and reference materials.

## National Library of Ireland

**Kildare Street, Dublin 2, Republic of Ireland**

- 00353 1 603 0200
- 00353 1 676 6690
- info@nli.ie
- www.nli.ie

**About** The National Library of Ireland has the world's largest collection of Irish documentary material, including books and periodicals, newspapers, photographs, prints and drawings and manuscripts.

## National Library of Scotland

**George IV Bridge, Edinburgh, EH1 1EW**

- 0131 623 3700
- 0131 623 3701
- enquiries@nls.uk
- www.nls.uk

**About** The National Library of Scotland is a treasure trove of information about Scotland. It holds collections of books, manuscripts and maps, which cover the nation's history and culture.

## National Library of Wales

**Aberystwyth, Ceredigion, SY23 3BU**

- 01970 632800
- 01970 615709
- Online contact form on the website, or cat@llgc.org.uk for catalogue comments and questions
- www.llgc.org.uk

**About** The National Library of Wales contains over four million printed volumes, including books, periodicals, newspapers, official publications and maps from many countries. The National Screen and Sound Archive of Wales is also part of the library (tel. 01972 632828, or email agssc@llgc.org.uk).

## National Meteorological Library

**Fitzroy Road, Exeter, Devon, EX1 3PB**

- 01392 884841
- metlib@metoffice.gov.uk
- www.metoffice.gov.uk/corporate/library

**About** Open to any member of the public with an interest in weather and climate, the library's holdings include the majority of published writing on meteorology in the UK over the last 150 years. There are weather reports for the UK, from 1 January 1869, to the present. From around the world, they hold the original Beaufort scale, marine weather logbooks (worldwide records from merchant and Royal Navy ships), and weather records from Scott's Antarctic expedition in 1911. The collection of historical meteorological literature has the great early writings on meteorology; these are maintained in cooperation with the Royal Meteorological Society.

## Natural History Museum, Library and Information Services

**Cromwell Road, London, SW7 5BD**

- 020 7942 5000
- Online form on the website
- www.nhm.ac.uk/research-curation/library

**About** The Natural History Museum Library and Archive holds the world's premier collections of literature, original drawings and manuscripts relating to natural history. The library is a reference source for the biological and earth sciences and is comprised of over one million books dating from 1469. It holds 25,000 periodical titles and half a million artworks, together with extensive map, manuscript and photographic collections. The museum archives are made up of over one million items, relating to the history and work of the museum. Much of the library catalogue is online. By appointment only, researchers should contact the relevant subject department and contact details are given on the website.

## Northern Poetry Library

**County Library, The Willows, Morpeth, Northumberland, NE61 1TA**

**☎** 01670 534524

**☻** www.northumberland.gov.uk/services/
libraries.htm

**About** Established in 1968, the Northern Poetry
Library aims to collect all poetry published from the
area, as well as UK wide contemporary poetry. A
postal lending service is available for members.

## Office for National Statistics
**1 Drummond Gate, London, SW1V 2QQ**

**☎** 020 7533 6266 (London)/01633 812129 (Newport)

**☻** library.enquiries@ons.gov.uk

**☻** www.statistics.gov.uk

**About** Provides information on 200 years of
government statistical publishing. A unique
collection of every publication produced by the
Office for National Statistics (ONS) and its
predecessors (Central Statistical Office and the Office
of Population Censuses and Surveys). Visits are by
appointment only. There are online catalogue and
many of the resources will be accessible through
local libraries.

## People's Network

**☻** www.peoplesnetwork.gov.uk

**About** People's Network is a national online
resource, managed by the Museums, Libraries and
Archives Council. To find your nearest public library
click on 'Discover' (where there is a searchable
database by postcode), there is also an online
enquiry service.

## The Poetry Library
**Level 5, Royal Festival Hall, London, SE1 8XX**

**☎** 020 7921 0943/0664

**☻** www.poetrylibrary.org.uk

**About** Founded in 1953, The Poetry Library is the
major library for modern and contemporary poetry,
with the most comprehensive collection of poetry in
the UK. They aim to stock all poetry titles published
in the UK, plus a representation of work from other
countries, including work in parallel text and English
translation. The library's holdings date back to 1912;
it currently has around 90,000 items.

## The Portico Library and Gallery
**57 Mosley Street, Manchester, M2 3HY**

**☎** 0161 236 6785

**☎** 0161 236 6803

**☻** librarian@theportico.org.uk

**☻** www.theportico.org.uk

**About** The Portico Library and Gallery was founded
in 1806 and still occupies its original site, its
collection reflects the literary and intellectual
interests of the 19th Century. There is a wide
selection of travel literature, novels, biographies and
history, with a good representative selection of
fiction, including a number of first editions. The
strong travel section covers the voyages of Captain
Cook, many Victorian women travellers, and
Victorian continental exploration. The topography
section includes 18th Century antiquarian surveys of
English counties, as well as contemporaneous
accounts. Students and researchers wishing to
access the library should contact the Librarian.

## Royal Geographical Society
**1 Kensington Gore, London, SW7 2AR**

**☎** 020 7591 3000 (Main switchboard); 020 7591 3044
(Foyle Reading Room)

**☻** Online contact form on the website

**☻** www.rgs.org

**About** The library collection of the Royal
Geographical Society (RGS), holds over 150,000
bound volumes. These date primarily from the
foundation of the Society in 1830 onwards, and
focus on the history and geography of places across
the world. The society also has one of the largest
private map collections in the world and a collection
of historical travel guides. The Society's Foyle
Reading Room is open to members of the public
(identification needed for registering) but there is a
charge for non-members.

## Royal Observatory Edinburgh
**Blackford Hill, Edinburgh, EH9 3HJ**

**☎** 0131 668 8395

**☎** 0131 668 8264

**☻** library@roe.ac.uk

**☻** www.roe.ac.uk/roe/library

**About** The Royal Observatory holds one of the most
important and comprehensive collections of
astronomical literature in existence. The Crawford
Collection of books and manuscripts is one of the
most valuable astronomical libraries in the world.
Donated by James Ludovic Lindsay, 26th Earl of
Crawford, in 1888, it consists of around 15,000 books,
pamphlets and manuscripts dating from the 13th
Century to the end of the 19th Century. Bona fide
researchers only, most publications can be searched
via the online catalogue.

## The Royal Society
**Library and Information Services, 6–9 Carlton House Terrace, London, SW1Y 5AG**
- ☎ 020 7451 2606
- ☎ 020 7930 2170
- ✆ www.royalsoc.ac.uk

**About** The Royal Society is the independent scientific academy of the UK and the Commonwealth. Its library is open on a reference basis to visitors from all over the world, and the library catalogue includes books and journals dating back to the foundation of the Society in 1660.

## Royal Society of Chemistry, Library and Information Centre
**Burlington House, Piccadilly, London, W1J 0BA**
- ☎ 020 7440 3373
- ☎ 020 7287 9798
- ✆ Online contact form on the website
- ✆ www.rsc.org/Library

**About** Europe's foremost chemical knowledge source, which has been a focus of research for over 160 years. RSC Virtual Library is a free of charge, searchable resource, for premium chemical sciences and business information.

## Saffron Walden Town Library
**2 King Street, Saffron Walden, Essex, CB10 1ES**
- ☎ 01799 523178
- ☎ 01799 513642
- ✉ information@townlib.org.uk
- ✆ www.townlib.org.uk

**About** Formerly the Saffron Walden Literary and Scientific Institution, the Town Library collection has more than 25,000 volumes. Although the earliest material dates back to the middle of the 14th Century, there is a major resource for the study of the Victorian and Edwardian periods.

## The Scottish Poetry Library
**5 Crichton's Close, Canongate, Edinburgh, EH8 8DT**
- ☎ 0131 557 2876
- ☎ 0131 557 8393
- ✉ reception@spl.org.uk
- ✆ www.spl.org.uk

**About** The emphasis of the library is on contemporary poetry written in Scotland, in Scots, Gaelic and English. It also houses historic Scottish poetry and international contemporary works. Postal borrowing is available, plus an interlibrary loan service. Reading room for members.

## Society of Antiquaries of London
**Burlington House, Piccadilly, London, W1J 0BE**
- ☎ 020 7479 7084
- ✉ library@sal.org.uk
- ✆ www.sal.org.uk/library

**About** The foremost and oldest archaeological research library in the UK. The Society of Antiquaries library collection includes British county histories, 18th and 19th Century books on the antiquities of Britain and other countries, plus a wide collection of international periodicals. The collection includes an outstanding collection of prints and drawings. Access to the general public is available for a limited period, after application.

## Society of Genealogists, Library and Education Centre
**14 Charterhouse Buildings, Goswell Road, London, EC1M 7BA**
- ☎ 020 7251 8799
- ☎ 020 7250 1800
- ✉ library@sog.org.uk
- ✆ www.sog.org.uk

**About** A large collection of family histories, civil registration and census material. Over 9,000 county sources are held, including local histories, poll books, directories and other topographical material. Membership is open to anyone with an interest in family and social history. Non-members, on payment of a search fee may use the library.

## St. Bride Library
**Bride Lane, Fleet Street, London, EC4Y 8EE**
- ☎ 020 7353 4660
- ✆ www.stbride.org

**About** St. Bride Library is the world's premier printing and graphic arts library. There are 200 special collections, these include cover printing and related subjects, paper and binding, graphic design and typography, typefaces and calligraphy, illustration and printmaking. They also hold collections on publishing and book selling, and the social and economic aspects of the printing, book, newspaper and magazine trades. Open to the public free of charge, no registration.

### St Deiniol's Residential Library (The Gladstone Memorial Library)
**Church Lane, Hawarden, Flintshire, CH5 3DF**
- 01244 532350
- 01244 520643
- deiniol.librarian@btconnect.com
- www.st-deiniols.org

**About** Britain's only prime ministerial library, the St. Deiniols' collection, although now holding around 250,000 printed items, is based around Gladstone's own collection of over 30,000 volumes (many of them annotated by Gladstone). With particular strengths in theology and 19th Century studies, the library has been recognised as the most important Welsh research library and collection, after the National Library of Wales. The purpose built library buildings also house an exhibition on Gladstone and offer overnight accommodation, as well as being a venue for conferences and other events.

### Tennyson Research Centre
**Lincoln Central Library, Free School Lane, Lincoln, LN2 1EZ**
- 01522 510800
- 01522 575011
- grace.timmins@lincolnshire.gov.uk
- www.lincolnshire.gov.uk

**About** The Tennyson Research Centre at Lincoln Central Library is a world renowned collection on Alfred, Lord Tennyson, his family and the Victorian era. The collection includes letters, over 3,000 books from Tennyson's own library, and around 700 volumes from his father's library. There are also proofs of Tennyson's poetry, and manuscripts.

### Theatre Museum Library and Archive Reading Room
**Blythe House, 23 Blythe Road, London, W14 0QX**
- tmenquiries@vam.ac.uk
- www.vam.ac.uk/vastatic/theatre

**About** To make an appointment to use the Theatre Museum's reading room, email with details of research requests and suitable dates.

### UK Libraries Plus
- www.uklibrariesplus.ac.uk

**About** UK Libraries Plus is a cooperative venture between higher education libraries, to enable students and staff to use libraries near their home or work.

### UK Public Libraries on the Web
- http://dspace.dial.pipex.com/town/square/ac940/weblibs.html

**About** A-Z and regional listing of UK public libraries.

### Vaughan Williams Memorial Library
**Cecil Sharp House, 2 Regents Park Road, London, NW1 7AY**
- 020 7485 2206
- 020 7284 0523
- library@efdss.org
- www.efdss.org

**About** The multimedia library of the English Folk Dance and Song Society has collections relating to British folk culture and British based cultures in other countries, particularly North America and Ireland. There is also information about other world cultures, as well as important works on social history and folklore. Reference only for non-members, who are charged a daily fee.

### The Waterways Trust
**7th Floor, Llanthony Warehouse, The Docks, Gloucester, GL1 2EH**
- 01452 318224
- 01452 318225
- bwarchive@thewaterwaystrust.net
- www.thewaterwaystrust.org.uk

**About** The UK's largest collection of inland waterways information with around 78,000 records, its archive can be searched online at www.virtualwaterways.co.uk Access to the archive is by appointment only.

### Wellcome Library
**210 Euston Road, London, NW1 2BE**
- 020 7611 8722
- 020 7611 8369
- library@wellcome.ac.uk
- http://library.wellcome.ac.uk

**About** With over 600,000 books and journals, an extensive range of manuscripts, archives and films, and more than 100,000 pictures, the Wellcome Library is one of the world's major resources for the study of medical history. The library also holds a growing collection of contemporary biomedical information resources, relating to consumer health, popular science, biomedical ethics and public understanding of science. Membership of the library is open to all.

## Westminster Reference Library
**35 St. Martin's Street, London, WC2H 7HP**
- 020 7641 1300
- 020 7641 4606
- Online contact form on the website
- www.westminster.gov.uk/libraries/findalibrary/westref.cfm

**About** Specialist public reference library, with key subject collections on business, UK official publications, the European union, art and design, performance art, and law.

## The Women's Library
**London Metropolitan University, Old Castle Street, London, E1 7NT**
- 020 7320 2222
- 020 7320 2333
- moreinfo@thewomenslibrary.ac.uk
- www.londonmet.ac.uk/thewomenslibrary

**About** The Women's Library contains the most extensive women's history archive in the UK. A variety of topics are covered, including women's rights, suffrage, sexuality, health, education and employment, reproductive rights, the family, and the home. Some international material is included. Access is open to all.

## The Zoological Society of London
**Regents Park, London, NW1 4RY**
- 020 7449 6293
- library@zsl.org
- www.zsl.org/info/library

**About** Founded in 1826, The Zoological Society of London's Library is one of the world's major zoological libraries, with more than 200,000 volumes and 5,000 journal titles on zoology and animal conservation. Books date from the 16th Century. The library is open to the general public (reference only for non-members) but bring identification on your first visit. Applications to consult rare books should be made in advance, consult the online catalogue in the first instance.

# ONLINE RESOURCES

# WRITER'S SITES

## ABC Writers Network
- www.abcwritersnetwork.co.uk

**About** A free, international writer's forum, originating from Ireland.

## All Books Review
- www.allbookreviews.com

**About** A review site, largely for self published books.

## Ascriber/Writer's Eyes
- www.writerseyes.org

**About** A showcase site for unpublished, or self published writers. For a small fee you may display your work on the site, which the team claim to actively promote. The site also has sections for news, competitions and events, all of which are free to post in.

## Ask About Writing
- www.askaboutwriting.net

**About** A site containing information on writer's awards and competitions. There is also advice on aspects of writing, and advertisements for other services of use to writers.

## Ask Oxford
- www.askoxford.com

**About** A spin off from the Oxford English Dictionary. Includes tips on spelling, grammar and producing better writing, as well as stories of interest from around the globe.

## Authorbank
- www.authorbank.com

**About** For a fee of £25, members can upload a synopsis to be viewed by publishers who are also registered. Publishers can then approach the writer through Authorbank, who can act as literary agents. Submissions stay on view for six months. Additional submissions incur an additional £25 fee.

## Author Network

ⓦ www.author-network.com

**About** A site with articles, tips and resources for writers.

## Author's Den

ⓦ www.authorsden.com

**About** A free author's community site. Content includes book reviews, articles, e-books and more. Members get a free biography page.

## BBC Get Writing

ⓦ www.bbc.co.uk/getwriting

**About** A site full of resources, links, mini courses, quizzes and other inspiration and advice to encourage people to write.

## BBC Writer's Room

ⓦ www.bbc.co.uk/writersroom

**About** Offers advice on writing for the BBC. Potential BBC writers can submit scripts for consideration.

## Bloomsbury Writers' Area

ⓦ www.bloomsbury.com/writersarea

**About** Resources for writers and readers, with advice on how to get published. The site includes an invitation to join the Bloomsbury reading club.

## Chapter One Promotions

ⓦ www.chapteronepromotions.com

**About** A writer's site, which is also a literary agency and consultancy. Writers and illustrators may display their work on the site for a fee. There are details of events and competitions, and a section on resources for children.

## Freelance Writing Organization International

ⓦ www.fwointl.com

**About** A Canadian based members site, which is free to join. Contains many resources for writers, including forums, markets, research resources and more.

## The Frontlist

ⓦ www.thefrontlist.com

**About** A site whereby users upload samples of their work, and in turn provide several critiques of others' work. Once the critiques have been done, their own work will be put up for critique. Pieces scoring above a certain threshold will be put forward to specialist editors and agents. The Friday Project has published recent high scoring additions to this site in print. A £10 charge is made to view the critiques of your own work. You do not have to view them if you do not wish to, but they will still be sent forward if they score highly enough.

## Great Writing

ⓦ www.greatwriting.co.uk

**About** Great Writing is a volunteer-run online writing community that was formed after the closure of much of the BBCs 'Get Writing' service. It is free to join and offers members a chance to submit their own writing to the site for peer review, as well as providing writing forums and chat areas, articles, news and the occasional competition.

## Hackwriters

ⓦ www.hackwriters.com

**About** A free internet magazine which accepts submissions of travel writing, fiction, lifestyle and social comment, but does not pay any fees.

## Hopeful Writer

ⓦ www.hopefulwriter.co.uk

**About** A site containing links to writer and poet resources. The site is fairly small and has a lot of US content.

## Internet Writing Journal

ⓦ www.internetwritingjournal.com

**About** A US based online journal for writers, with lots of articles on writing itself. Other sections of the site include news, blogs and links.

## Journalism UK

ⓦ www.journalismuk.co.uk

**About** A small directory site of interest to UK journalists working in print.

## Merriam Webster

ⓦ www.m-w.com

**About** A US dictionary site with added features such as 'word of the day' and word games.

## National Novel Writing Month

☎ www.nanowrimo.com

**About** US site which challenges people to write a 50,000 word novel between the 1st and 30th November each year. If you make the deadline, you are a 'winner'. The idea is to encourage fast writing and not necessarily to focus on quality.

## Novelists Inc.

☎ www.ninc.com

**About** US based membership site with advice and practical help for fiction writers. Members' only sections include an agent guide and an email list.

## nthPosition

☎ www.nthposition.com

**About** A free online magazine/e-zine with politics & opinion, travel writing, fiction & poetry, reviews and interviews.

## One of Us

☎ www.oneofus.co.uk

**About** A resource site with articles, writing tips and a discussion forum. Free to access.

## Plays on the Net

☎ www.playsonthenet.com

**About** An online shop, specialising in the sale of books, plays and audio books. The site advertises writing competitions and has the facility for new playwrights to submit their work for public view.

## The Poetry Archive

☎ www.poetryarchive.org

**About** A site for poetry readings by well known poets. Users can download audio clips, read poems and also purchase poetry CDs.

## Prize Magic

☎ www.prizemagic.co.uk

**About** A site which contains a useful directory of writing competitions and the links to them.

## Proof Postive Writing Contests

☎ www.proofpositive.com/contests/ writecontests.php

**About** A US site advertising many writing contests, including those that are open to UK residents.

## Publisher's Lunch

☎ www.caderbooks.com

**About** A subscription-based free daily newsletter of news and events in publishing (US based). Publishing professionals may sign up to the deluxe service for a fee.

## The Publishing Law Center

☎ www.publaw.com

**About** US site containing useful information for publishers, editors, agents and writers on all aspects of publishing and its legal issues. They also offer a free newsletter.

## Reactive Writing

☎ www.reactivewriting.co.uk

**About** A site dedicated to exploring creative writing on the internet.

## Screenwriters Online

☎ www.screenwriter.com

**About** A US site with input from major Hollywood screenwriters. Offers a newsletter, industry analysis, master classes and links to other services.

## Scriberazone

☎ www.scriberazone.co.uk

**About** A poetry website that accepts submissions from the public, for online publication.

## Shaw Guides

☎ http://writing.shawguides.com

**About** This US based portal site allows users to search for writers, conferences and workshops, including those based in the UK.

## Trace

☎ http://tracearchive.ntu.ac.uk

**About** A free online resource linked to Nottingham Trent University. Trace provides a space for writers to meet, communicate, discuss work and be creative. Also offered through the site are courses, a consultancy service and a children's area.

## UK Children's Books

☎ www.ukchildrensbooks.co.uk

**About** A large site containing links to many publishers and authors of children's books, as well as other helpful organisations. The site is affiliated with

Word Pool, a resource site centred on children's books.

## WordCounter
www.wordcounter.com
**About** A site that allows you to copy and paste text into a field and check for repetitions. In a separate field you may also check your writing for political leanings.

## Write4Kids
www.write4kids.com
**About** US site, with many free resources and advice on writing for children. The site also has a free newsletter.

## Write a Book Now
www.writeabooknow.com
**About** US site with a free email course on the various aspects of getting published. There is a strong emphasis on shortcuts and speediness. You may sign up for email newsletters, or read articles directly from the site.

## Write Away
www.writeaway.co.uk
**About** A membership site, which offers a writers' community forum, access to editors and library information staff, plus the option of paying for appraisal services. The team can also advise on self publishing and sell your books through the site. Lifetime membership from £17.75.

## Write Link
www.writelink.co.uk
**About** A membership site where work in progress is rated by other members. Once the work is at a certain level, it gets linked to the resources area, which contains information on paying markets. Each piece published in the resources area earns £20. There is a discussion forum and subscription is free, although if you want the chance to submit work for review, you must pay a fee.

## Writernet
www.writernet.co.uk
**About** A site dedicated to writers of drama, designed to act as a networking and resource site.

## Writers' Circles
www.writers-circles.com
**About** A directory of writer's circles across the country that is available to buy in print, or search online. The site links to other resources, such as writing competitions and contains small market directory sections, including agents and magazines.

## Writers Free Reference
www.writers-free-reference.com
**About** A free portal site containing links to many other sites, resources and articles of interest to writers.

## Writer's Market UK
www.writersmarket.co.uk
**About** The sister site to this book, packed with all the directory listings and hundreds more that we couldn't fit in the book, updated daily. Also contains writers' resources, articles, community features and current writing and publishing news, plus much more. Subscription fee.

## Writer's Market US
www.writersmarket.com
**About** A subscription based site with access to thousands of frequently updated US writing markets, plus advice, tips and resources.

## Writers Net
www.writers.net
**About** A US site, containing information for writers, editors, agents and publishers. The site contains lists of US contacts and has a discussion forum.

## Writers Promote
www.writerspromote.com
**About** A membership site, where for £48 per year writers in the UK and US can help each other promote and sell their books online and at bookfairs. Published and self published authors may join. Each person receives a web page and email address linked to the site.

## WritersReign
www.writersreign.co.uk
**About** A resources site for writers, containing a small directory of publishers, competitions, courses, links to other useful sites and advice on writing.

## Writers Services
⊕ www.writersservices.com
**About** A very full site with information, services and advice for writers.

## Writers Write
⊕ www.writerswrite.com
**About** US resource site, which contains articles and links of interest to writers.

## Writing World
⊕ www.writing-world.com
**About** A US site full of articles on writing and publishing. There are also links to freelance job opportunities and a book shop.

# RESEARCH & LANGUAGE SITES

## A2A
⊕ www.a2a.org.uk
**About** A site allowing users to search for information from 18th century archives in England and Wales. Potentially useful for historical and non-fiction writers.

## AbeBooks
⊕ www.abebooks.co.uk
**About** An online marketplace for books, particularly rare and out of print editions. Useful for research material and information on the independent bookselling world.

## Alt-X
⊕ www.altx.com
**About** A site dedicated to the various forms of online publishing. As well as the opportunity to buy e-books, the site contains comments and discussion on aspects of the online world, in particular how it meets the world of literature and publishing.

## Ananova
⊕ www.ananova.com
**About** A good resource for journalists, the site contains all the latest UK news headlines, as well as 'quirkies', a selection of more unusual stories.

## Ancestry
⊕ www.ancestry.com
**About** A site offering genealogical data. Potentially useful for historical fiction and non-fiction writers.

## Bartleby
⊕ www.bartleby.com
**About** A site containing many free resources, book extracts and quotations. Users can search through texts from fiction, non-fiction, verse and reference. Includes an online version of Roget's Thesaurus.

## Bible Gateway
⊕ www.biblegateway.com
**About** A site which allows you to search for extracts from the Bible.

## Bibliomania
⊕ www.bibliomania.com
**About** A research site featuring many free book extracts, study guides, articles, interviews and reference texts.

## British Library
⊕ www.bl.uk
**About** The British Library's vast site contains information about the Library, the scope of its collections, thousands of images and hundreds of sound samples. It offers free searches of major reference and document collections, and has areas for researchers and students.

## Channel 4 Ideas Factory
⊕ www.ideasfactory.com
**About** A site full of resources for those interested in the media, with a specific section on writing. Contains interviews, articles, videos and advice.

## CIA World Fact Book
⊕ www.cia.gov/cia/publications/factbook
**About** A useful, searchable resource, with information and statistics on individual countries. The publication is also available to download.

## The Complete Works of William Shakespeare
⊕ www-tech.mit.edu/shakespeare
**About** A fairly static site that contains full text versions of Shakespeare's complete works.

## Corsinet

ⓦ www.corsinet.com

**About** A site full of supposedly 'useless' information, including famous deathbed quotes, 'Brain Candy' and general trivia.

## Cross Ref

ⓦ www.crossref.org

**About** A membership website, which allows users to gain access to primary research sources and citations, by cross referencing with other people's work.

## Dictionary of Slang

ⓦ www.dictionaryofslang.co.uk

**About** A searchable dictionary of slang words.

## Encyclopaedia Britannica

ⓦ www.britannica.com

**About** A searchable encyclopaedia site full of general knowledge and specialist resources. Some parts of the site are free and others require a subscription. A free trial is offered.

## The English Server

ⓦ http://eserver.org

**About** A collection of online literary work. Also has a community support element.

## Etext

ⓦ www.etext.org

**About** An archive of past e-texts, including e-zines and online poetry.

## Frankfurt Book Fair

ⓦ www.frankfurt-book-fair.com

**About** The site that accompanies the Frankfurt Book Fair.

## Free Pint

ⓦ www.freepint.com

**About** An online community, with almost 80,000 researchers. Members receive a free newsletter with news and tips on researching and information sources. The Free Pint bar is a facility where specific questions can be posted. A good resource for those wanting to conduct large amounts of research, or Information gathering.

## The Good Web Guide

ⓦ www.thegoodwebguide.co.uk

**About** A review site, which lists thousands of websites and their ratings. A good starting place to check the reliability of websites for research.

## Guide to Grammar and Style

ⓦ www.andromeda.rutgers.edu/~jlynch/writing

**About** A US site, which contains many tips and resources on correct grammar and good writing style.

## Ingenta

ⓦ www.ingentaconnect.com

**About** A bibliographic database site for academic research. Membership is required, although access is often free through educational institutions if you are a student. Users may then search journals and articles and, depending on level of membership, gain access to either the abstract or the full text.

## Internet Classics Archive

ⓦ http://classics.mit.edu

**About** A database of classical writing in Greek, Latin, Chinese and Peruvian. All are translated into English, although many of the originals are available.

## Internet Movie Database

ⓦ www.imdb.com

**About** An enormous searchable database of actors, films, television programmes and other entertainment. Enter a search term and the site will pull up all references across all genres, and provide detailed information such as an actor's entire biography, or a film's entire credits. All are cross referenced.

## Internet Public Library

ⓦ www.ipl.org

**About** Started by students at The University of Michigan, the site has grown into a large set of resources for researchers. Users can search by topics, categories or keywords. Sections include magazines, encyclopaedias, dictionaries and blogs.

## Internet Writing Journal

🌐 www.internetwritingjournal.com

**About** A US online journal for writers, including many articles on writing itself. Other sections of the site include news, blogs and many links.

## Location Register of 20th Century English Literary Manuscripts and Letters

🌐 www.library.rdg.ac.uk/colls/projects/locreg.html

**About** A searchable site detailing the current homes of many literary manuscripts in Britain, as well as recordings and letters. The database includes small museums, as well as large institutions and is not limited to just well known pieces of work.

## London Book Fair

🌐 www.londonbookfair.co.uk

**About** Information on all aspects of Britain's largest trade book fair.

## Murder Files

🌐 www.murderfiles.com

**About** A site detailing murders, past and present. Users can pay for information on crimes they want to know more about. Particularly good for historical fiction and crime writers. The website also provides links to other useful sites.

## Oxford Text Archive

🌐 www.ota.ahds.ac.uk

**About** A collection of online texts in literature, arts and humanities. This site is not very regularly updated.

## Ref Desk

🌐 www.refdesk.com

**About** A large site full of weird and wonderful facts, trivia and links to other interesting sites.

## Rhyme Zone

🌐 www.rhymezone.com

**About** Type in a word and the site will come back with a list of words that rhyme with it.

## Rimbaud

🌐 www.rimbaud.org.uk

**About** Dee Rimbaud's site for writers looking to get their work published. Articles, advice, resources and listings are all part of the content.

## The Science Fiction Hub

🌐 www.sfhub.ac.uk

**About** A portal site for readers, writers and students of science fiction.

## Shakespeare at eNotes

🌐 www.shakespeare.com

**About** A portal to many Shakespeare resources, including notes and study guides.

## Sourcewire

🌐 http://sourcewire.com

**About** A site for business and technology journalists, featuring up to the minute press releases, and other resources such as industry events and jobs.

## They Work for You

🌐 www.theyworkforyou.com

**About** A site containing a vast amount of political information, including Hansard debates (House of Commons), and a searchable database of MPs and Lords. Good for providing general contextual information, as well as for specific research to inform political writing.

## United Kingdom Parliament

🌐 www.parliament.uk

**About** The site contains access to many research reports and general information on parliament.

## Virtual Perpetual Calendars

🌐 www.vpcalendar.net

**About** A site for checking dates and their corresponding days of the week, from 1900 onwards. Great for historical accuracy.

## WATCH

🌐 http://tyler.hrc.utexas.edu

**About** A limited site, which features a searchable database of who to contact, if using particular copyrighted material. Hosted in the UK by the

University of Reading and in the US by the University of Texas.

## What's on When

ⓦ www.whatsonwhen.com

**About** An international events calendar, possibly useful for journalists, reviewers, or general research.

## World Wide Words

ⓦ www.worldwidewords.org

**About** A site exploring the worldwide use of the English language, looked at from a British viewpoint. Contains definitions, language information and other resources.

## Write Brain

ⓦ www.write-brain.com

**About** As well as selling software, the website links to many other useful sites for researchers and writers. Users may search by research category.

# WRITING SOFTWARE

## ADM

ⓦ www.adm21.net

**About** An 'advanced data management' tool, that could be of use to research heavy projects such as academic writing, non-fiction, or historical fiction. Costs $129.99.

## Book Writer

ⓦ www.yadudigital.com

**About** A downloadable piece of software, designed to simplify and organise the process of writing a book. A free trial is granted for 30 days, after which you may buy a single user licence for $44.95.

## Dramatica

ⓦ www.dramatica.com

**About** A site selling screenwriting software. Costs $269.

## Dreamascript

ⓦ www.dreamascript.com

**About** Scriptwriting software. Costs around £120.

## Film Angel

ⓦ www.filmangel.co.uk

**About** A site for screenwriters. Writers may post synopses of their work on the site for a fee and potential investors, or 'angels' can request further information. Clients may also commission tailor made films, for a substantial fee, that may act as showcases for their writing, or acting talents.

## Final Draft

ⓦ www.finaldraft.com

**About** Downloadable, professional scriptwriting software. Costs $229.

## Idea Tracker

ⓦ www.intellectusenterprises.com/ideatracker.html

**About** An online application, a license for which can be bought for $39.95. Designed to help sort, organise and track ideas.

## New Novelist

ⓦ www.newnovelist.com

**About** A software package, which helps to write a novel, aiding with editing, structure, characterisation and plot. Costs around £30.

## Screenforge

ⓦ www.apotheosispictures.com

**About** A downloadable software package for scriptwriters, that works with Microsoft Word. An initial 45 day trial period is offered, after which the software must be registered for $45.

## Storycraft Pro

ⓦ www.storycraftpro.com

**About** A website offering a variety of packages, based around the Jarvis method of fiction writing. Prices range from $49–$129 and software is available as a CD, or a download.

## StyleWriter

ⓦ www.editorsoftware.com

**About** A word processor add on package that checks writing against a large database of style and usage issues, picking up on any inconsistencies, or poor practice in writing style. Costs £110 + VAT.

### Write Brain
🌐 www.write-brain.com

**About** A site selling a wide variety of software packages for writers, including screenwriting and novel writing aids.

### Write it Now
🌐 www.ravensheadservices.com

**About** A downloadable package designed to help write and store complete novels. After a free trial, the registration fee is £19.95, which allows users to download add ons from the website.

### Writer's Blocks
🌐 www.writersblocks.com

**About** A software package that allows writers to organise their notes, research and writing into 'blocks'. These can then be easily manipulated and amalgamated.

### Writer's Café
🌐 www.writerscafe.co.uk

**About** A storywriting software package, available as a CD or a download. Costs £32.90.

### Z-Write
🌐 www.stonetablesoftware.com

**About** A writing package solely for Macs, combining the functions of a word processor with a project manager. You may download Z-Write free of charge, but after two weeks it reverts to a demo version and you must pay to upgrade.

## STUDENT RESOURCES

# GENERAL STUDENT WEBSITES

### British Universities Sports Association
🌐 www.busa.org.uk

**About** Website of the British Universities Sports Association (BUSA). Includes news, fixtures and results from UK universities with BUSA membership.

### Fresh Direction
🌐 www.freshdirection.com

**About** General student information, news and discussion.

### HERO
🌐 www.hero.ac.uk

**About** Official gateway to universities, colleges and research organisations in the UK. The site is full of higher education information and links, including a comprehensive section on study skills.

### Lazy Student
🌐 www.lazystudent.co.uk

**About** Lazystudent is the UK's most comprehensive student website. It links to hundreds of other sites, with commentary and star ratings.

### National Union of Students
🌐 www.nusonline.co.uk

**About** Information about student campaigns, student life and discounts for NUS cardholders.

### NewStudent
🌐 www.newstudent.org

**About** Advice for new and prospective students.

### One Life
🌐 www.bbc.co.uk/radio1/onelife/

**About** BBC Radio One's online guide to life and key issues for young people. The site includes advice on health, relationships, sex, drugs, travel, work and education.

## Push Online

🌐 www.push.co.uk/

**About** A website that gives information on UK universities and advice about life as a student. Includes an excellent jargon buster.

## The Site

🌐 www.thesite.org

**About** Owned and run by YouthNet UK, this website offers support and guidance for young adults (age 16-24). It provides fact sheets and articles on the key issues they face. There is also an online community, offering peer to peer discussion and support.

## Student Accommodation UK

🌐 www.studentpad.co.uk

**About** A site that helps students find accommodation. It also includes advice and a comprehensive housing guide.

## Studentastic

🌐 www.studentastic.co.uk

**About** Founded in 2005 to offer a reference point on how to survive as a student. The site features articles written by experts on accommodation, work, relationships, and exams.

## Student Hampers

🌐 www.studenthampers.com

**About** A site offering student treats, delivered straight to the door.

## Student Health

🌐 www.studenthealth.com

**About** Dedicated health site for students.

## StudentUK.com

🌐 www.studentuk.com

**About** Help and advice for students on many topics, including studying, jobs, health, accommodation and travel. There are also chat forums and a guide to UK universities and colleges.

## Studentzone

🌐 www.studentzone.org.uk

**About** All round site offering information and links on studying, careers, legal issues and finance, health, sport and entertainment.

## Support4learning

🌐 www.support4learning.org.uk

**About** Resource links for advisors and students, or anyone involved in education and training. The site has information about finance and supporting education, training, career planning and job searching.

## Universities and Colleges Admissions Service for the UK

🌐 www.ucas.co.uk

**About** Comprehensive information about getting into higher education, and student issues. Includes a selection of information for parents.

## Woman Student

🌐 www.womanstudent.co.uk

**About** A site offering student and life issues, from a female perspective.

# LEARNING RESOURCES

## AskOxford.com

🌐 www.askoxford.com

**About** The site allows you to search the compact English Dictionary, ask a grammar question, or get spelling and grammar tips. It also offers a section where you can find out the meaning of your name, and get help with CV and job applications.

## Atlapedia Online

🌐 www.atlapedia.com

**About** Maps, key facts and statistics on countries of the world.

## Cambridge Dictionaries Online

🌐 http://dictionary.cambridge.org/

**About** Choose the dictionary you require and look up words and phrases.

## Foreignword.com

🌐 www.foreignword.com

**About** A global dictionary, which searches in 275 dictionaries on the internet. The site translates from 69 source languages, into 73 target languages.

### How to get a First
ⓦ www.howtogetafirst.co.uk
**About** Advice from a student who achieved a first class degree.

### The Internet Public Library
ⓦ www.ipl.org/
**About** A site founded by the University of Michigan School of Information. Extensive resources are available, including the 'Ask a Question' reference service.

### Intute:virtual training suite
ⓦ www.vts.intute.ac.uk
**About** Subject specific, the site offers free online tutorials, which are designed to improve internet information literacy.

### Presenters University
ⓦ www.presentersuniversity.com
**About** Tips and downloads for better presentations. The site is designed for businesses, but is useful for students too.

### Researchtogether.com
ⓦ www.researchtogether.com
**About** A useful site for researchers. Allows users to search for others doing similar work and compare notes.

### Skills4study
ⓦ www.palgrave.com/skills4study/index.asp
**About** Practical advice for studying more effectively in higher education, from one of the leading academic publishers.

### Thesaurus.com
ⓦ http://thesaurus.reference.com/
**About** Offers a thesaurus, dictionary, encyclopedia and general online reference.

### The UK Grad Programme
ⓦ www.grad.ac.uk
**About** Support and advice for postgraduates. The 'Just for Postgrads' section on the site gives information on managing research and careers.

### Using English for Academic Purposes
ⓦ www.uefap.com
**About** Advice for UK and international students, on writing and related study skills.

### VARK - a guide to learning styles
ⓦ www.vark-learn.com
**About** Allows you to find out your preferred learning style with its online questionnaire.

### Yourdictionary.com
ⓦ www.yourdictionary.com
**About** Free online dictionary and thesaurus, with definitions, audio pronunciation and correct grammar usage.

# STUDENTS WITH DISABILITIES

### Department for Work and Pensions (DWP)
ⓦ www.disability.gov.uk
**About** Information for disabled people and carers.

### National Bureau for Students with Disabilities
ⓦ www.skill.org.uk/
**About** A national charity promoting opportunities for young people with any kind of impairment in 16 plus education, training, or employment. The website offers comprehensive information, profiles and a series of free downloadable booklets.

### Ouch
ⓦ www.bbc.co.uk/ouch/lifefiles/student
**About** A BBC website about life as a student with disabilities.

# MONEY

### Department for Education and Skills
ⓦ www.dfes.gov.uk/studentsupport/
**About** Financial information for students in higher education, including a section for parents.

### Discounts for Students
🌐 www.discounts4students.net
**About** An online directory for students, with offers, services and discounts.

### HM Revenue & Customs
🌐 www.hmrc.gov.uk/taxandu
**About** Accessible information about student tax matters.

### S-k-i-n-t
🌐 www.s-k-i-n-t.co.uk
**About** Money savers, quizzes and competitions for students.

### Student Awards Agency for Scotland
🌐 www.student-support-saas.gov.uk
**About** Financial support and advice for Scottish students.

### Student Finance Direct
🌐 www.studentsupportdirect.co.uk
**About** Information about financial support for students in further, or higher education in England.

### Student Finance NI
🌐 www.studentfinanceni.co.uk
**About** Information about financial support for students in further, or higher education in Northern Ireland.

### Student Finance Wales
🌐 www.studentfinancewales.co.uk
**About** Information about financial support for students in further, or higher education in Wales.

### Student Free Stuff
🌐 www.studentfreestuff.com
**About** A site offering free deals for students. Also includes a student guide and lots of links to other student sites.

### Student Loans Company Ltd
🌐 www.slc.co.uk
**About** Access to key information about student loans and the Student Loans Company UK.

# BOOKS & MAGAZINES

### Academic Book Trade
🌐 www.academicbooktrade.co.uk
**About** Listing and information service for used academic books.

### Scrounge.it Books
🌐 http://books.scrounge.it
**About** Finds the best deals for buying books.

### Student Subscription Service
🌐 www.student-subscription-service.co.uk/
**About** Offers cheap magazine subscriptions for students and teachers.

### Student Subscription Service (Ireland)
🌐 www.student-subscription-service.ie
**About** Offers cheap magazine subscriptions for students in Ireland.

### Study Bookshop
🌐 www.studybookshop.com
**About** A second hand text book website.

# INTERNATIONAL STUDENTS

### British Council
🌐 www.britishcouncil.org
**About** Information on teaching English worldwide. The website also includes information about studying in the UK.

### Hobsons Study UK
🌐 www.studyuk.hobsons.com
**About** Information and advice for international students about living and studying in the UK.

### HostUK
🌐 www.hostuk.org.uk
**About** An organisation that brings international students at universities and colleges in the UK together with British residents, who then welcome students into their homes for a short visit.

### International Students Union
ⓦ www.isu.org.uk
**About** Founded in 2002 by a group of international students from several London universities, ISU is run by students and open to students all over the world.

### Okey Dokey
ⓦ www.okey-dokey.co.uk
**About** A free website for students learning English.

### Studystay.com
ⓦ www.studystay.com
**About** UK study guide for international students.

### UKCOSA: The Council for International Education
ⓦ www.ukcosa.org.uk
**About** Advice and guidance for international students (and their families) planning to study in the UK. The site also has information for UK students thinking about studying abroad.

### UK Student Life
ⓦ www.ukstudentlife.com
**About** A comprehensive guide and links to student life in the UK (aimed at international students).

# CAREERS & QUALIFICATIONS

### Everything You Wanted to Know
ⓦ www.everythingyouwantedtoknow.com
**About** Everything you wanted to know about university, sponsorship, placements and graduate opportunities. Offers advice on student finance, careers and how to make the most of university.

### Foundation Degree Forward
ⓦ www.fdf.ac.uk
**About** Information on foundation degrees; includes a student guide to this relatively new qualification.

### Graduate Prospects
ⓦ www.prospects.ac.uk
**About** The UK's official graduate careers website. Excellent, comprehensive careers advice and information on postgraduate studies.

### Mind Tools
ⓦ www.mindtools.com/
**About** Online career and learning tools.

# WORKING STUDENTS

### Department for Education and Skills
ⓦ www.dfes.gov.uk/international-students/wituk.shtml
**About** Information for international students on working in the UK.

### Morethanwork
ⓦ www.morethanwork.net
**About** A website for all working students. Identify your skills, build a CV and find out about employment rights.

### Trouble at Work
ⓦ www.troubleatwork.org.uk
**About** A website with up to date information and advice for working students with job problems.

### Work Smart
ⓦ www.worksmart.org.uk
**About** Guide to working, from the TUC. The site has a page of information for working students.

# TRAVEL

### Foreign & Commonwealth Office
ⓦ www.fco.gov.uk/
**About** This site has a country by country travel advice section, including a risk assessment of threats from terrorism. The FCO runs the 'Know Before You Go' campaign.

### Go Gap Year
ⓦ www.gogapyear.com
**About** Tips and useful hints on planning your gap year travels.

### Intern Abroad
ⓦ www.internabroad.com
**About** Lists overseas internship opportunities.

### Lonely Planet
🌐 www.lonelyplanet.com
**About** Travel advice, guidebooks and information for the independent traveller.

### Rough Guides
🌐 www.roughguides.com
**About** Online information for travel destinations.

### Tours4students
🌐 www.tours4students.co.uk
**About** Specialist student tour operator, for large or small groups.

### Travellers Worldwide
🌐 www.travellersworldwide.com/
**About** Voluntary work placements overseas.

### Travel Line
🌐 www.traveline.org.uk
**About** UK public transport information.

### Working Travel Directory
🌐 www.workingtravel.co.uk
**About** An online working travel directory, free to use.

# SECONDHAND BOOKS

### AbeBooks
**AbeBooks Europe GmbH, Ronsdorfer Strasse 77a, Germany, 40233 DŸsseldorf**
✉ info@abebooks.co.uk
🌐 www.abebooks.co.uk
**About** The world's largest site for new, second hand, rare and out of print books. Over 100,000,000 titles listed.

### A Book for All Reasons
**Rockville House, 6 Pakefield Road, Lowestoft, Suffolk, NR33 0HS**
🌐 www.2nd-hand-books.co.uk
**Contact** G. A. Michael Sims
**About** A resources site for booksellers and book collectors. Includes information on databases, repair services, book prizes and book searches.

### Academic Book Trade
**82 Prebend Street, London, N1 8PR**
🌐 www.academicbooktrade.co.uk
**About** An online marketplace for students and academics to trade used books. Includes a fully searchable database of all books for sale, as well as a 'wanted' facility.

### Alibris
🌐 www.alibris.co.uk
**About** A large international database of second hand, new, out of print, foreign language, and hard

to find titles. There are over 60,000,000 titles in the database.

### Amazon
🌐 www.amazon.co.uk
**About** As well as selling new books, Amazon also acts as a marketplace for used books worldwide.

### Barter Books
**Alnwick Station, Northumberland, NE66 2NP**
☎ 01665 604888
✉ bb@barterbooks.co.uk
🌐 www.barterbooks.co.uk
**About** A Northumberland based independent bookshop, with a large online catalogue and purchase facility. Sells both fiction and non-fiction books.

### Biblio.com
🌐 www.biblio.com
**About** A US based service, allowing users to search for used, rare, and out of print books from booksellers around the world. The list contains more than 45,000,000 books.

### Biblion
**Biblion Bookshop, Davies Mews, London, W1K 5AB**
🌐 http://biblion.co.uk

**About** A London bookshop with an online facility, allowing users to find dealers for second hand and rare books.

## Book Lovers
🌐 www.booklovers.co.uk
**About** Lists over 350,000 books from independent dealers. Also sells bibliographies and runs a book valuation service.

## The Bookshop
**17 North Main Street, Wigtown, DG8 9HL**
☎ 01988 402499
✉ mail@the-bookshop.com
🌐 www.the-bookshop.com
**About** A secondhand bookshop located in the Scottish national book town, Wigtown. It also has a fully searchable online catalogue, in conjunction with Biblio, www.biblio.com/bookstores/wigtown

## Byre Books
**24 South Main Street, Wigtown, DG8 9EH**
☎ 0845 458 3813
✉ enquiries@byrebooks.co.uk
🌐 www.byrebooks.co.uk
**About** A bookshop in Wigtown, the Scottish national book town. It specialises in books on folklore and mythology, theatre, film and television, and books of Scottish interest. The website can take secure orders and contains a large online catalogue.

## Discovery Bookshop
**52 Cwmamman Road, Garnant, Ammanford, South Wales, SA18 1LT**
☎ 01269 823839
🌐 www.discoverybookshop.co.uk
**About** A shop in South Wales, which has its web presence in conjunction with AbeBooks. The site sells second hand books, records, CDs, sheet music, videos, cassettes and reel to reel tapes.

## Dusty Books
**The Old Woollen Mill, Shortbridge Street, Llanidloes, Powys, SY18 6AD**
☎ 01686 411247
☎ 01686 411248
✉ scribe@dustybooks.co.uk
🌐 www.dustybooks.co.uk
**About** A searchable online shop of used, rare and out of print books.

## eBay
🌐 www.ebay.co.uk
**About** The auction site contains a category for books, comics and magazines, both new and used.

## Hay on Wye Bookshops
🌐 www.hay-on-wye.co.uk/bookshops
**About** A directory of the many second hand bookshops and booksellers in Hay on Wye, Hereford.

## Inprint/The Book Guide
**31 High Street, Stroud, GL5 1AJ**
☎ 01453 759731
✉ enquiries@inprint.co.uk
🌐 www.inprint.co.uk
**About** A bookshop selling second hand and out of print books, it also has a full online catalogue and purchase facility. They are specialists in out of print books about the cinema. The Book Guide is a resource area with a searchable database of second hand bookshops in the UK by region. Also contains information on book fairs and auctions.

## Mary Ward Books
**Blyford, Halesworth, Suffolk, IP19 9JR**
☎ 01986 875543
✉ sales@marywardbooks.com
**About** An independent online bookstore specialising in second hand books, out of print books and used books. As well as the online search facility, there are many titles offline that can be requested.

## UK Book World
🌐 www.ukbookworld.com
**About** Allows users to search databases containing 1,000,000 old and out of print books for dealers and sellers across the world.

## UK Christian Bookshops Directory
✉ ukcbd.enquiries@christianbookshops.org.uk
🌐 www.christianbookshops.org.uk
**Contact** Phil Groom
**About** A directory of UK Christian bookshops, including a list of those who stock second hand, rare and out of print books.

## Used Book Search

◉ contact@usedbooksearch.co.uk
ⓦ www.usedbooksearch.co.uk

**About** A large search facility, allowing users to locate second hand books from databases including AbeBooks, WH Smith, Amazon and Biblion.

## Word Power Bookshop

**43 West Nicolson Street, Edinburgh, EH8 9DB**

☎ 0131 662 9112
☎ 0131 662 9112
◉ books@word-power.co.uk
ⓦ www.word-power.co.uk

**About** An independent bookshop in Scotland with a fully developed online service which can source and deliver any book in print, as well as their core list of literature outside the mainstream. They aim to increase the profile of small presses and new writers by fostering debate and selling, at times, radical books.

## Zardiz Books

**20 Whitecroft, Dilton Marsh, Westbury, Wiltshire, BA13 4DJ**

☎ 01373 865371
☎ 01373 303984
◉ mflanagan@zardozbooks.co.uk
ⓦ www.zardozbooks.co.uk

**Contact** Maurice Flanagan

**About** A collectible and out of print book dealer. Also sells books via auction on eBay.

Bursaries, fellowships and awards are included here because they are often educational in the sense that they provide opportunities for work experience of many kinds. Many awards are directed specifically at new writers and new writing. Some are aimed at recent graduates. Courses include those specifically to do with writing, journalism, etc; read David Penfold's article in the front section of this book for ideas on related creative courses.

## BURSARIES, FELLOWSHIPS & GRANTS

### ABSW Student Journalism Bursaries
**Association of British Science Writers, Wellcome Wolfson Building, 165 Queen's Gate, London, SW7 5HD**

☎ 0870 770 3361

🌐 www.absw.org.uk/bursaries.htm

**About** Nine bursaries are offered to students taking a science communication course (seven for full time courses, two for part time). Bursaries are designed to cover course fees and living expenses. Candidates must be able to demonstrate a background in science, an aptitude for communication and a lack of alternative sources for funding. Applications should consist of a CV, a 500 word stated case for the bursary and completion of a set exercise. An application form is available on the website.

### The Airey Neave Trust
**PO Box 36800, 40 Bernard Street, London, WC1N 1WJ**

☎ 020 7833 4440

✉ hanthoc@aol.com

🌐 www.aireyneavetrust.org.uk

**Contact** Mrs. Hannah Scott

**About** Offers fellowships for scholars wishing to undertake research in the field of 'human freedom'. Masters and PhD students are discouraged from applying. There is no application form and applicants should submit a research plan for either one or two years, of not more than 500 words, giving a synopsis of the planned research and a more detailed account suitable for an expert referee's judgment.

### Alfred Bradley Bursary Award
**BBC Writers Room, 379–381 Euston Road, London, NW1 3AU**

🌐 www.bbc.co.uk/writersroom/opportunity

**About** A biennial radio drama award in memory of Alfred Bradley, a distinguished BBC radio writer. The winner is awarded a bursary of up to £6,000 and a commission for an afternoon play on BBC Radio 4. Applicants must have been born in the North of England, been bought up there, or currently live in the region. Applicants cannot have had a play produced by the BBC in the past. To apply, send a hardcopy of an original 45 minute play of around 7,000 words. Most recent closing date was November 2006. Previous winners include Julia Copus and Katie Douglas.

### The Authors' Foundation
**The Society of Authors, 84 Drayton Gardens, London, SW10 9SB**

☎ 020 7373 6642

☎ 020 7373 5768

✉ info@societyofauthors.org

🌐 www.societyofauthors.org

**About** Grants are available for writers who are already commissioned by a British publisher to write a full length work of fiction, poetry, or non-fiction. There are also grants for those that have been previously published and can demonstrate a strong likelihood they will be published in Britain again. Money is designed to assist with the research, travel and living costs that a publisher's advance may not cover. The twice-yearly grants, awarded in April and September, are normally between £1,000 and £2,000, and rarely exceed £4,000. Applicants should include: a brief history of their writing career; details of their current work; size of advance (if any); names of publishers already approached, or working with; overall financial position and why the grant is needed; details of past grants; and copies of past reviews (if any). Full application details are available on the website.

LISTINGS  EDUCATION

## BBC News Sponsorship Scheme

ⓦ www.bbc.co.uk/jobs/nss

**About** Open to current or past students of BJTC accredited courses in any aspect of journalism. A bursary of £5,000 is awarded for living expenses and course fees are paid, or reimbursed. Successful candidates will undertake work placements and training and will be assigned a mentor. Check the website for details of 2007 and 2008 schemes.

## British Academy Research Funding

**10 Carlton House Terrace, London, SW1Y 5AH**

ⓞ 020 7969 5217

ⓞ 020 7969 5414

ⓔ grants@britac.ac.uk

ⓦ www.britac.ac.uk

**About** Research grants are awarded at postdoctoral or equivalent level, for researchers in the humanities and social sciences fields. Application forms are available for both small (up to £7,500) and large (up to £100,000) awards, reflecting the size and scope of different research proposals.

## Charles Pick Fellowship

**School of Literature and Creative Writing, University of East Anglia, University Plain, Norwich, NR4 7TJ**

ⓞ 01603 592286

ⓞ 01603 507728

ⓔ charlespickfellowship@uea.ac.uk

ⓦ www.uea.ac.uk/eas/fellowships/pick.shtml

**About** A six month bursary of £10,000 in memory of Charles Pick, a publisher and literary agent. Applicants must be unpublished writers of fictional or non-fictional prose (excluding reports from academic research). Winners will be picked on the strength of their writing proposal and references from editors, agents or accredited creative writing teachers. Fellows must reside at the University of East Anglia. Shared office space and computer facilities will be made available for the Fellow in the School of Literature and Creative Writing. The Fellow will be required to submit written work to a nominated mentor and take part in Creative Writing Research Seminars, however there are no teaching duties.

## David T. K. Wong Fellowship

**School of Literature and Creative Writing, University of East Anglia, University Plain, Norwich, NR4 7TJ**

ⓞ 01603 592286

ⓞ 01603 507728

ⓔ davidtkwongfellowship@uea.ac.uk

ⓦ www.uea.ac.uk/eas/fellowships/wong/wong/shtml

**About** An annual grant of around £25,000 to enable a writer to spend a year based at the University of East Anglia writing a work of fiction incorporating an aspect of life in the Far East as a subject matter. Applicants may be of any nationality.

## E. M. Forster Award

**American Academy of Arts and Literature, 633 West 155th Street, New York, NY 10032**

ⓞ 001 212 368 5900

ⓦ www.artsandletters.org

**About** Proceeds from the royalties of Forster's novel Maurice are put towards an annual award of $15,000 for young British writer to stay in the United States.

## European Jewish Publication Society

**PO Box 19949, London, N3 3ZL**

ⓞ 020 8346 1668

ⓞ 020 8346 1776

ⓔ cs@ejps.org.uk

ⓦ www.ejps.org.uk

**Contact** Dr. Colin Shindler

**About** The society supplies grants to publishers of up to £3,000 for assistance in the publication of Jewish interest books, both fiction and non-fiction (£1,000 for poetry). Assistance is also given with the marketing and promotion of the title once published. Potential applicants must firstly approach a publisher, and then the publisher must contact the society. Recent examples of books include; Photographing the Holocaust by Janina Struck and The Arab-Israeli Cookbook by Robin Soans.

## Fulbright Awards

**The Fulbright Commission, Fulbright House, 62 Doughty Street, London, WC1N 2JZ**

ⓞ 020 7404 6880

ⓞ 020 7404 6834

ⓔ programme@fulbright.co.uk

ⓦ www.fulbright.co.uk

**Contact** British Programme Manager

**About** A set of postgraduate awards, one in journalism, to fund British students undertaking courses at American universities (first year only). Students must research and apply to each university course themselves. Either apply on the website, or send an S.A.E with enough postage to cover 100g.

Include a covering letter stating which award you require information on.

## The George Viner Memorial Fund Trust
**Headland House, 308–312 Grays Inn Road, London, WC1X 8DP**
- 020 7843 3723
- 020 7278 6617
- georgeviner@nuj.org.uk
- www.georgeviner.org.uk

**About** Sponsorship opportunities facilitated by the National Union of Journalists. They are granted once a year for potential students from ethnic minority backgrounds who have been accepted onto a course, but cannot accept for financial reasons. Check website for application details. Deadlines are normally in August.

## Guardian Research Fellowship
**Nuffield College, Oxford, OX1 1NF**
- 01865 278542
- 01865 278666

**Contact** Academic Administrator, S. Wright

**About** A year long fellowship, endowed by the Scott Trust, owner of the Guardian newspaper. The fellowship enables a media professional to put their experiences into a published report and give a lecture. Applicants include journalists, managers and broadcasters. The research proposals must be linked to working in the media.

## Hawthornden Literary Institute
**Hawthornden International Retreat for Writers, Lasswade, EH18 1EG**
- 0131 440 2180
- 0131 440 1989

**About** Hawthornden provides a quiet retreat for up to six writers to concentrate on their work. Writers that win access to this facility are known as Hawthornden fellows. Fellows become guests of the retreat once they have arrived, but no travel expenses are paid. Application forms can be requested by telephone or fax and must be returned by the end of November for retreats the following year.

## Jerwood Awards
**The Royal Society of Literature, Somerset House, Strand, London, WC2R 1LA**
- 020 7845 4676

- paulaj@rslit.org
- www.rslit.org

**Contact** Paula Johnson

**About** Three annual awards, one of £10,000 and two of £5,000, to authors engaged on their first major commissioned works of non-fiction. Open to first time writers resident in the UK or Ireland for at least three years and who have been firmly contracted to write a piece of non-fiction. Applicants should send a covering letter explaining the piece, a copy of the contract with the publisher, a synopsis of the book and a letter of recommendation from the editor confirming that the piece is the author's first, and is of literary merit.

## Journalists' Charity
**Dickens House, 35 Wathen Road, Dorking, Surrey, RH4 1JY**
- 01306 887511
- 01306 888212
- enquiries@journalistscharity.org.uk
- www.journalistscharity.org.uk

**About** A charity providing grants, bursaries and other financial assistance to journalists and their dependants. The charity also run retirement homes and can provide nursing care. Originally established in 1860, Charles Dickens was a founding member.

## Laurence Stern Fellowship
**Department of Journalism, City University, Northampton Square, London, EC1V OHB**
- 020 7040 8221
- a.r.mckane@city.ac.uk
- www.city.ac.uk

**Contact** Anna McKane

**About** An opportunity for a journalist with experience of working on national stories to intern at the Washington Post in the US for three months during the summer. Applicants may be working in print, radio, television, or web, but demonstrate relevant experience in print particularly. The intention is to send a young journalist, although there is no age limit. Applicants should attach a CV, two references, with at least one from a present or former editor or producer, and no more than three samples of their work. Television or radio journalists may submit scripts, or cite examples of their recent achievements. The fellowships normally start in July and the deadline is the previous February, check the website for more details.

## The Nico Colchester Journalism Fellowship

**1 Southwark Bridge, London, SE1 9HL**

- ☎ 020 7873 3000
- 🖷 020 7873 3076
- ✉ ncprize@ft.com
- 🖳 www.ft.com/nicocolchester

**About** Two internships are available, each for three months. One is for a British journalist at an Economist office in Europe and one for a European journalist at the Financial Times (FT) in London. Both winners receive a £4,000 bursary. Submit a 1,000-word article on the topic 'How can national economic interests be protected in this era of globalisation?' in English, together with a CV and covering letter.

## North East Literary Fellowship

**Arts Council England North East, Central Square, Forth Street, Newcastle upon Tyne, NE1 3PJ**

- ☎ 0191 255 8542
- ☎ 0191 230 1020
- 🖳 www.artscouncil.org.uk

**About** A fellowship in association with the University of Durham and the University of Newcastle. Contact the North East branch of Arts Council England for more details and how to apply.

## Northern Rock Foundation Writer's Award

**New Writing North, 2 School Lane, Wickham, Newcastle upon Tyne, NE16 4SL**

- ☎ 0191 488 8580
- 🖷 0191 488 8576
- ✉ mail@newwritingnorth.com
- 🖳 www.nr-foundationwriters.com

**About** An annual award of £60,000 split over three years to enable a writer to completely concentrate on writing. Applicants must have lived and worked in Tees Valley, Tyneside, County Durham, Northumberland or Cumbria for at least three years. The award is for writers who have already had two or more books published (self-publishing is excluded). It is open to writers of both literary and genre fiction, poetry, biography and children's literature. Apply with a sample of up to 6,000 words or 40 poems. The samples should be taken from your current work in progress. Work must be supported by the following items: an outline or synopsis; explanation of the stage the work is at i.e. commissioned, first draft etc. Also include a writing biography. Send five copies to

New Writing North. Deadline is 15th December 2007.

## PAWS (Public Awareness of Science) Drama Fund

**PAWS Office, Omni Communications, 1st Floor, 155 Regents Park Road, London, NW1 8BB**

- ☎ 020 7483 4545
- ✉ pawsomni@btconnect.com
- 🖳 www.pawsdrama.com

**About** Two levels of grants for dramatic writers in the field of science and technology. The first, at around £5,000 is for top writers whose ideas feature in some way women scientists or engineers in leading roles. The second level, around £1,000 to £2,000 is for writers who already have some interest in their work from a producer or broadcaster. There is no competitive element for the top grants. Any writer in these fields may approach PAWS directly about the application process.

## Pearson Playwrights' Scheme

**c/o Pearson Plc, 80 Strand, London, WC2R 0RL**

- ✉ playwrightsscheme@tiscali.co.uk
- **Contact** Jack Andrews MBE

**About** Five bursaries of £6,500 are awarded annually to scriptwriters. A theatre must make nominations in October each year and winners then gain a year's attachment with that theatre. An additional prize is awarded the following year for the best play emerging from the five winners.

## Peggy Ramsay Foundation

**Hanover House, 14 Hanover Square, London, W1S 1HP**

- ☎ 020 7667 5000
- 🖷 020 7667 5100
- ✉ laurence.harbottle@harbottle.com
- 🖳 www.peggyramsayfoundation.org
- **Contact** G. Laurence Harbottle

**About** A foundation borne out of the will of Peggy Ramsay, a play agent. Grants totalling around £200,000 per year are made directly to writers. The writer must show that they have had at least one full length play produced professionally for an adult audience, need time to write again for the stage and cannot otherwise afford to do so. Also considered from time to time, are organisations whose projects and awards may help new writing for the stage. Writers must be resident in Britain, but of no particular nationality. The trustees meet four to five times a year. Applications should be brief, made by the writer concerned, preferably in a simple letter stating the need and the amount requested. A full CV of the applicant must be enclosed. Scripts and previous publicity should not be sent.

## Peter Martin Fellowship
**1 Southwark Bridge, London, SE1 9HL,**
- 020 7873 3000
- 020 7873 3076
- pmfellow@ft.com
- www.ft.com/petermartin

**About** A three month internship in memory of Peter Martin, a former chief business columnist and deputy editor of the Financial Times. A bursary of £4,000 will be made to cover living expenses. Candidates must have a thorough grounding in economics, a first degree and possibly a postgraduate qualification. They must demonstrate an interest in the areas that interested Peter, particularly the impact of technology on the economy. Submit a CV and draft editorial piece of up to 5,000 words.

## The Richard Casement Internship
**The Economist, 25 St. James' Street, London, SW1A 1HG**
- 020 7830 7000
- casement@economist.com
- www.economist.com

**Contact** Science Editor, Geoffrey Carr
**About** A summer internship for a young person to spend three months working as a journalist in the science and technology section. Applicants should be under 25 and are more likely to succeed if they're a science student who wants to develop writing skills, rather than a writer who wants to learn about science. Details usually appear in the magazine and on the website in January or February.

## Robert Louis Stevenson Memorial Fellowship
**The National Library of Scotland, George IV Bridge, Edinburgh, EH1 1EW**
- 0131 226 6051
- 0131 225 9833
- help.desk@scottisharts.org.uk
- www.scottisharts.org.uk

**About** Winners receive two months self-catering accommodation at the Hotel Chevillon International Arts Centre in France, along with travel expenses and £2,400 living expenses. Applicants must be writers living in Scotland or be Scottish by birth.

Submit no more than 3,000 words of original work (in progress or recently published), along with a brief statement of how the fellowship would be useful and a short career history. An application form is downloadable from the website.

## The Royal Literary Fund
**3 Johnson's Court, off Fleet Street, London, EC4A 3EA**
- 020 7353 7159
- egunnrlf@globalnet.co.uk
- www.rlf.org.uk

**Contact** General Secretary, Eileen Gunn
**About** The Royal Literary Fund has been continuously helping authors since it was set up in 1790. It is funded by bequests and donations from writers who wish to help other writers. Its committee members come from all walks of literary life and include novelists, biographers, poets, publishers, lawyers and agents. Help is given to writers in many different situations where personal or professional setbacks have resulted in loss of income. Grants cannot be made for works in progress. Pensions are considered for older writers who have seen their earnings decrease. To apply, contact Eileen Gunn providing a list of your work, including names of publishers, dates, and whether sole author. Of special interest to all involved in writing in HE is Writing Matters, the RLF Report on Student Writing in Higher Education. It examines the difficulties many students face in writing effectively and proposes a range of measures to address these. The report argues that much greater attention should be paid to helping students adjust to the demands of writing at university and that writing development is a key factor for progress in the HE sector.

## The Royal Literary Fund Fellowship Scheme
**3 Johnson's Court, off Fleet Street, London, EC4A 3EA**
- 020 7353 7160
- rlitfund@btconnect.com
- www.rlf.org.uk

**Contact** Fellowship and Education Officer, Stephen Cook
**About** A fellowship scheme for professional, published writers of literary merit with at least two (sole-authored) books published of any genre, mainstream theatre works performed, or scripts broadcast. Applicants must be native English speakers and the resident of a commonwealth country. Citizens of other countries may apply if they

have been resident in the UK for at least three years. Fellows will be attached to a British University and will be paid a fee of around £14,000 for one academic year. There are two recruitment rounds per year. Contact Stephen Cook for an application pack (not usually available between April and November).

## Sander Thoenes Award
**1 Southwark Bridge, London, SE1 9HL**
- 020 7873 3000
- 020 7873 3076
- www.ft.com/sanderthoenes

**About** An annual award in memory of the former Jakarta correspondent for the Financial Times (FT), who was killed in East Timor in September 1999. The winner is offered a three month internship at the FT's headquarters in London and a bursary of £5,250 to cover accommodation and living expenses. Applicants are welcomed from all over the world, but must be fluent in written English and have no more than five years journalistic experience. Submit a CV, two references, an unpublished original article of 900 words max. on an issue relevant to emerging democracies, plus copies of two published articles, or an academic essay. Also send a covering letter of no more than 400 words explaining how you would benefit from winning.

## Scottish Arts Council Bursaries
**Grants Administration Department, 12 Manor Place, Edinburgh, EH3 7DD**
- 0131 226 6051
- 0131 225 9833
- help.desk@scottisharts.org.uk
- www.scottisharts.org.uk

**About** A range of grants, which are available for professionals working in the arts, including some in the literature and drama fields. Check the website for details of current offers and application procedures. Applicants should normally live in Scotland or work in Scotland.

## Scott Trust Bursaries
**60 Farringdon Road, London, EC1R 3GA**
- 020 7278 2332

**About** The Scott Trust, owners of the Guardian Media Group plc, offer four annual bursary places on the Postgraduate Diploma course in Newspaper Journalism at City University, London. Course fees are covered and contribution towards living expenses, plus work experience with the Guardian Media Group is offered. Preference is given to those who already have some work experience within newspapers. Ethnic minorities, disabled applicants and applicants with varied experience since graduating are encouraged to apply. The trust is also open to application for charitable donations.

## The Society of Authors Charitable Trusts
**The Society of Authors, 84 Drayton Gardens, London, SW10 9SB**
- 020 7373 6642
- 020 7373 5768
- info@societyofauthors.org
- www.societyofauthors.org

**Contact** Dorothy Sim

**About** There are currently three funds available for professional freelance writers who experience sudden, or temporary financial difficulty. The Francis Head Bequest is open to all writers, particularly those with unexpected health problems. The Authors' Contingency Fund is open to writers or their dependents that are in extreme financial difficulty. The John Masefield Memorial Trust is open to poets or their dependents that face sudden financial problems. Applications for all three may be made using the form available on the website.

## Tony Doyle Bursary for New Writing
**BBC NI Drama Department, Broadcasting House, Ormeau Avenue, Belfast, BT2 8HQ**
- 028 9033 8845
- tvdrama.ni@bbc.co.uk
- www.bbc.co.uk/northernireland/drama/writing_opps

**About** A bursary which encourages new scriptwriters to produce television drama about Ireland. The winner will receive £2,000 and an invitation to attend a residential seminar. This will consist of a series of intensive sessions with the BBC Northern Ireland development team and experienced practitioners - producers, directors, actors and fellow writers. Two runners up will also receive invitations. Submit a 60 or 90 minute script for a television drama, either a single piece, the first part of a series, serial or two parter. For anything other than a one off, also attach a synopsis of future storylines. No writers who have been produced for television or feature film are eligible. Independent films that have subsequently been broadcast are eligible. Check the website for deadlines. In 2007 the deadline was the end of January.

## Tony Godwin Memorial Trust

c/o 38 Lyttelton Court, Lyttelton Road, London, N2 0EB

- 020 8209 1613
- info@tgmt.org.uk
- www.tgmt.org.uk

**Contact** Iain Brown

**About** A biennial award (odd years) commemorating the life of Tony Godwin, a distinguished publisher from the 1960s and 70s. A grant of up to $5,000 allows the winner to spend to least a month working at an American publishing house and learning about international publishing.

## The Travelling Scholarships

The Society of Authors, 84 Drayton Gardens, London, SW10 9SB

- 020 7373 6642
- 020 7373 5768
- info@societyofauthors.org
- www.societyofauthors.org

**About** Honorary grants awarded to established writers nominated by the Society of Authors' committee of management. No submissions are accepted.

# WRITING & PUBLISHING COURSES

# FULL-TIME COURSES

## Anglia Ruskin University

East Road, Cambridge, CB1 1PT

- 0845 271 3333
- answers@anglia.ac.uk
- www.anglia.ac.uk

**Courses** BA Writing
BA Writing and Drama, English or Film Studies

## Bath Spa University

School of English and Creative Studies, Bath Spa University, Newton Park Campus, Bath, BA2 9BN

- 01225 875743
- 01225 875503
- www.bathspa.ac.uk

**Courses** BA Creative Writing (single or joint). Contact Richard Kerridge, r.kerridge@bathspa.ac.uk
MA Creative Writing. Contact Richard Kerridge, r.kerridge@bathspa.ac.uk
MA Writing for Young People. Contact Julia Green, j.a.green@bathspa.ac.uk
PhD Creative Writing. Contact Dr. Tracey Brain, t.brain@bathspa.ac.uk

## Birkbeck College

Malet Street, Bloomsbury, London, WC1E 7HX

- 020 7631 6000
- 020 7631 6270
- info@birkbeckmatters.com
- www.bbk.ac.uk

**Courses** MA Creative Writing. Contact office@eng.bbk.ac.uk

## Blackpool and The Fylde College

Ashfield Road, Bispham, Blackpool, FY2 0HB

- 01253 504343
- 01253 356127
- visitors@blackpool.ac.uk
- www.blackpool.ac.uk

**Courses** BA English Language, Literature and Writing

## Bournemouth University

Fern Barrow, Talbot Campus, Poole, Dorset, BH12 5BB

- 01202 524111
- 01202 962736
- enquiries@bournemouth.ac.uk
- www.bournemouth.ac.uk

**Courses** BA Scriptwriting for Film and Television. Contact kking@bournemouth.ac.uk
BA Multimedia Journalism. Kread@bournemouth.ac.uk
MA Journalism (International), Multimedia Journalism, or Magazine Journalism. Contact sbrownlee@bournemouth.ac.uk

## Brunel University

Uxbridge, Middlesex, UB8 3PH

- 01895 274000
- 01895 232806
- admissions@brunel.ac.uk
- www.brunel.ac.uk

**Courses** BA Creative Writing. Contact Rose Atfield, english.admissions@brunel.ac.uk

BA English with Creative Writing. Contact Rose Atfield, english.admissions@brunel.ac.uk
MA Creative and Professional Writing. Contact Donna White, donna.white@brunel.ac.uk
MA Creative Writing (the novel). Contact Donna White, donna.white@brunel.ac.uk
MA Journalism. Contact Donna White, donna.white@brunel.ac.uk

## Buckinghamshire Chilterns University College
**Queen Alexandra Road, High Wycombe, Buckinghamshire, HP11 2JZ**
- 01494 522141
- 01494 524392
- www.bcuc.ac.uk

**Courses** BA Creative Writing with Film Studies, Drama, English Literature, Media Studies, or Digital Video Production (or combinations)

## Canterbury Christchurch University
**North Holmes Road, Canterbury, Kent, CT1 1QU**
- 01227 767700
- 01227 470442
- admissions@canterbury.ac.uk
- www.canterbury.ac.uk

**Courses** MA Creative Writing. Contact Dr. Andrew Palmer
MA Journalism. Contact Kate Handley, kk23@canterbury.ac.uk

## Cardiff University
**Cardiff, Wales, CF10 3XQ**
- 029 2087 4000
- www.cardiff.ac.uk

**Courses** MA Journalism Studies. Contact Karin Wahl-Jorgensen, wahl-jorgensenK@cardiff.ac.uk
MA International Journalism. Contact Sara Hadwin, hadwins@cardiff.ac.uk
MA Teaching and Practice of Creative Writing. Contact encap@cardiff.ac.uk

## Central School of Speech and Drama
**Embassy Theatre, Eton Avenue, London, NW3 3HY**
- 020 7559 3901
- enquiries@cssd.ac.uk
- www.cssd.ac.uk

**Courses** MA Writing for Stage and Broadcast Media

## City University
**Northampton Square, London, EC1V 0HB**
- 020 7040 5060
- enquiries@city.ac.uk/journalism@city.ac.uk
- www.city.ac.uk

**Courses** BA Journalism and Contemporary History
BA Journalism and Social Science
MA Broadcast Journalism
MA Creative Writing (novels)
MA Creative Writing (plays & scripts)
MA Magazine, Newspaper or International Journalism
MA Publishing Studies

## Coventry University
**Priory Street, Coventry, CV1 5FB**
- 024 7688 7688
- info.rao@coventry.ac.uk
- www.coventry.ac.uk

**Courses** BA Journalism with English (joint)
BA Journalism and Media
MA Journalism (automotive/global/health). Contact postgraduate@coventry.ac.uk

## Cumbria Institute of Arts
**Brampton Road, Carlisle, CA3 9AY**
- 01228 400300
- 01228 514491
- info@cumbria.ac.uk
- www.cumbria.ac.uk

**Courses** BA Creative Writing. Contact Nick Pemberton
BA Journalism
MA Scriptwriting. Contact Dr. Fiona Powley, fiona.powley@cumbria.ac.uk

## Dartington College of Arts
**Dartington Hall Estate, Totnes, Devon, TQ9 6EJ**
- 01803 862224
- 01803 861666
- enquiries@dartington.ac.uk
- www.dartington.ac.uk

**Courses** BA Writing, Writing (scripted media) or Writing (contemporary practices)
MA Performance Writing

## De Montfort University
**The Gateway, Leicester, LE1 9BH**
- 0116 255 1551
- 0116 257 7533
- enquiry@dmu.ac.uk

www.dmu.ac.uk
**Courses** BA Creative Writing. Contact huadmiss@dmu.ac.uk
 BA Journalism (joint). Contact huadmiss@dmu.ac.uk
 MA Creative Writing and New Media. Contact Sue Thomas, hsspgrad@dmu.ac.uk
 PGDip Journalism. Contact hsspgrad@dmu.ac.uk
 PGDip Publishing and New Media. Contact hsspgrad@dmu.ac.uk
 MA Television Scriptwriting. Contact hsspgrad@dmu.ac.uk

## Doncaster College
**The Hub, Chappell Drive, Doncaster, DN1 2RF**
01302 553553
01302 553559
infocentre@don.ac.uk
www.don.ac.uk
**Courses** BA Scriptwriting

## Dublin City University
**Dublin 9, Republic of Ireland**
00353 1 700 5566
00353 1 836 0830
registry@dcu.ie
www.dcu.ie
**Courses** BA Journalism. Contact Martin Molony, martin.molony@dcu.ie
 MA Journalism. Contact John O'Sullivan, john.osullivan@dcu.ie

## Dublin Institute of Technology, School of Languages
**Fitzwilliam House, 30 Upper Pembroke Street, Dublin 2**
00353 1 402 3000
media@dit.ie
www.dit.ie
**Courses** BA Journalism with a Language

## Edge Hill University
**St. Helen's Road, Ormskirk, Lancashire, L39 4QP**
01695 575171
01695 579997
enquiries@edgehill.ac.uk
www.edgehill.ac.uk
**Courses** BA Creative Writing. Contact Dr. Ailsa Cox, coxa@edgehill.ac.uk
 BA Journalism
 MA Writing Studies. Contact Prof. Robert Sheppard

## Goldsmiths College
**University of London, New Cross, London, SE14 6NW**
020 7919 7171
admissions@gold.ac.uk
www.gold.ac.uk
**Courses** MA Creative and Life Writing. Contact english@gold.ac.uk
 MA Creative Writing. Contact english@gold.ac.uk
 MA Writing for Performance. Contact drama@gold.ac.uk
 MA Journalism. Contact media-comms@gold.ac.uk
 MA Scriptwriting. Contat media-comms@gold.ac.uk
 MA Feature Film. Contact media-comms@gold.ac.uk
 MA Radio. Contact media-comms@gold.ac.uk
 MA Filmaking. Contact media-comms@gold.ac.uk
 MA Screen Documentary. Contact media-comms@gold.ac.uk

## Griffith College
**Wellington House, 9–11 Patrick Hill, Cork, Republic of Ireland**
00353 21 450 7027
00353 21 450 7659
day@griffithcollegecork.ie
www.griffithcollegecork.ie
**Courses** BA Journalism

## Grimsby Institute of Further and Higher Education
**Nuns Corner, Grimsby, North East Lincolnshire, DN34 5BQ**
01472 311222
01472 879924
infocent@grimsby.ac.uk
www.grimsby.ac.uk
**Courses** BA Journalism
 BA Professional Writing

## King's College
**Strand, London, WC2R 2LS**
020 7836 5454
ceu@kcl.ac.uk
www.kcl.ac.uk
**Courses** MA Text and Performance Studies. Contact helene.hokland@kcl.ac.uk

## Kingston University
**River House, 53–57 High Street, Kinston upon Thames, Surrey, KT1 1LQ**

020 8547 2000
admissions-info@kingston.ac.uk
www.kingston.ac.uk
**Courses** BA Journalism. Contact hsundergrad-info@kingston.ac.uk
MA Creative, Fiction or Travel Writing. Contact Susan Henry, fasspostgrad-info@kingston.ac.uk
MA Writing for Children. Contact Susan Henry, hsundergrad-info@kingston.ac.uk
MA Poetry. Contact Susan Henry, hsundergrad-info@kingston.ac.uk
MA Publishing Studies. Contact Susan Henry, hsundergrad-info@kingston.ac.uk
MA Making Plays: Writing and Devising for the Stage. Contact Susan Henry, hsundergrad-info@kingston.ac.uk
MA The Creative Economy and Creative Writing, Publishing, Journalism, Film and Video, or Digital Media. Contact creativeindustries@kingston.ac.uk

## Lancaster University
**Lancaster, LA1 4YW**
01524 65201
www.lancaster.ac.uk
**Courses** BA English Language with Creative Writing. Contact l.williams5@lancaster.ac.uk
BA English Literature with Creative Writing. Contact k.elliott@lancaster.ac.uk
BA English Literature, Creative Writing and Practice. Contact k.elliott@lancaster.ac.uk
MA Creative Writing. Contact englishpg@lancaster.ac.uk

## Leeds Metropolitan University
**Civic Quarter, Leeds, LS1 3HE**
0113 283 3113
0113 283 3148
www.lmu.ac.uk
**Courses** MA Screenwriting: Fiction. Contact Chris Pugh, c.j.pugh@leedsmet.ac.uk

## Liverpool John Moores University
**Dean Walters Building, 1 St. James' Road, Liverpool, L1 7BR**
0151 231 2121
recruitment@ljmu.ac.uk
www.ljmu.ac.uk
**Courses** BA Imaginative Writing. Contact Julie Quine, j.quine@ljmu.ac.uk
BA Journalism. Contact Jane Finnen, j.finnen@ljmu.ac.uk
MA Writing. Contact Jim Friel, j.friel@ljmu.ac.uk

MA International Journalism. Contact Amanda Greening, mccamasters@livjm.ac.uk
MA Journalism. Contact Jane Finnen, j.finnen@ljmu.ac.uk
MA Screenwriting. Contact Amanda Greening, mccamasters@livjm.ac.uk

## London Metropolitan University
**166–220 Holloway Road, London, N7 8DB**
020 7133 4200/020 7133 4202
admissions@londonmet.ac.uk
www.londonmet.ac.uk
**Courses** BA Creative Writing (single or joint)
BA Creative Writing and English Literature
BA Journalism Studies
MA Professional Writing. Contact humanities@londonmet.ac.uk
MA Screenwriting. Contact Brian Dunnigan, b.dunnigan@lfs.org.uk

## London South Bank University
**90 London Road, London, SE1 6EN**
020 7815 7815
enquiry@lsbu.ac.uk
www.lsbu.ac.uk
**Courses** BA Writing for Media Arts. Contact Colin Harvey, harveycb@lsbu.ac.uk
BA Creative Writing
MA Writing for Media. Contact Dr. Anna Reading, readinam@lsbu.ac.uk

## Loughborough University
**Loughborough, Leicestershire, LE11 3TU**
01509 263171
www.lboro.ac.uk
**Courses** BA Publishing with English. Contact j.harrison@lboro.ac.uk
MA Creative Writing. Contact Dr. Jonathan Taylor, j.p.taylor1@lboro.ac.uk
MA Modern and Contemporary Writing. Contact Dr. Brian Jarvis, b.jarvis@lboro.ac.uk

## Manchester Metropolitan University
**All Saints Building, All Saints, Manchester, M15 6BH**
0161 247 2000
0161 247 6390
enquiries@mmu.ac.uk
www.mmu.ac.uk
**Courses** BA Creative Writing (single and joint). Contact adm.cheshire@mmu.ac.uk

BA English and Creative Writing. Contact english-hums@mmu.ac.uk

MA Creative Writing. Contact Heather Beck, h.beck@mmu.ac.uk

## Marjon: The College of St. Mark and St. John

**Derriford Road, Plymouth, Devon, PL6 8BH**
- 01752 636700
- admissions@marjon.ac.uk
- www.marjon.ac.uk

**Courses** BA Creative Writing (joint)
BA Writing for the Media

## Napier University

**Craig Lockhart Campus, Edinburgh, EH14 1DJ**
- 0845 260 6040
- info@napier.ac.uk
- www.napier.ac.uk

**Courses** BA Journalism
BA Publishing Media
MSc Journalism
MSc Publishing

## National Film and Television School

**Beaconsfield Studios, Station Road, Beaconsfield, Buckinghamshire, HP9 1LG**
- 01494 671234
- 01494 674042
- info@nftsfilm-tv.ac.uk
- www.nftsfilm-tv.ac.uk

**Courses** MA Screenwriting

## National University of Ireland, Galway

**University Road, Galway, Republic of Ireland**
- 00353 91 524411

**Courses** MA Literature and Publishing. Contact Julia Kilroy, julia.kilroy@nuigalway.ie

MA Journalism. Contact Bernadette O'Sullivan, bernadette.osullivan@nuigalway.ie

MA Writing. Contact Adrian Frazier, adrian.frazier@nuigalway.ie

MA Screenwriting. Contact Rod Stoneman, rod.stoneman@nuigalway.ie

## Newcastle University

**Newcastle upon Tyne, NE1 7RU**
- 0191 222 6000
- enquiries@ncl.ac.uk
- www.ncl.ac.uk

**Courses** MA Creative Writing

## Newman College of Higher Education

**Genners Lane, Bartley Green, Birmingham, B32 3NT**
- 0121 476 1181
- 0121 476 1196
- registry@newman.ac.uk
- www.newman.ac.uk

**Courses** Creative Writing (joint honours programmes). Contact Jenny Daniels, english@newman.ac.uk

## Northumbria University

**Ellison Place, Newcastle upon Tyne, NE1 8ST**
- 0191 232 6002
- 0191 227 4017
- ar.admissions@northumbria.ac.uk
- www.northumbria.ac.uk

**Courses** BA English and Creative Writing
BA Journalism
MA Creative Writing

## The Norwich School of Art and Design

**Francis House, 3–7 Redwell Street, Norwich, Norfolk, NR2 4SN**
- 01603 610561
- 01603 615728
- info@nsad.ac.uk
- www.nsad.ac.uk

**Courses** BA Creative Writing
MA Writing the Visual. Contact postgrad@nsad.ac.uk

## Nottingham Trent University

**Burton Street, Nottingham, NG1 4BU**
- 0115 941 8418
- cor.web@ntu.ac.uk/hum.undergrad@ntu.ac.uk/hum.postgard@ntu.ac.uk
- www.ntu.ac.uk

**Courses** BA English with Creative Writing
BA Print Journalism
BA Broadcast Journalism
MA Creative Writing
MA Newspaper Journalism
MA Radio Journalism
MA Television Journalism
MA Online Journalism

## Oxford Brookes University
**Gipsy Lane, Oxford, OX3 0BP**
- 01865 484848
- query@brookes.ac.uk
- www.brookes.ac.uk

**Courses** BA/BSc Publishing. Contact Lisa Atkinson, lisa.atkinson@brookes.ac.uk
 MA Publishing. Contact pgah@brookes.ac.uk
 MA Publishing and Language. Contact pgah@brookes.ac.uk
 MA Publishing, Interactive Media. Contact pgah@brookes.ac.uk

## Queen Mary University, University of London
**Department of History, London, E1 4NS**
- 020 7882 5016
- 020 8980 8400
- history@qmul.ac.uk
- www.qmul.ac.uk

**Courses** BA Journalism and Contemporary History

## Queen's University, Belfast
**University Road, Belfast, Northern Ireland, BT7 1NN**
- 028 9024 5133
- 028 9097 5137
- english@qub.ac.uk
- www.qub.ac.uk

**Courses** MA English (Creative Writing)

## The Robert Gordon University
**Schoolhill, Aberdeen, Scotland, AB10 1FR**
- 01224 262728
- 01224 262728
- admissions@rgu.ac.uk
- www.rgu.ac.uk

**Courses** BA Publishing with Journalism
 MSc Publishing with Journalism. Contact Dr. Sarah Pedersen, s.pedersen@rgu.ac.uk
 MSc Publishing Studies. Contact Dr. Sarah Pedersen, s.pedersen@rgu.ac.uk

## Roehampton University
**Erasmus House, Roehampton Lane, London, SW15 5PU**
- 020 8392 3232
- 020 8392 3470
- enquiries@roehampton.ac.uk
- www.roehampton.ac.uk

**Courses** BA Creative Writing (single or joint)

BA Journalism and News Media (joint)
 MA Creative and Professional Writing. Contact Jeff Hilson, j.hilson@roehampton.ac.uk
 MA Children's Literature. Contact Lisa Sainsbury, l.sainsbury@roehampton.ac.uk

## Royal Holloway, University of London
**Egham Hill, Egham, TW20 0EX**
- 01784 434455
- 01784 437520
- admissions@rhul.ac.uk
- www.rhul.ac.uk

**Courses** BA English and Creative Writing
 BA Drama and Creative Writing
 MA Creative Writing. Contact Prof. Andrew Motion, andrew.motion@rhul.ac.uk
 MA Feature Film Screenwriting. Contact mediaarts@rhul.ac.uk
 MA Screenwriting for Television and Film. Contact mediaarts@rhul.ac.uk

## Ruskin College, Oxford
**Walton Street, Oxford, OX1 2HE**
- 01865 310713
- 01865 554372
- enquiries@ruskin.ac.uk
- www.ruskin.ac.uk

**Courses** BA English Studies (Creative Writing and Critical Practice)

## Sheffield Hallam University
**City Campus, Howard Street, Sheffield, S1 1WB**
- 0114 225 5555
- 0114 225 4449
- enquiries@shu.ac.uk
- www.shu.ac.uk

**Courses** BA Journalism Studies
 MA Writing. Contact dsenquiry@shu.ac.uk
 MA Broadcast Journalism. Contact aces-info@shu.ac.uk
 MA International Broadcast Journalism. Contact aces-info@shu.ac.uk

## Southampton Solent University
**East Park Terrace, Southampton, SO14 0YN**
- 023 8031 9000
- 023 8022 2259
- postmaster@solent.ac.uk/fmas@solent.ac.uk
- www.ssu.ac.uk

**Courses** BA Journalism
 BA Magazine Journalism and Feature Writing

BA Media Writing
BA Online Journalism
BA Screenwriting
BA Writing Fashion and Culture
BA Writing Popular Fiction
MA Media Writing

## South East Essex College
**Luker Road, Southend on Sea, Essex, SS1 1ND**
- 01702 220400
- admissions@southend.ac.uk
- www.southend.ac.uk
**Courses** BA Journalism

## Staffordshire University
**Stoke on Trent, Staffordshire, ST4 2DE**
- 01782 294000
- admissions@staffs.ac.uk/amdadmissions@staffs.ac.uk
- www.staffs.ac.uk
**Courses** BA Creative Writing
BA Journalism (single or joint)
BA Broadcast Journalism
BA Sports Journalism

## Stirling University
**Stirling, FK9 4LA**
- 01786 473171
- infocentre@stir.ac.uk
- www.stir.ac.uk
**Courses** MLitt Publishing Studies. Contact english-pg@stir.ac.uk

## St. Martin's College
**Lancaster Campus, Bowerham Road, Lancaster, LA1 3JD**
- 01524 384384
- 01524 384385
- admissions@ucsm.ac.uk
- www.stmartins.ac.uk
**Courses** BA Drama and Creative Writing
BA English and Creative Writing

## St. Mary's College
**Waldergrave Road, Strawberry Hill, Twickenham, TW1 4SX**
- 020 8240 4000
- 020 8240 4255
- www.smuc.ac.uk
**Courses** BA Professional and Creative Writing.
Contact Peter Dewar, dewarp@smuc.ac.uk

## Trinity and All Saints
**Brownberrie Lane, Horsforth, Leeds, LS18 5HD**
- 0113 283 7100
- 0113 283 7200
- admissions@leedstrinity.ac.uk
- www.leedstrinity.ac.uk
**Courses** BA English and Writing
BA Journalism
MA Bi-media, Radio, or Print Journalism. Contact Graham Greer, g.greer@leedstrinity.ac.uk

## Trinity College, Carmarthen
**Carmarthen, Wales, SA31 3EP**
- 01267 676767
- 01267 676766
- registry@trinity-cm.ac.uk
- www.trinity-cm.ac.uk
**Courses** BA Creative Writing with English, Film Studies or Media Studies. Contact Paul Wright, p.wright@trinity-cm.ac.uk
MA Creative Writing. Contact Paul Wright, p.wright@trinity-cm.ac.uk

## Trinity College, Dublin
**College Green, Dublin 2, Republic of Ireland**
- 00353 1 896 1000
- oscar@tcd.ie
- www.tcd.ie
**Courses** MPhil Creative Writing

## University College, Falmouth
**Woodlane, Falmouth, Cornwall, TR11 1RH**
- 01326 211077
- 01326 213880
- admissions@falmouth.ac.uk
- www.falmouth.ac.uk
**Courses** BA English with Creative Writing. Contact 01326 214358
BA Journalism. Contact 01326 214370
MA/PgDip Professional Writing. Contact 01326 214374
MA International Journalism. Contact 01326 214389
MA/PgDip Broadcast Journalism. Contact 01326 214386

## University College, University of London
**Gower Street, London, WC1E 6BT**
- 020 7679 2000
- admissions@ucl.ac.uk
- www.ucl.ac.uk

**Courses** MA Publishing
MA Electronic Communication and Publishing

## University College for the Creative Arts
**Ashley Road, Epsom, KT18 5BE, Or, Falkner Road, Farnham, GU9 7DS**
- 01372 728811 (Epsom)/01252 722441 (Farnham)
- info@ucreative.ac.uk
- www.ucreative.ac.uk

**Courses** BA Fashion Journalism (Epsom Campus)
BA Journalism (Farnham Campus)

## University of Bedfordshire
**Park Square, Luton, Bedfordshire, LU1 3JU**
- 01234 400400
- www.bedfordshire.ac.uk

**Courses** BA Creative Writing
BA Journalism and Journalism with Public Relations
MA Creative Writing (by research). Contact Keith Jebb, keith.jebb@beds.ac.uk

## University of Birmingham
**Edgebaston, Birmingham, B15 2TT**
- 0121 414 3344
- 0121 414 3971
- english@bham.ac.uk
- www.bham.ac.uk

**Courses** BA English with Creative Writing. Contact english@bham.ac.uk
MPhil (B) Playwriting Studies. Contact Steve Waters, dramapg@contacts.bham.ac.uk

## University of Bolton
**Deane Road, Bolton, BL3 5AB**
- 01204 900600
- enquiries@bolton.ac.uk
- www.bolton.ac.uk

**Courses** BA Creative Writing (single or joint). Contact Matthew Welton, mw7@bolton.ac.uk
BA Media, Writing and Production. Contact Jenny Shepherd, jms3@bolton.ac.uk
MA Creative Writing (part time). Contact Jon Glover, jg5@bolton.ac.uk

## University of Central England
**Perry Barr, Birmingham, B42 2SU**
- 0121 331 5595
- 0121 331 7994
- info@ucechoices.com
- www.uce.ac.uk

**Courses** BA Media and Communication (Journalism)
MA Broadcast Journalism. Contact Diane Kemp, diane.kemp@uce.ac.uk
MA International Broadcast Journalism. Contact Diane Kemp, diane.kemp@uce.ac.uk

## University of Central Lancashire
**Preston, PR1 2HE**
- 01772 201201

**Courses** Combined Honours Creative Writing. Contact chonours@uclan.ac.uk
BA Journalism (single or joint). Contact Andrea Walker, alwalker1@uclan.ac.uk
BA Sports, International or Travel Journalism. Contact Andrea Walker, alwalker1@uclan.ac.uk

## University of Chester
**Parkgate Road, Chester, CH1 4BJ**
- 01244 511000
- 01244 511300
- enquiries@chester.ac.uk
- www.chester.ac.uk

**Courses** BA Creative Writing (joint honours). Contact Jen Mawson, j.mawson@chester.ac.uk
MA Creative and Critical Writing. Contact Dr. Ashley Chantler, a.chantler@chester.ac.uk

## University of Chichester
**Bishop Otter Campus, College Lane, Chichester, West Sussex, PO19 6PE**
- 01243 816000
- admissions@chi.ac.uk
- www.chiuni.ac.uk

**Courses** BA English and Creative Writing. Contact english.chiuni.ac.uk
MA Creative Writing. Contact english.chiuni.ac.uk

## University of Derby
**Kedleston Road, Derby, DE22 1GB**
- 01332 590500
- 01332 294861
- enquiries-admissions@debry.ac.uk
- www.derby.ac.uk

**Courses** BA Creative Writing (single and joint). Contact adtenquiry@derby.ac.uk
BA Media Writing (joint). Contact adtenquiry@derby.ac.uk

## University of Dundee
**Nethergate, Dundee, DD1 4HN**
- 01382 383000

☎ 01382 201604
✉ university@dundee.ac.uk
🌐 www.dundee.ac.uk
**Courses** MA Writing Culture. Contact Dr. K.B.
Williams, k.b.williams@dundee.ac.uk

## University of East Anglia
**Norwich, NR4 7TJ**
☎ 01603 456161
☎ 01603 458553
🌐 www.uea.ac.uk
**Courses** BA English Literature with Creative Writing.
Contact Dr. P Magrs, p.magrs@uea.ac.uk
 MA Creative Writing (prose). Contact Prof. Michele
Roberts, m.roberts@uea.ac.uk
 MA Creative Writing (poetry). Contact Prof. Denise
Riley, d.riley@uea.ac.uk
 MA Creative Writing (scriptwriting). Contact Val
Taylor, v.taylor@uea.ac.uk
 MA Life Writing. Contact Prof Janet Garton, j.garton@
uea.ac.uk

## University of East London
**Docklands Campus, 4–6 University Way, London
E16 2RD**
☎ 020 8223 3000
☎ 020 8590 7799
✉ admiss@uel.ac.uk
🌐 www.uel.ac.uk
**Courses** BA Creative and Professional Writing.
Contact Tessa McWatt, t.mcwatt@uel.ac.uk
 MA Journalism and Society. Contact Dr. Andrew
Calcutt, a.calcultt@uel.ac.uk
 MA Magazines. Contact Dr. Andrew Calcutt,
a.calcultt@uel.ac.uk
 MA Writing (imaginative practice). Contact Tessa
McWatt t.a.mcwatt@uel.ac.uk

## University of Edinburgh
**Old College, South Bridge, Edinburgh, EH8 9LY**
☎ 0131 650 1000
☎ 0131 650 2147
✉ communications.office@ed.ac.uk
🌐 www.ed.ac.uk
**Courses** MSc English Literature: Creative Writing.
Contact rajamieso@staffmail.ed.ac.uk

## University of Essex
**Wivenhoe Park, Colchester, CO4 3SQ**
☎ 01206 873333
☎ 01206 873598

✉ admit@essex.ac.uk, pgadmit@essex.ac.uk
🌐 www.essex.ac.uk
**Courses** BA Journalism
 BA Creative Writing
 MA Literature, Creative Writing
 MA/Diploma in Professional Theatre (writing,
directing, pedagogy)

## University of Exeter
**The Queen's Drive, Exeter, EX4 4QJ**
☎ 01392 263035
✉ admissions@exeter.ac.uk
**Courses** MA Creative Writing. Contact soe.pgoffice@
exeter.ac.uk

## University of Glamorgan
**Pontypridd, Wales, CF37 1DL**
☎ 0800 716925
☎ 01443 654040
🌐 www.glam.ac.uk
**Courses** BA Creative and Professional Writing
 MA Scriptwriting
 MPhil Writing

## University of Glasgow
**Glasgow, G12 8QQ**
☎ 0141 330 2000
✉ pgadmissions@admin.gla.ac.uk
🌐 www.glasgow.ac.uk
**Courses** MA Creative Writing. Contact Prof. Michael
Schmidt, M.Schmidt@englit.arts.gla.ac.uk
 MA Film Journalism. Contact Dr. Dimitris
Eleftheriotis, tfts.office@arts.gla.ac.uk
 MA Writing. Contact Tom Powell, t.pow@
crichton.gla.ac.uk

## University of Gloucestershire
**Albert Road, Cheltenham, GL52 3JG**
☎ 0870 721 0210
🌐 www.glos.ac.uk
**Courses** BA Creative Writing
 BA Broadcast Journalism
 BA Print Journalism
 BA Publishing
 MA Creative and Critical Writing. Contact Dr. Nigel
McLoughlin, humanities@glos.ac.uk
 MA Broadcast Journalism. Contact Claire Simmons,
csimmons@glos.ac.uk
 MA Print Journalism. Contact Sharon Wheeler,
swheeler@glos.ac.uk

## University of Greenwich
**Old Royal Navy College, Park Row, Greenwich, London, SE10 9LS**
- 020 8331 8000
- 020 8331 8145
- courseinfo@greenwich.ac.uk
- www.gre.ac.uk

**Courses** BA Creative Writing
BA Journalism, Public Relations and Marketing
BA Media Writing

## University of Hertfordshire
**College Lane, Hatfield, Hertfordshire, AL10 9AB**
- 01707 284000
- 01707 284115
- admissions@herts.ac.uk
- www.herts.ac.uk

**Courses** BA Film and Television Documentary, Fiction or Entertainment. Contact Prof. Alan Horrox, a.horrox@herts.ac.uk
BA Journalism (Humanities)
BA Digital Publishing (Humanities)
BA Creative Writing (Humanities)
MA Film and Television Screenwriting. Contact Prof. A Horrox, a.horrox@herts.ac.uk

## University of Huddersfield
**Queensgate, Huddersfield, HD1 3DH**
- 01484 422288
- admissions@hud.ac.uk
- www.huddersfield.ac.uk

**Courses** BA English, English Language or English Literature with Creative Writing. Contact englishadmissions@hud.ac.uk
BA English, English Language or English Literature with Journalism. Contact englishadmissions@hud.ac.uk
BA History with Journalism. Contact historyadmissions@hud.ac.uk
BA Media and Print, Radio, or Sports Journalism. Contact Andy Fox, a.fox@hud.ac.uk
BA Fine Art with Contemporary Writing. Contact Steven Swindells, s.p.swindells@hud.ac.uk
MA Writing for Performance. Contact Tim Moss, t.moss@hud.ac.uk

## University of Hull
**Hull, HU6 7RX**
- 01482 346311
- www.hull.ac.uk

**Courses** BA Creative Writing (joint honours)
MA Creative Writing

## University of Kent
**Department of English, Rutherford College, University of Kent, Canterbury, CT2 7NX**
- 01227 823054
- 01227 827001
- english@kent.ac.uk
- www.kent.ac.uk

**Courses** BA English and American Literature and Creative Writing
MA Creative Writing. Contact english-office@kent.ac.uk

## University of Leeds
**Leeds, LS2, 9JT**
- 0113 243 1751
- 0113 244 3923
- ask@leeds.ac.uk
- www.leeds.ac.uk

**Courses** MA Writing for Performance and Production. Contact admissions-pci@leeds.ac.uk

## University of Manchester
**Oxford Road, Manchester, M13 9PL**
- 0161 306 6000
- pg.admissions@manchester.ac.uk
- www.manchester.ac.uk

**Courses** MA Creative Writing. Contact pg-english@manchester.ac.uk

## University of Middlesex
**Bramely Road, London, N14 4YZ**
- 020 8411 5555
- admissions@mdx.ac.uk
- www.mdx.ac.uk

**Courses** BA Film, Creative and Media Writing, or Journalism and Communication, with Creative Writing
BA Publishing and Media
BA Creative and Media Writing
BA Television Journalism
BA Publishing, Journalism and Media
BA Publishing, Media and Cultural Studies
BA Publishing, Writing and Media
BA Writing and Publishing
BA Creative Writing and English Literature
BA Publishing, Media and English
BA Media and Cultural Studies with Journalism, or Journalism with Media and Cultural Studies

BA Journalism, Publishing and Media
BA Media, Publishing and Cultural Studies
BA Journalism and Communication
MA Writing

## University of Northampton
**Park Campus, Boughton Green Road, Northampton, NN2 7AL**
- 01604 735500
- study@northampton.ac.uk
- www.northampton.ac.uk

**Courses** BA Creative Writing (joint)
 BA Journalism

## University of Oxford
**Wellington Square, Oxford, OX1 2JD**
- 01865 270000
- 01865 270708
- www.ox.ac.uk

**Courses** MSc Creative Writing. Contact Dr. Clare Morgan, clare.morgan@conted.ox.ac.uk

## University of Plymouth
**Drake Circus, Plymouth, PL4 8AA**
- 01752 600600
- www.plymouth.ac.uk

**Courses** BA English with Creative Writing. Contact arts.admissions@plymouth.ac.uk
 MA Creative Writing. Contact artspostgrad@plymouth.ac.uk
 MA Publishing. Contact artspostgrad@plymouth.ac.uk

## University of Portsmouth
**University House, Winston Churchill Avenue, Portsmouth, Hampshire, PO1 2UP**
- 023 9284 8484
- 023 9284 3082
- info.centre@port.ac.uk
- www.port.ac.uk

**Courses** BA Creative Writing and Drama. Contact humanities.admissions@port.ac.uk
 BA Creative Writing (joint). Contact create.admissions@port.ac.uk
 MA Creative Writing. Contact create.admissions@port.ac.uk

## University of Salford
**Salford, Greater Manchester, M5 4WT**
- 0161 295 5000
- 0161 295 5999

- course-enquiries@salford.ac.uk
- www.salford.ac.uk

**Courses** BA English and Creative Writing. Conact Alex Farrell, a.l.farrell.salford.ac.uk
 BA Journalism and English (joint). Contact l.a.harris@salford.ac.uk
 MA Journalism. Contact Tom Gill, t.gill@salford.ac.uk

## University of Sheffield
**Western Bank, Sheffield, S10 2TN**
- 0114 222 2000
- www.sheffield.ac.uk

**Courses** BA Journalism Studies. Contact Celia Harvey, c.e.harvey@sheffield.ac.uk
 BA Journalism (joint). Contact Celia Harvey, c.e.harvey@sheffield.ac.uk

## University of St. Andrews
**St. Andrews, Fife, KY16 9AJ**
- 01334 476161
- admissions@st-andrews.ac.uk
- www.st-andrews.ac.uk

**Courses** MLitt Creative Writing. Contact Prof. Douglas Dunn, ded@st-andrews.ac.uk

## University of Strathclyde
**16 Richmond Street, Glasgow, G1 1XQ**
- 0141 552 4400
- 0141 552 0775
- contact-facultyofarts@strath.ac.uk
- www.strath.ac.uk

**Courses** BA Journalism and Creative Writing
 MLitt Journalism Studies

## University of Sunderland
**Edinburgh Building, City Campus, Chester Road, Sunderland, SR1 3SD**
- 0191 515 2000
- www.sunderland.ac.uk

**Courses** BA Broadcast Journalism. Contact 0191 515 2634
 BA Journalism. Contact 0191 515 2634
 MA Journalism. Contact Ian Blackhall, ian.blackhall@sunderland.ac.uk

## University of Sussex
**Sussex House, Brighton, BN1 9RH**
- 01273 606755
- 01273 678335
- pg.admissions@sussex.ac.uk
- www.sussex.ac.uk

**Courses** MA Creative Writing and Authorship.
Contact Dr. Sue Roe, s.m.roe@sussex.ac.uk
 MA Creative Writing and Personal Development.
Contact Dr. Celia Hunt, c.m.hunt@sussex.ac.uk
 MA Dramatic Writing. Contact Richard Crane,
r.a.crane@sussex.ac.uk

## University of Teeside
**Middlesborough, Tees Valley, TS1 3BA**
- 01642 218121
- 01642 384201
- hotline@tees.ac.uk/arts@tees.ac.uk
- www.tees.ac.uk

**Courses** BA Journalism and News Practice
(top up award)
 BA Multimedia Journalism Professional Practice

## University of the Arts, London
**65 Davies Street, London, W1K 5DA**
- 020 7514 6000
- info@arts.ac.uk
- www.lcc.arts.ac.uk

**Courses** BA Magazine Publishing with Public
Relations, Media and Cultural Studies, or Marketing
and Advertising. Contact info@lcc.arts.ac.uk
 BA Journalism. Contact info@lcc.arts.ac.uk
 BA Fashion Journalism. Contact enquiries@
fashion.arts.ac.uk
 MA Journalism. Contact info@lcc.arts.ac.uk
 MA Fashion Journalism. Contact enquiries@
fashion.arts.ac.uk
 MA Critical Writing and Curatorial Practice. Contact
enquiries@chelsea.arts.ac.uk
 MA Screenwriting. Contact info@lcc.arts.ac.uk
 MA Publishing. Contact Tina Stennet, t.stennett@
lcc.arts.ac.uk

## University of Ulster
**Coleraine Campus, Cromore Road, Co.
Londonderry, Northern Ireland, BT52 1SA**
- 0870 040 0700
- www.ulster.ac.uk

**Courses** BA Journalism and Publishing
Studies (joint)
 MA Journalism. Contact Colm Murphy, c.murphy@
ulster.ac.uk
 MA Written and Verbal Arts: Creativity in Practice

## University of Wales, Aberystwyth
**Department of English, University of Wales,
Hugh Owen Building, Aberystwyth, SY23 3DY**

- 01970 622534
- 01970 622530
- www.aber.ac.uk/english

**Courses** BA English Literature with Creative Writing.
Contact Dr. Sarah Prescott, scp@aber.ac.uk
 MA Creative Writing. Contact Dr. Rhys Williams, pg-
admissions@aber.ac.uk
 PhD Creative Writing subjects. Contact Dr.
Jem Poster

## University of Wales, Bangor
**University of Wales, Bangor, Gwynedd,
LL57 2DG**
- 01248 382005
- enquiries@bangor.ac.uk
- www.bangor.ac.uk

**Courses** BA English Language with Creative Writing.
contact Prof. Jenny Thomas, e.price@bangor.ac.uk
 BA English with Creative Writing. Contact Dr. Tony
Brown, els015@bangor.ac.uk
 BA English with Journalism. Contact Dr. Tony Brown,
els015@bangor.ac.uk
 BA Journalism with Media Studies. Contact
mediastudies@bangor.ac.uk
 BA Literature and Creative Writing (part time).
Contact doll@bangor.ac.uk
 MA Creative Studies. Contact Dr. Ian Gregson,
i.gregson@bangor.ac.uk
 PhD/MPhil Creative and Critical Writing. Contact Dr.
Ian Gregson, i.gregson@bangor.ac.uk

## University of Wales, Lampeter
**Ceredigion, Wales, SA48 7ED**
- 01570 422351
- 01570 42342
- www.lamp.ac.uk

**Courses** BA English with Creative Writing. Contact
Beryl Doyle, b.doyle@lamp.ac.uk
 MA Creative and Scriptwriting. Contact Dic Edwards,
d.edwards@lamp.ac.uk
 MA Screenwriting

## University of Wales, Newport
**Information Centre, Caerleon Campus, PO Box
101, Newport, NP18 3YH**
- 01633 432432
- 01633 432046
- uic@newport.ac.uk
- www.newport.ac.uk

**Courses** BA Creative Writing (joint)
 BA Cinema Studies and Scriptwriting
 BA Publishing Design

## University of Wales, Swansea
**Singleton Park, Swansea, SA2 8PP**
- 01792 205678
- 01792 295157
- www.swansea.ac.uk

**Courses** MA Creative and Media Writing. Contact Dr. Stevie Davis, stephanie.davies@swansea.ac.uk
 MA Professional Writing
 MA Comparative Journalism. Contact Mala Jagmohan, r.m.jagmohan@swan.ac.uk

## University of Wales Institute, Cardiff
**Howard Gardens, Cardiff, CF5 2YB**
- 029 2041 6070
- 029 2041 6286
- uwicinfo@uwic.ac.uk
- www.uwic.ac.uk

**Courses** BA Art and Creative Writing. Contact Dr. Clive Cazeaux, ccazeaux@uwic.ac.uk
 BA Writing for Media and the Arts. Contact Andrea Williams, abwilliams@uwic.ac.uk

## University of Warwick
**Coventry, CV4 7AL**
- 024 7652 3523
- 024 7646 1606
- ugadmissions@warwick.ac.uk, pgadmissions@warwick.ac.uk
- www.warwick.ac.uk

**Courses** BA English Literature and Creative Writing
 MA Writing
 MA Translation, Writing and Cultural Difference

## University of Westminster
**35 Marylebone Road, London, NW1 5LS**
- 020 7915 5511
- 020 7911 5858
- course-enquiries@wmin.ac.uk
- www.wmin.ac.uk

**Courses** BA English Literature and Creative Writing. Contact Paul O'Hanlon ohanlop@wmin.ac.uk
 BA Linguistics and Creative Writing. Contact Paul O'Hanlon, ohanlop@wmin.ac.uk
 BA Media Studies (Journalism). Contact Alan Greere, a.geere@westminster.ac.uk
 BA Medical Journalism
 MA Journalism
 MA Screenwriting and Producing for Film and Television. Contact Steve May, mays@westminster.ac.uk

## University of Winchester
**West Hill, Winchester, SO22 4NR**
- 01962 841515
- 01962 842280
- course.enquiries@winchester.ac.uk
- www.winchester.ac.uk

**Courses** BA Creative Writing
 BA Journalism
 MA Creative and Critical Writing
 MA Writing for Children

## University of Wolverhampton
**Millennium City Building, City Campus South, Wulfruna Street, Wolverhampton, WV1 1SB**
- 01902 321000
- enquiries@wlv.ac.uk
- www.wlv.ac.uk

**Courses** BA Creative and Professional Writing (joint)
 BA Journalism and Editorial Design

# PART-TIME COURSES

## 7:84 Summer School
**784 Theatre Company Ltd, 4 Summertown Road, Glasgow, G51 2LY**
- 0141 445 7245
- lorenzo@784theatre.com
- www.784theatre.com

**About** Run a four day summer school, on scripts and theatre writing.

## ACS Distance Education
**PO Box 4171, Stourbridge, DY8 2WZ**
- 0800 328 4723
- 020 7681 2702
- admin@acsedu.co.uk
- www.acsedu.co.uk

**About** Writing, publishing and journalism courses by correspondence.

## AD Services
**AD Services Scotland, The Beckford Business Centre Suite 15, 28 Beckford Street, Hamilton, ML3 0BT**
- 01698 307171
- 01698 307140
- training@ad-services-scotland.co.uk
- www.ad-services-scotland.co.uk

**About** Distance learning courses in fiction writing and journalism.

## Adult College, Lancaster

The Adult College, Whitecross Education Centre, Quarry Road, Lancaster, LA1 3SE

- ☎ 01524 60141
- ☎ 01524 581137
- ✉ adcollege.info@ed.lancscc.gov.uk
- 🌐 www.theadultcollege.org

**About** Part time creative writing courses.

## Alston Hall

Alston Hall, Alston Lane, Longridge, Preston, PR3 3BP

- ☎ 01772 784661
- ☎ 01772 785835
- ✉ alston.hall@ed.lancscc.gov.uk
- 🌐 www.alstonhall.com

**About** Range of day, evening and weekly courses on writing and literature.

## Ammerdown Conference and Retreat Centre

Ammerdown Park, Radstock, Bath, BA3 5SW

- ☎ 01761 433709
- ☎ 01761 433094
- ✉ centre@ammerdown.org.uk
- 🌐 www.ammerdown.org

**About** Various day and residential writing courses.

## Annual Writers' Writing Courses and Workshops

F*F Productions, 39 Raneleagh Road, Sandown, PO36 8NT

- ✉ contact@writeplot.co.uk
- 🌐 www.writeplot.co.uk

**About** Organises writers' retreats and conferences. Also run screenwriting courses. For these, contact admin@cityeye.co.uk

## Anthology Store

Anthology Books Dublin, Temple Bar, Dublin 2, Republic of Ireland

- ☎ 00353 1 635 1422
- ☎ 00353 1 635 1423
- ✉ info@anthologystore.com
- 🌐 www.anthologystore.com/#creative

**About** Run writing workshops.

## Arista

Arista Devlopment, 11 Wells Mews, London, W1T 3HD

- ☎ 020 7323 1775
- ☎ 020 7323 1772
- ✉ arista@aristotle.co.uk
- 🌐 www.aristotle.co.uk

**About** Professional courses and consultancy on script development.

## Arts Institute at Bournemouth

Wallisdown, Poole, Bournemouth, BH12 5HH

- ☎ 01202 363222
- ✉ scourses@aib.ac.uk
- 🌐 www.aib.ac.uk

**About** Short courses in copywriting, editing and journalism.

## Arvon Foundation

The Arvon Foundation, 42a Buckingham Palace Road, London, SW1 0RE

- 🌐 www.arvonfoundation.org

**About** Residential writing courses across four properties in Devon, Scotland, Shropshire and West Yorkshire.

## ASM Training Centre

345 Ballards Lane, North Finchley, London, N12 8LJ

- ✉ info@asmtraining.co.uk
- 🌐 http://asmtrainingcentre.co.uk

**About** Training courses in journalism.

## Aspiring Writers

47 Old Exeter Road, Tavistock, Devon, PL19 0JE

- ☎ 01822 615610
- ✉ info@aspiringwriters.co.uk
- 🌐 www.aspiringwriters.co.uk

**About** Courses and workshops on every aspect of writing. Residential weekends can also be arranged.

## Ballsbridge College of Further Education

Shelbourne Road, Dublin 4, Republic of Ireland

- ☎ 00353 1 668 4806
- ☎ 00353 1 668 2361
- ✉ info@ballsbridge.cdvec.ie
- 🌐 www.ballsbridgecollege.com

**About** Creative writing evening course.

## Ballyfermot College of Further Education
**Ballyfermot Road, Dublin 10, Republic of Ireland**
- 00353 1 626 9421
- 00353 1 626 6754
- night.school@bcfe.cdvec.ie
- www.bcfe.ie

**About** Evening classes in creative writing, journalism and screenwriting.

## Barry College of Further Education
**Colcot Road, Barry, CF62 8YJ**
- 01446 725000
- 01446 732667
- enquiries@barry.ac.uk
- www.barry.ac.uk

**About** Journalism and media access course.

## Beginning to Write
**United Reform Church, 30 Fisherton Street, Salisbury, SP2 7RG**
- susandown5@aol.com.

**About** Beginner's writing course. Wednesday evenings from 7–9pm, throughout October and November. Contact Susan Down.

## Belfast Institute
**c/o East Belfast Community Education Centre, 6–8 Finvoy Street, Belfast, Northern Ireland, BT5 5DH**
- 028 9026 5265
- central_admissions@belfastinstitute.ac.uk
- www.belfastinstitute.ac.uk

**About** Adult learning and vocational courses in writing, media and journalism.

## Belstead House Education and Conference Centre
**Belstead House, Sprites Lane, Ipswich, Suffolk, IP8 3NA**
- belstead.house@educ.suffolkcc.gov.uk

**About** Residential courses.

## Birkbeck College
**Birkbeck College, University of London, Malet Street, London, WC1E 7HX**
- 0845 601 0174
- 020 7631 6270
- imcdonagh@bbk.ac.uk
- www.bbk.ac.uk

**About** Short courses and adult learning classes for various types of writing.

## Blackpool and The Fylde College
**Ashfield Road, Bispham, Blackpool, Lancashire, FY2 0HB**
- 01253 352352
- 01253 356127
- visitors@blackpool.ac.uk
- www.blackpool.ac.uk

**About** Adult, community learning and access courses in creative writing.

## Bournemouth Adult Learning
**Ensbury Avenue, Bournemouth, Dorest, BH10 4HG**
- 01202 451950
- 01202 451989
- bal.enquiries@bournemouth.gov.uk

**About** Various adult learning courses.

## Bournville College
**Bristol Road South, Northfield, Birmingham, B31 2AJ**
- 0121 483 1111
- info@bournville.ac.uk
- www.bournville.ac.uk

**About** Media courses.

## Brighton Writers' Workshop
**Vardean College, Surrenden Campus, Surrenden Road, Brighton, BN1 6WQ**
- 01273 546604
- 01273 542950
- commed@varndean.ac.uk
- www.varndean.ac.uk

**About** Writing course for adults.

## Brockenhurst College
**Lyndhurst Road, Brockenhurst, Hampshire, SO42 7ZE**
- 01590 625555
- adulteducation@brock.ac.uk
- www.brock.ac.uk

**About** Wide range of adult courses, including an open college certificate in creative writing.

## Brooklands College
**Heath Road, Weybridge, Surrey, KT13 8TT**
- info@brooklands.ac.uk

ⓦ www.brooklands.ac.uk
**About** Diploma in publishing and journalism.

## BSY Group
**BSY Group, Stanhope Square, Holsworthy, Devon, EX22 6DF**
ⓣ 0800 731 9271
ⓔ info@bsygroup.co.uk
ⓦ www.bsygroup.co.uk
**About** Distance learning courses, including creative writing.

## Buckingham Adult Learning - Missenden Abbey
**Adult Learning Data Centre, Evreham, Swallow Street, Iver, SL0 0HS**
ⓔ studentenquiries@buckscc.gov.uk
ⓦ www.adultlearningbcc.ac.uk
**About** Adult creative writing courses.

## Burnley College
**Shorley Bank, off Ormerod Road, Burnley, Lancashire, BB11 2RX**
ⓣ 01282 711222
ⓣ 01282 711200
ⓔ student.services@burnley.ac.uk
ⓦ www.burnley.ac.uk
**About** Adult creative writing course.

## Burton Manor
**Burton Manor, Burton, Neston, Cheshire, CH64 5SJ**
ⓣ 0151 336 5172
ⓣ 0151 336 6586
ⓔ enquiry@burtonmanor.com
ⓦ www.burtonmanor.com
**About** Variety of short residential, or non-residential writing courses.

## Bury Adult and Community Learning Service
**Bury Adult Education Centre, 18 Haymarket Street, Bury, BL9 0AQ**
ⓣ 0161 253 7501
ⓔ student.services@bury.gov.uk
**About** Community courses in creative writing.

## Caboodle Retreats
**Caboodle Cottage, 69 Southwold Road, Beccles, Suffolk, NR34 8JE**
ⓣ 01502 676101
ⓣ 01502 676101
ⓔ info@caboodleretreats.co.uk
ⓦ www.caboodleretreats.co.uk
**About** Writing holidays.

## Cambridge University
**Institute of Continuing Education, University of Cambridge, Madingley Hall, Madingley, Cambridge, CB3 8AQ**
ⓔ registration@cont-ed.cam.ac.uk
ⓦ www.cont-ed.cam.ac.uk
**About** Wide variety of creative writing courses.

## Cambridge Women's Resource Centre
**Hooper Street, Cambridge, CB1 2NZ**
ⓣ 01223 321148
ⓔ admin@cwrc.org.uk
ⓦ www.cwrc.co.uk
**About** Creative writing course for women.

## Carlow College
**Carlow College, College Street, Carlow, Republic of Ireland**
ⓣ 00353 59 913 1114
ⓔ jamesheaney@carlowcollege.ie
ⓦ www.carlowcollege.ie
**About** Creative writing evening course.

## Castle College Nottingham
**Maid Marian Way, Nottingham, NG1 6AB**
ⓣ 0845 845 0500
ⓔ learn@castlecollege.ac.uk
ⓦ www.broxtowe.ac.uk
**About** Wide range of writing and journalism courses.

## Castle of Park
**Castle of Park, Cornhill, Aberdeenshire, AB45 2AX**
ⓣ 01466 751111
ⓔ info@castleofpark.net
ⓦ www.castleofpark.net/mainpages/writing.htm
**About** Wide range of residential courses on all types of writing.

## Castlereagh College
**Montgomery Road, Belfast, Northern Ireland, BT6 9JD**

☎ 028 9079 7144
🖷 028 9040 1820
🌐 www.castlereagh.ac.uk
**About** Creative writing courses, journalism and part time workshops.

## Central Saint Martins College of Art and Design
**Southampton Row, London, WC1B 4AP**
☎ 020 7514 7015
✉ shortcourse@csm.arts.ac.uk
🌐 www.csm.arts.ac.uk
**About** Evening and weekend courses on all types of writing.

## Chapter Centre
**Chapter Centre, Market Road, Cardiff, CF5 1QE**
☎ 029 2031 1050
✉ enquiry@chapter.org
🌐 www.chapter.org
**About** Writing workshops and competitions.

## Charles Street Community Education Centre
**16 Charles Street, Newport, NP20 1JU**
☎ 01633 656656
**About** Short courses in writing.

## Cheadle and Marple Sixth Form College
**Cheadle Road, Cheadle Hulme, Stockport, Cheshire, SK8 5HA**
☎ 0161 486 4600
🖷 0161 482 8129
✉ info@camsfc.ac.uk
🌐 www.camsfc.ac.uk
**About** Adult learning course in creative writing.

## Chesterfield College
**c/o Parish Centre, Christchurch Hall Stonegravels, Sheffield Road, Chesterfield, S41 7JH**
☎ 01246 500500
✉ advice@chesterfield.ac.uk
🌐 www.chesterfield.ac.uk
**About** Part time, adult and community courses.

## City College Brighton and Hove
**Pelham Street, Brighton, BN1 4FA**
☎ 01273 667788

☎ 01273 667703
✉ info@ccb.ac.uk
🌐 www.ccb.ac.uk
**About** Full and part time certificates and diplomas in writing and journalism.

## City Lit
**Keeley Street, Covent Garden, London, WC2B 4BA**
☎ 020 7492 2600
🖷 020 7492 2735
✉ humanities@citylit.ac.uk
🌐 www.citylit.ac.uk
**About** Range of writing and journalism short courses.

## City of Bath College
**Avon Street, Bath, BA1 1UP**
🌐 www.citybathcoll.ac.uk
**About** Part time creative writing courses.

## City of Bristol College
**College Green Centre, St. George's Road, Bristol, BS1 5UA**
☎ 0117 312 5000
🖷 0117 312 5051
✉ enquiries@cityofbristol.ac.uk
🌐 www.cityofbristol.ac.uk
**About** Part time adult courses in various types of writing, and diplomas in journalism.

## City of Wolverhampton College
**Paget Road Campus, Paget Road, Wolverhampton, West Midlands, WV6 0DU**
☎ 01902 836000
🖷 01902 423070
✉ mail@wolvcoll.ac.uk
🌐 www.wolverhamptoncollege.ac.uk
**About** Full and part time journalism courses.

## City University
**Northampton Square, London, EC1V 0HB**
☎ 020 7040 5060
🖷 020 7040 5070
✉ a.burns@city.ac.uk
🌐 www.city.ac.uk/conted/cfa.htm
**About** Courses for adults in writing and journalism. Contact Alison Burns.

## Cleland Thom Journalism Training Services

22 The Green, Swanfield, Chichester, West Sussex, PO19 6XN

- 07733 145620
- cleland.thom@tesco.net
- www.ctjt.biz

**About** Online journalism courses, workshops and training events.

## Clydebank College

Killbowie Road, Clydebank, G81 2AA

- 0141 952 7771
- 0141 951 1574
- info@clydebank.ac.uk
- www.clydebank.ac.uk

**About** Part time journalism course.

## Coleg Powys

Llanidloes Road, Newtown, Powys, Wales, SY16 4HU

- 0845 408 6200
- 01686 622246
- enquiries@coleg-powys.ac.uk
- www.coleg-powys.ac.uk

**About** Access courses in writing and literature.

## The College of Technical Authorship

PO Box 7, Cheadle, Stockport, SK8 3BY

- 0161 437 4235
- 0161 437 4235
- crossley@coltecha.com
- www.coltecha.com

**About** Technical authorship distance learning course.

## Comberton Village College

West Street, Comberton, Cambridgeshire, CB3 7DU

- 01223 262503
- 01223 264116
- thecollege@comberton.cambs.sch.ac.uk
- www.combertonvc.org

**About** Various community courses.

## The Complete Creative Writing Course

Groucho Club, Soho, London

- maggie@writingcourses.org.uk
- www.writingcourses.org.uk/home.php

**About** Original, advanced, intensive and residential writing courses.

## Conway Education Centre

Conway Mill, 5–7 Conway Street, Belfast, Northern Ireland, BT13 2DE

- 028 90 248543

**About** Various writing courses.

## Creative in Calvados

- steveharvey@creativeincalvados.co.uk
- www.creativeincalvados.co.uk

**About** Various writers' holidays, in a property in Normandy, France.

## The Creative Writers Workshop

The Studio, Ballycullen House, Ashford, Co. Wicklow, Republic of Ireland

- 00353 86 252 3428
- creativewriting@ireland.com
- www.thecreativewritersworkshop.com

**About** Creative writing workshops and retreats in locations across Ireland. Contact Irene Graham.

## Darlington College of Technology

Darlington Technology College, Cleveland Avenue, Darlington, Durham, DL3 7BB

- 01325 503050
- 01325 503000
- kwalker@darlington.ac.uk
- www.darlington.ac.uk

**About** Journalism short courses.

## Dillington House

Dillington House, Illminster, TA19 9DT

- 01460 258613
- jtharrison@somerset.gov.uk
- www.dillington.co.uk

**About** Residential and day courses in literature and creative writing.

## Dingle Writing Courses

Ballintlea, Ventry, Co. Kerry, Republic of Ireland

- 00353 66 915 9815
- 00353 66 915 9815
- info@dinglewritingcourses.ie
- www.dinglewritingcourses.ie

**About** Various weekend writing courses for all levels of experience.

## Doncaster College

Waterdale, Doncaster, South Yorkshire, DN1 3EX

- ☎ 01302 553553
- ☎ 01302 553559
- ✉ infocentre@don.ac.uk
- 🌐 www.don.ac.uk

**About** Introduction to creative writing course.

## Dublin College of Management and IT

Station House, Shankill, Co. Dublin, Republic of Ireland

- ☎ 00353 1 286 5783
- ☎ 00353 1 633 5544
- ✉ info@cmit.ie

**About** Distance learning courses in journalism and fiction writing.

## Dunstable College

Dubstable College, Kingsway, Dunstable, Bedfordshire, LU5 4HG

- ☎ 01582 477776
- ☎ 01582 478801
- ✉ enquiries@dunstable.ac.uk
- 🌐 www.dunstable.ac.uk

**About** Creative writing examination courses.

## The Earnley Concourse

Earnley Trust Ltd, Earnley, Chichester, West Sussex, PO20 7JL

- ☎ 01243 670392
- ☎ 01243 670832
- ✉ info@earnley.co.uk
- 🌐 www.earnley.co.uk

**About** Various residential writing courses.

## Eastleigh College

Chestnut Avenue, Eastleigh, SO50 5SF

- ☎ 023 8091 1000
- 🌐 www.eastleigh.ac.uk

**About** Part time creative writing course.

## Eastmoors Community Education Centre

Sanquahar Street, Splott, Cardiff, CE24 2AD

- ☎ 029 2046 2858
- ✉ eastmoorsac@cardiff.gov.uk

**About** Various community courses.

## East Surrey College

Claremont Road, Redhill, RH1 2JX

- ☎ 01737 772611
- ☎ 01737 788444
- ✉ studentservices@esc.ac.uk
- 🌐 www.esc.ac.uk

**About** Part time creative writing workshops.

## Edinburgh University

Office of Lifelong Learning, University of Edinburgh, 11 Buccleuch Place, Edinburgh, EH8 9LW

- ☎ 0131 650 4400
- ☎ 0131 662 0783
- ✉ oll@ed.ac.uk
- 🌐 www.lifelong.ed.ac.uk

**About** Wide variety of adult learning courses, including aspects of creative writing.

## Emerson College

Emerson College, Forest Row, East Sussex, RH18 5JX

- ☎ 01342 822238
- ☎ 01342 826055
- ✉ info@emerson.org.uk
- 🌐 www.emerson.org.uk

**About** Various weekend and short courses in literature and creative writing.

## Essex Live Literature Courses

Essex Libraries, Goldlay Gardens, Chelmsford, Essex, CM2 6WN

- ☎ 01245 436759
- ✉ malcolm.burgess@essexcc.gov.uk
- 🌐 www.essexlivelit.org.uk

**About** Various literature events, including writing courses. Contact Malcolm Burgess.

## Euroscript

PO Box 3117, Gloucester, GL4 0WW

- ☎ 07803 369414
- ✉ enquiries@euroscript.co.uk
- 🌐 www.euroscript.co.uk

**About** A range of scriptwriting and development workshops. Also provide a consultancy service.

## Exeter College

Victoria House, Queen Street, Exeter, EX4 3SR

- ☎ 01392 205222
- ✉ admissions@exe-coll.ac.uk

www.exe-coll.ac.uk
**About** Courses in 'writing for fun and publication' and creative writing. Print journalism certification course.

## Exeter Phoenix
**Exeter Phoenix Centre, Bradninch Place, Gandy Street, Exeter, EX4 3LS**
01392 667065
programming@exeterphoenix.org.uk
www.exeterphoenix.org.uk
**About** Various community classes and workshops.

## Falmouth College of Arts
**Woodlane, Falmouth, Cornwall, TR11 4RH**
01326 370444
business@falmouth.ac.uk
www.falmouth.ac.uk
**About** Summer schools on novel writing and writing for children.

## Farncombe Estate
**Farncombe Estate Centre, Broadway, Cotswolds, Worcestershire, WR12 7LJ**
0845 230 8590
01386 854350
enquiries@farncombeestate.co.uk
www.farncombeestate.co.uk
**About** Weekend courses on various types of writing and literature.

## Far West
**23 Chapel Street, Penzance, Cornwall, TR18 4AP**
angela@farwest.co.uk
www.farwest.co.uk
**About** Writing for connection' course, focusing on writing as a connection to dreams, adventure, healing and strength. Contact Angela Stoner.

## Fire in the Head
**PO Box 17, Yelverton, Devon, PL20 6YF**
01822 841081
roselleangwin@fire-in-the-head.co.uk
www.fire-in-the-head.co.uk
**About** Various residential and day courses for writers at locations across the south of England.

## Galway Arts Centre
**47 Dominick Street, Galway, Republic of Ireland**
00353 91 565886

00353 91 568642
info@galwayartscentre.ie
www.galwayartscentre.ie
**About** Various writing courses and events, as part of the literature and arts programme.

## Grimsby Institute of Further Education
**Nuns Corner, Grimsby, North East Lincolnshire, DN34 5BQ**
0800 315002
infocent@grimsby.ac.uk
www.grimsby.ac.uk
**About** Journalism courses.

## Guildford Institute
**Ward Street, Guildford, Surrey, GU1 4LH**
01483 562142
guildford-institute@surrey.ac.uk
www.guildford-institute.org.uk
**About** A range of part time writing courses.

## Harrow College
**Harrow on the Hill Campus, Harrow College, Lowlands Road, Harrow, HA1 3AQ**
020 8909 6000
enquiries@harrow.ac.uk
www.harrow.ac.uk
**About** Part time creative writing courses.

## Havering Adult College
**Scimitar House, 23 Eastern Road, Romford, Essex, RM1 3NH**
01708 433790
01708 379569
enquiries-adultcollege@havering.gov.uk
www.havering.gov.uk/index.cfm?articleid=654
**About** Adult learning courses in creative writing.

## Henry Cort Community College
**Hillson Drive, Fareham, Hampshire, PO15 6PH**
01329 843127
01329 846755
enquiries@henry-cort.hants.sch.uk
www.henry-cort.hants.sch.uk/
**About** Creative writing courses.

## Hereward College
**Bramston Crescent, Tile Hill Lane, Coventry, CV4 9SW**

- 024 7646 1231
- 024 7669 4305
- enquiries@hereward.ac.uk
- www.hereward.ac.uk

**About** Full and part time courses in media and creative studies. The college has a particularly well developed programme for disabled students.

## Higham Hall
**Higham Hall College, Bassenthwaite Lake, Cockermouth, CA13 9SH**
- 01768 776276
- 01768 776013
- admin@highamhall.com
- www.highamhall.com

**About** Day and residential courses in literature and writing.

## Highbury College Portsmouth
**Dovercourt Road, Cosham, Portsmouth, PO6 2SA**
- 023 9231 3373
- 023 9232 5551
- info@highbury.ac.uk
- www.highbury.ac.uk

**About** Adult learning and full time certification courses in journalism disciplines, media and publishing.

## Hull College
**Part Time Provision Office, Larkin Building, University of Hull, Hull, HU6 7RX**
- 01482 466605
- v.j.magee@hull.ac.uk
- www.hull.ac.uk

**About** Creative writing evening course.

## ICS Ltd
**Skypark 5, 1st Floor, 45 Finnieston Street, Glasgow, G3 8JU**
- 0800 056 3983
- icscourseadvisors@ics-uk.co.uk
- www.icslearn.co.uk

**About** Distance learning journalism, proofreading and writing courses.

## Indian King Arts
**Garmoe Cottage, 2 Trefrew Road, Camelford, Cornwall, PL32 9TP**
- indianking@btconnect.com

**About** Poetry courses and workshops.

## Institute of Copywriting
**Overbrook House, Poolbridge Road, Blackford, Wedmore, BS28 4PA**
- 0800 781 1715
- 01934 713492
- copy@inst.org
- www.inst.org/copy

**About** Distance learning copywriting courses, for beginners and professionals.

## The Institute of Creative Writing
**Overbrook Business Centre, Poolbrook Road, Blackford, Wedmore, BS28 4PA**
- 0800 781 1715
- 01934 713492
- creative_writing_main_index_page_uk@inst.org.uk
- www.inst.org/authors

**About** Distance course on creative writing and getting published.

## Irish Academy
**Academy House, 1 Newtown Park, Blackrock, Co. Dublin, Republic of Ireland**
- 00353 1 278 0802
- 00353 1 278 0251
- info@irishacademy.com
- www.irishacademy.com

**About** Diploma and higher diploma in journalism. Also runs distance learning journalism courses.

## Irish Writers Centre
**19 Parnell Square, Dublin 1, Republic of Ireland**
- 00353 1 872 1302
- courses@writerscentre.ie
- www.writerscentre.ie

**About** Wide range of part time courses on writing.

## Itchen College
**Middle Road, Bitterne, Southampton, SO19 7TB**
- 023 8043 5636
- 023 8042 1911
- info@itchen.ac.uk
- www.itchen.ac.uk

**About** Journalism diplomas and short courses.

## John Wilson's Writing Courses
**Gate Road, Froncysyllte, Wrexham, Wales**
- john.wilson@virgin.net
- www.argoedebooks.com/writing-courses.html

**About** Beginner, intermediate and advanced courses on all aspects of writing and publishing. Distance tuition is also available.

## Josiah Mason College
**Slade Road, Erdington, Birmingham, B23 7JH**
- 0121 603 4757
- 0121 377 6076
- enquiries@jmc.ac.uk
- www.jmc.ac.uk

**About** Full time adult courses in journalism and media.

## Journalism School
**PO Box 380, Grimsby, DN32 8XR**
- 07951 815885
- info@thejournalismschool.co.uk
- www.thejournalismschool.co.uk

**About** Distance learning courses in journalism.

## Keele University
**Centre for Continuing and Professional Education, Keele University, Freepost ST1666, Newcastle Under Lyme, ST5 5BR**
- 01782 583436
- enquiries@cpe.keele.ac.uk
- www.keele.ac.uk/courses/cpe

**About** Creative writing courses at a range of centres, within the Staffordshire area.

## Killaloe Hedge-School of Writing
**4 Riverview, Ballina, Killaloe, Co. Clare, Republic of Ireland**
- 00353 61 375217
- 00353 61 375487
- www.killaloe.ie/khs/

**About** Various weekend writing courses and workshops. Contact David Rice.

## Kilroys College
**26 York Street, London, W1U 6PZ**
- 0845 300 4259
- homestudy@kilroyscollege.ac.uk
- www.kilroyscollege.co.uk

**About** Distance learning courses in creative writing and journalism.

## Knowsley Community College
**Roby Campus, Robert Road, Roby, Liverpool, L36 9TD**
- 0845 155 1055
- info@knowsleycollege.ac.uk
- www.knowsleycollege.ac.uk

**About** A-level enhancement course on an 'Introduction to Journalism'.

## Knuston Hall Residential College
**Irchester, Wellingborough, NN29 7EU**
- 01933 312104
- 01933 357596
- enquiries@knustonhall.org.uk
- www.knustonhall.org.uk

**About** Residential college running various short writing courses.

## Lambeth College
**Brixton Centre, 56 Brixton Hill, Lambeth, London, SW2 1QS**
- 020 7501 5000
- courses@lambethcollege.ac.uk
- www.lambeth.ac.uk

**About** Pre-entry, foundation degrees and certification courses in journalism. A short, part time, creative writing course is also available.

## Lancaster University
**Department of Continuing Education, Lancaster University, Ash House, Lancaster, LA1 4YT**
- 01524 592623
- 01524 592448
- conted@lancaster.ac.uk
- www.lancs.ac.uk/users/conted/index.htm

**About** Various short courses and distance learning courses in creative writing.

## Learning Curve Home Study Ltd
**Leader Cottage, Nether Blainslie, Galashiels, TD1 2PR**
- 01896 860661
- edesk@learningcurve.uk.com
- www.learningcurve-uk.com

**About** Various correspondence courses in writing and copywriting.

## Leicester City Council
**Admissions Department, Marlborough House, 38 Welford Road, Leicester, LE2 7AA**
- 0116 229 4367
- lifelonglearning@leicester.gov.uk
- www.leicester.gov.uk/index.asp?pgid=3636

**About** Community classes in creative writing.

## Leicestershire County Council

**County Hall, Leicester Road, Glenfield, Leicester, LE3 8RA**

- 0116 265 6387
- 0116 265 6398
- communityed@leics.gov.uk
- www.leics.gov.uk

**About** Creative writing classes at various locations around Leicestershire. Contact Louise Robinson.

## Liberato

**9 Bishops Avenue, Bishops Stortford, Hertfordshire, CM23 3EJ**

- 01279 833690
- liberato@tesco.net
- www.liberato.co.uk

**About** Writing retreats and courses in Suffolk and Greece. Also provide editorial services.

## Liverpool Community College

**The Arts Centre, Myrtle Street, Liverpool, L7 7JA**

- 0151 252 4360
- peter.dutton@liv-coll.ac.uk
- www.liv-coll.ac.uk

**About** Foundation diplomas in journalism disciplines. Contact Peter Dutton.

## London Academy of Radio, Film and TV

**1 Lancing Street, London, NW1 1NA**

- 0870 850 4994
- www.media-courses.com

**About** Vocational part time and short courses for all broadcast and audio media, including scriptwriting.

## London College of Communication

**London Artscom Ltd, London College of Communication, Elephant and Castle, London, SE1 6SB**

- 020 7514 6569
- shourtcourses@lcc.arts.ac.uk
- www.lcc.arts.ac.uk/training

**About** Wide range of short courses in writing and journalism.

## London School of Journalism

**126 Shirland Road, Maida Vale, London, W9 2BT**

- 020 7289 7777
- 020 7432 8141
- info@lsjournalism.org

- www.learntowrite.org

**About** Distance learning and short courses in journalism and writing.

## The Lotus Foundation

**16 Lancaster Grove, Swiss Cottage, London, NW3 4PB**

- 020 7794 8880
- info@lotusfoundation.org.uk
- www.lotusfoundation.org.uk

**About** Courses, workshops, therapy and poetry groups.

## Manchester Adult Education Service

**Various venues across Manchester**

- 0800 083 2121
- adult-education@manchester.gov.uk
- www.manchester.gov.uk/education/adulted/

**About** Community creative writing courses across Manchester.

## Marlborough College Summer School

**Marlborough College, Marlborough, Wiltshire, SN8 1PA**

- 01672 892388
- 01672 892476
- admin@mcsummerschool.org.uk
- www.mcsummerschool.org.uk

**About** July summer school with adult courses and workshops in creative writing disciplines.

## Mary Immaculate College, University of Limerick

**Department of English and Literature, Mary Immaculate College, University of Limerick, Republic of Ireland**

- maeve.tynan@mic.ul.ie
- www.mic.ul.ie/creativewriting/creativewriting3.htm

**About** A creative writing course based around a series of workshops. Contact Maeve Tynan.

## Middlesex University Summer School

**Summer School Office Middlesex University, Trent Park, Bramley Road, London, N14 4YZ**

- 020 8411 5782
- 020 8411 2297
- sschool@mdx.ac.uk
- www.mdx.ac.uk/summer

**About** Summer school runs from June–August and includes several courses on writing for different types of media.

## Morley College
**61 Westminster Bridge, London, SE1 7HT**
- 020 7928 8501
- 020 7928 4074
- enquiries@morleycollege.ac.uk
- www.morleycollege.ac.uk

**About** Part time creative writing courses, for beginners.

## National Academy of Writing
**University of Central England, Perry Barr Campus, Birmingham, B42 2SU**
- 0121 331 5540
- samantha.malkin@uce.ac.uk
- www.thenationalacademyofwriting.org.uk

**About** Diploma in writing, covering various genres. There is a strict application process to be followed before being accepted onto the full diploma course.

## National Council for the Training of Journalists
**The New Granary, Station Road, Newport, Saffron Walden, CB11 3PL**
- 01799 544014
- 01799 544015
- ingo@nctj.com
- www.nctj.com

**About** Accredits journalism courses at many different centres. Runs distance learning courses in magazine and newspaper journalism, and editing.

## National Extension College
**The Michael Young Centre, Purbeck Road, Cambridge, CB2 8HN**
- 0800 389 2839
- courses@nec.ac.uk
- www.nec.ac.uk/courses/category-browse?usca_p=t&category_id=489

**About** Distance learning courses on creative writing, writing for money and writing short stories.

## National Film and Television School
**Beaconsfield Studios, Station Road, Beaconsfield, Buckinghamshire, HP9 1LG**
- 01494 677903
- 01494 678708
- shortcourses@nftsfilm-tv.ac.uk

- www.nftsfilm-tv.ac.uk

**About** Many short courses on film and television writing and producing.

## National Home Study College
**Cardinal Point, Park Road, Rickmansworth, Hertfordshire, WD3 1RE**
- 0870 242 7141
- enquiries@homestudynet.com
- www.homestudynet.com

**About** Distance learning journalism, television and film production courses.

## Newcastle under Lyme College
**Liverpool Road, Newcastle under Lyme, Staffordshire, ST5 2DF**
- 01782 715111
- info@nulc.ac.uk
- www.nulc.ac.uk

**About** Diploma in media techniques, with radio and journalism.

## Nightcourses
- www.nightcourses.com

**About** Search facility for courses of various types, including part time and evening courses in the Republic of Ireland.

## North Warwickshire and Hinckley College
**Hinckley Road, Nuneaton, Warwickshire, CV11 6BH**
- 024 7624 3154
- communitycollege@nwhc.ac.uk
- www.nwhc.ac.uk

**About** A range of certificated writing courses.

## North West Institute of Further and Higher Education
**Strand Road, Londonderry, Northern Ireland, BT48 7AL**
- 028 7127 6000
- info@nwifhe.ac.uk
- www.nwifhe.ac.uk

**About** Journalism GCSE (part time), and radio journalism certificate.

## North West Kent College
**Oakfield Lane, Dartford, DA1 2JT**
- 01322 629400

01332 629468

course.enquiries@nwkcollege.ac.uk

www.nwkcollege.ac.uk

**About** Part time foundation degree in professional writing. Contact Neil Nixon.

## noSWeat Journalism Training
**16–17 Clerkenwell Close, London, EC1R 0AN**

020 7490 2006

info@nosweatjt.co.uk

www.nosweatjt.co.uk

**About** Newspaper, magazine and broadcast journalism, also editing courses. Contact Stephen Ward.

## Oaklands College
**St. Albans Smallford Campus, Hatfield Road, St. Albans, AL4 0JA**

01727 737080

help.line@oaklands.ac.uk

www.oaklands.ac.uk

**About** Journalism and media studies A Level, and part time courses in fiction writing.

## Open College of the Arts
**Open College of the Arts, Freepost SF10678**

0800 731 2116

01226 730838

open.arts@ukonline.co.uk

www.oca-uk.com/courses/creativewriting/

**About** Beginners and advanced creative writing courses.

## Open Learning Centre International
**24 King Street, Carmarthen, SA31 1BS**

0800 393743

01267 238179

info@olci.info

www.olci.info

**About** Distance learning courses in creative writing, media and journalism.

## Open University
**Literature Department, The Open University, Walton Hall, Milton Keynes, MK7 6AA**

0870 333 4340

01908 654806

art-lit-enquiries@open.ac.uk

www.open.ac.uk/arts/literature/creative-writing.htm

**About** Short beginners courses in creative writing.

## Oxford University Summer School
**Oxford University Department for Continuing Education, Rewley House, 1 Wellington Square, Oxford, OX1 2JA**

01865 270360

01865 270309

oussa@conted.ox.ac.uk

www.conted.ox.ac.uk/oussa

**About** July summer school running a variety of writing courses and workshops.

## Palmers College
**Chadwell Road, Grays, Essex, RM17 5TD**

01375 370121

enquiries@palmers.ac.uk

www.palmers.ac.uk

**About** A-level enhancement courses in journalism, writing and getting published.

## Periodical Publishers Association
**Queens House, 28 Kings Way, Holborn, London, WC2A 3LJ**

020 7404 4166

020 7404 4167

www.ppa.co.uk

**About** Full day, half day and two day courses in every aspect of periodical publishing, writing and marketing.

## Perth College
**Creiff Road, Perth, PH1 2NX**

01738 877000

01738 877001

pc.enquiries@perth.uhi.ac.uk

www.perth.ac.uk

**About** Creative writing leisure courses.

## Peterborough Regional College
**Park Crescent, Peterborough, PE1 4DZ**

01733 767366

01733 767986

www.peterborough.ac.uk

**About** Part time journalism and creative writing courses.

## Pitman Training Centre

0800 220454

www.pitman-training.com

**About** Journalism courses at centres around the country.

## Plunket College

Swords Road, Whitehall, Dublin 9, Republic of Ireland

- ☎ 00353 1 837 1689
- ☎ 00353 1 836 8066
- ✉ info@plunketcollege.ie
- 🌐 www.plunketcollege.ie

**About** Short evening course in creative writing.

## PMA Training

PMA House, Free Churh Passage, St. Ives, Cambridge, PE27 5AY

- ☎ 020 7278 0606
- ☎ 01480 496022
- ✉ training@pma-group.com
- 🌐 www.pma-group.com

**About** Training courses in journalism, media and communications, from beginner to postgraduate level. Run at their centre in central London, or as in house training sessions throughout the UK.

## Queens University, Belfast School of Education

Lifelong Learning, School of Education, Queen's University Belfast, Northern Ireland, BT7 1LN

- ☎ 028 9097 3323/3539
- ☎ 028 9023 9263
- ✉ education@qub.ac.uk
- 🌐 www.qub.ac.uk/edu

**About** Open learning courses in creative writing.

## Regent Academy

6 John Street, London, WC1N 2ES

- ☎ 0800 378281
- ☎ 020 7430 8401
- ✉ info@regentacademy.com
- 🌐 www.regentacademy.com

**About** Distance learning courses in many aspects of writing, publishing and the media.

## Reid Kerr College

Renfrew Road, Paisley, PA3 4DR

- ☎ 0800 052 7343
- ✉ sservices@reidkerr.ac.uk
- 🌐 www.reidkerr.ac.uk

**About** Creative writing course.

## Richmond Adult Community College

Clifden Road, Twickenham, Richmond upon Thames, TW1 4LT

- ☎ 020 8843 7997
- ☎ 020 8332 6560
- ✉ enquiries@racc.ac.uk
- 🌐 www.racc.ac.uk

**About** Range of part time writing courses including screenwriting, creative writing and comedy writing.

## Rotherham College of Arts and Technology

Town Centre Campus, College Campus, Eastwood Lane, Rotherham, S65 1EG

- ☎ 08080 722777
- ✉ info@rotherham.ac.uk
- 🌐 www.rotherham.ac.uk

**About** Advanced creative writing course (part time).

## Scottish Universities International Summer School

21 Buccleuch Place, Edinburgh, EH8 9LN

- ☎ 0131 650 4369
- ☎ 0131 662 0275
- ✉ suiss@ed.ac.uk
- 🌐 www.arts.ed.ac.uk/suiss

**About** Annual summer school, which includes creative writing courses.

## Screenwriter's Workshop

NPA Film Centre, 1.07 Tea Building, 56 Shoreditch High Street, London, E1 6JJ

- ☎ 020 7613 0440
- ☎ 020 7729 1852
- ✉ queries@npa.org.uk
- 🌐 www.npa.org.uk

**About** Training and events for producers and film makers.

## The Script Factory

66–67 Wells Street, London, W1T 3PY

- ☎ 020 7323 1414
- ✉ general@scriptfactory.co.uk
- 🌐 www.scriptfactory.co.uk

**About** Training, masterclasses and workshops on scriptwriting and development.

## Sheffield College

Norton College Site, Dyche Lane, Sheffield, S20 8LY

- ☎ 0114 260 3603
- ☎ 0114 260 3655
- 🌐 http://my.sheffcol.ac.uk/

**About** Full time accredited journalism courses.

## Somerset College of Arts and Technology
**Wellington Road, Taunton, Somerset, TA1 5AX**
- ☎ 01823 366366
- ☎ 01823 366418
- ✉ enquiries@somerset.ac.uk
- 🌐 www.somerset.ac.uk

**About** Access to higher education course in teaching, history and journalism.

## South East Essex College
**Luker Road, Southend on Sea, SS1 1ND**
- ☎ 01702 220400
- ☎ 01702 432320
- ✉ weekend@southend.ac.uk
- 🌐 www.southend.ac.uk

**About** Diploma in advanced publishing, and weekend courses in creative writing and writing novels.

## South Nottingham College
**West Bridgford Centre, Greythorn Drive, West Bridgford, Nottingham, NG2 7GA**
- ☎ 0115 914 6400
- ☎ 0115 914 6444
- ✉ enquiries@snc.ac.uk
- 🌐 www.snc.ac.uk

**About** Part time creative writing courses.

## South Tyneside College
**St. George's Avenue, South Shields, Tyne and Wear, NE34 6ET**
- ☎ 0191 427 3500
- 🌐 www.stc.ac.uk

**About** Foundation degree in media design.

## Spread the Word
**77 Lambeth Walk, London, SE11 6DX**
- ☎ 020 7735 3111
- ☎ 020 7735 2666
- ✉ info@spreadtheword.org.uk
- 🌐 www.spreadtheword.org.uk

**About** Courses, workshops and advice for London writers.

## Stevenson College Edinburgh
**Bankhead Avenue, Edinburgh, EH11 4DE**
- ☎ 0131 535 4600
- ☎ 0131 535 4700
- ✉ info@stevenson.ac.uk
- 🌐 www.stevenson.ac.uk

**About** Open access creative writing courses.

## St. Helen's College
**Town Centre Campus, Brook Street, St. Helens, Merseyside, WA10 1PZ**
- ☎ 01744 733766
- ☎ 01744 623400
- ✉ enquire@sthelens.ac.uk
- 🌐 www.sthelens.ac.uk

**About** Adult workshops in creative writing and radio journalism.

## Stonebridge Associated Colleges
**Stonebridge House, Bude, Cornwall, EX23 8ST**
- ☎ 0845 230 6880Ê
- ☎ 01288 355799
- ✉ info@stonebridge.uk.com
- 🌐 www.stonebridge.uk.com

**About** Wide range of short distance courses in writing and journalism.

## Strode College
**Strode College, Church Road, Street, Somerset, BA16 0AB**
- ☎ 01458 844400
- ☎ 01458 844411
- ✉ course-info@strode-college.ac.uk
- 🌐 www.strode-college.ac.uk

**About** Part time creative writing course.

## Study House
**Writers College, 8 Hillswood Avenue, Kendal, Cumbria, LA9 5BT**
- ☎ 01539 724622
- ✉ info@study-house.com
- 🌐 www.study-house.com/Writers%20College/writer_college.htm

**About** Certificates in fiction writing and journalism.

## St. Vincent's College
**Mill Lane, Gosport, PO12 4QA**
- ☎ 023 9258 8311
- ☎ 023 9251 1186
- ✉ info@stvincent.ac.uk
- 🌐 www.stvincent.ac.uk

**About** Diploma in media techniques (journalism and radio).

### Sutton Coldfield College
34 Lichfield Road, Sutton Coldfield, West Midlands, B74 2NW
- 0121 355 5671
- 0121 355 0799
- infoc@sutcol.ac.uk
- www.sutcol.ac.uk

**About** Full and part time adult courses in journalism, media and publishing. Pre-entry certificate in journalism.

### Swanwick Writers' Summer School
Hayes Conference Centre, Alfreton, Swanwick, Derbyshire, DE55 1UY
- swanwick@neteireann.com
- www.wss.org.uk

**About** Two week summer school in August, dedicated to writing courses. For all levels of experience.

### Swarthmore Education Centre
2–7 Woodhouse Square, Leeds, West Yorkshire, LS3 1AD
- 0113 243 2210
- 0113 243 2210
- info@swarthmore.org.uk
- www.swarthmore.org.uk

**About** Creative writing courses.

### Training and Performance Showcase
Shepperton Studios, Shepperton, Middlesex, TW17 0QD
- 01932 592151
- 01932 592233
- jill@tapsnet.org
- www.tapsnet.org

**About** Masterclasses and workshops for British television and film scriptwriters.

### Travellers' Tales
92 Hillfield Road, London, NW6 1QA
- info@travellerstales.org
- www.travellerstales.org

**About** Residential courses, retreats, holidays and masterclasses in travel writing.

### Ty Newydd
National Writers Centre for Wales, Llanystumdwy, Criceth, Gwynedd, LL52 0LW
- 01766 522811
- post@tyneyd.org
- www.tynewydd.org

**About** Residential writing courses.

### UCD Adult Education Centre
Library Building, University College Dublin, Belfield, Dublin 4, Republic of Ireland
- 00353 1 716 7123
- 00353 1 716 7500
- adult.education@ucd.ie
- www.ucd.ie/adulted/courses

**About** Adult courses in creative writing.

### UK Open Learning
31 Chapel Street, Bigrigg, Egremont, Cumbria, CA22 2UU
- 0800 043 4288
- sales@uk-open-learning.com
- www.uk-open-learning.com

**About** Distance learning courses in writing, journalism and editing.

### University Centre Hastings
Havelock Road, Hastings, East Sussex, TN34 1DQ
- 0845 602 0607
- information@uch.ac.uk
- www.uch.ac.uk

**About** Print and radio journalism certification course, as well as short courses in writing, poetry and screenwriting.

### University of Bristol
Department of English, 3–5 Woodland Road, Bristol, BS8 1TB
- 0117 928 9000
- admissions@bristol.ac.uk
- www.bris.ac.uk

**About** Short courses and day courses in creative writing, contact Tom Sperlinger, tom.sperlinger@bris.ac.uk Part time diploma in creative writing, contact Hilary Betts, hilary.betts@bristol.ac.uk

### University of Derby
1 Devonshire Road, Buxton, Derbyshire, SK17 6RY
- 01298 28321
- adultedbuxton@derby.ac.uk
- www.derby.ac.uk

**About** Introduction to creative writing', part time adult course.

## University of Dundee

**Continuing Education, University of Dundee, Nethergate, Dundee, DD1 4HN**

- 01382 383000
- 01382 201604
- university@dundee.ac.uk
- www.dundee.ac.uk/learning/conted

**About** Adult creative writing courses.

## University of East Anglia

**Continuing Education, Faculty of Social Sciences, University of East Anglia, Norwich, NR4 7TJ**

- 01603 591451
- 01603 451999
- cont.ed@uea.ac.uk
- www.uea.ac.uk/contedu/

**About** Certificates and diplomas in creative writing, screenwriting, fiction and poetry. Also run creative writing and literature day schools.

## University of Glasgow

**St. Andrew's Building, 11 Eldon Street, Glasgow, G3 6NH**

- 0141 330 1835
- 0141 330 1829
- dace-query@educ.gla.ac.uk
- www.gla.ac.uk/adulteducation

**About** Creative writing and journalism part time courses.

## University of Hull

**Part Time Provision Office, Larkin Building, University of Hull, HU6 7RX**

- 01482 466605
- p.robinson@hull.ac.uk, v.j.magee@hull.ac.uk, j.ayres@hull.ac.uk
- www.hull.ac.uk

**About** Certificate and diploma in creative writing.

## University of Kent

**School of English, Rutherford College, University of Kent, Canterbury, CT2 7NX**

- 01227 823054
- 01227 827001
- part-time@kent.ac.uk
- www.kent.ac.uk

**About** Part time certificates and diplomas in creative writing subjects. Run at a range of locations across Kent.

## University of Liverpool

**Continuing Education, University of Liverpool, 126 Mount Pleasant, Liverpool, L69 3GR**

- 0151 794 2538
- conted@liv.ac.uk
- www.liv.ac.uk/conted

**About** Part time courses in creative writing and getting published. Contact Joan Squires.

## University of Newcastle

**School of English, Percy Building, Newcastle upon Tyne, NE1 7RU**

- 0191 222 7625
- 0191 222 8708
- v.a.aves@ncl.ac.uk
- www.ncl.ac.uk/elll/creative

**About** Short courses in various types of creative writing. Also run spring and summer schools on creative writing and host many other writing events, such as readings. Contact Viv Aves.

## University of Reading

**The School of Continuing Education, London Road, Reading, RG1 5AQ**

- 0118 378 8347
- continuing-education@reading.ac.uk
- www.reading.ac.uk/conted

**About** Day courses on writing for radio, screenwriting, picture writing and other writing topics.

## University of Sheffield

**Institute for Lifelong Learning, University of Sheffield, 196–198 West Street, Sheffield, S1 4ET**

- 0114 222 7000
- 0114 222 7001
- till@sheffield.ac.uk
- www.sheffield.ac.uk/till

**About** Certificate in creative writing. Contact Dr. Sandra Courtman, s.courtman@sheffield.ac.uk Also run a range of creative writing and general interest courses.

## University of St. Andrews

**University of St. Andrews Creative Writing Summer Program, St. Katharine's West, 16 The Scores, St. Andrews, KY16 9AX**

- 01334 462238
- 01334 462158
- crsp@st-andrews.ac.uk
- www.st-andrews.ac.uk

**About** Summer school for creative writing. Contact Dr. M.I.S. Hunter.

## University of Strathclyde
Centre for Lifelong Learning, Graham Hills Building, 40 George Street, Glasgow, G1 1QE
- 0141 548 4803
- janice.macwhirter@strath.ac.uk
- www.cll.strath.ac.uk

**About** Evening and weekend classes in many types of writing. Contact Janice MacWhirter.

## University of Sunderland
Centre for Lifelong Learning, Joseph Cowen House, Newcastle upon Tyne, NE1 7RU
- 0191 515 2800
- 0191 515 2890
- lifelong.learning@sunderland.ac.uk
- www.cll.sunderland.ac.uk

**About** Wide range of adult education courses in literature, writing and getting published.

## University of Sussex
Centre for Continuing Education, The Sussex Institute, Essex House, University of Sussex, Brighton, BN1 9QQ
- 01273 877888
- 01273 877534
- si-enquiries@sussex.ac.uk
- www.sussex.ac.uk

**About** Open courses in creative writing. Also teach a certificate in creative writing.

## University of the Arts, London
65 Davies Street, London, W1K 5DA
- 020 7514 6000
- info@arts.ac.uk
- www.arts.ac.uk

**About** Many short courses on writing, editing, journalism and publishing, at various centres in London.

## University of Warwick
Centre for Lifelong Learning, University of Warwick, Coventry, CV4 7AL
- 024 7652 4617
- 024 7652 4223
- cll@warwick.ac.uk
- www.warwick.ac.uk/cll/openstudies

**About** Adult short courses in creative writing, journalism and publishing.

## Upper Bann Institute of Further and Higher Education
Banbridge Campus, 36 Lurgan Road, Portadown, Co. Armargh, Northern Ireland, BT63 5BL
- enquiries@ubi.ac.uk
- www.ubi.ac.uk

**About** NVQ4 Journalism course. Contact Ms. G. McIvor, mcivorg@ubi.ac.uk

## Urchfont Manor College
Urchfont, Devizes, Wiltshire, SN10 4RG
- 01380Ê840495
- 01380 840005
- urchfontmanor@wiltshire.gov.uk
- www.urchfontmanor.co.uk

**About** Residential courses, day courses and study tours on creative writing topics.

## Wakefield Adult & Community Education Service
Manygates Education Centre, Manygates Lane, Sandal, Wakefield, WF2 7DQ
- 01924 303302
- aces@wakefield.gov.uk
- www.wakefieldaes.org.uk

**About** Creative writing community course. Contact Andrea Benson.

## Waterford Institute of Technology
Adult and Continuing Education Office, WIT College Street Campus, St. Dominic's, Waterford, Republic of Ireland
- 00353 51 302000
- info@wit.ie
- www.wit.ie

**About** Creative writing evening class.

## Wedgewood Memorial College
Station Road, Barlaston, Stoke on Trent, ST12 9DG
- 01782 372105
- 01782 372393
- wedgewood.memorial@swann.stoke.gov.uk
- www.sgfl.org.uk/wmc

**About** Residential and day courses on various writing topics.

## Weston College
Knightsone Road, Weston Super Mare, BS23 2AL
- 01934 411411

01934 411410
enquiries@weston.ac.uk
www.weston.ac.uk
**About** Part time creative writing courses.

## Workers Educational Association
**3rd Floor, 70 Clifton Street, London, EC2A 4HB**
020 7426 3450
020 7426 3451
national@wea.org.uk
www.wea.org.uk
**About** Voluntary provider of adult learning, including courses in creative writing, publishing and journalism. Search the website by location to find the nearest course.

## Write Away
**Arts Training Central, Arts Council East Midlands, 16 New Street, Leicester, LE1 5NR**
0116 242 5202
info@artstrainingcentral.co.uk
www.artstrainingcentral.co.uk
**About** Residential courses on writing, from Friday to Sunday afternoon. Held at Leicester University.

## The Write Coach
**2 Rowan Close, Wokingham, RG1 4BH**
0118 978 4904
info@thewritecoach.co.uk
www.thewritecoach.co.uk
**About** Courses, workshops and individual sessions on how to overcome writer's block and get motivated, from life coach and writer, Bekki Hill.

## Writers Academy
**Carrig on Bannow, Co. Wexford, Republic of Ireland**
00353 51 561789
thewritersacademy@eircom.net
www.thewritersacademy.net
**About** Correspondence courses and editorial services for writers.

## Writers Bureau
**Sevendale House, 7 Dale Street, Manchester, M1 1JB**
0845 345 5995
0161 236 9440
advisory@writersbureau.com
www.writersbureaucourse.com

**About** Home study courses on writing and getting published.

## Writers News
**1st Floor Victoria House, 143–145 The Headrow, Leeds, LS1 5RL**
0113 200 2917
0113 200 2928
rachel.bellerby@writersnews.co.uk
www.writersnews.co.uk
**About** Nine home based courses on writing and journalism.

## Write Words
**Writewords, PO Box 850, St. Albans, AL1 9BE**
admin@writewords.org.uk
www.writewords.org.uk
**About** Range of email correspondence courses on different types of writing and publishing.

## The Writing College
**16 Magdalen Road, Exeter, EX2 4SY**
0800 328 9396
01392 498008
enquiries@writingcollege.com
www.writingcollege.com
**About** The complete writer' correspondence course.

## Writing Life
**PO Box 4065, Braintree, Essex, CM7 9RJ**
info@creativewritinglife.co.uk
www.creativewritinglife.co.uk
**About** Teach-yourself' creative writing course. For £5 you are sent all the course materials.

## Written Words
**5 Queen Elisabeth Close, London, N16 0HL**
henrietta@writtenwords.net
www.writtenwords.net
**About** Intensive beginners, or advanced day courses for writers. Also runs workshops and private tutorials.

## Wye Valley Arts Centre
**The Coach House, Mork, St. Briavel's, Lydney, Gloucestershire, GL15 6QH**
01594 530214
01291 689463
wyearts@cwc.net

www.wyeart.cwc.net
**About** Workshops and residential courses on various types of writing.

## Yorkshire Art Circus
**School Lane, Glasshoughton, Castleford, WF10 4QH**
01977 550401
01977 512819
admin@artcircus.org.uk
www.artcircus.org.uk
**About** Courses and workshops in creative writing and publishing for writers throughout Yorkshire. Also run a young writer development programme. Contact beccy@artcircus.org.uk

The potential here to win seems huge, but a careful read will reveal that many of the competitions and prizes have very specific rules, and are often aimed at rewarding writing in specific areas. Many are not open, but are by nomination or by decision of the organisation behind the award. Writers should look to their publishers to submit their work in many instances as that is what the competitions will expect and accept.

## Academi Cardiff International Poetry Competition

**Academi, Mount Stuart House, Mount Stuart Square, Cardiff, CF10 5FQ**

- 029 2047 2266
- 029 2049 2930
- post@academi.org
- www.academi.org

**Competition/Award Director** Chief Executive, Peter Finch

**Established** 1986

**Insider Info** The competition is administered by Academi with the financial assistance of Cardiff Council. The competition takes place annually, with a first prize of £5,000; second prize of £500; third prize of £250 and five runner up prizes of £50 each. The competition is judged by three established poets, with one acting as a filter judge. Copyright will remain with the competitor, but Academi reserves the right to arrange the first publication or broadcast of selected poems as it sees fit. The competition is open to poets of all nationalities, they do not have to be resident in Wales.

**Genres** Poetry

**Submission Guidelines** Submissions should be received before January 26 each year and must be previously unpublished. Guidelines and entry forms are available with SAE. There is an entry fee of £5 per poem.

## Aeon Award

**8 Bachelor's Walk, Dublin 1, Republic of Ireland**

- fraslaw@yahoo.co.uk
- www.albedo1.com

**Insider Info** The Aeon Award is for the best submitted short story in the Science Fiction, Horror or Fantasy genres. Submissions are invited for four closing dates (end of September, December, March and June each year) and the shortlist is added to after each round is complete. The competition takes place annually, and the overall winner, chosen from the shortlist compiled after four rounds of submissions, wins €1,000. The top four will be published in *Albedo One* magazine and writer Ian Watson will judge the overall winner.

**Genres** Short Stories

**Submission Guidelines** Submission guidelines are available on the website. There is an entry fee of €5 per entry and stories must be previously unpublished. Email and postal submissions are welcome.

**Tips** Entries must be no longer than 8,000 words and be typed with double spacing.

## The Alexander Prize

**University College London, Gower Street, London, WC1E 6BT**

- 020 7387 7532
- 020 7387 7532
- rhs.info@rhs.ac.uk
- www.rhs.ac.uk

**Competition/Award Director** Executive Secretary

**Established** 1897

**Insider Info** Sponsored by the Royal Historical Society. Awarded annually for a published scholarly journal article or an essay based on original historical research. The award recognises the accomplishments of doctoral candidates and fledgling historians. The prize consists of £250 or a silver medal. Entrants must be doctoral students in history in a UK institution, or be within two years of having graduated from a doctoral degree course in history in a UK institution.

**Genres** Essays, Articles

**Submission Guidelines** Deadline for entries is the end of December. Previously published entries must have been published in an academic journal or an edited collection between January 1 and December 31.

**Tips** Submit two hard copies of the published item (not manuscript copies) with full information on the journal or volume in which it was published.

## The Alfred Fagon Award

**The Royal Court Theatre, Sloane Square, London, SW1W 8AS**

www.talawatheatrecompany.co.uk
**Established** 1997
**Insider Info** An award in memory of playwright Alfred Fagon designed to recognise a variety of writing talents in people of Caribbean descent, particularly playwrights. Awarded annually, winners receive £5,000. Writers must be of Caribbean descent and living in the UK.
**Genres** Scripts
**Submission Guidelines** The play need not have been produced.
**Tips** To apply send two copies of a script along with an author biography and covering letter by post before the deadline. Closing dates will be published on the website.

## ALPSP Awards and ALPSP/Charlesworth Awards
**47 Vicarage Road, Old Moulsham, Chelmsford, CM2 9BS**
01245 260571
01245 260935
events@alpsp.org
www.alpsp.org
**Competition/Award Director** Lesley Ogg
**Insider Info** Awards for achievements in learning and professional publishing. The award ceremony is held annually and takes place in September. Entries are judged by a panel of independent experts.
**Tips** The ALPSP Awards are open to publishers, societies and journals, either UK- or internationally-based. Includes commercial and not-for-profit organisations. Full details available on the website.

## The Amaury Talbot Prize for African Anthropology
**50 Fitzroy Street, London, W1T 5BT**
020 7387 0455
020 7388 8817
admin@therai.org.uk
www.therai.org.uk
**Competition/Award Director** Amaury Talbot Prize Coordinator
**Insider Info** Sponsored by the Royal Anthropological Institute. An award for non-fiction on anthropological research relating to Africa. Awarded annually, prize money is £500. Judges are appointed by the RAI Council.
**Genres** Non-fiction
**Submission Guidelines** Deadline for entries is end of March each year. Work should be published previously, between April 1 and March 31.

**Tips** Preference is given firstly to work relating to Nigeria and secondly to another part of West Africa or West Africa in general. Submit three copies of the book, work or article.

## The André Simon Memorial Book Awards
**1 Westbourne Gardens, Glasgow, G12 9XE**
0141 342 4929
katie@andresimon.co.uk
www.andresimon.co.uk
**Competition/Award Director** Sarah Jane Evans
**Established** 1975
**Insider Info** Awards for best food book and drink book that may include recipe books, biographies, guides, polemical works or reference books that focus from some angle on food and drink. Awarded annually, the winners in each category receive £2,000 with special commendations receiving £1,000.
**Genres** Non-fiction.
**Submission Guidelines** Deadline for entries is November; books must have been published in the previous year.
**Tips** Nominations are usually invited from publishers from April onwards although all books within the remit of the award will be considered.

## Angus Book Award
**County buildings, Forfar, DD8 3WF, Scotland**
01307 461460
01307 462590
cultural.services@angus.gov.uk
www.angus.gov.uk/bookaward
**Established** 1995
**Insider Info** A shortlist of five new paperback novels for teenagers are voted for by Angus secondary school children. This award is designed to encourage older children to take an active interest in books and is held annually. Sponsored by Angus Council.
**Genres** Fiction, Novels and Teenage Fiction
**Submission Guidelines** Titles must be previously published.
**Tips** To be eligible for this award books must have been written by UK authors.

## The Anthony Hecht Poetry Prize
**9 Woodstock Road, London, N4 3ET**
020 8374 5526
020 8374 5736
waywiserpress@aol.com

🌐 www.way-wiserpress.com

**Competition/Award Director** Philip Hoy

**Established** 2005

**Insider Info** Sponsored by the Waywiser Press. The prize is awarded annually to the best collection of poems in English submitted by an author who has no more than one previous collection of poems published. The purpose is to reward the author of the best collection with a cash prize of £1,750 as well as publication of his/her collection by The Waywiser Press in the UK and USA. In 2005, the judge was J. D. McClatchy, poet, critic and editor of the Yale Review, as well as Anthony Hecht's literary executure. In 2006, it was Mary Jo Salter, poet, anthologist and teacher at Mount Holyoke College. The prize winner will be offered a publishing contract with a standard set of royalties specified. Entrants must be 18 or over. They may not have published more than one previous collection of poems (though they may have published books belonging to other genres, and individual poems from the submission may have been published in magazines, journals, anthologies and chapbooks of 32 pages or less, or self-published books of 46 pages or less). No author who has a book published by or forthcoming from Waywiser may enter. Manuscripts must be in English, though as much as one third of the poems they contain can consist of public domain or permission-secured translations.

**Genres** Poetry

**Submission Guidelines** Deadline for entry is December; some small changes are possible and potential entrants are advised to consult the guidelines (available with entry forms via SAE). Entry fee is £15. Work should be unpublished.

**Tips** Feature poems from each of the people who get as far as the semi-finals appear on the website; the work is very diverse, but some idea of the standard required can be seen here.

## Arthur C. Clarke Award for Science Fiction

**60 Bournemouth Road, Folkestone, Kent, CT19 5AZ**

☎ 01303 252939

✉ clarkeaward@gmail.com

🌐 www.clarkeaward.com

**Competition/Award Director** Paul Billinger

**Established** 1986

**Insider Info** The Arthur C. Clarke Award for Science Fiction is presented for the best Science Fiction novel of the year, as selected from a shortlist. The award is presented annually and the prize consists of a trophy and £2,008 (for the 2008 award and

increasing by £1 annually). The winning book is picked by a jury panel. This competition is open to writers from any nationality, provided their book is in English and published in the UK.

**Genres** Science Fiction

**Submission Guidelines** Titles must be previously published in the UK between January 1 and December 31 in the current year.

**Tips** Novellas (less than 30,000 words) and short story collections are not eligible for this award. Entries should be made by the book's publishers.

## Arundel Theatre Trails Writers Competitions

**Drip Action Theatre, 13 King Street, Arundel, West Sussex, BN18 9BJ**

☎ 01903 885250

✉ dripactioninfo@btinternet.com

**Established** 2000

**Insider Info** Entries are invited to fill the slots designated for eight short plays at The Arundel Festival. Competition takes place annually. Eight winning plays will be performed at the festival and the overall winner will receive the Joy Gaun award. Each writer will also receive a £100 fee.

**Genres** Scripts

**Submission Guidelines** Submissions should be received before December 31 each year. There is a £5 fee for each script submitted.

**Tips** Scripts need to be 30–40 minutes long and suitable to be performed in the day with limited props and cast. Submit a hard copy by post, restricted to one play per entrant.

## Arvon Foundation International Poetry Competition

**2nd Floor, 42a Buckingham Palace Road, London, SW1W 0RE**

☎ 020 7931 7611

🖷 020 7963 0961

✉ comps@arvonfoundation.org

🌐 www.arvonfoundation.org

**Established** 1980

**Insider Info** This is a competition for unpublished poems in the English language. The competition is held annually with a first prize of £5,000, second prize of £2,500, third prize of £1,000 and three runner up prizes of £500 each. The judges change each year; the 2006 panel consisted of Sujata Bhatt, Edna Longley and Michael Symmons-Roberts. Worldwide copyright remains with the poets but Arvon may publish the poem or produce reading in all media platforms within 12 months of the prize-giving.

**Genres** Poetry

**Submission Guidelines** Submissions should be received between May and the end of September each year. Submission guidelines are available on the website. There is a fee of £7 for the first poem and £5 for each subsequent poem. Poems must be previously unpublished.

**Tips** Submit two hard copies of each poem on single-sided sheets, along with an entry form which is available on the website.

## Asham Award

**Lewes Town Hall, High Street, Lewes, East Sussex, BN7 2QS**

- 01273 483159
- camilla@ashamaward.com
- www.ashamaward.com

**Competition/Award Director** Carole Buchan (administrator)

**Established** 1995

**Insider Info** The Asham award is a short story competition open to women of any nationality, providing they have not previously had any short or full length fiction published. The award is designed to allow new women writers the same platform as more well-known authors. The competition is held every two years (odd years). Winners are published in an anthology of short stories and receive a share of £3,000 prize money. Winners also get advice from novelist Kate Pullinger and are given the chance to take part in writing workshops. The competition is open to female writers only, over the age of 18.

**Genres** Short Stories

**Submission Guidelines** Submissions must be previously unpublished.

**Tips** There is no set theme or genre for the stories. There are normally between 700 and 950 entries for the award every year.

## Author's Club First Novel Award

**40 Dover Street, London, W1S 4NP**

- 020 7499 8581
- 020 7409 0913
- authors@theartsclub.co.uk

**Competition/Award Director** Stella Kane

**Established** 1954

**Insider Info** The Author's Club award is presented to a promising work of fiction written by a British author and published in the UK. The award is presented annually, with prize money of £1,000.

**Genres** Novels

**Submission Guidelines** Submissions must be previously published full-length novels by first-time authors.

**Tips** Entries are usually nominated by publishers.

## BAAL Book Prize

**Department of Linguistics and English Language, Lancaster University, Lancaster, LA1 4YT**

- 01524 843085
- c.dembry@lancs.ac.uk
- www.baal.org.uk

**Insider Info** This prize is awarded to a book in the field of Applied Linguistics. This prize is offered annually and is open to any writer worldwide.

**Genres** Non-fiction and Lingustics.

**Submission Guidelines** Submissions should be received before December 13 each year. Guidelines are available on the website. There is a fee of £35 per title submitted. Titles must be previously published. Nominations must be made by the book's publishers and be accompanied by four hard copies of the book itself. Post to Claire Dembry at the above address.

**Tips** Linguistics is a broad term and can include sociolinguistics, discourse analysis, communication studies and education. If unsure about the work's eligibility, contact Veronika Koller, Publications Secretary: v.koller@lancaster.ac.uk.

## BA/Nielsen BookData Author of the Year

**The Booksellers Association of the UK and Ireland, 272 Vauxhall Bridge Road, London, SW1V 1BA**

- 020 7802 0801
- 020 7802 0803
- naomi.gane@booksellers.org.uk
- www.booksellers.org.uk

**Competition/Award Director** Naomi Gane

**Established** 1993

**Insider Info** Booksellers Association members vote for the writer who has made the biggest impact on their business in that year. This can be in a sales context or could reflect their personal tastes. This award is presented annually and consists of £1,000 and a trophy.

**Submission Guidelines** The title must be published within the preceding year.

**Tips** There are no entries invited as the winner is voted for entirely by BA members.

## BBC Four Samuel Johnson Prize for Non-fiction

**Colman Getty PR, 28 Windmill Street, London, W1T 2JJ**

- 020 7631 2666
- 020 7631 2699
- info@colmangettypr.co.uk
- www.bbc.co.uk/bbcfour/books/features/ samueljohnson

**Established** 1999

**Insider Info** Celebrates the best work of non-fiction published in the previous year. Competition takes place annually. The prize consists of £30,000 for the winner and smaller cash prizes for shortlisted books. 2006 judges included Robert Winston, Sir Richard Eyre, Pankaj Mishra, Cristina Odone and Michael Prodger.

**Genres** Non-fiction

**Submission Guidelines** Work should be previously published, having appeared between May 1 of the previous year and April 30 of the year of entry.

**Tips** Entries should be submitted by publishers only and can include non-fiction books on a wide range of topics.

## BBC Wildlife/Expert Africa Travel Writing Award

**14th Floor, Tower House, Fairfax Street, Bristol, BS1 3BN**

- 0117 314 8375
- jamesfair@bbcmagazinesbristol.com
- www.bbcwildlifemagazine.com

**Competition/Award Director** James Fair

**Insider Info** BBC Wildlife/Expert Africa Travel Writing Award is given to 800 words of travel writing that involves an intimate encounter with a wild animal, on foot or in a boat (but not in a car). The purpose of the competition is to showcase the best travel writing of BBC Wildlife (and other) readers and to offer them the chance to write about their nature experiences. This competition is held annually and the prize is a wildlife holiday for two supplied by Expert Africa. By entering the material in the competition, the writer grants BBC Wildlife the right to publish it in the magazine (only winning entries are published).

**Genres** Non-fiction

**Submission Guidelines** Submissions must be received by February 28 each year. Entry form is in the magazine. Any writer can enter but all entries must be previously unpublished.

**Tips** Read the magazine for more details.

## BBC Wildlife Magazine Poet of the Year Award

**Tower House, 14th Floor, Fairfax Street, Bristol, BS1 3BN**

- 0117 927 9009
- 0117 927 9008
- wildlifemagazine@bbcmagazinesbristol.com
- www.bbcwildlifemagazine.com

**Insider Info** This is an award for unpublished poetry on the subject of the natural world and/or our relationship to it. Details are published in the April edition of the magazine, which entrants are encouraged to buy. There are five categories: adult; age 15–17; age 12–14; age 8–11; and age 7 and under. This award is presented annually; first prize for adults consists of publication in the magazine and a trip to Lancashire. Young poets receive books as their prizes. By entering the competition, entrants grant, free of charge, the right for all or part of their poem to be published, broadcast, transmitted, and read in all media (now known or hereafter created), or on stage, including the right for the poems to be published in *BBC Wildlife Magazine* and any resulting anthology if the organizers wish.

**Genres** Poetry

**Submission Guidelines** Submissions must be received by the end of May each year. The poetry must be previously unpublished.

**Tips** Poems can take any form and could be, for example, a song of praise, an ode, or a lament and may be in rhyme, free verse or blank verse.

## BBC Wildlife Magazine Young Environmental Journalist of the Year Award

**14th Floor, Tower House, Fairfax Street, Bristol, BS1 3BN**

- 0117 927 9009
- 0117 933 8032
- www.bbcwildlifemagazine.com

**Insider Info** A national competition for people aged 18–25 who are interested in conservation journalism. Entrants must interview somebody who has been involved in conservation, and write a profile in less than 750 words. Competition takes place annually. The prize consists of publication in the magazine and an Earthwatch trip (flights included) where winners can choose to take part in conservation projects. Judges are: Richard Donkin, journalist and trustee of Earthwatch; Eva Carpenter, Director of Programmes for Earthwatch; James Fair, Environment Editor for BBC Wildlife; and Kate Humble, BBC presenter.

**Genres** Articles

**Submission Guidelines** Submissions should be received by the end of April each year. Further guidelines are available on the website. Entrants may be published before, but the article itself must not have been. Attach an entry form (available from the website).

**Tips** Articles should show a broader interest in the environment that goes beyond an interest in one person. Entries should be typed on single-sided sheets. Winners will be commissioned for a further article for BBC Wildlife magazine.

## Ben Pimlott Prize for Political Writing
**The Fabian Society, 11 Dartmouth Street, London, SW1H 9BN**
- 020 7227 4900
- 020 7676 7153
- www.guardian.co.uk/benpimlottprize

**Established** 2005

**Insider Info** This competition is sponsored by The Fabian Society and *The Guardian*. The Ben Pimlott Prize for Political Writing is an open competition for political essays on a particular theme and using a given title. The competition was started in memory of Ben Pimlott, political writer and regular contributor to *The Guardian*. The competition is held annually and the winner receives £3,000 and the essay is published in *The Guardian Review*.

**Genres** Political Essays

**Submission Guidelines** Submissions must be received by the end of March each year. Essays must be previously unpublished.

**Tips** Essays should be no longer than 3,000 words. Because the winning entry will be published in *The Guardian*, it may be useful to follow *The Guardian* style guide, available at www.guardian.co.uk/styleguide although this is not mandatory.

## The Bernard Levin Award
**Woodbourn Business Centre, 10 Jessell Street, Sheffield, S9 3HY**
- 0114 244 9561
- 0114 244 9563
- admin@indexers.org.uk
- www.indexers.org.uk

**Established** 2000

**Insider Info** Sponsored by The Society of Indexers. Awarded to an individual for outstanding services to The Society of Indexers. Competition held every one to two years.

**Tips** No submissions.

## Betty Trask Awards
**84 Drayton Gardens, London, SW10 9SB**
- 020 7373 6642
- 020 7373 5768
- info@societyofauthors.org
- www.societyofauthors.org

**Insider Info** These awards are sponsored by the Society of Authors and presented for the best first published, due to be published, or unpublished novel by a writer under the age of 35. Novels should be romantic or traditional and the prize will not be awarded to experimental fiction. Several prizes may be presented in one year and prize money totals £25,000 and should be used for periods of foreign travel.

**Genres** Fiction, Novels

**Submission Guidelines** Submissions must be received by the end of January each year. Guidelines and entry form is available on the website.Writers should be Commonwealth citizens and must not have had work published other than the novel submitted. Unpublished writers should submit a copy of the manuscript. Published writers should send a book, proof or manuscript via their publisher. Mark for the attention of Dorothy Sym.

## Bill Naughton Short Story Competition
**Box No 2006, Aghamore, Ballyhaunis, County Mayo, Republic of Ireland**
- 00353 94 9367019
- paulwdrogers@eircom.net
- www.aghamoreireland.com/kennynaughton/shortstory.htm

**Insider Info** This is an open short story competition for stories of up to 2,500 words on any subject matter or theme. The competition is held annually and €200 is awarded for 1st prize, €130 for 2nd prize and €65 for 3rd prize.

**Genres** Short Stories

**Submission Guidelines** Submissions must be received by the end of September each year. There is a £5 fee per story or £10 for three stories. Stories must be previously unpublished. There is no entry form but all entries must be postal.

## The Biographer's Club Prize
**119a Fordwych Road, London, NW2, 3NJ**
- 020 7222 7574
- 020 7222 7576
- lownie@globalnet.co.uk, anna@annaswan.co.uk
- www.biographersclub.co.uk

**Competition/Award Director** Andrew Lownie
**Established** 1999
**Insider Info** Sponsored by *The Daily Mail*. Created to finance and encourage new writers researching a biography. All previous winners have secured publishing contracts. Awarded annually, with prize money of £1,000. Judges change each year; for 2007: Rachel Holmes, Anne Sebba and Christopher Sinclair-Stevenson. Entrants must be previously unpublished, uncommisioned and must be proposing a biography.
**Genres** Biographies
**Submission Guidelines** Deadline for entries is August. Work should be previously unpublished.
**Tips** Submit a 15–20 page proposal to Anna Swan, competition administrator. Include an author's CV, information on sources, market competition and a synopsis of each chapter together with a sample of ten concurrent pages.

## Birdwatch Bird Book of the Year
**B403a The Chocolate Factory, 5 Clarendon Road, London, N22 6XJ**
☎ 020 8881 0550
✉ enquiries@birdwatch.co.uk
🌐 www.birdwatch.co.uk
**Established** 1992
**Insider Info** This award is sponsored by *Birdwatch Magazine* and is awarded to a publication dealing with ornithology that has appealed to a broad audience, rather than a niche market.
**Genres** Non-fiction
**Submission Guidelines** Submissions must be previously published.
**Tips** Nominations are only accepted from publishers only.

## Biscuit Poetry and Short Story Prizes
**PO Box 123, Washington, Newcastle Upon Tyne, NE37 2YW**
✉ info@biscuitpublishing.com
🌐 www.biscuitpublishing.com
**Insider Info** Biscuit Publishing run a variety of competitions that may change from year to year. The 2007 award was for poetry and short stories, the winners of each category (short fiction or poetry) win £1,000 cash. Runners up win a writer's retreat at Flanders Talbot House.
**Genres** Poetry, Short Stories and Story Collections
**Submission Guidelines** Submissions must be received by October 1 each year. Guidelines are available on the website. There is a fee of £12 per portfolio. Submit either three short stories of 1,000–

5,000 words or six poems along with a cover sheet. Writers can enter in both categories if they wish and can win in both. State on the cover sheet if the poetry or stories are intended for children, and what ages. Sheets should be single sided and double spaced. Include SAE for results and a postcard if acknowledgement is required. No email entries accepted.

## Blinking Eye Poetry Competition
**PO Box 549, North Shields, Tyne & Wear, NE30 2WT**
✉ poetry@blinking-eye.co.uk
🌐 www.blinking-eye.co.uk
**Insider Info** This competition is sponsored by Blinking Eye Publishing and is a poetry competition for the over fifties where writers are invited to submit a small collection of five poems in any style. The competition takes place annually. The overall winner will have a complete collection published by Blinking Eye and will receive 100 copies. The competition is open to any writer over the age of 50 on August 7 each year, regardless of nationality.
**Genres** Poetry
**Submission Guidelines** Submissions must be received by August 7 each year. Guidelines are available on the website. There is a fee of £10 per five poems. The five sample poems should be unpublished although online publication is acceptable. Poems must be in English. Only overseas entrants may submit online. UK writers should submit five poems by post, along with a cover sheet containing contact details. All sheets should be double spaced, single sided and typed.

## Blinking Eye Short Story Competition
**PO Box 549, North Shields, Tyne & Wear, NE30 2WT**
✉ poetry@blinking-eye.co.uk
🌐 www.blinking-eye.co.uk
**Insider Info** This competition is sponsored by Blinking Eye Publishing and is a competition for short stories of up to 5,000 words in any genre except Children's. The competition is designed to encourage older writers, and entrants must be over 50 years of age. The competition is held annually. The winner will have a collection of short stories published and receive 100 copies of the book. An anthology of other entries may be published and in this case contributors will receive a complimentary copy. Open to any writer over 50 on February 7 each year, regardless of nationality.
**Genres** Short Stories

**Submission Guidelines** Submissions must be received by February 7 each year. There is a fee of £7 per story. Stories must be previously unpublished. Overseas entrants may apply online, otherwise postal submissions are required. Stories should be in English, typed, double spaced and single sided, and accompanied by a cover sheet including contact details.

## Blue Peter Book Awards
c/o Awards Administrator, Fraser Ross Associates, 6 Wellington Place, Edinburgh, EH6 7EQ
☎ 0131 553 2759
☎ 0131 553 2759
✉ lindsey.fraser@tiscali.co.uk, kjross@tiscali.co.uk
🌐 www.bbc.co.uk/cbbc/bluepeter/bookclub/awards
**Established** 2000
**Insider Info** A shortlist of books for young people is put together by a panel of celebrity judges. The winners are then decided by a selection of young judges, chosen through a selection process. Categories are: The Best Book with Facts; The Book I Couldn't Put Down; and The Best Illustrated Book to Read Aloud. From these three winning titles, a Book of the Year is selected. These awards are presented annually, and winners receive a trophy.
**Genres** Children's Fiction and Non-fiction
**Submission Guidelines** The awards take place in June each year. Titles must be previously published.
**Tips** Previous winners include high profile books such as *Harry Potter and the Philosopher's Stone* by J.K Rowling and *Private Peaceful* by Michael Morpurgo.

## Boardman Tasker Prize
Pound House, Llangennith, Swansea, W Glamorgan, SA3 1JQ
☎ 01792 386 215
☎ 01792 386 215
✉ margaretbody@lineone.net
🌐 www.boardmantasker.com
**Competition/Award Director** Margaret Body (Hon. Sec.)
**Established** 1983
**Insider Info** This prize is sponsored by Boardman Tasker Charitable Trust and is for an original work in book form. Given in memory of climbers Peter Boardman and Joe Tasker, the prize honours the best literary work, whether fiction or non-fiction, the central theme of which is concerned with the mountain environment (not necessarily mountaineering). The competition is held annually

with a prize of £2,000 and is judged by a panel of three different people each year. Any published writer may enter via their publisher.
**Genres** Fiction, Non-fiction, Poetry, Essays, Novels, Story collections.
**Submission Guidelines** Submissions must be received by August 16 each year. Entry should be via publisher. The submitted work must be previously published between November 1 of the previous year and October 31 in the current year.

## The Bollinger Everyman Wodehouse Prize for Comic Fiction
c/o Colman Getty PR, Middlesex House, 32–42 Cleveland Street, London, W1T 4JE
☎ 020 7631 2666
☎ 020 7631 2699
✉ info@colmangettypr.co.uk; lois@colmangetty.co.uk
**Established** 2000
**Insider Info** A celebration of comic writing in the memory of P.G. Wodehouse. Awarded annually, the winner receives a bottle of Bollinger champagne, and a rare breed of pig is named after the novel.
**Genres** Comic fiction
**Submission Guidelines** Work should be published previously.
**Tips** Enquiries about nominating books should be directed to Colman Getty PR.

## The Booktrust Early Years Awards
Book House, 45 East Hill, Wandsworth, London, SW18 2QZ
☎ 020 8516 2972
☎ 020 8516 2978
✉ tarryn@booktrust.org.uk
🌐 www.booktrust.org.uk
**Established** 2004
**Insider Info** Sponsored by Booktrust. This annual award has three categories: Best book for babies under one year old; Best Picture Book for pre-school children up to five years of age; and Best New Illustrator, again up to five years old, for the illustrator's first ever published pre-school picture book. The winners will each receive a cheque for £2,000 (to be shared between author & illustrator if appropriate) and a crystal ornament, and in addition the Best New Illustrator will receive a specially commissioned award. Also, the publishers of the winning titles will be presented with an Award naming them as one of the Booktrust Early Years Awards Publishers of the Year. The aim of the prize is to celebrate, publicise and reward the exciting range

of books being published today for babies, toddlers and pre-school children. Also to promote and make these books accessible to as wide an audience as possible. The publishers of all three books will also receive a crystal ornament pronouncing them as one of the Booktrust Early Years Awards Publishers of the Year. There is a panel of five, chaired by Wendy Cooling, Children's Book Consultant. She is joined each year by a representative from the library service, the health service, a parent from the National Bookstart programme and a children's illustrator. The prize is only open to UK citizens, but other nationalities are eligible to enter as long as they have been in the British Isles for at least five years.

**Genres** Juvenile, Baby books

**Submission Guidelines** Deadline for entry is June; this date may change. There is no entry fee. Work should be published previously, between September 1 and August 31.

**Tips** Entries are invited from publishers only.

## Book Trust Teenage Prize
**Book House, 45 East Hill, London, SW18 2QZ**
- 020 8516 2986
- 020 8516 2978
- hannah@booktrust.org.uk
- www.bookheads.org.uk

**Established** 2003

**Insider Info** Recognises the best works of Teenage Fiction in the UK in the preceding year. The competition is held annually and the winner receives £2,500. It is open to residents of the UK as well as citizens of the UK. Works must be in English but can be in any genre, providing they are aimed at children.

**Genres** Story Collections and Fiction for 13–16 year olds

**Submission Guidelines** Submissions must be received by the end of March each year and should be previously published between July 1 of the previous year and June 30 of the current year.

**Tips** Entries are invited from publishers only.

## Bookworms Short Story Competition
**3 Yeomanry Road, Battlefield Enterprise Park, Shrewsbury, Shropshire, SY1 3EH**
- 01743 360573
- 01743 443388
- kazbamail-fern@yahoo.co.uk
- beanpolebooks.co.uk

**Competition/Award Director** Karen Lowe
**Established** 2006

**Insider Info** This competition is sponsored by Beanpole Books and involves submitting a 1,500 word short story suitable for general reading on a public website. The title is chosen from the crossword titles in *50 Bookworms Crosswords*, to give an opportunity to a new or little-published writer to share their work with a wider public. This competition takes place annually and the prize is £150 and publication on the Beanpole Books website for a year. Entries are judged by Karen Lowe and a guest judge (will vary each year). Entry to the competition assumes Beanpole Books has the right to publish the winning story on its website for twelve months. This competition is open to any UK based writer.

**Genres** Fiction and Short Stories

**Submission Guidelines** Submissions must be received by October 30. Entry form is included with purchase of *50 Bookworms Crosswords*, £3.99. Short stories must be previously unpublished.

**Tips** View the website to see previous winners. The story should be suitable for general viewing on a public website which may be accessed by children. No Science-Fiction, violence, explicit sex, or strong language. This is a new competition. Details may vary in future years.

## The Branford Boase Award
**Library & Information HQ, 81 North Walls, Winchester, SO23 8BY**
- 01962 826658
- anne.marley@tiscali.co.uk
- www.branfordboaseaward.org.uk

**Insider Info** Annually awarded for the most promising first novel by a new writer of a book for young people. The winner receives £1,000 and a handcrafted box. Writers may have been published before in other fields but must enter their first, unpublished, book for children.

**Genres** Fiction, Novels for young people aged 7+

**Submission Guidelines** Entry deadline is December. Guidelines available on website. Work should be published previously, between January 1 and December 31.

**Tips** Entries are invited from publishers, who may submit up to five books. No short story collections by multiple authors, poetry or picture books.

## Brian MacMahon Short Story Award
**Writer's Week, 24 the Square, Listowel, Co. Kerry, Republic of Ireland**
- 00353 682 1074
- 00353 682 2893

info@writersweek.ie
www.writersweek.ie

**Insider Info** This award is sponsored by The American Ireland Funds and is an open short story competition for stories of up to 3,000 words. The competition takes place annually and the winner receives €2,000. Writer's Week reserves the right to withhold or publish winning entries in the publication the *Winners Anthology*.

**Genres** Short Stories

**Submission Guidelines** Submissions must be received by the end of March. There is a fee of €10 per entry and the short stories must be previously unpublished.

**Tips** Entries must be either in English or Irish. Entrants may enter as many stories as they wish with the appropriate fees.

## Brian Way Award
**Theatre Centre, Shoreditch Town Hall, London, EC1V 9LT**
020 7729 3066
020 7739 9741
admin@theatre-centre.co.uk
www.theatre-centre.co.uk

**Established** 2000

**Insider Info** Formerly the Arts Council Children's Award. Named after the late Brian Way, founder of the Theatre Centre, and designed to celebrate the achievements and raise the profile of playwrights who write specifically for young people. The competition takes place annually and offers prize money of £6,000 for a 1st, 2nd or 3rd production of a play written within the last decade. Writers must either be resident in the UK or Republic of Ireland or have had a writing association with a UK theatre company or group.

**Genres** Plays for young people up to the age of 18.

**Submission Guidelines** Submissions must be received by November 30 each year and the play itself must be performed between July 1 the previous year and June 30 the current year. Postal submissions of scripts may come from agents or writers themselves. Also include details of where and when performances have taken place.

**Tips** Judges look for plays that demonstrate a special quality in the writing, that stimulate the imagination and use innovative languages and forms.

## The Bridport Prize
**Bridport Arts Centre, South Street, Bridport, Dorset, DT6 3NR**

frances@bridportprize.org.uk
www.bridportprize.org.uk

**Insider Info** An international creative writing competition for poetry of up to 42 lines and short stories of up to 5,000 words. Awarded annually, prizes consist of: 1st £5,000; 2nd £1,000; 3rd £500; and ten runner up prizes of £50 each. The poetry judge for 2007: Don Paterson; for short stories: Tracy Chevalier. Copyright remains with the author but the administration retains unrestricted rights to publish winning entries in the Bridport Anthology. Open to any writer over the age of 18 and resident in the UK..

**Genres** Poetry, Short stories

**Submission Guidelines** Deadline for entry is the end of June. Guidelines available on the website. Entry fee is £6 per poem or story. Work should be previously unpublished.

**Tips** Submit as many entries as you wish, either by post or online. Entry forms are available online. The judges' criteria for winning entries are published on the website.

## British Book Awards
**7 John Street, London, WC1N 2ES**
0870 870 2345
0870 870 0385
www.britishbookawards.com

**Established** 1990

**Insider Info** These awards are sponsored by *Publishing News* and are known as 'The Nibbies'. They are the publishing industry's equivalent of the BAFTAs, where awards in various categories are handed out at a televised awards ceremony. This takes place annually and trophies are awarded at the ceremony.

**Submission Guidelines** Submissions must be previously published.

**Tips** Each category is voted for by various groups based on books published in the previous year, therefore there is no opportunity for writers to submit unpublished works for consideration.

## British Czech & Slovak Association Writing Competition
**BCSA Prize Administrator, 24 Ferndale, Tunbridge Wells, Kent, TN2 3NS**
01892 543206
prize@bcsa.co.uk
www.bcsa.co.uk

**Competition/Award Director** Edward Peacock, Prize Administrator

**Established** 2002

**Insider Info** This competition is sponsored by the British Czech & Slovak Association. Fiction or non-fiction welcome, based on the links between Britain and the Czech and Slovak Republics, or on society in transition in those Republics since the Velvet Revolution in 1989. The competition is firstly for fun, and secondly to advance the BCSA's purpose in encouraging links between Britain and the Czech & Slovak Republics. The competition takes place annually offering £300 for the first prize, presented at BCSA Annual Dinner; £100 for the second prize and winning entries are published in *British Czech & Slovak Review*. A panel of expert judges is recruited each year. By entering, authors allow the BCSA to publish entries in their publications, but entrants retain the copyright to their entries. Submissions are invited from individuals of any age, nationality or educational background.

**Genres** Fiction, Non-fiction, Essays and Short Stories

**Submission Guidelines** Submissions must be received by June 30 each year. There is no entry fee. Guidelines and entry forms are available for self-addressed SAE. Submissions must be previously unpublished.

**Tips** Entries should be in English and should not exceed 2,000 words in length.

## British Fantasy Awards

**201 Reddish Road, South Reddish, Stockport, SK5 7HR**

- 0161 476 5368
- info@britishfantasysociety.org.uk
- www.britishfantasysociety.org.uk

**Insider Info** Sponsored by the British Fantasy Society. The awards are presented at an annual conference to recognise achievement in the Fantasy genre. Categories include best novel, best novella and best artist.

**Genres** Fantasy

**Submission Guidelines** Titles must be previously published.

**Tips** The awards are not an open competition for writers.

## British Press Awards

**Press Gazette, 10 Old Bailey, London, EC4M 7NG**

- 020 7038 1469
- 020 7038 1155
- www.britishpressawards.com

**Insider Info** A ceremony to award UK newspapers and journalists in various categories. Winners are voted for by industry professionals. The awards take place annually. Judges include 80 established journalists and a smaller grand jury from each of the national newspaper groups.

**Tips** Visit the website for details on how to enter the newspapers, journalists and articles categories.

## British Science Fiction Association Awards

**16 Napier Road, Oxford, OX4 3JA**

- 01865 749378
- bsfamail@gmail.com
- www.bsfa.co.uk

**Established** 1970

**Insider Info** These awards are presented at The British National Science Fiction Convention to recognise excellence in various categories within the genre. The awards take place annually and winners are voted for by BSFA members and members of the British National Science Fiction Convention (Eastercon).

**Genres** Science Fiction writing and artwork

**Submission Guidelines** Writing and artwork must be previously published.

**Tips** Entry is by nomination only. See website for details of how to nominate.

## British Sports Book Awards

**Café Royal, 68 Regent Street, London, W1B 5EL**

- 020 7437 0144
- 020 7437 5441
- david@nationalsportingclub.co.uk
- www.nationalsportingclub.co.uk

**Competition/Award Director** David Wilis

**Established** 2003

**Insider Info** The British Sports Book Awards is sponsored by the National Sporting Club. It is an awards ceremony to celebrate the best in Sports publishing. Categories include Best Autobiography, Best Biography, Best New Writer, Best Illustrated Title, Best Cricket Book, Best Football Book and Outstanding Contribution to Sports Publishing. The awards take place annually and judges are a panel made up of sports journalists and publishing professionals.

**Genres** Non-fiction, Sports Non-fiction and Biography

**Submission Guidelines** Submissions must be received by the end of November each year. Titles must be previously published.

**Tips** Entry is by nomination only.

## The Browning Society Poetry Prize

84 Addison Gardens, London, W14 0DR

☎ 020 7602 3094
☎ 020 7602 3771
✉ pamela.sington@tvdox.com
🌐 www.browningsociety.org

**Competition/Award Director** Pamela Neville Sington

**Insider Info** A poetry competition for young people. Entrants are split into two categories: 9–13 years, and 14–19 years. Inspiration for entries must be drawn from two specific poems published on the website. Poems should be up to 70 lines long. Awarded annually, the prize for the older category is £200. The younger winner receives £100. Both are invited to the annual wreath-laying ceremony in Poets' Corner, Westminster Abbey. Entrants must be citizens of, or residents in, the UK.

**Genres** Poetry

**Submission Guidelines** Deadline for entry is March. Work should be previously unpublished.

**Tips** Read the guidelines on the website carefully as they detail how to use the pre-selected poems as a starting point for entries.

## The Caine Prize for African Writing

Menier Chocolate Factory, 51 Southwark Street, London, SE1 1RU

☎ 020 7378 6234
☎ 020 7378 6234
✉ info@caineprize.com
🌐 www.caineprize.com

**Competition/Award Director** Nick Elam

**Established** 2000

**Insider Info** Sponsored by The Menier Gallery. An annual short story competition for African writers, designed to highlight African work that has dealt with African sensibilities. Awarded annually, prize money is £10,000 for the winner and a travel award for up to five shortlisted entrants. Writers must be from Africa, an African resident or have African parents. Work must be in English, or have been published in English translation.

**Genres** Short stories

**Submission Guidelines** Deadline for submission is end January each year. Work should be published previously, between February 1 (five years previously) and January 31 (year of the prize giving).

**Tips** Stories of over 3,000 words must be submitted by publishers. Submit six hard copies. Internet publications are eligible.

## Calvin and Rose G Hoffman Prize

Kings School Canterbury, 25 The Precincts, Canterbury, Kent, CT1 2ES

☎ 01227 595544
☎ 01227 595589

**Insider Info** Awarded to the best piece of written work on Christopher Marlowe and his relationship with William Shakespeare. The competition is held annually and the prize consists of £5,000.

**Genres** Non-fiction

**Submission Guidelines** Submissions must be received by September 1 each year. The scholarly work must be previously unpublished.

**Tips** This award is normally awarded to scholarly works of up to 5,000 words. Contact the administrator at the above address for more information.

## Carey Award

Woodbourn Business Centre, 10 Jessell Street, Sheffield, S9 3HY

☎ 0114 244 9561
☎ 0114 244 9563
✉ admin@indexers.org.uk
🌐 www.indexers.org.uk

**Established** 1977

**Insider Info** This award is sponsored by the Society of Indexers. It is an award presented occasionally by the Society to individuals who are deemed to have made a significant contribution to indexing. The award consists of a framed, illuminated parchment.

**Tips** This award is not open to submissions or nominations and winners are chosen by the Society as and when suitable candidates arise.

## Cartier Diamond Dagger

PO Box 273, Boreham Wood, WD6 2XA

✉ info@thecwa.co.uk
🌐 www.thecwa.co.uk

**Established** 1986

**Insider Info** This award is sponsored by the Crime Writers Association, it is a lifetime achievement award for a Crime writer that has made an outstanding contribution to Crime writing in the English language. The award is presented annually. The dagger may be awarded to writers regardless of nationality, age of gender.

**Genres** Crime Fiction

**Tips** There are no submissions, this award is voted for by a committee of the CWA based on nominations from members.

## CBI Bisto Book of the Year Award

**17 North Great Georges Street, Dubin 1, Republic of Ireland**

- ☎ 00353 1 872 7475
- ☎ 00353 1 872 8486
- ⌨ info@childrensbooksireland.com
- 🖥 www.childrensbooksireland.com

**Competition/Award Director** Mary Shine Thompson

**Established** 1990

**Insider Info** The awards consist of: CBI Bisto Book of the Year Award; three CBI Bisto Honour Awards (authors or illustrators); and The Eilís Dillon Award (for a first children's book). The awards are presented annually and the winner of the Book of the Year Award receives €10,000 as well as a perpetual trophy and framed certificate. Honour Awards winners share a prize fund of €6,000 and each receive a framed certificate. The Eilís Dillon winner wins €3,000, a trophy and a framed certificate. Writers and illustrators must be from Ireland or resident in Ireland at the time of publication.

**Genres** Children's Books

**Submission Guidelines** Submissions must be received by December 15 each year. Titles must have been published between January 1and December 31 each year. Entries must be submitted by publishers. Send 12 hard copies with an entry form.

## C. B. Oldman Prize

**Aberdeen University Library, Meston Walk, Aberdeen, AB24 3UE**

- ☎ 01224 272590
- ☎ 01224 487048
- ⌨ r.turbet@abdn.ac.uk
- 🖥 www.iaml-uk-irl.org

**Established** 1987

**Insider Info** Sponsored by the International Association of Music Libraries, Archives and Documentation Centres (IAML), United Kingdom and Ireland. The C. B. Oldman Prize is awarded for the best book on music bibliography, librarianship or reference published in the UK. The prize is given annually and the winner receives £200. Writers must be resident in the UK.

**Genres** Non-fiction

**Submission Guidelines** Submissions must be previously published.

## Chapter One Promotions Children's Short Story Competitions

**PO Box 43667, London, SE22 9XU**

- ☎ 0845 456 5364
- ☎ 0845 456 5347
- ⌨ kidskorner@chapteronepromotions.com
- 🖥 www.chapteronepromotions.com

**Insider Info** A short story competition for children writing stories of up to 1,000 words. Themes to choose from are published on the website. Individuals may enter, as may groups from particular schools or colleges. Age categories are: 7–9; 10–12; 13–15 and 16–18. In each category, 1st, 2nd and 3rd place winners will receive £150, £75 and £50 respectively. Open to any writer that either lives within the Commonwealth and is English speaking or an English national.

**Submission Guidelines** Submissions must ne received by May 31 each year. There is a fee of £5 per story. Schools, colleges and youth clubs can submit group entries of up to 30 stories for £50. Submissions may be made online or by post and may be typed or handwritten.

**Tips** Stories must relate to one of the set themes on the website.

## Chapter One Promotions International Novel Competition

**PO Box 43667, London, SE22 9XU**

- ☎ 0845 456 5364
- ☎ 0845 456 5347
- ⌨ info@chapteronepromotions.com
- 🖥 www.chapteronepromotions.com

**Insider Info** This is an open competition for unpublished novels. Only the first two chapters and the closing chapter are required, and the novel need not have been finished. The competition is held every four years. The winner will receive support in completing their work, which will be published and available through the Book Cellar and Amazon.

**Genres** Novels

**Submission Guidelines** Submissions must be received by February 28 each year. There is a fee of £20 per novel. Titles should be previously unpublished.

**Tips** There is no word count and entries may be submitted by post or online. Entrants must declare if their work has been submitted to any other competitions, agents or publishers.

## Chapter One Promotions International Open Poetry Competition

**PO Box 43667, London, SE22 9XU**
- 0845 456 5364
- 0845 456 5347
- poetry@chapteronepromotions.com
- www.chapteronepromotions.com

**Insider Info** An open competition for poems of up to 30 lines long in English. The competition is held annually and prizes consist of £1,000, £500 and £250 for 1st, 2nd and 3rd. The top 20 poems are selected by the poet Jacob Sam-La Roşe and are published on the website. Users then vote for their favourite. Entrants must be over 18.

**Genres** Poetry

**Submission Guidelines** Submissions must be received by June 30 each year. Entry guidelines are available on the website. There is a £5 fee per poem. Poems must be previously unpublished.

**Tips** Accepts handwritten or typed poems and both submissions and payments can be made either online or by post.

## Chapter One Promotions International Short Story Competition

**PO Box 43667, London, SE22 9XU**
- 0845 456 5364
- 0845 456 5347
- shortstory@chapteronepromotions.com
- www.chapteronepromotions.com

**Established** 2005

**Insider Info** An international competition for short stories of up to 2,500 words. The competition takes place annually and prizes are: £2,500 for the winner; £1,000 for 2nd place; and £500 for 3rd place. The 13 top ranking entries are published in an anthology.

**Genres** Short Stories

**Tips** Details of entry procedures will be available on the website. This competition is open to any writer.

## The Children's Laureate

**Book House, 45 East Hill, London, SW18 2QZ**
- 020 8516 2976
- 020 8516 2978
- childrenslaureate@booktrust.org.uk
- www.childrenslaureate.org

**Established** 1998

**Insider Info** Sponsored by Booktrust. A title awarded to a writer or illustrator for children's books that has made an outstanding contribution to children's publishing. 2005–2007 laureate is Jacqueline Wilson. Awarded every two years (odd years), the prize consist of the title, a medal and £10,000.

**Tips** Nominations are usually accepted from organisations representing librarians, critics, writers and booksellers. Contact Nikki Marsh at the above email address for further details.

## Cholmondeley Awards for Poets

**The Society of Authors, 84 Drayton Gardens, London, SW10 9SB**
- 020 7373 6642
- 020 7373 5768
- info@societyofauthors.org
- www.societyofauthors.org

**Established** 1966

**Insider Info** Founded by the late Dowager Marchioness of Cholmondeley to recognize the achievements of poets. These awards are honorary and submissions are not accepted. The winners are chosen by the board for their contribution to poetry. The awards are presented annually.

## CILIP Carnegie Medal

**7 Ridgmount Street, London, WC1E 7AE**
- 020 7255 0650
- 020 7255 0651
- ckg@cilip.org.uk
- www.carnegiegreenaway.org.uk

**Established** 1936

**Insider Info** Awarded to an outstanding children's book in any category. The award is presented annually and the winner receives a golden medal and £500 worth of books to donate to a library of their choice. Books must be in English and have had their first publication in the UK, or have had a co-publication within a three month time lapse.

**Genres** Children's Fiction or Non-fiction

**Submission Guidelines** Submissions must be previously published.

**Tips** Both e-books and short stories are eligible for this award. Nominations for the award are made by members of CILIP.

## CILIP Kate Greenaway Medal

**7 Ridgmount Street, London, WC1E 7AE**
- 020 7255 0650
- 020 7255 0651
- ckg@cilip.org.uk
- www.carnegiegreenaway.org.uk

**Established** 1955

**Insider Info** Awarded for excellence in children's book illustrating during the previous year. The award is presented annually and the winner receives a golden medal and £500 worth of books to donate to a library of their choice. Winners are also granted the Colin Mears Award, which is worth £5,000.

**Genres** Illustrated Children's Books

**Submission Guidelines** Submissions must be previously published.

**Tips** Nominations are taken from members of CILIP. Books for both older and younger children are included.

## Cinnamon Press Novella Award

**Meirion House, Glan yr afon, Tanygrisiau, Blaenau Ffestiniog, Gwynedd, LL41 3SU**

✉ jan@cinnamonpress.com

🌐 www.cinnamonpress.com

**Insider Info** This competition is aimed at bringing attention to novellas and promoting their publication. A novella is defined as being between 20,000 and 45,000 words. The award is offered twice yearly. The winner will receive £200 and a contract for their first novella to be published by Cinnamon Press. The competition is open to published and unpublished writers.

**Genres** Novellas

**Submission Guidelines** Submissions must be received by June 30 and November 30 each year. There is a fee of £16 per collection, £14 for subscribers to *Envoi* magazine.

**Tips** Submit the first 10,000 words only to start with. Entries should be typed, single sided and double spaced.

## Cinnamon Press Novel Writing Award

**Meirion House, Glan yr afon, Tanygrisiau, Blaenau Ffestiniog, Gwynedd, LL41 3SU**

✉ jan@cinnamonpress.com

🌐 www.cinnamonpress.com

**Insider Info** An award aimed at allowing new writers their first full-length novel publication. Writers are invited to submit the first 10,000 words of their work. The award is offered twice yearly. The top five based on the samples will be invited to submit their full novel. The winner receives £500 and a contract for their novel of between 60,000 and 80,000 words to published by Cinnamon Press. Open to any writer who has never had a full length novel published.

**Genres** Novels

**Submission Guidelines** Submissions must be receeved June 30 and November 30 each year.

Guidelines are available on the website. The entry fee is £20 per novel. Novels must be previously unpublished.

**Tips** Novels do not necessarily need to be finished at the closing date but writers need to be able to provide the full work within two months of the closing date if they are shortlisted. Work should be double spaced on single sided sheets. Handwritten entries will not be accepted.

## Cinnamon Press Poetry Collection Award

**Meirion House, Glan yr afon, Tanygrisiau, Blaenau Ffestiniog, Gwynedd, LL41 3SU**

✉ jan@cinnamonpress.com

🌐 www.cinnamonpress.com

**Insider Info** The award aims to give new writers the chance to publish a collection of poetry. Entrants are invited to submit ten poems of up to 40 lines each. Competition is offered twice yearly, and three shortlisted poets will be invited to submit ten further poems. The final winner will receive £100 and a contract with a view to publishing a collection of around 60 poems.

**Genres** Poetry

**Submission Guidelines** Deadlines are always June 30 and November 30. Guidelines available on website. Entry fee of £16 per collection – £14 for subscribers to *Envoi* magazine. May include poems that have been previously published in small press anthologies or magazines.

**Tips** When submitting, do not put your name on any of the poems. Include a separate sheet with contact details and titles of poems. Each poem should be on a separate sheet.

## Cinnamon Press Short Story Award

**Meirion House, Glan yr afon, Tanygrisiau, Blaenau Ffestiniog, Gwynedd, LL41 3SU**

✉ jan@cinnamonpress.com

🌐 www.cinnamonpress.com

**Insider Info** A competition aiming to encourage the writing of short fiction of between 2,000 and 4,000 words. The award is offered twice yearly. The winner receives £100 and the story is published by Cinnamon Press. Up to ten others will be published in an anthology. This competition is open to new and published writers.

**Genres** Short Stories

**Submission Guidelines** Submissions must be received June 30 and November 30 each year. Guidelines are available on the website. There is a fee of £16 per collection, £14 for subscribers to *Envoi* magazine.

**Tips** Accepts postal entries only, typed on single sided sheets.

## City of Derby Short Story and Poetry Competition

**PO Box 7065, Derby, Derbyshire, DE1 OAD**

**☏** 01332 725362

**✉** info@cityofderbywritingcompetition.org.uk

**✇** www.cityofderbywritingcompetition.org.uk

**Established** 2006

**Insider Info** This competition is sponsored by *The Independent*. Short stories are invited of up to 5000 words and poems of up to 40 lines. The primary purpose of the competition is to provide a vehicle for enabling new writers to receive recognition which they might not otherwise have known. Or, if their writing has been already recognized in some way, to give the writers in question further encouragement on the route to reaching a wider audience. The competition takes place annually. In each category of short stories/poetry there is a £350 1st prize, a £250 2nd prize and a £150 3rd prize. The judges are always established authors and poets. Entrants retain all rights to their work. Winning entries are published permanently on the competition website. The competition is open to all ages and nationalities.

**Genres** Poetry and Short Stories

**Submission Guidelines** Submissions must be received by 31 May each year. No entry form is required. Full entry details are contained within the website. There is a fee of £3 per entry. Poems and stories must be previously unpublished.

**Tips** Entries must be typed.

## Commonwealth Writers' Prize

**Marlborough House, Pall Mall, London, SW1Y 5HY**

**☏** +44 020 7747 6262

**☏** +44 02078398157

**✉** j.sobol@commonwealth.int

**✇** www.commonwealthfoundation.com/culturediversity/writersprize/

**Competition/Award Director** Jennifer Sobol

**Established** 1987

**Insider Info** The Commonwealth Writer's Prize is an annual award to reward and encourage the upsurge of new Commonwealth fiction. Any work of prose or fiction is eligible, i.e. a novel or collection of short stories. No drama or poetry. The work must be first written in English by a citizen of the Commonwealth and be first published in the year before its entry for the prize. Entries must be submitted by the publisher to the region of the writer's Commonwealth citizenship. The four regions are: Africa, Europe and South Asia, South East Asia and South Pacific, Caribbean and Canada. 2006 winner: Kate Grenville, *The Secret River* (Best Book Award); Mark McWatt, *Suspended Sentences: Fictions of Atonement* (Best First Book Award). The Commonwealth Writers' Prize is genuinely international in its character and administration. In practice it consists of ten prizes. In four Commonwealth regions two prizes of £1,000 are given out: one for the Best Book and one for the Best First Book. The regional winners then go through to the final phase of the competition, where a distinguished pan-Commonwealth panel meets to decide the overall Commonwealth winners for Best Book and Best First Book. There will be one award of £10,000 for the Overall Best Book and one award of £5,000 for the Overall Best First Book.

**Genres** Fiction, Novels, Story collections

**Submission Guidelines** Deadlines change each year – see the website for details. Accepts simultaneous submissions. Submissions must be previously published between December 1 of the previous year, and December 31 of the year of application.

**Tips** Please visit the CWP website for more information.

## Costa Book Awards

**Booksellers Association, Minster House, 272 Vauxhall Bridge Road, London, SW1V 1BA**

**☏** 020 7802 0802

**✉** dionne.parker@whitbread.com, naomi.gane@booksellers.org.uk

**✇** www.costabookawards.com

**Established** 1971

**Insider Info** These awards have been designed to celebrate British contemporary writing and were formerly known as the Whitbread Book Awards. There are five categories: Novel; First Novel; Biography; Poetry; and Children's Books. The awards are held annually and each of the category winners receives £5,000, and the overall winner receives a further £25,000. Writers must have been resident in the UK or Ireland for at least 6 months of each of the previous 3 years but do not necessarily have to be of UK or Irish nationality.

**Genres** Fiction and Non-fiction.

**Submission Guidelines** Submissions must be received by the end of June each year and must be previously published between 1 November of the previous year and 30 October in the current year.

**Tips** Short story collections are not accepted at present. Accepts submissions from publishers only. Contact the Booksellers Association for an application form.

## Country Ghost Story Competition
**14 The Park, Stow On The Wold, Cheltenham, Glos, GL54 1DX**

- 01451 831053
- sales@parkpublications.co.uk
- parkpublications.co.uk

**Competition/Award Director** David Howarth
**Established** 1999
**Insider Info** This competition is sponsored by Park Publications and is for ghost stories of up to 2000 words with a rural setting. The competition takes place annually and there are three prizes of £75, £25 and £15 plus publication in *Countryside Tales* magazine. The Editor of the magazine judges the competition. Guidelines and entry forms are available for self-addressed SAEs. Park Publications reserves the right for first publication but the copyright remains with the author. The competition is open to any writer.
**Genres** Fiction
**Submission Guidelines** Submissions must be received by 31 January each year. There is an entry fee of £3 per entry. Stories must be previously unpublished.
**Tips** Read the writers' guidelines on the website and/or the magazine.

## The CWA Gold Dagger for Non-fiction
**PO Box 273, Boreham Wood, WD6 2XA**

- info@thecwa.co.uk
- www.thecwa.co.uk

**Established** 1978
**Insider Info** Sponsored by the Crime Writers Association. Awarded annually to the best non-fiction crime book published in the previous year. The winner receives an ornamental dagger and £2,000. All judges have a publishing or legal background.
**Genres** Non-fiction, Real-life crime/criminology
**Submission Guidelines** Work should be published previously.
**Tips** Submissions by publishers only..

## The CWA Short Story Award
**PO Box 273, Boreham Wood, WD6 2XA**

- info@thecwa.co.uk
- www.thecwa.co.uk

**Established** 1995
**Insider Info** Sponsored by the Crime Writers Association. Awarded annually for short crime stories that may have been published in magazines or anthologies. Winners receive a gold pin of the CWA's crossed daggers emblem and £1,500. Judges are made up of authors, editors and agents.
**Genres** Short stories
**Submission Guidelines** Work should be published previously.
**Tips** Submissions by publishers only.

## The Dagger in the Library
**PO Box 273, Boreham Wood, WD6 2XA**

- info@thecwa.co.uk
- www.thecwa.co.uk

**Established** 1994
**Insider Info** Sponsored by the Crime Writers Association and Random House Group. Awarded annually to a living crime fiction author that is deemed to have given readers the most pleasure. Writers are nominated by UK libraries. The prize consist of £1,500 and an ornamental dagger. Judged by librarians.
**Submission Guidelines** Work should be published previously.
**Tips** No submissions.

## Dark Tales Short Story Competition
**P.O. Box 681, Worcester, WR3 8WB**

- www.darktales.co.uk

**Insider Info** This is a regular competition for stories of up to 3,000 words. The magazine is based around genre, fantasy and speculative fiction. The prizes are: £100 for 1st place; £30 for 2nd place; £20 for 3rd place and £5 for shortlisted entries. All winning entries are published in the magazine. The competition is open to any writer, UK or international.
**Genres** Short Stories
**Submission Guidelines** Submission guidelines are available on the website. There is a fee of £3 for non-subscribers and £1.50 for subscribers. Stories must be previously unpublished.
**Tips** Entrants are strongly advised to buy a copy of the magazine and look at previous winning articles. The competition is held regularly and details of

upcoming deadlines are published on the website. Entries may be made by post or online.

## David Berry Prize
**University College London, Gower Street, London, WC1E 6BT**
- 020 7387 7532
- 020 7387 7532
- www.rhs.ac.uk/prizes.htm#david

**Insider Info** This award is sponsored by the Royal Historical Society and is presented to the writer of an outstanding essay or academic article on Scottish history. The award is offered annually and consists of £250 prize money.

**Genres** Essays and Articles

**Submission Guidelines** Submissions must be received by 30 October each year.

**Tips** Essays must be up to a maximum word limit of 10,000.

## David Cohen Prize for Literature
**14 Great Peter Street, London, SW1P 3NQ**
- 020 7973 5325
- 020 7973 6983
- info.literature@artscouncil.org.uk
- www.artscouncil.org.uk

**Insider Info** This prize is sponsored by the Arts Council England and is awarded for a lifetime's achievement in British Literature. The award is presented every 2 years (odd years). An award of £40,000 is provided by the David Cohen Family Charitable Trust for the winner and an additional £12,500 (the Clarissa Luard Award) is provided by the Arts Council for the winner to give to an organization of their choice that helps develop young writers and readers.

**Tips** Submissions are not accepted.

## The David St. John Thomas Charitable Trust and Awards
**PO Box 6055, Nairn, IV12 4YB**
- 01667 453351
- 01667 452365
- dsjtcharitynairn@fsmail.net

**Competition/Award Director** Lorna Edwardson

**Insider Info** A range of prizes are awarded annually by the trust including the annual ghost story and love story awards, self-publishing awards, writers group anthology and poetry awards any many others. The prize money totals around £30,000. There are various other prizes including publication in *Writer's News* magazine for certain winners.

**Submission Guidelines** Guidelines, categories and entry forms available via large SAE.

**Tips** Limited details of past winners are published on www.writers news.co.uk

## The David Watt Prize
**6 St. James' Square, London, SW1Y 4LD**
- 01985 844613
- 01985 844002
- davidwattprize@riotinto.com
- www.riotinto.com

**Established** 1988

**Insider Info** Sponsored by Rio Tinto PLC. Awarded annually in memory of David Watt to a journalist who has made an outstanding contribution to national or global current affairs. The winner receives £10,000.

**Genres** Articles

**Submission Guidelines** Deadlines for entries in March. Work should be published previously.

**Tips** Shortlisted pieces tend to be from journalists in top national newspapers such as *The Guardian* and *The Economist*.

## Debut Dagger
**PO Box 165, Wirral, CH31 9BD**
- Debut.Dagger@thecwa.co.uk
- www.thecwa.co.uk/daggers/debut

**Insider Info** The Debut Dagger award is sponsored by the Crime Writer's Association. It is an award designed to help launch the careers of unpublished crime writers and is presented annually. The prize consists of £500 and two tickets to the CWA Duncan Lawrie Dagger Awards including a night's stay for two in a hotel. All shortlisted entrants receive a selection of crime novels and professional critiques of their entries and will also be invited to the awards dinner. The award is open to any writer who has not previously had a novel published. Previously published writers in non-crime fiction areas (including self-published writers) should email for advice on their individual eligibility.

**Genres** Crime Fiction

**Submission Guidelines** Submissions must be received by the end of April each year. Guidelines for submissions are available on the website. Submit the first 3,000 words and a 500–1000 word synopsis of the rest of the novel. Include a signed entry form, information for which is on the website. There is also the facility for online entry. There is a fee of £20 per story. The novel must be previously unpublished.

**Tips** Crime novels only, although 'crime' can be interpreted broadly. For a style guide and advice on writing Crime novels, visit the website. Entrants are advised to sign up for the newsletter, in which they will be sent advice on putting together their entry.

## Delphi Award for Automotive Technology Journalism

**Guild of Motoring Writers, 39 Beswick Avenue, Bournemouth, BH10 4EY**

☏ 01202 518808

☏ 01202 518808

✉ chris@whizzco.freeserve.co.uk

🌐 www.guildofmotoringwriters.co.uk

**Insider Info** This is awarded for excellence in writing technical articles in the field of motoring. The award is presented annually and the winner receives £1,000.

**Genres** Non-fiction, Essays and Articles

**Submission Guidelines** Articles must be previously published.

**Tips** Winning articles or series must be of particular interest to specialists in the field, but also be accessible and appealing to a wider readership with a more limited technical knowledge.

## The Dennis Potter Screenwriting Award

**BBC Broadcasting House, Whiteladies Road, Bristol, BS8 2LR**

☏ 0117 974 7586

**Established** 1995

**Insider Info** An annual award in memory of Dennis Potter in recognition of emerging screenwriters.

**Genres** Scripts

**Tips** Submissions are usually sought from the BBC TV drama department and winners are often already fairly high profile.

## Dingle Prize

**5 Woodcote Green, Fleet, GU51 4EY**

✉ bshs@bshs.org.uk

🌐 www.bshs.org.uk

**Established** 1997

**Insider Info** This prize is sponsored by the British Society for the History of Science and is awarded for the best book in the categories: History of Science and Technology and Medicine. The book must be printed in the English language. The aim is to encourage accessible writing whilst maintaining rigorous historical methods. The prize is awarded every 2 years (odd years), and winners receive £300.

**Genres** Non-fiction

**Submission Guidelines** Submissions must be received by the end of February each year. Books must have been published in the preceding 3 years to the award. Send three hard copies to Philip Crane, Executive Secretary at the above address.

**Tips** Nominations are accepted by publishers only.

## Dolman Best Travel Book Prize

**The Author's Club, 40 Dover Street, London, W1S 4NP**

☏ 020 7408 5092

☏ 020 7408 0913

✉ stella@authorsclub.co.uk

**Insider Info** This prize was initiated by William Dolman, a former Authors Club chairman. It is awarded for an excellent first Travel book published in Great Britain. The prize is offered annually and consists of £1,000. British writers only are eligible.

**Genres** Travel Literature

**Submission Guidelines** Submissions must be received by the end of January each year. Tiles must be previously published.

**Tips** Contact Stella Kane at Authors' Club for more details on how to submit.

## Drama Association of Wales One-Act Playwriting Competition

**The Old Library, Singleton Road, Splott, Cardiff, CF24 2ET**

☏ 029 2045 2200

☏ 029 2045 2277

✉ aled.daw@virgin.net

**Insider Info** An open competition for one-act plays in either Welsh or English. Aims to encourage the writing of material for amateur theatre. There are usually three categories: an open category; plays for performance by 16–25 year olds; and plays the Welsh language. The competition takes place annually. Winning plays are published and the writers receive £200.

**Genres** Scripts

**Tips** Plays must be 20–50 minutes long and have a minimum cast of two. Contact Teresa Hennessy at the Drama Association of Wales (see above for contact details) for an application form and for details of the next competition. Mark correspondence by email 'FAO Teresa'.

## The Duff Cooper Prize

**54 Saint Maur Road, London, SW6 4DP**

☏ 020 7736 3729

☏ 020 7731 7638

**Competition/Award Director** Artemis Cooper
**Insider Info** Awarded annually for a literary work of history, biography, politics or poetry published in English or French. The prize consist of £5,000, a magnum of champagne and a presentation copy of Duff Cooper's autobiography *Old Men Forget*.
**Genres** Non-fiction, Poetry
**Submission Guidelines** Work must have been published by a recognised British publisher within the preceding year.
**Tips** Only open to entries from publishers that fulfil the criteria.

## The Duke of Westminster's Medal for Military Literature
**Royal United Services Institute for Defence and Security Studies, Whitehall, London, SW1A 2ET**
☎ 020 7930 2602
☎ 020 7321 0943
🌐 www.rusi.org/westminstermedal
**Established** 1997
**Insider Info** Awarded to what is deemed to be the best book published on international or national security, or the military professions. The prize is a medal.
**Submission Guidelines** Submissions should be published or due to publish six months either side of the closing date.
**Tips** Work must be in English but there are no restrictions as to nationality, gender or age.

## The Duncan Lawrie Dagger
**PO Box 273, Boreham Wood, WD6 2XA**
✉ info@thecwa.co.uk
🌐 www.thecwa.co.uk
**Established** 2006
**Insider Info** Sponsored by the Crime Writers Association and Duncan Lawrie Private Bank. Replaces the Gold and Silver Daggers. Awarded annually for the best crime fiction novel written in English. The winner receives an ornamental dagger and £20,000.
**Submission Guidelines** Work should be previously published.
**Tips** Submissions from publishers only.

## The Duncan Lawrie International Dagger
**PO Box 273, Boreham Wood, WD6 2XA**
✉ info@thecwa.co.uk
🌐 www.thecwa.co.uk
**Established** 2006

**Insider Info** Sponsored by the Crime Writers Association and Duncan Lawrie Private Bank. Awarded annually to the year's best crime novel translated into English from another language. Formerly the Gold and Silver Daggers. Winners receive an ornamental dagger, £5,000 for the author and £1,000 for the translator.
**Submission Guidelines** Work should be published previously.
**Tips** Submissions by publishers only.

## Dylan Thomas Prize
**The Dylan Thomas Centre, Somerset Place, Swansea, SA1 1RR**
☎ 01792 474051
☎ 01792 463993
✉ tim@dylanthomasprize.com
🌐 www.dylanthomasprize.com
**Competition/Award Director** Tim Prosser
**Established** 2004
**Insider Info** This prize is sponsored by EDS. An Award of £60,000 will be given to the winner of this prize, which was established to encourage, promote and reward exciting new writing in the English-speaking world and to celebrate the poetry and prose of Dylan Thomas. Entrants should be the author of a published book (in English) and under the age of 30 (when the work was published). Writing must be within one of the following categories: poetry, novel, collection of short stories by one author, play that has been professionally performed, a broadcast radio play or a professionally produced screenplay that has resulted in a feature-length film. Authors need to be nominated by their publishers or producers in the case of performance art. The award of £60,000 is presented every 2 years (odd years), and winners participate in the Dylan Thomas Festival in Swansea. There is also a short residency programme for the winner at the University of Texas, Austin. An international panel is appointed for each prize.
**Genres** Fiction, Poetry, Scripts, Novels, Short stories, Story collections
**Submission Guidelines** Submissions must be received by 28 April each odd year. Guidelines and entry forms are available with self-addressed SAE. There is an entry fee of £100. Submissions must be previously published.
**Tips** The Judges are looking to reward an outstanding use of language.

## Earlyworks Press Competitions

**Creative Media Centre, 45 Robertson Street, Hastings, Sussex, TN34 1HL**

@ www.earlyworkspress.co.uk

**Insider Info** Earlyworks Press competitions offer at least three competitions a year and publish three resulting anthologies. Previous competitions include the Science Fiction Challenge, a Short Story competition and a Poetry competition. First prize in each competition is usually £100 and 1st place in the anthology. Runners up are published and receive a complimentary copy of the book. Copyright remains with the author although Earlyworks Press retains the right to publish entries in their anthologies. Writers must be over 16.

**Submission Guidelines** Submission guidelines are available on the website. Fee is dependant on word count, see website for details. Work must be previously unpublished and must not be simultaneously entered for other competitions.

**Tips** Details of each new competition are published on the website, along with comprehensive terms and conditions.

## Eleanor Farjeon Award

@ www.childrensbookscircle.org.uk

**Established** 1965

**Insider Info** This award is sponsored by the Children's Book Circle and is awarded to a teacher, publisher, bookseller, librarian, writer. artist or other person who has made an outstanding contribution to the world of children's books. The award is presented annually and the winner receives a cash sum of around £750.

**Tips** Nominations are from members of the Children's Book Circle only.

## The Elizabeth Goudge Trophy

@ jan@jan-jones.co.uk

@ www.rna-uk.org

**Insider Info** Sponsored by the Romantic Novelists' Association. An annual competition open to all RNA members attending the annual conference. Writers are invited to submit entries based on a romance theme set by the Chairman. The winner is presented with a silver bowl at the conference.

**Genres** Fiction

**Submission Guidelines** Work should be previously unpublished.

**Tips** RNA members only.

## The Elizabeth Longford Prize for Historical Biography

**The Society of Authors, 84 Drayton Gardens, London, SW10 9SB**

@ 020 7373 6642

@ 020 7373 5768

@ info@societyofauthors.org

@ www.societyofauthors.org

**Established** 2003

**Insider Info** Sponsored by Flora Fraser and Peter Soros. Founded in memory of Elizabeth Longford, a biographer, the prize is awarded annually to the best historical biography in the preceding year. The winner receives £3,000.

**Genres** Biography

**Submission Guidelines** Work should be published previously.

**Tips** No unsolicited submissions.

## The Ellis Peters Award

**PO Box 273, Boreham Wood, WD6 2XA**

@ info@thecwa.co.uk

@ www.thecwa.co.uk

**Established** 1999

**Insider Info** Sponsored by the Crime Writers Association, Estate of Ellis Peters, Hodder Headline and Little Brown. Awarded annually for a crime novel with a historical background. The setting may be any period up to the 1960s. Winners receive £3,000 and an ornamental dagger, The judging panel is made up of the previous year's winner, historians and reviewers.

**Genres** Historical crime novels

**Submission Guidelines** Work should be previously published.

**Tips** Submissions by publishers only.

## The Encore Award

**84 Drayton Gardens, London, SW10 9SB**

@ 020 7373 6642

@ 020 7373 5768

@ info@societyofauthors.org

@ www.societyofauthors.org

**Established** 1990

**Insider Info** Sponsored by the Society of Authors. Awarded every two years (odd years) for the best 2nd published novel for a writer from the previous two years. The winner receives £10,000. Writers must be a British or Commonwealth citizen.

**Genres** Novels

**Submission Guidelines** Deadline for entry end November the previous year. Guidelines and entry forms available on the website. Entries must have been published in the UK in the previous two years (eg 2005 and 2006 for the 2007 award).

**Tips** Entries from publishers only.

## Enid McLeod Prize

2 Dovetail Studios, 465 Battersea Park Road, London, SW11 4LR

**☎** 020 7924 3511
**✉** execsec@francobritishsociety.org.uk
**🌐** www.francobritishsociety.org.uk

**Competition/Award Director** Kate Brayn
**Established** 1982

**Insider Info** This award is sponsored by the Franco-British Society and is awarded to the writer of a book that is deemed to have contributed the most to Franco-British understanding. The award is presented annually and the winner receives £250. Any book published in English, and in the UK by a British or Commonwealth writer is eligible. Translations are also considered.

**Genres** Non-fiction

**Submission Guidelines** Titles must be previously published between 1 January and 31 December that year.

**Tips** Submissions are accepted from publishers only. Contact the Franco-British Society for more information.

## Envoi International Open Poetry Competition

Meirion House, Glan yr afon, Tanygrisiau, Blaenau Ffestiniog, Gwynedd, LL41 3SU

**🌐** www.cinnamonpress.com

**Insider Info** This competition is sponsored by *Envoi Magazine* and is a competition for poems of up to 40 lines written in any style. The competition takes place three times a year. The prizes are: £150 for 1st place; £100 for 2nd place; and £50 for 3rd place. Poems are published in the magazine and complimentary copies are offered to all winners. Three runners up receive a subscription to the magazine.

**Genres** Poetry

**Submission Guidelines** Submissions must be received by 20 February, 20 June and 20 October each year. Submission guidelines are available on the website. There is a fee of £3 per poem and £12 for five poems. Poems must be previously unpublished and must not have been submitted to any other competitions.

**Tips** Accepts postal entries only.

## The Eric Gregory Trust Fund Awards

The Society of Authors, 84 Drayton Gardens, London, SW10 9SB

**☎** 020 7373 6642
**📠** 020 7373 5768
**✉** info@societyofauthors.org
**🌐** www.societyofauthors.org

**Insider Info** Prizes for young poets in memory of Eric Gregory. Prize money totals £24,000. Winners will be invited to give a reading at the prestigious at the Ledbury Poetry Festival at the discretion of the Trustees, and may also be invited to take part in an event hosted and promoted by the renowned Poetry Society. Entrants must be British by birth (excluding Eire and British colonies) and be under the age of 30.

**Genres** Poetry

**Submission Guidelines** Entry forms are available on the website. Works may be unpublished or published previously.

**Tips** The work submitted may be drama-poems or belles-lettres as well as a volume of poetry. No more than 30 poems should be submitted. Poems should be submitted on numbered sheets of A4 paper with a contents page that states the author's name. Submissions of unpublished poems should not be stapled or bound together. If you would like an acknowledgement and/or the return of your poems you need to provide SAEs.

## Financial Times and Goldman Sachs Business Book of the Year Award

1 Southwark Bridge, London, SE1 9HL

**☎** 020 7873 3000
**📠** 020 7873 3072
**✉** bookaward@ft.com
**🌐** www.ft.com/bookaward

**Established** 2005

**Insider Info** Awarded to the best business book published during the previous year. Winning books will have presented an exciting insight into modern business issues including management, finance and economics. The award is presented annually and winners receive £30,000 and shortlisted writers receive £5,000 each. The judging panel is made up of business experts from around the world.

**Genres** Business Non-fiction

**Submission Guidelines** Submissions must be received by 30 June each year. Titles must be previously published between 31 October in the previous year and 1 November in the current year.

**Tips** Submissions are accepted from publishers only.

# Fish Awards

**Darrus, Bantry, County Cork, Republic of Ireland**
🄯 info@fishpublishing.com
🅦 www.fishpublishing.com

**Insider Info** These awards are sponsored by Fish Publishing and offers various Fiction writing competitions, the names and styles of which change every year. The core competition is the annual Fish Short Story Competition. Recent examples of competitions include The 1 Page Story Awards and The Fish International Poetry Prize. The competition takes place at various points throughout the year. Prizes vary with each award, however most consist of sums of money. Other prizes include publication in anthologies and writing courses. Judges are different with each award and are published on the website. Writers should normally be writing in English.

**Genres** Fiction

**Submission Guidelines** Submission guidelines are available on the website. There is an entry fee which varies.

**Tips** Full details of each new competition are published on the website. An editorial consultancy service is available for a fee for those entrants who are unsure of the quality of their work. Most awards are now online entry only.

# The Forward Prizes for Poetry

**Colman Getty PR, 28 Windmill Street, London, W1T 2JJ**
🄯 020 7631 2666
🄯 020 7631 2699
**Established** 1991

**Insider Info** Awards for poetry published in three categories: poetry collection of the year; first collection; and single poem. Awarded annually, winners receive: £10,000 for best collection; £5,000 for best first collection; and £1,000 for best single poem.

**Genres** Poetry

**Submission Guidelines** Work should be published previously.

**Tips** No submissions. Nominations may be made by publishers and editors.

# Frank O'Connor International Short Story Award

**The Munster Literature Centre, Frank O'Connor House, 84 Douglas Street, Co. Cork**
🄯 00353 21 4312955
🄯 munsterlit@eircom.net

🅦 www.munsterlit.ie

**Insider Info** Awarded for the best collection of short stories in English published anywhere in the world during the previous year. The award is presented at The Frank O'Connor International Short Story Festival. The award is presented annually and the winner will receive 35,000 Euros (split between author and translator for translations). Any living author is eligible.

**Genres** Translations and Story Collections

**Submission Guidelines** Submissions must be received by the end of March each year. The short stories must be previously published between September the previous year and August of the current year. Submit seven copies of the book or proofs and details of publication for books published after the closing date.

**Tips** Submissions accepted by publishers only.

# The Frogmore Poetry Prize

**42 Morehall Avenue, Folkestone, CT19 4EF**
🄯 07751 251689
🅦 www.frogmorepress.co.uk
**Established** 1987

**Insider Info** Sponsored by *The Frogmore Papers* magazine. An annual open poetry competition for poems no longer than 40 lines. The overall winner will receive 200 guineas and a two year subscription to *The Frogmore Papers*. 2nd and 3rd place winners receive 75 and 50 guineas respectively and a year's subscription to the papers. All winning and shortlisted poems will be published in the magazine. Copyright remains with the authors but the Frogmore Press reserves the right to publish all poems shortlisted for the prize.

**Genres** Poetry

**Submission Guidelines** Deadline for entry is the end of May. Guidelines available on the website. Entry fee is £2 per poem. Work should be previously unpublished.

**Tips** For a copy of the magazine with the 2006 shortlisted poems, send £3.50 to the above address. Poems must be in English.

# Geoffrey Faber Memorial Prize

**3 Queen Square, London, WC1N 3AU**
🄯 020 7465 0045
🄯 020 7465 0043
🄯 belinda.matthews@faber.co.uk
**Established** 1963

**Insider Info** This award is sponsored by Faber and Faber Ltd, and is awarded in alternate (even) years for a work of prose or poetry by a writer under 40.

Special attention is paid to its literary merit. The winner receives £1,000. Writers must be a resident of the UK, Republic of Ireland or South Africa.

**Genres** Fiction and Poetry

**Submission Guidelines** Entries must have been published in the UK in the preceding two years.

**Tips** Entry is by nomination only, no submissions.

## George Devine Award

**9 Lower Mall, Hammersmith, London, W6 9DJ**

**Competition/Award Director** Christine Smith

**Insider Info** A prize in memory of the former artistic director of the Royal Court Theatre awarded to a new playwright. Prize money is usually £10,000.

**Genres** Scripts

**Submission Guidelines** Submissions must be received by the end of March each year.

**Tips** Submissions are welcomed from individuals, contact Christine Smith in writing for details.

## The George Orwell Memorial Prize

**Blackwell Publishing, 9600 Garsington Road, Oxford, OX4 2DQ**

 01865 476255

 01865 471255

**Established** 1993

**Insider Info** Sponsored by the George Orwell Memorial Fund and *The Political Quarterly* journal. Founded in memory of George Orwell to recognise excellence in political writing. The prize is split into two categories: books and journalism. Awarded annually, the winners in each category receive £1,000 each.

**Genres** Fiction, Non-fiction, Articles

**Submission Guidelines** Work should be published previously.

**Tips** Political writing can include politics, economics, social studies, cultural studies and fictional writing. Particular attention is paid to work that treats the writing as art and makes it accessible to the general public.

## The Gladstone History Book Prize

**University College London, Gower Street, London, WC1E 6BT**

 020 7387 7532

 020 7387 7532

 rhsinfo@rhs.ac.uk

 www.rhs.ac.uk

**Established** 1998

**Insider Info** Sponsored by the Royal Historical Society. Awarded annually for an original work of

historical research and writing on any subject other than an aspect of British history. The work must be the writer's first sole publication. The winner receives £1,000. Writers should be normally resident in the UK.

**Genres** Non-fiction

**Submission Guidelines** Entry deadline is end of December. Work should have been published during the previous calendar year.

**Tips** Nominations from publishers only.

## Glenfiddich Food and Drink Awards

**c/o Wild Card PR, Burridges Barn, Crick, Northamptonshire, NN6 7TG**

 020 7355 0655

 deck@wildcard.co.uk

 www.glenfiddich.co.uk/foodanddrink

**Insider Info** Awards presented in recognition of excellence in writing, publishing and broadcasting in the area of food and drink. Categories include: Food Book; Drink Book; Food Writer; Cookery Writer; Drink/Bar Writer; Wine Writer; Restaurant Critic; Regional Writer; Broadcast; and Photography. The awards are presented annually and winners in each category receive an award, £1,000 and a bottle of Glenfiddich Single Malt Scotch Whisky. The overall winner receives The Glenfiddich Trophy, and another £3,000.

**Genres** Non-fiction

**Submission Guidelines** Submissions must be received by the end of January each year. Titles must be previously published between January 1 and December 31 in the previous year.

**Tips** Open to nominations but submissions must come from publishers only. Detailed guidelines for submitting in each category are available on the website.

## Golden PEN Award for Lifetime Distinguished Service to Literature

**6–8 Amwell Street, London, EC1R 1UQ**

 020 7713 0023

 020 7837 7838

 enquiries@englishpen.org

 www.englishpen.org

**Insider Info** This award is established by English PEN, and is awarded to an established writer who is deemed by their peers to have made an outstanding contribution to the literary world. The award is offered annually. The award is voted for by members of the PEN committee.

**Tips** Nominations come from English PEN only. The award is normally awarded to senior writers with a long publishing history.

## Goss First Novel Award
**c/o Tourist Information Centre, Tunsgate, Guildford, GU1 3QT**
- 01483 444334
- assistant@guildfordbookfestival.co.uk
- www.guildfordbookfestival.co.uk

**Insider Info** The award is sponsored by Guildford Book Festival and is awarded for the best first novel published in the year between Guildford Book Festivals, usually held in October. The winner receives £2,500. Entry is open to any writer whose first novel was published within the given time frame.
**Genres** Novels
**Submission Guidelines** Submissions must be previously published.
**Tips** Accepts submissions from publishers and agents only.

## Grace Dieu Writers' Circle
**c/o Rockside, 139 London Road, Coalville, Leicestershire, LE67 3JE**
- 01530 450203
- 01530 811495
- kshatri@ntlworld.com
- http://beehive.thisisleicestershire.co.uk/

**Competition/Award Director** Competition Organizer, Tony Gutteridge
**Established** 2004
**Insider Info** Annual short story and poetry competition to promote and challenge writing, and to provide reward both financially and by way of publication. £1 from each book sold will be donated to Rainbows Children's Hospice in Leicestershire. Short story prizes are £200/£100/£50/£25/£15, poetry prizes are £100/£75/£50/£25/£15. Short story judge will be Simon Whaley (published author), poetry judge will be Dr. Kerry Featherstone. Winners agree to publication in Grace Dieu's anthology and on the website. All entries must be written in English observing usual competition rules, and competition is open to all (2004 winner was resident in New Zealand).
**Genres** Fiction, Poetry
**Submission Guidelines** Submissions should be made by February 28 each year. Accepts simultaneous submissions and submissions from previously published authors. Entry fee for short story competition is £5, poetry fee is £3. Reduction for multiple entries (see website for further information). Submitted material must be unpublished.

## Grimm Magazine Competitions
**1 Howden Hall Road, Edinburgh, EH16 6PQ**
- ukeditor@grimmagazine.com
- www.grimmagazine.com

**Insider Info** Various competitions open to UK and Canadian writers and readers of *Grimm Magazine*. Previous competitions have included a Short Story competition on a set theme and a Poetry competition with an open theme. The prizes usually consist of $100 CDN, a 1 year subscription to the magazine, publication in the magazine, and a Grimm t-shirt for 1st place; 2nd and 3rd place winners win a year's subscription, publication and a Grimm t-shirt.
**Submission Guidelines** There is an entry fee that varies between competitions but is usually around $14 CDN. The short stories and Poems must be previously unpublished.
**Tips** *Grimm Magazine* does not accept simultaneous submissions or previously published work. Details of the latest competition and closing dates are published on the website.

## The Guardian Children's Fiction Award
**119 Farringdon Road, London, EC1R 3ER**
- 020 7239 9694
- 020 7239 9933
- books@guardian.co.uk

**Established** 1967
**Insider Info** Awarded annually to the best children's fiction book for children aged 7+. Picture books are not eligible. The winner receives £1,500. The award is decided by *The Guardian* Children's Book Editor and a selection of authors. Writers must be a resident of Britain or the Commonwealth.
**Genres** Children's fiction
**Submission Guidelines** Work should be published in the UK, in the year preceding the award.
**Tips** Submissions are usually made by publishers.

## Guardian First Book Award
**119 Farringdon Road, London, EC1R 3ER**
- 020 7239 9694
- books@guardian.co.uk

**Competition/Award Director** The Literary Editor
**Established** 1999

**Insider Info** Awarded for the best first book in the year preceding the award. Any type of book, fiction or non-fiction, is eligible except academic texts, children's books, TV or radio tie-ins, educational books, directories and reprints. The award is offered annually and the winner receives £10,000 and is offered an advertising package across *The Guardian* and *The Observer*. This award is open to books in English that have been published in the UK.
**Genres** Fiction and Non-fiction
**Submission Guidelines** Submissions must be previously published.
**Tips** Accepts submissions from publishers only.

## The Guild of Food Writers' Awards
**255 Kent House Road, Beckenham, Kent, BR3 1JQ**
☎ 020 8659 0422
✉ awards@gfw.co.uk
🌐 www.gfw.co.uk
**Established** 1997
**Insider Info** *The Derek Cooper Award for Campaigning and Investigative Food Writing.* This award honours the Guild's first president, the writer and broadcaster Derek Cooper. It highlights the increasing importance of the food writer in the field of food policy. This can include informing and educating the public about agricultural and manufacturing processes, or campaigning to raise standards in the food supply chain. It is a multimedia category, open to works for radio and television as well as print, and to works by single authors or by organisations.
*The Michael Smith Sward for Work on British Food.* Michael was a great supporter of British foods and food traditions, and this award was established in his memory. It goes to the writer or broadcaster who has contributed most to promoting British food, in whatever medium; the work may be specialised or wide-ranging, text-led or recipe-led.
*The Jeremy Round Award for Best First Book.* Jeremy was a brilliant original writer and journalist, and author of The Independent Cook. This award, which commemorates him, is given to a writer of any age or level of experience, provided that this is his or her first cookery book or book about food.
*Food Book of the Year.* This may be biographical, historical, topographical; a guidebook, encyclopaedia or compendium, even a technical handbook. Recipes, if they form part of the work, should serve to illuminate the text, rather than lead it.
*Cookery Book of the Year.* Recipes and, if appropriate, the practicalities of cooking should be the main focus. The subject may be any cuisine, historical period, specific ingredient or diet.
*Food Journalist of the Year.* This award is given to the writer of the best food-related articles published in a magazine, newspaper or newspaper supplement. Five pieces should be submitted; they may contain recipes, but recipes should not form the bulk of the text. Note that a comparable quantity of material from a website or websites may also be nominated for this award, provided that the author has been commissioned and paid for the work and it is not self-published. If website material is nominated, the nominator should supply jurors with the relevant web addresses of the specific articles.
*The Evelyn Rose Award for Cookery Journalist of the Year.* This award was renamed in honour of Evelyn Rose, a former chair of the Guild, who produced a weekly cookery column for over 40 years and was famed for her meticulous recipe writing. The award goes to the writer of the best recipe-led articles, columns or pages published in a magazine, newspaper, newspaper supplement or on the internet. Five such features should be submitted. Material from a website or websites may only be nominated if the author has been commissioned and paid for the work and it is not self-published. If website material is nominated, the nominator should supply jurors with the relevant web addresses of the specific articles.
*The Miriam Polunin Award for Work on Healthy Eating* Miriam Polunin was a much loved and respected member of the Guild, serving two terms on its committee, most recently as Treasurer, who died in tragic circumstances in 2005. As she was one the first food writers to succeed in communicating complex issues of nutrition to the general public and in conveying the idea that healthy food could also be delicious, the Guild last year instituted this award in her honour. It goes to the writer or broadcaster who has contributed most to promoting healthy food, in whatever medium; the work may be specialised or wide-ranging, text-led or recipe-led.
Awarded annually, the prize is a large wooden charger. Judges are randomly selected members of the Guild of Food Writers.
**Genres** Non-fiction, Articles, TV or Radio programmes or websites.
**Submission Guidelines** Deadline for entry is in February each year. Forms are available on the Guild's website. Work should be published previously, between January 1 and December 31.

## Hans Christian Andersen Awards

**British Section of IBBY, PO Box 20875, London, SE22 9WQ**

☎ 020 82 99 16 41

✉ ann@lazim.demon.co.uk

🌐 www.ibby.org

**Established** 1956

**Insider Info** This award is sponsored by IBBY and is an award made to a living writer and illustrator who is seen to have made a lasting contribution to children's literature. It is the highest international recognition in the field of children's books and her Majesty Queen Margrethe II of Denmark is the Patron. The award is offered every two years (even years). The prize consists of a gold medal and a diploma, presented during the biennial IBBY Congress.

**Genres** Illustrated Children's Books

**Submission Guidelines** Submissions must be previously published.

**Tips** Writer and illustrator prizes may be awarded separately but both must have an entire body of work that has influenced children's literature over a period of time.

## Harry Bowling Prize

**Storytracks, Coseley House, Munslow, Craven Arms, Shropshire, SY7 9ET**

🌐 www.harrybowlingprize.net

**Established** 2000

**Insider Info** An award for the best opening chapter and synopsis of a novel set in London. In memory of Harry Bowling, a successful writer who set much of his work in London. Every two (even) years, the overall winner receives £1,000 and runners up receive £100 each. Judges include Jane Morpeth (Harry Bowling's editor at Hodder Headline) and Laura Longrigg (his agent at MBA). Entrants must not have published any adult works of fiction before, however they may have published short stories, scripts for TV and radio, non-fiction and children's fiction and non-fiction.

**Genres** Fiction

**Submission Guidelines** Submissions should be received by March 31 each year. Guidelines are available online. Entry fee of £10.

**Tips** Submit up to 5,000 words and a 500 word synopsis by post, along with an entry form (available from the website), entry fee and SAE if receipt is required. A list of criteria that the judges are looking for is published on the website – read this thoroughly before entering. The next prize is in 2008.

## The Hawthornden Prize

**42a Hays Mews, Berkeley Square, London, W1X 7RU**

**Insider Info** Sponsored by the Hawthornden Trust. Awarded annually for what is deemed to be the best and most imaginative work of literature published in the UK in the preceding year.

**Submission Guidelines** Work should be published previously.

**Tips** No entries, winners are chosen from nominations.

## Henrietta Branford Writing Competition

**Glebe House, Weobly, Hereford, HR4 8SD**

☎ 01544 318901

✉ editor@youngwriter.org

🌐 www.branfordboaseaward.org.uk

**Insider Info** An annual competition for young writers up to the age of 19. Entrants must download two opening paragraphs from the website and finish the story in up to 1,500 words. Winners of the 2007 award are invited to meet Jacqueline Wilson at the Branford Boase Award party in London, and receive copies of the shortlisted books for the main awards. The competition is judged by Kate Jones, director of Young Writer Magazine, to which you should also send entries at the above postal or email addresses. Writers may enter from all over the world.

**Genres** Short stories

**Submission Guidelines** Submissions should be made by May each year. Further guidelines available on the website. Submission should be unpublished.

**Tips** Although there is a 1,500 word limit, stories that are much shorter are welcomed.

## The Hessell-Tiltman Prize for Lyrical Poetry

**6–8 Amwell Street, London, EC1R 1UQ**

☎ 020 7713 0023

☎ 020 7837 7838

✉ enquiries@englishpen.org

🌐 www.englishpen.org

**Established** 2002

**Insider Info** Sponsored by English PEN. Awarded annually for a history text that is deemed to have a wide audience appeal. The author of the winning book receives £3,000.

**Genres** Non-fiction.

**Submission Guidelines** Work should be published previously.

**Tips** Submissions by publishers only.

## The Ian Fleming Steel Dagger

**PO Box 273, Boreham Wood, WD6 2XA**

info@thecwa.co.uk

www.thecwa.co.uk

**Established** 2002

**Insider Info** Sponsored by the Crime Writers' Association and Ian Fleming (Glidrose) Publications Ltd. An annual award given for the best thriller novel published in the preceding year. The prize consists of an ornamental steel dagger and £2,000.

**Genres** Crime/thriller novels

**Submission Guidelines** Work should be published previously.

**Tips** Submissions by publishers only.

## The Independent Foreign Fiction Prize

**The Literature Department, Arts Council England, 14 Great Peter Street, London, SW1P 3NQ**

020 7973 5204

020 7973 6983

info.literature@artscouncil.org.uk, bethany.king@artscouncil.org.uk

www.artscouncil.org.uk

**Insider Info** Awarded annually for a contemporary work of fiction in translation. It is one of the only awards to honour the writer and translator in equal measure. The winning writer and translator receive £5,000 each. The judging panel changes each year. The author must be living at the time of publication and the work must have been published in the UK.

**Genres** Translations

**Submission Guidelines** Deadline for entry is end of December each year. Guidelines and entry forms are available on the website. Work should be published previously, between January 1 and December 31.

**Tips** Although the deadline is the end of each year, entries are accepted and encouraged much earlier than this. Send seven copies to Bethany King, administrator.

## The International Dundee Book Prize

**City of Discovery Campaign, 3 City Square, Dundee, DD1 3BA**

01382 434214

01382 434650

book.prize@dundeecity.gov.uk

www.dundeebookprize.com

**Established** 1996

**Insider Info** Sponsored by Birlinn Ltd and the University of Dundee. Normally awarded every two years: the 2009 award will be presented to an entry that was received by early 2008. The winning writer receives £10,000 and the publication of their novel.

**Genres** Fiction, Novels.

**Submission Guidelines** Deadline for entry is March every two years. Entrants must not have had a novel previously published. Children's novels are not eligible.

**Tips** There are no restrictions on theme or style. Entries may be made by post or by email, although online entries have an earlier closing date; see website for details.

## The International IMPAC Dublin Literary Award

**Dublin City Library & Archive, 138–144 Pearse Street, Dublin 2, Republic of Ireland**

00353 1 674 4802

00353 1 674 4879

literaryaward@dublincity.ie

www.impacdublinaward.ie

**Competition/Award Director** Eileen Hendrick

**Established** 1994

**Insider Info** Sponsored by Dublin City Council and IMPAC. Awarded every two years (odd years) to a work of fiction in English, including translations into English. The winning writer receives €100,000 and a crystal trophy. If the book is a translation, a €25,000 share goes to the translator.

**Genres** Fiction, Novels, Translations

**Submission Guidelines** Deadline for entries is August. Work should be previously published – see the website for further details and submission guidelines.

**Tips** Nominations are to be made by libraries in capital cities all over the world.

## International Playwriting Festival

**Warehouse Theatre, Dingwall Road, Croydon, CR0 2NF**

rose@warehousetheatre.co.uk

www.warehousetheatre.co.uk

**Established** 1986

**Insider Info** An annual competition for playwrights from all over the world aimed at encouraging new writing for the theatre. Scripts are invited for submission and later in the year four selected, winning plays are performed at the festival. The festival is twinned with Premio Candoni – Arta Terme in Italy.

**Genres** Scripts

**Submission Guidelines** Submissions should be made by June 30 each year. Guidelines and entry forms are available on the website. Plays must not have been previously produced, although amateur performances do not count.

**Tips** There are no limitations to cast size or restrictions on theme, although scripts should be roughly 50–100 pages long, or a full length, completed play. Translations are eligible but adaptations are not. Contact Rose Marie Vernon for more information.

## ISG Reference Awards
**Information Services Group c/o CILIP, 7 Ridgemount Street, London, WC1E 6BT**
- 020 7255 0500
- 020 7255 0501
- www.cilip.org.uk

**Established** 1970

**Insider Info** Annual competition, sponsored by Nielsen Bookscan, consisting of three awards to mark achievements in reference works – The Besterman McColvin award for first editions of print titles; The Besterman McColvin award for new electronic publications, and The Walford award for contribution to bibliography. For the Besterman/ McColvin awards, the prizes consist of £500 cash, a medal and a certificate. For the Walford award, the winner receives £500 and a certificate. Entries are judged by members of ISG, along with the multimedia Information and Technology Group for the electronic award. The Besterman/McColvin nominations must have been already published in the UK. The Walford nominees do not need to be resident in the UK.

**Genres** Non-fiction

**Submission Guidelines** Submissions should be made by January 31 each year. Guidelines available on website. Submissions should have been published between January 1 and December 31 of the previous year.

**Tips** Works are judged on the scope of the content, the layout and quality of information and knowledge, the index and references, look and feel, innovation and whether it represents value for money.

## James Cameron Award
**City University Department of Journalism, Northampton Square, London, EC1V 0HB**
- 020 7040 8221
- 020 7040 8594

**Established** 1985

**Insider Info** An annual award celebrating the UK journalist who is judged to have made an outstanding contribution to the media in the tradition of foreign correspondent, columnist and author James Cameron.

**Tips** This is not an open competition.

## James Tait Black Memorial prizes
**Department of English Literature, The University of Edinburgh, David Hume Tower, George Square, Edinburgh, EH8 9JX**
- 0131 650 3620
- 0131 650 6898
- www.englit.ed.ac.uk

**Established** 1919

**Insider Info** Annual award with two prizes awarded for outstanding works of fiction or biography written in English. The winners in each category receive £10,000. The same writer may win both awards but never the same award twice. Open to writers of any nationality.

**Genres** Fiction, Biography

**Submission Guidelines** Submissions should be made by January 31 of each year. Simultaneous submissions accepted. An information pamphlet may be downloaded from the website. Submissions should have been published between January 1 and December 31 of the previous year.

**Tips** Submissions are invited from publishers. Send one copy of the book as soon after its publication as possible, stating the exact date of publication. The award may also be presented to books that have not been submitted but have caught the judge's eye, however this is rare.

## Jerwood Aldeburgh First Collection Prize
**The Cut, 9 New Cut, Halesworth, IP19 8BY**
- 01986 835950
- 01986 835949
- info@thepoetrytrust.org
- www.thepoetrytrust.org

**Insider Info** An annual competition, sponsored by The Poetry Trust, awarded for the best first poetry collection published in Britain or the Republic of Ireland in the previous year. The winner receives £3,000, one week's paid writing time in Aldeburgh and a paid opportunity to read their poetry at the Aldeburgh Poetry Festival of the following year.

**Genres** Poetry

**Submission Guidelines** Submissions should be made by July 31 of each year. Submissions must have been published between August 31 and July 1 of the previous year.

**Tips** Submissions are invited from poets and publishers. Submit three bound copies along with publication details.

## The Joan Hessayon New Writers' Scheme Award

- gillroger@tiscali.co.uk
- www.rna-uk.org

**Competition/Award Director** Roger Sanderson

**Insider Info** Sponsored by the Romantic Novelists' Association. Awarded annually for a debut published romance novel from a member of the New Writers' Scheme. The writer must still be a member of the New Writers' Scheme at the time of the award and the winning novel in particular must have been developed through the scheme.

**Genres** Fiction, Novels

**Submission Guidelines** The book must either be published or under contract with a publisher.

**Tips** Any unpublished romantic novelist may apply to join the New Writers' Scheme. Entry forms are available from the website and fees are £90. Members will have access to all the events and services of the RNA and will be entitled to a manuscript appraisal service.

## John D. Criticos Prize

**The Hellenic Centre, 16–18 Paddington Street, London, W1U 5AS**

**Competition/Award Director** Mr George Rodopoulos

**Established** 1996

**Insider Info** An annual award, sponsored by The London Hellenic Society, awarded to an artist, writer, or researcher for a book on an aspect of Hellenic culture. Prize money totals £10,000.

**Genres** Non-fiction

**Tips** Particular areas of interest are archaeology, art, history and literature. Submissions are welcome from both individuals and publishers.

## The John Dryden Translation Competition

**School of Literature and Creative Writing, University of East Anglia, Norwich, NR4 7TJ**

- 01603 250599
- transcomp@uea.ac.uk
- www.bcla.org

**Established** 1983

**Insider Info** Sponsored by the British Comparative Literature Association and the British Centre for Literary Translation. Awarded annually for unpublished literary translations from any language into English. This can include prose, poetry or drama from any era. Winners will have their work published on the website, and extracts from winning entries may be published in the *Comparative Critical Studies* journal. Judges include: Peter Frost, editor of *The Oxford Guide to Literature in English Translation*; Stuart Gillespie, editor of *Translation and Literature*; Amanda Hopkinson, director of the British Centre for Literary Translation; and Elinor Shaffer, former editor of *Comparative Criticism*.

**Genres** Translations

**Submission Guidelines** Deadline for entries is February. entry fee is £5 per entry. Work should be previously unpublished.

**Tips** Writers may submit a maximum of three entries each, none of which may have been previously entered for competitions or been published.

## John Llewellyn Rhys Prize

**Book House, 45 East Hill, London, SW18 2QZ**

- 020 8516 2972
- 020 8516 2978
- tarryn@booktrust.org.uk
- www.booktrust.org.uk

Tarryn McKay

**Established** 1942

**Insider Info** An annual competition, sponsored by Booktrust, awarded for a work of either fiction or non-fiction by a British or Commonwealth writer under the age of 35. In memory of John Llewellyn, a writer killed in WW2. The winning author receives £5,000. Shortlisted writers recieve £500 each. Although the authors may be from any Commonwealth country, the book must be in English.

**Genres** Fiction, Non-fiction

**Submission Guidelines** Submissions must be previously published.

**Tips** Publisher submissions only.

## The John Whiting Award

**14 Great Peter Street, London, SW1P 3NQ**

- 020 7973 6480
- www.artscouncil.org.uk

**Established** 1965

**Insider Info** Sponsored by the Arts Council England. Awarded for a new play that bears reference to contemporary society whilst being innovative in writing style. The winner receives £6,000.

**Genres** Scripts

**Tips** The award may be given to a writer who has had some previous involvement with the Arts

Council such as winning a previous grant or award, or having their play produced in an Art Council-subsidised theatre.

## J. R Ackerley Prize

**English PEN, 6–8 Amwell Street, London, EC1R 1UQ**

☎ 020 7713 0023

☏ 020 7837 7838

✉ enquiries@englishpen.org

🌐 www.englishpen.org

**Established** 1982

**Insider Info** An annual competition awarded for an outstanding work of literary autobiography written in the previous year by a British writer. Prize money is £1,000.

**Genres** Autobiography

**Submission Guidelines** Submissions must be previously published.

**Tips** Nominations are from members of the judging panel and Ackerley trustees only. No public submissions.

## Katherine Briggs Folklore Award

**The Warburg Institute, Woburn Square, London, WC1H 0AB**

☎ 020 7862 8564

✉ susanvass@hotmail.com

🌐 www.folklore-society.com

**Insider Info** An annual competition, sponsored by the Folklore Society, created to encourage the study and publication of folklore in Britain and Ireland, and to commemorate the life and work of Katharine Mary Briggs (1898–1980; Society president 1969–1972).The prize consists of an engraved goblet and £200. There are three judges, one of whom is the Society's President, Vice-President or Publications Officer. Open to all books in English having their first publication in the United Kingdom and/or Republic of Ireland.

**Genres** Non-fiction

**Submission Guidelines** Submissions should be made by May 31 each year. Guidelines available on the website. Submissions must have been published between June 1 and May 31 of the previous year.

**Tips** Folklore can include all aspects of traditional and popular culture, narrative, beliefs, customs and folk arts, including studies with a literary, anthropological, linguistic, sociological or geographical slant. Entries are welcomed from both writers and publishers, as long as they meet all the criteria. Submit four hard copies, along with an application form, to the Convenor at the above address.

## Keats-Shelley Prize

**School of English, University of St Andrews, Scotland, KY16 9AL**

✉ hello@keats-shelley.co.uk

🌐 www.keats-shelley.com

**Competition/Award Director** A. N. Wilson, Chairman.

**Established** 1998

**Insider Info** An annual competition sponsored by Barclays Bank PLC, The School of English, University of St Andrew's and The Cowley Foundation. The award is in two categories: poems that take their inspiration from the style of the romantic poets, and essays on the life and work of Keats or Shelley. The specific theme for the poetry category is chosen by the judges each year. The winners and runners up in each category receive a share of £3,000. The critic and writer A. N. Wilson will judge the shortlisted entries. The competition is open to anyone, although it tends to be heavily promoted through universities.

**Genres** Poetry, Essays

**Submission Guidelines** Submissions should be made by June 30 each year. Simultaneous submissions accepted.

**Tips** Essays of 2,000–3,000 words (including quotations) may be on any aspect of the life or work of John Keats, P. B. Shelley, Mary Shelley or Lord Byron. Poems may be up to 50 lines long. For an information leaflet, contact Sandra McDevitt at the above address.

## Kelpies Prize

**15 Harrison Gardens, Edinburgh, EH11 1SH**

☎ 0131 337 2372

☏ 0131 347 9919

🌐 www.florisbooks.co.uk/kelpiesprize

**Insider Info** An annual competition, sponsored by Floris Books, for the best unpublished novel for children aged 9–12 set entirely, or mainly, in Scotland.Winners receive a cash prize and their novel will be published in the Kelpies series by Floris Books. Open to any writer, but the book must be set in Scotland. Writers may have been published before but the winning entry must not have been.

**Genres** Fiction, Novels, Older children/young teenage novels

**Submission Guidelines** Submissions should be made by February of each year. Guidelines are available on the website.

**Tips** The stories must appeal to both boys and girls within the relevant age group. Novels with animals as main characters and romantic novels are not generally recommended.

## Kent and Sussex Poetry Society annual competition

- info@kentandsussexpoetrysociety.org
- www.kentandsussexpoetrysociety.org

**Insider Info** Annual international competition, with £1,350 prize money. Submissions limited to 40 lines. Different, well known and respected judge each year. All entries should be submitted anonymously, and will be read by the judge. Total prize fund of £1,350, and winners will be published in the anthology.

**Genres** Poetry

**Submission Guidelines** Submissions should be made by January 31 each year. Simultaneous submissions accepted, but submitted pieces must be previously unpublished. Enter via the website or write to the competition organiser.

## Kerry Group Irish Fiction Award

**Writer's Week, 24 The Square, Listowel, Co. Kerry, Republic of Ireland**

- 00353 682 1074
- 00353 682 2893
- info@writersweek.ie
- www.writersweek.ie

**Insider Info** Annual competition, sponsored by the Kerry Group PLC, awarded to a published fiction book by an Irish writer. The results are linked in with the Writers Week festival in Listowel. The winner receives €10,000.

**Genres** Fiction

**Submission Guidelines** Submissions must be previously published. See the website for further details.

**Tips** Details of other competitions that run with each festival appear on the website.

## The Kim Scott Walwyn Prize

**Booktrust, Book House, 45 East Hill, London, SW18 2QZ**

- 020 8516 2972
- 020 8516 2978
- helen@booktrust.org.uk
- www.booktrust.org.uk

**Insider Info** An annual award to celebrate the achievements of women in publishing, in memory of Kim Scott Walwyn, former Director of Publishing

at Oxford University Press. The prize is presented to an individual who is deemed to have made an outstanding professional contribution to the publishing industry over a period of time. The winner receives £3,000. The judges are a panel of female professionals in the publishing industry including agents, editors and broadcasters.

**Submission Guidelines** Deadline for entry is February. Guidelines are available on the website.

**Tips** Nominations may be made by the entrants themselves, or by sponsors. Email entries are encouraged - see the website for details of how to apply and what to include. Winners may be from any area of the publishing industry including editorial, marketing, design, sales and production and should show potential for future achievements as well as substantial existing career successes.

## Kraszna-Krausz Book Awards

**The National Media Museum, Bradford, West Yorkshire, BD1 1NQ**

- mbrownevents@hotmail.com
- www.k-k.org.uk

**Established** 1985

**Insider Info** Annual awards that alternate between being for books on photography and books on the moving image. Books may be about any technical or creative aspect of these areas. Books may have been published in any country and be written in any language.

**Genres** Non-fiction

**Submission Guidelines** Submissions should be made by December of each year, and must be previously published.

**Tips** Nominations from publishers only. Entry forms and more details are available on the website.

## Lakeland Book of the Year Awards

**Windermere Road, Staveley, Cumbria, LA8 9PL**

- 01539 825052
- 01539 825076
- slindsay@cumbriatourism.org
- www.golakes.co.uk

**Competition/Award Director** Sheila Lindsay – Co-ordinator

**Established** 1984

**Insider Info** Annual competition, sponsored by Cumbria Tourism. Over the past 22 years the Lakeland Book of the Year Awards has established itself as a prestigious event on the literary calendar. Authors (be they first-time or previously published) and publishers are encouraged to enter. Last year's awards saw a large number of entries all competing

for the prestigious Hunter Davies Prize of The Lakeland Book of the Year. Categories are: Titus Wilson Prize for Guides, Walks, Places; Bookends Prize for Arts, Literature; Saint & Co Prize for Business, Industry; Bill Rollinson Prize for Landscape and Tradition; Dodd and Co Chartered Accountants Prize for Photographic; The New Bookshop Prize for Biographies and Autobiographies; The Hunter Davies Prize for the Book of the Year. Prize is £100, plus certificate and publicity for each category.
**Submission Guidelines** Submissions should be made by March 9 each year. Simultaneous submissions are accepted. Submissions must have been published between January and December of the previous year.

## Leaf Books Writing Competitions
**GTi Suite, Valleys Innovations Centre, Abercynon, CF45 4SN**
- 01443 665704
- contact@leafbooks.co.uk
- www.leafbooks.co.uk

**Competition/Award Director** Sam Burns
**Established** 2005
**Insider Info** Ongoing competitions for Fiction, Short Stories, Micro-fiction and Poetry. Each competition is run in order to get the winning entries into print. Leaf's aim is to get as many authors published as possible. Ongoing throughout the year. Prize consists of publication and £200. Judged by named judges or a panel of readers. Rights to submitted material remains with the author upon entry. Competition open to any writer.
**Genres** Fiction, Poetry, Short stories, microfiction
**Submission Guidelines** Guidelines and entry form available via SAE. Entry fee is £5. Work should be previously unpublished.
**Tips** Read the guidelines on the website.

## Legend Writing Award
**39 Emmanuel Road, Hastings, East Sussex, TN34 3LB**
- www.legendwritingaward.com

**Established** 2001
**Insider Info** An annual open competition for short stories of less than 2,000 words. Stories may be on any theme but children's stories and poetry are not accepted. Prizes consist of: 1st £500; 2nd £25; 3rd £100; three runners-up £50; and four shortlisted £25. Copyright remains with the author but the work may be published in the Hastings Writers Group Anthology. The entry must not have been previously entered for any other award or competition.

**Genres** Short stories.
**Submission Guidelines** Deadline for entry is end of August. Guidelines and entry forms are available on the website. entry fee is £5 per entry. Work should be previously unpublished.
**Tips** Postal entries only, including an entry form. They should be typed, single sided and double spaced.

## Lichfield and District Writers Short Story Competition
**133 Park Road, Barton-under-Needwood, Burton-on-Trent, DE13 8DD**
- lichfield_writers@yahoo.co.uk
- http://members.lycos.co.uk/Lichfield_Writers

**Insider Info** An annual open short story competition for pieces up to a maximum of 2,000 words. Prizes consist of: £125 for 1st place; £75 for 2nd place; and £25 for 3rd place. All short listed writers receive a certificate.
**Genres** Short stories.
**Submission Guidelines** Deadline for entries is November. Guidelines available on the website. entry fee is £3 for the first entry, £2 for subsequent entries. Work should be previously unpublished.
**Tips** Entrants are invited to include a further £4 per story if they would like a written appraisal. Entries should be typed and double spaced on single sided sheets. Details of future closing dates will be published on the website.

## London Press Club Awards
**St. Bride Institute, 14 Bride Lane, Fleet Street, London, EC4Y 8EQ**
- 020 7353 7086
- 020 7353 7087
- info@londonpressclub.co.uk
- www.londonpressclub.co.uk

**Insider Info** Awards are presented annually across a variety of categories to celebrate British journalism and journalists. Judges are made up of industry professionals from the journalism, media and communications industry.
**Tips** Awards are voted for by the judging panel and do not need submissions.

## London Writers Competition
**Room 224a, The Town Hall, Wandsworth High Street, London, SW18 2PU**
- 020 8871 8711
- 020 8871 7630
- arts@wandsworth.gov.uk

@ www.wandsworth.gov.uk

**Established** 1977

**Insider Info** sponsored by Wandsworth Council and Roehampton University. An annual competition designed to encourage people who work, live or study in London to write. The categories include poetry, story, play and fiction for children. There is a total prize fund of £5,000.

**Genres** Fiction, Poetry, Scripts, Children's fiction

**Submission Guidelines** Work should be previously unpublished.

**Tips** Details of closing dates for future competitions will be published in the arts events section of the Wandsworth Council website.

## Longman/History Today Book of the Year

**History Today, 20 Old Compton Street, London, W1V 5PE**

📞 020 7534 8000

📧 p.furtado@historytoday.com

@ www.historytoday.com

**Competition/Award Director** Peter Furtado

**Established** 1993

**Insider Info** Awarded annually for a writer's first or second historical non-fiction book. The winner receives £1,000.

**Genres** Non-fiction

**Submission Guidelines** Work should be published previously.

**Tips** Publisher submissions only.

## L. Ron Hubbard's Writer of the Future Contest

**PO Box 218, East Grinstead, RH19 4GH**

**Established** 1984

**Insider Info** Aimed at encouraging new writing in the science fiction, horror and fantasy genres. The annual competition consists of four quarterly mini-contests with an annual overall winner. The 1st, 2nd and 3rd placed winners in each quarter receive £640, £480 and £320 respectively. The overall winner each year wins £2,500.

**Genres** Short stories, Novelettes

**Submission Guidelines** Entrants must be previously unpublished.

**Tips** Write to adminstrator Andrea Grant-Webb at the above address for more details. Short stories of up to 10,000 words and novelettes of up to 17,000 words may be submitted.

## Macmillan Prize for a Children's Picture Book Illustration

**Macmillan Children's Books, 20 New Wharf Road, London, N1 9RR**

📞 020 7014 6124

📞 020 7014 6124

@ www.panmacmillan.com

**Insider Info** An annual competition to find the best original illustration for children's books. Entrants are invited to submit a 'mock book' based on their own story or an out of copyright text. Art and illustration students are usually invited to apply. The winner receives £1,000 and the possibility of being published with Macmillan.

**Submission Guidelines** Work should be previously unpublished.

**Tips** Details of the scheme are usually advertised through art colleges and the art departments of universities.

## The Mail on Sunday Novel Competition

**Associated Newspapers Limited, Northcliffe House, 2 Derry Street, London, W8 5TT**

@ www.mailonsunday.co.uk

**Insider Info** Sponsored by *The Mail on Sunday*. An annual award for the best new novel submitted. Prizes consist of book tokens and writing courses.

**Genres** Fiction, Novels

**Tips** Details of how to enter the competition appear in *The Mail on Sunday Newspaper* in late summer.

## The Man Booker International Prize

**c/o Colman Getty PR, 28 Windmill Street, London, W1T 2JJ**

📞 020 7631 2666

📞 020 7631 2699

📧 pr@colmangetty.co.uk

@ www.manbookerinternational.com

**Competition/Award Director** Ion Trewin

**Established** 2004

**Insider Info** Awarded every two years (odd years) to a fiction writer who is deemed to have made an outstanding contribution to international literature with work written in, or translated to the English language. The winner receives £60,000. Open to writers of any nationality.

**Genres** Fiction, Translations

**Submission Guidelines** Work should be published previously.

**Tips** Contenders for the prize are decided by a panel of judges that change every year. No unsolicited submissions.

## The Man Booker Prize for Fiction
**28 Windmill Street, London, W1T 2JJ**
- 020 7631 2666
- 020 7631 2699
- eleanor@colmangetty.co.uk
- www.themanbookerprize.com

**Established** 1968

**Insider Info** Sponsored by Colman Getty PR. Awards the best novel of the year written by a citizen of the Commonwealth or the Republic of Ireland. Prize is awarded annually. Prize money is £50,000. Judges change every year but normally include a literary critic, an academic, a literary editor and a novelist. Only open to writers of books published in the UK (incl. books that have also been published outside the UK).

**Genres** Fiction and Novels

**Submission Guidelines** Work should be published previously appearing between October 1 of the previous year and September 30 of the year of entry.

**Tips** Entrants must be nominated by UK publishers. Works must be in English. Please do not nominate any translations, short story collections, novellas or self-published books.

## Marsh Award for Children's Literature in Translation
**National Centre for Research in Children's Literature, Roehampton University, Froebel College, Roehampton Lane, London, SW15 5PJ**
- 020 8392 3008
- 020 8392 3819
- g.lathey@roehampton.ac.uk

**Competition/Award Director** Dr. Gillian Lathey

**Established** 1995

**Insider Info** Awarded to the best book translated into English and published by a British publisher. Competition takes place every two years (odd years); the winner receives £1,000.

**Genres** Fiction, Non-fiction, Children's books for ages four and over.

**Submission Guidelines** Work should be published previously.

**Tips** Encyclopedias, reference books, audio books and e-book are not eligible.

## Marsh Biography Award
**The English-Speaking Union, Dartmouth House, 37 Charles Street, London, W1J 5ED**
- 020 7529 1550
- 020 7495 6108
- esu@esu.org, gillian_parker@esu.org
- www.esu.org

**Established** 1985

**Insider Info** Awarded for the most influential biography published in Britain over the previous two years; competition takes place every two years (odd years). The winning biographer receives £4,000, a trophy and membership to the ESU. Writers must be British.

**Genres** Biography

**Submission Guidelines** Work should be published previously.

**Tips** The award is usually given to a thoroughly researched biography, often of a historical figure.

## Martha Gellhorn Trust Prize
**Rutherfords, Herbert Road, Torquay, TQ8 8HN**

**Insider Info** An award for journalism in honour of journalist Martha Gellhorn. Focuses on human interest stories and how people cope in the midst of larger scale news events. The competition takes place annually, and the winner receives £5,000.

**Genres** Articles

**Submission Guidelines** Work should be published previously.

**Tips** Postal submissions may be made. The deadline is usually in March.

## Mary Vaughan Jones Award
**Castell Brychan, Aberystwyth, SY23 2JB**
- 01970 624151
- 01970 625385
- wbc.children@wbc.org.uk
- www.wbc.org.uk

**Established** 1985

**Insider Info** Awarded to a person who has made a significant contribution to children's literature in Wales over a long period of time. Awarded every three years, with the next award in 2009. The winner receives a silver trophy.

**Tips** Not open to submissions.

## MCA Management Awards
**London Hilton, Park Lane, London**
- natalia.kay@mca.org.uk
- www.mca.org.uk/MCA/Awards/ThisYear.aspx

**Established** 1996

**Insider Info** The prestigious Management Awards are organised by the Management Consultancies Association (MCA), and run in association with *Management Today* – the most widely read monthly business magazine in Britain. The awards aim to identify the best case studies in each of ten categories, where organisations, in the private or public sector, have achieved a significant improvement in performance with the assistance of management consultants, either in-house or external. See the website for each year's categories and list of judges. Entries should show the problems faced by one client, the solutions developed and the ultimate benefits to the organisation. Entries should be jargon-free, underline quantifiable results and demonstrate the respective roles of the client and the consultants in the project.

**Genres** Non-fiction

**Submission Guidelines** Deadline for entry is October for the following year's award, and is the same time each year. Send SAE for guidelines and entry forms. Entry fee for members is £300 +VAT; entry fee for non-members is £1,000 +VAT.

**Tips** Top ten tips for a winning entry: 1. Use plain English, not management speak. 2. Don't spend too much time describing the project; stress what the benefits to the client were. 3. Include human interest – what did the people from the client's side get out of the project? What were their views? 4. Have a snappy executive summary or introduction, to gain the reader's interest. 5. Obtain client sign-off early to avoid last minute delays in the process. 6. Only one client organisation should be used in your case study. 7. Stick to the word limit – case studies have been disqualified in the past! 8. Could your client have done the work without you? If the answer is no, make sure you state what you did that was different. 9. Within the constraints of confidentiality, if possible indicate the net benefit/payback to the client. 10. Don't baffle your reader! Only include clearly designed tables and figures if they aid the reader in understanding your case study.

## McKitterick Prize

**84 Drayton Gardens, London, SW10 9SB**

- 020 7373 6642
- 020 7373 5768
- info@societyofauthors.org
- www.societyofauthors.org

**Insider Info** Sponsored by the Society of Authors. Awarded for a first full length novel by a writer over the age of 40. Awarded annually, the winner receives

£4,000. The writer must be over the age of 40 on the December 31 in the year of submission.

**Genres** Novels

**Submission Guidelines** Guidelines available on the website. Previously published entries must have appeared in print between January 1 and December 31 the previous year. Accepts unpublished entries.

**Tips** Send four copies of the book (if published), or the first 30 pages of the manuscript (if unpublished), to Dorothy Sym at the Society of Authors. Entries are normally invited from late summer.

## Medical Book Awards

**Society of Authors, 84 Drayton Gardens, London, SW10 9SB**

- 020 7373 6642
- 020 7373 5768
- sbaxter@societyofauthors.org
- www.societyofauthors.org

**Insider Info** Sponsored by the Royal Society of Medicine. Awards are given for books written either for the medical profession, or for the general public on a medical theme. There are a number of categories for new books, new editions, specialist and general books. Awarded annually. The prizes are different for each category but winner usually receives a cash prize. Each category has a different set of entry criteria. See the website for details.

**Genres** Non-fiction

**Submission Guidelines** Deadline for entry is April. Work should be published previously between May 1 and April 30.

**Tips** Entries from publishers only. Each publisher may submit ten books per imprint, per category.

## The Mercedes Benz Award for the Montagu of Beaulieu Trophy

**Guild of Motoring Writers, 39 Beswick Avenue, Bournemouth, BH10 4EY**

- 01202 518808
- 02102 518808
- chris@whizzco.freeserve.co.uk
- www.guildofmotoringwriters.co.uk

**Established** 1972

**Insider Info** Sponsored by Mercedes Benz UK. The award is made to an individual who has contributed to highlighting and recording the history of motoring or motorcycling. It originated when Lord Montagu introduced it to celebrate the opening of the National Motor Museum at Beaulieu. The award is given annually. The winner receives £1,000 and a trophy.

**Genres** Non-fiction, Essays, Scripts and Articles

**Tips** Multiple winners may be awarded in the same year. Books, TV broadcasts, films, radio broadcasts, essays, research documents and articles are all eligible as long as they are publicly accessible.

## Mere Literary Festival Open Competition

**Lawrence's, Old Hollow, Mere, Warminster, Wiltshire, BA12 6EG**

☎ 01747 860475

🌐 www.merewilts.org.uk

**Competition/Award Director** Mrs Adrienne Howell

**Insider Info** An open competition for both young people and adults. The subject may vary each year. The winners are announced at the festival which takes place annually.

**Genres** Short stories

**Submission Guidelines** Guidelines and entry forms are also available on the website. Work should be previously unpublished.

**Tips** Although the competition is open to writers living all over the country, entrants living within a ten mile radius of Mere are often simultaneously entered for a separate prize.

## Meyer-Whitworth Award

**Arts Council England, 14 Great Peter Street, London, SW1P 3NQ**

☎ 020 7973 6480

📧 charles.hart@artscouncil.org.uk

🌐 www.artscouncil.org.uk

**Insider Info** Awarded to a playwright who has had a play produced in the preceding year but no more than two produced in their career so far. The award is designed to help fully establish emerging writers for the theatre. Awarded annually, the winner receives £8,000. Plays must be in English and have been produced in the UK.

**Genres** Theatre productions

**Submission Guidelines** Work should be published previously.

**Tips** Nominations from theatre directors. Contact Charles Hart for more details.

## MIND Book of the Year Award

**Granta House, 15–19 Broadway, London, E15 4BQ**

☎ 020 8215 2301

☎ 020 8215 2269

🌐 www.mind.org.uk

**Established** 1981

**Insider Info** Awarded for a book published in the preceding year that has made significant advances in helping the public understanding of mental health issues. Awarded annually.

**Genres** Fiction, Non-fiction

**Submission Guidelines** Work should be published previously.

**Tips** Memoir, fiction and non-fiction are eligible as long as the book is publicly accessible and deals with issues in a way that appeals to general readers, rather than specialists.

## Mitsubishi Motors Regional Motoring Journalist of the Year Award

**Guild of Motoring Writers, 39 Beswick Avenue, Bournemouth, BH10 4EY**

☎ 01202 518808

☎ 01202 518808

📧 chris@whizzco.freeserve.co.uk

🌐 www.guildofmotoringwriters.co.uk

**Insider Info** Presented to a regional journalist, freelancers included, who have made contributions to the field of motoring journalism. Awarded annually, the winner receives £1,000.

**Genres** Non-fiction, Articles

**Submission Guidelines** Work should be published previously.

**Tips** The winners must be people who write for local press and do not earn their main income from writing for national newspapers.

## Momaya Press Short Story Competition

**Flat 1, 189 Balham High Road, London, SW12 9BE**

☎ 020 8673 9616

📧 infouk@momayapress.com

🌐 www.momayapress.com

**Insider Info** An open competition for any writer writing short stories in English up to 2,500 words long. Each year entrants are given a set theme on which to write. Awarded anually, prizes consist of: £110 for 1st place; £55 for 2nd place; and £30 for 3rd place. All winning stories are published in the Momaya Annual Review 2007. Judges are: Lucy Alexander, a writer and researcher at The Times Magazine; Claire Nozières, a literary agent; and Rosalind Porter, an assistant editor at Random House.

**Genres** Short stories

**Submission Guidelines** Deadline for entry is April. Guidelines available on the website. Entry fee is £6 per story. Submissions should be unpublished.

**Tips** Email entry only. Although there is a set theme, the style and subject matter are completely open.

## Mslexia Women's Poetry Competition

**Mslexia Publications, PO Box 656, Newcastle Upon Tyne, NE99 1PZ**

- 0191 2616656
- 0191 2616636
- postbag@mslexia.demon.co.uk
- www.mslexia.co.uk

**Competition/Award Director** Carol Seajay

**Established** 2004

**Insider Info** *Mslexia*, the magazine for women writers, invites poems in any style, of any length, on any subject by women. Awarded annually, with prizes of £1,000, £500 and £250 plus 22 other finalists; all winning poems will be published in *Mslexia* magazine. Names should not appear on entries. £5 entry fee allows you to enter five poems. Full competition rules on the website. Poems should be unpublished. Email submissions are accepted from outside the UK only. Purpose of the competition is to find the best contemporary poetry written by women. Judges were U. A. Fanthorpe and R. V. Baîley in 2007; previous judges have included Selima Hill, Jo Shapcott and Wendy Cope. Copyright remains with author. *Mslexia* should be credited if the poem appears elsewhere after publication. Submissions invited from women of all ages and nationalities.

**Genres** Poetry

**Submission Guidelines** Dealine for entry is always the end of April each year; the exact day varies. Entry fee is £5 for a group of five poems. Work should be unpublished.

## Nasen and TES Special Educational Needs Book Awards

**Nasen House, 4–5 Amber Business Village, Amber Close, Amington, Tamworth, B77 4RP**

- 01827 311500
- 01827 313005
- welcome@nasen.org.uk
- www.nasen.org.uk

**Insider Info** Awards to celebrate writers and publishers of books that help and encourage children with special educational needs, as well as teachers. Categories include: Academic Book Award; Books for Teaching and Learning; and Children's Award. Awarded annually, the winners in each category receive £500. Books must have been published in the UK.

**Genres** Fiction, Non-fiction, Children's special educational.

**Submission Guidelines** Deadline for entry is June. Work must be published previously.

**Tips** The awards usually take place in October with a shortlist announced in August. Books that portray special educational needs in a positive light are often successful, especially in the children's category.

## National Association of Writers Groups Creative Writing Competitions

**The Arts Centre, Biddick Lane, Washington, Tyne & Wear, NE38 2AB**

- nawg@tesco.net
- www.nawg.co.uk

**Insider Info** The NAWG run a variety of annual competitions including the NAWG/Writers' News short story competition. Other categories have included: Mini-Tale; Denise Robertson Trophy for the Best Group Anthology; Best Limerick; Free Verse Poem; Children's Poem; A Collection of Five Poems; Open Short Story; Short Story (with given last line); Children's Short Story; Novel (previously unpublished); Non-fictional Article in 'how-to' mode; and Fantasy/Science Fiction. Awarded annually, each category has different prizes but there are often small cash prizes, books and trophies on offer.

**Genres** Fiction, Non-fiction, Poetry, Novels, Articles, Short stories, Story collections.

**Submission Guidelines** There are various entry fees. Works should be unpublished.

**Tips** Details of further competitions, categories and closing dates will be published on the website along with shortlisted and winning entries from previous years.

## National Poetry Anthology

**United Press, Admail 3735, London, EC1B 1JB**

- 0870 240 6190
- 0870 240 6191
- www.unitedpress.co.uk

**Competition/Award Director** Peter Quinn

**Established** 1998

**Insider Info** An open poetry competition. Writers are invited to submit up to three poems of up to 20 lines or 160 words on any theme or subject. Awarded annually; winning entries are published in an anthology, a copy of which contributors receive for free. Every contributor then casts a vote for their favourite poem and the overall winner receives £1,000 and a trophy.

**Genres** Poetry

**Submission Guidelines** Deadline for entry is June each year. Guidelines and entry forms available via SAE. Work should be unpublished.

**Tips** You may submit three poems but no more. Winners will be informed by November.

## National Poetry Competition
**22 Betterton Street, London, WC2H 9BX**
- 020 7420 9895
- 020 7240 4818
- competition@poetrysociety.org.uk
- www.poetrysociety.org.uk

**Established** 1978

**Insider Info** Sponsored by The Poetry Society. An open competition for poets around the world, both published and unpublished. Entry forms are available from April. Awarded annually, prizes consist of: £5,000 for 1st place; £1,000 for 2nd place; £500 for 3rd place; and £50 for 10 runners up. All winners will also have the chance to read their poetry at the Ledbury Poetry Festival. Judges are Michael Schmidt, Penelope Shuttle and E A Markham.

**Genres** Poetry

**Submission Guidelines** Deadline for entry is October/Guidelines and entry form available via SAE. entry fee is £5 for the first poem and £3 per subsequent poem. Work should be unpublished.

**Tips** Entry forms will be available on the website or by post in April. No submissions without completed forms.

## The National Short Story Prize
**Booktrust, Book House, 45 East Hill, London, SW18 2QZ**
- story@booktrust.org.uk
- www.theshortstory.org.uk

**Established** 2005

**Insider Info** Sponsored by the National Endowment for Science, Technology and the Arts (NESTA) and supported by BBC Radio 4. The National Short Story Prize is the biggest single short story award in the world, designed to bring attention to the short story form. Stories should be a maximum of 8,000 words. The prize is awarded annually. Prizes consist of: £15,000 for the winner; £3,000 for 2nd place; and £500 for 3 shortlisted stories.

**Genres** Short stories

**Submission Guidelines** Submissions should be received by October 31. Submissions should be published previously having appeared between January 1 and December 31 of the previous year, or should be unpublished.

**Tips** Entrants are advised that they should have some history of creative writing and their work (although not necessarily the piece they are submitting) should have been published in book or magazine form. Details of the competition running for 2008 will be published on the Booktrust website.

## Nestle Children's Book Prize
**Book House, 45 East Hill, London, SW18 2QZ**
- 020 8516 2972
- 020 8516 2978
- query@booktrust.org.uk
- www.booktrusted.co.uk

**Established** 1985

**Insider Info** Booktrust, An award designed to stimulate interest and high standards in children's books. The prize is split into three categories by age: 5 years and under; 6–8 years; and 9–11 years. Awarded annually, Gold award winners in each category receive £2,500; Silver Award winners receive £1,500; Bronze award winners receive £500. Books are judged by an adult panel and three are shortlisted in each category. The Gold, Silver and Bronze prizes are decided by children who are selected after the completion of a task at selected schools, who judge the books for their own age category.

**Genres** Children's Fiction or Poetry

**Submission Guidelines** Deadline for entry is July. Work should be previously published.

**Tips** All work must be submitted by UK publishers.

## The New Blood Dagger
**PO Box 273, Boreham Wood, WD6 2XA**
- info@thecwa.co.uk
- www.thecwa.co.uk

**Established** 1973

**Insider Info** Sponsored by the Crime Writers Association and BBC Audio Books. It is awarded in memory of John Creasey, founder of the CWA, for first crime novels by previously unpublished writers. It was previously known as The John Creasey Memorial Award. The award is given annually. Winners receive an ornamental dagger and £1,000. Entries must be the first work of a writer who has no publishing history.

**Genres** Crime novels

**Tips** Submissions must be made by publishers only.

## The New Writer Prose and Poetry Prize

**PO Box 60, Cranbrook, TN17 2ZR**
- 01580 212226
- 01580 212041
- admin@thenewwriter.com
- www.thenewwriter.com

**Established** 1997

**Insider Info** Sponsored by *The New Writer* magazine. The prize is an open award for poets and writers. Categories include: factual (essays, articles and interviews); short stories (up to 4,000 words; Serials/Novellas (up to 20,000 words); single poems (up to 40 lines); and poetry collections (6–10 poems). Prize is awarded annually. For the factual category the prizes are £150, £100 and £50 for 1st, 2nd and 3rd respectively. For short stories the prizes are £300, £200, and £100. The winner of the serial/novella category receives £300. The single poem category prizes are £100, £75 and £50 and the poetry collection winners receive £300, £200 and £100. Winning entries may also be published in *The New Writer* 'Special Collection' anthology.

**Genres** Fiction, Non-fiction, Poetry, Essays, Articles and Short stories

**Submission Guidelines** Submissions should be received by November 30. The entry fees are: £4 for single poems, factual entries or short stories, £10 for poetry collections or serials/novellas. Magazine subscribers may submit two entries for the price of one in the £4 categories. Work should be unpublished.

**Tips** Short entries may be submitted online, but longer entries should be submitted by post. An online entry form and payment system are published on the website.

## New Writing North

**New Writing North, 2 School Lane, Wickham, Newcastle upon Tyne, NE16 4SL**
- 0191 488 8580
- 0191 488 8576
- mail@newwritingnorth.com
- www.nr-foundationwriters.com

**Insider Info** An annual award of £60,000 split over three years to enable a writer to completely concentrate on writing. Applicants must have lived and worked in Tees Valley, Tyneside, County Durham, Northumberland or Cumbria for at least three years. Open to writers of poetry, prose, children's fiction or biography who have published at least two novels, collections of poetry, short stories or biography (self-publishing is excluded).

**Submission Guidelines** Send up to 6,000 words of fiction or up to 40 pages of poems. This work should be taken from your current work in progress. Apply with a sample of up to 6,000 words or 40 poems. This work must be supported by the following items: an outline or synopsis; explanation of the stage the work is at i.e commissioned, first draft etc. Also include a writing biography. Send five copies to New Writing North.

## New Writing Ventures

**Booktrust, Book House, 45 East Hill, London, SW18 2QZ**
- 020 8516 2972
- 020 8516 2978
- tarryn@booktrust.org.uk
- www.booktrust.org.uk/prizes

**Established** 2005

**Insider Info** Sponsored by The New Writing Partnership (www.newwritingpartnership.org.uk). Awards in the categories of fiction, creative non-fiction and poetry, designed to encourage new writers to further their careers. Awarded annually, the winner in each category receives £5,000 and two runners up from each category win £1,000 each. All winners win a place on the Ventures Development Programme which offers workshops, one-to-one training and advice over the period of a year on an intermittent, part-time basis. Open to any UK writer.

**Genres** Fiction, Non-fiction, Poetry.

**Submission Guidelines** Deadline for entry is May. Work should be unpublished.

**Tips** No writing for children. Entrants must be prepared to commit to the full year's course as part of their prize.

## Nielsen Gold and Platinum Book Awards

**3rd Floor Midas House, 62 Goldsworth Road, Woking, GU21 6LQ**
- 01483 712222
- 01483 712220
- gold&platinumawards@nielsenbookscan.co.uk
- www.nielsenbookscan.co.uk

**Established** 2000

**Insider Info** Sponsored by Nielsen BookScan. Awarded for consumer sales of books in UK shops. Gold standard is 500,000 copies; platinum is 1 million. The award consists of a plaque presented to the writer by their publisher.

**Submission Guidelines** Work should be published previously.

## Noma Award for Publishing in Africa
**PO Box 128, Witney, Oxfordshire, OX8 5XU**
- 01993 775235
- 01993 709265
- maryljay@aol.com
- www.nomaaward.org

**Competition/Award Director** Mary Jay
**Established** 1979
**Insider Info** Sponsored by Kodansha Ltd, Japan. Annual US$10,000 award for a book by an African writer and published by an independent/autonomous African publishing house domiciled on the continent. Scholarly works, literature and children's books are eligible. Submission and entry must be made by publisher; maximum entries three. Purpose is to encourage African scholars and writers to publish with independent/autonomous African publishers, rather than abroad, with a view to strengthening African publishing. Judged by a panel of African and international scholars and book experts, chaired by Walter Bgoya, Tanzanian publisher. No entry fee. The writer must be an African national, wherever resident.
**Genres** Fiction, Non-fiction, Poetry, Essays, Juvenile, Novels, Short stories, Drama
**Submission Guidelines** Deadline for entry is March each year. Guidelines and entry forms do not need SAE; they can be posted, emailed, or downloaded from the website. Previously published entries must appear in print between January 1 and December 31 the previous year.
**Tips** If interpretation of guidelines gives rise to questions of eligibility, the Secretariat can advise.

## Olive Cook and Tom-Gallon Awards
**84 Drayton Gardens, London, SW10 9SB**
- 020 7373 6642
- 020 7373 5768
- info@societyofauthors.org
- www.societyofauthors.org

**Insider Info** Sponsored by the Society of Authors. Awarded by Miss Nellie Tom-Gallon in memory of her brother, and by Olive Cook in alternate years for short story writers who have had at least one piece of work accepted for publication. Writers must have serious ambitions to become professional and their financial circumstances will be taken into consideration. The winners receive £1,000. Entrants must be residents of the UK, Commonwealth or the Republic of Ireland.
**Genres** Short stories
**Submission Guidelines** Guidelines and entry form available on the website. Tom-Gallon award is presented bianually in odd years, the Olive Cook award in even years.
**Tips** The stories submitted must be traditional, rather than experimental and should be no longer than 5,000 words. Postal entries only, for the attention of Dorothy Sym.

## Orange Award for New Writers
**Booktrust, Book House, 45 East Hill, London, SW18 2QZ**
- 020 8516 2972
- 020 8516 2978
- tarryn@booktrust.org.uk
- www.orangeprize.co.uk

**Established** 2005
**Insider Info** An award for an emerging woman writer who has had her first work of fiction published and shows great potential. Awarded annually, the winner receives £10,000. Writers must be female and their first work must have been published in the UK.
**Genres** Fiction, Novels, Short stories, Story collections, Novellas.
**Submission Guidelines** Work should be published previously between 1st April and 31st March.
**Tips** Submissions from publishers only. Awarded on the basis of future potential shown in first published work.

## Orange Prize for Fiction
**Booktrust, Book House, 45 East Hill, London, SW18 2QZ**
- 020 8516 2972
- 020 8516 2978
- tarryn@booktrust.org.uk
- www.orangeprize.co.uk

**Established** 1996
**Insider Info** Awarded for a full length novel published in the UK by a female writer. Designed to celebrate and highlight the achievement of women in literature and publishing. Awarded annually, the winner receives £30,000 and a limited edition bronze figurine called the 'Bessie'. The judging panel changes each year and details are published on the website. Usually made up of media personalities, writers and publishing professionals. Not open to novels by men.
**Genres** Fiction, Novels
**Submission Guidelines** Work should be published previously, between April 1 and March 31.
**Tips** Submissions by publishers only.

## The Oscar Moore Screenwriting Prize

c/o Screen International, 33–39 Bowling Green Lane, London, EC1R 0DA

- ☏ 020 7505 8080
- ☏ 020 7505 8087
- ⊕ www.screendaily.com

**Established** 1997

**Insider Info** Sponsored by The Oscar Moore Foundation. The prize is awarded for a best first draft of a screenplay in memory of Oscar Moore, a *Guardian* columnist and editor of Screen International. The prize is awarded annually. The winner receives £10,000 and often other prizes such as scriptwriting courses and a live performance of the play.

**Genres** Scripts

**Submission Guidelines** Work should be unpublished.

**Tips** Each year the competition has a different theme. In 2004 it was thrillers and in 2006 it was comedy. Details are available from the Foundation. There was deemed to be no entry good enough to win in 2006 so no award was made.

## OWG Awards for Excellence

PO Box 520, Bamber Bridge, Preston, Lancashire, PR5 8LF

- ☏ 01772 321243
- ☏ 0870 137 8888
- ⊙ secretary@owg.org.uk
- ⊕ www.owg.org.uk

**Established** 1980

**Insider Info** Sponsored by the Outdoor Writers' Guild. Awards made in several categories including writing, journalism and broadcast about outdoor living and pursuits. Awarded annually.

**Genres** Non-fiction, Articles

**Submission Guidelines** Deadline for entry is July. Work should be published previously.

**Tips** OWG members only. To join, send a CV and samples of published/produced work to memsec@owg.org.uk.

## Oxford Weidenfeld Translation Prize

St Anne's College, Oxford, OX2 6HS

- ☏ 01865 274820
- ☏ 01865 274899
- ⊙ sandra.madley@st-annes.ox.ac.uk
- ⊕ www.stannes.ox.ac.uk/about/translationprize.html

**Competition/Award Director** Dr Matthew Reynolds

**Established** 1996

**Insider Info** Sponsored by St Anne's College, The Queen's College and New College, Oxford, and Lord Weidenfeld. The prize is for book-length English translations of fiction, poetry or drama written in any living European language by any author living or dead. Three copies of each translation must be submitted; it will not be possible to return them. The judges consider the quality of the translation as well as the importance of the original work, and the value of its being put into English. Aims to honour the craft of translation, and to recognise its cultural importance. Entries must be books, must have been published in the preceding calendar year, must be distributed in the UK, and may be the work of up to three translators. They must be submitted by the publisher rather than by the translator. Awarded annually, the prize £2,000 is awarded at an event at St Anne's College Oxford where all the shortlisted translators are invited to read from their work. The competition is judged by three Oxford academics and translators, plus a guest judge. The 2007 judges: Robert McCrum, literary editor of *The Observer* (guest judge); Dr Matthew Reynolds (chair); Dr Caroline Warman; Chris Miller. In 2008 the guest judge will be Helen Dunmore. No entry fee. Books must have been published in the preceding calendar year and must be distributed in the UK. Entries must be submitted by the publisher.

**Genres** Translations

**Submission Guidelines** Deadline for entry is the end of January each year. Publisher submission only. Work should be published previously between the beginning of January and the end of December.

## The Paul Foot Award

6 Carlisle Street, London, W1D 3BN

- ⊕ www.private-eye.co.uk

**Established** 2005

**Insider Info** Sponsored by *Private Eye* and *The Guardian*. Awarded in memory of Paul Foot for achievement in campaigning journalism. The award may be given to an individual, a team, or a newspaper for either a single article or an entire campaign. The award is given annually. 1st prize is £5,000 and five runners up will also receive £1,000.

**Submission Guidelines** Submissions should received by September 1. Work should be published previously having appeared between September 1 of the previous year and August 31 of the year of entry and either be in print or online.

**Tips** Application forms and details on how to submit material will be available on the *Private Eye* website during the period the competition is open. Please do not send any broadcast material.

## Peterloo Poets Open Poetry Competition

**The Old Chapel, Sand Lane, Calstock, Cornwall, PL18 9QX**

- 01822 833473
- info@peterloopoets.com
- www.peterloopoets.com

**Established** 1984

**Insider Info** An open competition for poems of any style, in English, of up to 40 lines. Awarded annually, the prizes consist of: £1,500 for 1st place; £1,000 for 2nd place; £500 for 3rd place; £100 for 4th place; £50 for 10 further runners up and £100 for 10 winners in the 15–19 year age group category. 2007 judges: John Mole, Carole Satyamurti, Peter Sansom, Harry Chambers. Copyright remains with the author, but they must agree to assign first publication rights to Peterloo Poets for inclusion in the Peterloo Competition Booklet.

**Genres** Poetry

**Submission Guidelines** Deadline for entry is March each year. Guidelines available on the website. Entry fee is £5 per poem and £2 for the 15–19 age category. Peterloo Poets members receive one free entry having submitted two paid-for ones. Work should be previously unpublished.

**Tips** Each writer may submit a maximum of ten poems. Enclose an entry form, available from the website.

## The Petra Kenney Poetry Competition

**PO Box 32, Filey, North Yorkshire, YO14 9YG**

- morgan@kenney.uk.net
- www.petrapoetrycompetition.co.uk

**Established** 1995

**Insider Info** A set of poetry awards in the memory of Petra Kenney. The categories include a general category, comic verse and young poets (14–18). The competition is held annually, The prizes for the general category consist of: £1,000 and publication in *Writers Magazine* for the winner; £500 for 2nd place; and £250 for 3rd place. All three also win a Royal Brierley Crystal Vase. The winner of the comic verse receives £250 and the Young Poet winner receives £250 whilst the runner up receives £150. Open to UK and international writers (see website for fees in $US).

**Genres** Poetry

**Submission Guidelines** Submissions should be received by December 31 each year. Guidelines are available on the website. The entry fee is £3 per poem. Work should be unpublished.

**Tips** Poems should be no more than 80 lines and should be typed on A4 paper.

## The Philip Good Memorial Prize

**1 Blake Close, Bilton, Rugby, CV22 7LJ**

- 01788 334302
- jo@qwfmagazine.co.uk
- www.qwfmagazine.co.uk

**Competition/Award**

**Director** Competition Secretary

**Established** 1998

**Insider Info** An international short story competition in memory of Philip Good who died in 1997 at the age of 34. The prize is given annually. Winners will be published in an anthology. Prize money consists of £300 for 1st prize, £150 for 2nd prize and £75 for 3rd prize. The judges are Jo Good, editor of *QWF* magazine and Sally Zigmond. Entrants must be over 18.

**Genres** Short stories

**Submission Guidelines** Submissions should be received by December 31. Guidelines are available on the website. The entry fees are: £5 for each story and £15 for an appraisal (optional). Work should be unpublished.

**Tips** Stories should be up to 5,000 words, in English, typed, double-spaced and single sided and stapled at the top left hand corner with no bindings and no recorded delivery. Manuscripts not requiring an appraisal will not be returned.

## P. J. O'Connor Radio Drama Awards

**RTÉ Radio Drama, Donnybrook, Dublin 4, Republic of Ireland**

- 00353 1 208 3111
- 00353 1 208 3304
- radiodrama@rte.ie
- www.rte.ie

**Insider Info** Sponsored by RTÉ, this competition aims to find the best radio drama script from an new writer. Plays must last 28 minutes and be in either Irish or English. Awarded annually, prizes consist of: €3,000 for the 1st place; €2,000 for 2nd; and €1,000 for 3rd. All three plays are also professionally produced. RTÉ Radio have the right to broadcast all winning plays twice before having to pay fees. Writers must be either unproduced or have had a maximum of one hour's radio professionally produced.

**Genres** Scripts

**Submission Guidelines** Deadline for entry is April. Guidelines are available on the website. Work should be previously unpublished.

## The Poetry Business Book & Pamphlet Competition

**The Studio, Byram Arcade, Westgate, Huddersfield, HD1 1ND**
☎ 01484 434840
☎ 01484 426566
🌐 www.poetrybusiness.co.uk

**Insider Info** Competition for poetry collections. The purpose of this contest is to find and publish new or less-well-known poets. The competition is held annually. The first set of winners will have their collection published in pamphlet form. These winners can submit an extended manuscript and one will be chosen to be published in a full length collection under the Smith/Doorstop imprint. Winners also share a cash prize. The competition is open to any adult writer.

**Genres** Poetry

**Submission Guidelines** Submissions should be received by October. Guidelines and entry forms are available with an SAE. The entry fee is £18.

**Tips** Please do not submit any poetry for children.

## Poetry London Competition

**1a Jewel Road, London, E17 4QU**
☎ 020 8521 0776
☎ 020 8521 0776
✉ editors@poetrylondon.co.uk
🌐 www.poetrylondon.co.uk

**Established** 2000

**Insider Info** Sponsored by *Poetry London* magazine, this annual poetry competition is judged by a guest judge each year. The judging process begins in July. Details of entry will be published in the magazine and on the website.

**Genres** Poetry

**Submission Guidelines** Work should be previously unpublished.

**Tips** Each year the judges write a report on what they found successful and unsuccessful about the competition and its entries. These are published on the website for entrants to read.

## The Portico Prize

**The Portico Library, 57 Mosley Street, Manchester, M2 3HY**
☎ 0161 236 6785
☎ 0161 236 6803

✉ librarian@theportico.org.uk
🌐 www.theportico.org.uk

**Established** 1985

**Insider Info** Sponsored by The Zochonis Charitable Trust. The prize is awarded for a book set wholly or mainly in the North West of England including Lancashire, Cheshire, the High Peak region of Derbyshire, Manchester, Liverpool and Cumbria. The book should be of general interest whilst maintaining literary quality. Fiction and non-fiction shortlists are drawn up but there is one overall winner. The prize is awarded every two years (even years). The overall winner receives £3,000.

**Genres** Fiction and Non-fiction.

**Submission Guidelines** Work should be published previously appearing between August 31 of two years before and August 31 of the year of entry.

**Tips** Contact Emma Marigliano at the above email address for more details. The shortlisted books are selected from a possible long list of 50.

## Practical Art Instruction Book of the Year

**PO Box 32, Huntingdon, PE28 0QX**
☎ 01832 710201
☎ 01832 710488
✉ award@acaward.com
🌐 www.acaward.com

**Insider Info** Sponsored by Artist's Choice book club, *The Leisure Painter* magazine and *The Artist* magazine, this is an annual award for best instructional art book. A shortlist is drawn up by the sponsors which is then voted for by readers of the magazines through the award's website.

**Genres** Non-fiction

**Submission Guidelines** Work should be published previously.

**Tips** No submissions; the magazine and book club editors shortlist their choice of books.

## Prose & Poetry Prizes

**PO Box 60, Cranbrook, Kent, TN17 2ZR**
☎ 01580 212626
☎ 01580 212041
✉ admin@thenewwriter.com
🌐 www.thenewwriter.com

**Competition/Award Director** Merric Davidson

**Established** 1997

**Insider Info** Sponsored by *The New Writer* magazine, this is an international prize for contemporary fiction and poetry, essays and articles, and an opportunity to bring your work to a wider audience. Looking for bold, incisive material in any genre that reflects writing today. Up to twenty prizes are presented as well as publication for the prize-winning writers in *The New Writer* 'Collection'. Annually awards over £2,000 in prizes plus publication for the winning and highly commended entries. Recent judges have included the novelists Robyn Young, Mimi Thebo and Phil Whitaker, and poets Robert Seatter, Jane Draycott and Ros Barber. First British serial rights other than that the rights remain with the author. Competition open to any writer.

**Genres** Non-fiction, Poetry, Essays, Articles, Short stories, Novellas

**Submission Guidelines** Deadline for entry is November every year. Guidelines and entry form available via SAE. Entry fee varies from £4 for a story/poem/article to £10 for a novella/collection of poems. Work should be previously unpublished.

**Tips** Original hard-hitting work greatly appreciated. It is suggested you read some of the stories published in *The New Writer* magazine, particularly the annual collection (see website for details).

## The Raymond Williams Community Publishing Prize

**The Literature Department, 14 Great Peter Street, London, SW1P 3NQ**

- 020 7973 5204
- info.literature@artscouncil.org.uk
- www.artscouncil.org.uk

**Insider Info** The prize is sponsored by the Arts Council England and is awarded for works published to highlight and reflect the experiences of a particular community. Open to not-for-profit publishing companies only. The prize is awarded annually. The prizes are usually £3,000 for the winners and £2,000 for the runners up.

**Submission Guidelines** Work should be published previously.

**Tips** At the time of going to press the award administration is under review and not open to submissions. New details and calls for submissions will be published on the website.

## The Reader Classic Rescue Prize

**English Department, University of Liverpool, Liverpool, L69 7ZR**

**Insider Info** The prize is sponsored by *The Reader*. Writers and readers are asked to review a classic book that they would save if all the world's libraries were burning down. The only criteria is that the book must be more than 75 years old. The prize is awarded monthly. The winning review will be published in each month's *Reader* magazine and

authors will receive 15 titles from Oxford World's Classic series.

**Genres** Book reviews

**Tips** Reviews should be kept to under 850 words and sent by post to the address above. Be sure to include plenty of quotations in the entry.

## Red House Children's Book Award

**The Old Malt House, Aldbourne, Marlborough, Wiltshire, SN8 2DW**

- 01672 540629
- 01672 541280
- marianneadey@aol.com
- www.redhousechildrensbookaward.co.uk

**Competition/Award Director** Marianne Adey

**Established** 1980

**Insider Info** Sponsored by The Federation of Children's Book Groups. This annual award voted for entirely by children is given in three categories: Books for Younger Children; Books for Young Readers; and Books for Older Children. The top 50 titles are published in Red House's Pick of the Year list. The top ten writers and illustrators receive sets of children's letters and pictures relating to their book. Winners in each category receive an engraved silver bowl and the overall winner receives an oak and silver trophy for a year and an engraved silver acorn to keep. Nominations are invited from children, writers, illustrators and publishers, and shortlisted books are published on the website. Children may then vote either individually or in groups through the website for the category winners and the overall winner. Books entered must have been published in the UK for the first time in the corresponding year.

**Genres** Children's fiction

**Submission Guidelines** Deadline for entry is December each year. Nomination forms and submissions guidelines are available on the website. Work should be published previously, between January 1 and December 31 the same year.

**Tips** To submit a book for consideration send 12 copies to the above address. The book must be original, although major re-workings of religious or folk stories are accepted.

## Reginald Taylor and Lord Fletcher Essay Prize

**Institute of Archaeology, 36 Beaumont Street, Oxford, OX1 2PG**

- www.britarch.ac.uk

**Competition/Award Director** Dr Martin Henig, Honorary Editor

**Insider Info** A prize for the best essay submitted in the areas of art history, archaeology or antiquarian subject. Awarded every two years (even years). The winning essay will be published in the *Journal of the British Archaeological Association* and read at a meeting.

**Genres** Essays

**Submission Guidelines** Deadline for entry is June. Work should be previously unpublished.

**Tips** Essay should be a maximum of 7,500 words. Contact The Hon. Editor for more details.

## Regional Press Awards

**Press Gazette, 10 Old Bailey, London, EC4M 7NG**
- 020 7038 1469
- 020 7038 1155
- franb@pressgazette.co.uk
- www.pressgazette.co.uk

**Insider Info** An annual awards ceremony to recognise regional newspapers and journalists. Freelancers and employees may be presented with prizes in a number of categories.

**Genres** Non-fiction, Articles

**Submission Guidelines** Work should be published previously.

**Tips** The ceremony is usually held in June or July. Details are published in the events section of the Press Gazette website.

## Renault UK Journalist of the Year Award

**Guild of Motoring Writers, 39 Beswick Avenue, Bournemouth, BH10 4EY**
- 01202 518808
- 01202 518808
- chris@whizzco.freeserve.co.uk
- www.guildofmotoringwriters.co.uk

**Insider Info** Awarded annually to an individual deemed to have made an outstanding contribution during the previous year to the field of motoring journalism. The winner receives £2,000.

**Genres** Non-fiction, Articles

**Submission Guidelines** Work should be previously published.

**Tips** The awarding judges are looking for initiative and endeavour over an entire year. Tends to be awarded to bodies of work and series.

## The Richard Imison Memorial Award

**84 Drayton Gardens, London, SW10 9SB**
- 020 7373 6642
- 020 7373 5768

- jhodder@societyofauthors.org
- www.societyofauthors.org

**Established** 1995

**Insider Info** Sponsored by The Society of Authors. The award was founded in memory of Richard Imison to encourage the writing of original radio drama by a writer or writers who have never previously been published or produced. The award is given annually. Winners receive £1,500. Judges are made up from the Broadcasting Committee of the Society of Authors. Entries may include a one-off drama or the first episode of a series of serial but adaptions are not eligible.

**Genres** Scripts

**Submission Guidelines** Submissions should be received by January. Guidelines are available on the website. Work mus have been previously broadcast having appeared between January 1 and December 31 of the previous year.

**Tips** Submissions may come from any source, including the writers themselves. Send three copies of the script along with its broadcast recording, a 250 word synopsis, an author biography and a completed entry form, to Jo Hodder at the address above.

## Romance Prize

**13 Makepeace Avenue, London, N6 6EL**
- normacurtisuk@yahoo.co.uk
- www.rna-uk.org

**Competition/Award Director** Norma Curtis

**Established** 2003

**Insider Info** Sponsored by the Romantic Novelists' Association, this is an award for category romances by members of the RNA. Category romances are defined as short romances with a strong emphasis on the central relationship. They are usually published in a standard format and several similar books published each month. Serials in magazines are also eligible for the prize. Awarded annually, the winner receives £1,000 and an enscribed cup. A panel of 'ordinary' members of the public read the entries between November and January, ranking the titles based on criteria such as most enjoyable, least able to put down, good plot and characters, would buy another book by that author. The shortlist that emerges from this process is then judged by a committee of editors and agents. Books must have been first published in the UK between the dates specified.

**Genres** Fiction, Novels

**Submission Guidelines** Deadline for entry is October. Entry forms and guidelines available on the website. Work should be published previously, between January 1 and December 31.

**Tips** No self-published or vanity novels. Send two copies along with an entry form to Norma Curtis.

## Romantic Novel of the Year
**RNA Award Organiser, PO Box 50421, London, W8 5XW**

- rnaawardorganiser@hotmail.com
- www.rna-uk.org

**Established** 1960

**Insider Info** Sponsored by the Romantic Novelists' Association, this awards the prize for the most romantic novel of the year. The purpose of the competition is to celebrate good writing and to encourage excellence within the genre. Awarded annually, the prize is a cheque for £5,000 and a small trophy to the winner. First round judging by ordinary readers/members of the public. Each book will get three reads and the 20 books with the highest scores are read a fourth time. From their total scores, the six with the highest marks are short listed. The books on the short list are then read by three specially selected judges. The competition is open to any writer, but the book must be written in the English language and only books first published in the UK are eligible. Novels may be submitted in hardback or paperback form, but the original version must have been published within the period stated.

**Genres** Novels

**Submission Guidelines** Deadline for entry is October every year. See RNA website for guidelines and entry form. Entries must be published in the UK between January 1 and December 31 of the year before the prize is awarded. Must be written in the English language.

## Rose Mary Crawshay Prize
**10 Carlton House Terrace, London, SW1Y 5AH**

- 020 7969 5200
- 020 7969 5300
- secretary@britac.ac.uk
- www.britac.ac.uk

**Established** 1888

**Insider Info** Sponsored by the British Academy. Presented to a women who has produced historical or critical writing on any aspect of English Literature, particularly one of the poets Byron, Shelley and Keats. Usually awarded twice yearly. Writers may be of any nationality.

**Genres** Non-fiction, Essays

**Submission Guidelines** Works should be published within three years prior to the award.

**Tips** Although preference is said to be given to work on the poets mentioned above, this has only been the case for one winner since 2003. A list of previous winners and their subject matters is published on the website.

## Royal Mail Awards for Scottish Children's Books
**Scottish Book Trust, Sandeman's House, Trunk's Close, Edinburgh, EH1 1SR**

- 0131 524 0160
- 0131 524 0161
- royalmailawards@braw.org.uk
- www.braw.org.uk

**Insider Info** Awards presented for children's books across three categories, 0–7 years, 8–11 years and 12–16 years. Primarily for Scottish writers and illustrators resident in Scotland. Awarded annually, a shortlist is drawn up from nominated books. The category winners and runners up are then voted on entirely by children who register through their schools.

**Genres** Fiction, Non-fiction, Poetry, Children's books

**Submission Guidelines** Deadline for entry is January each year. Work should be published previously between January 1 and December 31.

**Tips** Submissions by publishers only. Books may be in English or Scots but must be available to buy in Scotland and by authors and illustrators living in Scotland.

## The Royal Society of Literature Ondaatje Prize
**Somerset House, Strand, London, WC2R 1LA**

- 020 7845 4676
- 020 7845 4679
- paulaj@rslit.org
- www.rslit.org

**Insider Info** Awarded to a work written in English, published during the preceding year, that successfully evokes the spirit of a place. The prize is awarded annually. The winner receives £10,000. Writers must be resident in the UK, Ireland or the Commonwealth.

**Genres** Fiction, Non-fiction, Poetry

**Submission Guidelines** Submissions must be received by December each year. Guidelines are available on the website. Work should be published previously having appeared between January 1 and December 1 of the year of entry.

**Tips** Please do not submit short stories, novellas or children's literature. Submissions should be made by

publishers only; submit four copies to
Paula Johnson.

## The Royal Society Prizes for Science Books

**The Royal Society, 6–9 Carlton House Terrace, London, SW1Y 5AG**

☎ 020 7451 2576

☎ 020 7930 2170

🌐 www.royalsoc.ac.uk/sciencebooks

**Established** 1988

**Insider Info** The awards are aimed at encouraging the writing, publishing and reading of popular science books. There are two separate categories: The Junior Prize, for books written for the under-14s; and the General Prize, for books written for a general audience. The prizes are awarded annually. Prizes consist of £10,000 for each of the two category winners and £1,000 each for shortlisted books. Books must be in the English language and be distributed in the UK.

**Genres** Popular, accessible science books

**Submission Guidelines** Submissions should be received by January 31. Guidelines are available on the website. Work should be published for the first time in the previous year.

**Tips** No purely educational textbooks, encyclopedias or books for a specialist audience. The aim of the prize is to award writers whose books make science accessible to an unknowledgeable audience. Entries must be submitted by publishers only. Please send seven hard copies.

## RTÉ Radio 1 Short Story Competition

**RTÉ Radio Centre, Donnybrook, Dublin 4, Republic of Ireland**

☎ 00 353 1 208 3111

☎ 00 353 1 208 3304

🌐 www.rte.ie/radio1/francismacmanus

**Established** 1985

**Insider Info** An open competition for radio short stories to commemorate the life of Francis MacManus, writer and Head of Talks and Features in Radio Eireann. Awarded annually, the prizes consist of: €3,000 and a commemorative trophy for the overall winner; €2,000 for 2nd place; and €1,000 for 3rd. The three winners, plus a selection of shortlisted stories will be broadcast on RTÉ Radio 1.

**Genres** Short stories

**Submission Guidelines** Deadline for entries is October each year. Work should be unpublished.

**Tips** Entries may be in English or Irish, and should be by Irish writers or writers living in Ireland.

## Runciman Award

**Lady Fairweather, 39c Pembridge Villas, London, W11 3EP**

☎ 020 7221-5227

🌐 www.hellenicbookservice.com

**Established** 1985

**Insider Info** Sponsored by The National Bank of Greece and The Anglo-Hellenic League. Awarded for a book of any type, published in English anywhere in the world, that focuses wholly or mainly on Greece or Hellenism. The purpose of the award is to promote an understanding of Greek culture and its impact on civilisation. Awarded annually, the winner receives £9,000. Work must be available for purchase in the UK at the time of the award presentation.

**Genres** Fiction, Non-fiction, Poetry, Essays, Scripts, Novels, Articles, Short stories, Story collections, Biography

**Submission Guidelines** Deadline for entry is January each year. Work should be previously published.

**Tips** No works of translation. Other than this exception, no types of work are excluded. Work may reflect any time period from ancient Greece right up to present day life.

## Saga Award for Wit

**c/o Belinda Harley Associates, 22 South Audley Street, London, W1K 2NY**

☎ 020 7499 4979

☎ 020 7499 4068

📧 info@belindaharley.com

**Insider Info** Sponsored by Saga magazine. Awarded annually to a work of comedy written by an author over the age of 50. The winner receives £20,000.

**Genres** Fiction, Non-fiction

**Submission Guidelines** Work should be previously published.

**Tips** Nominations by publishers only.

## Saltire History Book of the Year Award

**9 Fountain Close, 22 High Street, Edinburgh, EH1 1TF**

☎ 0131 556 1836

☎ 0131 557 1675

📧 saltire@saltiresociety.org.uk

🌐 www.saltiresociety.org.uk

**Established** 1965

**Insider Info** Sponsored by The Saltire Society. An annual award in memory of Dr. Angus Mure

MacKenzie for a work of Scottish historical research published during the preceding year.

**Genres** Non-fiction

**Submission Guidelines** An entry form is available online. Work should be published previously.

**Tips** Nominations should be sent via the online form to the administrator.

## The Saltire Literary Award

**9 Fountain Close, 22 High Street, Edinburgh, EH1 1TF**

- 0131 556 1836
- 0131 557 1675
- saltire@saltiresociety.org.uk
- www.saltiresociety.org.uk

**Insider Info** The award is sponsored by The Saltire Society, Royal Mail Group, Faculty of Advocates and the National Library of Scotland. Prizes are awarded in two categories: Scottish Book of the Year and Scottish first Book of the Year. To qualify, the book must be by a writer born or living in Scotland, or of Scottish descent, or alternatively must deal with a Scottish theme, event or situation. The award is given annually. The winner of the book of the year title receives £5,000. The first book winner receives £1,500.

**Genres** Fiction, Non-fiction, Poetry, Essays, Scripts, Articles

**Submission Guidelines** Submissions should be received by September 8. Work should be published previously having appeared between September 1 of the previous year and August 31 of the year of entry.

**Tips** Nominations are invited from editors and reviewers working in Scotland, as well as producers of radio and television and publishers. Address nominations to Kathleen Munro, Administrator, at the above address.

## Samuel Pepys Award

**c/o Colman Getty PR, 34–42 Cleveland Street, London, W1T 4JE**

- 020 7631 2666
- 020 7631 2699
- hannah@colmangettypr.co.uk
- www.pepys-club.org.uk

**Established** 2003

**Insider Info** Awarded for a book that has increased the understanding of Samuel Pepys, his era, or his peers and encouraged further study. Awarded every two years (odd years), the winner receives £2,000 and a silver medal. Judges for 2007: Dr Richard Luckett, Pepys Librarian, Magadalene College; Roddy

Pryor, Chairman of the Samuel Pepys Club; Sir Keith Thomas, historian; Claire Tomalin, writer and literary journalist.

**Submission Guidelines** Deadline for 2007 entries July. Work should be published between July 1 2005 and June 31 2007.

**Tips** Submissions by publishers only. Send five copies to Hannah Blake at Colman Getty PR.

## Science Writer Awards

**PO Box 5824, Westcliff-on-Sea, Southend, SS1 9EW**

- 0845 094 6367
- enquiries@science-writer.co.uk
- www.science-writer.co.uk

**Competition/Award Director** Dr. Roger Highfield

**Established** 1987

**Insider Info** Sponsored by *The Daily Telegraph* and Bayer. A competition for science articles of around 700 words that successfully communicate a scientific subject in a clear and jargon-free way. There are two categories: 16–9 and 20–28. Awarded annually, the winner in each category receives £1,000, a work placement at *The Daily Telegraph*, Bayer or The Royal Society, a year's subscription to *Nature* and *New Scientist* magazines and the opportunity for their article to be published in the *Telegraph's* science section. The prize for 2nd place is £500, publication in the *Telegraph* and the magazine subscriptions. Nine runners up each receive £100.

**Genres** Non-fiction, Essays, Articles

**Submission Guidelines** Deadline for submission is June. Guidelines are available on the website. Work should be previously unpublished.

**Tips** There are extensive tips and guidelines on the website along with previous winning entries and advice from top science writers. Entries must not exceed 800 words.

## SciTalk Competitions

**Plumbland House, Plumbland, Aspatria, Cumbria, CA7 2HD**

- enquiries@scitalk.org.uk
- www.scitalk.org.uk

**Insider Info** SciTalk is an organisation that promotes the inclusion of science and scientists in literature without limiting them to science fiction. Occasional competitions are offered with this aim in mind. A recent example is The Short Story Challenge where writers were invited to talks and lab tours from scientists and then challenged to write a short story including the information they had gathered. Prizes will vary with competitions but have included publication in *The Guardian*.

**Tips** New competitions will be published in the events section on the website. The website may also be used as a research tool for writers and can put people in touch with scientists willing to help with information and ideas to be put into fiction writing.

## The Scotsman and Orange Short Story Award
**PO Box 105–6, Edinburgh, EH8 8YN**
- 0131 620 8613
- www.scotsman.com

**Insider Info** An open short story competition centred around a different theme each year. The theme for 2006 was 'work' but this is intended as a loose guideline, rather than a specific topic area. The award is given annually. The winner receives £7,500 and a trip, including travel and accommodation, to the Orange Prize for Fiction. Five runners up receive £500 each. Writers must have been born in Scotland or be a current Scottish resident.

**Genres** Short stories

**Submission Guidelines** Work should be unpublished.

**Tips** Stories should be up to 3,000 words, double-spaced and single-sided. Details of future competitions, closing dates and entry forms will be published in *The Scotsman* newspaper and website.

## Scribble Magazine Competitions
**14 The Park, Stow on the Wold, Cheltenham, GL54 1DX**
- 01451 831053
- sales@parkpublications.co.uk
- www.parkpublications.co.uk

**Insider Info** Sponsored by Park Publications. Several competitions are offered by the magazine including an ongoing quarterly short story competition for stories of up to 3,000 words. Details of various other one-off writing competitions are published on the website. The prizes consist of £75, £25, and £15 for the top 3 three published in each issue.

**Genres** Poetry, Articles, Short stories.

**Submission Guidelines** Guidelines and entry forms available via SAE. Entry fee of £3 per short story for the quarterly competition. Work should be previously unpublished.

**Tips** Guidelines are published on the submissions section of the website that advise writers how to best write for *Scribble's* audience. Subscribers to the magazine get free entry to competitions.

## Seventh Quark Competitions
**Kingfisher Barn, Lower Farm Court, Hambridge Lane, Newbury, Berkshire, RG14 5TH**
- 01635 34317
- alex.keegan@btconnect.com; info@7thquarkmagazine.com
- www.alexkeegan.com/7Q

**Competition/Award Director** Alex Keegan

**Insider Info** Literary magazine *7th Quark* runs various competitions to help source its content. Current examples include flash fiction and short story challenges. Prizes often consist of small cash sums and publication in the magazine.

**Genres** Fiction, Short stories.

**Submission Guidelines** Entry fees vary. Work should be previously unpublished.

**Tips** Potential entrants must register by email before submitting. Competitions and deadlines are subject to change depending on the level of response.

## The Shiva Naipaul Memorial Prize
**22 Old Queen Street, London, SW1H 9HP**
- 020 7961 0200
- www.spectator.co.uk

**Insider Info** The prize is sponsored by *The Spectator* and is awarded to a writer who is able to powerfully convey a visit to a foreign place or culture. The prize is awarded annually. The winner receives £3,000. Entry is open to any writer under 35 who writes in English.

**Genres** Non-fiction

**Submission Guidelines** Submissions should be received by May. Work should be unpublished.

**Tips** Although the award is essentially for travel writing, the judges look past this at how well a foreign culture is conveyed to the reader.

## Sid Chaplin Short Story Competition
**Shildon Town Council, Civic Hall Square, Shildon, DL4 1AH**
- 01388 772563
- 01388 775227
- council@shildon.gov.uk
- www.shildon.gov.uk

**Established** 1988

**Insider Info** A short story competition. Entries are invited of up to 3,000 words. Annually, 1st prize is £300, 2nd is £150 and 3rd is £75. Junior prizes will be split into various age groups from 8–17. There will also be a prize for the best entry from a resident of Shildon. Open to anyone aged 8+ years.

**Genres** Short stories

**Submission Guidelines** Deadline for entry end March.entry fee is £2.50 for adults, children free. Work should be previously unpublished.
**Tips** The competition is open to stories on any theme. For more details contact Shildon town council.

## Sir Banister Fletcher Award
**40 Dover Street, London, W1S 4NP**
☎ 020 7408 5092
☎ 020 7409 0913
✉ stella@theauthorsclub.co.uk
**Established** 1954
**Insider Info** Sponsored by the Author's Club, awarded for the best book on architecture or the arts published in Britain. The prize consist of £1,000. Open to any books written by British authors and published under a British imprint.
**Genres** Non-fiction.
**Submission Guidelines** Work should be published previously.
**Tips** No submissions.

## Sir William Lyons Award
**39 Beswick Avenue, Ensbury Park, Bournemouth, BH10 4EY**
☎ 01202 518808
☎ 01202 518808
✉ chris@whizzco.freeserve.co.uk
🌐 www.guildofmotoringwriters.co.uk
**Established** 1966
**Insider Info** Sponsored by The Guild of Motoring Writers, an award open to people under the age of 23 who are interested in motor journalism. To be eligible for the award the entrant has to complete a number of tasks, including conducting and writing up an interview with a person in the motoring industry. Awarded annually, winners receive a cash prize and membership to The Guild of Motoring Journalists. Open to people who are British by nationality or live in Britain.
**Submission Guidelines** Deadline for entries is September each year. Entry forms are usually available in late spring.
**Tips** There is a useful tips document from a previous award winner available on the website.

## Slingink Shorts
✉ shorts@slingink.co.uk, help@slingink.co.uk
🌐 www.slingink.co.uk
**Established** 2004

**Insider Info** A competition that invites submissions of short stories of less than 140 words (141 including the mandatory one word title). Awarded annually, the winning writer receives £75. If enough good entries are received they will be published in an anthology bearing the title of the winning story.
**Genres** Short stories
**Submission Guidelines** Deadline for entries is March. entry fee is £6 for between one and six stories by the same writer. Work should be previously unpublished.
**Tips** Entrants must register online before entering. The winner will be the most original, captivating, entertaining and polished story.

## Society of Theatre Research Book Prize
**c/o The Theatre Museum, 1e Tavistock Street, London, WC2E 7PR**
🌐 www.str.org.uk
**Established** 1998
**Insider Info** An award for the best piece of writing in English on British theatre published during the preceding year. Awarded annually, the winner receives £400. Writers may be of any nationality and the book does not have to have been published by a British publisher.
**Genres** Non-fiction
**Submission Guidelines** Work should be previously published.
**Tips** Submissions invited from publishers. Write to the administrator at the above address for more information.

## Somerset Maugham Awards
**The Society of Authors, 84 Drayton Gardens, London, SW10 9SB**
☎ 020 7373 6642
☎ 020 7373 5768
✉ info@societyofauthors.org
🌐 www.societyofauthors.org
**Insider Info** Awards for a British work of fiction or non-fiction by a young writer. The award should be spent on foreign travel. Awarded annually with up to £6,000 in prize money. Writers must be under the age of 35 and be British by birth (excluding Eire and British colonies). The work submitted must be a full length book published within the previous year in Britain.
**Genres** Fiction, Poetry, Novels, Criticism, Biography, History, Philosophy, Belles-lettres, Travel
**Submission Guidelines** Entry form on website. work should be published within the previous year.

**Tips** Entry is by publisher so if you are interested in entering, you should first contact your publisher to discuss.

## Sony Radio Academy Awards
**47–48 Chagford Street, London, NW1 6EB**
- 020 7723 0106
- 020 7724 6163
- info@radioawards.org, secretariat@radioawards.org
- www.radioawards.org

**Established** 1983
**Insider Info** An annual awards ceremony to recognise excellence in radio broadcast during the preceding year. The awards are split into various categories that are subject to review each year.
**Submission Guidelines** Deadline for entries is January. Entries must have been broadcast on FM, AM, digital terrestrial, satellite or cable, streamed or been downloadable between January 1 and December 31 the previous year.
**Tips** Entries may only be submitted by OFCOM (or similar) licensed radio stations, BBC production departments, independent production companies and BFBS. Clear guidelines are published on the website along with tips on how to submit winning entries and details of all individual prize categories.

## Southport Writers' Circle International Poetry Competition
**32 Dover Road, Birkdale, Southport, Merseyside, PR8 4TB**

**Insider Info** An open poetry competition for poetry of up to 40 lines. Awarded annually, the winning poet receives £200. 2nd prize is £100 and 3rd prize is £50. There are additional £25 prizes for a humorous poem and local poet.
**Genres** Poetry
**Submission Guidelines** Deadline for entry is April each year. Entry fee is £2 per poem. Work should be previously unpublished.
**Tips** Writers with Liverpool or Preston postcodes should mark their entries with an 'L' in the top right corner for entry into the local prize.

## Speakeasy Open Creative Writing Competition
**46 Wealdstone Place, Springfield, Miton Keynes, Buckinghamshire, MK6 3JG**
- 01908 663860
- speakeasy@writerbrock.co.uk
- www.mkweb.co.uk/speakeasy

**Competition/Award Director** Martin Brocklebank
**Established** 1996
**Insider Info** Sponsored by Speakeasy – Milton Keynes Writers' Group. Prizes in both short story and poetry awarded annually. 1st is £100, 2nd is £50 and 3rd is £25 in both short story and poetry. Judges vary each year. Open to all writers and poets 16 years and above; there is a separate Young Writers competition.
**Genres** Poetry, Short stories
**Submission Guidelines** Deadline for entry is end of October each year. Guidelines and entry forms available via SAE. Entry fee is £3 per poem or four for £10; £4 per short story or three for £10. Work should be previously unpublished.
**Tips** Please read the rules carefully and send in your entries with an entry form printed from the website.

## Strokestown International Poetry Competition
**Strokestown Poetry Festival Office, Strokestown, County Roscommon, Republic of Ireland**
- 00353 71 9633759
- petersirr@eircom.net
- www.strokestownpoetry.org

**Competition/Award Director** Peter Sirr
**Insider Info** Sponsored by Strokestown International Poetry Festival. A poetry competition established to promote excellence in poetry and participation in the reading and writing of it. There are three awards: for an unpublished poem in English; for an unpublished poem in Irish or Scottish Gaelic language; and smaller on-the-spot prizes for witty verses during the festival. Awarded annually, prizes are €4,000, €2,000 and €1,000 for the two main poetry categories and €500, €100, €80 for on-the-spot prizes. Poets may also be invited to read their poems at the festival for a fee and travel expenses. Judges are different for each category and are published on the website each year. Copyright remains with the poet, but Strokestown Community Development Association reserves the right to arrange first publication or broadcast of selected poems. Poems must be unpublished and the original work of a living poet..
**Genres** Poetry
**Submission Guidelines** Deadline for entry is end January. Guidelines on website. Entry fee is £4 for each poem. Work should be previously unpublished.
**Tips** Entries must be typed or written on single sided paper. No entries are returned.

## Sunday Times Young Writer of the Year Award

**84 Drayton Gardens, London, SW10 9SB**

☎ 020 7373 6642

☎ 020 7373 5768

✉ info@societyofauthors.org

🌐 www.societyofauthors.org

**Established** 1991

**Insider Info** Sponsored by the Society of Authors. Awarded annually to a young writer under the age of 35 for a full length British publication in the preceding year. The winner receives £5,000. Writers must be usually resident in Britain and their work must be in English.

**Genres** Fiction, Non-fiction, Poetry.

**Submission Guidelines** Deadline for entry is October. Guidelines are available on the website. Work should be published previously, between January 1 and December 31.

**Tips** Submissions are normally invited from August although details will be published on the Society of Authors' website. Four copies of the work are required.

## Sygenta ABSW Science Writers' Awards

**58 Greenhill Road, Moseley, Birmingham, B13 9SS**

☎ 07866 769381

✉ sciencewritersawards@clairejowett.com

🌐 www.sciencewritersawards.co.uk

**Established** 1966

**Insider Info** Sponsored by the Association of British Science Writers. Awards given annually across eight categories for excellence in science journalism, including writing and broadcasting. The winners in each category receive £2,000.

**Genres** Non-fiction, Essays, Scripts, Articles.

**Submission Guidelines** Guidelines and entry forms available on the website.

**Tips** Of particular interest to new science journalists is the New Voice Award (formerly the Young Broadcaster), open to journalists aged 30 or under. Detailed guidelines for all categories are published on the website.

## Templar Poetry Pamphlet & Collection Competition 2007

**Templar Poetry, PO Box 7082, Bakewell, Derbyshire, DE45 9AF**

☎ 01629 582500

✉ info@templarpoetry.co.uk

🌐 www.templarpoetry.co.uk

**Competition/Award Director** Alex McMillen

**Established** 2005

**Insider Info** Sponsored by Templar Poetry. The annual Templar Poetry Pamphlet & Collection competition is open to all poets writing in English. The competition aims to find and publish excellent poetry from new and previously published writers. Three winners have their pamphlets published in an exceptionally high quality perfect bound pamphlet. The three winners also receive a prize of £500 each and the option to submit a full collection for publication. There is also a competition anthology containing the best individual poems from the remaining submissions. All writers will have the option of recording an audio CD containing a selection of their poems to be included free with their pamphlet or collection. All entrants receive a complimentary copy of the anthology. Submissions are invited of between 18–25 A4 pages of poetry of up to 40 lines per page. The award ceremony is held in Derbyshire in late October or early November. A respected poet is appointed each year to carry out the judging; for the 2007 competition: Jean Sprackland, currently Education Director at the Poetry Archive. An anthology of the best individual poems is published alongside the three winners and there is an annual reading in Derbyshire in late autumn. Authors retain their rights according to copyright law, but grant the permission to publish their work in the pamphlets, anthology and collections in the usual way, again in accordance with copyright law. Translated poetry is not eligible. There are no residency requirements or limitations.

**Genres** Poetry

**Submission Guidelines** Closing date for submissions is the first week of May every year. Further information and rules are available on the Templar Poetry website. Individual poems may have been previously published, but not the submission as a whole. The entry fee is £16.

## Theakston's Old Peculier Prize for Crime Novel of the Year

**Festival Office, Raglan House, Raglan Street, Harrogate, HG1 1LE**

☎ 01423 562303

☎ 01423 521264

✉ crime@harrogate-festival.org.uk

🌐 www.harrogate-festival.org.uk

**Established** 2005

**Insider Info** Sponsored by Harrogate Crime Writing Festival and Theakston's Old Peculier. An award for a full length crime novel published in Britain and written by a British writer. Presented during the annual crime writing festival which takes place 19th–22nd July 2007. The winner receives £3,000 and a handmade, oak beer cask. A shortlist is advertised and members of the public are invited to vote for the winner.

**Genres** Fiction, Novels

**Submission Guidelines** Work should be published previously.

**Tips** The shortlist is usually published around April on the festival's website and tends to include several commercial successes by high profile writers such as Ian Rankin and Val McDermid.

## The Tir Na N-Og Award
**Castell Brychan, Aberystwyth, SY23 2JB**
- 01970 624151
- 01970 625385
- wbc.children@wbc.org.uk
- www.wbc.org.uk

**Established** 1976

**Insider Info** The award is sponsored by Cyngor Llyfrau Cymru (Welsh Books Council) and is an award for children's books. The award is split over three categories: English language books; Welsh language books, primary sector; and Welsh language books, secondary sector. The award is judged annually. The winner in each category receives £3,000.

**Genres** Children's books

**Submission Guidelines** Work should be published previously.

## The Translators Association Prizes
**84 Drayton Gardens, London, SW10 9SB**
- 020 7373 6642
- 020 7373 5768
- info@societyofauthors.org
- www.societyofauthors.org

**Insider Info** The prizes are sponsored by the Society of Authors. Awards are given for translations in several categories: Dutch/Flemish Translation, The Vondel Translation Prize; French Translation, The Scott Moncrieff Prize; German Translation, The Schlegel-Tieck Prize; Greek Translation, The Hellenic Foundation for Culture Translation Prize; Italian Translation, The John Florio Prize; Portuguese Translation, The Calouste Gulbenkian Prize; Spanish Translation, The Premio Valle Inclán; Swedish Translation, The Bernard Shaw Prize; and Arabic Translations, The Banipal Prize. Each prize may be given at different intervals. The prizes vary but are usually sums of £1,000 or £2,000.

**Genres** Translations

**Submission Guidelines** Submissions should be received by January 31 every year. Work should be published previously. Submissions should be made by publishers and five copies sent.

**Tips** For the criteria of each individual prize, visit the Society of Authors website.

## Trevor Reese Memorial Prize
**Institute of Commonwealth Studies, University of London, 28 Russell Square, London, WC1B 5DS**
- 020 7862 8844
- 020 7862 8820
- ics@sas.ac.uk
- www.commonwealth.sas.ac.uk/reese

**Established** 1979

**Insider Info** Awarded in memory of Trevor Reese, an academic in the field of Australian and Commonwealth history. Presented for a work which has made a significant contribution to the study of Imperial and Commonwealth History. The prize is awarded every two years (even years). The winner receives £1,000.

**Genres** Non-fiction and Essays

**Submission Guidelines** Submissions should be received by February of the year before entry. Works must have been published in the two years preceding the year in which the award is presented. Please send two copies of the entry to Dee Burn, Development and Marketing Officer, at the above address.

**Tips** Submissions are welcome from publishers or writers.

## Trollope Society Short Story Prize
**84 Addison Gardens, London, W14 0DR**
- pamela@tvdox.com
- www.trollopestoryprize.org

**Competition/Award Director** Dr Pamela Neville-Sington

**Established** 2001

**Insider Info** Prize is sponsored by The Trollope Society. Anthony Trollope was, he confessed, thoroughly miserable and 'always in disgrace' at school, yet he became a much loved author. To encourage interest in his work among young people, the Trollope Society has established an annual short story competition. The emphasis is on reading – and writing – for fun. Each year entrants are asked to base their stories on a particular novel or short story by Anthony Trollope. The prize is awarded annually. The winner receives £1,000 and publication in the Trollope Society's quarterly journal, 'Trollopiana', and on the website. The judges are: Dr Sophie Gilmartin of Royal Holloway, University of London; Dr Margaret Markwick of Exeter University; Professor David Skilton of Cardiff University; Pamela Neville-Sington, biographer of Fanny Trollope; and John Williams, sponsor of the Prize. Entrants should be Twenty-one years and younger. The competition is worldwide.

**Genres** Short stories

**Submission Guidelines** Submissions should be received by January 15 each year. Writer's wishing to enter the competition should make contact via email. Work should be unpublished.

**Tips** Use your imagination!

## Twisted Tongue Flash Fiction Competition

◉ twistedtongue@blueyonder.co.uk
◉ www.twistedtongue.co.uk
**Established** 2006

**Insider Info** Prize is awarded for the best short-story up to 500 words, based on any theme. The competition is held quarterly. The top three entries will be published and receive payment through Paypal. Payment depends on the amount of entries received, the minimum first place will receive is £20. There are five anonymous judges. The competition is open to all.

**Genres** Fiction

**Submission Guidelines** Submissions should be received by 1st of Jan, April, July and October. Please only send email entries only. Entry fee is £1.50 with a discount for bulk entries. Work should be unpublished.

**Tips** Ensure you double check your work for typos, and do not go over 500 words. To get an idea of what the judges prefer take a look at a back issue.

## Undiscovered Authors

**50 Albemarle Street, London, W1S 4BD**
◉ 0207 529 3747
◉ enquiries@undiscoveredauthors.co.uk
◉ www.undiscoveredauthors.co.uk
**Competition/Award Director** Graham Miller
**Established** 2005

**Insider Info** The competition is sponsored by Discovered Authors. The organisation looks for works in the categories of: General Fiction, Non-fiction and Academic. These three categories are open to unpublished writers, plus a new and separate category has been introduced for Previously Published Authors. There is a top National prize of £10,000 available, plus a publishing contract

with Discovered Authors. The competition is a search for new literary talent – giving new writer's an opportunities. The competition is held annually. The General Fiction category is split regionally across the UK and Ireland with a prize of £1,000 per region. All regional winners will be put forward to a National Final to win a top prize of £10,000, along with three wild card entries, which will be selected from the favourite losing entries. Regional 2nd and 3rd placed entrants will also win a prize of publication. The Non-fiction and Academic categories will be judged on a National level only – with the winners receiving a prize of £1,000. The Previously Published category is a new addition to the competition and is open to published writers – but the text they submit must be previously unpublished – The National winner in this category will win £2,500. A publication contract with Discovered Authors will be offered to all winners. Judges include: representatives from the publishing industry and bookstores, editors, and authors – Including John Murray and Hans Offringa. No rights will be acquired at entry. The competition is open to all writers.

**Genres** Fiction, Non-fiction, Poetry, Juvenile, Novels, Short stories, Story collections and Academic

**Submission Guidelines** Submissions should be received by the end of January every year. Guidelines and entry forms are available via email. A synopsis and completed work is required at entry. Registration details are available at www.undiscoveredauthors.co.uk. The entry fee is £10. Work should be unpublished.

## Verity Bargate Award

**21 Dean Street, London, W1D 3NE**
◉ 020 7287 5060
◉ 020 7287 5061
◉ writers@sohotheatre.com
◉ www.sohotheatre.com

**Insider Info** The award is sponsored by Soho Theatre Company and is a national competition to find the best play by a new or fledgling writer. The award is given every two years (odd years). The prize is £5,000 and a residency at the Soho Theatre. Open to writers resident in the UK or Republic of Ireland. The following are not eligible: writers with three or more professional productions to their credit; plays commissioned by Soho Theatre Company (STC); previous Verity Bargate Award winners; plays that have already be rejected by the STC literary department.

**Genres** Scripts

**Submission Guidelines** Submissions should be received by the July of the year of entry. Guidelines are available on the website. Work should be unpublished and unproduced.

**Tips** Submit one full-length play of at least 70 minutes on any subject. Include a title page with contact details and two SAEs for acknowledgement letter and manuscripts. Also please include a career history of all publications/productions.

## Ver Poets Open Competition
**181 Sandridge Road, St. Albans, Hertfordshire, AL1 4AH**

Ⓦ www.verpoets.org.uk

**Insider Info** An open competition for poetry of up to 30 lines on any theme or subject. The competition is held annually. The overall winner receives £500, 2nd place wins £300 and 3rd place wins £100. The copyright remains with the author.

**Genres** Poetry

**Submission Guidelines** Submissions should be received by April of each year. Entry fees are: £3 per poem, £10 for 4 poems and £2 each for the 11th poem onwards. Work should be unpublished.

**Tips** Submit twocopies of each poem with an application form, downloadable from the website. Please do not submit any translations or poems that have been entered in any other competition.

## Vogue Talent Contest
**Vogue House, Hanover Square, London, W1S 1JU**

Ⓦ www.vogue.co.uk

**Insider Info** A competition for young journalists, or potential journalists, under the age of 25. Entrants are invited to submit three pieces of writing on set subjects. Previous awards have required a 600 word autobiography, a 600 word arts review or comment on a fashion trend and an 800 word magazine-style profile of an important person in their life. The contest is held annually. The winner receives £1,000 and a month's paid work experience at *Vogue*. The runner up receives £500. Judges will include the editor of *Vogue*, senior magazine staff and guest writers and editors. Copyright of entries belongs to Condé Nast Publications Ltd. Writers must be under 25 on the January 1 in the year of the award presentation.

**Submission Guidelines** Submissions should be received by April. Entries should be unpublished.

**Tips** The judges state they are looking for 'creativity, wit and stylish writing'. Studying several copies of *Vogue* magazine may give an idea of the magazine's style of writing.

## VS Pritchett Memorial Prize
**Somerset House, Strand, London, WC2R 1LA**

Ⓞ 020 7845 4676

Ⓞ 020 7845 4679

Ⓔ info@rslit.org

Ⓦ www.rslit.org/pritchett.htm

**Established** 1999

**Insider Info** Prize is sponsored by the Royal Society of Literature and Chatto & Windus and is awarded for a short story of between 2,000 and 5,000 words in memory of VS Pritchett. The prize is awarded annually. The winner receives £1,000 and publication of their story in *The London Magazine*. Writers must be resident in the UK or Ireland.

**Genres** Short stories

**Submission Guidelines** Submissions should be received by January of each year. Writers wishing to enter the competition should email the above address for an entry form in November and it will be sent in the mail, alternatively the form is also available on the website. The cost for entry is £5 per story. Work should be unpublished.

**Tips** Entries should be double spaced on single sided A4 paper. Please do not send any handwritten entries. Entrants may read VS Pritchett's stories for inspiration.

## Wadsworth Prize for Business History
**Lloyds TSB Group Archives, 5th Floor, Princess House, 1 Suffolk Lane, London, EC4R 0AX**

Ⓞ 020 7489 3945

Ⓞ 020 7489 3945

Ⓦ www.businessarchivescouncil.org.uk

**Established** 1978

**Insider Info** Prize is sponsored by The Business Archives Council and is awarded to an individual who is deemed to have made an outstanding contribution to the study of business history in the preceding year. The prize is awarded annually.

**Genres** Non-fiction

**Submission Guidelines** Work should be previously published.

**Tips** Nominations should be by publishers only. All correspondence should be addressed to Karen Sampson at the above address.

## Ware Poets Open Poetry Competition
**48 Highbury Road, Hitchen, SG4 9SA**

Ⓦ www.rockingham-press.co.uk

**Insider Info** An open competition for poetry of up to 50 lines on any theme or subject. The competition is held annually. The prizes are: £500 for 1st place,

£200 for 2nd and £300 for 3rd. Winning entries will be published in the competition anthology.

**Genres** Poetry

**Submission Guidelines** Submissions should be received by April. Guidelines for the submission of entries are available on the website. Entry fees are: £3 per poem, £10 for four poems and £2.50 for the 11th poem onwards. Work should be unpublished.

**Tips** There is also a separate prize for sonnets, sponsored by Redwing. Sonnets may therefore be considered for both prizes and should be marked with an 'S' in the top right-hand corner.

## Wellington Town Council Short Story Competition

**Civic Offices, Larkin Way, Tan Bank, Wellington, Telford, TF1 1LX**

☎ 01952 567697

☎ 01952 567690

✉ welltowncl@aol.com

🌐 www.wellington-shropshire.gov.uk

**Competition/Award Director** Town Clerk, Derrick Drew

**Established** 1997

**Insider Info** Competition is sponsored by Wellington Town Council. The competition is open to persons regardless of age or location and it has no theme. Entries should not exceed 4,500 words. Prizes are awarded in the following three categories: Best story nationally: 1st, 2nd and 3rd prize; Best Story submitted by a Shropshire resident : 1st, 2nd and 3rd prize; Best Story written by a young person (aged 16 or younger): 1st, 2nd and 3rd prize. Competition is held annually. Cash prizes are awarded and there is a trophy for the winner of the Shropshire resident category and for that of the u16 category. The competition is judged by Write Associates (www.writeassociates.co.uk). The competition is open to anyone.

**Genres** Fiction, Children's and Short stories.

**Submission Guidelines** Submissions should be received by the end of August each year. The entry fee is £3 (in 2006). Guidelines and entry form are available with an SAE. Work should be unpublished.

## The Wheatley Medal

**Woodbourn Business Centre, 10 Jessell Street, Sheffield, S9 3HY**

☎ 0114 244 9561

☎ 0114 244 9563

✉ admin@indexers.org.uk

🌐 www.indexers.org.uk

**Insider Info** Sponsored by the Society of Indexers. The Wheatley Medal is an award that recognizes an outstanding index in any type of publication. The award is given annually. The winner receives £500 and a gold medal.

**Submission Guidelines** Work should be published previously.

**Tips** A set of criteria that the judges will use to make the award is published on the Society of Indexers website.

## Whitfield Prize

**University College London, Gower Street, London, WC1E 6BT**

☎ 020 7387 7532

☎ 020 7387 7532

✉ rhs.info@rhs.ac.uk

🌐 www.rhs.ac.uk

**Established** 1977

**Insider Info** Prize is sponsored by the Royal Historical Society. The Whitfield Prize is awarded for a first published book on British history published in the UK during the previous year. The prize is awarded annually. The winner receives £1,000. The submission must be the writer's first published history book.

**Genres** Non-fiction

**Submission Guidelines** Submissions should be received by the end of December of the previous year. The work should be published previously.

**Tips** Submissions by authors or publishers are welcome. Please send three copies before the closing date.

## The Wilfred Owen Award for Poetry

✉ woa@1914-18.co.uk

🌐 www.1914-18.co.uk/owen

**Established** 1988

**Insider Info** The award is sponsored by Faber & Faber and The Royal College of Art and is awarded for poetry that is deemed to reflect the intentions and feel of Wilfred Owen's own poetry. The award is judged annually. The winner is presented with a piece of art.

**Genres** Poetry

**Submission Guidelines** Work should be published previously.

**Tips** Do not send any submissions, the winner is selected by the Wilfred Owen Association. Winners and details of the award ceremony are published on the website.

## William Hill Sports Book of the Year

**William Hill, Greenside House, 50 Station Road, Wood Green, London, N22 7TP**
- 020 8918 3731
- 020 8918 3728
- pressoffice@williamhill.co.uk
- www.williamhillmedia.com

**Established** 1989

**Insider Info** Awarded for the best book on a sporting theme, known as 'The Bookie Prize'. The award is usually announced in November and is held annually. The winner receives £18,000, a free £2,000 bet, a specially commissioned hand-bound copy of their book and a day at the races.

**Genres** Sports books

**Submission Guidelines** Submissions should be received by September 11. Work should be published previously, having appeared between September 30 of the previous year and September 29 of the year of entry.

**Tips** Books must be nominated and entered by publishers.

## Wingate Literary Prize

**Jewish Quarterly, PO Box 37645, London, NW7 1WB**
- 020 8343 4675
- admin@jewishquarterly.org
- www.jewishquarterly.org

**Established** 1977

**Insider Info** Prize is sponsored by the Harold Hyam Wingate Foundation. The Wingate Literary Prize is an award designed to celebrate work that encourages an interest in Jewish themes and issues in a wider readership. The prize is awarded annually. The winner receives £5,000. Writers may be resident in the UK, the Commonwealth, Israel or the Republic of Ireland but books must be published in the UK.

**Genres** Fiction and Non-fiction

**Submission Guidelines** Work should be published previously.

**Tips** Translations and originals are eligible as long as they reflect Jewish concerns.

## W.J.M Mackenzie Book Prize

**Political Studies Association, Department of Politics, University of Newcastle, Newcastle Upon Tyne, NE1 7RU**
- 0191 222 8021
- 0191 222 3499
- psa@ncl.ac.uk
- www.psa.ac.uk

**Established** 1987

**Insider Info** Awarded for a political science book published in the preceding year. Prize is awarded annually.

**Genres** Non-fiction

**Submission Guidelines** Submissions should be received by October. Work should be published previously having appeared between January 1 and December 31 of the previous year.

**Tips** Nominees from members of the Political Studies Association only.

## Wolfson History Prizes

**8 Queen Anne Street, London, W1G 9LD**
- 020 7323 5730
- 020 7323 3241
- www.wolfson.org.uk

**Established** 1972

**Insider Info** Prizes are sponsored by the Wolfson Foundation. They are awarded to promote and encourage the writing of history for the general public. Prizes are given for two works published during the year, with an occasional general award for an individual's outstanding contribution to the writing of history. The prizes are awarded annually. The judges are Sir Keith Thomas FBA (Chairman), Professor Averil Cameron CBE FBA, Professor Richard Evans FBA and Professor David Cannadine FBA. Writers must be British and normally resident in Britain and the work must have also been published in Britain.

**Genres** Non-fiction

**Submission Guidelines** Work should be published previously.

**Tips** Books are selected by judges but suggestions for consideration may be made in writing. Books should be academic, yet remain accessible to a more general readership.

## Write a Story for Children Competition

**PO Box 95, Huntingdon, Cambridgeshire, PE28 5RR**
- 01487 832752
- 01487 832752
- enquiries@childrens-writers.co.uk
- www.childrens-writers.co.uk

**Competition/Award Director** Roger Dewar

**Established** 1985

**Insider Info** The competition is sponsored by the Academy of Children's Writers and is for a short story of up to 2,000 words aimed at children of any age. The author must be over 18 and previously unpublished. The competition is held annually. The 1st Prize is £2,000, 2nd Prize is £300 and 3rd Prize is £200. The competition is judged by an independent panel. The competition is open to all.

**Genres** Fiction, Juvenile and short stories

**Submission Guidelines** Submissions should be received by the end of March each year. Guidelines and entry forms are available with an SAE. The entry fee is £2.10, $5 or €5.

**Tips** Please read the rules and conditions, available on the website.

## The Writers Bureau Poetry and Short Story Competition
**Sevendale house, 7 Dale Street, Manchester, M1 1JB**

❶ 0161 228 2362
❶ 0161 228 3533
✉ studentservices@writersbureau.com
🌐 www.writersbureau.com

**Established** 1994

**Insider Info** An open poetry competition for poems of up to 40 lines and short stories of up to 2,000 words. The competition is held annually. Prizes are £1000, £400, £200 and £100 and 6 lots of £50 for 1st–5th place winners in each category. Judges for 2007 are Iain Pattison for short stories and Alison Chisholm for poems. Copyright remains with the author but first publication rights lay with The Writers Bureau once assigned from the writer, as does permission to include the work on The Writers Bureau website for up to 12 months.

**Genres** Poetry and Short stories

**Submission Guidelines** Submissions should be received by 30th June. Entry fee is £5 per entry. Work should be unpublished.

**Tips** Online and postal entries accepted but entries by email will not be accepted. All posted sheets should be single sided and double spaced.

## Writers Forum Poetry and Short Story Competitions
**PO Box 3229, Bournemouth, BH1 1ZS**

❶ 01202 589828
❶ 01202 587758
✉ editorial@writers-forum.com
🌐 www.writers-forum.com

**Insider Info** The competition is sponsored by *Writers Forum Magazine*. For the poetry competition, readers may submit a poem of up to 40 lines for a competition in each issue of the magazine. Similarly, readers may submit short stories of between 1,500 and 3,000 words for a competition each month and

an overall yearly prize. Competition is held annually. For the poetry competition there is a monthly 1st prize of £100 and three runner-up prizes. For the short story competition there is a minimum monthly 1st prize of £300, 2nd prize of £150 and 3rd prize of £100 with an annual trophy and a cheque for £1,000 for the yearly winner.

**Genres** Poetry and Short stories

**Submission Guidelines** Poetry entries should be received by the 15th of each month. Short stories should be received by the 5th of each month. Guidelines and entry form are available on the website. Entry fees are: £5 for one poem, £7 for two, £10 for each short story (a reading fee). Work should be previously unpublished.

**Tips** The guidelines state that by reading the magazine, writers are more likely to be successful.

## Writers Inc Writers-of-the-Year Competition
**14 Somerset Gardens, London, SE13 7SY**

❶ 020 8305 8844
❶ 020 8469 2147

**Established** 1993

**Insider Info** An open competition for poetry and prose across various categories. The 2007 categories are: poems; extended sequences of poems; short stories (50–2,500 words); and writing for children (8–12 years, up to 20,000 words). The competition is held annually. The prize money totals £3,000 and winners will be invited to read their work at a Writers Inc event. A portion of the prize fund may be allocated as bursaries, awarded to writers from London to attend a writing weekend at the Abbey in Sutton Courtenay, Oxfordshire. One winner will be submitted to the Forward Poetry Prize and in the category for writing for children, the winning entry will be read by a London literary agency. Judges may change each year. For 2007 the judges were Sue Hubbard, a freelance art critic, novelist and poet and Mario Petrucci former poet-in-residence at The Imperial War Museum and with BBC Radio 3. Copyright remains with the author but Writers Inc reserves the right to first publication after the closing date. The competition is open to any writer writing in English.

**Genres** Fiction, Poetry and Short stories

**Submission Guidelines** Submissions should be received by April. Guidelines and entry form are available on the website. Entry fees are: £3 for poems up to 60 lines, £5 for poems over 60 lines, £8 for a poetry sequence of up to 400 lines, £5 for a short story, £12 for three short stories and £4 for a children's story. Work should be previously unpublished.

**Tips** Competition categories may change from year to year so please check the website for new competition details.

---

## Young Minds Book Award
**48–50 St. John Street, London, EC1M 4DG**

- 020 7336 8445
- 020 7336 8446
- bookaward@youngminds.org.uk
- www.youngminds.org.uk/bookaward

**Insider Info** Awarded to a publication which highlights and explores the ways a child takes in and makes sense of the world and gives an insight into the minds of children. The competition is held annually. The winner receives £3,000.

**Genres** Fiction, Non-fiction, Poetry, Novels and Memoirs

**Submission Guidelines** Work should be published previously.

**Tips** The award tends be for an adult book that conveys childhood experiences, rather than a children's book or an academic study.

Literary festivals are more and more popular, and cater for all interests, from the general through to the most erudite and highbrow. Some will love the intimate atmosphere of the smaller festivals, which can feel more like family occasions than public gatherings. Writers can learn a lot from attending the talks and workshops run by publishing professionals. Some of the conferences focus on practical sessions and on hands-on sessions with writers. The highlight of the festival calendar is arguably *The Guardian* Hay Festival, held in early summer each year.

## The Aldeburgh International Poetry Festival

**The Poetry Trust, 9 New Cut, Halesworth, Suffolk, IP19 8BY**

☎ 01986 835950

✉ info@thepoetrytrust.org

🌐 www.thepoetrytrust.org

**Contact** Festival Director, Naomi Jaffa

**Dates** November

**About** A mixture of free and ticketed poetry readings and events with an attendance of around 3,800.

## Aspects Festival

**North Down Heritage Centre, Bangor, Co. Down, Northern Ireland**

☎ 028 9127 8032

🌐 www.northdown.gov.uk

**Dates** September

**About** A series of events to celebrate Irish writing. Many guest speakers across various genres of writing.

## Athlone Literary Festival

✉ literaryathlone@eircom.net

🌐 www.athlone.ie/literaryfestival

**Dates** Summer

**About** Formerly known as the John Broderick weekend, which celebrated the work of Broderick. It is now a broader literary festival. Guest speakers include writers, poets, agents and academics.

## Aurthur Miller Centre International Literary Festival

**School of English and American Studies, University of East Anglia, Norwich, NR4 7TJ**

☎ 01603 592810

☎ 01603 507728

✉ boxoffice@uea.ac.uk

🌐 www.uea.ac.uk/eas/events/intro.shtml

**Dates** September–December

**About** An annual festival of events and talks by well known writers.

## Ballymena Arts Festival

**Leisure and Events Unit, Ballymena Showgrounds, Warden Street, Ballymena, BT43 7DR Northern Ireland**

☎ 028 2563 9853

☎ 028 2563 8549

✉ rosalind.lowry@ballymena.gov.uk

🌐 www.ballymena.gov.uk

**Contact** Rosalind Lowry

**Dates** October

**About** A general arts festival that also includes literature events.

## Bath Literature Festival

**Festival Offices, Abbey Chambers, Kingston Buildings, Bath, BA1 1NT**

☎ 01225 463362

✉ info@bathfestivals.org.uk

🌐 www.bathlitfest.org.uk/pages

**Contact** Artistic Director, Sarah LeFanu

**Dates** Late February/early March each year.

**About** Ten days of literary events over a wide range of topics and genres.

## Belfast Festival at Queens

**Culture and Arts Unit, Queen's University, 8 Fitzwilliam Street, Belfast, BT9 6AW Northern Ireland**

☎ 028 9097 1034

✉ festival@qub.ac.uk

🌐 www.belfastfestival.com

**Contact** Box Office Manager, Michael Kelly

**Dates** October/November

**About** A festival of arts, including music, theatre, film and writing.

## Beverley Literature Festival

**Wordquake, Council Offices, Skirlaugh, East Riding of Yorkshire, HU11 5HN**

- 01482 392745
- john@bevlit.org
- www.beverley-literature-festival.org

**Contact** Festival Director, John Clarke

**Dates** October

**About** A series of literature events and readings, including some to live music. A children's programme runs alongside the main festival.

## Birmingham Book Festival

- 0121 246 2770
- www.birminghambookfestival.org

**Dates** October

**About** An annual festival of books and writing. Workshops are also run throughout the year, through a programme called Write On!.

## Book Now! Literature Festival

**Education and Children's Services, London Borough of Richmond upon Thames, 1st Floor, Regal House, London Road, Twickenham, TW1 3QB**

- www.richmond.gov.uk/literature

**Contact** Arts Programmer, Sarah Hinsley

**Dates** November

**About** A series of high-profile writers and media personalities give lectures on aspects of writing and literature.

## Brighton Festival

**12a Pavillion Buildings, Brighton, BN1 1EE**

- 01273 700747
- penny.sims@brightonfestival.org
- www.brightonfestival.org.uk

**Contact** Press Officer, Penny Sims

**Dates** May

**About** Events centred around the arts; including music, literature and performance.

## Bristol Poetry Festival

**Poetry Can, Unit 11, 20–22 Hepburn Road, Bristol, BS2 8UD**

- 01179 426976
- admin@poetrycan.co.uk
- www.poetrycan.co.uk

**Dates** September

**About** Poetry readings, open mic nights, seminars, talks, and workshops around Bristol. Organised by Poetry Can.

## The British and Irish Contemporary Poetry Conference

**St. Anne's College, Woodstock Road, Oxford, OX2 6HS**

- coordinator@poetryconference.org.uk
- www.poetryconference.org.uk

**Contact** Conference Coordinator, Clare Brown

**Dates** September

**About** A weekend conference for academics, designed to produce original, contemporary poetry.

## Buxton Festival

**3 The Square, Buxton, Derbyshire, SK17 6AZ**

- 01298 70395
- 01298 72289
- info@buxtonfestival.co.uk
- www.buxtonfestival.co.uk

**Contact** Artistic Director, Andrew Greenwood

**Dates** July

**About** A music and literature festival, with an emphasis on opera.

## Cambridge Conference of Contemporary Poetry

**Winstanley Lecture Hall, Trinity College Cambridge, Cambridge**

- 01223 332922
- lan22@cam.ac.uk
- www.cccp-online.org.uk

**Dates** April

**About** An annual weekend of poetry readings, performances, discussion and other events. The emphasis is on modernist poetry.

## Cambridge Wordfest

**ADC Theatre, Park Street, Cambridge, CB5 8AS**

- 01223 264404
- cam.wordfest@btinternet.com
- www.cambridgewordfest.co.uk

**Contact** Festival Director, Cathy Moore

**Dates** April

**About** A literature festival with events for adults and children.

## Canterbury Festival

**Festival Office, Christ Church Gate, The Precincts, Canterbury, CT1 2EE**

**☎** 01227 452853

**✆** www.canterburyfestival.co.uk

**Contact** Festival Director, Rosie Turner

**Dates** October

**About** A large, international festival of the arts. Includes talks from well known authors.

## The Charleston Festival/Small Wonder - Short Stories Festival
**The Charleston Trust, Charleston Firle, Lewes, East Sussex, BN8 6LL**

**☎** 01323 811265

**✉** info@charleston.org.uk

**✆** www.charleston.org.uk

**Dates** May/July

**About** Charleston (May): programme of literary events and readings. Small Wonder (July): short story workshops, challenges and speakers.

## Chaucer Festival
**Chaucer Heritage Trust, 22 St. Peter's Street, Canterbury, CT1 2BQ**

**☎** 01227 470379

**Dates** Spring/Summer/Autumn

**About** An annual festival taking place at various locations throughout London, Canterbury and Kent during the spring, summer and autumn. Includes medieval fairs, readings, performances and schools programmes based around the works of Chaucer.

## Chester Literature Festival
**Festival Office, Viscount House, River Lane, Saltney, Chester, CH4 8RH**

**☎** 01244 674020

**✉** info@chesterlitfest.org.uk

**✆** www.chester-literature-festival.org.uk

**Contact** Katherine Seddon

**Dates** September–November

**About** A literature festival with workshops, readings and other events.

## Chichester Festivities
**Canon Gate House, South Street, Chichester, West Sussex, PO19 1PU**

**☎** 01243 785718

**✉** info@chifest.org.uk

**✆** www.chifest.org.uk

**Dates** June–July

**About** An arts festival including many literary speakers at various venues in Chichester.

## City of London Festival
**12–14 Mason's Avenue, London, EC2V 5BB**

**☎** 020 7796 4949

**✉** admin@colf.org

**✆** www.colf.org

**Contact** Festival Director, Ian Ritchie

**Dates** June–July

**About** An arts festival offering a varied programme including: opera, literature, installations and exhibitions of visual arts, film screenings, architecture walks and talks.

## County Bookshop Peak Festival (Spring and Autumn)
**Countrybookshop, Hassop Station, Nr Bakewell, Derbyshire, DE45 1NW**

**✆** www.countrybookshop.co.uk/peakfestival

**Dates** May–June/October–November

**About** Two large literary festivals held in the Peak District with many well known authors. The Peak District Book of the Year award is also presented during the festival.

## The Cuirt International Festival of Literature
**Galway Arts Centre, 47 Dominick Street, Galway, Republic of Ireland**

**☎** 00353 91 565886

**✉** Maura@galwayartscentre.ie

**✆** www.galwayartscentre.ie/cuirt

**Contact** Programme Director, Maura Kennedy

**Dates** April

**About** A festival of around 6,000 visitors. Includes readings, signings and workshops.

## Derbyshire Literature Festival

**☎** 01773 831359

**✉** alison.betteridge@derbyshire.gov.uk

**✆** www.derbyshire.gov.uk

**Contact** Literature Development Officer, Alison Betteridge

**About** A biennial festival in June, of which the next is in 2008. The festival takes place in venues all over Derbyshire. It aims to encourage people to become involved in all kinds of literature and storytelling, from poetry to screenwriting.

## Dorchester Festival
**Festival Box Office, Dorchester Arts Centre, School Lane, The Grove, Dorchester, DT1 1XR**

**☎** 01305 266926

🖑 www.dorchesterarts.org.uk
**Dates** April–May
**About** A local arts festival with a few literary events.

## Dromineer Literary Festival
**Arts Office, North Tipperary County Council, Civic Offices, Limerick Road, Nenagh, Co. Tipperary, Republic of Ireland**
☎ 00353 87 753 5207
📧 festival@dromineer.net
🖑 www.festival.dromineer.net
**Contact** Eleanor Hooker
**Dates** September–October
**About** A weekend festival. The programme includes readings, storytelling and competitions.

## Dublin Writers Festival
**Dublin City Council Arts Office, The LAB, Foley Street, Dublin 1, Republic of Ireland**
☎ 00353 1 222 7847
📧 office@dublinwritersfestival.com
🖑 www.dublinwritersfestival.com
**Contact** Festival Director, Jack Gilligan
**Dates** June
**About** A writer's festival with readings, workshops and other events. Some events are specifically for children.

## Durham Literature Festival
**Durham City Arts, 2 The Cottages, Fowler's Yard, Back Silver Street, Durham City, DH1 3RA**
☎ 0191 375 0763
📧 durhamlitfest@btinternet.com
🖑 www.literaturefestival.co.uk
**Dates** October
**About** A range of literary events, readings and talks.

## The Dylan Thomas Festival
**The Dylan Thomas Centre, Somerset Place, Swansea, SA1 1RR**
☎ 01792 463980
☎ 01792 463993
📧 dylanthomas.lit@swansea.gov.uk
🖑 www.dylanthomas.org
**Dates** October–November
**About** An annual festival to celebrate the life and work of Dylan Thomas. The programme includes poetry readings, performances, films, talks and discussions. The Dylan Thomas Centre also organises year round literary events.

## Edinburgh International Book Festival
**5a Charlotte Square, Edinburgh, EH2 4DR**
☎ 0131 718 5666
☎ 0131 226 5335
📧 admin@edbookfest.co.uk
🖑 www.edbookfest.co.uk
**Contact** Festival Director, Catherine Lockerbie
**Dates** August
**About** A large festival of literature and books, with around 220,000 visitors. A children's programme also runs alongside the main festival.

## The Ennis Book Club Festival
**25 Willsgrove, Cahercalla, Ennis, Co. Clare, Republic of Ireland**
☎ 00353 87 972 3647/00353 85 775 8523
📧 info@ennisbookclubfestival.com
🖑 www.ennisbookclubfestival.com
**Dates** March
**About** A weekend festival celebrating books of all types and genres. Events include readings, lectures, music, workshops, exhibitions, cookery demonstrations and more.

## Essex Poetry Festival
📧 derek@essex-poetry-festival.co.uk
🖑 www.essex-poetry-festival.co.uk
**Contact** Derek Adams
**Dates** October
**About** A festival of poetry readings and talks. The festival incorporates the Young Essex Poet of the Year competition and an adult poetry competition.

## Exeter Festival (Summer & Autumn)
**Arts, Festivals and Events, Exeter City Council, Paris Street, Exeter, EX1 1JJ**
☎ 01392 265200
☎ 01392 265366
📧 general.festivals@exeter.gov.uk
🖑 www.exeter.gov.uk/festival
**About** Two festivals of arts (July and November), including literature, music, drama, workshops and exhibitions.

## Federation of Worker Writers and Community Publishers Festival of Writing
**Burslem School of Art, Queen Street, Stoke-on-Trent, Staffordshire, ST6 3EJ**
☎ 01782 822327

○ thefwwcp@tiscali.co.uk
ⓦ www.thefwwcp.org.uk
**Dates** Spring
**About** An annual festival for members of the FWWCP, which includes workshops, readings and opportunities to write. The federation is a not-for-profit members organisation for writers groups and community publishers.

## Festival at the Edge & Winter's Edge
**FATE, Rose Cottage, Church Road, Welshpool, SY21 7LN**
❶ 01939 236626
ⓦ www.festivalattheedge.org
**Contact** Ali Quarrell
**Dates** July/February
**About** Storytelling festivals in both the summer and winter in Much Wenlock, Shropshire. In the summer there is the option to camp at the site. Programmes include new commissions, workshops, readings and talks.

## Folkestone Literary Festival
**Festival Office, The Glassworks, Mill Bayt, Folkestone, CT20 1JG**
❶ 01303 211300
○ info@folkestonelitfest.co.uk
ⓦ www.folkestonelitfest.com
**Contact** Festival Organiser, John Prebble
**Dates** November
**About** Literary workshops and events. The festival also runs a short story competition and a series of children's events.

## Frome Festival
**Festival Office, 25 Market Place, Frome, BA11 1AH**
❶ 01373 453889
○ office@fromefestival.co.uk
ⓦ www.fromefestival.co.uk
**Contact** Festival Director, Martin Bax
**Dates** July
**About** A community festival with a literature element.

## The Guardian Hay Festival
**The Drill Hall, 25 Lion Street, Hay on Wye, HR3 5AD**
❶ 0870 990 1299
❶ 01497 821066
○ admin@hayfestival.com

ⓦ www.hayfestival.com
**Dates** May–June
**About** Hay on Wye is a paradise for lovers of secondhand books. The Guardian Hay Festival is a major UK festival, which includes talks from a number of famous literary personalities. Webcasts and podcasts of events are made available.

## Guildford Book Festival
❶ 01483 444334
○ director@guildfordbookfestival.co.uk
ⓦ www.guildfordbookfestival.co.uk
**Contact** Festival Director, Glenys Pycraft
**Dates** October
**About** Talks, workshops and events, in and around Guildford.

## Harrogate Crime Writing Festival
**Raglan House, Raglan Street, Harrogate, North Yorkshire, HG1 1LE**
❶ 01423 562303
❶ 01423 521264
○ crime@harrogate-festival.org.uk
ⓦ www.harrogate-festival.org.uk/crime
**Contact** Crime Festival Coordinator, Adina Watt
**Dates** July
**About** Discussions, seminars, workshops and talks on crime writing.

## Hull Literature Festival (HumberMouth)
**City Arts Unit, Central Library, Kingston Upon Hull, HU1 3TF**
❶ 01482 616961
❶ 01482 616827
○ maggie.hannan@hullcc.gov.uk
ⓦ www.humbermouth.org.uk
**Contact** Festival Director, Maggie Hannan
**Dates** June–July
**About** A programme of literature related events, including guest speakers.

## Ilkley Literature Festival
**Manor House, 2 Castle Hill, Ilkley, West Yorkshire, LS29 9DT**
❶ 01943 816714
❶ 01943 817079
○ admin@ilkleyliteraturefestival.org.uk
ⓦ www.ilkleyliteraturefestival.org.uk
**Contact** Festival Director, Rachel Feldberg
**Dates** September–October

**About** A literature festival sponsored by Skipton Building Society. The festival includes a free fringe programme and a children's programme.

## International Playwriting Festival
**Warehouse Theatre, Dingwall Road, Croydon, CR20 2NF**
- 020 8681 1257
- 020 8688 6699
- rose@warehousetheatre.co.uk
- www.warehousetheatre.co.uk/ipf.html

**Contact** Rose Marie Vernon
**Dates** November
**About** A two part playwriting festival, the first part being an international competition and the second being the festival itself. Twinned with the Italian festival Premio Candoni Arta Terme.

## Jewish Book Week
**Jewish Book Council, PO Box 38247, London, NW3 5YQ**
- 020 8343 4675
- 020 8343 4675
- jewishbookcouncil@btopenworld.com
- www.jewishbookweek.com

**Dates** February–March
**About** A week celebrating Jewish books and writing, with international speakers and events for children.

## King's Lynn Festival
**5 Thorseby Cottage, Queen Street, King's Lynn, Norfolk, PE30 1HX**
- 01553 767557
- 01533 767688
- www.kingslynnfestival.org.uk

**Contact** Artistic Director, Ambrose Miller
**Dates** July
**About** An arts festival with an emphasis on musical performance, although literature talks and events are also held.

## King's Lynn Literature Festivals
**Festival Chairman, Hawkins Solicitors, 19 Tuesday Market Place, King's Lynn, PE30 1JW**
- 01553 691661
- enquiries@lynnlitfests.com
- www.lynnlitfests.com

**Contact** Chairman, Anthony Ellis
**Dates** March/September

**About** A fiction festival in March and a poetry festival in September, both held over weekends. Programmes include presentations from international writers in different genres.

## King's Sutton Literary Festival
**Festival Tickets, 4 Church Avenue, King's Sutton, Banbury, OX17 3RJ**
- 01869 811001
- info@kslitfest.co.ukÊÊ
- http://kslitfest.co.uk

**Contact** Sara Allday
**Dates** March
**About** A festival of literary events, including readings and guest speakers.

## Knutsford Literature Festival
**76 Glebelands Road, Knutsford, Cheshire, WA16 9DZ**
- www.knutsfordlitfest.blogspot.com

**Dates** October
**About** A small friendly festival, offering a range of literary events.

## Latitude
**MFMG, 16–18 High Street, Harlesden, London, NW10 4LX**
- 020 8963 0940
- www.latitudefestival.co.uk

**Dates** July
**About** A weekend music festival with elements of drama, poetry and other literary events. A campsite is available.

## Ledbury Poetry Festival
- 0845 458 1743
- www.poetry-festival.com

**Dates** July
**About** Britain's largest poetry festival with a resident poet, and many events for both adults and children. A poetry competition is also held.

## Lewes Live Literature Festival
**PO Box 2766, Lewes, East Sussex, BN7 2WF**
- 01273 483181
- 01273 483181
- info@leweslivelit.co.uk
- www.leweslivelit.co.uk

**Contact** Artistic Director, Mark Hewitt
**Dates** October

**About** The festival programme includes: creative writing workshops, performances, readings, music, film and visual arts events.

## Lincoln Book Festival

- 01522 873844/01522 804305
- arts@lincoln.gov.uk
- www.lincolnbookfestival.co.uk

**Contact** Sara Bullimore/Karen Parsons
**Dates** May
**About** The programme includes talks, workshops, discussions, exhibitions and performances. There were over 6,000 visitors in 2006.

## Lit.com

- 01472 323382
- charlotte.bowen@nelincs.gov.uk
- www.nelincs.gov.uk

**Contact** Charlotte Bowen
**About** A festival of words and comedy, including live poetry and events, special film screenings, stand-up comedy, workshops and live music. Held at various venues across North East Lincolnshire.

## Lit Fest

**PO Box 751, Lancaster, Lancashire, LA1 9AJ**
- 01524 62166
- 0871 433 6449
- www.litfest.org

**Contact** Andy Darby
**Dates** November
**About** An annual festival focusing on literature and writing. Includes newly commissioned performances each year. Literature development continues throughout the year in Lancaster.

## Lowdham Book Festival

**The Bookcase, 50 Main Street, Lowdham, NG14 7BE**
- 0115 966 4143
- janestreeter@thebookcase.co.uk
- www.lowdhambookfestival.co.uk

**Contact** Jane Streeter/Ross Bradshaw
**Dates** June
**About** A book festival with many different arts events, including talks, readings and live music.

## Manchester Literature Festival

**24 Lever Street, Manchester, M1 1DZ**
- 0161 236 5725
- admin@mlfestival.co.uk
- www.manchesterliteraturefestival.co.uk

**Contact** Festival Manager, Fee Plumley
**Dates** October
**About** A series of literature events in Manchester, including readings and projects to become involved with.

## Maria Edgeworth Literary Festival

**Edgeworthstown Community Co-op, Ballymahon Road, Edgeworthstown, Co. Longford, Republic of Ireland**
- 00353 43 71801
- edgelocdev@eircom.net
- www.edgeworthliteraryfestival.com

**Dates** March
**About** A festival based around an annual literary competition, culminating in a gala weekend with events, readings, talks and discussions. Set in the town of Edgeworthstown.

## National Eisteddfod of Wales

**40 Parc Ty Glas, Llanisien, Cardiff, CF14 5WU**
- 029 2076 3777
- 029 2076 3737
- info@eisteddfod.org.uk
- www.eisteddfod.org.uk

**Dates** August
**About** A large festival of culture held in a different location in Wales every year. The location for 2007 is Mold. Events include performances, exhibitions and competitions in all the arts, including literature.

## NAWG Open Festival of Writing

- 01262 609228
- nawg@tesco.net
- www.nawg.co.uk

**Contact** Festival Coordinator, Mike Wilson
**Dates** September
**About** A residential festival that includes tutor led workshops for writers.

## Norfolk and Norwich Festival

**Festival Office, 1st Floor, Augustine Steward House, 14 Tombland, Norwich, NR3 1HF**
- 01603 877750
- 01603 877766
- info@nnfestival.org.uk
- www.n-joy.org.uk

**Contact** Festival Director, Jonathan Holloway
**Dates** May
**About** A festival of music, comedy and dance.

## Northern Children's Book Festival

**22 Highbury, Newcastle Upon Tyne, NE2 3DY**

☎ 0191 281 3289

🌐 www.ncbf.co.uk

**Contact** Ann Key

**Dates** November

**About** Europe's largest free children's book festival. Authors and poets visit schools throughout the north of England, culminating in a gala day of workshops, talks, seminars and activities for children and their families.

## Oundle Festival of Literature

**Ticket Sales, Oundle Tourist Information Centre, 14 West Street, Oundle**

☎ 01832 274333

✉ enquiries@oundlelitfest.org.uk

🌐 www.oundlelitfest.org.uk

**Contact** Chair, Nick Turnball

**Dates** January–March

**About** A festival of fiction, theatre, poetry, history, politics, travel, gardening, cuisine, environmental issues and a Community Events programme. Some events are free. Others are paid for.

## Poetry International

**Royal Festival Hall, South Bank Centre, Belvedere Road, London, SE1 8XX**

☎ 0870 380 4300

☎ 0870 163 3896

🌐 www.rfh.org.uk/poetryinternational

**About** A six day biennial festival of poetry, with readings, workshops and projects.

## proudWORDS

**PO Box 181, Newcastle Upon Tyne, NE6 5XG**

🌐 www.proudwords.org

**Dates** October

**About** An annual writing festival in Newcastle and Gateshead to promote gay and lesbian writing. Events include workshops, performances, talks and competitions.

## Quite Literary

**The Plough Arts Centre, 9–11 Fore Street, Torrington, Devon, EX38 8HQ**

☎ 01805 622522

☎ 01805 622113

🌐 www.plough-arts.org

**About** A year-round programme of literature events around Torrington. There are readings, workshops, and community events.

## Redbridge Book and Media Festival

**London Borough of Redbridge, Arts and Events Team, 8th Floor, Lynton House, 255–259 High Road, Ilford, IG1 1NY**

☎ 020 8708 3044

✉ mark.etherington@redbridge.gov.uk

🌐 www.redbridge.gov.uk/leisure/redbkmedfest.cfm

**Contact** Arts Development Officer, Mark Etherington

**Dates** May

**About** A festival of the written word in all its forms, including visits from well known writers and performers. The programme includes competitions, workshops, talks and performances. The media element to this festival, alongside the more traditional literature events makes it unique.

## Royal Court Young Writers' Festival

**The Royal Court Young Writer's Programme, Sloane Square, London, SW1W 8AS**

☎ 020 7565 5050

🌐 www.royalcourttheatre.com

**Dates** January–March

**About** A Biennial festival, the next of which will take place in 2008. Young people under the age of 26 may submit scripts to win the chance to see them developed and performed.

## Rye Arts Festival

**PO Box 33, Rye, East Sussex, TN31 7YB**

☎ 01797 22444

✉ info@ryeartsfestival.co.uk

🌐 www.ryefestival.co.uk

**Contact** Catherine Bingham

**Dates** September

**About** A festival of the arts, including writing, theatre and music.

## Salisbury International Arts Festival

**87 Crane Street, Salisbury, Wiltshire, SP1 2PU**

☎ 01722 332977

✉ info@salisburyfestival.co.uk

🌐 www.salisburyfestival.co.uk

**Contact** Festival Director, Jo Metcalfe

**Dates** May–June

**About** An annual arts festival focusing on dance, sport and theatre, with some literary events.

## Scottish Book Town Festivals (Spring and Autumn)
Freepost NAT3539, Wigtown, Newton Stuart, DG8 9JH
- 01988 403222
- mail@wigtownbookfestival.com
- www.wigtownbookfestival.com

**Contact** Festival Director, Michael McCreath
**Dates** May/September–October
**About** Two annual festivals in Wigtown, Scotland's national book town. Programme includes readings and events at various locations in Wigtown.

## Southern Writers Conference
Earnley Concourse, Earnley, Chichester, West Sussex, PO20 7JN
- 01243 670392
- 01243 670832
- admin@southernwriters.co.uk
- www.southernwriters.co.uk

**Contact** Chairman, Martin Hall
**Dates** June
**About** A residential conference for writers, which is based around talks and discussion groups. Anyone with a serious interest in writing is welcome, whether a beginner or experienced.

## StAnza: Scotland's Poetry Festival
Artistic Director, 57 Station Court, Leven, Fife, KY8 4RP
- info@stanzapoetry.org
- www.stanzapoetry.org

**Contact** Artistic Director, Eleanor Livingstone
**Dates** March
**About** An annual poetry festival with an international outlook. Programme includes workshops, master classes, readings, performances, discussions, exhibitions and much more. There is also a children's programme. Visiting poets come from all over the world.

## Stratford Upon Avon Poetry Festival
The Shakespeare Centre, Henley Street, Stratford Upon Avon, CV37 6QW
- 01789 204016
- info@shakespeare.org.uk
- www.shakespeare.org

**Dates** July–August
**About** An annual poetry festival with readings of poetry taking place, mainly on Sunday evenings, in various venues in Stratford. Famous actors read poems of the past, while contemporary poets present their work. There is also a children's event.

## The Sunday Times Oxford Literary Festival
Christ Church, Oxford, OX1 1DP
- 01865 514149
- info@sundaytimes-oxfordliteraryfestival.co.uk
- www.sundaytimes-oxfordliteraryfestival.co.uk

**Dates** March
**About** Workshops and talks on many literary topics, including writing in different genres and publishing.

## Swindon Festival of Literature
Lower Shaw Farm, Shaw, Swindon, Wiltshire, SN5 5PJ
- 01793 771080
- swindonlitfest@lowershawfarm.co.uk
- www.swindonfestivalofliterature.co.uk

**Contact** Festival Director, Matt Holland
**Dates** May
**About** Workshops, talks and speakers on literature and writing, in and around Swindon. Includes a family and children's weekend.

## The Times Cheltenham Literature Festival
Cheltenham Town Hall, Imperial Square, Cheltenham, Gloucestershire, GL50 1QA
- 01242 263494
- 01242 256457
- sarah.smyth@cheltenham.gov.uk
- www.cheltenhamfestivals.com

**Contact** Festival Director, Sarah Smyth
**Dates** October
**About** A series of literary workshops, events and performances, including some big name speakers. Podcasts are available on the Times website.

## Ty Newydd Festival
Ty Newydd, Llanystumdwy, Criccieth, Gwynedd, LL52 0LW
- 01766 522811
- post@tynewydd.org
- www.tynewydd.org

**Dates** April
**About** A biennial festival, the next of which will be held in 2007. It is a weekend festival with a poetry programme in both Welsh and English.

## Warwick International Festival

**Pageant House, Jury Street, Warwick, CV34 4EW**

☎ 01962 694277

🖥 www.warwickintfestival.org

**Dates** June–July

**About** A music and arts festival in and around Warwick, with some literary events.

## Warwick Words

**The Court House, Jury Street, Warwick, CV34 4EW**

☎ 01926 427056

🖥 www.warwickwords.co.uk

**Contact** Patron, Andrew Davies

**Dates** October

**About** A festival of literature and the spoken word. Workshops, talks, performances and children's events are part of the programme.

## Way With Words Literature Festivals

**Droridge Farm, Dartington, Totnes, Devon, TQ9 6JG**

☎ 01803 867373

☎ 01803 863688

✉ office@waywithwords.co.uk

🖥 www.wayswithwords.co.uk

**Contact** Victoria Patch

**Dates** March/July/November

**About** Runs literature festivals at several locations across the UK: Keswick (March); Dartington (July); Southwold (November). Also runs retreats and events overseas.

## Wellington Literary Festival

☎ 01952 222935

✉ welltowncl@aol.com

🖥 www.wellington-shropshire.gov.uk

**Dates** October

**About** A series of free events and talks in Wellington, with several guest speakers.

## Wells Festival of Literature

**Festival Office, Gable House, Parbrook, Glastonbury, BA6 8PB**

☎ 01749 670929

🖥 www.somersite.co.uk/wellsfest.htm

🖥 www.wlitf.co.uk

**Dates** October

**About** A series of lectures and workshops on various topics within literature and writing. Also run annual short story and poetry competitions.

## Welsh Writing in English Annual Conference

**Gregynog Hall, Newton, Powys, Wales**

☎ 029 20 875622

✉ gramichk@cardiff.ac.uk

**Contact** Conference Organiser, Dr. Katie Gramich

**Dates** March

**About** An annual weekend conference centred around Welsh writing in English, with a different theme every year. The 2007 theme is 'life writing in Wales'.

## West Cork Literary Festival

**15 Glengarriff Road, Bantry, Co. Cork, Republic of Ireland**

☎ 00353 27 61157

✉ info@westcorkliteraryfestival.ie

🖥 www.westcorkliteraryfestival.ie

**Dates** July

**About** A week of literary events for writers, including the annual launch of the Fish Publishing anthology and short story prize.

## Winchester Writer's Conference

**Faculty of Arts, University of Winchester, West Hill, Winchester, SO22 4NR**

☎ 01962 827238

✉ barbara.large@winchester.ac.uk

🖥 www.writersconference.co.uk

**Contact** Founder/Director, Barbara Large

**Dates** June–July

**About** A weekend of workshops, events and talks. Also run a book fair.

## Wonderful Words Book Festival

**Penzance Library, Morrab Road, Penzance, Cornwall, TR18 4EY**

☎ 0800 032 2345

☎ 01736 330644

✉ wonderfulwords06@yahoo.co.uk

🖥 http://db.cornwall.gov.uk/ww/ww

**Dates** Autumn

**About** A festival of workshops, talks, readings and events throughout Cornwall. Many of the visiting speakers are big name authors, or media personalities.

## Word

**Office of External Affairs, University of Aberdeen, King's College, Aberdeen, AB24 3FX**

☎ 01224 274444

- 01224 272086
- word@abdn.ac.uk
- www.abdn.ac.uk/word

**Contact** Artistic Director, Alan Spence

**Dates** May

**About** A large festival with over 10,000 visitors. Programme includes readings, workshops, music sessions, art exhibitions, children's activities and film screenings.

## World Book Day

- worldbookday@blueyonder.co.uk
- www.worldbookday.com

**Dates** March

**About** A day celebrating books and encouraging children to read. Special £1 books are created, and there are lots of events in schools throughout the country. The Bookseller and National Book Tokens Ltd host and sponsor the day.

## Writers Holiday at Caerleon

**School Bungalow, Church Road, Pontnewydd, Cwmbran, NP44 1AT**

- enquiries@writersholiday.net
- www.writersholiday.net

**Contact** Anne Hobbs

**Dates** July

**About** A six day residential conference for everyone from beginners to the more experienced. Around 150 delegates attend.

## Writers Week

**24 The Square, Listowel, Co. Kerry, Republic of Ireland**

- 00353 68 21074
- 00353 68 22893
- info@writersweek.ie
- www.writersweek.ie

**Contact** Chairperson, Joanna Keane O'Flynn

**Dates** May

**About** A major Irish writer's festival. Events include free workshops and competitions.

## Writing on the Wall

**60 Duke Street, Liverpool, L1 5AA**

- 0151 707 4313
- info@writingonthewall.org.uk
- www.writingonthewall.org.uk

**Contact** Festival Administrator, Janette Stowell

**Dates** May

**About** A not for profit organisation that runs a series of literature related events. These are designed to encourage young people and the wider community to take part.

## Young Readers Birmingham

**Children's Office, Central Library, Chamberlain Square, Birmingham, B3 3HQ**

- 0121 303 3368
- 0121 464 1004
- gena.gaynor@birmingham.gov.uk
- www.birmingham.gov.uk/youngreaders

**Contact** Gena Gaynor

**Dates** May–June

**About** An annual two week festival for children and young people, to encourage them to enjoy books and reading. There are around 150 events across Birmingham during the two week period.

**FESTIVALS AND CONFERENCES**

**LISTINGS**

**957**

**976**